THE PHILOSOPHER'S INDEX

1995 CUMULATIVE EDITION

VOLUME 29

The Philosopher's Index

An International Index
To Philosophical Periodicals and Books

1995 CUMULATIVE EDITION
VOLUME 29

Produced by:
Philosophy Documentation Center
Bowling Green State University
Bowling Green, OH 43403-0189
Phone: 419-372-2419

Published by:
Philosopher's Information Center
1616 East Wooster Street
Bowling Green, OH 43402-3466
Phone: 419-353-8830

THE PHILOSOPHER'S INDEX

Editor

Richard H. Lineback

Editorial Staff

Donald Callen, Assistant Editor
Bowling Green State University
Robert Goodwin, Assistant Editor
Bowling Green State University
Fred Miller, Assistant Editor
Bowling Green State University
Robert Wolf, Assistant Editor
Southern Illinois University

Frederick Rickey, Assistant Editor
Bowling Green State University
Mario Sáenz, Assistant Editor
LeMoyne College
Kartik Seshadri, Assistant Editor
Cardiff, CA

Table of Contents

The Philosopher's Index

The Philosopher's Index, ISSN 0031-7993, is a subject and author index with abstracts. Philosophy books and journals in English, French, German, Spanish, and Italian are indexed, along with selected books and journals in other languages and related interdisciplinary publications. This periodical is published quarterly and cumulated annually as a service to the philosophical community. Suggestions for improving this service are solicited and should be sent to the Editor.

Policies: Each quarterly issue of the *Index* includes the articles of journals and books that are received in the months prior to its publication. The dates on the journals indexed vary due to dissimiliar publishing schedules and to delays encountered in overseas mailing.

The following factors are weighed in selecting journals to be indexed: 1) the purpose of the journal, 2) its circulation, and 3) recommendations from members of the philosophic community. Articles in interdisciplinary journals are indexed only if they are related to philosophy.

Most of the journal articles and books cited in *The Philosopher's Index* can be obtained from the Bowling Green State University Library, through the Inter-Library Loan Department. The library, though, requests that you first try to locate the articles and books through your local or regional library facilities.

Subscriptions should be sent to the Philosopher's Information Center, 1616 East Wooster Street, Bowling Green, OH 43402-3456. The 1996 subscription price for 4 quarterly issues is $179 (Individuals $55). The price of any single quarterly issue is $50 (Individuals $16). An annual Cumulative Edition of *The Philosopher's Index* is published in the spring following the volume year. The 1995 Cumulative Edition is $189 (Individuals $65).

Abbreviations of Periodicals Indexed

(*Journal is no longer indexed and/or published. The abbreviation is included here for use in conjunction with DIALOG.)

Abraxas*	Abraxas
Acorn	The Acorn: Journal of the Gandhi-King Society
Acta Analytica	Acta Analytica: Philosophy and Psychology
Acta Phil	Acta Philosophica: Ateneo Romano della Santa Croce
Acta Phil Fennica	Acta Philosophica Fennica
Aesthetics	Aesthetics
Agora*	Agora: A Journal of the Humanities and the Social Sciences
Agora (Spain)	Agora: Papeles de Filosofía
Agr Human Values	Agriculture and Human Values
Aitia	Aitia: Philosophy-Humanities Magazine
Ajatus*	Ajatus: Yearbook of the Philosophical Society of Finland
Aletheia*	Aletheia: An International Journal of Philosophy
Alg Log*	Algebra and Logic
Alg Ned Tijdschr Wijs	Algemeen Nederlands Tijdschrift voor Wijsbegeerte
Amer Cath Phil Quart	American Catholic Philosophical Quarterly (formerly The New Scholasticism)
Amer J Philo	American Journal of Philology
Amer J Theol Phil	American Journal of Theology & Philosophy
Amer Phil Quart	American Philosophical Quarterly
An Cated Suarez	Anales de la Cátedra Francisco Suárez
An Seminar Hist Filosof	Anales del Seminario de Historia de la Filosofía
An Seminar Metaf	Anales del Seminario de Metafisica
Analisis Filosof	Análisis Filosófico
Analogia	Analogía Filosófica: Revista de Filosofía
Analysis	Analysis
Ancient Phil	Ancient Philosophy
Ann Esth*	Annales D'Esthétique
Ann Fac Lett Filosof	Annali della Facolta di Lettere e Filosofia
Ann Univ Mariae Curie-Phil	Annales Universitatis Mariae Curie-Skłodowska, Sectio I/Philosophia-Sociologia
Annals Math Log	Annals of Mathematical Logic (see Annals Pure Applied Log)
Annals Pure Applied Log	Annals of Pure and Applied Logic (formerly Annals of Mathematical Logic)
Annu Soc Christ Ethics	The Annual of the Society of Christian Ethics
Antioch Rev	The Antioch Review
Anu Filosof	Anuario Filosófico
Apeiron	Apeiron: A Journal for Ancient Philosophy and Science
Applied Phil	Applied Philosophy (see Int J Applied Phil)
Aquinas	Aquinas: Rivista Internazionale di Filosofia
Arch Begriff*	Archiv für Begriffsgeschichte
Arch Filosof*	Archivio di Filosofia
Arch Gesch Phil	Archiv für Geschichte der Philosophie
Arch Math Log*	Archiv für Mathematische Logik und Grundlagenforschung
Arch Phil	Archives de Philosophie
Arch Rechts Soz	Archiv für Rechts- und Sozialphilosophie
Arch Stor Cult	Archivio di Storia della Cultura
Arete	Areté: Revista de Filosofía
Argumentation*	Argumentation: An International Journal on Reasoning
Arion	Arion: A Journal of Humanities and the Classics
Aris Soc	The Aristotelian Society: Supplementary Volume
Asian J Phil	The Asian Journal of Philosophy
Asian Phil	Asian Philosophy
Augustin Stud	Augustinian Studies
Augustinus	Augustinus
Auslegung	Auslegung: A Journal of Philosophy
Austl J Phil	Australasian Journal of Philosophy
Behavior Phil	Behavior and Philosophy (formerly Behaviorism)
Behaviorism	Behaviorism (see Behavior Phil)
Berkeley News	Berkeley Newsletter
Between Species	Between the Species: A Journal of Ethics
Bigaku	Bigaku: The Japanese Journal of Aesthetics
Bijdragen	Bijdragen, Tijdschrift voor Filosofie en Theologie
Bioethics	Bioethics
Bioethics Quart	Bioethics Quarterly (see J Med Human)
Biol Phil	Biology & Philosophy
Boll Centro Stud Vichianl	Bollettino del Centro di Studi Vichiani
Boston Col Stud Phil*	Boston College Studies in Philosophy
Boundary 2*	Boundary 2: An International Journal of Literature and Culture
Brahmavadin*	Brahmavadin
Bridges	Bridges: An Interdisciplinary Journal of Theology, Philosophy, History, and Science
Brit J Aes	The British Journal of Aesthetics
Brit J Hist Phil	British Journal for the History of Philosophy
Brit J Phil Sci	British Journal for the Philosophy of Science
Bull Hegel Soc Gt Brit	Bulletin of the Hegel Society of Great Britain
Bull Santayana Soc	Overheard in Seville: Bulletin of the Santayana Society

Estud Filosof*	Estudios Filosóficos
Ethics	Ethics: An International Journal of Social, Political, and Legal Philosophy
Ethics Animals*	Ethics and Animals
Ethics Behavior	Ethics and Behavior
Ethics Med	Ethics and Medicine: An International Christian Perspective on Bioethics
Ethos*	Ethos: Revista de Filosofía Practica
Etud Phil*	Les Études Philosophiques
Etudes*	Etudes
Etyka	Etyka
Euridice	Eurídice
Euro J Phil	European Journal of Philosophy
Euthanasia Rev*	The Euthanasia Review
Exer Pat*	Exercices de la Patience
Exist Psychiat*	Existential Psychiatry
Explor Knowl	Explorations in Knowledge
Facta Univ	Facta Universitatis
Faith Phil	Faith and Philosophy: Journal of the Society of Christian Philosophers
Fem Stud	Feminist Studies
Fichte-Studien	Fichte-Studien
Filosofia	Filosofia
Filosof Cas	Filosofický Časopis
Filozof Istraz	Filozofska Istraživanja
Filozof Vestnik	Filozofski Vestnik
Filozofia	Filozofia
Found Lang	Foundations of Language (see Ling Phil)
Fran Stud	Franciscan Studies
Franciscanum	Franciscanum: Revista de las Ciencias del Espiritu
Free Inq	Free Inquiry
Frei Z Phil Theol	Freiburger Zeitschrift für Philosophie und Theologie
Fronesis	Fronesis: Revista de Filosofía Jurídica, Social y Política
Futurum*	Futurum
G Crit Filosof Ital	Giornale Critico della Filosofia Italiana
G Metaf	Giornale di Metafisica
Gnosis	Gnosis: A Journal of Philosophic Interest
Grad Fac Phil J	Graduate Faculty Philosophy Journal
Grazer Phil Stud	Grazer Philosophische Studien
Gregorianum	Gregorianum
Grund Kybor Geist*	Grundlagenstudien aus Kybernetik und Geisteswissenschaft
Harvard Rev Phil	The Harvard Review of Philosophy
Hastings Center Rep	Hastings Center Report (formerly Hastings Center Studies)
Hastings Center Stud	Hastings Center Studies (see Hastings Center Rep)
Hegel-Jrbh*	Hegel-Jahrbuch
Heidegger Stud	Heidegger Studies
Hermathena	Hermathena: A Dublin University Review
Heythrop J	The Heythrop Journal: A Quarterly Review of Philosophy and Theology
Hibbert J*	The Hibbert Journal: A Quarterly Review of Religion, Theology, and Philosophy
Hist Euro Ideas	History of European Ideas
Hist Human Sci	History of the Human Sciences
Hist Phil Life Sci	History and Philosophy of the Life Sciences
Hist Phil Log	History and Philosophy of Logic
Hist Phil Quart	History of Philosophy Quarterly
Hist Polit Thought	History of Political Thought
Hist Theor	History and Theory: Studies in the Philosophy of History
Hobbes Stud	Hobbes Studies
Horiz Phil	Horizons Philosophiques
Human Context*	The Human Context
Human Soc*	Humanities in Society
Human Stud	Human Studies: A Journal for Philosophy and the Social Sciences
Humanist	The Humanist: A Magazine of Critical Inquiry and Social Concern
Humanitas*	Humanitas: Journal of the Institute of Formative Spirituality
Humanitas (Mexico)*	Humanitas: Anuario del Centro de Estudios Humanisticos
Hume Stud	Hume Studies
Husserl Stud	Husserl Studies
Hypatia	Hypatia: A Journal of Feminist Philosophy
Ideal Stud	Idealistic Studies: An Interdisciplinary Journal of Philosophy
Ideas Valores	Ideas y Valores: Revista Colombiana de Filosofía
Il Protag	Il Protagora
Independ J Phil	Independent Journal of Philosophy
Indian J Phil*	Indian Journal of Philosophy
Indian Phil Cult*	Indian Philosophy and Culture
Indian Phil Quart	Indian Philosophical Quarterly: Journal of the Department of Philosophy - University of Poona
Inform Log	Informal Logic
Inquiry	Inquiry: An Interdisciplinary Journal of Philosophy
Inquiry (USA)	Inquiry: Critical Thinking Across the Disciplines
Int Dialog Z*	Internationale Dialog Zeitschrift
Int J Applied Phil	The International Journal of Applied Philosophy (formerly Applied Philosophy)
Int J Moral Soc Stud	International Journal of Moral and Social Studies
Int J Phil Relig	International Journal for Philosophy of Religion
Int J Phil Stud	International Journal of Philosophical Studies (formerly Philosophical Studies)
Int Log Rev	International Logic Review

Key to Abbreviations

List of Periodicals Indexed

(frequency of publication given in parentheses)

The Acorn: Journal of the Gandhl-King Society. No ISSN. (bi-ann) Box CB, St.Bonaventure University, St.Bonaventure, NY 14778, USA

Acta Analytica. ISSN 0353-5150 (bi-ann) Verlag Dr. Josef H. Röll, Postfach 9, D-97335 Dettelbach, Germany

Acta Philosophica: Ateno Romano della Santa Croce. ISSN 1121-2179. (3 times per yr) Armando Armando s.r.1., Viale Trastevere, 236, 00153 Rome, Italy

Acta Philosophica Fennica. ISSN 0355-1792. (irr) Academic Bookstore, Keskuskatu 1, 00100 Helsinki, Finland

Aesthetics. ISSN 0289-0895. (bi-enn) Japanese Society for Aesthetics, c/o Institute of Aesthetics, Faculty of Letters, University of Tokyo, Hongo 7-3-1, Bunkyo-ku, Tokyo 113, Japan

Agora: Papeles de Filosofía. ISSN 0211-6642. (bi-ann) Servicio de Publicaciones, Universidad de Santiago de Compostela, Santiago de Compostela 15701, Spain

Agriculture and Human Values. ISSN 0889-048X. (q) Managing Editor, 370 ASB, University of Florida, Gainesville, FL 32611, USA

Aitia: Philosophy-Humanities Magazine. ISSN 0731-5880. (3 times per yr) Knapp Hall 15, SUNY at Farmingdale, Farmingdale, NY 11735, USA

Algemeen Nederlands Tijdschrift voor Wijsbegeerte. ISSN 0002-5275. (q) Van Gorcum, Postbus 43, 9400 AA Assen, The Netherlands

American Catholic Philosophical Quarterly. ISSN 1051-3558. (q) American Catholic Philosophical Assoc., The Catholic University of America, Washington, DC 20064, USA

American Journal of Philology. ISSN 0002-9475. (q) The Johns Hopkins University Press, 701 West 40th Street, Suite 275, Baltimore, MD 21211, USA

American Journal of Theology & Philosophy. ISSN 0194-3448. (3 times per yr) W. Creighton Peden, Editor, Dept. of Philosophy, Augusta College, Augusta, GA 30910, USA

American Philosophical Quarterly. ISSN 0003-0481. (q) Philosophy Documentation Center, Bowling Green State University, Bowling Green, OH 43403-0189, USA

Anales de la Cátedra Francisco Suárez. ISSN 0008-7750. (ann) Departamento de Filosofía del Derecho, Moral y Política, Facultad de Derecho, Plaza de la Universidad, 3, 18071 Granada, Spain

Anales del Seminario de Historia de la Filosofía. ISSN 0211-2337. (ann) Editorial Complutense, C/ Donoso Cortés, 65, E-28015 Madrid, Spain

Anales del Seminario de Metafísica. ISSN 0580-8650. (ann) Editor, Universidad Complutense, Noviciado 3, 28015 Madrid, Spain

Análisis Filosófico. ISSN 0326-1301. (bi-ann) Bulnes 642, 1176 Buenos Aires, Argentina

Analogía Filosófica: Revista de Filsofía. ISSN 0188-896X (bi-ann) Dr. Gabriel Chico O.P., Apartado 23-161; Xochimilco, 16000 México D.F., Mexico

Analysis. ISSN 0003-2638. (q) Blackwell Publishers, 108 Cowley Road, Oxford OX4 1JF, United Kingdom (or 238 Main St., Cambridge, MA 02142, USA)

Ancient Philosophy. ISSN 0740-2007. (bi-ann) Prof. Ronald Polansky, Duquesne University, Pittsburgh, PA 15282, USA

Annales Universitatis Mariae Curie-Sklodowskiej, Sectio 1/Philosophia-Sociologia. ISSN 0137-2025. (ann) Biuro Wydawnictw, Uniwersytet Marii Curie-Sklodowskiej, Pl. Marii Curie-Sklodowskiej, 5, 20-031 Lublin, Poland

Annali della Facolta di Lettere e Filosofia. No ISSN. Pubblicazioni dell'Università di Studi di Bari, Palazzo Ateneo, 70100 Bari, Italy

Annals of Pure and Applied Logic. ISSN 0168-0072. (18 times per yr) Elsevier Science Publishers, Box 211, 1000 AE Amsterdam, The Netherlands

The Annual of the Society of Christian Ethics. ISSN 0732-4928. (ann) Georgetown University Press, P.O. Box 4866, Hampden Station, Baltimore, MD 21211, USA

Antioch Review. ISSN 0003-5769. (q) P.O. Box 148, Yellow Springs, OH 45387, USA

Anuario Filosófico. ISSN 0066-5215. Servicio de Publicaciones de la Universidad de Navarra, S.A. Edificio Bibliotecas, Campus Universitario, 31080 Pamplona, Spain

Apeiron: A Journal for Ancient Philosophy and Science. ISSN 0003-6390. (q) Academic Printing and Publishing, P.O. Box 4834, Edmonton, Alberta T6E 5G7, Canada

Aquinas: Rivista Internazionale de Filosofia. ISSN 0003-7362. (3 times per yr) Pontificia Universita Lateranense, Piazza S. Giovanni in Laterano 4, 00120 Città del Vaticano, Vatican City State

Archiv für Geschichte der Philosophie. ISSN 0003-9101. (3 times per yr) Walter de Gruyter, Genthiner Str. 13, D-10785 Berlin, Germany

Archiv für Rechts- und Sozialphilosophie. ISSN 0001-2343. (q) Franz Steiner Verlag Wiesbaden GmbH, Postfach 101526, D-70014 Stuttgart, Germany

Archives de Philosophie. ISSN 0003-9632. 72 rue des Saints-Pères, 75007 Paris, France

Archivio di Storia della Cultura. (ann) Morano Editore S.P.A., Vico S. Domenico Maggiore, 9-80134 Naples, Italy

Areté: Revista de Filosofía. ISSN 1016-913X. (bi-ann) Pontificia Universidad Católica del Perú, Fondo Editorial, Apartado 1761, Lima-100, Peru

Argumentation. ISSN 0920-427X. (q) Kluwer Academic Publishers, P.O. Box 322, 3300 AH Dordrecht, The Netherlands (or P.O.Box 358, Accord Station, Hingham, MA 02018-0358, USA)

Arion: A Journal of Humanities and the Classics. ISSN 0095-5809. (3 times per yr) 745 Commonwealth Avenue, Nr.435, Boston, MA 02215, USA

The Aristotelian Society: Supplementary Volume. ISSN 0309-7013. (ann) Members: The Aristotelian Society, Dept. of Philosophy, Birkbeck College, Malet Street, London WC1E 7HX, United Kingdom. Non- members: Blackwell Publishers, 108 Cowley Road, Oxford OX4 1JF, United Kingdom (or 238 Main St., Cambridge, MA 02142, USA)

The Asian Journal of Philosophy. No ISSN. (bi-ann) Prof. Tran Van Doan, Dept. of Philosophy, National Taiwan University, Roosevelt Road, Sec. 4, 10764 Taipei, Taiwan

Asian Philosophy. ISSN 0955-2367 (bi-ann) Carfax Publishing Co., P.O. Box 25, Abingdon, Oxfordshire OX14 3UE, United Kingdom

Augustinian Studies. ISSN 0094-5323. (ann) Tolentine Hall, P.O. Box 98, Villanova University, Villanova, PA 19085, USA

Augustinus. ISSN 0004-802X. (q) P. José Oroz Reta, General Dávila 5, Madrid 28003, Spain

Auslegung: A Journal of Philosophy. ISSN 0733-4311. (bi-ann) Editors, Dept. of Philosophy, University of Kansas, Lawrence, KS 66045, USA

Australasian Journal of Philosophy. ISSN 0004-8402. (q) Robert Young, Editor, Department of Philosophy, La Trobe University, Bundoora, Victoria 3083, Australia

Behavior and Philosophy. No ISSN. (bi-ann) Boyd Printing, 49 Sheridan Avenue, Albany, NY 12210, USA

Berkeley Newsletter. ISSN 0332-026X. (ann) The Editor, Dept. of Philosophy, Trinity College, Dublin 2, Ireland

Between the Species: A Journal of Ethics. No ISSN. (q) Schweitzer Center, San Francisco Bay Institute, P.O. Box 254, Berkeley, CA 94701, USA

Bigaku: The Japanese Journal of Aesthetics. ISSN 0520-0962. (q) The Japanese Society for Aesthetics, c/o Faculty of Letters, University of Tokyo, Bunkyo-Ku, Tokyo, Japan

Bijdragen, Tijdschrift voor Filosofie en Theologie. ISSN 0006-2278. (q) Administratie Bijdragen, Krips Repro B.V., Postbus 106, 7940 AC Meppel, The Netherlands

Bioethics. ISSN 0269-9702. (q) Blackwell Publishers, 108 Cowley Road, Oxford OX4 1JF, United Kingdom (or 238 Main St., Cambridge, MA 02142, USA)

Biology & Philosophy. ISSN 0169-3867. (q) Kluwer Academic Publishers, P.O. Box 322, 3300 AH Dordrecht, The Netherlands (or P.O.Box 358, Accord Station, Hingham, MA 02018-0358, USA)

Bollettino del Centro di Studi Vichiani. ISSN 0392-7334. (ann) Bibliopolis, Edizioni di Filosofia e Scienze, SpA, Via Arangio Ruiz 83, 80122 Naples, Italy

Bridges: An Interdisciplinary Journal of Theology, Philosophy, History, and Science. ISSN 1042-2234. (bi-ann) Robert S. Frey, Editor, 5702 Yellow Rose Court, Columbia, MD 21045, USA

The British Journal of Aesthetics. ISSN 0007-0904. (q) Oxford University Press, Pinkhill House, Southfield Road, Eynsham, Oxford OX8 1JJ, United Kingdom

British Journal for the History of Philosophy. ISSN 0960-8788. (bi-ann) Thoemmes Press, 11 Great George Street, Bristol, BS1 5RR, United Kingdom

British Journal for the Philosophy of Science. ISSN 0007-0882. (q) Oxford University Press, Pinkhill House, Southfield Road, Eynsham, Oxford OX8 1JJ, United Kingdom

Bulletin de la Société Française de Philosophie. ISSN 0037-9352. (q) 12 rue Colbert, 75002 Paris, France

Bulletin of the Hegel Society of Great Britain. ISSN 0263-5232. (bi-ann) H. Williams, Dept. of International Politics, University College of Wales, Penglais Aberystwyth, Dyfed SY23 3DB, United Kingdom

Bulletin of the Section of Logic. ISSN 0138-0680. (q) Managing Editor, Grzegorz Malinowski, 8 Marca 8, 90-365 Lodź, Poland

Bulletin of the Santayana Society. (ann) Santayana Edition, Dept. of Philosophy, Texas A & M University, College Station, TX 77843-4237, USA

The Bulletin of Symbolic Logic. ISSN 1079-8986. (q) Assoc. of Symbolic Logic, Journals Division UIP, 1325 South Oak St., Champaign, IL 61820, USA

Business Ethics Quarterly. ISSN 1052-150X. (q) Philosophy Documentation Center, Bowling Green State University, Bowling Green, OH 43403-0189, USA

Business & Professional Ethics Journal. ISSN 0277-2027. (q) Center for Applied Philosophy, 243 Dauer Hall, University of Florida, Gainesville, FL 32611, USA

Cadernos de História e Filosofia da Ciéncia. ISSN 0101-3424. (bi-ann) Editor, Centro de Lógica-Unicamp, C.P. 6133, 13.081 Campinas, São Paulo, Brazil

Cambridge Quarterly of Healthcare Ethics. ISSN 0963-1801. (q) Cambridge University Press, The Edinburgh Building, Shaftesbury Road, Cambridge CB2 2RU, United Kingdom (or 40 West 20th Street, New York, NY 10011-4211, USA)

Canadian Journal of Philosophy. ISSN 0045-5091. (q) University of Calgary Press, 2500 University Drive NW, Calgary, Alberta T2N 1N4, Canada

Canadian Philosophical Reviews. ISSN 0228-491X. (m) Academic Printing and Publishing, Box 4834, Edmonton, Alberta T6E 5G7, Canada

Il Cannocchiale: Rivista di Studi Filosofici. No ISSN. (3 times per yr) Il Cannocchiale. C.P. 12014, Roma 00100, Italy

Chinese Studies in Philosophy. ISSN 0023-8627. (q) M.E. Sharpe, 80 Business Park Drive, Armonk, NY 10504, USA

Christian Bioethics. ISSN 1380-3603. (3 times per yr) Swets and Zeitlinger, P.O.Box 825, 2160 SZ Lisse, The Netherlands

Clio: A Journal of Literature, History, and the Philosophy of History. ISSN 0884-2043. (q) Indiana University-Purdue University, Fort Wayne, IN 46805, USA

Communication and Cognition: An Interdisciplinary Quartrly Journal. ISSN 0378-0880. (q) Blandijnberg 2, B-9000 Ghent, Belgium

Communication and Cognition—Artifical Intelligence (CC-AI): The Journal for the Integrated Study of Artificial Intelligence, Cognitive Science and Applied Epistemology. ISSN 0773-4182. (q) Blandijnberg 2, B-9000 Ghent, Belgium

Conceptus: Zeitschrift für Philosophie. ISSN 0010-5155. (3 times per yr) Verband der wissenschaftlichen Gesellschaften Oesterreichs, Lindengasse 37, A-1070 Vienna, Austria

Conference: A Journal of Philosophy and Theory. ISSN 1072-1894 (bi-ann) Conference, c/o Dept. of Philosophy, 139 Collins Hall, Fordham University, Bronx, NY 10458, USA

Constellations: An International Journal of Critical and Democratic Theory. ISSN 0260-8448. (3 times per yr) Blackwell Publishers, 108 Cowley Road, Oxford OX4 1JF, United Kingdom (or 238 Main St., Cambridge, MA 02142, USA)

Contemporary Philosophy. No ISSN. (bi-m) P.O. Box 1373, Boulder, CO 80306, USA

Convivium: Revista de Filosofia. No ISSN. (3 times per yr) Redacció Administració, Dept. de Filosofia Teorètica i Pràtica, Facultad de Filosofia, Universitat de Barcelona, Carrer Baldiri Reixac, 1, 08028 Barcelona, Spain

Criminal Justice Ethics. ISSN 0731-129X. (bi-ann) The Institute for Criminal Justice Ethics, CUNY, John Jay College of Criminal Justice, 899 Tenth Avenue, New York, NY 10019, USA

Crítica: Revista Hispanoamericana de Filosofía. ISSN 0011-1503. (3 times per yr) Apartado 70-447, 04510 México, DF, Mexico

Critical Inquiry. ISSN 0093-1896. (q) The University of Chicago, Wieboldt Hall 202, 1050 East 59th Street, Chicago, IL 60637, USA

Critical Review: An Interdisciplinary Journal. ISSN 0891-3811. (q) P.O. Box 14528, Dept. 26A, Chicago, IL 60614, USA

Cuadernos de Etica. ISSN 0326-9523. (bi-ann) Asociación Argentina de Investigación Etica, Tte. Gral. J. D. Perón 2395-3° "G", 1040 Buenos Aires, Argentina

Cuadernos de Filosofía. ISSN 0590-1901. (bi-ann) Prof. Margarita Costa, Editor, Instituto de Filosofía, 25 de Mayo 217, 1002 Buenos Aires, Argentina

Cuadernos Sobre Vico. ISSN 1130-7498 (ann) Secretariado de Publicaciones de la Universidad de Sevilla, c/ Valparaíso, 5, E-41003 Sevilla, Spain

Daimon, Revista de Filosofía. ISSN 1130-0507. (bi-ann) Secretario de Daimon, Departamento de Filosofía y Lógica, Universidad de Murcia, E-30071 Espinardo-Murcia, Spain

Danish Yearbook of Philosophy. ISSN 0070-2749. (ann) Museum Tusculanum Press, Njalsgade 94, DK 2300 Copenhagen S, Denmark

Darshana International. No ISSN. Anurag Atreya, Managing Editor, Moradabad 244 001, India

Das Argument: Zeitschrift für Philosophie und Sozialwissenschaften. ISSN 0004-1157. (bi-m) Argument-Verlag, Rentzelstr. 1, D-20146 Hamburg, Germany

De Philosophia. ISSN 0228-412X. Editor, Dept. of Philosophy, University of Ottawa, Ottawa, Ontario K1N 6N5, Canada

Deutsche Zeitschrift für Philosophie. ISSN 0012-1045. (m) Akademie Verlag GmbH, Mühlenstr. 33-34, D-13187 Berlin, Germany

Dialectica: International Journal of Philosophy of Knowledge. ISSN 0012-2017. (q) P.O. Box 5907, CH-3001 Bern, Switzerland

Diálogo Filosófico. ISSN 0213-1196. (3 times per yr) Apartado 121, 28770 Colmenar Viejo, Madrid, Spain

Diálogos: Revista del Departamento de Filsofía Universidad de Puerto Rico. ISSN 0012-2122. (bi-ann) Box 21572, UPR Station, Río Piedras, PR 00931, USA

Dialogue: Journal of Phi Sigma Tau. ISSN 0012-2246. (bi-ann) Phi Sigma Tau, Dept. of Philosophy, Marquette University, Milwaukee, WI 53233, USA

Dialogue: Canadian Philosophical Review. ISSN 0012-2173. (q) Prof. Steven Davis, Editor, Dept. of Philosophy, Simon Fraser University, Burnaby, British Columbia V5A 1S6, Canada

Dialogue and Humanism: The Universalist Journal. ISSN 0324-8275. (q) Institute of Philosophy, Warsaw University, Krakowskie Przedmiescie 3, 00-047 Warsaw, Poland

Diánoia. ISSN 0185-2450. (ann) Instituto de Investigaciones Filosóficas, Dirección del Anuario de Filosofía, Circuito Mtro. Mario de la Cueva, Ciudad de la Investigación en Humanidades, Coyoacán 04510, México, DF, Mexico

Diogenes. ISSN 0392-1921. (q) Berg Publishers Ltd., 150 Cowley Road, Oxford OX4 1JJ, United Kingdom

Dionysius. ISSN 0705-1085. (ann) Dept. of Classics, Dalhousie University, Halifax, Nova Scotia B3H 3J5, Canada

Diotima: Review of Philosophical Research. (ann) Hellenic Society for Philosophical Studies, 40 Hypsilantou Street, Athens 11521, Greece

Discurso: Revista do Departamento de Filosofia. ISSN 0103-328X. (ann) Departamento de Filosofia-FFLCH, Universidade de São Paulo, 05508 São Paulo, Brazil

Economics and Philosophy. ISSN 0266-2671. (bi-ann) Cambridge University Press, The Edinburgh Building, Shaftesbury Road, Cambridge CB2 2RU, United Kingdom (or 40 West 20th Street, New York, NY 10011-4211, USA)

Educação e Filosofia. ISSN 0102-6801. (bi-ann) Revista "Educação e Filosofia", Universidade Federal de Uberlândia, Av. Universitaria, 155 C.P. 593, Campus Santa Monica, 38.400 Uberlândia MG, Brazil

Educational Philosophy and Theory. ISSN 0013-1857. (bi-ann) D.N. Aspin, Editor, Faculty of Education, Monash University, Clayton, Victoria 3168, Australia

Educational Studies. ISSN 0013-1946. (q) Richard LaBrecque, Editor, 131 Taylor Education Building, University of Kentucky, Lexington, KY 40506-0001, USA

Educational Theory. ISSN 0013-2004. (q) Education Building, University of Illinois, 1310 South 6th Street, Champaign, IL 61820, USA

Eidos: The Canadian Graduate Journal of Philosophy. ISSN 0707-2287. (bi-ann) Editors, Dept. of Philosophy, University of Waterloo, Waterloo, Ontario N2L 3G1, Canada

El Basilisco: Revista de Filosofía, Ciencias Humanas, Teoría de la Ciencia y de la Cultura. ISSN 0210-0088. (q) Apartado 360, 33080 Oviedo, Spain

Environmental Ethics: An Interdisciplinary Journal Dedicated to the Philosophical Aspects of Environmental Problems. ISSN 0163-4275. (q) Dept. of Philosophy, The University of North Texas, P.O. Box 13496, Denton, TX 76203-3496, USA

Environmental Values. ISSN 0963-2719. (q) The White Horse Press, 10 High Street, Knapwell, Cambridge CB3 8NR, United Kingdom

Epistemologia: Revista italiana di Filosofia della Scienza. (bi-ann) Tilgher-Genova s.a.s., via Assarotti 52, 16122 Genova, Italy

Epoche. No ISSN. (bi-ann) c/o Philosophy Dept., Jesse Knight Humanities Building, Brigham Young University, Provo, Utah 84602-6279, USA

Erkenntnis: An International Journal of Analytic Philosophy. ISSN 0165-0106. (6 times per yr) Kluwer Academic Publishers, P.O. Box 322, 3300 AH Dordrecht, The Netherlands (or P.O.Box 358, Accord Station, Hingham, MA 02018-0358, USA)

Escritos de Filosofía. ISSN 0325-4933. (ann) Centro de Estudios Filosoficos, Academia Nacional de Ciencias, Av. Alvear 1711, 3er. Piso, 1014 Buenos Aires, Argentina

Espíritu. ISSN 0014-0716. (ann) Durán y Bas Nr 9, Apartado 1382, 08080 Barcelona, Spain

Estetika. ISSN 0014-1291. (q) Helena Lorenzová, Editor, Institute of History & Theory of Art, Czech Academy of Sciences, Husova 4, 110 00 Praha 1, Czech Republic

Ethics: An International Journal of Social, Political, and Legal Philosophy. ISSN 0014-1704. (q) University of Chicago Press, P.O. Box 37005, Chicago, IL 60637, USA

Ethics and Behavior. ISSN 1050-8422. (q) Journal Subscription Dept., LEA, 365 Broadway, Hillsdale, NJ 07642, USA

Ethics and Medicine: An International Christian Perspective on Bioethics. ISSN 0226-688X. (3 times per yr) Paternoster Periodicals, P.O. Box 11127, Birmingham, AL 35202, USA

Etyka. ISSN 0014-2263. (bi-ann) Instytut Filozofii i Socjologii PAN, Nowy Swiat 72, pok 243, 00-330, Warsaw, Poland

Eurídice. ISSN 1131-6640. (ann) Secretario-Eurídice, Servicio de Publicaciones, UNED-Navarre, Apdo.409, E-31080 Pamplona (Navarre), Spain

European Journal of Philosophy. ISSN 0966-8373. (3 times per yr) Blackwell Publishers, 108 Cowley Road, Oxford OX4 1JF, United Kingdom (or 238 Main St., Cambridge, MA 02142, USA)

Explorations in Knowledge. ISSN 0261-1376. (bi-ann) David Lamb, Sombourne Press, 294 Leigh Road, Chandlers Ford, Eastleigh, Hants S05 3AU, United Kingdom

Facta Universitatis. ISSN 0354-4648. (ann) Facta Universitatis, University of Niš, TRG Bratsva i Jedinstva 2, 18000 Niš, Yugoslavia

Faith and Philosophy: Journal of the Society of Christian Philosophers. ISSN 0739-7046. (q) Michael Peterson, Managing Editor, Asbury College, Wilmore, KY 40390, USA

Feminist Studies. ISSN 0046-3663. (3 times per yr) Claire G. Moses, Women's Studies Program, University of Maryland, College Park, MD 20742, USA

Fichte-Studien. ISSN 0925-0166. (ann) Mr. Eric Van Broekhuizen, Editions Rodopi B. V., Keizersgracht 302-304, 1016 EX Amsterdam-Holland, The Netherlands

Filosofia. ISSN 0015-1823. (q) Piazzo Statuto 26, 10144 Turin, Italy

Filozofia. ISSN 0046-385X. (bi-m) Frantisek Novosád, Editor, Klemensova 19, 813 64 Bratislava, Slovakia

Filozofický Časopis. ISSN 0015-1831. (bi-m) Petr Horák, Editor, Institute of Philosophy & Sociology, Czech Academy of Sciences, Jilská 1, 110 00 Praha 1, Czech Republic

Filozofska Istraživanja. ISSN 0351-4706. Editor, Filozofski Fakultet, D. Salaja 3, p.p. 171, 41000 Zagreb, Croatia

Filozofski Vestnik. ISSN 0353-4510. (bi-ann) Filosofski Vestnik, ZRC SAZU, Gosposka ul. 13, SL-61000 Ljubljana, Slovenia

Franciscan Studies. ISSN 0080-5459. (ann) St. Bonaventure University, St. Bonaventure, NY 14778, USA

Franciscanum: Revista de las Ciencias del Espiritu. ISSN 0120-1468. (3 times per yr) Universidad de San Buenaventura, Calle 73 No. 10-45, Apartado Aéreo No. 52312, Bogota, Colombia

Free Inquiry. ISSN 0272-0701. (q) Paul Kurtz, Editor, Box 5, Central Park Station, Buffalo, NY 14215, USA

Freiburger Zeitschrift für Philosophie und Theologie. ISSN 0016-0725. (bi-ann) Editions St.-Paul, Perolles 42, CH-1700 Fribourg, Switzerland

Fronesis: Revista de Filosofía Jurídica, Social y Política. ISSN 1315-6268. Instituto de Filosofía del Recho "Dr. J. M. Delgado Ocando", Av. Guajira, Ciudad Universitaria "Dr. Antonio Borjas Romero", Facultad de Ciencias Jurídicas y Políticas, Universidad del Zulia, Maricaibo 4011, Venezuela

Giornale Critico della Filosofia Italiana. ISSN 0017-0089. (q) LICOSA, SpA, Subscription Dept., Via B. Fortini 120/10, 50125 Florence, Italy

Giornale di Metafisica. (3 times per yr) Tilgher-Genova s.a.s., via Assarotti 52, 16122 Genova, Italy

Gnosis: A Journal of Philosophic Interest. ISSN 0316-618X. (ann) Editor, Dept. of Philosophy, Concordia University, 1455 de Maisonneuve Boulevard West, Montreal, Québec H3G 1M8, Canada

Graduate Faculty Philosophy Journal. ISSN 0093-4240. (bi-ann) Editor, Dept. of Philosophy, New School for Social Research, 65 Fifth Avenue, New York, NY 10003, USA

Grazer Philosophische Studien. ISSN 0165-9227. (ann) Humanities Press International, Atlantic Highlands, NJ 07716, USA

Gregorianum. ISSN 0017-4114. (q) 4 Piazza della Pilotta, 1-00187 Rome, Italy

The Harvard Review of Philosophy. ISSN 1062-6239. (ann) Dept. of Philosophy, Harvard University, Emerson Hall, Cambridge, MA 02138, USA

Hastings Center Report. ISSN 0093-0334. (bi-m) The Hastings Center, 255 Elm Road, Briarcliff Manor, NY 10510, USA

Heidegger Studies. ISSN 0885-4580 (ann) Duncker & Humblot GmbH, Postfach 41 03 29, D-12113 Berlin, Germany

Hermathena: A Dublin University Review. ISSN 0018-0750. (bi-ann) The Editor, Trinity College, Dublin 2, Ireland

The Heythrop Journal: A Quarterly Review of Philosophy and Theology. ISSN 0018-1196. (q) The Manager, 11 Cavendish Square, London W1M 0AN, United Kingdom

History and Philosophy of Logic. ISSN 0144-5340. (bi-ann) Taylor & Francis, 4 John Street, London WC1N 2ET, United Kingdom

History and Philosophy of the Life Sciences. ISSN 0391-9114. (bi-ann) Taylor & Francis, 1900 Frost Road, Suite 101, Bristol, PA 19007, USA (or Rankine Road, Basingstoke, Hants RG24 0PR, United Kingdom)

History and Theory: Studies in the Philosophy of History. ISSN 0018-2656. (q) Julia Perkins, History and Theory, Wesleyan Station, Middletown, CT 06457, USA

History of European Ideas. ISSN 0191-6599. (bi-m) Pergamon Press, Headington Hill Hall, Oxford OX3 0BW, United Kingdom

History of Philosophy Quarterly. ISSN 0740-0675. (q) Philosophy Documentation Center, Bowling Green State University, Bowling Green, OH 43403-0189, USA

History of Political Thought. ISSN 0143-781X. (q) Imprint Academic, 32 Haldon Road, Exeter EX4 4DZ, United Kingdom

History of the Human Sciences. ISSN 0952-6951. (q) Sage Publications, LTD, 6 Bonhill Street, London, EC2A 4PU, United Kingdom

Hobbes Studies. (ann) Van Gorcum, P.O. Box 43, 9400 AA Assen, The Netherlands

Horizons Philosophiques. ISSN 0709-4469. (bi-ann) Service de l'Edition, College Edouard-Montpetit, 945 chemin Chambly, Longueuil, Québec J4H 3M6, Canada

Human Studies: A Journal for Philosophy and the Social Sciences. ISSN 0163-8548. (q) Martinus Nijhoff Publishers, P.O. Box 322, 3300 AH Dordrecht, The Netherlands

The Humanist: A Magazine of Critical Inquiry and Social Concern. ISSN 0018-7399. (bi-m) Frederick Edwords, American Humanist Assoc., 7 Harwood Drive, P.O. Box 1188, Amherst, NY 14226-7188, USA

Hume Studies. ISSN 0319-7336. (bi-ann) Editor, Dept. of Philosophy, University of Western Ontario, London, Ontario N6A 3K7, Canada

Husserl Studies. ISSN 0167-9848. (q) Kluwer Academic Publishers, P.O. Box 322, 3300 AH Dordrecht, The Netherlands (or P.O.Box 358, Accord Station, Hingham, MA 02018-0358, USA)

Hypatia: A Journal of Feminist Philosophy. ISSN 0887-5367. (3 times per yr) Linda Lopez McAlister, Editor, University of South Florida, SOC 107, Tampa, FL 33620-8100, USA

Idealistic Studies: An Interdisciplinary Journal of Philosophy. ISSN 0046-8541. (3 times per yr) Walter Wright, Editor, Dept. of Philosophy, Clark University, Worcester, MA 01610, USA

Ideas y Valores: Revista Colombiana de Filosofía. ISSN 0120-0062. (3 times per yr) Departamento de Filosofía, Universidad Nacional de Colombia, Ciudad Universitaria, Bogatá, Colombia

Il Protagora. (bi-ann) via A. Gidiuli 19, 73100 Lecce, Italy

The Independent Journal of Philosophy. ISSN 0378-4789. (irr) George Elliott Tucker, Editor, 47 Van Winkle Street, Boston, MA 02124, USA

Indian Philosophical Quarterly. ISSN 0376-415X. (q) The Editor, Dept. of Philosophy, University of Poona, Pune 411 007, India

Informal Logic. ISSN 0824-2577. (3 times per yr) Assistant to the Editors, Dept. of Philosophy, University of Windsor, Windsor, Ontario N9B 3P4, Canada

Inquiry: An Interdisciplinary Journal of Philosophy. ISSN 0020-174X. (q) Universitetsforlaget, P.O. Box 2959, Tøyen, 0608 Oslo 6, Norway

Inquiry: Critical Thinking Across the Disciplines. No ISSN. (q) Institute for Critical Thinking, Montclair State University, Upper Montclair, NJ 07043, USA

International Journal for Philosophy of Religion. ISSN 0020-7047. (q) Kluwer Academic Publishers, P.O. Box 322, 3300 AH Dordrecht, The Netherlands (or P.O.Box 358, Accord Station, Hingham, MA 02018-0358, USA)

International Journal of Applied Philosophy. ISSN 0739-098X. (bi-ann) Indian River Community College, Fort Pierce, FL 34981-5599, USA

International Journal of Moral and Social Studies. ISSN 0267-9655. (3 times per yr) Journals, One Harewood Row, London NW1 6SE, United Kingdom

International Journal of Philosophical Studies. ISSN 0967-2559. (bi-ann) Professor Dermot Moran, Editor, Dept. of Philosophy, University College Dublin, Dublin 4, Ireland

International Logic Review. (bi-ann) Editor, via Belmeloro 3, 40126 Bologna, Italy

International Philosophical Quarterly. ISSN 0019-0365. (q) Vincent Potter, S.J., Fordham University, Bronx, NY 10458, USA

International Studies in Philosophy. ISSN 0270-5664. (3 times per yr) Scholars Press, P.O. Box 15288, Atlanta, GA 30333, USA

International Studies in the Philosophy of Science. ISSN 0269-8595. (3 times per yr) Carfax Publishing Co., P.O. Box 25, Abingdon, Oxfordshire OX14 3UE, United Kingdom

Interpretation: A Journal of Political Philosophy. ISSN 0020-9635. (3 times per yr) Hilail Gildin, Editor-in-Chief, King Hall 101, Queens College, Flushing, NY 11367-0904, USA

Irish Philosophical Journal. ISSN 0266-9080. (bi-ann) Dr. Bernard Cullen, Editor, Dept. of Scholastic Philosophy, Queen's University, Belfast BT7 1NN, Northern Ireland, United Kingdom

Isegoria: Revista de Filosofía Moral y Política. ISSN 1130-2097. (q) Editorial Anthropos, Apartado 387, 08190 Sant Cugat del Valles, Spain

Itinerari Filosofici: Rivista di Filosofia. ISSN 1121-2772 (3 times per yr) Redazione di Itinerari Filosofici, Via Carlo Crivelli, 20, 20122-Milano, Italy

Iyyun: The Jerusalem Philosophical Quarterly. ISSN 0021-3306. (q) Manager, S.H. Bergman Centre for Philosophical Studies, Hebrew University of Jerusalem, Jerusalem 91905, Israel

Journal for General Philosophy of Science. ISSN 0925-4560. (bi-ann) Kluwer Academic Publishers, P.O. Box 322, 3300 AH Dordrecht, The Netherlands (or P.O.Box 358, Accord Station, Hingham, MA 02018-0358, USA)

Journal for the Theory of Social Behavior. ISSN 0021-8308. (q) Blackwell Publishers, 108 Cowley Road, Oxford OX4 1JF, United Kingdom (or 238 Main St., Cambridge, MA 02142, USA)

The Journal of Aesthetic Education. ISSN 0021-8510. (q) University of Illinois Press, 54 East Gregory Drive, Champaign, IL 61820, USA

The Journal of Aesthetics and Art Criticism. ISSN 0021-8529. (q) Philip A. Alperson, Editor, University of Louisville, Louisville, KY 40292, USA

Journal of Agricultural and Environmental Ethics. ISSN 0893-4282. (bi-ann) Room 039, MacKinnon Building, University of Guelph, Guelph, Ontario N1G 2W1, Canada

Journal of Applied Philosophy. ISSN 0264-3758. (bi-ann) Carfax Publishing Co., P.O. Box 25, Abingdon, Oxfordshire OX14 3UE, United Kingdom

Journal of Business Ethics. ISSN 0167-4544. Kluwer Academic Publishers, P.O. Box 322, 3300 AH Dordrecht, The Netherlands (or P.O.Box 358, Accord Station, Hingham, MA 02018-0358, USA)

Journal of Chinese Philosophy. ISSN 0301-8121. (q) Dialogue Publishing Co., P.O. Box 11071, Honolulu, HI 96828, USA

The Journal of Clinical Ethics. ISSN 1406-7690. (q) 107 East Church Street, Frederick, MD 21701, USA

Journal of Dharma. ISSN 0253-7222. (q) Center for the Study of World Religions, Dharmaram College, Bangalore 560029, India

The Journal of Hellenic Studies. ISSN 0075-4269. (ann) Secretary, The Hellenic Society, 31-34 Gordon Square, London WC1H 0PP, United Kingdom

Journal of Indian Council of Philosophical Research. ISSN 0970-7794. (3 times per yr) Indian Council of Philosophical Research, Rajendra Bhavan (4th floor), 210 Deen Dayal Upadhyaya Marg, New Delhi 110002, India

Journal of Indian Philosophy. ISSN 0022-1791. Kluwer Academic Publishers, P.O. Box 322, 3300 AH Dordrecht, The Netherlands (or P.O.Box 358, Accord Station, Hingham, MA 02018-0358, USA)

Journal of Information Ethics. ISSN 1061-9321. (bi-ann) McFarland and Co., Inc., Publishers, Box 611, Jefferson, NC 28640, USA

The Journal of Libertarian Studies. ISSN 0363-2873. (q) Center for Libertarian Studies, P.O. Box 4091, Burlingame, CA 94011, USA

Journal of Medical Ethics: The Journal of the Institute of Medical Ethics. ISSN 0306-6800. (q) Subscription Manager, Professional and Scientific Publications (JME), Tavistock House East, Tavistock Square, London WC1H 9JR, United Kingdom (or Professional and Scientific Publications, 1172 Commonwealth Avenue, Boston, MA 02134, USA)

The Journal of Medical Humanities. ISSN 1041-3545. (q) Human Sciences Press, 233 Spring Street, New York, NY 10013, USA

The Journal of Medicine and Philosophy. ISSN 0360-5310. (6 times per yr) Kluwer Academic Publishers, P.O. Box 322, 3300 AH Dordrecht, The Netherlands (or P.O.Box 358, Accord Station, Hingham, MA 02018-0358, USA)

The Journal of Mind and Behavior. ISSN 0271-0137. (q) Circulation Dept., P.O. Box 522, Village Station, New York, NY 10014, USA

Journal of Moral Education. ISSN 0305-7240. (3 times per yr) Carfax Publishing Co., P.O. Box 25, Abingdon, Oxfordshire OX14 3UE, United Kingdom

The Journal of Neoplatonic Studies. ISSN 1065-5840. (semi-ann) Dr. James Martin, Editor, Department of Philosophy, St. John's University, Jamaica, NY 11439, USA

The Journal of Non-Classical Logic. (bi-ann) Centro de Lógica-Unicamp, C.P. 6133, 13.081 Campinas, São Paulo, Brazil

Journal of Philosophical Logic. ISSN 0022-3611. Kluwer Academic Publishers, P.O. Box 322, 3300 AH Dordrecht, The Netherlands (or P.O.Box 358, Accord Station, Hingham, MA 02018-0358, USA)

Journal of Philosophical Research. ISSN 1053-8364. (ann) Philosophy Documentation Center, Bowling Green State University, Bowling Green, OH 43403-0189, USA

The Journal of Philosophy. ISSN 0022-362X. (m) 709 Philosophy Hall, Columbia University, New York, NY 10027, USA

Journal of Philosophy of Education. ISSN 0309-8249. (semi-ann) Carfax Publishing Co., P.O. Box 25, Abingdon, Oxfordshire OX14 3UE, United Kingdom

Journal of Pragmatics. ISSN 0378-2166. (bi-m) Elsevier Science Publishers, P.O. Box 211, 1000 AE Amsterdam, The Netherlands

The Journal of Religious Ethics. ISSN 0384-9694. (bi-ann) Scholars Press, P.O. Box 15288, Atlanta, GA 30333, USA

Journal of Semantics. ISSN 0167-5133. (q) Oxford University Press, Pinkhill House, Southfield Road, Eynsham, Oxford OX8 1JJ, United Kingdom

Journal of Social and Biological Structures . ISSN 1040-1750. (q) JAI Press, Inc., 55 Old Post Road-No. 2, Greenwich, CT 06836, USA (For the United Kingdom, Europe, Africa, and Asia: 118 Pentonville, Road, London N1 9JN, United Kingdom)

Journal of Social Philosophy. ISSN 0047-2786. (3 times per yr) Dr. Peter French, Editor, Trinity University, San Antonio, TX 78212, USA

The Journal of Speculative Philosophy. ISSN 0891-625X. (q) Pennsylvania State University Press, Suite C, 820 North University Drive, University Park, PA 16802, USA

The Journal of Symbolic Logic. ISSN 0022-4812. Association for Symbolic Logic, Dept. of Mathematics, University of Illinois, 1409 West Green Street, Urbana, IL 61801, USA

The Journal of the British Society for Phenomenology. ISSN 007-1773. (3 times per yr) Haigh & Hochland, JBSP Department, Precinct Centre, Manchester M13 9QA, United Kingdom

Journal of the History of Ideas. ISSN 0022-5037. (q) Donald R. Kelley, Executive Editor, 442 Rush Rhees Library, University of Rochester, Rochester, NY 14627, USA

Journal of the History of Philosophy. ISSN 0022-5053. (q) Business Office, Dept. of Philosophy, Washington University, St. Louis, MO 63130, USA

Journal of the Philosophy of Sport. ISSN 0094-8705. (ann) Human Kinetics Publishers, Box 5076, Champaign, IL 61820-9971, USA

Journal of Theoretical and Philosophical Psychology. ISSN 1068-8471. (bi-ann) Divisions Service Office, American Psychological Assoc., 750 First Street, NE, Washington, DC 20002-4242, USA

Journal of Thought. ISSN 0022-5231. (q) Dr. Robert M. Lang, Editor, College of Education, Leadership, and Educational Policy Studies, Northern Illinois University, Dekalb, IL 60115, USA

The Journal of Value Inquiry. ISSN 0022-5363. (q) Kluwer Academic Publishers, P.O. Box 322, 3300 AH Dordrecht, The Netherlands (or P.O.Box 358, Accord Station, Hingham, MA 02018-0358, USA)

Kant-Studien: Philosophische Zeitschrift der Kant-Gesellschaft. ISSN 0022-8877. (q) Walter de Gruyter, Genthiner Str. 13, D-10785 Berlin, Germany

Kennedy Institute of Ethics Journal. ISSN 1054-6863. (q) The Johns Hopkins University Press, Journals Publishing Division, 701 West 40th Street, Suite 275, Baltimore, MD 21211-2190, USA

Kennis en Methode: Tijdschrift voor Wetenschapsfilosofie en Wetenschapsonderzoek. ISSN 0165-1773. (q) Boompers, Postbus 400, 7940 AK Meppel, The Netherlands

Kinesis: Graduate Journal in Philosophy. ISSN 0023-1568. (bi-ann) Dept. of Philosophy, Southern Illinois University, Carbondale, IL 62901, USA

Kriterion: Revista de Filosofia. (bi-ann) Faculdade de Filosofia e Ciências Humanas, da UFMG, Av Antonio Carlos, C.P. 6627, Belo Horizonte, MG, Brazil

Kriterion: Zeitschrift für Philosophie. ISSN 1019-8288 (bi-ann) Institut für Philosophie, Franziskanergasse 1, A-5020 Salzburg, Austria

Kwartalnik Filozoficzny. ISSN 1230-405- (q) Polska Akademia Umiejtnoci, Sawkowska 17, 31-016 Kraków, Poland

Laval Théologique et Philosophique. ISSN 0023-9054. (3 times per yr) Service de Revues, Les Presses de l'Université Laval, C.P. 2447, Québec G1K 7R4, Canada

Law and Philosophy: An International Journal for Jurisprudence and Legal Philosophy. ISSN 0167-5249. (q) Kluwer Academic Publishers, P.O. Box 322, 3300 AH Dordrecht, The Netherlands (or P.O.Box 358, Accord Station, Hingham, MA 02018-0358, USA)

Legal Theory. ISSN 1352-3252. (q) Cambridge University Press, The Edinburgh Building, Shaftesbury Road, Cambridge CB2 2RU, United Kingdom (or 40 West 20th Street, New York, NY 10011-4211, USA)

Leibniz Society Review. ISSN 1069-5192. Dr. Glenn A. Hartz, Editor, Dept. of Philosophy, 1680 University Drive, Ohio State University, Mansfield, OH 44906-1599, USA

Lekton. ISSN 1180-2308. (q) Presses de l'Université du Québec, C.P. 250 Sillery, Québec G1T 2R1, Canada

Linguistics and Philosophy: A Journal of Natural Language Syntax, Semantics, Logic, Pragmatics, and Processing. ISSN 0165-0157. (6 times per yr) Kluwer Academic Publishers, P.O. Box 322, 3300 AH Dordrecht, The Netherlands (or P.O.Box 358, Accord Station, Hingham, MA 02018-0358, USA)

Listening: Journal of Religion and Culture. ISSN 0024-4414. (3 times per yr) P.O. Box 1108, Route 53, Romeoville, IL 60441-2298, USA

Literature and Aesthetics: The Journal of the Sydney Society of Literature and Aesthetics. ISSN 1036-9368. (ann) Dr. C. A. Runcie, Editor, Dept. of English, A20, University of Sydney, Sydney 2006, Australia

The Locke Newsletter: An Annual Journal of Locke Research. ISSN 0307-2606 (ann) Roland Hall, Editor, Summerfields, The Glade, Escrick, York YO4 6JH United Kingdom

Logique et Analyse. ISSN 0024-5836. (q) Professor Jean Paul Van Bendegem, Editor, U. G. Rozier 44, B-9000 Gent, Belgium

Logos: Revista de Filosofía. ISSN 0185-6375. (3 times per yr) Apartado Postal 18-907, Colonia Tacubaya, Delegación Miguel Hidalgo, C.P. 11800, México, DF, Mexico

Lua: The Journal of Philosophy and Sociology. ISSN 0352-4973. (bi-ann) Prof. Bogoljub Šjakovi, Filosofski fakultet, YU-81400 Nikši, Yugoslavia

Lyceum. (bi-ann) Saint Anselm College, Box 1698, 87 Saint Anselm Drive, Manchester, NH 03102-1310, USA

Magyar Filozófiai Szemle. ISSN 0025-0090. (bi-m) Kultura, P.O. Box 149, H-1389 Budapest 62, Hungary

Man and Nature/L'homme et la Nature: Yearbook of the Canadian Society for Eighteenth-Century Studies. (ann) Academic Printing and Publishing, P.O. Box 4834, South Edmonton, Alberta T6E 5G7, Canada

Man and World: An International Philosophical Review. ISSN 0025-1534. (q) Kluwer Academic Publishers, P.O. Box 322, 3300 AH Dordrecht, The Netherlands (or P.O.Box 358, Accord Station, Hingham, MA 02018-0358, USA)

Manuscrito: Revista Internacional de Filosofia. ISSN 0100-6045. (bi-ann) Circulation Dept., Centro de Lógica, Unicamp C.P. 6133, 13.081 Campinas, São Paulo, Brazil

Maritain Studies-Études Maritainiennes. ISSN 0826-9920 (ann) Canadian Jacques Maritain Assoc., c/o Dept. of Philosophy, 65 University Dr., University of Ottawa, ON K1N 6N5, Canada

Mediaeval Studies. ISSN 0076-5872. (ann) Dr. Ron B. Thomson, Director of Publications, Pontifical Institute of Mediaeval Studies, 59 Queen's Park Crescent East, Toronto, Ontario M5S 2C4, Canada

Medical Humanities Review. ISSN 0892-2772. (bi-ann) Institute for the Medical Humanities, University of Texas Medical Branch, Galveston, TX 77550, USA

Metaphilosophy. ISSN 0026-1068. Blackwell Publishers, 108 Cowley Road, Oxford OX4 1JF, United Kingdom (or 238 Main St., Cambridge, MA 02142, USA)

Method: Journal of Lonergan Studies. ISSN 0736-7392. (bi-ann) The Lonergan Institute, Boston College, Chestnut Hill, MA 02167, USA

Methodology and Science: International Journal for the Empirical Study of the Foundations of Science and their Methodology. ISSN 0543-6095. (q) Dr. P.H. Esser, Secretary and Editor, Beelslaan 20, 2012 PK Haarlem, The Netherlands

Midwest Studies in Philosophy. No ISSN. (ann/mono) Dr. Peter A. French, Editor, Dept. of Philosophy, Trinity University, San Antonio, TX 78212 USA

Mind: A Quarterly Review of Philosophy. ISSN 0026-4423. (q) Oxford University Press, Pinkhill House, Southfield Road, Eynsham, Oxford OX8 1JJ, United Kingdom

Mind & Language. ISSN 0268-1064. (q) Blackwell Publishers, 108 Cowley Road, Oxford OX4 1JF, United Kingdom (or 238 Main St., Cambridge, MA 02142, USA)

Minds and Machines: Journal for Artificial Intelligence, Philosophy, and Cognitive Science. ISSN 0924-6495. (q) Kluwer Academic Publishers, P.O. Box 322, 3300 AH Dordrecht, The Netherlands (or P.O.Box 358, Accord Station, Hingham, MA 02018-0358, USA)

The Modern Schoolman: A Quarterly Journal of Philosophy. ISSN 0026-8402. (q) William C. Charron, Editor, Dept. of Philosophy, St. Louis University, St. Louis, MO 63103, USA

Modern Theology. ISSN 0266-7177. (q) Blackwell Publishers, 108 Cowley Road, Oxford OX4 1JF, United Kingdom (or 238 Main St., Cambridge, MA 02142, USA)

The Monist: An International Quarterly Journal of General Philosophic Inquiry. ISSN 0026-9662. (q) The Hegler Institute, P.O. Box 600, La Salle, IL 61301, USA

NAO Revista de la Cultura del Mediterráneo. (3 times per yr) Mansilla 3344, 1° C, 1425 Capital Federal, Argentina

National Forum: Phi Kappa Phi Journal. ISSN 0162-1831. (q) Subscription Dept., 129 Quad Center, Auburn University, Auburn University, AL 36849, USA

Nature, Society, and Thought. ISSN 0890-6130. (q) University of Minnesota, 116 Church Street, S.E., Minneapolis, MN 55455, USA

Neue Hefte für Philosophie. ISSN H085-3917. (irr/ann) Vandenhoeck & Ruprecht, Postfach 3753, D-37027 Göttingen, Germany

New Vico Studies. ISSN 0733-9542. (ann) Institute for Vico Studies, 69 Fifth Avenue, New York, NY 10003, USA (or Humanities Press International, 171 First Avenue, Atlantic Highlands, NJ 07716, USA)

Nietzsche-Studien: Internationales Jahrbuch für die Nietzsche-Forschung.(ann) Walter de Gruyter, Genthiner Str. 13, D-10785 Berlin, Germany

Nomos: Yearbook of the American Society for Political and Legal Philosophy. No ISSN. (ann) Order Dept., New York University Press, 70 Washington Square South, New York, NY 10012, USA

Notre Dame Journal of Formal Logic. ISSN 0029-4527. (q) Business Manager, University of Notre Dame, Box 5, Notre Dame, IN 46556, USA

Notre Dame Journal of Law, Ethics & Public Policy. (bi-ann) Zigad I. Naccasha, Managing Editor, University of Notre Dame, Notre Dame, IN 46556, USA

Noûs. ISSN 0029-4624. (q) Dept. of Philosophy, 126 Sycamore Hall, Indiana University, Bloomington, IN 47405, USA

Nouvelles de la République des Lettres. ISSN 0392-2332. (bi-ann) C.C. 1794767/01, Banca Commerciale Italiana, AG3 Naples, Italy

The Owl of Minerva. ISSN 0030-7580. (bi-ann) Dept. of Philosophy, Villanova University, Villanova, PA 19085, USA

Pacific Philosophical Quarterly. ISSN 0279-0750. (q) Expediters of the Printed Word, 5155 Madison Avenue, New York, NY 10022, USA

Patristica et Mediaevalia. ISSN 0235-2280. (ann) Editor, Miembros del Centro de Estudios de Filosofía Medieval, 25 de Mayo 217, 2° Piso, 1002 Buenos Aires, Argentina

Pensamiento: Revista de Investigación e Información Filosófica. ISSN 0031-4749. (q) Administración, Pablo Aranda 3, 28006 Madrid, Spain

Per la Filosofia. ISSN 0394-4131. (3 times per yr) Editrice Massimo, Viale Bacchiglione, 20A, 20139 Milano, Italy

The Personalist Forum. ISSN 0889-065X. Editor, Dept. of Philosophy, Furman University, Greenville, SC 29613, USA

Philo-Logica: Rassenga di analisi linguistica ed ironia culturale. No ISSN. (bi-ann) Edizioni Zara, Via Portilia, 6, 43100 Parma, Italy

Philosopher: Revue de l'enseignment de la philosophie au Québec. ISSN 0827-1887. (ann) Pierre Cohen-Bacrie, Directeur, Département de Philosophie, Collège Montmorency, 475, Boulevard de l'Avenir, Laval, Québec H7N 5H9, Canada

Philosophia. ISSN 0031-8000. (ann) Editorial Office-Distribution, Research Center for Greek Philosophy, Academy of Athens, 14 Anagnostopoulou Street, Athens 106 73, Greece

Philosophia: Philosophical Quarterly of Israel. ISSN 0048-3893. (q) Bar-Ilan University, Subscriptions, Dept. of Philosophy, Ramat-Gan 52100, Israel

Philosophia: Revista de Filsofia. No ISSN. (bi-ann) Editora Universitária Champagnat, Rua Imaculada Conceição, 1155, Curitiba-Paraná, 80215-901 Brazil

Philosophia Mathematica. ISSN 0031-8019. (bi-ann) Journals Division, University of Toronto Press, 5201 Dufferin Street, Downsville, Ontario M3H 5T8, Canada

Philosophia Naturalis. ISSN 0031-8027. (bi-ann) Vittorio Klostermann GmbH, Postfach 90 06 01, Frauenlobstrasse 22, D-60487 Frankfurt/M, Germany

Philosophia Reformata. ISSN 0031-8035. (q) Centrum voor Reformatorische Wijsbegeerte, P.O. Box 368, 3500 AJ Utrecht, The Netherlands

Philosophic Exchange: Annual Proceedings. ISSN 0193-5046. (ann) Center for Philosophic Exchange, SUNY at Brockport, Brockport, NY 14420, USA

Philosophica. ISSN 0379-8402. (bi-ann) Rozier 44, B-9000 Gent, Belgium

Philosophica. (q) 38A/10 Belgachia Road, Calcutta 700037, India

Philosophica: Zborník Univerzity Komenského. (ann) Dr. Miroslav Marcelli, Editor, Department of Philosophy & History of Philosophy, Faculty of Arts, Comenius University, Gondova 8, 81801 Bratislava, Slovakia

Philosophical Books. ISSN 0031-8051. (q) Blackwell Publishers, 108 Cowley Road, Oxford OX4 1JF, United Kingdom (or 238 Main St., Cambridge, MA 02142, USA)

The Philosophical Forum. ISSN 0031-806X. (q) CUNY, Baruch College, Box 239, 17 Lexington Avenue, New York, NY 10010, USA

Philosophical Inquiry: An International Philosophical Quarterly. (q) Prof. D.Z. Andriopoulos, Editor, School of Philosophy, Aristotelian University of Thessaloniki, P.O. Box 84, Thessaloniki, Greece (or P.O. Box 61116, Maroussi, Athens, Greece)

Philosophical Investigations. ISSN 0190-0536. (q) Blackwell Publishers, 108 Cowley Road, Oxford OX4 1JF, United Kingdom (or 238 Main St., Cambridge, MA 02142, USA)

Philosophical Papers. ISSN 0556-8641. (3 times per yr) Dept. of Philosophy, Rhodes University, P.O. Box 94, Grahamstown 6140, South Africa

Philosophical Psychology. ISSN 0951-5089. (3 times per yr) Carfax Publishing Co., P.O. Box 25, Abingdon, Oxfordshire OX14 3UE, United Kingdom

The Philosophical Quarterly. ISSN 0031-8094. (q) Blackwell Publishers, 108 Cowley Road, Oxford OX4 1JF, United Kingdom (or 238 Main St., Cambridge, MA 02142, USA)

Philosophical Review. (ann) Editor-in-Chief, Dept. of Philosophy, National Taiwan University, Taipei 10764, Taiwan

The Philosophical Review. ISSN 0031-8103. (q) 327 Goldwin Smith Hall, Cornell University, Ithaca, NY 14853, USA

Philosophical Studies: An International Journal for Philosophy in the Analytic Tradition. ISSN 0031-8116. (12 times per yr) Kluwer Academic Publishers, P.O. Box 322, 3300 AH Dordrecht, The Netherlands (or P.O.Box 358, Accord Station, Hingham, MA 02018-0358, USA)

Philosophical Studies in Education: Proceedings of the Annual Meeting of the Ohio Valley Philosophy of Education Society. ISSN 0160-7561. (ann) Terence O'Connor, Indiana State University, Terre Haute, IN 47809, USA

Philosophical Topics. ISSN 0276-2080. (bi-ann) Christopher Hill, Editor, Dept. of Philosophy, University of Arkansas, Fayetteville, AR 72701, USA

Philosophie et Logique. ISSN 0035-4031. (q) Editura Academiei Republicii Socialiste Romania, Str. Gutenberg 3 bis, Sector 6, Bucaresti, Romania

Die Philosophin: Forum für feministische Theorie und Philosophie. ISSN 0936-7586 (bi-ann) Edition Diskord, Dr. G. Kimmerle, Schwärzlocherstr. 104/b, D-72070 Tübingen, Germany

Philosophique. ISSN 0980-0891. (ann) Faculté des Lettres et Sciences Humaines, Université de Franche-Comté, 30 rue Megevand, 25000 Besançon Cédex, France

Philosophiques. ISSN 0316-2923. (bi-ann) Les Editions Bellarmin, 165 rue Deslauriers, Saint-Laurent, Québec H4N 2S4, Canada

Philosophische Rundschau. ISSN 0031-8159. (q) J.C.B. Mohr (Paul Siebeck), Postfach 20 40, D-72010 Tübingen, Germany

Philosophy: The Journal of the Royal Institute of Philosophy. ISSN 0031-8191. (q plus 2 supps). Cambridge University Press, The Edinburgh Building, Shaftesbury Road, Cambridge, CB2 2RU, United Kingdom, (or 40 West 20th Street, New York, NY 10011-4211, USA)

Philosophy and Literature. ISSN 0190-0013. (semi-ann) The Johns Hopkins University Press, 701 West 40th Street, Suite 275, Baltimore, MD 21211-2190, USA

Philosophy and Phenomenological Research. ISSN 0031-8205. (q) Brown University, Box 1947, Providence, RI 02912, USA

Philosophy and Public Affairs. ISSN 0048-3915. (q) The Johns Hopkins University Press, 701 West 40th Street, Suite 275, Baltimore, MD 21211-2190, USA

Philosophy and Rhetoric. ISSN 0031-8213. (q) Dept. of Philosophy, The Pennsylvania State University, University Park, PA 16802, USA

Philosophy and Social Action. ISSN 0377 2772. (q) Business Editor, M-120 Greater Kailash-I, New Delhi 110048, India

Philosophy and Social Criticism. ISSN 0191-4537. (q) David M. Rasmussen, Editor, P.O. Box 368, Lawrence, KS 66044, USA

Philosophy and the History of Science. ISSN 1022-4874. (bi-ann) Dr. Yu-Houng, Managing Editor, Yuan-Liou Publishing Co., Ltd., 7F-5, 184, Sec. 3, Ding-Chou Road, Taipei, Taiwan

Philosophy and Theology: Marquette University Quarterly. ISSN 0-87462-559-9. (q) A. Tallon, Dept. of Philosophy and Theology, Marquette University, Milwaukee, WI 53233, USA

Philosophy East and West. ISSN 0031-8221. (q) The University of Hawaii Press, 2840 Kolowalu Street, Honolulu, HI 96822, USA

Philosophy in Science. ISSN 0277-2434. (ann) Pachart Publishing House, 1130 San Lucas Circle, Tucson, AZ 85704, USA

Philosophy in the Contemporary World. ISSN 1077-1999. (q) Jack Weir, Editor, UPO 662, Morehead State University, Morehead, KY 40351-1689, USA

Philosophy of Education: Proceedings of the Annual Meeting of the Philosophy of Education Society. No ISSN (ann) Philosophy of Education Society, Dept. of Teacher Education, San Jose State University, 1 Washington Square, San Jose, CA 95192

Philosophy of Music Education Review. ISSN 1063-5734. (bi-ann) Music Education Dept., SY405, School of Music, Indiana University, Bloomington, IN 47405, USA

Philosophy of Science. ISSN 0031-8248. (q) Executive Secretary, Philosophy of Science Assoc., Dept. of Philosophy, 114 Morrill Hall, Michigan State University, East Lansing, MI 48824-1036, USA

Philosophy of the Social Sciences. ISSN 0048-3931. (q) Sage Publications, 2455 Teller Road, Newbury Park, CA 91320, USA

Philosophy, Psychiatry, and Psychology. ISSN 1071-6076. (q) The Johns Hopkins University Press, Journals Publishing Division, P.O. Box 19966, Baltimore, MD 21211, USA

Philosophy Today. ISSN 0031-8256. (q) DePaul University, 802 West Belden Avenue, Chicago, IL 60614, USA

Phoenix: The Journal of the Classical Association of Canada. ISSN 0031-8299. (q) J. Schutz, Editorial Assistant, Trinity College, Larkin 339, University of Toronto, Toronto, Ontario M5S 1H8, Canada

Phronesis: A Journal for Ancient Philosophy. ISSN 0031-8868. (3 times per yr) Van Gorcum, P.O. Box 43, 9400 AA Assen, The Netherlands

Polis. (bi-ann) P. P. Nicholson, Dept. of Politics, University of York, York YO1 5DD, United Kingdom (or Prof. Kent F. Moors, Dept. of Political Science, Duquesne University, Pittsburgh, PA 15282-0001, USA)

Political Theory: An International Journal of Political Philosophy. ISSN 0090-5917. (q) Sage Publications, 2455 Teller Road, Newbury Park, CA 91320, USA

Pragmatics and Cognition. ISSN 0929-0907. (bi-ann) John Benjamins Publishing Co., Amsteldijk 44, P.O. Box 75577, 1070 AN Amsterdam, The Netherlands

Prilozi za Istraivanje Hrvatske Filozofske Baštine. ISSN 0350-2791 (bi-ann) Ljerka Schiffler-Premec, ed., Institut za Filosofiju, Ul. grada Vukovara 54, 41000 Zagreb, Croatia

Prima Philosophia. ISSN 0933-5749. (q) Traude Junghans Verlag, Flat 5, 21 Essex Rd., Dartford/Kent DA1 2AU, United Kingdom

Proceedings and Addresses of the American Philosophical Association. ISSN 0065-972X. (7 times per yr) The American Philosophical Assoc., University of Delaware, Newark, DE 19716, USA

Proceedings of the American Catholic Philosophical Association. ISSN 0065-7638. (ann) Treasurer, The American Catholic Philosophical Assoc., Catholic University of America, Washington, DC 20064, USA

Proceedings of the Aristotelian Society. ISSN 0066-7374. Members: The Aristotelian Society, Dept. of Philosophy, Birkbeck College, Malet Street, London WC1E 7HX, United Kingdom. Non-members: Blackwell Publishers, 108 Cowley Road, Oxford OX4 1JF, United Kingdom (or 238 Main St., Cambridge, MA 02142, USA)

Proceedings of the Biennial Meetings of the Philosophy of Science Association. ISSN 0270-8647. (ann) Philosophy of Science Assoc., 18 Morrill Hall, Michigan State University, East Lansing, MI 48824-1036, USA

Proceedings of the Boston Area Colloquium in Ancient Philosophy. (ann) Co-publishing Program, University Press of America, 4720 Boston Way, Lanham, MD 20706, USA

Proceedings of the Heraclitean Society. (irr) Dept. of Philosophy, Western Michigan University, Kalamazoo, MI 49008, USA

Proceedings of the South Atlantic Philosophy of Education Society. (ann) Joseph W. Congleton, School of Education, SAPES, East Carolina University, Greenville, NC 27858, USA

Process Studies. ISSN 0360-6503. (q) Center for Process Studies, 1325 North College Avenue, Claremont, CA 91711, USA

Professional Ethics: A Multidisciplinary Journal. ISSN 1063-6579. Center for Applied Philosophy, 331 Griffin-Floyd Hall, University of Florida, Gainesville, FL 32611, USA

Protosoziologie. ISSN 0940-4147 (bi-ann) Gerhard Preyer, ed., Dept. of Social Sciences, J.W.Goethe University, Stephan-Heise Str. 56, D-60488 Frankfurt/M, Germany

Public Affairs Quarterly. ISSN 0887-0373. (q) Philosophy Documentation Center, Bowling Green State University, Bowling Green, OH 43403-0189, USA

Quaderns de Filosofia i Ciència. ISSN 0213-5965. (irr) Societat de Filosofia del País Valencià, Facultat de Filosofia i Ciències de l'Educació, Universitat de València, Av. Blasco Ibáñez, 21-46010 València, Spain

Quest: Philosophical Discussions. ISSN 1011-226X. (bi-ann) Circulation Manager, P.O. Box 9114, 9703 LC Groningen, The Netherlands

Radical Philosophy: A Journal of Socialist and Feminist Philosophy. ISSN 0300-211X. (3 times per yr) Central Books (RP Subscriptions), 99 Wallis Rd., London E9 5LN, United Kingdom

Ratio: An International Journal of Analytic Philosophy. ISSN 0034-0066. (3 times per yr) Blackwell Publishers, 108 Cowley Road, Oxford OX4 1JF, United Kingdom (or 238 Main St., Cambridge, MA 02142, USA)

Ratio Juris: An International Journal of Jurisprudence and Philosophy of Law. ISSN 0952-1919. (3 times per year) Blackwell Publishers, 108 Cowley Rd., Oxford OX4 1JF, United Kingdom (or 238 Main St., Cambridge, MA 02142 USA)

Reason Papers: A Journal of Interdisciplinary Normative Studies. ISSN 0363-1893. (ann) Dept. of Philosophy, Auburn University, Auburn University, AL 36849, USA

Religious Humanism. ISSN 0034-4095. (q) Fellowship of Religious Humanists, P.O. Box 278, Yellow Springs, OH 42387, USA

Religious Studies: An International Journal for the Philosophy of Religion. ISSN 0034-4125. (q) Cambridge University Press, The Edinburgh Building, Shaftesbury Road, Cambridge, CB2 2RU, United Kingdom (or 40 West 20th Street, New York, NY 10011-4211, USA)

Reports on Mathematical Logic. ISSN 0137-2904. (ann) Centrala Handlu Zagranicznego "Ars Polona," ul. Krakowskie Przedmiescie 7, 00-068 Warsaw, Poland

Reports on Philosophy. ISSN 0324-8712. Elzbieta Paczkowska-Lagowska, Editor-in-Chief, Instytut Filozofii, ul. Grodzka 52, 31-044 Krakow, Poland

Research in Phenomenology. ISSN 0085-5553. (ann) Humanities Press International, Atlantic Highlands, NJ 07716, USA

Research in Philosophy and Technology. (ann) JAI Press, Inc., 55 Old Post Road-No. 2, Greenwich, CT 06836, USA

The Review of Metaphysics. ISSN 0034-6632. (q) Catholic University of America, Washington, DC 20064, USA

Revista de Filosofía. ISSN 0185-3481. (3 times per yr) Universidad Iberoamericana, Prolongación Paseo de la Reforma No. 880, Lomas de Santa Fé, 01210 México, DF, Mexico

Revista de Filosofía. No ISSN. (bi-ann) Centro de Estidios Filosóficos, Edificio Viyaluz Piso 8, Apartado 526, Maracaibo, Venezuela

Revista de Filosofía: Publicación de la Asociación de Estudios Filosóficos. ISSN 0326-8160. (bi-ann) Marcelo Diego Boeri, ADEF C.C. 3758 Correo Central, 1000 Capital Federal, Argentina

Revista de Filosofía de la Universidad de Costa Rica. ISSN 0034-8252. (bi-ann) Editor, Universidad de Costa Rica, Apartado 75-2060, San José, Costa Rica

Revista de Filosofie. ISSN 0034-8260. (bi-m) Rompresfilatelia, Calea Victoriei 125, 79717 Bucharest, Romania

Revista Española de Filosofía Medieval. ISSN 1133-0902. (ann) Servicio de Publicaciones, Edificio de Geológicas, Ciudad Universitaria, 50,009 Zaragoza, Spain

Revista Latinoamericana de Filosofía. ISSN 0325-0725. (3 times per yr) Box 1192, Birmingham, AL 35201, USA (or Casilla de Correo 5379, Correo Central, 1000 Buenos Aires, Argentina)

Revista Portuguesa de Filosofia. ISSN 0035-0400. (q) Faculdade de Filosofia, UCP, 4719 Braga, Portugal

Revue de Métaphysique et de Morale. ISSN 0035-1571. (q) 156 Avenue Parmentier, 75010 Paris, France

Revue de Théologie et de Philosophie. ISSN 0035-1784. (q) 7 ch. des Cèdres, CH-1004 Lausanne, Switzerland

Revue Internationale de Philosophie. ISSN 0048-8143. (q) Prof. Michael Meyer, Institut de Philosophie (CP/188), Université Libre de Bruxelles, Av. F. D. Roosevelt, 50, B-1050 Brussels, Belgium

Revue Philosophique de la France et de L'étranger. ISSN 0035-3833. (q) Redaction de la Revue Philosophique, 12 rue Jean-de-Beauvais, 75005 Paris, France

Revue Philosophique de Louvain. ISSN 0035-3841. (q) Editions Peeters, B.P. 41, B-3000 Leuven, Belgium

Revue Thomiste: Revue Doctrinale de Théologie et de Philosophie. ISSN 0035-4295. (q) Ecole de Théologie, Avenue Lacordaire, Cedex, 31078 Toulouse, France

Rivista di Filosofia. ISSN 0035-6239. (q) Societa Editrice Il Mulino, Strada Maggiore 37, 40125 Bologna, Italy

Rivista di Filosofia Neo-Scolastica. ISSN 0035-6247. (q) Pubblicazioni dell'Universita Cattolica del Sacro Cuore, Vita e Pensiero, Largo A. Gemelli, 20123 Milan, Italy

Rivista di Studi Crociani. ISSN 0035-659X. (q) Presso la Societa di Storia Partia, Piazza Municipio, Maschio Angiolino, 80133 Naples, Italy

Rivista Internazionale di Filosofia del Diritto. (q) Casa Editrice Dott. A. Giuffre, via Busto Arsizio 40, 20151 Milan, Italy

Russell: The Journal of the Bertrand Russell Archives. ISSN 0036-0163. (q) McMaster University Library Press, McMaster University, Hamilton, Ontario L8S 4L6, Canada

Russian Studies in Philosophy: A Journal of Translations. ISSN 0038-5883. (q) M.E. Sharpe, 80 Business Park Drive, Armonk, NY 10504, USA

S'vara: A Journal of Philosophy, Law, and Judaism. ISSN 1044-0011. (bi-ann) Business Manager, AFSHI, 280 Grand Avenue, Englewood, NJ 07631, USA

Sapientia. ISSN 0036-4703. (q) Bartolome Mitre 1869, 1039 Buenos Aires, Argentina

Sapienza. ISSN 0036-4711. (q) Vicoletto S. Pietro a Maiella, 4-80134 Naples, Italy

Schopenhauer-Jahrbuch. ISSN 0080-6935. (ann) Heinz Gerd Ingenkamp, Editor, Albertus-Magnus-Str. 35a, D-53177 Bonn, Germany

Science, Technology, and Human Values. ISSN 0162-2439. (q) Sage Publications, 2455 Teller Road, Newbury Park, CA 91320, USA

Social Epistemology: A Journal of Knowledge, Culture, and Policy. ISSN 0269-1728. (q) Taylor and Francis Ltd, 4 John St., London WC1N 2ET, United Kingdom (or Taylor & Francis Inc, 242 Cherry St., Philadelphia, PA 19106-1906, USA)

Social Indicators Research: An International and Interdisciplinary Journal for Quality-of-Life Measurement. ISSN 0303-8300. Kluwer Academic Publishers, P.O. Box 322, 3300 AH Dordrecht, The Netherlands (or P.O.Box 358, Accord Station, Hingham, MA 02018-0358, USA)

Social Philosophy and Policy. ISSN 0265-0525. (bi-ann) Cambridge University Press, The Edinburgh Building, Shaftesbury Road, Cambridge CB2 2RU, United Kingdom (or 40 West 20th Street, New York, NY 10011-4211, USA)

Social Theory and Practice: An International and Interdisciplinary Journal of Social Philosophy. ISSN 0037-802X. (3 times per yr) Dept. of Philosophy R-36C, 203 Dodd Hall, The Florida State University, Tallahassee, FL 32306-1054, USA

Sophia: A Journal for Philosophical Theology and Cross-Cultural Philosophy of Religion. ISSN 0038-1527. (3 times per yr) School of Humanities, Deakin University, Victoria 3217, Australia

Sorites: An International Electronic Quarterly of Analytic Philosophy. ISSN 1135-1349 (q) c/o Prof. Lorenzo Peña, CSIC-Institute of Philosophy, Pinar 25, E-28006 Madrid, Spain

South African Journal of Philosophy. ISSN 0258-0136. (q) Bureau for Scientific Publications, P.O. Box 1758, Pretoria 0001, South Africa

The Southern Journal of Philosophy. ISSN 0038-4283. (q) Editor, Department of Philosophy, Memphis State University, Memphis, TN 38152, USA

Southwest Philosophical Studies. ISSN 0885-9310. (3 times per yr) Jack Weir, Co-Editor, Department of Philosophy, Hardin-Simmons University, Abilene, TX 79698, USA (or Joseph D. Stamey, Co-Editor, Dept. of Philosophy, McMurry University, Abilene, TX 79697, USA)

Southwest Philosophy Review. ISSN 0897-2346. (bi-ann) Dept. of Philosophy, University of Central Arkansas, Conway, AR 72302, USA

Stromata. ISSN 0049-2353. (q) Universidad del Salvador, C.C. 10, 1663 San Miguel, Argentina

Studi Filosofici: Annali del Dipartimento di Filosofia e Politica, Istituto Universitario Orientale. No ISSN.(ann) Dip. di Filosofia e Politica, Via Dei Fiorentini Nr.10, 80133 Napoli, Italy

Studia Leibnitiana: Zeitschrift für Geschichte der Philosophie und der Wissenschaften. ISSN 0039-3185. (bi-ann) Franz Steiner Verlag Wiesbaden GmbH, Postfach 101526, D-70014 Stuttgart, Germany

Studia Logica. ISSN 0039-3215. Kluwer Academic Publishers, P.O. Box 322, 3300 AH Dordrecht, The Netherlands (or P.O.Box 358, Accord Station, Hingham, MA 02018-0358, USA)

Studia Philosophiae Christiane. ISSN 0585-5470. (bi-ann) ATK, ul. Dewajtis 5, 01-653 Warsaw, Poland

Studia Philosophica. (ann) Helmut Holzhey and Jean-Pierre Leyvraz, Editors, Verlag Paul Haupt, Falkenplatz 11/14, CH-3001 Berne, Switzerland

Studia Spinozana. ISSN 0179-3896. (ann) Douglas J. Den Uyl, Bellarmine College, Newburg Road, Louisville, KY 40205, USA

Studies in East European Thought. ISSN 0925-9392. Kluwer Academic Publishers, P.O. Box 322, 3300 AH Dordrecht, The Netherlands (or P.O.Box 358, Accord Station, Hingham, MA 02018-0358, USA)

Studi Filosofici: Annali del Dipartimento di Filosofia e Politica, Istituto Universitario Orientale. No ISSN (ann) Dip. di Filosofia e Politica, Via dei Fiorentini, 10, 80133 Napoli, Italy

Studies in History and Philosophy of Science. ISSN 0039-3681. (q) Pergamon Press, Maxwell House, Fairview Park, Elmsford, NY 10523, USA

Studies in Philosophy and Education. ISSN 0039-3746. (q) Kluwer Academic Publishers, P.O. Box 322, 3300 AH Dordrecht, The Netherlands (or P.O.Box 358, Accord Station, Hingham, MA 02018-0358, USA)

Synthese: An International Journal for Epistemology, Methodology, and Philosophy of Science. ISSN 0039-7857. (12 times per yr) Kluwer Academic Publishers, P.O. Box 322, 3300 AH Dordrecht, The Netherlands (or P.O.Box 358, Accord Station, Hingham, MA 02018-0358, USA)

Teaching Philosophy. ISSN 0145-5788. (q) Philosophy Documentation Center, Bowling Green State University, Bowling Green, OH 43403-0189, USA

Telos: Revista Iberoamericana de Estudios Utilitaristas. ISSN 1132-0877 (bi-ann) S.I.E.U., Facultad de Filosofía y CC.EE., Campus Sur, E-15706 Santiago de Compostela, Spain

Teoria: Rivista di Filosofia. (bi-ann) E.T.S., C.C.P. 12157566, Piazza Torricelli 4, 56100 Pisa, Italy

Thémata: Revista de Filosofía. ISSN 0210-8365. (ann) Servicio de Publicaciones de la Universidad de Sevilla, C. San Fernando 4, E-41004, Sevilla C, Spain

Theologie und Philosophie: Vierteljahresschrift. ISSN 0040-5655. (q) Schriftleitung, Offenbacher Landstrasse 224, D-60599 Frankfurt/M, Germany

Theoretical Medicine: An International Journal for the Philosophy and Methodology of Medical Research and Practice. ISSN 0167-9902. (q) Kluwer Academic Publishers, P.O. Box 322, 3300 AH Dordrecht, The Netherlands (or P.O.Box 358, Accord Station, Hingham, MA 02018-0358, USA)

Theoria. ISSN 0495-4548. (3 times per yr) Plaza de Pio XII, 1, 6°, 1ª, Apartado 1.594, 20.080 San Sebastian, Spain

Theoria: A Swedish Journal of Philosophy. ISSN 0040-5825. (3 times per yr) Filosofiska Institution, Kungshuset i Lundagard, S-223 50 Lund, Sweden

Theoria: Filosofsko Drustvo Srbije. ISSN 0351-2274. (q) Cika Ljubina 18-20, 11000 Beograd, Yugoslavia

Theory and Decision: An International Journal for Methods and Models in the Social and Decision Sciences. ISSN 0040-5833. (6 times per year) Kluwer Academic Publishers, P.O. Box 322, 3300 AH Dordrecht, The Netherlands (or P.O.Box 358, Accord Station, Hingham, MA 02018-0358, USA)

Theory, Culture and Society. ISSN 0263-2764. (q) Sage Publications, LTD, 6 Bonhill Street, London, EC2A 4PU, United Kingdom

Thinking: The Journal of Philosophy for Children. ISSN 0190-3330. (q) The Institute for the Advancement of Philosophy for Children, Montclair State College, Upper Montclair, NJ 07043, USA

The Thomist: A Speculative Quarterly Review. ISSN 0040-6325. (q) The Thomist Press, 487 Michigan Avenue NE, Washington, DC 20017, USA

Tijdschrift voor de Studie van de Verlichting en van Het Vrije Denken. ISSN 0774-1847. (q) Centrum voor de Studie van de Verlichting en van Het Vrije Denken, Vrije Universiteit Brussel, Pleinlaan 2-B416, 1050 Brussels, Belgium

Tijdschrift voor Filosofie. ISSN 0040-750X. (q) Kardinaal Mercierplein 2, B-3000 Leuven, Belgium

Tópicos: Revista de Filosofía. ISSN 0188-6649. (ann) Dr. Héctor Zagal, Editor, Facultad de Filosofía, Universidad Panamericana, A Rodin #498, Plaza de Mixcoac, 03910 México, DF, Mexico

Guidance on the Use of the Subject Index

The Subject Index lists in alphabetical order the significant subject descriptors and proper names that describe the content of the articles and books indexed. Since titles are frequently misleading, the editors read each article and book to determine which subject headings accurately describe it. Each entry under a subject heading includes the complete title of the book or article and the author's name.

Subject entries fall into the following classes:

1) proper names, such as Quine, Kant, and Hegel;
2) nationalities, such as American and German;
3) historical periods, which are: ancient, medieval, renaissance, modern, nineteenth-century, and twentieth-century;
4) major fields of philosophy, which are: aesthetics, axiology, education, epistemology, ethics, history, language, logic, metaphysics, philosophical anthropology, philosophy, political philosophy, religion, science, and social philosophy;
5) subdivisions of the major fields of philosophy, such as: utilitarianism, induction, realism, and nominalism;
6) other specific topics, such as grue, pain, paradox, and Turing-machine;
7) bibliographies, which are listed under "bibliographies," the person or subject, and the appropriate historical period.

The Subject Index is used like the index found in the back of a textbook. Scan the alphabetical listing of significant words until the desired subject is found. If the title confirms your interest, then locate the author's name, which occurs after the title, in the section entitled "Author Index with Abstracts." The title, in addition to suggesting the content of the article or book, indicates the language in which the document is written.

Although every effort is made to standardize subject headings, complete uniformity is impossible. Hence, check for various spellings of subject headings, particularly of proper names. Due consideration should be given to subject headings that sometimes are written with a space, a hyphen, or an umlaut. The following example illustrates some possibilities:

DE MORGAN
DE-MORGAN
DEMORGAN

Not only does the computer treat the above subject headings as different, but it may file other subject headings between them.

Generally, only the last names of famous philosophers are used as subject headings. Last names and first initials usually are used for other philosophers. The following list indicates who of two or more philosophers with the same last name is designated by last name only.

Alexander (Samuel)	James (William)
Austin (J L)	Jung (Carl G)
Bacon (Francis)	Lewis (C I)
Bradley (Francis H)	Mill (John Stuart)
Brown (Thomas)	Moore (G E)
Butler (Joseph)	Niebuhr (Reinhold)
Collins (Anthony)	Paul (Saint)
Darwin (Charles)	Price (Richard)
Eckhart (Meister)	Russell (Bertrand)
Edwards (Jonathan)	Schiller (Friedrich)
Green (Thomas H)	Toynbee (Arnold)
Hartmann (Edward von)	Wolff (Christian)
Huxley (T H)	

A POSTERIORI

El control experimental y la construcción del objeto científico. Ginebra i Molins, M P.

A PRIORI

Scheler's Critique of Kant's Ethics. Blosser, Philip.

Apriori Concepts. Kalsi, Marie-Luise Schubert.

Fine-Grained Opinion, Probability, and the Logic of Full Belief. Van Fraassen, Bas C.

La filosofía trascendental bajo la óptica de la teoría evolucionista del conocimiento. Hoyos Jaramillo, Luis Eduardo.

La Interpretación de Kant de Fernando Montero Moliner. Arenas Llopis, Luis.

Le sphinx de la connaissance: Husserl et l'énigme de l'*a priori* corrélationnel. Miskiewicz, Wioleta.

Notes on the "Lack of Foundation" in Theodor W Adorno Philosophy (in Portuguese). De Paiva Durate, Rodrigo Antonio.

Observações sobre a Concepção Kantiana do Espaço. Molina, Jorge Alberto.

Zwischen Apriorismus und Empirismus im Kontext der Isomorphie zweier Apriorismen: Zur Rekonstruktion von Fichtes philosophischer Konzeption. Kiss, Endre.

ABEL, G

Responses. Quine, W V.

ABELARD

A Teoria da Predicação de Pierre Abélard e a Semântica da Frase de Peter Von Polenz: Uma Tentativa de Aproximação. Chaves-Tannús, Marcio.

Disidencias de Pedro Abelardo. Brasa Díaz, Mariano.

Notabilia V. Imbach, Ruedi.

Old and New: The Body, Subjectivity, and Ethics. McAleer, Graham.

ABIDHARMA

How Innovative is the *Alayavijnana*?, Part II. Waldron, William S.

ABNORMALITY

Phenomenological Concepts of Normality and Abnormality. Steinbock, A J.

ABORIGINAL

"Rediscovering America: The *Two Treatises* and Aboriginal Rights" in *Locke's Philosophy, Rogers, G A J (ed)*. Tully, James.

"The Religious and Ethical Tradition of Ancient and Contemporary Australia" in *Ethics, Religion and Biodiversity, Hamilton, Lawrence S (ed)*. Senanayake, Ranil.

Strange Multiplicity: Constitutionalism in an Age of Diversity. Tully, James.

Transcending Race: Further Reflections on Australian Aboriginal Culture. Turner, David H.

ABORTION

"Disembodiment: Abortion and Gay Rights" in *Radical Philosophy of Law, Caudill, David S (ed)*. Colker, Ruth.

"How People Argue about Abortion and Capital Punishment in Europe and America..." in *Ethics on the Frontiers of Human Existence, Badham, Paul (ed)*. Davies, Christie.

"The Abortion Dilemma" in *The 1994 Annual of Hermeneutics and Social Concern, Lawler, Justus George (ed)*. Haag, Louis J.

Individuals, Humans, Persons: Questions of Life and Death. Kuhse, Helga and Singer, Peter.

Intervention and Reflection: Basic Issues in Medical Ethics (Fifth Edition). Munson, Ronald (ed).

Real Rights. Wellman, Carl P.

The Constructed Body: AIDS, Reproductive Technology, and Ethics. Murphy, Julien S.

Abortion and In Vitro Fertilization. Waller, Bruce N.

Abortion as Murder?: A Response. Stone, Jim.

Abortion Ethics: Rights and Responsibilities. Porter, Elisabeth.

Bioethik und Feminismus. Pauer-Studer, Herlinde.

Integrity, Abortion, and the Pro-Life Perinatologist. Thorp Jr, John M (& others).

Justifying the Rights of Pregnancy: The Interest View. Marquis, Don.

La Vida Humana, La Etica y la Ley. Ruiz Rodríguez, Virgilio.

Marquis' Argument Against Abortion: A Critique. Shirley, Edward S.

Rachels, Abortion, and the Seventeenth Century. Dombrowski, Daniel A.

Sex-Selective Abortion: A Relational Approach. Weiss, Gail.

The Pro-Life Maternal-Fetal Medicine Physician: A Problem of Integrity. Blustein, Jeffrey and Fleischman, Alan R.

Viability. Gert, Heather.

Women, Ectogenesis, and Ethical Theory. Cannold, Leslie.

ABRAHAM, N

Rhythms: On the Work, Translation, and Psychoanalysis of Nicolas Abraham. Rand, Nicholas T (ed) and Torok, Maria (ed).

ABSENCE

El misterio construido. Lapoujade, María Noel.

ABSOLUTE

see also Gods

"Ich aber fordere Sie auf, absolute Genesis ins Auge zu fassen!". Richli, Urs.

"Royce: The Absolute and the Beloved Community Revisited" in *Meaning, Truth, and God, Rouner, Leroy (ed)*. Smith, John E.

"The Status of *Vorstellung* in Hegel's Philosophy of Religion" in *Meaning, Truth, and God, Rouner, Leroy (ed)*. Ricoeur, Paul.

A Philosophy of History in Fragments. Heller, Agnes.

Civil Society, Civil Religion. Shanks, Andrew.

Elementa: L'argument Ontologique chez Saint Anselme et chez Hegel (Band 60). Girard, Louis, Berlinger, Rudolph (ed) and Schrader, Wiebke (ed).

Erinnerung, Retrait, Absolute Reflection: Hegel and Derrida. Kisner, Wendell.

Hegel: Phenomenology and System. Harris, H S.

The Owl at Dawn: A Sequel to Hegel's Phenomenology of Spirit. Curtrofello, Andrew.

The Production of Space. Lefebvre, Henri and Nicholson-Smith, Donald (trans).

Absolute Forms of Gödel's Incompleteness Theorem. Kim, Sangmun.

Amor Dei Intellectualis: Vernunft—und Gottesliebe in Gipfelsätzen neuzeitlicher Systembildungen (Spinoza, Hegel, Schelling, Fichte). Janke, Wolfgang.

Coleridge's "Ideal Realism": An Alternative to the "Doctors of the Absolute"?. Perkins, Mary Anne.

Consequentialism and Absolutism. Elliot, Robert.

Critical Notice of Raymond Bradley: *The Nature of All Being, A Study of Wittgenstein's Modal Absolutism*. Bogen, James.

Discernment in the Realm of Shadows: Absolute Knowing and Otherness. Williams, Robert R.

El Individuo y la Nación: El Sujeto y lo Absoluto en las Filosofías del Lenguaje de Humboldt y Fichte. Pérez, Jorge Navarro.

Fichte en 1804-1806: Arrebato y Entrega. Ciria, Alberto.

Fichtes Konzept absoluter Einheit (1804)—Ein performativer Selbstwiderspruch?. Lütterfelds, Wilhelm.

Individuo y Comunidad: Reflexiones Sobre el Eterno Círculo Fichteano. López-Domínguez, Virginia.

J G Fichte: l'affermazione dell'Assoluto. Gamarra, Daniel.

L'Esprit absolu de Hegel est-il Dieu?. Beauvais, Chantal.

La logique de l'auto-identité absolument contradictoire de Nishida. Tremblay, Jacynthe.

Lo stato moderno: profili storici e dottrinali. Catania, Alfonso.

Modernità e post-modernità dell'agostinismo. Penati, Giancarlo.

Newton sobre Movimento, Espaço e Tempo. Salles, Eduardo and Barra, Oliveira.

Prima Facie Obligation and Doing the Best One Can. Zimmerman, Michael J.

Realität und System: Das Realitätsproblem in Fichtes Theorie der Fünffachheit. Traub, Hartmut.

Relativity, Absoluteness and Observation. Janssen, H C I M.

Remarques sur l'histoire de la notion philosophique d'absolu. Huber, Gerhard.

Sophiology: A Human Reading of the Book of God. Mosolova, S V.

Springe's Argument for Absolute Idealism. Naik, A D.

Subjectivité et absolu dans les premiers écrits de Schelling (1794-1801). Marquet, Jean-François.

Teleo-logía y teo-logía en Edmund Husserl. Bello, Angela Ales.

The Role of the Absolute Infinite in Cantor's Conception of Set. Jané, Ignacio.

The Safeguarded Self. Mullin, Amy.

The Soteriocentrism of John Hick. Louw, Dirk J.

The Unity of Heaven and Man versus Absolute Unlikeness—Kierkegaard, European Thinker, Contra Chinese Philosophy. Zhou, Yiyun.

ABSOLUTISM

Francia, Spagna e Portogallo: Le Monarchie Europee "Qui Vont au Despotisme" Secondo Montesquieu. Felice, Domenico.

L'absolutisme dans la Philosophie: Politique de Thomas Hobbes. Gnanagbe, Gogoua.

Sobre la cuestión del método en el debate Modernidad-Postmodernidad. Esquirol, Josep M.

Tussen relativisme en absolutisme: Democratie en mensenrechten. Van Haute, Philippe.

Wittgenstein and Peirce on Meaning: The Evolution from Absolutism to Fallibilism. Boghossian, Peter G and Drewniak, Erik.

ABSTRACT

The Production of Space. Lefebvre, Henri and Nicholson-Smith, Donald (trans).

La Questione dell'Astratto e del Concreto fra il 1912 e il 1917. Sasso, Gennaro.

ABSTRACT LOGIC

Algebraic Study of Two Deductive Systems of Relevance Logic. Font, Josep Maria and Rodríquez, Gonzalo.

ABSTRACTION

Abstraction and the Real Distinction Between Mind and Body. Thomas, Bruce M.

Il Ritorno dell'Identità nel "Sistema di Logica" di G Gentile. Sainati, Vittorio.

ABSURD

How Can We Live in a World of the Absurd? The Humanism of Albert Camus. Lowen, Jeanette.

The Idea of the Absurd and the Moral Decision: Possibilities and Limits of a Physician's Actions in the View of the Absurd. Lengers, Frank P.

ABUSE

War, Battering, and Other Sports: The Gulf Between American Men and Women. McBride, James.

Baby Ryan and Virtual Futility. Capron, Alexander Morgan.

Clinical Ethics and Intervention in Domestic Violence. Ryan, Maura A.

Ethical and Legal Dilemmas in the Management of Family Violence. Bourne, Richard.

Family Violence and Family Systems: Who Is the Patient?. Gottlieb, Michael C.

Rights in Collision: A Non-Punitive, Compensatory Remedy for Abusive Speech. Meyers, Diana Tietjens.

The Severed Head and Existential Dread: The Classroom as Epistemic Community and Student Survivors of Incest. Potter, Nancy.

ACADEMIA

"Hate Speech, Freedom, and Discourse Ethics in the Academy" in *Radical Philosophy of Law, Caudill, David S (ed)*. Mann, Patricia S.

"Locke at Oxford" in *Locke's Philosophy, Rogers, G A J (ed)*. Milton, J R.

"Obstacles to Fruitful Discussion in the American Academy" in *European Philosophy and the American Academy, Smith, Barry (ed)*. Detmer, David J.

AESTHETICS

AFRICAN

see also South African

"Africa and the Africans" in *African Philosophy: Selected Readings, Mosley, Albert G (ed)*. Blyden, Edward W.

"Africa and the Imperative of Philosophy: A Skeptical Consideration" in *African Philosophy: Selected Readings, Appiah, Kwame Anthony*. Owomoyela, Oyekan.

"African Religions and Philosophy" in *African Philosophy: Selected Readings, Mosley, Albert G (ed)*. Mbiti, John.

"African Traditional Thought and Western Science" in *African Philosophy: Selected Readings, Appiah, Kwame Anthony*. Horton, Robin.

"An Essay on African Philosophical Thought—The Akan Conceptual Scheme" in *African Philosophy: Selected Readings, Mosley, Albert G (ed)*. Gyekye, Kwame.

"Bantu Philosophy" in *African Philosophy: Selected Readings, Mosley, Albert G (ed)*. Tempels, Placide.

"Contemporary Thought in French Speaking Africa" in *African Philosophy: Selected Readings, Appiah, Kwame Anthony*. Irele, Abiola.

"Custom and Morality" in *African Philosophy: Selected Readings, Mosley, Albert G (ed)*. Wiredu, Kwasi.

"Excerpts from Knowledge, Belief, and Witchcraft" in *African Philosophy: Selected Readings, Mosley, Albert G (ed)*. Hallen, Barry and Sodipo, J O.

"How Natives Think" in *African Philosophy: Selected Readings, Mosley, Albert G (ed)*. Levy-Bruhl, Lucien.

"How Not to Compare African Thought with Western Thought" in *African Philosophy: Selected Readings, Mosley, Albert G (ed)*. Wiredu, Kwasi.

"La Vraie Face de la Démocratie": A Note. Keita, Lansana.

"Morality, Art, and African Philosophy: A Response to Wiredu" in *African Philosophy: Selected Readings, Mosley, Albert G (ed)*. English, Parker and Hamme, Nancy Steele.

"Negritude, Nationalism, and Nativism: Racists or Racialists?" in *African Philosophy: Selected Readings, Appiah, Kwame Anthony*. Mosley, Albert G.

"On Negrohood: Psychology of the African Negro" in *African Philosophy: Selected Readings, Mosley, Albert G (ed)*. Senghor, Leopold S.

"On the Distinction between Modern and Traditional African Aesthetics" in *African Philosophy: Selected Readings, Mosley, Albert G (ed)*. Blocker, H Gene.

"The Conservation of Races" in *African Philosophy: Selected Readings, Mosley, Albert G (ed)*. Du Bois, William E B.

"The Particular and the Universal" in *African Philosophy: Selected Readings, Mosley, Albert G (ed)*. Hountondji, Paulin.

"'The Instruction of Any' and Moral Philosophy" in *African Philosophy: Selected Readings, Mosley, Albert G (ed)*. James, David.

African Philosophy: Selected Readings. Mosley, Albert G (ed).

Encountering the Other(s): Studies in Literature, History, and Culture. Brinker-Gabler, Gisela (ed).

I Am Because We Are: Readings in Black Philosophy. Hord, Fred Lee (ed) and Lee, Jonathan Scott (ed).

Readings in African Philosophy: An Akan Collection. Kwame, Safro (ed).

A Debate on African Philosophy. Rai, Chhaya.

A Practical Idea of Blackness. Kiros, Teodros.

Africa: The Role Model of Planetary Solidarity—Between All Humans and the Human Universum. Eboh, Marie Pauline.

Afro Images: Politics, Fashion, and Nostalgia. Davis, Angela Y.

Are There Cultural Universals?. Wiredu, Kwasi.

Black Socrates?. Critchley, Simon.

Bringing Women Back In: A Search for Alternative Historiographies. Ahikire, Josephine.

Conceptualizing Democracy in an African Context. Fortman, Bas de Gaay.

Critical Comments on Pearce, African Philosophy, and the Sociological Thesis. Bewaji, John A I.

Dialogue and Universalism: A Practical Application to Africa. Eboh, Marie Pauline.

Indeterminacy, Ethnophilosophy, Linguistic Philosophy, African Philosophy. Hallen, Barry.

La Tribu Contre l'Etat en Afrique. Dimi, Charles.

Language and Igbo Philosophy: Towards an Igbo Phenomenology of Language. Chukweulobe, Matthew C.

Las preguntas básicas sobre la filosofía-de-los sabios en Africa. Oruka, H Odera.

Le Syndrome Hampâté Bâ ou Comment Naissent les Proverbes. Konaté, Yacouba.

Rorty's Critique of Philosophy: The Implications for the Search for a Method in Contemporary African Philosophy. Irele, Dipo.

The House of the "INU": Keys to the Structure of a Yoruba Theory of the Self. Hallen, Barry and Sodipo, Olubi.

Towards an African (Yoruba) Perspective on Empirical Knowledge: A Critique of Hallen and Sodipo. Okè, Moses.

Truth and Ethics in African Thought: A Reply to Emmanuel Eze. Bewaji, Tunde.

Truth, Ethics and Divination in Igbo and Yoruba Traditions: A Reply to Emmanuel Eze. Uyanne, Frank.

AFRO-AMERICAN

Bad Faith and Antiblack Racism. Gordon, Lewis R.

Multiculturalism: A Critical Reader. Goldberg, David Theo.

Afro Images: Politics, Fashion, and Nostalgia. Davis, Angela Y.

By Any Means Necessary: John Locke and Malcolm X on the Right to Revolution. Gordon, Jill.

Mixed Black and White Race and Public Policy. Zack, Naomi.

Non-Cartesian *Sums*: Philosophy and the African-American Experience. Mills, Charles.

Pedagogy, Philosophy, and African-American Students. Martinez, Roy.

Preferential Hiring and Just War Theory. English, Parker.

Reflective Solidarity. Dean, Jodi.

AFROCENTRISM

"Cheikh Anta Diop, the 'Stolen Legacy,' and Afrocentrism" in *African Philosophy: Selected Readings, Mosley, Albert G (ed)*. Crawford, Jeffrey.

AGAMBEN, G

Idea of Prose. Agamben, Giorgio, Sullivan, Michael (trans) and Whitsitt, Sam (trans).

AGAPE

Perplexity and Ultimacy. Desmond, William.

Peirce's Agape and the Generality of Concern. Anderson, Douglas R.

AGE OF REASON

see Enlightenment

AGENCY

Algunas presuposiciones metafísicas de la acción humana. Haldane, John.

Browning and Two Traditions. Krecz, Charles A.

Deseos Distinguidos. Platts, Mark.

Doing and Refraining from Refraining. Xu, Ming.

Ethics and Agency Theory. French, Peter A.

Is Gerwin's Natural-Agency Theory a Viable Alternative to Hume?. Ward, Andrew.

Motivation and Moral Choice in Kant's Theory of Rational Agency. McCarty, Richard.

Neutralidad y relatividad agencial. Farrell, Martín D.

On the Basic Logic of STIT with a Single Agent. Xu, Ming.

Rational Agency and Objectively Practical Reason. Abrams, Edward L.

Reply to Krecz. Browning, Douglas.

Thomas Reid on Free Agency. O'Connor, Timothy.

AGENT

Comprensión e identidad: Encuentro entre filosofíade la historia y filosofía de la acción. Cruz, Manuel.

La Dualidad Personal: Autor y Actor. Choza, Jacinto.

Punishing Times: Reply to Smilansky. New, Christopher.

Santo Tomás y el *De Amina* (Comentario a los Caps. 4 y 5 del Libro III del *De Anima* de Aristóteles). Schmidt Andrade, Ciro E.

The Control of Actions by Agents. Vollmer, Fred.

Utilitarianism and Future Mistakes: Another Look. Curran, Angela.

AGGRESSION

Aggressiveness, Competition and Human Unity. Chatterjee, Amitava.

Das Aggressionsverhalten der subhumanan Primaten. Rosinski, Franciszek M.

AGING

A Buddhist Reflection on the Task of Elders. Nakasone, Ronald Y.

CQ Sources/Bibliography. Buehler, David A.

Dementia in Our Midst: The Moral Community. Post, Stephen G.

Ethics in an Aging Society. Holstein, Martha.

Health, Aging, and Death. Emson, Harry E.

Jessica Mitford Discusses Attitudes on Aging. Kushner, Thomasine.

AGNOSTICISM

Weak Agnosticism Defended. Oppy, Graham.

AGRARIAN

"Class Structure and Choice of Technology in an Agrarian Economy" in *Foundations of Analytical Marxism (Volume I), Roemer, John E (ed)*. Cabeza-Gutés, Maite.

AGREEMENT

El contractualismo libero de D Gauthier: Contratualismo vs Utilitarismo. González Altable, M Pilar.

Terms of Agreement. Bach, Kent.

AGRICOLA, R

Rudolf Agricola's *De inventione dialectica libri tres*. Van Der Poel, Marc.

AGRICULTURE

Amounts of Pesticides Reaching Target Pests: Environmental Impacts and Ethics. Pimentel, David.

Beyond the Terms of the Contract: Mothers and Farmers. Campbell, Mora.

Commentary—Social Justice and Sustainable Agriculture: Moving Beyond Theory. Clancy, Kate.

De wereld van de legbatterij. Van De Poel, Ibo.

Do Agriculturalists Need a New, an Ecocentric, Ethic? 1994 Presidential Address to the Agriculture, Food, and Human Values Society. Comstock, Gary L.

Ethics Perceptions of American Farmers: An Empirical Analysis. Rappaport, Allen and Himschoot, Robert A.

Journalists' Views of Advertiser Pressures on Agricultural News. Reisner, Ann and Walter, Gerry.

Off the Treadmill? Technology and Tourism in the North American Maple Syrup Industry. Hinrichs, C Clare.

Wes Jackson, Wendell Berry, and Bruce Colman (eds): *Meeting the Expectations of the Land: Essays in Sustainable Agriculture and Stewardship*. Houle, K.

AHARONOV, Y

The Aharonov-Bohm Effect and the Reality of Wave Packets. Liu, Chuang.

AHIMSA

Ahimsa, the Self, and Postmodernism: Jain, Vedantist, and Buddhist Perspectives. Gier, Nicholas F.

Ahimsa (Noninjury) Revisited. Fox, Michael W.

AHLBERG, L

On Analysing Analytic Aesthetics. Shusterman, Richard.

AIDS

Intervention and Reflection: Basic Issues in Medical Ethics (Fifth Edition). Munson, Ronald (ed).

AIDS

The Constructed Body: AIDS, Reproductive Technology, and Ethics. Murphy, Julien S.

AIDS, Confidentiality, and Ethical Models. Gorbett, Jason.

Going Early, Going Late: The Rationality of Decisions about Suicide in AIDS. Battin, Margaret P.

Health Care Workers with HIV and a Patient's Right To Know. Murphy, Timothy F.

HIV +/AIDS Related Bioethical Issues in Japan. Hoshino, Kazusama.

HIV Preventive Vaccine Research: Selected Ethical Issues. Grady, Christine.

Informed Consent and Anonymous Tissue Samples: The Case of HIV Seroprevalence Studies. Kopelman, Loretta M.

Legal Trends in Bioethics. Davis, Dena S.

Moving From Autonomy to Responsibility in HIV-Related Healthcare. Tuohey, John F.

Sida y confidencialidad: un problema complejo. Luna, Florencia.

Some Thoughts on AIDS and Death. Novick, Alvin.

The Moral Significance of AIDS. Murphy, Timothy F and Walters, LeRoy.

AIM

see Purpose

AJDUKIEWICZ

The Universal Scientific Methods. Krajewski, Wladyslaw.

AKAIKE, H

Forster and Sober on the Curve-Fitting Problem. Kukla, André.

AKAN

"An Essay on African Philosophical Thought—The Akan Conceptual Scheme" in *African Philosophy: Selected Readings, Mosley, Albert G (ed)*. Gyekye, Kwame.

Readings in African Philosophy: An Akan Collection. Kwame, Safro (ed).

AKRASIA

Aristotle and Augustine on Freedom: Two Theories of Freedom, Voluntary Action, and Akrasia. Chappell, T D J.

Akrasia. Wilkerson, Terence.

Non-Intentional Actions. Chan, David K.

AL-FARABI

Al-Fârâbî: El Concepto del Ser. Ramón, Rafael.

Los "Articulos de Necesario Conocimiento Para Quien se Inicie en el Arte de la Lógica" de ABU NASR AL-FARABI. Ramón Guerrero, Rafael.

AL-RAZI

Abu Bakr Al-Razi: Un Filósofo de una Antiguedad Tardía. Escobar, Santiago.

ALBERT THE GREAT

"Sinderesi, desidereio naturale e fondamento dell'agire morale nel pensiero medievale" in *L'etica e il suo Altro, Vigna, Carmelo (ed)*. Sciuto, Italo.

El *De animalibus* de Alberto Magno y la organización del discurso sobre los animales en el siglo XIII. De Asúa, Miguel.

La Relación Entre la Metafísica y la Teología en San Alberto Magno y Santo Tomás de Aquino. Andereggen, Ignacio E M.

Notabilia V. Imbach, Ruedi.

ALBRITTON, R

Free Willing: Comments on Hoffman's "Freedom and Strength of Will". Chappell, Vere.

Freedom and Strength of Will in Hoffman and Albritton. Watson, Gary.

Freedom and Strength of Will: Descartes and Albritton. Hoffman, Paul.

Responses to Chappell and Watson. Hoffman, Paul.

ALCHEMY

"Sali Nitri" de Vico y los Orígenes de la Civilización Pagana: La Dimensión Alquímica de la "Ciencia Nueva". Costa, Gustavo.

The Diffident Naturalist: Robert Boyle and the Philosophy of Experiment. Sargent, Rose-Mary.

The Hermetic Tradition: Symbols and Teachings of the Royal Art. Evola, Julius.

Il "Traicté du Feu et du Sel" di Blaise de Vigenère e una sua Sconosciuta Traduzione Italiana. Trabucco, Oreste.

ALCOHOLISM

see also Drunkenness

Liver Transplantation and Alcoholic Patients: When is it Justified to Just Say No?. Rutecki, Gregory W.

ALEXANDER OF APHRODISIAS

Alexander of Aphrodisias: Quaestiones 2.16-3.15. Sharples, R W (trans).

ALFONSI, P

'Potere' e 'ragione' nel *Dialogus* di Pietro Alfonsi (Mosà Sefardi): Linee preliminari per una ipotesi interpretativa. Arduini, Maria Lodovica.

ALFORD, C

Language, Narration and the Self. Staude, John-Raphael.

ALGAZEL

Una Cit de Algazel en la Filosofía del Sentido Común de Llorens y Barba. Anglés Cervelló, Misericordia.

ALGEBRA

see also Boolean Algebra

A Desperate Fix. Hale, Bob.

A Note on the Logical Dependence of Simple Quantifiers. Zuber, R.

Algebraic Study of Two Deductive Systems of Relevance Logic. Font, Josep Maria and Rodríquez, Gonzalo.

An Algebraic Characterization of Thomason's System Δ. Marconi, Diego.

An Algebraic Theory of Normal Forms. Ghilardi, Silvio.

Anneaux de Fonctions p-Adiques. Bélair, Luc.

Applications of Cohomology to Set Theory I: Hausdorff Gaps. Talayco, Daniel E.

Beniaminov Algebras Revised: One More Algebraic Version of First-Order Logic. Cirulis, Janis.

Chains and Antichans in Interval Algebras. Bekkali, M.

Cinque Esemplari Postillati della *Scienza Nuova*. Rotoli, Daniela.

Completeness Results for Intuitionistic and Modal Logic in a Categorical Setting. Makkai, M.

Connections Between Axioms of Set Theory and Basic Theorems of Universal Algebra. Kurucz, H Andréka and Németi, I.

Corps et Chirurgie. Pillay, Anand and Poizat, Bruno.

Diophantine Undecidability in Some Rings of Algebraic Numbers of Totally Real Infinite Extensions.... Shlapentokh, Alexandra.

Elimination des Quantificateurs dans des Paires de Corps. Leloup, G.

Even Tabular Modal Logics Sometimes do not have Independent Base for Admissible Rules. Rybakov, Vladimir V.

Fork Algebras are Representable. Frias, Marcelo F, Baum, Gabriel A and Haeberer, Armando M.

Grammar Formalisms Viewed as Evolving Algebras. Johnson, David E and Moss, Lawrence S.

Incremental Semantics for Propositional Texts. Vermeulen, C F M.

Is Algebraic Lorentz-Covariant Quantum Field Theory Stochastic Einstein Local?. Muller, F A and Butterfield, Jeremy.

Modal Fictionalism Cannot Deliver Possible World Semantics. Divers, John.

Modal Fictionalism Fixed. Rosen, Gideon.

Modal Fictionalism—a Simple Dilemma. Hale, Bob.

On a Generalization of Distributivity. Kanai, Yasuo.

On Jacob Klein's *Greek Mathematical Thought and the Origin of Algebra*. Gonda, Joseph.

On Some Operators on Pseudovarieties II. Graczynska, Ewa.

Representations for Small Relation Algebras. Andréka, Hajnal and Maddux, Roger D.

Semantics for First Degree Relatedness Logic. Paoli, Francesco.

Strict Coherence, Sigma Coherence and the Metaphysics of Quantity. Skyrms, Brian.

Superstable Quasi-Varieties. Hart, B and Starchenko, S.

Syntactic Refutations against Finite Models in Modal Logic. Skura, Tomasz.

The Data Type of Stack Algebras. Bergstra, J A and Tucker, J V.

The Model Theory of Unitriangular Groups. Belegradek, Oleg V.

Topological Structure of Diagonalizable Algebras and Corresponding Logical Properties of Theories. D'Agostino, Giovanna.

ALGERIAN

"Beauvoir and the Algerian War: Toward a Postcolonial Ethics" in *Feminist Interpretations of Simone de Beauvoir, Simons, Margaret A (ed)*. Murphy, Julien.

ALGORITHM

Reasoning about Knowledge. Fagin, Ronald (& others).

Changing the Theory of Theory Change: Towards a Computational Approach. Tennant, Neil.

Characterization of Realizable Space Complexities. Seiferas, Joel I and Meyer, Albert R.

Fixed-parameter Tractability and Completeness IV: On Completeness for W[P] and PSPACE Analogues. Abrahamson, K A (& others).

Logical Reasoning and Domain Specificity: A Critique of the Social Exchange Theory of Reasoning. Davies, Paul Sheldon, Fetzer, James H and Foster, Thomas R.

Reasoning, Logic and Computation. Shapiro, Stewart.

The Structure of the Honest Polynomial m-Degrees. Downey, Rod, Gasarch, William and Moses, Michael.

ALIEN

Rationality and Alien Cultures. Simon, Lawrence H.

ALIENATION

The Future of Alienation. Schacht, Richard.

Diferença entre Alienaçao e Estranhamento nos Manuscritos Econômico-Filosóficos (1844), de Karl Marx. Ferreira Chagas, Eduardo.

El Idealismo Práctico de Marx: Una Lectura de las *Thesen über Feuerbach*. Andrés Bonetti, José.

En torno a la ecuación desarrollo científico y tecnológico igual a progreso social. Cuello, César.

La alienación del trabajo según la perspectiva del marxismo analítico. Gallichio, Santiago.

Loneliness, Its Nature and Forms: An Existential Perspective. McGraw, John G.

ALLAIS, M

The Real Foundations of the Alleged Errors in Allais' Impossibility Theorem: Unceasingly Repeated Errors or Contraditions of Mark Machina. Allais, Maurice.

The Two Errors: A Summary. Machina, Mark J.

Two Errors in the 'Allais Impossibility Theorem'. Machina, Mark J.

ALLEN, D

Is Marx a Moral Consequentialist?. Vogel, Jeffrey S.

ALLIANCE

Agency and Alliance in Public Discourses About Sexualities. Jakobsen, Janet R.

ALLISON, H

Allison's Reading of Kant's Paradox of Inner Sense. Conard, Mark T.

ALLOY

Ideal Reaction Types and the Reactions of Real Alloys. Ramsey, Jeffry L.

ALONSO

Friar Alonso on the Logic of God. Redmond, Walter.

ALSTON, W

Alston and Hartshorne on the Concept of God. Dombrowski, Daniel A.

ALSTON, W

Alston on Direct Perception and Interpretation. Van Woudenberg, René.

Alstonian Foundationalism and Higher-Level Theistic Evidentialism. Sudduth, Michael L Czapkay.

Bi-Level Evidentialism and Reformed Apologetics. Suddith, Michael L Czapkay.

Perceptual Experience, Doxastic Practice, and the Rationality of Religious Commitment. Audi, Robert.

St Teresa, William Alston, and the Broadminded Atheist. Kretzmann, Norman.

Truth-Warranted Manifestation Beliefs. Zeis, John.

What's the Question?. Plantinga, Alvin.

Why Alston's Mystical Doxastic Practice Is Subjective. Gale, Richard.

ALTERITY

Anima hace hablar a la razón con una voz diferente: Nuevos nexos entre la tecnociencia y el mundo de la vida. Cañón Loyes, Camino.

La alteridad en el Sofista de Platón. Iglesias, Mercedes.

ALTHUSSER, L

"A Process Without a Subject or Goal(s)" in Marxism in the Postmodern Age, Callari, Antonio (ed). Montag, Warren.

Althusser: A Critical Reader. Elliott, Gregory (ed).

ALTRUISM

"Did Evolution Make Us Psychological Egoists?" in From a Biological Point of View, Sober, Elliott. Sober, Elliott.

"The Emotions of Altruism, East and West" in Emotions in Asian Thought, Marks, Joel (ed). Kupperman, Joel J.

Ayn Rand: The Russian Radical. Sciabarra, Chris Matthew.

Emotions in Asian Thought. Marks, Joel (ed) and Ames, Roger T (ed).

Evolution and Human Values. Wesson, Robert (ed) and Williams, Patricia A (ed).

A Critical Review of Philosophical Work on the Units of Selection Problem. Sober, Elliott and Wilson, David Sloan.

Aristotle on Loving Another for His Own Sake. Rogers, Kelly.

Caring for Whom? Moral Discussions between Early Confucians and Mohists. Defoort, Carine.

Design and Evaluation of a Programme to Promote Prosocial-Altruistic Behaviour in the School. Etxebarria, I (& others).

Egoism and Altruism in Ethics: Dispensing with Spurious Generality. Van Der Steen, Wim J.

Existence Value, Welfare and Altruism. Aldred, Jonathan.

From the Senses to Sense: The Hermeneutics of Love. Shafer, Ingrid H.

Language as a Community of Interacting Belief Systems: A Case Study Involving Conduct Toward Self and Others. Wilson, David Sloan.

Narratives of Volunteering. Paolicchi, Piero.

Nishitani and Nietzsche on the Selfless Self. Smith, Joel R.

Pangloss, L'Erreur et la Divergence. Laurier, Daniel.

Teaching Philanthropy Ethics. Martin, Mike W.

The Naturalness of Creation and Redemptive Interests in Theology, Science, and Technology. Richardson, Kurt Anders.

The Possibility of Communist Altruism. Jenkins, J L.

Was Ayn Rand a Humanist?. Walker, Jeff.

ALVAREZ, M

A Radical Interpretation of Davidson: Reply to Alvarez. Glock, Hans-Johann.

ALZHEIMER'S DISEASE

Commentary on "The Alzheimer's Disease Sufferer as Semiotic Subject". Hope, Tony.

Dementia in Our Midst: The Moral Community. Post, Stephen G.

The Alzheimer's Disease Sufferer as a Semiotic Subject. Sabat, Steven R and Harré, Rom.

AMBIGUITY

A Challenge to the Compound Lottery Axiom: A Two-Stage Normative Structure and Comparison to Other Theories. Davis, Donald B and Paté-Cornell, M Elisabeth.

Ambiguità e Semiosi. Morpurgo-Tagliabue, Guido.

Executing the Second Best Option. Pietroski, Paul M.

Regular, Ambiguo, Disposicional. Pérez de Tudela, Jorge.

Tras la postmodernidad. Innerarity, Daniel.

AMERICAN

see also Iberoamerica, Latin American

"American Philosophy and Its Lost Public" in Pragmatism: From Progressivism to Postmodernism, Hollinger, Robert (ed). Kuklick, Bruce.

"American Pragmatism and the Humanist Tradition" in Pragmatism: From Progressivism to Postmodernism, Hollinger, Robert (ed). Kolenda, Konstantin.

"In Defense of the French" in European Philosophy and the American Academy, Smith, Barry (ed). Garver, Newton.

"Obstacles to Fruitful Discussion in the American Academy" in European Philosophy and the American Academy, Smith, Barry (ed). Detmer, David J.

"On Writing Philosophy" in American Philosophy Today and Other Philosophical Studies, Rescher, Nicholas. Rescher, Nicholas.

"Public Philosophy and Public Theology in America Today" in Civil Religion and Political Theology, Rouner, Leroy S (ed). Bellah, Robert N.

"The Decline and Fall of French Nietzscheo-Structuralism" in European Philosophy and the American Academy, Smith, Barry (ed). Engel, Pascal.

"The Moral Justification of Systematic Education Reform in the United States" in Identity, Culture, and Education, Smeyers, Paul (ed). Bull, Barry.

"The Problem of Pragmatism in American History" in Pragmatism: From Progressivism to Postmodernism, Hollinger, Robert (ed). Hollinger, David A.

"The Unhinging of the American Mind: Derrida as Pretext" in European Philosophy and the American Academy, Smith, Barry (ed). Willard, Dallas.

"Tolerance" as an Excuse for Censorship on Campus. Levin, Michael.

"Vanishing Frontiers in American Philosophy: Two Dogmas of Idealism" in Pragmatism: From Progressivism to Postmodernism, Hollinger, Robert (ed). Sleeper, Ralph W.

A Companion to American Thought. Fox, Richard Wightman (ed) and Kloppenberg, James T (ed).

American Mixed Race: The Culture of Microdiversity. Zack, Naomi (ed).

American Philosophy Today and Other Philosophical Studies. Rescher, Nicholas.

An American Ethic: A Philosophy of Freedom Applied to Contemporary Issues. Gerken, John D.

Ernst Cassirer—Von Marburg nach New York: Eine philosophische Biographie. Paetzold, Heinz.

European Philosophy and the American Academy. Smith, Barry (ed).

Max Weber in Amerika: Wirkungsgeschichte und Rezeptionsgeschichte Webers in der anglo-amerikanischen Philosophie und Sozialwissenschaft. Erdelyi, Agnes.

Pragmatism: From Progressivism to Postmodernism. Hollinger, Robert (ed) and Depew, David (ed).

Racist Culture: Philosophy and the Politics of Meaning. Goldberg, David Theo.

Rational Individualism: The Perennial Philosophy of Legal Interpretation. Simonds, Roger T.

Too Much Liberty?: Perspectives on Freedom and the American Dream. Saari, David J.

Understanding History: An Introduction to Analytical Philosophy of History. Gorman, Jonathan.

A Comparison of Japanese and U S Corporate Financial Accountability and its Impact on the Responsibilties of Corporate Managers. Hazera, Alejandro.

A Critical Discussion of John E Smith's Communitarian Vision. Kruse, Felicia.

A Sounding of Walden's Philosophical Depth. Borjesson, Gary.

An Analysis of Public Interest Reporting: The Case of General Motors in South Africa. Malone, David and Roberts, Robin W.

Bribery and Extortion in International Business: Ethical Perceptions of Greeks Compared to Americans. Tsalikis, John and LaTour, Michael S.

Coercion and Long-Term Contraceptives. Steinbock, Bonnie.

Contraceptive Policy and Ethics: Illustrations from American History. Powderly, Kathleen E.

Conversing With Other Minds: A Symposium of Themes. Kaplan, Andrew.

Cornel West: American Radicalism. Osborne, Peter.

Distributive Justice and the Minnesota Health Access Initiative. Hull, Robert.

Does Legally Mandated Consent to Psychotherapy Ensure Ethical Appropriateness?: The Colorado Experience. Handelsman, Mitchell M (& others).

Egoist Theory and America's Individualist Anarchists: A Dilemma of Praxis. Brooks, Frank.

Ethical Perceptions of Organizational Politics: A Comparative Evaluation of American and Hong Kong Managers. Ralston, David A, Giacalone, Robert A and Terpstra, Robert H.

Ethics Perceptions of American Farmers: An Empirical Analysis. Rappaport, Allen and Himschoot, Robert A.

Extracto de "Libraos de Ultramaria". Bentham, Jeremy.

G H Mead: Linguistically Constituted Intersubjectivity and Ethics. Mendieta, Eduardo.

Hegel y América. Perez-Estevez, Antonio.

Historicism: The History and Meaning of the Term. Iggers, Georg G.

John Locke and the Fundamental Constitutions of Carolina. Milton, J R.

John Smith's America's Philosophical Vision: American and/or Philosophical?. Wallace, Kathleen.

Language, Action and Context: Linguistic Pragmatics in Europe and America. Nerlich, Brigitte and Clarke, David D.

Long-Acting Contraceptives: Rationale, Current Development, and Ethical Implications. Brown, George F.

Medalist's Address. Dougherty, Jude P.

Mixed Black and White Race and Public Policy. Zack, Naomi.

Negotiating the Moral Order: Paradoxes of Ethics Consultation. Crigger, Bette-Jane.

Nietzsche, Heidegger, and the Americanization of Defeat. Bergmann, Peter.

Oikophobia and Xenophilia. Scruton, Roger.

On the Motives for the New Sociology of Science. Fuller, Steve.

Philosophical Night Vision. Stuhr, John.

Philosophy of Liberation in the North American Context: Transforming Oppressor Consciousness. Lindemann, Kate.

Public Relations Ethics: Ivy Lee, Hill and Knowlton, and the Gulf War. Marlin, Randal.

Review of "The Community Reconstructs: The Meaning of Pragmatic Social Thought" by James Campbell. Golash, Deirdre.

Santo Tomás de Aquino como Inspirador de Francisco de Vitoria. Romero Baró, José María.

Teaching as a Moral Activity: Listening to Teachers in Russia and the United States. Higgins, Ann.

The Critical Aesthetics of Disney World. Berleant, Arnold.

The Family in Trouble: Why We Should Worry. Elshtain, Jean Bethke.

The New World Disorder: A Crisis of Philosophical Identity. Redpath, Peter A.

The United States Media and the Liberal Tradition. Bartkowiak, Julia J.

The University, Dialogue and Universalism. Brown, Charles S.

Top Executive Compensation: Equity or Excess? Implications for Regaining American Competitiveness. Walters, Bruce, Hardin, Tim and Schick, James.

Toward a Fuller Recovery of Living Reason. Colapietro, Vincent.

Trapped in a Metaphor. Sanday, Peggy Reeves.

Vico en Italia y en USA. Sevilla, José M.

ARISTOTLE

Readings in Ancient Greek Philosophy: From Thales to Aristotle. Cohen, S Marc (ed), Curd, Patricia (ed) and Reeve, C D C (ed).

Rhetorische Vernunft Oder: Das Design in der Philosophie. Mainberger, Gonsalv K.

Sachen und Zeichen: Zur Philosophie des Pragmatismus. Oehler, Klaus.

Substance and Separation in Aristotle. Spellman, Lynne.

The Cambridge Companion to Aristotle. Barnes, Jonathan (ed).

The Crossroads of Norm and Nature. Sim, May (Mui Hwa) (ed).

The Sciences in Greco-Roman Society (Apeiron 27-4). Barnes, Timothy D.

The Sea Battle and the Master Argument: Aristotle and Diodorus Cronus on the Metaphysics of the Future. Gaskin, Richard.

Time and Exteriority: Aristotle, Heidegger, Derrida. Protevi, John.

Tode Ti and *Toionde* in Metaphysics Z. Yu, Jiyuan.

Tommaso Campanella: Eine Philosophie der Ähnlichkeit. Hagengruber, Ruth.

Versus Trasimaco: E confutabile il detto "la giustizia non è altro che l'utile del più forte"?. Fiorillo, Vanda.

A Investigaçao sobre o Tempo na "Física" de Aristóteles. Quartim de Moraes, Joao.

Acting From Virtue. Audi, Robert.

Akrasia. Wilkerson, Terence.

Algunas consideraciones sobre "lo sensible" en *De Anima*. Mier y Terán, Rocío.

Algunas Precisiones Sobre el Lenguaje y la Paronimia en Aristóteles. Femenías, María Luisa.

An Ingenuous Account of the Doctrine of the Mean. Martin, Christopher.

Are There "Cont-Moral Virtues?". McCarty, Richard.

Argumentación y Método en la Etica Eudemia. Arreguín, Héctor Zagal.

Argumentaciones éticas a partir de la naturaleza: Aristóteles y después. Annas, Julia.

Aristote et l'Aristotélisme. Elders, Leo.

Aristoteles' "Politik" kommentieren. Höffe, Otfried.

Aristotle and Hellenistic Philosophy. Sharples, Bob.

Aristotle and the Political Role of Women. Mulgan, Richard.

Aristotle Meets Wall Street: The Case for Virtue Ethics in Business. Boatright, John R.

Aristotle nel Novecento. Mangiagalli, Maurizio.

Aristotle on Detective Fiction. Sayers, Dorothy L.

Aristotle on Dividing the Soul and Uniting the Virtues. Gottlieb, Paula.

Aristotle on Imagination: *De anima* iii 3. Turnbull, Kenneth.

Aristotle on Loving Another for His Own Sake. Rogers, Kelly.

Aristotle on Substance, Essence and Biological Kinds. Charles, David.

Aristotle on Tragedy: Rediscovering the *Poetics*. Howland, Jacob A.

Aristotle on Unqualified Knowledge: Do Referential Universals Solve the *Meno* Paradox?. Degnan, Michael.

Aristotle's Biology: Plain, But Not Simple. Lennox, James G.

Aristotle's Completeness Proof. Smiley, Timothy.

Aristotle's Method. McLeod, Owen.

Aristotle's Renaissance As an Example of the Essential Tension between Tradition and Innovation. Berti, Enrico.

Aristotle's Theology and Its Influence on the Philosophers of Islam, Judaism and Christianity. Georgiadis, Constantine.

Aristotle, Success, and Moral Luck. Farwell, Paul.

Aristotle: Philosophy and Politics, Theory and Practice. Thompson, Walter J.

Assertoric vs Modal Syllogistic. Striker, Gisela.

Autour du *Liber de causis*: Quelques réflexions sur la récente littérature. Pattin, Adriaan.

Biomedical Models of Reproduction in the Fifth Century BC and Aristotle's *Generation of Animals*. Coles, Andrew.

Chance and Teleology in Aristotle's *Physics*. Boeri, Marcelo D.

Commentary on Charles's "Aristotle on Substance, Essence and Biological Kinds". Gill, Mary Louise.

Commentary on Morrison's "The Place of Unity in Aristotle's Metaphysical Project". Pakaluk, Michael.

Commentary on Sherman's "The Role of Emotions in Aristotelian Virtue". Dustin, Christopher A.

Commentary on Smith's "What Use is Aristotle's *Organon*?". Hintikka, Jaakko.

Common Advantage and Common Good. Smith, Michael A.

Conceptualized and Unconceptualized Desire in Aristotle. Tuozzo, Thomas M.

Conflicting Parts of Happiness in Aristotle's Ethics. White, Nicholas P.

Consideraciones sobre el *De grammatico* de Anselmo de Canterbury. Corti, Enrique C.

Cuatro conceptos para un pensamiento no ilustrado (analogía, otredad, empatía y epimeleia). Llano, Carlos.

Cuerpo y Alma en el Helemorfismo de Santo Tomás. Beuchot, Mauricio.

Dialectic and the Syllogism. Smith, Robin.

Die Entdeckung Platons durch Schelling. Bubner, Rüdiger.

El ser de la verdad en la *Metafísica* de Aristóteles. Segura, Carmen.

El Significado de la Contrariedad. Sacchi, Mario Enrique.

Entre la Teoría Económica y la Economía Política: Estudio Sobre *Ética a Nicómaco* V.5 y *Política* I.8-10 de Aristóteles. Basañez, Frederico.

Epistemologie im Humanismus: Marsilio Ficino, Pietro Pomponazzi und Niklaus von Kues. Burkhard, Mojsisch.

Ethics and Aesthetics in Aristotle's *Poetics*. Crittenden, Paul.

Ethik und Freundschaft. Pazanin, Ante.

Evidencia de la naturaleza en Aristóteles. Morán y Castellanos, Jorge.

From Eternal to Perpetual Truths: A Note on the Medieval History of Aristotle, *De interpretatione*, Ch 1, 16a18. Kneepkens, C H.

Genus/Diferentia, Matter/Form, and Levels of Complexity. Freytag, Matthew.

Heidegger and Aristotle's Treatise on Time. Kane, Michael T.

Il Prologo al Commento a Giobbe di San Tommaso d'Aquino. Pandolfi, Carmelo.

In Defence of Aristotelian Honour. Putman, Daniel.

L'Élenchos del Principio nella Metafisica di Averroé. Roccaro, Giuseppe.

L'esclave, le travail et l'action: Aristote et Hegel. Faes, Hubert.

La définition et la démonstration dans la logique d'Aristote. Valois, Raynald.

La filosofia cristiana secondo Edith Stein. Tilliette, Xavier.

La Musica in Aristotele. Vetere, Lucia.

La perception du mouvement chez Aristote. Hubert, Bernard.

La riappropriazione di Aristotele nell'ultimo Ricoeur. Rizzacasa, Aurelio.

Le Glosse di Juan Ginés de Sepúlveda alle Traduzioni Latine di Aristotele. Coroleu, Alejandro.

Le Questioni Inedite. Conforti, Patrizia.

Metaphysik und Ontologie bei Aristoteles. Ambühl, Hans.

Modernità e post-modernità dell'agostinismo. Penati, Giancarlo.

Moralité privée et moralité publique chez Aristote. Rutten, Christian.

Movimiento y acto en Aristóteles. Lorite Mena, J.

Needs and Essence. Rotenstreich, Nathan.

Nota Acerca de las Precisiones Tomistas al Concepto Aristotélico de Ciencia Práctica y la Noción Contemporánea de Ciencias Sociales. Crespo, Ricardo F.

Nota Sobre el Estatuto Ontológico del Devenir en Aristóteles. Barrio Maestre, José María.

Nous y Phronesis: Un comentario a EN 1143a 35ss. Zagal, Héctor.

On Western Rationality and Its Alleged Relation to Aristotle. Evangeliou, Christos.

Ontologie und Politik: Quod racio principantes et subjecti sumitur ex racione actus et potencie. Flüeler, Christoph.

Per una Biografia Intellettuale di Marcel de Corte. Castellano, Danilo.

Relational Attributes in Aristotle. Morales, Fabio.

Roughing Out the Ground Rules: Reason and Experience in Practical Deliberation. Carr, David.

Santo Tomás y el *De Anima* (Comentario a los Caps. 4 y 5 del Libro III del *De Anima* de Aristóteles). Schmidt Andrade, Ciro E.

Sobre la Fortuna de Aristóteles en España. Escobar Chico, Angel.

Suchen, sich Verständigen, Kämpfen: das Umfeld der Sprache. Roberts, Julian.

Tavola Rotonda. Rossi, Pietro (& others).

The Becoming of Aristotelian Virtues. Sim, May (Mui Hwa).

The Definition of Philosophy, Revisited. Kainz, Howard P.

The Definition of Soul in Aristotle's *De anima* ii 1 Is Not Analogous to the Definition of Snub. Wehrle, Walter E.

The Discovery of the Imagination. Castoriadis, Cornelius.

The First Crisis in First Philosophy. Benardete, Seth.

The Founding of Logic. Corcoran, John.

The Keystone of the Aristotelian *Metaphysics*. Owens, Joseph J.

The Modern Misunderstanding of Aristotle's Theory of Motion. Balaban, Oded.

The Near Made Far Away: The Role of Cultural Criticism in Aristotle's Political Theory. Mara, Gerald.

The Ontological Status of Matter in Aristotle. Cresswell, M J.

The Place of Unity in Aristotle's Metaphysical Project. Morrison, Donald R.

The Problem of Dialectical Reasoning in Aristotle. Bolton, Robert.

The Role of Emotions in Aristotelian Virtue. Sherman, Nancy.

The Value of Passions in Plato and Aristotle. Leighton, Stephen.

The Value of Passions in Plato and Aristotle: Comments. Curzer, Howard J.

The Vocation to Be a Philosopher. Andrews, Philip.

Théorie Aristotélicienne du rôle de la quantité et de la qualité chez les êtres vivants (I). Bernier, Réjane.

Théorie Aristotélicienne du Rôle de la Quantité et de la Qualité chez les êtres Vivants (II). Bernier, Réjane.

Thirteenth-Century Discussions on Modal Terms. Spruyt, Joke.

Thomas Aquinas, Creation, and Two Historians. Dewan, Lawrence.

Tiempo, Verdad y Posibilidad en Aristóteles y la Filosofía Helenística. Weidemann, Hermann.

Tomás de Aquino, la voluntad y la Ética a Nicómaco. Gallagher, David M.

Tre Schede su Bruno e Oxford. Aquilecchia, Giovanni.

Una Pregunta Sobre la Noción de "Bien" en Aristóteles. Femenías, María Luisa.

Une étude sur l'aristotélisme réformé: L'édition Bodéüs de la Correspondance Leibniz-Thomasius. Duchesneau, François.

Vicisitudes de los Topicos. Pereda F, Carlos.

Virtue and Choice in Aristotle's *Ethics*. Tilley, John.

Vital Signs: The *Place* of Memory in Psychoanalysis. Shepherdson, Charles.

What Use is Aristotle's *Organon*?. Smith, Robin.

Wholes, Parts, and Sequences in Aristotle. Blyth, D J.

Why Ethics is Political Science for Aristotle. Gerson, L.

Why the Elements Imitate the Heaven: *Metaphysics* ix 8.1050b28-34. Lang, Helen S.

Zum Begriff des "Zuvorkommens" in der politischen Philosophie. Brieskorn, Norbert.

ARITHMETIC

Frege's Philosophy of Mathematics. Demopoulos, William (ed).

Parts of Classes. Lewis, David.

Selected Logic Papers: Enlarged Edition. Quine, W V.

Vie della scrittura: Frege e la svolta linguistica. Penco, Carlo.

A Feasible Theory for Analysis. Ferreira, Fernando.

A Model for Intuitionistic Non-standard Arithmetic. Moerdijk, I.

A Revision-Theoretic Analysis of the Arithmetical Hierarchy. Antonelli, Gian Aldo.

Almost Weakly 2-Generic Sets. Fenner, Stephen A.

Axiomatizing Higher-Order Kleene Realizability. Van Oosten, Jaap.

Counting on Number: Plato on the Goodness of *Arithmos*. Roochnik, David L.

Diophantine Undecidability in Some Rings of Algebraic Numbers of Totally Real Infinite Extensions.... Shlapentokh, Alexandra.

ASCETICISM
"Das Schöne, das Erhabene, die Askese und der Selbstmord" in *Naturzweckmässigkeit und ästhetische Kultur, Schwabe, Karl-Heinz (ed)*. Fischer, Peter.

ASHCRAFT, R
Liberalism and the Problem of Poverty: Reply to Ashcraft. Horne, Thomas A.
Radicalism, Capitalism and Historical Contexts: Not Only a Reply to Richard Ashcraft on John Locke. Wood, Ellen Meiksins.

ASIAN
see also Oriental
Emotions in Asian Thought. Marks, Joel (ed) and Ames, Roger T (ed).
Ethics and Australian International Business: Which Way to Asia?. Skubik, Daniel W.
On Heidegger's Other Sins of Omission: Asian Thought and Christian Philosophy. Bernasconi, Robert.
'Shame' as a Neglected Value in Schooling. Tombs, David.

ASIMOV, I
"Isaac Asimov's Contribution to Humanism" in *Contributors to the Philosophy of Humanism, Hillar, Marian (ed)*. Veley, Carl.

ASMIS, E
Commentary on Asmis's "Epicurean Poetics". Sider, David.

ASPECT
"The Marking of the Episodic/Generic Distinction in Tense-Aspect Systems" in *The Generic Book, Carlson, Gregory N (ed)*. Dahl, Östen.

ASSENT
Los dos tipos de asentimiento del escéptico y el problema de la posibilidad del conocimiento. Frede, Michael.

ASSERTION
Reasoning about Update Logic. Van Eijck, Jan and De Vries, Fer-Jan.
Truth, Assertion and Warrant. Teichmann, Roger.

ASSERTION LOGIC
Assertoric vs Modal Syllogistic. Striker, Gisela.

ASSESSMENT
Criterion-referenced Assessment and the Development of Knowledge and Understanding. Davis, Andrew.

ASSISTED SUICIDE
Beyond Theological Conflict in the Courts: The Issue of Assisted Suicide. Dyck, Arthur J.
Commentary on "But Is It Assisted Suicide?". Nelson, James Lindemann.
Conflicts of Conscience: Hospice and Assisted Suicide. Campbell, Courtney S (& others).
Physician Assisted Suicide: Its Challenge to the Prevailing Constitutional Paradigm. Robinson, John H.
Physician Assisted Suicide: New Developments in the Netherlands. Gevers, Sjef.
Physician-Assisted Suicide and the Profession's Gyrocompass. Miles, Steven H.
Professional Integrity and Physician-Assisted Death. Miller, Franklin G and Brody, Howard.
Reflections on the State of Current Debate Over Physician-Assisted Suicide and Euthanasia. Winkler, Earl.
The Role of Courts in the Debate on Assisted Suicide: A Communitarian Approach. Beschle, Donald L.
When the Majority Says You May Die: Aid-in-Dying Initiatives. Povelones Jr, Arthur A.

ASSOCIATION
Associació estable versus unió social: La concepció de la societat en Nozick i Rawls. Castiñera, Angel.
Axiomatizations of Commutative and Non-Associative Ajdukiewicz Calculus. Kandulski, Maciej.

ASSOCIATIONISM
Key Concepts: Associationism. Spitzer, Manfred.

ASSUMPTION
"Presuppositions in Science" in *Life, World and Meaning, Roux, A P J (ed)*. Kistner, Wietske.

ASTROLOGY
Adorno: The Stars Down to Earth and Other Essays on the Irrational in Culture. Crook, Stephen (ed) and Adorno, Theodor W.
Spinozismo e Libertinismo: A Proposito di due Recenti Libri su Boulainviller. Mori, Gianluca.

ASTRONOMY
"Das Naturverständnis Johannes Keplers" in *Naturauffassungen in Philosophie, Wissenschaft, Technik: Band II, Schäfer, Lothar (ed)*. Hoyer, Ulrich.
The Sciences in Greco-Roman Society (Apeiron 27-4). Barnes, Timothy D.
The Diagram H-R of Stars Displacement: Real Fact or Useful Research Instrument?. Zabierowski, Miroslaw.
The Scientific Revolution in the Renaissance—A Unique Phenomenon in the History of Mankind. Rosen, Edward.

ASYLUM
Asylum: A Moral Dilemma. Plaut, W Gunther.

ASYMMETRY
Difference and Repetition. Deleuze, Gilles and Patton, Paul (trans).
Asymmetry in Attitudes and the Nature of Time. Gallois, André.
Compatibilists Could Have Done Otherwise: Responsibility and Negative Agency. McIntyre, Alison.
Reinterpreting the Wheeler-Feynman Absorber Theory: Reply to Leeds. Price, Huw.
What's Right and What's Wrong with Transference Theories. Dowe, Phil.

ATHEISM
see also Theism
"Ricoeur on Atheism: A Critique" in *The Philosophy of Paul Ricoeur, Hahn, Lewis Edwin (ed)*. Detmer, David.
Analisi della Fede e Critica della Ragione nella Filosofia di Pierre Bayle. Paganini, Gianni.
Autonomie des Selbstbewusstseins: Eine Untersuchung zum Verhältnis von Bruno Bauer und Karl Marx (1835-1843). Waser, Ruedi.
Bridging the Sacred and the Secular. Hooper, J Leon (ed) and Murray, John Courtney.
Search for Community in a Withering Tradition: Conversations between a Marxian Atheist and a Calvinian Christian. Nielsen, Kai and Hart, Hendrik.
The Atheist Trap. Mixie, Joseph.
Anonymous or Analogous Christians? Rahner and von Balthasar on Naming the Non-Christian. Lamadrid, Lucas.
Appunti sulla Fortuna di Gabriel Naudé nella Germania del Primo Illuminismo. Mulsow, Martin.
Ateismo, filosofia e cristianesimo in Del Noce. Possenti, Vittorio.
Ateismo, scetticismo e fideismo. Penelhum, Terence.
De Sade o la subversión de/en la Ilustración. Mayos, Gonça.
Der Schöpfer als Wirklichkeit—Gegenüber dem Atheismus als nichtwissenschaftlicher Ideologie. Knappik, Georg J.
Heidegger's Understanding of the Atheism of Philosophy. Fehér, István M.
How Religion Impedes Moral Development. Clark, Brad.
Immanence and Transcendence in Modern Philosophy: Some Questions with Reference to Fichte's 'Dispute on Atheism' (in Dutch). Jonkers, P.
Sartre: Metodología del Problema de Dios. Ferrer, Gabriel.
Spinoza "athée & épicurien". Lagrée, Jacqueline.
Weak Agnosticism Defended. Oppy, Graham.

ATHENIAN
Achilles, Socrates, and Democracy. Holway, Richard.

ATKINS, P
Policing the Frontiers of Science. Velody, Irving.

ATOM
Atoms, Pleasure, Virtue: The Philosophy of Epicurus. Koen, Avraam.
Mind, Matter, and Quantum Mechanics. Stapp, Henry P.
Fork Algebras are Representable. Frias, Marcelo F, Baum, Gabriel A and Haeberer, Armando M.

ATOMISM
"Conceptual Connection and the Observation/ Theory Distinction" in *Holism: A Consumer Update, Fodor, Jerry A (ed)*. Anthony, Louise.
"Hegel on Galvinism" in *Hegel on the Modern World, Collins, Ardis B (ed)*. Burbidge, John W.
"Intentional Chemistry" in *Holism: A Consumer Update, Fodor, Jerry A (ed)*. Levine, Joseph.
"Solidity and Elasticity in the Seventeenth Century" in *Locke's Philosophy, Rogers, G A J (ed)*. Alexander, Peter.
Ancient Greek Philosophy: Its Development and Relevance to Our Time. Trundle, Robert C.
Ethics and Agency Theory. French, Peter A.
L'atomisme dans le monisme épicurien. Droz-Vincent, Gabriel.
Notas sobre la física epicúrea. Fallas, Luis A.
The Psychologist's Fallacy as a Persistent Framework in William James's Psychological Theorizing. Reed, Edward.
What is Wrong with an Atomistic Account of Mental Representation?. Hogan, Melinda.

ATONEMENT
"Leo Baeck: New Dimensions and Explorations" in *Thinkers and Teachers of Modern Judaism, Goldsmith, Emanuel S (ed)*. Friedlander, Albert H.

ATTENTION
Filosofía como arte y experiencia de la vida. Innerarity, Daniel.

ATTITUDE
see also Propositional Attitudes
"Radicalism or Historical Consciousness: On Breaks and Continuity in the Discussion of Basic Attitudes" in *Ecology, Technology, and Culture, Zweers, Wim (ed)*. Zweers, Wim.
Attitudes, Chaos, and the Connectionist Mind. Eiser, J Richard.
Attitudes as Nonentities. Baker, Lynne Rudder.
Discussions about the Use of Life-Sustaining Treatments: A Literature Review of Physicians' and Patients' Attitudes and Practices. Layson, Rita T (& others).
Etica y filosofía primera en E Levinas. Sanabria, José Rubén.
The Deontological Conception of Epistemic Justification and Doxastic Voluntarism. Kim, Kihyeon.

ATTRIBUTE
Relational Attributes in Aristotle. Morales, Fabio.
Substance et attribut chez Spinoza. Glausier, Richard.

ATTRIDGE, H
Commentary on Attridge's "Gnostic Platonism". Perkins, Pheme.

AUDARD, C
The Idea of Public Reason: Can It Fulfill Its Task?. Lehning, Percy B.

AUDI, R
Nondoxastic Faith: Audi on Religious Commitment. Radcliffe, Dana M.
Reply to Critics. Alston, William P.
Self-Deception and Belief Attribution. Hales, Steven D.

AUDITOR

Helps for CPAs in Dealing with Ethical Issues. Cooper, Robert W, Frank, Garry L and Heaston, Patrick H.

AUGUSTINE

"Gadamer and Augustine: On the Origin of the Hermeneutical Claim to Universality" in *Hermeneutics and Truth, Wachterhauser, Brice (ed)*. Grondin, Jean.

"La Teoría de los Géneros en San Agustín y S Tomás de Aquino" in *Temas Actuales de Filosofía, Palacios, María Julia (ed)*. Mendez, Julio R.

"Sinderesi, desidereio naturale e fondamento dell'agire morale nel pensiero medieval" in *L'etica e il suo Altro, Vigna, Carmelo (ed)*. Sciuto, Italo.

Aristotle and Augustine on Freedom: Two Theories of Freedom, Voluntary Action, and Akrasia. Chappell, T D J.

Augustine: Against the Academicians and *The Teacher*. King, Peter (trans).

Augustine. Clark, Mary T.

Christianity and the Classics: The Acceptance of a Heritage. Helleman, Wendy E (ed).

Confessions' Bliss: Postmodern Criticism as a Palimpsest of Augustine's *Confessions*. Fendt, Gene.

Itinerari del Volontarismo: Teologia e politica al tempo di Luis de León. Ferraro, Domenico.

Sources of Hermeneutics. Grondin, Jean.

Augustine on Prescience and Free Will. den Bok, Nico.

Beyond Infinity: Augustin and Cantor. Drozdek, Adam.

Dalla nostalgia di patria alla nostalgia del paradiso. Giardini, F.

Dialéctica de Casiciaco. Rosado, Juan.

Does Evil Have a Cause? Augustine's Perplexity and Thomas' Answer. Steel, Carlos.

Empty Time and the Eternality of God. Lodzinski, Don.

Foreknowledge and Human Freedom in Augustine. Morgan, Vance G.

Giustizia e carità nella dottrina dei padri, Il. Pizzorini, Reginaldo M.

Il Significato del Cuore nella Filosofia Giuridica di S Agostino e di Marsilio da Padova. Ancona, Elvio.

La risposta di S Agostino alle critiche contro il cristianesimo. De Falco, Enrico.

Modernità e post-modernità dell'agostinismo. Penati, Giancarlo.

Sexual Needs and Sexual Pleasures. Moore, Gareth.

St Augustine on Just War. Schmal, Dániel.

Totum Suscepit. den Bok, Nico.

Ultimate Reality According to Augustine of Hippo. Teske, Roland J.

Why are There Sinners? Augustine's Response to Mackie. You, Sung-Keun.

AUGUSTINISM

Primera aproximación al lenguaje. Weismann, Francisco J.

AURAL

"What is it Like to be Boring and Myopic?" in *Dennett and his Critics, Dahlbom, Bo (ed)*. Akins, Kathleen.

AUREOLI

Ontologie und Politik: Quod racio principantes et subjecti sumitur ex racione actus et potencie. Flüeler, Christoph.

What Am I Thinking About? John Duns Scotus and Peter Aureol on Intentional Objects. Perler, Dominik.

AUSTIN

Logic, Facts, and Representation: An Examination of R M Hare's Moral Philosophy. Ronnow-Rasmussen, Toni.

Philosophical Passages: Wittgenstein, Emerson, Austin, Derrida. Cavell, Stanley.

Appreciating a Situation. Decyk, Betsy Newell.

Demonstratives, Descriptions, and Knowledge: A Critical Study of Three Recent Books. Martens, David.

J L Austin: un análisis de la percepción desde la fenomenología lingüística. Reverter Bañón, Sonia.

Rhetoric and the Perlocutionary Field. Mason, Jeff.

AUSTRALIAN

"The Religious and Ethical Tradition of Ancient and Contemporary Australia" in *Ethics, Religion and Biodiversity, Hamilton, Lawrence S (ed)*. Senanayake, Ranil.

Business Ethics and Commercial Morality in Western Australia. Small, Michael W.

Business Ethics and Commercial Morality: Report of the Royal Commission into Commercial Activities. Small, Michael W.

Can We Talk About Ethics Anymore?. Hill, John.

Ethics and Australian International Business: Which Way to Asia?. Skubik, Daniel W.

Ethics as Excellence: A Strategic Management Perspective. Smith, John Milton.

Means or Ends? Ethical Decision Frameworks in the Western Australian Public Service. Peachment, Allan (& others).

Police Gratuities: What the Public Think. Prenzler, Tim and Mackay, Peta.

The Use of Stakeholder Analysis to Understand Ethical and Moral Issues in the Primary Resource Sector. Frost, Frederick A.

AUSTRIAN

"Heinrich Gomperz und die Österreichische Philosophie" in *Heinrich Gomperz, Karl Popper und die österreichische Philosophie, Seiler, Martin (ed)*. Haller, Rudolf.

"Nach Verschiedenen Zwischenfällen ist die Arbeit Schliesslich bei mir Gelandet" in *Die besten Geister der Nation, Korotin, Ilse (ed)*. Korotin, Ilse.

"Österreichische Wissenschaftsgeschichte: Erkenntnisprozess oder Verdrängung?" in *Der geistige Anschluss, Fischer, Kurt R (ed)*. Wegeler, Cornelia.

"Philosophiestudieren in den dreissiger Jahren" in *Der geistige Anschluss, Fischer, Kurt R (ed)*. Ekstein, Rudolf.

"Konservative Revolution und Philosophie in Österreich" in *Der geistige Anschluss, Fischer, Kurt R (ed)*. Dethloff, Klaus and Wimmer, Franz M (ed).

Der geistige Anschluss. Fischer, Kurt R (ed) and Wimmer, Franz M (ed).

Heinrich Gomperz, Karl Popper und die österreichische Philosophie. Seiler, Martin (ed) and Stadler, Friedrich (ed).

Bernard Bolzano and German Classical Philosophy. Pavlík, Ján.

The Importance of Being Austrian. Uebel, Thomas E.

AUTHENTICITY

Authenticities: Philosophical Reflections on Musical Performance. Kivy, Peter.

In Search of Authenticity: From Kierkegaard to Camus. Golomb, Jacob.

Authenticity and Autonomy in the Managed-Care Era: Forensic Psychiatric Perspectives. Bursztajn, Harold J and Brodsky, Archie.

Authenticity and the Project of Modernity. Ferrara, Alessandro.

Authenticity as a Foundational Principle of Medical Ethics. Welie, Jos V M.

Authenticity in Musical Performance: Personal or Historical?. O'Dea, Jane W.

Authenticity Naturalized. Waller, Bruce N.

Authenticity: From Philosophic Concept to Literary Character. Leahy, Robert.

Dropping: The "Subject" of Authenticity. *Being and Time* on Disappearing Existentials and True Friendship with Being. Visker, Rudi.

L'uso dell'*Index Thomisticus* nello studio delle fonti di Tommaso d'Aquino: considerazoni generali e questioni di metodo. Portalupi, Enzo.

Pursuing Truth in Narrative Research. O'Dea, Jane W.

Reply to Taylor. Rudinow, Joel.

So Black and Blue: Response to Rudinow. Taylor, Paul Christopher.

Towards Authentic Conversations: Authenticity in the Patient-Professional Relationship. Arnason, Vilhjalmur.

Von der Autonomie zur Authentizität der Freiheit: Die "Studie zur theologischen Ethik" als kaleidoskop gegenwärtiger Fundamentalmoral. Römelt, Josef.

AUTHOR

"Reconfiguring the Subject: Foucault's Analytics of Power" in *Reconstructing Foucault, Miguel-Alfonso, Ricardo (ed)*. Schrift, Alan D.

Author and Repression. Gracia, Jorge J E.

Kierkegaard and 1848. Kirmmse, Bruce H.

La Dualidad Personal: Autor y Actor. Choza, Jacinto.

Late-Marxist, Post-Poststructuralist Critical Nebulosity. Harris, Wendell V.

AUTHORITY

An Introduction to Historical Epistemology: The Authority of Knowledge. Tiles, Mary and Tiles, Jim.

Authenticities: Philosophical Reflections on Musical Performance. Kivy, Peter.

Authority and Its Enemies (New Edition). Molnar, Thomas.

Power: Its Forms, Bases, and Uses. Wrong, Dennis H.

Vindiciae, Contra Tyrannos: Or, Concerning the Legitimate Power of a Prince Over the People, and of the People Over a Prince. Garnett, George (ed).

Challenging Medical Authority: The Refusal of Treatment by Christian Scientists. May, Larry.

Conceptual and Moral Disputes about Futile and Useful Treatments. Kopelman, Loretta M.

Daniel Herwitz, *Making Theory/Constructing Art: On the Authority of the Avant-Garde*. Horowitz, Gregg.

Glaucon's Challenges. Phillips, D Z.

Intrinsic Evil, Truth, and Authority. O'Neill, John.

Is Toughness a Business Virtue?. van Wensveen, Louke M.

Kierkegaard on Authority and Leadership: Political Logic in Religious Thought. Khan, Abrahim H.

Leadership Ethics: Mapping the Territory. Ciulla, Joanne B.

On Therapeutic Authority: Psychoanalytical Expertise Under Advanced Liberalism. Miller, Peter and Rose, Nikolas.

Outrage and Authority. Fisk, Milton T.

Political Authority and Moral Education. Simpson, Peter.

The Epistemic Authority of Expertise. Pierson, Robert.

The Physician's Authority to Withhold Futile Treatment. Griener, Glenn G.

The Relative Heteronomy of Law. MacCormick, Neil.

Where Do Moral Theories Come From?. Walker, Margaret Urban.

AUTHORSHIP

La Máxima Hermenéutica "Comprender a un Autor..." en el Pensamiento de Dilthey. Trias, Susana.

The Authenticity of the Attribution to St Thomas Aquinas of *De natura materiae et dimensionibus interminatis/ De principio individuationis*. Morris, Nancy A.

AUTISM

"Autism and the 'Theory of Mind' Debate" in *Philosophical Psychopathology, Graham, George (ed)*. Gordon, Robert M and Barker, John A.

AUTOBIOGRAPHY

"Intellectual Autobiography of Paul Ricoeur" in *The Philosophy of Paul Ricoeur, Hahn, Lewis Edwin (ed)*. Ricoeur, Paul.

American Mixed Race: The Culture of Microdiversity. Zack, Naomi (ed).

Imagination and Time. Warnock, Mary.

Karl Jaspers: Basic Philosophical Writings. Ehrlich, Edith (& other eds).

Killing Time: The Autobiography of Paul Feyerabend. Feyerabend, Paul.

Mass Enlightenment: Critical Studies in Rousseau and Diderot. Simon, Julia.

The Lukács Reader. Kadarkay, Arpad (ed).

The Philosophy of Paul Ricoeur. Hahn, Lewis Edwin (ed).

Autobiography and Philosophy: Variations on a Theme of Wittgenstein. Szabados, Béla.

Freud: d'une *tension* autobiographique. Minassian, Marie-José.

On Giambattista Vico. Mali, Joseph.

Sartre and the Drug Connection. Haynes-Curtis, Carole.

Self-Reflection and Autobiography—Kierkegaard's Writings about Himself. Rosenau, Hartmut.

Selves, Interpreters, Narrators. Knight, Deborah.

AUTONOMY

"Autonomy and Preference Formation" in *In Harm's Way, Coleman, Jules L (ed)*. Arneson, Richard J.

"Autonomy" in *Concepts and Cases in Nursing Ethics, Yeo, Michael (& others)*. Yeo, Michael and Dalziel, Jean.

"The Autonomous Chooser and 'Reforms' in Education" in *Identity, Culture, and Education, Smeyers, Paul (ed)*. Marshall, James.

Autonomie des Selbstbewusstseins: Eine Untersuchung zum Verhältnis von Bruno Bauer und Karl Marx (1835-1843). Waser, Ruedi.

Autonomous Agents: From Self-Control to Autonomy. Mele, Alfred R.

Autonomy and Intervention: Parentalism in the Caring Life. Kultgen, John.

Concepts and Cases in Nursing Ethics. Yeo, Michael (& others).

Itinerari del Volontarismo: Teologia e politica al tempo di Luis de León. Ferraro, Domenico.

A Desperate Solution: Individual Autonomy and the Double-Blind Controlled Experiment. Logue, Gerald and Wear, Stephen.

A Educaçao e a Autonomia do Profesor: Caminhos para a Emancipaçao. Oaigen, Edson Roberto.

Approaches (and Possible Contraindications) to Enhancing Patients' Autonomy. Howe, Edmund G.

Auffassungen der Freiheit. Geuss, Raymond.

Authenticity and Autonomy in the Managed-Care Era: Forensic Psychiatric Perspectives. Bursztajn, Harold J and Brodsky, Archie.

Authenticity as a Foundational Principle of Medical Ethics. Welie, Jos V M.

Authenticity Naturalized. Waller, Bruce N.

Autonomía y Conducta Desviada: el Problema del Paternalismo en la Obra de John Stuart Mill. De Miguel Alvarez, Ana.

Autonomy and Blameworthiness. Haji, Ishtiyaque.

Autonomy and Commitment: Compatible Ideals. Aviram, Aharon.

Autonomy and Free Expression. Gomberg, Paul.

Autonomy and the Free Speech Principle. Easton, Susan.

Autonomy, Informed Consent, and Psychosurgery. Hundert, Edward M.

Autonomy, Value, and Conditioned Desire. Noggle, Robert.

Beyond Autonomy to the Person Coping with Illness. Thomasma, David C.

Distinguishing between Patients' Refusals and Requests. Gert, Bernard, Bernat, James L and Mogielnicki, R Peter.

Hegel's Critique of Kant in the Philosophy of Right. Lottenbach, Hans and Tenenbaum, Sergio.

In Defence of Autonomous Linguistics. Das Gupta, Amitabha.

Individual Autonomy and the Double-Blind Controlled Experiment: The Case of Desperate Volunteers. Minogue, Brendan P (& others).

Kant contra Spinoza?: Dos Éticas de la Autonomía. Fernández García, Eugenio.

Key Concepts: Autonomy. Agich, George J.

La Universalidad de la ley Moral. Rivera de Rosales, Jacinto.

Le Sujet Auto-Nome du Droit: Entretien avec Lukas Sosoe. Bacot, Jean-François.

Moral y Derecho en Bentham. Moncho, Josep.

Natural Freedom and Moral Autonomy: Emile as Parent, Teacher, and Citizen. Simon, Julia.

On Having a Sense of Responsibility. Troxell, Eugene A.

Penser l'Autonomie, Penser la Connaissance: l'Évolution d'un Centre de Recherche en Épistémologie. Lavallée, Alain.

Pufendorf tra Classicità e Modernità: Nota su un Libro di Simone Goyard-Fabre. Catteneo, Mario A.

Punishing Times: Reply to Smilansky. New, Christopher.

Rationalisme et Éthique Naturalisée. Quinn, Andrew.

Reworking Autonomy: Toward a Feminist Perspective. Donchin, Anne.

Ricoeur et la fiction de l'autonomie. Gagnon, Martin.

Rights, Duties, and Limits of Autonomy. Emson, H E.

Sind wir einzigartig? Zum Verhältnis von Selbstbewusstsein und Individualität. Löw-Beer, Martin.

Starke Wertungen, Wünsche zweiter Ordnung und intersubjektive Kritik: Überlegungen zum Begriff ethischer Autonomie. Anderson, Joel.

The Concept of Autonomy. May, Thomas.

Towards Authentic Conversations: Authenticity in the Patient-Professional Relationship. Arnason, Vilhjalmur.

Un Inedito di Bertrando Spaventa sul Concetto di Filosofia. Petrone, Giuseppe Landolfi.

Une approche déflationniste de la liberté de la volonté: un autre visage de Kant. Schroeter, François.

Volver a Kant Significa Avanzar. Funke, Gerhard.

Von der Autonomie zur Authentizität der Freiheit: Die "Studie zur theologischen Ethik" als kaleidoskop gegenwärtiger Fundamentalmoral. Römelt, Josef.

AUXTER, T

Introducing Philosophy Through Concepts of Ultimate Reality and Meaning. Krettek, Tom.

AVANT-GARDE

Daniel Herwitz, *Making Theory/Constructing Art: On the Authority of the Avant-Garde*. Horowitz, Gregg.

On Discourses on the "Failure of the Avant-garde". Toyama, Kikuko.

Postmodernism and the Artistic Avant-gardes. Erjavec, Ales.

AVERILL, E

Are Physical Properties Dispositions?. Reeder, Nick.

AVERROES

El Problema de la Causalidad en el *Tahafut* de Averroes. Maiza Ozcoidi, Idoia.

L'Élenchos del Principio nella Metafisica di Averroó. Roccaro, Giuseppe.

La Disputa Averroismo-Tomismo en el op "De Unitate Intellectus Contra Averroistas", de Tomás de Aquino. Barrio Maestre, José María.

AVICENNA

Ibn Sina's Contribution to Philosophy. Saleem, Mohammad Anwar.

Il soggetto della scienza prima. Roccaro, Giuseppe.

AWARENESS

see also Consciousness

On Love and Awareness. Wautischer, Helmut.

Poinsot on the Semiotics of Awareness. Raposa, Michael.

AXIOLOGY

see also Value

"The Function of Ontology and Experience in Roman Ingarden's Axiological Investigations" in *Kunst und Ontologie, Galewicz, Wlodzimierz (ed)*. Wegrzecki, Adam.

Nietzsche's Revaluation of Values: A Study in Strategies. Sleinis, E E.

Axiological Invariants. Reale, Miguel.

Juventud, valores y crisis de nuestro tiempo. Vegas, José M.

La intimidad como valor antropológico y social. Pallarés Gonzalez, José Luis.

Repairing the Reticulated Model of Scientific Rationality. Resnik, David.

Universal Metaphilosophy of Life and Universalist Ethics: An Axiological Approach. Grünberg, Ludwig.

Zubiri ante el problema del valor. Palacios, Juan Miguel.

AXIOM

Mathematics—The Music of Reason. Dieudonné, Jean, Dales, H G (trans) and Dales, J C (trans).

A General Framework for Priority Arguments. Lempp, Steffen and Lerman, Manuel.

A Note on Derivation Rules in Modal Logic. Goranko, Valentin.

A Partial Model of "NF" with E. Prati, N.

A System of Complete and Consistent Truth. Halbach, Volker.

Algebraic Study of Two Deductive Systems of Relevance Logic. Font, Josep Maria and Rodríquez, Gonzalo.

Applications of Cohomology to Set Theory I: Hausdorff Gaps. Talayco, Daniel E.

Axiom V and Hume's Principle in Frege's Foundational Project. Schirn, Matthias.

Bargaining with Reasonable Aspirations. Brunner, Johann K.

Combinatorics on Ideals and Axiom A. Sharp, James D.

Connections Between Axioms of Set Theory and Basic Theorems of Universal Algebra. Kurucz, H Andréka and Németi, I.

Cylindric Modal Logic. Venema, Yde.

Desire-as-Belief Implies Opinionation or Indifference. Costa, Horacio Arló, Collins, John and Levi, Isaac.

Discrete Tense Logic with Beginning and Ending Time: An Infinite Hierarchy of Complete Axiomatic Systems. Aqvist, Lennart.

Foundational Belief Change. Nayak, Abhaya C.

Four-Valued Semantics for Relevant Logics (and Some of Their Rivals). Restall, Greg.

Fragments of Martin's Axiom and Δ 1/3 Sets of Reals. Bagaria, Joan.

Hintikka Formulas as Axioms of Refutation Calculus, a Case Study. Inoué, Takao.

Is Gold-Putnam Diagonalization Complete?. Juhl, Cory.

Martin's Axiom and the Continuum. Judah, Haim and Roslanowski, Andrzej.

Measures: Back and Forth Between Point Sets and Large Sets. Goldring, Noa.

More About Relatively Lawless Sequences. Moschovakis, Joan Rand.

On the Equivalence of Certain Consequences of the Proper Forcing Axiom. Nyikos, Peter and Piatkiewicz, Leszek.

On the Independence of B from I, C, W, K' $_1$, and Karpenko's Formula X. Ulrich, Dolph E.

Predicative Foundations of Arithmetic. Feferman, Solomon and Hellman, Geoffrey.

Reasoning about Update Logic. Van Eijck, Jan and De Vries, Fer-Jan.

Reconciling Austinian and Russellian Accounts of the Liar Paradox. King, Paul John.

The Real Core Model and Its Scales. Cunningham, Daniel W.

The Single Axiom-Schema of March 8th. Inoué, Takao.

Uniformization Problems and the Cofinality of the Infinite Symmetric Group. Sharp, James D and Thomas, Simon.

AXIOM OF CHOICE

The Real Core Model and Its Scales. Cunningham, Daniel W.

AXIOMATIC

El significado de las constantes lógicas. Palau, Gladys.

AXIOMATIZABILITY

Finitely Axiomatizable $\aleph_1$ Categorical Theories. Hrushovski, Ehud.

AXIOMATIZATION

A Completeness Theorem for Open Maps. Joyal, A and Moerdijk, I.

Axiomatizations of Commutative and Non-Associative Ajdukiewicz Calculus. Kandulski, Maciej.

Semantics for First Degree Relatedness Logic. Paoli, Francesco.

AYER

A J Ayer's Notion of Philosophical Analysis. Balkrishnan P, Hemjith.

AYERS, M

Review Article on Ayers, 'Locke'. Milton, J R.

BABBAGE, C

Babbage's Intelligence: Calculating Engines and the Factory System. Schaffer, Simon.

BABY

Baby Ryan and Virtual Futility. Capron, Alexander Morgan.

When Is Birth Unfair to the Child?. Steinbock, Bonnie and McClamrock, Ron.

BACH, K

Actions and Events. Zimmerman, Michael.

BACHELARD

"Las XI Tesis No-Epistmológicas de Gastón Bachelard" in *Temas Actuales de Filosofía, Palacios, María Julia (ed)*. Diaz de Kobila, Esther.

La teoría del instante en Bachelard y el espacio onírico. Castillo, Roberto.

BEING

On Some Disputed Questions in Leibniz's Metaphysics. Mondadori, Fabrizio.

On the Existential Interpretation of Human Sciences. Ginev, Dimitri.

On the Metaphysical Foundations of Neo- and New Confucianism: Reflections on Lauren Pfister's Essay on Religious Confucianism. Ivanhoe, Philip J.

On the Way to an Ontological Ethics: Ethical Suggestions in Reading Heidegger. Benso, Silvia.

Ontología modal en la *Philosophia Prima*. Cuéllar, Hortensia.

Orden, Desorden, Azar. Bolzán, Juan Enrique and Larre, Olga L.

Originalità del pensiero filosofico di S Tommaso. Mondin, Battista.

Philosophy of Methodology in Heidegger's *Die Idee der Philosophie und das Weltanschuungsproblem* (1919). Fuchs, Yuval.

Poetizar y Pensar? Desde la Meditación Heideggeriana Hacia el *Topos* Histórico de Hölderlin. Zubiría, Martín.

Poinsot on Knowability of Beings of Reason. Doyle, John P.

Principialidad de las Facultades en el Orden del Ser. Mier y Terán, Rocío.

Reading Heidegger after Derrida. Strawser, Michael J.

Realismo fenomenológico y Metafisica. García-Baró, Miguel.

Refuting Kant's "Refutation of Idealism". Frangiotti, Marco Antonio.

Relations with Others in Sartre and Levinas: Assessing Some Implications for an Ethics of Proximity. Vetlesen, Arne Johan.

Reply: The Schellingian Alternative. Bowie, Andrew.

Sanc and Kozelj—Two Slovenian Philosophers in Croatia. Belic, Miljenko.

Sartre and the Drug Connection. Haynes-Curtis, Carole.

Sartrean Concept of Intersubjectivity. Sindhu, L.

Searle on Rediscovering the Mind. Burton, Robert G.

Six Heideggerian Figures. Wood, Robert E.

Sobre el origen del ser y la nada. Echauri, Raúl.

Sobre el Problema de la Filosofía (II). Zubiri, Xavier.

Social Being and the Human Essence: An Unresolved Issue in Soviet Philosophy. Bakhurst, David.

Staurologie. Crétella, Henri.

Suárez on the Analogy of Being: Some Historical Background. Ashworth, E J.

Substanz und Mensch: Spinozas Auffassung der Wirklichkeit. Graeser, Andreas.

Sympathy for the Devil: Edwards and Heidegger. McManus, Denis.

The Apprehension of the Act of Being in Aquinas. Gonzalez, Orestes J.

The Being of the Maybe: Husserl on Doubting. McCarthy, J C.

The Evolution of the Will. Norwood, Rick.

The Genetic Difference in Reading *Being and Time*. Kisiel, Theodore.

The Hermeneutics of the Emerging of Being (On Figal's Interpretation of Heidegger). Cibulka, Josef.

The History of Being and the History of Doctrine: An Influence of Heidegger on Theology. O'Meara, Thomas F.

The Importance of Dionysius for St Thomas Aquinas' Comprehension of Being. Pöltner, Günther.

The Last God—A Reading. Stenstad, Gail.

The Nietzsche Image in Heidegger's *Beiträge, Contributions to Philosophy (On the Event)*. Behler, Ernst.

The Philosophical Bases of Heidegger's Politics: A Response to Wolin. Sikka, Sonya.

The Philosophy of Nicolas Berdyaev. Sharma, Jyotirmaya.

The Place of Unity in Aristotle's Metaphysical Project. Morrison, Donald R.

The Primacy of Pure Practical Reason. Billings, Blake (trans) and Levinas, Emmanuel.

The Question of the Subject: Heidegger and the Transcendental Tradition. Carr, David.

The Topography of Heidegger's Concept of Conscience. Schalow, Frank.

The Unity of Theoretical and Practical Spirit in Hegel's Concept of Freedom. Houlgate, Stephen.

Theravada Buddhism and the Definition of Religion. Smart, Ninian.

Time, Eternity, and the Visual Moment (Augenblick): Heidegger and the Problem of a Theology of Time. Hoping, Helmut.

Traduire les *Beiträge zur Philosophie (Vom Ereignis)*. Fédier, François.

Truth and Control in Being and Language. Krummel, J.

Un Inedito di Bertrando Spaventa sul Concetto di Filosofia. Petrone, Giuseppe Landolfi.

Understanding the Difference of Being: On the Relationship between Metaphysics and Theology. Hoping, Helmut.

Unger's *Identity, Consciousness and Value*. Van Inwagen, Peter.

Universals and Infinite Modes in the Thought of Spinoza. Murthy, Viren.

Van Inwagen's *Material Beings*. Persson, Ingmar.

Virtual Reality and the Metaphysics of Self, Community, and Nature. Cooper, Wes.

Wat is metafysica?. Heyde, L.

Wholes, Parts, and Sequences in Aristotle. Blyth, D J.

Why Evil? Heidegger, Schelling, and the Tragic View of Being. Schalow, Frank.

Why Students of Heidegger Will Have to Read Emil Lask. Kisiel, Theodore.

Zarathustra's Dance: A Heideggerian Misstep?. Cristian, Alin.

BEING-IN-ITSELF

Remarques sur l'histoire de la notion philosophique d'absolu. Huber, Gerhard.

BELETSKII, Z

The Case of Professor Z la Beletskii: An Episode from the History of Soviet Philosophy. Batygin, Gennadii and Deviatko, Inna.

BELGIAN

Metafysica in Leuven. Jonkers, Peter.

Philosophy in Belgium. de Vos, Lou.

BELIEF

see also Faith

"A Response to Hartshorne" in *Peirce and Contemporary Thought: Philosophical Inquiries, Ketner, Kenneth Laine (ed)*. Potter, Vincent G.

"African Traditional Thought and Western Science" in *African Philosophy: Selected Readings, Appiah, Kwame Anthony*. Horton, Robin.

"Belief-forming Practices and the Social" in *Socializing Epistemology: The Social Dimensions of Knowledge, Schmitt, Frederick (ed)*. Alston, W P.

"Closure and Consistency" in *Modality, Morality, and Belief, Sinnott-Armstrong, Walter (ed)*. Levi, Isaac.

"De Re Belief, Action Explanations, and the Essential Indexical" in *Modality, Morality, and Belief, Sinnott-Armstrong, Walter (ed)*. Sosa, Ernest.

"Empirical Justification" in *Life, World and Meaning, Roux, A P J (ed)*. Malherbe, Jeanette.

"Excerpts from Knowledge, Belief, and Witchcraft" in *African Philosophy: Selected Readings, Mosley, Albert G (ed)*. Hallen, Barry and Sodipo, J O.

"Grounds for Believing in God's Existence" in *Meaning, Truth, and God, Rouner, Leroy (ed)*. Hartshorne, Charles.

"Hume and the Madness of Religion" in *Hume and Hume's Connexions, Stewart, M A (ed)*. Bernard, Christopher.

"Kant's Critique of Hume's Theory of Faith" in *Hume and Hume's Connexions, Stewart, M A (ed)*. Kuehn, Manfred.

"On the Existence of Witches" in *African Philosophy: Selected Readings, Mosley, Albert G (ed)*. Oluwole, Sophie.

"On the Projectable Predicates of Connectionist Psychology" in *Connectionism: Debates on Psychological Explanation, Macdonald, Cynthia (ed)*. Smolensky, Paul.

"Peirce and Religion: Between Two Forms of Religious Belief" in *Peirce and Contemporary Thought: Philosophical Inquiries, Ketner, Kenneth Laine (ed)*. Hartshorne, Charles.

"Pierre, Saul, Ruth, and Bob and a Puzzle about Belief" in *Modality, Morality, and Belief, Sinnott-Armstrong, Walter (ed)*. Fogelin, Robert.

"Pragmatic Reasons for Belief" in *Gambling on God: Essays on Pascal's Wager, Jordan, Jeffrey (ed)*. Foley, Richard.

"Putnam and the Skolem Paradox" in *Reading Putnam, Clark, Peter (ed)*. Hallett, Michael.

"Radiance and Religious Belief" in *Contributors to the Philosophy of Humanism, Hillar, Marian (ed)*. Suckiel, Ellen Kappy.

"Religious Belief and Scientific Method" in *American Philosophy Today and Other Philosophical Studies, Rescher, Nicholas*. Rescher, Nicholas.

"Remarks on Collective Belief" in *Socializing Epistemology: The Social Dimensions of Knowledge, Schmitt, Frederick F (ed)*. Gilbert, Margaret.

"Shamanic Nietzsche" in *Nietzsche: A Critical Reader, Sedgwick, Peter R (ed)*. Land, Nick.

"The Howson-Urbach Proofs of Bayesian Principles" in *Probability and Conditionals, Eells, Ellery (ed)*. Chihara, Charles S.

"The Justification of Group Beliefs" in *Socializing Epistemology: The Social Dimensions of Knowledge, Schmitt, Frederick F (ed)*. Schmitt, Frederick F.

"Viruses of the Mind" in *Dennett and his Critics, Dahlbom, Bo (ed)*. Dawkins, Richard.

"Wittgenstein on Necessity: Some Reflections" in *Reading Putnam, Clark, Peter (ed)*. Dummett, Michael.

"Introduction" Gambling on God: Essays on Pascal's Wager. Jordan, Jeffrey (ed).

A Companion to the Philosophy of Mind. Guttenplan, Samuel (ed).

Autonomous Agents: From Self-Control to Autonomy. Mele, Alfred R.

Desire: Its Role in Practical Reason and the Explanation of Action. Schueler, G F.

Explaining Attitudes: A Practical Approach to the Mind. Baker, Lynne Rudder.

Gambling on God: Essays on Pascal's Wager. Jordan, Jeffrey (ed).

Gott—Gebote—Ideale: Analytische Philosophie und theologische Ethik. Löhr, Gebbhard.

Logic and Representation. Moore, Robert C.

Meaning, Truth, and God. Rouner, Leroy (ed).

Mediaeval Reactions to the Encounter Between Faith and Reason. Wippel, John F.

Modality, Morality, and Belief. Sinnott-Armstrong, Walter (ed).

Morality, Normativity, and Society. Copp, David.

Natural Theories of Mind: Evolution, Development, and Simulation of Everyday Mindreading. Whiten, Andrew (ed).

Strands of System: The Philosophy of Charles Peirce. Anderson, Douglas R.

The Atheist Trap. Mixie, Joseph.

The Rational and the Moral Order: The Social Roots of Reason and Morality. Baier, Kurt.

The Wisdom of Religious Commitment. Tilley, Terrence W.

There are Two Errors In the the Title of This Book: A Sourcebook of Philosophical Puzzles, Problems, and Paradoxes. Martin, Robert M.

Universals and Property Instances: The Alphabet of Being. Bacon, John.

A Heuristic for Conceptual Change. Arntzenius, Frank.

An Apprentice Argument. Millgram, Elijah.

An Understanding of Contemporary Foundationalism. Lenka, Laxminarayan.

Anti-foundationalism, Hendrick Hart, and the Nature and Function of Religious Belief. Sweet, William.

Are Beliefs and Experiences Candidates for Elimination?. Pojman, Paul.

Are Beliefs Brain-States? And If They Are What Might That Explain?. Van Gulick, Robert.

Arthur Collins's *The Nature of Mental Things*. Moran, Richard.

Attitudes as Nonentities. Baker, Lynne Rudder.

Autonomy, Value, and Conditioned Desire. Noggle, Robert.

BIOETHICS

Ernst Cassirer—Von Marburg nach New York: Eine philosophische Biographie. Paetzold, Heinz.

Hegel In His Time: Berlin, 1818-1831. Burbidge, John W (trans) and D'Hondt, Jacques.

Spinoza's Ethica From Manuscript to Print: Studies on Text, Form, and Related Topics. Steenbakkers, Piet.

Strands of System: The Philosophy of Charles Peirce. Anderson, Douglas R.

The Cambridge Dictionary of Philosophy. Audi, Robert (ed).

The Heidegger Controversy: A Critical Reader. Wolin, Richard (ed).

A Debate on *The Passion of Michel Foucault*. Miller, James (& others).

Between Terrestriality and Aquacity: Miller's 'Limit Experience'. Luchte, James.

Cambridge Philosophers II: Ludwig Wittgenstein. Anscombe, G E M.

Ein Brief Johann Gottlieb Fichtes. Roser, Andreas and Schulten, Holger.

Ernesto Sábato: Físico Antes que Escritor. Fuertes, José Félix.

Fichte und die Freimaurerie. Hammacher, Klaus.

Fichtes Einfluss auf seine Studenten en Berlin zum Beginn der Befreiungskriege. Fuchs, Erich.

Homenaje a Octavio Paz. Aguayo Cruz, Enrique Ignacio.

Jan Patocka. Klibansky, Raymond.

La filosofia, el método y el hombre en el pensamiento de Adolfo Muñoz Alonso. González Miguel, Jesús Graciliano.

Relational Ethics in Writing a Woman's Life. Franklin, Betty and Townsend, Lucy.

Selves, Interpreters, Narrators. Knight, Deborah.

The Case of Professor Z la Beletskii: An Episode from the History of Soviet Philosophy. Batygin, Gennadii and Deviatko, Inna.

The Pariah and Her Shadow: Hannah Arendt's Biography of Rahel Varnhagen. Benhabib, Seyla.

What Was Plato's Real Name?. Irvine, Andrew D.

BIOLOGY

see also Darwinism, Evolution, Life, Psychobiology, Vitalism

"Anmerkungen zu einem möglichen Dialog Schellings mit der modernen Biologie" in *Schelling und die Selbstorganisation, Heuser-Kessler, Marie-Luise (ed)*. Schneider, Helmuth.

"Are Synergetic Systems (Including Brains) Machines?" in *The Machine as Metaphor and Tool, Haken, Hermann (ed)*. Haken, Hermann.

"Biological Diversity and Ethical Development" in *Ethics, Religion and Biodiversity, Hamilton, Lawrence S (ed)*. Goulet, Denis.

"Biology, Ethics and the Origins of Life: An Introduction" in *Biology, Ethics, and the Origins of Life, Rolston III, Holmes (ed)*. Rolston III, Holmes.

"Bionics Revisited" in *The Machine as Metaphor and Tool, Haken, Hermann (ed)*. Rosen, Robert.

"Darwinism and Postmodern Theism" in *Biology, Ethics, and the Origins of Life, Rolston III, Holmes (ed)*. Birch, Charles.

"Der Diskurs über Gen-Tätigkeit" in *Mythos Wertfreiheit?, Apel, Karl-Otto (ed)*. Keller, Evelyn Fox.

"Did Evolution Make Us Psychological Egoists?" in *From a Biological Point of View, Sober, Elliott*. Sober, Elliott.

"Evolutionary Ethics: A Defense" in *Biology, Ethics, and the Origins of Life, Rolston III, Holmes (ed)*. Ruse, Michael E.

"Explaining Homosexuality: Philosophical Issues, and Who Cares Anyhow?" in *Gay Ethics, Murphy, Timothy F (ed)*. Suppe, Frederick.

"Facing Nature" in *Biology, Ethics, and the Origins of Life, Rolston III, Holmes (ed)*. Margulis, Lynn and Sagan, Dorion.

"How Dare You Sport Thus with Life?": Frankensteinian Fictions as Case Studies in Scientific Ethics. Goldbort, Robert C.

"L'argumentation finaliste en biologie" in *Rhétoriques de la science, De Coorebyter, Vincent (ed)*. Duchesneau, François.

"Mass Extinction and Human Responsibility" in *Biology, Ethics, and the Origins of Life, Rolston III, Holmes (ed)*. Eldredge, Niles.

"Mathematical Machines" in *The Machine as Metaphor and Tool, Haken, Hermann (ed)*. Henry, Paul.

"Reply: A Bet with Peacocke" in *Philosophy of Psychology: Debates on Psychological Explanation, Macdonald, Cynthia (ed)*. Millikan, Ruth Garrett.

"The Adaptive Advantage of Learning and *A Priori* Prejudice" in *From a Biological Point of View, Sober, Elliott*. Sober, Elliott.

"The Biological Turn" in *Philosophy of Psychology: Debates on Psychological Explanation, Macdonald, Cynthia (ed)*. Macdonald, Graham.

"The Difference of Being Human" in *Biology, Ethics, and the Origins of Life, Rolston III, Holmes (ed)*. Ayala, Francisco J.

"When Natural Selection and Culture Conflict" in *Biology, Ethics, and the Origins of Life, Rolston III, Holmes (ed)*. Sober, Elliott.

"Wider Natur: Die Biologisierung sozialer Praxis im 'naturwissenschaftlichen Monismus'" in *Nationalsozialismus und Moderne, Welzer, Harald (ed)*. Hartmann, Frank.

A New Science of Life: The Hypothesis of Morphic Resonance. Sheldrake, Rupert.

A Philosophy of Matter and Mind: A New Look at an Old Major Topic in Philosophy. Wassermann, Gerhard D.

Biology, Ethics, and the Origins of Life. Rolston III, Holmes (ed).

Caring: An Essay in the Philosophy of Ethics. van Hooft, Stan.

Ethics, Religion and Biodiversity. Hamilton, Lawrence S (ed).

From a Biological Point of View. Sober, Elliott.

Instrumental Biology or the Disunity of Science. Rosenberg, Alexander.

Mapping the Human Genome: Reality, Morality, and Deity. Kent, Theodore C.

Mind and Cognition: A Reader. Lycan, William G (ed).

Reason, Regulation, and Realism: Toward a Regulatory Systems Theory of Reason and Evolutionary Epistemology. Hooker, C A.

The Immune Self: Theory or Metaphor?. Tauber, Alfred I.

The Sciences in Greco-Roman Society (Apeiron 27-4). Barnes, Timothy D.

A (Not-so-radical) Solution to the Species Problem. Wilson, Bradley E.

A Filosofia da Biologia à Luz da Biologia Molecular: Resolveu-se o Mistério?. Delouya, Daniel.

Are There Natural Laws Concerning Particular Biological Species?. Lange, Marc.

Aristotle on Substance, Essence and Biological Kinds. Charles, David.

Aristotle's Biology: Plain, But Not Simple. Lennox, James G.

Before I Was an Embryo, I Was a Pre-Embryo: Or Was I?. Jones, D Gareth and Telfer, Barbara.

Bioética y derechos humanos II: Aspectos formales y sustanciales para una normativa biomédica en un mundo biotecnológico. Golcher, Cristián.

Biological Realism and Social Constructivism. Sabini, John and Schulkin, Jay.

Characterizing Classifying: Explicating a Biological Distinction. Lambert, Karel and Simons, Peter.

Cognitive Value and the Advancement of Science. Levi, Isaac.

Commentary on Charles's "Aristotle on Substance, Essence and Biological Kinds". Gill, Mary Louise.

Commerce and Genetic Diagnostics. Silverman, Paul H.

Consciousness, Intentionality and Function: What Is the Right Order of Explanation?. Jacob, Pierre.

Consciousness, the Brain and the Connection Principle: A Reply. Searle, John R.

Defending Robustness: The Bacterial Mesosome as a Test Case. Culp, Sylvia.

Die biologischen Analogien und die erkenntnistheoretischen Alternativen in Kants Kritik der reinen Vernunft B 27. Ingensiep, Hans Werner.

Discussion: A Comment on Some Recent Arguments in Evolutionary Epistemology —and Some Counterarguments. Wuketits, Franz M.

Emergence of New Fields in Ecology: The Case of Life History Studies. Korfiatis, K J and Stamou, G P.

Ethical Considerations in the Use of Transgenic Animals. Giraud, Raymond.

Exorcising Laplace's Demon: Chaos and Antichaos, History and Metahistory. Shermer, Michael.

For Pluralism and Against Realism About Species. Stanford, P Kyle.

Function without Purpose: The Uses of Causal Role Function in Evolutionary Biology. Amundson, Ron and Lauder, George V.

Functional Language and Biological Discovery. Resnik, David B.

Global Idealism/Local Materialism. Matsuno, Koichiro and Salthe, Stanley N.

How Does the Teilhardian Vision of Evolution Compare with Contemporary Theories?. Galleni, Lodovico.

How to Perform a Reduction. Brooks, D H M.

Is Species Selection Dependent Upon Emergent Characters?. Stidd, Benton M and Wade, David L.

Leibniz and the Logic of Life. Wilson, Catherine.

Mental Causation in Searle's "Biological Naturalism". Kim, Jaegwon.

Mental Disorder, Illness and Biological Disfunction. Papineau, David.

Metaphors of Race: Theoretical Presuppositions Behind Racism. Asma, Stephen T.

Mixed Black and White Race and Public Policy. Zack, Naomi.

New Ways to Look at Fitness. Van Der Steen, Wim J.

Non-Reductionism and John Searle's *The Rediscovery of the Mind*. Garrett, Brian J.

Normality as a Biological Concept. Wachbroit, Robert.

Ontdekkingspraktijk in Plaats van Logica: Wetenschappelijk Ontdekken in Computer-Ondersteunde Ontdekkingsomgevingen. de Jong, Hidde and Rip, Arie.

Optimization in Evolutionary Ecology. Richardson, Robert C.

Philosophy in Biology. Esser, Piet Hein.

Précis of *The Advancement of Science*. Kitcher, Philip.

Reasons for the Failure of Theories. Mayr, Ernst.

Representations of Information Technology in Disciplinary Development: Disappearing Plants and Invisible Networks. Hine, Christine.

Screening-Off and the Levels of Selection. McClamrock, Ron.

Shaping Priorities in Genetic Medicine. Boyle, Philip J.

The Autonomy of Moral Education. Boss, Judith A.

The Boulder and the Sphere: Subjectivity and Implicit Values in Biology. Alpert, Peter.

The Cronin Controversy. Griffiths, Paul E.

The Misuse of Sober's Selection for/Selection of Distinction. Goode, R and Griffiths, P E.

The Origin of Vertebrates and the Principle of Succession of Functions: Genealogical Sketches by Anton Dohrm, 1875—An English Translation. Ghiselin, Michael T.

The Religious Dimensions of the Biological Narrative. Goodenough, Ursula W.

The Selection of Alleles and the Additivity of Variance. Sarkar, Sahotra.

The Super Bowl and the Ox-Phos Controversy: "Winner-Take-All" Competition in Philosophy of Science. Allchin, Douglas.

Theism, the Hypothesis of Indifference, and the Biological Role of Pain and Pleasure. Howard-Snyder, Daniel.

Towards Welfare Biology: Evolutionary Economics of Animal Consciousness and Suffering. Ng, Yew-Kwang.

Twenty Five Years of Theoretical Biology. Blandino, Giovanni.

Two Concepts of Constraint: Adaptationism and the Challenge from Developmental Biology. Amundson, Ron.

Understanding Life: Recent Work in Philosophy of Biology. Sterelny, Kim.

What Locke Should Have Believed about Real Essences. Danaher, James P.

Why the Connection Argument Doesn't Work. Van Gulick, Robert.

BIOMEDICAL RESEARCH

La Notion de Personne Selon Lucien Sève. Thérrien, Jean-Marie.

Les Séquences d'ADN Humain Peuvent-Elles Etre Brevetées?. Thérrien, Jean-Marie.

BIOTECHNOLOGY
The Biotechnology "Wheel of Fortune": Who Gives, Who Gets, Who Profits?. Davis, Elizabeth B (& others).

BIRKHOFF, G
Complete Metric Boolean Algebras. Jeffrey, Richard (trans) and Kolmogorov, A N.

BIRTH
Nietzsche (Past Masters). Tanner, Michael.
When Is Birth Unfair to the Child?. Steinbock, Bonnie and McClamrock, Ron.

BIRTH CONTROL
see also Contraception
"Birth Control and the Value of Human Life" in *Ethics on the Frontiers of Human Existence, Badham, Paul (ed)*. Kono, Shigemi.
Coercion and Long-Term Contraceptives. Steinbock, Bonnie.

BIVALENCE
"Verdad, Lógica y Bivalencia" in *Temas Actuales de Filosofía, Palacios, María Julia (ed)*. Faas, Horacio.
Multivalence and Vagueness: A Reply to Copeland. Simons, Peter.
Repuesta a E Barrio acerca de su defensa del realismo semántico. Legris, Javier.
Una defensa del realismo semántico. Barrio, Eduardo.
Vagueness and Bivalence: A Discussion of Williamson and Simons. Copeland, B J.

BLACK, M
Max Black on the Identity of Indiscernibles. Cross, Charles B.

BLACKBURN, S
"Comments and Replies" in *Reading Putnam, Clark, Peter (ed)*. Putnam, Hilary.
Shades of Realism. De Gaynesford, Max.
Supervenience and Moral Realism. Shafer-Landau, Russ.

BLACKMAIL
May We Stop Worrying About Blackmail?. Smilansky, Saul.

BLACKS
see also Negro
Bad Faith and Antiblack Racism. Gordon, Lewis R.
I Am Because We Are: Readings in Black Philosophy. Hord, Fred Lee (ed) and Lee, Jonathan Scott (ed).
A Practical Idea of Blackness. Kiros, Teodros.

BLAME
Assessing Responsibility: Fixing Blame versus Fixing Problems. Sanders, John T.
Consequentialis, Moral Responsibility, and the Intention/ Foresight Distinction. Oakley, Justin.
Forgiving as an Obligation of the Moral Life. Harvey, J.
Hyprocrisy and Moral Seriousness. Crisp, Roger and Cowton, Christopher.
Moral Beliefs and Blameworthiness. Fields, Lloyd.
Shame and Blame: The Self through Time and Change. Radden, Jennifer.
Supererogation and Ethical Methodology: A Reply to Mellema. Heyd, David.
Supererogation, Blame, and the Limits of Obligation. Mellema, Gregory.

BLAMEWORTHY
Autonomy and Blameworthiness. Haji, Ishtiyaque.
Zimmerman on Moral Responsibility, Obligation and Alternate Possibilities. Widerker, David and Katzoff, Charlotte.

BLANCHOT, M
The Blanchot Reader. Holland, Michael (ed).
On Deconstructing Nostalgia for Community within the West: The Debate between Nancy and Blanchot. Bernasconi, Robert.

BLASIUS, M
Political Philosophy as Political Action: A Response to Mark Blasius. Statham Jr, E Robert.

BLOCH, E
Das Feindbild der marxistisch-leninistischen Philosophie in der DDR 1945-1988. Kapferer, Norbert.
El Cristianismo como *A Priori* de la Revolución en la Filosofía de Ernst Bloch. Orsolic, Marco.

BLOCHMANN, E
Heidegger's Interpretation of the German "Revolution". Elder, Frank H W.

BLOM, T
Constructivisme, Epistemologie en Maatschappijtheorie: Een Reactie op Blom. Harbers, Hans.
What, Me Worry? I am but Mad North-North-West. Disco, Nil.

BLONDEL, M
Logica del Concreto ed Ermeneutica della Vita Morale: Newman, Blondel, Piovani. Jervolino, Domenico.
Blondel and Ignatius' Spiritual Exercises (in Dutch). Boey, K.
Blondel and the Tradition of the Innate Longing for God (in Dutch). Schrama, Martijn.
Blondel e la verità come "Adaequatio Realis". Bertoldi, Francesco.
Blondel's L'Action (1893) and Neo-Thomism's Metaphysics of Symbol. Fields, Stephen.

BLOOD
HIV +/AIDS Related Bioethical Issues in Japan. Hoshino, Kazusama.

BLUES
Reply to Taylor. Rudinow, Joel.
So Black and Blue: Response to Rudinow. Taylor, Paul Christopher.

BLUMENBERG, H
Blumenberg: Truly Memorable Memories. Hrachovec, Herbert and Turner, Charles (ed).

BLUSTEIN, J
Integrity, Abortion, and the Pro-Life Perinatologist. Thorp Jr, John M (& others).
Toward a Thick Theory of Moral Agency. Manning, Rita C.

BOATRIGHT, J
Conflict of Interest Revisited. Davis, Michael.

BODIN, J
Politischer Individualismus: Die Rekonstruktion einer Sozialtheorie unter Bezugnahme auf Machiavelli, Bodin, und Hobbes. Hegmann, Horst.

BODY
see also Minds
"Acerca de la Dificultad para Identificar Personas como Particulares Básicos en Strawson" in *Temas Actuales de Filosofía, Palacios, María Julia (ed)*. Skidelsky, Liza D.
"Aporie ed origini della teoria spinoziana dell'idea adequata" in *L'etica e il suo Altro, Vigna, Carmelo (ed)*. Marion, Jean-Luc.
"Beauvoir's Concept of Bodily Alienation" in *Feminist Interpretations of Simone de Beauvoir, Simons, Margaret A (ed)*. Arp, Kristana.
"Beauvoir's Two Senses of 'Body' in *The Second Sex*" in *Feminist Interpretations of Simone de Beauvoir, Simons, Margaret A (ed)*. Ward, Julie K.
"Bionics Revisited" in *The Machine as Metaphor and Tool, Haken, Hermann (ed)*. Rosen, Robert.
"Body and Soul" in *The Mind-Body Problem: A Guide to the Current Debate, Warner, Richard (ed)*. Swinburne, Richard.
"Intertheoretic Reduction: A Neuroscientist's Field Guide" in *The Mind-Body Problem: A Guide to the Current Debate, Warner, Richard (ed)*. Churchland, Paul M and Churchland, Patricia S.
"Language, Music, and the Body" in *Intersections: Nineteenth-Century Philosophy and Contemporary Theory, Rajan, Tilottama (ed)*. Rajan, Tilottama.
"Locke's Philosophy of Body" in *The Cambridge Companion to Locke, Chappell, Vere (ed)*. McCann, Edwin.
"Mathematical Machines" in *The Machine as Metaphor and Tool, Haken, Hermann (ed)*. Henry, Paul.
"Monte—Cuerpo: Enfoques Evolutivos" in *Temas Actuales de Filosofía, Palacios, María Julia (ed)*. Cornejo, Raquel (& others).
"Mind and Body" in *The Cambridge Companion to Husserl, Smith, Barry (ed)*. Smith, David Woodruff.
"Minds and Bodies" in *The Mind-Body Problem: A Guide to the Current Debate, Warner, Richard (ed)*. Heil, John.
"Stubborn Attachment, Bodily Subjection" in *Intersections: Nineteenth-Century Philosophy and Contemporary Theory, Rajan, Tilottama (ed)*. Butlor, Judith.
"The Mind-Body Problem and Contemporary Psychology" in *The Mind-Body Problem: A Guide to the Current Debate, Warner, Richard (ed)*. Macnamara, John.
"The Mind-Body Problem" in *The Mind-Body Problem: A Guide to the Current Debate, Warner, Richard (ed)*. Shoemaker, Sydney.
Dialectical Materialism and Modern Science. Cameron, Kenneth Neill.
Disertación sobre la Naturaleza y la Propagación del Fuego. de Châtelet, Marquesa.
Freud and the Politics of Psychoanalysis. Brunner, José.
Il Nyaya Sutra di Gautama. Arena, Leonardo Vittorio.
Knowledge and the Body-Mind Problem: In Defence of Interaction. Notturno, M A (ed) and Popper, Karl R.
Mental Reality. Strawson, Galen.
Mind's Bodies: Thought in the Act. Lang, Berel.
Reshaping the Female Body: The Dilemma of Cosmetic Surgery. Davis, Kathy.
Subjectivity and Reduction: An Introduction to the Mind-Body Problem. Hannan, Barbara.
The Book of the Body Politic. Forhan, Kate Langdon (ed & trans) and De Pizan, Christine.
The Broken Middle: Out of our Ancient Society. Rose, Gillian.
The Cambridge Companion to Husserl. Smith, Barry (ed) and Smith, David Woodruff (ed).
The Cambridge Companion to Locke. Chappell, Vere (ed).
The Constructed Body: AIDS, Reproductive Technology, and Ethics. Murphy, Julien S.
The Convergence of Machine and Human Nature: A Critique of the Computer Metaphor of Mind and Artificial Intelligence. McClintock, Alexander.
The Enigma of the Mind: The Mind-Body Problem in Contemporary Thought. Moravia, Sergio and Staton, Scott (trans).
The Mind-Body Problem: A Guide to the Current Debate. Warner, Richard (ed) and Szubka, Tadesz (ed).
The Site of Our Lives: The Self and the Subject from Emerson to Foucault. Hans, James S.
The Stop. Appelbaum, David.
The Undivided Universe: An Ontological Interpretation of Quantum Theory. Hiley, B J and Bohm, David.
Weltentwürfe: Ludwig Binswangers phänomenologische Psychologie. Herzog, Max.
What is a Human Being? A Heideggerian View. Olafson, Frederick A.
A Deadly Delight: Feldman on the Nature and Value of Death. Haji, Ishtiyaque.
Abstraction and the Real Distinction Between Mind and Body. Thomas, Bruce M.
Anthropology and the Theory of Medicine. von Uexküll, Thure.
Are Animal Displays Bodily Movements or Manifestations of the Animal's Mind. Smit, Harry.

BODY

Beauty and Breast Implantation: How Candidate Selection Affects Autonomy and Informed Consent. Parker, Lisa S.

Body and Environment. LaBossiere, Michael.

Commentary on Furley's "Some Points About Stoic Dynamics". Striker, Gisela.

Consciousness, Intentionality and Function: What Is the Right Order of Explanation?. Jacob, Pierre.

Coscienza e Corporeità. Cavaciuti, Santino.

Creative Agency and Fluid Images: A Revew of Iris Young's *Throwing Like a Girl and Other Essays in Feminist Philosophy and Social Theory*. Weiss, Gail.

Critical Comments. Wei-Hsun Fu, Charles.

Cuerpo e intencionalidad. Pfeiffer, María Luisa.

Cuerpo humano y visión integral del hombre. Lucas, Ramón Lucas.

Cuerpo y Alma en el Helemorfismo de Santo Tomás. Beuchot, Mauricio.

Death According to Descartes: Why the Soul Leaves the Body. Ablondi, Fred.

Decomposition vs Co-relation (in Hebrew). Barzel, Alexander.

Duplicity in the Flesh: Bergson and Current Philosophy of the Body. Mullarkey, John C.

Hartshorne's Response to Haugen and Keeling: "Hartshorne's Process Theism and Big Bang Cosmology". Hartshorne, Charles.

How Innovative is the *Alayavijnana*?, Part II. Waldron, William S.

Identificational Recruit: Between the Temptation of Nihilism and a Tie-In with the Body. Liubomirova, Nataly.

Immanenz als Falle des Lebens. Schmitz, Hermann.

In-Jestion: Intestinal Laughter in Kant and Nietzsche. Swift, Paul.

Individualism, Physicalism, and Spinoza on Minds and Bodies. Lantin, Robert.

Instruments and the Body: Sartre and Merleau-Ponty. Kujundzic, Nebojsa and Buschert, William.

La antropología prospectiva tomista. Castello Dubra, Julio A.

La dimensión natural del hombre en Santo Tomás de Aquino. Castello Dubra, Julio A.

Leibniz, Lamy, and 'The Way of Pre-Established Harmony'. Woolhouse, Roger S and Francks, Richard.

Malebranche on Descartes on Mind-Body Distinctness. Schmaltz, Tad M.

Mental Causation in Searle's "Biological Naturalism". Kim, Jaegwon.

Merleau-Ponty's Concept of Reason. Low, Douglas.

Mind, Body, and Ethics in Spinoza. Winch, Peter G.

Mind-Body Identity Revised. Li, Chenyang.

Minded Body/Embodied Mind. Seidel, George J.

Non-Reductionism and John Searle's *The Rediscovery of the Mind*. Garrett, Brian J.

Old and Now: The Body, Subjectivity, and Ethics. McAleer, Graham.

On the Uniqueness of Socrates. Schall, James V.

On What the Mind is Identical With. Rockwell, W Teed.

Paths to Perfection: Yoga and Confucian. Podgorski, Frank R.

Response. Gendlin, E T.

Response and Commentary on Iris Young's *Throwing Like a Girl and Other Essays in Feminist Philosophy and Social Theory*. Connolly, Maureen.

Some Points About Stoic Dynamics. Furley, David.

Springe's Argument for Absolute Idealism. Naik, A D.

The Body as "Sign and Tool" in Hegel's *Encyclopaedia*. Dodd, James.

The Communication of Cells Within the Body. Krans, H M J.

The Complexity of Bodily Feeling. Wallulis, Jerald T.

The Content of Cartesian Sensation and the Intermingling of Mind and Body. Aquila, Richard E.

The Sense of Society. Sandelands, Lloyd E.

The Whole Body, not Heart, as 'Seat of Consciousness': The Buddha's View. Sugunasiri, Suwanda H J.

Using the Human Body as a Paradigm for the Structure of Time: Some Reflections on Time's URAM. Modell, Stephen M.

Van Inwagen's *Material Beings*. Persson, Ingmar.

Von einer Ethik der Technik aus antinaturalistischem Geist. Betzler, Monika.

Why the Connection Argument Doesn't Work. Van Gulick, Robert.

William Poteat's Anthropology: "Mindbody In the World". Mead, Walter B.

Zarathustra's Dance: A Heideggerian Misstep?. Cristian, Alin.

BOECKLE, F

Von der Autonomie zur Authentizität der Freiheit: Die "Studie zur theologischen Ethik" als kaleidoskop gegenwärtiger Fundamentalmoral. Römelt, Josef.

BOER, S

Boër and Lycan's *Knowing Who*. Richard, Mark E.

BOESKY, I

Albert Schweitzer or Ivan Boesky? Why We Should Reject the Dichotomy Between Medicine and Business. Wicks, Andrew C.

BOETHIUS

Boethius und die Tradition. Sonderegger, Erwin.

Razón e Intelecto en Boecio. Lluch-Baixauli, Miguel.

The Text of Boethius' *De divisione*. Magee, John.

The Vanishing Person: A Century of the *Encyclopaedia Britannica* on the Meaning of "Person". O'Hara, Mary L.

BOGHOSSIAN, P

Externalism, Self-Knowledge, and the Prevalence of Slow Switching. Ludlow, Peter.

BOHM, D

Quantum Mechanics: Historical Contingency and the Copenhagen Hegemony. Cushing, James T.

David Bohm, físico y filósofo: In Memoriam. Herrero, Libia.

Decoherence in Unorthodox Formulations of Quantum Mechanics. Karakostas, Vassilios and Dickson, Michael.

Discussion: Why Bohm's Theory Solves the Measurement Problem. Maudlin, Tim.

Learning from the Bell-Inequalities: Causality, Locality and Realism. Tygat, Wim.

The Aharonov-Bohm Effect and the Reality of Wave Packets. Liu, Chuang.

The Bohmian Model of Quantum Cosmology. Callender, Craig and Weingard, Robert.

The Distribution Postulate in Bohm's Theory. Barrett, Jeffrey A.

Trouble-Shooting Creativity: A Critical Appraisal of David Bohm and F David Peat's 'Science Orders and Creativity'. Fisch, Menachem.

BOHR, N

Quantum Mechanics: Historical Contingency and the Copenhagen Hegemony. Cushing, James T.

La Philosophie de Niels Bohr. Bunge, Mario.

Locality/ Separability: Is This Necessarily a Useful Distinction?. Cushing, James T.

The Meaning of Complementarity. Held, Carsten.

BOLIVAR, S

Las relaciones entre Jeremías Bentham y S Bolívar. Schwartz, P and Rodríguez Braun, C.

BOLSHEVISM

The Lukács Reader. Kadarkay, Arpad (ed).

BOLZANO

Inhalts- oder Umfangslogik? Die Kontroverse zwischen E Husserl und A H Voigt. Hamacher-Hermes, Adelheid.

Bernard Bolzano and German Classical Philosophy. Pavlík, Ján.

BONDY, E

Egon Bondy's Place in the History of Metaphysics. Machovec, Milan.

BONJOUR, L

Perspectives in Virtue Epistemology: A Response to Dancy and BonJour. Sosa, Ernest.

Probability, Evidence, and the Coherence of the Whole Truth. Cross, Charles B.

The Incoherence of Coherence Theories. Fumerton, Richard.

BONTADINI, G

Omaggio a Bontadini: Osservazioni sulla Coerenza Interna e sugli Sviluppi del Pensiero Bontadininano. Turoldo, Fabrizio.

BOOLE

La Depsicologizzazione della Logica: Un confronto tra Boole e Frege. Vassallo, Nicla.

Interpretations of Boole's Alleged Psychologism. Vassallo, Nicla.

BOOLEAN

Forcing in Nonstandard Analysis. Ozawa, Masanao.

BOOLEAN ALGEBRA

Selected Logic Papers: Enlarged Edition. Quine, W V.

Vie della scrittura: Frege e la svolta linguistica. Penco, Carlo.

Boolean Algebras, Stone Spaces, and the Iterated Turing Jump. Jockusch Jr, Carl G and Soare, Robert I.

Chains and Antichans in Interval Algebras. Bekkali, M.

Complete Metric Boolean Algebras. Jeffrey, Richard (trans) and Kolmogorov, A N.

Filters and Large Cardinals. Levinski, Jean-Pierre.

Inference, Noncommutativity, and Determinateness in Quantum Mechanics. Bub, Jeffrey.

BOONIN-VAIL, D

Commentary on "Contractarianism Gone Wild: Carruthers and the Moral Status of Animals". Robinson, William S.

BOORSE, C

Ducking Harm and Sacrificing Others. Fischer, John Martin and Ravizza, Mark.

Ducking Trolleys. Boorse, Christopher.

BOOTSTRAP

Toward a Defensible Bootstrapping. Mitchell, Sam.

BORDER

Some Reflections on the Relevance of Karl Jaspers' Concept of Border Situation in Present-Day South Africa. Ally, Mashuq.

BOREL IDEALS

On Borel Ideals. Van Engelen, Fons.

BORGES, J

Scientific Sight and Embodied Knowledges: Social Circumstances in Science and Theology. Westhelle, Vítor.

BORMANN, A

Albert Bormann and John Dewey on Everyday Technology. Limper, Peter.

BORRADORI, G

Postmodernism and Contemporary Italian Philosophy. Silverman, Hugh J.

BOSANQUET

The Word 'Liberty' on the Chains of Galley-Slaves: Bosanquet's Theory of the General Will. Primoratz, Igor.

Was Bosanquet a Hegelian?. Sweet, William.

BOSKOVIC, R

Quantitas Inassignabilis: Language and Knowledge in Boskovic's Approach to Infinitesimals. Martinovic, Ivica.

BOSNJAK, B

Bosnjaks *Geschichte der Philosophie* und das geschichtliche Denken. Pazanin, Ante.

Bosnjaks Geschichte der Philosophie. Pejovic, Danilo.

Geschichte der Philosophie (als Wissenschaft) oder Entwicklung des Denkens in(nerhalb) der Idee des Ganzen. Despot, Branko.

BOTURINI, L

Boturini e la Diffusione di Vico in Spagna. Mestre, Antonio.

BRITISH

Political Writings: King James VI and I. Sommerville, Johann P (ed), James VI and James I.

The British Moralists and the Internal 'Ought': 1640-1740. Darwall, Stephen.

The Politics of English Jacobinism: Writings of John Thelwall. Thelwall, John and Claeys, Gregory (ed).

The Trace of Political Representation. Seitz, Brian.

The 'Arabick' Interest of the Natural Philosophers in Seventeenth-Century England. Russell, G A (ed).

Antecedentes del Utilitarismo en los moralistas británicos anteriores a Hume. Costa, Margarita.

British Hegelianism: A Non-Metaphysical View?. Stern, Robert.

British Idealism, the State, and International Relations. Boucher, David.

British Idealist International Theory. Boucher, David.

John Ruskin and the Ethical Foundations of Morris and Company, 1861-96. Harvey, Charles and Press, Jon.

Olympus Mislaid? A Profile of Perry Anderson. Elliot, Gregory.

Sympathy—Imitation—Metamorphosis (in Japanese). Aizawa, Teruaki.

The Impoverishment of Art. Kieran, Matthew.

Ultimate Reality and Ethical Meaning: Theological Utilitarianism in Eighteenth Century England. Forbes, Alexander M.

Was Bosanquet a Hegelian?. Sweet, William.

BROADIE, S

Aristotle and Hellenistic Philosophy. Sharples, Bob.

BROOME, J

Weighing Goods: Some Questions and Comments. Temkin, Larry S.

BROUNOWER, S

Manservant as Amanuensis: Sylvester Brounower. Milton, J R.

BROWN

The Religion of a Scientist: Explorations into Reality (*Religio philosophi naturalis*). Peacocke, Arthur.

BROWNING, D

A Reexamination of Browning's View of Experience. Pappas, Gregory.

All We Seem To Get Is Life Implicitness: The Practical As Ontological. McDermott, John J.

Browning and Two Traditions. Krecz, Charles A.

Browning's Ontology. Van de Vate, Dwight.

Remodelling Nature: The Roots of Pragmatic Theory. Hickman, Larry A.

Some Notes on Browning's *Ethical Notes*. Van de Vate, Dwight.

The Value of Passions in Plato and Aristotle. Leighton, Stephen.

BRUAIRE, C

Bedürfen und Vorstellungsdestrucktion. Kühn, Rolf.

BRUECKNER, A

Accepting the Consequences of Anti-Individualism. McKinsey, Michael.

Failing to Beg the Question. Steinitz, Yuval.

BRUMMER, V

Calvin and Bernard on Freedom and Necessity: A Reply to Brümmer. Helm, Paul.

BRUNI, L

La Rehabilitacíon del Humanismo Retórico: Considerando el Antihumanismo de Heidegger. Grassi, Ernesto.

BRUNO

Attualità di Bruno. Garin, Eugenio.

Le Fonti del "Sigillus Sigillorum" del Bruno, Ossia: Il Confronto con Ficino a Oxford Sull'anima Umana. Sturlese, Rita.

Tre Schede su Bruno e Oxford. Aquilecchia, Giovanni.

BUBER

"Buber's Socialist and Political Views: A Critique" in *Thinkers and Teachers of Modern Judaism, Goldsmith, Emanuel S (ed).* Uffenheimer, Benjamin.

"The Gate to God's Presence in Heschel, Buber, and Soloveitchik" in *Thinkers and Teachers of Modern Judaism, Goldsmith, Emanuel S (ed).* Zuesse, Evan M.

Philosophie als Dialogik: Frühe Schriften Werke 1. Goldschmidt, Hermann Levin.

The Levinas Reader. Hand, Seán.

Buber's Dialogic Personalism. Kowalczyk, Stanislaw.

Reciprocity and the Height of God: A Defence of Buber Against Levinas. Kelly, Andrew.

BUCHANAN, A

Breaking Up: An Essay on Secession. Gauthier, David.

Can There Be a Right to Secede?. Ewin, R E.

Marx and Rights. Corlett, J Angelo.

BUCHANAN, B

Medium AI and Experimental Science. Kukla, André.

BUCK-MORSS, S

"Überwindung von Schwierigem durch Häufung Desselben". Steiner, Uwe.

BUDD, M

Musical Beauty and Levels of Hearing. Yuktanandana, Aksak.

BUDDHISM

see also Karma, Mahayana, Zen Buddhism

"A Buddhist View of Human Rights" in *Human Rights and Religious Values, An-Na'im, Abdullahi A (& other eds).* Abe, Masao.

"Personal Rights and Contemporary Buddhism" in *Human Rights and the World's Religions, Rouner, Leroy (ed).* Unno, Taitetsu.

"Qing (Emotions) in Pre-Buddhist Chinese Thought" in *Emotions in Asian Thought, Marks, Joel (ed).* Hansen, Chad.

"Social and Cultural Rights in Buddhism" in *Human Rights and the World's Religions, Rouner, Leroy (ed).* Thurman, Robert A F.

"The Emotions of Altruism, East and West" in *Emotions in Asian Thought, Marks, Joel (ed).* Kupperman, Joel J.

"The Potential Contribution of Buddhism in Developing an Environmental Ethic..." in *Ethics, Religion and Biodiversity, Hamilton, Lawrence S (ed).* Sponsel, Leslie E and Natadecha-Sponsel, Poranee.

"Theoretical Perspectives on Emotions in Early Buddhism" in *Emotions in Asian Thought, Marks, Joel (ed).* De Silva, Padmasiri.

Ahimsa, the Self, and Postmodernism: Jain, Vedantist, and Buddhist Perspectives. Gier, Nicholas F.

Antologia del Buddhismo Ch'an. Arena, Leonardo Vittorio.

Emotions in Asian Thought. Marks, Joel (ed) and Ames, Roger T (ed).

Human Rights and the World's Religions. Rouner, Leroy (ed).

Seven Dilemmas in World Religions. Stephens, G Lynn and Pence, Gregory.

Sunyata, Textualism, and Incommensurability. Barnhart, Michael G.

The Art of Living: Aesthetics of the Ordinary in World Spiritual Traditions. Sartwell, Crispin.

The Divine Matrix: Creativity as Link between East and West. Bracken, Joseph A.

A Belated Response to Hu Shih and D T Suzuki. Sellmann, James D.

A Buddhist Reflection on the Task of Elders. Nakasone, Ronald Y.

A Case for Convergence in Tibetan and Vedāntin Meditative Practices. Liberman, Kenneth.

B-Series Temporal Order in Dogen's Theory of Time. Vorenkamp, Dirck.

Buddhism and Cognitivism: A Postmodern Appraisal. Pickering, John.

Buddhism: Gotamavada Versus Theravada. Bahm, Archie.

Critical Concept of Nothing. Seidel, Bradley.

De studie der Chinese wijsbegeerte in het Westen: Een bibliografisch overzicht. Van der Leeuw, Karel L.

Dharmakirti and Tibetans on *Adrsyanupalabdhihetu*. Tillemans, Tom J F.

Early Yogacara and Its Relationship with the Madhyamaka School. King, Richard.

Food in India. Olivelle, Patrick.

Nagarjuna's Appeal. Hayes, Richard P.

Person as Narration: The Dissolution of 'Self' and 'Other' in Ch'an Buddhism. Hershock, Peter D.

Personal Identity: In Buddhist and Whiteheadian Thought (An Exercise with an Intercultural Experience). Sarkar, Anil K.

Presence with a Difference: Buddhists and Feminists on Subjectivity. Klein, Anne C.

Selfhood and Identity in Confucianism, Taoism, Buddhism, and Hinduism: Contrasts With the West. Ho, David Y F.

The Buddhist Aesthetic Nature: A Challenge to Rationalism and Empiricism. Inada, Kenneth K.

The Buddhist Perspective on Business Ethics: Experiential Exercises for Exploration and Practice. Gould, Stephen J.

The Genesis of Buddhist Painting in Ancient India and Its Early Development. Sadakane, Keiji.

The Hermeneutics of Formal Analytics: The Case of Tibetan Philosophical Criticism. Liberman, Kenneth.

The Place of Buddhism in Santayana's Moral Philosophy. Michelsen, John Magnus.

The Provisional World: Existenthood, Causal Efficiency, and Sri Harsa. Ram-Prasad, C.

The Relationship Between Analysis and Insight (Prajñā) in Mādhyamika Buddhism: Some Western Interpretations. Dean, Colin.

The Turn Towards Buddhism. McGhee, Michael.

The Whole Body, not Heart, as 'Seat of Consciousness': The Buddha's View. Sugunasiri, Suwanda H J.

Theravada Buddhism and the Definition of Religion. Smart, Ninian.

Transmigration Without a Self. Datta, Rama.

Vallabha's Positive Response to Buddhism. Yadav, Bibhuti S.

Xunzi and the Confucian Answer to Titanism. Gier, Nicholas F.

'Critical Buddhism' and the Question of Philosophical Syncretism. Heine, Steven.

BUDGET

Multinational Capital Budgeting, Emerging Markets, and Managerial Agency: A Proposal for an Ethically Constrained Capital Budgeting Model. Stanley, Marjorie Thines.

BUDGETING

Global Budgeting in the Real World. Gold, Jay A.

The Ethics of Global Budgeting: Some Historically Based Observations. Baker, Robert B.

BULGAKOV, S

The Trinitarian Panentheism of Sergej Bulgakov. O'Donnell, John.

BULTMANN

Il Problema del Mito nel Dialogo Bultmann-Jaspers. Donadio, Francesco.

BURBIDGE, J

Recent Work on Hegel's Philosophy of Religion. Dickey, L.

BURBULES, N

Dialogue Needs a Point and Purpose. Robinson, Viviane M J.

BURDEN

To Save the Logic, the Facts Must Fit. Pellegrino, Edmund D.

BUREAUCRACY

Groupe et idéologie: A propos de *Fonctionnaires de Dieu* d'Eugen Drewermann. Saint-Germain, Christian.

BURGE, T

Burge's Literal Interpretation of Frege. Weiner, Joan.

CHAPPELL, T
God Had to Create the World. Pearl, Leon.

CHAPPELL, V
Responses to Chappell and Watson. Hoffman, Paul.

CHARACTER
"Butler and Hume on Habit and Moral Character" in *Hume and Hume's Connexions, Stewart, M A (ed)*. Wright, John P.

Aporie del Simbolo: Saggio su Otto Weininger. Manfreda, Luigi Antonio.

Aristotle's Rhetoric: An Art of Character. Garver, Eugene.

Character and Culture: Essays on East and West. Babbitt, Irving.

Practical Realism and Moral Psychology. Jacobs, Jonathan.

Woman and the History of Philosophy. Tuana, Nancy.

Character: The Framework for a Successful Life. Adams, E M.

El Concepto de Complexión y Alma en Tomás de Aquino y Galena. Martínez Sendra, María Carmen.

Emotions, Reason, and Character. Wilson, James Q.

Empirischer und intelligibler Charakter: Von Kant über Fries und Schelling zu Schopenhauer. Kossler, Matthias.

Le Rôle de la Notion de Caractère. Koana, Akiko.

Myth and Politics: Notes on the Concept of Destiny in the "Young" Benjamin (in Portuguese). Chaves, Ernani.

Not by Skill Alone: The Centrality of Character to Critical Thinking. Siegel, Harvey.

The Nature of Fictional Characters and The Referential Fallacy. Dauer, Francis W.

What Is Character?. Braun, David.

CHARACTERISTICS
Disertación sobre la Naturaleza y la Propagación del Fuego. de Châtelet, Marquesa.

CHARACTERIZATION
"Genericity: An Introduction" in *The Generic Book, Carlson, Gregory N (ed)*. Krifka, Manfred (& others).

CHARDIN, PIERRE TEILHARD DE
see Teilhard

CHARISMA
Fichte und die charismatische Verklärung der Vernunft. Villacañas, José L.

CHARITY
Locality and Practical Judgment: Charity and Sacrifice. Ross, Stephen David.

Egoism and Altruism in Ethics: Dispensing with Spurious Generality. Van Der Steen, Wim J.

Giustizia e carità nella dottrina dei padri, II. Pizzorini, Reginaldo M.

Indeterminacy and Interpretation. Abel, Günter.

Ingérence des États en temps de guerre: Action humanitaire des organisations bénévoles chrétiennes et témoignage de l'évangile. Joblin, Joseph.

La Polemica di Leroux contro Lacordaire e Malthus sulla Questione Sociale. Fiorentino, Fernando.

Loving God *and* One's Neighbor: Thomistic Charity. Adams, Don.

Pangloss, L'Erreur et la Divergence. Laurier, Daniel.

When to Terminate a Charitable Trust?. Landesman, Cliff.

Wong on Davidson. Potter, R Dennis.

CHARLES, D
Commentary on Charles's "Aristotle on Substance, Essence and Biological Kinds". Gill, Mary Louise.

CHARRON, P
Scepsi Moderna: Interpretazioni dello Scetticismo da Charron a Hume. Paganini, Gianni.

CHASTITY
"Über die Beziehung von Schamhaftigkeit, Öffentlichkeit und Geschlecht" in *Macht Geschlechter Differenz, Müller-Funk, Wolfgang (ed)*. Saurer, Edith.

CHATEAUBRIAND
D'Atala à Athéna: L'Itinéraire Poétique et Politique de Chateaubriand. Garguilo, René.

De l'Itinéraire à la Note sur la Grèce: Évolution et Constantes de l'Attitude de Chateaubriand Face à la Grèce. Antoine, Philippe.

CHATER, N
Systematicity Revisited: Reply to Chater and Christiansen and Niklasson and Van Gelder. Hadley, Robert F.

CHEATING
Estimating the Incidence of Wrongdoing and Whistle-Blowing: Results of a Study Using Randomized Response Technique. Burton, Brian K and Near, Janet P.

The Case of the Stolen Psychology Test: An Analysis of an Actual Cheating Incident. Faulkender, Patricia J (& others).

CHEMISTRY
see also Biochemistry

"Das Verständnis von Auslösung und Beschleunigung.." in *Naturauffassungen in Philosophie, Wissenschaft, Technik: Band III, Schäfer, Lothar (ed)*. Ruthenberg, Klaus.

"Prozeßstrukturen" in *Schelling und die Selbstorganisation, Heuser-Kessler, Marie-Luise (ed)*. Niedersen, Uwe.

A History of Scientific Thought: Elements of a History of Science. Serres, Michel (ed).

Knowledge and the Body-Mind Problem: In Defence of Interaction. Notturno, M A (ed) and Popper, Karl R.

A Filosofia da Biologia à Luz da Biologia Molecular: Resolveu-se o Mistério?. Delouya, Daniel.

Brain Water, the Ether, and the Art of Constructing Systems. Rueger, Alexander.

Could Theoretical Entities Save Realism?. Elsamahi, Mohamed.

Experiment, Speculation and Law: Faraday's Analysis of Arago's Wheel. Steinle, Friedrich.

Has Chemistry Been at Least Approximately Reduced to Quantum Mechanics?. Scerri, Eric R.

Ideal Reaction Types and the Reactions of Real Alloys. Ramsey, Jeffry L.

Meta-Química, Estética e Iluminación. Ocaña, Enrique.

Philosophers versus Chemists Concerning 'Laws of Nature'. Christie, Maureen.

Química y Salvación. Villacañas, José L.

Seeing and Paradigms in the Chemical Revolution. Shelton, Jim.

Some Considerations on the Reducibility of Chemistry to Physics. Mosini, Valeria.

Spectrometers as Analogues of Nature. Rothbart, Daniel.

The Exclusion Principle, Chemistry and Hidden Variables. Scerri, Eric R.

CHENEY, J
Caring Relationships with Natural and Artificial Environments. Field, Terri.

CHENG, C
On Chung-Ying Cheng's Onto-Hermeneutics. Derong, Pan and Xin, Katherine R.

CHERNYSHEVSKY
Concerning the National Uniqueness of Russian Philosophy. Boldyrev, I A.

CHILD ABUSE
Child Abuse and Embodiment from a Thomistic Perspective. Harak, G Simon.

Child Abuse or Acceptable Cultural Norms. Brant, Renée, Martin, Tony and Wyatt, Gail Elizabeth.

The Discourse of Denial: Cross-Examining Child Victim Witnesses. Brennan, Mark.

CHILDHOOD
Il Sogno, la Fanciullezza e l'Arte nel Pensiero di Giovanni Gentile. Stella, Vittorio.

Nietzsche and Music. Storr, Anthony.

CHILDREN
see also Infant

"Children Who Run: Ethics and Homelessness" in *Introducing Applied Ethics, Almond, Brenda (ed)*. Parker, Michael.

"Women and Children First" in *Medicine and Moral Reasoning, Fulford, K W M (ed)*. Gillett, Grant.

Autonomy and Intervention: Parentalism in the Caring Life. Kultgen, John.

Folk Psychology: The Theory of Mind Debate. Davies, Martin (ed) and Stone, Tony (ed).

Natural Theories of Mind: Evolution, Development, and Simulation of Everyday Mindreading. Whiten, Andrew (ed).

The Constructed Body: AIDS, Reproductive Technology, and Ethics. Murphy, Julien S.

Understanding Images: Finding Meaning in Digital Imagery. Marchese, Francis T (ed).

Adolescence as a Cultural Invention: Philippe Ariès and the Sociology of Youth. Ben-Amos, Ilana Krausman.

Children's Capacity to Agree to Psychological Research: Knowledge of Risks and Benefits and Voluntariness. Abramovitch, Rona (& others).

Clinical Ethics Consultations with Children. Orr, Robert D and Perkin, Ronald M.

Durkheim and Moral Education for Children: A Recently Discovered Lecture. Pickering, W S F.

Ethical Issues in Discharge Planning for Vulnerable Infants and Children. Cohen, Marsha H.

Ética y Bienestar. Griffin, James.

How Religion Impedes Moral Development. Clark, Brad.

Identity, Becoming, and Rights of Development. Covey, Edward.

Innocence. Richards, Norvin W.

Inventing 'Child Art': Franz Cizek and Modernism. Malvern, S B.

Is There a Moral Obligation to Have Children?. Smilansky, Saul.

On the Unavoidability of Power in Child-rearing: Is the Language of Rights Educationally Appropriate?. Smeyers, Paul.

Peer Pressure and Children's Religious Belief. Howe, Norma.

Qué es eso de la Filosofía para niños?. Cohen, Diana.

Réflexion sur *La Philosophie pour Enfants*. Tozzi, Michel.

Reports of Assent and Permission in Research With Children: Illustrations and Suggestions. Range, Lillian M and Cotton, C Randy.

The Friendship Model of Filial Obligations. Dixon, Nicholas.

The Primacy of Virtue in Children's Moral Development. Putman, Daniel.

When I Was a Child, I Thought as a Child: The Educational Philosophy of Paul K Feyerabend. Bossé, Michael J.

CHILDRESS, J
Rationality and Allocating Scarce Medical Resources. Forsberg, Ralph P.

CHINESE
see also Buddhism, Confucianism, Taoism

"Common Nouns: A Contrastive Analysis of Chinese and English" in *The Generic Book, Carlson, Gregory N (ed)*. Krifka, Manfred.

"Ecstasy and Epistemology" in *Emotions in Asian Thought, Marks, Joel (ed)*. Rouner, Leroy S.

"New *Lixue*" Metaphysics: Examination and Critique. Lai, Chen.

"Qing (Emotions) in Pre-Buddhist Chinese Thought" in *Emotions in Asian Thought, Marks, Joel (ed)*. Hansen, Chad.

"Rites as Rights: The Confucian Alternative" in *Human Rights and the World's Religions, Rouner, Leroy (ed)*. Ames, Roger T.

"The Concept of Emotion Revisited: A Critical Synthesis of Western and Confucian Thought" in *Emotions in Asian Thought, Marks, Joel (ed)*. Bockover, Mary I.

Amoral Politics: The Persistent Truth of Machiavellism. Scharfstein, Ben-Ami.

Scientism and Humanism: Two Cultures in Post-Mao China (1978-1989). Hua, Shiping.

CHINESE

The Epistemology of Comparative Philosophy: A Critique with Reference to P T Raju's Views. Kaipayil, Joseph.

The Tao Te Ching: A New Translation with Commentary. Chen, Ellen M.

A Few Problems Related to Nineteenth Century Chinese and Western Philosophies and their Cultural Interaction. Weishi, Yuan.

A Philosophical Correspondence with Li Rui. Yuanhua, Wang.

A Voice in Discussion About Mr Tsung-I Dow's Report. Nowicki, Andrzej.

Continuity—Guo Xiang, Chan, Cheng-Zhu *Lixue*, New Realism, and Marxism—Feng's Discernment of the Way. Obenchain, Diane B.

De studie der Chinese wijsbegeerte in het Westen: Een bibliografisch overzicht. Van der Leeuw, Karel L.

Derrida and Ideographic Poetics. Cheng, Jiewei.

Eine grundlegende konzeptionelle Denkfigur der altchinesischen Philosophie. Trauzettel, Rolf.

Feng Youlan and the Vienna Circle (A Synopsis). Shouchang, Wang.

Feng Youlan's Views on Chinese and Western Culture. Zhonghua, Li.

From Montague to Neo-Confucianism: Feng Youlan's "New *Lixue*" and Logical Analysis. Lujun, Yin.

Las ideas chinas en la conceptualización transcultural: La relevancia de la historia intelectual. Lee, Thomas H C.

Moral/Political Education in the People's Republic of China: Learning Through Role Models. Reed, Gay Garland.

Mourning Professor Feng Youlan by Engaging in Serious Philosophical Discussion Today. Zehou, Li.

Mourning Professor Feng Youlan: "Method of Abstract Inheriting" Should Not Be Denied. Disheng, Yang.

On Chung-Ying Cheng's Onto-Hermeneutics. Derong, Pan and Xin, Katherine R.

Recollecting Professor Feng's 1957 Lectures in the Spring. Pu, Pang.

Reflections on Song-Ming *Lixue* and the Philosophy of Harmony and Integration. Liwen, Zhang.

Taoism, Confucianism and the Chinese Self. Morris, Brian.

The "Zhi Yan" in Feng Youlan's *Xin Zhi Yan*. Yijie, Tang.

The *Tao* of Confucian Virtue Ethics. Bretzke, James T.

The Different Faces of Contemporary Religious Confucianism. Pfister, Lauren.

The Formation of New *Lixue*: Feng Youlan and New Realism. Juji, Azuma.

The Historical Significance of Feng Youlan's *Zhen Yuan Liu Shu*. Dainian, Zhang.

The Logic of Liu Hui and Euclid as Exemplified in Their Proofs of the Volume of a Pyramid. Crossley, J N and Lun, A W C.

The Unity of Heaven and Man versus Absolute Unlikeness—Kierkegaard, European Thinker, Contra Chinese Philosophy. Zhou, Yiyun.

Universality in Chinese Culture. Dow, Tsung-I.

Universals and Individuals: A Brief Discussion of New *Lixue*. Youguang, Tu.

White Horse not Horse: Making Sense of a Negative Logic. Lai, Whalen.

CHISHOLM, R

"Chisholm's Ontology of Things" in *American Philosophy Today and Other Philosophical Studies, Rescher, Nicholas*. Rescher, Nicholas.

Neutrals. Lemos, Noah M.

Religious Experience After the Demise of Foundationalism. Grube, Dirk-Martin.

Toward a Credible Agent-Causal Account of Free Will. Clarke, Randolph.

Why Is There Analytic Epistemology?. Vinci, Tom.

CHOICE

see also Decision

"Concretization Quandaries and Pragmatic Anomalies" in *American Philosophy Today and Other Philosophical Studies, Rescher, Nicholas*. Rescher, Nicholas.

"Dio e il male" in *L'etica e il suo Altro, Vigna, Carmelo (ed)*. Possenti, Vittorio.

"Simone de Beauvoir: Falling into (Ambiguous) Line" in *Feminist Interpretations of Simone de Beauvoir, Simons, Margaret A (ed)*. Le Doeuff, Michèle.

"The Quest for Identity" in *Identity, Culture, and Education, Smeyers, Paul (ed)*. Tamir, Yael.

"Wille" e "Willkür" in Fichte. Moiso, Francesco.

Hipparchia's Choice: An Essay Concerning Women, Philosophy, etc. Le Doeuff, Michèle.

Life Choices: A Hastings Center Introduction to Bioethics. Howell, Joseph H (ed) and Sale, William Frederick (ed).

Morality, Normativity, and Society. Copp, David.

Parts of Classes. Lewis, David.

Rationing Medicine. Blank, Robert H.

Reshaping the Female Body: The Dilemma of Cosmetic Surgery. Davis, Kathy.

A Rebuttal To Shelly Kagan's Attack on Options. Warenski, Lisa.

Double's *The Non-Reality of Free Will*. Kapitan, Tomis.

Equal Opportunity or Equal Social Outcome. Fleurbaey, Marc.

Ethical Standards, Attitudes Toward Risk, and Intentional Noncompliance: An Experimental Investigation. Ghosh, Dipankar and Crain, Terry L.

Ethics and Agency Theory. French, Peter A.

Forced Choices and Self-Defence. Montague, Phillip.

Four Dogmas of Environmental Economics. Sagoff, Mark.

Getting Our Options Clear: A Closer Look at Agent-Centered Options. Hurley, Paul E.

Hard Times, Hard Choices: Founding Bioethics Today. Gracia, Diego.

Healthcare Rationing through Global Budgeting: The Ethical Choices. Veatch, Robert M.

Het statistische argument. De Vries, Michiel S.

Impossible Choices: When Patients and Careproviders Face Impossible Decisions. Howe, Edmund G.

Judgement and Rational Theory-Choice. Sankey, Howard.

Motivation and Moral Choice in Kant's Theory of Rational Agency. McCarty, Richard.

On Not Confusing Necessity With Compulsion: A Reply to Paul Helm. Brümmer, Vincent.

On the Difficulty of Making Social Choices. Nurmi, Hannu.

Proving Too Little and Too Much: A Theistic Response to Tipler. Burns, Peter.

Rational Choice and Social Theory: A Comment. Hausman, Daniel M.

Reasonable Doubts about Rational Choice. Houghton, David.

Sexual Harassment in the Law: The Demarcation Problem. Hajdin, Mane.

Spinoza on Religious Choice. Cooper, Neil.

The Choice-Intention Principle. Goetz, Stewart C.

The Gulf Between: Surrogate Choices, Physician Instructions, and Informal Network Responses. Koch, Tom.

The Normative Nature of Coercion. Hankinson, Jennifer.

The Social Equation: Freedom and its Limits. Horvath, Charles M.

Theory Change and Theory Choice. Chalmers, Alan F.

Underdetermination and the Social Side of Science. Brown, James Robert.

Virtue and Choice in Aristotle's *Ethics*. Tilley, John.

CHOICE SEQUENCES

Doing and Refraining from Refraining. Xu, Ming.

CHOMSKY, N

"Tacit Knowledge and Subdoxastic States" in *Philosophy of Psychology: Debates on Psychological Explanation, Macdonald, Cynthia (ed)*. Davies, Martin.

A Companion to the Philosophy of Mind. Guttenplan, Samuel (ed).

Challenging Chomsky: The Generative Garden Game. Botha, Rudolf P.

Consumerism and Language Acquisition. Mercier, Adèle.

Dos Concepciones del Lenguaje. Tomasini Bassols, Alejandro.

Interview with Noam Chomsky On Linguistics and Politics. Grewendorf, Günther.

Language and Determinism: A Contribution to the Cognitivist Critique of Chomsky's Innateness Hypothesis. Jutronic-Tlhomirovic, Dunja.

The Seduction of Abduction: Peirce's Theory of Signs and Indeterminacy in Language. Melrose, Robin.

CHOREOGRAPHY

"Spaced Out or Folded In? Trends in Architectural Choreography" in *Philosophy and Architecture, Mitias, Michael H (ed)*. Donougho, Martin J.

CHRIST

Positives Paradox: Entwurf einer neostrukturalistischen Religionspädagogik. Beuscher, Bernd.

Zum Begriff der Trinität. Polemis, Michael.

Imitatio Christi: Ethical Problems of Some Christological Standpoints. Vidrányi, Katalin.

Sokrates und Christus in der Verfasserschaft Soren Kierkegaards: Eine Henologische Ganzheitsinterpretation. Wyller, Egil A.

CHRISTENSEN, D

Dialectic and the Advance of Science. Harris, Errol E.

Toward a Defensible Bootstrapping. Mitchell, Sam.

CHRISTIAN

La Dialéctica en el Cancionero de Baena. Sánchez-Romate, María José Gómez.

La Filosofia Cristiana nei Secoli XIX e XX. Scilironi, Carlo.

Nota Sobre la Poesía Algorítmica de Ramón Llull. Lizalde, Carlos Lorenza.

Razón e historia: La modernidad del postmodernismo. Koslowski, Peter.

Religious Toleration. Haldane, John.

Variaciones Isidorianas. Rodón, Eulalia.

CHRISTIANITY

see also Catholicism, Protestantism

"A Postmodern Trinity?" in *The 1994 Annual of Hermeneutics and Social Concern, Lawler, Justus George (ed)*. Sanders, Theresa.

"Birth Control and the Value of Human Life" in *Ethics on the Frontiers of Human Existence, Badham, Paul (ed)*. Kono, Shigemi.

"Christian Belief and the Ethics of In-vitro Fertilization Research" in *Ethics on the Frontiers of Human Existence, Badham, Paul (ed)*. Badham, Paul.

"Christian Concepts of the Responsible Self" in *Human Rights and the World's Religions, Rouner, Leroy (ed)*. Rendtorff, Trutz.

"Christianity is the Future of Paganism: Schelling's Philosophy of Religion, 1826-1854" in *Meaning, Truth, and God, Rouner, Leroy S (ed)*. O'Meara, Thomas F.

"From Civil Religion to Public Philosophy" in *Civil Religion and Political Theology, Rouner, Leroy S (ed)*. Neuhaus, Richard John.

"Hegel as Theologian" in *Meaning, Truth, and God, Rouner, Leroy (ed)*. Findlay, J N.

"How People Argue about Abortion and Capital Punishment in Europe and America..." in *Ethics on the Frontiers of Human Existence, Badham, Paul (ed)*. Davies, Christie.

"Hume's Historical View of Miracles" in *Hume and Hume's Connexions, Stewart, M A (ed)*. Stewart, M A.

"Loving, Appraising, and Bestowing" in *The Nature and Pursuit of Love, Goicoechea, David (ed)*. Vannoy, Russell C.

"Nietzsche and the Crisis of Nihilism" in *Meaning, Truth, and God, Rouner, Leroy S (ed)*. Fortin, Ernest L.

"Roman Suicide" in *Medicine and Moral Reasoning, Fulford, K W M (ed)*. Griffin, Miriam.

"Shamanic Nietzsche" in *Nietzsche: A Critical Reader, Sedgwick, Peter R (ed)*. Land, Nick.

"The Origins of Process Theology" in *Meaning, Truth, and God, Rouner, Leroy (ed)*. Cobb Jr, John B.

"The Politics of Christianity" in *Locke's Philosophy, Rogers, G A J (ed)*. Harris, Ian.

CITIZENSHIP

Culture, Citoyenneté, Humanité. Coutel, Charles.
Fichte y Ortega (II). Héroes o Ciudadanos. El Mito de Don Quijote. Molinuevo, José Luis.
L'Enseignement de la Philosophie et la Citoyenneté. Baillargeon, Jean.
La Philosophie Politique et la Formation du Citoyen. Norman, Wayne.
Leadership, Moral Development, and Citizenship Behavior. Graham, Jill W.
Mothers, Citizenship, and Independence: A Critique of Pure Family Values. Young, Iris Marion.
Organs for Undocumented Aliens? A Transplantation Dilemma. Gottlieb, Lawrence and Zucker, Mark J.
Psychosocial and Citizenship Status of Patients Needing Transplant. McCullough, Laurence B.
Reply to Michael Walzer. Bader, Veit.
Response to Veit Bader. Walzer, Michael.
The Eleatic Stranger's Socratic Condemnation of Socrates. Howland, Jacob A.
Toward a More Democratic Ethic of Technological Governance. Zimmerman, Andrew D.
Translating Samuel Pufendorf: On Two English Editions. Palladini, Fiammetta.

CITY

Ende der Geschichte, Ende der Stadt?. Flusser, Vilém.
A Key Topos in Thucydides: The Comparison of Cities and Individuals. Morrison, James V.

CIVICS

Civic Education and Social Diversity. Gutman, Amy.
Liberal Civic Education and Religious Fundamentalism: The Case of God v. John Rawls?. Macedo, Stephen.

CIVIL

"From Civil Religion to Public Philosophy" in Civil Religion and Political Theology, Rouner, Leroy S (ed). Neuhaus, Richard John.

CIVIL DISOBEDIENCE

"Some Philosophical Assessments of Environmental Disobedience" in Philosophy and the Natural Environment, Attfield, Robin (ed). List, Peter C.
The Transformation of Natural Philosophy: The Case of Philip Melanchthon. Kusukawa, Sachiko.
Civil Disobedience and Plato's Crito. Herrera, Christopher D.

CIVIL LAW

Bridging the Sacred and the Secular. Hooper, J Leon (ed) and Murray, John Courtney.

CIVIL RIGHT

"A Moral Justification for Gay and Lesbian Civil Rights Legislation" in Gay Ethics, Murphy, Timothy F (ed). Samar, Vincent J.
Environmental Justice: An Environmental Civil Rights Value Acceptable to All World Views. Hartley, Troy W.
Let's Get the L Out: Or Why Johnson Controls Is Not an Unequivocal Victory for Women. Callahan, Joan.

CIVIL SOCIETY

Civil Society, Civil Religion. Shanks, Andrew.
Rousseau (Past Masters). Wokler, Robert.
At the Crossroads: Hegel and the Ethics of bürgerliche Gesellschaft. Smith, Steven B.
Hermeneutics and Critical Theory: Enlightenment as Political (in Portuguese). Howard, Dick.
La vie éthique perdue dans ses extrêmes...Scission et réconciliation dans la théorie hégélienne de la Sittlichkeit. Kervégan, Jean-François.
Leviatán en los confines de la modernidad: Una crítica anarquista de la sociedad civil y el Estado. Jiménez, Jorge.
Nationalisme versus republikeinse burgerschapszin. Van Erp, Herman.

CIVILIZATION

Civilized Madness: Schizophrenia, Self-Consciousness and the Modern Mind. Sass, Louis A.
I Giganti in Vico. Mazzola, Roberto.
La Prospettiva Morale di Augusto Guzzo. Bosco, Nynfa.
Philosophy and General Education: "World Civilizations" as Virtue Ethics. Omundson, Bruce.
Religione, etica e politica nel pensiero di Ernst Troeltsch. Cantillo, Giuseppe.
Tavola Rotonda. Rossi, Pietro (& others).
The Royce-Howison Debate on the Conception of God. Skrupskelis, Ignas K.
Un colloquio filosofico su "rivoluzione" e "contraddizione". De Stafano, Rodolfo.
Vico y Sarmiento. Lértora Mendoza, Celina A.

CIXOUS, H

Fear, Truth, Writing: From Paper Village to Electronic Community. Brown, Alison Leigh.
On the Gift-Giving Virtue: Nietzsche's Unacknowledged Feminine Economy. Schrift, Alan D.

CIZEK, F

Inventing 'Child Art': Franz Cizek and Modernism. Malvern, S B.

CLACK, B

On Giving Practice Its Due—A Reply. Phillips, D Z.

CLARITY

El Principio de Causalidad en la Tercera Meditación. Chávez-Arvizo, Enrique.
La Claridad en el Pensamiento. Guerrero M, Luis.

CLARK, A

"Reply to Clark and Smolensky: Do Connectionist Minds Have Beliefs?" in Connectionism: Debates on Psychological Explanation, Macdonald, Cynthia (ed). Stich, Stephen and Warfield, Ted A.
The Virtues, Challenges and Implications of Connectionism. Stich, Stephen.

CLARK, M

May We Stop Worrying About Blackmail?. Smilansky, Saul.

CLARK, S

Applied Philosophy and Business Ethics. Kieran, Matthew.

CLARKE

"A Reply to My Critics and Friendly Commentators" in The Nature and Pursuit of Love, Goicoechea, David (ed). Singer, Irving.
Internal and External Causal Explanations of the Universe. Smith, Quentin.

CLASS

see also Set, Working Class
"Class Structure and Choice of Technology in an Agrarian Economy" in Foundations of Analytical Marxism (Volume I), Roemer, John E (ed). Cabeza-Gutés, Maite.
"La Filsofía va al Taller" in Temas Actuales de Filosofía, Palacios, María Julia (ed). Gonza, Guillermo.
"Max Weber and the Bourgeoisie" in The Barbarism of Reason, Horowitz, Asher (ed). Strong, Tracy B.
"Morality: Invention or Discovery?" in Medicine and Moral Reasoning, Fulford, K W M (ed). Urmson, James O.
"Post-Marxism and Class" in Marxism in the Postmodern Age, Callari, Antonio (ed). Sandler, Blair and Diskin, Jonathan.
"The Relevance of Marxist Theory for Understanding the Present World Crisis" in Marxism in the Postmodern Age, Callari, Antonio (ed). Mandel, Ernest.
Bad Faith and Antiblack Racism. Gordon, Lewis R.
Einführung in die Logik. Menne, Albert.
Feminism and Philosophy: Essential Readings in Theory, Reinterpretation, and Application. Tuana, Nancy (ed) and Tong, Rosemarie (ed).
Foundations of Analytical Marxism (Volume I). Roemer, John E (ed).
Parts of Classes. Lewis, David.
Power: Its Forms, Bases, and Uses. Wrong, Dennis H.
Racist Culture: Philosophy and the Politics of Meaning. Goldberg, David Theo.
Real Rights. Wellman, Carl P.
Socialism After Communism: The New Market Socialism. Pierson, Christopher.
The Book of the Body Politic. Forhan, Kate Langdon (ed & trans) and De Pizan, Christine.
Are Subclasses Parts of Classes?. Oliver, Alex.
Complete Problems for Fixed-Point Logics. Grohe, Martin.
Francis Hutcheson and the Problem of Conspicuous Consumption. Mortensen, Preben.
Justice and the Case for School Vouchers. Spoerl, Joseph.
La Società Concreta: Considerazioni su Fichte e Hegel. Fonnesu, Luca.
Las Personas y su Identidad. Sanfélix, Vicente.
On Countable Fractions from an Elementary Class. Ash, C J.
On Russell's Argument for Restricting Modes of Specification and Domains of Quantification. Weiss, Bernhard.
Paternalism and the Argument from Illiteracy. Luna, Florencia.
Power, Modernity and Morality in the Long Nineteenth Century. Goldblatt, David.
Scepticism About Legal Reasoning. Martin, Michael.

CLASSICAL ART

Hegel on Classical Art: a Reexamination. Winfield, Richard Dien.

CLASSICAL PHYSICS

"Quantum Cosmology and the Emergence of a Classical World" in Philosophy, Mathematics and Modern Physics, Rudolph, Enno (ed). Kiefer, Claus.
The Shaggy Steed of Physics: Mathematical Beauty in the Physical World. Oliver, David.
De la Excelencia y Fundamentos de la Filosofía Corpuscular o Mecánica. Boyle, Robert.
El buen relojero. Mataix, Carmen.
El Giro de la Nueva Ciencia: De Platón a Aristóteles. Mataix, Carmen.
Tautologías y circularidad en la Mecánica clásica. Mataix, Carmen.
Temporal Asymmetry in Classical Mechanics. Hutchison, Keith.

CLASSICISM

"Classicism v Connectionism" in Connectionism: Debates on Psychological Explanation, Macdonald, Cynthia (ed). Macdonald, Cynthia.

CLASSIFICATION

"Problems with the DSM Approach to Classifying Psychopathology" in Philosophical Psychopathology, Graham, George (ed). Poland, Jeffrey, Von Eckardt, Barbara and Spaulding, Will.
Characterizing Classifying: Explicating a Biological Distinction. Lambert, Karel and Simons, Peter.

CLAUDEL, P

Claudel philosophe. Tilliette, Xavier.

CLAUSE

From Syllogism to Predicate Calculus. McQuade, Thomas J.
The Function of LIKE in Dialogue. Miller, Jim and Weinert, Regina.
When Other Things Aren't Equal: Savings Ceteris Paribus Laws from Vacuity. Pietroski, Paul and Rey, Georges.

CLAUSEWITZ, C

Theoretical Limitlessness in War. Faitak, Joseph A.

CLIENT

National Survey of Social Workers' Sexual Attraction to Their Clients: Results, Implications, and Comparison to Psychologists. Bernsen, Ann, Tabachnick, Barbara G and Pope, Kenneth S.
Nonerotic Dual Relationships Between Therapists and Clients: The Effects of Sex, Theoretical Orientation, and Interpersonal Boundaries. Baer, Barbara E and Murdock, Nancy L.

COGNITION

Conoscenza e Normatività nella Filosofia Italiana Contemporanea. Carcaterra, Gaetano.

Content: Covariation, Control and Contingency. Maloney, J Christopher.

Dharmottara's Theory of Knowledge in His *Laghupramanyapariksa*. Krasser, Helmut.

Dispositional Beliefs and Dispositions to Believe. Audi, Robert.

El Mundo y el Arbol, Tareas de la Mirada. Ruiz Moreno, Luisa.

Emotion and Memory: The Second Cognitive Revolution. Harré, Rom.

Emotion as a Natural Kind: Towards a Computational Foundation for Emotion Theory. Charland, Louis C.

Epistemic Justification and the Possibility of Empirical Evidence. Karu, George.

Fichtes Lehre vom nicht bewussten Vernunfthandeln. Soller, Alois K.

History and Philosophy of Science Rapprochement: Shared Methodological Framework. Yaneva, Dominika A.

Il Problema della Natura Umana nella Filosofia Spagnola. Ballestros, Jesus.

Intuitionism and the Poverty of the Inference Argument. George, Alexander.

Is Cognitive Neuropsychology Possible?. Bub, Jeffrey.

James H Fetzer, *Philosophy and Cognitive Science*; Jay L Garfield (ed), *Foundations of Cognitive Science: The Essential Readings*. Causey, Robert L.

La Distinción *Narrow Content-Wide Content*. Vergara, Julia.

Langer on the Arts as Cognitive. Reimer, Bennett.

Los dos tipos de asentimiento del escéptico y el problema de la posibilidad del conocimiento. Frede, Michael.

Mind, Society, the Growth of Knowledge. Thagard, Paul.

Minimal Strong Functionalism. Ross, Don.

Non-Cartesian Explanations Meet the Problem of Mental Causation. Montgomery, Richard.

On the Methods of Cognitive Neuropsychology. Glymour, Clark.

On the Normative Aspect of Concepts as Rules: An Essay on Kant's Transcendental Deduction. Cicovacki, Predrag.

On the Quantum Mechanical Wave Function as a Link Between Cognition and the Physical World: A Role for Psychology. Snyder, Douglas M.

Quest Schemes in Analytical Models of Discourse. Ishmuratov, Anatoliy.

Razón e Intelecto en Boecio. Lluch-Baixauli, Miguel.

Reading as Understanding. Fitzpatrick, Joseph.

Representation and the Imperfect Ideal. Wallis, Charles.

Similarity: A Cognitive Foundation for Aritificial Intelligence. Downes, Stephen.

Simplicity, Cognition and Adaptation: Some Remarks on Marr's Theory of Vision. Gilman, Daniel.

Some Preliminary Remarks on "Cognitive Interest" in Husserlian Phenomenology. McCarthy, J C.

Studying Organisms with Basic Cognitive Capacities in Artificial Worlds. Exteberria, A, Merelo, J J and Moreno, A.

Testing Models of Cognition Through the Analysis of Brain-Damaged Performance. Bub, Jeffrey.

The "Explicit-Implicit" Distinction. Hadley, Robert F.

The Case Against Connectionism: Productivity and Systematicity. Marinov, Marin.

The Cognitive Culture System. Talmy, Leonard.

The Cognitive-Emotive Theory of Desire. Shibles, Warren A.

The Depersonalization of Creativity. Muscari, Paul G.

The Epistemological Incenization and the Problem of Time in the Conception of Recentivism. Banka, Jozef.

The Nonrationality and Noncognivity of the Belief in God's Existence. Herbert, Robert T.

The Secret Operations of the Mind. Traiger, Saul.

The Significance for Cognitive Realism of the Thought of John Poinsot. Rasmussen, Douglas B.

The Significance of Emotions. Helm, Bennett W.

The Virtues, Challenges and Implications of Connectionism. Stich, Stephen.

Thick or Thin? The Cognitive Content of Moral Education in a Plural Democracy. Haydon, Graham.

To What Extent Do Beliefs Affect Apparent Motion?. Wright, Richard D and Dawson, Michael R W.

Tre teorie sulle emozione: cognitiva, fenomenologica e comportamentistica (seconda parte). Malo, Antonio.

Truthlikeness Misapplied: A Reply to Ernest W Adams. Niiniluoto, Ilkka.

Turing, Wittgenstein and the Science of the Mind. Proudfoot, Diane and Copeland, B Jack.

Two Empirical Approaches to the Study of Reasoning. Finocchiaro, Maurice A.

Two Types of Theories: The Impact on Churchland's "Perceptual Plasticity". DesAutels, Peggy.

Vlastos on a Metaphysical Paradox. Code, Alan D.

What is a Category?. Hanzel, I, Cernik, V and Vicenik, J.

What Might Cognition Be, If Not Computation?. van Gelder, Tim.

Why Everything Doesn't Realize Every Computation. Chrisley, Ronald L.

Zu Husserls Wahrnehmungsbegriff. Orth, E W.

COGNITIVE

"Consciousness, Explanatory Inversion, & Cognitive Science" in *Philosophy of Psychology: Debates on Psychological Explanation, Macdonald, Cynthia (ed)*. Searle, John R.

"Reply: Consciousness and the Varieties of Aboutness" in *Philosophy of Psychology: Debates on Psychological Explanation, Macdonald, Cynthia (ed)*. Davies, Martin.

An Epistemological Foundation for Thinking: A Deweyian Approach. Holder Jr, John J.

Análisis gnoseológico de la psicología cognitiva. Blanco Martín, Carlos J.

Assessing the Application of Cognitive Moral Development Theory to Business Ethics. Fraedrich, John, Thorne, Debbie M and Ferrell, O C.

Cognitive Value and the Advancement of Science. Levi, Isaac.

Discovering Natural Kinds Through Inter-Theoretic Prototypes. Rothbart, Daniel.

Doing without Representing?. Clark, Andy and Toribio, Josefa.

Stich and the *De Dicto-De Re* Ambiguity. Kvart, Igal.

COGNITIVE DEVELOPMENT

Stages and Transitions in Cognitive Development. Johnson, M L.

COGNITIVE PSYCHOLOGY

"Connectionism and Cognitive Architecture: A Critical Analysis" in *Connectionism: Debates on Psychological Explanation, Macdonald, Cynthia (ed)*. Fodor, Jerry A and Pylyshyn, Zenon W.

"Constituent Structure and Explanation in..Cognitive Architecture" in *Connectionism: Debates on Psychological Explanation, Macdonald, Cynthia (ed)*. Smolensky, Paul.

Connectionism: Debates on Psychological Explanation. Macdonald, Cynthia (ed) and Macdonald, Graham (ed).

Cognitive Psychology: A Phenomenological Critique. Wertz, Frederick J.

Dato e interpretación: el problema de la base empírica del psicoanálisis. Guillermo Pissinis, C.

Lectura Epistemológica de la Teoría Unificada de la Cognición en Allen Newell. Monserrat, Javier.

Vigotsky and Artificial Intelligence: What Could Cognitive Psychology Possibly Be About?. Harré, Rom.

COGNITIVE SCIENCE

"Révolutions scientifiques et paradigmes: le cas des sciences cognitives" in *Rhétoriques de la science, De Coorebyter, Vincent (ed)*. Oléron, Pierre.

La Renovación Pragmatista de la Filosofía Analítica: Una Introducción a la Filosofía Contemporánea del Lenguaje. Nubiola, Jaime.

A Nonclassical Framework for Cognitive Science. Horgan, Terence and Tienson, John.

Cognitive Science and Hermeneutic Explanation: Symbiotic or Incompatible Frameworks?. Drury, John.

Compositionality in Cognitive Models: The Real Issue. Butler, Keith.

Explanation and Evaluation in Cognitive Science. Montgomery, Richard.

Folk Psychology and Cognitive Architecture. Egan, Frances.

Ingeniería del Conocimiento y Conocimiento Ordinario. Velarde Lombraña, Julián.

Inteligência Artificial e Caça aos Andróides. de Fernandes T, Joao.

Joyeuse Méditation Épistémologique sur la Modélisation Symbolisante de l'Intelligence. Le Moigne, Jean-Louis.

Kant's "Historicist" Alternative to Cognitive Science. McDonough, Richard.

L'Ancrage des Symboles dans le Monde *Analogique* à l'Aide de Réseaux Neuronaux: Un Modèle Hybride. Harnad, Steven.

L'Intelligence Artificielle: Au Confluent des Neurosciences et de l'Informatique. Jorion, Paul.

La Communication entre Sperber et Bateson: de l'Environnement Cognitif à l'Écologie de l'Esprit. Anspach, Mark R.

Le Problème de l'Architecture et le Débat entre l'Approche Connexionniste et les Approches "Classiques" de la Représentation. Lacharité, Normand.

Le Traitement Symbolique et non Symbolique dans les Réseaux Neuronaux: Un Problème de Catégorisation. Proulx, Robert.

Lectura Epistemológica de la Teoría Unificada de la Cognición en Allen Newell. Monserrat, Javier.

Natural Deduction in Connectionist Systems. Bechtel, William.

Réflexion Épistémologique sur l'Intelligence Artificielle et les Sciences Cognitives: à Quelles Conditions une Machine Pourrait-elle Connaître?. Robert, Serge.

Richesse, Tensions et Diversité des Sciences de la Cognition. Rialle, Vincent and Payette, Daniel.

Sémantique Interprétative et Compréhension du Langage. Rastier, François.

Soft Laws. Horgan, Terence and Tienson, John.

Suivre une règle: Wittgenstein et les sciences cognitives. Pinkas, Daniel.

Un Dérangement Modulaire de la Compétence Linguistique. Pietroski, Paul.

COGNITIVISM

see also Noncognitivism

"Algunos Aportes Sobre la Discusión entre Cognitivismo...y el Constuctivismo (Piaget) Acerca de la Adquis. de Concepto de Unsistema Repres." in *Temas Actuales de Filosofia, Palacios, María Julia (ed)*. Fernandez Acevedo, Yolanda.

Practical Realism and Moral Psychology. Jacobs, Jonathan.

Buddhism and Cognitivism: A Postmodern Appraisal. Pickering, John.

Language and Determinism: A Contribution to the Cognitivist Critique of Chomsky's Innateness Hypothesis. Jutronic-Tihomirovic, Dunja.

Noncognitivist Moral Realism. Waller, Bruce N.

Professional Codes of Practice and Ethical Conduct. Dawson, Angus James.

COHEN, G

Interpersonal Comparisons of Freedom. Carter, Ian.

COHEN, H

Die Botschaft des Judentums: Werke 3. Goldschmidt, Hermann Levin.

Philosophie als Dialogik: Frühe Schriften Werke 1. Goldschmidt, Hermann Levin.

Hermann Cohen's Concept of Judaic Universalism. Rosen, Henryk Zvi.

On the Anniversary of the First World War. Horák, Petr.

COHEN, J

"Some Philosophical Assessments of Environmental Disobedience" in *Philosophy and the Natural Environment, Attfield, Robin (ed)*. List, Peter C.

COHEN, M

Cohen on Einstein on Simultaneity. Walton, Gertrud.

COHERENCE

Evidence and Inquiry: Towards Reconstruction in Epistemology. Haack, Susan.

CONSCIOUSNESS

Embodiment and Responsibility: Merleau-Ponty and the Ontology of Nature. Russon, John.

Fichtes Lehre vom nicht bewussten Vernunfthandeln. Soller, Alois K.

General Method. McShane, Philip.

Grammacentrism and the Transformation of Rhetoric. Khushf, George.

Hegel and Fichte: Recognition, Otherness, and Absolute Knowing. Houlgate, Stephen.

How Can What I Perceive Be True?. Wahl, Russell.

How Innovative is the *Alayavijnana*?, Part II. Waldron, William S.

Husserl on the Ego and Its Eidos (*Cartesian Meditations*, IV). Ferrarin, Alfredo.

Husserl's Conception of Hume's Problem: Toward a Transcendental Hermeneutic of Hume's *Treatise*. Tagore, Saranindra N.

Identity, Self-Reflection and the Problem of Validating Standards. Raffel, Stanley.

Inside Time-Consciousness: Diagramming the Flux. Larrabee, M J.

Is There a Break in Sartre's Thought?. Singh, Ravindra M.

John Searle and Human Consciousness. Beards, Andrew.

Knowledge of One-Self and Other-Self. Alexander, Charles P.

La Dualidad Personal: Autor y Actor. Choza, Jacinto.

La fin de l'histoire serait-elle le commencement de la sagesse? L'aliénation de l'esprit dans la *Phénoménologie* de Hegel. Joós, Ernest.

La mirada errante: de la "Spaltung" en Lacan, al "caos-cosmos" de Deleuze. Gonzalo I Carbó, Antoni.

La paradoja de la narración: de los actos de habla a los actos de conciencia. Cofré, Juan O.

Liberating Dialogue: An Indian Perspective. Wilfred, Felix.

Locke on Personal Identity. Cicovacki, Predrag.

Machines and the Mental. Dretske, Frederick.

Materialism, Reduction, Replacement, and the Place of Consciousness in Science. Foss, Jeffrey E.

Merleau-Ponty's Metaphorical Philosophy. Review of *Merleau-Ponty and Metaphor* by Jerry H Gill. Compton, John J.

Mirror of Consciousness. Gupta, R K.

Monistic Idealism May Provide Better Ontology for Cognitive Science: A Reply to Dyer. Goswami, Amit.

On *Hume's Theory of Consciousness*. Wilson, Fred.

On the Distinction Between the Object and Content of Consciousness. Natsoulas, Thomas.

On the Language of Consciousness: Propositional Discourse and Moral Sensibility. Ray, G Thomas.

Quantum Physics and Consciousness, Creativity, Computers: A Commentary on Goswami's Quantum-Based Theory of Consciousness and Free Will. Dyer, Michael G.

Radical Empiricism and the New Science of Consciousness. Taylor, Eugene.

Reply to Carol Rovane's "Comment on McGinn's 'The Problem of Philosophy'". McGinn, Colin.

Requiem for the Identity Theory. Smythies, John R.

Searle on Rediscovering the Mind. Burton, Robert G.

Selbstbewusstsein: Ein Problem der Philosophie nach Kant. *Zum Verhältnis Reinhold-Hölderlin-Fichte.* Stolzenberg, Jürgen.

Some Comments on Professor R Sundararajan's Book Entitled *Towards a Critique of Cultural Reason*. Krishna, Daya.

Subjetividad y Privacidad. Hurtado, Guillermo.

Survival or Super-Psi?. Braude, Stephen E.

Synopsis of a Theory of Modernity. Ibañez-Noé, Javier A.

The Churchlands' Eliminative Materialism. Hunter, Geoffrey.

The Concept of Consciousness$_4$: The Reflective Meaning. Natsoulas, Thomas.

The Concept of Consciousness$_5$: The Unitive Meaning. Natsoulas, Thomas.

The Control of Actions by Agents. Vollmer, Fred.

The Ideological Involvement of Philosophy. Niznik, Jozef.

The Metaphoric Origins of Objectivity, Subjectivity, and Consciousness in the Direct Perception of Reality. Mulaik, Stanley A.

The Whole Body, not Heart, as 'Seat of Consciousness': The Buddha's View. Sugunasiri, Suwanda H J.

The World and 'I'. Phillips, D Z.

Thought and Qualia. Cole, David.

Universality in Chinese Culture. Dow, Tsung-I.

Van Inwagen's *Material Beings*. Persson, Ingmar.

Wat is metafysica?. Heyde, L.

What *Is* The Connection Principle?. Fodor, Jerry A and Lepore, Ernie.

What Is 'Consciousness'?. Carley, Adam L.

Why the Connection Argument Doesn't Work. Van Gulick, Robert.

CONSENSUS

Razón y poder: La radicalización simbólica de la razón liberal. Domingo Moratalla, Agustín.

Thresholds for Rights. Brennan, Samantha.

Validité et limites du consensus en éthique clinique. Malherbe, Jean-François, Rocchetti, Loretta and Boire-Lavigne, Anne-Marie.

CONSENT

Democracy and Social Injustice: Law, Politics, and Philosophy. Simon, Thomas W.

Reshaping the Female Body: The Dilemma of Cosmetic Surgery. Davis, Kathy.

Children's Capacity to Agree to Psychological Research: Knowledge of Risks and Benefits and Voluntariness. Abramovitch, Rona (& others).

Conceptual and Moral Disputes about Futile and Useful Treatments. Kopelman, Loretta M.

Der "consensus gentium"—fundamentaltheologische Erwägungen zu einem vernachlässigten Gottesbeweis. Rosenau, Hartmut.

Does Legally Mandated Consent to Psychotherapy Ensure Ethical Appropriateness?: The Colorado Experience. Handelsman, Mitchell M (& others).

Exploited Consent. Archard, David.

Issues of Consent: The Use of the Recently Deceased for Endotracheal Intubation Training. Hayes, Gregory J.

Patients' Perceptions of Consent. Shenk, Ian.

Reports of Assent and Permission in Research With Children: Illustrations and Suggestions. Range, Lillian M and Cotton, C Randy.

Sexual Harassment in the Law: The Demarcation Problem. Hajdin, Mane.

Should Hospital Policy Require Consent for Practicing Invasive Procedures on Cadavers?. Perkins, Henry S and Gordon, Anna M.

CONSEQUENCE

A Generalisation of the Tarski-Herbrand Deduction Theorem. Surma, S J.

Confianza y Racionalidad. Aguiar, Fernando.

El "Tractatus Consequentiarum" (1518) en la Lógica de Juan de Oria. Muñoz Delgado, Vicente.

Etchemendy and Logical Consequence. Priest, Graham.

The Logical Form of Determiners. Ludlow, Peter.

CONSEQUENT

A Case of Affirming the Consequent in International Law: UN Security Council Resolution 232 (1966)—Southern Rhodesia. Hund, John.

CONSEQUENTIALISM

Kant on Happiness in Ethics. Wike, Victoria S.

Adjusting Utility for Justice: A Consequentialist Reply to the Objection from Justice. Feldman, Fred.

Consecuencialismo e imparcialidad. Salcedo, Damián.

Consecuencialismo Restrictivo. Pettit, Philip and Brennan, Geoffrey.

Consecuencialismo: debate ético y jurídico. Nino, Carlos Santiago.

Consequentialis, Moral Responsibility, and the Intention/ Foresight Distinction. Oakley, Justin.

Consequentialism and Absolutism. Elliot, Robert.

Contra la sistetización en ética. Griffin, James.

Economic Consequentialism and Beyond. Friedman, Jeffrey.

Entre el Kantismo y el Consecuencialismo en la Filosofía Moral de T H Green. Weinstein, David.

Entrevista con Amartya Sen. Sen, Amartya.

Epistemic Value: Truth or Explanation?. Resnik, David B.

Group Action and Act Consequentialism. Fumerton, Richard.

Immoralist: That Means the Opposite of Consequentialist: Comment on Professor Hale's "Was Nietzsche a Consequentialist?". Crawford, Claudia.

Is Marx a Moral Consequentialist?. Vogel, Jeffrey S.

Is Rule-Consequentialism a Rubber Duck?. Hooker, Brad.

La justificación consecuencialista de las lealtades. Lara Sánchez, Francisco Damián.

Methods of Ethics: Wide Reflective Equilibrium and a Kind of Consequentialism. Nielsen, Kai.

Minimal Consequentialism. Caws, Peter.

Morality in the First Person Plural. Postema, Gerald J.

Observaciones y respuesta. Lara, Francisco, Salcedo, Damián and Gutiérrez, Gilberto.

Parfit und die Theorie C. Nimtz, Christian H.

Rational Choice: Extensions and Revisions. Nida-Rümelin, Julian.

Rule-Consequentialism, Incoherence, Fairness. Hooker, Brad.

The Heart of Consequentialism. Howard-Snyder, Frances.

Una aproximación al concepto de derecho a la intimidad en John Stuart Mill. García Añón, José.

Was Nietzsche a Consequentialist?. Hales, Steven D.

What is Consequentialism? A Proposal for a Systematic Classification (in Italian). Corradini, Antonella.

CONSERVATION

"Ecology and the Ethics of Environmental Restoration" in *Philosophy and the Natural Environment, Attfield, Robin (ed)*. Elliot, Robert.

"Solidity and Elasticity in the Seventeenth Century" in *Locke's Philosophy, Rogers, G A J (ed)*. Alexander, Peter.

"Special Overview: Role of Ethics, Culture, Religion in Conserving Biodiversity" in *Ethics, Religion and Biodiversity, Hamilton, Lawrence S (ed)*. Engel, J Ronald.

"The Potential Contribution of Buddhism in Developing an Environmental Ethic..." in *Ethics, Religion and Biodiversity, Hamilton, Lawrence S (ed)*. Sponsel, Leslie E and Natadecha-Sponsel, Poranee.

Earth Ethics: Environmental Ethics, Animal Rights, and Practical Applications. Sterba, James P (ed).

Environmental Ethics (Oxford Readings in Philosophy). Elliot, Robert (ed).

Comentarios Sobre la Teoría de las Cantidades Conservadas. Rodriguez, Victor.

Green Anarchism: Peter Marshall's *Nature's Web*. Welsh, Ian.

More Thoughts on Nature Conservation and the Voluntary Principle. Ratcliffe, Derek.

CONSERVATISM

"Liberal Neutrality and the Justification of Environmental Conservation" in *Ecology, Technology, and Culture, Zweers, Wim (ed)*. Musschenga, Bert.

"Some Moral Contradictions in the Conservative Educational Reform Discourse in the US" in *Identity, Culture, and Education, Smeyers, Paul (ed)*. Ray, G Thomas.

"*Konservative Revolution und Philosophie in Österreich*" in *Der geistige Anschluss, Fischer, Kurt R (ed)*. Dethloff, Klaus and Wimmer, Franz M (ed).

Der Katechon: Zu Carl Schmitts fundamentalistischer Kritik der Zeit. Meuter, Günter.

COSMOLOGICAL PROOF

"Leibniz's Ontological and Cosmological Arguments" in *The Cambridge Companion to Leibniz, Jolley, Nicholas (ed)*. Blumenfeld, David C.

The Cosmological and Ontological Arguments: How Saint Thomas Solved the Kantian Problem. Forgie, J William.

COSMOLOGY

"Quantum Cosmology and the Emergence of a Classical World" in *Philosophy, Mathematics and Modern Physics, Rudolph, Enno (ed)*. Kiefer, Claus.

"Science" in *The Cambridge Companion to Aristotle, Barnes, Jonathan (ed)*. Hankinson, R J.

"What Kind of Science is Cosmology?" in *Philosophy, Mathematics and Modern Physics, Rudolph, Enno (ed)*. Goenner, Hubert F M.

From Myth to Modern Mind: A Study of the Origins and Growth of Scientific Thought, Volume I. Schlagel, Richard H.

Inleiding Comparatieve Filosofie. Libbrecht, Ulrich.

On Naming the Present: God, Hermeneutics, and Church. Tracy, David.

The Cambridge Companion to Leibniz. Jolley, Nicholas (ed).

The Cosmology of Freedom (New Edition). Neville, Robert Cummings.

The Shape of Space (Second Edition). Nerlich, Graham.

The Undivided Universe: An Ontological Interpretation of Quantum Theory. Hiley, B J and Bohm, David.

Timaeus and Modern Cosmology. Petkovic, Tomislav.

A Critique of Quentin Smith's Atheistic Argument from Big Bang Cosmology. Lorca, Daniel.

Anthropic Explanations in Cosmology. Smith, Quentin.

Brain Water, the Ether, and the Art of Constructing Systems. Rueger, Alexander.

Contributions of Tipler's Omega Point Theory. Birtel, Frank T.

Cosmology from Alpha to Omega. Russell, Robert John.

Cosmology: A Philosophical Survey. Leslie, John.

Cosmology: An Empirical Science?. Anderson, John.

Creation Without a Creator: Reflections on Contemporary Scientific Cosmologies. Kozhamthadam, Job.

Hartshorne's Process Theism and Big Bang Cosmology. Haugen, David and Keeling, L Bryant.

Kant and the Eternity of the World: A Historico-critical Reading of the First Antinomy. van Veldhuijsen, Peter.

L'Istanza Cosmologica tra Scienzatecnica e Filosofia. Mazzarella, Eugenio.

La cosmologie contemporaine doit-elle intéresser les philosophes?. Merleau-Ponty, Jacques.

Locke and Gilles de Launay. Milton, J R.

Nemesis and Theory Evaluation. Boersema, David B.

Nietzschean Recurrence: The Science and the Moment. Goldberg, David W.

Objective Chance: Lonergan and Peirce on Scientific Generalization. Potter, Vincent G.

On Certain Consequence of the Temporal and Spatial Scale of the Universe: Comments on "How the Physical Sciences Discovered the Unity of Nature". Butryn, Stanislaw.

Platonismo, Rivoluzione Scientifica, Culti Solari: Un Tema da Riesaminare. Albanese, Luciano.

Quantum Fluctuation, Self-Organizing Biological Systems, and Human Freedom. Trundle, Robert C.

Should We Believe in the Big Bang?: A Critique of the Integrity of Modern Cosmology. Rhook, Graeme and Zangari, Mark.

Stephen Hawking's Cosmology and Theism. Smith, Quentin.

Teilhard's Vision of the World and Modern Cosmology. Heller, Michael.

Teoría metafísica de las propensiones y universo abierto en la filosofía de Popper. Queraltó Moreno, Ramón.

The Bohmian Model of Quantum Cosmology. Callender, Craig and Weingard, Robert.

The Idea of Eternal Life in Modern Cosmology: Its Ultimate Reality and Metaethical Meaning. Nesteruk, Alexei V.

The Problematic Status of Cosmology. De Gandt, François, Blau, Peter (trans) and Bergo, Bettina (trans).

Toward a Process-Relational Christian Eschatology. Wheeler, David L.

Uniformitarianism in Cosmology: Background and Philosophical Implications of the Steady-State Theory. Balashov, Yuri.

COSMOPOLITANISM

Métaphysique et Éthique au Fondement du Droit. Trigeaud, Jean-Marc.

Emancipation, Resistance and Cosmopolitanism. Del Aguila, Rafael.

Ist Fichtes Modell des Kosmopolitismus pluralistisch?. Radrizzani, Ives.

Nation, Weltbürgertum, und Synthesis der Geisterwelt. Schrader, Wolfgang H.

COSMOS

"The End of Anthropocentrism?" in *Philosophy and the Natural Environment, Attfield, Robin (ed)*. Midgley, Mary.

"Why the Elements Imitate the Heavens: *Metaphysics* IX.8 1050b28-34" in *The Crossroads of Norm and Nature, Sim, May (ed)*. Lang, Helen S.

Chaosmosis: An Ethico-Aesthetic Paradigm. Guattari, Félix, Bains, Paul (trans) and Pefanis, Julian (trans).

Inventing the Universe: Plato's Timaeus, The Big Bang, and the Problem of Scientific Knowledge. Brisson, Luc and Meyerstein, F Walter.

Plato's World: Man's Place in the Cosmos. Cropsey, Joseph.

The Sciences in Greco-Roman Society (Apeiron 27-4). Barnes, Timothy D.

Ahistorical Intentional Content. Kurthen, Martin.

Cosmic and Human Drama in Plato's *Statesman*: On Cosmos, God and Microcosm in the Myth. Carone, Gabriela Roxana.

Hartshorne's Response to Haugen and Keeling: "Hartshorne's Process Theism and Big Bang Cosmology". Hartshorne, Charles.

COST

Attitudes of Seriously Ill Patients toward Treatment that Involves High Costs and Burdens on Others. Schneiderman, Lawrence J (& others).

Citizens, Consumers and the Environment: Reflections on *The Economy of the Earth*. Keat, Russell.

Clear, Convincing, and Authentic Advance Directives in the Context of Managed Care?. Bursztajn, Harold J and Brodsky, Archie.

The Euthanasia Debate and Empirical Evidence: Separating Burdens to Others from One's Own Quality of Life. Ubel, Peter A and Arnold, Robert M.

The Practical and Ethical Costs of Corporate Reengineering. French, Peter A.

To Save the Logic, the Facts Must Fit. Pellegrino, Edmund D.

COST-BENEFIT ANALYSIS

The Moral Justification of Benefit/ Cost Analysis. Hubin, Donald C.

COSTARICAN

"Contributions to the Philosophy of Technology in Costa Rica" in *Philosophy of Technology in Spanish Speaking Countries, Mitcham, Carl (ed)*. Camacho Naranjo, Luis A.

COTTA, S

On the Existential Meaning of Violence. Santoni, Ronald E.

COTTINGHAM, J

Descartes in der angelsächsischen Diskussion. Perler, Dominik.

COUMAS, C

Agathon dans la Pensée de C M Coumas. Argyropoulos, R.

COUNSELING

Ethical and Legal Issues in Group Counseling. Corey, Gerald (& others).

Report on Applying Philosophy in Philosophical Counseling. Schuster, Shlomit C.

The Practice of Sartre's Philosophy in Philosophical Counseling and Existential Psychotherapy. Schuster, Shlomit C.

COUNTABLE

Diophantine Equivalence and Countable Rings. Shlapentokh, Alexandra.

On Countable Fractions from an Elementary Class. Ash, C J.

COUNTERFACTUAL

A Counterfactual Theory of Causal Explanation. Ruben, David-Hillel.

Are Physical Properties Dispositions?. Reeder, Nick.

Bell's Theorem in an Indeterministic Universe. Bedford, Donald and Stapp, Henry P.

Can Counterfactuals Save Mental Causation?. Kazez, Jean.

Causal Efficacy, Content and Levels of Explanation. Toribio, Josefa.

Classifying Conditionals: The Traditional Way is Right. Bennett, Jonathan.

Comment on 'Stapp's Theorem Without Counterfactual Commitment'. Stapp, Henry P.

Contrafácticos. Tomasini Bassols, Alejandro.

Counterfactuals: Ambiguities, True Premises, and Knowledge. Kvart, Igal.

Dispositions and Scientific Explanation. Lange, Marc.

Lewis on Causal Dependence. McDermott, Michael.

Lewis on 'Might' and 'Would' Counterfactual Conditionals. De Rose, Keith.

Might-counterfactuals and Gratuitous Differences. Heller, Mark.

Nonreductive Materialism and Mental Causation. Marras, Ausonio.

Pretend Play: Is It Metarepresentational?. Jarrold, Chris (& others).

The Attack on Methodological Solipsism. Duran, Jane.

The Miracle of Counterfactuals: Counterexamples to Lewis's World Ordering. Krasner, Daniel and Heller, Mark.

The Truth about Counterfactuals. Lowe, E J.

COURAGE

Locality and Practical Judgment: Charity and Sacrifice. Ross, Stephen David.

Categories of the Ethics of Sport. Krawczyk, Zbigniew.

COURT

see also Supreme Court

Constitution and Continuity, Part II: The Hungarian Case. Arato, Andrew.

Innocence. Richards, Norvin W.

The Role of Courts in the Debate on Assisted Suicide: A Communitarian Approach. Beschle, Donald L.

Una defensa del consecuencialismo en el Derecho. Bengoetxea, Joxerramon.

COUSIN, V

Reid and His French Disciples: Aesthetics and Metaphysics. Manns, James W.

COVARIATION

Representation and the Imperfect Ideal. Wallis, Charles.

COVERING

Covering Analytic Sets by Families of Closed Sets. Solecki, Slawomir.

COWEN, T

Law as a Private Good: A Response to Tyler Cowen on the Economics of Anarchy. Friedman, David D.

COX, C

Naturalizing the Epistemologist: The Final Shadow of the Dead God. Conway, Daniel W.

CRAIG, W

A Defense of a Principle of Sufficient Reason. Smith, Quentin.

Reply to Craig: Inverse Operations with Transfinite Numbers and the *Kalam* Cosmological Argument. Oppy, Graham.

CRANDALL, R

On Costs, Benefits, and Regulatory Success: Reply to Crandall. Sunstein, Cass R.

CREATION

"Creation and Relation" in *Medicine and Moral Reasoning, Fulford, K W M (ed)*. Soskice, Janet Martin.

CREATION

"Franz Rosenzweig's Doctrine of Creation" in *Thinkers and Teachers of Modern Judaism, Goldsmith, Emanuel S (ed)*. Samuelson, Norbert M.

"Galaxy Creation in a Non-Big-Bang Universe" in *Philosophy, Mathematics and Modern Physics, Rudolph, Enno (ed)*. Arp, Halton.

Arte y Ciencia: Una Visión Especular. Leyra, Ana María and Mataix, Carmen.

Augustine. Clark, Mary T.

Being and the Between. Desmond, William.

Essentials of Shinto: An Analytical Guide to Principal Teachings. Picken, Stuart D B.

Agostino Steuco y la *Perennis Philosophia*. Granada, Miquel A.

Anthropic Explanations in Cosmology. Smith, Quentin.

Comparative Law as Shock Treatment. Glendon, Mary Ann.

Cosmology: An Empirical Science?. Anderson, John.

Creación y origen del tiempo. Borrego, Enrique.

Creation Without a Creator: Reflections on Contemporary Scientific Cosmologies. Kozhamthadam, Job.

Dios en la filosofía de Malebranche. Fernández, José Luis.

Dos Concepciones del Lenguaje. Tomasini Bassols, Alejandro.

God Had to Create the World. Pearl, Leon.

How an Unsurpassable Being Can Create a Surpassable World. Howard-Snyder, Daniel and Howard-Snyder, Frances.

Kann die Theologie der naturwissenschaftlichen Vernunft die Welt Is Schöpfung verständlich machen?. Fischer, Johannes.

La Razón y la fe Ante la Creación Temporal del Mundo. Azcoaga Bengoechea, Ignatio M.

Mystery and Explanation in Aquinas's Account of Creation. Liccione, Michael.

Nature as Creation. Tanzella-Nitti, Giuseppe.

Nietzschean Self-Creation and the Critique of Liberal Institutions. Detwiler, Bruce.

Nota sulla "creazione". Messinese, Leonardo.

Professor Grünbaum on Creation. Craig, W L.

Repliek op Kal. te Velde, R.

Science and Art: Heuristic and Aesthetic Dimensions of Scientific Discovery. Wartofsky, Marx.

Should We Believe in the Big Bang?: A Critique of the Integrity of Modern Cosmology. Rhook, Graeme and Zangari, Mark.

Sobre el origen del ser y la nada. Echauri, Raúl.

The Existential Problem of Evil: Reflections on the Analogy Between Creation and Procreation. Menssen, Sandra L.

The Future of Teilhardian Theology. Schmitz-Moormann, Karl.

The Problem of Evil and a Plausible Defence. Murphy, Frank J.

Thomas Aquinas, Creation, and Two Historians. Dewan, Lawrence.

Uniformitarianism in Cosmology: Background and Philosophical Implications of the Steady-State Theory. Balashov, Yuri.

Universales Poéticos, Fantasía y Racionalidad. Sevilla, José M.

Van Participatie tot Zelflimitatie; Over Thomas' Filosofie van de Schepping. Kal, Victor.

CREATIONISM

The Methodological Isolation of Religious Belief. Schoen, Edward L.

CREATIVE

"An Investment Perspective on Creative Insight" in *The Nature of Insight, Sternberg, Robert J (ed)*. Sternberg, Robert J.

"Creative Insight and Preinventive Forms" in *The Nature of Insight, Sternberg, Robert J (ed)*. Finke, Ronald A.

"Creative Insight: The Social Dimension of a Solitary Moment" in *The Nature of Insight, Sternberg, Robert J (ed)*. Csikszentmihalyi, Mihaly and Sawyer, Keith.

Person to Person Inspiration. Kidd, James W and Kidd, Sunnie D.

CREATIVITY

"Too Thin a Self, Too Small a Human" in *Contributors to the Philosophy of Humanism, Hillar, Marian (ed)*. Kegley, Jacquelyn A K.

Anthropologie der Künste. Frey, Gerhard.

Creativity and God: A Challenge to Process Theology. Neville, Robert Cummings.

Syncope: The Philosophy of Rapture. O'Driscoll, Sally (trans), Clément, Catherine and Mahoney, Deirdre M (trans).

The Divine Matrix: Creativity as Link between East and West. Bracken, Joseph A.

The Educational Imperative: A Defence of Socratic and Aesthetic Learning. Abbs, Peter.

A Pragmatist Theory of Artistic Creativity. Leddy, Thomas W.

Dio nella modernità: Husserl. Rigobello, Armando.

El jardín de la ciencia. Escudero, Miguel.

Función de la Creatividad en la Filosofía de A N Whitehead. Oroz Ezcurra, Javier.

La teoría del instante en Bachelard y el espacio onírico. Castillo, Roberto.

Las preguntas básicas sobre la filosofía-de-los sabios en Africa. Oruka, H Odera.

Merleau-Ponty's View of Creativity and Its Philosophical Consequences. Hamrick, William S.

Music, Platonism and Performance: Some Ontological Strains. Sharpe, R A.

Quantum Physics and Consciousness, Creativity, Computers: A Commentary on Goswami's Quantum-Based Theory of Consciousness and Free Will. Dyer, Michael G.

Quine's Truth. Bergström, Lars.

Rebelión y goce: aproximación a la estética de Camus. Sanabria, Carolina.

The Depersonalization of Creativity. Muscari, Paul G.

The Religious Creativity of Modern Humanity: Some Observations on Eliade's Unfinished Thought. Rennie, B S.

Trouble-Shooting Creativity: A Critical Appraisal of David Bohm and F David Peat's 'Science Orders and Creativity'. Fisch, Menachem.

Value Inquiry—Aesthetic Value. Hein, Hilde.

CRESCINI, A

Expérience et métaphysique. Gilbert, Paul.

CREUZER, F

Quests for a Scientific Mythology: F Creuzer and K O Müller on History and Myth. Blok, Josine H.

CRICK, F

Francis Crick on the Workings of the Brain. Flynn, Thomas W and Madigan, Timothy J.

CRIME

"Benign and Malign Morality" in *In Harm's Way, Coleman, Jules L (ed)*. Gross, Hyman.

"Crime and Responsibility" in *Introducing Applied Ethics, Almond, Brenda (ed)*. Tam, Henry.

"Ethical Questions Facing Law Enforcement Agents" in *Introducing Applied Ethics, Almond, Brenda (ed)*. Kleinig, John.

"Force, Consent, and the Reasonable Woman" in *In Harm's Way, Coleman, Jules L (ed)*. McGregor, Joan L.

"Liberalism, Retribution and Criminality" in *In Harm's Way, Coleman, Jules L (ed)*. Hampton, Jean.

"Some Ruminations on Women, Violence, and the Criminal Law" in *In Harm's Way, Coleman, Jules L (ed)*. Murphy, Jeffrie G.

Punishment and the Death Penalty: The Current Debate. Baird, Robert M (ed) and Rosenbaum, Stuart E (ed).

Capital Punishment: An Act of Murder, Revenge, or Justice. Waters, Raphael T.

Degrees of Freedom. Van Zyl Smit, Dirk.

Discussion: Just Another Simi Valley Jury: The Supreme Court and the Death Penalty. Thomson, Ernie and Osbrun, Jerry R.

Justice and the Distribution of Fear. Burgess-Jackson, Keith.

Kant on Capital Punishment. Lind, Douglas.

Locke on the Death Penalty. Simmons, A John.

More on Race and Crime: Levin's Reply. Adler, Jonathan E.

Reply to Adler's "More on Race and Crime: Levin's Reply". Levin, Michael E.

The "New Syndrome Excuse Syndrome". Morse, Stephen J.

The Appearance of Official Impropriety and the Concept of Political Crime. Stark, Andrew.

The Retributive Paradox. Golash, Deirdre.

Vigilantism and the Common Good. Green, Steven.

CRIMINAL JUSTICE

"The Marxian Critique of Criminal Justice" in *Radical Philosophy of Law, Caudill, David S (ed)*. Reiman, Joffroy.

Moral Authority in Law and Criminal Justice: Some Reflections on Wilson's *The Moral Sense*. Tyler, Tom R and Kerstetter, Wayne.

The Quiddity of Mercy. Walker, Nigel.

CRIMINAL LAWS

"Self-Defense" in *In Harm's Way, Coleman, Jules L (ed)*. Schopp, Robert F.

Conscience (Rule) Utilitarianism and the Criminal Law. Brandt, Richard B.

Review Essay: Perfectionist Moral Theory, the Criminal Law, and the Liberal State— *Making Men Moral* by Robert P George. Richards, David A J.

Rights and the Criminal Law. Ellis, Anthony.

The Retributive Paradox. Golash, Deirdre.

CRISIS

A Bowie: Estética y Subjetividad. García García, Javier.

De la crisis de la racionalidad a la racionalidad de la crisis: Una nota sobre G Vico. Sevilla, José M.

En Torno al *Postcursorismo* Viquiano de la Modernidad Problemática. Sevilla, José M.

CRITERIA

Criteria: The State of the Debate. Addis, Mark.

The Irrelevance of Distribution for the Syllogism. Murphree, Wallace A.

Towards an Adequate Definition of Distribution for First-Order Logic. Friedman, Joel I.

CRITICAL

Kant's Early Metaphysics and the Origins of the Critical Philosophy. Laywine, Alison.

Actitud crítica y racionalidad en Popper. Marquéz, Gustavo.

The Critical Number of a Variable in a Function. Takeuti, Gaisi.

CRITICAL PHILOSOPHY

The Dialectic of System and Critique in Recent Interpretations of Kant's Critical Philosophy. Mikkelsen, Jon Mark.

CRITICAL RATIONALISM

Positivismusstreit: Die Auseinandersetzungen der Frankfurter Schule mit dem logischen Positivismus, dem Pragmatismus und dem kritischen Rationalismus. Dahms, Hans-Joachim.

Wahrheitskriterien im Kritischen Rationalismus. Gesang, Bernward.

K Popper: Racionalismo Critico, Metafisica y Metodologia de lo Inverificable. Velasco N, Ignacio Ruiz.

CRITICAL THEORY

"Carta Imaginaria de un Postmoderno 'Avant la Lettre'" in *Temas Actuales de Filosofía, Palacios, María Julia (ed)*. Alvarez de Toledo, Blanca I.

"Critical Analysis and Constructive Interpretation" in *In Harm's Way, Coleman, Jules L (ed)*. Lyons, David.

"Critical Theory and Technoculture: Habermas and Baudrillard" in *Baudrillard: A Critical Reader, Kellner, Douglas M (ed)*. Poster, Mark.

"Critical Theory as a Research Program" in *The Cambridge Companion to Habermas, White, Stephen K (ed)*. Dryzek, John S.

CRUELTY

Animal Welfare and Human Values. Preece, Rod and Chamberlain, Lorna.

Dworkin, Vague Constitutional Clauses, and the Eighth Amendment's Admonition Against "Cruel and Unusual Punishment". Neeley, G Steven.

Feminism and Vegetarianism: A Critique of Peter Singer. McKenna, Erin.

Feminism and Vegetarianism: A Response. Singer, Peter.

Moral Realism and Wanton Cruelty. Carlson, George R.

CUBE

A Geometric Proof of the Completeness of the Lukasiewicz Calculus. Panti, Giovanni.

CULPABILITY

Compensation and Culpability. Zimmerman, Michael J.

Rights, Compensation, and Culpability. Zimmerman, Michael J.

CULT

Die kultische Gebärde: Kunst, Politik, Religion im Denken Franz Rosenzweigs. Hufnagel, Cordula.

Dionysius: Myth and Cult. Otto, Walter F and Palmer, Robert B (trans).

CULTURAL ANTHROPOLOGY

Dimensione Transculturale dei Fenomeni Giuridici nella Ricerca Antropologica. Scillitani, Lorenzo.

CULTURAL CRITICISM

"The Limits of Pure Critique" in *After Postmodernism*, Simons, Herbert W (ed). Gergen, Kenneth J.

Character and Culture: Essays on East and West. Babbitt, Irving.

Cultural Materialism, Cultural and Post-Culturalism: The Legacy of Raymond Williams. Milner, Andrew.

Domination and Enlightenment: The Limits of Manipulation. Cook, Deborah.

Late-Marxist, Post-Poststructuralist Critical Nebulosity. Harris, Wendell V.

CULTURAL DIVERSITY

"General Education, Cultural Diversity, and Identity" in *Identity, Culture, and Education*, Smeyers, Paul (ed). Meijer, Wilna.

CULTURAL PLURALISM

L'enseignement de la Philosophie Devant l'approche-Programme et l'éducation Interculturelle. Turgeon, Marc.

CULTURAL RELATIVISM

Das Problem des Multikulturalismus in der politischen Ethik. Gutmann, Amy.

CULTURAL STUDIES

"Evading the Subject: The Poverty of Contingency Theory" in *After Postmodernism*, Simons, Herbert W (ed). Cole, Steven E.

"Inscription and Horizon: A Postmodern Civilizing Effect?" in *After Postmodernism*, Simons, Herbert W (ed). Angus, Ian.

"Teaching the Pedagogies: A Dialectical Approach to an Ideological Dilemma" in *After Postmodernism*, Simons, Herbert W (ed). Simons, Herbert W.

"'Socialism of the Mind': The New Age of Post-Marxism" in *After Postmodernism*, Simons, Herbert W (ed). Cloud, Dana L.

After Postmodernism. Simons, Herbert W (ed) and Billig, Michael (ed).

CULTURE

see also Custom, Habit, Popular Culture

"A Rethink in Political Philosophy" in *Life, World and Meaning*, Roux, A P J (ed). Postma-de Beer, Zach.

"Aesthetic Production and Cultural Politics: Baudrillard and Contemporary Art" in *Baudrillard: A Critical Reader, Kellner, Douglas M (ed)*. Luke, Timothy W.

"Architecture, Expression, and the Understanding of a Culture" in *Philosophy and Architecture, Mitias, Michael H (ed)*. Tilghman, B R.

"Buber's Socialist and Political Views: A Critique" in *Thinkers and Teachers of Modern Judaism, Goldsmith, Emanuel S (ed)*. Uffenheimer, Benjamin.

"Communicative Rationality and Cultural Values" in *The Cambridge Companion to Habermas, White, Stephen K (ed)*. Warnke, Georgia.

"Creative Insight: The Social Dimension of a Solitary Moment" in *The Nature of Insight, Sternberg, Robert J (ed)*. Csikszentmihalyi, Mihaly and Sawyer, Keith.

"Cultural Relativism and Universal Human Rights?" in *Human Rights and Religious Values, An-Na'im, Abdullahi A (& other eds)*. Droogers, André F.

"Decolonizing Liberalism" in *The End of "Isms"?, Shtromas, Alexsandras (ed)*. Parekh, Bhikhu.

"Entstehen und Werden allgemeinenschlicher Kulturuniversalien" in *Das geistige Erbe Europas, Buhr, Manfred (ed)*. Oisermann, Teodor I.

"Fatal Forms: Toward a (Neo) Formal Sociological Theory of Media Culture" in *Baudrillard: A Critical Reader, Kellner, Douglas M (ed)*. Epstein, Jonathan S and Epstein, Margarete J.

"Hermeneutic Listening: An Approach to Understanding in Multicultural Conversations" in *Identity, Culture, and Education, Smeyers, Paul (ed)*. Kimball, Stephanie and Garrison, Jim.

"In Search of an Ecological Culture: Environmental Philosophy in the 1990's" in *Ecology, Technology, and Culture, Zweers, Wim (ed)*. Zweers, Wim.

"Integración Cultural y Económica de América Latina: El Caso Argentina—Brasil" in *Temas Actuales de Filosofía, Palacios, María Julia (ed)*. Pérez Zavala, Carlos.

"Life and Society at Ancient Memphis According to the Saqqâra Texts" in *Life, World and Meaning, Roux, A P J (ed)*. Dreyer, H J.

"North American Theories of Postmodern Culture" in *Postmodernism and Social Inquiry, Dickens, David R (ed)*. Dickens, David R.

"Postmodernism and Deconstructionism" in *Postmodernism and Social Inquiry, Dickens, David R (ed)*. Denzin, Norman K.

"Semiotics and Postmodernism" in *Postmodernism and Social Inquiry, Dickens, David R (ed)*. Gottdiener, M.

"Social and Cultural Rights in Buddhism" in *Human Rights and the World's Religions, Rouner, Leroy (ed)*. Thurman, Robert A F.

"Technology and Politics: Toward Artificial History?" in *Philosophy of Technology in Spanish Speaking Countries, Mitcham, Carl (ed)*. García de la Huerta, Marcos.

"The Cross-Cultural Comparison of Emotion" in *Emotions in Asian Thought, Marks, Joel (ed)*. Solomon, Robert C.

"The Cultural Boycott: An Act of Censorship or a Tool of Liberation?" in *Life, World and Meaning, Roux, A P J (ed)*. Skawran, Karin M.

"The Cultural Justification of Unearned Income" in *Profits and Morality, Cowan, Robin (ed)*. Cooter, Robert D and Gordley, James.

"The Particular and the Universal" in *African Philosophy: Selected Readings, Mosley, Albert G (ed)*. Hountondji, Paulin.

"The Postmodernism That Failed" in *Postmodernism and Social Inquiry, Dickens, David R (ed)*. Goldman, Robert and Papson, Steven.

"The Problem of Cultural Imputation in History: Cultures Versus History" in *Historiography Between Modernism and Postmodernism, Topolski, Jerzy (ed)*. Wrzosek, Wojciech.

"The Quest for Identity" in *Identity, Culture, and Education, Smeyers, Paul (ed)*. Tamir, Yael.

"The Study of Rhetoric as an Approach to Cultural History: The Case of Hobbes" in *Main Trends in Cultural History, Melching, Willem (ed)*. Skinner, Quentin.

"Topología—Atopología del Saber" in *Temas Actuales de Filosofía, Palacios, María Julia (ed)*. Craia, Eladio Pablo C (& others).

"Tradition, Recognition, and Truth: Cultural Identity in the Eyes of the University" in *Identity, Culture, and Education, Smeyers, Paul (ed)*. Crawley, Francis P.

"World, Leisure and a Meaningful Life" in *Life, World and Meaning, Roux, A P J (ed)*. Du Toit, Pieter.

A Philosophy of History in Fragments. Heller, Agnes.

A Theory of Textuality: The Logic and Epistemology. Gracia, Jorge J E.

Adorno: The Stars Down to Earth and Other Essays on the Irrational in Culture. Crook, Stephen (ed) and Adorno, Theodor W.

Baudrillard: A Critical Reader. Kellner, Douglas M (ed).

Beast and Man: The Roots of Human Nature. Midgley, Mary.

Character and Culture: Essays on East and West. Babbitt, Irving.

Design & Systems: General Applications of Methodology. Collen, Arne (ed) and Gasparski, Wojciech W (ed).

Die Barbarei: Eine phänomenologische Kulturkritik. Henry, Michel.

Encountering the Other(s): Studies in Literature, History, and Culture. Brinker-Gabler, Gisela (ed).

Exploring Our Environmental Connections. Schuster, Eleanor A (ed) and Brown, Carolyn L (ed).

Free Spirits: Feminist Philosophers on Culture. Mehuron, Kate (ed) and Percesepe, Gary (ed).

Georg Lukács. Sim, Stuart.

Habermas: A Critical Introduction. Outhwaite, William.

Humane Medicine: A Leading Surgeon Examines What Doctors Do, What Their Patients Expect from Them, and How the Expectations of Both Are Not Being Met. Little, Miles.

Identity, Culture, and Education. Smeyers, Paul (ed).

Langdon Gilkey: Theologian for a Culture in Decline. Walsh, Brian J.

Life, World and Meaning. Roux, A J P (ed).

Liminal Postmodernisms: The Postmodern, the (Post-)Colonial, and the (Post-)Feminist. D'haen, Theo (ed) and Bertens, Hans (ed).

Main Trends in Cultural History. Melching, Willem (ed) and Velema, Wyger (ed).

Meaning and Development. Kebede, Messay.

Metapatterns: Across Space, Time, and Mind. Volk, Tyler.

Mythos Wertfreiheit?. Apel, Karl Otto (ed) and Kettner, Matthias (ed).

Naturzweckmässigkeit und ästhetische Kultur. Schwabe, Karl-Heinz (ed) and Thom, Martina (ed).

Nietzsche's Genealogy: Nihilism and the Will to Knowledge. Havas, Randall.

Normative Cultures. Neville, Robert Cummings.

On Hume and Eighteenth-Century Aesthetics: The Philosopher on a Swing. Carabelli, Giancarlo and Hall, Joan Krakover (trans).

Openness in Research: The Tension Between Self and Other. Maso, I (& other eds).

Philosophie im Vergleich der Kulturen. Mall, Ram Adhar.

Philosophy and Architecture. Mitias, Michael H (ed).

Philosophy of Technology in Spanish Speaking Countries. Mitcham, Carl (ed).

Post-Modernism and Anthropology: Theory and Practice. Geuijen, Karin (ed), Raven, Diederick (ed) and De Wolf, Jan (ed).

Postmodern Representations: Truth, Power, and Mimesis in the Human Sciences and Public Culture. Brown, Richard Harvey (ed).

Postmodernism and Social Inquiry. Dickens, David R (ed) and Fontana, Andrea (ed).

Race and Mixed Race. Zack, Naomi.

Racist Culture: Philosophy and the Politics of Meaning. Goldberg, David Theo.

Rousseau (Past Masters). Wokler, Robert.

Science and Culture: Popular and Philosophical Essays. von Helmholtz, Hermann and Cahan, David (ed).

The Conflict of Law and Justice in the Icelandic Sagas. Pencak, William.

The Decolonization of Imagination: Culture, Knowledge, and Power. Pieterse, Jan Nederveen (ed) and Parekh, Bhikhu (ed).

The Fragmented World of the Social: Essays in Social and Political Philosophy. Wright, Charles W (ed) and Honneth, Axel.

DESTINY
De cómo "el ser" devino época. Muñoz Delgado, Mercedes.
Implicaciones políticas de la eclesiología de Wyclif. Bertelloni, Francisco.
Myth and Politics: Notes on the Concept of Destiny in the "Young" Benjamin (in Portuguese). Chaves, Ernani.
Philosophy as Destiny?. Schiffler, Ljerka.
The Question of Truth in Religion. Ward, J S K.

DESTRUCTION
Death Drive. Lingis, Alphonso F.

DETERMINACY
see also Indeterminacy
Finito e infinito e l'idealismo della filosofia: La logica hegeliana dell'essere determinato: Parte Seconda. Movia, Giancarlo.
The Real Core Model and Its Scales. Cunningham, Daniel W.

DETERMINATION
see also Self-Determination
Finito e infinito e l'idealismo della filosofia: La logica hegeliana dell'essere determinato: Parte Prima. Movia, Giancarlo.

DETERMINER
The Logical Form of Determiners. Ludlow, Peter.

DETERMINISM
see also Fatalism, Indeterminism
"Qué Necesidad Hay?" in Temas Actuales de Filosofía, Palacios, María Julia (ed). Gaeta, Rodolfo.
Kausalität Determinismus und Zufall in der wissenschaftlichen Naturbeschreibung. Koch, Günter.
The Cosmology of Freedom (New Edition). Neville, Robert Cummings.
A Reply to Antony Flew's Discussion of "E O Wilson After 20 Years". Robinson, Peter.
Algunas presuposiciones metafísicas de la acción humana. Haldane, John.
Beyond Determinism and Indignity: A Reinterpretation of Operant Conditioning. Rockwell, W Teed.
Causal Troubles. Titiev, Robert.
Chance and Teleology in Aristotle's Physics. Boerl, Marcelo D.
Coscienza e Corporeità. Cavaciuti, Santino.
Descripteurs distaux et externalisme. Proust, Joëlle.
Determinism Al Dente. Pereboom, Derk.
Epicurus, Determinism, and the Security of Knowledge. Magill, Kevin.
Flew on Anti-Social Determinism. House, I W O.
Freedom and Determinism. Clarke, Randolph.
Holes and Determinism: Another Look. Leeds, Stephen.
La responsabilité de l'agent dans la philosophie analytique de l'action: une interprétation. Blais, François.
Language and Determinism: A Contribution to the Cognitivist Critique of Chomsky's Innateness Hypothesis. Jutronic-Tihomirovic, Dunja.
On the Transfer of Necessity. O'Connor, Timothy.
Responsabilidad y castigo. Skutch, Alexander F.
Sartre, Freedom, and the Gambler. Irwin, William.
Some Metaphysical Presuppositions of Agency. Haldane, John.
Sovereignty, Soft Determinism and Responsibility. Gooch, Paul W.
Spinoza: La Simultaneidad de los Tres Géneros del Conocimiento. Beltrán, Miquel.
The Distribution Postulate in Bohm's Theory. Barrett, Jeffrey A.
Twenty Five Years of Theoretical Biology. Blandino, Giovanni.
Uncertainty About Determinism: A Critical Review of Challenges to the Determinism of Modern Science. Fraley, Lawrence E.
Walter Benjamin and Marxism (in Portuguese). Löwy, Michael.
Which Universals are Laws?. Peterson, Philip.
Willensfreiheit: Zwei gute Argumente und eine schlechtes. Leder, Matthias.

DEVELOPMENT
Folk Psychology: The Theory of Mind Debate. Davies, Martin (ed) and Stone, Tony (ed).
Meaning and Development. Kebede, Messay.
Democrazia e sviluppo—La Democrazia alla prova. Thesing, Josef.
Entwicklungsdenken bei Piaget und Merleau-Ponty. Herzog, Maximilian.
Epistemological and Ethical Development for Human Resource Professionals. Payne, Stephen L.
Finito e infinito e l'idealismo della filosofia: La logica hegeliana dell'essere determinato: Parte Prima. Movia, Giancarlo.
Holistic Approach to Development. Michnowski, Leslaw.
Identity, Becoming, and Rights of Development. Covey, Edward.
Influence and Development: Two Basic Paradigms of Education. Oelkers, Jürgen.
La Politique du Développement Durable: Voie ou Impasse. Nguyen, Vinh-De.
Leadership and Ethical Development: Balancing Light and Shadow. Lichtenstein, Benyamin M, Smith, Beverly A and Torbert, William R.
On the Unavoidability of Power in Child-rearing: Is the Language of Rights Educationally Appropriate?. Smeyers, Paul.
Postille: 1)Pensiero Orientale Verticale e Pensiero Occidentale Orizzontale, 2)La Filsofia della Crisi. Del Vecchio, Dante.
Some Developmental Issues in Transpersonal Experience. Hunt, Harry T.
The Primacy of Virtue in Children's Moral Development. Putman, Daniel.

DEVIANCE
Morality, Normativity, and Society. Copp, David.

DEVIL
How to Tell God from the Devil: On the Way to Comedy. Eckardt, A Roy.
La Religión y el Mal: Gnosticismo y Satanismo. Bravo, Elia Nathan.

DEVITT, M
Semantic Realism. Shalkowski, Scott A.

DEWALD, C
Herodotus and the Rhetoric of Otherness. Gray, Vivienne.

DEWEY
"Community Without Fusion: Dewey, Mead, Tufts" in Pragmatism: From Progressivism to Postmodernism, Hollinger, Robert (ed). Campbell, James.
"Epistemology" Reburied. Dicker, Georges.
"John Dewey and the Roots of Democratic Imagination" in Recovering Pragmatism's Voice, Langsdorf, Lenore (ed). Alexander, Thomas M.
"Misreading Dewey: A Thesis and Exemplar" in Identity, Culture, and Education, Smeyers, Paul (ed). Stone, Lynda.
"Pragmatism Reconsidered: John Dewey and Michel Foucault on the Consequences of Inquiry" in Recovering Pragmatism's Voice, Langsdorf, Lenore (ed). Macke, Frank J.
"Pragmatism, Democracy, and the Imagination: Rethinking the Deweyan Legacy" in Pragmatism: From Progressivism to Postmodernism, Hollinger, Robert (ed). Gunn, Giles.
"Rorty's Dewey: Pragmatism, Education, and the Public Sphere" in Identity, Culture, and Education, Smeyers, Paul (ed). Neiman, Alven M.
(Re)searching Dewey for Feminist Imaginaries: Linguistic Continuity, Discourse and Gossip. Leach, Mary.
Dewey's Ethical Thought. Welchman, Jennifer.
Dewey's New Logic: A Reply to Russell. Burke, Tom.
John Dewey: An Intellectual Portrait. Hook, Sidney.
Understanding John Dewey: Nature and Cooperative Intelligence. Campbell, James.
Work, Education, and Leadership: Essays in the Philosophy of Education. Howard, V A and Scheffler, Israel.
A Reply to Christopher Kulp's "Dewey, Indeterminacy, and the Spectator Theory of Knowledge". Pratt, Scott L.
Albert Bormann and John Dewey on Everyday Technology. Limper, Peter.
An Epistemological Foundation for Thinking: A Deweyian Approach. Holder Jr, John J.
Applying the Term 'Mental' in a World without a Within: Dewey's Realism. Tiles, J E.
Constructionalism in Dewey's Theory of Knowing. Friend, Stacie.
Content and Criticism: The Aims of Schooling. Hare, William.
Démocratie et expérience: introduction à la démocratie créatrice de John Dewey. Leroux, François.
Dewey on Causation in Social Science. Stone, George C.
Dewey on Experience: Foundation or Reconstruction?. Shusterman, Richard.
Dewey's Metaphysics and the Self. Cunningham, Craig A.
Educating the Democratic Heart: Pluralism, Traditions and the Humanities. Alexander, Thomas M.
Educating the Moral Artist: Dramatic Rehearsal in Moral Education. Fesmire, Steven A.
Education and Democracy: Confronting the Postmodernist Challenge. Carr, Wilfred.
Education for Democracy. Tiles, J E.
Heaven's Partners or Nietzschean Free Spirits?. Frisina, Warren G.
If We Took Dewey's Aesthetics Seriously, How Would the Arts Be Taught?. Jackson, Philip W.
John Dewey: An "Old-Fashioned" Reformer. Boisvert, Raymond D.
John Dewey: Philosopher of Technology. Hickman, Larry A.
La démocratie créatrice: la tâche qui nous attend, John Dewey. Chaput, Sylvie (trans) and Dewey, John.
La Fortuna di Croce e Gentile negli Stati Uniti. Roberts, David D.
Nature and Culture. Manicas, Peter T.
On the Alleged Neutrality of Technology: A Study in Dewey's Experience and Nature. Blacker, David.
On What We May Hope: Rorty on Dewey and Foucault. Marshall, James D.
Practical Expressions of Natural Piety: Emerson and Dewey. Wilson, Eddy.
Pragmatism as a Pedagogy of Communicative Action. Biesta, Gert J J.
Science Education for a Life Curriculum. Hickman, Larry A.
The Beyond in the Midst: The Relevance of Dewey's Philosophy of Religion for Education. Miedema, Siebren.
What's A Philosopher To Do? A Deweyan Response. Teehan, John.

DHARMA
A Note on the Concepts of Nitya-karma, Naimittika-karma and Kamya-karma. Pandurangi, K T.
Culture and Cultures. Pande, G C.
How Innovative is the Alayavijnana?, Part II. Waldron, William S.
Universal Values: An Indian Perspective. Prasad, Ranjendra.

DHARMAKIRTI
Dharmakirti and Tibetans on Adrsyanupalabdhihetu. Tillemans, Tom J F.

DHARMOTTARA
Dharmottara's Theory of Knowledge in His Laghupramanyapariksa. Krasser, Helmut.

DIAGNOSIS
Causal Reasoning and the Diagnostic Process. Rizzi, Dominick A.
Commerce and Genetic Diagnostics. Silverman, Paul H.
'Ze zijn allemaal dood...' Over kennissystemen in de medische praktijk, voorvechters en critici, en het mysterieuze succes van onderzoeksprotocollen. Berg, Marc.

DIAGONALIZATION
Is Gold-Putnam Diagonalization Complete?. Juhl, Cory.
Topological Structure of Diagonalizable Algebras and Corresponding Logical Properties of Theories. D'Agostino, Giovanna.

DIAGRAM

Berkeley's Triangle. Szabó, Zoltán.
Degrees of Iconicity in the Lexicon. Waugh, Linda R.
Diagrams and Metaphors: Iconic Aspects in Language. Hiraga, Masako K.

DIALECTIC

"Aporía y Dialéctica en el *Teeteto*" in *Platón: Los Diálogos Tardíos, Lan, Conrado Eggers (ed)*. Hülsz Piccone, Enrique.
"Plato's Ghost: Consequences of Aristotelian Dialectic" in *The Crossroads of Norm and Nature, Sim, May (ed)*. DeMarco, C Wesley.
"Quand la science parle à vide: procédés dialectiques et métaphoriques chez Aristote" in *Rhétoriques de la science, De Coorebyter, Vincent (ed)*. Vegetti, Mario.
"Überwindung von Schwierigem durch Häufung Desselben". Steiner, Uwe.
"Working Through Puzzles with Aristotle" in *The Crossroads of Norm and Nature, Sim, May (ed)*. Cleary, John J.
Chronos and *Logos*: Rhetoric and the Rise of Philosophy. Houser, R Edward.
Commitment in Dialogue: Basic Concepts of Interpersonal Reasoning. Walton, Douglas N and Krabbe, Erik C W.
Of Problematology: Philosophy, Science, and Language. Meyer, Michel and Jamison, David (trans).
Rosmini et l'Idée de Progrès. Raschini, Maria-Adelaide and Rocher, Emmanuel (trans).
Absolu/Sujet. Jarczyk, Gwendoline and Labarrière, Pierre-Jean.
Analisi e Assiomatizzazione nella Dialettica di Platone. Ferrari, Franco.
Aspectos dialécticos en los primeros filósofos. Fallas, Luis A.
Being, Determination, and Dialectic: On the Sources of Metaphysical Thinking. Desmond, William.
Collingwood's Reform of Hegelian Dialectic. Peters, Rik.
De la Utilidad de la Dialéctica. Campos Benítez, Juan Manuel.
Dialectic and Dialogue. Anderson, Albert A.
Dialectic and the Advance of Science. Harris, Errol E.
Dialectic and the Syllogism. Smith, Robin.
Dialectic at a Standstill. Arsenault, Joseph and Brinkley, Tony.
Dialéctica Hegeliana de la Ilustración. Aranda Torres, Cayetano.
Dialéctica y Libertad. Aizpún, Teresa.
Dialectical Analogy: The Oscillating Center of Rahner's Thought. McDermott, John M.
Dialektik und Entschluss bei Fichte. Irie, Yukio.
Disidencias de Pedro Abelardo. Brasa Díaz, Mariano.
Fichtes praxologische Dialektik. Hammacher, Klaus.
Finito e infinito e l'idealismo della filosofia: La logica hegeliana dell'essere determinato: Parte Seconda. Movia, Giancarlo.
Galileu e a Dialética: Síntese pelo Experimento e Natureza como Domínio dos Objectos. Maar, Wolfgang Leo.
Habermas and the Force of Dialectical Argument. Hesse, Mary.
Hegel et Schelling: critique du formalisme et prise en charge de la contingence. Lardic, Jean-Marie.
Idealismo e Dialettica dell'Idea nell'Attualismo di Giovanni Gentile. Spanio, Davide.
Il Ritorno dell'Identità nel "Sistema di Logica" di G Gentile. Sainati, Vittorio.
Intellektuelle Anschauung und Dialektik. Nagasawa, Kunihiko.
Kontinuität oder Bruch? Zum Verhältnis von sokratischer und platonischer Dialektik. Mesch, Walter.
L'informe bergsoniano nella filosofia di Serres. Delcò, Alessandro.
La Dialéctica en el Cancionero de Baena. Sánchez-Romate, María José Gómez.
La Inferència Dialèctico-Especulativa a la *Ciència de la Lògica* de Hegel. Alegre I Biosca, Lluís.
Limitative Dialektik: Überlegungen im Anschluss an die Methodenreflexion in Fichtes *Grundlage* 1794/95. Janke, Wolfgang.
Logique théologique et logique systémique: Dialogue avec Edgar Morin. Kraege, Jean-Denis.
Los Campos de la Argumentación. Beuchot, Mauricio.
Marxism on Dialectical and Logical Contradiction. Goldstick, D.
Negative Dialektik als begriffliche Antithese zum Begriff. Tóth, Cvetka.
Plotinus and the Neoplatonic Conception of Dialectic. Anton, John P.
Protreptique et Dialectique. Leroux, Georges.
Rationality in Legal Discussions: A Pragma-Dialectical Perspective. Feteris, Eveline T.
The Concept of Dialectic. Stack, George J.
The Game that Looks Like Work in Plato's "Parmenides". Delgado De Torres, Olivia.
The Heirs of German Idealism (in Portuguese). Musse, Ricardo.
The Problem of Dialectical Reasoning in Aristotle. Bolton, Robert.

DIALECTICAL

"Hegel's Critique of Kant and Pre-Kantian Metaphysics" in *Hegel Reconsidered, Engelhardt Jr, H Tristram (ed)*. Brinkmann, Klaus.
Husserl e lo scetticismo. Savi, Cristina.
Dialéctica y Política. Fornari, Aníbal.

DIALECTICAL MATERIALISM

Dialectical Materialism and Modern Science. Cameron, Kenneth Neill.
Tre Improbabili Nani Sulle Spalle dei Giganti. Mastroianni, Giovanni.

DIALOGIC

Perspektiven der Dialogik: Zürcher Kolloquium zum 80. Geburtstag von Hermann Levin Goldschmidt. Goetschel, Willi (ed).
Philosophie als Dialogik: Frühe Schriften Werke 1. Goldschmidt, Hermann Levin.

DIALOGUE

"Hume and the Art of Dialogue" in *Hume and Hume's Connexions, Stewart, M A (ed)*. Malherbe, Michel.
"Per una razionalità practica dialogica" in *L'etica e il suo Altro, Vigna, Carmelo (ed)*. Cortella, Lucio.
Commitment in Dialogue: Basic Concepts of Interpersonal Reasoning. Walton, Douglas N and Krabbe, Erik C W.
Three Dialogues on Knowledge. Feyerabend, Paul.
Dialectic and Dialogue. Anderson, Albert A.
El misterio construido. Lapoujade, María Noel.
Pulsión y Símbolo. Mandrioni, Héctor D.
Rebelión y goce: aproximación a la estética de Camus. Sanabria, Carolina.
Sócrates: Filósofo en el Límite?.-Gómez-Lobo, Alfonso.
The Concept of Dialectic. Stack, George J.

DICHOTOMOUS

The Logic of Dichotomic Changes. Wajszczyk, Józef.

DICKER, G

Descartes in der angelsächsischen Diskussion. Perler, Dominik.

DICKSON, M

Comment on 'Stapp's Theorem Without Counterfactual Commitment'. Stapp, Henry P.

DICTIONARY

A Companion to Metaphysics. Kim, Jaegwon (ed) and Sosa, Ernest (ed).
A Descartes Dictionary. Cottingham, John.
A Hobbes Dictionary. Martinich, A P.
A Kant Dictionary. Caygill, Howard.
Dictionnaire des philosophes antiques, publié sous la direction de Richard Goulet, t.II Babélyca d'Argos á Dyscolius. Lafrance, Yvon.
The Blackwell Companion to the Enlightenment. Yolton, John W (& other eds).
The Cambridge Dictionary of Philosophy. Audi, Robert (ed).
The Oxford Companion to Philosophy. Honderich, Ted (ed).

DIDEROT

Mass Enlightenment: Critical Studies in Rousseau and Diderot. Simon, Julia.
Preliminary Discourse to the Encyclopedia of Diderot. D'Alembert, Jean Le Rond and Schwab, Richard N (trans).

DIEKS, D

Independently Motivating the Kochen-Dieks Modal Interpretation of Quantum Mechanics. Clifton, Robert.

DIENHART, J

A Theoretical Ground for the Practice of Business Ethics. Madsen, Peter.

DIESING, M

"Individual-Level Predicates as Inherent Generics" in *The Generic Book, Carlson, Gregory N (ed)*. Chierchia, Gennaro.
"Stage-Level and Individual-Level Predicates" in *The Generic Book, Carlson, Gregory N (ed)*. Kratzer, Angelika.

DIFFERENCE

"Deferring to Derrida's Difference" in *European Philosophy and the American Academy, Smith, Barry (ed)*. Margolis, Joseph.
"Sexuelle Differenz als eine Frage der Ethik" in *Macht Geschlechter Differenz, Müller-Funk, Wolfgang (ed)*. Butler, Judith.
"Von den Differenzen von Differenzen" in *Macht Geschlechter Differenz, Müller-Funk, Wolfgang (ed)*. Müller-Funk, Wolfgang.
Barth, Derrida, and the Language of Theology. Ward, Graham.
Difference and Repetition. Deleuze, Gilles and Patton, Paul (trans).
Identidad y Relación en Kant Los Juicios Sintéticos a Priori como Principios. Segura, Armando.
Immanuel Kant zur Geschlechterdifferenz: Aufklärerische Vorurteilskritik und bürgerliche Geschlechtsvormundschaft. Jauch, Ursula Pia.
Macht Geschlechter Differenz. Müller-Funk, Wolfgang (ed).
Philosophie in Sein und Zeit: Kritische Erwägungen zu Heidegger. Graeser, Andreas.
Race and Mixed Race. Zack, Naomi.
The Irigaray Reader. Whitford, Margaret (ed).
There are Two Errors In the the Title of This Book: A Sourcebook of Philosophical Puzzles, Problems, and Paradoxes. Martin, Robert M.
A Note on Justice, Care, and Immigration Policy. Baier, Annette C.
Annäherung an Derrida oder: Wer spät kommt, den belohnt das Lesen. Naumann-Beyer, Waltraud.
Commentary: Proliferating Conceptions of Truth: Comments on McGee and McLaughlin. Hyde, Dominic.
Dealing with Difference. Phillips, Anne.
Derrida and the Scene of Drawing: A Discussion of *Mémoires D'aveugle. L'Autoportrait et autres ruines* by Jacques Derrida. Newman, Michael.
Distinctions Without a Difference. McGee, Vann and McLaughlin, Brian.
Es negociable la diferencia?. Lorite Mena, José.
Is There Sexual Difference in the Work of Georges Bataille?. McWhorter, Ladelle.
Kierkegaard and the Problem of the Social Other. Matthis, Michael J.
La alteridad en el Sofista de Platón. Iglesias, Mercedes.
La Culture Amérindienne: Cette Inconnue (Entretien avec Robert Vachon). Landry, Cécile.
Philosophy, Sex and Gender: Mutual Interrogations. Kaplan, Morris B.
Race/Gender and the Ethics of Difference: A Reply to Okin's "Gender Inequality and Cultural Differences". Flax, Jane.
Rationality and the Politics of Gender Difference. Rooney, Phyllis A.
Rawls: Principio de diferencia y justicia intergeneracional. Amor, Claudio.
Reconciling Equality to Difference: Caring (F)or Justice For People With Disabilities. Silvers, Anita.
Response to Jane Flax. Okin, Susan Moller.

DISTRIBUTIVITY
On a Generalization of Distributivity. Kanai, Yasuo.

DIVERSITY
"Biological Diversity and Ethical Development" in *Ethics, Religion and Biodiversity*, Hamilton, Lawrence S (ed). Goulet, Denis.
"Toward the Possibility of a Global Community" in *Ethics, Religion and Biodiversity*, Hamilton, Lawrence S (ed). Weiming, Tu.
American Mixed Race: The Culture of Microdiversity. Zack, Naomi (ed).
Ethics, Religion and Biodiversity. Hamilton, Lawrence S (ed).
Nationalism (Fourth, Expanded Edition). Kedourie, Elie.
Strange Multiplicity: Constitutionalism in an Age of Diversity. Tully, James.
Adolescents, Post-Structuralism, and "Playing It Cool!". Merttens, Ruth.
Bayesianism and Diverse Evidence. Wayne, Andrew.
Can Justice as Fairness Accommodate Diversity? An Examination of the Representation of Minorities and Women in *A Theory of Justice*. Trout, Lara M.
Civic Education and Social Diversity. Gutman, Amy.
Dimensione Transculturale dei Fenomeni Giuridici nella Ricerca Antropologica. Scillitani, Lorenzo.
Diversity and Unity of Sciences as the Foundation of Universalism. Kuczynski, Janusz.
Diversity Stress as Morality Stress. André, Rae.
Ecumenism Between the World Religions. Charlesworth, Max.
Facing the Challenges of Diversity—A Reflection on the Role of Philosophy in South Africa Today. Van Der Merwe, W L.
Human Equality and Intra- as well as Intercultural Diversity. Holenstein, Elmar.
Kymlicka, Liberalism, and Respect for Cultural Minorities. Tomasi, John.
Legitimacy and Diversity: Dialectical Reflections on Analytical Distinctions. McCarthy, Thomas.
Montesquieu e il Problema del "Diversité". Courtney, C P.
Mothering, Diversity and Peace: Comments on Sara Ruddick's Feminist Maternal Peace Politics. Bailey, Alison.
The Diverse Community or the Unoppressive City: Which Ideal for a Transformative Politics of Difference?. Green, Judith M.
Two Concepts of Liberalism. Galston, William A.

DIVIDED LINE
Should Plato's Line Be Divided in the Mean and Extreme Ratio?. Balashov, Yuri V.

DIVINATION
HE MANTIKE TECHNE: *Statesman* 260e1 and 290c4-6. Brickhouse, Thomas C and Smith, Nicholas D.

DIVINE
J G Fichte: l'affermazione dell'Assoluto. Gamarra, Daniel.
Religious Pluralism and the Divine: Another Look at John Hick's Neo-Kantian Proposal. Eddy, Paul R.

DIVINITY
"The Only Diabological Thing about Women...": Luce Irigaray on Divinity. Deutscher, Penelope.
Creativity and God: A Challenge to Process Theology. Neville, Robert Cummings.
Gott—Gebote—Ideale: Analytische Philosophie und theologische Ethik. Löhr, Gebbhard.
Inhabiting the Earth: Heidegger, Environmental Ethics, and the Metaphysics of Nature. Foltz, Bruce V.
Lectures on Divine Humanity. Solovyov, Vladimir.
The Divine Matrix: Creativity as Link between East and West. Bracken, Joseph A.
The Human Shape of God: Religion in Hegel's "Phenomenology of Spirit". Jamros, Daniel P.
Transformations in Consciousness: The Metaphysics and Epistemology. Merrell-Wolff, Franklin.
Boturini e la Diffusione di Vico in Spagna. Mestre, Antonio.
Cartesian Causality, Explanation, and Divine Concurrence. Clatterbaugh, Kenneth.
Could There Be More Than One Lord?. Bartel, T W.
David Pailin's Theology of Divine Action. Middleton, Darren J N.
Divine Action: Is It Credible?. Nelson, James S.
Does Theological Fatalism Rest on an Equivocation?. Hunt, David P.
Epilogue: Prolegomenon to Future Feminist* Philosophies of Religion. Thie, Marilyn.
Gianni Vattimo's Hermeneutics and the Trace of Divinity. D'Isanto, Luca.
God with/out Being. Van Den Hengel, John.
Good, Beauty, and Eros in Dionysius' Doctrine of Divine Causality. Niarchos, C G.
Heidegger and Von Balthasar: A Lover's Quarrel over Beauty and Divinity. Daigler, Matthew A.
Hindu Titanism. Gier, Nicholas F.
Holiness as Service: *Therapeia* and *Hyperetike* in Plato's *Euthyphro*. Parry, David M.
I Believe in God the Father, Almighty. Clark, Kelly J.
Is God Essentially God?. Sennett, James F.
L'Infinité Divine dans l'Antiquité et au Moyen Age. Côté, Antoine.
Leibniz on Divine Foreknowledge of Future Contingents and Human Freedom. Murray, Michael J.
Molina on Divine Foreknowledge and the Principle of Bivalence. Gaskin, Richard.
Néant Divin et Théophanie: Erigène Disciple de Denys. Jeauneau, Édouard.
Of Angels, Oysters, and an Unchanging God: Aquinas on Divine Immutability. Dodds, Michael J.
On "Divine Simplicity: A New Defense". Miller, Barry.
On Property Self-Exemplification: Rejoinder to Miller. Vallicella, William F.
Sophiology: A Human Reading of the Book of God. Mosolova, S V.
The Metaphysical Foundation of Gnosiology in Neoplatonic Proclus (412-485). Térézis, Christos.

The Nature of Divine Love. Brümmer, Vincent.
The Need for Christian Philosophy. Owens, Joseph.
Time and Foreknowledge: A Critique of Zagzebski. Oaklander, L Nathan.
What did Pyrrho Think About "The Nature of the Divine and the Good"?. Bett, Richard.
Why the Philosophical Problems of Chalcedonian Christology Have Not Gone Away. Bartel, T W.
Xunzi and the Confucian Answer to Titanism. Gier, Nicholas F.

DIVISION
On Division in Plato's *Statesman*. Fattal, Michel.
Two Theories of Mental Division. Dunn, Robert L.

DIVORCE
Discussing Divorce in Introductory Ethics. Gould, James B.
Peoples and Secession. Ewin, R E.

DOCTOR-PATIENT RELATIONSHIP
Postmodernist Theory and the Physician-Patient Relationship. Tsouyopoulos, Nelly.
The Patient-Physician Relationship and the Allocation of Scarce Resources: A Law and Economics Approach. Mehlman, Maxwell J and Massey, Susan R.
Towards Authentic Conversations: Authenticity in the Patient-Professional Relationship. Arnason, Vilhjalmur.
Viktor Emil von Gebsattel on the Doctor-Patient Relationship. Welie, Jos V M.

DOCTRINE
The History of Being and the History of Doctrine: An Influence of Heidegger on Theology. O'Meara, Thomas F.

DOCUMENT
The Inalienable Right to Life and the Durable Power of Attorney. Wellman, Carl P.

DODGE, J
The Uniformity of the Causal Connection in the Second Analogy, or How Not to Dodge Beck. Wheeler, Mark.

DOGMA
"Remarks on 'Aesthetization' in Science on the Basis of History" in *Historiography Between Modernism and Postmodernism*, Topolski, Jerzy (ed). Kostyrko, Teresa.
The Letter of Apologetics and History and Dogma. Dru, Alexander (trans), Trethowan, Illtyd (trans) and Blondel, Maurice.
Are Quine's Two Dogmas Still Dogmas. Kanthamani, A.
Scriptural Logic: Diagrams for a Postcritical Metaphysics. Ochs, Peter.

DOGMATISM
Sócrates: Filósofo Dogmático? Una Réplica a Alfonso Gómez-Lobo. Nudler, Oscar.

DOHRM, A
The Origin of Vertebrates and the Principle of Succession of Functions: Genealogical Sketches by Anton Dohrm, 1875—An English Translation. Ghiselin, Michael T.

DOING
Doing and Refraining from Refraining. Xu, Ming.

DOMAIN
On Russell's Argument for Restricting Modes of Specification and Domains of Quantification. Weiss, Bernhard.

DOMINATING
Dominating Projective Sets in the Baire Space. Spinas, Otmar.

DOMINATION
Anima hace hablar a la razón con una voz diferente: Nuevos nexos entre la tecnociencia y el mundo de la vida. Cañón Loyes, Camino.
Critical Legal Theory and the Challenge of Feminism: A Philosophical Reconception. Kramer, Matthew H.
Ecology. Merchant, Carolyn (ed).
Race and Mixed Race. Zack, Naomi.
De Sade o la subversión de/en la Ilustración. Mayos, Gonça.
Domination and Enlightenment: The Limits of Manipulation. Cook, Deborah.
Equational Derivation vs Computation. Handley, W G and Wainer, S S.

DOMINO, B
Quantitative and Qualitative Abductive Inquiry. Bybee, Michael D.

DONAGAN, A
The Philosophical Papers of Alan Donagan: Volume II, Action, Reason, and Value. Malpas, J E (ed) and Donagan, Alan.

DONALDSON, T
A Critique of Social Contracts for Business. Conroy, Edward J.
Continuing the Social Contract Tradition. Keeley, Michael.
Decision-Making Processes on Ethical Issues: The Impact of a Social Contract Perspective. Robertson, Diana C and Ross Jr, William T.
Social Contract Theory and Gender Discrimination: Some Reflections on the Donaldson/Dunfee Model. Mayer, Don and Cava, Anita.
Social Contracting as a Trust-Building Process of Network Governance. Calton, Jerry M and Lad, Lawrence J.

DONNE, J
Christus Patiens and *Christus Victor*: John Donne's Ultimate Reality and Meaning. Labriola, Albert C.

DONNELLAN, K
Referenztheorien in der analytischen Philosophie. Kellerwessel, Wulf.

DONOR
Information Sharing in Donor Insemination: A Conflict of Rights and Needs. Daniels, Ken R.

DOOYEWEERD, H
Die uitdrukkingskracht van de transcendentale denkkritiek. Hoogland, J.

DUNN, J
The Political Thought of John Dunn and the Cambridge School. Hanzawa, Takamaro.

DUNNE, J
Roughing Out the Ground Rules: Reason and Experience in Practical Deliberation. Carr, David.

DUNS SCOTUS
Attualità nelle leggi logiche in Giovanni Duns Scoto. Olejnik, Roman M.
Poinsot on Knowability of Beings of Reason. Doyle, John P.
What Am I Thinking About? John Duns Scotus and Peter Aureol on Intentional Objects. Perler, Dominik.

DUPONT, P
Broadening the Picture of Science in Revolutionary France: Adding Du Pont and Restif to Lavoisier and Laplace. Conner, Clifford D.

DUPRE, J
Critical Notice of John Duprè The Disorder of Things: Metaphysical Foundations of the Disunity of Science. Ereshefsky, Marc.

DUPRE, L
Louis Dupré's "Passage to Modernity" (in Dutch). De Dijn, H.

DURABLE POWER OF ATTORNEY
The Inalienable Right to Life and the Durable Power of Attorney. Wellman, Carl P.

DURATION
see also Time
La teoría del instante en Bachelard y el espacio onírico. Castillo, Roberto.

DURKHEIM
Credere all Cose e Credere Agli Dei: Teorie della Credenza da Renouvier a Durkheim. Paoletti, Giovanni.
Durkheim and Moral Education for Children: A Recently Discovered Lecture. Pickering, W S F.
Education, Virtue and Democracy in the Work of Emile Durkheim. Cladis, Mark S.
Il Guardiano delle Soglia. Angelini, Pietro.
Weber and Durkheim: Beyond the Differences a Common Important Paradigm?. Boudon, Raymond.

DURRANT, M
"Describing God". Dombrowski, Daniel.

DUTCH
"Die Philosophielehre im neuen Europa—Bemerkungen zur niederländischen Perspektive" in Das geistige Erbe Europas, Buhr, Manfred (ed). Petry, Michael John.
"How Much 'Heimat' does a Human Being Need?" in Identity, Culture, and Education, Smeyers, Paul (ed). Levering, Bas.
De Disciplinering van het Hoger Onderwijs: Aantekeningen bij de Massa-Universiteit. Baggen, Peter and Maat, Harro.
Euthanasia in the Netherlands: Sliding Down the Slippery Slope?. Keown, John.
Johannes Tauler in den Niederlanden: Grundzüge eines philosophie- und rezeptionsgeschichtlichen Forschungsrogramms. Hoenen, Maarten.
Sociale theorie en wetenschapsonderzoek: hebben die wat aan elkaar?. Van El, Carla.
The Historiography of Dutch Philosophy: Problems and Perspectives (in Dutch). Wielema, M R.

DUTY
see also Obligation
"Duties and Rights in Hindu Society" in Human Rights and the World's Religions, Rouner, Leroy (ed). Carman, John B.
"Professional Codes and Kantian Duties" in Ethics and the Professions, Chadwick, Ruth (ed). Harris, Nigel G E.
Real Rights. Wellman, Carl P.
The Secret Chain: Evolution and Ethics. Bradie, Michael.
A Theory of Social Decisions. Baron, Jonathan.
Acceptance of Authority and the Duty to Comply with Just Institutions: A Comment on Waldron. Murphy, Mark C.
An Argument Against a Legal Duty to Rescue. Hunt, Lester H.
Causally Irrelevant Reasons and Action Solely from the Motive of Duty. Latham, Noa.
El tema de la virtud: recientes debates. Mauri, Margarita.
Four Problems of Professional Ethics. Wangerin, Paul T.
L'exigence morale. Granier, Jean.
La esencia del formalismo ético. Palacios, Juan Miguel.
Lo Obligatorio, lo Meritorio y Otras Nociones Deónticas en la Ética Formal de Kant. García Norro, Juan José.
Michael Oakeshott on Life: Waiting with Godot. Worthington, Glenn.
Political Obligation and the Natural Duties of Justice. Klosko, George.
Rights, Duties, and Limits of Autonomy. Emson, H E.
Sollen, Wollen, Tun. Lembeck, Karl-Heinz.
The Incoherence of the Moral 'Ought'. Richter, Duncan.
The Relation Between Ethical Codes and Moral Principles. Bersoff, Donald N and Koeppl, Peter M.
The Soldier as Conscientious Objector. Whitman, Jeffrey P.

DWORKIN, R
"Having a Voice and Getting a Hearing" in Identity, Culture, and Education, Smeyers, Paul (ed). White, Patricia.
Dworkin, Vague Constitutional Clauses, and the Eighth Amendment's Admonition Against "Cruel and Unusual Punishment". Neeley, G Steven.
Legal Adjudication and Democracy: Some Remarks on Dworkin and Habermas. Günther, Klaus.
On R Dworkin, Life's Dominion (in Hebrew). Ullmann-Margalit, Edna.

Pluralism, Integrity, and the Interpretive Model of Law. Golash, Deirdre.
The Independent Value of Freedom. Carter, Ian.
The Place of Equality in Habermas' and Dworkin's Theories of Justice. Gosepath, Stefan.
Two Essays in Public Philosophy: Callahan's The Troubled Dream of Life and Dworkin's Life's Dominion. Nelson, James Lindemann.

DYER, M
Monistic Idealism May Provide Better Ontology for Cognitive Science: A Reply to Dyer. Goswami, Amit.

DYING
see also Death
Dignity, Death and Modern Virtue. Meyer, Michael J.
El morir como pauta ética del empiricismo trascendental. Echeverría, José.
Pain Relief for Dying Persons: Dealing with Physicians' Fears and Concerns. Buchan, Melissa L and Tolle, Susan W.
Physician Aid in Dying and the Relief of Patients' Suffering: Physicians' Attitudes Regarding Patients' Suffering and End-of-Life Decisions. Huang, Frederick Y and Emanuel, Linda L.

DYNAMICS
A Dualistic Model of Ultimate Reality and Meaning: Self-Similarity in Chaotic Dynamics and Swedenborg. Baker, Gregory L.
Actualidad y Perennidad de Vico. Uscatescu, Jorge.
Changes in Preference. Hansson, Sven Ove.
Chaos, Clio, and Scientific Illusions of Understanding. Roth, Paul A and Ryckman, Thomas A.
Commentary on Furley's "Some Points About Stoic Dynamics". Striker, Gisela.
Concepts of Chaos: The Analysis of Self-Similarity and the Relevance of the Ethical Dimension. Modell, Stephen M.
Deterministisches Chaos: Einige Wissenschaftstheoretisch Interessante Aspekte. Düsberg, Klaus Jürgen.
Dynamic Dependency Grammar. Milward, David.
GRW and the Tails Problem. Lewis, Peter.
Inference, Noncommutativity, and Determinateness in Quantum Mechanics. Bub, Jeffrey.
Merging without Mystery or: Variables in Dynamics Semantics. Vermeulen, C F M.
Restabilizing Dynamics: Construction and Constraint in the History of Walrasian Stability Theory. Hands, D Wade.
Scientism without Tears: A Reply to Roth and Ryckman. Reisch, George.
Some Points About Stoic Dynamics. Furley, David.
The Renormalisation Group and Effective Field Theories. Huggett, Nick and Weingard, Robert.
What Might Cognition Be, If Not Computation?. van Gelder, Tim.

DYNAMISM
Intellectual Dynamism in Transcendental Thomism: A Metaphysical Assessment. Knasas, John F X.
La riappropriazione di Aristotele nell'ultimo Ricoeur. Rizzacasa, Aurelio.

EARMAN, J
Absolute vs Relational Theories of Space and Time: A Review of World Enough and Space-Time by John Earman. Rynasiewicz, Robert.
Earman on the Projectibility of Grue. Lange, Marc.
Holes and Determinism: Another Look. Leeds, Stephen.
Substance, Modality, and Spacetime. Healey, Richard.

EARTH
Inhabiting the Earth: Heidegger, Environmental Ethics, and the Metaphysics of Nature. Foltz, Bruce V.
A Vedantic Response to the Ecological Crisis. Manninezhath, Thomas.
Making Peace with the Earth: Indigenous Agriculture and the Green Revolution. Curtin, Deane.
Preparing for the 21st Century: A Philosophy for New Thinking. Parsons, Howard L.
Reverence for the Earth is Animal Rights Ethics. Pérez, Berta E.
The Unnatural Steward: Humanity's Relationship to Earth. Artson, Bradley Shavit.

EAST EUROPEAN
"John Locke and the Greek Intellectual Tradition" in Locke's Philosophy, Rogers, G A J (ed). Kitromilides, Paschalis M.
"The Modern World and the Individual: From the Metamorphosis of Eastern European Marxism to Marx's Errors" in Whither Marxism?, Magnus, Bernd (ed). Marga, Andrei.
The End of "Isms"?. Shtromas, Aleksandras (ed).
Constitution and Continuity in the Transitions: Part I. Arato, Andrew.
Constitution and Continuity, Part II: The Hungarian Case. Arato, Andrew.
Introduction: Reconstructing Philosophy in Eastern Europe. Ryder, John.
The Formation Approach and the Crisis of "Real Socialism". Juchler, Jakob.
The Post-Socialist Change in Eastern Europe: Specific Development or Universal Trend of Global History? A Formation Approach. Juchler, Jakob.

EASTERN
see also Oriental
"The Emotions of Altruism, East and West" in Emotions in Asian Thought, Marks, Joel (ed). Kupperman, Joel J.
On the Basis of Morality. Payne, E F J (trans) and Schopenhauer, Arthur.
The Bounds of Freedom: About the Eastern and Western Approaches to Freedom. Balaban, Oded and Erev, Anan.
The Divine Matrix: Creativity as Link between East and West. Bracken, Joseph A.
Some Notes on Emotion, "East and West". Solomon, Robert C.
Teilhard's Reflections on Eastern Religions Revisited. King, Ursula.

EASTERN

The Problem of Inter-Faith Studies. Matilal, Bimal K.

Towards Global Environmental Values: Lessons from Western and Eastern Experience. Sarre, Philip.

EASTHOPE, A

Reply to Easthope. Ryle, Martin.

EATING

Food in India. Olivelle, Patrick.

EBBS, G

Ebbs on Skepticism, Objectivity and Brains in Vats. Brueckner, Anthony.

ECCLESIOLOGY

Implicaciones políticas de la eclesiología de Wyclif. Bertelloni, Francisco.

ECKHART

Esse est Deus: Meister Eckharts christologische Versöhnung von Philosophie und Religion und ihre Ursprünge in der Tradition des Abendlandes. Manstetten, Reiner.

Beyond Subjectivity: Opening the Ego. Demkovich, Michael.

Emanation and Mysticism in the Writings of Meister Eckhart. Sells, Michael.

Intellektuelle Anschauung und Mystik. Omine, Akira.

Mechthild von Magdeburg und der frühe Meister Eckhart. Weiss, Bardo.

The Model of an Ethics of Being in Meister Eckhart and in the Structural Philosophy of Heinrich Rombach. Mieth, Dietmar.

The Way to Ultimate Meaning in Meister Eckhart's Mysticism. Kovacs, George.

ECLECTICISM

The Bullying of an Untheoretical History of Philosophy—Eclecticism Instead of Ideology. Zimmerli, Walther Christoph.

ECOFEMINISM

Exploring Our Environmental Connections. Schuster, Eleanor A (ed) and Brown, Carolyn L (ed).

Free Spirits: Feminist Philosophers on Culture. Mehuron, Kate (ed) and Percesepe, Gary (ed).

Postmodern Environmental Ethics. Oelschlaeger, Max (ed).

An Ordinal Context for Ecofeminism. Kruse, Felicia.

Is There an Ecofeminism-Deep Ecology "Debate"?. Slicer, Deborah.

Women-Animals-Machines: A Grammar for a Wittgensteinian Ecofeminism. Lee-Lampshire, Wendy.

ECOLOGY

"Can Liberal Democracy Help us to Survive the Environmental Crisis?" in Ecology, Technology, and Culture, Zweers, Wim (ed). Jacobs, Frans.

"Can Liberal Democracy Survive the Environmental Crisis? Sustainability, Liberal Neutrality, and Overlapping Consensus" in Ecology, Technology, and Culture, Zweers, Wim (ed). Achterberg, Wouter.

"First the Jew but also the Greek: In Search of the Roots of the Environmental Problem in Western Civilization" in Ecology, Technology, and Culture, Zweers, Wim (ed). Boersema, Jan J.

"In Search of an Ecological Culture: Environmental Philosophy in the 1990's" in Ecology, Technology, and Culture, Zweers, Wim (ed). Zweers, Wim.

"Liberal Neutrality and the Justification of Environmental Conservation" in Ecology, Technology, and Culture, Zweers, Wim (ed). Musschenga, Bert.

"Models and Modernism: Between Anxiety and Hubris" in Ecology, Technology, and Culture, Zweers, Wim (ed). Kwa, Chung Lin.

"Radicalism or Historical Consciousness: On Breaks and Continuity in the Discussion of Basic Attitudes" in Ecology, Technology, and Culture, Zweers, Wim (ed). Zweers, Wim.

"Science: A Modest Hope" in Ecology, Technology, and Culture, Zweers, Wim (ed). Schroevers, Pieter.

"Technology and the Ecological Crisis" in Ecology, Technology, and Culture, Zweers, Wim (ed). van der Wal, Koo.

"The Limits of Science" in Ecology, Technology, and Culture, Zweers, Wim (ed). Tennekes, Henk.

"The Mouse in the Cat's Claws: A Framework for a Hermeneutics of Nature" in Ecology, Technology, and Culture, Zweers, Wim (ed). Kockelkoren, Petran.

"The Technological Universe" in Ecology, Technology, and Culture, Zweers, Wim (ed). Tijmes, Pieter.

"Theological-Anthropological Reflections on the Environmental Issue" in Ecology, Technology, and Culture, Zweers, Wim (ed). van Dijk, Paul.

"Towards a Hermeneutics of Nature: On the Necessity of Enduring Distance" in Ecology, Technology, and Culture, Zweers, Wim (ed). Coolen, Maarten.

Angewandte Ethik im Spannungsfeld von Ökologie und Ökonomie. Neumaier, Otto (ed).

Chaosmosis: An Ethico-Aesthetic Paradigm. Guattari, Félix, Bains, Paul (trans) and Pefanis, Julian (trans).

Die Technik und die Schwäche: Ökologie nach Nietzsche, Heidegger und dem "schwachen" Denken. Schönherr, Hans-Martin.

Ecological Enlightenment: Essays on the Politics of the Risk Society. Beck, Ulrich and Ritter, Mark A (trans).

Ecology, Technology, and Culture. Zweers, Wim (ed) and Boersema, Jan J (ed).

Ecology. Merchant, Carolyn (ed).

Humanity, Environment, and God. Spurway, Neil.

Inhabiting the Earth: Heidegger, Environmental Ethics, and the Metaphysics of Nature. Foltz, Bruce V.

Philosophical Arguments. Taylor, Charles.

Philosophy and the Natural Environment. Attfield, Robin (ed) and Belsey, Andrew (ed).

Plenishment in the Earth. Ross, Stephen David.

Postmodern Environmental Ethics. Oelschlaeger, Max (ed).

The Greening of Ethics: From Human Chauvinism to Deep-Green Theory. Sylvan, Richard and Bennett, David.

The Metamorphosis of the Given: Toward an Ecology of Consciousness. Schwarzkopf, Friedemann-Eckart.

The Nationalism Reader. Dahbour, Omar (ed) and Ishay, Micheline R (ed).

The New Ecological Order. Ferry, Luc and Volk, Carol (trans).

A Philosophical Approach to the Ecological Crisis. Chethimattam, J B.

A Vedantic Response to the Ecological Crisis. Manninezhath, Thomas.

Against Methodological Solipsism: The Ecological Approach. Rowlands, Mark.

Beyond the Material and the Mechanical: Occam's Razor Is a Double-Edged Blade. Ulanowicz, Robert E.

Can There Be a "Humanistic" Ecology? A Debate Between Hegel and Heidegger on the Meaning of Ecological Thinking. Berthold-Bond, Daniel.

Das Gemeinsame von Ökologie und Bioethik. Halaczek, Bernard.

Eco-Ethics—The Key to Survival. Skolimowski, Henryk.

Ecological Explanation and the Population-Growth Thesis. Shrader-Frechette, Kristin.

Ecological Literacy for Moral Virtue: Orr on (Moral) education for postmodern sustainability. Prakash, Madhu Suri.

Ecology and Eschatology: Science and Theological Modeling. Klink, William H.

Ecology and Globalism: Response to Professor E H Cadwallader's Paper 'Ultimate Meaning and Reality in the Battle Between Globalism and Anti-Globalism. Kristiansen, Roald E.

Education, the Interpretive Agenda of Science, and the Obligation of Scientists to Promote this Agenda. Fox, Warwick.

Emergence of New Fields in Ecology: The Case of Life History Studies. Korfiatis, K J and Stamou, G P.

Environmental Destruction and the Public Sphere: On Habermas's Discursive Model and Political Ecology. Alario, Margarita.

Envisioning Ecological Sustainability: The Need and a Method. Carroll, John E.

Etretien Avec Michel Salomon. Landry, Cécile.

Failures of Explanation in Darwinian Ecological Anthropology: Part I. Vayda, Andrew P.

Feminism and Ecology: Realism and Rhetoric in the Discourses of Nature. Soper, Kate.

Finding Our Feminist Ways in Natural Philosophy and Religious Thought. Gatens-Robinson, Eugenie.

Freedom and the Environment: Reply to Critics. Anderson, Terry L and Leal, Donald R.

Hannah Arendt and Ecological Politics. Whiteside, Kerry H.

Healing the Ills of Unemployment, Societal Breakdown, and Ecological Degradation: Gandhi's Vision for a Sustainable Society. Gruzalski, Bart.

Human-Centered or Ecocentric Environmental Ethics?. Howie, John.

Individuality, Human and Natural Communities, and the Foundations of Ethics. DiZerega, Gus.

Is Daoism 'Green'?. Cooper, David E.

La Construction du Champ de l'Éthique en Environnement. Beauchamp, André.

Myth, Nature, and the Bureaucratic Experience. McGinnis, Michael V.

Ökologische Blindheit: Die Aporie der herrschenden Wirtschaftswissenschaft. Reheis, Fritz.

Real Patterns and the Ontological Foundations of Microeconomics. Ross, Don.

Skepsis und Praxis: Zur Grundlegung der praktischen Philosophie. Sitter-Liver, Beat.

The Crisis of Ecology: A Phenomenological Perspective. Howarth, J M.

Ultimate Reality and Meaning in the Conflict Between Globalism and Anti-Globalism. Cadwallader, Eva H.

Value Theory and Ecology in Environmental Ethics: A Comparison of Rolston and Niebuhr. Scoville, Judith N.

Value, Metaphysics, and Anthropocentrism. Morito, Bruce.

Why Psychology Is Mute about the Environmental Crisis. Kidner, David W.

ECONOMETRICS

"Economic Models and Their Applications" in Idealization VI: Idealization in Economics, Hamminga, Bert (ed). Janssen, Maarten C W.

"On Correspondence between Economic Theories" in Idealization VI: Idealization in Economics, Hamminga, Bert (ed). Nowakowa, Izabella and Nowak, Leszek.

"The Theory of Reduction in Econometrics" in Idealization VI: Idealization in Economics, Hamminga, Bert (ed). Cook, Steven and Hendry, David.

"Three Generalization Processes for Economic Models" in Idealization VI: Idealization in Economics, Hamminga, Bert (ed). Walliser, Bernard.

Idealization VI: Idealization in Economics. Hamminga, Bert (ed) and De Marchi, Neil B (ed).

ECONOMICS

"An Economic Theory of Natural Resources" in Ecology, Technology, and Culture, Zweers, Wim (ed). van der Straaten, Jan.

"Economic Models and Their Applications" in Idealization VI: Idealization in Economics, Hamminga, Bert (ed). Janssen, Maarten C W.

"Exchange Versus Influence: A Case of Idealization" in Idealization VI: Idealization in Economics, Hamminga, Bert (ed). Balzer, Wolfgang.

"Idealization and Empirical Adequacy in Economic Theory" in Idealization VI: Idealization in Economics, Hamminga, Bert (ed). García de la Sienra, Adolfo.

"Idealization and the Defence of Economics" in Idealization VI: Idealization in Economics, Hamminga, Bert (ed). Hamminga, Bert and De Marchi, Neil.

"Idealization and Transformation" in Idealization VI: Idealization in Economics, Hamminga, Bert (ed). Jorland, Gérard.

"Idealizations and Theory Development in Economics" in Idealization VI: Idealization in Economics, Hamminga, Bert (ed). Birner, Jack.

EDUCATION

"Coherence Lost": Education, Modernity, and Fractured Meaning. Gunter, Pete A Y.

"Common Sense as an Ingredient of the Self and the Community" in *Identity, Culture, and Education*, Smeyers, Paul (ed). Koch, Lutz.

"Como un Mirar que se Pregunta por Horizontes que Otro Traza" in *Temas Actuales de Filosofía, Palacios, María Julia* (ed). Carbajal, Sergio I.

"Education for European Citizenship: A Philosophical Critique" in *Identity, Culture, and Education*, Smeyers, Paul (ed). Williams, Kevin.

"Education for Freedom versus Socio-Technical Control..." in *Philosophy of Technology in Spanish Speaking Countries*, Mitcham, Carl (ed). Molina, Leopoldo.

"Education: Conserving Tradition" in *Introducing Applied Ethics*, Almond, Brenda (ed). Haldane, John.

"Enseñanga, Políticae Institución" in *Temas Actuales de Filosofía, Palacios, María Julia* (ed). Insua, Elda and Sardisco, Ana M.

"Evolving Conceptions of Self through Community or The Development and Overcoming of Prejudice" in *Identity, Culture, and Education*, Smeyers, Paul (ed). Noel, Jana.

"General Education, Cultural Diversity, and Identity" in *Identity, Culture, and Education*, Smeyers, Paul (ed). Meijer, Wilna.

"Having a Voice and Getting a Hearing" in *Identity, Culture, and Education*, Smeyers, Paul (ed). White, Patricia.

"Hermeneutic Listening: An Approach to Understanding in Multicultural Conversations" in *Identity, Culture, and Education*, Smeyers, Paul (ed). Kimball, Stephanie and Garrison, Jim.

"How Much 'Heimat' does a Human Being Need?" in *Identity, Culture, and Education*, Smeyers, Paul (ed). Levering, Bas.

"Identity, Education, and the Experience of Language" in *Identity, Culture, and Education*, Smeyers, Paul (ed). Larrosa, Jorge.

"Individualization, Singularization, and E-Ducation (Between Indifference and Responsibility)" in *Identity, Culture, and Education*, Smeyers, Paul (ed). Masschelein, Jan.

"Intellectuals and their Education" in *Identity, Culture, and Education*, Smeyers, Paul (ed). Weijers, Ido.

"Is Community Necessary: Quasi-Philosophical Ruminations" in *Identity, Culture, and Education*, Smeyers, Paul (ed). MacMillan, C J B.

"Late Capitalism and Postmodernism: Educational Problems and Possibilities" in *Identity, Culture, and Education*, Smeyers, Paul (ed). Brosio, Richard.

"Liberalism, Nationality, and Education" in *Identity, Culture, and Education*, Smeyers, Paul (ed). White, John.

"Los Seminarios en la Enseñanza de la Filosofía" in *Temas Actuales de Filosofía, Palacios, María Julia* (ed). Rabossi, Eduardo A, Stigol, Nora and González, María Cristina.

"Medical Education: Knowledge and Know-How" in *Ethics and the Professions*, Chadwick, Ruth (ed). Fulford, K W M.

"Misreading Dewey: A Thesis and Exemplar" in *Identity, Culture, and Education*, Smeyers, Paul (ed). Stone, Lynda.

"Moral Identity and Education in a Multicultural Society" in *Identity, Culture, and Education*, Smeyers, Paul (ed). Spiecker, Ben and Steutel, Jan.

"National Identity as Educational Problem: Towards a National System of Education in Belarus" in *Identity, Culture, and Education*, Smeyers, Paul (ed). Buiko, Tatyana.

"New Humanistic Curriculum: A Response to Education's Betrayal of the Need for Meaning" in *Identity, Culture, and Education*, Smeyers, Paul (ed). Aviram, Aharon.

"Philosophizing about Education in a Postmodern Society" in *Identity, Culture, and Education*, Smeyers, Paul (ed). Losito, William F.

"Relational Persons and Ethical Paradigms" in *Identity, Culture, and Education*, Smeyers, Paul (ed). Wells, Douglas.

"Rorty's Dewey: Pragmatism, Education, and the Public Sphere" in *Identity, Culture, and Education*, Smeyers, Paul (ed). Neiman, Alven M.

"Schools, Identity, and the Conception of the Good" in *Identity, Culture, and Education*, Smeyers, Paul (ed). de Ruyter, Doret J and Miedema, Siebren.

"Some Moral Contradictions in the Conservative Educational Reform Discourse in the US" in *Identity, Culture, and Education*, Smeyers, Paul (ed). Ray, G Thomas.

"Staying Alive": Intellectual and Spiritual Sustenance on the Journey for Critical Foundations Scholars-Teachers. Brosio, Richard A.

"Staying Dumb? Feminist Research and Pedagogy With/in the Postmodern" in *After Postmodernism, Simons, Herbert W* (ed). Lather, Patti.

"The Autonomous Chooser and 'Reforms' in Education" in *Identity, Culture, and Education*, Smeyers, Paul (ed). Marshall, James.

"The Moral Justification of Systematic Education Reform in the United States" in *Identity, Culture, and Education*, Smeyers, Paul (ed). Bull, Barry.

"The Quest for Identity" in *Identity, Culture, and Education*, Smeyers, Paul (ed). Tamir, Yael.

"Un Modelo Formal para la Enseñanza Filosófica en la Escuela Secundaria y un Ejemplo de Aplicacion del Mismo" in *Temas Actuales de Filosofía, Palacios, María Julia* (ed). Obiols, Guillermo A.

"Ways of Thinking and Being: Explorations in Ontologies" in *Identity, Culture, and Education*, Smeyers, Paul (ed). O'Loughlin, Marjorie.

"Zarathustra/Zarathustra as Educator" in *Nietzsche: A Critical Reader, Sedgwick, Peter R* (ed). Schacht, Richard.

(Re)searching Dewey for Feminist Imaginaries: Linguistic Continuity, Discourse and Gossip. Leach, Mary.

Blindness of Modern Science. Uus, Undo.

Design & Systems: General Applications of Methodology. Collen, Arne (ed) and Gasparski, Wojciech W (ed).

Die Sehnsucht nach dem Schönen, Guten und Wahren oder platonische Reminiszenzen in Rousseaus Menschenbild und Erziehungslehre. Burkert-Wepfer, Esther.

European Philosophy and the American Academy. Smith, Barry (ed).

For Education: Towards Critical Educational Inquiry. Carr, Wilfred.

Further Selections from the Prison Notebooks. Gramsci, Antonio and Boothman, Derek (ed & trans).

Identity, Culture, and Education. Smeyers, Paul (ed).

In Search of a Calling: The College's Role in Shaping Identity. Buford, Thomas O.

Intimacy and Spectacle: Liberal Theory as Political Education. Esquith, Stephen L.

John Dewey: An Intellectual Portrait. Hook, Sidney.

Multiculturalism: A Critical Reader. Goldberg, David Theo.

Natural Theories of Mind: Evolution, Development, and Simulation of Everyday Mindreading. Whiten, Andrew (ed).

Openness in Research: The Tension Between Self and Other. Maso, I (& other eds).

Philosophen im "Dritten Reich": Studie zu Hochschul- und Philosophiebetrieb im faschistischen Deutschland. Leske, Monika.

Positives Paradox: Entwurf einer neostrukturalistischen Religionspädagogik. Beuscher, Bernd.

Pragmatist Aesthetics: Living Beauty, Rethinking Art. Shusterman, Richard.

Reason in the Balance: The Case Against Naturalism in Science, Law, and Education. Johnson, Phillip E.

Rhetorical Mosaic for a Kaleidoscope of Sound: Poetry as a Road to Understanding the Prose Voice. Britt, John F.

Rousseau (Past Masters). Wokler, Robert.

The Educational Imperative: A Defence of Socratic and Aesthetic Learning. Abbs, Peter.

The Future of the Humanities: Teaching Art, Religion, Philosophy, Literature, and History (New Edition). Kaufmann, Walter Arnold.

The Genius of Language: Observations for Teachers. Steiner, Rudolf.

The Greening of Ethics: From Human Chauvinism to Deep-Green Theory. Sylvan, Richard and Bennett, David.

The Spirit of the Waldorf School. Steiner, Rudolf, Lathe, Robert F (trans) and Whittaker, Nancy Parsons (trans).

Understanding Images: Finding Meaning in Digital Imagery. Marchese, Francio T (ed).

University-Business Partnerships: An Assessment. Bowie, Norman E.

Utopie II ou Vers une Société des Personnes. Adam, E.

Values, Work, Education: The Meanings of Work. Natale, Samuel M (ed) and Rothschild, Brian M (ed).

Work, Education, and Leadership: Essays in the Philosophy of Education. Howard, V A and Scheffler, Israel.

A Critical Review of Allen Pearson, *The Teacher: Theory and Practice in Teacher Education*. O'Leary, Paul.

A Educaçao e a Autonomia do Profesor: Caminhos para a Emancipaçao. Oaigen, Edson Roberto.

A Lonerganian Critique of the Pragmatic Method of Education. Gilbert, Christopher.

A Model of Intervention for Improving Moral Reasoning: An Experiment in the Basque Country. Medrano, Concepción.

A Review of Samuel Scolnicov's *Plato's Metaphysics of Education*. Sichel, Betty A.

Aesthetic Music Education Revisited: Discourses of Exclusion and Oppression. Koza, Julia Eklund.

Aesthetics and Art Education. Delaruelle, Jacques.

Am I Wicked?. Gendin, Sidney.

An Epistemological Foundation for Thinking: A Deweyian Approach. Holder Jr, John J.

An Experiential Component in Teaching Philosophy of Science. Nissani, Moti.

An Impolite View of the Graduate Record Examination: Some Practical Reasons Why Most Studies Find This Test Has Low Predictive Validity. Oldfield, Kenneth.

Analyse d'Une Expérience de Pédagogie. Tozzi, Michel.

Apprendre et Enseigner la Philosophie. Coutel, Charles.

Arguments and Arguers. Gilbert, Michael A.

Art as Research, Research as Art. Phillips, D C.

Arts and Knowledge: A Discussion. Bresler, Liora and Davidson, Judith.

Attitudes of Students and Accounting Practitioners Concerning the Ethical Acceptability of Earnings Management. Fischer, Marilyn and Rosenzweig, Kenneth.

Authenticity: From Philosophic Concept to Literary Character. Leahy, Robert.

Autonomy and Commitment: Compatible Ideals. Aviram, Aharon.

Autonomy or Heteronomy? Levinas's Challenge to Modernism and Postmodernism. Child, Mark (& others).

Autopsie de l'approche par Compétences. Gendron, Diane.

Begging the Question: Is Critical Thinking Biased?. Alston, Kal.

Bodies of Knowledge. McCarty, Luise Prior.

Brandon Shaw, Neil Perry, and the Perils of Education. Calhoun, Laura.

Business Students' Ethical Perceptions of Retail Situations: A Microcultural Comparison. Burns, David J, Fawcett, Jeffrey K and Lanasa, John.

Can Virtue Be Bought?. Pullman, Daryl.

Case Study in the Ethics of Teaching Philosophy. Pence, Gregory.

Catching a Glimpse of the Palace of Reason: The Education of Moral Emotions. Roebben, Bert.

Ciencia, tecnología y sociedad. García Moriyón, Félix.

Citizens and Soldiers: Teaching Just War Theory. Whitman, Jeffrey P, Haight, Catherine and Tipton, Paul.

EDUCATION

Common Values and Value Conflicts in Environmental Education. Döbler, Matthias.

Competing Conceptions of the Educated Public. Wain, Kenneth.

Consideraciones Metodológicas Acerca de la Investigación en el Ambito de la Filosofía de la Educación (en Europa). Barrio Maestre, José María.

Content and Criticism: The Aims of Schooling. Hare, William.

Contribuiçao par as Discussoes ao Projeto de Implantaçao do Curso de Pedagogia na Fac de Ciências da Univ Estadual Paulista "Júlio de Mesquita Filho". Ghiraldelli Júnior, Paulo.

Creating Spaces for Reconstructing Knowledge in Feminist Pedagogy. Thompson, Audrey and Gitlin, Andrew.

Criterion-referenced Assessment and the Development of Knowledge and Understanding. Davis, Andrew.

Croce e Gentile nell'Epistolario di Fausto Nicolini. Rascaglia, Maria.

Current Educational Reform: "Shape-shifting" or Genuine Improvement in the Quality of Teaching and Learning?. Merchant, Betty.

De Disciplinering van het Hoger Onderwijs: Aantekeningen bij de Massa-Universiteit. Baggen, Peter and Maat, Harro.

De l'Avenir de la Philosophie au Cégep ou de la Résolution Possible d'un Paradoxe. Cohen-Bacrie, Pierre.

Department Reorganization and Faculty Status in Educational Administration. Norton, M Scott.

Design and Evaluation of a Programme to Promote Prosocial-Altruistic Behaviour in the School. Etxebarria, I (& others).

Developing Philosophical Literacy. Miller, Thomas G.

Dewey on Causation in Social Science. Stone, George C.

Dewey's Metaphysics and the Self. Cunningham, Craig A.

Dialogue Needs a Point and Purpose. Robinson, Viviane M J.

Discussing Divorce in Introductory Ethics. Gould, James B.

Do Senior Secondary Students Possess the Moral Maturity to Negotiate Class Rules?. Langford, Peter E, Lovegrove, Hildegard and Lovegrove, Malcolm N.

Durkheim and Moral Education for Children: A Recently Discovered Lecture. Pickering, W S F.

École et Pédagogie. Walsh, John-Pierre.

Ecological Literacy for Moral Virtue: Orr on (Moral) education for postmodern sustainability. Prakash, Madhu Suri.

Educating the Democratic Heart: Pluralism, Traditions and the Humanities. Alexander, Thomas M.

Educating the Moral Artist: Dramatic Rehearsal in Moral Education. Fesmire, Steven A.

Education and Democracy: Confronting the Postmodernist Challenge. Carr, Wilfred.

Education and the Archeology of Consciousness: Freire and Hegel. Torres, Carlos Alberto.

Education and the Educational Project I: The Atmosphere of Post-modernism. Smeyers, Paul.

Education and Work: Reflections on the Moral and Spiritual Dimensions of the Job Crisis. Books, Sue.

Education for Democracy. Tiles, J E.

Education, the Interpretive Agenda of Science, and the Obligation of Scientists to Promote this Agenda. Fox, Warwick.

Education, Virtue and Democracy in the Work of Emile Durkheim. Cladis, Mark S.

Enseigner et Apprendre chez Descartes. Gajano, Alberto.

Enseigner l'Éthique par l'Histoire. Marcil, Louise.

Enseigner l'Éthique Selon le Paradigme du "Moi Moralement Relié". Mullet, Sheila Mason.

Entretien avec Michel Morin. Bombardier, Denise.

Entretien avec Michel Tozzi. Cohen-Bacrie, Pierre.

Escola Pública: Trabalho Produtivo ou Improdutivo. Pizzi, Laura Cristina V.

Estudio introductorio a "De la educación moral del Hombre": Texto inédito en castellano de Claude Adrien Helvétius. Diego, Carmen Verde.

Ethics and Accounting Doctoral Education. Loeb, Stephen E.

Ethics in Undergraduate Accounting Education: An Empirical Study. Sisaye, Seleshi and Lackman, Conway.

Ethics of Business Students: Some Marketing Perspectives. Lane, J C.

Éthique et Enseignement. Carrier, André.

Évoluer en Enseignant la Philosophie. Chbat, Joseph.

Fallacious Reasoning. Goldstein, Laurence.

Feminism as Critique in Philosophy of Music Education. Lamb, Roberta.

Feminist Theory and the Displaced Music Curriculum: Beyond the "Add and Stir" Projects. Morton, Charlene.

Fichtes Einfluss auf seine Studenten en Berlin zum Beginn der Befreiungskriege. Fuchs, Erich.

Fichtes Erziehungslehre als erste logische Begründung der Vorbilderziehung. Kumamoto, Yasuhiro.

Filosofia e Pedagógica da Libertaçao Latinoamericana. Moreno Villa, Mariano.

Formation Fondamentale et Culture Humaniste dans les Études Collégiales. Talbot, Pierre.

Gender Bias in Critical Thinking: Continuing the Dialogue. Wheary, Jennifer and Ennis, Robert H.

Gender, Musical Meaning, and Education. Green, Lucy.

Getting Serious About the Questions of Democracy. Hostetler, Karl.

Getting the Whole Picture: The View From Here. Gould, Elizabeth S.

Grading. Weis, Gregory F.

Hearing New Music: Pedagogy from a Phenomenological Perspective. Lochhead, Judy.

Hermeneutic Issues in Qualitative Research. Ferrara, Lawrence.

Hirsch on Education and National Culture: A Critique. Grant, Robert.

HIV +/AIDS Related Bioethical Issues in Japan. Hoshino, Kazusama.

How Religion Impedes Moral Development. Clark, Brad.

If We Took Dewey's Aesthetics Seriously, How Would the Arts Be Taught?. Jackson, Philip W.

Il Programma e il Metodo dell'Insegnamento della Logica nei Seminari Maggiori. Olejnik, Roman M.

Il Sogno, la Fanciullezza e l'Arte nel Pensiero di Giovanni Gentile. Stella, Vittorio.

Influence and Development: Two Basic Paradigms of Education. Oelkers, Jürgen.

Instructions du 2 Septembre 1925. de Monzie, Anatole.

Interdisziplinarität und Wissensentwicklung: Wie Phänomene in interdisziplinärer Kommunikation wissenschaftlich bedeutsam werden. Lüdtke, Karlheinz.

Internationalizing the Business Ethics Curriculum: A Survey. Cowton, Christopher J and Dunfee, Thomas W.

Introducing Philosophy Through Concepts of Ultimate Reality and Meaning. Krettek, Tom.

Is Critical Thinking Biased? Clarifications and Implications. Bailin, Sharon.

Is Reading Plato Educational? Thoughts on Education, Prompted by a Reading of Plato's Meno. Weingartner, Rudolph H.

Is There a Queer Pedagogy? Or Stop Reading Straight. Britzman, Deborah P.

Is There Room for God in Education?. Auxier, Randall E.

James H Fetzer, Philosophy and Cognitive Science; Jay L Garfield (ed), Foundations of Cognitive Science: The Essential Readings. Causey, Robert L.

Jeremy Bentham y la educación jurídica en la Universidad de Salamanca durante el siglo XIX. Pérez Luño, Antonio-Enrique.

John Dewey: An "Old-Fashioned" Reformer. Boisvert, Raymond D.

Journal Writing in an Introductory Philosophy Course. Garns, Rudy.

Justice and the Case for School Vouchers. Spoerl, Joseph.

Knowledge and Truth in Religious Education. Carr, David.

Knowledge, Practice, Truth. Standish, Paul.

L'approche par Compétences (Entretien avec Michel Jean). Landry, Cécile.

L'enseignement de la Philosophie Devant l'approche-Programme et l'éducation Interculturelle. Turgeon, Marc.

L'Enseignement de la Philosophie et la Citoyenneté. Baillargeon, Jean.

La Formation Générale au Niveau Collégial. Sa Qualité Passe d'Abord par la Consolidation de la Formation de Base. Lévesque, Gérard.

La Formation Intellectualle. Després, Pierre.

La Philosophie: Une Présence Essentielle. Cohen-Bacrie, Pierre (& others).

La Réforme et le Rôle de la Philosophie dans la Formation Collégiale. Martineau, Jean-François.

Le savoir et sa transmission: De la volonté d'éduquer au désir de transmettre. Cornaz, Laurent.

Les comités d'éthique comme mécanisme de contrôle des activités de recherche: Le point de vue de la philosophie. Gendron, Pierre.

Liberal Philosophy of Education: A Paradigm Under Strain. Jonathan, Ruth.

Liberal Universalism and Multicultural Curricular Reform in the Social Studies: Issues to Consider. Malone, Patricia and Benson, Norman.

Limits to the Effectiveness of Accounting Ethics Education. Shaub, Michael K.

Líneas de Pensamiento Positivista y Antipositista en América. Romero Baró, José María.

Living (Not Learning) Ethics. Solberg, Joseph, Strong, Kelly C and McGuire Jr, Charles.

Locke's Educational Theories (and) the Woman Question. Lembcke, V L.

MacIntyre and the Idea of an Educated Public. Wain, Kenneth.

Make My Case: Ethics Teaching and Case Presentations. Kuczewski, Mark (& others).

Michel Foucault: Governmentality and Liberal Education. Marshall, James.

Moral Literacy. Cooper, David D.

Moral/Political Education in the People's Republic of China: Learning Through Role Models. Reed, Gay Garland.

Multicultural Education and Feminist Ethics. Friedman, Marilyn.

Musical Values Revisited: A Reply to Forest Hansen's "Values in Music Education". Elliott, David J.

Narratives of Volunteering. Paolicchi, Piero.

Nationale Erziehung und sittliche Bestimmung. Soller, Alois K.

O Método Paulo Freire: A Inter-Relaçao da Teoria do Conhecimento com a Teoria da Sociedade. Marinho Sampaio, Tânia Maria.

Oasis of Peace: A Community of Moral Education in Israel. Feuerverger, Grace.

On Teaching as a Profession. Götz, Ignacio L.

On the Language of Consciousness: Propositional Discourse and Moral Sensibility. Ray, G Thomas.

On the Unavoidability of Power in Child-rearing: Is the Language of Rights Educationally Appropriate?. Smeyers, Paul.

On Translating Locke, Berkeley, and Hume into English. Bennett, Jonathan.

On What We May Hope: Rorty on Dewey and Foucault. Marshall, James D.

Outlines for Success. Burnor, Richard.

Pedagogia Pelo e Para o Trabalho: Açao Disciplinadora da Burguesia e a Resistência dos trabalhadores. Rodrigues, Alcione.

Pedagogy, Philosophy, and African-American Students. Martinez, Roy.

Philosophie et technique autour de l'université. Iwano, Takuji.

Philosophy Discussions with Less B.S.. Thomason, Neil.

Philosophy of Music Education in a Slightly New Key. Hansen, Forest.

Philosophy, Education and the Quality of Life. Prasad, Rajendra.

Plato's School, the Academy. Baltes, Matthias.

Popular Art and Education. Shusterman, Richard.

Postmodernism and the Education of the Whole Person. Standish, Paul.

Pour un Enseignement Relativiste de l'Éthique. Martineau, Jean-François.

Power and Knowledge: Some Educational Implications of Foucault's Epistemology. Nuyen, A T.

EGOISM

"Egoism in Epistemology" in *Socializing Epistemology: The Social Dimensions of Knowledge, Schmitt, Frederick (ed)*. Foley, Richard.

Das Anfangsproblem bei Karl Leonhard Reinhold. Bondeli, Martin.

Egoism and Altruism in Ethics: Dispensing with Spurious Generality. Van Der Steen, Wim J.

Egoist Theory and America's Individualist Anarchists: A Dilemma of Praxis. Brooks, Frank.

Zur Konsistenz des soziobiologischen Begriffs "egoistisches Gen". Erbrich, Paul.

EGOTISM

El Utilitarismo de Hume. Costa, Margarita.

EGYPTIAN

"Ancient Temple Architecture" in *Homage to Pythagoras, Bamford, Christopher (ed)*. Lawlor, Robert.

The Sciences in Greco-Roman Society (Apeiron 27-4). Barnes, Timothy D.

Hegel and Ancient Egypt: History and Beocming. Lampert, Jay.

EIGHTEENTH CENTURY

see Modern

EINSTEIN

Quantum Mechanics: Historical Contingency and the Copenhagen Hegemony. Cushing, James T.

Cohen on Einstein on Simultaneity. Walton, Gertrud.

Is Algebraic Lorentz-Covariant Quantum Field Theory Stochastic Einstein Local?. Muller, F A and Butterfield, Jeremy.

Science and Art: Heuristic and Aesthetic Dimensions of Scientific Discovery. Wartofsky, Marx.

Spacetime Theory as Physical Geometry. Disalle, Robert.

Time in Philosophy and in Physics: From Kant and Einstein to Gödel. Wang, Hao.

EISELE, C

"Peirce at the Intersection of Mathematics and Philosophy" in *Peirce and Contemporary Thought: Philosophical Inquiries, Ketner, Kenneth Laine (ed)*. Pycior, Helena M.

EISNER, E

Art as Research, Research as Art. Phillips, D C.

Arts and Knowledge: A Discussion. Bresler, Liora and Davidson, Judith.

ELDERLY

Concepts and Cases in Nursing Ethics. Yeo, Michael (& others).

A Buddhist Reflection on the Task of Elders. Nakasone, Ronald Y.

Are the Elderly Really Machiavellian? A Reinterpretation of an Unexpected Finding. Mudrack, Peter E.

Are There Limits to Solidarity with the Elderly?. Ter Meulen, Ruud.

CQ Sources/Bibliography. Buehler, David A.

Dementia in Our Midst: The Moral Community. Post, Stephen G.

Ethics in an Aging Society. Holstein, Martha.

Should People Do unto Others as They Would Not Want Done unto Themselves:. Harrison, Christine (& others).

The Ethical Challenge of Providing Healthcare for the Elderly. Thomasma, David C.

The Ethics of Decision Making for the Critically Ill Elderly. Iris, Madelyn Anne.

The Limits of Proxy Decision Making: Undertreatment. Gillick, Muriel R and Fried, Terri.

User Rights and the Frail Aged. Gibson, Diane.

ELDRIDGE, R

Without Guilt, What's the Matter? How Tragedy Matters: Response to Richard Eldridge's "How Can Tragedy Matter For Us?". Haines, Victor Yelverton.

ELEATIC

HE MANTIKE TECHNE: *Statesman* 260e1 and 290c4-6. Brickhouse, Thomas C and Smith, Nicholas D.

Persuasion in an Empty Ontology: The Eleatic Synthesis of Philosophy, Poetry, and Rhetoric. Poster, Carol.

The Eleatic Stranger's Socratic Condemnation of Socrates. Howland, Jacob A.

ELECTIONS

Politics and Manipulation. Mills, Claudia.

ELECTRICITY

"Die Entwicklung der Elektrotechnik.." in *Naturauffassungen in Philosophie, Wissenschaft, Technik: Band III, Schäfer, Lothar (ed)*. Dienel, Hans-Liudger.

Discovering Natural Kinds Through Inter-Theoretic Prototypes. Rothbart, Daniel.

ELECTROMAGNETISM

Alternativen der Wissenschaftsgeschichte. Haney, Frank.

ELECTRONICS

Fear, Truth, Writing: From Paper Village to Electronic Community. Brown, Alison Leigh.

The Electronic Agora: Using a Mainframe Computer In Introductory Courses. Domino, Brian.

ELEMENT

"Why the Elements Imitate the Heavens: *Metaphysics* IX.8 1050b28-34" in *The Crossroads of Norm and Nature, Sim, May (ed)*. Lang, Helen S.

Beiträge zu Aristoteles' Naturphilosophie. Seidl, Horst.

A Representational Reconstruction of Carnap's Quasianalysis. Mormann, Thomas.

La presencia virtual de los elementos en la combinación química según Santo Tomás de Aquino. Sacchi, Mario Enrique.

ELEMENTARY

Elementary Descent Recursion and Proof Theory. Friedman, Harvey and Sheard, Michael.

Elementary Functions and Loop Programs. Damnjanovic, Zlatan.

On Countable Fractions from an Elementary Class. Ash, C J.

ELIADE, M

The Religious Creativity of Modern Humanity: Some Observations on Eliade's Unfinished Thought. Rennie, B S.

ELIMINATION

Elimination des Quantificateurs dans des Paires de Corps. Leloup, G.

ELIMINATIVISM

"Connectionism and Eliminativism" in *Connectionism: Debates on Psychological Explanation, Macdonald, Cynthia (ed)*. Macdonald, Cynthia.

Introducción a la Filosofía de las Emociones. Rodríguez, Mariano.

ELITISM

"Intellectuals and their Education" in *Identity, Culture, and Education, Smeyers, Paul (ed)*. Weijers, Ido.

Heidegger's Concept of *Volk*. Sikka, Sonya.

How Far Was Plato Concerned to Rebut the Claims of Cyrus the Great and Pisistratus to the Title of *Statesman*?. Tanner, R G.

In Defense of "Elitism". Shusterman, Ronald.

Review Essay: Robert B Pippin's *Modernism as a Philosophical Problem*. Chytry, Josef.

ELLACURIA, I

Filosofía e Historia Según I. Ellacuría. Martínez, José A.

ELLIOTT, C

Commentary on "Puppetmasters and Personality Disorders". Gillett, Grant.

ELLUL, J

Middle Level Theory in Ellul's Thought: Where Theory and Practice Meet. Wennemann, Daryl J.

EMANCIPATION

A Educaçao e a Autonomia do Professor: Caminhos para a Emancipaçao. Oaigen, Edson Roberto.

Emancipation, Resistance and Cosmopolitanism. Del Aguila, Rafael.

J Habermas: La crítica de la razón interesada. Carrascoso, Arce.

Notes on the "Lack of Foundation" in Theodor W Adorno Philosophy (in Portuguese). De Paiva Durate, Rodrigo Antonio.

EMBEDDING

Embedding Lattices into the *wtt*-Degrees Below 0'. Downey, Rod and Haught, Christine.

Reflections on "Difficult" Embeddings. Prijatelj, Andreja.

EMBRYO

"Embryo Experimentation: Public Policy in a Pluralist Society" in *Medicine and Moral Reasoning, Fulford, K W M (ed)*. Hare, Richard M.

"Moral Uncertainty and Human Embryo Experimentation" in *Medicine and Moral Reasoning, Fulford, K W M (ed)*. Oddie, Graham.

Medicine and Moral Reasoning. Fulford, K W M (ed), Gillett, Grant (ed) and Soskice, Janet Martin (ed).

At the Vortex of Controversy: Developing Guidelines for Human Embryo Research. Green, Ronald M.

Awe Diminished. Campbell, Courtney S.

Before I Was an Embryo, I Was a Pre-Embryo: Or Was I?. Jones, D Gareth and Telfer, Barbara.

Cloning without Prior Approval: A Response to Recent Disclosures of Noncompliance. Macklin, Ruth.

Human Identity and the Primitive Streak. Lockwood, Michael.

Report on Human Cloning through Embryo Splitting: An Amber Light. NABER Report.

Response to the HFEA Consultation Document on Research and Fertility Treatment. Sutton, Agneta.

Splitting Embryos on the Slippery Slope: Ethics and Public Policy. Macklin, Ruth.

Symbolic Issues in Embryo Research. Robertson, John A.

The Puzzle of Profound Respect. Callahan, Daniel.

The Status of the Embryo from a Christian Point of View. Folscheid, Dominique.

Totipotency and the Value of Embryonic Cells. Tindale, Christopher W.

EMBRYOLOGY

"Der Diskurs über Gen-Tätigkeit" in *Mythos Wertfreiheit?, Apel, Karl-Otto (ed)*. Keller, Evelyn Fox.

EMERGENCE

"Dynamik, Emergenz und Mathematik: Über Kontinua und Diskontinua" in *Schelling und die Selbstorganisation, Heuser-Kessler, Marie-Luise (ed)*. Eisenhardt, Peter.

Repräsentation und Identität. Vogeley, Kai.

EMERSON

Philosophical Passages: Wittgenstein, Emerson, Austin, Derrida. Cavell, Stanley.

The Site of Our Lives: The Self and the Subject from Emerson to Foucault. Hans, James S.

Practical Expressions of Natural Piety: Emerson and Dewey. Wilson, Eddy.

EMOTION

see also Feeling, Sentiment

"Dispassion and the Ethical Life" in *Emotions in Asian Thought, Marks, Joel (ed)*. Marks, Joel.

"Ecstasy and Epistemology" in *Emotions in Asian Thought, Marks, Joel (ed)*. Rouner, Leroy S.

"Emotion in Bengali Religious Thought: Substance and Metaphor" in *Emotions in Asian Thought, Marks, Joel (ed)*. McDaniel, June.

"Emotions in Western Thought: Some Background for a Comparative Dialogue" in *Emotions in Asian Thought, Marks, Joel (ed)*. Marks, Joel.

"Empfindung, Gefühl und Emotion: Zur Analyse von Bewertungen" in *Mythos Wertfreiheit?, Apel, Karl Otto (ed)*. Dorschel, Andreas.

EMOTION

"Ethics of Emotion: Some Indian Reflections" in *Emotions in Asian Thought, Marks, Joel (ed)*. Bilimoria, Purusottama.

"Need, Nurturance, and the Emotions on a Pacific Atoll" in *Emotions in Asian Thought, Marks, Joel (ed)*. Lutz, Catherine.

"Nietzsche and Zen Master Hakuin on the Roles of Emotion and Passion" in *Emotions in Asian Thought, Marks, Joel (ed)*. Parkes, Graham R.

"Qing (Emotions) in Pre-Buddhist Chinese Thought" in *Emotions in Asian Thought, Marks, Joel (ed)*. Hansen, Chad.

"The Concept of Emotion Revisited: A Critical Synthesis of Western and Confucian Thought" in *Emotions in Asian Thought, Marks, Joel (ed)*. Bockover, Mary I.

"The Cross-Cultural Comparison of Emotion" in *Emotions in Asian Thought, Marks, Joel (ed)*. Solomon, Robert C.

"Theoretical Perspectives on Emotions in Early Buddhism" in *Emotions in Asian Thought, Marks, Joel (ed)*. De Silva, Padmasiri.

Das Problem des Einen und Vielen in Platons "Philebos". Löhr, Gebbhard.

Emotion and Embodiment: Fragile Ontology. Mazis, Glen.

Emotions in Asian Thought. Marks, Joel (ed) and Ames, Roger T (ed).

L'Éducation Sentimentale. Robinson, Jenefer.

Music, Value, and the Passions. Ridley, Aaron.

Practical Guilt: Moral Dilemmas, Emotions, and Social Norms. Greenspan, P S.

Sehnsucht—Affekt und Antrieb: Begriff, Struktur und praktische Bedeutung. Häfner, Ansgar.

The Philosophy of the Visual Arts. Alperson, Philip (ed).

A Note on the Intentionality of Fear. Horowitz, Amir.

Being Dismissed: The Politics of Emotional Expression. Campbell, Sue.

Catching a Glimpse of the Palace of Reason: The Education of Moral Emotions. Roebben, Bert.

Commentary on "Normal Grief: Good or Bad? Health or Disease?". Wise, Thomas N.

Commentary on Sherman's "The Role of Emotions in Aristotelian Virtue". Dustin, Christopher A.

Emotion and Memory: The Second Cognitive Revolution. Harré, Rom.

Emotion as a Natural Kind: Towards a Computational Foundation for Emotion Theory. Charland, Louis C.

Emotional Responses to Fiction: Reply to Radford. Neill, Alex.

Emotions in Music (A Postscript). Goldman, Alan.

Emotions, Reason, and Character. Wilson, James Q.

Emphatic Speech Style With Special Focus on the Prosodic Signalling of Heightened Emotive Involvement in Conversation. Selting, Margret.

Estetica e politica in Rousseau: Il sentimento come movente di critica al modello sociale del "Bourgeois". Pallavidini, Renato.

Fear and Belief. Neill, Alex.

Feeling One's Emotions and Knowing Onself. Roberts, Robert C.

Gossip, Emotions, and Morality (in Hebrew). Ben-Ze'ev, Aaron.

Group Membership, Social Rules, and Power: A Social-Psychological Perspective on Emotional Communication. Gallois, Cynthia.

Hanslick on Hearing Beauty. Shibles, Warren A.

Humanistic Art. Shibles, Warren.

Informed Consent to Amnestics, or: What Sound Does a Tree Make in the Forest When It Falls on Your Head?. Mehlman, Maxwell J (& others).

Introducción a la Filosofía de las Emociones. Rodríguez, Mariano.

Las Emociones ante la Ficción. Bejarano, Teresa.

Metaphor and Monophony in the 20th-Century Psychology of Emotions. Gergen, Kenneth.

Musical Sympathies: The Experience of Expressive Music. Ridley, Aaron.

Nature's Moods. Howarth, J M.

Normal Grief: Good or Bad? Health or Disease?. Kopelman, Loretta M.

Rationele passies en intellectuele deugden: Een conceptuele analyse. Steutel, Jan and Spiecker, Ben.

Reconciling Emotions with Western Personhood. Fischer, Agneta H and Jansz, Jeroen.

Rejoinder: If Grief Is Not Bad, Is It Good?. Kopelman, Loretta M.

Science, Ethics, and Moral Status. Miller, Harlan B.

Sentiment and Sentimentality in Practical Ethics. Feinberg, Joel.

Some Notes on Emotion, "East and West". Solomon, Robert C.

Startle. Robinson, Jenefer M.

Still Hopeful: Reply to Karl and Robinson. Levinson, Jerrold.

Sympathy, Simulation, and the Impartial Spectator. Gordon, Robert M.

The Cognitive-Emotive Theory of Desire. Shibles, Warren A.

The Form of Feeling. Yob, Iris M.

The Heart of the Kantian Moral Agent. Nuyen, A T.

The Neuropsychology of Communication: Spontaneous and Symbolic Aspects. Buck, Ross.

The Paradox of Emotion and Fiction. Yanal, Robert J.

The Role of Emotions in Aristotelian Virtue. Sherman, Nancy.

The Significance of Emotions. Helm, Bennett W.

The Social Construction of Aesthetic Response. Eaton, Marcia Muelder.

The Status of Expressive Content. Kemp, Gary.

The Structure of Awareness: Contemporary Applications of William James' Forgotten Concept of "The Fringe". Galin, David.

The 'Passions of the Soul': Descartes' Shadow on Theories of the Emotions. Gorevan, Patrick.

Toward a Pragmatics of Emotive Communication. Caffi, Claudia and Janney, Richard W.

Toward a Thick Theory of Moral Agency. Manning, Rita C.

Tre teorie sulle emozione: cognitiva, fenomenologica e comportamentistica (seconda parte). Malo, Antonio.

EMPATHY

"Edith Stein, Theodor Lipps und die Einfühlungsproblematik" in *Studien zur Philosophie von Edith Stein, Fetz, Reto Luzius (ed)*. Fidalgo, António.

Cuatro conceptos para un pensamiento no ilustrado (analogía, otredad, empatía y epimeleia). Llano, Carlos.

Empathy and Universalizability. Deigh, John.

Empathy, Mind, and Morals. Goldman, Alvin.

EMPEDOCLES

Critical Note: Empedocles and his Interpreters. Mansfeld, Jaap.

Empedocles and his Interpreters: The Four-Element Doxography. Kingsley, Peter.

EMPIRE

Poder Político e Imperio en Dante Alighieri. Torres, Fernando.

EMPIRICAL

Denken im Modell: Theorie und Erfahrung im Paradigma eines pragmatischen Modellbegriffs. Wernecke, Jörg.

Elementos para una crítica del positivismo científico. Romero Baró, José.

Inconmensuralbilidad Empírica: Un Enfoque Macrológico. Moya, Eugenio.

La Interpretación de Kant de Fernando Montero Moliner. Arenas Llopis, Luis.

Los dos significados de *falsabilidad*. Popper, Karl R.

EMPIRICISM

see also Logic Empiricism, Pragmatism, Radical Empiricism

"Carnap's Principle of Tolerance, Empiricism, and Conventionalism" in *Reading Putnam, Clark, Peter (ed)*. Ricketts, Thomas.

"Empirical Justification" in *Life, World and Meaning, Roux, A P J (ed)*. Malherbe, Jeanette.

"Idealization and Empirical Adequacy in Economic Theory" in *Idealization VI: Idealization in Economics, Hamminga, Bert (ed)*. García de la Sienra, Adolfo.

"John Locke and the Polish Enlightenment" in *Locke's Philosophy, Rogers, G A J (ed)*. Rosicka, Janina.

"On the Assumption That Our Concepts 'Structure the Material of Our Experience'" in *Philosophy, Mathematics and Modern Physics, Rudolph, Enno (ed)*. Mühlhölzer, Felix.

"Reflexiones Sobre la Propuesta Epistém. Formulada por Quine en 'Dos Dogmas d. Empirismo'" in *Temas Actuales de Filosofía, Palacios, María Julia (ed)*. Saravia Sacchelli, Hugo O.

"Six Queries about Idealization in an Empirical Context" in *Idealization VI: Idealization in Economics, Hamminga, Bert (ed)*. Hoover, Kevin D.

"Sobre los Avatares Ontológicos del Empirismo y Trascendentalismo Jurídicos" in *Temas Actuales de Filosofía, Palacios, María Julia (ed)*. Ferraro, Agustín.

A Philosophical Testament. Grene, Marjorie.

Carnap and the Vienna Circle: Empiricism and Logical Syntax. Cirera, Ramon.

From a Biological Point of View. Sober, Elliott.

Idealization VI: Idealization in Economics. Hamminga, Bert (ed) and De Marchi, Neil B (ed).

Il Linguaggio Dell'Oggettività: Saggio su Meinong. Brigati, Roberto.

Reason, Regulation, and Realism: Toward a Regulatory Systems Theory of Reason and Evolutionary Epistemology. Hooker, C A.

The Context of Explanation. Bunzl, Martin.

The Metamorphosis of the Given: Toward an Ecology of Consciousness. Schwarzkopf, Friedemann-Eckart.

The Philosophy of Social Science: An Introduction. Hollis, Martin.

Understanding Social Science: A Philosophical Introduction to the Social Sciences. Trigg, Roger.

A Content-Independent Explanation of Science's Effectiveness. Quillian, M Ross.

A Hint at Peirce's Empirical Evidence for Tychism. Dearmont, David.

An Empirical Philosophy of Economic Theory. Backhouse, Roger E.

An Empirical Reply to Empiricism: Protective Measurement Opens the Door for Quantum Realism. Dickson, Michael.

An Erotetic Approach to Explanation by Specification. Kuipers, Theo A F and Wisniewski, Andrzej.

An Evaluation of Karl Popper's Criticism of Sociology of Knowledge. Mondal, Sunil Baran.

Are Some *Propositions* Empirically Necessary?. Peterson, Philip.

Artisanal Knowledge and Experimental Natural Philosophers: The British Response to J Fraunhofer and the Bavarian Usurpation of Their Optical Empire. Jackson, Myles W.

Background Independence and the Causation of Observations. Hudson, Robert G.

Cartwright on Probabilistic Causality: Types, Tokens, and Capacities. Eells, Ellery.

Constructive Empiricism. Leeds, Stephen.

Contentless Consciousness and Information-Processing Theories of Mind. Sullivan, Philip R.

Cosmology: An Empirical Science?. Anderson, John.

Del Empirismo al Humanismo: Clave de Lectura y Crítica de la Obra de P K Feyerabend. Tula Molina, Fernando.

Dennett's Conceptual Reform. Ross, Don.

Der Begriff der psychischen Krankheit aus der Sicht der Fichteschen Transzendentalphilosophie. Hoff, Paul.

Emergent Properties. O'Connor, Timothy.

Emotion as a Natural Kind: Towards a Computational Foundation for Emotion Theory. Charland, Louis C.

Empirical vs Rational Order in the History of Philosophy. Butler, Clark W.

Empiricism and the Epistemology of Instruments. Wilson, Fred.

Epistemic Competence and Contextualist Epistemology: Why Contextualism Is Not Just the Poor Person's Coherentism. Henderson, David K.

EPISTEMOLOGY

EPISTEMOLOGY

EPISTEMOLOGY

L'Istanza Cosmologica tra Scienzatecnica e Filosofia. Mazzarella, Eugenio.

L'optimisation est-elle un critère de rationalité individuelle?. Mongin, Philippe.

La Aproximación a la Verdad en Peirce. Herrera Ibáñez, Alejandro.

La Consideración de las ideas Innatas en Descartes y la Problemática del Conocimiento de lo Físico. García del Campo, Juan Pedro.

La Disputa Averroismo-Tomismo en el op "De Unitate Intellectus Contra Averroistas", de Tomás de Aquino. Barrio Maestre, José María.

La falsedad en el pensamiento y en el discurso: Comentarios al *Sofista* 259b al 265e. Sala, J F A.

La filosofía trascendental bajo la óptica de la teoría evolucionista del conocimiento. Hoyos Jaramillo, Luis Eduardo.

La Función de la Intuición Ockhamista. López Vázquez, J Ramón.

La Funzione Terapeutica del Mito: Un Problema di Psicologia Analitica. Procesi, Lidia.

La genesi della coscienza reale nella "Grundlage der gesamten Wissenschaftslehre" di Fichte. Metz, Wilhelm.

La liquidación de la Filosofía: Notas sobre la disputa entre R Rorty y J Habermas. Gómez Ibáñez, Vicente.

La Reivindicación de la Sabiduría Poética en G B Vico y A Machado. Ramírez Luque, Isabel.

La Teoría del Conocimiento de Francisco Sánchez y el Verum/Factum de Vico. Faur, José.

La Unidad Interna del Saber en G Kalinowski. Ballester, Manuel.

Langer, Language, and Art. Gill, Jerry H.

Language and the Etymological Turn of Thought. Schalow, Frank.

Language and World: Some Classical Indian Approaches *vis-a-vis* Analytical Western Approaches. Gokhale, Pradeep P.

Language as Empowerment. Kelkar, Ashok R.

Las Dificultades de la Noción de Acción. Crespo, Enrique Bocardo.

Las Emociones y la Naturalización de la Intencionalidad. Moya, Carlos J.

Lawlikeness. Lange, Marc.

Le caractère social du langage et de la pensée. Burri, Alex.

Le Paradigme Esthétique. Roumanes, Jacques Bernard.

Le Problème de L'analogie dans la *Critique de la Raison Pure*. Feron, Olivier.

Le Référentiel selon Ferdinand Gonseth, et ses aspects philosophiques. Thom, René.

Lectura Epistemológica de la Teoría Unificada de la Cognición en Allen Newell. Monserrat, Javier.

Leibniz and the Logic of Life. Wilson, Catherine.

Leibniz Konzeption der "characteristica universalis" zwischen 1677 und 1690. Schnelder, Martin.

Leibniz on the Principle of Continuity. Duchesneau, François.

Les paradoxes de la tortue (dans les récits de la pensée). Canty, Daniel.

Lewis on Causal Dependence. McDermott, Michael.

Limitative Dialektik: Überlegungen im Anschluss an die Methodenreflexion in Fichtes *Grundlage* 1794/95. Janke, Wolfgang.

Lion Talk. Luckhardt, C Grant.

Literary into Cultural Studies. Easthope, Antony.

Lo sviluppo della riduzione fenomenologica: dalla *Filosofia dell'aritmetica* a *Ideen*. Costa, Vincenzo.

Locke and the Preface Paradox. Odegard, Douglas.

Locke on Knowledge and Trifling Propositions. de Almeida, Claudio.

Locke on Reason, Probable Reasoning, and Opinion. Owen, David.

Locke's Arguments for the Resemblance Thesis Revisited. Heyd, Thomas.

Locke's Challenge to Innate Practical Principles Revisited. O'Connor, Peg.

Locke's Own. Mautner, Thomas.

Logic and Modal Intuitions. Tidman, Paul.

Logique et métaphysique dans le système critique: L'exemple de la causalité. Longuenesse, Béatrice.

Los dos tipos de asentimiento del escéptico y el problema de la posibilidad del conocimiento. Frede, Michael.

Los límites de una teoría del progreso. Molina, Francisco.

Lovejoy, Hartshorne, and Progress in Philosophy. Dombrowski, Daniel.

Maimons Versuch über Transzendentalphilosophie: Eine interpretierende Skizze der Grundgedanken. Krämer, Felix.

Making Comparisons. Katz, Bernard D.

Making Sense: The Work of Eugene Gendlin. Levin, David Michael.

Making Strange What Had Appeared Familiar. Elliott, Terri.

Marxism on Dialectical and Logical Contradiction. Goldstick, D.

Marxismo y Hermenéutica. Torrico, Vitaliano.

Más Problemas con el Realismo. Muñoz Veiga, Jacobo.

Materialism and Supervenience. Jack, Andrew.

Max Black on the Identity of Indiscernibles. Cross, Charles B.

Meaning Holism and Intentional Content. Silverberg, Arnold.

Meaning, Realism, and the Rejection of Analyticity. Liz, Manuel.

Meaning, Use and Truth. Horwich, Paul.

Meanings and their Nature. Schiffer, Stephen.

Melancholie—Sizze zur epistemologischen Deutung eines Topos. Krämer, Sybille.

Mental Causation for Dualists. Pietroski, Paul M.

Mental Images and their Ontology. Gozzano, Simone.

Mentalese Syntax: Between a Rock and Two Hard Places. Pessin, Andrew.

Merleau-Ponty's View of Creativity and Its Philosophical Consequences. Hamrick, William S.

Methodological Reflections on Two Kripkean Strategies. Ramachandran, Murali.

Methodology, Epistemology and Conventions: Popper's Bad Start. Preston, John.

Michael Faraday's Concept of Ultimate Reality and Meaning. Utke, Allen R.

Might-counterfactuals and Gratuitous Differences. Heller, Mark.

Modal Realism and Inductive Scepticism. Thomas, Holly.

Moderne, Modernisierung, Modernität. Makropoulos, Michael.

Moore's Paradox and Self-Knowledge. Shoemaker, Sydney.

Moore's Paradox, Asserting and Skepticism. Doran, Katheryn.

Murder on Moriah: A Paradoxical Representation. Dooley, Mark.

Must a Hermeneutical Psychoanalysis Exclude Science?. O'Grady, Paul, Rigby, Paul and Van Den Hengel, John.

Nāgārjuna and Deconstruction. Mabbett, Ian W.

Names, Natural Kind Terms, and Rigid Designation. Macbeth, Danielle.

Narrow Content: A Defence. Silverberg, Arnold.

Natural Deduction in Connectionist Systems. Bechtel, William.

Naturalism and Intentionality. Horgan, Terence.

Naturalized Epistemology and Epistemic Evaluation. Hookway, Christopher.

Naturalized Epistemology and 'First Philosophy'. Siegel, Harvey.

Neuere Interpretationen der Phänomenologie Husserls in Italien (1986-1992). Sinigaglia, Corrado.

Neuhousers Fichte-Deutung. Rohs, Peter.

Nietzsche-Deleuze: The Aesthetics and Ethics of Chance. Olkowski, Dorothea.

No Longer, Not Yet: Reading History Grammatically. Erickson, Stephen A.

No Rush to Judgment. Nelson, Jack and Nelson, Lynn Hankinson.

Noção de Estilo em Granger e Narrativa Histórica. Cardoso Jr, Hélio Rebello.

Nonconceptual Content: Kinds, Rationales and Relations. Peacocke, Christopher.

Not Much Trouble for Ultra-Externalism. McCulloch, Gregory.

Nota sobre las críticas al realismo semántico: el caso de los enunciados indecidibles. Legris, Javier.

Nota sullo scetticismo. Urbani Ulivi, L.

Notes on the "Lack of Foundation" in Theodor W Adorno Philosophy (in Portuguese). De Paiva Durate, Rodrigo Antonio.

Nothing Like Experience. Mellor, David Hugh.

Nozickian Tracking and Naturalization. Duran, Jane.

Obeying a Rule: Wittgenstein's Stress on Obedience in Sections 198-202 of the *Philosophical Investigations*. Susse, Jennifer.

Object-Dependent and Property-Dependent Contents. Bruns, Manfred and Soldati, Gianfranco.

Objective Knowledge and Psychologism. Chaudhury, Mahasweta.

Objectivism and the Evolutionary Value of Colour Vision. Dedrick, Don.

Objectivity and Interpretation. Stecker, Robert.

Objectivity in History. Bevir, Mark.

Observing Re-Entries. Luhmann, Niklas.

Of Epicycles and Elegance. Adams, Frederick.

Oltre l'Interpretazione: Ermeneutica e Nichilismo. D'Agostini, Franca.

On an Argument about Reference to Future Individuals. Oppy, Graham.

On an Argument Against Omniscience. Simmons, Keith.

On Conditionals. Edgington, Dorothy.

On Division in Plato's *Statesman*. Fattal, Michel.

On Fractal Thought: Derrida, Hegel, and Chaos Science. McRobert, Laurie.

On Subjective Truth. Barbiero, Daniel.

On the Alleged Neutrality of Technology: A Study in Dewey's *Experience and Nature*. Blacker, David.

On the Designated Student and Related Induction Paradoxes. Jacquette, Dale.

On the Evolution of Intentionality as Seen from the Intentional Stance. Foss, Jeffrey.

On the Explanation, the Justification, and the Interpretation of Action. Myers, Robert H.

On the Incompatability of Enduring and Perduring Entities. Merricks, Trenton.

On the Transfer of Necessity. O'Connor, Timothy.

On Western Rationality and Its Alleged Relation to Aristotle. Evangeliou, Christos.

Ontological Connivance (in French). Van Eynde, L.

Ontological Dependence. Fine, Kit.

Ontology, Epistemic Access, and the Sublime. Godlovitch, Stan.

Oración III Pronunciada el 18 de Octubre de 1701. Vico, G and Gómez, Francisco Navarro (trans).

Order Out of Messes: Akeel Bilgrami's *Belief and Meaning*. Travis, Charles.

Otto Neurath's Idealist Inheritance: *The Social and Economic Thought of Wilhelm Neurath*. Uebel, Thomas E.

Paksata in Navya-Nyaya. Rai, A K.

Paradoxes of Pure Curiosity. Tennant, Neil.

Paternalism and Rights. Brennan, Samantha.

Peacocke's Argument Against the Autonomy of Nonconceptual Representational Content. Bermúdez, José Luis.

Peirce's First Rule of Reason and the Bad Faith of Rortian Post-Philosophy. Migotti, Mark.

Penser l'Autonomie, Penser la Connaissance: l'Évolution d'un Centre de Recherche en Épistémologie. Lavallée, Alain.

Perceiving Particulars and Recollecting the Forms in the *Phaedo*. Osborne, Catherine.

Performativi in Jean-Louis Gardies: verità, verificabilità, vero-funzionalità. Rossetti, Andrea.

Personal Identity, 'R-Relatedness' and the Empty Question Argument. Chappell, Tim.

Perspectival Thoughts and Psychological Generalizations. Corazza, Eros.

Perspectives in Virtue Epistemology: A Response to Dancy and BonJour. Sosa, Ernest.

Phänomenologische Erschliessung der russischen Philosophie. Plotnikov, Nikolaj.

Philosophical Craftsmanship. Hansson, Sven Ove.

Philosophical Disappointment: Introduction. Light, Steve.

Philosophical Republicanism and Monarchism—and Republican and Monarchical Philosophy—in Kant and Hegel. Redding, Paul.

EPISTEMOLOGY

The "Tacit" and the "Personal": An Aesthetical Approach to the Nature of Knowledge. Ujlaki, Gabriella.

The 3D/4D Controversy and Non-Present Objects. Markosian, Ned.

The Allure of Connectionism Reexamined. McLaughlin, B P and Warfield, Ted A.

The Attack on Methodological Solipsism. Duran, Jane.

The Autonomy of Pure Reason in Kant. Troim, David.

The Body as "Sign and Tool" in Hegel's *Encyclopaedia*. Dodd, James.

The Churchlands' Eliminative Materialism. Hunter, Geoffrey.

The Common Need for Classical Epistemological Foundations: Against a Feminist Alternative. Thalos, Mariam.

The Content of Kant's Logical Functions of Judgment. Greenberg, Robert S.

The Creativity of Intellect: From Ontology to Meaning—The Transmutation of the Sensible and Intelligible Worlds in Kant's Critical Work. Gulick, Walter B.

The Deontological Conception of Epistemic Justification and Doxastic Voluntarism. Kim, Kihyeon.

The Dialectics of Scepticism: Comments on Gallois. Michael, Michaelis.

The End of Analysis. Bencivenga, Ermanno.

The Epistemic Conception of Vagueness. Wright, Crispin.

The Epistemological Incenization and the Problem of Time in the Conception of Recentivism. Banka, Jozef.

The Epistemology of the Uruguayan Philosopher Carlos Vaz Ferreira. Romero Baró, José María.

The Extent of Kierkegaard's Skepticism. Anderson, Thomas C.

The Failure of Expected-Utility Theory as a Theory of Reason. Hampton, Jean.

The First Person Perspective. Eilan, Naomi.

The Gettier Problem and the Parable of the Ten Coins. Levi, Don S.

The Governance of Big Science: On the Wisdom of Solomon. Fuller, Steve.

The Heirs of German Idealism (in Portuguese). Musse, Ricardo.

The Hermeneutic Medium. Bineham, Jeffery L.

The Hermeneutics of Formal Analytics: The Case of Tibetan Philosophical Criticism. Liberman, Kenneth.

The Idea of Eternal Life in Modern Cosmology: Its Ultimate Reality and Metaethical Meaning. Nesteruk, Alexei V.

The Incompatibility of Intuition and Constitution in Husserl's *The Idea of Phenomenology* (1907). Ryan, William F.

The Irony of Contingency and Solidarity. Cleveland, Timothy.

The Justification of Belief. Burke, T E.

The Language-of-Thought Relation and Its Implications. Schiffer, Stephen.

The Limits of Pragmatic Realism. Forster, Paul D.

The Logical Status of 'Exists'. Stirton, William R.

The Many Persons Problem. Chihara, Charles S.

The Market for Feminist Epistemology. Baber, Harriet.

The Metaphoric Origins of Objectivity, Subjectivity, and Consciousness in the Direct Perception of Reality. Mulaik, Stanley A.

The Mishap at Reichenbach Fall: Singular vs General Causation. Hitchcock, Christopher Read.

The Mutual Deteination of Wants and Benefits. Broome, John.

The Ontological Ground of the Alethic Modality. Shalkowski, Scott A.

The Palinode of the Analyst Rationality and Self in the *Euthyphro*. Glouberman, Mark.

The Philosophical Context of Collingwood's Re-Enactment Theory. van der Dussen, Jan.

The Place of Reason in Locke's *Essay*. Hall, Roland.

The Postmodern Spirit and The Status of God. Nikkel, David H.

The Presidential Address: Why there is really No Such Thing as the Theory of Motivation. Dancy, Jonathan.

The Problem of Generality (on Alan Millar's *Reasons and Experience*). Roddy, Bernard.

The Problem of Objectivity. Davidson, Donald.

The Problem of Philosophy. McGinn, Colin.

The Problem of Self-Identification. O'Brien, Lucy F.

The Provisional World: Existenthood, Causal Efficiency, and Sri Harsa. Ram-Prasad, C.

The Pseudo-Problem of Scepticism. Sweetman, B.

The Rationality of Human Communication: On the Relationship Between Consensual, Strategic, and Systems Rationality. Apel, Karl Otto.

The Refutation by Analogous Ectoqualia. Endicott, Ronald P.

The Relativity of Scientific Views of Reality. Puligandla, Ramakrishna.

The Representation of Causation and Hume's Two Definitions of 'Cause'. Garrett, Don.

The Revisionist Difference Principle. Williams, Andrew D.

The Rhetoric of Feminist Writings. Nuyen, A T.

The Role of Dissociation in Redeeming Knowledge Claims: Nineteenth-Century Shakers' Epistemological Resistance to Decline. Olson, Kathryn M.

The Role of Imagination in Integrative Knowledge: A Polanyian View. Shin, Un-Chol.

The Scope of Observation. Menuge, Angus.

The Shadow of the Other (Subject): Intersubjectivity and Feminist Theory. Benjamin, Jessica.

The Shoals of Language: Michael Dummett: *The Seas of Language*. Rosen, Gideon.

The Social Dynamics of Disrespect: On the Location of Critical Theory Today. Honneth, Axel.

The Sphere of Critical Thinking in a Post-Epistemic World. Fuller, Steve.

The Structure of the Skeptical Argument. Brueckner, Anthony.

The Substance of Knowing Is History: Absolute Knowing and History in Hegel's *Phenomenology*. De Nys, Martin J.

The Threshold Model of Scientific Change and the Continuity of Scientific Knowledge. Kuokkanen, Martti and Tuomivaara, Timo.

The Turing Test and the Argument from Analogy for Other Minds. Waterman, Craig M.

The Unstatability of Kripkean Scepticisms. Read, Rupert.

The Untruth in Relativism. Dustin, Christopher A.

The Virgin Paradigm. Sawaf, Ayman.

The Virtues, Challenges and Implications of Connectionism. Stich, Stephen.

Theaetetan Epistemology as Platonic Epistemology. O'Leary-Hawthorne, Diane.

Theories of Masses and Problems of Constitution. Zimmerman, Dean.

Things in Themselves. Thompson, Manley.

Thinking in Neurons: Comments on Stephen Schiffer's "The Language-of-Thought Relation and Its Implications". Yagisawa, Takashi.

Thomas Reid on Free Agency. O'Connor, Timothy.

Thought and Language: On the Line of Demarcation between Animal and Human Abilities. Strauss, D F M.

Three-Concept Monte: Explanation, Implementation and Systematicity. Matthews, Robert J.

Time and Change. Scott, Michael.

Tomberlin's *Philosophical perspectives, 5, Philosophy of Religion, 1991*. Grim, Patrick.

Toward a Credible Agent-Causal Account of Free Will. Clarke, Randolph.

Toward a Relational Theory of Meaning. Cherwitz, Richard A and Darwin, Thomas J.

Towards a Critical Ethnomethodology. McHoul, Alec.

Towards an African (Yoruba) Perspective on Empirical Knowledge: A Critique of Hallen and Sodipo. Okè, Moses.

Towards an Anthropology of Epistemology. Maffie, James.

Trabajo e Interacción como Intereses Rectores del Conocimiento. López Molina, Antonio M.

Transcendentaal-Pragmatiek en Semantiek. Sas, Peter.

Transcendental Idealism and Phenomenalism. Frangiotti, Marco Antonio.

Tras la postmodernidad. Innerarity, Daniel.

Truth Is a Thing of This World. Review of *Michel Foucault's Force of Flight: Toward an Ethics for Thought* by James W Bernauer. Flynn, Thomas R.

Truth Wronged (on Crispin Wright, *Truth and Objectivity*). Rumfitt, Ian.

Truth, Assertion and Warrant. Teichmann, Roger.

Truth, Correspondence, and Success. Leeds, Stephen.

Truth, Knowledge, and Reality. Lafont, Cristina.

Truth, Permanence, and the Regulation of Belief. Miller, Alexander,

Trying the Impossible: Reply to Adams. Ludwig, Kirk A.

Trying, Desire, and Desiring to Try. Adams, Frederick.

Trying: You've Got to Believe. Adams, Frederick.

Two (Related) World Views. Zalta, Edward N.

Two Cheers for Process Reliabilism. Hill, Christopher.

Two Concepts of Entailment. Lance, Mark.

Über die Unhaltbarkeit und die Unentbehrlichkeit des Skeptizismus bei Fichte. Breazeale, Daniel.

Über die Zeit als das Mittelglied zwischen dem Intelligiblen und dem Sinnlichen. Rohs, Peter.

Un ensayo de recomposición del protagorismo. Solana Dueso, José.

Un Esbozo de Solución a un Enigma de Kripke. Orayen, Raúl.

Un Unico Heidegger? Note sul *Systematischer Index* di Eduard Landolt. Salmeri, Giovanni.

Una Cit de Algazel en la Filsofía del Sentido Commún de Llorens y Barba. Anglés Cervelló, Misericordia.

Una defensa del realismo semántico. Barrio, Eduardo.

Undercutting and the Ramsey Test for Conditionals. Fuhrmann, André and Levi, Isaac.

Understanding Rules. Nemirow, Laurence E.

Une ou deux indéterminations. Laugier, Sandra.

Une Théorie Darwinienne de la Connaissance. Dumouchel, Paul.

Universales Poéticos, Fantasía y Racionalidad. Sevilla, José M.

Unsettled Problems with Vague Truth. Mills, Andrew.

Upon Nothing. Scruton, Roger.

Urteilsenthaltung und Glück: Eine Verteidigung ethisch motivierter Skepsis. Engstler, Achim.

Utilitarianism and Future Mistakes: Another Look. Curran, Angela.

Vagueness: Welcome to the Quicksand. Tye, Michael.

Vattimo and Literary Understanding: An Essay on Recent Hermeneutics. Melaney, William D.

Veranlasste die Universalienlehre Ockham, die Prädikation zuletzt ohne ein intentionales Moment zu verstehen?. Liske, Michael-Thomas.

Verdad Acrítica y Verdad Crítica: Viquianismo Diádico. Sevilla Fernández, José M.

Vico'1994. Bermudo, José M.

Vital Signs: The *Place* of Memory in Psychoanalysis. Shepherdson, Charles.

Vorzukunft. Hrachovec, Herbert.

Walter Burleigh on the Conclusion that You Are an Ass. Nuchelmans, Gabriel.

Was ist Philosophie? Die Antwort der realistischen Phänomenologie. Seifert, Josef.

Weyl, Reichenbach and the Epistemology of Geometry. Ryckman, Thomas A.

What Am I Thinking About? John Duns Scotus and Peter Aureol on Intentional Objects. Perler, Dominik.

What Can We Learn From the Paradox of Knowability?. Cozzo, Cesare.

What Could a *Feminist* Science Be?. Gross, Barry R.

What Does the Sociology of Scientific Knowledge Explain?: Or, When Epistemological Chickens Come Home to Roost. Roth, Paul A.

What is a Physical Event?. Drai, Dalia.

What is a Thought?. Wittgenstein, Ludwig.

EPISTEMOLOGY

What is Consequentialism? A Proposal for a Systematic Classification (in Italian). Corradini, Antonella.

What is Quine's View of Truth?. Davidson, Donald.

What Mathematical Knowledge Could Be. Katz, Jerrold J.

What Mathematics Is About. Edidin, Aron.

What's an Epistemologist to Do?. Edidin, Aron.

When Silence May Mean Derision. Akman, Varol.

Why Is There Analytic Epistemology?. Vinci, Tom.

Why Not Solipsism?. Sober, Elliott.

Why Plato Never Had a Theory of Forms. Sayre, Kenneth.

Why the World Cannot be Vague. Sainsbury, Mark.

Why We Need Proper Function. Plantinga, Alvin.

William James: Rationality as a Pragmatic Choice. Goodman, Robert F.

Wittgenstein on Private Language and Private Mental Objects. Jacquette, Dale.

Wittgenstein on Private Language: Exorcising the Ghost from the Machine. Hitchcock, Christopher Read.

Wittgenstein's Elephant and Closet Tortoise. Grant, Brian.

Wittgenstein, transzendentale Gründzüge und transzendentale Einschränkungen. Sacks, Mark.

Wittgenstein, Truth-Functions and Generality. Scanlan, Michael.

Wong on Davidson. Potter, R Dennis.

Wozu noch Erste Philosophie? Über das Wechselverhältnis von Subjektivität und raumzeitlicher Einzelnheit. Koch, Anton Friedrich.

Wright's *Truth and Objectivity*. Horgan, Terence.

Zur Rekonstruktion der Philosophischen Hermeneutik. Krämer, Hans.

Zwischen Apriorismus und Empirismus im Kontext der Isomorphie zweier Apriorismen: Zur Rekonstruktion von Fichtes philosophischer Konzeption. Kiss, Endre.

'Cupiditas Veri Videnti': Pierre Villemandy's Dogmatic versus Cicero's Sceptical Interpretation of 'Man's Desire to Know'. Floridi, Luciano.

'Idea' in Locke's Works. Hall, Roland.

'World' is not a Count Noun. Van Fraassen, Bas.

EPOCH

De cómo "el ser" devino época. Muñoz Delgado, Mercedes.

EPOCHE

Urteilsenthaltung und Glück: Eine Verteidigung ethisch motivierter Skepsis. Engstler, Achim.

EPSILON CALCULUS

The Epsilon Calculus' Problematic. Slater, B H.

EQUALITY

see also Egalitarianism, Inequality

"Having a Voice and Getting a Hearing" in *Identity, Culture, and Education, Smeyers, Paul (ed)*. White, Patricia.

"La Vraie Face de la Démocratie": A Note. Keita, Lansana.

"The Conservation of Races" in *African Philosophy: Selected Readings, Mosley, Albert G (ed)*. Du Bois, William E B.

Democracy and Social Injustice: Law, Politics, and Philosophy. Simon, Thomas W.

Emmanuel Levinas: The Genealogy of Ethics. Llewelyn, John (ed).

Immanuel Kant zur Geschlechterdifferenz: Aufklärerische Vorurteilskritik und bürgerliche Geschlechtsvormundschaft. Jauch, Ursula Pia.

Moral Theory: A Contemporary Overview. DeMarco, Joseph P.

No Harm: Ethical Principles for a Free Market. Burke, T Patrick.

Private Consciences and Public Reasons. Greenawalt, Kent.

Rational Individualism: The Perennial Philosophy of Legal Interpretation. Simonds, Roger T.

The Bounds of Freedom: About the Eastern and Western Approaches to Freedom. Balaban, Oded and Erev, Anan.

The Ethics of Our Climate: Hermeneutics and Ethical Theory. O'Neill, William.

The Rational and the Moral Order: The Social Roots of Reason and Morality. Baier, Kurt.

A Reply in Defense of Impartiality. Baker, Judith.

Adam, Eve and the Controversial Rib: Gender, Technology, Conflict and Universalism. Rosen, Aviva.

Chance and Order in Our Inorganic Universe. Blandino, Giovanni.

Charles Hall: Exploitation, Commercial Society and Political Economy. Cunliffe, John.

Conceptualizing Democracy in an African Context. Fortman, Bas de Gaay.

Conflicting Principles or Completing Counterparts? J S Mill on Political Economy and the Equality of Women. Green, Michele.

Consensus and Democracy: An Anglo-French Conference on John Rawls. Audard, Catherine.

Constitutionalism and Democracy. Dworkin, Ronald.

Democracy as a Reflection of Principles of Universalism. Riser, John J.

Democratic Equality and the Problem of Persistent Minorities. Christiano, Thomas.

Die Ehe als Ort gleichberechtigter Lust. Heinrichs, Thomas.

Equal Opportunity or Equal Social Outcome. Fleurbaey, Marc.

Equality, Property, and the Problem of Partisanship: The Lockean Constitution as Mixed Regime. Myers, Peter C.

Fathers' Rights, Mothers' Wrongs? Reflections on Unwed Fathers' Rights and Sex Equality. Shanley, Mary L.

Feminism and Empowerment: A Critical Reading of Foucault. Deveaux, Monique.

Feminismo y política en dos encrucijadas históricas: La modernidad madura. Ciriza, Alejandra.

Gregory Vlastos on Justice and Equality. Kraut, Richard H.

Human Equality and Intra- as well as Intercultural Diversity. Holenstein, Elmar.

Impairment, Disadvantage, and Equality: A Reply to Anita Silvers. Wasserman, David.

Individuum und Gemeinschaft in der WL zwischen 1796 und 1800. Perrinjaquet, Alain.

Ist Fürsorglichkeit mit Gleichbehandlung unvereinbar?. Nagl-Docekal, Herta.

John Stuart Mill and Harriet Taylor on Women and Marriage. Mendus, Susan.

Justice and the Case for School Vouchers. Spoerl, Joseph.

Justice toward Groups: Political Not Juridical. Williams, Melissa S.

Kierkegaard on Authority and Leadership: Political Logic in Religious Thought. Khan, Abrahim H.

Let's Get the L Out: Or Why *Johnson Controls* Is Not an Unequivocal Victory for Women. Callahan, Joan.

Mill's Principle of Liberty. Chopra, Y N.

Mismeasuring "Unfair Advantage": A Response to Michael Davis. Dolinko, David.

Nagel on the Grounds for Compensation. Smilansky, Saul.

Natureza e História: Os Sentidos da Liberdade e da Igualdade. Ribeiro Silva, Idalice.

Normal Forms in Combinatory Logic. Johann, Patricia.

Phenomenology, Universalism and Dialogue. Brown, Charles S.

Privatization and Just Health Care. Buchanan, Allen.

Rationality, Oppression and Excellence: A Response to Professor Gewirth. Neiman, Alven Michael.

Recognizing Rationalizations Among Responses to Hunger. Dandekar, Natalie.

Reconciling Equality to Difference: Caring (F)or Justice For People With Disabilities. Silvers, Anita.

Replies to Comments. Gewirth, Alan.

Should Trees Have Managerial Standing? Toward Stakeholder Status for Non-Human Nature. Starik, Mark.

Taking Dependency Seriously: The Family and Medical Leave Act Considered in Light of the Social Organization of Dependency Work and Gender Equality. Kittay, Eva Feder.

The Common Faith of Liberalism. Hampton, Jean.

The Dishwasher's Child: Education and the End of Egalitarianism. White, John.

The End of Dignity: Some Reflections 'Currente Calamo' on a Social and Ethical Problem. Ferreira da Cunha, Paulo.

The Limits of Contractual Equality: A Reply to Jacques Bidet. Cohen, Gerald A.

The Market for Feminist Epistemology. Baber, Harriet.

The Moral Basis of Liberal Education. Gewirth, Alan.

The Place of Equality in Habermas' and Dworkin's Theories of Justice. Gosepath, Stefan.

The University, Dialogue and Universalism. Brown, Charles S.

Towards a More Adequate Rawlsian Theory of Social Justice. Peffer, Rodney G.

Überwindung des Anthropozentrismus durch Gleichheit alles Lebendigen?. Kohlmann, Ulrich.

Una visión de mujer en el pensamiento de John Stuart Mill. Gil Ruiz, Juana María.

Utilitarianism, Deontology, and the Priority of Right. Freeman, Samuel.

Weighting Health States and Strong Evaluation. Edgar, Andrew.

Wild Justice. Wallace, Gerry.

EQUATION

A Note on Definability in Equational Logic. Weaver, George.

Construction by Reduction. Ramsey, Jeffry L.

Equational Derivation vs Computation. Handley, W G and Wainer, S S.

EQUILIBRIUM

A Theory of Forward Induction in Finitely Repeated Games. Al-Najjar, Nabil.

Axiomatic Considerations of Nash Equilibrium. Kaneko, Mamoru.

Convention as Correlated Equilibrium. Vanderschraaf, Peter.

Endogenous Correlated Equilibria in Noncooperative Games. Vanderschraaf, Peter.

Methods of Ethics: Wide Reflective Equilibrium and a Kind of Consequentialism. Nielsen, Kai.

The Foundations of Quantum Mechanics and the Approach to Thermodynamic Equilibrium. Albert, David Z.

Uncertainty and the Role of the Pawn in Extended Deterrence. Kilgour, D M and Zagare, F C.

EQUITY

Equity and Nuclear Waste Disposal. Shrader-Frechette, Kristin.

Liberal Philosophy of Education: A Paradigm Under Strain. Jonathan, Ruth.

Rawls: Principio de diferencia y justicia intergeneracional. Amor, Claudio.

EQUIVALENCE

Constructing Strongly Equivalent Nonisomorphic Models for Unsuperstable Theories, Part A. Hyttinen, Tapani and Shelah, Saharon.

Diophantine Equivalence and Countable Rings. Shlapentokh, Alexandra.

Fine-Grained Opinion, Probability, and the Logic of Full Belief. Van Fraassen, Bas C.

In welchem Sinne ist die Identität eine Äquivalenzrelation?. Pardey, Ulrich.

Incompatible Empirically Equivalent Theories: A Structural Explication. Mormann, Thomas.

Some Theorems on Equivalential Tense Logic. Malinowski, Jacek.

The Topological Vaught's Conjecture and Minimal Counterexamples. Becker, Howard.

EQUIVOCATION

L'analogia dell'ente in Domenico di Fiandra. Riva, Franco.

ERASMUS

Christianity and the Classics: The Acceptance of a Heritage. Helleman, Wendy E (ed).

Erasmus, Utopia, and the Jesuits: Essays on the Outreach of Humanism. Olin, John C.

Ateismo, scetticismo e fideismo. Penelhum, Terence.

ERHARD, J

"Recht zur Aufklärung und Sozialrechte—Zu J B Erhards Theorie der Menschenrechte" in *Das geistige Erbe Europas, Buhr, Manfred (ed)*. Colbois, Sylvie and Perrinjaquet, Alain.

ERIGENA
Néant Divin et Théophanie: Erigène Disciple de Denys. Jeauneau, Édouard.

ERIUGENA
El Lenguaje Sobre Dios en Juan Escoto Eriúgena. Murillo, Ildefonso.

EROS
"Psique y Eros en el *Fedro*" in *Platón: Los Diálogos Tardíos, Lan, Conrado Eggers (ed)*. Gonzáles, Juliana.
Aporie del Simbolo: Saggio su Otto Weininger. Manfreda, Luigi Antonio.
Die Sehnsucht nach dem Schönen, Guten und Wahren oder platonische Reminiszenzen in Rousseaus Menschenbild und Erziehungslehre. Burkert-Wepfer, Esther.
Il.luminar-te el Rostre, Estimat: Ressons de la Caverna al Cicle Rondallístic de l'Animal-Nuvi. Temporal Oleart, Josep.
Ecstatic and Emanating, Providential and Unifying: A Study of the Psuedo-Dionysian and Plotinian Concepts of *Eros*. Buckley, Lisa Marie Esposito.
Giustizia e carità nella dottrina dei padri, II. Pizzorini, Reginaldo M.
Reflexiones Zubirianas Sobre la Fruición y el Amor. Marquínez Argote, Germán.

EROTETIC LOGIC
An Erotetic Approach to Explanation by Specification. Kuipers, Theo A F and Wisniewski, Andrzej.
Aristotelian Problems. Lennox, James G.

EROTICISM
"Out from Under: Beauvoir's Philosophy of the Erotic" in *Feminist Interpretations of Simone de Beauvoir, Simons, Margaret A (ed)*. Bergoffen, Debra B.
"The Erotic Self-Sufficiency of Socrates" in *The Socratic Movement, Vander Waerdt, Paul A (ed)*. O'Connor, David K.
A Model to Explore the Ethics of Erotic Stimuli in Print Advertising. Henthorne, Tony L and La Tour, Michael S.
Does Courtly Love Have an Arabic Background?. Mrozek-Dumanowska, Anna.
On Love and Awareness. Wautischer, Helmut.

ERROR
Filosofía como arte y experiencia de la vida. Innerarity, Daniel.
Inneity in Descartes' Regulae. Barbone, Steven.
The New Experimentalism, Topical Hypotheses, and Learning from Error. Mayo, Deborah G.

ESCHATOLOGY
"The End of History" as a Sociosophical Problem. Rachkov, P A.
Language, Metaphysics, and Death (Second Edition). Donnelly, John (ed).
Ecology and Eschatology: Science and Theological Modeling. Klink, William H.
Some Problems of the Origin of the Idea of Progressive Historical Time. Czarnecki, Zdzislaw J.
Toward a Process-Relational Christian Eschatology. Wheeler, David L.

ESOTERISM
Commémoration du Centenaire de la Mort de Jules Lagneau: "Jules Lagneau, Professeur: L'Obscure Clarté de la Philosophie". Poirier, Jean-Louis.
En la confluencia de filosofía y esoterismo: Jean D'Encausse y la doctrina del "despertar". Saura, Emilio.

ESSE
see Being

ESSENCE
see also Form
"Individual Essence in Ingarden's Ontology" in *Kunst und Ontologie, Galewicz, Wlodzimierz (ed)*. Swiderski, Edward M.
"Senses of Essence" in *Modality, Morality, and Belief, Sinnott-Armstrong, Walter (ed)*. Fine, Kit.
"Teeteto. 201e-208b. Totalità (Holon) e Insieme (Pan): Un Problema di non Facile Soluzione" in *Platón: Los Diálogos Tardíos, Lan, Conrado Eggers (ed)*. Mazzara, Giuseppe.
"Wittgenstein on Grammar and Essence" in *Wittgenstein and Contemporary Philosophy, Teghrarian, Souren (ed)*. Hunter, J F M.
Aristotle on Substance, Essence and Biological Kinds. Charles, David.
Definición del Hombre en Términos de lo que Quiere Ser. López Ruiz, Isabel.
Edith Stein-fenomologia e/ o metafisica. Molinaro, Aniceto.
Edith Stein: l'Apprendistato Fenomenologico. Pezzella, Anna Maria.
Essence and Existence in Part 3 of Spinoza's "Ethics". Lucash, Frank.
La persona come apertura all'essere eterno secondo E Stein. D'Ambra, Michele.
La polémica en torno a la distinción de la esencia y la existencia entre Enrique de Gante y Gil de Roma. Beuchot, Mauricio.
La Relación Esencia-existencia en la Segunda de las Meditaciones Metafísicas de Descartes. Pérez, Gilles.
La respuesta Husserliana en las Investigaciones Lógicas a la aporía del antropologismo. García Norro, Juan José.
Le Questioni Inedite. Conforti, Patrizia.
Los Modos de Manifestación de la Alteridad y su Articulación en el Pensamiento de Emmanuel Levinas. Garrido-Maturano, Angel E.
Metafísica del ser y de la Vida en Santo Tomás. Torralba Roselló, Francesc.
Needs and Essence. Rotenstreich, Nathan.
Ontological Dependence. Fine, Kit.
Principialidad de las Facultades en el Orden del Ser. Mier y Terán, Rocío.
Real Essences in Particular. Phemister, Pauline.
Responding to Plato's Thrasymachus. Flew, Antony.
Se Ocupa el Fenomenólogo de la Metafísica?. da Silveira, Maria Joao C.
The Essence of Genuine Reference. Marti, Genoveva.
The Logic of Essence. Fine, Kit.
'Essence' and 'Accident' in Lamb's Elia Essays. Mulvihill, James.

ESSENTIALISM
"Esencilaismo y Conjuntivismo Mereológico" in *Temas Actuales de Filosofía, Palacios, María Julia (ed)*. Sabatés, Marcelo.
"The Rejection of the Identity Thesis" in *The Mind-Body Problem: A Guide to the Current Debate, Warner, Richard (ed)*. Bealer, George.
Artifacts and Constituents. Denkel, Arda.
Cientificismo, Kantismo y Esencialismo. Rodríguez Alcázar, Javier.
Direct Reference and Events. Berckmans, Paul.
Essentialism and the Market. O'Neill, John.
Essentialism, Mental Properties, and Causation. Jackson, Frank.
Feminist Misogyny: Mary Wollstonecraft and the Paradox of "It Takes One to Know One". Gubar, Susan.
K Popper: Racionalismo Critico, Metafisica y Metodologia de lo Inverificable. Velasco N, Ignacio Ruiz.
Kant, Natural Kind Terms, and Scientific Essentialism. Anderson, Erik.
La dimensione teologale dell'uomo e la teologia fondamentale in Xavier Zubiri. Savignano, Armando.
Leibnizian Freedom and Superessentialism. Lodzinski, Don.
On Some Disputed Questions in Leibniz's Metaphysics. Mondadori, Fabrizio.
On Some Failures of Nerve in Constructivist and Feminist Analyses of Technology. Grint, Keith and Woolgar, Steve.
Phenomenology and the Claiming of Essential Knowledge. Spader, Peter.

ESTEEM
Zubiri ante el problema del valor. Palacios, Juan Miguel.

ESTHETICS
see Aesthetics

ESTRANGEMENT
Diferencia entre Alienaçao e Estranhamento nos Manuscritos Econômico-Filosóficos (1844), de Karl Marx. Ferreira Chagas, Eduardo.

ETCHEMENDY, J
A Guide to Truth Predicates in the Modern Era. Sheard, Michael.
Etchemendy and Logical Consequence. Priest, Graham.
Reconciling Austinian and Russellian Accounts of the Liar Paradox. King, Paul John.
Tarski's Quantificational Semantics and Meinongian Object Theory Domains. Jacquette, Dale.

ETERNAL
Emanation and Mysticism in the Writings of Meister Eckhart. Sells, Michael.
From Eternal to Perpetual Truths: A Note on the Mediaeval History of Aristotle, *De interpretatione*, Ch 1, 16a18. Kneepkens, C H.
Javelli and Suárez on the Eternal Truths. Wells, Norman J.
La persona come apertura all'essere eterno secondo E Stein. D'Ambra, Michele.
Nietzsche's Future Perfect and the Eternal Return: Toward a Genealogy of Ideas. Boothroyd, David.
Pensare la religione: Modelli di filosofia della religione a confronto. Fabris, Adriano.
Platone e Vico: Una Reinterpretazione Platonica di Vico. Tucker, Aviezer.
The Creation of 'Eternal' Objects. Ford, Lewis S.

ETERNAL RECURRENCE
La mirada errante: de la "Spaltung" en Lacan, al "caos-cosmos" de Deleuze. Gonzalo I Carbó, Antoni.
Nietzschean Recurrence: The Science and the Moment. Goldberg, David W.
Zarathustra and the Progress of Sovereignty: From the Overman to the External Recurrence. White, Richard J.

ETERNALITY
Il Nyaya Sutra di Gautama. Arena, Leonardo Vittorio.
Eternità e tempo in Plotino. Ferretti, Silvia.

ETERNITY
Eternity and Freedom: A Critical Analysis of Divine Timelessness as a Solution to the Foreknowledge/Free Will Debate. Robinson, Michael D.
Nietzsche: The Ethics of an Immoralist. Berkowitz, Peter.
The Presence of the Past: Morphic Resonance and the Habits of Nature. Sheldrake, Rupert.
Time, Change, and Freedom: An Introduction to Metaphysics. Smith, Quentin and Oaklander, L Nathan.
A Contemporary Challenge to Religion: The Question of Eternity. Lowry, Atherton C.
Empty Time and the Eternality of God. Lodzinski, Don.
Kant and the Eternity of the World: A Historico-critical Reading of the First Antinomy. van Veldhuijsen, Peter.
L'eternità dell'essere nel pensiero di Emanuele Severino. Sperduto, D.
La Spécificité de la Conception Spinoziste de l'Eternité de l'Esprit. Jacquet, Chantal.
Providence, Eternity, and Human Freedom: A Reply to Stump and Kretzmann. Widerker, David.
The Manifold Attitude to Time and Eternity in a Single Culture. Suchodolski, Bogdan.
Time, Eternity, and the Visual Moment (Augenblick): Heidegger and the Problem of a Theology of Time. Hoping, Helmut.

ETHER
O Éter Luminoso como Espaço Absoluto. Oliveira, Maurício Pietrocola.

ETHICAL RELATIVISM
see also Relativism
Brauchen wir ein neues Weltethos? Universale Ethik in einer geschichtlichen Welt. Schockenhoff, Eberhard.
Pluralism of Norms and Values: On the Claim and Reception of the Universal. Klapwijk, J.

ETHICAL THEORY
The Ethics of Our Climate: Hermeneutics and Ethical Theory. O'Neill, William.
Warum Heidegger keine Ethik geschrieben hat. Brandner, Rudolf.

ETHICS

"War, Terrorism, and Ethical Consistency" in *Introducing Applied Ethics, Almond, Brenda (ed).* Wallace, Gerry.

"What Is Ethical Feminism?" in *Feminist Contentions, Benhabib, Seyla (& others).* Cornell, Drucilla.

"Wirkliche" und "philosophische" Anschauung: Formen der intellektuellen Anschauung in Fichtes *System der Sittenlehre* (1798). Perrinjaquet, Alain.

"'The Instruction of Any' and Moral Philosophy" in *African Philosophy: Selected Readings, Mosley, Albert G (ed).* James, David.

A Companion to Aristotle's Politics. Keyt, David and Miller, Fred D.

Adventures in Lesbian Philosophy. Card, Claudia F (ed).

African Philosophy: Selected Readings. Mosley, Albert G (ed).

Ahimsa, the Self, and Postmodernism: Jain, Vedantist, and Buddhist Perspectives. Gier, Nicholas F.

American Philosophy Today and Other Philosophical Studies. Rescher, Nicholas.

Amoral Politics: The Persistent Truth of Machiavellism. Scharfstein, Ben-Ami.

An American Ethic: A Philosophy of Freedom Applied to Contemporary Issues. Gerken, John D.

An Introduction to the Philosophy of Religion. Tilghman, B R.

Angewandte Ethik im Spannungsfeld von Ökologie und Ökonomie. Neumaier, Otto (ed).

Animal Welfare and Human Values. Preece, Rod and Chamberlain, Lorna.

Aristotle and Augustine on Freedom: Two Theories of Freedom, Voluntary Action, and Akrasia. Chappell, T D J.

Aristotle in Outline. Robinson, Timothy A.

Aristotle's Philosophy of Friendship. Stern-Gillet, Suzanne.

Aristotle's Rhetoric: An Art of Character. Garver, Eugene.

Aristotle: Selections. Irwin, Terence (trans) and Fine, Gail (trans).

Asylum: A Moral Dilemma. Plaut, W Gunther.

Atoms, Pleasure, Virtue: The Philosophy of Epicurus. Koen, Avraam.

Autonomous Agents: From Self-Control to Autonomy. Mele, Alfred R.

Autonomy and Intervention: Parentalism in the Caring Life. Kultgen, John.

Ayn Rand: The Russian Radical. Sciabarra, Chris Matthew.

Bad Faith and Antiblack Racism. Gordon, Lewis R.

Beast and Man: The Roots of Human Nature. Midgley, Mary.

Bioethics: A Committee Approach. Minogue, Brendan.

Biology, Ethics, and the Origins of Life. Rolston III, Holmes (ed).

Business Ethics (Fourth Edition). De George, Richard T.

Business Ethics at Work. Vallance, Elizabeth.

Caring: An Essay in the Philosophy of Ethics. van Hooft, Stan.

Cases in Ethics and the Conduct of Business. Boatright, John R.

Chaosmosis: An Ethico-Aesthetic Paradigm. Guattari, Félix, Bains, Paul (trans) and Pefanis, Julian (trans).

Character and Culture: Essays on East and West. Babbitt, Irving.

Civil Society, Civil Religion. Shanks, Andrew.

Classic Cases in Medical Ethics (Second Edition). Pence, Gregory E.

Computers, Ethics and Social Values. Johnson, Deborah G (ed) and Nissenbaum, Helen (ed).

Concepts and Cases in Nursing Ethics. Yeo, Michael (& others).

Contributors to the Philosophy of Humanism. Hillar, Marian (ed) and Prahl, Frank (ed).

Crazy Mountains: Learning from Wilderness to Weigh Technology. Strong, David.

Critical Legal Theory and the Challenge of Feminism: A Philosophical Reconception. Kramer, Matthew H.

Democracy and Social Injustice: Law, Politics, and Philosophy. Simon, Thomas W.

Der logische Unterschied theoretischer und praktischer Sätze und seine philosophische Bedeutung. Kümmel, Friedrich (ed) and König, Josef.

Desire: Its Role in Practical Reason and the Explanation of Action. Schueler, G F.

Dewey's Ethical Thought. Welchman, Jennifer.

Earth Ethics: Environmental Ethics, Animal Rights, and Practical Applications. Sterba, James P (ed).

Ecology. Merchant, Carolyn (ed).

Emmanuel Levinas: The Genealogy of Ethics. Llewelyn, John (ed).

Environmental Ethics (Oxford Readings in Philosophy). Elliot, Robert (ed).

Ernst Cassirer—Von Marburg nach New York: Eine philosophische Biographie. Paetzold, Heinz.

Essays on Bioethics by R M Hare. Crisp, Roger.

Essentials of Shinto: An Analytical Guide to Principal Teachings. Picken, Stuart D B.

Ethical Argument: Critical Thinking in Ethics. Curtler, Hugh Mercer.

Ethical Aspects of Information Technology. Spinello, Richard A.

Ethical Issues in Suicide. Battin, Margaret P.

Ethical Judgment: The Use of Science in Ethics. Edel, Abraham.

Ethics and the Professions. Chadwick, Ruth (ed).

Ethics from Experience. Caws, Peter.

Ethics of Scientific Research. Shrader-Frechette, Kristin.

Ethics on the Frontiers of Human Existence. Badham, Paul (ed).

Ethics, Killing and War. Norman, Richard.

Ethics, Religion and Biodiversity. Hamilton, Lawrence S (ed).

Ethik und Identität: Der ethische Ansatz in der Prozessphilosophie A N Whiteheads und seine Bedeutung für die gegenwärtige Ethik. Lachmann, Rolf.

Evolution and Human Values. Wesson, Robert (ed) and Williams, Patricia A (ed).

Exploring Our Environmental Connections. Schuster, Eleanor A (ed) and Brown, Carolyn L (ed).

Feminist Contentions. Benhabib, Seyla (& others).

Foucault and the Writing of History. Goldstein, Jan (ed).

Freiheit, Verantwortung und Folgen in der Wissenschaft. Sandkühler, Hans Jörg (ed).

From a Biological Point of View. Sober, Elliott.

Gott—Gebote—Ideale: Analytische Philosophie und theologische Ethik. Löhr, Gebbhard.

How Are We to Live? Ethics in an Age of Self-Interest. Singer, Peter.

Human Dignity and the Common Good in the Aristotelian-Thomistic Tradition. Smith, Michael A.

Human Rights and Religious Values. An-Na'im, Abdullahi A (& other eds).

Humane Medicine: A Leading Surgeon Examines What Doctors Do, What Their Patients Expect from Them, and How the Expectations of Both Are Not Being Met. Little, Miles.

Humanity, Environment, and God. Spurway, Neil.

Hume and Hume's Connexions. Stewart, M A (ed) and Wright, John P (ed).

Il Trapianto d'Organi: Contributi per un'analisi etica, psicologica e sociale del problema. Soricelli, Elisabetta.

In Harm's Way. Coleman, Jules L (ed) and Buchanan, Allen (ed).

In Search of Authenticity: From Kierkegaard to Camus. Golomb, Jacob.

Individuals, Humans, Persons: Questions of Life and Death. Kuhse, Helga and Singer, Peter.

Intervention and Reflection: Basic Issues in Medical Ethics (Fifth Edition). Munson, Ronald (ed).

Intrinsic Value: Concept and Warrant. Lemos, Noah M.

Introducing Applied Ethics. Almond, Brenda (ed).

Introduction to Ethics: Personal and Social Responsibility in a Diverse World. Percesepe, Gary.

John Cage: Composed in America. Perloff, Marjorie (ed) and Junkerman, Charles (ed).

Judaism and Modernity: Philosophical Essays. Rose, Gillian.

Kant on Happiness in Ethics. Wike, Victoria S.

Kant's Theory of Imagination: Bridging Gaps in Judgement and Experience. Gibbons, Sarah.

Karl Rosenkranz: Briefe 1827 bis 1850. Butzlaff, Joachim (ed).

L'etica e il suo Altro. Vigna, Carmelo (ed).

Lectures on Divine Humanity. Solovyov, Vladimir.

Legislative Intent and Other Essays on Law, Politics, and Morality. Singer, Marcus G (ed), MacCallum Jr, Gerald C and Martin, Rex (ed).

Levinas Beyond the Horizons of Cartesianism: An Inquiry into the Metaphysics of Morals. Beavers, Anthony F.

Life Choices: A Hastings Center Introduction to Bioethics. Howell, Joseph H (ed) and Sale, William Frederick (ed).

Life in Fragments: Essays in Postmodern Morality. Bauman, Zygmunt.

Locality and Practical Judgment: Charity and Sacrifice. Ross, Stephen David.

Logic, Facts, and Representation: An Examination of R M Hare's Moral Philosophy. Ronnow-Rasmussen, Toni.

Logica del Concreto ed Ermeneutica della Vita Morale: Newman, Blondel, Piovani. Jervolino, Domenico.

Lolita and Aristotle's Ethics. Levine, Peter.

Making Sense of Humanity and Other Philosophical Papers 1982-1993. Williams, Bernard.

Mapping the Human Genome: Reality, Morality, and Deity. Kent, Theodore C.

Media Ethics. Fink, Conrad C.

Medicine and Moral Reasoning. Fulford, K W M (ed), Gillett, Grant (ed) and Soskice, Janet Martin (ed).

Medicine, Money, and Morals: Physicians' Conflicts of Interest. Rodwin, Marc A.

Mill's Principle of Utility: A Defence of John Stuart Mill's Notorious Proof. Alican, Nejip Fikri.

Mind's Bodies: Thought in the Act. Lang, Berel.

Moral Issues In Business (Sixth Edition). Shaw, William H and Barry, Vincent.

Moral Theory: A Contemporary Overview. DeMarco, Joseph P.

Moral Voices, Moral Selves: Carol Gilligan and Feminist Moral Theory. Hekman, Susan J.

Morality, Normativity, and Society. Copp, David.

Narrative and the Natural Law: An Interpretation of Thomistic Ethics. Hall, Pamela M.

Narrative Ethics. Newton, Adam Zachary.

Nietzsche (Past Masters). Tanner, Michael.

Nietzsche's Genealogy: Nihilism and the Will to Knowledge. Havas, Randall.

Nietzsche: The Ethics of an Immoralist. Berkowitz, Peter.

Normative Cultures. Neville, Robert Cummings.

Nursing Ethics: Therapeutic Caring Presence. Bishop, Anne H and Scudder Jr, John R.

Objectivity, Communication, and the Foundation of Understanding. McKinzie, Bruce Wayne.

On the Basis of Morality. Payne, E F J (trans) and Schopenhauer, Arthur.

Other Minds: Critical Essays 1969-1994. Nagel, Thomas.

Philosophy and the Natural Environment. Attfield, Robin (ed) and Belsey, Andrew (ed).

Philosophy of Technology in Spanish Speaking Countries. Mitcham, Carl (ed).

Philosophy: A Beginner's Guide (Second Edition). Teichman, Jenny and Evans, Katherine C.

ETHICS

ETHICS

AIDS, Confidentiality, and Ethical Models. Gorbett, Jason.

Akrasia. Wilkerson, Terence.

Albert Schweitzer or Ivan Boesky? Why We Should Reject the Dichotomy Between Medicine and Business. Wicks, Andrew C.

Algunas Implicaciones Éticas del Psicoanálisis. Alvarez Argüelles, Luz María.

Allocation of Resources at the Bedside: The Intersection of Economics, Law, and Ethics. Pellegrino, Edmund D.

Ambivalence About Ambiguity. Review of Sartre's Political Theory by William L McBride. Flay, Joseph C.

Ambivalencias de Bentham en la lectura de Foucault. García, Francisco Vázquez.

Amnesia Instead of Anesthesia: Not Always a Question of Consent. Truog, Robert D and Waisel, David.

Amounts of Pesticides Reaching Target Pests: Environmental Impacts and Ethics. Pimentel, David.

An Algorithm for Determining Best Interest?. Gillick, Muriel R.

An Analysis of Public Interest Reporting: The Case of General Motors in South Africa. Malone, David and Roberts, Robin W.

An Answer to Lucretius' Symmetry Argument Against the Fear of Death. Kaufman, Frederik.

An Argument Against a Legal Duty to Rescue. Hunt, Lester H.

An Ethics Consult Team in Geriatric Long-Term Care. Chichin, Eileen R and Olson, Ellen.

An Immodest Proposal: Foucault, Hysterization, and the "Second Rape". Hengehold, Laura.

An Ingenuous Account of the Doctrine of the Mean. Martin, Christopher.

An Ordinal Context for Ecofeminism. Kruse, Felicia.

Análisis Económico del Derecho y Utilitarismo: Concordancias y Divergencias. Mercado Pacheco, Pedro.

Analogy, Evaluation, and Moral Disagreement. Post, Stephen G and Leisey, Robert G.

Annette Baier and the Context of Risk. Green, Stephen A.

Antecedentes del Utilitarismo en los moralistas británicos anteriores a Hume. Costa, Margarita.

Aportes Filosóficos para una Teoría y Práctica de Instituciones Justas. Scannone, J C.

Applied Philosophy and Business Ethics. Kieran, Matthew.

Applied Professional Ethics and Organized Religion. Battin, Margaret P.

Approaches (and Possible Contraindications) to Enhancing Patients' Autonomy. Howe, Edmund G.

Appropriate and Inappropriate Use of Advance Directives. Emanuel, Linda.

Aquinas, Vertitatis Splendor, and Contemporary Moral Theology. Krasevac, Edward L.

Are Coerced Acts Free?. Murray, Michael J and Dudrick, David F.

Are Deontology and Teleology Mutually Exclusive?. MacDonald, James E and Beck-Dudley, Caryn L.

Are Moral Intuitions Self-Evident Truths?. Shweder, Richard A.

Are the Elderly Really Machiavellian? A Reinterpretation of an Unexpected Finding. Mudrack, Peter E.

Are There "Cont-Moral Virtues?". McCarty, Richard.

Are There Limits to Solidarity with the Elderly?. Ter Meulen, Ruud.

Are Women More Ethical than Men?. Sikula Sr, Andrew and Costa, Adelmiro D.

Argumentación y Método en la Etica Eudemia. Arreguín, Héctor Zagal.

Argumentaciones éticas a partir de la naturaleza: Aristóteles y después. Annas, Julia.

Argumentation in Law and Politics. Weinberger, Ota.

Aristotle and Hellenistic Philosophy. Sharples, Bob.

Aristotle Meets Wall Street: The Case for Virtue Ethics in Business. Boatright, John R.

Aristotle on Dividing the Soul and Uniting the Virtues. Gottlieb, Paula.

Aristotle on Loving Another for His Own Sake. Rogers, Kelly.

Aristotle, Success, and Moral Luck. Farwell, Paul.

Aristotle: Philosophy and Politics, Theory and Practice. Thompson, Walter J.

Articulating the Aesthetic in the Ethical: Aesthetics and the Ethics of Care. Morris, Susan.

Aspetti Sistematici della "Filosofia del Diritto" di Gentile. Marini, Giuliano.

Assessing the Application of Cognitive Moral Development Theory to Business Ethics. Fraedrich, John, Thorne, Debbie M and Ferrell, O C.

Assimilative Moral Realism and Supervenience. Yasenchuk, Ken.

At the Vortex of Controversy: Developing Guidelines for Human Embryo Research. Green, Ronald M.

Attitudes of Seriously Ill Patients toward Treatment that Involves High Costs and Burdens on Others. Schneiderman, Lawrence J (& others).

Attitudes of Students and Accounting Practitioners Concerning the Ethical Acceptability of Earnings Management. Fischer, Marilyn and Rosenzweig, Kenneth.

Attitudes Towards Business Ethics of Business Students in Malaysia. Alam, Kazi Firoz.

Authenticity and Autonomy in the Managed-Care Era: Forensic Psychiatric Perspectives. Bursztajn, Harold J and Brodsky, Archie.

Authenticity as a Foundational Principle of Medical Ethics. Welie, Jos V M.

Authenticity: From Philosophic Concept to Literary Character. Leahy, Robert.

Autonomy and Blameworthiness. Haji, Ishtiyaque.

Autonomy and the Free Speech Principle. Easton, Susan.

Autonomy, Informed Consent, and Psychosurgery. Hundert, Edward M.

Autonomy, Value, and Conditioned Desire. Noggle, Robert.

Avoiding Mistakes in Reasoning about Naturalness: A Reply to Dalcourt. Sartorelli, Joseph J.

Awe Diminished. Campbell, Courtney S.

Axiological Invariants. Reale, Miguel.

Baby Ryan and Virtual Futility. Capron, Alexander Morgan.

Basic Values of Western Industrial Society: Feedback Effect of Rationality. Mineau, André.

Beatrice's 'Dante': Loving the Individual?. Nussbaum, Martha C.

Beauty and Breast Implantation: How Candidate Selection Affects Autonomy and Informed Consent. Parker, Lisa S.

Before I Was an Embryo, I Was a Pre-Embryo: Or Was I?. Jones, D Gareth and Telfer, Barbara.

Being Human, More or Less. Kohák, Erazim.

Being Morally Responsible for an Action Versus Acting Responsibly or Irresponsibly. Anderson, Susan Leigh.

Benedetto Croce Critico dell'Irrazionalismo. Tertulian, Nicolas.

Bentham: la ciencia del legislador. Bermudo Avila, José Manuel.

Bernard Williams, Shame and Necessity. Held, Dirk T D.

Between Ontology and Ethics. Dokulil, Milos.

Beyond Autonomy to the Person Coping with Illness. Thomasma, David C.

Beyond the Terms of the Contract: Mothers and Farmers. Campbell, Mora.

Beyond Theological Conflict in the Courts: The Issue of Assisted Suicide. Dyck, Arthur J.

Beyond World History: On Hegel's and Kierkegaard's Interests in Ethics and Religion. Cruysberghs, Paul.

Bien común y mal común. Inciarte, Fernando.

Bioethics and Family Values. Almond, Brenda.

Bioethics and Philosophy of Science. Veatch, Robert M.

Bioethics and the Challenge of the Post-Consensus Society. Cameron, Nigel M De S.

Bioethics and the Old-Time Religion: Response to Dena Davis. Freedman, Benjamin.

Bioethics in the Language of the Law. Schneider, Carl E.

Bioethics; Its Scope and Purpose. Fox, Michael W.

Bioethik und Feminismus. Pauer-Studer, Herlinde.

Bioética y derechos humanos II: Aspectos formales y sustanciales para una normativa biomédica en un mundo biotecnológico. Golcher, Cristián.

Biomedical Models of Reproduction in the Fifth Century BC and Aristotle's Generation of Animals. Coles, Andrew.

Blurring Distinctions between the Dying and the Dead: A Call for Discernment in Organ Donation. Rutecki, Gregory W.

Body and Environment. LaBossiere, Michael.

Brain Water, the Ether, and the Art of Constructing Systems. Rueger, Alexander.

Brandon Shaw, Neil Perry, and the Perils of Education. Calhoun, Laura.

Brauchen wir ein neues Weltethos? Universale Ethik in einer geschichtlichen Welt. Schockenhoff, Eberhard.

Breast Cancer Genetic Screening and Critical Bioethics' Gaze. Parker, Lisa S.

Brentano contra Kant: Sobre el imperativo categórico. Palacios, Juan Miguel.

Bribery and Extortion in International Business: Ethical Perceptions of Greeks Compared to Americans. Tsalikis, John and LaTour, Michael S.

Broadening Care, Discerning Worth: The Environmental Contributions of Minimalist Religious Naturalism. Stone, Jerome A.

Business Ethics and Commercial Morality in Western Australia. Small, Michael W.

Business Ethics and Commercial Morality: Report of the Royal Commission into Commercial Activities. Small, Michael W.

Business Ethics and Job-Related Constructs: A Cross-Cultural Comparison of Automotive Salespeople. Honeycutt, Earl D, Siguaw, Judy A and Hunt, Tammy G.

Business Ethics in a Competitive Market. Nelson, Julianne.

Business Ethics in Context: Researching with Case Studies. Brigley, Stephen.

Business Ethics in Developing Countries. Rossouw, Gedeon J.

Business Ethics: A Japanese View. Taka, Iwao.

Business Ethics: Restrictive or Empowering?. Kjonstad, Bjorn and Willmott, Hugh.

Business Intelligence Methods—How Ethical. Hallaq, John H and Steinhorst, Kirk.

Business Meta-Ethics: An Analysis of Two Theories. Brady, F Neil and Dunn, Craig P.

Business Policy, Ethics, and Society. Minkes, A L.

Business Students' Ethical Perceptions of Retail Situations: A Microcultural Comparison. Burns, David J, Fawcett, Jeffrey K and Lanasa, John.

Business's Environmental Responsibility in Taiwan—Moral, Legal or Negotiated. Sheng, Peihua, Chang, Linda and French, Warren A.

But Doctor, It's My Hip!: The Fate of Failed Medical Devices. Fielder, John H and Black, Jonathan.

Butler's Argument for the Natural Authority of Conscience. Brownsey, Paul.

Calling It Quits: Stopping Futile Treatment and Caring for Patients. Jecker, Nancy S.

Camus's Meursault and Sartrian Irresponsibility. Sherman, David.

Can a Good Man Know Himself?. Skillen, Anthony.

Can A Patient Refuse a Psychiatric Consultation to Evaluate Decision-Making Capacity?. Wenger, Neil S and Halpern, Jodi.

Can Human Genetic Enhancement be Prohibited?. Gardner, William.

Can One Justify Morality to Fooles?. DeBruin, Debra A.

Can There Be a "Humanistic" Ecology? A Debate Between Hegel and Heidegger on the Meaning of Ecological Thinking. Berthold-Bond, Daniel.

Can There Be a Right to Secede?. Ewin, R E.

Can We Talk About Ethics Anymore?. Hill, John.

Capital Punishment and the Sanctity of Life. Holyer, Robert.

Capital Punishment: An Act of Murder, Revenge, or Justice. Waters, Raphael T.

Capitalism, Environmentalism, and Mediating Structures. Collins, Denis and Barkdull, John.

Care as a Basis for Radical Political Judgements. Tronto, Joan C.

Care Ethics: A Concept in Search of a Framework. Loewy, Erich H.

Caring for Patients in Cross-Cultural Settings. Jecker, Nancy S (& others).

Caring for Whom? Moral Discussions between Early Confucians and Mohists. Defoort, Carine.

ETHICS

ETHICS

Determinism *Al Dente*. Pereboom, Derk.

Diagnosing the Naturalistic Fallacy: Principia Ethica Revisited. Wright, Darryl F.

Die Aufhebung der Ethik in der kroatischen Praxisphilosophie. Kukoc, Mislav.

Die Kant-Rezeption in der Sportwissenschaft. Court, Jürgen.

Die Moralität des antiken Menschen: Über Bernhard Williams Buch "Shame and Necessity". Rapp, Christof.

Die sogenannte freie Gewissheit und ihre ethischen Implikationen. Belic, Miljenko.

Die Wiederkehr der Tugend: Zur gegenwärtigen Diskussion der politischen Theorie über die moralischen. Kersting, Wolfgang.

Differences in the Ethical Decision-Making of Nursing Faculty and Nursing Staff. Martin, Shirley Davis.

Dignity, Death and Modern Virtue. Meyer, Michael J.

Dilemmas of Emergency Food: A Guide for the Perplexed. Poppendieck, Janet E.

Discourse and Narrative: Ethics after the Linguistics Turn. Sauer, James.

Discussing Divorce in Introductory Ethics. Gould, James B.

Discussion of Lazarus's "How Certain Boundaries and Ethics Diminish Therapeutic Effectiveness". Gutheil, Thomas G.

Discussion: Just Another Simi Valley Jury: The Supreme Court and the Death Penalty. Thomson, Ernie and Osbrun, Jerry R.

Discussions about the Use of Life-Sustaining Treatments: A Literature Review of Physicians' and Patients' Attitudes and Practices. Layson, Rita T (& others).

Diskursethik, schwere Fürsorge und leichte Fürsorge. White, Stephen K.

Distinguishing between Patients' Refusals and Requests. Gert, Bernard, Bernat, James L and Mogielnicki, R Peter.

Distributive Justice and the Minnesota Health Access Initiative. Hull, Robert.

Diversity Stress as Morality Stress. André, Rae.

Divine Commands and Arbitrariness. Rooney, Paul.

Do Agriculturalists Need a New, an Ecocentric, Ethic? 1994 Presidential Address to the Agriculture, Food, and Human Values Society. Comstock, Gary L.

Do Free-Market Governments Create Crisis-Ridden Societies?. Richardson, Bill and Curwen, Peter.

Docs on the Box: Or, How We Learned to Stop Worrying and Love the Tube. Elliott, Carl and Kahn, Jeffrey.

Does Christianity Make a Difference?. McCormick, Richard A.

Does Ethics Code Design Matter? Effects of Ethics Code Rationales and Sanctions on Recipients' Justice Perceptions and Content Recall. Weaver, Gary R.

Does Kant's Categorical Imperative Allow for a Concept of Mercy?. Lee, Peter H.

Does Legally Mandated Consent to Psychotherapy Ensure Ethical Appropriateness?: The Colorado Experience. Handelsman, Mitchell M (& others).

Does Physician Assisted Suicide Violate the Integrity of Medicine?. Momeyer, Richard.

Dr Kevorkian and the Struggle for Physician-Assisted Dying. Pence, Greg.

Ducking Harm and Sacrificing Others. Fischer, John Martin and Ravizza, Mark.

Ducking Trolleys. Boorse, Christopher.

Dworkin, Vague Constitutional Clauses, and the Eighth Amendment's Admonition Against "Cruel and Unusual Punishment". Neeley, G Steven.

É o principio da utilidade racional?. Brito, José De Sousa.

Ecclesioethics: Theologically Neutral But Morally Toothless. Quinn, Philip L.

Eco-Ethics—The Key to Survival. Skolimowski, Henryk.

Ecology and Globalism: Response to Professor E H Cadwallader's Paper 'Ultimate Meaning and Reality in the Battle Between Globalism and Anti-Globalism. Kristiansen, Roald E.

Economists' Preferences and the Preferences of Economists. Norton, Bryan G.

Educated Folly About Animal Minds and Animal Suffering. Landman, Willem A.

Education, the Interpretive Agenda of Science, and the Obligation of Scientists to Promote this Agenda. Fox, Warwick.

Egoism and Altruism in Ethics: Dispensing with Spurious Generality. Van Der Steen, Wim J.

Ein Anfang der Gerechtigkeit: Postmoderne Theorien des Politischen. Schönherr-Mann, Hans-Maring.

Ein Kommentar zum Heraklit. Zoumbos, A N.

El "Averroísmo" en la Filosofía Moral de Kant. Montero Moliner, Fernando.

El Combate entre el Mundo y la Razón Segun Pedro Compostelano. Dafonte, César Raña.

El contractualismo libero de D Gauthier: Contratualismo vs Utilitarismo. González Altable, M Pilar.

El escándalo del mal. Ricoeur, Paul.

El Fundamento de las Normas Morales Según Georges Kalinowski. Ballester, Manuel.

El Ideal de la Vida Filosófica Según Leibniz. Laliga, Rensoli.

El modelo utilitarista en la construcción y desarrollo de la bioética. Clotet, Joaquín.

El morir como pauta ética del empiricismo trascendental. Echeverría, José.

El Primer Principio del Conocimiento Práctico: Objeciones y Respuestas. Massini Correas, Carlos I.

El tema de la virtud: recientes debates. Mauri, Margarita.

El utilitarismo libertario de William Godwin. Adair, Phillipe.

Elements of Accounting Ethics: The Notion of "Fairness". Carpenter, David J.

Emotions, Reason, and Character. Wilson, James Q.

Empathy and Universalizability. Deigh, John.

Empathy, Mind, and Morals. Goldman, Alvin.

En Torno a la Noción de Pobreza Voluntaria. Salazar, Ignacio.

Enlightenment and Technology: Outline for a General Ethics of Technology. Hastedt, Heiner.

Enseigner l'Éthique par l'Histoire. Marcil, Louise.

Enseigner l'Éthique Selon le Paradigme du "Moi Moralement Relié". Mullet, Sheila Mason.

Entre el Kantismo y el Consecuencialismo en la Filosofía Moral de T H Green. Weinstein, David.

Environmental Destruction and the Public Sphere: On Habermas's Discursive Model and Political Ecology. Alario, Margarita.

Environmental Ethics and the Ideology of Meat Eating. Fox, Michael Allen.

Environmental Justice: An Environmental Civil Rights Value Acceptable to All World Views. Hartley, Troy W.

Environmental Quality and the Quality of our Way of Life. Boersema, Jan J.

Environmental Risk Assessment and Nuclear Waste Disposal. Shrader-Frechette, Kristin.

Environmental Security: Choices for the Twenty-First Century. Soroos, Marvin S.

Environmental Valuation: Some Problems of Wrong Questions and Misleading Answers. Knetsch, Jack L.

Environmentalism vs Value Subjectivism: Rejoinder to Anderson and Leal. Sagoff, Mark.

Envisioning Ecological Sustainability: The Need and a Method. Carroll, John E.

Épicurisme et saducéisme dans la communauté sépharade d'Amsterdam. Albiac, Gabriel.

Épicurisme et spinozisme: l'éthique. Bove, Laurent.

Epicurus as a Forerunner of Utilitarianism. Scarre, Geoffrey.

Epistemological and Ethical Development for Human Resource Professionals. Payne, Stephen L.

Equity and Nuclear Waste Disposal. Shrader-Frechette, Kristin.

Eric Voegelin: Le Ragioni e il Metodo della Conscienza. Sallusti, Marina.

Es trascendental la ética Kantiana?. De Maliandi, Graciela Fernandez.

Esthétique et pneumatologie philosophique chez Schleiermacher. Brito, Emilio.

Estimating the Incidence of Wrongdoing and Whistle-Blowing: Results of a Study Using Randomized Response Technique. Burton, Brian K and Near, Janet P.

Ethical and Legal Dilemmas in the Management of Family Violence. Bourne, Richard.

Ethical and Legal Issues in Group Counseling. Corey, Gerald (& others).

Ethical Aspects of an Urban Catastrophe. Argandoña, Antonio.

Ethical Aspects of Investor Behavior. Rivoli, Pietra.

Ethical Attitudes of Mental Health Practitioners: Balancing Therapeutic Practices and Treatments. Rawwas, Mohammed Y A, Strutton, David and Pelton, Lou.

Ethical Behaviours in Organizations: Directed by the Formal or Informal Systems?. Falkenberg, Loren and Herremans, Irene.

Ethical Challenges in the Leader-Follower Relationship. Hollander, Edwin P.

Ethical Concerns and Risk Perceptions Associated with Different Applications of Genetic Engineering. Frewer, Lynn J and Shepherd, Richard.

Ethical Concerns of Nonclinical Forensic Witnesses and Consultants. Pfeifer, Jeffrey E and Brigham, John C.

Ethical Congruency of Constituent Groups. Stephenson, Harriet Buckman, Galbraith, Sharon and Grimm, Robert B.

Ethical Considerations in the Use of Transgenic Animals. Giraud, Raymond.

Ethical Corporate Social Resonsibility: A Framework for Managers. L'Etang, Jacquie.

Ethical Decision Making, Boundaries, and Treatment Effectiveness: A Reprise. Gottlieb, Michael C.

Ethical Internalism and Moral Indifference. Sytsma, Sharon E.

Ethical Issues in Discharge Planning for Vulnerable Infants and Children. Cohen, Marsha H.

Ethical Perceptions of Organizational Politics: A Comparative Evaluation of American and Hong Kong Managers. Ralston, David A, Giacalone, Robert A and Terpstra, Robert H.

Ethical Standards, Attitudes Toward Risk, and Intentional Noncompliance: An Experimental Investigation. Ghosh, Dipankar and Crain, Terry L.

Ethics. Kolakowski, Leszak.

Ethics and Accounting Doctoral Education. Loeb, Stephen E.

Ethics and Aesthetics in Aristotle's *Poetics*. Crittenden, Paul.

Ethics and Agency Theory. French, Peter A.

Ethics and Australian International Business: Which Way to Asia?. Skubik, Daniel W.

Ethics and the Eucharist. Van Eijk, A H C.

Ethics and the Law: US Supreme Court Rulings on the Solicitation of Clients. Mintz, Steven M and Moffeit, Katherine S.

Ethics and the Problem of Time. Banajski, Ryszard.

Ethics as Excellence: A Strategic Management Perspective. Smith, John Milton.

Ethics Consultation: The *Most* Dangerous Profession: A Reply to Critics (CQ Vol 2, No 4). Scofield, Giles R.

Ethics in a Bicultural Context. Campbell, Alastair V.

Ethics in an Aging Society. Holstein, Martha.

Ethics in Organizations: A Framework for Theory and Research. Nicholson, Nigel.

Ethics in Undergraduate Accounting Education: An Empirical Study. Sisaye, Seleshi and Lackman, Conway.

Ethics of Business Students: Some Marketing Perspectives. Lane, J C.

Ethics Perceptions of American Farmers: An Empirical Analysis. Rappaport, Allen and Himschoot, Robert A.

Ethics vs Economics: The Issue of Free Trade with Mexico. Hosmer, LaRue Tone and Masten, Scott E.

Ethics, Incentives, and Conflicts of Interest: A Practical Solution. Kurland, Nancy B.

Ethics: Public and Private. Capron, Alexander Morgan.

Ethik und Freundschaft. Pazanin, Ante.

Éthique de la mort et droit à la mort: A propos d'un livre récent. Keating, Bernard.

Éthique et Enseignement. Carrier, André.

Éthique et Éthiques Appliquées. Parizeau, Marie-Hélène.

Éthique et fondation ultime de la raison: Considérations sur un ouvrage de V Hösle. Langlois, Luc.

Ethischer Gradualismus: Jenseits von Anthropozentrismus und Biozentrismus?. Skirbekk, Gunnar.

ETHICS

Ética y Bienestar. Griffin, James.

Etica y filosofia primera en E Levinas. Sanabria, José Rubén.

Etica y Racionalidad en Kant. Market, Oswaldo.

Éticas del don: Aporías y negociaciones. Peññalver Gómez, Patricio.

Etretien Avec Michel Salomon. Landry, Cécile.

Eudaimonism and the Appeal to Nature in the Morality of Happiness: Comments on Julia Annas, *The Morality of Happiness*. Cooper, John M.

Eugenics. Coutts, Mary Carrington and McCarrick, Pat Milmoe.

Euthanasia in the Netherlands: Sliding Down the Slippery Slope?. Keown, John.

Evaluating Religious Practices: Ecclesioethics Engendered. Callahan, Joan.

Evaluation of Employee Rule Violations: The Impact of Impression Management Effects in Historical Context. Giacalone, Robert A and Payne, Stephen L.

Even When the Devil Says He Is Telling the Truth, He Is Lying. Kolakowski, Leszek.

Evidence, Experts, and Legal Reasoning. Holmström-Hintikka, Ghita.

Excellence V Effectiveness: Macintyre's Critique of Business. Horvath, Charles M.

Exclusion and Emphasis Reframed as a Matter of Ethics. Daniel, Jessica Henderson.

Existence Value, Welfare and Altruism. Aldred, Jonathan.

Existentialism and Postmodernism: Continuities, Breaks, and Some Consequences for Medical Theory. Richter, Dirk.

Exploitation in the Use of Human Subjects for Medical Experimentation: A Re-Examination of Basic Issues. de Castro, Leonardo D.

Family Violence and Family Systems: Who Is the Patient?. Gottlieb, Michael C.

Fanaticism and Integrity. Newman, Jay.

Fear and Belief. Neill, Alex.

Feminism and Ecology: Realism and Rhetoric in the Discourses of Nature. Soper, Kate.

Feminism and Vegetarianism: A Critique of Peter Singer. McKenna, Erin.

Feminism and Vegetarianism: A Response. Singer, Peter.

Feminism, Social Policy, and Long-Acting Contraception. Nelson, Hilde Lindemann and Nelson, James Lindemann.

Fichte und die Freimaurerie. Hammacher, Klaus.

Filosofi a Bologna fra Ottocento e Novecento. Garin, Eugenio.

Filosofia e Religione nelle Pagine del Giovane Gentile. Malusa, Luciano.

Filosofie, Metafysica en Moraal van Karl Popper. Abbes, J K.

Flew on Anti-Social Determinism. House, I W O.

For Our Own Good. Archard, David.

Forced Choices and Self-Defence. Montague, Phillip.

Forgiveness. Lang, Berel.

Forgiving as an Obligation of the Moral Life. Harvey, J.

Formalism, Realism, and the Concept of Law. Stokes, Michael.

Fortunate Misfortune. Smilansky, Saul.

Four Dogmas of Environmental Economics. Sagoff, Mark.

Four Problems of Professional Ethics. Wangerin, Paul T.

Freedom and the Environment: Reply to Critics. Anderson, Terry L and Leal, Donald R.

Freedom for the Good: Thomistic Philosophy on Freedom in the Context of Linguistic-Analytic Reception. Koprek, Ivan.

Freedom in Christian Theological Ethics. Valkovic, Marijan.

Freedom, Understanding, and Therapy in Spinoza's Moral Psychology. Gabhart, Mitchell.

French's *Responsibility Matters*, Murphy's *Retribution Reconsidered*, and Sher's *Desert*. Zimmerman, Michael J.

From Biocentric Individualism to Biocentric Pluralism. Sterba, James P.

From Futility to Triage. Gatter Jr, Robert A and Moskop, John C.

From Natural Identity to Radical Democracy. Sandilands, Catriona.

From the Profane to the Sacred: Why We Need to Retrieve Christian Bioethics. Capaldi, Nicholas.

From the Senses to Sense: The Hermeneutics of Love. Shafer, Ingrid H.

Fuller's Internal Point of View. Schauer, Frederick.

Fumerton on Coherence Theories. BonJour, Laurence.

Fundamentación última y factidad: (Un intento de argumentar "con Apel contra Apel"). Saez Rueda, L.

Fundamentals of Taoist Thinking. Libbrecht, Ulrich J.

Futility and Bargaining Power. Spielman, Bethany.

Futility and Hospital Policy. Tomlinson, Thomas and Czlonka, Diane.

G H Mead: Linguistically Constituted Intersubjectivity and Ethics. Mendieta, Eduardo.

Gandhian Conception of Brahrmacharya. Tiwary, N P.

Gender Bias and Moral Decision Making: The Moral Orientations of Justice and Care. Sanchez, J Martin and Self, Donnie J.

Gender Issues in Health Care. McCarrick, Pat Milmoe.

Genetic Therapy, Identity and Person-Regarding Reasons. Persson, Ingmar.

Giudicare o Decidere: Il Senso della Funzione Giudiziaria. Ollero Tassara, Andrés.

Global Budgeting in the Real World. Gold, Jay A.

Going Early, Going Late: The Rationality of Decisions about Suicide in AIDS. Battin, Margaret P.

Good Ethics Is Good for Business: Ethical Attributions and Response to Environmental Advertising. Davis, Joel J.

Gossip and Morality (in Hebrew). Statman, Daniel.

Gossip, Emotions, and Morality (in Hebrew). Ben-Ze'ev, Aaron.

Green Anarchism: Peter Marshall's *Nature's Web*. Welsh, Ian.

Gregory Vlastos on Justice and Equality. Kraut, Richard H.

Grenzen der Verantwortung. Heidbrink, Ludger.

Habermas y el universalismo moral. Prior Olmos, Angel.

Hanfling on Loving My Neighbour, Loving Myself. Walton, Gertrud.

Hanfling on Neighbour Love. Radcliffe, Dana M.

Hanfling on Self-Love. Champlin, T S.

Hannah Arendt and Ecological Politics. Whiteside, Kerry H.

Hard Rules, Soft Rules, and Moral Vision: Models of Ethical Rationality. Haney, Mitchell R.

Hard Times, Hard Choices: Founding Bioethics Today. Gracia, Diego.

Harmony (He) and Gender in Early Chinese Thought. Hinsch, Bret.

Hawkeye Pierce and the Questionable Relevance of Medical Etiquette to Contemporary Medical Ethics and Practice. Sugarman, Jeremy.

Head-Heart Disparity Among Future Managers: Implications for Ethical Conduct. Kochunny, C M and Rogers, Hudson.

Health Care Workers with HIV and a Patient's Right To Know. Murphy, Timothy F.

Health Maintenance as Responsibility for Self. Kolcaba, Raymond and Kolcaba, Katharine.

Health, Aging, and Death. Emson, Harry E.

Healthcare as a Commons. Jecker, Nancy S and Jonsen, Albert R.

Healthcare Rationing through Global Budgeting: The Ethical Choices. Veatch, Robert M.

Hearing the Difference: Theorizing Connection. Gilligan, Carol.

Hegel on the Rationality and Priority of Ethical Life. Pippin, Robert B.

Heidegger's Anti-Anthropocentrism. Dombrowski, Daniel A.

Helping Ken and Marie Pines. Bonkovsky, Frederick O.

Helps for CPAs in Dealing with Ethical Issues. Cooper, Robert W, Frank, Garry L and Heaston, Patrick H.

Heteronomy and Spurious Principles of Morality in Kant's Groundwork. Sherline, Edward.

Historical Rights and Fair Shares. Simmons, A John.

Historicism, Social Practice, and Sustainability: Some Themes in Hegelian Ethical Theory. Pinkard, Terry P.

HIV +/AIDS Related Bioethical Issues in Japan. Hoshino, Kazusama.

HIV Preventive Vaccine Research: Selected Ethical Issues. Grady, Christine.

Homosexuality. Quinton, Anthony.

Honor Among Thieves: A Transaction-Cost Interpretation of Corruption in Third World Countries. Husted, Bryan W.

Honor Among Thieves: Some Reflections on Professional Codes of Ethics. Sanders, John T.

How Certain Boundaries and Ethics Diminish Therapeutic Effectiveness. Lazarus, Arnold A.

How Christian Ethics Became Medical Ethics: The Case of Paul Ramsey. Hauerwas, Stanley.

How Religion Impedes Moral Development. Clark, Brad.

How to Ground a Universalistic Ethics of Co-Responsibility for the Effects of Collective Actions and Activities?. Apel, Karl Otto.

How We Acquire a Sense of Morality. Eysenck, H J.

How Would you Like your 'Sustainability', Sir? Weak or Strong? A Reply to my Critics. Beckerman, Wilfred.

Human Flourishings: A Psychological Critique of Virtue Ethics. Terzis, George N.

Human Good does not Consist in Isolated Pleasures, but in Contentment. Rosmini, Antonio.

Human Growth Hormone: A Case Study in Treatment Priorities. Tauer, Carol A.

Human Identity and the Primitive Streak. Lockwood, Michael.

Human Rights as the Rights of the Poor: The Perspective from Liberation Theology. Aldunate, José.

Human Value of Sustainable Society. Dewan, M L.

Human-Centered or Ecocentric Environmental Ethics?. Howie, John.

Humanism as a Basis for Universalist Thinking. Cauchy, Venant.

Hume's Deontology. Flage, Daniel E.

Hume's Problem and the Possibility of Normative Ethics. Flage, Daniel E and Glass, Ronald J.

Humility. Snow, Nancy E.

Humor as Social Act: Ethical Issues. Harvey, J.

Hyprocrisy and Moral Seriousness. Crisp, Roger and Cowton, Christopher.

I Preliminari Logici. Gardies, Jean-Louis.

Iatrogenic Ethical Problems: A Commentary on "Can a Patient Refuse a Psychiatric Consultation to Evaluate Decision Making Capacity?". Stone, Alan A.

Identity and Quality of Life (in Dutch). Musschenga, A W.

Il problema della definizione generale del diritto. Bagolini, Luigi.

Il Problema della Natura Umana nella Filosofia Spagnola. Ballestros, Jesus.

Illness, the Problem of Evil, and the Analogical Structure of Healing: On the Difference Christianity Makes in Bioethics. Khushf, George.

Images of Corporate Executives in Recent Fiction. Sarachek, Bernard.

Imitatio Christi: Ethical Problems of Some Christological Standpoints. Vidrányi, Katalin.

Imperfect Markets: Business Ethics as an Easy Virtue. Sethi, S Prakash.

Implementing Business Ethics: Sexual Harassment. Crain, Karen A and Heischmidt, Kenneth A.

Implicit Law. Postema, Gerald J.

Impossible Choices: When Patients and Careproviders Face Impossible Decisions. Howe, Edmund G.

In Defence of Aristotelian Honour. Putman, Daniel.

In Defence of Sustainable Development. Skolimowski, Henryk.

In Defense of Active Pacifists. Cady, Duane L.

In Defense of Self-Determination. Philpott, Daniel.

In the Land of Omissions: An Opinionated Guide. Sistare, Christine T.

Incommensurability: Its Implications for the Patient/Physician Relation. Veatch, Robert M and Stempsey, William C.

Inconmensurabilidad y razonamiento jurídico. Raz, Joseph.

Indeterminism and Control. Clarke, Randolph.

ETHICS

ETHICS

ETHICS

Use and Then Prove, or Prove and Then Use? Some Thoughts on the Ethics of Mental Health Professionals' Courtroom Involvement. Faust, David.

User Rights and the Frail Aged. Gibson, Diane.

Util-izing Animals. LaFollette, Hugh and Shanks, Niall.

Utilidad, arte, virtud y riqueza en la Ilustración Escocesa. Itxaso, María Elósegui.

Utilitarianism and the Virtues. Foot, Philippa.

Utility, Subjectivism and Moral Ontology. Ross, Philip J.

Vagueness, Borderline Cases and Moral Realism. Shafer-Landau, Russ.

Validité et limites du consensus en éthique clinique. Malherbe, Jean-François, Rocchetti, Loretta and Boire-Lavigne, Anne-Marie.

Value Theory and Ecology in Environmental Ethics: A Comparison of Rolston and Niebuhr. Scoville, Judith N.

Value Theory and the Best Interests Standard. DeGrazia, David.

Value, Metaphysics, and Anthropocentrism. Morito, Bruce.

Values, Naturalism, and Teaching the Nature of Values. Jacobs, Jonathan.

Veatch and Brain Death: A Plea for Soul. Pentz, Rebecca D.

Verità ed etica nella *Dialectica* di Lorenzo Valla. Laffranchi, M.

Vers une Éthique de Responsabilité en Milieu Médical. Léry, Nicole.

Viability. Gert, Heather.

Vices and the Self. Taylor, Gabriele.

Victimes et utopies: Analyse d'une structure de notre conscience morale. Boss, Gilbert.

Vigilantism and the Common Good. Green, Steven.

Viktor Emil von Gebsattel on the Doctor-Patient Relationship. Welie, Jos V M.

Virtue and Choice in Aristotle's *Ethics*. Tilley, John.

Virtue and Truth in Clinical Science. Gillett, Grant.

Virtue as the Use of Other Goods. Annas, Julia.

Virtue Ethics and Contractarianism: Towards a Reconciliation. McCracken, Janet and Shaw, Bill.

Virtue Ethics and Psychology. Statman, Daniel.

Virtue without Knowledge: Socrates' Conception of Holiness in Plato's *Euthyphro*. Weiss, Roslyn.

Vlastos on Socratic and Platonic Forms. Fine, Gail.

Volver a Kant Significa Avanzar. Funke, Gerhard.

Von einer Ethik der Technik aus antinaturalistischem Geist. Betzler, Monika.

Was Ayn Rand a Humanist?. Walker, Jeff.

Was Hobbes a Legal Positivist?. Murphy, Mark C.

Weighing Goods: Some Questions and Comments. Temkin, Larry S.

Woighting Health States and Strong Evaluation. Edgar, Andrew.

Wes Jackson, Wendell Berry, and Bruce Colman (eds): *Meeting the Expectations of the Land: Essays in Sustainable Agriculture and Stewardship*. Houle, K.

What Do Animals Deserve?. Voice, Paul.

What is Mimetic Desire?. Livingston, Paisley.

What Is the Value of Rangitoto Island?. Vadnjal, Dan and O'Connor, Martin.

What Is Universalism?. Kuczynski, Janusz.

What is Wrong with Hypocrisy?. Benn, Piers.

What's Missing from Current Clinical Trial Guidelines? A Framework for Integrating Science, Ethics, and the Community Context. Sutherland, Heather J, Meslin, Eric M and Till, James E.

What's Wrong with Ethnic Cleansing?. Nickel, James W.

When Families Request That 'Everything Possible' Be Done. Jecker, Nancy S and Schneiderman, Lawrence J.

When Is Birth Unfair to the Child?. Steinbock, Bonnie and McClamrock, Ron.

When OPRR Comes Calling: Enforcing Federal Research Regulations. McCarthy, Charles R.

When the Majority Says You May Die: Aid-in-Dying Initiatives. Povelones Jr, Arthur A.

When to Terminate a Charitable Trust?. Landesman, Cliff.

Where Do Moral Theories Come From?. Walker, Margaret Urban.

Who Should a Utilitarian Be?. Smilansky, Saul.

Who Should be Committable?. Lavin, Michael.

Whose Patient Am I, Anyway?. Gorovitz, Samuel.

Whose Tradition? Which Enlightenment? What Content? Engelhardt, Hauerwas, Capaldi, and the Future of Christian Bioethics. McKenny, Gerald P.

Why are There No Objective Values? A Critique of Ethical Intuitionism from an Epistemological Point of View. Geiger, Gebhard.

Why Ethics is Political Science for Aristotle. Gerson, L.

Why Law—Efficacy, Freedom, or Fidelity?. Waldron, Jeremy.

Why Psychology Is Mute about the Environmental Crisis. Kidner, David W.

Why Theorize How to Live with Each Other?. Gibbard, Allan F.

Why?. Goldman, Michael.

Wild Beasts and Idle Humours: Legal Insanity and the Finding of Fault. Robinson, Daniel N.

Wild Justice. Wallace, Gerry.

Wilderness Philosophy. Gay, Hannah.

William Godwin y el anarquismo: A propósito de *Political Justice*. Alvarez, Antón Fernández.

Wittgenstein, the Self, and Ethics. Kelly, John C.

Women, Ectogenesis, and Ethical Theory. Cannold, Leslie.

Women-Animals-Machines: A Grammar for a Wittgensteinian Ecofeminism. Lee-Lampshire, Wendy.

Y a-t-il un Droit de Mourir?. Malherbe, Jean-François.

Yves Simon's Approach to Natural Law. Long, Steven A.

Zimmerman on Moral Responsibility, Obligation and Alternate Possibilities. Widerker, David and Katzoff, Charlotte.

'The Same Thing Therefore Ought To Be and Ought Not To Be': Anselm on Conflicting Oughts. O'Neill, John.

'The Unnatural Desire for More than one Needs': An Objection to James Tully's View. Kopton, K.

'We Good Europeans': Nietzsche's New Europe in *Beyond Good and Evil*. Martin, Nicholas.

ETHICS COMMITTEES

Bioethics: A Committee Approach. Minogue, Brendan.

Humane Medicine: A Leading Surgeon Examines What Doctors Do, What Their Patients Expect from Them, and How the Expectations of Both Are Not Being Met. Little, Miles.

Should Ethics Committees Study Themselves?. Danis, Marion.

Should Hospital Ethics Committees Do Research?. Sugarman, Jeremy.

ETHNICITY

American Mixed Race: The Culture of Microdiversity. Zack, Naomi (ed).

Moral Voices, Moral Selves: Carol Gilligan and Feminist Moral Theory. Hekman, Susan J.

Cultural Stereotypes and Positioning Theory. Van Langenhove, Luk and Harré, Rom.

Liberalism, Multiculturalism, and Minority Protection. Rickard, Maurice.

Reply to Michael Walzer. Bader, Veit.

So Black and Blue: Response to Rudinow. Taylor, Paul Christopher.

What's Wrong with Ethnic Cleansing?. Nickel, James W.

ETHNOCENTRISM

"On Ethnocentric Truth and Pragmatic Justice" in *Recovering Pragmatism's Voice, Langsdorf, Lenore (ed)*. Smith, Andrew R and Shyles, Leonard.

Post-Modernism and Anthropology: Theory and Practice. Geuijen, Karin (ed), Raven, Diederick (ed) and De Wolf, Jan (ed).

Cultural Universals as Endless Tasks: Phenomenology, Relativism, and Ethnocentrism. Noé, Keiichi.

ETHNOGRAPHY

"The Problem of Cultural Imputation in History: Cultures Versus History" in *Historiography Between Modernism and Postmodernism, Topolski, Jerzy (ed)*. Wrzosek, Wojciech.

Modernity and Identity. Lash, Scott (ed) and Friedman, Jonathan (ed).

Post-Modernism and Anthropology: Theory and Practice. Geuijen, Karin (ed), Raven, Diederick (ed) and De Wolf, Jan (ed).

The Decolonization of Imagination: Culture, Knowledge, and Power. Pieterse, Jan Nederveen (ed) and Parekh, Bhikhu (ed).

ETHNOLOGY

The Paradox of Levi-Strauss or Cultural Time Yesterday and Today. Krzemien-Ojak, Slaw.

ETHNOPHILOSOPHY

African Philosophy: Selected Readings. Mosley, Albert G (ed).

Readings in African Philosophy: An Akan Collection. Kwame, Safro (ed).

Indeterminacy, Ethnophilosophy, Linguistic Philosophy, African Philosophy. Hallen, Barry.

ETHOLOGY

Algunas Vías de Acceso a la Teoría Evolucionista del Conocimiento/Epistemología Evolucionista. Ursúa, Nicanor.

ETHOS

Das geschichtliche Ethos gegenüber der absolut gesetzten Freiheit. Brujic, Branka.

ETIQUETTE

Hawkeye Pierce and the Questionable Relevance of Medical Etiquette to Contemporary Medical Ethics and Practice. Sugarman, Jeremy.

ETYMOLOGY

Language and the Etymological Turn of Thought. Schalow, Frank.

EUCHARIST

Ethics and the Eucharist. Van Eijk, A H C.

EUCLID

The Logic of Liu Hui and Euclid as Exemplified in Their Proofs of the Volume of a Pyramid. Crossley, J N and Lun, A W C.

EUCLIDEAN

The Shape of Space (Second Edition). Nerlich, Graham.

EUDAIMONIAN

Two Extreme Approaches to Rights Versus an Aristotelian Mean. Fay, Thomas A.

EUDAIMONISM

Eudaimonism and the Appeal to Nature in the Morality of Happiness: Comments on Julia Annas, *The Morality of Happiness*. Cooper, John M.

Is Moderation a Virtue? Gregory Vlastos and the Toxins of Eudaemonism. Meister, Robert.

La Eudaimonía y las Bienaventuranzas. de Gayoso, Graciela L Ritacco.

Reply to Cooper. Annas, Julia.

EUGENICS

"Eugenische Utopien: Entwürfe für die Rationalisierung der menschlichen Entwicklung" in *Nationalsozialismus und Moderne, Welzer, Harald (ed)*. Weingart, Peter.

Das utopische Staatsmodell von Platons "Politeia" aus der Sicht von Orwells "Nineteen Eighty-Four". Otto, Dirk.

Eugenics. Coutts, Mary Carrington and McCarrick, Pat Milmoe.

EUROCENTRISM

"The Problem of Cultural Imputation in History: Cultures Versus History" in *Historiography Between Modernism and Postmodernism, Topolski, Jerzy (ed)*. Wrzosek, Wojciech.

Intercultural Understanding and the Role of Europe. Held, Klaus.

The World-System Perspective in the Construction of Economic History. Abu-Lughod, Janet.

Understanding Oriental Cultures. Gare, Arran E.

EUROPEAN

see also East European

"Der faustische Mensch—Die Wissenschaft als euripäisches Erbe" in *Das geistige Erbe Europas, Buhr, Manfred (ed).* Eriksson, Gunnar.

"Der griechische Anfang Europas und die Frage der Romanitas" in *Europa und die Philosophie, Gander, Hans-Helmuth (ed).* Chiereghin, Franco.

"Dialog der Religionen und Eurozentrismus" in *Das geistige Erbe Europas, Buhr, Manfred (ed).* Klein, Hans-Dieter.

"Die Brüche in der europäischen Philosophietradition" in *Das geistige Erbe Europas, Buhr, Manfred (ed).* D'Hondt, Jacques.

"Die Philosophielehre im neuen Europa—Bemerkungen zur niederländischen Perspektive" in *Das geistige Erbe Europas, Buhr, Manfred (ed).* Petry, Michael John.

"Die Viefalt Europas—Erbe und Zukunft" in *Das geistige Erbe Europas, Buhr, Manfred (ed).* Gadamer, Hans-Georg.

"Education for European Citizenship: A Philosophical Critique" in *Identity, Culture, and Education, Smeyers, Paul (ed).* Williams, Kevin.

"Europa als Thema und Aufgabe der Philosophie" in *Das geistige Erbe Europas, Buhr, Manfred (ed).* Baumgartner, Hans Michael.

"Europa und der 'andere Anfang'" in *Europa und die Philosophie, Gander, Hans-Helmuth (ed).* Dastur, Françoise.

"Europa und die interkulturelle Verständigung" in *Europa und die Philosophie, Gander, Hans-Helmuth (ed).* Held, Klaus.

"Europa und die Oikoumene" in *Europa und die Philosophie, Gander, Hans-Helmuth (ed).* Gadamer, Hans-Georg.

"Europa und die Philosophie" in *Europa und die Philosophie, Gander, Hans-Helmuth (ed).* Gander, Hans-Helmuth.

"Europas Identität und seine pilosophische Erbschaft" in *Das geistige Erbe Europas, Buhr, Manfred (ed).* Kluxen, Wolfgang.

"Heideggers europäische Wendung" in *Das geistige Erbe Europas, Buhr, Manfred (ed).* Riedel, Manfred.

"Heideggers europäische Wendung" in *Europa und die Philosophie, Gander, Hans-Helmuth (ed).* Riedel, Manfred.

"Rechtsfrieden als Grundlage der Einheit Europas—Überlegungen zu Kant und Fichte" in *Das geistige Erbe Europas, Buhr, Manfred (ed).* Schrader, Wolfgang H.

"Tradition, Recognition, and Truth: Cultural Identity in the Eyes of the University" in *Identity, Culture, and Education, Smeyers, Paul (ed).* Crawley, Francis P.

Amoral Politics: The Persistent Truth of Machiavellism. Scharfstein, Ben-Ami.

Das geistige Erbe Europas. Buhr, Manfred (ed).

Europa und die Philosophie. Gander, Hans-Helmuth (ed).

European Philosophy and the American Academy. Smith, Barry (ed).

Foucault and the Writing of History. Goldstein, Jan (ed).

Martin Heidegger and European Nihilism. Löwith, Karl, Wolin, Richard (ed) and Steiner, Gary (trans).

Rational Individualism: The Perennial Philosophy of Legal Interpretation. Simonds, Roger T.

Suchbild Europa—künstlerische Konzepte der Moderne. Wertheimer, Jürgen (ed).

The Beautiful Soul: Aesthetic Morality in the Eighteenth Century. Norton, Robert E.

The Decolonization of Imagination: Culture, Knowledge, and Power. Pieterse, Jan Nederveen (ed) and Parekh, Bhikhu (ed).

The Gift of Death. Wills, David (trans) and Derrida, Jacques.

Between Reform and Revolution: Three Hypotheses about the Nature of the Regime Change. Kis, János.

Classifications of Philosophy, the Sciences, and the Arts in Sixteenth- and Seventeeth-Century Europe. Freedman, Joseph S.

Concepts et Symboles du XVIIIe Siècle Européen: le Cas de la Grèce. Argyropoulos, Roxane D.

Consideraciones Metodológicas Acerca de la Investigación en el Ambito de la Filosofía de la Educación (en Europa). Barrio Maestre, José María.

Contributors to the Genesis of Europe: Gotthold Ephraim Lessing and His Followers. Ritchie, Gisela F.

Criterion-referenced Assessment and the Development of Knowledge and Understanding. Davis, Andrew.

Crítica de la filosofía global quinientos años después. Herra, Rafael Angel.

Does a Good Market Make a Good European?. Fuchs, Wolfgang W.

Europe, or How to Escape Babel. Olender, Maurice.

Hegel y América. Perez-Estevez, Antonio.

Identificational Recruit: Between the Temptation of Nihilism and a Tie-In with the Body. Liubomirova, Nataly.

Intercultural Understanding and the Role of Europe. Held, Klaus.

Language, Action and Context: Linguistic Pragmatics in Europe and America. Nerlich, Brigitte and Clarke, David D.

Living Poetically: Kierkegaard and German Romanticism. Walsh, Sylvia.

Moses Mendelssohn and the *End of Illusion Theory*: An Inquiry into Innovation in Aesthetics in the Middle of the Eighteenth-Century. Otabe, Tanehisa.

National Identity and National Consciousness. Tevzadze, Natia.

On the Concepts of the 'Other' and the 'Enemy'. Harle, Vilho.

On the Motives for the New Sociology of Science. Fuller, Steve.

Philosophy in Post-Communist Europe. Gordon, Dane R.

Propositions on 'The End of Socialism?'. Lovell, David W.

Review Essay: Robert B Pippin's *Modernism as a Philosophical Problem*. Chytry, Josef.

Speculations on Strauss' Political Intentions Suggested by *On Tyranny*. Glenn, Gary D.

The End of Humanism and Fichte's Concept of European Intellectualism. Fischer, Bernd.

The Image of Wisdom and the Wise Man in the History of European Philosophy. Semane, Tatjana.

The New World Disorder: A Crisis of Philosophical Identity. Redpath, Peter A.

The Pathos of European Political Philosophy After Marxism. McBride, William L.

The Philosophy of Nature and European Ontology. Funda, Otakar A.

The Rhetoric of Artifacts and the Decline of Classical Humanism: The Case of Josef Strzygowski. Marchland, Suzanne L.

The Unity of Heaven and Man versus Absolute Unlikeness—Kierkegaard, European Thinker, Contra Chinese Philosophy. Zhou, Yiyun.

Thinking the Post-Socialism: From Socialist Community to Pluralistic Society. Flego, Gvozden.

William James and the Development of Phenomenological Psychology in Europe. Herzog, Max.

Women as Mothers and the Making of the European Mind: A Contribution to the History of Developmental Psychology and Primary Socialization. Niestroj, Brigitte H E.

'We Good Europeans': Nietzsche's New Europe in *Beyond Good and Evil*. Martin, Nicholas.

EUTHANASIA

see also Letting Die

"The Right to Die" in *Ethics on the Frontiers of Human Existence, Badham, Paul (ed).* Smith, Patrick Nowell.

Ethical Issues in Suicide. Battin, Margaret P.

Ethics on the Frontiers of Human Existence. Badham, Paul (ed).

Individuals, Humans, Persons: Questions of Life and Death. Kuhse, Helga and Singer, Peter.

Attitudes of Seriously Ill Patients toward Treatment that Involves High Costs and Burdens on Others. Schneiderman, Lawrence J (& others).

Commentary on "But Is It Assisted Suicide?". Nelson, James Lindemann.

Conflicts of Conscience: Hospice and Assisted Suicide. Campbell, Courtney S (& others).

CQ Interview: Dr Boudewijn Chabot on Assisted Suicide in the Absence of Somatic Illness. Klotzko, Arlene Judith.

Distinguishing between Patients' Refusals and Requests. Gert, Bernard, Bernat, James L and Mogielnicki, R Peter.

Does Physician Assisted Suicide Violate the Integrity of Medicine?. Momeyer, Richard.

Dr Kevorkian and the Struggle for Physician-Assisted Dying. Pence, Greg.

Euthanasia in the Netherlands: Sliding Down the Slippery Slope?. Keown, John.

Going Early, Going Late: The Rationality of Decisions about Suicide in AIDS. Battin, Margaret P.

L'euthanasie: Enjeux Ethiques et Politiques. St-Arnaud, Jocelyne.

Physician Assisted Suicide: Its Challenge to the Prevailing Constitutional Paradigm. Robinson, John H.

Physician Assisted Suicide: New Developments in the Netherlands. Gevers, Sjef.

Physician-Assisted Suicide and the Profession's Gyrocompass. Miles, Steven H.

Professional Integrity and Physician-Assisted Death. Miller, Franklin G and Brody, Howard.

Reflections on the State of Current Debate Over Physician-Assisted Suicide and Euthanasia. Winkler, Earl.

Selling Death and Dignity. Hendin, Herbert.

The Ethics of Suicide Prevention. Cosculluela, Victor.

The Euthanasia Debate and Empirical Evidence: Separating Burdens to Others from One's Own Quality of Life. Ubel, Peter A and Arnold, Robert M.

The Euthanasia Debate in Germany—What's the Fuss?. Glock, Hans-Johann.

The Holocaust: Moral and Political Lessons. Lesser, A H.

The Physician-Assisted Suicide and Euthanasia Debate: An Annotated Bibliography of Representative Articles. Fins, Joseph J and Bacchetta, Matthew D.

The Role of Courts in the Debate on Assisted Suicide: A Communitarian Approach. Beschle, Donald L.

The State's Dr Death: What's Unethical About Physicians Helping at Executions?. Davis, Michael.

To Save the Logic, the Facts Must Fit. Pellegrino, Edmund D.

Trois discours de Pie XII et le débat sur l'euthanasie. Saint-Arnaud, Jocelyne.

When the Majority Says You May Die: Aid-in-Dying Initiatives. Povelones Jr, Arthur A.

Y a-t-il un Droit de Mourir?. Malherbe, Jean-François.

EVALUATION

Analogy, Evaluation, and Moral Disagreement. Post, Stephen G and Leisey, Robert G.

Deseos Distinguidos. Platts, Mark.

Expert Systems Evaluation. Juristo, N, Maté, J L and Pazos, J.

The Effects of Computerized Performance Monitoring: An Ethical Perspective. Hawk, Stephen R.

Using the Multitrait-Multimethod Matrix to Evaluate Knowledge-Based Systems. Adelman, Leonard and Riedel, Sharon L.

What Is Character?. Braun, David.

EVANGELISM

The Counterfeit Wisdom of Shallow Minds: A Critique of Some Leading Offenders of the 1980's. Habermehl, Lawrence.

Ingérence des États en temps de guerre: Action humanitaire des organisations bénévoles chrétiennes et témoignage de l'évangile. Joblin, Joseph.

EVANS, C

(Writing) About Writing About Kierkegaard. Cameron, W S K.

EXISTENCE

EXISTENTIAL

EXISTENTIAL IMPORT

EXISTENTIALISM

EXPERIENCE

Reply to Professor Cebik's "Secondary Language and Secondary Art". Tilghman, B R.

Response. Gendlin, E T.

Roughing Out the Ground Rules: Reason and Experience in Practical Deliberation. Carr, David.

Se Ocupa el Fenomenólogo de la Metafísica?. da Silveira, Maria Joao C.

Searle's Theory of Visual Experience. Wilkie, Sean.

Second Thoughts: Revoking Decisions Over One's Own Future. Radden, Jennifer.

Secondary Language and Secondary Art. Cebik, L B.

Should a Materialist Believe in Qualia?. Lewis, David.

Six Heideggerian Figures. Wood, Robert E.

Sobre la Experiencia y el Conocimiento del Alma. Quijano, Francisco.

Some Developmental Issues in Transpersonal Experience. Hunt, Harry T.

Some Peculiarities about Musical Aesthetic Qualities. Porter, Roosevelt.

Sport, the Aesthetic, and Narrative. Feezell, Randolph M.

Stages and Transitions in Cognitive Development. Johnson, M L.

Strawson's Analytic Salvage of Kant's Transcendental Deduction of the Categories. Tai, Hua Terence.

The Adequacy of Simple Ideas in Locke—A Rehabilitation of Berkeley's Criticisms. Bermúdez, José Luis.

The Aesthetic Value of Representation in Painting. Goldman, Alan H.

The Buddhist Perspective on Business Ethics: Experiential Exercises for Exploration and Practice. Gould, Stephen J.

The Earth Might be Round, But the World is Flat: The Groundwork for an Ethics of Relief. Ramsey, Ramsey Eric.

The End of History: Déjà-Vu All Over Again. Cooper, Barry.

The Linguistic and Personal Meaning of Metaphorical Speech. Gleeson, G P.

The Lived Experience of Disability. Toombs, S K.

The Palinode of the Analyst Rationality and Self in the *Euthyphro*. Glouberman, Mark.

The Philosophy of Samuel Frederick Hahnemann—A Perspective. Sinha, Shyam Deo Kumar.

The Structure of Awareness: Contemporary Applications of William James' Forgotten Concept of "The Fringe". Galin, David.

The Telos of Peirce's Realism. Hausman, Carl R and Anderson, Douglas R.

The Value of Music. Graham, Gordon.

What Is 'Consciousness'?. Carley, Adam L.

Why Pains Are Mental Objects. Langsam, Harold.

EXPERIMENT

"Logic, Quanta, and the Two-slit Experiment" in *Heading Putnam, Clark, Peter (ed)*. Redhead, Michael.

"Probability and the Understanding of Individual Differences" in *Probability in Theory-Building, Brzezinski, Jerzy (ed)*. Wahlsten, Douglas.

Animal Welfare and Human Values. Preece, Rod and Chamberlain, Lorna.

The Context of Explanation. Bunzl, Martin.

The Diffident Naturalist: Robert Boyle and the Philosophy of Experiment. Sargent, Rose-Mary.

The Undivided Universe: An Ontological Interpretation of Quantum Theory. Hiley, B J and Bohm, David.

Capacities, Tendencies and the Problem of Singular Causes. Morrison, Margaret.

Cartwright on Probabilistic Causality: Types, Tokens, and Capacities. Eells, Ellery.

Circularidades en la contrastación experimental. Garrido, Julián Garrido.

Cognitive Psychology: A Phenomenological Critique. Wertz, Frederick J.

Controversies in the Interpretation of Mendel's Discovery. Orel, Vitezslav and Hartl, Daniel L.

Critical Notice of Roy Sorensen *Thought Experiments*. Brown, James Robert.

Duhem, Quine, and the Multiplicity of Scientific Tests. Balashov, Yuri.

El Programa del Naturalismo Epistémico Evolucionista: Alcance y Límites. Pacho G, J.

Empirical Equivalence, Underdetermination, and Systems of the World. Hoefer, Carl and Rosenberg, Alexander.

Equipotential Recipes for Unambiguous Images: A Reply to Rollins. Reisberg, Daniel.

Experiment, Speculation and Law: Faraday's Analysis of Arago's Wheel. Steinle, Friedrich.

Experimentation and the Legitimacy of Idealization. Laymon, Ronald E.

Exploitation in the Use of Human Subjects for Medical Experimentation: A Re-Examination of Basic Issues. de Castro, Leonardo D.

Filosofía como arte y experiencia de la vida. Innerarity, Daniel.

Galileu e a Dialética: Síntese pelo Experimento e Natureza como Domínio dos Objectos. Maar, Wolfgang Leo.

Hacking's Experimental Realism. Resnik, David B.

Hacking's Experimental Realism: An Untenable Middle Ground. Reiner, Richard and Pierson, Robert.

Imaginary Science. Gooding, David.

In het land der doven is éénoog nog geen koning. Pieters, Toine.

Individual Autonomy and the Double-Blind Controlled Experiment: The Case of Desperate Volunteers. Minogue, Brendan P (& others).

Medium AI and Experimental Science. Kukla, André.

Objectivity in Experimental Inquiry: Breaking Data-Technique Circles. Culp, Sylvia.

Of Nulls and Norms. Godfrey-Smith, Peter.

On the Methods of Cognitive Neuropsychology. Glymour, Clark.

On the Paradoxical Aspects of New Quantum Experiments. Vaidman, Lev.

Philosophical Craftsmanship. Hansson, Sven Ove.

Re: Reinterpreting Images. Rollins, Mark.

Reply to Eells, Humphreys and Morrison. Cartwright, Nancy.

Scientists' Responses to Anomalous Data: Evidence from Psychology, History, and Philosophy of Science. Brewer, William F and Chinn, Clark A.

Testing Models of Cognition Through the Analysis of Brain-Damaged Performance. Bub, Jeffrey.

The Impossibility of Experimental Elicitation of Subjective Probabilities. Karni, Edi.

The New Experimentalism, Topical Hypotheses, and Learning from Error. Mayo, Deborah G.

The Super Bowl and the Ox-Phos Controversy: "Winner-Take-All" Competition in Philosophy of Science. Allchin, Douglas.

Theory Change and Theory Choice. Chalmers, Alan F.

Totipotency and the Value of Embryonic Cells. Tindale, Christopher W.

Two Empirical Approaches to the Study of Reasoning. Finocchiaro, Maurice A.

Two Models of Models in Biomedical Research. LaFollette, Hugh and Shanks, Niall.

Why There Can't Be a Logic of Induction. Glennan, Stuart S.

EXPERIMENTAL

El control experimental y la construcción del objeto científico. Ginebra i Molins, M P.

La herencia de Gadamer en K O Apel: hermenéutica experimental o hermenéutica trascendental?. Domingo Moratalla, A.

EXPERIMENTALISM

see also Pragmatism

Charles Peirce's Pragmatic Pluralism. Rosenthal, Sandra B.

EXPERIMENTATION

"Embryo Experimentation: Public Policy in a Pluralist Society" in *Medicine and Moral Reasoning, Fulford, K W M (ed)*. Hare, Richard M.

"Moral Uncertainty and Human Embryo Experimentation" in *Medicine and Moral Reasoning, Fulford, K W M (ed)*. Oddie, Graham.

EXPERT

"La rhétorique de l'expertise économique" in *Rhétoriques de la science, De Coorebyter, Vincent (ed)*. McCloskey, Donald N.

Evidence, Experts, and Legal Reasoning. Holmström-Hintikka, Ghita.

Filosofía del conocimiento y sistemas expertos. Lombraña, Julián Velarde.

Seven Issues in Conducting Forensic Assessments: Ethical Responsibilities in Light of New Standards and New Tests. Butcher, James N and Pope, Kenneth S.

Sócrates: Filósofo Dogmático? Una Réplica a Alfonso Gómez-Lobo. Nudler, Oscar.

EXPERT SYSTEM

Expert System Evaluation: A Review and Integrative Model. Liebowitz, Jay and Mata-Toledo, Ramon A.

Expert Systems Evaluation. Juristo, N, Maté, J L and Pazos, J.

The Post-Implementation Evaluation of Expert Systems: Enlightenment after Five Years in the Trenches. Sharma, R S and Conrath, D W.

EXPERT WITNESS

Ethical Concerns of Nonclinical Forensic Witnesses and Consultants. Pfeifer, Jeffrey E and Brigham, John C.

Institutional Constraints on the Ethics of Expert Testimony. Sales, Bruce D and Simon, Leonore.

EXPERTISE

Philosophical Craftsmanship. Hansson, Sven Ove.

The Epistemic Authority of Expertise. Pierson, Robert.

EXPLANATION

"Anti-Individualism and Psychological Explanation" in *Philosophy of Psychology: Debates on Psychological Explanation, Macdonald, Cynthia (ed)*. Macdonald, Cynthia.

"Causal Relevance and Explanatory Exclusion" in *Philosophy of Psychology: Debates on Psychological Explanation, Macdonald, Cynthia (ed)*. Macdonald, Cynthia and Macdonald, Graham.

"Does Meaning Matter?" in *Philosophy of Psychology: Debates on Psychological Explanation, Macdonald, Cynthia (ed)*. Dretske, Frederick.

"Explanatory Exclusion and the Problem of Mental Causation" in *Philosophy of Psychology: Debates on Psychological Explanation, Macdonald, Cynthia (ed)*. Kim, Jaegwon.

"Psychoanalytic Explanation" in *Philosophy of Psychology: Debates on Psychological Explanation, Macdonald, Cynthia (ed)*. Macdonald, Graham.

"Reply: Causal Relevance and Explanatory Exclusion" in *Philosophy of Psychology: Debates on Psychological Explanation, Macdonald, Cynthia (ed)*. Dretske, Frederick.

The Context of Explanation. Bunzl, Martin.

A Brief Guide to the Work of Carl Gustav Hempel. Jeffrey, Richard.

An Erotetic Approach to Explanation by Specification. Kuipers, Theo A F and Wisniewski, Andrzej.

Causal Efficacy, Content and Levels of Explanation. Toribio, Josefa.

Causality and Conserved Quantities: A Reply to Salmon. Dowe, Phil.

Causas. Leyes Naturales y Explicaciones Científicas. Flichman, Eduardo H.

Ceteris Paribus Laws and Psychological Explanations. Wallis, Charles.

Circular Justifications. Brown, Harold I.

Denken, Handeln, und Erklärung durch Gründe: Ein Diskussionsbeitrag. Röska-Hardy, Louise.

Discussion: Salmon on Explanatory Relevance. Hitchcock, Christopher Read.

Dispositions and Scientific Explanation. Lange, Marc.

Explicando la Explicación. Diéguez, Antonio J.

Glymour on Explanation. Yi, Byeonguk.

Historia y Hermenéutica. Alcalá Campos, Raúl.

Induçao, Acaso e Racionalidade. Monteiro, Joao Paulo.

Internal and External Causal Explanations of the Universe. Smith, Quentin.

Old Evidence and New Theories. Zynda, Lyle.

On the Explanation, the Justification, and the Interpretation of Action. Myers, Robert H.

Perception and Proper Explanatory Width. Rollins, Mark.

FAITH

Rethinking Metaphysics. Jones, L Gregory (ed) and Fowl, Stephen E (ed).

Search for Community in a Withering Tradition: Conversations between a Marxian Atheist and a Calvinian Christian. Nielsen, Kai and Hart, Hendrik.

The Human Shape of God: Religion in Hegel's "Phenomenology of Spirit". Jamros, Daniel P.

Thinkers and Teachers of Modern Judaism. Goldsmith, Emanuel S (ed) and Patai, Raphael (ed).

An Explosion of Dazzling Flashes: Teilhard's Unity of Faith and Science. King, Thomas M.

Blaise Pascals "Discours sur la religion": Zu einer neueren Ausgabe der "Pensées". Raffelt, Albert.

Challenging Medical Authority: The Refusal of Treatment by Christian Scientists. May, Larry.

Cinco Claves Para Comprender a Jacques Maritain. Burgos, Juan Manuel.

Critical Historical Judgment and Biblical Faith. Evans, C Stephen.

Der "consensus gentium"—fundamentaltheologische Erwägungen zu einem vernachlässigten Gottesbeweis. Rosenau, Hartmut.

Disidencias de Pedro Abelardo. Brasa Díaz, Mariano.

El escándalo del mal. Ricoeur, Paul.

En torno a la nueva edición de Schleiermacher. Ginzo, Arsenio.

Freedom and Faith in Kierkegaard's Philosophy. Shukla, Dipti.

Il Guardiano delle Soglia. Angelini, Pietro.

Inevitable Martyrdom: The Connection Between Faith and Suffering in Kierkegaard's Later Writings. Imbrosciano, Anthony.

Just the Facts. Oberdiek, Hans F.

Justice: An Inter-Faith Task. Pattery, George.

Kierkegaard and the Historians. Rae, Murray A.

L'Esprit absolu de Hegel est-il Dieu?. Beauvais, Chantal.

La Dialéctica en el Cancionero de Baena. Sánchez-Romate, María José Gómez.

La Razón y la fe Ante la Creación Temporal del Mundo. Azcoaga Bengoechea, Ignatio M.

La Tensión Razón-Fe en la Filosofía Judeomusulmana de Al-Andalus. Ayala, Jorge M.

Leaps and Circles: Kierkegaard and Newman on Faith and Reason. Ferreira, M Jamie.

Liberalism, Pluralism, and Lived Faith. Hart, Hendrick.

Method in Catholic Theology. Lonergan, Bernard J F.

Moral Faith. Adams, Robert Merrihew.

Nootomismo a Salerno: L'Ambiente Culturale in cui visse ed Operò Pasquale Naddeo. Gigante, Mario.

Nondoxastic Faith: Audi on Religious Commitment. Radcliffe, Dana M.

Personalist and Universalistic Aspects of the Idea of Development in the Encyclical *Sollicitudo rei socialis* by John Paul II. Kowalczyk, Stanislaw.

Propositional Faith as a Mode of Belief and a Gift of God. Creel, Richard.

Reason and Rationality: The Core Doctrines of Secular Humanism. D'Agostino, S Matthew.

Reason, History, and a Little Madness: Toward a Hermeneutics of Christian Historicality. Caputo, John D.

Religious Pluralism and Interfaith Dialogue: Beyond Universalism and Particularism. Huang, Yong.

Religious Plurality and Realist Christianity: Idolatry and the Testing of One's Faith. McLeod, Mark S.

Representation, Theology and Faith. Ayres, Lewis.

Science et foi: l'apport de l'herméneutique. Bühler, Pierre.

The Beyond in the Midst: The Relevance of Dewey's Philosophy of Religion for Education. Miedema, Siebren.

The Opening up of Natural Law. Kearns, Paul.

The Problem of Inter-Faith Studies. Matilal, Bimal K.

Two Dualisms. Mautner, Thomas.

Une réflexion sur les rapports entre science et foi. Rivier, Dominique.

Wagering Belief: Examining Two Objections to Pascal's Wager. Groothuis, D.

FALLACY

see also Genetic Fallacy, Intentionalist Fallacy, Naturalistic Fallacy

Mill's Principle of Utility: A Defence of John Stuart Mill's Notorious Proof. Alican, Nejip Fikri.

Understanding Logic. Flage, Daniel E.

A Case of Affirming the Consequent in International Law: UN Security Council Resolution 232 (1966)—Southern Rhodesia. Hund, John.

Begging the Question as a Pragmatic Fallacy. Walton, Douglas N.

Denying the Antecedent: A Common Fallacy?. Burke, Michael B.

Extensionalidad, Opacidad y Estructura Intensional: Un Análisis de las Falacias en Contextos Epistémicos. José Frápolli, María.

Fallacies and Alternative Interpretations. Adler, Jonathan E.

Fallacious Reasoning. Goldstein, Laurence.

Frans H van Eemeren and Rob Grootendorst Perelman and the Fallacies. van Eemeren, Frans H and Grootendorst, Rob.

Is There an Audience for this Argument? Fallacies, Theories, and Relativisms. Crosswhite, James.

William James, the Psychologist's Dilemma and the Historiography of Psychology: Cautionary Tales. Leary, David E.

FALLIBILISM

La Aproximación a la Verdad en Peirce. Herrera Ibáñez, Alejandro.

Le faillibilisme de Jürgen Habermas et ses difficultés: un faillibilisme conséquent est-il possible?. Courtois, Stéphane.

Wittgenstein and Peirce on Meaning: The Evolution from Absolutism to Fallibilism. Boghossian, Peter G and Drewniak, Erik.

FALSE

La falsedad en el pensamiento y en el discurso: Comentarios al *Sofista* 259b al 265e. Sala, J F A.

FALSIFIABILITY

"Sobre la 'Falsación' del Falsacionismo" in *Temas Actuales de Filosofía, Palacios, María Julia (ed)*. Lucero, Susana.

Los dos significados de *falsabilidad*. Popper, Karl R.

FALSIFICATION

"Sobre la 'Falsación' del Falsacionismo" in *Temas Actuales de Filosofía, Palacios, María Julia (ed)*. Lucero, Susana.

Criticism and the History of Science. Andersson, Gunnar.

Philosophy of Science in the Twentieth Century: Four Central Themes. Gillies, Donald.

Wahrheitskriterien im Kritischen Rationalismus. Gesang, Bernward.

Die Gottesbeweise als vermeintliche Stütze von Religion und Theologie. Morscher, Edgar.

Falsificationisme versus efficiënte waarheidsbenadering. Kuipers, Theo A F.

Kuipers over waarheidsgelijkenis en wetenschappelijk realisme. Derksen, Ton.

Lying During Crisis Negotiations: A Costly Means to Expedient Resolution. Burke Jr, Francis V.

FALSITY

Falsity without Negative Predication: On *Sophistes* 255e-263d. Van Eck, Job.

Nether Logic. Sobel, Jordan Howard.

The Miracle of Counterfactuals: Counterexamples to Lewis's World Ordering. Krasner, Daniel and Heller, Mark.

The Open Past. Markosian, Ned.

The Presidential Address: Why there is really No Such Thing as the Theory of Motivation. Dancy, Jonathan.

FAMILY

"Trouble with Families?" in *Introducing Applied Ethics, Almond, Brenda (ed)*. Midgley, Mary and Hughes, Judith.

Bertrand Russell. Slater, J G.

Concepts and Cases in Nursing Ethics. Yeo, Michael (& others).

Hegel In His Time: Berlin, 1818-1831. Burbidge, John W (trans) and D'Hondt, Jacques.

Introducing Applied Ethics. Almond, Brenda (ed).

After the Family Wage: Gender Equity and the Welfare State. Fraser, Nancy.

Bioethics and Family Values. Almond, Brenda.

Clinical Ethics and Intervention In Domestic Violence. Ryan, Maura A.

Ethical and Legal Dilemmas in the Management of Family Violence. Bourne, Richard.

Family Justice and Social Justice. Waldron, Jeremy.

Family Violence and Family Systems: Who Is the Patient?. Gottlieb, Michael C.

Futility and Bargaining Power. Spielman, Bethany.

Marx, Engels, and the Abolition of the Family. Weikart, Richard.

Mothers, Citizenship, and Independence: A Critique of Pure Family Values. Young, Iris Marion.

Recognizing and Respecting Family Judgment. Swigart, Valerie.

Taking Dependency Seriously: The Family and Medical Leave Act Considered in Light of the Social Organization of Dependency Work and Gender Equality. Kittay, Eva Feder.

The Family in Trouble: Why We Should Worry. Elshtain, Jean Bethke.

The Hermeneutical Project and Clinical Ethics. Potter, Robert Lyman.

The Will to Harmony and the Pursuit of Family. Neisser, Philip T.

When Families Request That 'Everything Possible' Be Done. Jecker, Nancy S and Schneiderman, Lawrence J.

FANATICISM

Eric Hoffer, Philosopher for the People. Arnold, Richard.

Fanaticism and Integrity. Newman, Jay.

FANCY

see Imagination

FANON, F

Journey to the Native Land: Violence and the Concept of the Self in Fanon and Gandhi. Federici, Silvia.

FANTASY

Aporie del Simbolo: Saggio su Otto Weininger. Manfreda, Luigi Antonio.

Universales Poéticos, Fantasía y Racionalidad. Sevilla, José M.

FANTIN-LATOUR, H

Between Realisms: From Derrida to Manet. Fried, Michael.

FARADAY, M

Experiment, Speculation and Law: Faraday's Analysis of Arago's Wheel. Steinle, Friedrich.

Michael Faraday's Concept of Ultimate Reality and Meaning. Utke, Allen R.

The Whewell-Faraday Exchange on the Application of the Concepts of Momentum and Inertia to Electromagnetic Phenomena. Anderson, Ronald.

FARM

Animal Welfare and Human Values. Preece, Rod and Chamberlain, Lorna.

FARMER

Ethics Perceptions of American Farmers: An Empirical Analysis. Rappaport, Allen and Himschoot, Robert A.

FARMING

Beyond the Terms of the Contract: Mothers and Farmers. Campbell, Mora.

Journalists' Views of Advertiser Pressures on Agricultural News. Reisner, Ann and Walter, Gerry.

Redemptive Communities: Indigenous Knowledge, Colonist Farming Systems, and Conservation of Tropical Forests. Browder, John O.

FARMING
Wes Jackson, Wendell Berry, and Bruce Colman (eds): *Meeting the Expectations of the Land: Essays in Sustainable Agriculture and Stewardship*. Houle, K.

FASCISM
"Anti-Semitism and Fascist Propaganda" in *Adorno: The Stars Down to Earth and Other Essays on the Irrational in Culture, Crook, Stephen (ed)*. Adorno, Theodor W.
"Die Rezeption der Philosophie Friedrich Nietzsches im deutschen Faschismus" in *Die besten Geister der Nation, Korotin, Ilse (ed)*. Zapata, Martha.
"Gescheitert—Der Versuch zur etablierung Nationalsozialistischer Philosophen an der Un. München" in *Die besten Geister der Nation, Korotin, Ilse (ed)*. Schorcht, Claudia.
"Research Project on Anti-Semitism" in *Adorno: The Stars Down to Earth and Other Essays on the Irrational in Culture, Crook, Stephen (ed)*. Adorno, Theodor W.
"Schopenhauer als Ahnherr einer faschistischen Anthropologie" in *Die besten Geister der Nation, Korotin, Ilse (ed)*. Klinger, Gerwin.
Adorno: The Stars Down to Earth and Other Essays on the Irrational in Culture. Crook, Stephen (ed) and Adorno, Theodor W.
Feminist Interpretations of Hannah Arendt. Honig, Bonnie (ed).
Philosophen im "Dritten Reich": Studie zu Hochschul- und Philosophiebetrieb im faschistischen Deutschland. Leske, Monika.
Philosophieverhältnisse im deutschen Faschismus. Laugstien, Thomas.
Preface to Modernism. Berman, Art.
The Broken Middle: Out of our Ancient Society. Rose, Gillian.
Blindingly Obvious Christian Anti-Semitism. Stump, Eleonore and Kretzmann, Norman.
Contextualising Carl Schmitt's Concept of *Grossraum*. Schwab, Georg.
Critical Theory and Pre-Fascist Social Thought. Stauth, Georg.
Die Kant-Studien im Dritten Reich. Leaman, George and Simon, Gerd.
Facts and Truth. Esser, Piet H.
Gentile Ritrovato? Note sui più Recenti Studi Gentiliani. Ferrari, Massimo.
Gnōthi Sauton: Heidegger's Problem Ours. Swazo, Norman K.
Heidegger, Nietzsche, Jünger, and the Interpretation of the Contemporary Age. Ibáñez-Noé, Javier A.
Hirsch on Education and National Culture: A Critique. Grant, Robert.
La Fortuna di Croce e Gentile negli Stati Uniti. Roberts, David D.
Lon L Fuller, Gustav Radbruch, and the "Positivist" Theses. Paulson, Stanley L.
On Brinks and Bridges in Heidegger. Fritsche, Johannes.
Rassegne Crociane: I. I Carteggi dell'Ultimo Decennio. II. Una Bibliografia "Ragionata". Miccolis, Stefano.
The End of Philosophy, the Time of Auschwitz, and the Bound Transcendence of Communities of Differences. Watson, James R.
The Philosophical Bases of Heidegger's Politics: A Response to Wolin. Sikka, Sonya.
Zur Geschichte der Israelitengemeinde von Prostejov (Prossnitz). Elias, Bohuslav.

FASHION
"Fashion and Signification in Baudrillard" in *Baudrillard: A Critical Reader, Kellner, Douglas M (ed)*. Tseëlon, Efrat.
Afro Images: Politics, Fashion, and Nostalgia. Davis, Angela Y.

FATALISM
The Ethical Primate: Humans, Freedom and Morality. Midgley, Mary.
Does Theological Fatalism Rest on an Equivocation?. Hunt, David P.
Schopenhauer im Spiegel der europäischen Literatur des 19 und 20 Jarhunderts. Ries, Wiebrecht.
The Open Past. Markosian, Ned.

FATE
Luck and the Enigmas of Fate. Rescher, Nicholas.
Reflections on the Perception of Time in Poland in the 16th and 17th Centuries. Bogucka, Maria.

FATHER
Fathers' Rights, Mothers' Wrongs? Reflections on Unwed Fathers' Rights and Sex Equality. Shanley, Mary L.

FAULCONER, J
Can Post-Newtonian Psychologists Find Happiness in a Pre-Paradigm Science?. Roth, Paul A.

FAULT
Wild Beasts and Idle Humours: Legal Insanity and the Finding of Fault. Robinson, Daniel N.

FAUSTIAN
"Der faustische Mensch—Die Wissenschaft als euripäisches Erbe" in *Das geistige Erbe Europas, Buhr, Manfred (ed)*. Eriksson, Gunnar.
"Der philosophische Aufstieg des faustischen Menschen" in *Das geistige Erbe Europas, Buhr, Manfred (ed)*. Gedö, András.

FEAR
see also Anxiety
Fear, Truth, Writing: From Paper Village to Electronic Community. Brown, Alison Leigh.
A Note on the Intentionality of Fear. Horowitz, Amir.
An Answer to Lucretius' Symmetry Argument Against the Fear of Death. Kaufman, Frederik.
Fear and Belief. Neill, Alex.
Justice and the Distribution of Fear. Burgess-Jackson, Keith.
Miedo e Incertidumbre. Hansberg, Olbeth.
Pain Relief for Dying Persons: Dealing with Physicians' Fears and Concerns. Buchan, Melissa L and Tolle, Susan W.
The *Fin De Siècle* Redux. London, Herb.

FECHNER, G
"Fechners Verhältnis zur Naturphilosophie Schellings" in *Schelling und die Selbstorganisation, Heuser-Kessler, Marie-Luise (ed)*. Heidelberger, Michael.

FECHNER, T
Le radici romantiche della simbolica di Otto Weininger. Lotito, Leonardo.

FEDER, J
"Beschrieene Dunkelheit" und "Seichtigkeit". Petrus, Helke.

FEDERAL
When OPRR Comes Calling: Enforcing Federal Research Regulations. McCarthy, Charles R.

FEDERALISM
Federalist Theory and World Peace. Newcombe, Hanna.

FEELING
see also Emotion
"Theoretical Perspectives on Emotions in Early Buddhism" in *Emotions in Asian Thought, Marks, Joel (ed)*. De Silva, Padmasiri.
Das Problem des Einen und Vielen in Platons "Philebos". Löhr, Gebbhard.
G W F Hegel: El *Fragmento de Tubinga*. del Carmen Paredes, María.
Hanslick on Hearing Beauty. Shibles, Warren A.
La Vivencia de lo Sublime y la Experiencia Moral en Kant. Ribeiro dos Santos, Leonel.
Reconsidering Pain. Nelkin, Norton.
Schopenhauer, Feeling and the Noumenon. Nicholls, Moira.
Sentiment and Sentimentality in Practical Ethics. Feinberg, Joel.
The Complexity of Bodily Feeling. Wallulis, Jerald T.
The Form of Feeling. Yob, Iris M.
The Significance of Emotions. Helm, Bennett W.
The Status of Expressive Content. Kemp, Gary.

FEIBLEMAN, J
Alice in Wittgenstein: Inside the Great Mirror. Gray, Christopher Berry.

FEIJOO, B
Fr Benito J Feijóo, profesor de filosofía escolástica. López Vázquez, J Ramón.

FEINBERG, J
"Benign and Malign Morality" in *In Harm's Way, Coleman, Jules L (ed)*. Gross, Hyman.
In Harm's Way. Coleman, Jules L (ed) and Buchanan, Allen (ed).
Religious Luck. Zagzebski, Linda.
Thresholds for Rights. Brennan, Samantha.
When Is Birth Unfair to the Child?. Steinbock, Bonnie and McClamrock, Ron.

FELDMAN, F
A Deadly Delight: Feldman on the Nature and Value of Death. Haji, Ishtiyaque.

FELDMAN, R
Why We Need Proper Function. Plantinga, Alvin.

FEMALE
see also Feminism, Woman, Women
"Male and Female in the Modern World" in *The Nature and Pursuit of Love, Goicoechea, David (ed)*. Mitterer, John.
Damenphilosophie und Männermoral: Von Abbé de Gérard bis Marquis de Sade Ein Versuch über die lächelnde Vernunft. Jauch, Ursula Pia.

FEMININE
On Calling God 'Mother'. Harper, William.

FEMININITY
Anima hace hablar a la razón con una voz diferente: Nuevos nexos entre la tecnociencia y el mundo de la vida. Cañón Loyes, Camino.

FEMINISM
see also Female, Woman
"Biologistische und Rassistische Tendenzen im spirituellen Öko-Feminismus" in *Der feministische "Sündenfall"?, Kohn-Ley, Charlotte (ed)*. Wölflingseder, Maria.
"Der Antifeminismus und Antisemitismus Otto Weiningers " in *Der feministische "Sündenfall"?, Kohn-Ley, Charlotte (ed)*. Schröder, Hannelore.
"Disembodiment: Abortion and Gay Rights" in *Radical Philosophy of Law, Caudill, David S (ed)*. Colker, Ruth.
"Feminism Without Guarantees" in *Marxism in the Postmodern Age, Callari, Antonio (ed)*. Stabile, Carol A.
"Feminist Legal Critics: The Reluctant Radicals" in *Radical Philosophy of Law, Caudill, David S (ed)*. Smith, Patricia.
"Feminist Queries and Metaphysical Musings" in *Rethinking Metaphysics, Jones, L Gregory (ed)*. Chopp, Rebecca S.
"For a Careful Reading" in *Feminist Contentions, Benhabib, Seyla (& others)*. Butler, Judith.
"Hermeneutics, Tradition, and the Standpoint of Women" in *Hermeneutics and Truth, Wachterhauser, Brice (ed)*. Warnke, Georgia.
"Je—Luce Irigaray": A Meeting with Luce Irigaray. Hirsh, Elizabeth and Olson, Gary A.
"Jungians, Archetypalists, and Fear of Feminism" in *The 1994 Annual of Hermeneutics and Social Concern, Lawler, Justus George (ed)*. Rigsby, Roberta K.
"Konfigurationen des Patriarchats, des Judentums und des Nazismus im deutschen feministischen Denken" in *Der feministische "Sündenfall"?, Kohn-Ley, Charlotte (ed)*. Heschel, Susannah.
"La Filosofía Sexista, la Epistemología Feminista y Otras Vicisitudes de la Razón" in *Temas Actuales de Filosofía, Palacios, María Julia (ed)*. Maffía, Diana Elena.
"Marriage, Law, and Gender: A Feminist Inquiry" in *Radical Philosophy of Law, Caudill, David S (ed)*. Hunter, Nan D.

FICHTE

Von der Reichweite mathematischen Denkens bei Fichte und Novalis. Csech, Werner.

Zur Geschichtserkenntnis nach der Transzendentalphilosophie. Ivaldo, Marco.

Zwischen Apriorismus und Empirismus im Kontext der Isomorphie zweier Apriorismen: Zur Rekonstruktion von Fichtes philosophischer Konzeption. Kiss, Endre.

FICINO

Epistemologie im Humanismus: Marsilio Ficino, Pietro Pomponazzi und Niklaus von Kues. Burkhard, Mojsisch.

Florence, 1492: Réapparaît Plotin. Saffrey, Henri Dominique.

Le Fonti del "Sigillus Sigillorum" del Bruno, Ossia: Il Confronto con Ficino a Oxford Sull'anima Umana. Sturlese, Rita.

Melancholie—Sizze zur epistemologischen Deutung eines Topos. Krämer, Sybille.

Notabilia IV: Hinweise auf wichtige Neuerscheinungen aus dem Bereich der mittelalterlichen Philosophie. Imbach, Ruedi.

Plotino, Ficino e noi stessi: alcuni riflessi etici. Rist, John M and Peroli, E (trans).

FICTION

"Fiktive Welt im literarischen Kunstwerk" in *Kunst und Ontologie, Wlodzimierz, Galewicz (ed)*. Ströker, Elisabeth.

"Getting the Story Straight: Narrative and Historical Knowledge" in *Historiography Between Modernism and Postmodernism, Topolski, Jerzy (ed)*. Carr, David.

"How Dare You Sport Thus with Life?": Frankensteinian Fictions as Case Studies in Scientific Ethics. Goldbort, Robert C.

"The Truth about Fiction" in *Kunst und Ontologie, Wlodzimierz, Galewicz (ed)*. Seifert, Joseph and Smith, Barry.

Lolita and Aristotle's Ethics. Levino, Peter.

Nietzsche's Aesthetic Turn: Reading Nietzsche after Heidegger, Deleuze, Derrida. Winchester, James J.

Race and Mixed Race. Zack, Naomi.

Syncope: The Philosophy of Rapture. O'Driscoll, Sally (trans), Clément, Catherine and Mahoney, Deirdre M (trans).

The 1994 Annual of Hermeneutics and Social Concern. Lawler, Justus George (ed).

Utopie II ou Vers une Société des Personnes. Adam, E.

A Desperate Fix. Hale, Bob.

Aristotle on Detective Fiction. Sayers, Dorothy L.

Beliefs and Fictional Narrators. Matravers, Derek.

Edward Said on Contrapuntal Reading. Wilson, George M.

Emotional Responses to Fiction: Reply to Radford. Neill, Alex.

Enjoying Horror Fictions: A Reply to Gaut. Carroll, Noël.

Fiction and the *De Se* Self. Vance, Robert D.

Fiction as "Grammatical" Investigation: A Wittgensteinian Account. Schalkwyk, David.

Fiction et Vérité. Sasaki, Ken-ichi.

Fiction, Pity, Fear, and Jealousy. Radford, Colin.

Film, Fiktion und psychoanalytische Theorie. Allen, Richard.

How Can We Live in a World of the Absurd? The Humanism of Albert Camus. Lowen, Jeanette.

Images of Corporate Executives in Recent Fiction. Sarachek, Bernard.

Kendall L Walton's *Mimesis as Make-Believe*. Carroll, Noël.

Las Emociones ante la Ficción. Bejarano, Teresa.

Max Black on the Identity of Indiscernibles. Cross, Charles B.

Merleau-Ponty and Literary Language. Morrison, James C.

Modal Fictionalism Cannot Deliver Possible World Semantics. Divers, John.

Modal Fictionalism Fixed. Rosen, Gideon.

Modal Fictionalism—a Simple Dilemma. Hale, Bob.

On the Leveling of the Genre Distinction Between Theory and Fiction. Weinstein, Jami.

Phenomenological Reflections on the Self and the Other—As Real, As Fictional. Paskow, Alan.

Science as Truth. Atkins, Peter.

Spinoza et le Totalitarisme: Fiction et Réalité. Rougemont, Jean-Daniel.

The Case of a Broken Cohesive Chain. Kurzon, Dennis.

The Enjoyment Theory of Horror: A Response to Carroll. Gaut, Berys.

The Logic of Fictional Descriptions. Kastin, Jonathan.

The Moral Psychology of Fiction. Currie, Gregory.

The Nature of Fictional Characters and The Referential Fallacy. Dauer, Francis W.

The Paradox of Emotion and Fiction. Yanal, Robert J.

The Paradox of Junk Fiction. Carroll, Noël.

The Value of Reading Fiction. Gleeson, Gerald.

Towards Discourse in the Public Domain: Adolescent Fictions in Moral and Political Education. Gooderham, David.

Unreliability Refigured: Narrative in Literature and Film. Currie, Gregory.

Who's Telling this Story, Anyway? Or, How to Tell the Gender of a Storyteller. Barwell, Ismay.

Worlds within Worlds? The Paradoxes of Embedded Fiction. Le Poidevin, Robin.

FIDEISM

Analisi della Fede e Critica della Ragione nella Filosofia di Pierre Bayle. Paganini, Gianni.

Ateismo, scetticismo e fideismo. Penelhum, Terence.

FIDELITY

Adultery and Fidelity. Martin, Mike W.

FIEDLER, C

On Artistic Process: Eye, Hand, Language. Nitta, Hiroë.

FIELD

Anneaux de Fonctions *p*-Adiques. Bélair, Luc.

Corps et Chirurgie. Pillay, Anand and Poizat, Bruno.

Diophantine Equivalence and Countable Rings. Shlapentokh, Alexandra.

Elimination des Quantificateurs dans des Paires de Corps. Leloup, G.

FIELD THEORY

A Formal Framework for Quantum Non-Individuality. Krause, Décio and French, Steven.

Interpretations of Quantum Field Theory. Huggett, Nick and Weingard, Robert.

Is Algebraic Lorentz-Covariant Quantum Field Theory Stochastic Einstein Local?. Muller, F A and Butterfield, Jeremy.

On the Field Aspect of Quantum Fields. Huggett, Nick and Weingard, Robert.

The Renormalisation Group and Effective Field Theories. Huggett, Nick and Weingard, Robert.

FIELD, H

Narrow Content: A Defence. Silverberg, Arnold.

FIFTHTEENTH CENTURY

see Renaissance

FIGAL, G

The Hermeneutics of the Emerging of Being (On Figal's Interpretation of Heidegger). Cibulka, Josef.

FIGURE

"Le figuré et le littéral dans le langage scientifique" in *Rhétoriques de la science, De Coorebyter, Vincent (ed)*. Kremer-Marietti, Angèle.

I principi matematici kantiani del mondo fisico, II. Pellecchia, Pasquale.

FILIPINO

Exploitation in the Use of Human Subjects for Medical Experimentation: A Re-Examination of Basic Issues. de Castro, Leonardo D.

FILLMORE, C

Whorf's Empty Gasoline Drum and the Pope's Missing Wife. Edwards, Derek.

FILM

"Postmodernism and Deconstructionism" in *Postmodernism and Social Inquiry, Dickens, David R (ed)*. Denzin, Norman K.

American Mixed Race: The Culture of Microdiversity. Zack, Naomi (ed).

The Counterfeit Wisdom of Shallow Minds: A Critique of Some Leading Offenders of the 1980's. Habermehl, Lawrence.

The Philosophy of the Visual Arts. Alperson, Philip (ed).

Brandon Shaw, Neil Perry, and the Perils of Education. Calhoun, Laura.

Der audio-visuelle Kontrakt—der Lärm um das Reale. Zizek, Slavoj.

Der Gedanke als Überblendung in der Folge der Bilder: Peirces visuelles Modell geistiger Prozesse. Pape, Helmut.

Film, Fiktion und psychoanalytische Theorie. Allen, Richard.

Fotografien sind wie Namen. Seel, Martin.

Lust und Weisheit des Scheines: Die Alptraumwelt Alfred Hitchcocks. Fink-Eitel, Hinrich.

Nachstellungen—Film und historischer Moment. Koch, Gertrud.

Schwerpunkt: Philosophie und Film—ein hundertjähriges Verhältnis. Koch, Gertrud.

The Nature of Fictional Characters and The Referential Fallacy. Dauer, Francis W.

Unreliability Refigured: Narrative in Literature and Film. Currie, Gregory.

FILTER

A Model for Intuitionistic Non-standard Arithmetic. Moerdijk, I.

Filters and Large Cardinals. Levinski, Jean-Pierre.

The Structure of Pleasant Ideals. Leary, Christopher C.

FINAL CAUSE

Metafísica de la finalidad natural: Su metamorfosis en la línea Kant-Schopenhauer-Nietzsche. Rodriguez Gonzalez, M.

FINALITY

"L'argumentation finaliste en biologie" in *Rhétoriques de la science, De Coorebyter, Vincent (ed)*. Duchesneau, François.

A Proposito de la Critica del Juicio. Labrada, María Antonia.

Analogia della legge: Uno studio su S Tommaso d'Aquino. Vendemiati, Aldo.

God as Final Cause in Spinoza (in Hebrew). Sigad, Ran.

L'idée de Finalité dans l'esthétique de Giovanni Gentile. Moutsopoulos, Evanghélos A.

Nietzsche: A Origem da Linguagem. Lessa da Fonseca, Thelma Silveira Mota.

'Potere' e 'ragione' nel *Dialogus* di Pietro Alfonsi (Mosà Sefardi): Linee preliminari per una ipotesi interpretativa. Arduini, Maria Lodovica.

FINANCE

Business Ethics at Work. Vallance, Elizabeth.

A Comparison of Japanese and U S Corporate Financial Accountability and its Impact on the Responsibilties of Corporate Managers. Hazera, Alejandro.

Accounting for Ethics: Where Does Ethics Fit into Accounting Theory and Accounting Practice?. Engström, Timothy H.

Elements of Accounting Ethics: The Notion of "Fairness". Carpenter, David J.

Ethics and Accounting Doctoral Education. Loeb, Stephen E.

Helps for CPAs in Dealing with Ethical Issues. Cooper, Robert W, Frank, Garry L and Heaston, Patrick H.

Limits to the Effectiveness of Accounting Ethics Education. Shaub, Michael K.

Possible Ethical Issues and Their Impact on The Firm: Perceptions Held by Public Accountants. David, Jeanne M, Kantor, Jeffrey and Greenberg, Ira.

Teaching Ethics in Accounting Curricula. Lampe, James C and Finn, Don W.

The Ethical Importance of Conflicts of Interest: Accounting and Finance Examples. Dilworth, John B.

FINE ART

Kant on Fine Art: Artistic Sublimity Shaped by Beauty. Wicks, Robert.

Kant's Confusion of Expression with Communication. Cantrick, Robert B.

FOLK PSYCHOLOGY

"Es la Psicología del Sentido Común (Folk Psychology) una Teoría?" in *Temas Actuales de Filosofía, Palacios, María Julia (ed)*. González, María Cristina.

Folk Psychology: The Theory of Mind Debate. Davies, Martin (ed) and Stone, Tony (ed).

A Corrective to the Ramsey-Lewis Account of Theoretical Terms. O'Leary-Hawthorne, John.

Connectionism and the Fate of Folk Psychology: A Reply to Ramsey, Stich and Garon. Forster, Malcolm and Saidel, Eric.

Dispositional Beliefs and Dispositions to Believe. Audi, Robert.

Intentionality and Economics. Cottrell, Allin.

FOLLESDAL, D

Do Modal Distinctions Collapse in Carnap's System?. Marti, Genoveva.

FOOD

Food: Multidisciplinary Perspectives. Harriss-White, Barbara (ed) and Hoffenberg, Raymond (ed).

Dilemmas of Emergency Food: A Guide for the Perplexed. Poppendieck, Janet E.

Do Agriculturalists Need a New, an Ecocentric, Ethic? 1994 Presidential Address to the Agriculture, Food, and Human Values Society. Comstock, Gary L.

Ethical Concerns and Risk Perceptions Associated with Different Applications of Genetic Engineering. Frewer, Lynn J and Shepherd, Richard.

Food in India. Olivelle, Patrick.

Off the Treadmill? Technology and Tourism in the North American Maple Syrup Industry. Hinrichs, C Clare.

Recognizing Rationalizations Among Responses to Hunger. Dandekar, Natalie.

FORCE

'Coordinative Definition' and Reichenbach's Semantic Framework: A Reassessment. Shapiro, Lionel Stefan.

FORCING

ω_1 as an Initial Segment of the *c*-Degrees. Groszek, Marcia.

A Simpler Proof of Jensen's Coding Theorem. Friedman, Sy D.

Boolean Algebras, Stone Spaces, and the Iterated Turing Jump. Jockusch Jr, Carl G and Soare, Robert I.

Chains and Antichans in Interval Algebras. Bekkali, M.

Coherent Sequences Versus Radin Sequences. Cummings, James.

Combinatorial Properties of Classical Forcing Notions. Brendle, Jörg.

Forcing in Nonstandard Analysis. Ozawa, Masanao.

Hechler Reals. Labedzki, Grzegorz and Repicky, Miroslav.

Martin's Axiom and the Continuum. Judah, Haim and Roslanowski, Andrzej.

More About Relatively Lawless Sequences. Moschovakis, Joan Rand.

On the Equivalence of Certain Consequences of the Proper Forcing Axiom. Nyikos, Peter and Piatkiewicz, Leszek.

Power Set Recursion. Moss, Lawrence S.

Regularity Properties for Dominating Projective Sets. Brendle, Jörg.

Semimorasses and Nonreflection at Singular Cardinals. Koszmider, Piotr.

The Consistency Strength of an Infinitary Ramsey Property. Kafkoulis, George.

Ultrafilters on Omega. Baumgartner, James E.

FORD, L

The Original Version of Process and Reality, Part V: A Tentative Reconstruction. Hurtubise, Denis.

FOREIGN POLICY

Inducing Fair Trade Out of Hegemonic Trade. Dacey, Raymond.

Mathematical Models of Foreign Policy Decision-Making: Compensatory vs Noncompensatory. Mintz, Alex, Geva, Nehemia and Derouen Jr, Karl.

FOREKNOWLEDGE

Eternity and Freedom: A Critical Analysis of Divine Timelessness as a Solution to the Foreknowledge/Free Will Debate. Robinson, Michael D.

The Sea Battle and the Master Argument: Aristotle and Diodorus Cronus on the Metaphysics of the Future. Gaskin, Richard.

Augustine on Prescience and Free Will. den Bok, Nico.

Foreknowledge and Human Freedom in Augustine. Morgan, Vance G.

Leibniz on Divine Foreknowledge. Sleigh, Robert.

Leibniz on Divine Foreknowledge of Future Contingents and Human Freedom. Murray, Michael J.

Molina on Divine Foreknowledge and the Principle of Bivalence. Gaskin, Richard.

Time and Foreknowledge: A Critique of Zagzebski. Oaklander, L Nathan.

FORENSICS

Ethical Concerns of Nonclinical Forensic Witnesses and Consultants. Pfeifer, Jeffrey E and Brigham, John C.

Seven Issues in Conducting Forensic Assessments: Ethical Responsibilities in Light of New Standards and New Tests. Butcher, James N and Pope, Kenneth S.

Social Responsibility Ethics: Doing Right, Doing Good, Doing Well. Clark, Charles R.

The Relation Between Ethical Codes and Moral Principles. Bersoff, Donald N and Koeppl, Peter M.

Use and Then Prove, or Prove and Then Use? Some Thoughts on the Ethics of Mental Health Professionals' Courtroom Involvement. Faust, David.

FORESIGHT

"Foresight in Insight? A Darwinian Answer" in *The Nature of Insight, Sternberg, Robert J (ed)*. Simonton, Dean Keith.

FOREST

Critical Environmental Hermeneutics. van Buren, John.

FORGETTING

La Ilustración y el problema del pasado: La reflexión de Nietzsche en torno a la memoria y el olvido. Avila Crespo, Remedios.

FORGIVENESS

Forgiveness. Lang, Berel.

Forgiving as an Obligation of the Moral Life. Harvey, J.

Moral Anger, Forgiving, and Condoning. Hughes, Paul M.

On Forgiving Oneself: A Reply to Snow. Hughes, Paul M.

FORKING

Meager Forking. Newelski, Ludomir.

FORM

see also Essence, Idea

"Existence, Location, and Function: The Appreciation of Architecture" in *Philosophy and Architecture, Mitias, Michael H (ed)*. Carlson, Allen.

"Is Architecture Art?" in *Philosophy and Architecture, Mitias, Michael H (ed)*. Davies, Stephen.

"On the Theoretical Form of Hegel's Aesthetics" in *Hegel Reconsidered, Engelhardt Jr, H Tristram (ed)*. Aschenberg, Reinhold.

"The Myth of Meaningful Forms" in *Philosophy and Architecture, Mitias, Michael H (ed)*. Weber, Ralf.

Aporie del Simbolo: Saggio su Otto Weininger. Manfreda, Luigi Antonio.

Beiträge zu Aristoteles' Naturphilosophie. Seidl, Horst.

Le Même et L'Autre dans la Structure Ontologique du Timée de Platon. Brisson, Luc (ed).

Philosophy and Architecture. Mitias, Michael H (ed).

Plato's Ethics. Irwin, Terence.

Pragmatist Aesthetics: Living Beauty, Rethinking Art. Shusterman, Richard.

The Platonic Odyssey: A Philosophical-Literary Inquiry into the "Phaedo". Gilead, Amihud.

Thinking About Logic: An Introduction to the Philosophy of Logic. Read, Stephen.

Absolute Forms of Gödel's Incompleteness Theorem. Kim, Sangmun.

Commentary on Sayre's "Why Plato Never Had a Theory of Forms". Griswold, Charles.

Forme e metafore dell'intuizione in Friedrich Hölderlin. Augello, Giuseppe.

Formes Métaphysiques et Etres Empiriques Selon Proclus. Térézis, Christos.

Genus/Diferentia, Matter/Form, and Levels of Complexity. Freytag, Matthew.

Logical Form and the Hidden-Indexical Theory: A Reply to Schiffer. Ludlow, Peter.

Perceiving Particulars and Recollecting the Forms in the *Phaedo*. Osborne, Catherine.

Plato on Self-Predication of "the fine"—*Hippias Major* 292, e6-7. Kato, Motoaki.

Should Plato's Line Be Divided in the Mean and Extreme Ratio?. Balashov, Yuri V.

The Creation of 'Eternal' Objects. Ford, Lewis S.

The Definition of Soul in Aristotle's *De anima* ii 1 Is Not Analogous to the Definition of Snub. Wehrle, Walter E.

The Modern Misunderstanding of Aristotle's Theory of Motion. Balaban, Oded.

Vlastos on Socratic and Platonic Forms. Fine, Gail.

Why Plato Never Had a Theory of Forms. Sayre, Kenneth.

Wittgenstein on Forms of Life: Towards a Transcendental Iperspective. Pradhan, R C.

FORMAL

The Undecidability of Formal Definitions in the Theory of Finite Groups. da Costa, Newton C A, Doria, Francisco A and Tsuji, Marcelo.

FORMAL LANGUAGE

"Das Problem der Sprache in der Philosophie" in *Die Sprache in den Wissenschaften, Weingartner, Paul (ed)*. Weingartner, Paul.

FORMAL LOGIC

Die Vollständigkeit der kantischen Urteilstafel. Wolff, Michael.

Nietzsche e il Nonsense. Arena, Leonardo Vittorio.

Attualità nelle leggi logiche in Giovanni Duns Scoto. Olejnik, Roman M.

Il predicato di dimostrabilità e la nozione di consistenza: alternative alla formulazione classica. Ballarino, Annamaria.

The Logic of Probability. Angell, Richard B (trans) and De Finetti, Bruno.

FORMALISM

"The Chaotic Indeterminacy of Tort Law: Between Formalism and Nihilism" in *Radical Philosophy of Law, Caudill, David S (ed)*. Brion, Denis J.

Appropriation and Interpretation. Sartwell, Crispin.

Consideraciones en Torno a la Esencia del Formalismo Ético. García Norro, Juan José.

Formalism of Kant's A Priori Versus Scheler's Material A Priori. Moosa, Imtiaz.

Formalism, Realism, and the Concept of Law. Stokes, Michael.

Gentile e Gödel. Sainati, Vittorio.

Grammar Formalisms Viewed as Evolving Algebras. Johnson, David E and Moss, Lawrence S.

La esencia del formalismo ético. Palacios, Juan Miguel.

La Etica en Husserl. Ferrer, Urbano.

Measurement and the Interpretation of Quantum Mechanics and Relativity Theory. De Muynck, W M.

Reasoning, Logic and Computation. Shapiro, Stewart.

The Domain of Set Valued Feature Structures. Moshier, M Andrew and Pollard, Carl J.

The Formal Sciences Discover the Philosophers' Stone. Franklin, J.

Whitehead's Early Philosophy of Mathematics. Henry, Granville C and Valenza, Robert J.

FORMALIZATION

A Note on Formalisations of First-Order Theories. Stepien, Teodor.

Formalization in Philosophical Logic. Jacquette, Dale.

On Formalization of Model-Theoretic Proofs of Gödel's Theorems. Kikuchi, Makoto and Tanaka, Kazuyuki.

FORMULA

In Defence of the Barcan Formula. Cresswell, M J.

FREEDOM

FUTURE

"Die Zukunft der Antike" in *Das geistige Erbe Europas, Buhr, Manfred (ed)*. Mittelstrass, Jürgen.

"The Future of Environmental Philosophy" in *Ecology, Technology, and Culture, Zweers, Wim (ed)*. Vermeersch, Etienne.

"The Future of Social Theory and the Limits of Postmodern Critique" in *Postmodernism and Social Inquiry, Dickens, David R (ed)*. Antonio, Robert J and Kellner, Douglas.

Imagination and Time. Warnock, Mary.

Powers of the Rational: Science, Technology, and the Future of Thought. Birmingham, Peg (trans), Janicaud, Dominique and Birmingham, Elizabeth (trans).

The Sea Battle and the Master Argument: Aristotle and Diodorus Cronus on the Metaphysics of the Future. Gaskin, Richard.

Vergangenheit als Zukunft. Haller, Michael (ed) and Habermas, Jürgen.

Categorical Desires and the Future. Yonah, Yossi.

Contemporary Property Rights, Lockean Provisos, and the Interests of Future Generations. Wolf, Clark.

Cosmopolitan Universalism: Prolegomena to a Future Ideology. Arnopoulos, Paris.

El Futuro Requiere de Pasado (Nota Para Una Hermenéutica de la Narración Histórica). Chico, Gabriel.

Envisioning Ecological Sustainability: The Need and a Method. Carroll, John E.

Gauthier, Property Rights, and Future Generations. Sauvé, Kevin.

How Should Future Opinion Affect Current Opinion?. Foley, Richard.

In and Out of Time. Gault, Richard.

La Democracia y el Futuro del Socialismo. Fernández del Riesgo, Manuel.

La posible contribución de la filosofía clásica rusa a la construcción de una sociedad humanista. Kline, Goerge L.

Nietzsche y el Problema del Lenguaje en la Perspectiva de la Musica. Cragnolini, Mónica B.

Nietzsche's Future Perfect and the Eternal Return: Toward a Genealogy of Ideas. Boothroyd, David.

On an Argument about Reference to Future Individuals. Oppy, Graham.

Philosophy and Future. Rorty, Richard.

Preparing for the 21st Century: A Philosophy for New Thinking. Parsons, Howard L.

Present Concerns and Future Interests. Magnell, Thomas.

Second Thoughts: Revoking Decisions Over One's Own Future. Radden, Jennifer.

The Death of Philosophy and the Future of Thought. Stellardi, Giuseppe A.

The Future Perfect and the Perfect Future: History has its Reasons. Flynn, Thomas R.

The Time-Space of Human Life. Cackowski, Zdzislaw.

The Universal and the Particular Reflections on the Future. Cauchy, Venant.

Vorzukunft. Hrachovec, Herbert.

What Time Is Not: Critical Remarks on Husserl's Analysis of Time. Wälde, Martin.

FUTURE GENERATION

"Verantwortung für zukünftige Generationen" in *Freiheit, Verantwortung und Folgen in der Wissenschaft, Sandkühler, Hans Jörg (ed)*. Birnbacher, Dieter.

FUZZINESS

The Philosophy of Fuzziness and the Mathematics of Randomness. Gerstenkorn, Tadeusz and Manko, Jacek.

FUZZY LOGIC

Modalities in Vector Logic. Mizraji, Eduardo.

GADAMER, H

"Emanation, Incarnation, and the Truth-Event in Gadamer's *Truth and Method*" in *Hermeneutics and Truth, Wachterhauser, Brice (ed)*. Carpenter, David.

"Gadamer and Augustine: On the Origin of the Hermeneutical Claim to Universality" in *Hermeneutics and Truth, Wachterhauser, Brice (ed)*. Grondin, Jean.

"Gadamer's Realism: The 'Belongingness' of Word and Reality" in *Hermeneutics and Truth, Wachterhauser, Brice (ed)*. Wachterhauser, Brice.

"Hermeneutics, Tradition, and the Standpoint of Women" in *Hermeneutics and Truth, Wachterhauser, Brice (ed)*. Warnke, Georgia.

"On the Ground of Understanding" in *Hermeneutics and Truth, Wachterhauser, Brice (ed)*. Bubner, Rüdiger.

"The Experience of Truth for Gadamer and Heidegger: Taking Time and Sudden Lightning" in *Hermeneutics and Truth, Wachterhauser, Brice (ed)*. Dostal, Robert J.

"The Remembrance of Truth: The Truth of Remembrance" in *Hermeneutics and Truth, Wachterhauser, Brice (ed)*. Risser, James C.

"Understanding Truth and Objectivity: A Dialogue between Davidson and Gadamer" in *Hermeneutics and Truth, Wachterhauser, Brice (ed)*. Stueber, Karsten R.

I Sentieri di Heidegger di Hans Georg Gadamer. Caracciolo, Alberto.

Sources of Hermeneutics. Grondin, Jean.

Sunyata, Textualism, and Incommensurability. Barnhart, Michael G.

Critique of Ideology: Hermeneutics or Critical Theory?. Nuyen, A I.

Denken, Sprechen und Verstehen bei Matthias Flacius Illyricus. Kordic, Ivan.

Gadamer and the Platonic *Eidos*. Kidder, Paulette.

Gadamer über Tradition. Auerochs, Bernd.

Gadamer Without Tears. Agassi, Joseph.

Habermas, Kohlberg, and the Myth of Expertise. Fairfield, Paul.

Heidegger urbanizado (Notas para una crítica de la hermenéutica). Racionero, Quintín.

Interview: Hans-Georg Gadamer. Rée, Jonathan and Gehron, Christiane.

L'évolution de la critique de l'herméneutique chez Habermas. Guillemot, Jean-Louis.

La herencia de Gadamer en K O Apel: hermenéutica experimental o hermenéutica trascendental. Domingo Moratalla, A.

Los conceptos de Arte y Belleza en H G Gadamer. Dacal Alonso, José Antonio.

Poetic Dwelling in Gadamer's Hermeneutics. Risser, James C.

Transzendentale Phänomenologie und das Problem der Geschichte. Chestanov, Ruslan Z.

Zur hermeneutischen Transformation der Sprachanalyse. Tietz, Udo.

GAGE, N

Process-Product Research on Teaching: Ten Years Later. Garrison, James W and Macmillan, C J B.

GALE, R

B-Series Temporal Order in Dogen's Theory of Time. Vorenkamp, Dirck.

Gale on God: The Return of Philo?. Hasker, William.

Reply to Commentators. Alston, William P.

GALEN

Commentary on Mansfeld's "The Idea of the Will in Chrysippus, Posidonius, and Galen". Sedley, David.

El Concepto de Complexión y Alma en Tomás de Aquino y Galena. Martínez Sendra, María Carmen.

The Idea of the Will in Chrysippus, Posidonius, and Galen. Mansfeld, Jaap.

GALEOTTI, A

A Problem with Headscarves: Contemporary Complexities of Political and Social Identity. Moruzzi, Norma Claire.

A Response to Galeotti's "A Problem with Theory". Moruzzi, Norma Claire.

GALILEO

"Das Naturverständnis bei Galilei" in *Naturauffassungen in Philosophie, Wissenschaft, Technik: Band II, Schäfer, Lothar (ed)*. Fischer, Klaus.

"'Neutrale Bewegung' beim jungen Galilei " in *Naturauffassungen in Philosophie, Wissenschaft, Technik: Band II, Schäfer, Lothar (ed)*. Wolff, Michael.

An Explosion of Dazzling Flashes: Teilhard's Unity of Faith and Science. King, Thomas M.

Arguments from Conceivability. Prudovsky, Gad.

Attualità di Bruno. Garin, Eugenio.

Circularity and the Paduan *Regressus*: From Pietro d'Abano to Galileo Galilei. Wallace, William A.

From Galileo to Leibniz: Motion, Qualities and Experience at the Foundation of Natural Science. Ranea, Alberto Guillermo.

Galileu e a Dialética: Síntese pelo Experimento e Natureza como Domínio dos Objectos. Maar, Wolfgang Leo.

Rehabilitación de Galileo?. Ponferrada, Gustavo Eloy.

Sherlock Holmes, Galileo, and the Missing History of Science. Thomason, Neil.

Um Teorema de Inércia e o Conceito de Velocidade nos *Discorsi* de Galileu. Vasconcelos, Júlio C R.

Valeriano Magni e la Discussione sul Vuoto in Italia. Bucciantini, Massimo.

GALLOIS, A

The Dialectics of Scepticism: Comments on Gallois. Michael, Michaelis.

GALSTON, W

Mothers, Citizenship, and Independence: A Critique of Pure Family Values. Young, Iris Marion.

GALVINISM

"Hegel on Galvinism" in *Hegel on the Modern World, Collins, Ardis B (ed)*. Burbidge, John W.

GAMBLING

The Ethics of Lottery Advertising: Issues and Evidence. Stearns, James M and Borna, Shaheen.

GAME

see also Language Game

Challenging Chomsky: The Generative Garden Game. Botha, Rudolf P.

The Philosophy of Social Science: An Introduction. Hollis, Martin.

Wittgensteinian Themes: Essays 1978-1989. Malcolm, Norman and von Wright, Georg Henrik (ed).

Axiomatic Considerations of Nash Equilibrium. Kaneko, Mamoru.

Combinatorics on Ideals and Axiom A. Sharp, James D.

Constructing Strongly Equivalent Nonisomorphic Models for Unsuperstable Theories, Part A. Hyttinen, Tapani and Shelah, Saharon.

Convention as Correlated Equilibrium. Vanderschraaf, Peter.

Fixed-parameter Tractability and Completeness IV: On Completeness for W[P] and PSPACE Analogues. Abrahamson, K A (& others).

Gauthier and the Rationality of Justice. Koons, Robert C.

Generalized Quantifiers and Pebble Games on Finite Structures. Kolaitis, Phokion G.

Is Gold-Putnam Diagonalization Complete?. Juhl, Cory.

Probabilism. Foley, Richard.

The Real Core Model and Its Scales. Cunningham, Daniel W.

Turing's Sexual Guessing Game. Genova, Judith.

Turing's Test and the Perils of Psychohistory. Anderson, James A.

GAME THEORY

A Theory of Forward Induction in Finitely Repeated Games. Al-Najjar, Nabil.

Apollo's Oracle: Strategizing for Peace. Seitz, Steven Thomas.

Bargaining with Reasonable Aspirations. Brunner, Johann K.

Constrained Maximization Reconsidered—An Elaboration and Critique of Gauthier's Modelling of Rational Cooperation in a Single Prisoner's Dilemma. Franssen, Maarten.

Darwin Meets *The Logic of Decision*: Correlation in Evolutionary Game Theory. Skyrms, Brian.

Democratic Voting and The Mixed-Motivation Problem. Wolff, Jonathan.

Endogenous Correlated Equilibria in Noncooperative Games. Vanderschraaf, Peter.

Hobbes, Spinoza, Kant, Highway Robbery and Game Theory. Marinoff, Louis.

Normalisation and Language-Games. De Queiroz Ruy, J G B.

Paradoxes of Rationality. Bicchieri, Cristina.

Postulates and Paradoxes of Relative Voting Power—A Critical Re-Appraisal. Felsenthal, Dan S and Machover, Moshé.

GOD

"Aporie ed origini della teoria spinoziana dell'idea adequata" in *L'etica e il suo Altro, Vigna, Carmelo (ed)*. Marion, Jean-Luc.

"Catholicism and the Value of Human Life" in *Ethics on the Frontiers of Human Existence, Badham, Paul (ed)*. Coughlan, Michael.

"Christianity is the Future of Paganism: Schelling's Philosophy of Religion, 1826-1854" in *Meaning, Truth, and God, Rouner, Leroy S (ed)*. O'Meara, Thomas F.

"Describing God". Dombrowski, Daniel.

"Dio e il male" in *L'etica e il suo Altro, Vigna, Carmelo (ed)*. Possenti, Vittorio.

"Dios en la Ontología del *Parménides*" in *Platón: Los Diálogos Tardíos, Lan, Conrado Eggers (ed)*. Eggers Lan, Conrado.

"Et 'Factum' et 'Verum' cum 'Verbo' Convertuntur": Lingua Divina e 'Prima Parlari' delle Nazioni in Vico. Agrimi, Mario.

"From Civil Religion to Public Philosophy" in *Civil Religion and Political Theology, Rouner, Leroy S (ed)*. Neuhaus, Richard John.

"God and Endangered Species" in *Ethics, Religion and Biodiversity, Hamilton, Lawrence S (ed)*. Rolston III, Holmes.

"Grounds for Believing in God's Existence" in *Meaning, Truth, and God, Rouner, Leroy (ed)*. Hartshorne, Charles.

"Hegel as Theologian" in *Meaning, Truth, and God, Rouner, Leroy (ed)*. Findlay, J N.

"Human Being, Beast, and God" in *The Crossroads of Norm and Nature, Sim, May (ed)*. Achtenberg, Deborah.

"Human In-vitro Fertilization" in *Ethics on the Frontiers of Human Existence, Badham, Paul (ed)*. Fishel, Simon.

"Leibniz's Ontological and Cosmological Arguments" in *The Cambridge Companion to Leibniz, Jolley, Nicholas (ed)*. Blumenfeld, David C.

"Locke's Philosophy of Religion" in *The Cambridge Companion to Locke, Chappell, Vere (ed)*. Wolterstorff, Nicholas.

"Moral Objections to Pascalian Wagering" in *Gambling on God: Essays on Pascal's Wager, Jordan, Jeffrey (ed)*. Quinn, Philip.

"Nietzsche and the Crisis of Nihilism" in *Meaning, Truth, and God, Rouner, Leroy S (ed)*. Fortin, Ernest L.

"Only a God Can Save Us Now". Heidegger, Martin.

"Shamanic Nietzsche" in *Nietzsche: A Critical Reader, Sedgwick, Peter R (ed)*. Land, Nick.

"Spiritus" e "Anima" in Bernardino Telesio. Bondì, Roberto.

"The Gate to God's Presence in Heschel, Buber, and Soloveitchik" in *Thinkers and Teachers of Modern Judaism, Goldsmith, Emanuel S (ed)*. Zuesse, Evan M.

"The Kingdom of God is at Hand!" (Did Kant Really Say *That*?). Palmquist, Stephen.

"The Many-Gods Objection" in *Gambling on God: Essays on Pascal's Wager, Jordan, Jeffrey (ed)*. Jordan, Jeffrey.

"The Only Diabological Thing about Women...": Luce Irigaray on Divinity. Deutscher, Penelope.

"The Status of *Vorstellung* in Hegel's Philosophy of Religion" in *Meaning, Truth, and God, Rouner, Leroy (ed)*. Ricoeur, Paul.

"The Wager in Pascal and Others" in *Gambling on God: Essays on Pascal's Wager, Jordan, Jeffrey (ed)*. Ryan, John K.

"The World Disenchanted, and the Return of Gods and Demons" in *The Barbarism of Reason, Horowitz, Asher (ed)*. Kontos, Alkis.

"Verification in Matters Religious" in *Meaning, Truth, and God, Rouner, Leroy (ed)*. Burrell, David.

"Wagering and the Evidence" in *Gambling on God: Essays on Pascal's Wager, Jordan, Jeffrey (ed)*. Morris, Thomas V.

...also muss auf Schelling zurückgegangen werden. Ehrhardt, Walter E.

An Introduction to the Philosophy of Religion. Tilghman, B R.

Aristotle and Augustine on Freedom: Two Theories of Freedom, Voluntary Action, and Akrasia. Chappell, T D J.

Aristotle in Outline. Robinson, Timothy A.

Augustine. Clark, Mary T.

Bad Faith and Antiblack Racism. Gordon, Lewis R.

Bridging the Sacred and the Secular. Hooper, J Leon (ed) and Murray, John Courtney.

Certainty. Westphal, Jonathan (ed).

Creativity and God: A Challenge to Process Theology. Neville, Robert Cummings.

Die Übermacht des Seins: Heideggers Auslegung des Bezuges von Mensch und Natur und Hölderlins Dichtung des Heiligen. Bohlen, Stephanie.

Esse est Deus: Meister Eckharts christologische Versöhnung von Philosophie und Religion und ihre Ursprünge in der Tradition des Abendlandes. Manstetten, Reiner.

Essentials of Shinto: An Analytical Guide to Principal Teachings. Picken, Stuart D B.

Eternity and Freedom: A Critical Analysis of Divine Timelessness as a Solution to the Foreknowledge/Free Will Debate. Robinson, Michael D.

Explorations in Metaphysics: Being-God-Person. Clarke, W Norris.

Gambling on God: Essays on Pascal's Wager. Jordan, Jeffrey (ed).

God and Plastic Surgery: Marx, Nietzsche, Freud and the Obvious. Barris, Jeremy.

God, Knowledge, and Mystery: Essays in Philosophical Theology. Van Inwagen, Peter.

Gott—Gebote—Ideale: Analytische Philosophie und theologische Ethik. Löhr, Gebbhard.

Grundzüge der Religionsphilosophie Edith Steins. Müller, Andreas Uwe.

Hegel: Phenomenology and System. Harris, H S.

How to Tell God from the Devil: On the Way to Comedy. Eckardt, A Roy.

Humanity, Environment, and God. Spurway, Neil.

Il Nyaya Sutra di Gautama. Arena, Leonardo Vittorio.

Innovation and Tradition in Religion: Towards an Institutional Theory. Disbrey, Claire (ed).

Itinerari del Volontarismo: Teologia e politica al tempo di Luis de León. Ferraro, Domenico.

La Tirania en la Grecia Antigua. Sánchez de la Torre, D Angel.

Lectures on Divine Humanity. Solovyov, Vladimir.

Leibniz and the Rational Order of Nature. Rutherford, Donald.

Maimonides and St Thomas on the Limits of Reason. Dobbs-Weinstein, Idit.

Meaning, Truth, and God. Rouner, Leroy (ed).

Mediaeval Reactions to the Encounter Between Faith and Reason. Wippel, John F.

Metafisica: Universalis Philosophiae SEU Metaphysicarum Rerum Iuxta Propria Dogmata, Liber I. Lamacchia, Ada (ed & trans), Ponzio, Paolo (ed & trans) and Campanella, Tommaso.

Modality, Probability, and Rationality. Sennett, James F.

Narrative and the Natural Law: An Interpretation of Thomistic Ethics. Hall, Pamela M.

Natural History of Religion. Fieser, James (ed) and Hume, David.

Nature's Causes. Connell, Richard J.

Nietzsche's Revaluation of Values: A Study in Strategies. Sleinis, E E.

Nihilism Before Nietzsche. Gillespie, Michael Allen.

Nuggets of Wisdom from Great Jewish Thinkers: From Biblical Times to the Present. Gerber, William.

On Naming the Present: God, Hermeneutics, and Church. Tracy, David.

Only a God Can Save Us: Disabling the Rational Subject in Heidegger's Reactionary Modernism. Anabtawi, Jehanne.

Platón: Los Diálogos Tardíos. Lan, Conrado Eggers (ed).

Reason in the Balance: The Case Against Naturalism in Science, Law, and Education. Johnson, Phillip E.

Relationality and the Concept of God. Jansen, Henry.

Roots of Wisdom: Speaking the Language of Philosophy. Mitchell, Helen Buss.

Saint Thomas Aquinas: On Evil. Oesterle, Jean (trans).

Scepsi Moderna: Interpretazioni dello Scetticismo da Charron a Hume. Paganini, Gianni.

Search for Community in a Withering Tradition: Conversations between a Marxian Atheist and a Calvinian Christian. Nielsen, Kai and Hart, Hendrik.

Seven Dilemmas in World Religions. Stephens, G Lynn and Pence, Gregory.

Spinoza's Ethica From Manuscript to Print: Studies on Text, Form, and Related Topics. Steenbakkers, Piet.

The Atheist Trap. Mixie, Joseph.

The Embodied Self: Friedrich Schleiermacher's Solution to Kant's Problem of the Empirical Self. Thandeka.

The Human Shape of God: Religion in Hegel's "Phenomenology of Spirit". Jamros, Daniel P.

The Levinas Reader. Hand, Seán.

The Lyotard Reader. Benjamin, Andrew (ed).

The Philosophy of Jonathan Edwards. Daniel, Stephen H.

The Philosophy of Religion and Advaita Vedānta: A Comparative Study in Religion and Reason. Sharma, Arvind.

The Sources of Christian Ethics. Pinckaers, Servais and Noble, Mary Thomas (trans).

The Transformation of Natural Philosophy: The Case of Philip Melanchthon. Kusukawa, Sachiko.

The Wisdom of Religious Commitment. Tilley, Terrence W.

Theophrastus Redivivus, Volumes 1 and 2. Canziani, Guido (ed) and Paganini, Gianni (ed).

There are Two Errors In the the Title of This Book: A Sourcebook of Philosophical Puzzles, Problems, and Paradoxes. Martin, Robert M.

Three Messengers for One God. Schlabach, Gerald W (& other trans) and Arnaldez, Roger.

Transzendenz-"Relation": Zum Transzendenzbezug in der Philosophie Emmanuel Levinas'. Esterbauer, Reinhold.

Understanding Our World: An Integral Ontology. Hart, Hendrik.

Varieties of Scientific Experience: Emotive Aims in Scientific Hypotheses. Feuer, Lewis S.

Without God or His Doubles: Realism, Relativism and Rorty. Vaden House, David.

A Contemporary Challenge to Religion: The Question of Eternity. Lowry, Atherton C.

A Critique of Quentin Smith's Atheistic Argument from Big Bang Cosmology. Lorca, Daniel.

A Defense of a Principle of Sufficient Reason. Smith, Quentin.

A Gross and Palpable Contradiction?: Incarnation and Consistency. Yandell, Keith E.

A Key to Heidegger's *Beiträge*. Seidel, George J.

A Language for the Description of God, Part I: A Unique Language for a Unique Object. Graves, David and Alon, Ilai.

A Moral Argument for Undertaking Theism. Drabkin, Douglas.

A Morning and Evening Star: Editor's Introduction. Deely, John.

A Note on the Relation of Pacifism and Just-War Theory: Is There a Thomistic Convergence?. Palmer-Fernandez, Gabriel.

A Scientist and a Theologian See the World: Compromise or Synthesis?. Gerhart, Mary and Russell, Allan Melvin.

Alston and Hartshorne on the Concept of God. Dombrowski, Daniel A.

Alston on Direct Perception and Interpretation. Van Woudenberg, René.

Alstonian Foundationalism and Higher-Level Theistic Evidentialism. Sudduth, Michael L Czapkay.

GOD

The Question of the Existence of God in the Book of Stephen Hawking "A Brief History of Time". Driessen, Alfred.

The Quiddity of Mercy. Walker, Nigel.

The Religion of a Scientist: Explorations into Reality (Religio philosophi naturalis). Peacocke, Arthur.

The Religious Dimensions of the Biological Narrative. Goodenough, Ursula W.

The Riddle of Religion in the Making. Ford, Lewis S.

The Teleological Argument. Mixie, Joseph.

The Tryambaka Mantra: Its Meaning and Significance. Jayashanmukham, N.

The Turn Towards Buddhism. McGhee, Michael.

The Vocation to Be a Philosopher. Andrews, Philip.

The Will as King over the Powers of the Soul: Uses and Sources of an Image in the Thirteenth Century. Teske, Roland J.

The 'Is/Ought' Relation in Hume. Barbone, Steven L.

The 'Passions of the Soul': Descartes' Shadow on Theories of the Emotions. Gorevan, Patrick.

Theism, the Hypothesis of Indifference, and the Biological Role of Pain and Pleasure. Howard-Snyder, Daniel.

Theological Study and the Pursuit of Truth. Wardlaw, Harry.

Theravada Buddhism and the Definition of Religion. Smart, Ninian.

Thinking the Post-Socialism: From Socialist Community to Pluralistic Society. Flego, Gvozden.

Thirteenth-Century Discussions on Modal Terms. Spruyt, Joke.

Time and Foreknowledge: A Critique of Zagzebski. Oaklander, L Nathan.

To Bet the Impossible Bet. Holcomb III, Harmon R.

Tomberlin's Philosophical perspectives, 5, Philosophy of Religion, 1991. Grim, Patrick.

Tradizione Biblica, Miti e Rivoluzioni Geologiche Negli "Anecdotes de la Nature" di Nicolas-Antoine Boulanger. Cristani, Giovanni.

Triangulating God. Palmquist, Stephen.

Truth-Warranted Manifestation Beliefs. Zeis, John.

Two Dualisms. Mautner, Thomas.

Two McFagues: Meaning, Truth, and Justification in Models of God. Reynolds, Terrence.

Understanding St Thomas on Christ's Immediate Knowledge of God. Mansini, Guy.

Universalism and the Meaning of History. Mitias, Michael H.

Universale and Infinito Modos in the Thought of Spinoza. Murthy, Viren.

Van Participatie tot Zelflimitatie; Over Thomas' Filosofie van de Schepping. Kal, Victor.

Vico e i 'Figliuoli di Dio': Ricerche sui Giganti nel Diritto universale e nella Scienza nuova Prima. Boschetto, Luca.

Violence and Post-Modernism. Jasper, David.

Wagering Belief: Examining Two Objections to Pascal's Wager. Groothuis, D.

Wahrheit in Herrlichkeit: Auf Balthasar hören. Splett, Jörg.

Weak Agnosticism Defended. Oppy, Graham.

What Did Lonergan Really Say about Aquinas's Theory of the Will?. Stebbins, J Michael.

Why Alston's Mystical Doxastic Practice Is Subjective. Gale, Richard.

Why the Philosophical Problems of Chalcedonian Christology Have Not Gone Away. Bartel, T W.

Wittgenstein's Elephant and Closet Tortoise. Grant, Brian.

Zur Geschichtlichkeit der Rede von Gott: Einflüsse zeitgenössischer Königsideologie auf die Trinitätslehre Wilhelms von Auxerre. Arnold, Johannes.

'The Same Thing Therefore Ought To Be and Ought Not To Be': Anselm on Conflicting Oughts. O'Neill, John.

'We Shall Bear the Image of the Man of Heaven': Theology and the Concept of Truth. Marshall, Bruce D.

GODDESS

Dismantling the Master's House: A Hestian/ Hermean Deconstruction of Classic Texts. Thompson, Patricia J.

Finding Our Feminist Ways in Natural Philosophy and Religious Thought. Gatens-Robinson, Eugenie.

Introduction: Prolegomenon to Future Feminist Philosophies of Religions. Frankenberry, Nancy.

The Idea of God in Feminist Philosophy. Suchocki, Marjorie Hewitt.

Women, Earth, and the Goddess: A Shākta-Hindu Interpretation of Embodied Religion. Patel, Kartikeya C.

GODEL

see Goedel

GODS

Lo spiritualismo indiano antico: Echi egizi nelle Upanisad. Masi, Giuseppe.

GODWIN

El utilitarismo libertario de William Godwin. Adair, Phillipe.

William Godwin y el anarquismo: A propósito de Political Justice. Alvarez, Antón Fernández.

GOEDEL

"Das Problem der Sprache in der Philosophie" in Die Sprache in den Wissenschaften, Weingartner, Paul (ed). Weingartner, Paul.

Absolute Forms of Gödel's Incompleteness Theorem. Kim, Sangmun.

Gentile e Gödel. Sainati, Vittorio.

Platonism and Mathematical Intuition in Kurt Gödel's Thought. Parsons, Charles.

The Replacement of Time. Savitt, Steven F.

Time in Philosophy and in Physics: From Kant and Einstein to Gödel. Wang, Hao.

What is Logic?. Wang, Hao.

GOEDEL THEOREM

On Formalization of Model-Theoretic Proofs of Gödel's Theorems. Kikuchi, Makoto and Tanaka, Kazuyuki.

On the Incompleteness Theorems. Kotlarski, Henryk.

GOETHE

Karl Rosenkranz: Briefe 1827 bis 1850. Butzlaff, Joachim (ed).

The Flight from Woman (New Edition). Stern, Karl.

Faust e Lust. La Guardia, Giovanni.

GOETSCHEL, W

Das Vermächtnis des deutschen Judentums: Werke 2. Goldschmidt, Hermann Levin.

Die Botschaft des Judentums: Werke 3. Goldschmidt, Hermann Levin.

Freiheit für den Widerspruch: Werke 6. Goldschmidt, Hermann Levin.

Philosophie als Dialogik: Frühe Schriften Werke 1. Goldschmidt, Hermann Levin.

GOFFMAN, E

Social Epistemology and Goffmanian Theory. Duran, Jane.

GOICOECHEA, D

"A Reply to My Critics and Friendly Commentators" in The Nature and Pursuit of Love, Goicoechea, David (ed). Singer, Irving.

GOLD, E

Is Gold-Putnam Diagonalization Complete?. Juhl, Cory.

GOLDEN RULE

La Règle d'Or: l'effet-radar. Hunyadi, Mark.

The Golden Rule as the Foundation of Universal Ethics. Eboh, Marie Pauline.

GOLDMAN, A

"The Mental Simulation Debate" in Objectivity, Simulation and the Unity of Consciousness, Peacocke, Christopher (ed). Davies, Martin.

GOLDSCHMIDT, H

Perspektiven der Dialogik: Zürcher Kolloquium zum 80. Geburtstag von Hermann Levin Goldschmidt. Goetschel, Willi (ed).

GOMPERZ, H

"Epistemologie, Sprachanalyse und Semiotik bei H Gomperz" in Heinrich Gomperz, Karl Popper und die österreichische Philosophie, Seiler, Martin (ed). Seiler, Martin.

"Heinrich Gomperz und die griechische Philosophie" in Heinrich Gomperz, Karl Popper und die österreichische Philosophie, Seiler, Martin (ed). Dönt, Eugen.

"Heinrich Gomperz und die Österreichische Philosophie" in Heinrich Gomperz, Karl Popper und die österreichische Philosophie, Seiler, Martin (ed). Haller, Rudolf.

"Heinrich Gomperz und die Psychoanalyse" in Heinrich Gomperz, Karl Popper und die österreichische Philosophie, Seiler, Martin (ed). Fischer, Kurt R.

"Heinrich Gomperz und Karl Popper im Kontext..." in Heinrich Gomperz, Karl Popper und die österreichische Philosophie, Seiler, Martin (ed). Stadler, Friedrich.

"Rechts- und Sozialphilosophie bei Heinrich Gomperz" in Heinrich Gomperz, Karl Popper und die österreichische Philosophie, Seiler, Martin (ed). Pfersmann, Otto.

"Zu Heinrich Gomperz: Die Wissenschaft und die Tat" in Heinrich Gomperz, Karl Popper und die österreichische Philosophie, Seiler, Martin (ed). Rutte, Heiner.

Heinrich Gomperz, Karl Popper und die österreichische Philosophie. Seiler, Martin (ed) and Stadler, Friedrich (ed).

GONSETH, F

Le Référentiel selon Ferdinand Gonseth, et ses aspects philosophiques. Thom, René.

Philosophie ouverte de F Gonseth et philosophie analytique. Emery-Hellwig, Eric.

GOOD

see also Common Good, Evil, Public Good, Right, Virtue

"Democracy and the Rechsstaat: Habermas's Faktizität und Geltung" in The Cambridge Companion to Habermas, White, Stephen K (ed). Baynes, Kenneth.

"Reply to Professor Roche" in The Crossroads of Norm and Nature, Sim, May (ed). Kraut, Richard H.

"Schools, Identity, and the Conception of the Good" in Identity, Culture, and Education, Smeyers, Paul (ed). de Ruyter, Doret J and Miedema, Siebren.

"Sui Rischi di un'Attitudine Troppo Benevola dell'Interprete verso il Testo" in Platón: Los Diálogos Tardíos, Lan, Conrado Eggers (ed). Rossetti, Livio.

"The Ultimate End of Action: A Critique of Richard Kraut's Aristotle on the Human Good" in The Crossroads of Norm and Nature, Sim, May (ed). Roche, Timothy.

"Zur moralphilosophischen Funktion des Prinzips vom höchsten Gut" in Naturzweckmässigkeit und ästhetische Kultur, Schwabe, Karl-Heinz (ed). Grünewald, Bernward.

Civil Society, Civil Religion. Shanks, Andrew.

Die Sehnsucht nach dem Schönen, Guten und Wahren oder platonische Reminiszenzen in Rousseaus Menschenbild und Erziehungslehre. Burkert-Wepfer, Esther.

Hume and Hume's Connexions. Stewart, M A (ed) and Wright, John P (ed).

Maimonides and St Thomas on the Limits of Reason. Dobbs-Weinstein, Idit.

Nietzsche: The Ethics of an Immoralist. Berkowitz, Peter.

Nursing Ethics: Therapeutic Caring Presence. Bishop, Anne H and Scudder Jr, John R.

Practical Realism and Moral Psychology. Jacobs, Jonathan.

Saint Thomas Aquinas: On Evil. Oesterle, Jean (trans).

Sartre and Evil: Guidelines for a Struggle. Gordon, Haim and Gordon, Rivca.

The High Road of Humanity: The Seven Ethical Ages of Western Man. Levi, Albert William, Verene, Donald Phillip (ed) and Verene, Molly Black (ed).

GOOD

The Rational and the Moral Order: The Social Roots of Reason and Morality. Baier, Kurt.

There are Two Errors In the the Title of This Book: A Sourcebook of Philosophical Puzzles, Problems, and Paradoxes. Martin, Robert M.

Thinkers Through Time: Reading Ethics With Literature. Curran, Mary Bernard.

Twentieth Century Ethical Theory. Cahn, Steven M (ed) and Haber, Joram G (ed).

Understanding John Dewey: Nature and Cooperative Intelligence. Campbell, James.

A Good Man is Hard to Find. Curley, Edwin.

A Rebuttal To Shelly Kagan's Attack on Options. Warenski, Lisa.

Absolute Safety. Ashdown, Lance.

Algunas presuposiciones metafísicas de la acción humana. Haldane, John.

Being Morally Responsible for an Action Versus Acting Responsibly or Irresponsibly. Anderson, Susan Leigh.

Can a Good Man Know Himself?. Skillen, Anthony.

Desire and the Human Good. Kraut, Richard H.

Dialéctica de Casiciaco. Rosado, Juan.

Entre el Kantismo y el Consecuencialismo en la Filosofía Moral de T H Green. Weinstein, David.

Faust e Lust. La Guardia, Giovanni.

Fichtes Erziehungslehre als erste logische Begründung der Vorbilderziehung. Kumamoto, Yasuhiro.

Finding Beauty. Lenman, James.

For Our Own Good. Archard, David.

Fortunate Misfortune. Smilansky, Saul.

Freedom and Good in the Thomistic Tradition. Loughran, Thomas.

Friedrich Nietzsche: His Christian Spirit. García-Bárcena, Rafael.

Full-Information Theories of Individual Good. Loeb, Don.

Good Ethics Is Good for Business: Ethical Attributions and Response to Environmental Advertising. Davis, Joel J.

John Rawls and the Search for Stability. Barry, Brian.

Justice and Good in the Political Liberalism of John Rawls. Velek, Josef.

Kalokagathia. Jaroszynski, Piotr.

La Estética del Romanticismo y su Análisis Dentro de la Filosofía Existencial (Kierkegaard y Dostoievsky). Rendón Rojas, Miguel Angel.

Law as a Private Good: A Response to Tyler Cowen on the Economics of Anarchy. Friedman, David D.

Le bien suprême est-il virtuellement réalisé dans le monde? Le jugement politique chez Jacques Poulain. Lanteigne, Josette.

Le juste et le bien: priorité ou complémentarité?. Berten, André.

Life, Science, and Wisdom According to Descartes. Peperzak, Adriaan.

Lonergan and Bellah: Social Science as Public Philosophy. Hoyt-O'Connor, Paul E.

Los Modos de Manifestación de la Alteridad y su Articulación en el Pensamiento de Emmanuel Levinas. Garrido-Maturano, Angel E.

Love: Its Universe and Universality. McGraw, John G.

Luck and the Enigmas of Fate. Rescher, Nicholas.

Moral Experience and the Internalist Argument Against Moral Realism. Tolhurst, William E.

Morality without Ethics. Bauman, Zygmunt.

Naturalism, Normativity, and the Open Question Argument. Rosati, Connie.

Neutrals. Lemos, Noah M.

Niccolò Machiavelli-Adviser of Princes. Kain, Philip J.

Osservazioni sul Problema del Male in Filosofia. Franchi, Alfredo.

Persons, Perspetives, and Full Information Accounts of the Good. Rosati, Connie.

Plato and the Scientific Spirit. Mollenhauer, B.

Platonic Politics and the Good. Reeve, C D C.

Post-Analytic Philosophy: Its Causes and Its Cure. Meynell, Hugo.

Rejoinder to David Friedman on the Economics of Anarchy. Cowen, Tyler.

Reply to Van de Vate. Browning, Douglas.

Responsibility and Necessity. Cockburn, David.

Revising the Substituted Judgment Standard. Baergen, Ralph.

Riding the Fiery Steed: *Von den Freuden-und Leidenschaften.* Coker, John C.

Socratic Goods and Socratic Happiness. Santas, Gerasimos.

Some Notes on Browning's *Ethical Notes.* Van de Vate, Dwight.

Straining the Quality of Mercy. Nuyen, A T.

Supervenience, Virtues, and Consequences: A Commentary on *Knowledge in Perspective.* Dancy, Jonathan.

The Concept of Morality. Pawlowska, Ija Lazari.

The Eleatic Stranger's Socratic Condemnation of Socrates. Howland, Jacob A.

The Multiplication of Utility. Nathan, N M L.

The Priority of Right and Ideas of the Good. Rawls, John.

The Species and Unity of the Moral Act. Ripperger, Chad.

The Structure of the Human Acting Subject in Thomas Aquinas. Delivoyatzis, S.

The Task of Philosophy. Szahaj, Andrzej.

The Work of Art as a Model of "The Open Whole". Kuczynski, Alicja.

Towards a Political Ethic: Exploring the Boundaries of a Moral Politics. De Wijze, Stephen.

Two Concepts of Utopia. Graybosch, A J.

Una Pregunta Sobre la Noción de "Bien" en Aristóteles. Femenías, María Luisa.

Universal Dimensions of Natural Law. Tokarczyk, Roman A.

Virtue as the Use of Other Goods. Annas, Julia.

Weighing Goods: Some Questions and Comments. Temkin, Larry S.

What did Pyrrho Think About "The Nature of the Divine and the Good"?. Bett, Richard.

What Does Hegel Make of the Jews?: A Scato-Logical Reading of Kafka's *Die Verwandlung.* Munk, Linda.

What is Wrong with Hypocrisy?. Benn, Piers.

What's an Epistemologist to Do?. Edidin, Aron.

'We Good Europeans': Nietzsche's New Europe in *Beyond Good and Evil.* Martin, Nicholas.

GOOD LIFE

"Etica e morale" in *L'etica e il suo Altro, Vigna, Carmelo (ed).* Ricoeur, Paul.

Aristotle and Augustine on Freedom: Two Theories of Freedom, Voluntary Action, and Akrasia. Chappell, T D J.

Private Consciences and Public Reasons. Greenawalt, Kent.

Revolutionary Rationality and the Good Life. Hughes, Paul M.

What is the Content of Education in a Democratic Society?. Haberman, Bonna Devora.

GOODIN, R

Needs versus Desires. Larson, Erica.

GOODMAN, N

"Expression in Architecture" in *Philosophy and Architecture, Mitias, Michael H (ed).* Mitias, Michael H.

Art Infraction: Goodman, Rap, Pragmatism. Shusterman, Richard.

Bildliche Sprechakte. Taube, Volkmar.

Earman on the Projectibility of Grue. Lange, Marc.

Gruesome Perceptual Spaces. Weir, Alan.

How Carnap Should Bite Goodman's Bullet. Paprzycka, Katarzyna.

Husserl and Goodman on the Role of Resemblance in Pictorial Representation. Drost, Mark P.

Learning from Art. Graham, Gordon.

Nelson Goodman's Assimilation of Literary and Scientific Knowledge. Campbell, Keith.

GOODNESS

Contro Gli Etici. Spinelli, Emidio (trans).

Kant's Theory of Imagination: Bridging Gaps in Judgement and Experience. Gibbons, Sarah.

Commentary on Patterson's "The Ascent in Plato's *Symposium.* Lawrence, Joseph P.

Interpreting Simone Weil: Presence and Absence in Attention. Pirruccello, Ann.

Moral Values and the Taoist Sage in the *Tao de Ching.* Allinson, Robert E.

Personal Goodness and Moral Facts. Sencerz, Stefan.

Spinoza's Democratic Turn: Chapter 16 of the *Theologico-Political Treatise.* Smith, Steven B.

The Ascent in Plato's *Symposium.* Patterson, Richard.

Whitehead and Heidegger on Technological Goodness. Grange, Joseph.

GOODS

Consuming Goods and the Goods of Consuming. Campbell, Colin.

Persona corriente y filosofía moral: reglas, virtudes y bienes. MacIntyre, Alasdair, Corral, Carmen (trans) and Román, Begoña (trans).

GOODWILL

Kant's Vision of the Moral Hero and the 'Laws of Arithmetic'. Temple, Dennis.

GORAYSKA, B

On Gorayska and Lindsay's Definition of Relevance. Mey, Jacob L.

On Putting Necessity in Its Place. Lindsay, R O and Gorayska, Barbara.

GORDON, A

Critical Response II: The No-Drop Rule. Michaels, Walter Benn.

Life Versus Death: Exposing a Misapplication of Ethical Reasoning. Iserson, Kenneth V.

Politically Correct Ethical Thinking and Intubation Practice on Cadavers. Orlowski, James P.

GORDON, R

"The Mental Simulation Debate" in *Objectivity, Simulation and the Unity of Consciousness, Peacocke, Christopher (ed).* Davies, Martin.

Miedo e Incertidumbre. Hansberg, Olbeth.

GOSPEL

The Transformation of Natural Philosophy: The Case of Philip Melanchthon. Kusukawa, Sachiko.

An Explosion of Dazzling Flashes: Teilhard's Unity of Faith and Science. King, Thomas M.

Marx, Moses, and the Pagans in the Secular City. Sunic, Tomislav.

GOSSIP

Gossip and Morality (in Hebrew). Statman, Daniel.

Gossip, Emotions, and Morality (in Hebrew). Ben-Ze'ev, Aaron.

GOSWAMI, A

On the Quantum Mechanical Wave Function as a Link Between Cognition and the Physical World: A Role for Psychology. Snyder, Douglas M.

Quantum Physics and Consciousness, Creativity, Computers: A Commentary on Goswami's Quantum-Based Theory of Consciousness and Free Will. Dyer, Michael G.

GOTTSCHALK

Implicaciones políticas de la eclesiología de Wyclif. Bertelloni, Francisco.

GOUHIER, H

Lettres d'Étienne Gilson à Henri Gouhier. Prouvost, Géry.

GOULD, C

On the Possibility of Feminist Philosophy. McAlister, Linda Lopez.

GOULD, S

Adaptationism or the Theory of Optimization. Janovic, Tomislav.

The Cronin Controversy. Griffiths, Paul E.

GOULET, R
Dictionnaire des philosophes antiques, publié sous la direction de Richard Goulet, t.II *Babélyca d'Argos á Dyscolius*. Lafrance, Yvon.

GOVERNANCE
Foucault and Law: Towards a Sociology of Law as Governance. Hunt, Alan and Wickham, Gary.

GOVERNMENT
see also Anarchism
Asylum: A Moral Dilemma. Plaut, W Gunther.
Democracy. Green, Philip (ed).
Dominations and Powers: Reflections on Liberty, Society, and Government. Santayana, George.
No Harm: Ethical Principles for a Free Market. Burke, T Patrick.
Political Theory and Christian Vision: Essays in Memory of Bernard Zylstra. Chaplin, Jonathan (ed) and Marshall, Paul (ed).
Privatizing Public Lands. Lehmann, Scott.
Rationing Medicine. Blank, Robert H.
Statesman (299b-d) and the Condemnation of Socrates. Dueso, José Solana.
Thomas Jefferson's Freethought Legacy: A Saying Per Day by the Sage of Monticello. Greeley, Roger E.
University-Business Partnerships: An Assessment. Bowie, Norman E.
Versus Trasimaco: E confutabile il detto "la giustizia non è altro che l'utile del più forte"?. Fiorillo, Vanda.
Autonomy and Free Expression. Gomberg, Paul.
Between Reform and Revolution: Three Hypotheses about the Nature of the Regime Change. Kis, János.
Defining Core Health Services: The New Zealand Experience. Campbell, Alastair V.
Do Free-Market Governments Create Crisis-Ridden Societies?. Richardson, Bill and Curwen, Peter.
Fugitive Democracy. Wolin, Sheldon.
Libertad constitucional y democracia reprsentativa. Rosen, Fred.
Locke's Early Political Reading. Milton, J R.
Michel Foucault: Governmentality and Liberal Education. Marshall, James.
Philosophy in Russian Today. Yulina, N S.
Popular Government and Effective Government. McNamara, Peter.
Private Bioethics Forums: Counterpoint to Government Bodies. Cohen, Cynthia B and McCloskey, Elizabeth Leibold.
Remaking the Corporation: The 1991 US Sentencing Guidelines. Rafalko, Robert J.
Selective Conscientious Objection and the Right Not to Kill. Ruesga, G Albert.
Systemic Rationality and the Effects of Financial Regulation: Rejoinder to Kindleberger. Horwitz, Steven.
The Contractarian Explanation of the State. Hampton, Jean.
The New 'Everyman' Edition of Locke's Two Treatises. Goldie, Mark.
Theory vs History: Reply to Horwitz. Kindleberger, Charles P.
Theory, Practice, Reality. Borgmann, Albert.

GRACE
Augustine. Clark, Mary T.
Itinerari del Volontarismo: Teologia e politica al tempo di Luis de León. Ferraro, Domenico.
Pensées and Other Writings: A New Translation by Honor Levi. Pascal, Blaise and Levi, Honor (trans).
Calvin and Bernard on Freedom and Necessity: A Reply to Brümmer. Helm, Paul.
Consciousness and Grace. Doran, Robert M.
El Cristianismo como A Priori de la Revolución en la Filosofía de Ernst Bloch. Orsolic, Marco.
Interpretación de K Rahner Sobre Tomás de Aquino. Schenk, Richard.
Métaphysique de l'être et théologie de la grâce dans le médiévalisme contemporain: É Gilson et M D Chenu entre H Bergson et A Gardeil. Conticello, C G.
Moral Content, Tradition, and Grace: Rethinking the Possibility of a Christian Bioethics. Engelhardt Jr, H Tristram.

GRACIAN, B
Las apariencias en Vladimir Jankélévitch. Trejos, Susana.

GRADING
Grading. Weis, Gregory F.

GRAECO-LATIN
see Greek, Latin

GRAHAM, A
White Horse not Horse: Making Sense of a Negative Logic. Lai, Whalen.

GRAHAM, G
Commentary on "Self-Consciousness, Mental Agency, and the Clinical Psychopathology of Thought Insertion". Wiggins, Osborne P.
Liberalism, Religion, and Politics Again: A Reply to Gordon Graham. Van Wyk, Robert N.

GRAMMAR
"Le discours linguistique: Etude comparée de textes" in *Rhétoriques de la science, De Coorebyter, Vincent (ed)*. Chevalier, Jean-Claude.
"Wittgenstein on Grammar and Essence" in *Wittgenstein and Contemporary Philosophy, Teghrarian, Souren (ed)*. Hunter, J F M.
"Wittgenstein on Psychological Verbs" in *Wittgenstein and Contemporary Philosophy, Teghrarian, Souren (ed)*. Vesey, Godfrey.
Challenging Chomsky: The Generative Garden Game. Botha, Rudolf P.
Dynamics of Meaning: Anaphora, Presupposition, and the Theory of Grammar. Chierchia, Gennaro.
Logic and Representation. Moore, Robert C.

Mentalistic Turn: A Critical Evaluation of Chomsky by Kalyan Sen Gupta. Devaraja, N K.
Reading Theory: An Introduction to Lacan, Derrida, and Kristeva. Payne, Michael.
Anscombe and the First Person. Garrett, Brian J.
Anscombe and the Self-Reference Rule. O'Brien, Lucy F.
Consumerism and Language Acquisition. Mercier, Adèle.
Discontinuity in Categorical Grammar. Morrill, Glyn.
Dynamic Dependency Grammar. Milward, David.
E-Type Pronouns, 1-Sums, and Donkey Anaphora. Lappin, Shalom and Francez, Nissim.
Feeling at Home in Language (What Makes Reading *Philosophical Investigations* Possible?). Minar, Edward H.
Fiction as "Grammatical" Investigation: A Wittgensteinian Account. Schalkwyk, David.
Formas Gramaticales, Formas Lógicas y Frases Denotativas: Sorpresas en la Historia de la Semántica. Piacenza, Eduardo.
From Compositional to Systematic Semantics. Zadrozny, Wlodek.
From Syllogism to Predicate Calculus. McQuade, Thomas J.
Grammacentrism and the Transformation of Rhetoric. Khushf, George.
Grammar Formalisms Viewed as Evolving Algebras. Johnson, David E and Moss, Lawrence S.
Iconic Manifestation of Interlocutor Distance in Russian. Yokoyama, Olga T.
Iconicity and Auxiliation. Kuteva, Tania.
Iconicity, Analogy, and Universal Grammar. Itkonen, Esa.
Intrinsic Constraints on Language: Grammar and Hermeneutics. Bickhard, Mark H.
La grammatica ed il problema degli universali nel Medioevo cristiano. Bertola, Ermenegildo.
Locke's Own. Mautner, Thomas.
Making Comparisons. Katz, Bernard D.
No Longer, Not Yet: Reading History Grammatically. Erickson, Stephen A.
On the Treatment of Complex Predicates in Categorial Grammar. Kang, Beom-Mo.
Such: Binding and the Pro-Adjective. Siegel, Muffy E A.
The Domain of Set-Valued Feature Structures. Moshier, M Andrew and Pollard, Carl J.
The Function of LIKE in Dialogue. Miller, Jim and Weinert, Regina.
The Sanskrit of Science. Staal, Frits.
Theories of Masses and Problems of Constitution. Zimmerman, Dean.
Transcendental Subjectivity Meets Transcendental Grammar. Pradhan, R C.
Vacuous Singular Terms. Adams, Fred and Stecker, Robert.
Vagueness and Utility: The Semantics of Common Nouns. Parikh, Rohit.
Vyadi and The Realist Theory of Meaning. Ganeri, Jonardon.
Walter Burleigh on the Conclusion that You Are an Ass. Nuchelmans, Gabriel.
Wittgenstein e o Domínio da Gramática: A Ruptura com o Tractatus. Vergilio G Cuter, Joao.

GRAMSCI, A
Further Selections from the Prison Notebooks. Gramsci, Antonio and Boothman, Derek (ed & trans).

GRANDY, R
Radical Translation and Animals: An Argument from the Principle of Humanity. Weir, Jack L.

GRANGER, G
Noção de Estilo em Granger e Narrativa Histórica. Cardoso Jr, Hélio Rebello.

GRAPH
On the Methods of Cognitive Neuropsychology. Glymour, Clark.
The Monadic Second-Order logic of Graphs VIII: Orientations. Courcelle, Bruno.

GRAPHIC
Understanding Images: Finding Meaning in Digital Imagery. Marchese, Francis T (ed).

GRASSENDI
Locke and Gilles de Launay. Milton, J R.

GRASSI, E
Profils d'Ernesto Grassi. Muller, Philippe.

GRATUITY
Police Gratuities: What the Public Think. Prenzler, Tim and Mackay, Peta.

GRAVITY
The Children of Time: Causality, Entropy, Becoming. Lestienne, Rémy and Neher, E C (trans).
Are Physical Properties Dispositions?. Reeder, Nick.
Capacities, Tendencies and the Problem of Singular Causes. Morrison, Margaret.
Cartwright on Probabilistic Causality: Types, Tokens, and Capacities. Eells, Ellery.
Reply to Eells, Humphreys and Morrison. Cartwright, Nancy.

GRAY, J
The Theory and Practice of Liberalism. Bellamy, Richard.

GREATNESS
Arte y Grandeza. Bertman, Martin A.

GRECO-ROMAN
The Sciences in Greco-Roman Society (Apeiron 27-4). Barnes, Timothy D.

GREED
How Are We to Live? Ethics in an Age of Self-Interest. Singer, Peter.
Cicero Versus Machiavelli: Does the End Justify the Means. Hancock, Curtis L.

GREEK
see also Ancient, Logos, Mimesis, Presocratics
"A Mind to Love: Friends and Lovers in Ancient Greek Philosophy" in *The Nature and Pursuit of Love, Goicoechea, David (ed)*. Gooch, Paul W.
"Der Antike Dionysos bei Friedrich Nietzsche und Walter Friedrich Otto" in *Die besten Geister der Nation, Korotin, Ilse (ed)*. Zwiauer, Charlotte.

HABERMAS, J

The Place of Equality in Habermas' and Dworkin's Theories of Justice. Gosepath, Stefan.

Trabajo e Interacción como Intereses Rectores del Conocimiento. López Molina, Antonio M.

Una Conversione della Teoria Critica? Sulla Teoria del Diritto e dello Stato di Habermas. Höffe, Otfried.

Unità e molteplicità in Juergen Habermas. Giovagnoli, Raffaela.

Zur hermeneutischen Transformation der Sprachanalyse. Tietz, Udo.

HABIT

"Butler and Hume on Habit and Moral Character" in *Hume and Hume's Connexions, Stewart, M A (ed)*. Wright, John P.

Difference and Repetition. Deleuze, Gilles and Patton, Paul (trans).

Lonergan and Bellah: Social Science as Public Philosophy. Hoyt-O'Connor, Paul E.

HACKING, I

Could Theoretical Entities Save Realism?. Elsamahi, Mohamed.

Hacking's Experimental Realism. Resnik, David B.

Hacking's Experimental Realism: An Untenable Middle Ground. Reiner, Richard and Pierson, Robert.

HACKING, J

Ground Truth and Virtual Reality: Hacking vs van Fraassen. Seager, William.

HAHN, L

Interview of Lewis E Hahn. Abbarno, John M.

HAINES, V

Response to Victor Yelverton Haines. Eldridge, Richard.

HAJEK, A

"Conditionals as Random Variables" in *Probability and Conditionals, Eells, Ellery (ed)*. Stalnaker, Robert and Jeffrey, Richard.

"Triviality on the Cheap?" in *Probability and Conditionals, Eells, Ellery (ed)*. Hájek, Alan.

HAKUIN EKAKU

"Nietzsche and Zen Master Hakuin on the Roles of Emotion and Passion" in *Emotions in Asian Thought, Marks, Joel (ed)*. Parkes, Graham R.

HALDEMAN-JULIUS, E

"Haldeman-Julius: Publisher, Freethinker, Humanist" in *Contributors to the Philosophy of Humanism, Hillar, Marian (ed)*. Prahl, Frank.

HALES, S

Immoralist: That Means the Opposite of Consequentialist: Comment on Professor Hale's "Was Nietzsche a Consequentialist?". Crawford, Claudia.

HALL, C

Charles Hall: Exploitation, Commercial Society and Political Economy. Cunliffe, John.

HALL, N

"Conditionals as Random Variables" in *Probability and Conditionals, Eells, Ellery (ed)*. Stalnaker, Robert and Jeffrey, Richard.

"Triviality on the Cheap?" in *Probability and Conditionals, Eells, Ellery (ed)*. Hájek, Alan.

HALLDEN COMPLETENESS

On Variable Separation in Modal Logics. Maksimova, Larisa.

HALLEN, B

Towards an African (Yoruba) Perspective on Empirical Knowledge: A Critique of Hallen and Sodipo. Okè, Moses.

HALPERN, J

Appropriate and Inappropriate Use of Advance Directives. Emanuel, Linda.

Clear, Convincing, and Authentic Advance Directives in the Context of Managed Care?. Bursztajn, Harold J and Brodsky, Archie.

The Capacity to Make Decisions in Advance and Borderline Personality Disorder. Ganzini, Linda, Lee, Melinda A and Heintz, Ronald T.

HAMANN

L'*anthropologia in nuce* de Kant et Hamann. Cohen-Halimi, Michèle.

HAMBLIN, C

Commitment in Dialogue: Basic Concepts of Interpersonal Reasoning. Walton, Douglas N and Krabbe, Erik C W.

HAMMACHER, K

Fichte und die hermetische Demokratie der Friemaurer. Lawatsch, Hans-Helmut.

HAMPATE BA, A

Le Syndrome Hampâté Bâ ou Comment Naissent les Proverbes. Konaté, Yacouba.

HAND

On Artistic Process: Eye, Hand, Language. Nitta, Hiroë.

HANDICAP

The Non-Identity Problem and Genetic Harm—The Case of Wrongful Handicaps. Brock, Dan W.

HANDICAPPED

"Hard Choices: Ethical Questions Raised by the Birth of Handicapped Infants" in *Ethics on the Frontiers of Human Existence, Badham, Paul (ed)*. Kuhse, Helga and Singer, Peter.

The Lived Experience of Disability. Toombs, S K.

HANFLING, O

Hanfling on Loving My Neighbour, Loving Myself. Walton, Gertrud.

Hanfling on Neighbour Love. Radcliffe, Dana M.

Hanfling on Self-Love. Champlin, T S.

Scepticism's Health Buoyant. Franklin, James.

HANSEN, F

Musical Values Revisited: A Reply to Forest Hansen's "Values in Music Education". Elliott, David J.

HANSLICK, E

Hanslick on Hearing Beauty. Shibles, Warren A.

HAPPINESS

see also Hedonism, Pleasure

"Aristotle's 'Exclusive' Account of Happiness" in *The Crossroads of Norm and Nature, Sim, May (ed)*. Burger, Ronna C.

"Azioni ed eventi in Aristotele" in *L'etica e il suo Altro, Vigna, Carmelo (ed)*. Natali, Carlo.

"Die promesse de bonheur in Kants *Kritik der Urteilskraft*" in *Naturzweckmässigkeit und ästhetische Kultur, Schwabe, Karl-Heinz (ed)*. Recki, Birgit.

"Perfection and Happiness in the Best Possible World" in *The Cambridge Companion to Leibniz, Jolley, Nicholas (ed)*. Blumenfeld, David C.

"Socrates in the Clouds" in *The Socratic Movement, Vander Waerdt, Paul A (ed)*. Vander Waerdt, Paul A.

Ancient Greek Philosophy: Its Development and Relevance to Our Time. Trundle, Robert C.

Contro Gli Etici. Spinelli, Emidio (trans).

Il Nyaya Sutra di Gautama. Arena, Leonardo Vittorio.

Kant on Happiness in Ethics. Wike, Victoria S.

Plato's Ethics. Irwin, Terence.

The Oracle of Wisdom: Towards Philosophic Equipoise. Akam, J B.

Theophrastus Redivivus, Volumes 1 and 2. Canziani, Guido (ed) and Paganini, Gianni (ed).

Thinkers Through Time: Reading Ethics With Literature. Curran, Mary Bernard.

Conflicting Parts of Happiness in Aristotle's Ethics. White, Nicholas P.

Dalla nostalgia di patria alla nostalgia del paradiso. Giardini, F.

Dialéctica de Casiciaco. Rosado, Juan.

En torno a la ecuación desarrollo científico y tecnológico igual a progreso social. Cuello, César.

Eudaimonism and the Appeal to Nature in the Morality of Happiness: Comments on Julia Annas, *The Morality of Happiness*. Cooper, John M.

Fortunate Misfortune. Smilansky, Saul.

Is Happiness a Trait? Tests of the Theory That a Better Society Does Not Make People Any Happier. Veenhoven, Ruut.

Kant's Ethics as a Philosophy of Happiness: Reflections on the *Reflexionen*. Römpp, Georg.

La Eudaimonía y las Bienaventuranzas. de Gayoso, Graciela L Ritacco.

Multiple-Discrepancies Theory Versus Resource Theory. Schulz, Wolfgang.

Neutralidad y relatividad agencial. Farrell, Martín D.

O interesse geral o e interesse de cada um. Sottomayor-Cardía, M.

Reply to Cooper. Annas, Julia.

Socratic Goods and Socratic Happiness. Santas, Gerasimos.

Test of Predictions Implied in Three Theories of Happiness: The Cross-National Pattern of Happiness. Veenhoven, Ruut and Ehrhardt, Joop.

The Road Not Taken: Friendship, Consumerism, and Happiness. Lane, Robert E.

Urteilsenthaltung und Glück: Eine Verteidigung ethisch motivierter Skepsis. Engstler, Achim.

Wealth and Happiness. Wilson, James Q.

Who Should a Utilitarian Be?. Smilansky, Saul.

Why I am so Happy. Schmidt, Dennis J.

HARAWAY, D

The Ethics of Hybrid Subjects: Feminist Constructivism According to Donna Haraway. Prins, Baukje.

HARDIN, C

Objectivism and the Evolutionary Value of Colour Vision. Dedrick, Don.

HARDING, S

Feminist Epistemology: Implications for Philosophy of Science. Pinnick, Cassandra L.

In Defense of Bacon. Soble, Alan.

Making Strange What Had Appeared Familiar. Elliott, Terri.

Should There Be Separatist Epistemologies?. Landau, Iddo.

The Market for Feminist Epistemology. Baber, Harriet.

What Could a *Feminist* Science Be?. Gross, Barry R.

HARDNESS

Fixed-parameter Tractability and Completeness IV: On Completeness for W[P] and PSPACE Analogues. Abrahamson, K A (& others).

HARDWIG, J

The Epistemic Authority of Expertise. Pierson, Robert.

HARE, R

"Se debe", entonces "yo debo": implicación?. Guariglia, Osvaldo.

Essays on Bioethics by R M Hare. Crisp, Roger.

Logic, Facts, and Representation: An Examination of R M Hare's Moral Philosophy. Ronnow-Rasmussen, Toni.

The Boundaries of Moral Discourse. Hajdin, Mane.

Cómo es posible aceptar sin contradecirse "debo hacer X" y no aceptar "se debe hacer X"?. Valdés, Margarita M.

Das Universalisierungsproblem in der Moralphilosophie. Meggle, Georg.

The Coherence of Two-Level Utilitarianism: Hare vs Williams. Levy, Sanford S.

The Importance of Examples for Moral Education: An Aristotelian Perspective. McDonough, Kevin.

HARM

Absolute Safety. Ashdown, Lance.

Compensation and Culpability. Zimmerman, Michael J.

Ducking Harm and Sacrificing Others. Fischer, John Martin and Ravizza, Mark.

Ducking Trolleys. Boorse, Christopher.

HEGEL

Das Feindbild der marxistisch-leninistischen Philosophie in der DDR 1945-1988. Kapferer, Norbert.

Elementa: L'argument Ontologique chez Saint Anselme et chez Hegel (Band 60). Girard, Louis, Berlinger, Rudolph (ed) and Schrader, Wiebke (ed).

Entgegensetzungen: Studien zu Fichte-Konfrontationen von Rousseau bis Kierkegaard. Janke, Wolfgang.

Erinnerung, Retrait, Absolute Reflection: Hegel and Derrida. Kisner, Wendell.

Hegel and Marx: Introductory Lectures. Kedourie, Elie.

Hegel In His Time: Berlin, 1818-1831. Burbidge, John W (trans) and D'Hondt, Jacques.

Hegel on the Modern World. Collins, Ardis B (ed).

Hegel Reconsidered. Engelhardt Jr, H Tristram (ed) and Pinkard, Terry (ed).

Hegel: Contra Sociology. Rose, Gillian.

Hegel: Phenomenology and System. Harris, H S.

Hegels "Wissenschaft der Logik": Eine internationale Bibliographie ihrer Rezeption im XX Jahrhundert. Hasselberg, Erwin (ed) and Radtke, Frank (ed).

Hegels Wissenschaft der Logik—metaphysische Letztbegründung oder Theorie logischer Formen?. Schick, Friedrike.

Heideggers Begriff der Geschichte und das neuzeitliche Geschichtsdenken. Brandner, Rudolf.

Karl Rosenkranz: Briefe 1827 bis 1850. Butzlaff, Joachim (ed).

On Hegel's Logic: Fragments of a Commentary. Burbidge, John W.

Philosophen im "Dritten Reich": Studie zu Hochschul- und Philosophiebetrieb im faschistischen Deutschland. Leske, Monika.

Philosophie und Totalitarismus: Zur Kritik dialektischer Diskursivität Eine Hegellektüre. Engelmann, Peter.

Rosmini et l'Idée de Progrès. Raschini, Maria-Adelaide and Rocher, Emmanuel (trans).

Sehnsucht—Affekt und Antrieb: Begriff, Struktur und praktische Bedeutung. Häfner, Ansgar.

Syncope: The Philosophy of Rapture. O'Driscoll, Sally (trans), Clément, Catherine and Mahoney, Deirdre M (trans).

The Future of Alienation. Schacht, Richard.

The Human Shape of God: Religion in Hegel's "Phenomenology of Spirit". Jamros, Daniel P.

The Owl at Dawn: A Sequel to Hegel's Phenomenology of Spirit. Curtrofello, Andrew.

Was ist Wahrnehmung?. Ziemke, Axel.

Zum Begriff der Trinität. Polemis, Michael.

A Critique of "Non-Instrumental Reason". Siemek, Marek J.

Absolu/Sujet. Jarczyk, Gwendoline and Labarrière, Pierre-Jean.

Amor Dei Intellectualis: Vernunft—und Gottesliebe in Gipfelsätzen neuzeitlicher Systembildungen (Spinoza, Hegel, Schelling, Fichte). Janke, Wolfgang.

At the Crossroads: Hegel and the Ethics of *bürgerliche Gesellschaft*. Smith, Steven B.

Bedeutung der Philosophiegeschichte: W Weischedel als Philosophie-Historiker. Mauro, Letterio.

Benedetto Croce Critico dell'Irrazionalismo. Tertulian, Nicolas.

Beyond World History: On Hegel's and Kierkegaard's Interests in Ethics and Religion. Cruysberghs, Paul.

British Hegelianism: A Non-Metaphysical View?. Stern, Robert.

Can There Be a "Humanistic" Ecology? A Debate Between Hegel and Heidegger on the Meaning of Ecological Thinking. Berthold-Bond, Daniel.

Coleridge's "Ideal Realism": An Alternative to the "Doctors of the Absolute"?. Perkins, Mary Anne.

Crítica y Defensa de lo Existente. Referencias de la Filosofía a la Realidad. Estudio Sobre la Filosofía Hegeliana del Derecho. Sandkühler, Hans Jörg.

De Sade o la subversión de/en la Ilustración. Mayos, Gonça.

Dialéctica Hegeliana de la Ilustración. Aranda Torres, Cayetano.

Die methodologische Funktion des Verhältnisses von "Herr und Knecht" in der Philosophie Hegels. Kumamoto, Yasuhiro.

Difficulté de l'hégélianisme. Apropos de l'ouvrage de Jean-François Kervégan: *Hegel, Carl Schmitt: le politique entre spéculation et positivité*. Gervais, Richard.

Education and the Archeology of Consciousness: Freire and Hegel. Torres, Carlos Alberto.

Filosofi a Bologna fra Ottocento e Novecento. Garin, Eugenio.

Finito e infinito e l'idealismo della filosofia: La logica hegeliana dell'essere determinato: Parte Prima. Movia, Giancarlo.

Finito e infinito e l'idealismo della filosofia: La logica hegeliana dell'essere determinato: Parte Seconda. Movia, Giancarlo.

G W F Hegel: El *Fragmento de Tubinga*. del Carmen Paredes, María.

Gentile e Jaja. Savorelli, Alessandro.

Go Figure! Refiguring *Disfuguring*. Shapiro, Gary.

Hegel and Ancient Egypt: History and Beocming. Lampert, Jay.

Hegel and Aquinas on Self-Knowledge and Historicity. Baur, Michael.

Hegel and Fichte: Recognition, Otherness, and Absolute Knowing. Houlgate, Stephen.

Hegel and Our Democracy. Znoj, Milan.

Hegel and the Hermeneutics of German Idealism. Rockmore, Tom.

Hegel and the Myth of Reason. Stewart, Jon.

Hegel dans *Soi-même comme un autre* de Paul Ricoeur. Brito, Emilio.

Hegel et la Grèce. Vieillard-Baron, Jean-Louis.

Hegel et Schelling: critique du formalisme et prise en charge de la contingence. Lardic, Jean-Marie.

Hegel on Classical Art: a Reexamination. Winfield, Richard Dien.

Hegel on Property and Recognition. Cristi, Renato.

Hegel on Saying and Showing. Hahn, Susan.

Hegel on the Bacchanalian Revel of Truth. Kainz, Howard P.

Hegel on the Rationality and Priority of Ethical Life. Pippin, Robert B.

Hegel or Schelling?. White, Alan.

Hegel und das Problem der Macht. Zenkert, Georg.

Hegel y América. Perez-Estevez, Antonio.

Hegel's *Phenomenology* and the Critique of the Enlightenment An Essay in Interpretation. DiGiovanni, George.

Hegel's Confessions; or, Why We Need a Sequel to the *Phenomenology of Spirit*. Cutrofello, Andrew.

Hegel's Critique of Kant in the Philosophy of Right. Lottenbach, Hans and Tenenbaum, Sergio.

Hegel, Marx and Idealistic Vapourizing. Ninnes, L E.

Historicism, Social Practice, and Sustainability: Some Themes in Hegelian Ethical Theory. Pinkard, Terry P.

How Philosophy *Instructs the World*. Harris, Henry S.

Il Primo Hegel in Traduzione Italiana. Masciarelli, Pasqualino.

Intellektuelle Anschauung und Dialektik. Nagasawa, Kunihiko.

Ist eine Selbstbescheidung der Philosophie aus sich heraus möglich?. Burkhardt, Bernd.

Kant and Hegel on War and Peace. Siebert, Rudolf J.

L'Ermeneutica e il Trascendentale. Cortella, Lucio.

L'esclave, le travail et l'action: Aristote et Hegel. Faes, Hubert.

L'Esprit absolu de Hegel est-il Dieu?. Beauvais, Chantal.

L'opposition de Hegel au conservatisme de Charles-Louis de Haller. Ponton, Lionel.

L'université d'état et ses contradictions philosophiques: Hegel et la création de l'université de Berlin. Reid, Jeffrey.

La Critique de l'ontologie et la Théorie Sociale de Hegel dans l'oeuvre de Herbert Marcuse. C-Mazaraki, A.

La fin de l'histoire serait-elle le commencement de la sagesse? L'aliénation de l'esprit dans la *Phénoménologie* de Hegel. Joós, Ernest.

La Inferència Dialèctico-Especulativa a la *Ciència de la Lògica* de Hegel. Alegre I Biosca, Lluís.

La lecture du journal selon Hegel: "une sorte de-prière du matin réaliste"?. Bienenstock, Myriam.

La Questione dell'Astratto e del Concreto fra il 1912 e il 1917. Sasso, Gennaro.

La Ruse de la Raison. D'Hondt, Jacques.

La Società Concreta: Considerazioni su Fichte e Hegel. Fonnesu, Luca.

La vie éthique perdue dans ses extrêmes...Scission et réconciliation dans la théorie hégélienne de la *Sittlichkeit*. Kervégan, Jean-François.

Labriola tra Croce e Gentile. Agrimi, Mario.

Lo spirito di serietà e l'ironia. Gallino, Guglielmo.

Logos y realidad (Evocación de Hegel). Blanco, José.

Nature, coutume et droit chez Hegel. Vieillard-Baron, Jean-Louis.

Needs and Essence. Rotenstreich, Nathan.

Neoidealismo ed Hegelismo Ortodosso nel Carteggio Croce-Mariano. Savorelli, Alessandro.

On Fractal Thought: Derrida, Hegel, and Chaos Science. McRobert, Laurie.

On the Memory of Last Things. Schmidt, Dennis.

On Translating Hegel's *Encyclopedia Logic*: A Response. Geraets, Theodore F and Harris, H S.

Philosophical Disappointment: Introduction. Light, Steve.

Philosophical Republicanism and Monarchism—and Republican and Monarchical Philosophy—in Kant and Hegel. Redding, Paul.

Philosophie hégélienne de l'actualité et actualité de la philosophie hégélienne. Bourgeois, Bernard.

Reason *as* Revolution. Maker, William.

Recent Work on Hegel's Philosophy of Religion. Dickey, L.

Reply: The Schellingian Alternative. Bowie, Andrew.

Selbstbewusstsein als Prinzip des neuzeitlichen Selbstverständnisses: Seine Grundstruktur und seine Schwierigkeiten. Gloy, Karen.

Spirit, Estrangement and Unification: Hegel's Philosophico-Religious Quest. Singh, R P.

T H Green's Doubts About Hegel's Political Philosophy. Nicholson, Peter.

Tentations et tentatives hégéliennes. Secretan, Philibert.

The Body as "Sign and Tool" in Hegel's *Encyclopaedia*. Dodd, James.

The Definition of Philosophy, Revisited. Kainz, Howard P.

The Safeguarded Self. Mullin, Amy.

The Sounds of the Ideal: Hegel's Aesthetic of Music. Etter, Brian K.

The Substance of Knowing Is History: Absolute Knowing and History in Hegel's *Phenomenology*. De Nys, Martin J.

The Unity of Theoretical and Practical Spirit in Hegel's Concept of Freedom. Houlgate, Stephen.

The Word 'Liberty' on the Chains of Galley-Slaves: Bosanquet's Theory of the General Will. Primoratz, Igor.

Um Comentário sobre a Filosofia da Natureza na Enciclopédia de Hegel. Pereira Jr, Alfredo.

Una Conversione della Teoria Critica? Sulla Teoria del Diritto e dello Stato di Habermas. Höffe, Otfried.

What Does Hegel Make of the Jews?: A Scato-Logical Reading of Kafka's *Die Verwandlung*. Munk, Linda.

Zur Aktualität des Deutschen Idealismus. Horstman, Rolf-Peter.

HEGELIANISM

"Atomism, Art, and Arthur: Danto's Hegelian Turn" in *Danto and his Critics*, Rollins, Mark (ed). Solomon, Robert C and Higgins, Kathleen M.

HISTORY

Scientism and Humanism: Two Cultures in Post-Mao China (1978-1989). Hua, Shiping.

Sed Amentes Sunt Isti: Against Michel Foucault's Account of Cartesian Skepticism. D'Amico, Robert D.

Slavery and the Catholic Tradition: Rights in the Balance. Brett, Stephen F.

Socialism After Communism: The New Market Socialism. Pierson, Christopher.

Sources of Hermeneutics. Grondin, Jean.

Spinoza's Ethica From Manuscript to Print: Studies on Text, Form, and Related Topics. Steenbakkers, Piet.

Starting with Foucault: An Introduction to Genealogy. Prado, C G.

Telemachus, Son of Ulysses. Fenelon, François and Riley, Patrick (ed & trans).

The 1994 Annual of Hermeneutics and Social Concern. Lawler, Justus George (ed).

The Atheist Trap. Mixie, Joseph.

The Barbarism of Reason. Horowitz, Asher (ed) and Maley, Terry (ed).

The Beautiful Soul: Aesthetic Morality in the Eighteenth Century. Norton, Robert E.

The Blanchot Reader. Holland, Michael (ed).

The Book of the Body Politic. Forhan, Kate Langdon (ed & trans) and De Pizan, Christine.

The British Moralists and the Internal 'Ought': 1640-1740. Darwall, Stephen.

The Broken Middle: Out of our Ancient Society. Rose, Gillian.

The Correspondence of Richard Price, Volume III: February 1786-February 1791. Peach, W Bernard (ed) and Price, Richard.

The Decolonization of Imagination: Culture, Knowledge, and Power. Pieterse, Jan Nederveen (ed) and Parekh, Bhikhu (ed).

The Defeat of the Mind. Friedlander, Judith (trans) and Finkielkraut, Alain.

The Development of German Aesthetic Theory from Kant to Schiller: A Philosophical Commentary on Schiller's Aesthetic Education of Man (1795). Murray, Patrick T.

The Diffident Naturalist: Robert Boyle and the Philosophy of Experiment. Sargent, Rose-Mary.

The Discourses of Science. Pera, Marcello and Botsford, Clarissa (trans).

The End of "Isms"?. Shtromas, Aleksandras (ed).

The Ends of Philosophy. Cahoone, Lawrence E.

The Epistemology of Comparative Philosophy: A Critique with Reference to P T Raju's Views. Kaipayil, Joseph.

The Erich Fromm Reader. Fromm, Erich and Funk, Rainer (ed).

The Flight from Woman (New Edition). Stern, Karl.

The Fragmented World of the Social: Essays in Social and Political Philosophy. Wright, Charles W (ed) and Honneth, Axel.

The Future of Alienation. Schacht, Richard.

The Future of the Humanities: Teaching Art, Religion, Philosophy, Literature, and History (New Edition). Kaufmann, Walter Arnold.

The Genius of Language: Observations for Teachers. Steiner, Rudolf.

The Heidegger Controversy: A Critical Reader. Wolin, Richard (ed).

The High Road of Humanity: The Seven Ethical Ages of Western Man. Levi, Albert William, Verene, Donald Phillip (ed) and Verene, Molly Black (ed).

The Ironist's Cage: Memory, Trauma, and the Construction of History. Roth, Michael S.

The Letter of Apologetics and History and Dogma. Dru, Alexander (trans), Trethowan, Illtyd (trans) and Blondel, Maurice.

The Lyotard Reader. Benjamin, Andrew (ed).

The Machine as Metaphor and Tool. Haken, Hermann (ed), Karlqvist, Anders (ed) and Svedin, Uno (ed).

The Names of History: On the Poetics of Knowledge. Rancière, Jacques and Melehy, Hassan (trans).

The Nature of Insight. Sternberg, Robert J (ed) and Davidson, Janet E (ed).

The New Ecological Order. Ferry, Luc and Volk, Carol (trans).

The Passionate Intellect: Essays on the Transformation of Classical Traditions. Ayres, Lewis (ed).

The Philosophical Papers of Alan Donagan: Volume I, Historical Understanding and the History of Philosophy. Malpas, J E (ed) and Donagan, Alan.

The Philosophy of Cynicism: An Annotated Bibliography. Navia, Luis E.

The Philosophy of the Visual Arts. Alperson, Philip (ed).

The Politics of English Jacobinism: Writings of John Thelwall. Thelwall, John and Claeys, Gregory (ed).

The Reputations of Socrates: The Afterlife of a Gadfly. Hulse, James W.

The Secret Chain: Evolution and Ethics. Bradie, Michael.

The Semiotic Self. Wiley, Norbert.

The Socratic Movement. Vander Waerdt, Paul A (ed).

The Sources of Christian Ethics. Pinckaers, Servais and Noble, Mary Thomas (trans).

The Trace of Political Representation. Seitz, Brian.

The Transformation of Natural Philosophy: The Case of Philip Melanchthon. Kusukawa, Sachiko.

The 'Arabick' Interest of the Natural Philosophers in Seventeenth-Century England. Russell, G A (ed).

Theorizing Masculinities. Brod, Harry (ed) and Kaufman, Michael (ed).

Thought as a System (New Edition). Bohm, David.

Time and Exteriority: Aristotle, Heidegger, Derrida. Protevi, John.

Too Much Liberty?: Perspectives on Freedom and the American Dream. Saari, David J.

Twentieth Century Ethical Theory. Cahn, Steven M (ed) and Haber, Joram G (ed).

Understanding History: An Introduction to Analytical Philosophy of History. Gorman, Jonathan.

University-Business Partnerships: An Assessment. Bowie, Norman E.

Utopia: Latin Text and English Translation. More, Thomas and Logan, George M (& other eds).

Ways of Knowing: Selected Readings (Second Edition). Dodson, Kevin E (ed) and Avery, Jon (ed).

A Critique of Western Philosophical Ethics: Multidisciplinary Alternatives for Framing Ethical Dilemmas. Carlin, William B and Strong, Kelly C.

A Few Problems Related to Nineteenth Century Chinese and Western Philosophies and their Cultural Interaction. Weishi, Yuan.

A Modern History Theory of Function. Godfrey-Smith, Peter.

A Perspective on Solidarity in a 'Post-Socialist' World. Steger, Manfred.

A Philosophical Correspondence with Li Rui. Yuanhua, Wang.

Abandoning Informed Consent. Veatch, Robert M.

About the Philosophical Style of Thinking. Panova, Elena.

Actualidad y Perennidad de Vico. Uscatescu, Jorge.

Algunas preguntas acerca de la Idea de Progreso. Peña, Vidal.

Allgemeine Arbeit. Haug, Wolfgang Fritz.

Alternativen der Wissenschaftsgeschichte. Haney, Frank.

Ambivalence About Ambiguity. Review of *Sartre's Political Theory* by William L McBride. Flay, Joseph C.

Ambivalencias de Bentham en la lectura de Foucault. García, Francisco Vázquez.

An Immodest Proposal: Foucault, Hysterization, and the "Second Rape". Hengehold, Laura.

Analytic Concept of History. Lonergan, Bernard J F.

Antecedentes del Utilitarismo en los moralistas británicos anteriores a Hume. Costa, Margarita.

Appunti sulla Fortuna di Gabriel Naudé nella Germania del Primo Illuminismo. Mulsow, Martin.

Aristotle's Biology: Plain, But Not Simple. Lennox, James G.

Armistice in the Recent Battle of the Books: Paul de Man, Claudio Guillén, and History. Milner, Earl.

Art, Society and 'Contrapuntal Criticism': A Review of Edward Said's *Culture and Imperialism*. Polan, Dana.

Artisanal Knowledge and Experimental Natural Philosophers: The British Response to J Fraunhofer and the Bavarian Usurpation of Their Optical Empire. Jackson, Myles W.

Authenticity in Musical Performance: Personal or Historical?. O'Dea, Jane W.

Author and Repression. Gracia, Jorge J E.

Axiological Invariants. Reale, Miguel.

B Croce—G Gentile: Bibliografia 1980-1993. Bonechi, Sara.

Bataille in the Street: The Search for Virility in the 1930s. Suleiman, Susan Rubin.

Bedeutung der Philosophiegeschichte. W Weischedel als Philosophie Historiker. Mauro, Letterio.

Before Nietzsche: Nihilism as a Critique of German Idealism. Cho, Stephen Wagner.

Being Human, More or Less. Kohák, Erazim.

Bernard Williams, *Shame and Necessity*. Held, Dirk T D.

Between Culture, Politics and Philosophy. Howard, Dick.

Beyond World History: On Hegel's and Kierkegaard's Interests in Ethics and Religion. Cruysberghs, Paul.

Black Socrates?. Critchley, Simon.

Blumenberg: Truly Memorable Memories. Hrachovec, Herbert and Turner, Charles (ed).

Boturini e la Diffusione di Vico in Spagna. Mestre, Antonio.

Bringing Women Back In: A Search for Alternative Historiographies. Ahikire, Josephine.

British Idealism, the State, and International Relations. Boucher, David.

Broadening the Picture of Science in Revolutionary France: Adding Du Pont and Restif to Lavoisier and Laplace. Conner, Clifford D.

Categories of the Ethics of Sport. Krawczyk, Zbigniew.

Catene di civiltà: La seconda fase del pensiero di Oswald Spengler. Conte, Domenico.

Catherine Wilson on Leibniz's Metaphysics. Okruhlik, M Kathleen.

Causality and Conserved Quantities: A Reply to Salmon. Dowe, Phil.

Chaos, Clio, and Scientific Illusions of Understanding. Roth, Paul A and Ryckman, Thomas A.

Charles Hall: Exploitation, Commercial Society and Political Economy. Cunliffe, John.

Cognitive Psychology: A Phenomenological Critique. Wertz, Frederick J.

Collingwood's Hermeneutic of Acts and Events in Historical Explanation. Mann, Doug.

Collingwood's Reform of Hegelian Dialectic. Peters, Rik.

Colonialism and Its Others: Considerations On Rights and Care Discourses. Narayan, Uma.

Colonialism and the Language Question: A Reply to Godfrey Tangwa. Uroh, Chris.

Commentary on Attridge's "Gnostic Platonism". Perkins, Pheme.

Commentary on Caston's "Toward a History of the Problem of Intentionality Among the Greeks". Matthews, Gareth B.

Comprensión e identidad: Encuentro entre filosofíade la historia y filosofía de la acción. Cruz, Manuel.

Conceptualizing Knowledge Used in Innovation: A Second Look at the Science-Technology Distinction and Industrial Innovation. Faulkner, Wendy.

Consolación Mediante la Historia: Cuatro *visiones* de la Historia Universal. Sevilla Fornández, José M.

Constitution and Continuity in the Transitions: Part I. Arato, Andrew.

Contextualising Carl Schmitt's Concept of *Grossraum*. Schwab, Georg.

HISTORY

HISTORY

Las Formas lógicas de la Sección Primera de El Capital. Delgado, Manuel.

Las ideas chinas en la conceptualización transcultural: La relevancia de la historia intelectual. Lee, Thomas H C.

Las Paradojas de la Modernidad. Castro López, Octavio.

Late Scholastic Philosophy: Introduction. Ashworth, E J.

Laws of Nature, Corpuscles, and Concourse: Non-Occasionalist Tendencies in the Natural Philosophy of Robert Boyle. Jacobs, Struan.

Le Dehors et le Dedans. Dagognet, M François (& others).

Le Forme Diffratte di Serres: Prolegomeni a una Nuova Filosofia della Storia. Delcò, Alessandro.

Le Syndrome Hampâté Bâ ou Comment Naissent les Proverbes. Konaté, Yacouba.

Leibniz and Brentano: Two Philosophers Concerning Catastrophes and their Solutions. Benedikt, Michael.

Leo Strauss and Classical Political Philosophy. Bolotin, David.

Let's Get the L Out: Or Why Johnson Controls Is Not an Unequivocal Victory for Women. Callahan, Joan.

Liberal Eugenics and the Vitalist Life Sciences: Incongruities in the German Human Sciences in the 19th Century. Whimster, Sam.

Liberal Tradition in the Cultural-Historical Experience of Russia. Novikova, L and Sizemskaia, I.

Literary into Cultural Studies. Easthope, Antony.

Living Poetically: Kierkegaard and German Romanticism. Walsh, Sylvia.

Locke's Antagonist, Jonas Proast. Vernon, Richard.

Locke's Educational Theories (and) the Woman Question. Lembcke, V L.

Locke's Political Sympathies. Pringle, Helen.

Lonergan and Analytic Philosophy of History. Beards, Andrew.

Long-Acting Contraceptives: Ethical Guidance for Policymakers and Health Care Providers. Moskowitz, Ellen H.

Long-Acting Contraceptives: Rationale, Current Development, and Ethical Implications. Brown, George F.

Los escritos póstumos de J P Sartre (II). Amorós, Celia.

Los Tratados Filosóficos de S Vicente Ferrer: Nota Histórica y Bibliográfica. García-Cuadrado, José Ángel.

Lyotard's Homeopathic Indeterminacy: The Medicinal Sublime. Miller-Frank, Felicia.

Madness, the Absence of Work. Foucault, Michel, Stastny, Peter (trans) and Sengel, Deniz (trans).

Manservant as Amanuensis: Sylvester Brounower. Milton, J R.

Marx, Moses, and the Pagans in the Secular City. Sunic, Tomislav.

Materials for an Analysis of a Just Universe. Herman, Arthur L.

Max Weber et le néo-Kantisme: Pour une politique de la modernité. Piché, Claude.

Medicine and History as Theoretical Tools in a Confucian Pragmatism. Birdwhistell, Anne D.

Medievo y Renacimiento, Ruptura o Continuidad?. González Fernández, Martín.

Metaphors of Race: Theoretical Presuppositions Behind Racism. Asma, Stephen T.

Michel Foucault: Governmentality and Liberal Education. Marshall, James.

Mixing Metaphors: Contemporary Views on the 'End' of Philosophy. Bredeck, Elizabeth.

Modernity, Post-Modernity, and the Philosophy of History. Carr, David.

Montesquieu on the Causes of Roman Greatness. Myers, Richard.

Montesquieu's Paradox on Freedom and Hungary's Constitutions 1790-1990. Péter, László.

Moral/Political Education in the People's Republic of China: Learning Through Role Models. Reed, Gay Garland.

Moralist or Therapist? Foucault and the Critique of Psychiatry. Matthews, Eric.

Moses Mendelssohn and the End of Illusion Theory: An Inquiry into Innovation in Aesthetics in the Middle of the Eighteenth-Century. Otabe, Tanehisa.

Mourning, Work, and Play. Comay, Rebecca.

Narrative, Irony, and Faith in Gibbon's Decline and Fall. Wootton, David.

Nathaniel Hawthorne and Conservatism's "Night of Ambiguity". Mendilow, Jonathan.

National Identification and the Transgression of National Boundaries: The Steps Toward Universalization. Kloskowska, Antonina.

National Identity and National Consciousness. Tevzadze, Natia.

National Past, Socialist Future. Geoghegan, Vincent.

Natura Umana e Conoscenza Storica in Vico: Sulle Recenti 'Riletture' Vichiane di Leon Pompa. Nuzzo, Enrico.

Natureza e História: Os Sentidos da Liberdade e da Igualdade. Ribeiro Silva, Idalice.

Nederman, Gerson, Conciliar Theory, and Constitutionalism: Sed Contra. Oakley, Francis.

Neitzsche and the Contemporary Writer: What does it all Mean?. Diethe, Carol.

Neo-Stoicism and the Transition to Modernity in Wilhelm Dilthey's Philosophy of History. Frohman, Larry.

Neoidealismo ed Hegelismo Ortodosso nel Carteggio Croce-Mariano. Savorelli, Alessandro.

Neutral Currents and the History of Scientific Ideas. Miller, Arthur I and Bullock, Frederick W.

New Perspectives on Teilhard Publications. Schmitz-Moormann, Nicole.

New Ways to Look at Fitness. Van Der Steen, Wim J.

Nietzsche and Epicurus. Vincenzo, Joseph P.

Nietzsche and Foucault: An Interpretation of Influence. Kissack, Michael.

Nietzsche and the Agenda of Post-Modernity. O'Sullivan, Noël.

Nietzsche's Future Perfect and the Eternal Return: Toward a Genealogy of Ideas. Boothroyd, David.

No Longer, Not Yet: Reading History Grammatically. Erickson, Stephen A.

Noção de Estilo em Granger e Narrativa Histórica. Cardoso Jr, Hélio Rebello.

Nota acerca del Rendimiento socio-cultural de la utopía: Sobre la necesidad de superar la mentalidad positivista. Barrio Maestre, José María.

Objectivity in History. Bevir, Mark.

Observaciones al Margen a la Investigación Viquiana en la España Contemporánea. Cacciatore, Giuseppe.

On Histoire de la folie as an Event. Canguilhem, Georges and Hobart, Ann (trans).

On a Mistake Commonly Made in Accounts of Sixteenth-Century Discussions of the Immortality of the Soul. Martin, Christopher.

On Brinks and Bridges in Heidegger. Fritsche, Johannes.

On Giambattista Vico. Mali, Joseph.

On Gilles Deleuze and Félix Guattari, A Thousand Plateaus. Negri, Antonio and Wolf, Charles (trans).

On Jacob Klein's Greek Mathematical Thought and the Origin of Algebra. Gonda, Joseph.

On Neitzsche's Enigmatic Anti-Kantian Categorical Imperative. Hodge, Roger D.

On the Competitive Structure of Problem-Solving. Fu, Daiwei.

On the Idealization of the Historical Past. Czarnecki, Zdzislaw J.

On the Possibility of Feminist Philosophy. McAlister, Linda Lopez.

On Various Faces of Postmodernist Philosophical Thinking. Morawski, Stefan.

Oportet Philosophari in Theologia (I). Fisichella, Rino.

Outrage and Authority. Fisk, Milton T.

Peirce on the Relation of Logic and Mathematics. Sumwalt, Vernon.

Periodizing World History. Green, William.

Phenomenology, Universalism and Dialogue. Brown, Charles S.

Phenomenotechnique in Historical Perspective: Its Origins and Implications for Philosophy of Science. Castelao-Lawless, Teresa.

Philosophie, Raison, Histoire. Glauser, Richard.

Philosophiegeschichte als Problemfeld der Wissenschaftslehre Fichtes. Stahl, Jürgen.

Philosophy in Post-Communist Europe. Gordon, Dane R.

Philosophy of Universalism and the Concept of Human Nature. Wiercinski, Andrzej.

Philosophy Under Fire: J F Lyotard Transcending the Trenches of Postmodernity. Brons, H R.

Popper Revisited, or What Is Wrong With Conspiracy Theories?. Pigden, Charles.

Popular Government and Effective Government. McNamara, Peter.

Poteat on Modern Culture and Critical Philosophy. Adams, E M.

Power, Modernity and Morality in the Long Nineteenth Century. Goldblatt, David.

Present Concerns and Future Interests. Magnell, Thomas.

Protestantism as a Transnational Ideology. Baskerville, Stephen.

Psychoanalysis and Ideology: Bakhtin, Lacan, and Zizek. Baker, Harold D.

Putting Ourselves Up for the Question: A Postmodern Critique of Richard Rorty's Postmodernist Bourgeois Liberalism. Hendley, Steven.

Qué es la Ilustración?. Foucault, Michel.

Quests for a Scientific Mythology: F Creuzer and K O Müller on History and Myth. Blok, Josine H.

R G Collingwood, The Idea of History. Levine, Joseph M.

Radicalism, Capitalism and Historical Contexts: Not Only a Reply to Richard Ashcraft on John Locke. Wood, Ellen Meiksins.

Rassegne Crociane: I. I Carteggi dell'Ultimo Decennio. II. Una Bibliografia "Ragionata". Miccolis, Stefano.

Rationalism and Irrationalism: A Nietzschean Perspective. Cauchi, Francesca.

Rationality, Gender, and History. Allen, Prudence.

Reason, History, and a Little Madness: Toward a Hermeneutics of Christian Historicality. Caputo, John D.

Reason, Truth, and Sacred History?. Haldane, John.

Reasoned Freedom: John Locke and Enlightenment. Losonsky, Michael.

Reflections on the Perception of Time in Poland in the 16th and 17th Centuries. Bogucka, Maria.

Reflective Solidarity. Dean, Jodi.

Regius's Fundamenta Physices. Verbeek, Theo.

Religione, etica e politica nel pensiero di Ernst Troeltsch. Cantillo, Giuseppe.

Religious Memory and the Pluralism of Readings: Reflections on Roberto de Nobili and the Taittiriya Upanisad. Clooney, Francis X.

Reply to Easthope. Ryle, Martin.

Reply to Michael Walzer. Bader, Veit.

Report from Mr Canguilhem on the Manuscript Filed by Mr Michel Foucault, Director of the Institut Français of Hamburg.... Canguilhem, Georges and Hobart, Ann (trans).

Response to Veit Bader. Walzer, Michael.

Restabilizing Dynamics: Construction and Constraint in the History of Walrasian Stability Theory. Hands, D Wade.

Retrieving the Point of the Realism-Instrumentalism Debate: Mach vs Planck on Science Education Policy. Fuller, Steve.

Review Article on Ayers, 'Locke'. Milton, J R.

Review Essay: Leon Pompa's Vico: A Study of the 'New Science'. Miller, Cecilia.

Review Essay: Philip Barker's Michel Foucault: Subversions of the Subject. Anchor, Robert.

Review Essay: Robert B Pippin's Modernism as a Philosophical Problem. Chytry, Josef.

Richard Rorty and Solidarity, or the Inconsequence of a Certain Capacity. Veroli, Nicolas.

Rosmini on Natural Law and Right. Cleary, Denis.

Saccheri's Postulate. Angelelli, Ignacio.

Santo Tomás y el Progreso Histórico en el Conocimiento de la Verdad. Luque Alcaide, Elisa.

Schelling: La formation de la conscience à travers la mythologie, ou l'origine mythologique de l'histoire. Challiol-Gillet, Marie-Christine.

Science and the Construction of the Cultural Sciences in Late Enlightenment Germany: The Case of Wilhelm von Humboldt. Reill, Peter Hanns.

HISTORY

HISTORY OF LOGIC

HISTORY OF PHILOSOPHY

Heidegger im Kontext: Gesamtüberblick zum NS-Engagement der Universitätsphilosophen. Leaman, George.

The Philosophical Papers of Alan Donagan: Volume I, Historical Understanding and the History of Philosophy. Malpas, J E (ed) and Donagan, Alan.

Woman and the History of Philosophy. Tuana, Nancy.

Bosnjaks *Geschichte der Philosophie* und das geschichtliche Denken. Pazanin, Ante.

Empirical vs Rational Order in the History of Philosophy. Butler, Clark W.

Geschichte der Philosophie (als Wissenschaft) oder Entwicklung des Denkens in(nerhalb) der Idee des Ganzen. Despot, Branko.

The Bullying of an Untheoretical History of Philosophy—Eclecticism Instead of Ideology. Zimmerli, Walther Christoph.

The Historiography of Dutch Philosophy: Problems and Perspectives (in Dutch). Wielema, M R.

HISTORY OF SCIENCE

"Discussion: Peirce and the History of Science" in *Peirce and Contemporary Thought: Philosophical Inquiries,* Ketner, Kenneth Laine (ed). Skagestad, Peter.

"Peirce and History of Science" in *Peirce and Contemporary Thought: Philosophical Inquiries,* Ketner, Kenneth Laine (ed). Dauben, Joseph W.

Criticism and the History of Science. Andersson, Gunnar.

HITCHCOCK, A

Lust und Weisheit des Scheines: Die Alptraumwelt Alfred Hitchcocks. Fink-Eitel, Hinrich.

HITLER

"Die Platon-Rezeption in Deutschland um 1933" in *Die besten Geister der Nation,* Korotin, Ilse (ed). Orozco, Teresa.

"Am Muttergeist soll die Welt genesen": Philosophische Dispositionen zum Frauenbild im Nationalsozialismus. Korotin, Ilse Erika.

Denker Denken Geschichte Erkundungen zu Philosophie und Nationalsozialismus. Hartmann, Frank.

Genozid und Heilserwartung: zum nationalsozialistischen Mord am europäischen Judentum. Ley, Michael.

Mein Leben in Deutschland vor und nach 1933. Löwith, Karl.

Philosophen im "Dritten Reich": Studie zu Hochschul- und Philosophiebetrieb im faschistischen Deutschland. Leske, Monika.

Philosophieverhältnisse im deutschen Faschismus. Laugstien, Thomas.

HOBBES

"Hegel and Hobbes Revised" in *Hegel on the Modern World, Collins, Ardis B (ed).* Peperzak, Adriaan.

"Hegel, Hobbes, Kant, and the Scienticization of Practical Philosophy" in *Hegel on the Modern World, Collins, Ardis B (ed).* Buchwalter, Andrew.

"Linguaggio e politica" in *L'etica e il suo Altro, Vigna, Carmelo (ed).* Bubner, Rüdiger.

"Marxism in the Shadow of Hobbes" in *Marxism in the Postmodern Age, Callari, Antonio (ed).* Sinisi, John.

"The Study of Rhetoric as an Approach to Cultural History: The Case of Hobbes" in *Main Trends in Cultural History, Melching, Willem (ed).* Skinner, Quentin.

A History of Modern Political Thought: Major Political Thinkers from Hobbes to Marx. Hampsher-Monk, Iain.

A Hobbes Dictionary. Martinich, A P.

Der Katechon: Zu Carl Schmitts fundamentalistischer Kritik der Zeit. Meuter, Günter.

Politischer Individualismus: Die Rekonstruktion einer Sozialtheorie unter Bezugnahme auf Machiavelli, Bodin, und Hobbes. Hegmann, Horst.

Studien zum Gedanken der Einheit des Staates: Über die rechtsphilosophische Auflösung der Einheit des Subjektes. Waechter, Kay.

Thomas Hobbes and the Science of Moral Virtue. Boonin-Vail, David.

Zur Begründung der Menschenrechte: Hobbes-Locke-Kant. König, Siegfried.

D Gauthier o Hobbes sin Leviatán. Montoya, José.

Estetica e politica in Rousseau: Il sentimento come movente di critica al modello sociale del "Bourgeois". Pallavidini, Renato.

Fear, Technology, and the State: Carl Schmitt, Leo Strauss, and the Revival of Hobbes in Weimar and National Socialist Germany. McCormick, John P.

Hobbes's Biblical Beasts: *Leviathan* and *Behemoth.* Springborg, Patricia.

Hobbes, Heresy, and the *Historia Ecclesiastica.* Springborg, Patricia.

Hobbes, Spinoza, Kant, Highway Robbery and Game Theory. Marinoff, Louis.

Justice as a Kind of Impartiality. Nielsen, Kai.

L'absolutisme dans la Philosophie: Politique de Thomas Hobbes. Gnanagbe, Gogoua.

Probleme der Wirtschaftsethik. Kersting, Wolfgang.

Speculations on Strauss' Political Intentions Suggested by *On Tyranny.* Glenn, Gary D.

The Rationality of Rule-Following: Hobbes's Dispute with the Foole. Kavka, Gregory S.

Vico y Hobbes: el "verum-factum". Bermudo, José M.

Was Hobbes a Legal Positivist?. Murphy, Mark C.

Worin unterscheiden sich die Gesellschaftsverträge der Schweizer-von jenen der Philosophiegeschichte?. Holenstein, Elmar.

HOCHBERG, H

Is the Absurd the Problem or the Solution? *The Myth of Sisyphus* Reconsidered. Sagi, Avi.

HOCHE, H

Sollen, Wollen, Tun. Lembeck, Karl-Heinz.

HOCUTT, M

Relativism, Evil, and Disagreement: A Reply to Hocutt. Sullivan, Stephen J.

HOELDERLIN

Die Übermacht des Seins: Heideggers Auslegung des Bezuges von Mensch und Natur und Hölderlins Dichtung des Heiligen. Bohlen, Stephanie.

Entgegensetzungen: Studien zu Fichte-Konfrontationen von Rousseau bis Kierkegaard. Janke, Wolfgang.

Syncope: The Philosophy of Rapture. O'Driscoll, Sally (trans), Clément, Catherine and Mahoney, Deirdre M (trans).

Was ist und wozu überhaupt-Philosophie? Vorübungen sich verändernden Denkens. Brandner, Rudolf.

Der Grund im Bewusstsein. Von Graevenitz, Gerhart.

Forme e metafore dell'intuizione in Friedrich Hölderlin. Augello, Giuseppe.

Heidegger on Hölderlin's *Der Rhein:* Some External Considerations. Grugan, Arthur A.

Hölderlin et la Question du Centre. Villani, Arnaud.

Poetizar y Pensar? Desde la Meditación Heideggeriana Hacia el *Topos* Histórico de Hölderlin. Zubiría, Martín.

Reading the *Poetics* after the *Remarks.* Fynsk, Christopher.

Selbstbewusstsein: Ein Problem der Philosophie nach Kant. *Zum Verhältnis Reinhold-Hölderlin-Fichte.* Stolzenberg, Jürgen.

Semiosis of Listening: The Other in Heidegger's Writings on Hölderlin and Celan's "The Meridian". Ziarek, Krzysztof.

The Instress of Being and the Coronach of Dasein in Hölderlin's *Germanien.* Grugan, Arthur A.

HOENIGSWALD, R

"Hönigswalds Neukant. u. Husserls Phänomenol. als Hintergrund d. Denkens von Stein" in *Studien zur Philosophie von Edith Stein, Fetz, Reto Luzius (ed).* Orth, Ernst Wolfgang.

HOFFER, E

Eric Hoffer, Philosopher for the People. Arnold, Richard.

HOFFMAN, F

'Critical Buddhism' and the Question of Philosophical Syncretism. Heine, Steven.

HOFFMAN, P

Free Willing: Comments on Hoffman's "Freedom and Strength of Will". Chappell, Vere.

HOFFMAN, R

What's in a Word? Bring on the Seals and the Sheep (In Response to Hoffmann). Edwards, Derek.

HOGARTH, M

Non-Turing Computers and Non-Turing Computability. Hogarth, Mark.

HOLE

Holes and Determinism: Another Look. Leeds, Stephen.

Spacetime and Holes. Brighouse, Carolyn.

HOLINESS

Como Pensar los Valores Morales a Partir de Kant?. Norbert, Bilbeny.

Holiness as Service: *Therapeia* and *Hyperetike* in Plato's *Euthyphro.* Parry, David M.

La Vivencia de lo Sublime y la Experiencia Moral en Kant. Ribeiro dos Santos, Leonel.

HOLISM

"A Critique of the Case for Semantic Holism" in *Holism: A Consumer Update, Fodor, Jerry A (ed).* Devitt, Michael.

"Conceptual Connection and the Observation/ Theory Distinction" in *Holism: A Consumer Update, Fodor, Jerry A (ed).* Anthony, Louise.

"Holism, Intrinsically, and the Ambition of Transcendence" in *Dennett and his Critics, Dahlbom, Bo (ed).* Rorty, Richard.

"Holism: The Polarized Spectrum" in *Holism: A Consumer Update, Fodor, Jerry (ed).* Peruzzi, Alberto.

"Holismo y el Problema de la Validación de las Teorías Científicas en la Perspectiva s Need-Stegmüller" in *Temas Actuales de Filosofía, Palacios, María Julia (ed).* Gonzalo de Aguirre, Adriana.

"Inferential Roles, Quine, and Mad Holism" in *Holism: A Consumer Update, Fodor, Jerry (ed).* Berg, Jonathan.

"Intentional Chemistry" in *Holism: A Consumer Update, Fodor, Jerry A (ed).* Levine, Joseph.

"Is Content Holism Incoherent?" in *Holism: A Consumer Update, Fodor, Jerry A (ed).* Ludwig, Kirk A.

"Meaning Holism Defended" in *Holism: A Consumer Update, Fodor, Jerry A (ed).* Harman, Gilbert.

"Replies" in *Holism: A Consumer Update, Fodor, Jerry (ed).* Fodor, Jerry A and LePore, Ernest.

"Semantic Holism Is Here To Stay" in *Holism: A Consumer Update, Fodor, Jerry A (ed).* Brandl, Johannes.

"The Cost of Meaning Solipsism" in *Holism: A Consumer Update, Fodor, Jerry (ed).* Yagisawa, Takashi.

"The Impossibility of Punctate Mental Representations" in *Holism: A Consumer Update, Fodor, Jerry (ed).* Bezuidenhout, Anne.

"The Unavailability of What We Mean: A Reply to Quine, Fodor and LePore" in *Holism: A Consumer Update, Fodor, Jerry A (ed).* Rey, Georges.

A Philosophy of Matter and Mind: A New Look at an Old Major Topic in Philosophy. Wassermann, Gerhard D.

Global Anti-realism. Young, James O.

Holism: A Consumer Update. Fodor, Jerry A (ed) and LePore, Ernest (ed).

HOLISM

Meaning and Argument: A Theory of Meaning Centred on Immediate Argumental Role. Cozzo, Cesare.

Mental Content. McGinn, Colin.

Wittgenstein on Mind and Language. Stern, David G.

A Development of Heidegger and Merleau-Ponty Towards a Holistic Conception of Health. Carey, Seamus.

An Argument for Holism. Block, Ned.

For Whom the Bell Arguments Toll. Hawthorne, James and Silberstein, Michael.

Holistic Approach to Development. Michnowski, Leslaw.

In Defense of Conceptual Holism: Reply to Fodor and Lepore. Pessin, Andrew.

Meaning Holism and Intentional Content. Silverberg, Arnold.

Scientific versus Mathematical Realism: The Indispensability Argument. Resnik, Michael D.

The Buddhist Perspective on Business Ethics: Experiential Exercises for Exploration and Practice. Gould, Stephen J.

The Relevance of Thomas Aquinas for Contemporary Issues in Spirituality. Fatula, Mary Ann.

Zweierlei Holismus: Überlegungen zur Interpretationstheorie D Davidsons. Siebelt, Frank.

'The Friend of My Enemy is My Enemy': Modeling Triadic Internation Relationships. Lee, S C, Muncaster, R G and Zinnes, D A.

HOLMES, R

Pacifism and Wartime Innocence. Vorobej, Mark.

HOLMES, S

Sherlock Holmes, Galileo, and the Missing History of Science. Thomason, Neil.

HOLOCAUST

Judaism and Modernity: Philosophical Essays. Rose, Gillian.

On Naming the Present: God, Hermeneutics, and Church. Tracy, David.

Perspektiven der Dialogik: Zürcher Kolloquium zum 80. Geburtstag von Hermann Levin Goldschmidt. Goetschel, Willi (ed).

Is It Possible to Misrepresent the Holocaust?. Lang, Berel.

Persons of Lesser Value: Moral Argument and the 'Final Solution'. Steiner, Hillel.

The Holocaust and Philosophy. Freeman, Michael.

The Holocaust: Moral and Political Lessons. Lesser, A H.

Universalism and Evil. Kamenka, Eugene.

HOLTON, R

Holton on Attitude Ascriptions and Intermediate Scope. Pickles, David.

HOLY

Die Übermacht des Seins: Heideggers Auslegung des Bezuges von Mensch und Natur und Hölderlins Dichtung des Heiligen. Bohlen, Stephanie.

Inhabiting the Earth: Heidegger, Environmental Ethics, and the Metaphysics of Nature. Foltz, Bruce V.

La Razón y lo Sagrado: Respuesta a Jacinto Choza. Arana, Juan.

Virtue without Knowledge: Socrates' Conception of Holiness in Plato's *Euthyphro*. Weiss, Roslyn.

HOME

Welzijn Zeggenschap en Eigendom. Hogervorst, S.

In Search of Home. Tucker, Aviezer.

On Translating Locke, Berkeley, and Hume into English. Bennett, Jonathan.

HOME CARE

The Technological Tether: An Introduction to Ethical and Social Issues in High-Tech Home Care. Arras, John (& others).

HOMELESSNESS

"Children Who Run: Ethics and Homelessness" in *Introducing Applied Ethics*, Almond, Brenda (ed). Parker, Michael.

HOMER

Die Moralität des antiken Menschen: Über Bernhard Williams Buch "Shame and Necessity". Rapp, Christof.

La Vision de la Mort en Tant que Principe d'une Éthique de l'action chez Homére. Vlachos, Georges.

HOMOPHOBIA

"Homophobia and the Moral Authority of Medicine" in *Gay Ethics*, Murphy, Timothy F (ed). Wilkerson, Abby.

HOMOSEXUALITY

"Coming Out, Being Out, and Acts of Virtue" in *Gay Ethics*, Murphy, Timothy F (ed). Barbone, Steven and Rice, Lee.

"Explaining Homosexuality: Philosophical Issues, and Who Cares Anyhow?" in *Gay Ethics*, Murphy, Timothy F (ed). Suppe, Frederick.

"Fixation and Regression in the Psychoanalytic Theory of Homosexuality—A Critical Evaluation" in *Gay Ethics*, Murphy, Timothy F (ed). Ferguson, Michael.

"Gay Marriage: A Civil Right" in *Gay Ethics*, Murphy, Timothy F (ed). Dean, Craig R.

"Homophobia and the Moral Authority of Medicine" in *Gay Ethics*, Murphy, Timothy F (ed). Wilkerson, Abby.

"Homosex/Ethics" in *Gay Ethics*, Murphy, Timothy F (ed). Murphy, Timothy F.

"Incorporating Queer Theory on the Left" in *Marxism in the Postmodern Age*, Callari, Antonio (ed). Hennessy, Rosemary.

"Outing, Truth-Telling, and the Shame of the Closet" in *Gay Ethics*, Murphy, Timothy F (ed). Chekola, Mark.

"Privacy and the Ethics of Outing" in *Gay Ethics*, Murphy, Timothy F (ed). Mayo, David J and Gunderson, Martin.

"The Military Ban and the ROTC: A Study in Closeting" in *Gay Ethics*, Murphy, Timothy F (ed). Card, Claudia.

Adventures in Lesbian Philosophy. Card, Claudia F (ed).

Gay Ethics. Murphy, Timothy F (ed).

Avoiding Mistakes in Reasoning about Naturalness: A Reply to Dalcourt. Sartorelli, Joseph J.

Heterosexual Utopianism. Soper, Kate.

Homosexuality. Quinton, Anthony.

Is it Wrong to Discriminate on the Basis of Homosexuality?. Jordan, Jeff.

Is There a Queer Pedagogy? Or Stop Reading Straight. Britzman, Deborah P.

Militant Gayes, Gayes in the Military, and Privacy as Social Freedom. Nunan, Richard.

Philosophy, Sex and Gender: Mutual Interrogations. Kaplan, Morris B.

Political Philosophy as Political Action: A Response to Mark Blasius. Statham Jr, E Robert.

Prejudice and Homosexuality: America's Experience. Mohr, Richard D.

Ruse on Gay Rights and Affirmative Action. Sartorelli, Joseph J.

Same-Sex Relations and the Law. Sunstein, Cass R.

The Gender Distinctions of Primeval History and a Christian Sexual Ethic. Tuohey, John F.

The Meaning and Status of Gay and Lesbian Political Philosophy: A Rejoinder to E Robert Statham Jr. Blasius, Mark.

HONDERICH, T

Causal Troubles. Titiev, Robert.

Epicurus, Determinism, and the Security of Knowledge. Magill, Kevin.

HONECKER, M

"Die Randnotizen Martin Honeckers zur Habilitationsschrift 'Potenz und Akt'" in *Studien zur Philosophie von Edith Stein, Fetz, Reto Luzius (ed)*. Ott, Hugo.

HONESTY

In Search of Authenticity: From Kierkegaard to Camus. Golomb, Jacob.

Politicians, Honesty and the Higher Amorality of Politics. Luhmann, Niklas.

Rationele passies en intellectuele deugden: Een conceptuele analyse. Steutel, Jan and Spiecker, Ben.

Two Practical Guidelines for Resolving Truth-Telling Problems. Hamilton III, J Brooke and Strutton, David.

HONG KONG

Ethical Perceptions of Organizational Politics: A Comparative Evaluation of American and Hong Kong Managers. Ralston, David A, Giacalone, Robert A and Terpstra, Robert H.

HONNETH, A

Autonomy, Recognition and Respect: Habermas, Benjamin, Honneth. Meehan, Johanna.

Derrida—Ein unvollendeter Habermas'?. Van Reijen, Willem.

Diskursethik, schwere Fürsorge und leichte Fürsorge. White, Stephen K.

Habermas und Derrida werden verheiratet. Critchley, Simon.

Ist Fürsorglichkeit mit Gleichbehandlung unvereinbar?. Nagl-Docekal, Herta.

HONOR

In Defence of Aristotelian Honour. Putman, Daniel.

HOOKER, R

Thomistic Law and the Moral Theory of Richard Hooker. Westberg, Daniel.

HOOKS, B

Interrogating Whiteness: Dialogue as a Pragmatist Tool for Postmodern Identity-Formation *or* Breaking Bread with Bell Hooks and Cornel West. Paris, Jeffrey.

HOOKWAY, C

Carnap and Quine: Internal and External Questions. Bird, Graham H.

Responses. Quine, W V.

The Laboratory-Trained Believer: Peirce on the Scientific Character of Belief. Staab, Janice.

HOPE

El Cristianismo como *A Priori* de la Revolución en la Filosofía de Ernst Bloch. Orsolic, Marco.

Hope at the End of the Century. Fehér, Ferenc.

La pobreza y los cambios sociales. Carranza, Salvador Abascal.

Las fuentes espirituales de la angustia y de la esperanza. Zubiri, Xavier.

HOPE, T

Commentary on "The Alzheimer's Disease Sufferer as Semiotic Subject". Greenberg, William M.

Mild Mania and the Theory of Health: A Response to "Mild Mania and Well-Being". Nordenfelt, Lennart.

The Trouble with Well-Being: A Response to "Mild Mania and Well-Being". Seedhouse, David.

HOPKINS, G

Hopkins and the Theory of Metaphor. Potts, Michael.

HORGAN, T

A WORLD without MIND: Comments on Terence Horgan's "Naturalism and Intentionality". Egan, Frances.

Commentary: Transvaluationism: Comments on Horgan. Raffman, Diana.

Representations without Rules, Connectionism and the Syntactic Argument. Aizawa, Kenneth.

HORIZON

Estética del límite: Transformaciones en la configuración literaria del horizonte. Innerarity, Daniel.

Sobre el problema de la filosofia. Zubiri, Xavier.

HORKHEIMER, M

Positivismusstreit: Die Auseinandersetzungen der Frankfurter Schule mit dem logischen Positivismus, dem Pragmatismus und dem kritischen Rationalismus. Dahms, Hans-Joachim.

HORMONE

Human Growth Hormone: A Case Study in Treatment Priorities. Tauer, Carol A.

HUMAN NATURE

HUMAN RESOURCES

HUMAN RIGHTS

HUMAN SCIENCES

HUMANENESS

HUMANISM

HUMANISM

Utopia: Latin Text and English Translation. More, Thomas and Logan, George M (& other eds).

Camus's Ideal of Authentic Life. Golomb, Jacob.

Can There Be a "Humanistic" Ecology? A Debate Between Hegel and Heidegger on the Meaning of Ecological Thinking. Berthold-Bond, Daniel.

Cinco Claves Para Comprender a Jacques Maritain. Burgos, Juan Manuel.

Cómo Volver a dar un Sentido a la Palabra "Humanismo"?. Giralt, Pau.

Del Empirismo al Humanismo: Clave de Lectura y Crítica de la Obra de P K Feyerabend. Tula Molina, Fernando.

El Humanismo de Santo Tomás Moro y sus Obras Desde la Torre. Martínez Esteruelas, Cruz.

El humanismo marxiano. Calvez, Jean-Yves.

Epistemologie im Humanismus: Marsilio Ficino, Pietro Pomponazzi und Niklaus von Kues. Burkhard, Mojsisch.

Florian Znaniecki's Concept of a Humanist All-Mankind Civilization. Szczepanski, Jan.

Formation Fondamentale et Culture Humaniste dans les Études Collégiales. Talbot, Pierre.

Humanism and Unity. Kelly, Michael.

Humanism as a Basis for Universalist Thinking. Cauchy, Venant.

Humanistic Art. Shibles, Warren.

L'équivoque de l'histoire: Ontologie ou philosophie des formes symboliques—Bloch et Merleau-Ponty. Raulet, Gérard.

L'Etre et les Sciences. Llosa-Vasquez, Vincenzo.

L'Humanitaire Entre l'Éthique et la Politique. Thérrien, Jean-Marie.

La pensée politique de Jean Jaurès. Drouin, Paul.

La Rehabilitacíon del Humanismo Retórico: Considerando el Antihumanismo de Heidegger. Grassi, Ernesto.

La Tradición de los Disticha Catonis, Entre la Auctoritas Medieval y la Renovatio Humanística. Sesé Sanz, Juan Carlos.

Late Scholastic Philosophy: Introduction. Ashworth, E J.

Les Éternels Galilées. Heilless, Hellem.

On the Way to an Ontological Ethics: Ethical Suggestions in Reading Heidegger. Benso, Silvia.

Peer Pressure and Children's Religious Belief. Howe, Norma.

Reading Machiavelli: Innocent Gentillet's Discourse on Method. Kahn, Victoria.

Reason and Rationality: The Core Doctrines of Secular Humanism. D'Agostino, S Matthew.

Ricordando Giovanni e Gianfrancesco Pico della Mirandola. Garin, Eugenio.

The Challenge of Exoevolution. Birx, H James.

The End of Humanism and Fichte's Concept of European Intellectualism. Fischer, Bernd.

The Open Society and the Open Mind. Madigan, Timothy J.

Un Pari Pour la Philosophie. Brès, Jean-Claude.

Universalism and the Meaning of History. Mitias, Michael H.

Universalism: Humanistic Principles and Antipodes. Minkevicius, Jokubas.

Vico o la Metafísica como Método de Fundamentación de la Naturaleza Humana. Pastor Pérez, Miguel A.

Víves, Calderón y Vico: Lenguaje Metafórico y Filosofar Ingenioso. Hidalgo-Serna, Emilio.

Was Ayn Rand a Humanist?. Walker, Jeff.

Xunzi and the Confucian Answer to Titanism. Gier, Nicholas F.

HUMANITARIANISM

Ingérence des États en temps de guerre: Action humanitaire des organisations bénévoles chrétiennes et témoignage de l'évangile. Joblin, Joseph.

HUMANITIES

Emotion and Embodiment: Fragile Ontology. Mazis, Glen.

Human Sciences or Humanities: The Case of Literature. Olafson, Frederick A.

The Future of the Humanities: Teaching Art, Religion, Philosophy, Literature, and History (New Edition). Kaufmann, Walter Arnold.

Chaos Theory Can Close the Gap Between the Sciences and the Humanities. Krieglstein, Werner.

Educating the Democratic Heart: Pluralism, Traditions and the Humanities. Alexander, Thomas M.

Gadamer Without Tears. Agassi, Joseph.

Liberal Neutralism and the Social-Democratic Project. Rosenberg, Paul.

Physicians Pursuing the Humanities: Benefits and Barriers. Brody, Howard (& others).

Rationality and the Humanities and Social Sciences. Sweet, William.

HUMANITY

"Awe and Humility: Intrinsic Value in Nature" in *Philosophy and the Natural Environment, Attfield, Robin (ed)*. Lee, Keekok.

"Life and Society at Ancient Memphis According to the Saqqâra Texts" in *Life, World and Meaning, Roux, A P J (ed)*. Dreyer, H J.

"Natur—Ästhetische Kultur—Humanitätsförderung" in *Naturzweckmässigkeit und ästhetische Kultur, Schwabe, Karl-Heinz (ed)*. Thom, Martina.

"Technology and Basic Needs" in *Philosophy of Technology in Spanish Speaking Countries, Mitcham, Carl (ed)*. Dussel, Enrique.

Creativity and God: A Challenge to Process Theology. Neville, Robert Cummings.

Environmental Ethics (Oxford Readings in Philosophy). Elliot, Robert (ed).

Foucault and Law: Towards a Sociology of Law as Governance. Hunt, Alan and Wickham, Gary.

Lectures on Divine Humanity. Solovyov, Vladimir.

Making Sense of Humanity and Other Philosophical Papers 1982-1993. Williams, Bernard.

Mapping the Human Genome: Reality, Morality, and Deity. Kent, Theodore C.

Mediaeval Reactions to the Encounter Between Faith and Reason. Wippel, John F.

Plato's World: Man's Place in the Cosmos. Cropsey, Joseph.

Powers of the Rational: Science, Technology, and the Future of Thought. Birmingham, Peg (trans), Janicaud, Dominique and Birmingham, Elizabeth (trans).

The Dawn of Historical Reason: The Historicality of Human Existence in the Thought of Dilthey, Heidegger and Ortega y Gasset. Tuttle, Howard N.

The Development of German Aesthetic Theory from Kant to Schiller: A Philosophical Commentary on Schiller's Aesthetic Education of Man (1795). Murray, Patrick T.

The High Road of Humanity: The Seven Ethical Ages of Western Man. Levi, Albert William, Verene, Donald Phillip (ed) and Verene, Molly Black (ed).

The Human Shape of God: Religion in Hegel's "Phenomenology of Spirit". Jamros, Daniel P.

The Machine as Metaphor and Tool. Haken, Hermann (ed), Karlqvist, Anders (ed) and Svedin, Uno (ed).

Thinking in Complexity: The Complex Dynamics of Matter, Mind, and Mankind. Mainzer, Klaus.

Africa: The Role Model of Planetary Solidarity—Between All Humans and the Human Universum. Eboh, Marie Pauline.

Agostino Steuco y la *Perennis Philosophia*. Granada, Miquel A.

Bacon and Pascal on Mastery Over Nature. Groothuis, Douglas.

Being Human, More or Less. Kohák, Erazim.

Bioethics; Its Scope and Purpose. Fox, Michael W.

Can We Have a Common Humanity?. Harris, R Baine.

Cinque Esemplari Postillati della *Scienza Nuova*. Rotoli, Daniela.

Consistent Bioethics and Christian Consistency. Jaki, Stanley.

Contributors to the Genesis of Europe: Gotthold Ephraim Lessing and His Followers. Ritchie, Gisela F.

Cosmic and Human Drama in Plato's *Statesman*: On Cosmos, God and Microcosm in the Myth. Carone, Gabriela Roxana.

Critical Notice of Hilary Putnam: *Realism With a Human Face* and *Renewing Philosophy*. Allen, Barry G.

Culture, Citoyenneté, Humanité. Coutel, Charles.

Deconstructing the Driving Forces of Human Knowledge: D P Chattopadhyaya's *Induction, Probability and Scepticism*. Pandit, G L.

Discretely Metaphysical: Refracting Metaphysical Light in Post-Metaphysical Prisms. Schenk, Richard.

Environmental Security: Choices for the Twenty-First Century. Soroos, Marvin S.

Foreknowledge and Human Freedom in Augustine. Morgan, Vance G.

Heidegger on the Work of Art and Human Existence (in Hebrew). Mansbach, A.

Human Equality and Intra- as well as Intercultural Diversity. Holenstein, Elmar.

Human Life as a Value in Anthropology of Old Judaism. Palubicki, Wladyslaw.

Human Value of Sustainable Society. Dewan, M L.

I Believe in God the Father, Almighty. Clark, Kelly J.

I Giganti in Vico. Mazzola, Roberto.

John Dewey: Philosopher of Technology. Hickman, Larry A.

John Searle and Human Consciousness. Beards, Andrew.

José Ortega y Gasset on Understanding Life as Ultimate Reality and Meaning. Weigart, Andrew J.

Kierkegaardian Meditations on First Philosophy: A Reading of *Johannes Climacus*. Strawser, Michael.

La Ontología de Lessing y las Metáforas de la Deshumanización. Andreu, Agustín.

La Presenza di Vico nella Poetica Spagnola del XVIII Secolo. Zacarés Pamblanco, Amparo.

La Riflessione sul Mito in Leopardi. Stella, Vittorio.

Making the Everyday. Allan, George.

Mind and Progress in Plato. Naddaf, Gerard.

Models of Nursing and Theories of Humanity: A Christian Perspective. Parfitt, Barbara and Williams, Stephen.

Montesquieu e il Problema del "Diversité". Courtney, C P.

On the Existential Interpretation of Human Sciences. Ginev, Dimitri.

On the Existential Meaning of Violence. Santoni, Ronald E.

Ortega e Vico. Cacciatore, Giuseppe.

Persons of Lesser Value: Moral Argument and the 'Final Solution'. Steiner, Hillel.

Present Concerns and Future Interests. Magnell, Thomas.

Putting Ourselves Up for the Question: A Postmodern Critique of Richard Rorty's Postmodernist Bourgeois Liberalism. Hendley, Steven.

Radical Translation and Animals: An Argument from the Principle of Humanity. Weir, Jack L.

Rekindling Humanity's Love Affair with Science and Technology. Flynn, Thomas W.

Some Comments on *Perfectionism*. Stocker, Michael.

Some Problems of Rationality, Understanding, and Universalistic Ethics in the Context of Habermas's Theory of Communicative Action. Ajzner, Jan.

Spinozismo e Libertinismo: A Proposito di due Recenti Libri su Boulainviller. Mori, Gianluca.

The Beginning of Sorrows: The Ecological Crisis and the Prospects of Human Survival. Smith, Joseph Wayne.

The Energetics of Spirituality and Human Sexuality. Kidd, James W and Zonneveld, Leo W.

The Hiddenness of God and the Problem of Evil. Keller, James A.

The Holocaust and Philosophy. Freeman, Michael.

The Horizons of the Organic Vision of the Universe and Humanity: Vladimir Solovyev Revisited in the Light of Process Theology. Gubman, Boris L.

The Ideas of Contemporary Universalim and Medicine. Imielinski, Christian.

I

La Exigencia Ontológica Radical en Fichte y su Necesaria Ruptura con el Criticismo. Market, Oswaldo.

La mirada errante: de la "Spaltung" en Lacan, al "caos-cosmos" de Deleuze. Gonzalo I Carbó, Antoni.

Las Tres Reseñas de Fichte del Otoño de 1793. Serrano, Vicente.

Lenzen vs Castañeda. Rohs, Peter.

Quintuplicatà e Individualità: La Construzione dell'io in WL 1807. Rametta, Gaetano.

Stellt Fichtes Theorie vom "Ich" in der WL von 1794/95 eine Produktionstheorie des "Ich" dar?. Hiltscher, Reinhard.

Sujeto y Realidad: Del Yo Analítico Substante al Yo Sintétoco Transcendental. Rivera de Rosales, Jacinto.

I-THOU

Husserls Theorie der Intersubjektivität. Iribarne, Julia V.

IAMBLICHUS

I nessi Strutturali tra Metafisica e Teurgia im Giamblico. Cocco, Giuseppe.

IBERIAN

Filsofía Jurídica e Política na Poesía Luso-árabe. Ferreira da Cunha, Paulo.

La Biblioteca de la Universidad de Santo Tomás en Manila, Filipinas: Una Nota Bibliográfica Sobre Libros Raros de Filosofía, 1500-1800. Felipe, Donald.

IBEROAMERICA

Ilustración y Utilitarismo en Iberoamérica. Rodríguez Braun, Carlos.

La recepción del Utilitarismo en el mundo hispánico: El caso de Ortega y Gasset. López Frías, Francisco.

Las relaciones entre Jeremías Bentham y S Bolívar. Schwartz, P and Rodríguez Braun, C.

IBN AL-JAWZI

A Refutation of Philosophy by a Medieval Arab Author: Ibn Al-Jawzi (d 1201). Budelli, Rosanna.

IBN-TUFAYL

"The Impact of the *Philosophus Autodidactus*" in *The 'Arabick' Interest of the Natural Philosophers...*, Russell, G A (ed). Russell, G A.

ICELANDIC

The Conflict of Law and Justice in the Icelandic Sagas. Pencak, William.

ICON

"Icons, Fragments, and Ironists" in *Recovering Pragmatism's Voice, Langsdorf, Lenore (ed).* Presnell, Mick.

Degrees of Iconicity in the Lexicon. Waugh, Linda R.

Diagrams and Metaphors: Iconic Aspects in Language. Hiraga, Masako K.

Iconic Manifestation of Interlocutor Distance in Russian. Yokoyama, Olga T.

Iconicity and Auxiliation. Kuteva, Tania.

Iconicity, Analogy, and Universal Grammar. Itkonen, Esa.

Representation(s). Rheinberger, Hans-Jörg.

The Problem of Iconicity. Radwanska-Williams, Joanna.

IDEA

see also Concept, Innate Idea

"Dios en la Ontología del *Parménides*" in *Platón: Los Diálogos Tardíos, Lan, Conrado Eggers (ed).* Eggers Lan, Conrado.

"Locke's Theory of Ideas" in *The Cambridge Companion to Locke, Chappell, Vere (ed).* Chappell, Vere.

Finitude and Transcendence in the Platonic Dialogues. Hyland, Drew A.

Hegels Wissenschaft der Logik—metaphysische Letztbegründung oder Theorie logischer Formen?. Schick, Friedrike.

Karl Marx's Theory of Ideas. Torrance, John.

Arnauld et Malebranche. Senofonte, Ciro.

Du calcul des idées à la sémantique formelle. Dominicy, Marc.

El Hegelianismo de la inédita *Filosofía Lógica* de Unamuno. García Casanova, Juan Francisco.

El jardín de la ciencia. Escudero, Miguel.

Homenaje a Octavio Paz. Aguayo Cruz, Enrique Ignacio.

Husserl on the Ego and Its Eidos (*Cartesian Meditations*, IV). Ferrarin, Alfredo.

Ideas, In and Before Descartes. Ariew, Roger and Grene, Marjorie.

Malebranche and Arnauld on Ideas. Watson, Richard A.

Mental Images and their Ontology. Gozzano, Simone.

Neutral Currents and the History of Scientific Ideas. Miller, Arthur I and Bullock, Frederick W.

Reid's Critique of Berkeley and Hume: What's the Big Idea?. Greco, John.

Sobre el 'Pensamiento Latinoamericano' y su Historiografía. Sasso, Javier.

Spiegeln Ideen die Natur? Zum Begriff der Repräsentation bei Descartes. Perler, Dominik.

The Adequacy of Simple Ideas in Locke—A Rehabilitation of Berkeley's Criticisms. Bermúdez, José Luis.

The Game that Looks Like Work in Plato's "Parmenides". Delgado De Torres, Olivia.

The New Way of Ideas: Plato, Locke, and their Romantic Readers. Douca-Kabitoglou, Catherina.

Transcendental Idealism and Phenomenalism. Frangiotti, Marco Antonio.

Tre lezioni su Platone e la scrittura della filosofia. Szlezák, T A.

'Idea' in Locke's Works. Hall, Roland.

IDEAL

"Sui Rischi di un'Attitudine Troppo Benevola dell'Interprete verso il Testo" in *Platón: Los Diálogos Tardíos, Lan, Conrado Eggers (ed).* Rossetti, Livio.

Anneaux de Fonctions *p*-Adiques. Bélair, Luc.

Combinatorics on Ideals and Axiom A. Sharp, James D.

Die Realität der Idee. de Vos, L.

El Ideal de la Vida Filosófica Según Leibniz. Laliga, Rensoli.

G W F Hegel: El *Fragmento de Tubinga.* del Carmen Paredes, María.

Hechler Reals. Labedzki, Grzegorz and Repicky, Miroslav.

How Philosophy *Instructs the World*. Harris, Henry S.

On a Generalization of Distributivity. Kanai, Yasuo.

On the Rationality of Irrational Ideals. Harriott, Howard.

Sociedad Real y Comunidad Ideal Según K-O Apel. García Leal, José.

The Structure of Pleasant Ideals. Leary, Christopher C.

Ultrafilters on Omega. Baumgartner, James E.

IDEALISM

"A Response to Savan" in *Peirce and Contemporary Thought: Philosophical Inquiries, Ketner, Kenneth Laine (ed).* Sfendoni-Mentzou, Demetra.

"Exchange Versus Influence: A Case of Idealization" in *Idealization VI: Idealization in Economics, Hamminga, Bert (ed).* Balzer, Wolfgang.

"German Idealism Under Fire: Fichte, Hegel, and 'Metacriticism'" in *Hegel on the Modern World, Collins, Ardis B (ed).* Surber, Jere Paul.

"Idealization and Empirical Adequacy in Economic Theory" in *Idealization VI: Idealization in Economics, Hamminga, Bert (ed).* García de la Sienra, Adolfo.

"Idealization and the Defence of Economics" in *Idealization VI: Idealization in Economics, Hamminga, Bert (ed).* Hamminga, Bert and De Marchi, Neil.

"Idealization and Transformation" in *Idealization VI: Idealization in Economics, Hamminga, Bert (ed).* Jorland, Gérard.

"Idealizations and Theory Development in Economics" in *Idealization VI: Idealization in Economics, Hamminga, Bert (ed).* Birner, Jack.

"Introduction" in *Hegel Reconsidered, Engelhardt Jr, H Tristram (ed).* Engelhardt Jr, H Tristram.

"Max Weber and the Legacy of Critical Idealism" in *The Barbarism of Reason, Horowitz, Asher (ed).* Lenhardt, Christian.

"Merke auf dich selbst" Das Verhältnis des Philosophen zu seinem Gegenstand nach dem *Versuch einer neuen Darstellung der Wissenschaftslehre.* Römelt, Johannes.

"Mill and Menger: Ideal Elements and Stable Tendencies" in *Idealization VI: Idealization in Economics, Hamminga, Bert (ed).* Cartwright, Nancy.

"Nowak on Explanation and Idealization in Marx's 'Capital'" in *Idealization VI: Idealization in Economics, Hamminga, Bert (ed).* Diederich, Werner.

"Paul Samuelson as Dr Frankenstein: When an Idealization Runs Amuck" in *Idealization VI: Idealization in Economics, Hamminga, Bert (ed).* Hausman, Daniel M.

"Peirce and Idealism" in *Peirce and Contemporary Thought: Philosophical Inquiries, Ketner, Kenneth Laine (ed).* Savan, David.

"Philosophischer Idealismus und Nationalsozialismus" in *Der geistige Anschluss, Fischer, Kurt R (ed).* Klein, Hans-Dieter.

"Pursuing Love with the Proper Map" in *The Nature and Pursuit of Love, Goicoechea, David (ed).* Madigan, Timothy J.

"The Idealization Methodology and Economics" in *Idealization VI: Idealization in Economics, Hamminga, Bert (ed).* Nowak, Leszek.

"The Other: F H Jacobi and German Idealism" in *Hegel on the Modern World, Collins, Ardis B (ed).* Williams, Robert R.

"Transcendental Idealism" in *The Cambridge Companion to Husserl, Smith, Barry (ed).* Philipse, Herman.

"Vanishing Frontiers in American Philosophy: Two Dogmas of Idealism" in *Pragmatism: From Progressivism to Postmodernism, Hollinger, Robert (ed).* Sleeper, Ralph W.

...also muss auf Schelling zurückgegangen werden. Ehrhardt, Walter E.

Autonomie des Selbstbewusstseins: Eine Untersuchung zum Verhältnis von Bruno Bauer und Karl Marx (1835-1843). Waser, Ruedi.

Das Feindbild der marxistisch-leninistischen Philosophie in der DDR 1945-1988. Kapferer, Norbert.

Der Zusammenhang der Wirklichkeit. Krämer, Felix.

Die Freiheit im Wissen: Eine Untersuchung zu Schellings Konzept der Rationalität. Peetz, Siegbert.

Entgegensetzungen: Studien zu Fichte-Konfrontationen von Rousseau bis Kierkegaard. Janke, Wolfgang.

Kant's Idealism. Neujahr, Philip J.

Philosophieverhältnisse im deutschen Faschismus. Laugstien, Thomas.

The Development of German Aesthetic Theory from Kant to Schiller: A Philosophical Commentary on Schiller's Aesthetic Education of Man (1795). Murray, Patrick T.

The Embodied Self: Friedrich Schleiermacher's Solution to Kant's Problem of the Empirical Self. Thandeka.

Transformations in Consciousness: The Metaphysics and Epistemology. Merrell-Wolff, Franklin.

Was ist Wahrnehmung?. Ziemke, Axel.

Work, Education, and Leadership: Essays in the Philosophy of Education. Howard, V A and Scheffler, Israel.

Before Nietzsche: Nihilism as a Critique of German Idealism. Cho, Stephen Wagner.

British Idealism, the State, and International Relations. Boucher, David.

British Idealist International Theory. Boucher, David.

Carta abierta al Dr Wessell. Pintor Ramos, A.

Comentario kafkiano en torno a la obra *Realidad y Verdad* de Antonio Pintor-Ramos. Wessell, L P.

Compromising with Convention. Hooker, Brad.

Croce e Gentile nell'Epistolario di Fausto Nicolini. Rascaglia, Maria.

Der Begriff der psychischen Krankheit aus der Sicht der Fichteschen Transzendentalphilosophie. Hoff, Paul.

Der Grund im Bewusstsein. Von Graevenitz, Gerhart.

IDENTITY

E J Lowe on Vague Identity and Quantum Indeterminacy. Noonan, Harold W.

Extensionalidad, Opacidad y Estructura Intensional: Un Análisis de las Falacias en Contextos Epistémicos. José Frápolli, María.

Fichte y Ortega (II). Héroes o Ciudadanos. El Mito de Don Quijote. Molinuevo, José Luis.

Fichtes Satz *Ich bin*: Argumentanalytische Überlegungen zu Paragraph 1 der *Grundlage der gesamten Wissenschaftslehre* von 1794-95. Stolzenberg, Jürgen.

From Natural Identity to Radical Democracy. Sandilands, Catriona.

Genetic Therapy, Identity and Person-Regarding Reasons. Persson, Ingmar.

How to Know the Inner-Self?. Esser, Piet Hein.

Human Identity and the Primitive Streak. Lockwood, Michael.

Identidad cultural, conflicto cultural y violencia. Vilas Nogueira, J.

Identität und Versprechen. Emrich, H M.

Identité et nationalisme irlandais. Sullivan, Timothy.

Identity and Quality of Life (in Dutch). Musschenga, A W.

Identity in World History: A Post-Modern Perspective. Wurgaft, Lewis.

Identity Politics and Dialectical Reason: Beyond an Epistemology of Provenance. Kruks, Sonia.

Identity, Becoming, and Rights of Development. Covey, Edward.

Identity, Knowledge, and Toni Morrison's *Beloved*: Questions about Understanding Racism. Babbitt, Susan E.

Identity, Self-Reflection and the Problem of Validating Standards. Raffel, Stanley.

Il fantasma di Turing e l'incancellabilità del soggetto. Turpia, Piero.

In Orbit. Lingis, Alphonso F.

In welchem Sinne ist die Identität eine Äquivalenzrelation?. Pardey, Ulrich.

Interrogating Whiteness: Dialogue as a Pragmatist Tool for Postmodern Identity-Formation *or* Breaking Bread with Bell Hooks and Cornel West. Paris, Jeffrey.

James on Self Identity Over Time. Gale, Richard M.

L'Ambiguità del non Essere e l'Inganno del Sofista: Una Nuova Edizione Francese del *Sofista* di Platone. Fronterotta, Francesco.

La alteridad en el Sofista de Platón. Iglesias, Mercedes.

La Funzione Terapeutica del Mito: Un Problema di Psicologia Analitica. Procesi, Lidia.

La logique de l'auto-identité absolument contradictoire de Nishida. Tremblay, Jacynthe.

La mo(n)stración abaddónica de Ernesto Sábato. Villalobos, Carlos Manuel.

La Teoría de las Distinciones en la Edad Media y su Influjo en la Edad Moderna. Beuchot, Mauricio.

Las Personas y su Identidad. Sanfélix, Vicente.

Les axiomes de l'identité et la démonstration des formules arithmétiques: "2+2=4". Fichant, Michel.

Living in Two Worlds: A Personal Appraisal. Ching, Julia.

Locke's Identity Meaning of Ownership. Zack, Naomi.

Lógica y Ontología: Verdad, Existencia e Identidad como Funciones de Segundo Nivel. Frápolli, María José.

Max Black on the Identity of Indiscernibles. Cross, Charles B.

Merleau-Ponty's Concept of Reason. Low, Douglas.

Michael Polanyi and Human Identity. Kettle, David.

Mind-Body Identity Revised. Li, Chenyang.

National Identification and the Transgression of National Boundaries: The Steps Toward Universalization. Kloskowska, Antonina.

National Identity and National Consciousness. Tevzadze, Natia.

Personal Identity, 'R-Relatedness' and the Empty Question Argument. Chappell, Tim.

Physicalism, Ordinary Objects, and Identity. Melnyk, Andrew.

Politics, Identity, and Social Change: Contested Grounds in Psychoanalytic Feminism. Elliot, Patricia.

Proof-Theoretical Semantics and Fregean Identity Criteria for Propositions. Sundholm, Göran.

Qué es Poesía?. Núñez Cea, Victoria Martha.

Re-monstrations: Heidegger, Derrida and Wittgenstein's Hand. Mulhall, Stephen.

Requiem for the Identity Theory. Smythies, John R.

Resistance and Insubordination. Nelson, Hilde Lindemann.

Ricoeur and Political Identity. Dauenhauer, Bernard.

Rotarians in a Changing World. Seidler, Leopold G and Kolek, Leszek S.

Some Considerations on the Status of the Psychic in "Freudian" Project (in Portuguese). Milidoni, Carmen Beatriz.

Sorites and Identity. Priest, Graham.

Staatsbürgerliche Identität und Selbstachtung im jüdischen Staat: Eine Rawls'che Perspektive. Brunner, José and Peled, Yoav.

The First-Person Perspective. Shoemaker, Sydney.

The Many Persons Problem. Chihara, Charles S.

The Problem of Self-Identification. O'Brien, Lucy F.

The Stoics on Identity and Individuation. Lewis, Eric.

Vague Identity and Quantum Indeterminacy. Lowe, E J.

Vague Identity and Quantum Non-Individuality. French, Steven and Krause, Décio.

Vagueness, Identity, and the World. Garrett, Brian.

Versuche die ersten Prinzipien in Frage zu stellen. Rutowski, Tadeusz.

What's Right and What's Wrong with Transference Theories. Dowe, Phil.

Who Should a Utilitarian Be?. Smilansky, Saul.

Worldly Indeterminacy of Identity. Parsons, Terence and Woodruff, Peter.

IDEOLOGY

"El Reconocimiento de Ideologías en un Discurso Político" in *Temas Actuales de Filosofía, Palacios, María Julia (ed)*. Carranza, Elena N and Debon, María C.

"Ideologiekritik und Psychoanalyse: Awei Seiten einer hermeneutischen Medaille?" in *Mythos Wertfreiheit?, Apel, Karl Otto (ed)*. Kettner, Matthias.

"La Identidad del Discurso Estético y la Crítica Ideológica en la Etapa Post-Estructuralista de Roland Barthes" in *Temas Actuales de Filosofía, Palacios, María Julia (ed)*. Peñafort, Juan J E.

"The Return of the Romantic" in *Intersections: Nineteenth-Century Philosophy and Contemporary Theory, Rajan, Tilottama (ed)*. Mileur, Jean-Pierre.

"The Romanticism of Contemporary Ideology" in *Intersections: Nineteenth- Century Philosophy and Contemporary Theory, Rajan, Tilottama (ed)*. Hamilton, Paul.

After Postmodernism. Simons, Herbert W (ed) and Billig, Michael (ed).

Die Barbarei: Eine phänomenologische Kulturkritik. Henry, Michel.

Karl Marx's Theory of Ideas. Torrance, John.

Algunas preguntas acerca de la Idea de Progreso. Peña, Vidal.

An Integrative Ideology for Russia. Kosolapov, N A.

Dialéctica y Política. Fornari, Aníbal.

Farewell to a Brilliant Dish Cleaner: Paul Feyerabend and the Merry Philosophy of Science. Cortois, P.

Groupe et idéologie: A propos de *Fonctionnaires de Dieu* d'Eugen Drewermann. Saint-Germain, Christian.

Ideas sobre Ortega y Gasset y el ocaso del marxismo. Pallotini, Michele.

Involvement in Linguistic Practice: An Ethnographic Appraisal. Besnier, Niko.

La evolución filosófica e ideológica de la Asociación Española para el Progreso de las Ciencias (1908-1979). Sierra, Pelayo García.

Leibniz and Brentano: Two Philosophers Concerning Catastrophes and their Solutions. Benedikt, Michael.

Marxism, 'Ideology,' and Moral Objectivism. Mills, Charles W.

Psychoanalysis and Ideology: Bakhtin, Lacan, and Zizek. Baker, Harold D.

Razón e historia: La modernidad del postmodernismo. Koslowski, Peter.

Ricoeur on Metaphor and Ideology. Gay, William C.

The Bullying of an Untheoretical History of Philosophy—Eclecticism Instead of Ideology. Zimmerli, Walther Christoph.

The Ideological Involvement of Philosophy. Niznik, Jozef.

Weiskel's Sublime and the Impasse of Knowledge. Quinney, Laura.

IDOLATRY

Ask and It Will Be Given to You. Murray, Michael J and Meyers, Kurt.

Religious Plurality and Realist Christianity: Idolatry and the Testing of One's Faith. McLeod, Mark S.

IGNATIUS OF LOYOLA

Blondel and Ignatius' Spiritual Exercises (in Dutch). Boey, K.

Saint Ignatius of Loyola's Search for Ultimate Reality and Meaning. Mester, Fiore.

'Auf die Kräfte des Leibes achten': Die Bedeutung der Gesundheit im Leben und Wirken des Ignatius von Loyola. Lutterbach, Hubertus.

IGNORANCE

The Defeat of the Mind. Friedlander, Judith (trans) and Finkielkraut, Alain.

Vértigos argumentales: Una ética de la disputa. Pereda, Carlos.

De ludo veritatis: L'esperienza del vero nel pensiero di Niccolò da Cusa. Egger, Jean-Luc.

The Intellectual Virtues. Cooper, Neil.

ILLENKOV, E

Not the "Human Factor" but the Person. Suvorov, Aleksandr V.

ILLITERACY

Paternalism and the Argument from Illiteracy. Luna, Florencia.

ILLNESS

see also Mental Illness

Advance Care Planning: Priorities for Ethical and Empirical Research. Teno, Joan M, Hill, T Patrick and O'Connor, Mary Ann.

Attitudes of Seriously Ill Patients toward Treatment that Involves High Costs and Burdens on Others. Schneiderman, Lawrence J (& others).

Beyond Autonomy to the Person Coping with Illness. Thomasma, David C.

CQ *Interview*: Dr Boudewijn Chabot on Assisted Suicide in the Absence of Somatic Illness. Klotzko, Arlene Judith.

Illness, the Problem of Evil, and the Analogical Structure of Healing: On the Difference Christianity Makes in Bioethics. Khushf, George.

Medical Technology: A Pandora's Box?. Hewa, Soma.

Morbus Hermeneuticus: Theses on a Philosophical Sickness. Schnädelbach, Herbert.

Personal Identity and Psychiatric Illness. Hope, Tony.

The Lived Experience of Disability. Toombs, S K.

ILLOCUTIONARY ACT

Es la uniformidad semántica una condición de corrección formal de una teoría del modo oracional?. Marqueze, Jorge R.

Formalisierungsversuch der Sprechakttheorie. Labude, Joachim.

ILLUMINATION

Augustine: Against the Academicians and *The Teacher*. King, Peter (trans).

ILLUSION

"Filling In: Why Dennett is Wrong" in *Dennett and his Critics, Dahlbom, Bo (ed)*. Churchland, P S and Ramachandran, V S.

Appearance and Reality: A Philosophical Investigation into Perception and Perceptual Qualities. Hacker, P M S.

Der Katechon: Zu Carl Schmitts fundamentalistischer Kritik der Zeit. Meuter, Günter.

Moses Mendelssohn and the *End of Illusion Theory*: An Inquiry into Innovation in Aesthetics in the Middle of the Eighteenth-Century. Otabe, Tanehisa.

The Layers of Artistic Illusion. Perricone, Christopher.

The Logic of Probability. Angell, Richard B (trans) and De Finetti, Bruno.

Truth and Illusion in *The Birth of Tragedy*. Klein, Wayne.

IMAGE

see also Mental Image

Understanding Images: Finding Meaning in Digital Imagery. Marchese, Francis T (ed).

INCOMMENSURABILITY

Incommensurabel, incompatibel, onvergelijkbaar. Raven, Diederick.

Incommensurability, Incomparability, Irrationality. Kindi, Vassiliki.

Incommensurability: Its Implications for the Patient/Physician Relation. Veatch, Robert M and Stempsey, William E.

Inconmensuralbilidad Empírica: Un Enfoque Macrológico. Moya, Eugenio.

Three Kinds of Incommensurability Thesis. Simmons, Lance.

INCOMPATIBILITY

Incommensurabel, incompatibel, onvergelijkbaar. Raven, Diederick.

INCOMPETENCE

The Incompetent Patient on the Slippery Slope. Dresser, Rebecca and Whitehouse, Peter J.

INCOMPLETENESS

see also Completeness

ω-Consistency and Löb's Theorem. Kim, S M.

A Smart Child of Peano's. Shavrukov, V Y.

Absolute Forms of Gödel's Incompleteness Theorem. Kim, Sangmun.

Gentile e Gödel. Sainati, Vittorio.

Incompleteness and the Barcan Formula. Cresswell, M J.

On the Incompleteness Theorems. Kotlarski, Henryk.

Paper Machines. Mundici, Daniele and Sieg, Wilfried.

INCONSISTENCY

A Small Reflection Principle for Bounded Arithmetic. Verbrugge, Rineke and Visser, Albert.

INCREMENTAL

Incremental Semantics for Propositional Texts. Vermeulen, C F M.

INDEFINITE

"Indefinites, Adverbs of Quantification, and Focus Semantics" in The Generic Book, Carlson, Gregory N (ed). Rooth, Mats.

Milesischer Anfang. Bremer, Dieter.

INDEPENDENCE

Las relaciones entre Jeremías Bentham y S Bolívar. Schwartz, P and Rodríguez Braun, C.

On the Independence of B from I, C, W, K' $_1$, and Karpenko's Formula X. Ulrich, Dolph E.

Spontaneität. Vossenkuhl, Wilhelm.

INDETERMINACY

The Facts of Causation. Mellor, D H.

A Reply to Christopher Kulp's "Dewey, Indeterminacy, and the Spectator Theory of Knowledge". Pratt, Scott L.

Ambiguity, Absurdity, and Reversibility: Responses to Indeterminacy. Weiss, Gail.

Bell's Theorem in an Indeterministic Universe. Bedford, Donald and Stapp, Henry P.

E J Lowe on Vague Identity and Quantum Indeterminacy. Noonan, Harold W.

For Whom the Bell Arguments Toll. Hawthorne, James and Silberstein, Michael.

Indeterminacy and Interpretation. Abel, Günter.

Indeterminacy, Ethnophilosophy, Linguistic Philosophy, African Philosophy. Hallen, Barry.

Lyotard's Homeopathic Indeterminacy: The Medicinal Sublime. Miller-Frank, Felicia.

On the Nature of Meaning and Its Indeterminacy: Davidson's View in Perspective. Hofmann, Alexander.

Rejoinder to Scott L Pratt. Kulp, Christopher B.

The Epistemic Conception of Vagueness. Wright, Crispin.

The Seduction of Abduction: Peirce's Theory of Signs and Indeterminacy in Language. Melrose, Robin.

Transcendentaal-Pragmatiek en Semantiek. Sas, Peter.

Una Posición Intermedia Entre el Fisicalismo y el Intencionalismo: Dennett. Saab, Salma.

Une ou deux indéterminations. Laugier, Sandra.

Vague Identity and Quantum Indeterminacy. Lowe, E J.

Vague Identity and Quantum Non-Individuality. French, Steven and Krause, Décio.

Vagueness, Borderline Cases and Moral Realism. Shafer-Landau, Russ.

Worldly Indeterminacy of Identity. Parsons, Terence and Woodruff, Peter.

INDETERMINATE

"Lo Apeiron de Anaximandro y lo Inconsciente Freudiano" in Temas Actuales de Filosofía, Palacios, María Julia (ed). Kohan, Walter O.

INDETERMINISM

Defensa de la Causalidad. Sanvisens Herreros, Alejandro.

Der Grund der Dualität der Materie und des Indeterminismus in der physikalischen Natur: Die Lösung eines quantenphysikalischen Rätsels. Mues, Albert.

Indeterminism and Control. Clarke, Randolph.

Indeterminism and the Direction of Time. Arntzenius, Frank.

Willensfreiheit: Zwei gute Argumente und eine schlechtes. Leder, Matthias.

INDEX

Ambiguità e Semiosi. Morpurgo-Tagliabue, Guido.

INDEXICALITY

"De Re Belief, Action Explanations, and the Essential Indexical" in Modality, Morality, and Belief, Sinnott-Armstrong, Walter (ed). Sosa, Ernest.

"Indexicality" in Peirce and Contemporary Thought: Philosophical Inquiries, Ketner, Kenneth Laine (ed). Sebeok, Thomas A.

(Direct) Reference. Napoli, Ernesto.

Indexikalische Gedanken: Über den Gegenstandsbezug in der raumzeitlichen Erkenntnis. Wyller, Truls.

Paradoxes (Second Edition). Sainsbury, R M.

Descriptions, Indexicals, and Belief Reports: Some Dilemmas (But Not the Ones You Expect). Schiffer, Stephen.

First Person Authority and Singular Thoughts. Wyller, Truls.

Logic Purified. Yagisawa, Takashi.

Rigor se Dice de muchas Maneras. Pereda, Carlos.

INDIAN

see also Buddhism, Hinduism, Jainism, Yoga

"Emotion in Bengali Religious Thought: Substance and Metaphor" in Emotions in Asian Thought, Marks, Joel (ed). McDaniel, June.

"Ethics of Emotion: Some Indian Reflections" in Emotions in Asian Thought, Marks, Joel (ed). Bilimoria, Purusottama.

Amoral Politics: The Persistent Truth of Machiavellism. Scharfstein, Ben-Ami.

The Bounds of Freedom: About the Eastern and Western Approaches to Freedom. Balaban, Oded and Erev, Anan.

The Epistemology of Comparative Philosophy: A Critique with Reference to P T Raju's Views. Kaipayil, Joseph.

A Concept of Indian Music. Roy, Tirthankar.

Bhartrhari's Solution to The Liar and Some Other Paradoxes. Houben, Jan E M.

Encounter of Hindus with the Ancient Thomas Christians in Kerala. Rao, S N.

La notion de Samskara. Chenet, François.

Language and World: Some Classical Indian Approaches vis-a-vis Analytical Western Approaches. Gokhale, Pradeep P.

Lo spiritualismo indiano antico: Echi egizi nelle Upanisad. Masi, Giuseppe.

Minded Body/Embodied Mind. Seidel, George J.

The Genesis of Buddhist Painting in Ancient India and Its Early Development. Sadakane, Keiji.

The Reception of German Philosophy in Contemporary Indian Thought. Herring, Herbert.

The Significance of Professor Matilal's Logical Illumination of Indian Mysticism in His Studies of Indian Philosophy. Chopra, Y N.

Theory and Practice in Indian Philosophy. Mohanty, J N.

Universal Values: An Indian Perspective. Prasad, Ranjendra.

Violation of Social Contract with Kashmiri People. Parthasarthy, Malini.

Wie indisch ist das Indienbild Schopenhauers?. Mall, Ram Adhar.

INDIFFERENCE

Contro Gli Etici. Spinelli, Emidio (trans).

Philosophical Anarchism and Legal Indifference. Murphy, Mark C.

INDIRECT

The Indirectness of Kierkegaard's Signed Writings. Strawser, Michael.

INDISCERNIBILITY

Max Black on the Identity of Indiscernibles. Cross, Charles B.

Tras la postmodernidad. Innerarity, Daniel.

Vagueness, Indiscernibility, and Pragmatics: Comments on Burns. Varzi, Achille C.

INDISPENSABILITY

Scientific versus Mathematical Realism: The Indispensability Argument. Resnik, Michael D.

INDIVIDUAL

see also Person

"Autonomy and Preference Formation" in In Harm's Way, Coleman, Jules L (ed). Arneson, Richard J.

"Besuch im Hades: Über Günther Anders' Geschichtsphilosophie des Individuums" in Nationalsozialismus und Moderne, Welzer, Harald (ed). Dobiesz, Stephanie.

"Individual Essence in Ingarden's Ontology" in Kunst und Ontologie, Galewicz, Wlodzimierz (ed). Swiderski, Edward M.

"Individual-Level Predicates as Inherent Generics" in The Generic Book, Carlson, Gregory N (ed). Chierchia, Gennaro.

"Individualization, Singularization, and E-Ducation (Between Indifference and Responsibility)" in Identity, Culture, and Education, Smeyers, Paul (ed). Masschelein, Jan.

"Individuum, Individualität und Individuation nach Edith Stein und Wilhelm Dilthey" in Studien zur Philosophie von Edith Stein, Fetz, Reto Luzius (ed). Secrétan, Philibert.

"Socializing Epistemology" in Socializing Epistemology: The Social Dimensions of Knowledge, Schmitt, Frederick (ed). Schmitt, Frederick F.

"The Image of the Human and the Rights of the Individual in Jewish Tradition" in Human Rights and the World's Religions, Rouner, Leroy (ed). Fishbane, Michael.

Aristotle and Augustine on Freedom: Two Theories of Freedom, Voluntary Action, and Akrasia. Chappell, T D J.

Heidegger Lesen. Marten, Rainer.

I Am Because We Are: Readings in Black Philosophy. Hord, Fred Lee (ed) and Lee, Jonathan Scott (ed).

Individuals, Humans, Persons: Questions of Life and Death. Kuhse, Helga and Singer, Peter.

Introduction to Ethics: Personal and Social Responsibility in a Diverse World. Percesepe, Gary.

Medieval Thought: An Introduction. Price, B B.

Nietzsche's Genealogy: Nihilism and the Will to Knowledge. Havas, Randall.

Relationality and the Concept of God. Jansen, Henry.

Universals and Property Instances: The Alphabet of Being. Bacon, John.

Aporien in den Konzepten der Freiheit. Bosto, Sulejman.

Corporate Moral Responsibility: When It Might Matter. Phillips, Michael J.

Der materiale Gehalt des Sittengesetzes nach Fichtes Sittenlehre. Rohs, Peter.

Die Identität der Person: Facetten eines Problems. Quante, Michael.

Do Individuals Exist?. Vallicella, William F.

Do Social Structures Govern Action?. Schatzki, Theodore R.

El Individuo y la Nación: El Sujeto y lo Absoluto en las Filosofías del Lenguaje de Humboldt y Fichte. Pérez, Jorge Navarro.

INDIVIDUAL

Free Agency and Self-Worth. Benson, Paul H.
Habermas and Mead: On Universality and Individuality. Aboulafia, Mitchell.
Hegel und das Problem der Macht. Zenkert, Georg.
Identidad cultural, conflicto cultural y violencia. Vilas Nogueira, J.
Il Livello Religioso Dell'intersoggettività nel Pensiero di Fichte. Ivaldo, Marco.
Individu, identiteit, soort. Lievers, Menno.
Individual and Community: Charles Murray's Political Philosophy. Hudson, James.
Individuelle Freiheit und soziale Bindung: Vom Nutzen und Nachteil der Institutionen für den Menschen. Schluchter, Wolfgang.
Individuum und Gemeinschaft in der WL zwischen 1796 und 1800. Perrinjaquet, Alain.
Intentions, Ends, and Joint Action. Miller, Seumas.
Kierkegaard, la recuperación del individuo existente y el discurso sobre lo histórico. Washburn, Jimmy.
Können Kollektive Berechtigte von Menschenrechten sein? Ein Aspekt des Themas "Extensionen von Menschenrechten". Witschen, Dieter.
Locke on Slavery and Inalienable Rights. Welchman, Jennifer.
On "Divine Simplicity: A New Defense". Miller, Barry.
On an Argument about Reference to Future Individuals. Oppy, Graham.
On Property Self-Exemplification: Rejoinder to Miller. Vallicella, William F.
Pruning the Tree of Life. Neander, Karen.
Psicologia delle folle e Scienza Politica in Italia alla Fine del XIX Secolo. Donzelli, Maria.
Ratifiability and the Logic of Decision. Skyrms, Brian.
Se Ocupa el Fenomenólogo de la Metafísica?. da Silveira, Maria Joao C.
The Ethics of Excess. Lamm, Richard D.
The Impossibility of Interpersonal Utility Comparisons. Hausman, Daniel M.
Universals and Individuals: A Brief Discussion of New *Lixue*. Youguang, Tu.

INDIVIDUALISM

"Anti-Individualism and Psychological Explanation" in *Philosophy of Psychology: Debates on Psychological Explanation, Macdonald, Cynthia (ed)*. Macdonald, Cynthia.
"Il sogno di un'alt(r)a morale: Considerazioni su *Les deux sources* di Henri Bergson" in *L'etica e il suo Altro, Vigna, Carmelo (ed)*. Goisis, Giuseppe L.
"The Modern World and the Individual: From the Metamorphosis of Eastern European Marxism to Marx's Errors" in *Whither Marxism?, Magnus, Bernd (ed)*. Marga, Andrei.
Cartesian Psychology and Physical Minds: Individualism and the Sciences of the Mind. Wilson, Robert A.
Philosophy of Psychology: Debates on Psychological Explanation. Macdonald, Cynthia (ed) and Macdonald, Graham (ed).
Politischer Individualismus: Die Rekonstruktion einer Sozialtheorie unter Bezugnahme auf Machiavelli, Bodin, und Hobbes. Hegmann, Horst.
Rational Individualism: The Perennial Philosophy of Legal Interpretation. Simonds, Roger T.
Social Science in Christian Perspective. Marshall, Paul A (ed) and Vandervennen, Robert E (ed).
Accepting the Consequences of Anti-Individualism. McKinsey, Michael.
Approaches to Liberty: Outline for a "Methodological Communitarianism". Ferry, Jean-Marc.
Citizenship, Individualism, and Democratic Politics. Fullinwider, Robert K.
Egoist Theory and America's Individualist Anarchists: A Dilemma of Praxis. Brooks, Frank.
Entre o Sociologismo e o Individualismo: Considerações sobre a Sociologia de Pierre Bourdieu. Vieira, Luiz Renato.
Healthcare as a Commons. Jecker, Nancy S and Jonsen, Albert R.
Individualism and Social Responsibility: Reflections on Recent Work by French and May. Smith, Patricia.
Individualism and Vision Theory. Egan, Frances.
Individualism, Physicalism, and Spinoza on Minds and Bodies. Lantin, Robert.
Individualism, Subjectivity, and Presence: A Response to Taylor Carman. Olafson, Frederick A.
Leibniz et le droit subjectif. Zarka, Yves-Charles.
Los argumentos del individualismo: En torno a la primera identidad liberal. M Rosales, J.
Pufendorf tra Classicità e Modernità: Nota su un Libro di Simone Goyard-Fabre. Catteneo, Mario A.
Qué Locke? Tradición y Cambio en la Historia del Liberalismo. Méndez Baiges, Victor.
Social Norms and Narrow Content. Williams, Meredith.
The Renaissance, Individualism, and the Portrait. Burke, Peter.
The Traditionalist Critique of Individualism in Post-Revolutionary France: The Case of Louis de Bonald. Reedy, W Jay.
Tocqueville y la dinámica de la democracia moderna: Entre la escisión individualista y la ética republicana. Vega, Jose Fernandez.
Ultimate Reality and Meaning in the Conflict Between Globalism and Anti-Globalism. Cadwallader, Eva H.
Universalism and Individualism. Buckle, Stephen.

INDIVIDUALITY

"Individuum, Individualität und Individuation nach Edith Stein und Wilhelm Dilthey" in *Studien zur Philosophie von Edith Stein, Fetz, Reto Luzius (ed)*. Secrétan, Philibert.
Das Problem der Individualität in Fichtes früher Ethik und Rechtslehre. Düsing, Edith.
E J Lowe on Vague Identity and Quantum Indeterminacy. Noonan, Harold W.
Individuo y Comunidad: Reflexiones Sobre el Eterno Círculo Fichteano. López-Domínguez, Virginia.

La Filosofia Tedesca del Secondo Ottocento tra Scienze dello Spirito e Scienze della Natura. Meschiari, Alberto.
Las Paradojas de la Modernidad. Castro López, Octavio.
Quintuplicatà e Individualità: La Construzione dell'io in WL 1807. Rametta, Gaetano.
Sind wir einzigartig? Zum Verhältnis von Selbstbewusstsein und Individualität. Löw-Beer, Martin.
Unità e molteplicità in Juergen Habermas. Giovagnoli, Raffaela.
Vague Identity and Quantum Non-Individuality. French, Steven and Krause, Décio.

INDIVIDUATION

"Individuum, Individualität und Individuation nach Edith Stein und Wilhelm Dilthey" in *Studien zur Philosophie von Edith Stein, Fetz, Reto Luzius (ed)*. Secrétan, Philibert.
Substance Among Other Categories. Hoffman, Joshua and Rosenkrantz, Gary S.
Logique et existence. Verley, Xavier.
The Spatio-Temporal Theory of Individuation. Potts, Michael.
The Stoics on Identity and Individuation. Lewis, Eric.

INDUCTION

"Induction According to Peirce" in *Peirce and Contemporary Thought: Philosophical Inquiries, Ketner, Kenneth Laine (ed)*. Levi, Isaac.
"Karl Popper und das Induktionsproblem" in *Heinrich Gomperz, Karl Popper und die österreichische Philosophie, Seiler, Martin (ed)*. Schurz, Gerhard.
"On Peirce on Induction: A Response to Levi" in *Peirce and Contemporary Thought: Philosophical Inquiries, Ketner, Kenneth Laine (ed)*. Ullian, Joseph S.
"Zu Heinrich Gomperz: *Die Wissenschaft und die Tat*" in *Heinrich Gomperz, Karl Popper und die österreichische Philosophie, Seiler, Martin (ed)*. Rutte, Heiner.
What is This Thing Called Science? (Second Edition). Chalmers, A F.
A Theory of Forward Induction in Finitely Repeated Games. Al-Najjar, Nabil.
An Inductivist Version of Critical Rationalism. Agassi, Joseph.
Aristote et l'Aristotélisme. Elders, Leo.
How I Almost Solved the Problem of Induction. Watkins, John.
Inducao, Acaso e Racionalidade. Monteiro, Joao Paulo.
Inductive Countersupport. Dorn, George J W.
Is Gold-Putnam Diagonalization Complete?. Juhl, Cory.
Modal Realism and Inductive Scepticism. Thomas, Holly.
On Grzegorczyk Induction. Cornaros, C.
On the Controversy between Poincaré and Russell about the Status of Complete Induction. Heinzmann, Gerhard.
On the Designated Student and Related Induction Paradoxes. Jacquette, Dale.
Science and Ethics: Toward a Theory of Ethical Value. Welch, John R.
The Speed-Optimality of Reichenbach's Straight Rule of Induction. Juhl, Cory F.
Thomas Reid and the Justification of Induction. Anstey, Peter.
Why There Can't Be a Logic of Induction. Glennan, Stuart S.

INDUCTIVE LOGIC

Gruesome Perceptual Spaces. Weir, Alan.

INDUSTRY

Ecological Enlightenment: Essays on the Politics of the Risk Society. Beck, Ulrich and Ritter, Mark A (trans).
The Myth of the Framework: In Defence of Science and Rationality. Popper, Karl R and Notturno, M A (ed).
Basic Values of Western Industrial Society: Feedback Effect of Rationality. Mineau, André.
Business Ethics and Job-Related Constructs: A Cross-Cultural Comparison of Automotive Salespeople. Honeycutt, Earl D, Siguaw, Judy A and Hunt, Tammy G.
Envisioning Capital: Political Economy on Display. Buck-Morss, Susan.
Industry Type, Culture, Mode of Entry and Perceptions of International Marketing Ethics Problems: A Cross-Cultural Comparison. Armstrong, Robert W and Sweeney, Jill.
John Ruskin and the Ethical Foundations of Morris and Company, 1861-96. Harvey, Charles and Press, Jon.
Moral Development in the Biographies of Skilled Industrial Workers. Lempert, Wolfgang.
Off the Treadmill? Technology and Tourism in the North American Maple Syrup Industry. Hinrichs, C Clare.
Organizational Characteristics and HRM Policies on Rights: Exploring the Patterns of Connections. Schwoerer, Catherine E (& others).
Rights Against Polluters. Kernohan, Andrew.
The Ethics of the Pharmaceutical Industry and the Need for a Dual Market System. Kreiner, Anna.
The Place of Ethics in Business: Shifting Paradigms?. Shepard, Jon M (& others).

INEQUALITY

Democracy. Green, Philip (ed).

INERTIA

The Whewell-Faraday Exchange on the Application of the Concepts of Momentum and Inertia to Electromagnetic Phenomena. Anderson, Ronald.
Um Teorema de Inércia e o Conceito de Velocidade nos *Discorsi* de Galileu. Vasconcelos, Júlio C R.

INFANT

"Hard Choices: Ethical Questions Raised by the Birth of Handicapped Infants" in *Ethics on the Frontiers of Human Existence, Badham, Paul (ed)*. Kuhse, Helga and Singer, Peter.
Ethical Issues in Discharge Planning for Vulnerable Infants and Children. Cohen, Marsha H.

INFECTION

Pollution and Infection: An Hypothesis Still-born. Hankinson, R J.

INFERENCE

Vision: Variations on Some Berkeleian Themes. Schwartz, Robert.
Argumentation im Kontext. Mans, Dieter.
Austere Realism and the Worldly Assumptions of Inferential Statistics. Trout, J D.
Classical Harmony: Rules of Inference and the Meaning of the Logical Constants. Milne, Peter.
Conditional Reasoning and Conditional Logic. Lycan, William G.
Filosofía del conocimiento y sistemas expertos. Lombraña, Julián Velarde.
In Defense of Deductive Inference. Kornblith, Hilary.
Induçao, Acaso e Racionalidade. Monteiro, Joao Paulo.
Inference to the Best Explanation and Other Minds. Melnyk, Andrew.
Inference to the Loveliest Explanation. Barnes, Eric.
Inference, Noncommutativity, and Determinateness in Quantum Mechanics. Bub, Jeffrey.
Intuitionism and the Poverty of the Inference Argument. George, Alexander.
La Inferència Dialèctico-Especulativa a la *Ciència de la Lògica* de Hegel. Alegre I Biosca, Lluís.
La subalternación y la conversión aristotélica de las proposiciones. Valadez, Leticia.
Nyaya Inference-Deductive-Inductive Pattern. Sen, Amit Kumar.
On Negation, Truth, and Warranted Assertibility. Tennant, Neil.
Paksata in Navya-Nyaya. Rai, A K.
Reply to Hilary Kornblith's "In Defense of Deductive Inference". Lycan, William G.
Two Concepts of Entailment. Lance, Mark.

INFERENCE RULE

A Note on Derivation Rules in Modal Logic. Goranko, Valentin.
A Note on Formalisations of First-Order Theories. Stepien, Teodor.
A Revision-Theoretic Analysis of the Arithmetical Hierarchy. Antonelli, Gian Aldo.
Axiomatizations of Commutative and Non-Associative Ajdukiewicz Calculus. Kandulski, Maciej.
Bisimulations and Predicate Logic. Fernando, Tim.
Even Tabular Modal Logics Sometimes do not have Independent Base for Admissible Rules. Rybakov, Vladimir V.
Extending Intuitionistic Linear Logic with Knotted Structural Rules. Hori, Ryuichi, Ono, Hiroakira and Schellinx, Harold.
Non-Well-Founded Sets via Revision Rules. Antonelli, Gian Aldo.
On the Atomic Formula Property of Härtig's Refutation Calculus. Inoué, Takao.

INFERTILITY

Infertility Treatment for Postmenopausal Patients: An Equity-Based Approach. Purviance, Susan M.

INFINITARY LOGIC

A Functorial Property of the Aczel-Buchholz-Feferman Function. Weiermann, Andreas.
A Model and Its Subset: The Uncountable Case. Newelski, Ludomir.
The Consistency Strength of an Infinitary Ramsey Property. Kafkoulis, George.

INFINITE

see also Finite
Dios en la filosofía de Malebranche. Fernández, José Luis.
From Finite to Infinite Lambda Calculi. Kennaway, Richard (& others).
L'Univers Infini: Les Interventions de Marin Mersenne et de Charles Sorel. Del Prete, Antonella.
Surveyability and the *Sorites* Paradox. Addis, Mark.
The Role of the Absolute Infinite in Cantor's Conception of Set. Jané, Ignacio.
The Structure of Amorphous Sets. Truss, J K.
Uniformization Problems and the Cofinality of the Infinite Symmetric Group. Sharp, James D and Thomas, Simon.

INFINITESIMAL

Quantitas Inassignabilis: Language and Knowledge in Boskovic's Approach to Infinitesimals. Martinovic, Ivica.

INFINITY

"Infinite Decision Theory" in *Gambling on God: Essays on Pascal's Wager, Jordan, Jeffrey (ed)*. Sorensen, Roy.
Alexander of Aphrodisias: Quaestiones 2.16-3.15. Sharples, R W (trans).
Difference and Repetition. Deleuze, Gilles and Patton, Paul (trans).
On Hegel's Logic: Fragments of a Commentary. Burbidge, John W.
Philoponus: On Aristotle's "Physics" 3. Edwards, M J (trans).
Selected Logic Papers: Enlarged Edition. Quine, W V.
The Divine Matrix: Creativity as Link between East and West. Bracken, Joseph A.
Time, Change, and Freedom: An Introduction to Metaphysics. Smith, Quentin and Oaklander, L Nathan.
Beyond Infinity: Augustin and Cantor. Drozdek, Adam.
Breviarium Principii: Prosènanchos Archèten. Incardona, Nunzio.
De la determinación del infinito a la inaccesibilidad en los cardinales transfinitos. Alvarez, Carlos.
Finding *Finity* and Motion for Zeno. Borejszo, Zee.
Finito e infinito e l'idealismo della filosofia: La logica hegeliana dell'essere determinato: Parte Seconda. Movia, Giancarlo.
Il Trattato Tomista sulle Proprietà Trascendentali dell'Essere. Ventimiglia, Giovanni.
L'Infinité Divine dans l'Antiquité et au Moyen Age. Côté, Antoine.
On Division in Plato's *Statesman*. Fattal, Michel.
Reluctant Transcendence: The Face to Face in Levinas' *Totality and Infinity*. Long, Christopher Philip.
Reply to Craig: Inverse Operations with Transfinite Numbers and the *Kalam Cosmological Argument*. Oppy, Graham.
The Quest for Infinity and the Synthesis of Science (An Interview with Professor Andrzej Kajetan Wróblewski). Bendyk, Edwin.

Tre Schede su Bruno e Oxford. Aquilecchia, Giovanni.
Universals and Infinite Modes in the Thought of Spinoza. Murthy, Viren.

INFLUENCE

Antecedentes Griegos y Medievales del Calculo Logico. Beuchot, Mauricio.
Domingo de Soto en el Origen de la Ciencia Moderna. Pérez Camacho, Juan José and Sols Lucía, Ignacio.
Martin Heidegger en la Perpectiva del Siglo xx: Sobre la *Gesamtausgabe* de Heidegger. Barash, Jeffrey Andrew.

INFORMAL FALLACY

Slippery Slope Arguments by Douglas Walton. Van Der Burg, Wiltbren.
The Appeal to Tradition: Cultural Evolution and Logical Soundness. Harpine, William D.

INFORMAL LOGIC

Slippery Slope Arguments by Douglas Walton. Van Der Burg, Wiltbren.
Defining the Term "Argument". Chittleborough, P and Newman, M E.
Denying the Antecedent: A Common Fallacy?. Burke, Michael B.
Not by Skill Alone: The Centrality of Character to Critical Thinking. Siegel, Harvey.
Rationality in Legal Discussions: A Pragma-Dialectical Perspective. Feteris, Eveline T.
The Appeal to Tradition: Cultural Evolution and Logical Soundness. Harpine, William D.

INFORMATION

"Generic Information and Dependent Generics" in *The Generic Book, Carlson, Gregory N (ed)*. Link, Godehard.
"The Brain's Software: The Natural Languages and Poetic Information Processing" in *The Machine as Metaphor and Tool, Haken, Hermann (ed)*. Johansson, S Ryan.
Ethical Aspects of Information Technology. Spinello, Richard A.
Logic and Information. Devlin, Keith.
A Critique of Information Processing Theories of Consciousness. Hardcastle, Valerie Gray.
Can Computers Carry Content 'Inexplicitly'?. Skokowski, Paul G.
Deutsche Positionen zur Informationstechnologie. Hrachovec, Herbert.
Effective Deliberation about What to Intend: Or Striking it Rich in a Toxin-Free Environment. Mele, Alfred R.
Full-Information Theories of Individual Good. Loeb, Don.
Information and Teleosemantics. Zawidzski Jr, Tad and Ross, Don.
Information et Référence. Assamoi, Bertin Y.
Las Emociones y la Naturalización de la Intencionalidad. Moya, Carlos J.
Markets, Information, and Benevolence. Brennan, Timothy J.
Reasoning about Update Logic. Van Eijck, Jan and De Vries, Fer-Jan.
Representations of Information Technology in Disciplinary Development: Disappearing Plants and Invisible Networks. Hine, Christine.
Something to do With Vagueness. Burns, Linda.
The Problem of Ultimate Reality and Meaning in the Context of Information Self-Organization and Isotopic Diversity. Berezin, Alexander A.
The Problems of Information in Approach to Systems. Dolega, Jósef.
Utopie in actie: wat verwachtingen in technologie doen. Van Lente, Harro.

INFORMED CONSENT

A Desperate Solution: Individual Autonomy and the Double-Blind Controlled Experiment. Logue, Gerald and Wear, Stephen.
Abandoning Informed Consent. Veatch, Robert M.
Amnesia Instead of Anesthesia: Not Always a Question of Consent. Truog, Robert D and Waisel, David.
Autonomy, Informed Consent, and Psychosurgery. Hundert, Edward M.
Changing the Paradigm for Informed Consent. Dagi, Teo Forcht.
Conscious Forgetting and Subconscious Remembering of Pain. Tinnin, Louis.
Individual Autonomy and the Double-Blind Controlled Experiment: The Case of Desperate Volunteers. Minogue, Brendan P (& others).
Informed Consent and Anonymous Tissue Samples: The Case of HIV Seroprevalence Studies. Kopelman, Loretta M.
Informed Consent to Amnestics, or: What Sound Does a Tree Make in the Forest When It Falls on Your Head?. Mehlman, Maxwell J (& others).
Informed Consent: Pondering a New Piece of the Puzzle. Jacobson, Jay A.
Patients' Perceptions of the Quality of Informed Consent for Common Medical Procedures. Sulmasy, Daniel P (& others).
Physicians' Ethical Responsibilities under Co-Pay Insurance: Should Potential Fiscal Liability Become Part of Informed Consent?. Turner, J F (& others).
Reconsidering "Psychosurgery": Issues of Informed Consent and Physician Responsibility. Stagno, Susan J (& others).
Shading the Truth in Seeking Informed Consent for Research Purposes. Bok, Sissela.
To Be or Not to Be: Waiving Informed Consent in Emergency Research. McCarthy, Charles R.
Trees and Heads: The Objective and the Subjective in Painful Procedures. Bennett, Henry L.

INGARDEN, R

"Art and Participation" in *Kunst und Ontologie, Wlodzimierz, Galewicz (ed)*. Strozewski, Wladyslaw.
"Das Problem des Seinsstatus der gegenständlichen Sinne und Ingardens Ontologie..." in *Kunst und Ontologie, Wlodzimierz, Galewicz (ed)*. Galewicz, Wlodzimierz.
"Ens multipliciter dicitur: The Ingardian Variant of an Old Thesis" in *Kunst und Ontologie, Wlodzimierz, Galewicz (ed)*. Haefliger, Gregor.
"Fiktive Welt im literarischen Kunstwerk" in *Kunst und Ontologie, Wlodzimierz, Galewicz (ed)*. Ströker, Elisabeth.

INGARDEN, R

"Individual Essence in Ingarden's Ontology" in *Kunst und Ontologie, Galewicz, Wlodzimierz (ed).* Swiderski, Edward M.

"Language as Bearer of Meaning: The Phenomenology of Roman Ingarden" in *Kunst und Ontologie, Wlodzimierz, Galewicz (ed).* Gumpel, Liselotte.

"Painting and the Structure of Consciousness: Remarks on Roman Ingarden's Theory of Painting" in *Kunst und Ontologie, Wlodzimierz, Galewicz (ed).* Poltawski, Andrzej.

"Sentences, Propositions and *Quasi*-Propositions" in *Kunst und Ontologie, Galewicz, Wlodzimierz (ed).* Wolenski, Jan.

"Strata in Ingarden's Ontology" in *Kunst und Ontologie, Wlodzimierz, Galewicz (ed).* Simons, Peter.

"The Function of Ontology and Experience in Roman Ingarden's Axiological Investigations" in *Kunst und Ontologie, Galewicz, Wlodzimierz (ed).* Wegrzecki, Adam.

"The Truth about Fiction" in *Kunst und Ontologie, Wlodzimierz, Galewicz (ed).* Seifert, Joseph and Smith, Barry.

"What Ingarden Has to Say to Painters" in *Kunst und Ontologie, Galewicz, Wlodzimierz (ed).* Taranczewski, Pawel.

Kunst und Ontologie. Wlodzimierz, Galewicz (ed), Ströker, Elisabeth (ed) and Strozewski, Wladyslaw (ed).

Reading Ingarden Read Husserl: Metaphysics, Ontology, and Phenomenological Method. Bostar, Leo J.

INHERENT

"Individual-Level Predicates as Inherent Generics" in *The Generic Book, Carlson, Gregory N (ed).* Chierchia, Gennaro.

INJECTIVE

Deissler Rank Complexity of Powers of Indecomposable Injective Modules. Chartrand, R and Kucera, T.

INNATE

Blondel and the Tradition of the Innate Longing for God (in Dutch). Schrama, Martijn.

INNATE IDEA

Inneity in Descartes' Regulae. Barbone, Steven.

La Consideración de las ideas Innatas en Descartes y la Problemática del Conocimiento de lo Físico. García del Campo, Juan Pedro.

Leibniz y la Tradición Neoplatónica: Estado Actual de la Cuestión. Orio, Bernardino.

INNATENESS

Locke's Challenge to Innate Practical Principles Revisited. O'Connor, Peg.

Moral Innatism, Connatural Ideas, and Impuissance in Daily Affairs: James Q Wilson's Acrobatic Dive into an Empty Pool. Geis, Gilbert.

Moral Sense and Utopian Sensibility. Fox, Robin.

INNOCENCE

Innocence. Richards, Norvin W.

INNOVATION

Innovation and Tradition in Religion: Towards an Institutional Theory. Disbrey, Claire (ed).

Aristotle's Renaissance As an Example of the Essential Tension between Tradition and Innovation. Berti, Enrico.

Crítica y propuesta a la distinción entre contexto de descubrimiento y contexto de justifición. Echeverría, Javier.

INQUIRY

Dewey's New Logic: A Reply to Russell. Burke, Tom.

Cognitive Value and the Advancement of Science. Levi, Isaac.

For a Better Understanding of Philosophy, For a Better Philosophical Method. Sanjeev, M P.

Is Gold-Putnam Diagonalization Complete?. Juhl, Cory.

INSANITY

Wild Beasts and Idle Humours: Legal Insanity and the Finding of Fault. Robinson, Daniel N.

INSIDER TRADING

Insider Trading and the Social Contract. Salbu, Steven R.

INSIGHT

"An Investment Perspective on Creative Insight" in *The Nature of Insight, Sternberg, Robert J (ed).* Sternberg, Robert J.

"Cognitive and Affective Components of Insight" in *The Nature of Insight, Sternberg, Robert J (ed).* Gick, Mary L and Lockhart, Robert S.

"Constraints on Thinking in Insight and Invention" in *The Nature of Insight, Sternberg, Robert J (ed).* Isaak, Matthew I and Just, Marcel Adam.

"Creative Insight and Preinventive Forms" in *The Nature of Insight, Sternberg, Robert J (ed).* Finke, Ronald A.

"Creative Insight: The Social Dimension of a Solitary Moment" in *The Nature of Insight, Sternberg, Robert J (ed).* Csikszentmihalyi, Mihaly and Sawyer, Keith.

"Demystification of Cognitive Insight" in *The Nature of Insight, Sternberg, Robert J (ed).* Seifert, Colleen M (& others).

"Foresight in Insight? A Darwinian Answer" in *The Nature of Insight, Sternberg, Robert J (ed).* Simonton, Dean Keith.

"Getting Into and Out of Mental Ruts: A Theory of Fixation, Incubation, and Insight" in *The Nature of Insight, Sternberg, Robert J (ed).* Smith, Steven M.

"How Scientists Really Reason: Scientific Reasoning in Real-World Laboratories" in *The Nature of Insight, Sternberg, Robert J (ed).* Dunbar, Kevin.

"Insight and Affect in the History of Science" in *The Nature of Insight, Sternberg, Robert J (ed).* Gruber, Howard E.

"Insight and Problem Solving" in *The Nature of Insight, Sternberg, Robert J (ed).* Dominowski, Roger L and Dallob, Pamela.

"Insight in Minds and Genes" in *The Nature of Insight, Sternberg, Robert J (ed).* Perkins, David N.

"Prolegomena to Theories of Insight in Problem Solving: A Taxonomy of Problems" in *The Nature of Insight, Sternberg, Robert J (ed).* Weisberg, Robert W.

"Putting Insight into Perspective" in *The Nature of Insight, Sternberg, Robert J (ed).* Schooler, Jonathan W (& others).

"The Inception of Insight" in *The Nature of Insight, Sternberg, Robert J (ed).* Ippolito, Maria F and Tweney, Ryan D.

"The Search for Insight: Grappling with Gestalt Psychology's Unanswered Questions" in *The Nature of Insight, Sternberg, Robert J (ed).* Mayer, Richard E.

"The Suddenness of Insight" in *The Nature of Insight, Sternberg, Robert J (ed).* Davidson, Janet E.

The Nature of Insight. Sternberg, Robert J (ed) and Davidson, Janet E (ed).

Commentary on "Insight, Delusion, and Belief". Loizzo, Joseph.

Insight, Delusion, and Belief. Gillett, Grant.

Spinozas Gedanke, dass Einsicht befreit. Bittner, Rüdigner.

The Relationship Between Analysis and Insight (Prajñā) in Mādhyamika Buddhism: Some Western Interpretations. Dean, Colin.

INSPIRATION

Person to Person Inspiration. Kidd, James W and Kidd, Sunnie D.

The Dynamic Aspects of Inspiration: An Essay on the Phenomenon of Authentically Being Inspired. Kidd, Sunnie D and Kidd, James W.

INSTANT

Aquí y Ahora, Desde la Hermenéutica. Duque, Félix.

La teoría del instante en Bachelard y el espacio onírico. Castillo, Roberto.

INSTINCT

Nietzsche: A Origem da Linguagem. Lessa da Fonseca, Thelma Silveira Mota.

INSTITUTION

"Enseñanga, Políticae Institución" in *Temas Actuales de Filosofía, Palacios, María Julia (ed).* Insua, Elda and Sardisco, Ana M.

A Theory of Social Decisions. Baron, Jonathan.

Acceptance of Authority and the Duty to Comply with Just Institutions: A Comment on Waldron. Murphy, Mark C.

Conflicts of Obligation. Forrester, James William.

In Orbit. Lingis, Alphonso F.

Institutional Constraints on the Ethics of Expert Testimony. Sales, Bruce D and Simon, Leonore.

Institutional Excuses and Neutrality. Ewin, R E.

The Emerging Practice of Institutional Apologies. Harvey, J.

The Ethical Life of Health Care Organizations. Reiser, Stanley Joel.

INSTRUCTION

see Teaching

INSTRUMENT

Empiricism and the Epistemology of Instruments. Wilson, Fred.

Instruments and the Body: Sartre and Merleau-Ponty. Kujundzic, Nebojsa and Buschert, William.

Knowledge and the Trustworthiness of Instruments. Lehrer, Keith.

Spectrometers as Analogues of Nature. Rothbart, Daniel.

INSTRUMENTAL

Instrumental Rationality. Airaksinen, Timo and Kaalikoski, Katri.

INSTRUMENTALISM

see also Pragmatism

Anima hace hablar a la razón con una voz diferente: Nuevos nexos entre la tecnociencia y el mundo de la vida. Cañón Loyes, Camino.

Ciencia y relativismo cognitivo: una crítica del pragmatismo. Cassini, Alejandro.

Il predicato di dimostrabilità e la nozione di consistenza: alternative alla formulazione classica. Ballarino, Annamaria.

INSURANCE

The Ethics of Excess. Lamm, Richard D.

INTEGRATION

Reflections on Song-Ming *Lixue* and the Philosophy of Harmony and Integration. Liwen, Zhang.

INTEGRITY

"Integrity" in *Concepts and Cases in Nursing Ethics, Yeo, Michael (& others).* Yeo, Michael and Ford, Ann.

Ressentiment, Evaluation, and Integrity. Reginster, Bernard.

Does Physician Assisted Suicide Violate the Integrity of Medicine?. Momeyer, Richard.

Fanaticism and Integrity. Newman, Jay.

Integrity, Abortion, and the Pro-Life Perinatologist. Thorp Jr, John M (& others).

Law and the Virtues: Developing a Legal Theory for Business Ethics. Nesteruk, Jeffrey.

Liberale Integrität. Rinderle, Peter.

Moral Integrity of Professions. Griener, Glenn G.

Old Guards, Young Turks, and the $64,000 Question: What is Business Ethics?. Olson, Steven.

Standing for Something. Calhoun, Cheshire.

The Pro-Life Maternal-Fetal Medicine Physician: A Problem of Integrity. Blustein, Jeffrey and Fleischman, Alan R.

INTELLECT

see also Reason

The Passionate Intellect: Essays on the Transformation of Classical Traditions. Ayres, Lewis (ed).

La Disputa Averroismo-Tomismo en el op "De Unitate Intellectus Contra Averroistas", de Tomás de Aquino. Barrio Maestre, José María.

INTERSUBJECTIVITY

"Per una razionalità practica dialogica" in *L'etica e il suo Altro, Vigna, Carmelo (ed)*. Cortella, Lucio.

Husserls Theorie der Intersubjektivität. Iribarne, Julia V.

Weltentwürfe: Ludwig Binswangers phänomenologische Psychologie. Herzog, Max.

Dio nella modernità: Husserl. Rigobello, Armando.

Il Livello Religioso Dell'intersoggettività nel Pensiero di Fichte. Ivaldo, Marco.

Intersubjektivität und Objektivität der moralischen Werte. Corradini, Antonella.

Presente eterno y dolor: La tematización unamuniana de la estructura temporal de la existencia y el problema de la intersubjectividad. Padilla Rodríguez, J Teresa.

Starke Wertungen, Wünsche zweiter Ordnung und intersubjektive Kritik: Überlegungen zum Begriff ethischer Autonomie. Anderson, Joel.

INTERVAL

Chains and Antichans in Interval Algebras. Bekkali, M.

INTERVENTION

"Nationalism and Intervention" in *Introducing Applied Ethics, Almond, Brenda (ed)*. Coady, C A J.

Autonomy and Intervention: Parentalism in the Caring Life. Kultgen, John.

Intervention and Reflection: Basic Issues in Medical Ethics (Fifth Edition). Munson, Ronald (ed).

Deciding Whether to Intervene. Howe, Edmund G.

Military Intervention as a Moral Duty. Tan, Kok-Chor.

INTERVIEW

"Irving Singer on the History of Love" in *The Nature and Pursuit of Love, Goicoechea, David (ed)*. Fulford, Robert.

"Je—Luce Irigaray": A Meeting with Luce Irigaray. Hirsh, Elizabeth and Olson, Gary A.

A Debate on *The Passion of Michel Foucault*. Miller, James (& others).

An Interview with Niklas Luhmann. Sciulli, David.

Between Terrestriality and Aquacity: Miller's 'Limit Experience'. Luchte, James.

CQ *Interview*: Dr Boudewijn Chabot on Assisted Suicide in the Absence of Somatic Illness. Klotzko, Arlene Judith.

Interview of Lewis E Hahn. Abbarno, John M.

Interview of Ludwig Grünberg. Abbarno, John M.

Interview: Hans-Georg Gadamer. Rée, Jonathan and Gehron, Christiane.

Investigative Interviewing: A Phenomenological Approach to a Universal Method. Kidd, James W.

The Deconstruction of Actuality: An Interview with Jacques Derrida. Rée, Jonathan (trans).

INTIMACY

La intimidad como valor antropológico y social. Pallarés Gonzalez, José Luis.

INTOLERANCE

On the Intolerable. Leiser, Burton M.

INTRINSIC

"Holism, Intrinsicality, and the Ambition of Transcendence" in *Dennett and his Critics, Dahlbom, Bo (ed)*. Rorty, Richard.

Intrinsic Value: Concept and Warrant. Lemos, Noah M.

Bhavaviveka's *Prajñapradipa*. Ames, William L.

Intrinsic Constraints on Language: Grammar and Hermeneutics. Bickhard, Mark H.

Locality/ Separability: Is This Necessarily a Useful Distinction?. Cushing, James T.

Neutrals. Lemos, Noah M.

Supervenience Unthwarted: Rejoinder to Wicks. Zangwill, Nick.

The Concept of Consciousness$_4$: The Reflective Meaning. Natsoulas, Thomas.

The Intrinsic, Non-Supervenient Nature of Aesthetic Properties. Eaton, Marcia Mulder.

Zubiri ante el problema del valor. Palacios, Juan Miguel.

INTUITION

"Anschauung als Quelle von Erkenntnis: Erbe und Neubewertung" in *Das geistige Erbe Europas, Buhr, Manfred (ed)*. Andreas-Grisebach, Manon.

"Wirkliche" und "philosophische" Anschauung: Formen der intellektuellen Anschauung in Fichtes *System der Sittenlehre* (1798). Perrinjaquet, Alain.

Aesthetic as Science of Expression and General Linguistic. Croce, Benedetto and Ainslie, Douglas (trans).

On Hegel's Logic: Fragments of a Commentary. Burbidge, John W.

Perspectives on Quine. Barrett, Robert (ed) and Gibson, Roger (ed).

Tempo e Intuizione: Alle origini dello slancio vitale nel pensiero di Henri Bergson. Taroni, Paolo.

An Intuition About Self-Knowledge: A Challenge to Fodor. Goldberg, Sandy.

Chiose alle "Regole" Cartesiane. Caleo, Marcello.

Construction and Mathematical Schematism: Kant on the Exhibition of a Concept in Intuition. Ferrarin, Alfredo.

Constructive Thinking: Personal Voice. Thayer-Bacon, Barbara.

En torno a la nueva edición de Schleiermacher. Ginzo, Arsenio.

Física Cuántica y Filosofía. Chevalley, Catherine.

Imaginary Science. Gooding, David.

Intellektuelle Anschauung und Dialektik. Nagasawa, Kunihiko.

Intellektuelle Anschauung und Gewissen: Aufriss eines Begründngsproblems. Janke, Wolfgang.

Intellektuelle Anschauung und Mystik. Omine, Akira.

Intuition and Reason. Fricker, Miranda.

Intuition, Involvement, Interrogation: The Meaning of Self-Making. Sloboda, Myron.

Intuitionistic Mathematics Does Not Need *Ex Falso Quodlibet*. Tennant, Neil.

Kant and Lonergan on Insight Into the Sensible. Sala, Giovanni B.

Knowledge of Proofs. Pagin, Peter.

La Función de la Intuición Ockhamista. López Vázquez, J Ramón.

La genesi della coscienza reale nella "Grundlage der gesamten Wissenschaftslehre" di Fichte. Metz, Wilhelm.

La justificación consecuencialista de las lealtades. Lara Sánchez, Francisco Damián.

Le pragmatisme: Solution au problème moral de la modernité?. Poltier, Hugues.

Logic and Modal Intuitions. Tidman, Paul.

Mysticism and Phenomenology. Neblett, William.

Nous y Phronesis: Un comentario a EN 1143a 35ss. Zagal, Héctor.

Observaçoes sobre a Concepçao Kantiana do Espaço. Molina, Jorge Alberto.

Platonism and Mathematical Intuition in Kurt Gödel's Thought. Parsons, Charles.

Poinsot on the Semiotics of Awareness. Raposa, Michael.

Quintuplicatà e Individualità: La Construzione dell'io in WL 1807. Rametta, Gaetano.

Temporal and Atemporal Truth in Intuitionistic Mathematics. Martino, Enrico and Usberti, Gabriele.

The "Explicit-Implicit" Distinction. Hadley, Robert F.

The Incompatibility of Intuition and Constitution in Husserl's *The Idea of Phenomenology* (1907). Ryan, William F.

INTUITIONISM

A Model for Intuitionistic Non-standard Arithmetic. Moerdijk, I.

Antirrealismo y Verdad: La Realidad del Pasado. L Prades, Josep.

Are Moral Intuitions Self-Evident Truths?. Shweder, Richard A.

De zaak van de dieren. Melle, Ullrich.

Enumerators of Lambda Terms are Reducing Constructively. Barendregt, H.

Etchemendy and Logical Consequence. Priest, Graham.

Herman Weyl's Intuitionistic Mathematics. van Dalen, Dirk.

Heyting's Contribution to the Change in Research into the Foundations of Mathematics. Franchella, Miriam.

Intuitionism and the Poverty of the Inference Argument. George, Alexander.

Intuitionists Are Not (Turing) Machines. Wright, Crispin.

K Popper: Racionalismo Critico, Metafisica y Metodologia de lo Inverificable. Velasco N, Ignacio Ruiz.

La Lógica Intuicionista Como una Lógica del Conocimiento Matemático. Legris, Javier.

More About Relatively Lawless Sequences. Moschovakis, Joan Rand.

Never Say Never. Williamson, Timothy.

On the Intuitionistic Solution of the Sorites Paradox. Mott, Peter.

Strictly Primitive Recursive Realizability, I. Damnjanovic, Zlatan.

The Foundation of Ethics in Late Confucianism. Kern, Iso.

Why are There No Objective Values? A Critique of Ethical Intuitionism from an Epistemological Point of View. Geiger, Gebhard.

Wright on the Non-Mechanizability of Intuitionist Reasoning. Detlefsen, Michael.

INTUITIONISTIC LOGIC

Vie della scrittura: Frege e la svolta linguistica. Penco, Carlo.

Completeness Results for Intuitionistic and Modal Logic in a Categorical Setting. Makkai, M.

Extending Intuitionistic Linear Logic with Knotted Structural Rules. Hori, Ryuichi, Ono, Hiroakira and Schellinx, Harold.

Hypergraphs and the Intuitionistic Propositional Calculus. Kolany, Adam.

Models of Intuitionistic TT and NF. Dzierzgowski, Daniel.

Natural Deduction for Intuitionistic Linear Logic. Troelstra, A S.

Operators Defined by Propositional Quantification and Their Interpretation Over Cantor Space. Polacik, Tomasz.

Reflections on "Difficult" Embeddings. Prijatelj, Andreja.

The Decidability of Dependency in Intuitionistic Propositional Logic. De Jongh, Dick and Chagrova, L A.

INVARIANCE

"A Most General Principle of Invariance" in *Philosophy, Mathematics and Modern Physics, Rudolph, Enno (ed)*. Scheibe, Erhard.

Completeness Results for Intuitionistic and Modal Logic in a Categorical Setting. Makkai, M.

INVENTION

"Constraints on Thinking in Insight and Invention" in *The Nature of Insight, Sternberg, Robert J (ed)*. Isaak, Matthew I and Just, Marcel Adam.

INVESTIGATION

Cuestiones Metodológicas en la Investigación Filosófica. Rivera de Rosales, Jacinto.

La Discusión Lakatos-Kuhn. Alcalá Campos, Raúl.

INVESTING

Ethical Aspects of Investor Behavior. Rivoli, Pietra.

INVESTMENT

"An Investment Perspective on Creative Insight" in *The Nature of Insight, Sternberg, Robert J (ed)*. Sternberg, Robert J.

INVOLUNTARY ACTION

Libertad y revocabilidad. Martin, Christopher.

IRANIAN

Abu Bakr Al-Razi: Un Filósofo de una Antiguedad Tardía. Escobar, Santiago.

IRAQI

Public Relations Ethics: Ivy Lee, Hill and Knowlton, and the Gulf War. Marlin, Randal.

IRIGARAY, L

"Je—Luce Irigaray": A Meeting with Luce Irigaray. Hirsh, Elizabeth and Olson, Gary A.

"The Only Diabological Thing about Women...": Luce Irigaray on Divinity. Deutscher, Penelope.

The Irigaray Reader. Whitford, Margaret (ed).

Beauvoir, Irigaray, and the Mystical. Hollywood, Amy M.

IRIGARY, L

Is There Sexual Difference in the Work of Georges Bataille?. McWhorter, Ladelle.

JAMESON, F
"Late Capitalism and Postmodernism: Jameson/Mandel" in *Marxism in the Postmodern Age, Callari, Antonio (ed)*. Norton, Bruce.

JANKELEVITCH, V
Las apariencias en Vladimir Jankélévitch. Trejos, Susana.

JAPANESE
see also Buddhism, Zen Buddhism
"Lieu": Nishida, Nishitani, Derrida. Elberfeld, Rolf.
"Vernunft und Selbstbewusstsein—Zur Fichte-Rezeption in Japan" in *Das geistige Erbe Europas, Buhr, Manfred (ed)*. Kumamoto, Chukei.
Essentials of Shinto: An Analytical Guide to Principal Teachings. Picken, Stuart D B.
How Are We to Live? Ethics in an Age of Self-Interest. Singer, Peter.
Values, Work, Education: The Meanings of Work. Natale, Samuel M (ed) and Rothschild, Brian M (ed).
A Comparison of Japanese and U S Corporate Financial Accountability and its Impact on the Responsibilties of Corporate Managers. Hazera, Alejandro.
Business Ethics: A Japanese View. Taka, Iwao.
Content and Criticism: The Aims of Schooling. Hare, William.
Fichtes Erziehungslehre als erste logische Begründung der Vorbilderziehung. Kumamoto, Yasuhiro.
Fukuzawa Yukichi and Religion. Koizumi, Takashi.
HIV +/AIDS Related Bioethical Issues in Japan. Hoshino, Kazusama.
Japanese Aesthetics: The Construction of Meaning. Marra, Michele.
Karl Löwith et le nihilisme japonais. Stevens, Bernard.
L'ontologie structurale et le dialogue des mondes. Rombach, Heinrich.
Milieu et logique du lieu chez Watsuji. Berque, Augustin.
Nishida Kitarô, l'école de Kyôto et l'ultra-nationalisme. Lavelle, Pierre.
Patients' Rights in Japan: Progress and Resistance. Morikawa, Isao.
Spontanéité et nature: le cas d'Andô Shôeki: Comparatisme et récupération. Joly, Jacques.
Sur la personne et l'oeuvre de Hajime Tanabe. Laube, Johannes.
Sushi, Science, and Spirituality: Modern Japanese Philosophy and Its Views of Western Science. Kasulis, Thomas P.
The Function of the Subject Complex in *Tanka*. Amagasaki, Akira.
Zeami's Concept of "Flower" in Noh Performance. Aoki, Takao.
'Critical Buddhism' and the Question of Philosophical Syncretism. Heine, Steven.

JARDINE, N
The Limits of Pragmatic Realism. Forster, Paul D.

JASPERS
Karl Jaspers: Basic Philosophical Writings. Ehrlich, Edith (& other eds).
Commentary on "Karl Jaspers and Edmund Husserl". Chadwick, Ruth F.
Der Begriff der psychischen Krankheit aus der Sicht der Fichteschen Transzendentalphilosophie. Hoff, Paul.
Il Problema del Mito nel Dialogo Bultmann-Jaspers. Donadio, Francesco.
Jaspers en discusión con el pensamiento de su época. Barrio, Jaime Franco.
Karl Jaspers and Edmund Husserl—I: The Perceived Convergence. Walker, Chris.
Karl Jaspers and Edmund Husserl—II: The Divergence. Walker, Chris.
Karl Jaspers and Edmund Husserl—III: Jaspers as a Kantian Phenomenologist. Walker, Chris.
Some Reflections on the Relevance of Karl Jaspers' Concept of Border Situation in Present-Day South Africa. Ally, Mashuq.
The Image of Socrates in the Mirror of Jaspers. Erickson, Stephen A.

JAVELLI, C
Javelli and Suárez on the Eternal Truths. Wells, Norman J.

JAYNES, J
The Metaphoric Origins of Objectivity, Subjectivity, and Consciousness in the Direct Perception of Reality. Mulaik, Stanley A.

JEFFERSON
Thomas Jefferson's Freethought Legacy: A Saying Per Day by the Sage of Monticello. Greeley, Roger E.

JEFFREY, R
Newcomblike Problems. Sobel, Jordan Howard.
Ratifiability and the Logic of Decision. Skyrms, Brian.

JESUITS
Erasmus, Utopia, and the Jesuits: Essays on the Outreach of Humanism. Olin, John C.
Jesuit Science Between Texts and Contexts. Biagioli, Mario.
'Auf die Kräfte des Leibes achten': Die Bedeutung der Gesundheit im Leben und Wirken des Ignatius von Loyola. Lutterbach, Hubertus.

JESUS
see Christ

JEWISH
see also Hebraic, Judaism
"Überwindung von Schwierigem durch Häufung Desselben". Steiner, Uwe.
Feminist Interpretations of Hannah Arendt. Honig, Bonnie (ed).
Nuggets of Wisdom from Great Jewish Thinkers: From Biblical Times to the Present. Gerber, William.
Bioethics and the Old-Time Religion: Response to Dena Davis. Freedman, Benjamin.
Fichtes Stellung zum Judentum. Fuchs, Erich.
Freud and the Torah. Weed, Laura E.
La Tensión Razón-Fe en la Filosofía Judeomusulmana de Al-Andalus. Ayala, Jorge M.
One of These Mornings I'm Going to Rise Up Singing: The Necessity of the Prophetic Voice in Jewish Bioethics. Zoloth-Dorfman, Laurie.

Richard Rorty and the Righteous Among the Nations. Geras, Norman.
Setting Up a Straw Man: Commentary on Dena Davis. Rosner, Fred.
Staatsbürgerliche Identität und Selbstachtung im jüdischen Staat: Eine Rawls'che Perspektive. Brunner, José and Peled, Yoav.
The End of Philosophy, the Time of Auschwitz, and the Bound Transcendence of Communities of Differences. Watson, James R.
The Holocaust and Philosophy. Freeman, Michael.
The Pariah and Her Shadow: Hannah Arendt's Biography of Rahel Varnhagen. Benhabib, Seyla.
Universalistic Aspects of Jewish Culture and Religion. Minkevicius, Jokubas.
Variaciones Isidorianas. Rodón, Eulalia.
What Does Hegel Make of the Jews?: A Scato-Logical Reading of Kafka's *Die Verwandlung*. Munk, Linda.

JOB
Education and Work: Reflections on the Moral and Spiritual Dimensions of the Job Crisis. Books, Sue.

JOHN
Henologische Perspektiven I/I-II: Platon—Johannes—Cusanus. Wyller, Egil A.

JOHN OF ORIA
El "Tractatus Consequentiarum" (1518) en la Lógica de Juan de Oria. Muñoz Delgado, Vicente.

JOHN OF SALISBURY
Titles and Subtitles of the *Policraticus*: A Proposal. Van Laarhoven, Jan.

JOHN OF THE CROSS
San Juan de la Cruz y el Problema Místico. Ferraro, Joseph.

JOHN PAUL II
John Paul II's Manifesto on Labor and Vision of a Universal Society. Kuczynski, Janusz.
Karol Wojtyla—John Paul II's Idea of Ultimate Reality and Meaning. Ramos, Alice.
Personalist and Universalistic Aspects of the Idea of Development in the Encyclical *Sollicitudo rei socialis* by John Paul II. Kowalczyk, Stanislaw.

JOHNSON, C
Law in Virtue Ethics. Slote, Michael.
Learning from the Law for Regulatory Science. Cranor, Carl F.
Morality in the First Person Plural. Postema, Gerald J.

JOHNSON, M
The Metaphoric Origins of Objectivity, Subjectivity, and Consciousness in the Direct Perception of Reality. Mulaik, Stanley A.

JOHNSON, P
On Calling God 'Mother'. Harper, William.

JOHNSTON, M
"Reply: Irrationality, Interpretation, and Division" in *Philosophy of Psychology: Debates on Psychological Explanation, Macdonald, Cynthia (ed)*. Hopkins, James.
Self-Deception and Belief Attribution. Hales, Steven D.

JOKE
How to Tell God from the Devil: On the Way to Comedy. Eckardt, A Roy.
Involvement and Joking in Conversation. Norrick, Neal R.

JONAS, H
Hans Jonas's Diagnosis of Nihilism: The Case of Heidegger. Vogel, Lawrence.
L'analyse philosophique jonassienne de la théorie de l'évolution: aspects problématiques. Foppa, Carlo.

JONKES, G
Das unendliche Altern der Moderne: Untersuchungen zur Romantrilogie Gert Jonkes. Schönherr, Ulrich.

JONSEN, A
Ethics Consultation: The *Most* Dangerous Profession: A Reply to Critics (CQ Vol 2, No 4). Scofield, Giles R.

JOURNAL
Journal Writing in an Introductory Philosophy Course. Garns, Rudy.
Manservant as Amanuensis: Sylvester Brounower. Milton, J R.
Toward a Phenomenology of Music: A Musician's Composition Journal. Smith, F Joseph.

JOURNALISM
"Accuracy in Journalism: An Economic Approach" in *Socializing Epistemology: The Social Dimensions of Knowledge, Schmitt, Frederick F (ed)*. Cox, James C and Goldman, Alvin I.
Journalists' Views of Advertiser Pressures on Agricultural News. Reisner, Ann and Walter, Gerry.

JOWETT, B
Plato's Gorgias. Plato and Jowett, Benjamin (trans).

JOY
Rebelión y goce: aproximación a la estética de Camus. Sanabria, Carolina.

JOYCE
The Transfiguration of Everyday Life. Nussbaum, Martha C.

JUAN DE SEGOVIA
William of Ockham, Juan de Segovia, and Heretical Pertinacity. Mann, Jesse D.

JUDAISM
"Buber's Socialist and Political Views: A Critique" in *Thinkers and Teachers of Modern Judaism, Goldsmith, Emanuel S (ed)*. Uffenheimer, Benjamin.
"Franz Rosenzweig's Doctrine of Creation" in *Thinkers and Teachers of Modern Judaism, Goldsmith, Emanuel S (ed)*. Samuelson, Norbert M.

KNOWLEDGE

KOHL, M

"A Reply to My Critics and Friendly Commentators" in *The Nature and Pursuit of Love, Goicoechea, David (ed)*. Singer, Irving.

KOHLBERG, L

Business Ethics: Restrictive or Empowering?. Kjonstad, Bjorn and Willmott, Hugh.

De Piaget á Habermas et Rawls: les Problèmes de la Reconstruction Rationnelle du Jugement Moral chez Kohlberg. Mortier, Freddy.

Habermas, Kohlberg, and the Myth of Expertise. Fairfield, Paul.

Limits to the Effectiveness of Accounting Ethics Education. Shaub, Michael K.

Utilitarismo y Teoría del Desarrollo Moral (I): Análisis crítico de las teorías cognitivas del desarrollo moral y de sus fundamentos Kantianos. Tasset, José Luis.

KOJEVE, A

God, Nature and the End of History. Bedford, David.

KOLAKOWSKI, L

On Leszek Kolakowski's Philosophizing. Morawski, Stefan.

KOLB, D

Recent Work on Hegel's Philosophy of Religion. Dickey, L.

KOLENDA, K

"Konstantin Kolenda: His Life and Times" in *Contributors to the Philosophy of Humanism, Hillar, Marian (ed)*. Kolenda, Pauline.

"Radiance and Religious Belief" in *Contributors to the Philosophy of Humanism, Hillar, Marian (ed)*. Suckiel, Ellen Kappy.

"The Contribution to Humanism of Konstantin Kolenda" in *Contributors to the Philosophy of Humanism, Hillar, Marian (ed)*. Burch, Robert W.

"Too Thin a Self, Too Small a Human" in *Contributors to the Philosophy of Humanism, Hillar, Marian (ed)*. Kegley, Jacquelyn A K.

KONINCK, C

Human Dignity and the Common Good in the Aristotelian-Thomistic Tradition. Smith, Michael A.

KONNER, M

Response to Rottschaefer, Beckley, and Konner. Gustafson, James M.

KOPELMAN, L

Commentary on "Normal Grief: Good or Bad? Health or Disease?". Wise, Thomas N.

KORAN

Islam and the Concept of Tolerance and Co-Existence. Sho'ala, Abdulnabi Al.

KORCZAK, J

Positives Paradox: Entwurf einer neostrukturalistischen Religionspädagogik. Beuscher, Bernd.

KORNBLITH, H

Reply to Hilary Kornblith's "In Defense of Deductive Inference". Lycan, William G.

KOTARBINSKI, T

Even When the Devil Says He Is Telling the Truth, He Is Lying. Kolakowski, Leszek.

Tadeusz Kotarbinski's Independent Ethics. Kotarbinska, Janina.

KOZELJ, I

Sanc and Kozelj—Two Slovenian Philosophers in Croatia. Belic, Miljenko.

KRAEMER, H

Platons Hypomnemata: Die Genese des Platonismus aus dem Gedächtnis der Schrift. Thiel, Detlef.

KRATOCHVIL, J

The Philosophy and the History of Philosophy in the Neoscholastic Interpretation of Josef Kratochvil. Glombik, Czeslaw.

KRATZER, A

"Individual-Level Predicates as Inherent Generics" in *The Generic Book, Carlson, Gregory N (ed)*. Chierchia, Gennaro.

KRAUT, R

"The Ultimate End of Action: A Critique of Richard Kraut's *Aristotle on the Human Good*" in *The Crossroads of Norm and Nature, Sim, May (ed)*. Roche, Timothy.

KRECZ, C

Reply to Krecz. Browning, Douglas.

KRETZMANN, N

CODA. Griffiths, Paul J.

Providence, Eternity, and Human Freedom: A Reply to Stump and Kretzmann. Widerker, David.

Reply to Critics. Alston, William P.

KRIECK, E

Heidegger im Kontext: Gesamtüberblick zum NS-Engagement der Universitätsphilosophen. Leaman, George.

KRIPKE, S

"Pierre, Saul, Ruth, and Bob and a Puzzle about Belief" in *Modality, Morality, and Belief, Sinnott-Armstrong, Walter (ed)*. Fogelin, Robert.

"Wittgenstein, Kripke, and the 'Paradox' of Meaning" in *Wittgenstein and Contemporary Philosophy, Teghrarian, Souren (ed)*. Teghrarian, Souren.

Referenztheorien in der analytischen Philosophie. Kellerwessel, Wulf.

A Guide to Truth Predicates in the Modern Era. Sheard, Michael.

Dónde se Encuentra el Enigma Sobre la Creencia?. Sosa, David.

El Enigma de Kripke: Una Solución Formal-Intensional. Ramos, Pedro.

Gemeinschaft, Normativität, Praxis: Debatte zu L Wittgenstein's Regelbegriff. Nießen, Peter.

Methodological Reflections on Two Kripkean Strategies. Ramachandran, Murali.

On an Argument about Reference to Future Individuals. Oppy, Graham.

Spikes on Kripke. Sartorelli, Joseph J.

Suivre une règle: Wittgenstein et les sciences cognitives. Pinkas, Daniel.

The Problem of Rule-Following in Compositional Semantics. Shogenji, Tomoji.

The Unstatability of Kripkean Scepticisms. Read, Rupert.

Un Esbozo de Solución a un Enigma de Kripke. Orayen, Raúl.

KRISTEVA, J

Reading Theory: An Introduction to Lacan, Derrida, and Kristeva. Payne, Michael.

The Philosophy of Jonathan Edwards. Daniel, Stephen H.

X-Sample: Gespräche am Rande der Zeit. Miessgang, Thomas.

KRUEGER, F

Heidegger im Kontext: Gesamtüberblick zum NS-Engagement der Universitätsphilosophen. Leaman, George.

KRUSE, F

Response. Smith, John E.

KUCZYNSKI, J

Dialogue and Universalism: A Practical Application to Africa. Eboh, Marie Pauline.

Philosophy of Universalism and the Concept of Human Nature. Wiercinski, Andrzej.

Positive Universalism: The Universal Language of Science Used to Construct a Universal Metatheory. Hubert, Jerzy Z.

The Ideas of Contemporary Universalim and Medicine. Imielinski, Christian.

Universalism and the Meaning of History. Mitias, Michael H.

KUHLMANN, W

Ist die Tranzendentalpragmatik letztebegründet oder holistisch?. Bremer, Manuel E.

KUHN, T

Das Jenseits der Philosophie: Wider das dualistische Erkenntnisprinzip. Mitterer, Josef and Engelmann, Peter (ed).

El Cambio Científico y el Modelo de Solución de Problemas de L Laudan. Martínez de Velasco, Jesús.

Kuhn's *The Structure of Scientific Revolutions* Revisited. Kindi, Vasso P.

La Discusión Lakatos-Kuhn. Alcalá Campos, Raúl.

Post-positivisme en de ontwikkeling van wiskunde. Glas, Eduard.

Rahner, Popper and Kuhn: A Note on Some Critical Parallels in Science and Theology. Guarino, Thomas G.

Seeing and Paradigms in the Chemical Revolution. Shelton, Jim.

Three Kinds of Incommensurability Thesis. Simmons, Lance.

Underdetermination. McMullin, Ernan.

KUIPERS, T

Kuipers over waarheidsgelijkenis en wetenschappelijk realisme. Derksen, Ton.

KULP, C

"Epistemology" Reburied. Dicker, Georges.

A Reply to Christopher Kulp's "Dewey, Indeterminacy, and the Spectator Theory of Knowledge". Pratt, Scott L.

Rejoinder to Scott L Pratt. Kulp, Christopher B.

KUNDERA

Old and New: The Body, Subjectivity, and Ethics. McAleer, Graham.

KUNG, H

Reflections on World Peace through Peace among Religions—A Confucian Perspective. Liu, Shu-Hsien.

KURZON, D

Indefinite Noun Phrases in Legal Texts: Use, Function and Construction of Mental Spaces. Lundquist, Lita.

When Silence May Mean Derision. Akman, Varol.

KUSSER, A

The Mutual Deteination of Wants and Benefits. Broome, John.

KUWAITI

Public Relations Ethics: Ivy Lee, Hill and Knowlton, and the Gulf War. Marlin, Randal.

KYBURG, H

"Closure and Consistency" in *Modality, Morality, and Belief, Sinnott-Armstrong, Walter (ed)*. Levi, Isaac.

KYMLICKA, W

Can Liberalism Be Communitarian?. Taylor, Charles.

Kymlicka, Liberalism, and Respect for Cultural Minorities. Tomasi, John.

Revising the Self. Beiner, Ronald.

The Independent Value of Freedom. Carter, Ian.

The Value of Cultural Belonging: Expanding Kymlicka's Theory. Nickel, James.

Transformation oder Verteidigung: Zu Will Kymlickas liberaler politischer Philosophie. Frank, Martin.

Utilitarianism, Deontology, and the Priority of Right. Freeman, Samuel.

LABOR

"Constituting the Modern State" in *Radical Philosophy of Law, Caudill, David S (ed)*. Swidorski, Carl.

"El Marxismo Analítico y el Problema Moral del Trabajo" in *Temas Actuales de Filosofía, Palacios, María Julia (ed)*. Gallichio, Santiago.

"Fichtes und Prodhons Begriff des Eigentums als Recht auf Arbeit" in *Das geistige Erbe Europas, Buhr, Manfred (ed)*. Hahn, Karl.

"Post-Marxism and Class" in *Marxism in the Postmodern Age, Callari, Antonio (ed)*. Sandler, Blair and Diskin, Jonathan.

"Situating the Capitalist State" in *Marxism in the Postmodern Age, Callari, Antonio (ed)*. Lebowitz, Michael A.

"The Nature and Role of Professional Codes in Modern Society" in *Ethics and the Professions, Chadwick, Ruth (ed)*. Häyry, Heta and Häyry, Matti.

Foundations of Analytical Marxism (Volume I). Roemer, John E (ed).

Idéer om Arbete. Hansson, Sven Ove.

Logik und Arbeit. Hartmann, Bruno.

LABOR

Socialism After Communism: The New Market Socialism. Pierson, Christopher.

Values, Work, Education: The Meanings of Work. Natale, Samuel M (ed) and Rothschild, Brian M (ed).

Die methodologische Funktion des Verhältnisses von "Herr und Knecht" in der Philosophie Hegels. Kumamoto, Yasuhiro.

Diferença entre Alienação e Estranhamento nos Manuscritos Econômico-Filosóficos (1844), de Karl Marx. Ferreira Chagas, Eduardo.

John Paul II's Manifesto on Labor and Vision of a Universal Society. Kuczynski, Janusz.

La alienación del trabajo según la perspectiva del marxismo analítico. Gallichio, Santiago.

Marx and German Idealism: Labour and the Transcendental Synthesis. Moggach, Douglas.

That a Worker's Labour Cannot be a Commodity. Nelson, John O.

What's Wrong with Exploitation?. Schwartz, Justin K.

LABRIOLA, A

Frammenti Politici di Antonio Labriola con una Postilla Bibliografica. Miccolis, Stefano.

LACAN, J

"Postmodern Law and Subjectivity: Lacan and the Linguistic Turn" in *Radical Philosophy of Law, Caudill, David S (ed)*. Milovanovic, Dragan.

"Vom Omphalos zum Phallus" in *Macht Geschlechter Differenz, Müller-Funk, Wolfgang (ed)*. Bronfen, Elisabeth.

"Weibliche" Ästhetik? Möglichkeiten und Grenzen einer Subversion von Codes. Lummerding, Susanne.

Althusser: A Critical Reader. Elliott, Gregory (ed).

Auflösen, Untersuchen, Aufwecken: Psychoanalyse und andere Analysen. Ruhs, August (ed) and Seitter, Walter (ed).

Positives Paradox: Entwurf einer neostrukturalistischen Religionspädagogik. Beuscher, Bernd.

Reading Theory: An Introduction to Lacan, Derrida, and Kristeva. Payne, Michael.

Sinn, Unsinn, Sein: Philosophische Studien über Psychoanalyse, Dekonstruktion und Genealogie. Gerlich, Siegfried.

Der audio-visuelle Kontrakt—der Lärm um das Reale. Zizek, Slavoj.

Hypostatizing Thanatos: Lacan's Analysis of the Ego. Whitebook, Joel.

La mirada errante: de la "Spaltung" en Lacan, al "caos-cosmos" de Deleuze. Gonzalo I Carbó, Antoni.

Lacan and the Enlightenment: Antigone's Choice. Richardson, William J.

Lacan, Kant, and Sade. Sample, Ruth.

Political Action and the Unconscious: Arendt and Lacan on Decentering the Subject. Dolan, Frederick M.

Psychoanalysis and Ideology: Bakhtin, Lacan, and Zizek. Baker, Harold D.

Vital Signs: The *Place* of Memory in Psychoanalysis. Shepherdson, Charles.

LACHS, J

Santayana and Making Claims on the Spiritual Truth about Matters of Fact. Levinson, Henry Samuel.

LACORDAIRE, H

La Polemica di Leroux contro Lacordaire e Malthus sulla Questione Sociale. Fiorentino, Fernando.

LAIRD, J

John Laird and *The Idea of Value*. Attfield, Robin.

LAKATOS, I

La Discusión Lakatos-Kuhn. Alcalá Campos, Raúl.

Post-positivisme en de ontwikkeling van wiskunde. Glas, Eduard.

LAKOFF, G

The Metaphoric Origins of Objectivity, Subjectivity, and Consciousness in the Direct Perception of Reality. Mulaik, Stanley A.

LAMB, C

'Essence' and 'Accident' in Lamb's Elia Essays. Mulvihill, James.

LAMBDA CALCULUS

Enumerators of Lambda Terms are Reducing Constructively. Barendregt, H.

From Finite to Infinite Lambda Calculi. Kennaway, Richard (& others).

Normal Forms in Combinatory Logic. Johann, Patricia.

Some Results on Numeral Systems in Lambda-Calculus. Intrigila, Benedetto.

Strong Normalization in Type Systems: A Model Theoretic Approach. Terlouw, Jan.

LAMONT, C

"The Philosophy of Corliss Lamont" in *Contributors to the Philosophy of Humanism, Hillar, Marian (ed)*. Lattie, George.

LAND

Privatizing Public Lands. Lehmann, Scott.

LANDSCAPE

Cultural Landscapes and Environmental Ethics: The Case of Puslinch Township's Historic Roadside Trees. Pollock-Ellwand, Nancy.

LANE, R

Wealth and Happiness. Wilson, James Q.

LANGAN, T

Investigative Interviewing: A Phenomenological Approach to a Universal Method. Kidd, James W.

LANGER, S

Communion and its Limits: Expression and Communication in Susanne Langer's Aesthetics. McGandy, Michael.

Does Knowledge Entail Justification?. Carrier, L S.

Langer on the Arts as Cognitive. Reimer, Bennett.

Langer, Language, and Art. Gill, Jerry H.

Philosophy in a New Key: An Interpretation. Price, Kingsley.

Philosophy of Music Education in a Slightly New Key. Hansen, Forest.

Susanne K Langer's Conception of 'Symbol'—Making Connections through Ambiguity. Nelson, Beatrice K.

Susanne Langer's Theory of Symbolism: An Analysis and Extension. Reichling, Mary J.

The Form of Feeling. Yob, Iris M.

LANGUAGE

see also Adjective, Formal Language, Metalanguage, Natural Language, Noun, Pronoun, Religious Language, Semantics, Sign Language, Verb

"1879?" in *Reading Putnam, Clark, Peter (ed)*. Boolos, George.

"A Central Problem for a Speech-Dispositional Account of Logic and Language" in *Perspectives on Quine, Barrett, Robert (ed)*. Berger, Alan.

"A Good Rhetoric Is Possible" in *The Philosophy of Paul Ricoeur, Hahn, Lewis Edwin (ed)*. Lanigan, Richard L.

"Acciones Complejas e Indiferencias Adverbiales" in *Temas Actuales de Filosofía, Palacios, María Julia (ed)*. Oller, Carlos A.

"Acerca de la Distinción entre Reglas Constitutivas y Reglas Regulativas" in *Temas Actuales de Filosofía, Palacios, María Julia (ed)*. Gentile, Nélida.

"Archive of Pure Language" in *The 1994 Annual of Hermeneutics and Social Concern, Lawler, Justus George (ed)*. Britt, Brian.

"Aspectos Semióticos del Tractatus" in *Temas Actuales de Filosofía, Palacios, María Julia (ed)*. Maltese Guerra, Luis F.

"Back in the CCCP" in *Probability and Conditionals, Eells, Ellery (ed)*. Hall, Ned.

"Carnap's Principle of Tolerance, Empiricism, and Conventionalism" in *Reading Putnam, Clark, Peter (ed)*. Ricketts, Thomas.

"Changing the Subject: Rorty and Contemporary Rhetorical Theory" in *Recovering Pragmatism's Voice, Langsdorf, Lenore (ed)*. Horne, Janet S.

"De Re Belief, Action Explanations, and the Essential Indexical" in *Modality, Morality, and Belief, Sinnott-Armstrong, Walter (ed)*. Sosa, Ernest.

"El Lenguaje como Límite en el 2do. Wittgenstein" in *Temas Actuales de Filosofía, Palacios, María Julia (ed)*. Scotto, Silvia C.

"Ens multipliciter dicitur: The Ingardian Variant of an Old Thesis" in *Kunst und Ontologie, Wlodzimierz, Galewicz (ed)*. Haefliger, Gregor.

"Epistemologie, Sprachanalyse und Semiotik bei H Gomperz" in *Heinrich Gomperz, Karl Popper und die österreichische Philosophie, Seiler, Martin (ed)*. Seiler, Martin.

"Foucault: The Twofold Games of Language" in *Reconstructing Foucault, Miguel-Alfonso, Ricardo (ed)*. De Peretti, Cristina.

"Gadamer's Realism: The 'Belongingness' of Word and Reality" in *Hermeneutics and Truth, Wachterhauser, Brice (ed)*. Wachterhauser, Brice.

"History as Theory: One Linguist's View" in *Peirce and Contemporary Thought: Philosophical Inquiries, Ketner, Kenneth Laine (ed)*. Shapiro, Michael.

"Holism: The Polarized Spectrum" in *Holism: A Consumer Update, Fodor, Jerry (ed)*. Peruzzi, Alberto.

"Identity, Education, and the Experience of Language" in *Identity, Culture, and Education, Smeyers, Paul (ed)*. Larrosa, Jorge.

"Inferential Roles, Quine, and Mad Holism" in *Holism: A Consumer Update, Fodor, Jerry (ed)*. Berg, Jonathan.

"Intellectual Autobiography of Paul Ricoeur" in *The Philosophy of Paul Ricoeur, Hahn, Lewis Edwin (ed)*. Ricoeur, Paul.

"Is Content Holism Incoherent?" in *Holism: A Consumer Update, Fodor, Jerry A (ed)*. Ludwig, Kirk A.

"Is Intentional Ascription Intrinsically Normative?" in *Dennett and his Critics, Dahlbom, Bo (ed)*. Fodor, Jerry A and Lepore, Ernest.

"Language as Bearer of Meaning: The Phenomenology of Roman Ingarden" in *Kunst und Ontologie, Wlodzimierz, Galewicz (ed)*. Gumpel, Liselotte.

"Language, Music, and the Body" in *Intersections: Nineteenth-Century Philosophy and Contemporary Theory, Rajan, Tilottama (ed)*. Rajan, Tilottama.

"Locke on Meaning and Signification" in *Locke's Philosophy, Rogers, G A J (ed)*. Losonsky, Michael.

"Locke's Philosophy of Language" in *The Cambridge Companion to Locke, Chappell, Vere (ed)*. Guyer, Paul.

"Ludwig Wittgenstein, los Juegos del Lenguaje y la Etica" in *Temas Actuales de Filosofía, Palacios, María Julia (ed)*. Ambrosini, Cristina.

"Meaning and Language" in *The Cambridge Companion to Husserl, Smith, Barry (ed)*. Simons, Peter.

"Naive and Sentimental Hermeneutics: Keeping Language Open" in *The Philosophy of Paul Ricoeur, Hahn, Lewis Edwin (ed)*. Rudnick, Hans H.

"On Ricoeur's Analysis of Time and Narration" in *The Philosophy of Paul Ricoeur, Hahn, Lewis Edwin (ed)*. Stevens, Bernard.

"Paul Ricoeur and Literary Theory" in *The Philosophy of Paul Ricoeur, Hahn, Lewis Edwin (ed)*. Valdés, Mario J.

"Peirce and Communication" in *Peirce and Contemporary Thought: Philosophical Inquiries, Ketner, Kenneth Laine (ed)*. Habermas, Jürgen.

"Peirce on Language and Reference" in *Peirce and Contemporary Thought: Philosophical Inquiries, Ketner, Kenneth Laine (ed)*. Hilpinen, Risto.

"Philosophy and Language in Leibniz" in *The Cambridge Companion to Leibniz, Jolley, Nicholas (ed)*. Rutherford, Donald.

"Philosophy of Language and Philosophy of Communication" in *Recovering Pragmatism's Voice, Langsdorf, Lenore (ed)*. Langsdorf, Lenore.

"Pragmatism, Feminism, and the Linguistic Turn" in *Feminist Contentions, Benhabib, Seyla (& others)*. Fraser, Nancy.

"Predicados y Propiedades" in *Temas Actuales de Filosofía, Palacios, María Julia (ed)*. Stigol, Nora.

LANGUAGE

The Philosophy of Paul Ricoeur. Hahn, Lewis Edwin (ed).

The Platonic Odyssey: A Philosophical-Literary Inquiry into the "Phaedo". Gilead, Amihud.

The Semiotic Self. Wiley, Norbert.

The Site of Our Lives: The Self and the Subject from Emerson to Foucault. Hans, James S.

The Stop. Appelbaum, David.

Thinking About Logic: An Introduction to the Philosophy of Logic. Read, Stephen.

Thinking. Kirby, Gary R and Goodpaster, Jeffery R.

Transzendenz-"Relation": Zum Transzendenzbezug in der Philosophie Emmanuel Levinas'. Esterbauer, Reinhold.

Truth: A Primer. Schmitt, Frederick F.

Understanding Logic. Flage, Daniel E.

Understanding Vision: An Interdisciplinary Perspective. Humphreys, Glyn W (ed).

Vie della scrittura: Frege e la svolta linguistica. Penco, Carlo.

Ways of Worldmaking. Goodman, Nelson.

Without God or His Doubles: Realism, Relativism and Rorty. Vaden House, David.

Wittgenstein and Contemporary Philosophy. Teghrarian, Souren (ed).

Wittgenstein on Mind and Language. Stern, David G.

Wittgensteinian Themes: Essays 1978-1989. Malcolm, Norman and von Wright, Georg Henrik (ed).

Work, Education, and Leadership: Essays in the Philosophy of Education. Howard, V A and Scheffler, Israel.

A Form of Metaphysical Realism. Smart, J J C.

A J Ayer's Notion of Philosophical Analysis. Balkrishnan P, Hemjith.

A Language for the Description of God, Part I: A Unique Language for a Unique Object. Graves, David and Alon, Ilai.

A Modern History Theory of Function. Godfrey-Smith, Peter.

A New Look at Personal Identity. Hamilton, Andy.

A Note about a Quinean Argument against Direct Reference. Oppy, Graham.

A Note on Frege's and Russell's Influence on Wittgenstein's *Tractatus*. McDonough, Richard.

A Paradox of Meaning. Schiffer, Stephen.

A Problem in the Frege-Church Theory of Sense and Denotation. Salmon, Nathan.

A Problem with the Minimalist Theory of Truth. Mikel, Anton.

A Prototype View of Context and Linguistic Behavior: Context Prototypes and Talk. Glover, Kelly D.

A Radical Interpretation of Davidson: Reply to Alvarez. Glock, Hans-Johann.

A Revised Formulation of the Logic of Sense and Denotation: Alternative (1). Church, Alonzo.

Against Rationalistic Pragmatics. Kopytko, Roman.

Algunas Precisiones Sobre el Lenguaje y la Paronimia en Aristóteles. Femenías, María Luisa.

Alice in Wittgenstein: Inside the Great Mirror. Gray, Christopher Berry.

All'inizio è il linguaggio. Moriconi, Enrico.

Ambiguità e Semiosi. Morpurgo-Tagliabue, Guido.

An Argument for Holism. Block, Ned.

An Understanding of Contemporary Foundationalism. Lenka, Laxminarayan.

Anaphoric Pronouns in Very Late Medieval Supposition Theory. Parsons, Terence.

Andersonian Deontic Logic. Mares, Edwin D.

Annäherung an Derrida oder: Wer spät kommt, den belohnt das Lesen. Naumann-Beyer, Waltraud.

Anscombe and the First Person. Garrett, Brian J.

Anscombe and the Self-Reference Rule. O'Brien, Lucy F.

Aproximación al Morfema: Romanticismo Alemán. Market, Oswaldo.

Are Quine's Two Dogmas Still Dogmas. Kanthamani, A.

Are Some *Propositions* Empirically Necessary?. Peterson, Philip.

Armistice in the Recent Battle of the Books: Paul de Man, Claudio Guillén, and History. Miner, Earl.

Art and Family Resemblances. Beardsmore, R W.

Art and Reality. Dilman, Ilham.

Art, Pleasure, and Play. Graham, Gordon.

Assertoric vs Modal Syllogistic. Striker, Gisela.

Asymmetry in Attitudes and the Nature of Time. Gallois, André.

Autobiography and Philosophy: Variations on a Theme of Wittgenstein. Szabados, Béla.

B-Series Temporal Order in Dogen's Theory of Time. Vorenkamp, Dirck.

Bachtins Polyphonie der Stimmen: Ein Dialogkonzept zwischen Moderne und Postmoderne. Friedrich, Clemens.

Begging the Question as a Pragmatic Fallacy. Walton, Douglas N.

Begriff und Gegenstand. Frege, Gottlob.

Being of Two Minds: Belief with Doubt. Salmon, Nathan.

Belief, Knowledge and the Origins of Content. Guttenplan, Samuel.

Belief, Substitution, and Logical Structure. Taschek, William.

Beyond Reductionism in Rhetorical Theories of Meaning. Cherwitz, Richard A and Darwin, Thomas J.

Bhartrhari's Philosophy of Relation between Word and Meaning. Tiwari, D N.

Biblical Speech and Modern Consciousness in the Post-Modern Age: The Double Paradox of Modernism. Zelechow, Bernard.

Bildliche Sprechakte. Taube, Volkmar.

Bioethics in the Language of the Law. Schneider, Carl E.

Boër and Lycan's *Knowing Who*. Richard, Mark E.

Bradley's Regress, the Copula and the Unity of the Proposition. Gaskin, Richard.

Cambridge Philosophers II: Ludwig Wittgenstein. Anscombe, G E M.

Carlos Moya's Regress-Problem. Vermazen, Bruce.

Characterizing Classifying: Explicating a Biological Distinction. Lambert, Karel and Simons, Peter.

Ciencia Nueva y Escritura: Nota Sobre Una Nota de Derrida, en Torno a Vico. Busom Zabala, Rais.

Classifying Conditionals: The Traditional Way is Right. Bennett, Jonathan.

Cognitive Processes and Prosodic Encoding: Speakers' Adaptation to Discourse Conditions. Caelen-Haumont; G.

Cognitive Processes and Social Norms in Natural Discourse at the Marketplace. Lindenfeld, Jacqueline.

Colonialism and the Language Question: A Reply to Godfrey Tangwa. Uroh, Chris.

Comment on Professor Johnson's Article on Computer Language. Sundararajan, Louise.

Commentary on Sayre's "Why Plato Never Had a Theory of Forms". Griswold, Charles.

Commentary: On Vague Objects, Fuzzy Logic, and Fractal Boundaries. Copeland, B Jack.

Commentary: Proliferating Conceptions of Truth: Comments on McGee and McLaughlin. Hyde, Dominic.

Commentary: Some Remarks on Vagueness and a Dynamic Conception of Language. Tappenden, Jamie.

Commentary: The Epistemic Conception of Vagueness: Comments on Wright. Sorensen, Roy.

Comments on "Moore's Paradox and Self-Knowledge". Albritton, Rogers.

Common Sources for the Semiotic of Charles Peirce and John Poinsot. Beuchot, Mauricio and Deely, John.

Compositionality in Cognitive Models: The Real Issue. Butler, Keith.

Concept Development and Computation of Meaning Thought and Language by Vygotsky. Forest, F and Siksou, M.

Conditional Reasoning and Conditional Logic. Lycan, William G.

Conservatism in Epistemology. Christensen, David.

Consumerism and Language Acquisition. Mercier, Adèle.

Conversational Implicature. Bach, Kent.

Conversing With Other Minds: A Symposium of Themes. Kaplan, Andrew.

Counterfactuals: Ambiguities, True Premises, and Knowledge. Kvart, Igal.

Counting on Number: Plato on the Goodness of *Arithmos*. Roochnik, David L.

Criteria: The State of the Debate. Addis, Mark.

Critique of Pure Capacity. Segerdahl, Pär.

Das Metasprachenproblem und die Bedingungen einer welterschliessenden, formal selbständigen Sprache. Ofsti, Audun.

Das Wort Im Leben und das Wort in der Poesie. Volosinov, Valentin N.

Davidson's Sentences and Wittgenstein's Builders. Perry, John.

De la Utilidad de la Dialéctica. Campos Benítez, Juan Manuel.

De ludo veritatis: L'esperienza del vero nel pensiero di Niccolò da Cusa. Egger, Jean-Luc.

Definiteness and Knowability. Williamson, Timothy.

Degrees of Iconicity in the Lexicon. Waugh, Linda R.

Derrida and Ideographic Poetics. Cheng, Jiewei.

Descriptions, Indexicals, and Belief Reports: Some Dilemmas (But Not the Ones You Expect). Schiffer, Stephen.

Descriptions, référence et anaphore. Vallée, Richard.

Diagrams and Metaphors: Iconic Aspects in Language. Hiraga, Masako K.

Dialectic and the Syllogism. Smith, Robin.

Dialectic at a Standstill. Arsenault, Joseph and Brinkley, Tony.

Die Idee der Nation als Implikat der Interpersonalitäts- und Geschichtstheorie. Hahn, Karl.

Die Rationalitätsbegriffe des Handelns: Eine Grundlegung zu einer Typologie sozialen Handelns. Preyer, Gerhard.

Die Verneinung. Frege, Gottlob.

Die Zurückführung des Möglichen auf das Wirkliche. Kügler, Peter.

Direct Deductive Computation on Discourse Representation Structures. Reyle, Uwe and Gabbay, Dov M.

Direct Reference, Mental Causation and Consciousness: Old Wine in New Bottles. Palmer, Anthony.

Disambiguation of Language: The Ultimate Reality and Meaning of Computer Studies. Johnson, Julia A.

Discontinuity in Categorical Grammar. Morrill, Glyn.

Displacing Descartes: Philosophical Hermeneutics and Rhetorical Studies. Bineham, Jeffery L.

Disquotational Truth and Factually Defective Discourse. Field, Hartry.

Does Knowledge Entail Justification?. Carrier, L S.

Dónde se Encuentra el Enigma Sobre la Creencia?. Sosa, David.

Dos Concepciones del Lenguaje. Tomasini Bassols, Alejandro.

Dos Nociones de Objeto en el *Tractatus*. Tomasini Bassols, Alejandro.

Dynamic Dependency Grammar. Milward, David.

E-Type Pronouns, 1-Sums, and Donkey Anaphora. Lappin, Shalom and Francez, Nissim.

El Concepto, Como Signo Natural: Una Polémica Acerca de Ockham. Velázquez, Lorena.

El Enigma de Kripke: Una Solución Formal-Intensional. Ramos, Pedro.

El Frege Kantiano. Rosado Haddock, Guillermo E, Hjorth, Greg and Spinas, Otmar.

El Individuo y la Nación: El Sujeto y lo Absoluto en las Filosofías del Lenguaje de Humboldt y Fichte. Pérez, Jorge Navarro.

El Lenguaje Sobre Dios en Juan Escoto Eriúgena. Murillo, Ildefonso.

El Mundo y el Arbol, Tareas de la Mirada. Ruiz Moreno, Luisa.

Emphatic Speech Style—With Special Focus on the Prosodic Signalling of Heightened Emotive Involvement in Conversation. Selting, Margret.

Empty Names. Braun, David.

Es la Matemática un lenguaje?. Quesada, Daniel.

LANGUAGE

The Idea of God in Feminist Philosophy. Suchocki, Marjorie Hewitt.

The Idea of Social Life. Sandelands, Lloyd E.

The Influence of the Rhetoric on the Ethics. Rigotti, Francesca.

The Language of Thought and Connectionism. Jutronic-Tihomirovic, Dunja.

The Language-of-Thought Relation and Its Implications. Schiffer, Stephen.

The Languages of Thought. Kaye, Lawrence J.

The Logic of Essence. Fine, Kit.

The Logical Status of 'Exists'. Stirton, William R.

The Metaphoric Nature of Coding: Toward a Theory of Utterance. Zaitseva, Valentina.

The Miracle of Counterfactuals: Counterexamples to Lewis's World Ordering. Krasner, Daniel and Heller, Mark.

The Mishap at Reichenbach Fall: Singular vs General Causation. Hitchcock, Christopher Read.

The Nature of Mathematics: Towards a Social Constructivist Account. Ernest, Paul.

The Neuropsychology of Communication: Spontaneous and Symbolic Aspects. Buck, Ross.

The Problem of Iconicity. Radwanska-Williams, Joanna.

The Problem of Objectivity. Davidson, Donald.

The Problem of Rule-Following in Compositional Semantics. Shogenji, Tomoji.

The Problem of Self-Identification. O'Brien, Lucy F.

The Problem of the Many, Many Composition Questions, and Naive Mereology. Sanford, David H.

The Ramsey Test Revisited. Lindström, Sten and Rabinowicz, Wlodzimierz.

The Rationality of Human Communication: On the Relationship Between Consensual, Strategic, and Systems Rationality. Apel, Karl Otto.

The Representation of Causation and Hume's Two Definitions of 'Cause'. Garrett, Don.

The Rhetoric of Feminist Writings. Nuyen, A T.

The Right of Silence: A Socio-Pragmatic Model of Interpretation. Kurzon, Dennis.

The Role of Dissociation in Redeeming Knowledge Claims: Nineteenth-Century Shakers' Epistemological Resistance to Decline. Olson, Kathryn M.

The Sanskrit of Science. Staal, Frits.

The Script Rose. Catalano, Joseph S.

The Seduction of Abduction: Peirce's Theory of Signs and Indeterminacy in Language. Melrose, Robin.

The Sense of Communication. Heck Jr, Richard G.

The Shoals of Language: Michael Dummett: *The Seas of Language*. Rosen, Gideon.

The Social Stance. Gärdenfors, Peter.

The Sphota Doctrine of Bhartrhari. Pathiraj R.

The Structure of the Skeptical Argument. Brueckner, Anthony.

The Vocation to Be a Philosopher. Andrews, Philip.

Thinking in Neurons: Comments on Stephen Schiffer's "The Language-of-Thought Relation and Its Implications". Yagisawa, Takashi.

Thought and Language: On the Line of Demarcation between Animal and Human Abilities. Strauss, D F M.

Three-Concept Monte: Explanation, Implementation and Systematicity. Matthews, Robert J.

Time and Change. Scott, Michael.

Tolerance and Metalanguages in Carnap's *Logical Syntax of Language*. DeVidi, David and Solomon, Graham.

Toward a Defensible Bootstrapping. Mitchell, Sam.

Toward a Pragmatics of Emotive Communication. Caffi, Claudia and Janney, Richard W.

Toward a Relational Theory of Meaning. Cherwitz, Richard A and Darwin, Thomas J.

Towards a Winograd/Flores Semantics. Mott, Peter.

Transcendental Subjectivity Meets Transcendental Grammar. Pradhan, R C.

Translation as a Cultural-Philosophical Problem: Towards a Phenomenology of Culture. Ogawa, Tadashi.

Transvaluationism: A Dionysian Approach to Vagueness. Horgan, Terence.

Truth and Control in Being and Language. Krummel, J.

Truth Wronged (on Crispin Wright, *Truth and Objectivity*). Rumfitt, Ian.

Truth, Correspondence, and Success. Leeds, Stephen.

Truth, Knowledge, and Reality. Lafont, Cristina.

Truthlikeness, Translation, and Approximate Causal Explanation. Barnes, Eric.

Two (Related) World Views. Zalta, Edward N.

Un Dérangement Modulaire de la Compétence Linguistique. Pietroski, Paul.

Understanding Rules. Nemirow, Laurence E.

Une crítica al realismo desde la teoría del significado. Toribio, Josefa.

Unsettled Problems with Vague Truth. Mills, Andrew.

Uses and Misuses of Frege's Ideas. Hintikka, Jaakko and Sandu, Gabriel.

Utilitarianism and Future Mistakes: Another Look. Curran, Angela.

Vacuous Singular Terms. Adams, Fred and Stecker, Robert.

Vagueness and Utility: The Semantics of Common Nouns. Parikh, Rohit.

Vagueness, Indiscernibility, and Pragmatics: Comments on Burns. Varzi, Achille C.

Vagueness: Welcome to the Quicksand. Tye, Michael.

Validità sintattica vs invalidità sintattica in Geiger. Cabrera, Carlos Alarcón.

Van Inwagen's New Clothes. Bigelow, John.

Veranlasste die Universalienlehre Ockham, die Prädikation zuletzt ohne ein intentionales Moment zu verstehen?. Liske, Michael-Thomas.

Vico y la Poética de la Modernidad. Zacarés Pamblanco, Amparo.

Vigotsky and Artificial Intelligence: What Could Cognitive Psychology Possibly Be About?. Harré, Rom.

Vives, Calderón y Vico: Lenguaje Metafórico y Filosofar Ingenioso. Hidalgo-Serna, Emilio.

Vyadi and The Realist Theory of Meaning. Ganeri, Jonardon.

Was leister die semantische Interpretation der Wahrheit. Padilla-Gálvez, Jesús.

Was sind reflexive Sprechhandlungen? Bemerkungen zum Verhältnis von Reflexion und Sprache. Ulfig, Alexander.

What *Is* The Connection Principle?. Fodor, Jerry A and Lepore, Ernie.

What Is Character?. Braun, David.

What is Quine's View of Truth?. Davidson, Donald.

What Mathematics Is About. Edidin, Aron.

What's in a Word? Bring on the Seals and the Sheep (In Response to Hoffmann). Edwards, Derek.

When Is If?. Yoes Jr, M G.

When Silence May Mean Derision. Akman, Varol.

Whorf's Empty Gasoline Drum and the Pope's Missing Wife. Edwards, Derek.

Why Plato Never Had a Theory of Forms. Sayre, Kenneth.

Wittgenstein and Aesthetics. Armstrong, D M.

Wittgenstein and Peirce on Meaning: The Evolution from Absolutism to Fallibilism. Boghossian, Peter G and Drewniak, Erik.

Wittgenstein Bibliographie 1992-93. Haller, Rudolf, Henrichs, Norbert and Roser, Andreas.

Wittgenstein e o Domínio da Gramática: A Ruptura com o Tractatus. Vergílio G Cuter, Joao.

Wittgenstein on Private Language: Exorcising the Ghost from the Machine. Hitchcock, Christopher Read.

Wittgenstein, ill Linguaggio e l'Interpretazione. Perissinotto, Luigi.

Wittgenstein, Truth-Functions and Generality. Scanlan, Michael.

Women and Language in Susan Griffin's *Woman and Nature: The Roaring Inside Her*. Cantrell, Carol H.

Worldly Indeterminacy of Identity. Parsons, Terence and Woodruff, Peter.

Zur hermeneutischen Transformation der Sprachanalyse. Tietz, Udo.

Zweierlei Holismus: Überlegungen zur Interpretationstheorie D Davidsons. Siebelt, Frank.

'Do You Understand What You are Reading?'. Sharpe, Eric J.

'Essence' and 'Accident' in Lamb's Elia Essays. Mulvihill, James.

'We Shall Bear the Image of the Man of Heaven': Theology and the Concept of Truth. Marshall, Bruce D.

LANGUAGE GAME

Philosophische Praxis. Stastny, Roland.

Lenguaje religioso y racionalidad argumentativa. Ortiz, Gustavo.

LAPLACE

Broadening the Picture of Science in Revolutionary France: Adding Du Pont and Restif to Lavoisier and Laplace. Conner, Clifford D.

LARGE CARDINALS

A Dilemma in the Philosophy of Set Theory. Schindler, Ralf-Dieter.

Filters and Large Cardinals. Levinski, Jean-Pierre.

Possible Behaviours for the Mitchell Ordering II. Cummings, James.

Ultrafilters Generated by a Closed Set of Functions. Bishop, Greg.

LARMORE, C

Political Liberalism: Neutrality and the Political. Mouffe, Chantal.

LASK, E

Why Students of Heidegger Will Have to Read Emil Lask. Kisiel, Theodore.

LASLETT, P

Locke's Early Political Reading. Milton, J R.

The New 'Everyman' Edition of Locke's *Two Treatises*. Goldie, Mark.

LATIN

Spinoza's Ethica From Manuscript to Print: Studies on Text, Form, and Related Topics. Steenbakkers, Piet.

What Happened to Philosophy Between Aquinas and Descartes?. Deely, John N.

LATIN AMERICAN

"Acerca de la Filosofía en Latinoamérica" in *Temas Actuales de Filosofía, Palacios, María Julia (ed)*. Puló de Ortiz, Mercedes.

"Contributions to the Philosophy of Technology in Costa Rica" in *Philosophy of Technology in Spanish Speaking Countries, Mitcham, Carl (ed)*. Camacho Naranjo, Luis A.

"Integración Cultural y Económica de América Latina: El Caso Argentina—Brasil" in *Temas Actuales de Filosofía, Palacios, María Julia (ed)*. Pérez Zavala, Carlos.

"Para Pensar Latinoaméerica" in *Temas Actuales de Filosofía, Palacios, María Julia (ed)*. Liendo, María Cristina.

"Posmodernidad y Arte desde América" in *Temas Actuales de Filosofía, Palacios, María Julia (ed)*. Navamuel de Figueroa, Leonor.

"Technology and Basic Needs" in *Philosophy of Technology in Spanish Speaking Countries, Mitcham, Carl (ed)*. Dussel, Enrique.

Painting on the Page: Interartistic Approaches to Modern Hispanic Texts. Geisdorfer Feal, Rosemary and Feal, Carlos.

Aportes Filosóficos para una Teoría y Práctica de Instituciones Justas. Scannone, J C.

El Conflicto de los Proyectos Históricos en la Perspectiva de Leopoldo Zea. Ibáñez, Alfonso.

El Positivismo en el Caribe Hispano. Osorio, Carlos Rojas.

Extracto de "Libraos de Ultramaria". Bentham, Jeremy.

Filosofía e Historia Según I. Ellacuría. Martínez, José A.

Filosofia e Pedagógica da Libertaçao Latinoamericana. Moreno Villa, Mariano.

Hay una Filosofía Latinoamericana?. Sanabria, José Rubén.

Hegel y América. Perez Estevez, Antonio.

Homenaje a Octavio Paz. Aguayo Cruz, Enrique Ignacio.

Líneas de Pensamiento Positivista y Antipositista en América. Romero Baró, José María.

LAW

Giuridicità e durata. Marinelli, Vincenzo.

Grenzen der Verantwortung. Heidbrink, Ludger.

Historical Rights and Fair Shares. Simmons, A John.

Il problema della definizione generale del diritto. Bagolini, Luigi.

Implicit Law. Postema, Gerald J.

In the Land of Omissions: An Opinionated Guide. Sistare, Christine T.

Kant's Denial of Absolute Sovereignty. Arntzen, Sven.

Killing a Chinese Mandarin: The Moral Implications of Distance. Ginzburg, Carlo.

La esencia del formalismo ético. Palacios, Juan Miguel.

La Obligación en el Positivismo: El Caso de H L A Hart. Hernández, Héctor H.

Las "ciencias normativas" y la "ciencia del derecho". Vega, Jesús Fernández.

Law and Politics in Plato's *Statesman*. Samberg, Mark.

Law as a Private Good: A Response to Tyler Cowen on the Economics of Anarchy. Friedman, David D.

Law in Virtue Ethics. Slote, Michael.

Laws and Coincidences Contrasted. Daly, Chris.

Learning from the Law for Regulatory Science. Cranor, Carl F.

Legislating the Moral Law. Reath, Andrews.

Leyes Causales Intencionales? Sobre los Argumentos de Fodor en Favor de las Leyes Intencionales. Pérez, Diana Inés.

Logical Content of Two Legal Principles. Wolenski, Jan.

Lying During Crisis Negotiations: A Costly Means to Expedient Resolution. Burke Jr, Francis V.

May We Stop Worrying About Blackmail?. Smilansky, Saul.

Moral Authority in Law and Criminal Justice: Some Reflections on Wilson's *The Moral Sense*. Tyler, Tom R and Kerstetter, Wayne.

Moral y Derecho en Bentham. Moncho, Josep.

Naturaleza del principio de la debida discreción de juicio en el consentimiento matrimonial (segunda y última parte). Moncada, Jesús Salvador.

On the Internal Relation Between the Rule of Law and Democracy. Habermas, Jürgen.

On the Interpretation of Facts. Aarnio, Aulis.

On the Tasks of the Contemporary Philosophy of Law. Novgorodtsev, P I.

Physician Assisted Suicide: Its Challenge to the Prevailing Constitutional Paradigm. Robinson, John H.

Pluralism, Integrity, and the Interpretive Model of Law. Golash, Deirdre.

Politically Correct Ethical Thinking and Intubation Practice on Cadavers. Orlowski, James P.

Practical Reason and Possible Community: A Reply to Jean-Marc Ferry. O'Neill, Onora.

Putting Interpretation in its Place. Endicott, Timothy A O.

Rawls and the Claims of Liberal Legitimacy. Gaut, Berys.

Reply to Paul Ricoeur's "The Plurality of Sources of Law". Dworkin, Ronald.

Resolving Environmental Disputes: Litigation, Mediation, and the Courting of Ethical Community. Kahn Jr, Peter H.

Self-Defense Theory. Gardner, Martin R.

Splitting Embryos on the Slippery Slope: Ethics and Public Policy. Macklin, Ruth.

Suchen, sich Verständigen, Kämpfen: das Umfeld der Sprache. Roberts, Julian.

Taking Drugs and Rights Seriously. Gaus, Gerald F.

The "New Syndrome Excuse Syndrome". Morse, Stephen J.

The Combat Exclusion and the Role of Women in the Military. DeCew, Judith Wagner.

The Development of the Roman Catholic Teachings on Suicide. Barry, Robert.

The Dispersion of Genetic Technologies and the Law. Clayton, Ellen Wright.

The Effects of Professional Education on Values and the Resolution of Ethical Dilemmas: Business School versus Law School Students. McCabe, Donald L, Dukerich, Janet M and Dutton, Jane E.

The Idea of Law in the Philosophy of V S Solov'ev. Novgorodtsev, P I.

The Moral *Prima Facie* Obligation to Obey the Law. Wilkins, Burleigh T.

The Normative Nature of Coercion. Hankinson, Jennifer.

The Plurality of Sources of Law. Ricoeur, Paul.

The Problem of the Origin of Pragmatism. Mendell, Mark.

The Rationality of Rule-Following: Hobbes's Dispute with the Foole. Kavka, Gregory S.

The Relative Heteronomy of Law. MacCormick, Neil.

The Role of Courts in the Debate on Assisted Suicide: A Communitarian Approach. Beschle, Donald L.

Thomistic Law and the Moral Theory of Richard Hooker. Westberg, Daniel.

Uberto Scarpelli, Giurista e Filosofo. Jori, Mario.

Um Teorema de Inércia e o Conceito de Velocidade nos *Discorsi* de Galileu. Vasconcelos, Júlio C R.

Una Lógica del Compromiso Social. Redmond, Walter.

Universalism in Morality, Ethics and Law. Lang, Wieslaw.

Verhaal en beslissing: Notities bij Bert van Roermunds *Recht, verhaal en werkelijkheid*. Tindemans, Klaas.

When Is If?. Yoes Jr, M G.

When the Majority Says You May Die: Aid-in-Dying Initiatives. Povelones Jr, Arthur A.

Why Law—Efficacy, Freedom, or Fidelity?. Waldron, Jeremy.

Wild Beasts and Idle Humours: Legal Insanity and the Finding of Fault. Robinson, Daniel N.

LAWLESS

More About Relatively Lawless Sequences. Moschovakis, Joan Rand.

LAWS

see also Civil Law, Common Law, Criminal Laws, Moral Laws, Natural Law

Ethical Issues in Suicide. Battin, Margaret P.

Statesman. Plato, Annas, Julia (& other eds) and Waterfield, Robin (trans).

Values, Work, Education: The Meanings of Work. Natale, Samuel M (ed) and Rothschild, Brian M (ed).

Acts, Omissions, and Constitutionalism. Schauer, Frederick.

Análisis Económico del Derecho y Utilitarismo: Concordancias y Divergencias. Mercado Pacheco, Pedro.

Bentham's Social and Political Thoughts: A Brief Account. Shafiquil Alam, M.

Bódog Somló's Theory of Values. Szegó, Katalin.

Circularidades en la contrastación experimental. Garrido, Julián Garrido.

De Winst van Tranen: Over de Aarzeling als Methode. Benschop, Ruth, Hendriks, Ruud and Nelis, Annemiek.

Dimensione Transculturale dei Fenomeni Giuridici nella Ricerca Antropologica. Scillitani, Lorenzo.

Ethical and Legal Dilemmas in the Management of Family Violence. Bourne, Richard.

Ethical Concerns of Nonclinical Forensic Witnesses and Consultants. Pfeifer, Jeffrey E and Brigham, John C.

Family Violence and Family Systems: Who Is the Patient?. Gottlieb, Michael C.

Giudicare o Decidere: Il Senso della Funzione Giudiziaria. Ollero Tassara, Andrés.

Hard and Soft Accidental Uniformities. Flichman, Eduardo H.

Ideal Reaction Types and the Reactions of Real Alloys. Ramsey, Jeffry L.

Il Significato del Cuore nella Filosofia Giuridica di S Agostino e di Marsilio da Padova. Ancona, Elvio.

La Funzione Legislativa. Trigeaud, Jean-Marc.

La Legge e il Diritto. Montanari, Bruno.

La Teoria e la Pratica del Diritto. De Pascale, Carla.

La Vida Humana, La Etica y la Ley. Ruiz Rodríguez, Virgilio.

Lawlikeness. Lange, Marc.

Laws of Nature, Corpuscles, and Concourse: Non-Occasionalist Tendencies in the Natural Philosophy of Robert Boyle. Jacobs, Struan.

Le juste Politique est-Il selon Platon Supérior aux Lois?. Maraguianou, E.

Let's Get the L Out: Or Why *Johnson Controls* Is Not an Unequivocal Victory for Women. Callahan, Joan.

Montesquieu e il Problema dell "Diversité". Courtney, C P.

Note sul Rapporto Violenza/Diritto/Comunicazione. Andronico, Alberto.

Oltre l'Interpretazione: Ermeneutica e Nichilismo. D'Agostini, Franca.

Oración Il Pronunciada el 18 de Octubre de 1700. Vico, G y Gómez, Francisco Navarro (trans).

Organ Transplantation: Contemporary Sunni Muslim Legal and Ethical Perspectives. Ebrahim, Abul Fadl Moshin.

Persuasion in Plato's *Laws*. Stalley, R F.

Physician Assisted Suicide: New Developments in the Netherlands. Govors, Sjof.

Presidential Address: Is the Sanctity of Life Terminally Ill?. Singer, Peter.

Remaking the Corporation: The 1991 US Sentencing Guidelines. Rafalko, Robert J.

Same-Sex Relations and the Law. Sunstein, Cass R.

Seven Issues in Conducting Forensic Assessments: Ethical Responsibilities in Light of New Standards and New Tests. Butcher, James N and Pope, Kenneth S.

Sexual Harassment in the Law: The Demarcation Problem. Hajdin, Mane.

Simetrías versus leyes? Apostilla a Van Fraassen sobre la representación. Ibarra, Andoni and Mormann, Thomas.

Social Responsibility Ethics: Doing Right, Doing Good, Doing Well. Clark, Charles R.

Students and Legal Obedience. Rich, John Martin.

The Inalienable Right to Life and the Durable Power of Attorney. Wellman, Carl P.

The Lies Remain the Same: A Reply to Chalmers. Clarke, Steve.

The Limits of Proxy Decision Making: Undertreatment. Gillick, Muriel R and Fried, Terri.

The Relation Between Ethical Codes and Moral Principles. Bersoff, Donald N and Koeppl, Peter M.

Use and Then Prove, or Prove and Then Use? Some Thoughts on the Ethics of Mental Health Professionals' Courtroom Involvement. Faust, David.

When OPRR Comes Calling: Enforcing Federal Research Regulations. McCarthy, Charles R.

When Other Things Aren't Equal: Savings *Ceteris Paribus* Laws from Vacuity. Pietroski, Paul and Rey, Georges.

Which Universals are Laws?. Peterson, Philip.

LAWYER

"Accountability and Lawyers" in *Ethics and the Professions, Chadwick, Ruth (ed)*. Tur, Richard H S.

"Hume and the Natural Lawyers: A Change of Landscape" in *Hume and Hume's Connexions, Stewart, M A (ed)*. Westerman, Pauline C.

Problems and Materials on Professional Responsibility (Sixth Edition). Morgan, Thomas D and Rotunda, Ronald D.

LAYSON, R

"How Do You Catch a Cloud and Pin It Down?" (With Apologies to Rogers and Hammerstein): A Commentary on Layson and Colleagues. Povar, Gail J.

LAZARUS, A

Concrete Boundaries and the Problem of Literal-Mindedness: A Response to Lazarus. Brown, Laura S.

Discussion of Lazarus's "How Certain Boundaries and Ethics Diminish Therapeutic Effectiveness". Gutheil, Thomas G.

Ethical Decision Making, Boundaries, and Treatment Effectiveness: A Reprise. Gottlieb, Michael C.

Maintaining Therapeutic Boundaries: The Motive Is Therapeutic Effectiveness, not Defensive Practice. Borys, Debra S.

Response to Lazarus's "How Certain Boundaries and Ethics Diminish Therapeutic Effectiveness". Bennett, Bruce E, Bricklin, Patricia M and VandeCreek, Leon.

Teetering on the Precipice: A Commentary on Lazarus's "How Certain Boundaries and Ethics Diminish Therapeutic Effectiveness". Gabbard, Glen O.

LEACH, J

On Not Taking Sides. Gross, Alan G.

LIFE

Anima hace hablar a la razón con una voz diferente: Nuevos nexos entre la tecnociencia y el mundo de la vida. Cañón Loyes, Camino.

Biology, Ethics, and the Origins of Life. Rolston III, Holmes (ed).

Contro Gli Etici. Spinelli, Emidio (trans).

Der Aufbau der Logik auf dem Boden der Philosophie des Lebens. Kühne-Bertram, Gudrun (ed), Misch, Georg (ed) and Rodi, Frithjof (ed).

Dilthey and the Narrative of History. Owensby, Jacob.

Environmental Ethics (Oxford Readings in Philosophy). Elliot, Robert (ed).

Ethics, Killing and War. Norman, Richard.

Il Trapianto d'Organi: Contributi per un'analisi etica, psicologica e sociale del problema. Soricelli, Elisabetta.

Individuals, Humans, Persons: Questions of Life and Death. Kuhse, Helga and Singer, Peter.

Language, Metaphysics, and Death (Second Edition). Donnelly, John (ed).

Life Choices: A Hastings Center Introduction to Bioethics. Howell, Joseph H (ed) and Sale, William Frederick (ed).

Life, World and Meaning. Roux, A J P (ed).

Nietzsche: Truth and Redemption. Sadler, Ted.

Philosophy as a Way of Life: Spiritual Exercises from Socrates to Foucault. Hadot, Pierre, Davidson, Arnold I (ed) and Chase, Michael (trans).

Pragmatist Aesthetics: Living Beauty, Rethinking Art. Shusterman, Richard.

Tempo e Intuizione: Alle origini dello slancio vitale nel pensiero di Henri Bergson. Taroni, Paolo.

The Children of Time: Causality, Entropy, Becoming. Lestienne, Rémy and Neher, E C (trans).

The Gift of Death. Wills, David (trans) and Derrida, Jacques.

Theophrastus Redivivus, Volumes 1 and 2. Canziani, Guido (ed) and Paganini, Gianni (ed).

Thinking in Complexity: The Complex Dynamics of Matter, Mind, and Mankind. Mainzer, Klaus.

A Deadly Delight: Feldman on the Nature and Value of Death. Haji, Ishtiyaque.

A Life Satisfaction Measure: Additional Validation Data for the Congruity Life Satisfaction Measure. Sirgy, M Joseph (& others).

Abortion and In Vitro Fertilization. Waller, Bruce N.

An Algorithm for Determining Best Interest?. Gillick, Muriel R.

Art and Life: Models for Understanding Music. Hermerén, Göran.

Awe Diminished. Campbell, Courtney S.

Character: The Framework for a Successful Life. Adams, E M.

Designing Babies: Morally Permissible Ways to Modify the Human Genome. Agar, Nicholas.

Discourse on Artificiality: A Unifying Framework for the Artificial Sciences. Ali, S M and Zimmer, R M.

Eco-Ethics—The Key to Survival. Skolimowski, Henryk.

El Ideal de la Vida Filosófica Según Leibniz. Laliga, Rensoli.

Emergence of New Fields in Ecology: The Case of Life History Studies. Korfiatis, K J and Stamou, G P.

Environmental Quality and the Quality of our Way of Life. Boersema, Jan J.

Evolution in Thermodynamic Perspective: A Historical and Philosophical Angle. Fry, Iris.

Filosofía como arte y experiencia de la vida. Innerarity, Daniel.

Human Identity and the Primitive Streak. Lockwood, Michael.

Human Life as a Value in Anthropology of Old Judaism. Palubicki, Wladyslaw.

Identity and Quality of Life (in Dutch). Musschenga, A W.

Identity and the Narrative Structure of Life. Hattingh, Herselman and van Veuren, Pieter.

Intentionality in Artificial Life. Schmidt, William C.

José Ortega y Gasset on Understanding Life as Ultimate Reality and Meaning. Weigart, Andrew J.

La "Filosofia Positiva" di Bruno Forte. Scilironi, Carlo.

La Concepción de la Metafísica en Gabriel Marcel. Tomar Romero, Francisca.

La Riflessione sul Mito in Leopardi. Stella, Vittorio.

La Vida Humana, La Etica y la Ley. Ruiz Rodríguez, Virgilio.

La vie et la Mort Selon Platon et Plotin. Kélessidou, Anna.

La Vie, Catégorie Ontologique chez Proclus et Denys. Térézis, Christos.

Lacan, Kant, and Sade. Sample, Ruth.

Le Syndrome Hampâté Bâ ou Comment Naissent les Proverbes. Konaté, Yacouba.

Life Versus Death: Exposing a Misapplication of Ethical Reasoning. Iserson, Kenneth V.

Life, Science, and Wisdom According to Descartes. Peperzak, Adriaan.

Meditations On the Shared Life. Haddox, Bruce.

Mono- und poligenischer Ursprung des Lebens. Wojciechowski, Tadeusz.

Natural Law as the Defense for Human Life. McLean, Edward B.

Nemesis and Theory Evaluation. Boersema, David B.

Non-Heart-Beating Organ Donation: A Reply to Campbell and Weber. DeVita, Michael A (& others).

On R Dworkin, *Life's Dominion* (in Hebrew). Ullmann-Margalit, Edna.

Physician Aid in Dying and the Relief of Patients' Suffering: Physicians' Attitudes Regarding Patients' Suffering and End-of-Life Decisions. Huang, Frederick Y and Emanuel, Linda L.

Protreptique et Dialectique. Leroux, Georges.

Quintuplicatà e Individualità: La Construzione dell'io in WL 1807. Rametta, Gaetano.

Real Essences in Particular. Phemister, Pauline.

Sacrificing One to Save Many. Clark, Michael.

Some Thoughts on AIDS and Death. Novick, Alvin.

Studying Organisms with Basic Cognitive Capacities in Artificial Worlds. Exteberria, A, Merelo, J J and Moreno, A.

The Church as the Axis of Convergence in Teilhard's Theology and Life. Trennert-Helwig, Mathias.

The Idea of Social Life. Sandelands, Lloyd E.

The Inalienable Right to Life and the Durable Power of Attorney. Wellman, Carl P.

The Metaphysics of Brain Death. McMahan, Jeff.

The Status of the Embryo from a Christian Point of View. Folscheid, Dominique.

Tom Regan's Seafaring Dog and (Un)Equal Inherent Worth. Edwards, Rem B.

Understanding Life: Recent Work in Philosophy of Biology. Sterelny, Kim.

Universal Metaphilosophy of Life and Universalist Ethics: An Axiological Approach. Grünberg, Ludwig.

Verontrustende vriendschappen: Foucault, Nietzsche en de bestaansesthetiek. Huijer, Marli.

Well-Being, Categorical Deprivation and the Role of Education. Yonah, Yossi.

Why Theorize How to Live with Each Other?. Gibbard, Allan F.

Wittgenstein on Forms of Life: Towards a Transcendental lperspective. Pradhan, R C.

LIFE AFTER DEATH

see Immortality

LIFE SCIENCE

El programa reduccionista en las Ciencias de la vida (1910-1944). González Recio, José Luis.

LIFE SUPPORT

"The Appropriate Medical Care of the Terminally Ill" in *Ethics on the Frontiers of Human Existence, Badham, Paul (ed)*. Kryspin, Jan and Phillips, Heather.

Blurring Distinctions between the Dying and the Dead: A Call for Discernment in Organ Donation. Rutecki, Gregory W.

Commentary on Discussions About Life-Sustaining Treatments. Emanuel, Ezekiel J.

Discussions about the Use of Life-Sustaining Treatments: A Literature Review of Physicians' and Patients' Attitudes and Practices. Layson, Rita T (& others).

LIFE WORLD

"La Primacía de la Percepción y del mundo Vivido" in *Temas Actuales de Filosofía, Palacios, María Julia (ed)*. Pochelú, Alicia G.

LIFTON, R

"Dopplung als Leugnung: Zur Theorie von Robert J Lifton" in *Nationalsozialismus und Moderne, Welzer, Harald (ed)*. Sedghi, Darjosh.

LIGHT

"Pythagorean Number as Form, Color, and Light" in *Homage to Pythagoras, Bamford, Christopher (ed)*. Lawlor, Robert.

Aristotle on Imagination: *De anima* iii 3. Turnbull, Kenneth.

Science and Art: Heuristic and Aesthetic Dimensions of Scientific Discovery. Wartofsky, Marx.

Valeriano Magni e la Discussione sul Vuoto in Italia. Bucciantini, Massimo.

LIMBAUGH, R

Logic and Mr Limbaugh: A Dittohead's Guide to Fallacious Reasoning. Perkins Jr, Raymond K.

LIMITS

"El Lenguaje como Límite en el 2do. Wittgenstein" in *Temas Actuales de Filosofía, Palacios, María Julia (ed)*. Scotto, Silvia C.

"The Limits of Science" in *Ecology, Technology, and Culture*, Zweers, Wim (ed). Tennekes, Henk.

El Estatuto Noético del Primum Cognitum: Una Aproximación desde Tomás de Aquino. Romera Oñate, Luis.

Estética del límite: Transformaciones en la configuración literaria del horizonte. Innerarity, Daniel.

Gentile e Gödel. Sainati, Vittorio.

Paper Machines. Mundici, Daniele and Sieg, Wilfried.

Pulsión y Símbolo. Mandrioni, Héctor D.

Sócrates: Filósofo Dogmático? Una Réplica a Alfonso Gómez-Lobo. Nudler, Oscar.

Sócrates: Filósofo en el Límite. Nudler, Oscar.

Sócrates: Filósofo en el Límite?. Gómez-Lobo, Alfonso.

LINDBECK, G

Schleiermacher *contra* Lindbeck on the Status of Doctrinal Sentences. Behrens, Georg.

LINDSAY, R

On Gorayska and Lindsay's Definition of Relevance. Mey, Jacob L.

On Putting Necessity in Its Place. Lindsay, R O and Gorayska, Barbara.

LINE

"Peirce's Continuum" in *Peirce and Contemporary Thought: Philosophical Inquiries, Ketner, Kenneth Laine (ed)*. Putnam, Hilary.

LINEAR

A Comparison between Two Different Tarski-Style Semantics for Linear Logic. Piazza, Mario.

Well Ordered Subsets of Linearly Ordered Sets. Höft, Harmut and Howard, Paul.

LINEAR LOGIC

A Modal View of Linear Logic. Martini, Simone and Masini, Andrea.

Axiomatizations of Commutative and Non-Associative Ajdukiewicz Calculus. Kandulski, Maciej.

Extending Intuitionistic Linear Logic with Knotted Structural Rules. Hori, Ryuichi, Ono, Hiroakira and Schellinx, Harold.

Natural Deduction for Intuitionistic Linear Logic. Troelstra, A S.

Reflections on "Difficult" Embeddings. Prijatelj, Andreja.

Semantics of Weakening and Contraction. Jacobs, Bart.

Sequent Reconstruction in LLM—A Sweepline Proof. Banach, R.

LINGUISTIC ANALYSIS

Ist eine Deutung der Welt als Wille und Vorstellung heute noch möglich? Schopenhauer nach der Sprachanalytischen Philosophie. Weimer, Wolfgang.

LINGUISTICS

"Common Nouns: A Contrastive Analysis of Chinese and English" in *The Generic Book, Carlson, Gregory N (ed)*. Krifka, Manfred.

"Focus and the Interpretation of Generic Sentences" in *The Generic Book, Carlson, Gregory N (ed)*. Krifka, Manfred.

"Genericity: An Introduction" in *The Generic Book, Carlson, Gregory N (ed)*. Krifka, Manfred (& others).

"Indefinites, Adverbs of Quantification, and Focus Semantics" in *The Generic Book, Carlson, Gregory N (ed)*. Rooth, Mats.

"Individual-Level Predicates as Inherent Generics" in *The Generic Book, Carlson, Gregory N (ed)*. Chierchia, Gennaro.

"Le discours linguistique: Etude comparée de textes" in *Rhétoriques de la science, De Coorebyter, Vincent (ed)*. Chevalier, Jean-Claude.

"Not More Medical Ethics" in *Medicine and Moral Reasoning, Fulford, K W M (ed)*. Fulford, K William M.

"Paul Ricoeur's Place in the Hermeneutic Tradition" in *The Philosophy of Paul Ricoeur, Hahn, Lewis Edwin (ed)*. Ihde, Don.

"Postmodern Law and Subjectivity: Lacan and the Linguistic Turn" in *Radical Philosophy of Law, Caudill, David S (ed)*. Milovanovic, Dragan.

"Rorty's Pragmatism and the Linguistic Turn" in *Pragmatism: From Progressivism to Postmodernism, Hollinger, Robert (ed)*. Donovan, Rickard.

"Semantic Constraints on Type-Shifting Anaphora" in *The Generic Book, Carlson, Gregory N (ed)*. ter Meulen, Alice.

"Stage-Level and Individual-Level Predicates" in *The Generic Book, Carlson, Gregory N (ed)*. Kratzer, Angelika.

"The Marking of the Episodic/Generic Distinction in Tense-Aspect Systems" in *The Generic Book, Carlson, Gregory N (ed)*. Dahl, Östen.

"The Semantics of the Common Noun *Kind*" in *The Generic Book, Carlson, Gregory N (ed)*. Wilkinson, Karina.

"Truth Conditions of Generic Sentences: Two Contrasting Views" in *The Generic Book, Carlson, Gregory N (ed)*. Carlson, Gregory N.

"What Some Generic Sentences Mean" in *The Generic Book, Carlson, Gregory N (ed)*. Asher, Nicholas and Morreau, Michael.

Dynamics of Meaning: Anaphora, Presupposition, and the Theory of Grammar. Chierchia, Gennaro.

I Sentieri di Heidegger di Hans Georg Gadamer. Caracciolo, Alberto.

La Renovación Pragmatista de la Filosofía Analítica: Una Introducción a la Filosofía Contemporánea del Lenguaje. Nubiola, Jaime.

La Sémiotique Empiriste Face au Kantisme. Formigari, Lia.

Mentalistic Turn: A Critical Evaluation of Chomsky by Kalyan Sen Gupta. Devaraja, N K.

The Generic Book. Carlson, Gregory N (ed) and Pelletier, Francis Jeffry (ed).

A Language for the Description of God, Part I: A Unique Language for a Unique Object. Graves, David and Alon, Ilai.

A Paradox of Meaning. Schiffer, Stephen.

A Problem in the Frege-Church Theory of Sense and Denotation. Salmon, Nathan.

A Prototype View of Context and Linguistic Behavior: Context Prototypes and Talk. Glover, Kelly D.

A Revised Formulation of the Logic of Sense and Denotation: Alternative (1). Church, Alonzo.

Anaphoric Pronouns in Very Late Medieval Supposition Theory. Parsons, Terence.

Are Some *Propositions* Empirically Necessary?. Peterson, Philip.

Boër and Lycan's *Knowing Who*. Richard, Mark E.

Cognitive Processes and Social Norms in Natural Discourse at the Marketplace. Lindenfeld, Jacqueline.

Common Sources for the Semiotic of Charles Peirce and John Poinsot. Beuchot, Mauricio and Deely, John.

Consideraciones sobre el *De grammatico* de Anselmo de Canterbury. Corti, Enrique C.

Consumerism and Language Acquisition. Mercier, Adèle.

Could There Be A Science of Rationality?. Davidson, Donald.

Davidson's Sentences and Wittgenstein's Builders. Perry, John.

Direct Deductive Computation on Discourse Representation Structures. Reyle, Uwe and Gabbay, Dov M.

Discontinuity in Categorial Grammar. Morrill, Glyn.

Discourse and Narrative: Ethics after the Linguistics Turn. Sauer, James.

Displacing Descartes: Philosophical Hermeneutics and Rhetorical Studies. Bineham, Jeffery L.

E-Type Pronouns, 1-Sums, and Donkey Anaphora. Lappin, Shalom and Francez, Nissim.

Emphatic Speech Style—With Special Focus on the Prosodic Signalling of Heightened Emotive Involvement in Conversation. Selting, Margret.

Empty Names. Braun, David.

Even: The Conventional Implicature Approach Reconsidered. Francescotti, Robert M.

Fallacies and Alternative Interpretations. Adler, Jonathan E.

Foregrounding Structures in American Sign Language. Wilbur, Ronnie B.

From Compositional to Systematic Semantics. Zadrozny, Wlodek.

From Königsberg to Vienna: Coffa on the Rise of Modern Semantics. Creath, Richard.

Group Membership, Social Rules, and Power: A Social-Psychological Perspective on Emotional Communication. Gallois, Cynthia.

How to Lose the Soul of Language. Gorayska, Barbara.

Iconic Manifestation of Interlocutor Distance in Russian. Yokoyama, Olga T.

In Defence of Autonomous Linguistics. Das Gupta, Amitabha.

Interpreting Malapropisms. Fatic, Aleksandar.

Interpreting Malapropisms: On Donald Davidson's Theory of Interpretation. Fatic, Aleksandar.

Interview with Noam Chomsky On Linguistics and Politics. Grewendorf, Günther.

Involvement and Joking in Conversation. Norrick, Neal R.

Involvement in Linguistic Practice: An Ethnographic Appraisal. Besnier, Niko.

Involvement with Language and In Language. Danes, Frantisek.

J L Austin: un análisis de la percepción desde la fenomenología lingüística. Reverter Bañón, Sonia.

L'Esilio Ou-topico dell'Etica: L Wittgenstein. Pellecchia, Pasquale.

Language, Action and Context: Linguistic Pragmatics in Europe and America. Nerlich, Brigitte and Clarke, David D.

Le caractère social du langage et de la pensée. Burri, Alex.

Let Bachelors and Lacking Wives Rest! (In Reaction to Edwards, 1994). Hofmann, T R.

Linguistic Competence and Moral Development: Some Parallels. Mckie, John R.

Mass and Count Quantifiers. Higginbotham, Jim.

MAY and Meaning$_{SN}$. Nicoloff, Franck.

Notes on the "Lack of Foundation" in Theodor W Adorno Philosophy (in Portuguese). De Paiva Durate, Rodrigo Antonio.

On the Necessity of Distinguishing between (Un)Boundedness and (A)Telicity. Depraetere, Ilse.

On the Treatment of Complex Predicates in Categorial Grammar. Kang, Beom-Mo.

Peirce's First Rule of Reason and the Bad Faith of Rortian Post-Philosophy. Migotti, Mark.

Quantity, Volubility, and Some Varieties of Discourse. Green, Mitchell S.

Quine and the Linguistic Doctrine of Logical Truth. Akiba, Ken.

Ricoeur on Metaphor and Ideology. Gay, William C.

Signo, Texto y Contexto: Alcance y conexiones filosóficas de las Teoría Semiótica. Knabenschuh de Porta, Sabine.

Simbolización Lingüística de la Realidad. Chamizo Domínquez, Pedro José.

Such: Binding and the Pro-Adjective. Siegel, Muffy E A.

Term-Labeled Categorial Type Systems. Oehrle, Richard T.

The Existential Perspective of Language and Meaning. Pal, Santosh Kumar.

The Feasibility of Historical Pragmatics. Jucker, Andreas H.

The Linguistic and Personal Meaning of Metaphorical Speech. Gleeson, G P.

The Metaphoric Nature of Coding: Toward a Theory of Utterance. Zaitseva, Valentina.

The Sanskrit of Science. Staal, Frits.

The Sphota Doctrine of Bhartrhari. Pathiraj R.

Theories of Masses and Problems of Constitution. Zimmerman, Dean.

Toward a Pragmatics of Emotive Communication. Caffi, Claudia and Janney, Richard W.

Translation as a Cultural-Philosophical Problem: Towards a Phenomenology of Culture. Ogawa, Tadashi.

Un Dérangement Modulaire de la Compétence Linguistique. Pietroski, Paul.

Vacuous Singular Terms. Adams, Fred and Stecker, Robert.

What *Is* The Connection Principle?. Fodor, Jerry A and Lepore, Ernie.

What Happened to Philosophy Between Aquinas and Descartes?. Deely, John N.

What's in a Word? Bring on the Seals and the Sheep (In Response to Hoffmann). Edwards, Derek.

'World' is not a Count Noun. Van Fraassen, Bas.

LIPPS, T

"Edith Stein, Theodor Lipps und die Einfühlungsproblematik" in *Studien zur Philosophie von Edith Stein, Fetz, Reto Luzius (ed)*. Fidalgo, António.

LIPTEN, P

Inference to the Loveliest Explanation. Barnes, Eric.

LISTENING

Semiosis of Listening: The Other in Heidegger's Writings on Hölderlin and Celan's "The Meridian". Ziarek, Krzysztof.

LITERACY

Platons Hypomnemata: Die Genese des Platonismus aus dem Gedächtnis der Schrift. Thiel, Detlef.

Developing Philosophical Literacy. Miller, Thomas G.

Ecological Literacy for Moral Virtue: Orr on (Moral) education for postmodern sustainability. Prakash, Madhu Suri.

MacIntyre and the Idea of an Educated Public. Wain, Kenneth.

Phonological Awareness in Learning Literacy. Jimenez Glez, J E and Del Rosario, M.

LITERAL

"Le figuré et le littéral dans le langage scientifique" in *Rhétoriques de la science, De Coorebyter, Vincent (ed)*. Kremer-Marietti, Angèle.

LITERARY

Liminal Postmodernisms: The Postmodern, the (Post-)Colonial, and the (Post-)Feminist. D'haen, Theo (ed) and Bertens, Hans (ed).

Mito e Linguaggio Letterario nell'Italia di fine Secolo. De Caprio, Caterina.

LITERARY CRITICISM

"The Rigors of Deconstruction" in *European Philosophy and the American Academy, Smith, Barry (ed)*. Evans, J Claude.

A Theory of Textuality: The Logic and Epistemology. Gracia, Jorge J E.

Narrative Ethics. Newton, Adam Zachary.

Fiction, Pity, Fear, and Jealousy. Radford, Colin.

Hermeneutics and Postmodernism: Can We Have a Radical Reader-Response Theory? Part II. Noble, Paul R.

LITERARY CRITICISM

Levels of Interpretation of a Legal Text. Sarkowicz, Ryszard.

Our Best Rhetorologist. Booth, Wayne C.

Rhetoric and Philosophy. Warner, Martin.

Scienza del Mito e Critica Letteraria: Conoscere per Composizione. Cottone, Margherita.

The Author of Common Law Texts. Glass, Arthur.

The Function of the Subject Complex in *Tanka*. Amagasaki, Akira.

The Nature of Fictional Characters and The Referential Fallacy. Dauer, Francis W.

Value-Judgements and Literature. Brooks, David.

Worlds within Worlds? The Paradoxes of Embedded Fiction. Le Poidevin, Robin.

LITERARY THEORY

"Getting the Story Straight: Narrative and Historical Knowledge" in *Historiography Between Modernism and Postmodernism*, Topolski, Jerzy (ed). Carr, David.

"Paul Ricoeur and Literary Theory" in *The Philosophy of Paul Ricoeur*, Hahn, Lewis Edwin (ed). Valdés, Mario J.

Althusser: A Critical Reader. Elliott, Gregory (ed).

Idea of Prose. Agamben, Giorgio, Sullivan, Michael (trans) and Whitsitt, Sam (trans).

L'Éducation Sentimentale. Robinson, Jenefer.

Liminal Postmodernisms: The Postmodern, the (Post-)Colonial, and the (Post-) Feminist. D'haen, Theo (ed) and Bertens, Hans (ed).

Montaigne: A Collection of Essays, Volume 1—Montaigne's Message and Method. Berven, Dikka (ed).

Montaigne: A Collection of Essays, Volume 3—Montaigne's Rhetoric. Berven, Dikka (ed).

Preface to Modernism. Berman, Art.

Syncope: The Philosophy of Rapture. O'Driscoll, Sally (trans), Clément, Catherine and Mahoney, Deirdre M (trans).

The Discourses of Science. Pera, Marcello and Botsford, Clarissa (trans).

The War Lover: A Study of Plato's Republic. Craig, Leon Harold.

Author and Repression. Gracia, Jorge J E.

Camus's Ideal of Authentic Life. Golomb, Jacob.

Fiction et Vérité. Sasaki, Ken-ichi.

In Defense of "Elitism". Shusterman, Ronald.

Intention and Representation: Searle's 'Internal' Thesis. Goodrich, R A.

Late-Marxist, Post-Poststructuralist Critical Nebulosity. Harris, Wendell V.

Literary into Cultural Studies. Easthope, Antony.

Literary Theory and Intellectual Kitsch. Dutton, Denis.

Must a Hermeneutical Psychoanalysis Exclude Science?. O'Grady, Paul, Rigby, Paul and Van Den Hengel, John.

Nelson Goodman's Assimilation of Literary and Scientific Knowledge. Campbell, Keith.

On the Leveling of the Genre Distinction Between Theory and Fiction. Weinstein, Jami.

Phenomenological Reflections on the Self and the Other—As Real, As Fictional. Paskow, Alan.

Reply to Easthope. Ryle, Martin.

Some Peculiarities about Musical Aesthetic Qualities. Porter, Roosevelt.

The Meaning of *Express* in Aesthetics: The Reconstruction of Literature. Shibles, Warren.

The Value of Reading Fiction. Gleeson, Gerald.

Unreliability Refigured: Narrative in Literature and Film. Currie, Gregory.

Vattimo and Literary Understanding: An Essay on Recent Hermeneutics. Melaney, William D.

LITERATURE

see also Fiction, Novel

"*Paradise Lost* and the Materialism Debate" in *The 1994 Annual of Hermeneutics and Social Concern*, Lawler, Justus George (ed). Fallon, Stephen M.

"Accessories (*Ecce Homo*, 'Why I Write Such Good Books', 'The Untimelies', 3)" in *Nietzsche: A Critical Reader*, Sedgwick, Peter R (ed). Kofman, Sarah.

"Fiktive Welt im literarischen Kunstwerk" in *Kunst und Ontologie*, Wlodzimierz, Galewicz (ed). Ströker, Elisabeth.

"François Rabelais as Humanist" in *Contributors to the Philosophy of Humanism*, Hillar, Marian (ed). Finch, Sheila A.

"How Dare You Sport Thus with Life?": Frankensteinian Fictions as Case Studies in Scientific Ethics. Goldbort, Robert C.

"La Epistemología de Emile Zola" in *Temas Actuales de Filosofía*, Palacios, María Julia (ed). Mari, Enrique E.

"Not Exactly Making Believe: An Essay in the Philosophy of Literature" in *Life, World and Meaning*, Roux, A P J (ed). Wilkinson, Jennifer.

"The Contributions to Humanism of Mark Twain" in *Contributors to the Philosophy of Humanism*, Hillar, Marian (ed). Prahl, Frank.

"The Truth about Fiction" in *Kunst und Ontologie*, Wlodzimierz, Galewicz (ed). Seifert, Joseph and Smith, Barry.

"'The Necessary Heritage of Darkness'" in *Intersections: Nineteenth-Century Philosophy and Contemporary Theory*, Rajan, Tilottama (ed). Clark, David L.

Adventures in Lesbian Philosophy. Card, Claudia F (ed).

Aesthetic as Science of Expression and General Linguistic. Croce, Benedetto and Ainslie, Douglas (trans).

Color Codes: Modern Theories of Color in Philosophy, Painting and Architecture, Literature, Music, and Psychology. Riley II, Charles A.

Das unendliche Altern der Moderne: Untersuchungen zur Romantniologie Gert Jonkes. Schönherr, Ulrich.

Encountering the Other(s): Studies in Literature, History, and Culture. Brinker-Gabler, Gisela (ed).

God and Plastic Surgery: Marx, Nietzsche, Freud and the Obvious. Barris, Jeremy.

Human Sciences or Humanities: The Case of Literature. Olafson, Frederick A.

Idea of Prose. Agamben, Giorgio, Sullivan, Michael (trans) and Whitsitt, Sam (trans).

Kant als Schriftsteller. Goetschel, Willi.

L'Éducation Sentimentale. Robinson, Jenefer.

Life, World and Meaning. Roux, A J P (ed).

Liminal Postmodernisms: The Postmodern, the (Post-)Colonial, and the (Post-) Feminist. D'haen, Theo (ed) and Bertens, Hans (ed).

Montaigne: A Collection of Essays, Volume 2—Sources of Montaigne's Thought. Berven, Dikka (ed).

Montaigne: A Collection of Essays, Volume 3—Montaigne's Rhetoric. Berven, Dikka (ed).

Montaigne: A Collection of Essays, Volume 4—Language and Meaning. Berven, Dikka (ed).

Montaigne: A Collection of Essays, Volume 5—Reading Montaigne. Berven, Dikka (ed).

Narrative Ethics. Newton, Adam Zachary.

Nietzsche's Aesthetic Turn: Reading Nietzsche after Heidegger, Deleuze, Derrida. Winchester, James J.

On Hume and Eighteenth-Century Aesthetics: The Philosopher on a Swing. Carabelli, Giancarlo and Hall, Joan Krakover (trans).

Painting on the Page: Interartistic Approaches to Modern Hispanic Texts. Geisdorfer Feal, Rosemary and Feal, Carlos.

Paradoxism's Main Roots. Vasiliu, Florin and Benea, Stefan (trans).

Pathognostica: Aufsätze zur Theorie und Anwendung genealogischer Philosophie. Petersen, Karl Thomas.

Preface to Modernism. Berman, Art.

Rhetorical Mosaic for a Kaleidoscope of Sound: Poetry as a Road to Understanding the Prose Voice. Britt, John F.

Solitudes: From Rimbaud to Heidegger. Froment-Meurice, Marc and Walsh, Peter (trans).

Suchbild Europa—künstlerische Konzepte der Moderne. Wortheimer, Jürgen (ed).

Syncope: The Philosophy of Rapture. O'Driscoll, Sally (trans), Clément, Catherine and Mahoney, Deirdre M (trans).

The 1994 Annual of Hermeneutics and Social Concern. Lawler, Justus George (ed).

The Atheist Trap. Mixie, Joseph.

The Blanchot Reader. Holland, Michael (ed).

The Conflict of Law and Justice in the Icelandic Sagas. Pencak, William.

The Future of the Humanities: Teaching Art, Religion, Philosophy, Literature, and History (New Edition). Kaufmann, Walter Arnold.

The Lukács Reader. Kadarkay, Arpad (ed).

The Platonic Odyssey: A Philosophical-Literary Inquiry into the "Phaedo". Gilead, Amihud.

The War Lover: A Study of Plato's Republic. Craig, Leon Harold.

Thinkers Through Time: Reading Ethics With Literature. Curran, Mary Bernard.

Toward the Post-Modern. Lyotard, Jean-François, Harvey, Robert (ed) and Roberts, Mark S (ed).

Utopie II ou Vers une Société des Personnes. Adam, E.

William James, Public Philosopher. Cotkin, George.

A Sounding of *Walden's* Philosophical Depth. Borjesson, Gary.

A Taste of Madeleine: Notes Toward a Philosophy of Place. Malpas, Jeff.

Aristotle on Detective Fiction. Sayers, Dorothy L.

Aristotle on Tragedy: Rediscovering the *Poetics*. Howland, Jacob A.

Armistice in the Recent Battle of the Books: Paul de Man, Claudio Guillén, and History. Miner, Earl.

Authenticity: From Philosophic Concept to Literary Character. Leahy, Robert.

Bakhtin, Rabelais, and Utopia. Skorobogatov-Gray, Yevgenia.

Belief and the Problem of Ulysses and the Sirens. Van Fraassen, Bas.

Camus's Ideal of Authentic Life. Golomb, Jacob.

Camus's Meursault and Sartrian Irresponsibility. Sherman, David.

Claire Loves Julie: Reading the Story of Women's Friendship in *La Nouvelle Héloïse*. Disch, Lisa.

Commentary on Rowe's "Philosophy and Literature: The Arguments of Plato's *Phaedo*". Tuozzo, Thomas M.

Concerning the National Uniqueness of Russian Philosophy. Boldyrev, I A.

Das Paradox des Schweigens: Über den Begriff der Kunst Sören Kierkegaards seit seiner Kritik der romantischen Ironie. Okabayashi, Hiroshi.

Der Begriff der Ironie und die Kunsttheorie des frühen Friedrich Schlegels (in Japanese). Ogawa, Nobuko.

Die kroatische Ästhetik des 17 Jahrhunderts: Die Epoche der Gegenreformation, des Rationalismus und des Empirismus. Barock und Klassizismus. Posavac, Zlatko.

Die philosophische und literarische Rezeption des Kommunismus. Kukoc, Mislav.

Divisio Scientiarum: Ein bisher unveröffentlichtes Wissenschaftsmodell in der Clavis Compendii des Johannes von Garlandia. Haye, Thomas.

Edward Said on Contrapuntal Reading. Wilson, George M.

Emotional Responses to Fiction: Reply to Radford. Neill, Alex.

Enjoying Horror Fictions: A Reply to Gaut. Carroll, Noël.

Ethics and Aesthetics in Aristotle's *Poetics*. Crittenden, Paul.

Everyday Surface Aesthetic Qualities: "Neat," "Messy," "Clean," "Dirty". Leddy, Thomas.

Fiction and the *De Se* Self. Vance, Robert D.

Fiction et Vérité. Sasaki, Ken-ichi.

Heidegger After the Fall. Review of *Heidegger and the Poets* by Véronique M Fóti. Lysaker, John T.

Hopkins and the Theory of Metaphor. Potts, Michael.

LOGIC

Gangesa and Mathuranatha on Simhavyaghralaksana of *Vyapti*. Wada, Toshihiro.

Gaps and Gluts: Reply to Parsons. Priest, Graham.

Generalized Quantifiers and Pebble Games on Finite Structures. Kolaitis, Phokion G.

Gentile e Gödel. Sainati, Vittorio.

Geometric Conventionalism and Carnap's Principle of Tolerance. DeVidi, David and Solomon, Graham.

Geometry and Generality in Frege's Philosophy of Arithmetic. Tappenden, Jamie.

Glymour on Explanation. Yi, Byeonguk.

Grzegorcyk's Hierarchy and *lep* E $_1$. Takeuti, Gaisi.

Hechler Reals. Labedzki, Grzegorz and Repicky, Miroslav.

Hempel Meets Wason. Humberstone, I L.

Hereditary Undecidability of Some Theories of Finite Structures. Willard, Ross.

Herman Weyl's Intuitionistic Mathematics. van Dalen, Dirk.

Heyting's Contribution to the Change in Research into the Foundations of Mathematics. Franchella, Miriam.

Hilbert and the Internal Logic of Mathematics. Gauthier, Yvon.

Hintikka Formulas as Axioms of Refutation Calculus, a Case Study. Inoué, Takao.

Hobbes, Spinoza, Kant, Highway Robbery and Game Theory. Marinoff, Louis.

How Carnap Should Bite Goodman's Bullet. Paprzycka, Katarzyna.

How I Almost Solved the Problem of Induction. Watkins, John.

How to get Something from Nothing. Orenstein, Alex.

Humean Supervenience and Enduring Things. Haslanger, Sally.

Husserl in discussione. Orlando, Teodosio.

Hypergraphs and the Intuitionistic Propositional Calculus. Kolany, Adam.

Il predicato di dimostrabilità e la nozione di consistenza: alternative alla formulazione classica. Ballarino, Annamaria.

Il Programma e il Metodo dell'Insegnamento della Logica nei Seminari Maggiori. Olejnik, Roman M.

Il Ritorno dell'Identità nel "Sistema di Logica" di G Gentile. Sainati, Vittorio.

Impossible Propositions and the Forms of Objects in Wittgenstein's *Tractatus*. Wahl, Russell.

In Defence of the Barcan Formula. Cresswell, M J.

In Defense of Deductive Inference. Kornblith, Hilary.

In Search of a Pointless Decision Principle. Bandyopadhayay, Prasanta S.

Incompatible Empirically Equivalent Theories: A Structural Explication. Mormann, Thomas.

Incompleteness and the Barcan Formula. Cresswell, M J.

Incremental Semantics for Propositional Texts. Vermeulen, C F M.

Inducing Fair Trade Out of Hegemonic Trade. Dacey, Raymond.

Inductive Countersupport. Dorn, George J W.

Inference to the Loveliest Explanation. Barnes, Eric.

Initial Segments of the Lattice of Ideals of R E Degrees. Weber, Frank P.

Intentionality in John Poinsot. Beuchot, Mauricio.

Intentions, Ends, and Joint Action. Miller, Seumas.

Intuitionistic Mathematics Does Not Need *Ex Falso Quodlibet*. Tennant, Neil.

Intuitionists Are Not (Turing) Machines. Wright, Crispin.

Is Even Minimal Negation Constructive?. Hazen, A P.

Is Gold-Putnam Diagonalization Complete?. Juhl, Cory.

Is there any Logik in Madness? Linguistic Reflections on an Interpersonal Theory of Mental Illness. Fischer, Rudi.

Iterated Belief Change Based on Epistemic Entrenchment. Nayak, Abhaya C.

Jensen's Σ* Theory and the Combinatorial Content of $V = L$. Friedman, Sy D.

Jeronimo Pardo on the Necessity of Scientific Propositions. Coombs, Jeffrey.

Kant's Dynamic Constructions. Westphal, Kenneth R.

Kant, Heidegger e la logica filosofica. Messinese, Leonardo.

Kants Philosophie und moderne Logik: Eine Tagung in Swetlogorsk. Bryuschinkin, W.

Kernel Contraction. Hansson, Sven Ove.

Knowledge of Proofs. Pagin, Peter.

La "Confusa" Suposición Sólo Confusa. Muñoz García, Angel.

La Crítica de Vico a Descartes. Muñoz-Alonso López, Gemma.

La définition et la démonstration dans la logique d'Aristote. Valois, Raynald.

La Fundamentación de la Matemática y la Génesis de la Metódica Fenomenológico-Reductiva. García Prada, Ovidio.

La Lógica Intuicionista Como una Lógica del Conocimiento Matemático. Legris, Javier.

La logique hier, les logiques aujourd'hui. Largeault, Jean.

La Partícula Medieval "Vel": Excluyente o no Excluyente?. Muñoz García, Angel.

La Recucción al Absurdo: Una Aproximación Histórica. Vega, Luis.

La respuesta Husserliana en las Investigaciones Lógicas a la aporía del antropologismo. García Norro, Juan José.

La subalternación y la conversión aristotélica de las proposiciones. Valadez, Leticia.

La Teoria de la Argumentacion y el Circulo de Viena. Gonzáles R, Edgar.

Legitimizing Chance: The Best-System Approach to Probabilistic Laws in Physical Theory. Halpin, John F.

Leibniz on Intension and Extension. Swoyer, Chris.

Leibniz's Calculus of Real Addition. Swoyer, Chris.

Les axiomes de l'identité et la démonstration des formules arithmétiques: "2+2=4". Fichant, Michel.

Les Mathématiques Sont-Elles une Syntaxe du Langage?. Gödel, Kurt, Fagnot, Dominique (trans) and Heinzmann, Gerhard (trans).

Lewis on Causal Dependence. McDermott, Michael.

Lewis on 'Might' and 'Would' Counterfactual Conditionals. De Rose, Keith.

Lo sviluppo della riduzione fenomenologica: dalla *Filosofia dell'aritmetica* a *Ideen*. Costa, Vincenzo.

Locke and Gilles de Launay. Milton, J R.

Logic and Cognitive Science: Frege's Anti-Psychologism. Barbosa De Oliveira, Marcos.

Logic and Modal Intuitions. Tidman, Paul.

Logic for Contingent Beings. Deutsch, Harry.

Logic Purified. Yagisawa, Takashi.

Lógica en Razonamiento Ordinário: Razonamiento Práctico. Péres Antia, Jesús A.

Logical Content of Two Legal Principles. Wolenski, Jan.

Logical Form and the Hidden-Indexical Theory: A Reply to Schiffer. Ludlow, Peter.

Logik der Sozialwissenschaften—150 Jahre nach J St Mills System of Logic. Eberlein, Gerald L.

Logique et existence. Verley, Xavier.

Logique et métaphysique dans le système critique: L'exemple de la causalité. Longuenesse, Béatrice.

Los "Articulos de Necesario Conocimiento Para Quien se Inicie en el Arte de la Lógica" de ABU NASR AL-FARABI. Ramón Guerrero, Rafael.

Los Campos de la Argumentación. Beuchot, Mauricio.

MacColl, Russell, the Existential Import of Propositions, and the Null-Class. Radford, Colin.

Making Sense of 'On Denoting'. Makin, Gideon.

Martin's Axiom and the Continuum. Judah, Haim and Roslanowski, Andrzej.

Mathematical Modeling of the Effects of 'Capability' and 'Intent' on the Stability of a Competitive International System. Saperstein, Alvin M.

Mathematical Models of Foreign Policy Decision-Making: Compensatory vs Noncompensatory. Mintz, Alex, Geva, Nehemia and Derouen Jr, Karl.

Meager Forking. Newelski, Ludomir.

Meaning, Realism, and the Rejection of Analyticity. Liz, Manuel.

Measures: Back and Forth Between Point Sets and Large Sets. Goldring, Noa.

Merging without Mystery or: Variables in Dynamics Semantics. Vermeulen, C F M.

Mixed Systems. Ash, C J and Knight, J F.

Modal Fictionalism Cannot Deliver Possible World Semantics. Divers, John.

Modal Fictionalism Fixed. Rosen, Gideon.

Modal Fictionalism—a Simple Dilemma. Hale, Bob.

Modal Supervenience and Modal Realism. Divers, John.

Modal-Epistemic Variants of Shapiro's System of Epistemic Arithmetic. Horsten, Leon.

Modalities in Vector Logic. Mizraji, Eduardo.

Model Completions and Omitting Types. Millar, Terrence.

Model Theory of Modules Over a Serial Ring. Eklof, Paul C and Herzog, Ivo.

Modellings for Belief Change: Prioritization and Entrenchment. Rott, Hans.

Models of Arithmetic and Upper Bounds for Arithmetic Sets. Lachlan, Alistair H and Soare, Robert I.

Models of Intuitionistic TT and NF. Dzierzgowski, Daniel.

Moralische Dilemmas in der deontischen Logik als Systeme der epistemischen Logik. Brkic, Slavko.

More About Relatively Lawless Sequences. Moschovakis, Joan Rand.

Multivalence and Vagueness: A Reply to Copeland. Simons, Peter.

Naive Mereology, Admissable Valuations, and Other Matters. Van Inwagen, Peter.

Natural Deduction Based upon Strict Implication for Normal Modal Logics. Cerrato, Claudio.

Natural Deduction for Intuitionistic Linear Logic. Troelstra, A S.

Natural Deduction in Connectionist Systems. Bechtel, William.

Natural Deduction System for Tense Logics. Indrzejczak, Andrzej.

Natural Kinds and Projectible Predicates. Mueller, Axel.

Nether Logic. Sobel, Jordan Howard.

Never Say Never. Williamson, Timothy.

Newcomblike Problems. Sobel, Jordan Howard.

Non-Bayesian Foundations for Statistical Estimation, prediction, and the Ravens Example. Forster, Malcolm R.

Non-Empirical Theoretical Virtues and the Argument from Undertermination. Kukla, André.

Non-Uniqueness of Normal Proofs for Minimal Formulas in Implication-Conjunction Fragment of BCK. Aoto, Takahito and Ono, Hiroakira.

Non-Well-Founded Sets via Revision Rules. Antonelli, Gian Aldo.

Nonreductive Materialism and Mental Causation. Marras, Ausonio.

Normal Forms in Combinatory Logic. Johann, Patricia.

Normalisation and Language-Games. De Queiroz Ruy, J G B.

Not by Skill Alone: The Centrality of Character to Critical Thinking. Siegel, Harvey.

Nota Vichiana. Agrimi, Mario.

Nozick's *The Nature of Rationality*. Christensen, David.

Numbers Can Be Just What They Have To. McLarty, Colin.

Nyaya Inference-Deductive-Inductive Pattern. Sen, Amit Kumar.

Of Nulls and Norms. Godfrey-Smith, Peter.

Old Evidence and New Theories. Zynda, Lyle.

On a Generalization of Distributivity. Kanai, Yasuo.

On a Point of Logic. Dudman, V H.

On Artifacts and Works of Art. Hilpinen, Risto.

On Borel Ideals. Van Engelen, Fons.

On Classes and Higher-Order Logic: A Critique of W V O Quine. Cocchiarella, Nino B.

On Completeness of Intermediate Predicate Logics with Respect to Kripke Semantics. Shimura, Tatsuya.

On Conditionals. Edgington, Dorothy.

On Countable Fractions from an Elementary Class. Ash, C J.

On Gödel's Theorems on Lengths of Proofs I: Number of Lines and Speedup for Arithmetics. Buss, Samuel R.

On Grzegorczyk Induction. Cornaros, C.

On Jacob Klein's *Greek Mathematical Thought and the Origin of Algebra*. Gonda, Joseph.

LOGIC

LOGICAL ATOMISM

LOGICAL CONSTANT

LOGICAL EMPIRICISM

LOGICAL FORM

LOGICAL NECESSITY

LOGICAL POSITIVISM

LOGICAL TRUTH

LOGICISM

LOGOCENTRISM

LOGOS

LOMBARDI, L

LONELINESS

LUCAS, J
Intuitionists Are Not (Turing) Machines. Wright, Crispin.

LUCK
"Instigating the Unpredisposed: Bad Luck in Law and Life" in *Modality, Morality, and Belief, Sinnott-Armstrong, Walter (ed)*. Feinberg, Joel.
The Act Itself. Bennett, Jonathan.
A Second Paradox Concerning Responsibility and Luck. Greco, John.
Aristotle, Success, and Moral Luck. Farwell, Paul.
Luck and the Enigmas of Fate. Rescher, Nicholas.
Religious Luck. Zagzebski, Linda.

LUCRETIUS
Epicurean Poetics. Asmis, Elizabeth.

LUDWIG, K
Rationality, Norms and the Primitively Compelling: A Reply to Kirk Ludwig. Peacocke, Christopher.

LUEBKE, N
Conflict of Interest Revisited. Davis, Michael.

LUGONES, M
Standing for Something. Calhoun, Cheshire.

LUHMANN, N
An Interview with Niklas Luhmann. Sciulli, David.
Moderne, Modernisierung, Modernität. Makropoulos, Michael.
The Fascination of Amorality: Luhmann's Theory of Morality and its Resonances among German Intellectuals. Neckel, Sighard and Wolf, Jürgen.

LUKACS, G
"Am Muttergeist soll die Welt genesen": Philosophische Dispositionen zum Frauenbild im Nationalsozialismus. Korotin, Ilse Erika.
Das Feindbild der marxistisch-leninistischen Philosophie in der DDR 1945-1988. Kapferer, Norbert.
Georg Lukács. Sim, Stuart.
The Lukács Reader. Kadarkay, Arpad (ed).
Reproduction and Ontology in Lukács (in Portuguese). Lessa, Sergio.
Two Ways of Coming Back to Reality: Kierkegaard and Lukács. Hannay, Alastair.

LUKASIEWICZ
Philosophy and Science in Jan Lukasiewicz (in Italian). Coniglione, Francesco.

LULL
Nota Sobre la Poesía Algorítmica de Ramón Llull. Lizalde, Carlos Lorenza.

LUNG, K
White Horse not Horse: Making Sense of a Negative Logic. Lai, Whalen.

LUNG-SUN LUNG
"Common Nouns: A Contrastive Analysis of Chinese and English" in *The Generic Book, Carlson, Gregory N (ed)*. Krifka, Manfred.

LUNTLEY, M
Kant's Refutation of Anti-Realism. Blatnik, Edward.

LUST
Faust e Lust. La Guardia, Giovanni.

LUTHER
The Transformation of Natural Philosophy: The Case of Philip Melanchthon. Kusukawa, Sachiko.

LUTZ, C
"Ecstasy and Epistemology" in *Emotions in Asian Thought, Marks, Joel (ed)*. Rouner, Leroy S.

LUZAN, I
La Presencia de Giambattista Vico en la Cultura Española (I). Sevilla Fernández, José M.

LYCAN, W
Boër and Lycan's *Knowing Who*. Richard, Mark E.
Criteria: The State of the Debate. Addis, Mark.
In Defense of Deductive Inference. Kornblith, Hilary.

LYING
"The Primacy of Truth-Telling and the Evolution of Lying" in *From a Biological Point of View, Sober, Elliott*. Sober, Elliott.
"Truthfulness, Lies, and Moral Philosophers" in *The Tanner Lectures on Human Values, Volume 16, Peterson, Grethe B (ed)*. MacIntyre, Alasdair.
Lying During Crisis Negotiations: A Costly Means to Expedient Resolution. Burke Jr, Francis V.
The Game that Looks Like Work in Plato's "Parmenides". Delgado De Torres, Olivia.

LYNCH, J
Commentary on "Is Animal Pain Conscious?". Duran, Jane.

LYNCH, M
Representation(s). Rheinberger, Hans-Jörg.

LYOTARD, J
Ästhetik des Erhabenen: Burke, Kant, Adorno, Lyotard. Peña Aguado, María Isabel.
The Lyotard Reader. Benjamin, Andrew (ed).
Toward the Post-Modern. Lyotard, Jean-François, Harvey, Robert (ed) and Roberts, Mark S (ed).
Autonomy or Heteronomy? Levinas's Challenge to Modernism and Postmodernism. Child, Mark (& others).
J G Fichte und das postmoderne Denken (Jean-François Lyotard). Schrader, Wolfgang H.
Lyotard's Homeopathic Indeterminacy: The Medicinal Sublime. Miller-Frank, Felicia.

Lyotard's Peregrination: Three (and-a-half) Responses to the Call of Justice. Dalton, Stuart.
Philosophy Under Fire: J F Lyotard Transcending the Trenches of Postmodernity. Brons, H R.
Plato Visits Postmodernity: Reflections on Narrative Philosophy. Bowery, Anne-Marie.
Postmodern Theology After the Decline of the Mastery Story of Christianity, Inspired by Lyotard's Critical Theory of Postmodernity (in Dutch). Boeve, Lieven.
Violence and Post-Modernism. Jasper, David.

MABBOTT, J
The Morality of legal Retribution. Gaffney, Paul.

MACCOLL, H
MacColl, Russell, the Existential Import of Propositions, and the Null-Class. Radford, Colin.

MACDONALD, C
"Does Meaning Matter?" in *Philosophy of Psychology: Debates on Psychological Explanation, Macdonald, Cynthia (ed)*. Dretske, Frederick.
"Explanatory Exclusion and the Problem of Mental Causation" in *Philosophy of Psychology: Debates on Psychological Explanation, Macdonald, Cynthia (ed)*. Kim, Jaegwon.
"Reply: Causation and Two Kinds of Laws" in *Philosophy of Psychology: Debates on Psychological Explanation, Macdonald, Cynthia (ed)*. Block, Ned.

MACH
Retrieving the Point of the Realism-Instrumentalism Debate: Mach vs Planck on Science Education Policy. Fuller, Steve.

MACHADO, A
La Reivindicación de la Sabiduría Poética en G B Vico y A Machado. Ramírez Luque, Isabel.

MACHAMER, P
Author's Response. Kitcher, Philip.

MACHIAVELLI
Amoral Politics: The Persistent Truth of Machiavellism. Scharfstein, Ben-Ami.
Montaigne: A Collection of Essays, Volume 2—Sources of Montaigne's Thought. Berven, Dikka (ed).
Politischer Individualismus: Die Rekonstruktion einer Sozialtheorie unter Bezugnahme auf Machiavelli, Bodin, und Hobbes. Hegmann, Horst.
A Metastructural Reinterpretation of the Rawlsian Theory: From Rawls to Machiavelli. Bidet, Jacques.
Cicero Versus Machiavelli: Does the End Justify the Means. Hancock, Curtis L.
Machiavelli, Harrington, and the Character of Modern Utopia. Linker, Damon.
Niccolò Machiavelli-Adviser of Princes. Kain, Philip J.
Reading Machiavelli: Innocent Gentillet's Discourse on Method. Kahn, Victoria.
Some Reflections on Descartes and Machiavelli (in Portuguese). Araújo, Cícero.

MACHIAVELLIAN
Are the Elderly Really Machiavellian? A Reinterpretation of an Unexpected Finding. Mudrack, Peter E.
On Individual Amorality as the Background to Machiavellism. Scharfstein, Ben-Ami.

MACHINA, M
Allais' Rejoinder. Allais, Maurice.
The Real Foundations of the Alleged Errors in Allais' Impossibility Theorem: Unceasingly Repeated Errors or Contradictions of Mark Machina. Allais, Maurice.

MACHINE
see also Technology
"Are Synergetic Systems (Including Brains) Machines?" in *The Machine as Metaphor and Tool, Haken, Hermann (ed)*. Haken, Hermann.
"From Clocks to Chaos: Humanizing the Mechanistic World-View" in *The Machine as Metaphor and Tool, Haken, Hermann (ed)*. Toulmin, Stephen.
"La machine de l'exemple ou la comparison chez Descartes" in *Rhétoriques de la science, De Coorebyter, Vincent (ed)*. Hallyn, Fernand.
"Mathematical Machines" in *The Machine as Metaphor and Tool, Haken, Hermann (ed)*. Henry, Paul.
"The Mechanization of Time" in *The Machine as Metaphor and Tool, Haken, Hermann (ed)*. Lundmark, Lennart.
Artificial Intelligence: A Philosophical Introduction. Copeland, B Jack.
The Convergence of Machine and Human Nature: A Critique of the Computer Metaphor of Mind and Artificial Intelligence. McClintock, Alexander.
The Machine as Metaphor and Tool. Haken, Hermann (ed), Karlqvist, Anders (ed) and Svedin, Uno (ed).
The Problem of Consciousness: Essays Towards a Resolution. McGinn, Colin.
A Critique of Information Processing Theories of Consciousness. Hardcastle, Valerie Gray.
Artificial Intelligence, Feminist and Otherwise. Keith, William.
Blumenberg: Truly Memorable Memories. Hrachovec, Herbert and Turner, Charles (ed).
Computation as an Intrinsic Property. Boyle, C Franklin.
Computation, Among Other Things, Is Beneath Us. Bringsjord, Selmer.
Les variétés des hybrides dans les récits de la pensée. Canty, Daniel.
Machines and the Mental. Dretske, Frederick.
Marcel Duchamp, la musique et les machines. Raymond, François.
Materialism, Reduction, Replacement, and the Place of Consciousness in Science. Foss, Jeffrey E.
Paper Machines. Mundici, Daniele and Sieg, Wilfried.
Réflexion Épistémologique sur l'Intelligence Artificielle et les Sciences Cognitives: à Quelles Conditions une Machine Pourrait-elle Connaître?. Robert, Serge.

MACHINE

Response to Anderson and Keith. Genova, Judith.

The Case Against Connectionism: Productivity and Systematicity. Marinov, Marin.

The Church-Turing Thesis and Effective Mundane Procedures. Horsten, Leon.

The Semantics of Flang. Mantsivoda, Andrei.

Turing and the Origins of AI. Shanker, Stuart.

Turing's Test and the Perils of Psychohistory. Anderson, James A.

Why Everything Doesn't Realize Every Computation. Chrisley, Ronald L.

Women-Animals-Machines: A Grammar for a Wittgensteinian Ecofeminism. Lee-Lampshire, Wendy.

MACINTYRE, A

"After Virtue? On Distorted Philosophical Narratives" in *The 1994 Annual of Hermeneutics and Social Concern, Lawler, Justus George (ed)*. Ruprecht Jr, Louis A.

Innovation and Tradition in Religion: Towards an Institutional Theory. Disbrey, Claire (ed).

Competing Conceptions of the Educated Public. Wain, Kenneth.

Excellence V Effectiveness: Macintyre's Critique of Business. Horvath, Charles M.

Identity and the Narrative Structure of Life. Hattingh, Herselman and van Veuren, Pieter.

Justice and Moral Conflict. Sims, Jesse.

Macintyre and the Idea of an Educated Public. Wain, Kenneth.

Macintyre's Conservatism and Its Cure: The Formal Structure of Traditions. Freytag, Matthew.

Moral Provincialism. Kent, Bonnie.

Rationalité des traditions et possibilité d'une éthique universelle: discussion de la position de Macintyre. Müller, Denis.

Recent Work on Liberalism and Communitarianism. Shapiro, Daniel.

The *Tao* of Confucian Virtue Ethics. Bretzke, James T.

The Politics of Communitarianism. Friedman, Jeffrey.

Topische Paradoxien der kommunitaristischen Argumentation. Giusti, Miguel.

MACKIE, J

Mackie's Paradox and the Free Will Defence. Khamara, Edward J.

Moral Realism, Objective Values, and J L Mackie. Mizzoni, John.

Natural Fact, Moral Reason. Passell, Dan.

Why are There Sinners? Augustine's Response to Mackie. You, Sung-Keun.

MACKINNON, C

"Having a Voice and Getting a Hearing" in *Identity, Culture, and Education, Smeyers, Paul (ed)*. White, Patricia.

Pornography: The Theory. Ferguson, Frances.

MACKLIN, R

When OPRR Comes Calling: Enforcing Federal Research Regulations. McCarthy, Charles R.

MACNAMARA, M

"Life and Society at Ancient Memphis According to the Saqqâra Texts" in *Life, World and Meaning, Roux, A P J (ed)*. Dreyer, H J.

Life, World and Meaning. Roux, A J P (ed).

MADDY, P

Scientific versus Mathematical Realism: The Indispensability Argument. Resnik, Michael D.

MADHYAMAKA

The Relationship Between Analysis and Insight (Prajñā) in Mādhyamika Buddhism: Some Western Interpretations. Dean, Colin.

MADHYAMIKA

Bhavaviveka's *Prajñapradipa*. Ames, William L.

MADISON

The Trouble with Transformational Leadership: Toward a Federalist Ethic for Organizations. Keeley, Michael.

MADISON, J

"Our Complicated System": James Madison on Power and Liberty. Read, James H.

MADNESS

The Blanchot Reader. Holland, Michael (ed).

Beyond Liberation: Michel Foucault and the Notion of a Critical Psychiatry. Bracken, Patrick J.

Civilized Madness: Schizophrenia, Self-Consciousness and the Modern Mind. Sass, Louis A.

Is there any Logik in Madness? Linguistic Reflections on an Interpersonal Theory of Mental Illness. Fischer, Rudi.

Madness, the Absence of Work. Foucault, Michel, Stastny, Peter (trans) and Sengel, Deniz (trans).

Mind and Madness: New Directions in the Philosophy of Psychiatry. Fulford, K W M.

Moralist or Therapist? Foucault and the Critique of Psychiatry. Matthews, Eric.

Remembering My Own Madness: A Hermeneutics of That Which is Prior to Rationality. Jones, Michael Ponder.

Report from Mr Canguilhem on the Manuscript Filed by Mr Michel Foucault, Director of the Institut Français of Hamburg.... Canguilhem, Georges and Hobart, Ann (trans).

MAGIC

"At the Crossroads of Positivism and Magic:" Benjamin, Baudelaire, and the Shock of the Sublime. Wood, Gillen.

"Magic, Witchcraft, and ESP: A Defence of Scientific and Philosophical Skepticism" in *African Philosophy: Selected Readings, Mosley, Albert G (ed)*. Bodunrin, P O.

African Philosophy: Selected Readings. Mosley, Albert G (ed).

Appunti sulla Fortuna di Gabriel Naudé nella Germania del Primo Illuminismo. Mulsow, Martin.

The Presuppositions of Jaimini and the Vedāntins. De Smet, Richard.

MAGLIOLA, R

"A Postmodern Trinity?" in *The 1994 Annual of Hermeneutics and Social Concern, Lawler, Justus George (ed)*. Sanders, Theresa.

MAGNETISM

Experiment, Speculation and Law: Faraday's Analysis of Arago's Wheel. Steinle, Friedrich.

The Whewell-Faraday Exchange on the Application of the Concepts of Momentum and Inertia to Electromagnetic Phenomena. Anderson, Ronald.

MAGRITTE, R

René Magritte, Constructivism, and the Researcher as Interpreter. Stake, Robert and Kerr, Dale.

MAHAYANA

Early Yogacara and Its Relationship with the Madhyamaka School. King, Richard.

Nāgārjuna and Deconstruction. Mabbett, Ian W.

MAIMON

The Antinomy of Thought: Maimonian Skepticism and the Relation between Thoughts and Objects. Bransen, Jan.

Maimons Versuch über Transzendentalphilosophie: Eine interpretierende Skizze der Grundgedanken. Krämer, Felix.

MAIMONIDES

Maimonides and St Thomas on the Limits of Reason. Dobbs-Weinstein, Idit.

MAISTRE, J

Considerations on France: Joseph de Maistre. Lebrun, Richard A (ed & trans) and De Maistre, Joseph.

MAKI, U

"The Idealization Methodology and Economics" in *Idealization VI: Idealization in Economics, Hamminga, Bert (ed)*. Nowak, Leszek.

MAKINSON, D

Towards an Adequate Definition of Distribution for First-Order Logic. Friedman, Joel I.

MALAMENT, D

Non-Turing Computers and Non-Turing Computability. Hogarth, Mark.

MALAYSIAN

Attitudes Towards Business Ethics of Business Students in Malaysia. Alam, Kazi Firoz.

MALCOLM X

By Any Means Necessary: John Locke and Malcolm X on the Right to Revolution. Gordon, Jill.

Preferential Hiring and Just War Theory. English, Parker.

MALCOLM, N

Consciousness, Dreams, and Virtual Realities. Revonsuo, Antti.

MALE

see also Men

"Male and Female in the Modern World" in *The Nature and Pursuit of Love, Goicoechea, David (ed)*. Mitterer, John.

Damenphilosophie und Männermoral: Von Abbé de Gérard bis Marquis de Sade Ein Versuch über die lächelnde Vernunft. Jauch, Ursula Pia.

MALEBRANCHE

Arnauld et Malebranche. Senofonte, Ciro.

Choosing a Theodicy: The Leibniz-Malebranche-Arnauld Connection. Nadler, Steven.

Dios en la filosofía de Malebranche. Fernández, José Luis.

Malebranche and Arnauld on Ideas. Watson, Richard A.

Malebranche on Descartes on Mind-Body Distinctness. Schmaltz, Tad M.

Recenti Studi su Antoine Arnauld. Donnici, Rocco.

MALENESS

Woman and the History of Philosophy. Tuana, Nancy.

MALLARME, S

Solitudes: From Rimbaud to Heidegger. Froment-Meurice, Marc and Walsh, Peter (trans).

MALPRACTICE

Malpractice Arising From Negligent Psychotherapy: Ethical, Legal, and Clinical Implications of *Osheroff vs Chestnut Lodge*. Packman, Wendy L, Cabot, Mithran G and Bongar, Bruce.

MALTHUS

La Polemica di Leroux contro Lacordaire e Malthus sulla Questione Sociale. Fiorentino, Fernando.

Malthus on Colonization and Economic Development: A Comparison with Adam Smith. Pullen, J M.

MAMARDASCHWILI, M

Ist Philosophie auf Russisch möglich?. Malachov, Vladimir.

MAN

see also Human, Individual, Person, Philosophical Anthropology

"Dappertutto e in Nessun Luogo": Volontà e Potenza di un'edizione Nietzscheana. Brusotti, Marco and Gerratana, Federico.

Itinerari del Volontarismo: Teologia e politica al tempo di Luis de León. Ferraro, Domenico.

Tode Ti and *Toionde* in Metaphysics Z. Yu, Jiyuan.

Cinque Esemplari Postillati della *Scienza Nuova*. Rotoli, Daniela.

El humanismo marxiano. Calvez, Jean-Yves.

Ermeneutica, Metafisica e Nichilismo in Heidegger. Sciuto, Italo.

Estetica e politica in Rousseau: Il sentimento come movente di critica al modello sociale del "Bourgeois". Pallavidini, Renato.

Filosofi a Bologna fra Ottocento e Novecento. Garin, Eugenio.

MAN

La dimensión natural del hombre en Santo Tomás de Aquino. Castello Dubra, Julio A.

La dimensione teologae dell'uomo e la teologia fondamentale in Xavier Zubiri. Savignano, Armando.

La Divinisation de l'Homme selon Denys. De Andia, Ysabel.

La Polemica di Leroux contro Lacordaire e Malthus sulla Questione Sociale. Fiorentino, Fernando.

Le Fonti del "Sigillus Sigillorum" del Bruno, Ossia: Il Confronto con Ficino a Oxford Sull'anima Umana. Sturlese, Rita.

M Heidegger (e U Eco) contro la definizione di uomo come animale razionale. Chitarin, Luigi.

Modern Man and Man *Tout Court*: The Flight from Nature and the Modern Difference, Review Essay on *La Cité de l'homme*, by Pierre Manent. Mahoney, Daniel J.

Osservazioni sul Problema del Male in Filosofia. Franchi, Alfredo.

Per un Servizio Sapienziale della Filosofia nella Chiesa. Sánchez Sorondo, Marcello.

Postille: 1)Pensiero Orientale Verticale e Pensiero Occidentale Orizzontale, 2)La Filsofia della Crisi. Del Vecchio, Dante.

Sobre el Problema de la Filosofía (II). Zubiri, Xavier.

Sul Vico di Piovani. Vasoli, Cesare.

Tre Improbabili Nani Sulle Spalle dei Giganti. Mastroianni, Giovanni.

Una Ricerca sullo Stato di Edith Stein. D'Agostino, Francesco.

Versuche die ersten Prinzipien in Frage zu stellen. Rutowski, Tadeusz.

Vico e i 'Figliuoli di Dio': Ricerche sui Giganti nel *Diritto universale* e nella *Scienza nuova Prima*. Boschetto, Luca.

Why Students of Heidegger Will Have to Read Emil Lask. Kisiel, Theodore.

MANAGED CARE

Authenticity and Autonomy in the Managed-Care Era: Forensic Psychiatric Perspectives. Bursztajn, Harold J and Brodsky, Archie.

MANAGEMENT

A Management Perspective on Business Ethics. Soutar, Geoffrey N (& others).

Attitudes of Students and Accounting Practitioners Concerning the Ethical Acceptability of Earnings Management. Fischer, Marilyn and Rosenzweig, Kenneth.

Creating Common Ground: A Lesson from the Past. Acklin, David and King, Jonathan.

Ethical Challenges in the Leader-Follower Relationship. Hollander, Edwin P.

Ethical Perceptions of Organizational Politics: A Comparative Evaluation of American and Hong Kong Managers. Ralston, David A, Giacalone, Robert A and Terpstra, Robert H.

Ethics as Excellence: A Strategic Management Perspective. Smith, John Milton.

Evaluation of Employee Rule Violations: The Impact of Impression Management Effects in Historical Context. Giacalone, Robert A and Payne, Stephen L.

Head-Heart Disparity Among Future Managers: Implications for Ethical Conduct. Kochunny, C M and Rogers, Hudson.

Leadership and Ethical Development: Balancing Light and Shadow. Lichtenstein, Benyamin M, Smith, Beverly A and Torbert, William R.

Leadership Ethics: Mapping the Territory. Ciulla, Joanne B.

Leadership, Moral Development, and Citizenship Behavior. Graham, Jill W.

Leadership: A Discussion About Ethics. Rost, Joseph C.

Managerial Ethical Leadership: Examples Do Matter. Murphy, Patrick E and Enderle, Georges.

Means or Ends? Ethical Decision Frameworks in the Western Australian Public Service. Peachment, Allan (& others).

Should Trees Have Managerial Standing? Toward Stakeholder Status for Non-Human Nature. Starik, Mark.

The Social Construction of Genetic Abnormality: Ethical Implications for Managerial Decisions in the Workplace. Strudler, Alan.

The Trouble with Transformational Leadership: Toward a Federalist Ethic for Organizations. Keeley, Michael.

Top Executive Compensation: Equity or Excess? Implications for Regaining American Competitiveness. Walters, Bruce, Hardin, Tim and Schick, James.

Toward an Understanding of Ethical Climate: Its Relationship to Ethical Behavior and Supervisory Influence. Wimbush, James C and Shepard, Jon M.

Unethical Behaviour in Procurement: A Perspective on Causes and Solutions. Badenhorst, J A.

MANAGER

Ethical Corporate Social Resonsibility: A Framework for Managers. L'Etang, Jacquie.

Head-Heart Disparity Among Future Managers: Implications for Ethical Conduct. Kochunny, C M and Rogers, Hudson.

Professional Responsibilities of Corporate Managers. Machan, Tibor R.

MANDEL, E

"Late Capitalism and Postmodernism: Jameson/Mandel" in *Marxism in the Postmodern Age, Callari, Antonio (ed)*. Norton, Bruce.

MANDELBROT, B

Reply to H Stapp's Comment. Dickson, Michael.

MANENT, P

Modern Man and Man *Tout Court*: The Flight from Nature and the Modern Difference, Review Essay on *La Cité de l'homme*, by Pierre Manent. Mahoney, Daniel J.

MANET, E

Between Realisms: From Derrida to Manet. Fried, Michael.

MANFREDA, L

Aporie del Simbolo: Saggio su Otto Weininger. Manfreda, Luigi Antonio.

MANIA

Mild Mania and Well-Being. Moore, Andrew, Hope, Tony and Fulford, K W M.

MANIPULATION

Politics and Manipulation. Mills, Claudia.

MANKIND

Thinking in Complexity: The Complex Dynamics of Matter, Mind, and Mankind. Mainzer, Klaus.

MANN, T

"Die Verführerische Marionette" in *Die besten Geister der Nation, Korotin, Ilse (ed)*. Stockreiter, Karl.

MANSFELD, J

Commentary on Mansfeld's "The Idea of the Will in Chrysippus, Posidonius, and Galen". Sedley, David.

MANY

see also Pluralism

Plotino, Ficino e noi stessi: alcuni riflessi etici. Rist, John M and Peroli, E (trans).

The Game that Looks Like Work in Plato's "Parmenides". Delgado De Torres, Olivia.

MANY-VALUED LOGICS

A Geometric Proof of the Completeness of the Lukasiewicz Calculus. Panti, Giovanni.

Even Tabular Modal Logics Sometimes do not have Independent Base for Admissible Rules. Rybakov, Vladimir V.

Remarks on a Theorem of McGee. Adams, Ernest W.

Sheffer's Stroke for Prime Numbers. Karpenko, Alexander S.

Subformula Property in Many-Valued Modal Logics. Takano, Mitio.

The Strong Completeness of a System Based on Kleene's Strong Three-Valued Logic. Aoyama, Hiroshi.

Wittgenstein—Ein Wegbereiter der Mehrwertigen Logik?. Strehle, Peter.

MAO

A Philosophical Correspondence with Li Rui. Yuanhua, Wang.

Subjectivity: Marxism and "The Spiritual" in China Since Mao. Tongqi, Lin and Minghua, Li.

MAOISM

Scientism and Humanism: Two Cultures in Post-Mao China (1978-1989). Hua, Shiping.

MAORI

Ethics in a Bicultural Context. Campbell, Alastair V.

Maori Environmental Virtues. Patterson, John.

MAP

A Completeness Theorem for Open Maps. Joyal, A and Moerdijk, I.

MARCEL

La Concepción de la Metafísica en Gabriel Marcel. Tomar Romero, Francisca.

MARCUS, R

"Closure and Consistency" in *Modality, Morality, and Belief, Sinnott-Armstrong, Walter (ed)*. Levi, Isaac.

"Marcus and the Problem of Nested Deontic Modalities" in *Modality, Morality, and Belief, Sinnott-Armstrong, Walter (ed)*. Belnap Jr, Nuel D and Bartha, Paul.

"Moral Dilemmas Revisited" in *Modality, Morality, and Belief, Sinnott-Armstrong, Walter (ed)*. Foot, Philippa.

"Perspectival Guilt" in *Modality, Morality, and Belief, Sinnott-Armstrong, Walter (ed)*. Greenspan, Patricia.

"Pierre, Saul, Ruth, and Bob and a Puzzle about Belief" in *Modality, Morality, and Belief, Sinnott-Armstrong, Walter (ed)*. Fogelin, Robert.

"Ruth Barcan Marcus and the Barcan Formula" in *Modality, Morality, and Belief, Sinnott-Armstrong, Walter (ed)*. Parsons, Terence.

"The Interaction of Modality with Quantification and Identity" in *Modality, Morality, and Belief, Sinnott-Armstrong, Walter (ed)*. Stalnaker, Robert.

"The Kant-Frege-Russell View of Existence" in *Modality, Morality, and Belief, Sinnott-Armstrong, Walter (ed)*. Wiggins, David.

Modality, Morality, and Belief. Sinnott-Armstrong, Walter (ed).

MARCUSE, H

Max Weber in Amerika: Wirkungsgeschichte und Rezeptionsgeschichte Webers in der anglo-amerikanischen Philosophie und Sozialwissenschaft. Erdelyi, Agnes.

La Critique de l'ontologie et la Théorie Sociale de Hegel dans l'oeuvre de Herbert Marcuse. C-Mazaraki, A.

Marx, Stalin, Marcuse: Die kritische Theorie in ideengeschichtlicher Sicht. Aleksandrowicz, Dariusz.

The Theory of Social Change with Introduction by Bill Scheuerman. Marcuse, Herbert and Neumann, Franz.

MARECHAL, J

Blondel's L'Action (1893) and Neo-Thomism's Metaphysics of Symbol. Fields, Stephen.

MARECHAL, L

La belleza y los esteticismos. Corti, Enrique.

MARGOLIS, J

Contra Margolis' Peircean Constructivism: A Peircean Pragmatic *Logos*. Wells, Kelley J.

Relativism About Interpretation. Stecker, Robert.

Relativism in Interpretation. Davies, Stephen.

The Telos of Peirce's Realism. Hausman, Carl R and Anderson, Douglas R.

MARIANO, R

Neoidealismo ed Hegelismo Ortodosso nel Carteggio Croce-Mariano. Savorelli, Alessandro.

MARITAIN

Human Dignity and the Common Good in the Aristotelian-Thomistic Tradition. Smith, Michael A.

MARITAIN

Cinco Claves Para Comprender a Jacques Maritain. Burgos, Juan Manuel.

La fundamentación filosófica de los derechos humanos en Jacques Maritain. Beuchot, Mauricio.

Per una Biografia Intellettuale di Marcel de Corte. Castellano, Danilo.

The Problem of Thing and Object in Maritain. Cahalan, John C.

Una Ricerca sullo Stato di Edith Stein. D'Agostino, Francesco.

MARKET

Idealization VI: Idealization in Economics. Hamminga, Bert (ed) and De Marchi, Neil B (ed).

Socialism After Communism: The New Market Socialism. Pierson, Christopher.

D Gauthier o Hobbes sin Leviatán. Montoya, José.

Does a Good Market Make a Good European?. Fuchs, Wolfgang W.

Environmental Valuation: Some Problems of Wrong Questions and Misleading Answers. Knetsch, Jack L.

Essentialism and the Market. O'Neill, John.

Four Dogmas of Environmental Economics. Sagoff, Mark.

Imperfect Markets: Business Ethics as an Easy Virtue. Sethi, S Prakash.

Las Formas lógicas de la Sección Primera de El Capital. Delgado, Manuel.

Markets, Information, and Benevolence. Brennan, Timothy J.

Moralizing Markets. Bellamy, Richard.

Ökologische Blindheit: Die Aporie der herrschenden Wirtschaftswissenschaft. Reheis, Fritz.

On Costs, Benefits, and Regulatory Success: Reply to Crandall. Sunstein, Cass R.

On Morals and Markets. Schwartz, Barry.

Rights and Interests in a Participatory Market Society. van Luijk, Henk.

Selling Death and Dignity. Hendin, Herbert.

Systemic Rationality and the Effects of Financial Regulation: Rejoinder to Kindleberger. Horwitz, Steven.

The Economic Organization of Science, the Firm, and the Marketplace. Wible, James R.

The Ethics of the Pharmaceutical Industry and the Need for a Dual Market System. Kreiner, Anna.

Theory vs History: Reply to Horwitz. Kindleberger, Charles P.

Wealth and Happiness. Wilson, James Q.

MARKETING

Business Ethics at Work. Vallance, Elizabeth.

Ethics of Business Students: Some Marketing Perspectives. Lane, J C.

Ethics, Incentives, and Conflicts of Interest: A Practical Solution. Kurland, Nancy B.

Industry Type, Culture, Mode of Entry and Perceptions of International Marketing Ethics Problems: A Cross-Cultural Comparison. Armstrong, Robert W and Sweeney, Jill.

MARMOR, A

Putting Interpretation in its Place. Endicott, Timothy A O.

MARQUAND, D

"Premature Obituaries: A Comment on O'Sullivan, Minogue, and Marquand" in The End of "Isms"?, Shtromas, Alexsandras (ed). Callinicos, Alex.

MARQUIS, D

Marquis' Argument Against Abortion: A Critique. Shirley, Edward S.

MARR, D

A Nonclassical Framework for Cognitive Science. Horgan, Terence and Tienson, John.

Individualism and Vision Theory. Egan, Frances.

Perception and Proper Explanatory Width. Rollins, Mark.

Simplicity, Cognition and Adaptation: Some Remarks on Marr's Theory of Vision. Gilman, Daniel.

MARRIAGE

"Gay Marriage: A Civil Right" in Gay Ethics, Murphy, Timothy F (ed). Dean, Craig R.

"Male-Order" Brides: Immigrant Women, Domestic Violence, and Immigration Law. Narayan, Uma.

"Marriage, Law, and Gender: A Feminist Inquiry" in Radical Philosophy of Law, Caudill, David S (ed). Hunter, Nan D.

Adultery and Fidelity. Martin, Mike W.

Die Ehe als Ort gleichberechtigter Lust. Heinrichs, Thomas.

Discussing Divorce in Introductory Ethics. Gould, James B.

John Stuart Mill and Harriet Taylor on Women and Marriage. Mendus, Susan.

Naturaleza del principio de la debida discreción de juicio en el consentimiento matrimonial (segunda y última parte). Moncada, Jesús Salvador.

MARSILIUS OF PADUA

Il Significato del Cuore nella Filosofia Giuridica di S Agostino e di Marsilio da Padova. Ancona, Elvio.

MARTIN, M

Reading Religions: A Reply to Callahan, Martin, and Quinn. Battin, Margaret P.

MARTIN, R

The Philosophical Context of Collingwood's Re-Enactment Theory. van der Dussen, Jan.

MARTIN, V

Resistance and Insubordination. Nelson, Hilde Lindemann.

MARX

"Nowak on Explanation and Idealization in Marx's 'Capital'" in Idealization VI: Idealization in Economics, Hamminga, Bert (ed). Diederich, Werner.

A History of Modern Political Thought: Major Political Thinkers from Hobbes to Marx. Hampsher-Monk, Iain.

After Marxism. Aronson, Ronald.

Autonomie des Selbstbewusstseins: Eine Untersuchung zum Verhältnis von Bruno Bauer und Karl Marx (1835-1843). Waser, Ruedi.

Dialectical Materialism and Modern Science. Cameron, Kenneth Neill.

God and Plastic Surgery: Marx, Nietzsche, Freud and the Obvious. Barris, Jeremy.

Hegel and Marx: Introductory Lectures. Kedourie, Elie.

Karl Marx's Theory of Ideas. Torrance, John.

Marx's Theory of the Social Formation. Duan, Zhongqiao.

Marxism and Spirituality: An International Anthology. Page, Benjamin B (ed).

Political Identity: Thinking Through Marx. Meister, Robert.

Rhetoric and Marxism. Aune, James Arnt.

Spectres de Marx: Entretien avec Jacques Derrida. Boissinot, Christian.

The Future of Alienation. Schacht, Richard.

Vergangenheit als Zukunft. Haller, Michael (ed) and Habermas, Jürgen.

Was ist und wozu überhaupt-Philosophie? Vorübungen sich verändernden Denkens. Brandner, Rudolf.

A Critique of "Non-Instrumental Reason". Siemek, Marek J.

Derrida and Habermas on the Aporia of the Politics of Identity and Difference: Towards Radical Democratic Multiculturalism. Matustík, Martin J.

Diferencia entre Alienaçao e Estranhamento nos Manuscritos Econômico-Filosóficos (1844), de Karl Marx. Ferreira Chagas, Eduardo.

El humanismo marxiano. Calvez, Jean-Yves.

El Idealismo Práctico de Marx: Una Lectura de las Thesen über Feuerbach. Andrés Bonetti, José.

Hegel, Marx and Idealistic Vapourizing. Ninnes, L E.

Ideas sobre Ortega y Gasset y el ocaso del marxismo. Pallotini, Michele.

Il Guardiano delle Soglia. Angelini, Pietro.

Is Marx a Moral Consequentialist?. Vogel, Jeffrey S.

Ist Philosophie auf Russisch möglich?. Malachov, Vladimir.

Karl Marx und die soziale Wirklichkeit. Epple, Moritz.

La alienación del trabajo según la perspectiva del marxismo analítico. Gallichio, Santiago.

La Riflessione sul Mito in Leopardi. Stella, Vittorio.

Las Formas lógicas de la Sección Primera de El Capital. Delgado, Manuel.

Marx and Engels on Democracy. Doveton, Daniel.

Marx and German Idealism: Labour and the Transcendental Synthesis. Moggach, Douglas.

Marx and Rights. Corlett, J Angelo.

Marx, Engels, and the Abolition of the Family. Weikart, Richard.

Marx, Moses, and the Pagans in the Secular City. Sunic, Tomislav.

Marx, Stalin, Marcuse: Die kritische Theorie in ideengeschichtlicher Sicht. Aleksandrowicz, Dariusz.

Technology as Art and the "Spheres of Freedom and Necessity". Evans, Fred.

The Greek Matrix of Marx's Critique of Political Economy. Katz, Claudio.

Tre Improbabili Nani Sulle Spalle dei Giganti. Mastroianni, Giovanni.

What's Wrong with Exploitation?. Schwartz, Justin K.

MARXISM

"A Process Without a Subject or Goal(s)" in Marxism in the Postmodern Age, Callari, Antonio (ed). Montag, Warren.

"Beyond Democracy: The Politics of Empowerment" in Marxism in the Postmodern Age, Callari, Antonio (ed). Levins, Richard.

"Class Structure and Choice of Technology in an Agrarian Economy" in Foundations of Analytical Marxism (Volume I), Roemer, John E (ed). Cabeza-Gutés, Maite.

"Consenting to Whiteness" in Marxism in the Postmodern Age, Callari, Antonio (ed). Williams, Rhonda M.

"Die verlorene Wette—Versuch über die Krisen des 'realen' Sozialismus" in Das geistige Erbe Europas, Buhr, Manfred (ed). Labica, Georges.

"El Marxismo Analítico y el Problema Moral del Trabajo" in Temas Actuales de Filosofía, Palacios, María Julia (ed). Gallichio, Santiago.

"Europa und sein geistiges Erbe" in Das geistige Erbe Europas, Buhr, Manfred (ed). Buhr, Manfred.

"Feminism Without Guarantees" in Marxism in the Postmodern Age, Callari, Antonio (ed). Stabile, Carol A.

"Has 'the World' Changed?" in Marxism in the Postmodern Age, Callari, Antonio (ed). Balibar, Etienne.

"Late Capitalism and Postmodernism: Jameson/Mandel" in Marxism in the Postmodern Age, Callari, Antonio (ed). Norton, Bruce.

"Lessons from the USSR: Taking Marxian Theory the Next Step" in Whither Marxism?, Magnus, Bernd (ed). Resnick, Stephen and Wolff, Richard.

"Liberty or Community? Defining the Post-Marxist Agenda" in Introducing Applied Ethics, Almond, Brenda (ed). Almond, Brenda.

"Marxism and Sexuality: The Body as Battleground" in Marxism in the Postmodern Age, Callari, Antonio (ed). Baxandall, Rosalyn.

"Marxism and Spirituality" in Marxism in the Postmodern Age, Callari, Antonio (ed). Kovel, Joel.

"Marxism in the New World Order: Crisis and Possibilities" in Marxism In the Postmodern Age, Callari, Antonio (ed). Callari, Antonio.

"Marxism in the Shadow of Hobbes" in Marxism in the Postmodern Age, Callari, Antonio (ed). Sinisi, John.

"Marxism: From Scientific to Utopian" in Whither Marxism?, Magnus, Bernd (ed). Longxi, Zhang.

"Morality: Invention or Discovery?" in Medicine and Moral Reasoning, Fulford, K W M (ed). Urmson, James O.

"Notizen über eine Erfahrung: Der Weg zum Marxismus" in Das geistige Erbe Europas, Buhr, Manfred (ed). Chitas, Eduardo.

"Post-Marxism and Class" in Marxism in the Postmodern Age, Callari, Antonio (ed). Sandler, Blair and Diskin, Jonathan.

MARXISM

"Postmodernism, Marxism, and the Critique of Modern Economic Thought" in *Marxism in the Postmodern Age, Callari, Antonio (ed)*. Amariglio, Jack and Ruccio, David F.

"Postwar Panics and the Crisis of Masculinity" in *Marxism in the Postmodern Age, Callari, Antonio (ed)*. Epstein, Barbara.

"Refiguring Values, Power, Knowledge: Or Foucault's Disavowal of Marx" in *Whither Marxism?, Magnus, Bernd (ed)*. Janmohamed, Abdul.

"Retrieval and Renewal" in *Marxism in the Postmodern Age, Callari, Antonio (ed)*. Rowbotham, Sheila.

"Situating the Capitalist State" in *Marxism in the Postmodern Age, Callari, Antonio (ed)*. Lebowitz, Michael A.

"Spinoza's Democracy: The Passions of Social Assemblages" in *Marxism in the Postmodern Age, Callari, Antonio (ed)*. Hardt, Michael.

"Supplementing Marxism" in *Whither Marxism?, Magnus, Bernd (ed)*. Spivak, Gayatri Chakravorty.

"The Analytic Defense of Functional Marxism and Law" in *Radical Philosophy of Law, Caudill, David S (ed)*. Gold, Steven Jay.

"The End of Orthodox Marxism" in *Marxism in the Postmodern Age, Callari, Antonio (ed)*. Kellner, Douglas M.

"The Legacy of Marxist Jurisprudence" in *Radical Philosophy of Law, Caudill, David S (ed)*. Belliotti, Raymond A.

"The Marxian Critique of Criminal Justice" in *Radical Philosophy of Law, Caudill, David S (ed)*. Reiman, Jeffrey.

"The Modern World and the Individual: From the Metamorphosis of Eastern European Marxism to Marx's Errors" in *Whither Marxism?, Magnus, Bernd (ed)*. Marga, Andrei.

"The Obsolescence of Marxism?" in *Whither Marxism?, Magnus, Bernd (ed)*. Kellner, Douglas M.

"The Relevance of Marxist Theory for Understanding the Present World Crisis" in *Marxism in the Postmodern Age, Callari, Antonio (ed)*. Mandel, Ernest.

"The Second Sex: From Marxism to Radical Feminism" in *Feminist Interpretations of Simone de Beauvoir, Simons, Margaret A (ed)*. Simons, Margaret A.

"What's Left of Marx?" in *The Cambridge Companion to Habermas, White, Stephen K (ed)*. Love, Nancy S.

"Zum Gebrauch von Traditionen" in *Das geistige Erbe Europas, Buhr, Manfred (ed)*. Merker, Nicolao.

"'Socialism of the Mind': The New Age of Post-Marxism" in *After Postmodernism, Simons, Herbert W (ed)*. Cloud, Dana L.

After Marxism. Aronson, Ronald.

After Postmodernism. Simons, Herbert W (ed) and Billig, Michael (ed).

Althusser: A Critical Reader. Elliott, Gregory (ed).

Critical Theory and Political Possibilities: Conceptions of Emancipatory Politics in the Works of Horkheimer, Adorno, Marcuse, and Habermas. Alway, Joan.

Das Feindbild der marxistisch-leninistischen Philosophie in der DDR 1945-1988. Kapferer, Norbert.

Das utopische Staatsmodell von Platons "Politeia" aus der Sicht von Orwells "Nineteen Eighty-Four". Otto, Dirk.

Foundations of Analytical Marxism (Volume I). Roemer, John E (ed).

Georg Lukács. Sim, Stuart.

Hegel and Marx: Introductory Lectures. Kedourie, Elie.

Humanism and its Aftermath: The Shared Fate of Deconstruction and Politics. Martin, Bill.

Karl Marx's Theory of Ideas. Torrance, John.

Marxism and Spirituality: An International Anthology. Page, Benjamin B (ed).

Marxism in the Postmodern Age. Callari, Antonio (ed), Cullenberg, Stephen (ed) and Biewener, Carole (ed).

Mass Enlightenment: Critical Studies in Rousseau and Diderot. Simon, Julia.

Meaning and Development. Kebede, Messay.

Philosophieverhältnisse im deutschen Faschismus. Laugstien, Thomas.

Positivismusstreit: Die Auseinandersetzungen der Frankfurter Schule mit dem logischen Positivismus, dem Pragmatismus und dem kritischen Rationalismus. Dahms, Hans-Joachim.

Rhetoric and Marxism. Aune, James Arnt.

S L Frank: The Life and Work of A Russian Philosopher, 1877-1950. Boobbyer, Philip.

Search for Community in a Withering Tradition: Conversations between a Marxian Atheist and a Calvinian Christian. Nielsen, Kai and Hart, Hendrik.

The Lukács Reader. Kadarkay, Arpad (ed).

The Lyotard Reader. Benjamin, Andrew (ed).

The Real World of Democracy Revisited and Other Essays on Democracy and Socialism. Cunningham, Frank.

Whither Marxism?. Magnus, Bernd (ed) and Cullenberg, Stephen (ed).

A Critique of "Non-Instrumental Reason". Siemek, Marek J.

A Metastructural Reinterpretation of the Rawlsian Theory: From Rawls to Machiavelli. Bidet, Jacques.

An Integrative Ideology for Russia. Kosolapov, N A.

Continuity—Guo Xiang, Chan, Cheng-Zhu *Lixue*, New Realism, and Marxism— Feng's Discernment of the Way. Obenchain, Diane B.

Contribuiçao par as Discussoes ao Projeto de Implantaçao do Curso de Pedagogia na Fac de Ciências da Univ Estadual Paulista "Júlio de Mesquita Filho". Ghiraldelli Júnior, Paulo.

Cultural Materialism, Cultural and Post-Culturalism: The Legacy of Raymond Williams. Milner, Andrew.

Das Wort im Leben und das Wort in der Poesie. Volosinov, Valentin N.

El Cristianismo como *A Priori* de la Revolución en la Filosofía de Ernst Bloch. Orsolic, Marco.

El humanismo marxiano. Calvez, Jean-Yves.

Escola Pública: Trabalho Produtivo ou Improdutivo. Pizzi, Laura Cristina V.

Fashion in Ruins: History After the Cold War. Buck-Morss, Susan.

Feminism as Critique in Philosophy of Music Education. Lamb, Roberta.

Feminist Social Criticism and Marx's Theory of Religion. Newman, Amy.

Histoire, mémorie et oubli chez Walter Benjamin. Gagnebin, Jeanne-Marie.

Ideas sobre Ortega y Gasset y el ocaso del marxismo. Pallotini, Michele.

Karl Popper, 1902-1994. Agassi, Joseph (& others).

La alienación del trabajo según la perspectiva del marxismo analítico. Gallichio, Santiago.

La posible contribución de la filosofía clásica rusa a la construcción de una sociedad humanista. Kline, Goerge L.

Labriola tra Croce e Gentile. Agrimi, Mario.

Late-Marxist, Post-Poststructuralist Critical Nebulosity. Harris, Wendell V.

Leviatán en los confines de la modernidad: Una crítica anarquista de la sociedad civil y el Estado. Jiménez, Jorge.

Marxism on Dialectical and Logical Contradiction. Goldstick, D.

Marxism, 'Ideology,' and Moral Objectivism. Mills, Charles W.

Marxismo y Hermenéutica. Torrico, Vitaliano.

Not the "Human Factor" but the Person. Suvorov, Aleksandr V.

Ökologische Blindheit: Die Aporie der herrschenden Wirtschaftswissenschaft. Reheis, Fritz.

Olympus Mislaid? A Profile of Perry Anderson. Elliot, Gregory.

Philosophy in Russian Today. Yulina, N S.

Rassegne Crociane: I. I Carteggi dell'Ultimo Decennio. II. Una Bibliografia "Ragionata". Miccolis, Stefano.

Razón e historia: La modernidad del postmodernismo. Koslowski, Peter.

Reaction to Marek Siemek's "Critique of 'Non-Instrumental Reason'". Mayer, J R A.

Russian Philosophy as an Area of Study and as a Spiritual Value. Kuvakin, V A.

Social Being and the Human Essence: An Unresolved Issue in Soviet Philosophy. Bakhurst, David.

Storia e Politica nel Pensiero di Benedetto Croce. Lönne, Karl-Egon.

Subjectivity: Marxism and "The Spiritual" in China Since Mao. Tongqi, Lin and Minghua, Li.

Synopsis of a Theory of Modernity. Ibañez-Noé, Javier A.

Tactics, Ethics, or Temporality? Heidegger's Politics Reviewed. Osborne, Peter.

The Concept of Dialectic. Stack, George J.

The Heirs of German Idealism (in Portuguese). Musse, Ricardo.

The Pathos of European Political Philosophy After Marxism. McBride, William L.

The Political Thought of John Dunn and the Cambridge School. Hanzawa, Takamaro.

The Possibility of Communist Altruism. Jenkins, J L.

The Relative Heteronomy of Law. MacCormick, Neil.

The Social Philosophy of P I Novgorodtsev. Zhukov, V N.

The Sundered Totality: Adorno's Freudo-Marxism. Cook, Deborah.

Un'idea alla Ricerca di un Partito: L'eredità di Silvio Spaventa nel Liberalismo di Fine Ottocento. Ricci, Saverio.

Walter Benjamin and Marxism (in Portuguese). Löwy, Michael.

Wesensmerkmale der russischen Philosophie. Losskij, Nikolaj O.

What Can We Learn From Art?. Diffey, T J.

Whither Universalism?. Bhate, Anilkumar.

Zwischen 'Kritik der bürgerlichen Ideologie' und 'integralem Marxismus': Zur Rexeption der Frankfurter Schule in der DDR. Bialas, Wolfgang.

'The World Spirit on the Fins of a Rocket': Adorno's Critique of Progress. Löwy, Michael and Varikas, Eleni.

MASARYK, T

Concrete Logic—The Lifelong Subject of T G Masaryk. Olsovsky, Jirí.

MASCULINITY

"Postmodernism and the Interrogation of Masculinity" in *Theorizing Masculinities, Brod, Harry (ed)*. Gutterman, David S.

"Postwar Panics and the Crisis of Masculinity" in *Marxism in the Postmodern Age, Callari, Antonio (ed)*. Epstein, Barbara.

"Theorizing Masculinities in Contemporary Social Science" in *Theorizing Masculinities, Brod, Harry (ed)*. Coltrane, Scott.

Theorizing Masculinities. Brod, Harry (ed) and Kaufman, Michael (ed).

L'homme en quête de lui-même—A propos du livre d'Elisabeth Badinter: *XY: De l'identité masculine*. Bouchard, Guy.

MASK

Las máscaras del demonio: Nietzsche y la hermenéutica. Conill, Jesus.

MASS

Il mondo "Pesante" di Newton. Infante, Giancarlo.

MASSEN, J

"Ethics of Emotion: Some Indian Reflections" in *Emotions in Asian Thought, Marks, Joel (ed)*. Bilimoria, Purusottama.

MASSES

Hannah Arendt and the Question of Mass Society. Lima, Joseph.

Theories of Masses and Problems of Constitution. Zimmerman, Dean.

MASSEY, S

Allocation of Resources at the Bedside: The Intersection of Economics, Law, and Ethics. Pellegrino, Edmund D.

MASTER-SLAVE

Die methodologische Funktion des Verhältnisses von "Herr und Knecht" in der Philosophie Hegels. Kumamoto, Yasuhiro.

MATERIAL

Kant's Early Metaphysics and the Origins of the Critical Philosophy. Laywine, Alison.

MATERIAL CAUSE

Théorie Aristotélicienne du rôle de la quantité et de la qualité chez les êtres vivants (I). Bernier, Réjane.

MATERIAL WORLD

Descartes und der Traumskeptizismus. Imlay, Robert A.

MATERIALISM

see also Atomism, Dialectical Materialism, Matter

"*Homo Homini Deus Est*: Feuerbach's Religious Materialism" in *Meaning, Truth, and God*, Rouner, Leroy (ed). Wartofsky, Marx W.

"*Paradise Lost* and the Materialism Debate" in *The 1994 Annual of Hermeneutics and Social Concern*, Lawler, Justus George (ed). Fallon, Stephen M.

"*Juan Huarte de San Juan: Un Materialista Español del Siglo XVI*" in *Temas Actuales de Filosofía*, Palacios, María Julia (ed). Femenías, María Luisa.

"Marxism and Spirituality" in *Marxism in the Postmodern Age*, Callari, Antonio (ed). Kovel, Joel.

"Mind and Brain" in *The Mind-Body Problem: A Guide to the Current Debate*, Warner, Richard (ed). Dretske, Fred.

"On the Assumption That Our Concepts 'Structure the Material of Our Experience'" in *Philosophy, Mathematics and Modern Physics*, Rudolph, Enno (ed). Mühlhölzer, Felix.

A Philosophy of Matter and Mind: A New Look at an Old Major Topic in Philosophy. Wassermann, Gerhard D.

Farben und Phänomenales Wissen. Nida-Rümelin, Martine.

Marx's Theory of the Social Formation. Duan, Zhongqiao.

Subjectivity and Reduction: An Introduction to the Mind-Body Problem. Hannan, Barbara.

The 1994 Annual of Hermeneutics and Social Concern. Lawler, Justus George (ed).

The Enigma of the Mind: The Mind-Body Problem in Contemporary Thought. Moravia, Sergio and Staton, Scott (trans).

The Erich Fromm Reader. Fromm, Erich and Funk, Rainer (ed).

The Problem of Consciousness: Essays Towards a Resolution. McGinn, Colin.

Beyond the Material and the Mechanical: Occam's Razor Is a Double-Edged Blade. Ulanowicz, Robert E.

Croce e Gentile nell'Epistolario di Fausto Nicolini. Rascaglia, Maria.

Cultural Materialism, Cultural and Post-Culturalism: The Legacy of Raymond Williams. Milner, Andrew.

David Hume: la révolution praxologique du matérialisme. Grandjean, Fabien.

El Idealismo Práctico de Marx: Una Lectura de las *Thesen über Feuerbach*. Andrés Bonetti, José.

El Materialismo de Feuerbach: Un Estudio de sus Escritos. Barata-Moura, José.

Eléments pour un matérialisme dynamique. Andrieu, Bernard.

Global Idealism/Local Materialism. Matsuno, Koichiro and Salthe, Stanley N.

Kim on Multiple Realizability and Causal Types. McClamrock, Ron.

La Percepción Jeráquica de la Realidad. Sánchez del Río, Carlos.

Marxism on Dialectical and Logical Contradiction. Goldstick, D.

Material Minds: On Materialism (in Dutch). Cuypers, S E.

Materialism and Supervenience. Jack, Andrew.

Materialism and the "Problem" of Quantum Measurement. Mulhauser, Gregory R.

Materialism, Reduction, Replacement, and the Place of Consciousness in Science. Foss, Jeffrey E.

Matérialisme et neuro-sciences: la question des localisations cérébrales. Missa, Jean-Noël.

Nonreductive Materialism and Mental Causation. Marras, Ausonio.

Notas sobre la física epicúrea. Fallas, Luis A.

On Gilles Deleuze and Félix Guattari, *A Thousand Plateaus*. Negri, Antonio and Wolf, Charles (trans).

Positivismo e Metafisica in Russia in uno Scritto di Vladimir Solov'ev. Mastroianni, Giovanni.

Revisionary Materialism: A Critique of Stich. Roe, John H.

Should a Materialist Believe in Qualia?. Lewis, David.

The Churchlands' Eliminative Materialism. Hunter, Geoffrey.

The Materialist Mentality Revisited. Dov Lerner, Berel.

Transzendentale Basis, Materialismus, und Religion. Lauth, Reinhard.

Two Cheers for Reductionism: Or, the Dim Prospects for Non-Reductive Materialism. Melnyk, Andrew.

What Is Universalism?. Kuczynski, Janusz.

MATERIALITY

Substance Among Other Categories. Hoffman, Joshua and Rosenkrantz, Gary S.

The Substantial Unity of Material Substances According to John Poinsot. Kronen, John D.

Van Inwagen's *Material Beings*. Persson, Ingmar.

MATHEMATICS

see also Addition, Algebra, Calculus, Geometry

"A Problem in Possible-World Semantics" in *Modality, Morality, and Belief*, Sinnott-Armstrong, Walter (ed). Kaplan, David B.

"Charles S Peirce, Mathematician" in *Peirce and Contemporary Thought: Philosophical Inquiries*, Ketner, Kenneth Laine (ed). Eisele, Carolyn.

"Dynamik, Emergenz und Mathematik: Über Kontinua und Diskontinua" in *Schelling und die Selbstorganisation*, Heuser-Kessler, Marie-Luise (ed). Eisenhardt, Peter.

"Logic, Mind, and Mathematics" in *Dennett and his Critics*, Dahlbom, Bo (ed). McGinn, Colin.

"Mathematical Machines" in *The Machine as Metaphor and Tool*, Haken, Hermann (ed). Henry, Paul.

"Mathematics" in *The Cambridge Companion to Husserl*, Smith, Barry (ed). Tieszen, Richard.

"Mathématiques: la couleur des preuves" in *Rhétoriques de la science*, De Coorebyter, Vincent (ed). Dubucs, Jacques and Dubucs, Monique.

"On the Mathematical Overdetermination of Physics" in *Philosophy, Mathematics and Modern Physics*, Rudolph, Enno (ed). Scheibe, Erhard.

"Part-Whole" in *The Cambridge Companion to Husserl*, Smith, Barry (ed). Fine, Kit.

"Peirce at the Intersection of Mathematics and Philosophy" in *Peirce and Contemporary Thought: Philosophical Inquiries*, Ketner, Kenneth Laine (ed). Pycior, Helena M.

"Pythagorean Number as Form, Color, and Light" in *Homage to Pythagoras*, Bamford, Christopher (ed). Lawlor, Robert.

"Questions Concerning Theory and Experience and the Role of Mathematics..." in *Philosophy, Mathematics and Modern Physics*, Rudolph, Enno (ed). Stamatescu, I O.

"Structuralism and the Concept of Set" in *Modality, Morality, and Belief*, Sinnott-Armstrong, Walter (ed). Parsons, Charles.

"The Limited Lure of Arabic Mathematics" in *The 'Arabick' Interest of the Natural Philosophers in Seventeenth-Century England*, Russell, G A (ed). Molland, George.

"The Mathematical Frame of Quantum Field Theory" in *Philosophy, Mathematics and Modern Physics*, Rudolph, Enno (ed). Fredenhagen, Klaus.

"The Role of Mathematics in Contemporary Theoretical Physics" in *Philosophy, Mathematics and Modern Physics*, Rudolph, Enno (ed). Münster, Gernot.

"The Two Lights" in *Homage to Pythagoras*, Bamford, Christopher (ed). Zajonc, Arthur.

"Was kann die heutige Mathematik von Schelling lernen?" in *Schelling und die Selbstorganisation*, Heuser-Kessler, Marie-Luise (ed). Radbruch, Knut.

A History of Scientific Thought: Elements of a History of Science. Serres, Michel (ed).

Aristotle's Theory of Actuality. Bechler, Zev.

Continuity and Change in the Development of Russell's Philosophy. Hager, Paul J.

Denken im Modell: Theorie und Erfahrung im Paradigma eines pragmatischen Modellbegriffs. Wernecke, Jörg.

Die Musik als scientia mathematica von der Spätantike bis zum Barock. Hirtler, Eva.

Die Sprache in den Wissenschaften. Weingartner, Paul (ed).

Frege's Philosophy of Mathematics. Demopoulos, William (ed).

Homage to Pythagoras. Bamford, Christopher (ed).

La Depsicologizzazione della Logica: Un confronto tra Boole e Frege. Vassallo, Nicla.

Ludwig Wittgenstein: Wiener Ausgabe/Vienna Edition—Band 1: Philosophische Bemerkungen. Nedo, Michael (ed) and Wittgenstein, Ludwig.

Ludwig Wittgenstein: Wiener Ausgabe/Vienna Edition—Band 2: Philosophische Betrachtungen, Philosophische Bemerkungen. Nedo, Michael (ed) and Wittgenstein, Ludwig.

Mathematics—The Music of Reason. Dieudonné, Jean, Dales, H G (trans) and Dales, J C (trans).

On Knowing—The Natural Sciences. McKeon, Richard, Owen, David B (ed) and McKeon, Zahava K (ed).

Paradoxism's Main Roots. Vasiliu, Florin and Benea, Stefan (trans).

Philosophical Naturalism. Papineau, David.

Philosophy, Mathematics and Modern Physics. Rudolph, Enno (ed) and Stamatescu, I O (ed).

Projective Probability. Logue, James.

Spinoza's Ethica From Manuscript to Print: Studies on Text, Form, and Related Topics. Steenbakkers, Piet.

Strands of System: The Philosophy of Charles Peirce. Anderson, Douglas R.

The Shaggy Steed of Physics: Mathematical Beauty in the Physical World. Oliver, David.

The 'Arabick' Interest of the Natural Philosophers in Seventeenth-Century England. Russell, G A (ed).

Vie della scrittura: Frege e la svolta linguistica. Penco, Carlo.

A Case for Realism in Mathematics. Drozdek, Adam and Keagy, Tom.

A Formal Framework for Quantum Non-Individuality. Krause, Décio and French, Steven.

Absolute Forms of Gödel's Incompleteness Theorem. Kim, Sangmun.

Analisi e Assiomatizzazione nella Dialettica di Platone. Ferrari, Franco.

Boturini e la Diffusione di Vico in Spagna. Mestre, Antonio.

Chaos Theory, the End of Physicalism?. Schopman, Joop.

Chaos, Clio, and Scientific Illusions of Understanding. Roth, Paul A and Ryckman, Thomas A.

Commentary on Sayre's "Why Plato Never Had a Theory of Forms". Griswold, Charles.

Commentary on Smith's "What Use is Aristotle's *Organon*?". Hintikka, Jaakko.

Comments on Smolarski's 'Finding Meaning in Mathematics'. Johnson, Julia A.

Connectionism and the Mind: An Introduction to Parallel Processing in Networks. Ohayon, Elan Liss.

Construction and Mathematical Schematism: Kant on the Exhibition of a Concept in Intuition. Ferrarin, Alfredo.

Construction et Structure Dynamique des Théories Physiques. Gauthier, Yvon.

MECHANISM

Newton, Science, and Causation. Faulconer, James E.

Paper Machines. Mundici, Daniele and Sieg, Wilfried.

Prediction Versus Retrodiction in Mill. Steinitz, Yuval.

Reasoning, Logic and Computation. Shapiro, Stewart.

Temporal Asymmetry in Classical Mechanics. Hutchison, Keith.

The Correspondence Principle and the Closure of Theories: Two Incompatible Aspects of Heisenberg's Philosophy of Science. Weinert, Friedel.

The Evolution of the Will. Norwood, Rick.

Turing and the Origins of AI. Shanker, Stuart.

Two Logical Patterns of the Reduction of Theories: Comments on Józef Werle's Paper "How the Physical Sciences Discovered the Unity of Nature". Krajewski, Wladyslaw.

Wright on the Non-Mechanizability of Intuitionist Reasoning. Detlefsen, Michael.

MECHANIZATION

"The Mechanization of Time" in *The Machine as Metaphor and Tool*, Haken, Hermann (ed). Lundmark, Lennart.

MECHTHILD OF MAGDEBURG

Mechthild von Magdeburg und der frühe Meister Eckhart. Weiss, Bardo.

MEDIA

"Ethics, Law, and the Quality of the Media" in *Introducing Applied Ethics*, Almond, Brenda (ed). Belsey, Andrew.

"Fatal Forms: Toward a (Neo) Formal Sociological Theory of Media Culture" in *Baudrillard: A Critical Reader*, Kellner, Douglas M (ed). Epstein, Jonathan S and Epstein, Margarete J.

"Symbolic Exchange in Hyperreality" in *Baudrillard: A Critical Reader*, Kellner, Douglas M (ed). Cook, Deborah.

Media Ethics. Fink, Conrad C.

The Counterfeit Wisdom of Shallow Minds: A Critique of Some Leading Offenders of the 1980's. Habermehl, Lawrence.

Docs on the Box: Or, How We Learned to Stop Worrying and Love the Tube. Elliott, Carl and Kahn, Jeffrey.

Journalists' Views of Advertiser Pressures on Agricultural News. Reisner, Ann and Walter, Gerry.

The United States Media and the Liberal Tradition. Bartkowiak, Julia J.

MEDIATION

"Immediacy, Opposition, and Mediation" in *Recovering Pragmatism's Voice*, Langsdorf, Lenore (ed). Colapietro, Vincent M.

An Introduction to the Philosophy of Giuseppe Capograssi. Pagallo, Ugo.

From Adjudication to Mediation: Third Party Discourse in Conflict Resolution. Maley, Yon.

MEDICAL

Locke's Medical Notebook, 'Adversaria 3'. Meynell, Guy.

MEDICAL DEVICE

But Doctor, It's My Hip!: The Fate of Failed Medical Devices. Fielder, John H and Black, Jonathan.

MEDICAL ETHICS

see also Abortion, Bioethics, Clinical Ethics, Euthanasia

"Creation and Relation" in *Medicine and Moral Reasoning*, Fulford, K W M (ed). Soskice, Janet Martin.

"Dependency: The Foundational Value in Medical Ethics" in *Medicine and Moral Reasoning*, Fulford, K W M (ed). Campbell, Alastair V.

"Letting Patients Die: Legal and Moral Reflections" in *In Harm's Way*, Coleman, Jules L (ed). Kadish, Sanford H.

"Medical Ethics, Moral Philosophy and Moral Tradition" in *Medicine and Moral Reasoning*, Fulford, K W M (ed). Murray, Thomas H.

"Not More Medical Ethics" in *Medicine and Moral Reasoning*, Fulford, K W M (ed). Fulford, K William M.

"Wann ist ein Mensch tot?" Bemerkungen zum Streit um den menschlichen Tod. Quante, Michael.

Classic Cases in Medical Ethics (Second Edition). Pence, Gregory E.

Humane Medicine: A Leading Surgeon Examines What Doctors Do, What Their Patients Expect from Them, and How the Expectations of Both Are Not Being Met. Little, Miles.

Life Choices: A Hastings Center Introduction to Bioethics. Howell, Joseph H (ed) and Sale, William Frederick (ed).

Nursing Ethics: Therapeutic Caring Presence. Bishop, Anne H and Scudder Jr, John R.

AIDS, Confidentiality, and Ethical Models. Gorbett, Jason.

Approaches (and Possible Contraindications) to Enhancing Patients' Autonomy. Howe, Edmund G.

Authenticity as a Foundational Principle of Medical Ethics. Welie, Jos V M.

Bioethik und Feminismus. Pauer-Studer, Herlinde.

Chemins et Impasses de l'Éthique à l'Hôpital. Malherbe, Jean-François.

Commentary on Discussions About Life-Sustaining Treatments. Emanuel, Ezekiel J.

Ethical Issues in Discharge Planning for Vulnerable Infants and Children. Cohen, Marsha H.

Hawkeye Pierce and the Questionable Relevance of Medical Etiquette to Contemporary Medical Ethics and Practice. Sugarman, Jeremy.

How Christian Ethics Became Medical Ethics: The Case of Paul Ramsey. Hauerwas, Stanley.

La Bioéthique, une Interface entre Théorie et Pratique?. Leclerc, Bruno.

La Bioéthique: d'Une Révolution à l'Autre. Mélançon, Marcel J.

La Notion de *Personne* Selon Lucien Sève. Thérrien, Jean-Marie.

Les Séquences d'ADN Humain Peuvent-Elles Etre Brevetées?. Thérrien, Jean-Marie.

Literature as Mirror or Lamp? Commentary on "Literature, Medical Ethics, and 'Epiphanic Knowledge'". Jones, Anne Hudson.

Literature, Medical Ethics, and "Epiphanic Knowledge". Hawkins, Anne Hunsaker.

Make My Case: Ethics Teaching and Case Presentations. Kuczewski, Mark (& others).

Negotiating the Moral Order: Paradoxes of Ethics Consultation. Crigger, Bette-Jane.

Oppressive Limits: Callahan's Foundation Myth. Dixon, Kathleen Marie.

Sida y confidencialidad: un problema complejo. Luna, Florencia.

The Idea of the Absurd and the Moral Decision: Possibilities and Limits of a Physician's Actions in the View of the Absurd. Lengers, Frank P.

The Physician-Assisted Suicide and Euthanasia Debate: An Annotated Bibliography of Representative Articles. Fins, Joseph J and Bacchetta, Matthew D.

The Role of Empirical Research in Medical Ethics: Asking Questions or Answering Them?. Braddock III, Clarence H.

The Word "Bioethics": Its Birth and the Legacies of Those Who Shaped Its Meaning. Reich, Warren Thomas.

Towards a Just, Courageous, and Honest Resolution of the Futility Debate. Tong, Rosemarie.

Validité et limites du consensus en éthique clinique. Malherbe, Jean-François, Rocchetti, Loretta and Boire-Lavigne, Anne-Marie.

Vers une Éthique de Responsabilité en Milieu Médical. Léry, Nicole.

MEDICINE

"Accountability and Nursing" in *Ethics and the Professions*, Chadwick, Ruth (ed). Tadd, Win.

"Common Codes: Divergent Practices" in *Ethics and the Professions*, Chadwick, Ruth (ed). Jackson, Jennifer.

"Homophobia and the Moral Authority of Medicine" in *Gay Ethics*, Murphy, Timothy F (ed). Wilkerson, Abby.

"Human In-vitro Fertilization" in *Ethics on the Frontiers of Human Existence*, Badham, Paul (ed). Fishel, Simon.

"Krankheit als Tat-Sache" in *Mythos Wertfreiheit?*, Apel, Karl-Otto (ed). Pawelzik, Markus.

"Lebensqualitätsbewertung im Gesundheitswesen als Problem der Medizin und der Ökonomie" in *Mythos Wertfreiheit?*, Apel, Karl-Otto (ed). Schöffski, Oliver.

"Medical Education: Knowledge and Know-How" in *Ethics and the Professions*, Chadwick, Ruth (ed). Fulford, K W M.

"Narrating Social Work" in *Ethics and the Professions*, Chadwick, Ruth (ed). Edgar, Andrew.

"Not More Medical Ethics" in *Medicine and Moral Reasoning*, Fulford, K W M (ed). Fulford, K William M.

"The Appropriate Medical Care of the Terminally Ill" in *Ethics on the Frontiers of Human Existence*, Badham, Paul (ed). Kryspin, Jan and Phillips, Heather.

"The Nature and Role of Professional Codes in Modern Society" in *Ethics and the Professions*, Chadwick, Ruth (ed). Häyry, Heta and Häyry, Matti.

"The Placebo Concept in Medicine and Psychiatry" in *Philosophical Psychopathology*, Graham, George (ed). Erwin, Edward.

"Was heisst es, den Tod zu definieren?" in *Freiheit, Verantwortung und Folgen in der Wissenschaft*, Sandkühler, Hans Jörg (ed). Bayertz, Kurt.

"'Wanted' and 'Unwanted' Life" in *Ethics on the Frontiers of Human Existence*, Badham, Paul (ed). Kittrie, Nicholas.

Bioethics: A Committee Approach. Minogue, Brendan.

Classic Cases in Medical Ethics (Second Edition). Pence, Gregory E.

Concepts and Cases in Nursing Ethics. Yeo, Michael (& others).

Essays on Bioethics by R M Hare. Crisp, Roger.

Ethical Argument: Critical Thinking in Ethics. Curtler, Hugh Mercer.

Ethical Issues in Suicide. Battin, Margaret P.

Ethics on the Frontiers of Human Existence. Badham, Paul (ed).

Exploring Our Environmental Connections. Schuster, Eleanor A (ed) and Brown, Carolyn L (ed).

Freud and the Politics of Psychoanalysis. Brunner, José.

Humane Medicine: A Leading Surgeon Examines What Doctors Do, What Their Patients Expect from Them, and How the Expectations of Both Are Not Being Met. Little, Miles.

Intervention and Reflection: Basic Issues in Medical Ethics (Fifth Edition). Munson, Ronald (ed).

Life Choices: A Hastings Center Introduction to Bioethics. Howell, Joseph H (ed) and Sale, William Frederick (ed).

Medicine and Moral Reasoning. Fulford, K W M (ed), Gillett, Grant (ed) and Soskice, Janet Martin (ed).

Medicine, Money, and Morals: Physicians' Conflicts of Interest. Rodwin, Marc A.

Rationing Medicine. Blank, Robert H.

The Diffident Naturalist: Robert Boyle and the Philosophy of Experiment. Sargent, Rose-Mary.

The Immune Self: Theory or Metaphor?. Tauber, Alfred I.

A Memo from the Central Office: The "Ethical and Religious Directives for Catholic Health Care Services". Wildes, Kevin William.

A Motivational Approach to Confirmation: An Interpretation of Dysphagic Patients' Experiences. Gustafsson, Barbro and Pörn, Ingmar.

Advance Care Planning: Priorities for Ethical and Empirical Research. Teno, Joan M, Hill, T Patrick and O'Connor, Mary Ann.

Albert Schweitzer or Ivan Boesky? Why We Should Reject the Dichotomy Between Medicine and Business. Wicks, Andrew C.

Anthropology and the Theory of Medicine. von Uexküll, Thure.

Anxiety: A Pseudo-Concept. Shibles, Warren.

Appropriate and Inappropriate Use of Advance Directives. Emanuel, Linda.

METAPHYSICS

METAPHYSICS

Fenomenología y metafísica. Lobato, Abelardo.

Fichte en 1804-1806: Arrebato y Entrega. Ciria, Alberto.

Fichte's Rhetoric of Deception: Reflections on the Early Fichte in the Spirit of Jacobi. Di Giovanni, George.

Fichtean Circularity, Antifoundationalism, and Groundless System. Rockmore, Tom.

Fichtes genetische Deduktion von Raum und Zeit in Differenz zu Kant. Metz, Wilhelm.

Fichtes Lehre vom nicht bewussten Vernunfthandeln. Soller, Alois K.

Filosofia cristiana, fenomenologia e metafisica secondo E Stein. Mondin, Battista.

Filosofía e Historia Según I. Ellacuría. Martínez, José A.

Filosofía y Traducción. Casares, Angel J.

Filosofie, Metafysica en Moraal van Karl Popper. Abbes, J K.

Final Causality in Contemporary Physics. Quay, Paul M.

Finding *Finity* and Motion for Zeno. Borejszo, Zee.

Finito e infinito e l'idealismo della filosofia: La logica hegeliana dell'essere determinato: Parte Prima. Movia, Giancarlo.

Finito e infinito e l'idealismo della filosofia: La logica hegeliana dell'essere determinato: Parte Seconda. Movia, Giancarlo.

Following Edmund Husserl on One of the Paths Leading to the Transcendental Reduction. Kortooms, Toine.

Formes Métaphysiques et Etres Empiriques Selon Proclus. Térézis, Christos.

Four Practical Challenges of the Mature Royce to Californians and Others. Oppenheim, Frank.

Free Willing: Comments on Hoffman's "Freedom and Strength of Will". Chappell, Vere.

Freedom and Determinism. Clarke, Randolph.

Freedom and Faith in Kierkegaard's Philosophy. Shukla, Dipti.

Freedom and Strength of Will in Hoffman and Albritton. Watson, Gary.

Freedom and Strength of Will: Descartes and Albritton. Hoffman, Paul.

Freud: d'une *tension* autobiographique. Minassian, Marie-José.

From a Restricted to a General Economy of Play: Heidegger's Critique of Metaphysics. Küchler, T.

From Montague to Neo-Confucianism: Feng Youlan's "New *Lixue*" and Logical Analysis. Lujun, Yin.

From Ontology to Text in *Being and Time*. Kaplan, David.

From Relations to Practice in the Empiricism of Gilles Deleuze. Hayden, Patrick.

From the Chariot: The Katha and the Phaedrus. Johnson, Lawrence E.

Función de la Creatividad en la Filosofía de A N Whitehead. Oroz Ezcurra, Javier.

Gassendi contre Spinoza selon Bayle: ricochets de la critique de l'âme du monde. Darmon, Jean-Charles.

Gegenwärtige Diskussionen über eine Konzeption der Naturphilosophie. Hajduk, Zygmunt.

Geist und Psyche in tiefenpsychologischer und phänomenologischer Perspektive. Weier, Winfried.

General Method. McShane, Philip.

Genres of Jain History. Cort, John E.

Genus/Diferentia, Matter/Form, and Levels of Complexity. Freytag, Matthew.

Giuseppe Rensi e la lettura antimetafisica della teologia di Spinoza. Siena, R M.

Going on Knowing? The Development of the Idea of Living Liberation in the Upanisads. Fort, Andrew O.

Grammacentrism and the Transformation of Rhetoric. Khushf, George.

Habermas and Mead: On Universality and Individuality. Aboulafia, Mitchell.

Hacia un Nuevo Concepto de Trascendentalismo?. Recas Bayón, Javier.

Hans Jonas's Diagnosis of Nihilism: The Case of Heidegger. Vogel, Lawrence.

Harry Frankfurt: El agente moral y la noción de incondicionalidad. Beltrán, Miquel.

Haunting Resonances at the Threshold of Contemporary Philosophy. Review of *Echoes: After Heidegger* by John Sallis. Brogan, Walter.

Hegel and Fichte: Recognition, Otherness, and Absolute Knowing. Houlgate, Stephen.

Hegel and the Myth of Reason. Stewart, Jon.

Hegel or Schelling?. White, Alan.

Hegel's Confessions; or, Why We Need a Sequel to the *Phenomenology of Spirit*. Cutrofello, Andrew.

Hegel, Marx and Idealistic Vapourizing. Ninnes, L E.

Heidegger and Aristotle's Treatise on Time. Kane, Michael T.

Heidegger on Hölderlin's *Der Rhein*: Some External Considerations. Grugan, Arthur A.

Heidegger y la otra historia de Occidente: Notas Kantianas para una lectura de los *Beiträge zur Philosophie*. Callejo, M José.

Heidegger's "Time and Being": A Draft of the Third Section of "Being and Time" (in Dutch). De Boer, Karin.

Heidegger's Appropriation of Schelling. Sikka, Sonya.

Heidegger's Early Freiburg Courses, 1915-1923. van Buren, John.

Heidegger's Hermeneutic Circle. Fisher, Linda.

Heidegger's Virtue is Knowledge: Being-With and Solicitude in Chapter 26 of *Being and Time*. Shapiro, Joel B.

Heidegger, Early and late: The Vanishing of the Subject. Hodge, Joanna.

Heidegger, lector de Nietzsche. Rodríguez, Amán Rosales.

Hermenéutica y Realismo Científico. Alcalá Campos, Raúl.

Het monisme van Herman Berger. Kal, Victor.

Holiness as Service: *Therapeia* and *Hyperetike* in Plato's *Euthyphro*. Parry, David M.

How (Not) to Read Heidegger. Sheehan, Thomas.

How Can What I Perceive Be True?. Wahl, Russell.

How Innovative is the *Alayavijnana*?, Part II. Waldron, William S.

How Narrow is Narrow Content?. Recanati, François.

How Should Future Opinion Affect Current Opinion?. Foley, Richard.

How to Know the Inner-Self?. Esser, Piet Hein.

How to Start and Stop: Walter Burley on the Instant of Transition. Spade, Paul Vincent.

Hume's Actual Argument Against Belief in Miracles. Armstrong Jr, Benjamin F.

Hume's View on External Object: A Critical Analysis. Pandey, Indu.

Humean Supervenience and Enduring Things. Haslanger, Sally.

Husserl and Sartre: A Question of Reason. Mensch, James R.

Husserl on the Ego and Its Eidos (*Cartesian Meditations*, IV). Ferrarin, Alfredo.

Husserl's Conception of Hume's Problem: Toward a Transcendental Hermeneutic of Hume's *Treatise*. Tagore, Saranindra N.

Husserl, Heidegger, Cassirer: Trois philosophies de crise. Lofts, Steve.

Husserl, Schutz, "Paul" and Me: Reflections on Writing Phenomenology. Bentz, Valerie Malhotra.

I nessi Strutturali tra Metafisica e Teurgia im Giamblico. Cocco, Giuseppe.

Identidad Personal y yo Moral en David Hume. Clotet, Joaquín.

Identity, Self-Reflection and the Problem of Validating Standards. Raffel, Stanley.

If Wittgenstein Had Read Poinsot: Recasting the Problem of Signs and Mental States. Cahalan, John C.

Il carattere illusorio della critica di Jacques Derrida alla metafisica. Traversa, Guido.

Il Cominciamento e la Costituzione della Fattualità. Tagliavia, Grazia.

Il Rapporto tra i Concetti di *Possibile* ed *Esistente* nel Quadro della Teoria Leibniziana dei Mondi Possibili. Auletta, Gennaro.

Il soggetto della scienza prima. Roccaro, Giuseppe.

Il soggetto e la prassi nell'ermeneutica di Paul Ricoeur. Brezzi, Francesca.

Il Trattato Tomista sulle Proprietà Trascendentali dell'Essere. Ventimiglia, Giovanni.

Immoralist: That Means the Opposite of Consequentialist: Comment on Professor Hale's "Was Nietzsche a Consequentialist?". Crawford, Claudia.

Immutability of God: Metaphysical Inconsistency or Essential Grounding for Human Transcendence. Ebert, Howard.

In Search for "Historical Time": Time—Culture—History. Wrzosek, Wojciech.

Individu, identiteit, soort. Lievers, Menno.

Individualism, Physicalism, and Spinoza on Minds and Bodies. Lantin, Robert.

Individualism, Subjectivity, and Presence: A Response to Taylor Carman. Olafson, Frederick A.

Individuo y Comunidad: Reflexiones Sobre el Eterno Círculo Fichteano. López-Domínguez, Virginia.

Inside Time-Consciousness: Diagramming the Flux. Larrabee, M J.

Instruments and the Body: Sartre and Merleau-Ponty. Kujundzic, Nebojsa and Buschert, William.

Inteligência Artificial e Caça aos Andróides. de Fernandes T, Joao.

Intellectual Dynamism in Transcendental Thomism: A Metaphysical Assessment. Knasas, John F X.

Introducción a la Filosofía de las Emociones. Rodríguez, Mariano.

Introducción a un tratado de filosofía primera. García-Baró, Miguel.

Intuition, Involvement, Interrogation: The Meaning of Self-Making. Sloboda, Myron.

Is Gerwin's Natural-Agency Theory a Viable Alternative to Hume?. Ward, Andrew.

Is Knowing a State of Mind?. Williamson, Timothy.

Is the Absurd the Problem or the Solution? *The Myth of Sisyphus* Reconsidered. Sagi, Avi.

Is the Experienced World a Determinate Totality? Vācaspati on *Anyathakhyativada* and *Anirvacaniyakhyativada*. Ram-Prasad, C.

Is the Skeptic Defeated by Putnam's "Transcendental Argument"?. Frangiotti, Marco Antonio.

Is There a Break in Sartre's Thought?. Singh, Ravindra M.

J G Fichte: l'affermazione dell'Assoluto. Gamarra, Daniel.

Jalons pour poursuivre l'effort d'Étienne Gilson en noétique. Wéber, É H.

James on Self Identity Over Time. Gale, Richard M.

James's Conception of Psychology as a Natural Science. Skrupskelis, Ignas K.

Jan Patocka: Negative Platonism. Kiss, Róbert Szemán.

Japanese Aesthetics: The Construction of Meaning. Marra, Michele.

Javelli and Suárez on the Eternal Truths. Wells, Norman J.

Je est un Autre. Corazza, Eros.

John Searle and Human Consciousness. Beards, Andrew.

José Ortega y Gasset on Understanding Life as Ultimate Reality and Meaning. Weigart, Andrew J.

Kann Schellings Philosophie von 1804 als System bestehen?. Lauth, Reinhard.

Kant and Analogy: Categories as Analogical Equivocals. Ess, Charles M and Gulick, Walter B.

Kant and Lonergan on Insight Into the Sensible. Sala, Giovanni B.

Kant and the Eternity of the World: A Historico-critical Reading of the First Antinomy. van Veldhuijsen, Peter.

Kant on the Possibility of Thought: Universals without Language. Waxman, Wayne.

Kant's "Historicist" Alternative to Cognitive Science. McDonough, Richard.

Kant's Argument for Causality in the Second Analogy. Steinhoff, Gordon.

Kant's Doctrine of the Categories: Some Problems. Krishna, Daya.

Kant's Dynamic Constructions. Westphal, Kenneth R.

Kant's Refutation of Anti-Realism. Blatnik, Edward.

Kant's View of the Transcendental Imagination in the First *Critique*. Hickey, Lance P.

Kant, Fichte, and *The Interests of Reason*. Breazeale, Daniel.

Kant, la razza e la storia. Pellecchia, Pasquale.

Kant, Levinas, and the Thought of the "Other". Surber, Jere Paul.

Kants Philosophie in Rumänien. Schuster-Stein, Paul.

Kants's Critical Model of the Experiencing Subject. Mosser, Kurt.

Karl Jaspers and Edmund Husserl—III: Jaspers as a Kantian Phenomenologist. Walker, Chris.

Karl Löwith et le nihilisme japonais. Stevens, Bernard.

Kierkegaard and the Problem of the Social Other. Matthis, Michael J.

Kierkegaard, la recuperación del individuo existente y el discurso sobre lo histórico. Washburn, Jimmy.

METAPHYSICS

METAPHYSICS

METHOD

Philosophy as a Way of Life: Spiritual Exercises from Socrates to Foucault. Hadot, Pierre, Davidson, Arnold I (ed) and Chase, Michael (trans).

The Real World of Democracy Revisited and Other Essays on Democracy and Socialism. Cunningham, Frank.

Thinking About Social Thinking (Second Edition). Flew, Antony.

Wittgenstein on Mind and Language. Stern, David G.

Consideraciones Metodológicas Acerca de la Investigación en el Ambito de la Filosofía de la Educación (en Europa). Barrio Maestre, José María.

De Winst van Tranen: Over de Aarzeling als Methode. Benschop, Ruth, Hendriks, Ruud and Nelis, Annemiek.

Der Übergang von der *Grundlage* zur *Wissenschaftslehre nova methodo.* Radrizzani, Ives.

Descartes's Theory of Modality. Bennett, Jonathan.

Disciplining Clio: The Rhetoric of Positivism. Carrard, Philippe.

Discoursing on Method in the University World of Descartes's France. Brockliss, Laurence.

Dónde se Encuentra el Enigma Sobre la Creencia?. Sosa, David.

El hacha niveladora: Donoso Cortés y Vico. Villalobos, José.

Foucault's Genealogical Method. Gutting, Gary.

Historia y Hermenéutica. Alcalá Campos, Raúl.

How Carnap Should Bite Goodman's Bullet. Paprzycka, Katarzyna.

La Máxima Hermenéutica "Comprender a un Autor..." en el Pensamiento de Dilthey. Trias, Susana.

O Método Paulo Freire: A Inter-Relaçao da Teoria do Conhecimento com a Teoria da Sociedade. Marinho Sampaio, Tânia Maria.

Patients' Perceptions of the Quality of Informed Consent for Common Medical Procedures. Sulmasy, Daniel P (& others).

Philosophie und Struktur: Über die Notwendigkeit strukturtheoretischer Reflexionen in den hermeneutischen Wissenschaften. Müller, Ulrich.

Por qué aún Filosofía de las Matemáticas?. Avila del Palacio, Alfonso.

Rorty's Critique of Philosophy: The Implications for the Search for a Method in Contemporary African Philosophy. Irele, Dipo.

Sobre la cuestión del método en el debate Modernidad-Postmodernidad. Esquirol, Josep M.

Unnatural Science. Elgin, Catherine Z.

Vico'1994. Bormudo, José M.

Wetenschapsfilosofie en wetenschapsonderzoek: op weg naar een vruchtbare latrelatie?. Radder, Hans.

What Use is Aristotle's *Organon*?. Smith, Robin.

METHODOLOGY

"By Indirections Find Directions Out": Kierkegaard's Socratic Attractor. Easterbrook, Neil.

"On Writing Philosophy" in *American Philosophy Today and Other Philosophical Studies, Rescher, Nicholas*. Rescher, Nicholas.

"Soviet Historiography as a 'Normal Science'" in *Historiography Between Modernism and Postmodernism, Topolski, Jerzy (ed)*. Zalejko, Gwidon.

"The Depth and Breadth of Paul Ricoeur's Philosophy" in *The Philosophy of Paul Ricoeur, Hahn, Lewis Edwin (ed)*. Jervolino, Domenico.

"The Idealization Methodology and Economics" in *Idealization VI: Idealization in Economics, Hamminga, Bert (ed)*. Nowak, Leszek.

"'Die Wende der Philosophie': Wittgenstein's New Logic of 1928" in *Wittgenstein and Contemporary Philosophy, Teghrarian, Souren (ed)*. Hintikka, Jaakko.

Bertrand Russell. Slater, J G.

Blindness of Modern Science. Uus, Undo.

Design & Systems: General Applications of Methodology. Collen, Arne (ed) and Gasparski, Wojciech W (ed).

For Education: Towards Critical Educational Inquiry. Carr, Wilfred.

Foucault and the Writing of History. Goldstein, Jan (ed).

Ludwig Wittgenstein: Wiener Ausgabe/Vienna Edition—Introduction. Nedo, Michael (ed).

Montaigne: A Collection of Essays, Volume 1—Montaigne's Message and Method. Berven, Dikka (ed).

Nietzsche: A Critical Reader. Sedgwick, Peter R (ed).

The Context of Explanation. Bunzl, Martin.

A Behaviorist Alternative to *Theory* and *Simulation* Theories of Folk Psychology. Stemmer, Nathan.

A Heuristic for Conceptual Change. Arntzenius, Frank.

Against Methodological Solipsism: The Ecological Approach. Rowlands, Mark.

An Empirical Philosophy of Economic Theory. Backhouse, Roger E.

Analisi e Assiomatizzazione nella Dialettica di Platone. Ferrari, Franco.

Aristotle's Method. McLeod, Owen.

Austere Realism and the Worldly Assumptions of Inferential Statistics. Trout, J D.

Circularity and the Paduan *Regressus*: From Pietro d'Abano to Galileo Galilei. Wallace, William A.

Creating Common Ground: A Lesson from the Past. Acklin, David and King, Jonathan.

Europe, or How to Escape Babel. Olender, Maurice.

Experimentation and the Legitimacy of Idealization. Laymon, Ronald E.

False Idealisation: A Philosophical Threat to Scientific Method. Cartwright, Nancy.

For a Better Understanding of Philosophy, For a Better Philosophical Method. Sanjeev, M P.

Formalism of Kant's A Priori Versus Scheler's Material A Priori. Moosa, Imtiaz.

Fukuyama's Hegelianism—Historical Exhaustion or Philosophical Closure. Grumley, John.

General Method. McShane, Philip.

Harvey Sacks's Primitive Natural Science. Lynch, Michael and Bogen, David.

How I Almost Solved the Problem of Induction. Watkins, John.

Indeterminacy, Ethnophilosophy, Linguistic Philosophy, African Philosophy. Hallen, Barry.

La Fundamentación de la Matemática y la Génesis de la Metódica Fenomenológico-Reductiva. García Prada, Ovidio.

Medicine and History as Theoretical Tools in a Confucian Pragmatism. Birdwhistell, Anne D.

Methodological Cynicism in Ethics. Smilansky, Saul.

Methodological Reflections on Two Kripkean Strategies. Ramachandran, Murali.

Methodology, Epistemology and Conventions: Popper's Bad Start. Preston, John.

Normality as a Biological Concept. Wachbroit, Robert.

Notes on Some Methodological Aspects of Rawls' Theory of Justice. Tugendhat, Ernst.

On the Scientific Method, Its Practice and Pitfalls. Ayala, Francisco J.

On Wittgenstein's Way of Doing Philosophy. Gupta, Narendra Nath.

Otto Neurath's Idealist Inheritance: *The Social and Economic Thought of Wilhelm Neurath*. Uebel, Thomas E.

Phenomenology as a Methodology for Universalism. Brown, Charles S.

Philosophy of Methodology in Heidegger's *Die Idee der Philosophie und das Weltanschuungsproblem* (1919). Fuchs, Yuval.

Teaching 'Inference to the Best Explanation'. Eflin, Juli.

The "Zhi Yan" in Feng Youlan's *Xin Zhi Yan*. Yijie, Tang.

The Attack on Methodological Solipsism. Duran, Jane.

The Ends of Metaphysics. Markus, György.

The Methodological and Metaphysical Peculiarities of the Human Sciences. Margolis, Joseph.

The Philosophical Context of Collingwood's Re-Enactment Theory. van der Dussen, Jan.

The Post-Implementation Evaluation of Expert Systems: Enlightenment after Five Years in the Trenches. Sharma, R S and Conrath, D W.

Towards a Critical Ethnomethodology. McHoul, Alec.

Towards an Anthropological Psychiatry. Mooij, Anton.

Vico y Hobbes: el "verum-factum". Bermudo, José M.

When Psychology Looks Like a "Soft" Science, It's for Good Reason!. Howard, George S.

METRICS

Complete Metric Boolean Algebras. Jeffrey, Richard (trans) and Kolmogorov, A N.

MEXICAN

Ethics vs Economics: The Issue of Free Trade with Mexico. Hosmer, LaRue Tone and Masten, Scott E.

MEYER, L

Values in Music Education. Hansen, Forest.

MICHAELS, W

In Defense of "Elitism". Shusterman, Ronald.

MICROECONOMICS

Real Patterns and the Ontological Foundations of Microeconomics. Ross, Don.

The Microeconomic Interpretation of Games. LaCasse, Chantale and Ross, Don.

MILITARY

"The Military Ban and the ROTC: A Study in Closeting" in *Gay Ethics, Murphy, Timothy F (ed)*. Card, Claudia.

Just War in the Balkans?. Quirk, Michael J.

Militant Gayes, Gayes in the Military, and Privacy as Social Freedom. Nunan, Richard.

Military Intervention as a Moral Duty. Tan, Kok-Chor.

The Combat Exclusion and the Role of Women in the Military. DeCew, Judith Wagner.

The Soldier as Conscientious Objector. Whitman, Jeffrey P.

MILL

"Decolonizing Liberalism" in *The End of "Isms"?, Shtromas, Alexsandras (ed)*. Parekh, Bhikhu.

"Mill and Menger: Ideal Elements and Stable Tendencies" in *Idealization VI: Idealization in Economics, Hamminga, Bert (ed)*. Cartwright, Nancy.

"The Lot of Gifted Ladies Is Hard": A Study of Harriet Taylor Mill Criticism. Jacobs, Jo Ellen.

A History of Modern Political Thought: Major Political Thinkers from Hobbes to Marx. Hampsher-Monk, Iain.

John Stuart Mill och socialismen. Hansson, Sven Ove.

Mill's Principle of Utility: A Defence of John Stuart Mill's Notorious Proof. Alican, Nejip Fikri.

The Correspondence of John Stuart Mill and Auguste Comte. Haac, Oscar A (ed & trans).

Varieties of Scientific Experience: Emotive Aims in Scientific Hypotheses. Feuer, Lewis S.

Actitud crítica y racionalidad en Popper. Marquéz, Gustavo.

An Empirical Philosophy of Economic Theory. Backhouse, Roger E.

Autonomía y Conducta Desviada: el Problema del Paternalismo en la Obra de John Stuart Mill. De Miguel Alvarez, Ana.

Conflicting Principles or Completing Counterparts? J S Mill on Political Economy and the Equality of Women. Green, Michele.

El liberalismo frente a Bentham y Mill. Farrell, Martín Diego.

Inference to the Loveliest Explanation. Barnes, Eric.

John Stuart Mill and Harriet Taylor on Women and Marriage. Mendus, Susan.

Logik der Sozialwissenschaften—150 Jahre nach J St Mills System of Logic. Eberlein, Gerald L.

Mill's Principle of Liberty. Chopra, Y N.

Por qué son necesarias inútiles las virtudes específicamente religiosas?. Sastre, Gerardo López.

MODALITY

MODE

MODEL

MODERNISM

Review Essay: Robert B Pippin's *Modernism as a Philosophical Problem*. Chytry, Josef.

The Crisis of Ecology: A Phenomenological Perspective. Howarth, J M.

The Impoverishment of Art. Kieran, Matthew.

MODERNITY

"Coherence Lost": Education, Modernity, and Fractured Meaning. Gunter, Pete A Y.

"Critical Theory as a Research Program" in *The Cambridge Companion to Habermas*, White, Stephen K (ed). Dryzek, John S.

"Foucault Deudor de Kant" in *Temas Actuales de Filosofía, Palacios, María Julia (ed)*. Caponi, Sandra N.

"La Modernidad entre los Demonios y el Inconsciente" in *Temas Actuales de Filosofía, Palacios, María Julia (ed)*. Barale, Griselda C.

"Paul Ricoeur and the Conflict of Interpretations" in *The Philosophy of Paul Ricoeur, Hahn, Lewis Edwin (ed)*. Lavine, Thelma Z.

"Reason, Modernity, and Democracy" in *The Cambridge Companion to Habermas*, White, Stephen K (ed). White, Stephen K.

"The End of Orthodox Marxism" in *Marxism in the Postmodern Age, Callari, Antonio (ed)*. Kellner, Douglas M.

"The Politics of Time: Subjectivity and Modernity in Max Weber" in *The Barbarism of Reason, Horowitz, Asher (ed)*. Maley, Terry.

After Marxism. Aronson, Ronald.

Anima hace hablar a la razón con una voz diferente: Nuevos nexos entre la tecnociencia y el mundo de la vida. Cañón Loyes, Camino.

Arte y Ciencia: Una Visión Especular. Leyra, Ana María and Mataix, Carmen.

Critical Theory and Political Possibilities: Conceptions of Emancipatory Politics in the Works of Horkheimer, Adorno, Marcuse, and Habermas. Alway, Joan.

Das Vermächtnis des deutschen Judentums: Werke 2. Goldschmidt, Hermann Levin.

Ecological Enlightenment: Essays on the Politics of the Risk Society. Beck, Ulrich and Ritter, Mark Λ (trans).

Foucault and Law: Towards a Sociology of Law as Governance. Hunt, Alan and Wickham, Gary.

Habermas: A Critical Introduction. Outhwaite, William.

Hegel on the Modern World. Collins, Ardis B (ed).

Historiography Between Modernism and Postmodernism. Topolski, Jerzy (ed).

Judaism and Modernity: Philosophical Essays. Rose, Gillian.

Langdon Gilkey: Theologian for a Culture in Decline. Walsh, Brian J.

Mass Enlightenment: Critical Studies in Rousseau and Diderot. Simon, Julia.

Meaning and Development. Kebede, Messay.

Modernity and Identity. Lash, Scott (ed) and Friedman, Jonathan (ed).

Poetics of Modernity: Toward a Hermeneutic Imagination. Kearney, Richard.

Political Theory, Modernity, and Postmodernity: Beyond Enlightenment and Critique. Rengger, N J.

Solitudes: From Rimbaud to Heidegger. Froment-Meurice, Marc and Walsh, Peter (trans).

Temas Actuales de Filosofía. Palacios, María Julia (ed).

The Barbarism of Reason. Horowitz, Asher (ed) and Maley, Terry (ed).

The Cambridge Companion to Habermas. White, Stephen K (ed).

A Bowie: Estética y Subjetividad. García García, Javier.

A Modest Reason. Seguin, Eve.

A Proposito de la Critica del Juicio. Labrada, María Antonia.

Ateismo, filosofia e cristianesimo in Del Noce. Possenti, Vittorio.

Authenticity and the Project of Modernity. Ferrara, Alessandro.

Beyond the Philosophy of the Subject and Beyond the Economics of Choice: Sociology in a Changed World. Schwengel, Hermann.

Cinco Claves Para Comprender a Jacques Maritain. Burgos, Juan Manuel.

Civilized Madness: Schizophrenia, Self-Consciousness and the Modern Mind. Sass, Louis A.

De cómo "el ser" devino época. Muñoz Delgado, Mercedes.

De la crisis de la racionalidad a la racionalidad de la crisis: Una nota sobre G Vico. Sevilla, José M.

De Winst van Tranen: Over de Aarzeling als Methode. Benschop, Ruth, Hendriks, Ruud and Nelis, Annemiek.

Education and Democracy: Confronting the Postmodernist Challenge. Carr, Wilfred.

El concepto de Bildung en el primer romanticismo alemán. Sánchez Meca, Diego.

El Conflicto de los Proyectos Históricos en la Perspectiva de Leopoldo Zea. Ibáñez, Alfonso.

En Torno al *Postcursorismo* Viquiano de la Modernidad Problemática. Sevilla, José M.

Éticas del don: Aporías y negociaciones. Peñalver Gómez, Patricio.

Feminismo y política en dos encrucijadas históricas: La modernidad madura. Ciriza, Alejandra.

Hermeneutics and Critical Theory: Enlightenment as Political (in Portuguese). Howard, Dick.

Historia de la Filosofía e Historia: Notas Para un Debate. Sanz, Víctor.

Historical Studies between Modernity and Postmodernity. Rüsen, Jörg.

Il Problema del Mito nel Dialogo Bultmann-Jaspers. Donadio, Francesco.

L'éthique dans un monde désenchanté. Bruguès, Jean-Louis.

La Declaración de los Derechos del Hombre de 1789 y la Tradición Judeo-Cristiana. Camacho, Ramón Kuri.

La Historia de los Vencidos (Un Ensayo de Filosofía de la Historia Contra las Ontologías del Presente). Mate, Reyes.

La liquidación de la Filosofía: Notas sobre la disputa entre R Rorty y J Habermas. Gómez Ibáñez, Vicente.

Las Paradojas de la Modernidad. Castro López, Octavio.

Lectura ética del pensamiento ilustrado. Bello, Eduardo.

Louis Dupré's "Passage to Modernity" (in Dutch). De Dijn, H.

Modernity, Post-Modernity, and the Philosophy of History. Carr, David.

Neitzsche and the Contemporary Writer: What does it all Mean?. Diethe, Carol.

Neo-Stoicism and the Transition to Modernity in Wilhelm Dilthey's Philosophy of History. Frohman, Larry.

Nietzsche's Post-Modern Identity: From *Epoch to Ethos*. Ansell-Pearson, Keith.

Ontological Connivance (in French). Van Eynde, L.

Poteat on Modern Culture and Critical Philosophy. Adams, E M.

Prudence and Morality in Ancient and Modern Ethics. Annas, Julia.

Qué es la ilustración?. Foucault, Michel.

Química y Salvación. Villacañas, José L.

Razón e historia: La modernidad del postmodernismo. Koslowski, Peter.

Sobre el problema de la filosofia. Zubiri, Xavier.

Sobre la cuestión del método en el debate Modernidad-Postmodernidad. Esquirol, Josep M.

Sociology and the Diagnosis of the Times or: The Reflexivity of Modernity. Lichtblau, Klaus.

Sull'Ermeneutica della Secolarizzazione. Iervolino, Domenico.

Synopsis of a Theory of Modernity. Ibañez-Noé, Javier A.

The End of History, Five Years Later. Fukuyama, Francis.

The Image of Wisdom and the Wise Man in the History of European Philosophy. Semane, Tatjana.

The Mirror of Modernity and Spiritual Resources for the Global Community. Wei-Ming, Tu.

The Political Logic of Economics and the Economic Logic of Modernity in Max Weber. Breiner, Peter.

The Post-Modern Challenge to Community. Mellos, Koula.

The Will to Harmony and the Pursuit of Family. Neisser, Philip T.

Tras la postmodernidad. Innerarity, Daniel.

Two Theories of Modernity. Taylor, Charles.

MODESTY

Humility. Snow, Nancy E.

MODULARITY

Meager Forking. Newelski, Ludomir.

MODULE

Deissler Rank Complexity of Powers of Indecomposable Injective Modules. Chartrand, R and Kucera, T.

Model Theory of Modules Over a Serial Ring. Eklof, Paul C and Herzog, Ivo.

MOHAMMEDANISM

see Islam

MOHISM

Caring for Whom? Moral Discussions between Early Confucians and Mohists. Defoort, Carine.

MOHR, H

"Springflut des Bösen". Briese, Olaf.

MOHR, R

"Privacy and the Ethics of Outing" in *Gay Ethics, Murphy, Timothy F (ed)*. Mayo, David J and Gunderson, Martin.

MOLECULE

Instrumental Biology or the Disunity of Science. Rosenberg, Alexander.

Two Logical Patterns of the Reduction of Theories: Comments on Józef Werle's Paper "How the Physical Sciences Discovered the Unity of Nature". Krajewski, Wladyslaw.

MOLINA

Molina on Divine Foreknowledge and the Principle of Bivalence. Gaskin, Richard.

MOLYNEUX

"The Real Molyneux Question and the Basis of Locke's Answer" in *Locke's Philosophy, Rogers, G A J (ed)*. Bolton, Martha Brandt.

MOMENT

Aquí y Ahora, Desde la Hermenéutica. Duque, Félix.

MOMENTUM

The Whewell-Faraday Exchange on the Application of the Concepts of Momentum and Inertia to Electromagnetic Phenomena. Anderson, Ronald.

MONAD

Leibniz y la Tradición Neoplatónica: Estado Actual de la Cuestión. Orio, Bernardino.

MONADIC

The Monadic Second-Order logic of Graphs VIII: Orientations. Courcelle, Bruno.

MONADOLOGY

Husserls Theorie der Intersubjektivität. Iribarne, Julia V.

Zum Wandel der Leibniz-Rezeption im Denken Heideggers. Sakai, Kiyoshi.

MONADS

Content and Sensitivity. Horowitz, Amir.

MONARCHY

Francia, Spagna e Portogallo: Le Monarchie Europee "Qui Vont au Despotisme" Secondo Montesquieu. Felice, Domenico.

Philosophical Republicanism and Monarchism—and Republican and Monarchical Philosophy—in Kant and Hegel. Redding, Paul.

MONET, C

Is Hermeneutics 'Philosophy'? Interpretation and Overinterpretation of the Past. Lucas Jr, George R.

MONETARY

Theory vs History: Reply to Horwitz. Kindleberger, Charles P.

MONEY

Die berechnende Vernunft: Über das Ökonomische in allen Lebenslagen. Müller-Funk, Wolfgang (ed).

Money, Monetary Crisis, and the Doctrine of Being. Meaney, Mark E.

'The Unnatural Desire for More than one Needs': An Objection to James Tully's View. Kopton, K.

MONISM

A Companion to the Philosophy of Mind. Guttenplan, Samuel (ed).

Confessions' Bliss: Postmodern Criticism as a Palimpsest of Augustine's *Confessions*. Fendt, Gene.

The Bounds of Freedom: About the Eastern and Western Approaches to Freedom. Balaban, Oded and Erev, Anan.

The Philosophy of Religion and Advaita Vedānta: A Comparative Study in Religion and Reason. Sharma, Arvind.

Das Programm des methodologischen Monismus Subjekttheoretische und methodologische Aspekte der Elementarphilosophie K L Reinholds. Stamm, Marcelo.

From Montague to Neo-Confucianism: Feng Youlan's "New *Lixue*" and Logical Analysis. Lujun, Yin.

Het monisme van Herman Berger. Kal, Victor.

Ist eine reine Inhaltslogik möglich? Zu Leibniz' Begriffstheorie. Liske, Michael-Thomas.

L'atomisme dans le monisme épicurien. Droz-Vincent, Gabriel.

Lovejoy, Hartshorne, and Progress in Philosophy. Dombrowski, Daniel.

Materialism and Supervenience. Jack, Andrew.

Monism and Pluralism. Krapiec, Mieczyslaw Albert.

Moral Monism in Environmental Ethics Defended. Callicott, J Baird.

Notes sur le Relativisme et le Monisme en Éthique. Weinstock, Daniel M.

On the Theological Roots of Spinoza's Argument for Monism. Carriero, John.

P F Strawson and the Ghost of F H Bradley. Glouberman, Mark.

Repliek. Berger, Herman.

The Demise of Monism and Pluralism in Environmental Ethics. Van Der Steen, Wim J.

MONOTHEISM

On Naming the Present: God, Hermeneutics, and Church. Tracy, David.

MONTAGUE, R

Holes and Determinism: Another Look. Leeds, Stephen.

MONTAGUE, W

From Montague to Neo-Confucianism: Feng Youlan's "New *Lixue*" and Logical Analysis. Lujun, Yin.

MONTAIGNE

Montaigne: A Collection of Essays, Volume 1—Montaigne's Message and Method. Berven, Dikka (ed).

Montaigne: A Collection of Essays, Volume 2—Sources of Montaigne's Thought. Berven, Dikka (ed).

Montaigne: A Collection of Essays, Volume 3—Montaigne's Rhetoric. Berven, Dikka (ed).

Montaigne: A Collection of Essays, Volume 4—Language and Meaning. Berven, Dikka (ed).

Montaigne: A Collection of Essays, Volume 5—Reading Montaigne. Berven, Dikka (ed).

The Wisdom of Religious Commitment. Tilley, Terrence W.

Ateismo, scetticismo e fideismo. Penelhum, Terence.

Montaigne et la Valeur de la Voix (Sur Une Influence Stoïcienne dans l'écriture des Essais). Protopapas, Maria.

MONTESQUIEU

Montesquieu e il Problema dell "Diversité". Courtney, C P.

Montesquieu on the Causes of Roman Greatness. Myers, Richard.

Montesquieu's Paradox on Freedom and Hungary's Constitutions 1790-1990. Péter, László.

MOOD

Mild Mania and the Theory of Health: A Response to "Mild Mania and Well-Being". Nordenfelt, Lennart.

Mild Mania and Well-Being. Moore, Andrew, Hope, Tony and Fulford, K W M.

Nature's Moods. Howarth, J M.

The Concept of Rasa According to Abhinavgupta. Ghosh, Raghunath.

MOODY, H

Ethics in an Aging Society. Holstein, Martha.

MOORE

Comments on "Moore's Paradox and Self-Knowledge". Albritton, Rogers.

Diagnosing the Naturalistic Fallacy: Principia Ethica Revisited. Wright, Darryl F.

Kant y la Falacia Naturalista. Chacón Fuertes, Pedro.

Moore's Paradox and Self-Knowledge. Shoemaker, Sydney.

Moore's Paradox, Asserting and Skepticism. Doran, Katheryn.

Self-Knowledge and Moore's Paradox. Rosenthal, David M.

Wittgenstein, Truth-Functions and Generality. Scanlan, Michael.

MOORE, A

Mild Mania and the Theory of Health: A Response to "Mild Mania and Well-Being". Nordenfelt, Lennart.

The Trouble with Well-Being: A Response to "Mild Mania and Well-Being". Seedhouse, David.

MORAL

"Moral Philosophy—Another 'Disabling Profession?'" in *Ethics and the Professions*, Chadwick, Ruth (ed). Parker, Jenneth.

"Sinderesi, desidereio naturale e fondamento dell'agire morale nel pensiero medievale" in *L'etica e il suo Altro*, Vigna, Carmelo (ed). Sciuto, Italo.

"'The Instruction of Any' and Moral Philosophy" in *African Philosophy: Selected Readings*, Mosley, Albert G (ed). James, David.

Logic, Facts, and Representation: An Examination of R M Hare's Moral Philosophy. Ronnow-Rasmussen, Toni.

Consecuencialismo e imparcialidad. Salcedo, Damián.

El escándalo del mal. Ricoeur, Paul.

La Obligación en el Positivismo: El Caso de H L A Hart. Hernández, Héctor H.

Moralischer Minimalismus. Walzer, Michael.

Tugend und Moraltheorie. Schroeter, Francois.

Tugendhat, der Prinz und die Moral. Thomä, Dieter.

MORAL AGENT

"Immediacy and Dissolution" in *Intersections: Nineteenth-Century Philosophy and Contemporary Theory*, Rajan, Tilottama (ed). Pfau, Thomas.

Harry Frankfurt: El agente moral y la noción de incondicionalidad. Beltrán, Miquel.

Identidad Personal y yo Moral en David Hume. Clotet, Joaquín.

The Heart of the Kantian Moral Agent. Nuyen, A T.

MORAL DEVELOPMENT

Assessing the Application of Cognitive Moral Development Theory to Business Ethics. Fraedrich, John, Thorne, Debbie M and Ferrell, O C.

How Religion Impedes Moral Development. Clark, Brad.

L'Enseignement de l'Éthique comme Activité de Formation Morale. Bégin, Luc.

Moral Addicts. Cunningham, Anthony.

Moral Development in the Biographies of Skilled Industrial Workers. Lempert, Wolfgang.

Utilitarismo y Teoría del Desarrollo Moral (I): Análisis crítico de las teorías cognitivas del desarrollo moral y de sus fundamentos Kantianos. Tasset, José Luis.

MORAL EDUCATION

A Lonerganian Critique of the Pragmatic Method of Education. Gilbert, Christopher.

A Model of Intervention for Improving Moral Reasoning: An Experiment in the Basque Country. Medrano, Concepción.

Can Virtue Be Bought?. Pullman, Daryl.

Catching a Glimpse of the Palace of Reason: The Education of Moral Emotions. Roebben, Bert.

Design and Evaluation of a Programme to Promote Prosocial-Altruistic Behaviour in the School. Etxebarria, I (& others).

Do Senior Secondary Students Possess the Moral Maturity to Negotiate Class Rules?. Langford, Peter E, Lovegrove, Hildegard and Lovegrove, Malcolm N.

Durkheim and Moral Education for Children: A Recently Discovered Lecture. Pickering, W S F.

Ecological Literacy for Moral Virtue: Orr on (Moral) education for postmodern sustainability. Prakash, Madhu Suri.

Educating the Moral Artist: Dramatic Rehearsal in Moral Education. Fesmire, Steven A.

Education, Virtue and Democracy in the Work of Emile Durkheim. Cladis, Mark S.

La actualización en la enseñanza de la moral propuesta por la Veritatis Splendor. Alonso, Luz García.

Liberal Education *Is* Moral Education. McCabe, David.

Moral Development in the Biographies of Skilled Industrial Workers. Lempert, Wolfgang.

Moral/Political Education in the People's Republic of China: Learning Through Role Models. Reed, Gay Garland.

Narratives of Volunteering. Paolicchi, Piero.

Oasis of Peace: A Community of Moral Education in Israel. Feuerverger, Grace.

Political Authority and Moral Education. Simpson, Peter.

Teaching as a Moral Activity: Listening to Teachers in Russia and the United States. Higgins, Ann.

The Autonomy of Moral Education. Boss, Judith A.

The Importance of Examples for Moral Education: An Aristotelian Perspective. McDonough, Kevin.

The Primacy of Virtue in Children's Moral Development. Putman, Daniel.

Thick or Thin? The Cognitive Content of Moral Education in a Plural Democracy. Haydon, Graham.

Toward a Fair Community of Scholars: Moral Education as the Negotiation of Classroom Practices. Thorkildsen, Theresa A.

Towards Discourse in the Public Domain: Adolescent Fictions in Moral and Political Education. Gooderham, David.

MORAL JUDGMENT

Making Sense of Social Experiences and Moral Judgments. Turiel, Elliot.

MORAL LAWS

Brentano contra Kant: Sobre el imperativo categórico. Palacios, Juan Miguel.

MORAL PHILOSOPHY

"Truthfulness, Lies, and Moral Philosophers" in *The Tanner Lectures on Human Values, Volume 16*, Peterson, Grethe B (ed). MacIntyre, Alasdair.

Ethics from Experience. Caws, Peter.

A Reckoning of Sorts on the Prospects of Moral Philosophy. Margolis, Eric.

MORAL REASONING

Los ejemplos literario en la filosofia moral: Comentario al trabajo de Osvaldo Guariglia. Lima, María Herrera.

Respuesta a algunas objeciones. Guariglia, Osvaldo.

MORAL RESPONSIBILITY

Consequentialis, Moral Responsibility, and the Intention/ Foresight Distinction. Oakley, Justin.

Responsibility and the Principle of Possible Action. Glannon, Walter.

MORAL SENTIMENT

La Vivencia de lo Sublime y la Experiencia Moral en Kant. Ribeiro dos Santos, Leonel.

MORAL THEORY

"Competition and Moral Philosophy (1975)" in *Legislative Intent and Other Essays on Law, Politics, and Morality*, Singer, Marcus G (ed). MacCallum Jr, Gerald C.

MORAL THEORY

Atoms, Pleasure, Virtue: The Philosophy of Epicurus. Koen, Avraam.
Ethics from Experience. Caws, Peter.
Moral Theory: A Contemporary Overview. DeMarco, Joseph P.
The Fragmented World of the Social: Essays in Social and Political Philosophy. Wright, Charles W (ed) and Honneth, Axel.
Conscience and the Moral Law: A Critical Review of Antonio Rosmini's Moral Thought. Killoran, John.
Consequentialism and Absolutism. Elliot, Robert.
Contra la sistetización en ética. Griffin, James.
Hume's Deontology. Flage, Daniel E.
Moral Decision-Making and the Role of the Moral Question. Melchin, Kenneth R.
Moral Theory, Its Scope and Limits: Bernard Gert and Richard T De George. Magnell, Thomas.
Moral Theory: Understanding and Disagreement. Scanlon, Thomas M.
On the Nature of Moral Principles. Sheng, C L.
Review Essay: Perfectionist Moral Theory, the Criminal Law, and the Liberal State— Making Men Moral by Robert P George. Richards, David A J.
Simulation and Interpersonal Utility. Goldman, Alvin I.
Thomistic Law and the Moral Theory of Richard Hooker. Westberg, Daniel.
Where Do Moral Theories Come From?. Walker, Margaret Urban.
Why Theorize How to Live with Each Other?. Gibbard, Allan F.

MORALISM

The British Moralists and the Internal 'Ought': 1640-1740. Darwall, Stephen.

MORALITY

"A Moral Justification for Gay and Lesbian Civil Rights Legislation" in *Gay Ethics, Murphy, Timothy F (ed)*. Samar, Vincent J.
"Accountability and Lawyers" in *Ethics and the Professions, Chadwick, Ruth (ed)*. Tur, Richard H S.
"Accountability: The Obligation to Lay Oneself Open to Criticism" in *Ethics and the Professions, Chadwick, Ruth (ed)*. Holdsworth, Dick.
"After Virtue? On Distorted Philosophical Narratives" in *The 1994 Annual of Hermeneutics and Social Concern, Lawler, Justus George (ed)*. Ruprecht Jr, Louis A.
"Butler and Hume on Habit and Moral Character" in *Hume and Hume's Connexions, Stewart, M A (ed)*. Wright, John P.
"Christian Belief and the Ethics of In-vitro Fertilization Research" in *Ethics on the Frontiers of Human Existence, Badham, Paul (ed)*. Badham, Paul.
"Coming Out, Being Out, and Acts of Virtue" in *Gay Ethics, Murphy, Timothy F (ed)*. Barbone, Steven and Rice, Lee.
"Custom and Morality" in *African Philosophy: Selected Readings, Mosley, Albert G (ed)*. Wiredu, Kwasi.
"Dependency: The Foundational Value in Medical Ethics" in *Medicine and Moral Reasoning, Fulford, K W M (ed)*. Campbell, Alastair V.
"Deserving Profits" in *Profits and Morality, Cowan, Robin (ed)*. Narveson, Jan.
"Discourse and Democratic Practices" in *The Cambridge Companion to Habermas, White, Stephen K (ed)*. Chambers, Simone.
"El Marxismo Analítico y el Problema Moral del Trabajo" in *Temas Actuales de Filosofía, Palacios, María Julia (ed)*. Gallichio, Santiago.
"Enlarging the Community: Companion Animals" in *Introducing Applied Ethics, Almond, Brenda (ed)*. Clark, Stephen R L.
"Ethics" in *The Cambridge Companion to Aristotle, Barnes, Jonathan (ed)*. Hutchinson, D S.
"Etica e morale" in *L'etica e il suo Altro, Vigna, Carmelo (ed)*. Ricoeur, Paul.
"Genethics" in *Philosophy of Technology in Spanish Speaking Countries, Mitcham, Carl (ed)*. Sanmartín, José.
"Hard Choices: Ethical Questions Raised by the Birth of Handicapped Infants" in *Ethics on the Frontiers of Human Existence, Badham, Paul (ed)*. Kuhse, Helga and Singer, Peter.
"Homophobia and the Moral Authority of Medicine" in *Gay Ethics, Murphy, Timothy F (ed)*. Wilkerson, Abby.
"Human Rights from the Perspective of..Religious Morality" in *Human Rights and Religious Values, An-Na'im, Abdullahi A (& other eds)*. Reinders, Johannes S.
"Hume and Hutcheson" in *Hume and Hume's Connexions, Stewart, M A (ed)*. Moore, James.
"Hume and the Invention of Utilitarianism" in *Hume and Hume's Connexions, Stewart, M A (ed)*. Darwall, Stephen L.
"Hume and the Natural Lawyers: A Change of Landscape" in *Hume and Hume's Connexions, Stewart, M A (ed)*. Westerman, Pauline C.
"Identity Matters" in *Medicine and Moral Reasoning, Fulford, K W M (ed)*. Lockwood, Michael.
"Integrity" in *Concepts and Cases in Nursing Ethics, Yeo, Michael (& others)*. Yeo, Michael and Ford, Ann.
"Is Psychopathy a Moral Concept?" in *Introducing Applied Ethics, Almond, Brenda (ed)*. Bavidge, Michael and Cole, Andrew J.
"Justice and Adversary Proceedings (1977)" in *Legislative Intent and Other Essays on Law, Politics, and Morality, Singer, Marcus G (ed)*. MacCallum Jr, Gerald C.
"Kant and the Moral Considerability of Non-Rational Beings" in *Philosophy and the Natural Environment, Attfield, Robin (ed)*. Hayward, Tim.
"Know Thyself": Socratic Companionship and Platonic Community. Avnon, Dan.
"Leibniz's Moral Philosophy" in *The Cambridge Companion to Leibniz, Jolley, Nicholas (ed)*. Brown, Gregory.
"Letting Patients Die: Legal and Moral Reflections" in *In Harm's Way, Coleman, Jules L (ed)*. Kadish, Sanford H.

"Locke's Moral Philosophy" in *The Cambridge Companion to Locke, Chappell, Vere (ed)*. Schneewind, J B.
"Love and Personal Relationships" in *Introducing Applied Ethics, Almond, Brenda (ed)*. Gregory, Paul.
"Love's Moral and Religious Implications: Irving Singer's Trilogy" in *The Nature and Pursuit of Love, Goicoechea, David (ed)*. Nota, John.
"Medical Ethics, Moral Philosophy and Moral Tradition" in *Medicine and Moral Reasoning, Fulford, K W M (ed)*. Murray, Thomas H.
"Moral Dilemmas Revisited" in *Modality, Morality, and Belief, Sinnott-Armstrong, Walter (ed)*. Foot, Philippa.
"Moral Identity and Education in a Multicultural Society" in *Identity, Culture, and Education, Smeyers, Paul (ed)*. Spiecker, Ben and Steutel, Jan.
"Moral Objections to Pascalian Wagering" in *Gambling on God: Essays on Pascal's Wager, Jordan, Jeffrey (ed)*. Quinn, Philip.
"Moral Uncertainty and Human Embryo Experimentation" in *Medicine and Moral Reasoning, Fulford, K W M (ed)*. Oddie, Graham.
"Morality, Art, and African Philosophy: A Response to Wiredu" in *African Philosophy: Selected Readings, Mosley, Albert G (ed)*. English, Parker and Hamme, Nancy Steele.
"Morality: Invention or Discovery?" in *Medicine and Moral Reasoning, Fulford, K W M (ed)*. Urmson, James O.
"Nietzsche's Attitude toward Socrates" in *Nietzsche: A Critical Reader, Sedgwick, Peter R (ed)*. Kaufmann, Walter.
"Not More Medical Ethics" in *Medicine and Moral Reasoning, Fulford, K W M (ed)*. Fulford, K William M.
"Perspectival Guilt" in *Modality, Morality, and Belief, Sinnott-Armstrong, Walter (ed)*. Greenspan, Patricia.
"Quality of Life and Health Care" in *Medicine and Moral Reasoning, Fulford, K W M (ed)*. Crisp, Roger.
"Reconciling Business Imperatives and Moral Virtues" in *Introducing Applied Ethics, Almond, Brenda (ed)*. Jackson, Jennifer.
"Roman Suicide" in *Medicine and Moral Reasoning, Fulford, K W M (ed)*. Griffin, Miriam.
"Sittlichkeit and Post-Modernity" in *Hegel Reconsidered, Engelhardt, Jr, H Tristram (ed)*. Engelhardt Jr, H Tristram.
"Some Moral Contradictions in the Conservative Educational Reform Discourse in the US" in *Identity, Culture, and Education, Smeyers, Paul (ed)*. Ray, G Thomas.
"The Cultural Boycott: An Act of Censorship or a Tool of Liberation?" in *Life, World and Meaning, Roux, A P J (ed)*. Skawran, Karin M.
"The Gene Revolution" in *Introducing Applied Ethics, Almond, Brenda (ed)*. Chadwick, Ruth.
"The Nature of Profits: Some Economic Insights and Their Ethical Implications" in *Profits and Morality, Cowan, Robin (ed)*. Kirzner, Israel M.
"The Primacy of Truth-Telling and the Evolution of Lying" in *From a Biological Point of View, Sober, Elliott*. Sober, Elliott.
"The Value of In-vitro Research" in *Ethics on the Frontiers of Human Existence, Badham, Paul (ed)*. Winston, Robert.
"The Virtues in a Professional Setting" in *Medicine and Moral Reasoning, Fulford, K W M (ed)*. May, William F.
"Trouble with Families?" in *Introducing Applied Ethics, Almond, Brenda (ed)*. Midgley, Mary and Hughes, Judith.
"Why Take Rights Seriously? A Confucian Critique" in *Human Rights and the World's Religions, Rouner, Leroy (ed)*. Rosemont Jr, Henry.
"Women and Children First" in *Medicine and Moral Reasoning, Fulford, K W M (ed)*. Gillett, Grant.
"Xenophon's Socrates as Teacher" in *The Socratic Movement, Vander Waerdt, Paul A (ed)*. Morrison, Donald R.
American Philosophy Today and Other Philosophical Studies. Rescher, Nicholas.
Amoral Politics: The Persistent Truth of Machiavellism. Scharfstein, Ben-Ami.
An American Ethic: A Philosophy of Freedom Applied to Contemporary Issues. Gerken, John D.
Ancient Greek Philosophy: Its Development and Relevance to Our Time. Trundle, Robert C.
Aristotle's Rhetoric: An Art of Character. Garver, Eugene.
Asylum: A Moral Dilemma. Plaut, W Gunther.
Augustine. Clark, Mary T.
Autonomy and Intervention: Parentalism in the Caring Life. Kultgen, John.
Business Ethics (Fourth Edition). De George, Richard T.
Caring: An Essay in the Philosophy of Ethics. van Hooft, Stan.
Classic Cases in Medical Ethics (Second Edition). Pence, Gregory E.
Computers, Ethics and Social Values. Johnson, Deborah G (ed) and Nissenbaum, Helen (ed).
Damenphilosophie und Männermoral: Von Abbé de Gérard bis Marquis de Sade Ein Versuch über die lächelnde Vernunft. Jauch, Ursula Pia.
Democracy and Social Injustice: Law, Politics, and Philosophy. Simon, Thomas W.
Desire: Its Role in Practical Reason and the Explanation of Action. Schueler, G F.
Dewey's Ethical Thought. Welchman, Jennifer.
Earth Ethics: Environmental Ethics, Animal Rights, and Practical Applications. Sterba, James P (ed).
Emmanuel Levinas: The Genealogy of Ethics. Llewelyn, John (ed).
Essays on Bioethics by R M Hare. Crisp, Roger.
Ethical Argument: Critical Thinking in Ethics. Curtler, Hugh Mercer.
Ethical Issues in Suicide. Battin, Margaret P.

MORALITY

MORALITY

MORALITY

MORRIS, W
John Ruskin and the Ethical Foundations of Morris and Company, 1861-96. Harvey, Charles and Press, Jon.
William Morris and Anti-Parliamentarism. Kinna, Ruth.

MORRISON, D
Commentary on Morrison's "The Place of Unity in Aristotle's Metaphysical Project". Pakaluk, Michael.

MORRISON, T
Identity, Knowledge, and Toni Morrison's *Beloved*: Questions about Understanding Racism. Babbitt, Susan E.

MORTALITY
Il Nyaya Sutra di Gautama. Arena, Leonardo Vittorio.
Opening Address: The Fifth Freedom. Kincaid-Smith, Priscilla.
Two Essays in Public Philosophy: Callahan's *The Troubled Dream of Life* and Dworkin's *Life's Dominion*. Nelson, James Lindemann.

MORTON, C
Pythagoras' Rib Or, What Does Music Education Want?. Bogdan, Deanne.

MORUZZI, N
A Problem with Theory: A Rejoinder to Moruzzi. Galeotti, Anna Elisabetta.

MOSES
Marx, Moses, and the Pagans in the Secular City. Sunic, Tomislav.

MOSSELMAN, E
Teleologie en fysica, en een reactie van A A Derksen op Th Kuipers over waarheidsbenadering. Van Luipen, Hans.

MOTHERHOOD
"Fetal-Maternal Conflicts" in *In Harm's Way, Coleman, Jules L (ed)*. Smith, Holly M.
Woman and the History of Philosophy. Tuana, Nancy.
Mothers, Citizenship, and Independence: A Critique of Pure Family Values. Young, Iris Marion.
Women as Mothers and the Making of the European Mind: A Contribution to the History of Developmental Psychology and Primary Socialization. Niestroj, Brigitte H E.

MOTHERING
Fathers' Rights, Mothers' Wrongs? Reflections on Unwed Fathers' Rights and Sex Equality. Shanley, Mary L.
Mothering, Diversity and Peace: Comments on Sara Ruddick's Feminist Maternal Peace Politics. Bailey, Alison.

MOTION
"Passive Materie und bewegende Kraft" in *Naturauffassungen in Philosophie, Wissenschaft, Technik: Band II, Schäfer, Lothar (ed)*. Carrier, Martin.
"'Neutrale Bewegung' beim jungen Galilei " in *Naturauffassungen in Philosophie, Wissenschaft, Technik: Band II, Schäfer, Lothar (ed)*. Wolff, Michael.
Aristotle's Theory of Actuality. Bechler, Zev.
Beiträge zu Aristoteles' Naturphilosophie. Seidl, Horst.
On Knowing—The Natural Sciences. McKeon, Richard, Owen, David B (ed) and McKeon, Zahava K (ed).
Arguments from Conceivability. Prudovsky, Gad.
Commentary on Furley's "Some Points About Stoic Dynamics". Striker, Gisela.
De la Excelencia y Fundamentos de la Filosofía Corpuscular o Mecánica. Boyle, Robert.
Deterministisches Chaos: Einige Wissenschaftstheoretisch Interessante Aspekte. Düsberg, Klaus Jürgen.
Domingo de Soto en el Origen de la Ciencia Moderna. Pérez Camacho, Juan José and Sols Lucía, Ignacio.
Entre a Sabedoria Silenciosa e a Fala sem Fim. Rodrigo, Lidia Maria.
Finding *Finity* and Motion for Zeno. Borejszo, Zee.
From Galileo to Leibniz: Motion, Qualities and Experience at the Foundation of Natural Science. Ranea, Alberto Guillermo.
Il mondo "Pesante" di Newton. Infante, Giancarlo.
Indexical Reference and Causal Diagrams in Intentional Action. Castañeda, Héctor-Neri.
L'Ambiguità del non Essere e l'Inganno del Sofista: Una Nuova Edizione Francese del *Sofista* di Platone. Fronterotta, Francesco.
La perception du mouvement chez Aristote. Hubert, Bernard.
Le Glosse di Juan Ginés de Sepúlveda alle Traduzioni Latine di Aristotle. Coroleu, Alejandro.
Movimiento y acto en Aristóteles. Lorite Mena, J.
Newton and Leibniz: Rivalry in the Family. Feist, Richard.
Newton sobre Movimento, Espaço e Tempo. Salles, Eduardo and Barra, Oliveira.
Nota Sobre el Estatuto Ontológico del Devenir en Aristóteles. Barrio Maestre, José María.
O Éter Luminoso como Espaço Absoluto. Oliveira, Maurício Pietrocola.
On What It Takes to Be a World. Albert, David Z and Barrett, Jeffrey A.
Platonismo, Rivoluzione Scientifica, Culti Solari: Un Tema da Riesaminare. Albanese, Luciano.
Some Points About Stoic Dynamics. Furley, David.
The Modern Misunderstanding of Aristotle's Theory of Motion. Balaban, Oded.
To What Extent Do Beliefs Affect Apparent Motion?. Wright, Richard D and Dawson, Michael R W.
Um Teorema de Inércia e o Conceito de Velocidade nos *Discorsi* de Galileu. Vasconcelos, Júlio C R.
Why the Elements Imitate the Heaven: *Metaphysics* ix 8.1050b28-34. Lang, Helen S.

MOTIVATION
A Motivational Approach to Confirmation: An Interpretation of Dysphagic Patients' Experiences. Gustafsson, Barbro and Pörn, Ingmar.
Humean Motivation and Humean Rationality. van Roojen, Mark.
Intention and Motivational Strength. McCann, Hugh.
Marc Neuberg's *Philosophie de l'action*. Antoniol, Lucie.
Moral Functionalism and Moral Motivation. Jackson, Frank and Pettit, Philip.
Motivation and Moral Choice in Kant's Theory of Rational Agency. McCarty, Richard.
Must We Care About Morality?. Thomas, Laurence.
Self-Control and Belief. Mele, Alfred R.
The Gadfly Business Ethics Project. Reeves, M Francis.
The Presidential Address: Why there is really No Such Thing as the Theory of Motivation. Dancy, Jonathan.
What is Mimetic Desire?. Livingston, Paisley.

MOTIVE
Desire: Its Role in Practical Reason and the Explanation of Action. Schueler, G F.
Sehnsucht—Affekt und Antrieb: Begriff, Struktur und praktische Bedeutung. Häfner, Ansgar.
Die Trieblehre bei Fichte. De Pascale, Carla.
Motive and Obligation in Hume's Ethics. Darwall, Stephen L.

MOTOR
The Divine Matrix: Creativity as Link between East and West. Bracken, Joseph A.

MOUFFE, C
In Defense of Political Liberalism. Barry, Brian.

MOVEMENT
Are Animal Displays Bodily Movements or Manifestations of the Animal's Mind. Smit, Harry.

MOVIE
see Film

MOYA, C
Carlos Moya's Regress-Problem. Vermazen, Bruce.

MULHOLLAND, L
Leslie Mulholland on Kant's *Rechtslehre*. Gregor, Mary J.

MULLER, K
Quests for a Scientific Mythology: F Creuzer and K O Müller on History and Myth. Blok, Josine H.

MULTICULTURALISM
"Hermeneutic Listening: An Approach to Understanding in Multicultural Conversations" in *Identity, Culture, and Education, Smeyers, Paul (ed)*. Kimball, Stephanie and Garrison, Jim.
"Moral Identity and Education in a Multicultural Society" in *Identity, Culture, and Education, Smeyers, Paul (ed)*. Spiecker, Ben and Steutel, Jan.
Multiculturalism: A Critical Reader. Goldberg, David Theo.
Philosophie im Vergleich der Kulturen. Mall, Ram Adhar.
The Defeat of the Mind. Friedlander, Judith (trans) and Finkielkraut, Alain.
Das Problem des Multikulturalismus in der politischen Ethik. Gutmann, Amy.
Democratic Multicultures and Cosmopolis: Beyond the Aporias of the Politics of Identity and Difference. Matustik, Martin J.
Derrida and Habermas on the Aporia of the Politics of Identity and Difference: Towards Radical Democratic Multiculturalism. Matustík, Martin J.
Faktizität und "liberale Gemeinschaften". Lohmann, Georg.
Liberal Universalism and Multicultural Curricular Reform in the Social Studies: Issues to Consider. Malone, Patricia and Benson, Norman.
Liberalism, Multiculturalism, and Minority Protection. Rickard, Maurice.
Multicultural Education and Feminist Ethics. Friedman, Marilyn.
Multiculturalism and Welfare Reform. Jones, John D.
Multikulturalismus, Demokratie, Nation: Zur Philosophie der deutschen Einheit. Thomä, Dieter.
Multikulturalismus: eine liberale Perspektive. Raz, Joseph.
Otto's Idea of the 'Numinous': A Crosscultural Reappraisal. O'Meley, Serena.
Philosophy and General Education: "World Civilizations" as Virtue Ethics. Omundson, Bruce.
The Disputation of Hate: Speech Codes, Pluralism, and Academic Freedoms. Cox, Philip N.
The Secular Model of the Multi-cultural State. Tännsjö, Torbjörn.
The Sociopolitical Implications of Multiculturalism. Valadez, Jorge M.
Validité et limites du consensus en éthique clinique. Malherbe, Jean-François, Rocchetti, Loretta and Boire-Lavigne, Anne-Marie.

MULTINATIONAL
International Business Ethics. De George, Richard T.
Multinational Capital Budgeting, Emerging Markets, and Managerial Agency: A Proposal for an Ethically Constrained Capital Budgeting Model. Stanley, Marjorie Thines.

MULTIPLE PERSONALITY
Multiple Personality and Computational Models. Boden, Margaret A.

MULTIPLICITY
An Introduction to the Philosophy of Giuseppe Capograssi. Pagallo, Ugo.
Aristotle nel Novecento. Mangiagalli, Maurizio.
Unità e molteplicità in Juergen Habermas. Giovagnoli, Raffaela.

MUNOZ ALONSO, A
La filosofía, el método y el hombre en el pensamiento de Adolfo Muñoz Alonso. González Miguel, Jesús Graciliano.

MUNOZ, M
Fundamentos Filosóficos del Concepto Muñocista de la Libertad. Rivera, José.

MURDER

Ethics, Killing and War. Norman, Richard.
The Rational and the Moral Order: The Social Roots of Reason and Morality. Baier, Kurt.
Abortion as Murder?: A Response. Stone, Jim.
Capital Punishment and the Sanctity of Life. Holyer, Robert.
Is Killing No Worse than Letting Die?. Nesbitt, Winston.
Sacrificing One to Save Many. Clark, Michael.
Selective Conscientious Objection and the Right Not to Kill. Ruesga, G Albert.
Self-Defense Theory. Gardner, Martin R.

MURPHY, J

French's *Responsibility Matters*, Murphy's *Retribution Reconsidered*, and Sher's *Desert*. Zimmerman, Michael J.

MURRAY, C

Individual and Community: Charles Murray's Political Philosophy. Hudson, James.

MUSGRAVE, A

An Inductivist Version of Critical Rationalism. Agassi, Joseph.

MUSIC

see also Rock Music

"John Cage's Approach to the Global" in *John Cage: Composed in America, Perloff, Marjorie (ed)*. Herwitz, Daniel A.
"La Cuestión del Género en la Cultura Popular: Del Tango al Rock" in *Temas Actuales de Filosofía, Palacios, María Julia (ed)*. Cabrera, Mónica and Vidiella, Graciela.
"Language, Music, and the Body" in *Intersections: Nineteenth-Century Philosophy and Contemporary Theory, Rajan, Tilottama (ed)*. Rajan, Tilottama.
"Logik der Musikforschung: K Poppers methodischer Beitrag" in *Heinrich Gomperz, Karl Popper und die österreichische Philosophie, Seiler, Martin (ed)*. Blaukopf, Kurt.
"Poethics: John Cage and Stanley Cavell at the Crossroads of Ethical Theory" in *John Cage: Composed in America, Perloff, Marjorie (ed)*. Bruns, Gerald L.
"Weber, Niotzsche, and Music" in *Nietzsche: A Critical Reader, Sedgwick, Peter R (ed)*. Edgar, Andrew.
Augen.Blick: Eine Skizze zu Bildern Arnold Schönbergs und Texten Theodor W Adornos. Hansbauer, Severin.
Authenticities: Philosophical Reflections on Musical Performance. Kivy, Peter.
Color Codes: Modern Theories of Color in Philosophy, Painting and Architecture, Literature, Music, and Psychology. Riley II, Charles A.
Die Musik als scientia mathematica von der Spätantike bis zum Barock. Hirtler, Eva.
John Cage: Composed in America. Perloff, Marjorie (ed) and Junkerman, Charles (ed).
Music, Value, and the Passions. Ridley, Aaron.
On Hume and Eighteenth-Century Aesthetics: The Philosopher on a Swing. Carabelli, Giancarlo and Hall, Joan Krakover (trans).
The Sciences in Greco-Roman Society (Apeiron 27-4). Barnes, Timothy D.
A Concept of Indian Music. Roy, Tirthankar.
Art and Life: Models for Understanding Music. Hermerén, Göran.
Authenticity in Musical Performance: Personal or Historical?. O'Dea, Jane W.
Emotions in Music (A Postscript). Goldman, Alan.
Esthétique musicale et éthique humaine. Piguet, J Claude.
Feyerabend, the Ancient Quarrel and the Problem of Aesthetic Criteria. Couvalis, George.
Gender, Musical Meaning, and Education. Green, Lucy.
General Theories of Art versus Music. Davies, Stephen.
Giulio Bajamonti, un Vichiano Dalmata. Roic, Sanja.
Hanslick on Hearing Beauty. Shibles, Warren A.
Hearing New Music: Pedagogy from a Phenomenological Perspective. Lochhead, Judy.
Hermeneutic Issues in Qualitative Research. Ferrara, Lawrence.
If the Semantics of Music Theorizing is Broke, Let's Fix it. Cantrick, Robert B.
Interdisciplinary and Intercultural Aspects of Music. Heimes, Klaus F.
Kierkegaard: La Seduzione, l'Interiorità, l'Ironia. Gallino, Guglielmo.
La Fonction de la Musique chez les Contemporains du Denys Authentique. Witt, Richard.
La Musica in Aristotele. Vetere, Lucia.
Langer on the Arts as Cognitive. Reimer, Bennett.
Le Rôle de la Notion de Caractère. Koana, Akiko.
Les aspects mythologieques de la musique (le passage du modernisme au post-modernisme). Hofman-Veselinovic, Mijana.
Levinson on Hope in *The Hebrides*. Karl, Gregory and Robinson, Jenefer.
Lyotard's Homeopathic Indeterminacy: The Medicinal Sublime. Miller-Frank, Felicia.
Marcel Duchamp, la musique et les machines. Raymond, François.
Music Criticism and Musical Meaning. Herzog, Patricia.
Music, Platonism and Performance: Some Ontological Strains. Sharpe, R A.
Musical Beauty and Levels of Hearing. Yuktanandana, Aksak.
Musical Sympathies: The Experience of Expressive Music. Ridley, Aaron.
Musical Values Revisited: A Reply to Forest Hansen's "Values in Music Education". Elliott, David J.
Nietzsche and Music. Storr, Anthony.
Nietzsche y el Problema del Lenguaje en la Perspectiva de la Musica. Cragnolini, Mónica B.
Philodemus Resartus: Progress in Reconstructing the Philosophical Papyri from Herculaneum. Janko, Richard.
Philosophy of Music Education in a Slightly New Key. Hansen, Forest.
Reply to Taylor. Rudinow, Joel.

Schutz, Music, and Temporality: A Wittgensteinian Assessment. Costelloe, Timothy M.
So Black and Blue: Response to Rudinow. Taylor, Paul Christopher.
Some Peculiarities about Musical Aesthetic Qualities. Porter, Roosevelt.
Sound, Society, and Music "Proper". Bowman, Wayne D.
Sounds Before Symbols: What Does Phenomenology Have to Say?. Bartholomew, Douglas.
Still Hopeful: Reply to Karl and Robinson. Levinson, Jerrold.
The Birth of Cadential-Harmonic Music from the Spirit of Modern Idealism. Nussbaum, Charles.
The Challenge of History. Rainbow, Bernarr.
The Form of Feeling. Yob, Iris M.
The Music Goes Round and Round: How Music Means in School. Erickson, Frederick.
The Orchestral Workplace. Fischer, Marilyn M.
The Sounds of the Ideal: Hegel's Aesthetic of Music. Etter, Brian K.
The Value of Music. Graham, Gordon.
Toward a Phenomenology of Music: A Musician's Composition Journal. Smith, F Joseph.
Toward an Integrated Aesthetic and the Implications for Music Education. Palmer, Anthony J.
Values in Music Education. Hansen, Forest.
Why Pains Are Mental Objects. Langsam, Harold.

MUSIC CRITICISM

If the Semantics of Music Theorizing is Broke, Let's Fix it. Cantrick, Robert B.
Music Criticism and Musical Meaning. Herzog, Patricia.

MUSIC EDUCATION

Aesthetic Music Education Revisited: Discourses of Exclusion and Oppression. Koza, Julia Eklund.
Feminism as Critique in Philosophy of Music Education. Lamb, Roberta.
Feminist Theory and the Displaced Music Curriculum: Beyond the "Add and Stir" Projects. Morton, Charlene.
Gender, Musical Meaning, and Education. Green, Lucy.
Getting the Whole Picture: The View From Here. Gould, Elizabeth S.
Musical Values Revisited: A Reply to Forest Hansen's "Values in Music Education". Elliott, David J.
Philosophy of Music Education in a Slightly New Key. Hansen, Forest.
Pythagoras' Rib Or, What Does Music Education Want?. Bogdan, Deanne.
Sound, Society, and Music "Proper". Bowman, Wayne D.
Sounds Before Symbols: What Does Phenomenology Have to Say?. Bartholomew, Douglas.
Susanne Langer's Theory of Symbolism: An Analysis and Extension. Reichling, Mary J.
Toward an Integrated Aesthetic and the Implications for Music Education. Palmer, Anthony J.
Values in Music Education. Hansen, Forest.

MUSICIAN

Toward a Phenomenology of Music: A Musician's Composition Journal. Smith, F Joseph.

MUSICOLOGY

Alexius Meinong und Guido Adler: Eine Freundschaft in Briefen. Eder, Gabriele Johanna (ed).
Music, Value, and the Passions. Ridley, Aaron.
Levinson on Hope in *The Hebrides*. Karl, Gregory and Robinson, Jenefer.

MUSLIM

see also Islam

La Tensión Razón-Fe en la Filosofía Judeomusulmana de Al-Andalus. Ayala, Jorge M.

MYSTERY

Das geheimnisvolle Verschwinden des Geheimnisses. Voigts, Manfred.
God, Knowledge, and Mystery: Essays in Philosophical Theology. Van Inwagen, Peter.
Bedürfen und Vorstellungsdestrucktion. Kühn, Rolf.
El misterio construido. Lapoujade, María Noel.
Mystery and Explanation in Aquinas's Account of Creation. Liccione, Michael.
The Ethics of *Formale Anzeige* in Heidegger. Van Buren, John.
Wahrheit in Herrlichkeit: Auf Balthasar hören. Splett, Jörg.

MYSTICISM

"Demystification of Cognitive Insight" in *The Nature of Insight, Sternberg, Robert J (ed)*. Seifert, Colleen M (& others).
"How Natives Think" in *African Philosophy: Selected Readings, Mosley, Albert G (ed)*. Levy-Bruhl, Lucien.
"On Negrohood: Psychology of the African Negro" in *African Philosophy: Selected Readings, Mosley, Albert G (ed)*. Senghor, Leopold S.
"Von der Kritik zur Mystik: Edith Stein und der Marburger Neukantianismus" in *Studien zur Philosophie von Edith Stein, Fetz, Reto Luzius (ed)*. Lembeck, Karl-Heinz.
Das geheimnisvolle Verschwinden des Geheimnisses. Voigts, Manfred.
Inleiding Comparatieve Filosofie. Libbrecht, Ulrich.
Nuggets of Wisdom from Great Jewish Thinkers: From Biblical Times to the Present. Gerber, William.
Person to Person Inspiration. Kidd, James W and Kidd, Sunnie D.
The Bounds of Freedom: About the Eastern and Western Approaches to Freedom. Balaban, Oded and Erev, Anan.
The Young Heidegger: Rumor of the Hidden King. Van Buren, E John.
Three Messengers for One God. Schlabach, Gerald W (& other trans) and Arnaldez, Roger.

MYSTICISM

NARRATIVE

Discourse and Narrative: Ethics after the Linguistics Turn. Sauer, James.

El Futuro Requiere de Pasado (Nota Para Una Hermenéutica de la Narración Histórica). Chico, Gabriel.

Identity and the Narrative Structure of Life. Hattingh, Herselman and van Veuren, Pieter.

Is It Possible to Misrepresent the Holocaust?. Lang, Berel.

La paradoja de la narración: de los actos de habla a los actos de conciencia. Cofré, Juan O.

Las Emociones ante la Ficción. Bejarano, Teresa.

Must a Hermeneutical Psychoanalysis Exclude Science?. O'Grady, Paul, Rigby, Paul and Van Den Hengel, John.

Nachstellungen—Film und historischer Moment. Koch, Gertrud.

Narrative Time: The Inherently Perspectival Structure of the Human World. Wolff, Robert Paul.

Narrative, Irony, and Faith in Gibbon's *Decline and Fall*. Wootton, David.

No Longer, Not Yet: Reading History Grammatically. Erickson, Stephen A.

Noçao de Estilo em Granger e Narrativa Histórica. Cardoso Jr, Hélio Rebello.

Phenomenology and the Possibility of Narrative. Steeves, H Peter.

Plato Visits Postmodernity: Reflections on Narrative Philosophy. Bowery, Anne-Marie.

Postmodern Feminist Reflections on Reading Wolff. Hinkle, Gisela J.

Pursuing Truth in Narrative Research. O'Dea, Jane W.

R G Collingwood, *The Idea of History*. Dray, William H.

Rhetoric and the Narration of Conscience. Black, David.

Sport, the Aesthetic, and Narrative. Feezell, Randolph M.

The Kinds of Time in Historical Narration. Topolski, Jerzy.

The Value of Reading Fiction. Gleeson, Gerald.

The World-System Perspective in the Construction of Economic History. Abu-Lughod, Janet.

Towards Discourse in the Public Domain: Adolescent Fictions in Moral and Political Education. Gooderham, David.

Tradition, Insight and Constraint. Wolterstorff, Nicholas.

Unreliability Refigured: Narrative in Literature and Film. Currie, Gregory.

Verhaal en beslissing: Notities bij Bert van Roermunds *Recht, verhaal en werkelijkheid*. Tindemans, Klaas.

Who's Telling this Story, Anyway? Or, How to Tell the Gender of a Storyteller. Barwell, Ismay.

'Do You Understand What You are Reading?'. Sharpe, Eric J.

NATION

Pensando la nación. Polakovic, Stefan.

Racist Culture: Philosophy and the Politics of Meaning. Goldberg, David Theo.

The Politics of English Jacobinism: Writings of John Thelwall. Thelwall, John and Claeys, Gregory (ed).

Die Idee der Nation als Implikat der Interpersonalitäts- und Geschichtstheorie. Hahn, Karl.

El Individuo y la Nación: El Sujeto y lo Absoluto en las Filosofías del Lenguaje de Humboldt y Fichte. Pérez, Jorge Navarro.

Fichte und Humboldt—Zur Frage der Nationalsprache. Hennigfeld, Jochem.

History's Forgotten Doubles. Nandy, Ashis.

Multikulturalismus, Demokratie, Nation: Zur Philosophie der deutschen Einheit. Thomä, Dieter.

Nation, Weltbürgertum, und Synthesis der Geisterwelt. Schrader, Wolfgang H.

National Identification and the Transgression of National Boundaries: The Steps Toward Universalization. Kloskowska, Antonina.

Philosophy and the Self-Determination of Nation and Person Today. Pavlov, Dejan.

Power, Modernity and Morality in the Long Nineteenth Century. Goldblatt, David.

Richard Rorty and the Righteous Among the Nations. Geras, Norman.

NATIONAL

National Justice, International Justice, World Justice: Dialogues. Ginsberg, Robert.

NATIONAL SECURITY

Raíces ideológicas de la "guerra suicia" en América latina (en especial Argentina). Spitta, Arnold.

NATIONAL SOCIALISM

"...wirkliche Möglichkeiten für eine nationalsozialistische Philosophie?" in *Der geistige Anschluss, Fischer, Kurt R (ed)*. Heiss, Gernot.

"Das Institut für Philosophie der Universität Wien: Der Status quo und seine Genese" in *Der geistige Anschluss, Fischer, Kurt R (ed)*. Nagl-Docekal, Herta.

"Der Antike Dionysos bei Friedrich Nietzsche und Walter Heinrich Otto" in *Die besten Geister der Nation, Korotin, Ilse (ed)*. Zwiauer, Charlotte.

"Der Nationalsozialismus und die Idee der Welthistorischen Krise" in *Die besten Geister der Nation, Korotin, Ilse (ed)*. Sluga, Hans.

"Deutsche Philosophen und das 'Amt Rosenberg'" in *Die besten Geister der Nation, Korotin, Ilse (ed)*. Leaman, George.

"Die mythische Wirklichkeit eines Volkes" in *Der feministische "Sündenfall"?, Kohn-Ley, Charlotte (ed)*. Korotin, Ilse.

"Die Platon-Rezeption in Deutschland um 1933" in *Die besten Geister der Nation, Korotin, Ilse (ed)*. Orozco, Teresa.

"Die Rezeption der Philosophie Friedrich Nietzsches im deutschen Faschismus" in *Die besten Geister der Nation, Korotin, Ilse (ed)*. Zapata, Martha.

"Die verfehlte Sendung: Die Philosophie und der Nationalsozialismus" in *Der geistige Anschluss, Fischer, Kurt R (ed)*. Sluga, Hans.

"Die Verführerische Marionette" in *Die besten Geister der Nation, Korotin, Ilse (ed)*. Stockreiter, Karl.

"Dopplung als Leugnung: Zur Theorie von Robert J Lifton" in *Nationalsozialismus und Moderne, Welzer, Harald (ed)*. Sedghi, Darjosh.

"Erinnern ohne Gedenken" in *Nationalsozialismus und Moderne, Welzer, Harald (ed)*. Kannonier-Finster, Waltraud and Ziegler, Meinrad.

"Eugenische Utopien: Entwürfe für die Rationalisierung der menschlichen Entwicklung" in *Nationalsozialismus und Moderne, Welzer, Harald (ed)*. Weingart, Peter.

"Frauen und Rechtsextremismus: 'Kampfgefährtin' oder 'Heimchen am Herd'?" in *Nationalsozialismus und Moderne, Welzer, Harald (ed)*. Knapp, Gudrun-Axeli.

"Geistiger Anschluss? Das Wiener Philosophische Institut und der Nationalsozialismus" in *Der geistige Anschluss, Fischer, Kurt R (ed)*. Hartmann, Frank.

"Gescheitert—Der Versuch zur etablierung Nationalsozialistischer Philosophen an der Un. München" in *Die besten Geister der Nation, Korotin, Ilse (ed)*. Schorcht, Claudia.

"Höss lesen" in *Nationalsozialismus und Moderne, Welzer, Harald (ed)*. Montau, Robert.

"Komplizenschaft über Generationen" in *Nationalsozialismus und Moderne, Welzer, Harald (ed)*. Müller-Hohagen, Jürgen.

"Konfigurationen des Patriarchats, des Judentums und des Nazismus im deutschen feministischen Denken" in *Der feministische "Sündenfall"?, Kohn-Ley, Charlotte (ed)*. Heschel, Susannah.

"Männer der Praxis: Zur Sozialpsychologie des Verwaltungsmassenmordes" in *Nationalsozialismus und Moderne, Welzer, Harald (ed)*. Welzer, Harald.

"Nach Auschwitz kein Gedicht?: Ist Adornos Diktum übertrieben, überholt und widerlegt?" in *Nationalsozialismus und Moderne, Welzer, Harald (ed)*. Claussen, Detlev.

"Nach Verschiedenen Zwischenfällen ist die Arbeit Schliesslich bei mir Gelandet" in *Die besten Geister der Nation, Korotin, Ilse (ed)*. Korotin, Ilse.

"Österreichische Wissenschaftsgeschichte: Erkenntnisprozess oder Verdrängung?" in *Der geistige Anschluss, Fischer, Kurt R (ed)*. Wegeler, Cornelia.

"Philosophie in Wien zwischen "Anschluss" und Befreiung, Mythos, Affekt und Praktischer Vernunft" in *Der geistige Anschluss, Fischer, Kurt R (ed)*. Pfersmann, Otto.

"Philosophie und Drittes Reich" in *Der geistige Anschluss, Fischer, Kurt R (ed)*. Hartmann, Frank.

"Philosophiestudieren in den dreissiger Jahren" in *Der geistige Anschluss, Fischer, Kurt R (ed)*. Ekstein, Rudolf.

"Philosophischer Idealismus und Nationalsozialismus" in *Der geistige Anschluss, Fischer, Kurt R (ed)*. Klein, Hans-Dieter.

"Prolegomena zu einer National-Sozialistischen Rechtsphilosophie" in *Die besten Geister der Nation, Korotin, Ilse (ed)*. Ley, Michael.

"Reine Rechtslehre und schmutzige Verfassungstricks" in *Der geistige Anschluss, Fischer, Kurt R (ed)*. Graf, Georg.

"Schopenhauer als Ahnherr einer faschistischen Anthropologie" in *Die besten Geister der Nation, Korotin, Ilse (ed)*. Klinger, Gerwin.

"Wider Natur: Die Biologisierung sozialer Praxis im 'naturwissenschaftlichen Monismus'" in *Nationalsozialismus und Moderne, Welzer, Harald (ed)*. Hartmann, Frank.

"Zwischen Orthodoxie und gesellschaftlicher Sichtbarkeit" in *Der geistige Anschluss, Fischer, Kurt R (ed)*. Nemeth, Elisabeth.

"'Die Staatgründende Tat'—Alfred Baeumler und die Politisierung der Ästhetik" in *Die besten Geister der Nation, Korotin, Ilse (ed)*. Ross, Martin Michael.

"Am Muttergeist soll die Welt genesen": Philosophische Dispositionen zum Frauenbild im Nationalsozialismus. Korotin, Ilse Erika.

Denker Denken Geschichte Erkundungen zu Philosophie und Nationalsozialismus. Hartmann, Frank.

Der feministische "Sündenfall"?. Kohn-Ley, Charlotte (ed) and Korotin, Ilse (ed).

Der geistige Anschluss. Fischer, Kurt R (ed) and Wimmer, Franz M (ed).

Die besten Geister der Nation. Korotin, Ilse (ed).

Genozid und Heilserwartung: zum nationalsozialistischen Mord am europäischen Judentum. Ley, Michael.

Mein Leben in Deutschland vor und nach 1933. Löwith, Karl.

Nationalsozialismus und Moderne. Welzer, Harald (ed).

Philosophen im "Dritten Reich": Studie zu Hochschul- und Philosophiebetrieb im faschistischen Deutschland. Leske, Monika.

Philosophie an den bayerischen Universitäten 1933-1945. Schorcht, Claudia.

Die Kant-Studien im Dritten Reich. Leaman, George and Simon, Gerd.

NATIONALISM

"For the Nation! How Street Gangs Problematize Patriotism" in *After Postmodernism, Simons, Herbert W (ed)*. Conquergood, Dwight.

"How Much 'Heimat' does a Human Being Need?" in *Identity, Culture, and Education, Smeyers, Paul (ed)*. Levering, Bas.

"Liberalism, Nationality, and Education" in *Identity, Culture, and Education, Smeyers, Paul (ed)*. White, John.

"National Identity as Educational Problem: Towards a National System of Education in Belarus" in *Identity, Culture, and Education, Smeyers, Paul (ed)*. Buiko, Tatyana.

"Nationalism and Intervention" in *Introducing Applied Ethics, Almond, Brenda (ed)*. Coady, C A J.

"Nationalism: Ambiguous Legacies and Contingent Futures" in *The End of "Isms"?, Shtromas, Alexsandras (ed)*. Kamenka, Eugene.

"Negritude, Nationalism, and Nativism: Racists or Racialists?" in *African Philosophy: Selected Readings, Appiah, Kwame Anthony*. Mosley, Albert G.

Freud and the Politics of Psychoanalysis. Brunner, José.

Nationalism (Fourth, Expanded Edition). Kedourie, Elie.

Pensando la nación. Polakovic, Stefan.

The Nationalism Reader. Dahbour, Omar (ed) and Ishay, Micheline R (ed).

The New Ecological Order. Ferry, Luc and Volk, Carol (trans).

Whither Marxism?. Magnus, Bernd (ed) and Cullenberg, Stephen (ed).

NATIONALISM

Boturini e la Diffusione di Vico in Spagna. Mestre, Antonio.

Democrazia e sviluppo—La Democrazia alla prova. Thesing, Josef.

Der Primat Deutschlands bei Fichte. De Pascale, Carla.

Die Rezeption der politischen Philosophie Fichtes in Frankreich. Espagne, Michel.

En Deçà de la Souveraineté. Pestieau, Joseph.

Fichte y Ortega (II). Héroes o Ciudadanos. El Mito de Don Quijote. Molinuevo, José Luis.

Fichtes Nationalstaatsgedanke auf der Grundlage unveröffentlichter Manuskripte von 1807. Schottky, Richard.

Fichtes Stellung zum Judentum. Fuchs, Erich.

Hirsch on Education and National Culture: A Critique. Grant, Robert.

Identité et nationalisme irlandais. Sullivan, Timothy.

Il Debutto Politico di Gentile: Introduzione agli Scritti sulla Prima Guerra Mondiale. Galasso, Giuseppe.

Is Liberal Nationalism an Oxymoron? An Essay for Judith Shklar. Levinson, Sanford.

Ist Fichtes Modell des Kosmopolitismus pluralistisch?. Radrizzani, Ives.

Justice: An Inter-Faith Task. Pattery, George.

La posible contribución de la filosofía clásica rusa a la construcción de una sociedad humanista. Kline, Goerge L.

National Identification and the Transgression of National Boundaries: The Steps Toward Universalization. Kloskowska, Antonina.

National Identity and National Consciousness. Tevzadze, Natia.

National Past, Socialist Future. Geoghegan, Vincent.

Nationale Erziehung und sittliche Bestimmung. Soller, Alois K.

Nationalism, Patriotism, and Toleration. Nathanson, Stephen.

Nationalisme versus republikeinse burgerschapszin. Van Erp, Herman.

Nationalsprache und Sprachnation: Zur Gegenwartsbedeutung von Fichtes *Reden an die deutsche Nation*. Heinrichs, Johannes.

Nishida Kitarô, l'école de Kyôto et l'ultra-nationalisme. Lavelle, Pierre.

Patriotism and Political Obligation. Montague, Phillip.

Patriotism: Virtue or Vice?. Gaffney, James.

Positive Universalism: The Universal Language of Science Used to Construct a Universal Metatheory. Hubert, Jerzy Z.

Protestantism as a Transnational Ideology. Baskerville, Stephen.

Should Communitarians be Nationalists?. O'Neill, John.

NATIVE AMERICAN

Can There Be a Right to Secede?. Ewin, R E.

NATIVES

"How Natives Think" in *African Philosophy: Selected Readings, Mosley, Albert G (ed)*. Levy-Bruhl, Lucien.

NATSOULAS, T

The Concept of Consciousness$_5$: The Unitive Meaning. Natsoulas, Thomas.

NATURAL

"Putnam's Doctrine of Natural Kind Words and Frege's Doctrines of Sense, Reference, and Extension" in *Reading Putnam, Clark, Peter (ed)*. Wiggins, David.

The Problem of Consciousness: Essays Towards a Resolution. McGinn, Colin.

Argumentaciones éticas a partir de la naturaleza: Aristóteles y después. Annas, Julia.

Caring Relationships with Natural and Artificial Environments. Field, Terri.

Cognitive Processes and Social Norms in Natural Discourse at the Marketplace. Lindenfeld, Jacqueline.

Computation as an Intrinsic Property. Boyle, C Franklin.

Discontinuity in Categorical Grammar. Morrill, Glyn.

Emotion as a Natural Kind: Towards a Computational Foundation for Emotion Theory. Charland, Louis C.

Metafísica de la finalidad natural: Su metamorfosis en la línea Kant-Schopenhauer-Nietzsche. Rodriguez Gonzalez, M.

Names, Natural Kind Terms, and Rigid Designation. Macbeth, Danielle.

Resources and Environmental Policy. Narveson, Jan.

NATURAL DEDUCTION

Natural Deduction Based upon Strict Implication for Normal Modal Logics. Cerrato, Claudio.

Natural Deduction for Intuitionistic Linear Logic. Troelstra, A S.

Natural Deduction System for Tense Logics. Indrzejczak, Andrzej.

Uniformization Problems and the Cofinality of the Infinite Symmetric Group. Sharp, James D and Thomas, Simon.

NATURAL HISTORY

"Die Sprache in den (Natur-) historischen Wissenschaften" in *Die Sprache in den Wissenschaften, Weingartner, Paul (ed)*. Boné, Edouard.

Natural History of Religion. Fieser, James (ed) and Hume, David.

Religion's 'Foundation in Reason': The Common Sense of Hume's Natural History. Ferreira, M Jamie.

NATURAL LANGUAGE

"The Brain's Software: The Natural Languages and Poetic Information Processing" in *The Machine as Metaphor and Tool, Haken, Hermann (ed)*. Johansson, S Ryan.

Dewey's New Logic: A Reply to Russell. Burke, Tom.

Logical Form and the Hidden-Indexical Theory: A Reply to Schiffer. Ludlow, Peter.

NATURAL LAW

"Socrates and Stoic Natural Law" in *The Socratic Movement, Vander Waerdt, Paul A (ed)*. DeFilippo, Joseph G and Mitsis, Phillip T.

"Universales, Particulares, Simetría, Leyes Naturales" in *Temas Actuales de Filosofía, Palacios, María Julia (ed)*. Flichman, Eduardo Héctor.

"Zeno's *Republic* and the Origins of Natural Law" in *The Socratic Movement, Vander Waerdt, Paul A (ed)*. Vander Waerdt, Paul A.

"'Wanted' and 'Unwanted' Life" in *Ethics on the Frontiers of Human Existence, Badham, Paul (ed)*. Kittrie, Nicholas.

Métaphysique et Éthique au Fondement du Droit. Trigeaud, Jean-Marc.

Narrative and the Natural Law: An Interpretation of Thomistic Ethics. Hall, Pamela M.

Actualidad de un Filósofo del Siglo XVI: Francisco de Vitoria. Ocaña García, Marcelino.

Analogia della legge: Uno studio su S Tommaso d'Aquino. Vendemiati, Aldo.

Are There Natural Laws Concerning Particular Biological Species?. Lange, Marc.

Critical Notice of 'Questions concerning the Law of Nature'. Stewart, M A.

Derecho Natural o Derecho Racional?. García-Huidobro, Joaquín.

Kant: Ilustración jurídica versus razón de Estado. Villacañas, José L.

Killing a Chinese Mandarin: The Moral Implications of Distance. Ginzburg, Carlo.

L'opposition de Hegel au conservatisme de Charles-Louis de Haller. Ponton, Lionel.

La Dualidad Personal: Autor y Actor. Choza, Jacinto.

Miracles in the Best of All Possible Worlds: Leibniz's Dilemma and Leibniz's Razor. Brown, Gregory.

Natural Law as the Defense for Human Life. McLean, Edward B.

Philosophers versus Chemists Concerning 'Laws of Nature'. Christie, Maureen.

Rosmini on Natural Law and Right. Cleary, Denis.

Rousseau's Pufendorf: Natural Law and the Foundations of Commercial Society. Wokler, Robert.

Simetrías versus leyes? Apostilla a Van Fraassen sobre la representación. Ibarra, Andoni and Mormann, Thomas.

The Opening up of Natural Law. Kearns, Paul.

Translating Samuel Pufendorf: On Two English Editions. Palladini, Fiammetta.

Truth, Ethics and Divination in Igbo and Yoruba Traditions: A Reply to Emmanuel Eze. Uyanne, Frank.

Universal Dimensions of Natural Law. Tokarczyk, Roman A.

Was Hobbes a Legal Positivist?. Murphy, Mark C.

Yves Simon's Approach to Natural Law. Long, Steven A.

NATURAL PHILOSOPHY

"Socrates in the Clouds" in *The Socratic Movement, Vander Waerdt, Paul A (ed)*. Vander Waerdt, Paul A.

Leibniz and the Rational Order of Nature. Rutherford, Donald.

The Transformation of Natural Philosophy: The Case of Philip Melanchthon. Kusukawa, Sachiko.

Gegenwärtige Diskussionen über eine Konzeption der Naturphilosophie. Hajduk, Zygmunt.

Le Glosse di Juan Ginés de Sepúlveda alle Traduzioni Latine di Aristotle. Coroleu, Alejandro.

Metafisica Teologica e Filosofia Naturale in Roberto Grossatesta. Sannino, Antonella.

NATURAL RESOURCES

"An Economic Theory of Natural Resources" in *Ecology, Technology, and Culture, Zweers, Wim (ed)*. van der Straaten, Jan.

How Would you Like your 'Sustainability', Sir? Weak or Strong? A Reply to my Critics. Beckerman, Wilfred.

In Defence of Sustainable Development. Skolimowski, Henryk.

Off the Treadmill? Technology and Tourism in the North American Maple Syrup Industry. Hinrichs, C Clare.

Sustainable Development, Capital Substitution and Economic Humility: A Response to Beckerman. Jacobs, Michael.

NATURAL RIGHT

"Are There Natural Rights?—Hegel's Break with Kant" in *Hegel on the Modern World, Collins, Ardis B (ed)*. Tunick, Mark.

"Das Erbe der Freiheit" in *Das geistige Erbe Europas, Buhr, Manfred (ed)*. Zarka, Yves-Charles.

Para la Paz Perpetua de Kant y el *Fundamento del Derecho Natural* de Fichte: Encuentros y Desencuentros. Oncina, Faustino.

Zur Begründung der Menschenrechte: Hobbes-Locke-Kant. König, Siegfried.

A Proposito di 'Filosofia del Diritto'. Bello, Angela Ales.

Ilustración política y teoría del estado en Leibniz (Materiales para una reflexión contemporánea). Racionero, Quintín.

La fundamentación filosófica de los derechos humanos en Jacques Maritain. Beuchot, Mauricio.

Le Epistole Vichiane e la Nascita dell'idea di Scienza Nuova. Sanna, Manuela.

Leibniz et le droit subjectif. Zarka, Yves-Charles.

Leslie Mulholland on Kant's *Rechtslehre*. Gregor, Mary J.

Montesquieu e il Problema dell'"Diversité". Courtney, C P.

Pufendorf tra Classicità e Modernità: Nota su un Libro di Simone Goyard-Fabre. Catteneo, Mario A.

NATURAL SCIENCES

Naturwissenschaftliche Untersuchungen. Seneca, L Annaeus and Brok, M F A (ed & trans).

On Knowing—The Natural Sciences. McKeon, Richard, Owen, David B (ed) and McKeon, Zahava K (ed).

Platonism and Positivism in Psychology. Adler, Mortimer.

Science and Culture: Popular and Philosophical Essays. von Helmholtz, Hermann and Cahan, David (ed).

Ways of Knowing: Selected Readings (Second Edition). Dodson, Kevin E (ed) and Avery, Jon (ed).

About the Philosophical Style of Thinking. Panova, Elena.

Blurred Boundaries: Recent Changes in the Relationship Between Economics and the Philosophy of Natural Science. Hands, D Wade.

Does Kant's *Metaphysical Foundations of Natural Science* Fill a Gap in the *Critique of Pure Reason*?. Westphal, Kenneth R.

Epistemology of the Value-Judgements. Markakis, Manolis.

NATURE

NEED

"Need, Nurturance, and the Emotions on a Pacific Atoll" in *Emotions In Asian Thought, Marks, Joel (ed)*. Lutz, Catherine.

Cicero Versus Machiavelli: Does the End Justify the Means. Hancock, Curtis L.

Doing What One Wants Less: A Reappraisal of the Law of Desire. Clarke, Randolph.

Information Sharing in Donor Insemination: A Conflict of Rights and Needs. Daniels, Ken R.

Needs and Essence. Rotenstreich, Nathan.

Needs versus Desires. Larson, Erica.

Sexual Needs and Sexual Pleasures. Moore, Gareth.

The Earth Might be Round, But the World is Flat: The Groundwork for an Ethics of Relief. Ramsey, Ramsey Eric.

What Do Women Want? Rewriting the Social Contract. Thompson, Janna.

'The Unnatural Desire for More than one Needs': An Objection to James Tully's View. Kopton, K.

NEEDHAM, J

Understanding Oriental Cultures. Gare, Arran E.

NEGATION

On Beings of Reason (De Entibus Rationis) Metaphysical Disputation LIV. Suárez, Francisco and Doyle, John P (trans).

Transformations in Consciousness: The Metaphysics and Epistemology. Merrell-Wolff, Franklin.

A Star-Free Semantics for R. Mares, Edwin D.

Cessation and Integration in Classical Yoga. Whicher, Ian.

Classical Harmony: Rules of Inference and the Meaning of the Logical Constants. Milne, Peter.

Conditional Negation on the Positive Logic. Geisler, Jacek and Nowak, Marek.

Denegating God. Taylor, Mark C.

Die Verneinung. Frege, Gottlob.

Finito e infinito e l'idealismo della filosofia: La logica hegeliana dell'essere determinato: Parte Prima. Movia, Giancarlo.

Intuitionists Are Not (Turing) Machines. Wright, Crispin.

Is Even Minimal Negation Constructive?. Hazen, A P.

Ist eine reine Inhaltslogik möglich? Zu Leibniz' Begriffstheorie. Liske, Michael-Thomas.

On Negation, Truth, and Warranted Assertibility. Tennant, Neil.

Paraconsistent Logics. Slater, B H.

The Concept of Dialectic. Stack, George J.

The Dimension of the Negation of Transitive Closure. McColm, Gregory L.

Transmigration Without a Self. Datta, Rama.

Wright on the Non-Mechanizability of Intuitionist Reasoning. Detlefsen, Michael.

NEGATIVE

Proposiciones con Términos Negativos. Muñoz García, Angel.

White Horse not Horse: Making Sense of a Negative Logic. Lai, Whalen.

NEGATIVITY

"Ich aber fordere Sie auf, absolute Genesis ins Auge zu fassen!". Richli, Urs.

Dasein and the Ground of Negativity: A Note on the Fourth Movement in the *Beiträge*-Symphony. Richardson, William J.

NEGLIGENCE

Malpractice Arising From Negligent Psychotherapy: Ethical, Legal, and Clinical Implications of *Osheroff vs Chestnut Lodge*. Packman, Wendy L, Cabot, Mithran G and Bongar, Bruce.

NEGOTIATION

Lying During Crisis Negotiations: A Costly Means to Expedient Resolution. Burke Jr, Francis V.

NEGRO

see also Blacks

"On Negrohood: Psychology of the African Negro" in *African Philosophy: Selected Readings, Mosley, Albert G (ed)*. Senghor, Leopold S.

NEIGHBOR

A Note on Justice, Care, and Immigration Policy. Baier, Annette C.

Hanfling on Loving My Neighbour, Loving Myself. Walton, Gertrud.

Hanfling on Neighbour Love. Radcliffe, Dana M.

NEILL, A

Fiction, Pity, Fear, and Jealousy. Radford, Colin.

NEIMAN, A

Replies to Comments. Gewirth, Alan.

NELSON, M

Infinite Utility and Temporal Neutrality. Vallentyne, Peter.

NEMESIUS

Henologische Perspektiven I/I-II: Platon—Johannes—Cusanus. Wyller, Egil A.

NEO-CONFUCIANISM

"Neo-Confucianism and Human Rights" in *Human Rights and the World's Religions, Rouner, Leroy (ed)*. De Bary, W Theodore.

NEO-KANTIANISM

"Hönigswalds Neukant. u. Husserls Phänomenol. als Hintergrund d. Denkens von Stein" in *Studien zur Philosophie von Edith Stein, Fetz, Reto Luzius (ed)*. Orth, Ernst Wolfgang.

"Von der Kritik zur Mystik: Edith Stein und der Marburger Neukantianismus" in *Studien zur Philosophie von Edith Stein, Fetz, Reto Luzius (ed)*. Lembeck, Karl-Heinz.

Studien zur Philosophie von Edith Stein. Fetz, Reto Luzius (ed), Rath, Matthias (ed) and Schulz, Peter (ed).

Die uitdrukkingskracht van de transcendentale denkkritiek. Hoogland, J.

Jaspers en discusión con el pensamiento de su época. Barrio, Jaime Franco.

La Ontologia Anti-Metafisica de Nicolai Hartmann. Cuéllar P, Hortensia.

NEO-PLATONISM

Augustine. Clark, Mary T.

Die Musik als scientia mathematica von der Spätantike bis zum Barock. Hirtler, Eva.

S L Frank: The Life and Work of A Russian Philosopher, 1877-1950. Boobbyer, Philip.

Cognition and Human Actualization in Plotinus and Aristotle. Husain, Martha.

Empedocles and his Interpreters: The Four-Element Doxography. Kingsley, Peter.

Florence, 1492: Réapparaît Plotin. Saffrey, Henri Dominique.

Il "Traicté du Feu et du Sel" di Blaise de Vigenère e una sua Sconosciuta Traduzione Italiana. Trabucco, Oreste.

L'État Actuel des Recherches Dionysiennes. Bénakis, Linos.

La Fonction Catalytique de l'Echaiphnes chez Denys. Moutsopoulos, Evanghélos.

Le Dieu Transcendant dans le Néoplatonisme et chez Denys. Garcia Bazán, Francisco.

Leibniz y la Tradición Neoplatónica: Estado Actual de la Cuestión. Orio, Bernardino.

Neoplatonism in Christianity, Judaism and Islam. Harris, R Baine.

Plotinus and the Neoplatonic Conception of Dialectic. Anton, John P.

Roger Bacon (1214-94): Ética y Reforma. Boadas-Llavat, Agustí.

The Metaphysical Foundation of Gnosiology in Neoplatonic Proclus (412-485). Térézis, Christos.

The Neoplatonic Interpretation as to the Teaching of Divine Love in Dionysius. Manos, Andreas.

NEO-THOMISM

Das Feindbild der marxistisch-leninistischen Philosophie in der DDR 1945-1988. Kapferer, Norbert.

Neotomismo a Salerno: L'Ambiente Culturale in cui visse ed Operò Pasquale Naddeo. Gigante, Mario.

NEOPOSITIVISM

Zur gesellschaftlichen Stellung der Kunst zwischen Natur und Technik (Band 2). Knoell, Dieter Rudolf.

NEOSCHOLASTICISM

The Philosophy and the History of Philosophy in the Neoscholastic Interpretation of Josef Kratochvil. Glombik, Czeslaw.

NETWORK

"Connectionism and Eliminativism" in *Connectionism: Debates on Psychological Explanation, Macdonald, Cynthia (ed)*. Macdonald, Cynthia.

Connectionism and the Mind: An Introduction to Parallel Processing in Networks. Bechtel, William and Abrahamsen, Adele.

Cognition without Neurones: Adaptation, Leanring and Memory in the Immune System. Stewart, J.

Connectionism and Psychiatry: A Brief Review. Park, S B G and Young, A H.

Connectionism and the Mind: An Introduction to Parallel Processing in Networks. Ohayon, Elan Liss.

Connectionist Hysteria: Reducing a Freudian Case Study to a Network Model. Lloyd, Dan.

Social Contracting as a Trust-Building Process of Network Governance. Calton, Jerry M and Lad, Lawrence J.

The "Explicit-Implicit" Distinction. Hadley, Robert F.

NEUHOUSER, F

Neuhousers Fichte-Deutung. Rohs, Peter.

NEUMANN, F

The Theory of Social Change with Introduction by Bill Scheuerman. Marcuse, Herbert and Neumann, Franz.

NEUMANN, I

On the Concepts of the 'Other' and the 'Enemy'. Harle, Vilho.

NEURAL

How the Self Controls Its Brain. Eccles, John C.

Connectionism and Psychiatry: A Brief Review. Park, S B G and Young, A H.

The "Explicit-Implicit" Distinction. Hadley, Robert F.

NEURATH, O

Philosophie aus Wien. Fischer, Kurt Rudolf.

Otto Neurath's Idealist Inheritance: *The Social and Economic Thought of Wilhelm Neurath*. Uebel, Thomas E.

NEUROBIOLOGY

Repräsentation und Identität. Vogeley, Kai.

NEUROLOGY

A Neural Network Approach to Obsessive-Compulsive Disorder. Stein, Dan J and Hollander, Eric.

How the Brain Gives Rise to Mathematics in Ontogeny and in Culture. Vandervert, Larry R.

NEURON

Mind, Matter, and Quantum Mechanics. Stapp, Henry P.

Cognition without Neurones: Adaptation, Leanring and Memory in the Immune System. Stewart, J.

Some Considerations on the Status of the Psychic in "Freudian" Project (in Portuguese). Milidoni, Carmen Beatriz.

NEUROPSYCHOLOGY

Is Cognitive Neuropsychology Possible?. Bub, Jeffrey.

On the Methods of Cognitive Neuropsychology. Glymour, Clark.

Testing Models of Cognition Through the Analysis of Brain-Damaged Performance. Bub, Jeffrey.

The Neuropsychology of Communication: Spontaneous and Symbolic Aspects. Buck, Ross.

NIETZSCHE

NIETZSCHEAN

NIHILISM

NIJENHUIS, J

NIKLASSON, L

NINETEENTH

NINETEENTH

Absolu/Sujet. Jarczyk, Gwendoline and Labarrière, Pierre-Jean.

At the Crossroads: Hegel and the Ethics of *bürgerliche Gesellschaft*. Smith, Steven B.

Difficulté de l'hégélianisme. Apropos de l'ouvrage de Jean-François Kervégan: *Hegel, Carl Schmitt: le politique entre spéculation et positivité*. Gervais, Richard.

Filosofi a Bologna fra Ottocento e Novecento. Garin, Eugenio.

Hegel dans *Soi-même comme un autre* de Paul Ricoeur. Brito, Emilio.

Hegel et la Grèce. Vieillard-Baron, Jean-Louis.

Hegel et Schelling: critique du formalisme et prise en charge de la contingence. Lardic, Jean-Marie.

Hegel on Property and Recognition. Cristi, Renato.

Hegel's *Phenomenology* and the Critique of the Enlightenment An Essay in Interpretation. DiGiovanni, George.

How Philosophy *Instructs the World*. Harris, Henry S.

Interpretations of Boole's Alleged Psychologism. Vassallo, Nicla.

Kierkegaard e l'ironia socratica. Gallino, Guglielmo.

Kierkegaard: La Seduzione, l'Interiorità, l'Ironia. Gallino, Guglielmo.

L'opposition de Hegel au conservatisme de Charles-Louis de Haller. Ponton, Lionel.

L'université d'état et ses contradictions philosophiques: Hegel et la création de l'université de Berlin. Reid, Jeffrey.

La Filosofia Cristiana nei Secoli XIX e XX. Scilironi, Carlo.

La fin de l'histoire serait-elle le commencement de la sagesse? L'aliénation de l'esprit dans la *Phénoménologie* de Hegel. Joós, Ernest.

La lecture du journal selon Hegel: "une sorte de-prière du matin réaliste"?. Bienenstock, Myriam.

La matière illusoire de la médecine mentale au XIXe siècle. Lantéri-Laura, Georges.

La Ruse de la Raison. D'Hondt, Jacques.

La vie éthique perdue dans ses extrêmes...Scission et réconciliation dans la théorie hégélienne de la *Sittlichkeit*. Kervégan, Jean-François.

Las máscaras del demonio: Nietzsche y la hermenéutica. Conill, Jesus.

Les Raisons du Coeur: Lectures de la Relation de Comte à Clotilde. Giolito, Christophe.

Max Weber et le néo-Kantisme: Pour une politique de la modernité. Piché, Claude.

Max Weber und das Problem der Weltanschauung. Rossi, Pietro.

Nature, coutume et droit chez Hegel. Vieillard-Baron, Jean-Louis.

O Éter Luminoso como Espaço Absoluto. Oliveira, Maurício Pietrocola.

On Translating Hegel's *Encyclopedia Logic*: A Response. Geraets, Theodore F and Harris, H S.

Philosophie hégélienne de l'actualité et actualité de la philosophie hégélienne. Bourgeois, Bernard.

Psicologia delle folle e Scienza Politica in Italia alla Fine del XIX Secolo. Donzelli, Maria.

Zeitgemässe Unzeitgemässe: Von Friedrich Nietzsche über Georg Simmel zu Max Weber. Schluchter, Wolfgang.

NISHITANI, K

Nishitani and Nietzsche on the Selfless Self. Smith, Joel R.

NOBILITY

The Book of the Body Politic. Forhan, Kate Langdon (ed & trans) and De Pizan, Christine.

Moral Leadership in Society: Some Parallels between the Confucian "Noble Man" and the Jewish *Zaddik*. Goldman, René.

NODDINGS, N

Clinical Ethics and Nursing: "Yes" to Caring, But "No" to a Female Ethics of Care. Kuhse, Helga.

NOH THEATER

Zeami's Concept of "Flower" in Noh Performance. Aoki, Takao.

NOMINALISM

The Facts of Causation. Mellor, D H.

El "Tractatus Consequentiarum" (1518) en la Lógica de Juan de Oria. Muñoz Delgado, Vicente.

El Concepto, Como Signo Natural: Una Polémica Acerca de Ockham. Velázquez, Lorena.

Roger Bacon (1214-94): Ética y Reforma. Boadas-Llavat, Agustí.

Una Pregunta Sobre la Noción de "Bien" en Aristóteles. Femenías, María Luisa.

NON-CHRISTIAN

Bringing into Captivity Every Thought: Capita Selecta in the History of Christian Evaluations of Non-Christian Philosophy. Klapwijk, Jacob (ed) and Griffioen, Sander (ed) and Groenewoud, Gerben (ed).

NONCOGNITIVISM

"Metaethischer Nonkognitivismus und moralische Aufmerksamkeit" in *Mythos Wertfreiheit?, Apel, Karl Otto (ed)*. Leist, Anton.

NONCONTRADICTION

Principio di Non-Contraddizione e Modalità Originaria dell'Archè-Fondamento. Bosio, Franco.

NONREDUCTIVE

Causal Relevance and Nonreductive Physicalism. Barrett, Jonathan.

NONSENSE

Nietzsche e il Nonsense. Arena, Leonardo Vittorio.

Carta abierta al Dr Wessell. Pintor Ramos, A.

Comentario kafkiano en torno a la obra *Realidad y Verdad* de Antonio Pintor-Ramos. Wessell, L P.

NONSTANDARD ANALYSIS

A Constructive Approach to Nonstandard Analysis. Palmgren, E.

Flat Sets. Grainger, Arthur D.

Forcing in Nonstandard Analysis. Ozawa, Masanao.

NONSTANDARD LOGICS

A Model for Intuitionistic Non-standard Arithmetic. Moerdijk, I.

NONSTANDARD MODELS

The Isomorphism Property for Nonstandard Universes. Schmerl, James H.

The Thickness Lemma..... Yang, Yue.

NONVIOLENCE

Ahimsa (Noninjury) Revisited. Fox, Michael W.

NOOSPHERE

Noospheric Synarchy: From an Ancient Hellenic Democracy to the Aristocracy of Spirit. Gromow, Ivan G and Kuvakina, Olga D.

NORM

"Concepts and Norms in a Natural World" in *Philosophy of Psychology: Debates on Psychological Explanation, Macdonald, Cynthia (ed)*. Peacocke, Christopher.

"Etica e morale" in *L'etica e il suo Altro, Vigna, Carmelo (ed)*. Ricoeur, Paul.

Moral Theory: A Contemporary Overview. DeMarco, Joseph P.

Norm and Context in the Social Sciences. Griffioen, Sander (ed) and Verhoogt, Jan (ed).

Practical Guilt: Moral Dilemmas, Emotions, and Social Norms. Greenspan, P S.

The Crossroads of Norm and Nature. Sim, May (Mui Hwa) (ed).

Brentano contra Kant: Sobre el imperativo categórico. Palacios, Juan Miguel.

Compromising with Convention. Hooker, Brad.

Conoscenza e Normatività nella Filosofia Italiana Contemporanea. Carcaterra, Gaetano.

Contingenza delle Norme e Soluzione delle Controversie. D'Agostino, Francesco.

Critical Notice of Roger Shiner *Norm and Nature: The Movements of Legal Thought*. Schauer, Frederick.

De-Individualizing Norms of Rationality. Tanney, Julia.

Giudicare o Decidere: Il Senso della Funzione Giudiziaria. Ollero Tassara, Andrés.

Giuridicità e durata. Marinelli, Vincenzo.

Il Problema della Natura Umana nella Filosofia Spagnola. Ballestros, Jesus.

Integrative Social Contracts Theory. Donaldson, Thomas and Dunfee, Thomas W.

Neutralidad y relatividad agencial. Farrell, Martín D.

Of Nulls and Norms. Godfrey-Smith, Peter.

Pluralism of Norms and Values: On the Claim and Reception of the Universal. Klapwijk, J.

Social Norms and Narrow Content. Williams, Meredith.

The Normative Nature of Coercion. Hankinson, Jennifer.

NORMAL

Natural Deduction Based upon Strict Implication for Normal Modal Logics. Cerrato, Claudio.

Syntactic Refutations against Finite Models in Modal Logic. Skura, Tomasz.

The Concept of Morality. Pawlowska, Ija Lazari.

NORMAL FORMS

An Algebraic Theory of Normal Forms. Ghilardi, Silvio.

Normal Forms in Combinatory Logic. Johann, Patricia.

Paper Machines. Mundici, Daniele and Sieg, Wilfried.

NORMALITY

Es negociable la diferencia?. Lorite Mena, José.

Normality as a Biological Concept. Wachbroit, Robert.

On *Histoire de la folie* as an Event. Canguilhem, Georges and Hobart, Ann (trans).

Phenomenological Concepts of Normality and Abnormality. Steinbock, A J.

NORMALIZATION

Natural Deduction for Intuitionistic Linear Logic. Troelstra, A S.

Strong Normalization in Type Systems: A Model Theoretic Approach. Terlouw, Jan.

NORMATIVE

Morality, Normativity, and Society. Copp, David.

Normative Cultures. Neville, Robert Cummings.

Normative Systeme. Alchourrón, Carlos E, Bulygin, Eugenio and Schmitt, Annette (& other trans).

Basing 'Ought' On 'Is'. Singer, Beth J.

De Sade o la subversión de/en la Ilustración. Mayos, Gonça.

Fundamentación última y factidad: (Un intento de argumentar "con Apel contra Apel"). Saez Rueda, L.

Hume's Problem and the Possibility of Normative Ethics. Flage, Daniel E and Glass, Ronald J.

Las "ciencias normativas" y la "ciencia del derecho". Vega, Jesús Fernández.

Naturalism, Normativity, and the Open Question Argument. Rosati, Connie.

Persons, Perspetives, and Full Information Accounts of the Good. Rosati, Connie.

Qu'est-ce que la pensée du politique? Une introduction au projet philosophique de Claude Lefort. Poltier, Hugues.

NORMATIVE ETHICS

Argumentaciones éticas a partir de la naturaleza: Aristóteles y después. Annas, Julia.

Hume's Problem and the Possibility of Normative Ethics. Flage, Daniel E and Glass, Ronald J.

NORMATIVE JUDGMENT

Conoscenza e Normatività: Una Prospettiva Metafisica. Cotta, Sergio.

I Preliminari Logici. Gardies, Jean-Louis.

NORMATIVITY

"Die hermeneutische Dimension von Sozialwissenschaft und ihre normative Grundlage" in *Mythos Wertfreiheit?, Apel, Karl Otto (ed)*. Apel, Karl Otto.

NORTON, B

"Natural Capital" in *Philosophy and the Natural Environment, Attfield, Robin (ed)*. Holland, Alan.

Contextualism and Norton's Convergence Hypothesis. Steverson, Brian K.

NORTON, J

Substance, Modality, and Spacetime. Healey, Richard.

OAKLEY, J

Toward a Thick Theory of Moral Agency. Manning, Rita C.

OBEDIENCE

L'Obiezione di Coscienza: A Proposito di un Recente Convegno. Troncarelli, Barbara.

Lo stato moderno: profili storici e dottrinali. Catania, Alfonso.

Obeying a Rule: Wittgenstein's Stress on Obedience in Sections 198-202 of the *Philosophical Investigations*. Susse, Jennifer.

OBJECT

see also Aesthetic Object, Mental Object

"Chisholm's Ontology of Things" in *American Philosophy Today and Other Philosophical Studies, Rescher, Nicholas*. Rescher, Nicholas.

"Objects and Objectivity" in *Objectivity, Simulation and the Unity of Consciousness, Peacocke, Christopher (ed)*. Campbell, John.

"Thoughts about Objects, Places and Times" in *Objectivity, Simulation and the Unity of Consciousness, Peacocke, Christopher (ed)*. Brewer, Bill.

Inleiding Comparatieve Filosofie. Libbrecht, Ulrich.

Kant's Idealism. Neujahr, Philip J.

The Antinomy of Thought: Maimonian Skepticism and the Relation between Thoughts and Objects. Bransen, Jan.

Actos básicos y actos fundados. Serrano, Agustín.

Adrian Stokes and Venice. Newman, Geoffrey.

Artifacts and Constituents. Denkel, Arda.

Begriff und Gegenstand. Frege, Gottlob.

Commentary: On Vague Objects, Fuzzy Logic, and Fractal Boundaries. Copeland, B Jack.

Dos Nociones de Objeto en el *Tractatus*. Tomasini Bassols, Alejandro.

El control experimental y la construcción del objeto científico. Ginebra i Molins, M P.

El Ente Como Objeto Formal de la Metafísica. Forment, Eudaldo.

Galileu e a Dialética: Síntese pelo Experimento e Natureza como Domínio dos Objectos. Maar, Wolfgang Leo.

Holton on Attitude Ascriptions and Intermediate Scope. Pickles, David.

Hume's View on External Object: A Critical Analysis. Pandey, Indu.

Humean Supervenience and Enduring Things. Haslanger, Sally.

Hutcheson and Mill on Evaluating Actions and Characters. Strasser, Mark.

Malebranche and Arnauld on Ideas. Watson, Richard A.

Object-Dependent and Property-Dependent Contents. Bruns, Manfred and Soldati, Gianfranco.

On Artifacts and Works of Art. Hilpinen, Risto.

On the Distinction Between the Object and Content of Consciousness. Natsoulas, Thomas.

On the Paradoxical Aspects of New Quantum Experiments. Vaidman, Lev.

Perspectival Thoughts and Psychological Generalizations. Corazza, Eros.

Scepticism and the Justification of Transcendental Idealism. Bermúdez, José Luis.

Semiosis y Objetos: Los Objetos Naturales. Prada Oropeza, Renato.

Some Issues in the Theory of Artifacts: Defining 'Artifact' and Related Notions. Dipert, Randall R.

The 3D/4D Controversy and Non-Present Objects. Markosian, Ned.

The Creation of 'Eternal' Objects. Ford, Lewis S.

The Problem of Reconciliation. Denkel, Arda.

The Problem of Thing and Object in Maritain. Cahalan, John C.

Théories de la pensée, de ses objets et de son discours chez Guillaume d'Occam. Karger, Élizabeth.

Truth as an Object. Magdziak, Marek.

Vyadi and The Realist Theory of Meaning. Ganeri, Jonardon.

What Am I Thinking About? John Duns Scotus and Peter Aureol on Intentional Objects. Perler, Dominik.

Zalta's Intensional Logic and the Metaphysics of Intentionality. Swoyer, Chris.

OBJECTIVE

"La doble Tensión y el Concepto Primitivo de Persona" in *Temas Actuales de Filosofía, Palacios, María Julia (ed)*. Baringoltz, Eleonora.

Kierkegaard, la recuperación del individuo existente y el discurso sobre lo histórico. Washburn, Jimmy.

OBJECTIVISM

"Unity and Objectivity" in *Objectivity, Simulation and the Unity of Consciousness, Peacocke, Christopher (ed)*. Hurley, Susan.

Colours: Their Nature and Representation. Maund, Barry.

Ethical Argument: Critical Thinking in Ethics. Curtler, Hugh Mercer.

An Objectivist Account of Theory Change. Soles, David E.

El Primer Principio del Conocimiento Práctico: Objeciones y Respuestas. Massini Correas, Carlos I.

Frictionless Philosophy: Paul Feyerabend and Relativism. Preston, John.

La Inevitabilidad del Objetivismo Etico. Massini, Carlos Ignacio.

Marxism, 'Ideology,' and Moral Objectivism. Mills, Charles W.

Objective Chance: Lonergan and Peirce on Scientific Generalization. Potter, Vincent G.

Was Ayn Rand a Humanist?. Walker, Jeff.

OBJECTIVITY

see also Impartiality

"Consciousness and Objective Reality" in *The Mind-Body Problem: A Guide to the Current Debate, Warner, Richard (ed)*. Nagel, Thomas.

"Evading the Subject: The Poverty of Contingency Theory" in *After Postmodernism, Simons, Herbert W (ed)*. Cole, Steven E.

"Objects and Objectivity" in *Objectivity, Simulation and the Unity of Consciousness, Peacocke, Christopher (ed)*. Campbell, John.

"Thoughts about Objects, Places and Times" in *Objectivity, Simulation and the Unity of Consciousness, Peacocke, Christopher (ed)*. Brewer, Bill.

"Understanding Truth and Objectivity: A Dialogue between Davidson and Gadamer" in *Hermeneutics and Truth, Wachterhauser, Brice (ed)*. Stueber, Karsten R.

A Philosophy of Matter and Mind: A New Look at an Old Major Topic in Philosophy. Wassermann, Gerhard D.

Hegels Wissenschaft der Logik—metaphysische Letztbegründung oder Theorie logischer Formen?. Schick, Friedrike.

Husserl e lo scetticismo. Savi, Cristina.

Il Linguaggio Dell'Oggettività: Saggio su Meinong. Brigati, Roberto.

La Depsicologizzazione della Logica: Un confronto tra Boole e Frege. Vassallo, Nicla.

Mythos Wertfreiheit?. Apel, Karl Otto (ed) and Kettner, Matthias (ed).

Objectivity, Communication, and the Foundation of Understanding. McKinzie, Bruce Wayne.

Objectivity, Simulation and the Unity of Consciousness. Peacocke, Christopher (ed).

Practical Reasoning about Final Ends. Richardson, Henry S.

The Ironist's Cage: Memory, Trauma, and the Construction of History. Roth, Michael S.

The Truth About Relativism. Margolis, Joseph.

Understanding Social Science: A Philosophical Introduction to the Social Sciences. Trigg, Roger.

Absolute vs Relational Theories of Space and Time: A Review of *World Enough and Space-Time* by John Earman. Rynasiewicz, Robert.

Anticipación de la naturaleza y giro copernicano: La naturaleza de la explicación científica en Bacon y en Kant. López Fernández, Alvaro.

Beyond Reductionism In Rhetorical Theories of Meaning. Cherwitz, Richard A and Darwin, Thomas J.

Constant Colors in the Head. McGilvray, James A.

Die Hermeneutik-Debatte in der italienischen Philosophie der Gegenwart. Bianco, Franco.

Edith Stein: l'Apprendistato Fenomenologico. Pezzella, Anna Maria.

En torno a los "estados de cosas": una investigación ontológico-formal. Crespo, Mariano.

Epistemic Competence. Henderson, David K.

Epistemic Justification and the Possibility of Empirical Evidence. Karu, George.

Feministinnen und Philosophie. Nussbaum, Martha C.

Fractured Subjectivity. Boyne, Roy.

Gender, Objectivity, and Realism. Soble, Alan.

Heidegger urbanizado (Notas para una crítica de la hermenéutica). Racionero, Quintín.

Husserl in discussione. Orlando, Teodosio.

Intersubjektivität und Objektivität der moralischen Werte. Corradini, Antonella.

Introducción a un tratado de filosofía primera. García-Baró, Miguel.

Objective Knowledge and Psychologism. Chaudhury, Mahasweta.

Objectivism and the Evolutionary Value of Colour Vision. Dedrick, Don.

Objectivity and Interpretation. Stecker, Robert.

Objectivity in Experimental Inquiry: Breaking Data-Technique Circles. Culp, Sylvia.

Objectivity in History. Bevir, Mark.

On What We May Hope: Rorty on Dewey and Foucault. Marshall, James D.

Putnam und Rorty über Objektivität und Wahrheit. Allen, Barry G.

Questionable Objectivity. Ripstein, Arthur.

Rational Agency and Objectively Practical Reason. Abrams, Edward L.

Sceptical Insulation and Sceptical Objectivity. Hetherington, Stephen Cade.

Scepticism About Legal Reasoning. Martin, Michael.

The Metaphoric Origins of Objectivity, Subjectivity, and Consciousness in the Direct Perception of Reality. Mulaik, Stanley A.

The Problem of Objectivity. Davidson, Donald.

The Untruth in Relativism. Dustin, Christopher A.

Theory Change and Theory Choice. Chalmers, Alan F.

Tras la postmodernidad. Innerarity, Daniel.

Truth Wronged (on Crispin Wright, *Truth and Objectivity*). Rumfitt, Ian.

Un Unico Heidegger? Note sul *Systematischer Index* di Eduard Landolt. Salmeri, Giovanni.

Uncertainty About Determinism: A Critical Review of Challenges to the Determinism of Modern Science. Fraley, Lawrence E.

Wright's *Truth and Objectivity*. Horgan, Terence.

Zur Rekonstruktion der Philosophischen Hermeneutik. Krämer, Hans.

Zwischen "objektiver Gültigkeit" und "subjektiv-notwendigem Probierstein" der Wahrheit. Köveker, Dietmar.

OBLIGATION

see also Duty

"Etica e morale" in *L'etica e il suo Altro, Vigna, Carmelo (ed)*. Ricoeur, Paul.

"Obligation Dynamics and Deontic Metamorphosis" in *American Philosophy Today and Other Philosophical Studies, Rescher, Nicholas*. Rescher, Nicholas.

Universals and Property Instances: The Alphabet of Being. Bacon, John.

A Threat or a Promise. Seligman, David B.

Acceptance of Authority and the Duty to Comply with Just Institutions: A Comment on Waldron. Murphy, Mark C.

Conflicts of Obligation. Forrester, James William.

Forgiving as an Obligation of the Moral Life. Harvey, J.

Hume's Problem and the Possibility of Normative Ethics. Flage, Daniel E and Glass, Ronald J.

Is There a Moral Obligation to Have Children?. Smilansky, Saul.

La Ética desde la Izquierda. Bueno, Gustavo.

La Obligación en el Positivismo: El Caso de H L A Hart. Hernández, Héctor H.

Lo Obligatorio, lo Meritorio y Otras Nociones Deónticas en la Ética Formal de Kant. García Norro, Juan José.

PARTICIPATION
Eternità e tempo in Plotino. Ferretti, Silvia.

Il Sogno, la Fanciullezza e l'Arte nel Pensiero di Giovanni Gentile. Stella, Vittorio.

La alteridad en el Sofista de Platón. Iglesias, Mercedes.

Repliek op Kal. te Velde, R.

Van Participatie tot Zelflimitatie; Over Thomas' Filosofie van de Schepping. Kal, Victor.

PARTICLE
The Exclusion Principle, Chemistry and Hidden Variables. Scerri, Eric R.

PARTICULAR
"Espacio, Tiempo y Particulares" in *Temas Actuales de Filosofía, Palacios, María Julia (ed).* Rodríguez Larreta, Juan.

"Universales, Particulares, Simetría, Leyes Naturales" in *Temas Actuales de Filosofía, Palacios, María Julia (ed).* Flichman, Eduardo Héctor.

La Función de la Intuición Ockhamista. López Vázquez, J Ramón.

PARTICULARISM
"Universalismo y Particularismo en la Etica Contemporánea" in *Temas Actuales de Filosofía, Palacios, María Julia (ed).* Guariglia, Osvaldo.

Universalismo y Particularismo en la Ética Contemporánea. Guariglia, Osvaldo.

PARTICULARS
"Acerca de la Dificultad para Identificar Personas como Particulares Básicos en Strawson" in *Temas Actuales de Filosofía, Palacios, María Julia (ed).* Skidelsky, Liza D.

Davidson, la relación causal y los eventos particulares. Pérez, Diana Inés.

La subalternación y la conversión aristotélica de las proposiciones. Valadez, Leticia.

PARTITION
A Modified Sentence Unprovable in "PA". Gordeev, L.

Effective Versions of Ramsey's Theorem: Avoiding the Cone Above 0'. Hummel, Tamara Lakins.

On a Generalization of Distributivity. Kanai, Yasuo.

The Consistency Strength of an Infinitary Ramsey Property. Kafkoulis, George.

PARTNERSHIP
University-Business Partnerships: An Assessment. Bowie, Norman E.

PASCAL
Pensées and Other Writings: A New Translation by Honor Levi. Pascal, Blaise and Levi, Honor (trans).

Arnauld et Pascal. Le Guern, Michel.

Ateismo, scetticismo e fideismo. Penelhum, Terence.

Between Finitude and Infinity: Hegelian Reason and the Pascalian Heart. Desmond, William.

Bishop Pierre-Daniel Huet's Remarks on Pascal. Maia Neto, José R and Popkin, Richard H.

Blaise Pascals "Discours sur la religion": Zu einer neueren Ausgabe der "Pensées". Raffelt, Albert.

Combating the Noetic Effects of Sin: Pascal's Strategy for Natural Theology. Cuneo, Terrence D.

Du Beau et du Sublime chez Pascal. Bouchilloux, Hélène.

La "clef" de Job—Pascal: la liberté/le mal. Leduc-Fayette, Denise.

La Catégorie Pascalienne de l'Hérésie. Leduc-Fayette, Denise.

Pascal and Descartes on First Ideas. Yhap, Jennifer.

Pascal on Certainty and Utility. McCarthy, John C.

Pascal: el hombre ante la perspectiva de la nueva ciencia. Domínguez, Virginia López.

Time and the Tragic. Pluzanski, Tadeusz.

PASCAL'S WAGER
"A Central Theistic Argument" in *Gambling on God: Essays on Pascal's Wager, Jordan, Jeffrey (ed).* Schlesinger, George.

"Infinite Decision Theory" in *Gambling on God: Essays on Pascal's Wager, Jordan, Jeffrey (ed).* Sorensen, Roy.

"Moral Objections to Pascalian Wagering" in *Gambling on God: Essays on Pascal's Wager, Jordan, Jeffrey (ed).* Quinn, Philip.

"Pascal's Wager and Finite Decision Theory" in *Gambling on God: Essays on Pascal's Wager, Jordan, Jeffrey (ed).* McClennen, Edward.

"Pragmatic Reasons for Belief" in *Gambling on God: Essays on Pascal's Wager, Jordan, Jeffrey (ed).* Foley, Richard.

"The Logic Of Pascal's Wager" in *Gambling on God: Essays on Pascal's Wager, Jordan, Jeffrey (ed).* Hacking, I.

"The Many-Gods Objection" in *Gambling on God: Essays on Pascal's Wager, Jordan, Jeffrey (ed).* Jordan, Jeffrey.

"The Wager in Pascal and Others" in *Gambling on God: Essays on Pascal's Wager, Jordan, Jeffrey (ed).* Ryan, John K.

"Wagering and the Evidence" in *Gambling on God: Essays on Pascal's Wager, Jordan, Jeffrey (ed).* Morris, Thomas V.

"Introduction" Gambling on God: Essays on Pascal's Wager. Jordan, Jeffrey (ed).

Gambling on God: Essays on Pascal's Wager. Jordan, Jeffrey (ed).

The Wisdom of Religious Commitment. Tilley, Terrence W.

Betting Against Pascal's Wager. Mougin, Gregory and Sober, Elliott.

On Pascal's Wager and Infinite Utilities. Byl, John.

Recent Criticisms and Defenses of Pascal's Wager. Anderson, Robert.

Wagering Belief: Examining Two Objections to Pascal's Wager. Groothuis, D.

PASSION
"Loving, Appraising, and Bestowing" in *The Nature and Pursuit of Love, Goicoechea, David (ed).* Vannoy, Russell C.

"Nietzsche and Zen Master Hakuin on the Roles of Emotion and Passion" in *Emotions in Asian Thought, Marks, Joel (ed).* Parkes, Graham R.

"Oltre l'etica: Il rapporto tra morale e sovramorale in Soren Kierkeggard" in *L'etica e il suo Altro, Vigna, Carmelo (ed).* Bettiolo, Isabella Adinolfi.

Music, Value, and the Passions. Ridley, Aaron.

Action et passion. Wetzel, Marc.

De la passionnalité. Kremer-Marietti, Angèle.

Descartes et Spinoza: de l' admiration au désir. Timmermans, Benoît.

Human Good does not Consist in Isolated Pleasures, but in Contentment. Rosmini, Antonio.

Introduction: De l'importance et de la résurgence des passions. Meyer, Michel.

Le timbre de l'affect et les tonalités affectives. Parret, Herman.

Les problèmes des passions chez Saint Thomas d'Aquin. Meyer, Michel.

Modalisations et modulations passionnelles. Fontanille, Jacques.

Noterelle in Margine a due Convegni su Plutarco. Santaniello, Carlo.

Reason, Passion, and Action. Chappell, T D J.

The Role of Emotions in Aristotelian Virtue. Sherman, Nancy.

The Value of Passions in Plato and Aristotle. Leighton, Stephen.

The Value of Passions in Plato and Aristotle: Comments. Curzer, Howard J.

PAST
The Presence of the Past: Morphic Resonance and the Habits of Nature. Sheldrake, Rupert.

The Sea Battle and the Master Argument: Aristotle and Diodorus Cronus on the Metaphysics of the Future. Gaskin, Richard.

Vergangenheit als Zukunft. Haller, Michael (ed) and Habermas, Jürgen.

Antirrealismo y Verdad: La Realidad del Pasado. L Prades, Josep.

El Futuro Requiere de Pasado (Nota Para Una Hermenéutica de la Narración Histórica). Chico, Gabriel.

History's Forgotten Doubles. Nandy, Ashis.

In Search for "Historical Time": Time—Culture—History. Wrzosek, Wojciech.

La Historia de los Vencidos (Un Ensayo de Filosofía de la Historia Contra las Ontologías del Presente). Mate, Reyes.

La Ilustración y el problema del pasado: La reflexión de Nietzsche en torno a la memoria y el olvido. Avila Crespo, Remedios.

Mourning, Work, and Play. Comay, Rebecca.

On the Idealization of the Historical Past. Czarnecki, Zdzislaw J.

On the Memory of Last Things. Schmidt, Dennis.

The Time-Space of Human Life. Cackowski, Zdzislaw.

Time and the Tragic. Pluzanski, Tadeusz.

What Time Is Not: Critical Remarks on Husserl's Analysis of Time. Wälde, Martin.

PATANJALI
Cessation and Integration in Classical Yoga. Whicher, Ian.

Is There a Moral Perspective in Patañjali's Yogasutras?. Gokhale, Pradeep P.

Vyadi and The Realist Theory of Meaning. Ganeri, Jonardon.

PATERNALISM
"Truthfulness" in *Concepts and Cases in Nursing Ethics, Yeo, Michael (& others).* Yeo, Michael and Mitchell, Sandra.

Autonomía y Conducta Desviada: el Problema del Paternalismo en la Obra de John Stuart Mill. De Miguel Alvarez, Ana.

Changing the Paradigm for Informed Consent. Dagi, Teo Forcht.

For Our Own Good. Archard, David.

Paternalism and Rights. Brennan, Samantha.

Paternalism and the Argument from Illiteracy. Luna, Florencia.

The Inherent Paternalism in Clinical Practice. Wulff, Henrik R.

PATHOLOGY
see also Psychopathology

Mild Mania and Well-Being. Moore, Andrew, Hope, Tony and Fulford, K W M.

PATIENT
"How Do You Catch a Cloud and Pin It Down?" (With Apologies to Rogers and Hammerstein): A Commentary on Layson and Colleagues. Povar, Gail J.

"Letting Patients Die: Legal and Moral Reflections" in *In Harm's Way, Coleman, Jules L (ed).* Kadish, Sanford H.

Humane Medicine: A Leading Surgeon Examines What Doctors Do, What Their Patients Expect from Them, and How the Expectations of Both Are Not Being Met. Little, Miles.

Idéer om Ägande. Hansson, Sven Ove (ed).

The Boundaries of Moral Discourse. Hajdin, Mane.

Abandoning Informed Consent. Veatch, Robert M.

Allocation of Resources at the Bedside: The Intersection of Economics, Law, and Ethics. Pellegrino, Edmund D.

Amnesia Instead of Anesthesia: Not Always a Question of Consent. Truog, Robert D and Waisel, David.

Approaches (and Possible Contraindications) to Enhancing Patients' Autonomy. Howe, Edmund G.

Attitudes of Seriously Ill Patients toward Treatment that Involves High Costs and Burdens on Others. Schneiderman, Lawrence J (& others).

But Doctor, It's My Hip!: The Fate of Failed Medical Devices. Fielder, John H and Black, Jonathan.

Calling It Quits: Stopping Futile Treatment and Caring for Patients. Jecker, Nancy S.

Can A Patient Refuse a Psychiatric Consultation to Evaluate Decision-Making Capacity?. Wenger, Neil S and Halpern, Jodi.

Caring for Patients in Cross-Cultural Settings. Jecker, Nancy S (& others).

Changing the Paradigm for Informed Consent. Dagi, Teo Forcht.

Clinical Ethics Consultations with Children. Orr, Robert D and Perkin, Ronald M.

Commentary on "But Is It Assisted Suicide?". Nelson, James Lindemann.

Commentary on "Helping Ken and Marie Pines". Grodin, Michael.

Commentary on "The Forgetful Mourner". Yang-Lewis, Tony.

Commentary on Discussions About Life-Sustaining Treatments. Emanuel, Ezekiel J.

PERCEPTION

Alston on Direct Perception and Interpretation. Van Woudenberg, René.

Artistic Expression and Contemplation: Some Reflections Based on the Epistemology of Michael Polanyi. Baumgarten, Barbara Bennett.

Biases in the Perception of Mirror-Image Reversal. Yates, David J.

Conceptualized and Unconceptualized Desire in Aristotle. Tuozzo, Thomas M.

Constant Colors in the Head. McGilvray, James A.

Content and Causation in Perception. Pendlebury, Michael.

Dalla nostalgia di patria alla nostalgia del paradiso. Giardini, F.

Evidencia de la naturaleza en Aristóteles. Morán y Castellanos, Jorge.

Experiences in the Cave, the Closet, and the Vat—and in Bed. Stevenson, Leslie F.

Explanation and Evaluation in Cognitive Science. Montgomery, Richard.

Gruesome Perceptual Spaces. Weir, Alan.

How Can What I Perceive Be True?. Wahl, Russell.

How Should Future Opinion Affect Current Opinion?. Foley, Richard.

Hutchenson and Mill on Evaluating Actions and Characters. Strasser, Mark.

Individualism and Vision Theory. Egan, Frances.

Is Seeing Believing?. Hilbert, David.

Kimball on Whitehead and Perception. Hildebrand, David L.

La Percepción Jeráquica de la Realidad. Sánchez del Río, Carlos.

Las apariencias en Vladimir Jankélévitch. Trejos, Susana.

Leibniz on Apperception and Animal Souls. Miles, M L.

Lo sviluppo della riduzione fenomenologica: dalla *Filosofia dell'aritmetica* a *Ideen*. Costa, Vincenzo.

Locke on Personal Identity. Cicovacki, Predrag.

Mental Images and their Ontology. Gozzano, Simone.

Nonconceptual Content: Kinds, Rationales and Relations. Peacocke, Christopher.

Not Much Trouble for Ultra-Externalism. McCulloch, Gregory.

Patients' Perceptions of Consent. Shenk, Ian.

Peacocke's Argument Against the Autonomy of Nonconceptual Representational Content. Bermúdez, José Luis.

Perception and Causation. Byrne, Alex and Hilbert, David.

Perception and Mystical Experience. Pappas, George S.

Perception and Proper Explanatory Width. Rollins, Mark.

Perceptual Experience, Doxastic Practice, and the Rationality of Religious Commitment. Audi, Robert.

Phänomenologische Erschliessung der russischen Philosophie. Plotnikov, Nikolaj.

Poétique de la Perception. Maillard, Chantal.

Précis of *Perceiving God*. Alston, William P.

Reference and Unity in Kant's Theory of Judgement. Gibson, Martha I.

Religious Disagreements and Doxastic Practices. Adams, Robert M.

Representation, Self-Representation, and the Passions in Descartes. Schmitter, Amy Morgan.

Seeing That and Seeing As. Kvart, Igal.

Simplicity, Cognition and Adaptation: Some Remarks on Marr's Theory of Vision. Gilman, Daniel.

Some Preliminary Remarks on "Cognitive Interest" in Husserlian Phenomenology. McCarthy, J C.

The Problem of Reconciliation. Denkel, Arda.

The Role of Imagination in Integrative Knowledge: A Polanyian View. Shin, Un-Chol.

Theaetetan Epistemology as Platonic Epistemology. O'Leary-Hawthorne, Diane.

To What Extent Do Beliefs Affect Apparent Motion?. Wright, Richard D and Dawson, Michael R W.

Two Types of Theories: The Impact on Churchland's "Perceptual Plasticity". DesAutels, Peggy.

Über die Zeit als das Mittelglied zwischen dem Intelligiblen und dem Sinnlichen. Rohs, Peter.

Why Pains Are Mental Objects. Langsam, Harold.

PEREGRIN, J

Towards One Review from Two. Cmorej, Pavel.

PERELMAN, C

Frans H van Eemeren and Rob Grootendorst Perelman and the Fallacies. van Eemeren, Frans H and Grootendorst, Rob.

Is There an Audience for this Argument? Fallacies, Theories, and Relativisms. Crosswhite, James.

PERFECTION

"Perfection and Happiness in the Best Possible World" in *The Cambridge Companion to Leibniz, Jolley, Nicholas (ed)*. Blumenfeld, David C.

Statesman (299b-d) and the Condemnation of Socrates. Dueso, José Solana.

The Beautiful Soul: Aesthetic Morality in the Eighteenth Century. Norton, Robert E.

Divine Poiesis and Abstract Entities. Power, William L.

El Principio de Causalidad en la *Tercera* Meditación. Chávez-Arvizo, Enrique.

Paths to Perfection: Yoga and Confucian. Podgorski, Frank R.

Some Comments on *Perfectionism*. Stocker, Michael.

The Future Perfect and the Perfect Future: History has its Reasons. Flynn, Thomas R.

The Nature and the Impossibility of Moral Perfection. Conee, Earl.

Why Evil? Heidegger, Schelling, and the Tragic View of Being. Schalow, Frank.

PERFORMANCE

Authenticities: Philosophical Reflections on Musical Performance. Kivy, Peter.

Authenticity in Musical Performance: Personal or Historical?. O'Dea, Jane W.

Es la uniformidad semántica una condición de corrección formal de una teoría del modo oracional?. Marqueze, Jorge R.

Performativi in Jean-Louis Gardies: verità, verificabilità, vero-funzionalità. Rossetti, Andrea.

Some Peculiarities about Musical Aesthetic Qualities. Porter, Roosevelt.

Zeami's Concept of "Flower" in Noh Performance. Aoki, Takao.

PERIOD

Periodizing World History. Green, William.

PERKINS, D

Two Empirical Approaches to the Study of Reasoning. Finocchiaro, Maurice A.

PERKINS, H

Life Versus Death: Exposing a Misapplication of Ethical Reasoning. Iserson, Kenneth V.

Politically Correct Ethical Thinking and Intubation Practice on Cadavers. Orlowski, James P.

PERMANENCE

"Ricoeur, Kant, and the Permanence of Time" in *The Philosophy of Paul Ricoeur, Hahn, Lewis Edwin (ed)*. Godlove Jr, Terry F.

Certainty. Westphal, Jonathan (ed).

Kierkegaard, la recuperación del individuo existente y el discurso sobre lo histórico. Washburn, Jimmy.

La logique hier, les logiques aujourd'hui. Largeault, Jean.

PEROVICH, A

Triangulating God. Palmquist, Stephen.

PERPLEXITY

Perplexity and Ultimacy. Desmond, William.

PERRY, J

Indexikalische Gedanken: Über den Gegenstandsbezug in der raumzeitlichen Erkenntnis. Wyller, Truls.

PERRY, N

Brandon Shaw, Neil Perry, and the Perils of Education. Calhoun, Laura.

PERSISTENCE

Humean Supervenience and Enduring Things. Haslanger, Sally.

What's Right and What's Wrong with Transference Theories. Dowe, Phil.

PERSON

see also Human, Individual

"Acerca de la Dificultad para Identificar Personas como Particulares Básicos en Strawson" in *Temas Actuales de Filosofía, Palacios, María Julia (ed)*. Skidelsky, Liza D.

"La doble Tensión y el Concepto Primitivo de Persona" in *Temas Actuales de Filosofía, Palacios, María Julia (ed)*. Baringoltz, Eleonora.

"Relational Persons and Ethical Paradigms" in *Identity, Culture, and Education, Smeyers, Paul (ed)*. Wells, Douglas.

Explorations in Metaphysics: Being-God-Person. Clarke, W Norris.

Exploring Philosophy: The Philosophical Quest (Second Edition). Almond, Brenda.

God, Knowledge, and Mystery: Essays in Philosophical Theology. Van Inwagen, Peter.

Il Nyaya Sutra di Gautama. Arena, Leonardo Vittorio.

Individuals, Humans, Persons: Questions of Life and Death. Kuhse, Helga and Singer, Peter.

Métaphysique et Éthique au Fondement du Droit. Trigeaud, Jean-Marc.

Person to Person Inspiration. Kidd, James W and Kidd, Sunnie D.

Philosophical Arguments. Taylor, Charles.

Relationship Morality. Kellenberger, J.

A Naturalist View of Persons. Baier, Annette.

A Proposito di 'Filosofia del Diritto'. Bello, Angela Ales.

Affect, Agency, and Engagement: Conceptions of the Person in Philosophy, Neuropsychiatry, and Psychotherapy. Binns, Peter.

Anscombe and the First Person. Garrett, Brian J.

Becoming a Changed Person. Bastow, David.

Commentary on "Affect, Agency, and Engagement". Caws, Peter.

Die Identität der Person: Facetten eines Problems. Quante, Michael.

Fundamento ontológico de la persona: Immanencia y transcendencia. Arellano, Joaquín Ferrer.

Integrity, Boundary and the Ecology of Personal Processes. Binns, Peter.

Juventud, valores y crisis de nuestro tiempo. Vegas, José M.

La dimensione teologale dell'uomo e la teologia fondamentale in Xavier Zubiri. Savignano, Armando.

La fenomenologia, uno sguardo sulla verità. Bettinelli, Carla.

La filosofia cristiana secondo Edith Stein. Tilliette, Xavier.

La intimidad como valor antropológico y social. Pallarés Gonzalez, José Luis.

La Notion de *Personne* Selon Lucien Sève. Thérrien, Jean-Marie.

La persona come apertura all'essere eterno secondo E Stein. D'Ambra, Michele.

La persona nell'itinerario filosofico ermeneutico di P Ricoeur. Rizzacasa, Aurelio.

Libertà umana e dono ontologico: La penultima filosofia di Luigi Pareyson. Ciglia, Francesco Paolo.

Max Scheler's Practical Ethics and the Model Person. Spader, Peter.

Metafísica de la Persona y Análisis Existencial. Martínez Porcell, Juan.

Not the "Human Factor" but the Person. Suvorov, Aleksandr V.

Per un Servizio Sapienziale della Filosofia nella Chiesa. Sánchez Sorondo, Marcello.

Person and Ethics in Thomas Aquinas. Gallagher, David M.

Persons of Lesser Value: Moral Argument and the 'Final Solution'. Steiner, Hillel.

Philosophy and the Self-Determination of Nation and Person Today. Pavlov, Dejan.

Plotino, Ficino e noi stessi: alcuni riflessi etici. Rist, John M and Peroli, E (trans).

Postmodernism and the Education of the Whole Person. Standish, Paul.

Rawls' Conception of a Person. Muquim, M.

The First Person Perspective. Eilan, Naomi.

The Impossibility of Interpersonal Utility Comparisons. Hausman, Daniel M.

PHENOMENOLOGY

PHENOMENON

PHILANTHROPY

PHILLIPS, D

PHILODEMUS

PHILOLOGY

PHILOPONUS

PHILOSOPHER

PHILOSOPHER

Ethical Writings: Ethics and *Dialogue between a Philosopher, a Jew, and a Christian.* Abelard, Peter and Spade, Paul Vincent (trans).

Hegel In His Time: Berlin, 1818-1831. Burbidge, John W (trans) and D'Hondt, Jacques.

Killing Time: The Autobiography of Paul Feyerabend. Feyerabend, Paul.

S L Frank: The Life and Work of A Russian Philosopher, 1877-1950. Boobbyer, Philip.

The Cambridge Dictionary of Philosophy. Audi, Robert (ed).

The Correspondence of John Stuart Mill and Auguste Comte. Haac, Oscar A (ed & trans).

Thinkers and Teachers of Modern Judaism. Goldsmith, Emanuel S (ed) and Patai, Raphael (ed).

Cambridge Philosophers I: F P Ramsey. Mellor, D H.

Entrevista: Carlos R Braun dialoga con Pedro Schwartz. Schwartz, Pedro and Braun, Carlos Rodríguez.

Homenaje a Octavio Paz. Aguayo Cruz, Enrique Ignacio.

Interview of Lewis E Hahn. Abbarno, John M.

Interview of Ludwig Grünberg. Abbarno, John M.

John Dewey: An "Old-Fashioned" Reformer. Boisvert, Raymond D.

Mourning Professor Feng Youlan by Engaging in Serious Philosophical Discussion Today. Zehou, Li.

Mourning Professor Feng Youlan: "Method of Abstract Inheriting" Should Not Be Denied. Disheng, Yang.

Nietzsche and Music. Storr, Anthony.

Philosophy from an Antiphilosopher: Paul Valéry. Bouveresse, Jacques, Fournier, Christian (trans) and Laugier, Sandra (trans).

The Philosophy of Samuel Frederick Hahnemann—A Perspective. Sinha, Shyam Deo Kumar.

The Social Philosophy of P I Novgorodtsev. Zhukov, V N.

The Vocation to Be a Philosopher. Andrews, Philip.

What Was Plato's Real Name?. Irvine, Andrew D.

PHILOSOPHER-KING

"Sui Rischi di un'Attitudine Troppo Benevola dell'Interprete verso il Testo" in *Platón: Los Diálogos Tardíos, Lan, Conrado Eggers (ed).* Rossetti, Livio.

PHILOSOPHICAL ANTHROPOLOGY

Definición del Hombre en Términos de lo que Quiere Ser. López Ruiz, Isabel.

El humanismo marxiano. Calvez, Jean-Yves.

Fundamento ontológico de la persona: Immanencia y transcendencia. Arellano, Joaquín Ferrer.

Il fantasma di Turing e l'incancellabilità del soggetto. Turpia, Piero.

La dimensión natural del hombre en Santo Tomás de Aquino. Castello Dubra, Julio A.

La Dualidad Personal: Autor y Actor. Choza, Jacinto.

La Estética del Estado en la Polis Clásica. Gutiérrez, Ramón Mandado.

Metafísica de la Persona y Análisis Existencial. Martínez Porcell, Juan.

Pascal: el hombre ante la perspectiva de la nueva ciencia. Domínguez, Virginia López.

Santo Tomás y el *De Amina* (Comentario a los Caps. 4 y 5 del Libro III del *De Anima* de Aristóteles). Schmidt Andrade, Ciro E.

Sobre la Experiencia y el Conocimiento del Alma. Quijano, Francisco.

Tre teorie sulle emozione: cognitiva, fenomenologica e comportamentistica (seconda parte). Malo, Antonio.

PHILOSOPHIZING

En la confluencia de filosofía y esoterismo: Jean D'Encausse y la doctrina del "despertar". Saura, Emilio.

Heidegger y la otra historia de Occidente: Notas Kantianas para una lectura de los *Beiträge zur Philosophie.* Callejo, M José.

Las preguntas básicas sobre la filosofía-de-los sabios en Africa. Oruka, H Odera.

Sobre el problema de la filosofía. Zubiri, Xavier.

PHILOSOPHY

see also Metaphilosophy, Natural Philosophy

"...wirkliche Möglichkeiten für eine nationalsozialistische Philosophie?" in *Der geistige Anschluss, Fischer, Kurt R (ed).* Heiss, Gernot.

"A Brief Survey of Adams' Contributions to Philosophy" in *Probability and Conditionals, Eells, Ellery (ed).* Suppes, Patrick.

"Acerca de la Filosofía en Latinoamérica" in *Temas Actuales de Filosofía, Palacios, María Julia (ed).* Puló de Ortiz, Mercedes.

"African Religions and Philosophy" in *African Philosophy: Selected Readings, Mosley, Albert G (ed).* Mbiti, John.

"American Philosophy and Its Lost Public" in *Pragmatism: From Progressivism to Postmodernism, Hollinger, Robert (ed).* Kuklick, Bruce.

"Bantu Philosophy" in *African Philosophy: Selected Readings, Mosley, Albert G (ed).* Tempels, Placide.

"By Indirections Find Directions Out": Kierkegaard's Socratic Attractor. Easterbrook, Neil.

"Can a Woman Be a Philosopher? Reflections of a Beauvoirian Housemaid" in *Feminist Interpretations of Simone de Beauvoir, Simons, Margaret A (ed).* Holveck, Eleanore.

"Cheikh Anta Diop, the 'Stolen Legacy,' and Afrocentrism" in *African Philosophy: Selected Readings, Mosley, Albert G (ed).* Crawford, Jeffrey.

"Danto as Systematic Philosopher or *comme on lit Danto en français*" in *Danto and his Critics, Rollins, Mark (ed).* Carrier, David.

"Das Institut für Philosophie der Universität Wien: Der Status quo und seine Genese" in *Der geistige Anschluss, Fischer, Kurt R (ed).* Nagl-Docekal, Herta.

"Der Rückgang in den Grund des Eigenen als Bedingung für ein Verstehen des Anderen im Denken Heideggers" in *Europa und die Philosophie, Gander, Hans-Helmuth (ed).* Thurnher, Rainer.

"Die Brüche in der europäischen Philosophietradition" in *Das geistige Erbe Europas, Buhr, Manfred (ed).* D'Hondt, Jacques.

"Die Schrift 'Einführung in die Philosophie'" in *Studien zur Philosophie von Edith Stein, Fetz, Reto Luzius (ed).* Schulz, Peter.

"Emotions in Western Thought: Some Background for a Comparative Dialogue" in *Emotions in Asian Thought, Marks, Joel (ed).* Marks, Joel.

"Ens multipliciter dicitur: The Ingardian Variant of an Old Thesis" in *Kunst und Ontologie, Wlodzimierz, Galewicz (ed).* Haefliger, Gregor.

"Europa und die Philosophie" in *Europa und die Philosophie, Gander, Hans-Helmuth (ed).* Gander, Hans-Helmuth.

"Filosofía, para qué?" in *Temas Actuales de Filosofía, Palacios, María Julia (ed).* Palacios, María Julia.

"Freud, Philosophy, and Interpretation" in *The Philosophy of Paul Ricoeur, Hahn, Lewis Edwin (ed).* Smith, John E.

"From Civil Religion to Public Philosophy" in *Civil Religion and Political Theology, Rouner, Leroy S (ed).* Neuhaus, Richard John.

"G W Leibniz, Life and Works" in *The Cambridge Companion to Leibniz, Jolley, Nicholas (ed).* Ariew, Roger.

"Haldeman-Julius: Publisher, Freethinker, Humanist" in *Contributors to the Philosophy of Humanism, Hillar, Marian (ed).* Prahl, Frank.

"Hegel, Hobbes, Kant, and the Scienticization of Practical Philosophy" in *Hegel on the Modern World, Collins, Ardis B (ed).* Buchwalter, Andrew.

"How Not to Compare African Thought with Western Thought" in *African Philosophy: Selected Readings, Mosley, Albert G (ed).* Wiredu, Kwasi.

"Hume and the Art of Dialogue" in *Hume and Hume's Connexions, Stewart, M A (ed).* Malherbe, Michel.

"In Defense of the French" in *European Philosophy and the American Academy, Smith, Barry (ed).* Garver, Newton.

"Intellectual Autobiography of Paul Ricoeur" in *The Philosophy of Paul Ricoeur, Hahn, Lewis Edwin (ed).* Ricoeur, Paul.

"Introduction" in *The Cambridge Companion to Leibniz, Jolley, Nicholas (ed).* Jolley, Nicholas.

"Klaus Hartmann and G W F Hegel: A Personal Postscript" in *Hegel Reconsidered, Engelhardt, Jr, H Tristram (ed).* Engelhardt Jr, H Tristram.

"Konstantin Kolenda: His Life and Times" in *Contributors to the Philosophy of Humanism, Hillar, Marian (ed).* Kolenda, Pauline.

"La Filosofía en Tiempos del Cólera" in *Temas Actuales de Filosofía, Palacios, María Julia (ed).* Simesen de Bielke, Ana and Leonardi de Herran, Teresa.

"Life and Work" in *The Cambridge Companion to Aristotle, Barnes, Jonathan (ed).* Barnes, Jonathan.

"Locke at Oxford" in *Locke's Philosophy, Rogers, G A J (ed).* Milton, J R.

"Locke's Influence" in *The Cambridge Companion to Locke, Chappell, Vere (ed).* Aarsleff, Hans.

"Los Seminarios en la Enseñanza de la Filosofía" in *Temas Actuales de Filosofía, Palacios, María Julia (ed).* Rabossi, Eduardo A, Stigol, Nora and González, María Cristina.

"Not Exactly Making Believe: An Essay in the Philosophy of Literature" in *Life, World and Meaning, Roux, A P J (ed).* Wilkinson, Jennifer.

"On Renormalization in Quantum Field Theory and the Structure of Space-Time" in *Philosophy, Mathematics and Modern Physics, Rudolph, Enno (ed).* Stamatescu, I O.

"On the Dialogue Between Physics and Philosophy" in *Philosophy, Mathematics and Modern Physics, Rudolph, Enno (ed).* Rudolph, Enno and Stamatescu, I O.

"On Writing Philosophy" in *American Philosophy Today and Other Philosophical Studies, Rescher, Nicholas.* Rescher, Nicholas.

"Para Pensar Latinoaméerica" in *Temas Actuales de Filosofía, Palacios, María Julia (ed).* Liendo, María Cristina.

"Peirce's Logic" in *Peirce and Contemporary Thought: Philosophical Inquiries, Ketner, Kenneth Laine (ed).* Quine, W V.

"Philosophie und Drittes Reich" in *Der geistige Anschluss, Fischer, Kurt R (ed).* Hartmann, Frank.

"Philosophiestudieren in den dreissiger Jahren" in *Der geistige Anschluss, Fischer, Kurt R (ed).* Ekstein, Rudolf.

"Philosophizing about Education in a Postmodern Society" in *Identity, Culture, and Education, Smeyers, Paul (ed).* Losito, William F.

"Philosophy and Logic" in *The Cambridge Companion to Leibniz, Jolley, Nicholas (ed).* Parkinson, G H R.

"Philosophy, Technology, and Society" in *Philosophy of Technology in Spanish Speaking Countries, Mitcham, Carl (ed).* Medina, Manuel.

"Public Philosophy and Public Theology in America Today" in *Civil Religion and Political Theology, Rouner, Leroy S (ed).* Bellah, Robert N.

"Responses and Replies" in *Danto and his Critics, Rollins, Mark (ed).* Danto, Arthur C.

"Simone de Beauvoir: Falling into (Ambiguous) Line" in *Feminist Interpretations of Simone de Beauvoir, Simons, Margaret A (ed).* Le Doeuff, Michèle.

"Socrates in the Clouds" in *The Socratic Movement, Vander Waerdt, Paul A (ed).* Vander Waerdt, Paul A.

"Space and Time" in *Philosophy, Mathematics and Modern Physics, Rudolph, Enno (ed).* Lurçat, François.

"The Contribution to Humanism of Konstantin Kolenda" in *Contributors to the Philosophy of Humanism, Hillar, Marian (ed).* Burch, Robert W.

PHYSICS

A History of Scientific Thought: Elements of a History of Science. Serres, Michel (ed).

A New Science of Life: The Hypothesis of Morphic Resonance. Sheldrake, Rupert.

Aristotle: Selections. Irwin, Terence (trans) and Fine, Gail (trans).

Die Sprache in den Wissenschaften. Weingartner, Paul (ed).

Human Will: The Search for Its Physical Basis. Harkavy, Allan Abraham.

Knowledge and the Body-Mind Problem: In Defence of Interaction. Notturno, M A (ed) and Popper, Karl R.

On Knowing—The Natural Sciences. McKeon, Richard, Owen, David B (ed) and McKeon, Zahava K (ed).

Philosophie als Dialogik: Frühe Schriften Werke 1. Goldschmidt, Hermann Levin.

Philosophy of Science in the Twentieth Century: Four Central Themes. Gillies, Donald.

Philosophy, Mathematics and Modern Physics. Rudolph, Enno (ed) and Stamatescu, I O (ed).

Platón: Los Diálogos Tardíos. Lan, Conrado Eggers (ed).

Quantum Mechanics: Historical Contingency and the Copenhagen Hegemony. Cushing, James T.

The Conscious Universe: Part and Whole in Modern Physical Theory. Kafatos, Menas and Nadeau, Robert.

The Myth of the Framework: In Defence of Science and Rationality. Popper, Karl R and Notturno, M A (ed).

The Philosophy Behind Physics. De La Peña, Luis (ed), Hodgson, Peter E (ed) and Brody, Thomas A.

The Shaggy Steed of Physics: Mathematical Beauty in the Physical World. Oliver, David.

The Undivided Universe: An Ontological Interpretation of Quantum Theory. Hiley, B J and Bohm, David.

Timaeus and Modern Cosmology. Petkovic, Tomislav.

A Filosofia da Biologia à Luz da Biologia Molecular: Resolveu-se o Mistério?. Delouya, Daniel.

A Investigaçao sobre o Tempo na "Física" de Aristóteles. Quartim de Moraes, Joao.

Alternativen der Wissenschaftsgeschichte. Haney, Frank.

Anthropic Explanations in Cosmology. Smith, Quentin.

Bell's Theorem in an Indeterministic Universe. Bedford, Donald and Stapp, Henry P.

Breaking a Taboo: Frank Tipler's *Physics of Immortality*. Pannenberg, Wolfhart.

Causalité et Physique Moderne. Marchildon, Louis.

Change, Action and Causality. Jadacki, Jacek Juliusz.

Construction et Structure Dynamique des Théories Physiques. Gauthier, Yvon.

Contributions of Tipler's Omega Point Theory. Birtel, Frank T.

Cosmology: An Empirical Science?. Anderson, John.

Could Theoretical Entities Save Realism?. Elsamahi, Mohamed.

Creation Without a Creator: Reflections on Contemporary Scientific Cosmologies. Kozhamthadam, Job.

Das neue Erkenntnisproblem: Erkenntniskritische Überlegungen zum "anthropoischen Prinzip" in der neueren Physik. Willems, Klaas.

Deterministisches Chaos: Einige Wissenschaftstheoretisch Interessante Aspekte. Düsberg, Klaus Jürgen.

Dispositions and Scientific Explanation. Lange, Marc.

Divine Action: Is It Credible?. Nelson, James S.

Domingo de Soto en el Origen de la Ciencia Moderna. Pérez Camacho, Juan José and Sols Lucía, Ignacio.

Épicure et Spinoza: la physique. Moreau, Pierre-François.

Ernesto Sábato: Físico Antes que Escritor. Fuertes, José Félix.

Exorcising Laplace's Demon: Chaos and Antichaos, History and Metahistory. Shermer, Michael.

Extraterrestrial Intelligence and UFOs: Challenges to Physics, Metaphysics, and Theology?. Trundle, Robert C.

Field or Print. Groenewold, Hip.

Final Causality in Contemporary Physics. Quay, Paul M.

Fisica e Filosofia nella Cultura Italiana dei Primi due Decenni del Novecento. Maiocchi, Roberto.

How the Physical Sciences Discovered the Unity of Nature. Werle, Jozef.

How to Interpret Quantum Mechanics. Bub, Jeffrey.

How to Perform a Reduction. Brooks, D H M.

How Unified is Physics Itself?: Comments on Józef Werle's Paper "How the Physical Sciences Discovered the Unity of Nature". Strawinski, Witold.

I Giganti in Vico. Mazzola, Roberto.

I principi matematici kantiani del mondo fisico. Pellecchia, Pasquale.

I principi matematici kantiani del mondo fisico, II. Pellecchia, Pasquale.

Ideation und Projektion. Stekeler-Weithofer, Pirmin.

Independently Motivating the Kochen-Dieks Modal Interpretation of Quantum Mechanics. Clifton, Robert.

Interpretations of Quantum Field Theory. Huggett, Nick and Weingard, Robert.

Is Classical Mechanics Time Reversal Invariant?. Savitt, Steven F.

Kants zweite Antinomie und die Physik. Falkenburg, Brigitte.

L'Épistemologie de Helmholtz et la Question du Réalisme Scientifique. Leroux, Jean.

L'esthétique scientifique: commentaire sur la Grande Unification. Durand, Stéphane.

La Consideración de las ideas Innatas en Descartes y la Problemática del Conocimiento de lo Físico. García del Campo, Juan Pedro.

La Philosophie de Niels Bohr. Bunge, Mario.

Le livre de la nature dans l'écrit de la culture: Cassirer et le Nouvel esprit scientifique. Sandkühler, Hans Jörg (& others).

Making Sense of Approximate Decoherence. Bacciagaluppi, Guido and Hemmo, Meir.

Metafisica ed Esistenza di Dio nel Periodo Precritico di Kant. Nicolosi, Salvatore.

Michael Faraday's Concept of Ultimate Reality and Meaning. Utke, Allen R.

Micro-Chaos and Idealization in Cartesian Physics. Nelson, Alan.

Nature as Creation. Tanzella-Nitti, Giuseppe.

Nemesis and Theory Evaluation. Boersema, David B.

Notas sobre la fisica epicúrea. Fallas, Luis A.

On the Field Aspect of Quantum Fields. Huggett, Nick and Weingard, Robert.

On the Paradoxical Aspects of New Quantum Experiments. Vaidman, Lev.

On the Quantum Mechanical Wave Function as a Link Between Cognition and the Physical World: A Role for Psychology. Snyder, Douglas M.

On What It Takes to Be a World. Albert, David Z and Barrett, Jeffrey A.

Ortega e Vico. Cacciatore, Giuseppe.

Platone e Vico: Una Reinterpretazione Platonica di Vico. Tucker, Aviezer.

Relativity, Absoluteness and Observation. Janssen, H C I M.

Representation and the Imperfect Ideal. Wallis, Charles.

Representation, Similarity, and the Chorus of Prototypes. Edelman, Shimon.

Rückehr zu Kants Kritik der reinen Vernunft für Erkenntnisforschritt in der mathematischen Physik. Adler, Norbert.

Science as Truth. Atkins, Peter.

Sober on Brandon on Screening-Off and the Levels of Selection. Brandon, Robert N.

Some Considerations on the Reducibility of Chemistry to Physics. Mosini, Valeria.

Sul Vico di Piovani. Vasoli, Cesare.

Teleologie en fysica, en een reactie van A A Derksen op Th Kuipers over waarheidsbenadering. Van Luipen, Hans.

Temporal Asymmetry in Classical Mechanics. Hutchison, Keith.

The Foundations of Quantum Mechanics and the Approach to Thermodynamic Equilibrium. Albert, David Z.

The Lies Remain the Same: A Reply to Chalmers. Clarke, Steve.

The Modern Misunderstanding of Aristotle's Theory of Motion. Balaban, Oded.

The Ontological Status of Matter in Aristotle. Cresswell, M J.

The Problematic Status of Cosmology. De Gandt, François, Blau, Peter (trans) and Bergo, Bettina (trans).

The Quest for Infinity and the Synthesis of Science (An Interview with Professor Andrzej Kajetan Wróblewski). Bendyk, Edwin.

The Scientific Revolution in the Renaissance—A Unique Phenomenon in the History of Mankind. Rosen, Edward.

The Suggestive Properties of Quantum Mechanics Without the Collapse Postulate. Barrett, Jeffrey A.

The 'Decoherence' Approach to the Measurement Problem in Quantum Mechanics. Elby, Andrew.

Theories of Probability. Howson, Colin.

Thomas Reid and the Justification of Induction. Anstey, Peter.

Three Measurement Problems. Maudlin, Tim.

Time in Philosophy and in Physics: From Kant and Einstein to Gödel. Wang, Hao.

Time, Quantum Mechanics, and Decoherence. Saunders, Simon.

Two Logical Patterns of the Reduction of Theories: Comments on Józef Werle's Paper "How the Physical Sciences Discovered the Unity of Nature". Krajewski, Wladyslaw.

Uniformitarianism in Cosmology: Background and Philosophical Implications of the Steady-State Theory. Balashov, Yuri.

Using the Human Body as a Paradigm for the Structure of Time: Some Reflections on Time's URAM. Modell, Stephen M.

Wavefunction Tails in the Modal Interpretation. Dickson, Michael.

Weyl, Reichenbach and the Epistemology of Geometry. Ryckman, Thomas A.

Why the Elements Imitate the Heaven: *Metaphysics* ix 8.1050b28-34. Lang, Helen S.

'Coordinative Definition' and Reichenbach's Semantic Framework: A Reassessment. Shapiro, Lionel Stefan.

PHYSIOLOGY

F J J Buytendijk's Concept of an Anthropological Physiology. Dekkers, Wim J M.

Francis Crick on the Workings of the Brain. Flynn, Thomas W and Madigan, Timothy J.

The Communication of Cells Within the Body. Krans, H M J.

The Philosophy of Samuel Frederick Hahnemann—A Perspective. Sinha, Shyam Deo Kumar.

PIAGET

"Algunos Aportes Sobre la Discusión entre Cognitivismo...y el Constuctivismo (Piaget) Acerca de la Adquis. de Concepto de Unsistema Repres." in *Temas Actuales de Filosofía, Palacios, María Julia (ed)*. Fernandez Acevedo, Yolanda.

"Les mystères de la douleur divine": Une "prière" du jeune Jean Piaget pour l'année 1916. Vidal, Fernando.

Reason, Regulation, and Realism: Toward a Regulatory Systems Theory of Reason and Evolutionary Epistemology. Hooker, C A.

A Comparison between Evolutionary and Genetic Epistemology or: Jean Piaget's Contribution to a Post-Darwinian Epistemology. Kesselring, Thomas.

Entwicklungsdenken bei Piaget und Merleau-Ponty. Herzog, Maximilian.

Resolución de problemas: de Piaget a otros autores. Fallas, Jackeline García.

Utilitarismo y Teoría del Desarrollo Moral (I): Análisis crítico de las teorías cognitivas del desarrollo moral y de sus fundamentos Kantianos. Tasset, José Luis.

PICASSO

"Sobre Picasso y Algunos Retratos Femeninos" in *Temas Actuales de Filosofía, Palacios, María Julia (ed)*. Plaza Müller, Elsa.

PICKLES, D

Sources and Leapfrogging: Reply to Pickles. Holton, Richard.

PICO

Ricordando Giovanni e Gianfrancesco Pico della Mirandola. Garin, Eugenio.

PLEASURE

Feminist Heterosexuality and Its Politically Incorrect Pleasures. Gaines, Jane.

Fichtes Erziehungslehre als erste logische Begründung der Vorbilderziehung. Kumamoto, Yasuhiro.

Francis Hutcheson and the Problem of Conspicuous Consumption. Mortensen, Preben.

Human Good does not Consist in Isolated Pleasures, but in Contentment. Rosmini, Antonio.

Is Happiness a Trait? Tests of the Theory That a Better Society Does Not Make People Any Happier. Veenhoven, Ruut.

Kant on Pleasure in the Agreeable. Zangwill, Nick.

Learning from Art. Graham, Gordon.

Sexual Needs and Sexual Pleasures. Moore, Gareth.

Tertullian und das Vergnügen in *De spectaculis*. Kessler, Andreas.

The Multiplication of Utility. Nathan, N M L.

The Value of Music. Graham, Gordon.

Theism, the Hypothesis of Indifference, and the Biological Role of Pain and Pleasure. Howard-Snyder, Daniel.

Time and Value from Aristippus to Plotinus. Lackey, Douglas.

PLINY

Pliny on Cicero and Oratory: Self-Fashioning in the Public Eye. Riggsby, Andrew M.

PLOTINUS

"Vernunft im abendländischen Denken: Wandel und Konstanz" in *Das geistige Erbe Europas, Buhr, Manfred (ed)*. Kremer, Klaus.

Cognition and Human Actualization in Plotinus and Aristotle. Husain, Martha.

Du Parfait et de l'Un. Connexions Entre les Pensées Plotinienne et Dionysienne. Kélessidou, Anna.

Du Parfait et de l'Un. Sur Quelques Connexions de la Pensée Plotinienne et de la Théologie de Denys. Kélessidou, Anna.

Eternità e tempo in Plotino. Ferretti, Silvia.

Florence, 1492: Réapparaît Plotin. Saffrey, Henri Dominique.

La vie et la Mort Selon Platon et Plotin. Kélessidou, Anna.

Osservazioni sul Problema del Male in Filosofia. Franchi, Alfredo.

Platons und Plotins Zugang zur transzendenten Wesenheit. Skledar, Nikola.

Plotin et la Thèse de L'incorruptibilité du Monde. Kélessidou, Anna.

Plotino, Ficino e noi stessi: alcuni riflessi etici. Rist, John M and Peroli, E (trans).

Plotinus and the Neoplatonic Conception of Dialectic. Anton, John P.

Plotinus on the Souls of Beasts. Cole, Eve Browning.

Time and Value from Aristippus to Plotinus. Lackey, Douglas.

Transcendance et Inconnaissance chez Plotin et Denys. Lang, André.

PLURALISM

see also Cultural Pluralism, Many

"Embryo Experimentation: Public Policy in a Pluralist Society" in *Medicine and Moral Reasoning, Fulford, K W M (ed)*. Hare, Richard M.

"New" New History: A *Longue Durée* Structure. Olábarri, Ignacio.

American Mixed Race: The Culture of Microdiversity. Zack, Naomi (ed).

Aristotle's Rhetoric: An Art of Character. Garver, Eugene.

Character and Culture: Essays on East and West. Babbitt, Irving.

Charles Peirce's Pragmatic Pluralism. Rosenthal, Sandra B.

Moral Theory: A Contemporary Overview. DeMarco, Joseph P.

Multiculturalism: A Critical Reader. Goldberg, David Theo.

Political Theory and Christian Vision: Essays in Memory of Bernard Zylstra. Chaplin, Jonathan (ed) and Marshall, Paul (ed).

Strange Multiplicity: Constitutionalism in an Age of Diversity. Tully, James.

The Defeat of the Mind. Friedlander, Judith (trans) and Finkielkraut, Alain.

The Myth of the Framework: In Defence of Science and Rationality. Popper, Karl R and Notturno, M A (ed).

The Politics of Culture: Race, Violence, and Democracy. Choi, Jung Min, Callaghan, Karen A and Murphy, John W.

Thinking. Kirby, Gary R and Goodpaster, Jeffery R.

Understanding Social Science: A Philosophical Introduction to the Social Sciences. Trigg, Roger.

Vértigos argumentales: Una ética de la disputa. Pereda, Carlos.

Adolescents, Post-Structuralism, and "Playing It Cool!". Merttens, Ruth.

Consensus and Democracy: An Anglo-French Conference on John Rawls. Audard, Catherine.

Culture and Cultures. Pande, G C.

Del Empirismo al Humanismo: Clave de Lectura y Crítica de la Obra de P K Feyerabend. Tula Molina, Fernando.

Democratic Multicultures and Cosmopolis: Beyond the Aporias of the Politics of Identity and Difference. Matustik, Martin J.

Desire and the Human Good. Kraut, Richard H.

Diversity and Unity of Sciences as the Foundation of Universalism. Kuczynski, Janusz.

Educating the Democratic Heart: Pluralism, Traditions and the Humanities. Alexander, Thomas M.

Existence and Non-Existence in Haribhadra Suri's Anekanta-Jaya-Pataka. van den Bossche, Frank.

Facing the Challenges of Diversity—A Reflection on the Role of Philosophy in South Africa Today. Van Der Merwe, W L.

For Pluralism and Against Realism About Species. Stanford, P Kyle.

From Biocentric Individualism to Biocentric Pluralism. Sterba, James P.

God's Action in the Human World: Our Intellectual Humility and Dialogue between Religions. Grzegorczyk, Andrzej.

Il problema della filosofia spagnola. Savignano, Armando.

In Defense of Political Liberalism. Barry, Brian.

Ist Fichtes Modell des Kosmopolitismus pluralistisch?. Radrizzani, Ives.

John Rawls, Mikhail Bakhtin, and the Praxis of Toleration. Walker, Brian.

Las ambigüedades de la democracia y los enfoques postmodernistas. Mansilla, H C F.

Liberal and Totalitarian Morality. Almond, Brenda.

Liberal Justice: Political and Metaphysical. Bellamy, Richard and Hollis, Martin.

Liberalism, Multiculturalism, and Minority Protection. Rickard, Maurice.

Liberalism, Pluralism, and Lived Faith. Hart, Hendrick.

Māya and the Pluralist Predicament. Forrest, Peter.

Marx and Engels on Democracy. Doveton, Daniel.

Monism and Pluralism. Krapiec, Mieczyslaw Albert.

Multikulturalismus: eine liberale Perspektive. Raz, Joseph.

Observaciones y respuesta. Lara, Francisco, Salcedo, Damián and Gutiérrez, Gilberto.

Otto's Idea of the 'Numinous': A Crosscultural Reappraisal. O'Meley, Serena.

Pluralism of Norms and Values: On the Claim and Reception of the Universal. Klapwijk, J.

Pluralism, Integrity, and the Interpretive Model of Law. Golash, Deirdre.

Pluralisme et théologisme, Deux aspects doctrinaux de la correspondance Gilson-Labourdette. Bonino, Serge-Thomas.

Profiles of the Virtues. Swanton, Christine.

Public Reason and Cultural Pluralism: Political Liberalism and the Problem of Moral Conflict. Bohman, James F.

Rahner, Popper and Kuhn: A Note on Some Critical Parallels in Science and Theology. Guarino, Thomas G.

Reflective Solidarity. Dean, Jodi.

Religious Memory and the Pluralism of Readings: Reflections on Roberto de Nobili and the *Taittiriya Upanisad*. Clooney, Francis X.

Religious Pluralism and Interfaith Dialogue: Beyond Universalism and Particularism. Huang, Yong.

Religious Pluralism and the Divine: Another Look at John Hick's Neo-Kantian Proposal. Eddy, Paul R.

Religious Plurality and Realist Christianity: Idolatry and the Testing of One's Faith. McLeod, Mark S.

Reply to Paul Ricoeur's "The Plurality of Sources of Law". Dworkin, Ronald.

Response. Smith, John E.

Sobre la cuestión del método en el debate Modernidad-Postmodernidad. Esquirol, Josep M.

Sociality as a Philosophically Significant Category. Gilbert, Margaret.

Structure Not Substance: Theological Realism for a Pluralistic Age. Knight, Christopher.

The 3D/4D Controversy and Non-Present Objects. Markosian, Ned.

The Demise of Monism and Pluralism in Environmental Ethics. Van Der Steen, Wim J.

The Diverse Community or the Unoppressive City: Which Ideal for a Transformative Politics of Difference?. Green, Judith M.

The Economic Organization of Science, the Firm, and the Marketplace. Wible, James R.

The Pluralist Constellation. Parens, Erik.

The Plurality of Philosophical and Religious Traditions and Principles of Freedom and Peace. McLean, George F.

The Plurality of Sources of Law. Ricoeur, Paul.

The Problem of Inter-Faith Studies. Matilal, Bimal K.

The Puzzle of Profound Respect. Callahan, Daniel.

The Question of Truth in Religion. Ward, J S K.

The Royce-Howison Debate on the Conception of God. Skrupskelis, Ignas K.

The Rushdie Affair: Tolerance, Pluralism, or Secularism?. Rule, Paul.

The Sociopolitical Implications of Multiculturalism. Valadez, Jorge M.

Thick or Thin? The Cognitive Content of Moral Education in a Plural Democracy. Haydon, Graham.

Thinking the Post-Socialism: From Socialist Community to Pluralistic Society. Flego, Gvozden.

Tolerance and the Possibility of Pluralism in Judaism. Sagi (Schweitzer), Avi.

Two Theories of Modernity. Taylor, Charles.

William James: Rationality as a Pragmatic Choice. Goodman, Robert F.

Winch and Instrumental Pluralism. Dov Lerner, Berel.

PLURALITY

"Teoría Social y Pluralidad Teórica" in *Temas Actuales de Filosofía, Palacios, María Julia (ed)*. Morey, Patricia S.

Kant's Doctrine of the Categories: Some Problems. Krishna, Daya.

L'Élenchos del Principio nella Metafisica di Averroé. Roccaro, Giuseppe.

Plural Worlds in Anaximander. Finkelberg, Aryeh.

PLUTARCH OF CHAERONEA

Noterelle in Margine a due Convegni su Plutarco. Santaniello, Carlo.

POCOCK, J

Historical Contextualism: The New Historicism?. King, Preston.

POCOCKE, E

"The Impact of the *Philosophus Autodidactus*" in *The 'Arabick' Interest of the Natural Philosophers..., Russell, G A (ed)*. Russell, G A.

PODGORSKI, F

Critical Comments. Wei-Hsun Fu, Charles.

The Coin and the Mirror. Yadav, Bibhuti S.

POET

Homenaje a Octavio Paz. Aguayo Cruz, Enrique Ignacio.

POETICS

Das Wort im Leben und das Wort in der Poesie. Volosinov, Valentin N.

Forme e metafore dell'intuizione in Friedrich Hölderlin. Augello, Giuseppe.

Poétique de la Perception. Maillard, Chantal.

POETRY

"*Paradise Lost* and the Materialism Debate" in *The 1994 Annual of Hermeneutics and Social Concern, Lawler, Justus George (ed)*. Fallon, Stephen M.

"At the Crossroads of Positivism and Magic:" Benjamin, Baudelaire, and the Shock of the Sublime. Wood, Gillen.

"How Much 'Heimat' does a Human Being Need?" in *Identity, Culture, and Education, Smeyers, Paul (ed)*. Levering, Bas.

"Rhetoric and Poetics" in *The Cambridge Companion to Aristotle, Barnes, Jonathan (ed)*. Barnes, Jonathan.

Aristotle: Selections. Irwin, Terence (trans) and Fine, Gail (trans).

Christus Patiens and *Christus Victor*: John Donne's Ultimate Reality and Meaning. Labriola, Albert C.

Die Übermacht des Seins: Heideggers Auslegung des Bezuges von Mensch und Natur und Hölderlins Dichtung des Heiligen. Bohlen, Stephanie.

Grundzüge der Religionsphilosophie Edith Steins. Müller, Andreas Uwe.

Montaigne: A Collection of Essays, Volume 1—Montaigne's Message and Method. Berven, Dikka (ed).

Montaigne: A Collection of Essays, Volume 3—Montaigne's Rhetoric. Berven, Dikka (ed).

Montaigne: A Collection of Essays, Volume 5—Reading Montaigne. Berven, Dikka (ed).

Phaedrus. Plato, Woodruff, Paul (trans) and Nehamas, Alexander (trans).

Poetics of Modernity: Toward a Hermeneutic Imagination. Kearney, Richard.

Reading Theory: An Introduction to Lacan, Derrida, and Kristeva. Payne, Michael.

Rhetorical Mosaic for a Kaleidoscope of Sound: Poetry as a Road to Understanding the Prose Voice. Britt, John F.

The Conflict of Law and Justice in the Icelandic Sagas. Pencak, William.

The Educational Imperative: A Defence of Socratic and Aesthetic Learning. Abbs, Peter.

The Passionate Intellect: Essays on the Transformation of Classical Traditions. Ayres, Lewis (ed).

The Platonic Odyssey: A Philosophical-Literary Inquiry into the "Phaedo". Gilead, Amihud.

A Taste of Madeleine: Notes Toward a Philosophy of Place. Malpas, Jeff.

Archè come Fondamento e Origine in Martin Heidegger. Penati, Giancarlo.

Boturini e la Diffusione di Vico in Spagna. Mestre, Antonio.

Commentary on Asmis's "Epicurean Poetics". Sider, David.

Derrida and Ideographic Poetics. Cheng, Jiewei.

Die kroatische Ästhetik des 17 Jahrhunderts: Die Epoche der Gegenreformation, des Rationalismus und des Empirismus. Barock und Klassizismus. Posavac, Zlatko.

Drawing upon Levinas to Sketch Out a Heterotopic Poetics of Art and Tragedy. Anderson, Travis.

Epicurean Poetics. Asmis, Elizabeth.

Ethics and Aesthetics in Aristotle's Poetics. Crittenden, Paul.

Feyerabend, the Ancient Quarrel and the Problem of Aesthetic Criteria. Couvalis, George.

Filsofía Jurídica e Política na Poesía Luso-árabe. Ferreira da Cunha, Paulo.

Flowers as 'Free Beauties of Nature'. Hutchings, Patrick.

Giulio Bajamonti, un Vichiano Dalmata. Roic, Sanja.

Heidegger After the Fall. Review of Heidegger and the Poets by Véronique M Fóti. Lysaker, John T.

Heidegger and Heaney: Poetry and Possibility. Wright, Terrence C.

Hopkins and the Theory of Metaphor. Potts, Michael.

Interview: Hans-Georg Gadamer. Rée, Jonathan and Gehron, Christiane.

La Filosofía de los Poetas en la Fundación Fernando Rielo. Sánchez-Gay Venegas, Juana.

La Perduta Prossimità del dio: Mito e Poesia in Walter Otto. Moretti, Giampiero.

La Presenza di Vico nella Poetica Spagnola del XVIII Secolo. Zacarés Pamblanco, Amparo.

La Reivindicación de la Sabiduría Poética en G B Vico y A Machado. Ramírez Luque, Isabel.

La Riflessione sul Mito in Leopardi. Stella, Vittorio.

Living Poetically: Kierkegaard and German Romanticism. Walsh, Sylvia.

Martin Heidegger and Franz Rosenzweig on the Limits of Language as Poetry. Greenberg, Yudit Kornberg.

Paul Celan's Uncanny Speech. Del Caro, Adrian.

Persuasion in an Empty Ontology: The Eleatic Synthesis of Philosophy, Poetry, and Rhetoric. Poster, Carol.

Phenomenology and the Possibility of Narrative. Steeves, H Peter.

Philosophical Disappointment: Introduction. Light, Steve.

Poetic Dwelling in Gadamer's Hermeneutics. Risser, James C.

Poetizar y Pensar? Desde la Meditación Heideggeriana Hacia el Topos Histórico de Hölderlin. Zubiría, Martín.

Purusarthas in Aesthetics. Patnaik, Tandra.

Qué es Poesía?. Núñez Cea, Victoria Martha.

Reading the Poetics after the Remarks. Fynsk, Christopher.

Ricordando Giovanni e Gianfrancesco Pico della Mirandola. Garin, Eugenio.

The First Crisis in First Philosophy. Benardete, Seth.

The Function of the Subject Complex in Tanka. Amagasaki, Akira.

The Instress of Being and the Coronach of Dasein in Hölderlin's Germanien. Grugan, Arthur A.

Titles and Subtitles of the Policraticus: A Proposal. Van Laarhoven, Jan.

Vico in Spagna: Per Introdurre. Martínez Bisbal, Josep.

Vico y la Poética de la Modernidad. Zacarés Pamblanco, Amparo.

Von der Reichweite mathematischen Denkens bei Fichte und Novalis. Csech, Werner.

Wallace Stevens and Metaphysics: The Plain Sense of Things. Gardner, Sebastian.

POINCARE

On the Controversy between Poincaré and Russell about the Status of Complete Induction. Heinzmann, Gerhard.

POINSOT, J

A Morning and Evening Star: Editor's Introduction. Deely, John.

A Prospect of Postmodernity. Deely, John.

Being-as-First-Known in Poinsot: A Priori or Aporia?. Guagliardo, Vincent.

Common Sources for the Semiotic of Charles Peirce and John Poinsot. Beuchot, Mauricio and Deely, John.

If Wittgenstein Had Read Poinsot: Recasting the Problem of Signs and Mental States. Cahalan, John C.

Intentionality in John Poinsot. Beuchot, Mauricio.

John Poinsot on Created Eternal Truths vs Vasquez, Suárez and Descartes. Wells, Norman J.

John Poinsot on How To Be, Know, and Love a Non-Existent Possible. Coombs, Jeffrey.

Language, Communication, and Representation in the Semiotic of John Poinsot. Murphy, James B.

Poinsot and the Mental Imagery Debate. Dalcourt, Gerard J.

Poinsot on Knowability of Beings of Reason. Doyle, John P.

Poinsot on the Semiotics of Awareness. Raposa, Michael.

The Significance for Cognitive Realism of the Thought of John Poinsot. Rasmussen, Douglas B.

The Substantial Unity of Material Substances According to John Poinsot. Kronen, John D.

POLANYI, M

Visual Art as Theology. Baumgarten, Barbara Dee Bennett.

Artistic Expression and Contemplation: Some Reflections Based on the Epistemology of Michael Polanyi. Baumgarten, Barbara Bennett.

Michael Polanyi and Human Identity. Kettle, David.

The Role of Imagination in Integrative Knowledge: A Polanyian View. Shin, Un-Chol.

William Poteat's Anthropology: "Mindbody In the World". Mead, Walter B.

POLARITY

The Logical Form of Determiners. Ludlow, Peter.

POLENZ, P

A Teoria da Predicaçao de Pierre Abélard e a Semântica da Frase de Peter Von Polenz: Uma Tentativa de Aproximaçao. Chaves-Tannús, Marcio.

POLICE

"Ethical Questions Facing Law Enforcement Agents" in *Introducing Applied Ethics, Almond, Brenda (ed)*. Kleinig, John.

Police Gratuities: What the Public Think. Prenzler, Tim and Mackay, Peta.

The Justified Scoundrel: The Structural Genesis of Corruption. Anechiarico, Frank and Kuo, Lenore.

POLICY

see also Public Policy

Food: Multidisciplinary Perspectives. Harriss-White, Barbara (ed) and Hoffenberg, Raymond (ed).

Business Policy, Ethics, and Society. Minkes, A L.

Does Clinical Decision Analysis Change the Subject?. Douard, John W.

Economists' Preferences and the Preferences of Economists. Norton, Bryan G.

Futility and Hospital Policy. Tomlinson, Thomas and Czlonka, Diane.

Het statistische argument. De Vries, Michiel S.

Long-Acting Contraceptives: Ethical Guidance for Policymakers and Health Care Providers. Moskowitz, Ellen H.

Resources and Environmental Policy. Narveson, Jan.

Should Hospital Policy Require Consent for Practicing Invasive Procedures on Cadavers?. Perkins, Henry S and Gordon, Anna M.

The Dishwasher's Child: Education and the End of Egalitarianism. White, John.

POLIS

"Epichereîn..Katà Pólin Therapeían Téchnei Gnorízein" in *Platón: Los Diálogos Tardíos, Lan, Conrado Eggers (ed)*. Schmidt Osmanczik, Ute.

"La Ley en el Pensamiento Platónico" in *Platón: Los Diálogos Tardíos, Lan, Conrado Eggers (ed)*. Gómez Robledo, Antonio.

Aristotle in Outline. Robinson, Timothy A.

A la sombra de Artemis: Reflexión sobre los espacios mítico e histórico de "La República". Luri, Gregorio.

Laques: la dialéctica del coraje. Cappelletti, Angel J.

The Greeks and Us (in Portuguese). Alves dos Santos, Maris Carolina.

POLISH

"John Locke and the Polish Enlightenment" in *Locke's Philosophy, Rogers, G A J (ed)*. Rosicka, Janina.

"Konstantin Kolenda: His Life and Times" in *Contributors to the Philosophy of Humanism, Hillar, Marian (ed)*. Kolenda, Pauline.

Bibliografia Prac: Romana Andrzeja Tokarczyka. Tokarczyk, Roman A.

Die Tugend der Toleranz in Polen nach dem Zerfall des Kommunismus. Lazari-Pawlowska, Ija.

Mieczyslaw Lubanskis Leben und Werk. Latawiec, Anna, Lemanska, Anna and Slaga, Szczepan W.

Philosophy of Science in Poland. Krajewski, Wladyslaw.

Reflections on the Perception of Time in Poland in the 16th and 17th Centuries. Bogucka, Maria.

The Idea of Universalism in the Polish Romantic Tradition. Walicki, Andrzej.

The Philosophy of Fuzziness and the Mathematics of Randomness. Gerstenkorn, Tadeusz and Manko, Jacek.

The Philosophy of Science and Women's Issues in Poland: Possibilities and Obstacles Today (A Personal Account). Pakszys, Elzbieta.

Time in Old Polish Culture. Tazbir.

POLITICS

"Global Environmental Justice" in *Philosophy and the Natural Environment,* Attfield, Robin (ed). Jamieson, Dale.

"Homosex/Ethics" in *Gay Ethics, Murphy, Timothy F (ed).* Murphy, Timothy F.

"La Epistemología de las Ciencias Sociales: Sus Políticas Inexpresas" in *Temas Actuales de Filosofía, Palacios, María Julia (ed).* Lovisolo, Jorge.

"Liberalism and Collectivism in the 20th Century" in *The End of "Isms"?, Shtromas, Alexsandras (ed).* Ebeling, Richard M.

"Liberalism and Group Rights" in *In Harm's Way, Coleman, Jules L (ed).* Buchanan, Allen.

"Liberalism and the New Skeptics" in *In Harm's Way, Coleman, Jules L (ed).* Morawetz, Thomas.

"Locke's Political Philosophy" in *The Cambridge Companion to Locke, Chappell, Vere (ed).* Ashcraft, Richard.

"Max Weber and the Liberal Political Tradition" in *The Barbarism of Reason, Horowitz, Asher (ed).* Beetham, David.

"Philosophical Foundations of Political Theology" in *Civil Religion and Political Theology, Rouner, Leroy S (ed).* McCarthy, Thomas A.

"Political Integration, the Limited State, and the Philosophy of Postmodernism" in *The End of "Isms"?, Shtromas, Alexsandras (ed).* O'Sullivan, Noel.

"Political Rights Versus Social Rights" in *Human Rights and the World's Religions, Rouner, Leroy (ed).* Markovic, Mihailo.

"Politics" in *The Cambridge Companion to Aristotle, Barnes, Jonathan (ed).* Taylor, C C W.

"Racism, Genocide, and Resistance: The Politics of Language and International Law" in *Marxism in the Postmodern Age, Callari, Antonio (ed).* James, Joy.

"Rediscovering America: The *Two Treatises* and Aboriginal Rights" in *Locke's Philosophy, Rogers, G A J (ed).* Tully, James.

"Research Project on Anti-Semitism" in *Adorno: The Stars Down to Earth and Other Essays on the Irrational in Culture, Crook, Stephen (ed).* Adorno, Theodor W.

"Retrieval and Renewal" in *Marxism in the Postmodern Age, Callari, Antonio (ed).* Rowbotham, Sheila.

"Romantik der Arbeit" Perspektiven des frühromantischen Arbeitsbegriffs. Arndt, Andreas.

"Socrates in the Context of Xenophon's Political Writings" in *The Socratic Movement, Vander Waerdt, Paul A (ed).* Pangle, Thomas L.

"Some Reflections on the Temporal Structure of Conceptual Change" in *Main Trends in Cultural History, Melching, Willem (ed).* Koselleck, Reinhart.

"Sui Rischi di un'Attitudine Troppo Benevola dell'Interprete verso il Testo" in *Platón: Los Diálogos Tardíos, Lan, Conrado Eggers (ed).* Rossetti, Livio.

"Teaching the Pedagogies: A Dialectical Approach to an Ideological Dilemma" in *After Postmodernism, Simons, Herbert W (ed).* Simons, Herbert W.

"Technology and Politics: Toward Artificial History?" in *Philosophy of Technology in Spanish Speaking Countries, Mitcham, Carl (ed).* García de la Huerta, Marcos.

"The Aesthetics of Architecture and the Politics of Space" in *Philosophy and Architecture, Mitias, Michael H (ed).* Sparshott, Francis.

"The Closet and the Ethics of Outing" in *Gay Ethics, Murphy, Timothy F (ed).* McCarthy, Jeremiah.

"The Concept of Fundamentalism" in *The End of "Isms"?, Shtromas, Alexsandras (ed).* Parekh, Bhikhu.

"The Dilemmas of Islamic Identity" in *Human Rights and the World's Religions, Rouner, Leroy (ed).* Mayer, Ann Elizabeth.

"The Drama of Theory: Vengeful Objects and Wily Props" in *Baudrillard: A Critical Reader, Kellner, Douglas (ed).* Genosko, Gary.

"The New Politics of the Workplace: Ideology and Other Unobtrusive Controls" in *After Postmodernism, Simons, Herbert W (ed).* Deetz, Stanley.

"The Obsolescence of Marxism?" in *Whither Marxism?, Magnus, Bernd (ed).* Kellner, Douglas M.

"The Perils of Personality: Lewis Mumford and Politics After Liberalism" in *Pragmatism: From Progressivism to Postmodernism, Hollinger, Robert (ed).* Blake, Casey Nelson.

"The Politics of Christianity" in *Locke's Philosophy, Rogers, G A J (ed).* Harris, Ian.

"The State, Gender and Sexual Politics: Theory and Appraisal" in *Power/Gender, Radtke, H Lorraine (ed).* Connell, R W.

"Theory, Pragmatisms, and Politics" in *Pragmatism: From Progressivism to Postmodernism, Hollinger, Robert (ed).* West, Cornel.

"Universalism and the Situated Critic" in *The Cambridge Companion to Habermas, White, Stephen K (ed).* Pensky, Max.

A Companion to Aristotle's Politics. Keyt, David and Miller, Fred D.

A History of Modern Political Thought: Major Political Thinkers from Hobbes to Marx. Hampsher-Monk, Iain.

A Hobbes Dictionary. Martinich, A P.

Adventures in Lesbian Philosophy. Card, Claudia F (ed).

Althusser: A Critical Reader. Elliott, Gregory (ed).

Amoral Politics: The Persistent Truth of Machiavellism. Scharfstein, Ben-Ami.

An American Ethic: A Philosophy of Freedom Applied to Contemporary Issues. Gerken, John D.

Aristotle's Rhetoric: An Art of Character. Garver, Eugene.

Aristotle: Selections. Irwin, Terence (trans) and Fine, Gail (trans).

Asylum: A Moral Dilemma. Plaut, W Gunther.

Autonomous Agents: From Self-Control to Autonomy. Mele, Alfred R.

Bad Faith and Antiblack Racism. Gordon, Lewis R.

Baudrillard: A Critical Reader. Kellner, Douglas M (ed).

Bertrand Russell. Slater, J G.

Carnap and the Vienna Circle: Empiricism and Logical Syntax. Cirera, Ramon.

Civil Religion and Political Theology. Rouner, Leroy S (ed).

Considerations on France: Joseph de Maistre. Lebrun, Richard A (ed & trans) and De Maistre, Joseph.

Constructive Sociological Theory. Imber, Jonathan B (ed), Woolfolk, Alan (ed) and Masaryk, Thomas G.

Contributors to the Philosophy of Humanism. Hillar, Marian (ed) and Prahl, Frank (ed).

Critical Theory and Political Possibilities: Conceptions of Emancipatory Politics in the Works of Horkheimer, Adorno, Marcuse, and Habermas. Alway, Joan.

Dewey's Ethical Thought. Welchman, Jennifer.

Die kultische Gebärde: Kunst, Politik, Religion im Denken Franz Rosenzweigs. Hufnagel, Cordula.

Die Sehnsucht nach dem Schönen, Guten und Wahren oder platonische Reminiszenzen in Rousseaus Menschenbild und Erziehungslehre. Burkert-Wepfer, Esther.

Dominations and Powers: Reflections on Liberty, Society, and Government. Santayana, George.

Ecological Enlightenment: Essays on the Politics of the Risk Society. Beck, Ulrich and Ritter, Mark A (trans).

Ecology. Merchant, Carolyn (ed).

Ende der Geschichte, Ende der Stadt?. Flusser, Vilém.

Ernst Cassirer—Von Marburg nach New York: Eine philosophische Biographie. Paetzold, Heinz.

Ethics, Killing and War. Norman, Richard.

Evolution and Human Values. Wesson, Robert (ed) and Williams, Patricia A (ed).

Feminism and Philosophy: Essential Readings in Theory, Reinterpretation, and Application. Tuana, Nancy (ed) and Tong, Rosemarie (ed).

Feminist Contentions. Benhabib, Seyla (& others).

Feminist Interpretations of Hannah Arendt. Honig, Bonnie (ed).

FI Interview: Camille Paglia on Freethought, Feminism, and Iconoclasm. Madigan, Timothy J.

Free Spirits: Feminist Philosophers on Culture. Mehuron, Kate (ed) and Percesepe, Gary (ed).

Freud and the Politics of Psychoanalysis. Brunner, José.

Gay Ethics. Murphy, Timothy F (ed).

Georg Lukács. Sim, Stuart.

Hegel In His Time: Berlin, 1818-1831. Burbidge, John W (trans) and D'Hondt, Jacques.

Hegel on the Modern World. Collins, Ardis B (ed).

Hegel: Contra Sociology. Rose, Gillian.

Hipparchia's Choice: An Essay Concerning Women, Philosophy, etc. Le Doeuff, Michèle.

Human Rights and Religious Values. An-Na'im, Abdullahi A (& other eds).

Humanism and its Aftermath: The Shared Fate of Deconstruction and Politics. Martin, Bill.

Idea of Prose. Agamben, Giorgio, Sullivan, Michael (trans) and Whitsitt, Sam (trans).

Idéer om Arbete. Hansson, Sven Ove.

In Search of Authenticity: From Kierkegaard to Camus. Golomb, Jacob.

Intimacy and Spectacle: Liberal Theory as Political Education. Esquith, Stephen L.

Introducing Applied Ethics. Almond, Brenda (ed).

Is Hermeneutics 'Philosophy'? Interpretation and Overinterpretation of the Past. Lucas Jr, George R.

John Dewey: An Intellectual Portrait. Hook, Sidney.

Jung and the Jungians on Myth: An Introduction. Walker, Steven F.

Justice. Fisk, Milton (ed).

Legislative Intent and Other Essays on Law, Politics, and Morality. Singer, Marcus G (ed), MacCallum Jr, Gerald C and Martin, Rex (ed).

Liberals and Communitarians. Mulhall, Stephen and Swift, Adam.

Life in Fragments: Essays in Postmodern Morality. Bauman, Zygmunt.

Locality and Practical Judgment: Charity and Sacrifice. Ross, Stephen David.

Logic and Mr Limbaugh: A Dittohead's Guide to Fallacious Reasoning. Perkins Jr, Raymond K.

Main Trends in Cultural History. Melching, Willem (ed) and Velema, Wyger (ed).

Martin Heidegger and European Nihilism. Löwith, Karl, Wolin, Richard (ed) and Steiner, Gary (trans).

Marx's Theory of the Social Formation. Duan, Zhongqiao.

Medieval Thought: An Introduction. Price, B B.

Modernity and Identity. Lash, Scott (ed) and Friedman, Jonathan (ed).

Moral Voices, Moral Selves: Carol Gilligan and Feminist Moral Theory. Hekman, Susan J.

Multiculturalism: A Critical Reader. Goldberg, David Theo.

Nationalism (Fourth, Expanded Edition). Kedourie, Elie.

Nietzsche: The Ethics of an Immoralist. Berkowitz, Peter.

Other Minds: Critical Essays 1969-1994. Nagel, Thomas.

Pensando la nación. Polakovic, Stefan.

Philosophical Arguments. Taylor, Charles.

Philosophie und Totalitarismus: Zur Kritik dialektischer Diskursivität Eine Hegellektüre. Engelmann, Peter.

Plato's World: Man's Place in the Cosmos. Cropsey, Joseph.

Platón: Los Diálogos Tardíos. Lan, Conrado Eggers (ed).

Political Identity: Thinking Through Marx. Meister, Robert.

POLITICS

POSTMODERNISM

POSTMODERNISM

Postmodernism and Contemporary Italian Philosophy. Silverman, Hugh J.
Postmodernism and Politics: Skepticism or Pragmatism?. Briand, Michael.
Postmodernism and the Artistic Avant-gardes. Erjavec, Ales.
Postmodernism and the Education of the Whole Person. Standish, Paul.
Postmodernism and the Gender Relations in Feminist Theory. Flax, Jane.
Postmodernist Theory and the Physician-Patient Relationship. Tsouyopoulos, Nelly.
Power's Blind Struggle for Existence: Foucault, Genealogy and Darwinism. Atterton, Peter.
Putting Ourselves Up for the Question: A Postmodern Critique of Richard Rorty's Postmodernist Bourgeois Liberalism. Hendley, Steven.
Qué es la ilustración?. Foucault, Michel.
Razón e historia: La modernidad del postmodernismo. Koslowski, Peter.
Reason and Utopia: Richard Bernstein and the Rage against Reason. Nevo, Isaac.
Rekindling Humanity's Love Affair with Science and Technology. Flynn, Thomas W.
Reply to Bruce Caldwell: Can Subjectivism Be Non-Hermeneutic?. Burczak, Theodore A.
Sobre la cuestión del método en el debate Modernidad-Postmodernidad. Esquirol, Josep M.
Sociology and the Diagnosis of the Times or: The Reflexivity of Modernity. Lichtblau, Klaus.
Somewhere Under the Rainbow: The Postmodern Politics of Art Education. Grumet, Madeleine R.
Style and Responsibility: Medicine in Postmodernity. Wiesing, Urban.
Subjektivität und Theologie: Eine hartnäckige Rückfrage. Müller, Klaus.
The End of History, Five Years Later. Fukuyama, Francis.
The Ends of Metaphysics. Markus, György.
The Future of Art and the Theory of Post-Philosophical Culture. Grünberg, Ludwig.
The Impoverishment of Art. Kieran, Matthew.
The Post-Modern Challenge to Community. Mellos, Koula.
The Post-Modern Leo Strauss?. Smith, Gregory Bruce.
The Postmodern Spirit and The Status of God. Nikkel, David H.
The Postmodern Sublime: Kant and Tony Smith's Anecdote of the Cube. Beidler, Paul G.
The Shifting Concept of the Self. Burkitt, Ian.
Violence and Post-Modernism. Jasper, David.
Why a Philosophy of Architecture? The Importance of Harries's Contribution. Olivier, Bert.

POSTMODERNITY

"Posmodernidad y Arte desde América" in Temas Actuales de Filosofía, Palacios, María Julia (ed). Navamuel de Figueroa, Leonor.
Is the Postmodern World a Nietzschean World?. Bermúdez, José Luis.

POSTSTRUCTURALISM

"Can There Be Definitive Interpretations?" in European Philosophy and the American Academy, Smith, Barry (ed). Gracia, Jorge J E.
"La Identidad del Discurso Estético y la Crítica Ideológica en la Etapa Post-Estructuralista de Roland Barthes" in Temas Actuales de Filosofía, Palacios, María Julia (ed). Peñafort, Juan J E.
"Pragmatism, Feminism, and the Linguistic Turn" in Feminist Contentions, Benhabib, Seyla (& others). Fraser, Nancy.
"The Decline and Fall of French Nietzscheo-Structuralism" in European Philosophy and the American Academy, Smith, Barry (ed). Engel, Pascal.
Pathognostica: Aufsätze zur Theorie und Anwendung genealogischer Philosophie. Petersen, Karl Thomas.
Adolescents, Post-Structuralism, and "Playing It Cool!". Merttens, Ruth.
Hypostatizing Thanatos: Lacan's Analysis of the Ego. Whitebook, Joel.
The Reflexive Politics of Constructivism. Fuller, Steve.

POSTULATE

Postulates and Paradoxes of Relative Voting Power—A Critical Re-Appraisal. Felsenthal, Dan S and Machover, Moshé.

POTEAT, W

Poteat on Modern Culture and Critical Philosophy. Adams, E M.
William Poteat's Anthropology: "Mindbody In the World". Mead, Walter B.

POTENCY

Nota sulla "creazione". Messinese, Leonardo.
Totipotency and the Value of Embryonic Cells. Tindale, Christopher W.

POTENTIAL

The Role of the Absolute Infinite in Cantor's Conception of Set. Jané, Ignacio.

POTENTIALITY

Nota Sobre el Estatuto Ontológico del Devenir en Aristóteles. Barrio Maestre, José María.

POTTER, K

Historical Bibliography of Upanisads in Translation. Renard, Philip.

POTTER, V

The Word "Bioethics": The Struggle Over Its Earliest Meanings. Reich, Warren Thomas.

POVERTY

"Rich and Poor" in Introducing Applied Ethics, Almond, Brenda (ed). Trusted, Jennifer.
Ecology. Merchant, Carolyn (ed).
The Politics of Culture: Race, Violence, and Democracy. Choi, Jung Min, Callaghan, Karen A and Murphy, John W.
The Tanner Lectures on Human Values, Volume 16. Peterson, Grethe B (ed).
Death Drive. Lingis, Alphonso F.
Dilemmas of Emergency Food: A Guide for the Perplexed. Poppendieck, Janet E.
Economic Disparity: A Philosophic Response. Manimala, Varghese.

En Torno a la Noción de Pobreza Voluntaria. Salazar, Ignacio.
Exclusive and Inclusive Theories of Property Rights: Rejoinder to Horne. Ashcraft, Richard.
La pobreza y los cambios sociales. Carranza, Salvador Abascal.
Liberalism and the Problem of Poverty: Reply to Ashcraft. Horne, Thomas A.
Multiculturalism and Welfare Reform. Jones, John D.
Recognizing Rationalizations Among Responses to Hunger. Dandekar, Natalie.
T H Green's Doubts About Hegel's Political Philosophy. Nicholson, Peter.
The Roots of Economic Disparity and Poverty. Panthanmackel, George.

POWER

"Dappertutto e in Nessun Luogo": Volontà e Potenza di un'edizione Nietzscheana. Brusotti, Marco and Gerratana, Federico.
"Demokratie, Macht und Legitimität" in Mythos Wertfreiheit?, Apel, Karl Otto (ed). Munnichs, Geert.
"Force, Consent, and the Reasonable Woman" in In Harm's Way, Coleman, Jules L (ed). McGregor, Joan L.
"Foucault's Fallacy" in Reconstructing Foucault, Miguel-Alfonso, Ricardo (ed). Ryan, Michael.
"Into the Realm of the Fearful: Power, Identity and the Gender Problematic" in Power/Gender, Radtke, H Lorraine (ed). Kerfoot, Deborah and Knights, David.
"Macht als Wesen und Widersacher der Liebe" in Macht Geschlechter Differenz, Müller-Funk, Wolfgang (ed). Dux, Günter.
"Modernity, Ethics and Irony: The Return of the Subject in the Later Works of Foucault" in Reconstructing Foucault, Miguel-Alfonso, Ricardo (ed). Jones, Kath Renark.
"Nietzsche and Weber: When Does Reason Become Power?" in The Barbarism of Reason, Horowitz, Asher (ed). Warren, Mark E.
"On War: The Space of Knowledge, Knowledge of Space" in Reconstructing Foucault, Miguel-Alfonso, Ricardo (ed). Campillo, Antonio.
"Our Complicated System": James Madison on Power and Liberty. Read, James H.
"Problematizing Pleasure: Radical Feminist Deconstructions of Sexuality and Power" in Power/Gender, Radtke, H Lorraine (ed). Kitzinger, Celia.
"Putting Nietzsche to Work: The Case of Gilles Deleuze" in Nietzsche: A Critical Reader, Sedgwick, Peter R (ed). Schrift, Alan D.
"Reconfiguring the Subject: Foucault's Analytics of Power" in Reconstructing Foucault, Miguel-Alfonso, Ricardo (ed). Schrift, Alan D.
"Refiguring Values, Power, Knowledge: Or Foucault's Disavowal of Marx" in Whither Marxism?, Magnus, Bernd (ed). Janmohamed, Abdul.
"Resistance: Lessons from Foucault and Feminism" in Power/Gender, Radtke, H Lorraine (ed). Faith, Karlene.
"The Female Subject after the Death of Man" in Reconstructing Foucault, Miguel-Alfonso, Ricardo (ed). Rodríguez, Rosa M.
"Why Foucault No Longer Matters" in Reconstructing Foucault, Miguel-Alfonso, Ricardo (ed). O'Hara, Daniel T.
Authority and Its Enemies (New Edition). Molnar, Thomas.
Contested Knowledge: Social Theory in the Postmodern Era. Seidman, Steven.
Critical Legal Theory and the Challenge of Feminism: A Philosophical Reconception. Kramer, Matthew H.
Critique, Action, and Liberation. Marsh, James.
Democracy and Social Injustice: Law, Politics, and Philosophy. Simon, Thomas W.
Dominations and Powers: Reflections on Liberty, Society, and Government. Santayana, George.
Ethics from Experience. Caws, Peter.
Foucault and the Writing of History. Goldstein, Jan (ed).
Foundations of Analytical Marxism (Volume I). Roemer, John E (ed).
Intimacy and Spectacle: Liberal Theory as Political Education. Esquith, Stephen L.
Macht Geschlechter Differenz. Müller-Funk, Wolfgang (ed).
Music, Value, and the Passions. Ridley, Aaron.
Postmodern Representations: Truth, Power, and Mimesis in the Human Sciences and Public Culture. Brown, Richard Harvey (ed).
Power/Gender. Radtke, H Lorraine (ed) and Stam, Henderikus J (ed).
Power: Its Forms, Bases, and Uses. Wrong, Dennis H.
Powers of the Rational: Science, Technology, and the Future of Thought. Birmingham, Peg (trans), Janicaud, Dominique and Birmingham, Elizabeth (trans).
Racist Culture: Philosophy and the Politics of Meaning. Goldberg, David Theo.
Reconstructing Foucault. Miguel-Alfonso, Ricardo (ed) and Caporale-Bizzini, Silvia (ed).
Starting with Foucault: An Introduction to Genealogy. Prado, C G.
The Decolonization of Imagination: Culture, Knowledge, and Power. Pieterse, Jan Nederveen (ed) and Parekh, Bhikhu (ed).
The Irigaray Reader. Whitford, Margaret (ed).
The Site of Our Lives: The Self and the Subject from Emerson to Foucault. Hans, James S.
Versus Trasimaco: E confutabile il detto "la giustizia non è altro che l'utile del più forte"?. Fiorillo, Vanda.
Vértigos argumentales: Una ética de la disputa. Pereda, Carlos.
Whither Marxism?. Magnus, Bernd (ed) and Cullenberg, Stephen (ed).
Das Problem der Gewaltenteilung bei Rousseau und Fichte. Schottky, Richard.
Deissler Rank Complexity of Powers of Indecomposable Injective Modules. Chartrand, R and Kucera, T.
Existe en Zubiri una protopolítica?. Marquinez Argote, Germán.
Feminism and Empowerment: A Critical Reading of Foucault. Deveaux, Monique.
Foucault's Reconception of Power. Weberman, David.

PRIVACY

"Privacy and the Ethics of Outing" in *Gay Ethics, Murphy, Timothy F (ed)*. Mayo, David J and Gunderson, Martin.

Computers, Ethics and Social Values. Johnson, Deborah G (ed) and Nissenbaum, Helen (ed).

Constitutional Domains: Democracy, Community, Management. Post, Robert C.

Ethical Aspects of Information Technology. Spinello, Richard A.

Constitutional Privacy. Johnson, Jeffery L.

Data Privacy and Legal Argumentation. Elgesem, Dag.

Deception Methods in Psychology: Have They Changed in 23 Years?. Sieber, Joan E, Iannuzzo, Rebecca and Rodriguez, Beverly.

Informed Consent and Anonymous Tissue Samples: The Case of HIV Seroprevalence Studies. Kopelman, Loretta M.

Militant Gayes, Gayes in the Military, and Privacy as Social Freedom. Nunan, Richard.

Subjetividad y Privacidad. Hurtado, Guillermo.

PRIVATE

Private Consciences and Public Reasons. Greenawalt, Kent.

The Idea of Private Law. Weinrib, Ernest J.

El concepto de propiedad privada en el Derecho Constitucional Venezolano. Peña, Angel Bustillos.

Ethics: Public and Private. Capron, Alexander Morgan.

Moralité privée et moralité publique chez Aristote. Rutten, Christian.

Public Vices, Private Benefits. Commers, Ronald.

PRIVATE EXPERIENCE

Wittgenstein on Private Language and Private Mental Objects. Jacquette, Dale.

PRIVATE LANGUAGE

The Wittgenstein Reader. Wittgenstein, Ludwig and Kenny, Anthony (ed).

A New Exposition of the 'Private Language Argument': Wittgenstein's 'Notes for the "Philosophical Lecture"'. Stern, David G.

External and Internal Private Language Arguments. Stevenson, Leslie.

La anotación de las Investigaciones Filosóficas de Wittgenstein. Rodríguez Pereyra, Gonzalo.

Le caractère social du langage et de la pensée. Burri, Alex.

Obeying a Rule: Wittgenstein's Stress on Obedience in Sections 198-202 of the *Philosophical Investigations*. Susse, Jennifer.

Origins of the Private Language Argument. Dejnozka, Jan.

Wittgenstein on Private Language and Private Mental Objects. Jacquette, Dale.

Wittgenstein on Private Language: Exorcising the Ghost from the Machine. Hitchcock, Christopher Read.

PRIVATE PROPERTY

Idéer om Ägande. Hansson, Sven Ove (ed).

Waldron on Special Rights *in rem*. Cristi, Renato.

PRIVATIZATION

Privatization and Just Health Care. Buchanan, Allen.

PRO CHOICE

"The Abortion Dilemma" in *The 1994 Annual of Hermeneutics and Social Concern, Lawler, Justus George (ed)*. Haag, Louis J.

PROAST, J

Locke's Antagonist, Jonas Proast. Vernon, Richard.

PROBABILISM

Bayesian Epistemology: Probabilistic Confirmation and Rational Decision. Eells, Ellery.

Probabilism. Foley, Richard.

PROBABILITY

"A Brief Survey of Adams' Contributions to Philosophy" in *Probability and Conditionals, Eells, Ellery (ed)*. Suppes, Patrick.

"A Mediational Model of Research Artifacts" in *Probability in Theory-Building, Brzezinski, Jerzy (ed)*. Strohmetz, David B and Rosnow, Ralph L.

"A Theoretical and Experimental Inquiry Into the Relation of Theoretical Concepts..." in *Probability in Theory-Building, Brzezinski, Jerzy (ed)*. Heyer, Dieter and Mausfeld, Rainer.

"Adams Conditionals" in *Probability and Conditionals, Eells, Ellery (ed)*. Skyrms, Brian.

"Back in the CCCP" in *Probability and Conditionals, Eells, Ellery (ed)*. Hall, Ned.

"Conditionals as Random Variables" in *Probability and Conditionals, Eells, Ellery (ed)*. Stalnaker, Robert and Jeffrey, Richard.

"Contrast Analysis in Behavioral Research" in *Probability in Theory-Building, Brzezinski, Jerzy (ed)*. Koutstaal, Wilma and Rosenthal, Robert.

"Dimensions of the Diagnostic Space" in *Probability in Theory-Building, Brzezinski, Jerzy (ed)*. Brzezinski, Jerzy.

"Learning the Impossible" in *Probability and Conditionals, Eells, Ellery (ed)*. McGee, Vann.

"Letter to Brian Skyrms" in *Probability and Conditionals, Eells, Ellery (ed)*. Stalnaker, Robert.

"Modeling Cognitive Learning Steps" in *Probability in Theory-Building, Brzezinski, Jerzy (ed)*. Krause, Bodo.

"Probability and the Understanding of Individual Differences" in *Probability in Theory- Building, Brzezinski, Jerzy (ed)*. Wahlsten, Douglas.

"Reichenbach Falls (Or Only Stumbles?)" in *American Philosophy Today and Other Philosophical Studies, Rescher, Nicholas*. Rescher, Nicholas.

"Rough Set Methods in Psychology" in *Probability in Theory-Building, Brzezinski, Jerzy (ed)*. Iwinski, Tadeusz B.

"Some Questions about Adams' Conditionals" in *Probability and Conditionals, Eells, Ellery (ed)*. Suppes, Patrick.

"Statistical Dependencies, Statements and the Idealizational Theory of Science" in *Probability in Theory-Building, Brzezinski, Jerzy (ed)*. Gaul, Marek.

"The Howson-Urbach Proofs of Bayesian Principles" in *Probability and Conditionals, Eells, Ellery (ed)*. Chihara, Charles S.

"The Hypothesis of the Conditional Construal of Conditional Probability" in *Probability and Conditionals, Eells, Ellery (ed)*. Hájek, Alan and Hall, Ned.

"Triviality on the Cheap?" in *Probability and Conditionals, Eells, Ellery (ed)*. Hájek, Alan.

Modality, Probability, and Rationality. Sennett, James F.

Probability and Conditionals. Eells, Ellery (ed) and Skyrms, Brian (ed).

Probability in Theory-Building. Brzezinski, Jerzy (ed).

Projective Probability. Logue, James.

The Facts of Causation. Mellor, D H.

The Mind of David Hume: A Companion to Book I of 'A Treatise of Human Nature'. Johnson, Oliver A.

The Philosophy Behind Physics. De La Peña, Luis (ed), Hodgson, Peter E (ed) and Brody, Thomas A.

The Shaggy Steed of Physics: Mathematical Beauty in the Physical World. Oliver, David.

A Natural Prior Probability Distribution Derived from the Propositional Calculus. Paris, J B, Vencovská, A and Wilmers, G M.

A New Theory of Content I: Basic Content. Gemes, Kenneth.

A Note on the Decidability of De Finetti's Coherence. Corielli, Francesco.

An Inverse of Bell's Theorem. Hansen, Kaj B.

Believing the Improbable. Kaplan, Mark.

Chance and Order in Our Inorganic Universe. Blandino, Giovanni.

Conditioning and Intervening. Meek, Christopher and Glymour, Clark.

Convex Models of Uncertainty: Applications and Implications. Ben-Haim, Yakov.

Could the Probability of Doom Be Zero or One?. Krieger, Martin H.

Desire-as-Belief Implies Opinionation or Indifference. Costa, Horacio Arló, Collins, John and Levi, Isaac.

Earman on the Projectibility of Grue. Lange, Marc.

Economic Choice in Generalized Expected Utility Theory. Quiggin, John.

Fine-Grained Opinion, Probability, and the Logic of Full Belief. Van Fraassen, Bas C.

Flexibility, Endogenous Risk, and the Protection Premium. Lence, Sergio H and Babcock, Bruce A.

How I Almost Solved the Problem of Induction. Watkins, John.

In Search of a Pointless Decision Principle. Bandyopadhayay, Prasanta S.

Inference, Noncommutativity, and Determinateness in Quantum Mechanics. Bub, Jeffrey.

Legitimizing Chance: The Best-System Approach to Probabilistic Laws in Physical Theory. Halpin, John F.

Locke and the Preface Paradox. Odegard, Douglas.

Old Evidence and New Theories. Zynda, Lyle.

On the Nature of Bayesian Convergence. Hawthorne, James.

On the Probabilties of Conditionals. Döring, Frank.

Optimization in Evolutionary Ecology. Richardson, Robert C.

Probabilities for New Theories. Maher, Patrick.

Probability in Rational Decision-Making. Moser, Paul K and Mulder, D Hudson.

Probability Reparation: The Problem of New Explanation. Jeffrey, Richard.

Probability, Evidence, and the Coherence of the Whole Truth. Cross, Charles B.

Realism, Convergence, and Additivity. Juhl, Cory and Kelly, Kevin T.

Screening-Off and the Levels of Selection. McClamrock, Ron.

Sober on Brandon on Screening-Off and the Levels of Selection. Brandon, Robert N.

Some Steps Towards a General Theory of Relevance. Cohen, L Jonathan.

Stephen Hawking's Cosmology and Theism. Smith, Quentin.

Stronger Evidence. Achinstein, Peter.

Subjective Probability and Acceptance. Lance, Mark Norris.

The Extent of Dilation of Sets of Probabilities and the Asymptotics of Robust Bayesian Inference. Herron, Timothy, Seidenfeld, Teddy and Wasserman, Larry.

The Impossibility of Experimental Elicitation of Subjective Probabilities. Karni, Edi.

The Logic of Probability. Angell, Richard B (trans) and De Finetti, Bruno.

The Mishap at Reichenbach Fall: Singular vs General Causation. Hitchcock, Christopher Read.

The New Experimentalism, Topical Hypotheses, and Learning from Error. Mayo, Deborah G.

The Second Law of Probability Dynamics. Barrett, Martin and Sober, Elliott.

The Speed-Optimality of Reichenbach's Straight Rule of Induction. Juhl, Cory F.

The Theory of Random Propositions. Norton, John D.

The Two-Envelope Paradox. Broome, John.

Theories of Probability. Howson, Colin.

Toward a Defensible Bootstrapping. Mitchell, Sam.

PROBLEM

Of Problematology: Philosophy, Science, and Language. Meyer, Michel and Jamison, David (trans).

Complete Problems for Fixed-Point Logics. Grohe, Martin.

Contraposition and Existential Import. Perry, Clifton B and Jolley, Kelly D.

Fixed-parameter Tractability and Completeness IV: On Completeness for W[P] and PSPACE Analogues. Abrahamson, K A (& others).

The Gettier Problem and the Parable of the Ten Coins. Levi, Don S.

The Problem of Philosophy. McGinn, Colin.

PROBLEM SOLVING

"Insight and Problem Solving" in *The Nature of Insight, Sternberg, Robert J (ed)*. Dominowski, Roger L and Dallob, Pamela.

"Prolegomena to Theories of Insight in Problem Solving: A Taxonomy of Problems" in *The Nature of Insight, Sternberg, Robert J (ed)*. Weisberg, Robert W.

PSYCHOLOGY

"Connectionism and the Problem of Systematicity" in *Connectionism: Debates on Psychological Explanation, Macdonald, Cynthia (ed)*. Fodor, Jerry A and McLaughlin, Brian P.

"Connectionism, Constituency, and the Language of Thought" in *Connectionism: Debates on Psychological Explanation, Macdonald, Cynthia (ed)*. Smolensky, Paul.

"Connectionism, Eliminativism, and the Future of Folk Psychology" in *Connectionism: Debates on Psychological Explanation, Macdonald, Cynthia (ed)*. Ramsey, William, Stich, Stephen and Garon, Joseph.

"Connectionist Minds" in *Connectionism: Debates on Psychological Explanation, Macdonald, Cynthia (ed)*. Clark, Andy.

"Consciousness, Explanatory Inversion, & Cognitive Science" in *Philosophy of Psychology: Debates on Psychological Explanation, Macdonald, Cynthia (ed)*. Searle, John R.

"Contrast Analysis in Behavioral Research" in *Probability in Theory-Building, Brzezinski, Jerzy (ed)*. Koutstaal, Wilma and Rosenthal, Robert.

"Die Stellung Edith Steins im Psychologismusstreit" in *Studien zur Philosophie von Edith Stein, Fetz, Reto Luzius (ed)*. Rath, Matthias.

"Dimensions of the Diagnostic Space" in *Probability in Theory-Building, Brzezinski, Jerzy (ed)*. Brzezinski, Jerzy.

"Does Meaning Matter?" in *Philosophy of Psychology: Debates on Psychological Explanation, Macdonald, Cynthia (ed)*. Dretske, Frederick.

"How to be Psychologically Relevant" in *Philosophy of Psychology: Debates on Psychological Explanation, Macdonald, Cynthia (ed)*. Macdonald, Cynthia and Macdonald, Graham.

"Introduction to *Philosophical Essays on Freud*" in *Philosophy of Psychology: Debates on Psychological Explanation, Macdonald, Cynthia (ed)*. Hopkins, James.

"La Enseñanza de la Epistemología en la Carrera de Psicología o Técnicas Para Desvestir a una Invitada Molesta" in *Temas Actuales de Filosofía, Palacios, María Julia (ed)*. Feldman, Susana B and Krichmar, Fernando Gabriel.

"Modeling Cognitive Learning Steps" in *Probability in Theory-Building, Brzezinski, Jerzy (ed)*. Krause, Bodo.

"On Negrohood: Psychology of the African Negro" in *African Philosophy: Selected Readings, Mosley, Albert G (ed)*. Senghor, Leopold S.

"On the Proper Treatment of Connectionism" in *Connectionism: Debates on Psychological Explanation, Macdonald, Cynthia (ed)*. Smolensky, Paul.

"Probability and the Understanding of Individual Differences" in *Probability in Theory-Building, Brzezinski, Jerzy (ed)*. Wahlsten, Douglas.

"Problems with the *DSM* Approach to Classifying Psychopathology" in *Philosophical Psychopathology, Graham, George (ed)*. Poland, Jeffrey, Von Eckardt, Barbara and Spaulding, Will.

"Psychoanalytic Explanation" in *Philosophy of Psychology: Debates on Psychological Explanation, Macdonald, Cynthia (ed)*. Macdonald, Graham.

"Psychological Externalism" in *The Mind-Body Problem: A Guide to the Current Debate, Warner, Richard (ed)*. Owens, Joseph.

"Psychology" in *The Cambridge Companion to Aristotle, Barnes, Jonathan (ed)*. Everson, Stephen.

"Reply: A Bet with Peacocke" in *Philosophy of Psychology: Debates on Psychological Explanation, Macdonald, Cynthia (ed)*. Millikan, Ruth Garrett.

"Reply: Causation and Two Kinds of Laws" in *Philosophy of Psychology: Debates on Psychological Explanation, Macdonald, Cynthia (ed)*. Block, Ned.

"Reply: Consciousness and the Varieties of Aboutness" in *Philosophy of Psychology: Debates on Psychological Explanation, Macdonald, Cynthia (ed)*. Davies, Martin.

"Rough Set Methods in Psychology" in *Probability in Theory-Building, Brzezinski, Jerzy (ed)*. Iwinski, Tadeusz B.

"Supervenient Causation" in *Philosophy of Psychology: Debates on Psychological Explanation, Macdonald, Cynthia (ed)*. Macdonald, Cynthia and Macdonald, Graham.

"Tacit Knowledge and Subdoxastic States" in *Philosophy of Psychology: Debates on Psychological Explanation, Macdonald, Cynthia (ed)*. Davies, Martin.

"Tacit Knowledge" in *Philosophy of Psychology: Debates on Psychological Explanation, Macdonald, Cynthia (ed)*. Macdonald, Graham.

"The Biological Turn" in *Philosophy of Psychology: Debates on Psychological Explanation, Macdonald, Cynthia (ed)*. Macdonald, Graham.

"The Mind-Body Problem and Contemporary Psychology" in *The Mind-Body Problem: A Guide to the Current Debate, Warner, Richard (ed)*. Macnamara, John.

"The Mind-Body Problem" in *The Mind-Body Problem: A Guide to the Current Debate, Warner, Richard (ed)*. Fodor, Jerry A.

"Wittgenstein on Psychological Verbs" in *Wittgenstein and Contemporary Philosophy, Teghrarian, Souren (ed)*. Vesey, Godfrey.

(Direct) Reference. Napoli, Ernesto.

Anthroposophy in Everyday Life. Steiner, Rudolf.

Auflösen, Untersuchen, Aufwecken: Psychoanalyse und andere Analysen. Ruhs, August (ed) and Seitter, Walter (ed).

Cartesian Psychology and Physical Minds: Individualism and the Sciences of the Mind. Wilson, Robert A.

Color Codes: Modern Theories of Color in Philosophy, Painting and Architecture, Literature, Music, and Psychology. Riley II, Charles A.

Connectionism: Debates on Psychological Explanation. Macdonald, Cynthia (ed) and Macdonald, Graham (ed).

Explaining Attitudes: A Practical Approach to the Mind. Baker, Lynne Rudder.

Husserl e lo scetticismo. Savi, Cristina.

Il Linguaggio Dell'Oggettività: Saggio su Meinong. Brigati, Roberto.

Instrumental Biology or the Disunity of Science. Rosenberg, Alexander.

La Depsicologizzazione della Logica: Un confronto tra Boole e Frege. Vassallo, Nicla.

La Renovación Pragmatista de la Filosofía Analítica: Una Introducción a la Filosofía Contemporánea del Lenguaje. Nubiola, Jaime.

La Sémiotique Empiriste Face au Kantisme. Formigari, Lia.

Mental Reality. Strawson, Galen.

Mental Representation: A Reader. Stich, Stephen P (ed) and Warfield, Ted A (ed).

On Naming the Present: God, Hermeneutics, and Church. Tracy, David.

Philosophical Psychopathology. Graham, George (ed) and Stephens, G Lynn (ed).

Philosophy of Psychology: Debates on Psychological Explanation. Macdonald, Cynthia (ed) and Macdonald, Graham (ed).

Platonism and Positivism in Psychology. Adler, Mortimer.

Practical Realism and Moral Psychology. Jacobs, Jonathan.

Probability in Theory-Building. Brzezinski, Jerzy (ed).

Repräsentation und Identität. Vogeley, Kai.

Subjectivity and Reduction: An Introduction to the Mind-Body Problem. Hannan, Barbara.

Tertium datur? Reflections on Owen Flanagan's Consciousness Reconsidered. Cottrell, Allin.

The Common Mind: An Essay on Psychology, Society, and Politics by Philip Pettit. Price, Huw.

The Sciences of Cognition: Theory and Research in Psychology and Artificial Intelligence. Wagman, Morton.

Weltentwürfe: Ludwig Binswangers phänomenologische Psychologie. Herzog, Max.

A Behaviorist Alternative to *Theory* and *Simulation* Theories of Folk Psychology. Stemmer, Nathan.

A Critique of Information Processing Theories of Consciousness. Hardcastle, Valerie Gray.

A Neural Network Approach to Obsessive-Compulsive Disorder. Stein, Dan J and Hollander, Eric.

A Note on the Intentionality of Féar. Horowitz, Amir.

A Scientific Psychologistic Foundation for Theories of Meaning. Kaye, Lawrence J.

Against Methodological Solipsism: The Ecological Approach. Rowlands, Mark.

Análisis gnoseológico de la psicología cognitiva. Blanco Martín, Carlos J.

Animal Concepts: Content and Discontent. Chater, Nick and Heyes, Cecilia.

Anxiety: A Pseudo-Concept. Shibles, Warren.

Beliefs, Functionally Discrete States, and Connectionist Networks: A Comment on Ramsey, Stich, and Garon. Botterill, George.

Beyond Determinism and Indignity: A Reinterpretation of Operant Conditioning. Rockwell, W Teed.

Bibliography of Structuralism II (1989-1994 and Additions). Diederich, Werner, Ibarra, Andoni and Mormann, Thomas.

Buddhism and Cognitivism: A Postmodern Appraisal. Pickering, John.

Can Post-Newtonian Psychologists Find Happiness in a Pre-Paradigm Science?. Roth, Paul A.

Ceteris Paribus Laws and Psychological Explanations. Wallis, Charles.

Children's Capacity to Agree to Psychological Research: Knowledge of Risks and Benefits and Voluntariness. Abramovitch, Rona (& others).

Cognition Without Classical Architecture. Garson, James W.

Commentary on "Affect, Agency, and Engagement". Caws, Peter.

Commentary on "Connectionist Hysteria". Phillips, James and Woody, J Melvin.

Commentary on "Kant, Thought Insertion, and Mental Unity". Stephens, G Lynn and Graham, George.

Commentary on "The Alzheimer's Disease Sufferer as Semiotic Subject". Hope, Tony.

Could There Be A Science of Rationality?. Davidson, Donald.

Cultural Stereotypes and Positioning Theory. Van Langenhove, Luk and Harré, Rom.

Deceived Versus Nondeceived Participants' Perceptions of Scientific and Applied Psychology. Soliday, Elizabeth and Stanton, Annette L.

Deception Methods in Psychology: Have They Changed in 23 Years?. Sieber, Joan E, Iannuzzo, Rebecca and Rodriguez, Beverly.

Dennett's Conceptual Reform. Ross, Don.

Discussion of Lazarus's "How Certain Boundaries and Ethics Diminish Therapeutic Effectiveness". Gutheil, Thomas G.

Dispositional Beliefs and Dispositions to Believe. Audi, Robert.

Distributed Representation and Causal Modularity: A Rejoinder to Forster and Saidel. Ramsey, William.

Edith Stein: l'Apprendistato Fenomenologico. Pezzella, Anna Maria.

Electric Brain Fields and Memory Traces: Wittgenstein and Gestalt Psychology. Hark, Michael.

Emotion and Memory: The Second Cognitive Revolution. Harré, Rom.

Emotion as a Natural Kind: Towards a Computational Foundation for Emotion Theory. Charland, Louis C.

Entwicklungsdenken bei Piaget und Merleau-Ponty. Herzog, Maximilian.

Equipotential Recipes for Unambiguous Images: A Reply to Rollins. Reisberg, Daniel.

Ethical Concerns of Nonclinical Forensic Witnesses and Consultants. Pfeifer, Jeffrey E and Brigham, John C.

Ethical Decision Making, Boundaries, and Treatment Effectiveness: A Reprise. Gottlieb, Michael C.

Exclusion and Emphasis Reframed as a Matter of Ethics. Daniel, Jessica Henderson.

Explanation and Evaluation in Cognitive Science. Montgomery, Richard.

QUANTUM THEORY

Philosophy, Mathematics and Modern Physics. Rudolph, Enno (ed) and Stamatescu, I O (ed).

Quantum Mechanics: Historical Contingency and the Copenhagen Hegemony. Cushing, James T.

The Conscious Universe: Part and Whole in Modern Physical Theory. Kafatos, Menas and Nadeau, Robert.

The Undivided Universe: An Ontological Interpretation of Quantum Theory. Hiley, B J and Bohm, David.

Thinking in Complexity: The Complex Dynamics of Matter, Mind, and Mankind. Mainzer, Klaus.

A Formal Framework for Quantum Non-Individuality. Krause, Décio and French, Steven.

A Formal System for Classical Particle Mechanics, Its Model-Theoretic Applications and Space-Time Structure. Ishigaki, Toshio.

An Inverse of Bell's Theorem. Hansen, Kaj B.

Comment on 'Stapp's Theorem Without Counterfactual Commitment'. Stapp, Henry P.

Computation Is Just Interpretable Symbol Manipulation; Cognition Isn't. Harnad, Stevan.

Constructive Empiricism. Leeds, Stephen.

Creation Without a Creator: Reflections on Contemporary Scientific Cosmologies. Kozhamthadam, Job.

David Bohm, físico y filósofo: In Memoriam. Herrero, Libia.

E J Lowe on Vague Identity and Quantum Indeterminacy. Noonan, Harold W.

Further Adventures of Wigner's Friend. Albert, David Z and Putnam, Hilary.

Has Chemistry Been at Least Approximately Reduced to Quantum Mechanics?. Scerri, Eric R.

Interpretations of Quantum Field Theory. Huggett, Nick and Weingard, Robert.

Is Algebraic Lorentz-Covariant Quantum Field Theory Stochastic Einstein Local?. Muller, F A and Butterfield, Jeremy.

La Philosophie de Niels Bohr. Bunge, Mario.

Legitimizing Chance: The Best-System Approach to Probabilistic Laws in Physical Theory. Halpin, John F.

Locality/ Separability: Is This Necessarily a Useful Distinction?. Cushing, James T.

Making Sense of Approximate Decoherence. Bacciagaluppi, Guido and Hemmo, Meir.

Neutral Currents and the History of Scientific Ideas. Miller, Arthur I and Bullock, Frederick W.

On the Field Aspect of Quantum Fields. Huggett, Nick and Weingard, Robert.

On the Paradoxical Aspects of New Quantum Experiments. Vaidman, Lev.

Relativistic Hidden Variable Theories?. Arntzenius, Frank.

Temporal Gestalt: A Concept for Quantum Theory. McKee, Patrick L and Quinn, Carol.

The Aharonov-Bohm Effect and the Reality of Wave Packets. Liu, Chuang.

The Bohmian Model of Quantum Cosmology. Callender, Craig and Weingard, Robert.

The Correspondence Principle and the Closure of Theories: Two Incompatible Aspects of Heisenberg's Philosophy of Science. Weinert, Friedel.

The Quest for Infinity and the Synthesis of Science (An Interview with Professor Andrzej Kajetan Wróblewski). Bendyk, Edwin.

The Renormalisation Group and Effective Field Theories. Huggett, Nick and Weingard, Robert.

The Suggestive Properties of Quantum Mechanics Without the Collapse Postulate. Barrett, Jeffrey A.

The 'Decoherence' Approach to the Measurement Problem in Quantum Mechanics. Elby, Andrew.

Theories Between Theories: Asymptotic Limiting Intertheoretic Relations. Batterman, Robert W.

Vague Identity and Quantum Indeterminacy. Lowe, E J.

Vague Identity and Quantum Non-Individuality. French, Steven and Krause, Décio.

Wavefunction Tails in the Modal Interpretation. Dickson, Michael.

QUEBEC

Peoples and Secession. Ewin, R E.

QUESTION

Was ist und wozu überhaupt-Philosophie? Vorübungen sich verändernden Denkens. Brandner, Rudolf.

Carnap and Quine: Internal and External Questions. Bird, Graham H.

Why?. Goldman, Michael.

QUINE

"Inferential Roles, Quine, and Mad Holism" in *Holism: A Consumer Update, Fodor, Jerry (ed).* Berg, Jonathan.

"James, Quine, and Analytic Pragmatism" in *Pragmatism: From Progressivism to Postmodernism, Hollinger, Robert (ed).* Nevo, Isaac.

"Meaning Holism Defended" in *Holism: A Consumer Update, Fodor, Jerry A (ed).* Harman, Gilbert.

"Reflexiones Sobre la Propuesta Epistém. Formulada por Quine en 'Dos Dogmas d. Empirismo'" in *Temas Actuales de Filosofía, Palacios, María Julia (ed).* Saravia Sacchelli, Hugo O.

"The Unavailability of What We Mean: A Reply to Quiine, Fodor and LePore" in *Holism: A Consumer Update, Fodor, Jerry A (ed).* Rey, Georges.

"Wittgenstein Vs Quine on Logical Necessity" in *Wittgenstein and Contemporary Philosophy, Teghrarian, Souren (ed).* Glock, Hans-Johann.

In Mediis Rebus. Dreben, Burton.

Perspectives on Quine. Barrett, Robert (ed) and Gibson, Roger (ed).

Referenztheorien in der analytischen Philosophie. Kellerwessel, Wulf.

Sunyata, Textualism, and Incommensurability. Barnhart, Michael G.

A Biopsy of Recent Analytic Philosophy. Margolis, Joseph.

A Note about a Quinean Argument against Direct Reference. Oppy, Graham.

Are Quine's Two Dogmas Still Dogmas. Kanthamani, A.

Carnap and Quine: Internal and External Questions. Bird, Graham H.

Duhem, Quine, and the Multiplicity of Scientific Tests. Balashov, Yuri.

Externalism and Analyticity. Preti, Consuelo.

Incompatible Empirically Equivalent Theories: A Structural Explication. Mormann, Thomas.

Indeterminacy and Interpretation. Abel, Günter.

Naturalized Epistemology and Epistemic Evaluation. Hookway, Christopher.

On Classes and Higher-Order Logic: A Critique of W V O Quine. Cocchiarella, Nino B.

Proxy Functions and Inscrutability of Reference. Reynolds, Steven L.

Quine and Davidson: Two Naturalized Epistemologists. Gibson, Roger F.

Quine and Logical Positivism. Van Evra, James.

Quine and the Linguistic Doctrine of Logical Truth. Akiba, Ken.

Quine and Verificationism. Prawitz, Dag.

Quine's Pragmatic Ontology. McHenry, Leemon.

Quine's Truth. Bergström, Lars.

Quine, le continuisme et la fin de l'épistémologie néo-positiviste. Largeault, Jean.

Radical Translation and Animals: An Argument from the Principle of Humanity. Weir, Jack L.

Statements and Modality: Strawson, Quine and Wolfram. Millican, Peter.

The Common Need for Classical Epistemological Foundations: Against a Feminist Alternative. Thalos, Mariam.

Transcendentaal-Pragmatiek en Semantiek. Sas, Peter.

Une ou deux indéterminations. Laugier, Sandra.

W V Quine: Pursuit of Truth. Alcázar, Javier R.

What is Quine's View of Truth?. Davidson, Donald.

QUINET, E

Edgar Quinet, Chantre de "La Grèce Moderne". Guichardet, Jeannine.

QUINN, P

Reading Religions: A Reply to Callahan, Martin, and Quinn. Battin, Margaret P.

QUINN, W

Revising the Doctrine of Double Effect. McMahan, Jeff.

RABELAIS, F

"François Rabelais as Humanist" in *Contributors to the Philosophy of Humanism, Hillar, Marian (ed).* Finch, Sheila A.

RACE

"The Conservation of Races" in *African Philosophy: Selected Readings, Mosley, Albert G (ed).* Du Bois, William E B.

American Mixed Race: The Culture of Microdiversity. Zack, Naomi (ed).

Bad Faith and Antiblack Racism. Gordon, Lewis R.

I Am Because We Are: Readings in Black Philosophy. Hord, Fred Lee (ed) and Lee, Jonathan Scott (ed).

Justice. Fisk, Milton (ed).

Moral Voices, Moral Selves: Carol Gilligan and Feminist Moral Theory. Hekman, Susan J.

Postmodern Environmental Ethics. Oelschlaeger, Max (ed).

Race and Mixed Race. Zack, Naomi.

The Politics of Culture: Race, Violence, and Democracy. Choi, Jung Min, Callaghan, Karen A and Murphy, John W.

The Tanner Lectures on Human Values, Volume 16. Peterson, Grethe B (ed).

A Practical Idea of Blackness. Kiros, Teodros.

Cultural Relativism: Some Comments. Otakpor, Nkeonye.

Facing the Challenges of Diversity—A Reflection on the Role of Philosophy in South Africa Today. Van Der Merwe, W L.

Interrogating Whiteness: Dialogue as a Pragmatist Tool for Postmodern Identity-Formation *or* Breaking Bread with Bell Hooks and Cornel West. Paris, Jeffrey.

Mixed Black and White Race and Public Policy. Zack, Naomi.

Race/Gender and the Ethics of Difference: A Reply to Okin's "Gender Inequality and Cultural Differences". Flax, Jane.

Reply to Taylor. Rudinow, Joel.

Response to Jane Flax. Okin, Susan Moller.

So Black and Blue: Response to Rudinow. Taylor, Paul Christopher.

Transcending Race: Further Reflections on Australian Aboriginal Culture. Turner, David H.

RACHELS, J

Rachels, Abortion, and the Seventeenth Century. Dombrowski, Daniel A.

RACISM

"Biologistische und Rassistische Tendenzen im spirituellen Öko-Feminismus" in *Der feministische "Sündenfall"?, Kohn-Ley, Charlotte (ed).* Wölflingseder, Maria.

"Consenting to Whiteness" in *Marxism in the Postmodern Age, Callari, Antonio (ed).* Williams, Rhonda M.

"Deutsche Philosophen und das 'Amt Rosenberg'" in *Die besten Geister der Nation, Korotin, Ilse (ed).* Leaman, George.

"Die verfehlte Sendung: Die Philosophie und der Nationalsozialismus" in *Der geistige Anschluss, Fischer, Kurt R (ed).* Sluga, Hans.

"Frauen und Rechtsextremismus: 'Kampfgefährtin' oder 'Heimchen am Herd'?" in *Nationalsozialismus und Moderne, Welzer, Harald (ed).* Knapp, Gudrun-Axeli.

"Höss lesen" in *Nationalsozialismus und Moderne, Welzer, Harald (ed).* Montau, Robert.

"Komplizenschaft über Generationen" in *Nationalsozialismus und Moderne, Welzer, Harald (ed).* Müller-Hohagen, Jürgen.

"Männer der Praxis: Zur Sozialpsychologie des Verwaltungsmassenmordes" in *Nationalsozialismus und Moderne, Welzer, Harald (ed).* Welzer, Harald.

REALITY

see also Being, Existence, Ontology

"Art in a Box" in *Danto and his Critics, Rollins, Mark (ed)*. Shusterman, Richard.

"Bantu Philosophy" in *African Philosophy: Selected Readings, Mosley, Albert G (ed)*. Tempels, Placide.

"Consciousness and Objective Reality" in *The Mind-Body Problem: A Guide to the Current Debate, Warner, Richard (ed)*. Nagel, Thomas.

"Does Technology 'Construct' Scientific Reality?" in *Philosophy of Technology in Spanish Speaking Countries, Mitcham, Carl (ed)*. Queraltó Moreno, Ramón.

"Enchanting Views" in *Reading Putnam, Clark, Peter (ed)*. Blackburn, Simon.

"Gadamer's Realism: The 'Belongingness' of Word and Reality" in *Hermeneutics and Truth, Wachterhauser, Brice (ed)*. Wachterhauser, Brice.

"How Scientists Really Reason: Scientific Reasoning in Real-World Laboratories" in *The Nature of Insight, Sternberg, Robert J (ed)*. Dunbar, Kevin.

"Ich aber fordere Sie auf, absolute Genesis ins Auge zu fassen!". Richli, Urs.

"Symbolic Exchange in Hyperreality" in *Baudrillard: A Critical Reader, Kellner, Douglas M (ed)*. Cook, Deborah.

"The Commodification of Reality and the Reality of Commodification" in *Baudrillard: A Critical Reader, Kellner, Douglas M (ed)*. Best, Steven.

"The Philosophic Background of Aristotle's *Aitia*" in *The Crossroads of Norm and Nature, Sim, May (ed)*. Moravcsik, Julius.

A Companion to Metaphysics. Kim, Jaegwon (ed) and Sosa, Ernest (ed).

Antologia del Buddhismo Ch'an. Arena, Leonardo Vittorio.

Appearance and Reality: A Philosophical Investigation into Perception and Perceptual Qualities. Hacker, P M S.

Attitudes, Chaos, and the Connectionist Mind. Eiser, J Richard.

Blindness of Modern Science. Uus, Undo.

Das unendliche Altern der Moderne: Untersuchungen zur Romantrilogie Gert Jonkes. Schönherr, Ulrich.

Der Katechon: Zu Carl Schmitts fundamentalistischer Kritik der Zeit. Meuter, Günter.

Der Zusammenhang der Wirklichkeit. Krämer, Felix.

Il Nyaya Sutra di Gautama. Arena, Leonardo Vittorio.

Inventing the Universe: Plato's Timaeus, The Big Bang, and the Problem of Scientific Knowledge. Brisson, Luc and Meyerstein, F Walter.

Kant's Idealism. Neujahr, Philip J.

Leibniz and the Rational Order of Nature. Rutherford, Donald.

Making Sense of Humanity and Other Philosophical Papers 1982-1993. Williams, Bernard.

Mapping the Human Genome: Reality, Morality, and Deity. Kent, Theodore C.

Mental Content. McGinn, Colin.

Mental Reality. Strawson, Galen.

Nietzsche e il Nonsense. Arena, Leonardo Vittorio.

Parts of Classes. Lewis, David.

Phänomenale Realität und Erkenntnis: Umrisse einer Theorie im Ausgang von der eigentümlichen Natur des Qualia-Begriffs. Pohlenz, Gerd.

Roots of Wisdom: Speaking the Language of Philosophy. Mitchell, Helen Buss.

Science, Reality, and Language. Marsonet, Michele.

The Metamorphosis of the Given: Toward an Ecology of Consciousness. Schwarzkopf, Friedemann-Eckart.

The Production of Space. Lefebvre, Henri and Nicholson-Smith, Donald (trans).

Understanding History: An Introduction to Analytical Philosophy of History. Gorman, Jonathan.

Ways of Worldmaking. Goodman, Nelson.

Writings on Logic and Metaphysics. Bradley, F H, Allard, James W (ed) and Stock, Guy (ed).

A Contemporary Challenge to Religion: The Question of Eternity. Lowry, Atherton C.

A Dualistic Model of Ultimate Reality and Meaning: Self-Similarity in Chaotic Dynamics and Swedenborg. Baker, Gregory L.

A New Challenge for the Physicalist: Indistinguishability. Lahav, Ran.

A Search for Ultimate Reality and Meaning in a Universe of Possibilities. Tallet, J A.

Aesthetic Order. Haines, Victor Yelverton.

Appunti di Lettura sul Cartesianesimo Napoletano tra '600 e '700. Cantillo, Clementina.

Art and Reality. Dilman, Ilham.

B-Series Temporal Order in Dogen's Theory of Time. Vorenkamp, Dirck.

Bradley's Regress, the Copula and the Unity of the Proposition. Gaskin, Richard.

British Hegelianism: A Non-Metaphysical View?. Stern, Robert.

Browning's Ontology. Van de Vate, Dwight.

Cognitive and Communicative Development in Reality Free Representation. Dietrich, O.

Comentario kafkiano en torno a la obra *Realidad y Verdad* de Antonio Pintor-Ramos. Wessell, L P.

Comment on Professor Johnson's Article on Computer Language. Sundararajan, Louise.

Comments on Smolarski's 'Finding Meaning in Mathematics'. Johnson, Julia A.

Crítica y Defensa de lo Existente. Referencias de la Filosofía a la Realidad. Estudio Sobre la Filosofía Hegeliana del Derecho. Sandkühler, Hans Jörg.

Critique of Pure Capacity. Segerdahl, Pär.

Deflating "the Real": Project for a Metaphysical Reconstruction of Time. Calore, Gary.

Der Begriff der Ironie und die Kunsttheorie des frühen Friedrich Schlegels (in Japanese). Ogawa, Nobuko.

Der Übergang von der *Grundlage* zur *Wissenschaftslehre nova methodo*. Radrizzani, Ives.

Descartes und der Traumskeptizismus. Imlay, Robert A.

Die Realität der Idee. de Vos, L.

Die Unterscheidung der Realität in Fichtes *Wissenschaftslehre* von 1794. Jürgensen, Sven.

Disambiguation of Language: The Ultimate Reality and Meaning of Computer Studies. Johnson, Julia A.

Double's *The Non-Reality of Free Will*. Kapitan, Tomis.

Ecology and Globalism: Response to Professor E H Cadwallader's Paper 'Ultimate Meaning and Reality in the Battle Between Globalism and Anti-Globalism. Kristiansen, Roald E.

El Principio de Causalidad en la *Tercera* Meditación. Chávez-Arvizo, Enrique.

Experiences in the Cave, the Closet, and the Vat—and in Bed. Stevenson, Leslie F.

Finding Meaning in Mathematics. Smolarski, Dennis C.

Historia de la Filosofía e Historia: Notas Para un Debate. Sanz, Víctor.

Historical Knowledge and Historical Reality: A Plea for "Internal Realism". Lorenz, Chris.

Hume's Pragmaticist Argument for the Reality of God. Beach, Dennis (trans) and Deuser, Hermann.

I principi matematici kantiani del mondo fisico. Pellecchia, Pasquale.

Il Problema del Mito nel Dialogo Bultmann-Jaspers. Donadio, Francesco.

Is Gerwin's Natural-Agency Theory a Viable Alternative to Hume?. Ward, Andrew.

Just the Facts. Oberdiek, Hans F.

Kant and Analogy: Categories as Analogical Equivocals. Ess, Charles M and Gulick, Walter B.

Kant's Doctrine of the Categories: Some Problems. Krishna, Daya.

Kant's Ideas About Ultimate Reality and Meaning in Relation to His Moral Theory: Critique of an Enlightenment Ideal. Crosby, Donald A.

Karl Marx und die soziale Wirklichkeit. Epple, Moritz.

La Percepción Jeráquica de la Realidad. Sánchez del Rio, Carlos.

Langer, Language, and Art. Gill, Jerry H.

Las apariencias en Vladimir Jankélévitch. Trejos, Susana.

Lo spiritualismo indiano antico: Echi egizi nelle Upanisad. Masi, Giuseppe.

Logos y realidad (Evocación de Hegel). Blanco, José.

Metafisica e *Archè*, nel Pensiero Greco più Antico: Causalità e Temporalità in Quanto Categorie Presocratiche. Zeppi, Stelio.

Michael Faraday's Concept of Ultimate Reality and Meaning. Utke, Allen R.

Mirror of Consciousness. Gupta, R K.

New Work for Counterpart Theorists: Determinism. Belot, Gordon.

On Artifacts and Works of Art. Hilpinen, Risto.

Philosophy and Science in Jan Lukasiewicz (in Italian). Coniglione, Francesco.

Plotinus and the Neoplatonic Conception of Dialectic. Anton, John P.

Positivismo e Metafisica in Russia in uno Scritto di Vladimir Solov'ev. Mastroianni, Giovanni.

Pretend Play: Is It Metarepresentational?. Jarrold, Chris (& others).

Razón e Intelecto en Boecio. Lluch-Baixauli, Miguel.

Real Essences in Particular. Phemister, Pauline.

Realismo sin Empirismo. Defez i Martín, Antoni.

Realität und System: Das Realitätsproblem in Fichtes Theorie der Fünffachheit. Traub, Hartmut.

Realität und Tätigkeit im ersten Teil von Fichtes *Grundlage*, beurteilt aus der Sicht Whiteheads. Krämer, Felix.

Reason and Reality. Rescher, Nicholas.

Reason and the Real. Burbidge, John W.

Scienza del Mito e Critica Letteraria: Conoscere per Composizione. Cottone, Margherita.

Simbolización Lingüística de la Realidad. Chamizo Domínquez, Pedro José.

The Existential Perspective of Language and Meaning. Pal, Santosh Kumar.

The Idea of Eternal Life in Modern Cosmology: Its Ultimate Reality and Metaethical Meaning. Nesteruk, Alexei V.

The Ideality of Time. Frangiotti, Marco Antonio.

The Layers of Artistic Illusion. Perricone, Christopher.

The Metaphoric Origins of Objectivity, Subjectivity, and Consciousness in the Direct Perception of Reality. Mulaik, Stanley A.

The Original Version of Process and Reality, Part V: A Tentative Reconstruction. Hurtubise, Denis.

The Problem of Ultimate Reality and Meaning in the Context of Information Self-Organization and Isotopic Diversity. Berezin, Alexander A.

The Relativity of Scientific Views of Reality. Puligandla, Ramakrishna.

The Religion of a Scientist: Explorations into Reality (*Religio philosophi naturalis*). Peacocke, Arthur.

The Riddle of *Religion in the Making*. Ford, Lewis S.

The Virgin Paradigm. Sawaf, Ayman.

The Way to Ultimate Meaning in Meister Eckhart's Mysticism. Kovacs, George.

The World and 'I'. Phillips, D Z.

Theravada Buddhism and the Definition of Religion. Smart, Ninian.

Truth, Knowledge, and Reality. Lafont, Cristina.

Two Ways of Coming Back to Reality: Kierkegaard and Lukács. Hannay, Alastair.

Unsettled Problems with Vague Truth. Mills, Andrew.

Vlastos on a Metaphysical Paradox. Code, Alan D.

Wallace Stevens and Metaphysics: The Plain Sense of Things. Gardner, Sebastian.

What Can We Learn From the Paradox of Knowability?. Cozzo, Cesare.

Why the World Cannot be Vague. Sainsbury, Mark.

REALIZABILITY

Axiomatizing Higher-Order Kleene Realizability. Van Oosten, Jaap.

Strictly Primitive Recursive Realizability, I. Damnjanovic, Zlatan.

REALIZATION

see Self-Realization

REASON

REFORM

"The Autonomous Chooser and 'Reforms' in Education" in *Identity, Culture, and Education, Smeyers, Paul (ed)*. Marshall, James.

"The Moral Justification of Systematic Education Reform in the United States" in *Identity, Culture, and Education, Smeyers, Paul (ed)*. Bull, Barry.

Current Educational Reform: "Shape-shifting" or Genuine Improvement in the Quality of Teaching and Learning?. Merchant, Betty.

The Ethical Challenge of Providing Healthcare for the Elderly. Thomasma, David C.

REFORMATION

Reformation Thought: An Introduction (Second Edition). McGrath, Alister E.

Roger Bacon (1214-94): Ética y Reforma. Boadas-Llavat, Agustí.

REFRAINING

Doing and Refraining from Refraining. Xu, Ming.

REFUGEE

Asylum: A Moral Dilemma. Plaut, W Gunther.

REFUSAL

Can A Patient Refuse a Psychiatric Consultation to Evaluate Decision-Making Capacity?. Wenger, Neil S and Halpern, Jodi.

REFUSAL OF TREATMENT

Challenging Medical Authority: The Refusal of Treatment by Christian Scientists. May, Larry.

Distinguishing between Patients' Refusals and Requests. Gert, Bernard, Bernat, James L and Mogielnicki, R Peter.

REFUTATION

Hintikka Formulas as Axioms of Refutation Calculus, a Case Study. Inoué, Takao.

On the Atomic Formula Property of Härtig's Refutation Calculus. Inoué, Takao.

Syntactic Refutations against Finite Models in Modal Logic. Skura, Tomasz.

REGAN, T

Tom Regan's Seafaring Dog and (Un)Equal Inherent Worth. Edwards, Rem B.

REGIUS, H

Regius's *Fundamenta Physices*. Verbeek, Theo.

REGULAR

On Some Operators on Pseudovarieties II. Graczynska, Ewa.

REGULARITY

Regularity Properties for Dominating Projective Sets. Brendle, Jörg.

REGULATION

"Acerca de la Distinción entre Reglas Constitutivas y Reglas Regulativas" in *Temas Actuales de Filosofía, Palacios, María Julia (ed)*. Gentile, Nélida.

No Harm: Ethical Principles for a Free Market. Burke, T Patrick.

Reason, Regulation, and Realism: Toward a Regulatory Systems Theory of Reason and Evolutionary Epistemology. Hooker, C A.

Zur Regulation der "Harmonia": Der Regelkreis als Modell ganzheitlicher Organisation unter dem Aspekt des Bewusstseins. Düll, Rupprecht.

Bentham: la ciencia del legislador. Bermudo Avila, José Manuel.

Ethics and the Law: US Supreme Court Rulings on the Solicitation of Clients. Mintz, Steven M and Moffeit, Katherine S.

Learning from the Law for Regulatory Science. Cranor, Carl F.

On Costs, Benefits, and Regulatory Success: Reply to Crandall. Sunstein, Cass R.

Systemic Rationality and the Effects of Financial Regulation: Rejoinder to Kindleberger. Horwitz, Steven.

To Be or Not to Be: Waiving Informed Consent in Emergency Research. McCarthy, Charles R.

REHABILITATION

"Rehabilitating Nature and Making Nature Habitable" in *Philosophy and the Natural Environment, Attfield, Robin (ed)*. Attfield, Robin.

Punishment and the Death Penalty: The Current Debate. Baird, Robert M (ed) and Rosenbaum, Stuart E (ed).

Rehabilitación de Galileo?. Ponferrada, Gustavo Eloy.

REICHENBACH

"Reichenbach Falls (Or Only Stumbles?)" in *American Philosophy Today and Other Philosophical Studies, Rescher, Nicholas*. Rescher, Nicholas.

Certainty. Westphal, Jonathan (ed).

A Note on Von Bretzel's Solution to an Alleged Problem with Reichenbach's Definition of Time Direction. Paprzycka, Katarzyna.

Spacetime Theory as Physical Geometry. Disalle, Robert.

The Speed-Optimality of Reichenbach's Straight Rule of Induction. Juhl, Cory F.

Time Direction, Philosophy of Technology, and Technology Assessment. Tondl, Ladislav.

Weyl, Reichenbach and the Epistemology of Geometry. Ryckman, Thomas A.

'Coordinative Definition' and Reichenbach's Semantic Framework: A Reassessment. Shapiro, Lionel Stefan.

REID

"Hume, Reid and the Science of the Mind" in *Hume and Hume's Connexions, Stewart, M A (ed)*. Wood, P B.

Reid and His French Disciples: Aesthetics and Metaphysics. Manns, James W.

Reid's Critique of Berkeley and Hume: What's the Big Idea?. Greco, John.

Thomas Reid and the Justification of Induction. Anstey, Peter.

Thomas Reid on Free Agency. O'Connor, Timothy.

REIMAN, J

Strengthening Social Contract Theory: *Justice and Modern Moral Philosophy*, by Jeffrey Reiman. Morrisey, Will.

REIMER, B

Aesthetic Music Education Revisited: Discourses of Exclusion and Oppression. Koza, Julia Eklund.

REINACH, A

"Edith Stein und Adolf Reinach" in *Studien zur Philosophie von Edith Stein, Fetz, Reto Luzius (ed)*. Schuhmann, Karl.

REINCARNATION

see Immortality, Rebirth

REINHOLD

Das Anfangsproblem bei Karl Leonhard Reinhold. Bondeli, Martin.

Das Programm des methodologischen Monismus Subjekttheoretische und methodologische Aspekte der Elementarphilosophie K L Reinholds. Stamm, Marcelo.

Las Tres Reseñas de Fichte del Otoño de 1793. Serrano, Vicente.

Rückkehr zur Metaphysik? Reinholds Abkehr von der Philosophie Fichtes. Aschoff, Frank.

Selbstbewusstsein: Ein Problem der Philosophie nach Kant. *Zum Verhältnis Reinhold-Hölderlin-Fichte*. Stolzenberg, Jürgen.

REISM

Contrarréplica a una Valoración Sobre mi Crítica al Realismo Radical de Xavier Zubiri. Wessell Jr, Leonard P.

RELATEDNESS

Semantics for First Degree Relatedness Logic. Paoli, Francesco.

RELATION

see also International Relation, Social Relations

-Completeness of a Fragment of the Theory of Trees with Subtree Relation. Cintioli, P and Tulipani, S.

Einführung in die Logik. Menne, Albert.

Quid sit natura prius? La conception leibnizienne de l'ordre. Rauzy, Jean-Baptiste.

A Note on Anti-Cyclic Properties of Complete Binary Relations. Hansson, Sven Ove.

Correspondances Philosophiques et Techniques Argumentatives au XVIIe Siècle. Abiteboul, Olivier.

Fine-Grained Opinion, Probability, and the Logic of Full Belief. Van Fraassen, Bas C.

Fork Algebras are Representable. Frias, Marcelo F, Baum, Gabriel A and Haeberer, Armando M.

From Ternary to Tetrary?. Vasyukov, Vladimir L.

Orden, Desorden, Azar. Bolzán, Juan Enrique and Larre, Olga L.

Pi^1_1 Wellfounded Relations. Hjorth, Greg.

Relational Attributes in Aristotle. Morales, Fabio.

Representations for Small Relation Algebras. Andréka, Hajnal and Maddux, Roger D.

Simple Termination of Rewrite Systems. Middeldorp, Aart and Zantema, Hans.

The Consistency Strength of an Infinitary Ramsey Property. Kafkoulis, George.

The First-Order Coding of Models in Models with a Single Binary Relation. Pazdyka, Pawel.

The Topological Vaught's Conjecture and Minimal Counterexamples. Becker, Howard.

Un ensayo de recomposición del protagorismo. Solana Dueso, José.

RELATIONAL

Beniaminov Algebras Revised: One More Algebraic Version of First-Order Logic. Cirulis, Janis.

RELATIONSHIP

"How Do You Catch a Cloud and Pin It Down?" (With Apologies to Rogers and Hammerstein): A Commentary on Layson and Colleagues. Povar, Gail J.

"Love and Personal Relationships" in *Introducing Applied Ethics, Almond, Brenda (ed)*. Gregory, Paul.

Relationship Morality. Kellenberger, J.

Confucian Moral Thinking. Lai, Karyn L.

Relations with Others in Sartre and Levinas: Assessing Some Implications for an Ethics of Proximity. Vetlesen, Arne Johan.

Tests of the Causal Directions of.Global-Life Facet Satisfaction Relationships. Lance, Charles E, Mallard, Alison G and Michalos, Alex C.

The Energetics of Spirituality and Human Sexuality. Kidd, James W and Zonneveld, Leo W.

Whose Patient Am I, Anyway?. Gorovitz, Samuel.

RELATIVISM

see also Cultural Relativism, Ethical Relativism

"Cultural Relativism and Universal Human Rights?" in *Human Rights and Religious Values, An-Na'im, Abdullahi A (& other eds)*. Droogers, André F.

"Esquemas Conceptuales: Relativismo y Ontología" in *Temas Actuales de Filosofía, Palacios, María Julia (ed)*. Rabossi, Eduardo.

"Reliability, Realism, and Relativism" in *Reading Putnam, Clark, Peter (ed)*. Kelly, Kevin, Juhl, Cory and Glymour, Clark.

Das Jenseits der Philosophie: Wider das dualistische Erkenntnisprinzip. Mitterer, Josef and Engelmann, Peter (ed).

Ethical Argument: Critical Thinking in Ethics. Curtler, Hugh Mercer.

Ethical Judgment: The Use of Science in Ethics. Edel, Abraham.

Moral Theory: A Contemporary Overview. DeMarco, Joseph P.

Morality, Normativity, and Society. Copp, David.

Reading Putnam. Clark, Peter (ed) and Hale, Bob (ed).

The Boundaries of Moral Discourse. Hajdin, Mane.

The Ends of Philosophy. Cahoone, Lawrence E.

The Philosophy of Social Science: An Introduction. Hollis, Martin.

The Truth About Relativism. Margolis, Joseph.

Truth: A Primer. Schmitt, Frederick F.

What is This Thing Called Science? (Second Edition). Chalmers, A F.

Without God or His Doubles: Realism, Relativism and Rorty. Vaden House, David.

Ciencia y relativismo cognitivo: una crítica del pragmatismo. Cassini, Alejandro.

Communicative Universals. Mihayara, Isamu.

Cultural Relativism: Some Comments. Otakpor, Nkeonye.

RELIGION

RELIGION

John Paul II's Manifesto on Labor and Vision of a Universal Society. Kuczynski, Janusz.

John Poinsot on Created Eternal Truths vs Vasquez, Suárez and Descartes. Wells, Norman J.

John Poinsot on How To Be, Know, and Love a Non-Existent Possible. Coombs, Jeffrey.

Judaism, Christianity, Islam and Universalism. Krajewski, Stanislaw.

Just War in the Balkans?. Quirk, Michael J.

Justice and Mercy: A Reply to Thomas Talbott. Holyer, Robert.

Justice: An Inter-Faith Task. Pattery, George.

Kann die Theologie der naturwissenschaftlichen Vernunft die Welt Is Schöpfung verständlich machen?. Fischer, Johannes.

Kant: La Religión como *Veneración Moral Pura de Dios*. Jimenez, Jose D.

Karol Wojtyla—John Paul II's Idea of Ultimate Reality and Meaning. Ramos, Alice.

Kierkegaard and the Feminine Self. Howe, Leslie A.

Kierkegaard and the Historians. Rae, Murray A.

Kierkegaard on Authority and Leadership: Political Logic in Religious Thought. Khan, Abrahim H.

Kierkegaardian Suspicion and Properly Basic Beliefs. Williams, Clifford.

Knowledge and Truth in Religious Education. Carr, David.

La "clef" de Job—Pascal: la liberté/le mal. Leduc-Fayette, Denise.

La actualización en la enseñanza de la moral propuesta por la Veritatis Splendor. Alonso, Luz García.

La antropología prospectiva tomista. Castello Dubra, Julio A.

La Belleza como Camino Hacia Dios (Santo Tomás de Aquino). Schmidt Andrade, Ciro E.

La Catégorie Pascalienne de l'Hérésie. Leduc-Fayette, Denise.

La Estética del Romanticismo y su Análisis Dentro de la Filosofía Existencial (Kierkegaard y Dostoievsky). Rendón Rojas, Miguel Angel.

La filosofia cristiana secondo Edith Stein. Tilliette, Xavier.

La notion de Samskara. Chenet, François.

La Ontología de Lessing y las Metáforas de la Deshumanización. Andreu, Agustín.

La Pensée Comme Rédemption. Marcondes Cesar, Constança.

La Problématique de Denys sur Dieu: Théologie ou Philosophie?. Koutlouka, Maria.

La Prospettiva Religiosa di Augusto Guzzo. Mathieu, Vittorio.

La Razón y lo Sagrado: Respuesta a Jacinto Choza. Arana, Juan.

La Relación Entre la Metafísica y la Teología en San Alberto Magno y Santo Tomás de Aquino. Andereggen, Ignacio E M.

La Religión y el Mal: Gnosticismo y Satanismo. Bravo, Elia Nathan.

La Riflessione sul Mito in Leopardi. Stella, Vittorio.

La risposta di S Agostino alle critiche contro il cristianesimo. De Falco, Enrico.

La Spécificité de la Conception Spinoziste de l'Eternité de l'Esprit. Jacquet, Chantal.

La Ténèbre chez Denys: Sources du Chapître I de la *Théologie Mystique*. Gobry, Ivan.

La Théologie Apophatique de Denys et la Théodicée de Leibniz. Gabaude, Jean-Marc.

Language, Communication, and Representation in the Semiotic of John Poinsot. Murphy, James B.

Le Combat de Kierkegaard. Grelot, Pierre.

Le Discours de la Théologie Face à L'Indicible chez Denys. Lang, Démètre.

Le problème de la connaissance dans la doctrine philosophique de Fr H Jacobi (II). Strauss, Leo, Hartje, Hans (trans) and Guglielmina, Pierre (trans).

Leaps and Circles: Kierkegaard and Newman on Faith and Reason. Ferreira, M Jamie.

Leibniz on Cartesian Omnipotence and Contingency. Werther, David.

Leibniz on Divine Foreknowledge. Sleigh, Robert.

Leibniz on Divine Foreknowledge of Future Contingents and Human Freedom. Murray, Michael J.

Leibniz's "Examination of the Christian Religion". Adams, Robert Merrihew.

Lenguaje religioso y racionalidad argumentativa. Ortiz, Gustavo.

Liberal Civic Education and Religious Fundamentalism: The Case of God v. John Rawls?. Macedo, Stephen.

Liberalism, Pluralism, and Lived Faith. Hart, Hendrick.

Liberalism, Religion, and Politics Again: A Reply to Gordon Graham. Van Wyk, Robert N.

Liberating Dialogue: An Indian Perspective. Wilfred, Felix.

Líneas de Pensamiento Positivista y Antipositista en América. Romero Baró, José María.

Living in Two Worlds: A Personal Appraisal. Ching, Julia.

Locke's 'Observations' on Boyle. Stewart, M A.

Logique théologique et logique systémique: Dialogue avec Edgar Morin. Kraege, Jean-Denis.

Lonergan on Consciousness: Is There a Fifth Level?. Vertin, Michael.

Lonergan's "Philosophy and the Religious Phenomenon": A Commentary. Crysdale, Cynthia S W.

Lonergan's Universalist View of Religion. Crowe, Frederick E.

Loving God *and* One's Neighbor: Thomistic Charity. Adams, Don.

Lumière et Ténèbre chez Denys. Palamiotou, Constantina.

Mackie's Paradox and the Free Will Defence. Khamara, Edward J.

Mal y Muerte: Notas Sobre los Apologistas. Cercós Soto, José.

Malebranche and Arnauld on Ideas. Watson, Richard A.

Martin Heidegger's Catholic Origins. Ott, Hugo.

Marx, Moses, and the Pagans in the Secular City. Sunic, Tomislav.

Materials for an Analysis of a Just Universe. Herman, Arthur L.

Max Scheler's Practical Ethics and the Model Person. Spader, Peter.

Max Weber und das Problem der Weltanschauung. Rossi, Pietro.

Max Weber y la racionalización, desmagificación y remagificación del mundo. Prado, José Hernández.

Meanings and Ways of Reconciliation. Przelecki, Marian.

Mechthild von Magdeburg und der frühe Meister Eckhart. Weiss, Bardo.

Medalist's Address. Dougherty, Jude P.

Metaphysics and Phenomenology: A Relief for Theology. Carlson, Thomas A (trans) and Marion, Jean-Luc.

Métaphysique de l'être et théologie de la grâce dans le médiévalisme contemporain: É Gilson et M D Chenu entre H Bergson et A Gardeil. Conticello, C G.

Method in Catholic Theology. Lonergan, Bernard J F.

Middle Knowledge and Christian Exclusivism. Craig, William Lane.

Molina on Divine Foreknowledge and the Principle of Bivalence. Gaskin, Richard.

Monism and Pluralism. Krapiec, Mieczyslaw Albert.

Moral Content, Tradition, and Grace: Rethinking the Possibility of a Christian Bioethics. Engelhardt Jr, H Tristram.

Moral Faith. Adams, Robert Merrihew.

Moral Provincialism. Kent, Bonnie.

Moral Values and the Taoist Sage in the *Tao de Ching*. Allinson, Robert E.

Mystery and Explanation in Aquinas's Account of Creation. Liccione, Michael.

Narrative, Irony, and Faith in Gibbon's *Decline and Fall*. Wootton, David.

Nature as the Image of God: Reflections on the Signs of the Sacred. Gilkey, Langdon.

Néant Divin et Théophanie: Erigène Disciple de Denys. Jeauneau, Édouard.

Necessary Beings. Steinitz, Yuval.

Neoplatonism in Christianity, Judaism and Islam. Harris, R Baine.

Neotomismo a Salerno: L'Ambiente Culturale in cui visse ed Operò Pasquale Naddeo. Gigante, Mario.

New Perspectives on Teilhard Publications. Schmitz-Moormann, Nicole.

Nietzsche, Hebraism, Hellenism. Cohen, Martin.

Nietzsche: *Das religiöse Wesen*. Rethy, Robert A.

Nondoxastic Faith: Audi on Religious Commitment. Radcliffe, Dana M.

Noospheric Synarchy: From an Ancient Hellenic Democracy to the Aristocracy of Spirit. Gromow, Ivan G and Kuvakina, Olga D.

Nota Sobre la Poesía Algorítmica de Ramón Llull. Lizalde, Carlos Lorenza.

Of Angels, Oysters, and an Unchanging God: Aquinas on Divine Immutability. Dodds, Michael J.

Omnipotence and the Transfer of Power. Glannon, Walter.

Omnipotence, Feminism, and God. Byrne, Peter.

On "Divine Simplicity: A New Defense". Miller, Barry.

On a Mistake Commonly Made in Accounts of Sixteenth-Century Discussions of the Immortality of the Soul. Martin, Christopher.

On Calling God 'Mother'. Harper, William.

On Giving Practice Its Due—A Reply. Phillips, D Z.

On Heidegger's Other Sins of Omission: Asian Thought and Christian Philosophy. Bernasconi, Robert.

On Leszek Kolakowski's Philosophizing. Morawski, Stefan.

On Neitzsche's Enigmatic Anti-Kantian Categorical Imperative. Hodge, Roger D.

On Not Confusing Necessity With Compulsion: A Reply to Paul Helm. Brümmer, Vincent.

On Pascal's Wager and Infinite Utilities. Byl, John.

On Property Self-Exemplification: Rejoinder to Miller. Vallicella, William F.

On Some Paradigms of Ecumenical Dialogue. Toeplitz, Karol.

On the Metaphysical Foundations of Neo- and New Confucianism: Reflections on Lauren Pfister's Essay on Religious Confucianism. Ivanhoe, Philip J.

On the Radical Distinction between the *Krsna* and the *Sukla Yajurveda* and *Professor Heesterman's Remarks Thereon*. Krishna, Daya.

On the Theological Roots of Spinoza's Argument for Monism. Carriero, John.

One of These Mornings I'm Going to Rise Up Singing: The Necessity of the Prophetic Voice in Jewish Bioethics. Zoloth-Dorfman, Laurie.

Oportet Philosophari in Theologia (I). Fisichella, Rino.

Origenes and Numenios. Somos, Róbert.

Otto's Idea of the 'Numinous': A Crosscultural Reappraisal. O'Meley, Serena.

Pascal on Certainty and Utility. McCarthy, John C.

Paths to Perfection: Yoga and Confucian. Podgorski, Frank R.

Peer Pressure and Children's Religious Belief. Howe, Norma.

Peirce's Agape and the Generality of Concern. Anderson, Douglas R.

Pensare la religione: Modelli di filosofia della religione a confronto. Fabris, Adriano.

Per un Servizio Sapienziale della Filosofia nella Chiesa. Sánchez Sorondo, Marcello.

Perception and Mystical Experience. Pappas, George S.

Perceptual Experience, Doxastic Practice, and the Rationality of Religious Commitment. Audi, Robert.

Person as Narration: The Dissolution of 'Self' and 'Other' in Ch'an Buddhism. Hershock, Peter D.

Personalist and Universalistic Aspects of the Idea of Development in the Encyclical *Sollicitudo rei socialis* by John Paul II. Kowalczyk, Stanislaw.

Perspectivism: Aquinas and Nietzsche on Intellect and Will. Thompson, Walter J.

Philosophy and the Religious Phenomenon. Lonergan, Bernard J F.

Platonism as a Common Element of Different Religious Axiologies. Przelecki, Marian.

Pluralisme et théologisme, Deux aspects doctrinaux de la correspondance Gilson-Labourdette. Bonino, Serge-Thomas.

Poinsot on Knowability of Beings of Reason. Doyle, John P.

Poinsot on the Semiotics of Awareness. Raposa, Michael.

Points of Convergence between Judaism, Christianity and Islam. Eboh, Marie Pauline.

Por qué son necesariamente inútiles las virtudes específicamente religiosas?. Sastre, Gerardo López.

Post-Hegelian Elements in Lonergan's Philosophy of Religion. Morelli, Elizabeth.

Postmodern Theology After the Decline of the Mastery Story of Christianity, Inspired by Lyotard's Critical Theory of Postmodernity (in Dutch). Boeve, Lieven.

RELIGION

REPRESENTATION

Was ist Wahrnehmung?. Ziemke, Axel.

Wittgenstein on Mind and Language. Stern, David G.

Análisis gnoseológico de la psicología cognitiva. Blanco Martín, Carlos J.

Consciousness: A Connectionist Manifesto. Lloyd, Dan.

Das Problem der Gewaltenteilung bei Rousseau und Fichte. Schottky, Richard.

Doing without Representing?. Clark, Andy and Toribio, Josefa.

Field or Print. Groenewold, Hip.

Husserl and Goodman on the Role of Resemblance in Pictorial Representation. Drost, Mark P.

Intention and Representation: Searle's 'Internal' Thesis. Goodrich, R A.

Judgments as Meta-Representations in the *Critique of Pure Reason*. Cuonzo, Margaret.

Kendall L Walton's *Mimesis as Make-Believe*. Carroll, Noël.

L'impossible naturalisme de la psychosémantique de Fodor. Cuypers, Stefaan E.

Language, Communication, and Representation in the Semiotic of John Poinsot. Murphy, James B.

Le Paradigme Esthétique. Roumanes, Jacques Bernard.

Le Problème de l'Architecture dans le Débat entre l'Approche Connexionniste et les Approches "Classiques" de la Représentation. Lacharité, Normand.

Messages in Art. Levinson, Jerrold.

Messages 'In' and Messages 'Through' Art. Novitz, David.

Nonconceptual Content: Kinds, Rationales and Relations. Peacocke, Christopher.

Peacocke's Argument Against the Autonomy of Nonconceptual Representational Content. Bermúdez, José Luis.

Pictorial Realism. Lopes, Dominic.

Power Set Recursion. Moss, Lawrence S.

Pretend Play: Is It Metarepresentational?. Jarrold, Chris (& others).

Projected Actuality. Williams, Quentin.

Realisme zonder representatie. Slors, Marc.

Relativism Hot and Cold. Turner, Stephen.

Representation and the Imperfect Ideal. Wallis, Charles.

Representation(s). Rheinberger, Hans-Jörg.

Representation, Self-Representation, and the Passions in Descartes. Schmitter, Amy Morgan.

Representation, Similarity, and the Chorus of Prototypes. Edelman, Shimon.

Representational Trajectories in Connectionist Learning. Clark, Andy.

Representations for Small Relation Algebras. Andréka, Hajnal and Maddux, Roger D.

Representations versus Regularities: Does Computation Require Representation?. Bailey, Andrew.

Scare Quoted "Seeing". Slater, Hartley.

Some Considerations on the Status of the Psychic in "Freudian" Project (in Portuguese). Milidoni, Carmen Beatriz.

Systematicity Revisited: Reply to Chater and Christiansen and Niklasson and Van Gelder. Hadley, Robert F.

The Aesthetic Value of Representation in Painting. Goldman, Alan H.

Transcendental Idealism and Phenomenalism. Frangiotti, Marco Antonio.

What is Wrong with an Atomistic Account of Mental Representation?. Hogan, Melinda.

What What It's Like is Really Like. Tye, Michael.

REPRESENTATIONALISM

Beyond Representationalism: Ontological Alternatives in Heidegger and Lonergan. Kililis, George.

Simetrías versus leyes? Apostilla a Van Fraassen sobre la representación. Ibarra, Andoni and Mormann, Thomas.

Spiegeln Ideen die Natur? Zum Begriff der Repräsentation bei Descartes. Perler, Dominik.

REPRODUCTION

The Constructed Body: AIDS, Reproductive Technology, and Ethics. Murphy, Julien S.

Bioethics and Family Values. Almond, Brenda.

Biomedical Models of Reproduction in the Fifth Century BC and Aristotle's *Generation of Animals*. Coles, Andrew.

Ethics in a Bicultural Context. Campbell, Alastair V.

Infertility Treatment for Postmenopausal Patients: An Equity-Based Approach. Purviance, Susan M.

Norplant and Irresponsible Reproduction. Robertson, John A.

Parenting Ethics and Reproductive Technologies. Hartwig, Michael J.

Private Bioethics Forums: Counterpoint to Government Bodies. Cohen, Cynthia B and McCloskey, Elizabeth Leibold.

Reproduction and Ontology in Lukács (in Portuguese). Lessa, Sergio.

Reproductive Responsibility and Long-Acting Contraceptives. Arras, John D and Blustein, Jeffrey.

Reproductive Technologies in Developing Countries. Macklin, Ruth.

The Ethics of Babymaking. Sherwin, Susan.

REPUBLIC

Frammenti Politici di Antonio Labriola con una Postilla Bibliografica. Miccolis, Stefano.

Francia, Spagna e Portogallo: Le Monarchie Europee "Qui Vont au Despotisme" Secondo Montesquieu. Felice, Domenico.

REPUBLICANISM

Liberale Integrität. Rinderle, Peter.

Nationalisme versus republikeinse burgerschapszin. Van Erp, Herman.

Philosophical Republicanism and Monarchism—and Republican and Monarchical Philosophy—in Kant and Hegel. Redding, Paul.

Reading Machiavelli: Innocent Gentillet's Discourse on Method. Kahn, Victoria.

Response to Spitz's "The Concept of Liberty in 'A Theory of Justice' and Its Republican Version". Swift, Adam.

The Concept of Liberty in "A Theory of Justice" and Its Republican Version. Spitz, Jean-Fabien.

RESCHER, N

"Peirce on the Reliability of Science: A Response to Rescher" in *Peirce and Contemporary Thought: Philosophical Inquiries, Ketner, Kenneth Laine (ed)*. Delaney, Cornelius J.

RESEARCH

"A Mediational Model of Research Artifacts" in *Probability in Theory-Building, Brzezinski, Jerzy (ed)*. Strohmetz, David B and Rosnow, Ralph L.

"Contrast Analysis in Behavioral Research" in *Probability in Theory-Building, Brzezinski, Jerzy (ed)*. Koutstaal, Wilma and Rosenthal, Robert.

"Ethical Considerations in Genetic Testing" in *Medicine and Moral Reasoning, Fulford, K W M (ed)*. Brandt, Jason.

"Human In-vitro Fertilization" in *Ethics on the Frontiers of Human Existence, Badham, Paul (ed)*. Fishel, Simon.

"On Writing Philosophy" in *American Philosophy Today and Other Philosophical Studies, Rescher, Nicholas*. Rescher, Nicholas.

(Re)searching Dewey for Feminist Imaginaries: Linguistic Continuity, Discourse and Gossip. Leach, Mary.

Ethics of Scientific Research. Shrader-Frechette, Kristin.

For Education: Towards Critical Educational Inquiry. Carr, Wilfred.

Humane Medicine: A Leading Surgeon Examines What Doctors Do, What Their Patients Expect from Them, and How the Expectations of Both Are Not Being Met. Little, Miles.

Medicine and Moral Reasoning. Fulford, K W M (ed), Gillett, Grant (ed) and Soskice, Janet Martin (ed).

Openness in Research: The Tension Between Self and Other. Maso, I (& other eds).

A Desperate Solution: Individual Autonomy and the Double-Blind Controlled Experiment. Logue, Gerald and Wear, Stephen.

Alternativen der Wissenschaftsgeschichte. Haney, Frank.

Animal Concepts: Content and Discontent. Chater, Nick and Heyes, Cecilia.

Art as Research, Research as Art. Phillips, D C.

Assessing the Application of Cognitive Moral Development Theory to Business Ethics. Fraedrich, John, Thorne, Debbie M and Ferrell, O C.

At the Vortex of Controversy: Developing Guidelines for Human Embryo Research. Green, Ronald M.

Awe Diminished. Campbell, Courtney S.

Before I Was an Embryo, I Was a Pre-Embryo: Or Was I?. Jones, D Gareth and Telfer, Barbara.

Children's Capacity to Agree to Psychological Research: Knowledge of Risks and Benefits and Voluntariness. Abramovitch, Rona (& others).

Clinical Practice Guidelines as Tools of Public Policy: Conflicts among Purpose, Issues of Autonomy, and Justice. Redman, Barbara K.

Coercion and Long-Term Contraceptives. Steinbock, Bonnie.

Commerce and Genetic Diagnostics. Silverman, Paul H.

Contraceptive Policy and Ethics: Illustrations from American History. Powderly, Kathleen E.

Deceived Versus Nondeceived Participants' Perceptions of Scientific and Applied Psychology. Soliday, Elizabeth and Stanton, Annette L.

Deception Methods in Psychology: Have They Changed in 23 Years?. Sieber, Joan E, Iannuzzo, Rebecca and Rodriguez, Beverly.

Department Reorganization and Faculty Status in Educational Administration. Norton, M Scott.

El modelo utilitarista en la construcción y desarrollo de la bioética. Clotet, Joaquín.

Ethical Concerns and Risk Perceptions Associated with Different Applications of Genetic Engineering. Frewer, Lynn J and Shepherd, Richard.

Ethics in Organizations: A Framework for Theory and Research. Nicholson, Nigel.

Feminism, Social Policy, and Long-Acting Contraception. Nelson, Hilde Lindemann and Nelson, James Lindemann.

Folk Psychology and Cognitive Architecture. Egan, Frances.

Gender, Sexuality Research, and the Flight from Complexity. Longino, Helen E.

Hermeneutic Issues in Qualitative Research. Ferrara, Lawrence.

HIV Preventive Vaccine Research: Selected Ethical Issues. Grady, Christine.

Human Growth Hormone: A Case Study in Treatment Priorities. Tauer, Carol A.

Human Identity and the Primitive Streak. Lockwood, Michael.

Informed Consent and Anonymous Tissue Samples: The Case of HIV Seroprevalence Studies. Kopelman, Loretta M.

Issues of Consent: The Use of the Recently Deceased for Endotracheal Intubation Training. Hayes, Gregory J.

La Bioéthique: d'Une Révolution à l'Autre. Mélançon, Marcel J.

Les comités d'éthique comme mécanisme de contrôle des activités de recherche: Le point de vue de la philosophie. Gendron, Pierre.

Long-Acting Contraceptives: Ethical Guidance for Policymakers and Health Care Providers. Moskowitz, Ellen H.

Long-Acting Contraceptives: Rationale, Current Development, and Ethical Implications. Brown, George F.

Norplant and Irresponsible Reproduction. Robertson, John A.

On the Scientific Method, Its Practice and Pitfalls. Ayala, Francisco J.

Physicians' Quantitative Assessments of Medical Futility. Van McCrary, S (& others).

Politically Correct Ethical Thinking and Intubation Practice on Cadavers. Orlowski, James P.

Pursuing Truth in Narrative Research. O'Dea, Jane W.

Rationalität und Reproduzierbarkeit. Mittelstrass, Jürgen.

RESTORATION

"Ecology and the Ethics of Environmental Restoration" in *Philosophy and the Natural Environment, Attfield, Robin (ed)*. Elliot, Robert.

RESTRICTION

El concepto de propiedad privada en el Derecho Constitucional Venezolano. Peña, Angel Bustillos.

RESURRECTION

Zum Begriff der Trinität. Polemis, Michael.
La antropología prospectiva tomista. Castello Dubra, Julio A.

RETRIBUTION

"Liberalism, Retribution and Criminality" in *In Harm's Way, Coleman, Jules L (ed)*. Hampton, Jean.
Kant on Capital Punishment. Lind, Douglas.
The Retributive Paradox. Golash, Deirdre.

REVELATION

Innovation and Tradition in Religion: Towards an Institutional Theory. Disbrey, Claire (ed).
Cuerpo e intencionalidad. Pfeiffer, María Luisa.
Interventi nel Dibattito. De Palma, Armando.
La Dialéctica en el Cancionero de Baena. Sánchez-Romate, María José Gómez.
Mito, tragedia, reivelazione: Sulla presenza di Franz Rosenzweig nell'opera di Benjamin. Mottolese, Maurizio.
Per un Servizio Sapienziale della Filosofia nella Chiesa. Sánchez Sorondo, Marcello.

REVENGE

Wild Justice. Wallace, Gerry.

REVERENCE

Reverence for the Earth is Animal Rights Ethics. Pérez, Berta E.

REVERSE MATHEMATICS

A Feasible Theory for Analysis. Ferreira, Fernando.
Connections Between Axioms of Set Theory and Basic Theorems of Universal Algebra. Kurucz, H Andréka and Németi, I.
Effective Versions of Ramsey's Theorem: Avoiding the Cone Above 0'. Hummel, Tamara Lakins.

REVIEW

El Frege Kantiano. Rosado Haddock, Guillermo E, Hjorth, Greg and Spinas, Otmar.

REVISION

A Revision-Theoretic Analysis of the Arithmetical Hierarchy. Antonelli, Gian Aldo.
Foundational Belief Change. Nayak, Abhaya C.
Non-Well-Founded Sets via Revision Rules. Antonelli, Gian Aldo.

REVISIONISM

"Elizabeth Cady Stanton: Free Thinker and Radical Revisionist" in *Contributors to the Philosophy of Humanism, Hillar, Marian (ed)*. Leuchtag, Alice.
Realism, Meaning, and Truth (Second Edition). Wright, Crispin.
The Revisionist Difference Principle. Williams, Andrew D.

REVOLUTION

see also Scientific Revolution

"Revolution as Foundation of Political Philosophy" in *Hegel Reconsidered, Engelhardt Jr, H Tristram (ed)*. Howard, Dick.
Between Reform and Revolution: Three Hypotheses about the Nature of the Regime Change. Kis, János.
By Any Means Necessary: John Locke and Malcolm X on the Right to Revolution. Gordon, Jill.
El Cristianismo como *A Priori* de la Revolución en la Filosofía de Ernst Bloch. Orsolic, Marco.
El Idealismo Práctico de Marx: Una Lectura de las *Thesen über Feuerbach*. Andrés Bonetti, José.
Frammenti Politici di Antonio Labriola con una Postilla Bibliografica. Miccolis, Stefano.
Heidegger's Interpretation of the German "Revolution". Elder, Frank H W.
Metabole and Revolution: The Myth of the Platonic *Statesman* and the Modern Concept of Revolution. Steiner, Peter.
Reason *as* Revolution. Maker, William.
The Scientific Revolution in the Renaissance—A Unique Phenomenon in the History of Mankind. Rosen, Edward.
Towards a Politics of Judgement. Howard, Dick.
Tre Improbabili Nani Sulle Spalle dei Giganti. Mastroianni, Giovanni.
Un colloquio filosofico su "rivoluzione" e "contraddizione". De Stafano, Rodolfo.
Un'idea alla Ricerca di un Partito: L'eredità di Silvio Spaventa nel Liberalismo di Fine Ottocento. Ricci, Saverio.

REWARD

"The Moral Status of Profits and Other Rewards: A Perspective from Modern Welfare Economics" in *Profits and Morality, Cowan, Robin (ed)*. Hammond, Peter J.
Praise: More Than Just Social Reinforcement. Delin, Catherine R and Baumeister, Roy F.

REWRITTEN

Simple Termination of Rewrite Systems. Middeldorp, Aart and Zantema, Hans.

RHETORIC

"Changing the Subject: Rorty and Contemporary Rhetorical Theory" in *Recovering Pragmatism's Voice, Langsdorf, Lenore (ed)*. Horne, Janet S.
"From Enthymeme to Abduction" in *Recovering Pragmatism's Voice, Langsdorf, Lenore (ed)*. Lanigan, Richard L.
"Rhetoric and Poetics" in *The Cambridge Companion to Aristotle, Barnes, Jonathan (ed)*. Barnes, Jonathan.
"The Study of Rhetoric as an Approach to Cultural History: The Case of Hobbes" in *Main Trends in Cultural History, Melching, Willem (ed)*. Skinner, Quentin.

"Une rhétorique optimale du discours scientifique" in *Rhétoriques de la science, De Coorebyter, Vincent (ed)*. Thinès, Georges.
Aristotle's Rhetoric: An Art of Character. Garver, Eugene.
Aristotle: Selections. Irwin, Terence (trans) and Fine, Gail (trans).
Chronos and *Logos*: Rhetoric and the Rise of Philosophy. Houser, R Edward.
Henologische Perspektiven I/I-II: Platon—Johannes—Cusanus. Wyller, Egil A.
Montaigne: A Collection of Essays, Volume 1—Montaigne's Message and Method. Berven, Dikka (ed).
Montaigne: A Collection of Essays, Volume 3—Montaigne's Rhetoric. Berven, Dikka (ed).
Montaigne: A Collection of Essays, Volume 5—Reading Montaigne. Berven, Dikka (ed).
Rhetoric and Marxism. Aune, James Arnt.
Rhetorical Mosaic for a Kaleidoscope of Sound: Poetry as a Road to Understanding the Prose Voice. Britt, John F.
Rhétoriques de la science. De Coorebyter, Vincent (ed).
Rhetorische Vernunft Oder: Das Design in der Philosophie. Mainberger, Gonsalv K.
Spinoza's Ethica From Manuscript to Print: Studies on Text, Form, and Related Topics. Steenbakkers, Piet.
The Discourses of Science. Pera, Marcello and Botsford, Clarissa (trans).
Beyond Reductionism in Rhetorical Theories of Meaning. Cherwitz, Richard A and Darwin, Thomas J.
Cicero on Rhetoric and Philosophy: *Tusculan Disputations* i. Schrenk, Lawrence.
Counting on Number: Plato on the Goodness of *Arithmos*. Roochnik, David L.
De la passionnalité. Kremer-Marietti, Angèle.
De quelques emplois médiévaux du verbe "convincere" au sens moderne du mot. Patfoort, Albert.
Death and Furniture: The Rhetoric, Politics, and Theology of Bottom Line Arguments against Relativism. Edwards, Derek, Ashmore, Malcolm and Potter, Jonathan.
Disciplining Clio: The Rhetoric of Positivism. Carrard, Philippe.
Displacing Descartes: Philosophical Hermeneutics and Rhetorical Studies. Bineham, Jeffery L.
Frans H van Eemeren and Rob Grootendorst Perelman and the Fallacies. van Eemeren, Frans H and Grootendorst, Rob.
Grammacentrism and the Transformation of Rhetoric. Khushf, George.
Hegel on the Bacchanalian Revel of Truth. Kainz, Howard P.
Heidegger's Hermeneutics and the Rhetoric of Biblical Theology. Scult, Allen.
Herodotus and the Rhetoric of Otherness. Gray, Vivienne.
Hesse and Rorty on Metaphor: Rhetoric in Contemporary Philosophy. Gal, Ofer.
Is There an Audience for this Argument? Fallacies, Theories, and Relativisms. Crosswhite, James.
La Rehabilitacíon del Humanismo Retórico: Considerando el Antihumanismo de Heidegger. Grassi, Ernesto.
Los Campos de la Argumentación. Beuchot, Mauricio.
Meaning in Nature: Rhetoric, Phenomenology, and the Question of Environmental Value. Maxcy, David J.
Moral Literacy. Cooper, David D.
On the Category of the Controversial: An Approach through Schleiermacher's Dialectic. Gutenberg, Norbert and Johnstone Jr, Henry W.
Our Best Rhetorologist. Booth, Wayne C.
Persuasion in an Empty Ontology: The Eleatic Synthesis of Philosophy, Poetry, and Rhetoric. Poster, Carol.
Persuasive Design in Cicero's *De oratore*. Hall, Jon.
Politische Philosophie oder Demagogie? Zur rhetorischen Metakritik von Fichtes *Reden an die deutsche Nation*. Oesterreich, Peter L.
Quantitative and Qualitative Abductive Inquiry. Bybee, Michael D.
Rhetoric and Philosophy. Warner, Martin.
Rhetoric and the Narration of Conscience. Black, David.
Rhetoric and the Perlocutionary Field. Mason, Jeff.
Rhetoric, Environmentalism, and Environmental Ethics. Bruner, Michael and Oelschlaeger, Max.
Science and Rhetoric in the Middle Ages: The Natural Philosophy of William of Conches. Cadden, Joan.
The Call of Conscience: Heidegger and the Question of Rhetoric. Hyde, Michael J.
The Influence of the Rhetoric on the Ethics. Rigotti, Francesca.
The Rhetoric of Feminist Writings. Nuyen, A T.
The Role of Dissociation in Redeeming Knowledge Claims: Nineteenth-Century Shakers' Epistemological Resistance to Decline. Olson, Kathryn M.
Toward a Relational Theory of Meaning. Cherwitz, Richard A and Darwin, Thomas J.
Verità ed etica nella *Dialectica* di Lorenzo Valla. Laffranchi, M.
Vives, Calderón y Vico: Lenguaje Metafórico y Filosofar Ingenioso. Hidalgo-Serna, Emilio.

RICH

"Rich and Poor" in *Introducing Applied Ethics, Almond, Brenda (ed)*. Trusted, Jennifer.

RICH, A

"Post-Modernizing Gender: From Adrienne Rich to Judith Butler" in *Power/Gender, Radtke, H Lorraine (ed)*. Weir, Lorraine.

RICHARDS, T

Towards an Adequate Definition of Distribution for First-Order Logic. Friedman, Joel I.

RICOEUR, P

"A Good Rhetoric Is Possible" in *The Philosophy of Paul Ricoeur, Hahn, Lewis Edwin (ed)*. Lanigan, Richard L.

RICOEUR, P

"Act, Sign, and Consciousness: Thinking Along with Ricoeur" in *The Philosophy of Paul Ricoeur, Hahn, Lewis Edwin (ed)*. Tong, Lik Kuen.

"Bibliography of Paul Ricoeur" in *The Philosophy of Paul Ricoeur, Hahn, Lewis Edwin (ed)*. Vansina, Frans D and Ricoeur, Paul.

"Ethics and Narrativity" in *The Philosophy of Paul Ricoeur, Hahn, Lewis Edwin (ed)*. Kemp, Peter.

"Freud, Philosophy, and Interpretation" in *The Philosophy of Paul Ricoeur, Hahn, Lewis Edwin (ed)*. Smith, John E.

"From the Ego to the Self: A Philosophical Itinerary" in *The Philosophy of Paul Ricoeur, Hahn, Lewis Edwin (ed)*. Blamey, Kathleen.

"Intellectual Autobiography of Paul Ricoeur" in *The Philosophy of Paul Ricoeur, Hahn, Lewis Edwin (ed)*. Ricoeur, Paul.

"Metaphor, Hermeneutics, and Situations" in *The Philosophy of Paul Ricoeur, Hahn, Lewis Edwin (ed)*. Townsend, Dabney.

"Naive and Sentimental Hermeneutics: Keeping Language Open" in *The Philosophy of Paul Ricoeur, Hahn, Lewis Edwin (ed)*. Rudnick, Hans H.

"On Ricoeur's Analysis of Time and Narration" in *The Philosophy of Paul Ricoeur, Hahn, Lewis Edwin (ed)*. Stevens, Bernard.

"Paul Ricoeur and Literary Theory" in *The Philosophy of Paul Ricoeur, Hahn, Lewis Edwin (ed)*. Valdés, Mario J.

"Paul Ricoeur and the Conflict of Interpretations" in *The Philosophy of Paul Ricoeur, Hahn, Lewis Edwin (ed)*. Lavine, Thelma Z.

"Paul Ricoeur's Aesthetics: On How to Read a Metaphor" in *The Philosophy of Paul Ricoeur, Hahn, Lewis Edwin (ed)*. Kaelin, Eugene F.

"Paul Ricoeur's Place in the Hermeneutic Tradition" in *The Philosophy of Paul Ricoeur, Hahn, Lewis Edwin (ed)*. Ihde, Don.

"Philosophical Imagination: Paul Ricoeur as the Singer of Ruins" in *The Philosophy of Paul Ricoeur, Hahn, Lewis Edwin (ed)*. Philibert, Michel.

"Razón Imaginativa y Etica: Reflexiones a Partir de la Obra de Paul Ricoeur" in *Temas Actuales de Filosofía, Palacios, María Julia (ed)*. Cragnolini, Mónica B.

"Ricoeur and the Hermeneutics of the Subject" in *The Philosophy of Paul Ricoeur, Hahn, Lewis Edwin (ed)*. Madison, G B.

"Ricoeur and the Problem of Evil" in *The Philosophy of Paul Ricoeur, Hahn, Lewis Edwin (ed)*. Tyman, Stephen T.

"Ricoeur as Social Philosopher" in *The Philosophy of Paul Ricoeur, Hahn, Lewis Edwin (ed)*. Bien, Joseph.

"Ricoeur on Atheism: A Critique" in *The Philosophy of Paul Ricoeur, Hahn, Lewis Edwin (ed)*. Detmer, David.

"Ricoeur on Religious Language" in *The Philosophy of Paul Ricoeur, Hahn, Lewis Edwin (ed)*. Stewart, David.

"Ricoeur, Kant, and the Permanence of Time" in *The Philosophy of Paul Ricoeur, Hahn, Lewis Edwin (ed)*. Godlove Jr, Terry F.

"The Depth and Breadth of Paul Ricoeur's Philosophy" in *The Philosophy of Paul Ricoeur, Hahn, Lewis Edwin (ed)*. Jervolino, Domenico.

"The Idea of a Hermeneutical Ethics" in *The Philosophy of Paul Ricoeur, Hahn, Lewis Edwin (ed)*. Klein, Ted.

"The Limits of Ricoeur's Hermeneutics of Existence" in *The Philosophy of Paul Ricoeur, Hahn, Lewis Edwin (ed)*. Bourgeois, Patrick L.

"The Live Metaphor" in *The Philosophy of Paul Ricoeur, Hahn, Lewis Edwin (ed)*. Gerhart, Mary.

"The Symbol Gave Rise to Thought" in *The Philosophy of Paul Ricoeur, Hahn, Lewis Edwin (ed)*. Pellauer, David.

"Words and Deeds: The Semantics of Actions" in *The Philosophy of Paul Ricoeur, Hahn, Lewis Edwin (ed)*. Reagan, Charles E.

Poetics of Modernity: Toward a Hermeneutic Imagination. Kearney, Richard.

Rhetorische Vernunft Oder: Das Design in der Philosophie. Mainberger, Gonsalv K.

The Philosophy of Paul Ricoeur. Hahn, Lewis Edwin (ed).

Acciones básicas y teoría del conocimiento: una tesis de P Ricoeur sobre de la teoría de A Danto. Brunsteins, Patricia C and García, Pablo Sebastián.

Discourse and Narrative: Ethics after the Linguistics Turn. Sauer, James.

Hegel dans *Soi-même comme un autre* de Paul Ricoeur. Brito, Emilio.

Hermenéutica y Realismo Científico. Alcalá Campos, Raúl.

Identity and the Narrative Structure of Life. Hattingh, Herselman and van Veuren, Pieter.

Il soggetto e la prassi nell'ermeneutica di Paul Ricoeur. Brezzi, Francesca.

La Règle d'Or: l'effet-radar. Hunyadi, Mark.

La riappropriazione di Aristotele nell'ultimo Ricoeur. Rizzacasa, Aurelio.

Multiple Foreignness. Ricoeur, Paul.

Reply to Paul Ricoeur's "The Plurality of Sources of Law". Dworkin, Ronald.

Ricoeur and Political Identity. Dauenhauer, Bernard.

Ricoeur et la fiction de l'autonomie. Gagnon, Martin.

Ricoeur on Metaphor and Ideology. Gay, William C.

Tre teorie sulle emozione: cognitiva, fenomenologica e comportamentistica (seconda parte). Malo, Antonio.

RIGHT

see also Good, Left, Natural Right, Personal Right, Virtue

La Tirania en la Grecia Antigua. Sánchez de la Torre, D Angel.

Questions of Judgment: Determining What's Right. Low-Beer, F H.

Staat en Welzijn: Het belang van een vernieuwde conceptie van de Minimale Staat. Hogervorst, S.

The Rational and the Moral Order: The Social Roots of Reason and Morality. Baier, Kurt.

Zur Begründung der Menschenrechte: Hobbes-Locke-Kant. König, Siegfried.

Das Problem der Individualität in Fichtes früher Ethik und Rechtslehre. Düsing, Edith.

Ethics. Kolakowski, Leszak.

How Philosophy *Instructs the World*. Harris, Henry S.

L'Orientamento della Filosofia del Diritto in Francia. Terré, François.

La justicia en Kant. Brandt, Reinhard.

La Teoria e la Pratica del Diritto. De Pascale, Carla.

La victima y el "No-sujeto de derecho". Messuti de Zabala, Ana.

Le juste et le bien: priorité ou complémentarité?. Berten, André.

Le Sujet Auto-Nome du Droit: Entretien avec Lukas Sosoe. Bacot, Jean-François.

Moral y Derecho en Bentham. Moncho, Josep.

Nature, coutume et droit chez Hegel. Vieillard-Baron, Jean-Louis.

The Emerging Practice of Institutional Apologies. Harvey, J.

The Priority of Right and Ideas of the Good. Rawls, John.

RIGHT TO DIE

"The Right to Die" in *Ethics on the Frontiers of Human Existence, Badham, Paul (ed)*. Smith, Patrick Nowell.

Éthique de la mort et droit à la mort: A propos d'un livre récent. Keating, Bernard.

L'euthanasie: Enjeux Ethiques et Politiques. St-Arnaud, Jocelyne.

Y a-t-il un Droit de Mourir?. Malherbe, Jean-François.

RIGHTS

see also Civil Right, Human Rights

"Archäologie des Rechtsstaates" in *Das geistige Erbe Europas, Buhr, Manfred (ed)*. De Pascale, Carla.

"Autonomy" in *Concepts and Cases in Nursing Ethics, Yeo, Michael (& others)*. Yeo, Michael and Dalziel, Jean.

"Common Codes: Divergent Practices" in *Ethics and the Professions, Chadwick, Ruth (ed)*. Jackson, Jennifer.

"Deserving Profits" in *Profits and Morality, Cowan, Robin (ed)*. Narveson, Jan.

"Fetal-Maternal Conflicts" in *In Harm's Way, Coleman, Jules L (ed)*. Smith, Holly M.

"Gay Marriage: A Civil Right" in *Gay Ethics, Murphy, Timothy F (ed)*. Dean, Craig R.

"Homosex/Ethics" in *Gay Ethics, Murphy, Timothy F (ed)*. Murphy, Timothy F.

"Justice" in *Concepts and Cases in Nursing Ethics, Yeo, Michael (& others)*. Yeo, Michael and Donner, Gail.

"Liberalism and Group Rights" in *In Harm's Way, Coleman, Jules L (ed)*. Buchanan, Allen.

"Neo-Confucianism and Human Rights" in *Human Rights and the World's Religions, Rouner, Leroy (ed)*. De Bary, W Theodore.

"Perversions of Justice: Examining the Doctrine of U.S. Rights to Occupancy in North America" in *Radical Philosophy of Law, Caudill, David S (ed)*. Churchill, Ward.

"Rediscovering America: The *Two Treatises* and Aboriginal Rights" in *Locke's Philosophy, Rogers, G A J (ed)*. Tully, James.

"Religions and Rights: Local Values and Universal Declarations" in *Human Rights and Religious Values, An-Na'im, Abdullahi A (& other eds)*. Clayton, John.

"Responsibility for Consequences" in *In Harm's Way, Coleman, Jules L (ed)*. Fischer, John Martin and Ravizza, Mark.

"Rights to Natural Talents and Pure Profits: A Critique of Gauthier on Rights and Economic Rent" in *Profits and Morality, Cowan, Robin (ed)*. Mack, Eric.

"Rites as Rights: The Confucian Alternative" in *Human Rights and the World's Religions, Rouner, Leroy (ed)*. Ames, Roger T.

"Social and Cultural Rights in Buddhism" in *Human Rights and the World's Religions, Rouner, Leroy (ed)*. Thurman, Robert A F.

"The Abortion Dilemma" in *The 1994 Annual of Hermeneutics and Social Concern, Lawler, Justus George (ed)*. Haag, Louis J.

"The Closet and the Ethics of Outing" in *Gay Ethics, Murphy, Timothy F (ed)*. McCarthy, Jeremiah.

"Why Take Rights Seriously? A Confucian Critique" in *Human Rights and the World's Religions, Rouner, Leroy (ed)*. Rosemont Jr, Henry.

Adventures in Lesbian Philosophy. Card, Claudia F (ed).

Autonomy and Intervention: Parentalism in the Caring Life. Kultgen, John.

Constitutional Domains: Democracy, Community, Management. Post, Robert C.

Democracy. Green, Philip V.

Ethical Argument: Critical Thinking in Ethics. Curtler, Hugh Mercer.

Ethics from Experience. Caws, Peter.

Feminism and Philosophy: Essential Readings in Theory, Reinterpretation, and Application. Tuana, Nancy (ed) and Tong, Rosemarie (ed).

Food: Multidisciplinary Perspectives. Harriss-White, Barbara (ed) and Hoffenberg, Raymond (ed).

Gay Ethics. Murphy, Timothy F (ed).

Hegel In His Time: Berlin, 1818-1831. Burbidge, John W (trans) and D'Hondt, Jacques.

Human Dignity and the Common Good in the Aristotelian-Thomistic Tradition. Smith, Michael A.

In Harm's Way. Coleman, Jules L (ed) and Buchanan, Allen (ed).

Intervention and Reflection: Basic Issues in Medical Ethics (Fifth Edition). Munson, Ronald (ed).

Intimacy and Spectacle: Liberal Theory as Political Education. Esquith, Stephen L.

Modern Political Thought. Plant, Raymond.

Moral Voices, Moral Selves: Carol Gilligan and Feminist Moral Theory. Hekman, Susan J.

Real Rights. Wellman, Carl P.

Relationship Morality. Kellenberger, J.

Responsibility and the Moral Sentiments. Wallace, R Jay.

RIGHTS

Slavery and the Catholic Tradition: Rights in the Balance. Brett, Stephen F.

Strange Multiplicity: Constitutionalism in an Age of Diversity. Tully, James.

The Blanchot Reader. Holland, Michael (ed).

The Constructed Body: AIDS, Reproductive Technology, and Ethics. Murphy, Julien S.

The Erich Fromm Reader. Fromm, Erich and Funk, Rainer (ed).

The Ethical Primate: Humans, Freedom and Morality. Midgley, Mary.

The Idea of Private Law. Weinrib, Ernest J.

The Irigaray Reader. Whitford, Margaret (ed).

The New Ecological Order. Ferry, Luc and Volk, Carol (trans).

Thomas Jefferson's Freethought Legacy: A Saying Per Day by the Sage of Monticello. Greeley, Roger E.

Too Much Liberty?: Perspectives on Freedom and the American Dream. Saari, David J.

A Proposito di 'Filosofia del Diritto'. Bello, Angela Ales.

A Theory of Social Decisions. Baron, Jonathan.

Abortion and In Vitro Fertilization. Waller, Bruce N.

Abortion as Murder?: A Response. Stone, Jim.

Abortion Ethics: Rights and Responsibilities. Porter, Elisabeth.

Aspetti Sistematici della "Filosofia del Diritto" di Gentile. Marini, Giuliano.

Autonomy and the Free Speech Principle. Easton, Susan.

Beyond Theological Conflict in the Courts: The Issue of Assisted Suicide. Dyck, Arthur J.

Bioethics; Its Scope and Purpose. Fox, Michael W.

Can There Be a Right to Secede?. Ewin, R E.

Citizenship: A European Wager. La Torre, Massimo.

Colonialism and Its Others: Considerations On Rights and Care Discourses. Narayan, Uma.

Commentary on "Contractarianism Gone Wild: Carruthers and the Moral Status of Animals". Robinson, William S.

Commentary on "The Forgetful Mourner". Moody, Harry R.

Commentary on Discussions About Life-Sustaining Treatments. Emanuel, Ezekiel J.

Commentary—Social Justice and Sustainable Agriculture: Moving Beyond Theory. Clancy, Kate.

Communitarianism, Liberalism, and Superliberalism. Kymlicka, Will.

Contractarianism Gone Wild: Carruthers and the Moral Status of Animals. Doonin-Vail, David.

Corporate Democracy. Caste, Nicholas J.

Das Problem der Gewaltenteilung bei Rousseau und Fichte. Schottky, Richard.

Deciding Whether to Intervene. Howe, Edmund G.

Degrees of Freedom. Van Zyl Smit, Dirk.

Derecho Natural o Derecho Racional?. Garcia-Huidobro, Joaquín.

Distributive Justice and the Complex Structure of Ownership. Christman, John P.

Droits individuels, bien commun et vertu civique dans la querelle des libéraux et des communautariens. Ossipow, William.

El concepto de propiedad privada en el Derecho Constitucional Venezolano. Peña, Angel Bustillos.

El utilitarismo libertario de William Godwin. Adair, Phillipe.

Ethics in a Bicultural Context. Campbell, Alastair V.

Fathers' Rights, Mothers' Wrongs? Reflections on Unwed Fathers' Rights and Sex Equality. Shanley, Mary L.

Feminismo y política en dos encrucijadas históricas: La modernidad madura. Ciriza, Alejandra.

Fuentes del Derecho y del sistema jurídico. López Ruiz, Francisco.

Harrison and Hick on God and Animal Pain. Lynch, Joseph J.

Health Care Workers with HIV and a Patient's Right To Know. Murphy, Timothy F.

How Far Was Plato Concerned to Rebut the Claims of Cyrus the Great and Pisistratus to the Title of *Statesman*?. Tanner, R G.

Human Rights and Human Nature. Possenti, Vittorio.

Il problema della definizione generale del diritto. Bagolini, Luigi.

Information Sharing in Donor Insemination: A Conflict of Rights and Needs. Daniels, Ken R.

Intrinsic Limitations of Property Rights. Elegido, J M.

Is Redistribution to Help the Needy Unjust?. Davies, Stephen.

Is There a Moral Obligation to Have Children?. Smilansky, Saul.

Justifying the Rights of Pregnancy: The Interest View. Marquis, Don.

L'Obiezione di Coscienza: A Proposito di un Recente Convegno. Troncarelli, Barbara.

La Funzione Legislativa. Trigeaud, Jean-Marc.

La Legge e il Diritto. Montanari, Bruno.

La Polemica di Leroux contro Lacordaire e Malthus sulla Questione Sociale. Fiorentino, Fernando.

Las "ciencias normativas" y la "ciencia del derecho". Vega, Jesús Fernández.

Le Epistole Vichiane e la Nascita dell'idea di Scienza Nuova. Sanna, Manuela.

Liberties, Not Rights: Gauthier and Nozick on Property. Torek, Paul.

Locke on Slavery and Inalienable Rights. Welchman, Jennifer.

Marquis' Argument Against Abortion: A Critique. Shirley, Edward S.

Marx and Rights. Corlett, J Angelo.

Militant Gayes, Gayes in the Military, and Privacy as Social Freedom. Nunan, Richard.

Mill's Principle of Liberty. Chopra, Y N.

More on Race and Crime: Levin's Reply. Adler, Jonathan E.

Naturalità del Diritto e Universali Giuridici. Cosi, Giovanni.

Note sul Rapporto Violenza/Diritto/Comunicazione. Andronico, Alberto.

Obligations of Physicians to Patients and Third-Party Payers. Holleman, Warren L (& others).

On the Unavoidability of Power in Child-rearing: Is the Language of Rights Educationally Appropriate?. Smeyers, Paul.

Organizational Characteristics and HRM Policies on Rights: Exploring the Patterns of Connections. Schwoerer, Catherine E (& others).

Paternalism and Rights. Brennan, Samantha.

Political Philosophy as Political Action: A Response to Mark Blasius. Statham Jr, E Robert.

Pornography: An Uncivil Liberty?. Carse, Alisa L.

Private Bioethics Forums: Counterpoint to Government Bodies. Cohen, Cynthia B and McCloskey, Elizabeth Leibold.

Reply to Adler's "More on Race and Crime: Levin's Reply". Levin, Michael E.

Reproductive Responsibility and Long-Acting Contraceptives. Arras, John D and Blustein, Jeffrey.

Reproductive Technologies in Developing Countries. Macklin, Ruth.

Research Participation as a Contract. Lawson, Craig.

Reverence for the Earth is Animal Rights Ethics. Pérez, Berta E.

Rights Against Polluters. Kernohan, Andrew.

Rights and Interests in a Participatory Market Society. van Luijk, Henk.

Rights and Power: A Feminist Rethinking of Liberal Rights. Kelly, Michaeleen J.

Rights and the Criminal Law. Ellis, Anthony.

Rights in Collision: A Non-Punitive, Compensatory Remedy for Abusive Speech. Meyers, Diana Tietjens.

Rights, Compensation, and Culpability. Zimmerman, Michael J.

Rights, Duties, and Limits of Autonomy. Emson, H E.

Rights, Neutrality, and the Oppressive Power of the State. Sher, George.

Rosmini on Natural Law and Right. Cleary, Denis.

Ruse on Gay Rights and Affirmative Action. Sartorelli, Joseph J.

Statistical Victims and Their Rights. Hanks, Donald K.

Suicidio y fiesta del yo: el suicidio como transgresión moral definitiva: A propósito de "On Suicide" de David Hume. Tasset, José Luis.

Taking Drugs and Rights Seriously. Gaus, Gerald F.

Taking Rites Seriously. Weithman, Paul J.

The *Right* Approach. Cordero, Ronald A.

The Ethic of Care vis-à-vis the Ethic of Rights: A Problem for Contemporary Moral Theory. Kroeger-Mappes, Joy.

The Inalienable Right to Life and the Durable Power of Attorney. Wellman, Carl P.

The Meaning and Status of Gay and Lesbian Political Philosophy: A Rejoinder to E Robert Statham Jr. Blasius, Mark.

The Moral *Prima Facie* Obligation to Obey the Law. Wilkins, Burleigh T.

The Moral Basis of Liberal Education. Gewirth, Alan.

The Realm of Rights. Baier, Kurt.

The Reflections of Linus: The Contradictions of Plato. Weiss, Daniel A.

Thresholds for Rights. Brennan, Samantha.

Two Extreme Approaches to Rights Versus an Aristotelian Mean. Fay, Thomas A.

Uberto Scarpelli, Giurista e Filosofo. Jori, Mario.

Un colloquio filosofico su "rivoluzione" e "contraddizione". De Stafano, Rodolfo.

Una aproximación al concepto de derecho a la intimidad en John Stuart Mill. García Añón, José.

Una Conversione della Teoria Critica? Sulla Teoria del Diritto e dello Stato di Habermas. Höffe, Otfried.

Una Lógica del Compromiso Social. Redmond, Walter.

Una Ricerca sullo Stato di Edith Stein. D'Agostino, Francesco.

User Rights and the Frail Aged. Gibson, Diane.

Value Theory and the Best Interests Standard. DeGrazia, David.

Waldron on Political Legitimacy and the Social Minimum. Weithman, Paul.

Waldron on Special Rights *in rem*. Cristi, Renato.

What Do Animals Deserve?. Voice, Paul.

When Is Birth Unfair to the Child?. Steinbock, Bonnie and McClamrock, Ron.

William Godwin y el anarquismo: A propósito de *Political Justice*. Alvarez, Antón Fernández.

Women, Ectogenesis, and Ethical Theory. Cannold, Leslie.

Zwei Seiten der Kantschen Begründung von Eigentum und Staat. Baumann, Peter.

RIGORISM

Rigor se Dice de muchas Maneras. Pereda, Carlos.

RIMBAUD, A

Solitudes: From Rimbaud to Heidegger. Froment-Meurice, Marc and Walsh, Peter (trans).

RING

Anneaux de Fonctions p-Adiques. Bélair, Luc.

Diophantine Equivalence and Countable Rings. Shlapentokh, Alexandra.

Diophantine Undecidability in Some Rings of Algebraic Numbers of Totally Real Infinite Extensions.... Shlapentokh, Alexandra.

Model Theory of Modules Over a Serial Ring. Eklof, Paul C and Herzog, Ivo.

The Model Theory of Unitriangular Groups. Belegradek, Oleg V.

RISK

Ecological Enlightenment: Essays on the Politics of the Risk Society. Beck, Ulrich and Ritter, Mark A (trans).

A Strong (Ross) Characterization of Multivariate Risk Aversion. Grant, Simon.

A Survey of Ethical Conduct in Risk Management: Environmental Economists. Goldberg, Laura and Greenberg, Michael.

Environmental Risk Assessment and Nuclear Waste Disposal. Shrader-Frechette, Kristin.

Ethical Standards, Attitudes Toward Risk, and Intentional Noncompliance: An Experimental Investigation. Ghosh, Dipankar and Crain, Terry L.

Exploitation in the Use of Human Subjects for Medical Experimentation: A Re-Examination of Basic Issues. de Castro, Leonardo D.

Flexibility, Endogenous Risk, and the Protection Premium. Lence, Sergio H and Babcock, Bruce A.

RISK

More Theoretical Risks. Henley, Tracy B.

Risk, Autonomy, and Responsibility: Informed Consent for Prenatal Testing. Press, Nancy and Browner, C H.

The Two-Envelope Paradox. Broome, John.

RISK ANALYSIS

Annette Baier and the Context of Risk. Green, Stephen A.

RITE

"Rites as Rights: The Confucian Alternative" in *Human Rights and the World's Religions, Rouner, Leroy (ed).* Ames, Roger T.

RITUAL

Essentials of Shinto: An Analytical Guide to Principal Teachings. Picken, Stuart D B.

A Note on the Concepts of *Nitya-karma, Naimittika-karma* and *Kamya-karma.* Pandurangi, K T.

Dr Kansara's Comments. Kansara, N M.

On the Radical Distinction between the *Krsna* and the *Sukla Yajurveda* and *Professor Heesterman's Remarks Thereon. Krishna, Daya.*

Ritual Action (*Li*) in Confucius and Hsun Tzu. Martin, Michael R.

'Brahmin, Ritual and Renouncer' A Comment by Dr Fateh Singh. Singh, Fateh.

RIVERA, J

Fundamentos Filosóficos del Concepto Muñocista de la Libertad. Rivera, José.

ROBERTSON, J

The Ethics of Babymaking. Sherwin, Susan.

ROBINSON, A

Reply to Craig: Inverse Operations with Transfinite Numbers and the *Kalam* Cosmological Argument. Oppy, Graham.

ROBINSON, J

Still Hopeful: Reply to Karl and Robinson. Levinson, Jerrold.

ROBINSON, W

Reply to the Commentary on "Contractarianism Gone Wild: Carruthers and the Moral Status of Animals". Boonin-Vail, David.

ROBOT

Movements, Actions, the Internal, and *Hauser Robots.* Gunderson, Keith.

Propositional Actitudes: Reply to Gunderson. Hauser, Larry.

ROBOTICS

Artificial Intelligence: A Philosophical Introduction. Copeland, B Jack.

ROCHE, T

"Reply to Professor Roche" in *The Crossroads of Norm and Nature, Sim, May (ed).* Kraut, Richard H.

ROCK MUSIC

Between Rock and a Harp Place. Young, James O.

Music for the Young at Heart. Baugh, Bruce.

ROGERS, G

Review of *Drafts for the Essay Concerning Human Understanding, and Other Philosophical Writings*, Volume 1: Drafts A and B. Milton, J R.

ROLLINS, M

Equipotential Recipes for Unambiguous Images: A Reply to Rollins. Reisberg, Daniel.

ROLSTON, H

Value Theory and Ecology in Environmental Ethics: A Comparison of Rolston and Niebuhr. Scoville, Judith N.

ROMAN

Rational Individualism: The Perennial Philosophy of Legal Interpretation. Simonds, Roger T.

The Reputations of Socrates: The Afterlife of a Gadfly. Hulse, James W.

Cicero on Rhetoric and Philosophy: *Tusculan Disputations* i. Schrenk, Lawrence.

Edward Gibbon and the Anti-Miracle Man: Hume's 'Of Miracles' at Work in the *Decline and Fall of the Roman Empire.* Foster, Stephen P.

Montesquieu on the Causes of Roman Greatness. Myers, Richard.

The Rhetoric of Politics in Cicero's Fourth Catilinarian. Cape Jr, Robert W.

ROMAN CATHOLICISM

see Catholicism

ROMANES, G

The Many Perils of Ejective Anthropomorphism. Thompson, Nicholas S.

ROMANIAN

Interview of Ludwig Grünberg. Abbarno, John M.

Kants Philosophie in Rumänien. Schuster-Stein, Paul.

ROMANTICISM

"Reconstructing Aesthetic Education" in *Intersections: Nineteenth-Century Philosophy and Contemporary Theory, Rajan, Tilottama (ed).* Meyer, Eric.

"Richard Rorty's Romantic Pragmatism" in *Pragmatism: From Progressivism to Postmodernism, Hollinger, Robert (ed).* Nevo, Isaac.

"Romantik der Arbeit" Perspektiven des frühromantischen Arbeitsbegriffs. Arndt, Andreas.

"The Return of the Romantic" in *Intersections: Nineteenth-Century Philosophy and Contemporary Theory, Rajan, Tilottama (ed).* Mileur, Jean-Pierre.

"The Romanticism of Contemporary Ideology" in *Intersections: Nineteenth-Century Philosophy and Contemporary Theory, Rajan, Tilottama (ed).* Hamilton, Paul.

"'Non-Identity'" in *Intersections: Nineteenth-Century Philosophy and Contemporary Theory, Rajan, Tilottama (ed).* Bowie, Andrew.

Genozid und Heilserwartung: zum nationalsozialistischen Mord am europäischen Judentum. Ley, Michael.

Para la Paz Perpetua de Kant y el *Fundamento del Derecho Natural* de Fichte: Encuentros y Desencuentros. Oncina, Faustino.

Preface to Modernism. Berman, Art.

Rhetoric and Marxism. Aune, James Arnt.

Aproximación al Morfema: Romànticismo Alemán. Market, Oswaldo.

Considérations Rétrospectives. Moutsopoulos, Evanghélos.

Das Paradox des Schweigens: Über den Begriff der Kunst Sören Kierkegaards seit seiner Kritik der romantischen Ironie. Okabayashi, Hiroshi.

De Sade o la subversión de/en la Ilustración. Mayos, Gonça.

Edgar Quinet, Chantre de "La Grèce Moderne". Guichardet, Jeannine.

El concepto de Bildung en el primer romanticismo alemán. Sánchez Meca, Diego.

Fuite et Nostalgie Romantiques de la Grèce. Moutsopoulos, Evanghélos.

Gleichzeitigkeit des Ungleichzeitigen: zur Frühen Lessingrezeption bei Friedrich Schlegel. Münster, Reinhold.

Heidegger's Concept of *Volk.* Sikka, Sonya.

Hölderlin et la Question du Centre. Villani, Arnaud.

Ilustración y Romanticismo en la *Scienza Nuova*: La Racionalidad del Mito y el Mito de la Racionalidad. Marín Casanova, José A.

Jewish Mysticism in Romantic Medicine? Indirect Incorporation of Kabbalistic Elements in the Work of Gotthilf Heinrich Schubert. Roelcke, Volker.

La Estética del Romanticismo y su Análisis Dentro de la Filosofía Existencial (Kierkegaard y Dostoievsky). Rendón Rojas, Miguel Angel.

Lamartine et la Grèce. Court, Antoine.

Le Pessimisme Romantique et le Pessimisme Dionysiaque des Hellènes Selon Nietzsche. Lang, André.

Le Romantisme de M de Guérin et la Grèce. Gabaude, Jean-Marc.

Le Romantisme des Premiers Lyriques Grecs. Galy, Jean-Michel.

Le Romantisme Grec. Richer, Renée.

Living Poetically: Kierkegaard and German Romanticism. Walsh, Sylvia.

Prométhée, Personnage Romantique. Thivel, Antoine.

Quests for a Scientific Mythology: F Creuzer and K O Müller on History and Myth. Blok, Josine H.

Résurgences Grecques au fil du Romantisme Anglais. Tschumi, Raymond.

The Idea of Universalism in the Polish Romantic Tradition. Walicki, Andrzej.

Über das Malerische oder Pittoreske. Kambayashi, Tsunemichi.

'Essence' and 'Accident' in Lamb's Elia Essays. Mulvihill, James.

ROMBACH, H

The Model of an Ethics of Being in Meister Eckhart and in the Structural Philosophy of Heinrich Rombach. Mieth, Dietmar.

ROQUENTIN, A

Sport, the Aesthetic, and Narrative. Feezell, Randolph M.

RORTY, R

"Changing the Subject: Rorty and Contemporary Rhetorical Theory" in *Recovering Pragmatism's Voice, Langsdorf, Lenore (ed).* Horne, Janet S.

"Icons, Fragments, and Ironists" in *Recovering Pragmatism's Voice, Langsdorf, Lenore (ed).* Presnell, Mick.

"Postmodern Pragmatism: Nietzsche, Heidegger, Derrida, and Rorty" in *Pragmatism: From Progressivism to Postmodernism, Hollinger, Robert (ed).* Magnus, Bernd.

"R Rorty: Pragmatismo, Horizonte Postfilosófico y Conversación" in *Temas Actuales de Filosofía, Palacios, María Julia (ed).* Páez, Alicia.

"Richard Rorty's Romantic Pragmatism" in *Pragmatism: From Progressivism to Postmodernism, Hollinger, Robert (ed).* Nevo, Isaac.

"Rorty's Dewey: Pragmatism, Education, and the Public Sphere" in *Identity, Culture, and Education, Smeyers, Paul (ed).* Neiman, Alven M.

"Rorty's Pragmatism and the Linguistic Turn" in *Pragmatism: From Progressivism to Postmodernism, Hollinger, Robert (ed).* Donovan, Rickard.

"Talking-With as a Model for Writing-About: Implications of Rortyean Pragmatism" in *Recovering Pragmatism's Voice, Langsdorf, Lenore (ed).* Bochner, Arthur P and Waugh, Joanne B.

"The 'Spider's Web' and the 'Tool': Nietzsche *vis-à-vis* Rorty on Metaphor" in *Nietzsche: A Critical Reader, Sedgwick, Peter R (ed).* Tanesini, Alessandra.

"William James and Richard Rorty: Context and Conversation" in *Pragmatism: From Progressivism to Postmodernism, Hollinger, Robert (ed).* Cotkin, George.

L'homme Spéculaire. Hébert, Robert.

Recovering Pragmatism's Voice. Langsdorf, Lenore (ed) and Smith, Andrew R (ed).

Without God or His Doubles: Realism, Relativism and Rorty. Vaden House, David.

Cultural Relativism: Some Comments. Otakpor, Nkeonye.

Half-Hearted Pragmatism. Mozur, Gerald.

Heaven's Partners or Nietzschean Free Spirits?. Frisina, Warren G.

Hesse and Rorty on Metaphor: Rhetoric in Contemporary Philosophy. Gal, Ofer.

La liquidación de la Filosofía: Notas sobre la disputa entre R Rorty y J Habermas. Gómez Ibáñez, Vicente.

On What We May Hope: Rorty on Dewey and Foucault. Marshall, James D.

Our World Views (May Be) Incommensurable: Now What?. Bayley, Carol.

Peirce's First Rule of Reason and the Bad Faith of Rortian Post-Philosophy. Migotti, Mark.

Philosophical Progress and the Theory of Action. Donagan, Alan.

Pragmatism According to Rorty: A Disaster Area. Nelson, John O.

Putnam und Rorty über Objektivität und Wahrheit. Allen, Barry G.

Putting Ourselves Up for the Question: A Postmodern Critique of Richard Rorty's Postmodernist Bourgeois Liberalism. Hendley, Steven.

Realisme zonder representatie. Slors, Marc.

Richard Rorty and Solidarity, or the Inconsequence of a Certain Capacity. Veroli, Nicolas.

SCIENCE

"Fertile Ground: Pragmatism, Science, and Logical Positivism" in *Pragmatism: From Progressivism to Postmodernism, Hollinger, Robert (ed)*. Wilson, Daniel J.

"From World3 to the Social Assessment of Technology" in *Philosophy of Technology in Spanish Speaking Countries, Mitcham, Carl (ed)*. Sanmartín, José.

"Hegel, Hobbes, Kant, and the Scienticization of Practical Philosophy" in *Hegel on the Modern World, Collins, Ardis B (ed)*. Buchwalter, Andrew.

"How Dare You Sport Thus with Life?": Frankensteinian Fictions as Case Studies in Scientific Ethics. Goldbort, Robert C.

"How Scientists Really Reason: Scientific Reasoning in Real-World Laboratories" in *The Nature of Insight, Sternberg, Robert J (ed)*. Dunbar, Kevin.

"Hume, Reid and the Science of the Mind" in *Hume and Hume's Connexions, Stewart, M A (ed)*. Wood, P B.

"Insight and Affect in the History of Science" in *The Nature of Insight, Sternberg, Robert J (ed)*. Gruber, Howard E.

"Isaac Asimov's Contribution to Humanism" in *Contributors to the Philosophy of Humanism, Hillar, Marian (ed)*. Veley, Carl.

"Las XI Tesis No-Epistmológicas de Gastón Bachelard" in *Temas Actuales de Filosofía, Palacios, María Julia (ed)*. Diaz de Kobila, Esther.

"Leibniz: Physics and Philosophy" in *The Cambridge Companion to Leibniz, Jolley, Nicholas (ed)*. Garber, Daniel.

"Magic, Witchcraft, and ESP: A Defence of Scientific and Philosophical Skepticism" in *African Philosophy: Selected Readings, Mosley, Albert G (ed)*. Bodunrin, P O.

"Meaning Holism Defended" in *Holism: A Consumer Update, Fodor, Jerry A (ed)*. Harman, Gilbert.

"Merke auf dich selbst" Das Verhältnis des Philosophen zu seinem Gegenstand nach dem *Versuch einer neuen Darstellung der Wissenschaftslehre*. Römelt, Johannes.

"Metaphysics, Science, and Self-Control: A Response to Apel" in *Peirce and Contemporary Thought: Philosophical Inquiries, Ketner, Kenneth Laine (ed)*. Hookway, Christopher.

"Modelos de Procesos Justificatorios" in *Temas Actuales de Filosofía, Palacios, María Julia (ed)*. Horenstein, Norma.

"Natur u. ihre Wissenschaft in der Philosophie des 19.Jhr." in *Naturauffassungen in Philosophie, Wissenschaft, Technik: Band III, Schäfer, Lothar (ed)*. Ströker, Elisabeth.

"Observaciones sobre la Noción Popperiana de Análisis Conceptual" in *Temas Actuales de Filosofía, Palacios, María Julia (ed)*. Caponi, Gustavo A.

"Österreichische Wissenschaftsgeschichte: Erkenntnisprozess oder Verdrängung?" in *Der geistige Anschluss, Fischer, Kurt R (ed)*. Wegeler, Cornelia.

"On the Dialogue Between Physics and Philosophy" in *Philosophy, Mathematics and Modern Physics, Rudolph, Enno (ed)*. Rudolph, Enno and Stamatescu, I O.

"On the Mathematical Overdetermination of Physics" in *Philosophy, Mathematics and Modern Physics, Rudolph, Enno (ed)*. Scheibe, Erhard.

"Peirce on the Reliability of Science: A Response to Rescher" in *Peirce and Contemporary Thought: Philosophical Inquiries, Ketner, Kenneth Laine (ed)*. Delaney, Cornelius J.

"Peirce on the Validation of Science" in *Peirce and Contemporary Thought: Philosophical Inquiries, Ketner, Kenneth Laine (ed)*. Rescher, Nicholas.

"Philosophy of Science" in *The Cambridge Companion to Aristotle, Barnes, Jonathan (ed)*. Hankinson, R J.

"Potter's Bull and Castrated Pigs: Considering the Impossibility of a Hermeneutic Natural Science" in *Ecology, Technology, and Culture, Zweers, Wim (ed)*. Lijmbach, Susanne.

"Presuppositions in Science" in *Life, World and Meaning, Roux, A P J (ed)*. Kistner, Wietske.

"Putting Insight into Perspective" in *The Nature of Insight, Sternberg, Robert J (ed)*. Schooler, Jonathan W (& others).

"Quantum Theory—A Window to the World Beyond Physics" in *Philosophy, Mathematics and Modern Physics, Rudolph, Enno (ed)*. Squires, E J.

"Questions Concerning Theory and Experience and the Role of Mathematics..." in *Philosophy, Mathematics and Modern Physics, Rudolph, Enno (ed)*. Stamatescu, I O.

"Remarks on 'Aesthetization' in Science on the Basis of History" in *Historiography Between Modernism and Postmodernism, Topolski, Jerzy (ed)*. Kostyrko, Teresa.

"Sali Nitri" de Vico y los Orígenes de la Civilización Pagana: La Dimensión Alquímica de la "Ciencia Nueva". Costa, Gustavo.

"Science and the Civic Spirit of Liberal Democracy" in *Civil Religion and Political Theology, Rouner, Leroy S (ed)*. Ezrahi, Yaron.

"Science" in *The Cambridge Companion to Aristotle, Barnes, Jonathan (ed)*. Hankinson, R J.

"Science, Technology, History, and Philosophy..." in *Philosophy of Technology in Spanish Speaking Countries, Mitcham, Carl (ed)*. García Bacca, Juan David.

"Science: A Modest Hope" in *Ecology, Technology, and Culture, Zweers, Wim (ed)*. Schroevers, Pieter.

"Service and Science in Professional Life" in *Ethics and the Professions, Chadwick, Ruth (ed)*. Airaksinen, Timo.

"Sobre la 'Falsación' del Falsacionismo" in *Temas Actuales de Filosofía, Palacios, María Julia (ed)*. Lucero, Susana.

"Sobre las Explicaciones Evolucionistas de la Razón" in *Temas Actuales de Filosofía, Palacios, María Julia (ed)*. Prado, José Julián.

"Statistical Dependencies, Statements and the Idealizational Theory of Science" in *Probability in Theory-Building, Brzezinski, Jerzy (ed)*. Gaul, Marek.

"The Fate of Knowledge in Social Theories of Science" in *Socializing Epistemology: The Social Dimensions of Knowledge, Schmitt, Frederick F (ed)*. Longino, Helen E.

"The Inception of Insight" in *The Nature of Insight, Sternberg, Robert J (ed)*. Ippolito, Maria F and Tweney, Ryan D.

"The Limits of Science" in *Ecology, Technology, and Culture, Zweers, Wim (ed)*. Tennekes, Henk.

"The Mathematical Frame of Quantum Field Theory" in *Philosophy, Mathematics and Modern Physics, Rudolph, Enno (ed)*. Fredenhagen, Klaus.

"The Origin of Life and the Value of Life" in *Biology, Ethics, and the Origins of Life, Rolston III, Holmes (ed)*. Cech, Thomas R.

"The Real Molyneux Question and the Basis of Locke's Answer" in *Locke's Philosophy, Rogers, G A J (ed)*. Bolton, Martha Brandt.

"The Relevance of Scientific Research About Sexual Orientation to Lesbian and Gay Rights" in *Gay Ethics, Murphy, Timothy F (ed)*. Stein, Edward.

"The Revenge of the Sacred: Technology and Re-enchantment" in *The Barbarism of Reason, Horowitz, Asher (ed)*. Germain, Gilbert G.

"Une rhétorique optimale du discours scientifique" in *Rhétoriques de la science, De Coorebyter, Vincent (ed)*. Thinès, Georges.

"Ursprung und Wiederholung" in *Europa und die Philosophie, Gander, Hans-Helmuth (ed)*. Vetter, Helmuth.

"What Is Truth?" in *Hermeneutics and Truth, Wachterhauser, Brice (ed)*. Gadamer, Hans-Georg.

"What Kind of Science is Cosmology?" in *Philosophy, Mathematics and Modern Physics, Rudolph, Enno (ed)*. Goenner, Hubert F M.

"Wissenschaft und Technik aus paneuropäischer Sicht" in *Das geistige Erbe Europas, Buhr, Manfred (ed)*. Erpenbeck, John.

"Wissenschaft und Technik" in *Naturauffassungen in Philosophie, Wissenschaft, Technik: Band I, Schäfer, Lothar (ed)*. Ströker, Elisabeth.

"Words Lie in Our Way". MacLennan, Bruce J.

"Zu Heinrich Gomperz: *Die Wissenschaft und die Tat*" in *Heinrich Gomperz, Karl Popper und die österreichische Philosophie, Seiler, Martin (ed)*. Rutte, Heiner.

"'Wertneutralität'—Wie frei von Werten darf Wissenschaft sein?" in *Freiheit, Verantwortung und Folgen in der Wissenschaft, Sandkühler, Hans Jörg (ed)*. Alheit, Peter.

A History of Scientific Thought: Elements of a History of Science. Serres, Michel (ed).

A New Science of Life: The Hypothesis of Morphic Resonance. Sheldrake, Rupert.

A Philosophy of Matter and Mind: A New Look at an Old Major Topic in Philosophy. Wassermann, Gerhard D.

American Philosophy Today and Other Philosophical Studies. Rescher, Nicholas.

An Introduction to the Philosophy of Religion. Tilghman, B R.

Anima hace hablar a la razón con una voz diferente: Nuevos nexos entre la tecnociencia y el mundo de la vida. Cañón Loyes, Camino.

Aristotle in Outline. Robinson, Timothy A.

Aristotle's Theory of Actuality. Bechler, Zev.

Arte y Ciencia: Una Visión Especular. Leyra, Ana María and Mataix, Carmen.

Artificial Intelligence: A Philosophical Introduction. Copeland, B Jack.

Attitudes, Chaos, and the Connectionist Mind. Eiser, J Richard.

Auflösen, Untersuchen, Aufwecken: Psychoanalyse und andere Analysen. Ruhs, August (ed) and Seitter, Walter (ed).

Beast and Man: The Roots of Human Nature. Midgley, Mary.

Bertrand Russell. Slater, J G.

Biology, Ethics, and the Origins of Life. Rolston III, Holmes (ed).

Blindness of Modern Science. Uus, Undo.

Cartesian Psychology and Physical Minds: Individualism and the Sciences of the Mind. Wilson, Robert A.

Civil Religion and Political Theology. Rouner, Leroy S (ed).

Connectionism and the Mind: An Introduction to Parallel Processing in Networks. Bechtel, William and Abrahamsen, Adele.

Connectionism: Debates on Psychological Explanation. Macdonald, Cynthia (ed) and Macdonald, Graham (ed).

Contested Knowledge: Social Theory in the Postmodern Era. Seidman, Steven.

Criticism and the History of Science. Andersson, Gunnar.

Das geistige Erbe Europas. Buhr, Manfred (ed).

Denken aan al wat is: Een hedendaagse fundamentele wijsbegeerte. Van der Veken, J.

Dialectical Materialism and Modern Science. Cameron, Kenneth Neill.

Die Barbarei: Eine phänomenologische Kulturkritik. Henry, Michel.

Die Sprache in den Wissenschaften. Weingartner, Paul (ed).

Disertación sobre la Naturaleza y la Propagación del Fuego. de Châtelet, Marquesa.

Eternity and Freedom: A Critical Analysis of Divine Timelessness as a Solution to the Foreknowledge/Free Will Debate. Robinson, Michael D.

Ethical Judgment: The Use of Science in Ethics. Edel, Abraham.

Ethics of Scientific Research. Shrader-Frechette, Kristin.

Evolution and Human Values. Wesson, Robert (ed) and Williams, Patricia A (ed).

Explaining Attitudes: A Practical Approach to the Mind. Baker, Lynne Rudder.

Folk Psychology: The Theory of Mind Debate. Davies, Martin (ed) and Stone, Tony (ed).

For Education: Towards Critical Educational Inquiry. Carr, Wilfred.

Freiheit, Verantwortung und Folgen in der Wissenschaft. Sandkühler, Hans Jörg (ed).

Freud and the Politics of Psychoanalysis. Brunner, José.

From a Biological Point of View. Sober, Elliott.

SCIENCE

SCIENCE

SCIENCE

The Ontological Status of Matter in Aristotle. Cresswell, M J.

The Origin of Vertebrates and the Principle of Succession of Functions: Genealogical Sketches by Anton Dohrm, 1875—An English Translation. Ghiselin, Michael T.

The Philosophy of Science and Women's Issues in Poland: Possibilities and Obstacles Today (A Personal Account). Pakszys, Elzbieta.

The Post-Implementation Evaluation of Expert Systems: Enlightenment after Five Years in the Trenches. Sharma, R S and Conrath, D W.

The Practice of Sartre's Philosophy in Philosophical Counseling and Existential Psychotherapy. Schuster, Shlomit C.

The Problem of Reconciliation. Denkel, Arda.

The Problem of Ultimate Reality and Meaning in the Context of Information Self-Organization and Isotopic Diversity. Berezin, Alexander A.

The Problematic Status of Cosmology. De Gandt, François, Blau, Peter (trans) and Bergo, Bettina (trans).

The Progress of Technology and the Philosophical Myth of Progress. McBride, William L.

The Psychologist's Fallacy as a Persistent Framework in William James's Psychological Theorizing. Reed, Edward.

The Quest for Infinity and the Synthesis of Science (An Interview with Professor Andrzej Kajetan Wróblewski). Bendyk, Edwin.

The Relativity of Scientific Views of Reality. Puligandla, Ramakrishna.

The Religion of a Scientist: Explorations into Reality (*Religio philosophi naturalis*). Peacocke, Arthur.

The Religious Claim of Technology. Tzamalikos, Panayiotis.

The Renormalisation Group and Effective Field Theories. Huggett, Nick and Weingard, Robert.

The Replacement of Time. Savitt, Steven F.

The Scientific Community as the Ideal of the Universal Human Community. Krajewski, Wladyslaw.

The Scientific Revolution in the Renaissance—A Unique Phenomenon in the History of Mankind. Rosen, Edward.

The Scientific Status of Research on Teaching. Gage, N L.

The Scope of Psychology. Butler, Keith.

The Second Law of Probability Dynamics. Barrett, Martin and Sober, Elliott.

The Selection of Alleles and the Additivity of Variance. Sarkar, Sahotra.

The Single-Mind and Many-Minds Versions of Quantum Mechanics. Barrett, Jeffrey A.

The Social Standing of Science: Some Contemporary History. Christie, John.

The Specification of "Specification". Partridge, Derek and Galton, Antony.

The Structure of Awareness: Contemporary Applications of William James' Forgotten Concept of "The Fringe". Galin, David.

The Suggestive Properties of Quantum Mechanics Without the Collapse Postulate. Barrett, Jeffrey A.

The Super Bowl and the Ox-Phos Controversy: "Winner-Take-All" Competition in Philosophy of Science. Allchin, Douglas.

The Threshold Model of Scientific Change and the Continuity of Scientific Knowledge. Kuokkanen, Martti and Tuomivaara, Timo.

The Trouble with Well-Being: A Response to "Mild Mania and Well-Being". Seedhouse, David.

The Unconscious: A Perspective from Sociohistorical Psychology. Ratner, Carl.

The Universal Scientific Methods. Krajewski, Wladyslaw.

The Virtues of a Psychology of Personal Morality. Punzo, Vincent A and Meara, Naomi M.

The Whewell-Faraday Exchange on the Application of the Concepts of Momentum and Inertia to Electromagnetic Phenomena. Anderson, Ronald.

The 'Decoherence' Approach to the Measurement Problem in Quantum Mechanics. Elby, Andrew.

Theories Between Theories: Asymptotic Limiting Intertheoretic Relations. Batterman, Robert W.

Theories of Probability. Howson, Colin.

Theory Change and Theory Choice. Chalmers, Alan F.

There are More Things in Heaven and Earth, Horatio, Than are Dreamt of in Your Philosophy: A Dialogue on Realism and Constructivism. Nola, Robert.

Thought and Language: On the Line of Demarcation between Animal and Human Abilities. Strauss, D F M.

Three Measurement Problems. Maudlin, Tim.

Time Direction, Philosophy of Technology, and Technology Assessment. Tondl, Ladislav.

Time in Philosophy and in Physics: From Kant and Einstein to Gödel. Wang, Hao.

Time, Quantum Mechanics, and Decoherence. Saunders, Simon.

To What Extent Do Beliefs Affect Apparent Motion?. Wright, Richard D and Dawson, Michael R W.

Toward a Defensible Bootstrapping. Mitchell, Sam.

Toward a More Democratic Ethic of Technological Governance. Zimmerman, Andrew D.

Towards an Anthropological Psychiatry. Mooij, Anton.

Towards Welfare Biology: Evolutionary Economics of Animal Consciousness and Suffering. Ng, Yew-Kwang.

Tradizione Biblica, Miti e Rivoluzioni Geologiche Negli "Anecdotes de la Nature" di Nicolas-Antoine Boulanger. Cristani, Giovanni.

Tre Schede su Bruno e Oxford. Aquilecchia, Giovanni.

Trouble-Shooting Creativity: A Critical Appraisal of David Bohm and F David Peat's 'Science Orders and Creativity'. Fisch, Menachem.

Troubles for Direct Proper Functions. Davies, Paul Sheldon.

Truthlikeness, Translation, and Approximate Causal Explanation. Barnes, Eric.

Turing's Sexual Guessing Game. Genova, Judith.

Turing's Test and the Perils of Psychohistory. Anderson, James A.

Turing, Wittgenstein and the Science of the Mind. Proudfoot, Diane and Copeland, B Jack.

Twenty Five Years of Theoretical Biology. Blandino, Giovanni.

Two Cheers for Reductionism: Or, the Dim Prospects for Non-Reductive Materialism. Melnyk, Andrew.

Two Concepts of Constraint: Adaptationism and the Challenge from Developmental Biology. Amundson, Ron.

Two Logical Patterns of the Reduction of Theories: Comments on Józef Werle's Paper "How the Physical Sciences Discovered the Unity of Nature". Krajewski, Wladyslaw.

Two Types of Theories: The Impact on Churchland's "Perceptual Plasticity". DesAutels, Peggy.

Um Comentário sobre a Filosofia da Natureza na Enciclopédia de Hegel. Pereira Jr, Alfredo.

Um Teorema de Inércia e o Conceito de Velocidade nos *Discorsi* de Galileu. Vasconcelos, Júlio C R.

Una Pregunta Sobre la Noción de "Bien" en Aristóteles. Femenías, María Luisa.

Uncertainty About Determinism: A Critical Review of Challenges to the Determinism of Modern Science. Fraley, Lawrence E.

Underdetermination. McMullin, Ernan.

Underdetermination and the Social Side of Science. Brown, James Robert.

Understanding Life: Recent Work in Philosophy of Biology. Sterelny, Kim.

Une réflexion sur les rapports entre science et foi. Rivier, Dominique.

Unification and the History of Science: Comments on Józef Werle's Paper "How the Physical Sciences Discovered the Unity of Nature". Pietruska-Madej, Elzbieta.

Uniformitarianism in Cosmology: Background and Philosophical Implications of the Steady-State Theory. Balashov, Yuri.

Unnatural Science. Elgin, Catherine Z.

Using the Human Body as a Paradigm for the Structure of Time: Some Reflections on Time's URAM. Modell, Stephen M.

Using the Multitrait-Multimethod Matrix to Evaluate Knowledge-Based Systems. Adelman, Leonard and Riedel, Sharon L.

Utopie in actie: wat verwachtingen in technologie doen. Van Lente, Harro.

Vague Identity and Quantum Indeterminacy. Lowe, E J.

Valeriano Magni e la Discussione sul Vuoto in Italia. Bucciantini, Massimo.

Van Fraassen e os Limites da Observabilidade. Henrique, Luiz and Dutra, Araújo.

Vico e i 'Figliuoli di Dio': Ricerche sui Giganti nel *Diritto universale* e nella *Scienza nuova Prima*. Boschetto, Luca.

Vico y Hobbes: el "verum-factum". Bermudo, José M.

Vigotsky and Artificial Intelligence: What Could Cognitive Psychology Possibly Be About?. Harré, Rom.

Virtue and Truth in Clinical Science. Gillett, Grant.

Vital Signs: The *Place* of Memory in Psychoanalysis. Shepherdson, Charles.

Von der Reichweite mathematischen Denkens bei Fichte und Novalis. Csech, Werner.

Waiting for Newton. Leahey, Thomas H.

Was Cartesian Science Ever Meant to Be A Priori? A Comment on Hatfield. Raftopoulos, Athanasse.

Wavefunction Tails in the Modal Interpretation. Dickson, Michael.

Wetenschap, Filosofische Hermeneutiek, Metafysica. Heldring, Ottho G.

Weyl, Reichenbach and the Epistemology of Geometry. Ryckman, Thomas A.

What Could a *Feminist* Science Be?. Gross, Barry R.

What Does the Sociology of Scientific Knowledge Explain?: Or, When Epistemological Chickens Come Home to Roost. Roth, Paul A.

What is a Category?. Hanzel, I, Cernik, V and Vicenik, J.

What is Mimetic Desire?. Livingston, Paisley.

What Is Wrong with an Atomistic Account of Mental Representation?. Hogan, Melinda.

What Is 'Consciousness'?. Carley, Adam L.

What Locke Should Have Believed about Real Essences. Danaher, James P.

What Might Cognition Be, If Not Computation?. van Gelder, Tim.

When Other Things Aren't Equal: Saving *Ceteris Paribus* Laws from Vacuity. Pietroski, Paul and Rey, Georges.

When Psychology Looks Like a "Soft" Science, It's for Good Reason!. Howard, George S.

Who Should be Committable?. Lavin, Michael.

Why Everything Doesn't Realize Every Computation. Chrisley, Ronald L.

Why the Connection Argument Doesn't Work. Van Gulick, Robert.

Why There Can't Be a Logic of Induction. Glennan, Stuart S.

William James's Scientific Education. Croce, Paul Jerome.

William James, the Psychologist's Dilemma and the Historiography of Psychology: Cautionary Tales. Leary, David E.

Wisdom Updated. Falk, Arthur.

Wittgenstein and Aesthetics. Armstrong, D M.

Wonder as Source of Philosophy and of Science: A Comparison. George, Marie I.

Works on Teilhard, 1980-1994: An Annotated Bibliography. Salmon, James F and King, Thomas M.

Zur Konsistenz des soziobiologischen Begriffs "egoistisches Gen". Erbrich, Paul.

Zur Rekonstruktion der Philosophischen Hermeneutik. Krämer, Hans.

'Coordinative Definition' and Reichenbach's Semantic Framework: A Reassessment. Shapiro, Lionel Stefan.

'Ze zijn allemaal dood...' Over kennissystemen in de medische praktijk, voorvechters en critici, en het mysterieuze succes van onderzoeksprotocollen. Berg, Marc.

SCIENCE FICTION

Computer-Neue Flügel des Geistes?. Mainzer, Klaus.

SCIENTIFIC

Anticipación de la naturaleza y giro copernicano: La naturaleza de la explicación científica en Bacon y en Kant. López Fernández, Alvaro.

SHAPERE, D
Author's Response. Kitcher, Philip.

SHAPIN, S
Cultural History of Science: An Overview with Reflections. Dear, Peter.

SHAREHOLDER
Ethical Aspects of Investor Behavior. Rivoli, Pietra.

SHARING
Meditations On the Shared Life. Haddox, Bruce.
Walking Together: A Paradigmatic Social Phenomenon. Gilbert, Margaret.
Why Theorize How to Live with Each Other?. Gibbard, Allan F.

SHARMA, A
Response to Professor Arvind Sharma. Rambachan, Anantanand.

SHARPE, R
Back to the Future: A Reply to Sharpe. McFee, Graham.

SHAW, B
Brandon Shaw, Neil Perry, and the Perils of Education. Calhoun, Laura.

SHEFFER FUNCTIONS
Sheffer's Stroke for Prime Numbers. Karpenko, Alexander S.

SHELLEY, J
Hume's True Judges. Wieand, Jeffrey.

SHERMAN, N
Commentary on Sherman's "The Role of Emotions in Aristotelian Virtue". Dustin, Christopher A.

SHIH, H
A Belated Response to Hu Shih and D T Suzuki. Sellmann, James D.

SHINER, R
Critical Notice of Roger Shiner *Norm and Nature: The Movements of Legal Thought*. Schauer, Frederick.

SHINTOISM
Essentials of Shinto: An Analytical Guide to Principal Teachings. Picken, Stuart D B.

SHKLAR, J
Is Liberal Nationalism an Oxymoron? An Essay for Judith Shklar. Levinson, Sanford.

SHOEKI, A
Spontanéité et nature: le cas d'Andô Shôeki: Comparatisme et récupération. Joly, Jacques.

SHOEMAKER, S
Comments on "Moore's Paradox and Self-Knowledge". Albritton, Rogers.
Time and Change. Scott, Michael.

SHOTO, H
Interpreting Simone Weil: Presence and Absence in Attention. Pirruccello, Ann.

SHOWING
Hegel on Saying and Showing. Hahn, Susan.

SICHEL, B
Socrates, Plato and the Development of Reason: A Rejoinder to Professor Sichel. Scolnicov, Samuel.

SICKNESS
In-Jestion: Intestinal Laughter in Kant and Nietzsche. Swift, Paul.

SIDGWICK
El modelo utilitarista en la construcción y desarrollo de la bioética. Clotet, Joaquín.

SIEGEL, H
Circular Justifications. Brown, Harold I.
Sustaining and Responding to Charges of Bias in Critical Thinking. Norris, Stephen P.

SIEMEK, M
Reaction to Marek Siemek's "Critique of 'Non-Instrumental Reason'". Mayer, J R A.

SIGHT
The Stop. Appelbaum, David.
Understanding Vision: An Interdisciplinary Perspective. Humphreys, Glyn W (ed).
Vision: Variations on Some Berkeleian Themes. Schwartz, Robert.

SIGN
see also Symbol
"Act, Sign, and Consciousness: Thinking Along with Ricoeur" in *The Philosophy of Paul Ricoeur*, Hahn, Lewis Edwin (ed). Tong, Lik Kuen.
"Das Problem der Sprache in der Philosophie" in *Die Sprache in den Wissenschaften, Weingartner, Paul (ed)*. Weingartner, Paul.
"Ricoeur and the Hermeneutics of the Subject" in *The Philosophy of Paul Ricoeur, Hahn, Lewis Edwin (ed)*. Madison, G B.
"The Live Metaphor" in *The Philosophy of Paul Ricoeur, Hahn, Lewis Edwin (ed)*. Gerhart, Mary.
"The Symbol Gave Rise to Thought" in *The Philosophy of Paul Ricoeur, Hahn, Lewis Edwin (ed)*. Pellauer, David.
A Theory of Textuality: The Logic and Epistemology. Gracia, Jorge J E.
Aporie del Simbolo: Saggio su Otto Weininger. Manfreda, Luigi Antonio.
Consciousness and the Play of Signs. Innis, Robert E.
La Sémiotique Empiriste Face au Kantisme. Formigari, Lia.
Mind's Bodies: Thought in the Act. Lang, Berel.
Philosophy of the Sign. Simon, Josef and Heffernan, George (trans).
Sachen und Zeichen: Zur Philosophie des Pragmatismus. Oehler, Klaus.
Semiological Reductionism: A Critique of the Deconstructionist Movement in Postmodern Thought. Dillon, Martin C.
The Lyotard Reader. Benjamin, Andrew (ed).

The Stop. Appelbaum, David.
Ambiguità e Semiosi. Morpurgo-Tagliabue, Guido.
El Concepto, Como Signo Natural: Una Polémica Acerca de Ockham. Velázquez, Lorena.
Essay on Nature's Semeiosis. Falk, Arthur.
Fotogene Enttäuschungen. Hrachovec, Herbert.
If Wittgenstein Had Read Poinsot: Recasting the Problem of Signs and Mental States. Cahalan, John C.
La Filosofía Escolástica en los Orígenes de la Semiótica de Peirce. Beuchot, Mauricio.
Ockham: Suposición y Ontología. Valdivia, Benjamín.
Paintings and their Places. Feagin, Susan L.
Precedentes Ockhamistas de la Significación. Velásquez, Lorena.
Primera aproximación al lenguaje. Weismann, Francisco J.
Regular, Ambiguo, Disposicional. Pérez de Tudela, Jorge.
The Body as "Sign and Tool" in Hegel's *Encyclopaedia*. Dodd, James.
The Seduction of Abduction: Peirce's Theory of Signs and Indeterminacy in Language. Melrose, Robin.
Veranlasste die Universalienlehre Ockham, die Prädikation zuletzt ohne ein intentionales Moment zu verstehen?. Liske, Michael-Thomas.
Wittgenstein and Peirce on Meaning: The Evolution from Absolutism to Fallibilism. Boghossian, Peter G and Drewniak, Erik.
Wittgenstein, ill Linguaggio e l'Interpretazione. Perissinotto, Luigi.

SIGN LANGUAGE
Foregrounding Structures in American Sign Language. Wilbur, Ronnie B.

SIGNIFICANCE
All'inizio è il linguaggio. Moriconi, Enrico.
Ambiguità e Semiosi. Morpurgo-Tagliabue, Guido.
La fenomenologia, uno sguardo sulla verità. Bettinelli, Carla.
The Historical Significance of Feng Youlan's *Zhen Yuan Liu Shu*. Dainian, Zhang.

SIGNIFICATION
"Act, Sign, and Consciousness: Thinking Along with Ricoeur" in *The Philosophy of Paul Ricoeur, Hahn, Lewis Edwin (ed)*. Tong, Lik Kuen.
"Fashion and Signification in Baudrillard" in *Baudrillard: A Critical Reader, Kellner, Douglas M (ed)*. Tseëlon, Efrat.
"Locke on Meaning and Signification" in *Locke's Philosophy, Rogers, G A J (ed)*. Losonsky, Michael.
"Semiotics and Postmodernism" in *Postmodernism and Social Inquiry, Dickens, David R (ed)*. Gottdiener, M.
Consciousness and the Play of Signs. Innis, Robert E.
Philosophy of the Sign. Simon, Josef and Heffernan, George (trans).
Semiological Reductionism: A Critique of the Deconstructionist Movement in Postmodern Thought. Dillon, Martin C.
The Semiotic Self. Wiley, Norbert.
Berkeley, Causality, and Signification. Brook, Richard.
Diagrams and Metaphors: Iconic Aspects in Language. Hiraga, Masako K.
Essay on Nature's Semeiosis. Falk, Arthur.
From Relations to Practice in the Empiricism of Gilles Deleuze. Hayden, Patrick.
Iconicity, Analogy, and Universal Grammar. Itkonen, Esa.
Il carattere illusorio della critica di Jacques Derrida alla metafisica. Traversa, Guido.
La respuesta Husserliana en las Investigaciones Lógicas a la aporía del antropologismo. García Norro, Juan José.
Messages in Art. Levinson, Jerrold.
Susanne K Langer's Conception of 'Symbol'—Making Connections through Ambiguity. Nelson, Beatrice K.
The Hermeneutics of Formal Analytics: The Case of Tibetan Philosophical Criticism. Liberman, Kenneth.
The Old and the New Sublimes: Do They Signify? God?. Hutchings, Patrick.
The Problem of Iconicity. Radwanska-Williams, Joanna.

SILENCE
Qué es Poesía?. Núñez Cea, Victoria Martha.
The Case of a Broken Cohesive Chain. Kurzon, Dennis.
The Right of Silence: A Socio-Pragmatic Model of Interpretation. Kurzon, Dennis.
When Silence May Mean Derision. Akman, Varol.

SILVERS, A
Impairment, Disadvantage, and Equality: A Reply to Anita Silvers. Wasserman, David.

SIMILARITY
Tommaso Campanella: Eine Philosophie der Ähnlichkeit. Hagengruber, Ruth.
Les fondements d'une éthique de la similitude. Matheron, Alexandre.

SIMMEL, G
"Am Muttergeist soll die Welt genesen": Philosophische Dispositionen zum Frauenbild im Nationalsozialismus. Korotin, Ilse Erika.
Introduction to the Simmel Texts. Frisby, David.
Zeitgemässe Unzeitgemässe: Von Friedrich Nietzsche über Georg Simmel zu Max Weber. Schluchter, Wolfgang.

SIMMIAS
The Death of Socrates and the Life of Philosophy: An Interpretation of Plato's Phaedo. Ahrensdorf, Peter J.

SIMON, J
Philosophy of the Sign. Simon, Josef and Heffernan, George (trans).

SIMON, Y
Yves Simon's Approach to Natural Law. Long, Steven A.

SIMONS, P
"A Response to a Letter from Peg Simons, December 1993" in *Feminist Interpretations of Simone de Beauvoir, Simons, Margaret A (ed)*. Allen, Jeffner.
Vagueness and Bivalence: A Discussion of Williamson and Simons. Copeland, B J.

SOCIAL PHIL

Critical Theory and Political Possibilities: Conceptions of Emancipatory Politics in the Works of Horkheimer, Adorno, Marcuse, and Habermas. Alway, Joan.

Critique, Action, and Liberation. Marsh, James.

Das Vermächtnis des deutschen Judentums: Werke 2. Goldschmidt, Hermann Levin.

Democracy and Social Injustice: Law, Politics, and Philosophy. Simon, Thomas W.

Der feministische "Sündenfall"?. Kohn-Ley, Charlotte (ed) and Korotin, Ilse (ed).

Die Barbarei: Eine phänomenologische Kulturkritik. Henry, Michel.

Die berechnende Vernunft: Über das Ökonomische in allen Lebenslagen. Müller-Funk, Wolfgang (ed).

Die Technik und die Schwäche: Ökologie nach Nietzsche, Heidegger und dem "schwachen" Denken. Schönherr, Hans-Martin.

Dominations and Powers: Reflections on Liberty, Society, and Government. Santayana, George.

Ecological Enlightenment: Essays on the Politics of the Risk Society. Beck, Ulrich and Ritter, Mark A (trans).

Encountering the Other(s): Studies in Literature, History, and Culture. Brinker-Gabler, Gisela (ed).

Ethics and the Professions. Chadwick, Ruth (ed).

Ethique IV propositions 70-71. Macherey, Pierre.

Feminism and Philosophy: Essential Readings in Theory, Reinterpretation, and Application. Tuana, Nancy (ed) and Tong, Rosemarie (ed).

Feminist Contentions. Benhabib, Seyla (& others).

Feminist Interpretations of Hannah Arendt. Honig, Bonnie (ed).

Feminist Interpretations of Simone de Beauvoir. Simons, Margaret A (ed).

FI Interview: Camille Paglia on Freethought, Feminism, and Iconoclasm. Madigan, Timothy J.

Food: Multidisciplinary Perspectives. Harriss-White, Barbara (ed) and Hoffenberg, Raymond (ed).

Foucault and Law: Towards a Sociology of Law as Governance. Hunt, Alan and Wickham, Gary.

Foundations of Analytical Marxism (Volume I). Roemer, John E (ed).

Free Spirits: Feminist Philosophers on Culture. Mehuron, Kate (ed) and Percesepe, Gary (ed).

Freiheit für den Widerspruch: Werke 6. Goldschmidt, Hermann Levin.

Freud and the Politics of Psychoanalysis. Brunner, José.

Gay Ethics. Murphy, Timothy F (ed).

Georg Lukács. Sim, Stuart.

Gesamtausgabe (III Abteilung): Unveröffentlichte Abhandlungen. Heidegger, Martin.

Habermas: A Critical Introduction. Outhwaite, William.

Hipparchia's Choice: An Essay Concerning Women, Philosophy, etc. Le Doeuff, Michèle.

How Are We to Live? Ethics in an Age of Self-Interest. Singer, Peter.

Human Sciences or Humanities: The Case of Literature. Olafson, Frederick A.

Humanism and its Aftermath: The Shared Fate of Deconstruction and Politics. Martin, Bill.

I Am Because We Are: Readings in Black Philosophy. Hord, Fred Lee (ed) and Lee, Jonathan Scott (ed).

Idéer om Arbete. Hansson, Sven Ove.

Immanuel Kant zur Geschlechterdifferenz: Aufklärerische Vorurteilskritik·und bürgerliche Geschlechtsvormundschaft. Jauch, Ursula Pia.

In Harm's Way. Coleman, Jules L (ed) and Buchanan, Allen (ed).

Intersections: Nineteenth-Century Philosophy and Contemporary Theory. Rajan, Tilottama (ed) and Clark, David L (ed).

Intimacy and Spectacle: Liberal Theory as Political Education. Esquith, Stephen L.

Justice. Fisk, Milton (ed).

La Décadence. Roux, Yvon.

Liberals and Communitarians. Mulhall, Stephen and Swift, Adam.

Locality and Practical Judgment: Charity and Sacrifice. Ross, Stephen David.

Locke's Philosophy. Rogers, G A J (ed).

Logic and Mr Limbaugh: A Dittohead's Guide to Fallacious Reasoning. Perkins Jr, Raymond K.

Logik und Arbeit. Hartmann, Bruno.

Macht Geschlechter Differenz. Müller-Funk, Wolfgang (ed).

Making Sense of Humanity and Other Philosophical Papers 1982-1993. Williams, Bernard.

Marx's Theory of the Social Formation. Duan, Zhongqiao.

Marxism in the Postmodern Age. Callari, Antonio (ed), Cullenberg, Stephen (ed) and Biewener, Carole (ed).

Mass Enlightenment: Critical Studies in Rousseau and Diderot. Simon, Julia.

Max Weber in Amerika: Wirkungsgeschichte und Rezeptionsgeschichte Webers in der anglo-amerikanischen Philosophie und Sozialwissenschaft. Erdelyi, Agnes.

Meaning and Development. Kebede, Messay.

Mein Leben in Deutschland vor und nach 1933. Löwith, Karl.

Modern Technology in the Heideggerian Perspective, Volume I. Lovitt, William and Lovitt, Harriet Brundage.

Modern Technology in the Heideggerian Perspective, Volume II. Lovitt, William and Lovitt, Harriet Brundage.

Modernity and Identity. Lash, Scott (ed) and Friedman, Jonathan (ed).

Multiculturalism: A Critical Reader. Goldberg, David Theo.

Nationalism (Fourth, Expanded Edition). Kedourie, Elie.

No Harm: Ethical Principles for a Free Market. Burke, T Patrick.

Norm and Context in the Social Sciences. Griffioen, Sander (ed) and Verhoogt, Jan (ed).

Normative Cultures. Neville, Robert Cummings.

Openness in Research: The Tension Between Self and Other. Maso, I (& other eds).

Pensando la nación. Polakovic, Stefan.

Perspektiven der Dialogik: Zürcher Kolloquium zum 80. Geburtstag von Hermann Levin Goldschmidt. Goetschel, Willi (ed).

Perversion and Utopia: A Study in Psychoanalysis and Critical Theory. Whitebook, Joel.

Philosophical Arguments. Taylor, Charles.

Philosophie als Dialogik: Frühe Schriften Werke 1. Goldschmidt, Hermann Levin.

Philosophie im Vergleich der Kulturen. Mall, Ram Adhar.

Philosophy of Technology in Spanish Speaking Countries. Mitcham, Carl (ed).

Plenishment in the Earth. Ross, Stephen David.

Positivismusstreit: Die Auseinandersetzungen der Frankfurter Schule mit dem logischen Positivismus, dem Pragmatismus und dem kritischen Rationalismus. Dahms, Hans-Joachim.

Post-Modernism and Anthropology: Theory and Practice. Geuijen, Karin (ed), Raven, Diederick (ed) and De Wolf, Jan (ed).

Postmodern Ethics. Bauman, Zygmunt.

Postmodern Representations: Truth, Power, and Mimesis in the Human Sciences and Public Culture. Brown, Richard Harvey (ed).

Postmodernism and Social Inquiry. Dickens, David R (ed) and Fontana, Andrea (ed).

Power/Gender. Radtke, H Lorraine (ed) and Stam, Henderikus J (ed).

Power: Its Forms, Bases, and Uses. Wrong, Dennis H.

Powers of the Rational: Science, Technology, and the Future of Thought. Birmingham, Peg (trans), Janicaud, Dominique and Birmingham, Elizabeth (trans).

Practical Guilt: Moral Dilemmas, Emotions, and Social Norms. Greenspan, P S.

Practical Reasoning about Final Ends. Richardson, Henry S.

Pragmatism: From Progressivism to Postmodernism. Hollinger, Robert (ed) and Depew, David (ed).

Privatizing Public Lands. Lehmann, Scott.

Race and Mixed Race. Zack, Naomi.

Racist Culture: Philosophy and the Politics of Meaning. Goldberg, David Theo.

Real Rights. Wellman, Carl P.

Reason in the Balance: The Case Against Naturalism in Science, Law, and Education. Johnson, Phillip E.

Reason, History, and Politics: The Communitarian Grounds of Legitimation in the Modern Age. Ingram, David.

Reshaping the Female Body: The Dilemma of Cosmetic Surgery. Davis, Kathy.

Rousseau (Past Masters). Wokler, Robert.

Sartre and Evil: Guidelines for a Struggle. Gordon, Haim and Gordon, Rivca.

Schelling und die Selbstorganisation. Heuser-Kessler, Marie-Luise (ed) and Jacobs, Wilhelm G (ed).

Scientism and Humanism: Two Cultures in Post-Mao China (1978-1989). Hua, Shiping.

Socializing Epistemology: The Social Dimensions of Knowledge. Schmitt, Frederick F (ed).

Spirits Hovering Over the Ashes: Legacies of Postmodern Theory. Hix, H L.

Statesman (299b-d) and the Condemnation of Socrates. Dueso, José Solana.

Strange Multiplicity: Constitutionalism in an Age of Diversity. Tully, James.

Subjective Agency: A Theory of First-person Expressivity and its Social Implications. Altieri, Charles. ·

The Barbarism of Reason. Horowitz, Asher (ed) and Maley, Terry (ed).

The Blackwell Companion to the Enlightenment. Yolton, John W (& other eds).

The Blanchot Reader. Holland, Michael (ed).

The Book of the Body Politic. Forhan, Kate Langdon (ed & trans) and De Pizan, Christine.

The Broken Middle: Out of our Ancient Society. Rose, Gillian.

The Conflict of Law and Justice in the Icelandic Sagas. Pencak, William.

The Constructed Body: AIDS, Reproductive Technology, and Ethics. Murphy, Julien S.

The Convergence of Machine and Human Nature: A Critique of the Computer Metaphor of Mind and Artificial Intelligence. McClintock, Alexander.

The Cosmology of Freedom (New Edition). Neville, Robert Cummings.

The Counterfeit Wisdom of Shallow Minds: A Critique of Some Leading Offenders of the 1980's. Habermehl, Lawrence.

The Decolonization of Imagination: Culture, Knowledge, and Power. Pieterse, Jan Nederveen (ed) and Parekh, Bhikhu (ed).

The Defeat of the Mind. Friedlander, Judith (trans) and Finkielkraut, Alain.

The Erich Fromm Reader. Fromm, Erich and Funk, Rainer (ed).

The Flight from Woman (New Edition). Stern, Karl.

The Fragmented World of the Social: Essays in Social and Political Philosophy. Wright, Charles W (ed) and Honneth, Axel.

The Future of Alienation. Schacht, Richard.

The Greening of Ethics: From Human Chauvinism to Deep-Green Theory. Sylvan, Richard and Bennett, David.

The Irigaray Reader. Whitford, Margaret (ed).

The Nationalism Reader. Dahbour, Omar (ed) and Ishay, Micheline R (ed).

The Philosophy of Social Science: An Introduction. Hollis, Martin.

The Politics of English Jacobinism: Writings of John Thelwall. Thelwall, John and Claeys, Gregory (ed).

SOCIAL THEORY

After Postmodernism. Simons, Herbert W (ed) and Billig, Michael (ed).

Contested Knowledge: Social Theory in the Postmodern Era. Seidman, Steven.

Socializing Epistemology: The Social Dimensions of Knowledge. Schmitt, Frederick F (ed).

The Fragmented World of the Social: Essays in Social and Political Philosophy. Wright, Charles W (ed) and Honneth, Axel.

A Theory of Social Decisions. Baron, Jonathan.

Actualidad del tema del hombre: los estudios de la mujer. Santa Cruz, María Isabel.

Consuming Goods and the Goods of Consuming. Campbell, Colin.

Creative Agency and Fluid Images: A Revew of Iris Young's *Throwing Like a Girl and Other Essays in Feminist Philosophy and Social Theory*. Weiss, Gail.

Husserl, Schutz, "Paul" and Me: Reflections on Writing Phenomenology. Bentz, Valerie Malhotra.

Language, Narration and the Self. Staude, John-Raphael.

Rational Choice and Social Theory: A Comment. Hausman, Daniel M.

Response and Commentary on Iris Young's *Throwing Like a Girl and Other Essays in Feminist Philosophy and Social Theory*. Connolly, Maureen.

Sociale theorie en wetenschapsonderzoek: hebben die wat aan elkaar?. Van El, Carla.

SOCIAL WORK

"Narrating Social Work" in *Ethics and the Professions*, Chadwick, Ruth (ed). Edgar, Andrew.

National Survey of Social Workers' Sexual Attraction to Their Clients: Results, Implications, and Comparison to Psychologists. Bernsen, Ann, Tabachnick, Barbara G and Pope, Kenneth S.

SOCIALISM

"After Socialism" in *The End of "Isms"?*, Shtromas, Alexsandras (ed). Marquand, David.

"Buber's Socialist and Political Views: A Critique" in *Thinkers and Teachers of Modern Judaism*, Goldsmith, Emanuel S (ed). Uffenheimer, Benjamin.

"Das Erbe der Aufklärung: Mut zum Denken, Mut zum Handeln" in *Das geistige Erbe Europas*, Buhr, Manfred (ed). Besse, Guy.

"Die verlorene Wette—Versuch über die Krisen des 'realen' Sozialismus" in *Das geistige Erbe Europas*, Buhr, Manfred (ed). Labica, Georges.

"Marxism: From Scientific to Utopian" in *Whither Marxism?*, Magnus, Bernd (ed). Longxi, Zhang.

"The Modern World and the Individual: From the Metamorphosis of Eastern European Marxism to Marx's Errors" in *Whither Marxism?*, Magnus, Bernd (ed). Marga, Andrei.

"What's Left of Marx?" in *The Cambridge Companion to Habermas*, White, Stephen K (ed). Love, Nancy S.

"'Socialism of the Mind': The New Age of Post-Marxism" in *After Postmodernism*, Simons, Herbert W (ed). Cloud, Dana L.

Critique, Action, and Liberation. Marsh, James.

John Stuart Mill och socialismen. Hansson, Sven Ove.

Logik und Arbeit. Hartmann, Bruno.

Marxism and Spirituality: An International Anthology. Page, Benjamin B (ed).

Socialism After Communism: The New Market Socialism. Pierson, Christopher.

The Owl at Dawn: A Sequel to Hegel's Phenomenology of Spirit. Curtrofello, Andrew.

The Real World of Democracy Revisited and Other Essays on Democracy and Socialism. Cunningham, Frank.

Vergangenheit als Zukunft. Haller, Michael (ed) and Habermas, Jürgen.

A Perspective on Solidarity in a 'Post-Socialist' World. Steger, Manfred.

Democrazia e sviluppo—La Democrazia alla prova. Thesing, Josef.

Essentialism and the Market. O'Neill, John.

Fear, Technology, and the State: Carl Schmitt, Leo Strauss, and the Revival of Hobbes in Weimar and National Socialist Germany. McCormick, John P.

Gnōthi Sauton: Heidegger's Problem Ours. Swazo, Norman K.

Holotechnodemocracy: An Alternative to Capitalism and Socialism. Bunge, Mario.

La Democracia y el Futuro del Socialismo. Fernández del Riesgo, Manuel.

La pensée politique de Jean Jaurès. Drouin, Paul.

Labriola tra Croce e Gentile. Agrimi, Mario.

Lenin, Kautsky and Working-Class Consciousness. Mayer, Robert.

Lyotard's Peregrination: Three (and-a-half) Responses to the Call of Justice. Dalton, Stuart.

Moral/Political Education in the People's Republic of China: Learning Through Role Models. Reed, Gay Garland.

National Past, Socialist Future. Geoghegan, Vincent.

Pedagogia Pelo e Para o Trabalho: Açao Disciplinadora da Burguesia e a Resistência dos trabalhadores. Rodrigues, Alcione.

Propositions on 'The End of Socialism?'. Lovell, David W.

Socialism and Democracy: Elaborations of the Idea of a Self-Governing Community. Hindess, Barry.

The Formation Approach and the Crisis of "Real Socialism". Juchler, Jakob.

The Post-Socialist Change in Eastern Europe: Specific Development or Universal Trend of Global History? A Formation Approach. Juchler, Jakob.

The Sundered Totality: Adorno's Freudo-Marxism. Cook, Deborah.

The Theory of Social Change with Introduction by Bill Scheuerman. Marcuse, Herbert and Neumann, Franz.

The University of Liberal Capitalism and the Possibility of Renewed Socialism: Reflections on the Soviet Coup of August 1991. Lawler, James M.

Thinking the Post-Socialism: From Socialist Community to Pluralistic Society. Flego, Gvozden.

Transzendentale Basis, Materialismus, und Religion. Lauth, Reinhard.

SOCIALITY

Sociality as a Philosophically Significant Category. Gilbert, Margaret.

SOCIALIZATION

On the Coerciveness of Sexist Socialization. Burgess-Jackson, Keith.

SOCIETY

see also Civil Society

"A Conservative Approach to Social Epistemology" in *Socializing Epistemology: The Social Dimensions of Knowledge, Schmitt, Frederick (ed)*. Kornblith, Hilary.

"A Theory of Social Injustice" in *Radical Philosophy of Law, Caudill, David S (ed)*. Simon, Thomas W.

"Architecture and the Aesthetics of Continuity" in *Philosophy and Architecture, Mitias, Michael H (ed)*. Berleant, Arnold.

"Beziehung ohne Beziehung": Bemerkungen zur Gesellschafts- und Gemeinschaftskritik von Emmanuel Lévinas. Wenzel, U J.

"Capitalism and the Code: A Critique of Baudrillard's Third Order Simulacrum" in *Baudrillard: A Critical Reader, Kellner, Douglas M (ed)*. Schoonmaker, Sara.

"Commercial Society and Political Theory in the Eighteenth Century" in *Main Trends in Cultural History, Melching, Willem (ed)*. Hont, Istvan.

"Community Without Fusion: Dewey, Mead, Tufts" in *Pragmatism: From Progressivism to Postmodernism, Hollinger, Robert (ed)*. Campbell, James.

"Contrasting Conceptions of Social Epistemology" in *Socializing Epistemology: The Social Dimensions of Knowledge, Schmitt, Frederick F (ed)*. Kitcher, Philip.

"Enlightenment and the Institution of Society: Notes for a Conceptual History" in *Main Trends in Cultural History, Melching, Willem (ed)*. Baker, Keith Michael.

"From World3 to the Social Assessment of Technology" in *Philosophy of Technology in Spanish Speaking Countries, Mitcham, Carl (ed)*. Sanmartín, José.

"Hegel and Hobbes Revised" in *Hegel on the Modern World, Collins, Ardis B (ed)*. Peperzak, Adriaan.

"La Filsofia va al Taller" in *Temas Actuales de Filosofía, Palacios, María Julia (ed)*. Gonza, Guillermo.

"Life and Society at Ancient Memphis According to the Saqqâra Texts" in *Life, World and Meaning, Roux, A P J (ed)*. Dreyer, H J.

"Max Weber and the Bourgeoisie" in *The Barbarism of Reason, Horowitz, Asher (ed)*. Strong, Tracy B.

"Perspectivas Epistemológicas para un Modelo Macrosocial" in *Temas Actuales de Filosofía, Palacios, María Julia (ed)*. José, Elena Teresa.

"Philosophy, Technology, and Society" in *Philosophy of Technology in Spanish Speaking Countries, Mitcham, Carl (ed)*. Medina, Manuel.

"Political Rights Versus Social Rights" in *Human Rights and the World's Religions, Rouner, Leroy (ed)*. Markovic, Mihailo.

"Remarks on Collective Belief" in *Socializing Epistemology: The Social Dimensions of Knowledge, Schmitt, Frederick F (ed)*. Gilbert, Margaret.

"Responsibility for Consequences" in *In Harm's Way, Coleman, Jules L (ed)*. Fischer, John Martin and Ravizza, Mark.

"Ricoeur as Social Philosopher" in *The Philosophy of Paul Ricoeur, Hahn, Lewis Edwin (ed)*. Bien, Joseph.

"Socializing Epistemology: A Bibliography" in *Socializing Epistemology: The Social Dimensions of Knowledge, Schmitt, Frederick F (ed)*. Schmitt, Frederick F and Spellman, James.

"Staying Alive": Intellectual and Spiritual Sustenance on the Journey for Critical Foundations Scholars-Teachers. Brosio, Richard A.

"The Justification of Group Beliefs" in *Socializing Epistemology: The Social Dimensions of Knowledge, Schmitt, Frederick F (ed)*. Schmitt, Frederick F.

"Universalism and the Situated Critic" in *The Cambridge Companion to Habermas, White, Stephen K (ed)*. Pensky, Max.

"Wittgenstein and 'Mainstream' Contemporary Philosophy" in *Wittgenstein and Contemporary Philosophy, Teghrarian, Souren (ed)*. Schwyzer, Hubert.

A Companion to Aristotle's Politics. Keyt, David and Miller, Fred D.

A Philosophy of History in Fragments. Heller, Agnes.

Chaosmosis: An Ethico-Aesthetic Paradigm. Guattari, Félix, Bains, Paul (trans) and Pefanis, Julian (trans).

Danto and his Critics. Rollins, Mark (ed).

Dominations and Powers: Reflections on Liberty, Society, and Government. Santayana, George.

Ecological Enlightenment: Essays on the Politics of the Risk Society. Beck, Ulrich and Ritter, Mark A (trans).

Emmanuel Levinas: The Genealogy of Ethics. Llewelyn, John (ed).

Foucault and Law: Towards a Sociology of Law as Governance. Hunt, Alan and Wickham, Gary.

Foucault and the Writing of History. Goldstein, Jan (ed).

Hegel and Marx: Introductory Lectures. Kedourie, Elie.

Hegel In His Time: Berlin, 1818-1831. Burbidge, John W (trans) and D'Hondt, Jacques.

How Are We to Live? Ethics in an Age of Self-Interest. Singer, Peter.

I Am Because We Are: Readings in Black Philosophy. Hord, Fred Lee (ed) and Lee, Jonathan Scott (ed).

Identity, Culture, and Education. Smeyers, Paul (ed).

Introduction to Ethics: Personal and Social Responsibility in a Diverse World. Percesepe, Gary.

Kant on Happiness in Ethics. Wike, Victoria S.

La Tirania en la Grecia Antigua. Sánchez de la Torre, D Angel.

Lectures on Divine Humanity. Solovyov, Vladimir.

SOUL

Theophrastus Redivivus, Volumes 1 and 2. Canziani, Guido (ed) and Paganini, Gianni (ed).

Zum Begriff der Trinität. Polemis, Michael.

A Practical Idea of Blackness. Kiros, Teodros.

Appunti di Lettura sul Cartesianesimo Napoletano tra '600 e '700. Cantillo, Clementina.

Aristotle on Dividing the Soul and Uniting the Virtues. Gottlieb, Paula.

Aristotle: Philosophy and Politics, Theory and Practice. Thompson, Walter J.

Coscienza e Corporeità. Cavaciuti, Santino.

Cuerpo y Alma en el Helemorfismo de Santo Tomás. Beuchot, Mauricio.

Death According to Descartes: Why the Soul Leaves the Body. Ablondi, Fred.

El Concepto de Complexión y Alma en Tomás de Aquino y Galena. Martínez Sendra, María Carmen.

En Busca de la Lógica Viquiana. Costa, Gustavo.

Eternità e tempo in Plotino. Ferretti, Silvia.

Form und Materie bei Leibniz: die mittleren Jahre. Adams, Robert Merrihew.

From the Chariot: The Katha and the Phaedrus. Johnson, Lawrence E.

Gassendi contre Spinoza selon Bayle: ricochets de la critique de l'âme du monde. Darmon, Jean-Charles.

Geist und Psyche in tiefenpsychologischer und phänomenologischer Perspektive. Weier, Winfried.

Holiness as Service: *Therapeia* and *Hyperetike* in Plato's *Euthyphro*. Parry, David M.

Il fantasma di Turing e l'incancellabilità del soggetto. Turpia, Piero.

Il soggetto della scienza prima. Roccaro, Giuseppe.

Kant's View of the Transcendental Imagination in the First *Critique*. Hickey, Lance P.

La belleza y los esteticismos. Corti, Enrique.

La Musica in Aristotele. Vetere, Lucia.

La persona come apertura all'essere eterno secondo E Stein. D'Ambra, Michele.

Le Fonti del "Sigillus Sigillorum" del Bruno, Ossia: Il Confronto con Ficino a Oxford Sull'anima Umana. Sturlese, Rita.

Leibniz on Apperception and Animal Souls. Miles, M L.

Leibniz, Lamy, and 'The Way of Pre-Established Harmony'. Woolhouse, Roger S and Francks, Richard.

Memoro-Politics, Trauma and the Soul. Hacking, Ian.

Neotomismo a Salerno: L'Ambiente Culturale in cui visse ed Operò Pasquale Naddeo. Gigante, Mario.

On a Mistake Commonly Made in Accounts of Sixteenth-Century Discussions of the Immortality of the Soul. Martin, Christopher.

Platonismo, Rivoluzione Scientifica, Culti Solari: Un Tema da Riesaminare. Albanese, Luciano.

Plotinus on the Souls of Beasts. Cole, Eve Browning.

Religious Belief and Philosophical Inquiry. Prasad, M.

Sobre la Experiencia y el Conocimiento del Alma. Quijano, Francisco.

Sophocles' *Oedipus the King*: Art and the Mystery of Human Existence. Georgiadis, Constantine.

Teleology and Evil in *Laws* 10. Carone, Gabriela Roxana.

The Content of Cartesian Sensation and the Intermingling of Mind and Body. Aquila, Richard E.

The Definition of Soul in Aristotle's *De anima* ii 1 Is Not Analogous to the Definition of Snub. Wehrle, Walter E.

The Peace of the Soul...(Harmonizing Techniques in the World-religions). Karvalics, László Z.

The Will as King over the Powers of the Soul: Uses and Sources of an Image in the Thirteenth Century. Teske, Roland J.

The 'Passions of the Soul': Descartes' Shadow on Theories of the Emotions. Gorevan, Patrick.

The 'Soul': Modern Psychological Interpretations. Hunt, Morton.

Tortuous Dualism. Levin, Michael.

Transmigration Without a Self. Datta, Rama.

Veatch and Brain Death: A Plea for Soul. Pentz, Rebecca D.

Von einer Ethik der Technik aus antinaturalistischem Geist. Betzler, Monika.

Why Ethics is Political Science for Aristotle. Gerson, L.

'Town Criers of Inwardness' or Reflections on Rorty. Fitzpatrick, Joseph.

SOUND

Authenticities: Philosophical Reflections on Musical Performance. Kivy, Peter.

Philosophy of the Sign. Simon, Josef and Heffernan, George (trans).

Rhetorical Mosaic for a Kaleidoscope of Sound: Poetry as a Road to Understanding the Prose Voice. Britt, John F.

Der audio-visuelle Kontrakt—der Lärm um das Reale. Zizek, Slavoj.

Music, Platonism and Performance: Some Ontological Strains. Sharpe, R A.

Sound, Society, and Music "Proper". Bowman, Wayne D.

Sounds Before Symbols: What Does Phenomenology Have to Say?. Bartholomew, Douglas.

SOUNDNESS

Discrete Tense Logic with Beginning and Ending Time: An Infinite Hierarchy of Complete Axiomatic Systems. Aqvist, Lennart.

Four-Valued Semantics for Relevant Logics (and Some of Their Rivals). Restall, Greg.

Reasoning about Update Logic. Van Eijck, Jan and De Vries, Fer-Jan.

SOURCE

L'uso dell'*Index Thomisticus* nello studio delle fonti di Tommaso d'Aquino: considerazoni generali e questioni di metodo. Portalupi, Enzo.

SOUTH AFRICAN

An Analysis of Public Interest Reporting: The Case of General Motors in South Africa. Malone, David and Roberts, Robin W.

Facing the Challenges of Diversity—A Reflection on the Role of Philosophy in South Africa Today. Van Der Merwe, W L.

Interdisciplinary and Intercultural Aspects of Music. Heimes, Klaus F.

Some Reflections on the Relevance of Karl Jaspers' Concept of Border Situation in Present-Day South Africa. Ally, Mashuq.

The Philosophical Anthropology of Alfred North Whitehead. Prozesky, Martin.

SOVEREIGNTY

Der Katechon: Zu Carl Schmitts fundamentalistischer Kritik der Zeit. Meuter, Günter.

Aristoteles' "Politik" kommentieren. Höffe, Otfried.

En Deçà de la Souveraineté. Pestieau, Joseph.

Kant's Denial of Absolute Sovereignty. Arntzen, Sven.

Sovereignty, Soft Determinism and Responsibility. Gooch, Paul W.

SOVIET

"Die verlorene Wette—Versuch über die Krisen des 'realen' Sozialismus" in *Das geistige Erbe Europas*, Buhr, Manfred (ed). Labica, Georges.

"Ideology after the Collapse of Communism" in *The End of "Isms"?*, Shtromas, Alexsandras (ed). Minogue, Kenneth.

"Lessons from the USSR: Taking Marxian Theory the Next Step" in *Whither Marxism?*, Magnus, Bernd (ed). Resnick, Stephen and Wolff, Richard.

"Soviet Historiography as a 'Normal Science'" in *Historiography Between Modernism and Postmodernism*, Topolski, Jerzy (ed). Zalejko, Gwidon.

"The End of History" as a Sociosophical Problem. Rachkov, P A.

S L Frank: The Life and Work of A Russian Philosopher, 1877-1950. Boobbyer, Philip.

The End of "Isms"?. Shtromas, Aleksandras (ed).

Concerning the National Uniqueness of Russian Philosophy. Boldyrev, I A.

Democracy and Tyranny in Modern and Recent Times. Medushevskii, A N.

East and West: Russian Renewal and the Future. Borodaj, Jurij and Nikiforov, Aleksandr.

Liberal Tradition in the Cultural-Historical Experience of Russia. Novikova, L and Sizemskaia, I.

On the Tasks of the Contemporary Philosophy of Law. Novgorodtsev, P I.

Philosophy in Moscow in the Fifties and Sixties. Sadovskii, V N.

Philosophy in Russian Today. Yulina, N S.

Raíces ideológicas de la "guerra suicia" en América latina (en especial Argentina). Spitta, Arnold.

Russian Philosophy as an Area of Study and as a Spiritual Value. Kuvakin, V A.

Social Being and the Human Essence: An Unresolved Issue in Soviet Philosophy. Bakhurst, David.

The Case of Professor Z la Beletskii: An Episode from the History of Soviet Philosophy. Batygin, Gennadii and Deviatko, Inna.

The Idea of Law in the Philosophy of V S Solov'ev. Novgorodtsev, P I.

The Trinitarian Panentheism of Sergej Bulgakov. O'Donnell, John.

The University of Liberal Capitalism and the Possibility of Renewed Socialism: Reflections on the Soviet Coup of August 1991. Lawler, James M.

SOVIET UNION

An Integrative Ideology for Russia. Kosolapov, N A.

Identificational Recruit: Between the Temptation of Nihilism and a Tie-In with the Body. Liubomirova, Nataly.

Not the "Human Factor" but the Person. Suvorov, Aleksandr V.

Sophiology: A Human Reading of the Book of God. Mosolova, S V.

The Philosophy of Pavel Florenskii and the Future of Russian Culture. Sidorov, Igor.

Toward a Nontraditional Understanding. Sokolova, R I.

SPACE

"Constituent Structure and Explanation in..Cognitive Architecture" in *Connectionism: Debates on Psychological Explanation*, Macdonald, Cynthia (ed). Smolensky, Paul.

"Dimensions of the Diagnostic Space" in *Probability in Theory-Building*, Brzezinski, Jerzy (ed). Brzezinski, Jerzy.

"Espacio, Tiempo y Particulares" in *Temas Actuales de Filosofía*, Palacios, María Julia (ed). Rodríguez Larreta, Juan.

"Is Conscious Awareness Consistent with Space-Time Descriptions?" in *Philosophy, Mathematics and Modern Physics*, Rudolph, Enno (ed). Penrose, Roger.

"On Renormalization in Quantum Field Theory and the Structure of Space-Time" in *Philosophy, Mathematics and Modern Physics*, Rudolph, Enno (ed). Stamatescu, I O.

"On the Origin of Structure in the Universe" in *Philosophy, Mathematics and Modern Physics*, Rudolph, Enno (ed). Barbour, Julian B.

"Para una Relectura Posible de la Epistemología Kantiana" in *Temas Actuales de Filosofía*, Palacios, María Julia (ed). Rechach, Carmen Alicia.

"Space and Time" in *Philosophy, Mathematics and Modern Physics*, Rudolph, Enno (ed). Lurçat, François.

"Spaced Out or Folded In? Trends in Architectural Choreography" in *Philosophy and Architecture*, Mitias, Michael H (ed). Donougho, Martin J.

"The Aesthetics of Architecture and the Politics of Space" in *Philosophy and Architecture*, Mitias, Michael H (ed). Sparshott, Francis.

"Topología—Atopología del Saber" in *Temas Actuales de Filosofía*, Palacios, María Julia (ed). Craia, Eladio Pablo C (& others).

Continuity and Change in the Development of Russell's Philosophy. Hager, Paul J.

Eternity and Freedom: A Critical Analysis of Divine Timelessness as a Solution to the Foreknowledge/Free Will Debate. Robinson, Michael D.

From Myth to Modern Mind: A Study of the Origins and Growth of Scientific Thought, Volume I. Schlagel, Richard H.

SPACE

Humanity, Environment, and God. Spurway, Neil.

Imagination and Time. Warnock, Mary.

Indexikalische Gedanken: Über den Gegenstandsbezug in der raumzeitlichen Erkenntnis. Wyller, Truls.

Kant's Idealism. Neujahr, Philip J.

Le Même et L'Autre dans la Structure Ontologique du Timée de Platon. Brisson, Luc (ed).

Metapatterns: Across Space, Time, and Mind. Volk, Tyler.

On Knowing—The Natural Sciences. McKeon, Richard, Owen, David B (ed) and McKeon, Zahava K (ed).

Other Minds: Critical Essays 1969-1994. Nagel, Thomas.

Paradoxes (Second Edition). Sainsbury, R M.

Substance Among Other Categories. Hoffman, Joshua and Rosenkrantz, Gary S.

The Children of Time: Causality, Entropy, Becoming. Lestienne, Rémy and Neher, E C (trans).

The Mind of David Hume: A Companion to Book I of 'A Treatise of Human Nature'. Johnson, Oliver A.

The Production of Space. Lefebvre, Henri and Nicholson-Smith, Donald (trans).

The Shaggy Steed of Physics: Mathematical Beauty in the Physical World. Oliver, David.

The Shape of Space (Second Edition). Nerlich, Graham.

A Formal System for Classical Particle Mechanics, Its Model-Theoretic Applications and Space-Time Structure. Ishigaki, Toshio.

Absolute vs Relational Theories of Space and Time: A Review of *World Enough and Space-Time* by John Earman. Rynasiewicz, Robert.

Accessibility, Kinds, and Laws: A Structural Explication. Mormann, Thomas.

Algumas Observaçoes sobre a Lógica Espacial. Alves, Elias Humberto.

Boolean Algebras, Stone Spaces, and the Iterated Turing Jump. Jockusch Jr, Carl G and Soare, Robert I.

Characterization of Realizable Space Complexities. Seiferas, Joel I and Meyer, Albert R.

Cosmology: A Philosophical Survey. Leslie, John.

Covering Analytic Sets by Families of Closed Sets. Solecki, Slawomir.

Dominating Projective Sets in the Baire Space. Spinas, Otmar.

Extraterrestrial Intelligence and UFOs: Challenges to Physics, Metaphysics, and Theology?. Trundle, Robert C.

Fichtes genetische Deduktion von Raum und Zeit in Differenz zu Kant. Metz, Wilhelm.

Fixed-parameter Tractability and Completeness IV: On Completeness for W[P] and PSPACE Analogues. Abrahamson, K A (& others).

General Method. McShane, Philip.

Gruesome Perceptual Spaces. Weir, Alan.

Haunting Resonances at the Threshold of Contemporary Philosophy. Review of *Echoes: After Heidegger* by John Sallis. Brogan, Walter.

Hechler Reals. Labedzki, Grzegorz and Repicky, Miroslav.

Historia de la Filosofía e Historia: Notas Para un Debate. Sanz, Víctor.

Hume's Aesthetic Psychology of Distance, Greatness and the Sublime. Jacquette, Dale.

Il mondo "Pesante" di Newton. Infante, Giancarlo.

Kants zweite Antinomie und die Physik. Falkenburg, Brigitte.

L'informe bergsoniano nella filosofia di Serres. Delcò, Alessandro.

La notion d'Espace Cosmique et des origines de l'Univers. Vieillard-Baron, Jean-Louis.

Modalities in Vector Logic. Mizraji, Eduardo.

New Work for Counterpart Theorists: Determinism. Belot, Gordon.

Newton sobre Movimento, Espaço e Tempo. Salles, Eduardo and Barra, Oliveira.

Non-Turing Computers and Non-Turing Computability. Hogarth, Mark.

O Éter Luminoso como Espaço Absoluto. Oliveira, Maurício Pietrocola.

Observaçoes sobre a Concepçao Kantiana do Espaço. Molina, Jorge Alberto.

On Certain Consequence of the Temporal and Spatial Scale of the Universe: Comments on "How the Physical Sciences Discovered the Unity of Nature". Butryn, Stanislaw.

On the Field Aspect of Quantum Fields. Huggett, Nick and Weingard, Robert.

Operators Defined by Propositional Quantification and Their Interpretation Over Cantor Space. Polacik, Tomasz.

Particulars *as* Universals: Russell's Ontological Assay of Particularity and Phenomenological Space-Time. Hochberg, Herbert.

Pi$^1_1$ Wellfounded Relations. Hjorth, Greg.

Platonismo, Rivoluzione Scientifica, Culti Solari: Un Tema da Riesaminare. Albanese, Luciano.

Regularity Properties for Dominating Projective Sets. Brendle, Jörg.

Relativity, Absoluteness and Observation. Janssen, H C I M.

Requiem for the Identity Theory. Smythies, John R.

Space Curvature and Repeatable Properties, Almost No Problems With a Peaceful Coexistence. Mormann, Thomas.

Space-time in Philosophy and Physics (Melchior Palágyi's Theory on Space-time and the Einstein-Minkowski Theory of Relativity). Székely, László.

Spacetime and Holes. Brighouse, Carolyn.

The Bohmian Model of Quantum Cosmology. Callender, Craig and Weingard, Robert.

The Diagram H-R of Stars Displacement: Real Fact or Useful Research Instrument?. Zabierowski, Miroslaw.

The Discontinuity of Space and Time. Cekic, Miodrag.

The Logic of Relations and the Ideality of Space. Macbeth, Danielle.

The Neglected Alternative in Kant's Philosophy Revisited. Katz, Claire Elise.

The Spatio-Temporal Theory of Individuation. Potts, Michael.

The Time-Space of Human Life. Cackowski, Zdzislaw.

SPACE-TIME

Spacetime Theory as Physical Geometry. Disalle, Robert.

Substance, Modality, and Spacetime. Healey, Richard.

Wozu noch Erste Philosophie? Über das Wechselverhältnis von Subjektivität und raumzeitlicher Einzelnheit. Koch, Anton Friedrich.

SPANISH

"Juan Huarte de San Juan: Un Materialista Español del Siglo XVI" in *Temas Actuales de Filosofía, Palacios, María Julia (ed)*. Femenías, María Luisa.

"Technology and Human Nature" in *Philosophy of Technology in Spanish Speaking Countries, Mitcham, Carl (ed)*. García-Merita, María Luisa.

Painting on the Page: Interartistic Approaches to Modern Hispanic Texts. Geisdorfer Feal, Rosemary and Feal, Carlos.

Philosophy of Technology in Spanish Speaking Countries. Mitcham, Carl (ed).

Slavery and the Catholic Tradition: Rights in the Balance. Brett, Stephen F.

Actualidad de un Filósofo del Siglo XVI: Francisco de Vitoria. Ocaña García, Marcelino.

De Vicios y Virtudes en Algunos Textos Castellanos del Siglo XV. Salinas Espinosa, Concepción.

Estudio introductorio a "De la educación moral del Hombre": Texto inédito en castellano de Claude Adrien Helvétius. Diego, Carmen Verde.

Extracto de "Libraos de Ultramaria". Bentham, Jeremy.

Fr Benito J Feijóo, profesor de filosofía escolástica. López Vázquez, J Ramón.

Ideas sobre Ortega y Gasset y el ocaso del marxismo. Pallotini, Michele.

Il problema della filosofia spagnola. Savignano, Armando.

Jeremy Bentham y la educación jurídica en la Universidad de Salamanca durante el siglo XIX. Pérez Luño, Antonio-Enrique.

La evolución filosófica e ideológica de la Asociación Española para el Progreso de las Ciencias (1908-1979). Sierra, Pelayo García.

La Filosofía de los Poetas en la Fundación Fernando Rielo. Sánchez-Gay Venegas, Juana.

La filosofía, el método y el hombre en el pensamiento de Adolfo Muñoz Alonso. González Miguel, Jesús Graciliano.

La Presencia de Giambattista Vico en la Cultura Española (II). Sevilla Fernández, José M.

Nota Sobre la Poesía Algorítmica de Ramón Llull. Lizalde, Carlos Lorenza.

Observaciones al Margen a la Investigación Viquiana en la España Contemporánea. Cacciatore, Giuseppe.

Phonological Awareness in Learning Literacy. Jimenez Glez, J E and Del Rosario, M.

Razón Vital y Fenomenología (Génesis del Raciovitalismo Orteguiano). Pozo, Antonio Gutierrez.

Sobre la Fortuna de Aristóteles en España. Escobar Chico, Angel.

Variaciones Isidorianas. Rodón, Eulalia.

Zur Situation der Philosophie in Spanien. Rühle, Volker.

SPARSHOTT, F

Aristotle and Hellenistic Philosophy. Sharples, Bob.

SPATIALITY

Estética del límite: Transformaciones en la configuración literaria del horizonte. Innerarity, Daniel.

SPAVENTA, B

Un Inedito di Bertrando Spaventa sul Concetto di Filosofia. Petrone, Giuseppe Landolfi.

SPAVENTA, S

Un'idea alla Ricerca di un Partito: L'eredità di Silvio Spaventa nel Liberalismo di Fine Ottocento. Ricci, Saverio.

SPEAKER

The Metaphoric Nature of Coding: Toward a Theory of Utterance. Zaitseva, Valentina.

SPEAKING

"Public and Private Speaking in Plato's Later Dialogues" in *Platón: Los Diálogos Tardíos, Lan, Conrado Eggers (ed)*. Rowe, Christopher.

Semiosis of Listening: The Other in Heidegger's Writings on Hölderlin and Celan's "The Meridian". Ziarek, Krzysztof.

SPECIES

The Evolution of Evil. Anders, Timothy.

A (Not-so-radical) Solution to the Species Problem. Wilson, Bradley E.

A Critical Review of Philosophical Work on the Units of Selection Problem. Sober, Elliott and Wilson, David Sloan.

Are There Natural Laws Concerning Particular Biological Species?. Lange, Marc.

Contemporary Non-Conventional Evolutionary Theories. Urbanek, Adam.

For Pluralism and Against Realism About Species. Stanford, P Kyle.

Is Species Selection Dependent Upon Emergent Characters?. Stidd, Benton M and Wade, David L.

Language as a Community of Interacting Belief Systems: A Case Study Involving Conduct Toward Self and Others. Wilson, David Sloan.

Ostensive Definitions of the Names of Species and Clades. Ghiselin, Michael T.

Reasons for the Failure of Theories. Mayr, Ernst.

The Argument from Marginal Cases: Is Speciesism Defensible?. Feezell, Randolph M and Stephens, William O.

The Definitions of Species and Clade Names: A Reply to Ghiselin. de Queiroz, Kevin.

Two Concepts of Constraint: Adaptationism and the Challenge from Developmental Biology. Amundson, Ron.

SPECIFICATION

L'ontologie de la spécificité. Martineau, Emmanuel.

On Russell's Argument for Restricting Modes of Specification and Domains of Quantification. Weiss, Bernhard.

The Specification of "Specification". Partridge, Derek and Galton, Antony.

SPECTROMETER

Spectrometers as Analogues of Nature. Rothbart, Daniel.

SPECULATION

La Inferència Dialèctico-Especulativa a la *Ciència de la Lògica* de Hegel. Alegre I Biosca, Lluís.

SPECULATIVE

Absolu/Sujet. Jarczyk, Gwendoline and Labarrière, Pierre-Jean.

SPEECH

"A Central Problem for a Speech-Dispositional Account of Logic and Language" in *Perspectives on Quine, Barrett, Robert (ed)*. Berger, Alan.

"Et 'Factum' et 'Verum' cum 'Verbo' Convertuntur": Lingua Divina e 'Prima Parlari' delle Nazioni in Vico. Agrimi, Mario.

Constitutional Domains: Democracy, Community, Management. Post, Robert C.

God and Plastic Surgery: Marx, Nietzsche, Freud and the Obvious. Barris, Jeremy.

Perspectives on Quine. Barrett, Robert (ed) and Gibson, Roger (ed).

Phaedrus. Plato, Woodruff, Paul (trans) and Nehamas, Alexander (trans).

The Names of History: On the Poetics of Knowledge. Rancière, Jacques and Melehy, Hassan (trans).

A Prototype View of Context and Linguistic Behavior: Context Prototypes and Talk. Glover, Kelly D.

Biblical Speech and Modern Consciousness in the Post-Modern Age: The Double Paradox of Modernism. Zelechow, Bernard.

By Any Means Necessary: John Locke and Malcolm X on the Right to Revolution. Gordon, Jill.

De cómo "el ser" devino época. Muñoz Delgado, Mercedes.

De la Croyance Morale à la Parole Éthique. Legault, Georges A.

Emphatic Speech Style—With Special Focus on the Prosodic Signalling of Heightened Emotive Involvement in Conversation. Selting, Margret.

Es la uniformidad semántica una condición de corrección formal de una teoría del modo oracional?. Marqueze, Jorge R.

Foregrounding Structures in American Sign Language. Wilbur, Ronnie B.

If a Lion Could Talk. Burns, Steven A M.

In Defence of Autonomous Linguistics. Das Gupta, Amitabha.

Incommensurability, Incomparability, Irrationality. Kindi, Vassiliki.

Interpreting Malapropisms. Fatic, Aleksandar.

Involvement with Language and In Language. Danes, Frantisek.

Is Thinking a Kind of Speaking?. Schroeder, Severin.

La anotación de las Investigaciones Filosóficas de Wittgenstein. Rodríguez Pereyra, Gonzalo.

Paul Celan's Uncanny Speech. Del Caro, Adrian.

Pornography: An Uncivil Liberty?. Carse, Alisa L.

Religione Parola Scrittura. Bello, Angela Ales.

Rights in Collision: A Non-Punitive, Compensatory Remedy for Abusive Speech. Meyers, Diana Tietjens.

Scare Quoted "Seeing". Slater, Hartley.

Sprache und ästhetische Terminologie: Kunst und Sprachwissenschaft in der Funktion der Zerstörung von Leben und Geistigkeit. Posavac, Zlatko.

Sprachebenen und Sprachliche Einheiten in Ludwig Wittgenstein's Tractatus Logico-Philosophicus. Reifarth, G T.

The Feasibility of Historical Pragmatics. Jucker, Andreas H.

The Languages of Thought. Kaye, Lawrence J.

The Linguistic and Personal Meaning of Metaphorical Speech. Gleeson, G P.

The Music Goes Round and Round: How Music Means in School. Erickson, Frederick.

The Right of Silence: A Socio-Pragmatic Model of Interpretation. Kurzon, Dennis.

The Speech of Facts and Logic. Kolár, Petr.

Vallabha's Positive Response to Buddhism. Yadav, Bibhuti S.

SPEECH ACT

Logic, Facts, and Representation: An Examination of R M Hare's Moral Philosophy. Ronnow-Rasmussen, Toni.

Basing 'Ought' On 'Is'. Singer, Beth J.

Bildliche Sprechakte. Taube, Volkmar.

Es la uniformidad semántica una condición de corrección formal de una teoría del modo oracional?. Marqueze, Jorge R.

Formalisierungsversuch der Sprechakttheorie. Labude, Joachim.

Formalizing the Theory of Intentionality. Brassac, Christian and Trognon, Alain.

Intention and Representation: Searle's 'Internal' Thesis. Goodrich, R A.

Is a Science of Language Possible? The Derrida-Searle Debate. Gross, Alan G.

La paradoja de la narración: de los actos de habla a los actos de conciencia. Cofré, Juan O.

Let the Audience De-Side: Possibilities for Postmodern Discourse Ethics. Leach, Joan.

Ökonomisches Handeln. Kummert, Michael.

On Not Taking Sides. Gross, Alan G.

Some Issues in the Theory of Artifacts: Defining 'Artifact' and Related Notions. Dipert, Randall R.

Sprechen, Sprache, Handeln. Röska-Hardy, Louise.

Taking Sides: Science, Language, and Debate after Derrida, Searle, and Alan Gross. Leach, Joan.

The Presuppositions of Jaimini and the Vedantins. De Smet, Richard.

Was sind reflexive Sprechhandlungen? Bemerkungen zum Verhältnis von Reflexion und Sprache. Ulfig, Alexander.

SPENCER

Herbert Spencer, Bertrand Russell, and the Shape of Early Analytic Philosophy. Cunningham, Suzanne.

SPENGLER

Catene di civiltà: La seconda fase del pensiero di Oswald Spengler. Conte, Domenico.

SPENGLER, O

L'iper-razionalismo di Oswald Spengler e l'interpretazione di Otto Neurath del Tramonto dell'Occidente. Ingravalle, Francesco.

SPERBER, D

Fitting Pragmatics into the Mind: Some Issues in Mentalist Pragmatics. Sinclair, Melinda.

SPHERE

On Knowing—The Natural Sciences. McKeon, Richard, Owen, David B (ed) and McKeon, Zahava K (ed).

SPIKES, M

Spikes on Kripke. Sartorelli, Joseph J.

SPINOSA, C

Explaining Old Worlds. Kersh, Rogan.

Marketing Heidegger: Entrepreneurship and Corporate Practices. Solomon, Robert C.

Must New Worlds Also be Good?. Grant, Robert.

On 'Disclosing New Worlds'. Taylor, Charles.

Politics, Democratic Action, and Solidarity. Mouffe, Chantal.

Skillful Solidarity. Hoy, David Couzens.

The Secular Model of the Multi-cultural State. Tännsjö, Torbjörn.

SPINOZA

"Aporie ed origini della teoria spinoziana dell'idea adequata" in *L'etica e il suo Altro, Vigna, Carmelo (ed)*. Marion, Jean-Luc.

"Spinoza's Democracy: The Passions of Social Assemblages" in *Marxism in the Postmodern Age, Callari, Antonio (ed)*. Hardt, Michael.

Ethique IV propositions 70-71. Macherey, Pierre.

Making Sense of Nietzsche: Reflections Timely and Untimely. Schacht, Richard.

Spinoza's Ethica From Manuscript to Print: Studies on Text, Form, and Related Topics. Steenbakkers, Piet.

The Philosophical Papers of Alan Donagan: Volume I, Historical Understanding and the History of Philosophy. Malpas, J E (ed) and Donagan, Alan.

Varieties of Scientific Experience: Emotive Aims in Scientific Hypotheses. Feuer, Lewis S.

VIX (Ethique IV Appendice chapitre 7) ou peut-on se sauver tout seul?. Beyssade, Jean-Marie.

Amor Dei Intellectualis: Vernunft—und Gottesliebe in Gipfelsätzen neuzeitlicher Systembildungen (Spinoza, Hegel, Schelling, Fichte). Janke, Wolfgang.

Correspondances Philosophiques et Techniques Argumentatives au XVIIe Siècle. Abiteboul, Olivier.

Descartes et Spinoza: de l' admiration au désir. Timmermans, Benoît.

Épicure et Spinoza: la physique. Moreau, Pierre-François.

Épicurisme et saducéisme dans la communauté sépharade d'Amsterdam. Albiac, Gabriel.

Épicurisme et spinozisme: l'éthique. Bove, Laurent.

Essence and Existence in Part 3 of Spinoza's "Ethics". Lucash, Frank.

Fichte's Rhetoric of Deception: Reflections on the Early Fichte in the Spirit of Jacobi. Di Giovanni, George.

Finito e infinito e l'idealismo della filosofia: La logica hegeliana dell'essere determinato Parte Prima. Movia, Giancarlo.

Freedom, Understanding, and Therapy in Spinoza's Moral Psychology. Gabhart, Mitchell.

Gassendi contre Spinoza selon Bayle: ricochets de la critique de l'âme du monde. Darmon, Jean-Charles.

Giuseppe Rensi e la lettura antimetafisica della teologia di Spinoza. Siena, R M.

God as Final Cause in Spinoza (in Hebrew). Sigad, Ran.

Hobbes, Spinoza, Kant, Highway Robbery and Game Theory. Marinoff, Louis.

Individualism, Physicalism, and Spinoza on Minds and Bodies. Lantin, Robert.

John Toland et l'épicurisme. Lurbe, Pierre.

Kant contra Spinoza?: Dos Éticas de la Autonomía. Fernández García, Eugenio.

La Filosofia Tedesca del Secondo Ottocento tra Scienze dello Spirito e Scienze della Natura. Meschiari, Alberto.

La notion de puissance dans son rapport à la *causa sui* chez les stoïciens et dans la philosophie de Spinoza. Narbonne, Jean-Marc.

La philosophie de Spinoza, l'éthique et la vérité. Gendron, Pierre.

La riappropriazione di Aristotele nell'ultimo Ricoeur. Rizzacasa, Aurelio.

La Spécificité de la Conception Spinoziste de l'Eternité de l'Esprit. Jacquet, Chantal.

Le modèle de l'homme libre. Temkine, Pierre.

Les fondements d'une éthique de la similitude. Matheron, Alexandre.

Libertad Necedad? Sobre los estoicos antiguos y Spinoza. Barquero, Elizabeth Muñoz.

Mind, Body, and Ethics in Spinoza. Winch, Peter G.

On the Theological Roots of Spinoza's Argument for Monism. Carriero, John.

Rôle et fonction des valeurs à l'origine des sociétés. Pezzillo, Lelia.

Schopenhauers Ethik—die Konsequenz. Schulz, Ortrun.

Should Franciscus van den Enden's Role in the Outset of Spinozism Be Reconsidered? (in Dutch). Mertens, F.

Spinoza "athée & épicurien". Lagrée, Jacqueline.

Spinoza et le Totalitarisme: Fiction et Réalité. Rougemont, Jean-Daniel.

Spinoza on Religious Choice. Cooper, Neil.

Spinoza's Democratic Turn: Chapter 16 of the *Theologico-Political Treatise*. Smith, Steven B.

Spinoza, lecteur des *Objections* de Gassendi à Descartes. Rousset, Bernard.

Spinoza: La Simultaneidad de los Tres Géneros del Conocimiento. Beltrán, Miquel.

Spinozas Gedanke, dass Einsicht befreit. Bittner, Rüdiger.

Spinozismo e Libertinismo: A Proposito di due Recenti Libri su Boulainviller. Mori, Gianluca.

STATE

"Political Integration, the Limited State, and the Philosophy of Postmodernism" in *The End of "Isms"?*, Shtromas, Alexsandras (ed). O'Sullivan, Noel.

"Politics" in *The Cambridge Companion to Aristotle*, Barnes, Jonathan (ed). Taylor, C C W.

"Politische Aufklärung und Staatstheorie bei Leibniz" in *Das geistige Erbe Europas*, Buhr, Manfred (ed). Racionero, Quintín.

"Situating the Capitalist State" in *Marxism in the Postmodern Age*, Callari, Antonio (ed). Lebowitz, Michael A.

"Socrates in the Context of Xenophon's Political Writings" in *The Socratic Movement*, Vander Waerdt, Paul A (ed). Pangle, Thomas L.

"The State, Gender and Sexual Politics: Theory and Appraisal" in *Power/Gender*, Radtke, H Lorraine (ed). Connell, R W.

Aristotle in Outline. Robinson, Timothy A.

Aristotle's Philosophy of Friendship. Stern-Gillet, Suzanne.

Communitas Liberorum: En Torno a *Sententia Libri Politicorum* de Tomás de Aquino. Lorca, Andres Martinez.

Habermas: A Critical Introduction. Outhwaite, William.

Hegel and Marx: Introductory Lectures. Kedourie, Elie.

Justice. Fisk, Milton (ed).

Nationalism (Fourth, Expanded Edition). Kedourie, Elie.

Plato's World: Man's Place in the Cosmos. Cropsey, Joseph.

Political Identity: Thinking Through Marx. Meister, Robert.

Political Theory and Christian Vision: Essays in Memory of Bernard Zylstra. Chaplin, Jonathan (ed) and Marshall, Paul (ed).

Staat en Welzijn: Het belang van een vernieuwde conceptie van de Minimale Staat. Hogervorst, S.

Studien zum Gedanken der Einheit des Staates: Über die rechtsphilosophische Auflösung der Einheit des Subjektes. Waechter, Kay.

Too Much Liberty?: Perspectives on Freedom and the American Dream. Saari, David J.

A Proposito di 'Filosofia del Diritto'. Bello, Angela Ales.

Autonomía y Conducta Desviada: el Problema del Paternalismo en la Obra de John Stuart Mill. De Miguel Alvarez, Ana.

British Idealism, the State, and International Relations. Boucher, David.

British Idealist International Theory. Boucher, David.

Civil Disobedience and Plato's *Crito*. Herrera, Christopher D.

Community in the Minimal State. Tomasi, John.

Das Problem der Gewaltenteilung bei Rousseau und Fichte. Schottky, Richard.

East and West: Russian Renewal and the Future. Borodaj, Jurij and Nikiforov, Aleksandr.

Edith Stein fenomenologa. Pezzella, Anna Maria.

Fichtes *Aufhebung* des Rechtsstaates. Geismann, Georg.

Frammenti Politici di Antonio Labriola con una Postilla Bibliografica. Miccolis, Stefano.

Hegel dans *Soi-même comme un autre* de Paul Ricoeur. Brito, Emilio.

How Far Was Plato Concerned to Rebut the Claims of Cyrus the Great and Pisistratus to the Title of *Statesman*?. Tanner, R G.

Ilustración política y teoría del estado en Leibniz (Materiales para una reflexión contemporánea). Racionero, Quintín.

Kant's Denial of Absolute Sovereignty. Arntzen, Sven.

Kant: Ilustración jurídica versus razón de Estado. Villacañas, José L.

L'état et l'état des choses: Le choc des conformismes. Baribeau, Jean-Serge.

L'opposition de Hegel au conservatisme de Charles-Louis de Haller. Ponton, Lionel.

La Estética del Estado en la Polis Clásica. Gutiérrez, Ramón Mandado.

La Società Concreta: Considerazioni su Fichte e Hegel. Fonnesu, Luca.

La Teoria e la Pratica del Diritto. De Pascale, Carla.

La vie éthique perdue dans ses extrêmes...Scission et réconciliation dans la théorie hégélienne de la *Sittlichkeit*. Kervégan, Jean-François.

Leviatán en los confines de la modernidad: Una crítica anarquista de la sociedad civil y el Estado. Jiménez, Jorge.

Liberalism, State, and Community. Simpson, Peter.

Lo stato moderno: profili storici e dottrinali. Catania, Alfonso.

Needs and Essence. Rotenstreich, Nathan.

On Costs, Benefits, and Regulatory Success: Reply to Crandall. Sunstein, Cass R.

Oración IV Pronunciada el 18 de Octubre de 1704. Vico, G and Gómez, Francisco Navarro (trans).

Outrage and Authority. Fisk, Milton T.

Psicologia delle folle e Scienza Politica in Italia alla Fine del XIX Secolo. Donzelli, Maria.

Rawls and the Claims of Liberal Legitimacy. Gaut, Berys.

Rechtsstaat und Kulturstaat bei Fichte: Eine Erwiderung. Schottky, Richard.

Reflections on the State of Current Debate Over Physician-Assisted Suicide and Euthanasia. Winkler, Earl.

Rights, Neutrality, and the Oppressive Power of the State. Sher, George.

The Contractarian Explanation of the State. Hampton, Jean.

The Ethics of Lottery Advertising: Issues and Evidence. Stearns, James M and Borna, Shaheen.

The Moral Neutrality of the Liberal State. Sadurski, Wojciech.

The Rhetoric of Politics in Cicero's Fourth Catilinarian. Cape Jr, Robert W.

The Secular Model of the Multi-cultural State. Tännsjö, Torbjörn.

The Single-Mind and Many-Minds Versions of Quantum Mechanics. Barrett, Jeffrey A.

The State as a Work of Art: Petrarch and His *Speculum Principis* (SEN, XIV, 1). Bejczy, István P.

Un'idea alla Ricerca di un Partito: L'eredità di Silvio Spaventa nel Liberalismo di Fine Ottocento. Ricci, Saverio.

Una Conversione della Teoria Critica? Sulla Teoria del Diritto e dello Stato di Habermas. Höffe, Otfried.

Una Ricerca sullo Stato di Edith Stein. D'Agostino, Francesco.

Zwei Seiten der Kantschen Begründung von Eigentum und Staat. Baumann, Peter.

STATE OF NATURE

"Linguaggio e politica" in *L'etica e il suo Altro*, Vigna, Carmelo (ed). Bubner, Rüdiger.

STATEMENT

Statements and Modality: Strawson, Quine and Wolfram. Millican, Peter.

What is Quine's View of Truth?. Davidson, Donald.

STATHAM, E

The Meaning and Status of Gay and Lesbian Political Philosophy: A Rejoinder to E Robert Statham Jr. Blasius, Mark.

STATIONARY

Possible Behaviours of the Reflection Ordering of Stationary Sets. Witzany, Jirí.

STATISTICS

"De l'homme moyen à la moyenne des hommes" in *Rhétoriques de la science*, De Coorebyter, Vincent (ed). Javeau, Claude.

"Statistical Dependencies, Statements and the Idealizational Theory of Science" in *Probability in Theory-Building*, Brzezinski, Jerzy (ed). Gaul, Marek.

Probability in Theory-Building. Brzezinski, Jerzy (ed).

The Undivided Universe: An Ontological Interpretation of Quantum Theory. Hiley, B J and Bohm, David.

Austere Realism and the Worldly Assumptions of Inferential Statistics. Trout, J D.

Het statistische argument. De Vries, Michiel S.

Locke and Hume Contrasted. Malpas, R M P.

Non-Bayesian Foundations for Statistical Estimation, prediction, and the Ravens Example. Forster, Malcolm R.

Normality as a Biological Concept. Wachbroit, Robert.

Probability in Rational Decision-Making. Moser, Paul K and Mulder, D Hudson.

Statistical Victims and Their Rights. Hanks, Donald K.

Vom Ursprung der Soziologie aus der posttridentinischen Theologie. Knebel, Sven K.

STEIN, E

"Die Randnotizen Martin Honeckers zur Habilitationsschrift 'Potenz und Akt'" in *Studien zur Philosophie von Edith Stein*, Fetz, Reto Luzius (ed). Ott, Hugo.

"Die Schrift 'Einführung in die Philosophie'" in *Studien zur Philosophie von Edith Stein*, Fetz, Reto Luzius (ed). Schulz, Peter.

"Die Stellung Edith Steins im Psychologismusstreit" in *Studien zur Philosophie von Edith Stein*, Fetz, Reto Luzius (ed). Rath, Matthias.

"Edith Stein und Adolf Reinach" in *Studien zur Philosophie von Edith Stein*, Fetz, Reto Luzius (ed). Schuhmann, Karl.

"Edith Stein und die analogia entis" in *Studien zur Philosophie von Edith Stein*, Fetz, Reto Luzius (ed). Hedwig, Klaus.

"Edith Stein und Freiburg" in *Studien zur Philosophie von Edith Stein*, Fetz, Reto Luzius (ed). Ott, Hugo.

"Edith Stein und H Conrad-Martius: Eine menschliche und intellektuelle Begegnung" in *Studien zur Philosophie von Edith Stein*, Fetz, Reto Luzius (ed). Bello, Angela Ales.

"Edith Stein, Theodor Lipps und die Einfühlungsproblematik" in *Studien zur Philosophie von Edith Stein*, Fetz, Reto Luzius (ed). Fidalgo, António.

"Hönigswalds Neukant. u. Husserls Phänomenol. als Hintergrund d. Denkens von Stein" in *Studien zur Philosophie von Edith Stein*, Fetz, Reto Luzius (ed). Orth, Ernst Wolfgang.

"Ich, Seele, Selbst: Edith Steins Theorie personaler Identität" in *Studien zur Philosophie von Edith Stein*, Fetz, Reto Luzius (ed). Fetz, Reto Luzius.

"Individuum, Individualität und Individuation nach Edith Stein und Wilhelm Dilthey" in *Studien zur Philosophie von Edith Stein*, Fetz, Reto Luzius (ed). Secrétan, Philibert.

"Von der Kritik zur Mystik: Edith Stein und der Marburger Neukantianismus" in *Studien zur Philosophie von Edith Stein*, Fetz, Reto Luzius (ed). Lembeck, Karl-Heinz.

Grundzüge der Religionsphilosophie Edith Steins. Müller, Andreas Uwe.

Studien zur Philosophie von Edith Stein. Fetz, Reto Luzius (ed), Rath, Matthias (ed) and Schulz, Peter (ed).

Edith Stein fenomenologa. Pezzella, Anna Maria.

Edith Stein—Anlässe und Anfänge einer philosophischen Neubesinnung. Ströker, Elisabeth.

Edith Stein-fenomenologia e/ o metafisica. Molinaro, Aniceto.

Edith Stein: l'Apprendistato Fenomenologico. Pezzella, Anna Maria.

Fenomenología y metafísica. Lobato, Abelardo.

Filosofia cristiana, fenomenologia e metafisica secondo E Stein. Mondin, Battista.

La fenomenologia, uno sguardo sulla verità. Bettinelli, Carla.

La filosofia cristiana secondo Edith Stein. Tilliette, Xavier.

La persona come apertura all'essere eterno secondo E Stein. D'Ambra, Michele.

Una Ricerca sullo Stato di Edith Stein. D'Agostino, Francesco.

STEIN, H

Scientific Abstraction and the Realist Impulse. Bunzl, Martin.

STEINER, R

Intuitive Thinking as a Spiritual Path. Steiner, Rudolf.

Living Thinking. Anderson, Tyson.

STEINITZ, Y

Reply to Steinitz's "Failing to Beg the Question". Brueckner, Anthony.

Scepticism and the Causal Theory of Reference. Brueckner, Anthony.

STEMMER, P

Kontinuität oder Bruch? Zum Verhältnis von sokratischer und platonischer Dialektik. Mesch, Walter.

SUBJECTIVITY

Epistemic Competence. Henderson, David K.
Fractured Subjectivity. Boyne, Roy.
Fundamento ontológico de la persona: Immanencia y transcendencia. Arellano, Joaquín Ferrer.
G H Mead: Linguistically Constituted Intersubjectivity and Ethics. Mendieta, Eduardo.
How Subjectivity is Truth in the *Concluding Unscientific Postscript*. Hughes, Edward J.
Husserl in discussione. Orlando, Teodosio.
Immanenz als Falle des Lebens. Schmitz, Hermann.
Individualism, Subjectivity, and Presence: A Response to Taylor Carman. Olafson, Frederick A.
Introducción a un tratado de filosofía primera. García-Baró, Miguel.
Ist eine Selbstbescheidung der Philosophie aus sich heraus möglich?. Burkhardt, Bernd.
Judgement and Intersubjectivity in Kant and Habermas's Ethics. Kattago, Siobhan.
La mirada errante: de la "Spaltung" en Lacan, al "caos-cosmos" de Deleuze. Gonzalo I Carbó, Antoni.
La persona nell'itinerario filosofico ermeneutico di P Ricoeur. Rizzacasa, Aurelio.
Lo spiritualismo indiano antico: Echi egizi nelle Upanisad. Masi, Giuseppe.
Materialism and the "Problem" of Quantum Measurement. Mulhauser, Gregory R.
Neuhousers Fichte-Deutung. Rohs, Peter.
Old and New: The Body, Subjectivity, and Ethics. McAleer, Graham.
Postkonventionelle Selbstverwirklichung: Überlegungen zur praktischen Subjektivität. Cooke, Maeve.
Presence with a Difference: Buddhists and Feminists on Subjectivity. Klein, Anne C.
Razón Vital y Fenomenología (Génesis del Raciovitalismo Orteguiano). Pozo, Antonio Gutierrez.
Representation, Self-Representation, and the Passions in Descartes. Schmitter, Amy Morgan.
Review Essay: Philip Barker's *Michel Foucault: Subversions of the Subject*. Anchor, Robert.
Sartrean Concept of Intersubjectivity. Sindhu, L.
Skepticism and Subjectivity: Two Critiques of Traditional Epistemology Reconsidered. Bermúdez, José Luis.
Subjectividad y Racionalidad Communicativa en J Habermas. Arce Carrascoso, José Luis.
Subjectivité et absolu dans les premiers écrits de Schelling (1794-1801). Marquet, Jean-François.
Subjektivität und Theologie: Eine hartnäckige Rückfrage. Müller, Klaus.
Subjetividad y Privacidad. Hurtado, Guillermo.
Sujeto y Realidad: Del Yo Analítico Substante al Yo Sintétoco Transcendental. Rivera de Rosales, Jacinto.
The Boulder and the Sphere: Subjectivity and Implicit Values in Biology. Alpert, Peter.
The Definition of Philosophy, Revisited. Kainz, Howard P.
The Impossibility of Experimental Elicitation of Subjective Probabilities. Karni, Edi.
The Question of the Subject: Heidegger and the Transcendental Tradition. Carr, David.
The Shadow of the Other (Subject): Intersubjectivity and Feminist Theory. Benjamin, Jessica.
The Subjectivity of Welfare. Sumner, L W.
Tras la postmodernidad. Innerarity, Daniel.
Two Ways of Coming Back to Reality: Kierkegaard and Lukács. Hannay, Alastair.
Wozu noch Erste Philosophie? Über das Wechselverhältnis von Subjektivität und raumzeitlicher Einzelnheit. Koch, Anton Friedrich.

SUBLIME

"Das Schöne, das Erhabene, die Askese und der Selbstmord" in *Naturzweckmässigkeit und ästhetische Kultur, Schwabe, Karl-Heinz (ed)*. Fischer, Peter.
"Moments of Discipline" in *Intersections: Nineteenth-Century Philosophy and Contemporary Theory, Rajan, Tilottama (ed)*. Cheetham, Mark A.
Ästhetik des Erhabenen: Burke, Kant, Adorno, Lyotard. Peña Aguado, María Isabel.
Kant's Theory of Imagination: Bridging Gaps in Judgement and Experience. Gibbons, Sarah.
Kants Metaphysik: Welt und Freiheit. Effertz, Dirk.
Beauty, Sublimity, and Expression: Reply to Wicks and Cantrick. Guyer, Paul.
Du Beau et du Sublime chez Pascal. Bouchilloux, Hélène.
Faust e Lust. La Guardia, Giovanni.
Hume's Aesthetic Psychology of Distance, Greatness and the Sublime. Jacquette, Dale.
Kant on Fine Art: Artistic Sublimity Shaped by Beauty. Wicks, Robert.
Kant's Confusion of Expression with Communication. Cantrick, Robert B.
La Vivencia de lo Sublime y la Experiencia Moral en Kant. Ribeiro dos Santos, Leonel.
Los Creadores de Ficciones Sublimes. Zárate, Marla.
Ontology, Epistemic Access, and the Sublime. Godlovitch, Stan.
Paul Crowther and the Experience of the Sublime. Hund, William B.
The Kantian Sublime and the Nostalgia for Violence. Huhn, Thomas.
The Old and the New Sublimes: Do They Signify? God?. Hutchings, Patrick.
The Postmodern Sublime: Kant and Tony Smith's Anecdote of the Cube. Beidler, Paul G.
Weiskel's Sublime and the Impasse of Knowledge. Quinney, Laura.

SUBSTANCE

see also Attribute, Matter

"Substance as Function" in *Philosophy, Mathematics and Modern Physics, Rudolph, Enno (ed)*. Rudolph, Enno.

"The Foundations of Knowledge and the Logic of Substance" in *Locke's Philosophy, Rogers, G A J (ed)*. Ayers, Michael.
"The Substance of Aristotle's Ethics" in *The Crossroads of Norm and Nature, Sim, May (ed)*. Halper, Edward C.
Esse est Deus: Meister Eckharts christologische Versöhnung von Philosophie und Religion und ihre Ursprünge in der Tradition des Abendlandes. Manstetten, Reiner.
Hegels Wissenschaft der Logik—metaphysische Letztbegründung oder Theorie logischer Formen?. Schick, Friedrike.
Leibniz and the Rational Order of Nature. Rutherford, Donald.
Substance Among Other Categories. Hoffman, Joshua and Rosenkrantz, Gary S.
Substance and Separation in Aristotle. Spellman, Lynne.
Tode Ti and *Toionde* in Metaphysics Z. Yu, Jiyuan.
Aristotle on Substance, Essence and Biological Kinds. Charles, David.
Boethius und die Tradition. Sonderegger, Erwin.
Commentary on Charles's "Aristotle on Substance, Essence and Biological Kinds". Gill, Mary Louise.
Cosmology: A Philosophical Survey. Leslie, John.
Dos Nociones de Objeto en el *Tractatus*. Tomasini Bassols, Alejandro.
Expérience et métaphysique. Gilbert, Paul.
La grammatica ed il problema degli universali nel Medioevo cristiano. Bertola, Ermenegildo.
Los Predicamentos o Categorías en el Cardenal Cayetano. Beuchot, Mauricio.
Materia prima y cmabio substancial, Hoy. Speranza, J L.
Plotino, Ficino e noi stessi: alcuni riflessi etici. Rist, John M and Peroli, E (trans).
Principialidad de las Facultades en el Orden del Ser. Mier y Terán, Rocío.
Relational Attributes in Aristotle. Morales, Fabio.
Substance et attribut chez Spinoza. Glausier, Richard.
Substance, Modality, and Spacetime. Healey, Richard.
Substances and Substrata. LaBossiere, Michael C.
Substanz und Mensch: Spinozas Auffassung der Wirklichkeit. Graeser, Andreas.
Tertiary Qualities in Locke's 'Essay'. Goodin, Susanna.
The Substantial Unity of Material Substances According to John Poinsot. Kronen, John D.
Wholes, Parts, and Sequences in Aristotle. Blyth, D J.

SUBSTITUTION

An Algebraic Theory of Normal Forms. Ghilardi, Silvio.

SUCCESS

Character: The Framework for a Successful Life. Adams, E M.
Fortunate Misfortune. Smilansky, Saul.
On the Danger of Half-Truths. Osherson, Daniel and Weinstein, Scott.
Outlines for Success. Burnor, Richard.
Truth, Correspondence, and Success. Leeds, Stephen.

SUFFERING

Ethics, Killing and War. Norman, Richard.
The New Ecological Order. Ferry, Luc and Volk, Carol (trans).
A Response to David Cockburn. Long, Ann.
Action et passion. Wetzel, Marc.
Ahimsa (Noninjury) Revisited. Fox, Michael W.
Buddhism: Gotamavada Versus Theravada. Bahm, Archie.
De zaak van de dieren. Melle, Ullrich.
Educated Folly About Animal Minds and Animal Suffering. Landman, Willem A.
Genetic and Other Engineering. Clark, Stephen R L.
Harrison and Hick on God and Animal Pain. Lynch, Joseph J.
Il Prologo al Commento a Giobbe di San Tommaso d'Aquino. Pandolfi, Carmelo.
Inevitable Martyrdom: The Connection Between Faith and Suffering in Kierkegaard's Later Writings. Imbrosciano, Anthony.
Is Animal Pain Conscious?. Lynch, Joseph J.
Justice is Strife. Hampshire, Stuart.
Physician Aid in Dying and the Relief of Patients' Suffering: Physicians' Attitudes Regarding Patients' Suffering and End-of-Life Decisions. Huang, Frederick Y and Emanuel, Linda L.
Suffering unto God. Ashley, J Matthew (trans) and Metz, Johann Baptist.
The Earth Might be Round, But the World is Flat: The Groundwork for an Ethics of Relief. Ramsey, Ramsey Eric.
The Problem of Evil and a Plausible Defence. Murphy, Frank J.
The Protection Laboratory Animals: A Response to Stephenson. Parker, James.
Towards Welfare Biology: Evolutionary Economics of Animal Consciousness and Suffering. Ng, Yew-Kwang.
Util-izing Animals. LaFollette, Hugh and Shanks, Niall.

SUFFICIENT REASON

A Defense of a Principle of Sufficient Reason. Smith, Quentin.
Leibniz on the Principle of Continuity. Duchesneau, François.

SUFI

El Pensamiento Irracional Islámico: El Sufismo de Sohrawardi. Aragués, Juan Manuel.

SUGARMAN, J

Should Ethics Committees Study Themselves?. Danis, Marion.

SUICIDE

"Das Schöne, das Erhabene, die Askese und der Selbstmord" in *Naturzweckmässigkeit und ästhetische Kultur, Schwabe, Karl-Heinz (ed)*. Fischer, Peter.
"Roman Suicide" in *Medicine and Moral Reasoning, Fulford, K W M (ed)*. Griffin, Miriam.
"The Right to Die" in *Ethics on the Frontiers of Human Existence, Badham, Paul (ed)*. Smith, Patrick Nowell.
Ethical Issues in Suicide. Battin, Margaret P.

SUICIDE

CQ *Interview*: Dr Boudewijn Chabot on Assisted Suicide in the Absence of Somatic Illness. Klotzko, Arlene Judith.

Does Physician Assisted Suicide Violate the Integrity of Medicine?. Momeyer, Richard.

Dr Kevorkian and the Struggle for Physician-Assisted Dying. Pence, Greg.

Going Early, Going Late: The Rationality of Decisions about Suicide in AIDS. Battin, Margaret P.

Selling Death and Dignity. Hendin, Herbert.

Suicidio y fiesta del yo: el suicidio como transgresión moral definitiva: A propósito de "On Suicide" de David Hume. Tasset, José Luis.

The Development of the Roman Catholic Teachings on Suicide. Barry, Robert.

The Ethics of Suicide Prevention. Cosculluela, Victor.

The Physician-Assisted Suicide and Euthanasia Debate: An Annotated Bibliography of Representative Articles. Fins, Joseph J and Bacchetta, Matthew D.

The State's Dr Death: What's Unethical About Physicians Helping at Executions?. Davis, Michael.

SULLIVAN, P

Commentary on "Contentless Consciousness". Binns, Peter.

SULLIVAN, S

Relativism and Moral Judgements: A Reply to Sullivan. Hocutt, Max.

SULLIVAN, T

Can Everything Come to Be Without a Cause?. Smith, Quentin.

Existence vs Being: An All-important Matter of Terminology. Nijenhuis, John.

SULMASY, D

Informed Consent: Pondering a New Piece of the Puzzle. Jacobson, Jay A.

SUMMUM BONUM

"Zur moralphilosophischen Funktion des Prinzips vom höchsten Gut" in *Naturzweckmässigkeit und ästhetische Kultur, Schwabe, Karl-Heinz (ed)*. Grünewald, Bernward.

SUNNI

Organ Transplantation: Contemporary Sunni Muslim Legal and Ethical Perspectives. Ebrahim, Abul Fadl Moshin.

SUNSTEIN, C

Acts, Omissions, and Constitutionalism. Schauer, Frederick.

SUPERNATURAL

Ateismo, filosofia e cristianesimo in Del Noce. Possenti, Vittorio.

SUPERSTITIONS

Analisi della Fede e Critica della Ragione nella Filosofia di Pierre Bayle. Paganini, Gianni.

A Tale of Two Cultures and Other Higher Superstitions. Fuller, Steve.

Appunti sulla Fortuna di Gabriel Naudé nella Germania del Primo Illuminismo. Mulsow, Martin.

SUPERVENIENCE

"Supervenience, Recognition, and Consciousness" in *The Mind-Body Problem: A Guide to the Current Debate, Warner, Richard (ed)*. Wagner, Steven J.

"Supervenient Causation" In *Philosophy of Psychology: Debates on Psychological Explanation, Macdonald, Cynthia (ed)*. Macdonald, Cynthia and Macdonald, Graham.

Mentale Verursachung: Eine Theorie aus der Perspektive des semantischen Anti-Realismus. Brüntrup, Godehard.

Naturalizing the Mind. Dretske, Frederick.

Philosophical Naturalism. Papineau, David.

A WORLD without MIND: Comments on Terence Horgan's "Naturalism and Intentionality". Egan, Frances.

Account for Macro-level Causation. Henderson, David K.

Assimilative Moral Realism and Supervenience. Yasenchuk, Ken.

Causal Efficacy, Content and Levels of Explanation. Toribio, Josefa.

Content and Causal Powers. Saidel, Eric.

Dretske on the Causal Efficacy of Meaning. García-Carpintero, Manuel.

Humean Supervenience and Enduring Things. Haslanger, Sally.

Materialism and Supervenience. Jack, Andrew.

Mental Causation in Searle's "Biological Naturalism". Kim, Jaegwon.

Mentale Verursachung und metaphysischer Realismus. Brüntrup, Godehard.

Modal Supervenience and Modal Realism. Divers, John.

Naturalism and Intentionality. Horgan, Terence.

Principles of Supervenience. Bovens, Luc.

Reply to Egan's "A WORLD without MIND". Horgan, Terence.

Supervenience and Moral Realism. Shafer-Landau, Russ.

Supervenience Unthwarted: Rejoinder to Wicks. Zangwill, Nick.

The Intrinsic, Non-Supervenient Nature of Aesthetic Properties. Eaton, Marcia Mulder.

The Supervenience of the Mental on the Physical (in Hebrew). Drai, Dalia.

SUPERVISION

Toward an Understanding of Ethical Climate: Its Relationship to Ethical Behavior and Supervisory Influence. Wimbush, James C and Shepard, Jon M.

SUPPOSITION

Aspectos Gnoseológicos de la *Suppositio Naturalis* de San Vicente Ferrer. García-Cuadrado, José Angel.

Fine-Grained Opinion, Probability, and the Logic of Full Belief. Van Fraassen, Bas C.

La "Confusa" Suposición Sólo Confusa. Muñoz García, Angel.

SUPREME COURT

"Constituting the Modern State" in *Radical Philosophy of Law, Caudill, David S (ed)*. Swidorski, Carl.

Constitutional Privacy. Johnson, Jeffery L.

Discussion: Just Another Simi Valley Jury: The Supreme Court and the Death Penalty. Thomson, Ernie and Osbrun, Jerry R.

Ethics and the Law: US Supreme Court Rulings on the Solicitation of Clients. Mintz, Steven M and Moffeit, Katherine S.

Euthanasia in the Netherlands: Sliding Down the Slippery Slope?. Keown, John.

The Combat Exclusion and the Role of Women in the Military. DeCew, Judith Wagner.

Who Should be Committable?. Lavin, Michael.

SURGERY

see also Psychosurgery

Reshaping the Female Body: The Dilemma of Cosmetic Surgery. Davis, Kathy.

Beauty and Breast Implantation: How Candidate Selection Affects Autonomy and Informed Consent. Parker, Lisa S.

Trees and Heads: The Objective and the Subjective in Painful Procedures. Bennett, Henry L.

SURI, H

Existence and Non-Existence in Haribhadra Suri's Anekanta-Jaya-Pataka. van den Bossche, Frank.

SURROGACY

The Gulf Between: Surrogate Choices, Physician Instructions, and Informal Network Responses. Koch, Tom.

SURROGATE

The Best-Interest Standard: Surrogate Decision Making and Quality of Life. Drane, James F and Coulehan, John.L.

SURVEYABILITY

Surveyability and the *Sorites* Paradox. Addis, Mark.

'Surveyability' Should not be Formalized. Kielkopf, Charles F.

SURVIVAL

Eugenics. Coutts, Mary Carrington and McCarrick, Pat Milmoe.

New Ways to Look at Fitness. Van Der Steen, Wim J.

Survival or Super-Psi?. Braude, Stephen E.

The Beginning of Sorrows: The Ecological Crisis and the Prospects of Human Survival. Smith, Joseph Wayne.

Unger's *Identity, Consciousness and Value*. Van Inwagen, Peter.

Viability. Gert, Heather.

SUSPICION

Kierkegaardian Suspicion and Properly Basic Beliefs. Williams, Clifford.

SUSTAINABILITY

"The Lie of Sustainability" in *Ecology, Technology, and Culture, Zweers, Wim (ed)*. Achterhuis, Hans.

Envisioning Ecological Sustainability: The Need and a Method. Carroll, John E.

How Would you Like your 'Sustainability', Sir? Weak or Strong? A Reply to my Critics. Beckerman, Wilfred.

SUSTENANCE

Human Value of Sustainable Society. Dewan, M L.

In Defence of Sustainable Development. Skolimowski, Henryk.

On Wilfred Beckerman's Critique of Sustainable Development. Daly, Herman E.

Sustainable Development, Capital Substitution and Economic Humility: A Response to Beckerman. Jacobs, Michael.

SUZUKI, D

A Belated Response to Hu Shih and D T Suzuki. Sellmann, James D.

SWEDENBORG

A Dualistic Model of Ultimate Reality and Meaning: Self-Similarity in Chaotic Dynamics and Swedenborg. Baker, Gregory L.

SWEENEY, L

L'Infinité Divine dans l'Antiquité ét au Moyen Age. Côté, Antoine.

SWISS

Worin unterscheiden sich die Gesellschaftsverträge der Schweizer-von jenen der Philosophiegeschichte?. Holenstein, Elmar.

SYDENHAM, T

Locke as Author of *Anatomia* and *De Arte Medica*. Meynell, Guy.

SYLLOGISM

"Logic" in *The Cambridge Companion to Aristotle, Barnes, Jonathan (ed)*. Smith, Robin.

A Venn-Euler Test for Categorical Syllogisms. Bennett, James and Nolt, John.

Aristotle's Completeness Proof. Smiley, Timothy.

Assertoric vs Modal Syllogistic. Striker, Gisela.

Attualità nelle leggi logiche in Giovanni Duns Scoto. Olejnik, Roman M.

Begging the Question as a Pragmatic Fallacy. Walton, Douglas N.

Circularity and Amphiboly in Some Anselmian Ontological Proofs: A Syllogistic Inquiry. Kelly, Charles J.

Contraposition and Existential Import. Perry, Clifton B and Jolley, Kelly D.

Dialectic and the Syllogism. Smith, Robin.

Fallacies and Alternative Interpretations. Adler, Jonathan E.

Syllogistic Reasoning Pattern in Turkish Adolescent. Celeri, Nermin.

The Immediate Premises of Aristotelian Demonstration. Ferejohn, Michael T.

The Irrelevance of Distribution for the Syllogism. Murphree, Wallace A.

The Problem of Dialectical Reasoning in Aristotle. Bolton, Robert.

SYLLOGISTIC

Einführung in die Logik. Menne, Albert.

Distribution and Proportion. Peterson, Philip L.

La définition et la démonstration dans la logique d'Aristote. Valois, Raynald.

SYMBOL

"The Symbol Gave Rise to Thought" in *The Philosophy of Paul Ricoeur, Hahn, Lewis Edwin (ed)*. Pellauer, David.

Artificial Intelligence: A Philosophical Introduction. Copeland, B Jack.

The Hermetic Tradition: Symbols and Teachings of the Royal Art. Evola, Julius.

TASTE

On Hume and Eighteenth-Century Aesthetics: The Philosopher on a Swing. Carabelli, Giancarlo and Hall, Joan Krakover (trans).

Contemplazione e Interpretazione: L'Estetica Kantiana Nell'Analisi di Luigi Pareyson. Russo, Francesco.

De la Nature au Social. Peterson, Michel.

Francis Hutcheson and the Problem of Conspicuous Consumption. Mortensen, Preben.

Hume's Deontology. Flage, Daniel E.

Hume's Double Standard of Taste. Shelley, James.

Hume's True Judges. Wieand, Jeffrey.

La découverte de la faculté de juger réfléchissante. Dumouchel, Daniel.

Rule and Verdict. Shelley, James.

The Possibility of Aesthetics. Hogan, Patrick Colm.

TAULER, J

Johannes Tauler in den Niederlanden: Grundzüge eines philosophie- und rezeptionsgeschichtlichen Forschungsrogramms. Hoenen, Maarten.

TAUTOLOGY

Tautologías y circularidad en la Mecánica clásica. Mataix, Carmen.

Wittgenstein, ill Linguaggio e l'Interpretazione. Perissinotto, Luigi.

TAXATION

Ethical Standards, Attitudes Toward Risk, and Intentional Noncompliance: An Experimental Investigation. Ghosh, Dipankar and Crain, Terry L.

Public Goods and the Paying Public. Byrne, Edmund F.

TAXONOMY

Representations of Information Technology in Disciplinary Development: Disappearing Plants and Invisible Networks. Hine, Christine.

TAYLOR, C

Charles Taylor, Strong Hermeneutics and the Politics of Difference. Smith, Nick.

Foucault's Reconception of Power. Weberman, David.

Goods and Life Forms: Relativism in Charles Taylor's Political Philosophy. Rosa, Hartmut.

Identity and Quality of Life (in Dutch). Musschenga, A W.

Language, Narration and the Self. Staude, John-Raphael.

Morality, Ethical Life and the Persistence of Universalism. O'Neill, Shane.

Realisme zonder representatie. Slors, Marc.

Recent Work on Liberalism and Communitarianism. Shapiro, Daniel.

Richard Rorty's Inquiry Monism. Crawford, Michael Sean.

The Politics of Communitarianism. Friedman, Jeffrey.

Weighting Health States and Strong Evaluation. Edgar, Andrew.

TAYLOR, H

John Stuart Mill and Harriet Taylor on Women and Marriage. Mendus, Susan.

Una visión de mujer en el pensamiento de John Stuart Mill. Gil Ruiz, Juana María.

TAYLOR, M

"A Postmodern Trinity?" in *The 1994 Annual of Hermeneutics and Social Concern, Lawler, Justus George (ed).* Sanders, Theresa.

Go Figure! Refiguring *Disfiguring.* Shapiro, Gary.

Immutability of God: Metaphysical Inconsistency or Essential Grounding for Human Transcendence. Ebert, Howard.

TAYLOR, P

Against Biospherical Egalitarianism. French, William C.

From Biocentric Individualism to Biocentric Pluralism. Sterba, James P.

Reply to Taylor. Rudinow, Joel.

TAYLOR, R

Toward a Credible Agent-Causal Account of Free Will. Clarke, Randolph.

TEACHER

"La Filsofía va al Taller" in *Temas Actuales de Filosofía, Palacios, María Julia (ed).* Gonza, Guillermo.

"Staying Alive": Intellectual and Spiritual Sustenance on the Journey for Critical Foundations Scholars-Teachers. Brosio, Richard A.

A Critical Review of Allen Pearson, *The Teacher: Theory and Practice in Teacher Education.* O'Leary, Paul.

A Educaçao e a Autonomia do Profesor: Caminhos para a Emancipaçao. Oaigen, Edson Roberto.

Am I Wicked?. Gendin, Sidney.

On the Language of Consciousness: Propositional Discourse and Moral Sensibility. Ray, G Thomas.

Teaching as a Practice: A Rejoinder. Pearson, Allen T.

The Nature of Philosophy of Education Reconsidered. Higgs, Philip.

There Must be Some Way Out of Here: A Case Study in the Teaching of Critical Thinking. Drewett, Michael.

TEACHING

"Education: Conserving Tradition" in *Introducing Applied Ethics, Almond, Brenda (ed).* Haldane, John.

"La Enseñanza de la Epistemología en la Carrera de Psicología o Técnicas Para Desvestir a una Invitada Molesta" in *Temas Actuales de Filosofía, Palacios, María Julia (ed).* Feldman, Susana B and Krichmar, Fernando Gabriel.

"Los Seminarios en la Enseñanza de la Filosofía" in *Temas Actuales de Filosofía, Palacios, María Julia (ed).* Rabossi, Eduardo A, Stigol, Nora and González, María Cristina.

"Reconstructing Social Theory after the Postmodern Critique" in *After Postmodernism, Simons, Herbert W (ed).* Brown, Richard Harvey.

"Unwritten Teachings" in the *Parmenides.* Miller, Mitchell.

"Xenophon's Socrates as Teacher" in *The Socratic Movement, Vander Waerdt, Paul A (ed).* Morrison, Donald R.

For Education: Towards Critical Educational Inquiry. Carr, Wilfred.

How to Write a Philosophy Paper. Stramel, James S.

Identity, Culture, and Education. Smeyers, Paul (ed).

The Educational Imperative: A Defence of Socratic and Aesthetic Learning. Abbs, Peter.

The Future of the Humanities: Teaching Art, Religion, Philosophy, Literature, and History (New Edition). Kaufmann, Walter Arnold.

The Logic Course. DeHaven, Stephen Lee.

The Teachings of Don Von: A Turnkey Way of Knowledge. Abellera, Tom.

Work, Education, and Leadership: Essays in the Philosophy of Education. Howard, V A and Scheffler, Israel.

A Educaçao e a Autonomia do Profesor: Caminhos para a Emancipaçao. Oaigen, Edson Roberto.

A Lonerganian Critique of the Pragmatic Method of Education. Gilbert, Christopher.

An Experiential Component in Teaching Philosophy of Science. Nissani, Moti.

Analyse d'Une Expérience de Pédagogie. Tozzi, Michel.

Apprendre et Enseigner la Philosophie. Coutel, Charles.

Arguments and Arguers. Gilbert, Michael A.

Art as a Means of Understanding in the Teaching of Philosophy. Fürst, Maria.

Bodies of Knowledge. McCarty, Luise Prior.

Brandon Shaw, Neil Perry, and the Perils of Education. Calhoun, Laura.

Case Study in the Ethics of Teaching Philosophy. Pence, Gregory.

Common Values and Value Conflicts in Environmental Education. Döbler, Matthias.

Current Educational Reform: "Shape-shifting" or Genuine Improvement in the Quality of Teaching and Learning?. Merchant, Betty.

De l'Avenir de la Philosophie au Cégep ou de la Résolution Possible d'un Paradoxe. Cohen-Bacrie, Pierre.

Developing Philosophical Literacy. Miller, Thomas G.

Do Senior Secondary Students Possess the Moral Maturity to Negotiate Class Rules?. Langford, Peter E, Lovegrove, Hildegard and Lovegrove, Malcolm N.

Education for Democracy. Tiles, J E.

Enseigner l'Éthique par l'Histoire. Marcil, Louise.

Enseigner l'Éthique Selon le Paradigme du "Moi Moralement Relié". Mullet, Sheila Mason.

Entretien avec Michel Tozzi. Cohen-Bacrie, Pierre.

Éthique et Enseignement. Carrier, André.

Évoluer en Enseignant la Philosophie. Chbat, Joseph.

Fallacious Reasoning. Goldstein, Laurence.

Grading. Weis, Gregory F.

How to Teach Philosophy in High Schools. Schlegelová, Jaroslava.

If We Took Dewey's Aesthetics Seriously, How Would the Arts Be Taught?. Jackson, Philip W.

Instructions du 2 Septembre 1925. de Monzie, Anatole.

Introducing Philosophy Through Concepts of Ultimate Reality and Meaning. Krettek, Tom.

Is Reading Plato Educational? Thoughts on Education, Prompted by a Reading of Plato's *Meno.* Weingartner, Rudolph H.

I 'Enseignement de l'Éthique comme Activité de Formation Morale. Bégin, Luc.

L'Enseignement de l'Histoire de l'Éthique. Leydet, Dominique.

La Formation Générale au Niveau Collégial. Sa Qualité Passe d'Abord par la Consolidation de la Formation de Base. Lévesque, Gérard.

La Formation Intellectualle. Després, Pierre.

La Philosophie: Une Présence Essentielle. Cohen-Bacrie, Pierre (& others).

La Réforme et le Rôle de la Philosophie dans la Formation Collégiale. Martineau, Jean-François.

Living (Not Learning) Ethics. Solberg, Joseph, Strong, Kelly C and McGuire Jr, Charles.

Make My Case: Ethics Teaching and Case Presentations. Kuczewski, Mark (& others).

On Teaching as a Profession. Götz, Ignacio L.

On Translating Locke, Berkeley, and Hume into English. Bennett, Jonathan.

Outlines for Success. Burnor, Richard.

Pedagogy, Philosophy, and African-American Students. Martinez, Roy.

Philosophy Discussions with Less B.S.. Thomason, Neil.

Plato's School, the Academy. Baltes, Matthias.

Process-Product Research on Teaching: Ten Years Later. Garrison, James W and Macmillan, C J B.

Quelques Pistes de Réflexion sur l'Avenir de l'Enseignement Collégial de la Philosophie. Marsolais, Arthur.

Réflexions sur l'Enseignement de l'Éthique. Paris, Claude.

Representing Philosophy to Students. Chambers, Ellie.

Science Education for a Life Curriculum. Hickman, Larry A.

Socrates and Self-Knowledge. Rappe, Sara L.

Students and Legal Obedience. Rich, John Martin.

Teaching as a Moral Activity: Listening to Teachers in Russia and the United States. Higgins, Ann.

Teaching as Applied Philosophy. Kaplan, Laura Duhan.

Teaching Foundations...or Foundationalizing Teaching. Healy, Seán D.

Teaching in the Shadow of Socrates. Biel, Joseph.

Teaching Philanthropy Ethics. Martin, Mike W.

Teaching Philosophical Analysis with Nota Bene 3.0. Stypinski, Andrew B.

Teaching the Liberal-Communitarian Debate. Lowe, Scott.

Teaching 'Inference to the Best Explanation'. Eflin, Juli.

The Challenge of History. Rainbow, Bernarr.

The Electronic Agora: Using a Mainframe Computer In Introductory Courses. Domino, Brian.

The Scientific Status of Research on Teaching. Gage, N L.

TRANSCENDENTAL

Der Begriff der psychischen Krankheit aus der Sicht der Fichteschen Transzendentalphilosophie. Hoff, Paul.

Die Signatur der Zeit—Zum 80, Geburstag von Gerhard Funke. Kopper, Joachim.

Die transzendentale Freiheit bei Fichte. Kumamoto, Chukei.

Die uitdrukkingskracht van de transcendentale denkkritiek. Hoogland, J.

El morir como pauta ética del empiricismo trascendental. Echeverría, José.

Es trascendental la ética Kantiana?. De Maliandi, Graciela Fernandez.

Fichtes Wissenschaftslehre im Aufbrechen der Paradigmen mechanizistischen Denkens. Stahl, Jürgen.

Following Edmund Husserl on One of the Paths Leading to the Transcendental Reduction. Kortooms, Toine.

Fundamentación última y factidad: (Un intento de argumentar "con Apel contra Apel"). Saez Rueda, L.

Het monisme van Herman Berger. Kal, Victor.

Husserl und das Erbe der Tranzendentalphilosophie. Siemek, Marek J.

Il Trattato Tomista sulle Proprietà Trascendentali dell'Essere. Ventimiglia, Giovanni.

J Habermas: La crítica de la razón interesada. Carrascoso, Arce.

Kants Philosophie und moderne Logik: Eine Tagung in Swetlogorsk. Bryuschinkin, W.

L'Ermeneutica e il Trascendentale. Cortella, Lucio.

La "Crítica de la Razón Práctica" como saber Transcendental. Bastons i Prat, Miquel.

La Estética de Kant como Filosofía de la Cultura. Fontán, Manuel.

La filosofía trascendental bajo la óptica de la teoría evolucionista del conocimiento. Hoyos Jaramillo, Luis Eduardo.

La herencia de Gadamer en K O Apel: hermenéutica experimental o hermenéutica trascendental?. Domingo Moratalla, A.

La Interpretación de Kant de Fernando Montero Moliner. Arenas Llopis, Luis.

Maimons Versuch über Transzendentalphilosophie: Eine interpretierende Skizze der Grundgedanken. Krämer, Felix.

Notes on the "Lack of Foundation" in Theodor W Adorno Philosophy (in Portuguese). De Paiva Durate, Rodrigo Antonio.

Observaçoes sobre a Concepçao Kantiana do Espaço. Molina, Jorge Alberto.

Philosophiegeschichte als Problemfeld der Wissenschaftslehre Fichtes. Stahl, Jürgen.

Pragmatism and the Transcendental Turn in Truth and Ethics. Misak, Cheryl.

Quintuplicatà e Individualità: La Construzione dell'io in WL 1807. Rametta, Gaetano.

Racionalidad Común. Serrano, Manuel G.

Razón Vital y Fenomenología (Génesis del Raciovitalismo Orteguiano). Pozo, Antonio Gutierrez.

Reflexiones Acerca del Papel de las *Eigne Meditationen* para la Formación del Sistema Transcendental de Fichte. Marín, Vicente Serrano.

Repliek. Berger, Herman.

Scepticism and the Justification of Transcendental Idealism. Bermúdez, José Luis.

System des transzendentalen Idealismus bei Kant? Offene Fragen der—und an die —Kritik der Urteilskraft. Tuschling, Burkhard.

Trabajo e Interacción como Intereses Rectores del Conocimiento. López Molina, Antonio M.

Transcendentaal-Pragmatiek en Semantiek. Sas, Peter.

Transzendentale Basis, Materialismus, und Religion. Lauth, Reinhard.

Transzendentale Phänomenologie und das Problem der Geschichte. Chestanov, Ruslan Z.

Über die Unhaltbarkeit und die Unentbehrlichkeit des Skeptizismus bei Fichte. Breazeale, Daniel.

Wittgenstein, transzendentale Gründzüge und transzendentale Einschränkungen. Sacks, Mark.

Zur Geschichtserkenntnis nach der Transzendentalphilosophie. Ivaldo, Marco.

TRANSCENDENTAL DEDUCTION

Schritte auf dornichten Pfaden: Zu neuerer Kantliteratur. Klotz, Christian.

Self-Understanding in Kant's Transcendental Deduction. Pereboom, Derk.

TRANSCENDENTAL DEDUCTISM

System des transzendentalen Idealismus bei Kant? Offene Fragen der—und an die —Kritik der Urteilskraft. Tuschling, Burkhard.

TRANSCENDENTAL EGO

Sujeto y Realidad: Del Yo Analítico Substante al Yo Sintétoco Transcendental. Rivera de Rosales, Jacinto.

TRANSCENDENTALISM

"Sobre los Avatares Ontológicos del Empirismo y Trascendentalismo Jurídicos" in *Temas Actuales de Filosofía, Palacios, María Julia (ed)*. Ferraro, Agustín.

Hacia un Nuevo Concepto de Trascendentalismo?. Recas Bayón, Javier.

Transcendental Subjectivity Meets Transcendental Grammar. Pradhan, R C.

TRANSFERENCE

What's Right and What's Wrong with Transference Theories. Dowe, Phil.

TRANSFORMATION

Heidegger, Early and late: The Vanishing of the Subject. Hodge, Joanna.

O Método Paulo Freire: A Inter-Relaçao da Teoria do Conhecimento com a Teoria da Sociedade. Marinho Sampaio, Tânia Maria.

The Project of Ethical Renewal and Critique: Edmund Husserl's Early Phenomenology of Culture. Steinbock, Anthony J.

TRANSFUSION

HIV +/AIDS Related Bioethical Issues in Japan. Hoshino, Kazusama.

TRANSITIVITY

Fine-Grained Opinion, Probability, and the Logic of Full Belief. Van Fraassen, Bas C.

The Dimension of the Negation of Transitive Closure. McColm, Gregory L.

TRANSLATION

Further Selections from the Prison Notebooks. Gramsci, Antonio and Boothman, Derek (ed & trans).

Heraclitus: Translation and Analysis. Sweet, Dennis.

Idea of Prose. Agamben, Giorgio, Sullivan, Michael (trans) and Whitsitt, Sam (trans).

On Beings of Reason (De Entibus Rationis) Metaphysical Disputation LIV. Suárez, Francisco and Doyle, John P (trans).

Outlines of Scepticism. Annas, Julia (trans), Barnes, Jonathan (trans) and Sextus Empiricus.

Phaedrus. Plato, Woodruff, Paul (trans) and Nehamas, Alexander (trans).

Plato's Gorgias. Plato and Jowett, Benjamin (trans).

Preliminary Discourse to the Encyclopedia of Diderot. D'Alembert, Jean Le Rond and Schwab, Richard N (trans).

Solitudes: From Rimbaud to Heidegger. Froment-Meurice, Marc and Walsh, Peter (trans).

Telemachus, Son of Ulysses. Fénelon, François and Riley, Patrick (ed & trans).

The Book of the Body Politic: Forhan, Kate Langdon (ed & trans) and De Pizan, Christine.

The Names of History: On the Poetics of Knowledge. Rancière, Jacques and Melehy, Hassan (trans).

The Spirit of the Waldorf School. Steiner, Rudolf, Lathe, Robert F (trans) and Whittaker, Nancy Parsons (trans).

The Tao Te Ching: A New Translation with Commentary. Chen, Ellen M.

Critical Notice of 'Questions concerning the Law of Nature'. Stewart, M A.

Estudio introductorio a "De la educación moral del Hombre": Texto inédito en castellano de Claude Adrien Helvétius. Diego, Carmen Verde.

Franz Rosenzweig on Nation, Translation, and Judaism. Hollander, Dana.

From Eternal to Perpetual Truths: A Note on the Mediaeval History of Aristotle, *De interpretatione*, Ch 1, 16a18. Kneepkens, C H.

Historical Bibliography of Upanisads in Translation. Renard, Philip.

How (Not) to Read Heidegger. Sheehan, Thomas.

Incommensurabel, incompatibel, onvergelijkbaar. Raven, Diederick.

Introduction to the Simmel Texts. Frisby, David.

Las ideas chinas en la conceptualización transcultural: La relevancia de la historia intelectual. Lee, Thomas H C.

On Brinks and Bridges in Heidegger. Fritsche, Johannes.

On Giambattista Vico. Mali, Joseph.

On Translating Hegel's *Encyclopedia Logic*: A Response. Geraets, Theodore F and Harris, H S.

On Translating Locke, Berkeley, and Hume into English. Bennett, Jonathan.

Philosophy from an Antiphilosopher: Paul Valéry. Bouveresse, Jacques, Fournier, Christian (trans) and Laugier, Sandra (trans).

Rudolf Agricola's *De inventione dialectica libri tres*. Van Der Poel, Marc.

Semantic Competency (Yogyata). Vattanky, John.

The *Gesamtausgabe* Nietzsche: An Exercise in Translation and Thought. Schalow, Frank.

The Diffusion of Sextus Empiricus's Works in the Renaissance. Floridi, Luciano.

The Origin of Vertebrates and the Principle of Succession of Functions: Genealogical Sketches by Anton Dohrm, 1875—An English Translation. Ghiselin, Michael T.

Traduire les *Beiträge zur Philosophie (Vom Ereignis)*. Fédier, François.

Translating Samuel Pufendorf: On Two English Editions. Palladini, Fiammetta.

Translation as a Cultural-Philosophical Problem: Towards a Phenomenology of Culture. Ogawa, Tadashi.

Truthlikeness, Translation, and Approximate Causal Explanation. Barnes, Eric.

Zu Fragen der Interpretation und Entzifferung der Grundlagen der Gesamtausgabe Martin Heideggers. Emad, Parvis.

TRANSMIGRATION

Transmigration Without a Self. Datta, Rama.

TRANSPERSONAL

Some Developmental Issues in Transpersonal Experience. Hunt, Harry T.

TRANSPLANT

Sacrificing One to Save Many. Clark, Michael.

TRANSPLANTATION

Blurring Distinctions between the Dying and the Dead: A Call for Discernment in Organ Donation. Rutecki, Gregory W.

Liver Transplantation and Alcoholic Patients: When is it Justified to Just Say No?. Rutecki, Gregory W.

TRANSVALUATION

Commentary: Transvaluationism: Comments on Horgan. Raffman, Diana.

Las máscaras del demonio: Nietzsche y la hermenéutica. Conill, Jesus.

Transvaluationism: A Dionysian Approach to Vagueness. Horgan, Terence.

TRAUMA

Exclusion and Emphasis Reframed as a Matter of Ethics. Daniel, Jessica Henderson.

Reply to Daniel's "Exclusion and Emphasis Reframed as a Matter of Ethics". Herman, Judith Lewis.

TRAVEL

The Birth of Reason and Other Essays. Cory, Daniel (ed) and Santayana, George.

TRAVERSE

Bhavaviveka's *Prajñapradipa*. Ames, William L.

TREATMENT

Should People Do unto Others as They Would Not Want Done unto Themselves:. Harrison, Christine (& others).

The Physician's Authority to Withhold Futile Treatment. Griener, Glenn G.

TREE

-Completeness of a Fragment of the Theory of Trees with Subtree Relation. Cintioli, P and Tulipani, S.

Chains and Antichans in Interval Algebras. Bekkali, M.

UTILITARIANISM

Mathematics—The Music of Reason. Dieudonné, Jean, Dales, H G (trans) and Dales, J C (trans).

Modern Political Thought. Plant, Raymond.

Twentieth Century Ethical Theory. Cahn, Steven M (ed) and Haber, Joram G (ed).

A Critique of Western Philosophical Ethics: Multidisciplinary Alternatives for Framing Ethical Dilemmas. Carlin, William B and Strong, Kelly C.

A Proposito di 'Filosofia del Diritto'. Bello, Angela Ales.

A Role for Virtue Ethics in the Analysis of Business Practice. Koehn, Daryl.

Act-Utilitarianism and Coordination: A Critique of Allan Gibbard's View. Rahman, Lutfor.

Análisis Económico del Derecho y Utilitarismo: Concordancias y Divergencias. Mercado Pacheco, Pedro.

Antecedentes del Utilitarismo en los moralistas británicos anteriores a Hume. Costa, Margarita.

Are Deontology and Teleology Mutually Exclusive?. MacDonald, James E and Beck-Dudley, Caryn L.

Bentham's Social and Political Thoughts: A Brief Account. Shafiquil Alam, M.

Bentham: la ciencia del legislador. Bermudo Avila, José Manuel.

Business Meta-Ethics: An Analysis of Two Theories. Brady, F Neil and Dunn, Craig P.

Collective Rationality and Simple Utilitarian Theories. Almeida, Michael J.

Compromising with Convention. Hooker, Brad.

Conscience (Rule) Utilitarianism and the Criminal Law. Brandt, Richard B.

Consecuencialismo e imparcialidad. Salcedo, Damián.

Consecuencialismo: debate ético y jurídico. Nino, Carlos Santiago.

Contemporary Non-Conventional Evolutionary Theories. Urbanek, Adam.

Das Universalisierungsproblem in der Moralphilosophie. Meggle, Georg.

É o principio da utilidade racional?. Brito, José De Sousa.

El liberalismo frente a Bentham y Mill. Farrell, Martín Diego.

El modelo utilitarista en la construcción y desarrollo de la bioética. Clotet, Joaquín.

El Utilitarismo de Hume. Costa, Margarita.

El utilitarismo libertario de William Godwin. Adair, Phillipe.

Entre el Kantismo y el Consecuencialismo en la Filosofía Moral de T H Green. Weinstein, David.

Entrevista con Amartya Sen. Sen, Amartya.

Entrevista: Carlos R Braun dialoga con Pedro Schwartz. Schwartz, Pedro and Braun, Carlos Rodríguez.

Epicurus as a Forerunner of Utilitarianism. Scarre, Geoffrey.

Es Bentham utilitarista?. Rosen, Fred.

Extracto de "Libraos de Ultramaria". Bentham, Jeremy.

Filosofie, Metafysica en Moraal van Karl Popper. Abbes, J K.

From Biocentric Individualism to Biocentric Pluralism. Sterba, James P.

Fukuzawa Yukichi and Religion. Koizumi, Takashi.

Gibbard's Evolutionary Theory of Rationality and Its Ethical Implications. Ball, Stephen W.

Grenzen der Verantwortung. Heidbrink, Ludger.

Human Flourishings: A Psychological Critique of Virtue Ethics. Terzis, George N.

Human Rights Reaffirmed. Machan, Tibor R.

Ilustración y Utilitarismo en Iberoamérica. Rodríguez Braun, Carlos.

Inconmensurabilidad y razonamiento jurídico. Raz, Joseph.

Infinite Utility and Temporal Neutrality. Vallentyne, Peter.

Intersubjektivität und Objektivität der moralischen Werte. Corradini, Antonella.

Jeremy Bentham y la educación jurídica en la Universidad de Salamanca durante el siglo XIX. Pérez Luño, Antonio-Enrique.

La Disparité des Morales. Cloutier, Éric.

La recepción del Utilitarismo en el mundo hispánico: El caso de Ortega y Gasset. López Frías, Francisco.

La utilitat com a objecte amable de la relació. Ferrer, Joana.

Las reflexiones sobre la moral en Italia entre la Ética teórica y la Ética aplicada. Lecaldano, Eugenio.

Libertad constitucional y democracia reprsentativa. Rosen, Fred.

Moral y Derecho en Bentham. Moncho, Josep.

Neutralidad y relatividad agencial. Farrell, Martín D.

O interesse geral o e interesse de cada um. Sottomayor-Cardía, M.

Obedience to Rules and Berkeley's Theological Utilitarianism. Häyry, Matti and Häyry, Heta.

Observaciones y respuesta. Lara, Francisco, Salcedo, Damián and Gutiérrez, Gilberto.

On the Nature of Moral Principles. Sheng, C L.

Politeo's "Brown Note Book" (1860): Morality—Freedom. Festini, Heda.

Por qué son necesariamente inútiles las virtudes específicas religiosas?. Sastre, Gerardo López.

Rawls' Conception of a Person. Muquim, M.

Repugnant Desires and the Two-Tier Conception of Utility. Powers, Madison.

Should Utilitarianism Accommodate Moral Dilemmas?. Norcross, Alastair.

Social Justice and Individual Ethics. Van Parijs, Philippe.

Stuart Mill. Pardo Bazán, Emilia.

Students and Legal Obedience. Rich, John Martin.

The Coherence of Two-Level Utilitarianism: Hare vs Williams. Levy, Sanford S.

The Distinction Between Criterion and Decision Procedure: A Reply to Madison Powers. Griffin, James.

The Multiplication of Utility. Nathan, N M L.

The Problem of Endless Joy: Is Infinite Utility Too Much for Utilitarianism?. Garcia, Jorge L A and Nelson, M T.

The Quiddity of Mercy. Walker, Nigel.

Tugend und Moraltheorie. Schroeter, Francois.

Una aproximación al concepto de derecho a la intimidad en John Stuart Mill. García Añón, José.

Utilidad y autonomía de la dogmática jurídica. Muñiz, Joaquín R T.

Utilitarianism and Future Mistakes: Another Look. Curran, Angela.

Utilitarianism and the Virtues. Foot, Philippa.

Utilitarianism, Deontology, and the Priority of Right. Freeman, Samuel.

Utilitarismo y Teoría del Desarrollo Moral (I): Análisis crítico de las teorías cognitivas del desarrollo moral y de sus fundamentos Kantianos. Tasset, José Luis.

When to Terminate a Charitable Trust?. Landesman, Cliff.

Who Should a Utilitarian Be?. Smilansky, Saul.

Why Theorize How to Live with Each Other?. Gibbard, Allan F.

UTILITY

Autonomy and Intervention: Parentalism in the Caring Life. Kultgen, John.

Mental Content. McGinn, Colin.

Mill's Principle of Utility: A Defence of John Stuart Mill's Notorious Proof. Alican, Nejip Fikri.

Versus Trasimaco: E confutabile il detto "la giustizia non è altro che l'utile del più forte"?. Fiorillo, Vanda.

Work, Education, and Leadership: Essays in the Philosophy of Education. Howard, V A and Scheffler, Israel.

Allais' Rejoinder. Allais, Maurice.

Confianza y Racionalidad. Aguiar, Fernando.

De la Utilidad de la Dialéctica. Campos Benítez, Juan Manuel.

Economic Choice in Generalized Expected Utility Theory. Quiggin, John.

Entre la Teoría Económica y la Economía Política: Estudio Sobre *Ética a Nicómaco* V.5 y *Política* I.8-10 de Aristóteles. Basañez, Frederico.

Is Futility a Futile Concept?. Brody, Baruch A and Halevy, Amir.

La utilitat com a objecte amable de la relació. Ferrer, Joana.

On Pascal's Wager and Infinite Utilities. Byl, John.

Pascal on Certainty and Utility. McCarthy, John C.

Simulation and Interpersonal Utility. Goldman, Alvin I.

The Failure of Expected-Utility Theory as a Theory of Reason. Hampton, Jean.

The Impossibility of Interpersonal Utility Comparisons. Hausman, Daniel M.

The Two Errors: A Summary. Machina, Mark J.

Two Errors in the 'Allais Impossibility Theorem'. Machina, Mark J.

Utilidad, arte, virtud y riqueza en la Ilustración Escocesa. Itxaso, María Elósegui.

Utility, Subjectivism and Moral Ontology. Ross, Philip J.

When to Terminate a Charitable Trust?. Landesman, Cliff.

UTOPIA

"Eugenische Utopien: Entwürfe für die Rationalisierung der menschlichen Entwicklung" in *Nationalsozialismus und Moderne*, Welzer, Harald (ed). Weingart, Peter.

"La Filosofía en Tiempos del Cólera" in *Temas Actuales de Filosofía*, Palacios, María Julia (ed). Simesen de Bielke, Ana and Leonardi de Herran, Teresa.

"Marxism: From Scientific to Utopian" in *Whither Marxism?*, Magnus, Bernd (ed). Longxi, Zhang.

A Philosophy of History in Fragments. Heller, Agnes.

Apocalypse Theory and the Ends of the World. Bull, Malcolm (ed).

Das utopische Staatsmodell von Platons "Politeia" aus der Sicht von Orwells "Nineteen Eighty-Four". Otto, Dirk.

Erasmus, Utopia, and the Jesuits: Essays on the Outreach of Humanism. Olin, John C.

Finitude and Transcendence in the Platonic Dialogues. Hyland, Drew A.

Perversion and Utopia: A Study in Psychoanalysis and Critical Theory. Whitebook, Joel.

The Broken Middle: Out of our Ancient Society. Rose, Gillian.

The Evolution of Evil. Anders, Timothy.

Utopia: Latin Text and English Translation. More, Thomas and Logan, George M (& other eds).

Utopie II ou Vers une Société des Personnes. Adam, E.

A Critique of "Non-Instrumental Reason". Siemek, Marek J.

Ambivalencias de Bentham en la lectura de Foucault. García, Francisco Vázquez.

Bakhtin, Rabelais, and Utopia. Skorobogatov-Gray, Yevgenia.

Contribuiçao par as Discussoes ao Projeto de Implantaçao do Curso de Pedagogia na Fac de Ciências da Univ Estadual Paulista "Júlio de Mesquita Filho". Ghiraldelli Júnior, Paulo.

El Humanismo de Santo Tomás Moro y sus Obras Desde la Torre. Martínez Esteruelas, Cruz.

Heterosexual Utopianism. Soper, Kate.

Ideas sobre Ortega y Gasset y el ocaso del marxismo. Pallotini, Michele.

Machiavelli, Harrington, and the Character of Modern Utopia. Linker, Damon.

Max Weber et le néo-Kantisme: Pour une politique de la modernité. Piché, Claude.

Moral Sense and Utopian Sensibility. Fox, Robin.

Reason and Utopia: Richard Bernstein and the Rage against Reason. Nevo, Isaac.

Techniek als utopie. Achterhuis, Hans.

The Ideal of Social Disillusionment. Simpson, Evan and Williams, Mark.

Two Concepts of Utopia. Graybosch, A J.

Utopie in actie: wat verwachtingen in technologie doen. Van Lente, Harro.

Victimes et utopies: Analyse d'une structure de notre conscience morale. Boss, Gilbert.

Visionen für das 21 Jahrhundert?. Mayer, Günter.

UTOPIANISM

Actualidad del tema del hombre: los estudios de la mujer. Santa Cruz, María Isabel.

VACCINE

HIV Preventive Vaccine Research: Selected Ethical Issues. Grady, Christine.

VACUUM

Valeriano Magni e la Discussione sul Vuoto in Italia. Bucciantini, Massimo.

VADAS, M
Simulation and the Reproduction of Injustice: A Reply. Hopkins, Patrick D.

VAGUE
Why the World Cannot be Vague. Sainsbury, Mark.

VAGUENESS
Normative Cultures. Neville, Robert Cummings.
Paradoxes (Second Edition). Sainsbury, R M.
Commentary: On Vague Objects, Fuzzy Logic, and Fractal Boundaries. Copeland, B Jack.
Commentary: Proliferating Conceptions of Truth: Comments on McGee and McLaughlin. Hyde, Dominic.
Commentary: Some Remarks on Vagueness and a Dynamic Conception of Language. Tappenden, Jamie.
Commentary: The Epistemic Conception of Vagueness: Comments on Wright. Sorensen, Roy.
Commentary: Transvaluationism: Comments on Horgan. Raffman, Diana.
Distinctions Without a Difference. McGee, Vann and McLaughlin, Brian.
E J Lowe on Vague Identity and Quantum Indeterminacy. Noonan, Harold W.
Multivalence and Vagueness: A Reply to Copeland. Simons, Peter.
Science and Ethics: Toward a Theory of Ethical Value. Welch, John R.
Something to do With Vagueness. Burns, Linda.
The Epistemic Conception of Vagueness. Wright, Crispin.
Transvaluationism: A Dionysian Approach to Vagueness. Horgan, Terence.
Unsettled Problems with Vague Truth. Mills, Andrew.
Vague Identity and Quantum Non-Individuality. French, Steven and Krause, Décio.
Vagueness and Bivalence: A Discussion of Williamson and Simons. Copeland, B J.
Vagueness and Utility: The Semantics of Common Nouns. Parikh, Rohit.
Vagueness, Borderline Cases and Moral Realism. Shafer-Landau, Russ.
Vagueness, Identity, and the World. Garrett, Brian.
Vagueness, Indiscernibility, and Pragmatics: Comments on Burns. Varzi, Achille C.
Vagueness: Welcome to the Quicksand. Tye, Michael.

VAISESIKA
Anomolies of the Nyaya-Vaisesika Concept of Self. Dravid, N S.

VALERY, P
Faust e Lust. La Guardia, Giovanni.
Philosophy from an Antiphilosopher: Paul Valéry. Bouveresse, Jacques, Fournier, Christian (trans) and Laugier, Sandra (trans).

VALIDATION
"Holismo y el Problema de la Validación de las Teorías Científicas en la Perspectiva s Need-Stegmüller" in *Temas Actuales de Filosofía, Palacios, María Julia (ed)*. Gonzalo de Aguirre, Adriana.
Semántica de actualización. Veltman, Frank.

VALIDITY
"Verdad y Validez" in *Temas Actuales de Filosofía, Palacios, María Julia (ed)*. Santillán, Miguel Angel and del Valle Manzur, Analía.
An Impolite View of the Graduate Record Examination: Some Practical Reasons Why Most Studies Find This Test Has Low Predictive Validity. Oldfield, Kenneth.
El Programa del Naturalismo Epistémico Evolucionista: Alcance y Límites. Pacho G, J.
On Moral Relativism. Phillips, David.
Protosoziologie und Diskurstheorie. Ulfig, Alexander.
Remarks on a Theorem of McGee. Adams, Ernest W.
The Irrelevance of Distribution for the Syllogism. Murphree, Wallace A.
Validità sintattica vs invalidità sintattica in Geiger. Cabrera, Carlos Alarcón.
What Is Character?. Braun, David.
Zwischen "objektiver Gültigkeit" und "subjektiv-notwendigem Probierstein" der Wahrheit. Köveker, Dietmar.

VALLABHA
Vallabha's Positive Response to Buddhism. Yadav, Bibhuti S.

VALLENTYNE, P
The Problem of Endless Joy: Is Infinite Utility Too Much for Utilitarianism?. Garcia, Jorge L A and Nelson, M T.

VALLICELLA, W
Does the Ontological Argument Beg the Question?. McGrath, P J.
On "Divine Simplicity: A New Defense". Miller, Barry.

VALUATION
"Empfindung, Gefühl und Emotion: Zur Analyse von Bewertungen" in *Mythos Wertfreiheit?, Apel, Karl Otto (ed)*. Dorschel, Andreas.
Il problema della definizione generale del diritto. Bagolini, Luigi.
Truth as an Object. Magdziak, Marek.

VALUE
"Awe and Humility: Intrinsic Value in Nature" in *Philosophy and the Natural Environment, Attfield, Robin (ed)*. Lee, Keekok.
"Justified Warfare and the Relative Value of Human Life" in *Ethics on the Frontiers of Human Existence, Badham, Paul (ed)*. Van Den Dungen, Peter.
"Value in Nature and the Nature of Value" in *Philosophy and the Natural Environment, Attfield, Robin (ed)*. Rolston III, Holmes.
"Values, Reasons and the Environment" in *Philosophy and the Natural Environment, Attfield, Robin (ed)*. Crisp, Roger.
"Wertproblematik und Begründungsstruktur im Recht" in *Mythos Wertfreiheit?, Apel, Karl Otto (ed)*. Garm, Heino.
"Wertsphären, argumentative Vernunft und die gesellschaftliche Bewältigung von wissenschaftlicher und moralisch-ethischer Unsicherheit " in *Mythos Wertfreiheit?, Apel, Karl Otto (ed)*. von Schomberg, René.

Animal Welfare and Human Values. Preece, Rod and Chamberlain, Lorna.
Environmental Ethics (Oxford Readings in Philosophy). Elliot, Robert (ed).
Ethics from Experience. Caws, Peter.
For Education: Towards Critical Educational Inquiry. Carr, Wilfred.
Intrinsic Value: Concept and Warrant. Lemos, Noah M.
Kant on Happiness in Ethics. Wike, Victoria S.
Mill's Principle of Utility: A Defence of John Stuart Mill's Notorious Proof. Alican, Nejip Fikri.
Music, Value, and the Passions. Ridley, Aaron.
Nietzsche's Revaluation of Values: A Study in Strategies. Sleinis, E E.
Poetics of Modernity: Toward a Hermeneutic Imagination. Kearney, Richard.
Pragmatist Aesthetics: Living Beauty, Rethinking Art. Shusterman, Richard.
Private Consciences and Public Reasons. Greenawalt, Kent.
The Boundaries of Moral Discourse. Hajdin, Mane.
The Philosophical Papers of Alan Donagan: Volume II, Action, Reason, and Value. Malpas, J E (ed) and Donagan, Alan.
The Tanner Lectures on Human Values, Volume 16. Peterson, Grethe B (ed).
Values, Work, Education: The Meanings of Work. Natale, Samuel M (ed) and Rothschild, Brian M (ed).
A Pragmatist Theory of Artistic Creativity. Leddy, Thomas W.
Algunas preguntas acerca de la Idea de Progreso. Peña, Vidal.
Análisis Económico del Derecho y Utilitarismo: Concordancias y Divergencias. Mercado Pacheco, Pedro.
Autonomy, Value, and Conditioned Desire. Noggle, Robert.
Axiological Invariants. Reale, Miguel.
Basic Values of Western Industrial Society: Feedback Effect of Rationality. Mineau, André.
Bayesian Inference Given Data 'Significant at α': Tests of Point Hypothesis. Johnstone, D J and Lindley, D V.
Being and Value: Heidegger contra Nietzsche. Young, Julian.
Benedetto Croce Critico dell'Irrazionalismo. Tertulian, Nicolas.
Bioethics and Family Values. Almond, Brenda.
Bódog Somló's Theory of Values. Szegó, Katalin.
Cognitive Value and the Advancement of Science. Levi, Isaac.
Common Values and Value Conflicts in Environmental Education. Döbler, Matthias.
Como Pensar los Valores Morales a Partir de Kant?. Norbert, Bilbeny.
De la teoría general del valor a una ética de fines en Husserl. Ferrer, Urbano.
Democracy and Right in Habermas's Theory of Facticity and Value. Williams, Howard.
Dialéctica de Casiciaco. Rosado, Juan.
Dialogue sur un dialogue: A propos du *Dialgoue* d'Ernest Joós *avec Heidegger sur les valeurs*. Giroux, Laurent.
Do Agriculturalists Need a New, an Ecocentric, Ethic? 1994 Presidential Address to the Agriculture, Food, and Human Values Society. Comstock, Gary L.
Environmental Valuation: Some Problems of Wrong Questions and Misleading Answers. Knetsch, Jack L.
Existence Value, Welfare and Altruism. Aldred, Jonathan.
Explanation and Evaluation in Cognitive Science. Montgomery, Richard.
For Our Own Good. Archard, David.
Human Value of Sustainable Society. Dewan, M L.
Humility. Snow, Nancy E.
Inconmensurabilidad y razonamiento jurídico. Raz, Joseph.
Intersubjektivität und Objektivität der moralischen Werte. Corradini, Antonella.
John Laird and *The Idea of Value*. Attfield, Robin.
Juventud, valores y crisis de nuestro tiempo. Vegas, José M.
Kanean Libertarianism. Bernstein, Mark H.
Kant, Heidegger e la logica filosofica. Messinese, Leonardo.
Knowledge of Value. Sarin, Indu.
La Comprensión Científica en el Siglo Veinte. Salmon, W.
La intimidad como valor antropológico y social. Pallarés Gonzalez, José Luis.
Learning from Art. Graham, Gordon.
Los Valores en el Pensamiento de F Nietzsche. Alvarez Argüelles, Luz María.
Moral Realism, Objective Values, and J L Mackie. Mizzoni, John.
Moral Standing, Value, and Environmental Ethics. Landman, Willem A.
Musical Values Revisited: A Reply to Forest Hansen's "Values in Music Education". Elliott, David J.
Neutrals. Lemos, Noah M.
Nietzsche and Feminism: Transvaluing Women in *Thus Spoke Zarathustra*. Lorraine, Tamsin.
Observaciones y respuesta. Lara, Francisco, Salcedo, Damián and Gutiérrez, Gilberto.
Otto Neurath's Idealist Inheritance: *The Social and Economic Thought of Wilhelm Neurath*. Uebel, Thomas E.
Philosophy, Education and the Quality of Life. Prasad, Rajendra.
Plotino, Ficino e noi stessi: alcuni riflessi etici. Rist, John M and Peroli, E (trans).
Pluralism of Norms and Values: On the Claim and Reception of the Universal. Klapwijk, J.
Priest's Paraconsistent Arithmetic. Denyer, Nicholas.
Reply to Van de Vate. Browning, Douglas.
Response to Victor Yelverton Haines. Eldridge, Richard.
Rôle et fonction des valeurs à l'origine des sociétés. Pezzillo, Lelia.
Science and Ethics: Toward a Theory of Ethical Value. Welch, John R.
Some Notes on Browning's *Ethical Notes*. Van de Vate, Dwight.
Standing for Something. Calhoun, Cheshire.
Stronger Evidence. Achinstein, Peter.
The *Fin De Siècle* Redux. London, Herb.

VISUAL

Distinctions Without a Difference. McGee, Vann and McLaughlin, Brian.

Do We See with Microscopes?. Pacherie, Elisabeth.

Epistemology of Visual Thinking in Elementary Real Analysis. Giaquinto, Marcus.

Husserl and Goodman on the Role of Resemblance in Pictorial Representation. Drost, Mark P.

Perception and Proper Explanatory Width. Rollins, Mark.

Phenomenal Character. Shoemaker, Sydney.

Searle's Theory of Visual Experience. Wilkie, Sean.

The 3D/4D Controversy and Non-Present Objects. Markosian, Ned.

The Aesthetic Value of Representation in Painting. Goldman, Alan H.

The Experiential Text and the Limits of Visual Understanding. Denzin, Norman K.

The Three Ages of Looking. Rauth, Eric (trans) and Debray, Régis.

Why Pains Are Mental Objects. Langsam, Harold.

VISUAL ART

The Philosophy of the Visual Arts. Alperson, Philip (ed).

Visual Art as Theology. Baumgarten, Barbara Dee Bennett.

Afro Images: Politics, Fashion, and Nostalgia. Davis, Angela Y.

Appropriation and Interpretation. Sartwell, Crispin.

On Artistic Process: Eye, Hand, Language. Nitta, Hiroë.

Pictorial Realism. Lopes, Dominic.

Reflections on Art, Culture and Universalism. Kamenka, Eugene.

The Picture Frame: An Aesthetic Study. Simmel, Georg and Ritter, Mark (trans).

VITALISM

La Filosofia Tedesca del Secondo Ottocento tra Scienze dello Spirito e Scienze della Natura. Meschiari, Alberto.

On Gilles Deleuze and Félix Guattari, *A Thousand Plateaus*. Negri, Antonio and Wolf, Charles (trans).

VITORIA, F

Actualidad de un Filósofo del Siglo XVI: Francisco de Vitoria. Ocaña García, Marcelino.

Santo Tomás de Aquino como Inspirador de Francisco de Vitoria. Romero Baró, José María.

VLASTOS, G

Gregory Vlastos on Justice and Equality. Kraut, Richard H.

Is Moderation a Virtue? Gregory Vlastos and the Toxins of Eudaemonism. Meister, Robert.

Kontinuität oder Bruch? Zum Verhältnis von sokratischer und platonischer Dialektik. Mesch, Walter.

Pagan Justice and Christian Love. Williams, Bernard.

Plato's Philosopher. Davidson, Donald.

Plato's Politic of Narcissism. Lear, Jonathan.

Self-Censorship in Plato's Republic. Blundell, Mary Whitlock.

Socratic Goods and Socratic Happiness. Santas, Gerasimos.

Virtue as the Use of Other Goods. Annas, Julia.

Vlastos on a Metaphysical Paradox. Code, Alan D.

Vlastos on Socratic and Platonic Forms. Fine, Gail.

'Say What You Believe'. Irwin, T H.

VOCATION

The Vocation to Be a Philosopher. Andrews, Philip.

VOEGELIN, E

Eric Voegelin: Le Ragioni e il Metodo della Conscienza. Sallusti, Marina.

VOGEL, C

"Springflut des Bösen". Briese, Olaf.

VOICE

Rhetorical Mosaic for a Kaleidoscope of Sound: Poetry as a Road to Understanding the Prose Voice. Britt, John F.

VOIGT, A

Inhalts- oder Umfangslogik? Die Kontroverse zwischen E Husserl und A H Voigt. Hamacher-Hermes, Adelheid.

VOLTAIRE

"'Ich bin der Apostel und Märtyrer der Engländer gewesen'" in *Naturauffassungen in Philosophie, Wissenschaft, Technik: Band II*, Schäfer, Lothar (ed). Wahsner, Renate.

Voltaire y la Enciclopedia: La Génesis del Nuevo Campo Epistémico de la Historia. Mudrovcic, María Inés.

VOLUNTARISM

Itinerari del Volontarismo: Teologia e politica al tempo di Luis de León. Ferraro, Domenico.

The Deontological Conception of Epistemic Justification and Doxastic Voluntarism. Kim, Kihyeon.

VOLUNTARY

En Torno a la Noción de Pobreza Voluntaria. Salazar, Ignacio.

VOLUNTARY ACTION

Libertad y revocabilidad. Martin, Christopher.

VOLUNTEERISM

Narratives of Volunteering. Paolicchi, Piero.

VON BALTHASAR, H

Anonymous or Analogous Christians? Rahner and von Balthasar on Naming the Non-Christian. Lamadrid, Lucas.

VON BRETZEL, P

A Note on Von Bretzel's Solution to an Alleged Problem with Reichenbach's Definition of Time Direction. Paprzycka, Katarzyna.

VON GARLANDIA, J

Divisio Scientiarum: Ein bisher unveröffentlichtes Wissenschaftsmodell in der Clavis Compendii des Johannes von Garlandia. Haye, Thomas.

VON GEBSATTEL, V

The Meaning of Medical Practice. von Gebsattel, Victor E and Welie, Jos V M (trans).

Viktor Emil von Gebsattel on the Doctor-Patient Relationship. Welie, Jos V M.

VON LAUE, T

Identity in World History: A Post-Modern Perspective. Wurgaft, Lewis.

VON WEIZSACKER, V

The Anthropological Tradition in the Philosophy of Medicine. Ten Have, Henk.

VOROBEJ, M

Pacifism and Wartime Innocence: A Response. Holmes, Robert L.

VOTING

Democratic Voting and The Mixed-Motivation Problem. Wolff, Jonathan.

On the Difficulty of Making Social Choices. Nurmi, Hannu.

Postulates and Paradoxes of Relative Voting Power—A Critical Re-Appraisal. Felsenthal, Dan S and Machover, Moshé.

VYGOTSKY, L

Concept Development and Computation of Meaning Thought and Language by Vygotsky. Forest, F and Siksou, M.

G H Mead and L S Vygotsky on Meaning and the Self. Koczanowicz, Leszek.

The Unconscious: A Perspective from Sociohistorical Psychology. Ratner, Carl.

WAGE

see Compensation, Income

WAGNER

"Accessories (*Ecce Homo*, 'Why I Write Such Good Books', 'The Untimelies', 3)" in *Nietzsche: A Critical Reader*, Sedgwick, Peter R (ed). Kofman, Sarah.

The Complete Works of Friedrich Nietzsche: Volume 2: Unfashionable Observations. Nietzsche, Friedrich, Colli, Giorgio (ed) and Montinari, Mazzino (ed).

Liebe, Tod, Erlösung: Richard Wagners "Tristan" und der Einfluss Schopenhauers. Steiger, Karsten.

WAGNER, S

A Note about a Quinean Argument against Direct Reference. Oppy, Graham.

WAKING

En la confluencia de filosofía y esoterismo: Jean D'Encausse y la doctrina del "despertar". Saura, Emilio.

WALDORF SCHOOL

The Spirit of the Waldorf School. Steiner, Rudolf, Lathe, Robert F (trans) and Whittaker, Nancy Parsons (trans).

WALDRON, J

Acceptance of Authority and the Duty to Comply with Just Institutions: A Comment on Waldron. Murphy, Mark C.

Waldron on Political Legitimacy and the Social Minimum. Weithman, Paul.

Waldron on Special Rights *in rem*. Cristi, Renato.

WALKER, C

Commentary on "Karl Jaspers and Edmund Husserl". Chadwick, Ruth F.

WALKER, N

Recent Work on Punishment. Ellis, Anthony.

WALKER, R

Ralph C S Walker, *The Coherence Theory of Truth: Realism, Anti-Realism, Idealism*. Wright, Crispin.

WALLACE, K

Response. Smith, John E.

WALLACE, W

Jesuit Science Between Texts and Contexts. Biagioli, Mario.

WALTON, D

Slippery Slope Arguments by Douglas Walton. Van Der Burg, Wiltbren.

WALTON, K

Fiction and the *De Se* Self. Vance, Robert D.

General Theories of Art versus Music. Davies, Stephen.

Kendall L Walton's *Mimesis as Make-Believe*. Carroll, Noël.

Sculpture. Vance, Robert D.

WALZER, M

Reply to Michael Walzer. Bader, Veit.

The Politics of Communitarianism. Friedman, Jeffrey.

WANG YANG-MING

De studie der Chinese wijsbegeerte in het Westen: Een bibliografisch overzicht. Van der Leeuw, Karel L.

The Foundation of Ethics in Late Confucianism. Kern, Iso.

WANGLIE, H

When Families Request That 'Everything Possible' Be Done. Jecker, Nancy S and Schneiderman, Lawrence J.

WAR

see also Cold War

"Beauvoir and the Algerian War: Toward a Postcolonial Ethics" in *Feminist Interpretations of Simone de Beauvoir*, Simons, Margaret A (ed). Murphy, Julien.

"Justified Warfare and the Relative Value of Human Life" in *Ethics on the Frontiers of Human Existence*, Badham, Paul (ed). Van Den Dungen, Peter.

"On War: The Space of Knowledge, Knowledge of Space" in *Reconstructing Foucault*, Miguel-Alfonso, Ricardo (ed). Campillo, Antonio.

"War, Terrorism, and Ethical Consistency" in *Introducing Applied Ethics*, Almond, Brenda (ed). Wallace, Gerry.

Ethics, Killing and War. Norman, Richard.

Gesamtausgabe (III Abteilung): Unveröffentlichte Abhandlungen. Heidegger, Martin.

WELFARE

Accepting the Consequences of Anti-Individualism. McKinsey, Michael.

After the Family Wage: Gender Equity and the Welfare State. Fraser, Nancy.

El óptimo de Pareto frente al utilitarismo. Carreras, Mercedes.

Entrevista con Amartya Sen. Sen, Amartya.

Existence Value, Welfare and Altruism. Aldred, Jonathan.

Four Dogmas of Environmental Economics. Sagoff, Mark.

Las ambigüedades de la democracia y los enfoques postmodernistas. Mansilla, H C F.

Multiculturalism and Welfare Reform. Jones, John D.

Social Justice and Individual Ethics. Van Parijs, Philippe.

The Meshing of Care and Justice. Held, Virginia.

The Subjectivity of Welfare. Sumner, L W.

WELL-BEING

Nursing Ethics: Therapeutic Caring Presence. Bishop, Anne H and Scudder Jr, John R.

Staat en Welzijn: Het belang van een vernieuwde conceptie van de Minimale Staat. Hogervorst, S.

Welzijn Zeggenschap en Eigendom. Hogervorst, S.

Abandoning Informed Consent. Veatch, Robert M.

Autonomy and Commitment: Compatible Ideals. Aviram, Aharon.

La Eudaimonía y las Bienaventuranzas. de Gayoso, Graciela L Ritacco.

La justificación consecuencialista de las lealtades. Lara Sánchez, Francisco Damián.

Mild Mania and the Theory of Health: A Response to "Mild Mania and Well-Being". Nordenfelt, Lennart.

Mild Mania and Well-Being. Moore, Andrew, Hope, Tony and Fulford, K W M.

National Differences in Reported Subjective Well-Being: Why Do They Occur?. Diener, Ed (& others).

The Impossibility of Interpersonal Utility Comparisons. Hausman, Daniel M.

The Trouble with Well-Being: A Response to "Mild Mania and Well-Being". Seedhouse, David.

Well-Being, Categorical Deprivation and the Role of Education. Yonah, Yossi.

WELSH, J

On the Concepts of the 'Other' and the 'Enemy'. Harle, Vilho.

WENGER, N

Appropriate and Inappropriate Use of Advance Directives. Emanuel, Linda.

Clear, Convincing, and Authentic Advance Directives in the Context of Managed Care?. Bursztajn, Harold J and Brodsky, Archie.

The Capacity to Make Decisions in Advance and Borderline Personality Disorder. Ganzini, Linda, Lee, Melinda A and Heintz, Ronald T.

WENZ, P

Rawls and Environmental Ethics: A Critical Examination of the Literature. Thero, Daniel P.

The Demise of Monism and Pluralism in Environmental Ethics. Van Der Steen, Wim J.

WERLE, J

How Unified is Physics Itself?: Comments on Józef Werle's Paper "How the Physical Sciences Discovered the Unity of Nature". Strawinski, Witold.

On Certain Consequence of the Temporal and Spatial Scale of the Universe: Comments on "How the Physical Sciences Discovered the Unity of Nature". Butryn, Stanislaw.

Two Logical Patterns of the Reduction of Theories: Comments on Józef Werle's Paper "How the Physical Sciences Discovered the Unity of Nature". Krajewski, Wladyslaw.

Unification and the History of Science: Comments on Józef Werle's Paper "How the Physical Sciences Discovered the Unity of Nature". Pietruska-Madej, Elzbieta.

WESSELL, L

Carta abierta al Dr Wessell. Pintor Ramos, A.

WEST, C

Cornel West: American Radicalism. Osborne, Peter.

Interrogating Whiteness: Dialogue as a Pragmatist Tool for Postmodern Identity-Formation *or* Breaking Bread with Bell Hooks and Cornel West. Paris, Jeffrey.

WESTERN

see also Occidental

"African Traditional Thought and Western Science" in *African Philosophy: Selected Readings, Appiah, Kwame Anthony*. Horton, Robin.

"Emotions in Western Thought: Some Background for a Comparative Dialogue" in *Emotions in Asian Thought, Marks, Joel (ed)*. Marks, Joel.

"How Not to Compare African Thought with Western Thought" in *African Philosophy: Selected Readings, Mosley, Albert G (ed)*. Wiredu, Kwasi.

"The Emotions of Altruism, East and West" in *Emotions in Asian Thought, Marks, Joel (ed)*. Kupperman, Joel J.

Antologia del Buddhismo Ch'an. Arena, Leonardo Vittorio.

Classics of Western Philosophy (Fourth Edition). Cahn, Steven M (ed).

The Bounds of Freedom: About the Eastern and Western Approaches to Freedom. Balaban, Oded and Erev, Anan.

The Divine Matrix: Creativity as Link between East and West. Bracken, Joseph A.

The High Road of Humanity: The Seven Ethical Ages of Western Man. Levi, Albert William, Verene, Donald Phillip (ed) and Verene, Molly Black (ed).

The Machine as Metaphor and Tool. Haken, Hermann (ed), Karlqvist, Anders (ed) and Svedin, Uno (ed).

A Few Problems Related to Nineteenth Century Chinese and Western Philosophies and their Cultural Interaction. Weishi, Yuan.

A Reckoning of Sorts on the Prospects of Moral Philosophy. Margolis, Eric.

Eine grundlegende konzeptionelle Denkfigur der altchinesischen Philosophie. Trauzettel, Rolf.

Feng Youlan and the Vienna Circle (A Synopsis). Shouchang, Wang.

Feng Youlan's Views on Chinese and Western Culture. Zhonghua, Li.

Islam and the West. Danecki, Janusz.

L'occidentalité de la Philosophie. Bucio, Francisco.

Language and World: Some Classical Indian Approaches *vis-a-vis* Analytical Western Approaches. Gokhale, Pradeep P.

On Western Rationality and Its Alleged Relation to Aristotle. Evangeliou, Christos.

Reconciling Emotions with Western Personhood. Fischer, Agneta H and Jansz, Jeroen.

Some Notes on Emotion, "East and West". Solomon, Robert C.

The Problem of Inter-Faith Studies. Matilal, Bimal K.

The Social Equation: Freedom and its Limits. Horvath, Charles M.

The Turn Towards Buddhism. McGhee, Michael.

Towards Global Environmental Values: Lessons from Western and Eastern Experience. Sarre, Philip.

WESTERN CIVILIZATION

El Siglo XIII de París: Nuevo Rumbo para la Filosofía Occidental. Zapater, José María.

Sócrates: Filósofo en el Límite. Nudler, Oscar.

WEYL, H

Herman Weyl's Intuitionistic Mathematics. van Dalen, Dirk.

Weyl, Reichenbach and the Epistemology of Geometry. Ryckman, Thomas A.

WHEELER, J

Reinterpreting the Wheeler-Feynman Absorber Theory: Reply to Leeds. Price, Huw.

WHEWELL, W

It's *All* Necessarily So: William Whewell on Scientific Truth. Snyder, Laura J.

The Whewell-Faraday Exchange on the Application of the Concepts of Momentum and Inertia to Electromagnetic Phenomena. Anderson, Ronald.

WHISTLEBLOWING

A Critical Examination of the AICPA Code of Professional Conduct. Collins, Allison and Schultz, Norm.

Estimating the Incidence of Wrongdoing and Whistle-Blowing: Results of a Study Using Randomized Response Technique. Burton, Brian K and Near, Janet P.

WHITE

Interrogating Whiteness: Dialogue as a Pragmatist Tool for Postmodern Identity-Formation *or* Breaking Bread with Bell Hooks and Cornel West. Paris, Jeffrey.

WHITE, A

Reply: The Schellingian Alternative. Bowie, Andrew.

WHITE, G

Jeremy Bentham's Panopticon as Metaphor: Science and Supervision in Tobias Smollett and Gilbert White. Chalmers, Rachel.

WHITE, N

Prudence and Morality in Greek Ethics. Irwin, T H.

WHITE, P

Knowledge, Practice, Truth. Standish, Paul.

WHITE, T

Toward the Feminine Firm: An Extension to Thomas White. Dobson, John and White, Judith.

WHITEHEAD

Der Zusammenhang der Wirklichkeit. Krämer, Felix.

Ethik und Identität: Der ethische Ansatz in der Prozessphilosophie A N Whiteheads und seine Bedeutung für die gegenwärtige Ethik. Lachmann, Rolf.

Browning and Two Traditions. Krecz, Charles A.

Función de la Creatividad en la Filosofía de A N Whitehead. Oroz Ezcurra, Javier.

Kimball on Whitehead and Perception. Hildebrand, David L.

Matter and God in Rahner and Whitehead. Doud, Robert E.

Personal Identity: In Buddhist and Whiteheadian Thought (An Exercise with an Intercultural Experience). Sarkar, Anil K.

Realität und Tätigkeit im ersten Teil von Fichtes *Grundlage*, beurteilt aus der Sicht Whiteheads. Krämer, Felix.

Reply to Krecz. Browning, Douglas.

The Creation of 'Eternal' Objects. Ford, Lewis S.

The Original Version of Process and Reality, Part V: A Tentative Reconstruction. Hurtubise, Denis.

The Philosophical Anthropology of Alfred North Whitehead. Prozesky, Martin.

The Relevance of Foucault to Whiteheadian Environmental Ethics. McGee, Glenn.

The Riddle of *Religion in the Making*. Ford, Lewis S.

Whitehead and Heidegger on Technological Goodness. Grange, Joseph.

Whitehead's Early Philosophy of Mathematics. Henry, Granville C and Valenza, Robert J.

WHITNEY, W

The Sanskrit of Science. Staal, Frits.

WICKS, R

Beauty, Sublimity, and Expression: Reply to Wicks and Cantrick. Guyer, Paul.

Supervenience Unthwarted: Rejoinder to Wicks. Zangwill, Nick.

WIEAND, J

Hume's Double Standard of Taste. Shelley, James.

Rule and Verdict. Shelley, James.

WIELAND, C

Shopenhauers Ästhetik bei Wieland. Ingenkamp, Heinz Gerd.

WIENER, N

The Ontology of the Enemy: Norbert Wiener and the Cybernetic Vision. Galison, Peter.

WIGGINS, D
"Comments and Replies" in *Reading Putnam, Clark, Peter (ed)*. Putnam, Hilary.
Moral Realism and Wanton Cruelty. Carlson, George R.
Three Kinds of Incommensurability Thesis. Simmons, Lance.

WIGNER, E
The Applicabilities of Mathematics. Steiner, Mark.

WILDERNESS
Postmodern Environmental Ethics. Oelschlaeger, Max (ed).
Wilderness Philosophy. Gay, Hannah.

WILL
see also General Will
"Dappertutto e in Nessun Luogo": Volontà e Potenza di un'edizione Nietzscheana. Brusotti, Marco and Gerratana, Federico.
"Locke on the Freedom of the Will" in *Locke's Philosophy, Rogers, G A J (ed)*. Chappell, Vere.
"Oltre l'etica: Il rapporto tra morale e sovramorale in Soren Kierkeggard" in *L'etica e il suo Altro, Vigna, Carmelo (ed)*. Bettiolo, Isabella Adinolfi.
"Wille" e "Willkür" in Fichte. Moiso, Francesco.
"Yo Pienso" y "Yo Quiero": Razones de una Asimetría. V Arregui, Jorge.
A Companion to the Philosophy of Mind. Guttenplan, Samuel (ed).
A Philosophy of History in Fragments. Heller, Agnes.
Blindness of Modern Science. Uus, Undo.
Human Will: The Search for Its Physical Basis. Harkavy, Allan Abraham.
Itinerari del Volontarismo: Teologia e politica al tempo di Luis de León. Ferraro, Domenico.
Nietzsche's Genealogy: Nihilism and the Will to Knowledge. Havas, Randall.
Other Minds: Critical Essays 1969-1994. Nagel, Thomas.
Scepsi Moderna: Interpretazioni dello Scetticismo da Charron a Hume. Paganini, Gianni.
Tempo e Intuizione: Alle origini dello slancio vitale nel pensiero di Henri Bergson. Taroni, Paolo.
The Philosophical Papers of Alan Donagan: Volume II, Action, Reason, and Value. Malpas, J E (ed) and Donagan, Alan.
Belief and the Problem of Ulysses and the Sirens. Van Fraassen, Bas.
Commentary on Mansfeld's "The Idea of the Will in Chrysippus, Posidonius, and Galen". Sedley, David.
Definición del Hombre en Términos de lo que Quiere Ser. López Ruiz, Isabel.
Eternità e tempo in Plotino. Ferretti, Silvia.
Faust e Lust. La Guardia, Giovanni.
Fichte y Ortega (II). Héroes o Ciudadanos. El Mito de Don Quijote. Molinuevo, José Luis.
Four Practical Challenges of the Mature Royce to Californians and Others. Oppenheim, Frank.
Free Willing: Comments on Hoffman's "Freedom and Strength of Will". Chappell, Vere.
Freedom and Strength of Will in Hoffman and Albritton. Watson, Gary.
Freedom and Strength of Will: Descartes and Albritton. Hoffman, Paul.
Habermas y el universalismo moral. Prior Olmos, Angel.
Hegel's Critique of Kant in the Philosophy of Right. Lottenbach, Hans and Tenenbaum, Sergio.
How to Read Religion within the Limits of Reason Alone. Davidovich, Adina.
Il Livello Religioso Dell'intersoggettività nel Pensiero di Fichte. Ivaldo, Marco.
Interés es Aquello por lo Cual la Razón se Hace Práctica. Carmo Ferreira, Manuel J.
Kant, la razza e la storia. Pellecchia, Pasquale.
L'eternità dell'essere nel pensiero di Emanuele Severino. Sperduto, D.
La domanda speculativa fondamentale: Il linguaggio della filosofia come forme di invocazione. Bosio, Franco.
La Etica en Husserl. Ferrer, Urbano.
Miedo e Incertidumbre. Hansberg, Olbeth.
Morality, Practical Knowledge, and Will. Wallace, James D.
Naturalizing the Epistemologist: The Final Shadow of the Dead God. Conway, Daniel W.
Nietzsche, Naturalism, and Interpretation. Cox, Christoph.
On Being Moved by Desire. Hertzberg, Lars.
On Neitzsche's Enigmatic Anti-Kantian Categorical Imperative. Hodge, Roger D.
On Nietzsche's Perspectivism. Li, Hon-Lam.
Perspectivism: Aquinas and Nietzsche on Intellect and Will. Thompson, Walter J.
Probleme der Kantischen Ethik: Überlegungen im Anschluss an Paul Menzers kritische Betrachtung. Wichmann, Heinz.
Pufendorf tra Classicità e Modernità: Nota su un Libro di Simone Goyard-Fabre. Catteneo, Mario A.
Responses to Chappell and Watson. Hoffman, Paul.
Schopenhauer im Spiegel der europäischen Literatur des 19 und 20 Jarhunderts. Ries, Wiebrecht.
Schopenhauer, Feeling and the Noumenon. Nicholls, Moira.
Schopenhauers Ethik—die Konsequenz. Schulz, Ortrun.
Sollen, Wollen, Tun. Lembeck, Karl-Heinz.
The Disappearance of Tradition in Weber. Turner, Stephen P and Factor, Regis A.
The Evolution of the Will. Norwood, Rick.
The Idea of the Will in Chrysippus, Posidonius, and Galen. Mansfeld, Jaap.
The Kantian Inheritance and Schopenhauer's Doctrine of Will. Nicholls, Moira.
The Nature of the Will and its Place in Schopenhauer's Philosophy. Hall, Roland.
The Nietzsche Image in Heidegger's *Beiträge, Contributions to Philosophy (On the Event)*. Behler, Ernst.
Una Polemica su Gentile alle Origini dello Stalinismo Filosofico. Mastroianni, Giovanni.

Une approche déflationniste de la liberté de la volonté: un autre visage de Kant. Schroeter, François.
What Did Lonergan Really Say about Aquinas's Theory of the Will?. Stebbins, J Michael.
Wie indisch ist das Indienbild Schopenhauers?. Mall, Ram Adhar.
Wille und Wunsch in der Handlung bei Wittgenstein. Ule, Andrej.

WILL TO POWER
Nietzsche e il nichilismo. Penzo, Giorgio.
Nietzsche's Will to Power as a Doctrine of the Unity of Science. Anderson, R Lanier.
The *Gesamtausgabe* Nietzsche: An Exercise in Translation and Thought. Schalow, Frank.

WILLIAM OF AUXERRE
Zur Geschichtlichkeit der Rede von Gott: Einflüsse zeitgenössischer Königsideologie auf die Trinitätslehre Wilhelms von Auxerre. Arnold, Johannes.

WILLIAM OF CONCHES
Science and Rhetoric in the Middle Ages: The Natural Philosophy of William of Conches. Cadden, Joan.

WILLIAMS, B
Aristotle, Success, and Moral Luck. Farwell, Paul.
Bernard Williams, *Shame and Necessity*. Held, Dirk T D.
Categorical Desires and the Future. Yonah, Yossi.
Die Moralität des antiken Menschen: Über Bernhard Williams Buch "Shame and Necessity". Rapp, Christof.
Moral Incapacity. Taylor, Craig.
Questionable Objectivity. Ripstein, Arthur.
Rational Agency and Objectively Practical Reason. Abrams, Edward L.
The Argument from Marginal Cases: Is Speciesism Defensible?. Feezell, Randolph M and Stephens, William O.
The Coherence of Two-Level Utilitarianism: Hare vs Williams. Levy, Sanford S.
Three Kinds of Incommensurability Thesis. Simmons, Lance.
Wittgenstein, transzendentale Gründzüge und transzendentale Einschränkungen. Sacks, Mark.

WILLIAMS, C
Lógica y Ontología: Verdad, Existencia e Identidad como Funciones de Segundo Nivel. Frápolli, María José.

WILLIAMS, J
Belief-In Revisited: A Reply to Williams. MacIntosh, J J.

WILLIAMS, M
A Reply in Defense of Impartiality. Baker, Judith.

WILLIAMS, R
Civilized Madness: Schizophrenia, Self-Consciousness and the Modern Mind. Sass, Louis A.
Cultural Materialism, Cultural and Post-Culturalism: The Legacy of Raymond Williams. Milner, Andrew.
Hegel and Fichte: Recognition, Otherness, and Absolute Knowing. Houlgate, Stephen.

WILLIAMSON, T
Multivalence and Vagueness: A Reply to Copeland. Simons, Peter.
Vagueness and Bivalence: A Discussion of Williamson and Simons. Copeland, B J.

WILSON, A
Teaching as Applied Philosophy. Kaplan, Laura Duhan.

WILSON, C
Catherine Wilson on Leibniz's Metaphysics. Okruhlik, M Kathleen.

WILSON, D
Fitting Pragmatics into the Mind: Some Issues in Mentalist Pragmatics. Sinclair, Melinda.

WILSON, E
A Reply to Antony Flew's Discussion of "E O Wilson After 20 Years". Robinson, Peter.
Explaining and Valuing: An Exchange between Theology and the Human Sciences. Gustafson, James M.

WILSON, J
Are Moral Intuitions Self-Evident Truths?. Shweder, Richard A.
How We Acquire a Sense of Morality. Eysenck, H J.
Making Sense of Social Experiences and Moral Judgments. Turiel, Elliot.
Moral Authority in Law and Criminal Justice: Some Reflections on Wilson's *The Moral Sense*. Tyler, Tom R and Kerstetter, Wayne.
Moral Innatism, Connatural Ideas, and Impuissance in Daily Affairs: James Q Wilson's Acrobatic Dive into an Empty Pool. Geis, Gilbert.
Moral Sense and Utopian Sensibility. Fox, Robin.
On Morals and Markets. Schwartz, Barry.
Sentiments, Evaluations, and Claims. Gaus, Gerald F.
The Immoral Sense. Gewirth, Alan.
The Moral Sense: Ancient and Modern. Saxonhouse, Arlene W.
Trapped in a Metaphor. Sanday, Peggy Reeves.
Universalism and Individualism. Buckle, Stephen.

WINCH, P
Los ejemplos literario en la filosofia moral: Comentario al trabajo de Osvaldo Guariglia. Lima, María Herrera.
Winch and Instrumental Pluralism. Dov Lerner, Berel.

WINOGRAD, T
Towards a Winograd/Flores Semantics. Mott, Peter.

WINTERHALDER, B
Failures of Explanation in Darwinian Ecological Anthropology: Part I. Vayda, Andrew P.

WOMEN

Power/Gender. Radtke, H Lorraine (ed) and Stam, Henderikus J (ed).

Reshaping the Female Body: The Dilemma of Cosmetic Surgery. Davis, Kathy.

Simone de Beauvoir: The Making of an Intellectual Woman. Moi, Toril.

The 1994 Annual of Hermeneutics and Social Concern. Lawler, Justus George (ed).

The Constructed Body: AIDS, Reproductive Technology, and Ethics. Murphy, Julien S.

The Flight from Woman (New Edition). Stern, Karl.

The Irigaray Reader. Whitford, Margaret (ed).

Values, Work, Education: The Meanings of Work. Natale, Samuel M (ed) and Rothschild, Brian M (ed).

War, Battering, and Other Sports: The Gulf Between American Men and Women. McBride, James.

Woman and the History of Philosophy. Tuana, Nancy.

A Postmodern Feminist View of "Reasonableness" in Hostile Environment Sexual Harassment. Paetzold, Ramona L.

A Reply in Defense of Impartiality. Baker, Judith.

Abortion and In Vitro Fertilization. Waller, Bruce N.

Abortion Ethics: Rights and Responsibilities. Porter, Elisabeth.

Actualidad del tema del hombre: los estudios de la mujer. Santa Cruz, María Isabel.

Adam, Eve and the Controversial Rib: Gender, Technology, Conflict and Universalism. Rosen, Aviva.

Are Women More Ethical than Men?. Sikula Sr, Andrew and Costa, Adelmiro D.

Aristotle and the Political Role of Women. Mulgan, Richard.

Articulating the Aesthetic in the Ethical: Aesthetics and the Ethics of Care. Morris, Susan.

Beauty and Breast Implantation: How Candidate Selection Affects Autonomy and Informed Consent. Parker, Lisa S.

Beauvoir, Irigaray, and the Mystical. Hollywood, Amy M.

Being Dismissed: The Politics of Emotional Expression. Campbell, Sue.

Between Discrimination and Differentiation: Introductory Reflections. Gould, Carol C.

Bioethics and Philosophy of Science. Veatch, Robert M.

Breast Cancer Genetic Screening and Critical Bioethics' Gaze. Parker, Lisa S.

Bringing Women Back In: A Search for Alternative Historiographies. Ahikire, Josephine.

Can Justice as Fairness Accommodate Diversity? An Examination of the Representation of Minorities and Women in *A Theory of Justice*. Trout, Lara M.

Claire Loves Julie: Reading the Story of Women's Friendship in *La Nouvelle Héloïse*. Disch, Lisa.

Clinical Ethics and Intervention in Domestic Violence. Ryan, Maura A.

Clinical Ethics and Nursing: "Yes" to Caring, But "No" to a Female Ethics of Care. Kuhse, Helga.

Conflicting Principles or Completing Counterparts? J S Mill on Political Economy and the Equality of Women. Green, Michele.

Enlightenment Calculations. Daston, Lorraine.

Epilogue: Prolegomenon to Future Feminist* Philosophies of Religion. Thie, Marilyn.

Ethical and Legal Dilemmas in the Management of Family Violence. Bourne, Richard.

Family Violence and Family Systems: Who Is the Patient?. Gottlieb, Michael C.

Feminism and Empowerment: A Critical Reading of Foucault. Deveaux, Monique.

Feminism and Modernity. Braidotti, Rosi.

Feminism as Critique in Philosophy of Music Education. Lamb, Roberta.

Feminism, Fundamentalism, and Liberal Legitimacy. Exdell, John B.

Feminist Misogyny: Mary Wollstonecraft and the Paradox of "It Takes One to Know One". Gubar, Susan.

Feminist Philosophy and the Women's Movement. Addelson, Kathryn Pyne.

Feminist Theory and the Displaced Music Curriculum: Beyond the "Add and Stir" Projects. Morton, Charlene.

Four Problems of Professional Ethics. Wangerin, Paul T.

Gender Discrimination Today: A Philosophical Response. Mannath, Joe.

Gender Issues in Health Care. McCarrick, Pat Milmoe.

Gender, Musical Meaning, and Education. Green, Lucy.

Herodotus and the Rhetoric of Otherness. Gray, Vivienne.

How to Be Postmodern Without Being a Feminist. Hesse, Mary.

Identity, Knowledge, and Toni Morrison's *Beloved*: Questions about Understanding Racism. Babbitt, Susan E.

Implementing Business Ethics: Sexual Harassment. Crain, Karen A and Heischmidt, Kenneth A.

In Search of Feminist Epistemology. Longino, Helen E.

Infertility Treatment for Postmenopausal Patients: An Equity-Based Approach. Purviance, Susan M.

Is There an Ecofeminism-Deep Ecology "Debate"?. Slicer, Deborah.

John Stuart Mill and Harriet Taylor on Women and Marriage. Mendus, Susan.

Justice toward Groups: Political Not Juridical. Williams, Melissa S.

Justifying the Rights of Pregnancy: The Interest View. Marquis, Don.

Kierkegaard and the Feminine Self. Howe, Leslie A.

Let's Get the L Out: Or Why *Johnson Controls* Is Not an Unequivocal Victory for Women. Callahan, Joan.

Locke's Educational Theories (and) the Woman Question. Lembcke, V L.

Long-Acting Contraceptives: Ethical Guidance for Policymakers and Health Care Providers. Moskowitz, Ellen H.

Making Strange What Had Appeared Familiar. Elliott, Terri.

Marquis' Argument Against Abortion: A Critique. Shirley, Edward S.

Mulheres em Transiçao nos EUA Hoje: Escolhas e Conflitos. Cangemi, Joseph P.

Nietzsche and Feminism: Transvaluing Women in *Thus Spoke Zarathustra*. Lorraine, Tamsin.

Nietzsche Was No Feminist.... Bergoffen, Debra B.

Nietzsche's Misogyny. Clark, Maudemarie.

Nomad, Come Home. Klein, Ellen R.

On Feminist Nomadism. Smith, Barry.

On the Possibility of Feminist Philosophy. McAlister, Linda Lopez.

Opening Address: The Fifth Freedom. Kincaid-Smith, Priscilla.

Pornography and the Justifiability of Restricting Freedom of Expression. Orser, Mari E.

Pornography: An Uncivil Liberty?. Carse, Alisa L.

Presence with a Difference: Buddhists and Feminists on Subjectivity. Klein, Anne C.

Private Bioethics Forums: Counterpoint to Government Bodies. Cohen, Cynthia B and McCloskey, Elizabeth Leibold.

Rape, Group Responsibility, and Trust. Davion, Victoria.

Relational Ethics in Writing a Woman's Life. Franklin, Betty and Townsend, Lucy.

Reply to Patrick Hopkins. Vadas, Melinda.

Reply to Victoria Davion's Comments on May and Strikwerda. May, Larry and Strikwerda, Robert.

Reproductive Technologies in Developing Countries. Macklin, Ruth.

Rights and Power: A Feminist Rethinking of Liberal Rights. Kelly, Michaeleen J.

Sexual Harassment: Why the Corporate World Still Doesn't "Get It". Feary, Vaughana Macy.

Should There Be Separatist Epistemologies?. Landau, Iddo.

Taking Dependency Seriously: The Family and Medical Leave Act Considered in Light of the Social Organization of Dependency Work and Gender Equality. Kittay, Eva Feder.

The Combat Exclusion and the Role of Women in the Military. DeCew, Judith Wagner.

The Ethic of Care vis-à-vis the Ethic of Rights: A Problem for Contemporary Moral Theory. Kroeger-Mappes, Joy.

The Gender Closet: Lesbian Disappearance under the Sign "Women". Calhoun, Cheshire.

The Market for Feminist Epistemology. Baber, Harriet.

The Match and Other Agents of Liberation: The Role of Technology in the Social Thought of Louise Otto. Soudek, Ingrid H and Neeley, Kathryn A.

The Pariah and Her Shadow: Hannah Arendt's Biography of Rahel Varnhagen. Benhabib, Seyla.

The Philosopher's Seduction: Hume and the Fair Sex. Sapp, Vicki J.

The Philosophy of Science and Women's Issues in Poland: Possibilities and Obstacles Today (A Personal Account). Pakszys, Elzbieta.

Toward the Feminine Firm: An Extension to Thomas White. Dobson, John and White, Judith.

Twenty Years of Feminist Philosophy. Ferguson, Ann.

What Do Women Want? Rewriting the Social Contract. Thompson, Janna.

What Foucault Fails to Acknowledge...: Feminists and *The History of Sexuality*. Still, Judith.

Women and Language in Susan Griffin's *Woman and Nature: The Roaring Inside Her*. Cantrell, Carol H.

Women and Power in Eighteenth-Century France: Actresses at the Comédie-Française. Berlanstein, Lenard R.

Women as Mothers and the Making of the European Mind: A Contribution to the History of Developmental Psychology and Primary Socialization. Nicstroj, Brigitto H E.

Women, Earth, and the Goddess: A Shākta-Hindu Interpretation of Embodied Religion. Patel, Kartikeya C.

Women, Ectogenesis, and Ethical Theory. Cannold, Leslie.

Women-Animals-Machines: A Grammar for a Wittgensteinian Ecofeminism. Lee-Lampshire, Wendy.

WOMEN'S LIBERATION

Feminismo y política en dos encrucijadas históricas: La modernidad madura. Ciriza, Alejandra.

WONDER

Wonder as Source of Philosophy and of Science: A Comparison. George, Marie I.

WONG, W

Wong on Davidson. Potter, R Dennis.

WOOLGAR, S

Representation(s). Rheinberger, Hans-Jörg.

WORD

"Gadamer's Realism: The 'Belongingness' of Word and Reality" in *Hermeneutics and Truth, Wachterhauser, Brice (ed)*. Wachterhauser, Brice.

"Words Lie in Our Way". MacLennan, Bruce J.

Mind's Bodies: Thought in the Act. Lang, Berel.

Ways of Worldmaking. Goodman, Nelson.

A Note on Some Meanings of the Term 'Aesthetic'. Diffey, T J.

Bhartrhari's Philosophy of Relation between Word and Meaning. Tiwari, D N.

Davidson's Sentences and Wittgenstein's Builders. Perry, John.

Degrees of Iconicity in the Lexicon. Waugh, Linda R.

Even: The Conventional Implicature Approach Reconsidered. Francescotti, Robert M.

Foregrounding Structures in American Sign Language. Wilbur, Ronnie B.

Incommensurability, Incomparability, Irrationality. Kindi, Vassiliki.

Involvement and Joking in Conversation. Norrick, Neal R.

Locke and Hume Contrasted. Malpas, R M P.

Lonergan and the Later Wittgenstein. Fitzpatrick, Joseph.

On the Structure of Lexical Competence. Marconi, Diego.

Precedentes Ockhamistas de la Significación. Velásquez, Lorena.

Primera aproximación al lenguaje. Weismann, Francisco J.

Rhetoric and the Perlocutionary Field. Mason, Jeff.

Whorf's Empty Gasoline Drum and the Pope's Missing Wife. Edwards, Derek.

WORK

"Romantik der Arbeit" Perspektiven des frühromantischen Arbeitsbegriffs. Arndt, Andreas.

"World, Leisure and a Meaningful Life" in *Life, World and Meaning, Roux, A P J (ed)*. Du Toit, Pieter.

Business Ethics at Work. Vallance, Elizabeth.

Idéer om Arbete. Hansson, Sven Ove.

Logik und Arbeit. Hartmann, Bruno.

Values, Work, Education: The Meanings of Work. Natale, Samuel M (ed) and Rothschild, Brian M (ed).

Welzijn Arbeid en Zekerheid. Hogervorst, S.

Welzijn Zeggenschap en Eigendom. Hogervorst, S.

Work, Education, and Leadership: Essays in the Philosophy of Education. Howard, V A and Scheffler, Israel.

Allgemeine Arbeit. Haug, Wolfgang Fritz.

Diferença entre Alienação e Estranhamento nos Manuscritos Econômico-Filosóficos (1844), de Karl Marx. Ferreira Chagas, Eduardo.

Education and Work: Reflections on the Moral and Spiritual Dimensions of the Job Crisis. Books, Sue.

Escola Pública: Trabalho Produtivo ou Improdutivo. Pizzi, Laura Cristina V.

G Vico: Oración I (1669). Rodríguez Donís, Marcelino.

Just Another Day at the Office: The Ordinariness of Professional Ethics. Welch, Don.

L'esclave, le travail et l'action: Aristote et Hegel. Faes, Hubert.

Mulheres em Transição nos EUA Hoje: Escolhas e Conflitos. Cangemi, Joseph P.

Reconstructing Artifacts, Reconstructing Work: From Textual Edition to On-Line Databank. Ruhleder, Karen.

Reproduction and Ontology in Lukács (in Portuguese). Lessa, Sergio.

That a Worker's Labour Cannot be a Commodity. Nelson, John O.

The Pariah and Her Shadow: Hannah Arendt's Biography of Rahel Varnhagen. Benhabib, Seyla.

Trabajo e Interacción como Intereses Rectores del Conocimiento. López Molina, Antonio M.

WORK OF ART

The Intentional Fallacy. Calhoun, Laurie.

WORKER

Lenin, Kautsky and Working-Class Consciousness. Mayer, Robert.

WORKING CLASS

Pedagogia Pelo e Para o Trabalho: Ação Disciplinadora da Burguesia e a Resistência dos trabalhadores. Rodrigues, Alcione.

WORKPLACE

"The New Politics of the Workplace: Ideology and Other Unobtrusive Controls" in *After Postmodernism, Simons, Herbert W (ed)*. Deetz, Stanley.

The Impact of Personal Values on Judgments of Ethical Behaviour in the Workplace. Finegan, Joan.

The Orchestral Workplace. Fischer, Marilyn M.

WORKS

The Fine Awareness of Martha Nussbaum. Todd, D D.

WORLD

see also External World

"Putnam's Doctrine of Natural Kind Words and Frege's Doctrines of Sense, Reference, and Extension" in *Reading Putnam, Clark, Peter (ed)*. Wiggins, David.

"World-Picture and Conscience" in *Hermeneutics and Truth, Wachterhauser, Brice (ed)*. Simon, Josef.

Amoral Politics: The Persistent Truth of Machiavellism. Scharfstein, Ben-Ami.

Apocalypse Theory and the Ends of the World. Bull, Malcolm (ed).

Blindness of Modern Science. Uus, Undo.

Character and Culture: Essays on East and West. Babbitt, Irving.

Encountering the Other(s): Studies in Literature, History, and Culture. Brinker-Gabler, Gisela (ed).

Husserls Theorie der Intersubjektivität. Iribarne, Julia V.

Kants Metaphysik: Welt und Freiheit. Effertz, Dirk.

Life, World and Meaning. Roux, A J P (ed).

Post-Modernism and Anthropology: Theory and Practice. Geuijen, Karin (ed), Raven, Diederick (ed) and De Wolf, Jan (ed).

The Enigma of the Mind: The Mind-Body Problem in Contemporary Thought. Moravia, Sergio and Staton, Scott (trans).

Understanding Our World: An Integral Ontology. Hart, Hendrik.

Weltentwürfe: Ludwig Binswangers phänomenologische Psychologie. Herzog, Max.

Actitud crítica y racionalidad en Popper. Marquéz, Gustavo.

Anthropic Explanations in Cosmology. Smith, Quentin.

Aporias of Löwith's Return to "The Natural World". Covic, Ante.

Applying the Term 'Mental' in a World without a Within: Dewey's Realism. Tiles, J E.

Aquinas on the Past Possibility of the World's Having Existed Forever. Wilks, Ian.

Armistice in the Recent Battle of the Books: Paul de Man, Claudio Guillén, and History. Miner, Earl.

Beyond World History: On Hegel's and Kierkegaard's Interests in Ethics and Religion. Cruysberghs, Paul.

Bigelow, Possible Worlds and The Passage of Time. Oaklander, L Nathan.

Brauchen wir ein neues Weltethos? Universale Ethik in einer geschichtlichen Welt. Schockenhoff, Eberhard.

Business Ethics and Job-Related Constructs: A Cross-Cultural Comparison of Automotive Salespeople. Honeycutt, Earl D, Siguaw, Judy A and Hunt, Tammy G.

Cinque Esemplari Postillati della *Scienza Nuova*. Rotoli, Daniela.

Cosmopolitan Universalism: Prolegomena to a Future Ideology. Arnopoulos, Paris.

Cultura y Filosofía. Dacal Alonso, Jose Antonio

Descartes and the Dream Argument. Odegard, Douglas.

Die Weltgeschichte beim späten Fichte. Metz, Wilhelm.

Ecumenism Between the World Religions. Charlesworth, Max.

El buen relojero. Mataix, Carmen.

El Combate entre el Mundo y la Razón Según Pedro Compostelano. Dafonte, César Raña.

El Método de la Simulación: Ocaso del Método Experimental?. Larre, Olga L.

Environmental Justice: An Environmental Civil Rights Value Acceptable to All World Views. Hartley, Troy W.

Expérience et métaphysique. Gilbert, Paul.

Federalist Theory and World Peace. Newcombe, Hanna.

Filosofía e Historia Según I. Ellacuría. Martínez, José A.

Following Edmund Husserl on One of the Paths Leading to the Transcendental Reduction. Kortooms, Toine.

Función de la Creatividad en la Filosofía de A N Whitehead. Oroz Ezcurra, Javier.

Honor Among Thieves: A Transaction-Cost Interpretation of Corruption in Third World Countries. Husted, Bryan W.

How an Unsurpassable Being Can Create a Surpassable World. Howard-Snyder, Daniel and Howard-Snyder, Frances.

How Can We Live in a World of the Absurd? The Humanism of Albert Camus. Lowen, Jeanette.

Il mondo "Pesante" di Newton. Infante, Giancarlo.

Kant on the Third Antinomy, Is Freedom Possible in a World of Natural Necessity?. Naticchia, Chris.

Knowing the World and Knowing Our Minds. Warfield, Ted A.

La Comprensión Científica en el Siglo Veinte. Salmon, W.

La fenomenología como vía de acceso al mundo griego. Brague, Rémi.

La Science Contemporaine Connaît-elle Vraiment le Monde?. Lane, Gilles.

Language and World: Some Classical Indian Approaches *vis-a-vis* Analytical Western Approaches. Gokhale, Pradeep P.

Le Forme Diffratte di Serres: Prolegomeni a una Nuova Filosofia della Storia. Delcò, Alessandro.

Leyendo a Rudolf Carnap. Medina F, Nelson.

Living in Two Worlds: A Personal Appraisal. Ching, Julia.

Miracles in the Best of All Possible Worlds: Leibniz's Dilemma and Leibniz's Razor. Brown, Gregory.

Monism and Pluralism. Krapiec, Mieczyslaw Albert.

Nation, Weltbürgertum, und Synthesis der Geisterwelt. Schrader, Wolfgang H.

On the Existential Meaning of Violence. Santoni, Ronald E.

On the Prohibitive Cost of Indiscernable Concrete Possible Worlds. Divers, John.

On the Quantum Mechanical Wave Function as a Link Between Cognition and the Physical World: A Role for Psychology. Snyder, Douglas M.

On What It Takes to Be a World. Albert, David Z and Barrett, Jeffrey A.

Otto's Idea of the 'Numinous': A Crosscultural Reappraisal. O'Meley, Serena.

Pascal and Descartes on First Ideas. Yhap, Jennifer.

Periodizing World History. Green, William.

Philosophy and General Education: "World Civilizations" as Virtue Ethics. Omundson, Bruce.

Plotin et la Thèse de L'incorruptibilité du Monde. Kélessidou, Anna.

Postille: 1)Pensiero Orientale Verticale e Pensiero Occidentale Orizzontale, 2)La Filsofia della Crisi. Del Vecchio, Dante.

Preparing for the 21st Century: A Philosophy for New Thinking. Parsons, Howard L.

Realismo sin Empirismo. Defez i Martín, Antoni.

Reflections on World Peace through Peace among Religions—A Confucian Perspective. Liu, Shu-Hsien.

Reply to Egan's "A WORLD without MIND". Horgan, Terence.

Rotarians in a Changing World. Seidler, Leopold G and Kolek, Leszek S.

Semiosis y Objetos: Los Objetos Naturales. Prada Oropeza, Renato.

Skills, Historical Disclosing, and the End of History: A Response to Our Critics. Spinosa, Charles (& others).

Sobre el origen del ser y la nada. Echauri, Raúl.

Teilhard's Vision of the World and Modern Cosmology. Heller, Michael.

The 3D/4D Controversy and Non-Present Objects. Markosian, Ned.

The Changing Shape of World History. McNeill, William H.

The Earth Might be Round, But the World is Flat: The Groundwork for an Ethics of Relief. Ramsey, Ramsey Eric.

The Ethics of *Formale Anzeige* in Heidegger. Van Buren, John.

The Problem of No Best World. Rowe, William L.

The World and 'I'. Phillips, D Z.

The World, the Flesh and the Argument from Design. Boos, William.

The World-System Perspective in the Construction of Economic History. Abu-Lughod, Janet.

Theory, Practice, Reality. Borgmann, Albert.

Towards Global Environmental Values: Lessons from Western and Eastern Experience. Sarre, Philip.

Two (Related) World Views. Zalta, Edward N.

Vagueness, Identity, and the World. Garrett, Brian.

Vagueness: Welcome to the Quicksand. Tye, Michael.

What Philosophy Does the World Need?. Bahm, Archie J.

Why Students of Heidegger Will Have to Read Emil Lask. Kisiel, Theodore.

Why the World Cannot be Vague. Sainsbury, Mark.

William Poteat's Anthropology: "Mindbody In the World". Mead, Walter B.

World Philosophy Methodology for Considering World Philosophy. Bahm, Archie J.

Worlds within Worlds? The Paradoxes of Embedded Fiction. Le Poidevin, Robin.

'World' is not a Count Noun. Van Fraassen, Bas.

ZIZEK, S

X-Sample: Gespräche am Rande der Zeit. Miessgang, Thomas.

Psychoanalysis and Ideology: Bakhtin, Lacan, and Zizek. Baker, Harold D.

ZNANIECKI, F

Florian Znaniecki's Concept of a Humanist All-Mankind Civilization. Szczepanski, Jan.

ZOLA, E

"La Epistemología de Emile Zola" in *Temas Actuales de Filosofía, Palacios, María Julia (ed)*. Mari, Enrique E.

ZOLO, D

The Importance of Being Austrian. Uebel, Thomas E.

ZOVKO, J

Wem schlägt die Glocke?. Barbaric, Damir.

ZUBIRI, X

Contrarréplica a una Valoración Sobre mi Crítica al Realismo Radical de Xavier Zubiri. Wessell Jr, Leonard P.

Existe en Zubiri una protopolítica?. Marquinez Argote, Germán.

Reflexiones Zubirianas Sobre la Fruición y el Amor. Marquínez Argote, Germán.

Zubiri ante el problema del valor. Palacios, Juan Miguel.

ZYLSTRA, B

Political Theory and Christian Vision: Essays in Memory of Bernard Zylstra. Chaplin, Jonathan (ed) and Marshall, Paul (ed).

ZYNDA, L

Probability Reparation: The Problem of New Explanation. Jeffrey, Richard.

Guidance on the Use of the Author Index With Abstracts

Each entry in this section begins with the author's name and contains the complete title of the article or book, other bibliographic information, and an abstract if available. The list is arranged in alphabetical order with the author's last name first. Articles by multiple authors are listed under each author's name. Names preceded by the articles De, La, Le, etc. or the prepositions Da, De, Van, Von, etc. are treated as if the article or preposition were a part of the last name.

The vast majority of abstracts are provided by the authors of the articles and books; where an abstract does not appear, it was not received from the author prior to the publication of this edition. The staff of the *Index* prepares some abstracts. These abstracts are followed by "(edited)".

In order to locate all the articles and books written by a given author, various spellings of the author's name should be checked. This publication uses the form of the author's name given in the articles and books. Because some authors have changed the form of their name that they attach to articles and because some editors took liberties with the proper name submitted, variations of an author's name may occur in this index. Particular care should be given to names that have a space, a dash, or an apostrophe in their surnames. Because the computer sorts on each character, the names of other authors may be "filed" between different spellings of a given author's name.

A-Bourloyianni, A. Seeds in Epicurus Ontology. *Philosophia (Athens)*, 23-24, 190-195, 1993-94.

According to the classic Lucretius' interpretation of Epicurean seeds (*Letter to Herodotus*, 32) they are considered to be "semina certa" of all living beings, able to put a limit to the chance coming-to-be of anything from anything else. Yet this indeed ambiguous term "seeds" is used here in a very general, let's say, anaxagorean sense, as seeds of all things, that is as elementary entities capable to "reproduce"—in a clearly metaphorical sense—all composite things similar to them. Such a hypothesis leads to the conclusion that Epicurus in his ontology, apart from the use of the atoms, he also accepts the seeds as structural entities of the formally definite things.

Aarnio, Aulis. On the Interpretation of Facts. *Commun Cog*, 28(1), 77-86, 1995.

In legal decisions, a general norm is applied to the facts of the case. Hence, there may exist uncertainty about two basic kinds of problems. The person who decides the case may be uncertain about the *contents of the norms* or about the *evidence* concerning the facts. The uncertainty about the normative side may concern 1) The vagueness, ambiguity or openness of the normative language (the case of interpretation), 2) Gaps, 3) Contradictions of the normative basis or 4) Redundancy. This time I am interested only in the gap situations which are very well pointed out in Alchourrón's and Bulygin's discussions of the concept of legal gap. Before I proceed to examine the pertinent problems of legal justification from this perspective, I will take a look at their treatment of the problem.

Aarsleff, Hans. "Locke's Influence" in *The Cambridge Companion to Locke, Chappell, Vere (ed)*, 252-289. New York, Cambridge Univ Pr, 1994.

This essay gives the main thrust of Locke's influence to his radical arguments in favor of the autonomy of thought of each individual and its ability to gain understanding in religion, politics, and the knowledge of nature, thus setting us free from the burden of authority and tradition. The eighteenth century gets the most space, with attention to personal identity, thinking matter, Molyneux's problem, and to Condillac's powerful argument that the Cartesian and Lockeian ideal of the wordless discourse of the mind is a chimera: instead language is seen as being constitutive of thought as understood within a global theory of human expression that embraces both aesthetics and epistemology, art and science, poetry and prose. The essay has citations and an extensive bibliography.

Abbarno, John M. Interview of Lewis E Hahn. *J Value Inq*, 29(2), 255-268, Je 95.

Interview of Lewis E Hahn of Southern Illinois University inquires into the origin and continued success of the Library of Living Philosophers series. Lewis E Hahn is the editor of the reputed book series which was founded in 1938 by Paul Arthur Schilpp. Hahn comments on the format of the exchange between philosophers in the book series which includes Einstein, Dewey, Sartre, Russell, and Ayer. The interview informs the reading audience of why some philosophers, such as Wittgenstein and Heidegger do not have designated volumes despite their influence on the direction of philosophy. As for the future L L P Lewis Hahn discusses what may be the role of video production in serving wider philosophical audiences, at the turn of the century. This expanded medium for philosophy reflects the vision and imagination central to philosophy's enterprise.

Abbarno, John M. Interview of Ludwig Grünberg. *J Value Inq*, 29(1), 115-123, Mr 95.

The interview of Ludwig Grunberg is one in a series of interviews of international philosophers in the Journal of Value Inquiry. Ludwig Grunberg cited the influence of fellow Romanian Camill Petrescu for his interest in value theory. Husserl, however, figures a key role in his own methodological treatment of value phenomena. Grunberg dedicated his life to developing an axio-centric ontology of the human condition. His comments reflect the hope axio-centric ontology reveals about reconciling dualistic theories. Grunberg illustrates the need for such a theory among inventive and creative ethical perspectives of the twentieth century. His framework maps a direction for value inquiry for the third millennium; it is here he believes "culture" and "universalism" must be studied for their irreducible values. In his own words "...the human condition starts from the presence and purpose of the general human values..."

Abbes, J K. Filosofie, Metafysica en Moraal van Karl Popper. *Alg Ned Tijdschr Wijs*, 87(2), 97-111, Ap 95.

This article presents a new interpretation of Popper's works. It is possible to see Popper's works as a kind of metaphysics "in a wider sense", that is to say as a "world view". This metaphysics is the basis of his ethics: the rational and humanitarian attitude, and his negative utilitarianism, the minimalisation of suffering. Popper's "world view" has the same structure as religion and it may be an alternative for religious world views which is better adapted to modern science than religion ever could be.

Abbs, Peter. *The Educational Imperative: A Defence of Socratic and Aesthetic Learning*. Bristol, Falmer Pr, 1994.

The author opens by examining the true and fitting ends of education. He contends that the ends of education are seldom discussed, only the means. This has lead to a profound loss of purpose and to the identification of education with certification and training. He outlines a positive conception of education as an initiation into critical enquiry and the personal art of learning. In place of the current progressive and prescriptive approaches Abbs proposes a further paradigm for the teaching of the arts. He argues that the creativity of the individual and the creativity of the culture must be brought into a permanent, exacting and living fusion. The final section examines some of the intellectual forces shaping current arguments, and offers critical appraisals of some influential figures in the field.

Abe, Masao. "A Buddhist View of Human Rights" in *Human Rights and Religious Values, An-Na'im, Abdullahi A (& other eds)*, 144-153. Grand Rapids, Eerdmans, 1995.

Abel, Günter. Indeterminacy and Interpretation. *Inquiry*, 37(4), 403-419, D 94.

This paper contains a discussion of Quine's thesis of indeterminacy of translation within the more general thesis that using and understanding a language are to be

conceived of as a creative and interpretative-constructional activity. Indeterminacy is considered to be ineliminable. Three scenarios are distinguished concerning, first, the reasons for indeterminacy, second, the kinds of indeterminacy, and third, different levels of a general notion of recursive interpretation. Translational hypotheses are seen as interpretational constructs. The indeterminacy thesis turns out to be a consequence of the externalizing of language, meaning, and epistemology. By means of a three-leveled interpretation model one can substantiate the crucial aspects, first, that indeterminacy is not an indeterminacy of facts of the matter and second, that there is a signification difference between indeterminacy and underdetermination. In addition, the relationship between indeterminacy, interpretation, and charity is elucidated. Indeterminacy is seen not as an obstacle to but as a condition for communication. Charity and empathy in dialogue are conditional upon indeterminacy. All three components reveal the interpretative-constructional character of the inseparable connection of meaning and experience.

Abelard, Peter and Spade, Paul Vincent (trans). *Ethical Writings: Ethics and Dialogue between a Philosopher, a Jew, and a Christian*. Indianapolis, Hackett, 1995.

Abellera, Tom. *The Teachings of Don Von: A Turnkey Way of Knowledge*. Kansas City, Stochos, 1994.

This book solves four things: 1) It summarizes the nuts and bolts Theory and Information as originally developed by Claude Shannon; 2) It explains the apparent glamour of information theory; 3) It smuggles in mass quantities of popular culture to make information theory accessible to all undergraduate students; and 4) It illustrates sidebar topics to the nuts and bolts Theory of Information suitable for classroom discussion.

Abiteboul, Olivier. Correspondances Philosophiques et Techniques Argumentatives au XVIIe Siècle. *Philosopher*, 17, 129-136, 1995.

Ablondi, Fred. Death According to Descartes: Why the Soul Leaves the Body. *Iyyun*, 44, 47-54, Ja 95.

From a Cartesian standpoint, it would seem that a change in the figure of the human body or cessation of heat in the heart would not be sufficient to occasion the soul's departure from that body as Descartes claims. I argue that an answer to this problem must take into account the notion of 'proper purpose' in Descartes, and I conclude that once the soul, as a result of changes to the body, is no longer able to direct the body to receive sensations and avoid what is harmful, there is in effect no more union, and the soul departs.

Aboulafia, Mitchell. "George Herbert Mead and the Many Voices of Universality" in *Recovering Pragmatism's Voice, Langsdorf, Lenore (ed)*, 179-194. Albany, SUNY Pr, 1995.

George Herbert Mead, along with other progessives of his day, was committed to the Enlightenment's ideals of universalism and progress. Not only did he believe in progress, he thought that it depended in part on the wide spread application of what he took to be the democratic methodology of the empirical sciences. Yet his universalism was tempered by a commitment to particularity that showed itself in his interest in the novel and unique. His theory of intersubjectivity grounded in linguistic interaction can be viewed as an attempt to negotiate a path between the twin dangers of abstract universalism and romantic particularism. This paper addresses Mead's approach with an eye toward clarifying why he thought increased understanding between diverse groups possible. It suggests that the concept of the generalized other can serve as a key to Mead's qualified universalism, as well as to his non-positivistic interpretation of science.

Aboulafia, Mitchell. Habermas and Mead: On Universality and Individuality. *Constellation*, 2(1), 94-113, Ap 95.

For a number of years now Jürgen Habermas has viewed George Herbert Mead as a forerunner of his own thought. In a relatively recent extended article, "Individuation through Socialization: On George Herbert Mead's Theory of Subjectivity," he has argued for the affinity between his own model of subjectivity and Mead's. While there are a good many similarities between these two thinkers, I argue in this piece that Habermas has in fact given an overly Kantian reading of Mead, which thereby diminishes the novelty of Mead's own pragmatic orientation and the potential impact of the latter's mode of thought on contemporary issues in ethics and social theory.

Abrahamsen, Adele and Bechtel, William. *Connectionism and the Mind: An Introduction to Parallel Processing in Networks*. Cambridge, Blackwell, 1991.

This book offers an elementary exposition of the operation of feedforward connectionist networks and explores a number a conceptual and philosophical issues raised by connectionism. Among these issues are the problem of modeling intentionality and the question of whether cognition requires explicit symbols and operation performed upon them. The potential of connectionism to transform various cognitive science disciplines is also examined.

Abrahamson, K A (& others). Fixed-parameter Tractability and Completeness IV: On Completeness for W[P] and PSPACE Analogues. *Annals Pure Applied Log*, 73(3), 235-276, Je 95.

We describe new results in parametrized complexity theory. In particular, we prove a number of concrete hardness results for W[P], the top level of the hardness hierarchy introduced by Downey and Fellows in a series of earlier papers. We also study the parametrized complexity of analogues of PSPACE via certain natural problems concerning k-move games. Finally, we examine several aspects of the structural complexity of W[P] and related classes. For instance, we show that W[P] can be characterized in terms of the DTIME $(2^{o(n)})$ and NP.

Abramovitch, Rona (& others). Children's Capacity to Agree to Psychological Research: Knowledge of Risks and Benefits and Voluntariness. *Ethics Behavior*, 5(1), 25-48, 1995.

A series of studies investigated the capacity of children between the ages of 7 and 12 to give free and informed consent to participation in psychological research. Children were reasonably accurate in describing the purpose of studies, but many did not understand the possible benefits or especially the possible risks of participating. In several studies children's consent was not affected by the knowledge that their parents had given their permission or by the parents saying that they would not be upset if the children refused. In contrast, other studies found that children were much more likely to stop their participation if the experimenter said explicitly that she would not be upset if they stopped. We suggest that experimenters should pay more attention to describing the possible risks and benefits of participation in research and that they should also make it clearer to children that they are free to stop once they have begun.

Abrams, Edward L. Rational Agency and Objectively Practical Reason. *Conference*, 4(2), 31-53, Fall 93.

Abu-Lughod, Janet. The World-System Perspective in the Construction of Economic History. *Hist Theor*, 34(2), 86-98, 1995.

This essay examines the experience of rewriting historical narratives from a world-system perspective, drawing on the author's attempt to construct an integrated image of the world economy in the thirteenth century. Searching for an intermediate epistemological path between unanchored postmodern hermeneutics and overconfident positivism, the author argues that three apparent deviations from the "ideals of positivist social science", which she ironically labels eccentricity, namely, recognizing perspectives other than those that conventionally view the world through the eyes of the West, can help historians to escape from ethnocentrism or Eurocentrism. Ideology, more conventionally called theory, is essential if historians are to select and integrate new material. And idiosyncrasy in the interests and backgrounds of historians can often be the source of the re-vision so essential for challenging earlier historical narratives. The author alludes to parallels with ethnographic research methods and cautions against substituting these three aids to research for rigorous attention to empirical sources and "the real world".

Achinstein, Peter. Stronger Evidence. *Phil Sci*, 61(3), 329-350, S 94.

According to a standard account of evidence, one piece of information is stronger evidence for an hypothesis than is another if and only if the probability of the hypothesis on the one is greater than it is on the other. This condition, I argue, is neither necessary nor sufficient because various factors can strengthen the evidence for a hypothesis without increasing (and even decreasing) its probability. Contrary to what probabilists claim, I show that this obtains even if a probability function can take these evidential factors into account in ways they suggest and yield a unique probability value. Nor will the problem be solved by appealing to second-order probabilities.

Achtenberg, Deborah. "Human Being, Beast, and God" in *The Crossroads of Norm and Nature*, Sim, May (ed), 29-50. Lanham, Rowman & Littlefield, 1995.

Achterberg, Wouter. "Can Liberal Democracy Survive the Environmental Crisis? Sustainability, Liberal Neutrality, and Overlapping Consensus" in *Ecology, Technology, and Culture*, Zweers, Wim (ed), 135-157. Cambridge, White Horse, 1994.

Achterhuis, Hans. "The Lie of Sustainability" in *Ecology, Technology, and Culture*, Zweers, Wim (ed), 198-203. Cambridge, White Horse, 1994.

The promise of sustainable development by way of the embedding of the economy, is unmasked as a lie from two different perspectives. The first one is developed out of Hannah Arendt's major work 'The Human Condition' in which she shows that the traditional idea of the durability of the works of homo faber, was destroyed by the economic process of labor and consumption. In the second place the modern social construction of scarcity pushed modern economy forward in a process that seems to be unable to fix limits to economic growth, even when this growth turns out to be unsustainable nature.

Achterhuis, Hans. Techniek als utopie. *Kennis Methode*, 19(1), 9-28, 1995.

In The myth of Prometheus as told in Plato's Protagoras technology and utopia are closely linked together. Socrates' answer on the question 'how to save our lives' can be found in the construction of a techné of measurement that makes possible an ideal society. In 'Utopia' of Thomas More and 'Nova Atlantis' of Francis Bacon we find the same linkage. The happiness of the inhabitants is assured by technical means. In the light of these observations the role of technology in our modern society that can be described as 'a realized utopia' is considered in a critical discussion with Nussbaum's interpretation of Protagoras.

Acklin, David and King, Jonathan. Creating Common Ground: A Lesson from the Past. *J Bus Ethics*, 14(1), 1-16, Ja 95.

Orthodox business ethics, conventional management theory, and a great deal of higher education embody the overriding emphasis accorded to "analysis" by yesteryear's science. An alternative strategy, exemplified by the war stories told by a Confederate General, is more consistent with late twentieth century science in general and soft systems methodology in particular.

Adair, Phillipe. El utilitarismo libertario de William Godwin. *Telos (Spain)*, 2(2), 71-92, D 93.

The French Revolution is used as the background of the work of Godwin. Hereafter his work is analyzed with the aim of showing the difficulties and paradoxes that his defense of Calvinism and natural rights as well as his altruist and perfectionist utilitarianism arise. The author discusses the controversy over Godwin's work both in his and our time. Reference is made to Godwin's liberalism as well as to his rejection of social contract and political coercion. According to the author, Godwin fails when trying to make utilitarianism the sole foundation of social order because he makes use of the notion of *virtue* in order to make plausible his argument, something that, in the author's view a utilitarian writer should not do.

Adam, E. *Utopie II ou Vers une Société des Personnes*. Montréal, Les Press D'Amer, 1994.

Utopie II is a radical social critique. In Part I, E Adam pinpoints a fundamental flaw of every developed country: in spite of a superficial appearance of rationality, almost every social structure and policies—in politics, economics, education, health—are left to chance. The result is a chaos where persons are deprived of consideration. In Part II, the author shows how *respect for persons* as a principle would realistically improve social life.

Adam, Michel. Actualité de Rosmini. *Rev Phil Fr*, 2, 195-202, Ap-Je 94.

Adams, Don. Loving God *and* One's Neighbor: Thomistic Charity. *Faith Phil*, 11(2), 207-223, Ap 94.

St Thomas Aquinas defines charity (*caritas*) as a "friendship of a person for God" and he claims that charity "extends itself to sinners, whom we love from charity because of God (*propter Deum*)" (*Summa Theologiae* q 23 a 1 and ad 3). However, it is not clear what it means to love someone "because of God," nor is it clear how a friendship which is "for God" can "extend itself" to someone other than God. This paper clarifies what Aquinas means here by focusing on three questions. 1) Is charity for a sinner anything more than an insipid, kindly attitude? 2) If charity is *by definition* "for God," then can a human being count as a genuine cause of charity? 3) If with charity we love our fellow human beings only "because of God," then is charity a genuine form of friendship between human beings?

Adams, E M. Character: The Framework for a Successful Life. *S J Phil*, 33(1), 1-17, Spr 95.

Adams, E M. Poteat on Modern Culture and Critical Philosophy. *Tradition Discovery*, 21(1), 45-50, 1994-95.

While agreeing with Poteat that the modern Western culture has gone awry in a humanly destructive way, the paper contends that the culprit was not, as Poteat claims, Enlightenment critical philosophy, but the materialistic values of the bourgeois form of life and the puritanical view of knowledge and the naturalistic worldview that they generated. Accordingly, the solution proposed is not Poteat's unreflected experience and commonsense worldview but a shift to a humanistic culture-generating stance and a critical humanistic philosophy.

Adams, Ernest W. Remarks on a Theorem of McGee. *J Phil Log*, 24(4), 343-348, Ag 95.

McGee, *Journal of Philosophical Logic*, 10, 1981, pp.349-351, showed that no many-valued logic can yield the same validities for inferences involving conditionals as the modal theories of R Stalnaker and D Lewis, or the probabilistic theory of E Adams. These remarks show that McGee's result holds when validity is defined not just in the standard way in many-valued logic, but in terms of any "excluded combination" of truth-values in the premisses and conclusion of an inference, as is the case in recent theories of *conditional event algebra*.

Adams, Fred and Stecker, Robert. Vacuous Singular Terms. *Mind Lang*, 9(4), 387-401, D 94.

We offer direct reference solutions to two problems presented by vacuous singular terms: the semantics of sentences or thoughts containing vacuous terms and the explanation of behavior employing vacuous terms. We argue that the content of "Fa", where 'a' is vacuous, is the content of the open sentence 'x is F', and the content of "a exists" is the content of 'there is an x such that x = y' where y cannot be identified. We also argue that the syntax of sentences or thoughts plus the semantics of the associated thoughts or sentences explains behavior involving vacuous terms. We contrast our view with those of Braun, Burge, Donnellan, and Segal.

Adams, Frederick. Of Epicycles and Elegance. *Can J Phil*, 24(4), 637-641, D 94.

This paper replies to criticism of my account of the relationship between trying, desire, and desiring to try. After replying to criticisms of my view, I suggest that one ought to choose between competing views based upon the overall elegance of one's theory of intentional behavior. While other views (epicycles and all) may save the phenomena of intentional activity, not all are equally elegant (nor equally likely to be true). My theory of intentional action explains that one intentionally does (or tries) to do A only if one desires to do A. I defend this view against attack and competitors.

Adams, Frederick. Trying, Desire, and Desiring to Try. *Can J Phil*, 24(4), 613-626, D 94.

Can one try to do A without desiring to do A? Might one desire only to try to do A (to try to solve, but not to solve a puzzle)? The answer depends upon the nature of attempts. Attempts to do A may themselves require desires to do A? Then desires to try to A would not be sufficient to produce attempts to A. The desire to do A that is part of the very attempt would also be required. This paper develops a cognitive theory of trying that articulates the relationship between trying, desire, and desiring to try.

Adams, Frederick. Trying: You've Got to Believe. *J Phil Res*, 20, 549-561, 1995.

Sue knows that, unaided, she cannot lift the 1,000 pound weight, but surely she can try. Can she not? For even if she believes it is impossible to succeed in lifting the weight, trying to lift the weight need not involve success. So surely, it would seem that nothing could be easier than for Sue to give lifting the weight a try. In this paper, I argue that, appearances aside, it is not possible for someone to try to do what that person believes to be impossible. So, on this view, perhaps surprisingly, not only would it be impossible for Sue to lift the weight, but it would be impossible for her to try (as long as she believed her lifting it to be impossible). I defend this view in the context of a package of related claims and a functional account of trying and intentional action.

Adams, Robert M. Religious Disagreements and Doxastic Practices. *Phil Phenomenol Res*, 54(4), 885-890, D 94.

Adams, Robert Merrihew. Form und Materie bei Leibniz: die mittleren Jahre. *Stud Leibniz*, 25(2), 132-152, 1993.

Recent influential interpreters have argued that the philosophy of body that prevails in Leibniz's writings from the 1680's to about 1704 is both more Aristotelian and less idealistic than the 'monadology' of his last years. It is argued here that the Aristotelian terminology of matter and (especially) form which is undoubtedly prominent in the work of Leibniz's 'middle years' was understood by him in a sense that is consistent with the monadology. The monadology is foreshadowed, moreover, in important arguments against the Cartesian thesis that extension is the essence of corporeal substance. Leibniz can be seen as a sort of realist in physics, in contrast with occasionalists. But what is important in that contrast is not so much the reality of (what Leibniz called) matter, as the reality of form, which Leibniz interpreted in terms of the active powers of soul-like substances.

Adams, Robert Merrihew. Leibniz's "Examination of the Christian Religion". *Faith Phil*, 11(4), 517-546, Oct 94.

Leibniz, though a lifelong member of the Lutheran church, left us a complete, Roman Catholic systematic theology. The present paper explores the questions this raises for our understanding of his life and religious thought, placing him in the context of the Calixtine Lutheran theology dominant in Lower Saxony in his time. The work is shown to be neither a platform for church reunion nor Leibniz's personal confession of faith, but it does reflect his own views regarding a theology of love and the practical nature of theology.

Adams, Robert Merrihew. Moral Faith. *J Phil*, 92(2), 75-95, F 95.

Addelson, Kathryn Pyne. Feminist Philosophy and the Women's Movement. *Hypatia*, 9(3), 216-224, Sum 94.

Feminist philosophy is now an established subdiscipline, but it began as an effort to transform the profession. Academics and activists worked together to make the new courses, and feminist theory was tested in the streets. As time passed, the "second wave" receded, but core elements of feminist theory were preserved in the academy. How can feminist philosophers today continue the early efforts of changing profession and the society, hand in hand with women outside the academy.

Addis, Mark. Criteria: The State of the Debate. *J Phil Res*, 20, 139-174, 1995.

The article presents a review of the current literature on Wittgenstein's notion of a criterion. It essentially deals with developments since Lycan's survey article on the topic and examines the most important pieces contemporary with or prior to it. Different views on various aspects of criteria are considered and summarized. Particular attention is paid to the role criteria play in the philosophy of mind. A framework in which criteria are regarded as states of affairs is used to provide uniformity in the presentation of the accounts. The connections between and implications of various positions on aspects of criteria are assessed. No overall perspective on criteria is given and the question of whether the proposed accounts in the literature are adequate interpretations of Wittgenstein's texts is not covered.

Addis, Mark. Surveyability and the *Sorites* Paradox. *Phil Math*, 3(2), 157-165, My 95.

This paper aims to explore issues raised for the strict finitist by the notion of surveyability and how it is represented mathematically. Wright considers the sense in which the positive integers are surveyable and suggests that their structure will be a weakly finite, but weakly infinite totality. One way to expose the incoherence of this account is by applying Wittgenstein's distinction between intensional and extensional to it. Criticism of the idea of a surveyable proof shows the notion's lack of clarity. It is suggested that this concept should be replaced by that of a feasible operation.

Adeigbo, F A. The Metaphysical Presuppositions of the Concept of Teleology in the Nicomachean Ethics. *Quest*, 8(2), 71-81, D 94.

Dans cet article l'auteur constate que le concept de téléologie est fondamental pour la théorie éthique d'Aristote. Partant de cette constatation, il recherche les racines de ce concept dans la Métaphysique du philosophe. Il remarque que dans cette oeuvre le concept subit un changement subtil quand à sa signification sans qu'un changement correspondant ait lieu du point de vue de la terminologie. Il identifie les différentes manières qu'a Aristote de concevoir une action ou acte comme détenteur d'une valeur. Après une analyse attentive de la théorie de causalité d'Aristote il montre que l'idée de finalité constitue la racine métaphysique de la téléologie dans l'Ethique. C'est la raison pour laquelle l'oeuvre éthique la plus populaire d'Aristote, l'Ethique à Nicomaque, commence par l'affirmation métaphysique énigmatique que la conduite humaine doit avoir une fin tout d'abord définie comme bonheur mais finalement identifiée comme activité contemplative.

Adelman, Leonard and Riedel, Sharon L. Using the Multitrait-Multimethod Matrix to Evaluate Knowledge-Based Systems. *Commun Cog—AI*, 11(3), 277-297, 1994.

This paper presents empirical data illustrating how the multitrait-multimethod matrix can be applied to assess the adequacy of knowledge-based systems in difficult but common evaluation settings, where there is only one problem scenario, experts who disagree, and no accuracy measures.

Adler, Jonathan E. Fallacies and Alternative Interpretations. *Austl J Phil*, 72(3), 271-281, S 94.

A natural practice of argument evaluation is to conclude that if an argument has a plausible, nonfallacious interpretation, then any interpretation of it as a fallacy is strongly disfavored, if not ruled out. I analyze two lines of reasoning toward this and related conclusions, and then proceed to systematically and critically examine them.

Adler, Jonathan E. More on Race and Crime: Levin's Reply. *J Soc Phil*, 25(2), 105-114, Fall 94.

A reply to M Levin's response to various critiques of his article, which argued that the high rate of crime among young black males justifies differential judgment and treatment of them, including by police (e.g., selective preventive interrogation). I reinforce my primary complaint about his original article which depended upon the assumption that screening criteria relevant for ethical, epistemic and legal purposes could depend only on informational value (e.g., probability), not causal relevance. Further arguments of his are also discussed.

Adler, Mortimer. *Platonism and Positivism in Psychology*. New Brunswick, Transaction Books, 1994.

Adler, Norbert. Rückehr zu Kants Kritik der reinen Vernunft für Erkenntnisforschritt in der mathematischen Physik. *Kantstudien*, 85(3), 309-336, 1994.

The topic is the determination of a nonmechanistic objective concept drawn out of the phenomena discovered by physics in the 20th century. Natural cognition for the general human being is not yet reached. This problem is solved according to Kant's "double use of understanding"; the mathematical case by construction of concepts and the philosophical one by concepts. This leads to the objective concept of substance characterized by "dynamic filling of space" based on inner forces. The time-depending intensity of them causes once its field-state and once its partical-state. Harmonization is made with Lorentz-transformation, non-Euclidic geometry and Heisenberg's uncertainty-relation.

Adolphi, Rainer. "Wertbeziehung: Die Mehrschichtigkeit von wissenschaftlichen Wert-Problemen (im Anschluss an Max Weber)" in *Mythos Wertfreiheit?, Apel, Karl Otto (ed)*, 77-107. Frankfurt, Campus Verlag, 1994.

The article attempts to reconstruct Weber's theory of "Wertbeziehung". 1) It first clarifies the significance of the question of the extent to which knowledge is bound to "values" or other subjective components (interests, etc) in the social sciences and humanities, and it outlines various answers to this question raised by Nietzsche. 2) "Wertbeziehung"—i.e., the selective structuring of empirical questions (hermeneutical impossibility of completely "descriptive" concepts)—refers to a view of cultural dependency of knowledge which does not detract from rationality, but provides its very foundation. This concept is contrasted with its Neo-Kantian origins and with its application in contemporary debates on positivism (value-free, objective knowledge) and relativism.

Adorno, Theodor W. "Anti-Semitism and Fascist Propaganda" in *Adorno: The Stars Down to Earth and Other Essays on the Irrational in Culture, Crook, Stephen (ed)*, 162-171. New York, Routledge, 1994.

Adorno, Theodor W. "Research Project on Anti-Semitism" in *Adorno: The Stars Down to Earth and Other Essays on the Irrational in Culture, Crook, Stephen (ed)*, 135-161. New York, Routledge, 1994.

Adorno, Theodor W and Crook, Stephen (ed). *Adorno: The Stars Down to Earth and Other Essays on the Irrational in Culture*. New York, Routledge, 1994.

Agamben, Giorgio and Sullivan, Michael (trans) and Whitsitt, Sam (trans). *Idea of Prose*. Albany, SUNY Pr, 1985.

Agar, Nicholas. Designing Babies: Morally Permissible Ways to Modify the Human Genome. *Bioethics*, 9(1), 1-15, Ja 95.

My focus in this paper is the question of the moral acceptability of attempts to modify the human genome. Much of the debate in this area has revolved around the distinction between supposedly therapeutic modification on the one hand, and eugenic modification on the other. In the first part of the paper I reject some recent arguments against genetic engineering. In the second part I seek to distinguish between permissible and impermissible forms of intervention in such a way that does not appeal to the therapeutic/eugenic distinction. If I am right much of what we would intuitively call eugenic intervention will be morally acceptable. Central to my argument is an asymmetry in the way genetic engineers can influence a person's capacities on the one hand and life-goals on the other. Forms of genetic intervention that have a high probability of producing a mismatch of life-goals and capacities will be ruled out.

Agassi, Joseph. An Inductivist Version of Critical Rationalism. *Phil Soc Sci*, 24(4), 458-465, D 94.

Alan Musgrave superbly contrasts Hume's and Popper's views about science and about rationality, thereby exhibiting the logical weaknesses of Hume's view that initially looks logically watertight. He then offers a version of the theory of rational belief that he claims is Popperian, yet Popper's view of rationality links it with criticism, not with belief.

Agassi, Joseph. Gadamer Without Tears. *Phil Soc Sci*, 24(4), 485-505, D 94.

The chief feature of Gadamer's philosophy is his claim that the humanities obey their own rules concerning reading texts and ensuring certitude. The promise of certitude is illusory, however, and the discourses on interpretation by him and his leading disciples are too confused to instruct the reader. His own sketch of his philosophy, published in his autobiographic *Philosophical Apprenticeship*, and its reflection in *Gadamer and Hermeneutics* (Hugh J Silverman, ed), shows this and reveals him as still too insensitive to the national tragedy of the Third Reich, which he witnessed.

Agassi, Joseph (& others). Karl Popper, 1902-1994. *Rad Phil*, 70, 2-8, Mr-Ap 95.

Popper has opened a new era in philosophy by showing some of the force of his proposal to replace the demand for justification of ideas with the attempt to criticize them. This is a philosophy for the autonomous thinker with implications in many fields.

Agich, George J. Key Concepts: Autonomy. *Phil Psychiat Psych*, 1(4), 267-269, D 94.

Various key meanings and uses of the term autonomy are discussed with an eye toward research in philosophy of psychiatry. A brief history of the usage of the concept of autonomy is reviewed. Difficulties associated with defining autonomy are reviewed and it is concluded that the meaning of autonomy involves a set of family resemblances based on its use in a variety of contexts or language games. Five meanings of autonomy are outlined with reference to psychiatric considerations: becoming autonomous, being autonomous, choosing autonomously, being recognized as autonomous, or being respected as an autonomous agent.

Agis, Domingo Fernández. La venganza de Espinosa: Caos en el orden y orden en el caos. *El Basilisco*, 16, 19-21, Ap-Je 94.

Agrimi, Mario. "Et 'Factum' et 'Verum' cum 'Verbo' Convertuntur": Lingua Divina e 'Prima Parlari' delle Nazioni in Vico. *G Crit Filosof Ital*, 72(3), 437-452, S-D 93.

Agrimi, Mario. Labriola tra Croce e Gentile. *G Crit Filosof Ital*, 73(2-3), 184-204, My-D 94.

Agrimi, Mario. Nota Vichiana. *Stud Filosofici*, 185-193, 1991-92.

Aguayo Cruz, Enrique Ignacio. Homenaje a Octavio Paz. *Logos (Mexico)*, 22(66), 151-155, S-D 94.

El homenaje a Octavio Paz se centra en la exposición breve de un tema importante de su filosofía: el amor y la política que son elementos deleje de nuestra civilización: la persona. En ésta el amor brota de lo profundo de su ser, manifestándose hacia las demás personas. El arraigo delamor en el interior de cada hombre es provocado por el otro. El amor deambos da una convivencia humana pacífica y fraterna. Otros temas de su pensamiento son filosofía de la poesía, de la historia, de la política, del lenguaje y del instante.

Agud, Ana. Sueño Metafísco y Vigilia Pronominal. *Daimon Rev Filosof*, 8, 169-177, 1994.

AUTHOR INDEX WITH ABSTRACTS 419 Albiac, Gabriel

Aguiar, Fernando. Confianza y Racionalidad. *Educ Filosof*, 8(16), 239-245, Jl-D 94.

The aim of this article is to analyze trust as a device to reduce uncertainty in our relationships with other people and with abstract systems (institutions). After criticizing the standard rational choice approach to trust, and proposing a redefinition of the concept in terms of bounded rationality, it is showed that trust could be a very useful concept to understand social problems such as charisma, collective action or democractic behavior.

Ahikire, Josephine. Bringing Women Back In: A Search for Alternative Historiographies. *Quest*, 8(2), 3-20, D 94.

Dans cet article l'auteur met en avant certains points concernant les études féministes dans le contexte de l'Ouganda. La principale supposition est que les études féministes ne peuvent pas n'être qu'une addition au status quo mais, bien plutôt, qu'il existe des problèmes théoriques qui ont besions d'être soumis à des débats et à une réflexion critique. La position des femmes dans l'histoire et le besoin de redonner une légitimité aux discours différents sont mis à l'oeuvre afin d'illustrer cette supposition.

Ahrensdorf, Peter J. *The Death of Socrates and the Life of Philosophy: An Interpretation of Plato's Phaedo*. Albany, SUNY Pr, 1995.

While the *Phaedo* is most famous for its moving portrayal of Socrates' death and its arguments for the immortality of the soul, this book argues that the dialogue is primarily devoted to presenting Socrates' final defense of the philosophic life against the theoretical and political challenge of religion. Through an analysis of both the historical context of the *Phaedo* and the arguments and drama of the dialogue, Ahrensdorf argues that Socrates' defense of rationalism is singularly undogmatic and that a study of that defense can lead us to a clearer understanding and a deeper and richer appreciation of the case both for and against rationalism.

Ainslie, Douglas (trans) and Croce, Benedetto. *Aesthetic as Science of Expression and General Linguistic*. New Brunswick, Transaction Books, 1995.

Airaksinen, Timo. "Service and Science in Professional Life" in *Ethics and the Professions, Chadwick, Ruth (ed)*, 1-13. Brookfield, Avebury, 1994.

Airaksinen, Timo and Kaalikoski, Katri. Instrumental Rationality. *Protosoz*, 6, 151-159, 1994.

The standard view of rationality distinguishes between instrumental rationality and the rationality of ends. We discuss this conception briefly before introducing an alternative theory. According to it, means and ends are interconnected so that the means will produce the ends. In other words, the means are used to shape our ends. We describe and discuss this view, asking whether it can be called rationality. It is clear that this alternative view has many irrational features. But at the same time it is clear that much of our technological culture is based on this view so that also it is hampered by the emerging irrationality. We conclude by discussing the case of genetic engineering as a technology we cannot possibly accept. Its characteristic ends may be of a wrong type.

Aizawa, Kenneth. Representations without Rules, Connectionism and the Syntactic Argument. *Synthese*, 101(3), 465-492, D 94.

Terry Horgan and John Tienson have suggested that connectionism might provide a framework within which to articulate a theory of cognition according to which there are mental representations without rules (RWR) (Horgan and Tienson 1988, 1989, 1991, 1992). In essence, RWR states that cognition involves representations in a language of thought, but that these representations are not manipulated by the sort of rules that have traditionally been posited. In the development of RWR, Horgan and Tienson attempt to forestall a particular line of criticism, the *Syntactic Argument*, which would show RWR to be inconsistent with connectionism. In essence, the argument claims that the node-level rules of connectionist networks, along with the semantic interpretations assigned to patterns of activation, serve to determine a set of representation-level rules incompatible with the RWR conception of cognition. The present paper argues that the Syntactic Argument can be made to show that RWR is inconsistent with connectionism.

Aizawa, Teruaki. Sympathy—Imitation—Metamorphosis (in Japanese). *Bigaku*, 45(2), 1-11, Autumn 94.

Adam Smith says that when we sympathize with others, we exchange with them not only our "circumstances" but also our "persons and characters". Or, in the words of Samuel Taylor Coleridge, sympathy contains the dynamic element of "mental metamorphosis". My purpose in this paper is to demonstrate how, in the eighteenth century, there existed a theory of literary creation to the effect that dramatist or novelist writing in direct speech can be, for some moments, sympathetically identified with even an evil person, and make a speech in the character of that person. (edited)

Aizpún, Teresa. Dialéctica y Libertad. *Topicos*, 4(7), 33-42, 1994.

Spirit, Freedom and *Dialectic* are frequently explained as if they were a whole. The spiritual movement, namely *Freedom*, is shown as a *dialectical* process. Apparently, there is no other solution when the *Spirit* is conceived as *truth*, as a plenitude that belongs to *Spirit*, but that it does not have and it must acquire. That's because *dialectic* is usually understood as a necessary consequence of the axiom: *truth is interiority*, and is therefore *identity*. And if this axiom were false?

Ajzner, Jan. Some Problems of Rationality, Understanding, and Universalistic Ethics in the Context of Habermas's Theory of Communicative Action. *Phil Soc Sci*, 24(4), 466-484, D 94.

The arguments presented in this discussion point to some problems in the theory of communicative action considered as a starting point for a sociological theory with both normative and explanatory aspirations. It is argued that Habermas's notion of consensus is not sufficiently developed to constitute a foundation of the ethics of public debates; that *both* social action and communicative action are grounded in social actors' references to the same three worlds, which makes the coordination of actions by means of understanding achieved in speech possible; that the criteria of rationality underlying use of language in the communicative action are ultimately those that are made explicit and consciously worked out in science; and that, finally, it is Parsons' solution to the Hobbesian problem and his concept of social action that provide a possible foundation for universalistic ethics.

Akam, J B. *The Oracle of Wisdom: Towards Philosophic Equipoise*. Enugu, Snaap Pr Lim, 1995.

Akiba, Ken. Quine and the Linguistic Doctrine of Logical Truth. *Phil Stud*, 78(3), 237-256, Je 95.

Akins, Kathleen. "What is it Like to be Boring and Myopic?" in *Dennett and his Critics, Dahlbom, Bo (ed)*, 124-160. Cambridge, Blackwell, 1995.

In "What is it Like to be a Bat?", Thomas Nagel claimed that we could never understand, through "objective" science, the phenomenal experience of a creature with an entirely different sensory system. This article begins with a review of the empirical literature on bat echolocation and then asks what insight about bat phenomenology has been gained. The conclusion is that, while it seems likely that bats do not have a sonar "point of view" at all, questions of "subjectivity" and phenomenology are intimately tied to questions about representational capacities.

Akman, Varol. When Silence May Mean Derision. *J Prag*, 22(2), 211-212, Ag 94.

In an interesting squib ("When Silence May Mean Power", *Journal of Pragmatics*, 18, 92-95, 1992), Dennis Kurzon shows that silence does not necessarily mean lack of power: the silent response to a question may well be aiming at gaining control of a situation, viz., exercising power. In this squib, I extend Kurzon's analysis and argue (via two examples which display some close parallels to real-life incidents that I am familiar with) that at times silence may mean derision or ridicule.

Al-Najjar, Nabil. A Theory of Forward Induction in Finitely Repeated Games. *Theor Decis*, 38(2), 173-193, Mr 95.

A forward induction solution for finitely repeated games with complete information is developed. This notion is motivated in terms of its implications on the way deviations affect the opponent's expectations about the future behavior of the deviating player. We argue that the inability of the notion of perfect equilibrium to take account of forward induction is a key factor responsible for a number of difficulties encountered in the use of perfect equilibria in repeated games. It is then shown that the solution proposed in this paper remedies some of these problems in the study of three important classes of repeated games: i) finitely repeated coordination games; ii) repeated games where one long-term player plays a sequence of short-term players; iii) repeated battle of the sexes games.

Aladjem, Terry K. Of Truth and Disagreement: Habermas, Foucault, and Democratic Discourse. *Hist Euro Ideas*, 20(4-6), 909-914, F 95.

There is a paradigm of 'argument-unto-agreement' deeply imbedded in the liberal theories of discourse from Mill's to Habermas's. While democracy thrives on argument and a plurality of different voices, it is justified in such theories by the hope that argument leads not only to agreement but to *truth*. While the participant in this scheme is implicitly a truth-*seeker*, it is argued that Foucault's emphasis on the Parrhesiast, the 4th century truth-*teller* considered in his last seminar, challenges this paradigm and reveals the more anxious, wishful assumptions about agreement within it which pose risks for pluralism.

Alam, Kazi Firoz. Attitudes Towards Business Ethics of Business Students in Malaysia. *J Bus Ethics*, 14(4), 309-313, Ap 95.

The main objective of this paper is to assess the attitude of a group of Malaysian business students towards business ethics. The survey results indicate that the respondents in general are of the opinion that the businesses in Malaysia consider ethics as secondary. A greater emphasis on ethical values in the business curricular has been strongly supported by the respondents. Moreover, the majority of the respondents believe that moral/ethical education and top management attitudes are the most important factors influencing ethical standards in business practices.

Alario, Margarita. Environmental Destruction and the Public Sphere: On Habermas's Discursive Model and Political Ecology. *Soc Theor Pract*, 20(3), 327-341, Fall 94.

Habermas's *Structural Transformation of the Public Sphere* (1989), offers a singular edge to environmentalists by reconstructing the public sphere as a discursively mediated arena of political participation. What needs to be added to a model of the public sphere that focuses on the formal structural denominator among individuals and their situations, is a discussion of the concrete instances of public intervention that reveals how the environmental discourse has been assembled and collective actors have incrementally gained *access* to the public sphere. For resources—such as knowledge, money, time, technological access, and so on—are not equally available to all grieving groups, strategic considerations need to be included. From the political ecological point of view this represents the double burden of inducing public discussion on the ecological agenda fully embracing the social question.

Albanese, Luciano. Platonismo, Rivoluzione Scientifica, Culti Solari: Un Tema da Riesaminare. *Stud Filosofici*, 79-105, 1991-92.

Albert, David Z. The Foundations of Quantum Mechanics and the Approach to Thermodynamic Equilibrium. *Erkenntnis*, 41(2), 191-206, S 94.

Albert, David Z and Barrett, Jeffrey A. On What It Takes to Be a World. *Topoi*, 14(1), 35-37, Mr 95.

A many-worlds interpretation is of quantum mechanics tells us that the linear equations of motion are the true and complete laws for the time-evolution of every physical system and that the usual quantum-mechanical states provide complete descriptions of all possible physical situations. Such an interpretation, however, denies the standard way of understanding quantum-mechanical states. When the pointer on a measuring device is in a superposition of pointing many different directions, for example, we are to understand this as many pointers, each in a different *world*, each pointing in a different determinate direction. We ask here whether such talk makes any genuinely intelligible sense of the term "world". We conclude that it does not.

Albert, David Z and Putnam, Hilary. Further Adventures of Wigner's Friend. *Topoi*, 14(1), 17-22, Mr 95.

Albiac, Gabriel. Épicurisme et saducéisme dans la communauté sépharade d'Amsterdam. *Arch Phil*, 57(3), 503-512, Jl-S 94.

Albrecht, Michael. Kants Maximenethik und ihre Begründung. *Kantstudien*, 85(2), 129-146, 1994.

A new approach to understanding Kant's conception of 'Maxime', based on his quasi-synonymous use of 'Maxime' and 'Grundsatz'. Maxims do not depend on habit, but on man's freedom. To act virtuously means to act according to virtuous maxims.

Albritton, Rogers. Comments on "Moore's Paradox and Self-Knowledge". *Phil Stud*, 77(2-3), 229-239, Mr 95.

Alcalá Campos, Raúl. Hermenéutica y Realismo Científico. *Analogia*, 4(2), 161-172, 1990.

Alcalá Campos, Raúl. Historia y Hermenéutica. *Analogia*, 7(1), 115-129, 1993.

Alcalá Campos, Raúl. La Discusión Lakatos-Kuhn. *Analogia*, 8(1), 79-101, 1994.

Alcázar, Javier R. W V Quine: Pursuit of Truth. *Rev Filosof (Spain)*, 4(5), 229-235, 1991.

This is a discussion in Spanish of Quine's *Pursuit of Truth*. I argue that this book favors the reading of Quine as a *systematic* philosopher and of *naturalism* as the basic ingredient of the system. Then I analyze the novel elements in the book: (i) Quine insists in preferring "observation conditionals" to "observation categoricals"; (ii) stresses the normative side of naturalized epistemology; (iii) incorporates *observation sentences*; (iv) sounds slightly more conciliatory when talking about intensions; (v) chooses, after some hesitations, a *secretarian* rather than an *ecumenical* stance on the topic of empirically equivalent theory formulations.

Alchourrón, Carlos E and Bulygin, Eugenio and Schmitt, Annette (& other trans). *Normative Systeme*. Freiburg, Alber, 1994.

Aldred, Jonathan. Existence Value, Welfare and Altruism. *Environ Values*, 3(4), 381-402, Wint 94.

Existence value has become an increasingly important concept as the use of cost benefit analysis has spread from traditional applications to attempts to place monetary value on, for instance, a rare wetland habitat. Environmental economists have generally accepted the tensions arising in the existence value concept from the range of recent applications, but it is argued here that their various attempts to resolve the difficulties have largely failed. Critics from outside economics, on the other hand, typically claim that the very notion of existence value as understood in economics is flawed, and urge its abandonment altogether. This paper suggests instead a fundamental redefinition of existence value, which, it is argued, i) explains a number of diverse problems posed by the usual meaning of the term in economics; ii) does not strain the intentions of respondents to 'willingness-to-pay' surveys; iii) is consistent with a more realistic model of rational choice in environmental decision-making; and iv) is sensitive to criticisms from environmental ethics.

Aldunate, José. Human Rights as the Rights of the Poor: The Perspective from Liberation Theology. *J Moral Educ*, 23(3), 297-303, 1994.

Alegre I Biosca, Lluís. La Inferència Dialèctico-Especulativa a la *Ciència de la Lògica* de Hegel. *Convivium*, 7, 5-14, 1995.

One of the serious problems on Hegel's *Logics Science* is the transition between the categories that is, the speculative-dialectical inference. This inference is carried out from the word being and its indetermination. Speaking about being to expose its meaning and significance as a form of logical and systematical construction involves the use of the metaphor, if one sets that the inference or the transition between the categories has to be immanent and must not include any other presupposition apart from the indetermination of the being itself, as concept content and as reference of the philosophical and scientific experience. The use of the metaphor enriches the contents of Hegelian speculation, full of suggestions, but at the same time its logic perfection become liable, by means of the construction of a system without cracks. (edited)

Aleksandrowicz, Dariusz. Marx, Stalin, Marcuse: Die kritische Theorie in ideengeschichtlicher Sicht. *Stud East Euro Thought*, 46(4), 287-314, D 94.

Both critical theory and communist philosophy arise from the post-Hegelian theory of salvation. Critical theory undertook the effort to preserve the core of this theoretical background and at the same time criticized the totalitarian consequences the communist ideology had derived from it. The crucial point of the new-leftist criticism of the Stalinist ideology was the rejection of a central claim of the latter according to which the salvation predicted in the leftist-revolutionary tradition had found its actual fulfillment in the institutional framework of the Soviet state. The relative achievements of critical theory lie in the damage it has caused to the two foundations of the totalitarian ideology, i.e.,: 1) its authority over tradition and 2) its authority over language. (edited)

Alemán, Anastasio. La Noción de Convención en Wittgenstein. *Rev Filosof (Spain)*, 7(12), 369-381, 1994.

In this paper I attempt to elucidate what is meant when it is said that a rule is conventional. Rules of chess in contrast to rules of cooking constitute, for Wittgenstein, a paradigmatic case of such type of rules. Later on it is showed that grammatical rules are conventional rules too, and some objections against that thesis are discussed.

Alexander, Charles P. Knowledge of One-Self and Other-Self. *Darshana Int*, 32(3/127), 12-16, Jl 92.

This work is a fresh attempt at understanding self; both one-self and other-self. Self has been a subject of dispute and enquiry since time immemorial. In this article 'Knowledge of One-Self and Other-Self', the common denominator self is a capsuled term, which is neither body nor mere function of electro-chemical waves. Pure self transcends our empirical understanding of it, because a person is not the sum total of an individual's parts alone, but an aggregate sum total of individual parts: the value of which is more than the sum total of different parts. Hence, to understand self is to take into account not just the behavior of the person, but the socio-culturally programmed individual experience concepts.

Alexander, Peter. "Solidity and Elasticity in the Seventeenth Century" in *Locke's Philosophy*, Rogers, G A J (ed), 143-164. New York, Oxford Univ Pr, 1994.

Locke provisionally accepted Boyle's Corpuscularian view of matter. The aim of this paper is to throw light on the question whether they hold that the corpuscles of their hypothesis were *absolutely* solid. Accepting or rejecting this raised problems about rebounding on collision and the explanation of elasticity. The controversy about this continued through the seventeenth century into the nineteenth century involving many distinguished philosophers and scientists. The paper claims that the nature of this controversy made it reasonable for intelligent people to take either view according to what more basic principles of explanation and intelligibility they accepted.

Alexander, Thomas M. "John Dewey and the Roots of Democratic Imagination" in *Recovering Pragmatism's Voice*, Langsdorf, Lenore (ed), 131-154. Albany, SUNY Pr, 1995.

Is pluralism a benefit or a necessity for democracy? Most democratic theories see it as a difficulty to be overcome, or, at best, a means for preventing power coalitions (e.g., Madison). I argue that Dewey's theory of democracy sees pluralism as the necessary condition for the kind of political intelligence that democracy needs. This form of intelligence uses emotion and imagination as well as reason.

Alexander, Thomas M. Educating the Democratic Heart: Pluralism, Traditions and the Humanities. *Stud Phil Educ*, 13(3-4), 243-259, 1994-95.

This essay argues that pluralism is essential toward developing a democratic use of the humanities. Contrary to the views of E D Hirsch, Alastair MacIntyre and others, I show that John Dewey's views support such a pluralistic outlook without succumbing to the celebration of pure difference and relativism.

Alexandrakis, Aphrodite. The Classical Conception of Beauty in Byzantine Art. *Diotima*, 23, 157-161, 1995.

Alheit, Peter. "'Wertneutralität'—Wie frei von Werten darf Wissenschaft sein?" in *Freiheit, Verantwortung und Folgen in der Wissenschaft*, Sandkühler, Hans Jörg (ed), 97-110. New York, Lang, 1994.

Ali, S M and Zimmer, R M. Discourse on Artificiality: A Unifying Framework for the Artificial Sciences. *Ideal Stud*, 24(3), 201-226, Fall 94.

This paper presents a unifying framework for the study of artificial life, intelligence and reality. By providing this framework we can give a clear and concise introduction to the fundamental arguments of all three artificial sciences and facilitate the translation of arguments from any one domain to the other two. The framework is based on a variant of functionalism that does not exclude the role of the observer.

Alican, Nejip Fikri. *Mill's Principle of Utility: A Defence of John Stuart Mill's Notorious Proof*. Amsterdam, Rodopi, 1994.

This book is a thoroughgoing analysis, interpretation, and defense of John Stuart Mill's proof of the principle of utility. The primary aim is to show, against long-standing criticism, that Mill proceeds intelligibly and systematically in pursuing a well-defined project in the fourth chapter of *Utilitarianism*, and that he successfully defends what he sets out to establish in his proof of the principle of utility. To this end, the book analyzes and refutes historically popular and persistently enduring charges against Mill's proof. The central chapters address the traditional charges that Mill commits the fallacy of equivocation, the fallacy of composition, and the naturalistic fallacy in the proof.

Allais, Maurice. Allais' Rejoinder. *Theor Decis*, 38(3), 309-311, My 95.

Allais, Maurice. The Real Foundations of the Alleged Errors in Allais' Impossibility Theorem: Unceasingly Repeated Errors or Contradictions of Mark Machina. *Theor Decis*, 38(3), 251-299, My 95.

The Impossibility Theorem rests on five fundamental properties. On each of them Machina has confirmed his agreement over and over again between 1984 and 1986. The proof of the Impossibility Theorem is mathematically and rigorously correct. The alleged Machina's demonstration of the Allais's two errors *is indeed only grounded on a series of errors* and it is *in total contradiction* with the interpretations *explicitly* given by Machina from 1982 to 1986 of his local utility theory in the discrete case, especially in his letters. In fact one cannot but ask if Machina really understands the meaning and the implications of his formulation of the local utility, and what is really in question. In any case it would be without any doubt eminently desirable that before hastily concluding that the others are making mistakes, Machina should begin by seriously asking himself if he is not himself into error.

Allan, George. Making the Everyday. *Res Phil Technol*, 14, 175-187, 1994.

Humans construct social worlds as instruments for fulfilling their desires; these creations unavoidably involve technologies. The ethical issue is not whether but how technological enhancements of human creative powers are utilized, what the moral resources are for directing their use in ways that deepen rather than trivialize the goods they help make available. All our cultural resources are a legacy from the past. If that legacy is debased, technologically or otherwise, so then are our chances for fulfillment. Even the "wild" can serve as a source of societal renewal only through the societal traditions that give us access to it.

Allard, James W (ed) and Bradley, F H and Stock, Guy (ed). *Writings on Logic and Metaphysics*. New York, Oxford Univ Pr, 1994.

Allchin, Douglas. The Super Bowl and the Ox-Phos Controversy: "Winner-Take-All" Competition in Philosophy of Science. *Proc Phil Sci Ass*, 1, 22-33, 1994.

Several diagrams and tables from review articles during on Ox-Phos Controversy serve as an occasion to assess the nature of competition in models of theory choice in science. Many models follow "Super-Bowl" principles of polar, either-or, winner-take-all competition. A significant alternative highlighted by this episode, however, is the differentiation of domains. Incommensurability and the partial divergence of overlapping domains serve both as signals and context for shifting frameworks of competition. Appropriate strategies may thus help researchers diagnose the status of competition and shape their research accordingly.

Allen, Barry G. Critical Notice of Hilary Putnam: *Realism With a Human Face* and *Renewing Philosophy*. *Can J Phil*, 24(4), 665-688, D 94.

This article provides a survey of Putnam's principle arguments against "metaphysical realism", as well as a view of the constructive effort of his work in the last ten years. It argues that Putnam's recent work systematically shifts concepts of truth and objectivity away from metaphysics and epistemology toward ethics and politics and also argues that Putnam's animadversions against Rorty wrongly suggest more difference than there is between Putnam's pragmatic realism and Rorty's ethnocentric pragmatism.

Allen, Barry G. Putnam und Rorty über Objektivität und Wahrheit. *Deut Z Phil*, 42(6), 989-1005, 1994.

Allen, Colin. It Isn't What You Think: A New Idea about Intentional Causation. *Nous*, 29(1), 115-126, Mr 95.

I analyze a standard argument for the conclusion that intentional properties are irrelevant to causal explanations of behavior. I then analyze an analogous argument for the conclusion that the property of genuineness is irrelevant to causal explanations of the effects that twenty-dollar bills have on human agents, and I indicate a way in which this argument fails. I then apply the lessons learned from the example of genuineness to articulate a defense for the causal relevance of intentional properties. I end the paper by discussing several objections to this defense.

Allen, Jeffner. "A Response to a Letter from Peg Simons, December 1993" in *Feminist Interpretations of Simone de Beauvoir*, Simons, Margaret A (ed), 113-135. University Park, Penn St Univ Pr, 1995.

This study presents 1) reinterpretation of Beauvoir in the light of the recent publication of her journals, and 2) discussion of Beauvoir's relation to existentialism and to feminist philosophy.

Allen, Prudence. Rationality, Gender, and History. *Amer Cath Phil Quart*, 68(Supp), 271-288, 1994.

Three basic theories of the relation of rationality and gender are identified: 1) *sex unity*: or no significant differences between men's and women's rationality; 2) *sex polarity*: or significant sex and gender differences in rational capacities and data, and either men's rationality or women's rationality is superior; and 3) *sex complementarity*: or an equality of rational capacities in men and women, with some data of consciousness being sex and gender differentiated. After tracing specific histories of these three theories this paper argues that contemporary Catholic philosophy ought to base a theory of rationality on a premise of integral complementarity.

Allen, Richard. Film, Fiktion und psychoanalytische Theorie. *Deut Z Phil*, 43(3), 507-519, 1995.

This paper assesses the coherence of influential psychoanalytic explanations of film spectatorship. Their credibility turns on the application of the concepts of fetishism and disavowal to the cinema that relies upon an untenable conception of cinematic representation as a form of illusion and of fiction as an institution that elicits a form of imaginative engagement that is essentially pathological in its structure. I conclude that psychoanalysis cannot explain what cinema or fiction prescribes us to imagine, it can at most provide an explanation of what individual genres or films prescribe us to imagine.

Allinson, Robert E. Moral Values and the Taoist Sage in the *Tao de Ching*. *Asian Phil*, 4(2), 127-136, 1994.

The theme of this paper is that while there are four seemingly contradictory classes of statements in the *Tao de Ching* regarding moral values and the Taoist sage, these statements can be interpreted to be consistent with each other. There are statements which seemingly state or imply that nothing at all can be said about the Tao; there are statements which appear to attribute moral behaviour to the Taoist sage and there are statements which appear to attribute moral behaviour to the Taoist sage and there are statements which appear to attribute amoral or immoral behaviour to the Taoist sage. A consistent interpretation of these different statements can be found first by qualifying the assertion that the Tao is not capable of description to the less absolute assertion that nothing absolutely true can be said about the Tao; second, by arguing that the statements that appear to make all values relative refer to the correlativity of concepts, not the equality of values. (edited)

Allis, Victor and Koetsier, Teun. One Some Paradoxes of the Infinite II. *Brit J Phil Sci*, 46(2), 235-247, Je 95.

In an earlier paper the authors discussed some super-tasks by means of a kinematical interpretation. In the present paper we show a semi-formal way that a more abstract treatment is possible. The core idea of our approach is simple: if a super-task can be considered as a union of (finite) tasks, it is natural to define the effect of the super-task as the union of the effects of the finite tasks it consists of. We show that this approach enables us to handle two of the three super-tasks that we discussed earlier. We also argue that recent objections against our original kinematical interpretation do not hold water. One of our arguments is based on the construction of an elegant correspondence between the first of those three super-tasks and Zeno's *Achilles and the Tortoise*.

Ally, Mashuq. Some Reflections on the Relevance of Karl Jaspers' Concept of Border Situation in Present-Day South Africa. *S Afr J Phil*, 14(2), 48-53, My 95.

In this article the author considers Karl Jaspers's concept of border situation. This seminal idea of Jaspers is elucidated and shown to be central to his concept of self-realization. The derivation of certain moral and political norms from this concept demonstrates its practical significance. The application of the concept of border situation to socio-political conditions in present-day South Africa is a further demonstration of this significance. In tracing certain connections between the various forms of border situation and these conditions the author suggests ways in which reflection upon Jaspers's concept of border situation may help us to come to terms with our present predicament.

Almeida, Michael J. Collective Rationality and Simple Utilitarian Theories. *Dialogue (Canada)*, 33(3), 363-375, Sum 94.

I consider several counterexamples to simple, additive, utilitarian theories designed to show that universal conformity to such theories in contexts of independent choice can be collectively irrational: a group G of utilitarian agents would be better off,

collectively, if one or more agents were to fail to fulfill their simple utilitarian obligations in certain cases. I show that there is no context of independent choice in which universal conformity to one's actual, utilitarian obligations leaves a group worse off than it would have been had one of more agents failed to fulfill their actual obligations. Simple utilitarianism is not collectively irrational.

Almond, Brenda. "Liberty or Community? Defining the Post-Marxist Agenda" in *Introducing Applied Ethics*, Almond, Brenda (ed), 247-259. Cambridge, Blackwell, 1995.

Liberalism is under challenge for its moral neutralism and the practical decline this has brought about in social conditions (e.g., crime, family breakdown and deteriorating cultural and moral standards). There are also global problems, environmental and economic with which many believe liberalism is ill-equipped to deal. This chapter argues that this critique and consequent moves to welfare and communitarian alternatives to liberalism, are valid only against a mistaken conception of liberalism which, even in its minimalist classical formulation can deal with these ills on the basis of supporting individual rights, i.e., protecting the individual from internal and external threats and enforcing contracts between individuals.

Almond, Brenda. Bioethics and Family Values. *J Applied Phil*, 12(1), 107-108, 1995.

Discusses recent book on bioethics, particularly concerned with aspects of reproductive medicine, relating the issue to broader social questions, including its impact on the family, and the effect of interpreting liberalism as a demand for publicly financed freedoms.

Almond, Brenda. *Exploring Philosophy: The Philosophical Quest (Second Edition)*. Cambridge, Blackwell, 1995.

New revised edition of *The Philosophical Quest*. Includes chapters on moral philosophy, political and social philosophy, forms of argument (logic and philosophy of science), language and meaning, philosophy of mind and the self, and a brief introduction to metaphysics, with the Stoics and Spinoza taken as exemplars. Last chapter relates issues to ongoing debates (Quine, Rorty, Putnam) and to the issues of truth and virtue, reflective first-person presentation. Emphasis is "applied" touching on abortion, toleration, and environment, while overall a liberal rights (as opposed to utilitarian) approach is adopted.

Almond, Brenda (ed). *Introducing Applied Ethics*. Cambridge, Blackwell, 1995.

Specially commissioned chapters each treating a topic in applied ethics and, through a system of Reading-Guides and Notes introducing the reader to the debate within that field. Includes an extensive introdution on the relation between ethical theory and ethical practice, followed by sections on personal issues, including family relationships and homelessness; professional issues in education, journalism, business, law enforcement, medicine, including psychiatry, science and genetics; broad social and political issues, including health and welfare, community, liberty, and capitalism; and international and global issues, including war, terrorism, poverty and wealth, relations between humans and animals, and the ethics of environmentalism.

Almond, Brenda. Liberal and Totalitarian Morality. *Filozof Istraz*, 14(2-3), 283-293, 1994.

The author contrasts liberalism and totalitarianism, not as two political systems, but rather as two opposed types of morality. Ethical systems as different as Marxism, fascism, and Benthamite utilitarianism exhibit three basic traits which the author takes as definitive of totalitarian morality: 1) They replace the plurality of values by a single value; 2) They are partisan rather than impartial in their application; 3) They put the advancing of a cause above respect for the individual. Liberal morality, on the other hand, can be defined not only negatively, in terms of its opposition to various excesses of the totalitarian mind, but also positively, in terms of its basic traits, which are contrasted with the defining traits of totalitarian moral outlook. This, together with value pluralism, disposes the liberal to toleration in its proper form—not to the toleration of evil and intolerance, but to a sympathetic understanding of those confronting genuine ethical problems. Liberal impartiality, on the other hand, leads to a rejection of the partisan conception of toleration advanced in Marcuse's "critique of pure tolerance".

Almond, Brenda. The Retreat from Liberty. *Crit Rev*, 8(2), 235-246, Spr 94.

In *What's the Matter with Liberalism?* Ronald Beiner diagnoses the ills of liberalism along the three broad fronts where it is now widely challenged: its pretensions to moral neutrality; its lack of cultural standards; and its inability to deal with crime, unemployment, family breakdown, homelessness, rampant consumerism, and global environmental and economic problems. But even in its minimalist classical formulation, liberalism entails a substantive moral position, and is committed to resisting the violations of rights that lead to the crises with which Beiner is concerned.

Alon, Ilai and Graves, David. A Language for the Description of God, Part I: A Unique Language for a Unique Object. *Int J Phil Relig*, 36(3), 169-186, D 94.

Alonso, Luz García. La actualización en la enseñanza de la moral propuesta por la Veritatis Splendor. *Logos (Mexico)*, 22(66), 107-119, S-D 94.

Alperson, Philip (ed). *The Philosophy of the Visual Arts*. New York, Oxford Univ Pr, 1992.

This book provides a systematic introduction to philosophical problems concerning the visual arts and the institutions that sustain them. Stressing conceptual and theoretical issues, the collection examines the notion of "the visual arts." It then investigates philosophical issues raised by various art forms, starting with painting, the paradigmatic visual art, and taking up questions about form and representation and the relationship between the pictorial arts and other human domains (psychology, religion, politics and society). The book then turns to other visual arts including architecture, sculpture, the more controversial modern forms of photography and film, and the borders of the arts spectrum, including kitsch, dance, the circus, body beautification, and the appreciation of the natural environment.

Alpert, Peter. The Boulder and the Sphere: Subjectivity and Implicit Values in Biology. *Environ Values*, 4(1), 3-16, F 95.

Science is inherently subjective. The experience of dissertation research in ecology showed how intuitively derived hypotheses and assumptions define the questions one asks and the variables one measures and how idealized forms and generalized types facilitate analysis but distort interpretation. Because these conceptual tools are indispensable to science, subjectivity is ineluctable. This has moral implications. Scientists are responsible for the particular abstractions they select and must therefore accept some moral responsibility for the way their results are used. Those who use scientific results have an equal responsibility to acknowledge the significance of the methods and not just of the conclusions. In biology, subjectivity may also have a positive side. A wide consensus of ecological biologists accept, on the apparently neutral grounds of accumulated study, a set of generalizations that society at large treats more as philosophical beliefs. This category of implicit values in biology holds much promise for improving our relations with nature and each other.

Alston, Kal. Begging the Question: Is Critical Thinking Biased?. *Educ Theor*, 45(2), 225-233, Spr 95.

This article looks at questions raised by Ennis, Norris, and Bailin regarding bias in critical thinking. The author attempts to situate the question of bias in profession, texts, and theories related to critical thinking traditions. She examines the claim that the forms of argument, logic, and rationality utilized in the tradition at the least ignore or minimized other forms used by women or groups outside the European center. The author suggests that strenuous argument on either side grants the critical thinking tradition a centrality which can only be earned by situating thinking and rationality into a more holistic frame.

Alston, W P. "Belief-forming Practices and the Social" in *Socializing Epistemology: The Social Dimensions of Knowledge*, Schmitt, Frederick (ed), 29-51. Lanham, Rowman & Littlefield, 1994.

This paper is concerned with the role of social considerations in the epistemic assessment of doxastic (belief forming) practices, particularly the determination of their reliability or unreliability. Three grades of social involvement of such assessment are distinguished. 1) Since doxastic practices are themselves ineluctably social, facts about them are social facts. 2) Some reasons for reliability have to do with results that are obtained by social processes. 3) The degree of social establishment of doxastic practices is itself relevant to their epistemic assessment.

Alston, William P. Précis of *Perceiving God*. *Phil Phenomenol Res*, 54(4), 863-868, D 94.

Alston, William P. Reply to Commentators. *Phil Phenomenol Res*, 54(4), 891-899, D 94.

Alston, William P. Reply to Critics. *J Phil Res*, 20, 67-81, 1995.

Altieri, Charles. *Subjective Agency: A Theory of First-person Expressivity and its Social Implications*. Cambridge, Blackwell, 1994.

Subjective Agency relies on Hegelian expressivist theory, interpreted through Wittgenstein, as its means of countering are the debilitating binaries shaping treatments of this topic in contemporary literary theory and cultural studies. Part one develops a version of "logical existentialism" based on asymmetries between first and third person discourse, while Part 2 turns from the constitution of subjectivity to the ethical and political stances defensible in relation to the overall model. Ultimately Kantian aesthetics provides a framework for establishing ethical purposiveness, and the indeterminacy of decision-making provides grounds for restating liberal political commitments.

Alvarez, Antón Fernández. William Godwin y el anarquismo: A propósito de *Political Justice*. *Telos (Spain)*, 2(2), 93-106, D 93.

When analyzing the fundamentals of libertarian ideology in general, many authors consider anarchism as the "culmination of liberal ideology". The personality and work of William Godwin can be very useful for us in pointing out and understanding the possible relationships between both ideologies (i.e., between anarchism and liberal ideology). With this aim in mind, we will go over part of the various ideas and main principles of Godwin's *Political Justice* in order to delimit the similarities and/or differences which will allow us to draw the dividing or connecting line between classical liberalism and Godwin's incipient "anarchism".

Alvarez, Carlos. De la determinación del infinito a la inaccesibilidad en los cardinales transfinitos. *Critica*, 26(78), 27-71, D 94.

In this paper I deal with two problems in mathematical philosophy: the question about the nature of infinity and the possible answer to this question after Cantor's theory of transfinite numbers. In the first part of this paper I discuss Cantorian theory of transfinite numbers and his particular point of view about this matter. The second part gives a general view of this development and of the theory of the inaccessible cardinal numbers in order to make clear my point of view concerning Aristotelian potential infinity. (edited)

Alvarez Argüelles, Luz María. Algunas Implicaciones Éticas del Psicoanálisis. *Analogia*, 8(1), 169-175, 1994.

Alvarez Argüelles, Luz María. Los Valores en el Pensamiento de F Nietzsche. *Analogia*, 9(1), 193-204, 1995.

Alvarez de Toledo, Blanca I. "Carta Imaginaria de un Postmoderno 'Avant la Lettre'" in *Temas Actuales de Filosofía*, Palacios, María Julia (ed), 49-61. Buenos Aires, Univ Nacional Salta, 1993.

Alves, Elias Humberto. Algumas Observaçoes sobre a Lógica Espacial. *Cad Hist Filosof Cie*, 3(1-2), 151-162, Ja-D 93.

We discuss the question of spatial logic, a topic which, in contrast to temporal logic, has received very little attention from logicians. Arguments presented in Taylor (1976) are used to show that contrary to much traditional thought, spatial and temporal relations have fundamental similarities. In addition, it is shown that many of Taylor's ideas are already implicit in Rescher and Gasson (1968), where various systems of temporal logic are discussed from the point of view of topological logic. We conclude by suggesting that the construction of systems of spatial logic may be capable of clarifying some of the complex philosophical problems raised by the proliferation of temporal systems.

Alves dos Santos, Maris Carolina. The Greeks and Us (in Portuguese). *Trans/Form/Acao*, 17, 133-141, 1994.

This article gives an affirmative answer to the recurrent question concerning the effective contribution brought by the study of the political thought of the ancient Greeks to the problems faced by modern democratic societies.

Alway, Joan. *Critical Theory and Political Possibilities: Conceptions of Emancipatory Politics in the Works of Horkheimer, Adorno, Marcuse, and Habermas*. Westport, Greenwood Pr, 1995.

Amagasaki, Akira. The Function of the Subject Complex in *Tanka*. *Aesthetics*, 3, 91-100, Mr 88.

We can postulate two modes of *tanka* composition in terms of "subject complex." One is to refer to some concrete object to communicate a state of mind around the main topic, i.e., some *representation* of a certain content or experience. The other is to use the main topic as "pretext" to support a display of an unexpected construction of words or images, namely, the "presentation" of a *sugata*. In the former there are also two cases. One is to *project the taste* of the concrete object on the main topic. The other is to *tinge the image* of the concrete object with a certain feeling grounded in the main topic, in other words, to make the object a symbol. We cannot say which is the better, for both modes yielded many excellent *tanka*. We can, however, say that while the communication of content or experience is possible (to at least some degree) in both prose and poetry, but the presentation of *sugata* is a privilege of poetry. *Kabuki* audiences are sometimes brought to ecstasy by beautiful lines even without understanding their content, just like viewers of modern art who are often deeply impressed without understanding what the subject is. This is the effect of *sugata*. (edited)

Amariglio, Jack and Ruccio, David F. "Postmodernism, Marxism, and the Critique of Modern Economic Thought" in *Marxism in the Postmodern Age*, Callari, Antonio (ed), 13-23. New York, Guilford, 1994.

The essay discusses the effects of modernist notions of cognition, behavior, subjectivity, and social determination on Marxian economic theory, such as capitalism vs. socialism, present capitalism as disordered, alienating, socially fragmented, and mystifying, and socialism as socially ordered, organically unified, and subjectively whole. The essay teases out the postmodern notions of disorder, decentering, and uncertainty that are implicit in the oppositions of classical Marxism and contends that the modernist faith in the inherent rationality of socialist economy be replaced by the recognition that capitalism has no unique purchase on disorder, decentering, and uncertainty.

Ambrosini, Cristina. "Ludwig Wittgenstein, los Juegos del Lenguaje y la Etica" in *Temas Actuales de Filosofía*, Palacios, María Julia (ed), 63-73. Buenos Aires, Univ Nacional Salta, 1993.

Ambühl, Hans. Metaphysik und Ontologie bei Aristoteles. *Frei Z Phil Theol*, 41(1-2), 223-228, 1994.

This is a review of five articles on Aristotelian Metaphysics (*Revue Philosophique de Louvain*, 90, November 92). Main results are: 1) there is no conflict between ontology and theology, because in its object the latter also comprises the causes of the being qua being. 2) In the formula "being qua being" the "qua being" does not stand for a specific reality, but for a formal point of view directing the investigation. 3) The train of thought in Book Z leads to the establishment of the fundamental structure of being, i.e., the "being in itself". 4) Ontology and henology (theory of the one) complement each other; the former relates to reality, the latter provides the corresponding methodical structure. 5) The application of stylometric methods and an in-depth analysis of Book K show certain traditional interpretations in a new light.

Ames, Roger T. "Rites as Rights: The Confucian Alternative" in *Human Rights and the World's Religions*, Rouner, Leroy (ed), 199-216. Notre Dame, Univ Notre Dame Pr, 1988.

Ames, Roger T (ed) and Marks, Joel (ed). *Emotions in Asian Thought*. Albany, SUNY Pr, 1995.

In recent years emotion has become the focus of intensive theoretical work among philosophers of the West, but what is striking to a comparative philosopher is the almost total lack of references to non-Western thought. This book redresses that situation. Beginning with an overview of recent work in the West, the inquiry preceeds to the main business of scrutinizing various relevant issues from both Asian and comparative perspectives, including original essays by June McDaniel, Purushottama Bilimoria, Leroy Rouner, Joel Kupperman, Joel Marks, Mary Bockover, Chad Hansen, and Graham Parkes. The book concludes with an extensive overview by Robert Solomon.

Ames, William L. Bhavaviveka's *Prajñapradipa*. *J Indian Phil*, 23(3), 295-365, S 95.

This article is an annotated translation of chapter two of Bhavaviveka's *Prajñapradipa*, a commentary on Nagarjuna's *Mula-madhyamka-karika*, the fundamental text of the Madhyamaka school of Mahayana Buddhist philosophy. Chapter Two is a critique of the idea of motion, titled "Examination of the Traverser, the Untraversed, and that which is being Traversed." Bhavaviveka (c. 500-570) was the founder of the Svatantrika-Madhyamaka subschool and pioneered the use of the Indian formal logic in expounding the Madhyamka. He also discusses the views of the other Buddhist and non-Buddhist schools of his day.

Amor, Claudio. Rawls: Principio de diferencia y justicia intergeneracional. *Rev Filosof (Argentina)*, 8(1-2), 3-18, N 93.

The principle of just saving is proposed by Rawls as a response to the question of how the charges involved in the reconstruction of a materially just society should be distributed among various generations. The theoretical status of that principle is central to the theory: it is only on the basis of its plausibility that the satisfactibility of the intragenerational principles of justice can be grounded. In particular, the satisfactibility of the principle of difference depends on it. In this paper we will try to show that Rawls' version of the relation between the principle of just saving and the principle of difference gives rise to unsurmountable problems. In the general framework of justice as fairness, we try to develop an alternative approach.

Amorós, Celia. Los escritos póstumos de J P Sartre (II). *Rev Filosof (Spain)*, 4(5), 133-161, 1991.

Amsterdamska, Olga. W(h)ither Philosophy? W(h)ither Sociology?. *Kennis Methode*, 18(2-3), 179-184, 1994.

AUTHOR INDEX WITH ABSTRACTS 423 **Anderson-Gold, Sharon**

Amundson, Ron. Two Concepts of Constraint: Adaptationism and the Challenge from Developmental Biology. *Phil Sci*, 61(4), 556-578, D 94.

The so-called "adaptationism" of mainstream evolutionary biology has been criticized from a variety of sources. One, which has received relatively little philosophical attention, is developmental biology. Developmental constraints are said to be neglected by adaptationists. This paper explores the divergent methodological and explanatory interests that separate mainstream evolutionary biology from its embryological and developmental critics. It will focus on the concept of *constraint* itself; even this central concept is understood differently by the two sides of the dispute.

Amundson, Ron and Lauder, George V. Function without Purpose: The Uses of Causal Role Function in Evolutionary Biology. *Biol Phil*, 9(4), 443-469, O 94.

Philosophers of evolutionary biology favor the so-called "etiological concept" of function according to which the function of trait is its evolutionary purpose, defined as the effect for which that trait was favored by natural selection. We term this the selected effect (SE) analysis of function. An alternative account of function was introduced by Robert Cummins in a nonevolutionary and nonpurposive context. Cummins's account has received attention but little support from philosophers of biology. This paper will show that a similar nonpurposive concept of function, which we term causal role (CR) function, is crucial to certain research programs in evolutionary biology, and that philosophical criticisms of Cummins's concept are ineffective in this scientific context. (edited)

An-Na'im, Abdullahi A (& other eds). *Human Rights and Religious Values*. Grand Rapids, Eerdmans, 1995.

Varying interpretations of religious values and basic human rights have given rise to a number of conflicts throughout the world in recent years. This volume seeks to establish a relationship between these values and rights. The eighteen essays collected here respond to the central question: Can human rights be interpreted from within religious traditions such that they are apprehended as the "common core" of a universal morality among these traditions? Clearly reflecting the diverse religious backgounds of their authors—Hinduism, Buddhism, Christianity, and Islam—these essays demonstrate that religious ideals of human life differ considerably. They offer a realistic approach to these differences and serve to facilitate open and critical dialogue on this important topic.

Anabtawi, Jehanne. *Only a God Can Save Us*: Disabling the Rational Subject in Heidegger's Reactionary Modernism. *Heythrop J*, 36(2), 190-201, Ap 95.

Anchor, Robert. Review Essay: Philip Barker's *Michel Foucault: Subversions of the Subject*. *Hist Theor*, 34(1), 122-132, 1995.

Ancona, Elvio. Il Significato del Cuore nella Filosofia Giuridica di S Agostino e di Marsilio da Padova. *Riv Int Filosof Diritto*, 71(4), 201-215, 1994.

Andereggen, Ignacio E M. La Relación Entre la Metafísica y la Teología en San Alberto Magno y Santo Tomás de Aquino. *Sapientia*, 49(193-4), 229-240, 1994.

Anders, Timothy. *The Evolution of Evil*. Peru, Open Court, 1994.

According to Anders, the root of all human suffering, and hence of all evil, is to be found in the historical process by which human life was created: evolution by natural selection. The simplicity of this explanation has been overlooked because of several widely-held misconceptions, notably the view that evolution favors the good and eliminates the bad, or that evolution favors an inexorable ascent to 'higher', more intelligent, and more complex forms. At the heart of these misconceptions lie prejudices such as anthropocentrism—the view that humankind is the 'point' of the universe, and that things therefore tend to be arranged for humanity's benefit; the assumption that nature is essentially benevolent toward humans; and political utopianism, which proclaims that it is possible to bring about a perfect or nearly perfect society. (edited)

Anderson, Albert A. Dialectic and Dialogue. *Dialogue Hum*, 3(2), 103-117, 1993.

Anderson, Albert A. Universal Love. *Dialogue Hum*, 4(5), 65-77, 1994.

Anderson, Albert A. Universal Love: The Source of Philosophy. *Dialogue Hum*, 4(2-3), 65, 1994.

Anderson, David L. A Dogma of Metaphysical Realism. *Amer Phil Quart*, 32(1), 1-11, Ja 95.

There is a dogma about metaphysical realism that is well nigh universal: *If one is a metaphysical realist about the external world, then one ought to be a semantic realist about (all) external-world statements*. I argue that this dogma should be rejected. It is possible for a metaphysical realist to be a *semantic dualist*, holding that some middle-sized object statements receive a realist interpretation, but that most such statements require an antirealist interpretation. To show that a semantically dual language is at least possible, I describe a possible world (The Land of Subscript) whose inhabitants speak a version of English that is syntactically dual. Further I argue that English in the *actual world* is itself semantically dual.

Anderson, Douglas R. Peirce's Agape and the Generality of Concern. *Int J Phil Relig*, 37(2), 103-112, Ap 95.

This essay examines the general nature of C S Peirce's conception of *agape* and the import of this generality for what we now call environmental concerns.

Anderson, Douglas R. *Strands of System: The Philosophy of Charles Peirce*. West Lafayette, Purdue Univ Pr, 1995.

This book is an introduction to the systematic thinking of Charles Peirce. It includes a brief biography, an overview of Peirce's philosophy, and two of Peirce's essays accompanied by commentaries. The essays are "The Fixation of Belief" and "A Neglected Argument for the Reality of God."

Anderson, Douglas R and Hausman, Carl R. The Telos of Peirce's Realism. *Trans Peirce Soc*, 30(4), 825-838, Fall 94.

The paper is intended to show how Joseph Margolis's critique of Charles Peirce's unique kind of realism treats Peirce's "reality" as static rather than dynamic and evolutionary. This overlooking of the unique features of Peirce's realism seems to be the product of assuming the ultimacy of analytic presuppositions, especially a Cartesian notion of reason that Peirce argued against.

Anderson, Erik. Kant, Natural Kind Terms, and Scientific Essentialism. *Hist Phil Quart*, 11(4), 355-373, O 94.

What, for Kant, is the semantic status of the proposition: Water is H_2O? Is it analytic or synthetic? Based on textual evidence, I attribute to Kant the position that natural kind terms are indexical like, and I give a plausible interpretation according to which, for Kant, the proposition mentioned above is analytic. I then go on to show that, although Kant's semantics of natural kind terms closely resembles that of contemporary scientific essentialists, it nevertheless does not commit him to an essentialist position.

Anderson, James A. Turing's Test and the Perils of Psychohistory. *Soc Epistem*, 8(4), 327-332, O-D 94.

Anderson, Joel. Starke Wertungen, Wünsche zweiter Ordnung und intersubjektive Kritik: Überlegungen zum Begriff ethischer Autonomie. *Deut Z Phil*, 42(1), 97-119, 1994.

Anderson, John. Cosmology: An Empirical Science?. *Phil Sci (Tucson)*, 6, 47-75, 1995.

Anderson, R Lanier. Nietzsche's Will to Power as a Doctrine of the Unity of Science. *Stud Hist Phil Sci*, 25(5), 729-750, O 94.

Nietzsche's will to power is apparently an *a priori* metaphysical doctrine incompatible with his perspectivism (which insists that beliefs have at best provisional validity). This paper resolves the difficulty, reading the doctrine as a provisional interpretation which attempts to explain how results in various sciences cohere under a single conceptual system, based on a central concept of power. Particular scientific results are the empirical evidence against which any proposed unifying conceptual system must test itself. Nietzsche's appeals to the will to power in particular explanations are thus attempts to confirm his doctrine empirically by showing how it unifies scientific results.

Anderson, Robert. Recent Criticisms and Defenses of Pascal's Wager. *Int J Phil Relig*, 37(1), 45-56, F 95.

Recently Pascal's wager has attracted a few defenders, though its critics still remain more numerous. Recent defenses of the wager, however, only defend weaker versions of the argument or only defend it against weaker objections. A stronger version of the wager construes it as a decision problem under risk where probabilities can be very small, and a stronger defense of the wager must answer the many-gods objection and many-practices objection cause for the wager admit of a general solution. But I also raise a new objection which spells serious trouble even for the stronger version of the wager.

Anderson, Ronald. The Whewell-Faraday Exchange on the Application of the Concepts of Momentum and Inertia to Electromagnetic Phenomena. *Stud Hist Phil Sci*, 25(4), 577-594, Ag 94.

Anderson, Susan Leigh. Being Morally Responsible for an Action Versus Acting Responsibly or Irresponsibly. *J Phil Res*, 20, 451-462, 1995.

In her article "Asymmetrical Freedom," and more recently in her book *Freedom Within Reason*, Susan Wolf claims to have given us a new theory to account for when we can be held morally responsible for our actions. I believe that she has confused "being morally responsible for an action" with "acting responsibly or irresponsibly." I will argue that Wolf has given us a nice analysis of the latter concepts, but not of the former one as she intended. I do not believe that she is alone in not appreciating the distinction between these different concepts, but I will focus on her work as being a particularly good example of how confusing them can lead to an incorrect account of moral responsibility.

Anderson, Terry L and Leal, Donald R. Freedom and the Environment: Reply to Critics. *Crit Rev*, 8(3), 461-465, Sum 94.

Two fundamental principles are overlooked by critics. First, environmental quality is a good that is increasingly demanded as incomes rise, and incomes rise as a result of market forces. Second, environmental quality is more likely to be supplied in cases where well-specified property rights provide positive incentives for the human actors. Free market environmentalism, which focuses on voluntary action, is the only sure way of accounting for subject values, material or aesthetic. For the environmentalist who is not libertarian, it is a pragmatic way of improving resource stewardship. For the libertarian who is not an environmentalist, it maximizes freedom.

Anderson, Thomas C. The Extent of Kierkegaard's Skepticism. *Man World*, 27(3), 271-289, Jl 94.

Although Kierkegaard stresses the limitations of human knowledge, especially in *Postscript*, he does not set forth an epistemology that is as thoroughly skeptical about human cognitive powers as many maintain. Also, although much of the epistemology presented by Johannes Climacus, the "writer" of *Fragments* and *Postscript*, is Kierkegaard's own, his position differs from that of his pseudonymous author in significant respects. Finally, I show that some of Kierkegaard's (not Climacus') views, especially his belief that the ontological distance between beings can be bridged by passion, allows for a concrete knowledge of other beings and thereby moves Kierkegaard beyond even the mitigated skepticism that he espouses.

Anderson, Travis. Drawing upon Levinas to Sketch Out a Heterotopic Poetics of Art and Tragedy. *Res Phenomenol*, 24, 69-96, 1994.

Anderson, Tyson. Living Thinking. *J Indian Counc Phil Res*, 11(3), 1-23, My-Ag 94.

Rudolf Steiner's idea of "living thinking" reconciles the scientific, religious, and artistic aspects of life. Thinking normally operates out of a condition of *avidya* and bondage. As "imagination" in the broad sense, living thinking is the fundamental activity of our understanding. It liberates people from bondage, discloses the harmony between thinking as it operates in the humanities and in the sciences, and opens the way for cross-cultural understanding.

Anderson-Gold, Sharon. Kant's Ethical Anthropology and the Critical Foundation of the Philosophy of History. *Hist Phil Quart*, 11(4), 405-419, O 94.

Andersson, Gunnar. *Criticism and the History of Science*. Leiden, Brill, 1994.

The work deals with two key problems in the philosophy of science: the problem created by the fact that observation are theory-impregnated and, hence, test statements fallible, and the problem of how to test complex theoretical systems. To solve them the author shows how problematic test statements can be criticised and whole theoretical systems falsified. In this way he refines and develops the falsificationist conception of science and makes it possible to understand science and its history better.

André, Rae. Diversity Stress as Morality Stress. *J Bus Ethics*, 14(6), 489-496, Je 95.

In multicultural situations it is common for people to feel that their usual modes of coping are insufficient. They experience what is here called "diversity stress". Today diversity stress is widely experienced in part because key management assumptions involving moral judgments are changing. Understanding diversity stress as a type of morality stress suggests particular patterns of causation, and of productive and counterproductive reactions on the part of individuals and organizations.

Andreas-Grisebach, Manon. "Anschauung als Quelle von Erkenntnis: Erbe und Neubewertung" in *Das geistige Erbe Europas, Buhr, Manfred (ed)*, 387-399. Napoli, Vivarium, 1994.

Andréka, Hajnal and Maddux, Roger D. Representations for Small Relation Algebras. *Notre Dame J Form Log*, 35(4), 550-562, Fall 94.

There are eighteen isomorphism types of finite relation algebras with eight or fewer elements, and all of them are representable. We determine all the cardinalities of sets on which these algebras have representations.

Andrés Bonetti, José. El Idealismo Práctico de Marx: Una Lectura de las *Thesen über Feuerbach*. *Analogia*, 7(2), 115-124, 1993.

Andreu, Agustín. La Ontología de Lessing y las Metáforas de la Deshumanización. *Daimon Rev Filosof*, 8, 39-54, 1994.

This article exposes and analyzes G E Lessing's social ontology, especially as it appears in the *Dramatic Poem Nathan the Wise*. Human life and affairs are characterized by a polarity between the essential human condition and the various religious and national peculiarities. Religious and patriotic fanatisms deform true humanity and make those different paths lead against each other, while they should instead carry mankind to the same haven, that of the sense of humanness. Lessing addresses this problematique by using metaphors, many of them in the form of parables or allegories: *clothes and ministries* for civic virtues; *colors and perfumes* for pedagogical and local facilities; *coins* for the truth; *a building with numerous windows for illumination and doors for free entrance* for wise and tolerant government; etc. Lessing places in the forfront of his discussion the problems of intolerance between the three Abrahamic religions and their hearty and mutual enmity.

Andrews, Philip. The Vocation to Be a Philosopher. *Aquinas*, 37(2), 425-431, My-Ag 94.

Andrieu, Bernard. Eléments pour un matérialisme dynamique. *Rev Phil Fr*, 1, 71-82, Ja-Mr 95.

Andronico, Alberto. Note sul Rapporto Violenza/Diritto/Comunicazione. *Riv Int Filosof Diritto*, 71(4), 315-325, 1994.

Anechiarico, Frank and Kuo, Lenore. The Justified Scoundrel: The Structural Genesis of Corruption. *J Soc Phil*, 26(1), 147-161, Spr 95.

Angelelli, Ignacio. Saccheri's Postulate. *Vivarium*, 33(1), 98-111, My 95.

In modern terminology, Saccheri (ca. 1700) thought that the existence of appropriate interpretations of the predicate variables, as needed for instance to prove that the particular negative (Some A is not B) is not convertible, cannot be just taken for granted and must be "postulated". Even better, or "more noble" (*nobilior*) for Saccheri is to be able to proceed without such an existential postulate. In his attempt to establish syllogistic metatheorems in a postulate-free manner, he sometimes goes even further, applying the remarkable type of indirect argument that has been called "admirable consequence" or "law of Clavius".

Angelini, Pietro. Il Guardiano delle Soglia. *Stud Filosofici*, 215-228, 1991-92.

Angell, Richard B (trans) and De Finetti, Bruno. The Logic of Probability. *Phil Stud*, 77(1), 181-190, Ja 95.

This is a translation from the French of de Finetti's 1935 article "La Logique de la Probability". In defending his subjective theory of probability against frequency theories (specifically Reichenbach) de Finetti proposed a logic based on the betting model. Though he claimed not to depart from basic two-valued logic, for conditional probabilities he proposed three values, adding a null value. That a bet on a horse is won is true if and only if the race is run and the horse wins; it is false if the race is run and the horse loses; if the race is not run and in all other cases the statement is null—neither true nor false.

Anglés Cervelló, Misericordia. Una Cit de Algazel en la Filsofía del Sentido Commún de Llorens y Barba. *Rev Espan Filosof Med*, 0, 9-13, 1993.

Angus, Ian. "Inscription and Horizon: A Postmodern Civilizing Effect?" in *After Postmodernism, Simons, Herbert W (ed)*, 79-100. Newbury Park, Sage, 1994.

The postmodern turn in cultural studies seems to require denying the concept of critique in favor of a cultural relativism. By periodizing the historical development of cultural studies, the postmodern stream of discourse can be analyzed through the *medium* of communication that retrieves its critical edge.

Ankersmit, Frank R. "The Origins of Postmodernist Historiography" in *Historiography Between Modernism and Postmodernism, Topolski, Jerzy (ed)*, 87-117. Amsterdam, Rodopi, 1994.

It is argued that postmodernism in historical theory can best be seen as a radicalization of the nineteenth century historism. Nevertheless, this radicalization requires us to abandon the transcendentalist and objectivist assumptions that had remained unquestioned within the historical tradition. What is philosophically most interesting in the practice of history (as is correctly recognized in postmodernist historical theory), is its implicit critique of transcendentalism and of the metaphors suggested by transcendentalism in its effort to offer a foundation of (historical) knowledge. The consequences of an anti-transcendentalist position for both historical writing itself and the history of historical writing are investigated.

Annas, Julia. Argumentaciones éticas a partir de la naturaleza: Aristóteles y después. *Rev Latin de Filosof*, 20(2), 221-236, 1994.

Discussing Aristotle in detail as an example, I argue that ethical arguments from nature have two aspects: appeal to a normative ideal, opposed to a mere convention, and appel to what is customary or usual; it is only the latter which has conservative implications.

Annas, Julia. Prudence and Morality in Ancient and Modern Ethics. *Ethics*, 105(2), 241-257, Ja 95.

Annas, Julia. Reply to Cooper. *Phil Phenomenol Res*, 55(3), 599-610, S 95.

The reply shows that eudaimonist ethical theories need not essentially include claims of a metaphysical sort. Ancient ethical theories debate with one another (as in Cicero) without being trapped in their own larger theories; hence it is legitimate to reconstruct ancient ethical theories from ancient ethical debates.

Annas, Julia. Virtue as the Use of Other Goods. *Apeiron*, 26(3-4), 53-66, S-D 93.

The article examines an influential passage in Plato's *Euthydemus*, in which wisdom (identified with virtue) is said to be the only good thing, other things being good only insofar as put to correct use by wisdom. This passage, influential on stoic ethics, is rendered problematic by a later part of the dialogue which produces paradoxical conclusions from the idea of a wisdom which is supposed to benefit us and yet is supposed to be good in itself apart from its results.

Annas, Julia (trans) and Barnes, Jonathan (trans) and Sextus Empiricus. *Outlines of Scepticism*. New York, Cambridge Univ Pr, 1994.

Annas, Julia (& other eds) and Plato and Waterfield, Robin (trans). *Statesman*. New York, Cambridge Univ Pr, 1995.

Anscombe, G E M. Cambridge Philosophers II: Ludwig Wittgenstein. *Philosophy*, 70(273), 395-407, Jl 95.

Ansell-Pearson, Keith. Nietzsche's Post-Modern Identity: From *Epoch to Ethos*. *Hist Euro Ideas*, 20(1-3), 117-123, Ja 95.

Anspach, Mark R. La Communication entre Sperber et Bateson: de l'Environnement Cognitif à l'Écologie de l'Esprit. *Horiz Phil*, 2(2), 155-166, Spring 92.

Anstey, Peter. Thomas Reid and the Justification of Induction. *Hist Phil Quart*, 12(1), 77-93, Ja 95.

This paper outlines Thomas Reid's positive views on induction. It is argued that Reid's view of induction is very close to that which is widely held today, namely that inductive inferences are fallible, but rational. Further, Reid does offer a solution to the problem of induction. Inductive inferences are not justified by appeal to laws of nature as in some modern accounts. Rather they are justified by appeal to certain first principles of the mind. These principles are self-evident and mutually confirming. They include a 'principle of uniformity' and a principle regarding the trustworthiness of our rational faculties.

Anthony, Louise. "Conceptual Connection and the Observation/ Theory Distinction" in *Holism: A Consumer Update, Fodor, Jerry A (ed)*, 135-161. Amsterdam, Rodopi, 1993.

Fodor and LePore's reconstruction of the semantic holism debate in terms of "atomism" and "anatomism" is inadequate: it fails to highlight the important issue of how intentional contents are individuated, and excludes or obscures several possible positions on the metaphysics of content. One such position, "weak sociabilism" is important because it addresses concerns of Fodor and LePore's molecularist critics about conditions for possession of concepts, without abandoning atomism about content individuation. Properties like *democracy* may be "theoretical" in the following sense: only devices capable of inference can come to be selectively sensitive to such properties. Thus, such concepts cannot be punctate, although their contents are individuated, as atomism requires, independently of their conceptual connections.

Antognazza, Maria Rosa. Die Rolle der Trinitäts-und Mensch-werdungsdiskussionen für die Entstehung von Leibniz' Denken. *Stud Leibniz*, 26(1), 56-75, 1994.

Leibniz's repeated interventions in the Trinitarian polemics widespread throughout Europe in the seventeenth and eighteenth centuries cannot merely be read as scholastic exercises or concessions to the conventions of his time. On the contrary, they involved reflection on issues fundamental to Leibniz's philosophical doctrines: issues such as the relationship between faith and reason, the limitations of the human intellect and the various grades of human knowledge, and the significance of the 'analogia Trinitatis' reconsidered in light of the concept of harmony. This paper concentrates on the writings of the young Leibniz before his visit to Paris and aims to examine the role played by contemporary discussions concerning the Trinity and the Incarnation in the formation of Leibniz's thought.

Antoine, Philippe. De l'Itinéraire à la Note sur la Grèce: Évolution et Constantes de l'Attitude de Chateaubriand Face à la Grèce. *Diotima*, 22, 71-78, 1994.

Anton, John P. Plotinus and the Neoplatonic Conception of Dialectic. *J Neoplatonic Stud*, 1(1), 3-30, Fall 92.

Plato and Plotinus identified *dialektike* as the proper method of philosophy yet their respective conceptions of its practice and purpose served different axiological and ontological ends. Plotinus' position is discussed to identify the novel elements he introduced when redesigning Platonism. As a Neo-Platonist, he used dialectic as preparatory to the return to the One through the comprehension of the hierarchy of Being, of Nous as the realm of the Forms ensuring the intelligibility of the world, and of the nature of the soul. By making dialectic become the search for true Being he expanded the scope of traditional Greek philosophy.

Antonelli, Gian Aldo. A Revision-Theoretic Analysis of the Arithmetical Hierarchy. *Notre Dame J Form Log*, 35(2), 204-218, Spr 94.

This paper used Revision Rules as a general method to represent sets of increasing complexity in the arithmetical hierarchy. Revision Rules, as developed by Gupta and Belnap, provide a general theory of possibly circular definitions, whose primary application is in the theory of truth. The paper describes a procedure in which a recursive operator is "revised" transfinitely in such way as to establish a correspondence between the arithmetical complexity of the set being represented and the ordinal length of the corresponding revision process.

Antonelli, Gian Aldo. Non-Well-Founded Sets via Revision Rules. *J Phil Log*, 23(6), 633-679, D 94.

This paper uses Revision Rules to obtain general results in the model-theory of non-well-founded sets. Revision Rules, as developed by Gupta and Belnap, provide a general theory of possibly circular definitions, whose primary application is in the theory of truth. The paper applies Revision Rules as a general method to construct models of set theory containing non-well-founded sets that satisfy certain given constraints. On close scrutiny, this approach can be seen to be providing a congruence relation over the original universe of sets: this relation is then formally defined, and some of its formal properties are investigated.

Antonio, Robert J and Kellner, Douglas. "The Future of Social Theory and the Limits of Postmodern Critique" in *Postmodernism and Social Inquiry, Dickens, David R (ed)*, 127-152. New York, Guilford, 1994.

This essay addresses postmodern criticism of modern social theory, and especially its relevance for later nineteenth and early twentieth century theories with a sociological and historical thrust. We explore "critical" and "dogmatic" features of these approaches and argue that some of their most central critical themes anticipated postmodern criticism. We contend that postmodernists contribute to advancing a critique of enlightenment that began in modern theory, but, in their effort to shed the tradition's dogmatic elements, they also abandon its critical "social" resources stressing interdependence, cooperation, and solidarity. We conclude with a discussion of postmodernism and critical theory.

Antoniol, Lucie. Marc Neuberg's *Philosophie de l'action*. *Rev Int Phil*, 48(188), 255-259, 1994.

Antony, Michael V. Against Functionalist Theories of Consciousness. *Mind Lang*, 9(2), 105-123, Ju 94.

The paper contains an argument against functionalist theories of consciousness. The argument exploits an intuition to the effect that parts of an individual's brain that are not in use at a time t can have no bearing on whether that individual is conscious at t. The argument presented, it is then defended against various possible objections.

Aoki, Takao. Zeami's Concept of "Flower" in Noh Performance. *Aesthetics*, 3, 101-113, Mr 88.

Aoto, Takahito and Ono, Hiroakira. Non-Uniqueness of Normal Proofs for Minimal Formulas in Implication-Conjunction Fragment of BCK. *Bull Sec Log*, 23(3), 104-112, O 94.

Y Komori asked whether normal proofs of minimal formulas are unique in the implicational fragments of natural deduction systems for the intuitionistic logic and the logic BCK. It was already shown that the answer is positive for BCK, while it is negative for the intuitionistic logic. We show normal proofs for minimal formulas are not necessarily unique for the implication-conjunction fragment of BCK. This result contrasts sharply with the uniqueness of normal proofs of balanced formulas for the implication-conjunction fragment of the intuitionistic logic.

Aoyama, Hiroshi. The Strong Completeness of a System Based on Kleene's Strong Three-Valued Logic. *Notre Dame J Form Log*, 35(3), 355-368, Sum 94.

The present work, which was inspired by Kripke and McCarthy, is about a non-classical predicate logic system containing a truth predicate symbol. In this system, each sentence *A* is referred to not by a Gödel number but by its quotation name "*A*".

Apel, Karl Otto. "Die hermeneutische Dimension von Sozialwissenschaft und ihre normative Grundlage" in *Mythos Wertfreiheit?, Apel, Karl Otto (ed)*, 17-47. Frankfurt, Campus Verlag, 1994.

Apel, Karl Otto. "Transcendental Semiotic Hypothetical Metaphys. of Evolution" in *Peirce and Contemporary Thought: Philosophical Inquiries, Ketner, Kenneth Laine (ed)*, 366-397. New York, Fordham Univ Pr, 1995.

Apel, Karl Otto. How to Ground a Universalistic Ethics of Co-Responsibility for the Effects of Collective Actions and Activities?. *Philosophica*, 52(2), 9-29, 1993.

The paper is to expose the need for a novel concept of responsibility, namely: co-responsibility for the effects of collective actions or activities. After outlining the aporias of traditional ethics vis a vis the novel problems the paper tries to show that a transcendental-pragmatic foundation of discourse ethics can provide an answer to the novel problems.

Apel, Karl Otto. Illokutionäre Bedeutung und normative Gültigkeit: Die transzendentalpragmatische Begründung der uneingeschränkten kommunikativen Verständigung. *Protosoz*, 2, 2-15, Ja 92.

The paper tries first to show that P Strawson's and J Searle's proposal of explicating the illocutionary meaning of speech-acts (or corresponding explicit sentences) in terms of the *conditions of fulfillment or satisfaction* (with regard to the underlying intentional states of mind) is unsatisfactory. It provides no full understanding of the meaning of speech-acts, at least not of nonconstative acts, as, e.g., order, requests, demands, confessions, promises, etc.; for, through its quasiverficationist horizon, it provides no understanding of the illocutionary force in terms of the *conditions of accepting the validity-claims* that are connected with the performance of the act. Thus far the paper complies with Habermas' approach. There remains however an ambiguity with regard to the *good reasons for accepting* a speech-act. The paper argues that this suggestive contention cannot be proved, i.e., grounded by a descriptive analysis of the *normal* function of communicative actions in the life-world but only—indeed—by *transcendental pragmatic reflection on the normative conditions of argumentative discourse* which cannot be denied without committing a performative self-contradiction. (edited)

Apel, Karl Otto. The Rationality of Human Communication: On the Relationship Between Consensual, Strategic, and Systems Rationality. *Grad Fac Phil J*, 18(1), 1-25, 1995.

Apel, Karl Otto (ed) and Kettner, Matthias (ed). *Mythos Wertfreiheit?*. Frankfurt, Campus Verlag, 1994.

Apel, Karl Otto and Krois, John Michael (trans). *Charles S Peirce: From Pragmatism to Pragmaticism*. Atlantic Highlands, Humanities Pr, 1995.

Appelbaum, David. *The Stop*. Albany, SUNY Pr, 1995.

An exploration of a blinded, organically situated awareness, as it presented itself to thinkers of the Enlightenment. Specifically, a study, centered on Descartes's *Dioptrics*, of the equation of light with knowledge and sight with virtue, the aim of which is to show that the halting, discontinuous, effortful perception of the blind in fact enjoys an ontological priority. Reference is made to the rediscovery of linear perspective.

Aquila, Richard E. The Content of Cartesian Sensation and the Intermingling of Mind and Body. *Hist Phil Quart*, 12(2), 209-226, Ap 95.

The capacity of sensation to "teach" us concerning the "intermingling" of mind and body is explained in terms of its possession of an intermingled objective reality. As interpreted, the doctrine of objective reality says that the intentional content of a mental state is determined by the medium through which it occurs. Classically, this medium consists of the essence of a possible individual, or a combination of such essences. I suggest that Descartes broadened this to include modes, and combinations of modes, of essences as well. I argue that this is fully in the spirit of Descartes's basic ontology of essence and mode. A number of Descartes's claims about the content of sensation can then be explained on the supposition that sensations are mental states whose medium is a combination of mental and physical modes.

Aquilecchia, Giovanni. Tre Schede su Bruno e Oxford. *G Crit Filosof Ital*, 72(3), 376-393, S-D 93.

Aqvist, Lennart. Discrete Tense Logic with Beginning and Ending Time: An Infinite Hierarchy of Complete Axiomatic Systems. *Log Anal*, 34, 359-401, S-D 91.

The purpose of the paper is to give semantically sound and complete axiomatizations of all members in a certain infinite heirarchy of systems of *discrete* (linear) tense logic with *beginning* and *ending time*. Those systems differ from all current treatments of tense logic in having, in their primitive logical vocabulary, a special set of so-called *systematic frame constants*, which play a crucial role in our axiomatization. Those constants are foreshadowed by Prior's "world-state propositions" and by Gabbay's treatment of the problem of *irreflexivity* in tense logic.

Aragués, Juan Manuel. El Pensamiento Irracional Islámico: El Sufismo de Sohrawardi. *Rev Espan Filosof Med*, 0, 15-19, 1993.

Arana, Juan. El debate sobre la teología física en el siglo XVIII. *Pensamiento*, 198(50), 419-434, S-D 94.

La teologí física constituye al mismo tiempo un estilo apologético y un género literario que tuvo un enorme éxito a fines del siglo XVII y comienzos del siglo XVIII. Filósofos como Hume y Kant han considerado además que es la única forma de teología filosófica respetable. Todavía hoy en día mantiene su popularidad entre el público en general, aunque haya decaído el interés hacia ella entre los profesionales de la teología. El presente artículo contiene un breve examen de sus raíces y una discusión sobre su posible valor, apoyada en el pensamiento del que tal vez fue su crítico más agudo: P L M de Maupertuis.

Arana, Juan. La Razón y lo Sagrado: Respuesta a Jacinto Choza. *Themata*, 13, 231-247, 1995.

As a reply to a former paper by Professor Jacinto Choza, this one tries to establish whether reason is, or is not, a sufficient instrument to deal with such a topic as "the sacred" or "the holy". After discussing the very idea of reason, a formalistic conception of it will be asserted, and a vindication of its value for theological research will be finally advanced.

Aranda Torres, Cayetano. Dialéctica Hegeliana de la Ilustración. *Rev Filosof (Daimon)*, 7, 103-115, 1993.

This paper studies the function of the speculative notion of "Enlightenment" in Hegel's dialectics of the spirit, as it is exposed in the "Phenomenology of the Spirit". It concerns an episode of the abstract subjectivity of the spirit, which does not comprehend the part of the self as a result of its own doing, and which, consequently, remains locked in the world of representation, in a world where there is no dissonance or discontinuity between the things and their orderly reconstruction and empirical classification. On the other hand Hegel places knowledge outside the area of representation and sends it to the inside of a consciousness which speaks and works. The usefulness in terms of truth of the Enlightenment allows the "internalization" of knowledge as categorical thought by which subject and object are "equivalent".

Arato, Andrew. Constitution and Continuity in the Transitions: Part I. *Constellations*, 1(1), 92-112, Ap 94.

Arato, Andrew. Constitution and Continuity, Part II: The Hungarian Case. *Constellation*, 1(2), 306-325, O 94.

Araújo, Cícero. Some Reflections on Descartes and Machiavelli (in Portuguese). *Trans/Form/Acao*, 17, 113-132, 1994.

In this paper two of Descartes's letters on Machiavelli are examined. First, following the philosophers' own suggestions in the letters, Descartes's and Machiavelli's thoughts are contrasted, from which a distinction between morals and politics (in Descartes) arises. Next, the Cartesian morals is explained in order to point out the roots of this distinction.

Arce Carrascoso, José Luis. Subjectividad y Racionalidad Communicativa en J Habermas. *An Seminar Metaf*, 28, 59-84, 1994.

This study holds that Habermas's work, from *Knowledge and Interest* until *Postmetaphysical Thought*, effectively involves a notion of subjectivity in accordance with his critical project and his particular "linguistic turn". This notion is fundamental not only initially, with the idea of the "subject determined by transcendental interests", but also in subsequent works. A theory of rationality in the field of a linguistically mediated intersubjectivity still requires a transformed concept of subjectivity, which exempts us from "having to choose between Kant and Hegel" (*P.T.*)

Archard, David. Exploited Consent. *J Soc Phil*, 25(3), 92-101, Wint 94.

The article considers whether a professional's sexual relations with a client are wrong, even if the client's consent is not coerced, incapacitated or manipulated, the impartial conduct of professional affairs is not interfered with, and there are no damaged third parties. It argues that consent may be *exploited* if it is forthcoming only due to the occupancy of respective positions within an unequal relationship whose scope excludes such intimacy. The article explains the use of the term, 'exploited', and exposes those features of a professional relationship which make such exploitation both possible and unjustified.

Archard, David. For Our Own Good. *Austl J Phil*, 72(3), 283-293, S 94.

This article argues that individuals, short of a serious failure of will, misrecognize what is for their own good, and that others may do no wrong, indeed do right, in trying to promote what they can better recognize to be for the other's good. It criticizes the standard grounds for anti-paternalism, provides reasons for thinking individuals misrecognize their own good, rebuts claims which obscure the issues, and outlines limits to any justified paternalism. In conclusion, a suggestion is offered as to why I may be impossible to recognize that we ourselves might be the beneficiaries of the paternalism of others.

Archie, Lee. The No-Alternative Paradox and the Possibility of Metaphysics. *Cont Phil*, 17(1), 13-20, Ja-F 95.

A fundamental question of metaphysics, "Why is there something rather than nothing?," is shown to be subject to the no-alternative paradox. The no-alternative paradox is a philosophical argument that covertly excludes in its premises the possibility of refutation by either including in itself all possible purported counter-examples or by rendering proposed counter-examples meaningless. Indeed, the refutation of metaphysics cannot stand or fall on logical grounds.

Arduini, Maria Lodovica. 'Potere' e 'ragione' nel *Dialogus* di Pietro Alfonsi (Mosà Sefardi): Linee preliminari per una ipotesi interpretativa. *Riv Filosof Neo-Scolas*, 86(2), 219-286, Ap-Je 94.

Si stabiliscono le date biografiche di Alfonsi e del suo *Dialogus*. Si dimostra che fu Alfonso VI di Castigilia e Leòn, e non Alfonso I d'Aragona, il padrino del suo Battesimo (29 Giugno 1106). Il *Dialogus* si rivela *de facto* una sorta di discussione-confessione autobiografica: Alfonsi che si confronta con Mosè Sefardi, il se stesso di prima della conversione, ed appartiene al genere letterario, di antichissime origini, della *disputatio* tra cristiani ed ebrei per ragioni di fede. Dal confronto con il trattatello *De adventu Messiae* di Rabbi Samuel marochianus (che divenne cristiano a Toledo nel 1085), emerge una accentuata attitudine alla forza autoritativa della *ratio* nel *Dialogus*. Esso si colloca così in quella linea della *disputandi vis* che da Agostino, A Giovanni Scoto Eriugena, ad Anselmo di Aosta e Canterbury a Ruperto di Deutz, Abelardo, Adelardo di Bath, e tanti altri autori fino almeno a Cusano, ha rivelato di essere la colonna portante del sistema rzionale di pensiero del Medioevo Latino. (edited)

Arellano, Joaquín Ferrer. Fundamento ontológico de la persona: Immanencia y transcendencia. *Anu Filosof*, 27(3), 893-922, 1994.

Millán-Puelles justifies classic realism on the basis of the human person's dignity, analyzing subjectivity as one of conscience and volition. The author suggests that Millán-Puelles recognize in the relational openness, equally constitutive of the person, the formal reason of the subsistence of its immanent perfection.

Arena, Leonardo Vittorio. *Antologia del Buddhismo Ch'an*. Milan, Arnoldo Mondadori, 1994.

This book is a translation and an exhaustive commentary of six basic works of Ch'an school, from its beginning to golden age. In *Introduction* the theoretical bases of Ch'an are described from the viewpoint of comparative philosophy, and references are made to other Buddhist schools and philosophical Taoism. The same conviction permeates all the different masters' works: reality may only be seen through the mind. Thus, you must train the latter, so that all rational and emotional hindrances may be removed. Another kind of logic emerges, no more based upon dualistic ways, and Western thought can treasure it.

Arena, Leonardo Vittorio. *Il Nyaya Sutra di Gautama*. Rome, Ed Asram Vidya, 1994.

This book is a translation and commentary of the Nyaya Sutra, the principal treatise of Indian logic. Sanskrit text, and extensive introduction to the topics of Gautama's book, a bibliographical appendix, and a lexicon of all Sanskrit words are included. The author aims to show the peculiarities of a logic completely independent of the Western one. Through reasoning and debate, Indian philosophers wanted to reach enlightenment. Logic has an instrumental value for them, and it is not an end in itself. It is the means to establish a special, ethico-epistemological perspective, being completely new in the West.

Arena, Leonardo Vittorio. *Nietzsche e il Nonsense*. Milano, FrancoAngeli, 1994.

Nietzsche's whole work is analyzed, for the first time, on the basis of the category of nonsense, so that its antihermeneutical, antidogmatic facets may be underlined. It may be noticed that Nietzsche has overcome the perspective of "overturned Platonism," thence his thought cannot be conceived in the terms of Heideggerian interpretation; furthermore, Nietzsche's way of thinking is marked by an essential *impasse*, that cannot be solved by formal logic but may be practically experienced from a pragmatic point of view. The category of nonsense leads us to another kind of reality, which ordinary historiography cannot fathom.

Arenas Llopis, Luis. La Interpretación de Kant de Fernando Montero Moliner. *An Seminar Metaf*, 28, 331-336, 1994.

In Kant's philosophy, the possibility of science would find its limits between these two moments: just after the empirical stuff had lost its contingency (because of the space-time *a priori* and the pure concepts of understanding) and just before the ideas of reason (like the idea of mind) systematize the whole knowledge by going beyond of objective reality as a whole. The works of Fernando Montero Moliner about Kant's philosophy try to coordinate both views: In *El empirismo kantiano* Montero holds that the elements *a priori* in the *Kritik der reinen Vernunft* allow Kant to coordinate the presence of the ideal with the factual fulfillment of the ideal in the empirical stuff of experience. In *Mente y sentido interno en la Critica de la razón pura* the idea of mind (*Gemüt*) would be the key point of the architectonic systematization in Kant's first Critique.

Arends, J F M. Survival, War and Unity of the Polis in Plato's *Statesman*. *Polis*, 12(1-2), 154-187, 1993.

Argandoña, Antonio. Ethical Aspects of an Urban Catastrophe. *J Bus Ethics*, 14(7), 511-530, Jl 95.

As a consequence of the collapse of a building in Barcelona, in December 1990, it was discovered that a large number of dwellings, mainly in Barcelona but also in other towns of Catalonia, were affected by a structural defect known as "aluminosis", consisting of a deterioration of the reinforced concrete manufactured using aluminous cement, which considerably reduced its strength and that of the steel embedded in the concrete. This brought to light a series of economic, social, political and also moral problems, such as the use of the aluminous cement itself—a quality product but which requires careful handling—, the lack of regulation concerning the product and its use in construction, the poor state of repair of the buildings affected, the careless manner in which they had been built, the lag in technical knowledge, the financial situation of the people affected by the aluminosis, etc. This document provides a full account of the events and their historical, technical, economic and legal background, paying particular attention to the ethical problems created by the situation.

Argyropoulos, R. Agathon dans la Pensée de C M Coumas. *Philosophia (Athens)*, 23-24, 224-230, 1993-94.

C'est en 1814, que C M Coumas publie sa traduction en grec moderne de l'*Agathon* de Wieland. Cette démarche n'est pas sans signification pour son propre itinéraire intellectuel, ainsi que les dificultés qu'il rencontre lors de son séjour à Smyrne, en ce qui concerne la réalisation des idées pédagogiques des Lumières. En se référant au personnage d'Agathon, il adresse une critique aux Sophistes de l'Antiquité qui s'applique également aux 'sophistes' de son temps et se prononce contre leur subjectivisme. Coumas s'oriente vers une morale de l'art de vivre et s'éloigne de l'éthique kantienne qu'il propose dans son *Syntagma Philosophias* quelques années plus tard.

Argyropoulos, Roxane D. Concepts et Symboles du XVIIIe Siècle Européen: le Cas de la Grèce. *Philosophia (Athens)*, 23-24, 341-346, 1993-94.

The aim of this paper is the study of the correlation and the contrast between concepts such as light-darkness as well as nature-civilization. These concepts were predominent in the scholarship of the Enlightenment and provoqued many discussions between Greek scholars of this period. It is impossible to understand Greek intellectual history of that time without remembering the important part played by the idea of perfectibility borrowed from Condorcet. One can see and explain the relation between these concepts and the revival of Greek thought in eighteenth century as also with the struggle for the political independence of the Greek nation.

Arias, J Adolfo. La filosofía como hecho histórico y la prospectividad de la filisofía. *Rev Filosof (Spain)*, 4(6), 377-400, 1991.

Ariew, Roger. "G W Leibniz, Life and Works" in *The Cambridge Companion to Leibniz, Jolley, Nicholas (ed)*, 18-42. New York, Cambridge Univ Pr, 1994.

This is a biographical chapter to a book on Leibniz's philosophy, broadly interpreted to include his theology, philosophy of language, physics, psychology, as well as the more traditional areas of metaphysics, theory of knowledge, logic, and ethics and political philosophy. Thus, the chapter pays particular attention to some of Leibniz's more unusual interests, from his political interests, to his poetry, to his geology and history, and to his theology, including his thoughts about the philosophy and theology of the Chinese religion.

Ariew, Roger and Grene, Marjorie. Ideas, In and Before Descartes. *J Hist Ideas*, 56(1), 87-106, Ja 95.

We ask how the term "idea" was used in the seventeenth century before Descartes and consider in the light of this evidence both the possible sources for Descartes's usage and the true originality in his conception. Descartes appears to be drawing on a current literary usage, in which ideas are not just exemplars in God's mind, but actual psychological events in our minds, while at the same time refusing the identification of idea and image that the new literary sense suggests. So we ask, further, where did the current image-oriented use appear in the philosophical as against the literary works of the period, and on the other hand, how does the conceptual (nonimage) use Descartes was to devise relate to the philosophical use of "idea" in general? We suggest answers to such questions by referring to a number of early seventeenth century philosophical writers: Eustachius a Sancto Paulo, Jean Crassot, Charles François d'Abra de Raconis, and Rudolph Goclenius.

Armstrong, D M. Wittgenstein and Aesthetics. *Lit Aes*, 3, 108-115, Spr 93.

Armstrong, Mary Beth. Confidentiality: A Comparison Across the Professions of Medicine, Engineering and Accounting. *Prof Ethics*, 3(1), 71-88, Spr 94.

When should professionals keep client/patient confidences, and when does the threat of public harm outweigh the duty of confidentiality?.The paper discusses some philosophical considerations relating to professional confidentiality, and then traces the evolution of professional guidance concerning confidentiality in three professions: medicine, law, and accounting. The author concludes that changes in public expectations necessitate a complete rethinking of and reformulation of present confidentiality guidance by professional groups, from the ground floor up.

Armstrong, Robert W and Sweeney, Jill. Industry Type, Culture, Mode of Entry and Perceptions of International Marketing Ethics Problems: A Cross-Cultural Comparison. *J Bus Ethics*, 13(10), 775-785, O 94.

The authors investigate the differences in ethical perceptions of Australian and Hong Kong international managers. Ethical perceptions are measured with respect to different industry types, cultures and modes of entry into international markets. Mode of entry refers to how firms select to enter foreign markets. Modes of entry include: exporting (indirect or direct), contractual methods (licensing and franchising) and via direct foreign investment (joint ventures and wholly-owned subsidiaries). It was determined that culture and mode of entry have a significant effect on the perception of ethical problems.

Armstrong Jr, Benjamin F. Hume's Actual Argument Against Belief in Miracles. *Hist Phil Quart*, 12(1), 65-76, Ja 95.

Arnaldez, Roger and Schlabach, Gerald W (& other trans). *Three Messengers for One God*. Notre Dame, Univ Notre Dame Pr, 1994.

Roger Arnaldez's *Three Messengers for One God* summarizes a lifetime of scholarship into matter Islamic to offer a comparative approach to the three religions which espouse an active revelation of God. His doctoral studies included a second dissertation on Philo, so that he is better qualified than most Islamicists to incorporate Jewish thought as well. Without seeking a common denominator, he rather emphasizes differences, finding in the respective mystical traditions a kind of rapprochement which is never reductive yet can be seen to be mutually illuminating for each tradition's search for the face of God.

Arnason, Vilhjalmur. Towards Authentic Conversations: Authenticity in the Patient-Professional Relationship. *Theor Med*, 15(3), 227-242, S 94.

The purpose of this paper is to evaluate the significance of the existential notion of authenticity for medical ethics. This is done by analyzing authenticity and examining its implications for the patient-professional relationship and for ethical decision-making in medical situations. It is argued that while authenticity implies important demand for individual responsibility, which has therapeutic significance, it perpetuates ideas which are antithetical both to authentic interaction between patients and professionals and to fruitful deliberation of moral dilemmas. In order to counteract those consequences, an alternative idea of authenticity is introduced. According to this idea, authenticity is not regarded primarily as individual sovereignty, but as an ability to participate in a dialogue in which the subjectivity of both partners is respected. Such practice, based on mutual trust and responsibility, would enhance common decision-making and overcome the alienation between patients and professionals.

Arnau, Pablo and Arregui, Jorge V. Shaftesbury: Father or Critic of Modern Aesthetics?. *Brit J Aes*, 34(4), 350-362, O 94.

Contrary to the view that sees Shaftesbury as the father of modern aesthetics, the paper claims that Shaftesbury is the first great critic of modernity remembering that his claims were directed against the first characteristically modern views and stressing his criticism of the modern reduction of aesthetics to a decorative accessory in a mechanical world. His assertion of the role of aesthetics' in man's life and his demonstration of the cognitive value of the perception of beauty entails a break early modern thought in its typical identification of positive science, truth and the objective on the one hand, and the aesthetic, the apparent and the subjective on the other.

Arndt, Andreas. "Romantik der Arbeit" Perspektiven des frühromantischen Arbeitsbegriffs. *Das Argument*, 207, 883-896, N-D 94.

The concept of the "Romanticism of Work" allows another side of the philosophy of the early Romantics to be given its due alongside the "Romanticism of Alienation". Consideration of the objective conditions of the labor process transforms liberation *through work* into liberation *from work*, in the sense of an "economy of time". In an "empire of freedom", nonalienated, moral-political socialization can succeed on the basis of work, of the "empire of necessity". This conception, developed with reference to Novalis, Schleiermacher, and Friedrich Schlegel, has parallels in Marx as well as contemporary parallels which go beyond Marx.

Arneil, Barbara. Trade, Plantations, and Property: John Locke and the Economic Defense of Colonialism. *J Hist Ideas*, 55(4), 591-609, O 94.

Arneson, Richard J. "Autonomy and Preference Formation" in *In Harm's Way, Coleman, Jules L (ed)*, 42-75. New York, Cambridge Univ Pr, 1994.

Arnold, Johannes. Zur Geschichtlichkeit der Rede von Gott: Einflüsse zeitgenössischer Königsideologie auf die Trinitätslehre Wilhelms von Auxerre. *Theol Phil*, 69(3), 342-372, 1994.

In his "Summa Aurea", William of Auxerre (+1231) illustrates the Trinity by comparisons with profane, specifically French kingship. They reflect the final acceptance of hereditary monarchy in France since about 1200 and allow the various versions of the Summa to be dated more precisely. In De Trinitate Richard of St Victor seems to refer to the coregency of the King's eldest son—a practice followed until 1179. In England, the simultaneous regency of Henry II and his son Henry (+1183) and of the divine persons appear to be paralleled in the initials to Psalm 109 in the Winchester Bible.

Arnold, Richard. Eric Hoffer, Philosopher for the People. *Free Inq*, 15(1), 26-27, Wint 94-95.

Arnold, Robert M and Ubel, Peter A. The Euthanasia Debate and Empirical Evidence: Separating Burdens to Others from One's Own Quality of Life. *J Clin Ethics*, 5(2), 155-158, Sum 94.

Arnopoulos, Paris. Cosmopolitan Universalism: Prolegomena to a Future Ideology. *Dialogue Hum*, 4(2-3), 197-214, 1994.

This paper looks into the recent trends leading towards a renewed world order and proposes some distinct ways to promote it. The contemporary global *problematique* is symptomatic of a revolutionary period of transition from the modern to the post-modern era. During this time of upheaval and instability, many outdated structures are being dismantled and various innovative systems are being attempted. Only when the winners have been determined and the major choices made, will the new social system settle down into a relative peace once again.

Arntzen, Sven. Kant's Denial of Absolute Sovereignty. *Pac Phil Quart*, 76(1), 1-16, Mr 95.

Although Kant denies that the subjects in civil society can have coercive rights against the sovereign, he does not thereby embrace a doctrine of absolute sovereignty. His statements concerning what the state cannot do with respect to the subjects indicate that he regards sovereignty as limited according to the principle of humanity as an end in itself. This principle expresses a conceptual limitation of sovereignty, since the concept of a sovereign implies an obligation on the part of the subject, and being subject to obligation requires that one be regarded as endowed with humanity.

Arntzenius, Frank. A Heuristic for Conceptual Change. *Phil Sci*, 62(3), 357-369, S 95.

One of our more fundamental beliefs is that causal chains are continuous in time: we believe that every influence from the past upon the future runs through the present. I argue that this tenet, given certain data, can force conceptual changes upon us. I attempt to formulate a heuristic for discovery, based as explicitly as possible upon this tenet, and illustrate it by means of several examples, one of which is Mendel's discovery of genes.

Arntzenius, Frank. Indeterminism and the Direction of Time. *Topoi*, 14(1), 67-81, Mr 95.

Many phenomena in the world display a striking time-asymmetry: the forwards transition frequencies are approximately invariant while the backwards ones are not. I argue in this paper that theories of such phenomena will entail that time has a direction, and that quantum mechanics in particular entails that the future is objectively different from the past.

Arntzenius, Frank. Relativistic Hidden Variable Theories?. *Erkenntnis*, 41(2), 207-231, S 94.

I show that for any quantum dynamics and any choice of observables as hidden variables an adequate hidden variable theory always exists. I argue that hidden variable theories have no more problems in reconciling nonlocality with relativity than no-hidden-variable theories.

Aronson, Jerrold L and Harré, Rom and Way, Eileen Cornell. *Realism Rescued: How Scientific Progress Is Possible*. Peru, Open Court, 1995.

A full-blown version of convergent realism is defined and defended by replacing the logicist technique for analyzing scientific theories with one found in knowledge representation, the dynamic type hierarchy. The authors use these hierarchies to provide an analysis of models that displays their indispensable role in science. They go on to use this analysis to develop a semantics for verisimilitude, truth and modalities. An inductive justification for convergent realism is then presented, one which, the authors contend, is not open to the objections that anti-realists have made against the inference to the best explanation defense.

Aronson, Ronald. *After Marxism*. New York, Guilford, 1994.

Marxism is over as a movement of societal transformation. Whatever its continuing theoretical uses it has now decisively lost its practice. In exploring when, how, and why this happened, it, Marxism is shown to be a determinate historical outlook, arising at a specific moment and now decisively bypassed by events and trends. Insisting that radical social change remains necessary, the book explores how any movement for radical change will have to understand itself after Marxism—capable of eschatological change, irreducibly plural, lacking any commanding theoretical outlook, rooted in morality, and struggling within a time span of hundreds of years.

Arp, Halton. "Galaxy Creation in a Non-Big-Bang Universe" in *Philosophy, Mathematics and Modern Physics, Rudolph, Enno (ed)*, 132-143. New York, Springer-Verlag, 1994.

Observational evidence against the Big Bang is reviewed. It is shown that evidence for continuing bursts of galaxy creation is one of the most direct disproofs of the instantaneous creation of the whole universe. Empirically younger galaxies and quasars are found to have high intrinsic (nonvelocity) redshifts which contradict the assumption of an expanding universe. There are now more general solutions of the Einstein field equations which require creation of high redshift matter from a zero mass state in a flat space-time, non expanding universe.

Arp, Kristana. "Beauvoir's Concept of Bodily Alienation" in *Feminist Interpretations of Simone de Beauvoir, Simons, Margaret A (ed)*, 161-177. University Park, Penn St Univ Pr, 1995.

Arp, Kristana. Husserl and Putnam on the Human Sciences versus the Natural Sciences. *S J Phil*, 32(4), 355-366, Wint 94.

Arras, John (& others). The Technological Tether: An Introduction to Ethical and Social Issues in High-Tech Home Care. *Hastings Center Rep*, 24(5), Supp 1-28, S-O 94.

Arras, John D and Blustein, Jeffrey. Reproductive Responsibility and Long-Acting Contraceptives. *Hastings Center Rep*, 25(1), S27-S29, Jan-Feb 95.

Arregui, Jorge V. La Teleología de la Belleza en Shaftesbury y Hutcheson. *Themata*, 13, 11-35, 1995.

Teleology of Beauty according Shaftesbury and Hutcheson. 1) Teleological Conception of Nature according Shaftesbury. 2) Realism of the Teleology of Shaftesbury. 3) Conception of Nature according F Hutcheson. 4) Teleology of Beauty according Shaftesbury and Hutcheson.

Arregui, Jorge V and Arnau, Pablo. Shaftesbury: Father or Critic of Modern Aesthetics?. *Brit J Aes*, 34(4), 350-362, O 94.

Contrary to the view that sees Shaftesbury as the father of modern aesthetics, the paper claims that Shaftesbury is the first great critic of modernity remembering that his claims were directed against the first characteristically modern views and stressing his criticism of the modern reduction of aesthetics to a decorative accessory in a mechanical world. His assertion of the role of aesthetics' in man's life and his demonstration of the cognitive value of the perception of beauty entails a break early modern thought in its typical identification of positive science, truth and the objective on the one hand, and the aesthetic, the apparent and the subjective on the other.

Arreguín, Héctor Zagal. Argumentación y Método en la Etica Eudemia. *Topicos*, 4(7), 43-65, 1994.

Here I try to show the role of *éndoxa* and *aporiai* in *Eudemian Ethics* and in the rest of Aristotelian ethics as practical knowledge. *To know ethics* is *to be ethical*. Therefore, rhetorical argumentation (which implies action, and whose main strategies are mentioned above) has a relevant place in ethical argumentation.

Arrigo, Bruce A. "Rethinking the Language of Law, Justice, and Community: Postmodern Feminist Jurisprudence" in *Radical Philosophy of Law, Caudill, David S (ed)*, 88-107. Atlantic Highlands, Humanities Pr, 1995.

Arsenault, Joseph and Brinkley, Tony. Dialectic at a Standstill. *Int Stud Phil*, 27(1), 1-20, 1995.

Artëmov, Sergei and Montagna, Franco. Our First-Order Theories with Provability Operator. *J Sym Log*, 59(4), 1139-1153, D 94.

In this paper the modal operator "X is provable in Peano Arithmetic" is incorporated into first-order theories. A provability extension of a theory is defined. Presburger Arithmetic of addition, Skolem Arithmetic of multiplication, and some first order theories of partial consistency statements are shown to remain decidable after natural provability extensions. It is also shown that natural provability extensions of a decidable theory may be undecidable.

Artigas, Mariano and Price, Colin. Evolution: Science and Metaphysics—A Commentary on Michel Delsol's Article. *Laval Theol Phil*, 50(3), 595-600, O 94.

Neo-Darwinism does appear like an island between on the one hand physics and on the other metaphysics. The purpose of this article is to help fill out the anomalies from both sides.

Artson, Bradley Shavit. The Unnatural Steward: Humanity's Relationship to Earth. *Nat Forum*, 75(1), 10-12,19, Wint 95.

Asanuma, Keiji. Littérature et Imprimerie. *Aesthetics*, 3, 75-90, Mr 88.

The purpose of this article is to elucidate the aesthetic significance of the printing by comparing three genres of literature: the oral, the written and the printed. The printing changed the attitude of *reader* by disseminating books into vast space and also caused the birth of modern *author* and *critic*. It made impossible to identify the origin of the enunciation and brought an essential change to the narrative structure of literary *work*. Thus a new relation among four elements of literary process was formed: a new literary institution.

Aschenberg, Reinhold. "On the Theoretical Form of Hegel's Aesthetics" in *Hegel Reconsidered, Engelhardt Jr, H Tristram (ed)*, 79-101. Dordrecht, Kluwer, 1994.

Aschoff, Frank. Rückkehr zur Metaphysik? Reinholds Abkehr von der Philosophie Fichtes. *Fichte-Studien*, 6, 345-354, 1994.

Ash, C J. On Countable Fractions from an Elementary Class. *J Sym Log*, 59(4), 1410-1413, D 94.

This paper considers the class of countable structures obtained as relativized reducts of members of an elementary class.

Ash, C J and Knight, J F. Mixed Systems. *J Sym Log*, 59(4), 1383-1399, D 94.

This paper gives a metatheorem designed to handle priority constructions with infinitely many requirements at different levels. The new metatheorem extends results of Ash in which either all of the requirements were at one (top) level, or, in the special case where the top level was a limit ordinal, there was one requirement at each level in a recursive sequence converging to the top.

Ash, C J and Knight, J F. Ramified Systems. *Annals Pure Applied Log*, 70(3), 205-221, D 94.

This paper extends a metatheorem of Ash for nested priority constructions (see Ash, C J, "Recursive labelling systems and stability of recursive structures in hyperarithmetical degrees," *Trans of the Amer Math Soc*, 1986, pp 497-514; corrections, ib, 1988, p 851). The new result involves enumerating sets at various levels, while the original result involved enumerating a set at the recursive level only. The paper includes sample problems where the new metatheorem yields results, and the original metatheorem, and other variants, do not apply.

Ashcraft, Richard. "Locke's Political Philosophy" in *The Cambridge Companion to Locke, Chappell, Vere (ed)*, 226-251. New York, Cambridge Univ Pr, 1994.

Ashcraft, Richard. Exclusive and Inclusive Theories of Property Rights: Rejoinder to Horne. *Crit Rev*, 8(3), 435-440, Sum 94.

Contrary to Thomas Horne's propensity to consider arguments concerning property rights and poverty as exclusive and self-contained topics within the political discourse of liberalism, they should be seen as part of the defense of democratic and market institutions that is central to the historical development of liberalism. The problems arising from the relationship of property rights to poverty, therefore, need to be included in any assessment of the success or failure of the institutions of a democratic market society to realize their objectives.

Ashdown, Lance. Absolute Safety. *Phil Invest*, 18(2), 162-172, Ap 95.

Peter Winch and D Z Phillips construe statements of the form 'I am absolutely safe' as predictions. Both agree that predictions of this sort are problematic because they show a blindness on the part of the speaker to the possible loss of moral character. Because Socrates, for example, may well lose his moral spirit, he is not entitled to claim absolute safety for himself. I try to show that 'I am absolutely safe', when spoken in the appropriate context, expresses an absolute willingness to face life's contingencies which does not entail any sort of prediction.

Asher, Nicholas and Morreau, Michael. "What Some Generic Sentences Mean" in *The Generic Book, Carlson, Gregory N (ed)*, 300-338. Chicago, Univ of Chicago Pr, 1995.

Ashley, David. "Postmodernism and Antifoundationalism" in *Postmodernism and Social Inquiry, Dickens, David R (ed)*, 53-75. New York, Guilford, 1994.

Ashley, J Matthew (trans) and Metz, Johann Baptist. Suffering unto God. *Crit Inquiry*, 20(4), 611-622, Sum 94.

Ashmore, Malcolm and Edwards, Derek and Potter, Jonathan. Death and Furniture: The Rhetoric, Politics, and Theology of Bottom Line Arguments against Relativism. *Hist Human Sci*, 8(2), 25-49, My 95.

Ashworth, E J. Late Scholastic Philosophy: Introduction. *Vivarium*, 33(1), 1-8, My 95.

Late scholastic philosophy coexisted with humanism, Renaissance philosophy, and early modern philosophy from the late fifteenth to the late seventeenth century. It was characterized by its relation to institutions of higher learning, its method of presentation, its focus on Aristotle, and its explicit concern with problems stemming from the work of medieval philosophers.

Ashworth, E J. Suárez on the Analogy of Being: Some Historical Background. *Vivarium*, 33(1), 50-75, My 95.

I argue that Suàrez is best read as part of a tradition which predates Cajetan with respect to the classification of types of analogy, and which to some extent predates Scotus in its insistence on a concept of being which is both one and analogical. I draw on three fifteenth century philosophers and theologians, Capreolus, Dominic of Flanders, and Soncinas, and one sixteenth century writer, Domingo de Soto.

Asma, Stephen T. Metaphors of Race: Theoretical Presuppositions Behind Racism. *Amer Phil Quart*, 32(1), 13-29, Ja 95.

This paper seeks to explore the important role of deep metaphors in the shaping of racist discourse. Two opposing metaphors of causal agency (the internal and external metaphors) have provided foundations for racial theory, and the article explores the manner in which these metaphors can potentiate specific prejudices. The metaphors of agency that arise in modern philosophy's debate between rationalism and empiricism are traced through the nineteenth century and into the racially charged genocidal theories of the twentieth century. The article focuses specifically upon the transition from the internalism of a Cartesian concept of agency, which some scholars have considered to be inherently less racist than empiricism, to a pernicious form of racism that eventually evolved out of that internal metaphor. As might be expected, Asma frequently crosses the boundaries of biology and philosophy throughout the article.

Asmis, Elizabeth. Epicurean Poetics. *Proc Boston Colloq Anc Phil*, 7, 63-93, 1991.

This paper traces the Epicurean views of poetry from Epicurus to Lucretius. It is argued that Epicurus rejected poetry as a form of education, but welcomed it as entertainment. Some of his followers tried to reconcile their devotion to poetry with Epicurus' position by arguing that although poetry cannot provide any moral training in itself, philosophical study allows a person to cancel out the harm that poetry would otherwise do and to extract some moral lessons. Lucretius stands apart from all other Epicureans in using poetry as a means of imparting philosophical truths.

Aspe A, Virginia. El Concepto de Mimesis en la Filosofia del Arte de Platon. *Topicos*, 1(1), 175-182, 1991.

This article gives a general introduction to the different characteristics of art activity of the countries where freedom is defended and on the countries that freedom in art is denied. It makes the analogy between these concepts of art and Plato's theory of art that conceives it as part of theoretical knowledge whereas Aristotle puts it as coming from practical knowledge, that means from liberty.

Assamoi, Bertin Y. Information et Référence. *Philosopher*, 15, 53-67, 1994.

Atkins, Peter. Science as Truth. *Hist Human Sci*, 8(2), 97-102, My 95.

The paper argues that conventional science is the only way to truth about the whole range of existence. It argues that science is able to answer the deep questions of existence, and that objections to this view are largely based on fear and superstition. Issue is taken with those who assert that the knowledge emerging from scientific investigations are manifestations of social dimensions.

Atterton, Peter. Power's Blind Struggle for Existence: Foucault, Genealogy and Darwinism. *Hist Human Sci*, 7(4), 1-20, N 94.

Attfield, Robin. "Ethics and the Environment: The Global Perspective" in *Introducing Applied Ethics, Almond, Brenda (ed)*, 331-342. Cambridge, Blackwell, 1995.

This essay surveys environmental ethics, which seeks to remedy deficiencies in traditional philosophy's treatment of the natural world. Thus Arne Naess proposes a global, long-term environmental ethic. However, with Richard Sylvan, I find Naess's biotic egalitarianism inadequate as an action-guide. Against Tom Regan's animal-rights stance, I argue for an Equal-Interests Principle. On the issue of wilderness and human intervention, I argue for a blend of preservation and restoration. On the issues of whether an environmental ethic can give practical environmental guidance, or provide for sustainability, I conclude that a comprehensive ethic can discharge both these tasks.

Attfield, Robin. "Rehabilitating Nature and Making Nature Habitable" in *Philosophy and the Natural Environment, Attfield, Robin (ed)*, 45-57. New York, Cambridge Univ Pr, 1994.

This chapter sifts claims about rehabilitating nature and wilderness. Katz's view that restorations are invariably artifacts is rejected. A restored area could have equal value to its wild predecessor; likewise nature can retain its value when transplanted into culture. Discussing the Callicott/Rolston debate, I conclude (with Rolston) that wilderness cannot be managed, and that valuations are capable of objectivity; but (with Callicott) that sustainable development need not be anthropocentric. The obligation to foster sustainable development is stronger than to enhance the value of natural areas. Humanity has the role of making nature habitable, besides that of rehabilitating it.

Attfield, Robin. John Laird and *The Idea of Value*. *J Value Inq*, 29(1), 103-114, Mr 95.

In this "classics revisited" essay on John Laird's *Ideas of Value*, three central theories of value presented by Laird are examined: "natural election" (whatever matters to anything is of (dis)value to that thing); "the appreciative theory" (value is generated by conscious appreciation); and "the timological theory" (value consists in being objectively valuable). Laird's concept of natural election is argued to conflate diverse concepts incoherently. His suspicion of the appreciative theory is well grounded, despite his last-minute defence that it answers to the distinct concept of value as valuedness. His historical and analytical defence of the timological theory deserves continuing recognition.

Attfield, Robin (ed) and Belsey, Andrew (ed). *Philosophy and the Natural Environment*. New York, Cambridge Univ Pr, 1994.

This proceedings volume of the 1993 Royal Institute of Philosophy Conference aims to further the debate among philosophers and environmentalists about the concepts of nature, value, bioethics and environmental and global justice, and their contemporary application. It helps rectify the comparative neglect by philosophers of the concepts of nature and of the environment, and also contributes to ethics, metaphysics, and social and political philosophy. Contributors include Dale Jamieson, Frederick Ferré, Peter List, Homes Rolston (USA), Robert Elliot (Australia), Stephen Clark, Roger Crisp, Nigel Dower, Tim Hayward, Alan Holland, Keekok Lee, Mary Midgley, Ruth McNally and Peter Wheale, plus the editors (UK).

Attridge, Harold W. Gnostic Platonism. *Proc Boston Colloq Anc Phil*, 7, 1-29, 1991.

Christian Gnostics of the second and third centuries provide evidence of several types of appropriation of Platonic categories. The most complex and thoughtful appropriation is to be found in the remains of the second-century teacher Valentinus, particularly in the *Gospel of Truth*, in which Platonic epistemology is used to develop a Christian doctrine of revelation. In the third century a fragmentary text, the *Allogenes*, provides evidence of a late phase of "Sethian" Gnosticism, which uses ontological distinctions common in later neo-Platonism in order to explain its understanding of the relationship of the transcendent Godhead to the phenomenal world.

Aubrey, Jean-Christian. La Tolérance: Pour une Démocratie plus Humanisante. *Philosopher*, 15, 107-115, 1994.

Audard, Catherine. Consensus and Democracy: An Anglo-French Conference on John Rawls. *Ratio Juris*, 7(3), 267-271, D 94.

Audard, Catherine. The Idea of "Free Public Reason". *Ratio Juris*, 8(1), 15-29, Mr 95.

In this paper the nature and the role of Rawls's idea of a "free public reason" are examined with an emphasis on the divide between the private and the public spheres, a divide which is the hallmark of a liberal democracy. Criticisms from both the so-called Continental tradition and the Communitarian opponents to liberalism insist on the ineffectiveness of such a conception, on its inability to establish a political consensus on democracy. But it would be a mistake to see a contractarian theory of justice, such as Rawls's justice as fairness, as grounding the social contract in a public use of reason. Such a contract would indeed be susceptible to endless conflicts and renegotiations and would never achieve consensus. Therefore, a distinction must be made between the *values of justice* that are present in and through the "original" contractual positions and the *values of public reason* that regulate the public sphere and guarantee its stability.

Audi, Robert. Acting From Virtue. *Mind*, 104(415), 449-471, Jl 95.

Audi, Robert. Dispositional Beliefs and Dispositions to Believe. *Nous*, 28(4), 419-434, D 94.

Audi, Robert. Perceptual Experience, Doxastic Practice, and the Rationality of Religious Commitment. *J Phil Res*, 20, 1-18, 1995.

This paper is a constructive critical study of William P Alston's *Perceiving God*. It explores his account of perception of God, his doxastic practice epistemology, and his overall integration of faith and reason. In dealing with the first, it distinguishes some possible cases of theistic perception that have not generally been sorted out in the literature. In examining doxastic practices, it explores both the sense in which it is rational to engage in them and the epistemic status of beliefs formed through them. Concerning the integration between faith and reason, it proposes a conception of faith in which, contrary to the prevailing tradition, belief is not central; distinguishes rationality from justification; and argues that the rationality of faith so conceived need not meet the same standard appropriate to the justification, or even the rationality, of the corresponding religious beliefs.

Audi, Robert (ed). *The Cambridge Dictionary of Philosophy*. New York, Cambridge Univ Pr, 1995.

Auerochs, Bernd. Gadamer über Tradition. *Z Phil Forsch*, 49(2), 294-311, Ap-Je 95.

The paper tries to prove that Gadamer's concept of tradition derives from the mega-subjects of German idealism such as "weltgeist" or "history". But tradition has different forms in different symbolic forms. The prototype of Gadamer's concept of tradition can be found in religious tradition where the believer is necessarily inferior to the holy texts. On the other side, philosophy and science are characterized by the effort to start anew; everyone may take part in a debate which leaves origins behind. Therefore, the "Geisteswissenschaften" do not unconsciously continue tradition, their task is the critical reflection on culture.

Augello, Giuseppe. Forme e metafore dell'intuizione in Friedrich Hölderlin. *G Metaf*, 16(1-2), 199-210, Ja-Ag 94.

Auletta, Gennaro. Il Rapporto tra i Concetti di *Possibile* ed *Esistente* nel Quadro della Teoria Leibniziana dei Mondi Possibili. *Filosofia*, 45(3), 275-289, S-D 94.

Aune, James Arnt. *Rhetoric and Marxism*. Boulder, Westview Pr, 1994.

This book analyzes the relationship between Marxism and the rhetorical tradition. It finds that the classical texts of Marx and Engels wavered incoherently between positivist and romantic views of language and communication—views made possible by decline of the rhetorical tradition as a cultural force. It examines the work of Herbert Marcuse, Raymond Williams, and Jurgen Habermas as attempts to resolve the incoherence of classical Marxism. The book concludes by proposing a rhetoricized Marxism, in which the study of the rhetorical history of the labor movement becomes a central project.

Auxier, Randall E. Is There Room for God in Education?. *Pub Affairs Quart*, 9(1), 1-13, Ja 95.

This paper addresses the issue of whether there is any culturally sensitive, noncoercive way that belief in God can inform the standards and pedagogical practices of the public school teacher. The problem is approached through a comparison of Dewey and Niebuhr on the question of what "God" is, and how this affects practical values. It is argued that Dewey and Niebuhr have similar conceptions of God, and that both place great emphasis upon the value on inclusivity on the basis of their understanding of God. It is shown that Niebuhr's theism and

Dewey's religious humanism can be cashed out in very similar concrete methods for teaching. It is concluded that so long as inclusivity is the central value one derives from one's belief in God, there is no difficulty asserting that belief in God can play a formal role in constituting standards for public moral education—standards which are both culturally sensitive and non-coercive.

Auxier, Randy. "The Decline of Evolutionary Naturalism in Later Pragmatism" in *Pragmatism: From Progressivism to Postmodernism, Hollinger, Robert (ed)*, 180-207. Westport, Praeger, 1995.

This essay marks out a distinction between middle pragmatism (represented by Dewey and Mead), later pragmatism (represented by C I Lewis and Quine), and neo-pragmatism (represented by Rorty). Various tensions within middle pragmatism (as they diverged) gave rise to widely variant viewpoints in later pragmatism. It is argued that later pragmatism and neo-pragmatism are not genuine forms of evolutionary naturalism (being neither fully evolutionary nor fully naturalistic), and that genuine evolutionary thinking is all but dead in contemporary American philosophy. Recommendations are made for how to revive evolutionary naturalism.

Avery, Jon (ed) and Dodson, Kevin E (ed). *Ways of Knowing: Selected Readings (Second Edition)*. Dubuque, Kendall/Hunt, 1994.

Avila Crespo, Remedios. La Ilustración y el problema del padaso: La reflexión de Nietzsche en torno a la memoria y el olvido. *Rev Filosof (Daimon)*, 7, 117-132, 1993.

In this paper I want to qualify Nietzsche's place within the framework of the Enlightenment tradition taking into account two significant clues to it: the meaning to Zarathustra and Nietzsche's attitude to past and memory. A careful consideration of them will bring me to emphasize that Nietzsche's philosophical thought can be seen both as a prolongation of the Enlightenment and, at the same time, as a specific reply to its main contentions.

Avila del Palacio, Alfonso. Por qué aún Filosofía de las Matemáticas?. *Analogia*, 8(2), 97-116, 1994.

The purpose of this paper is to understand the impact of the foundations crisis in philosophy of mathematics. For this purpose, the author believes that it is necessary to distinguish between mathematical perspective and philosophical perspective. And he concludes that in face at same question, the mathematicians look for different answers, than the philosophers do. In this way, one can see the foundations crisis like problem only in the meta-mathematics, but not really in the philosophy of mathematics.

Aviram, Aharon. "New Humanistic Curriculum: A Response to Education's Betrayal of the Need for Meaning" in *Identity, Culture, and Education, Smeyers, Paul (ed)*, 97-104. Leuven, Leuven Univ Pr, 1994.

The paper presents and defends the following claims: 1) Throughout its long history the Liberal Curriculum has relied on two justifications: the theoretical and the practical. The theoretical justification presented the curriculum as portraying, or leading towards, Truth, knowledge of which was conceived as the ultimate aim of life; or at least as portraying culturally accepted truths. The practical justification presented the curriculum (mainly) as guaranteeing high social and economic status. 2) These justifications rendered the learning of this purely theoretical curriculum (boring but) meaningful for students throughout the last 2400 years. 3) Two processes characterizing postmodernity—the expansion of relativism and over-education, undermine these justifications. 4) Thus, the 2400 year old curriculum is rendered meaningless for our postmodern world. 5) We need to form new curricular concepts that will be meaningful in postmodernity. The paper ends by suggesting such concepts on both the theoretical and practical levels.

Aviram, Aharon. Autonomy and Commitment: Compatible Ideals. *J Phil Educ*, 29(1), 61-73, March 95.

Fears of alienation and anomie in liberal societies have driven many writers to emphasize care and commitment as essential ingredients of human well-being and as educational aims. Conceiving autonomy to be incompatible with these values, they have concluded that autonomy should be replaced with alternative conceptions of human well-being and of education that emphasize care and commitment. The claim I will try to defend in this paper is that, in contrast to these views, there is no contradiction between autonomy on the one hand and care and commitment on the other; hence acknowledgment of the importance of the latter pair of values need not lead to the rejection of the ideal of autonomy.

Avnon, Dan. "Know Thyself": Socratic Companionship and Platonic Community. *Polit Theory*, 23(2), 304-329, My 95.

Plato's portrayal of the Socratic elenchus includes "double communication," a dimension of inter-personal relationship that directs the interlocutors to discern possibilities of self-knowledge present in inter-personal dialogue. Analysis of three elentic encounters in the dialogue *Gorgias* shows how, at bottom, Socrates intends to awaken in his interlocutors a *gnosis* way of knowing self that is qualitatively more refined than *epistemic* forms of knowledge. Interpreting the *Republic* along the lines of analysis developed in the essay, we discover that a philosophical companion and not a fellow citizen, a community and not a city, a school and not a state guide Plato's edifying project in the *Republic*. Plato seeks to institutionalize the way to self-knowledge, and not to define the definitive statement regarding either the nature of self-knowledge or of moral conduct.

Ayala, Francisco J. "The Difference of Being Human" in *Biology, Ethics, and the Origins of Life, Rolston III, Holmes (ed)*, 113-136. Boston, Jones & Bartlett, 1995.

Literature, art, science, technology, and other behavioral features may have come about not because they were adaptively favored in human evolution, but because they are expressions of some other attribute present in modern humans. This attribute may have been favored by natural selection (its "target") rather than any one of those particular activities. I argue here that ethical behavior (the proclivity to judge human actions as either good or evil) has evolved as a distinctive trait of human behavior not because it was adaptive in itself, but rather as a pleiotropic consequence of the high intelligence characteristic of humans. I point out that the question of whether ethical behavior is biologically determined may refer either to the *capacity* for ethics (i.e., the proclivity to judge human actions as either right or wrong) or to the moral *norms* accepted by human beings for guiding their actions. My theses are: 1) that the capacity for ethics is a necessary attribute of human nature; and 2) that moral norms are products of cultural evolution, not of biological evolution.

Ayala, Francisco J. On the Scientific Method, Its Practice and Pitfalls. *Hist Phil Life Sci*, 16(2), 205-240, Ag 94.

This paper sets forth a familiar theme, that science essentially consists of two interdependent episodes, one imaginative, the other critical. Hypotheses and other imaginative conjectures are the initial stage of scientific inquiry because they provide the incentive to seek the truth and a clue as to where to find it. But scientific conjectures must be subject to critical examination and empirical testing. There is a dialogue between the two episodes; observations made to test a hypothesis are the inspiration for new conjectures. Inductive generalizations may also inspire hypotheses, but cannot validate them. A hypothesis is empirically tested by ascertaining whether or not predictions about the world of experience deduced from the hypothesis agree with what is actually observed. This has been appropriately considered the 'criterion of demarcation' that distinguishes science from other knowledge. But scientific hypotheses must satisfy other tests as well. I briefly explore such issues as verifiability and falsifiability, empirical content and truthfulness, contingency and certainty, fact and theory, error and fraud. (edited)

Ayala, Jorge M. La Tensión Razón-Fe en la Filosofía Judeomusulmana de Al-Andalus. *Rev Espan Filosof Med*, 0, 21-29, 1993.

Philosophy does not arise in the three monotheistic religions (Judaism, Christianity and Islamic) as an original phenomenon but as a shock with the Hellenistic "conformatio mentis". We examine here the tension "faith-reason" in the Medieval Yewish and Moslem Philosophers of Al-Andalus.

Ayers, Michael. "The Foundations of Knowledge and the Logic of Substance" in *Locke's Philosophy, Rogers, G A J (ed)*, 49-73. New York, Oxford Univ Pr, 1994.

The paper aims to show Locke's foundationalist empiricism and his theory of substance as two sides of a consistent anti-dogmatic system, each intelligible in the light of the other, and in the light of its sources in earlier philosophy. The former, taking perceptual knowledge of the existence of physical things as basic, was carefully developed, over a period, from ancient empiricism and its early-modern manifestations. The latter constituted a sophisticated critique of seventeenth-century dogmatic theory as well as of the Aristotelian tradition. Together they raise issues which deserve revival in the face of present-day conceptualism.

Ayres, Lewis. "Representation, Theology, and Faith" in *Rethinking Metaphysics, Jones, L Gregory (ed)*, 23-46. Cambridge, Blackwell, 1995.

Ayres, Lewis. Representation, Theology and Faith. *Mod Theol*, 11(1), 23-46, Ja 95.

Ayres, Lewis (ed). *The Passionate Intellect: Essays on the Transformation of Classical Traditions*. Cambridge, Blackwell, 1995.

Azcoaga Bengoechea, Ignatio M. La Razón y la fe Ante la Creación Temporal del Mundo. *Rev Espan Filosof Med*, 0, 31-38, 1993.

The temporal creation of the world is a question that has been debated for many philosophers, above all, in the Middle Ages. Saint Augustine, against the "maniqueos", has demonstrated that the temporal creation of the world, revealed in the Holy Bible, it is not impossible. Saint Thomas disputes with Saint Bonaventura. For this, the finite duration of the world is in dependence of the creation. For Saint Thomas, the distinction between "contingentia" and "temporalitas", and the possibility of the infinite "in potential", it allow to demonstrate the creation of the world without considering their "temporalitas".

Babbitt, Irving. *Character and Culture: Essays on East and West*. New Brunswick, Transaction Books, 1995.

This volume is a representative sampling of the ideas of Irving Babbitt, the leader of the intellectual and cultural movement called American Humanism or the New Humanism. First published together posthumously in 1940 under the misleading title *Spanish Character*, these essays span his scholarly career. The diverse topics discussed here—aesthetics, ethics, religion, politics, literature—are illuminated by the unifying vision of human existence that informs and structures all of Babbitt's writing. (edited)

Babbitt, Susan E. Identity, Knowledge, and Toni Morrison's *Beloved*: Questions about Understanding Racism. *Hypatia*, 9(3), 1-18, Sum 94.

In discussing Drucilla Cornell's remarks about Toni Morrison's *Beloved*, I consider epistemological questions raised by the acquiring of understanding of racism, particularly the deep-rooted racism embodied in social norms and values. I suggest that questions about understanding racism are, in part, questions about personal and political identities and that questions about personal and political identities are often, importantly, epistemological questions.

Babbitt, Susan E. Political Philosophy and the Challenge of the Personal: From Narcissism to Radical Critique. *Phil Stud*, 77(2-3), 293-318, Mr 95.

Babcock, Bruce A and Lence, Sergio H. Flexibility, Endogenous Risk, and the Protection Premium. *Theor Decis*, 38(1), 29-49, Ja 95.

We introduce two types of protection premia. The unconstrained protection premium, π^u, is the individual's willingness to pay for certain protection efficiency given flexibility to adjust optimally the investment in protection. The constrained protection premium, π^c, measures willingness to pay for certain protection efficiency given no flexibility to adjust the investment in protection. π^u depends on tastes and wealth as well as protection technology whereas π^c depends only on technology. We show that π^c cannot exceed π^u and develop necessary conditions for $\pi^c = \pi^u$. Optimal protection for an individual with decision flexibility may be larger or smaller than that desired under no flexibility.

Baber, Harriet. The Market for Feminist Epistemology. *Monist*, 77(4), 403-423, O 94.

Bacchetta, Matthew D and Fins, Joseph J. The Physician-Assisted Suicide and Euthanasia Debate: An Annotated Bibliography of Representative Articles. *J Clin Ethics*, 5(4), 329-340, Wint 94.

Bacciagaluppi, Guido and Hemmo, Meir. Making Sense of Approximate Decoherence. *Proc Phil Sci Ass*, 1, 345-354, 1994.

In realistic situations where a macroscopic system interacts with an external environment, decoherence of the quantum state, as derived in the decoherence approach, is only approximate. We argue that this can still give rise to facts, provided that during the decoherence process states that are, respectively, always close to eigenvectors of pointer position and record observable are correlated. We show in a model that this is always the case.

Bach, Kent. "Emotional Disorder and Attention" in *Philosophical Psychopathology, Graham, George (ed)*, 51-72. Cambridge, MIT Pr, 1993.

Attention is generally commensurate with emotion, but in emotional disorder there is a disruptive disparity between the two, involving irrationality, loss of control, and distress. Some domain of experience may overly capture one's attention (obsessive disorder) or, alternatively, be trivialized and even escape one's attention altogether (repressive disorder). Specific types of each may be classified partly by the kind of emotion involved, e.g., worry, suspicion, fear, anger, or shame. Emotional health involves being able to manage one's attention, to bring things to mind when need be, and to keep things from intruding when they do not warrant consideration. The latter requires an effective use of *exclusionary categories*, ways of categorizing actual and possible objects of attention so as to justify treating them as not worthy of attention.

Bach, Kent. Conversational Impliciture. *Mind Lang*, 9(2), 124-162, Ju 94.

To explain how what a speaker means can go beyond what he says, we should distinguish not only the implied from the explicit but the implicit from the implied. In Gricean implic-ature, one says and communicates one thing and also communicates something else; in what I call "implic-i-ture", one communicates simply an enriched version of what one says. This can happen because either 1) the sentence is *semantically underdeterminate*, so that its utterance does not (even after disambiguation and reference-fixing) express a complete proposition just by virtue of linguistic meaning and a process of *completion* is required to produce a full proposition, or 2) even though the utterance does express a complete proposition, what is communicated is some enriched version of that proposition, yielded by a process of *expansion*. Assorted examples illustrate how impliciture works and how pervasive it is.

Bach, Kent. Terms of Agreement. *Ethics*, 105(3), 604-612, Ap 95.

Margaret Gilbert has recently challenged the orthodox view that an agreement is an exchange of promises. She argues that regardless of the form or content of the exchanged promises, their exchange does not qualify as an agreement. Whether unconditional, conditional, or mutually conditional, they either fail to be interdependent, as the commitments in an agreement should be, or else are too weak. I suggest that her argument relies on an attenuated sense of "exchange" and that there is a fuller sense in which arguments are exchanges of promises. This is the sense in which a trade is an exchange. Just as trade is an exchange of goods, so an agreement is an exchange of commitments. The obligations thus created are not mutually conditional but reciprocal and, because they are exchanged, are interdependent.

Backhouse, Roger E. An Empirical Philosophy of Economic Theory. *Brit J Phil Sci*, 46(1), 111-121, Mr 95.

A review of Daniel M Hausman's *The Inexact and Separate Science of Economics* (1992). The paper argues that Hausman's modified version of J S Mill's inexact a priori method succeeds brilliantly in characterizing much contemporary economics, it fits only part of the field, but that a wider view of economics would have resulted in a different perspective. It is also suggested and that the criticisms of modern economics that Hausman wishes to make fit less comfortably with his modified Millian methodology than with the Popperian/Lakatosian methodology he emphatically rejects.

Bacon, John. *Universals and Property Instances: The Alphabet of Being*. Cambridge, Blackwell, 1995.

Universals are bundles of like property instances, or tropes. Individuals are chains of bundles of i-concurrent tropes (i = 1,...). A possible world is any set of tropes together with a likeness and a concurrence relation. Thus some tropes may not be in the actual world. The hypothesis is defended that tropes are ontologically basic, "the very alphabet of being", in D C Williams's phrase. But they could be structured complexes of some sort, such as possible facts. The resulting theory is extended to relational tropes, compound universals, and modality and applied to belief, time, causation, and obligation.

Bacot, Jean-François. Le Rationnel et le Raisonnable. *Philosopher*, 17, 73-102, 1995.

Bacot, Jean-François. Le Sujet Auto-Nome du Droit: Entretien avec Lukas Sosoe. *Philosopher*, 14, 7-31, 1993.

Bacot, Jean-François. Morale et Démocratie (Entretien avec Catherine Audard). *Philosopher*, 17, 281-296, 1995.

Badenhorst, J A. Unethical Behaviour in Procurement: A Perspective on Causes and Solutions. *J Bus Ethics*, 13(9), 739-745, S 94.

This article focuses on ethics, procurement or purchasing ethics, and unethical behavior among purchasers in general, as well as more specifically on the situation in South Africa, and makes recommendations for establishing codes of conduct, other procedures and policies for improving the situation of the purchaser in the enterprise. (edited)

Bader, Veit. Citizenship and Exclusion: Radical Democracy, Community, and Justice. Or, What is Wrong with Communitarianism?. *Polit Theory*, 23(2), 211-246, My 95.

Walzer tries to defend his focus on the 'nation-state' by two additional arguments: 1) With respect to 'physical and cultural survival' I think that one should not discuss state formations and 'alternative formations' as exclusive alternatives but rather as security formations which can supplement and mutually help and criticize each other. 2) With respect to 'welfare', 'ethnicity' and nationhood are, empirically as well as normatively, ambivalent resources for solidarity. My proposal to disentangle democratic citizenship from all ascriptive identities, particularly from ethnicity, is —contrary to Walzer's suggestion—not a typically American project. It is ever more important for all modern states which, in an age of migration, increasingly become multi-ethnic and culturally very diverse.

Bader, Veit. Reply to Michael Walzer. *Polit Theory*, 23(2), 250-252, My 95.

Michael Walzer's discussion of membership has contributed to correct the neglect of exclusionary effects of citizenship in political philosophy. Nevertheless, his arguments for a qualified closure of orders draw heavily on communitarian assumptions. As a moral philosopher, I criticize the blend of realist, prudential and thick eth(n)ic arguments in favor of closed borders from a moral point of view. As a sociologist, I focus on the superposition of ethnicity, culture, nation and state, trying to show that communitarian assumptions in favor of the state are highly implausible or false. As a political philosopher, I try to show that we have to rethink sovereignty and citizenship drastically if we want to avoid the exclusionary effects which seem to be inherent in 'strong'-democratic or (neo-)republican conceptions of politics. The leading idea in this repect is a sharp conceptual and practical distinction between low threshhold concepts of legal citizenship and thicker conceptions of constitution, citizenship, and politics.

Badham, Paul. "Christian Belief and the Ethics of In-vitro Fertilization Research" in *Ethics on the Frontiers of Human Existence, Badham, Paul (ed)*, 51-64. New York, Paragon House, 1992.

The chapter challenges Christian hostility towards in vitro fertilization research and argues from the perspective of the Bible, from Christian tradition prior to the 19th Century, and from the need for internal coherence in Christian belief that an unformed fetus cannot be a person. Christian attitudes have changed in other areas of medicine and change in possible here too. If a zygote already possessed personhood this would present insuperable problems for Christian beliefs about the meaning of life and the hope for immortality. The author is Dean of Theology at the University of Wales Lampeter.

Badham, Paul (ed). *Ethics on the Frontiers of Human Existence*. New York, Paragon House, 1992.

The book's purpose is to explore moral problems of life and death from in-vitro fertilization, abortion, and the care of desperately handicapped babies at the one end of life, to euthanasia versus palliative care of the dying at the other. Other related topics include capital punishment and warfare. The contributors are leading international experts in their respective disciplines of medicine, sociology, philosophy, theology, and peace studies.

Baer, Barbara E and Murdock, Nancy L. Nonerotic Dual Relationships Between Therapists and Clients: The Effects of Sex, Theoretical Orientation, and Interpersonal Boundaries. *Ethics Behavior*, 5(2), 131-145, 1995.

We surveyed 223 APA members to investigate the roles of therapists' sex, theoretical orientation, interpersonal boundaries, and clients' sex in predicting therapists' assessments of the ethicality of nonerotic dual relationships with their clients. Results indicated that therapists' sex, interpersonal boundaries, and theoretical orientation influenced ethical judgments of these relationships. Theoretical and practical implications of our findings are discussed.

Baergen, Ralph. Revising the Substituted Judgment Standard. *J Clin Ethics*, 6(1), 30-38, Spr 95.

The substituted judgment standard (SJS), which is used in certain circumstances to make medical decisions on behalf of incompetent patients, is usually formulated in unsatisfactory ways. The proposed revision of the SJS avoids the usual problems (notably, it does away with an unintended sensitivity to depression, denial, etc.); two sample cases illustrate this. Also, this revision makes more clear the relationship between the SJS and other decision-guiding principles used by surrogates.

Bagaria, Joan. Fragments of Martin's Axiom and Δ 1/3 Sets of Reals. *Annals Pure Applied Log*, 69(1), 1-25, S 94.

We strengthen a result of Harrington and Shelah (1985) by showing that, unless w_1 is an inaccessible cardinal in *L*, a relatively weak fragment of Martin's axiom implies that there exists a Δ1/3 set of reals without the property of Baire.

Baggen, Peter and Maat, Harro. De Disciplinering van het Hoger Onderwijs: Aantekeningen bij de Massa-Universiteit. *Kennis Methode*, 19(2), 194-219, 1995.

Few attempts have been made to connect social studies of sciences with related areas of investigation, such as higher education studies. Discussing the work of Wittrock and Elzinga, 1985, the authors focus on the rise and possible decline of 'disciplines' within Dutch higher education. Disciplines are usually seen as the constituting element of universities because of the education-research junction they provide. Furthermore, most analyses emphasize the epistemic characteristics of disciplines. In this article it is argued that disciplines are primarily structures for the educational function of the university. For a proper analysis of disciplines, besides the epistemic component, attention must be paid to the educational and pedagogical features. Applying such analysis to the Dutch universities shows that the importance of disciplines in higher education is much more contingent than generally assumed.

Bagolini, Luigi. Aspetti della Filosofia Brasiliana nell'Ultimo Libro di Miguel Reale. *Riv Int Filosof Diritto*, 71(4), 335-337, 1994.

Bagolini, Luigi. Il problema della definizione generale del diritto. *Riv Int Filosof Diritto*, 71(3), 385-400, 1994.

Bahm, Archie. Buddhism: Gotamavada Versus Theravada. *Darshana Int*, 32(2/126), 1-24, Ap 92.

My Fulbright research report, *Philosophy of the Buddha*, 1955, claimed that the philosophy of Gotama, The Buddha, centered about a single psychological principle which anyone can test, and involved explicit rejection of doctrines attributed to him by Theravadins. The issues were reviewed with A D T E Perera, Editor of *World Buddhism*, Sri Lanka, while visiting in the University of New Mexico. Gotama's view: desire for what will not be attained ends in frustration. To avoid frustration, avoid desiring what will not be attained. Gotama did not originate the Eight-fold Path, *anicca* and *anatta, paticcasamutpadda*, or an order of monks.

Bahm, Archie J. What Philosophy Does the World Need?. *Cont Phil*, 17(1), 11-12, Ja-F 95.

The world needs a philosophy that promotes love of wisdom, happiness, solving life's problems, and understanding. The philosophical method critically examining presuppositions helps to achieve understanding by removing misunderstandings due to obsolescence of accepted traditions and hasty generalizations of contemporary credulous specialists. Presuppositions of Western, Indian, and Chinese civilizations support both virtues and vices, both universal truths and conflicting falsities. The world needs a philosophy emphasizing support for a comprehensive synthesis of all virtues and elimination of all vices and conflicting contradiction. Philosophy itself, by its nature, has these aims. So, the philosophy the world needs is more of philosophy itself. Willingness to practice philosophy so conceived embodies love of wisdom.

Bahm, Archie J. World Philosophy Methodology for Considering World Philosophy. *Method Sci*, 26(4), 191-194, 1993.

World philosophy, one that everyone can agree upon, is an ideal implicit in the philosophies of many philosophers and religions. It is unattainable unless some agency with world status can pursue suitable methods for critically examining their presuppositions and conclusions and demonstrating their deficiencies and virtues. A methodology of four levels is proposed: essentials (agreeable to all), cultural claims (candidates for essentials), museums (accepted traditions not essential), freedoms (unrestricted unaccepted claims). Recommended agency: UNESCO Division of Philosophy and Ethics, or the United Nations University. A World Society of Responsible philosophers may be needed to prod these agencies.

Baier, Annette. A Naturalist View of Persons. *Proc Amer Phil Ass*, 65(3), 5-17, N 91.

Baier, Annette C. A Note on Justice, Care, and Immigration Policy. *Hypatia*, 10(2), 150-152, Spr 95.

Should a "caring" immigration policy give special treatment to would-be immigrants who are near neighbors? It is argued that, while those on our borders requesting entry have some special claim, it should not drown out the claims of more distant applicants for citizenship.

Baier, Kurt. *The Rational and the Moral Order: The Social Roots of Reason and Morality*. Peru, Open Court, 1994.

Baier, Kurt. The Realm of Rights. *Dialogue (Canada)*, 33(2), 283-296, Spr 94.

Bailey, Alison. Mothering, Diversity and Peace: Comments on Sara Ruddick's Feminist Maternal Peace Politics. *J Soc Phil*, 26(1), 162-182, Spr 95.

Bailey, Andrew. Representations versus Regularities: Does Computation Require Representation?. *Eidos*, 12(1), 47-58, Je 94.

A fundamental issue in the philosophy of mind is the partially concealed debate between those who think of cognition as being a *rule-guided* activity (i.e., conscious or unconscious pattern-matching of behavior to mental representations of rules), and those who see cognition as merely *rule-describable*. Kripke's reading of Wittgenstein's private language argument calls into doubt the coherence of rule-following thought mental representations, and Searle's Chinese Room thought-experiment demonstrates the 'intuitive' unsatisfactoriness of mere cognition-as-complex-regularity. A future full account of intentionality may constrain which way we should jump, probably in favor of rule-describability and the nonrepresentational theorists.

Bailin, Sharon. Is Critical Thinking Biased? Clarifications and Implications. *Educ Theor*, 45(2), 191-197, Spr 95.

Baillargeon, Jean. L'Enseignement de la Philosophie et la Citoyenneté. *Philosopher*, 16, 241-245, 1994.

This short paper is organized around a conception of citizenship borrowed from Rousseau and Rawls, in which citizens have a duty to justify their political choices to one another in light of public reasons. I argue that by encouraging critical reflection and communal inquiry, philosophy courses at the CEGEP level can help foster practices identified by this conception as having special significance. The paper concludes with the idea that understanding the egalitarian framework of the system of rights is an important component of liberal education, as well as being an integral part of membership in the liberal political community.

Baily, Mary Ann. The Democracy Problem. *Hastings Center Rep*, 24(4), 39-42, Jl-Ag 94.

Bains, Paul (trans) and Guattari, Félix and Pefanis, Julian (trans). *Chaosmosis: An Ethico-Aesthetic Paradigm*. Bloomington, Indiana Univ Pr, 1995.

Baird, Robert M (ed) and Rosenbaum, Stuart E (ed). *Punishment and the Death Penalty: The Current Debate*. Buffalo, Prometheus, 1995.

These essays raise two questions: What justifies punishment in general? What justifies capital punishment? Essays by Mabbot, Rawls, Menninger, Wasserstrom, Morris, and Dagger consider such questions as: Should we distinguish between justifying the institution of punishment and justifying punishment of particular individuals? Can punishment be best justified by retributive or utilitarian arguments? Should punishment be replaced by therapy? Essays by Bedau, van den Haag, Nathanson, Justices Blackmun and Scalia, and others focus on capital punishment. This debate too pits retributivists against utilitarians, the former tending to support capital punishment and the latter frequently opposing it. Additional issues are involved, however, and the essays capture many of these.

Baker, Gregory L. A Dualistic Model of Ultimate Reality and Meaning: Self-Similarity in Chaotic Dynamics and Swedenborg. *Ultim Real Mean*, 17(3), 184-196, S 94.

In the search for ultimate reality and meaning, science and religion have often held conflicting positions. Yet both themes speak to deep human needs: the need to know and the need for purpose, and as such both seem important to the human view of reality. In an attempt to make one connection between science and religion I describe the concept of Self-Similarity as found in certain aspects of science and religion. Self-similarity—the sameness of objects at different magnifications—is ubiquitous in chaotic dynamics, a new and developing interdisciplinary study of motion. The geometry of chaotic dynamics leads to structures called fractals. Yet the general concept of self-similarity as repetition of pattern is old. In particular, Emanuel Swedenborg (1688-1772) described a theology that rested heavily on this view of the structure of reality. In this paper I illustrate the essential features of self-similarity by examples from chaotic dynamics. These features are then compared to the "layering" structure in the Swedenborgian reality.

Baker, Harold D. Psychoanalysis and Ideology: Bakhtin, Lacan, and Zizek. *Hist Euro Ideas*, 20(1-3), 499-504, Ja 95.

This article proposes the paradigmatic series as a basis for contrasting social-historical and psychoanalytical frames of reference: in the former, typified by Mikhail Bakhtin, society is a paradigmatic series of persons; in the latter, typified by Jacques Lacan, language (or the Symbolic Order) is a paradigmatic series of signifiers. These positions are in conflict: Lacan critiques the notion of individual identity at the level of the subject, and Bakhtin critiques the notions of monadic utterance and transcendent sign system. Slavoj Zizek's concept of ideological "quilting" combines Lacan's concept of a hegemonic Symbolic Order with Bakhtin's historical pragmatics of signification.

Baker, John A. Philosophy and Artificial Intelligence in Canada. *Eidos*, 12(1), 87-160, Je 94.

Baker, Judith. A Reply in Defense of Impartiality. *Polit Theory*, 23(1), 92-100, F 95.

The failure of seemingly impartial standards of justice to secure equality for minority and marginal groups has led to them advocating a political role in the determination of principles of right and justice. But the criticism that epistemic defects of impartial judgment make impartiality impossible fails to appreciate the general nature of theories as revisable and of revision itself. Moreover, it threatens to undermine the position it seeks to support, for it competes with an understanding of what legitimates democracy and the proper role in a democracy of citizens' representatives.

Baker, Keith Michael. "Enlightenment and the Institution of Society: Notes for a Conceptual History" in *Main Trends in Cultural History, Melching, Willem (ed)*, 95-120. Amsterdam, Rodopi, 1994.

For the philosopher defined in the *Encyclopédie*, civil society was "a divinity...on earth." Exploring elements of that claim, this paper finds a critical shift in the meaning of *société* in French dictionaries of the late seventeenth century, when earlier voluntaristic associations of the term were joined by a more general definition of society as the essential condition of human existence. After considering some recent discussions of the issue (Dumont, Gauchet), the paper advances the hypothesis that the Enlightenment instituted society as the ontological frame of human existence in response to the epistemological, moral, religious, and political dimensions of a generalized seventeenth-century crisis of values.

Baker, Lynne Rudder. Attitudes as Nonentities. *Phil Stud*, 76(2-3), 175-203, D 94.

Many philosophers assume that the causal-explanatoriness of belief requires that beliefs be constituted by brain states. The aim of this paper is to challenge that assumption, and then to sketch a view that allows beliefs to be causally explanatory without being brain states.

Baker, Lynne Rudder. *Explaining Attitudes: A Practical Approach to the Mind*. New York, Cambridge Univ Pr, 1995.

Baker, Lynne Rudder. Reply to Van Gulick's "Are Beliefs Brain-States?". *Phil Stud*, 76(2-3), 217-221, D 94.

Baker, Robert B. The Ethics of Global Budgeting: Some Historically Based Observations. *J Clin Ethics*, 5(4), 343-346, Wint 94.

Robert Veatch and other philosophers have speculated that global budgets are morally dangerous because they require rationing decisions in the absence of formal public discussion. The rationalization and rationing practices of the globally-budgeted British National Health Service are analyzed to show that the NHS engages in unpublicized and unconsented forms of implicit rationing (through idiosyncratic characterizations of "necessary care", and through waiting lists). The author concludes that globally-budgeted healthcare institutions should be held accountable to their clients by a *principle of public consultation* that will protect patients' collective interests just as the principle of informed consent protects their individual interests.

Bakhurst, David. Social Being and the Human Essence: An Unresolved Issue in Soviet Philosophy. *Stud East Euro Thought*, 47(1-2), 3-60, Je 95.

This is a transcription of a debate on the concept of a person conducted in Moscow in 1983. David Bakhurst argues that Evald Ilyenkov's social constructivist conception of personhood, founded on Marx's thesis that the human essence is "the ensemble of social relations", is either false or trivially true. F T Mikhailov, V S Bibler, V A Lektorsky and V V Davydov critically assess Bakhurst's arguments, elucidate and contextualize Ilyenkov's views, and defend, in contrasting ways, the claim that human individuals are socially constituted beings. Issues discussed include: the concepts of activity (*dejatel'nost'*) and community (*obscenija*) and their relevance to the notions of mind and personhood; self-consciousness and its relation to personal identity; naturalism in Soviet thought. Translated from the Russian.

Balaban, Oded. The Modern Misunderstanding of Aristotle's Theory of Motion. *J Gen Phil Sci*, 26(1), 1-10, 1995.

In the *Physics*, Aristotle defined motion as "the actuality of what is potentially, qua potential" (Phys. 201b5). This definition has been interpreted countless times and has been the subject of heated controversy. At issue today is whether refers to motions as a process or a state. Accordingly, if the idea of is believed to refer to a process, it is translated to mean actualization. If on the other hand it is taken to refer to a state, it is translated as meaning actuality. In the first instance, known as the "state-view", a change is defined as being the *state* of a changing object when it is actually potentially F, for some F^1. In the second, or "process-view", a change is defined as the *actualization* of a potentially.

Balaban, Oded and Erev, Anan. *The Bounds of Freedom: About the Eastern and Western Approaches to Freedom*. New York, Lang, 1995.

This is an attempt to systematize different concepts of freedom in reference to the figures of Zeus, Prometheus, and Epimetheus in the Protagoras myth. Prometheus represents the freedom of purposeful production; Zeus, freedom as moral self-determination; and Epimetheus, freedom in the sense of spontaneously giving way to one's desires and needs. It is within the context and on the basis of this conception that the aim is put forward of arriving at a complementary synthesis, by way of intensive communication, between the positions represented by Zeus, Prometheus, and Epimetheus. Such a synthesis would assist the East in overcoming deficiency and want, and the West in guarding against the excesses that derive from the Promethean outlook.

Balashov, Yuri. Duhem, Quine, and the Multiplicity of Scientific Tests. *Phil Sci*, 61(4), 608-628, D 94.

Duhem's and Quine's holistic theses, when properly understood, allow methodologically responsible ways of resolving a conflict between a theoretical system and experience; they only deny the possibility of doing it in an epistemically persuasive way. By developing a "string" model of scientific tests I argue that the pattern of interaction between the elements of a theoretical system arising in response to multiple adverse data can be helpful in locating a "weak spot" in it. Combining this model with antiholistic arguments of Popper, Greenwood, and Lakatos significantly reinforces their joint power.

Balashov, Yuri. Uniformitarianism in Cosmology: Background and Philosophical Implications of the Steady-State Theory. *Stud Hist Phil Sci*, 25(6), 933-958, D 95.

Philosophical considerations have been essentially involved in the origin and development of the steady-state cosmological theory (SST). These considerations include an explicit *uniformitarian* methodology and implicit metaphysical views concerning the status of natural laws in a changing universe. I shall examine the foundations of SST by reconstructing its early history. Whereas the strong uniformitarian methodology of SST found no support in the subsequent development of cosmology, the idea of a possible influence the global structure of the universe may have on the laws of physics operative in it has been assimilated by the standard big bang theory as it made its remarkable progress in recent decades.

Balashov, Yuri V. Should Plato's Line Be Divided in the Mean and Extreme Ratio?. *Ancient Phil*, 14(2), 283-295, Fall 94.

Balázs, Zoltán. The Interpretations of an Interpretation (Leo Strauss on Locke). *Magyar Filozof Szemle*, 5-6, 711-747, 1994.

This paper aims at reconstructing the philosophical differences between scholars of John Locke and their interpretations of him, especially that of Leo Strauss. First his general philosophy is discussed and demonstrated that it is not a traditionalist but rather a Nietzschean one. In the second part Strauss's review essay about Locke's Essays about the *Law of Nature* (ELN) is analyzed. The third part deals with his general interpretation of Locke in his *Natural Rights and History* (NRH) and the different criticisms and responses he received. Whereas Strauss's suggestions concerning the ELN are rejected, his understanding of Locke in the NRH is defended, not as an interpretation but rather as a legitimate criticism of Locke which has not been satisfactorily reflected upon so far. His philosophical views, however, which are and remain largely unsupported and too arbitrary, are not shared by the author.

Balibar, Etienne. "Has 'the World' Changed?" in *Marxism in the Postmodern Age, Callari, Antonio (ed)*, 405-414. New York, Guilford, 1994.

Balkrishnan P, Hemjith. A J Ayer's Notion of Philosophical Analysis. *Indian Phil Quart*, 21/3(Supp), 11-20, Jl 94.

An attempt is made to reconstruct Ayer's mid-period reconciliation between linguistic phenomenalism and sophisticated realism in a number of logical steps.

Ball, Stephen W. Gibbard's Evolutionary Theory of Rationality and Its Ethical Implications. *Biol Phil*, 10(2), 129-180, Ap 95.

Gibbard's theory of rationality is "evolutionary" in terms of its result as well as its underpinning argument. The result is that judgments about what is "rational" are analyzed as being similar to judgments of morality—in view of what Darwin suggests concerning the latter. According to the Darwinian theory, moral judgments are based on sentiments which evolve to promote the survival and welfare of human societies. On Gibbard's theory, rationality judgments should be similarly regarded as expressing emotional attachments to behavioral norms which originate and function to coordinate social interaction. Consequently, Gibbard's theory of rationality might be used to illuminate Darwin's theory of morality, and vice versa. Additionally, as argued in the present essay, both can be further elaborated, and defended, by developing related themes in philosophical ethics: viz., connected with Hume and 20th-century emotivists. The main problem is that this general Darwinian approach faces widespread opposition nowadays, not only in ethics but in philosophy of science. The purpose of this essay is to analyze Gibbard's theory, critically and constructively, with emphasis on the pertinent commonalities in Darwin, Hume and the emotivists, while also critically addressing their common enemies. The pervasive methodological orientation is to relate this analysis to (philosophy of) science in general, and biological science in particular.

Ballarino, Annamaria. Il predicato di dimostrabilità e la nozione di consistenza: alternative alla formulazione classica. *Riv Filosof Neo-Scolas*, 86(2), 358-385, Ap-Je 94.

Ballester, Manuel. El Fundamento de las Normas Morales Según Georges Kalinowski. *Sapientia*, 49(193-4), 307-326, 1994.

Ballester, Manuel. La Unidad Interna del Saber en G Kalinowski. *Daimon Rev Filosof*, 8, 131-141, 1994.

This paper studies the Kalinowski's thought in a genetic perspective. Maybe his best approach to the philosophical topic consists in his intellectual process, specially in the transit from the logic to the metaphysic thought, this transit required a rigorous search of the fundament of all the topics of the human knowledge, thus in the philosophical and so in the scientific thought.

AUTHOR INDEX WITH ABSTRACTS 433 Barnes, Eric

Ballestros, Jesus. Il Problema della Natura Umana nella Filosofia Spagnola. *Riv Int Filosof Diritto*, 71(4), 704-715, 1994.

The aim of this paper is to show how ethical cognotivism is postulated by the main Spanish thinkers of the twentieth century. Thus, despite of his sentence "man has not nature but history", Ortega must be interpreted as a cognitivist philosopher. His statement does not deny human nature but its atemporality. Zubiri defines human beings according to their demands of connection, openness to reality, exit from themselves and the overcoming of instantaneity. Spanish legal philosophers under Zubiri's influence (Legaz, Recasens, Corts) conceive human freedom as interdependence: dependence from God, fraternity with other human beings and care of nature.

Baltes, Matthias. Plato's School, the Academy. *Hermathena*, 150, 5-26, Wint 93.

Balzer, Wolfgang. "Exchange Versus Influence: A Case of Idealization" in *Idealization VI: Idealization in Economics, Hamminga, Bert (ed)*, 189-203. Amsterdam, Rodopi, 1994.

The intertheoretical relation between economic equilibrium theory and a theory of social institutions is studied in reduced form, i.e., by comparing the central primitives rather than the full formal models. It is shown that equilibrium can be regarded as a limit of institutions with ever more symmetrical power relations. Economic equilibrium theory thus is shown to be an idealization of the theory of social institutions. A privisonary topology which gives substance to the notion of a limit is defined "internally", i.e., by reference to items occurring in the models only. The meta-scientific status of idealization is briefly discussed.

Bamford, Christopher (ed). *Homage to Pythagoras*. Hudson, Lindisfarne Pr, 1994.

Banach, R. Sequent Reconstruction in LLM—A Sweepline Proof. *Annals Pure Applied Log*, 73(3), 277-295, Je 95.

An alternative proof is given that to each LLM proof net there corresponds at least one LLM sequent proof. The construction is inspired by the sweepline technique from computational geometry and includes a treatment of the multiplicative constants and of proof boxes.

Banajski, Ryszard. Ethics and the Problem of Time. *Dialogue Hum*, 4(1), 57-66, 1994.

Bandyopadhayay, Prasanta S. In Search of a Pointless Decision Principle. *Proc Phil Sci Ass*, 1, 260-269, 1994.

I advance a decision principle called the "weak dominance principle" (WDP) based on the interval notion of probability to deal with the Ellsberg type paradox (ETP). Given ETP, I explain three things: i) Why WDP is a better principle than many principles, e.g., Kyburg's principle and Gardenfors and Sahlin's principle, ii) Why one should not, contrary to many principles, expect a unique solution in ETP, and iii) What is the relationship between WDP and the principles mentioned above. I prove also that WDP induces a strict partial ordering on the intervals to which it is applied.

Banka, Jozef. A Comment on Ryszard Banajski's "Ethics and the Problem of Time". *Dialogue Hum*, 4(1), 67-68, 1994.

Banka, Jozef. The Epistemological Incenization and the Problem of Time in the Conception of Recentivism. *Dialogue Hum*, 4(1), 36-56, 1994.

Barale, Griselda C. "La Modernidad entre los Demonios y el Inconsciente" in *Temas Actuales de Filosofía, Palacios, María Julia (ed)*, 75-81. Buenos Aires, Univ Nacional Salta, 1993.

Barash, Jeffrey Andrew. Martin Heidegger en la Perpectiva del Siglo xx: Sobre la *Gesamtausgabe* de Heidegger. *Rev Filosof (Spain)*, 7(11), 275-303, 1994.

This article presents a critical examination of the collected edition of Martin Heidegger's works, which is currently being published by B Klostermann in Frankfurt, Germany. Over forty volumes have already been published. The author examines the significance of Martin Heidegger's philosophical production in the larger perspective of 20th century thought. It deals with three general areas of investigation: 1) Heidegger's "deconstruction" (*Abbau*) of Western intellectual and cultural traditions; 2) the relation between Heidegger's thought in *Being and Time* and his later involvement with Nazism; 3) Heidegger's challenge to the heritage of scientific rationality.

Barata-Moura, José. El Materialismo de Feuerbach: Un Estudio de sus Escritos. *An Seminar Hist Filosof*, 11, 95-128, 1994.

Con base en una investigación de la obra completa de Feuerbach, se buscan los matices de la comprensión feuerbachiana del materialismo a lo largo de la evolución de su pensamiento. En contra de los dualismos exaltados. Feuerbach quiere fundar un materialismo antropológico y racional, en el marco del reconocimiento de la Naturaleza, de la intuición y del amor. Desde el punto de vista ontológico, queda, sin embargo, en cierto modo, abierta la cuestión de si ese materialismo es consecuente, sobre todo en lo que respecta al papel de la praxis y de la subjetividad como condición de posibilidad de la materialidad.

Barbaric, Damir. Wem schlägt die Glocke?. *Filozof Istraz*, 14(2-3), 593-605, 1994.

Im Text werden die von Jure Zovko vorgebrachten Anschuldigungen ("Philologische Barbarismen", *Filozofska istrazivanja* 51, 1993, s 967-982) hinsichtlich meines Kommentars von Platons *Politeia VI* und *VII* Punkt für Punkt als unbegründet, absichtlich verfälschend und ausserphilosophisch bzw. ausserwissenschaftlich motiviert zurückgewiesen.

Barbiero, Daniel. On Subjective Truth. *Phil Today*, 38(4), 356-368, Wint 94.

Kierkegaard's notion of subjective truth is a useful heuristic for an investigation of the doxic and/or affective quality of the relation between a person and a thing, idea, other person, etc. I show how subjective truth can be analyzed in terms of speech act theory's sincerity condition, and how it differs from a propositional attitude. I argue that subjective truth is intelligible as a mode of appropriation, or generalized quality of response, and as such is not necessarily bound to reflective or other first-person states.

Barbone, Steven. Inneity in Descartes' Regulae. *Tijdschr Filosof*, 57(2), 297-307, Je 95.

This essay explores the question of a possible difference between innate and implanted ideas in the *Regulae ad directionem ingenii*. I maintain that, in this work, in order to avoid metaphysical difficulties in his account of error, Descartes introduces into the mind an implanted ability which, while allowing for universal science, does not inherently rely on external objects for verification. Such a solution suspends metaphysics in favor of epistemology.

Barbone, Steven and Rice, Lee. "Coming Out, Being Out, and Acts of Virtue" in *Gay Ethics, Murphy, Timothy F (ed)*, 91-110. New York, Haworth Pr, 1994.

We examine three philosophical models for (gay) self-identity: utilitarianism (exemplified by Eichberg), deontologism (Mohr), and individualism (Spinoza). The first two, we argue, overlook the personal and multi-faceted nature of social relations. We argue that the framework of methodological individualism is better suited to deal with the issues of self-identity as they affect questions of whether, when, and how to come out, and being out. This framework suggests that there is no moral principle which could apply universally in regard to being out and that there are common situations in which it is not morally appropriate to come out or to be out at all.

Barbone, Steven L. The 'Is/Ought' Relation in Hume. *Indian Phil Quart*, 21(2), 129-146, Ap 94.

I offer an interpretation of Hume's *Treatise* III.I.i which supports his claim that morality is both based on an empirical relation and also has no basis in reason alone. Under this interpretation 'ought' statements are not logically derivable from statements of fact, though the former may be certain despite their independence from what Hume calls the philosophical relations. In one aspect this interpretation represents a return to the traditional claim that Hume rejected an ethics based upon the 'naturalistic fallacy'.

Barbosa De Oliveira, Marcos. Logic and Cognitive Science: Frege's Anti-Psychologism. *Manuscrito*, 17(2), 65-96, O 94.

The paper's purpose is to contribute to the rehabilitation of psychologism as a doctrine about the foundations of logic. Psychologism is defined as consisting in two tenets: 1) Facts about human reasoning are relevant to the choice of principles that are prescribed by normative logic, and 2) Logical entities (concepts, propositions, arguments, etc) are mental entities. Only the second tenet is discussed in the paper. There is first an argument to the effect that Frege's Platonism is incompatible with his view of logic as a normative discipline. Then refutations are presented of Frege's anti-mentalist arguments.

Barbour, Ian G. Experiencing and Interpreting Nature in Science and Religion. *Zygon*, 29(4), 457-487, D 94.

I trace three paths from nature to religious interpretation. The first starts from religious experience in the context of nature; examples are drawn from nature poets, reflective scientists, and exponents of creation spirituality. The second, "Natural Theology", uses scientific findings concerning cosmology or evolution to develop an argument from design—or alternatively to defend evolutionary naturalism. The third, "Theology of Nature", starts from traditional religious beliefs about God and human nature and reformulates them in the light of current science. I point to examples of each of these paths in papers by other participants in this symposium, and suggest that all three paths can contribute to the task of relating science and religion today.

Barbour, Julian B. "On the Origin of Structure in the Universe" in *Philosophy, Mathematics and Modern Physics, Rudolph, Enno (ed)*, 120-131. New York, Springer-Verlag, 1994.

Barendregt, H. Enumerators of Lambda Terms are Reducing Constructively. *Annals Pure Applied Log*, 73(1), 3-10, May 95.

Baribeau, Jean-Serge. L'état et l'état des choses: Le choc des conformismes. *Horiz Phil*, 5(2), 98-108, 1995.

Baringoltz, Eleonora. "La doble Tensión y el Concepto Primitivo de Persona" in *Temas Actuales de Filosofía, Palacios, María Julia (ed)*, 83-91. Buenos Aires, Univ Nacional Salta, 1993.

The aim of this paper consists of evaluating the possibility to neutralise the tension affecting the concept of person when the latter is seen as from dialectical focus, such as the one we are involved in when dealing with it from two standpoints namely "objective" and "subjective" points of view. The study of the Strawsonian integrating proposal reveal as a conclusion that its appealing to the concept of person as a primitive one, promising though does not successfull satisfying us due to the objections affecting it as that related to the criteria of adscription of the states of consciousness.

Barkdull, John and Collins, Denis. Capitalism, Environmentalism, and Mediating Structures. *Environ Ethics*, 17(3), 227-244, Fall 95.

How can an environmental ethic be developed that encompasses the concerns of both free and market proponents and environmentalists? In this article we approach the environment-market debate using Adam Smith's writings in *The Theory of Moral Sentiments, The Wealth of Nations, and Lectures on Jurisprudence*. Smith's guiding principle for solving prominent conflicts of self-interest is that government intervention is required when the economic activities of some cause bring harm to others. The solution that follows from Smith's analysis is a government-funded, independent, democratically controlled, and democratically accountable mediating structure that derives impartial decisions and is authorized to impose its just and fair decisions on affected parties. In practical terms, this analysis provides the ethical foundation for the wide-ranging development of stakeholder panels composed of public interest group representatives and business representatives and empowered to develop solutions to public conflicts arising out of environmental problems.

Barker, John A and Gordon, Robert M. "Autism and the 'Theory of Mind' Debate" in *Philosophical Psychopathology, Graham, George (ed)*, 163-181. Cambridge, MIT Pr, 1993.

Barnes, Eric. Explaining Brute Facts. *Proc Phil Sci Ass*, 1, 61-68, 1994.

I aim to show that one way of testing the mettle of a theory of scientific explanation is to inquire what that theory entails about the status of brute facts. Here I consider the nature of brute facts, and survey several contemporary accounts of explanation vis a vis this subject (the Freidman-Kitcher theory of explanatory unification, Humphrey's causal theory of explanation, and Lipton's notion of 'explanatory loveliness'). One problem with these accounts is that they seem to entail that brute facts represent a gap in scientific understanding. I argue that brute facts are nonmysterious and indeed are even explainable by the lights of Salmon's ontic conception of explanation (which I endorse here). The plausibility of various models of explanation, I suggest, depends to some extent on the tendency of their proponents to focus on certain examples of explananda—I ponder brute facts qua explananda here as a way of helping us to recognize this dependency.

Barnes, Eric. Inference to the Loveliest Explanation. *Synthese*, 103(2), 251-278, My 95.

Barnes, Eric. Truthlikeness, Translation, and Approximate Causal Explanation. *Phil Sci*, 62(2), 215-226, Je 95.

D Miller's demonstrations of the language dependence of truthlikeness raise a profound problem for the claim that scientific progress is objective. In two recent papers (Barnes 1990, 1991) I argue that the objectivity of progress may be grounded on the claim that the aim of science is not merely truth by knowledge; progress thus construed is objective in an epistemic sense. In this paper I construct a new solution to Miller's problem grounded on the notion of "approximate causal explanation" which allows for linguistically invariant progress outside an epistemic context. I suggest that the notion of "approximate causal explanation" provides the resources for a more robust theory of progress than that provided by the notion of "approximate truth."

Barnes, Jonathan. "Life and Work" in *The Cambridge Companion to Aristotle*, Barnes, Jonathan (ed), 1-26. New York, Cambridge Univ Pr, 1995.

Barnes, Jonathan. "Metaphysics" in *The Cambridge Companion to Aristotle*, Barnes, Jonathan (ed), 66-108. New York, Cambridge Univ Pr, 1995.

Barnes, Jonathan. "Rhetoric and Poetics" in *The Cambridge Companion to Aristotle*, Barnes, Jonathan (ed), 259-285. New York, Cambridge Univ Pr, 1995.

Barnes, Jonathan (ed). *The Cambridge Companion to Aristotle*. New York, Cambridge Univ Pr, 1995.

Barnes, Jonathan (trans) and Annas, Julia (trans) and Sextus Empiricus. *Outlines of Scepticism*. New York, Cambridge Univ Pr, 1994.

Barnes, Timothy D. *The Sciences in Greco-Roman Society (Apeiron 27-4)*. Edmonton, Academic, 1994.

Barnhart, Michael G. Sunyata, Textualism, and Incommensurability. *Phil East West*, 44(4), 647-658, O 94.

Textualism is defined as the view that all knowledge of the world is essentially contextual, a commonly accepted contemporary philosophical position which raises questions regarding the possible incommensurability of divergent cognitive contexts. Two contextualist philosophical strategies for resolving this issue, that of recent neopragmatism and Madhyamika Buddhism (of Nagarjuna), are compared and contrasted. Just as neopragmatism insists on both the openendedness and contextuality of all objective knowledge, so Buddhism insists on both the conventional and transcendental nature of all religious truth. However, Buddhism's insistence on "higher" truth is defended over neopragmatism's tepid accounts of human rationality.

Baron, Jonathan. A Theory of Social Decisions. *J Theor Soc Behav*, 25(2), 103-114, Je 95.

Barone, Francesco. Augusto Guzzo (1894-1986)—La Prospettiva Teoretica. *Filosofia*, 45(1), 9-25, Ja-Ap 94.

The paper was delivered at a symposium on Augusto Guzzo (1894-1986), professor of theoretical philosophy at the University of Turin (1939-1964), on the occasion of his centenary. It aims at sketching the meaning and scope of Guzzo's theoretical perspective in the Italian philosophy of the 20th century. The usual evaluation of Guzzo as a representative of "Catholic Spiritualism" is shown to be narrow: he was a Catholic, but his *Weltanschauung* insists on the human power of "creating cultural forms". His books on morality, science, art, philosophy and religion are still provocative for whoever is sympathetic with an analytical approach to philosophy.

Barquero, Elizabeth Muñoz. Libertad Necedad? Sobre los estoicos antiguos y Spinoza. *Rev Filosof (Costa Rica)*, 31(75-76), 97-154, D 93.

The assumptions of moral value judgments are rationality, freedom and responsibility. We consider that such assumptions, in turn, originate from a specific conception of the relationship between man and nature, by which it is usual to ascribe a freeing power to reason. In this work we examine if and how such a power can be found in the concept of nature, and the basis of moral responsibility in the ancient Stoics and Spinoza.

Barra, Oliveira and Salles, Eduardo. Newton sobre Movimento, Espaço e Tempo. *Cad Hist Filosof Cie*, 3(1-2), 85-115, Ja-D 93.

Analysis of the origins of the Newtonian doctrine about the absolute movement, space and time, in which is shown that this doctrine originates in the consolidation of the first ideas of Newton about the dynamics of circular movements. This analysis emphasizes both the meaning of the criticism to the Cartesian relativism present in the texts in which Newton exposes his doctrine and the possibility of interpreting these texts having as a starting point the exigencies of the Newtonian system of the "rational mechanics".

Barrett, Jeffrey A. The Distribution Postulate in Bohm's Theory. *Topoi*, 14(1), 45-54, Mr 95.

On Bohm's formulation of quantum mechanics particles always have determinate positions and follow continuous trajectories. Bohm's theory, however, requires a postulate that says that particles are initially distributed in a special way: particles are randomly distributed so that the probability of their positions being represented by a point in any region *R* in configuration space is equal to the square of the wave-function integrated over *R*. If the distribution postulate were false, then the theory would generally fail to make the right statistical predictions. Further, if it were false, then there would at least in principle be situations where a particle would approach an eigenstate of having one position but in fact always be somewhere very

different. Indeed, we will see how this might happen even if the distribution postulate were true. This will help to show how loose the connection is between the wave-function and the positions of particles in Bohm's theory and what the precise role of the distribution postulate is. Finally, we will briefly consider two attempts to formulate a version of Bohm's theory without the distribution postulate.

Barrett, Jeffrey A. The Single-Mind and Many-Minds Versions of Quantum Mechanics. *Erkenntnis*, 42(1), 89-105, Ja 95.

There is a long tradition of trying to find a satisfactory interpretation of Everett's relative-state formulation of quantum mechanics. Albert and Loewer recently described two new ways of reading Everett: one we will call the single-minded theory and the other the many-minds theory. I will briefly describe these theories and present some of their merits and problems. Since both are no-collapse theories, a significant merit is that they can take advantage of certain properties of the linear dynamics, which Everett apparently considered to be important, to constrain their statistical laws.

Barrett, Jeffrey A. The Suggestive Properties of Quantum Mechanics Without the Collapse Postulate. *Erkenntnis*, 41(2), 233-252, S 94.

Everett proposed resolving the quantum measurement problem by dropping the nonlinear collapse dynamics from quantum mechanics and taking what is left as a complete physical theory. If one takes such a proposal seriously, then the question becomes how much of the predictive and explanatory power of the standard theory can one recover without the collapse postulate and without adding anything else. Quantum mechanics without the collapse postulate has several suggestive properties, which we will consider in some detail. While these properties are not enough to make it acceptable given the usual standards for a satisfactory physical theory, one might want to exploit these properties to cook up a satisfactory no-collapse formulation of quantum mechanics. In considering how this might work, we will see why any no-collapse theory must generally fail to satisfy a least one of two plausible-sounding conditions.

Barrett, Jeffrey A and Albert, David Z. On What It Takes to Be a World. *Topoi*, 14(1), 35-37, Mr 95.

A many-worlds interpretation is of quantum mechanics tells us that the linear equations of motion are the true and complete laws for the time-evolution of every physical system and that the usual quantum-mechanical states provide complete descriptions of all possible physical situations. Such an interpretation, however, denies the standard way of understanding quantum-mechanical states. When the pointer on a measuring device is in a superposition of pointing many different directions, for example, we are to understand this as many pointers, each in a different *world*, each pointing in a different determinate direction. We ask here whether such talk makes any genuinely intelligible sense of the term "world". We conclude that it does not.

Barrett, Jonathan. Causal Relevance and Nonreductive Physicalism. *Erkenntnis*, 42(3), 339-362, My 95.

It has been argued that nonreductive physicalism leads to epiphenominalism about mental properties; the view that mental events cannot cause behavioral effects by virtue of their mental properties. Recently, attempts have been made to develop accounts of causal relevance for irreducible properties to show that mental properties need not be epiphenomenal. In this paper, I primarily discuss the account of Frank Jackson and Philip Pettit. I show how it can be developed to meet several obvious objections and to capture our intuitive conception of degrees of causal relevance. However, I argue that the account requires large-scale miraculous coincidence for there to be causally relevant mental properties. I also argue that the same problem arises for two apparently very different accounts of causal relevance. I suggest that this result does not show that these accounts, on appropriate readings, are false. Therefore, I tentatively conclude that we have reason to believe that irreducible mental properties are causally irrelevant. Moreover, given that there is at least *prima facie* evidence that mental properties can be causally relevant, my conclusion casts doubt on nonreductive physicalist theories of mental properties.

Barrett, Martin and Sober, Elliott. The Second Law of Probability Dynamics. *Brit J Phil Sci*, 45(4), 941-953, D 94.

When the probability of causes, and the probability of effects, given causes, are each randomly assigned, entropy 'usually' increases.

Barrett, Robert (ed) and Gibson, Roger (ed). *Perspectives on Quine*. Cambridge, Blackwell, 1993.

Barrio, Eduardo. Una defensa del realismo semántico. *Rev Filosof (Argentina)*, 9(1-2), 87-94, N 94.

Barrio, Jaime Franco. Jaspers en discusión con el pensamiento de su época. *Anu Filosof*, 27(3), 1025-1040, 1994.

Jaspers, using Weber as a model, makes a negative critique of phenomenology, neo-Kantism and modern human sciences, although he admires the discipline and clarity of thought of the two first philosophic movements.

Barrio Maestre, José María. Alegato contra la razón Pragmática: Pragmatismo geopolítico y cultura de la paz. *Logos (Mexico)*, 22(66), 63-70, S-D 94.

Barrio Maestre, José María. Consideraciones Metodológicas Acerca de la Investigación en el Ambito de la Filosofía de la Educación (en Europa). *Analogia*, 8(1), 137-149, 1994.

This article deals with the four classical epistemological models of the Philosophy of Education, especially with the theory of the action (praxis). Education is not only an object to analyze but a duty to do. Considering this, the article questions phenomenological methodology and hermeneutic's advantages and disadvantages, as well as the kind of truth which philosophical knowledges of education seek: Philosophy of Education, Philosophical Anthropology of Education, and Ethics and Politics of Education.

Barrio Maestre, José María. La Disputa Averroismo-Tomismo en el op "De Unitate Intellectus Contra Averroistas", de Tomás de Aquino. *An Seminar Hist Filosof*, 6, 131-141, 1986-89.

This work includes the commented translation to Spanish of the more relevant parts of this text of Aquinas. The classical debate about the matter of the double truth (one for the faith, another for the reason: between Tomismus and Averroismus is presented in this work. It explains Aristotelic theory about *intellectus patiens* and criticizes the traditional Arabic interpretation of the subject.

Barrio Maestre, José María. Nota acerca del Rendimiento socio-cultural de la utopía: Sobre la necesidad de superar la mentalidad positivista. *Rev Filosof (Costa Rica)*, 31(75-76), 211-216, D 93.

Positivist thought worked, in the context of the occidental culture, a reduction of the expectatives for human improvement, specially in the field of ethics and politics. With its imperative of reduction to 'facts', it has formented a conformism, apparently realist, that makes impossible all authentic progress. The necessity of proclaiming an authentic sense of Utopia arise from noticing that human reality can be better in the future.

Barrio Maestre, José María. Nota Sobre el Estatuto Ontológico del Devenir en Aristóteles. *Analogia*, 7(1), 179-189, 1993.

Barris, Jeremy. *God and Plastic Surgery: Marx, Nietzsche, Freud and the Obvious*. Brooklyn, Autonomedia, 1990.

The book presents the logic of relating incommensurable positions and its implications for social responsibility. It focuses on pluralism which, consistently, respects nonpluralistic positions. Since this logic is partly performative, the book is partly performative. Section one begins with the assumption that knowledge is a form of power, and shows how that assumption transforms itself into a contrasting one. This exhibition is taken as a model for the logic, justice and method of mutual justification of incommensurable positions. Section two reads Freud closely as offering a similar model. Section three applies this model to romantic and anti-romantic positions.

Barry, Brian. In Defense of Political Liberalism. *Ratio Juris*, 7(3), 325-330, D 94.

In response to a paper by Chantal Mouffe, liberalism is defended from the claim that it seeks to eliminate political conflict. Rather, it seeks to locate consensus in the framework of political decision-making, leaving most issues to be decided by the ordinary processes of politics.

Barry, Brian. John Rawls and the Search for Stability. *Ethics*, 105(4), 874-915, Jl 95.

Rawls claims in *Political Liberalism* (PL) that *A Theory of Justice* (TJ) was defective in resting the case for the principles of justice on a "comprehensive view", but it does not. What is true is that chapter 9 made stability depend on congruence between justice and each person's good, which could be guaranteed only by the "Kantian interpretation", which *is* a "comprehensive view". PL contains a freestanding "political" argument for justice which includes adequate motivation (corresponding to chapter 8 of TJ in the form of stability as an "overlapping consensus" of "comprehensive views". This move is unsuccessful and unnecessary.

Barry, Robert. The Development of the Roman Catholic Teachings on Suicide. *Notre Dame J Law Ethics*, 9(2), 449-501, 1995.

This article reviews the Old Testament and New Testament teachings about the morality of suicide. It examines the development of the Roman Catholic objections to suicide in antiquity and the Middle Ages and reviews the collapse of moral objections to suicide in the modern era. It concludes by examining the contemporary Roman Catholic position on rational suicide to show how it has advanced in the twentieth century.

Barry, Vincent and Shaw, William H. *Moral Issues In Business (Sixth Edition)*. Belmont, Wadsworth, 1995.

Moral Issues in Business is a textbook for use in business ethics classes. There are chapters on the nature of morality, normative theories of ethics, justice and economic distribution, the nature of capitalism, corporations, issues in the workplace, moral choices facing employees, job discrimination, consumers, and the environment. Forty-three case studies and thirty-three readings by other authors supplement the main text.

Bartel, T W. Could There Be More Than One Lord?. *Faith Phil*, 11(3), 357-378, Jl 94.

In this article I defend the Social Trinitarian—someone who maintains that the Trinity consists of three distinct divine individuals—against the objection that it is metaphysically impossible for each member of a Social Trinity to exercise the kind of sovereignity over the created world that traditional theists attribute to a divine being. I consider what I take to be the most forceful argument for this objection, and construct a reply which, though not conclusive, poses a serious challenge to those who believe that the argument has much force against the Social Trinitarianism.

Bartel, T W. Why the Philosophical Problems of Chalcedonian Christology Have Not Gone Away. *Heythrop J*, 36(2), 153-172, Ap 95.

Traditional Christology faces noteworthy philosophical objections to its assertion that Jesus of Nazareth is one and the same person as the fully-divine Son of God. The vast majority of those who have recently discussed these objections have confidently claimed that they are insurmountable, or that they are easily refuted. I argue that both of these claims are premature.

Bartha, Paul and Belnap Jr, Nuel D. "Marcus and the Problem of Nested Deontic Modalities" in *Modality, Morality, and Belief, Sinnott-Armstrong, Walter (ed)*, 174-197. New York, Cambridge Univ Pr, 1994.

In "Iterated Deontic Modalities" (1966), Marcus argued that deontic logic should be able to make sense of nesting one deontic modality inside another, as in the statement, "Parking on highways ought to be forbidden." We show how Belnap and Perloff's modal logic of agency ("stit theory") can shed light here. We suggest a grammar for representing prescriptions and prohibitions, and a semantics that builds on Belnap's semantics for "seeing-to-it-that." Our analysis allows for the serious use of quantifiers in deontic contexts, and shows that there are several subtly different ways to construe prohibitions such as Marcus' example.

Bartholomew, Douglas. Sounds Before Symbols: What Does Phenomenology Have to Say?. *Phil Music Educ Rev*, 3(1), 3-9, Spr 95.

Bartkowiak, Julia J. The United States Media and the Liberal Tradition. *J Soc Phil*, 25(3), 123-134, Wint 94.

Bartlett, Steven J. The Loss of Permanent Realities: Demoralization of University Faculty in the Liberal Arts. *Method Sci*, 27(1), 25-39, 1994.

Bartlett, Steven J. The Loss of Permanent Realities: Demoralization of University Faculty in the Liberal Arts. *Method Sci*, 27(2), 133-148, 1994.

Examines a largely unrecognized mental disorder that is a disability of values. The resulting intellectual, moral, and spiritual impairment of students today renders them incapable of apprehending the *permanent realities* that are the *raison d'être* of traditional liberal arts faculty. It is their daily contact with this pathology that leads many university faculty to demoralization. Demoralization among these faculty is a second-order phenomenon, due to the encounter between a professional group representing classical culture, and a population whose exclusionary values vitiate the range of their concerns, aptitudes, and capabilities.

Bartolomei V, Teresa. "Das narrative Sinnverstehen und die Grenzen der Hermeneutik" in *Mythos Wertfreiheit?, Apel, Karl Otto (ed)*, 133-156. Frankfurt, Campus Verlag, 1994.

Barwell, Ismay. Who's Telling this Story, Anyway? Or, How to Tell the Gender of a Storyteller. *Austl J Phil*, 73(2), 227-238, Je 95.

In this paper I am interested in trying to make clear how one might explain and justify a claim that a particular narrative expresses a gendered point of view where this is not determined by the gender of either the actual storyteller or the fictional storyteller, if there is one. I argue that the process of understanding a series of events as a story requires the postulation of a narrating activity, and thus, a narrator. This narrator will be constituted out of a bundle of selection principles (and other things). In these selection principles a gendered point of view may be realized.

Barzel, Alexander. Decomposition vs Co-relation (in Hebrew). *Iyyun*, 43, 445-451, O 94.

Basañez, Frederico. Entre la Teoría Económica y la Economía Política: Estudio Sobre *Ética a Nicómaco* V.5 y *Política* I.8-10 de Aristóteles. *Themata*, 13, 37-72, 1995.

This article analyses Aristotle's "economic texts", mainly *Nicomachean Ethics* V.5 and *Politics* I.8-10. We deal then with "utility friendship", "fairness as reciprocity", the *aspháleia* of the *pólis* and the possible openness to the future of the Aristotelian reflections on economic matters. We finish with a note on the current significance of the Aristotelian Philosophy of Economics.

Baskerville, Stephen. Protestantism as a Transnational Ideology. *Hist Euro Ideas*, 18(6), 901-911, N 94.

The Reformation is often seen as contributing to the rise of the nation-state. But in England, Calvinism was used during the Revolution of the 1640s to encourage transnational identification with co-religionists rather than compatriots. Puritan preachers repeatedly set religious above national loyalty and spoke disdainfully of the nation as unworthy of the allegiance of true believers. They interpreted international politics in ideological terms, urging the Long Parliament to aid the Protestant cause in conflicts in Ireland, Germany, and Bohemia and trying to organize an international crusade against the papal Antichrist. This fervor helped dissolve attachments to secular political institutions, including the monarchy, and contributed directly to the Revolution.

Bastons i Prat, Miquel. La "Crítica de la Razón Práctica" como saber Transcendental. *An Seminar Hist Filosof*, 9, 89-97, 1992.

Desde la actual teoría general de la acción se han levantado objeciones contra la validez como saber transcendental de la *Crítica de la razón práctica*. Se la acusa de haber deducido la libertad del "Faktum" moral en vez de deducir la moralidad de una libertad moralmente neutra y transcendentalmente ya asentada en el desarrollo crítico teórico. Un estudio antento de la obra revela, sin embargo, que en ella no se abandona la *reflexión* crítica y es justamente por ello que la moralidad puede entenderse como la doctrina transcendental de la libertad.

Bastow, David. Becoming a Changed Person. *Phil Invest*, 18(1), 49-64, Ja 95.

An important part of what it is to be a person is to have long term aims or intentions. Each of these guiding intentions will give rise to an intention system, leading in the end to the intention to do something specific at a particular time and place. A person's 'intention structure' will be made up of one or more of these intention systems—they may complement or conflict with one another. This structure may be brought into existence, changed, abandoned, intentionally. Discussion of the complexities of some religious examples raises further general points about second-order intentions to change intention structures.

Batterman, Robert W. Theories Between Theories: Asymptotic Limiting Intertheoretic Relations. *Synthese*, 103(2), 171-201, My 95.

This paper addresses a relatively common "scientific" (as opposed to philosophical) conception of intertheoretic reduction between physical theories. This is the sense of reduction in which one (typically newer and more refined) theory is said to reduce to another (typically older and "coarser") theory in the limit as an appropriate small parameter tends to zero. It is argued that whether or not a genuine reductive relationship obtains between such a pair of theories depends crucially on the nature of the limiting relationship—on whether it is regular or singular. Several examples are discussed in detail.

Battin, Margaret P. Applied Professional Ethics and Organized Religion. *Prof Ethics*, 3(2), 5-15, Sum 94.

Battin, Margaret P. *Ethical Issues in Suicide*. Englewood Cliffs, Prentice Hall, 1994.

Battin, Margaret P. Going Early, Going Late: The Rationality of Decisions about Suicide in AIDS. *J Med Phil*, 19(6), 571-594, D 94.

This paper makes a central assumption that where assistance in suicide is available, it is the moral obligation of others to protect and enhance as much as possible the rationality of that choice. Four components are identified in a rational choice about suicide in AIDS. Phrased as questions a person with AIDS might as him- or herself, they are: 1) "Is suicide an option I want to consider?" 2) "Shall I hold out for the chance of a cure?" 3) "How shall I time my suicide?" 4) "What weight shall I give to the welfare and interests of others?" Although physicians often make assertions relevant to 1), they are appropriately involved only in 3); and although friends or intimate partners often provide the patient with anecdotal information relevant to 3), they should be involved primarily in 1). (edited)

Battin, Margaret P. Reading Religions: A Reply to Callahan, Martin, and Quinn. *Prof Ethics*, 3(2), 71-87, Sum 94.

Batygin, Gennadii and Deviatko, Inna. The Case of Professor Z la Beletskii: An Episode from the History of Soviet Philosophy. *Russian Stud Phil*, 33(2), 73-96, Fall 94.

Baugh, Bruce. Music for the Young at Heart. *J Aes Art Crit*, 53(1), 81-83, Wint 95.

I argue against James Young's contention that rock music is less sophisticated and more limited in its modes of expression than classical music. The standards of rock music performance and evaluation are as rigorous as for any other type of music, but these standards are not formalizable. Rather, these standards are handed down from practitioner to practitioner through practice, most notably, through live or recorded performances.

Baum, Gabriel A and Frias, Marcelo F and Haeberer, Armando M. Fork Algebras are Representable. *Bull Sec Log*, 24(2), 64-75, Je 95.

Fork algebras are extensions of relation algebras by a new binary operator, *fork*. The expressiveness of fork algebras is known to encompass that of first order logic with equality, i.e., in any proper fork algebra (a standard model) every binary relation that is first-order definable is also denoted by a fork term. Here we complement this result by a representation theorem: every atomic abstract fork algebra is isomorphic to a proper one. This gives a framework specially adequate for program specification and development within relational calculi.

Bauman, Zygmunt. *Life in Fragments: Essays in Postmodern Morality*. Cambridge, Blackwell, 1995.

This sequel to *Postmodern Ethics* (Blackwell 1993), concerned with the possibility of ethical discourse under postmodern conditions, explores impact of postmodern condition on daily morality. In particular, it considers the changing forms of interpersonal relations, the new ethical position of the human body, the influences of biological science and electronic revolution on the issues of mortality and immortality, old and new forms of violence and redeployment of violence in shaping basing units of social integration, and various expressions of newly emerging neotribal moralities. These analyses lead to the question of the ways and means of the ethical extension of moral impulses and intuitions of the interpersonal level through politics—to match the enormity of contemporary intrasocietal, intersocietal and global ethical problems.

Bauman, Zygmunt. Morality without Ethics. *Theor Cult Soc*, 11(4), 1-34, N 94.

Aporias of moral life are rooted in the primal scene of encounter with the Other, not in conflicts between ethical codes. Ethical legislation was an effort to eliminate that primal ambivalence or reduce its psychical costs. With the postmodern crisis of ethical/normative regulation, the moral self is thrown back upon responsibility for its own responsibility—which makes the postmodern condition simultaneously a threat and a chance to moral life.

Bauman, Zygmunt. *Postmodern Ethics*. Cambridge, Blackwell, 1993.

Baumann, Peter. Zwei Seiten der Kantschen Begründung von Eigentum und Staat. *Kantstudien*, 85(2), 147-159, 1994.

Kant offers two independent arguments in favor of private property (not only one, as is usually assumed): the first argument is based on a conception of freedom whereas the second argument is based on his 'Rechtsprinzip'. This double aspect of individualistic and social elements also explains why Kant gives two concurring characterizations of the state's function (guarantee or constitution of rights) and why the status of the citizens' rights remains unclear. The combination of individualistic and social elements is a characteristic trait of Kant's philosophy of law. However, it also leads to problems in his conception of the state.

Baumeister, Roy F and Delin, Catherine R. Praise: More Than Just Social Reinforcement. *J Theor Soc Behav*, 24(3), 219-241, S 94.

In this article we present an analysis of the effects of praise. We begin by considering how to define praise. Next, we examine the view of praise as social reinforcement, a conception which roots praise firmly within an empiricist framework; this appears to have been the predominant theoretical view guiding previous research on praise. We conclude, however, that this view is conceptually inadequate to account for the empirical evidence. Because of that conclusion, our next step is to provide a novel examination of the likely processes and consequences involved in praise. The remainder of the article is then devoted to examining, where it is available, empirical evidence relevant to our analysis. (edited)

Baumgarten, Barbara Bennett. Artistic Expression and Contemplation: Some Reflections Based on the Epistemology of Michael Polanyi. *Tradition Discovery*, 21(2), 11-15, 1994-95.

An exploration of the relationship between imagination and intuition and the workings of visual perception, in light of Polanyi's epistemology, helps us to understand aesthetic seeing. The artist and contemplative learn to see anew and accordingly grasp extraordinary coherences of meaning.

Baumgarten, Barbara Dee Bennett. *Visual Art as Theology*. New York, Lang, 1994.

Visual Art as Theology is a post-critical aesthetics for theology based on the epistemology of Michael Polanyi. This aesthetics is employed in examining Paul Tillich's philosophy of art. Polanyi's epistemology is extended into an aesthetics which moves beyond the impasse left by Tillich's work in art and theology. This book demonstrates an appreciation of the possibilities and problems of Tillich's thought, and moves beyond Tillich towards a more integrative program. Baumgarten develops three characteristics of art in its relation to religion and the task of the art theologian.

Baumgartner, Hans Michael. "Europa als Thema und Aufgabe der Philosophie" in *Das geistige Erbe Europas, Buhr, Manfred (ed)*, 101-120. Napoli, Vivarium, 1994.

By reflections on philosophy of law and history, the essay sketches the possibility of a philosophical consideration of the historical and political situation in Europe. At first, based on a critical-transcendental conception of philosophy as a "Platzhalter" of the conditio humana, the function of philosophy in general and with respect to politics in particular is discussed. The second chapter sketches the fundamentals of a philosophy of politics, the third one regards the situation in Europe with respect to the chances and preconditions for a unification of the European countries. Finally, the present position of Germany within Europe is discussed from the point of view of the actual political situation.

Baumgartner, James E. Ultrafilters on Omega. *J Sym Log*, 60(2), 624-639, Je 95.

We study the *I*-ultrafilters on omega, where *I* is a collection of subsets of a set *X*, usually R or omega sub 1. The *I*-ultrafilters usually contain the *P*-points, often as a small proper subset. We study relations between *I*-ultrafilters for various *I*, and closure of *I*-ultrafilters under ultrafilter sums. We consider, but do not settle, the question whether *I*-ultrafilters always exist.

Baur, Michael. Hegel and Aquinas on Self-Knowledge and Historicity. *Amer Cath Phil Quart*, 68(Supp), 125-134, 1994.

Hegel argues that genuine self-knowledge is necessarily social and historical, while Aquinas says nothing about history or society in his account of self-knowledge. The aim of this paper is to uncover some of the systematic and philosophical reasons for this difference between the two thinkers. In seeking to illuminate this difference, this paper touches upon an underlying similarity between Hegel and Aquinas: their common Aristotelian background.

Bavidge, Michael and Cole, Andrew J. "Is Psychopathy a Moral Concept?" in *Introducing Applied Ethics, Almond, Brenda (ed)*, 185-196. Cambridge, Blackwell, 1995.

The article examines the changing terminology associated with anti-social personality disorder which has proved unstable for both medical and philosophical reasons. A major objection to terms such as "psychopathy" is that they confuse moral and clinical considerations. However, disruptive anti-social behaviour inevitably evokes moral responses and can only be described in moral terms. This is as true within the clinic as it is outside, as the experience of psychiatrists shows. Psychopathy is a hybrid concept because the clinician cannot avoid taking up a position at which moral and clinical considerations intersect.

Baxandall, Rosalyn. "Marxism and Sexuality: The Body as Battleground" in *Marxism in the Postmodern Age, Callari, Antonio (ed)*, 235-245. New York, Guilford, 1994.

Bayertz, Kurt. "Was heisst es, den Tod zu definieren?" in *Freiheit, Verantwortung und Folgen in der Wissenschaft, Sandkühler, Hans Jörg (ed)*, 111-127. New York, Lang, 1994.

Bayley, Carol. Our World Views (May Be) Incommensurable: Now What?. *J Med Phil*, 20(3), 271-283, Je 95.

In focusing their view on Kuhn, Robert Veatch and William Stempsey ignore alternative sources of insight from other voices that could help move us beyond incommensurability. Richard Rorty and Helen Longino, for example, offer another view of science and objectivity with constructive insight for the practice of science and medicine.

Baynes, Kenneth. "Democracy and the *Rechsstaat*: Habermas's *Faktizität und Geltung*" in *The Cambridge Companion to Habermas, White, Stephen K (ed)*, 201-232. New York, Cambridge Univ Pr, 1995.

Beach, Dennis (trans) and Deuser, Hermann. Hume's Pragmaticist Argument for the Reality of God. *J Speculative Phil*, 9(1), 1-13, 1995.

The author examines Hume's *Dialogues Concerning Natural Religion* to discover a variant of the usual teleological argument that abandons reliance on analogical reasoning. This second version, never refuted in the *Dialogues*, is termed "pragmaticist" in Peirce's sense. It relies upon an *abductive* hypothesis that claims not logical proof but the power of instinctual conviction. The *Dialogues'* espousal of sound common sense may then be viewed as an imperfectly articulated precursor of Peirce's pragmaticist argument for the reality rather than the existence of God.

Bealer, George. "The Rejection of the Identity Thesis" in *The Mind-Body Problem: A Guide to the Current Debate, Warner, Richard (ed)*, 355-388. Cambridge, Blackwell, 1994.

Beards, Andrew. John Searle and Human Consciousness. *Heythrop J*, 35(3), 281-295, Jl 94.

Beards, Andrew. Lonergan and Analytic Philosophy of History. *Method*, 11(2), 155-198, Fall 93.

Beardsmore, R W. Art and Family Resemblances. *Phil Invest*, 18(3), 199-215, Jl 95.

Beauchamp, André. La Construction du Champ de l'Éthique en Environnement. *Philosopher*, 16, 125-132, 1994.

L'émergence d'une éthique relative à l'environnement origine dans ce que l'on appelle la crise de l'environnement, laquelle est une interprétation d'un certain nombre d'observations scientifiques. Pour l'instant, cette éthique se résume davantage en une série de bonnes questions que dans la mise en place d'une résponse d'ensemble cohérente. Au contraire de la bioéthique, l'éthique relative à l'environnement reste globale et incertaine. L'objet de l'éthique de l'environnement c'est de cerner à la fois les rapports de l'être humain en milieu écologique (domaine oú a tendance à se confiner l'"Environmental Ethics" américaine) mais aussi les relations entre les humains suite aux contraintes générées par la crise.

Beauvais, Chantal. L'Esprit absolu de Hegel est-il Dieu?. *De Phil*, 10, 1-20, 1993.

How are we to interpret Hegel's use of religious imagery and Christian theological terms to characterize absolute spirit? Two possible approaches to this question are considered, that of P J Labarrière, who sees the absolute spirit of Hegel's dialectic as having a purely logical burden, with none of the resonances that "absolute spirit" would have in the Christian onto-theological tradition, and that of Quentin Laurer, who sees Hegel insisting on the continuity between religion and philosophy. The author attempts to clarify the controversy by way of an original reflection of the relations between faith and knowledge.

AUTHOR INDEX WITH ABSTRACTS 437 Bejczy, István P

Beavers, Anthony F. *Levinas Beyond the Horizons of Cartesianism: An Inquiry into the Metaphysics of Morals*. New York, Lang, 1995.

This book presents the ethical thought of Emmanuel Levinas as the moral completion of Cartesianism. It begins by presenting Descartes's views on mind and body and the relationship between them in light of the question of how consciousness relates to a world beyond it. Secondly, it presents a complete sketch of Levinas's ethical metaphysics showing how Levinas adopts many elements of Descartes's philosophy, including the idea of infinity and a philosophy of sensibility, and uses them to push Cartesianism to its moral conclusions.

Bechler, Zev. *Aristotle's Theory of Actuality*. Albany, SUNY Pr, 1995.

Bechtel, William. Natural Deduction in Connectionist Systems. *Synthese*, 101(3), 433-463, D 94.

I have argued elsewhere that the systematicity of human thought might better be explained as resulting from the fact that we have learned natural languages which are themselves syntactically structured. According to this view, symbols of natural language are external to the cognitive processing system and what the cognitive system must learn to do is produce and comprehend such symbols. In this paper I pursue that idea by arguing that ability in natural deduction itself may rely on pattern recognition abilities that enable us to operate on external symbols rather than encodings of rules that might be applied to internal representations. To support this suggestion, I present a series of experiment with connectionist networks that have been trained to construct simple natural deductions in sentential logic. (edited)

Bechtel, William and Abrahamsen, Adele. *Connectionism and the Mind: An Introduction to Parallel Processing in Networks*. Cambridge, Blackwell, 1991.

This book offers an elementary exposition of the operation of feedforward connectionist networks and explores a number a conceptual and philosophical issues raised by connectionism. Among these issues are the problem of modeling intentionality and the question of whether cognition requires explicit symbols and operation performed upon them. The potential of connectionism to transform various cognitive science disciplines is also examined.

Beck, Heinrich. The Contribution of Ontology to the Foundation of a Rational and Peaceful System of Peoples. *Magyar Filozof Szemle*, 5-6, 817-823, 1994.

Beck, Ulrich and Ritter, Mark A (trans). *Ecological Enlightenment: Essays on the Politics of the Risk Society*. Atlantic Highlands, Humanities Pr, 1995.

Ecological Enlightenment examines the politics of the risk society. The book considers the ecological issue—viewed both politically and sociologically—as a systematic, legalized violation of fundamental civil rights and argues that the ecological conflict is the successor to the industrial conflict. It concludes with the plaidoyer for the unfinished democracy: Can we survive in freedom? This may be the most significant question before us. Democracy has to be rethought and rebuilt towards a global ecological citizenship.

Beck-Dudley, Caryn L and MacDonald, James E. Are Deontology and Teleology Mutually Exclusive?. *J Bus Ethics*, 13(8), 615-623, Ag 94.

Current discussions of business ethics usually only consider deontological and utilitarian approaches. What is missing is a discussion of traditional teleology, often referred to as "virtue ethics". While deontology and teleology are useful, they both suffer insufficiencies. Traditional teleology, while deontological in many respects, does not object to utilitarian style calculations as long as they are contained within a moral framework that is not utilitarian in its origin. It contains the best of both approaches and can be used to focus on the individual's role within an organization. More work is needed in exposing students and faculty to traditional teleology and its place in business ethic's discussions.

Becker, Howard. The Topological Vaught's Conjecture and Minimal Counterexamples. *J Sym Log*, 59(3), 757-784, S 94.

Beckerman, Wilfred. How Would you Like your 'Sustainability', Sir? Weak or Strong? A Reply to my Critics. *Environ Values*, 4(2), 169-179, May 95.

This article concentrates on the Jacobs and Daly criticisms (*Environmental Values*, Spring 1994) of my earlier article in the same journal (Autumn 1994) criticising the concept of 'sustainable development'. Daly and Jacobs agreed with my criticisms of 'weak' sustainability, but defended 'strong' sustainability on the grounds that natural and manmade capital were 'complements' in the productive process and that economists were wrong, therefore in assuming that they are infinitely substitutable. This article maintains that they are confusing different concepts of 'complementarity' and 'substitutability'. It is also argued that, in fact, they do both sell crucial passes in their defence of strong sustainability without providing any clear abandonment of it in certain cases. It is also denied that the fact that environmental services may provide different satisfactions from those obtained from other goods and services elevates it to the status of some over-riding moral value, or that discounting future costs and benefits is 'unfair' to future generations.

Beckley, Harlan. A Raft That Floats: Experience, Tradition, and Sciences in Gustafson's Theocentric Ethics. *Zygon*, 30(2), 201-209, Je 95.

Although James Gustafson's use of the Christian Bible and tradition is not fully displayed in the essays published here, Bible and tradition are a crucial part of a composite rationale, which includes experience and the sciences, for his theocentric ethics. Gustafson's theocentric ethics employs the sciences to back, inform, and correct the Christian tradition and offers grounds for respecting the natural piety and morality of "nonreligious" persons while explaining and justifying why Christians draw on major themes and metaphors from their tradition that should penetrate their piety and morality. His proposal should reorient the thinking of theological ethics more than it has thus far.

Bedard, Katherine A. Partial Denotations of Theoretical Terms. *Nous*, 27(4), 499-511, D 93.

In "How to Define Theoretical Terms", Lewis argues that a theoretical term is implicitly defined by the theory from which the term comes. Otherwise, the term is denotationless. I argue that such terms are not denotationless. If a theory is false, its subtheories implicitly define the theoretical terms, and a theoretical term partially denotes, to varying degrees, each of the entities picked out by the subtheories. If a theory allows more than one entity to be the possible denotation of a term, that term partially denotes each of these entities.

Bedford, David. God, Nature and the End of History. *Hist Euro Ideas*, 19(1-3), 371-376, Jl 94.

The paper argues that Alexandre Kojève's reading of Hegel, especially his now famous view that with Hegel history ends, is critical for understanding modernity. By historicizing Spinoza's pantheism Hegel stripped the modern world of its embeddedness in the God-nature matrix. Borrowing from the philosophy of Charles Hartshorne the paper points to a possible metaphysical reconceptualization of nature which can serve as the way out of the mixture of vanity and despair that characterize the psyche and politics of modernity.

Bedford, Donald and Stapp, Henry P. Bell's Theorem in an Indeterministic Universe. *Synthese*, 102(1), 139-164, Ja 95.

A variation of Bell's theorem that deals with the indeterministic case is formulated and proved within the logical framework of Lewis's theory of counterfactuals. The no-faster-than-light-influence condition is expressed in terms of Lewis 'would' counterfactual conditionals. Objections to this procedure raised by certain philosophers of science are examined and answered. The theorem shows that the incompatibility between the predictions of quantum theory and the idea of no faster-than-light-influence cannot be ascribed to any auxiliary or tacit assumption of either determinism or the related idea that outcomes of unperformed measurements are determinate within nature. In addition, the theorem provides an example of an application of Lewis's theory of counterfactuals in a rigorous scientific context.

Bednar, Miloslav. Problèmes Contemporains de la Démocratie. *Philosopher*, 15, 87-94, 1994.

Beetham, David. "Max Weber and the Liberal Political Tradition" in *The Barbarism of Reason, Horowitz, Asher (ed)*, 99-112. Toronto, Univ of Toronto Pr, 1994.

Bégin, Luc. L'Enseignement de l'Éthique comme Activité de Formation Morale. *Philosopher*, 16, 39-48, 1994.

In this article the author maintains that when teaching ethics as a subject in a general education curriculum, the teacher's ultimate objective ought to be to develop the students' autonomy and responsibility. To attain this objective, teaching ethics needs to be seen as being in itself an exercise of moral development. Therefore, emphasis should be placed on classroom procedures that 1) arouse the students' awareness of their own universe of moral conceptions, and that 2) develop their ability to deliberate and to be reflexive about their choices of action and about the motivations that orient their choices. This approach is compared to a more classic conception of teaching ethics to college students and to future professionals.

Behler, Ernst. The Nietzsche Image in Heidegger's *Beiträge, Contributions to Philosophy (On the Event)*. *Int Stud Phil*, 27(3), 85-94, 1995.

Behrens, Georg. Schleiermacher *contra* Lindbeck on the Status of Doctrinal Sentences. *Relig Stud*, 30(4), 399-417, D 94.

Lindbeck has devised what he calls a 'regulative theory' of doctrinal sentences, which he considers to be superior to its main rivals 'propositionalism' and 'experiential-expressivism'. For Lindbeck, Schleiermacher is the classical expressivist. I argue that Schleiermacher is more properly classified as a propositionalist, though he does have expressivist inclinations. According to Schleiermacher, doctrinal sentences express propositions about God, the world, and human self-consciousness, and they can be the objects of cognitive states. At the same time, there is sense in which they 'express' pious self-consciousness. I also argue that Schleiermacher's account of doctrinal sentences is superior to Lindbeck's, because it provides a better basis for understanding ecumenical dialogue.

Beidler, Paul G. The Postmodern Sublime: Kant and Tony Smith's Anecdote of the Cube. *J Aes Art Crit*, 53(2), 177-186, Spr 95.

Beiner, Ronald. Revising the Self. *Crit Rev*, 8(2), 247-256, Spr 94.

The liberal political morality developed in Will Kymlicka's *Liberalism, Community and Culture* is in various respects stronger and more coherent than many theories of Kymlicka's liberal predecessors and contemporaries, but it still suffers from important weaknesses that characterize other liberalisms. By ridding liberal theory of unnecessary defects, Kymlicka helps to clarify why even a liberalism capable of repelling the communitarian challenge will continue to be subject to theoretical criticism.

Beiser, Frederick C. Bowie on Schelling. *Bull Hegel Soc Gt Brit*, 30, 1-5, Autumn-Wint 94.

Bejarano, Teresa. Las Emociones ante la Ficción. *Themata*, 13, 73-95, 1995.

How can we be moved by a narrative which we know to be fictitious? (Redford's paradox). Taking into consideration the symbolic game of children, I reject the solutions connected with meta-belief, and turn to the evolutionary path of imitation. The ability to imitate in latent fashion—to learn—motor sequences that are new for the subject, would require two registrations to be kept apart, each one for a different movement and environment. In this way, as well as finding a solution to the paradox, we discover that imagining oneself, only oneself, but in different circumstances from one's own, would form the basis of another, much more fundamental capacity—the ability to imitate, not only different circumstances, but also another person, another way of seeing the same world.

Bejczy, István P. The State as a Work of Art: Petrarch and His *Speculum Principis* (*SEN*, XIV, 1). *Hist Polit Thought*, 15(3), 313-322, Autumn 94.

Jacob Burckhardt introduced the concept of 'the state as a work of art' as a characterization of practical politics in fourteenth- and fifteenth-century Italy. Yet his concept may just as well characterize tendencies in Renaissance political thought that have perhaps more to do with utopian dreams. Petrarch's letter to Francesco da Carrara on the qualities of a good ruler (1373) develops a politico-aesthetical ideal which bears a clearly Renaissance character. The cultural ideal of the restoration of antiquity is turned into a political program of national rejuvenation. An analysis of the letter enables us to see Petrarch as the begetter of Renaissance political thought.

Bekkali, M. Chains and Antichans in Interval Algebras. *J Sym Log*, 59(3), 860-867, S 94.

Bélair, Luc. Anneaux de Fonctions *p*-Adiques. *J Sym Log*, 60(2), 484-497, Je 95.

We study first-order properties of the rings obtained by taking the ring of p-adic valued continuous definable functions on some affine p-adic variety and going to the quotient by some prime ideal. We use the representation of the prime ideal as a nonstandard point of the variety. We show that the rings obtained are integrally closed henselian local rings, with a p-adically closed residue field and field of fractions, and they are not valuation rings rings in general but always have the property that of any two elements at least one divides the square of the other.

Belegradek, Oleg V. The Model Theory of Unitriangular Groups. *Annals Pure Applied Log*, 68(3), 225-261, Ag 94.

The model theory of groups of unitriangular matrices over rings is studied. An important tool is a new algebraic notion of a quasi-T_n-group. The models of the theory of all UT_n-groups are algebraically characterized; all they are quasi-UT_n-groups. If *R* and *S* are domains or commutative rings then two quasi-UT_n-groups groups over *R* and *S* are isomorphic only if *R* and *S* are isomorphic or antiisomorphic. The models of $Th(UT_n(R))$ are studied. An example is constructed which shows the spectrum functions of $Th(UT_n(R))$ and $Th(R)$ can differ; for a commutative *R* it is impossible.

Belic, Miljenko. Die sogenannte freie Gewissheit und ihre ethischen Implikationen. *Filozof Istraz*, 14(1), 41-46, 1994.

Im vorliegenden Artikel wird zunächst das Faktum der sogenannten freien Gewissheit hervorgehoben. Sodann ist von Mechanismen innerhalb der Vernunft (des Verstandes) und des Willens die Rede, welche zur freien Gewissheit führen. Sie haben ihren Ursprung im Menschen, und zwar insofern als dieser ein individuelles Wesen oder Mitglied der Gemeinschaft ist. Obwohl der Mensch in seinem Erkennen frei ist, behalten die ausserrationalen Komponenten nicht die Oberhand, vielmehr werden sie selbst im Rahmen der Vernunft konstituiert. Freie Gewissheit führt zu negativen Folgen und partieller Inobjektivität in der Erkenntnis und zu Einseitigkeiten im Streben. Diese negativen Folgen sind jedoch grossenteils überwindbar; ja sogar durch diese Überwindung bieten sie Gelegenheit zu neuen Positivitäten wie Bereicherung der Erkenntnis, Charakterausbau des Individuums und Veredelung des Zusammenlebens.

Belic, Miljenko. Sanc and Kozelj—Two Slovenian Philosophers in Croatia. *Filozof Istraz*, 14(2-3), 453-471, 1994.

Franjo Sanc (1882-1953) and Ivan Kozelj (1896-1982), Slovenian philosophers who lived and worked among Croatians as Jesuit philosophers, were professors of philosophy at Sarajevo and Zagreb (Sanc) and Zagreb (Kozelj). According to Sanc's results, Aristotle speaks of *hyle* (and it's corresponding *morphé*) with two different analogous meanings: the physical and metaphysical order. By means of this distinction Sanc rejects objections to Aristotle's doctrine of matter and form (especially E Zeller's criticism), and opens up the possibility for new insights into certain important themes of classical metaphysics. Kozelj experienced certain insecurities regarding human speculative approaches to truth, especially philosophical observations of Being. This position oriented him towards a personal conception of truth and life through truth, which is carried out by a free orientation of confiding in Being, the Absolute, the Truth, God in Jesus Christ and great personal endeavour.

Bélisle, Marc. Genèse du Concept de Vérité Esthétique. *Horiz Phil*, 4(1), 91-107, Autumn 93.

Bell, Vikki. Dreaming and Time in Foucault's Philosophy. *Theor Cult Soc*, 11(2), 151-163, My 94.

Bellah, Robert N. "Public Philosophy and Public Theology in America Today" in *Civil Religion and Political Theology, Rouner, Leroy S (ed)*, 79-97. Notre Dame, Univ Notre Dame Pr, 1986.

Bellamy, Richard. Moralizing Markets. *Crit Rev*, 8(3), 341-357, Sum 94.

The Austrian school tends to associate the morality of the market with its efficient operation. Consequently, it criticizes attempts to offer an ethical evaluation of the market for not understanding how the market works. This criticism proves correct with regard to those who would seek to run an economy according to a set of predetermined moral criteria, such as socialist advocates of central planning or Victorian moralists who regarded the market as the embodiment of the desert ethic. However, if the market trades on moral resources it does not create, this may justify placing it within a more substantive moral framework that establishes its ethical basis and limits.

Bellamy, Richard. The Theory and Practice of Liberalism. *Hist Euro Ideas*, 18(5), 753-756, S 94.

This article reviews works by Beine and Gray on liberalism. (edited)

Bellamy, Richard and Hollis, Martin. Liberal Justice: Political and Metaphysical. *Phil Quart*, 45(178), 1-19, Ja 95.

Metaphysics is necessary to determine those minimum standards of just conduct which liberals insist are owed to all human beings. Politics enables us both to appreciate these basic obligations by bringing us into communication with our fellow citizens and makes possible practical agreements that go beyond this bare minimum by providing the extensive public services necessary to the functioning of a well-ordered modern state. Liberal justice needs to be both metaphysical and political.

Belliotti, Raymond A. "The Legacy of Marxist Jurisprudence" in *Radical Philosophy of Law, Caudill, David S (ed)*, 3-31. Atlantic Highlands, Humanities Pr, 1995.

First, this article explains basic Marxist notions such as alienation, exploitation, historical materialism, false consciousness, and dialectic method. Second, it explains and examines the Marxist critique of liberal-capitalist jurisprudence. Third, it advances criticisms of Marxist jurisprudence and Marxism's responses to those criticisms. Finally, it discusses the legacy of Marxist jurisprudence as reflected in Legal Realism, Feminism, Critical Legal Studies, and Critical Race Theory.

Bello, Angela Ales. "Edith Stein und H Conrad-Martius: Eine menschliche und intellektuelle Begegnung" in *Studien zur Philosophie von Edith Stein, Fetz, Reto Luzius (ed)*, 256-284. Freiburg, Alber, 1993.

Bello, Angela Ales. A Proposito di 'Filosofia del Diritto'. *Aquinas*, 37(3), 623-627, S-D 94.

The primary aim of the essay is that to establish the validity of the Philosophy of Law. To perform this intent an important help comes from the book written by Francesco D'Agostino *Filosofia del Diritto* (Torino, 1993), who reflects on the meaning of "that expression of the human praxis" called law. The Author compares the way in which D'Agostino intendes the jusnaturalistic perspective—dealing, according to him, with the "personalistic paradigm"—with the phenomenological approach proposed by Adolf Reinach and Edith Stein. The two positions come to a common view, even if they have different starting points.

Bello, Angela Ales. Religione Parola Scrittura. *Aquinas*, 36(3), 609-611, S-D 93.

Bello, Angela Ales. Teleo-logía y teo-logía en Edmund Husserl. *Anu Filosof*, 28(1), 11-18, 1995.

The problem of God is tackled by E Husserl and can be found in some passages of his phenomenological analysis. Though he is interested more to perform his method of research rather than to discuss that particular topic, it is possible to pinpoint that for him teo-logy—in the sense of the rational way to deal with the problem of the Absolute—is linked up with teleo-logy. As in Kant's speculation, but more under the influence of Leibniz and Fichte, in Husserl's inquiry we find that the finality of natural processes and the ultimate meaning of human being's behavior compels us to admit an absolute aim and a goal of all things. And that can be nothing else than God.

Bello, Eduardo. Lectura ética del pensamiento ilustrado. *Rev Filosof (Daimon)*, 7, 169-178, 1993.

Has the modern ethical program any current importance? Firstly the post-modern criticism does not invalidate the significance of such a program, even if it is relevant to differentiate this program from the philosophical background in which it has been generated. Secondly we should add the concept of tolerance—nowadays indispensable—to those central concepts translating the program (reason, criticism, autonomy, human nature, humanity, freedom, solidarity, equality, justice and emancipation) that have been studied by C Thiebaut, ed (1991). Thirdly we should oppose the post-modern voices with the Enlightenment-inspired arguments: Rawls, Habermas, Heller, Foucault.

Bello, Eduardo. Libertad Soñada y Libertad Concreta en la Época Ilustrada. *Cuad Vico*, 4, 103-123, 1994.

Is freedom an eighteenth century invention? Such a question could be analyzed involving the artistic, the "libertin" and the political aspects of the experience of freedom. Here, the political one is considered only, not only from the perspective of Locke's "Glorious Revolution" dealt with in *Two Essays of Government", but in the light of the "Du contrat social" theorically anticipated French Revolution as well, and also from the perspective of Kant's "dreamt goal".*

Belnap Jr, Nuel D and Bartha, Paul. "Marcus and the Problem of Nested Deontic Modalities" in *Modality, Morality, and Belief, Sinnott-Armstrong, Walter (ed)*, 174-197. New York, Cambridge Univ Pr, 1994.

In "Iterated Deontic Modalities" (1966), Marcus argued that deontic logic should be able to make sense of nesting one deontic modality inside another, as in the statement, "Parking on highways ought to be forbidden." We show how Belnap and Perloff's modal logic of agency ("stit theory") can shed light here. We suggest a grammar for representing prescriptions and prohibitions, and a semantics that builds on Belnap's semantics for "seeing-to-it-that." Our analysis allows for the serious use of quantifiers in deontic contexts, and shows that there are several subtly different ways to construe prohibitions such as Marcus' example.

Belot, Gordon. New Work for Counterpart Theorists: Determinism. *Brit J Phil Sci*, 46(2), 185-195, Je 95.

Recently Carolyn Brighouse and Jeremy Butterfield have argued that David Lewis's counterpart theory makes it possible both to believe in the reality of spacetime points and to consider general relativity to be a deterministic theory, thus avoiding the "hole argument" of John Earman and John Norton. Butterfield's argument relies on Lewis's own counterpart-theoretic analysis of determinism. In this paper, I argue that this analysis is inadequate. This leaves a gap in the Butterfield-Brighouse defence against the hole argument.

Belsey, Andrew. "Chaos and Order, Environment and Anarchy" in *Philosophy and the Natural Environment, Attfield, Robin (ed)*, 157-167. New York, Cambridge Univ Pr, 1994.

The distinction between chaos and order has been central to Western metaphysics and politics. The paper examines some cosmological and ethical issues in the pre-Socratics and Plato, and concludes that the anarchist tradition, which rejects Plato and looks back more to pre-Socratic ideas, offers a worthwhile framework for considering global environmental issues. The central part of the paper considers and criticizes David Cooper's claim that environmental thinking should be "local" not "global".

Belsey, Andrew. "Ethics, Law, and the Quality of the Media" in *Introducing Applied Ethics, Almond, Brenda (ed)*, 89-103. Cambridge, Blackwell, 1995.

Given the role of the media in the democratic process, the quality, in an ethical sense, of the media is an important issue. This paper contrasts the situation in the USA, where there is the First Amendment guarantee of press freedom, with that in the United Kingdom, where neither governments nor courts have shown much commitment to press freedom. The conclusions are that the UK situation is detrimental to media quality, and that the promotion of media quality is a matter of ethics, operating within a benign rather than a hostile legal framework.

Belsey, Andrew (ed) and Attfield, Robin (ed). *Philosophy and the Natural Environment*. New York, Cambridge Univ Pr, 1994.

This proceedings volume of the 1993 Royal Institute of Philosophy Conference aims to further the debate among philosophers and environmentalists about the concepts of nature, value, bioethics and environmental and global justice, and their contemporary application. It helps rectify the comparative neglect by philosophers of the concepts of nature and of the environment, and also contributes to ethics, metaphysics, and social and political philosophy. Contributors include Dale Jamieson, Frederick Ferré, Peter List, Homes Rolston (USA), Robert Elliot (Australia), Stephen Clark, Roger Crisp, Nigel Dower, Tim Hayward, Alan Holland, Keekok Lee, Mary Midgley, Ruth McNally and Peter Wheale, plus the editors (UK).

Beltrán, Miquel. Harry Frankfurt: El agente moral y la noción de incondicionalidad. *Convivium*, 6, 91-103, 1994.

In this paper the author critically analyzes Frankfurt's theory of a split-level self. The initial aim is to establish the advantages that Frankfurt's conception of self-determination takes with respect to classical compatibilistic accounts of moral agency (those of Hobbes and Locke), trying nevertheless to describe its weakness. The author gives also an account of some critical considerations of the split-level self theory by other defenders of compatibilism such as Gary Watson and Susan Wolf, particularly referred to the notion of wholeheartedness, a main key in Frankfurt's defense of his conception of the moral agent.

Beltrán, Miquel. Spinoza: La Simultaneidad de los Tres Géneros del Conocimiento. *An Seminar Metaf*, 28, 319-330, 1994.

Ben-Amos, Ilana Krausman. Adolescence as a Cultural Invention: Philippe Ariès and the Sociology of Youth. *Hist Human Sci*, 8(2), 69-89, My 95.

Ben-Haim, Yakov. Convex Models of Uncertainty: Applications and Implications. *Erkenntnis*, 41(2), 139-156, S 94.

Modern engineering has included the basic sciences and their accompanying mathematical theories among its primary tools. The theory of probability is one of the more recent entries into standard engineering practice in various technological disciplines. Probability and statistics serve useful functions in the solution of many engineering problems. However, not all technological manifestations of uncertainty are amenable to probabilistic representation. In this paper we identify the conceptual limitations of probabilistic representation. In this paper we identify the conceptual limitations of probabilistic and related theories as they occur in a wide range of engineering tasks. We discuss the structure and properties of an alternative, nonprobabilistic, method—convex modeling—for quantitatively representing uncertain phenomena.

Ben-Ze'ev, Aaron. Gossip, Emotions, and Morality (in Hebrew). *Iyyun*, 43, 417-426, O 94.

Both gossip and emotions are often criticized from a moral point of view; nevertheless, it is argued that they play an important role in morality. They express our care and interest in others. A society without gossip and emotions will be less humane. Only excessive forms of gossip and emotions are quite harmful and should be avoided. The maliciousness and lack of concern that are commonly attributed to gossip and emotions do not reflect their true nature.

Bénakis, Linos. L'État Actuel des Recherches Dionysiennes. *Diotima*, 23, 17-24, 1995.

Benardete, Seth. The First Crisis in First Philosophy. *Grad Fac Phil J*, 18(1), 237-248, 1995.

Aristotle's *Metaphysics* is split between philosophy and wisdom. Something like that split operates in Hesiod's *Theogony*, where the progressive solution to the problem of genesis—it is finally overcome in the birth of Athena as wisdom out of wisdom through wisdom—is played against the ambiguity of the narrative authority of the Muses. The combination of an account of the being of the gods with the meaning of the gods, which Hesiod establishes for the Muses, distorts the temporal order: the Muses are at the beginning of the poem but were not at the beginning. Desire (Himeros) is the only god without an origin.

Bencivenga, Ermanno. The End of Analysis. *Phil Forum*, 26(2), 149-155, Wint 94.

Building on the author's previous "Theories and Practices", this paper provides an account of how it is possible that psychoanalytic therapy be effective. The account must navigate a difficult course between the practical syllogism (psychoanalytic knowledge per se does *not* cure) and sheer hypnotic suggestion (which would make the specific psychoanalytic techniques irrelevant).

Bendyk, Edwin. The Quest for Infinity and the Synthesis of Science (An Interview with Professor Andrzej Kajetan Wróblewski). *Dialogue Hum*, 3(3), 115-120, 1993.

Benea, Stefan (trans) and Vasiliu, Florin. *Paradoxism's Main Roots*. Phoenix, Xiquan Pub House, 1994.

Benedikt, Michael. Leibniz and Brentano: Two Philosophers Concerning Catastrophes and their Solutions. *Hist Euro Ideas*, 20(4-6), 931-936, F 95.

Leibniz in his works around Theodizee and "Monadology" (disregarding his "vinculum substantiale") and the middle Brentano in his works on Philosophy of History of Philosophy as well as in epistemologico-moral treatises present models of an epistemically well-founded nature transformed into theories of history. Whereas Leibniz interprets catastrophies as necessary phases—candidates for a turning-point to the better and the best world,—Brentano's outlook is more modest in contrasting uprising stages with pitfalls of pragmatism, skepticism, and mysticism. Either philosopher in his respective world-view cannot, however, cope with an "anthropodizee", the defence of human dignity against man's own aggressive products.

Bengoetxea, Joxerramon. Una defensa del consecuencialismo en el Derecho. *Telos (Spain)*, 2(2), 31-68, D 93.

The main idea of this paper is the reiteration of a common sense truth concerning the appeal of the Courts of Justice to consequentialistic arguments when making judicial decisions and even, in some cases, when justifying a judicial decision. There is an attempt here to verify it by means of some instances. The author also tries to explain and analyze it from a philosophy of law that has an analytical and sociological basis. A difference is noted between two different meanings of *consequences*, a) consequences as a structural element of rules and b) consequences relating to the predictable effects of judicial decisions. The author uses consequences in the second sense and takes into consideration how they work along the different stages of judicial decisions-making.

Benhabib, Seyla. "Subjectivity, Historiography, and Politics" in *Feminist Contentions, Benhabib, Seyla (& others)*, 107-125. New York, Routledge, 1994.

Benhabib, Seyla. Deliberative Rationality and Models of Democratic Legitimacy. *Constellations*, 1(1), 26-52, Ap 94.

Benhabib, Seyla. Ein deliberatives Modell demokratischer Legitimität. *Deut Z Phil*, 43(1), 3-29, 1995.

Benhabib, Seyla (& others). *Feminist Contentions*. New York, Routledge, 1994.

Benhabib, Seyla. The Pariah and Her Shadow: Hannah Arendt's Biography of Rahel Varnhagen. *Polit Theory*, 23(1), 5-24, F 95.

Benjamin, Andrew (ed). *The Lyotard Reader*. Cambridge, Blackwell, 1993.

Benjamin, Jessica. The Shadow of the Other (Subject): Intersubjectivity and Feminist Theory. *Constellation*, 1(2), 231-254, O 94.

Benn, Piers. What is Wrong with Hypocrisy?. *Int J Moral Soc Stud*, 8(3), 223-235, Autumn 93.

The article asks what hypocrisy is and whether it is objectionable in itself. It is apparently possible to seem to be good when really one is not, and a Kantian account of what moral worth consists in can show how this is possible. Hypocrisy involves a discrepancy between actual conduct or motives and appearances, but such discrepancy is not sufficient for hypocrisy, as is shown by cases of *akrasia* and sincere error. There are also hypocrites who appear to believe in their own virtue; how they manage this is explained by reference to *de re* and *de dicto* belief. The article then considers some implausible criticisms of hypocrisy and defends certain kinds of politeness against this charge. Hypocrisy is most defensible when it is morally motivated and involves presenting certain complex moral considerations as if they constitute deontological constraints, when really they do not.

Bennett, Bruce E and Bricklin, Patricia M and VandeCreek, Leon. Response to Lazarus's "How Certain Boundaries and Ethics Diminish Therapeutic Effectiveness". *Ethics Behavior*, 4(3), 263-266, 1994.

Bennett, David and Sylvan, Richard. *The Greening of Ethics: From Human Chauvinism to Deep-Green Theory*. Cambridge, White Horse, 1994.

This text sets out what environmental ethics is and is not, tracks main movements in environmental ethics is proceeding and developing, provides suggestions on how environmental ethics can reach a wider audience, and recommends methods and actions of inculcating and promoting environmental ethics. The unifying theme is a greening of ethics and applications of this greening. The text also plays with the conception of an environmental ethic as good, as a focus of an intellectual business venture, theoretical ethics becoming a branch of economics. This suggests that there is no neat boundary between ethics and economics.

Bennett, Henry L. Trees and Heads: The Objective and the Subjective in Painful Procedures. *J Clin Ethics*, 5(2), 149-151, Sum 94.

Bennett, James and Nolt, John. A Venn-Euler Test for Categorical Syllogisms. *Teach Phil*, 17(1), 41-55, Mr 94.

We present a method for testing the validity of standard form categorical syllogisms, which differs from the Venn diagram test in two basic respects: it uses Euler's way of representing universal statements, although it retains Venn's way of representing particular ones, and it seeks a counter-example to the argument, by attempting to represent the antilogism. After presenting the test, we discuss its advantages over the Venn diagram test and two other, alternative methods.

Bennett, Jonathan. "Locke's Philosophy of Mind" in *The Cambridge Companion to Locke, Chappell, Vere (ed)*, 89-114. New York, Cambridge Univ Pr, 1994.

The topics covered in this chapter are as follows. Locke's acceptance of Descartes's view that there is a radical separation between the world's mental and its physical aspects. His view of the cognitive aspects and the conative aspects of the mind. What Locke said about the possibility that "matter thinks". The question of whether all thought could be entirely caused by changes in the physical world. What it is for a single mind to last through time. What it is for a mind to exist at a time when it is not doing anything.

Bennett, Jonathan. Classifying Conditionals: The Traditional Way is Right. *Mind*, 104(414), 331-354, Ap 95.

Several philosophers have argued that conditionals like 1) "If Booth doesn't kill Lincoln, someone else will" belong in the same fundamental category as 2) "If Booth hadn't killed Lincoln, someone else would have" rather than that of 3) "If Booth didn't kill Lincoln, someone else did". They have noted that 1) may be asserted on evidence that later supports 2) rather than 3). In this paper it is pointed out that 1) may properly be asserted on grounds like those for 3); and it is argued that the use of 1) to express what 2) expresses is, though common, an improper use of language.

Bennett, Jonathan. Descartes's Theory of Modality. *Phil Rev*, 103(4), 639-667, O 94.

Descartes propounded the allegedly "strange", "peculiar", "curious" and "incoherent" doctrine that necessary truths are made true by God's voluntary act. It is generally held that this doctrine must be kept out of sight while other Cartesian topics are being discussed. This paper offers an interpretation of this Cartesian doctrine under which it comes out as reasonable, consistent with the rest of his philosophy, and possible even true. According to this interpretation—which is more respectful of and close to Descartes's text than is the customary one—Descartes equated the alethic modalities with facts about human intellectual limitations, somewhat in the manner of Wittgenstein. Thus, God created modalities creating humans in the way he did.

Bennett, Jonathan. Mind and Brain in the 17th Century. *Phil Exch*, 24-25, 81-92, 1993-94.

Bennett, Jonathan. On Translating Locke, Berkeley, and Hume into English. *Teach Phil*, 17(3), 261-269, S 94.

This paper describes, and invites participation in, a current project in which some of the English language early modern classics are rendered into English which the average contemporary undergraduate has some chance of being able to read. The underlying thesis is that when we present undergraduates with the original texts and demand that they read them, we do them positive serious harm: just because they *cannot* actually *read* these texts, they are reinforced in the idea that they are already getting from so many sources that reading is skimming to get a general impression.

Bennett, Jonathan. *The Act Itself*. New York, Clarendon/Oxford Pr, 1995.

Benoist, Jocelyn. Egología y donación: primera aproximación a la cuestión de la presencia. *Anu Filosof*, 28(1), 109-141, 1995.

Husserl's theory of 'transcendental ego' is often read as a metaphysical absolute idealism. The author attempts to fight this view and to give its phenomenological meaning to the 'ego'. It is the name of the 'presence' the consciousness-life owns, beyond all metaphysical construction. So Husserl gives a new chance to ecology, related to the frame of phenomenality itself. In this way a nonmetaphysical rereading of the Cartesian cogito seems authorized.

Benschop, Ruth and Hendriks, Ruud and Nelis, Annemiek. De Winst van Tranen: Over de Aarzeling als Methode. *Kennis Methode*, 19(2), 220-227, 1995.

Benso, Silvia. On the Way to an Ontological Ethics: Ethical Suggestions in Reading Heidegger. *Res Phenomenol*, 24, 159-188, 1994.

Benson, Norman and Malone, Patricia. Liberal Universalism and Multicultural Curricular Reform in the Social Studies: Issues to Consider. *J Thought*, 30(2), 9-20, Sum 95.

Liberal universalism's doctrine of political equality as an effective limitation on multicultural presentations of American history is linked to debates over the social studies curriculum. The liberal refusal to recognize cultural maintenance as a primary good in a liberal society and pluralists' objections to it are clarified. Modifications of liberal universalism are discussed. Teachers of American history are urged to emphasize the historical struggle between social groups to define the public culture as a unifying theme, to foster an understanding of the society as a whole and to allow minorities to be seen as active contestants in producing mainstream culture.

Benson, Paul H. Free Agency and Self-Worth. *J Phil*, 91(12), 650-668, D 94.

Most contemporary theories of free agency have characterized freedom in terms of the absence of various kinds of impediment or restraint. This has yielded "content-neutral," or procedurally defined, conditions of freedom. I argue that such conditions cannot secure an important, nonneutral component of free agency which concerns the agent's sense of her own worthiness to act. This paper describes this neglected component of freedom, argues that it avoids the difficulties which normally attend normative conditions of freedom, and suggests that this component helps to explain the value of free agency for persons.

Bentham, Jeremy. Extracto de "Libraos de Ultramaria". *Telos (Spain)*, 1(3), 11-43, O 92.

Benton, L M. Selling the Natural or Selling Out? Exploring Environmental Merchandising. *Environ Ethics*, 17(1), 3-22, Spr 95.

In the twenty years since the first Earth Day, the environmental movement has become increasingly "commercialized." In this paper, I examine why many environmental organizations now offer an array of products through catalogs and magazines, or manage stores and outlets. I conclude that environmental products are contradictory because environmental merchandise is juxtaposed uneasily between environmental ideological rhetoric and material ambition. Environmental organizations must recognize this ambiguity before they can deal with the problem effectively. (edited)

Bentz, Valerie Malhotra. Husserl, Schutz, "Paul" and Me: Reflections on Writing Phenomenology. *Human Stud*, 18(1), 41-62, Ja 95.

This paper is a reflection on the boundaries of academic discourse as I came to be acutely aware of them while attempting to teach a graduate seminar in qualitative research methods. The purpose of the readings in Husserl and Schutz and the writing exercises was to assist students trained in quantitative methods and steeped in positivistic assumptions about research to write phenomenological descriptions of lived experience. "Paul" could not write the assigned papers due to a diagnosed writing "disability" but he did submit fictional stories and sketches which beautifully illustrated the concepts of Husserl and Schutz. Paul's disability presented a natural "bracketing" experiment which brought the positivistic assumptions surrounding academic research and writing to the fore front. I engaged in verbal dialogues with Paul in which he discussed the philosophical ideas. My work with Paul highlighted the extent to which the academic lifeworld marginalizes those who seek to write from the heart, disguising even the work of those philosophers who wish to uncover direct experiences.

Bercic, Boran. On Tolerance. *Filozof Istraz*, 14(1), 119-136, 1994.

This paper has two main parts. In the first part, the author presents and discusses two formulations of the alleged paradox of tolerance. He draws the conclusion that there is nothing paradoxical in the concept of tolerance and that there is no such thing as a "principle of tolerance". In the second part of the paper, three general strategies for the justification of tolerance are exposed; the relativistic, the skeptical and the fallibilistic. It is argued that the relativistic and the skeptical strategies are necessarily untenable, and that the fallibilistic strategy is promising.

Berckmans, Paul. Direct Reference and Events. *Dialogos*, 30(66), 43-58, Jl 95.

Berezin, Alexander A. The Problem of Ultimate Reality and Meaning in the Context of Information Self-Organization and Isotopic Diversity. *Ultim Real Mean*, 17(4), 295-309, D 94.

The Problem of Ultimate Reality and Meaning is discussed in a context of some novel ideas of physics of information. The prime focus is on the experiential nature of information when it is put in a context of a cosmic and biological evolution. Special attention is given to the enrichment of informational dynamics through the quantum effects stemming from isotopic diversity of chemical elements (the phenomenon of isotopicity). The prime issues are: 1) information as a universal pattern-forming factor (*IN*-formation) and 2) the ultimate cosmic nondestructibility (and/or destructibility) of information. Eternalization problem is further linked to quantum physics of consciousness, personal identity problem and the underlying exhibition of the issue of the reality of the Platonic (numerological) world.

Berg, Anne-Jorunn and Lie, Merete. Feminism and Constructivism: Do Artifacts Have Gender?. *Sci Tech Human Values*, 20(3), 332-351, Sum 95.

This article explores possibilities for establishing dialogues between feminism and constructivism in the field of technology studies. Based on an overview of Norwegian feminist debates about technology, it indicates several points where feminism and constructivism meet and can mutually benefit from each other. The article critically examines feminist studies questioning the problems of technological determinism, social determinism, and essentialism. It criticizes constructivism for a lack of concern for gender and politics but holds that it is still possible to use theoretical tools from constructivism in feminist analyses. Fruitful dialogues require the application of the principle of symmetry to the dialogues and sharing some common ground and mutual recognition of each other's strengths and weaknesses.

Berg, Jonathan. "Inferential Roles, Quine, and Mad Holism" in *Holism: A Consumer Update, Fodor, Jerry (ed)*, 283-301. Amsterdam, Rodopi, 1993.

Jerry Fodor and Ernie LePore argue against inferential role semantics on the grounds that either it relies on analytic/synthetic distinction vulnerable to Quinean objections, or else it leads to a variety of meaning holism frought with absurd consequences. However, the slide from semantic atomism to meaning holism might be prevented by distinctions not affected by Quine's arguments against analyticity; and the absurd consequences Fodor and LePore attribute to meaning holism obtain only on an implausible construal of inferential roles.

Berg, Marc. 'Ze zijn allemaal dood...' Over kennissystemen in de medische praktijk, voorvechters en critici, en het mysterieuze succes van onderzoeksprotocollen. *Kennis Methode*, 18(4), 361-391, 1994.

This paper deals with the failure of knowledge-based computer systems to have a meaningful impact on medical practice. Although advocates have argued since the early 1970s that computers for 'decision support' would thoroughly transform medicine, they are currently rarely being used as such. This paper argues that this is not due to either 'resistances' in medical practices, as advocates would have it, nor to the 'essential weaknesses' of these tools, as critics as Dreyfus and Collins would have it. Rather (and here the paper draws upon actor-network theory), 'success' or 'failure' are the outcome of *converging networks* of practices *and* tools—convergences in which both tool and practice transform each other.

Berger, Alan. "A Central Problem for a Speech-Dispositional Account of Logic and Language" in *Perspectives on Quine, Barrett, Robert (ed)*, 17-35. Cambridge, Blackwell, 1993.

First, I argue that Quine's speech-dispositional account of language cannot provide a successful defense of his rejection of alternative logics. The speech-dispositional defense can succeed only to the extent that it makes implicit use of such notions as (non-dispositional) meaning, a priority or other notions whose legitimacy Quine has rejected. Second, I argue more generally that any attempt to make sense of a speech-dispositional account of language must itself rely on one or another of these rejected notions. Although I address my objections primarily to Quine's formulations of a speech-dispositional account of logic and language, it should be clear that my central criticisms can be generalized to apply to any speech dispositional account. If my first claim is correct, this may count against rejecting notions such as non-dispositional meaning or a priority. For Quine's position on 'alternative logics', modified in a manner *not* available to him, seems to me to be attractive on its own. If my second claim is correct, Quine or anyone who offers a speech-dispositional account of language must either admit a rejected notion or give up any hope of developing an account of language.

Berger, Herman. Repliek. *Alg Ned Tijdschr Wijs*, 86(3), 239-245, Jl 94.

Bergmann, Peter. Nietzsche, Heidegger, and the Americanization of Defeat. *Int Stud Phil*, 27(3), 73-84, 1995.

As a child of the defeated revolution of 1848, Nietzsche rejected the Forty-Eighter theory of world Americanization in his 1865 lecture on the German churches in North America. He later championed Renaissance individualism over his erstwhile Emersonianism, and proclaimed, "No American future!" Nietzscheanism and Americanism became competing ideologies in interwar Germany with Heidegger denouncing Eduard Baumgarten's revival of the Emerson-Nietzsche connection. Heidegger turned to Nietzsche when he embraced Nazism, identifying them as one and the same just as he identified Americanism with Bolshevism. Heidegger sought to mobilize Nietzsche in the Nazi war against defeatism. In defeat he repudiated Nietzsche.

Bergo, Bettina (trans) and Blau, Peter (trans) and De Gandt, François. The Problematic Status of Cosmology. *Grad Fac Phil J*, 18(1), 51-64, 1995.

Bergoffen, Debra B. "Out from Under: Beauvoir's Philosophy of the Erotic" in *Feminist Interpretations of Simone de Beauvoir, Simons, Margaret A (ed)*, 179-192. University Park, Penn St Univ Pr, 1995.

Drawing on *The Ethics of Ambiguity's* discussion of intentionality, the situation and childhood, and opening toward the "Must We Burn Sade?" essay's analyses of the ethical risks and implications of the erotic, I see *The Second Sex* developing the ideas of the flesh, and the other, and posing the question: Can there be an ethics of the erotic?

Bergoffen, Debra B. Nietzsche Was No Feminist.... *Int Stud Phil*, 26(3), 23-31, 1994.

I do not intend to make Nietzsche a feminist. By examining the question of *Beyond Good and Evil*, "Supposing truth is a woman—what then?", however, I suggest that we align Nietzsche's concept of truth with the idea of flirtation, and take up the following thought: Nietzsche, by entangling the questions of truth, psychology, Zarathustra, the death of god, the ascetic ideal and the eternal recurrence with questions of the feminine, shows that the question of woman, far from treading at the margins of philosophy, lies close to its heart.

Bergstra, J A and Tucker, J V. The Data Type of Stack Algebras. *Annals Pure Applied Log*, 73(1), 11-36, May 95.

We define and study the class of all stack algebras as the class of all minimal algebras in a variety defined by an infinite recursively enumerable set of equations. Among a number of results, we show that the initial model of the variety is computable, that its equational theory is decidable, but that its equational deduction problem is undecidable. We show that it cannot be finitely axiomatised by equations, but it can be finitely axiomatised by equations with a hidden sort and functions. This class of all stack algebras, together with its specifications, can be used to survey the many models in the literature on stacks in a systematic way, and hence give the study of the stack some mathematical coherence.

Bergström, Lars. Quine's Truth. *Inquiry*, 37(4), 421-435, D 94.

W V Quine has made statements about truth which are not obviously compatible and his statements have been interpreted in more than one way. For example, Donald Davidson claims that Quine has an epistemic theory of truth, but Quine himself often says that truth is just disquotational. This paper argues that Quine should recognize two different notions of truth. One of these is disquotational, the other is empiricist. There is nothing wrong with recognizing two different notions of truth. Both may be perfectly legitimate, even though, to some extent, they may be applicable in different contexts. Roughly speaking, a sentence is true in the empiricist sense if it belongs to a theory which entails all observation sentences which would be assented to by the speakers of the language in question (and no observation sentences which would be dissented from by these speakers). Various objections to this idea are discussed and rejected.

Berkowitz, Peter. *Nietzsche: The Ethics of an Immoralist*. Cambridge, Harvard Univ Pr, 1995.

This book challenges the postmodern view that Nietzsche effects a radical break with traditional moral and political philosophy. It argues instead that in his major books Nietzsche relentlessly explores the best life. In characterizing the highest type, Nietzsche radicalizes modern notions about knowledge, freedom, and mastery, but on the basis of convictions about the virtues and an intelligible moral order more characteristic of ancient philosophy. Nietzsche's explorations, this book shows, expose the ground of, and the harshness, defects, and disadvantages that inhere in, the modern and postmodern imperative to become the absolutely free and exclusive author of one's existence.

Berlanstein, Lenard R. Women and Power in Eighteenth-Century France: Actresses at the Comédie-Française. *Fem Stud*, 20(3), 475-506, Fall 94.

Were the Enlightenment and the French Revolution essentially antifeminist? This essay shifts through the claims and counter-claims by examining the responses to the power wielded by actresses over an eminent cultural institution, the French Theater. We find that neither moderate nor radical Enlightenment figures accepted women's influence as legitimate. Neither did voices from within the absolute public sphere. Virtually all representations of women with power were constructed around female sexuality. We conclude that the Enlightenment and Revolution were masculinist, but breaks with the patriarchy of the Old Regime were not so clear-cut as is often suggested.

Berleant, Arnold. "Architecture and the Aesthetics of Continuity" in *Philosophy and Architecture, Mitias, Michael H (ed)*, 21-30. Amsterdam, Rodopi, 1994.

Instead of building an account based on differences and oppositions, this discussion of the aesthetics of architecture identifies resemblances and develops continuities. From an awareness of the physical and social context of a building, through the integration of beauty and use, the building and its site, the human and the natural, and architecture and the city, we arrive at a connection between city, landscape, and region, where similar concepts can apply. Structures that do not interpose themselves or mediate between humans and the natural environment, but that articulate the continuities that bind people to their landscape, achieve the ultimate integration of the architectural and the human.

Berleant, Arnold. Aesthetics and Community. *J Value Inq*, 28(2), 257-272, Je 94.

The usual approach to social order is a political one, classification by governmental form, by the pattern in which power is distributed. This paper proposes a grouping of communities based instead on the character and quality of human relations. The rational, the moral, and the aesthetic communities, the forms it identifies, are not pure nor are they logically exclusive, yet they distinguish different kinds of social understanding and experience. An examination of the philosophical and moral presuppositions and implications of each supports the concept of an aesthetic community.

Berleant, Arnold. The Critical Aesthetics of Disney World. *J Applied Phil*, 11(2), 171-180, 1994.

An analysis of Disney World as an aesthetic environment provides important insights. Its many distinct areas constitute a multiplicity of environments—futuristic, ethnic, fantasy, adventure. Each shapes time, space, and movement in distinctive ways, making Disney World a microcosm of America's cultural pluralism and at the same time the kitsch of postmodernism. The aesthetic analysis of Disney's worlds, by showing how realities are created and subverted, confronts us with the pervasiveness of the normative and the inseparability of the moral and the aesthetic. The challenge of our time is to reform knowledge and value in a way that is pluralistic and open-ended, and yet provides the basis for both decision and action. (edited)

Berlinger, Rudolph (ed) and Girard, Louis and Schrader, Wiebke (ed). *Elementa: L'argument Ontologique chez Saint Anselme et chez Hegel (Band 60)*. Amsterdam, Rodopi, 1995.

L'exposé cartésien de l'argument ontologique s'écarte radicalement de l'esprit originaire de la preuve, chez Saint Anselme. Le Dieu de Descartes, parfait parce que tout-puissant, est bien différent du Dieu de *Proslogion*, "Celui qui est tel que rien de plus grande ne puisse être pensé", fin de la pensée et du désir humains. La preuve d' Anselme conceptualise une expérience humaine qui se pense comme l'expérience chrétienne orthodoxe, décrivant, de ce fait, l'homme en sa vérité. Mais on n'entrera pleinement dans la pensée spéculative que si l'aspiration à Dieu en l'homme est considérée comme l'envers dialectique de l'amour, créateur de l'homme, en Dieu. Chez Hegel, ce n'est pas l'esprit fini qui accomplit la preuve ontologique, mais l'Esprit dans sa totalité. Ce mouvement de l'Esprit vers soi à travers sa division d'avec soi n'est pas un simple processus logique; en sa profondeur, il est le mouvement de réconciliation de la liberté humaine avec la liberté divine, créatrice et rédemptrice. La vérité de la Totalité, et donc, aussi, de l'histoire, dans le Concept, dit également la libre unification de l'homme et de Dieu dans et par la figure historique du Christ. Hegel pense le christianisme sans le réduire, parce qu'il le pense à partir de l'acte préalable de la foi, par lequel la liberté humaine s'ouvre à l'amour divin, posant ainsi l'unité dialectique du Tout. Que la foi puisse être rationnellement exposée ne l'empêche pas d'être la foi, c'est-à-dire la vie en union au Christ, Logos éternel et homme crucifié. On a dit: "Un Dieu compris n'est plus un Dieu". Cela n'est vrai que des faux dieux.

Berman, Art. *Preface to Modernism*. Champaign, Univ of Illinois Pr, 1994.

The aesthetic movement named *modernism* began as an importation of the Romantic aesthetic into *modernity* (the empiricist-Enlightenment world view) when Romanticism itself, originally an idealism-based counteraction to modernity, became no longer feasible. This process refashions art and literature, and also concepts of history, time, selfhood, community, nature, and politics. Modernism is positioned in relation to previous aesthetic movements, like the Renaissance, and also to science, nationalism, capitalism, socialism, fascism, creativity, psychoanalysis, the notion of talent in the work place, and various philosophical controversies. When the initial Romantic impetus eventually proves unsustainable, modernism adopts formalism to justify its aesthetic.

Bermúdez, José Luis. Is the Postmodern World a Nietzschean World?. *Int Stud Phil*, 27(2), 1-14, 1995.

This paper criticizes appropriations of Nietzsche by leading theorists of the postmodern, including Foucault, Baudrillard and Lyotard. It argues that, despite superficial similarities of formulation, Nietzsche cannot be seen as a recursor of postmodern theory in the way that is often claimed. Although important strands of Nietzsche's thought attack Enlightenment conceptions of truth, rationality and explanation, his critique of the Enlightenment is rooted in concerns that are fundamentally psychological and ethical.

Bermúdez, José Luis. Peacocke's Argument Against the Autonomy of Nonconceptual Representational Content. *Mind Lang*, 9(4), 402-418, D 94.

The idea that there might be states with nonconceptual representational content has potential applications in philosophy as well as in several areas of psychology. This paper outlines some of these possible applications and suggests that the notion of nonconceptual content will be most fruitfully employed if it is conceded that a creature might be in such contentful states even though it possesses no concepts at all. This possibility is defended against Peacock's claim that being in states with nonconceptual content requires certain basic forms of conceptual mastery.

Bermúdez, José Luis. Scepticism and the Justification of Transcendental Idealism. *Ratio*, 8(1), 1-23, Ap 95.

In this paper I explore a justification for transcendental idealism that emerges from the dialogue with philosophical scepticism in which Kant is on and off engaged throughout the *Critique of Pure Reason*. Many commentators have claimed that transcendental idealism is an unfortunate addition to the *Critique*, one that can profitably be excised in the interests of clarity and coherence. Against this general picture I urge that transcendental idealism is in fact a very natural consequence of some of the central doctrines of the Critical Philosophy. Nonetheless, I argue that Kant's employment of transcendental idealism against the sceptic is seriously compromised by his postulating the existence of unknowable things-in-themselves. In the final section of the paper I suggest that the only possible escape from this difficulty would be to rule out the possibility of affirming that unknowable things-in-themselves exist. (edited)

Bermúdez, José Luis. Skepticism and Subjectivity: Two Critiques of Traditional Epistemology Reconsidered. *Int Phil Quart*, 35(2), 141-158, Ju 95.

Philosophers from both the continental and analytic traditions have argued that epistemological scepticism is a pseudo-problem that makes sense only in the context of certain mistaken presuppositions about subjectivity and the mind. This paper considers two such lines of argument, drawn from Heidegger and Wittgenstein, and shows that they fail to neutralise the sceptical challenge. The conclusion is drawn that epistemological scepticism remains a threat even if Heidegger's analysis of *Dasein* and Wittgenstein's Private Language Argument are accepted. The sceptical challenge is more durable than it is often given credit for.

Bermúdez, José Luis. Syntax, Semantics, and Levels of Explanation. *Phil Quart*, 45(180), 361-367, Jl 95.

John McDowell has recently used the distinction between personal and sub-personal explanation to argue that cognitive science cannot elucidate propositional attitude psychology—because syntactic sub-personal explanation is concerned only with the 'enabling conditions' of semantic explanation at the personal level. This paper argues, first, that it is untenable to mark the distinction between levels in terms of a distinction between syntax and semantics, because no purely syntactic account of sub-personal events is possible. Second, even if some principled account can be given of the distinction, restricting sub-personal explanation to 'enabling conditions' cannot be maintained.

Bermúdez, José Luis. The Adequacy of Simple Ideas in Locke—A Rehabilitation of Berkeley's Criticisms. *Locke News*, 23, 25-58, 1992.

This paper challenges the popular view that Berkeley completely misunderstood Locke and that his criticisms of Locke should be ignored. It argues that Locke's attempt to combine a representative theory of perception with a naive perceptual realism rests crucially on his view that simple ideas are adequate. What Berkeley's criticism of the primary/secondary qualities distinction succeeds in showing is that there can be no adequate simple ideas in the sense that Locke requires.

Bermúdez, José Luis. The Unity of Apperception in the *Critique of Pure Reason*. *Euro J Phil*, 2(3), 213-240, D 94.

This paper distinguishes two readings of the unity of apperception, according to their degrees of ontological commitment. It is argued that the principle of the unity of apperception can only be reconciled with the Paralogisms if it is read regulatively, in a way that is neutral on the existence of a single thinking subject. Although the unity of apperception demands that suitably unified thought be *ascribable* to a single thinking subject, it is compatible with there being a succession of such subjects, or no subject at all. This does not require abandoning the idea the 'I' can function as a referring expression. The implications of this for the interpretation of the Transcendental Analytic are discussed.

Bermudo, José M. Vico y Hobbes: el "verum-factum". *Cuad Vico*, 1, 135-153, 1991.

Although Vico makes several references to Hobbes, we are of the opinion that he never really had a narrow knowledge of the English philosopher. We do not think it worth to look for similarities through some selected passages or some general coincidences. But we do think it interesting to compare both methodological attitudes, their common efforts to establish the bases of a civil science by reversing the <jerachy of evidence>, that is, by bringing the level of social science to that of mathematics and shifting the natural sciences to the rank of hypothesis. These coincidences, even if they are not enough to allow an intellectual approach between Vico and Hobbes, allow a better understanding of their philosophical projects.

Bermudo, José M. Vico'1994. *Cuad Vico*, 4, 9-26, 1994.

In this paper, attention will be focused mainly on the *De nostri temporis studiorum rationis*, and it will be analised also the treatment which has been due to il verosimile's criterium somewhat as an antecedent for that which is contained in the *Scienza Nuova's* axioms. It will be pointed out how the attention which has been given to "il verosimile" has been kept straightforward along the lines of Vico's works and it stands as much as a basis for his epistemological project as well as global methodological attitude.

Bermudo Avila, José Manuel. Bentham: la ciencia del legislador. *Telos (Spain)*, 1(2), 63-79, Je 92.

Bentham's project is to draw an "Art of the Legislation", which in his times is equivalent to an "art of governing". Bentham looks for a rational criterium for political activity, common to the judge as well as to the legislator, which allows the establishment of a community ruled by the *artificial harmony of interests*. This political character of his project should not hide Bentham's interest towards the "private ethics". Such an interest is better understood from a functional typology, which allows the understanding of the individual as a man, as a citizen and, occasionally, as a legislator. The two former functions, related with prudence, probity and beneficence, would fall within the "private ethics", which Bentham strongly values. (edited)

Bernard, Christopher. "Hume and the Madness of Religion" in *Hume and Hume's Connexions, Stewart, M A (ed)*, 224-238. University Park, Penn St Univ Pr, 1995.

Bernasconi, Robert. On Deconstructing Nostalgia for Community within the West: The Debate between Nancy and Blanchot. *Res Phenomenol*, 23, 3-21, 1993.

Jean-Luc Nancy's notion of a community without communion is examined in the light of his debate with Maurice Blanchot and, by implication, with Emmanuel Levinas. It seems that Nancy's denial of the radical alterity of the Other leads him to maintain the privilege of the Occident and of Western philosophy. Not only does Nancy's deconstruction of community fail to attend to the history of the thought of community, as deconstruction demands, but it also reflects certain inherent prejudices within deconstruction already apparent in Derrida's early essays.

Bernasconi, Robert. On Heidegger's Other Sins of Omission: Asian Thought and Christian Philosophy. *Amer Cath Phil Quart*, 69(2), 333-350, Spr 95.

Heidegger's insistence that philosophy is Greek in origin and essence was not merely the reassertion of a consensus first formed at the end of the eighteenth century. Heidegger apparently recognized but chose to downplay the role of Asian thought in the formation of early Greek thought. He denied the genuineness not only of Chinese or Indian philosophy, but also of what passed for Christian philosophy. This essay finds the explanation for these decisions in his preparation for another beginning of thinking that was inspired by his contested reading of Hölderlin and addressed specifically to the Germans.

Bernat, James L and Gert, Bernard and Mogielnicki, R Peter. Distinguishing between Patients' Refusals and Requests. *Hastings Center Rep*, 24(4), 13-15, Jl-Ag 94.

Not distinguishing between patient requests and patient refusals, but referring to them both as choices or decisions and then talking of patient autonomy, has resulted in both theoretical and practical confusion. Patient refusals must be honored when they represent the rational decisions of competent patients even when physicians know death will result. Honoring such refusals is not killing; it is, at most, allowing to die. In contrast, there is no moral requirement to honor patient requests when physicians know death will result.

Bernet, Rudolf. An Intentionality Without Subject or Object?. *Man World*, 27(3), 231-255, Jl 94.

Husserl's theory of intentionality has often been criticized for its subjectivism or its objectivism. A closer reading of the texts shows that Husserl's introduction of the transcendental ego is not the mark of solipsism but was motivated by the analysis of other minds and of a subject that is divided in itself. Far from ignoring a form of intentionality that precedes the relation to an object, Husserl considers it to be the source of all objectifying intentionality and sees it at work in the temporal and bodily self-affection of the subject, in its feelings and also in its relation to the world.

Bernier, Réjane. Théorie Aristotélicienne du rôle de la quantité et de la qualité chez les êtres vivants (I). *Arch Phil*, 58(1), 3-34, Ja-Mr 95.

In an age when science has accorded pride of place to quantitative and qualitative approaches to natural beings, I thought it opportune to investigate Aristotle's position concerning the role of quantity and quality in the formation of material substances. I have therefore analyzed the relations which exist between the quantity and quality of various objects and their forms. This study takes as its point of departure *De Generatione et Corruptione* to study the generation of element and the production of homoeomeria. It then proceeds to a review of the biological treatises as far as these

concern the formation of anhomoeomeria and the structures of complex organisms. It also deals with the fundamental ontological problems of essence and the action of the four causes in the formation and the organic functioning of living things. These problems will be developed in the second part of this work, to be continued in the next issue.

Bernier, Réjane. Théorie Aristotélicienne du Rôle de la Quantité et de la Qualité chez les êtres Vivants (II). *Arch Phil*, 58(2), 177-197, Ap-Je 95.

Our previous study (see the preceding issue) of the scientific works of Aristotle, such as *On Generation* and *Corruption* and the biological treatises, demonstrated the need to reexamine some of the contemporary interpretations of the ontological thought of this philosopher. Questions arising from the scientific works about essentialism, hylemorphism, reductionism and the predominance of teleology within living things are confronted with the notion of form as a proportion of the various composing parts. The role of quantity and of quality in the determination of form and nature of the material being obliges one to take into account the material and the formal causes, along with the final cause, for any explication of the living being. In effect, for Aristotle, the exercise of a function depends upon the nature of a being, which depends in turn not only upon its form but also upon its material constitution.

Bernsen, Ann and Tabachnick, Barbara G and Pope, Kenneth S. National Survey of Social Workers' Sexual Attraction to Their Clients: Results, Implications, and Comparison to Psychologists. *Ethics Behavior*, 4(4), 369-388, 1994.

A survey form sent to psychologists (Pope, Keith-Spiegel, and Tabachnick, 1986) was adapted and sent to 1,000 clinical social workers (return rate = 45%). Most participants reported sexual attraction to a client, causing (for most) guilt, anxiety, or confusion. Some reported having sexual fantasies about a client while engaging in sex with someone other than a client. Relatively few (3.6% men; 0.5% women) reported sex with a client; training was related to likelihood of offending, though the effect is small and complex. An analysis of eight national studies (data from 5,148 therapists) found significant effects for gender (more male offenders) and year of study (about 10% annual decrease in reported offenses since 1977) but not profession (i.e., no difference among psychiatrists, psychologists, and social workers). Most social workers reported no graduate training whatsoever about sexual attraction; only 10% reported adequate training.

Bernstein, Mark H. Kanean Libertarianism. *SW Phil Rev*, 11(1), 151-157, Ja 95.

Although Robert Kane, in a book and a series of articles, has presented perhaps the most powerful case yet for a viable libertarian theory of free will, I argue that, ultimately, his view succumbs to a constant thorn in the side of such theories. I argue that in Kane's libertarian world, one in which indeterminism is embraced, let alone begrudgingly accepted, personal control over one's actions is precluded. As such Kane fails to provide us with a libertarianism with which we can find comfort.

Berque, Augustin. Milieu et logique du lieu chez Watsuji. *Rev Phil Louvain*, 92(4), 495-507, N 94.

With the aim of supporting the conviction that there exists, at the meeting-point of corporeity (explored especially by European phenomenology) and of mediance (explored particularly by Japanese thought), a dimension of the real, the scientific analysis of which is only starting, the author inquires what Japanese thought can contribute to his own fundamental project of "mesology". At this point Berque, returning to the founding era of Japanese consciousness (the years 1920-1930), studies the Japanese notions of *fûdo* (environment) and of *basho* (situation, order, position, place)—the former of which was worked out by Watsuji (who discusses the theory of the influence of the environment on the manner of being of a people and of man in general), and the latter by Nishida (who worked out a "logic of place"). In both cases the aim is to surmount the difficulties arising from the dichotomy subject-object, and to inquire into the finitude and vulnerability of the terrestrial household.

Bersoff, Donald N and Koeppl, Peter M. The Relation Between Ethical Codes and Moral Principles. *Ethics Behavior*, 3(3-4), 345-357, 1993.

We describe the application of fundamental moral principles, with particular emphasis on prima facie duties, to formal codes of ethics that regulate the conduct of forensic psychologists who act as expert witnesses. Then we discuss the American Psychological Association's (1992) "Ethical Principles of Psychologists and Code of Conduct" and the Committee on Ethical Guidelines for Forensic Psychologist's "Specialty Guidelines for Forensic Psychologists" (1991) and critically appraise how these documents translate basic moral principles. We conclude that, in many ways, the documents exemplify ethical obligations such as nonmaleficence, beneficence, and justice, but they fall short in many other ways, particularly with regard to autonomy and fidelity.

Bertelloni, Francisco. Implicaciones políticas de la eclesiología de Wyclif. *Pat Med*, 15, 45-58, 1994.

This paper deals with the political consequences of Wyclif's ecclesiological thought, in particular of his extreme theory about divine predestination. The paper is organized in three parts: 1) Starting from a short analysis of Gottschalk's (IX century) predestination theory, 2) he analyzes the basis of Wyclif's ecclesiology, and 3) her utopian consequences.

Berten, André. Le juste et le bien: priorité ou complémentarité?. *Stud Phil (Switzerland)*, 53, 9-33, 1994.

Bertens, Hans (ed) and D'haen, Theo (ed). *Liminal Postmodernisms: The Postmodern, the (Post-)Colonial, and the (Post-)Feminist*. Amsterdam, Rodopi, 1994.

Liminal Postmodernisms (Postmodern Studies 8), concentrates on the various intersections between "The Postmodern", the "(Post-)Colonial", and the "(Post-)Feminist". Central to all the essays, by Robert Young, Sylvia Söderlind, John Thieme, Steven Connor, Richard Todd, Chantal Zabus, Hena Maes-Jelinek, Christine Levecq, Maria Del Sapio Garbero, R J Ellis, Allen Thiher, Annemarie Kemeny, Michael Gronow, Allen E Hibbard, and Julia Martin are the issues of liminality, of borders and boundaries both separating and joining races, genders, and nationalities, of definitions and discourses establishing others and selves. Philosophers regularly referred to include Deleuze and Guattari, Derrida, Foucault, and Lacan.

Berthold-Bond, Daniel. Can There Be a "Humanistic" Ecology? A Debate Between Hegel and Heidegger on the Meaning of Ecological Thinking. *Soc Theor Pract*, 20(3), 279-309, Fall 94.

The article engages the current debate between 'humanistic' and 'anti-humanistic' alternatives for an ecological philosophy by putting Heidegger and Hegel into dialogue. It is argued that Heidegger's portrait of Hegel's philosophy as a form of 'humanism' which foreshadows the modern logic of domination and exploitation of nature is highly misleading. Hegel's 'humanistic' position can allow for a genuinely ecological vision of nature, which, while not as radically ecological as Heidegger's, may in fact avoid some of the problems of Heidegger's view.

Berti, Enrico. Aristotle's Renaissance As an Example of the Essential Tension between Tradition and Innovation. *Phil Inq*, 16(3-4), 26-37, Sum-Fall 94.

As Thomas S Kuhn has shown, the tension between tradition and innovation is essential for the development of science. The most evident proof of his theory was the dialectical opposition between Padua Aristotelianism and Galileian science in the XVII century. An example of the same tension is the survival of Aristotelian tradition in the XXth century, which has produced many new ways of thinking. These are the Heideggerian thought, the analytical philosophy of Austin, Ryle, Strawson, Wiggins and others, the hermeneutics of Gadamer, the new rhetoric of Perelman, the "rehabilitation of practical philosophy" of J Ritter, Bubner, the neo-Aristotelianism of MacIntyre, Williams, Sen and Jonas, the new epistemology of Kuhn, Prigogine and Thom.

Bertman, Martin A. Arte y Grandeza. *Logos (Mexico)*, 22(66), 121-134, S-D 94.

Bertola, Ermenegildo. La grammatica ed il problema degli universali nel Medioevo cristiano. *Riv Filosof Neo-Scolas*, 86(3), 491-505, Jl-S 94.

Bertoldi, Francesco. Blondel e la verità come "Adaequatio Realis". *Sapienza*, 47(3), 337-355, 1994.

Bertolet, Rod. Conventions and Coreferentiality. *J Phil Res*, 19, 257-262, 1994.

In *Frege's Puzzle*, Nathan Salmon takes it to be obvious that the fact that names such as 'Hesperus' and 'Phosphorus' are coreferential is purely a matter of arbitrary linguistic convention, while the fact that Hesperus is Phosphorus is by no means a conventional matter. Salmon also takes these points to be ones to which Frege appeals in the opening paragraph of "On Sense and Reference," and hence finds it ironic that these points undercut the theory of sense that Frege develops in that paper. It is argued that the thesis that the coreferentiality of a pair of proper names is purely a matter of arbitrary linguistic convention is inconsistent with *any* plausible theory of reference. Salmon's reading of Frege's argument is also called into question.

Bertrand, Pierre. Critique de la Raison: Pour la Philosophie. *Philosopher*, 14, 155-169, 1993.

Berven, Dikka (ed). *Montaigne: A Collection of Essays, Volume 1—Montaigne's Message and Method*. New York, Garland, 1995.

Scholarship on Montaigne has moved in several directions in the twentieth century. Early studies of the *Essais* stress the development and evolution of Montaigne's thought. Scholars based their studies in large part on conclusion drawn from Montaigne's process of continually adding to his text, additions which are represented in successive editions of the *Essais* and which are now designated in most modern editions as the A, B and C layers of the text. Much valuable research resulted from the assumption that the *Essais* represents Montaigne's ideas on the many subject matters he treats throughout the work. More recent literary criticism has shifted its focus, giving greater emphasis to the written text than to its writer—all the while admitting the difficulties inherently associated with the study of a text by an author who describes himself as consubstantial with his book. Montaigne's form is open, his method unresolving, yet critics have described a coherence and deep sense of order and purpose in his text.

Berven, Dikka (ed). *Montaigne: A Collection of Essays, Volume 2—Sources of Montaigne's Thought*. New York, Garland, 1995.

Recent critical work on Montaigne's sources, while indebted to earlier studies which have identified and dated Montaigne's borrowed material, emphasizes the function of his sources in the text of the *Essais*. Analysis of Montaigne's skillful method of quoting, misquoting, concealing quotes, or camouflaging them has revealed at work in the *Essais* a new idea about the nature of language and written discourse, as well as new perceptions of the multiplicity of meanings inherent in shifting contexts. Articles in this volume provide insight into Montaigne's complex world of literary allusions.

Berven, Dikka (ed). *Montaigne: A Collection of Essays, Volume 3—Montaigne's Rhetoric*. New York, Garland, 1995.

Montaigne's *Essais* has been described as the most personal book in world literature. His claim to be of the same substance as his book, and the perpetual sense of his presence in the pages of the *Essais*, have led to much valuable scholarship on Montaigne's personal intellectual history. Recent trends in Montaigne's criticism reveal a shift away from the writer toward an interest in uncovering rhetorical and compositional strategies used by Montaigne. Articles in this volume demonstrate that the engaging artfulness of Montaigne's natural style belies his modest pretense that he writes as he would speak. Lately critics have proclaimed that the success of the self-portrait of the *Essais* may very well be due to Montaigne's unequalled rhetorical abilities.

Berven, Dikka (ed). *Montaigne: A Collection of Essays, Volume 4—Language and Meaning*. New York, Garland, 1995.

Modern readers in need of a precise understanding both of the changes in the French language over the last 400 years since the *Essais* was written and of the idiosyncracies of Montaigne's usage, will appreciate these articles exploring the nuances and fluctuations in the meaning of many of Montaigne's words. These critical studies of Montaigne's vocabulary and its shifting contexts will aid in understanding how Montaigne's choice of words reflects his ability to take elements from his background of wide-ranging, life-long classical reading and blend them with his own original unflagging curiosity and speculation about matters relating to contemporary life.

Berven, Dikka (ed). *Montaigne: A Collection of Essays, Volume 5—Reading Montaigne*. New York, Garland, 1995.

Critics have discovered in the pages of the *Essais* that Montaigne's views on reading and writing are surprisingly modern and relevant to present-day interests in the origins of meaning. Articles in this volume explore the nature of the relationship between the text of the *Essais* and its reader, and between writer and reader. Montaigne is, as Terence Cave has put it, in search of a reader who falls into no pre-existing category, a reader fashioned to a certain extent by Montaigne himself. Ultimately, such studies as the articles included in this volume assist the reader's understanding of the *Essais* and his role in it, and they pertain as well to the more general issue of the role of the reader before all written discourse.

Beschle, Donald L. The Role of Courts in the Debate on Assisted Suicide: A Communitarian Approach. *Notre Dame J Law Ethics*, 9(2), 367-405, 1995.

Besnier, Niko. Involvement in Linguistic Practice: An Ethnographic Appraisal. *J Prag*, 22(3-4), 279-299, O 94.

This paper is a critical examination of 'involvement' as an analytic category in sociolinguistics and discourse analysis. The discussion first identifies a variety of conceptual problems associated with the nature and locus of involvement. Then a number of ethnographic studies focusing on the relationship between language use, emotionality, society, and culture are described, and the usefulness of involvement as a descriptive and theoretical tool is evaluated. This paper shows that involvement, a notion which assumes Western views of interaction, emotionality, and personhood, does not adequately capture the essence of the interactional dynamics described in these ethnographic reports. An alternative agenda is outlined, in which the relationship between emotionality and linguistic practices is solidly grounded in a critical examination of the cultural and social dynamics in which it is embedded.

Besse, Guy. "Das Erbe der Aufklärung: Mut zum Denken, Mut zum Handeln" in *Das geistige Erbe Europas, Buhr, Manfred (ed)*, 272-276. Napoli, Vivarium, 1994.

Best, Steven. "Foucault, Postmodernism, and Social Theory" in *Postmodernism and Social Inquiry, Dickens, David R (ed)*, 25-52. New York, Guilford, 1994.

The author attempts to situate Foucault's work in relation to postmodern theory and sociology. He provides an overview of Foucault's work in its changes and overall themes. Foucault's work is distinguished from more radical postmodernists like Baudrillard and assessed for its potential value to sociology.

Best, Steven. "The Commodification of Reality and the Reality of Commodification" in *Baudrillard: A Critical Reader, Kellner, Douglas M (ed)*, 41-67. Cambridge, Blackwell, 1994.

In this essay, I critically compare the work of Karl Marx, Guy Debord, and Jean Baudrillard. I analyze the movement from the society of the *commodity*, to the society of the *spectacle*, to the society of the *simulacrum*, tracing a process of abstraction that Baudrillard claims leads to the end of reality in a mass-media generated "hyperreality."

Betegh, Gábor. The Sun and the Foot: Heraclitus in the Derveni Papyrus. *Magyar Filozof Szemle*, 1-2, 71-84, 1994.

We have finally at our disposal the first two columns of the highly awaited critical edition of the Derveni Papyrus by K Tsantsanoglou and G M Parássoglou (published in the *Studi e Testi per il corpo dei papiri filosofici greci e latini* and with some slight modifications in the *Corpus dei papiri Filosofici Grecie Latini*). This edition approves of W Burkert's proposition: the Derveni author quotes Heraclitus by name. Furthermore, this text provides the Heraclitean scholarship with a most surprising lesson: as the editors put it, "What had been known up to the present as two distinct and independent fragments (B3 and B94 DK = 57 and 52 M) appear now as one continuous fragment". (edited)

Bett, Richard. What did Pyrrho Think About "The Nature of the Divine and the Good"?. *Phronesis*, 39(3), 303-337, 1994.

A fragment of Timon of Phlius, quoted by Sextus Empiricus (*M* XI.20), represents someone speaking of "the nature of the divine and the good" as somehow the key to a trouble-free life. The speaker was always assumed to be Pyrrho, and the fragment was thought crucial in reconstructing his views—yet problematic because of its apparently anti-skeptical tone. The article argues that the view expressed cannot be squared with what we know about Pyrrho, but that there is no reason to think that the speaker was Pyrrho; a conundrum in early history of Greek scepticism is thereby removed.

Bettinelli, Carla. La fenomenologia, uno sguardo sulla verità. *Aquinas*, 37(2), 403-408, My-Ag 94.

Bettiolo, Isabella Adinolfi. "Oltre l'etica: Il rapporto tra morale e sovramorale in Soren Kierkeggard" in *L'etica e il suo Altro, Vigna, Carmelo (ed)*, 150-188. Milano, FrancoAngeli, 1994.

Betzler, Monika. Von einer Ethik der Technik aus antinaturalistischem Geist. *Phil Rundsch*, 42(1), 60-68, Mr 95.

Beuchot, Mauricio. Antecedentes Griegos y Medievales del Calculo Logico. *Topicos*, 1(1), 13-23, 1991.

Beuchot, Mauricio. Cuerpo y Alma en el Helemorfismo de Santo Tomás. *Rev Espan Filosof Med*, 0, 39-46, 1993.

Beuchot, Mauricio. Intentionality in John Poinsot. *Amer Cath Phil Quart*, 68(3), 279-296, Sum 94.

Beuchot, Mauricio. La Filosofía Escolástica en los Orígenes de la Semiótica de Peirce. *Analogia*, 5(2), 155-166, 1991.

Beuchot, Mauricio. La fundamentación filosófica de los derechos humanos en Jacques Maritain. *Topicos*, 3(4), 9-26, 1993.

The author shows how the relation between natural rights and human rights has some arguments with an idea of human rights in the Thomist philosophy, according to Maritain's stand point of view.

Beuchot, Mauricio. La polémica en torno a la distinción de la esencia y la existencia entre Enrique de Gante y Gil de Roma. *Rev Filosof (Argentina)*, 8(1-2), 47-58, N 93.

Beuchot, Mauricio. La Teoría de las Distinciones en la Edad Media y su Influjo en la Edad Moderna. *Rev Espan Filosof Med*, 1, 37-48, 1994.

Beuchot, Mauricio. Los Campos de la Argumentación. *Rev Filosof (Mexico)*, 28(82), 61-87, Ja-Ap 95.

Beuchot, Mauricio. Los Predicamentos o Categorías en el Cardenal Cayetano. *Analogia*, 8(1), 41-78, 1994.

Beuchot, Mauricio and Deely, John. Common Sources for the Semiotic of Charles Peirce and John Poinsot. *Rev Metaph*, 48(3), 539-566, Mr 95.

Beuscher, Bernd. *Positives Paradox: Entwurf einer neostrukturalistischen Religionspädagogik*. Vienna, Passagen, 1993.

Beuschers Studie kreist um die zentralen Begriffe der Geschöpflichkeit (fragmentarische Identität unterwegs), Gelassenheit (Konfirmation als Entsicherung des Glaubens), Angewiesenheit (das/der Fremde als Spiegel der Selbsterkenntnis), Getriebenheit (Angst als Index von Welt) und Getrostheit (Paradox der Gnade). Dabei wird sowohl die strukturale Psychoanalyse Jacques Lacans auf ihre theologische Relevanz hin befragt als auch das Werk des des 1942 in Treblinka umgekommenen Pädagogen Janusz Korczak als Realutopie gewürdigt. (edited)

Bevir, Mark. Objectivity in History. *Hist Theor*, 33(3), 328-344, 1994.

Many philosophers have rejected the possibility of objective historical knowledge on the grounds that there is no given past against which to judge rival interpretations. Their reasons for doing so are valid. But this does not demonstrate that we must give up the concept of historical objectivity as such. The purpose of this paper is to define a concept of objectivity based on criteria of comparison, not on a given past. Objective interpretations are those which best meet rational criteria of accuracy, comprehensiveness, consistency, progressiveness, fruitfulness, and openness. Finally, the nature of our being in the world is shown to give us a good reason to regard such objective interpretations as moving towards truth understood as a regulative ideal.

Bewaji, John A I. Critical Comments on Pearce, African Philosophy, and the Sociological Thesis. *Phil Soc Sci*, 25(1), 99-119, Mr 95.

Pearce's "African Philosophy and the Sociological Thesis" makes very interesting reading. Why it is interesting is not because it advances the frontiers of philosophical discourse in Africa or globally but because it shows that certain unwarranted dispositions die hard and that deliberate ignorance, if that is what is displayed, is hard to cure. In this article the author comments on the following contentions made by Pearce: 1) philosophy has no social relevance and/or responsibility; 2) philosophy is purely a linguistic activity concerned with analysis of concepts and examination; 3) philosophy derives from religion; 4) because African philosophy cannot supplant world philosophy, it lacks locus and legitimacy; 5) African philosophy pursues intellectual apartheid through an ethnophilosophical agenda; and 6) African philosophy is vulnerable to the Sociological Thesis and is voided by it. The author's rebuttal consists of a critical and analytic examination of Pearce's views, counterfactual illustrations, and elicitation of enthymemic presuppositions.

Bewaji, Tunde. Truth and Ethics in African Thought: A Reply to Emmanuel Eze. *Quest*, 8(1), 76-89, Je 94.

In an attempt to provide an analysis of "truth" and "ethics" on "African thought" Professor E Eze gave certain novel interpretations of the Yoruba Ifa literary corpus and divination system which are very curious as well as fantastic. I argue that while some of these interpretations might be appropriate to the Igbo Afa system, and among other societies where these divination system might be practiced, this does not represent the situation in the Yoruba epistemic, moral, cultural and religious practice of Ifa. I use extant literature and my personal research already in print to show some of the discrepancies.

Beyssade, Jean-Marie. *VIX (Ethique* IV Appendice chapitre 7) ou peut-on se sauver tout seul?. *Rev Metaph Morale*, 99(4), 493-503, O-D 94.

Bezuidenhout, Anne. "The Impossibility of Punctate Mental Representations" in *Holism: A Consumer Update, Fodor, Jerry (ed)*, 197-212. Amsterdam, Rodopi, 1993.

In *Holism: A Shopper's Guide* Fodor and LePore contend that there could be punctate minds; minds capable of being in only a single type of representational state. The Kantian idea that the construction of perceptual representations requires the synthesizing activity of the mind is invoked to argue against the possibility of punctate minds. Fodor's commitment to an inferential theory of perception is shown to share crucial assumptions with the Kantian view and hence to lead to the same conclusion. The argument from the need for synthesis is then extended beyond the perceptual case to mental representation in general.

Bhate, Anilkumar. Whither Universalism?. *Dialogue Hum*, 3(2), 83-87, 1993.

Bhave, S M. Remarks on Wittgenstein's Philosophy of Mathematics. *Indian Phil Quart*, 21(2), 147-160, Ap 94.

Transfinite numbers are made mysterious by attaching wrong pictures to them. By undertaking artificial revision of mathematics the logicists attempt to legitimise these wrong pictures. For Wittgenstein, mathematics begins as a technique which conceptualises several empirical processes that constitute the form of life for a community. The processes that constitute the form of life for a community. The processes develop into a technique because there is a spontaneous and universal consensus on its results. Mathematics grows by forming new concepts and enlarging the old ones. Mankind is completely free to carry out this activity. Therefore there is no pre-determined mathematical reality which acts as a control on mathematics.

Biagioli, Mario. Jesuit Science Between Texts and Contexts. *Stud Hist Phil Sci*, 25(4), 637-646, Ag 94.

Bialas, Wolfgang. Gemeinschaft und Gesellschaft: Deutsch-deutsche Variationen zum Thema. *Deut Z Phil*, 43(2), 365-374, 1995.

Bialas, Wolfgang. Zwischen 'Kritik der bürgerlichen Ideologie' und 'integralem Marxismus': Zur Rexeption der Frankfurter Schule in der DDR. *Deut Z Phil*, 43(1), 131-142, 1995.

Bianco, Franco. Die Hermeneutik-Debatte in der italienischen Philosophie der Gegenwart. *Z Phil Forsch*, 48(4), 595-613, 1994.

Bicchieri, Cristina. Paradoxes of Rationality. *Midwest Stud Phil*, 15, 65-79, 1990.

Bickhard, Mark H. Intrinsic Constraints on Language: Grammar and Hermeneutics. *J Prag*, 23(5), 541-554, My 95.

Functional and pragmatic approaches to grammar, and to language more broadly, are well known. All of these approaches, however, accept a core aspect of sentences, or utterances, as consisting of encodings of propositions. They proceed on their functional and pragmatic explorations with this much, at least, taken for granted. I wish to argue, to the contrary, that the functional characteristics of utterances penetrate even to the level of the structure—the grammar—of supposed propositional encodings. More specifically, I argue that the structure that is taken as a structure of propositional encodings is not that at all, but is instead a structure of functionally organized action. *Constraints* on such structures, in turn—constraints on grammars—emerge as intrinsic constraints on that functional organization. My point will of necessity be made programmatically, since to fill it out completely would be to complete a functional version of universal grammar.

Bidet, Jacques. A Metastructural Reinterpretation of the Rawlsian Theory: From Rawls to Machiavelli. *Ratio Juris*, 8(1), 68-84, Mr 95.

In the framework of a reinterpretation of Marxism and Rawlsianism which aims at a non-ecletic integration of both these theories, the author presents a transformation of the Rawlsian principles of justice into principles of political struggle with a view to establishing a just society. He deduces this normative development from a general theory of the modern world, proposed in his recent book (Bidet 1990).

Biel, Joseph. Teaching in the Shadow of Socrates. *Teach Phil*, 17(4), 345-350, D 94.

The article suggests that, for a Socratic-like dialogue to develop successfully in the classroom, it is necessary to establish an appropriate context for dialogue. Classical rhetorical theory provides concepts and terms that are useful for understanding and discussing the context of the Socratic dialogues.

Bien, Joseph. "Ricoeur as Social Philosopher" in *The Philosophy of Paul Ricoeur, Hahn, Lewis Edwin (ed)*, 287-305. Peru, Open Court, 1994.

The essay's purpose is to understand Ricoeur's different perspectives on social activity. Part One deals with his attempt to elucidate the willing of the self especially as understood in terms of consent. Major reference is made to *The Voluntary and the Involuntary* wherein he approaches the matter in an existential/phenomenological manner. Part Two points to the dialectical relationship between man and nature and the resultant emergence of freedom. Part Three deals with the hermeneutical approach to the question of ideology, especially Marxist ideology.

Bienenstock, Myriam. La lecture du journal selon Hegel: "une sorte de-prière du matin réaliste"?. *Arch Phil*, 57(4), 669-681, O-D 94.

Hegel always remained very interested in the minutest events of his time, yet never stopped to be a philosopher. The following paper clarifies the meaning of this attitude towards history and politics by examining his Jena *Notes and Fragments* (1803-1806) and, more particularly, by trying to answer the following questions: did Hegel approve of the expanding fashion, in his time, of newspaper-reading? Why did he require from philosophers to speak in their own language?

Biesta, Gert J J. Pragmatism as a Pedagogy of Communicative Action. *Stud Phil Educ*, 13(3-4), 273-290, 1994-95.

This paper gives an interpretation of the educational philosophy of John Dewey. Pragmatism understands education in terms of communication; communication is understood in terms of action. It is argued that the pragmatic understanding of communication is not just a different understanding of communication. Communication is an anthropological concept meant as an alternative for the Cartesian philosophy of consciousness. From the latter perspective, communicative pedagogy is a contradiction in terms, as education is seen as the process which brings about the competency to communicate. It is shown how this "communication paradox" is dissolved from a pragmatic point of view.

Biewener, Carole (ed) and Cullenberg, Stephen (ed) and Callari, Antonio (ed). *Marxism in the Postmodern Age*. New York, Guilford, 1994.

Fifty-three multidisciplinary essays which explore how Marxist theory is critically rethinking its conditions and objects of analysis. Situated in the context of changing national and international conditions, including the collapse of really existing socialism, the book captures a dialogue, carried on non-essentialist ground, between established Marxist concepts (of class and of economic interests) and other social identities and forms of oppression and resistence. The essays, many of which are by well-known contemporary figures, probe for an imaginary of social transformation capable of going beyond the established dichotomies of the modernist age, and chart a vast analytical terrain for a post-orthodox Marxism.

Bigelow, John. Van Inwagen's New Clothes. *Dialogue (Canada)*, 33(2), 297-304, Spr 94.

Bílek, Josef. Where Do We Start. *Filozof Cas*, 43(1), 136-138, 1995.

Bilimoria, Purushottama. Duhkha & Karma: The Problem of Evil and God's Omnipotence. *Sophia (Australia)*, 34(1), 92-119, Mr-Ap 95.

Bilimoria, Purusottama. "Ethics of Emotion: Some Indian Reflections" in *Emotions in Asian Thought, Marks, Joel (ed)*, 65-89. Albany, SUNY Pr, 1995.

A conundrum informs the inquiry: how is it that the Indian aesthetics identified forty-eight emotions common in human life, while about half of these are recognized as emotions, distinguished from sensations, feelings, affect, by Western theorists of emotions? A phenomenological survey and analysis of classical Indian thinking on the emotions, in philosophy, literary theory, in drama, dance and musical repertoire reveals more. The opening battle scene of Bhagavadgita where despondent Arjuna submits to his guru-analyst Krishna is re-interpreted to uncover the ethical and moral sensibilities of the culture reflected and inexorably intertwined, it is argued, with cultural expressions of the emotions.

Billig, Michael. "Sod Baudrillard! Or Ideology Critique in Disney World" in *After Postmodernism, Simons, Herbert W (ed)*, 150-171. Newbury Park, Sage, 1994.

This article discusses the work of Jean Baudrillard, especially his notion that in contemporary conditions there is little possibility of making ideology-critiques. This issue is discussed in relation to the possibility of an ideological critique of Disney World. Part of the argument involves criticising Baudrillard's style of writing and his 'fiction theory'. A more humane way of writing is proposed. As part of this recommendation, the article includes its own fictional vignettes of Disney World.

Billig, Michael (ed) and Simons, Herbert W (ed). *After Postmodernism*. Newbury Park, Sage, 1994.

Billings, Blake (trans) and Levinas, Emmanuel. The Primacy of Pure Practical Reason. *Man World*, 27(4), 445-453, O 94.

Bineham, Jeffery L. Displacing Descartes: Philosophical Hermeneutics and Rhetorical Studies. *Phil Rhet*, 27(4), 300-312, 1994.

Several communication scholars have worked to identify the influences of Cartesian dualism in rhetorical and communication studies and to call for the displacement of the Cartesian paradigm. One suggestion has been to move away from epistemology and toward philosophical hermeneutics as a framework for research. This essay, the second part of which is published in the next issue of *Philosophy & Rhetoric*, takes up that suggestion by examining how philosophical hermeneutics can obviate the problems of Cartesian dualism which plague rhetorical and communication studies. The paper argues, more specifically, that a focus on the hermeneutic medium, which emphasizes the ontological and social dimensions of language and tradition, can provide an escape from the Cartesian legacy in rhetoric and communication.

Bineham, Jeffery L. The Hermeneutic Medium. *Phil Rhet*, 28(1), 1-16, Ja 95.

Several communication scholars have worked to identify the influences of Cartesian dualism in rhetorical and communication studies, and to call for the displacement of the Cartesian paradigm. One suggestion has been to move away from epistemology and toward philosophical hermeneutics as a framework for research. The first part of this essay, which is published in the previous issue of *Philosophy and Rhetoric*, takes up that suggestion by examining how philosophical hermeneutics can obviate the problems of Cartesian dualism which plague rhetorical and communication studies. The paper argues, more specifically, that a focus on the hermeneutic medium, which emphasizes the ontological and social dimensions of language and tradition, can provide an escape from the Cartesian legacy in rhetoric and communication.

Binns, Peter. Affect, Agency, and Engagement: Conceptions of the Person in Philosophy, Neuropsychiatry, and Psychotherapy. *Phil Psychiat Psych*, 1(1), 13-23, Mr 94.

This paper is a critical account, centered on the views of a contemporary analytic philosopher, Derek Parfit, of concepts of the person which reduce personal processes to the mental content that they contain. It is argued that 1) the "split-brain" thought experiments that Parfit sees as undermining the unity of the person in fact only reveal some nonpathological divisions in its executive functions; 2) the reductionist analysis that Parfit offers fails to take account of the socially constituted dimension of personal life, producing a one-sidedly psychologistic analysis; 3) even within the realm of the psychological, this analysis fails to capture a central feature of personal processes; and 4) this is revealed through an examination of Korsakoff's syndrome patients. (edited)

Binns, Peter. Commentary on "Contentless Consciousness". *Phil Psychiat Psych*, 2(1), 61-63, Mr 95.

This is a commentary on Sullivan's "Contentless Consciousness and Information-Processing Theories" (Phil Psychiat Psych, 2(1), 51-59). It supports the latter's view that informational content and the way it is processed, is not a sufficient criterion for consciousness. However, it questions the way that the theory of functionalism has been criticized on the basis of this premise. It also questions the assumption that unmediated experience must be free of all cultural and social determinants.

Binns, Peter. Integrity, Boundary and the Ecology of Personal Processes. *Philosophy*, 37(Supp), 83-101, 1994.

Birch, Charles. "Darwinism and Postmodern Theism" in *Biology, Ethics, and the Origins of Life, Rolston III, Holmes (ed)*, 191-216. Boston, Jones & Bartlett, 1995.

Bird, Graham H. Carnap and Quine: Internal and External Questions. *Erkenntnis*, 42(1), 41-64, Ja 95.

Carnap's complex set of distinctions between internal and external questions from his paper "Empiricism, Semantics, and Ontology"[1] has been influential but is now widely regarded as erroneous and long since refuted. It is not at all fanciful to trace one major source, perhaps *the* major source, of that verdict to Quine's comments in his paper "On Carnap's Views on Ontology" and in *Word and Object*.[2] For, although many others have commented unfavourably on Carnap's distinctions, most of these criticisms post-date Quine's comments and many of them are consciously influenced by Quine.[3] Nevertheless, despite this consensus I want to argue that Quine's criticisms leave Carnap's central points quite untouched. (edited)

Birdwhistell, Anne D. Medicine and History as Theoretical Tools in a Confucian Pragmatism. *Phil East West*, 45(1), 1-28, Ja 95.

The purpose of this article is to examine how the metaphor of medicine and a particular view of the past helped to establish a pragmatic theoretical position within Confucian philosophy. The thought of Li Yong (1627-1705) is used as a particular example. Li viewed the teachings of specific philosophers as prescriptions aimed at treating the "illness" of social, political, and moral disorder, and he used the Confucian view of the past as "evidence" to show the effectiveness of past teachings (prescriptions) in healing social illnesses. He rejected the biological or generative metaphor as appropriate for conceptualizing Confucian teachings.

Birmingham, Elizabeth (trans) and Janicaud, Dominique and Birmingham, Peg (trans). *Powers of the Rational: Science, Technology, and the Future of Thought*. Bloomington, Indiana Univ Pr, 1994.

Birmingham, Peg (trans) and Janicaud, Dominique and Birmingham, Elizabeth (trans). *Powers of the Rational: Science, Technology, and the Future of Thought*. Bloomington, Indiana Univ Pr, 1994.

Birnbacher, Dieter. "Verantwortung für zukünftige Generationen" in *Freiheit, Verantwortung und Folgen in der Wissenschaft, Sandkühler, Hans Jörg (ed)*, 79-95. New York, Lang, 1994.

The contribution gives an outline of the main problems of a future ethics and draws attention to the ethical problem of future discounting in economic planning models. Hare's argument that future discounting is incompatible with the principle of universalizability is questioned and an independent metaethical argument against discounting proposed. The final section applies future ethics of the problem of climate change and draws some practical conclusions for climate protection and energy conservation policy.

Birner, Jack. "Idealizations and Theory Development in Economics" in *Idealization VI: Idealization in Economics, Hamminga, Bert (ed)*, 277-301. Amsterdam, Rodopi, 1994.

How are idealized theories related to models that are closer to the reality of existing economics? Historical background of the method, and the problem, providing the framework for discussing some recent analyses, especially Nancy Cartwright's. The problem must be seen as a part of the context of the logic of discovery. The relation between idealizing theories and factual models can be fruitfully analyzed in terms of a presupposition relation.

Birtel, Frank T. Contributions of Tipler's Omega Point Theory. *Zygon*, 30(2), 315-327, Je 95.

An attempt to discover what can be learned from the recent work of Frank Tipler on the Omega Point theory requires an analysis of his framework of understanding from scientific, philosophical, and theological perspectives. A critique of his crucial ideas, and of the salient points raised by some of his critics, can then be undertaken within the compass of his strengths. A critique of the critiques of Tipler's work allows one to evaluate the extent and limitations of his contributions.

Birx, H James. The Challenge of Exoevolution. *Free Inq*, 15(1), 32-34, Wint 94-95.

In the history of explanations for live on earth, the materialist writings of Charles Darwin established the fact of organic evolution to account for the emergence, diversity, and extinction of species on this planet. In fact, life forms and intelligent beings may also exist on other worlds. Furthermore, exobiology implies exoevolution: the origin, differential reproduction, and adaptive radiation of species on various planets throughout this cosmos and/or in other universes. Secular humanists may even anticipate the future science of comparative exoevolution. The far-reaching consequences of such a new perspective will challenge all earth-bound and human-centered worldviews.

Bishop, Anne H and Scudder Jr, John R. *Nursing Ethics: Therapeutic Caring Presence*. Boston, Jones & Bartlett, 1996.

The authors challenge the applied approach to nursing ethics by contending that nursing ethics articulates the moral sense inherent in nursing practice and assesses its fulfillment, appraises its adequacy, and explores new possibilities for fulfilling and expanding its moral sense. Through interpreting exemplars of nursing excellence, they disclose the integral relationship of care as practice with care a motive in good nursing practice and develop an ethics of therapeutic caring presence. The goal of their ethics is to help practicing nurses fulfill the moral sense of nursing by making ethics integral to nursing practice rather than applying detached expertise to it.

Bishop, Greg. Ultrafilters Generated by a Closed Set of Functions. *J Sym Log*, 60(2), 415-430, Je 95.

Bishop, John. Deciding to Believe: The Ethics and Rationality of Religious Belief. *Sophia (Australia)*, 34(1), 9-31, Mr-Ap 95.

A Jamesian defence of a moderate fideism which holds that acceptance of (religious) belief beyond, though not contrary to, the evidence is morally permissible—though only under quite tight conditions, which, I argue, include the requirement that the "passional basis" for such acceptance must itself be morally admirable. The claim that "suprarational" faith is virtuous thus remains open, even though vindicated against the objection that believing beyond the evidence is always vicious. I also explore the extent to which the proposal that what makes a belief religious is that it can be accepted only by suprarational faith imposes constraints on the possible content of religious belief.

Bishop, John D. Adam Smith's Invisible Hand Argument. *J Bus Ethics*, 14(3), 165-180, Mr 95.

Adam Smith is usually thought to argue that the result of everyone pursuing their own interests will be the maximization of the interests of society. Smith does use the invisible hand argument; however, a close reading of the *Wealth of Nations* reveals that Smith thought the interests of merchants and manufacturers were fundamentally opposed to those of society in general, and that they had an inherent tendency to deceive and oppress society while pursuing their own interests. It is argued that the invisible hand argument when applied to merchants and manufacturers is extremely restrictive, and that similar restrictions must apply to the moral corollary. (edited)

Bishop, Laura Jane and Coutts, Mary Carrington. Religious Perspectives on Bioethics, Part 2. *Kennedy Inst Ethics J*, 4(4), 357-386, D 94.

The many religions of the world bring diverse, and occasionally divergent, attitudes to bioethical issues. These beliefs often guide patients and health professionals in the health care setting. To further understanding of religious beliefs in our pluralistic and global society, this annotated bibliography identifies literature by major religious groups on topics in bioethics including: attitudes to health/health care, physician-patient relationship, treatment refusal, abortion, contraception, sterilization, reproductive technologies, genetics, mental health, human experimentation, organ donation/transplantation, death, euthanasia, and prolongation of life. Part 2, scope note 26, covers Native American religious traditions, Protestantism (generally and for 18 specific denominations), and Roman Catholicism.

Bittner, Rüdigner. Spinozas Gedanke, dass Einsicht befreit. *Deut Z Phil*, 42(6), 963-971, 1994.

Spinoza claims that freedom, the highest accomplishment of human beings, can be reached through rational insight. A proof of this basic tenet of enlightenment would be important. The article analyzes the argument offered in the *Ethics*, and reaches the conclusion that only the metaphysical conception of human minds as parts of the divine mind supports the claim in question.

Black, David. Rhetoric and the Narration of Conscience. *Phil Rhet*, 27(4), 359-373, 1994.

This paper suggests that rhetoric must be viewed not merely as an art of *persuasion* but as an archetypal art of *orientation*. Utilizing the work of Vico, the author claims that the orientational function of rhetoric is manifest in the narrative energy of foundational moral motifs and that Vico's philosophical tale about Jove and the *giganti* points to the rhetorical origin of human conscience.

Black, Jonathan and Fielder, John H. But Doctor, It's My Hip!: The Fate of Failed Medical Devices. *Kennedy Inst Ethics J*, 5(2), 113-131, Je 95.

It is difficult to study failed medical devices because of a lack of data. Routine device retrieval and analysis (DRA) is essential to performance evaluation, which, in turn, is essential to good patient care. We argue for the development of a national DRA program and medical device database and discuss the major ethical and policy issues associated with this proposal.

Blackburn, Simon. "Enchanting Views" in *Reading Putnam, Clark, Peter (ed)*, 12-30. Cambridge, Blackwell, 1995.

In this paper I argue that various kinds of 'internal' (or anthropocentric or perspectival) realism are incoherent. I then apply the result to the common view that we can escape problems of indeterminacy of radical translation by 'acquiescing' in a home language, arguing that this too cannot work.

Blacker, David. On the Alleged Neutrality of Technology: A Study in Dewey's *Experience and Nature*. *J Speculative Phil*, 8(4), 297-317, 1994.

This article explores how Dewey's magnum opus may contain the outlines for a philosophy of technology. Dewey's instrumentalism is quite singular and interesting in this regard, and is not reducible to the crude form in which it is sometimes presented. It is argued that for Dewey, if it is understood properly technology is not value-neutral in any simple, mechanistic sense. More accurately, it is nonneutral, in that it preconditions any valuation whatsoever. Some connections are made with certain aspects of Heidegger's account, as well as with Dewey's own educational theory.

Blais, François. La responsabilité de l'agent dans la philosophie analytique de l'action: une interprétation. *Dialogue (Canada)*, 33(4), 643-660, Fall 94.

It is impossible to separate our comprehension of "action" from "responsibility for this action". This thesis has been defended by H L A Hart and I propose now a new formulation of it. The text has two parts. In the first one, I make a survey of some important discussions about "agency" in contemporary philosophy of action. I conclude this survey by the consensus about the impossibility to naturalize the language of action. In the second part, I attempt to illustrate the reasons for this intrinsic relation between "action" and "responsibility". The language of action has an explicative and a normative function. In these two fundamental roles, we need to represent ourselves as distinct entities from the world.

Blake, Casey Nelson. "The Perils of Personality: Lewis Mumford and Politics After Liberalism" in *Pragmatism: From Progressivism to Postmodernism, Hollinger, Robert (ed)*, 88-106. Westport, Praeger, 1995.

Blamey, Kathleen. "From the Ego to the Self: A Philosophical Itinerary" in *The Philosophy of Paul Ricoeur, Hahn, Lewis Edwin (ed)*, 571-603. Peru, Open Court, 1994.

Blanco, José. Logos y realidad (Evocación de Hegel). *Rev Filosof (Spain)*, 4(5), 53-63, 1991.

Blanco Martín, Carlos J. Análisis gnoseológico de la psicología cognitiva. *El Basilisco*, 15, 29-48, Ja-Mr 94.

The idea of mental representation is analyzed here through the gnoseological tools of the philosophy of Gustavo Bueno. A rational elucidation of some concepts on mental representation is intended here. Mental imagery, schemata, frames, propositional representations and Co., are central notions in cognitive psychology and cognitive sciences. But, from a materialist view they are mentalistic ones. Specially, "Symbolic Representations" are not but mentalistic formats in psychology, so far away from computer programs and formal languages. Recently, subsymbolic systems are presented like a scientific revolution, but a global metaphysics (computational functionalism) is shared with classical architectures.

Blandino, Giovanni. Chance and Order in Our Inorganic Universe. *Aquinas*, 37(1), 209-224, Ja-Ap 94.

Blandino, Giovanni. Twenty Five Years of Theoretical Biology. *Aquinas*, 36(3), 527-537, S-D 93.

Blank, Robert H. *Rationing Medicine*. New York, Columbia Univ Pr, 1989.

Blasius, Mark. The Meaning and Status of Gay and Lesbian Political Philosophy: A Rejoinder to E Robert Statham Jr. *Polit Theory*, 23(3), 520-526, Ag 95.

Blatnik, Edward. Kant's Refutation of Anti-Realism. *J Phil Res*, 19, 127-146, 1994.

In *Language, Logic, and Experience*, Michael Luntley successfully employs a Kantian-style transcendental argument to refute Michael Dummett's anti-realist view that we are incapable of grasping

"recognition-transcendent" truth-conditions. But he also contends that his own purified version of anti-realism is immune to this sort of attack. This version is purified because it is concerned solely with the question of whether a given statement possesses a determinate truth *value*, and thus with whether the reality it is about exists determinately. I show that Kant's original version of the argument (in the "Transcendental Analytic") does in fact amount to a refutation of Luntleyan anti-realism. In particular, it demonstrates that the determinate existence of all past

and present naturalistic states and events is a necessary condition of thought. Sicne Luntleyan anti-realism entails that many such states and events are indeterminate, it must be rejected.

Blau, Peter (trans) and De Gandt, François and Bergo, Bettina (trans). The Problematic Status of Cosmology. *Grad Fac Phil J*, 18(1), 51-64, 1995.

Blaukopf, Kurt. "Logik der Musikforschung: K Poppers methodischer Beitrag" in *Heinrich Gomperz, Karl Popper und die österreichische Philosophie, Seiler, Martin (ed)*, 181-200. Amsterdam, Rodopi, 1994.

Popper's early music studies gave rise to ideas that went into his Logic of Scientific Discovery. Their relevance to a Logic of Musicology becomes apparent in Popper's theory about the rise of occidental polyphony (very similar to that of Max Weber); in Popper's concept of sociological laws and situational analysis; and in the identification of losses in artistic possibilities due to progressive artistic innovation. The positioning of music within the "three worlds" has led Popper to considerations about musical activity which tally with recent results of brain research.

Blecha, Ivan. The End of Ontology?. *Filozof Cas*, 42(6), 1034-1036, 1994.

Der Aufsatz gibt eine Antwort auf die Rundfrage, ob im gegenwärtigen philosophischen Diskurs noch eine Ontologie möglich ist und wenn ja, was für ein Charakter sie haben sollte. Der Aufsatz lehnt die traditionelle Substanzontologie ab, die das Sein nur aus Position einer idealen Subjektivität und nur als eine Sammlung von der aus den einzelnen Seienden abstrahierten Eigenschaften beschriebn hat, und nimmt eine phänomenologische Ontologie an, die besser imstande sein wird, die Erscheinungen von Sein /also die Seienden/ zum Sein selbst verweisen zu lassen und dabei der menschlichen Existenz als etwas zu verstehen, durch das diese Verweisung geschieht.

Bleicher, J (trans) and Tenbruck, Friedrich. Internal History of Science or Universal History?. *Theor Cult Soc*, 11(1), 75-93, F 94.

Blitz, Mark. Plato's *Alcibiades I*. *Interpretation*, 22(3), 339-358, Spr 95.

The paper is a commentary on Plato's Alcibiades I. The commentary is intended to make clear how Socrates' explicit arguments, the shortcomings of these arguments, and the dramatic details of the conversation combine to illuminate the basic problems that are the Alcibiades' underlying subject. The dialogue, I state, is divided into seven parts, the first three paralleling the last three, and Socrates, I argue, is, among other things, exploring the limits of phenomena such as sophistry, tyranny, and the arts insofar as they may claim to be fully comprehensive and self-sufficient.

Block, Ned. "Can the Mind Change the World?" in *Philosophy of Psychology: Debates on Psychological Explanation, Macdonald, Cynthia (ed)*, 29-59. Cambridge, Blackwell, 1995.

Block, Ned. "Reply: Causation and Two Kinds of Laws" in *Philosophy of Psychology: Debates on Psychological Explanation, Macdonald, Cynthia (ed)*, 78-83. Cambridge, Blackwell, 1995.

Block, Ned. An Argument for Holism. *Proc Aris Soc*, 95, 151-169, 1994-95.

This paper gives an argument from some relatively uncontroversial premises about identity and difference in narrow content at a single time to squeeze out a conclusion to the effect that one's narrow contents can be expected to change when one reads the newspaper all the way through.

Blocker, H Gene. "On the Distinction between Modern and Traditional African Aesthetics" in *African Philosophy: Selected Readings, Mosley, Albert G (ed)*, 428-438. Englewood Cliffs, Prentice Hall, 1995.

Blok, Josine H. Quests for a Scientific Mythology: F Creuzer and K O Müller on History and Myth. *Hist Theor*, 33(4), 26-52, 1994.

In the quests for a scientific mythology, K O Müller (1797-1840) was often regarded as an opponent of F Creuzer (1771-1858). Yet an analysis of their published work and of their private documents shows that they had much in common, a fact they both appreciated. In particular they held similar, deeply Romantic views on the religious origin of culture, in Müller's case inspired by Peitism, in Creuzer's by neo-Platonism. (edited)

Blom, Tannelie. Een Constructivistische Radicalisering van het Sociaal Constructivisme. *Kennis Methode*, 19(2), 160-180, 1995.

Blondel, Maurice and Trethowan, Illtyd (trans) and Dru, Alexander (trans). *The Letter of Apologetics and History and Dogma*. Grand Rapids, Eerdmans, 1994.

Blosser, Philip. *Scheler's Critique of Kant's Ethics*. Athens, Ohio Univ Pr, 1995.

Blosser analyzes Scheler's unique challenge to Kantian ethics, showing how, well before postmodernism, it called into question some of the most cherished myths of the Enlightenment, while avoiding the ethical skepticism of current deconstructionist approaches. Scheler, he argues, has more in common with MacIntyre than a naive "foundationalist", and his intricate criticisms of Kant's notions of "practical rationality", "moral feeling", and "duty" place his work squarely in the context of current debates about the nature of reason and virtue. Blosser offers a long-overdue examination of Scheler's project that is both historically informed and current, and opens up fresh interpretations of Kant, the phenomenological movement, and current debates about the nature of moral inquiry.

Blumenfeld, David C. "Leibniz's Ontological and Cosmological Arguments" in *The Cambridge Companion to Leibniz, Jolley, Nicholas (ed)*, 353-381. New York, Cambridge Univ Pr, 1994.

Blumenfeld, David C. "Perfection and Happiness in the Best Possible World" in *The Cambridge Companion to Leibniz, Jolley, Nicholas (ed)*, 382-410. New York, Cambridge Univ Pr, 1994. .

Blundell, Mary Whitlock. Self-Censorship in Plato's Republic. *Apeiron*, 26(3-4), 17-36, S-D 93.

Blustein, Jeffrey and Arras, John D. Reproductive Responsibility and Long-Acting Contraceptives. *Hastings Center Rep*, 25(1), S27-S29, Jan-Feb 95.

Blustein, Jeffrey and Fleischman, Alan R. The Pro-Life Maternal-Fetal Medicine Physician: A Problem of Integrity. *Hastings Center Rep*, 25(1), 22-26, Jan-Feb 95.

Blyden, Edward W. "Africa and the Africans" in *African Philosophy: Selected Readings, Mosley, Albert G (ed)*, 7-29. Englewood Cliffs, Prentice Hall, 1995.

AUTHOR INDEX WITH ABSTRACTS 447 **Bogen, David**

Blyth, D J. Wholes, Parts, and Sequences in Aristotle. *Int Phil Quart*, 34(4), 453-463, D 94.

Metaphysics XII.1, 1069a19-21, arguing that substance is primary whether everything forms a whole or a sequence, requires interpretation vis-à-vis Aristotle's own views and account of his predecessors. Conceiving substance as part of a cosmic whole suits the physical principles of the presocratics and eidetic principles of Plato and himself. The alternative suggests the categories, although they are not strictly sequential, being more loosely ordered *pros hen*, with a rough three level hierarchy. This contrasts with Platonic forms and also Speusippus, implying counterfactually that if the cosmos formed a sequence it would be of kinds of being and thus of categories, not mathematical principles, although actually sequentiality is too strict a criterion of order.

Boadas-Llavat, Agustí. Roger Bacon (1214-94): Ética y Reforma. *Convivium*, 7, 81-102, 1995.

The moral philosophy held by the English Franciscan Roger Bacon is at the top of his philosophical purpose. In recent times it has been studied deeply, in order to link not only the Neoplatonic tradition of the Oxford University and the premodern nominalism, but also to connect the spiritual movement such as Joachinism and history of ideas. This study sketches Bacon's moral aim of *reformatio* and its philosophical background.

Boatright, John R. Aristotle Meets Wall Street: The Case for Virtue Ethics in Business. *Bus Ethics Quart*, 5(2), 353-359, Ap 95.

This is a review article of Robert C Soloman, *Ethics and Excellence: Cooperation and Integrity in Business*, which explores the strengths and weaknesses of an Aristotelian approach to business ethics.

Boatright, John R. *Cases in Ethics and the Conduct of Business*. Englewood Cliffs, Prentice Hall, 1995.

Cases in Ethics and the Conduct of Business is a collection of cases that is intended to be a companion volume to the textbook *Ethics and the Conduct of Business* (also published by Prentice Hall). The 29 cases in the casebook cover the range of ethical issues in a standard business ethics course and include some well-known cases that have become classics as well as some that are published here for the first time. Most of the cases are fairly lengthy and detailed in order to reveal the complexity of decision making in a modern corporate setting, and they are designed to pose difficult decision-making situations for members of business organizations at all levels.

Boatright, John R. Conflict of Interest: A Response to Michael Davis. *Bus Prof Ethics J*, 12(4), 43-46, Wint 93.

This paper defends a definition of conflict of interest offered in John R Boatright, "Conflict of Interest: An Agency Analysis," in *Ethics and Agency Theory*, edited by N E Bowie and R E Freeman (New York: Oxford University Press) against criticisms by Michael Davis. In particular, the claims that competitive employments, abuse of position, and misappropriation may constitute conflict of interest are defended, and the inadequacy of Davis's definition is shown with respect to the rule in legal ethics on conflict of interest with former clients.

Bochner, Arthur P and Waugh, Joanne B. "Talking-With as a Model for Writing-About: Implications of Rortyean Pragmatism" in *Recovering Pragmatism's Voice, Langsdorf, Lenore (ed)*, 211-233. Albany, SUNY Pr, 1995.

This essay takes issue with traditional social science conceptions of communication as a research object and questions the validity of appropriations of writing as a model for speaking. The authors focus on ways in which the exemplary status of the scientist as a "moral exemplar" hinges on fixing language as an object out of which meaning can be found. The authors trace how from Plato on philosophical speech became parasitic on a conception of writing that claims a power external to our own. In response to the failed notion that nature can inscribe itself as an object, the authors propose an interpretative conception of language based on Davidson's notion of a "passing theory" that inspires a quite different conception of communication, one that blurs divisions between the narrative genres of literature and social science.

Bockover, Mary I. "The Concept of Emotion Revisited: A Critical Synthesis of Western and Confucian Thought" in *Emotions in Asian Thought, Marks, Joel (ed)*, 161-180. Albany, SUNY Pr, 1995.

The overall aim of this article is to provide a critical synthesis of current Western and ancient Chinese lines of thought, in light of a new way of understanding the emotions. In section one, two prominent (and antithetical) views of emotion from Western philosophy are critiqued. In section two, some timeless Confucian insights into the nature of human "goodness" are examined. Finally, in section three, I offer my own view of emotion in light of these Confucian insights, arguing that the "inner/outer" distinction that philosophy and psychology have come so heavily to rely on actually obscures some of the finer points about the nature of conscious experience.

Boden, Margaret A. Multiple Personality and Computational Models. *Philosophy*, 37(Supp), 103-114, 1994.

Multiple personality disorder (MPD) has reached "epidemic" proportions in the USA. It shows an extreme mental dissociation, with the same body presenting different cognitive-motivational streams of behavior and experience at different times. It may be due to suggestibility and/or hypnosis, being an artifact (of therapy and media-publicity) rather than a genuine syndrome. Even so, we need to understand how it is possible for it to appear, and why it is that we are tempted to describe it in terms of "multiple personality". The latter question can be answered in terms of the cognitive-motivational integration criterial of "personality". If this is apparently split into two relatively distinct and internally coherent intentionalistic streams, the concept can still be applied—but with more, and more fleeting, alternates this becomes increasingly indefensible. However, neither the clinical facts nor our normal concepts suggest multiple kinds. Proponents of computational psychology need to explain its possibility (if not its aetiology) in computational terms. Various ideas within the computational literature are discussed which might be helpful for such a project.

Bodunrin, P O. "Magic, Witchcraft, and ESP: A Defence of Scientific and Philosophical Skepticism" in *African Philosophy: Selected Readings, Mosley, Albert G (ed)*, 371-385. Englewood Cliffs, Prentice Hall, 1995.

The belief in witches and witchcraft is rampant in many parts of the world. Albert Mosley and Sopie Oluwole attempt to argue in support of the rationality of such a belief. I argue in this article that most of the occurrences that have been attributed to witches and witchcraft can be explained otherwise. I hold that it is better to admit that there are some as yet unexplained phenomena than to attribute them to unverifiable causal agents.

Boeri, Marcelo D. Chance and Teleology in Aristotle's *Physics*. *Int Phil Quart*, 35(1), 87-96, Mr 95.

Boersema, David B. Nemesis and Theory Evaluation. *Method Sci*, 27(4), 209-224, 1994.

The Nemesis hypothesis is the hypothesis that periodic mass extinctions of life on Earth have been caused by the relatively near-approach of Nemesis, a 'companion' star to our sun. This paper examines the current debates concerning the Nemesis hypothesis, particularly as these debates relate to theory evaluation, with an emphasis on the views of Kuhn, Lakatos, and Laudan. After an evaluation of these views is made, there are offered some normative remarks regarding theory evaluation in general.

Boersema, Jan J. "First the Jew but also the Greek: In Search of the Roots of the Environmental Problem in Western Civilization" in *Ecology, Technology, and Culture,* Zweers, Wim (ed), 20-55. Cambridge, White Horse, 1994.

Boersema, Jan J. Environmental Quality and the Quality of our Way of Life. *Environ Values*, 4(2), 97-108, May 95.

Today, sustainable development is generally accepted as a guiding principle. The present relation societies have with the natural environment is considered as being not-sustainable. However this presupposes some idea about the quality of the environment and of activities affecting the environment and, as a consequence, of the quality of life. In this article I defend the proposition that the limited progress made with respect to the environment—despite all the good intentions—could be due to the potential conflict between 'quality' and sustainable development. In other words: our interpretation of the concept of 'quality' is not compatible with the aims of sustainability. Some consequences for research and policy of accepting this proposition are discussed.

Boersema, Jan J (ed) and Zweers, Wim (ed). *Ecology, Technology, and Culture*. Cambridge, White Horse, 1994.

Boeve, Lieven. Postmodern Theology After the Decline of the Mastery Story of Christianity, Inspired by Lyotard's Critical Theory of Postmodernity (in Dutch). *Bijdragen*, 55(3), 269-295, 1994.

J F Lyotard is well known as the French philosopher who coined the vocabulary of postmodernity. According to him, we live in a postmodern condition, where the master-stories of modernity proved themselves to have failed and lost relevance. Christianity and Christian theology, as the reflection on Christian faith, functioned historically (and even today function) as a master-story. With the decline of all master-stories, the master-story of Christianity comes under suspicion. Nevertheless, Christianity does not have to disappear with the master-story. There remains a chance for Christianity and Christian theology to become more than relevant, if conceived along the concept of the 'open story'. A more careful study of Christian tradition shows already elements that prove that Christianity as an 'open story' is even more appropriate to signify its core: the event of grace. (edited)

Boey, K. Blondel and Ignatius' Spiritual Exercises (in Dutch). *Bijdragen*, 55(4), 399-411, 1994.

The Jesuits have paid a notably large amount of attention to Blondel's *Action* (1893), because many of them recognized some affinity between Blondel's thesis and Ignatius' *Spiritual Exercises*. Blondel demonstrated that is it possible for Christian faith to stand the test of the legitimate demands imposed by reason in their time. He calls on philosophical rationality for this. Unlike a number of his friends 'in the crisis of the modernism,' Blondel, throughout all difficulties, keeps to what Ignatius named: "the true conviction we have to share within the Church militant." (edited)

Bogard, William. "Baudrillard, Time, and the End" in *Baudrillard: A Critical Reader, Kellner, Douglas (ed)*, 313-333. Cambridge, Blackwell, 1994.

This essay examines Baudrillard's views on time and the end of history from the framework of his analysis of simulation. It suggests that we must interpret Buadrillard's work as an effort to work through the ideas of simulated time and simulated history, and that the recent debate over the end of history must be reformulated and critiqued in terms of how contemporary virtual technologies structure time. Along the way, the essay also defends Baudrillard against what have been some critical misinterpretations of his thought, viz., mistaken notions that it is apocalyptic, nihilistic, melancholy, and even postmodern.

Bogdan, Deanne. Pythagoras' Rib Or, What Does Music Education Want?. *Phil Music Educ Rev*, 2(2), 122-131, Fall 94.

This paper considers musical apologetics from the perspective of poetic apologetics. Building on questions raised in Charlene Morton's, "Feminist Theory and the Displaced Music Curriculum: Beyond the 'Add and Stir' Projects," it borrows key concepts from literature and literary criticism in mounting a defense of the educational value of musical experience. Drawing on the insights of Toni Morrison, Virginia Woolf, and Northrop Frye, it poses questions about the ethical import of music and the relationship between sense and sound, between musical and "real" experience, and between power hierarchies and musical effects.

Bogen, David and Lynch, Michael. Harvey Sacks's Primitive Natural Science. *Theor Cult Soc*, 11(4), 65-104, N 94.

Starting in the 1960's, Harvey Sacks developed a unique approach to the analysis of natural language use, which later became known as conversation analysis. Unlike most innovators in the social sciences, Sacks did not try to emulate the natural sciences; instead, he argued that an incipient 'natural observational science of human behavior' was already part of successful sciences. Scientists describe how to do observations as well as features of the things they observe, and the adequacy of such descriptions demonstrates the possibility of making replicable descriptions of human actions. Sacks aimed to expand this program of scientific description to cover a full range of ordinary communicative 'methods'. This paper is a critical appreciation of conversation analysis which tries to account for how Sacks's practical philosophy of science was turned into an empiricist research program.

Bogen, James. Critical Notice of Raymond Bradley: *The Nature of All Being, A Study of Wittgenstein's Modal Absolutism*. *Can J Phil*, 24(4), 643-664, D 94.

Boghossian, Peter G and Drewniak, Erik. Wittgenstein and Peirce on Meaning: The Evolution from Absolutism to Fallibilism. *Dialogos*, 30(65), 173-188, Ja 95.

Bogucka, Maria. Reflections on the Perception of Time in Poland in the 16th and 17th Centuries. *Dialogue Hum*, 4(1), 137-148, 1994.

The aim of the work was to analise the patterns of the "learned" as well as of popular time's conceptions in Poland in the early modern period. The time's conceptions were shaped by agricultural way of life linked to the Nature (ca 80 per cent of the population in the countryside) as well as by the liturgical year with its Holydays and celebrations recurring with seasons (Christmas, Easter, Advent). It promoted a circular conception of time rather than a linear one. The new, linear conception of time grew, however, because of the secularisation of time's perception among intellectual elites since the end of the 16th century as well as because of the development of urban life: market economy, trade-and credit-relations, salaried work, which phenomena were connected to some concrete linear time figures and time realisations and were based on the new technical invention: mechanical watch.

Bohlen, Stephanie. *Die Übermacht des Seins: Heideggers Auslegung des Bezuges von Mensch und Natur und Hölderlins Dichtung des Heiligen*. Berlin, Duncker Humblot, 1993.

Bohm, David. *Thought as a System (New Edition)*. New York, Routledge, 1994.

In *Thought as a System*, David Bohm takes as his subject the role of thought and knowledge at every level of human affairs, from our private reflections on personal identity to our collective efforts to fashion a tolerable civilization. Elaborating upon principles of the relationship between mind and matter first put forward in *Wholeness and the Implicate Order*, Bohm rejects the notion that our thinking processes neutrally report on what is 'out there' in an objective world. He explores the manner in which thought actively participates in forming our perceptions, our sense of meaning and one daily action. (edited)

Bohm, David and Hiley, B J. *The Undivided Universe: An Ontological Interpretation of Quantum Theory*. New York, Routledge, 1995.

Bohman, James F. Public Reason and Cultural Pluralism: Political Liberalism and the Problem of Moral Conflict. *Polit Theory*, 23(2), 253-279, My 95.

Appeals to an "overlapping consensus" and to religious tolerance hide a tension in contemporary liberalism: that between irreconcilable value pluralism and shared democratic citizenship. There are two main dilemmas of pluralist politics: "communitarian" dilemmas of trade-offs between unity and diversity within a polity; and "liberal," each/all dilemmas of intergroup conflicts. Although the conception of public reason in neither Rawls nor Habermas escapes these dilemmas, it can provide the normative standards for deliberating democratically about cultural conflict. Such deliberation requires that public reason become both dynamic and pluralistic, in its use in revising the interpretation of constitutional essentials and in forming distinctly moral compromises.

Boire-Lavigne, Anne-Marie and Rocchetti, Loretta and Malherbe, Jean-François. Validité et limites du consensus en éthique clinique. *Laval Theol Phil*, 50(3), 531-543, O 94.

Le caractère multiculturel qui marque profondément nos systèmes de valeurs rend difficile la référence à des normes reconnues par tous lorsqu'il est nécessaire de prendre une décision qui engage de multiples acteurs sociaux. Cette difficulté est particulèrement sensible lorsqu'il s'agit de prendre des décisions à l'égard de la mise en oeuvre des techniques biomédicales. Face à cette difficulté bien réelle, une tendance est apparue de fonder de telles décisions sur le consensus des personnes les plus directement concernées. L'objet de la présente discussion est d'évaluer la validité et les limites d'un tel recours au consensus. Le consensus auguel vise la discussion rationnelle entre les sujets éthiques à propos de la critique des normes particulières comme de l'application des normes universelles et particulières aux situations singulières, constitue une indispensable garantie à l'encontre de bien des arbitraires qui tendraient à s'emparer du pouvoir. Mais le refus inconditionnel de reconnaître l'existence de *dissensus avérés* aurait pour conséquence immédiate de restaurer subrepticement une forme d'arbitraire particulièrement subtile puisqu'elle se cacherait derrière le masque de la rationalité.

Boissinot, Christian. *Spectres de Marx*: Entretien avec Jacques Derrida. *Laval Theol Phil*, 50(3), 619-627, O 94.

Boisvert, Raymond D. John Dewey: An "Old-Fashioned" Reformer. *Stud Phil Educ*, 13(3-4), 325-341, 1994-95.

This essay provides an overview of Dewey's philosophy of education. Its interpretive center involves the claim that although Dewey broke with assumptions of "modern" philosophy, he does not fit neatly into any characterization as "post-modern,"pre-modern,"or "modern." He rather blends insights from "modern" and "pre-modern" philosophy, while adding his own creative dimension. The essay discusses the way Dewey moves beyond the assumptions of "modern man," indicates how for him education is not preparation, and discusses the importance of education in a democracy, an importance that is other than the usually cited need for a well-educated electorate.

Bok, Sissela. Shading the Truth in Seeking Informed Consent for Research Purposes. *Kennedy Inst Ethics J*, 5(1), 1-17, Mr 95.

I want to argue for two propositions. First, I suggest that what some researchers may take to be a simple trade-off between minor violations of the truth for the sake of access to far greater truths represents a profound miscalculation with far-reaching and cumulative reverberations. Second, I submit that today's research environment, as demanding, competitive, and sometimes bewildering as it is, offers genuine scope for what Murdoch calls truth-seeking, for imagining and questioning, and for relating to facts through both truth and truthfulness; but that, in so doing, it presents hard choices with respect to methods, and, in turn, to personal integrity—not only in particular research projects but also with respect to that fragile research environment in its own right.

Boldyrev, I A. Concerning the National Uniqueness of Russian Philosophy. *Metaphilosophy*, 25(2-3), 138-142, Ap-Jl 94.

Bole III, Thomas J. "The Cogency of the *Logic's* Argumentation" in *Hegel Reconsidered, Engelhardt Jr, H Tristram (ed)*, 103-117. Dordrecht, Kluwer, 1994.

Bolender, John. Is Multiple Realizability Compatable With Antireductionism?. *S J Phil*, 33(2), 129-142, Sum 95.

Bolotin, David. Leo Strauss and Classical Political Philosophy. *Interpretation*, 22(1), 129-142, Fall 94.

Bolotin, David (& other eds). Two Lectures by Leo Strauss. *Interpretation*, 22(3), 301-338, Spr 95.

Bolton, Martha Brandt. "The Real Molyneux Question and the Basis of Locke's Answer" in *Locke's Philosophy, Rogers, G A J (ed)*, 75-99. New York, Oxford Univ Pr, 1994.

Bolton, Robert. The Problem of Dialectical Reasoning in Aristotle. *Ancient Phil*, 14, 99-132, 1994.

Bolzán, Juan Enrique and Larre, Olga L. Orden, Desorden, Azar. *Sapientia*, 49(193-4), 327-336, 1994.

Bombardier, Denise. Entretien avec Michel Morin. *Philosopher*, 15, 11-26, 1994.

Bondeli, Martin. *Das Anfangsproblem bei Karl Leonhard Reinhold*. Frankfurt/M, Klostermann, 1995.

The book gives a systematic and historic description and a critical interpretation of Reinhold's philosophical development from his Kantian period of "Elementarphilosophie" (1789/90) to the end of the relevant phase of his new theory after 1800 called "Rationaler Realisms". The focus of interest is on Reinhold's attempt to create a post-Kantian system based on a first principle and especially on the difficulty of this attempt, which lead Reinhold to several revisions of the "Elementarphilosophie", to a confession to Fichte's view of a philosophical foundation and finally to a concept of hypothetical beginning, which had an obvious influence on the "Anfangsproblem" in Hegel's mature works.

Bondì, Roberto. "Spiritus" e "Anima" in Bernardino Telesio. *G Crit Filosof Ital*, 72(3), 405-417, S-D 93.

Boné, Edouard. "Die Sprache in den (Natur-) historischen Wissenschaften" in *Die Sprache in den Wissenschaften, Weingartner, Paul (ed)*, 145-178. Freiburg, Alber, 1993.

This chapter is part of a more complete discussion of the Institute for Interdisciplinary Research, in its annual (1992) meeting, concerned with the use of language in the various sciences. The present contribution deals with the approach of the natural (historical) sciences, more especially biology and paleontology. State of development of the human knowledge and interdependence of parallel sciences, limitations, role and influence of the observer: such are, a o limits to the language available to a particular discipline.

Bonechi, Sara. B Croce—G Gentile: Bibliografia 1980-1993. *G Crit Filosof Ital*, 73(2-3), 529-660, My-D 94.

Bongar, Bruce and Cabot, Mithran G and Packman, Wendy L. Malpractice Arising From Negligent Psychotherapy: Ethical, Legal, and Clinical Implications of *Osheroff vs Chestnut Lodge*. *Ethics Behavior*, 4(3), 175-197, 1994.

Traditionally, there have been few legal actions brought against psychotherapists that allege negligent psychotherapy and negligent treatment of psychiatric disorders. However, in the case of *Osheroff v Chestnut Lodge*, a patient-physician (Dr Osheroff) sued Chestnut Lodge, a private psychiatric facility, for negligence based on the staff's decision to apply a psychodynamic model of treatment (through psychotherapy) and not a biological model. The case sparked a heated debate between adherents of the psychodynamic model and those of the biological model. This article explores the implications of the *Osheroff* litigation for mental health professionals. It is proposed that an interactive informed consent process be used to protect psychotherapists against *Osheroff*-type litigation.

Bonino, Serge-Thomas. Pluralisme et théologisme, Deux aspects doctrinaux de la correspondance Gilson-Labourdette. *Rev Thomiste*, 94(3), 530-553, Jl-S 94.

BonJour, Laurence. Fumerton on Coherence Theories. *J Phil Res*, 19, 103-108, 1994.

I argue that while Fumerton's criticisms of pure coherence theories of truth are both important and extremely cogent, their application both to the main historical views usually identified as coherence theories of truth, *viz.* the views of the absolute idealists, and to contemporary anti-realism is more problematic. In addition, while Fumerton is again undeniably correct in his objection to pure coherence theories of justification, an impure coherence theory of justification may still be defensible.

BonJour, Laurence. Sosa on Knowledge, Justification, and Aptness. *Phil Stud*, 78(3), 207-220, Je 95.

Bonkovsky, Frederick O. Helping Ken and Marie Pines. *J Clin Ethics*, 5(2), 126, Sum 94.

Boobbyer, Philip. *S L Frank: The Life and Work of A Russian Philosopher, 1877-1950*. Athens, Ohio Univ Pr, 1995.

Books, Sue. Education and Work: Reflections on the Moral and Spiritual Dimensions of the Job Crisis. *J Thought*, 29(4), 31-45, Wint 94.

This article 1) draws a distinction between *work* in the broad sense of what one most fundamentally is about in the world and *jobs*, contractual relationships that ideally, but not necessarily, support one's work; 2) advocates a spiritual conception of work; and 3) speculates on how educators can respond to the culture's confusion about the meaning of work. Confusing students' need for good jobs with their need for a sense of meaning and purpose in life only clouds the educational issue: Learning to do a job well is not synonymous with learning to appropriate meaningful work.

AUTHOR INDEX WITH ABSTRACTS 449 Botsford, Clarissa

Boolos, George. "1879?" in *Reading Putnam, Clark, Peter (ed)*, 31-48. Cambridge, Blackwell, 1995.

Boonin-Vail, David. Contractarianism Gone Wild: Carruthers and the Moral Status of Animals. *Between Species*, 10(1-2), 39-48, Win-Spr 94.

Boonin-Vail, David. Reply to the Commentary on "Contractarianism Gone Wild: Carruthers and the Moral Status of Animals". *Between Species*, 10(1-2), 52-54, Win-Spr 94.

Boonin-Vail, David. Response—Parsimony Made Simple: Rosenfeld on Harrison and Animal Pain. *Between Species*, 9(3), 137-140, Sum 93.

Boonin-Vail, David. *Thomas Hobbes and the Science of Moral Virtue*. New York, Cambridge Univ Pr, 1994.

Influential modern interpretations of Hobbes's moral theory have portrayed him as either an amoralist, a moral contractarian, a rule-egoist, or a divine-command theorist. This work challenges these standard views and defends a novel and unorthodox interpretation of Hobbes's ethics. The book shows that Hobbes is best understood as embracing a theory of virtue concerned with the development of good character traits rather than with rules of behavior. It also analyzes how Hobbes grounds his theory of moral virtue in a more general science of human nature, explaining how for Hobbes ethics is part of natural philosophy.

Boorse, Christopher. Ducking Trolleys. *J Soc Phil*, 25(3), 146-152, Wint 94.

Boos, William. The World, the Flesh and the Argument from Design. *Synthese*, 101(1), 15-52, O 94.

Booth, Wayne C. Our Best Rhetorologist. *Phil Lit*, 19(1), 116-126, Ap 95.

This review-article celebrates Eugene Garver's *Aristotle's Rhetoric: An Art of Character* (Chicago: University of Chicago Press, 1994). The book is not only an original and challenging account of the *Rhetoric*. It is one of the most responsible encounters ever with philosophical, political, and ethical issues raised by the theory and practice of rhetoric. What's more, Garver grapples so well with how Aristotle's problems differ from ours, and how his solutions do not quite fit what we most need, that he might be called our "best rhetorologist": one of those rare comparativists of rhetorics who probe how disparate rhetorical practices and theories compete and are finally related.

Boothman, Derek (ed & trans) and Gramsci, Antonio. *Further Selections from the Prison Notebooks*. Minneapolis, Univ of Minn Pr, 1995.

Boothroyd, David. Nietzsche's Future Perfect and the Eternal Return: Toward a Genealogy of Ideas. *Hist Euro Ideas*, 20(1-3), 125-133, Ja 95.

Borejszo, Zee. Finding *Finity* and Motion for Zeno. *S Afr J Phil*, 13(4), 199-203, N 94.

Known for 2500 years as a paradox of motion, this famous riddle was thought up by Zeno of Elea and has vexed the most prominent thinkers until today by leading them inexorably to the conclusion that motion is impossible! The Achilles-Tortoise paradox is about an infinite number of distances, that arises mysteriously in a race between Achilles and a tortoise. Believing that the ideas, contained in widely scattered languages, are complementary, this author finds the correct tense for a terminated activity in the *perfective aspect or finitive form* of the verb, a feature of slavonic languages for pointing to *finite* events. A complete view of the race is produced, in the pictographic script of Japanese, from the terms for 'two competitors'. The assembly of this information reveals the *one, finite distance* that Achilles actually has to run! (edited)

Borges dos Santos, Silvia Gombi. Violência e Poder em Hannah Arendt. *Educ Filosof*, 8(16), 119-128, Jl-D 94.

Ao examinar o tema da violência e suas relaçoes com o poder a partir das idéias de Hannah Arendt, este estudo aborda o controvertido papel do intelectual frente a estes fenomenos e problematiza a perspectiva otimista da pensadora alema quanto à realizaçao da *vita activa*, como forma de superaçao da violência no mundo atual.

Borgmann, Albert. Artificial Intelligence and Human Personality. *Res Phil Technol*, 14, 271-283, 1994.

Borgmann, Albert. Theory, Practice, Reality. *Inquiry*, 38(1-2), 143-156, Je 95.

"Disclosing New Worlds" represents an extraordinarily fruitful response to the radically changed social and intellectual conditions of the late twentieth century. Its focus on skillful practice yields a social theory thicker than most. Yet in remaining aloof of material reality it retains an ambiguity that contemporary culture prevailingly resolves into a style of life largely devoid of skill and excellence. Consideration of material reality, however, discloses hopeful if inconspicuous practices as well, practices that are at the center of the good life and constitute the wellspring of solidarity. University teaching can be a vigorous introduction to that sort of life.

Borjesson, Gary. A Sounding of *Walden's* Philosophical Depth. *Phil Lit*, 18(2), 287-308, O 94.

This work is a synoptic interpretation of *Walden*'s philosophical substance. Thoreau's sensibility is kin to the ancients of Western and Eastern traditions. *Walden* is a logos of philosopher's desire to see all things, including one's own life, in light of the whole. This desire is incommensurate with transcendentalism generally, and with Emerson and Cavell's thought in particular. Thoreau's so-called transcendentalism is thus challenged, and the contrast between his spirit and the modern spirit of transcendentalism—its skepticism and concomitant obsession with subjectivity—is examined.

Borna, Shaheen and Stearns, James M. The Ethics of Lottery Advertising: Issues and Evidence. *J Bus Ethics*, 14(1), 43-51, Ja 95.

After a discussion of the evolution and criticisms of state run lotteries, this article examines the ethics of lottery advertising. A discussion of the appeals used by lottery advertisers is followed by evidence concerning the impact of expected value information on lottery purchase intentions. Findings point toward less emphasis on the lottery as a solution to financial and job problems and more emphasis on information about the actual value of a lottery bet. Using accepted standards from the marketing literature, lottery advertising is found to be deceptive.

Borodaj, Jurij and Nikiforov, Aleksandr. East and West: Russian Renewal and the Future. *Stud East Euro Thought*, 47(1-2), 61-116, Je 95.

Two philosophers and prominent public figures explore the spiritual and cultural framework within which Russia's crisis and prospects for social renewal must be understood. Their discussion ranges over several main areas of concern in Russia today: the nature of the person and her capacities as social actor, the forms of sociality Russia has known as seen against the background of Orthodoxy and Communism, and Russia's tragedy during the seventy-five years of Communism. A "third path" is envisaged for Russian renewal based on geopolitical, cultural, and spiritual constants in the history of the nation.

Borrego, Enrique. Creación y origen del tiempo. *Dialogo Filosof*, 10(2), 239-253, My-Ag 94.

Origen del tiempo no equivale a origen del ser ni a origen de la materia. Sólo desde una perspectiva gnoseológica discutible puede señalarse un "cuando" de la Creación. la idea de un universo en expansión no determina límite alguno sobre cuándo fue creado el universo, sino que sólo señala "el estado" inicial a partir del cual comienza a tener sentido para la inteligencia humana. Desde esta perspectiva criticamos las confusiones y ambigüedades de la *Historia del tiempo* de Stephen W Hawking.

Borys, Debra S. Maintaining Therapeutic Boundaries: The Motive Is Therapeutic Effectiveness, not Defensive Practice. *Ethics Behavior*, 4(3), 267-273, 1994.

Boschetto, Luca. Vico e i 'Figliuoli di Dio': Ricerche sui Giganti nel *Diritto universale* e nella *Scienza nuova Prima*. *Boll Centro Stud Vichiani*, 24-25, 79-95, 1994-95.

Bosco, Nynfa. La Prospettiva Morale di Augusto Guzzo. *Filosofia*, 45(1), 63-80, Ja-Ap 94.

Bosio, Franco. La domanda speculativa fondamentale: Il linguaggio della filosofia come forme di invocazione. *G Metaf*, 16(1-2), 25-30, Ja-Ag 94.

Bosio, Franco. Principio di Non-Contraddizione e Modalità Originaria dell'Archè-Fondamento. *G Metaf*, 16(3), 335-340, S-D 94.

Boss, Gilbert. Victimes et utopies: Analyse d'une structure de notre conscience morale. *Laval Theol Phil*, 50(3), 481-497, O 94.

Cette réflexion sur la structure morale reliant les idées de victime et d'utopie se développe en douze temps: 1) Le terme de victime comme foyer d'une structure du sentiment moral; 2) De la conception du pécheur à celle de la victime; 3) Victime et dépendance; 4) Victime et justice; 5) Le procès des bourreaux; 6) La justice et les utopies; 7) Le sens usuel de la notion de victime; 8) Le scandale de la distance par rapport à l'idéal; 9) Le problème de la définition de l'utopie; 10) L'action de la victime; 11) La forme de vie de la victime; 12) Pardelà la victime et le pécheur.

Boss, Judith A. The Autonomy of Moral Education. *Educ Theor*, 44(4), 399-416, Fall 94.

Traditional psychologists have maintained that there is a single intelligence and that moral reasoning is a function of this intelligence. This belief has been supported by a philosophical tradition which defines intelligence in terms of reason, and ignores the epistemological role of emotions and intuition. Others, such as Howard Gardner, argue that there are several relatively independent intelligences. The possibility is explored in the article that moral intelligence is an autonomous, intelligence with its own symbol system, developmental stages and biological basis, rather than being dependent on stage of cognitive development. Implications of this position for moral education are discussed.

Bossé, Michael J. When I Was a Child, I Thought as a Child: The Educational Philosophy of Paul K Feyerabend. *J Thought*, 29(4), 7-29, Wint 94.

Bostar, Leo J. Reading Ingarden Read Husserl: Metaphysics, Ontology, and Phenomenological Method. *Husserl Stud*, 10(3), 211-236, 1993-94.

Bosto, Sulejman. Aporien in den Konzepten der Freiheit. *Filozof Istraz*, 14(1), 85-98, 1994.

In diesem Text versucht der Autor, einige Schwierigkeiten der bestehenden Freiheitskonzepte zu zeigen, die er als eigenartige "Aporetik" versteht. Das "Aporetische" zeigt sich in der Widersprüchlickeit des "individualistischen" und des "kommunaristischen" Konzeptes der Freiheit, die in den gegenwärtigen philosophischen Diskussionen sowie in den politischen Wirklichkeiten zur Sprache kommt. Der Autor hat dabei in Sicht, dass bei diesen Streitigkeiten eine uralte Kluft zwischen dem normativen Sinne der menschlichen Freiheit und dem Verwirklichungsanspuch besteht. Vor diesem Hintergrund erweist sich die "Aporie" der Freiheit, sowohl theoretisch als auch praktisch, als ein Widerspruch des "Individualismus" der Freiheit (d.h. der grundlegenden Rolle des Individuums im Freiheitsraum) und des "Kollektivismus" der Freiheit (d.h. der grunlegenden Rolle des Allgemeinen, des gemeinsamen, intersubjektiven Lebens des Menschen im praktischen Freiheitsraum). Diese "Aporetik" ensteht aber nur dann, wenn man lediglich eine dieser Perspektiven einseitig als absolut geltende anzunehmen versucht. In der geschichtlichen Wirklichkeit der Freiheit sollte aber die Freiheit nur durch die Komplementarität beider Perspektiven betrachtet und durch ihre wechselseitige Bewegung und "situative" oder "kontextualistische" Auslegungsperspektive immer wieder neu verstanden werden.

Botha, Rudolf P. *Challenging Chomsky: The Generative Garden Game*. Cambridge, Blackwell, 1992.

Botsford, Clarissa (trans) and Pera, Marcello. *The Discourses of Science*. Chicago, Univ of Chicago Pr, 1994.

The book suggests a remedy for the "Cartesian syndrome"—the fixation on method shared by both the "standard" and "new" philosophy of science. Examining Galileo's *Dialogue*, Darwin's *Origin*, and the Big Bang-Steady State controversy, it develops a general picture according to which scientific research is not just an interchange between nature and the inquiring mind, but a dialogical game with *three* players, nature, the inquiring mind, and a community which, through the process of attack and defense determines what scientific knowledge is. Rhetoric, then, taken as the practice of argumentation, is an essential element of science; and dialectics, taken as the logic of scientific rhetoric, is the organon of science.

Botterill, George. Beliefs, Functionally Discrete States, and Connectionist Networks: A Comment on Ramsey, Stitch, and Garon. *Brit J Phil Sci*, 45(3), 899-906, S 94.

Ramsey, Stitch and Garon have suggested there is an incompatibility between the propositional modularity of common sense psychology and the holistic distribution of information in certain connectionist networks. However, the alleged incompatibility disappears as soon as we introduce a distinction between active beliefs (or occurrent thoughts) and beliefs as dispositions. This distinction is no *ad hoc* maneuver. So as yet we have no reason to suppose that connectionism will show that folk psychology is radically mistaken.

Bouchard, Guy. L'homme en quête de lui-même—A propos du livre d'Elisabeth Badinter: *XY: De l'identité masculine*. *Laval Theol Phil*, 51(1), 159-181, F 95.

There are three main difficulties with Badinter's book. First, her monolithic conception of Men's Studies: she does not seem to be aware of the many trends in the study of masculinities. Second, terminological and conceptual problems: the French adjectives "masculin" and "féminin" are misleadingly used at the level both of sex and of gender, and the way the concepts of masculinity and feminity are dealt with is highly problematic. Finally, the social context of the emergence of a new masculinity is undervalued. Nonetheless, if one reads the book less for its answers than for its inventory of the problems surrounding masculinity, this reading should be rewarding.

Boucher, David. British Idealism, the State, and International Relations. *J Hist Ideas*, 55(4), 671-694, O 94.

Boucher, David. British Idealist International Theory. *Bull Hegel Soc Gt Brit*, 31, 73-89, Spr-Sum 95.

Bouchilloux, Hélène. Du Beau et du Sublime chez Pascal. *Rev Phil Fr*, 2, 191-210, Ap-Je 95.

La catégorie de sublime est empruntée a Kant afin de rendre compte de la réflexion pascalienne sur la disproportion de l'homme dans l'infinité de la nature. En outre, chez Pascal comme chez Kant, le sublime est à rattacher au beau et à la problématique de l'esthétique. Il y a bien une esthétique de Pascal, qu'on doit reconstituer à travers la dispersion des textes. On s'aperçiot alors que l'esthétique de la proportion naturelle bascule, du fait de la dénaturation de l'homme, dans une esthétique de l'impossible justesse dont l'appréhension du sublime livre la clé.

Boudon, Raymond. Weber and Durkheim: Beyond the Differences a Common Important Paradigm?. *Rev Int Phil*, 49(192), 221-239, 1995.

Bourgeois, Bernard. Philosophie hégélienne de l'actualité et actualité de la philosophie hégélienne. *Laval Theol Phil*, 51(2), 229-238, Je 95.

La philosophie hégélienne de l'actualité est telle qu'elle reste actuelle, non seulement en sa forme, mais encore, pour une bonne part, en son contenu même, au point que, en son originalité même, notre époque continue de hégélianiser.

Bourgeois, Patrick and Rosenthal, Sandra B. Deconstruction or Reconstruction of The Living Present: Derrida or Merleau-Ponty and Mead. *Int Stud Phil*, 26(4), 1-17, 1994.

Bourgeois, Patrick L. "The Limits of Ricoeur's Hermeneutics of Existence" in *The Philosophy of Paul Ricoeur, Hahn, Lewis Edwin (ed)*, 549-566. Peru, Open Court, 1994.

Bourne, Richard. Ethical and Legal Dilemmas in the Management of Family Violence. *Ethics Behavior*, 5(3), 261-271, 1995.

Boutot, Alain. Est-il vrai que la science ne pense pas?. *Rev Phil Fr*, 2, 145-166, Ap-Je 94.

Bouveresse, Jacques. Leibniz et le problème de la "science moyenne". *Rev Int Phil*, 48(188), 99-126, 1994.

Bouveresse, Jacques and Fournier, Christian (trans) and Laugier, Sandra (trans). Philosophy from an Antiphilosopher: Paul Valéry. *Crit Inquiry*, 21(2), 354-381, Wint 95.

Bove, Laurent. Épicurisme et spinozisme: l'éthique. *Arch Phil*, 57(3), 471-484, Jl-S 94.

Bovens, Luc. Principles of Supervenience. *Austl J Phil*, 72(3), 294-301, S 94.

I present a categorization of a set of supervenience principles and lay out the logical connections between them. Some isolated pieces of this puzzle have been put together by Kim, Klagge and McFetridge. I sketch the current state of the puzzle and fill in the remaining part in a systematic fashion. In particular, I a) respond to McFetridge's appeal that the logical status of the set of principles of determination be examined, b) determine the role of complementation and comprehension principles with respect to alternative supervenience principles, and c) provide a solution to a problem first raised by Klagge involving a curious lack of entailment between supervenience principles.

Bowery, Anne-Marie. Plato Visits Postmodernity: Reflections on Narrative Philosophy. *SW Phil Rev*, 11(1), 135-142, Ja 95.

In this paper, I refer to Richard Rorty, Anthony Kerby, and Jean-Francois Lyotard in order to establish the narrative aspects of postmodern philosophy. Then I interpret Plato's *Symposium* from a narratological perspective. Third, I argue that although narration pervades the *Symposium* its prevalence does not necessarily entail Plato's approval of the phenomenon. Plato writes the *Symposium* to criticize those who practice philosophy as a narrative activity because it cultivates philosophical discipleship instead of serious philosophical reflection. Finally, I suggest that those philosophers sympathetic to postmodernism can benefit from this Platonic perspective on narrative philosophy.

Bowie, Andrew. "'Non-Identity'" in *Intersections: Nineteenth-Century Philosophy and Contemporary Theory, Rajan, Tilottama (ed)*, 243-260. Albany, SUNY Pr, 1995.

Bowie, Andrew. Reply: The Schellingian Alternative. *Bull Hegel Soc Gt Brit*, 30, 23-42, Autumn-Wint 94.

Bowie, Norman E. The Clash Between Academic and Business Values. *Bus Prof Ethics J*, 12(4), 3-19, Wint 93.

Bowie, Norman E. *University-Business Partnerships: An Assessment*. Lanham, Rowman & Littlefield, 1994.

After providing a brief history of university-business partnerships, the book describes the advantages and disadvantages of these partnerships and evaluates the arguments for and against them. Special consideration is given to issues of profitability and economic risks, conflicts of interest, constraints on publication, the clash between business values and academic values and issues of distributive justice. The concluding assessment is that university-business partnerships should be entered into with great caution and that most universities and industrial sponsors have not received the anticipated benefits. A readings section includes defenses of the various positions and documents of historical interest.

Bowman, Wayne D. Sound, Society, and Music "Proper". *Phil Music Educ Rev*, 2(1), 14-24, Spr 94.

Boyer, Alain. Democracy and Disagreement. *Ratio Juris*, 8(1), 1-8, Mr 95.

According to Popper's critical rationalism, the possibility of disagreement is at the heart of open societies. If this is assumed to be true, is it not illiberal to try to justify principles of justice, which can be regarded as the subject of an unending collective deliberation? I suggest that it is not, using an analogy with scientific progress. Moreover, I try to show that Rawls's achievement is misunderstood if one forgets that it is supposed to overcome the antinomy between "la liberté des Modernes" and "la liberté des Anciens." In this respect, I insist on some unnoticed similarities between Rawls's and Popper's points of views. I conclude on the idea of the "neutrality" of the theory of justice, suggesting a link between Rawls's approach and the French republican tradition.

Boyle, C Franklin. Computation as an Intrinsic Property. *Mind Mach*, 4(4), 451-467, N 94.

In an effort to uncover fundamental differences between computers and brains, this paper identifies computation with a particular kind of physical process, in contrast to interpreting the behaviors of physical systems as one or more abstract computations. That is, whether or not a system is computing depends on how those aspects of the system we consider to be informational physically cause change rather than on our capacity to describe its behaviors in computational terms. A physical framework based on the notion of "causal mechanism" is used to distinguish different kinds of information processing in a physically-principled way; each information processing type is associated with a particular causal mechanism. The causal mechanism associated with computation is pattern matching, which is *physically* defined as the fitting of physical structures such that they cause a different than pattern matching so defined, implying that brains do not compute, at least not in the physical sense that digital computers do. This casual difference may also mean that computers cannot have mental states.

Boyle, Philip J. Shaping Priorities in Genetic Medicine. *Hastings Center Rep*, 25(3), S2-S8, My-Je 95.

This Special Supplement grows out of a three-year investigation in how to set priorities for emerging genetic technologies. The supplement examines social influences on genetic priorities, case examples, and the normative problems embedded in any attempt to set priorities.

Boyle, Robert. De la Excelencia y Fundamentos de la Filosofía Corpuscular o Mecánica. *Themata*, 13, 277-296, 1995.

Boyman, Anne (trans) and Cache, Bernard and Speaks, Michael (ed). *Earth Moves: The Furnishing of Territories*. Cambridge, MIT Pr, 1995.

Boyne, Roy. Fractured Subjectivity. *Hist Human Sci*, 8(2), 51-68, My 95.

Georg Baselitz struggles with the contemporary subject. His 'fracture paintings' (1966-1969) hover between visions of exploded subjects, and camouflaged intimations of the absolute. Using the concept of the differend, the exploded fracture paintings are shown as signifiers of fragmented subjectivity, the horizontally lined fracture paintings as cultural dissections. These paintings did not ask how an artist could be-in-an-exploded-world. The expression of that dilemma is inversion. The fragmented ego cannot be faithful as mirror of the world. Still the desire to express remains powerful. Picturing upside down liberates representation from the arrogance that ego can grasp the world entire.

Bracken, Joseph A. *The Divine Matrix: Creativity as Link between East and West*. Maryknoll, Orbis, 1995.

The notion of the infinite as the transcendant source and goal of all human activity is common to virtually all the major world religions. Bracken proposes that the infinite is experienced, properly speaking, not as an entity (not even God as the Supreme Being), but as an ongoing activity which serves as the nature or immanent principle of activity for all entities, God included. Understood as the act of being or in Whitehead's metaphysics creativity, this activity links the Godhead in Christian theology with the notion of *Brahman* in Hinduism, Emptiness in Buddhism, and the *Tao* in Chinese philosophy.

Bracken, Patrick J. Beyond Liberation: Michel Foucault and the Notion of a Critical Psychiatry. *Phil Psychiat Psych*, 2(1), 1-13, Mr 95.

Philosophical disputes in psychiatry and psychoanalysis have traditionally been formulated in positivist ("medical model") versus anti-positivist (mainly existential and hermeneutic) frameworks. Foucault's critique of positivist psychiatry, uncovering the historical, political and cultural contexts in which its basic concepts and practices were developed, is well known. This paper examines his corresponding, though less well known, critique of anti-positivism, focusing in particular on the hermeneutic re-interpretation of psychoanalytic theory developed within critical theory by Habermas. (edited)

Braddock III, Clarence H. The Role of Empirical Research in Medical Ethics: Asking Questions or Answering Them?. *J Clin Ethics*, 5(2), 144-147, Sum 94.

Bradie, Michael. *The Secret Chain: Evolution and Ethics*. Albany, SUNY Pr, 1994.

An evolutionary concept of human nature has implications for both epistemology and ethics. The roots of Darwin's moral theory and the nineteenth century treatments of evolutionary ethics are traced to the arguments and models of the eighteenth century

British moral theorists. There is a critical discussion of recent sociobiological analyses of ethics and of attempts to use Darwinian considerations to expand the moral circle to include nonhuman animals. It is concluded that evolutionary approaches can provide valuable insights into moral phenomena although the extremist view that biology provides the basis for a complete analysis of ethics is rejected.

Bradley, F H and Allard, James W (ed) and Stock, Guy (ed). *Writings on Logic and Metaphysics*. New York, Oxford Univ Pr, 1994.

Brady, F Neil and Dunn, Craig P. Business Meta-Ethics: An Analysis of Two Theories. *Bus Ethics Quart*, 5(3), 385-398, Jl 95.

The main purpose of this paper is to defend traditional ethical theory (utilitarianism and deontology) for its application in business against a more recent model consisting of utility, rights, and justice. This is done in three parts: First, we provide a conceptual argument for the superiority of the traditional model; second, we demonstrate these points through an examination of three short cases; and third, we argue for the capability of the traditional model to account for universals and particulars in ethics.

Brague, Rémi. La fenomenología como vía de acceso al mundo griego. *Rev Filosof (Spain)*, 4(6), 401-427, 1991.

Spanish translation of an article originally published in French: "La phénoménologie comme voie d'accès au monde grec. Note sur la critique de la *Vorhandenheit* comme modèle ontologique dans la lecture Heideggerienne d'Aristote", in J-L Marion/G Planty-Bonjour, *Phénoménologie et Métaphysique* (Paris: P U F, 1984), 247-273, with a postscript of march 1991. A study on Heidegger's claim that Aristotle's ontology assumes as its paradigm the way of being of what is present-at-hand (*vorhanden*).

Braidotti, Rosi. Feminism and Modernity. *Free Inq*, 15(2), 23-29, Spr 95.

Braine, David. Reply to Cockburn's "Braine on the Mind". *Relig Stud*, 30(3), 353-360, S 94.

Brajicic, Rudolf. Les Principes Éthiques en tant que les Jugements Existants et la Liberté: Dans le Contexte de L'Éthique de la Situation. *Filozof Istraz*, 14(1), 27-32, 1994.

L'auteur affirme que tous les principes éthiques, de même que les principes les plus universaux, ne se dérivent pas de la nature humaine abstraite mais de celle existante. La nature humaine existante change, mais dans tous les changements elle reste identique à soi-même, et comme telle elle est le fondement des principes éthiques invariables. Vivant sa propre histoire dans son modèle individuel et dans le modèle des diverses situations, l'homme reste toujours obligé à sa nature existante invariable dans ses variations. Les principes éthiques invariables se prononcent en forme des jugements synthétiques *a priori*. Ces jugements manquent d'une évidence nécessitante et ils offrent la certitude libre. Cette liberté existe avant la liberté de faire du bein ou du mal et elle se réalise par l'acceptation libre des principes éthiques eux-mêmes.

Brand, Myles. Hornsby on Trying. *J Phil Res*, 20, 541-547, 1995.

In "Reasons for Trying" (*JPR*, 1995), Jennifer Hornsby rejects several views about trying, including the volitional account, which identifies trying with an 'inner' uniform mental occurrence leading to action and the instrumental view, which explicates trying as doing one thing is order to accomplish something else. She proffers, rather, an explication, which I label 'the capacity view,' that identifies trying with the agent doing all that she can to accomplish the goal. In this note, I argue, first, that Hornsby's approach more nearly captures our intuitions on trying, but, second, only if it is amended and expanded in critical ways. In particular, trying also involves overcoming perceived resistance.

Brand, Myles and Brand, Peg. "Surface and Deep Interpretation" in *Danto and his Critics, Rollins, Mark (ed)*, 55-69. Cambridge, Blackwell, 1993.

Brand, Peg and Brand, Myles. "Surface and Deep Interpretation" in *Danto and his Critics, Rollins, Mark (ed)*, 55-69. Cambridge, Blackwell, 1993.

Brandl, Johannes. "Semantic Holism Is Here To Stay" in *Holism: A Consumer Update, Fodor, Jerry A (ed)*, 1-16. Amsterdam, Rodopi, 1993.

Critically reflecting some theses of Fodor and LePore's *Holism*, it is argued that semantic holism in spite of all their criticism is not defeated. As a consequence of the rejection of the analytic-synthetic distinction, a first result is that they do not take traditional holism, as it originates from Frege and Wittgenstein, serious at all. Whereas a weak anatomism, inspired with views of traditional holism, might be an interesting alternative to atomism and holism even for Quine and neo-Fregeans like Dummett. Concerning the principle of compositionality and ambiguity between recurrence and functional compositionality is localized that relativizes their critique of Davidson. And finally versions of content- and belief-holism in combination with adequate charity-principles are discussed as a basis for squaring intentional realism with Brentano's thesis.

Brandner, Rudolf. *Heidegger Sein und Wissen: Eine Einführung in sein Denken*. Vienna, Passagen, 1993.

Das Erstaunlichste an Heidegger ist wohl, dass und wie er das Denken selbst umdenkt und verwandelt. Es verhält sich anders zu seinem Gedachten, als wir es unmittelbar an uns selbst finden und aus der Überlieferung der abendländischen Metaphysik gewohnt sind. Dies gelingt ihm nur, indem er das Verhältnis von Sein und Wissen grundsätzlich überdenkt und neu bestimmt. Der Ort dieser Bestimmung ist der Begriff der *Aletheia*. Die vorstehende "Einführung" in Heideggers Denken versucht, das im Begriff der *Aletheia* neu gedachte Verhältnis von Sein und Wissen auf seine konstitutiven Memente hin auseinanderzulegen. (edited)

Brandner, Rudolf. *Heideggers Begriff der Geschichte und das neuzeitliche Geschichtsdenken*. Vienna, Passagen, 1994.

Zum Phänomen der neuzeitlichen Vergeschichtlichung des Denkens gehört das seiner Entwirklichung, die sich in den Historisierungs- und Ästhetisierungsprozessen der Moderne niederschlägt. Entwirklichung aber verweist auf die subjektzentrierte Modifikation des Naturverhältnisses, der das neuzeitliche Geschichtsdenken allererst entspringt. Deshalb schliesst die Frage nach der geschichtlichen Konstitution des Denkens die Frage nach seinem konstitutiven Naturbezug mit ein. Infrage steht das, was heute ist—und mit ihm dieses Fragen selbst. Der Begriff der Geschichte wird damit zum Zentrum der Auseinandersetzung um Möglichkeit und Notwendigkeit philosophischen Denkens in der Moderne: und es ist dieses Zentrum, das es auf seine Momente hin auseinanderzulegen gilt.

Brandner, Rudolf. *Warum Heidegger keine Ethik geschrieben hat*. Vienna, Passagen, 1992.

Das geschichtliche Bedürfnis nach einer 'Ethik' unterstellt dem, was von der Philosophie heute noch übrig geblieben ist, eine gesellschaftliche Führungsfunktion in der Abwehr der technologischen Aushöhlung des Menschseins und seiner Selbstverständnisse insgesamt. Die Philosophie, ohnehin in 'Legitimationsnot', antwortet beflissen mit der 'Rehabilitation der praktischen Philosophie'. Die 'Ethik' wird zum vermittelbaren Marktwert eines Denkens, dem seine *'raison d'être'* abhanden gekommen ist, ohne dass seine geschichtliche Grundproblematik, wie sie an erster Stelle von Nietzsche, dann von Heidegger auseinandergesetzt wurde, noch eigens bedacht würde. (edited)

Brandner, Rudolf. *Was ist und wozu überhaupt-Philosophie? Vorübungen sich verändernden Denkens*. Vienna, Passagen, 1992.

Es ist längst zu einer fraglosen Selbstverständlichkeit der Gegenwartsphilosophie geworden, im Hinweis auf verschiedene "Ansätze" des Philosophierens jede Auseinandersetzung um das Philosophieren schon im "Ansatz" zu ersticken. Und dies paradoxerweise angesichts einer geschichtlich erfahrenen Fragwürdigkeit der Philosophie selbst, die nur noch im gelangweilten Hinweis auf den ausgemachten geschichtlichen Vollzug der Moderne Erwähnung findet. So hat ein jeder seinen Ansatz und ist es zufrieden. Die Frage nach der Philosophie versucht demgegenüber, das im "Ansatz" verschluckte Potential des Denkens zu reaktivieren und eine auseinandersetzung um die geschichtliche Situation zugänglich zu machen.

Brandom, Robert. Expressing and Attributing Beliefs. *Phil Phenomenol Res*, 54(4), 905-912, D 94.

This piece is a contribution to a symposium on Arthur Collins' book *The Nature of Mental Things*. Collins' argument from the observation that 'there is no state of belief that the subject might report without asserting that *p*' to the conclusion that beliefs are not inner states is expounded and critically assessed.

Brandon, Robert N. Sober on Brandon on Screening-Off and the Levels of Selection. *Phil Sci*, 61(3), 475-486, S 94.

Sober (1992) has recently evaluated Brandon's (1982, 1990; see also 1985, 1988) use of Salmon's (1971) concept of screening-off in the philosophy of biology. He critiques three particular issues, each of which will be considered in this discussion.

Brandt, Jason. "Ethical Considerations in Genetic Testing" in *Medicine and Moral Reasoning, Fulford, K W M (ed)*, 41-59. New York, Cambridge Univ Pr, 1994.

Brandt, Reinhard. La justicia en Kant. *Rev Filosof (Daimon)*, 7, 19-33, 1993.

En el seno de la ética kantiana la justicia no es examinada como una virtud específica, y los *Principios metafísicos de la doctrina del derecho* sólo parecen tratar del derecho privado y público, mas no de la justicia. En realidad, la ética expuesta en las tres *Críticas* depende de una *iustitia distributiva* de Dios merced al bien supremo, y la institución jurídica del Estado será descrita como "justicia pública". Este trabajo se propone clarificar esta conexión y realizar una contribución al tema señalado en el título.

Brandt, Richard B. Conscience (Rule) Utilitarianism and the Criminal Law. *Law Phil*, 14(1), 65-89, F 95.

A rule-utilitarian appraisal of criminal law requires that the total system, including punishments, is justified only if it will expectably maximize public benefit, including its stigmatizing some behaviors as "offenses" and its prescribed punishment of these, such as imprisonment, with (possible) deterrent effects. In view of the paucity of evidence about the deterrent effect of prison sentences, some changes seem to be in order: reduction in the length of incarceration, replacement of prison by fines or restrictions on the convicted such as house arrest for many hours of a day, intensive supervision, required community service (say thirty hours in place of a month in prison), enrollment in a drug program or therapy in the case of sex offenses, and so on. An evaluation of such proposals should be based on statistics and the psychology of criminal behavior.

Bransen, Jan. Anthropocentrism in Favourable Circumstances (Philip Pettit, *The Common Mind: An Essay on Psychology, Society, and Politics*). *Inquiry*, 37(3), 339-347, S 94.

This is an appreciative though still challenging review of Philip Pettit, *The Common Mind*. I emphasize the central importance of Pettit's ethnocentric account of rule-following for a satisfactory philosophy of the humanities. According to this account people are able to live their lives because of their habits of response and practices of negotiation, which lead, in favorable circumstances, to successful convergence. But I question Pettit's attempt to provide a naturalistic underpinning of this account, and I point out an aporia that follows from an unescapable ambiguity in the notion of 'favorable circumstances'.

Bransen, Jan. *The Antinomy of Thought: Maimonian Skepticism and the Relation between Thoughts and Objects*. Dordrecht, Kluwer, 1991.

This book provides an interpretation and defense of the post-Kantian skepticism of Salomon Maimon (1752-1800). It is argued that the structure of our articulations of the relation between thoughts and objects has an intrinsically aporetic character. The point of such skeptical arguments is that a *theory* is the wrong thing to look for as regards the relation between thoughts and objects—an adequate account of this relation will have to take the form of a *problem*. In order to show the actual importance of Maimonian skepticism it is argued that the failure of some contemporary American accounts of thought (those of Rosenberg, Rorty and Nagel) can be explained in terms of their ignorance of the antimony of thought.

Brant, Renée and Martin, Tony and Wyatt, Gail Elizabeth. Child Abuse or Acceptable Cultural Norms. *Ethics Behavior*, 5(3), 283-292, 1995.

Brasa Díaz, Mariano. Disidencias de Pedro Abelardo. *Rev Espan Filosof Med*, 1, 109-131, 1994.

On rereading the *Historia Calamitatum Mearum* by Peter Abelard, I was struck this time by a few passages in which the dissenting individual makes his appearance, where there is a clear break with tradition. The philosopher who had always sought freedom to communicate had become a dissident within the established order. He who had preferred philosophy to a military career, seeking in dialectics what students clamored for—reasons, valid argument, one not based solely on authority—, is condemned as a heretic because he cannot adapt to the norms that somebody or other had capriciously established. (edited)

Brassac, Christian and Trognon, Alain. Formalizing the Theory of Intentionality. *J Prag*, 23(5), 555-562, My 95.

Braude, Stephen E. Survival or Super-Psi?. *Darshana Int*, 32(4/128), 8-28, O 92.

Even the most sophisticated discussions of the evidence for post-mortem survival underestimate the difficulties facing the survival hypothesis. One major challenge is posed by the rival "super-psi" hypothesis, which posits refined psychic functioning among the living, and which most writers fail to confront in its most plausible and potent form. Once the super-psi hypothesis is taken seriously, two major weaknesses in discussions of survival stand out clearly. First, analyses of apparently anomalous knowledge—that tend to be fatally superficial in their treatment of subject psychodynamics. And second, analyses of apparently anomalous abilities and skills trade on an impoverished and naive conception of the nature of human abilities.

Braun, Carlos Rodríguez and Schwartz, Pedro. Entrevista: Carlos R Braun dialoga con Pedro Schwartz. *Telos (Spain)*, 1(1), 167-182, F 92.

En la presente entrevista Carlos Rodríguez Braun, socio fundador de la SIEU, destacado profesor de economía, Subdirector de Cambio 16, y uno de los más importantes investigadores del utilitarismo en el ámbito iberoamericano entrevista a Pedro Schwartz, presidente honorario de la SIEU, pionero de los estudios utilitaristas en el mundo iberoamericano en el presente siglo, una de las mentes más lúcidas de nuestro panorama intelectual que analiza con rigor las aportaciones del utilitarismo, y sus relaciones con el pensamiento liberal y socialista. La lúcida acidez de Pedro Schwartz es un magnífico estimulante para comenzar nuestra andadura como investigadores y críticos del utilitrismo. *Telos* agradece al entrevistador y el entrevistado sus punzantes e inteligentes preguntas y respuestas.

Braun, David. Empty Names. *Nous*, 27(4), 449-469, D 93.

The Theory of Direct Reference says (roughly) that a proper name has no semantic value other than its referent. In this paper I describe the apparent problems that empty names (proper names that fail to refer) raise for this theory. I then describe two theories that deal with these problems in ways which are consistent with direct reference. The first theory says that sentences that contain empty names fail to express propositions, and attempts to explain away the unintuitive results. The second theory says that sentences containing empty names express structured propositions containing unfilled positions.

Braun, David. What Is Character?. *J Phil Log*, 24(3), 227-240, Je 95.

In "Demonstratives", David Kaplan argues that indexicals have two sorts of meanings: character and content. In this paper, I point out a number of problems with Kaplan's theory of character. I first show that there is an inconsistency, of a certain sort, between Kaplan's informal description of character and his formal definition of character. I then argue that his theory fails to make certain "fine-grained" distinctions in character. Finally, I argue that we need two revisions in Kaplan's theory in order to handle the problems that I find with it.

Braun, Ingo. The Technology-Culture Spiral: Three Examples of Technological Developments in Everyday Life. *Res Phil Technol*, 14, 93-118, 1994.

Bravo, Elia Nathan. La Religión y el Mal: Gnosticismo y Satanismo. *Analogia*, 4(1), 83-104, 1990.

Braybrooke, David. How Do I Presuppose Thee? Let Me Count the Ways: The Relation of Regularities to Rules in Social Science. *Midwest Stud Phil*, 15, 80-93, 1990.

Social rules, given some combination of evidence about conformity, enforcement, and point, always imply causal regularities, indeed, causal regularities that are their exact counterparts. The implication the other way fails: Not all social regularities have counterparts in social rules; not all of them presuppose social rules just by involving actions. However, those that do not have a doubtful claim to belong to social science. Social science as it stands falls under a modally powerful thesis that would make of anything answering to the name something that treats only regularities that human beings have the freedom to change by changing social rules.

Brazier, Margaret. Commentary on "Who Should Be Committable?". *Phil Psychiat Psych*, 2(1), 49-50, Mr 95.

Breazeale, Daniel. Kant, Fichte, and *The Interests of Reason*. *Daimon Rev Filosof*, 9, 81-98, 1994.

Kant distinguishes the interest of theoretical reason from the interest of practical reason and tries both to the interest of reason as such, which he conceives of as ultimately "practical". Fichte links the interest of practical and of theoretical reason more closely than does Kant and connects his account of the fundamental interest of reason to this general theory of the "divided self" always struggling for an (inobtainable) unity. For Fichte, there is no real conflict between the interests of theoretical and of practical reason, nor can there be any genuine conflict between reason and interest. On the contrary, reason is always "interested", and the "life of reason" is one of active engagement with the world in a process of endless striving.

Breazeale, Daniel. Philosophy and the Divided Self: On the "Existential" and "Scientific" Tasks of the Jena *Wissenschaftslehre*. *Fichte-Studien*, 6, 117-147, 1994.

Breazeale, Daniel. Über die Unhaltbarkeit und die Unentbehrlichkeit des Skeptizismus bei Fichte. *Fichte-Studien*, 5, 7-19, 1993.

Breazeale, Kathyln A. Don't Blame It on the Seeds: Toward a Feminist Process Understanding of Anthropology, Sin, and Sexuality. *Process Stud*, 22(2), 71-83, Sum 93.

Bredeck, Elizabeth. Mixing Metaphors: Contemporary Views on the 'End' of Philosophy. *Hist Euro Ideas*, 20(1-3), 531-536, Ja 95.

In much recent discussion about the 'end' of philosophy, the discipline or *Fach* of philosophy is often described with one or more of the following metaphors: as one voice in a larger conversation, as a language game, or as a kind of writing. After summarizing the use of these related metaphors, the paper draws on the work of Lyotard to highlight some unsettling implications of pluralism and its metaphors. Finally, it considers the metaphor of 'orderly disorder' (borrowed from research into chaotic systems) as an alternative way to think about philosophy in a post-philosophical culture.

Breeur, Roland. De Dodendans en de Pianola. *Tijdschr Filosof*, 57(2), 221-249, Je 95.

This article attempts to frame Proust's treatment of the "mémoire involontaire" within a general concept of human being that prevails throughout the *Recherche*, and which is characterized by *non-coïncidence*. Proust always portrays the vicissitudes of a subject that never falls together with the world, the other or itself. "Mémoire involontaire" is itself, following Proust's description of love, jealously and art, the pre-eminent experience of this *non-coïncidence*. Finally, the general concept of human being allows us to approach and to put into question the classic parallel with Bergson's conception of memory.

Breeur, Roland (ed). Randbemerkungen Husserls zu Heideggers *Sein und Zeit* und *Kant und das Problem der Metaphysik*. *Husserl Stud*, 11(1-2), 3-63, 1994.

Breger, Herbert. Die mathematische-physikalische Schönheit bei Leibniz. *Rev Int Phil*, 48(188), 127-140, 1994.

The article discusses the role of mathematical and physical beauty according to Leibniz. For him not only theories, but nature itself is beautiful. Beauty is a final argument to justify those parts of a theory, which cannot be justified otherwise; so for Leibniz beauty has a function similar to simplicity in modern philosophy of science. Furthermore the role of beauty as an example for the role of tacit knowledge (Polanyi) in science is discussed.

Breiner, Peter. The Political Logic of Economics and the Economic Logic of Modernity in Max Weber. *Polit Theory*, 23(1), 25-47, F 95.

Interpreters have seen Max Weber as merely providing a sociological account of economics that complements the formal theory of price based on marginal utility theory. However, when we examine Weber's argument for the unavoidable use of the ideal type in economics and his substantive account of the rational capitalist economy, we discover that he undermines most of marginal utility theory's central claim. Weber constructs a new political economy in which maximizing conduct based on the law of final utility collides with a number of other logics that deflect or even disrupt the simple causality so central to marginal utility theory in which consumer behavior drives production. In particular, it collides with a logic of power and a logic of formal rationality that makes the modern capitalist market look similar to the realm of politics without being reducible to it. Only losers in the struggle for markets adhere to the law of final utility. This account is part of a broad notion of political economy that functions to measure the costs of systematic action in all the life-spheres that characterize modernity including the political one.

Bremer, Dieter. Milesischer Anfang. *Phil Rundsch*, 41(3), 204-211, Je 94.

Bremer, Manuel E. Ist die Tranzendentalpragmatik letztebegründet oder holistisch?. *J Gen Phil Sci*, 26(1), 153-168, 1995.

Transcendental pragmatics as developed by Karl-Otto Apel has been the object of various criticisms. Against the fallibilists' claim (Albert) that argumentation is at last either dogmatic, axiomatic or circular, the transcendental pragmatists have given an argument that ultimate foundation ('Letzbegründung') cannot be proved to be impossible. But this clarification of their claims leaves open the questions whether their method can establish universal statements, and whether they prove statements which are synthetic *a priori*. Against the claim of the reconstructive scientist (Habermas) they have to restate their view, and take into account an element of fallibilism. Here we encounter a first element of holism. With regard to the question whether there can be ultimate foundation without ultimate foundation of the method of ultimate foundation holism breaks in. The distinction between a vicious and a transcendental circle, used against Albert, is of no use in the establishment of the transcendental circle.

Brendle, Jörg. Combinatorial Properties of Classical Forcing Notions. *Annals Pure Applied Log*, 73(2), 143-170, Je 95.

Brendle, Jörg. Regularity Properties for Dominating Projective Sets. *Annals Pure Applied Log*, 72(3), 291-307, Ap 95.

Brennan, Geoffrey and Pettit, Philip. Consecuencialismo Restrictivo. *Telos (Spain)*, 3(2), 73-97, D 94.

While it might be appropriate to evaluate options by the criterion of maximizing probable value, it need not be sensible to select them on that basis. To satisfy the criterion of evaluation may often be to restrict or forswear its application, relying rather on some other criterion of choice. Consequentialists must be restrictive in choosing actions, avoiding the calculative evaluation of options, whenever calculation undermines maximazation of objectively probable value. Restrictive consequentialism is a real possibility when the pursued benefit is *calculatively elusive* and *calculatively vulnerable*. The disposition to satisfice is a more interesting case, since it may be extrapolated to three derived cases where the consequence of deliberation, not the deliberation itself, is what undermines the benefit. (edited)

Brennan, Mark. The Discourse of Denial: Cross-Examining Child Victim Witnesses. *J Prag*, 23(1), 71-91, Ja 95.

Child victim witnesses, when being cross-examined in adult criminal court, are subjected to a range of punitive linguistic strategies. The meaning and essence of their own experiences are systematically denied. Credibility is reduced and all problems are made, as in soap operas, personal rather than systemic or social. This process is created by and viewable through linguistic activity. Language as a social human activity has itself to become the focus of our attention and critique. Interview, observation, and transcript data have been analysed and cross-referenced to define and describe the 'strange language' to which child victim witnesses are subjected during their court appearance. Further, the process of cross-examination is shown to be grounded in a specificable discourse...the 'discourse of denial'. This punitive linguistic style has everything to do with the battle for credibility and little to do with the administration of justice. The specific tactics and strategies are identified.

Brennan, Samantha. Paternalism and Rights. *Can J Phil*, 24(3), 419-439, S 94.

Brennan, Samantha. Thresholds for Rights. *S J Phil*, 33(2), 143-168, Sum 95.

A moral right with a threshold is one which can justifiably be infringed when enough is at stake for those who will benefit from the infringement. A structure for rights thresholds is developed, according to which the threshold of a right is made up of three conditions: the total requirement, the universal constraint and the existential constraint. The total specifies the amount that must be at stake while the existential and universal constraints specify how that amount must be distributed. Using this framework I analyze Judith Thomson's account of thresholds for rights as developed in *The Realm of Rights*.

Brennan, Timothy J. Markets, Information, and Benevolence. *Econ Phil*, 10(2), 151-168, O 94.

Brès, Jean-Claude. Un Pari Pour la Philosophie. *Philosopher*, 15, 179-184, 1994.

Bresler, Liora and Davidson, Judith. Arts and Knowledge: A Discussion. *Educ Theor*, 45(1), 63-70, Wint 95.

Brett, Stephen F. *Slavery and the Catholic Tradition: Rights in the Balance*. New York, Lang, 1994.

Bretzke, James T. The *Tao* of Confucian Virtue Ethics. *Int Phil Quart*, 35(1), 25-41, Mr 95.

This article investigates the key aspects of the Confucian virtue ethics such as the *chün-tzu* (Superior Person), the Five Relationships of society, the particular Confucian virtues of *jen* (benevolence) and *li* (propriety), the moral vision of the *tao* (Way), and the understanding of the *t'ien-ming* (Mandate of Heaven). The thesis of the article is that the moral matrix provided by the web of social relationships allows the Confucian ethics of virtue to function well, and that a consideration of this Confucian moral matrix may illuminate the Western debate on the ethics of virtue vs the ethics of duty.

Breuer, Thomas. The Impossibility of Accurate State Self-Measurements. *Phil Sci*, 62(2), 197-214, Je 95.

It is shown that it is impossible for an observer to distinguish all present states of a system in which he or she is contained, irrespective of whether this system is a classical or a quantum mechanical one and irrespective of whether the time evolution is deterministic or stochastic. As a corollary, this implies that it is impossible for an observer to measure the EPR-correlations between himself or herself and an outside system. Implications of the main result are discussed for how we have to conceive of universally valid theories.

Brewer, Bill. "Thoughts about Objects, Places and Times" in *Objectivity, Simulation and the Unity of Consciousness, Peacocke, Christopher (ed)*, 21-34. New York, Oxford Univ Pr, 1994.

I argue that a person's engaged egocentric perspective on the world may suffice to meet Campbell's structural conditions on object perception and self-consciousness. If not, it is not clear how thought about times is supposed to help. In any case, he fails to establish any asymmetry between spatial and temporal thought in this regard.

Brewer, William F and Chinn, Clark A. Scientists' Responses to Anomalous Data: Evidence from Psychology, History, and Philosophy of Science. *Proc Phil Sci Ass*, 1, 304-313, 1994.

This paper presents an analysis of the forms of response that scientists make when confronted with anomalous data. We postulate that there are seven ways in which an individual who currently holds a theory can respond to anomalous data: 1) ignore the data; 2) reject the data; 3) exclude the data from the domain of the current theory; 4) hold the data in abeyance; 5) reinterpret the data; 6) make peripheral changes to the current theory; or 7) change the theory. We analyze psychological experiments and cases from the history of science to support this proposal. Implications for the philosophy of science are discussed.

Brezzi, Francesca. Il soggetto e la prassi nell'ermeneutica di Paul Ricoeur. *Aquinas*, 36(3), 643-654, S-D 93.

Briand, Michael. Postmodernism and Politics: Skepticism or Pragmatism?. *J Speculative Phil*, 9(2), 111-124, 1995.

We can identify two broad categories of post-modernist political views: a "weak" view and a "strong" view. The latter cannot support a practice of democratic politics. In contrast, the "weak" view is compatible with a conception of democratic politics that is pluralistic, liberal, and pragmatic. The central issue over which the two views part ways is whether human beings have enough in common to permit mutual comprehension. The strong view implies that they do not, and for this reason must be rejected. Within the weak view, disagreements are really a matter of emphasis: When and in what circumstances should we emphasize difference rather than commonality?

Briand, Michael K. Democratic Public Judgment: The Role of "Mutual Comprehension". *Phil Cont World*, 1(3), 1-7, Fall 94.

The need to choose between good things in conflict lies at the heart of politics. Only citizens deliberating together can authoritatively form the democratic public judgment necessary to resolve such conflicts. The key step to arriving at a sound, widely supported public judgment is getting all members of the public to "comprehend"—to understand and appreciate—the goods in conflict. Mutual comprehension enables us to combine our individual perspectives without loss, thereby providing the basis for collective deliberation. Such comprehension is essential because the mutual respect between citizens upon which democratic politics depends is impossible without it. Mutual comprehension is possible because we share a common human nature that, despite our manifest and irreducible differences is built around a limited and universal set of human needs and dispositions.

Brickhouse, Thomas C and Smith, Nicholas D. HE MANTIKE TECHNE: *Statesman* 260e1 and 290c4-6. *Polis*, 12(1-2), 37-51, 1993.

In this paper, we shall consider what Plato's view of divination. We shall argue that, recent interpretations to the contrary, Plato is consistent throughout the dialogues in portraying the diviner as possessing a genuine, though relatively meager, form of knowledge. We shall approach our topic anachronistically—beginning with what Plato's Stranger has to say in the *Politicus* about the diviner's craft, and then comparing that to the pronouncements of Plato's Socrates in the earlier dialogues.

Bricklin, Patricia M and Bennett, Bruce E and VandeCreek, Leon. Response to Lazarus's "How Certain Boundaries and Ethics Diminish Therapeutic Effectiveness". *Ethics Behavior*, 4(3), 263-266, 1994.

Briese, Olaf. "Springflut des Bösen". *Phil Rundsch*, 41(3), 245-255, Je 94.

Brieskorn, Norbert. Zum Begriff des "Zuvorkommens" in der politischen Philosophie. *Theol Phil*, 69(3), 321-341, 1994.

The article explains the concept of forestalling (f) (preventing and expected or feared event *and* bringing one's own end about in doing so) what is not to be equated with "acting against", "preventing" and "anticipating". The tension charged process of the concept's history is: the f action of the individual (first step) has been set limits by the modern state—through his own form of f (second step). Against this f of the state's might on the other hand there unfolds a f (third step) as protective law (human rights). Especially Plato and Aristotle, Hobbes, Locke, Rousseau and Kant handle this concept of f.

Brigati, Roberto. *Il Linguaggio Dell'Oggettività: Saggio su Meinong*. Turin, Thema Ed, 1992.

Meinong's theory of objects is supported by a partially latent epistemology and by a substantially implicit view of language. The coercion of a specific form of linguistic representation is transferred onto both the formal-ontological and the descriptive-psychological level. Having outlined Meinong's views, it is argued that his notion of object can be referred to a form of discourse which is identified as "objective use of language". His theory of "incomplete objects" is criticized and amended.

Brigham, John C and Pfeifer, Jeffrey E. Ethical Concerns of Nonclinical Forensic Witnesses and Consultants. *Ethics Behavior*, 3(3-4), 329-343, 1993.

Current research suggests that nonclinical forensic psychologists are appearing increasingly more often in the legal arena. We argue that many of the ethical dilemmas that face these psychologists differ from those encountered by clinical forensic psychologists. To test the accuracy of this assertion, 37 nonclinical forensic psychologists were surveyed to identify some of the ethical issues and dilemmas they have encountered while engaging in expert testimony or pretrial consulting. Respondents were asked also about how they have resolved these ethical issues and whether they were aware of the "Specialty Guidelines for Forensic Psychologists" (Committee on Ethical Guidelines for Forensic Psychologists, 1991). Results of the survey are discussed in terms of the need for additional regulatory guidelines or professional standards that speak directly to the ethical issues confronting nonclinical, forensic expert witnesses and consultants.

Brighouse, Carolyn. Spacetime and Holes. *Proc Phil Sci Ass*, 1, 117-125, 1994.

John Earman and John Norton have argued that substantivalism leads to a radical form of indeterminism within local spacetime theories. I compare their argument to more traditional arguments typical in the Relationist/Substantivalist dispute and show that they all fail for the same reason. All these arguments ascribe to the substantivalist a particular way of talking about possibility. I argue that the substantivalist is not committed to the modal claims required for the arguments to have any force, and show that this naturally leads to an alteration in the way determinism is characterized for local spacetime theories.

Brighouse, M Harry. Is There Any Such Thing As Political Liberalism?. *Pac Phil Quart*, 75(3-4), 318-332, S-D 94.

Brigley, Stephen. Business Ethics in Context: Researching with Case Studies. *J Bus Ethics*, 14(3), 219-226, Mr 95.

This paper discusses criticisms of survey research in business ethics as conceptually naive and methodologically unsound. A query is raised about the neglect of case-study methods by business ethics researchers—probably for prudential and ideological reasons. It is argued that the case-study approach is more appropriate to inquiries into the complex, diverse contents and contexts of business ethics. Investigatory case study in particular can do much to rectify the inadequacies of the prevailing positivist paradigm by evolving grounded theoretical questions for further research. Case study offers an alternative to the measurement of ethical behavior, i.e., naturalistic generalization which is rooted in the context of organizational cultures and economic systems. It results in enhanced conceptual understanding of the interaction between ethical beliefs of individuals and corporate and market pressures on business decision-taking.

Bringsjord, Selmer. Computation, Among Other Things, Is Beneath Us. *Mind Mach*, 4(4), 469-488, N 94.

What's computation? The received answer is that computation is a computer at work and a computer at work is that which can be modelled as a Turing machine at work. Unfortunately, as John Searle has recently argued, and as others have agreed, the received answer appears to imply that AI and Cog Sci are a royal waste of time. The argument here is alarmingly simple: AI and Cog Sci (of the "Strong" sort, anyway) are committed to the view that cognition is computation (or brains are computers); but *all* processes are computations (or *all* physical things are computers); so AI and Cog Sci are positively silly. I refute this argument herein, in part by defining the locutions 'x is a computer' and c is a computation' in a way that blocks Searle's argument but exploits the hard-to-deny link between What's Computation; and the theory of computation. However, I also provide at the end of this essay, an argument which, it seems to me, implies not that AI and Cog Sci are silly, but that they're based on a form of computation that is well "beneath" human person.

Brinker-Gabler, Gisela (ed). *Encountering the Other(s): Studies in Literature, History, and Culture*. Albany, SUNY Pr, 1995.

Brinkley, Tony and Arsenault, Joseph. Dialectic at a Standstill. *Int Stud Phil*, 27(1), 1-20, 1995.

Brinkmann, Klaus. "Hegel's Critique of Kant and Pre-Kantian Metaphysics" in *Hegel Reconsidered, Engelhardt Jr, H Tristram (ed)*, 57-78. Dordrecht, Kluwer, 1994.

Defends Hegel's rejection of the Kantian "transcendental distinction" between appearance and thing-in-itself and analyzes Hegel's critique of the subject-predicate proposition as well as his conception of objective thought in the *Encyclopedia*. Attempts a systematic interpretation of the Hegelian concept of representation (*Vorstellung*) as word meaning, focussing specifically on *Encyclopedia*, sections 451-464.

Brion, Denis J. "The Chaotic Indeterminacy of Tort Law: Between Formalism and Nihilism" in *Radical Philosophy of Law, Caudill, David S (ed)*, 179-199. Atlantic Highlands, Humanities Pr, 1995.

Because judicial doctrine is indeterminant, what courts do violates the formalist conceptualization of law and opens the legal process to the charge that it functions instrumentally to the power elite. The emerging scientific concept of Chaos (or Complexity) Theory provides, however, a powerful analogy—although the outcomes of judicial decisions, like natural phenomena, are not strictly predictable, these outcomes will fall into one or another of a set of patterns; and this set of patterns is itself predictable, much as natural phenomena fall into the patterns of the strange attractors of Chaos Theory. This analogy provides a way of understanding that formalism misconceives the nature of the law, and that the legal process can function autonomously of the powerful.

Brisson, Luc (ed). *Le Même et L'Autre dans la Structure Ontologique du Timée* de Platon. Sankt Augustin, Academia, 1994.

This book provides a close analysis of Plato's text which yields a detailed and consistent view of the philosophy of the *Timaeus*. Very different from the piecemeal interpretations provided by other scholars, Brisson's detailed discussion of the most important interpretations put forward in antiquity and in modern times gives the reader a good idea of the history of Platonism from the old Academy to the present day. His commentary provides an introduction to the most important problems of Plato's philosophy, and especially to the vexed questions of Plato's account of the origin of the universe, of man and of society. The book was first published in 1974 and has been out of print for many years. This new edition contains many important changes, covering 80 pages, including corrigenda, addenda, revised indexes, a postface and an up-to-date bibliography of modern scholarship on the *Timaeus*.

Brisson, Luc and Meyerstein, F Walter. *Inventing the Universe: Plato's Timaeus*, The Big Bang, and the Problem of Scientific Knowledge. Albany, SUNY Pr, 1995.

The "extra-logical gap" between perception and scientific explanation can be appraised historically. Three stages are to be distinguished. 1) Plato's *Timaeus* furnishes the first example of a scientific cosmology dealing with a realm of ideality which cannot be derived from immediate sensible perception. A list of presuppositions or axioms is first set down, then their consequences are expressed mathematically, and finally the degree of correspondence between this theoretical construction and the data of observation is established. But Plato refuses a naively operational interpretation of this correspondence, according to which a scientific explanation would be exhausted when predictions based on a theorem turn out to be appropriate. 2) Just as the world-order fashioned by the demiurge according to Plato manifests itself as symmetry, the Big Bang model is also mainly constituted on the basis of the geometrical notion of symmetry. Furthermore, the two cosmologies, whose overall parallelism is shown to be striking, take simplicity for granted. The list of axioms of Big Bang cosmology begins with metrical considerations. The Friedmann-Robertson-Walker metric for a homogeneous and isotropic universe is derived, and the various problems (theoretical and observational) associated with it are discussed. 3) In the more recent Algorithmic Information Theory, the analysis of the purely symbolic language expressing physical reality reveals the level of complexity of any given theory formulated in this language. The result is that the probability that the universe is actually in conformity with simple mathematics is zero.

Brito, Emilio. Esthétique et pneumatologie philosophique chez Schleiermacher. *Arch Phil*, 57(4), 645-667, O-D 94.

Having put forward Schleiermacher's conception of the place of the critical discipline of aesthetics within the system of the sciences, and of the place of art, as individual symbolization, within the context of ethics, the present study goes on to characterize Schleiermacher's understanding of art (the theory of production and expression) as an aesthetic of the self-manifestation of the spirit, and asks finally about its actuality.

Brito, Emilio. Hegel dans *Soi-même comme un autre* de Paul Ricoeur. *Laval Theol Phil*, 51(2), 389-404, Je 95.

Ricoeur reste très proche de la tentative hégélienne dans la mesure où celle-ci se dresse contre l'atomisme politique. Mais l'opposition entre *Sittlichkeit* et *Moralität* devient inutile, selon lui, si, d'une part, on donne à la règle de justice un champ d'application plus vaste que celui que lui assignait la doctrine hégélienne du droit abstrait, et si, d'autre part, on dissocie les analyses hégéliennes de la *Sittlichkeit* de l'ontologie de l'esprit qui transforme la médiation institutionnelle de l'État en instance capable de se penser elle-même.

Brito, José De Sousa. É o principio da utilidade racional?. *Telos (Spain)*, 1(1), 55-72, F 92.

Britt, Brian. "Archive of Pure Language" in *The 1994 Annual of Hermeneutics and Social Concern, Lawler, Justus George (ed)*, 59-80. New York, Continuum, 1994.

"The Bible", wrote Walter Benjamin, "in regarding itself as a revelation, must necessarily evolve the fundamental linguistic facts". This essay explicates Benjamin's theory of sacred text in light of his philosophy of language and argues that, according to Benjamin, the sacred text is an archive of pure language.

Britt, John F. *Rhetorical Mosaic for a Kaleidoscope of Sound: Poetry as a Road to Understanding the Prose Voice*. New York, Lang, 1994.

This work employs drama and imagination to guide the reader to the discovery of voice. Through this consciousness, the reader is involved in the role of poetry and rhetoric in the comprehension of prose from Homer, Plato and the Bible to John Henry Newman, James Joyce and Norman Mailer and in the role of autobiography in developing a philosophy of life. From these an interest in methods develops. Voice and image unite to challenge today's visual orthodoxy by moving the reader beyond typography to a secondary oralify described by Walter Ong in the work's inspiration, *Orality and Literacy*.

Britzman, Deborah P. Is There a Queer Pedagogy? Or Stop Reading Straight. *Educ Theor*, 45(2), 151-165, Spr 95.

Rather than reading queer theory, psychoanalysis, and the writing of AIDS activists as a content, this essay engages their methods in order to rethink the grounds of knowledge, pedagogy, and identity in education. Three methods are brought to bear on pedagogy: the study of limits, the study of ignorance, and the study of reading practices. The methods work to problematize how normality becomes the grounds of the thinkable in education and how discourses of inclusivity, toleration, and empathy provoke exclusion, intolerance, and disavowel. Such strange methods as problematics not as application, allow for the exploration of what might constitute the ethical grounds of curriculum and pedagogy.

Brkic, Slavko. Moralische Dilemmas in der deontischen Logik als Systeme der epistemischen Logik. *Filozof Istraz*, 14(1), 105-118, 1994.

Das Hauptziel dieses Aufsatzes ist die Betrachtung der deontischen Logik, d.h. ihrer Fähigkeiten, moralische Dilemmas zu lösen. Da sich im moralischen Bereich um die Werte geht, stellt der Verfasser fest, dass es nötig wäre, in diesen Fragenkomplex eine Wissens- oder epistemische Logik einzuführen, die jene Paradoxe lösen sollte, welche die deontische Logik nicht lösen kann. Dabei stellt der Verfasser einerseits die Probleme der deontischen Logik (als logischer Untersuchung des normativen Sprachgebrauchs), ihre axiomatische Grundlage und die Struktur ihrer Paradoxe und andererseits die epistemische Logik dar. Diese wird als Modalitätenlogik, in der statt der intensionalen Operatoren (Notwendigkeit, Möglichkeit) persönliche (epistemische), monadische Operatoren (Wissen, Glauben) kommen, dargestellt. Auf dieser Grundlage ist dann die epistemischlogische Versicherung der moralischen Beurteilung, die sich durch den Begriff des "rationalen Glaubens" zeigt, möglich.

Brkic, Slavko. The Role of Presuppositions in the Logic of Belief Change. *Filozof Istraz*, 13(4), 809-823, 1993.

In the logical analysis of intensional contexts, presuppositions are given an important role. Expressing the relation between classical and freely quantified modal logic as a framework of analysis, Fuhrmann's style of the logic of belief change is proposed, as a logic which is close to free logic. In this framework, presuppositions are analysed in the same role as Gärdenfors's definition of expectation in the theory of belief change. The only difference is that in the proposed analysis presuppositions have clear logical support. In other words, the theory of belief change in the analysis is not presented as a basis for logic. At the end, the significance of the exhausted and systematic representation of presuppositions are emphasized in the context of the logic of belief change.

Brock, Dan W. The Non-Identity Problem and Genetic Harm—The Case of Wrongful Handicaps. *Bioethics*, 9(3-4), 269-275, Jl 95.

The Human Genome Project will produce information permitting increasing opportunities to prevent genetically transmitted harms, most of which will be compatible with a life worth living, through avoiding conception or terminating a pregnancy. Failure to prevent these harms when it is possible for parents to do so without substantial burdens or costs to themselves or others are what I call "wrongful handicaps". Derek Parfit has developed a systematic difficulty for any such cases being wrongs—when the harm could be prevented only by preventing the existence of the individual who would have a worthwhile life even with the handicap, then bringing him into existence with the handicap does not make him worse off and so does not wrong him. I argue that a non "person-affecting" principle requiring the avoidance of suffering and limited opportunity correctly accounts for cases of wrongful handicaps without requiring that the individuals with the handicap have been made worse off and therefore wronged. It is an advantage, not a difficulty, of this account that it does not imply that the person with the handicap has been wronged or is a victim with a special moral complaint.

Brockliss, Laurence. Discoursing on Method in the University World of Descartes's France. *Brit J Hist Phil*, 3(1), 3-28, F 95.

Brod, Harry (ed) and Kaufman, Michael (ed). *Theorizing Masculinities*. Newbury Park, Sage, 1994.

Brodsky, Archie and Bursztajn, Harold J. Authenticity and Autonomy in the Managed-Care Era: Forensic Psychiatric Perspectives. *J Clin Ethics*, 5(3), 237-242, Fall 94.

Brodsky, Archie and Bursztajn, Harold J. Clear, Convincing, and Authentic Advance Directives in the Context of Managed Care?. *J Clin Ethics*, 5(4), 364-366, Wint 94.

Bursztajn and Brodsky, in the context of a clinical case discussion, raise the question of whether "Advance Directives" for treatment (living wills) can be reliably elicited, interpreted, and implemented in a managed care context. Questions which need to be addressed in order to ensure reliability include whether such directives are made autonomously, whether they authentically reflect the patient's wishes, and whether they are not merely the by-product of transient despair, an institutional emphasis on cost containment, or milieu psychopathology and the acting of clinical countertransference. A subspecialist, a forensic psychiatrist trained in psychodynamics, can be a useful consultant to the treating clinician, the patient, and the clinical ethicist in addressing each of these questions.

Brody, Baruch A and Halevy, Amir. Is Futility a Futile Concept?. *J Med Phil*, 20(2), 123-144, Ap 95.

This paper distinguishes four major types of futility (physiological, imminent demise, lethal condition, and qualitative) that have been advocated in the literature either in a patient dependent or a patient independent fashion. It proposes five criteria (precision, prospective, social acceptability, significant number, and non-agreement) that any definition of futility must satisfy if it is to serve as the basis for unilaterally limiting futile care. It then argues that none of the definitions that have been advocated meet the criteria, primarily because their proponents have not paid sufficient attention to the problematic nature of the data supporting the use of their definitions.

Brody, Howard (& others). Physicians Pursuing the Humanities: Benefits and Barriers. *J Med Human*, 15(3), 163-169, Fall 94.

We surveyed selected physician members of the Society for Health and Human Values (SHHV) to study the benefits and problems of combining a medical career with a strong scholarly interest in the humanities. The 19 usable narrative responses characterized major benefits as experiential base and teaching opportunities. Barriers were numerous and fell under the general headings of: lack of time; lack of institutional rewards; lack of money for research and scholarship; lack of support from humanities peers; lack of support from medical colleagues; personal financial sacrifice; and lack of training. Some respondents offered creative solutions to these problems, including assertive negotiation of a job description, identification of helpful mentors, and various networking and administrative strategies. The survey results, while preliminary, suggest ways in which SHHV can assist clinicians who wish to develop a serious commitment to humanities study and teaching.

Brody, Howard. The Multiple Facets of Futility. *J Clin Ethics*, 5(2), 142-144, Sum 94.

Brody, Howard and Miller, Franklin G. Professional Integrity and Physician-Assisted Death. *Hastings Center Rep*, 25(3), 8-17, My-Je 95.

This article discusses physician-assisted death from the perspective of professional integrity. After introducing the concept of personal integrity, we develop an account of the professional integrity of physicians, which is tied to ethically appropriate ends and means of medicine. We identify three goals of medicine—healing, promoting health, and helping patients die peacefully—and four basic duties constraining medical practice—competence, avoiding harm, refraining from fraudulent misrepresentation, and fidelity. In the light of this account we conclude that the practice of voluntary physician-assisted death as a last resort is morally problematic but does not necessarily violate professional integrity.

Brody, Thomas A and Hodgson, Peter E (ed) and De La Peña, Luis (ed). *The Philosophy Behind Physics*. New York, Springer-Verlag, 1993.

In this work, Thomas Brody was concerned to remove the barriers between physics and philosophy by discovering the philosophy implicit in the actual process of scientific research. He developed the theory of 'active epistemic cycles' to explain how we come to know things. This theory does justice to the richness and complexity of scientific research, in contrast to the superficial and bloodless accounts current among philosophers of science who have no experience of scientific research. He applied his ideas to a wide range of problems in the philosophy of physics, especially probability theory and quantum mechanics, giving special attention to the Bell inequalities and the ensemble interpretation.

Brogan, Walter. Haunting Resonances at the Threshold of Contemporary Philosophy. Review of *Echoes: After Heidegger* by John Sallis. *Res Phenomenol*, 23, 186-193, 1993.

John Sallis's book is about listening and writing "after" Heidegger. It is a text that owes its drift to Heidegger, but does not simply represent Heidegger's thought. *Echoes* offers a series of essays that follow certain central themes in Heidegger's work: time, the sensible, metontology, the effacement of imagination, death, art and poetics. Each essay has four parts that carefully trace the movement of Heidegger's thought and conclude by freeing Heidegger's text into the space of what Sallis calls a doubling return, a return to what is not said but able to be heard echoing in Heidegger's texts.

Brogan, Walter. Zarathustra: The Tragic Figure of the Last Philosopher. *Res Phenomenol*, 24, 42-56, 1994.

Nietzsche says often that he is the disciple of the philosopher Dionysus. After the death of god and the exhaustion of Socratism and philosophy, suddenly Dionysus, the god of tragedy, becomes a philosopher. My aim in this paper is to explore the character of this tragic philosopher who wears the mask of the god whom, Nietzsche claims, was unmasked by Socrates. If we are to take Nietzsche's claim seriously that with *Zarathustra* tragedy begins, then *Zarathustra* can be seen to begin with the overcoming of Socratism. In a sense, then, *Zarathustra* begins at the time of and with the announcement of the death of Socratic philosophy. This is a kind of double overturning; it is the death of the death of tragedy.

Brogan, Walter (trans) and Heidegger, Martin and Warnek, Peter (trans). *Aristotle's Metaphysics* Theta 1-3: On the Essence and Actuality of Force. Bloomington, Indiana Univ Pr, 1995.

Brok, M F A (ed & trans) and Seneca, L Annaeus. *Naturwissenschaftliche Untersuchungen*. Darmstadt, Wiss Buchgesell, 1995.

Bronfen, Elisabeth. "Vom Omphalos zum Phallus" in *Macht Geschlechter Differenz, Müller-Funk, Wolfgang (ed)*, 128-151. Vienna, Picus, 1994.

In this article I present a theoretical divergence from and a debt to Freud's discussion of castration, for which the Oedipus complex is the linchpin. For in the psychoanalytic model, the issue of having or not having the phallus is the pivotal indication for the position one can take within culture. I suggest adding a second somatic sign, the *Omphalos*, Greek for navel, to the discussion of the subject's position within culture. The crux of my argument is that beyond the issue of having or not having a culturally privileged sexual organ, what is at stake in representations of feminine death is the failed repression of the unencompassable body of materiality-maternity-mortality, whose anatomical sign is the navel. The argument begins with a return to Freud's formulation of the castration complex and a re-reading of Sophocles' *Oedipus Rex*, so as to shed light on a moment in this play Freud chose not to read, namely the death of Jocaste, which shifts the interpretation from incest and patricide to failed matricide. It highlights how, in Freud's early work on hysteria, the prevailing trauma is connected with scenes of death and mourning, and how the discussion of phallic monism ultimately screens out a recognition of death. My countermove begins by tracing the mythopoetic discussion of the navel, especially the omphalos at Delphi, and ends with a reading of Hitchcock's *Psycho*, with Norman Bates a modern Oedipus, succeeding at the matricide his mythic forefather was unable to fulfill.

Brons, H R. Philosophy Under Fire: J F Lyotard Transcending the Trenches of Postmodernity. *Hist Euro Ideas*, 20(4-6), 785-790, F 95.

Brook, Richard. Berkeley, Causality, and Signification. *Int Stud Phil*, 27(2), 15-31, 1995.

The purpose of the paper is to show that Berkeley has two conflicting views of efficient causality, 1) His explicit view that sense data ("ideas") lack causal efficacy, and 2) A view implicit in this theory of signs, that sense data (qua signs) are the causes of propositional attitudes such as expectations. The paper demonstrates that attempts to save the doctrine of the "passivity of ideas," from the challenge of 2), while remaining within the Berkelian system, are failures. At the end of the paper I suggest some consequences of this failure for Berkeley's view that "causal" relations embodied in natural laws should be thought of as a "natural language".

Brooks, D H M. How to Perform a Reduction. *Phil Phenomenol Res*, 54(4), 803-814, D 94.

The reductionist wishes to show that everything ontologically *is* physical, everything is ultimately determined by the physical and finally that everything is ultimately explicable in terms of physics. The Nagel model of reduction was based on the classical positivist hypothetico-deductive model of explanation. This model does not extend to biology, because of the crucial notion of a biological function. I wish to argue that those who argue for the irreducibility of biology and psychology are basing their arguments on an outmoded model of reduction.

Brooks, David. Value-Judgements and Literature. *Lit Aes*, 1, 39-59, Spr 91.

This article offers to defend the making of value-judgments in literary criticism and to reconcile an evaluative conception of literature with a Marxist conception of history. It outlines a theory of value as the satisfaction of needs, and connects it with a theory of general human nature and the modification of human nature in history. It defends a conception of literature as expression or representation against Catherine Belsey, correcting Belsey's account of Saussure, and showing against Belsey how Althusser's theory of art presupposes a hermeneutic-evaluative conception of literature.

Brooks, Frank. Egoist Theory and America's Individualist Anarchists: A Dilemma of Praxis. *Hist Polit Thought*, 15(3), 403-422, Autumn 94.

In *Liberty*, the preeminent journal of America's individualist anarchists in the late nineteenth century, radicals faced a "dilemma of praxis" as they considered egoist theory. In theoretical terms, these individualists debated whether their anarchist principles of individual sovereignty and equal liberty could be grounded in egoism. In strategic terms, they disputed whether egoist anarchists could do anything to advance anarchism while maintaining their own freedom. Some advocated passive resistance or agitation, but critics argued that these strategies were more suitable for guarding individual freedom than for achieving anarchy. The foolish consistency of this egoist anarchist praxis contributed to the decline of individualist anarchism.

Broome, John. Fairness versus Doing the Most Good. *Hastings Center Rep*, 24(4), 36-39, Jl-Ag 94.

When medical resources have to be rationed, the aim of fairness sometimes conflicts with the aim of doing the most good. This paper provides a theoretical analysis of fairness and its conflict with food. As an example, it discusses the Oregon plan and its treatment of disabilities.

Broome, John. The Mutual Deteination of Wants and Benefits. *Theor Decis*, 37(3), 333-338, N 94.

The degree to which I want something often affects the amount of pleasure or other benefit it will bring me if I get it. This, in turn, should affect the degree to which I want it. In the *Journal of Philosophy*, 89 (1992) 10-29, Anna Kusser and Wolfgang Spohn argue that decision theory cannot cope with this mutual determination of wants and benefits. This paper argues, to the contrary, that decision theory can cope with it easily.

Broome, John. The Two-Envelope Paradox. *Analysis*, 55(1), 6-11, Ja 95.

It has been suggested that the two-envelope paradox will not arise for a Bayesian who attaches a prior probability distribution to the sums of money contained in the two envelopes. This paper shows this is incorrect; it describes some prior distributions that generate the paradox. It shows a connection between the two-envelope paradox and the St Petersburg paradox, and argues that the two-envelope paradox has not yet been satisfactorily solved.

Brose, Karl. Religion und Ethik beim spaeten Wittgenstein: Zu Themen in Ueber Gewissheit. *Wittgenstein Stud*, n.a., 1994.

Wittgenstein macht in seinen letzten Aufzeichnungen in UEBER GEWISSHEIT bis unmittelbar vor seinem Tod am 29. April 1951 Aussagen zu Themen von Religion und Ethik, die das Gefuege seines Spaetwerks ueberschreiten und neue, unabgeschlossene Horizonte eroeffnen. Ja, diese zentralen Aeusserungen in UEBER GEWISSHEIT koennen als Summe aehnlicher Aussagen in seinen vorhergehenden Werken gelten, auf die sie sich zum Teil zurueckbeziehen lassen: von den fruehen TAGEBUCH-Notizen der Jahre 1914-1916 und dem ETHIK-Vortrag von 1929 ueber die VORLESUNGEN UEBER DEN RELIGIOeSEN GLAUBEN von 1938 bis zu den PHILOSOPHISCHEN UNTERSUCHUNGEN der Jahre 1947-1949. Aus den Aufzeichnungen in UEBER GEWISSHEIT sind im folgenden Strukturen herauszuarbeiten, die den spaeten und letzten Wittgenstein als einen eigenstaendigen und auch eigenwilligen Religionsphilosophen und Ethiker zeigen; und zwar nicht nur aufgrund seiner Aeusserungen ueber Religion und Glauben, sondern auch ueber Zweifel, Wissen und Gewissheit. Dabei wird auch eine religions-ERZIEHERISCHE Komponente sichtbar. Unter diesen Voraussetzungen zeigt sich der ueber die bisherige Philosophie hinausfuehrende PRAKTISCHE Charakter der Religionsphilosophie und Ethik Wittgensteins bis in die Gegenwart.

Brosio, Richard. "Late Capitalism and Postmodernism: Educational Problems and Possibilities" in *Identity, Culture, and Education, Smeyers, Paul (ed)*, 105-117. Leuven, Leuven Univ Pr, 1994.

This work analyzes certain aspects of postmodernist thought and argues that, although its adherents effectively challenge foundationalism as well as supporting marginalized persons and ideas, most postmodernist intellectuals have not been helpful in supporting the secular, radical democratic project subscribed to by the author. Putative postmodernist radicalism has not been directed against the regime(s) of capital; therefore, it is not clear how it can be useful to projects that are predicated upon the incompatibilities between capitalism and bona fide democracy. In spite of some important postmodernist contributions to schooling, this is not an adequate substitute for broad structural changes.

Brosio, Richard A. "Staying Alive": Intellectual and Spiritual Sustenance on the Journey for Critical Foundations Scholars-Teachers. *J Thought*, 30(3), 19-32, Fall 95.

This work addresses the sources of sustenance relied upon by the author as a critical Foundations of Education scholar-teacher. In this personal essay—anchored to critical scholarship—the reader learns of a tradition rooted in the *Piemontesi* working-class milieu of Italy: one grounded in refusal to succumb to oppressors. By maintaining transgenerational memory-solidarity, the author connects with a radical project that informs his own critical pedagogy. The key influence of Gramsci is discussed in the context of a Mediterranean tradition represented by Silone, Camus and Kazantzakis. The spirituality referred to is not equated with organized religion.

Brougham, Richard L. Ontological Hermeneutics: An Overlooked Bergsonian Perspective. *Process Stud*, 22(1), 37-41, Spr 93.

Bergson's writings appear to be inchoate and unsystematic. But one neglected article presages the whole-part mutual modification that can be found in Whitehead's concrescence and Lazlo's Systems "feed-back". Hermeneutic whole-part interplay is usually considered "epistemic". But Bergson located whole-part reciprocity at the heart of the nature of things: both efficient and final causation are exaggerated extremes of its operation. Bergson's ontological hermeneutics, not confined to this 1902 article, ought to be revisited and given serious scrutiny. It may hold the key to a more viable process metaphysics.

Browder, John O. Redemptive Communities: Indigenous Knowledge, Colonist Farming Systems, and Conservation of Tropical Forests. *Agr Human Values*, 12(1), 17-30, Winter 95.

This essay critically examines the emerging view among some ethnologists that replicable models of sustainable management of tropical forests may be found within the knowledge systems of contemporary indigenous peoples. As idealized epistemological types, several characteristics distinguishing "indigenous" from "modern" knowledge systems are described. Two culturally distinctive land use systems in Latin America are compared, one developed by an indigenous group, the Huastec Maya, and the other characteristic of colonist farms in Rondonia, Brazil. While each of these systems reflects a different cultural-historical tradition, I argue that the process of knowledge formation and cultural adaption is coevolutionary and continuous in both cases. The very concept of "indigenous" as a discrete analytic category is questioned; indigenicity alone cannot explain local adaption of farming systems. Rather than dichotomize indigenous and colonist knowledge as inherently different categories, differences in land use patterns between such social groups may be more accurately viewed as reflecting different points on a single epistemological continuum.

Brown, Alison Leigh. *Fear, Truth, Writing: From Paper Village to Electronic Community*. Albany, SUNY Pr, 1995.

Cultural production exposes the selves an individual works to mask with a presented self. Some acts of cultural production turn out to be political acta against authority. Cultural consumption is the act allowed us if we have the means to consume. This allowance has an effect of keeping most people "in their place" or in the subject positions created them by various ideologies. I show that cultural consumption turns out to be an important production when different groups find ways to overcome the fears attending creation. The form my book takes parodies dominant genres of expression.

Brown, Carolyn L (ed) and Schuster, Eleanor A (ed). *Exploring Our Environmental Connections*. New York, NLN Pr, 1994.

This is a collection of peer reviewed papers which, for the first time, expresses what the discipline of professional nursing has to say about health, healing, environment and wholeness. It represents a paradigm shift toward an expanded awareness of environment and prevention of illness. The common thread throughout is the issue of the nature of our relationships: with self, with one another, with earth and with all other inhabitants of the planet. Perspectives of twenty-four international nurse scholars are presented. The forward, by the futurist Hazel Henderson, places the work in the contexts of the present and the future.

Brown, Charles S. Phenomenology as a Methodology for Universalism. *Dialogue Hum*, 3(2), 118-124, 1993.

This paper explores the possibility of intercultural dialogue and understanding by examining Husserl's notions of transcendental subjectivity and life-world. It is argued that Husserl has a way out of the relativism which assumes that rationality is an internal feature of particular culture bound discourses by phenomenologically uncovering the structures of a common life world. Since the notions of life-world and transcendental subjectivity seem to collapse into each other as the cultural achievements of one generation become taken for granted frames of reference for succeeding generations, Husserl's dream of a context free, universally valid critique of rationality becomes threatened. The paper then searches for something common to all human experience which may serve as a starting point for dialogue between seeming incommensurable world worldviews.

Brown, Charles S. Phenomenology, Universalism and Dialogue. *Dialogue Hum*, 3(1), 53-69, 1993.

This paper argues that the only forms of universalism which are presently possible are ones which begin with the recognition of a robust plurality of worldviews, traditions, and discourses, and accepts the thesis that none of them can or should be seen as a privileged representation of the world. Since phenomenology begins with a philosophical absentation from everyday metaphysical commitments, phenomenological thinking offers a point of view free from ideological naivete and thereby may facilitate inter-cultural dialogue.

Brown, Charles S. The University, Dialogue and Universalism. *Dialogue Hum*, 4(2-3), 157-165, 1994.

Brown, George F. Long-Acting Contraceptives: Rationale, Current Development, and Ethical Implications. *Hastings Center Rep*, 25(1), S12-S15, Jan-Feb 95.

Brown, Gregory. "Leibniz's Moral Philosophy" in *The Cambridge Companion to Leibniz, Jolley, Nicholas (ed)*, 411-441. New York, Cambridge Univ Pr, 1994.

Brown, Gregory. Miracles in the Best of All Possible Worlds: Leibniz's Dilemma and Leibniz's Razor. *Hist Phil Quart*, 12(1), 19-39, Ja 95.

In the first section of this paper I discuss what Leibniz meant by a miracle and why Leibniz's definition of the best of all possible worlds implies that it is a world in which miracles are minimized. In the second part of the paper I argue that human happiness within the best of all possible worlds also requires, on Leibniz's principles, that miracles must there be minimized. In the third section of the paper I consider what, if any, miracles actually remain possible for Leibniz within the best of all possible worlds. In the final section I discuss one important kind of event upon which Leibniz vacillated whether it required miraculous intervention—namely, the elevation of the sensitive soul to rationality—and some speculation about the cause of this vacillation in Leibniz is offered.

Brown, Harold I. Circular Justifications. *Proc Phil Sci Ass*, 1, 406-414, 1994.

The thesis of this paper is that philosophers are often too hasty in rejecting justifications because the argument that yields the justification is circular. Circularity is distinguished from vicious circularity and several examples are examined in which a proposed justification is circular in a precise sense, but not viciously circular. These include an observational procedure which could yield a velocity in excess of the velocity of light even though the impossibility of such velocities is assumed at a key step in analyzing the data, and an argument that uses a specific argument form to show that that form is invalid.

Brown, Harold I. Reason, Judgement and Bayes's Law. *Phil Sci*, 61(3), 351-369, S 94.

This paper argues that when used judiciously Bayes's law has a role to play in the evaluation of scientific hypotheses. Several examples are presented in which a rational response to evidence requires a judgment whether to apply Bayes's law or whether, for example, to redistribute prior probabilities. The paper concludes that reflection of Bayes's law illustrates how an adequate account of the rational evaluation of hypotheses requires an account of judgment—a point which several philosophers have noted despite few attempts to develop an adequate theory of judgment.

Brown, James Robert. Critical Notice of Roy Sorensen *Thought Experiments*. *Can J Phil*, 25(1), 135-142, Mr 95.

This book adds to the growing literature on thought experiments. There are numerous examples drawn from the sciences and philosophy. The principle claim is that thought experiments are a limiting case of real experiments. It is a moderate empiricist view, in contrast to, e.g., the Platonism of Brown or the strict empiricism of Norton. Highly recommended.

Brown, James Robert. Underdetermination and the Social Side of Science. *Dialogue (Canada)*, 34(1), 147-161, Wint 95.

This paper criticizes one of the leading arguments for a social approach to science, the argument from underdetermination. This serves, in part, as a vehicle for replying to various reviewers and critics of my *The Rational and the Social* (1989).

Brown, Laura S. Concrete Boundaries and the Problem of Literal-Mindedness: A Response to Lazarus. *Ethics Behavior*, 4(3), 275-281, 1994.

Brown, Richard Harvey. "Reconstructing Social Theory after the Postmodern Critique" in *After Postmodernism, Simons, Herbert W (ed)*, 12-37. Newbury Park, Sage, 1994.

This essay explores major epistemological and political problems of post-modernist critique, and seeks to escape the destructive pessimism of some forms of postmodernism. The author suggests that the emancipatory postmodernist can reject judgemental relativism while championing epistemological relativism. The latter, he says, in no way precludes principled political action. Alongside the post-modernist's habitual 'hermeneutics of suspicion', a 'hermeneutics of affirmation' is required. Rather than a view of 'truth' as an outmoded relic of modernism, one may develop a sense of truth in language. The entire reconstruction can be intellectually playful but must be politically serious.

Brown, Richard Harvey (ed). *Postmodern Representations: Truth, Power, and Mimesis in the Human Sciences and Public Culture*. Champaign, Univ of Illinois Pr, 1995.

The concept of "postmodern representation" derives from new methodologies of textwork and new critiques theorizations of theory and society. All these converge in a indicate the possibilities of a rhetorical social theory of representation that accepts the complexities of language and the limitations of human knowledge. The essays in this volume define and extend this general project, drawing from, even as they reconceptualize, the disciplines of sociology, anthropology and ethnography, literary criticism, Soviet studies, film and media studies, and social theory. All these essays take a critical rhetorical approach to describe and illustrate postmodern representations, and to reveal interchanges of truth, power, and mimesis in the human sciences and public culture.

Brown, Stuart. "The Seventeenth-Century Intellectual Background" in *The Cambridge Companion to Leibniz, Jolley, Nicholas (ed)*, 43-66. New York, Cambridge Univ Pr, 1994.

Browner, C H and Press, Nancy. Risk, Autonomy, and Responsibility: Informed Consent for Prenatal Testing. *Hastings Center Rep*, 25(3), S9-S12, My-Je 95.

Why is informed consent required for noninvasive prenatal screening, such as maternal serum alphafetoprotein (MSAFP) testing? Consent is routinely sought, but examination of its implementation suggests a need to reconceptualize both the risks and responsibilities involved in offering and accepting prenatal testing. This work traces the history of informed consent and the different, sometimes contradictory logics of ethics and law driving it. It concludes with a consideration of how to conceptualize informed consent in the face of a patient's desire *not to know* and asks whether informed consent for prenatal testing might imply patient obligations as well as rights.

Browning, Douglas. Reply to Krecz. *SW Phil Rev*, 11(Supp), 131-135, Mr 95.

After giving an excellent overview of my work, Krecz points out, correctly, that 1) my attacks on the substance and process traditions for their inadequacy to acts and agents have not resulted in my proposing an alternative metaphysical system and 2) my repudiation of the category of process has left me with the special problem of handling by other means what it accommodates. I respond that, since each category in a system can be understood only in that system, no alternative system can adopt it. A new system must be built from the ground up. I also point out that I'm still working at this.

Browning, Douglas. Reply to Lemos. *SW Phil Rev*, 11(Supp), 75-81, Mr 95.

Lemos examines two of my arguments about value. The first, which he sees as a proposal about the *meaning* of statements of the form 'x is good', I point out as being, rather, an attempt to evaluate Everett Hall's ideal language project of *showing* by the structure of a value judgment the existence-intentionality of values themselves. I defend the second, which he correctly interprets as a defense of a contextualist view of intrinsic value against G E Moore's view, and I further argue against the view which Lemos proposes as a reformulation of Moore's view.

Browning, Douglas. Reply to Pappas. *SW Phil Rev*, 11(Supp), 109-116, Mr 95.

Pappas levels three criticisms against my writings on the moral stance. The first is that I tend to relegate the practical situation to a place of secondary importance. I respond that he has misunderstood me and attempt to set the record straight. The second is that I introduce normative considerations into my purported nonnormative description of the moral stance. I respond by attempting to show that I do not. The third is that I refuse to appeal to practical considerations in arguing for the primacy of the practical. I reply that such a defense would be question-begging.

Browning, Douglas. Reply to Van de Vate. *SW Phil Rev*, 11(Supp), 93-96, Mr 95.

Regarding my *Ontology and the Practical Arena* Van de Vate asks, "Why does Browning the honest ontological observer need Browning the systemist?" And he suggests that the "we" to whom I appeal in considering how a system is built is none other than the entrenched club of professional philosophers themselves. I point out in response that the central point of my book was to show the viability of the ontological enterprise in a manner in which the "we" who consider the issue are, not members of a professional group, but actual philosophers engaged in dialogue.

Brownsey, Paul. Butler's Argument for the Natural Authority of Conscience. *Brit J Hist Phil*, 3(1), 57-87, F 95.

Previous commentators differ widely about what Butler's argument for the natural authority of conscience is; several attribute to him a mixture of several arguments. The present paper argues that all the relevant passages in Butler point to a single argument whose nature has not previously been grasped. Its gist: reflection on the idea of a life corresponding to our nature requires us to say that conscience could have no other part in such a life than to be obeyed.

Brueckner, Anthony. Ebbs on Skepticism, Objectivity and Brains in Vats. *Pac Phil Quart*, 75(2), 77-87, Je 94.

Brueckner, Anthony. Reply to Steinitz's "Failing to Beg the Question". *Phil Quart*, 45(179), 205-206, Ap 95.

Brueckner, Anthony. Scepticism and the Causal Theory of Reference. *Phil Quart*, 45(179), 199-201, Ap 95.

Brueckner, Anthony. The Structure of the Skeptical Argument. *Phil Phenomenol Res*, 54(4), 827-835, D 94.

A *closure principle* for knowledge is thought to be required by a now standard formulation of the Cartesian skeptic's argument to show that one lacks knowledge about the external world. It is argued that another epistemic principle is also required, an *underdetermination principle* that renders closure superfluous.

Brühlmeier, Daniel. Libertatis splendor. *Stud Phil (Switzerland)*, 53, 95-108, 1994.

This contribution contains a defense of classical, Hobbesian and Smithian liberalism against modern, communitarian attacks. The author pleads for negative liberty: he takes a sceptical stand and questions the implicit priority of truth over liberty inherent in all communitarian writings, in particular in the encyclical letter *Veritatis Splendor* of Pope John Paul II. Furthermore, the author pleads for a resolute advocacy of liberalism, a liberalism that does not try too hard to find a common platform with communitarianism. Liberal social philosophy should emphasize its superior analytic powers in coping with the realities of a global economy at the end of the twentieth century.

Brümmer, Vincent. Calvin, Bernard and the Freedom of the Will. *Relig Stud*, 30(4), 437-455, D 94.

In his *Institutes* 2.2.5 Calvin declares that he 'willingly accepts' the distinction between freedom from necessity, from sin and from misery originally developed by St Bernard. It is remarkable that a determinist like Calvin seems here to accept a libertarian view of human freedom. In this paper I set out Bernard's doctrine of the three kinds of freedom and show that all its basic elements can in fact be found in Calvin's argument in chapters 2 and 3 of the *Institutes* part II. Towards the end of chapter 3, however, Calvin's doctrine of 'perseverance' makes him revert to a deterministic view of the divine-human relationship. I show that the considerations which prompt Calvin to this can be adequately met on the basis of Bernard's libertarian concept of human freedom.

Brümmer, Vincent. On Not Confusing Necessity With Compulsion: A Reply to Paul Helm. *Relig Stud*, 31(1), 105-109, Mr 95.

This paper responds to Helms rebuttal of Brümmer's account of Bernard and Calvin in *Religious Studies*, 30, 4. It contends that Helm confuses *in*determinism with *non*determinism and that a clear distinction between freedom from necessity and freedom from compulsion must be drawn. *Contra* Helm, there is still a contradiction between Calvin's defense of freedom from compulsion and his account of the perseverance of God's grace.

Brümmer, Vincent. The Nature of Divine Love. *S Afr J Phil*, 14(1), 1-8, F 95.

Talk about the love of God requires a *relational* concept of love, expressing the complex relationship between God and human persons. In the Christian tradition, however, love has generally been taken to be an attitude of one person toward another, rather than as a relation between persons. This generated various rival views on the nature of love, each of which picks out a different attitude as expressing the essence of love. Thus love is sometimes considered as an attitude of a romantic lover to his or her beloved: as exclusive attention to the beloved (Ortega y Gasset); as an ecstatic experience of a union with the beloved (nuptual mysticism); as passionate suffering in relation to the beloved (courtly love). Sometimes love is looked on as an attitude to other persons in general: *eros* (Plato and Augustine) or *agape* (Nygren). This article first discusses the most important attitudinal views, then shows how love could be looked on as a personal relationship involving all these various attitudes. Finally it shows what this entails for the nature of divine love and the ways in which this differs from human love.

Brüntrup, Godehard. Mentale Verursachung und metaphysischer Realismus. *Theol Phil*, 70(2), 203-223, 1995.

Brüntrup, Godehard. *Mentale Verursachung: Eine Theorie aus der Perspektive des semantischen Anti-Realismus*. Stuttgart, Kohlhammer, 1994.

Two assumptions characterize most positions in contemporary analytic philosophy of mind: 1) the physical realm is causally closed, 2) mental properties or events are causally efficacious. The "standard theories" (type-identity, token-identity, functionalism and supervenience) try to show that these seemingly contradictory assumptions can be reconciled. It is argued that none of these theories succeeds in providing satisfactory account of the causal efficacy of the mental. It is also argued that it is exactly the metaphysical-realist picture implicit in these theories that renders mental entities epiphenomenal. Only by giving up metaphysical realism, assumption 1 and 2 may be reconciled. An anti-realist or internal-realist interpretation of causality and explanation allows for a duality of independent explanatory schemes or paradigms. The problem of "explanatory exclusion" is thereby resolved.

Brugués, Jean-Louis. L'éthique dans un monde désenchanté. *Rev Thomiste*, 94(2), 195-210, Ap-Je 94.

Bruin, John. Heidegger and Two Kinds of Art. *J Aes Art Crit*, 52(4), 447-457, Fall 94.

In *The Origin of the Work of Art*, Heidegger at one point says he is dealing not with 'representational art', but rather with 'great art' only. Although it doesn't tell us what he means by the two terms, how he uses them can easily give the wrong impression that this is what he has in mind: The one term refers to those works which are imitative, the other to these works whose artistic merit is not in question. I propose that the terms have to do not so much with the works themselves, but rather with two distinctive ways of 'looking' at them.

Brujic, Branka. Das geschichtliche Ethos gegenüber der absolut gesetzten Freiheit. *Filozof Istraz*, 14(1), 67-83, 1994.

Es ist grundsätzlich unmöglich, dass die bunteste inhaltliche Ausfüllung der Grundwertarten und ihrer Modalitäten und die für sie geltende Rangordnung je an einer Stelle verwirklicht wird. In solchem Sachverhalt einerseits und in der Spontaneität und Freiheit der Person andererseits liegt die Geschichtlichkeit des Ethos. Da das Ethos als faktische Wertschätzung dem Werdeprozess der Welt die Richtung gibt, in dem sich die im *ens a se* enthaltenen Potenzen durch die menschlichen geistigen Akte realisieren, ist sie Scheler zufolge sogar der Kern der Geschichte. (edited)

Bruner, Michael and Oelschlaeger, Max. Rhetoric, Environmentalism, and Environmental Ethics. *Environ Ethics*, 16(4), 377-396, Wint 94.

The growth of environmental ethics as an academic discipline has not been accompanied by any cultural movement toward sustainability. Indices of ecological degradation steadily increase, and many of the legislative gains made during the 1970s have been lost during the Reagan-Bush anti-environmental revolution. This situation gives rise to questions about the efficacy of ecophilosophical discourse. We argue 1) that these setbacks reflect, on the one hand, the skillful use of rhetorical tools by anti-environmental factions and, on the other, the indifference (even hostility) of the ecophilosophical community toward rhetoric, 2) that since the linguistic turn in philosophy, no rigid line of demarcation can be maintained between rhetoric and philosophy, and 3) that rhetoric offers resources to the ecophilosophical community that increase its potential to effect change in society.

Brunner, Johann K. Bargaining with Reasonable Aspirations. *Theor Decis*, 37(3), 311-321, N 94.

Consider bargaining situations with two persons, where both have a specific idea of what would be an equitable outcome. In case these ideas differ, a procedure is needed which leads to a compromise between the different views. In the present paper the axioms of restricted homogeneity and of relative monotonicity are introduced, each of which, together with other standard conditions, allows one to determine a solution for this class of bargaining problems. An extension of this solution to bargaining problems with more than two persons is formulated.

Brunner, José. *Freud and the Politics of Psychoanalysis*. Cambridge, Blackwell, 1995.

Brunner argues that the categories of Freud's thought belong by their nature to modern political discourse. He reveals the politics hidden in Freud's early writings on hysteria and shows how Freud's metapsychology transposes the vocabulary of imperial court procedures into the psyche. He examines the role which class, gender and education played in the origins of Freud's therapeutic endeavours and probes into the dynamics of authority and power in the analytic setting. Finally, he traces the ideological ramifications of the way in which Freud applied his notion of the Oedipus complex to religion, history and modern society.

Brunner, José and Peled, Yoav. Staatsbürgerliche Identität und Selbstachtung im jüdischen Staat: Eine Rawls'che Perspektive. *Deut Z Phil*, 43(2), 329-348, 1995.

This essay examines the Israeli-Palestinian conflict from the vantage point of John Rawls's notions of respect and self-respect. 1) It provides a critical analysis of the pivotal role of these notions in Rawls's theorizing. 2) It considers the extent to which aspects of Israeli-Palestinian relations are compatible with—or even corroborate—Rawls's empirical hypotheses and normative claims concerning the interdependence of respect and self-respect. 3) It establishes where the values entailed in Rawls's perspective on respect and self-respect would place a Rawlsian vis-a-vis some issues of the Israeli-Palestinian question.

Bruns, Gerald L. "Poethics: John Cage and Stanley Cavell at the Crossroads of Ethical Theory" in *John Cage: Composed in America*, Perloff, Marjorie (ed), 206-225. Chicago, Univ of Chicago Pr, 1994.

This essay examines the conceptual coherence between the philosopher Stanley Cavell and the avant-garde musician John Cage—both very creative readers of H D Thoreau. The upshot is that neither music nor philosophy should be sealed off from they are not, specifically the ordinary and everyday, the random and contingent. The affinities between Cage and Cavell stand out sharply when seen against a background formed by the opposition between two traditions of ethical theory, characterized here in terms of Martha Nussbaum's subject-centered "morality of perception" and the other-centered ethics of responsibility developed by Emmanuel Levinas. One sees how both Cage and Cavell reconceptualize subjectivity away from perception toward reception, listening, acknowledgment, and openness to the nonidentical.

Bruns, Manfred and Soldati, Gianfranco. Object-Dependent and Property-Dependent Contents. *Dialectica*, 48(3-4), 185-208, 1994.

In a theory of representational or intentional states content is generally supposed to play various roles. It has to be the bearer of a truth-value, it has to determine the way a representation is about something (its mode of presentation), and finally it has to be used in order to give intra- and interpersonal psychological explanations. It has been argued that no unique kind of content can play all these roles. What criterion should one adopt in order to draw the dividing line? We suggest that the divide be based on ontological considerations related to the way content depends on external factors. There is a fundamental difference, we submit, between object-dependent and property-dependent contents. The requirements concerning modes of presentation as well as cognitive significance can be met by one kind of content. This content, it will appear, is property-dependent, but never object dependent.

Brunsteins, Patricia C and García, Pablo Sebastián. Acciones básicas y teoría del conocimiento: una tesis de P Ricoeur sobre de la teoría de A Danto. *Rev Filosof (Argentina)*, 8(1-2), 79-84, N 93.

In this paper, we have tried to present the main lines of Danto's theory of basic actions alone with the criticisms of that theory advanced by Ricoeur. We also put forward some objections to Ricoeur's criticisms, without meaning thereby a full-blooded defense of Danto's theory. Moreover, we point out some difficulties in the theory of basic actions.

Brusotti, Marco and Gerratana, Federico. "Dappertutto e in Nessun Luogo": Volontà e Potenza di un'edizione Nietzscheana. *G Crit Filosof Ital*, 72(3), 513-529, S-D 93.

Bruton, Garry D and Chrisman, James J. The Professional Ethics of the Academic Consultant. *Prof Ethics*, 3(1), 89-102, Spr 94.

This article addresses three primary ethical issues that face academic consultants: objective analysis of data; fiduciary responsibilities, and responsibility to society. We illustrate the complexities and interrelationships among these issues and argue that the objectivity of the academic consultant should be the highest priority. Next the academic consultant, in the role of an agent must emphasize their fiduciary responsibilities to the firm. Finally, the academic's perception of social responsibility should be addressed.

Bruzina, Ronald (trans) and Fink, Eugen. *Sixth Cartesian Meditation: The Idea of a Transcendental Theory of Method*. Bloomington, Indiana Univ Pr, 1995.

Bryuschinkin, W. Kants Philosophie und moderne Logik: Eine Tagung in Swetlogorsk. *Kantstudien*, 85(1), 85-87, 1994.

The purpose of the article is to describe a recently established at the Kaliningrad University tradition, which combines studies in Kant's philosophy and modern logic. This research direction consists of: 1) application of heuristic potential of Kant's philosophy to development of modern logic, 2) application of modern logical and linguistic tools to structural analysis of Kant's texts, 3) studies of the role of Kant's philosophy in creating and developing modern logical theories. The series of seminars in Kaliningrad sponsored by Russian Kant-Society was devoted to this research point. The article describes the third seminar in the series, which took place in the small recreation town Svetlogorsk on the Baltic sea shore and in which logicians and Kant scholars from Russia, Ukraine, Germany, Belgium, and Hungary participated. In the seminar's papers the results on different domains from philosophy of classical logic to quantum logic and artificial intelligence were represented.

Brzezinski, Jerzy. "Dimensions of the Diagnostic Space" in *Probability in Theory-Building*, Brzezinski, Jerzy (ed), 197-223. Amsterdam, Rodopi, 1994.

Brzezinski, Jerzy (ed). *Probability in Theory-Building*. Amsterdam, Rodopi, 1994.

Bub, Jeffrey. How to Interpret Quantum Mechanics. *Erkenntnis*, 41(2), 253-273, S 94.

I formulate the interpretation problem of quantum mechanics as the problem of identifying all possible maximal sublattices of quantum propositions that can be taken as simultaneously determinate, subject to certain constraints that allow the representation of quantum probabilities as measures over truth possibilities in the standard sense, and the representation of measurements in terms of the linear dynamics of the theory. The solution to this problem yields a modal interpretation that I show to be a generalized version of Bohm's hidden variable theory. I argue that unless we alter the dynamics of quantum mechanics, or accept a 'for all practical purposes' solution, this generalized Bohmian mechanics is the unique solution to the problem of interpretation.

Bub, Jeffrey. Inference, Noncommutativity, and Determinateness in Quantum Mechanics. *Topoi*, 14(1), 39-43, Mr 95.

I consider to what extent the phenomenon of interference precludes the possibility of attributing simultaneously determinate values to noncommuting observables, and I show that, while all observables can in principle be taken as simultaneously determinate, it suffices to take a suitable privileged observable as determinate to solve the measurement problem.

Bub, Jeffrey. Is Cognitive Neuropsychology Possible?. *Proc Phil Sci Ass*, 1, 417-427, 1994.

The aim of cognitive neuropsychology is to articulate the functional architecture underlying normal cognition, on the basis of cognitive performance data involving brain-damaged subjects. Glymour (forthcoming) formulates a discovery problem for cognitive neuropsychology, in the sense of formal learning theory, concerning the existence of a reliable methodology, and argues that the problem is insoluble: granted certain apparently plausible assumptions about the form of neuropsychological theories and the nature of the available evidence, a reliable methodology does not exist! I argue for a reformulation of the discovery problem in terms of an alternative characterization of relevant evidence in neuropsychology.

Bub, Jeffrey. Testing Models of Cognition Through the Analysis of Brain-Damaged Performance. *Brit J Phil Sci*, 45(3), 837-855, S 94.

The aim of cognitive neuropsychology is to articulate the functional architecture underlying normal cognition, on the basis of cognitive performance data involving brain-damaged subjects. Throughout the history of the subject, questions have been raised as to whether the methods of neuropsychology are adequate to its goals. The question has been reopened by Glymour (1994), who formulates a *discovery problem* for cognitive neuropsychology, in the sense of formal learning theory, concerning the existence of a reliable methodology. It appears that the discovery problem may be insoluble in principle! I propose a modified formulation of Glymour's discovery problem and argue that a skeptical conclusion about the possibility of cognitive neuropsychology as an empirical science is not warranted.

Bubner, Rüdiger. "Linguaggio e politica" in *L'etica e il suo Altro*, Vigna, Carmelo (ed), 228-239. Milano, FrancoAngeli, 1994.

Language plays a different role according to the underlying concept of politics. This is shown with regard to Aristotle's political community, the functioning machinery of Hobbes's Leviathan and Habermas's democratic ideal of mutual understanding.

Bubner, Rüdiger. "On the Ground of Understanding" in *Hermeneutics and Truth*, Wachterhauser, Brice (ed), 68-82. Evanston, Northwestern Univ Pr, 1994.

In Heidegger's hermeneutics the question of a ground of understanding cannot find an answer. The fact that it turns in a circle should be taken as reference to "Being." Gadamer's modification directs the unanswerable question to historical tradition. It is argued for the philosophical plausibility of this move.

Bubner, Rüdiger. Die Entdeckung Platons durch Schelling. *Neue Hefte Phil*, 35, 32-55, 1995.

New material in the "Nachlass" shows that Schelling had studied Plato before entering the discussion of Idealism. In 1972 he picks up Plato's ironical praise of enthusiasm (Ion), in 1794 he combines Kant's transcendental epistemology with the myth of world creation (Timaeus). Here lies the origin of his later efforts to overcome the Fichtean position and find his own way in philosophy.

Bucciantini, Massimo. Valeriano Magni e la Discussione sul Vuoto in Italia. *G Crit Filosof Ital*, 73(1), 73-91, Ja-Ap 94.

Buchan, Melissa L and Tolle, Susan W. Pain Relief for Dying Persons: Dealing with Physicians' Fears and Concerns. *J Clin Ethics*, 6(1), 53-61, Spr 95.

Buchanan, Allen. "Liberalism and Group Rights" in *In Harm's Way, Coleman, Jules L (ed)*, 1-15. New York, Cambridge Univ Pr, 1994.

Buchanan, Allen. Privatization and Just Health Care. *Bioethics*, 9(3-4), 220-239, Jl 95.

When advocates of insurance-privatization consider whether private insurance-dominated systems achieve justice at all, they tend to rely on an incomplete set of criteria for a just healthcare system. They also mistakenly assume that it is enough to show that justice is *in principle* achievable within a private insurance-dominated system. This essay offers a more complete set of criteria for a just healthcare system. It then argues that the motivational assumptions needed to make insurance-privatization at all plausible (on grounds of choice, efficiency, and quality of care) are inconsistent with the motivational assumptions needed to show that in practice a private insurance-dominated system will achieve justice. A private insurance-dominated system can be expected to satisfy the criteria for just healthcare only if 1) there is extensive and effective regulation to constrain the normal competitive behavior of private insurers or if 2) generous public funds are provided to fill the gaps in access left by the private insurance market. Yet the assumptions about the motivations and abilities of the public, regulators, and public officials needed to satisfy conditions 1 or 2 contradict the privatization advocate's explanations of how privatization will maximize efficiency, choice, and quality of care.

Buchanan, Allen (ed) and Coleman, Jules L (ed). *In Harm's Way*. New York, Cambridge Univ Pr, 1994.

Buchwalter, Andrew. "Hegel, Hobbes, Kant, and the Scienticization of Practical Philosophy" in *Hegel on the Modern World, Collins, Ardis B (ed)*, 177-198. Albany, SUNY Pr, 1995.

Bucio, Francisco. L'occidentalité de la Philosophie. *Philosopher*, 13, 109-142, 1992.

Many examples of thought from advertising to conventional wisdom purport to be philosophical but very few really are. Philosophy is a discourse that goes back to reason as the last instance of truth and certainty. In acknowledging this characteristic feature we not only avoid much unfortunate and persistent confusion, but also we trace philosophy's Western roots. If philosophy clearly belongs to the Western tradition it is not because it cannot flourish in other civilizations, but rather because philosophy began in Greece, became a component of Western civilization and, historically, has only developed in the West.

Buck, Ross. The Neuropsychology of Communication: Spontaneous and Symbolic Aspects. *J Prag*, 22(3-4), 265-278, O 94.

The neuropsychological bases of communication are reviewed, with emphasis upon spontaneous communication as forming an emotional basis for the communication process as a whole, including the linguistic communication process. Evidence presented for emotional preattunements, involving innate knowledge of the 'meaning' of the display. The neurological bases for displays are discussed in terms of the Jurgens-Ploog hierarchical model, which is compatible with the Arndt and Janney (1991) distinction of emotional, emotive, and cognitive communication. Cerebral lateralization is discussed—the lateralization both of the temporal limbic system and of the neocortex—with implications for the relationship of language and emotion.

Buck-Morss, Susan. Envisioning Capital: Political Economy on Display. *Crit Inquiry*, 21(2), 434-467, Wint 95.

Buck-Morss, Susan. Fashion in Ruins: History After the Cold War. *Rad Phil*, 68, 10-17, Autumn 94.

Buckle, Stephen. Universalism and Individualism. *Crim Just Ethics*, 13(2), 15-19, Sum-Fall 94.

Buckley, Lisa Marie Esposito. Ecstatic and Emanating, Providential and Unifying: A Study of the Psuedo-Dionysian and Plotinian Concepts of *Eros*. *J Neoplatonic Stud*, 1(1), 31-61, Fall 92.

Budelli, Rosanna. A Refutation of Philosophy by a Medieval Arab Author: Ibn Al-Jawzi (d 1201). *Philosophia (Athens)*, 23-24, 213-222, 1993-94.

This article points out an important tendency in Arab culture that opposed the study and the development of philosophy within the Islamic world. This aversion to philosophy started at the beginning of the spreading of Greek philosophy in the Middle Ages. Ibn al-Jawzi is a prominent religious leader whose influence upon later scholars was rather deep. Speculation is accepted by Islam as long as it does not contrast Revelation. According to the Arab writer, philosophy must not deal with metaphysics at all because, in this field, it is destined to fail. For this reason, only the exact sciences are reliable.

Buehler, David A. CQ Sources/Bibliography. *Cambridge Quart Healthcare Ethics*, 4(2), 193-196, Spr 95.

"CQ Sources" Bibliography covering approximately 100 items on "Designs of Life", choice, control, and responsibility in genetic manipulation.

Bühler, Pierre. Science et foi: l'apport de l'herméneutique. *Rev Theol Phil*, 126(2), 143-153, 1994.

S'inspirant de travaux menés à l'Institut de recherches herméneutiques et systématiques de Neuchâtel, l'article esquisse quelques implications résultant d'une approche herméneutique du dialogue entre science et foi. Partant de l'extension du phénomène de l'interprétation, il réfléchit aux conditions du travail interdisciplinaire et à l'accent interactionnel qui en résulte. Il aborde ensuite la question d'un tiers d'ancrage pour science et foi, ce qui le conduit à une réflexion sur la dialectique entre Ecriture et expérience.

Buekens, Filip. Externalism, Content, and Causal Histories. *Dialectica*, 48(3-4), 267-280, 1994.

Externalism in philosophy of mind is usually taken to be faced with the following difficulty: from the fact that meanings are externally individuated, it follows that the subjective character of mental states and events (their accessibility for the person who "has" them) becomes problematic. On the basis of a well-founded approach to similar problems in the philosophy of action, I propose a solution based on two connected issues: (a) we should think of mental states not as beliefs, but as (defeasible) states of knowledge, and (b) thought experiments, designed to strip off the contribution of the world from the subject's contribution to the contents of his mental states are doomed to fail. The allegedly subjective character of a propositional contentful states (beliefs, desires, meanings) is that they are agent-specific states. Agent-specificity is not in contradiction with mental states or intentional actions having a circumstantial nature.

Bueno, Gustavo. La Ética desde la Izquierda. *El Basilisco*, 17, 3-36, Ju-De 94.

Buford, Thomas O. *In Search of a Calling: The College's Role in Shaping Identity*. Macon, Mercer Univ Pr, 1995.

Colleges and universities abandoned their traditional role to educate for callings and adopted the role of educating for careers. Initially calling exercised a formative influence. Since the late nineteenth century influenced by technical rationality and the professions they have morally truncated students, routinized their educational lives, and rationalized their behavior. To reclaim their heritage they can appeal to two traditions: biblical religion and renaissance humanism. Therein lies a new view of the person and of calling. To achieve this task obstacles in the academic and administrative life of institutions must be faced.

Buhr, Manfred. "Europa und sein geistiges Erbe" in *Das geistige Erbe Europas*, Buhr, Manfred (ed), 165-174. Napoli, Vivarium, 1994.

Buhr, Manfred (ed). *Das geistige Erbe Europas*. Napoli, Vivarium, 1994.

Buhr, Manfred (ed). *Philosophische Weisheiten aus zweieinhalb Jahrtausenden*. Hanau, Werner Dausien, 1986.

Buiko, Tatyana. "National Identity as Educational Problem: Towards a National System of Education in Belarus" in *Identity, Culture, and Education*, Smeyers, Paul (ed), 119-128. Leuven, Leuven Univ Pr, 1994.

The paper argues that the idea of nation in its liberal interpretation can be and must be one of the main foundations of education. This thesis seems trivial for educators and philosophers of education from national states of Western Europe but it is quite controversial in Belarus now. There is opinion among our educators and policy makers that the idea of nation is disastrous for education because it limits our cultural horizons. This paper consists of a story about the development of Belarusian school and a discussion of the aims of education in connection with the problem of national identity.

Buksinski, Tadeusz. From Imposed Reason to Immanent Reason. *Metaphilosophy*, 25(2-3), 205-213, Ap-Jl 94.

In the article the point is made that in Eastern Europe, while Marxist thought was the official perspective of "society," it never really understood the nature and role of "community," and thus could never adequately accommodate to reality. Solidarity was a community movement based on emotion, values and prejudices and its victory was victory of community over the system. There is a paradox which characterizes post-communist societies. At the very introductory stage of the implementation of democratic and liberal institutions occurs the process of their alienation. It seems that for the democracy in Eastern Europe the main problem is how to reconcile liberty and community values. Philosophy can play an important role in the process of reconciliation.

Bull, Barry. "The Moral Justification of Systematic Education Reform in the United States" in *Identity, Culture, and Education*, Smeyers, Paul (ed), 129-138. Leuven, Leuven Univ Pr, 1994.

Bull, Malcolm (ed). *Apocalypse Theory and the Ends of the World*. Cambridge, Blackwell, 1995.

This book is a collection of historical and theoretical essays exploring the links between religious and secular versions of eschatology and teleology from Zoroaster to the present day. It examines the relationship between ends as purposes and ends as terminations, and challenges Blumenberg's argument that secular philosophies of history were developed independently of Christian apocalyptic. The book engages with postmodern debates about the end of history, and contains essays dealing with the work of Bacon, Kant, Cieszkowski, Adorno, Foucault, and Derrida.

Bullock, Frederick W and Miller, Arthur I. Neutral Currents and the History of Scientific Ideas. *Stud Hist Phil Sci*, 25(6), 895-932, D 95.

Bulygin, Eugenio and Alchourrón, Carlos E and Schmitt, Annette (& other trans). *Normative Systeme*. Freiburg, Alber, 1994.

Bungay, Stephen. "The Hegelian Project" in *Hegel Reconsidered*, Engelhardt Jr, H Tristram (ed), 19-42. Dordrecht, Kluwer, 1994.

Bunge, Mario. Holotechnodemocracy: An Alternative to Capitalism and Socialism. *Magyar Filozot Szemle*, 5-6, 869-876, 1994.

Savage capitalism is no less bankrupt than state socialism. The way out of this dilemma is integral democracy (biological, political, cultural and economic) informed by technology, in particular sociotechnology (management science, normative macroeconomics, etc.). Biological democracy means equality of sexes and races. Political democracy means not just voting once in awhile but intensive popular participation in the design of policies. Cultural democracy means universal access to the cultural fund and to the sources of cultural wealth. And economic democracy means more than equal opportunity: it means cooperative ownership and self-management—as proposed by J S Mill in his *Principles of Political Economy*, conveniently ignored by both Marxists and latter day neoliberals. The proposed social order, called 'technoholodemocracy', fits in with a systematic view of the world and society—a view that incorporates the valid components of individualism and holism.

Bunge, Mario. La Philosophie de Niels Bohr. *Horiz Phil*, 2(2), 27-50, Spring 92.

Niels Bohr exerted a decisive influence on the development of the quantum theory and its interpretations. He was subjectivist, holist, and somewhat irrationalist. In fact, he held that physical objects spring into existence out of the act of observation. He also regarded the system composed by the object, the observer and his observation instruments as a sealed unit. Finally, he maintained that truth and depth are mutually "complementary", i.e., exclusive. The paper argues that these three features of Bohr's philosophy are unsound and must be rejected in order to obtain purely physical (rather than psychological) interpretation of the quantum theory.

Bunzl, Martin. Meaning's Reach. *J Theor Soc Behav*, 24(3), 267-280, S 94.

What are the prospects for a realist account of meaning that is not in the head? This paper uses some case studies to demonstrate the difficulty that any such account faces is how to rule out letting an account of meaning in the head in through the back door. As illustrated, one way a cognitivist account can come back into the picture is by no way of appeals to 'reasonableness'. Another is by way of questions of what is termed the 'reach' of meaning.

Bunzl, Martin. Scientific Abstraction and the Realist Impulse. *Phil Sci*, 61(3), 449-456, S 94.

In a series of important papers, A Fine has developed and defended the view that the proper reading of scientific practice is neither realist nor antirealist. Instead, he argues that realism and antirealism both add something extra to a core position *which is neither*. In this discussion I reexamine his claim in the light of some criticisms. Fine's position contains an important insight, but to draw that point out requires shifting the way in which Fine poses the argument. I do so by examining an argument by H Stein.

Bunzl, Martin. *The Context of Explanation*. Dordrecht, Kluwer, 1993.

The author argues that given the variety of interests that prompt explanations in science, if a comprehensive account of explanation obtains it will range over specific models, one step removed from them. Conditions of adequacy for such an account are developed relying on the twin notions of explanatory conception and explanatory connection. The author applies the account to both the context of a finished theory and the context of a theory that is under development.

Burbidge, John W. "Hegel on Galvinism" in *Hegel on the Modern World*, Collins, Ardis B (ed), 111-124. Albany, SUNY Pr, 1995.

In his Remark to section 330 of the *Philosophy of Nature* Hegel refers to two contemporary chemists. Berzelius, active in the international scientific community, developed the modern chemical symbols. Pohl, Hegel's colleague at Berlin, claimed that the electricity of the Voltaic cell changed water into oxygen. Strangely, Hegel sided with Pohl against Berzelius. This paper explores the reasons for his doing so, and thereby throws some lights on what Hegel was attempting to do in his Philosophy of Nature. While keeping up with new developments, he used the logic to determine which phenomena to consider and which theories were genuinely explanatory.

Burbidge, John W. *On Hegel's Logic: Fragments of a Commentary*. Atlantic Highlands, Humanities Pr, 1981.

Burbidge, John W. Reason and the Real. *Bull Hegel Soc Gt Brit*, 30, 6-13, Autumn-Wint 94.

Both Schelling and Hegel produced philosophies of the real world—of nature and of history. During their early collaboration philosophy constructed a model of the real. The late Schelling dismisses a deductive scheme to develop a philosophy in which possibilities were developed conceptually but only experience could show that the possibilities had been actualized in history. In contrast, Hegel's logical thought at every stage finds that the real frustrates its projects. So the philosophy of nature can only anticipate a logical skeleton but relies on the givens of science to give it flesh.

Burbidge, John W (trans) and D'Hondt, Jacques. *Hegel In His Time: Berlin, 1818-1831*. Peterborough, Broadview Pr, 1988.

In this work Jacques D'Hondt explores "the philosophy of right whose maxims Hegel actually followed in his daily life." Using Hegel's letters and contemporary documents he shows that Hegel's patrons were the liberals in the Prussian regime; that he was constantly under suspicion from reactionaries; that he attacked the demagoguery and xenophobic chauvinism of the student movement while supporting and encouraging its liberal leaders; and that his closest contacts were with progressive figures in both France and Germany. The negative assessment by Marx and Engels reflects a later time when liberalism was no longer at the forefront of progress.

Burch, Robert W. "The Contribution to Humanism of Konstantin Kolenda" in *Contributors to the Philosophy of Humanism, Hillar, Marian (ed)*, 7-15. Pasadena, Humanists Houston, 1994.

The article argues that the humanism of Konstantin Kolenda is more favorable toward religious attitudes than is usually expected of humanism. Nevertheless, Kolenda's humanism is not any sort of superstitious commitment to organized religious doctrines.

Burczak, Theodore A. "Subjectivism and Democratic Firms" in *Marxism in the Postmodern Age, Callari, Antonio (ed)*, 169-177. New York, Guilford, 1994.

Burczak, Theodore A. Reply to Bruce Caldwell: Can Subjectivism Be Non-Hermeneutic?. *Econ Phil*, 10(2), 315-317, O 94.

Burge, Tyler. "Reply: Intentional Properties and Causation" in *Philosophy of Psychology: Debates on Psychological Explanation, Macdonald, Cynthia (ed)*, 226-235. Cambridge, Blackwell, 1995.

Burger, Ronna C. "Aristotle's 'Exclusive' Account of Happiness" in *The Crossroads of Norm and Nature, Sim, May (ed)*, 79-98. Lanham, Rowman & Littlefield, 1995.

The "exclusive" conception of happiness as contemplation, in *Nicomachean Ethics* X, seems to be at odds with a conception more inclusive of the range of human experience discussed in the course of the *Ethics* and implied, perhaps, by the first book. Missing from the contemporary debate is the possibility that this tension, which is not simply at work in Aristotle's account of the human good, is a deliberate one. Operating on that assumption, the contemplative wise man held up in Bk. X is found to be an image, both illuminating and distorting, which the political philosopher projects of himself for the non-philosopher.

Burgess-Jackson, Keith. Justice and the Distribution of Fear. *S J Phil*, 32(4), 367-391, Wint 94.

Philosophers have unduly neglected the distribution of socially created burdens, focusing instead on benefits. I try to rectify this by addressing the distribution of a particular burden, fearfulness. Social-scientific literature shows that fear of crime (my immediate topic) is distributed in patterns, not haphazardly. Women, for example are significantly more fearful than men, in large part because women but not men are victimized by rape. I argue that this state of affairs is unjust and that, since the distribution of fear can be rectified by collective action, it must be. I consider and dismiss several objections to this argument.

Burgess-Jackson, Keith. On the Coerciveness of Sexist Socialization. *Pub Affairs Quart*, 9(1), 15-27, Ja 95.

Is sexist socialization coercive? That is, are processes, mechanisms, and structures that channel males and females into different roles and occupations coercive? H E Baber has argued that the answer is "No". I criticize her argument, showing that on her own analysis of coercion (which I accept for purposes of argument), together with a proper (which is to say sensitive) understanding of the facts of women's lives, sexist socialization is coercive. My larger aim is to show that, from a radical-feminist point of view, the focus on coercion is misplaced. The debate over coercion highlights the difference between liberal and radical feminism.

Burgin, Mark and Kuznetsov, Vladimir. Scientific Problems and Questions from a Logical Point of View. *Synthese*, 100(1), 1-28, Jl 94.

Scientific knowledge systems function as effective and specialized apparatus for formulating, analyzing and solving scientific problems. In science, problems become internal parts of the knowledge systems; thus they acquire new forms and properties in comparison with common-sense problems. Definite theoretical structures connected with problems and questions appear in the theory. Among them are erotetic expressions and languages, calculi and algebras of problems. On the basis of the structure-nominative reconstruction of a theory, the unified treatment of these structures is given. Methods of the theory of named sets are used in the logical analysis of problems and their systems. As a consequence a new formalized model of the problem part of theory is constructed.

Burgio, Alberto. "Rassenkonflikt und Klassenkampf—Zur Theorie des gegenwärtigen europäischen Rassismus" in *Das geistige Erbe Europas, Buhr, Manfred (ed)*, 797-808. Napoli, Vivarium, 1994.

Burgos, Juan Manuel. Cinco Claves Para Comprender a Jacques Maritain. *Acta Phil*, 4(1), 5-25, 1995.

L'attuale rinascita e sviluppo degli studi maritainiani viene a volte ostacolata da una insufficiente conoscenza e valutazione della lunga e complessa evoluzione del suo pensiero. L'articolo sviluppa cinque aspetti ritenuti particolarmente rilevanti per la comprensione di questo percorso e la cui conoscenza può aiutare a evitare sia malintesi che giudizi imprecisi. Tali aspetti sono: 1) la conversione; 2) il tomismo; 3) la modernità; 4) l'*Umanesimo integrale* e 5) gli anni del post-concilio. Lo studio di questi aspetti mette in evidenza un Maritain fortemente coerente con i suoi principi più profondi (il cristianesimo e il tomismo) ma allo stesso tempo in una complessa evoluzione imperniata sul dialogo e il confronto con la cultura moderna.

Burian, Richard M and Trout, J D. Ontological Progress in Science. *Can J Phil*, 25(2), 177-201, Je 95.

In this paper we advance and defend four theses: 1) The ontology of science is intensely compositional and hierarchical; 2) Although much science is reductionistic, the reductionism in question is generally not eliminative; 3) Current philosophers' treatment of the ontology (or ontologies) of science are far too intimately tied to the latest or the "best" theory; and 4) A central form of ontological progress in science consists in obtaining significant contact with, and accurate characterizations of, theoretical entities further and further removed from those that are perceptually available to us. We believe that the fragmentary arguments we advance cumulate to an explanatory potent version of scientific realism.

Burke, Michael B. Denying the Antecedent: A Common Fallacy?. *Inform Log*, 16(1), 23-30, Wint 94.

An argumentative passage that might appear to be an instance of denying the antecedent will generally admit of an alternative interpretation, one on which the conditional contained by the passage is a preface to the argument rather than a premise of it. On this interpretation, which generally is a more charitable one, the conditional plays a certain dialectical role and, in some cases, a rhetorical role as well. Assuming only a very weak principle of exigetical charity, I consider what it would take in a given case to justify accepting the less charitable interpretation. I then present evidence that those conditions are seldom met. Indeed, I was unable to find a single published argument that can justifiably by charge with denying antecedent.

Burke, Peter. The Renaissance, Individualism, and the Portrait. *Hist Euro Ideas*, 21(3), 393-400, My 95.

What have the Renaissance, individualism and the portrait to do with one another? In order to answer this question methodically, this paper is divided into three parts. It begins with the problem of Renaissance individualism, then turns to a case-study of the Renaissance portrait, and finally considers a further case-study within the first case-study, examining the historical portrait, whether painted or engraved.

Burke, T E. The Justification of Belief. *Wittgenstein Stud*, n.a., 1994.

'Religion', according to Wittgenstein, says: 'DO THIS! THINK LIKE THAT! but it cannot justify this...' This paper analyses Wittgenstein's remarks on religious belief in CULTURE AND VALUE, and considers the senses in which he is right in saying that religion can offer no justifications; it then goes on to show that this need not mean that the adoption of religious belief is something purely arbitrary or subjective.

Burke, T Patrick. *No Harm: Ethical Principles for a Free Market*. New York, Paragon House, 1994.

Burke, Tom. *Dewey's New Logic: A Reply to Russell*. Chicago, Univ of Chicago Pr, 1994.

This work is an analysis of the debate between John Dewey and Bertrand Russell which followed the publication of Dewey's 1938 book *Logic: The Theory of Inquiry*. A number of Russell's criticisms are examined, along with Dewey's replies. Russell's renditions of Dewey's views are shown to be mistaken or misleading, and his negative evaluation of Dewey's philosophy of logic is shown to be ill-founded. An effort is made to present Dewey's views in a more positive light, with an eye on their relevance to recent developments in logic, epistemology, and the philosophy of mind.

Burke Jr, Francis V. Lying During Crisis Negotiations: A Costly Means to Expedient Resolution. *Crim Just Ethics*, 14(1), 49-62, Wint-Spr 95.

Philosophical cost-benefit analysis of utilizing deception, specifically lying, during crisis-hostage negotiations. Moral theories of Kant, Grotious, and Bok are surveyed along with their applicability to the peaceful resolution of life-threatening situations to include, hostage-takings, barricaded subjects, and suicidal individuals. Considers long-range, negative effects of a hasty resort to deception (lying) for the benefit of expendiency. The perspective is from that of a practitioner who is a career police officer and experienced crisis negotiator which concludes that law enforcement officials should refrain from lying or employing deceptive tactics as long as reasonable alternatives exist.

Burkert-Wepfer, Esther. *Die Sehnsucht nach dem Schönen, Guten und Wahren oder platonische Reminiszenzen in Rousseaus Menschenbild und Erziehungslehre*. Berne, Haupt, 1995.

Wie erklären Platon und Rousseau die menschliche Sehnsucht nach den ewigen moralischen Werten des Schönen, Guten und Wahren? Verständlich und wissenschaftlich fundiert gibt die vorliegende Untersuchung auf diese Frage eine Antwort. Sie umfasst drei moralphilosophische Themen, denen je ein in sich geschlossener Teil gewidmet ist. Der erste Teil analysiert die zerstörerischen und geistig beflügelndenAspekte der Liebe. Im zweiten wird die innere Zerrissenheit zwischen sinnlich-leiblichen Begierden und seelisch-geistigem Streben thematisiert und im dritten steht die sittliche Vervollkommnung durch Einsicht und Liebe der ewigen Werte im Vordergrund. In einem ersten Schritt stellt die Autorin jeweils die Gedanken Rousseaus, in einem zweiten diejenigen Platons und in einem dritten inhaltliche Parallelen zwischen diesen beiden Denkern dar.

Burkhard, Mojsisch. Epistemologie im Humanismus: Marsilio Ficino, Pietro Pomponazzi und Niklaus von Kues. *Frei Z Phil Theol*, 42(1-2), 152-171, 1995.

This essay explores the interconnections among the epistemological theories of Ficino, Pomponazzi and Cusansus apparent in the context of their reception of ancient Greek and medieval philosophy. It shows that preceding the opposition between the (neo-)Platonic scheme of knowledge favored by Ficino and the Aristotelian account of intellect championed by Pomponazzi, Cusanus attempted to articulate the nature of the mind as such which all modes of knowledge presuppose. Concluding remarks expound upon the principal significance of the thought of nothing, which fundamentally defines the relation to self and other and therewith the horizon of the possible truth of knowledge.

Burkhardt, Bernd. Ist eine Selbstbescheidung der Philosophie aus sich heraus möglich?. *Theol Phil*, 69(4), 537-555, 1994.

Based on a close reading of the book, *Eins von Allem: Die Selbstbescheidung des Idealismus in Schellings Spätphilosophie* by Thomas Buchheim (Hamburg 1992), the article shows (1) that a precise re-reading and interpretation of Schelling's texts are required if one is to establish the truth of his claims; (2) that no critique of Shelling, especially of his late philosophy, can be successful without following the principles of immanent interpretation; and (3) that (and why) the program of Schelling's late philosophy is burdened with insoluble inconsistencies, insofar as the criteria he employs are incompatible with the final results that he attains based upon them.

Burkitt, Ian. The Shifting Concept of the Self. *Hist Human Sci*, 7(2), 7-28, My 94.

Burnor, Richard. Outlines for Success. *Teach Phil*, 18(1), 59-71, Mr 95.

Burns, David J and Fawcett, Jeffrey K and Lanasa, John. Business Students' Ethical Perceptions of Retail Situations: A Microcultural Comparison. *J Bus Ethics*, 13(9), 667-679, S 94.

Due in part to a growing realization of the importance of the role that retailing plays in the marketing channel, and to the increasing numbers of college graduates being employed by retailers, growing attention is being placed on business students' ethical perceptions of retailing practices. This study continues this focus by examining the ethical perceptions of collegiate business students attending two different universities which likely represent two different microcultures—conservative evangelical Protestant and secular. The results suggest that ethical perceptions may vary between the students attending two universities which likely represent differing microcultures. (edited)

Burns, Linda. Something to do With Vagueness. *S J Phil*, 33(Supp), 23-47, 1995.

An account is given of the kind of vagueness exemplified in the title of the paper in terms of contextually determined requirements on informational content. The relation of this to the more philosophically familiar "borderline case" vagueness is discussed, and it is argued that "vague" is vague, rather than ambiguous. This account of the common sources of kinds of vagueness is shown to have some bearing on the origins of the sorites paradox.

Burns, Peter. Proving Too Little and Too Much: A Theistic Response to Tipler. *Heythrop J*, 35(3), 303-312, Jl 94.

The physicist Tipler attempts an ingenious though implausible argument against theism using the suggestion that there is only one logically possible physics, which itself is necessarily instantiated. He bases this idea on that of a 'perfect computer simulation' of the universe, the 'program' for which consists in mathematical entities whose existence is logically necessary. I argue, 1) Tipler proves too little, for he never successfully takes us beyond the truism that theism is false if the world exists of necessity, and 2) he proves too much, since a plausible way of reconstructing his argument implicitly posits a reality with theistic attributes.

Burns, Steven A M. If a Lion Could Talk. *Wittgenstein Stud*, n.a., 1994.

This paper treats Wittgenstein's aphorism, "If a lion could talk, we could not understand him," not as absurd, nor as a comment about sensation reports, as various commentators have explained it. Rather, it is argued that an examination of its context (Section xi of Part II of PHILOSOPHICAL INVESTIGATIONS) demands an account first of perception (and of objectivity and subjectivity in the case of 'seeing-as'), and then of meaning (which is not itself an experience, but which otherwise is richly analogous to 'seeing-as'). The concept of 'social space' is then employed to explain the lion's meaning and our (mis-)understanding of him.

Burnyeat, M and Parellada, Ricardo (trans). El escéptico en su lugar y su tiempo. *An Seminar Metaf*, 27, 273-306, 1993.

Burrell, David. "Verification in Matters Religious" in *Meaning, Truth, and God, Rouner, Leroy (ed)*, 34-51. Notre Dame, Univ Notre Dame Pr, 1982.

This essay attempts to overcome Clifford-type objections to verification in matters religious, which have long bedeviled philosophical discussion of truth in relation to faith, by reminding us that engagement is ever a pre-condition for inquiry, so that "prospective" verification is an unrealistic ideal in any intellectual endeavor. The contrary approach of "retrospective" verification is at once more realistic epistemologically and more promising to faith traditions. This strategy was suggested in the last century by John Henry Newman in his *Essay in Aid to a Grammar of Assent*, whose merits this more modest essay attempts to retrieve.

Burri, Alex. Le caractère social du langage et de la pensée. *Dialectica*, 48(3-4), 337-352, 1994.

I argue that (i) language is a social phenomenon and that (ii) thoughts take place in a linguistic medium of representation. Davidson's private language ("idiolectic") approach to communication is reviewed and criticised in sections 2 and 3, respectively. It is shown that Dretske's recent definition of thought is not narrow enough to exclude algorithmic symbol manipulations done by computers from being thoughts. The difference between mere algorithmic symbol manipulation and thought is to be found in the human ability to infer the truth value of certain self-referential representations such as Gödel sentences (sections 4 and 5). Section 4 also contains an argument to the effect that only universal linguistic systems allow for the construction of such decidable self-referential representations and are, therefore, the appropriate media of thought. Some speculations on the relation between thought and internal symbol manipulation follow. The whole issue discussed in this essay indicates that some form of externalism is required to account for thought.

Bursztajn, Harold J and Brodsky, Archie. Authenticity and Autonomy in the Managed-Care Era: Forensic Psychiatric Perspectives. *J Clin Ethics*, 5(3), 237-242, Fall 94.

Bursztajn, Harold J and Brodsky, Archie. Clear, Convincing, and Authentic Advance Directives in the Context of Managed Care?. *J Clin Ethics*, 5(4), 364-366, Wint 94.

Bursztajn and Brodsky, in the context of a clinical case discussion, raise the question of whether "Advance Directives" for treatment (living wills) can be reliably elicited, interpreted, and implemented in a managed care context. Questions which need to be addressed in order to ensure reliability include whether such directives are made autonomously, whether they authentically reflect the patient's wishes, and whether they are not merely the by-product of transient despair, an institutional emphasis on cost containment, or milieu psychopathology and the acting of clinical countertransference. A subspecialist, a forensic psychiatrist trained in psychodynamics, can be a useful consultant to the treating clinician, the patient, and the clinical ethicist in addressing each of these questions.

Burton, Brian K and Near, Janet P. Estimating the Incidence of Wrongdoing and Whistle-Blowing: Results of a Study Using Randomized Response Technique. *J Bus Ethics*, 14(1), 17-30, Ja 95.

Student cheating and reporting of that cheating represents one form of organizational wrongdoing and subsequent whistle-blowing, in the context of an academic organization. An innovative method, the Randomized Response Technique (RRT), was used here to assess the validity of reported incidences of wrongdoing and whistle-blowing. Surprisingly, our findings show that estimates of these incidences did not vary significantly when RRT questionnaire results were compared to those obtained from standard surveys. (edited)

Burton, Robert G. Searle on Rediscovering the Mind. *Man World*, 28(2), 163-174, Ap 95.

In this paper I outline and assess Searle's critique of the dominant approaches to the study of mind as well as his own positive account of consciousness. Searle's critique of cognitive reason is flawed in several ways. There are both conceptual and empirical reasons for rejecting his connection principle. His denial of any form of privileged access denies something that is essential to his own research program, and his irreducibility claim turns out to be very weak and, therefore, not very interesting. In contrast to Searle, I argue that the differing approaches to the study of mind are interdependent.

Buschert, William and Kujundzic, Nebojsa. Instruments and the Body: Sartre and Merleau-Ponty. *Res Phenomenol*, 24, 206-215, 1994.

We argue that no sharp boundary can be drawn between the "authentic" human body and its instruments. In contrast to some other theorists of the continental canon—notably Heidegger and the Frankfurt school—Sartre and Merleau-Ponty can be read as asserting that the body (transitively) *lives* its instruments, weaving with them an intricate web of habitual actions and experiences. For Merleau-Ponty especially, the human body and its instruments are capable of complementing, supplementing, and melting into one another.

Busom Zabala, Rais. Ciencia Nueva y Escritura: Nota Sobre Una Nota de Derrida, en Torno a Vico. *Cuad Vico*, 1, 155-164, 1991.

The analysis starts from an indication given by Derrida on the relationship Vico-Rousseau, which credits the former for stating the contemporary origin of speech and writing. A reading of the *New Science* demonstrates that this thesis is based upon a more extensive conception of writing than the usual one. Consequently, Vico's concept of sign is not much saussurian, since it implicates a connection between myth and logos. As a conclusion from those points, Vico's project of the founding and grounding of a human science appears as absolutely alternative to the actual development of the human sciences, as we know them today.

Buss, Samuel R. On Gödel's Theorems on Lengths of Proofs I: Number of Lines and Speedup for Arithmetics. *J Sym Log*, 59(3), 737-756, S 94.

This paper discusses lower bounds for proof length, especially as measured by number of steps (inferences). We give the first publicly known proof of Gödels's claim that there is superrecursive (in fact, unbounded) proof speedup of (i + 1)st-order arithmetic over ith-order arithmetic, where arithmetic is formalized in Hilbert-style calculi with + and $\cdot$ as function symbols or with the language of PRA. The same results are established for any weakly schematic formalization of higher-order logic: this allows all tautologies as axioms and allows all generalizations of axioms as axioms. Our first proof of Gödel's claim is based on self-referential sentences: we give a second proof that avoids the use of self-reference based loosely on a method of Statman.

Bussmann, Hans. Eine systemanalytische Betrachtung des Schematismuskapitels in der Kritik der reinen Vernunft. *Kantstudien*, 85(4), 394-418, 1994.

The purpose of the work is to demonstrate the clearness and strictness of the schematism-chapter. In accordance with Kant's arguments it is proved that schematism is nothing else than an accomplished consciousness about judgment's own activity in time and space. Beginning with an extensive interpretation of the plate-circle-example the process of "Schematisieren", the "Schema" as a result of this process and the "Schematismus" as a product of a reflexive abstraction over the former two in unfolded. The second part of the article demonstrates the possibility to model Kant's doctrine of the transcendental schematism as a recursive control circuit: "Schematismus" has got its symbolic representation.

Butcher, James N and Pope, Kenneth S. Seven Issues in Conducting Forensic Assessments: Ethical Responsibilities in Light of New Standards and New Tests. *Ethics Behavior*, 3(3-4), 267-288, 1993.

The publication of a new ethics code for the American Psychological Association (1992), new guidelines (Committee on Ethical Guidelines for Forensic Psychologists, 1991), and two new versions of the Minnesota Multiphasic Personality Inventory (the MMPI-2, Butcher, Dahlstrom, Graham, Tellegen, and Kaemmer, 1989; and the MMPI-A, Butcher et al., 1992) provide an opportunity to review ethical aspects of forensic assessment. Seven major issues—appropriate graduate training, competence in the use of standardized tests, using tests that fit the task, using tests that fit the individual, administering tests correctly, using computers appropriately in forensic assessment, and assessing and reporting factors that may affect the meaning of test findings—are discussed. The revision of the MMPI is used to illustrate some of these issues.

Butchvarov, Panayot. "Wittgenstein and Scepticism with Regard to the Senses" in *Wittgenstein and Contemporary Philosophy, Teghrarian, Souren (ed)*, 131-159. Bristol, Thoemmes, 1994.

Wittgenstein's familiar arguments against skepticism with regard to the senses are inadequate but suggest a different argument he might have agreed with. It is that any such skepticism, to deserve attention, must be philosophical, i.e., grounded in the philosophical tradition. But the latter consists of philosophers, their books, lectures, etc., all of which are material objects knowable only through the senses. Therefore, to be taken seriously, skepticism must presuppose the reality of what it questions.

Butler, Clark W. Empirical vs Rational Order in the History of Philosophy. *Owl Minerva*, 26(1), 29-34, Fall 94.

Butler, Judith. "For a Careful Reading" in *Feminist Contentions*, Benhabib, Seyla (& others), 127-143. New York, Routledge, 1994.

Butler, Judith. "Sexuelle Differenz als eine Frage der Ethik" in *Macht Geschlechter Differenz*, Müller-Funk, Wolfgang (ed), 91-111. Vienna, Picus, 1994.

Butler, Judith. "Stubborn Attachment, Bodily Subjection" in *Intersections: Nineteenth-Century Philosophy and Contemporary Theory*, Rajan, Tilottama (ed), 173-196. Albany, SUNY Pr, 1995.

Butler, Keith. Compositionality in Cognitive Models: The Real Issue. *Phil Stud*, 78(2), 125-151, My 95.

Butler, Keith. The Scope of Psychology. *Proc Phil Sci Ass*, 1, 428-436, 1994.

Descartes' conception of the mind as a private entity, separable (in various ways) from the body and the world around it, has come under increasingly vigorous attack in recent years. A new and very different sort of expansion of the scope of psychology has recently been advanced by John Haugeland, who argues quite ingeniously that the Cartesian divisions between mind, body, and world are psychologically otiose. I demure, citing several traditional individuative criteria that are immune to Haugeland's case.

Butryn, Stanislaw. On Certain Consequence of the Temporal and Spatial Scale of the Universe: Comments on "How the Physical Sciences Discovered the Unity of Nature". *Dialogue Hum*, 3(3), 133-135, 1993.

The purpose of the work is to reveal a certain consequence of the immense temporal and spatial scale of the universe. In the opinion of the author this consequence is following: Creation of a cosmological model of the whole universe is in principle impossible because in its areas and scales the matter is qualitatively differential and its capability of creation of ever new forms being inexhaustible, since the universe has evolutionary character, and so every cosmological model may be but a model of some finite fragment of the universe and characterize its physical state within a finite temporal interval.

Butterfield, Jeremy and Muller, F A. Is Algebraic Lorentz-Covariant Quantum Field Theory Stochastic Einstein Local?. *Phil Sci*, 61(3), 457-474, S 94.

The general context of this paper is the locality problem in quantum theory. In a recent issue of this journal, Rédei (1991) offered a proof of the proposition that algebraic Lorentz-covariant quantum field theory is past stochastic Einstein local. We show that Rédei's proof is either spurious or circular, and that it contains two deductive fallacies. Furthermore, we prove that the mentioned theory meets the *stronger* condition of stochastic Haag locality.

Butzlaff, Joachim (ed). *Karl Rosenkranz: Briefe 1827 bis 1850*. Hawthorne, de Gruyter, 1994.

Bybee, Michael D. Quantitative and Qualitative Abductive Inquiry. *Phil Rhet*, 27(4), 415-417, 1994.

A recent analysis suggests that we may adequately describe abductive inferences' suasive import by ascribing to them a single, highly relevant common condition (a "clincher"). This cannot be true. An adequate account of abductive inferences must consider that the number of comparative conditions and the relevance of those conditions both determine the persuasiveness of an inference. Although some abductive inferences might persuade critical audiences with a single, highly relevant comparative condition (a "clincher"), most actual abductive inferences persuade their audiences by compiling many, albeit marginally relevant, comparative conditions.

Byl, John. On Pascal's Wager and Infinite Utilities. *Faith Phil*, 11(3), 467-473, Jl 94.

In this paper I discuss some objections to Pascal's Wager based on the notion of an infinite utility. It is alleged that infinite utilities result in decisional and mathematical indeterminancies that invalidate Pascal's Wager. Although various resolutions to these objections have been proposed, these in turn have shortcomings. It is argued that the indeterminacies can be readily avoided by treating the infinities as limits. It is suggested that, in situations where only one bet can be placed, the expected utility should be replaced by the most probable average utility. By this standard the Wager is found to fall short if the probability of God's existence is taken to be small.

Byrd, Michael. Part V of The Principles of Mathematics. *Russell*, 14(1), 47-86, Sum 94.

Byrne, Alex and Hilbert, David. Perception and Causation. *J Phil*, 92(6), 323-329, Je 95.

A defence of the causal analysis of perception, rebutting the arguments against it given by John Hyman [in "Vison and Power", Journal of Philosophy, XCI, 5 (May 1994): 236-52].

Byrne, Edmund F. Public Goods and the Paying Public. *J Bus Ethics*, 14(2), 117-123, F 95.

This paper proposes a way to undercut anarchist objections to taxation without endorsing an authoritarian justification of government coercion. I recommend a shareholder addendum to the doctrine of public goods. This recommendation involves modifying the public goods argument for government coercion to include a contributor-specific compensation proviso, thinking of contributors as investors, and including among the latter those whose investment is in the form not of a market transaction strictly speaking but of sacrifice. (edited)

Byrne, Edmund F. The Two-Tiered Ethics of EDP. *J Bus Ethics*, 14(1), 53-61, Ja 95.

Ethical questions regarding access to and use of electronically generated data are (if asked) commonly resolved by distinguishing in Lockean fashion between raw (unworked) and refined (worked) data. The former is thought to belong to no one, the latter to the collector and those to whom the collector grants access. Comparative power separates free riders from rightful owners. The resulting two-tiered ethics of access is here challenged on the grounds that it inequitably establishes a rule of law

for the strong while leaving the weak in a Hobbesian state of nature. Efforts at legislative constraints are reviewed; but such constraints are found to afford inadequate protections of privacy if a data subject may not prohibit others under ordinary circumstances from using recognizably name-linked data.

Byrne, Patrick H. Analogical Knowledge of God and the Value of Moral Endeavor. *Method*, 11(2), 103-135, Fall 93.

Byrne, Peter. Omnipotence, Feminism, and God. *Int J Phil Relig*, 37(3), 145-165, Je 95.

This paper reviews the feminist case for saying that the traditional concept of God is a projection or valorisation of the male desire for power. It concentrates upon arguments to the effect that the attribute of omnipotence in the traditional concept suggests that the notion of God serves this purpose. It contends that if the doctrine of omnipotence is understood alright, it does not serve to make the concept of God gendered in the manner alleged. Central to the paper is an exploration of the relations between omnipotence and goodness and between omnipotence and the moral and political order.

C-Mazaraki, A. La Critique de l'ontologie et la Théorie Sociale de Hegel dans l'oeuvre de Herbert Marcuse. *Philosophia (Athens)*, 23-24, 268-290, 1993-94.

Avant de devenir le penseur "planétaire" que l'on sait, Herbert Marcuse a été l'auteur de deux ouvrages de philosophie "universitaires" consacrés au système de Hegel. Le premier, *Hegels Ontologie und die Grundlegung einer Theorie der Geschichtlichkeit*, publié en 1932 à un moment qui déjà en Allemagne n'était plus favorable à la réflexion philosophique, n'a pas bénéficié du délai nécessaire à tout écrit sérieux pour pénétrer dans le public restreint auquel s'adresse le sérieux. Le second, *Reason and Revolution: Hegel and the Rise of Social Theory*, paru en 1941 à New York, fut longtemps considéré comme étant l'ouvrage représentatif de l'hégélianisme progressiste, une sorte de contrepoint à l'hégélianisme conservateur représenté par l'*Introduction à la lecture de Hegel* de Kojève et par les livres d'Eric Weil. Si on le reprend cependant aujourd'hui on s'aperçoit que c'est un livre fort peu dialectique qui, à travers un langage hégélien et de multiples citations de Hegel, représente un retour vers une position kantienne et fichtéenne actualisée et radicalisée. (edited)

Cabeza-Gutés, Maite. "Class Structure and Choice of Technology in an Agrarian Economy" in *Foundations of Analytical Marxism (Volume I)*, Roemer, John E (ed), 80-96. Aldershot, Elgar, 1994.

Cabot, Mithran G and Packman, Wendy L and Bongar, Bruce. Malpractice Arising From Negligent Psychotherapy: Ethical, Legal, and Clinical Implications of Osheroff vs Chestnut Lodge. *Ethics Behavior*, 4(3), 175-197, 1994.

Traditionally, there have been few legal actions brought against psychotherapists that allege negligent psychotherapy and negligent treatment of psychiatric disorders. However, in the case of *Osheroff v Chestnut Lodge*, a patient-physician (Dr Osheroff) sued Chestnut Lodge, a private psychiatric facility, for negligence based on the staff's decision to apply a psychodynamic model of treatment (through psychotherapy) and not a biological model. The case sparked a heated debate between adherents of the psychodynamic model and those of the biological model. This article explores the implications of the *Osheroff* litigation for mental health professionals. It is proposed that an interactive informed consent process be used to protect psychotherapists against *Osheroff*-type litigation.

Cabrera, Carlos Alarcón. Validità sintattica vs invalidità sintattica in Geiger. *Riv Int Filosof Diritto*, 71(3), 373-384, 1994.

Syntactic deontic validity, applied to the norms understood as deontic status (i.e., as extralinguistic facts with which deontic sentences deal: obligations, prohibitions, permissions), is the validity relative to constitutive rules on validity, to a legal order constitutive rules which determine the syntax of validity of that legal order. Within the legal order, it is relative to the basic norm, which is a logic condition of thinkability of the normative phenomena.

Cabrera, Mónica and Vidiella, Graciela. "La Cuestión del Género en la Cultura Popular: Del Tango al Rock" in *Temas Actuales de Filosofía*, Palacios, María Julia (ed), 93-98. Buenos Aires, Univ Nacional Salta, 1993.

This paper intends to establish a comparison between the way of developing the gender subject in two significant expressions of the popular art in Buenos Aires city: the "tango" (1900-1940) and the Argentine rock (since 1960). The "tango" conforms the femininity with a suspicious glance: the woman is the other, the intruder in the male universe. She always provokes infidelity, abandon, deceit, or perdition. Since the 1960's, the female presence in the Argentine rock is not a question (matter) and the women conforms an integral image that inspires friendships, maternal tenderness, and sexuality. By these comparisons on try to bild the women as subjectivity and to get her recognition, but not her objectivity.

Cacciatore, Giuseppe. Observaciones al Margen a la Investigación Viquiana en la España Contemporánea. *Cuad Vico*, 4, 75-81, 1994.

Cacciatore, Giuseppe. Ortega e Vico. *Boll Centro Stud Vichiani*, 24-25, 236-246, 1994-95.

Cache, Bernard and Boyman, Anne (trans) and Speaks, Michael (ed). *Earth Moves: The Furnishing of Territories*. Cambridge, MIT Pr, 1995.

Cackowski, Zdzislaw. Social-Cultural Time and the Problem of Universalism. *Dialogue Hum*, 4(1), 5-8, 1994.

The human development leading to the formation of global, universal community was accompanied and conditioned by the adequate development of the global (more and more abstract) forms of articulation of the human/social time; the study of the processes of creating more and more global/abstract forms of time's articulation is and should be a constitutive part of the process of the universalization/globalization of the human community.

Cackowski, Zdzislaw. The Peculiarities of Human Time. *Dialogue Hum*, 4(1), 16-30, 1994.

Time of evolution (biological time) and time of history (human/social time): acceleration of historical time due to its extrabiological (technological) substratum; polyphony of human time; the process of abstraction of the human time; domination of present phase in the tirade: past, present, future.

AUTHOR INDEX WITH ABSTRACTS 463 **Callari, Antonio**

Cackowski, Zdzislaw. The Time-Space of Human Life. *Dialogue Hum*, 4(1), 69-76, 1994.

If the present phase (phases of the physical time: past, present, future) of the human time is creative, then it opens up to the future, and in this case the human life is being realized just in two phases of time: present and future. If the present phase of the human time is miserable and barren, when it is devoid of the orientation towards the future, then it is supplemented by the past.

Cadden, Joan. Science and Rhetoric in the Middle Ages: The Natural Philosophy of William of Conches. *J Hist Ideas*, 56(1), 1-24, Ja 95.

Cadwallader, Eva H. Ultimate Reality and Meaning in the Conflict Between Globalism and Anti-Globalism. *Ultim Real Mean*, 17(3), 232-245, S 94.

Metaphysical foundations of globalism and anti-globalism are examined. The globalist ethos is a future-oriented valuational attitude with two main aspects: humanitarian and ecological, connected by respect and responsibility. A paradigm-shift to the globalist ethos is urged if human and planetary disasters are to be averted. Anti-globalism is seen as resting upon six errors: atomistic individualism, an economic approach to life, greed, misunderstanding of happiness, rejection of Gaia, and endorsement of domination. Grounded on a metaphysics of relatedness, globalism rejects the domination and exploitation of some people by others, and of the Earth by humanity.

Cady, Duane L. In Defense of Active Pacifists. *J Soc Phil*, 25(2), 89-91, Fall 94.

In "Are Active Pacifists Really Just-Warists in Disguise?" Paula Smithka refines and develops a pacifist-warist continuum building on her reading of my book, *From Warism to Pacifism: A Moral Continuum*. Smithka argues that just-warists and pacifists differ in that the latter capitulate to evil when challenged. In this essay I defend pacifism from this charge by pointing to the range of nonviolent yet *active* options open to pacifists. Pacifism is not passivism. Smithka also objects to my linking *jus ad bellum* principles of just-warism with *jus in bello* principles, claiming that nations must be allowed to undertake wars when the first conditions are met even if the second are not. I argue that such a move relieves just-warism of its own moral restraint rules of engagement.

Caelen-Haumont, G. Cognitive Processes and Prosodic Encoding: Speakers' Adaptation to Discourse Conditions. *Commun Cog—AI*, 11(1-2), 153-179, 1994.

This article concerns linguistic and psychological aspects of prosodic encoding in reading. We intend to show, in the framework of 36 readings of a text, that once past their comprehension (or learning) phase, speakers adapt their prosody rather accurately to the linguistic content of the significates and to the communicative situation: this defines the frame of the personal interpretation that the speaker invests in the text. (edited)

Caffi, Claudia and Janney, Richard W. Toward a Pragmatics of Emotive Communication. *J Prag*, 22(3-4), 325-373, O 94.

The task of developing a unified pragmatics of emotive communication poses many interesting challenges for future research. This paper outlines some areas in which more work could be done to help coordinate present linguistic research. After briefly reviewing some pioneering historical work on language and affect, the paper discusses the following concepts, all of which seem to be in need of further clarification: 'emotive meaning', 'involvement', 'emotive markedness', 'degree of emotive divergence', 'objects of emotive choice', '*loci* of emotive choice', and 'outer vs. inner deixis'. Competing categories of emotive devices in current studies of language and affect are reviewed, and a simplified framework is proposed, consisting of: 1) evaluation devices, 2) proximity devices, 3) specificity devices, 4) evidentiality devices, 5) volitionality devices, and 6) quantity devices. (edited)

Cahalan, John C. If Wittgenstein Had Read Poinsot: Recasting the Problem of Signs and Mental States. *Amer Cath Phil Quart*, 68(3), 297-319, Sum 94.

Cahalan, John C. The Problem of Thing and Object in Maritain. *Thomist*, 59(1), 21-46, Ja 95.

Cahan, David (ed) and von Helmholtz, Hermann. *Science and Culture: Popular and Philosophical Essays*. Chicago, Univ of Chicago Pr, 1995.

Science and Culture: Popular and Philosophical Essays presents a new edition of Hermann von Helmholtz's essays. As physiologist, physicist, and philosopher Helmholtz was one of the leading figures of nineteenth-century European intellectual life. From the 1850 to the 1890s, he delivered more than two dozen popular and general academic lectures. The editor, David Cahan, has selected fifteen of these lectures, including those on the origins of the planetary system, the relation of natural science to science in general, the aim and progress of the physical sciences, the problems of perception, and academic freedom in German universities. Cahan has also introduced these essays by setting them in their broader context.

Cahn, Steven M (ed). *Classics of Western Philosophy (Fourth Edition)*. Indianapolis, Hackett, 1995.

The fourth edition contains six major additions: Book I of Plato's *Republic*, an abridgment of Aristotle's *On the Soul*, Gaunilo's reply to Anselm and Anselm's response, Berkeley's *Treatise* (through section 33), the introduction and opening chapter of Hegel's *Phenomenology*, and an abridgment of Nietzsche's *Twilight of the Idols*. Also included are new introductory essays by Charles Guignon, Patricia Kitcher, William E Mann, and Derk Pereboom.

Cahn, Steven M (ed) and Haber, Joram G (ed). *Twentieth Century Ethical Theory*. Englewood Cliffs, Prentice Hall, 1995.

Twentieth Century Ethical Theory is a compilation of the complete texts of many of the most influential or provocative papers in twentieth-century, Anglo-American ethical theory beginning with G E Moore's "The Subject-Matter of Ethics" and concluding with Judith Thomson's Presidential Address for the 89th Annual Eastern Division Meeting of the American Philosophical Association. Selections from some major books of the period also have been included. The readings are presented chronologically in order to clarify and emphasize their historical sequence. The book also contains an overview of twentieth century ethical theory written by James Rachels exclusively for this volume.

Cahoone, Lawrence E. *The Ends of Philosophy*. Albany, SUNY Pr, 1995.

Caldwell, Bruce. Hayek's Scientific Subjectivism. *Econ Phil*, 10(2), 305-313, O 94.

In an earlier paper, Theodore Burczak argues that certain of the writings of the Austrian economist F A Hayek display a nascent hermeneutic postmodernism. In my comment I argue that though Hayek's work contains such elements, he ultimately resisted taking the "interpretative turn" towards hermeneutics. The note supplements Burczak's paper by providing some context for Hayek's anti-modernist statements, and by showing why Hayek might have resisted taking the step from anti-modernism to postmodernism. In the final section Burczak's characterization of Hayek's views on the operation of a free market is challenged.

Caldwell, Peter. Ernst Forsthoff and the Legacy of Radical Conservative State Theory in the Federal Republic of Germany. *Hist Polit Thought*, 15(4), 615-641, Wint 94.

The works of Ernst Forsthoff, administrative lawyer and student of Carl Schmitt, reveal a continuity in his political theory from the Weimar Republic, through Nazism, and into the Federal Republic of Germany. Before 1945, Forsthoff viewed the individual as subordinated either to the "total state" or to the "Volk". After 1945, he turned to a functionalist social theory: he now saw the individual as subordinated to the demands of technology. The continuity in radical conservative political theory lies in this notion that humans are radically alienated from the systems (Volk, State, Industrial Society) in which they live.

Cálek, Oldrich. Home and Upbringing. *Filozof Cas*, 42(5), 841-854, 1994.

The author does not articulate the home as a defined concept but as a phenomenon in the sense of M Heidegger and that of Czech philosopher Jan Patocka. Cálek rejects strictly the bio-ecological concept of the human home as an animal biotop. Also, he sees as insufficient to interpret the home as what is intimately well-known for the certain human being(s). The home is a way of the "being in the world"; in his opinion it means the taking care and responsibility of a concrete area of reality. The home is an existential tunedness of the world-relationship. In conclusion the study deals with the possibility to open and cultivate this human tunedness through the upbringing.

Caleo, Marcello. Chiose alle "Regole" Cartesiane. *Sapienza*, 47(3), 313-336, 1994.

Calhoun, Cheshire. Standing for Something. *J Phil*, 92(5), 235-260, My 95.

I sketch three common pictures of integrity—as the integration of "parts" of oneself into a whole, as fidelity to projects and principles constitutive of one's core identity, and as purity of agency. All three reduce integrity to something else with which it is not equivalent—to the conditions for unified agency, or for continuing as the same self, or for having reason to refuse cooperating with evil. Their analysis of why integrity is a virtue is also limited by the assumption that integrity is solely a personal virtue. I argue that integrity is the social virtue of standing before others for what, in one's best judgement, is worth person's doing.

Calhoun, Cheshire. The Gender Closet: Lesbian Disappearance under the Sign "Women". *Fem Stud*, 21(1), 7-34, Spr 95.

Can one theorize the lesbian within a feminist frame? I argue that a difference sensitive feminist frame closets lesbians because (1) heterosexist oppression has been undertheorized and thus gender analyses fail to intersect with sexual orientation analyses, (2) feminist values and goals have worked against representing lesbian difference from heterosexual women, and (3) difference sensitive feminism requires that lesbians be representable as *women* with a different sexuality and not as a "third sex", not-women, not-men, i.e., not through the very image through which lesbians historically were made conceivable.

Calhoun, Laura. Brandon Shaw, Neil Perry, and the Perils of Education. *J Thought*, 30(2), 43-59, Sum 95.

Calhoun, Laurie. The Intentional Fallacy. *Phil Lit*, 18(2), 337-338, O 94.

In this paper I try to make an important point, that "the intentional fallacy" is indeed a fallacy, in a new and succinct way.

Callaghan, Karen A and Choi, Jung Min and Murphy, John W. *The Politics of Culture: Race, Violence, and Democracy*. Westport, Praeger, 1995.

The protests in Los Angeles during the spring of 1992 signaled that the United States is a troubled society. Specifically, although American society is becoming increasingly diverse, many people are not close to experiencing democracy. Certain powerful interests constrict the American policy in very important ways. Clearly stated, conservatives have manipulated symbols and other cultural factors to maintain social control. Postmodernism exposes the limitations of the conservative project while introducing a new mode of order conducive to sustaining a democratic society.

Callahan, Daniel. The Puzzle of Profound Respect. *Hastings Center Rep*, 25(1), 39-40, Jan-Feb 95.

Callahan, Joan. Evaluating Religious Practices: Ecclesioethics Engendered. *Prof Ethics*, 3(2), 37-56, Sum 94.

Callahan, Joan. Let's Get the L Out: Or Why *Johnson Controls* Is Not an Unequivocal Victory for Women. *J Soc Phil*, 25(3), 65-75, Wint 94.

Callari, Antonio. "Marxism in the New World Order: Crisis and Possibilities" in *Marxism in the Postmodern Age, Callari, Antonio (ed)*, 1-10. New York, Guilford, 1994.

Callari, Antonio (ed) and Cullenberg, Stephen (ed) and Biewener, Carole (ed). *Marxism in the Postmodern Age*. New York, Guilford, 1994.

Fifty-three multidisciplinary essays which explore how Marxist theory is critically rethinking its conditions and objects of analysis. Situated in the context of changing national and international conditions, including the collapse of really existing socialism, the book captures a dialogue, carried on non-essentialist ground, between established Marxist concepts (of class and of economic interests) and other social identities and forms of oppression and resistence. The essays, many of which are by well-known contemporary figures, probe for an imaginary of social transformation capable of going beyond the established dichotomies of the modernist age, and chart a vast analytical terrain for a post-orthodox Marxism.

Callaway, H G. Review of "The Community Reconstructs: The Meaning of Pragmatic Social Thought" by James Campbell. *J Value Inq*, 29(2), 279-284, Je 95.

Callejo, M José. Heidegger y la otra historia de Occidente: Notas Kantianas para una lectura de los *Beiträge zur Philosophie*. *An Seminar Metaf*, 27, 59-109, 1993.

Callender, Craig and Weingard, Robert. The Bohmian Model of Quantum Cosmology. *Proc Phil Sci Ass*, 1, 218-227, 1994.

A realist causal model of quantum cosmology (QC) is developed. By applying the de Broglie-Bohm interpretation of quantum mechanics to QC, we resolve the notorious 'problem of time' in QC, and derive exact equations of motion for cosmological dynamical variables. Due to this success, it is argued that if the situation in QC is used as a yardstick by which other interpretations are measured, the de Broglie-Bohm theory seems uniquely fit as an interpretation of quantum mechanics.

Callicott, J Baird. Moral Monism in Environmental Ethics Defended. *J Phil Res*, 19, 51-60, 1994.

In dealing with concern for fellow human beings, sentient animals, and the environment, Christopher D. Stone suggests that a single agent adopt a different ethical theory—e.g., Kant's, Bentham's, Leopold's—for each domain. Ethical theories, however, and their attendant rules and principles are embedded in moral philosophies. Employing Kant's categorical imperative in this case, Bentham's hedonic calculus in that, and Leopold's land ethic in another, a single agent would therefore have either simultaneously or cyclically to endorse contradictory moral philosophies. Instead, I suggest that different and sometimes conflicting duties and obligations are generated by an agent's membership in multiple moral communities. Peter Wenz, Gary Varner, Andrew Brennan, Anthony Weston, and Eugene Hargrove, among others, variously misunderstand either what is at issue in the monism versus pluralism debate in environmental ethics or my suggested communitarian alternative to the sort of pluralism that Stone recommends.

Callinicos, Alex. "Premature Obituaries: A Comment on O'Sullivan, Minogue, and Marquand" in *The End of "Isms"?, Shtromas, Alexsandras (ed)*, 59-67. Cambridge, Blackwell, 1994.

Callon, Michel. Is Science a Public Good?. *Sci Tech Human Values*, 19(4), 395-424, Autumn 94.

Should governments accept the principle of devoting a proportion of their resources to funding basic research? From the standpoint of economics, science should be considered as a public good and for that reason it should be protected from market forces. This article tries to show that this result can only be maintained at the price of abandoning arguments traditionally deployed by economists themselves. It entails a complete reversal of our habitual ways of thinking about public goods. In order to bring this reversal about, this article draws on the central results obtained by the anthropology and sociology of science and technology over the past several years. Science is a public good, not because of its intrinsic properties but because it is a source of diversity and flexibility.

Calore, Gary. Deflating "the Real": Project for a Metaphysical Reconstruction of Time. *Int Phil Quart*, 35(2), 175-192, Ju 95.

Calton, Jerry M and Lad, Lawrence J. Social Contracting as a Trust-Building Process of Network Governance. *Bus Ethics Quart*, 5(2), 271-295, Ap 95.

Social contracting has a long and important place in the history of political philosophy (Hardin, 1991; Waldron, 1989) and as a theory of justice (Baynes, 1989; Rawls, 1971). More recently, it has been developed into an individual rights based-theory of organizations (Keeley, 1980, 1988), and as a way to integrate ethics and moral legitimacy into corporate strategy and action (Donaldson, 1982; Freeman and Gilbert, 1988). Currently, it is being proposed as an integrative theory of economic ethics (Donaldson and Dunfee, forthcoming). This paper will extend the Donaldson and Dunfee approach by arguing that *social contracting can best be understood and applied in organizational settings if it is perceived and treated as a network governance process*. This insight can benefit management scholars and practitioners alike, since it calls attention to the processes by which trust is created and sustained in on-going contractual relationships. It also strongly suggests that a new approach to applying managerial discretion, as *moral agency*, is needed to realize the full competitive and ethical potential of emerging network forms.

Calvez, Jean-Yves. El humanismo marxiano. *Stromata*, 50(1-2), 127-133, Ja-Je 94.

Camacho, Ramón Kuri. La Declaración de los Derechos del Hombre de 1789 y la Tradición Judeo-Cristiana. *Analogia*, 9(1), 51-78, 1995.

Camacho Naranjo, Luis A. "Contributions to the Philosophy of Technology in Costa Rica" in *Philosophy of Technology in Spanish Speaking Countries, Mitcham, Carl (ed)*, 71-80. Dordrecht, Kluwer, 1994.

The Philosophy of Technology has a long history in Costa Rica. The journal *Prometeo*, published in the early 70's, seems to have been the first of its kind in the world. This article traces the origins of the discipline in Costa Rica back to the pioneering work of Constantino Láscaris Conmeno (+1979) and, earlier yet, to the national commitment to science and technology which can be detected already in the late XIXth century. Its main conclusion is that such developments set the stage for the debate preceding the drafting and approval of the recently promulgated "Law for Scientific and Technological Development."

Cameron, Kenneth Neill. *Dialectical Materialism and Modern Science*. New York, Intl Publ, 1994.

Cameron, W S K. (Writing) About Writing About Kierkegaard. *Phil Today*, 39(1), 56-66, Spr 95.

Given both Kierkegaard's spoofs of scholarly endeavor and the carefully distanced posture his pseudonyms adopt, it is no wonder that many academic authors begin with more or less sheepish apologies for writing. This paper explores the legitimacy of this concern by rooting out the epistemology implicit in the pseudonymous work. As it turns out, this epistemology does disqualify some motives for writing, but it does not rule out our commentary altogether. The rationale for our work is no stronger, but it is just as strong, as that pragmatically presupposed by primary work of the pseudonymous authors themselves.

Camerson, Nigel M De S. Bioethics and the Challenge of the Post-Consensus Society. *Ethics Med*, 11(1), 1-7, Spr 95.

Campanale, Domenico. Metafisica dell'Arché. *G Metaf*, 16(3), 327-334, S-D 94.

Campanella, Tommaso and Ponzio, Paolo (ed & trans) and Lamacchia, Ada (ed & trans). *Metafisica: Universalis Philosophiae SEU Metaphysicarum Rerum Iuxta Propria Dogmata, Liber I*. Bari, Levante Ed, 1994.

"Mirifica nondum promulgata doctrina, nisi in nostris Metaphysicis". Thus, Tommaso Campanella (1568-1639) denotes his *Philosophia Universalis*, the monumental text published, now, in critical edition, with parallel Italian translation. The *Metaphysics*, in fact, published in 1638, is never more edited in integral form or in critical edition. With the present text, the first of eighteen books that constitute the opera omnia, we hope to take part in the knowledge of metaphysics arguments of Tommaso Campanella in his profundity and entirety.

Campbell, Alastair V. "Dependency: The Foundational Value in Medical Ethics" in *Medicine and Moral Reasoning, Fulford, K W M (ed)*, 184-192. New York, Cambridge Univ Pr, 1994.

In opposition to some current powerful trends in bioethics it is argued that respect for dependency should be the foundational principle of health care. The need to respect autonomy (and to prevent heteronomy) is accepted as also morally important. But the normative human state, from infancy to old age, is that of dependency on one's fellow humans. Thus a communal commitment to care for the vulnerable should be the first priority, ahead of the rewarding of individual initiative and independence. Examples are drawn from situation of chronic illness and disability to illustrate the point that the crisis situations of acute hospital medicine are not the only challenges to an adequate health care ethics.

Campbell, Alastair V. Defining Core Health Services: The New Zealand Experience. *Bioethics*, 9(3-4), 252-258, Jl 95.

The New Zealand health service has been extensively changed over the past four years, with the introduction of four new Regional Health Authorities, required to purchase services on behalf of the Government from a range of providers. In order to ensure fairness across the four regions a Core Services Committee has been set up to define which services must be purchased. However, no clear agreement has emerged about a "core" and no list, either positive (inclusions) or negative (exclusions) has been defined. Instead general criteria have been suggested and steps have been taken to consult the community on their priorities. This paper describes seven workshops run by the author in an effort to discover how the community would reach decisions on the rationing of scarce resources. The outcome of these workshops is that there is virtually no community support for an approach based on the social utility of individuals in need.

Campbell, Alastair V. Ethics in a Bicultural Context. *Bioethics*, 9(2), 149-154, Ap 95.

The distinctiveness of bioethics in New Zealand stems in part from a renewal of emphasis of Maori rights, based on the Treaty of Waitangi, the foundation document of the New Zealand state. Increasingly, committees dealing with health research ethics and with the ethics of assisted reproductive technology have to incorporate Maori values and perspectives.

Campbell, Colin. Consuming Goods and the Goods of Consuming. *Crit Rev*, 8(4), 503-520, Fall 94.

The tendency to denigrate consumerism derives from the widespread acceptance of sociological theories that represent consumers as prompted by such reprehensible motives as greed, pride, or envy. These theories are largely unsubstantiated and fail to address the distinctive features of modern consumption, such as the apparent insatiability of wants and the preference for the novel over the familiar. A more plausible view of consumerism regards it as an aspect of hedonism, and links consumption to the widespread practice of daydreaming. Seen in this light, one can discern an idealistic dimension to modern consumption.

Campbell, Courtney S. Awe Diminished. *Hastings Center Rep*, 25(1), 44-46, Jan-Feb 95.

Campbell, Courtney S (& others). Conflicts of Conscience: Hospice and Assisted Suicide. *Hastings Center Rep*, 25(3), 36-43, My-Je 95.

Campbell, James. "Community Without Fusion: Dewey, Mead, Tufts" in *Pragmatism: From Progressivism to Postmodernism, Hollinger, Robert (ed)*, 56-71. Westport, Praeger, 1995.

This paper considers the problem of social fusion—the ability of the group to absorb individuals into its collective actions—from the perspective of the Americal thinkers John Dewey, George Herbert Mead, and James Hayden Tufts. It explores the ways in which their social understanding of the self offers us both a means of understanding the problems of social fusion and a means of attempting to address it.

Campbell, James. *Understanding John Dewey: Nature and Cooperative Intelligence*. Peru, Open Court, 1995.

This volume is an attempt to portray, in a broad and detailed fashion, Dewey's philosophical work. The introduction offers biographical information and places him within the stream of American social history and the pragmatic movement in philosophy. Part I examines Dewey's general philosophical perspective, considering humans and their natural home: as evolutionary emergents, as essentially social beings, and as problem solvers. Part II examines Dewey's social vision. Here, his ethical thought sets the stage for efforts to advance human well-being. Some of his suggestions are fundamentally intellectual in nature, others are more practical. After exploring his assumptions about the efficacy of cooperative inquiry as a social method, I explore a series of challenges, especially the social criticism of C Wright Mills. The final chapter explores Dewey's religious perspective, especially his understanding of religion as a means to build a more fully human community.

Campbell, John. "Objects and Objectivity" in *Objectivity, Simulation and the Unity of Consciousness, Peacocke, Christopher (ed)*, 3-20. New York, Oxford Univ Pr, 1994.

Campbell, Keith. Nelson Goodman's Assimilation of Literary and Scientific Knowledge. *Lit Aes*, 4, 7-15, O 94.

This paper explores that issue of what is to be learned from works of fiction. It recognizes then sets aside the incidental information which many works provide. It then recognizes, and sets aside, various proposals as to the distinguishing mark of fictional knowledge. The contrast between creation and discovery does seem to indicate an important contrast between fiction and nonfictional descriptive writing: but it is this very contrast which Goodman has challenged. Goodman's metaphysical pluralism of 'versions' and the implicit 'portrait' metaphor is expounded. The claim that all categories are free human impositions is rejected. *Explanatory purpose* is identified as what marks off the nonfictive from the fictional. The distinctive contribution of fiction is to present portraits of the alternative forms human sensibility can take.

Campbell, Margaret L and Weber, Leonard J. Procuring Organs From a Non-Heart-Beating Cadaver: Commentary on a Case Report. *Kennedy Inst Ethics J*, 5(1), 35-42, Mr 95.

Procurement of organs from non-heart-beating cadaver donors raises concerns. Standards for optimal patient care during withdrawal of life-sustaining therapy are evolving and continue to be debated and studied. Consensus on specific procedures and methods has not been attained, however, and protocols for the procurement of organs from patients following the withdrawal of life-sustaining therapies may compromise the evolving standards and harm the patient and the attendant family. In addition, there is little evidence to suggest that such protocols will significantly increase the number of organs procured. "Non-heart-beating cadaver" protocols that do not give comprehensive attention to optimal patient/family care at the time of withdrawal of life-sustaining therapy ought not to be endorsed.

Campbell, Mora. Beyond the Terms of the Contract: Mothers and Farmers. *J Agr Environ Ethics*, 7(2), 205-220, 1994.

At the heart of the recent Canadian agricultural policy review, *Growing Together*, is the concept of partnership. The formation of partnerships between various members of the agri-food sector, it is claimed, will provide a framework in which all parties will benefit. I describe the contractarian assumptions inherent in this proposal, and show how their application jeopardizes the economic survival and values of many household farmers. Drawing on the work of philosophers Virginia Held and Sara Ruddick, I outline strong connections between the practices of mothering persons and household farmers, arguing that the values arising out of the practice of household farming are best articulated under a feminist ethic of care. I conclude that agricultural ethics must be contextualized to encompass all of the moral relations in agriculture.

Campbell, Richard. Anselm's Three-Stage Argument—Twenty Years On. *Sophia (Australia)*, 34(1), 32-41, Mr-Ap 95.

Campbell, Robert. "Life, Death, and the Law" in *Introducing Applied Ethics, Almond, Brenda (ed)*, 197-211. Cambridge, Blackwell, 1995.

"Life, Death and the Law" looks at the question of how far it is permissible or desirable to prolong the lives of those who are in one sense or another close to death. It considers the UK cases of *Bland and Cox* in the context of a critical examination of the principles governing euthanasia, suicide and the care of the critically ill. It argues that we need to be clear that a distinction exists between a duty of care and a duty to treat. In the cases considered there is always the former but not necessarily the latter.

Campbell, Sue. Being Dismissed: The Politics of Emotional Expression. *Hypatia*, 9(3), 46-65, Sum 94.

My intent is to bring a key group of critical terms associated with the emotions—bitterness, sentimentality, and emotionality—to greater feminist attention. These terms are used to characterize emoters on the basis of how we express ourselves, and they characterize us in ways that we need no longer be taken seriously. I analyze the ways in which these terms of emotional dismissal can be put to powerful political use.

Campillo, Antonio. "On War: The Space of Knowledge, Knowledge of Space" in *Reconstructing Foucault, Miguel-Alfonso, Ricardo (ed)*, 277-299. Amsterdam, Rodopi, 1994.

In Foucault's work, the war is the *model* that explains the history of the knowledge-powers, but it is also a *social practice*, a knowledge-power that favors the "disciplining" of individuals in modern societies. The study of military practices, which is not developed by Foucault, would allow us to understand not only the *birth of the subject* and of the "human sciences but also the *birth of space* and of the "natural sciences". The *eco-political* dominion over the populations and territories has had two phases: the "military revolution" (16th-17th centuries) and the "industrialization of war" (since the 19th century).

Campos Benítez, Juan Manuel. De la Utilidad de la Dialéctica. *Analogia*, 8(1), 161-168, 1994.

Canfield, John V. "The Phenomena of Thinking" in *Wittgenstein and Contemporary Philosophy, Teghrarian, Souren (ed)*, 109-130. Bristol, Thoemmes, 1994.

Cangemi, Joseph P. Mulheres em Transiçao nos EUA Hoje: Escolhas e Conflitos. *Educ Filosof*, 8(16), 129-150, Jl-D 94.

This article concerns itself with the current state of transition in which we find a great number of women in the United States. The traditional role of women, wife, mother, homemaker is fast disappearing. The new awareness of women of their talent and potential for success in the business world has developed a perspective virtually unknown amongst women barely two decades ago. While numerous women today are focusing on careers outside the home, they have found that it is not a simple matter in going to school, becoming educated, and getting involved in a career. A company and career choice, women are finding, have numerous conflicts. This article explores some of these conflicts, as well as the treatment of women in society, particularly in the workplace. Research and observations are presented to give the reader a balanced view of the choices and conflicts facing women today in the United States.

Canguilhem, Georges and Hobart, Ann (trans). Introduction to *Penser la folie: Essais sur Michel Foucault*. *Crit Inquiry*, 21(2), 287-289, Wint 95.

Canguilhem, Georges and Hobart, Ann (trans). On *Histoire de la folie* as an Event. *Crit Inquiry*, 21(2), 282-286, Wint 95.

Canguilhem, Georges and Hobart, Ann (trans). Report from Mr Canguilhem on the Manuscript Filed by Mr Michel Foucault, Director of the Institut Français of Hamburg.... *Crit Inquiry*, 21(2), 277-281, Wint 95.

Cannold, Leslie. Women, Ectogenesis, and Ethical Theory. *J Applied Phil*, 12(1), 55-64, 1995.

The nature of two influential theories on the moral status of abortion logically commits them to welcoming the advent of ectogenesis (the gestation of human beings outside the womb) as a solution to the abortion conflict. However, qualitative research into women's response to ectogenesis reveals that both women in favour and women opposed to abortion rights reject the technology on surprisingly similar grounds. The abortion framework which led women to reject ectogenesis as an ethical resolution to unwanted pregnancy is contrasted with the moral framework which shapes formal ethical discussions of abortion. It is argued that the need for ethical relevance requires the views of ethicists to move closer to those of women.

Cañón Loyes, Camino. *Anima* hace hablar a la razón con una voz diferente: Nuevos nexos entre la tecnociencia y el mundo de la vida. *Dialogo Filosof*, 11(1), 43-59, Ja-Ap 95.

El descubrimiento y desarrollo del poder instrumental de la razón en Occidente desde Galileo y Descartes se ha producido de modo unilateral: dominador, constructivo y, por tanto, encubridor de algunas de sus dimensiones esenciales. De esta forma, la ciencia, trocada en tecnociencia, se ha extrañado del mundo de la vida y la amenaza. Sólo haciendo oír la "otra voz" de la razón, su modulación femenina, el *anima*, podrán corregirse aquella parcialidades y volver a establecer los vínculos necesarios entre ciencia, tecnociencia y mundo de la vida.

Cantillo, Clementina. Appunti di Lettura sul Cartesianesimo Napoletano tra '600 e '700. *Boll Centro Stud Vichiani*, 24-25, 183-194, 1994-95.

Cantillo, Giuseppe. Religione, etica e politica nel pensiero di Ernst Troeltsch. *Arch Stor Cult*, 7, 115-140, 1994.

The essay investigates the "compromise" between wordly ethical goods and Christian ethical purpose, which is Troeltsch the place of an interaction between the normative subjective and the theological objective element of ethics. According to the kind of sociological configuration of the Christian idea the Christian natural right undergoes conservative or radical changes. Troeltsch's theory of state is the effort of a synthesis of the two basic ethical-political principles of modernity—democracy and conservativism—which agrees with the Christian task of a mutual limitation of the ideal of personality and the necessity of authority, an ethical destination of politics which is up to every single Christian conscience.

Cantrell, Carol H. Women and Language in Susan Griffin's *Woman and Nature: The Roaring Inside Her*. *Hypatia*, 9(3), 225-238, Sum 94.

In *Woman and Nature: The Roaring Inside Her*, Susan Griffin's embedding of language and culture within the natural world implicitly offers a critique of widespread assumptions, shared by many feminists, that language belongs only to the powerful and that it is inherently violent. Griffin's depiction of the process through which women come to speech is illuminated by V N Volosinov's work on the multiaccentuality of language and by Trinh Minh-ha's characterizations of oral traditions. Both authors stress the constant re-creation of language by speakers and listeners.

Cantrick, Robert B. If the Semantics of Music Theorizing is Broke, Let's Fix it. *Brit J Aes*, 35(3), 239-253, Jl 95.

Cantrick, Robert B. Kant's Confusion of Expression with Communication. *J Aes Art Crit*, 53(2), 193-194, Spr 95.

Guyer broaches a difficult question without appearing to recognize its difficulty: are 'expression' and 'communication' analogous terms? He says that they are for Kant, and leaves the matter at that. I agree with Guyer that conceiving expression to be the relation between form and content, such that the former expresses the latter, is as persuasive an idea today as when Kant wrote it. However, I submit that Kant's analogy with "the kind of expression which men use in speech" is incoherent. There is a semantic relation between communicating and what communicating is about, namely the aboutness relation. If the relation between artistic form and content cannot be reduced to aboutness, Kant's analogy with ordinary language is questionable.

Canty, Daniel. Les paradoxes de la tortue (dans les récits de la pensée). *Horiz Phil*, 5(1), 47-55, Autumn 94.

The first part of this essay deals with Zeno's paradox of Achille and the Tortoise through the figure of Jaromir Hladik (Borges). Hladik is viewed as emblematic of the "récits de la pensée" (Pierre Ouellet), whose characters try to substitute for the traditional modes of knowledge a way of thinking that is at the same time a perception of the whole range of the possible. Through Zeno's paradox, their relations to the continuum are investigated. In the second part, Zeno's paradox is interpretated through the figure of the labyrinth and its treatment in an episode of Italo's Calvino *Palomar*. The coupling of turtles in a garden motivates the use of objects belonging to cybernetics (Grey Walter's turtles) and topology (the labyrinth), as well as an evocation of the relations between automata and characters such as Palomar.

Canty, Daniel. Les variétés des hybrides dans les récits de la pensée. *Horiz Phil*, 5(2), 132-141, 1995.

This essay pursues the reflection began in "Les paradoxes de la tortue". The relation of the characters of the "récits de la pensée" (P Ouellet) to automata is explored through the figure of the hybrid or "quasi-object" (Serres and Latour). The characters of "réde la pensée" are literary hybrids. Beings wholly absorbed in the task of computing potentialities, they occupy an interstitial space homologous to that which the creatures of artificial life are bound to explore. The author, through a re-reading of Descartes's epistemology, terms them surrational automata, and establishes a metaphorical link between Descartes's philosophical queries, the technological endeavours of artificial life researchers, and the literary practice of Calvino, Pinget, Roegiers and Valéry.

Canziani, Guido (ed) and Paganini, Gianni (ed). *Theophrastus Redivivus, Volumes 1 and 2*. Firenze, La Nuova Ital Ed, 1981.

Capaldi, Nicholas. From the Profane to the Sacred: Why We Need to Retrieve Christian Bioethics. *Christian Bioethics*, 1(1), 65-83, Mr 95.

Christianity has been crucial in the conceptualization and articulation of the moral framework of the Western tradition. The social sciences, including ethics, were modeled on physical science. However, the Enlightenment project inculcated a metaphysics and an epistemology that reduced the subject to an object and thus undermined the conditions of freedom, agency and an accessible cosmic order; all of which are essential to morality. Competing value claims were shunted into a political context for resolution but the politicalized morality itself requires a framework for evaluating resolutions. While neither the Enlightenment nor post-modernism can provide such a framework, Christian tradition can, in fact, provide just such a framework and response.

Cape Jr, Robert W. The Rhetoric of Politics in Cicero's Fourth Catilinarian. *Amer J Philo*, 116(2), 255-277, Sum 95.

This article reinterprets Cicero's *Fourth Oration Against Catiline* as an example of Roman politics as practiced during the late Republic. It analyzes the speech in light of the particular political exigencies that beset Cicero when he delivered it rather than according to abstract rhetorical principles as described in ancient rhetorical handbooks. The goal of the speech is to portray Cicero as a prudent leader who consults rather than coerces the Senate, though the form of Cicero's expression indicates that he is arguing vigorously for a particular decision. The article concludes that oratory should figure more prominently in accounts of Roman politics.

Caponi, Gustavo A. "Observaciones sobre la Noción Popperiana de Análisis Conceptual" in *Temas Actuales de Filosofía, Palacios, María Julia (ed)*, 99-103. Buenos Aires, Univ Nacional Salta, 1993.

Caponi, Sandra N. "Foucault Deudor de Kant" in *Temas Actuales de Filosofía, Palacios, María Julia (ed)*, 105-110. Buenos Aires, Univ Nacional Salta, 1993.

Caporale-Bizzini, Silvia (ed) and Miguel-Alfonso, Ricardo (ed). *Reconstructing Foucault*. Amsterdam, Rodopi, 1994.

Cappelletti, Angel J. Laques: la dialéctica del coraje. *Rev Filosof (Costa Rica)*, 32(77), 71-80, Jl 94.

The 'Laches' supposes Plato's confrontation against Socrates' ethical point of view. It is, on one hand, an exposition of dialectical method; on the other hand, it is an inquiry about a fundamental moral virtue for Greek 'polis', in a historical time in which Athens' political and military decadence begins. Its aporethical conclusion seems to represent a way in order to avoid the Socratic thesis about virtue as science, displaying some contradictions implicated in it.

Capron, Alexander Morgan. Baby Ryan and Virtual Futility. *Hastings Center Rep*, 25(2), 20-21, Mr-Ap 95.

Capron, Alexander Morgan. Ethics: Public and Private. *Hastings Center Rep*, 24(6), 26-27, N-D 94.

Caputo, John D. Reason, History, and a Little Madness: Toward a Hermeneutics of Christian Historicality. *Amer Cath Phil Quart*, 68(Supp), 27-44, 1994.

If we ask the *New Testament* to say something to philosophical reason, what would it tell us about time and history? I propose we do this as way of letting philosophy breathe the air of prephilosophical sources. I have no wish to replace reason with faith, but to ferment reason with a little divine madness. What is the temporality and historicality of what is called in the *New Testament* "the kingdom of God"? What can we learn about time and history if we let philosophical reason listen to the sapiential sayings about the kingdom?

Carabelli, Giancarlo and Hall, Joan Krakover (trans). *On Hume and Eighteenth-Century Aesthetics: The Philosopher on a Swing*. New York, Lang, 1995.

This study is an original approach to the notion of "golden mean" in eighteenth-century culture. It bravely combines intellectual history and material history, spanning the field so philosophy, aesthetics, painting, sociology, optics, music, theater and garden history in an effort to cross the borders of academic writing, in the stylistic treatment of the subject. Giancarlo Carabelli examines the "golden mean" both in one of the highlights of Enlightenment philosophy—David Hume's essays and his discussion of the middle station of life and of the standard of taste—and in a modest artifact, "intermediate structure" par excellence: the invisible fence of the ha-ha, that magical "middle", that "simple enchantment", as Walpole called it, that was typical of eighteenth-century "modern garden".

Caracciolo, Alberto. *I Sentieri di Heidegger* di Hans Georg Gadamer. *Stud Filosofici*, 5-13, 1991-92.

Caramuta, Ersilia. Metafisica e Archè: Fine Senza Fine. *G Metaf*, 16(3), 383-396, S-D 94.

But if is the same thinking and the reason because there is the thought, it is not possible to annul the distance between power (noein) and act (noema), between the thinking and the reason of thought. Because if acting and undergoing are the same, the essence of this identity is not able to be expressed by a single definition. But it is able to keep the distance between the first and the second term, the distance has been taken off in the memory of thinking. In the memory, where the constant presence of the object confuses "before" and "after", and the beginning: the point to start or by to go on, it is an imperceptible access to the inaccessible.

Carbajal, Sergio I. "Como un Mirar que se Pregunta por Horizontes que Otro Traza" in *Temas Actuales de Filosofía, Palacios, María Julia (ed)*, 111-114. Buenos Aires, Univ Nacional Salta, 1993.

Carcaterra, Gaetano. Conoscenza e Normatività nella Filosofia Italiana Contemporanea. *Riv Int Filosof Diritto*, 71(4), 716-740, 1994.

Card, Claudia. "The Military Ban and the ROTC: A Study in Closeting" in *Gay Ethics, Murphy, Timothy F (ed)*, 117-146. New York, Haworth Pr, 1994.

This article examines reasons for university involvement in protesting ROTC policies discriminatory toward lesbians and gay men. The formal exclusion of lesbians and gay men from the military permits not only the abuses in selective enforcement of the policy and considerable economic costs to maintain it, but also contributes to the perpetuation of the closet. Closeting is not a phenomenon chosen by lesbians and gay men for reasons of their own, and it rewards deceit, penalizes honesty, blames lesbians and gays for the mistrust of others, and effects a psychological division ("doubling") of individual identity and corrupts individual responsibility. For these reasons, university educators, as committed to the advance of truth, have an obligation to protest ROTC compliance with discriminatory policies.

Card, Claudia F (ed). *Adventures in Lesbian Philosophy*. Bloomington, Indiana Univ Pr, 1994.

Papers in this anthology reflect on sadomasochism, ritual abuse, the meaning of "lesbian," the meaning of "lesbian philosophy," eros, motherhood, Descartes, Queer ethics, lesbian ethics, postmodernism, Simone de Beauvoir's relationships with girls, the journal *Lesbian Ethics*, lesbian writings of Jeffner Allen, Gloria Anzaldua's *Borderlands/La Frontera*, and Jewish lesbian writing. The conclusions reflect a variety of feminist perspectives. All but two pieces previously appeared in *Hypatia* 7:4, special Issue on Lesbian Philosophy. There is a new introduction by the editor, a 10-page analytical bibliography (expanded and updated), and a section of brief notes on contributors.

Cardoso Jr, Hélio Rebello. Noçao de Estilo em Granger e Narrativa Histórica. *Manuscrito*, 17(1), 145-153, Ap 94.

We have tried to summarize some elements of Granger's Philosophy of Style in an attempt to draw up its perspectives concerning epistemology of human sciences. As a matter of fact, the problem of historical narrativity, as we shall see, provides us such an opportunity to check out the concept of 'style' along with the general characters of a regional stilistic for historical knowledge. This case was not specified by Granger.

Carey, Seamus. A Development of Heidegger and Merleau-Ponty Towards a Holistic Conception of Health. *Conference*, 5(1), 49-62, Spr 94.

Carl, Wolfgang. *Frege's Theory of Sense and Reference: Its Origins and Scope*. New York, Cambridge Univ Pr, 1994.

Carley, Adam L. What Is 'Consciousness'?. *Free Inq*, 14(4), 26-30, Fall 94.

Carlin, William B and Strong, Kelly C. A Critique of Western Philosophical Ethics: Multidisciplinary Alternatives for Framing Ethical Dilemmas. *J Bus Ethics*, 14(5), 387-396, My 95.

American discourse in business ethics is steeped in the traditional ethical theories of Western philosophies, specifically the Greek classics, Kant, and the British Utilitarians. These theories may be largely uninterpretable or unacceptable to non-Western populations owing to different traditions, religious beliefs, or cultural histories. As economic boundaries collapse and markets become more global in scope, traditional Western ethical thought may lead to clashes among Western ethical thought may lead to clashes among Western organizations and companies from differing cultural settings. Such clashes could lead to alienation of foreign customers, firms and governments and resultant competitive disadvantage, or to an abandonment of ethical considerations altogether in the struggle to compete internationally. This paper puts forward two general alternatives to Western ethical philosophies as useful frameworks for the analysis of international ethical dilemmas. The first alternative uses new organizational economics, while the second emphasizes role relationships and organizational citizenship.

Carlson, Allen. "Existence, Location, and Function: The Appreciation of Architecture" in *Philosophy and Architecture, Mitias, Michael H (ed)*, 141-164. Amsterdam, Rodopi, 1994.

This essay explores the aesthetic appreciation of architecture by considering three questions which are typically posed by works of architecture and not by traditional artworks: the questions of why the work of architecture exists, of why it exists where it does, and of what its function is. It is argued that in appropriate appreciation of architecture contemplation of all three questions is vital and that in such appreciation the answer to the latter question is the key to the answers to the other two—and thus appropriate appreciation proceeds from the question of function to those of location and existence.

Carlson, George R. Moral Realism and Wanton Cruelty. *Philosophia (Israel)*, 24(1-2), 49-56, D 94.

Moral realists have not untypically utilized the obvious wrongness of wanton cruelty to support their belief in the existence of real moral truths, facts, or observations. However, in "Moral Realism and Wanton Cruelty", the author holds that the self-evidence of 'wanton cruelty is wrong' depends upon its meaning different, sometimes incompatible, things to different persons. As against moral realism, it is further argued that the one (nontautologous) interpretation of 'wanton cruelty is wrong', which is best supported by the psychological facts about sensory pain, is anti-realist.

Carlson, Gregory N. "Truth Conditions of Generic Sentences: Two Contrasting Views" in *The Generic Book, Carlson, Gregory N (ed)*, 224-237. Chicago, Univ of Chicago Pr, 1995.

Carlson, Gregory N (ed) and Pelletier, Francis Jeffry (ed). *The Generic Book*. Chicago, Univ of Chicago Pr, 1995.

Two types of linguistic phenomena have been called "generics": reference to a kind (or genus) and the attribution of a general property (which might admit exceptions) to an individual or to a kind. An example of the former type is "The horse was introduced to North America by the conquistadors", where 'the horse' clearly does not refer to any particular horse; an example of the latter type is "The horse has four legs and stands between 10 and 22 hands tall", which is true despite the existence of three-legged horses and horses that are not in this height range—it is only that the typical, or normal, or important horses have the properties ascribed. This book addresses the many problems surrounding these types of statements. The seven-authored, 125 page introductory chapter surveys the history and state of the field, and presents various directions for further research. The remaining chapters are by individual researchers, and take one or another of these topics further than has been done before. The book ends with a comprehensive bibliography of work done on generics, especially from the philosophical, linguistic, and computational realms. The book is available in hard and soft cover. (edited)

Carlson, Thomas A (trans) and Marion, Jean-Luc. Metaphysics and Phenomenology: A Relief for Theology. *Crit Inquiry*, 20(4), 572-591, Sum 94.

Carman, John B. "Duties and Rights in Hindu Society" in *Human Rights and the World's Religions, Rouner, Leroy (ed)*, 113-128. Notre Dame, Univ Notre Dame Pr, 1988.

Carmo Ferreira, Manuel J. Interés es Aquello por lo Cual la Razón se Hace Práctica. *An Seminar Hist Filosof*, 9, 107-113, 1992.

El concepto kantiano de "interés de la razón" significa en el orden teórico el impulso hacia un saber integral de las condiciones y de la voluntad de sistema, a la vez que se funde con el sentimiento de necesidad de la razón de una unidad y totalidad incondicionadas. Caracteriza así a la subjetividad finita. En el orden práctico, el interés de la razón en el cumplimiento de un orden de fines se considera la instauración de la realidad ética, mediante la cual el individuo se apropia de la universalidad de la ley. Determina así el *status* de la subjetividad libre, aunque sensible. Este concepto permite, por tanto, una comprensión íntegra y radical de la subjetividad humana en el horizonte de una filosofía del espíritu como impulso de autorrealización.

Carone, Gabriela Roxana. Cosmic and Human Drama in Plato's *Statesman*: On Cosmos, God and Microcosm in the Myth. *Polis*, 12(1-2), 99-121, 1993.

This paper intends to show that intimate relation of cosmology to anthropology and politics in the *Statesman*. Firstly, it argues against a literal interpretation of cycles of increasing cosmic disorder in the myth, through highlighting some elements of cosmological importance, particularly as regards the notion of God. Secondly, it is argued that the mythical cosmic picture of disorderly cycles is an anthropomorphic projection of actual human disorder. It is shown how the relation of the world to God in the myth stands for the relations of human beings with God as a model for human behavior and as a model for politicians to follow.

Carone, Gabriela Roxana. Teleology and Evil in *Laws* 10. *Rev Metaph*, 48(2), 275-298, D 94.

This paper analyses the status and causes of evil within a finalistic arrangement of the cosmos in Plato's *Laws* 10. It attempts to provide an interpretation of 896e-897b that makes both World-Soul and human souls as responsible for cosmic order, and discards the existence of any evil soul at a cosmic level. It is argued that, in the context of *Laws* 10, only human souls appear as responsible for all sorts of evil, including natural evil. Particular stress falls therefore on the cosmic influence of human behavior and the importance of our cooperation with god for the fulfillment of teleology.

Carpenter, David. "Emanation, Incarnation, and the Truth-Event in Gadamer's *Truth and Method*" in *Hermeneutics and Truth, Wachterhauser, Brice (ed)*, 98-122. Evanston, Northwestern Univ Pr, 1994.

Carpenter, David J. Elements of Accounting Ethics: The Notion of "Fairness". *Bus Prof Ethics J*, 13(1-2), 57-77, Spr-Sum 94.

Carr, David. "Getting the Story Straight: Narrative and Historical Knowledge" in *Historiography Between Modernism and Postmodernism, Topolski, Jerzy (ed)*, 119-133. Amsterdam, Rodopi, 1994.

This paper concerns the relation between historical narrative and the historical reality it is about. It carries forward a debate on the nature and role of narrative in history to which I contributed in some earlier writings. There I attacked Louis Mink, Hayden White, and to some extent Paul Ricoeur, for claiming that narrative imposes an alien structure on human events, such that narrative will always produce a distorted picture of reality. According to this skeptical view, the truth-telling pretensions of history, which distinguish it from fiction, are undercut. In the first part of the paper I recount briefly my objections to this view. I argue, on the contrary, that historical reality, consisting of people's plans, actions and experiences, has an intrinsically narrative character from the start, and that historical narrative is a continuation by other means of the very reality it portrays. If I am right this argument undercuts the formal reasons advanced against the truth-telling capacity of history, but it does not go far enough. It does not account for how historical narrative differs from other forms of social narrative and how its truth-telling aspirations can be realized. The main body of the paper is devoted to this question. (edited)

Carr, David. Knowledge and Truth in Religious Education. *J Phil Educ*, 28(2), 221-238, Wint 94.

It is reasonable to expect, with regard to any traditional academic subject, that it should be capable of being made good sense of as a rational form of knowledge or enquiry focused upon the discernment of truths of one sort or another concerning the world or human affairs. One curriculum area which has generally been held to be problematic in this respect, for a mixture of epistemological, social, ethical and pedagogical reasons, is that of religious education. In the first place, then, this paper is concerned to expose some of the confusions which have been allowed to obscure the nature of religious enquiry as a viable rational enterprise. Second, however, the paper also attempts to develop a coherent and workable account of the nature and operations of knowledge and truth in religious enquiry.

Carr, David. Modernity, Post-Modernity, and the Philosophy of History. *Amer Cath Phil Quart*, 68(Supp), 45-57, 1994.

Carr, David. Roughing Out the Ground Rules: Reason and Experience in Practical Deliberation. *J Phil Educ*, 29(1), 137-147, March 95.

Carr, David. The Question of the Subject: Heidegger and the Transcendental Tradition. *Human Stud*, 17(4), 403-418, 1994-95.

Carr, Wilfred. Education and Democracy: Confronting the Postmodernist Challenge. *J Phil Educ*, 29(1), 75-91, March 95.

This paper takes seriously the claim that postmodernism has seriously undermined our "modern" understanding of what the role of education in a democratic society should be. It therefore seeks to reinterpret this role in a way that confronts the challenge that postmodernism has posed. In order to do this the paper clarifies how postmodernism has now discredited the "modern" assumptions on which our view of the relationship between education and democracy has been erected. Drawing on the philosophy of John Dewey, it then reconstructs the relationship between education and democracy so as effectively to resist the challenge that postmodernism has posed.

Carr, Wilfred. *For Education: Towards Critical Educational Inquiry*. Milton Keynes, Open Univ Pr, 1995.

For Education provides a comprehensive justification for reconstructing educational theory and research as a form of critical theory. It confronts a number of important philosophical questions. What is educational theory? What is an educational practice? How are theory and practice related? Is a genuinely educational science possible? By appealing to developments in critical theory, the philosophy of science and the philosophy of the social sciences, the book provides answers to these questions which indicate the idea of an educational science that is not 'on' or 'about' education but 'for education'—a science genuinely committed to promoting educational values and ideals.

Carranza, Elena N and Debon, María C. "El Reconocimiento de Ideologías en un Discurso Político" in *Temas Actuales de Filosofía, Palacios, María Julia (ed)*, 115-123. Buenos Aires, Univ Nacional Salta, 1993.

Carranza, Salvador Abascal. La pobreza y los cambios sociales. *Rev Filosof (Mexico)*, 27(81), 508-514, S-D 94.

Carrard, Philippe. Disciplining Clio: The Rhetoric of Positivism. *Clio*, 24(2), 189-204, Wint 95.

Carrascoso, Arce. J Habermas: La crítica de la razón interesada. *Convivium*, 5, 40-62, 1993.

The main aim of this work is to draw attention to the connection of Habermas's critical theory with the phenomenological approach and the critical movement of the modern day. We bear in mind the deep seated differences that separate "traditional critical theory" from the "theory of knowledge as a critique of society". We establish the general framework in which the problem is posed, analyze the "new Habermasian transcendental approach", and study "interest" as constitutive parts of reason, in particular the "emancipative interest".

Carreras, Mercedes. El óptimo de Pareto frente al utilitarismo. *Telos (Spain)*, 1(2), 127-139, Je 92.

Pareto's contribution to social reform in the XIX century is examined here. His criticism on Benthamite's utilitarian approach can be seen as the origin of contemporary welfare-economics. He sets the grounds for the rejection of interpersonal utility comparisons, proposing an alternative criterion. Áfter reviewing his redefinition of the concept of *utility* in economics and its measure, the paper focuses on the genesis of Pareto's optimal from his approach of the maximum of *ophelimité* for society.

Carrier, André. Éthique et Enseignement. *Philosopher*, 16, 49-62, 1994.

Carrier, David. "Danto as Systematic Philosopher or *comme on lit Danto en français*" in *Danto and his Critics, Rollins, Mark (ed)*, 13-27. Cambridge, Blackwell, 1993.

Carrier, L S. Does Knowledge Entail Justification?. *Int Phil Quart*, 34(4), 413-418, D 94.

Most epistemologists have been unaware of two untoward consequences that follow from assuming that knowledge entails justification: 1) knowledge becomes indistinguishable from true belief, and 2) one is forced into either dogmatism or skepticism, depending on whether the justificatory belief is supposed to amount to knowledge or not. Rejecting the assumption not only removes these blemishes, but it allows us to confine questions of justification to how well our evidence supports the likelihood of our believing something because it is so; that is, to how well it supports the likelihood of our having knowledge.

Carrier, Martin. "Passive Materie und bewegende Kraft" in *Naturauffassungen in Philosophie, Wissenschaft, Technik: Band II, Schäfer, Lothar (ed)*, 217-241. Freiburg, Alber, 1994.

Newton's philosophy of nature is analyzed with particular emphasis on his philosophy of matter. Newton conceived of matter as a "passive entity" which is subject to the action of nonmaterial forces ("active principles"). The forces arise from the density differences in the ether. Regarding the structure of matter, Newton's elaboration of the foundations of affinity theory is described. Finally, Newton's views on the overall decay of the universe are portrayed.

Carriero, John. On the Theological Roots of Spinoza's Argument for Monism. *Faith Phil*, 11(4), 626-644, Oct 94.

I compare Spinoza's treatment of philosophical monism (the thesis that there is only one substance) with traditional arguments for theological monism (the thesis that there is only one God). First, I consider arguments that Spinoza presents in his correspondence, where his debt to traditional theology is most obvious, and then show how traditional ways of reasoning are present in the *Ethics* itself. Second, I suggest that a common objection to Spinoza's argument underestimates the importance of divine simplicity in Spinoza's (as in most standard) conceptions of a divine being. Finally, I consider Spinoza's reasons for attributing *necessary existence*, a property traditionally reserved for God, to substance as such.

Carroll, John E. Envisioning Ecological Sustainability: The Need and a Method. *Environ Values*, 4(2), 167-168, May 95.

We have an envisioning problem, for we cannot envision an ecological or a sustainable future. We may resolve this problem by establishing our vision of a "composite paradise". Such a composite paradise is based on an inventory of local nearby places which engender inspiration and celebrate sustainability. A circle is then drawn on a map representing an hour or so drive from an epicenter, selecting places meeting the above criteria, drawn many times by multiple people to gain consensus. A "consensual paradise" results, providing a collective vision of what is required to achieve both sustainability and satisfaction. (edited)

Carroll, Noël. "Essence, Expression, and History: Arthur Danto's Philosophy of Art" in *Danto and his Critics, Rollins, Mark (ed)*, 79-106. Cambridge, Blackwell, 1993.

Carroll, Noël. Danto, Style, and Intention. *J Aes Art Crit*, 53(3), 251-257, Sum 95.

Carroll, Noël. Enjoying Horror Fictions: A Reply to Gaut. *Brit J Aes*, 35(1), 67-72, Ja 95.

Carroll, Noël. Kendall L Walton's *Mimesis as Make-Believe*. *Phil Quart*, 45(178), 93-99, Ja 95.

Carroll, Noël. The Paradox of Junk Fiction. *Phil Lit*, 18(2), 225-241, O 94.

People read junk fictions for their stories though the stories in question are notoriously formulaic. This seems paradoxical because the stories are so formulaic that that would seem to preclude interest in them. This essay attempts to explain why it is rational for audiences to read stories that they in some sense already know.

Carse, Alisa L. Pornography: An Uncivil Liberty?. *Hypatia*, 10(1), 155-182, Wint 95.

Pornographic speech harms women by playing a key role in sustaining the social conditions through which women's liberty and equality are undercut. Though there is a principled moral and constitutional basis for pursuing a legal strategy in fighting pornography, we should not overestimate the effectiveness of the law or underestimate its potential dangers. The struggle against pornography must be waged through education, expressive exploration, and protest, not through the law.

Carson, Ronald A. Thinking about Cases as Stories. *J Clin Ethics*, 5(4), 347-348, Wint 94.

Case stories, told by students, recommend themselves to ethics teaching because they convey what Oliver Sacks has aptly called "the real and full presence of the patients themselves." The teacher's task is to support students' moral response by helping them to reconstruct the story, to reflect on its significance, and to hold it out for comment and query by other students, who may see things that the presenters missed and who stand to learn vicariously from the story. Thus does one encourage productive use of the moral imagination.

Carter, Alan. Knowledge and Hyperbole. *Heythrop J*, 36(1), 46-64, Ja 95.

Carter, Ian. Interpersonal Comparisons of Freedom. *Econ Phil*, 11(1), 1-23, Ap 95.

A number of authors have suggested implicitly that the question of whether an agent is free to perform a particular action is a purely empirical matter, but that the idea of an agent having an overall degree of freedom is nevertheless a value-laden one. This leads to grave problems of interpersonal comparability of degrees of freedom, and to an implausible account of the relationship between freedom and other goods. Only on a purely empirical account of interpersonal comparisons of overall freedom can these problems be overcome consistently with the demands of contemporary welfare economics and liberal theories of justice.

Carter, Ian. The Independent Value of Freedom. *Ethics*, 105(4), 819-845, Jl 95.

This paper argues that liberals see freedom as having value independently of the value of the particular things agents are free to do, i.e., that liberals value freedom as such. This is important, because it implies that principles of justice prescribing a particular distribution of freedom (e.g., maximal, equal or maximin freedom) need to be taken literally, rather than as elliptical for principles that prescribe certain "important freedoms" (as Dworkin, Kymlicka and the later Rawls have claimed), and that liberals therefore assume overall freedom to be measurable.

Carter, William S and Hestevold, H Scott. On Passage and Persistence. *Amer Phil Quart*, 31(4), 269-283, O 94.

Cartwright, Nancy. "Mill and Menger: Ideal Elements and Stable Tendencies" in *Idealization VI: Idealization in Economics, Hamminga, Bert (ed)*, 171-188. Amsterdam, Rodopi, 1994.

This paper starts from a discussion of the opinion of John Stuart Mill and Karl Menger on idealization in economics. How can we get from studies of economic actors as ideal or quasi-ideal reasoners to policy recommendations? The focus is on the transition from the so-called "ideal" to the real (from *a priori* principles to accounts of empirical phenomena), especially when the theory of the ideal proceeds mathematically, with at best small glances at data.

Cartwright, Nancy. *Précis of Nature's Capacities and Their Measurement*. *Phil Phenomenol Res*, 55(1), 153-155, Mr 95.

Three levels of causal claims are pointed out: singular claims, causal laws, and ascriptions of capacities. Singular causal facts are primary. The relation between probabilities and causal laws cannot be characterized correctly without referring to such facts. Causal laws describe what causal relations obtain in specified situations. However generic causal claims are best thought of as ascriptions of capacities. Capacities describe what kinds of causal laws can obtain across different kinds of situations. If laws are mere regularities then all laws are *ceteris paribus* laws, hence causal law do not have the same fundamental status as ascriptions of capacities, since in order to get a regularity we must first have an arrangement with an appropriate capacity.

Cartwright, Nancy. False Idealisation: A Philosophical Threat to Scientific Method. *Phil Stud*, 77(2-3), 339-352, Mr 95.

This paper argues that idealisation can be harmful in many ways. Two examples are considered which raise problems not for theory but for method in that the idealisations involved give us wrong tools with which to change the world. The first example concerns casual influences. It is shown that the commonly assumed screening-off condition does not hold in cases of probabilistic causation. The second example deals with casual modelling. It is argued that these models make sense only relative to a fixed substructure; and that standard methodology for establishing them only applies to the superstructure.

Cartwright, Nancy. Reply to Eells, Humphreys and Morrison. *Phil Phenomenol Res*, 55(1), 177-187, Mr 95.

Humphreys points out that only some theoretical activities within modern science are committed to abstraction and concretization and not science as a whole. Cartwright does not claim the contrary: The model of explanation by concretization can argue in favor of an ontology of tendencies only in domains that use its analytic method.

Contrary to Morrison's concerns, capacity claims can be tested by looking for their characteristic contributions in well-understood settings. Furthermore, ascriptions of capacities need not be universal; they may hold across restricted domains. Eell's proposal of counterfactually-defined properties serves as well as singular causes in treating the probabilistic relation between a cause and its effect when intermediate factors appear. However this approach doesn't seem to work for the problem of mixed capacities.

Cartwright, Richard L. Speaking of Everything. *Nous*, 28(1), 1-20, Mr 94.

Casanovas, Enrique. Compactly Expandable Models and Stability. *J Sym Log*, 60(2), 673-683, Je 95.

We study the notions of expandability and compactness for expandability. They correspond to a kind of completeness and compactness of the logic associated to a model in the same way as omega-logic is associated to the natural numbers. Among other things, we show that for countable models as well as for arbitrary models of an omega-stable theory without the finite cover property, the notions of expandability, saturation and compactness for expandability agree. We conjecture that there are compactly expandable models which are not expandable.

Casares, Angel J. Filosofía y Traducción. *Dialogos*, 30(66), 173-183, Jl 95.

To translate Plato or Aristotle is always to translate Greece. This is not to make them say what, today, we understand them to have said: it is to have them say what they said in their own time so that we can understand them today. Heidegger repeatedly denounced the distortion that the Greek world suffered in the Latin versions, a process which culminated in St Thomas's development of the idea of God from Aristotle's theós, and in the unintelligence of his doctrine of causes as the basis of transubstantiation. Western philosophy would do well to review the translations of his works with a critical eye.

Case, Jennifer. Rorty and Putnam: Separate and Unequal. *S J Phil*, 33(2), 169-184, Sum 95.

Rorty defends his philosophical stance and anti-relativistic strategy against criticism levelled by Putnam. Rorty attempts to undermine some of Putnam's criticism, and he disregards another of Putnam's charges, implying that it applies reflexively to Putnam himself. Furthermore, Rorty insists that his philosophical stance and anti-relativistic strategy are the ones Putnam is poised to embrace. I argue that Rorty is wrong on all counts. In light of my argument, I draw distinctions among relativism, conventionalism, and conceptual relativity. Relativism is pluralistic conventionalism, Rorty's philosophical stance is conventionalistic but not pluralistic, and Putnam's doctrine of conceptual relativity is pluralistic but not conventionalistic.

Cassini, Alejandro. Ciencia y relativismo cognitivo: una crítica del pragmatismo. *Rev Filosof (Argentina)*, 9(1-2), 99-112, N 94.

The aim of this note is to show that Laudan's pragmatism gives no satisfactory answer to the problems of cognitive relativism. The first part outlines Laudan's arguments and some of his assumptions. The second part offers a criticism of these arguments. Then, it points out the limits of the pragmatist instrumental rationality. Finally, it concludes that, although the pragmatist program is not directly refuted by the facts, it has low probabilities of success.

Castañeda, Héctor-Neri. Indexical Reference and Causal Diagrams in Intentional Action. *Phil Hist Sci*, 1(1), 1-29, O 92.

Caste, Nicholas J. Corporate Democracy. *J Soc Phil*, 25(2), 168-177, Fall 94.

Castelao-Lawless, Teresa. Phenomenotechnique in Historical Perspective: Its Origins and Implications for Philosophy of Science. *Phil Sci*, 62(1), 44-59, Mr 95.

This article provides an overview of the historical and philosophical context from which originated G Bachelard's concept of "phenomenotechnique". It analyzes why phenomenotechnique is crucial for science studies. By incorporating the concept of phenomenotechnique into Hacking's and Galison's models of science, I argue that we can avoid the radicalism of both while also preventing the analysis of scientific practices from collapsing into the interpretive frames mandated by social constructivists.

Castellano, Danilo. Per una Biografia Intellettuale di Marcel de Corte. *Sapienza*, 48(1), 67-73, 1995.

Castello Dubra, Julio A. La antropología prospectiva tomista. *Pat Med*, 15, 59-75, 1994.

The article deals with some aspects of Aquinas's treatment of the resurrection of the bodies. The anthropology concerning the final condition of man is viewed as a confirmation of the anthropology of the present condition, especially in what concerns with the comprehensive conception of man as a natural being, which is characteristic of St Thomas.

Castello Dubra, Julio A. La dimensión natural del hombre en Santo Tomás de Aquino. *Rev Filosof (Argentina)*, 8(1-2), 59-78, N 93.

The aim of this article is to point out Thomas Aquinas's position in favor of the integration of man into the realm of nature and the recovery of corporality as a nonseparable element of his essence. This is done through the analysis of some topics concerning the relation between body and soul.

Castilho Piqueira, José Roberto. Non-Linearities: From the Dynamics of the Simple to the Dynamics of the Complex (in Portuguese). *Trans/Form/Acao*, 17, 143-150, 1994.

Some concepts related to the utilization of Dynamical Systems Theory on complex systems problems are presented. Using these concepts, we suggest that two dynamics can be established: a short-term one and a long-term one, and both of them are connected to the system's organization processes.

Castillo, Roberto. La teoría del instante en Bachelard y el espacio onírico. *Rev Filosof (Costa Rica)*, 32(77), 109-116, Jl 94.

The present paper contrasts two positions concerning the reality of time: those of Bergson and Bachelard. the theory of duration and the theory of the instant opposes each other and it is from this opposition that Bachelard draws his concept of creative imagination.

Castiñera, Angel. Associació estable versus unió social: La concepció de la societat en Nozick i Rawls. *Convivium*, 5, 99-117, 1993.

This article compares critically Robert Nozick's and John Rawls's understandings of society. It starts from the characterization of the stable association derived from Nozick's utopian libertarian model and Rawls's social union as described in *A Theory of Justice*.

Caston, Victor. Toward a History of the Problem of Intentionality Among the Greeks. *Proc Boston Colloq Anc Phil*, 9, 213-245, 1993.

Castoriadis, Cornelius. The Discovery of the Imagination. *Constellation*, 1(2), 183-213, O 94.

The essay traces the discovery of the imagination to Aristotle, treatise *de anima*. It distinguishes two kinds of imagination discussed in this treatise, a commonplace and a radical one, and explores the relation of the latter to Kant's transcendental imagination.

Castro López, Octavio. Las Paradojas de la Modernidad. *Analogia*, 8(2), 159-173, 1994.

The transition from the medieval world to the modern implies the loss of a stabilizing element: God, the earth, Rome. Modernity has the sense of liberating. Dejected man takes on the responsibility of building his world completely: history, society, state, science, economy. He is the sole bestower of good sense and master of nature. Individuality and subjectivity are to the fore. Excessive confidence in reasoning. Results of the modern world: man finds himself a prisoner and his life hollow. He does not control nature, but damages it. Capitalism favours individual liberties, but paralyzes and exploits. In decisive issues, the individual is a number. Postmodernism questions freedom and defends the *status quo*.

Catalano, Joseph S. Reinventing the Transcendental Ego. *Man World*, 28(1), 101-111, Ja 95.

This review essay of Peter Caws's, *Yorick's World*, focuses on Caws's claim that the transcendental ego constitutes the world of our immediate experience, the life world, but not the world beyond our possible experience, the real world. Giving a Sartrean slant to Husserl's *Crisis*, and I find a broad context in which I can approve of the later Husserl and Caws. I reject the traditional view of the transcendental ego as an idealistic constitution of the world, but I hint at an anthropocentrism in which the world is the way it is because our body is the way it is.

Catalano, Joseph S. The Script Rose. *Phil Lit*, 19(1), 85-93, Ap 95.

I introduce a case for seeing writing as a genuine form of language independent of speech. The crafting of the written marks of an orthography no doubt began as a means of representing speech, but they became more than that. Writing should be seen as the result of a long and arduous craftsmanship in which marks were made to be meaningful of themselves.

Catania, Alfonso. Lo stato moderno: profili storici e dottrinali. *Riv Int Filosof Diritto*, 71(3), 401-437, 1994.

Catt, Isaac E. "The 'Cash-Value' of Communication: An Interpretation of William James" in *Recovering Pragmatism's Voice, Langsdorf, Lenore (ed)*, 97-114. Albany, SUNY Pr, 1995.

This paper argues that empiricism, which grounds competency research, has co-opted the study of communication and sells itself as the pragmatic paradigm. Tracing the historic roots of American pragmatism to William James, it is discovered that he was actually a phenomenologist. His view of pragmatism contrasts sharply with competency researchers. He would dismiss their attempt to integrate the human sciences as impractical because their position is essentially non-empirical. The richness and complexity of James' phenomenology is sketched and shown to be the precursor of modern communication theories. The latter critical-interpretative approaches are exemplified and their potential contribution on the competency issue demonstrated.

Catteneo, Mario A. Pufendorf tra Classicità e Modernità: Nota su un Libro di Simone Goyard-Fabre. *Riv Int Filosof Diritto*, 71(4), 753-761, 1994.

Cauchi, Francesca. Rationalism and Irrationalism: A Nietzschean Perspective. *Hist Euro Ideas*, 20(4-6), 937-943, F 95.

Focusing on three related forms of rational dogmatism—conceptual, moral and philosophical—the paper aims to expose the false rationality that fashions antitheses. Daunted by the manifold of perception, reason disingenuously planks over the flux of existence. Reason, mind and spirit are, through the prejudices of translators, seen to be interchangeable abstractions signifying nothing *in particular*. Through the lense of luxuriating pluralism, the moral binaries of body/soul, good/evil, rational/irrational dissolve into relations of affective force. And these ever-shifting relations, driven by an inexorable will to power, affectively belie the philosophical concepts of unity, substance and duration.

Cauchy, Venant. Humanism as a Basis for Universalist Thinking. *Dialogue Hum*, 3(2), 170-175, 1993.

Cauchy, Venant. The Universal and the Particular Reflections on the Future. *Dialogue Hum*, 4(5), 13-19, 1994.

The paper stresses the necessity of correctly defining universalism as a human ideal, and mainly of avoiding definitions which take for granted its identification with forms of living (acquistiveness, selfjustification by power etc.) accounting in large part for the paramount position of Western style societies in today's world.

Caudill, David S. "Re-Returning to Freud: Critical Legal Studies as Cultural Psychoanalysis" in *Radical Philosophy of Law, Caudill, David S (ed)*, 45-53. Atlantic Highlands, Humanities Pr, 1995.

This article surveys the use of Freudian theory by American critical legal scholars, and concludes that some neo-Freudian theorists, such as Marcuse and Lacan, are particularly helpful in the critique of legal processes and institutions.

Caudill, David S (ed) and Gold, Steven Jay (ed). *Radical Philosophy of Law*. Atlantic Highlands, Humanities Pr, 1995.

This volume is a collection of essays by scholars from various disciplines engaged in the critical evaluation of contemporary legal processes and institutions. Part I includes examples of radical theories, such as Marxism, critical psychoanalytic social theory, radical feminism, and postmodern literary theory, while Part II includes exemplary analyses of criminal law, tort law, contract law, Native American rights, Gay Rights, and Hate Speech.

Causey, Robert L. James H Fetzer, *Philosophy and Cognitive Science*; Jay L Garfield (ed), *Foundations of Cognitive Science: The Essential Readings*. *Mind Mach*, 4(3), 345-352, Ag 94.

This is a discussion review of the two books mentioned in the title. The Garfield anthology is reviewed briefly, with an assessment of its usefulness as a text. The Fetzer book is also a text, but includes Fetzer's own critical analysis of standard computational cognitive models and his preference for a theory based on ideas from Peirce's semiotics, and connectionist computational architectures. These views are critically analyzed.

Cava, Anita and Mayer, Don. Social Contract Theory and Gender Discrimination: Some Reflections on the Donaldson/Dunfee Model. *Bus Ethics Quart*, 5(2), 257-270, Ap 95.

This paper relates Donaldson and Dunfee's Integrative Social Contracts Theory to the problem of gender discrimination. We make the assumption that multinational managers might seek some guidance from ISCT to resolve ethical issues of gender discrimination in countries indifferent or hostile to gender equality. The role of Donaldson and Dunfee's "hypernorms" seems especially crucial, and we find that, under their writings thus far, no "hypernorms" exist to make unethical the most blatant acts of sex discrimination in a host country whose local norms tolerate such discrimination. The genesis of "hypernorms" as "global moral minimums" is recounted, and specific application of ISCT to a familiar ethics case ("A Foreign Assignment") is provided.

Cavaciuti, Santino. Coscienza e Corporeità. *Convivium*, 6, 5-14, 1994.

The central thesis of the article is that of presence, in man, at the same time, both of *necessity* (characteristic of the body) and of *freedom* (characteristic of the conscience), where, however, the conscience is essentially tied to the body, in that it explains and realizes itself *moving* (freely) the body. The relation which is being examined finds a particularly meaningful expression in the language, that is in the relation between the *thought* and the *word*, and can be expressed also with other formulas, such as: subjective body, incarnation of the spirit in the body, noninstrumentality of the body, etc. Its most supreme and significant moment is, however, that of *love*. (edited)

Cavanagh, Gerald F (& others). Making Business Ethics Practical. *Bus Ethics Quart*, 5(3), 399-418, Jl 95.

Our critics confuse the role normative ethical theory can take in business ethics. We argue that as a practical discipline, business ethics must focus on norms, not the theories from which the norms derive. It is true that our original work is defective, but not in its form, but in its neglect of contemporary advances in feminist ethics.

Cavell, Stanley. *Philosophical Passages: Wittgenstein, Emerson, Austin, Derrida*. Cambridge, Blackwell, 1995.

This most recent collection of Cavell's writing contains sustained readings of Emerson's "Fate," Derrida's response to Austin in "Signature Event Context," and Wittgenstein's *Philosophical Investigations*. The reading of "Fate" continues Cavell's investigations of Emerson's concepts of thinking and of patience. The reply to Derrida on Austin works to renew interest in Austin's theory of performative utterances among philosophers by challenging the dominant view of that theory in Literary Studies in part by placing it in the context of Austin's other writings. "Notes and Afterthoughts on the Opening of Wittgenstein's *Investigations*," a set of lecture notes from 1960-1975 on the first few dozen sections of the *Investigations*, interspersed with an almost equal amount of comments from 1991, look back on, and offer a new way of arriving at, the opening pages of his *The Claim of Reason*.

Caws, Peter. Commentary on "Affect, Agency, and Engagement". *Phil Psychiat Psych*, 1(1), 25-26, Mr 94.

This brief comment stresses the inescapability of a subjective point of view even for those who seek to eliminate it (e.g., Parfit). It comments on the mutual blindness of contemporary philosophers on the two sides of this debate.

Caws, Peter. *Ethics from Experience*. Boston, Jones & Bartlett, 1996.

This original inquiry into the foundations of ethics shows that individuals are capable of arriving at tested moral conclusions on the basis of experiences that anyone can have. The development of moral theory is worked out in conjunction with an account of scientific theory and method; moral agency operates in a world whose structure and behavior must be known if action is to be responsible. Most of the major problems of the field are referred to but the position finally arrived at is consequentialist (though not utilitarian). The value that morality is taken to serve is that of complex freedom.

Caws, Peter. Minimal Consequentialism. *Philosophy*, 70(273), 313-339, Jl 95.

This article deals with what makes acts morally permissible. It distinguishes between deontological, teleological, and consequentialist views, distancing the last of these from Utilitarianism. It defends consequentialism against unreasonable demands on the part of its critics. It points out that moral theories presuppose values that are not themselves moral, and argues via an analysis of intentionality that "complex freedom" is a value which in conjunction with consequentialism leads to a robust though exigent moral position. The resulting view is minimal because it makes no assumptions about the general good but limits itself to providing a test for particular acts.

Caygill, Howard. *A Kant Dictionary*. Cambridge, Blackwell, 1995.

A Kant Dictionary contains over 300 entries on all aspects of Kant's philosophy. Entries review the history of a philosophical concept, the use Kant put it to, and its subsequent development. Philosophical concepts are situated with respect to the history of philosophy as well as to other areas of "nonphilosophy" such as law, medicine and natural science. The book has a long introductory essay on "Kant and its Age of Criticism" a full bibliography of Kant's writings, a select bibliography of Kant research and indexes of philosophers and concepts.

Cebik, L B. Secondary Language and Secondary Art. *J Aes Art Crit*, 52(4), 459-464, Fall 94.

In "But Is It Art?", B R Tilghman holds that aesthetic descriptions are secondary descriptions or uses of words in a senses or senses indicated by Wittgenstein. Thus, art loses its self-sufficiency. Unfortunately, the case suffers from unconvincing examples. More significantly, it ignores the more productive view of language which sees social realms as dominating the uses of certain words and descriptions. In this way, such realms realize a degree of self-sufficiency that frees it of artificial impositions of criteria of sense from outside the realm.

Cech, Thomas R. "The Origin of Life and the Value of Life" in *Biology, Ethics, and the Origins of Life, Rolston III, Holmes (ed)*, 15-38. Boston, Jones & Bartlett, 1995.

Cekic, Miodrag. The Discontinuity of Space and Time. *Darshana Int*, 32(4/128), 1-2, O 92.

Celeri, Nermin. Syllogistic Reasoning Pattern in Turkish Adolescent. *Darshana Int*, 32(2/126), 62-68, Ap 92.

The purpose of this study is to compare the reasoning pattern of Turkish University Students accustomed to abstract syllogistic processes and the reasoning pattern of young industrial workers unaccustomed to abstract syllogistic processes. The subjects were 50 adolescents with an age range 18-22 years from low economic status. They were asked to solve twenty syllogistic problems (from simple to complex). The data are interpreted as follows: Formal training influence is more effective on syllogistic reasoning pattern.

Cercós Soto, José. Mal y Muerte: Notas Sobre los Apologistas. *Rev Espan Filosof Med*, 1, 133-139, 1994.

In this article, we study in what sense Grecian and Latin apologists consider two fundamental questions, namely, evil and death. In conclusion, as far as this ancient Christian thought is concerned, the understanding of its two questions is reached by the declaration of a rational creature's freedom and unfinished nature. All this allows the splitting of God, disorder, disproportion, the must-not-be, as well as the reverse way.

Cercós Soto, José. Naturaleza, Muerte y Mal: Notas Sobre Tomás de Aquino. *Rev Espan Filosof Med*, 0, 47-55, 1993.

Let us examine briefly, first of all, what evil is itself. Secondly, the causes of evil and death. Thirdly, the sense of evil and death. According to Thomas of Aquinas's ontological optimism, evil can only be apprehended when some good occurs, taking at the same time good referred to the whole of the universe as its frame. That is where the limits imposed on things find their meaning and make possible the existence of evil and death: perfection requires variety, perfection requires imperfection.

Cernik, V and Hanzel, I and Vicenik, J. What is a Category?. *Metaphilosophy*, 25(2-3), 181-193, Ap-Jl 94.

The task of this paper is to analyze the problems connected with philosophical categories as well as with systems of philosophical categories. We begin with some meta-reflections on the internal structure of philosophy. We then scrutinize the logical categories of cognition. Finally we explicate the concepts "philosophical category" and "system of philosophical categories", as well as the relation of categories to the history of human thinking.

Cerrato, Claudio. Natural Deduction Based upon Strict Implication for Normal Modal Logics. *Notre Dame J Form Log*, 35(4), 471-495, Fall 94.

We present systems of natural deduction based on strict implication for the main normal modal logics between *K* and *S5*. In this work we consider strict implication as the main modal operator, and establish a natural correspondence between strict implication and strict subproofs.

Chacón Fuertes, Pedro. Kant y la Falacia Naturalista. *An Seminar Hist Filosof*, 9, 157-168, 1992.

En un fingido diálogo, Hume, Kant y Moore exponen sus concepciones sobre el problema de una fundamentación racional de la moral que no implique la deducción ilegítima de lo que debe ser a partir de lo que es. La revisión del modelo de racionalidad científica operada en el pensamiento contemporáneo podría justificar un planteamiento diferente del que subyace a sus propuestas, que concibiera conjuntamente la verdad y lo bueno como ideales regulativos y en el que la metáfora del fundamento fuera sustituida por la de horizonte.

Chadwick, Ruth. "The Gene Revolution" in *Introducing Applied Ethics, Almond, Brenda (ed)*, 118-129. Cambridge, Blackwell, 1995.

Advances in human genome analysis raise issues connected with the acquisition (through screening and testing), control (e.g., in counseling), applications (medical uses) and implications (for our understanding of human life). New paradigms of human beings also have implications for ethics: developments in genetics have led to the suggestion that what are required are new ways of approaching the clinical issues, morally speaking. In particular genetics brings to the fore the tension between autonomy and community.

Chadwick, Ruth (ed). *Ethics and the Professions*. Brookfield, Avebury, 1994.

Ethics and the Professions is a collection of essays concerning different aspects of three main themes in professional ethics. The first theme examines the nature of professions; the second, the importance of accountability as a defining characteristic of the professional; the third, the nature and significance of professional codes, which are sometimes seen as a *sine qua non* of a professional group.

Chadwick, Ruth F. Commentary on "Karl Jaspers and Edmund Husserl". *Phil Psychiat Psych*, 2(1), 83-84, Mr 95.

Chris Walker argues against conventional interpretations of Jaspers that there is a considerable debt to Kant in his work, specifically that concepts such as "appearance" and "representation" are pivotal to Jaspers's phenomenology. He makes a detailed analysis of the use of such concepts in Jaspers and develops a convincing case for a Kantian influence in the employments of such distinctions as form and content, concept and intuition. The degree of such influence, however, is less clear. Walker's discussion of Kant and Jaspers brings out some of the difficulties in Kantian interpretation.

Chadwick, Ruth F. Kant, Thought Insertion, and Mental Unity. *Phil Psychiat Psych*, 1(2), 105-113, Je 94.

Two approaches to the phenomenon of thought insertion are considered: an agency account of thinking, as in the work of Stephens and Graham, and a cognitive account, as in Patricia Kitcher's reading of Kant. The latter departs from Kantian criticism that seeks to bypass the transcendental psychology in Kant's *Critique of Pure Reason*. It is argued, however, both that this is illuminating for a consideration of thought insertion and that the clinical phenomena have implications for Kantian exegesis. The cognitive account as presented here is found to be insufficient as an interpretative framework for thought insertion but points the way to questions that need to be addressed in further examination of the clinical phenomena.

Chaffin, Deborah. "The Logic of Contingency" in *Hegel Reconsidered, Engelhardt Jr, H Tristram (ed)*, 143-161. Dordrecht, Kluwer, 1994.

Chagrova, L A and De Jongh, Dick. The Decidability of Dependency in Intuitionistic Propositional Logic. *J Sym Log*, 60(2), 498-504, Je 95.

A definition is given for formulae $A_1,...A_n$ in some theory *T* which is formalized in a propositional calculus *S* to be (in)dependent with respect to *S*. It is shown that, for intuitionistic propositional logic *IPC*, dependency (with respect to *IPC* itself) is decidable. This is almost immediate consequence of Pitts' uniform interpolation theorem for *IPC*. A reasonably simple infinite sequence of *IPC*-formulae $F_n(p,q)$ is given such that *IPC*-formulae *A* and *B* are dependent if and only if at least on of the $F_n(A, B)$ is provable.

Chakrabarti, Arindam. *The Dark Mother Flying Kites*: Sri Ramakrishna's Metaphysic of Morals. *Sophia (Australia)*, 33(3), 14-29, N 94.

Chakrabarti, Arindam. Testimony: A Philosophical Study. *Phil Phenomenol Res*, 54(4), 965-972, D 94.

Chakrabarti, Susanta. Some Comments Concerning Popper's Definition of Corroboration. *J Indian Counc Phil Res*, 11(2), 111-112, Ja-Ap 94.

I argued against the sufficiency and necessity of Popper's final modified definition of corroboration, and tried to modify it in ways that make it sufficient and necessary. The insufficiency has been shown by considering the corroboration of a quantitative hypothesis for which we need to calculate the interval of experimental errors of each of the quantities occurring in the hypothesis. Next, to show a fallacy in the necessity condition of the definition, I have dwelt on some examples from the history of science. The modification suggested takes into account Popper's definition and the issue of intervals of experimental errors.

Challiol-Gillet, Marie-Christine. Schelling: La formation de la conscience à travers la mythologie, ou l'origine mythologique de l'histoire. *Arch Phil*, 58(1), 123-143, Ja-Mr 95.

According to Schelling, the formation of the human consciousness is the story of a progressive liberation over against the one, exclusive God with whom it was originally blindly identical. The parade of polytheistic mythologies among the various cultures is thus to be understood as a process of distancing. History in the strict sense does not begin until humankind in no longer haunted by the struggles of the gods. This latter does have an objective reality, if one wholly confined within the human spirit. Mythology thus gives rise to history and endows it with meaning, since human consciousness arrives finally at its fullest liberty only by means of a knowledge of the God triune, the fruit of positive philosophy.

Chalmers, A F. *What is This Thing Called Science? (Second Edition)*. Indianapolis, Hackett, 1994.

Chalmers, Alan F. Theory Change and Theory Choice. *Method Sci*, 27(3), 161-165, 1994.

Many of the problems involved in attempts to understand scientific change stem from the inappropriate identification of theory change with theory choice on the part on individual scientists. Philosophers have sought in vain for a definitive account of the criteria guiding theory choice. What is more, the choices of scientists are typically influenced by a range of personal factors not relevant for an understanding of the growth of science whilst the unintended and unanticipated consequences of those choices are of central importance to that growth.

Chalmers, David J. On Implementing a Computation. *Mind Mach*, 4(4), 391-402, N 94.

To clarify the notion of computation and its role in cognitive science, we need an account of implementation, the nexus between abstract computations and physical systems. I provide such an account, based on the idea that a physical system implements a computation if the causal structure of the system mirrors the formal structure of the computation. The account is developed for the class of combinatorial-state automata, but is sufficiently general to cover all other discrete computational formalism. The implementation relation is nonvacuous, so that criticisms by Searle and others fail. This account of computation can be extended to justify the foundational role of computation in artificial intelligence and cognitive science.

Chalmers, Rachel. Jeremy Bentham's Panopticon as Metaphor: Science and Supervision in Tobias Smollett and Gilbert White. *Lit Aes*, 4, 71-78, O 94.

Chamberlain, Lorna and Preece, Rod. *Animal Welfare and Human Values*. Waterloo, Wilfrid Laurier U Pr, 1995.

Grounding their ideas in Wordsworth's 'primal sympathy' and Jung's 'unconscious identity' with animals, the authors discuss the most contentious issues in animal welfare disputes—animal experimentation, fur-farming and trapping, the use of animals for human entertainment, and the conditions under which animals are raised for human consumption. The authors argue that 'community' and 'belonging' rather than 'individuality' and the pleasure-pain continuum are the appropriate categories through which to understand our relationships to other species. They conclude that common sense and compromise are the surest paths to the goals of respect and consideration which must underlie a sound conception of animal welfare.

Chambers, Ellie. Representing Philosophy to Students. *Teach Phil*, 17(3), 195-221, S 94.

The paper draws upon research into UK Open University undergraduates' study of an introductory course in philosophy. Students' expectations of such study are explored, and some of the difficulties they experience subsequently when trying to read philosophical texts and to speak and write within the conventions that govern philosophy as an academic discipline. Recommendations are made regarding appropriate teaching strategies. The paper is relevant to teachers in conventional institutions, who may also wish to consider the extent to which issues surrounding the education of adults differ from those involved in educating conventional undergraduates.

Chambers, Simone. "Discourse and Democratic Practices" in *The Cambridge Companion to Habermas, White, Stephen K (ed)*, 233-259. New York, Cambridge Univ Pr, 1995.

Chamizo Domínquez, Pedro José. Simbolización Lingüística de la Realidad. *Analogia*, 7(1), 91-113, 1993.

The purpose of this paper is to show how speakers use linguistic expressions to conceptualize the reality, as well as the reality of an audience. In order to do this the paper will analyze how we structure our reality through language in four different ways: 1) Through words used literally; 2) Through metaphors and euphemisms; 3) Through proper names; and 4) Through lexicalized phrases used as idioms.

Champlin, T S. Hanfling on Self-Love. *Philosophy*, 70(271), 107-110, Ja 95.

O Hanfling argues that the injunction to love others as oneself cannot be obeyed because the concept of self-love is incoherent. But Hanfling's objections to self-love have as much—and as little—force against other reflexives, such as self-respect, whose existence cannot be doubted. Perhaps what complicates the discussion is that there is sometimes a difference between loving oneself and self-love, as there is between deceiving oneself and self-deception. Perhaps self-love and self-deception are always morally bad. I describe what learning to love oneself, which might not be a case of self-love, would amount to.

Chan, David K. Non-Intentional Actions. *Amer Phil Quart*, 32(2), 139-151, Ap 95.

The aim of the paper is to show that there are actions which are non-intentional. An account is first given which links intentional and unintentional action to acting for a reason, or appropriate causation by an intention. Mannerisms and habitual actions are then presented as examples of behavior which are actions, but which are not done in the course of acting for a reason. This account has advantages over that of Hursthouse's "arational actions," which are allegedly intentional actions done for no reason at all. Finally, one consequence of neglecting non-intentional action is discussed to illustrate its importance.

Chandler, David H (ed) and Tonelli, Giorgio. *Kant's "Critique of Pure Reason" within the Tradition of Modern Logic: A Commentary on its History*. Hildesheim, Olms, 1995.

The world of Kant scholarship was electrified in 1974, when Giorgio Tonelli presented a brief summary of his life's work. His was a meticulous study; the plethora of sources shaping Kant's world, particularly the nature and scope of logic. Tonelli found widely held interpretations of Kant to be inadequate, even wrong. At the end of that brief summary, given at the Fourth International Kant Congress in Mainz, Tonelli promised to publish a book with the detailed justification for this rethinking of Kant. Here is that book. Tragically Tonelli's life was cut short. Though he had hoped to include more chapters, the evidence Tonelli provides is ample in the three he was able to complete. Kant scholars will find it necessary to reconsider received interpretations and assumptions in light of this ground-breaking work.

Chang, Linda and Sheng, Peihua and French, Warren A. Business's Environmental Responsibility in Taiwan—Moral, Legal or Negotiated. *J Bus Ethics*, 13(11), 887-897, N 94.

This study explores both the negotiating styles and moral reasoning processes of business people and governmental officials in Taiwan, so as to provide a footing for "outsiders" when negotiating with Taiwanese over environmental concerns. Findings imply that Taiwanese business people and governmental officials can and will reason both at the conventional level and at the postconventional level of moral judgment. But, results of this study also indicate that Taiwanese negotiating styles do not necessarily match their levels of moral reasoning. With respect to pollution concerns, Taiwanese seem unwillingly to accept responsibility as autonomous individuals. Instead, responsibility is accepted when mandated by the law.

Chaplin, Jonathan (ed) and Marshall, Paul (ed). *Political Theory and Christian Vision: Essays in Memory of Bernard Zylstra*. Lanham, Univ Pr of America, 1994.

This is a compilation of articles in political theory written from a Christian perspective and published in memory of Bernard Zylstra, who taught at the Institute for Christian Studies in Toronto. Its aim is to illustrate the fruitfulness of Christian political theorizing across a range of contemporary subjects. The first part deals with foundational themes including law and grace, the basis of rights, and the link between normative and empirical theory. The second explores a Christian conception of the state with special reference to its implications for cultural pluralism and inter-state relations. The final part addresses themes in political economy.

Chappell, T D J. *Aristotle and Augustine on Freedom: Two Theories of Freedom, Voluntary Action, and Akrasia*. New York, St Martin's Pr, 1995.

Both Aristotle and Augustine aim, not so much to prove that there is freedom, but by describing it to point out how much different things would be if there were no freedom. Both take it that free action and voluntary action are very closely connected. Moreover, both hold that voluntary actions must be 1) uncompelled, 2) not ignorant, and 3) done in pursuit of perceived goods. This raises the problem of akrasia, which both take to be inexplicable. But Aristotle infers from akrasia's inexplicability to its nonoccurence (in full-blown form); whereas Augustine, having a 'theory of will', does not.

Chappell, T D J. Reason, Passion, and Action. *Philosophy*, 70(273), 453-459, Jl 95.

Hume famously argues that "Reason" alone cannot motivate. But neither can "Passion". Nor can Reason and Passion together—unless the agent *sees* their belief/desire complexes as giving them a motive to act, they will do no action. This suggests a third condition on voluntary action, not about belief or ignorance, nor about free action or compulsion, but about practical reason or its absence—about seeing how to combine beliefs and desires in decisions. The ability to do this at all is

practical reason; the ability to do it well is practical wisdom. Without practical reason there can be no action; without practical wisdom there can be no virtue.

Chappell, Tim. Personal Identity, 'R-Relatedness' and the Empty Question Argument. *Phil Quart*, 45(178), 88-92, Ja 95.

Chappell, Vere. "Locke on the Freedom of the Will" in *Locke's Philosophy, Rogers, G A J (ed)*, 101-121. New York, Oxford Univ Pr, 1994.

In this paper I consider the question, treated by Locke in the *Essay* chapter "Of Power", whether, apart from the free actions we perform, the volitions by which (in Locke's view) we perform them are free. In the first edition of the *Essay* Locke advanced arguments designed to show that they are not: I examine these arguments. I then consider Locke's "second thoughts" on freedom, expressed in the second edition. Among these is a new "doctrine of suspension" (DS), according to which deliberating agents are sometimes able to suspend the operation of their wills. Some critics, including Locke's friend van Limborch, have taken DS to be incompatible with his original volitional determinism (VD), even though the latter remained in the second edition. I argue, however, that there are grounds for affirming as well as for denying the consistency of DS and VD. Nonetheless, Locke himself, at van Limborch's urging, repudiated VD in the *Essay's* fifth edition. I conclude by showing that this admission by Locke, though not entailed by his (revised) view of freedom, is perfectly compatible with it.

Chappell, Vere. "Locke's Theory of Ideas" in *The Cambridge Companion to Locke, Chappell, Vere (ed)*, 26-55. New York, Cambridge Univ Pr, 1994.

This essay presents a detailed account of Locke's conception of ideas, and of the various different types of ideas that he distinguished and characterized: simple and complex, abstract and general, images and concepts. Attention also is given to the representative function of ideas. The aim is primarily expository, but some imperative issues of current scholarly concern are considered as well; exception is taken, inter alia, to views recently expressed by John Yolton and Michael Ayers.

Chappell, Vere. Free Willing: Comments on Hoffman's "Freedom and Strength of Will". *Phil Stud*, 77(2-3), 273-281, Mr 95.

In these comments I present and defend an account of free volition that is different from Hoffman's (and Albritton's). On this account, which is based on Locke's account of free action (i.e., action "consecutive to volition"), an agent y is free to will to do something z if and only if y is both able to will to do z and able not to will to do z. I then use this account to correct (what I claim are) some mistakes in Hoffman's discussion of an example involving a master and a slave.

Chappell, Vere (ed). *The Cambridge Companion to Locke*. New York, Cambridge Univ Pr, 1994.

This volume consists of ten specially-commissioned essays covering the whole spread of Locke's philosophy: his theory of ideas, his philosophies of body, mind, language, and religion, his theory of knowledge, his ethics, and his political philosophy. There is also a chapter on Locke's life and times and one on his subsequent influence. The authors are distinguished scholars: Aarsleff, Ashcraft, Bennett, Chappell, Guyer, McCann, Milton, Schneewind, Wolterstorff, and Woolhouse. Collectively their work, while meant to be accessible to nonspecialists, provides a conspectus of recent developments in the study and interpretation of Locke's philosophy.

Chaput, Sylvie (trans) and Dewey, John. La démocratie créatrice: la tâche qui nous attend, John Dewey. *Horiz Phil*, 5(2), 41-48, 1995.

Charland, Louis C. Emotion as a Natural Kind: Towards a Computational Foundation for Emotion Theory. *Phil Psych*, 8(1), 59-84, 1995.

In this paper I link two hitherto disconnected sets of results in the philosophy of emotions and explore their implications for the computational theory of mind. The argument of the paper is that, for just the same reasons that some computationalists have thought that cognition may be a natural kind, so the same can plausibly be argued of emotion. The core of the argument is that emotions are a representation-governed phenomenon and that the explanation of how they figure in behaviour must as such be undertaken in those terms. I conclude with some interdisciplinary reflections in defence of the hypothesis that emotions might be more fundamental in the organization of behaviour than cognition; that, in effect, we may be *emoters* before we are *cognizers*. The aim of the paper is: 1) to introduce a number of promising results in philosophical and empirical emotion theory to a wider audience; and 2) to begin the task of organizing those results into a computational theoretical framework.

Charles, David. Aristotle on Substance, Essence and Biological Kinds. *Proc Boston Colloq Anc Phil*, 7, 227-261, 1991.

Charles-Saget, Annick. De la Structure du don chez Proclus et Denys. *Diotima*, 23, 77-80, 1995.

Charlesworth, Max. Ecumenism Between the World Religions. *Sophia (Australia)*, 34(1), 140-160, Mr-Ap 95.

Chartrand, R and Kucera, T. Deissler Rank Complexity of Powers of Indecomposable Injective Modules. *Notre Dame J Form Log*, 35(3), 398-402, Sum 94.

Minimality ranks in the style of Deissler are one way of measuring the structural complexity of minimal extensions of first-order structures. In particular, *positive Deissler rank* measures the complexity of the injective envelope of a module as an extension of that module. In this paper we solve a problem of the second author by showing that certain injective envelopes have the maximum possible Deissler rank complexity. The proof shows that this complexity naturally reflects the internal structure of the injective extension in the form of the levels of the Matlis hierarchy.

Chase, Michael (trans) and Davidson, Arnold I (ed) and Hadot, Pierre. *Philosophy as a Way of Life: Spiritual Exercises from Socrates to Foucault*. Cambridge, Blackwell, 1995.

Chater, Nick and Heyes, Cecilia. Animal Concepts: Content and Discontent. *Mind Lang*, 9(3), 209-246, S 94.

We argue that the notion of concept that is used in research on animal concepts research has no analog in human concepts research. Animal concepts researchers study discriminative abilities, whereas human concepts research focuses on internal mental structures. We also argue that discrimination data alone leaves the category that the animal has learned underdetermined.

Chatterjee, Amitava. Aggressiveness, Competition and Human Unity. *Darshana Int*, 32(2/126), 69-76, Ap 92.

It has been observed that aggressiveness is the *raison d'etre* for wanton violence and destruction in human society since pre-historic days to modern civilized century. From physical evolutionary point of view it has been concluded that aggressiveness being an inherent instinct can be kept under control but can never be completely cured. However, the metaphysical concept of evolution suggests that by human effort aggressiveness can be channelised to competition, an acquired instinct of lesser destructive mode. Competition, through its positive re-direction to an aspiring motive for joy and love and beauty will act as the implicit force for transforming human vital instinct of survival by fight and divisiveness to self-fulfilling joy of cooperation and unity.

Chaudhury, Mahasweta. Objective Knowledge and Psychologism. *J Indian Counc Phil Res*, 12(1), 1-27, S-D 94.

Popper has often mentioned "psychologism" in connection with empiricist theory of knowledge. He denounces (like Kant) psychologistic theories because they fall short of the requirements of knowledge, although he holds (unlike Kant) that knowledge can never be justified. I shall argue that although the alleged trace of 'psychodogism' found in Popper's own philosophy can be explained in various ways, psycholgism in a certain sense is not incompatible with an objective theory of knowledge. In fact, the 'information processing' model of knowledge involves a kind of 'psychologism' in the Popperian sense but is an adequate theory of knowledge which also endorses Popper's own view.

Chaves, Ernani. Myth and Politics: Notes on the Concept of Destiny in the "Young" Benjamin (in Portuguese). *Trans/Form/Acao*, 17, 15-30, 1994.

The concept of myth is one of the keys to understand the thought of Walter Benjamin. The aim of this paper is to follow its genesis from the first formulations of the concept of "destiny", as presented in Destiny and Character, written in 1919. The present paper is divided in two parts. The first reconstructs Benjamin's arguments, showing them to be within the domain of the theory of rights and their necessary insertion in a "temporality" mode, defined by "repetition"; the second part attempts to demonstrate that Benjamin's positions were closely linked to a political stand: their aim was, in name of an avowed anarchism, to fight against all nationalist "myths" (that brought Germany to war) and the need of "leaders" (Führer) for the people. Examples of this political bias, based on Benjamin's confrontation with Zionism, are presented.

Chaves-Tannús, Marcio. A Teoria da Predicaçao de Pierre Abélard e a Semântica da Frase de Peter Von Polenz: Uma Tentativa de Aproximaçao. *Educ Filosof*, 8(16), 229-237, Jl-D 94.

The purpose of this paper is to suggest that some aspects and findings in Abélard's predication theory are not only useful today but are also significant for contemporary logic and linguistic investigations of the semantics of the sentence. A representative sample of such aspects and findings is the author's conceptions of the verb "be" when it functions as copula. The examples presented throughout this study reveal that there are similarities between his point of view and those of contemporary logic followed by Polenz. Additionally, Abélard's work presents perspectives that could lead to further research.

Chávez-Arvizo, Enrique. El Principio de Causalidad en la *Tercera* Meditación. *Sapientia*, 49(193-4), 357-364, 1994.

This article provides a detailed examination of Descartes' general causal maxim which appears in the Third Meditation, namely, 'there must be as much in the cause as in the effect'. It argues that the maxim should be interpreted as 'there must be as much "reality" in the cause as in the effect' as opposed to 'there must be as much "of any particular property" in the cause as in the effect'.

Chbat, Joseph. Évoluer en Enseignant la Philosophie. *Philosopher*, 15, 189-208, 1994.

Cheetham, Mark A. "Moments of Discipline" in *Intersections: Nineteenth-Century Philosophy and Contemporary Theory, Rajan, Tilottama (ed)*, 349-362. Albany, SUNY Pr, 1995.

Chekola, Mark. "Outing, Truth-Telling, and the Shame of the Closet" in *Gay Ethics, Murphy, Timothy F (ed)*, 67-90. New York, Haworth Pr, 1994.

This essay examines the nature of being in the closet, coming out, and the practice of outing. It is argued that no general rule against outing can be maintained since outing others may be defensible as one pursues one's own legitimate legal and moral interests. Neither does privacy extend to all aspects of human life which someone may wish to keep secret, especially if information about sexual orientation is not obtained in any immoral way. Withholding information about sexual orientation may sometimes by justified but on grounds of secrecy and not in a way that always forbids outing. The shame and degradation of the closet are evils, but outing is not necessarily their solution, though any loss of "privacy" entailed by coming out of the closet can be more than compensated by the rewards of casting off implications of worthlessness.

Chen, Ellen M. *The Tao Te Ching: A New Translation with Commentary*. New York, Paragon House, 1989.

Chenet, François. La notion de Samskara. *Rev Phil Fr*, 2, 203-216, Ap-Je 94.

Cheng, Jiewei. Derrida and Ideographic Poetics. *Brit J Aes*, 35(2), 134-144, Ap 95.

Cherwitz, Richard A and Darwin, Thomas J. Beyond Reductionism in Rhetorical Theories of Meaning. *Phil Rhet*, 27(4), 313-329, 1994.

Cherwitz, Richard A and Darwin, Thomas J. Toward a Relational Theory of Meaning. *Phil Rhet*, 28(1), 17-29, Ja 95.

Chestanov, Ruslan Z. Transzendentale Phänomenologie und das Problem der Geschichte. *Deut Z Phil*, 43(1), 75-88, 1995.

Chethimattam, J B. A Philosophical Approach to the Ecological Crisis. *J Dharma*, 20(1), 17-25, Ja-Mr 95.

Today no one questions the fact that our earth's ecological system is in real crisis. The nonrenewable resources of nature are running out at a fast pace. We can fully agree with the statement that the present ecological crisis is mostly due to man's ignorance, greed, aggression, and arrogance, and that an inadequate understanding of the natural world and its laws is the potent cause of the environmental disaster. The only way open to us is to educate people on the root causes of the present rape of nature, so that they will change their attitudes and habits before it is too late. (edited)

Chevalier, Jean-Claude. "Le discours linguistique: Etude comparée de textes" in *Rhétoriques de la science, De Coorebyter, Vincent (ed)*, 211-230. Paris, Pr Univ France, 1994.

Chevalley, Catherine. Física Cuántica y Filosofía. *Rev Filosof (Spain)*, 7(12), 477-492, 1994.

Chichin, Eileen R and Olson, Ellen. An Ethics Consult Team in Geriatric Long-Term Care. *Cambridge Quart Healthcare Ethics*, 4(2), 178-185, Spr 95.

Chico, Gabriel. El Futuro Requiere de Pasado (Nota Para Una Hermenéutica de la Narración Histórica). *Analogia*, 5(2), 65-73, 1991.

Chierchia, Gennaro. "Individual-Level Predicates as Inherent Generics" in *The Generic Book, Carlson, Gregory N (ed)*, 176-223. Chicago, Univ of Chicago Pr, 1995.

This paper concerns the difference between predicates that express episodic properties of individuals, like *be on the roof*, (known in the literature as "stage-level predicates") and predicates that express tendentially stable properties, like *be tall* (known as "individual-level predicates"). It is argued that individual level predicates must have in their argument structure a generic operator, and in this sense they genericity built in from the start. Specific assumptions on the semantics and syntax of genericity are made. All the many grammatical features that differentiate stage-level predicates from individual-level ones are argued to be reduceable to this single difference in their argument structure.

Chierchia, Gennaro. *Dynamics of Meaning: Anaphora, Presupposition, and the Theory of Grammar*. Chicago, Univ of Chicago Pr, 1995.

Chiereghin, Franco. "Der griechische Anfang Europas und die Frage der Romanitas" in *Europa und die Philosophie, Gander, Hans-Helmuth (ed)*, 197-223. Frankfurt/M, Klostermann, 1993.

Heidegger's severe opinion on "Romanitas" is known. He considered it as responsible for the weakening of the original capacity of conveying meaning of the Greek words once translated in the Latin language. A more attentive cultural historical consideration of the origin of some key-words of "Romanitas" (such as *pietas, fides, religio*) could have enabled Heidegger to discover unexpected affinities with the most authentic roots of his thought.

Chihara, Charles S. "The Howson-Urbach Proofs of Bayesian Principles" in *Probability and Conditionals, Eells, Ellery (ed)*, 161-178. New York, Cambridge Univ Pr, 1994.

In their book *Scientific Reasoning*, C Howson and P Urbach claim to demonstrate the fundamental principles of Bayesianism. In this paper, I examine their "proof" of the Bayesian thesis that an agent's degrees of belief ought to be *coherent*. I also analyze their attempted proof of the *Principle of Conditionalization*. I conclude that neither of these "proofs" are successful.

Chihara, Charles S. The Many Persons Problem. *Phil Stud*, 76(1), 45-49, O 94.

In "Identity, Essence, and Indiscernibility", Stephen Yablo adopts a "two-thing" position regarding the puzzle of the statue and the lump of clay. Yablo is then driven to postulate an infinity of distinct entities occupying exactly the same portion of space-time. This paper concerns the problem that arises when Yablo's position is carried over to the case of persons. According to Yablo's views, there are infinitely many distinct things that occupy exactly the space-time region that I occupy. Now which of these infinitely many things is the one that is identical to me?"

Child, Mark (& others). Autonomy or Heteronomy? Levinas's Challenge to Modernism and Postmodernism. *Educ Theor*, 45(2), 167-189, Spr 95.

Ching, Julia. Living in Two Worlds: A Personal Appraisal. *Sophia (Australia)*, 34(1), 188-203, Mr-Ap 95.

Chinn, Clark A and Brewer, William F. Scientists' Responses to Anomalous Data: Evidence from Psychology, History, and Philosophy of Science. *Proc Phil Sci Ass*, 1, 304-313, 1994.

This paper presents an analysis of the forms of response that scientists make when confronted with anomalous data. We postulate that there are seven ways in which an individual who currently holds a theory can respond to anomalous data: 1) ignore the data; 2) reject the data; 3) exclude the data from the domain of the current theory; 4) hold the data in abeyance; 5) reinterpret the data; 6) make peripheral changes to the current theory; or 7) change the theory. We analyze psychological experiments and cases from the history of science to support this proposal. Implications for the philosophy of science are discussed.

Chitarin, Luigi. M Heidegger (e U Eco) contro la definizione di uomo come animale razionale. *Aquinas*, 37(2), 433-450, My-Ag 94.

Chitas, Eduardo. "Notizen über eine Erfahrung: Der Weg zum Marxismus" in *Das geistige Erbe Europas, Buhr, Manfred (ed)*, 159-164. Napoli, Vivarium, 1994.

Chittleborough, P and Newman, M E. Defining the Term "Argument". *Inform Log*, 15(3), 189-207, Fall 93.

Informal logic has expanded the concept of an 'argument' beyond that presented traditionally by formal logicians—to include arguments as encountered in 'real-life'. Existent definitions of argument structure are argued to be inadequate by failing to fully recognize that, ultimately, arguments have a human source. Accordingly, a new definition is proposed which appeals to relevant cognitive and behavioral factors. The definition retains some traditional concepts, but introduces the term 'supportive' as a modification to 'premiss'. The concept of a 'persuader' is also developed. The definition is argued to capture more fully the intricacies, subtleties and rich diversity of informal arguments.

Cho, Kah Kyung. "Der Abstieg über den Humanismus: West-Östliche Wege im Denken Heideggers" in *Europa und die Philosophie, Gander, Hans-Helmuth (ed)*, 143-174. Frankfurt/M, Klostermann, 1993.

Heidegger's hint at proximity of his thought to East Asian tradition is in garbled language and precious little of it is in print. The author articulates the true extent of Heidegger's encounter with Lao Tzu by interpreting three events around 1946 coherently, when *Letter on Humanism* suggested "mysterious rapports with the East", *Der Spruch des Anaximander* groped beyond the Occidental bounds for "a more pristine origin" of the history of Being, and Heidegger privately translated passages of *Tao Te Ching* with the help of Paul Hsiao. The experience of the basic word *Way* emerged as pointing to such common origin.

Cho, Stephen Wagner. Before Nietzsche: Nihilism as a Critique of German Idealism. *Grad Fac Phil J*, 18(1), 205-232, 1995.

The concept of nihilism first enters the broader philosophical discussion in Europe toward the end of the eighteenth century as a critique of German idealism, above all of Kant and Fichte. Although fundamental scholarship on this early history has long been available in German, it has remained largely neglected by discussions of nihilism in English. The article seeks to address this crucial gap by tracing the early philosophical development of nihilism in the works of 1) Obereit, 2) Jenisch, 3) Jacobi, and 4) Fichte, Hegel, Schelling. It is derived from a larger study, *The Historical Origins of Nihilism before Nietzsche* (Edwin Mellen, forthcoming).

Choi, Jung Min and Callaghan, Karen A and Murphy, John W. *The Politics of Culture: Race, Violence, and Democracy*. Westport, Praeger, 1995.

The protests in Los Angeles during the spring of 1992 signaled that the United States is a troubled society. Specifically, although American society is becoming increasingly diverse, many people are not close to experiencing democracy. Certain powerful interests constrict the American policy in very important ways. Clearly stated, conservatives have manipulated symbols and other cultural factors to maintain social control. Postmodernism exposes the limitations of the conservative project while introducing a new mode of order conducive to sustaining a democratic society.

Chomsky, Noam. Language and Nature. *Mind*, 104(413), 1-61, Ja 95.

Chopp, Rebecca S. "Feminist Queries and Metaphysical Musings" in *Rethinking Metaphysics, Jones, L Gregory (ed)*, 47-63. Cambridge, Blackwell, 1995.

Chopp, Rebecca S. Feminist Queries and Metaphysical Musings. *Mod Theol*, 11(1), 47-63, Ja 95.

Chopra, Y N. Mill's Principle of Liberty. *Philosophy*, 69(270), 417-441, O 94.

Mill intended his *Essay* to be read as a self-contained work. In this paper the Principle of Liberty propounded by him in it is examined autarchically while seeking to by-pass the question whether in arguing his case he successfully preserved his Utilitarian commitments. Mill's failure to take into account the relevance of the personal in any defense of liberty is the principle weakness of the *Essay*. Therefore although he rightly treated protection against harm by others as his central notion he failed to recognize the important conceptual limits this implied on societal intervention to provide protection against harm. When due importance is given to this notion Mill's use of the distinction between advanced societies and others to justify restricting the scope of his Principle to the former loses its justification.

Chopra, Y N. The Significance of Professor Matilal's *Logical Illumination of Indian Mysticism* in His Studies of Indian Philosophy. *J Indian Counc Phil Res*, 12(1), 79-105, S-D 94.

Choudhary, A K and Singh, D. A Note on the Relevance of Relevance Implication. *J Indian Counc Phil Res*, 11(2), 113-118, Ja-Ap 94.

The paper attempts to counteract a number of explications presented in defense of material implication. It argues that opinions like 'inferentially harmless', 'pernicious' and the like do not apply to material implication. It advances the argument that exploiting the intentional dimension would remain an undiminable premise underlying any genuine attempt at comprehending the relation of implication. The seminal idea of the paper is, relevance requires that as disjunctions and negated conjunctions are instinctively intentional, they need to be represented by intentional connectives.

Chowdhury, Ambar and Pillay, Anand. On the Number of Models of Uncountable Theories. *J Sym Log*, 59(4), 1285-1300, D 94.

The main result established in this paper is that if T is a complete first-order theory which is uncountable, then T has infinitely many pairwise nonisomorphic models having the same cardinality as T.

Chowers, Eyal. Disciplining the 'Personality': Self and Social Critique in Max Weber's Work. *Hist Polit Thought*, 15(3), 447-460, Autumn 94.

Choza, Jacinto. La Dualidad Personal: Autor y Actor. *Themata*, 13, 97-120, 1995.

Personal duality: Author and actor. 1) The first inhabitants of the Self. 2) The witness of the consciousness. I am we. 3) Threshold of lying and truth of one self. 4) Prejudices of judgments. The natural law and the feigned person.

Chrisley, Ronald L. Why Everything Doesn't Realize Every Computation. *Mind Mach*, 4(4), 403-420, N 94.

Some have suggested that there is no fact to the matter as to whether or not a particular physical system realizes a particular computational description. This suggestion has been taken to imply that computational states are not "real", and cannot, for example, provide a foundation for the cognitive sciences. In particular, Putnam has argued that every ordinary open physical system realizes every abstract finite automaton, implying that the fact that a particular computational characterization applies to a physical system does not tell one *anything* about the nature of that system. Putnam's argument is scrutinized, and found inadequate because, among other things, it employs a notion of causation that is too weak. I argue that if one's view of computation involves embeddedness (inputs and outputs) and full causality, one can avoid the universal realizability results. Therefore, the fact that a particular system realizes a particular automaton is not a vacuous one, and is often explanatory. Furthermore, I claim that computation would not necessarily be an explanatorily vacuous notion even if it were universally realizable.

Chrisman, James J and Bruton, Garry D. The Professional Ethics of the Academic Consultant. *Prof Ethics*, 3(1), 89-102, Spr 94.

This article addresses three primary ethical issues that face academic consultants: objective analysis of data; fiduciary responsibilities, and responsibility to society. We illustrate the complexities and interrelationships among these issues and argue that the objectivity of the academic consultant should be the highest priority. Next the academic consultant, in the role of an agent must emphasize their fiduciary responsibilities to the firm. Finally, the academic's perception of social responsibility should be addressed.

Christensen, David. Conservatism in Epistemology. *Nous*, 28(1), 69-89, Mr 94.

A wide range of prominent epistemological theories include a principle of conservatism. Such principles take the face that an agent currently holds a certain belief to constitute at least some measure of epistemic justification for her to maintain that belief. I examine the main arguments that have been made in conservatism's behalf, and find them unsound. Most interestingly, conservatism does not fall out of confirmational holism (the view that the justification of each of our beliefs is in part determined by our other beliefs). I argue that conservatism is a mild form of dogmatism, and should be abandoned.

Christensen, David. Nozick's *The Nature of Rationality*. *Nous*, 29(2), 259-274, Je 95.

This study examines several key suggestions made in Nozick's provocative book. It argues that the book's decision-theoretic proposal to accommodate divergent intuitions in Newcomb's problem by weighting both causal *and* epistemic expected utilities is not well motivated. The study reflects the proposed addition to decision theory of a special dimension representing *symbolic* utility, arguing that the symbolic values of acts are already captured in standard decision theory. It also criticizes the book's new probabilistic measure of explanatory support, and finds unpersuasive the book's proposal for making the pragmatic value of holding belief a key determinant of the belief's rationality.

Christiano, Thomas. Democratic Equality and the Problem of Persistent Minorities. *Phil Papers*, 23(3), 169-190, N 94.

Christie, John. The Social Standing of Science: Some Contemporary History. *Hist Human Sci*, 8(2), 103-108, My 95.

Christie, Maureen. Philosophers versus Chemists Concerning 'Laws of Nature'. *Stud Hist Phil Sci*, 25(4), 613-629, Ag 94.

The law of definite proportions and the law of multiple proportions are two of the important laws of chemistry associated with the development of the atomic theory in the early nineteenth century. A detailed study of these laws shows that they have characters which cannot be reconciled with philosophers' accounts of laws of nature. They are nonuniversal, and one of them is imprecise. Philosophers have approached an account of laws of nature by trying to fit their character to a particular model. Contrary to standard accounts, laws of nature are a diverse group of dicta, of widely varying character. Unlike philosophers, chemists have recognized this diversity for at least a hundred years. The analysis will show that *some* laws are approximations, while others are exact; and that some laws are purely formal, but not all of them. But on a more revolutionary note, it will also show that many quite respectable laws of science are nonuniversal, and even that there are a few that cannot be formulated as precise propositions. (edited)

Christman, John P. Distributive Justice and the Complex Structure of Ownership. *Phil Pub Affairs*, 23(3), 225-250, Sum 94.

In most discussions of distributive justice, ownership is either viewed as a monolithic bundle of rights that must be held together if ownership is recognized at all, or it is viewed as a package that can be disaggregated into its components, each of which can be allocated or traded separately. In this article I put aside both these views and present an alternative model of ownership, one where the different functions of ownership are analyzed. I claim that rights to control the asset and rights to trade and gain income from it protect different social and personal interests and therefore should be kept separate in any analysis of the proper structure of ownership in a just society.

Christofidou, Andrea. First Person: The Demand for Identification-Free Self-Reference. *J Phil*, 92(4), 223-234, Ap 95.

I defend an irreducibility account of "I"-thoughts as developed by Evans and McDowell, arguing that first-person reference is direct yet consistent with the Fregean conception of sense and reference: it is the sense of "I" which is behind the phenomenology of the first person. I consider whether a neo-Lockean analysis for first-person thoughts, which depends upon the idea that self-reference is meditated by a description, can be sustained. I conclude that such an analysis fails to accommodate the motivational role of "I"-thoughts, and leads to the loss of immunity to error through misidentification.

Chukwuelobe, Matthew C. Language and Igbo Philosophy: Towards an Igbo Phenomenology of Language. *Phil Today*, 39(1), 25-30, Spr 95.

Church, Alonzo. A Revised Formulation of the Logic of Sense and Denotation: Alternative (1). *Nous*, 27(2), 141-157, Je 93.

Churchill, Ward. "Perversions of Justice: Examining the Doctrine of U.S. Rights to Occupancy in North America" in *Radical Philosophy of Law, Caudill, David S (ed)*, 200-220. Atlantic Highlands, Humanities Pr, 1995.

The essay explores basis of U S claims to possession of legal title over its North American landbase. Beginning with an articulation of the principles of Discovery Doctrine and its subset, the Rights of Conquest, the manner in which Chief Justice of the Supreme Court John Marshall inverted these elements of the international legal system through a series of opinions during the first third of the nineteenth century (*Peck, Johnson, Worcester, Cherokee*) to arrive at a "legal" predication for U S conquest and colonization of American Indian territories. From there, the evolution of "American Indian Law" in the United States—a doctrine built on foundations of sand—is traced through the present moment.

Churchland, P S and Ramachandran, V S. "Filling In: Why Dennett is Wrong" in *Dennett and his Critics, Dahlbom, Bo (ed)*, 28-52. Cambridge, Blackwell, 1995.

Churchland, Patricia S and Churchland, Paul M. "Intertheoretic Reduction: A Neuroscientist's Field Guide" in *The Mind-Body Problem: A Guide to the Current Debate, Warner, Richard (ed)*, 41-54. Cambridge, Blackwell, 1994.

Churchland, Paul M. *The Engine of Reason, the Seat of the Soul: A Philosophical Journey into the Brain*. Cambridge, MIT Pr, 1995.

Churchland, Paul M and Churchland, Patricia S. "Intertheoretic Reduction: A Neuroscientist's Field Guide" in *The Mind-Body Problem: A Guide to the Current Debate, Warner, Richard (ed)*, 41-54. Cambridge, Blackwell, 1994.

Chytry, Josef. Review Essay: Robert B Pippin's *Modernism as a Philosophical Problem*. *Hist Theor*, 34(1), 106-121, 1995.

Cibulka, Josef. The Hermeneutics of the Emerging of Being (On Figal's Interpretation of Heidegger). *Filozof Cas*, 42(4), 583-597, 1994.

Das erste Kapitel der vorliegenden Studie thematisiert eine bestimmte Spannung zwischen zwei Momenten des Selbstzeigens des Seins bei Heidegger: Wir müssen das, was sich zeigt, so wie es sich von ihm selbst her zeigt, von ihm selbst her sehen lassen. Zugleich aber müssen wir das Gegenteil der Naivität eines zufälligen, unmittelbaren und unbedachten Schauens gelangen und mit Hilfe der fundamentalontologischen philosophischen Theorie das Dasein aus seiner Verdecktheit in der Dimension des Besorgens herausreissen, um sein authentisches Sein zurückzugewinnen. Das zweite Kapitel *Die Destruktion des Nichtauthentischen und die Optik der Möglichkeit* versucht das Motiv einer "Möglichkeit als Möglichkeit", einer Unbestimmtheit des entstehenden Seins zu etablieren. Das Dritte Kapitel beschreibt die zentrale Idee des Buches von Günter Figal: Um den Charakter einer "Möglichkeit als Möglichkeit" zu restituieren, ist Figal bestrebt unsere entworfene Projekte "zurückzuhmen", diese Projekte in ihre ursprüngliche Dimension einer Antwort auf die entsthenden Möglichkeiten zurückzubringen. (edited)

Cicenia, Salvatore. The Foundational Problems of Geometry in N I Lobacevskij's Thought (in Italian). *Epistemologia*, 17(1), 13-33, Ja-Je 94.

The importance of Lobacevskij's geometry not only consists in the solution of the ancient problem of parallel straight lines, but in the original contribute Lobacevskij gives to the foundational problems of geometry too. The Russian geometer rejects the Platonic aspects of Euclidean geometry and the metaphysics of ruler and compasses, which characterized the Euclidean geometrical tradition, and founds his geometry from an empirical point of view. The Lobacevskijan geometry is not based on axioms; particularly, his Untersuchungen Geometrishe zur Theorie der Parallelilien (1840) is based on the problem of how many parallel straight lines there are through a point to a given straight line. (edited)

Cicovacki, Predrag. Locke on Personal Identity. *Locke News*, 22, 57-70, 1991.

Cicovacki, Predrag. On the Normative Aspect of Concepts as Rules: An Essay on Kant's Transcendental Deduction. *Ideal Stud*, 25(1), 25-49, Wint 95.

The author reconstructs and defends the conclusion of the transcendental deduction in terms of Kant's understanding of concepts as rules. Kant's claim that categories are not arbitrary rules is defended by comparing categories with Searle's constitutive rules. By means of categories we construct cognizable properties for items of perceptual encounters; they must conform to categories because only by means of the application of categories can any of them become an object of cognition. The role of constitutive rules proves the legitimate right of categories to be employed in cognition.

Cifuentes, Carlos Llano. La idea práctica en la acción práctica. *Topicos*, 3(4), 61-84, 1993.

The author tries to recover the practice validity of Aristotelic philosophy, making emphasis in the study of formalism of the exemplar idea and in the inadequate use of analogy.

Ciglia, Francesco Paolo. Libertà umana e dono ontologico: La penultima filosofia di Luigi Pareyson. *Filosofia*, 45(2), 177-216, My-Ag 94.

Cintioli, P and Tulipani, S. -Completeness of a Fragment of the Theory of Trees with Subtree Relation. *Notre Dame J Form Log*, 35(3), 426-432, Sum 94.

Ciomos, Virgil. Philosophia Perennis: Anton Dumitriu (1905-1992). *Arch Phil*, 57(4), 693-698, O-D 94.

Cipra, Marijan. Der Gott der Philosophie: Mein Mit Lesen eines Buches in zwei Bänden. *Filozof Istraz*, 13(4), 911-916, 1993.

Anhand der Lektüre von Wilhelm Weischedels Buch *Der Gott der Philosophen* betrachtet der Verfasser in seiner Arbeit auf einzigartige Weise eine der grundlegenden philosophischen Fragen—die Frage nach Gott. Wahrhaftiges Philosophieren, so der Autor, kann tatsächlich nur Gott gewidmet sein. Den einen und ewigen Gott erahnte die Philosophie, noch bevor das Christentum in Erscheinung trat, noch vor der Verkörperung des göttlichen Logos. Der Verfasser erstellt einen Aufriss der Gottesauffassungen in den verschiedenen Geschichtsepochen—vom antiken Griechenland über das alte Judentum, das lateinische Mittelalter und die Renaissance bis zur Apokalipse des Endes des 20. Jahrhunderts. Als Lösung wird das "Manifest einer Philosophie des Ganzen", eine universale Synthese angeboten. Wahr ist, was notwendig *ist*. Solange der Teufel als reine Potenz und als schlechte Endlosigkeit, von Sein und Wesen losgerissen und abgesondert, bezeichnet wird, gilt: *Wahrheit, Sein* (kroat. bitak), *Sein* (kroat. biti) *ist*—ist *ein* und *dasselbe*. Der Verfasser gibt Antwort auf Kants "3+1" Frage (für die Philosophie) und kommt zum Schluss, dass "der Mensch... der neuzeitliche, faustische Mensch ist—eine Marionette in den Händen Satans". Es gibt aber einen Ausweg. Die Philosophie muss zur Philotheosophie und Ontotheosophie werden. In Ermangelung einer solchen Weisheit gibt es jedoch auch augenblickliche Hilfe. Diese befindet sich in der *Kirche*, u.zw. in der *Katholischen Kirche*. Mit ihrer Hilfe ist der Erde und der Menschheit die wahrhaftige *Auferstehung* gewiss.

Cirera, Ramon. *Carnap and the Vienna Circle: Empiricism and Logical Syntax*. Amsterdam, Rodopi, 1994.

This book follows the evolution of Carnap's thought during the period from the Aufbau to "Testability and Meaning", that is, the period during which Carnap worked or at least interacted frequently with the members of the Vienna Circle. The book discusses the influences on the Carnap of Schlick, Wittgenstein, Neurath and Popper, and sheds light on the transition from phenomenalism to physicalism and the syntactic point of view.

Ciria, Alberto. Fichte en 1804-1806: Arrebato y Entrega. *Themata*, 13, 121-155, 1995.

Fichte's mind since 1804 till 1806 is analyzed. In this period, after six years of silence, he wrote four words, strongly related one to other: *Die Wissenschaftslehre 1804* and three series of lectures. We attend to the notion of being raged (*Ergriffenheit*) and surrender. The notion of representation meant the subject refers to Nature unifying it, in such a way that this unicity is constitutive of its own interiority. And it means the unity of Man is granted to Nature and, at the same time, is acknowledged in it. What the subject makes with Nature in this act of contemplation is equivalent to what the Absolute makes with man in the act of appealing, call or range.

Ciriza, Alejandra. Feminismo y política en dos encrucijadas históricas: La modernidad madura. *Rev Filosof (Costa Rica)*, 32(77), 41-50, Jl 94.

This paper attempts to establish the articulation between feminism, as a theoretical and political discourse, and the constitution of women subject in two crossroads: mature modernity and it's crisis. Under the conditions of mature modernity feminist discourse interpolates women appealing to the collation between feminist emancipation and equality of rights and liberty. Modernity crisis would produce maladjustments on the inside of that discourse. We not only recover equality, but also difference.

Cirulis, Janis. Beniaminov Algebras Revised: One More Algebraic Version of First-Order Logic. *Bull Sec Log*, 23(4), 140-145, D 94.

Beniaminov algebras, a kind of algebras of finitary relations, arose in the abstract database theory. They have an elegant mathematical structure which differs, however, in several aspects from the structure of algebras traditionally studied in algebraic logic. The aim of this note is to show that a slightly restricted class of Beniaminov algebras is equivalent, as a category, to that of locally finite cylindric algebras (of a fixed infinite dimension).

Ciulla, Joanne B. Leadership Ethics: Mapping the Territory. *Bus Ethics Quart*, 5(1), 5-28, Ja 95.

In this paper I argue that a greater understanding of the part of ethics in leadership will improve leadership studies. Debates over the definition of leadership are really debates over what researchers think constitutes good leadership. The ultimate question is not "What is leadership?" but "What is good leadership?" The word *good* refers to both ethics and competence. Research into leadership ethics would explore the ethical issues of current leadership research, serve as a critical study of the field, analyze and expand normative theories of leadership, and develop new theories, research questions and ways of thinking about leadership.

Clack, Brian R. D Z Phillips, *Wittgenstein and Religion*. *Relig Stud*, 31(1), 111-120, Mr 95.

This is an article-length review of D Z Phillips's collection of essays *Wittgenstein and Religion*, focusing primarily on Phillips's accounts of magic and primitive religion and of those elements of ritual he labels 'superstitious'. It is argued that the distinction he draws between religion and superstition is unworkable and hides a prescriptive purpose. Contrasting Phillips's treatment of primitive religion with that of Wittgenstein, and by centering specifically on the scapegoat practice, it is further contended that Phillips fails adequately to apply Wittgenstein's insights concerning the nature and depth of ritual. Readers should consider Phillips's response to this review (*Relig Stud*, 31, 1, pp 121-127).

Cladis, Mark S. Education, Virtue and Democracy in the Work of Emile Durkheim. *J Moral Educ*, 24(1), 37-52, 1995.

A condition for a flourishing liberal society, I believe, is a public education similar to that recommended by Durkheim. Its heterogeneous character, embracing critical thought and shared traditions, autonomy and community, human diversity and social unity, provides a powerful support for and challenge to liberal, democratic institutions. Durkheim mingled standard liberal and communitarian values—values supporting individual rights and critical thought, on one hand, and values supporting the common good and tradition on the other. On my reading, Durkheim forged a middle way between liberalism and communitarianism, thereby rescuing us from the forced option that is often erected—defend "the individual" or protect "the community". He championed various authoritative perspectives from society's shared understanding as a means to cultivate, in students, dispositions for social criticism. Tradition and critical thought go hand in hand, in Durkheim's view, because social critics, faced with changing circumstances, draw deeply from their social inheritance as they forge new paths and criticize some old ones.

Claeys, Gregory (ed) and Thelwall, John. *The Politics of English Jacobinism: Writings of John Thelwall*. University Park, Penn St Univ Pr, 1995.

Clancy, Kate. Commentary—Social Justice and Sustainable Agriculture: Moving Beyond Theory. *Agr Human Values*, 11(4), 77-83, Fall 94.

One of the ongoing debates in the sustainable agriculture community is whether its platform should include social justice issues like farmworker rights, economic concentration, and hunger. The commentary describes the evolution of this controversy and places it in the context of competing and complicated moral theories that turn out to be of somewhat limited use in political arguments. The essay also outlines ways in which the present political climate is presenting a challenge to sustainable agriculture proponents, who, in response, are building new linkages with urban interests, including anti-hunger organizations. Despite abstract philosophical and more real political problems, a community food security agenda is being crafted, joining the interests of small farms, family farm, and sustainability advocates, and anti-hunger groups. Their focus is community and economic development as a way to improve the quality and availability of inner city food supplies, and to develop new markets and political allies for farmers.

Clark, Andy. "Connectionist Minds" in *Connectionism: Debates on Psychological Explanation, Macdonald, Cynthia (ed)*, 339-356. Cambridge, Blackwell, 1995.

If the mind turns out to be as connectionism paints it, could belief/desire explanation be undetermined? I analyse and reject one argument, by Ramsey, Stick, and Garon, which argues in favor of such a result.

Clark, Andy. Representational Trajectories in Connectionist Learning. *Mind Mach*, 4(3), 317-332, Ag 94.

The paper considers the problems involved in getting neural networks to learn about highly structured task domains. A central problem concerns the tendency of networks to learn only a set of shallow (nongeneralizable) representations for the task, i.e., to 'miss' the deep organizing features of the domain. Various solutions are examined, including task specific network configuration and incremental learning. The latter strategy is the more attractive, since it holds out the promise of task-independent solution to the problem. Once we see exactly how the solution works, however, it become clear that it is limited to a special class of cases in which 1) statistically driven undersampling is (luckily) equivalent to task decomposition, and 2) the dangers of unlearning are somehow being minimized. The technique is suggestive nonetheless, for a variety of developmental factors may yield the functional equivalent of both statistical AND 'informed' undersampling in early learning.

Clark, Andy and Toribio, Josefa. Doing without Representing?. *Synthese*, 101(3), 401-431, D 94.

Connectionism and classicism, it generally appears, have at least this much in common: both place some notion of internal representation at the heart of a scientific study of mind. In recent years, however, a much more radical view has gained increasing popularity. This view calls into question the commitment to internal representation itself. More strikingly still, this new wave of anti-representationalism is rooted not in 'armchair' theorizing but in practical attempts to model and understand intelligent, adaptive behavior. In this paper we first present, and then critically assess, a variety of recent anti-representationalist treatments. We suggest that so far, at least, the sceptical rhetoric outpaces both evidence and argument. Some probable causes of this premature scepticism are isolated. Nonetheless, the anti-representationalist challenge is shown to be both important and progressive insofar as it forces us to see beyond the bare representational/nonrepresentational dichotomy and to recognize instead a rich continuum of degrees and types of representationality.

Clark, Brad. How Religion Impedes Moral Development. *Free Inq*, 14(3), 23-25, Sum 94.

Clark, Charles R. Social Responsibility Ethics: Doing Right, Doing Good, Doing Well. *Ethics Behavior*, 3(3-4), 303-327, 1993.

The ethics of social responsibility is discussed in reference to six case vignettes drawn from forensic psychology. A definitional model of social responsibility is proposed, and two unequal components of the concept—respect for the individual and concern for social welfare—are identified. The sources of ethical conflict in regard to social responsibility are enumerated. Scholarly criticism of the value orientation of forensic psychology is reviewed, and forensic psychology is contrasted with social policy advocacy efforts made by organized psychology. The social responsibility obligations of psychologists in the microethical sphere, where their actions affect individuals, are differentiated from the obligations psychology has when operating in the macroethical sphere of social policy. The ethical problems inherent in policy advocacy brought about by individual psychologists working with individuals are underscored: the inevitable element of deception, the violation of role integrity, and the circumvention of social structures and institutions that safeguard the rights of individuals.

Clark, David L. "'The Necessary Heritage of Darkness'" in *Intersections: Nineteenth-Century Philosophy and Contemporary Theory, Rajan, Tilottama (ed)*, 79-146. Albany, SUNY Pr, 1995.

Clark, David L (ed) and Rajan, Tilottama (ed). *Intersections: Nineteenth-Century Philosophy and Contemporary Theory*. Albany, SUNY Pr, 1995.

This collection of essays defines "theory" as a field that emerges after Kant, and attempts to reconceive nineteenth-century and contemporary theory through each other. The collection thus looks at intersections between contemporary theory and a number of nineteenth-century thinkers: Hegel, Schelling, Nietzsche, Schopenhauer, Kierkegaard. Contributors include Tilottama Rajan, David Clark, John Sallis, Christopher Noris, Stanley Corngold, Judith Butler and others.

Clark, Kelly J. I Believe in God the Father, Almighty. *Int Phil Quart*, 35(1), 59-69, Mr 95.

The theist affirms God's paternal care and his unsurpassable ability. If God is Father, he is obliged to prevent harms in a manner similar to earthly fathers; but he has not. This essay refutes the claim that God has obligations closely analogous to those of earthly parents. The essay is a conceptual analysis of what the father/child relationship entails with respect to moral obligations and permissions. The dissimilarities between the divine and human parent create differences in obligation so great as to nullify judgments that the atheologian makes about what is to believe about the obligations and goodness of God.

Clark, Mary T. *Augustine*. Washington, Georgetown Univ Pr, 1994.

A comprehensive introduction to the main teachings of one of the most influential thinkers of all time, this book shows how Augustine developed his ideas in the search for harmony between faith and understanding, religion and philosophy. It presents Augustine's conclusions on central philosophical and theological issues with account taken of the most recently published scholarship and lately discovered letters. Intended for students and the general reader, it gives a chronology of Augustine's writings with the Latin editions and English translations indicated, and provides a sense of his writings as a whole.

Clark, Maudemarie. Nietzsche's Misogyny. *Int Stud Phil*, 26(3), 3-12, 1994.

Clark, Michael. Sacrificing One to Save Many. *J Applied Phil*, 12(2), 189-200, 1995.

Attempts to solve the Trolley Problem by means of a single principle have proved unpersuasive. Nor can the intuition about transplant be adequately grounded in the hypothetical dissent of rational contractors. It is explained by the initial liability principle, that loss should lie where it falls unless there is sufficient reason to shift it. If we did not think we should accept misfortune in such cases and thought that minimising loss of life was sufficient reason to shift the loss we should not be according others the minimum respect and treatment we feel is their due. The intuition about Trolley is explained by the affinity of that case to the pure case where the choice is between saving many and saving fewer, where minimising misfortune is the only credible option. But these considerations are not yet enough to accommodate the cases that lie between the extremes of Trolley and Transplant. We can handle the intermediate cases by attempting to assimilate them to one or other paradigm and to one another with a sensitivity to morally relevant and irrelevant differences that seeks initially to be faithful to the values reflected by our moral intuitions. Those intuitive judgements are unlikely to survive such an examination wholly unmodified.

Clark, Peter (ed) and Hale, Bob (ed). *Reading Putnam*. Cambridge, Blackwell, 1995.

The volume contains nine essays on major themes of Putnam's thought with a tenth chapter containing replies and comments by Putnam. The essays comprise: Simon Blackburn on internal realism; George Boolos on Peirce, Dedekind and Boole; Michael Dummett on Wittgenstein on Necessity; Michael Hallett on the model theoretic argument; Kevin Kelly, Cory Juhl and Clark Glymour on reliabilism; Michael Redhead on the Quantum Logic programme; Thomas Ricketts on Carnap and The Principle of Tolerance; David Wiggins on Natural Kinds and Crispin Wright on Putnam's Proof that we are not brains in a vat.

Clark, Stephen R L. "Enlarging the Community: Companion Animals" in *Introducing Applied Ethics, Almond, Brenda (ed)*, 318-330. Cambridge, Blackwell, 1995.

The better known relic of Stoicism is the thought that only rational beings deserve respect. Another strand founds moral judgment on natural sentiment. In the absence of good biological or metaphysical reasons to believe in clear species boundaries or specific essences, we can admit such sentiment, and personal attachment, as reasons to care for our companions (of whatever species) and the living world. The history of humanism is of betrayal; a return to the better sort of Stoicism would help us all.

Clark, Stephen R L. "Global Religion" in *Philosophy and the Natural Environment, Attfield, Robin (ed)*, 113-128. New York, Cambridge Univ Pr, 1994.

Only a 'religious spirit', a willed and eager commitment to a larger whole, can give us the strength to make the sacrifices and adjustments we must make to avoid ecological catastrophe. The question is: *which* spirit? I argue that we should blame our past errors on nothing more ideological than the wish to improve our lives. We do not need to abandon Judaic monotheism, nor adopt a romantic paganism of the sort currently fashionable amongst 'deep' environmentalists. Judaic monotheism, on the contrary, has the potential to alter our ways.

Clark, Stephen R L. Genetic and Other Engineering. *J Applied Phil*, 11(2), 233-237, 1994.

A survey on some recent work on genetic engineering, especially of nonhuman animals, together with suggestions about the moral issues that are usually ignored in professional discussion. Philosophers are urged to take any ordinary proccupations more seriously: notably the integrity of nature, and the sacredness of actually existing forms.

Clarke, David D and Nerlich, Brigitte. Language, Action and Context: Linguistic Pragmatics in Europe and America. *J Prag*, 22(5), 439-463, N 94.

Pragmatics is considered to be a fairly recent addition to the sciences of language, dating back to the works of Austin, Searle and Grice. However, this apparently new approach to language has its roots in the philosophical, psychological and linguistic traditions of the past. This is true of all four approaches to pragmatics which one can distinguish in Europe and America: the Anglo-Saxon one which emerged from Ordinary Language Philosophy and which has dominated the field until the present; the French one which is based on the theory of enunciation elaborated by Benveniste; the German one which wants to study pragmatics as part of a general theory of action; and the American one of pragmatism. To varying degrees all these strands of thought are blind to their own history, and have cut themselves off from a wealth of ideas, developed during the 19th century, of how language and the mind work. In this article we want to give an overview of the evolution of these traditions and stimulate discussion among colleagues in all fields and disciplines which are based in one way or another on linguistic pragmatics.

Clarke, David S. Does Acceptance Entail Belief?. *Amer Phil Quart*, 31(2), 145-155, Ap 94.

This paper asserts the "entailment thesis" that to accept a proposition as true necessitates believing that it is true. This thesis is defended against arguments proposed by Stalnaker, Bratman, and L J Cohen. Stalnaker and Bratman appeal to the context relativity of acceptance, the fact that what we accept will vary with purposes for which the accepted proposition is to be used. I argue that they misdescribe situations that suggest independence of belief from acceptance, and propose alternative descriptions. Cohen appeals to scientific practice. I argue his objections to the entailment thesis can be accommodated by restricting the thesis to terminal acceptance, which is contrasted to provisional acceptance in science.

Clarke, Randolph. Doing What One Wants Less: A Reappraisal of the Law of Desire. *Pac Phil Quart*, 75(1), 1-11, Mr 94.

Many proponents of causal theories of action assert what I call the Law of Desire (LOD), roughly, the thesis that whenever an agent acts, she does what she most strongly desires (at that time) to do. I argue that LOD is not a necessary truth—it may be violated in both indeterministic and deterministic worlds—and that it is probably not contingently true. I conclude that a causal theory of action need not lose explanatory power should it turn out that LOD is false.

Clarke, Randolph. Freedom and Determinism. *Phil Books*, 36(1), 9-18, Ja 95.

This paper surveys work on free will and determinism from the mid-1980's to 1995. Topics covered include: whether the ability to do otherwise is compatible with determinism; what determinism is and whether it appears to be true; libertarian accounts of free will; compatibilist accounts of the freedom requisite for moral responsibility; and what the implications might be if we lack free will.

Clarke, Randolph. Indeterminism and Control. *Amer Phil Quart*, 32(2), 125-138, Ap 95.

Free will is often said to be not only compatible with determinism but dependent upon it. This paper examines a version of this thesis, viz., the claim that an agent's control over her behavior is diminished to the extent to which her actions are not causally determined by prior conditions that include her having certain desires and beliefs. The author argues that, on the contrary, indeterminism need not diminish to any extent an agent's control. By the same token, it is argued, indeterminism itself does not increase to any extent an agent's control over her behavior.

Clarke, Randolph. Toward a Credible Agent-Causal Account of Free Will. *Nous*, 27(2), 191-203, Je 93.

According to agent-causal accounts, when an agent acts with free will, the agent causes her action, and causation by the agent does not consist in causation by events. Such accounts face two main objections: they have failed to provide for the rationality and rational explicability of free actions, and they have failed to render the notion of agent causation intelligible. This paper argues that the first objection can be met by combining agent causation with universal, probabilistic event causation. Progress is made toward a solution to the second objection by appeal to realist or a nonreductionist account of causation.

Clarke, Stanley G. "Can Scientists Make Love?" in *The Nature and Pursuit of Love, Goicoechea, David (ed)*, 236-247. Buffalo, Prometheus, 1995.

Irving Singer suggests, in *The Nature of Love*, that scientists will provide a unified, comprehensive theory of love. This paper argues against this possibility. It does so in two stages. The first is to show that love is better understood as a process than as a state. Scientific theories, both psychological and social, are appropriately placed as applying to elements of this process. The second is to argue that this process, as a whole, is an historical one in which the language of love is partly constitutive of it. It follows that no unified theory of love is possible.

Clarke, Steve. The Lies Remain the Same: A Reply to Chalmers. *Austl J Phil*, 73(1), 152-155, Mr 95.

Alan Chalmers charges that Cartwright holds an apparently contradictory position in *Nature's Capacities and their Measurement*. I defend Cartwright against this charge. Against Chalmers I hold that it is possible to be both realist about nature's capacities and anti-realist about the fundamental laws of nature. This combination of views can be consistent when fundamental laws are read as licenses to export information about capacities from ideal, simple situations to complex, worldly ones.

Clarke, W Norris. *Explorations in Metaphysics: Being-God-Person*. Notre Dame, Univ Notre Dame Pr, 1995.

This is a collection of ten of the author's best known articles and essays over the last forty years, dealing with basic topics of metaphysics in the contemporary Thomistic tradition. Reworked in what the author describes as a "creative retrieval", sometimes even a "creative completion", of Aquinas's own seminal ideas. The content is not just a random collection, but moves systematically through the central areas of being, God, and person, dealing with: the starting point of metaphysics; action as the self-revelation of being; participation in being; analogy; substance-in-relation; the existence and immutability of God; the relation of person to being.

Clatterbaugh, Kenneth. Cartesian Causality, Explanation, and Divine Concurrence. *Hist Phil Quart*, 12(2), 195-207, Ap 95.

David Hume notes that Descartes "insinuates" the doctrine of occasionalism, although Descartes is wise enough not to "insist" upon it. This paper briefly reviews the grounds for Descartes's insinuations of occasionalism and explores, in more detail, why Descartes does not insist upon it. It is Descartes's very rich notion of 'cause' that seems to allow Descartes a way to deny occasionalism by saying that *both* God and created things collaborate in producing effects; that is, both occur as premises in scientific explanations. But, this solution only helps to make the insinuations of occasionalism in Descartes. Thus, Descartes does not insist on occasionalism because he does not see that he insinuates it.

Claussen, Detlev. "Nach Auschwitz kein Gedicht?: Ist Adornos Diktum übertrieben, überholt und widerlegt?" in *Nationalsozialismus und Moderne, Welzer, Harald (ed)*, 240-247. Tübingen, Ed Diskord, 1993.

Clay, Diskin. "The Origins of the Socratic Dialogue" in *The Socratic Movement, Vander Waerdt, Paul A (ed)*, 23-47. Ithaca, Cornell Univ Pr, 1994.

Clayton, Ellen Wright. The Dispersion of Genetic Technologies and the Law. *Hastings Center Rep*, 25(3), S13-S15, My-Je 95.

Clayton, John. "Religions and Rights: Local Values and Universal Declarations" in *Human Rights and Religious Values, An-Na'im, Abdullahi A (& other eds)*, 259-266. Grand Rapids, Eerdmans, 1995.

Cleary, Denis. Rosmini on Natural Law and Right. *Vera Lex*, 13(1-2), 6-10, 1993.

The article provides an outline of the views of Antonio Rosmini (1797-1855) on natural law and right(s), prefaced by a description of his teaching on knowledge. All knowledge is based ultimately on the objective light of being. Natural law, or moral law related to human nature, requires an act of will by which persons, rooted in the dignity of being, acknowledge what they know for what they know it to be. Within the ambit of natural law, right is constituted by persons having something proper to self, and by others who must respect this possession for what it is.

Cleary, John J. "Working Through Puzzles with Aristotle" in *The Crossroads of Norm and Nature, Sim, May (ed)*, 175-220. Lanham, Rowman & Littlefield, 1995.

With specific reference to Aristotle's discussion of the mode of being of mathematical objects in *Metaphysics* III and XIII, I argue that a complete dialectical inquiry in first philosophy has four stages: 1) statement of the aporia; 2) review of the difficulties; 3) elenchus or breaking the impasse; 4) euporia or resolution of the aporia. These stages constitute a single aporetic method of inquiry which fulfills Aristotle's criteria for an adequate dialectical proof; i.e., that all the difficulties associated with a problem are first reviewed and then resolved so as to preserve the truth of the most reputable opinions.

Cleland, Carol E. Effective Procedures and Computable Functions. *Mind Mach*, 5(1), 9-23, F 95.

Horsten and Roelants have raised a number of important questions about my analysis of effective procedures and my evaluation of the Church-Turing thesis. They suggest that, on my account, effective procedures cannot enter the mathematical world because they have a built-in component of causality, and, hence, that my arguments against the Church-Turing thesis miss the mark. Unfortunately, however, their reasoning is based upon a number of misunderstandings.

Clément, Catherine and O'Driscoll, Sally (trans) and Mahoney, Deirdre M (trans). *Syncope: The Philosophy of Rapture*. Minneapolis, Univ of Minn Pr, 1994.

Cleveland, Timothy. The Irony of Contingency and Solidarity. *Philosophy*, 70(272), 217-241, Ap 95.

The political philosophy of Richard Rorty and his figure of the liberal ironist is the subject of this critique. Can one embrace the contingencies which the ironist philosophy emphasizes without undermining liberalism? The tensions between the idea that truth is created and the demands of liberalism are especially unbearable and make a positive response dubious. Liberalism limits concessions to contingency.

Clifton, Robert. Independently Motivating the Kochen-Dieks Modal Interpretation of Quantum Mechanics. *Brit J Phil Sci*, 46(1), 33-57, Mr 95.

The distinguishing feature of 'modal' interpretations of quantum mechanics is their abandonment of the orthodox eigenstate-eigenvalue rule, which says that an observable possesses a definite value if and only if the system is in an eigenstate of that observable. Kochen's and Dieks's new biorthogonal decomposition rule for picking out which observables have definite values is designed specifically to overcome the chief problem generated by orthodoxy's rule, the measurement problem, while avoiding the no-hidden-variable theorems. Otherwise, their new rule seems completely *ad hoc*. The *ad hoc* charge can only be laid to rest if there is some way to give Kochen's and Dieks's rule for picking out which observables have definite values some independent motivation. And there is, or so I will argue here. Specifically, I shall show that theirs is the *only* rule able to save Schrödinger's cat from a fate worse than death, and sidestep the Bell-Kochen-Specker no-hidden-variables theorem, once we impose four independently natural conditions on such rules.

Clooney, Francis X. Religious Memory and the Pluralism of Readings: Reflections on Roberto de Nobili and the *Taittiriya Upanisad*. *Sophia (Australia)*, 34(1), 204-225, Mr-Ap 95.

Clotet, Joaquín. El modelo utilitarista en la construcción y desarrollo de la bioética. *Telos (Spain)*, 2(1), 101-124, Je 93.

This paper attempts to examine the contribution that the utilitarian model has furnished and continues to furnish to bioethics. Utilitarianism assists the growth of bioethics in two important topics: first, the issue of veracity or truth-telling, formerly discussed by the utilitarian moral philosopher Henry Sidgwick; and secondly, the sphere of sensibility as a moral threshold of living beings that regulates the use of animals in biomedical research. (edited)

Clotet, Joaquín. Identidad Personal y yo Moral en David Hume. *Telos (Spain)*, 3(2), 17-28, D 94.

The question of personal identity, treated in *A Treatise of Human Nature* (T), offers disconcerting positions because of their inconsistency. Can a writer who will concentrate an important part of Hume's philosophy on ethics doubt or not even take into account the self, subject of morality? The concept of identity offers the possibility of different meanings and this seems to allow for a solution. One of the possible meanings can be reached through a critique of the substance and of the functional dynamism of the perceptions. (edited)

Cloud, Dana L. "'Socialism of the Mind': The New Age of Post-Marxism" in *After Postmodernism, Simons, Herbert W (ed)*, 222-251. Newbury Park, Sage, 1994.

This essay constructs an analogy between the philosophical assumptions of the New Age spirituality-lifestyle movement and post-Marxist/poststructuralist political philosophy. An analysis of the writings of post-Marxist theorists alongside a critical reading of New Age texts shows that despite claims to radical, oppositional, and revolutionary import, poststructuralism's contributions to political theory and practice are undergirded by the same idealist/textualist, liberal humanist, and relativist assumptions as the New Age movement. To the extent that the New Age is obviously a conservative set of practices, the political philosophy of post-Marxism is also called into question.

Cloutier, Éric. La Disparité des Morales. *Philosopher*, 17, 237-249, 1995.

Cmorej, Pavel. Towards One Review from Two. *Filozof Cas*, 42(4), 661-672, 1994.

Coady, C A J. "Nationalism and Intervention" in *Introducing Applied Ethics, Almond, Brenda (ed)*, 272-285. Cambridge, Blackwell, 1995.

Coady, C A J. "Speaking of Ghosts" in *Socializing Epistemology: The Social Dimensions of Knowledge, Schmitt, Frederick (ed)*, 75-92. Lanham, Rowman & Littlefield, 1994.

Cobb Jr, John B. "The Origins of Process Theology" in *Meaning, Truth, and God, Rouner, Leroy (ed)*, 91-111. Notre Dame, Univ Notre Dame Pr, 1982.

The roots of process theology can be traced in two ways: through the philosophy of Alfred North Whitehead and through the socio-historical school at the University of Chicago Divinity School. The former points to the revolutionary changes in physics early in this century which led to Whitehead's complex, speculative cosmology. The latter developed into the radical empiricism of Henry Nelson Wieman and the rationalistic metaphysics of Charles Hartshorne. All these roots are naturalistic in distinction from both idealistic and supernaturalistic. All reject substance thinking and dualism.

Cocchiarella, Nino B. On Classes and Higher-Order Logic: A Critique of W V O Quine. *Phil Hist Sci*, 2(1), 23-50, Ap 93.

The problematic features of Quine's set theories NF and ML result from compressing the higher-order predicate logic of type theory into a first-order logic of membership, and can be resolved by turning to a second-order predicate logic with nominalized predicates as abstract singular terms. A modified Fregean position, called conceptual realism, is described in which the concepts (unsaturated cognitive structures) that predicates stand for are distinguished from the extensions (or intensions) that their nominalizations denote as abstract singular terms. Quine's view that conceptualism cannot account for impredicative concept-formation is rejected, and a holistic conceptual realism is compared with Quine's class Platonism.

Cocco, Giuseppe. I nessi Strutturali tra Metafisica e Teurgia im Giamblico. *Riv Filosof Neo-Scolas*, 87(1), 3-50, Ja-Mr 95.

Cockburn, David. Braine on the Mind. *Relig Stud*, 30(3), 343-351, S 94.

In his book *The Human Person* David Braine aims to restore the vision of us as living beings having mental and physical aspects. He appeals to the causal criterion of reality in defense of his claim that our ontology of 'human beings' is the *correct* one. But this appeal fails. He also argues that the person transcends the body, in a way which leaves room for personal survival of death, on the grounds that linguistic understanding is an activity which does not 'involve the body'. There is, however, no reading of this phrase which will yield his conclusion.

Cockburn, David. Responsibility and Necessity. *Philosophy*, 70(273), 409-427, Jl 95.

Is there a logical tension between necessity and responsibility? The idea of 'logical tension' suggested by Wittgenstein's later thought will lead us to ask: 'What is it seriously to think that a person was responsible for what happened?' We see this in a diverse range of reactions to people—as opposed to a supposed underlying judgement—on account of what they have done. On the other side, talk of 'causal necessity' has its sense within a context of a concern to predict and control events. This leads to a version of incompatabilism which is markedly different from familiar forms.

Code, Alan D. Vlastos on a Metaphysical Paradox. *Apeiron*, 26(3-4), 85-98, S-D 93.

This paper explores Gregory Vlastos's attribution to Plato of a theory of degrees of reality according to which the Form of F-ness is really real whereas its instances are less real in that they are both F and not F. Vlastos's interpretation combines two different and inconsistent conceptions of what it is for a sensible instance of a Form to be both F and not F: 1) failing to possess all of the defining features of an F it is *imperfectly* F; 2) combining the defining features of an F with those of its opposite it is *impurely* F.

Cofré, Juan O. La paradoja de la narración: de los actos de habla a los actos de conciencia. *Rev Filosof (Spain)*, 4(6), 311-333, 1991.

Cohen, Bradley. Patterns Lost: Indeterminacy and Dennett's Realism About Beliefs. *Pac Phil Quart*, 76(1), 17-31, Mr 95.

I examine Daniel C Dennett's "Real Patterns," his most recent comprehensive attempt to establish a 'mild' realism about beliefs. At the heart of that attempt is the claim that patterns of intentionality are real patterns, objectively there in the world to be missed or discovered. I argue that the notion of a *real* pattern is problematic. Even granting that notion in general, if we accept indeterminacy (as Dennett does), then a view of intentional patterns as patterns that are imposed upon—as opposed to discovered in—the world is compelling. Finally, even if there are real intentional patterns to be discovered, the reality of such patterns confers no ontological status upon beliefs.

Cohen, Cynthia B and McCloskey, Elizabeth Leibold. Private Bioethics Forums: Counterpoint to Government Bodies. *Kennedy Inst Ethics J*, 4(3), 283-289, S 94.

Cohen, Diana. Qué es eso de la Filosofía para niños?. *Rev Filosof (Argentina)*, 8(1-2), 85-89, N 93.

Cohen, Gerald A. The Limits of Contractual Equality: A Reply to Jacques Bidet. *Ratio Juris*, 8(1), 85-90, Mr 95.

According to Jacques Bidet, "w[e] can bring together what's true in Rawls with what's true in Marx. The condition of doing so is that we interpret the modern system of class domination as the subversion of the contractual relation affirmed by modern consciousness". I argue, against Bidet, that since modern consciousness is a consciousness that is able to endorse the institutions of the capitalist welfare state, modern consciousness goes beyond affirmation of the contractual relation, in an egalitarian direction. I also argue that Karl Marx was wrong when he claimed that, in the contract between the capitalist and the proletarian, the equality and freedom of the contractual relation are inverted, that the labour contract subverts the normative presuppositions of the contractual relation.

Cohen, L Jonathan. Some Steps Towards a General Theory of Relevance. *Synthese*, 101(2), 171-185, N 94.

The classical analysis of relevance in probabilistic terms does not fit legal, moral or conversational relevance, and, though analysis in terms of a psychological model may fit conversational relevance, it certainly does not fit legal, moral or evidential relevance. It is important to notice here that some sentences are ambiguous between conversational and nonconversational relevance. But, if and only if *R* is relevant to a question *Q*, *R* is a reason, though not necessarily a complete or conclusive reason, for accepting or rejecting something as an answer to *Q*. Reasons of this kind are governed by appropriate covering laws or principled probabilities and a number of questions thus arise about the relationship between relevance and certain formal-logical properties.

Cohen, Marsha H. Ethical Issues in Discharge Planning for Vulnerable Infants and Children. *Ethics Behavior*, 5(1), 1-13, 1995.

Discharge planning for vulnerable infants and children is a collaborative, interdisciplinary, decision-making activity that is grounded in the ethical complexities of clinical practice. Although it is a psychosocial intervention that frequently causes moral distress for professionals and has the potential to inflict harm on children and their families, the process has received little attention from ethicists. An ongoing study of the transition of technology-dependent children from hospital to home suggests that the ethical issues embedded in the discharge-planning process maybe concealed by dominant cultural values, institutional policies, clinical standards, historical precedents, and legal regulations.

Cohen, Martin. Nietzsche, Hebraism, Hellenism. *Int Stud Phil*, 26(3), 45-65, 1994.

Cohen, S Marc (ed) and Curd, Patricia (ed) and Reeve, C D C (ed). *Readings in Ancient Greek Philosophy: From Thales to Aristotle*. Indianapolis, Hackett, 1995.

Extensive selections from the most important philosophical texts of ancient Greece from the Presocratics through Aristotle. Includes introductions, headnotes, maps, a concordance to the Presocratic fragments, an Aristotle glossary, and many new translations. 1) Presocratics and Sophists: Thales, Anaximander, Anaximenes, Pythagoras, Philolaus, Xenophanes, Heraclitus, Parmenides, Anaxagoras, Empedocles, Zeno, Leucippus, Democritus, Melissus, Protagoras, Gorgias, Antiphon, Critias. 2) Plato's dialogues: Euthyphro, Apology, Crito, Protagoras, Gorgias, Meno, Phaedo, Symposium, Republic, Parmenides, Timaeus. 3) Aristotle's treatises: Categories, De Interpretatione, Topics, Posterior Analytics, Physics, Generation and Corruption, On the Heavens, Meteorologica, Parts of Animals, Metaphysics, De Anima, Nicomachean Ethics, Politics.

Cohen-Bacrie, Pierre. De l'Avenir de la Philosophie au Cégep ou de la Résolution Possible d'un Paradoxe. *Philosopher*, 14, 173-179, 1993.

Cohen-Bacrie, Pierre. Entretien avec Michel Tozzi. *Philosopher*, 15, 39-49, 1994.

Cohen-Bacrie, Pierre (& others). La Philosophie: Une Présence Essentielle. *Philosopher*, 14, 205-217, 1993.

Cohen-Halimi, Michèle. *L'anthropologia in nuce* de Kant et Hamann. *Rev Metaph Morale*, 99(3), 313-326, Jl-S 94.

A singular event—the appearance in 1764 of a so-called "savage man" in the forests of Königsberg—gave Kant and Hamann the opportunity to taste their points of view concerning the intelligibility of both naturality, and human factuality. This confrontation, which appeared in the *Political and Literary Gazette* of Königsberg in the form of two articles (translated here), goes rapidly over the anecdote to arrive at a parting of the ways—that of Hamann: the theological interpretation; and that of Kant (although still in germination) the application of experimental methodology to anthropology.

Coker, John C. Riding the Fiery Steed: *Von den Freuden-und Leidenschaften*. *Int Stud Phil*, 26(3), 117-135, 1994.

This essay offers an interpretation of the section, "On Enjoying and Suffering the Passions" ("*Von den Freuden-und Leidenschaften*") in Nietzsche's *Thus Spoke Zarathustra*. This interpretation is developed in critical response to Lester Hunt's interpretation in his *Nietzsche and the Origin of Virtue*. At issue is the nature of and relation between passion and virtue.

Colapietro, Vincent. "Tell Your Friend Giulliano...": Jamesian Enthusiasms and Peircean Reservations. *Trans Peirce Soc*, 30(4), 897-926, Fall 94.

This paper explores the debate among the Italian pragmatists (especially Papini, Prezzolini, and Calderoni) over the nature of pragmatism and ultimately of philosophy itself. It explores this debate in reference to both the first-generation American pragmatists Peirce and James *and* our own contemporary philosophical scene (for the questions and concerns so prominent in the first decade of this century are equally prominent in the last decade). Also, some attempt is made to contrast the different cultural contexts in which pragmatism was championed; and, in this connection, possible links between *pragmatismo* and *fascismo* are discussed.

Colapietro, Vincent. Toward a Fuller Recovery of Living Reason. *Trans Peirce Soc*, 31(1), 21-39, Wint 95.

This paper is a contribution to a "symposium" on John E Smith's *America's Philosophical Vision*. It is one of four papers addressed to interpretive and substantive philosophical issues connected with Smith's work. As part of this "symposium" Smith himself offers a detailed response to each paper. Colapietro's contribution focuses on Smith's highly suggestive notion of "living reason" (as distinct from—among other things—purely formal and also purely instrumental reason). After highlighting several key features of Smith's thought (above all, his interrelated notions of experience and rationality), Colapietro poses several questions concerning Smith's account of living reason and of closely allied topics (including concrete selfhood, to whom living reason is most properly ascribed, and ultimate importance, with which such reason is characteristically concerned).

Colapietro, Vincent M. "Immediacy, Opposition, and Mediation" in *Recovering Pragmatism's Voice, Langsdorf, Lenore (ed)*, 23-48. Albany, SUNY Pr, 1995.

This paper offers a sketch of a distinctively Peircean approach to human communication. It explores some of the principal ways in which Peirce's categories of firstness, secondness, and thirdness help us to see how immediacy, opposition (or alterity), and mediation are irreducible aspects of our communicative practices. Moreover, particular attention is paid to the similarities and differences between Peirce's emphasis on secondness and Derrida's celebration of *différance*.

Colbois, Sylvie and Perrinjaquet, Alain. "Recht zur Aufklärung und Sozialrechte—Zu J B Erhards Theorie der Menschenrechte" in *Das geistige Erbe Europas, Buhr, Manfred (ed)*, 558-572. Napoli, Vivarium, 1994.

Cole, Andrew J and Bavidge, Michael. "Is Psychopathy a Moral Concept?" in *Introducing Applied Ethics, Almond, Brenda (ed)*, 185-196. Cambridge, Blackwell, 1995.

The article examines the changing terminology associated with anti-social personality disorder which has proved unstable for both medical and philosophical reasons. A major objection to terms such as "psychopathy" is that they confuse moral and clinical considerations. However, disruptive anti-social behaviour inevitably evokes moral responses and can only be described in moral terms. This is as true within the clinic as it is outside, as the experience of psychiatrists shows. Psychopathy is a hybrid concept because the clinician cannot avoid taking up a position at which moral and clinical considerations intersect.

Cole, David. Thought and Qualia. *Mind Mach*, 4(3), 283-302, Ag 94.

I present a theory of the nature and basis of the conscious experience characteristic of occurent propositional attitudes: thinking this or that. As a preliminary I offer an extended criticism of Paul Schweizer's treatment of such consciousness as unexplained secondary qualities of neural events. I also attempt to rebut arguments against the possibility of functionalist account of conscious experience and qualia.

Cole, Eve Browning. Plotinus on the Souls of Beasts. *J Neoplatonic Stud*, 1(1), 63-90, Fall 92.

When we look closely at what Plotinus has to say about the differences between the souls of humans and of beasts, we uncover two contradictory pictures: according to one, humans are distinguished from other animals in the possession of higher-order cognitive capacities, and this distinction is stable and absolute. According to the other though, humans and animals have rather a lot in common, and the boundary between the human domain and the realm of the beasts is crossed over in at least two ways: 1) by humans whose moral failings have been so severe as to erode their humanity, rendering them beasts in human shape; and 2) by humans who are reincarnated in animal form, rendering them humans in the shapes of beasts. I trace this duality of view to Aristotle, in whose writings a similar duality can be found, and I attempt to resolve the contradiction. I also show exactly where in Plotinus' teachings Porphyry may have found a philosophical basis for vegetarianism.

Cole, Steven E. "Evading the Subject: The Poverty of Contingency Theory" in *After Postmodernism, Simons, Herbert W (ed)*, 38-57. Newbury Park, Sage, 1994.

Colella, E Paul. Giuseppe Prezzolini's Pragmatist Interlude: A Reply to Colapietro. *Trans Peirce Soc*, 30(4), 927-938, Fall 94.

This paper is a reply to Vincent Colapietro's commentary on my "Two Faces of Italian Pragmatism: The Prezzolini—Calderoni Debate, 1904-1905", both of which appear in this same issue of the *Transactions of the Charles S Peirce Society*). Several of the terms raised by Colapietro's commentary, especially as they pertain to the flaws resident in Prezzolini's radically creative interpretation of the Will to Believe are discussed at some length. In addition, this reply suggests a continuity between the pragmatism of Giuseppe Prezzolini and his later conversion to Crocean idealism. A brief discussion follows in which the weaknesses in his pragmatism, as Colapietro identifies them, are to some degree remedied as a result of this conversion.

Colella, E Paul. Two Faces of Italian Pragmatism: The Prezzolini-Calderoni Debate, 1904-1905. *Trans Peirce Soc*, 30(4), 861-896, Fall 94.

This paper explores a debate which took place in the pages of Leonardo during 1904 and 1905 on the nature of pragmatism. The authors, Mario Calderoni and Giuseppe Prezzolini, were members of the small circle of Florentine pragmatists whose "leader", Giovanni Papini, won effusive praise from William James. Claderoni defined pragmatism in terms of the centrality of Peirce's pragmatic maxim. Similarly, he understood its scope to reside within the narrower limits of the clarification of ideas. Prezzolini on the other hand, developed a militant version of the Will to Believe which had its roots in Bergson, Schiller and James. In his pragmatism, human creative power was raised to a quasi-divine level. The debate is followed with care and in the process, the variety that existed within Italian pragmatism—a variety barely suggested by James's account of it—is more fully revealed.

Coleman, Jules L. "Tort Liability and the Limits of Corrective Justice" in *In Harm's Way, Coleman, Jules L (ed)*, 139-158. New York, Cambridge Univ Pr, 1994.

Coleman, Jules L (ed) and Buchanan, Allen (ed). *In Harm's Way*. New York, Cambridge Univ Pr, 1994.

Coleman, Wil. Simon Glynn on a Unified Epistemology of the Natural Human/Sciences. *J Brit Soc Phenomenol*, 26(1), 94-96, Ja 95.

Coles, Andrew. Biomedical Models of Reproduction in the Fifth Century BC and Aristotle's *Generation of Animals*. *Phronesis*, 40(1), 48-88, 1995.

Coles, Romand. "Identity and Difference in the Ethical Positions of Adorno and Habermas" in *The Cambridge Companion to Habermas, White, Stephen K (ed)*, 19-45. New York, Cambridge Univ Pr, 1995.

Colker, Ruth. "Disembodiment: Abortion and Gay Rights" in *Radical Philosophy of Law, Caudill, David S (ed)*, 234-254. Atlantic Highlands, Humanities Pr, 1995.

Collen, Arne (ed) and Gasparski, Wojciech W (ed). *Design & Systems: General Applications of Methodology*. New Brunswick, Transaction Books, 1995.

This third volume in a series consists of a set of contributions to the methodological study of design from a wide representation of disciplines and professions. Informed by general systems theory and praxiological-systemic perspectives, the contributors of this collection convey a variety of applications of theoretical and generic import, but with special concern for the effectiveness, purposive action, efficiency, and efficiency of methodology for design and systems.

Colli, Giorgio (ed) and Nietzsche, Friedrich and Montinari, Mazzino (ed). *The Complete Works of Friedrich Nietzsche: Volume 2: Unfashionable Observations*. Stanford, Stanford Univ Pr, 1995.

Collins, Allison and Schultz, Norm. A Critical Examination of the AICPA Code of Professional Conduct. *J Bus Ethics*, 14(1), 31-41, Ja 95.

The American Institute of Certified Public Accountants (AICPA) is responsible for the Code of Professional Conduct that governs the actions of CPAs. In 1988, the Code was revised by the AICPA, but a number of issues still remain unresolved. These issues are examined in light of the profession's stated commitment to the public good. (edited)

Collins, Ardis B (ed). *Hegel on the Modern World*. Albany, SUNY Pr, 1995.

Collins, Arthur W. Précis of *The Nature of Mental Things*. *Phil Phenomenol Res*, 54(4), 901-903, D 94.

Collins, Arthur W. Reply to Commentators. *Phil Phenomenol Res*, 54(4), 929-945, D 94.

Collins, Denis and Barkdull, John. Capitalism, Environmentalism, and Mediating Structures. *Environ Ethics*, 17(3), 227-244, Fall 95.

How can an environmental ethic be developed that encompasses the concerns of both free and market proponents and environmentalists? In this article we approach the environment-market debate using Adam Smith's writings in *The Theory of Moral Sentiments, The Wealth of Nations, and Lectures on Jurisprudence*. Smith's guiding principle for solving prominent conflicts of self-interest is that government intervention is required when the economic activities of some cause bring harm to others. The solution that follows from Smith's analysis is a government-funded, independent, democratically controlled, and democratically accountable mediating structure that derives impartial decisions and is authorized to impose its just and fair decisions on affected parties. In practical terms, this analysis provides the ethical foundation for the wide-ranging development of stakeholder panels composed of public interest group representatives and business representatives and empowered to develop solutions to public conflicts arising out of environmental problems.

Collins, John and Costa, Horacio Arló and Levi, Isaac. Desire-as-Belief Implies Opinionation or Indifference. *Analysis*, 55(1), 2-5, Ja 95.

The anti-Humean proposal of constructing desire as belief about what would be good must be abandoned on pain of triviality. Our central result shows that if an agent's belief-desire state is represented by Jeffrey's expected value theory enriched with the Desire as Belief Thesis (DAB), then, provided that three pairwise inconsistent propositions receive nonzero probability, the agent must view with indifference any proposition whose probability is greater than zero. Unlike previous results against DAB our Opinionation or Indifference Theorem is a purely synchronic one that depends in no way of the properties of Jeffrey conditionalization.

Coltrane, Scott. "Theorizing Masculinities in Contemporary Social Science" in *Theorizing Masculinities, Brod, Harry (ed)*, 39-60. Newbury Park, Sage, 1994.

Comay, Rebecca. Mourning, Work, and Play. *Res Phenomenol*, 23, 105-130, 1993.

Cometti, Jean-Pierre (trans) and Elgin, Catherine Z and Goodman, Nelson. *Reconceptions en philosophie*. Paris, Pr Univ France, 1994.

Commers, Ronald. Public Vices, Private Benefits. *Philosophica*, 52(2), 31-44, 1993.

Compton, John J. Merleau-Ponty's Metaphorical Philosophy. Review of *Merleau-Ponty and Metaphor* by Jerry H Gill. *Res Phenomenol*, 23, 221-226, 1993.

The contribution of Gill's book is to allow us to see how deeply metaphor informs Merleau-Ponty's thought, how it shapes his ontology and his view of philosophy itself. After presenting a nice analytical concordance of Merleau's metaphorical texts, Gill shows that, despite the fact the Merleau does not explicitly analyze metaphorical language, he may properly be said to have a theory of metaphor. Metaphor, for him, discloses the metaphorical (mediational) character of reality itself as a symbiosis of the knower and the known. The reviewer argues, further, that it is not only the use of metaphor as such, but Merleau's particular metaphors, which yield this important result.

Comstock, Gary L. Do Agriculturalists Need a New, an Ecocentric, Ethic? 1994 Presidential Address to the Agriculture, Food, and Human Values Society. *Agr Human Values*, 12(1), 2-16, Winter 95.

In 1973, Richard Sylvan began his seminal essay, "Do We Need a New, an Environmental Ethic?" with these words: "It is increasingly said that...Western civilization...stands in need of a new ethic...setting out people's relations to the natural environment." In the intervening years, it has increasingly been said that Western civilization is in need of ecocentrism, an ethic according to which a thing's value is derived from its contribution to the integrity, stability, and beauty of ecosystems. Do those interested in agricultural ethics need a new, an ecocentric, ethic? I argue that the answer is no. Agriculturalists must look elsewhere for an adequate ethic setting out our relations to the natural environment.

Conard, Mark T. Allison's Reading of Kant's Paradox of Inner Sense. *Phil Today*, 38(3-4), 317-325, Fall 94.

Conee, Earl. Against an Epistemic Dilemma. *Austl J Phil*, 72(4), 475-481, D 94.

A person is in an epistemic dilemma if believing, disbelieving, and withholding judgment on a proposition all go against the person's epistemic reasons. There seem to be examples of this, because there are cases in which believing or proposition would foreseeably undermine what otherwise is conclusive epistemic reason to believe it. It is argued that in such cases withholding judgment is uniquely epistemically reasonable. This position is derived from the nature of epistemic reasons and defended against objections.

Conee, Earl. The Nature and the Impossibility of Moral Perfection. *Phil Phenomenol Res*, 54(4), 815-825, D 94.

It is argued that a morally perfect agent is one who is ideal in every morally relevant respect. On the basis of this conception it is argued that morally perfect agency is impossible.

Conforti, Patrizia. Le Questioni Inedite. *Aquinas*, 37(3), 581-595, S-D 94.

The article is an abstract of the doctoral thesis discussed at the Pontifical University of Lateran (Rome, 1994). The thesis consists of the edition of an anonymous commentary (end XVth century) to distinction VIII, question I of Book I of *Defensiones Theologiae Divi Thomae Aquinatis* by John Capreolus, Dominican (dead 1444). This commentary is an interesting "treatise" on the Thomistic doctrine of the distinction between essence and existence. The abstract does not contain the edition, it rather introduces the text and gives an idea of its historical and doctrinal background. Finally, it establishes the general infidelity of "Thomistic tradition" to Saint Thomas.

Coniglione, Francesco. Philosophy and Science in Jan Lukasiewicz (in Italian). *Epistemologia*, 17(1), 73-100, Ja-Je 94.

Lukasiewicz is better known as a logician than as a philosopher: in this essay we outline synthetically the second aspect of his intellectual activity in the Lwow-Warsaw School. (edited)

Conill, Jesus. Las máscaras del demonio: Nietzsche y la hermenéutica. *Pensamiento*, 198(50), 407-417, S-D 94.

Es provechoso afrontar el reto nietzscheano en nuestro contexto cutural y filosófico, debido a su crítica radical de la ontología y la ética; e igualmente insertarlo en el marco del pensamiento hermenéutico, a fin de completar su historia contemporánea desde Schleiermacher con el enfoque de Nietzsche. Para superar ciertas interpretaciones (a veces hasta panfletarias) y presentar el sentido profundo de la peculiar hermenéutica nietzscheana, se toma como motivo central la expresión "las máscaras del demonio". El análisis y exposición de los textos relacionados con ella nos permitirá entender mejor el significado práctico de la "transvaloración" ofrecida por Nietzsche.

Connell, R W. "The State, Gender and Sexual Politics: Theory and Appraisal" in *Power/Gender, Radtke, H Lorraine (ed)*, 136-173. Newbury Park, Sage, 1994.

Gender and sexuality are major areas of state action; more, they are constitutive of the state. Conventional state theory acknowledges this only indirectly, feminist theories more directly but so far within a limited framework. A new framework is proposed, centering on these themes: the state is the central institutionalization of the power relations of gender; states are characterized by their internal gender regimes; states regulate gender relations in the wider society; states constitute gender categories; states are a major stake in gender and sexual politics; crisis tendencies in gender orders allow new political possibilities.

Connell, Richard J. *Nature's Causes*. New York, Lang, 1995.

This work shows that the four causes first described by Aristotle are actually employed in the natural sciences. It begins with a description of prevailing views of causality, presents Aristotle's analysis of coming to be, then treats the four causes in the following order: material cause, species or formal cause, moving and active cause, and final cause or purpose. Structural explanation, chance events, and the anthropic principle are also discussed. Much use is made of scientific data, and contemporary authors are the principal sources quoted. A major issue is the origin of species and the relation of purpose or final cause to evolution.

Conner, Clifford D. Broadening the Picture of Science in Revolutionary France: Adding Du Pont and Restif to Lavoisier and Laplace. *Phil Hist Sci*, 3(1), 29-70, Ap 94.

The history of French science in the era of the Revolution has traditionally focused upon the ideas and activities of famous scientists such as Lavoisier and Laplace. This has produced a distorted view, making the scientific thought of the period appear more modern than it really was. As a corrective, it is useful to consider what science meant to some of the many prominent intellectuals of the 1780s and 90s who were prolific authors of works of natural philosophy. (edited)

Connolly, Maureen. Phenomenology, Physical Education, and Special Populations. *Human Stud*, 18(1), 25-40, Ja 95.

This paper attempts to show the complementarity between phenomenology and physical education as human sciences, and discusses how a consideration of this relation might inform the questions we ask and the methods we use in our research and teaching. We enter the common ground shared by phenomenology and physical education by way of three sensitizing concepts: lived experience, intersubjectivity, and 'insiders' stories. Using examples from physical education and phenomenology, the paper shows the connections between these two increasingly compatible partners, emphasizes the primary connection—the body—and shows the practical and heuristic applications of phenomenology in the lifeworld of physical education.

Connolly, Maureen. Response and Commentary on Iris Young's *Throwing Like a Girl and Other Essays in Feminist Philosophy and Social Theory*. *Human Stud*, 17(4), 463-469, 1994-95.

This article provides response to and commentary on Iris Young's work from a physical education perspective. The author, writing from a feminist orientation, draws on phenomenology and somatics to support her stance on the primacy of the body in physical education and the lifeworld. Salient features include description of Young's format and content, stories from physical education contexts, and biomechanical and qualitative movement analysis. Conclusions reached are that the body is the first and best teacher and that women connect with the wisdom of the body and try to make sense of that connection through movement that feels authentic.

Connolly, William E. Tocqueville, Territory and Violence. *Theor Cult Soc*, 11(1), 19-41, F 94.

Conquergood, Dwight. "For the Nation! How Street Gangs Problematize Patriotism" in *After Postmodernism, Simons, Herbert W (ed)*, 200-221. Newbury Park, Sage, 1994.

Conrath, D W and Sharma, R S. The Post-Implementation Evaluation of Expert Systems: Enlightenment after Five Years in the Trenches. *Commun Cog—AI*, 11(3), 257-275, 1994.

We present a retrospective analysis of a five-year project on investigating methodologies for determining the quality of expert systems. More specifically, a multiple-criteria and multiple-stakeholder based subjective assessment technique is proposed as a sound and viable alternative to current practices. In short, the proposed approach elicits from users, developers and managers, their evaluations of an operational expert system along thirty-nine dimensions of quality spanning the various aspects of task, technology, people and organization. The underlying framework of the evaluation is based on a socio-technical model of quality. The intended contribution of our research efforts was to provide an assessment tool for knowledge engineers in the development of expert systems. Such a potential has been field-tested and confirmed.

Conroy, Edward J. A Critique of Social Contracts for Business. *Bus Ethics Quart*, 5(2), 187-212, Ap 95.

This article evaluates the social contract theorizing of Professors Thomas Donaldson, Thomas Dunfee and Michael Keeley. This theorizing is tested with G E Morres's concept of moral authority, with moral psychology, and by managerial utility. Both strengths and weaknesses are found in the theories and the author concludes that while there is great potential, much work in theory development remains.

Conte, Domenico. Catene di civiltà: La seconda fase del pensiero di Oswald Spengler. *Arch Stor Cult*, 7, 141-181, 1994.

Conticello, C G. Métaphysique de l'être et théologie de la grâce dans le médiévalisme contemporain: É Gilson et M D Chenu entre H Bergson et A Gardeil. *Rev Thomiste*, 94(3), 431-459, Jl-S 94.

Conway, Daniel W. "Returning to Nature: Nietzsche's *Götterdämmerung*" in *Nietzsche: A Critical Reader, Sedgwick, Peter R (ed)*, 31-52. Cambridge, Blackwell, 1995.

Conway, Daniel W. Naturalizing the Epistemologist: The Final Shadow of the Dead God. *Int Stud Phil*, 27(3), 19-23, 1995.

Conway, Jeremiah. Transforming Stories: *The Death of Ivan Ilyich*, The Birth of a Reflective Life. *Phil Cont World*, 1(3), 8-14, Fall 94.

The problem addressed by this paper concerns the responsibility of higher education in the growing thoughtlessness of culture. By "thoughtlessness" is meant not the abscence of mental "busyness," but indifference to the self-reflective life. How do we cope with the fact that, for so many, the educative act has little or nothing to do with the cultivation of self-reflection, especially when this indifference is amply represented within higher education as well as the wider culture? The paper unfolds in three sections. First, it explores the factors complicating the search for effective materials by which to instigate and encourage the transformation to a self-reflective life. Second, it argues that stories, particularly what it calls "transforming stories," play an important role in provoking and providing insight into the "turning around of the soul" from unreflective to reflective living. Finally, it illustrates how one such transforming story, *The Death of Ivan Illyich*, by Leo Tolstoy, helps accomplish this goal.

Cook, Deborah. "Symbolic Exchange in Hyperreality" in *Baudrillard: A Critical Reader, Kellner, Douglas M (ed)*, 150-167. Cambridge, Blackwell, 1994.

John Fiske and Jean Baudrillard have each put forward a version of the limited effects theory. Part of the essay is devoted to a discussion and critical assessment of Baudrillard's claims about the silent revolt of the majority and Fiske's ideas about the silent resistance of minority groups. In the final part of the essay, Baudrillard's proposal for radically restructuring the media-permitting symbolic exchange-is contrasted to Hans Magnus Enzensberger's endorsement of circuit reversal. Both writers ultimately praise collectively organized and operated media. The essay ends with an evaluation of the prospects for collective production.

Cook, Deborah. Domination and Enlightenment: The Limits of Manipulation. *J Brit Soc Phenomenol*, 26(1), 17-26, Ja 95.

Cook, Deborah. The Sundered Totality: Adorno's Freudo-Marxism. *J Theor Soc Behav*, 25(2), 191-215, Je 95.

Adorno used Marx's critique of the political economy of capitalism to develop his analysis of reification and the "fatherless society" under late capitalism. Freud's theory of instincts provided him with insights into the narcissism that often afflicts individuals today. The social totality is sundered into these two mutually exclusive, but equally material, parts: the economy of late capitalism with its debilitating effects on the psyche and the individual instincts with their potentially resistive force. Adorno's unique pairing of Marx and Freud formed the paradigm that explained the culture industry's principal characteristics, techniques and ideology as well as the individual's reception of its products.

Cook, Steven and Hendry, David. "The Theory of Reduction in Econometrics" in *Idealization VI: Idealization in Economics, Hamminga, Bert (ed)*, 71-100. Amsterdam, Rodopi, 1994.

Analysis of a number of types of reduction to be used in 'general to specific' modelling in econometric methodology. Specification of measures for the loss of information resulting from every type of reduction. Based upon this analysis, the formulation of criteria for model design in econometrics.

Cooke, Maeve. Postkonventionelle Selbstverwirklichung: Überlegungen zur praktischen Subjektivität. *Deut Z Phil*, 42(1), 61-72, 1994.

Cooke, Maeve. Selfhood and Solidarity. *Constellations*, 1(3), 337-357, Jan 95.

Two types of solidarity are discussed, one based on esteem and one based on respect. Each, arguably, is important for the development of postconventional selves, although problematic when considered purely on its own terms. The importance of esteem-based solidarity is shown through reference to a formal account of self-realization and supported by the respective work of Ricoeur and Honneth. Its limitations, however, suggest the need for respect-based solidarity. The latter, as conceived, for example, by Habermas, usefully supplements the former but ultimately fails to respond to a central concern this articulates. Consequently, learning processes in both dimensions of solidarity are required.

Coolen, Maarten. "Towards a Hermeneutics of Nature: On the Necessity of Enduring Distance" in *Ecology, Technology, and Culture,* Zweers, Wim (ed), 118-126. Cambridge, White Horse, 1994.

Cools, Kees and Hamminga, Bert and Kuipers, Theo A F. "Truth Approximation by Concretization in Capital Structure Theory" in *Idealization VI: Idealization in Economics, Hamminga, Bert (ed)*, 205-228. Amsterdam, Rodopi, 1994.

This paper supplies a structuralist reconstruction of the Modigliani-Miller theory and shows that the economic literature following their results reports on research with an implicit strategy to come "closer-to-the-truth" in the modern technical sense in philosophy of science.

Coombs, Jeffrey. Jeronimo Pardo on the Necessity of Scientific Propositions. *Vivarium*, 33(1), 9-26, My 95.

I examine the views of Jerónimo Pardo, a logic professor at the University of Paris in the early sixteenth century, concerning how scientific propositions which refer to contingent entities can be necessary. Pardo discusses this problem in relation to term "ampliation." I present the notion of ampliation, Pardo's discussion of various attempts to preserve the necessity of scientific propositions, followed by his solution. Pardo postulates that the necessity of scientific propositions is based on a possible connection or "string" between the referents of the terms of the propositions. I conclude that Pardo's solution raises more questions than it answers.

Coombs, Jeffrey. John Poinsot on How To Be, Know, and Love a Non-Existent Possible. *Amer Cath Phil Quart*, 68(3), 321-335, Sum 94.

The paper presents John Poinsot's view of three problems: what is the ontological basis of nonexistent possibles, how does God have knowledge of them, and does God love them? John Poinsot holds that the ontological basis for possibilities is "formally" God's intellect, the divine ideas. God knows of nonexistent possibles by means of an "abstractive" knowledge which derives from God's "intuitive" knowledge of the divine ideas. God, however, does not love nonexistent possibles which are never actual since they lack any intrinsic goodness. Finally, I conclude that Poinsot accepts "photo-exemplarism", a view which James Ross believes Aquinas rejects.

Cooper, Barry. The End of History: Déjà-Vu All Over Again. *Hist Euro Ideas*, 19(1-3), 377-383, Jl 94.

Analysis of F Fukuyama's notion of the end of history as a recurring second reality with its own history.

Cooper, David D. Moral Literacy. *J Value Inq*, 28(2), 297-312, Je 94.

Moral literacy encompasses discourse imagery used to articulate aspiration, commitment, and identity as we search for inner meaning and truth within the context of interpersonal commitments and wider obligations to society. The argument refutes objections to the term "moral Literacy" based on two lines of criticism: first, the social uses of literacy, and second, definitions of morality. Literacy practices that reinforce the refinement of moral discourse help foster a recovery of community by 1) placing individual actions and decisions in the context of ethical consequences, and 2) immersing individuals in their culture's enduring vocabularies of commitment.

Cooper, David E. Is Daoism 'Green'?. *Asian Phil*, 4(2), 119-125, 1994.

Contemporary advocates of 'deep ecology' often appeal to daoist ideals as an early expression of 'respect' for nature. This appeal is inspired, presumably, by daoist attacks on 'convention' or 'artifice' which, as Zhuang Zi puts it, 'has been the ruin of primordial nature...the ruin of the world'. But there are problems with this appeal. Daoists are extremely selective in the aspects of nature which they admire, and it is as much the skilled artisan as the person 'at one with nature' who is the daoist ideal. Nevertheless, daoist literature does have implications—albeit rather complicated—for proper environmental attitudes.

Cooper, David E. Science, Society, and Rationality. *Hist Human Sci*, 8(2), 109-115, My 95.

Cooper, John M. Eudaimonism and the Appeal to Nature in the Morality of Happiness: Comments on Julia Annas, *The Morality of Happiness*. *Phil Phenomenol Res*, 55(3), 587-598, S 95.

Cooper, Neil. Spinoza on Religious Choice. *Philosophy*, 69(270), 443-458, O 94.

Cooper, Neil. The Intellectual Virtues. *Philosophy*, 69(270), 459-469, O 94.

Cooper, Robert W and Frank, Garry L and Heaston, Patrick H. Helps for CPAs in Dealing with Ethical Issues. *Bus Prof Ethics J*, 13(1-2), 165-183, Spr-Sum 94.

The paper reports the findings of a study of CPAs designed to determine whether they tend to find factors related to their professional environment (especially the guides to professional conduct of the American Institute of Certified Public Accountants) to be more helpful than factors related to their business environment when faced with ethics problems. Like internal auditors surveyed earlier, the CPAs tend to view a number of factors in their business environment to be even more helpful than factors related to their professional environment in dealing with ethical dilemmas. Implications for CPAs as individuals and for their professional associations are discussed.

Cooper, Wes. Virtual Reality and the Metaphysics of Self, Community, and Nature. *Int J Applied Phil*, 9(2), 1-14, Wint-Spr 95.

Cooter, Robert D and Gordley, James. "The Cultural Justification of Unearned Income" in *Profits and Morality, Cowan, Robin (ed)*, 150-175. Chicago, Univ of Chicago Pr, 1995.

Copeland, B J. Vagueness and Bivalence: A Discussion of Williamson and Simons. *Proc Aris Soc*, 95, 193-200, 1994-95.

Copeland, B Jack. *Artificial Intelligence: A Philosophical Introduction*. Cambridge, Blackwell, 1995.

Copeland, B Jack. Commentary: On Vague Objects, Fuzzy Logic, and Fractal Boundaries. *S J Phil*, 33(Supp), 83-96, 1995.

Copeland, B Jack and Proudfoot, Diane. Turing, Wittgenstein and the Science of the Mind. *Austl J Phil*, 72(4), 497-519, D 94.

Copp, David. *Morality, Normativity, and Society*. New York, Oxford Univ Pr, 1995.

Under what conditions would a moral claim be true? The "society-centered" theory presented in this book is designed to underwrite the truth of moral "realism", "naturalism", and "externalism" while also explaining, without mystery, the normativity of moral claims. The theory says that a moral propostion is true only if a relevant moral standard is appropriately "justified". It argues that a moral standard is appropriately justified just in case its currency in society would serve the needs of society. The theory implies that moral properties are actually complex relations, with one of the relata being the relevant society.

Corazza, Eros. Je est un Autre. *Arch Phil*, 58(2), 199-212, Ap-Je 95.

The central issue is the mental practice of imagining to be another person. The paper's thesis is that in such practice we put our I-*buffer* in a relationship with the mental life labelled by the name of the person we imagine to be. The nature of the relationship is investigated and it is argued that such a relation is not a relation of identity.

Corazza, Eros. Perspectival Thoughts and Psychological Generalizations. *Dialectica*, 48(3-4), 307-336, 1994.

Against an externalist view popularized, among others, by Evans and McDowell I shall show that object-dependent thoughts are psychologically spurious. This version of externalism is contrasted with the picture that thoughts are object-independent. It is argued that object-independent thoughts are perspectival and context-sensitive and that these perspectival thoughts, unlike object-dependent thoughts: (i) deal with delusion in an intuitive and elegant way; (ii) support psychological generalizations in a straightforward way; (iii) do not need to be fully articulated and, as such, fit with an economical rule governing our thinking activity. To state my point I shall mainly concentrate on perceptual thoughts and emphasize how they are contextually restated to the external world.

Corcoran, John. The Founding of Logic. *Ancient Phil*, 14, 9-24, 1994.

Cordero, Ronald A. The *Right* Approach. *Sorites*, 46-50, Ap 95.

While discussions about improving society are commonly conducted in terms of human rights, there are serious drawbacks to this approach. People may differ as to the relative importance or the very existence of specific rights, and there are no generally accepted methods for the rational resolution of such disagreements. These difficulties can be avoided if proposed social changes are discussed with respect to a generally accepted end, rather than with respect to a set of rights. And agreement on such an end already exists, inasmuch as most advocates of social improvements want to see social arrangements changed in such a way that everyone will be able to lead a satisfying existence.

Corey, Gerald (& others). Ethical and Legal Issues in Group Counseling. *Ethics Behavior*, 5(2), 161-183, 1995.

Legal and ethical issues involved in group work are reviewed and discussed. Variations in different professional ethics codes are discussed. Recommendations for consideration by group leaders are made.

Corielli, Francesco. A Note on the Decidability of De Finetti's Coherence. *Theor Decis*, 38(1), 121-129, Ja 95.

To check the de Finetti coherence of a putative probability assigned to a class *A* of events, we must know the possible combinations of truth values (constituents) of any finite class of events in *A*. Even for a very simple, finite, *A* this can be impossible. In this case the notion of DF coherence cannot be applied to some or all the putative probabilities on this class of events.

Corlett, J Angelo. Marx and Rights. *Dialogue (Canada)*, 33(3), 377-389, Sum 94.

It is often either assumed or argued that political liberalism respects rights, while Marxism does not. In fact, many believe that the omission of rights in communism counts decisively against the viability of Karl Marx's social philosophy. Is there room for rights in Marx's social philosophy? This paper examines a popular interpretation of Marx's critique of rights. contrary to this popular interpretation, this paper argues that Marx's critique of rights is limited rather than comprehensive in scope. Moreover, part of a foundation of a Marxian theory of rights is set forth.

Cornaros, C. On Grzegorczyk Induction. *Annals Pure Applied Log*, 74(1), 1-21, Je 95.

Cornaz, Laurent. Le savoir et sa transmission: De la volonté d'éduquer au désir de transmettre. *Rev Theol Phil*, 126(3), 193-214, 1994.

Pour l'auteur, le projet moderne et européen d'éducation qui se réfère à la philosophie des Lumières est institutionnellement en crise depuis la fin des années soixante. Cette crise est analysée comme le symptôme d'une autre crise, plus ancienne et plus profonde: celle de la science comme "savoir vrai", crise banalisée depuis le début du siècle notamment en physique et en mathématiques. La fracture entre science et vérité pose de façon inédite et radicale la question des conditions de possibilité de la transmission du savoir. Cette question portant sur la nature et le pouvoir de la raison, le détour par le mythe s'avère ici nécessaire. Analysant la fable de La Fontaine "Le Laboureur et ses enfants", l'auteur montre que la transmission obéit à une logique inconsciente qu'ignorent les techniques de la communication et qui interdit de penser que l'écriture du savoir pourrait garantir sa transmission. Comment dès lors poursuivre aujourd'hui le projet moderne d'une éducation rationnelle, sinon en se refusant à réduire l'acte éducatif aux techniques de la communication et en prenant le risque de laisser ouverte la question de la vérité du savoir à transmettre?

Cornejo, Raquel (& others). "Mente—Cuerpo: Enfoques Evolutivos" in *Temas Actuales de Filosofía, Palacios, María Julia (ed)*, 125-130. Buenos Aires, Univ Nacional Salta, 1993.

The mind-body problem is a recurrent subject in different disciplines like Biology and Phylosophy. Traditionally, the discussion has been centered on two principal and contradictory trends: monisms and dualisms. During the last decades, the incorporation of new knowledge.from different areas of research into this debate, like the Theory of Evolution, shows new facets of the problem. In that sense, Popper grounds its interactivist dualism on the evolutionary theory. On the other hand, National Sciences with monist and materialistic traditional have been renewed with the incorporation of the General Systems Theory and Cybernetics. In that context positions appeared like Laborit's which is here discussed. There are many objections to monisms and dualisms and the inclusion of new elements, instead of simplifying the problem, makes it more complex and open new questions. This work is part of a major interdisciplinary project carried out by Human Sciences (Gnoseology and Phylosophic Anthropology) and Natural Sciences Faculties (Ecology and Evolution).

Cornell, Drucilla. "Rethinking the Time of Feminism" in *Feminist Contentions, Benhabib, Seyla (& others)*, 145-156. New York, Routledge, 1994.

Cornell, Drucilla. "What Is Ethical Feminism?" in *Feminist Contentions, Benhabib, Seyla (& others)*, 75-106. New York, Routledge, 1994.

Corngold, Stanley. "On Death and the Contingency of Criticism" in *Intersections: Nineteenth-Century Philosophy and Contemporary Theory, Rajan, Tilottama (ed)*, 363-377. Albany, SUNY Pr, 1995.

Coroleu, Alejandro. Le Glosse di Juan Ginés de Sepúlveda alle Traduzioni Latine di Aristotle. *G Crit Filosof Ital*, 73(1), 16-32, Ja-Ap 94.

Corradini, Antonella. Intersubjektivität und Objektivität der moralischen Werte. *Frei Z Phil Theol*, 41(1-2), 137-154, 1994.

Most of contemporary ethical theories refuse to acknowledge objectivity of values, if these are understood as properties somehow inherent in reality. Objectivity in this strong sense is substituted by objectivity in a weaker sense, i.e., as *intersubjectivity*. In utilitarianism, for example, the intersubjective validity of a value is ensured by the formal method of universalization. The aim of this work is to show that intersubjectivity cannot replace objectivity for almost two reasons: 1) Application of universalization presupposes the acceptance of substantive moral principles, the objectivity of which does not coincide with their intersubjective validity; 2) (Weak) Objectivity always requires for its justification objectivity in the stronger sense.

Corradini, Antonella. What is Consequentialism? A Proposal for a Systematic Classification (in Italian). *Epistemologia*, 17(1), 117-148, Ja-Je 94.

The aim of this paper is to distinguish between different forms of consequentialistic theory. The first form (C1) focuses on the *intended consequences* of an action and is typical of many teleological theories, as for example virtue or value ethics. Consequentialistic theories usually called (C2) are, by contrast, *outcome moralities*: morally relevant characteristics are constituted not only by the intended, but also by the *caused consequences* of an action. Supporters of C1 disagree on this point. While accepting teleology, they follow deontology in rejection of C2. The author argues that objections against C2 depend mainly on the fact that teleologists interpret C2 in its *welfaristic* version (C2a). There is another possibility, however, namely the construction of, in Sen's terminology, a *nonwelfaristic* consequentialistic system (C2b). (edited)

Corral, Carmen (trans) and MacIntyre, Alasdair and Román, Begoña (trans). Persona corriente y filosofía moral: reglas, virtudes y bienes. *Convivium*, 5, 63-80, 1993.

Cort, John E. Genres of Jain History. *J Indian Phil*, 23(4), 469-506, D 95.

This essay uses material from the Jain tradition to address the often-repeated claim, first advanced by Hegel, that the people of India have no sense of history. The author argues that an examination of the rich textual tradition of the Svetambara Murtipujaka Jains of western India shows that they have several distinctive theories of history. These theories are expressed in genres different from European theories of history, and only rarely exhibit the concern with facticity that is a hallmark of European theories. By looking at the genres in which Jain histories have been written, and exploring the ways in which the genres have shaped these histories, we can begin to see some of the ways in which Western theories of history are themselves limited and culture-bound.

Cortella, Lucio. "Per una razionalità practica dialogica" in *L'etica e il suo Altro, Vigna, Carmelo (ed)*, 69-91. Milano, FrancoAngeli, 1994.

Cortella, Lucio. L'Ermeneutica e il Trascendentale. *Teoria*, 14(2), 63-86, 1994.

Corti, Enrique. La belleza y los esteticismos. *Stromata*, 50(1-2), 119-126, Ja-Je 94.

Corti, Enrique C. Consideraciones sobre el *De grammatico* de Anselmo de Canterbury. *Pat Med*, 15, 27-38, 1994.

"De Grammatico" Anselm of Canterbury's booklet, is a work that tends towards to the understanding of the introduction of Aristotle's categories into occidental thinking. Its merits, however, are not exclusively of cultural historical character. This thesis can not be sustained starting with the D P Henry's works dedicated to "De Grammatico" from the S Lesniewsky's ontology. In this article beginning with a story on structural reexamination established besides the textual plane and the different levels of articulation (material-thematic-argumental) two assertions: 1) it deals with an impeccable logic and linguistic treatment of the relations between natural language and philosophical language which including a reinterpretation of the famous Aristotelian text beginning chapter 4 of "On Categories"; 2) that Anselm advances beyond the logic linguistic ground, demanding a contexting of it which anticipates the revaluation of the experience operated after by the introduction to Aristotelic naturalism.

Cortois, P. Farewell to a Brilliant Dish Cleaner: Paul Feyerabend and the Merry Philosophy of Science. *Tijdschr Filosof*, 57(1), 91-110, Mr 95.

In this commemorative article the significance of Paul Feyerabend's work for philosophy of science in general is reviewed. Its unifying perspective is identified as the fight against any possible constraint on imagination (i.e., on the capacity of generating alternatives). This alternative-maximizing search was already central in Feyerabend's "pre-anarchistic" studies. In fact, I claim that the really significant theses and arguments, as far as the intrinsic debate within the philosophy of science is concerned, were present in these earlier studies (criticism of the conditions of consistency and meaning invariance, pragmatic theory of observation, incommensurability thesis...). The context of the "historical turn" is sketched in which these arguments were developed as a response to current views on science. But these arguments do possess an independent normative significance.

Cortois, Paul. Quelques aspects du programme épistémologique de Cavaillès. *Dialectica*, 48(2), 125-141, 1994.

Cette étude essaie de réunir quelques éléments en vue d'une interprétation plus complète du programme épistémologique contenu de façon extrêmement elliptique dans l'ouvrage posthume de Jean Cavaillès, publié en 1947 par G Canguilhem et C Ehresmann sous le titre *Sur la logique et la théorie de la science* (désigné ci-aprés par "S"). Afin d'arriver, plus particulièrement à une articulation plus développée du contenu des fameuses dernières phrases de ce texte, où la "nécessité génératrice" d'une dialectique conceptuelle est évoquée, il faudra rappeler quelques aspects connus ainsi que quelques aspects moins connus de cheminement philosophique de Cavaillès. (edited)

Cory, Daniel (ed) and Santayana, George. *The Birth of Reason and Other Essays*. New York, Columbia Univ Pr, 1995.

Cosculluela, Victor. The Ethics of Suicide Prevention. *Int J Applied Phil*, 9(1), 35-41, Sum-Fall 94.

This paper considers the conditions under which coercive suicide prevention measures are permissible or obligatory. It begins by objecting to various arguments for the coercive prevention of all suicide, such as the argument that suicide must always be prevented because suicidal desires are products of mental illness. The paper then develops conditions which justify or require suicide prevention measures.

Cosi, Giovanni. Naturalità del Diritto e Universali Giuridici. *Riv Int Filosof Diritto*, 71(4), 216-242, 1994.

Costa, Adelmiro D and Sikula Sr, Andrew. Are Women More Ethical than Men?. *J Bus Ethics*, 13(11), 859-871, N 94.

This article reports that the idea that women are more ethical than men is not supported by the empirical data of this particular study of a large sample of California State University college-aged students. This study uses four different value measures and four different nonparametric statistical tests of probability and significance to conclude that women are *not* more ethical than men. They may have historically been so inclined, and perhaps even today may still be when fully matured. But among today's youth of normal college age, there are no significant differences between the ethical values of male and female students (in this sample of Northern California university enrollees).

Costa, Gustavo. "Sali Nitri" de Vico y los Orígenes de la Civilización Pagana: La Dimensión Alquímica de la "Ciencia Nueva". *Cuad Vico*, 2, 11-19, 1992.

Vico adopts a scientific basis in his anthropological theory regarding the primeval step from men to beasts and from beasts to men, shaping to his own theory of the "sali nitri" and the origin of giants certain aspects of scientific knowledge of his age, which pertain as much to medicine as to alchemy, and assuming various coprological theses typical of traditional pharmacology. In this Vichian evolutionist explanation certain vestiges of the alchemist tradition can be recognised.

Costa, Gustavo. En Busca de la Lógica Viquiana. *Cuad Vico*, 3, 7-52, 1993.

The concept of 'reason' in Vico forms itself through the Medieval debate, and its development in the Renaissance concerning 'rationality' and the 'soul'. In confronting the issues concerning the problems posed by 'reason' to the Renaissance and Theologists such as Suárez, the concept of a rational soul (a concept of Platonic-Aristotelian tradition) becomes established; whilst Vico, through Renaissance 'Pampsiquism', directs his interpretation towards the primitive mentality. The frequent use of Renaissance text had a propedeutical function in the formation of Vico's thought, helping him to better understand the classical sources of modern thought and preparing him to debate with the representatives of seventeenth and eighteenth century European philosophy.

Costa, Horacio Arló and Collins, John and Levi, Isaac. Desire-as-Belief Implies Opinionation or Indifference. *Analysis*, 55(1), 2-5, Ja 95.

The anti-Humean proposal of constructing desire as belief about what would be good must be abandoned on pain of triviality. Our central result shows that if an agent's belief-desire state is represented by Jeffrey's expected value theory enriched with the Desire as Belief Thesis (DAB), then, provided that three pairwise inconsistent propositions receive nonzero probability, the agent must view with indifference any proposition whose probability is greater than zero. Unlike previous results against DAB our Opinionation or Indifference Theorem is a purely synchronic one that depends in no way of the properties of Jeffrey conditionalization.

Costa, Margarita. Antecedentes del Utilitarismo en los moralistas británicos anteriores a Hume. *Telos (Spain)*, 2(1), 9-14, Je 93.

This paper deals with certain ideas found in the so-called British moralists of the seventeenth century and the first half of the eighteenth century, which anticipate strikingly some of the moral tenets of later utilitarian philosophers. Special emphasis is placed on one aspect of these doctrines: the idea of the possibility of a rational calculus concerning moral right and wrong. The chief aim is to show that the "principle of utility" was developed in a new atmosphere in which morality depended exclusively upon reason and/or feeling though continuing to incorporate a strong appeal to religion.

Costa, Margarita. El Utilitarismo de Hume. *Telos (Spain)*, 3(2), 9-15, D 94.

By analyzing some relevant passages of Hume's *Enquiry Concerning the Principles of Morals*, I try to show to what extent this philosopher supported a utilitarian point of view. In this connection, the two main points developed here are: the relation between the public good and the individual's private good and the utility of justice as an 'artificial' virtue.

Costa, Vincenzo. Lo sviluppo della riduzione fenomenologica: dalla *Filosofia dell'aritmetica* a *Ideen*. *Riv Filosof Neo-Scolas*, 86(3), 506-572, Jl-S 94.

Costelloe, Timothy M. Schutz, Music, and Temporality: A Wittgensteinian Assessment. *Phil Soc Sci*, 24(4), 439-457, D 94.

In his account of musical interaction and temporality, Schutz's outer-inner distinction appears to capture a component of everyday experience. But engagement with Wittgensteinian philosophy reveals Schutz's false contrast between literal and metaphorical components of language, a series of philosophical confusions stemming from reifications of mental verbs, and the attribution of genuine duration to phenomena that have life as linguistic objects. Consequently, Schutz's intended account of social interaction comes to rest upon a radically private concept of the subject. A sociology of time, it is concluded, can avoid these conceptual traps by attending to the linguistic component of temporality.

Côté, Antoine. L'Infinité Divine dans l'Antiquité et au Moyen Age. *Dialogue (Canada)*, 34(1), 119-137, Wint 95.

Cotkin, George. "William James and Richard Rorty: Context and Conversation" in *Pragmatism: From Progressivism to Postmodernism, Hollinger, Robert (ed)*, 38-55. Westport, Praeger, 1995.

Richard Rorty shares more affinities perhaps with William James than with John Dewey, but their cultural politics are strikingly different. Both shared a fear of a "desiccated" private sphere, but James's philosophy far more than Rorty's presents the individual with a public sphere that is exciting and creative. James is placed within the context of turn of the century social and philosophical concerns; Rorty is contextualized as responding to ideas associated with the New York intellectuals of the 1940s and 1950s. Rorty's rather strict division between the public and private is strongly criticized.

Cotkin, George. *William James, Public Philosopher*. Champaign, Univ of Illinois Pr, 1994.

Cotta, Sergio. Conoscenza e Normatività: Una Prospettiva Metafisica. *Riv Int Filosof Diritto*, 71(4), 555-568, 1994.

Cottier, Georges. Liberté et vérité. *Rev Thomiste*, 94(2), 179-194, Ap-Je 94.

Cottingham, John. *A Descartes Dictionary*. Cambridge, Blackwell, 1993.

This volume expounds Descartes's central ideas and concepts in metaphysics, epistemology, the philosophy of science, psychology and ethics, explaining his terminology and the influences behind his thought, unfolding the structure of his most important arguments, and discussing the principal areas of philosophical difficulty and controversy. Topics covered in the alphabetically arranged articles include the Cogito, method, mind and body, the passions and free will, as well as many lesser known aspects of Descartes scientific and philosophical system. Also included are a general introduction describing Descartes life and works, and a detailed bibliography of primary and secondary literature.

Cotton, C Randy and Range, Lillian M. Reports of Assent and Permission in Research With Children: Illustrations and Suggestions. *Ethics Behavior*, 5(1), 49-66, 1995.

This study ascertained reports of assent (affirmative agreement) and permission (agreement by an adult fully capable of being informed) in 114 children's research articles in 1990 in *Child Development (CD), Journal of Consulting and Clinical Psychology (JCCP), Journal of Pediatric Psychology*, and *Journal of Clinical Child Psychology*. Of the research projects, 43% failed to specify permission, and 68.5% failed to specify assent. *JCCP* reported assent significantly more than *CD*. Assent was reported significantly more in research with older children than with younger children. This lack of sensitivity to assent and permission suggests that many authors, reviewers, and editors consider reporting assent and permission unessential. We recommend specifying assent and permission in all manuscripts, highlighting children's research issues in graduate training, and using specific safeguards when conducting research with children.

Cottone, Margherita. Scienza del Mito e Critica Letteraria: Conoscere per Composizione. *Stud Filosofici*, 229-237, 1991-92.

Cottrell, Allin. *Tertium datur?* Reflections on Owen Flanagan's *Consciousness Reconsidered*. *Phil Psych*, 8(1), 85-103, 1995.

Owen Flanagan's arguments concerning qualia constitute an intermediate position between Dennett's "disqualification" of qualia and the thesis that qualia represent an insurmountable obstacle to constructive naturalism. This middle ground is potentially attractive, but it is shown to have serious problems. This is brought out via consideration of several classic areas of dispute connected with qualia, including the inverted spectrum, Frank Jackson's thought experiment, blindsight, and epiphenomenalism. An attempt is made to formulate the basis for a less vulnerable variant on the "middle ground".

Cottrell, Allin. Intentionality and Economics. *Econ Phil*, 11(1), 159-176, Ap 95.

Coughlan, Michael. "Catholicism and the Value of Human Life" in *Ethics on the Frontiers of Human Existence, Badham, Paul (ed)*, 65-80. New York, Paragon House, 1992.

Coulehan, John L and Drane, James F. The Best-Interest Standard: Surrogate Decision Making and Quality of Life. *J Clin Ethics*, 6(1), 20-29, Spr 95.

Through the disciplines of law and ethics, American culture provides clear standards for surrogate decision makers who know an incompetent patient's wishes and interests. Surrogates, however, often have to decide based on what is medically best for the incompetent patient. Burdens and benefits have to be weighed and then judiciously balanced. This article attempts to provide more objective indicators for making difficult life and death decisions for other persons whose personal wishes are unknown. Quality of life considerations are listed and suggestions are made for evaluating these in a a more objective way. The purpose of this article is to protect incompetent patients against overaggressive medical interventions while protecting them as well against the danger of being set aside. Decisional guidelines are provided for reasonable and defensible best interest judgments.

Courcelle, Bruno. The Monadic Second-Order logic of Graphs VIII: Orientations. *Annals Pure Applied Log*, 72(2), 103-143, Mr 95.

In every undirected graph or, more generally, in every undirected hypergraph of bounded rank, one can specify an orientation of the edges or hyperedges by monadic second-order formulas using quantifications on sets of edges or hyperedges. The proof uses an extension to hypergraphs of the classical notion of a depth-first spanning tree. Applications are given to the characterization of the classes of graphs and hypergraphs having decidable monadic theories.

Court, Antoine. Lamartine et la Grèce. *Diotima*, 22, 95-110, 1994.

Court, Jürgen. Die Kant-Rezeption in der Sportwissenschaft. *Kantstudien*, 85(2), 198-221, 1994.

In his article the author analyzes how Kant is interpreted in the sport science. By concentrating on the ethics of sports he points out that most interpreters of Kant simply repeat traditional misunderstandings of his moral philosophy. Especially it is claimed that Kant's ethics is only formal and does not take into regard the consequences of actions. Against that the author shows that a sufficient ethics of sport can only be constructed if it corrects these images of Kant and replaces it by differentiating interpretations.

Courtney, C P. Montesquieu e il Problema dell "Diversité". *Riv Int Filosof Diritto*, 71(4), 243-269, 1994.

Courtois, Stéphane. Le faillibilisme de Jürgen Habermas et ses difficultés: un faillibilisme conséquent est-il possible?. *Dialogue (Canada)*, 33(2), 253-282, Spr 94.

Coutel, Charles. Apprendre et Enseigner la Philosophie. *Philosopher*, 15, 119-140, 1994.

Coutel, Charles. Culture, Citoyenneté, Humanité. *Philosopher*, 17, 103-127, 1995.

Coutts, Mary Carrington and Bishop, Laura Jane. Religious Perspectives on Bioethics, Part 2. *Kennedy Inst Ethics J*, 4(4), 357-386, D 94.

The many religions of the world bring diverse, and occasionally divergent, attitudes to bioethical issues. These beliefs often guide patients and health professionals in the health care setting. To further understanding of religious beliefs in our pluralistic and global society, this annotated bibliography identifies literature by major religious groups on topics in bioethics including: attitudes to health/health care, physician-patient relationship, treatment refusal, abortion, contraception, sterilization, reproductive technologies, genetics, mental health, human experimentation, organ donation/transplantation, death, euthanasia, and prolongation of life. Part 2, scope note 26, covers Native American religious traditions, Protestantism (generally and for 18 specific denominations), and Roman Catholicism.

Coutts, Mary Carrington and McCarrick, Pat Milmoe. Eugenics. *Kennedy Inst Ethics J*, 5(2), 163-178, Je 95.

Eugenics, Scope Note 28 in the National Reference Center for Bioethics Literature, Kennedy Institute of Ethics series, offers a source to recent literature about eugenics as well as a brief background history of this controversial topic which has been both praised and scorned in the twentieth century. The series provides overviews to topics in biomedical ethics and includes annotated citations to books, journal articles, and government documents.

Couvalis, George. Feyerabend, the Ancient Quarrel and the Problem of Aesthetic Criteria. *Phil Inq*, 16(1-2), 1-19, Wint-Spr 94.

The focus of the paper is whether works which meet certain aesthetic criteria are philosophically valuable. I claim that Feyerabend's defence of the theatre of the absurd is inadequate, and he only shows Brechtian drama to be of minor philosophical interest. However, he is correct in arguing that without using arguments, fine theatre and film can bring into serious question the value of a life steeped in intellectual debate. Thus, theatre and film can counter Plato's question begging comparison of argument and poetry. So Feyerabend goes beyond Aristotle and others by showing that philosophy needs to defend itself poetically.

Covey, Edward. Identity, Becoming, and Rights of Development. *Int J Moral Soc Stud*, 8(3), 197-209, Autumn 93.

The concept of becoming is often used loosely in moral arguments by philosophers as well as others. Here it is argued that we must distinguish among three related, but logically and morally separable senses in which it can be true that something, x, 'becomes' an individual of a certain kind: 1) x comes to form the composition of a thing of that kind; 2) x is superseded by an individual of that kind, but is not identical with that subsequent individual; 3) x acquires the property of being an individual of that kind, while preserving its original identity. Of these, 3) is often the sense on which ethical potentiality arguments depend, and it should not be conflated with 1) or 2).

Covic, Ante. Aporias of Löwith's Return to "The Natural World". *Filozof Istraz*, 13(4), 955-965, 1993.

This article considers Löwith's world-view and the difficulties related to it. Löwith reconstructs the ancient world-view according to which the world is equated with nature. The world always includes the relation to God and man, and therefore Löwith marks the periods of world history as theism, deism and atheism. In the parallel course, philosophical history passes through the stages of cosmotheology, anthropology and the philosophy of the emancipation of man. Löwith finds in the philosophy of Nietzsche possibilities for the reversal to the original, i.e., ancient state, and not only in philosophical history but also in world history. Thus, it turns out that the main difficulties of Löwith's philosophical position proceed exactly from the indistinguishable nature of the reflexive level from the level of the subject-matter.

Cowan, Robin and Rizzo, Mario J. "Fundamental Issues in the Justification of Profits" in *Profits and Morality, Cowan, Robin (ed)*, 1-21. Chicago, Univ of Chicago Pr, 1995.

This paper discusses some of the more prominent arguments for and against the justification of profits. Early in the paper several different types of profit are distinguished to set the stage for normative evaluation. Then arguments like utilitarianism and Pareto-efficiency, evolutionism, rights and free exchange, fair exchange, "sweat-of-the-brow", and discovery are analyzed. The paper raises the important issues with which any normative theory of profits must deal.

Cowan, Robin (ed) and Rizzo, Mario J (ed). *Profits and Morality*. Chicago, Univ of Chicago Pr, 1995.

This book of papers addresses the issue of the moral justification of profits. Presenting arguments for and against the morality of profit-making, the contributors examine the nature of profits and the ethical theories that can support them. Two essays address economic aspects of profits: one explores entrepreneurship as a legitimate source of profits; the other argues that recent advances in welfare economics weaken the case for the morality of profits. The other chapters focus on ethical theory, covering the right to profit from economic rent; the morality of how profits are used; and whether or not profits are deserved.

Cowen, Robert H. Combinatorial Analytic Tableaux. *Rep Math Log*, 27, 29-39, 1993.

A tableau method similar to the Analytic Tableaux of Raymond Smullyan is introduced in a hypergraph setting and used to solve a number of combinatorial satisfiability problems, including satisfiability of conjunctive normal forms in propositional logic, graph coloring, and property B. A general duality principle for satisfiability in a hypergraph is utilized to obtain a dual tableau method as well.

Cowen, Tyler. Rejoinder to David Friedman on the Economics of Anarchy. *Econ Phil*, 10(2), 329-332, O 94.

The paper rebuts Friedman's response to Cowen's original argument in "Law as a Public Good: The Economics of Anarchy", published in *Economics and Philosophy*, Fall 1992, 8, 249-267. The original piece argued that private protection agencies would collude in a state of nature; that is, libertarian market anarchy would tend to reevolve into government. The original paper argued that if private protection agencies can produce the public good of dispute adjudication amongst themselves, they can also collude and institute coercive rule.

Cowton, Christopher and Crisp, Roger. Hyprocrisy and Moral Seriousness. *Amer Phil Quart*, 31(4), 343-349, O 94.

This paper argues that recent discussion of hypocrisy has failed to recognize its distinct forms. We identify four: 1) pretence; 2) blame; 3)inconsistency; 4)complacency. We then consider what these different forms have in common. We reject the linguistic argument based on the claim that biblical 'hypocrisy' is to be understood as 'wickedness'. We deny also Wittgensteinean and Aristotelian understandings, as well as any attempt to set hypocrisy in opposition to integrity. Finally, we argue that hypocrisy is a failure to possess a 'metavirtue' and to take morality seriously.

Cowton, Christopher J and Dunfee, Thomas W. Internationalizing the Business Ethics Curriculum: A Survey. *J Bus Ethics*, 14(5), 331-338, My 95.

This article reports on a telephone survey of business school faculty in the United Kingdom, Asia and North America concerning efforts to internationalize the teaching of business ethics. International dimensions of business ethics are currently given only limited coverage in the business school curriculum with over half of the faculty surveyed indicating that less than 10% of their ethics teaching focuses on global issues. Teaching objectives vary widely with some faculty emphasizing a relativistic, diversity oriented perspective while others stress the universality of values. The respondents identified a great need to develop teaching materials based upon non-U.S. corporations and/or non-U.S. incidents.

Cox, Christoph. Nietzsche, Naturalism, and Interpretation. *Int Stud Phil*, 27(3), 3-18, 1995.

This essay shows that Nietzsche's rejection of the epistemological ideal of a "God's eye view" leads him to a thoroughly naturalistic conception of knowing and being. Yet it shows that Nietzsche also comes to reject the corollary to the "God's eye view": the notion of an absolute ontology. It argues that Nietzsche regards ontologies as always relative to background interpretations and maintains that interpretations can only be challenged by alternative interpretations, not by recourse to brute facts. Nonetheless, Nietzsche's naturalism is seen as providing him with compelling, if not final, reasons for maintaining that some interpretations are better than others.

Cox, James C and Goldman, Alvin I. "Accuracy in Journalism: An Economic Approach" in *Socializing Epistemology: The Social Dimensions of Knowledge*, Schmitt, Frederick F (ed), 189-215. Lanham, Rowman & Littlefield, 1994.

Cox, Philip N. The Disputation of Hate: Speech Codes, Pluralism, and Academic Freedoms. *Soc Theor Pract*, 21(1), 113-144, Spr 95.

A variety of arguments have recently been made in behalf of academic "speech codes", or hate speech statutes. From a strictly legal point of view, I suggest that speech codes may be constitutionally sound, if the public policy logic that supports anti-discrimination law (notions of discriminatory conduct and relational harm) is extended to the educational arena. Nevertheless, I argue against attempts to regulate hate speech, on the grounds of the uneasy distinction between public and private speech, the reliance on a problematic notion of "social consensus", and the contradictions in artificially distinct group categories (mandating tolerance for intolerant beliefs, etc.).

Cozzo, Cesare. *Meaning and Argument: A Theory of Meaning Centred on Immediate Argumental Role*. Stockholm, Almqvist & Wiksell, 1994.

This study presents and develops the argumental conception of meaning. The two basic principles of the argumental conception of meaning are: 1) To know (implicitly) the sense of a *word* is to know (implicitly) all the argumentation rules concerning that word; ii) To know the sense of a *sentence* is to know the syntactic structure of that sentence and to know the senses of the words occurring in it. Acceptance of the argumental conception of meaning and of an epistemic conception of truth leads to a rejection of the idea of analytic truth. The argumental conception is *pluralistic* with respect to the understandability of different logic, and *neutral* with respect to their correctness. (edited)

Cozzo, Cesare. What Can We Learn From the Paradox of Knowability?. *Topoi*, 13(2), 71-78, S 94.

The intuitionistic conception of truth defended by Dummett, Martin Löf and Prawitz, according to which the notion of proof is conceptually prior to the notion of truth, is a particular version of the epistemic conception of truth. The paradox of knowability (first published by Frederic Fitch in 1963) has been described by many authors as an argument which threatens the epistemic, and the intuitionistic, conception of truth. In order to establish whether this is really so, one has to understand what the epistemic conception of truth really is. So I shall start in *part I* with a description of the matter at issue between the *epistemic* conception of truth and the opposite position, the *realistic* conception of truth. In *part II* I shall very briefly describe the paradox. In *part III* I shall try to answer the question which appears in the title of this paper: "What can we learn from the paradox of knowability?". My conclusion will be that the paradox of knowability is not a refutation of the epistemic conception of truth, but helps us to better formulate (and understand) such a view.

Craemer-Ruegenberg, Ingrid. "Das Naturverständnis von Aristoteles" in *Naturauffassungen in Philosophie, Wissenschaft, Technik: Band I*, Schäfer, Lothar (ed), 85-106. Freiburg, Alber, 1993.

Cragnolini, Mónica B. "Razón Imaginativa y Etica: Reflexiones a Partir de la Obra de Paul Ricoeur" in *Temas Actuales de Filosofía, Palacios, María Julia (ed)*, 131-139. Buenos Aires, Univ Nacional Salta, 1993.

Cragnolini, Mónica B. Nietzsche y el Problema del Lenguaje en la Perspectiva de la Musica. *Rev Latin de Filosof*, 21(1), 107-130, Fall 95.

The subject of music in Nietzsche's philosophy opens up valuable suggestions for an analysis of possibilities of the language after the death of the Grammar-God. Against the interpretation of Nietzsche's philosophy only as a loss into the fragmentary, this paper intends to show, based on a reflexion over the relationship Nietzsche-Shönberg established in Thomas Mann *Doktor Faustus*, the importance of the construction of senses for future nihilism. Such building is possible because of the *Wille zure Macht*, understood here as "imaginative rationality".

Craia, Eladio Pablo C (& others). "Topología—Atopología del Saber" in *Temas Actuales de Filosofía, Palacios, María Julia (ed)*, 141-146. Buenos Aires, Univ Nacional Salta, 1993.

Craig, Leon Harold. *The War Lover: A Study of Plato's Republic*. Toronto, Univ of Toronto Pr, 1994.

Craig, W L. Professor Grünbaum on Creation. *Erkenntnis*, 40(3), 325-341, My 94.

In a number of recent publications, Adolf Grünbaum (1989, 1990, 1991) has criticized the application of the theological notion of *creatio ex nihilo* to the origination of the universe. Since I have elsewhere responded to his covey of objections to the traditional cosmological argument for a chronologically first cause of the origin of the universe (Craig, 1991, 1992), I shall in this paper confine myself to an examination of Grünbaum's arguments "that pseudo-explanations offered in response to pseudo-problems vitiate current attempts to harness the influential cosmological models of recent decades in support of theological creationism". (Grünbaum, 1991, p 236) Two questions arise in assessing the alleged support lent by recent cosmological models to theological creationism: 1) Is the question of the creation of the universe a pseudo-problem, and 2) Is the response of theological creationism a pseudo-explanation? Let us address each in turn.

Craig, William Lane. Middle Knowledge and Christian Exclusivism. *Sophia (Australia)*, 34(1), 120-139, Mr-Ap 95.

It is shown that David Hunt's objection to a middle knowledge perspective on Christian exclusivism are based on a misunderstanding of that perspective and that his proposed alternative, in ascribing deceit to God, is plausibly regarded as broadly logically impossible.

Craig, William Lane. Robert Adams's New Anti-Molinist Argument. *Phil Phenomenol Res*, 54(4), 857-861, D 94.

Crain, Karen A and Heischmidt, Kenneth A. Implementing Business Ethics: Sexual Harassment. *J Bus Ethics*, 14(4), 299-308, Ap 95.

Sexual harassment is a problem for many organizations. Organizations must understand that sexual harassment lies within the broader context of sex discrimination and inequality of opportunity in the workplace. Sexual harassment is both an illegal and unethical practice. Companies need to implement a policy which respects the rights of individual employees by prohibiting sexual harassment. This policy needs to be clearly stated in the company Code of Ethics and enforced rigorously.

Crain, Terry L and Ghosh, Dipankar. Ethical Standards, Attitudes Toward Risk, and Intentional Noncompliance: An Experimental Investigation. *J Bus Ethics*, 14(5), 353-365, My 95.

Prior research has investigated the influence of decision maker characteristics on decision choice. This research examines the effect two personality traits of taxpayers, attitude towards risk and ethical standards, on intentional noncompliance. A taxpayer who is more (less) ethical will have lower (greater) intentional noncompliance, while a taxpayer who is more (less) risk averse will have lower (greater) intentional noncompliance. However, this study also found significant correlation between risk attitudes and ethical standards. This is because tax evasion is not just a gamble which can be explained by merely considering the risk variable. To understand tax evasive behavior better requires incorporation of noneconomic factors in the analysis, such as ethical standards, although risk attitudes may be an important explanatory factor. The current research suggests that individuals with lower ethical standards will have more intentional noncompliance. However, since ethical standards are correlated with attitude toward risk, the Internal Revenue Service (IRS) can partially overcome the influence of ethics by making the tax audit environment more uncertain. Thus, the research results justify the decision of the IRS no to release all its audit parameters because it makes the audit environment less uncertain.

Cranor, Carl F. Learning from the Law for Regulatory Science. *Law Phil*, 14(1), 115-145, F 95.

Crawford, Claudia. Immoralist: That Means the Opposite of Consequentialist: Comment on Professor Hale's "Was Nietzsche a Consequentialist?". *Int Stud Phil*, 27(3), 35-42, 1995.

In this article three specific arguments are elaborated in an effort to demonstrate Nietzsche's antiutilitarian stance in questions of moral value. The first argument points to Nietzsche's two worlds: the Dionysian world of physiology and will to power, and the semiotic world of humanly created values. On the semiotic level of common language Nietzsche can often "sound" consequentialist, but on the Dionysian level he is clearly antiutilitarian. The second argument shows Nietzsche questioning the very notions of causality and free will. If neither is taken for granted, utilitarianism is undone. The third argument against Nietzsche being taken for a consequentialist is that while on the semiotic level he speaks of good and evil and hierarchies of values, on the Dionysian level value oppositions disappear, and with *amour fati, all* of life's actions are affirmed.

Crawford, Jeffrey. "Cheikh Anta Diop, the 'Stolen Legacy,' and Afrocentrism" in *African Philosophy: Selected Readings, Mosley, Albert G (ed)*, 128-146. Englewood Cliffs, Prentice Hall, 1995.

The article summarizes Diop's work, particularly his 'Stolen Legacy Theory,' which holds that Egyptian intellectual developments (philosophy) have been attributed to the Greeks for racist reasons. The author argues that Diop's version of the theory avoids weaknesses of other versions, and concludes that whether one accepts Diop's interpretation of Egyptian material as philosophy, Diop's case deserves more attention than it has received. The article concludes that Afrocentrism encompasses divergent tendencies and that Diop's work is likely to further a process through which various Afrocentric positions are worked out in greater detail.

Crawford, Michael Sean. Richard Rorty's Inquiry Monism. *Eidos*, 11(1-2), 93-110, Je-D 93.

Crawley, Francis P. "Tradition, Recognition, and Truth: Cultural Identity in the Eyes of the University" in *Identity, Culture, and Education, Smeyers, Paul (ed)*, 139-144. Leuven, Leuven Univ Pr, 1994.

The article provides a genealogy of the origin of the university. It situates the underlying impetus of university education in the medieval notion of truth and the modern idea of identity. The text argues that Nietzsche provides a point of critique for the tradition of European culture and the idea of autonomy. The contemporary debate around multiculturalism is shown to undermine the traditional reflexive goal of singularity. Reference is made to Jacques Derrida, Michael Oakeshott, Martin Heidegger, Charles Taylor, and Alisdair MacIntyre.

Creath, Richard. From Königsberg to Vienna: Coffa on the Rise of Modern Semantics. *Dialogue (Canada)*, 34(1), 113-118, Wint 95.

Creel, Richard. Propositional Faith as a Mode of Belief and a Gift of God. *J Phil Res*, 19, 243-256, 1994.

Some people use "faith" to refer to an action, some to a passion, and some to a composite of the two. "Faith" is also sometimes used interchangeably with "belief". This paper is an effort to identify and overcome some of the problems caused by these facts. I pursue this end by distinguishing several meanings of "belief", and by distinguishing actional faith, passional faith, and faithfulness from one another. I argue that much can be gained by restricting the meaning of "faith" to the concept of a non-evidential doxastic passion that can be caused by any number of things, including God, if God exists.

Crespo, Enrique Bocardo. Las Dificultades de la Noción de Acción. *Cuad Vico*, 4, 27-38, 1994.

The paper starts with a quick perusal of Francisco Sánchez's sceptical criticism and sets forth a tentative definition of his epistemological principle. Shortly after Vico's principle *verum esse ipsum factum* is examined in connexion with Sánchez's esceptical thesis. A new definition of truth is considered and finally two theories on human action (those of von Wright's and Davidson's) are compared with Vico's principle.

Crespo, Mariano. En torno a los "estados de cosas": una investigación ontológico-formal. *Anu Filosof*, 28(1), 143-156, 1995.

The states of affairs are one of the basic categories of the formal ontology in the Husserlian sense of this word. They are objective correlates of judgements and they have an existence independent of propositions and of acts of judging. Their form is "the being-b of A". States of affairs have different properties. One of the most important is that they are bearers of ontological modalities. In this respect the analysis of the different classes of modalities needs to be completed for ontological investigations which make clear the several types of essences and the laws which are grounded in these essences.

Crespo, Ricardo F. Nota Acerca de las Precisiones Tomistas al Concepto Aristotélico de Ciencia Práctica y la Noción Contemporánea de Ciencias Sociales. *Sapientia*, 49(193-4), 297-305, 1994.

Crespo de Blaquier, Carola. "La Facultad Kantiana del Gusto Puro: Una Reflexión sin Conceptos" in *Temas Actuales de Filosofía, Palacios, María Julia (ed)*, 147-156. Buenos Aires, Univ Nacional Salta, 1993.

Cresswell, M J. In Defence of the Barcan Formula. *Log Anal*, 34, 271-282, S-D 91.

The paper argues that since the possible worlds semantics for quantified modal logic already assumes that we have a domain of possible objects, not all of which actually exist, there is no metaphysical bar to quantifying over them, and that considerations of naturalness, expressibility, and axiomatizability as extensions of standard axiomatic predicate logic, all strongly indicate that we should. In consequence it is systems possessing the Barcan Formula which should be taken as basic in modal predicate logic.

Cresswell, M J. Incompleteness and the Barcan Formula. *J Phil Log*, 24(4), 379-403, Ag 95.

A (normal) system of propositional modal logic is said to be complete if it is characterized by a class of (Kripke) frames. When we move to modal predicate logic the question of completeness can again be raised. It is not hard to prove that if a predicate modal logic is complete then it is characterized by the class of all frames for the propositional logic on which it is based. Nor is it hard to prove that if a propositional modal logic is incomplete then so is the predicate logic based on it. But the interesting question is whether a complete propositional modal logic can have an incomplete extension. In 1967 Kripke announced the incompleteness of a predicate extension of S4. The purpose of the present article is to present several such systems. In the first group it is the systems *with* the Barcan Formula which are incomplete, while those without are complete. In the second group it is those *without* the Barcan Formula which are incomplete, while those with the Barcan Formula are complete. But all these are based on propositional systems which are characterized by frames satisfying in each case a single first-order sentence.

Cresswell, M J. The Ontological Status of Matter in Aristotle. *Theoria*, 58(2-3), 116-130, 1992.

The paper uses Quine's criterion of ontological commitment in order to see whether Aristotle's doctrine of substantial change requires him to quantift over matter, or whether he can get away with having only substances and their accidents as the metaphysics in a first-order language. It is argued that he can avoid commitment to matter by using a four-place predicate meaning: the matter of x at t_1, is the same as (or alternatively, perhaps, overlaps) the matter of y at t_2.

Cresswell, Maxwell. "S1 Is Not So Simple" in *Modality, Morality, and Belief, Sinnott-Armstrong, Walter (ed)*, 29-40. New York, Cambridge Univ Pr, 1994.

Crétella, Henri. Staurologie. *Heidegger Stud*, 9, 63-75, 1993.

The aim of the article is to show that there are *two* meanings of the Heideggerian thinking. The "first"—ontological—has been studied for years. But the "second"—theological—remains quite neglected in its *basic* bearing. The article describes it as "staurological", that is to say: *cross-shaped*. This allows to prove—on the one hand—the original Christianity": (*Christlichkeit*, not *Christentum*) of the Heideggerian thinking; but that gives also—on the other hand—the reason of its essential importance for psychoanalysis as Lacan practiced and conceived it. This double issue should be now meditated in its *future origin*.

Crigger, Bette-Jane. Negotiating the Moral Order: Paradoxes of Ethics Consultation. *Kennedy Inst Ethics J*, 5(2), 89-112, Je 95.

Ethics consultation at the bedside has been hailed as a better way than courts and ethics committees to empower patients and make explicit the value components of treatment decisions. But close examination of the practice of ethics consultation reveals that it in fact risks subverting those ends by interpolating a third (expert) party into the doctor-patient encounter. In addition, the practice of bioethics through consultation does the broader cultural work of fashioning a shared moral order in the face of manifestly plural individual commitments. In doing so, however, bioethics furthers medicine's position as a privileged domain of public moral discourse in contemporary American society.

Crisp, Roger. "Quality of Life and Health Care" in *Medicine and Moral Reasoning, Fulford, K W M (ed)*, 171-183. New York, Cambridge Univ Pr, 1994.

This paper is largely a discussion of the notion of the Quality-Adjusted-Life-Year (QALY), as it is used in decisions concerning the allocation of medical resources. It is argued that the QALY overvalues health, and that quality of life should be understood in terms of an 'objective list' of goals. It is concluded that, because of problems arising from the discontinuity of values, a theory which makes room for fairness is more attractive than a QALY-maximising theory.

Crisp, Roger. "Values, Reasons and the Environment" in *Philosophy and the Natural Environment, Attfield, Robin (ed)*, 75-87. New York, Cambridge Univ Pr, 1994.

This paper considers the nature of the value of the environment, and the reasons to act grounded in this value. It defends a G E Moorean account of intrinsic value, drawing a distinction between 'good' and 'good for'. The domain of value is divided into three: aesthetic, welfare, and moral. Limits on maximizing value are outlined. The paper concludes that there are important practical links between development and the environments.

Crisp, Roger. *Essays on Bioethics* by R M Hare. *Bioethics*, 9(2), 155-163, Ap 95.

Hare's theory is outlined. He is charged with formalism, and a Sidgwickian alternative is suggested. It is argued that Hare could state his claims without employing the notion of harm to possible people.

Crisp, Roger and Cowton, Christopher. Hyprocrisy and Moral Seriousness. *Amer Phil Quart*, 31(4), 343-349, O 94.

This paper argues that recent discussion of hypocrisy has failed to recognize its distinct forms. We identify four: 1) pretence; 2) blame; 3)inconsistency; 4)complacency. We then consider what these different forms have in common. We reject the linguistic argument based on the claim that biblical 'hypocrisy' is to be understood as 'wickedness'. We deny also Wittgensteinean and Aristotelian understandings, as well as any attempt to set hypocrisy in opposition to integrity. Finally, we argue that hypocrisy is a failure to possess a 'metavirtue' and to take morality seriously.

Crispini, Ines. Parsimonia, frugalità, decoro: Sombart e l'antropologia del "borghese virtuoso". *Arch Stor Cult*, 7, 223-243, 1994.

This work analyses the most important aspects of the "bourgeois spirit" found in the anthropologic thinking of Werner Sombart. The "bourgeois spirit" is characterised by methodical approach, rationality and the relentless pursuit of ends. These characteristies become principles rules and finally virtues. Of these virtues, the most important is that of economy, namely parsimony in the administration of property, human resource and time. This principle of economy implies the other cardinal bourgeois virtues: industry and frugality. This analysis therefore allows definition of the meaning of life and mentality of the "bourgeois" which is penetrated in the "Weltanschauung" of the Western world.

Cristani, Giovanni. Tradizione Biblica, Miti e Rivoluzioni Geologiche Negli "Anecdotes de la Nature" di Nicolas-Antoine Boulanger. *G Crit Filosof Ital*, 73(1), 92-123, Ja-Ap 94.

Cristi, Renato. Hegel on Property and Recognition. *Laval Theol Phil*, 51(2), 335-344, Je 95.

The state, Hegel reiterates, "is by no means a contract, and its substantial essence does not consist unconditionally in the protection and safeguarding of the lives and property of individuals as such." An instrumental state whose sole function was the protection of private property would be contractually bound to civil society. This would weaken it considerably for this would deplete the autonomy, independence and neutrality required to protect property effectively.

Cristi, Renato. Waldron on Special Rights *in rem*. *Dialogue (Canada)*, 33(2), 183-190, Spr 94.

Cristian, Alin. Zarathustra's Dance: A Heideggerian Misstep?. *Man World*, 28(2), 145-162, Ap 95.

The ontological status of corporeal expressions cannot be reduced to an ecstatic temporality without important omissions. As the artistic "material" of dance, bodily movements do not possess that self-secluding character which alone, according to Heidegger, can sustain the world of the artwork. Their most original openness toward the others suggests an unprojective corporeal understanding at work within the very foundation of meaning. Moreover, such an *inconspicuous* kind of openness undermines the inaugural character of a key Heideggerian concept, i.e., *resolute* openness. This might explain a certain bias in Heidegger's appropriation of Nietzsche as metaphysician.

Critchley, Simon. Black Socrates?. *Rad Phil*, 69, 17-26, Ja-F 95.

Critchley, Simon. Habermas und Derrida werden verheiratet. *Deut Z Phil*, 42(6), 1025-1036, 1994.

This essay is a response to Axel Honneth's 'Der Andere der Gerechtigkeit' where he tries to show how the Habermasian program of Discourse Ethics stands in need of supplementations by a Derridian concept of justice, based in the asymmetrical respect for the other. With certain large reservations as to the questions of phenomenological method and normativity and the passage from ethics to politics, my essay endorses this marriage between Habermas and Derrida as a possible new future for philosophical debate beyond the state antagonisms of modernity versus postmodernity.

Critchlow, Keith. "The Platonic Tradition on the Nature of Proportion" in *Homage to Pythagoras, Bamford, Christopher (ed)*, 133-168. Hudson, Lindisfarne Pr, 1994.

Crittenden, Paul. Ethics and Aesthetics in Aristotle's *Poetics*. *Lit Aes*, 1, 15-27, Spr 91.

Croce, Benedetto and Ainslie, Douglas (trans). *Aesthetic as Science of Expression and General Linguistic*. New Brunswick, Transaction Books, 1995.

Croce, Paul Jerome. William James's Scientific Education. *Hist Human Sci*, 8(1), 9-28, F 95.

William James's disgust for scientific arrogance was not in defiance of his early education in science, but because of it. In particular, James was influenced by the probabilistic method of Charles Darwin's theory of natural selection, especially as interpreted by Charles Sanders Peirce. Peirce, who was James's most immediate scientific influence, maintained an unresolved ambiguity between a probabilistic scientific fallibilism and a confidence in science's quest for certainty, while James emphasized the fallibilism of science as the crowning evidence for epistemological uncertainties. Despite his disagreement with scientific certainty, James fully supported science as a fallible, useful means of inquiry.

Crook, Stephen (ed) and Adorno, Theodor W. *Adorno: The Stars Down to Earth and Other Essays on the Irrational in Culture*. New York, Routledge, 1994.

Cropsey, Joseph. *Plato's World: Man's Place in the Cosmos*. Chicago, Univ of Chicago Pr, 1995.

This book interprets seven consecutive Platonic dialogues that are set in the last months of Socrates' life. Regarding them as a dramatic entity because of their chronological continuity, they are presented as the Platonic/Socratic conception of human existence in a world in which gods and nature leave humanity exposed in ways that discourage utopianism.

Crosby, Donald A. Kant's Ideas About Ultimate Reality and Meaning in Relation to His Moral Theory: Critique of an Enlightenment Ideal. *Ultim Real Mean*, 17(2), 117-136, Ju 94.

Kant's claim that morality leads ineluctably to religion conflicts with compelling evidence that his culturally inherited religious assumptions provide essential background and inspiration for his moral theory. Neither his moral theory nor the religious ideas he professes to derive from it can be said to be independent of cultural conditioning. It is also argued that the Enlightenment notion that claims to truth and value, in order to be cogent, must be rooted in necessary and universal principles—and thus be wholly free of the influence of particular cultural assumptions—is itself patently unreasonable (as well as impossible to achieve).

Cross, Charles B. Max Black on the Identity of Indiscernibles. *Phil Quart*, 45(180), 350-360, Jl 95.

I give a critique of the argument against the Identity of Indiscernibles found in Max Black's dialogue "The Identity of Indiscernibles". I begin by postulating and giving existence and individuation conditions for actually existent thought experiment characters on analogy with fictional characters as postulated in Peter van Inwagen's "Creatures of Fiction". I then show that Black's two-spheres thought experiment raises not one but two discernibility questions: 1) Is it true in the two-spheres thought experiment that there exist two indiscernible spheres? NO. 2) Is it true in the actual world that there are two indiscernible sphere-characters? YES.

Cross, Charles B. Probability, Evidence, and the Coherence of the Whole Truth. *Synthese*, 103(2), 153-170, My 95.

The coherence of the whole truth is a presupposition of any holistic coherence theory of justification that postulates a positive connection between justification and truth, for unless the whole truth is itself systemically coherent there is no reason to look for systemic coherence when deciding whether one is justified in accepting a given body of beliefs as true. This paper develops a formal model of holistic evidential coherence and uses this model to formalize and defend the claim that the whole truth must be coherent in an evidential sense.

Crossley, J N and Lun, A W C. The Logic of Liu Hui and Euclid as Exemplified in Their Proofs of the Volume of a Pyramid. *Phil Hist Sci*, 3(1), 11-27, Ap 94.

We present a comparison of the logic employed in Euclid's *Elements* in the West and the *Jiu Zhang Suan Shu* in China. Previously it has been said that Chinese mathematics was algorithmic and practical, as opposed to the logical and theoretical Euclidean mathematics. We point out that Euclid uses logic which either is, or could be, as constructive as that of Liu Hui and has a number of points of contact even though the traditions are very different.

Crosswhite, James. Is There an Audience for this Argument? Fallacies, Theories, and Relativisms. *Phil Rhet*, 28(2), 134-145, 1995.

Crowe, Frederick E. Lonergan's Universalist View of Religion. *Method*, 12(2), 147-179, Fall 94.

Crowther, Paul. Sociological Imperialism and the Field of Cultural Production: The Case of Bourdieu. *Theor Cult Soc*, 11(1), 155-169, F 94.

Cruysberghs, Paul. Beyond World History: On Hegel's and Kierkegaard's Interests in Ethics and Religion. *Hist Euro Ideas*, 20(1-3), 155-160, Ja 95.

Why did Kierkegaard consider Hegel's philosophy of world history to be without any ethical relevance, whereas for Hegel world history has an eminent ethical and even religious significance? I argue that Kierkegaard's critical position over against the Hegelian conception of world history has something to do with what I call a loss of substance. I try to show that for Kierkegaard the actual social and political world has lost its substantial character. Kierkegaard's thought is an attempt to compensate for this loss of substance. It claims to offer an alternative for Hegelianism in an age that does not believe anymore in the reasonableness of world history.

Cruz, Manuel. Comprensión e identidad: Encuentro entre filosofíade la historia y filosofía de la acción. *Rev Latin de Filosof*, 20(2), 237-258, 1994.

The purpose of this study is to show—slightly toning down Hayden White's category—the links between what we could call the "metahistoric discourse" and the discourse of action. We begin by analyzing some aspects of the so called *Verstehen* process. The problem of comprehension allows for transit from one sphere to the other with no undue theoretical violence. The formula stating that the history of philosophy is nothing but the philosophy of past action becomes understandable if what both aim at is to make the conduct of others intelligible. The parallelism is worked out by showing that the central category of *subject* in the historicistic approaches finds its correlation in the notion of *agent* in today's action theorists. The correlation is, of course, not without difficulties, which explains the references to Parfit.

Cruz, Manuel. Comprensión Histórica, Acción e Identidad. *An Seminar Metaf*, 28, 85-101, 1994.

Crysdale, Cynthia S W. Lonergan's "Philosophy and the Religious Phenomenon": A Commentary. *Method*, 12(2), 181-204, Fall 94.

Csech, Werner. Von der Reichweite mathematischen Denkens bei Fichte und Novalis. *Theol Phil*, 70(1), 41-61, 1995.

Das moderne Leben ist vom mathematischen Denken beherrscht, dessen Präzision eine paradigmatische Funktion für alle Wissenschaft und sogar die Philosophie erhalten hat. Steht aber nicht die Philosophie wissenschaftstheoretisch über der Mathematik? Es werden Fichtes und Novalis' Auffassungen darüber untersucht. Schon früh versucht Fichte, die philosophischen Zusammenhänge in mathematischen Formeln auszusprechen. Bald erkannte er, dass die Evidenz des zu vermittelnden Inhalts nicht formalisiert werden kann. Im Gegenteil muss der Philosoph über den Sinn formaler Strukturen Rechenschaft geben. Ähnlich unterscheidet Novalis eine "Mathematik der Philosophie" von der "Philosophie der Mathematik", welche gemeinsam gipfeln in einer rein geistigen Beziehungswissenschaft. Diese ist kein Faktum, sondern eine Aufgabe der Menschheit.

Csikszentmihalyi, Mihaly and Sawyer, Keith. "Creative Insight: The Social Dimension of a Solitary Moment" in *The Nature of Insight, Sternberg, Robert J (ed)*, 329-363. Cambridge, MIT Pr, 1995.

Cuéllar, Hortensia. Ontología modal en la *Philosophia Prima*. *Topicos*, 3(4), 27-60, 1993.

Being is an analogical notion in Aristotle. There are several meanings of being, and some of them were misunderstood by the Latter Scholastic.

Cuéllar P, Hortensia. La Ontologia Anti-Metafisica de Nicolai Hartmann. *Topicos*, 1(1), 159-173, 1991.

In Nicolai Harmann's philosophical thought the modal category of *effectiveness* (*Wirklichkeit*, to which the remainder modalities, *Möglichkeit, Notwendigkeit*, and *Zufälligkeit* are related) reduces the wide field of the *real* to the narrow path of the *possible*, and thus, to that even narrower of the *contingent*. This progressive constriction yields a new edition of the Megaric theory of possibility which rejects an analogical treatment of *being* in the way Aristotle presents it, and the subsequent searching of the last foundation of reality. On the contrary, an Aristotelian approach to modality allows the achieving of both goals.

Cuello, César. En torno a la ecuación desarrollo científico y tecnológico igual a progreso social. *Rev Filosof (Costa Rica)*, 32(77), 61-69, Jl 94.

In almost four centuries of evolution, the ideal of social progress based on the development of science and technology has not brought to the majority of humankind the well-being and happiness it has promised. Such an ideal, on the contrary, became an alienating ideology that erases existence in the present tense in favor of a future lacking precise human goals and limits.

Cullenberg, Stephen (ed) and Callari, Antonio (ed) and Biewener, Carole (ed). *Marxism in the Postmodern Age*. New York, Guilford, 1994.

Fifty-three multidisciplinary essays which explore how Marxist theory is critically rethinking its conditions and objects of analysis. Situated in the context of changing national and international conditions, including the collapse of really existing socialism, the book captures a dialogue, carried on non-essentialist ground, between established Marxist concepts (of class and of economic interests) and other social identities and forms of oppression and resistence. The essays, many of which are by well-known contemporary figures, probe for an imaginary of social transformation capable of going beyond the established dichotomies of the modernist age, and chart a vast analytical terrain for a post-orthodox Marxism.

Cullenberg, Stephen (ed) and Magnus, Bernd (ed). *Whither Marxism?*. New York, Routledge, 1994.

What is living and what is dead in Marxism? Has the collapse of communism also spelled the death of Marxism, and of Marx as an important political thinker? Have we reached "the end of history" as Fukayama has argued, where pluralistic democracies and capitalist economies reign supreme? Is the future now a choice between Scandinavian style social democracy and unrestrained free market capitalism? Given the plight of the homeless, the lack of adequate health care, environmental degradation, racism, enormous national debt burdens, what sort of model for the future do we have? What is one to make of the violent nationalisms, ethnocentrism and xenophobia perhaps not seen since Hitler's Germany? What is the status of Marxist social goals such as the egalitarian distribution of income, increased workplace democracy, the end of economic exploitation and the eradication of class differences? Does the "end of history" also portend the end of Marxist theory? The *Whither Marxism* volumes raise these and related questions in an international and interdisciplinary context. (edited)

Culp, Sylvia. Defending Robustness: The Bacterial Mesosome as a Test Case. *Proc Phil Sci Ass*, 1, 46-57, 1994.

Rasmussen (1993) argues that, because electron microscopists did not use robustness and would not have been warranted in using it as a criterion for the reality or the artifactuality of mesosomes, the bacterial mesosome serves as a test case for robustness that it fails. I respond by arguing that a more complete reading of the research literature on the mesosome shows that ultimately the more robust body of data did not support the mesosome and that electron microscopists used and were warranted in using robustness as a criterion for the artifactuality of mesosomes.

Culp, Sylvia. Objectivity in Experimental Inquiry: Breaking Data-Technique Circles. *Phil Sci*, 62(3), 438-458, S 95.

I respond to H M Collin's claim (1985, 1990, 1993) that experimental inquiry cannot be objective because the only criterium experimentalists have for determining whether a technique is "working" is the production of "correct" (i.e., the expected) data. Collins claims that the "experimenters' regress," the name he gives to this data-technique circle, cannot be broken using the resources of experiment alone. I argue that the data-technique circle, can be broken even though any interpretation of the raw data produced by techniques is theory-dependent. However, it is possible to break this circle by eliminating dependence on even those theoretical presuppositions that are shared by an entire scientific community through the use of multiple independently theory-dependent techniques to produce robust bodies of data. Moreover, I argue, that it is the production of robust bodies of data that convinces experimentalists of the objectivity of their data interpretations.

Cummings, James. Coherent Sequences Versus Radin Sequences. *Annals Pure Applied Log*, 70(3), 223-241, D 94.

We attempt to make a connection between the sequences of measures used to define Radin forcing and the coherent sequences of extenders which are the basis of modern inner model theory. We show that in certain circumstances we can read off sequences of measures as defined by Radin from coherent sequences of extenders, and that we can define Radin forcing directly from a coherent extender sequence and a sequence of ordinals; this generalizes Mitchell's construction of Radin forcing from a coherent sequence of measures.

Cummings, James. Possible Behaviours for the Mitchell Ordering II. *J Sym Log*, 59(4), 1196-1209, D 94.

Cuneo, Terrence D. Combating the Noetic Effects of Sin: Pascal's Strategy for Natural Theology. *Faith Phil*, 11(4), 645-662, Oct 94.

Pascal is traditionally thought to be a fideist and a severe critic of natural theology. In this essay, I argue that though Pascal is certainly an anti-evidentialist he nonetheless envisions natural theology to play a unique epistemic role in acquiring faith. Natural theology is useful for combating the epistemic results of sin. Pascal draws upon a rich psychology to show both how sin stunts some of our natural belief forming tendencies and how natural theology can stymie the effects of sin by moving our volition away from love of self to love of God, thereby facilitating the movement of God's grace.

Cunliffe, John. Charles Hall: Exploitation, Commercial Society and Political Economy. *Hist Polit Thought*, 15(4), 535-553, Wint 94.

Hall's intellectual position is located in the intense controversy over economic modernization in the late eighteenth-century. His diagnosis of the ills of commercial society is based on a new emphasis on economic exploitation rather than political oppression as the major cause of mass poverty. This 'modern' theory of exploitative wage contracts is combined, firstly, with a broader view of the property relations which rendered all laborers vulnerable to such exploitation, and secondly, with an attack on the political system which sustained them. Hall's prescription called for the complete abolition of commercial society in favor of a system of equal individual property.

Cunningham, Anthony. Moral Addicts. *Dialogue (Canada)*, 33(2), 223-236, Spr 94.

Cunningham, Craig A. Dewey's Metaphysics and the Self. *Stud Phil Educ*, 13(3-4), 343-360, 1994-95.

This article explores the relationship between John Dewey's evolving metaphysics and his evolving conception of the self. I rely on Dewey's major ethical writings (including the two *Ethics* of 1908 and 1932) and Dewey's explicitly metaphysical writings (especially the 1915 "Subject Matter of Metaphysical Discourse" and the 1925 *Experience and Nature*). My article shows that despite a declaration in 1893 that metaphysics had no place in ethics, Dewey needed metaphysics to provide a scientific basis for values and for such concepts as potentiality, individuality, temporality, and the generic traits of existences of all kinds.

Cunningham, Daniel W. The Real Core Model and Its Scales. *Annals Pure Applied Log*, 72(3), 213-289, Ap 95.

Cunningham, Frank. *The Real World of Democracy Revisited and Other Essays on Democracy and Socialism*. Atlantic Highlands, Humanities Pr, 1994.

The essays in this collection join current efforts to integrate socialism and democracy. Beginning with C B Macpherson's *The Real World of Democracy* and sharing Macpherson's focus on political culture, a selection of problematic issues are addressed: contested conceptions of democracy and socialism; the status of Marxism after the collapse of communism; radical politics and the new social movements; and the nature of socialist egalitarianism (explicated in a critical interpretation of Marx's *Critique of the Gotha Program*). In addition democratic-socialist approaches are recommended regarding: communitarianism and individualism, philosophical foundationism, and global "sustainable development." An interview with Macpherson on Marxism is appended.

Cunningham, Henri-Paul. Darwin et le "transformisme des auteurs classiques". *Laval Theol Phil*, 50(2), 389-413, Ju 94.

Le jugement de Darwin déclarant: "En comparaison du vieil Aristote", Linné et Cuvier font figure "de simples enfants d'école", soulève de nombreuses difficultés. Passant en revue celles qui nous semblent les plus importantes, nous concluons que Darwin, après avoir exclu Spencer, a très justement inclus Aristote à la suite de Maupertius, Malthus et Wallace dans la liste des précurseurs scientifiques de sa théorie. S'il avait mieux connu les conclusions fort remarquables de la jeune science des fossiles, il aurait très certainement maintenu, croyonsnous, son évaluation du "transformisme classique"!

Cunningham, Suzanne. Herbert Spencer, Bertrand Russell, and the Shape of Early Analytic Philosophy. *Russell*, 14(1), 7-29, Sum 94.

It is widely agreed that Bertrand Russell's rejection of British Idealism helped to shape his version of analytic philosophy. In this paper I argue that Russell's objections to Herbert Spencer's views, particularly to his "evolutionism," also contributed in important ways to the shape that his philosophy took. Russell's preference for timeless truth, his insistence on mathematical physics rather than biology as the science relevant to philosophy, and his particular versions of atomism, all show that influence of his rejection of the Spencerian philosophy.

Cuonzo, Margaret. Judgments as Meta-Representations in the *Critique of Pure Reason*. *Conference*, 5(2), 71-78, Wint 94-95.

One of Kant's lesser known definitions of "judgment" says that a judgment is a "representation of a representation" of an object (B 93). On first reflection, such a definition is almost nonsensical given the vast number of entities that Kant classifies as presentations (e.g., concepts, sensations, intuitions). In "Judgments as Meta-Representations in the *Critique of Pure Reason*," I analyze this definition and argue that, despite first impressions, the definition is cogent, compatible with the other definitions, and one that in fact plausibly represents the nature of judgment.

Cupani, Alberto. A Filosofia da Ciência de Larry Laudan e a Crítica do "Positivismo". *Manuscrito*, 17(1), 91-143, Ap 94.

This paper analyses Larry Laudan's contribution to surmounting the "positivistic legacy" in philosophy of science. Espousing the historical view initiated by Thomas Kuhn, Laudan defends the view that the solution of cognitive problems characterizes science, and questions traditional theses such as the definition of science by the search for truth, epistemic realism and the impossibility of justifying axiological choices. At the same time, Laudan tries to avoid irrationalism and extreme relativism, showing the permanent value of some "positivistic" theses.

Curd, Patricia (ed) and Cohen, S Marc (ed) and Reeve, C D C (ed). *Readings in Ancient Greek Philosophy: From Thales to Aristotle*. Indianapolis, Hackett, 1995.

Extensive selections from the most important philosophical texts of ancient Greece from the Presocratics through Aristotle. Includes introductions, headnotes, maps, a concordance to the Presocratic fragments, an Aristotle glossary, and many new translations. 1) Presocratics and Sophists: Thales, Anaximander, Anaximenes, Pythagoras, Philolaus, Xenophanes, Heraclitus, Parmenides, Anaxagoras, Empedocles, Zeno, Leucippus, Democritus, Melissus, Protagoras, Gorgias, Antiphon, Critias. 2) Plato's dialogues: Euthyphro, Apology, Crito, Protagoras, Gorgias, Meno, Phaedo, Symposium, Republic, Parmenides, Timaeus. 3) Aristotle's treatises: Categories, De Interpretatione, Topics, Posterior Analytics, Physics, Generation and Corruption, On the Heavens, Meteorologica, Parts of Animals, Metaphysics, De Anima, Nicomachean Ethics, Politics.

Curley, Edwin. A Good Man is Hard to Find. *Proc Amer Phil Ass*, 65(3), 29-45, N 91.

Curran, Angela. Utilitarianism and Future Mistakes: Another Look. *Phil Stud*, 78(1), 71-85, Ap 95.

Curran, Mary Bernard. *Thinkers Through Time: Reading Ethics With Literature*. Bell Buckle, Iris Pr, 1993.

This book combines an explication of the teachings of a number of major philosophers from ancient times to the present on a number of key themes related to the ethical life with illustrations of how these themes were treated in contemporaneous works of literature. "Literature offers an experience of moral values that is immediate. Ordinarily, the reader participates in the literary more emotionally than he does in the philosophical." The first and larger section of the book selects the key themes of justice, happiness, morality, intention, person, communion, transcendence, and mercy. The philosophical and literary pairings are Plato and Sophocles; Aristotle and Sophocles; Aquinas and Dante; Kant and Ibsen; Scheler and Percy; Marcel and Wojtyla; Levinas and Camus; Wojtyla and Endo. In the second part of the book the same themes are presented more discursively in light of the thought of Aquinas and Wojtyla, permitting further reflection on the themes earlier treated more concretely.

Currie, Gregory. The Moral Psychology of Fiction. *Austl J Phil*, 73(2), 250-259, Je 95.

What can we learn from fiction? I argue that we can learn about the consequences of a certain course of action by projecting ourselves, in imagination, into the situation of the fiction's characters.

Currie, Gregory. Unreliability Refigured: Narrative in Literature and Film. *J Aes Art Crit*, 53(1), 19-29, Wint 95.

I argue for four theses: 1) That narrative unreliability is a concept separable from the concept of an unreliable narrator; 2) That narrative unreliability requires for its explanation the concept of an implied author; 3) That narrative unreliability bears close and interesting connections to the importantly distinct concept of an ambiguous narrative; 4) That we can explain the prevalence of certain devices in narrative in terms of the ease or difficulty of the reader's task in figuring out whether and how those devices are being used. These theses are intended to apply both to literary and to filmic narratives, but I also argue that each medium offers its own distinctive opportunities for narrative unreliability.

Curtin, Deane. Making Peace with the Earth: Indigenous Agriculture and the Green Revolution. *Environ Ethics*, 17(1), 59-74, Spr 95.

Since its inception in the years following World War II, the green revolution has been defended, not just as a technical program designed to alleviate world hunger, but on moral grounds as a program to achieve world peace. In this paper, I dispute the moral claim to a politics of peace, arguing instead that the green revolution is warist in its treatment of the environment and indigenous communities, and that the agricultural practices that the green revolution was designed to supplant—principally indigenous women's agriculture—are forms of ecological peacemaking, akin to pacifism. I argue as well, that the warist intentions of the green revolution are characteristic of a form of domination called developmentalism. A complete understanding of domination necessitates linking developmentalism with other forms of domination such as racism, sexism, and naturism.

Curtler, Hugh Mercer. *Ethical Argument: Critical Thinking in Ethics*. New York, Paragon House, 1993.

This is a "core" text that introduces students to basic argument skills that are then applied to complex ethical issues. The book seeks to exhibit what it teaches by directing a sustained argument against relativism in ethics. At every point the student is encouraged to question, disagree, and formulate counter-arguments using the skills presented in the text and incorporated into the main argument itself. Thus, the book seeks to involve the student in the activity of doing philosophy while learning about how philosophers approach ethical problem-solving. The book includes dozens of cases in five topic areas and is short enough to be used with primary sources or more elaborate case studies in such areas as business, medicine, or the professions.

Curtrofello, Andrew. *The Owl at Dawn: A Sequel to Hegel's Phenomenology of Spirit*. Albany, SUNY Pr, 1995.

Curwen, Peter and Richardson, Bill. Do Free-Market Governments Create Crisis-Ridden Societies?. *J Bus Ethics*, 14(7), 551-560, Jl 95.

The paper is concerned with the potential or actual impact that free-market governmental principles and policies might have, or might have had, in helping to create a more crisis-prone world. It is concerned with organizationally-induced crises where organizations and their environment interact to create disasters. The nature of the crisis-prone organization is discussed in the context of the relevant management literature. It is argued that the disastrous interaction of such an organization with its environment is promoted by a laisser-faire attitude on the part of the authorities. This is illustrated in the context of two recent British disasters involving the King's Cross Underground fire and the sinking of the Herald of Free Enterprise.

Curzer, Howard J. The Value of Passions in Plato and Aristotle: Comments. *SW Phil Rev*, 11(Supp), 57-62, Mr 95.

According to Leighton, Plato says that we should avoid certain passions and that reason should master the rest because otherwise the passions master reason. But Aristotle denies that we should reject or restrict the passions because he believes that reason and the passions can integrate. I maintain that both the *Republic* and Aristotle agree that we should avoid certain passions and that reason should integrate with rather than master the remaining passions. The *Phaedo* says that reason should master passions, but that is because the *Phaedo* describes philosophers under ordinary circumstances rather than under the ideal circumstances of the *Republic*.

Cushing, James T. Locality/ Separability: Is This Necessarily a Useful Distinction?. *Proc Phil Sci Ass*, 1, 107-116, 1994.

In the philosophy of science, we are to assess critically and on their intrinsic merits various proposals for a consistent interpretation of quantum mechanics, including resolutions of the measurement problem and accounts of the long-range Bell correlations. In this paper I suggest that the terms of debate may have been so severely and unduly constrained by the reigning orthodoxy that we labor unproductively with an unhelpful vocabulary and set of definitions and distinctions. I present an alternative conceptual framework, free of many of the standard conundrums.

Cushing, James T. *Quantum Mechanics: Historical Contingency and the Copenhagen Hegemony*. Chicago, Univ of Chicago Pr, 1994.

Cutrofello, Andrew. Hegel's Confessions; or, Why We Need a Sequel to the *Phenomenology of Spirit*. *Owl Minerva*, 26(1), 21-28, Fall 94.

In the *Phenomenology of Spirit*, Hegel presents a series of confessional scenes, the eventual culmination of which should represent the mutual recognition of subjects who recognize and respect their differences. During this process, however, a crucial confessional structure involves an elision of gender differences. This elision suggests that Hegel's narrative is incomplete. I articulate some of the conditions that would need to be met to continue Hegel's narrative, a project which I take up in my forthcoming book, *The Owl at Dawn: a Sequel to Hegel's Phenomenology of Spirit* (New York: State University of New York Press, 1995).

Cuypers, S E. Material Minds: On Materialism (in Dutch). *Tijdschr Filosof*, 56(4), 693-716, D 94.

Is the idea of a material mind intelligible? Or, to put it another way, is the hypothesis that the mind is the brain believable? This paper, *firstly*, claims that the materialistic project in contemporary philosophy of mind can only be accepted if both the general outlook of scientism and a specific scientific methodology to address the mind-body problem are taken for granted. The basic question—how are intentionality and consciousness possible, given mechanistic physicalism?—has a prima facie plausibility on the presumption of scientistic naturalism. However, it is shown, *secondly*, that materialism is neither successful in the execution of its project nor ultimately intelligible or believable because its fundamental naturalistic presuppositions are in no way mandatory or compulsory. *Finally*, in order to evade the pitfalls of dualistic mystification after having criticized the materialistic project an alternative Wittgensteinian attitude to the mind-body problem is suggested.

Cuypers, Stefaan E. L'impossible naturalisme de la psychosémantique de Fodor. *Dialectica*, 48(3-4), 231-248, 1994.

Dans *A Theory of Content* Jerry Fodor fait déboucher sa théorie représentationnelle de l'esprit sur une psychosémantique physicaliste et atomiste. Cette théorie externaliste de la signification—the *Asymmetric Dependency Theory*—fournit une solution entièrement naturalisée au second problème de Brentano, c'est-à-dire celui de l'objet référentiel. En m'appuyant sur le réalisme interne de Hilary Putnam, je critique deux éléments essentiels de la solution proposée par Fodor, à savoir la relation de dépendance asymétrique et l'individuation des objects de la référence. Cette critique vise à montrer que le problème de la naturalisation et celui de la détermination sémantique ne sauraient être résolus simultanément. En outre, la détermination ontologique des objects de la référence implique inévitablement le principe de relativité conceptuelle. L'impossibilité de la psychosémantique naturalisée de Fodor corrobore donc la thèse de Brentano selon laquelle les phénomènes de sémanticité et d'intentionnalité sont primitifs.

Czapkay Sudduth, Michael L. The Prospects for 'Mediate' Natural Theology in John Calvin. *Relig Stud*, 31(1), 53-68, Mr 95.

In the present paper I consider the plausibility of a mediate natural theology in John Calvin. First, utilizing Robert Audi's distinction between 'episodically' and 'structurally' inferential beliefs, I show that a plausible case can be made for the compatibility of a mediate theology corresponding to both these forms of inferential belief with salient features of Calvin's theology. Second, I apply Calvin's view on arguments for Scripture to theistic belief and suggest a way of construing natural theology as a intra-faith practice aimed at satisfying the cognitive desideratum of reflective nationality—a Calvinistic project of *fides quaerens intellectum*.

Czarnecki, Zdzislaw J. On the Idealization of the Historical Past. *Dialogue Hum*, 4(1), 77-78, 1994.

Czarnecki, Zdzislaw J. Some Problems of the Origin of the Idea of Progressive Historical Time. *Dialogue Hum*, 4(1), 90-100, 1994.

Czlonka, Diane and Tomlinson, Thomas. Futility and Hospital Policy. *Hastings Center Rep*, 25(3), 28-35, My-Je 95.

Decisions to withhold futile resuscitation without the consent of patients or families are defensible on ethical grounds, but the concerns frequently expressed against such authority suggest a number of safeguards necessary for implementing a trustworthy hospital policy on futile CPR. The article concludes with an outline of an ideal policy.

D'Agostini, Franca. Oltre l'Interpretazione: Ermeneutica e Nichilismo. *Filosofia*, 45(3), 357-368, S-D 94.

D'Agostino, Francesco. Contingenza delle Norme e Soluzione delle Controversie. *Riv Int Filosof Diritto*, 71(4), 666-678, 1994.

D'Agostino, Francesco. Una Ricerca sullo Stato di Edith Stein. *Aquinas*, 37(2), 409-415, My-Ag 94.

D'Agostino, Fred. The Ethics of Social Science Research. *J Applied Phil*, 12(1), 65-76, 1995.

Ethical thinking about social science research is dominated by a biomedical model whose salient features are the assumption that only potential harms to subjects of research are relevant in the ethical evaluation of that research, and in the emphasis on securing informed consent in order to establish ethical probity. A number of counter-examples are considered to the assumption, a number of defences against these counter-examples are examined, and an alternative model is proposed for the ethical evaluation of social science research: a model which can cope with the systemic harms (harms other than those to participants as particpants) which have been identified. This model is based on John Rawls's idea of original position reasoning and treats social science research as an institutional feature of the basic structure of society.

D'Agostino, Giovanna. Topological Structure of Diagonalizable Algebras and Corresponding Logical Properties of Theories. *Notre Dame J Form Log*, 35(4), 563-572, Fall 94.

This paper studies the topological duality between diagonalizable algebras and bitopological spaces. In particular, the correspondence between algebraic properties of a diagonalizable algebra and topological properties of its dual space is investigated. Since the main example of a diagonalizable algebra is the Lindenbaum algebra of an r.e. theory extending Peano Arithmetic, endowed with an operator defined by means of the provability predicate of the theory, this duality gives the possibility to study arithmetical properties of theories from a topological point of view. (edited)

D'Agostino, S Matthew. Reason and Rationality: The Core Doctrines of Secular Humanism. *Free Inq*, 15(1), 47-50, Wint 94-95.

D'Alembert, Jean Le Rond and Schwab, Richard N (trans). *Preliminary Discourse to the Encyclopedia of Diderot*. Chicago, Univ of Chicago Pr, 1995.

D'Ambra, Michele. La persona come apertura all'essere eterno secondo E Stein. *Aquinas*, 37(1), 179-195, Ja-Ap 94.

D'Amico, Robert D. *Sed Amentes Sunt Isti*: Against Michel Foucault's Account of Cartesian Skepticism. *Phil Forum*, 26(1), 33-48, Fall 94.

This article is a criticism of Michel Foucault's reading of a passage of Descartes' *Meditations*. I argue that Foucault's account of Descartes on madness fails both as an account of the passage and as an account of the skeptical doubt raised by the possibility of madness. However, Foucault's stress on the importance of Descartes's physiological-medical theory of madness does support a traditional reading of this brief passage in the *Meditations*.

D'Amour, Stéphan. Architecture et Rationalité: Walter Gropius. *Philosopher*, 17, 137-160, 1995.

In "La tête de l'architecte" (Antonia Soulez ed., *L'architecte et le philosophie*, Brussels, P Mardaga), Maurice Lagueux briefly suggested that the sort of rationality underlying the architectoral theory of *Walter Gropius, or at* least some aspects of it, might be quite similar to what F A Hayek called constructivist rationalism. This paper argues, among other things, that Gropius's constructivist attitude (in Hayek's sense) springs from his using in architecture organic analogies that emphasize the structure and functions of the living instead of its spontaneity.

D'Amour, Stéphan. La Conception du Sujet Selon Sandel. *Philosopher*, 15, 69-80, 1994.

D'Andrea, Thomas D. Towards an Understanding of Aquinas's Self-Understanding of His Work. *Topicos*, 4(7), 19-31, 1994.

This paper tries to provide an attempt of explanation of St Thomas Aquinas's intellectual aims as they are revealed in some texts of *Summa contra Gentiles* and a few minor works.

D'haen, Theo (ed) and Bertens, Hans (ed). *Liminal Postmodernisms: The Postmodern, the (Post-)Colonial, and the (Post-)Feminist*. Amsterdam, Rodopi, 1994.

Liminal Postmodernisms (Postmodern Studies 8), concentrates on the various intersections between "The Postmodern", the "(Post-)Colonial", and the "(Post-)Feminist". Central to all the essays, by Robert Young, Sylvia Söderlind, John Thieme, Steven Connor, Richard Todd, Chantal Zabus, Hena Maes-Jelinek, Christine Levecq, Maria Del Sapio Garbero, R J Ellis, Allen Thiher, Annemarie Kemeny, Michael Gronow, Allen E Hibbard, and Julia Martin are the issues of liminality, of borders and boundaries both separating and joining races, genders, and nationalities, of definitions and discourses establishing others and selves. Philosophers regularly referred to include Deleuze and Guattari, Derrida, Foucault, and Lacan.

D'Hondt, Jacques. "Die Brüche in der europäischen Philosophietradition" in *Das geistige Erbe Europas, Buhr, Manfred (ed)*, 221-235. Napoli, Vivarium, 1994.

L'existence d'une tradition philosophique européenne est incontestable. Elle manifeste, conjointement à une permanence dans l'espace, une continuité de développement dans le temps. On ne peut cependant se dissimuler la profondeur et parfois la brutalité des ruptures, des changements qualitatifs qui s'y sont produits. Les philosophies s'y succèdent en s'enchaînant positivement ou négativement les unes aux autres et cependant sans se ressembler entièrement. Il faut donc, à leur propos, parvenir à l'idée d'une histoire et d'une logique de la liaison intime des moments d'une discontinuité.

D'Hondt, Jacques. La Ruse de la Raison. *Laval Theol Phil*, 51(2), 293-310, Je 95.

Bien que la ruse soit généralement réprouvée par les moralistes, Hegel a donné à sa philosophie une résonance populaire en forgeant l'image fascinante d'une *ruse de la raison* qui régirait le monde humain. Elle illustre une pensée complexe et dissimulée. Pour la comprendre, il convient de distinguer d'abord deux instances que Hegel semble parfois confondre: une ruse de l'homme (son activité, son travail) à l'égard de la nature, et une ruse universelle s'exerçant sur les hommes pour les constituer en société historique. Cette ruse universelle reste-t-elle immanente à la vie sociale, ou bien doit-elle être imputée à un être transcendant? Hegel exprime alternativement ces deux conceptions incompatibles.

D'Hondt, Jacques and Burbidge, John W (trans). *Hegel In His Time: Berlin, 1818-1831*. Peterborough, Broadview Pr, 1988.

In this work Jacques D'Hondt explores "the philosophy of right whose maxims Hegel actually followed in his daily life." Using Hegel's letters and contemporary documents he shows that Hegel's patrons were the liberals in the Prussian regime; that he was constantly under suspicion from reactionaries; that he attacked the demagoguery and xenophobic chauvinism of the student movement while supporting and encouraging its liberal leaders; and that his closest contacts were with progressive figures in both France and Germany. The negative assessment by Marx and Engels reflects a later time when liberalism was no longer at the forefront of progress.

D'Isanto, Luca. Gianni Vattimo's Hermeneutics and the Trace of Divinity. *Mod Theol*, 10(4), 361-381, O 94.

In this article, I argue that Gianni Vattimo's postmodern ontological hermeneutics responds to metaphysical violence by practicing a patient, self-critical exercise of *pietas* that accompanies metaphysics towards its destiny of dissolution. I also suggest that Vattimo's hermeneutics discloses a fragile sense of emancipation which is lost in other postmodern thinkers, and helps clarify the internal discourse of theological hermeneutics. In particular, I argue that the task of theological hermeneutics is to inscribe the word "God" upon the occurrence of the cross and consequently upon every human event, without destroying the difference between divine and worldly being.

d'Ors, Angel and García-Clavel, Manuel. Sobre las *Obligationes* de Robert Fland: Antiqua et Nova Responsio. *Rev Filosof (Spain)*, 7(11), 51-88, 1994.

da Costa, Newton C A and Doria, Francisco A and Tsuji, Marcelo. The Undecidability of Formal Definitions in the Theory of Finite Groups. *Bull Sec Log*, 24(2), 56-63, Je 95.

In this paper a set of *explicit* expressions for a family of finite groups will be constructed in the language of Zermelo-Fraenkel *plus* the Axiom of Choice set theory in such a way that there is no general procedure to decide whether a given expression of this set is representing a finite solvable group or not.

da Silveira, Maria Joao C. Se Ocupa el Fenomenólogo de la Metafísica?. *Aquinas*, 37(3), 655-664, S-D 94.

Dacal Alonso, Jose Antonio. Cultura y Filosofía. *Logos (Mexico)*, 23(67), 11-49, Ja-Ap 95.

Se estudian los componentes históricos, antropológicos, gnoseológicos, metafísicos, ontológicos, axiológicos, éticos, políticos, vitales y educativos de una filosofía de la cultura. Se analiza el papel del mito, las creencias, las utopías y las ideologías en la configuración de la cultura. Así como la importancia de Ernst Cassi rer en torno a la cultura. Los anteriores son los ejes-criterio para intentar evaluar una filosofía de la cultura, lo cual es muy difícil, pues se trata no del estudio de un hecho particular, sino de encontrar el objeto formal universal de la cultura como fenómeno esencial al ser humano.

Dacal Alonso, José Antonio. Los conceptos de Arte y Belleza en H G Gadamer. *Logos (Mexico)*, 22(66), 95-103, S-D 94.

Gadamer busca comprender todas las formas de expresión artísticas, aún las opuestas a su ideario. Utiliza para ese fin el método fenomenológico y hermenéutico. La realidad del arte, permite buscar y alcanzar su verdad, a través de la reflexión y el símbolo, que desciende a mayores niveles de profundidad. El arte es vía de conocimiento de acuerdo a la verdad que busca y lo sustenta. Esa verdad se sostiene en el contenido de la obra de art y en su forma de expresión.

Dacey, Raymond. Inducing Fair Trade Out of Hegemonic Trade. *Synthese*, 100(3), 497-504, S 94.

This paper provides a model of the transition from hegemonic trade to contemporary (or fair) trade. Hegemonic trade is an instance of the two player game called Bully (Poundstone 1992) and Called Bluff (Snyder and Diesing 1977); contemporary trade is an instance of Prisoner's Dilemma (Krugman and Obstfeld 1991). In this paper, I show that a nation under the thumb of a hegemon, called the conciliatory nation, can induce fair trade. Further, I show that to induce fair trade, the conciliatory nation must not be timid.

Dafonte, César Raña. El Combate entre el Mundo y la Razón Según Pedro Compostelano. *Rev Espan Filosof Med*, 1, 27-36, 1994.

Dafonte, César Raña. Problemática en Torno a la Obra "De Conslatione Rationis" de Petrus Compostellanus. *Rev Espan Filosof Med*, 0, 165-168, 1993.

Dagi, Teo Forcht. Changing the Paradigm for Informed Consent. *J Clin Ethics*, 5(3), 246-250, Fall 94.

The purpose of this essay is to examine the purpose of obtaining informed consent in the light of empirical observations suggesting that many patients who sign attestations of consent may not actually comprehend the procedure(s) in question or their therapeutic options. A distinction is drawn between informed consent as a *process* and informed consent as a *result*. From a historical perspective, the obligation to engage patients in discussions regarding the treatment(s) they were about to receive physicians and scientists to disclose their intentions and the risks of the therapeutic or experimental regimen proposed, and an obligation to obtain the patients' explicit consent to proceed. There was no explicit requirement that the two be linked in the sense that the first process, that of disclosure, successfully conveyed to the patient the material risks and alternatives of treatment, and the patient based consent on such knowledge a concept of consent linked a measure of adequate knowledge on that patients' part represents a new and important evolution in the idea of informed consent.

Dagognet, M François (& others). Le Dehors et le Dedans. *Bull Soc Fr Phil*, 88(2), 39-63, Ap-Je 94.

We propose examining a concept of the world which divides it into two: on the one hand, the container, which serves only as an envelope, with the qualities of solidness, of consistence and of compactness; on the other hand, the contents which are thus carefully protected. Geosciences help to criticize this duality: we show with the help of the history of geology and its multiple branches how this discipline is semiological. This division between outside and inside also appears to apply to living creatures. We show that it is possible to propose an intelligence of a kind different from organic functioning, as if life should be understood in another way and set at its own periphery. (edited)

Dahbour, Omar (ed) and Ishay, Micheline R (ed). *The Nationalism Reader*. Atlantic Highlands, Humanities Pr, 1995.

The National Reader provides a wide selection of important writings on nationalism for the Enlightenment to the present, with emphasis on key figures, both nationalist and internationalist, from the history of thought. Thinkers from various ideologies—liberal, conservative, socialist, fascist, and anticolonial—and from different cultures—European, American, Asian, Islamic, and African—are represented. Many selections—including those by Mazzini, Acton, Renan, Ranke, Bauer, and Bourne—are out-of-print or hard to find and several are reproduced in their entirety. The volume concludes with some recent assessments of the revival of nationalism at the end of the twentieth century.

Dahl, Östen. "The Marking of the Episodic/Generic Distinction in Tense-Aspect Systems" in *The Generic Book, Carlson, Gregory N (ed)*, 412-425. Chicago, Univ of Chicago Pr, 1995.

Dahlbom, Bo. "Mind is Artificial" in *Dennett and his Critics, Dahlbom, Bo (ed)*, 161-183. Cambridge, Blackwell, 1995.

Dahlbom, Bo (ed). *Dennett and his Critics*. Cambridge, Blackwell, 1995.

Dahlstrom, Daniel O. *Das logische Vorurteil: Untersuchungen zur Wahrheitstheorie des frühen Heidegger*. Vienna, Passagen, 1994.

Das logische Vorurteil ist der Hang, den "Logos" im Sinne einer Aussage oder eines Urteils als den "Ort" der Wahrheti aufzufassen und die Anwesenheit des Gegenstandes oder Sachverhaltes, die durch eine wahre Aussage aufgewiesen wird, für den Sinn des Seins zu erklären. Anhand der Marburger Vorlesungen verfolgt diese Studie zunächst Heideggers Entwicklung seiner Auffassungen von Wahrheit und Sein durch eine Auseinandersetzung mit echten und angeblichen Vertretern dieses Vorturteils, nämlich Lotze, Husserl und Aristoteles. (edited)

Dahms, Hans-Joachim. *Positivismusstreit: Die Auseinandersetzungen der Frankfurter Schule mit dem logischen Positivismus, dem Pragmatismus und dem kritischen Rationalismus*. Frankfurt, Suhrkamp, 1994.

Daigler, Matthew A. Heidegger and Von Balthasar: A Lover's Quarrel over Beauty and Divinity. *Amer Cath Phil Quart*, 69(2), 375-394, Spr 95.

Both Martin Heidegger and Hans Urs von Balthasar explore the inseparable connection between beauty and Being, arguing that beauty is the supreme radiance of a thing, holding sway over the totality of Being. They further agree that beauty is holy, a manifestation of divinity. But while Heidegger ultimately subordinates the God of Christianity to Being, as simply one more manifestation of the holy, Balthasar sees in the glory of the Cross the ultimate clue to the meaning of Being as self-abandoning love. This serves to explain their fundamental disagreement over the question of the "gift of Being".

Dainian, Zhang. The Historical Significance of Feng Youlan's *Zhen Yuan Liu Shu*. *J Chin Phil*, 21(3-4), 283-301, S-D 94.

Dalcourt, Gerard J. Poinsot and the Mental Imagery Debate. *Mod Sch*, 72(1), 1-12, N 94.

In this century Ryle, Canto, Sartre, Casey and Brann have presented conflicting views as to the nature and existence of mental images. Here it is argued that a more adequate explanation of them is to be found in the theory of signs of Jean Poinsot (1589-1647), which holds images to be formal signs, i.e., entities that we may not be aware of but through which we become aware of that for which they stand, while the forementioned writers take images to be instrumental signs, i.e., signs first known by themselves and by which we can then know that which they represent.

Dales, H G (trans) and Dieudonné, Jean and Dales, J C (trans). *Mathematics —The Music of Reason*. New York, Springer-Verlag, 1992.

Dales, J C (trans) and Dales, H G (trans) and Dieudonné, Jean. *Mathematics —The Music of Reason*. New York, Springer-Verlag, 1992.

Dallmayr, Fred. "Max Weber and the Modern State" in *The Barbarism of Reason, Horowitz, Asher (ed)*, 49-67. Toronto, Univ of Toronto Pr, 1994.

Dallob, Pamela and Dominowski, Roger L. "Insight and Problem Solving" in *The Nature of Insight, Sternberg, Robert J (ed)*, 33-62. Cambridge, MIT Pr, 1995.

This essay considers insight as a form of understanding of a problem and its solution, which results from restructuring, a change in perception of a problem. Distinctions are made between insightful problem solving and remembering, between reproductive and productive thinking, and among types of insight problems. By definition, insight problems suggest incorrect representations; erroneous solutions might reflect inadequate mental monitoring, which is readily corrected, or more serious fixation on a wrong idea. Insightful solutions occur abruptly; solutions accompanied by understanding are remembered well. Insightful behavior can be promoted by training, although the generality of training effects is presently unclear.

Dalton, Stuart. Lyotard's Peregrination: Three (and-a-half) Responses to the Call of Justice. *Phil Today*, 38(3-4), 227-242, Fall 94.

I consider four stages in Lyotard's work—beginning with the articles for *Socialisme ou Barbarie* and concluding with *Differend* and *Heidegger and "the Jews"*—in terms of the theory of justice that they offer. I argue that there is a certain development in Lyotard's response to the problem of justice, and that some critics have dismissed Lyotard's work without fully appreciating this development, especially as it is represented in the later work, from *Differend* on.

Daly, Chris. Laws and Coincidences Contrasted. *Analysis*, 54(2), 98-104, Ap 94.

I defend the Dretske-Tooley-Armstrong theory of laws against an objection by L J Cohen. This theory explains the intensionality of law statements in terms of relations between universals. Cohen objects that since statements like, 'it is a coincidence that all Fs and Gs', are also intensional, they must be similarly explained, thereby collapsing the distinction between laws and coincidences. But 1) a'coincidence relation' need not exist merely because there are true statements about coincidences, 2) waiving this, such a relation would relate particulars, not universals, and would not be irreducibly second-order, unlike monic relations, and 3) the intensionality of such statements can be explained without this relation.

Daly, Herman E. On Wilfred Beckerman's Critique of Sustainable Development. *Environ Values*, 4(1), 49-56, F 95.

Dalziel, Jean and Yeo, Michael. "Autonomy" in *Concepts and Cases in Nursing Ethics, Yeo, Michael (& others)*, 54-85. Peterborough, Broadview Pr, 1991.

Damiani, Alberto. Teoría y Praxis en *De Nostri Temporis Studiorum Ratione*. *Cuad Vico*, 3, 53-66, 1993.

Mathematics are for Vico the only science man can cultivate since it produces its own object. Therefore neither the natural reality nor the social one can be subject of scientific consideration, since the first one is a divine product and the second, showing the hazardous character of human affairs, does not allow to explain them through universal scientific laws. The human faculty of knowledge being so restricted, makes social parxis become relevant and it can only be grapsed by means of *prudentia*. *De Ratione* denies the possibility of a scientific approach to the public and civil world, but at the same time, the conditions of possibility of such a knowledge are there posed.

Damiani, Alberto M. El *Arbor Scientiae* y la Vigencia de la Filosofía Viquiana. *Cuad Vico*, 4, 169-171, 1994.

Damnjanovic, Zlatan. Elementary Functions and Loop Programs. *Notre Dame J Form Log*, 35(4), 496-522, Fall 94.

The paper studies a hierarchy of Kalmar elementary functions on integers, based on a classification of LOOP programs of limited complexity, namely those in which the depth of nestings of LOOP commands does not exceed two. It is proved that n-place functions at the k-th level of the hierarchy can be enumerated by a single function at level k+2, and that the resulting hierarchy of elementary predicates (i.e., functions with 0, 1-values) is proper. The rudimentary predicates of Smullyan are classified as belonging to level 2.

Damnjanovic, Zlatan. Strictly Primitive Recursive Realizability, I. *J Sym Log*, 59(4), 1210-1227, D 94.

A realizability notion that employs only primitive recursive functions is defined, and, relative to it, the soundness of the fragment of Heyting Arithmetic (HA) in which induction is restricted to E0/1 formulae is proved. A dual concept of falsifiability is proposed and an analogous soundness result is established for a further restricted fragment of HA.

Danaher, James P. What Locke Should Have Believed about Real Essences. *Locke News*, 23, 83-103, 1992.

Locke claimed that the essences we use to denominate material substances are nominal and the product of human judgment. He also believed that material substances had real essences which were their internal corpuscular structures. These internal corpuscular structures were insensible in Locke's day and therefore could not be used to denominate substances into species. If such a corpuscular structure could be explored in the future (i.e., better microscopes) Locke seems to suggest that they would be a better basis for denominating species. I argue that real essences are no more real and are as much the product of human judgment as nominal essences.

Dancy, Jonathan. Supervenience, Virtues, and Consequences: A Commentary on *Knowledge in Perspective*. *Phil Stud*, 78(3), 189-205, Je 95.

This a critical commentary on E Sosa's *Knowledge in Perspective* (Cup, 1991). I try to make two points. First, that there are mistakes in Sosa's appeal to supervenience in formulating his notion of formal foundationalism. Second, that although he makes appeal to the idea of intellectual virtue, he is really a consequentialist in epistemology.

Dancy, Jonathan. The Presidential Address: Why there is really No Such Thing as the Theory of Motivation. *Proc Aris Soc*, 95, 1-18, 1994-95.

This paper challenges recent attempts to marry realism in the theory of value with Humeanism in the theory of motivation—that is, realism about justifying reasons and Humeanism about motivating reasons. It is argued that this combination is incoherent, and that value-realists should abandon Humean conceptions of motivation—conceptions which inform the very idea of a theory of motivation.

Dandekar, Natalie. Recognizing Rationalizations Among Responses to Hunger. *Agr Human Values*, 11(4), 28-37, Fall 94.

In this article I undertake to discover the extent to which five distinct philosophical arguments for "hardhearted" responses to hunger are rationalizations. In each case, I consider the prima facie appeal and then consider the extent to which these appeals can be answered or overcome by principles promoting policies of food equity. I pay special attention to the appeal that pits political self-determination against food equity, because I believe it is especially important to determine the extent to which respect for sovereignty and political self-determination is to be seen as compatible with promoting policies of food equity.

Danecki, Janusz. Islam and the West. *Dialogue Hum*, 3(3), 103-106, 1993.

Danes, Frantisek. Involvement with Language and In Language. *J Prag*, 22(3-4), 251-264, O 94.

In section 1, the ways in which people are involved with their own language are dealt with. The Prague School functional concept of 'experiencing one's language' (being a parallel to 'involvement') is presented, and the following points discussed: different attitudes of users toward language, characteristic features of their involvement with the text processes of speaking-writing and listening-reading, and the range of different experiential modes implied in the users' involvement. Section 2 is devoted to emotion as the most typical and natural manifestation of people's involvement in language. Emotion is treated as a specific dimension of the human mind and experience; its vast field is surveyed and contrasted with the dimension of cognition. The two dimensions (or, rather, aspects) are interwoven and mutually conditioned, both in our life and in linguistic expression. Further, the ways emotion enters discourse, and various types and means of its manifestation in communication are examined. Moreover, different functional positions of emotion in communication are discussed, and also a brief comparison of the emotional content of speech and music is sketched.

Daniel, Jessica Henderson. Exclusion and Emphasis Reframed as a Matter of Ethics. *Ethics Behavior*, 4(3), 229-235, 1994.

Judith Lewis Herman's Trauma and Recovery (1992) is reviewed using the Ethical Principles of Psychologists and the Code of Conduct (American Psychological Association 1992) as the criteria. The three ethical principles and the violations are as follows: 1) Principle B: Integrity: The presentation of a revisionist portrayal of history; 2) Principle D: Respect for People's Rights and Dignity: In two ways, emphasis on stereotype and the failure to attend to the intersection of race, gender and class in the case of rape; and 3) Principle F: Social Responsibility: Miseducation about the connection of psychological trauma and political movements.

Daniel, Stephen H. *The Philosophy of Jonathan Edwards*. Bloomington, Indiana Univ Pr, 1994.

This comprehensive analysis and redefinition of the philosophy of Jonathan Edwards indicates how he relies on principles radically at odds with modern rationalists and empiricists. Drawing on work by Peirce, Foucault, and Kristeva, the book shows how the Stoic-Renaissance theory of signatures (thematized by Paracelsus and Peter Ramus) provides Edwards and his contemporaries with a powerful alternative to the ideas of Descartes and Locke and to the modern dismissal of the language of nature. It demonstrates how Edwards's reasoning about typology, God, creation, Trinity, mind and body, original sin, freedom, moral agency, knowledge, and beauty assumes this ontology of signs or semiotics.

Daniel, Stephen H. The Semiotic Ontology of Jonathan Edwards. *Mod Sch*, 71(4), 285-304, My 94.

Jonathan Edwards' marginalization in modern philosophy stems from his refusal to endorse the predicational logic and substantialist ontology of the rationalist-empiricist debate. Instead, he appeals to a communicative, semiotic logic of propositions grounded in Stoic thought and thematized by Peter Ramus and his Puritan followers. That alternative logic displays an "ontology of supposition" that guarantees God's existence, justifies typological, magical, and even astrological inferences, undermines modernist dichotomies (e.g., between mind and matter), and invalidates efforts to speak of Edwards' thought in terms of idealism or immaterialism.

Daniels, Ken R. Information Sharing in Donor Insemination: A Conflict of Rights and Needs. *Cambridge Quart Healthcare Ethics*, 4(2), 217-224, Spr 95.

This paper's focus is on the psychological and ethical aspects of information sharing between participants in Donor Insemination. It outlines who these participants are, the roles that they have traditionally played and the information that has been shared between them. It looks at how the participants can claim to have rights to either gain access to or not to reveal information and at how these rights can come into conflict. It outlines how these issues have been responded to in various countries and at the effect that legislation and changes in participants attitudes have had on patterns of information sharing.

Daniels, Norman. Four Unsolved Rationing Problems: A Challenge. *Hastings Center Rep*, 24(4), 27-29, Jl-Ag 94.

Danis, Marion. Should Ethics Committees Study Themselves?. *J Clin Ethics*, 5(2), 159-162, Sum 94.

Danto, Arthur C. "Responses and Replies" in *Danto and his Critics, Rollins, Mark (ed)*, 193-216. Cambridge, Blackwell, 1993.

Danto, Arthur C. Die Kunstwelt. *Deut Z Phil*, 42(5), 907-919, 1994.

Dardis, Anthony. How the Radically Interpreted Make Mistakes. *Dialogue (Canada)*, 33(3), 415-435, Sum 94.

Meaning involves normativity: a word has meaning only if some of its uses are correct and some are incorrect. A philosophical theory of meaning must explain the normativity of meaning. Many offer an explanation in terms of conventions for the use of words. Donald Davidson argues that communication does not require linguistic conventions. Ian Hacking objects that without conventions there is no normativity, and hence that Davidson in unable to explain the possibility of error. This paper gives a Davidsonian explanation of how it is possible, without linguistic conventions, to say or to believe something false.

Darmon, Jean-Charles. Gassendi contre Spinoza selon Bayle: ricochets de la critique de l'âme du monde. *Arch Phil*, 57(3), 523-540, Jl-S 94.

Daros, W R. El Hecho de Conocer y el ser del Conocer (Problemática Entre A Rosmini y J Balmes). *Pensamiento*, 199(51), 101-128, Ja-Ap 95.

Sensistas, empiristas y positivista no tienen otro horizonte frente al hecho del concocer que describirlo, dándolo como un dato de experiencia. Rosmini se plantea el fundamento y raíz última de ese hecho. Lo encuentra en la condición humana que nace y vive con la *idea de ser*, indefinida, infinita, anterior y condición de todo ser (ente) determinado, base de la posibilidad, universalización y abstracción de todo conocimiento. Tras la exposición de la teoría epistemológica de Rosmini, se da un apunte de su evolución y se contrasta con la teoría de Balmes que se ha quedado en la idea también primigenia del *ente*.

Darwall, Stephen. *The British Moralists and the Internal 'Ought': 1640-1740*. New York, Cambridge Univ Pr, 1995.

Uncovers the roots of "internalism", the idea that any binding 'ought' must be based in the motives of a deliberating agent, as this notion developed in the thought of British philosophers writing in the period from Hobbes through Hume. An empirical naturalist tradition, comprising Hobbes, Locke, Cumberland, Hutcheson, and Hume, held obligation to consist in the practical force empirical discoveries can acquire in the process of deliberation. A second, "autonomist" tradition, including Cudworth, Shaftesbury, Butler, and, in some moments, Locke, viewed obligation as inconceivable without autonomous will and sought (well before Kant) to develop interdependent accounts of autonomous agency and obligation.

Darwall, Stephen L. "Hume and the Invention of Utilitarianism" in *Hume and Hume's Connexions, Stewart, M A (ed)*, 58-82. University Park, Penn St Univ Pr, 1995.

Hutcheson provided the first English formulation of the greatest happiness principle, but he derived it from a more fundamental view about benevolence's moral goodness. In its now familiar, teleological guise, philosophical utilitarianism was originated by Bentham. This paper discussed Hume as a crucial transitional figure. Although his basic ethical framework is similar to Hutcheson's, Hume's sympathy-driven account of moral sentiment, according to which approbation and disapprobation derive from reflection on immediate and distant nonmoral goods that traits realize or cause in agents and patients, was a crucial departure in the direction of Bentham's view.

Darwall, Stephen L. Motive and Obligation in Hume's Ethics. *Nous*, 27(4), 415-448, D 93.

Hume distinguishes natural obligation, the motive of self-interest, from moral obligation, the sentiment of approbation and disapprobation. I argue that his discussion of justice makes use of a third notion, in addition to the other two: rule-obligation. For Hume, the just person regulates her conduct by mutually advantageous rules of justice. Rule-obligation is the notion she requires to express her acceptance of these rules in so regulating herself. I place these ideas in relation to Hume's official theory of the will and to early modern thinking about obligation and the will more generally.

Darwin, Thomas J and Cherwitz, Richard A. Beyond Reductionism in Rhetorical Theories of Meaning. *Phil Rhet*, 27(4), 313-329, 1994.

Darwin, Thomas J and Cherwitz, Richard A. Toward a Relational Theory of Meaning. *Phil Rhet*, 28(1), 17-29, Ja 95.

Das Gupta, Amitabha. In Defence of Autonomous Linguistics. *J Indian Counc Phil Res*, 11(2), 96-110, Ja-Ap 94.

Daston, Lorraine. Enlightenment Calculations. *Crit Inquiry*, 21(1), 182-202, Autumn 94.

Dastur, Françoise. "Europa und der 'andere Anfang'" in *Europa und die Philosophie, Gander, Hans-Helmuth (ed)*, 185-196. Frankfurt/M, Klostermann, 1993.

Datta, Rama. Transmigration Without a Self. *Darshana Int*, 32(1/125), 32-37, Ja 92.

In section XII of the appendix to Vasubandhu's Abhidharmakosa, Vatsiputriya introduces the perplexing question that has haunted Buddhism from very early times, viz how to reconcile the doctrine of no-self (anātta or, anātman) with the belief in transmigration. If there is no individual existing, who is it that transmigrates? The present paper examines the Buddhist concept of transmigration and finds out that it has a special meaning in the Buddhist vocabulary. The paper also considers the Buddhist idea of moral responsibility and actions and explores the theory of transmission of consequences from one cycle to another.

Dauben, Joseph W. "Peirce and History of Science" in *Peirce and Contemporary Thought: Philosophical Inquiries, Ketner, Kenneth Laine (ed)*, 146-195. New York, Fordham Univ Pr, 1995.

This paper is one of the invited plenary lectures delivered at the Sequicentenary meeting in honor of the birth of Charles Sanders Peirce (1839-1914) held at Harvard Unviersity in June of 1989. The article begins with examples to show that it is virtually impossible to assess Peirce's thought accurately if one only relies upon the sometimes highly inaccurate versions abridged and "edited" as his "Collected Papers." The second half of this article is concerned primarily with the interest Peirce showed throughout his life in the History of Science. As an admirer of William Whewell, Peirce believed that the history of science was a useful record that might well hold the key to understanding the nature of human thought and its uncanny ability to understand the physical world.

Dauenhauer, Bernard. Ricoeur and Political Identity. *Phil Today*, 39(1), 47-55, Spr 95.

In this essay, I argue that Paul Ricoeur's analysis of the constitution of personal identity sheds lights on what can count as a defensible political identity. At the very least, for any particular political identity to be defensible, its holders must recognize that it is always both in need of reform and in danger of degeneration. Further, they must admit that inhabitants of other bodies politic can embrace a political identity that is no less defensible than their own.

Dauer, Francis W. The Nature of Fictional Characters and The Referential Fallacy. *J Aes Art Crit*, 53(1), 31-38, Wint 95.

The paper urges: Fictional characters have an ontology of their own in virtue of having both referential properties (relating to how it might be with actual persons) and formal properties (relating to the function the character plays in a work of art). This is argued by engaging in film criticism relating to Walter Kerr's claims about the character Chaplin plays in his silent comedies, and Kerr is seen to commit the referential fallacy of interpreting a fictional character's formal properties as referential properties.

Daukas, Nancy. Scepticism and the Framework-Relativity of Enquiry. *Ratio*, 7(2), 95-110, D 94.

Many argue that skeptical enquiry is incoherent insofar as it requires a detachment from and assessment of the framework judgments that constitute our practice of enquiry. This paper accepts that enquiry is relative to a framework, but argues that the Cartesian skeptical enquiry is consistent with that relativity. Part I presents Marie McGinn's Wittgensteinian anti-skeptical argument, comparing its view of enquiry to Carnap's. Part II clarifies the sense in which Wittgenstein's 'Moore-type' framework judgments could be unquestionable, and argues that McGinn's anti-skeptical argument fails. Part III shows that the skeptical enquiry finds all our beliefs to lack justification by suspending our normal nonskeptical framework judgment regarding perception in a way that is consistent with the framework-relativity of enquiry, and encouraged by normal standards. The paper closes by recommending a view of skepticism as a stimulus for enquiry.

David, Anthony S. Commentary on "Insight, Delusion, and Belief". *Phil Psychiat Psych*, 1(4), 237-239, D 94.

David, Jeanne M and Kantor, Jeffrey and Greenberg, Ira. Possible Ethical Issues and Their Impact on The Firm: Perceptions Held by Public Accountants. *J Bus Ethics*, 13(12), 919-937, D 94.

The accounting profession is concerned with the ethical beliefs of its members. To this end, the authors surveyed public accountants, questioning them about the AICPA's "Code of Professional Conduct" and their perceptions of how potentially unethical behaviors impact the firm. The paper focuses on respondents' perceptions of the impact on the firm's practice, image and degree of concern. (edited)

David, Pascal. Der Hirt des Seins. *Heidegger Stud*, 9, 53-62, 1993.

This essay in interpretation endeavours to show how far it is up to us to be 'shepherds of Being' rather than 'Lords of being', according to the essential distinction made by Heidegger in his *Letter on humanism*. How is it possible to let the shepherd of Being awake in us? The shepherd of Being lets Being be.

Davidovich, Adina. How to Read Religion within the Limits of Reason Alone. *Kantstudien*, 85(1), 1-14, 1994.

Central concepts and arguments of *Religion* acquire clarity and force only when we recognize their basis in Kant's theory of reflective judgment, as developed in the *Third Critique*, and only when we read that discussion as an attempt to establish fundamental harmony between the constructs of theoretical and practical reason but rather as a capacity that becomes possible through the faculty of judgment. It does not substitute divine intervention for moral choice but enables moral agents to contemplate the conduciveness of nature to virtue.

Davidson, Arnold I (ed) and Hadot, Pierre and Chase, Michael (trans). *Philosophy as a Way of Life: Spiritual Exercises from Socrates to Foucault*. Cambridge, Blackwell, 1995.

Davidson, Donald. Could There Be A Science of Rationality?. *Int J Phil Stud*, 3(1), 1-16, Mr 95.

Logic, semantic theories of truth in Tarski's style, and theories of decision-making under uncertainty can, when combined, be taken to describe the beliefs, values, and linguistic knowledge of an ideally rational agent. Such a unified theory is comparable to an axiomatized theory in the natural sciences. It differs from such theories, if it does, in the degree of idealization; the problems of empirical interpretation are considerable.

Davidson, Donald. Knowing One's Own Mind. *Proc Amer Phil Ass*, 60(3), 441-458, Ja 87.

A number of philosophers have argued that if the contents of thoughts are in part determined by social or other factors external, and perhaps unknown, to the thinker, then the intuition that we know what we think, special cases aside, must be false. This is a mistake; externalism neither shows that 'meanings ain't in the head' nor that we do not know what we think. The argument to this conclusion depends on the view that thinking does not require inner objects before the mind.

Davidson, Donald. Plato's Philosopher. *Apeiron*, 26(3-4), 179-194, S-D 93.

The approach to ethics in the *Philebus*, despite the innovative metaphysics, represents a return to the methodology of the earlier dialogues. When Plato had reworked the theory of ideas as a consequence of the explorations and criticisms of the *Parmenides, Sophist, Theaetetus*, and *Politicus*, he realized that the theory no longer could be deployed as the main support of an ethical position, as it had been in the *Republic* and elsewhere. This explains Plato's reversion to the Socratic elenchus, and makes sense of the startling reappearance of Socrates as the leading voice in the *Philebus*.

Davidson, Donald. The Problem of Objectivity. *Tijdschr Filosof*, 57(2), 203-220, Je 95.

Since Descartes, epistemology has been based on first person knowledge. We must begin, according to the usual story, with what is most certain: knowledge of our own sensations and thoughts. In one way or another we then progress, if we can, to knowledge of an objective external world. There is then the final, tenuous, step to knowledge of other minds.

Davidson, Donald. What is Quine's View of Truth?. *Inquiry*, 37(4), 437-440, D 94.

Two questions are raised about Quine's view of truth. He has recently said that ontology is relative to a translation manual: is this the same as relativizing it to a language? The same question may be asked about truth. Should we think there is one concept of truth which is relative to a language, or is there a separate concept for each language (or speaker)? The second question concerns Quine's repeated endorsements of the 'disquotational' account of truth. Does he think this account limits a truth predicate to application to a single language, or can translation (or Tarski's methods) allow us to apply a truth predicate in one language to sentences in other languages? If the latter, can Quine still contend that the disquotational account is a 'full' account of the concept of truth? The answer would tell us whether Quine can be counted among those who would deflate the concept of truth.

Davidson, Janet E. "The Suddenness of Insight" in *The Nature of Insight, Sternberg, Robert J (ed)*, 125-155. Cambridge, MIT Pr, 1995.

Davidson, Janet E (ed) and Sternberg, Robert J (ed). *The Nature of Insight*. Cambridge, MIT Pr, 1995.

Davidson, Judith and Bresler, Liora. Arts and Knowledge: A Discussion. *Educ Theor*, 45(1), 63-70, Wint 95.

Davidson, Larry. Commentary on "Insight, Delusion, and Belief". *Phil Psychiat Psych*, 1(4), 243-244, D 94.

This commentary highlights the valuable approach adopted by Gillet in his essay on the formation of delusional beliefs. In drawing attention to the domain of tacit, interpersonal skills and experiences through which individuals constitute beliefs, Gillett reconceptualizes the patient as an agent and encourages consideration of how affect, meaning, and life experience influence the formation and maintainance of delusional beliefs as one manifestation of a person's active involvement in the process of making sense of his or her experiences. This commentary outlines the implications for clinical theory and practice suggested by this alternative view of the nature of delusional beliefs.

Davies, Christie. "How People Argue about Abortion and Capital Punishment in Europe and America..." in *Ethics on the Frontiers of Human Existence, Badham, Paul (ed)*, 101-135. New York, Paragon House, 1992.

Davies, David. Le Défi Pédagogique du Relativisme en Éthique. *Philosopher*, 16, 207-212, 1994.

The arguments generally employed in critical discussions of ethical relativism when teaching classes lacking philosophical training are philosophically flawed. Yet we must somehow counter the unreflective relativism that many students bring to the classroom if we are to engage them in other ethical debates. The difficulty arises because such classes lack the philosophical background to appreciate the anti-relativist arguments that we ourselves take seriously. We solve this dilemma by distinguishing two elements in unreflective relativism—'pluralism' and an 'uncritical' approach to moral issues. It is the latter that we must, and can, counter to achieve our pedagogical goals.

Davies, David. Putnam's Brain-Teaser. *Can J Phil*, 25(2), 203-227, Je 95.

Anthony Brueckner has offered a dilemmatic formulation of Putnam's 'brain in a vat' (BIV) argument that is purportedly sound and apparently establishes the desired conclusion. In defending his formulation, however, Brueckner violates a general principle for assessing indicative conditionals of the sort that occur as premisses in the BIV argument. Nonetheless, Brueckner's version of the argument is sound, for the general principle in question fails to apply in this case. After identifying the distinctive feature of the BIV hypothesis that explains this failure, a reading of Putnam's argument grounded in this feature is defended, and its philosophical significance assessed.

Davies, Martin. "Reply: Consciousness and the Varieties of Aboutness" in *Philosophy of Psychology: Debates on Psychological Explanation, Macdonald, Cynthia (ed)*, 356-392. Cambridge, Blackwell, 1995.

Davies, Martin. "Tacit Knowledge and Subdoxastic States" in *Philosophy of Psychology: Debates on Psychological Explanation, Macdonald, Cynthia (ed)*, 309-330. Cambridge, Blackwell, 1995.

Davies, Martin. "The Mental Simulation Debate" in *Objectivity, Simulation and the Unity of Consciousness, Peacocke, Christopher (ed)*, 99-127. New York, Oxford Univ Pr, 1994.

I sketch the two opposed positions in the current form of the mental simulation debate: the *theory theory* and the *simulation alternative*, and give a brief review of some of the empirical literature. Then, I focus upon the particular development of the simulation theory that has been offered by Alvin Goldman. I use this exposition both as a way of motivating a particular way of delineating the two opposed views, and as a way of introducing the idea that simulation cannot be employed to give a philosophically fundamental account of our use of mental concepts. In the final section, I raise the question whether Robert Gordon's development of the simulation view presents a more promising prospect.

Davies, Martin (ed) and Stone, Tony (ed). *Folk Psychology: The Theory of Mind Debate*. Cambridge, Blackwell, 1995.

With little or no formal teaching, human beings develop the capacity to deploy psychological concepts in predicting and explaining the actions and mental states of other members of the species. Many philosophers and psychologists argue that this everyday ability reflects the fact that normal adult human beings possess a primitive or 'folk' psychological theory. Recently, however, this *theory theory* has come under challenge from the *simulation alternative* which says that human beings are able to predict and explain each others' actions by using the resources of their own minds to simulate the psychological aetiology of the actions of others. The thirteen essays in this volume present the foundations of the theory of mind debate, and are accompanied by an extensive Introduction.

Davies, Paul Sheldon. Troubles for Direct Proper Functions. *Nous*, 28(3), 363-381, S 94.

The aim of this paper is to raise a problem for theories of evolutionary functions. Evolutionary functions are functional properties acquired as a consequence of evolution by natural selection. Such theories are intended to apply to the traits of sexual organisms, amongst others, and hence such theories must specify (i) conditions of identity of traits in such a way that any instance of a trait today is of the same kind as that upon which selection acted in the past and (ii) conditions compatible with the creative and destructive, as well as systematic and holistic, forces involved in sexual reproduction. My thesis is that available theories of evolutionary functions do not satisfy (i) and (ii). I focus upon Millikan's (1984) theory of direct proper functions, since her's is the most sophisticated version of evolutionary functions to date. I explicate details of Millikan's theory and then show that it fails to satisfy (i) and (ii).

Davies, Paul Sheldon and Fetzer, James H and Foster, Thomas R. Logical Reasoning and Domain Specificity: A Critique of the Social Exchange Theory of Reasoning. *Biol Phil*, 10(1), 1-37, Ja 95.

The social exchange theory of reasoning, which is championed by Leda Cosmides and John Tooby, falls under the general rubric "evolutionary psychology" and asserts that human reasoning is governed by content-dependent, domain-specific, evolutionarily-derived algorithms. According to Cosmides and Tooby, the presumptive existence of what they call "cheater-detection" algorithms disconfirms the claim that we reason via general-purpose mechanisms or via inductively acquired principles. We contend that the Cosmides/Tooby arguments in favor of domain-specific algorithms or evolutionarily-derived mechanisms fail and that the notion of a social exchange rule, which is central to their theory, is not correctly characterized. As a consequence, whether or not their conclusion is true cannot be established on the basis of the arguments they have presented.

Davies, Stephen. "Is Architecture Art?" in *Philosophy and Architecture, Mitias, Michael H (ed)*, 31-47. Amsterdam, Rodopi, 1994.

I argue that the artistic product of the architect's craft is a building, not a plan, and attempt to characterize what it is for something to be a building. I suggest that some buildings are artworks and that usually they are the artworks of their architects, but I deny that architecture is an artform. Architectural artworks are contrasted with other kinds that are temporal, multiple, and for performance.

Davies, Stephen. General Theories of Art versus Music. *Brit J Aes*, 34(4), 315-325, O 94.

Most theories of art concentrate on literature and painting. As an abstract, performing art frequently discussed in technical terms, music's peculiarities easily can be overlooked in theories that claim to concern the arts in general. I argue that three general theories of art—Danto's Hegelian end of art thesis, Goodman's theory of expression, and Walton's theory of artworks as representations—do not readily apply to the case of music.

Davies, Stephen. Is Redistribution to Help the Needy Unjust?. *Analysis*, 55(1), 50-60, Ja 95.

Davies, Stephen. Relativism in Interpretation. *J Aes Art Crit*, 53(1), 8-13, Wint 95.

Literary works seemingly admit contradictory interpretations. Many theories attempt to remove the contradiction—the interpretations are not asserted, one interpretation is false, the work is internally ambiguous or contradictory, and so on. I prefer to remove the contradiction by regarding interpretations as having the implicit form: "the work can be read as..." It can be true that a work lends itself to contradictory readings. In a different vein, Joseph Margolis argues that the culturally emergent ontology of artworks requires a multivalent logic within which contradictions can take a high truth-value. I suggest that the ontology Margolis favors generates no such requirement and that the logic he outlines departs significantly from standard many-valued logics.

Davion, Victoria. Rape, Group Responsibility, and Trust. *Hypatia*, 10(2), 153-156, Spr 95.

In this paper I link the very interesting analysis of responsibility provided by Larry May and Robert Strikwerda in "Men in Groups: Collective Responsibility for Rape" (May and Strikwerda 1994) to some strategies for helping women for helping women avoid rape. In addition, I call for some clarification on May and Strikwerda's claim that rapists are fully responsible for their actions and that it is largely a matter of luck which men actually turn out to be rapists.

Davis, Andrew. Criterion-referenced Assessment and the Development of Knowledge and Understanding. *J Phil Educ*, 29(1), 3-21, March 95.

The paper argues that no criterion-referenced assessment system can achieve both reliability and validity at one and the same time. It shows that the reasons for this are conceptual, and hence that empirical research into the "problem" is a waste of money and effort. Considerable discussion is devoted to ideas of knowledge and understanding, and to proper educational objectives pertaining to these. Much reference is made to the current National Curriculum context in the United Kingdom, and conclusions are drawn for appropriate educational policy in this area.

Davis, Angela Y. Afro Images: Politics, Fashion, and Nostalgia. *Crit Inquiry*, 21(1), 37-45, Autumn 94.

Davis, Dena S. It Ain't Necessarily So: Clinicians, Bioethics, and Religious Studies. *J Clin Ethics*, 5(4), 315-319, Wint 94.

Davis, Dena S. Legal Trends in Bioethics. *J Clin Ethics*, 5(3), 267-272, Fall 94.

Davis, Donald B and Paté-Cornell, M Elisabeth. A Challenge to the Compound Lottery Axiom: A Two-Stage Normative Structure and Comparison to Other Theories. *Theor Decis*, 37(3), 267-309, N 94.

This paper examines references among uncertain prospects when the decision maker is uneasy about his assignment of subjective probabilities. It proposes a two-stage lottery framework for the analysis of such prospects, where the first stage represents an assessment of the vagueness (ambiguity) in defining the problem's randomness and the second stage represents an assessment of the problem for each hypothesized randomness condition. Standard axioms of rationality are prescribed for each stage, including weak ordering, continuity, and strong independence. The 'Reduction of Compound Lotteries' axiom is weakened, however, so that the two lottery stages have consistent, but not collapsible, preference structures. (edited)

Davis, Elizabeth B (& others). The Biotechnology "Wheel of Fortune": Who Gives, Who Gets, Who Profits?. *J Med Human*, 16(1), 23-38, Spr 95.

Davis, Joel J. Good Ethics Is Good for Business: Ethical Attributions and Response to Environmental Advertising. *J Bus Ethics*, 13(11), 873-885, N 94.

Researchers have used attribution theory as a basis for exploring the relationship between consumers' inferences of advertiser motivation (attributions) and advertising response. This study postulated the existence of two new types of attributions which relate to the perceived ethics of the advertiser (advertiser ethical attributions) and the advertising message (message ethical attributions). (edited)

Davis, Kathy. *Reshaping the Female Body: The Dilemma of Cosmetic Surgery*. New York, Routledge, 1995.

Re-shaping the Female Body is about women's involvement in cosmetic surgery. Whereas traditional explanations have tended to look to the female propensity toward narcissism, lack of self-esteem, or susceptibility to the lures of consumer capitalism and the myth of eternal youth or perfect beauty, this book situates cosmetic surgery in a feminist analysis of the cultural constraints of femininity. At the same time, it argues against the notion that women who have cosmetic surgery are victims of ideological manipulation, blindly complying with cultural definitions of feminine beauty. Cosmetic surgery is less about beauty than about being ordinary. It is a way to refuse to suffer beyond what is fair. Paradoxically, cosmetic surgery can be a way for some women to become embodied subjects who by reshaping their bodies can remake their lives. Rather than condemning cosmetic surgery as inherently repressive and, therefore, 'politically incorrect', and argument is made for exploring the unease which cosmetic surgery invokes, while taking the reasons of women seriously who see it as their only option under the circumstances.

Davis, Michael. Conflict of Interest Revisited. *Bus Prof Ethics J*, 12(4), 21-41, Wint 93.

A decade ago I analyzed conflict of interest as a concern tending to interfere with the proper exercise of judgment in another's service. This paper responds to two important critics of that analysis, Neil Luebke and John Boatright. Luebke's alternative is so narrow it can't deal with important issues in professional ethics; Boatright's is (in part so broad that it confuses conflict of interest with disloyalty, abuse of privilege, etc. Because Boatright's tries to make conflict of interest a failure of agency, it must also rule out conflict of interest in, e.g., members of corporate board of directors.

Davis, Michael. The State's Dr Death: What's Unethical About Physicians Helping at Executions?. *Soc Theor Pract*, 21(1), 31-60, Spr 95.

While physicians have been present at executions for well over a century, the increasing popularity of execution by lethal injection seems to have increased the importance of their participation and provoked official statements from a number of important medical organizations declaring unethical all participation—except the issuing of a death certificate. What arguments are in fact used to justify these statements? What arguments could justify them? Answering these questions sheds much light on the foundations of medical ethics in particular and professional ethics in general.

Davis, Richard B. The Principlism Debate: A Critical Overview. *J Med Phil*, 20(1), 85-105, F 95.

Clouser and Gert's 'A Critique of Principlism' (1990) has ignited debate over the adequacy of substituting principlism for moral theory as a means for dealing with biomedical dilemmas. Clouser and Gert argue that this sort of substitution is not adequate to the task. I examine their argument in light of recent defenses of principlism on this score, those of B Andrew Lustig (1992), David Degrazia (1992), and Beauchamp and Childress (1994). I argue that both sides in the debate have assumed differing conceptions of a moral theory that virtually guarantee their respective conclusions. These differing conceptions are motivated by antecedent epistemological commitments. The present debate over principlism is therefore inconclusive. Future discussion should focus on the underlying epistemological issues.

Davison, Scott A. Dretske on the Metaphysics of Freedom. *Analysis*, 54(2), 115-123, Ap 94.

In a recent article, Fred Dretske argues that a so-called 'component' theory of action provides compatibilists about freedom and determinism with a promising response to a traditional worry concerning human autonomy. In this paper, first I examine the problem for compatibilism which Dretske wishes to address, along with Dretske's reasons for rejecting one ('orthodox') compatibilist response to this problem. Then I explore Dretske's alternative ('component') theory of action. Finally, I argue that Dretske's approach fails to provide a compatibilist response which is any more plausible than the traditional approach which he rejects.

Dawkins, Richard. "Viruses of the Mind" in *Dennett and his Critics, Dahlbom, Bo (ed)*, 13-27. Cambridge, Blackwell, 1995.

Dawson, Angus James. Professional Codes of Practice and Ethical Conduct. *J Applied Phil*, 11(2), 145-153, 1994.

This essay is an attempt to examine the idea that a professional code of practice can entail ethical conduct. It is focused around two differing perspectives on ethics. It will be argued that the professions have, perhaps too hastily, adopted one theory without considering the merits, or the objections offered by the alternative account. This alternative, a 'cognitivist' theory, is sketched, and the possible advantages of such an approach are discussed. Such a perspective means adopting a radically different approach to the nature of ethics and what it is to be a moral agent, and could have interesting consequences for professional practice. Even if a cognitivist account is ultimately unconvincing, it does provide a number of worrying arguments for those professionals who believe that ethical conduct is generated by following a code of practice, and these arguments need to be addressed.

Dawson, Michael R W and Wright, Richard D. To What Extent Do Beliefs Affect Apparent Motion?. *Phil Psych*, 7(4), 471-491, 1994.

A number of studies in the apparent motion literature were examined using the cognitive penetrability criterion to determine the extent to which beliefs affect the perception of apparent motion. It was found that the interaction between the perceptual processes mediating apparent notion and higher order processes appears to be limited. In addition, perceptual and inferential beliefs appear to have different effects on perceived notion optimality and direction. Our findings suggest that the system underlying apparent motion perception has more than one stage and is informationally encapsulated from cognitive factors.

de Almeida, Claudio. Locke on Knowledge and Trifling Propositions. *Locke News*, 22, 31-55, 1991.

De Andia, Ysabel. La Divinisation de l'Homme selon Denys. *Diotima*, 23, 86-91, 1995.

De Asúa, Miguel. El *De animalibus* de Alberto Magno y la organización del discurso sobre los animales en el siglo XIII. *Pat Med*, 15, 3-26, 1994.

Discourse on animals in the thirteenth century was organized around a certain number of literary genres. Each of them resulted from the transformation of the materials received from Antiquity, embedded an epistemological project and answered to an especific rhetorical demand. Albert the Great's commentary on *De animalibus* is taken here as a synthesis between different ways of talking about animals. This paper considers 1) how Albert's *De animalibus* aims at the articulation on the medical and philosophical discourses on animals, 2) in what way Albert solves the problem of the integration of the discourse *De natura rerum* within the framework of the Aristotelian commentary. The first issue is analyzed focusing on the controversies between physicians and philosophers about the origin of the veins, the existence of the female sperm and the ultimate components of the living beings. The second section discusses the way Albert modified Thomas of Cantimpré's *De natura rerum* in order to include its material into his own commentary.

De Bary, W Theodore. "Neo-Confucianism and Human Rights" in *Human Rights and the World's Religions, Rouner, Leroy (ed)*, 183-198. Notre Dame, Univ Notre Dame Pr, 1988.

This essay discusses those concepts and value orientations in Confucianism that bear a resemblance of the terms in which human rights are formulated in the West. It discusses the religious dimensions of Confucianism on the basis of which self-cultivation and human relations were developed, with the concepts of humanity and rites as the framework within which respect for self and others was to be practiced. The bulk of the essay is devoted to the specific forms in which these values were institutionalized by a major Neo-Confucian scholar-official and prime exponent of Chu Hsi's teaching, Chen Te-hsiu (1178-1235).

de Beistegui, Miguel. Of the Gift That Comes to Thinking. *Res Phenomenol*, 24, 98-112, 1994.

De Boer, Karin. Heidegger's "Time and Being": A Draft of the Third Section of "Being and Time" (in Dutch). *Tijdschr Filosof*, 56(3), 427-468, S 94.

Heidegger often stressed that the analysis of *Dasein* in *Being and Time* should be understood as a mere preliminary investigation. That this analysis indeed prepares the investigation into the relationship between time, the understanding of Being and ontology, can only become clear when some light is thrown on the never published third section of *Being and Time*. In this section Heidegger would have explicated in what sense time can be understood as condition of possibility for every kind of ontology. When *Being and Time* is read with such a focus on the third section, the often used distinction between the early and the later Heidegger looses much of its sharpness if not its relevance: it is already in *Being and Time* itself that Heidegger tries to decenter the human being in behalf of a temporality that constitutes meaningful openness as such. (edited)

De Buzon, Frédéric. L'harmonie: métaphysique et phénoménalité. *Rev Metaph Morale*, 98(1), 95-120, Ja-Mr 95.

Varietas identitate compensata, diversity compensated by identity: this phrase defines the concept of harmony which Leibniz conceived in his very first philosophical works and upheld afterwards with some variations. This article deals with the progressive emergence and the factors of universal harmony, the value of harmony in law and sciences and the status of preestablished harmony. Then the status of dissonances raises the question of the consistency of Leibniz's doctrine, which leads me to distinguish two types of beauty. I examine some aspects of Leibniz's "aesthetics" and try to show that it eludes the intellectualism it is classically opposed to.

De Caprio, Caterina. Mito e Linguaggio Letterario nell'Italia di fine Secolo. *Stud Filosofici*, 239-250, 1991-92.

de Castro, Leonardo D. Exploitation in the Use of Human Subjects for Medical Experimentation: A Re-Examination of Basic Issues. *Bioethics*, 9(3-4), 259-268, Jl 95.

Relatively subtle forms of exploitation of human subjects may arise from the inefficiency or incompetence of a researcher, from the existence of a power imbalance between principal and subject, or from the uneven distribution of research risks among various segments of the population. A powerful and knowledgeable person (or institution) may perpetrate the exploitation of an unempowered and ignorant individual even without intending to. There is an ethical burden on the former to protect the interests of the vulnerable. Excessive or insufficient compensation may be exploitative. However, genuine economic imperatives motivating needy volunteers have to be considered. These forms of exploitation should be appreciated in the context of social and cultural factors suggesting that the relationship between researcher and subject cannot properly be appraised as a contractual undertaking. While compliance with pertinent codes and regulations minimises the exploitative potential, they cannot be enforced in a way that does not recognise a society's peculiar characteristics. The experience with some Filipino cultural traits illustrates this point.

de Chatêlet, Marquesa. *Disertación sobre la Naturaleza y la Propagación del Fuego*. Madrid, Carmen Mataix, 1994.

De Coorebyter, Vincent. "Hypothèse auxiliaire et pétition de principle: entre Popper et Feyerabend" in *Rhétoriques de la science, De Coorebyter, Vincent (ed)*, 91-16. Paris, Pr Univ France, 1994.

De Coorebyter, Vincent (ed). *Rhétoriques de la science*. Paris, Pr Univ France, 1994.

Mais les auteurs sollicités par V de Coorebyter vont plus loin en allant au coeur même de l'épistémologie contemporaine, là où résonnent les noms de Feyerabend, de Popper ou de Kuhn, sans jamais oublier d'interroger les grands textes scientifiques dans leur mode de pensée, conscient ou inconscient. On retrouvera ainsi Freud et Einstein, Aristote et Descartes, Copernic et Lamarck pour n'en citer que quelques-uns. Ce livre original s'addresse aussi bien aux scientifiques qu'aux philosophes. Son ampleur et sa richesse d'analyse en font un ouvrage incontournable pour tous ceux qui s'intéressent à la rationalité et à ses oeuvres, par-delà les clivages entre sciences de la nature et sciences de l'homme. (edited)

De Dijn, H. Louis Dupré's "Passage to Modernity" (in Dutch). *Tijdschr Filosof*, 56(3), 552-555, S 94.

De Falco, Enrico. La risposta di S Agostino alle critiche contro il cristianesimo. *Sapienza*, 47(4), 477-482, O-D 94.

de Fernandes T, Joao. Inteligência Artificial e Caça aos Andróides. *Cad Hist Filosof Cie*, 4(1), 61-91, Ja-Je 94.

The paper analyzes two major explanatory models developed by contemporary cognitive science and shows how they can possibly conflict. Part I presents such models, namely the functionalist and the evolutionary model, and how they account for cognitive phenomena such as the nature of intentional states. Part II and part III discuss, in a mental experiment, the possibility of a replica of a human being without an evolutionary past develop intentional states, thus leading to a conflict between the functionalist and the evolutionary account. Part IV and the conclusion present a conciliatory view between those two different approaches.

De Finetti, Bruno and Angell, Richard B (trans). The Logic of Probability. *Phil Stud*, 77(1), 181-190, Ja 95.

This is a translation from the French of de Finetti's 1935 article "La Logique de la Probability". In defending his subjective theory of probability against frequency theories (specifically Reichenbach) de Finetti proposed a logic based on the betting model. Though he claimed not to depart from basic two-valued logic, for conditional probabilities he proposed three values, adding a null value. That a bet on a horse is won is true if and only if the race is run and the horse wins; it is false if the race is run and the horse loses; if the race is not run and in all other cases the statement is null—neither true nor false.

De Gandt, François and Blau, Peter (trans) and Bergo, Bettina (trans). The Problematic Status of Cosmology. *Grad Fac Phil J*, 18(1), 51-64, 1995.

De Gaynesford, Max. Shades of Realism. *Phil Books*, 36(1), 1-9, Ja 95.

Simon Blackburn's quasi-realism is investigated as an extension and defense of Humean projectivism. As regards extension, particular attention is paid to Blackburn on rule-following, error theory, the bivalence principle, moral realism and Hume's notion of 'standards'. As regards defense, Blackburn's various distinctions between our right to express ourselves as a realist might from our explanation of what that discourse amounts to are explored. The conclusion is that quasi-realism is caught uncomfortably between legitimating both the flexibility of evaluative notions and the objectivity of discourse. So its claim to being a substantial and independent position, at least, is dubious.

de Gayoso, Graciela L Ritacco. La Eudaimonía y las Bienaventuranzas. *Sapientia*, 49(193-4), 201-215, 1994.

De George, Richard T. *Business Ethics (Fourth Edition)*. Englewood Cliffs, Prentice Hall, 1995.

De George, Richard T. International Business Ethics. *Bus Ethics Quart*, 4(1), 1-9, Ja 94.

International business ethics cannot be national in character, but different nations can take different approaches to it. The American is characterized by the socio-economic-political problem American businesses face. Nonetheless, despite differences throughout the globe, some common moral norms exist and the development of mutually accepted international rules and guidelines are possible.

de Jong, Hidde and Rip, Arie. Ontdekkingspraktijk in Plaats van Logica: Wetenschappelijk Ontdekken in Computer-Ondersteunde Ontdekkingsomgevingen. *Kennis Methode*, 19(2), 131-159, 1995.

The idea that computer programs might be able to make scientific discoveries provides a challenging perspective for both computer scientists and philosophers. Discussions on discovery programs often depart from the assumption that these programs should be seen as autonomous super scientists in which a certain logic of discovery has been embodied. In this article an alternative view will be elaborated, namely a view in which discovery programs are understood as supporting tools in a scientific practice. These supporting discovery programs are integrated with other computer tools and conventional tools in a computer-supported discovery environment. In order to illustrate the power of such a discovery environment, a realistic scenario is sketched describing the route to a discovery in molecular biology. In conclusion, the consequences of the introduction of a computer-supported discovery environment for scientific practices are discussed.

De Jongh, Dick and Chagrova, L A. The Decidability of Dependency in Intuitionistic Propositional Logic. *J Sym Log*, 60(2), 498-504, Je 95.

A definition is given for formulae $A_1,...A_n$ in some theory *T* which is formalized in a propositional calculus *S* to be (in)dependent with respect to *S*. It is shown that, for intuitionistic propositional logic *IPC*, dependency (with respect to *IPC* itself) is decidable. This is almost immediate consequence of Pitts' uniform interpolation theorem for *IPC*. A reasonably simple infinite sequence of *IPC*-formulae $F_n(p,q)$ is given such that *IPC*-formulae *A* and *B* are dependent if and only if at least on of the $F_n(A, B)$ is provable.

De La Peña, Luis (ed) and Hodgson, Peter E (ed) and Brody, Thomas A. *The Philosophy Behind Physics*. New York, Springer-Verlag, 1993.

In this work, Thomas Brody was concerned to remove the barriers between physics and philosophy by discovering the philosophy implicit in the actual process of scientific research. He developed the theory of 'active epistemic cycles' to explain how we come to know things. This theory does justice to the richness and complexity of scientific research, in contrast to the superficial and bloodless accounts current among philosophers of science who have no experience of scientific research. He applied his ideas to a wide range of problems in the philosophy of physics, especially probability theory and quantum mechanics, giving special attention to the Bell inequalities and the ensemble interpretation.

De Maistre, Joseph and Lebrun, Richard A (ed & trans). *Considerations on France: Joseph de Maistre*. New York, Cambridge Univ Pr, 19ed.

De Maliandi, Graciela Fernandez. Es trascendental la ética Kantiana?. *Cuad Etica*, 14, 9-17, D 92.

Did Kant fail when attempting to find a transcendental foundation for ethics? This paper argues against K O Apel's statement, which sustains that Kant could not bring such a foundation, although this had been his purpose. It is showed that, in an historical sense, there has not existed such an intention in Kant's program. However, no matter the historical motive aduced by Kant to exclude ethics from the field of transcendental research, a transcendental presentation of ethics and politics is possible. This later must deepen the study of the elements, the re-constructive aspects and the theories on which it is based, and must not polarize the attention around the refutation of scepticism.

De Marchi, Neil and Hamminga, Bert. "Idealization and the Defence of Economics" in *Idealization VI: Idealization in Economics, Hamminga, Bert (ed)*, 11-40. Amsterdam, Rodopi, 1994.

Illustrates and compares the opinions of the economists J R McCulloch (1825), J S Mill (1836), K Marx (1864), L Robbins (1932) and M Friedman (1953) on the problem of idealization in economics, both from a logical point of view (the structure of economic theories) and from a social point of view (idealizational methodology as a defense of theory against sceptical outsiders).

De Marchi, Neil B (ed) and Hamminga, Bert (ed). *Idealization VI: Idealization in Economics*. Amsterdam, Rodopi, 1994.

This book explores the different ways in which economic theories can be viewed as idealizations, and the consequences of these views for the methodology of economics and econometrics as well as for the nature of the epistemic claims of its theories. It starts with an inspection and comparison of the explicit views on the subject by some important authors in the history of economics. The contributors to the volume use their expertise in both economics, econometrics and philosophy of science.

De Marneffe, Peter. Rawls's Idea of Public Reason. *Pac Phil Quart*, 75(3-4), 232-250, S-D 94.

This paper makes two observations about Rawls's idea of public reason as presented in *Political Liberalism*. First: Rawls suggests that liberal political values can be accepted from within every reasonable comprehensive doctrine as the basis of strong moral claims on the basic structure of society, but his stated methods of identifying the content of public reason seems to allow that the liberal values of autonomy and individuality might be political values even though they could not be so accepted. Second: The content of public reason as Rawls has so far specified it does not yet make possible a decisive case for abortion rights and gay rights.

de Medici, Cristina B and Maidana, Susana H. "La Posmodernidad en la Encrucijada Argentina" in *Temas Actuales de Filosofía, Palacios, María Julia (ed)*, 359-365. Buenos Aires, Univ Nacional Salta, 1993.

The presence of postmodernism and its contradictions in Latin American countries is shown in this work. While in central countries it is necessary to pay attention to consumerism and high technology, we are struggling against illiteracy, infant mortality and unemployment. The Latin American man has to face a hard choice: either his "belonging" to a rich culture, full of mysteries and myths, or his "alienation" in view of the speed of changes. His true challenge will be to root himself into the mythological universe which is his by nature, and at the same time venture the new paths of present culture.

De Miguel Alvarez, Ana. Autonomía y Conducta Desviada: el Problema del Paternalismo en la Obra de John Stuart Mill. *Telos (Spain)*, 3(2), 59-70, D 94.

This article deals with the debate about whether John Stuart Mill defends any kind of paternalism, weak or strong, in his work *On Liberty*. Laseva's thesis about the coherence of on antipaternalist attitude in Mill is accepted here. The importance of this attitude is also developed, showing its influence in modern sociology of deviance and especially in the conceptualization of the, so-called, "crimes without victim". Finally, it is argued, through the case of prostitution, that the defense of a strong antipaternalism does not, as conservative liberalism pretends, ignore the important role of the State in promoting citizens' autonomy.

De Monticelli, Roberta. Nel Vivo dell'Essere: Per un Dialogo sull'Ontologia. *Teoria*, 14(2), 5-28, 1994.

de Monzie, Anatole. Instructions du 2 Septembre 1925. *Philosopher*, 15, 141-154, 1994.

De Muynck, W M. Measurement and the Interpretation of Quantum Mechanics and Relativity Theory. *Synthese*, 102(2), 293-318, F 95.

The axiomatic approaches of quantum mechanics and relativity theory are compared with approaches in which the theories are thought to descriptive readings of certain measurement operations. The usual axioms are shown to correspond with classes of ideal measurements. The necessity is discussed of generalizing the formalisms of both quantum and relativity theory so as to encompass more realistic nonideal measurements. It is argued that this generalization favours an empiricist interpretation of the mathematical formalisms over a realist one.

De Nys, Martin J. "Self-Consciousness and the Concept in Hegel's Appropriation of Kant" in *Hegel on the Modern World, Collins, Ardis B (ed)*, 143-158. Albany, SUNY Pr, 1995.

De Nys, Martin J. The Substance of Knowing Is History: Absolute Knowing and History in Hegel's *Phenomenology*. *Amer Cath Phil Quart*, 68(Supp), 135-144, 1994.

De Olaso, Ezequiel. Respuesta a Villoro. *Rev Latin de Filosof*, 20(2), 333-336, 1994.

De Paiva Durate, Rodrigo Antonio. Notes on the "Lack of Foundation" in Theodor W Adorno Philosophy (in Portuguese). *Trans/Form/Acao*, 17, 39-49, 1994.

Habermas "re-reads" Adorno and Horkheimer from his own perspective, that is, from the point of view of the "linguistic paradigm", which substitutes the transforming praxis for argumentation. Hence, Habermas cannot see that Adorno's competence in communication is subordinated to something essentially different, to an impulse towards emancipation. The characteristics of this rationally mediated transcendental *a priori* must be searched not in *Dialectics of enlightenment* but in Minima moralia.

De Palma, Armando. Interventi nel Dibattito. *Filosofia*, 45(1), 129-132, Ja-Ap 94.

De Pascale, Carla. "Archäologie des Rechtsstaates" in *Das geistige Erbe Europas, Buhr, Manfred (ed)*, 489-505. Napoli, Vivarium, 1994.

De Pascale, Carla. Der Primat Deutschlands bei Fichte. *Fichte-Studien*, 3, 68-85, 1991.

The *Trieb* in Fichte's philosophy refers not only to the natural side of limited rational being, but also to the whole being. There is a very close link between *Trieb* and *Streben*; the last one plays a theoretical—as well as a practical—important part. We must see the whole *Trieb* system to understand the *Trieb*. Therefore you can find in the article a complete map of *Trieb* that induce men to act: from the *Trieb zur Vorstellung* to the *Naturtrieb*, from the *blinden Trieb* to the *Trieb nach Glückeligkeit* and *nach Geselligkeit*, from the *reinen Trieb* to the *sittlechen Trieb*.

De Pascale, Carla. Die Trieblehre bei Fichte. *Fichte-Studien*, 6, 229-251, 1994.

De Pascale, Carla. La Teoria e la Pratica del Diritto. *Daimon Rev Filosof*, 9, 275-288, 1994.

The science of Right, as a particular science, is a constant object of Fichte's interest, from the early *Revolutionsschriften* to the latest writings. The comparison between the main works on this subject—the *Grundlage des Naturrechts* and the lessons on the *Rechtslehre*—shows that some problems of this science (i.e., the need for the certainty of Right and the necessity of a control over the central power) continue to be of extreme importance and salience. Through the modifications of Fichte's solution to this question, the tension between the progressive extension of the central power perogatives and the ideal striving of the State towards its own extinction is more and more evident.

De Peretti, Cristina. "Foucault: The Twofold Games of Language" in *Reconstructing Foucault, Miguel-Alfonso, Ricardo (ed)*, 35-49. Amsterdam, Rodopi, 1994.

De Pizan, Christine and Forhan, Kate Langdon (ed & trans). *The Book of the Body Politic*. New York, Cambridge Univ Pr, 1994.

de Queiroz, Kevin. The Definitions of Species and Clade Names: A Reply to Ghiselin. *Biol Phil*, 10(2), 223-228, Ap 95.

The definitions of species and clade names can in fact be stated in terms of logically necessary properties. Contrary arguments raised by Ghiselin (1995 Biology and Philosophy 10:219-222) either confuse the means used to specify defining properties with the defining properties themselves or rest on a false dichotomy between intentional and ostensive definitions. By conceptualizing defining properties as biological relationships rather than organismal traits, new definitions of species and clade names reveal several false dichotomies in the philosophy of taxonomy and permit a sythesis of formerly opposing views concerning the nature of biological taxa and the definitions of their names.

De Queiroz Ruy, J G B. Normalisation and Language-Games. *Dialectica*, 48(2), 83-123, 1994.

The question of finding a suitable formal account of meaning for (primitive) logical signs has troubled many philosophers and logicians since the early days of formal logic. Here I attempt to show how two *operational* (as opposed to *denotational*, or *truth*-based) approaches to the problem can still be shown to be 'technically' equivalent, despite having emerged from two different readings of a single philosophical account, and being essentially distinct with respect to the role of 'will' in mathematical activity: on the one hand, the 'semantics of use', my own reformulation of P Martin-Löf's *Intuitionistic Type Theory* canonical-values based semantics and, on the other hand, J Hintikka's *Game-Theoretical Semantics*. The philosophical account from which both emerge is precisely Wittgenstein's later account of propositions, where the notion of 'language-games' is introduced as a key semantical device. (edited)

De Rose, Keith. Lewis on 'Might' and 'Would' Counterfactual Conditionals. *Can J Phil*, 24(3), 413-418, S 94.

De Rose, Keith. Solving the Skeptical Problem. *Phil Rev*, 104(1), 1-52, Ja 95.

de Ruyter, Doret J and Miedema, Siebren. "Schools, Identity, and the Conception of the Good" in *Identity, Culture, and Education, Smeyers, Paul (ed)*, 145-156. Leuven, Leuven Univ Pr, 1994.

Schools have an important contribution to the formation of a child's identity. Identity can be divided into three aspects, namely those characteristics, values, and ideals a person describes to herself that she has derived from 1) her person; 2) the communities she is part of; 3) the society she lives in. In denominational schools frictions can arise regarding the contribution to the development of the child's societal identity and of her communital identity. Regarding this friction we take the stance that as the schools are fully subsidized by the state that makes freedom and diversity in (religious) identity possible, the state has the right to make freedom of choice for children possible as well. Thus, the balance tips to the societal identity.

De Silva, Padmasiri. "Theoretical Perspectives on Emotions in Early Buddhism" in *Emotions in Asian Thought, Marks, Joel (ed)*, 109-121. Albany, SUNY Pr, 1995.

De Smet, Richard. The Presuppositions of Jaimini and the Vedāntins. *J Indian Counc Phil Res*, 11(2), 77-87, Ja-Ap 94.

This paper argues to show that Jaimini's decision to escape the Buddhists' criticisms was responsible for the belief in the eternity of the sruti and that the diversity of the Vedantins's interpretations of the same works depends on the diversity of their *paratextual* conceptions of what a sentence does.

De Stafano, Rodolfo. Un colloquio filosofico su "rivoluzione" e "contraddizione". *Riv Int Filosof Diritto*, 71(3), 506-516, 1994.

De Vlieghere, Martin. A Reappraisal of Friedrich A Hayek's Cultural Evolutionism. *Econ Phil*, 10(2), 285-304, O 94.

de Vos, L. Die Realität der Idee. *Fichte-Studien*, 6, 367-397, 1994.

In der Diskussion des Atheismusstreites richtet sich die philosophische Frage auf das Verhältnis von Wesen, objektiver Gültigkeit und (objektiver) Realität der Idee Gottes. Damit wird die auch bei Kant schwierige Sachlage des Status der Ideen von Seiten der neupietistischen Öffentlichkeit gegen die Transzendentalphilosophie auf- und ausgespielt. Besonders das Verhältnis von objektiver Gültigkeit und Realität der müssigen Ideen ist—nach diesem tragischen Ereignis—Gegenstand der philosophischen Auseinandersetzung und der erneuten Untersuchung von Seiten Fichtes. Wie die interne Gliederung der Ideen schon vorher, in der *Grundlage*, bestimmt wurde, und wie der Jenaer Fichte die Idee Gottes aufnahm und nachher selbst mit dem Prädikat der objektiven Gültigkeit versah—was für einen rechten Kantianer doch seltsam ist—wird Gegenstand dieses Vortrags sein. (edited)

de Vos, Lou. Philosophy in Belgium. *Magyar Filozof Szemle*, 5-6, 859-864, 1994.

De Vries, Fer-Jan and Van Eijck, Jan. Reasoning about Update Logic. *J Phil Log*, 24(1), 19-45, F 95.

De Vries, Michiel S. Het statistische argument. *Kennis Methode*, 18(4), 341-360, 1994.

In dit artikel wordt ingegaan op de vergelijking tussen intuïtief genomen beslissingen en beslissingen op basis van statistische evaluaties. Na een verkenning van de eisen waaraan keuzen zouden moeten voldoen en een weergave van de problemen bij het nemen van beslissingen in het algemeen, volgt een exposé over de mate waarin statistische beslissingsondersteunende technieken aan die eisen voldoen. Dit wordt toegelicht aan de hand van twee statistische technieken, de multi attribute utility analysis en nonparametrische toetsen. Geconcludeerd wordt dat het gebruik van zulke technieken slechts een relatief voordeel kan geven en dat de logica achter zulke technieken een andere is dan die van een individuele besluitvormer.

De Wachter, Frans. Contextualism and Universalism in Postmodern Ethics. *Dialogue Hum*, 4(2-3), 81-91, 1994.

Post-modernity produced a contextual type of ethics that is anti-foundational and anti-universalistic. This development is evaluated from a moral point of view. Particularistic moral sensitivity can only play a heuristic role. There are moral arguments for not renouncing universalism completely. A universalistic outlook is not a rationalistic abstraction, but the reminder that our norms are of an ethical nature, and not just actual psychological sentiments and preferences.

De Wijze, Stephen. Towards a Political Ethic: Exploring the Boundaries of a Moral Politics. *Phil Papers*, 23(3), 191-215, N 94.

This paper argues for an ethic to provide a guide for political behaviour. The demands of political office require that the boundaries of a personal morality be redefined. I argue for three principles which when applied to examples taken from actual political conduct fit with our deeply held considered convictions about the rightness or wrongness of certain types of political conduct. I conclude by showing that this ethic, under certain carefully defined conditions, licenses some deceitful and violent acts and also obliges a politician to sometimes act against what would normally be unacceptable from a personal moral perspective.

De Wolf, Jan (ed) and Raven, Diederick (ed) and Geuijen, Karin (ed). *Post-Modernism and Anthropology: Theory and Practice*. Assen, Gorcum, 1995.

During the nineteen eighties the term *post-modern* started to be applied to tendencies within the field of cultural and social anthropology. To many post-modernism appeared not merely as another theoretical paradigm but as an ill conceived attempt to put the whole discipline on its head. In this volume the contributors want to consider two important questions which are crucial to a reasoned assessment of the ensuing debates. First, to what extent and in which way does post-modernism in anthropology differ from existing, 'modern' approaches? Secondly, what consequences does post-modernism have for the presentation of that quintessential anthropological experience: participant-observation in field work?

Dean, Carolyn J. The Productive Hypothesis: Foucault, Gender, and the History of Sexuality. *Hist Theor*, 33(3), 271-296, 1994.

This article addresses Michel Foucault's challenge to historians by historicizing his work on the history of sexuality. First, it summarizes recent scholarly literature about sexuality by historians and literary critics in order to clarify the theoretical and historical groundwork that has thus far been laid. It also places interdisciplinary scholarship in a framework historians will find meaningful. Second, the essay argues that Foucault's work is the product of crises in male subjectivity originating after the Great War. In so doing, it seeks to explain the absence of gender as a category of analysis in his own work, as well as his inability to account for the historical processes through which sexuality is produced.

Dean, Colin. The Relationship Between Analysis and Insight (Prajñā) in Mādhyamika Buddhism: Some Western Interpretations. *Indian Phil Quart*, 21(4), 347-353, O 94.

This article sets out for the first time what Western scholars say is the relationship between analysis and insight, or wisdom in Madhyamika Buddhism. This article shows that there is a wide range of opinion amongst Western scholars on this point. Theses are different for views regarding Nagarjuna's *Chandrakirti's* and the Geluk-ba *Prasangika* ideas about the relationship, as seen by certain Western scholars. This article both brings the issue of the relationship to the attention of a wider readership and shows the danger of making universalistic generalizations about the Madhyamika.

Dean, Craig R. "Gay Marriage: A Civil Right" in *Gay Ethics, Murphy, Timothy F (ed)*, 111-115. New York, Haworth Pr, 1994.

This article describes the author's efforts to secure marriage rights for same-sex couples in the District of Columbia. The importance of such rights are described in terms of their benefits to partners in areas such as inheritance, taxation, and benefit to society. It is argued that refusal to recognize same-sex marriages is not justified by statute and that discrimination on the basis of sex violates the District's Human Rights Act. Certain prior court cases, moreover, affirm the moral logic for extending marriage rights to same-sex couples.

Dean, Jodi. Reflective Solidarity. *Constellation*, 2(1), 114-140, Ap 95.

Dear, Peter. Cultural History of Science: An Overview with Reflections. *Sci Tech Human Values*, 20(2), 150-170, Spr 95.

The increased popularity of the label "cultural" within science studies, especially in relation to "cultural studies", invites consideration of how it is and can be used in historical work. A lot more seems now to be invested in the notion of "cultural history". This article examines some recent historiography of science as a means of considering what counts as cultural history in that domain and attempts to coordinate it with the sociologically informed studies of the past ten or fifteen years. The label "sociocultural" seems a more useful term by which to capture recent developments.

Dearmont, David. A Hint at Peirce's Empirical Evidence for Tychism. *Trans Peirce Soc*, 31(1), 185-204, Wint 95.

This paper explores tychism, Peirce's evolutionary theory of physical laws. In "Design and Chance," Peirce hypothesizes that absolute chance and habit-taking can account for both regularity and heterogeneity in nature. To motivate his argument, Peirce supplies a mental experiment and a sketch of the result. Using a computer simulation, I show that Peirce's claim is correct. I suggest that the empirical evidence Peirce claimed to have for tychism is grounded in the effects of absolute chance and habit-taking, and suggest what the empirical evidence might be, and how Peirce might have arrived at this evidence.

Debon, María C and Carranza, Elena N. "El Reconocimiento de Ideologías en un Discurso Político" in *Temas Actuales de Filosofía, Palacios, María Julia (ed)*, 115-123. Buenos Aires, Univ Nacional Salta, 1993.

Debray, Régis and Rauth, Eric (trans). The Three Ages of Looking. *Crit Inquiry*, 21(3), 529-555, Spr 95.

This essay translates chapter 8 in Debray's *Vie et mort de l'image*. It marks the first appearance in English of "mediology," since *Teachers, Writers, Celebrities*. Mediological history of the Western eye explores social groups of producers, theologians, critics, viewing subjects, and technologies that "mediate" representation and viewing of visual forms. Successive horizons of ocular expectation have linked practices of looking with belief. Idols (="indices") overcome death with eternity and miracle; icons (="Art") cultivate aesthetics and taste; the "visual" divinizes novelty, economy, influence. Their relation to inscription technologies (writing, print, computer-graphics) clarifies understanding of images *and* signs in culture and modernity.

DeBruin, Debra A. Can One Justify Morality to Fooles?. *Can J Phil*, 25(1), 1-32, Mr 95.

Why should one be moral? There is a very strong tradition in moral philosophy of attempting to answer this question by trying to demonstrate that we are rationally required to be moral. The aim of this paper is to question the viability of this rationalist project. I suggest that rationalism has an ultimate aim: to justify the obligatory force of morality. But what must rationalism do to meet this goal, and can it succeed? I argue that rationalism cannot succeed in justifying the obligatory force of morality. If rationalism fails, we must either admit that there is no obligation to be moral, or we must seek alternative modes of justification in ethics.

DeCew, Judith Wagner. The Combat Exclusion and the Role of Women in the Military. *Hypatia*, 10(1), 56-73, Wint 95.

I first discuss reasons for feminists to attend to the role of women in the military, despite past emphasis on antimilitarism. I then focus on the exclusion of women from combat duty, reviewing its sanction by the US Supreme Court and the history of its adoption. I present arguments favoring the exclusion, defending strong replies to each, and demonstrate that reasoning from related cases and feminist analyses of equality explain why exclusion remains entrenched.

Decker, Roy T. "Tactility and Imagination: Considerations of Aesthetic Experience in Architecture" in *Philosophy and Architecture, Mitias, Michael H (ed)*, 203-219. Amsterdam, Rodopi, 1994.

Decossas, Béatrice. Les exigences de la causalité créatrice selon l'*Expositio in Librum de causis* de Thomas d'Aquin. *Rev Thomiste*, 94(2), 241-272, Ap-Je 94.

Decyk, Betsy Newell. Appreciating a Situation. *J Soc Phil*, 25(2), 139-167, Fall 94.

Dedrick, Don. Objectivism and the Evolutionary Value of Colour Vision. *Dialogue (Canada)*, 34(1), 35-44, Wint 95.

Deely, John. A Morning and Evening Star: Editor's Introduction. *Amer Cath Phil Quart*, 68(3), 259-277, Sum 94.

Deely, John. A Prospect of Postmodernity. *Listening*, 30(1), 7-14, Wint 95.

Deely, John and Beuchot, Mauricio. Common Sources for the Semiotic of Charles Peirce and John Poinsot. *Rev Metaph*, 48(3), 539-566, Mr 95.

Deely, John N. What Happened to Philosophy Between Aquinas and Descartes?. *Thomist*, 58(4), 543-568, O 94.

Deetz, Stanley. "The New Politics of the Workplace: Ideology and Other Unobtrusive Controls" in *After Postmodernism, Simons, Herbert W (ed)*, 172-199. Newbury Park, Sage, 1994.

The essay describes why ideology and other unobtrusive forms of power are of such interest in the workplace and demonstrates how a communication-based analysis focused on the construction of identity can be more useful than traditional ideology critique. Traditional conceptions of both domination and democracy in the workplace are shown to overlook or take for granted the social processes by which group divisions are produced, individuals acquire identity, and different individuals acquire specific experiences and interests. In this analysis power is considered "within" such social producations. Communication-based analysis shows the practical manner by which this hidden power is deployed and potential workplace conflicts are suppressed in identity productions.

Defez i Martín, Antoni. Realismo sin Empirismo. *An Seminar Metaf*, 28, 13-25, 1994.

DeFilippo, Joseph G and Mitsis, Phillip T. "Socrates and Stoic Natural Law" in *The Socratic Movement, Vander Waerdt, Paul A (ed)*, 252-271. Ithaca, Cornell Univ Pr, 1994.

Defoort, Carine. Caring for Whom? Moral Discussions between Early Confucians and Mohists. *Tijdschr Filosof*, 57(1), 36-50, Mr 95.

Beginning with a dialogue written in the *Menicus* (late 4th c. B.C.), this article traces an old discussion in Chinese philosophy concerning the question of whom one should take care of. Confucius (551-479 B.C.) values the capacity for empathy or "likening to oneself". He thereby promotes, without explicitly arguing for it, a reevaluation and extension of the traditional attitude of gradual concern, starting from close relatives and radiating outward. The first opposition to this attitude comes from the Mohists (5-4th c. B.C.), who promote "concern for everybody", with stringent argumentation by analogy. Menicus, finally, reluctantly enters the discussion to defend the Confucian attitude. Although the Confucian and Mohist attitudes may seem to resemble Western discussions between ethical universalism and particularism, both opponents take spontaneous emotions as their starting-point and both argue by reasoning in the form of presenting analogies. While Menicus relies mainly on the emotions being conducted by a convincing analogy, the Mohists give primacy to the structure of infallible analogical reasoning, forcing the emotions towards morality.

Degnan, Michael. Aristotle on Unqualified Knowledge: Do Referential Universals Solve the *Meno* Paradox?. *Amer Cath Phil Quart*, 68(Supp), 145-158, 1994.

In the *Origins of Aristotelian Science* Michael Ferejohn argues that Aristotle solves the paradox of learning raised in Plato's *Meno* by distinguishing between "merely universal knowledge" and "knowledge in the unqualified sense." Unqualified knowledge of generalization entails knowledge of its application to all its corresponding instances. Ferejohn calls these existentially loaded generalizations, "referential universals." Degnan argues that referential universals cannot be consistently expressed and do the work Ferejohn expects. Even if the concept were coherent, Degnan shows that it fails to resolve the paradox. Degnan interprets unqualified knowledge in a way that escapes the difficulties of Ferejohn's reading.

Degnin, Francis Dominic. Laughter and Metaphysics: Interruptions of Levinas and Nietzsche. *Phil Today*, 39(1), 31-46, Spr 95.

This essay argues that Levinas's and Nietzsche's thought have far more in common—precisely in how each interrupts metaphysical systems—than has hitherto been recognized. This has led to a failure to recognize resources which could support each thinker's project and has obscured the more subtle differences between them. For example, it is possible that Levinas has articulated a transformation of values toward which Nietzsche dimly groped, while at the same time betraying his own project via a subtle remnant of the ascetic ideal. In terms of ethical thought, this essay is suggestive of the directions taken by thinkers like Derrida, Lyotard, Alphonso Lingis, and Charles Scott.

DeGrazia, David. Value Theory and the Best Interests Standard. *Bioethics*, 9(1), 50-61, Ja 95.

The idea of a patient's best interests raises issues in prudential value theory—the study of what makes up an individual's ultimate (nonmoral) good or well-being. While this connection may strike a philosopher as obvious, the literature on the best interests standard reveals almost no engagement of recent work in value theory. There seems to be a growing sentiment among bioethicists that their work is independent of philosophical theorizing. Is this sentiment wrong in the present case? Does value theory make a significant difference in interpreting best interests? In pursuing this question, I begin with a quick sketch of broad kinds of value theories, identifying representatives that are plausible enough to count as contenders. I then explore what each account suggests in 1) neonatal treatment decisions, and 2) decisions for patients in persistent vegetative states. I conclude that while these accounts converge somewhat in their interpretations of best interests, they also have importantly different implications.

DeHaven, Stephen Lee. *The Logic Course*. Peterborough, Broadview Pr, 1995.

The Logic Course combines an accessible textbook for courses in critical thinking or introductory logic with an exercise workbook and with a practical software package. The software, which the author has adapted from the highly-acclaimed LogicWorks program, has been very carefully structured to work with the text and workbook as a fully integrated package. (edited)

Deigh, John. Empathy and Universalizability. *Ethics*, 105(4), 743-763, Jl 95.

The paper examines the question of whether a person could know the difference between right and wrong and have the capacity to control his or her conduct yet not be moved by his or her knowledge of right or wrong. It proceeds by considering psychopathy and inquiring into the nature of the psychopath's cognitive deficits, if any. One possibility is that psychopaths are inconsistent in the sense of Kant's test of universalizability. This possibility is rejected after considerable argument. A second possibility is that psychopaths are incapable of empathy. Consideration of recent work in developmental psychology leads to the conclusion that this possibility remains open.

Dejnozka, Jan. Origins of the Private Language Argument. *Dialogos*, 30(66), 59-78, Jl 95.

The private language arguments of the analytic tradition may be understood best in terms of their historical origins. There are at least eight origins: verificationism, naturalism-pragmatism, materialism, projective geometry, justificationism, realism versus nominalism, the thesis that language and thought are identical, and "no entity without identity" theory. Anticipators include Dewey, James, Peirce, Helmholtz, Müller, Hamann, Herder, Humboldt, Marx, Engels, Feuerbach, Hegel, Schelling, Schopenhauer, Kant, Tooke, Hobbes, Bonald, Lamettrie, Arnobius, Cicero, Plato, 19th century opticians and geometers, and the Renaissance painters. Thus an enormous private-language dialogue flourished long before any analysts appeared on the scene.

Dekkers, Wim J M. F J J Buytendijk's Concept of an Anthropological Physiology. *Theor Med*, 16(1), 15-39, Mr 94.

In his concept of an anthropological physiology, F J J Buytendijk has tried to lay down the theoretical and scientific foundations for an anthropologically-oriented medicine. The aim of anthropological physiology is to demonstrate, empirically, what being specifically human is in the most elementary physiological functions. This article contains a sketch of Buytendijk's life and work, an overview of his philosophical-anthropological presuppositions, an outline of his idea of an anthropological physiology and medicine, and a discussion of some epistemological and methodological problems. It is demonstrated that Buytendijk's design of an anthropological physiology is fragmentary and programmatic and that his methodology offers few points of contact for specific anthropological experimental research. Notwithstanding, it is argued that Buytendijk's description of the subjective, animated body forms a pre-eminent point of reference for all research in physiology and psychology in which the specific human aspect is not ignored beforehand.

Del Aguila, Rafael. Emancipation, Resistance and Cosmopolitanism. *Grad Fac Phil J*, 18(1), 27-50, 1995.

The political practice of the left is going through a deep crisis, an important part of which is connected to the crisis of modernity and to the doubt cast upon some of its basic concepts. The present work will analyze one of these, the concept of emancipation, and its relation to two contemporary concepts: the ideal of resistance in Foucault and the idea of cosmopolitanism in Rorty. The thesis are the following: 1) part of the modern legacy inscribed in the concept of emancipation is still alive in the Foucauldian left and in Rorty's pragmatic liberalism; 2) certain reflective tools of emancipation and modernity are still indispensable for the creation of a nonconformist political alternative; 3) in the task of the creation of a public ethos capable of undertaken the transformation of our reality, we must assume the existence of a strategic and noncommunicative residue which may constitute our main theoretical problem at the present time.

del Carmen Paredes, María. G W F Hegel: El *Fragmento de Tubinga*. *Rev Filosof (Spain)*, 7(11), 139-176, 1994.

Translation into Spanish of Hegel's so-called *Tübinger Fragment*, based "on Text 16 from G W F Hegel" *Gesammelte Werke*, Düsseldorf 1989, Band 1 (83-114). The object of this essay is, as Hegel says, not to investigate what religious doctrines are most appealing to the soul, but rather what arrangements are requisite in order that the doctrines and the force of religion should enter into the web of human feelings. The essay was written by Hegel in 1793, during the last year of his stay in Tubingen.

Del Caro, Adrian. Paul Celan's Uncanny Speech. *Phil Lit*, 18(2), 211-223, O 94.

A distinguishing feature of Paul Celan's language is its uncanniness. "Uncanny" is German *unheimlich*, from *heim* (home) and *heimlich* (homely, secretive). After an intellectual-historical discussion of the uncanny we can better understand why it becomes a major concern of Celan after the Holocaust, which deprived millions of Jews of a home in the earth. Uncanny and the uncanny nature of Celan's "open" are defined and analyzed. Post-Holocaust discourses and our relation to language in general exhibit signs of the uncanny.

Del Prete, Antonella. L'Univers Infini: Les Interventions de Marin Mersenne et de Charles Sorel. *Rev Phil Fr*, 2, 145-164, Ap-Je 95.

Giordani Bruno's cosmological hypothesis that the universe is infinite and is made up infinite worlds, provokes Marin Mersenne's apologetical reply. His confutation (*L'impiété des Déostes*, 1626) does not deal with the astronomical side of Bruno's thought, but focuses on theological aspects. In defense of God's freedom and transcendence, he condemns the new cosmological theories, which he recognizes as dangerous only after reading Bruno. In his *La Science Universelle* (1660) Charles Sorel analyses Bruno's philosophy and cautiously defends the Copernicanism, but he reverses Mersenne's arguments in a partial rehabilitation of Bruno's theses.

Del Rosario, M and Jimenez Glez, J E. Phonological Awareness in Learning Literacy. *Commun Cog—AI*, 11(1-2), 127-152, 1994.

The present research examines accessibility to different levels of phonological awareness and their relationship to the mastery of the alphabetic code in Spanish language. The results obtained suggest that the pre-reader subjects are more sensitive to syllabic units than to intra-syllabic and phonemic units. Similarly, a greater mastery of the alphabetic code is associated with higher levels of intra-syllabic and phonemic awareness. (edited)

del Valle Manzur, Analía and Santillán, Miguel Angel. "Verdad y Validez" in *Temas Actuales de Filosofía, Palacios, María Julia (ed)*, 563-569. Buenos Aires, Univ Nacional Salta, 1993.

Del Vecchio, Dante. Postille: 1)Pensiero Orientale Verticale e Pensiero Occidentale Orizzontale, 2)La Filsofia della Crisi. *Sapienza*, 48(1), 105-109, 1995.

1) Eastern philosophy contemplates the man like spiritual creature, inclined toward the sky. Western philosophy examines the man like a rational being through course of events in the history. This philosophy bases oneself on mental faculties, supposed, but not proved and unfailing. 2) When a philosophical system passes through a crisis, the philosopher pays his attention to single man, not to the totality of men. The 'egologia' aims at discovering again the man and determining some essential finality in interior life.

Delaney, Cornelius J. "Peirce on the Reliability of Science: A Response to Rescher" in *Peirce and Contemporary Thought: Philosophical Inquiries, Ketner, Kenneth Laine (ed)*, 113-119. New York, Fordham Univ Pr, 1995.

Delaruelle, Jacques. Aesthetics and Art Education. *Lit Aes*, 4, 109-116, O 94.

Delcò, Alessandro. L'informe bergsoniano nella filosofia di Serres. *Filosofia*, 45(2), 217-50, My-Ag 94.

Delcò, Alessandro. Le Forme Diffratte di Serres: Prolegomeni a una Nuova Filosofia della Storia. *Filosofia*, 45(3), 369-400, S-D 94.

Deleuze, Gilles and Patton, Paul (trans). *Difference and Repetition*. New York, Columbia Univ Pr, 1994.

This brilliant exposition of the critique of identity is a classic in contemporary philosophy and one of Deleuze's most important words. Of fundamental importance to literary critics and philosophers, the book develops two central concepts—pure difference and complex repetition—and shows how the two concepts are related. While difference implies divergence and decentering, repetition is associated with displacement and disguising. Central in initiating the shift in French thought away from Hegel and Marx and toward Nietzsche and Freud, the book moves deftly to establish a fundamental critique of Western metaphysics.

Delgado, Manuel. Las Formas lógicas de la Sección Primera de El Capital. *Rev Filosof (Costa Rica)*, 31(75-76), 237-243, D 93.

A detailed research about the logical forms applied by Karl Marx in the study of society can be done from the analysis of the structure of the First Section of the First Book of Capital. Marx starts his analysis from the more abstract form, commodity and his market ("an immense accumulation of commodities"), to the highest forms of developing of history. Doing that, he shows the importance of the "historical method" in social analysis.

Delgado De Torres, Olivia. The Game that Looks Like Work in Plato's "Parmenides". *Dialogos*, 30(65), 33-48, Ja 95.

Delin, Catherine R and Baumeister, Roy F. Praise: More Than Just Social Reinforcement. *J Theor Soc Behav*, 24(3), 219-241, S 94.

In this article we present an analysis of the effects of praise. We begin by considering how to define praise. Next, we examine the view of praise as social reinforcement, a conception which roots praise firmly within an empiricist framework; this appears to have been the predominant theoretical view guiding previous research on praise. We conclude, however, that this view is conceptually inadequate to account for the empirical evidence. Because of that conclusion, our next step is to provide a novel examination of the likely processes and consequences involved in praise. The remainder of the article is then devoted to examining, where it is available, empirical evidence relevant to our analysis. (edited)

Delivoyatzis, S. The Structure of the Human Acting Subject in Thomas Aquinas. *Phil Inq*, 16(3-4), 56-61, Sum-Fall 94.

Delkeskamp-Hayes, Corinna. Towards a Non-Ecumentical Interchange: Engelhardt, Hauerwas, and Ramsey on Christian Bioethics. *Christian Bioethics*, 1(1), 48-64, Mr 95.

Does a nonecumenical journal on Christian bioethics make sense? Taking issue with Stanley Hauerwas's critique of Ramsey, the author argues 1) interdenominational exchange should not be construed as contest, and 2) the attempt on the part of Christians to address secular issues in secular terms should not be mistrusted or viewed as a contamination hazard. Instead 1) an awareness of human limits should render adherents of different traditions willing to learn from each other and 2) one should see in the love-of-neighbor principle an obligation to serve the world. Addressing the communication problem, the author recommends different language for intra-group and ever more encompassing inter-group exchanges.

Delouya, Daniel. A Filosofia da Biologia à Luz da Biologia Molecular: Resolveu-se o Mistério?. *Cad Hist Filosof Cie*, 4(1), 51-59, Ja-Je 94.

In view of the last 25 years of developments in molecular biology, many scientists and philosophers either reject the classical problematics of reducing biology to physico-chemistry and the related causality versus teleology dispute, or they believe this "life mystery" is solved. Most of these trends are inspired by the famous Jacque Monod's Le hasard et la necéssité. Reconsidering these questions we show that one cannot make these problematics disappear or vanish by simply introducing new cybernetic concepts or relying on molecular knowledge, the mystery is still alive.

DeMarco, C Wesley. "Plato's Ghost: Consequences of Aristotelian Dialectic" in *The Crossroads of Norm and Nature, Sim, May (ed)*, 151-174. Lanham, Rowman & Littlefield, 1995.

I describe the form of Aristotle's thinking about first principles. This is a kind of dialectic, one that owes much to Plato. I show how the large-scale structure of this dialectic determines the large-scale structure of Aristotle's *Ethics* and *Metaphysics*. In due course, exact correspondences between the *Ethics* and *Metaphysics* emerge, and some longstanding interpretative difficulties are dissolved. I conclude by sketching certain problems internal to Aristotelian thinking, and suggest that these problems arise from Aristotle's struggle with dialectical transcendence.

DeMarco, Joseph P. *Moral Theory: A Contemporary Overview*. Boston, Jones & Bartlett, 1996.

This text covers a full range of theoretical positions, from extreme particularism to moral ideals. The strengths and weaknesses of each is examined in order to show how typically opposed theories can jointly aid moral decision making. The text is organized from theories relying on concrete moral responses to those based in abstract values and principles. An initial survey of moral experience explores ways a moral problem may be resolved and how moral theories may be evaluated. Traditional theories are covered as are such topics as ideals, exemplars, norms, utopian thinking, role morality, virtues, casuistry, feminist ethics, and political philosophy.

Demkovich, Michael. Beyond Subjectivity: Opening the Ego. *Listening*, 29(3), 162-173, Fall 94.

This work addresses subjective autonomy and asks if such autonomy is an adequate ethic for human existence. Drawing inspiration from the fourteenth century Dominican mystic Meister Eckhart, this article explores his notion of the "pure self," or open ego, as a way to move beyond subjectivity. The open ego calls for the self simultaneously to be self- and other-centered, at the same time lodging and dislodging subjectivity. Thomas J J Altizer's "radical reversal of Christian consciousness" as a solution to autonomous existence is critiqued by Eckhart's "open ego" which exposes the underlying egoism of Altizer's Oriental vision of "egolessness."

Demopoulos, William (ed). *Frege's Philosophy of Mathematics*. Cambridge, Harvard Univ Pr, 1995.

This collection of essays addresses three main developments in recent work on Frege's philosophy of mathematics: the emerging interest in the intellectual background to his logicism; the rediscovery of Frege's theorem; and the reevaluation of the mathematical content of *The Basic Laws of Arithmetic*. Each essay attempts a sympathetic, if not uncritical, reconstruction, evaluation, or extension of a facet of Frege's theory of arithmetic. Together they form an accessible and authoritative introduction to aspects of Frege's thought that have, until now, been largely missed by the philosophical community.

Demopoulos, William. Frege, Hilbert, and the Conceptual Structure of Model Theory. *Hist Phil Log*, 15(2), 211-225, 1994.

This paper attempts to confine the preconceptions that prevented Frege from appreciating Hilbert's *Grundlagen der Geometrie* to two: i) Frege's reliance on what, following Wilfrid Hodges, I call a Frege-Peano language, and ii) Frege's view that the sense of an expression wholly determines its reference. I argue that these two preconceptions prevented Frege from achieving the conceptual structure of model theory, whereas Hilbert, at least in his practice, was quite close to the model-theoretic point of view. Moreover, the issues that divided Frege and Hilbert did not revolve around whether one or the other allowed metalogical notions. Frege, e.g., succeeded in formulating the notion of logical consequence, at least to the extent that Bolzano did; the point is rather that even though Frege had certain semantic concepts, he did not articulate them model-theoretically, whereas, in some limited sense, Hilbert did.

Demuijnck, Geert. Justice as a Competence. The Normative Relevance of Empirical Research on Judgments of 'Greatness'. *Philosophica*, 53(1), 39-56, 1994.

den Bok, Nico. Augustine on Prescience and Free Will. *Bijdragen*, 56(1), 40-60, 1995.

Augustine's analysis and solution of the classical problem of free will and foreknowledge—as given in *De libero arbitrio* III 4-10 and *De civitate Dei* V 8-10—stand out in their brevity and simplicity. His texts carry formulations which show an astonishing clarity not only in what they explicitly say, but also in what is implicitly said in them. Most recent discussions of Augustine's view, however, are unclear about this clarity, at least partly because they tend to a deterministic position; they probably sense, unwillingly, that Augustine intends to rule that position out. In the discussions on the problem a dilemma seems to be unavoidable; one can only cling to one of its horns. Either God knows the future and then human volitions cannot be free (the deterministic position), or the human will is free but then God cannot know its future volitions (Cicero's position).

den Bok, Nico. Totum Suscepit. *Bijdragen*, 56(2), 156-186, 1995.

The christological analysis of this article hinges on Augustine's thoughts about the predestination of Christ. These thoughts are developed within an anthropological context, in the quest for gratuitous grace; the analysis does not focus on this idea, however, but on the view of the nature of Christ's human willing which is entailed in it. The example of Christ's predestination shows, almost by the way, that very important anthropological distinctions return in a christological context. For in Christ too, human nature consists of body and mind and, within the mind, of knowing and willing and, within will, of disposition ("voluntas") and consent ("liberum arbitrium").

Dengerink, J D. In het krachtveld van het Scheppingswoord—Over de modaliteiten: haar fundamentele verscheidenheid, samenhang en eenheid. *Phil Reform*, 59(2), 137-157, 1994.

The focus is on the idea of the modes of reality, which determine basically and qualitatively everything in reality. Though they differ radically, they can only exist together. Each is marked by an original, nuclear moment, e.g., consistence, justice, harmony, solidarity, clarity, reasonableness, vitality, physicality, spatiality, numerality, temporality. Within them one should distinguish between (modal) laws and the subjects under these laws. For man they hold a mandate and a promise: keep the law and you will have peace. Their origin is the creation-word of God, which guarantees their unity. They function as nuclear words within this word.

Denkel, Arda. Artifacts and Constituents. *Phil Phenomenol Res*, 55(2), 311-322, Je 95.

Is this paper the author argues that a restricted form of artifact-essentialism is tenable. The essence of an artifact is the structure that gives it the same function in every possible world nomologically equivalent to the actual. The author refutes the claim that the reasons for regarding an artifact and the piece of stuff constituting it as nonidentical entities are inadequate, and demonstrates that an ontology intermediate between artifact-essentialism and its antithesis cannot be consistent. Failing to be an essentialist commits one to a full-fledged anti-essentialism in the same respect.

Denkel, Arda. The Problem of Reconciliation. *Phil Papers*, 24(1), 23-50, Ap 95.

The author questions how consistent it is to maintain scientific realism alongside with a common-sense realism. Considering accounts defending that the two tenets are consistent, and hence that the microphysical theory can be reconciled with "the manifest image", he argues that these attempts are all flawed. The remaining alternatives are, first, the relegation of the world as perceived to the status of appearance, and second, the abandonment of scientific realism in favour of an instrumentalism, constructive empiricism of relativism. The second alternative is to be favoured, for adopting the first will leave the microphysical theory without an empirical basis.

Dennett, Daniel. "Back from the Drawing Board" in *Dennett and his Critics, Dahlbom, Bo (ed)*, 203-235. Cambridge, Blackwell, 1995.

Denyer, Nicholas. Priest's Paraconsistent Arithmetic. *Mind*, 104(415), 567-575, Jl 95.

Priest's paraconsistent arithmetic is a theory which contains all of classical arithmetic, together with the negations of some of it. By using a logic in which not everything follows from a contradiction, it confines its disagreements with classical arithmetic to numbers too big to be encountered in any actual computation. Priest claims that, unlike classical arithmetic, paraconsistent arithmetic is categorical, decidable, and capable of containing its own truth predicate. I show that these claims are wrong; and also that, if Priest's "proof" of paraconsistent arithmetic is correct, then its disagreements with classical arithmetic are not confined to big numbers alone.

Denzin, Norman K. "Postmodernism and Deconstructionism" in *Postmodernism and Social Inquiry, Dickens, David R (ed)*, 182-202. New York, Guilford, 1994.

Denzin, Norman K. The Experiential Text and the Limits of Visual Understanding. *Educ Theor*, 45(1), 7-18, Wint 95.

Depew, David (ed) and Hollinger, Robert (ed). *Pragmatism: From Progressivism to Postmodernism*. Westport, Praeger, 1995.

This collection of essays examines American pragmatism in cultural and historical context, beginning with Progressivism and running through the era of Post-World War II positivism up to contemporary postmodernism. A main thesis of the essays is that Dewey's evolutionary metaphysics is a necessary ingredient of his vision of a democratic culture.

Depraetere, Ilse. On the Necessity of Distinguishing between (Un)Boundedness and (A)Telicity. *Ling Phil*, 18(1), 1-19, F 95.

It is argued that two different types of concept are often intermingled in discussions of Aktionsart. The most common type of classification is one of situation types, relating to the potential actualization of a situation, although some of the definitions have to do with the actual realization of the situation. This distinction, adequately captured by the notions *a) telicity* and *(un)boundedness* (Declerck 1989), is explored and it is shown how NPs, PPs and tense influence a sentence's classification as (un)bounded.

Depraz, Natalie. Edmund Husserl, *Adversus haereses mystikes?*. *Laval Theol Phil*, 50(2), 327-347, Ju 94.

Comment rendre raison de ce qui apparaît souvent comme une contradiction dans l'évolution du fondateur de la phénoménologie, entre sa position initiale de scientificité rigoureuse et son intérêt final pour une métaphysique transcendantale? L'hypothèse de l'article qui suit est que cette contradiction n'est qu'apparente, mais ne peut également être levée que par la vertu d'une distinction méthodologique radicale entre mystique et gnose, c'est-à-dire aussi entre théologie et métaphysique. Pratiquer cette distinction dans toute sa rigueur exige de maintenir fermement la force de la réduction phénoménologique, et ce à tous les niveaux de l'expérience. Il importe par là même—là réside l'opérateur méthodique du parcours—de mener une réduction effective de la mystique en gnose phénoménologique.

Der Derian, James. "Simulation: The Highest Stage of Capitalism?" in *Baudrillard: A Critical Reader, Kellner, Douglas M (ed)*, 189-207. Cambridge, Blackwell, 1994.

Derksen, Ton. Kuipers over waarheidsgelijkenis en wetenschappelijk realisme. *Alg Ned Tijdschr Wijs*, 86(4), 294-305, O 94.

Derong, Pan and Xin, Katherine R. On Chung-Ying Cheng's Onto-Hermeneutics. *J Chin Phil*, 22(2), 215-231, Je 95.

Chung-Ying Cheng's onto-hermeneutics not only embraced traditional Chinese thinking, but also assimilated ideas from the Western hermeneutical tradition and analytical thought. It is the offspring of the conflicts between and combination of Chinese and Western cultures. The very existence of onto-hermeneutics declares the possibility of the mutual understanding, penetration, and combination of Chinese and Western cultural systems. Society's important issues forces us to regard the world as globalizes totality. Onto-hermeneutics, with roots in both Chinese and Western cultures, provides a path for philosophical retrospection and reflection, helping improve our understanding.

Derouen Jr, Karl and Geva, Nehemia and Mintz, Alex. Mathematical Models of Foreign Policy Decision-Making: Compensatory vs Noncompensatory. *Synthese*, 100(3), 441-460, S 94.

There are presently two leading foreign policy decision-making paradigms in vogue. The first is based on the classical or rational model originally posited by von Neumann and Morgenstern to explain microeconomic decisions. The second is based on the cybernetic perspective whose groundwork was laid by Herbert Simon in his early research on bounded rationality. In this paper we introduce a third perspective—the *poliheuristic* theory of decision-making—as an alternative to the rational actor and cybernetic paradigms in international relations. This theory is drawn in large part from research on heuristics done in experimental cognitive psychology. According to the poliheuristic theory, policy makers use poly (many) heuristics while focusing on a very narrow range of options and dimensions when making decisions. Among them, the political dimension is noncompensatory. The paper also delineates the mathematical formulations of the three decision-making models.

Derrida, Jacques and Wills, David (trans). *The Gift of Death*. Chicago, Univ of Chicago Pr, 1995.

This book is the translation of an essay first published in French in 1992. It deals with questions raised in a number of earlier texts concerning the gift, sacrifice and responsibility, examining those issues through the work of Patocka, Heidegger, Kierkegaard, and the New Testament. Responsibility is discussed as a form of *aporia* whose complexity is represented by the French phrase *donner la mort*, meaning "to grant death" in the senses of putting to death and offering a gift of death. The text amounts to Derrida's most sustained consideration of religion to date.

DesAutels, Peggy. Two Types of Theories: The Impact on Churchland's "Perceptual Plasticity". *Phil Psych*, 8(1), 25-33, 1995.

In this paper I argue that because Churchland does not adequately address the distinction between high-level cognitive theories and low-level embodied theories, Churchland's claims for theory-laden perception lose their epistemological significance. I propose that Churchland and others debating the theory-ladenness of perception should distinguish carefully between two main ways in which perception is plastic: through modifying our high-level theories directly and through modifying our low-level theories using training experiences. This will require them to attend to two very different types of constraints on the modification of our perceptions.

Desmond, William. "Between Finitude and Infinity: Hegelian Reason and the Pascalian Heart" in *Hegel on the Modern World, Collins, Ardis B (ed)*, 1-28. Albany, SUNY Pr, 1995.

Hegel and Pascal are very different thinkers yet both share a recognition that the human being is situated between finitude and infinity. I examine the nature of that space between finitude and infinity, and the interplay of the two, as differently interpreted by Hegel and Pascal. I examine the following issues: the contrast of Hegel's dialectical approach and his sublation *Aufhebung of finitude in infinity and Pascal's more fragmentary approach; the recalcitrance of historic singularity to philosophical universalization; the scope of reason, especially regarding the limits of its philosophical form; the appropriate form of philosophical discourse itself.*

Desmond, William. *Being and the Between*. Albany, SUNY Pr, 1995.

As Plato told us long ago, the human being is neither a god nor a beast, but someone in between. What is the being of the between? *Being and the Between* seeks to answer the question in the most comprehensive terms possible. It offers a metaphysical rethinking of the fundamental senses of being, namely, the univocal, the equivocal, the dialectical and the metaxological senses. Part I focuses on the nature of metaphysics and the question of being in terms of the fourfold sense. Part II develops a metaphysics, relative to our basic perplexities, concerning origin, creation, things, intelligibilities, selves, communities, being true, being good.

Desmond, William. Being, Determination, and Dialectic: On the Sources of Metaphysical Thinking. *Rev Metaph*, 48(4), 731-769, Je 95.

In this paper I explore the connection of dialectic and determination in light of different claims about the end of metaphysics in Hegel's wake. I deny that Hegel embodies the culmination of metaphysics. I explore the equivocal legacy of dialectic in some of Hegel's successors. I give an account of the sources of metaphysical thinking in agapeic astonishment and erotic perplexity. Since the sources are never behind us, metaphysics will always continue to be reborn, beyond every claim to determinate completion. I offer suggestions concerning the contemporary renewal of metaphysics along the lines more fully developed in my *Being and the Between*.

Desmond, William. Between Finitude and Infinity: Hegelian Reason and the Pascalian Heart. *J Speculative Phil*, 9(2), 83-110, 1995.

Hegel and Pascal are very different thinkers yet both share a recognition that the human being is situated between finitude and infinity. I examine the nature of that space between finitude and infinity, and the interplay of the two, as differently interpreted by Hegel and Pascal. I examine the following issues: the contrast of Hegel's dialectical approach and his sublation (*Aufhebung*) of finitude in infinity and Pascal's more fragmentary approach; the recalcitrance of historic singularity to philosophical universalization; the scope of reason, especially regarding the limits of its philosophical form; the appropriate form of philosophical discourse itself.

Desmond, William. *Perplexity and Ultimacy*. Albany, SUNY Pr, 1995.

Perplexity and Ultimacy explores the nature of metaphysical perplexity in relation to ultimacy. It claims that such perplexity cannot be identified with scientific or commonsense curiosity. Chapter 1 is by way of introduction, both existential and systematic, to Desmond's notion of the between. Chapter 2 takes up the issue of perplexity relative to the experience of being at a loss, as manifested in the tragic. Chapter 3 takes up what is called the idiocy of being, where "idiocy" carries its Greek sense of the "intimate." The enigmatic singularity of selfhood is explored, as well as the field of communication. Chapter 4 is devoted to the meaning of agapeic mindfulness to be radically self-transcending, and to be mindful of the other as other. Chapter 5 is on ultimacy and perplexity, especially in relation to questions about groundlessness, contingency, absurdity, God. Chapter 6 is on agapeic being and addresses the question of ultimacy in relation to being and the good. The book complements (in a way less constrained by systematic considerations) Desmond's systematic work of metaphysics, *Being and the Between* (1995).

Despot, Branko. Geschichte der Philosophie (als Wissenschaft) oder Entwicklung des Denkens in(nerhalb) der Idee des Ganzen. *Filozof Istraz*, 14(2-3), 503-505, 1994.

Die *Geschichte der Philosophie* von Prof Dr Branko Bosnjak (3 Bände, NZMH, Zagreb 1993, cca 1600 Seiten) erörtert den Gegenstand und die Methode und gibt eine philosophische Darstellung der Sache. Philosophieren wird dabei als Denken, Denken als Transzendieren, Transzendieren als das denkende Hervorbringen des Noch-Nicht der nie zu erschöpfenden, aber immer schon seienden Idee des Ganzen verstanden. Das Sein des Seienden (im Ganzen) und das Sein des Denkenden geschehen als Geschichte (der Philosophie) und werden als solche philosophierend dargestellt.

Despotopoulos, K. Platon und die Deutsche Philosophie. *Philosophia (Athens)*, 23-24, 297-306, 1993-94.

The author discusses the reception of Platonism by German philosophy and the influence of Plato's dialogues on certain German philosophers. He investigates the intellectual and philosophical background of Germany, which prepared the acceptance and influence of Plato's ideas, and outlines the periods of Plato's reception. Plato's philosophy finds major acceptance by Leibniz, Mendelssohn, Eberhard, Engel, Tennemann, Hamann, Kleuker, Jacobi, Schlosser, Kant, Hölderlin, Schlegel, Schelling, Schleiermacher, Hegel, and Nietzsche.

Després, Pierre. La Formation Intellectualle. *Philosopher*, 15, 185-188, 1994.

Dessureault, Robert. Intervention. *Philosopher*, 15, 171-177, 1994.

Dethloff, Klaus and Wimmer, Franz M (ed). *"Konservative Revolution und Philosophie in Österreich" in Der geistige Anschluss, Fischer, Kurt R (ed)*. Wien, WUV Univ, 1993.

Detlefsen, Michael. Wright on the Non-Mechanizability of Intuitionist Reasoning. *Phil Math*, 3(1), 103-118, Ja 95.

In his paper, 'Intuitionists are not (Turing) Machines', Crispin Wright joins the ranks of those who have sought to refute mechanist theories of mind by invoking Gödel's incompleteness theorems. His predecessors include Gödel himself, J R Lucas and, most recently, Roger Penrose. The aim of this essay is to show that, like his predecessors, Wright, too, fails to make his case, and that, indeed, he fails to do so even when judged by standards of success which he himself lays down.

Detmer, David. "Ricoeur on Atheism: A Critique" in *The Philosophy of Paul Ricoeur, Hahn, Lewis Edwin (ed)*, 477-493. Peru, Open Court, 1994.

As a self-professed Christian, Ricoeur ultimately rejects atheism. But he accepts much of the critique of religion provided by such atheists as Nietzsche and Freud, and attempts to defend a version of Christian faith which can withstand such a critique. In this paper I argue 1) That the atheistic critique that Ricoeur accepts is unsound; 2) That he ignores stronger atheistic *arguments* against his position; 3) That the meaning of Ricoeur's version of Christian faith is sufficiently unclear as to render it indistinguishable from atheism; and 4) That he offers no reasons to accept this faith.

Detmer, David J. "Obstacles to Fruitful Discussion in the American Academy" in *European Philosophy and the American Academy, Smith, Barry (ed)*, 55-65. Peru, Open Court, 1994.

This article offers a partial analysis of the low quality of current debates over deconstruction. After noting the ill-informed and anti-intellectual nature of popular critiques of deconstruction, I go on to concentrate on ten rhetorical stratagems that are frequently used in defenses of deconstruction. I argue that all of these stratagems are objectionable because they immunize deconstruction from criticisms by rendering it (and everyting else) incapable of being discussed meaningfully. Thus, the article is intended, not as a sweeping denunciation of deconstruction, but as a criticism of rhetorical stratagems which stand as obstacles to an intelligent critical assessment of deconstruction.

Detwiler, Bruce. Nietzschean Self-Creation and the Critique of Liberal Institutions. *Int Stud Phil*, 27(3), 43-53, 1995.

Deuser, Hermann and Beach, Dennis (trans). Hume's Pragmaticist Argument for the Reality of God. *J Speculative Phil*, 9(1), 1-13, 1995.

The author examines Hume's *Dialogues Concerning Natural Religion* to discover a variant of the usual teleological argument that abandons reliance on analogical reasoning. This second version, never refuted in the *Dialogues*, is termed "pragmaticist" in Peirce's sense. It relies upon an *abductive* hypothesis that claims not logical proof but the power of instinctual conviction. The *Dialogues'* espousal of sound common sense may then be viewed as an imperfectly articulated precursor of Peirce's pragmaticist argument for the reality rather than the existence of God.

Deutsch, Harry. Logic for Contingent Beings. *J Phil Res*, 19, 273-329, 1994.

One of the logical problems with which Arthur Prior struggled is the problem of finding, in Prior's own phrase, a "logic for contingent beings." The difficulty is that from minimal modal principles and classical quantification theory, it appears to follow immediately that every possible object is a necessary existent. The historical development of quantified modal logic (QML) can be viewed as a series of attempts—due variously to Kripke, Prior, Montague, and the fee-logicians to solve this problem. In this paper, I review the extant solutions, finding them all wanting. Then I suggest a new solution inspired by Kripke's theory of rigid designation and Kaplan's logic of demonstratives, the latter in particular. It turns out that the basic mechanism of Kaplan's logic can be exploited to yield a version of QML that will serve as a viable logic for contingent beings. This result, as I show, sheds new light on the problems of singular negative existential propositions, the question of actualism, the question of the existence of the contingent a priori, the relation between logical truth and necessity, and various modal problems and paradoxes going back to Chrysippus, Ramsey, and Moore.

Deutscher, Penelope. "The Only Diabological Thing about Women...": Luce Irigaray on Divinity. *Hypatia*, 9(4), 88-111, Fall 94.

Luce Irigaray's argument that women need a feminine divine is placed in the context of her analyses of the interconnection between man's appropriation of woman as his "negative alter ego" and his identification with the impossible ego ideal represented by the figure of God. As an alternative, the "feminine divine" is conceived as a realm with which women would be continuous. It would allow mediation between humans, and interrupt cannibalizing appropriations of the other.

Devaraja, N K. *Mentalistic Turn: A Critical Evaluation of Chomsky* by Kalyan Sen Gupta. *J Indian Counc Phil Res*, 11(3), 119-132, My-Ag 94.

Devaraja, N K. The Artist's Intention. *J Indian Counc Phil Res*, 11(3), 114-118, My-Ag 94.

Deveaux, Monique. Feminism and Empowerment: A Critical Reading of Foucault. *Fem Stud*, 20(2), 223-247, Sum 94.

This article examines three waves of appropriations of Foucault's work on power by feminist theorists. It suggests that both Foucault's early, "docile bodies" thesis on power and his later, agonistic conception of power obscure many important experiences specific to women, due in part to Foucault's sharp distinction between violence and power. Nor can his theory provide us with an effective account of human agency, for it leaves untouched issues surrounding personal and social empowerment. Writing by such thinkers as Patricia Hill Collins, bell hooks, and Audre Lorde suggest compelling ways to think about the connections between power, self-understanding, and agency.

Deveaux, Monique. New Directions in Feminist Ethics. *Euro J Phil*, 3(1), 86-96, Ap 95.

Deveaux, Monique. Shifting Paradigms: Theorizing Care and Justice in Political Theory. *Hypatia*, 10(2), 115-119, Spr 95.

The following is an introduction to a roundtable panel of the American Political Science Association meeting (Normative Political Theory Division) held September 2, 1994, in New York City. I set out some main themes in the "care/justice debate," and suggest that the impasse between care proponents and liberal, neo-Kantian thinkers is perpetuated by caricatured construals of these theories; salient differences come into relief by addressing the ethical and political applications of these moral perspectives.

Deviatko, Inna and Batygin, Gennadii. The Case of Professor Z Ia Beletskii: An Episode from the History of Soviet Philosophy. *Russian Stud Phil*, 33(2), 73-96, Fall 94.

DeVidi, David and Solomon, Graham. Geometric Conventionalism and Carnap's Principle of Tolerance. *Stud Hist Phil Sci*, 25(5), 773-783, O 94.

We discuss in this paper the question of the scope of the principle of tolerance about languages promoted in Carnap's *The Logical Syntax of Language* and the nature of the analogy between it and the rudimentary conventionalism purportly exhibited in the work of Poincaré and Hilbert. We take it more or less for granted that Poincaré and Hilbert do argue for conventionalism. We begin by sketching Coffa's historical account, which suggests that tolerance be interpreted as a conventionalism that allows us complete freedom to select whatever language we wish—an interpretation that generalizes the conventionalism promoted by Poincaré and Hilbert which allows us complete freedom to select whatever axiom system we wish for geometry. We argue that such an interpretation saddles Carnap with a theory of meaning that has unhappy consequences, a theory we believe he did not hold. We suggest that the principle of linguistic tolerance in fact has a more limited scope; but within that scope the analogy between tolerance and geometric conventionalism is quite right.

DeVidi, David and Solomon, Graham. Tolerance and Metalanguages in Carnap's *Logical Syntax of Language*. *Synthese*, 103(1), 123-139, Ap 95.

Michael Friedman has recently argued that Carnap's *Logical Syntax of Language* is fundamentally flawed in a way that reveals "the ultimate failure of logical positivism". Friedman's argument depends crucially on two claims: 1) That Carnap was committed to the view that there is a universal metalanguage and 2) That given what Carnap wanted from a metalanguage, in particular given that he wanted a definition of "analytic" for an object language, he was in fact committed to a hierarchy of stronger and stronger metalanguages. We argue that neither of these claims need be accepted. We show that there is not textual evidence for (1) and that if metalanguages are to be used for merely descriptive and not also justificatory purposes, Carnap does not need to define analyticity sufficiently for proving consistency, and so could have given definition that does not entail a hierarchy of metalanguages.

DeVita, Michael A (& others). Non-Heart-Beating Organ Donation: A Reply to Campbell and Weber. *Kennedy Inst Ethics J*, 5(1), 43-50, Mr 95.

In the preceding commentary, Campbell and Weber raise two valid and important issues concerning non-heart-beating organ donation (NHBOD). We agree that attention to the important details of caring for the dying are, and must be, the primary concern of all health care workers caring for those individuals. Ensuring the patients' comfort, dignity, and autonomy, and providing for family and social support are the mainstays of this care. All policies for NHBOD should clearly support and mandate these concepts. Regarding the second concern, we agree that NHBOD is currently rare; however, evidence is increasing that this type of donation has great potential. (edited)

Devitt, Michael. "A Critique of the Case for Semantic Holism" in *Holism: A Consumer Update, Fodor, Jerry A (ed)*, 17-60. Amsterdam, Rodopi, 1993.

At its most extreme, semantic holism is the doctrine that all the inferential properties of an expression constitute its meaning. Holism is supported by the consideration that there is no principled basis for localism's distinction among these properties. The paper rejects four arguments for this. 1) The argument from confirmation holism is dismissed quickly because it rests on verificationism. 2) The argument from the rejection of analyticity fails because it saddles the localist with unacceptable epistemic assumptions. Localism is not committed to a priori knowledge or to knowledge that is in any interesting sense unrevisable. 3) The argument from psychological explanation fails because it begs the question. 4) The argument from functionalism needs to be accompanied by a further argument that functionalism is essentially holistic. In any case it could only establish a very mild holism.

Devlin, Keith. *Logic and Information*. New York, Cambridge Univ Pr, 1995.

A comprehensive account of situation theory, with applications to the semantics of natural language and the philosophy of mind. Situation theory is a foundational theory of information introduced by Barwise and Perry in 1981, and subsequently developed by the author and others. Among the technical results presented in the book are a resolution of the Liar Paradox and an analysis of some well-known problems with conditionals.

Dewan, Lawrence. Thomas Aquinas, Creation, and Two Historians. *Laval Theol Phil*, 50(2), 363-387, Ju 94.

Étienne Gilson held that Thomas Aquinas was aware that Aristotle's doctrine of divine causality of being was not a doctrine of creation. Gilson thus had to provide a meaning for those passages in which Thomas attributes to Aristotle, and even to Plato, a knowledge of the cause of being in all its universality. In doing so, Gilson actually gave a distorted interpretation of texts of Thomas. He could do so only because his own understanding of Thomas's conception of created being was faulty. Anton Pegis agreed with Gilson that Thomas did not attribute creation to Aristotle. However, he sees Thomas as thinking that Aristotle's principles should lead him to a doctrine of creation. Unlike Gilson, he tried to deal with Thomas's presentation of Plato and Aristotle in the *Treatise on Separate Substances*. I show that he seriously misleads readers about Thomas's attitude towards Plato and Aristotle in that work (and in other texts as well).

Dewan, M L. Human Value of Sustainable Society. *Darshana Int*, 32(3/127), 82-86, Jl 92.

Human values play a great role in effective peoples participation and any work in the field of soil conservation and watershed management, environmental control and in rural/urban development so much hinges on the understanding and practices of the human values which go to form a sustainable society. The sustainable development is to allow for future generations our remaining resources and rehabilitate the resources that have been treated carelessly in the past. Human values are ones in which we include truth, right action (the moral code), peace, love, and non-violence. These are the cornerstones of the entire philosophy of life and give us the basis for the concept of education that we wish to present.

Dewdney, A K. "Misled by Metaphors: Two Tools that Don't Always Work" in *The Machine as Metaphor and Tool, Haken, Hermann (ed)*, 77-86. New York, Springer-Verlag, 1993.

Dewey, John and Chaput, Sylvie (trans). La démocratie créatrice: la tâche qui nous attend, John Dewey. *Horiz Phil*, 5(2), 41-48, 1995.

Dews, Peter. Morality, Ethics, and 'Postmetaphysical Thinking': New Books by Jürgen Habermas. *Int J Phil Stud*, 3(1), 164-173, Mr 95.

This article traces Habermas's views on the nature of moral discourse and the distinction between morality and ethics, from *The Structural Transformation of the Public Sphere* (1962) to his current writings. It explores certain problems raised by Habermas's contrast between a universalist morality and culture-specific conceptions of the good, and questions his claim to deal with these issues without recourse to metaphysical assumptions.

di Giovanni, George. "Hegel, Jacobi, and "Crypto-Catholicism" or Hegel in Dialogue with the Enlightenment" in *Hegel on the Modern World, Collins, Ardis B (ed)*, 53-72. Albany, SUNY Pr, 1995.

The confrontation between the Enlightenment rationalist and the believer in Chapter 6 of the *Phenomenology* is based on a historical court case involving the freedom of the press to investigate deemed "popish" threats to liberal institutions. In the polemic surrounding the case Jacobi sided with the believer. Hegel seems to be doing the same. In fact, he gives reason the last word—a reason, however, which, unlike that of the typical *Aufklärer*, has a social dimension. But Jacobi also put his trust in social reason. Hegel's affinity with him thus turns out to be deeper than would appear at first.

Di Giovanni, George. Fichte's Rhetoric of Deception: Reflections on the Early Fichte in the Spirit of Jacobi. *Rev Int Phil*, 49(191), 59-78, 1995.

Jacobi's attack on philosophy was implicitly also a criticism of Goethe's early romanticism. Jacobi's use of Spinoza in this polemic was conceptually and historically misplaced. Jacobi was however justified in maintaining that in his contemporaries' universe, no less than in Spinoza's, there was no room for human freedom. Influenced by Jacobi, Fichte sought to add a "subjective" dimension to Spinoza by capitalizing on elements of Kant's critique and the new romanticism. In fact, as Jacobi argued, Fichte only succeeded in devising a language of false subjectivity—the only subjectivity in fact possible in a world where reflection is the principle.

Diaz de Kobila, Esther. "Las XI Tesis No-Epistmológicas de Gastón Bachelard" in *Temas Actuales de Filosofía, Palacios, María Julia (ed)*, 157-163. Buenos Aires, Univ Nacional Salta, 1993.

Dickens, David R. "North American Theories of Postmodern Culture" in *Postmodernism and Social Inquiry, Dickens, David R (ed)*, 76-100. New York, Guilford, 1994.

Dickens, David R (ed) and Fontana, Andrea (ed). *Postmodernism and Social Inquiry*. New York, Guilford, 1994.

Dickenson, Donna. "Is Efficiency Ethical? Resource Issues in Health Care" in *Introducing Applied Ethics, Almond, Brenda (ed)*, 229-246. Cambridge, Blackwell, 1995.

Rarely has either faction in the debate over market provision of health services challenged the assumption that efficiency advances the interests of both individuals and society. Anti-marketeers contest the effectiveness of market systems, but agree that there is more than a merely prudential obligation to seek efficiency gains, that efficiency promotes distributive justice by minimising resource scarcity. This chapter examines the markets' ethical basis and practical effect in US and UK health systems, arguing that no one is morally or rationally obliged to accept the market criterion of greater efficiency if it disadvantages her. Weighing against each other clinical, social and ethical criteria, the chapter considers alternative means of resource allocation and concludes that only deliberate randomisation treats equals equally.

Dicker, Georges. "Epistemology" Reburied. *Trans Peirce Soc*, 31(1), 167-184, Wint 95.

In a work called *Dewey's Theory of Knowing (Philosophical Monographs*, 1976), I argued that Dewey's attack on traditional epistemologies, which he collectively dubbed "The Spectator Theory of Knowledge," has considerable merit, and that Dewey's own theory of knowing provides an illuminating alternative to the Spectator Theory. In a recent (1992) book *The End of Epistemology: Dewey and his Current Allies on the Spectator Theory of Knowledge*, Christopher Kulp endorses my interpretation of Dewey's position, but criticizes my defense of Dewey. In this article, I respond to Kulp's criticisms.

Dickey, L. Recent Work on Hegel's Philosophy of Religion. *Phil Quart*, 45(180), 368-374, Jl 95.

Dickie, George. "A Tale of Two Artworlds" in *Danto and his Critics, Rollins, Mark (ed)*, 73-78. Cambridge, Blackwell, 1993.

Dickie, George T and Wilson, W Kent. The Intentional Fallacy: Defending Beardsley. *J Aes Art Crit*, 53(3), 233-250, Sum 95.

Dickson, Michael. An Empirical Reply to Empiricism: Protective Measurement Opens the Door for Quantum Realism. *Phil Sci*, 62(1), 122-140, Mr 95.

Quantum mechanics has sometimes been taken to be an empiricist (vs realist) theory. I state the empiricist's argument, then outline a recently noticed type of measurement—protective measurement—that affords a good reply for the realist. This paper is a reply to scientific empiricism (about quantum mechanics), but is neither a refutation of that position, nor an argument in favor of scientific realism. Rather, my aim is to place realism and empiricism on an even score in regards to quantum theory.

Dickson, Michael. Reply to H Stapp's Comment. *Stud Hist Phil Sci*, 25(6), 965-966, D 95.

Dickson, Michael. Wavefunction Tails in the Modal Interpretation. *Proc Phil Sci Ass*, 1, 366-376, 1994.

I review the modal interpretation of quantum mechanics, some versions of which rely on the biorthonormal decomposition of a statevector to determine which properties are physically possessed. Some have suggested that these versions fail in the case of inaccurate measurements, i.e., when one takes tails of the wavefunction into account. I show that these versions of the modal interpretation are satisfactory in such cases. I further suggest that a more general result is possible, namely, that these versions of the modal interpretation never encounter the sort of trouble that has been claimed to arise in the case of inaccurate measurement.

Dickson, Michael and Karakostas, Vassilios. Decoherence in Unorthodox Formulations of Quantum Mechanics. *Synthese*, 102(1), 61-96, Ja 95.

The conceptual structure of orthodox quantum mechanics has not provided a fully satisfactory and coherent description of natural phenomena. With particular attention to the measurement problem, we review and investigate two unorthodox formulations. First, there is the model advanced by GRWP, a stochastic modification of the standard Schrödinger dynamics admitting statevector reduction as a real physical process. Second, there is the ontological interpretation of Bohm, a causal reformulation of the usual theory admitting no collapse of the statevector. Within these two seemingly quite different approaches, we discuss in a comparative manner, several points: The meaning of the state vector, the status of quantum probability, the legitimacy of attributing macro objective properties to physical systems, and the possibility of retrieving the classical limit. Finally, we consider aspects on non-locality and relevant difficulties with formulating a relativistic generalization of the two approaches.

Dickson, Paul. The Phenomenology of Evil. *J Value Inq*, 29(1), 5-17, Mr 95.

The central investigation of this essay is the interconnection between ideas about who and what God is and freedom in evil. To synopsize, evil's qualities are: 1) a solitary quest to become God freedom, 2) total separation from the victim because the evildoers deny the similarity of relation of true freedom, 3) creation of a victim by temporary or permanent destruction of the victim's freedom.

Dickson, W Michael. Is There *Really* No Projection Postulate in the Modal Interpretation?. *Brit J Phil Sci*, 46(2), 197-218, Je 95.

Modal interpretations of quantum mechanics admit two kinds of state: physical states, which specify the values of observables on a system, and theoretical states, which specify a probability distribution over possible physical states. They appear to use this distinction to deny the projection postulate, claiming that collapse corresponds only to a change from discussing the theoretical state to discussing the physical state. I argue that modal interpretations should adopt a projection postulate at the level of the theoretical state. However, other features of modal interpretations might render the projection postulate immune from the usual objections.

Diederich, Werner. "Nowak on Explanation and Idealization in Marx's 'Capital'" in *Idealization VI: Idealization in Economics, Hamminga, Bert (ed)*, 255-264. Amsterdam, Rodopi, 1994.

Compares the Nowak model of concretization with another view, considered to be more appropriate, in which the categories for the concretized law arise during the development of the law, and thus are not, as in Nowak's reconstruction, present from the start in the idealized form of the law.

Diederich, Werner and Ibarra, Andoni and Mormann, Thomas. Bibliography of Structuralism II (1989-1994 and Additions). *Erkenntnis*, 41(3), 403-418, N 94.

Five years have passed since our "Bibliography of Structuralism" has been published in this journal (*Erkenntnis*, 30, 1989). The aim of the present bibliography is twofold: First, we list a number of titles up to 1989 which we regretfully failed to include five years ago. Second, we augment the bibliography by titles which have appeared since 1989.

Diego, Carmen Verde. Estudio introductorio a "De la educación moral del Hombre": Texto inédito en castellano de Claude Adrien Helvétius. *Telos (Spain)*, 2(2), 109-146, D 93.

The brief but important text by Helvétius contained in Chapter VII of his work *De L'homme, de ses facultées intelectuelles et de son education* is translated into Spanish for the first time here. A critical introduction precedes the chapter by Helvétius. An analysis of the author—his works and philosophy—is made to some extent, emphasizing the relevance of the posthumous work *De L'homme*, and its particular value as it shows the author's true radical ideas—not revealed in his previous works—concerning the Church and the King as actual hindrances for an enlightened system of education. His arguments are grounded on an ethical approach that clearly anticipates the main tenets of utilitarianism. (edited)

Diéguez, Antonio J. Explicando la Explicación. *Daimon Rev Filosof*, 8, 83-107, 1994.

The three main models that have been proposed to account for scientific explanation are here analyzed and evaluated: the covering-law model, the statistical-relevance model (completed with the causal-mechanical model) and the erotetic model. These models follow each other in a process of increasing conceptual refinement. The last two have solved some of the problems that the covering-law model presented, but they have given rise to others. None of them achieve to establish the necessary and sufficient conditions to determine when we face a scientific explanation, but taken as idealizations, they do not lack utility.

Dienel, Hans-Liudger. "Die Entwicklung der Elektrotechnik.." in *Naturauffassungen in Philosophie, Wissenschaft, Technik: Band III, Schäfer, Lothar (ed)*, 71-120. Freiburg, Alber, 1995.

Dienel, Hans-Liudger. "Herrschaft über die Natur?" in *Naturauffassungen in Philosophie, Wissenschaft, Technik: Band III, Schäfer, Lothar (ed)*, 121-148. Freiburg, Alber, 1995.

Two facts led engineers to a cautious and sensible nature concept in the 19th century. Firstly these concepts were part of the emanicipation of engineering from science. Since 1860, engineering was looking for an independent profile against science, as science emancipated from romantic natural philosophy half a century earlier. Thus, engineers criticized materialistic and mechanical nature-concepts and stressed the noncalculatable elements of nature. Secondly, engineers were forced by their every day work experience to perceipt a complex and systematic nature. Only seldomly, it was possible to reduce nature to ideal and calculatable conditions.

Diener, Ed (& others). National Differences in Reported Subjective Well-Being: Why Do They Occur?. *Soc Indic Res*, 34(1), 7-32, Ja 95.

There are marked variations between nations in reported subjective well-being (SWB), but the explanations for this diversity have not been fully explored. It is possible that the differences are entirely due to true variability in SWB, but it is also reasonable that the differences may be due to factors related to self-report measurement such as variation across nations in whether it is desirable to say one is happy. At a substantive level, there might be differences in the norms governing the experience of emotion such that cultural differences in SWB are due to affective regulation. (edited)

Dienhart, John. Rationality, Ethical Codes, and an Egalitarian Justification of Ethical Expertise: Implications for Professions and Organizations. *Bus Ethics Quart*, 5(3), 419-450, Jl 95.

In order to understand the nature of ethical evaluation as promoted by ethical codes and as practiced by ethicists, we need to understand the notions of rationality and judgment in terms of which codes are developed and ethical pronouncements are made. Although this paper focuses on what might be called "professional contexts" of ethical evaluation, the proposed view of rationality and judgment is argued to be common to all defensible ethical judgments. The paper begins by examining a classical interpretation of rationality which asserts that rational judgments are universal, necessary, and rule-guided. This is contrasted with a more robust and arguably superior view of rationality articulated by Norman Brown.

Dieter, Richard C. Secondary Smoke Surrounds the Capital Punishment Debate. *Crim Just Ethics*, 13(1), 2,82-84, Wint-Spr 94.

Diethe, Carol. Neitzsche and the Contemporary Writer: What does it all Mean?. *Hist Euro Ideas*, 20(1-3), 135-139, Ja 95.

Nietzsche's investigations into the hidden recesses of language sets him poles apart from postmodernist textual strategy (Derrida), where Nietzsche's ideas are utilized for a different agenda. Amongst contemporary writers there is a sharp division between those who admire Nietzsche's challenge to conventional thought, and those who see him as tainted by an undemocratic elitism. Marxists have been most likely to be strongly hostile to Nietzsche. Indeed, to embrace the ideas of Nietzsche became a subtle way of undermining Communism (Kundera). Set against this, we have the "outsider" faction spearheaded by Colin Wilson (*The Outsider*, 1956), which includes Thomas Bernhard and Sebastian Barker and is at least as interested in Nietzsche the man as in his ideas, even when the writer takes issue with many of those ideas (Iragaray).

Dietrich, O. Cognitive and Communicative Development in Reality Free Representation. *Commun Cog—AI*, 11(1-2), 55-89, 1994.

Under the aspect of constructivism evolution generates the varying boundary conditions to which evolution itself then is subject. This applies for organic as well as for cognitive evolution. The currently valid conditions for cognitive evolution we describe as laws of nature brought about by an independent reality. Within the constructivist evolutionary epistemology (CEE), however, the regularities we perceive and which we condense to the laws of nature are seen as the invariants of phylogenetically formed cognitive operators. The extension of the inborn operators by means of experimental operators (i.e., by measurement facilities) will lead to the consolidation of the classical world picture if both are commutable. Likewise mathematical and logical structures can be seen as invariants of cognitive operators. (edited)

Dieudonné, Jean and Dales, H G (trans) and Dales, J C (trans). *Mathematics—The Music of Reason*. New York, Springer-Verlag, 1992.

Diffey, T J. A Note on Some Meanings of the Term 'Aesthetic'. *Brit J Aes*, 35(1), 61-66, Ja 95.

"Aesthetic" is distinguished from "aesthetics". The meanings and relationships between the two terms are discussed. Brief etymologies and histories of the words are given and in conclusion some suggestions are offered about the current meaning of "aesthetic".

Diffey, T J. Art and the Transcendent. *Brit J Aes*, 34(4), 326-336, O 94.

Not all art expresses the transcendent but some does and is valued for that. What does the claim mean that art can express the transcendent? The purpose of the article is to analyze this question in the course of which various suggestions are made, including; 1) distinguishing the noumenally transcendent (what cannot be present to experience) from the phenomenally transcendent (what happens not to be present in current experience); 2) commenting on the unusual position of modern art as the art of secular societies; 3) the proposal that art constitutes rather than reproduces knowledge of the transcendent.

Diffey, T J. What Can We Learn From Art?. *Austl J Phil*, 73(2), 204-211, Je 95.

A modified version of Stolnitz's view is advocated that art has nothing peculiar to its own domain to teach. The modifications are that nothing distinctive is to be learned from art if "learn" is taken in the narrow sense of factual learning; this because works of art are in mediums which show without asserting. For art to be a source of factual knowledge requires the further premiss that cannot be stated within the work itself that it does indeed refer to the world.

DiGiovanni, George. Hegel's *Phenomenology* and the Critique of the Enlightenment An Essay in Interpretation. *Laval Theol Phil*, 51(2), 251-270, Je 95.

The *Phenomenology* has often been criticized for being an unfortunate mixture of logic and history. This paper argues that the work ought to be read as a "philosophical novel," and that, as so read, it has conceptual and artistic integrity. This new form of philosophical production was possible because Hegel had overcome some of the limitations of rationality as conceived by the Enlightenment. In their now famous critique of the Enlightenment, Adorno and Horkheimer used the myth of Odysseus to illustrate the manipulative and self-deceptive practices to which Enlightenment reason is necessarily given. This paper argues that myth-making is itself one of these practices; that Kant's idealizations of reason are a kind of myths; and that neither Kant nor Adorno/Horkheimer escaped the need for myth-making, in effect the limitations of Enlightenment rationality, the *Phenomenology* stands as an object lesson of how it is possible to derive universal meanings and values out of history without thereby escaping into the unreal time/space of myth.

Dillon, Martin C. *Semiological Reductionism: A Critique of the Deconstructionist Movement in Postmodern Thought*. Albany, SUNY Pr, 1995.

This book interprets Derrida and looks beyond deconstructionism. It is a critique that identifies a pervasive flaw in Derrida's thinking: the semiological reduction that permeates deconstructionist theory and postmodernism in general. The critique focuses on Derrida, but its conclusions may be applied to other major figures in the postmodern tradition who espouse the variant of Saussurean semiology that reduces all meaning to the signification of signs. This book challenges the philosophy of deconstruction at its roots, and does so on the basis of a diligent reading of central texts and an understanding of the tradition of Continental philosophy providing the context for Derridian thought.

Dilman, Ilham. Art and Reality. *Phil Invest*, 18(3), 264-280, Jl 95.

The paper is concerned with the question: what does saying, learning, understanding and truth amount to in connection with the arts: literature, painting and music. 1) It indicates how the arts and or interest in the arts grow out of natural activities we take part in since our childhood. 2) It discusses how the sense in which what is said in the arts is to be seen *in* the work and how the work, in turn, makes us see what we meet in life in its *particularity*. 3) It discusses the uniqueness of each work of art in the sense that how it says what it says cannot be said another way. 4) It tries to bring out how the saying differs with different forms of art—literature, painting, music—and what "saying" means in the different cases. 5) Finally it says something about the sense in which the arts contribute not only to our apprehension of reading but to its very constitution.

Dilworth, Craig. Principles, Laws, Theories and the Metaphysics of Science. *Synthese*, 101(2), 223-247, N 94.

In this paper an outline of a metaphysical conception of modern science is presented in which a fundamental distinction is drawn between scientific principles, laws and theories. On this view, ontological *principles*, rather than, e.g., empirical data, constitute the core of science. The most fundamental of these principles are a) the principle of the uniformity of nature, b) the principle of the perpetuity of substance, and c) the principle of causality. These three principles set basic constraints on the methodology of both empirical and theoretical science. The uniformity principle is central to the empirical aspect of science, suggesting a methodology consisting in the attempt to discover empirical *laws*, while the causality principle is central to the theoretical aspect of science, suggesting the postulation of scientific *theories* capable of indicating the causal basis of the laws. And the perpetuity principle functions so as to form a bridge between the theories and the laws. (edited)

Dilworth, John B. The Ethical Importance of Conflicts of Interest: Accounting and Finance Examples. *Bus Prof Ethics J*, 13(1-2), 25-40, Spr-Sum 94.

Dimi, Charles. La Tribu Contre l'Etat en Afrique. *Quest*, 8(1), 44-58, Je 94.

The colonial state is the transposition of the European state on African soil. Its function was at the same time to undermine and to enhance intertribal antagonism.

AUTHOR INDEX WITH ABSTRACTS 501 **Dodds, Michael J**

The colonial state denaturalized the tribe, adapting it to the new conditions of the state. But a solid foundation for the state in Africa can only be achieved by building it upon African tradition.

Dipert, Randall R. "Peirce's Underestimated Place in the History of Logic" in *Peirce and Contemporary Thought: Philosophical Inquiries, Ketner, Kenneth Laine (ed)*, 32-58. New York, Fordham Univ Pr, 1995.

Dipert, Randall R. Some Issues in the Theory of Artifacts: Defining 'Artifact' and Related Notions. *Monist*, 78(2), 119-135, Ap 95.

Disalle, Robert. Spacetime Theory as Physical Geometry. *Erkenntnis*, 42(3), 317-337, My 95.

Discussions of the metaphysical status of spacetime assume that a spacetime theory offers a causal explanation of phenomena of relative motion, and that the fundamental philosophical question is whether the inference to that explanation is warranted. I argue that those assumptions are mistaken, because they ignore the essential character of spacetime theory as a kind of physical geometry. As such, a spacetime theory does not *causally explain* phenomena of motion, but uses them to construct physical *definitions* of basic geometrical structures by coordinating them with dynamical laws. I suggest that this view of spacetime theories leads to a clearer view of the philosophical foundations of general relativity and its place in the historical evolution of spacetime theory. I also argue that this view provides a much clearer and more defensible account of what is entailed by realism concerning spacetime.

Disbrey, Claire (ed). *Innovation and Tradition in Religion: Towards an Institutional Theory*. Brookfield, Avebury, 1995.

By applying an innovative approach to an unusual topic, this book makes a major contribution to our understanding of religion, particularly the tensions between tradition and innovation and between religions and the cultures in which they are embedded. A critical look at current theories of religion find empiricist theories and those emerging from the Wittgensteinian tradition inadequate in accounting for the radical innovation so characteristic in the history of religions. A search for a different kind of theory ends with the beginnings of a new theory of religion inspired by, but substantially different from, the institutional theories found in aesthetics.

Disch, Lisa. Claire Loves Julie: Reading the Story of Women's Friendship in *La Nouvelle Héloïse*. *Hypatia*, 9(3), 19-45, Sum 94.

Rousseau's *Julie, ou La Nouvelle Héloïse* is two novels in one: a story of wifely virtue and a counterstory of women's friendship. Whereas the virtue story exemplifies what feminist readers since Mary Wollstonecraft have considered to be the most oppressive of Rousseau's prescriptions for women, the friendship counterstory questions the ethical foundations and social manifestations of the model of patriarchal authority that Rousseau ordinarily defends. In this essay, I read the novel with an eye for both stories and the tensions between them.

Disch, Lisa Jane. *Hannah Arendt and the Limits of Philosophy*. Ithaca, Cornell Univ Pr, 1994.

Disco, Nil. What, Me Worry? I am but Mad North-North-West. *Kennis Methode*, 19(2), 189-193, 1995.

Disheng, Yang. Mourning Professor Feng Youlan: "Method of Abstract Inheriting" Should Not Be Denied. *J Chin Phil*, 21(3-4), 407-430, S-D 94.

China has an age-old traditional culture. All the way along, how to inherit traditional culture has been an important question which has not been handled well. In 1957, Feng Youlan put forward the concept of "method of abstract inheriting". It caused extensive and sharp discussing and criticizing, which lasted till the sixties and the seventies. This paper approves the basic viewpoints, and considers abstract inheritance as one of the necessary manners in the domain of philosophy. Otherwise, it is in actuality to deny the possibility of inheritance in theory. But, never mind whether consciously or unconsciously, actually every person is inheriting, and acts in an abstract inheriting manner. In his life, Feng Youlan wrote two books on the history of Chinese philosophy, and established his own philosophy system. He absorbed nutrition from forerunners' philosophy to set up his own philosophy. His method is the very "abstract inheriting". He proceeded to the future by means of connecting to the past. As a matter of fact, we all act in the same way. Otherwise, mankind could not have possessed the modern civilization.

Diskin, Jonathan and Sandler, Blair. "Post-Marxism and Class" in *Marxism in the Postmodern Age, Callari, Antonio (ed)*, 178-187. New York, Guilford, 1994.

Divers, John. Modal Fictionalism Cannot Deliver Possible World Semantics. *Analysis*, 55(2), 81-89, Ap 95.

Gideon Rosen's fictionalist interpretation of possible world discourse is aimed at securing all of the benefits associated with the applications of the discourse without incurring the ontological cost of commitment to the existence of nonactual things. Prominent among the supposed benefits associated with the application of possible world discourse is the provision of a "possible worlds" semantics for "ordinary" modal statements. I argue that Rosen's fictionalist interpretation of possible world discourse does not afford a genuine possible worlds semantics since it does not afford an analytic and extensional semantics for ordinary modal statements.

Divers, John. Modal Supervenience and Modal Realism. *Theoria*, 58(2-3), 99-115, 1992.

Colin McGinn proposes that acceptance of the supervenience of the modal on the actual is the natural form of expression of a non-objectual realism about modality. Here, some of the difficulties that arise in applying theses of supervenience to the modal-actual case are discussed. It is then argued: 1)that the truth of many such theses is determined on uncontroversial modal logical and conceptual grounds, and 2) that this and other independent considerations render it highly implausible that the affirmation of modal-actual supervenience amounts to a modal realism.

Divers, John. On the Prohibitive Cost of Indiscernable Concrete Possible Worlds. *Austl J Phil*, 72(3), 384-389, S 94.

Two arguments against Lewis's agnosticism about indiscernible concrete worlds are presented and examined from a genuine modal realist standpoint. The Argument from Individuation should fail to convince a genuine modal realist who accepts standard counterpart-theoretic analyses. However, the Argument from Economy (contra Lewis) allows the genuine modal realist to reject indiscernible worlds and does so without undermining the realist's claim that a hypothesis of a plurality of nonduplicated worlds is good value.

Divers, John and Miller, Alex. Platitudes and Attitudes: A Minimalist Conception of Belief. *Analysis*, 55(1), 37-44, Ja 95.

The claim that minimalism about truth-aptitude successfully undercuts traditional expressivism about value has been resisted on the grounds that: 1) a conception of truth-aptitude can be adequate and minimalist only if there is a supporting conception of belief which is adequate and minimalist; and 2) no minimalist conception of belief is adequate, since none can account for all of the nonsemantic platitudes about belief. We accept 1) but reject 2), arguing that a minimalist conception of belief can account for what is platitudinous about belief, and that what the minimalist conception can't account for isn't platitudinous.

Dixon, Kathleen Marie. Oppressive Limits: Callahan's Foundation Myth. *J Med Phil*, 19(6), 613-637, D 94.

Daniel Callahan has not simply proposed alterations of important features of the health economy. He has constructed a blue print for society drawing on concepts of what is natural and appropriate to human beings. He is, in effect, establishing a new social order. Like any social order, Callahan's system has its justificatory schemes or founding myths. This paper offers a feminist examination of the functions that these four myths—the concept of a whole of life; the stages of life; a tolerable death; and a reconstruction of the meaning of the aged in terms of sacrifice—fulfill in Callahan's new social order. Callahan's concept of a whole of life reflects the power he assigns to nature, and the futility and harm he associates with attempts to repudiate biological imperatives. It introduces the stages of human life, tolerable death, and aging. The paper critically examines these concepts.

Dixon, Nicholas. The Friendship Model of Filial Obligations. *J Applied Phil*, 12(1), 77-87, 1995.

This paper is a defence of a modified version of Jane English's model of filial obligations based on adult children's friendship with their parents. 1) Unlike the more traditional view that filial obligations are a *repayment* for parental sacrifices, the friendship model puts filial duties in the appealing context of voluntary, loving relationships. 2) Contrary to English's original statement of this view, which is open to the charge of tolerating filial ingratitude, the friendship model can generate obligations to help our parents even if we are no longer friendly with them. 3) Joseph Kupfer has pointed our several ways in which parent-child relationships differ from peer friendships; but his arguments do not preclude our enjoying a *type* of friendship with our parents. 4) In response to Christina Hoff Sommers, who objects that feelings of friendship toward our parents are too flimsy a ground for filial duties, the friendship model can provide a plausible, robust account of filial obligations. 5) As for adult children who have never formed friendships with their loving, caring parents, and refuse to give them much-needed assistance, they can be criticised by moral considerations independent of but compatible with the friendship model.

DiZerega, Gus. Individuality, Human and Natural Communities, and the Foundations of Ethics. *Environ Ethics*, 17(1), 23-38, Spr 95.

An ecologically informed view of ethics focuses upon individuals considered in relation to the communities within which they live. Such a view holds that ethics is rooted in the fundamental relationships characterizing particular types of communities. From this perspective, the different communities of the polity, family, and ecosystem superficially appear to have very different ethical systems. In fact, however, all are characterized by respect for community members. Respect is the fundamental ethical insight. This view suggests a way of harmonizing modern society's relationship with the natural world and of bringing ethical theory into closer harmony with humankind's most timeless insights.

Dobbs-Weinstein, Idit. *Maimonides and St Thomas on the Limits of Reason*. Albany, SUNY Pr, 1995.

Through an examination of diverse philosophical *aporiae*, the author determines the degree of philosophical compatibility between Maimonides and Aquinas, and where disagreement is evident, its origin, nature and philosophical consequences. She argues that Maimonides' and Aquinas's philosophical confrontations with questions, such as providence and creation, make manifest the limits of demonstration, indicating that a recognition of these limits is a necessary condition for further understanding. She concludes that rethinking occluded aspects of Maimonides' and Aquinas's "dialogues" renders possible a better understanding of each thinker and provides a richer vocabulary for discussions of the relation between different modes of knowing and acting.

Dobiesz, Stephanie. "Besuch im Hades: Über Günther Anders' Geschichtsphilosophie des Individuums" in *Nationalsozialismus und Moderne, Welzer, Harald (ed)*, 12-25. Tübingen, Ed Diskord, 1993.

Dobson, John and White, Judith. Toward the Feminine Firm: An Extension to Thomas White. *Bus Ethics Quart*, 5(3), 463-478, Jl 95.

This paper concerns the influence of gender on a firm's moral and economic performance. It supports Thomas White's intimation of a male gender bias in the value system underlying extant business theory. We suggest that this gender bias may be corrected by drawing on the concept of substantive rationality inherent in virtue-ethics theory. This feminine-oriented relationship-based value system complements the essential nature of the firm as a nexus of relationships between stakeholders. Not only is this feminine firm morally desirable, but it also economically more efficient in that trust becomes a more feasible implicit contractual enforcement mechanism. In an organizational context, therefore, from both a moral and an economic perspective, long established economic man is dominated by nascent economic woman.

Dodd, James. The Body as "Sign and Tool" in Hegel's *Encyclopaedia*. *Int Stud Phil*, 27(1), 21-32, 1995.

Dodds, Michael J. Of Angels, Oysters, and an Unchanging God: Aquinas on Divine Immutability. *Listening*, 30(1), 35-49, Wint 95.

Though many theologians argue that an immutable God cannot be the object of religious devotion, Christian prayer continues to extoll God as "unchanging". To explain this anomaly, this article explores various connotations of the notion of immutability in the works of Thomas Aquinas, a theologian noted for his teaching on divine immutability. Observing its connotations in many contexts, as applied to everything from oysters to angels, we can understand its analogical nature, discover its meaning as applied to God, and see why worshipers may be more in touch than many theologians with the true significance of divine immutability.

Dodson, Kevin E (ed) and Avery, Jon (ed). *Ways of Knowing: Selected Readings (Second Edition)*. Dubuque, Kendall/Hunt, 1994.

Döbert, Rainer. "Evolution, Verstehen und Wertung bei Max Weber" in *Mythos Wertfreiheit?, Apel, Karl Otto (ed)*, 109-130. Frankfurt, Campus Verlag, 1994.

Döbler, Matthias. Common Values and Value Conflicts in Environmental Education. *Hist Euro Ideas*, 21(1), 37-46, Ja 95.

The article discusses the importance of values for environmental education. It is argued that both the philosophical as well as psychological assumptions about individual as well as social efforts to create and sustain moral identity and meaning have to be considered in educational theory and practice. By using an episode from Homer's Odyssey and linking the interpretation with constructivist-developmental research (Kegan) impacts for conceptual innovations in the teaching of values are discussed. It is concluded that 'context' and 'identity' are major schemes in environmental values education, helping to investigate the abilities, aspirations and limitations of the educational subjects.

Dönt, Eugen. "Heinrich Gomperz und die griechische Philosophie" in *Heinrich Gomperz, Karl Popper und die österreichische Philosophie, Seiler, Martin (ed)*, 69-81. Amsterdam, Rodopi, 1994.

Döring, Frank. On the Probabilties of Conditionals. *Phil Rev*, 103(4), 689-699, O 94.

Suppose that i) the semantic value of a conditional 'If p, then q' is a proposition (a total function from possible worlds into truth values); ii) this value is independent of the probabilities assigned to the sentences in the language, iii) 'If p, then q' is consistent with not p if p and q are logically independent. Then the following weak condition on the probabilities of conditional cannot be secured throughout any class of "reasonable" probability functions: If Pr(if p, then q) is greater than Pr(not-(if p, then q)), then Pr(p and q) is greater than Pr(p and not q), provided Pr(p) is greater than 0. Consequently, the stronger *Stalnaker hypothesis* that the probability of a conditional equals the associated conditional probability where the latter is defined cannot be secured either. Unlike in earlier objections to Stalnaker's hypothesis by Lewis and others, no assumption is made about the interpretation of conditionals containing nested conditionals.

Dokulil, Milos. Between Ontology and Ethics. *Filozof Cas*, 42(4), 675-681, 1994.

The article is an attempt at giving a general picture of a whole year of "The Review of Metaphysics" (1991-92), trying to depict its thematic peaks in form of a structured review. The author is sure that, in the contemporary modern—postmodern confrontation, philosophers again aim at postulating the objectivity of being and some reliable value scales of human behavior. This double challenge has been illustrated by quoting the contributors of the cited volume in two corresponding parts. From the initial doubts concerning metaphysics (I) passing over to "moral ontology" (II) the article shows a potentially fruitful feedback link between ethics and metaphysics.

Dolan, Frederick M. Political Action and the Unconscious: Arendt and Lacan on Decentering the Subject. *Polit Theory*, 23(2), 330-352, My 95.

This essay explores the extent to which Lacan's description of the subject of the unconscious can be employed to develop Arendt's conception of the personality uniquely revealed in authentic political action. A personality undetermined by consciousness or will, for Arendt and Lacan, is embedded in the linguistic character of human interaction; Lacan, however, relies upon a well-developed theory of language while Arendt does not, or does so only implicitly. This suggests that Lacan's reformulation of Saussurian linguistics might serve as a basis for Arendt's claims about the political actor, but doing so, the essay concludes, risks obscuring other valuable features political action, in particular the dimensions of creativity, openness, advent, and redemption as Arendt appreciates them.

Dolega, Jósef. The Problems of Information in Approach to Systems. *Stud Phil Christ*, 30(2), 65-72, 1994.

The information has been expressed as a discrete greatness which can be kept in some objects, transformed there and used for steering them. Of course, the object should be understood living organisms, technical things and the systems of those objects. The problem of information has been discussed in the world of nature and culture. In the world of nature, information has been found both in the world of the animate and inanimate nature, but in the world of culture, information has been noticed in the human world and in technical things. There has been an essential philosophical problem taken up related to information, viz: what is connexion of information with a structure of matter or with a structure of the matter being.

Dolinko, David. Mismeasuring "Unfair Advantage": A Response to Michael Davis. *Law Phil*, 13(4), 493-524, N 94.

One prominent contemporary retributivist theory is built on the notion that crime yields an "unfair advantage" over law-abiding citizens which punishment removes or nullifies. Michael Davis has defended this theory by constructing a market model of "unfair advantage" that he contends answers critics' objections to the retributivist enterprise. I seek to demonstrate the inadequacy of Davis's approach, arguing in particular that the market model rests on an incoherent notion of "demand" and would not, even if coherent, link "unfair advantage" to the seriousness of crimes in any acceptable fashion. The salience of traditional objections to retributivism is thus unaffected by Davis's theory.

Dombrowski, Daniel. "Describing God". *Phil Inq*, 16(3-4), 74-82, Sum-Fall 94.

Michael Durrant defends three theses in his essay "The Meaning of God." I agree with two of these theses, but I use the thought of Charles Hartshorne to disagree with Durrant's view that previous efforts to reconcile the description of the God of the philosophers and the description of the God of religion have failed.

Dombrowski, Daniel. Lovejoy, Hartshorne, and Progress in Philosophy. *Metaphilosophy*, 25(4), 335-347, O 94.

In 1990 at the age of 93, Charles Hartshorne published his intellectual autobiography, *The Darkness and the Light*. In this work he comments on A O Lovejoy's 1916 Presidential Address to the APA on some conditions of progress in philosophical inquiry. In the present article I comment on the reasons why philosophy has not progressed to the extent that it should have progressed from the time of Lovejoy to Hartshorne.

Dombrowski, Daniel A. Alston and Hartshorne on the Concept of God. *Int J Phil Relig*, 36(3), 129-146, D 94.

In this article two pieces by William Alston are examined that deal with the concept of God in the thought of Charles Hartshorne. Alston makes some concessions to Hartshorne's neoclassical, dipolar theism, but for the most part Alston remains a monopolar theist and a classical theist. I indicate the superiority of Hartshorne's view.

Dombrowski, Daniel A. Heidegger's Anti-Anthropocentrism. *Between Species*, 10(1-2), 26-38, Win-Spr 94.

The purpose of this article is to argue that Heidegger does not succeed in developing a convincing case for his type of anti-anthropocentrism; indeed there is someting odious about his critique of anthropocentrism. The interpreter of Heidegger who is primarily engaged is Michael Zimmerman.

Dombrowski, Daniel A. Rachels, Abortion, and the Seventeenth Century. *Int J Applied Phil*, 9(2), 35-41, Wint-Spr 95.

The purpose of this article is to use the thought of James Rachels, who is not a Catholic, to highlight the complexity of Catholic thought on abortion and to claim that the stance of the Church at present is based on certain mistakes made in seventeenth century science. At the end of the article I compare my view to that of Thomas Shannon and Allan Wolter.

Domingo Moratalla, A. La herencia de Gadamer en K O Apel: hermenéutica experimental o hermenéutica trascendental?. *Pensamiento*, 197(50), 253-266, My-Ag 94.

El objetivo del presente artículo es realizar una primera aproximación a la herencia de la fenomenología hermenéutica de H G Gadamer (hermenéutica experiencial) que pervive en la propuesta filosófica de K O Apel (hermenéutica trascendental). Si para Apel la propuesta de Gadamer es necesaria pero no suficiente debemos preguntarnos si la re-trascendentalización que Apel pretende no conlleva la transmutación de una "hermenéutica de máximos" en una "hermenéutica de mínimos", siempre dependiente de la famosa "parte B" de la ética discursiva referida a la historia.

Domingo Moratalla, Agustín. Razón y poder: La radicalización simbólica de la razón liberal. *Dialogo Filosof*, 10(3), 363-376, S-D 94.

El presente artículo tiene como finalidad profundizar en los presupuestos que sostienen la *razón liberal*. Esta profundización pretende esclarecer el tipo de *razón social* conel que legitimar el poder en las democracias llamadas "liberales". Tal legitimación, bien sea por la vía del "consenso" o del "conflicto", nos acercará a los enfoques posibles del problema. Elegiremos un enfoque donde el poder no es planteado sólo en clave de "dominación" sino en clave de "integración". Esta perspectiva de integración (o desintegración) social reclamará la atención de dimensiones que la "razón liberal" no se plantea con radicalidad; a saber, la estructura simbólica de la razón humana y, por consiguiente, la *mediación simbólica* del poder.

Domínguez, Virginia López. Pascal: el hombre ante la perspectiva de la nueva ciencia. *Rev Latin de Filosof*, 20(2), 259-282, 1994.

This article studies the most important notions of Blaise Pascal's anthropology considering them as a result of his peculiar scientific practice. From this point of view tries to harmonize the contradictions characteristic of this tragic thought, whose culmination is the betting for a hidden God.

Dominicy, Marc. Du calcul des idées à la sémantique formelle. *Rev Int Phil*, 48(190), 485-503, 1994.

Most theses of the Port-Royal *Logique* can be viewed as semantic metatheorems. In modern reconstructions of Arnauld's logico-grammatical theory, natural language is translated into an intermediate logical language (Leibniz's "calculus of ideas") which both supports inference and allows for an explicit semantic treatment. However, this strategy gives rise to serious problems, due to the fact that the Boolean structure of the "calculus of ideas" includes some operations which do not play any role in the deductive apparatus of the *Logique*. Therefore, one has to favor an alternative approach, where natural language is directly interpreted in model-theoretic terms.

Dominion, Jack. Commentary on "Normal Grief: Good or Bad? Health or Disease?". *Phil Psychiat Psych*, 1(4), 221-222, D 94.

Domino, Brian. The Electronic Agora: Using a Mainframe Computer In Introductory Courses. *Teach Phil*, 18(2), 115-123, Je 95.

Dominowski, Roger L and Dallob, Pamela. "Insight and Problem Solving" in *The Nature of Insight, Sternberg, Robert J (ed)*, 33-62. Cambridge, MIT Pr, 1995.

This essay considers insight as a form of understanding of a problem and its solution, which results from restructuring, a change in perception of a problem. Distinctions are made between insightful problem solving and remembering, between reproductive and productive thinking, and among types of insight problems. By definition, insight problems suggest incorrect representations; erroneous solutions might reflect inadequate mental monitoring, which is readily corrected, or more serious fixation on a wrong idea. Insightful solutions occur abruptly; solutions accompanied by understanding are remembered well. Insightful behavior can be promoted by training, although the generality of training effects is presently unclear.

Donadio, Francesco. Il Problema del Mito nel Dialogo Bultmann-Jaspers. *Stud Filosofici*, 251-265, 1991-92.

Donagan, Alan. Philosophical Progress and the Theory of Action. *Proc Amer Phil Ass*, 55(1), 25-52, S 81.

Donagan, Alan and Malpas, J E (ed). *The Philosophical Papers of Alan Donagan: Volume I, Historical Understanding and the History of Philosophy.* Chicago, Univ of Chicago Pr, 1994.

This volume contains papers from 1957-1993 (two previously unpublished) on the methodology of historical research, the problems of historical understanding, and topics in the history of philosophy including a number of papers on Descartes, Spinoza, Collingwood and Wittgenstein. The volume contains an editorial introduction and a foreword by Stephen Toulmin.

Donagan, Alan and Malpas, J E (ed). *The Philosophical Papers of Alan Donagan: Volume II, Action, Reason, and Value.* Chicago, Univ of Chicago Pr, 1994.

This volume contains papers from 1974-1991 (one previously unpublished) on the philosophy of action and moral philosophy. With papers on Kant, Von Wright, Sellars and Chisholm, the volume also addresses a range of issues in applied ethics from just war theory to the nature of legal practice. The volume includes a complete bibliography of Alan Donagan's published work as well as an editorial introduction and a foreword by Donald Davidson.

Donaldson, Thomas and Dunfee, Thomas W. Contractarian Business Ethics: Current Status and Next Steps. *Bus Ethics Quart*, 5(2), 173-186, Ap 95.

Social contract is rapidly becoming one of the significant alternatives for analyzing ethical issues in business. Contractarian approaches emphasizing consent as a means of justifying principles can provide needed context for rendering normative judgements concerning economic behaviors. Current research issues include developing tests of consent for both hypothetical and extant social contracts, and empirically testing the assumptions of the major contractarian approaches. Open questions include exploring the relationship between contractarian business ethics and other approaches, such as stakeholder management and virtue based ethics; and analysis of the intersection of contractarian approaches with the findings and assumptions of the field of moral psychology. Finally, the managerial utility of social contract based approaches needs to be explored with emphasis on identifying "translator" concepts.

Donaldson, Thomas and Dunfee, Thomas W. Integrative Social Contracts Theory. *Econ Phil*, 11(1), 85-112, Ap 95.

Donati, Pierpaolo. Sociologia e Teologia di Fronte al Futuro: Un Approccio Relazionale. *Acta Phil*, 4(1), 27-49, 1995.

The author examines the forms of relationship between theology and sociology in recent decades. Such forms exhibit mutual lack of understanding, despite the fact that both disciplines speak of the same reality: man and his society. A conceptual framework is therefore proposed which allows for significant interaction between the two disciplines, while safeguarding their respective autonomy. Such a framework is called relational. By means of it, a meta-theory can be developed which makes it possible to manage the mutual relationships and boundaries. (edited)

Donchin, Anne. Reworking Autonomy: Toward a Feminist Perspective. *Cambridge Quart Healthcare Ethics*, 4(1), 44-55, Wint 95.

A critique of the conception of personal autonomy imbedded in principalist approaches to bioethical theory. The paradigm of the autonomous individual derived from contractualist political theory fosters a misleading ideal of the autonomous patient, ignoring people's social and gendered nature and intensifying the disadvantaged position of women and other marginalized groups within health care. As a corrective, health care practice needs to be guided by a reconfigured principle of autonomy that recognizes both 1) The generalized respect for all that undergirds informed consent requirements and 2) The distinctive identity of each that is manifested in patient-specific informational, psychological, and social needs.

Donís, Marcelino Rodríguez. El Epicureísmo y su Repercusión Histórica. *Themata*, 13, 175-195, 1995.

This paper aims to establish the persistence of Epicureanism in Greek and Latin cultures, mainly through Cicero, Seneca, Horace, Virgil and Ovid, but also through Lucian, Celsus and others. Although Renaissance regains interest for Greek culture, and for Epicurean doctrines and its ethical elements in particular, the original Epicurean texts were mostly unknown in those times. A good knowledge of them could nevertheless be obtained from the interpretation offered by Cicero and Plutarch, an above all by Seneca—even if Seneca himself didn't deal with first hand texts and took just Ethics into account. The aim of this paper will therefore be to compare true Epicurean doctrine as preserved in tests with its popular (mis)interpretation, and it will be contended here that the later quite often leaves texts aside and thus ascribes to Epicure some doctrines he never ever sustained.

Donneaud, Henry. Correspondance Étienne Gilson. *Rev Thomiste*, 94(3), 479-529, JI-S 94.

Donnelly, John (ed). *Language, Metaphysics, and Death (Second Edition).* Bronx, Fordham Univ Pr, 1994.

Donner, Gail and Yeo, Michael. "Justice" in *Concepts and Cases in Nursing Ethics, Yeo, Michael (& others)*, 147-183. Peterborough, Broadview Pr, 1991.

Donnici, Rocco. Recenti Studi su Antoine Arnauld. *Stud Filosofici*, 157-175, 1991-92.

Donougho, Martin J. "Spaced Out or Folded In? Trends in Architectural Choreography" in *Philosophy and Architecture, Mitias, Michael H (ed)*, 165-182. Amsterdam, Rodopi, 1994.

This article asks how concepts of architectural space bear upon its "lived experience". Starting with Benjamin on "tacit" reception in art, it moves to a general discussion of spatial form, asking how that is related to experience. Reviewing views held by Giedion, Zevi, Riegl, Wöllflin, Langer, and Heidegger, it concludes by assessing two recent attempts to theorize "postmodern" space: Derrida's "deconstructivism", and "the fold" (Deleuze), arguing that these operate in theory, and in schools of architecture, but not in lived practice.

Donovan, Rickard. "Rorty's Pragmatism and the Linguistic Turn" in *Pragmatism: From Progressivism to Postmodernism, Hollinger, Robert (ed)*, 208-223. Westport, Praeger, 1995.

Donzelli, Maria. Psicologia delle folle e Scienza Politica in Italia alla Fine del XIX Secolo. *Stud Filosofici*, 15-41, 1991-92.

Dooley, Mark. Murder on Moriah: A Paradoxical Representation. *Phil Today*, 39(1), 67-82, Spr 95.

Doran, Katheryn. Moore's Paradox, Asserting and Skepticism. *SW Phil Rev*, 11(1), 41-48, Ja 95.

I argue that we cannot explain the oddness of Moore's paradox sentences—sentences of the form "p but I don't believe that p," or "p but I believe that not p"—without an explicit account of the practice of asserting. What's peculiarly interesting about Moore's paradox sentences is at the level of what is *said*. And so I embed an account of Moore's Paradox sentences in Robert Brandom's account of assertion. Finally, I argue that on this understanding of asserting the skeptic is guilty of inconsistency.

Doran, Robert M. Consciousness and Grace. *Method*, 11(1), 51-75, Spr 93.

Doria, Francisco A and da Costa, Newton C A and Tsuji, Marcelo. The Undecidability of Formal Definitions in the Theory of Finite Groups. *Bull Sec Log*, 24(2), 56-63, Je 95.

In this paper a set of *explicit* expressions for a family of finite groups will be constructed in the language of Zermelo-Fraenkel *plus* the Axiom of Choice set theory in such a way that there is no general procedure to decide whether a given expression of this set is representing a finite solvable group or not.

Dorn, George J W. Inductive Countersupport. *J Gen Phil Sci*, 26(1), 187-189, 1995.

The basic idea by means of which Popper and Miller proved the non-existence of inductive probabilistic support in 1983/1985/1987, is used to prove that inductive probabilistic countersupport does exist. So it seems that after falsification has won over verification on the deductive side of science, countersupport wins over support on the inductive side.

Dorschel, Andreas. "Empfindung, Gefühl und Emotion: Zur Analyse von Bewertungen" in *Mythos Wertfreiheit?, Apel, Karl Otto (ed)*, 157-173. Frankfurt, Campus Verlag, 1994.

Dorschel, Andreas. The Anthropological Argument in Practical Philosophy and the Logic of Comparison. *De Phil*, 10, 21-42, 1993.

Arnold Gehlen's attempt to give anthropological grounds for morality stems from Kant's idea that being freed from the compulsion of instinct left human beings in need of compensation for the loss of the practical guidance which instinct had hitherto provided. Whereas Kant thought this compensation was to be found only in reasoned morality, Gehlen would argue that morality provides recompense by becoming a quasi-instinct that functions without reflection and that needs to be bred into human beings. The author maintains that in comparing animals and human beings, Gehlen posits will as a deficient instinct and instinct as deficient will; because each side is characterized as the negative of the other. Gehlen's starting point fails to meet the conditions for a valid comparison.

Dostal, Robert J. "The Experience of Truth for Gadamer and Heidegger: Taking Time and Sudden Lightning" in *Hermeneutics and Truth, Wachterhauser, Brice (ed)*, 47-67. Evanston, Northwestern Univ Pr, 1994.

Gadamer's notion of truth is importantly based on Heidegger's notion of truth as *Unverborgenheit* (unconcealment). Nonetheless the metaphor for the experience of truth in Heidegger becomes the flash of lightning, while Gadamer treats the experience of truth as an experience of tarrying (*Verweilen*). The source of Gadamer's concept of "tarrying" may be the early Heidegger. Intuition and dialectic are the two poles of the experience of truth for Heidegger and Gadamer. Gadamer would have us resist the Heideggerian temptation to seek the original behind these two poles and would have us accept where we find ourselves in the play between them.

Douard, John W. Does Clinical Decision Analysis Change the Subject?. *Prof Ethics*, 2(3-4), 149-172, Fall-Wint 93.

Doublait, S and Lelouche, R. Proposal for a Multi-Agent Model with a Human-Assisted Adaptation and Learning Mechanism. *Commun Cog—AI*, 11(1-2), 91-125, 1994.

Very few attempts have been made to address the problem of modeling and adapting complex mental attitudes in multi-agent environments. In this paper, we introduce the tile concept of scene static description and propose a categorization of actors' mental and physical attitudes, based on the concepts of role, status, and behaviour. We also model background knowledge of a scene through spatial and temporal statements. (edited)

Douca-Kabitoglou, Catherina. The New Way of Ideas: Plato, Locke, and their Romantic Readers. *Philosophia (Athens)*, 23-24, 232-250, 1993-94.

Plato's theory of Ideas has left such deep traces on the history of European philosophy (and literature) that it was almost inevitable for Locke, the forerunner of British empiricism, to adopt the term "idea" in his attempt to denote the content of mind—fully aware, however, of the "new way" of conception and usage to which he was putting a word that had been a central term of reference in the birth and development of philosophical thinking. Despite the obvious divergence of doctrine between the Greek idealist and the British empiricist philosophers, a community of method is detected in their work in the effort to "clear away" the mind from given presuppositions. The interest of the Romantic poets in both thinkers is evidence of their intense engagement with epistemological, aesthetic, and metaphysical problems, their attraction to different or antagonistic philosophical systems, but also their characteristic "romantic" attitude to cancel the traditional barriers in the categories of thinking and being.

Doud, Robert E. Matter and God in Rahner and Whitehead. *Phil Theol*, 8(1), 63-81, Autumn 93.

The sciences and popular views generally consider matter from the bottom up, that is, as the least common denominator underlying all of its various forms and realizations. In Rahner sensibility is matter looked at from the top down, that is, with a view to the highest realization of matter in human beings, and in Christ. In Whitehead creativity is matter, not inert or static but spontaneous and active, and creativity is matter viewed in light of its highest realizations in humans and in God. So, in Rahner and in Whitehead, matter is viewed in much the same way, called sensibility in Rahner, and creativity in Whitehead, and defined in terms of its actualization in human nature.

Dougherty, Jude P. Medalist's Address. *Amer Cath Phil Quart*, 68(Supp), 19-26, 1994.

Jacques Maritain was once denied appointment to the faculty of philosophy of the University of Chicago in spite of then President Robert M Hutchins's endorsement, because in the judgment of the faculty "Maritain is not a good philosopher." It is that assertion which prompts this inquiry, what is a good philosopher? The essay is an attempt to describe the kind of knowledge required and the methodology to be followed if one is to claim to be a "lover of wisdom."

Dov Lerner, Berel. The Materialist Mentality Revisited. *Human Stud*, 17(4), 449-459, 1994-95.

Peter Winch has criticized the anthropologist E E Evans-Pritchard's interpretation of the mystical beliefs and practices of the Sudanese Azande. Here I consider the difficulties inherent in the attempt by a philosopher lacking field-work experience to criticize cultural interpretations made by anthropologists who have first-hand experience of the society in question. In particular, I address this issue in the light of the restatement of Winch's position (and of Ludwig Wittgenstein's position in his remarks on James Frazer's *The Golden Bough*) offered by W W Sharrock and R J Anderson in their article "Magic Witchcraft and the Materialist Mentality".

Dov Lerner, Berel. Winch and Instrumental Pluralism. *Phil Soc Sci*, 25(2), 180-191, Je 95.

Peter Winch and Ludwig Wittgenstein have opposed the idea that traditional religion and magic are practiced in order to gain practical, instrumental ends. Their argument rests on interpretive charity: other cultures would have to be unbelievably irrational to believe in magic's practical effectiveness. In this paper, I show that Winch's own philosophical doctrine makes room for the possibility of *instrumental pluralism*, the notion that different societies may possess different criteria of instrumental rationality. Judged in terms of a native criterion, the instrumental use of magic and religion may be rational.

Doveton, Daniel. Marx and Engels on Democracy. *Hist Polit Thought*, 15(4), 555-591, Wint 94.

Dow, Tsung-I. Universality in Chinese Culture. *Dialogue Hum*, 4(2-3), 215-229, 1994.

Chinese culture may be identified as Confucian in that the ideas initiated by Confucius and reinterpreted by Confucius' defenders have overwhelmingly molded the Chinese way of life since the Han dynasty. There are elements which, in the long evolutionary process in both theory and practice, can be considered universal in terms of sustaining, enjoying and searching for the meaning of life. This paper attempts to single out such characteristics in Chinese culture for references for universality. They are: 1) the twofold complementary and contradictory world view, 2) the concept of self-realization of the creative mind to practice reciprocity in resolving human relations, and 3) the attempt to establish a universal state, and 4) the potential of Chinese written characters as a universal computer language.

Dow, Tsung-I. Zero State of Mind in Thinking. *Dialogue Hum*, 3(2), 65-82, 1993.

Suffice it to say that research in the new physics has discovered a twofold structure in a polar relationship constituting the being and becoming of the phenomenal world. Recent studies of the brain and the computer also reveal the totality of the mind which unites, harmonizes, and synthesizes the seemingly contradictory yet complementary nature to generate and create the cognition process. The meta sign, zero, not only reflects the infinite creative power of the mind to transcend the wholeness yet discriminate among the process of thinking but also reaffirms the notion: with emptiness, everything is possible; without it, nothing is possible.

Dowe, Phil. Causality and Conserved Quantities: A Reply to Salmon. *Phil Sci*, 62(2), 321-333, Je 95.

In a recent paper (1994) Wesley Salmon has replied to criticisms (e.g., Dowe 1992c, Kitcher 1989) of his (1984) theory of causality, and has offered a revised theory which, he argues, is not open to those criticisms. The key change concerns the characterization of causal processes, where Salmon has traded "the capacity for mark transmission" for "the transmission" of an invariant quantity". Salmon argues against the view presented in Dowe (1992c), namely that the concept of "possession of a conserved quantity" is sufficient to account for the difference between causal and pseudo processes. Here that view is defended, and important questions are raised about the notion of transmission and about gerrymandered aggregates.

Dowe, Phil. What's Right and What's Wrong with Transference Theories. *Erkenntnis*, 42(3), 363-374, My 95.

This paper examines the Transference Theory of causation, developed originally by Aronson (1971) and Fair (1979). Three difficulties for that theory are presented: firstly, problems associated with the direction of transference and causal asymmetry; secondly, the case of persistence as causation, for example where a body's own inertia is the cause of its motion; and thirdly the problematic notion of identity through time of physical quantities such as energy or momentum. Finally, the theory is compared with the Conserved Quantity Theory (Dowe 1992c), and it is shown that that account embodies the modifications that the transference theory needs to adopt.

Dower, Nigel. "The Idea of the Environment" in *Philosophy and the Natural Environment, Attfield, Robin (ed)*, 143-156. New York, Cambridge Univ Pr, 1994.

This chapter identifies two senses of the idea of the environment, namely an environment as a meaningful field of significance and an environment as an objective system of causes and effects. Theoretically, the idea of the environment necessarily has these two faces (in part linked to the appearance/reality distinction). At a practical level, our environmental problems stem partly from the mismatch between people's fields of significance and what is happening in the physical world. The challenge is to adjust the former, and this includes our moral environment.

Dowling, Keith. The Justification of Democracy. *S Afr J Phil*, 13(4), 161-166, N 94.

In this article I want to make some quite general points about the justification of democracy. I will begin by arguing that any kind of democratic system requires a deliberative process in which political decisions are the outcome of rational discussion. I will go on to argue that such a process may be justified since we believe that in political contexts a) no one can claim to have incontrovertible knowledge; and at the same time, it meets our desires b) for self-determination and c) for equality of influence when we are affected by political decisions. I will then argue that a)-c) are predicated on d) an ideal of self-improvement. I will go on to show that in a representative democracy these desiderata cannot be met. However I will offer two proposals for a system in which they can. They both require a devolution of power into small regional governments. (edited)

Downes, Stephen. Similarity: A Cognitive Foundation for Aritificial Intelligence. *Eidos*, 12(1), 9-24, Je 94.

Downey, Rod and Gasarch, William and Moses, Michael. The Structure of the Honest Polynomial m-Degrees. *Annals Pure Applied Log*, 70(2), 113-139, D 94.

A language A is said to be honest polynomial time m-reducible to a language B iff there is a polynomial p and a polynomial time computable function f such that $f \varepsilon A$ iff $f(x)\ \alpha\ B$ and $|f(x)|$ is less than or equal to $P(|x|)$. The paper at hand explores the structure of the recursive sets partitioned by the ordering induced by honest polynomial time reductions.

Downey, Rod and Haught, Christine. Embedding Lattices into the *wtt*-Degrees Below 0'. *J Sym Log*, 59(4), 1360-1382, D 94.

The authors prove that every finite lattice can be embedded into the weak truth table degrees below 0' preserving 0 and 1.

Doyle, John P. Another God, Chimerae, Goat-Stags, and Man-Lions: A Seventeenth-Century Debate about Impossible Objects. *Rev Metaph*, 48(4), 771-808, Je 95.

This article concerns a 17th century debate over whether there are self-contradictory impossible objects of understanding or whether there is no intellectual object which is not some actual or possible being. The debate, which has its roots in the Greek and Scholastic traditions, is presented especially between two Jesuits: Thomas Compton Carleton and John Morawski, respectively, a proponent and an opponent of impossible objects. The article itself does not take sides in the debate, but, inasmuch as he wrote later, Morawski is presented as espousing his own view and answering arguments in support of Carleton's position.

Doyle, John P. Poinsot on Knowability of Beings of Reason. *Amer Cath Phil Quart*, 68(3), 337-362, Sum 94.

Doyle, John P (trans) and Suárez, Francisco. *On Beings of Reason (De Entibus Rationis) Metaphysical Disputation LIV*. Milwaukee, Marquette Univ Pr, 1995.

Drabkin, Douglas. A Moral Argument for Undertaking Theism. *Amer Phil Quart*, 31(2), 169-175, Ap 94.

The following argument is presented and defended: We ought to aspire to become as good as we can be, and this requires that we do good deeds with not just any emotional attitude, but with joy (a lively, hopeful feeling), even in difficult circumstances. Theism (of the right sort) offers us the best prospects for achieving a fully joyful moral life. And so it is morally good for those of us who are not theists to undertake theism—to commit ourselves to the religious project of coming to believe that God exists.

Drai, Dalia. The Supervenience of the Mental on the Physical (in Hebrew). *Iyyun*, 43, 363-374, O 94.

Drai, Dalia. What is a Physical Event?. *Phil Papers*, 23(2), 129-135, Ag 94.

In 'Mental Events' Davidson proves that every mental event has a physical description. The move from this claim to the identity thesis—that every mental event is identical to a physical event—lacks justification. A justification for this passage can be supplied by a proper definition of a physical event: An event is physical iff a *sortal* physical predicate applies it.

Drane, James F and Coulehan, John L. The Best-Interest Standard: Surrogate Decision Making and Quality of Life. *J Clin Ethics*, 6(1), 20-29, Spr 95.

Through the disciplines of law and ethics, American culture provides clear standards for surrogate decision makers who know an incompetent patient's wishes and interests. Surrogates, however, often have to decide based on what is medically best for the incompetent patient. Burdens and benefits have to be weighed and then judiciously balanced. This article attempts to provide more objective indicators for making difficult life and death decisions for other persons whose personal wishes are unknown. Quality of life considerations are listed and suggestions are made for evaluating these in a a more objective way. The purpose of this article is to protect incompetent patients against overaggressive medical interventions while protecting them as well against the danger of being set aside. Decisional guidelines are provided for reasonable and defensible best interest judgments.

Dravid, N S. Anomolies of the Nyaya-Vaisesika Concept of Self. *Indian Phil Quart*, 22(1), 1-12, Ja 95.

Dray, William H. R G Collingwood, *The Idea of History*. *Clio*, 24(1), 81-84, Fall 94.

Dreben, Burton. *In Mediis Rebus*. *Inquiry*, 37(4), 441-447, D 94.

For Quine all talk is *in mediis rebus*, is itself a physical phenomenon. To grasp what a sentence is, its relation to a language, and what it is for a sentence to be true is to be invited to see that notions of shared meaning across languages, of truth, even of knowledge, are far from what they are ordinarily taken to be. To read Quine reflectively is to plunge with him into the midst of things, shunning the vain support of purported transcendental certainties of Archimedean points, and spurning claims of the intuitive clarity of meaning, thought, and belief, for in the midst of things they themselves are what are most lacking in clarity.

Dresser, Rebecca and Whitehouse, Peter J. The Incompetent Patient on the Slippery Slope. *Hastings Center Rep*, 24(4), 6-12, Jl-Ag 94.

This paper focuses on issues arising in decisions on life-sustaining treatment for conscious incompetent patients when there is no clear evidence of their former preferences and values as competent persons. Using persons diagnosed with dementia as an example, the authors analyze the steps involved in applying the so-called best interests test (also known as the benefit-burden or reasonable person test). They discuss ways to improve the observer's ability to assess the subjective experiences of individual dementia patients and describe situations in which treatment could be withheld or withdrawn under a best interests approach.

Dretske, Fred. "Mind and Brain" in *The Mind-Body Problem: A Guide to the Current Debate, Warner, Richard (ed)*, 131-136. Cambridge, Blackwell, 1994.

Dretske, Fred. Reply to Slater and García-Carpintero. *Mind Lang*, 9(2), 203-208, Ju 94.

In criticism of my view of concept formation, Slater argues that it is not indication (information in my sense) but contingency that is necessary for discrimination learning. I agree, but deny that this is a criticism. I was interested in a certain type of discrimination learning—concept formation—and for this process (I argue) indication is necessary. Garcia-Carpintero questions my use of the distinction between triggering and structuring causes of behavior. He thinks that structuring causes can only be invoked to explain certain kinds of processes (those it has the function of producing). I deny that the idea of structuring cause needs to be restricted in this way.

Dretske, Frederick. "Does Meaning Matter?" in *Philosophy of Psychology: Debates on Psychological Explanation, Macdonald, Cynthia (ed)*, 107-120. Cambridge, Blackwell, 1995.

Since the meaning or content of an intentional state (like belief) is most plausibly construed as an extrinsic (relational) property of that state, the only way beliefs, *qua* beliefs, can figure in the explanation of a person's behavior is if an object's relational properties can help to explain the behavior of the system of which that object is a part. Conceiving of behavior as a causal process having bodily movements (and other more remote events) as their product is a way of doing this. The relational properties (content) of the belief explains not why the bodily movements occur, but why a process having those bodily movements as products (i.e., behavior) occurs.

Dretske, Frederick. "Reply: Causal Relevance and Explanatory Exclusion" in *Philosophy of Psychology: Debates on Psychological Explanation, Macdonald, Cynthia (ed)*, 142-151. Cambridge, Blackwell, 1995.

Kim (in his critique of "Does Meaning Matter") is right. The dual explananda strategy solves some problems (the explanatory relevance of mental content) but not others (the explanatory exclusion problem). It was only intended to solve one problem—the first. The explanatory exclusion problem—how mental content can explain something that physical facts also explain—is solved, as Kim suggests it might be, by *identifying* content with certain physical facts; the relational facts that constitute representational content. This is reductionism, yes, but *wide* reductionism (a form of externalism): a reduction of content to the relational (physical) facts on which content supervenes.

Dretske, Frederick. Machines and the Mental. *Proc Amer Phil Ass*, 59(1), 23-33, S 85.

Dretske, Frederick. *Naturalizing the Mind*. Cambridge, MIT Pr, 1995.

An analysis of qualitative experience—the what-it-is-like aspect of our mental life—in representational terms where representation is understood in a purely naturalistic way. Qualia are identified with the properties internal (physical) states represent, and the properties they represent are those internal states have the natural, the biological, function of indicating. These properties are generally properties of external physical objects (colors, shapes, movements, etc.) and sometimes (in the case of pain, thirst, etc.) of various internal conditions of the body. The final chapter is a defense of this externalistic theory of the mind against the more obvious objections.

Drewett, Michael. There Must be Some Way Out of Here: A Case Study in the Teaching of Critical Thinking. *S Afr J Phil*, 14(2), 72-76, My 95.

This article examines the growing problem which critical thinking poses to students entering the social sciences and arts at Rhodes University, South Africa. While the ability to think and write critically is an underlying requirement of many courses, students tend to lack confidence and feel insecure when expected to evaluate or present an argument. This article analyzes attempts by the Rhodes Unviersity Academic Development Programme (ADP) and the Department of Sociology and Industrial Sociology to teach critical thinking to students. It explains that the venture so far has not been entirely successful because of the uncritical environment in which such courses have been taught. Finally, it is argued that a deep-level holistic approach which draws on all areas of departmental teaching is required if future critical thinking projects are to be successful.

Drewniak, Erik and Boghossian, Peter G. Wittgenstein and Peirce on Meaning: The Evolution from Absolutism to Fallibilism. *Dialogos*, 30(65), 173-188, Ja 95.

Dreyer, H J. "Life and Society at Ancient Memphis According to the Saqqâra Texts" in *Life, World and Meaning, Roux, A P J (ed)*, 46-55. Pretoria, Univ of S Africa, 1990.

Driessen, Alfred. The Question of the Existence of God in the Book of Stephen Hawking "A Brief History of Time". *Acta Phil*, 4(1), 83-93, 1995.

In this study an attempt is given to unveil the philosophical concepts and steps that lead Hawking to his view on the existence of God. Especially his concept of causality is analyzed. Thereafter the classical Aristotelian-Thomistic proof of the existence of God is presented and compared with Hawking's approach, who ends up with a very restricted role of a possible creator. It is shown, that neither from the philosophical nor the scientific point of view his conclusions about the existence of God are strictly convincing, a position Hawking himself seems to be aware of.

Droogers, André F. "Cultural Relativism and Universal Human Rights?" in *Human Rights and Religious Values, An-Na'im, Abdullahi A (& other eds)*, 78-90. Grand Rapids, Eerdmans, 1995.

Drost, Mark P. Husserl and Goodman on the Role of Resemblance in Pictorial Representation. *Int Stud Phil*, 26(4), 17-27, 1994.

A common plaint among some critics who concede that resemblance is a necessary condition of pictorial representation is that the thesis is uninformative. Resemblance is such a broad ranging phenomenon that all things resemble one another in some way. However, these critics fail to distinguish the concept of resemblance *simpliciter* from the concept of *recognized* resemblance as it is appropriate to the pictorial attitude. The phenomenon of recognized resemblance is a necessary condition of the intentionality which operates within the pictorial attitude. The phenomenological fact of the pictorial attitude is that we do not regard the represented independently of the referent that is recognized through resemblance.

Drost, Mark P. In the Realm of the Senses: St Thomas Aquinas on Sensory Love, Desire, and Delight. *Thomist*, 59(1), 47-58, Ja 95.

Aquinas characterizes delight as a state in which we are in "union with some good". Further on he says "we are not without the good we love, but are at rest in its possession". Concerning love Aquinas says, "love remains whether the object is present or absent". However, Aquinas also says that when we love an object, "we are already in some kind of communion with it. Love therefore involves union". These statements are *prima facie* inconsistent unless Aquinas acknowledges that there are unions in which the object is not possessed. I contend that love is a case of being intentionally directed to a good, but it is not identical to the union which is a result of possessing a good.

Drouin, Paul. La pensée politique de Jean Jaurès. *Horiz Phil*, 5(2), 84-97, 1995.

In a time where it is easy to forget that socialism rhymes with democracy and secular humanism (*laïcité*), the political thought of Jean Jaurès (1859-1914) cannot leave us unconcerned. Jaurès's life and thought help us to identify the essential values of the modern democratic state and give us an insight into the ethical presuppositions of socialism, which remains, whatever might be said, a major political philosophy for the understanding of the outcomes of our actual political debate. Jaurès stresses the fact that the democratic movement developed itself, throughtout the world, in interaction with socialist political philosophy and action. Of course, Leninists and Stalinists completely evacuated democracy and liberties from socialism. Jaurès holds that socialism must widen the spaces of liberty and is, therefore, contrary to sanguinary dictatorship. That is why the socialism that Jaurès advocates still stands before us.

Droz-Vincent, Gabriel. L'atomisme dans le monisme épicurien. *Rev Phil Fr*, 1, 3-17, Ja-Mr 95.

Drozdek, Adam. Beyond Infinity: Augustin and Cantor. *Laval Theol Phil*, 51(1), 127-140, F 95.

It is argued in this paper that for Augustine 1) infinity is an inborn concept which is a prerequisite of any knowledge; 2) mathematics—because it relies on the concept of infinity—is the best tool of acquiring knowledge about God, and 3) God is neither finite nor infinite and his greatness is beyond infinity. Augustine is original in combining these three aspects in his philosophy, and all three aspects can again be found in Cantor.

Drozdek, Adam and Keagy, Tom. A Case for Realism in Mathematics. *Monist*, 77(3), 329-344, Jl 94.

The paper takes issue with anti-realist position in philosophy of mathematics, which denies an existence of mathematical entities independent of the cognitive subject. Anti-realism has appeared in various forms, and some of the arguments are discussed (Brouwer, Kitcher, Machover). The paper opts for realism and gives both philosophical arguments substantiating this position and an example of mathematical proof which was possible only due to the realist view (the proof concerns a transform of Levin to be used in approximating the limit of a sequence).

Dru, Alexander (trans) and Trethowan, Illtyd (trans) and Blondel, Maurice. *The Letter of Apologetics and History and Dogma*. Grand Rapids, Eerdmans, 1994.

Drury, John. Cognitive Science and Hermeneutic Explanation: Symbiotic or Incompatible Frameworks?. *Phil Psychiat Psych*, 1(1), 41-50, Mr 94.

No less than causal explanations, explanations in terms of meanings or interpretations must be validated. But how can an arguably interpretative framework such as psychoanalysis choose between equally plausible interpretations when all it can validate them with is further interpretations? Three possible solutions to this hermeneutic circle are described: the rationalist, the postmodernist, and the empiricist. Empiricist cognitive science already utilizes both causal and interpretative discourse in its own explanations; the approach is frequently an attempt to demonstrate that some interpretative explanations are justified because they accurately reflect an underlying reality beyond interpretations. This suggests that cognitive science could serve as an objective "anchor" for hermeneutic explanations in psychoanalysis. It is argued, however, that by privileging science over cognition, cognitive science ultimately represents the negation of interpretative knowledge rather than its justification.

Dryzek, John S. "Critical Theory as a Research Program" in *The Cambridge Companion to Habermas, White, Stephen K (ed)*, 97-119. New York, Cambridge Univ Pr, 1995.

Du Bois, William E B. "The Conservation of Races" in *African Philosophy: Selected Readings, Mosley, Albert G (ed)*, 30-39. Englewood Cliffs, Prentice Hall, 1995.

Du Toit, Pieter. "World, Leisure and a Meaningful Life" in *Life, World and Meaning, Roux, A P J (ed)*, 30-45. Pretoria, Univ of S Africa, 1990.

This article examines the assumption that deprivation of work infringes on the worthiness of human beings from three perspectives: the historico-cultural aspect, recent research on work, and the meaningful life. Ancient Greek and contemporary African work ethics is discussed, as well as the views of Hegel, Marx and certain Christian thinkers. It is argued that a stage may be reached where people may not be required to work at all. It is concluded that meaningful work need not be the primary basis of self-respect in people's lives, as other activities can provide this self-respect and self-realization.

Duan, Zhongqiao. *Marx's Theory of the Social Formation*. Brookfield, Avebury, 1995.

This book holds that the kernel of historical materialism concerns two questions: the structure of society and the stages of the development of society. By reconstructing Marx's theory of the social formation, it united Marx's expositions regarding these two questions and makes them form an integrated theory. It also offers a fundamental reinterpretation of some important concepts of historical materialism through historical and logical analyses of the expositions given by Marx himself, such as that human beings are not only carriers of social relations but also their subjects and that the development of human society appears as the successive replacement of three great social formations, i.e., pre-capitalism, capitalism and communism.

Dubucs, Jacques and Dubucs, Monique. "Mathématiques: la couleur des preuves" in *Rhétoriques de la science, De Coorebyter, Vincent (ed)*, 231-249. Paris, Pr Univ France, 1994.

Dubucs, Monique and Dubucs, Jacques. "Mathématiques: la couleur des preuves" in *Rhétoriques de la science, De Coorebyter, Vincent (ed)*, 231-249. Paris, Pr Univ France, 1994.

Duchesneau, François. "L'argumentation finaliste en biologie" in *Rhétoriques de la science, De Coorebyter, Vincent (ed)*, 189-210. Paris, Pr Univ France, 1994.

Teleological arguments play a strategic role in biological theories. Biologists cannot dispense with describing and expressing phenomena in functional terms; but, correlatively, explanations cannot but rely on analytic nonfunctional models. The combination of the two approaches is specific of some of the major biological research programs. The modalities of such a combination ought to be further explored from the methodological viewpoint.

Duchesneau, François. Leibniz on the Principle of Continuity. *Rev Int Phil*, 48(188), 141-160, 1994.

For Leibniz, the principle of continuity provides means for linking together sequences of empirical determinations. It forms an instrument for theoretical invention and demonstration as well as for discarding inadequate explanations. It ties up with Leibniz's notion of a method of analogical progression and discovery in the mathematical and natural sciences. It affords one of the main architectonic devices in Leibniz's theory of science proper.

Duchesneau, François. Une étude sur l'aristotélisme réformé: L'édition Bodéüs de la Correspondance Leibniz-Thomasius. *Dialogue (Canada)*, 33(3), 457-472, Sum 94.

The discussion about Bodéüs's interpretation of the correspondence Leibniz-Thomasius bears on the extent to which Leibniz adhered to a reformed philosophy that aimed to harmonize Aristotle's metaphysics with the mechanistic philosophy of the modern. Even when Leibniz restores the scholastic substantial forms, he does so in a significantly deviant fashion in line with the teachings of his dynamics.

Dudley, Michael Kioni. "Traditional Native Hawaiian Environmental Philosophy" in *Ethics, Religion and Biodiversity, Hamilton, Lawrence S (ed)*, 176-182. Cambridge, White Horse, 1994.

Dudman, V H. On a Point of Logic. *Analysis*, 54(4), 208-214, O 94.

The point alluded to is that whether something or other *will* happen has nothing to do with what will happen if it *does*. For instance 1) and 2) are logically indifferent: 1) If the bough breaks the cradle will fall; 2) The bough will break. Yet many semantic theories of conditionals treat 2) as a factor of 1). This article seeks to explain what prompts this inadvertance, and why some of these theories still work.

Dudrick, David F and Murray, Michael J. Are Coerced Acts Free?. *Amer Phil Quart*, 32(2), 109-123, Ap 95.

This article begins by describing a conception of coercion that differs from other accounts in the literature. The account offered is, it is argued, indifferent between libertarian and compatibilist accounts of freedom. The article then discusses the way in which the libertarian rendering of "could have done otherwise" applies to coerced act as characterized, concluding that such acts should be counted as free. The final section of the article contains a discussion of how such a libertarian might address the objection that, on this account, one should be held morally responsible for all acts performed under coercion.

Düll, Rupprecht. *Zur Regulation der "Harmonia": Der Regelkreis als Modell ganzheitlicher Organisation unter dem Aspekt des Bewusstseins*. Sankt Augustin, Academia, 1994.

The work tries to explain with help of a technic model how higher quality comes into existence by holistic organization. Some surprising connections between the phenomena of life and technic systems get clearer. It turns out that the regulation of feedback has a holistic nature. This regulation protects not only anything living, but is also the source of self-organizing processes. The whole system is illustrated by the "model of the hyperbola" which makes possible to arrange a quality of better proportions for the living and for the technic sphere. The work also refers to the fact, that open systems without adequate mechanisms of regulation get into stiffness, if it is too perfect.

Düsberg, Klaus Jürgen. Deterministisches Chaos: Einige Wissenschaftstheoretisch Interessante Aspekte. *J Gen Phil Sci*, 26(1), 11-24, 1995.

Düsing, Edith. Das Problem der Individualität in Fichtes früher Ethik und Rechtslehre. *Fichte-Studien*, 3, 29-50, 1991.

In der *Grundlage les Naturrechts* von 1796 vertritt Fichte allem Anschein nach die Auffassung, das Prinzip der Konstitution von Individualität sei der Leib; damit setzt er in verwandelter Weise das traditionelle Theorem fort, das *principium individuationis* sie die Materie. Es erhebt sich jedoch die Frage, ob diese Auffassung das einzige, ja überhaupt das entscheidende Kriterium für Individualität darstellt. Anhand der frühen Rechtslehre kann gezeigt werden, dass sich durch den Akt wechselseitiger Anerkennung freie Rechtspersonen in ihrem Selbstbewusstsein konstituieren, die gerade in ihrer Freiheit als Einzelwesen anzusehen sind (II). Schwieriger noch ist die Frage der Einzelheit geistigen Daseins in der frühen *Sittenlehre* zu entscheiden (III), in der Fichte Überlegungen aus der *Bestimmung des Gelehrten* (I) fortführt. Doch lässt sich m E auch hier zeigen, dass die intelligible Welt, die für Fichte substantieller Grund sittlichen Selbstbewusstseins und Handelns ist, zumindest den Fichteschen Voraussetzungen nach eine pluralistische intersubjektive Welt von sittlichen freien Wesen ist, die in ihrer Freiheit und Sittlichkeit als selbständige einzelne Personen

anzusehen sind. Schliesslich gilt es zu fragen, ob die Einzelheit der Rechtsperson der Einzelheit einer sittlich freien Person kongruent is oder nicht.

Dueso, José Solana. *Statesman* (299b-d) and the Condemnation of Socrates. *Polis*, 12(1-2), 52-63, 1993.

While many scholars see in *Statesman* 299b-d a clear reference to the Socratic activity and trial, they do not use it in order to solve the enigma of the historic Socrates. This paper holds up that this passage contains a Platonic view contradictory with that of the earlier dialogues. If *Crito* or *Apology* offer a passionate apology of his master, in the *Statesman* the Socratic activity is placed in the frame of a central problem of the middle-ages and old Plato: how to pass of the really existent systems to a perfect political one. From this point of view, the Platonic judgment about the activity of Socrates undergoes a basic variation.

Dukerich, Janet M and McCabe, Donald L and Dutton, Jane E. The Effects of Professional Education on Values and the Resolution of Ethical Dilemmas: Business School versus Law School Students. *J Bus Ethics*, 13(9), 693-700, S 94.

Prior research on the impact of ethics education within the business curriculum has yielded mixed results. Although the impact is often found to be positive, it appears to be both small and short-lived. Interpretation of these results, however, is subject to important methodological limitations. The present research employed a longitudinal methodology to evaluate the impact of an MBA program versus a law program on the values and ethical decision making behavior of a cohort of students at two major universities in the northeast. The results suggest that the MBA curriculum remains a value-neutral experience for most students. In contrast, the law school program had a significant impact on both values and ethical decision making.

Dumais-Lévesque, Louis-Blaise. Quelles Sont les Exigences et les Limites de la Tolérance en Démocratie?. *Philosopher*, 15, 97-106, 1994.

Dummett, Michael. "Wittgenstein on Necessity: Some Reflections" in *Reading Putnam, Clark, Peter (ed)*, 49-65. Cambridge, Blackwell, 1995.

Dumouchel, Daniel. La découverte de la faculté de juger réfléchissante. *Kantstudien*, 85(4), 419-442, 1994.

Dumouchel, Daniel. Théorie Kantienne du Génie dans l'Esthétique des Lumières. *Horiz Phil*, 4(1), 77-89, Autumn 93.

Dumouchel, Paul. Une Théorie Darwinienne de la Connaissance. *Horiz Phil*, 2(2), 131-153, Spring 92.

Dunbar, Kevin. "How Scientists Really Reason: Scientific Reasoning in Real-World Laboratories" in *The Nature of Insight, Sternberg, Robert J (ed)*, 365-395. Cambridge, MIT Pr, 1995.

Dunfee, Thomas W. Introduction to the Special Issue on Social Contracts and Business Ethics. *Bus Ethics Quart*, 5(2), 167-171, Ap 95.

One of the most promising of the new research paradigms indigenous to the academic field of business ethics is social contract, the subject of this special issue of the *Business Ethics Quarterly*. Articles critique contractarian approaches, introduce new concepts, empirically test contractarian assumptions, and identify key areas for future research. The articles demonstrate that social contract theory offers a realistic, contextual basis for making normative judgments. The realism is supported by the consistency of contractarian assumptions with empirical literature in the social sciences and moral psychology, and recent evidence demonstrating that contractarian concepts are familiar to managers and influence behavior.

Dunfee, Thomas W and Cowton, Christopher J. Internationalizing the Business Ethics Curriculum: A Survey. *J Bus Ethics*, 14(5), 331-338, My 95.

This article reports on a telephone survey of business school faculty in the United Kingdom, Asia and North America concerning efforts to internationalize the teaching of business ethics. International dimensions of business ethics are currently given only limited coverage in the business school curriculum with over half of the faculty surveyed indicating that less than 10% of their ethics teaching focuses on global issues. Teaching objectives vary widely with some faculty emphasizing a relativistic, diversity oriented perspective while others stress the universality of values. The respondents identified a great need to develop teaching materials based upon non-U.S. corporations and/or non-U.S. incidents.

Dunfee, Thomas W and Donaldson, Thomas. Contractarian Business Ethics: Current Status and Next Steps. *Bus Ethics Quart*, 5(2), 173-186, Ap 95.

Social contract is rapidly becoming one of the significant alternatives for analyzing ethical issues in business. Contractarian approaches emphasizing consent as a means of justifying principles can provide needed context for rendering normative judgements concerning economic behaviors. Current research issues include developing tests of consent for both hypothetical and extant social contracts, and empirically testing the assumptions of the major contractarian approaches. Open questions include exploring the relationship between contractarian business ethics and other approaches, such as stakeholder management and virtue based ethics; and analysis of the intersection of contractarian approaches with the findings and assumptions of the field of moral psychology. Finally, the managerial utility of social contract based approaches needs to be explored with emphasis on identifying "translator" concepts.

Dunfee, Thomas W and Donaldson, Thomas. Integrative Social Contracts Theory. *Econ Phil*, 11(1), 85-112, Ap 95.

Dunn, Craig P and Brady, F Neil. Business Meta-Ethics: An Analysis of Two Theories. *Bus Ethics Quart*, 5(3), 385-398, Jl 95.

The main purpose of this paper is to defend traditional ethical theory (utilitarianism and deontology) for its application in business against a more recent model consisting of utility, rights, and justice. This is done in three parts: First, we provide a conceptual argument for the superiority of the traditional model; second, we demonstrate these points through an examination of three short cases; and third, we argue for the capability of the traditional model to account for universals and particulars in ethics.

Dunn, Robert L. Two Theories of Mental Division. *Austl J Phil*, 72(3), 302-316, S 94.

Dupuis-Déri, Francis. Qu'est-ce que la démocratie?. *Horiz Phil*, 5(1), 84-95, Autumn 94.

Duque, Félix. Aquí y Ahora, Desde la Hermenéutica. *Daimon Rev Filosof*, 8, 55-61, 1994.

This paper transcripts a conference given at Naples in which, through a simple reflection about the use of adverbial terms, the impossibility of an isomorphy between language and reality is revealed. This is due to the repeated perspective shiftings, which point to the definitive breakdown of the metaphysical ideal of a 'constant presence', focused from a dominant subjectivity. This way, one's own 'I' is asymptotically rejected in the play of being's finitude and speaker's mortality.

Duque, Félix. L'ermeneutica qui ed ora. *Teoria*, 14(1), 69-79, 1994.

Duran, Jane. Commentary on "Is Animal Pain Conscious?". *Between Species*, 10(1-2), 8-9, Win-Spr 94.

It is argued that Lynch's counter to the theorists who contend that animals do not feel pain is not quite strong enough. Their contentions rest on a series of conflations between Freudian and ordinary uses of the term "conscious" and their arguments can easily be refuted.

Duran, Jane. Nozickian Tracking and Naturalization. *Metaphilosophy*, 25(4), 326-334, O 94.

The standard counterarguments to Nozickian tracking are presented, and it is concluded that the entire debate suffers from a lack of naturalization. The notion that the debate is less *au couvant* than it could be is supported by allusion to cognitive science, and the work of Luper-Foy and others is cited.

Duran, Jane. Positivism's Heir. *J Gen Phil Sci*, 26(1), 25-34, 1995.

Duran, Jane. Russell on Pragmatism. *Russell*, 14(1), 31-37, Sum 94.

Russell's views on the pragmatists are briefly contrasted, largely with Dewey's views, on two major points—an epistemological account of truth, and the importance of the notion of "desire" for theory of value. It is concluded that the burst in interest in the work of the pragmatists has done a disservice to Russell's original criticisms, and that a particularly salient part of Russell's commentary revolves around his trenchant attack on the motivations behind pragmatist doctrine.

Duran, Jane. Social Epistemology and Goffmanian Theory. *J Phil Res*, 19, 185-192, 1994.

The notion that epistemology can be naturalized by advertence to areas of the social sciences other than psychology—by employment of sociolinguistics, for example—is supported by three lines of argument. The first asks us to note that sociolinguistics provides information that would help us delineate the constraints of the process of epistemic justification as engaged in by a speaker/listener. The second asks us to take into account the sociology of language work of Erving Goffmann, who has written extensively on "face-saving" strategies and other non-verbal devices. The third repeats a constructed naturalized justification set from previous work in epistemology and asks us to envision this set with riders from Goffmanian theory. It is concluded that naturalized epistemology can and should draw from many areas of the social sciences.

Duran, Jane. The Attack on Methodological Solipsism. *Philosophica*, 53(1), 81-90, 1994.

Attacks on the Fodorian research strategy—by Baker and by Tuomela—are examined, and Baker's attack fully set out. Tuomela's criticisms of Baker's well-known counterexample to token-type identity are examined, and it is concluded that, even if Baker's counterexample does not completely go through, any assessment of its strength does not bode well for Fodor's overall position. An evaluation of what MS actually requires as a strategy is provided, and it is concluded that (as Fodor seems to admit), it cannot operate as a research position based merely on nomic regularity or psychological laws.

Durand, Guy. Coordonnées de base de l'éthique. *Laval Theol Phil*, 50(3), 467-480, O 94.

Cet article veut présenter les coordonnées de base de l'éthique (et de la morale), c'est-á-dire les éléments qui entrent dans l'élaboration du discours, de la réflexion et du jugement éthiques. Plutôt que proposer une solution ou justifier un système, il vise á èclairer l'horizon et à présenter les diverses facettes et les divers volets de la question.

Durand, Stéphane. L'esthétique scientifique: commentaire sur la Grande Unification. *Horiz Phil*, 5(1), 31-46, Autumn 94.

Au-delà des mathématiques, au-delà de l'explication des phénomènes, au-delà des expériences, il y a aussi, en physique, la beauté des structures. Nous tenterons d'illustrer cette esthétique scientifique dans le contexte des théories de Grande Unification.

Durbin, Paul T. Ferment in Philosophy of Science Revisited. *Thomist*, 58(4), 655-675, O 94.

This is a survey of recent work in philosophy of science, focusing on approximately 50 books. About half represent traditional approaches to philosophy of science, either general topics or philosophies of particular sciences. The other half are critical of traditional philosophy of science, representing postmodernist, feminist, and political critiques. The thesis of the paper is that philosophy of science is currently in a state of ferment, and exciting contributions are being made from all sorts of perspectives.

Dussel, Enrique. "Technology and Basic Needs" in *Philosophy of Technology in Spanish Speaking Countries, Mitcham, Carl (ed)*, 101-109. Dordrecht, Kluwer, 1994.

Dustin, Christopher A. Commentary on Sherman's "The Role of Emotions in Aristotelian Virtue". *Proc Boston Colloq Anc Phil*, 9, 34-56, 1993.

This commentary questions Sherman's attempt to fill the gaps in Aristotle's account of emotion and its connection to virtue. It seeks to clarify the sense in which emotions are ethically relevant, and considers the problem of objectivity raised by an account of the emotions that would give them a cognitive foundation and see them as a mode of recognizing value. Aristotle promises a solution, but Sherman's approach fails to capture it. She seeks to defend Aristotle against Kantian worries about control, but a concern for controlling emotion is un-Aristotelian. Aristotle's contribution to the debate over the rationality of emotion, and to our understanding of moral agency, will be missed if we try to make sense of it from a Kantian perspective.

Dustin, Christopher A. The Untruth in Relativism. *Int J Phil Stud*, 3(1), 17-53, Mr 95.

Dutra, Araújo and Henrique, Luiz. Van Fraassen e os Limites da Observabilidade. *Cad Hist Filosof Cie*, 3(1-2), 133-150, Ja-D 93.

This paper discusses the difference between the classical empiricist view on the limits of observability, such as exposed in Locke's work, and the contemporary naturalist view on this topic, which is defended by van Fraassen's constructive empiricism. According to van Fraassen, the problem of the limits of observability is to be answered not by philosophy, but by empirical science, which can furnish a simpler answer; but this doesn't seem to be the case if we consider the different scientific solutions to the problem.

Dutton, Denis. Literary Theory and Intellectual Kitsch. *Lit Aes*, 2, 23-34, Spr 92.

That postmodernism is a general cultural mood and a style in art, architecture, and literature is uncontroversial. But does postmodernism present a coherent *intellectual* doctrine or theory of politics, art, or life? In the discussion which follows, I will concentrate on two aspects of the intellectual pretensions of postmodernism. First, I examine the postmodernist claim to justify the idea that the postmodern world is characterized by a general indeterminacy of meaning. Next I will look at aspects of the postmodernist contention that the present age has witnessed the decline of individuality.

Dutton, Jane E and Dukerich, Janet M and McCabe, Donald L. The Effects of Professional Education on Values and the Resolution of Ethical Dilemmas: Business School versus Law School Students. *J Bus Ethics*, 13(9), 693-700, S 94.

Prior research on the impact of ethics education within the business curriculum has yielded mixed results. Although the impact is often found to be positive, it appears to be both small and short-lived. Interpretation of these results, however, is subject to important methodological limitations. The present research employed a longitudinal methodology to evaluate the impact of an MBA program versus a law program on the values and ethical decision making behavior of a cohort of students at two major universities in the northeast. The results suggest that the MBA curriculum remains a value-neutral experience for most students. In contrast, the law school program had a significant impact on both values and ethical decision making.

Dux, Günter. "Macht als Wesen und Widersacher der Liebe" in *Macht Geschlechter Differenz, Müller-Funk, Wolfgang (ed)*, 43-62. Vienna, Picus, 1994.

Dworkin, Gerald. Contracting Justice. *Phil Books*, 36(1), 19-26, Ja 95.

This is an essay-review of *Political Justice* by John Rawls. I discuss the differences in the nature and scope of the problem, the conception of political philosophy and the main concepts between this work and *A Theory of Justice*. I try to fill in some details as to how the arguments for an overlapping consensus might go for various comprehensive doctrines. I argue that although the scope and ambition of this work are reduced compared to the earlier book, it still serves a valuable function.

Dworkin, Ronald. Constitutionalism and Democracy. *Euro J Phil*, 3(1), 2-11, Ap 95.

Dworkin, Ronald. Reply to Paul Ricoeur's "The Plurality of Sources of Law". *Ratio Juris*, 7(3), 287-290, D 94.

Dybikowski, James C. Critical Notice of Myles Burnyeat*The* Theaetetus *of Plato*. *Can J Phil*, 25(1), 119-134, Mr 95.

Dyck, Arthur J. Beyond Theological Conflict in the Courts: The Issue of Assisted Suicide. *Notre Dame J Law Ethics*, 9(2), 503-535, 1995.

This article analyzes three theological/philosophical perspectives (Hobbesian, Millian, Christian) found in judicial opinions as to whether a given case of refusing treatment violates existing laws against assisted suicide. The author found: 1) That these perspectives generally concur in supporting a right to refuse medical treatment and in denying a right to physician-assisted suicide; 2) That maintaining this consensus provides the protection requisite for individual and communal life; and 3) That a "streamlined" version of Mill currently used to declare a constitutional right to physician-assisted suicide would, if it became the law of the land, divisively destroy the existing, longstanding consensus in common law and previous court decisions.

Dyer, Michael G. Quantum Physics and Consciousness, Creativity, Computers: A Commentary on Goswami's Quantum-Based Theory of Consciousness and Free Will. *J Mind Behav*, 15(3), 265-290, Sum 94.

Goswami (1990, 1993) proposes to replace the current scientific paradigm of *physical realism* with that of a *quantum-based monistic idealism* and, in the process, accomplish the following goals: a) establish a basis for explaining consciousness, b) reintegrate spirituality, mysticism, morality, a sense that the universe is meaningful, etc., with scientific discoveries and the scientific enterprise, and c) support the assumption that humans possess free will—i.e., that they are not controlled by the apparently inexorable causality of the physical laws that govern the functioning of their brains. Here, we critically examine this approach, from an artificial intelligence and neural network perspective, and point out what appear to be some inherent weaknesses in Goswami's arguments.

Dyk, Wieslaw. A Break Symmetry—The Principle of the Evolution of Universe. *Stud Phil Christ*, 30(2), 73-82, 1994.

The main aim of the article is to show a creative role of the breaking symmetry phenomenon, starting from a quantum leap out of an ideal vacuum to the physical one. The break in the ideal symmetry (supersymmetry) of the primitive universe and a transition through the inflation phase led in an unbalance state and caused to become matter-cooled. Creative features of time are brought to the process of acting by a lack of stability and becoming primitive puree cooled. The symmetrical laws of nature are being acted in the spreading universe but an evolutionary matter submits their operation with a large retardation. The retardation is a basis of the following formation unbalance sources, breaking symmetry and consequently, it is the source of more and more processes, arranged, organized matter and origin of life.

Dzierzgowski, Daniel. Models of Intuitionistic TT and NF. *J Sym Log*, 60(2), 640-653, Je 95.

Let us define the *intuitionistic part* of classical theory T as the intuitionistic theory whose proper axioms are identical with the proper axioms of T. For example, Heyting arithmetic HA is the intuitionistic part of classical Peano arithmetic PA. It's a well-known fact, proved by Heyting and Myhill, that ZF is identical with its intuitionistic part. In this paper, we mainly prove that TT, Russell's Simple Theory of Types, and NF, Quine's "New Foundations," are not equal to their intuitionistic part. So, an intuitionistic version of TT or NF seems more naturally definable than an intuitionistic version of ZF. In the first section, we present a simple technique to build Kripke models of the intuitionistic part of TT (with short examples showing bad properties of finite sets if they are defined in the usual classical way). In the remaining sections, we show how models of intuitionistic NF_2 and NF can be obtained from well-chosen classical ones. In these models, the excluded middle will not be satisfied for some non-stratified sentences.

Easterbrook, Neil. "By Indirections Find Directions Out": Kierkegaard's Socratic Attractor. *Phil Rhet*, 28(2), 89-104, 1995.

One motif of poststructural thought is its confrontation with the philosophical conceit of a rigorous distinction between philosophy and its multiple others: rhetoric, literature, politics, and so on. Derrida, for instance, argues against the possibility of a non-ironical philosophy, a position now commonplace in poststructuralism but which is *prefigured* by Kierkegaard. Like Derrida, Kierkegaard sought to break apart prereflective conceptions of signification, which following Barthes's term could be called *semioclasm*. Kierkegaard's rhetorical "excess," his privileging of irony as philosophy's master trope (fully articulated in the image of the Socratic attractor) is the rhetorical basin of his *The Concept of Irony*. Drawing on an analogy to the "strange attractors" of chaos science, this article shows how Kierkegaard anticipates many of the notions we now associate with poststructural rhetoric.

Easthope, Antony. Literary into Cultural Studies. *Rad Phil*, 70, 29-32, Mr-Ap 95.

Easton, Susan. Autonomy and the Free Speech Principle. *J Applied Phil*, 12(1), 27-39, 1995.

Autonomy may be used to justify free speech claims where the right is raised against the state but also to justify state intervention intended to promote autonomy which may entail restraints on others' speech. The appeal to diversity and autonomy may be used by both sides of the pornography and censorship debate. Although autonomy may be invoked in defence of pornography as part of the general defence of free speech, it is argued that autonomy favours the regulation of pornography. The "free speech" defence of pornography is critically examined here and an alternative argument advanced for regulation.

Eaton, Marcia Muelder. The Social Construction of Aesthetic Response. *Brit J Aes*, 35(2), 95-107, Ap 95.

Social constructionists argue that emotions are learned, culture-bound, and socially prescribed and proscribed. The author argues that these characteristics are also true of aesthetic response.

Eaton, Marcia Mulder. The Intrinsic, Non-Supervenient Nature of Aesthetic Properties. *J Aes Art Crit*, 52(4), 383-397, Fall 94.

Properties relevant to aesthetic judgments are intrinsic to objects or events. By explaining 'intrinsic' epistemologically rather than metaphysically (as has usually been the case), one can avoid entanglements that characterize explanations of aesthetic properties in terms of supervenience.

Ebeling, Richard M. "Liberalism and Collectivism in the 20th Century" in *The End of "Isms"?, Shtromas, Alexsandras (ed)*, 69-84. Cambridge, Blackwell, 1994.

Eberlein, Gerald L. Logik der Sozialwissenschaften—150 Jahre nach J St Mills System of Logic. *Protosoz*, 6, 229-240, 1994.

J Stuart Mill's System of Logic (1843) is reexamined from the perspective of present-day analytical philosophy of the social sciences. His naturalistic epistemology, "state", "general/universal laws", "social statics/dynamics" are discussed, as well as his four methods. His nomological-behavioral position is analysed, along with his theoretical approach.

Ebert, Howard. Immutability of God: Metaphysical Inconsistency or Essential Grounding for Human Transcendence. *Phil Theol*, 8(1), 41-61, Autumn 93.

Mark Lloyd Taylor in *God is Love: A Study in the Theology of Karl Rahner* charges that Rahner's understanding of the essential immutability of God renders his theology incoherent. An assessment of the validity of Taylor's process-informed critique requires a careful examination of Rahner's understanding of analogy. Analogy, for Rahner is not based on a conceptual or semantic distinction but on the ontological constitution of human transcendence. From Rahner's perspective, Taylor's critique is faulty because it springs from an impoverished view of Being and a diminished sense of the radical nature of human transcendence.

Eboh, Marie Pauline. Africa: The Role Model of Planetary Solidarity—Between All Humans and the Human Universum. *Dialogue Hum*, 4(2-3), 233-245, 1994.

Eboh, Marie Pauline. Dialogue and Universalism: A Practical Application to Africa. *Dialogue Hum*, 3(3), 85-90, 1993.

Eboh, Marie Pauline. Points of Convergence between Judaism, Christianity and Islam. *Dialogue Hum*, 3(1), 61-70, 1993.

Eboh, Marie Pauline. The Golden Rule as the Foundation of Universal Ethics. *Dialogue Hum*, 4(4), 65-72, 1994.

Ebrahim, Abul Fadl Moshin. Organ Transplantation: Contemporary Sunni Muslim Legal and Ethical Perspectives. *Bioethics*, 9(3-4), 291-302, Jl 95.

The problems that organ transplantation poses to the Muslim mind may be summarized as follows: firstly, a muslim believes that whatever he owns or possesses has been given to him as an *amanah* (trust) from *Allah*. Would it not be a breach of trust to give consent for the removal of parts of one's body, while still alive, for transplantation to benefit one's child, sibling or parent? Secondly, the *Shari'ah* (Islamic Law) emphasizes the sacredness of the human body, tantamount to its mutilation, if organs were to be removed after death for the purpose of transplantation? In this paper I attempt to illustrate how the Muslim jurists have tried to resolve the dilemma of Muslims by providing them with certain guidelines based on the original sources of Islam, namely, the *Qur'an* and the Prophetic tradition. In order to assist the followers of other religious traditions to grasp the gravity of the problem posed by organ transplantation to the Muslim mind, I begin by discussing the opinions of Muslim jurists on the issue of utilization of human parts. Thereafter, I touch upon the resolutions taken by the various Islamic Juridical Academies on the issue in question. Finally, I shed light upon the inclusion of organ donation in a Muslim Will and the enforceable nature of such a will.

Eccles, John C. *How the Self Controls Its Brain*. New York, Springer-Verlag, 1994.

The purpose of the book is given in the title. Each of us is a self-conscious self, which is a unique human existence and throughout life the self brings about desired actions by acting on the brain. The book shows that this action transcends the philosophical materialist belief by using quantum physics. In this way the conscious self introduces a new philosophical level of dualism based on neuroscience of the brain.

Echauri, Raúl. Sobre el origen del ser y la nada. *Acta Phil*, 2(3), 315-326, 1994.

Echeverría, Javier. Crítica y propuesta a la distinción entre contexto de descubrimiento y contexto de justifición. *Rev Latin de Filosof*, 20(2), 283-302, 1994.

This paper criticizes Reichenbach's distinction between context of discovery and context of justification. The crisis of the *received view* in the philosophy of science is commented, together with some alternative proposals. The author claims that philosophy of science should consider not only scientific knowledge, but also scientific activities. Furthermore, a renewed philosophy of science must study and analyze the present *technoscience*, in addition to classical scientific theories. The positivistic distinction between discovery and justification does not provide an adequate conceptual framework to understand the complexity and plurality of technoscientific activities. Consequently, a new distinction of four contexts of scientific activities is proposed: the *contexts of learning, innovation, evaluation and application*.

Echeverría, José. El morir como pauta ética del empiricismo trascendental. *Dialogos*, 30(65), 111-171, Ja 95.

Eckardt, A Roy. *How to Tell God from the Devil: On the Way to Comedy*. New Brunswick, Transaction Books, 1995.

Eco, Umberto. "Unlimited Semeiosis and Drift: Pragmaticism vs 'Pragmatism'" in *Peirce and Contemporary Thought: Philosophical Inquiries, Ketner, Kenneth Laine (ed)*, 205-221. New York, Fordham Univ Pr, 1995.

Eddy, Paul R. Religious Pluralism and the Divine: Another Look at John Hick's Neo-Kantian Proposal. *Relig Stud*, 30(4), 467-478, D 94.

This study focuses upon the heart of John Hick's pluralistic philosophy of religion—his neo-Kantian response to the problem of conflicting inter-religious conceptions of the divine. Hick attempts to root his proposal in two streams of tradition: 1) the inter-religious awareness of the distinction between the divine in itself vs. the divine as humanly experiences, and 2) a Kantian epistemology. In fact, these attempts are problematic in that his hypothesis introduces a radical subjectivizing element at both junctures. In the end, I contend that Hick's neo-Kantian proposal undermines his decades-long effort to defend some form of religious realism.

Edel, Abraham. *Ethical Judgment: The Use of Science in Ethics*. New Brunswick, Transaction Books, 1995.

Edel, Abraham. Naturalism and the Concept of Moral Change. *Proc Amer Phil Ass*, 60(5), 821-840, Je 87.

This essay, the first Romanell Lecture at the APA, examines naturalism's challenge to prevalent philosophical neglect of moral change. Morality became refined in evolutionary theory as itself growing and variable among different peoples. The ethical consequences of this changed view are: the need to integrate inquiries from different fields, from the biological to the social; the study of constancy and variation of moral outlooks over time; a shift from moral rules to moral decision-making; naturalization of the normative and an end to its isolation; a deeper understanding of the cultural functions of ethical theories themselves.

Edelman, Shimon. Representation, Similarity, and the Chorus of Prototypes. *Mind Mach*, 5(1), 45-68, F 95.

It is proposed to conceive of representation as an emergent phenomenon that is supervenient on patterns of activity of coarsely tuned and highly redundant feature detectors. The computational underpinnings of the outlined concept of representation are 1) the properties of collections of overlapping graded receptive fields, as in the biological perceptual systems that exhibit hyperacuity-level performance, and 2) the sufficiency of a set of proximal distances between stimulus representations for the recovery of the corresponding distal contrasts between stimuli, as in multidimensional scaling. The present preliminary study appears to indicate that this concept of representation is computationally viable, and is compatible with psychological and neurobiological data.

Eder, Gabriele Johanna (ed). *Alexius Meinong und Guido Adler: Eine Freundschaft in Briefen*. Amsterdam, Rodopi, 1995.

Edgar, Andrew. "Narrating Social Work" in *Ethics and the Professions, Chadwick, Ruth (ed)*, 125-135. Brookfield, Avebury, 1994.

The codes of ethics of the National Association of Social Work and the British Association of Social Work are compared using a narrative theory derived from Paul Ricoeur. Codes of ethics are treated as frameworks that at once facilitate and restrict the ethical narratives that social work practitioners can present as legitimations of their practice. The American and British codes are seen to provide distinct formulations of the character of professionals and clients, of the nature of moral problems in social work, and of the relationship of the individual practitioner to the profession as a whole.

Edgar, Andrew. "Weber, Nietzsche, and Music" in *Nietzsche: A Critical Reader, Sedgwick, Peter R (ed)*, 84-103. Cambridge, Blackwell, 1995.

Max Weber's *Rational and Social Foundations of Music* is interpreted in the light of Nietzsche's *The Birth of Tragedy*. Weber traces the rationalisation of Occidental music theory, and its relationship to non-Western theory. His relationship to Nietzsche is then characterised through four themes: the need for meaning in the face of suffering and irrationality; the problem of grounding science; the justification of Occidental and German culture; and the nature of personal identity. Weber's own later interpretations of his sociology of music serve to demonstrate the manner in which he increasingly suppressed the Nietzschean concerns of his early work.

Edgar, Andrew. Weighting Health States and Strong Evaluation. *Bioethics*, 9(3-4), 240-251, Jl 95.

The problem of public consultation over the allocation of health care resources is addressed by considering the role that quality of life measures, such as QALYs and the Nottingham Health Profile, could play. Such measures are typically grounded in social surveys, and as such may reflect public preferences for health care priorities. Using Charles Taylor's concepts of "weak" and "strong" evaluation, it is suggested that current quality of life measures are inadequate, insofar as they typically presuppose that survey respondents are mere "weak evaluators," who express only inarticulate preferences. Respondents may, conversely, be understood as strong evaluators, with deeper visions of human nature and the good life informing their health preferences. Space is then created for such respondents to be asked to defend their preferences, and so be encouraged to reflect critically and publicly on the beliefs and prejudices that ground their view of health care priorities.

Edgington, Dorothy. On Conditionals. *Mind*, 104(414), 235-329, Ap 95.

Edidin, Aron. What Mathematics Is About. *Phil Stud*, 78(1), 1-31, Ap 95.

Edidin, Aron. What's an Epistemologist to Do?. *Amer Phil Quart*, 31(4), 285-296, O 94.

Edie, James M. The Philosophical Framework of Sartre's Theory of the Theater. *Man World*, 27(4), 415-444, O 94.

This article situates Sartre's writings on the theater, as well as his plays, within the context of his philosophy of action, an existential ethics, as a whole. It goes on to discuss his theory of "empathy" in so far as it applies in the theater and compares it to the theories of Aristotle, Stanislavski and Brecht to show that Sartre's theory is by far superior to the others.

Edsall, John T. On Margot O'Toole and the Baltimore Case: A Personal Note on the Evolution of My Involvement. *Ethics Behavior*, 4(3), 239-247, 1994.

The article by Serge Lang (1993) in this journal on the Baltimore case is, I believe, a major contribution to the understanding of that extremely complex and important case. Lang's views on matters of ethics and scientific responsibility are generally in close accord with mine. On one point, relating to myself, I will offer a correction of a perfectly natural, and indeed flattering, inference that he has drawn concerning my conduct. Like him, I now strongly support the validity of Margot O'Toole's challenge that called for a published correction to the disputed paper in *Cell* (Weaver, et al., 1986) and thereby initiated the controversy that remains officially unresolved.

Edwards, Derek. What's in a Word? Bring on the Seals and the Sheep (In Response to Hoffmann). *J Prag*, 23(4), 451-453, Ap 95.

Edwards, Derek. Whorf's Empty Gasoline Drum and the Pope's Missing Wife. *J Prag*, 22(2), 215-218, Ag 94.

Edwards, Derek and Ashmore, Malcolm and Potter, Jonathan. Death and Furniture: The Rhetoric, Politics, and Theology of Bottom Line Arguments against Relativism. *Hist Human Sci*, 8(2), 25-49, My 95.

Edwards, Jim. The Universal Quantifier and Dummett's Verificationist Theory of Sense. *Analysis*, 55(2), 90-97, Ap 95.

The author argues that a verificationist theory of meaning, as conceived by Michael Dummett most perspicuously his "The Logical Basis of Metaphysics" (London, Duckworth, 1991) cannot be carried through in the case of the universal quantifier. It cannot be carried through because Dummett's introduction rule for the universal quantifier makes covert appeal on the input side to a judgement of an equal or a higher order of complexity than the sentence which is the output of the introduction rule, which violates a condition developed in the article for a verificationist theory of meaning to be a theory of understanding.

Edwards, M J (trans). *Philoponus: On Aristotle's "Physics" 3*. Ithaca, Cornell Univ Pr, 1994.

Edwards, Rem B. Tom Regan's Seafaring Dog and (Un)Equal Inherent Worth. *Between Species*, 9(4), 231-235, Fall 93.

Tom Regan maintains that all year-old or more mammals, including humans, are equal as subjects-of-a-life, in inherent worth, and in rights; but their satisfactions may differ. Where four humans and a dog vie to be saved in a life raft for four, the dog, with fewer opportunities for future satisfactions, should be thrown overboard. I contend that (1) in analyzing the harms of death, Regan ignores the loss of the (supposedly) equal inherent worth of the dog and the person, and (2) there are degrees of being the subject-of-a-life and thus of inherent worth, which is where the dog loses.

Edwards, Steve. *Externalism in the Philosophy of Mind*. Brookfield, Avebury, 1994.

The book constitutes an enquiry into an externalist theory of intentional content which is constrained by a token physicalist theory of mind. In part one, epistemic, ontological, and explanatory motivations for both internalism and externalism are set out and assessed. It is concluded that externalism is the more plausible thesis. In part two externalism is defended from the charge that it is not compatible with the phenomenon of first person authority. Finally, in part three, externalist accounts and individuation conditions of demonstrative and natural kind thoughts are put forward.

Eells, Ellery. Bayesian Epistemology: Probabilistic Confirmation and Rational Decision. *Protosoz*, 6, 38-60, 1994.

This paper distinguishes between "descriptive" and "normative" conceptions of Bayesian principles of rationality, both in the context of inference and in the context of decision (which of course are not unrelated). I emphasize an idea according to which, "You have to work with what you have to work with"—that is, that rationality is a relation among old beliefs, new information, and new beliefs (in the case of inference) and among beliefs, desires, preferences, and choices (in the case of decision). According to this conception of rationality, one's current beliefs and desires are not themselves subject to evaluation as to their rationality (except for some minimal, basically logical and "coherentist" constraints). From this perspective, rationality is about how we move from old beliefs (whatever they are) to new beliefs

when confronted with evidence, and about how our preferences are structured given what we believe and what we want (whatever we currently happen to believe and want). I present some formal details of this perspective and discuss several criticisms of it.

Eells, Ellery. Cartwright on Probabilistic Causality: Types, Tokens, and Capacities. *Phil Phenomenol Res*, 55(1), 169-175, Mr 95.

As part of a book symposium on Nancy Cartwright's *Nature's Capacities and their Measurement* (Oxford, 1989), the issues addressed have to do with generic and singular probabilistic causation, and with the relationship between theories at the two levels. In her book, Cartwright argues that singular causation is basic—that the theory of generic probabilistic causation depends on the idea of singular causation. Although we have come to agree about many fine points involved in theories and examples, I argue that she has not established the direction of dependence, and I allude to arguments of my own that the direction is opposite.

Eells, Ellery (ed) and Skyrms, Brian (ed). *Probability and Conditionals*. New York, Cambridge Univ Pr, 1994.

This is a collection of essays on the relation between conditional probabilities and probabilities of conditionals. Many of the essays provide new negative results concerning the natural idea that the probability of a conditional coincides with the corresponding conditional probability (i.e., concerning the relation between the probability of a statement of the form "if X, then Y" and the corresponding probability of Y given X). The essays in this volume elaborate on, advance, and evaluate the theories of Ernest Adams, a founder of this field of philosophical and logical investigation, whose important work in these areas is the main focus of the essays.

Effertz, Dirk. *Kants Metaphysik: Welt und Freiheit*. Freiburg, Alber, 1994.

Diese Untersuchung legt den Kreisgang der Kantischen Philosophie durch den Blick auf das System der Ideen als ihren "eigentlichen Zweck" (B 395) frei. Nucleus der Untersuchung ist die Frage nach dem systematischen Ort der Freiheitsidee und ihre Subsumtion unter die Weltidee in der ersten Kritik. Die Klärung dieses Sachverhalts führt auf eine Gesamtanalyse der Kritik der Urteilskraft, welche die Transformation der im System der Kritik—scheinbar—verschwindenden Vernunft-Idee der Welt in eine Vorstellung der Urteilskraft als Haupthese ausarbeitet. Damit einhergehend erschliesst sich der logische Bau der dritten Kritik als durch die Denkform der Disjunktion geprägt und zugleich in seinen auffälligen Asymmetrien begründbar.

Eflin, Juli. Teaching 'Inference to the Best Explanation'. *Teach Phil*, 17(2), 151-160, Je 94.

The nature of explanation is rarely discussed in introductory philosophy or critical reasoning courses. Yet we expect students to provide explanations and evaluate those that are offered. This paper discusses teaching Inference to the Best Explanation as an argument form. Using an in-class exercise, students increase their understanding from rudimentary common sense explanations to complex ones that face anomalies.

Egan, Frances. A WORLD without MIND: Comments on Terence Horgan's "Naturalism and Intentionality". *Phil Stud*, 76(2-3), 327-338, D 94.

Egan, Frances. Folk Psychology and Cognitive Architecture. *Phil Sci*, 62(2), 179-196, Je 95.

It has recently been argued that the success of the connectionist programs in cognitive science would threaten folk psychology. I articulate and defend a "minimalist" construal of folk psychology that comports well with empirical evidence on the folk understanding of belief and is compatible with even the most radical developments in cognitive science.

Egan, Frances. Individualism and Vision Theory. *Analysis*, 54(4), 258-264, O 94.

A psychological theory is *individualistic* just in case it taxonomizes psychological states without essential reference to the environment of the subject possessing them. It is *intentional* just in case it taxonomizes states by reference to their representational contents. This paper defends an individualist and nonintentional construal of David Marr's theory of vision against recent criticisms by Peter Morton.

Egger, Jean-Luc. De ludo veritatis: L'esperienza del vero nel pensiero di Niccolò da Cusa. *Sapienza*, 47(4), 387-438, O-D 94.

Eggerman, Richard W. Competition and the Categorical Imperative. *SW Phil Rev*, 11(1), 59-68, Ja 95.

Onora O'Neill claims that, for Kantian ethics, sporting and economic competition are to be judged morally unworthy because their maxims are nonuniversalizable. I agree that their maxims are nonuniversalizable, but attempt to avoid the harshly counterintuitive judgment of their unworthiness. I do this by arguing that such competitions do not necessarily violate the second formulation of the imperative. This approach commits me to denying the equivalence of the first and second formulations of the imperative.

Eggers Lan, Conrado. "Dios en la Ontología del *Parménides*" in *Platón: Los Diálogos Tardíos*, Lan, Conrado Eggers (ed), 49-56. Sankt Augustin, Academia, 1986.

Ehrhardt, Joop and Veenhoven, Ruut. Test of Predictions Implied in Three Theories of Happiness: The Cross-National Pattern of Happiness. *Soc Indic Res*, 34(1), 33-68, Ja 95.

Predictions about level and dispersion of happiness in nations are derived from three theories of happiness: comparison-theory, folklore-theory and livability-theory. The predictions are tested on two cross national data-sets: a comparative survey among university students in 38 nations in 1985 and a collection of comparable general population surveys in 28 nations around 1980. Most predictions of comparison-theory and folklore-theory are defied by the data. The predictions of livability-theory are all confirmed.

Ehrhardt, Walter E. ...also muss auf Schelling zurückgegangen werden. *Phil Rundsch*, 42(1), 1-10, Mr 95.

Ehrlich, Edith (& other eds). *Karl Jaspers: Basic Philosophical Writings*. Atlantic Highlands, Humanities Pr, 1986.

Eichler, Margrit. Sieben Weisen, den Sexismus zu erkennen. *Das Argument*, 207, 941-954, N-D 94.

This article identifies seven distinct types of sexist problems that may occur at any and each stage of the research process, including the title, language used, concepts employed, the research design, methods, data interpretation and policy recommendations. A simple diagnostic tool is presented that allows the identification of problems and suggests solutions. The approach is applicable regardless of subject area, discipline, or cultural context.

Eilan, Naomi. The First Person Perspective. *Proc Aris Soc*, 95, 51-66, 1994-95.

Eisele, Carolyn. "Charles S Peirce, Mathematician" in *Peirce and Contemporary Thought: Philosophical Inquiries, Ketner, Kenneth Laine (ed)*, 120-131. New York, Fordham Univ Pr, 1995.

Eisenhardt, Peter. "Dynamik, Emergenz und Mathematik: Über Kontinua und Diskontinua" in *Schelling und die Selbstorganisation, Heuser-Kessler, Marie-Luise (ed)*, 39-54. Berlin, Duncker Humblot, 1994.

The paper is concerned with a mathematical theory of emergence. Every object theory of emergence is faced with a problem, namely to find the precise mathematical representation of the transformation (which must not conserve specific structures) of the pre-state into the emerging (relative) end-state not reducible to the former and bearing new qualities. I work out such a transformation ("antimorphism") in the language of nonstandard topology. The basics are outlined; an updated English version will appear in: *From Simplicity to Complexity: Information, Interaction, Emergence*.

Eiser, J Richard. *Attitudes, Chaos, and the Connectionist Mind*. Cambridge, Blackwell, 1994.

This book examines the implications for attitude theory and social psychology of recent advances in cognitive science, many of these ideas can be traced back to the philosophy of Hume and the other empiricists. From this perspective it is argued that human attitudes should not be regarded merely as simple evaluative judgments but rather as attractors in a complex dynamical system, while the processes of attitude formation and change may be computable. The content of attitudes may not be since attitudes imply intentionality and awareness of other minds, they may provide an important test of the differences between machine intelligence and human intelligence.

Eklof, Paul C and Herzog, Ivo. Model Theory of Modules Over a Serial Ring. *Annals Pure Applied Log*, 72(2), 145-176, Mr 95.

We use the Drozd-Warfield structure theorem for finitely presented modules over a serial ring to investigate the model theory of modules over a serial ring, in particular, to give a simple description of pp-formulas and to classify the pure-injective indecomposable modules. We also study the question of whether every pure-injective indecomposable module over a valuation ring is the hull of a uniserial module.

Ekstein, Rudolf. "Philosophiestudieren in den dreissiger Jahren" in *Der geistige Anschluss, Fischer, Kurt R (ed)*, 123-129. Wien, WUV Univ, 1993.

Elberfeld, Rolf. "Lieu": Nishida, Nishitani, Derrida. *Rev Phil Louvain*, 92(4), 474-494, N 94.

Nishida's thought on place, as developed in 1926 in his explanation of Plato and Aristotle, opens new possibilities for a far-Eastern thought working in particular to overcome the subjectocentrism of Western philosophy. Nishitani, a pupil of Nishida, sought to work out this viewpoint setting out from Zen Buddhism and seeks then to determine the fountain-head of knowledge. Derrida, a critic of ethnocentrism, returns to the Platonic notion of "Chora", which Nishida had used for his view of place. It appears, thus, that Nishida, Nishitani and Derrida, each in a different way, seek to give an indication in the direction of the same seat of the nonapparent.

Elby, Andrew. The 'Decoherence' Approach to the Measurement Problem in Quantum Mechanics. *Proc Phil Sci Ass*, 1, 355-365, 1994.

Decoherence results from the dissipative interaction between a quantum system and its environment. As the system and environment become entangled, the reduced density operator describing the system "decoheres" into a mixture (with the interference terms damped out). This formal result prompts some to exclaim that the measurement problem is solved. I will scrutinize this claim by examining how modal and relative-state interpretations can use decoherence. Although decoherence cannot rescue these interpretations from general metaphysical difficulties, decoherence may help these interpretations to pick out a preferred basis. I will explore whether decoherence solves nagging technical problems associated with selecting a preferred basis.

Elder, Frank H W. Heidegger's Interpretation of the German "Revolution". *Res Phenomenol*, 23, 153-171, 1993.

Elders, Leo. Aristote et l'Aristotélisme. *Rev Thomiste*, 94(4), 653-660, O-D 94.

Eldredge, Niles. "Mass Extinction and Human Responsibility" in *Biology, Ethics, and the Origins of Life, Rolston III, Holmes (ed)*, 63-88. Boston, Jones & Bartlett, 1995.

Eldridge, Richard. Response to Victor Yelverton Haines. *J Aes Art Crit*, 53(2), 188-189, Spr 95.

Elegido, J M. Intrinsic Limitations of Property Rights. *J Bus Ethics*, 14(5), 411-416, My 95.

Many people take for granted an absolute conception of property rights. According to this conception, if I own a piece of property I have a moral right to do with it as I please, irrespective of the needs of others. This paper articulates an argument against this conception of property rights. First, it shows that there are many possible conceptions of property rights, and that there are significant differences among the models of ownership which have prevailed in different societies. Then, it argues that there are decisive grounds to refuse to grant that property owners have a moral right to exercise absolute control over their property, and that ownership implies not only rights but also duties and limits.

Elgesem, Dag. Data Privacy and Legal Argumentation. *Commun Cog*, 28(1), 91-111, 1995.

The paper tries to give a characterization of the principles of privacy protection that underlay modern data privacy legislation. The three notions of epistemic, practical and normative control, and their interrelations, are central in this characterization of data privacy. It is argued that what characterizes data privacy *violations* is that features of the way personal information is processed leads to both a decision that is wrong and harmful for the individual concerned, and that his legitimate expectation for a better outcome is frustrated. The relationship between modern data privacy and privacy as the control over the flow of intimate information is also discussed.

Elgin, Catherine Z. Unnatural Science. *J Phil*, 92(6), 289-302, Je 95.

Hilary Putnam claims to prove that any ideal theory is true. David Lewis urges that only elite properties figure in reference. Models containing plebian properties are not truth-makers. This circumvents Putnam's result, but does not square with scientific practice. Science favors ideal theories, whether their properties are elite or not. Still, Putnam's result is unsettling. It shows truth to be a mere side-effect of satisfying scientific ideals, practically whatever those ideals may be. The cognitive value of science lies not in its capacity to yield truths, but in its capacity to yield truths of a certain kind. The question is what sorts of truths are worth seeking?

Elgin, Catherine Z and Goodman, Nelson and Cometti, Jean-Pierre (trans). *Reconceptions en philosophie*. Paris, Pr Univ France, 1994.

Elias, Bohuslav. Zur Geschichte der Israelitengemeinde von Prostejov (Prossnitz). *Husserl Stud*, 10(3), 237-247, 1993-94.

Elias, Norbert. *Time: An Essay*. Cambridge, Blackwell, 1992.

Elliot, Gregory. Olympus Mislaid? A Profile of Perry Anderson. *Rad Phil*, 71, 5-19, My-Je 95.

This article attempts a synoptic account of the intellectual career of a thinker whose own writings, and whose editorial direction of *New Left Review* over two decades have rendered him one of the most influential figures in contemporary Anglophone Marxist culture. Utilizing unpublished source material, the article charts the vicissitudes of Anderson's theoretico-political project, from 1960 to the present, examining the crystallization, problematization and renunciation of a revolutionary-Marxist perspective. It concludes that Anderson's own evolution conforms to the pattern identified by him in his *Considerations on Western Marxism*.

Elliot, Patricia. Politics, Identity, and Social Change: Contested Grounds in Psychoanalytic Feminism. *Hypatia*, 10(2), 41-55, Spr 95.

This essay engages in a debate with Nancy Fraser and Dorothy Leland concerning the contribution of Lacanian-inspired psychoanalytic feminism to feminist theory and practice. Teresa Brennan's analysis of the impasse in psychoanalysis and feminism and Judith Butler's proposal for a radically democratic feminism are employed in examining the issues at stake. I argue, with Brennan, that the impasse confronting psychoanalysis and feminism is the result of different conceptions of the relationship between the psychical and the social. I suggest Lacanian-inspired feminist conceptions are useful and deserve our consideration.

Elliot, Robert. "Ecology and the Ethics of Environmental Restoration" in *Philosophy and the Natural Environment, Attfield, Robin (ed)*, 31-43. New York, Cambridge Univ Pr, 1994.

Elliot, Robert. Consequentialism and Absolutism. *Austl J Phil*, 73(1), 145-151, Mr 95.

It is shown that consequentialist ethics cannot ultimately be made to mimic deontological ethics by means of the device of attributing infinite values or disvalues to certain kinds of acts. Absolutist pacificism is the example used to make the point.

Elliot, Robert (ed). *Environmental Ethics (Oxford Readings in Philosophy)*. New York, Oxford Univ Pr, 1995.

Elliott, Carl. Puppetmasters and Personality Disorders: Wittgenstein, Mechanism, and Moral Responsibility. *Phil Psychiat Psych*, 1(2), 91-100, Je 94.

In this essay I suggest that psychiatrists have at least two different ways of speaking about persons: the language of mechanism and the language of ordinary life. I explore Wittgenstein's suggestion that when we look at something mechanistically we take up an attitude of "fatalism", the attitude that things could not have happened otherwise, and I argue that we are inclined to take up a similar attitude when we look at certain types of psychiatric patients. I also argue that both biological and psychodynamic explanations of human behavior embed deterministic assumptions, which may further undermine ordinary notions of moral responsibility. (edited)

Elliott, Carl and Kahn, Jeffrey. Docs on the Box: Or, How We Learned to Stop Worrying and Love the Tube. *Hastings Center Rep*, 24(6), 22-23, N-D 94.

Elliott, David J. Musical Values Revisited: A Reply to Forest Hansen's "Values in Music Education". *Phil Music Educ Rev*, 3(1), 52-55, Spr 95.

Elliott, Gregory (ed). *Althusser: A Critical Reader*. Cambridge, Blackwell, 1994.

Elliott, Terri. Making Strange What Had Appeared Familiar. *Monist*, 77(4), 424-433, O 94.

What is it about *being oppressed* that gives oppressed classes a privileged point of view from which to see the strangeness of the social relations in which they find themselves? Historical materialism offers a framework within which we might understand the epistemic priviledge of *particular* oppressed groups only. In "Making Strange What Had Appeared Familiar" a discourse is developed which characterizes the experience of "making strange" for all marginalized people. This discourse takes as its starting point reflection on various cases of insight into oppression and considers them in light of the Heideggerian distinction between *readiness-to-hand* and *presence-to-hand*.

Ellis, Anthony. Recent Work on Punishment. *Phil Quart*, 45(179), 225-233, Ap 95.

This article surveys some of the more important work in the philosophy of punishment in past ten years or so.

Ellis, Anthony. Rights and the Criminal Law. *Analysis*, 54(2), 79-83, Ap 94.

Judith Jarvis Thomson has argued that any acceptable—and perhaps even imaginable—legal system must assign to citizens certain rights not to be aggressed against. I argue that this is not so. Typical legal systems certain assign duties of nonaggression; but the criminal branches of those systems do not assign corresponding rights. The civil branches may, but not to an extent that supports Thomson's thesis.

Elsamahi, Mohamed. Could Theoretical Entities Save Realism?. *Proc Phil Sci Ass*, 1, 173-180, 1994.

Hacking and other entity realists suggest a strategy to build scientific realism on a stronger foundation than inference to the best explanation. They argue that if beliefs in the existence of theoretical entities are derived from experimentation rather than theories, they can escape the antirealist's criticism and provide a stronger ground for realism. In this paper, an outline and a critique of entity realism are presented. It will be argued that entity realism cannot stand as a separate position from classical realism. Thus, entity realism cannot avoid the problems facing classical realism.

Elshtain, Jean Bethke. The Family in Trouble: Why We Should Worry. *Nat Forum*, 75(1), 25-28, 32, Wint 95.

Emad, Parvis. Zu Fragen der Interpretation und Entzifferung der Grundlagen der Gesamtausgabe Martin Heideggers. *Heidegger Stud*, 9, 161-171, 1993.

It is the purpose of this paper to reconsider Heidegger's guidelines for the editing of the *Complete Edition (Gesamtausgabe)* of the work in order to reject the criticism recently leveled at this edition. This paper attempts to resent the fundamental connection between the process of editing *and* the ontological core of language in order to establish the thesis that translating a text is claimed by this core in a way which is not the case when editing a text. Considering this claim the recent criticism of the editing of the *Complete Edition* of Heidegger's work proves to be biased and unfounded.

Emanuel, Ezekiel J. Commentary on Discussions About Life-Sustaining Treatments. *J Clin Ethics*, 5(3), 250-252, Fall 94.

Emanuel, Linda. Appropriate and Inappropriate Use of Advance Directives. *J Clin Ethics*, 5(4), 357-359, Wint 94.

Advance directives provide a skilled intervention with defined purposes, but with risks and alternatives. Informed consent by competent patients and appropriate careful use are, therefore, necessary. Toward that end, the major and additional benefits of advance directives have been delineated; three important risks have also been itemized, along with their precautions for each. Patients with borderline competence should be assessed specifically for advance planning competence. Since all patients would do well to have some physician involvement, I support the recommendation that all advance directives be co-signed by a physician whenever possible.

Emanuel, Linda L and Huang, Frederick Y. Physician Aid in Dying and the Relief of Patients' Suffering: Physicians' Attitudes Regarding Patients' Suffering and End-of-Life Decisions. *J Clin Ethics*, 6(1), 62-67, Spr 95.

Emerson, Roger L. "The 'Affair' at Edinburgh and the 'Project' at Glasgow" in *Hume and Hume's Connexions, Stewart, M A (ed)*, 1-22. University Park, Penn St Univ Pr, 1995.

This article attempts to understand Hume's failure to obtain a professorship by looking at the politics of Scottish university appointments and at Hume's "political connexion" 1744-51. It argues that he failed at Edinburgh because his political backers were not strong enough to secure the post and that at Glasgow the Duke of Argyll saw no reason to support a man whose appointment would loco him influence in that city. It ends by saying that Hume's candidacies supposed a man with more religion than Hume appears now to have possessed.

Emery-Hellwig, Eric. Philosophie ouverte de F Gonseth et philosophie analytique. *Dialectica*, 48(2), 143-155, 1994.

L'intention de l'auteur du présent article est de montrer que des liens manifestes peuvent s'établir entre la philosophie de F Gonseth et celle de L Wittgenstein de même que celles de trois penseurs représentatifs de la philosophie dite analytique: J L Austin, W V Quine et J Searle. Il importe en effet de dénoncer certaines mises en opposition fallacieuses et de souligner le bénéfice à tirer d'un dialogue entre le courant de pensée anglo-saxon et celui d'Europe occidentale. En toile de fond, la philosophie du language! On se souviendra à det égard que F Gonseth a sans cesse défendu la thèse qu'un jeu de prêté-rendus s'établit en recherches scientifiques comme en recherches philosophiques sur le front de l'énonciation et sur le front de l'expérimentation. Il en résulte que la mise à l'épreuve de la pertinence du langage ne s'effectue correctement que si l'on prononce un verdict sur le complexe discours-activités. C'est dire l'importance accordée par F Gonseth à l'insertion non seulement des mots, mais de l'expression discursive en sa globalité dans des contextes précisants.

Emrich, H M. Identität und Versprechen. *Fichte-Studien*, 6, 179-193, 1994.

Bezieht man Fichtes Dichotomie von Einheit und Mannigfaltigkeit auf die Gegenwart, so erscheint postmodernes Denken, postmodernes Lebensgefühl als Bejahung der Mannigfaltigkeit, und der Einheitsgedanke wird in die Romantik zurückverwiesen. Wie aber ist unter solchen Bedingungen so etwas wie ein Versprechen sinnvoll möglich? Der Zusammenhang zwischen Identität und Versprechen scheint dabei dem performativen Selbstwidersspruch zu ähneln, den Lütterfelds in Fichtes Konzept der aboluten Einheit dargestellt hat, der aber eben—das ist die Pointe—die Eigenschaft hat, eine realistische Beschreibung der Situation zu sein, in der wir uns vorfinden.

Emson, H E. Rights, Duties, and Limits of Autonomy. *Cambridge Quart Healthcare Ethics*, 4(1), 7-11, Wint 95.

Emson, Harry E. Health, Aging, and Death. *Cambridge Quart Healthcare Ethics*, 4(2), 163-166, Spr 95.

This paper discusses the relationship between the natural aging process of the metazoan human which culminates inevitably in death, the effects of natural aging, and the concept of health as a function of age. If all or a significant proportion of the disadvantageous effects of aging can be prevented, it should be possible for death to occur in a state of health, and the curve of age against health effectively to be squared. The function of health care is not to strive for maximum length of life, but for optimal function characteristic for age.

Enderle, Georges and Murphy, Patrick E. Managerial Ethical Leadership: Examples Do Matter. *Bus Ethics Quart*, 5(1), 117-128, Ja 95.

The central role of corporate leaders in setting the ethical tone for their organization is widely accepted. Four well known former CEOs are profiled to illustrate how their managerial ethical leadership not only influenced their firms but also the practice of business. Insights are drawn from their writings and speeches as well as other sources which examine demonstrated leadership abilities. Their behavior not only provides examples of leadership but also is exemplary from an ethical point of view. The article concludes with five common themes that describe these individuals and the essence of managerial ethical leadership.

Endicott, Ronald P. The Refutation by Analogous Ectoqualia. *S J Phil*, 33(1), 19-30, Spr 95.

Endicott, Timothy A O. Putting Interpretation in its Place. *Law Phil*, 13(4), 451-479, N 94.

What can a philosophical analysis of the concept of interpretation contribute to legal theory? In his recent book, *Interpretation and Legal Theory*, Andrei Marmor proposes a complex and ambitious analysis as groundwork for his positivist assault on "interpretive" theories of law and language. I argue 1) that the crucial element in Marmor's analysis of interpretation is his treatment of Ludwig Wittgenstein's remarks on following rules, and 2) that a less ambitious analysis of interpretation than Marmor's can take better advantage of those insights about rules. I explore some implications of such an analysis for the role of interpretation in legal reasoning.

Engel, J Ronald. "Special Overview: Role of Ethics, Culture, Religion in Conserving Biodiversity" in *Ethics, Religion and Biodiversity, Hamilton, Lawrence S (ed)*, 183-214. Cambridge, White Horse, 1994.

Engel, Pascal. "The Decline and Fall of French Nietzscheo-Structuralism" in *European Philosophy and the American Academy, Smith, Barry (ed)*, 21-41. Peru, Open Court, 1994.

The aim of this paper is to describe a set of dogmas of what I call French Nietzscheo-structuralism (and especially the philosophy of Ailles Deleuze): the attack against truth, knowledge, rationality and other philosophical values. It is argued that none of these attacks succeed and that French Nietzscheo-structuralism is bound to fail on its own terms.

Engel, Pascal. Causalité mentale et niveaux de causalité. *Rev Phil Fr*, 1, 55-69, Ja-Mr 95.

This paper examines the problem of mental causation, and especially the notion of levels of causal explanation. It describes various attempts to solve the problem of the competition between explanatory levels, in particular those using the notion of supervenience, and the model of "program explanation" by Pettit and Jackson. None of them is found satisfactory.

Engelhardt Jr, H Tristram. "Introduction" in *Hegel Reconsidered, Engelhardt Jr, H Tristram (ed)*, 1-18. Dordrecht, Kluwer, 1994.

Hegel has been regarded as a metaphysician. His political works appeared to be devoid of moral claims and to canonize the existing ruling power. It is argued that a nonmetaphysical interpretation of Hegel's argument, following Klaus Hartmann's reassessment of Hegel, secures grounds of significance for Hegel's systematic claims. Hegel is revealed as a philosopher who can help in the rational assessment of ontology and political theory. Hegel's dialectic is an invitation to ontological criticism in which ontological categories are assessed in terms of how categorially understood content can be related and how thought about reality can be consistently understood.

Engelhardt Jr, H Tristram. "Klaus Hartmann and G W F Hegel: A Personal Postscript" in *Hegel Reconsidered, Engelhardt, Jr, H Tristram (ed)*, 225-229. Dordrecht, Kluwer, 1994.

There is a sense, felt by some, that the intellectual life of the academy is weakening. If the academic intellectual life is to be sustained, it will only be secured by individuals who imbue students with the excitement of ideas and the importance of serious scholarly investigation. The intellectual life need not be solitary, rather, fellowship in the sharing and exploration of ideas makes the life of the mind manifestly pleasurable. Klaus Hartmann's resonance between Hegel on the one hand and his students on the other yielded intellectual probity in the realm and relationship of ideas.

Engelhardt Jr, H Tristram. "Sittlichkeit and Post-Modernity" in *Hegel Reconsidered, Engelhardt, Jr, H Tristram (ed)*, 211-224. Dordrecht, Kluwer, 1994.

Hegel's development of the concept of Sittlichkeit and his criticism of Kant acknowledge that content-full morality is provided only in particular communities and thus disclose the roots of the post-modern predicament. Hegel offers an escape from the cacophony of moral visions through an account of objective moral volition in the state. Rather than supporting an argument for authoritarianism, Hegel's architectonic supports a categorial justification of a political unity. Thus the state, as a limited democracy, is the unity of a morally pluralistic society it overcomes moral pluralism in a higher level outcome which does not itself require further moral content.

Engelhardt Jr, H Tristram. Moral Content, Tradition, and Grace: Rethinking the Possibility of a Christian Bioethics. *Christian Bioethics*, 1(1), 29-47, Mr 95.

Birth, suffering, disability, disease and death were by medicine's successes placed within a context of seemingly novel challenges that cried out for new responses. Secular bioethics rose in response to the demands of these new biomedical technologies in the context of a culture fragmented in moral pluralism. While secular bioethics promised to unite persons separated by diverse religious and moral assumption, this is a promise that could not be fulfilled. Reason alone cannot provide canonical, content-full moral guidance or justify a moral community capable of binding all persons. Christian bioethics, as part of a way of life embedded in authentic worship, offers content, meaning and understanding where secular bioethics has failed. For Christians, resolution of bioethical controversies will not be found through appeals to foundational rational arguments or isolated scriptural quotations, but only in a Christan community united in authentic faith.

Engelhardt Jr, H Tristram. Towards a Christian Bioethics. *Christian Bioethics*, 1(1), 1-10, Mr 95.

Rather than revealing itself as a single, unified, ecumenical faith, Christianity is sundered with Christians united neither in one communion nor in one baptism. *Christian Bioethics* seeks to examine the traditional content-full moral commitments which the Christian faiths bring to life, sexuality, suffering, illness and death within the contexts of medicine and health care. Seeking to understand the differences which separate the bioethics of Roman Catholics, Protestants and the Orthodox, *Christian Bioethics* explores the manners in which the faiths diverge. The failure of the Enlightenment project to disclose a content-full communality that would bind mankind has left much to be reconsidered by Christians who face new ethical dilemmas in the novel guise of advances in health care technologies.

Engelhardt Jr, H Tristram (ed) and Pinkard, Terry (ed). *Hegel Reconsidered*. Dordrecht, Kluwer, 1994.

Hegel's thought influenced much of contemporary political theory, social thought and philosophy. Described as both a metaphysician and a narrator whose irony anticipated philosophy after metaphysics, Hegel has been characterized as both a defender of freedom and an enemy of the liberal state. This volume reassesses Hegel's work, building on the thought of Klaus Hartmann, and goes beyond considerations of metaphysics and the authoritarian state. It explores a nonmetaphysical reading of Hegel's philosophy and shows how Hegel's thought supports a liberal democratic state. This volume provides a basis for utilizing Hegel's work in the reassessment of ontology, aesthetics and revolution.

Engelmann, Peter. *Philosophie und Totalitarismus: Zur Kritik dialektischer Diskursivität Eine Hegellektüre*. Vienna, Passagen, 1990.

Wenn es uns um den *Widerstand* gegen totalitäre Gesellschaftsformen geht, müssen wir das Verhältnis von Philosophie und Totalitarismus auch über den Fall Heideggers hinaus untersuchen. In detaillierten Analysen des Anfangs der *Phänomenologie des Geistes* und der *Einleitungen* fragt Engelmann im vorliegenden Buch deshalb nach der Geltung des Heterogenen im Rahmen der systematischen Fassung der neuzeitlichen Philosophei durch Hegel. Einerseits erweist sich dabei Hegels Korrektur des neuzeitlichen Ansatzes als Versuch, dessen Ziele zu realisieren. Andererseits führt die Lektüre der *Einleitungen* zu der überraschenden Erkenntnis, dass der Hegelsche Text seine systematische Strategie selbst wieder durchkreuzt. (edited)

Engelmann, Peter (ed) and Mitterer, Josef. *Das Jenseits der Philosophie: Wider das dualistische Erkenntnisprinzip*. Vienna, Passagen, 1992.

Der Autor kritisiert das dualistische Erkenntnisprinzip im Rahmen einer nichtdualisierenden Argumentationsweise, die ein Jenseits des Diskurses als Diskursregulativ und Erkenntnisziel weder voraussetzt noch hervorbringt. (edited)

English, Parker. Preferential Hiring and Just War Theory. *J Soc Phil*, 25(2), 119-138, Fall 94.

Section one of this paper discusses two classic criticisms of preferential hiring, that it fails to compensate those who deserve it most (older African-Americans) and that those who bear most of its costs (younger whites) deserve these costs less than do older whites. Section two uses just war theory to explicate these criticisms. Section three shows how typical forms of preferential hiring can be modified to meet these criticisms. Section four discusses this modified form of preferential hiring.

English, Parker and Hamme, Nancy Steele. "Morality, Art, and African Philosophy: A Response to Wiredu" in *African Philosophy: Selected Readings, Mosley, Albert G (ed)*, 407-420. Englewood Cliffs, Prentice Hall, 1995.

This work discusses Kwasi Wiredu's claim that traditional Akan moral thought is less supernaturalistically authoritarian than is contemporary Western moral thought. We recognize that no written records of the traditional Akan exist with which to examine this claim. Instead, we focus on the preserved record found in the art artifacts and associated legends produced by traditional Akan societies, and then demonstrated that these societies were substantially authoritarian because of their supernaturalistic beliefs. We also endorse Wiredu's more general suggestion that traditional African moral thought be compared with traditional Western moral thought while contemporary African moral thought be compared with contemporary Western moral thought.

Engstler, Achim. Urteilsenthaltung und Glück: Eine Verteidigung ethisch motivierter Skepsis. *Z Phil Forsch*, 49(2), 194-219, Ap-Je 95.

Can the pyrrhonian sceptic act? And can he act according to the laws and customs of his nation? The aim of this paper is to point out that there is a strategy for the pyrrhonian sceptic to show his ability to act correctly, while preserving his *epoché*. In developing this argument, recent approaches to the problem (Burnyeat, Frede, Hossenfelder) are discussed.

Engström, Timothy H. Accounting for Ethics: Where Does Ethics Fit into Accounting Theory and Accounting Practice?. *Bus Prof Ethics J*, 13(1-2), 41-55, Spr-Sum 94.

Ennis, Robert H and Wheary, Jennifer. Gender Bias in Critical Thinking: Continuing the Dialogue. *Educ Theor*, 45(2), 213-224, Spr 95.

This paper reviews three sorts of claims that current conceptions of critical thinking reflect a male bias. The types discussed are 1) discrimination against females in educational settings where critical thinking is taught or observed; 2) neglect of females in research about thinking; and 3) an emphasis on typically male characteristics (such as rationality, judgment, and guidance by a set of universal principles) over typically female characteristics (such as emotion, attention to contextuality, a link between self and object, caring, and personal voice). The paper seeks to initiate dialogue about these claims by discussing: 1) their meaning, 2) their implications for conceptions of critical thinking and for critical thinking instruction, and 3) ways in which the claims need to be clarified or amended in order to be more helpful to those working in the area of critical thinking.

Enskat, Rainer. "Kausalitätsdiagnosen" in *Naturauffassungen in Philosophie, Wissenschaft, Technik: Band III, Schäfer, Lothar (ed)*, 149-223. Freiburg, Alber, 1995.

Epple, Moritz. Karl Marx und die soziale Wirklichkeit. *Z Phil Forsch*, 48(4), 518-542, 1994.

Epstein, Barbara. "Postwar Panics and the Crisis of Masculinity" in *Marxism in the Postmodern Age, Callari, Antonio (ed)*, 246-255. New York, Guilford, 1994.

Epstein, Jonathan S and Epstein, Margarete J. "Fatal Forms: Toward a (Neo) Formal Sociological Theory of Media Culture" in *Baudrillard: A Critical Reader, Kellner, Douglas M (ed)*, 135-149. Cambridge, Blackwell, 1994.

The purpose of this text is to offer the beginnings of a formal sociological theory of the mass media. It is contended throughout this paper that two of the most frequently debated theories of the media, that of Marshall McLuhan and that of Jean Baudrillard, can be understood as operating within the framework of philosopher Georg Simmel's formal sociology. In order to make this argument, we will first outline Simmel's formal sociology, demonstrate its presence in the work of McLuhan, and then present its extension, through McLuhan, into the work of Baudrillard. When understood in light of formal sociology, both McLuhan and Baudrillard have significant contributions to make to the sociology of culture. Baudrillard, in particular, offers a radical formal sociology that defines the shift into the postmodern at the fin de siecle.

Epstein, Margarete J and Epstein, Jonathan S. "Fatal Forms: Toward a (Neo) Formal Sociological Theory of Media Culture" in *Baudrillard: A Critical Reader, Kellner, Douglas M (ed)*, 135-149. Cambridge, Blackwell, 1994.

The purpose of this text is to offer the beginnings of a formal sociological theory of the mass media. It is contended throughout this paper that two of the most frequently debated theories of the media, that of Marshall McLuhan and that of Jean Baudrillard, can be understood as operating within the framework of philosopher Georg Simmel's formal sociology. In order to make this argument, we will first outline Simmel's formal sociology, demonstrate its presence in the work of McLuhan, and then present its extension, through McLuhan, into the work of Baudrillard. When understood in light of formal sociology, both McLuhan and Baudrillard have significant contributions to make to the sociology of culture. Baudrillard, in particular, offers a radical formal sociology that defines the shift into the postmodern at the fin de siecle.

Erbrich, Paul. Zur Konsistenz des soziobiologischen Begriffs "egoistisches Gen". *Theol Phil*, 70(1), 78-91, 1995.

Modern genetics don't look at the organism as a whole, but only as a mosaic of traits ("anti-essentialism" according to Ernst Mayr). From this it follows ultimately that genes are seeking goals, not organisms. Genes are pursuing their own replication by means of organisms which they have built for this purpose ("egoistic" genes according to Richard Dawkins). This article shows that, if we do no longer consider genes as mere passive carriers of information or programmes, we will end up in a kind of "animism of genes". To replace the "egoistic" genes by the "own" genes of an idividual in opposition of "their" genes (of relatives of that individual in the sense given by William Hamilton) is no way out.

Erdelyi, Agnes. *Max Weber in Amerika: Wirkungsgeschichte und Rezeptionsgeschichte Webers in der anglo-amerikanischen Philosophie und Sozialwissenschaft*. Vienna, Passagen, 1992.

Die Wirkungsgeschichte der Weberschen Ideen in den englisch sprechenden Ländern fing in einer politisch und intellektuell äusserst ungünstigen Situation an, in der alles verdächtig war, was mit deutschen Ideen, deutscher Philosophie assoziiert wurde. Der erste Teil des vorliegenden Buches untersucht daher wie die Weberschen Ideen aus ihrer eigenen, deutschen philosophischen Tradition herausgehoben wirkten und im Kontext der anglo-amerikanischen Philosophie interpretiert wurden. Der zweite Teil bietet einen historischen Überblick über die Rezeptionsgeschichte von dem Moment an, da Weber Amerika besuchte bis zu den letzten Entwicklungen der neoweberianischen historischen Soziologie in den späten 80er Jahren.

Ereshefsky, Marc. Critical Notice of John Duprè The Disorder of Things: Metaphysical Foundations of the Disunity of Science. *Can J Phil*, 25(1), 143-158, Mr 95.

Erev, Anan and Balaban, Oded. *The Bounds of Freedom: About the Eastern and Western Approaches to Freedom*. New York, Lang, 1995.

This is an attempt to systematize different concepts of freedom in reference to the figures of Zeus, Prometheus, and Epimetheus in the Protagoras myth. Prometheus represents the freedom of purposeful production; Zeus, freedom as moral self-determination; and Epimetheus, freedom in the sense of spontaneously giving way to one's desires and needs. It is within the context and on the basis of this conception that the aim is put forward of arriving at a complementary synthesis, by way of intensive communication, between the positions represented by Zeus, Prometheus, and Epimetheus. Such a synthesis would assist the East in overcoming deficiency and want, and the West in guarding against the excesses that derive from the Promethean outlook.

Erickson, Frederick. The Music Goes Round and Round: How Music Means in School. *Educ Theor*, 45(1), 19-34, Wint 95.

Erickson, Glenn and Fossa, John. O Número Nupcial no Livro VIII da República. *Cad Hist Filosof Cie*, 4(1), 9-23, Ja-Je 94.

A new interpretation of Plato's nuptial number (geometrical number), which is described in Book VIII of the Republic, is described herein. The geometric figure corresponding to the nuptial number is reconstructed. The figure is a Pythagorean triangle, that is, a triangle whose sides are in the proportion 3:4:5; the triangle is partioned into various similar triangles. The perimeters of the triangle determine those periods in which human reproduction will result in a man of gold, a man of silver, or a man of bronze and iron.

Erickson, Stephen A. No Longer, Not Yet: Reading History Grammatically. *Man World*, 28(1), 83-99, Ja 95.

Erickson, Stephen A. The Image of Socrates in the Mirror of Jaspers. *Phil Today*, 38(3-4), 285-293, Fall 94.

Eriksson, Gunnar. "Der faustische Mensch—Die Wissenschaft als euripäisches Erbe" in *Das geistige Erbe Europas, Buhr, Manfred (ed)*, 585-594. Napoli, Vivarium, 1994.

Erjavec, Ales. Postmodernism and the Artistic Avant-gardes. *Magyar Filozof Szemle*, 5-6, 749-758, 1994.

In the period after the World War II the so-called neo-avant-gardes used procedures started and advanced by the historical artistic avant-gardes. The works from the fifties, sixties and even seventies in many ways resounded the ways of the twenties and thirties. One also should not forget that many movements, considered to be avant-garde, continued from the before the war period, especially surrealism and expressionism. Also, other prewar avant-gardes survived, although in a marginal way: Italian futurism is still being executed in Italy under that name and the same goes for French surrealism, among others. With the advent of postmodernism it seemed that the period of the avant-gardes was over. (edited)

Ernest, Paul. The Nature of Mathematics: Towards a Social Constructivist Account. *Epistemologia*, 17(2), 179-196, Ju-De 94.

Two dichotomies in the philosophy of mathematics are discussed: the prescriptive-descriptive distinction, and the process-product distinction. By focusing on prescriptive matters, and on mathematics as a product, standard philosophy of mathematics has overlooked legitimate and pedagogically rewarding questions that highlight mathematics as a process of knowing which has social dimensions. In contrast the social-constructivist view introduced here can affect the aims, content, teaching approaches, implicit values, and assessment of the mathematics curriculum, and above all else, the beliefs and practices of the mathematics teacher.

Erpenbeck, John. "Wissenschaft und Technik aus paneuropäischer Sicht" in *Das geistige Erbe Europas*, Buhr, Manfred (ed), 717-729. Napoli, Vivarium, 1994.

Erwin, Edward. "The Placebo Concept in Medicine and Psychiatry" in *Philosophical Psychopathology*, Graham, George (ed), 261-284. Cambridge, MIT Pr, 1993.

Escobar, Santiago. Abu Bakr Al-Razi: Un Filósofo de una Antiguedad Tardía. *Rev Espan Filosof Med*, 0, 57-60, 1993.

This article is devoted to a brief analysis of the original mood of Abu Bakr Al-Razi's philosophic work—phisik Rhazes for the Latins—showing how his eclecticism and strong rationalism detrives in last terms from the most varied ancient origins (as well Greco-Roman as Iranian) and how, being already a philosoph living in a Muslim society, his devotion and attitude still in a great part so features characteristics of the antiquity. Undoubtfully, the same as happens with some Architectonic manifestations, he is a philosoph of transition between the ancient and the new philosophy.

Escobar Chico, Angel. Sobre la Fortuna de Aristóteles en España. *Rev Espan Filosof Med*, 1, 141-148, 1994.

The aim of this paper is to study from a methodological point of view the different ways to inquire into the manuscript and printed tradition of the *Corpus Aristotelicum* in Spain, as well as the influence of this legacy (philosophy, science and literature) on the cultural production of this country during the Middle Ages and the Renaissance.

Escudero, Miguel. El jardín de la ciencia. *Convivium*, 5, 121-124, 1993.

Creativity requires owning both ideas and imagination. Thus, it is worth finding out how they can be promoted. Science history registers countless examples of fruitful grafts obtained by means of apparently different ideas and results. Around that, this note considers several points of view of some living scientists.

Espagne, Michel. Die Rezeption der politischen Philosophie Fichtes in Frankreich. *Fichte-Studien*, 2, 193-222, 1990.

Fichtes Werk gehört zu den ausländischen Geistesprodukten, an denen sich im Frankreich des 19. Jahrhunderts das Selbstverständnis der französischen Geisteswissenschaften konstituiert. Dies hat bestimmt damit zu tun, dass Fichte einerseits das grundlegende Ereignis der modernen französischen Geschichte, die französische Revolution, interpretierte und billigte, andererseits den nationalistischen Konsequenzen der Revolution Einhalt gebieten wollte, und schliesslich durch seine rein philosophischen Schriften das ersehnte Pendant zur französischen Tat zu verkörpern schien. (edited)

Esquirol, Josep M. Sobre la cuestión del método en el debate Modernidad-Postmodernidad. *Convivium*, 5, 125-131, 1993.

We would like to indicate the different role assigned to the method by the modern philosophy and by the postmodern philosophy. In the first one, it was the most important question, but, now, in the second one, it is of secondary nature. In this writing we argue the optimality of the *methodological pluralism* and, so, of the convenience of reviewing, on the one hand, the modern tendency to make absolute one method and, on the other hand, the postmodern rejection of the method and the fundamental.

Esquith, Stephen L. *Intimacy and Spectacle: Liberal Theory as Political Education*. Ithaca, Cornell Univ Pr, 1994.

This interpretation of liberal theory has two parts. The first is critical: liberal theory has played an active but neglected role in the making of liberal citizens into clients and consumers and the evolution of power into expert authority in liberal societies. The second goal is more prospective. Through an Emersonian reading of power I describe how a more democratic political theory can disrupt both the intimacy of professional-client relations and the consumption of political spectacles. The argument against liberal theory as political education concentrates primarily on the work of John Stuart Mill and John Rawls.

Ess, Charles M and Gulick, Walter B. Kant and Analogy: Categories as Analogical Equivocals. *Ultim Real Mean*, 17(2), 89-99, Ju 94.

Kant's critical philosophy is hobbled by a charge of contradiction regarding his central notion of the thing-in-itself. Textual analysis shows, however, that Kant's use of the categories—including the fundamental category of causality—intentionally takes up analogical predication to allow for a primary meaning of the category to refer phenomena, while a secondary meaning refers to the relationship between things-in-themselves and phenomena. This use of analogical predication preempts the familiar charge of contradiction and allows Kant to speak coherently of the things-in-themselves, including human freedom and (the idea of) God.

Esser, Piet H. Facts and Truth. *Method Sci*, 27(4), 197-208, 1994.

Esser, Piet Hein. How to Know the Inner-Self?. *Method Sci*, 26(4), 161-169, 1993.

The purpose is to write on Kierkegaard's view of life, e.g., to show the necessity to make a choice. Liberalism annihilates the inner-self. One should be a riddle to others and to one self. There is but one, man should be afraid of: God. Impressions of childhhood you never forget, they are extremely important, God has only one passion: to love and wanting to be loved. Kierkegaard's spheres of existence are the esthetic, ethics, and religion with two confines: irony and humor.

Esser, Piet Hein. Philosophy in Biology. *Method Sci*, 27(1), 1-11, 1994.

The purpose of this paper is how to study nature. In 1831 Robert Brown discovered a *nucleus* in the cellular juice of the orchid. Structure and function of cells are studied by *microscopes*. The nucleus is, except for bacteria, bounded by a membrane. In plants *cellulose* is characteristic. It does not affect permeability. Membranes are useful for the synthesis of steroids including hormones. Korzybski found reality structured and discovered the electro-colloidal character of our nervous system. Humanity is time-binding. He has a choice, which animals lack. Szondi's and Nietzsche's work are mentioned. To kill cancer-cells a temperature higher than 41 degrees C is needed.

Esterbauer, Reinhold. *Transzendenz-"Relation": Zum Transzendenzbezug in der Philosophie Emmanuel Levinas'*. Vienna, Passagen, 1992.

Das Buch stellt die Levinas'sche Konzeption des ethischen "Gegenüber" von Anderem beziehungsweise Gott und Ich als "Un-Bezug" vor, der mit herkömmlichen Auffassungen von Relation nicht beschreibbar ist. Es erweist sich vielmehr eine neue Sprache als erforderlich, um auszusagen, sie sich der Andere in seinem Angesicht zum Ich verhält. In der Auseinandersetzung mit diesem Denken werden das Zukunftsweisende, aber auch die Probleme des Levinas'schen Ansatzes nachgezeichnet und zur Diskussion gestellt. (edited)

Étienne, Alexandre. Une autre vision de la philosophie médiévale. *Rev Theol Phil*, 126(3), 253-262, 1994.

L'*Introduction à la philosophie médiévale* de K Flasch nous ouvre à la philosophie du Moyen Age par le biais de conflits marquants qui opposèrent philosophes et théologiens de ce temps. C'est l'oeuvre d'un médiéviste qui a pu, par sa longue pratique des textes, se libérer d'une conception trop monolithique de la pensée médiévale. En refusant de juger celle-ci à la lumière d'un seul philosophe, l'A propose une vision de la philosophie médiévale différente et respectueuse de la variété des positions défendues. De plus, en représentant la philosophie à son lieu de naissance, l'A adopte une perspective qui, malgré un caractère très personnel, gagne en précision historique.

Etter, Brian K. The Sounds of the Ideal: Hegel's Aesthetic of Music. *Owl Minerva*, 26(1), 47-58, Fall 94.

This article reexamines Hegel's aesthetic of music, seeking to demonstrate that it did conform to the general understanding of musical practice in the nineteenth century, and that if formed a coherent part of Hegel's larger system of aesthetics. Since by his day music was commonly regarded as expressive, with a clearly developed language of expressive gestures, Hegel's emphasis on expression was not misplaced. Therefore, it was possible for him to show that music was indeed capable of expressing the ideal of human character in the ordering of feeling. Such an understanding necessarily challenges the modern, ahistorical ways of understanding music.

Etxebarria, I (& others). Design and Evaluation of a Programme to Promote Prosocial-Altruistic Behaviour in the School. *J Moral Educ*, 23(4), 409-425, 1994.

This article describes a programme of educational intervention aimed at the development of prosocial-altruistic behaviour, and presents a study which evaluated its efficacy. The sample comprised 110 subjects, aged between 10 and 12 years, from four class-groups. The intervention, which consisted of a series of activities intended to encourage empathy, perspective-taking, having the concept of a person, and co-operation, was carried out by the teacher-tutor of each group in 15 weekly sessions. The pre-test/post-test comparisons showed a significant increase in prosocial-altruistic behaviour (measured by a sociogram on "Consoling and Defending" behaviour and a questionnaire on Prosocial behaviour), as well as an improvement in the capacity for perspective-taking and in the climate in the classroom.

Euler, Werner and Stiening, Gideon. "...und nie der Pluralität widersprach"? Zur Bedeutung von Immanuel Kants Amtsgeschäften. *Kantstudien*, 86(1), 54-69, 1995.

Usually in philosophic-historical research Kant's official business at the University of Königsberg is described as being of less importance in relation either to his biography or to his scientific work. In contrast to this prepossession it's designed a new portrait of Kant that shows, how he was acting for some periods of universitary administration: he didn't deny responsibility, labour and democratic exposition in this context, concerning a great variety of universitary, cultural and political aspects; on the contrary he constructively made replies to the most important questions that had to be discussed and decided by the committees of the Albertina. Kant did not only influence his colleagues with innovative ideas but also produced plurality in the republic of letters that protected the autonomy of university and science against the authorities of the Prussian state. The thesis is demonstrated by help of unknown archival materials about the history of the University of Königsberg, recently discovered and explored in archives of Germany and Poland.

Evangeliou, Christos. On Western Rationality and Its Alleged Relation to Aristotle. *J Indian Counc Phil Res*, 12(1), 49-77, S-D 94.

It has been recently argued by philosophers and sociologists that the roots of the "myth" that rationality is a characteristic unique to "Western society" go back to Aristotle who has, thus, been turned into a champion of Western rationalism and Imperialism. Concurring with the "diagnosis" that the Western rationalistic picture of Aristotle's philosophy is incomplete, I suggest that, like all good Platonists, Aristotle is convinced that the love of wisdom, working slowly upon the life of the ascending philosopher, can bring in contact what is divine in us (*nous*) and God (*Nous*). Thus Aristotle's "road to enlightenment" bridges the East/West gap.

Evans, C Stephen. Critical Historical Judgment and Biblical Faith. *Faith Phil*, 11(2), 184-206, Ap 94.

Hans Frei has argued that the gospels contain "realistic narrative" that is "history-like" even if not historical. Many would regard the historicity of the narrative as dubious because of the miraculous and supernatural elements contained within it. I argue that the reasons commonly given for rejecting miracles and the supernatural by Troeltsch and Harvey are weak. The principles of critical historiography they advance gain their plausibility from a platitudinous reading, but the principles only cut against miracles and the supernatural when they are read in a less-plausible manner that presupposes dubious and controversial naturalistic assumptions. One should not reject the historicity of the gospel narratives simply because of miraculous and supernatural elements.

Evans, Fred. Technology as Art and the "Spheres of Freedom and Necessity". *Res Phil Technol*, 14, 219-234, 1994.

I argue that work is a form of communication (of Bakhtinian dialogism) as well as a means to produce goods and to reproduce society. This implies that we should repudiate Marx's (and also Habermas's and Gorz's) sharp distinction between a "sphere of freedom" (the political realm) and a "sphere of necessity" (the realm of immediate production) and instead develop what Marx indicates more generally: that a nonalienated or free society must be democratic and should produce in the creative manner usually associated with artistic endeavors. I illustrate this communicative and artistic dimension of production in terms of Zuboff's distinction between "automating" and "informating" strategies in relation to the new information technologies.

Evans, J Claude. "The Rigors of Deconstruction" in *European Philosophy and the American Academy, Smith, Barry (ed)*, 81-98. Peru, Open Court, 1994.

Evans, Katherine C and Teichman, Jenny. *Philosophy: A Beginner's Guide (Second Edition)*. Cambridge, Blackwell, 1995.

Everson, Stephen. "Psychology" in *The Cambridge Companion to Aristotle, Barnes, Jonathan (ed)*, 168-194. New York, Cambridge Univ Pr, 1995.

Evola, Julius. *The Hermetic Tradition: Symbols and Teachings of the Royal Art*. Rochester, Inner Traditions, 1995.

Ewin, R E. Can There Be a Right to Secede?. *Philosophy*, 70(273), 341-362, Jl 95.

This paper argues that a right to secede could apply only in the least interesting cases, viz. a state seceding in recognized fashion from a federation. What secedes us *a* people, not people; what exercises a right must be capable of a unitary will and decision; the people that has a right must, therefore, already be organized as an artificial person.

Ewin, R E. Institutional Excuses and Neutrality. *Int J Applied Phil*, 9(2), 67-75, Wint-Spr 95.

The lawyer's justification for helping the person charged with wrongdoing is simply reference to the function of lawyers. David Luban (in *Lawyers and Justice*) argues that this sort of institutional excuse works only if the institution in question (e.g., the adversarial legal system) itself produces sufficient good. This paper argues that it is sufficient if the institution provides a neutral way of resolving the dispute at issue.

Ewin, R E. Peoples and Secession. *J Applied Phil*, 11(2), 225-231, 1994.

Kai Nielsen (*Secession: The Case of Quebec*, Journal of Applied Philosophy, Volume 10, No 1), as did Allen Buchanan in *Secession* (Boulder: Westview Press, 1991), discusses secession on an analogy with no-fault divorce. Both these writers fail to distinguish between what it is to be a person and what it is to be a people, where peoples are the items that secede. The issue of what constitutes a people is thus crucial to the theory of secession (for similar reasons to those that made it crucial to seventeenth century debate about the right of resistance to the monarch). It is also the case that what makes a group of persons a people is often the fact that they are a particular racial group that has suffered unfair discrimination from the prevailing government or that they came to live where they do live by virtue of incidents that affect the justice of their relations with that government. Issues of justice thus enter the matter of the people's identity in a way that rules out the justifiability of unilateral no-fault secession.

Exdell, John B. Feminism, Fundamentalism, and Liberal Legitimacy. *Can J Phil*, 24(3), 441-463, S 94.

The aim of this essay is to determine whether John Rawl's *Political Liberalism* provides the foundation for a feminist critique of the traditional family, or whether it offers accomodation with the anti-feminist understanding of the religious right. In his discussion of the boundaries between the public and the personal Rawl's theory is systematically indecisive between these alternatives. However, the potential for incorporating feminist insights into liberal philosophy is finally negated by Rawl's doctrine of "public reason". Political liberalism, he says, does not admit controversial social theory into the deliberations concluding the constitutional contract, or into subsequent public political debates about issues of basic justice. On this basis political liberalism would exclude the divisive idea that the gendered division of labor within the family is a primary cause of social and political inequality between men and women.

Exteberria, A and Merelo, J J and Moreno, A. Studying Organisms with Basic Cognitive Capacities in Artificial Worlds. *Commun Cog—AI*, 11(1-2), 31-53, 1994.

In this paper we pose the problem of how to study basic cognitive processes in the frame of simulations of artificial worlds of the style of Artificial Life. The main difficulty of simulating biologically grounded cognitive processes lies in the search for forms of organisms suitable to establish functional relationships with their environments and co-evolve with them. In order to attempt this, we study the properties of autonomous systems at different degrees of complexity and the origin of cognitive processes as a sophistication of primitive sensori-motor loops of living systems. (edited)

Eysenck, H J. How We Acquire a Sense of Morality. *Crim Just Ethics*, 13(2), 53-60, Sum-Fall 94.

Experimental evidence supports the theory that (1) socialized behaviour is maintained largely by a person's "conscience". (2) Conscience is the product of Pavlovian conditioning. (3) Individuals differ genetically with respect to conditionability. (4) Personality is correlated with conditionability, and also with criminality and anti-social conduct generally. (5) Criminality has been shown to be strongly determined by genetic factors, presumably through personality and conditionability, themselves strongly determined by heredity. This theory accounts for differences in morality, in conjunction with environmental factors, i.e., conditioning experiences.

Ezrahi, Yaron. "Science and the Civic Spirit of Liberal Democracy" in *Civil Religion and Political Theology, Rouner, Leroy S (ed)*, 59-75. Notre Dame, Univ Notre Dame Pr, 1986.

Faas, Horacio. "Verdad, Lógica y Bivalencia" in *Temas Actuales de Filosofía, Palacios, María Julia (ed)*, 165-171. Buenos Aires, Univ Nacional Salta, 1993.

From the standpoint that every finite valued truth-functionally complete logic may be represented as a lattice with implication as the ordering relation, this paper shows how to get the usual rules of inference of a system of logic, e.g., the natural deduction cues; and discusses the purported preeminence of two-valued logic.

Fabris, Adriano. Pensare la religione: Modelli di filosofia della religione a confronto. *Teoria*, 14(1), 81-92, 1994.

The essay discusses four books (J Greisch, ed, *Penser la religion*; J F Courtine, ed, *Phénoménologie et théologie*; B Casper/W Sparn, eds, *Alltag und Transzendenz*; R D Geivett/B Sweetmen, eds, *Contemporary Perspectives on Religious Epistemology*) and describes three patterns of philosophy of religion: phenomenological, hermeneutical and analytical philosophy of religion. Finally the work outlines a new method for this discipline (the author is writing a handbook of philosophy of religion, forthcoming by Laterza Publishers, Rome).

Factor, Regis A and Turner, Stephen P. The Disappearance of Tradition in Weber. *Midwest Stud Phil*, 15, 400-424, 1990.

Late nineteenth century thinkers like Durkheim and Tönnies had the idea that morality was a societal force that impinged on individuals but was experienced as conscience or a sense of obligation. The idea is not found in Weber, who was an individualist. But it is instructive to ask what Weber did with the phenomena that these thinkers took to prove the insufficiency of individualism. The answer is to be found in Weber's classification of action. The phenomena are divided up, and each is explained under different individualist headings, such as habit, but in such a way that nothing remains.

Faes, Hubert. L'esclave, le travail et l'action: Aristote et Hegel. *Arch Phil*, 58(1), 97-121, Ja-Mr 95.

Even if Hegel had no intention of constructing a social or a political theory in the fourth section of *The Phenomenology of the Spirit*, a comparison of the famous dialectic between the master and the slave with the beginning of Aristotle's *Politics* allows one to see the modern specificity of the Hegelian conception of work and action. First of all, it supposes a relationship not of natural belonging but rather a relationship of recognition. It understands work not as the operation of the slave within the context of the activity of the master but rather as an entirely distinct action which permits the subject to produce him/herself in objectivity and to express him/herself as a subject. The question remains as to whether this conception of action, so important for modernity, remains satisfactory today.

Fagin, Ronald (& others). *Reasoning about Knowledge*. Cambridge, MIT Pr, 1995.

Reasoning About Knowledge is the first book to provide a general discussion of approaches to reasoning about knowledge and its applications to distributed systems, artificial intelligence, and game theory. It brings ten years of work by the authors into a cohesive framework for understanding and analyzing reasoning about knowledge that is intuitive, mathematically well founded, useful in practice, and widely applicable. The book is self-contained and should be accessible to readers in a variety of disciplines, including computer science, artificial intelligence, linguistics, philosophy, cognitive science, and game theory. Each chapter includes exercises and bibliographic notes.

Fagnot, Dominique (trans) and Gödel, Kurt and Heinzmann, Gerhard (trans). Les Mathématiques Sont-Elles une Syntaxe du Langage?. *Dialogue (Canada)*, 34(1), 3-34, Wint 95.

Fairfield, Paul. Habermas, Kohlberg, and the Myth of Expertise. *Eidos*, 11(1-2), 77-91, Je-D 93.

This paper concerns Jürgen Habermas's recruitment of Lawrence Kohlberg's moral developmental psychology as a key element in his reconstruction of the foundations of critical theory. Situating this discussion within the context of the debate between critical theory and philosophical hermeneutics, I address the question of whether Habermas's turn toward moral psychology renders critical theory less vulnerable to the criticisms advanced against Habermas by Hans-Georg Gadamer. I argue that Habermas's Kohlbergian turn renders his project still more vulnerable to the series of objections which Gadamer advanced, and that the reconstruction of historical materialism inadvertently rehabilitates the myth of moral expertise.

Faitak, Joseph A. Theoretical Limitlessness in War. *Dialogue (PST)*, 37(1), 25-34, O 94.

I argue that the conduct of (waging of) war and the conduct in war are interdependent. I also examine the notion of total war by Carl von Clausewitz and its bearing on morality in war. This analysis is then applied to historical facts of World War II to suggest that WWII was unjustly fought by both the Axis and Allied powers.

Faith, Karlene. "Resistance: Lessons from Foucault and Feminism" in *Power/Gender, Radtke, H Lorraine (ed)*, 36-66. Newbury Park, Sage, 1994.

This essay juxtaposes the work of Michel Foucault with processes of feminist resistances—as a forging of ethical and political challenges. The links between resistance and power are examined vis-à-vis marginalization; individuality and collectivity; exclusion; power relations; the state and rights discourse; the idea of truth; and the female body as a strategic site of power and resistance.

Fajkus, Bretislav. Ontology Today. *Filozof Cas*, 42(4), 647-651, 1994.

Fales, Evan. Are Christians Obliged to Be Pacifists?. *Faith Phil*, 11(2), 298-301, Ap 94.

This note contributes to an exchange between J Kellenberger and S Bringsjord over whether a religiously based ethics is committed to pacifism. I argue that Bringsjord's objection to Kellenberger's defense of pacifism is misplaced. I them briefly examine the scriptural basis for Christian pacifism.

Falk, Arthur. Essay on Nature's Semeiosis. *J Phil Res*, 20, 297-348, 1995.

In this two-part essay I develop a theory of natural signs. Since even primordial signs signify values, in the first part I develop the theory's valuative aspect. Goods are as primary in nature as facts are, and together facts and values generate semeiosis in all life without excess extrapolation from human psychology. To ward off over-extrapolating on values, I defend a major discontinuity between man and nature on the goods of ethics. In the essay's second part I develop the semeiotic dimensions of the negative feedback model of purposive systems. I provide tests for the truth and falsity of the primitive representations in these systems. I account for the holism of representational systems of their nonextensionality, and I define functions. I solve this important definitional problem by inverting the usual mode of thinking: Functions I defend this theory's way of understanding the continuity between human beings and the rest of living nature against several criticisms.

Falk, Arthur. Wisdom Updated. *Phil Sci*, 62(3), 389-403, S 95.

Given the personalist's latitudinarian conception of rationality, what is progress toward wisdom? An answer is in C I Lewis's concept of the "congruence" of propositions, propositions so related that the antecedent probability of any one of them will be increased if the remainder can be assumed. This effect can be modelled in the probability calculus with due attention to the temporal sequencing of our learning of contingent propositions without ever becoming certain of them, as Jeffrey proposes. A diachronic bootstrapping effect is obtained for Ockham's razor and premises of arguments about a god's existence. As a theory's probability rises with increased evidence, the probability of our earlier evidence rises too.

Falkenberg, Loren and Herremans, Irene. Ethical Behaviours in Organizations: Directed by the Formal or Informal Systems?. *J Bus Ethics*, 14(2), 133-143, F 95.

Past research has focused on individual culpability with the assumption that individuals will further their own self interest over that of the organization, given an appropriate opportunity. In contrast this research shifts the focus from individual motivation to the influence of the formal and informal control systems of organizations on ethical behaviors. An open-ended interview approach was used to collect data. It was found that pressures within the informal system were the dominant influence in the resolution of ethical issues. The dominance of the informal system, however, varies according to the economic position of the organization.

Falkenburg, Brigitte. Kants zweite Antinomie und die Physik. *Kantstudien*, 86(1), 4-25, 1995.

The logical and semantic structure of Kant's second antinomy of pure reason is analyzed in detail. The logically relevant parts of the thesis and antithesis (*every/no composed substance is made up of atoms*) are contrary rather than contradictory; the antinomy arises from semantic presuppositions concerning the concepts of a composed substance. In the proof of the thesis, however, Kant proved less than he claimed: the antinomy is due to his views of space, of relations and of the continuum. The known physical theories of ultimate parts of matter avoid such antinomy by presupposing space as a *composition reale*.

Fallas, Jackeline García. Resolución de problemas: de Piaget a otros autores. *Rev Filosof (Costa Rica)*, 32(77), 131-138, Jl 94.

This article is devoted to the analysis of epistemological expositions about problem solving. It reviews the literature from Piaget to later positions, like Brown's, Brandsford's, Ferrara's, Deloache's and Papert's. This article concludes that in problem solving it is necessary to carry out analysis and synthesis in knowledge processes.

Fallas, Luis A. Aspectos dialécticos en los primeros filósofos. *Rev Filosof (Costa Rica)*, 32(77), 81-92, Jl 94.

This article highlights some of the characteristics of dialectic thought in Anaximander, Pythagorism, Heraclitus and the Eleatism. The diversity among these schools shows how presocratic thought was in a state of constant flux.

Fallas, Luis A. Notas sobre la física epicúrea. *Rev Filosof (Costa Rica)*, 31(75-76), 227-235, D 93.

In an attempt to liberate us from ignorance, Epicurus defends a remake of atomist physics. Nevertheless, his materialist ontology, whose presocratic support is evident, is at fault when not being able to avoid some of the rigorous Aristotelic schemes, those that he was precisely dealing with in order to refute them.

Fallon, Stephen M. "*Paradise Lost* and the Materialism Debate" in *The 1994 Annual of Hermeneutics and Social Concern, Lawler, Justus George (ed)*, 174-203. New York, Continuum, 1994.

The metaphysical debates of the mid-seventeenth century carried profound implications for one of Milton's central concerns, the freedom of the will. Incorporealists viewed themselves as defending freedom of the will from attacks by materialist, determinist philosophies such as Hobbes's. Milton, taking a different route to defend free will, developed an idiosyncratic animist materialism. The angels in *Paradise Lost* embody Milton's animist materialism, while the devils represent those mechanist philosophies that evoked it. Milton presents the devils as alternately surrounding themselves with Cartesian and Hobbesian spaces and as being forcibly recalled to the monist truth.

Farganis, Sondra. "Postmodernism and Feminism" in *Postmodernism and Social Inquiry, Dickens, David R (ed)*, 101-126. New York, Guilford, 1994.

Several questions are posed: Can feminist theorists be postmodernists? Can feminists be sociologists? By reading key texts in feminist theory, we look to see what it is in postmodernism that is attractive to writers in the "women's movement". We also examine the consequences for the movement if it embraces a theory that may not lend itself to a feminist politics. The dialogue between feminism and postmodernism is rich in epistemological nuances (the idea of a self, the presuppositions of identity and identity politics, the political underpinnings of categorizing on the basis of gender). American in focus, we offer a brief history of developments in feminist theory and in postmodern theorizing and how each may limit or expand the other.

Farrell, Brian. "The Meaning of Life: A Psycho-Logical Exploration" in *Life, World and Meaning, Roux, A P J (ed)*, 1-8. Pretoria, Univ of S Africa, 1990.

The conceptual conflicts which generate the question (What is the meaning of life?) center around our compulsion to take a key expression, such as "Why are ...? (in, for example, the sentence: Why are we here?) out of its "home" use, and so leave it confusingly without sense. If we answer the question by resorting to the purposes of a personal God, we take the word "person" out of its "home" contexts, with similar results. The answer which a person accepts as "correct" is one which gives him/her a sustainable conceptual equilibrium. My own remarks are analogous to a description by a psychiatrist of the pathology of an obsessional compulsion and difficulty.

Farrell, Martín D. Neutralidad y relatividad agencial. *Telos (Spain)*, 2(1), 45-83, Je 93.

A new terminology has been employed for a traditional philosophical problem, the terminology of agent-neutral and agent-relative reasons. This article begins with an examination of the subject in authors like Nagel, Parfit, Sen and Broome. It identifies utilitarianism with agent-neutrality, defining an agent-neutral reason as one which considers the general happiness impartially. There are two types of agent-relative reasons: reasons of autonomy that limit the utilitarian calculus, and deontological reasons that try to eliminate that calculus. The word "reason" is employed in the paper in the sense of justifying something, more precisely in the sense of justifying norms. But there are agent-relative norms based on agent-neutral reasons and *vice versa*. A truly agent-neutral norm is a norm based on agent-neutral reasons. (edited)

Farrell, Martín Diego. El liberalismo frente a Bentham y Mill. *Telos (Spain)*, 1(1), 23-54, F 92.

There are many differences between the theories of Bentham and Stuart Mill specially in the ways in which both characterize the concept of pleasure. The concept, in turn, obviously has great influence on the utilitarian calculus. I am concerned in this paper with the issue of which of the two versions is most compatible with the liberal doctrine. In the process of establishing the compatibility of both versions with the liberal doctrine serious difficulties cannot be avoided, but these difficulties can be resolved easily in Bentham's theory. (edited)

Farwell, Paul. Aristotle, Success, and Moral Luck. *J Phil Res*, 19, 37-50, 1994.

My point of departure is Bernard Williams's "moral luck" thesis and its claim that luck and success are an integral part of ethics. Some scholars think Aristotle's ethics lends support to a version of the moral luck thesis. My claim is the exact opposite: Aristotle gives a subtle and interesting argument for keeping luck and ethics distinct. Luck plays little role since the moral worth of action lies in the agent's choice, *proairesis*, not merely in the quality of the act itself and even less the outcome or success of the action. Further, virtue and success are not equatable: although the courageous person must act with practical wisdom—he must know who his enemy is and when to fight—virtue does not require victory in a battle.

Fatic, Aleksandar. Interpreting Malapropisms. *Method Sci*, 27(1), 13-24, 1994.

Fatic, Aleksandar. Interpreting Malapropisms: On Donald Davidson's Theory of Interpretation. *Phil Inq*, 16(1-2), 44-54, Wint-Spr 94.

The article addresses Davidson's assumption that, in order to successfully explain the fact that communication succeeds even in cases where linguistic expressions breach conventional rules, one must presuppose the existence of a deeply divided, two-part mental structure. I argue in the article that Davidson's assumption is mistaken, and in addition that it springs from not taking language as a conventional system for communication very seriously. I start from Davidson's startling remark that in fact 'there is no such thing as language', and proceed to argue that this is more than just a colourful metaphor—namely, that Davidson's explanation appears required only if one dispenses with the notion of language. In this vein, I echo the arguments of people such as Michael Dummett and Ian Hacking, who argued that, is one already assumes that there is a plausible mentalistic explanation of communication (in terms of mental structures), then there is no reason to assume that this structure is divided. (edited)

Fattal, Michel. On Division in Plato's *Statesman*. *Polis*, 12(1-2), 64-76, 1993.

Why does division in the *Statesman* present "a contrasting picture" which surprisingly mingles comedy and seriousness, precision and confusion? In order to understand such an ambiguity, it must be seen that Plato wants to expose three kinds of division: the unregulated division which arouses irony and joke; the division based on median dichotomies, with its provisional, uncertain and approximate rules; and lastly, the division as exact as possible, which is an ideal to be reached, towards which Plato strives. It is the constant movement from one of these divisions to another which gives us the impression that Plato's account is confused and ambiguous.

Fatula, Mary Ann. The Relevance of Thomas Aquinas for Contemporary Issues in Spirituality. *Listening*, 30(1), 64-75, Wint 95.

Faukner Nogues, Frañco. "La Realización Humana en la Filosofía de Ortega y Gasset" in *Temas Actuales de Filosofía, Palacios, María Julia (ed)*, 173-178. Buenos Aires, Univ Nacional Salta, 1993.

Faulconer, James E. Newton, Science, and Causation. *J Mind Behav*, 16(1), 77-86, Wint 95.

Contrary to common belief, acceptance of Newtonian causation does not commit one to a mechanistic, materialistic, or deterministic understanding of the world. I argue that the Newtonian view can be assimilated to contemporary theoretical alternatives in psychology. This means that, given the Newtonian understanding of causation, it is possible for such alternatives to be scientific—to treat causes—without requiring either mechanism, materialism, or mathematical formalizations. I argue that we best understand Newtonian causation as formal causation. I do this by discussing the history of Newton's theory of causation and comparing his theory to Bacon's. I also compare Newton's theory of causation to Aristotle's, arguing that when we speak of formal causes we speak of our descriptions rather than the nature of things. We may (or may not) accurately impute various elements of our scientific descriptions to the nature of things, but when we speak of formal causes, we are speaking of the patterns we use to describe the changes we observe rather than the nature of things themselves. Since any science must use such patterns, even alternative psychologies use Newtonian causation—if they are genuinely scientific alternatives. However, mathematics is not the only discipline that offers such patterned explanations. Moral explanations offer an alternate model for causal explanation.

Faulkender, Patricia J (& others). The Case of the Stolen Psychology Test: An Analysis of an Actual Cheating Incident. *Ethics Behavior*, 4(3), 209-217, 1994.

We examined the attitudes of 600 students in large introductory algebra and psychology classes toward an actual or hypothetical cheating incident and the subsequent retake procedure. Overall, 57% of students in one class and 49% in the other reported that they either cheated or would have cheated if given the opportunity. More men (59%) than women (53%) reported cheating or potential cheating. Students who had actually experienced a retake procedure to handle cheating were more satisfied with such a procedure than others were about a hypothetical situation. Despite having a retake, cheaters were significantly more likely than noncheaters to predict that they would cheat again. Results suggest that instructors who require a retake following extensive cheating should devote class time to a discussion of the issue and all possible alternatives.

Faulkner, Wendy. Conceptualizing Knowledge Used in Innovation: A Second Look at the Science-Technology Distinction and Industrial Innovation. *Sci Tech Human Values*, 19(4), 425-458, Autumn 94.

This article reviews empirical and conceptual material from two distinct research traditions: on the science-technology relation and on industrial innovation. It aims both to shed new light on an old debate—the distinction between scientific and technological knowledge—and to refine our conceptualizations of the knowledge used by companies in the course of research and development leading to innovation. On the basis of three empirical studies, a composite categorization of different types of knowledge used in innovation is proposed, as part of a broader framework encompassing two further taxonomic dimensions. It is hoped that this typology and framework might provide useful research tools in furthering our understanding of the knowledge transfers and transformations that occur in the course of innovation. It could also prove useful for organizations and groups facing difficult strategic choices about technology.

Faur, José. La Teoría del Conocimiento de Francisco Sánchez y el Verum/Factum de Vico. *Cuad Vico*, 4, 83-99, 1994.

As to the general view of the *verum/factum* principle as a revolutionary formula of implication embodied in Vico's philosophy, this paper aims to examine the main thesis of F Sánchez's *Quod Nihil Scitur* in order to show that the principle, far from being a casual or incidental idea, lies on the bottom of his epistemological theory. In fact, this paper intends to present the Vichian formula as a response to the esceptical crisis which came out from Sánchez's very own theory of knowledge. Once the basic assumption of skepticism has been retorted, Vico brought to an end the skeptical crisis.

Faust, David. Use and Then Prove, or Prove and Then Use? Some Thoughts on the Ethics of Mental Health Professionals' Courtroom Involvement. *Ethics Behavior*, 3(3-4), 359-380, 1993.

Psychologists' courtroom involvement and testimony should not be dictated solely by what the judge or court allows but also require the application of personal or professional standards. This article explores various standards that might be used to determine whether psychological evidence is ready for courtroom application, whether or which evaluative procedures should be performed prior to courtroom use, and the potential tensions between personal validation or impression and formal scientific evidence. Although determining just how tough our professional standards ought to be involves complex issues, the field should take a strong stance against testimony that is based largely on personal validation and that lacks scientific support or conflicts with research evidence. Much of current testimony violates this minimal standard.

Fawcett, Jeffrey K and Burns, David J and Lanasa, John. Business Students' Ethical Perceptions of Retail Situations: A Microcultural Comparison. *J Bus Ethics*, 13(9), 667-679, S 94.

Due in part to a growing realization of the importance of the role that retailing plays in the marketing channel, and to the increasing numbers of college graduates being employed by retailers, growing attention is being placed on business students' ethical perceptions of retailing practices. This study continues this focus by examining the ethical perceptions of collegiate business students attending two different universities which likely represent two different microcultures—conservative evangelical Protestant and secular. The results suggest that ethical perceptions may vary between the students attending two universities which likely represent differing microcultures. (edited)

Fay, Thomas A. Two Extreme Approaches to Rights Versus an Aristotelian Mean. *Vera Lex*, 13(1-2), 41-42, 1993.

Feagin, Susan L. Paintings and their Places. *Austl J Phil*, 73(2), 260-268, Je 95.

The question "Can art give us knowledge?", when asked of painting and sculpture, presupposes a separation between art and life that is a constituent in many traditional theories of art and the aesthetic. I discuss some recent work in art history that challenges the assumption of this distance between art and life which is so fundamental to much aesthetic theory. Art becomes a part of life, rather than something through which we learn about life. When the presuppositions of our questioning are not satisfied, the inquiry itself comes to look peculiar and inappropriate, revealing the narrowness of the ways we have been thinking about the visual arts.

Feal, Carlos and Geisdorfer Feal, Rosemary. *Painting on the Page: Interartistic Approaches to Modern Hispanic Texts*. Albany, SUNY Pr, 1995.

Painting on the Page devises critical strategies that combine psychoanalysis, feminism, semiotics, and philosophy to examine late 19th- and 20th-century Spanish and Spanish-American literature in relation to painting and to larger questions of art and literary history. The authors widen the theoretical lines to Hispanism, where approaches of this kind are rare. The book raises crucial concerns that relocate the art works and texts in question beyond the historical or aesthetic framework in which they have been traditionally placed.

Feary, Vaughana Macy. Sexual Harassment: Why the Corporate World Still Doesn't "Get It". *J Bus Ethics*, 13(8), 649-662, Ag 94.

This paper shows that in order to understand and to resolve the problem of sexual harassment in the workplace, the corporate world will have to relinquish some myths. Sexual harassment does not result from ignorance about fact or law. It is not merely a cultural, gender, or communication problem. It is a problem which will be resolved only when the corporate world recognizes that sexual harassment is a moral problem and provides moral education for employees. Until then, it will remain an explosive problem for communication specialists.

Federici, Silvia. Journey to the Native Land: Violence and the Concept of the Self in Fanon and Gandhi. *Quest*, 8(2), 47-69, D 94.

Dans cet article l'auteur analyse le concept du même chez Fanon et Gandhi et en particulier les implications de ce concept pour leur manière d'envisager le rôle de la violence dans le combat pour la libération. Les thèses suivantes sont développées: a) La prise de position de Fanon pour la violence doit être comprise dans le contexte de sa conviction que la destruction de pouvoir colonial est pour le colonisé logiquement parlant la condition sine qua non d'autodétermination et d'autovalorisation; b) La non-violence de Ghandi fait intégralement partie d'une croyance philosophique dans l'existence d'une essence humaine éternelle offrant la possibilité d'une reconnaissance de soi mutuelle entre les colonisateurs et les colonisés.

Fédier, François. Traduire les *Beiträge zur Philosophie (Vom Ereignis)*. *Heidegger Stud*, 9, 15-33, 1993.

Feezell, Randolph M. Sport, the Aesthetic, and Narrative. *Phil Today*, 39(1), 93-104, Spr 95.

Feezell, Randolph M and Stephens, William O. The Argument from Marginal Cases: Is Speciesism Defensible?. *Cont Phil*, 16(4), 7-16, Jl-Ag 94.

We discuss various attempts to resist the conclusions offered by critics of speciesism who argue that many criteria of moral concern actually raise many nonhuman animals above some "marginal cases" of human beings. The appeal to ridicule, the appeal to ignorance, the argument from no-consciousness, the argument from self-interest, and the argument from religious appeals we contend are popular, but less philosophically serious responses. The more serious responses are the argument from kinds/norms, the argument from moral sentiments, and the argument from rule utility. We conclude that none of these responses refutes the argument from marginal cases.

Feferman, Solomon and Hellman, Geoffrey. Predicative Foundations of Arithmetic. *J Phil Log*, 24(1), 1-17, F 95.

Fehér, Ferenc. Hope at the End of the Century. *Magyar Filozof Szemle*, 3-4, 377-388, 1994.

Already Kant raised the question of what we can know, do and hope for. In dealing with hopes, Kant did not apply any qualification. Man can hope for literally everything; for human perfection, the immortality of the soul or for grasping the goal of the universe. Reason has no censorship role in this regard, or else man's autonomy would be dangerously curtailed. But there is a special "rational" kind of hope which should even be favoured. We hope rationally for something about which we have no knowledge because it is beyond our time/space horizon, but about which we would like to gain knowledge. In the case of rational hopes, hope stands for the mobilization of our energies, for the readiness to invest them into tasks the fulfillment of which may or may not guide us toward the sought-for objective, but about which it can be stated with some certainty that they will not mislead us.

Fehér, István M. "Heidegger und Kant—Heidegger und die Demokratie" in *Europa und die Philosophie, Gander, Hans-Helmuth (ed)*, 105-127. Frankfurt/M, Klostermann, 1993.

Fehér, István M. Heidegger's Understanding of the Atheism of Philosophy. *Amer Cath Phil Quart*, 69(2), 189-228, Spr 95.

Fehér, István M. Sartre and Hermeneutics. *Man World*, 28(1), 65-81, Ja 95.

Although the terms "hermeneutics," "hermeneutical," turn up just haphazardly in Sartre's works some of the leading insights and strategies of hermeneutic philosophy (of the Heideggerian-Gadamerian sort) are very much at work in his works *Critique of Dialectical Reason* (CRD), and in *Being and Nothingness* (BN). After summing up, first, those aspects of hermeneutics philosophy relevant for selecting Sartrean parallels, it is shown how these devices work i) in what can be called Sartre's hermeneutical critique of Marxism in CRD centering around the claim that the source of Marxist dogmatism is closure in front of the claim of the other; and ii) in what is claimed to be the anticipation of his critique in the parts of BN treating the problem of Being-for-others. If the basic hermeneutic comportment from Heidegger to Rorty is typically seen to be in openness to the strange, to the unfamiliar, then, it is argued, this kind of openness is very much at work in Sartre's description of the "look" in BN. Finally I briefly assess Sartre's hermeneutic relevance in contemporary American pragmatism, i.e., in Rorty.

Feinberg, Joel. "Instigating the Unpredisposed: Bad Luck in Law and Life" in *Modality, Morality, and Belief, Sinnott-Armstrong, Walter (ed)*, 152-173. New York, Cambridge Univ Pr, 1994.

Feinberg, Joel. Sentiment and Sentimentality in Practical Ethics. *Proc Amer Phil Ass*, 56(1), 19-46, S 82.

Feist, Richard. Newton and Leibniz: Rivalry in the Family. *De Phil*, 10, 59-70, 1993.

The debate between Newton and Leibniz as to whether there is absolute motion is distorted when it is interpreted from the perspective of today's science. The author proposes an interpretation of the Newton-Leibniz debate that allows these thinkers to be the children of their own time and that precludes one or the other being crowned the victor by modern developments in space-time theory.

Feldman, Fred. Adjusting Utility for Justice: A Consequentialist Reply to the Objection from Justice. *Phil Phenomenol Res*, 55(3), 567-585, S 95.

Traditional forms of consequentialism are open to objections based on considerations of justice. Classic cases such as the Small Southern Town, the Organ Harvest, the Colosseum, etc. show that such forms of consequentialism, focussing exclusively on the total value of available outcomes, are insensitive to questions about the manner in which that value is distributed among the various recipients in the outcome. As a result, such theories sometimes permit serious injustices. In this paper, I formulate an axiology that is sensitive to justice, and combine it with a consequentialist normative theory. I try to show that the resulting view generates correct results in cases involving justice.

Feldman, Fred. Desert: Reconsideration of Some Received Wisdom. *Mind*, 104(413), 63-77, Ja 95.

I consider two bits of received wisdom about desert. The first links desert to time: if you deserve in virtue of some fact, then that fact must be in the past. The second links desert to responsibility: if you deserve in virtue of some fact, then you must bear responsibility for that fact. After showing that many philosophers endorse these doctrines, I try to show that each bit of received wisdom is false. I speculate about the popularity of the views.

Feldman, Richard. "Good Arguments" in *Socializing Epistemology: The Social Dimensions of Knowledge, Schmitt, Frederick F (ed)*, 159-188. Lanham, Rowman & Littlefield, 1994.

In this paper I argue that the core notion of a good argument is an epistemological one. In the first section, I discuss logical accounts of good arguments, holding that good arguments are deductively or inductively sound. However, arguments having epistemically unjustified premises are not good arguments that emphasize the social role of arguments and I argue that they conflate persuasiveness and other interpersonal factors with rational merit. In the final section I explain and defend the view that an argument is a good argument for a person provided the conjunction of its premises are justified for the person, the person is justified in believing that the premises are "properly connected" to the conclusion, and the argument is "undefeated" for the person.

Feldman, Richard. Proper Functionalism. *Nous*, 27(1), 34-50, Mr 93.

In this paper I reply to some objections Alvin Plantinga raises to recent theories of epistemic justification in *Warrant: The Current Debate* and I raise objections to the theory Plantinga defends in *Warrant and Proper Function*. Plantinga's view is roughly that a belief has epistemic warrant provided it has been produced by properly functioning cognitive faculties in an appropriate environment. I argue that this theory is subject to a problem similar to the generality problem that affects reliabilism. I also argue that given Plantinga's view that something is functioning properly when it is functioning as it supposed or designed to function, his theory runs into objections arising from consideration of poorly designed beings.

Feldman, Susana B and Krichmar, Fernando Gabriel. "La Enseñanza de la Epistemología en la Carrera de Psicología o Técnicas Para Desvestir a una Invitada Molesta" in *Temas Actuales de Filosofía, Palacios, María Julia (ed)*, 179-185. Buenos Aires, Univ Nacional Salta, 1993.

Felice, Domenico. Francia, Spagna e Portogallo: Le Monarchie Europee "Qui Vont au Despotisme" Secondo Montesquieu. *G Crit Filosof Ital*, 74(1), 20-41, Ja-Ap 95.

Felipe, Donald. La Biblioteca de la Universidad de Santo Tomás en Manila, Filipinas: Una Nota Bibliográfica Sobre Libros Raros de Filosofía, 1500-1800. *Analogia*, 7(2), 169-188, 1993.

This article presents a bibliography of a rich collection of rare philosophy books published from 1500-1880, held at the University of Santo Tomas in Manila, Philippines. The bibliography indirectly documents active philosophical studies in the Philippines during the Spanish colonial period.

Felsenthal, Dan S and Machover, Moshé. Postulates and Paradoxes of Relative Voting Power—A Critical Re-Appraisal. *Theor Decis*, 38(2), 195-229, Mr 95.

This paper re-evaluates the problem of measuring the *a priori* relative voting power of a voter in an assembly. We propose several new intuitively compelling postulates that any reasonable index of voting power ought to satisfy. At the same time we argue that most of the paradoxes of voting power discussed in the literature are paradoxical only in a weak sense, if at all. This leaves three crippling paradoxes—the well-known paradox of *weighted voting*, and two new ones presented here: the *bloc* and *donation* paradoxes. We evaluate the four main relative power indices discussed in the literature with respect to these three severe paradoxes. The Shapley-Shubik index is seen to be immune to all three paradoxes, while the Deegan-Packel index is vulnerable to all three. The Banzhaf and the Johnston indices are demonstrably immune to the paradox of weighted voting. However, they are shown to suffer from both the bloc and the donation paradoxes. We argue that this seriously undermines these indices in a hitherto unsuspected way. Several other theoretical issues relating to voting power are discussed.

Felt, James W. Relational Realism and the Great Deception of Sense. *Mod Sch*, 71(4), 305-316, My 94.

This is, first of all, a systematic attack on representational epistemology (RE) such as is found in Hobbes, Locke, and very many others. The essay then suggests an alternative view, a "relational realism", that mediates between RE, in which the direct object of perceiving is one's perceptions, and naive realism. The direct object of perceiving is argued to be neither one's own perceptions nor the object in itself but the *perceived object*, which is a function both of the perceiver and of the object in itself. One thus finds oneself living in an *appearing world* rather than in a world of appearances.

Femenías, María Luisa. "Juan Huarte de San Juan: Un Materialista Español del Siglo XVI" in *Temas Actuales de Filosofía, Palacios, María Julia (ed)*, 195-203. Buenos Aires, Univ Nacional Salta, 1993.

Juan Huarte de San Juan, a Spanish medical doctor, wrote in 1575 *Examen de Ingenios*. The French translation (*L'Anacrise*) is considered to have very much influenced, at least, on Montaigne, Descartes, and perhaps not directly, on Hobbes. This article aims to introduce this nearly unknown but important figure.

Femenías, María Luisa. Algunas Precisiones Sobre el Lenguaje y la Paronimia en Aristóteles. *Analogia*, 7(1), 167-178, 1993.

This article criticizes Delgado-Antolín interpretation of *paronyma* and intends to show Aristotle different conception of *homonyma* and *synonyma* on the one hand and *paronyma* on the other.

Femenías, María Luisa. Una Pregunta Sobre la Noción de "Bien" en Aristóteles. *Analogia*, 4(2), 173-180, 1990.

This article intends to put in evidence the importance of "good" as a *pros hen homonyma* from an ontological/ethical point of view and its relation to *healthy* and *one*.

Fendt, Gene. *Confessions'* Bliss: Postmodern Criticism as a Palimpsest of Augustine's *Confessions*. *Heythrop J*, 36(1), 30-45, Ja 95.

This paper reads through some contemporary literary critical problems and theorizing about textuality to Augustine's *Confessions*, to the enrichment, if not the ecstasy of both contemporary and medieval thinking. It shows that Augustine is both aware of much that passes as new in theorizing about language, and that his text is argumentatively and rhetorically structured to set difference at play. Like Augustine's writing, this article is a performance piece: besides arguing, it acknowledges; beside demonstration, it questions; besides telling, it shows; it would not be called a study of texuality in Augustine, but a performance of texuality with (in) Augustine.

Fendt, Gene. Libidinal Economy and the Life of Logos. *Phil Lit*, 18(2), 320-325, O 94.

This article uses Lyotard's concept of the differend to show that logos makes a creature aware that there are two possible libidinal economies—the economy of permanently attempted gain, which is the general realm of politics, and the economy of voluntary loss, which is the general realm of religion. It shows how these two economies interact in *Republic*, and closes by arguing that Nietzsche must choose the second, for the first is a form of *ressentiment*.

Fénelon, François and Riley, Patrick (ed & trans). *Telemachus, Son of Ulysses*. New York, Cambridge Univ Pr, 1994.

Fenner, Stephen A. Almost Weakly 2-Generic Sets. *J Sym Log*, 59(3), 868-887, S 94.

Ferejohn, Michael T. The Immediate Premises of Aristotelian Demonstration. *Ancient Phil*, 14, 79-97, 1994.

This paper investigates Aristotle's insistence in *Posterior Analytics* A2 that the first principles of scientific demonstrations must be "immediate". Earlier interpretations are considered and rejected. It is argued that Aristotle addresses this condition in *Posterior Analytics* A4 by requiring that the predicate of a scientific principle be true of its subject "*qua* (that subject) itself", and that immediacy in this context is nothing more than a set-theoretical notion of immediate inclusion between subject and predicate: "S is P" is immediate if P includes S, and there is no intervening term, P, which both includes S and is included by P.

Ferguson, Ann. Twenty Years of Feminist Philosophy. *Hypatia*, 9(3), 197-215, Sum 94.

This paper provides an overview of twenty years of feminist philosophy in North American. The professionalization of feminist theory that has occurred through the mainstreaming of feminist philosophy creates a danger of a gap between theory and practice that creates the danger of co-optation. Three stages of feminist philosophizing are outlined, including the radical critique, gender difference and difference/post-modernist stages. The last stage, it is argued, leads to a conceptual impasse about feminist strategies for social change.

Ferguson, Frances. Pornography: The Theory. *Crit Inquiry*, 21(3), 670-695, Spr 95.

Ferguson, Michael. "Fixation and Regression in the Psychoanalytic Theory of Homosexuality—A Critical Evaluation" in *Gay Ethics, Murphy, Timothy F (ed)*, 309-327. New York, Haworth Pr, 1994.

This essay evaluates the notions of fixation and regression in the psychoanalytic theoretical conceptualization of homosexuality. Charles Socarides has had a central role in formulating the most prominent and influential psychoanalytic metapsychological understanding of homosexuality in recent years and for that reason this essay focuses principally on him. The concepts of fixation and regression are central to his understanding and I argue that the evolution of these concepts in contemporary usage renders them irrelevant to formulating the current psychoanalytic understanding of homosexuality and that their continued use by analysts reflects a negative attitude toward homosexual behavior on the part of Socarides and many other analysts that stems from an extremely narrow and idealized conception of human development.

Fernández, José Luis. Dios en la filosofía de Malebranche. *Acta Phil*, 2(3), 227-246, 1994.

Secondo Malebranche la nostra conoscenza di Dio è immediata e ciò ci obbliga a rivedere sia le prove *a priori* che *a posteriori* per il fatto che tutte e due sono discorsive. Ma immediatezza non vuol dire che la nostra conoscenza della Natura Divina sia perfetta. La stessa nozione di infinito, che si trova aldilà delle nostre capacità, ce lo impedisce. Ciò è valido per tutti gli attributi, compreso quello della Potenza Divina. Per questa ragione, anche se l'unica causa che esiste è la Causalità Divina, noi non la possiamo comprendere perfettamente, cioè dal punto di vista di Dio.

Fernandez Acevedo, Yolanda. "Algunos Aportes Sobre la Discusión entre Cognitivismo...y el Constuctivismo (Piaget) Acerca de la Adquis. de Concepto de Unsistema Repres." in *Temas Actuales de Filosofía, Palacios, María Julia (ed)*, 187-193. Buenos Aires, Univ Nacional Salta, 1993.

The purpose of this work is to argue in favor of the idea that it is possible for a dialogue between Piaget's thesis that concepts are evolutive constructs and Fodor's thesis that concepts are innate; because, in spite of the important differences in the "hard core" of the programmes of these authors, for the innatism it makes no sense to speak of "a beginning" and for the constructivism it is not necessary that there be "a beginning".

Fernández Beites, Pilar. Evidencia y verdad: Un problema en la fenomenología de E Husserl. *An Seminar Metaf*, 27, 195-215, 1993.

Fernández del Riesgo, Manuel. La Democracia y el Futuro del Socialismo. *Rev Filosof (Spain)*, 7(11), 219-263, 1994.

Fernández del Valle, Agustín Basave. Ciencia, Técnica y Sabiduría. *Logos (Mexico)*, 22(66), 137-147, S-D 94.

Fernández García, Eugenio. G E Lessing: Una Ilustración Radical e Insatisfecha. *An Seminar Hist Filosof*, 6, 111-130, 1986-89.

En los últimos años se ha avivado la discusión sobre el significado de la Ilustración y el alcance de la modernidad. El debate, que agudiza sus aristas en el enfrentamiento entre modernos y posmodernos, se está convirtiendo en un intercambio de rechazos, entre otras razones porque se toma como referencia una modernidad acartonada e inerte. En este contexto resulta especialmente interesante volver la mirada a Lessing, uno de los ilustrados más lúcido, crítico y apasionante, que, justamente por ello, conserva mayor viveza.

Fernández García, Eugenio. Kant contra Spinoza?: Dos Éticas de la Autonomía. *An Seminar Hist Filosof*, 9, 139-155, 1992.

No se pretende hacer una comparación entre la filosofía de Kant y la de Spinoza, sino más bien mostrar un punto de encuentro, en el que ambas se cruzan sin reconocerse. El análisis de tal encrucijada gira en torno a la autonomía y al conocimiento racional como acción libre. Después de esbozar la imagen filosófica que Kant tenía del Spinozismo y su crítica a éste como antítesis del criticismo, a pesar del carácter de racionalismo crítico que, sin embargo, posee, se muestra en una breve exposición de las líneas maestras de ambas éticas, como entre disonancias y malentendidos se produce una convergencia en lo esencial: una ética lúcida y sin sumisiones, a la vez que un enfrentamiento en cuanto a la naturaleza y función del deseo.

Fernández Moreno, Luis. Tarski y la Noción Carnapiana de Significado. *Rev Filosof (Spain)*, 7(12), 403-420, 1994.

This paper examines Tarski's remarks on Carnap's conception of synonymity and meaning in Carnap's *Introduction to Semantics* (1942). Carnap's conception of meaning and his definitions of synonymity and L-synonymity in this work are analyzed in detail. It is argued that only Carnap's definition of synonymity and not his definition of L-synonymity could have been accepted by Tarski.

Fernando, Tim. Bisimulations and Predicate Logic. *J Sym Log*, 59(3), 924-944, S 94.

Elementary (first-order) and nonelementary (set-theoretic) aspects of the largest bisimulation are considered with a view toward analyzing operational semantics from the perspective of predicate logic. The notion of a bisimulation is employed in two distinct ways: 1) as an extensional notion of equivalence on programs (or processes) generalizing input/output equivalence (at a cost exceeding Π 1/1 over certain transition predicates computable in log space), and 2) as a tool for analyzing the dependence of transitions on data (which can be shown to be elementary or nonelementary, depending on the formulation of the transitions).

Feron, Olivier. Le Problème de L'analogie dans la *Critique de la Raison Pure*. *Daimon Rev Filosof*, 8, 179-188, 1994.

Ferrara, Alessandro. Authenticity and the Project of Modernity. *Euro J Phil*, 2(3), 241-273, D 94.

Ferrara, Lawrence. Hermeneutic Issues in Qualitative Research. *Phil Music Educ Rev*, 3(1), 10-20, Spr 95.

Underlying qualitative research designs are numerous philosophical issues regarding the interpretive actions of the "researcher-as-tool." Qualitative research is context bound by the cultural and linguistic biases of the researcher with correctness and truth of findings understood as relative criteria. Conversations between human subjects embody interlocutional overtones that cannot be strictly formalized. Varieties of interpretation of similar educational contexts suggests richness, not chaos. One interprets human subjects' causal powers (dispositions and force), the constitution and particularlity of their agentic acts, and their impact on an educational setting. One strives to understand the constituent elements of a site in terms of the whole.

Ferrari, Franco. Analisi e Assiomatizzazione nella Dialettica di Platone. *Stud Filosofici*, 43-78, 1991-92.

Ferrari, Massimo. Gentile Ritrovato? Note sui più Recenti Studi Gentiliani. *G Crit Filosof Ital*, 73(2-3), 489-528, My-D 94.

Ferrarin, Alfredo. Construction and Mathematical Schematism: Kant on the Exhibition of a Concept in Intuition. *Kantstudien*, 86(2), 131-174, 1995.

Ferrarin, Alfredo. Husserl on the Ego and Its Eidos (*Cartesian Meditations*, IV). *J Hist Phil*, 32(4), 645-659, O 94.

This paper discusses the difficulties intrinsic to Husserl's theory of the eidos ego in the fourth Cartesian Meditation. After sketching the leading threads of the evolution in Husserl's conception of the ego, the notions of sedimentation, of abiding properties and of the substrate of habitualities are examined, and their historical antecedents, in particular Aristotle, are pointed out. The article then turns to the problem of synthesis of time for and in consciousness, stresses the basic ambiguity underlying it and argues that the foundation of Husserl's theory of the ego is aporetic. The consequences drawn by Sartre are legitimate. However, as long as consciousness is defined in terms of intentionality, self-consciousness may be secured, but the ego is made entirely dispensable. This solution leaves the problem of the self-ascription of Erlebnisse, and obviously of the identity of the ego, untouched.

Ferrarin, Alfredo. Kant's Productive Imagination and Its Alleged Antecedents. *Grad Fac Phil J*, 18(1), 65-92, 1995.

Ferraro, Agustín. "Sobre los Avatares Ontológicos del Empirismo y Trascendentalismo Jurídicos" in *Temas Actuales de Filosofía, Palacios, María Julia (ed)*, 205-216. Buenos Aires, Univ Nacional Salta, 1993.

Ferraro, Domenico. *Itinerari del Volontarismo: Teologia e politica al tempo di Luis de León*. Milano, FrancoAngeli, 1995.

Ferraro, Joseph. San Juan de la Cruz y el Problema Místico. *Analogia*, 4(1), 149-167, 1990.

Ferré, Frederick. "Highlights and Connections" in *Philosophy and the Natural Environment, Attfield, Robin (ed)*, 227-232. New York, Cambridge Univ Pr, 1994.

This concluding reflection aims to clarify and reinforce issues important to the author in light of positions taken by various companion essays. Illustrated in epistemological, metaphysical, and ethical contexts, the overall theme warns against "premature disjunction". It is tempting—but wrong—to fall into "all-or-nothing", "either-to" patterns of thinking. Holistic epistemology must not exclude analytical rigor; "natural" and "artificial" are not antonyms but come in degrees; we need not choose between the subjectivist axiom that "values require a valuer" and robust nonanthropocentric recognition of values in objective nature. Environmental ethics should lead the fight against "binary bias".

Ferré, Frederick. "Personalistic Organicism: Paradox or Paradigm?" in *Philosophy and the Natural Environment, Attfield, Robin (ed)*, 59-73. New York, Cambridge Univ Pr, 1994.

Organicism, rejecting anthropocentrism, rightly stresses the links between humans and other species; personalism, rejecting ecofascism, rightly celebrates every center of personhood. It seems there is a fundamental incompatibility between ethics grounded in one outlook or in the other. Nevertheless, beyond initial tensions lie still more important strands of continuity. Personal traits come in degrees and may be traced deep into the natural order; organic values are necessary conditions for persons. Personalistic organicism as paradigm of synthesis can ground an environmental ethic respecting types and grades of nonanthropocentric value in nature without falling into misanthropy or the confusions of "biocentric egalitarianism".

Ferré, Frederick. *Hellfire and Lighting Rods: Liberating Science, Technology, and Religion*. Hertfordshire, Orbis, 1993.

Science and religion must learn how to learn from each other. Mainstream religions evolve too reluctantly under pressure from scientific understanding; the modern scientistic worldview is too short on respect for the intuitions of value that underlie great world religions. This has led to "value-free" technologies whose quantitatively-immense but quality-disregarding successes are leading to environmental and social collapse. Needed postmodern technologies can rise from personalistic organicism, and integrated worldview combining the best of modern science (interpreted ecologically) with perennial religious values (respect for personal qualities and the self-limiting wisdom of healthy life).

Ferreira, Fernando. A Feasible Theory for Analysis. *J Sym Log*, 59(3), 1001-1011, S 94.

We construct a weak second-order theory of arithmetic which includes Weak König's Lemma (WKL) for trees defined by bounded formulae. The provably total functions of this theory are the polynomial time computable functions. It is shown that the first-order strength of this version of WKL is exactly that of the scheme of collection for bounded formulae.

Ferreira, M Jamie. Leaps and Circles: Kierkegaard and Newman on Faith and Reason. *Relig Stud*, 30(4), 379-397, D 94.

Soren Kierkegaard (in the Climacus writings) and John Henry Newman have starkly opposed formulations of the relation between faith and reason. In this essay I focus on a possible convergence in their respective understandings of the transition to religious belief or faith, as embodied in metaphors they use for a qualitative transition. I explore the ways in which attention to the legitimate dimension of discontinuity highlighted by the Climacan metaphor of the 'leap' can illuminate Newman's use of the metaphor of a 'polygon inscribed in a circle', as well as the ways in which Newman's metaphor can illuminate the dimension of continuity operative in the Climacan appreciation of qualitative transition.

Ferreira, M Jamie. Religion's 'Foundation in Reason': The Common Sense of Hume's Natural History. *Can J Phil*, 24(4), 565-581, D 94.

I examine Hume's claim in the *Natural History of Religion* that religion has a "foundation in reason" and that such belief is held by a "rational enquirer", suggesting that Hume's formulation of the answer to the question of religion's "foundation in reason" suggests not only the inability to suspend belief, but also (what is less often recognized) the lack of reasonable warrant for suspending it. I explore the parallel with Hume's view of the relation between reflection and 'natural beliefs', and I suggest one way in which "argument" can play a role in this "foundation in reason" without destroying the parallel with 'natural beliefs'.

Ferreira Chagas, Eduardo. Diferençia entre Alienaçao e Estranhamento nos Manuscritos Econômico-Filosóficos (1844), de Karl Marx. *Educ Filosof*, 8(16), 23-33, Jl-D 94.

Ferreira da Cunha, Paulo. Filsofía Jurídica e Política na Poesía Luso-árabe. *Rev Espan Filosof Med*, 0, 61-82, 1993.

Ferreira da Cunha, Paulo. The End of Dignity: Some Reflections 'Currente Calamo' on a Social and Ethical Problem. *Vera Lex*, 13(1-2), 26-27, 1993.

Purpose: analysis of some aspects of the relations between Dignity and Law nowadays. *Conclusions*: There are three kinds of dignity. The one that society in general must attribute to the individual; that the individuals must pay to each person; and that is self-reflexive—from one human being towards himself. Nowadays, when we speak of dignity, we generally forget the last two dimensions. We think everything would be solved if society or the State considers, or doesn't attack unfairly, the citizens. But that's not only a problem of citizenship. Nor it is only a matter of law, as we also tend to believe. Dignity comes from inside, from a personal ethical attitude. Law is only a mask. If the face lost its dignity, the farce will become tragedy.

Ferreira-Ross, Jeanette and Macnamara, Michael. "Drama and the Notion of Scheme-Role Meaning" in *Life, World and Meaning, Roux, A P J (ed)*, 121-157. Pretoria, Univ of S Africa, 1990.

Ferrell, O C and Thorne, Debbie M and Fraedrich, John. Assessing the Application of Cognitive Moral Development Theory to Business Ethics. *J Bus Ethics*, 13(10), 829-838, O 94.

Cognitive moral development (CMD) theory has been accepted as a construct to help explain business ethics, social responsibility and other organizational phenomena. This article critically assesses CMD as a construct in business ethics by presenting the history and criticisms of CMD. The value of CMD is evaluated and problems with using CMD as one predictor of ethical decisions are addressed. Researchers are made aware of the major criticisms of CMD theory including disguised value judgments, invariance of stages, and gender bias in the initial scale development. Implications for business ethics research are discussed and opportunities for future research delineated.

Ferrer, Gabriel. Sartre: Metodología del Problema de Dios. *Analogia*, 9(1), 31-47, 1995.

Ferrer, Joana. La utilitat com a objecte amable de la relació. *Convivium*, 5, 22-39, 1993.

The purpose of this article is to try to answer the question which describes the title: can the utilitarian relationship be another form of human friendship? Is it appropriate to call this friendship when there is a utilitarian relationship between two or more subjects? The negative answer to this question omits the complete sense of the *philia* term. On the other hand, the affirmative answer teaches the complete meaning of the *philia* reality and, in this way, it places the utilitarian object between the group of the moral elements which permits us to understand and test better the complete reality of ethics.

Ferrer, Urbano. De la teoría general del valor a una ética de fines en Husserl. *Anu Filosof*, 28(1), 41-60, 1995.

In this first stage of his ethics, Husserl stresses on the theory of value. The teleology seems necessary to him to form the concept of not objectivant act. Nevertheless since the essays after the second world war the striving and voluntary end will be more and more central in this ethical thought.

Ferrer, Urbano. La Etica en Husserl. *Rev Filosof (Spain)*, 4(6), 457-467, 1991.

The paper focuses on the main contributions of Husserl to the ethics in his first stage. The examination of formal axiological laws includes their parallelment with logical laws, but also their axiological peculiarities. The correlation between the objects and the acts motivated by them leads later to detach the acts of will (desire, will, decide...) and elucidate their essential connection. Finally the reestablishment of the teleological unity of the genre act by Husserl is examined, in which the objectifiant and nonobjectifiant modalities enter.

Ferretti, Silvia. Eternità e tempo in Plotino. *Filosofia*, 44(3), 371-392, S-D 93.

The purpose of the article is to study the meaning of the relation between time and eternity in Plotinus, *Enneades* III 7. It analyzes the nature of the reference to Plato, particularly the intellectual way to explain the myth in *Timaeus*. Two main concepts are pointed out: *unlikeness* as an idea of unlike coming from Plato's *Sophistes*) and *homonymy* (describing the peculiar relation between ideas and their images in the world soul). The article comes to the conclusion that Plotinus holds fast to the traditional Greek point of view: time is bounded to the eternal cosmic becoming. Nevertheless, we point out the originality of Plotinian hermeneutics on ancient philosophy, and his typical wavering between two conflicting points of view: the first conceiving time through eternal ideas or concepts; the second one realizing that the same concepts are transformed when applied to the field of becoming.

Ferry, Jean-Marc. Approaches to Liberty: Outline for a "Methodological Communitarianism". *Ratio Juris*, 7(3), 291-307, D 94.

In this paper, the author gives an account of the French perspective on the debate between an "individualist" and a "communitarian" conception of liberty. He argues that, despite the dominant tendency within recent French political philosophy to assume that the individualist conception of liberty is the only truly modern form of liberty, communitarian principles are present within the enlightenment tradition. He demonstrates the inadequacies of the individualist approach in an analysis of Rawls, and also rejects the type of communitarianism developed by MacIntyre, which depends upon a substantive concept of the community. With reference to theories of communication, he describes how we can elaborate a *communitarian* approach to *individual* freedom.

Ferry, Luc and Volk, Carol (trans). *The New Ecological Order*. Chicago, Univ of Chicago Pr, 1995.

Fesmire, Steven A. Educating the Moral Artist: Dramatic Rehearsal in Moral Education. *Stud Phil Educ*, 13(3-4), 213-227, 1994-95.

This essay articulates a Deweyan theory of moral understanding that makes our social commitments and moral valuations intelligible. Questions addressed are: What is the nature of moral deliberation? Given the psychology of thinking, how might we deliberate more effectively? Are there empirically warranted ideals that could fruitfully direct moral education? How might such ideals integrate the aesthetic dimension of growth? In order to contribute to a coherent and experimentally testable theory of the aims of moral education, Dewey's neglected conception of deliberation as imaginative *dramatic rehearsal* is examined alongside such concepts as "democracy," habit," "imagination," "the aesthetic," and "an experience."

Festini, Heda. Juraj Politeo: Language and Thought. *Filozof Istraz*, 13(4), 803-808, 1993.

Politeo, born in Split, the philosopher in Venice in 19th century, had original stand-point about relation between language and thought, because they did not reduce each other. After Politeo, the being of soul is the source of them, but partly with the contrast result. They are paralleled by their degrees of developments and they occur by common law which is formed under different circumstances and different places. "The code soul's enigma" seems that the language decodes; first as language of lower emotion getting the symbolic language which is today also the language of art, and that means, after Politeo, that the language is close to soul. From instinctive to higher level, the thought behaves in language through intuitive processes, it becomes the language of 'translates'—the cognitive language. when the language and the thought are on the higher level, then it decodes less the soul's enigma, i.e., the intuitive processes cease to be their medium; saying in modern terms, it becomes the decoding of the code by the thought. Politeo's treatment of such problem permits parallels with the recent comprehension of language (e.g., with Wittgenstein) and of thought (Clark, 1989; Bechtel, Lycan, 1990).

Festini, Heda. Politeo's "Brown Note Book" (1860): Morality—Freedom. *Filozof Istraz*, 14(1), 137-142, 1994.

In a thus far unpublished manuscript, Politeo further developed his theory of morality based on his nine lectures at the University of Padua in 1878/79, which were not published until 1919. What is clearer in the note book is the origins of this theory from Bentham-Mill's utilitarianism (main terms: pleasure, happiness, good, freedom) as well as still more definite differences (terms: love, egoism). The center of gravity of Politeo's conception is that authentic personality, utilitarianism, solidarity and the community. There is a great difference in the conceptions of freedom (unrestraint of tendencies and instincts) to its positive aspect through religion (inner struggle and self-determination). Given that utilitarianism is the basis for liberal democracy, Politeo's conception encounters Christian democracy, which demonstrates his present actuality. The possibility of asking the question about a third type of democracy is examined in passing.

Feteris, Eveline T. Rationality in Legal Discussions: A Pragma-Dialectical Perspective. *Inform Log*, 15(3), 179-188, Fall 93.

The central question addressed in this contribution is that of the procedures and rules in law which guarantee that a legal dispute will be resolved in a rational way. Taking the pragma-dialectical theory of van Eemeren and Grootendorst as a starting point for general conception of a system of procedures and rules for rational discussion, the procedures and rules for the resolution of legal disputes are compared with the pragma-dialectical rules. It is established which legal procedures and rules are necessary and sufficient to guarantee a rational acceptable resolution in a legal context.

Fetz, Reto Luzius. "Ich, Seele, Selbst: Edith Steins Theorie personaler Identität" in *Studien zur Philosophie von Edith Stein, Fetz, Reto Luzius (ed)*, 286-319. Freiburg, Alber, 1993.

Fetz, Reto Luzius (ed) and Rath, Matthias (ed) and Schulz, Peter (ed). *Studien zur Philosophie von Edith Stein*. Freiburg, Alber, 1993.

Fetzer, James H and Davies, Paul Sheldon and Foster, Thomas R. Logical Reasoning and Domain Specificity: A Critique of the Social Exchange Theory of Reasoning. *Biol Phil*, 10(1), 1-37, Ja 95.

The social exchange theory of reasoning, which is championed by Leda Cosmides and John Tooby, falls under the general rubric "evolutionary psychology" and asserts that human reasoning is governed by content-dependent, domain-specific, evolutionarily-derived algorithms. According to Cosmides and Tooby, the presumptive existence of what they call "cheater-detection" algorithms disconfirms the claim that we reason via general-purpose mechanisms or via inductively acquired principles. We contend that the Cosmides/Tooby arguments in favor of domain-specific algorithms or evolutionarily-derived mechanisms fail and that the notion of a social exchange rule, which is central to their theory, is not correctly characterized. As a consequence, whether or not their conclusion is true cannot be established on the basis of the arguments they have presented.

Feuer, Lewis S. *Varieties of Scientific Experience: Emotive Aims in Scientific Hypotheses*. New Brunswick, Transaction Books, 1995.

Feuerverger, Grace. Oasis of Peace: A Community of Moral Education in Israel. *J Moral Educ*, 24(2), 113-141, 1995.

On a rocky hill some 30 kilometres west of Jerusalem rests the village of *Neve Shalom/Wahat Al-Salam*. It is a co-operative community where Jewish and Arab families are involved in a highly innovative endeavour of peacemaking through education. This study focuses on the bilingual/bicultural/binational elementary school as a "moral community" embedded within the larger social organisation of the village. The aim was to explore the ways in which discussion, moral negotiation, and collaborative decision-making formed a basis for creating a spirit of community within the village and in the school. This school exemplifies a genuine attempt at partnership between two peoples whose cultures are in geo-political and socio-historic conflict. Through case study and narrative methodology, the author tries to make sense of the personal as well as professional experiences of her participants in their quest for intercultural harmony. The narratives explore the complex nature of their moral responses to one another and to themselves. The lived experiences of the children, parents and teachers were documented through in-depth interviews, conversations, and participant-observation techniques. The findings of this study could potentially provide a new and global dimension for exploring moral issues in education within a context of conflict resolution and peacemaking.

Feyerabend, Paul. *Killing Time: The Autobiography of Paul Feyerabend*. Chicago, Univ of Chicago Pr, 1995.

Feyerabend, Paul. *Three Dialogues on Knowledge*. Cambridge, Blackwell, 1992.

Fichant, Michel. De la puissance à l'action. *Rev Metaph Morale*, 98(1), 49-81, Ja-Mr 95.

The circumstances which led Leibniz to resort to the neologism of "Dynamics" (1690) highlight the novelty of the conceptual systems—compared to the previous conceptions based on the notion of *force*—resulting from interference of motive action. The *a priori* demonstration of the preservation of action does not transform dynamics into a mathematical science of necessary truths nor does it obliterate its dependence on metaphysical principles. The stylistic singularity of the concept of action becomes apparent in its dual constitution which associates extensive quantity and intensive quantity: thus Leibniz's dynamics revived the medieval doctrines of *intensio*; moreover as it endowed bodies with a true "action on themselves", in correlation with archaic understanding of inertia, it was originally irreducible to the paradigm of classical mechanics.

Fichant, Michel. Les axiomes de l'identité et la démonstration des formules arithmétiques: "2+2=4". *Rev Int Phil*, 48(188), 175-211, 1994.

Fidalgo, António. "Edith Stein, Theodor Lipps und die Einfühlungsproblematik" in *Studien zur Philosophie von Edith Stein, Fetz, Reto Luzius (ed)*, 90-106. Freiburg, Alber, 1993.

Field, Hartry. Disquotational Truth and Factually Defective Discourse. *Phil Rev*, 103(3), 405-452, Jl 94.

"Factually defective discourse" includes discourse that involves vague or referentially indeterminate expressions, as well as discourse for which some sort of nonfactualist account is appropriate. (Evaluative discourse and discourse involving indicative and/or subjunctive conditionals might be examples.) There seems to be a difficulty in making sense of factually defective discourse, and in explaining the division between it and other discourse, if one holds that the basic notion of truth is disquotational; so disquotationalists tend to deny that discourse can be factually defective, and believers in factually defective discourse tend to deny that the basic notion of truth is disquotational. But the author argues that a disquotationalist can recognize and account for each of these forms of factually defective discourse.

Field, Terri. Caring Relationships with Natural and Artificial Environments. *Environ Ethics*, 17(3), 307-320, Fall 95.

A relational-self theory claims that one's self is constituted by one's relationships. The type of ethics that is said to arise from this concept of self is often called an *ethics of care*, whereby the focus of ethical deliberation is on preserving and nurturing those relationships. Some environmental philosophers advocating a relational-self theory tend to assume that the particular relationships that constitute the self will prioritize the natural world. I question this assumption by introducing the problem of *artificial relationships*. It is unclear whether a relational-self theory recognizes relationships with the artificial world as being meaningful in any moral sense, and whether such relationships, if they can exist, should be accorded equal value to relationships with the natural world.

Fielder, John H and Black, Jonathan. But Doctor, It's My Hip!: The Fate of Failed Medical Devices. *Kennedy Inst Ethics J*, 5(2), 113-131, Je 95.

It is difficult to study failed medical devices because of a lack of data. Routine device retrieval and analysis (DRA) is essential to performance evaluation, which, in turn, is essential to good patient care. We argue for the development of a national DRA program and medical device database and discuss the major ethical and policy issues associated with this proposal.

Fields, Lloyd. Moral Beliefs and Blameworthiness. *Philosophy*, 69(270), 397-415, O 94.

Does moral ignorance excuse? An account is offered of a formal, classificatory use of "moral". In this sense of "moral", a person's acceptance of certain moral principles is a constituent of his character. So a person who accepts morally bad moral principles has, to that extent, a defect of character. It is a sufficient condition of an agent's being morally responsible for his action that his action be indicative of a defect of character. Thus, a person who acts in accordance with morally bad moral principles shows a defect of character and is therefore morally responsible for what he has done.

Fields, Stephen. Blondel's L'Action (1893) and Neo-Thomism's Metaphysics of Symbol. *Phil Theol*, 8(1), 25-40, Autumn 93.

The first three sections of this study explain the debt that Karl Rahner's metaphysics of symbol owed to the influence of Maurice Blondel and Joseph Maréchal. The concluding section suggests that a Blondel-inspired renewal of the metaphysics of symbol could challenge the restricted claim for reason offered by secular and religious post-modernity.

Fieser, James. Hume's Concealed Attack on Religion and His Early Critics. *J Phil Res*, 20, 431-449, 1995.

Like Hume scholars today, Hume's 18th century critics recognized his use of literary devices in his religious writings. Indeed, the early commentaries on Hume's religious writings are dominated by attempts to identify and decode Hume's concealed religious views. Little work has been done in Hume scholarship to understand the nature and scope of this aspect of his early critics. The purpose of the present essay is to resurrect the discussions of the "Natural History" and the *Dialogues* in which Hume's 18th century critics attempt to uncover his concealed meanings. I begin by discussing the limited value of 18th century anecdotes about Hume's personal religious views. After examining Hume's general strategy of concealment in his religious writings, I catalog and interpret individual passages from Hume's critics which acknowledge Hume's technique of concealment. I conclude by noting that their overall assessment of Hume's concealed religious views was more skeptical than the assessment of many contemporary commentators.

Fieser, James (ed) and Hume, David. *Natural History of Religion*. New York, Macmillan, 1992.

This annotated edition of Hume's *Natural History of Religion* follows the posthumous 1777 edition which includes Hume's final alterations; spelling and punctuation have not been modernized. The text restores two controversial passages which originally appeared in the unpublished edition of *Five Dissertations* (1756). The editor's introduction discusses the intellectual background of the *Natural History*, the problems of censorship which Hume faced, and 18th century reactions to the work.

Filatov, Alexander. Unethical Business Behavior in Post-Communist Russia: Origins and Trends. *Bus Ethics Quart*, 4(1), 11-15, Ja 94.

Russian is presently in a transition stage between the old centrally administered command economy and a market economy. The result is uncertainty and instability. In such a situation there is both little room and little concern for business ethics. The objective conditions for this include distortions in the systems of supply and exchange, political instability, and judicial ineffectiveness. The subjective conditions include the breakdown of morality under the communist system, and the wide acceptance of "wild" capitalism as a necessary stage in the development of a capitalist market system.

Filipec, Jindrich. "Der Mensch und die Zeit" in *Das geistige Erbe Europas, Buhr, Manfred (ed)*, 786-796. Napoli, Vivarium, 1994.

Finch, Robert D. "Aristotle's Ethics" in *Contributors to the Philosophy of Humanism, Hillar, Marian (ed)*, 43-50. Pasadena, Humanists Houston, 1994.

Finch, Robert D. "The Philosophy of Sir Karl Popper" in *Contributors to the Philosophy of Humanism, Hillar, Marian (ed)*, 133-152. Pasadena, Humanists Houston, 1994.

Finch, Sheila A. "François Rabelais as Humanist" in *Contributors to the Philosophy of Humanism, Hillar, Marian (ed)*, 83-89. Pasadena, Humanists Houston, 1994.

Findlay, J N. "Hegel as Theologian" in *Meaning, Truth, and God, Rouner, Leroy (ed)*, 177-194. Notre Dame, Univ Notre Dame Pr, 1982.

Fine, Arthur. Causes of Variability: Disentangling Nature and Nuture. *Midwest Stud Phil*, 15, 94-113, 1990.

This essay has two objectives: to investigate the extent to which one can apportion individual differences (especially personality traits) to the effects of heredity or environment, and to investigate the extent to which the causal order and realism over the causes of behavior. The results of the study are largely negative, and prompt one to question the viability of the framework of nature and nurture.

Fine, Gail. Vlastos on Socratic and Platonic Forms. *Apeiron*, 26(3-4), 67-83, S-D 93.

Fine, Gail (trans) and Irwin, Terence (trans). *Aristotle: Selections*. Indianapolis, Hackett, 1995.

Fine, Kit. "Part-Whole" in *The Cambridge Companion to Husserl, Smith, Barry (ed)*, 463-485. New York, Cambridge Univ Pr, 1995.

I attempt to provide a systematic exposition of Husserl's theory of dependent and independent part.

Fine, Kit. "Senses of Essence" in *Modality, Morality, and Belief, Sinnott-Armstrong, Walter (ed)*, 53-73. New York, Cambridge Univ Pr, 1994.

The notion of essence is clarified in an attempt to provide a firm foundation for the theory of essence.

Fine, Kit. Ontological Dependence. *Proc Aris Soc*, 95, 269-290, 1994-95.

The usual account of ontological dependence in terms of necessity is criticized; and an alternative account of terms of essence is proposed. Different notions of dependence are seen to correspond to different notions of essence.

Fine, Kit. The Logic of Essence. *J Phil Log*, 24(3), 241-273, Je 95.

Essence is construed as an indexed form of modality. Axioms are laid down and theorems are established.

Finegan, Joan. The Impact of Personal Values on Judgments of Ethical Behaviour in the Workplace. *J Bus Ethics*, 13(9), 747-755, S 94.

This study examines how our personal values influence our judgment of the morality of some workplace behaviors. Sixty-nine undergraduates were asked to rank order separately Rokeach's instrumental and terminal values in terms of their importance as guiding principles in their life. People with different value hierarchies perceived the targeted behavior differently. While the ranking of the instrumental value *honesty* was the best predictor of people's judgements about the morality of the behavior, their ranking of the instrumental value *ambition* was the best predictor of their behavioral intentions. (edited)

Fink, Conrad C. *Media Ethics*. Needham Heights, Allyn Bacon, 1995.

The book is designed to stimulate study and discussion of mass media ethical practices among two groups—media "consumers" (readers, listeners, viewers) and journalism students. Goals include consciousness-raising through case studies of media performance and illustration of how media professionals handle crucial ethical issues. A principal thrust is a step-by-step decision-making process that media professionals can use to decide how to handle ethical challenges. Included is a detailed examination of the influence advertising and "countinghouse" pressures have on newsroom performance in newsrooms of newspapers, magazines, radio and television.

Fink, Eugen and Bruzina, Ronald (trans). *Sixth Cartesian Meditation: The Idea of a Transcendental Theory of Method*. Bloomington, Indiana Univ Pr, 1995.

Fink-Eitel, Hinrich. Lust und Weisheit des Scheines: Die Alptraumwelt Alfred Hitchcocks. *Deut Z Phil*, 43(3), 539-547, 1995.

Finke, Ronald A. "Creative Insight and Preinventive Forms" in *The Nature of Insight, Sternberg, Robert J (ed)*, 255-280. Cambridge, MIT Pr, 1995.

Two forms of creative insight are distinguished. Convergent insight refers to the discovery of general principles or the solutions to problems by taking information from various sources and seeing the underlying connections or structures. Divergent insight refers to the discovery of creative implication and possibilities from structures that are already generated or provided. A particular class of structures, called preinventive forms, can often stimulate the discovery of new inventions, products, and creative concepts. Experimental studies reveal the value of using preinventive forms to promote divergent insight in creative thinking.

Finkelberg, Aryeh. Plural Worlds in Anaximander. *Amer J Philo*, 115(4), 485-506, Wint 94.

A synoptic examination of doxographical sources leads to the conclusion that the attribution of the theory of plural worlds to Anaximander can be traced back to Theophrastus and that Theophrastus meant these worlds to be single successive ones. Critical analysis exposes the invalidity of scholarly arguments against this attribution, including the contention that it would be inconsistent with Anaximander's fragment. The testimony not only proves intrinsically credible but finds independent support in certain other of Anaximander's conceptions as reported by Theophrastus.

Finkielkraut, Alain and Friedlander, Judith (trans). *The Defeat of the Mind*. New York, Columbia Univ Pr, 1995.

Finn, Don W and Lampe, James C. Teaching Ethics in Accounting Curricula. *Bus Prof Ethics J*, 13(1-2), 89-128, Spr-Sum 94.

The purpose of this study has been to determine the impact on auditors if educational interventions were successfully implemented to raise students' levels of post-conventional principled reasoning as measured by the Defining Issues Test (DIT). Data concerning attitudes, decision responses to auditor dilemmas, and DIT responses were collected from over 300 auditing students, recent graduates, and experienced audit practitioners. Conclusions are that: 1) differing interventions lead to different levels of moral development, 2) differing levels of moral development generate different decisions, and 3) students' levels of moral reasoning and decisions are different from those of both staff and experienced auditors.

Finocchiaro, Maurice A. Two Empirical Approaches to the Study of Reasoning. *Inform Log*, 16(1), 1-21, Wint 94.

David N Perkins has studied everyday reasoning by an experimental-critical approach involving tape interviews during which subjects reflect on controversial issues and articulate their reasoning on both sides. The present author has studied scientific reasoning in natural language by an historical-textual approach involving the reconstruction and evaluation of the arguments in Galileo's *Two Chief World Systems*. They have, independently, reached the strikingly similar substantive conclusion that the most common flaw of informal reasoning is the failure to consider lines of argument supporting conclusions contrary to the one in fact reached. This article describes, compares, and contrasts their respective approaches, results, and theoretical frameworks.

Fins, Joseph J and Bacchetta, Matthew D. The Physician-Assisted Suicide and Euthanasia Debate: An Annotated Bibliography of Representative Articles. *J Clin Ethics*, 5(4), 329-340, Wint 94.

Fins, Joseph J and Viederman, Milton. Commentary on "But Is It Assisted Suicide?". *Hastings Center Rep*, 25(3), 24-25, My-Je 95.

Fiorentino, Fernando. La Polemica di Leroux contro Lacordaire e Malthus sulla Questione Sociale. *Sapienza*, 48(1), 31-65, 1995.

While Marx and Malthus propose violent solutions to problems regarding the social question, in France Pierre Leroux (1797-1870) proposes a "peaceful way" with the intent of going beyond *laissenz-faire* or collectivist theories. In this undertaking, which is an explicit attempt to reconcile the rights of society, asserted in the name of "égalité", the French philosopher, (to whom we owe the terms "socialism" and "solidarity"), locates the possibility of reconciliation in the concept of "fraternité", no longer understood in a Christian sense. In this article only a segment of Leroux's proposal is presented, part of his polemic against the Dominican P Lacordaire.

Fiorillo, Vanda. *Versus* Trasimaco: E confutabile il detto "la giustizia non è altro che l'utile del più forte"?. *Riv Int Filosof Diritto*, 71(3), 499-50, 1994.

Firth, Roderick. Epistemic Merit, Intrinsic and Instrumental. *Proc Amer Phil Ass*, 55(1), 5-23, S 81.

Fisch, Menachem. Trouble-Shooting Creativity: A Critical Appraisal of David Bohm and F David Peat's 'Science Orders and Creativity'. *Hist Phil Life Sci*, 16(1), 141-153, Ja 94.

Fischer, Agneta H and Jansz, Jeroen. Reconciling Emotions with Western Personhood. *J Theor Soc Behav*, 25(1), 59-80, Mr 95.

It has often been taken for granted that Western everyday conceptions characterize emotions as irrational, involuntary, primitive bodily forces. This view of emotions is at odds with the main features of the cultural ideal of a person, here referred to as Western personhood. In this article we focus on the question of whether Western personhood really clashes with everyday conceptions of emotions. We will argue that this is not the case. Our claim will be supported by illustrating how Western persons make sense of their emotions, and more specifically how they reconcile their emotional experiences and expressions with Western personhood. People account for their feelings by telling a narrative in which emotions are presented as normal, intentional and appropriate reactions. Drawing from interviews about anger and fear, we show that people generally do not see their emotions as irrational and primitive forces, but as rational and functional responses in a particular situation. Thus, Western persons often hold a rationalized view on emotions. This bounded emotionality does not clash with the dominant form of Western personhood.

Fischer, Bernd. The End of Humanism and Fichte's Concept of European Intellectualism. *Hist Euro Ideas*, 20(4-6), 915-921, F 95.

Fischer, Johannes. Kann die Theologie der naturwissenschaftlichen Vernunft die Welt ls Schöpfung verständlich machen?. *Frei Z Phil Theol*, 41(3), 491-514, 1994.

Fischer, John Martin and Ravizza, Mark. "Responsibility for Consequences" in *In Harm's Way, Coleman, Jules L (ed)*, 183-208. New York, Cambridge Univ Pr, 1994.

We seek to give the conditions for moral responsibility for the consequences of one's actions. We employ the notion of control in a certain way. An agent can be held morally responsible for a consequence (on our approach), even though he could not have prevented it from obtaining.

Fischer, John Martin and Ravizza, Mark. Ducking Harm and Sacrificing Others. *J Soc Phil*, 25(3), 135-144, Wint 94.

There is a descriptive distinction between ducking harm and sacrificing others. But does this distinction have normative force? We suggest not; at least it is unclear that the distinction has the sort of moral consequences sometimes attributed to it.

Fischer, Josef L. The Eternal and Passing Tasks of Philosophy. *Filozof Cas*, 43(1), 99-110, 1995.

Fischer, Klaus. "Das Naturverständnis bei Galilei" in *Naturauffassungen in Philosophie, Wissenschaft, Technik: Band II, Schäfer, Lothar (ed)*, 149-183. Freiburg, Alber, 1994.

Fischer, Kurt R. "Heinrich Gomperz und die Psychoanalyse" in *Heinrich Gomperz, Karl Popper und die österreichische Philosophie, Seiler, Martin (ed)*, 83-93. Amsterdam, Rodopi, 1994.

Fischer, Kurt R (ed) and Wimmer, Franz M (ed). *Der geistige Anschluss*. Wien, WUV Univ, 1993.

Fischer, Kurt Rudolf. *Philosophie aus Wien*. Vienna, Geyer Ed, 1991.

Fischer, Marilyn and Rosenzweig, Kenneth. Attitudes of Students and Accounting Practitioners Concerning the Ethical Acceptability of Earnings Management. *J Bus Ethics*, 14(6), 433-444, Je 95.

There are many ways that accountants and managers can influence the reported accounting results of their organizational units. When such influence is directed at changing the amount of reported earnings, it is known as earnings management. The purpose of this paper is to present the results of surveys of undergraduate students, MBA students, and practicing accountants concerning their attitudes on the ethical acceptability of earnings management. Analysis of the survey results reveals how the attitudes of the three groups differ and what variables are associated with these differences. Based on the analysis, the authors suggest changes in accounting education curriculum and ethics awareness programs in business which might increase students' and practitioner's sensitivity to the ethical ramifications of earnings management.

Fischer, Marilyn M. The Orchestral Workplace. *J Soc Phil*, 25(3), 26-39, Wint 94.

Hierarchical power relations between conductor and musicians are an inherent structural feature of orchestral workplace, built right into the orchestral score. Marx's concept of alienated labor is used to show how these relations stand in the way of musical responsiveness. While Plato's "Republic" can serve as a metaphor for an orderly orchestral workplace, the "myth of the charismatic conductor" fails to sustain musicians' commitment.

Fischer, Peter. "Das Schöne, das Erhabene, die Askese und der Selbstmord" in *Naturzweckmässigkeit und ästhetische Kultur, Schwabe, Karl-Heinz (ed)*, 117-131. Sankt Augustin, Academia, 1993.

Fischer, Rudi. Is there any Logik in Madness? Linguistic Reflections on an Interpersonal Theory of Mental Illness. *Wittgenstein Stud*, n.a., 1994.

Wittgenstein's legacy does not consist in conceiving a systematic philosophy, but in a certain kind, a method of thinking. This thinking focuses on philosophical problems as illnesses of thinking and tries to cure these by means of philosophy/therapy. This approach with all its implications is certainly one of the reasons why Wittgenstein is practically ignored by a large number of academic philosophers. The therapeutic impetus of Wittgenstein's philosophy can be understood against the background of his own psychological problems. Throughout many years of his life he himself felt threatened by insanity. If one takes his descriptions of himself seriously, these apprehensions seem justified. He had an early desire to become a psychiatrist, as his friend Drury later on, and this can be interpreted as an attempt to achieve a metaposition vis-a-vis illness. However, Wittgenstein finally decided in favour of philosophy and realised his therapeutic ambitions in that field.

Fishbane, Michael. "The Image of the Human and the Rights of the Individual in Jewish Tradition" in *Human Rights and the World's Religions, Rouner, Leroy (ed)*, 17-32. Notre Dame, Univ Notre Dame Pr, 1988.

Fishel, Simon. "Human In-vitro Fertilization" in *Ethics on the Frontiers of Human Existence, Badham, Paul (ed)*, 1-43. New York, Paragon House, 1992.

This paper briefly examines the interest in procreation by men and women throughout the ages, leading to the birth of the first child conceived extracorporeally. It examines the arguments pertaining to the nature of the human conceptus from a scientific viewpoint and why many people feel so uneasy about the status of the human conceptus. The current practice of "high-technology pregnancies" for the alleviation of infertility is discussed. Finally, the current and future areas of research are also examined, with speculations on the possible advances for the future and with the discounting of some of the more fanciful and sensational but improbably claims, such as ectogenesis and cloning. (edited)

Fisher, David H. Philosophical Prejudice. *Proc Amer Phil Ass*, 60(5), 867-872, Je 87.

Fisher, David H and Fowler, Sarah B. Reimaging Moral Leadership in Business. *Bus Ethics Quart*, 5(1), 29-42, Ja 95.

In this paper we explore challenges facing leadership in a culture of "all consuming images" from a perspective which claims that images have a moral or normative dimension. The cumulative effect of contemporary image saturation is increased resistance to the normative power of an image. We also suggest that in a culturally diverse global economy, it is necessary to expand the moral aspects of good business leadership beyond providing a basis for productive, coherent group identity within a firm at the expense of seeing outsiders as "others". We also explore what imagining leadership in business might be like in a world in which visual images shape our understandings of individual and group identity. While our focus is on leadership in business, we also use examples from the political arena. We also suggest that imagining business leadership in the ways we propose may be helpful to women, providing them with an image of business leadership more closely reflective of their experience of corporate culture, its limits, and possibilities.

Fisher, Linda. Heidegger's Hermeneutic Circle. *Eidos*, 11(1-2), 7-17, Je-D 93.

Heidegger's discussion of the hermeneutic circle in *Being and Time* constitutes one of the more significant contemporary formulations of this key hermeneutical concept. In examining his formulation and appropriation of the circle, I trace the extent to which the circle represents not only a suggestive metaphor, but an important constitutive analysis in the disclosure of the fundamentally ontological and circular structure of understanding. As such, I argue that the hermeneutic circle functions as exemplar both for the account of hermeneutical understanding and for Heidegger's larger project, helping to encode the development of his thought.

Fisichella, Rino. Oportet Philosophari in Theologia (I). *Gregorianum*, 76(2), 221-262, 1995.

La théologie s'explicite à la lumière d'une compréhension toujours plus grande du mystère de la foi. Cet aspect détermine son rapport avec le savoir philosophique qu'il semble valoir la peine, aujourd'hui spécialement, de reconsidérer en vue d'une compréhension plus cohérente de l'autonomie des deux sciences. L'objet de l'article est d'esquisser une voie à travers laquelle il devienne possible de mettre en évidence le fondement épistémologique du savoir théologique par rapport à la philosophie. Dans cette première partie de l'étude, on se concentre sur les questions de méthode et sur les principes nécessaires pour un usage correct de la philosophie en théologie. Le panorama historique qui est présenté tente de montrer le rapport entre foi et raison tel qu'il s'est concrétisé aux moments plus significatifs de l'histoire de la pensée théologique.

Fisk, Milton (ed). *Justice*. Atlantic Highlands, Humanities Pr, 1993.

Fisk, Milton T. Outrage and Authority. *Phil Hist Sci*, 2(2), 1-25, O 93.

Fitzpatrick, Joseph. Lonergan and the Later Wittgenstein. *Method*, 10(1), 27-50, Spr 92.

The article compares Wittgenstein's notion of understanding, one of picturing or pointing, with Lonergan's notion of understanding and concludes that Lonergan provides a correction of the Wittgensteinian account. Since Wittgenstein's migration to the realm of public discourse is motivated by a mistaken understanding of understanding, Lonergan's account of understanding, the role it plays in knowing and its relation to language provide an alternative to Wittgenstein's program for philosophy. Where Wittgenstein invests normativity in the linguistic-social matrix, Lonergan invests it in the intentional operations we perform when coming to know, thus overcoming some of the outstanding problems of linguistic analysis.

Fitzpatrick, Joseph. Reading as Understanding. *Method*, 12(1), 37-61, Spr 94.

The article compares what Frank Smith has to say about reading as a process with what Bernard Lonergan has to say about the process of coming to understand in any context. There is a large measure of agreement, particularly in respect of the notions that we bring meaning to the text; that meaning is not in the printed or the spoken word; that meaning is what is intended. The importance of questioning, predicting and intending are all brought out. the two authors agree about reading as understanding but Lonergan could help save Smith from the embarrassments of the "homunculus fallacy".

Fitzpatrick, Joseph. 'Town Criers of Inwardness' or Reflections on Rorty. *Method*, 13(1), 1-33, Spr 95.

The article compares Richard Rorty's interpretation of the history of Western philosophy with that of Bernard Lonergan. It summarises the position of each, and diagnoses a contradiction between the "Whiggish" turn of Rorty's argument and his forthright contention that the history of philosophy is a series of accidents. It maintains that Rorty's interpretation overlooks an epistemological tradition other than the dominant one, for which Lonergan is probably the major spokesperson in English today. The article draws attention to Galileo's role in the Western epistemological tradition and sees Rorty's epistemological behaviorism as, in some ways, a fulfillment of the Galilean influence.

Flage, Daniel E. Hume's Deontology. *Int Stud Phil*, 26(4), 29-46, 1994.

Flage, Daniel E. *Understanding Logic*. Englewood Cliffs, Prentice Hall, 1995.

Understanding Logic is a comprehensive introduction to logic. It examines the functions of language, definitions, and informal fallacies. It covers categorical logic. It covers symbolic logic through the first-order predicate calculus with identity, and allows the instructor to choose between a system of natural deduction and the truth-tree technique. The discussions of induction include analogy, Mill's Methods, statistical reasoning, and the scientific method. There are over 1700 exercises with solutions included to all the odd-numbered problems. The discussions of issues are easily accessible to undergraduates, and the text is generously sprinkled with bits of humor.

Flage, Daniel E and Glass, Ronald J. Hume's Problem and the Possibility of Normative Ethics. *J Value Inq*, 29(2), 231-239, Je 95.

The essay shows that if the covering law model of moral justification is correct, Hume's "is"-"ought" paragraph calls the possibility of a justifiable theory of moral obligation into doubt. The doubts are delineated through a careful examination of the "is"-"ought" paragraph, and a skeptical solution to the doubts is presented.

Flanagan, Owen. "Multiple Identity, Character Transformation, and Self-Reclamation" in *Philosophical Psychopathology, Graham, George (ed)*, 135-162. Cambridge, MIT Pr, 1993.

Flanagan, Owen. Deconstructing Dreams: The Spandrels of Sleep. *J Phil*, 92(1), 5-27, Ja 95.

Flax, Jane. Postmodernism and the Gender Relations in Feminist Theory. *Filozof Cas*, 42(5), 745-761, 1994.

A central object of feminist theory is to analyze gender—its multiple meanings, the ways it is constituted and changes over time in one and in many societies, its effects on apparently non-gendered activities such as thinking, and its interactions with and interdependence on other social relations such as class and race. In insisting on the social constitution and instability of gender, feminist theorists join in the decentering of subjectivity which is also an important project for postmodernists. While feminists' attention to relations of domination makes them sceptical about the potential gender biases in postmodernism, the epistemological conflicts within feminist discourses also indicate that they have much to gain from closer attention to postmodern ones.

Flax, Jane. Race/Gender and the Ethics of Difference: A Reply to Okin's "Gender Inequality and Cultural Differences". *Polit Theory*, 23(3), 500-510, Ag 95.

Flay, Joseph C. Ambivalence About Ambiguity. Review of *Sartre's Political Theory* by William L McBride. *Res Phenomenol*, 23, 212-221, 1993.

Fleck, Christian. "Sieg der *Offenen Gesellschaft*?" in *Heinrich Gomperz, Karl Popper und die österreichische Philosophie, Seiler, Martin (ed)*, 201-222. Amsterdam, Rodopi, 1994.

Fleck, Leonard M. Just Caring: Oregon, Health Care Rationing, and Informed Democratic Deliberation. *J Med Phil*, 19(4), 367-388, Ag 94.

This essay argues that our national efforts at health reform ought to be informed by eleven key lessons for Oregon. Specifically, we must learn that the need for health care rationing is inescapable, that any rationing process must be public and visible and that fair rationing protocols must be self-imposed through a process of rational democratic deliberation. Part I of this essay notes that rationing is a ubiquitous feature of our health care system at present, but it is mostly hidden rationing, which is presumptively unjust. Part II argues that the need for health care rationing is inescapable. Although Oregon is flawed as a model of health rationing, it gives us worthy moral lessons for health reform at the national level, which I analyze and defend in Part III. The most significant of these lessons is the importance of rational democratic deliberation in articulating fair rationing protocols for a community. In Part IV I sketch the philosophic justification for this approach and respond to some important criticisms from Daniels.

Flego, Gvozden. Thinking the Post-Socialism: From Socialist Community to Pluralistic Society. *J Phil Res*, 20, 499-509, 1995.

The author discusses some aspects of the problem how to transform the former socialist into democratic states. In the first part he argues that the 'socialist societies' were not societies in the modern sense but organized in the way of traditional community without (civil) society. In the second part the author warns that the realization of the "European way of life," as a basic program of changes in Europe in 1989, was misunderstood because it was conceived as a fixed content and not as a procedure of attaining agreement. In the third part he concludes that nationalism and fervent religiosity, which predominate in several ex-socialist countries, are main obstacles of the transformation of the former socialism because of their exclusion of the different. (edited)

Fleischman, Alan R and Blustein, Jeffrey. The Pro-Life Maternal-Fetal Medicine Physician: A Problem of Integrity. *Hastings Center Rep*, 25(1), 22-26, Jan-Feb 95.

Fletcher, David B. Response to Nigel M de S Cameron's "Bioethics and the Challenge of the Post-Consensus Society". *Ethics Med*, 11(1), 7-12, Spr 95.

In this paper I examine the views of evangelical bioethicist Nigel M de S Cameron, who believes that the secular bioethics establishment is at the leading edge of a movement in medicine and society characterized by a rejection of traditional Christian and Hippocratic values, a movement toward what he calls "post-consensus medicine". In my paper I challenge important elements of his criticisms of the methods of secular bioethics and present my own assessment of the proper role of philosophical bioethical method. In this connection I consider the recent discussion of bioethical method by Edmund Pellegrino. I conclude that this method is a valid and essential resource for the rational discussion of bioethical issues in a pluralistic society, and in particular defend the principle of autonomy and the informed consent requirement against his criticisms.

Fleurbaey, Marc. Equal Opportunity or Equal Social Outcome. *Econ Phil*, 11(1), 25-55, Ap 95.

This paper critically examines recent proposals made by R Arneson and G Cohen to seek equality of opportunity in society. It points out many conceptual and ethical problems with this goal, and proposes another way to introduce individual responsibility into the formulation of egalitarianism.

Flew, Antony. Responding to Plato's Thrasymachus. *Philosophy*, 70(273), 436-447, Jl 95.

In *The Republic* of Plato Thrasymachus, in debunking mode, offers "the advantage of the stronger" as his definition of the word 'justice'. But if that was truly the meaning of the word there would be no falsehood or hypocrisy in hypocritical pretensions to be acting justly. In his response Socrates tries to make out that their justice is always advantageous to the just themselves. To do this he presents his vision of an ideal city state. That is, of course, strictly irrelevant. And in the actual world the contribution which Socrates tries to defend neither is nor could be true.

Flew, Antony. *Thinking About Social Thinking (Second Edition)*. Amherst, Prometheus, 1995.

This introduction to the philosophy of the social sciences insists that they must, because of the nature of their subject, differ fundamentally from the natural and the biological. For instance: since people can and cannot but make choices, and since choosers as such cannot be inescapably necessitated to choose in the senses in which they do choose, there cannot be natural laws of human action. This second edition adds: both a treatment of the promise of the socialist project and its failure; and a review of scandalous dishonesties in the work of Marx and of some later professing social scientists.

Flichman, Eduardo H. Causas. Leyes Naturales y Explicaciones Científicas. *Rev Latin de Filosof*, 21(1), 37-52, Fall 95.

During the last years it has been developed a philosophical stream which supports the idea that scientific explanations are based, at least partially, in *causal processes*, whose roots must be looked for in contemporary physical theories. Phil Dowe, for instance, bases the typical asymmetry of causal processes in irreversible processes tied to the second principle of thermodynamics and to the decay of the *k* mesons. I try to object such ideas by pointing out that the explication of the notion of a *causal process* is a nominally or conventionally necessary statement which transcends the theories and that, hence, cannot be tied to a fixed theory and fail in others. Previously I discuss the notion of *scientific explanation*.

Flichman, Eduardo H. Hard and Soft Accidental Uniformities. *Phil Sci*, 62(1), 31-43, Mr 95.

I discuss some aspects of the epistemological distinction between laws of nature and accidental uniformities. In order that the exposition be self-contained I briefly provide a taxonomy proposed in another work for statements that appear in a scientific theory. Once this taxonomy has been presented I attempt to prove two very different types of accidental uniformities: hard and soft. The distinction is fundamental because the latter have frequently been confused with laws of nature. I try to justify why I believe that these statements are accidental uniformities and not laws of nature.

Flichman, Eduardo Héctor. "Universales, Particulares, Simetría, Leyes Naturales" in *Temas Actuales de Filosofía, Palacios, María Julia (ed)*, 225-232. Buenos Aires, Univ Nacional Salta, 1993.

This paper outlines a first part of a theory of universals needed to develop ideas about laws of nature. Universals *emerge* from members of bundles of particulars and particulars *emerge* from members of bundles of universals without vicious circularity. Reality is a conjunctive state of affairs (that does not imply existence of atomic ones). Universals and particulars are not autonomous. Each requires the other in order to exist. Reality is an *auto-supported web* of states of affairs, where universals support particulars and conversely. Symmetry is not complete. Laws of nature describe the structure of some special bundles of particulars.

Flores Ortiz, Roberto. La Admiración en Tomás de Aquino y el *Diccionario de Autoridades*—Análisis Semiótico—(II). *Analogia*, 5(2), 49-63, 1991.

Floridi, Luciano. The Diffusion of Sextus Empiricus's Works in the Renaissance. *J Hist Ideas*, 56(1), 63-85, Ja 95.

The article provides a comprehensive examination of all the available evidence concerning the recovery and influence of Sextus Empiricus' works on Renaissance culture. Two previously unstudied manuscripts are analysed, Paéz de Castro's translation of the *Outlines* and a Renaissance copy of Lorenzi's translation. A new study of the extant Greek manuscripts containing portions of Sextus Empiricus' works is also offered. On the basis of the scholarly work, it is argued that although Pyrrhonian arguments were not widely used in philosophy during the Renaissance, Sextus Empiricus' works were better known among the humanists than has been previously suspected, and that therefore we should speak of a Renaissance lack of interest in the anti-epistemological function of Pyrrhonian arguments, rather than infer from the absence of "influence" a corresponding absence of knowledge of the skeptical literature during the fifteenth and sixteenth centuries.

Floridi, Luciano. '*Cupiditas Veri Videnti*': Pierre Villemandy's Dogmatic versus Cicero's Sceptical Interpretation of 'Man's Desire to Know'. *Brit J Hist Phil*, 3(1), 29-56, F 95.

Dogmatists and sceptics usually agree on the fact that "the desire to know is innate in man", and on interpreting this as the ideal force inspiring the search for knowledge. According to the sceptic, however, knowledge remains unattainable quite independently of the fact that man desires it, while according to the dogmatist the desire to know governing the search for knowledge is an innate *conatus*, which it would be unreasonable to suppose intrinsically unfulfillable. In order to clarify the discrepancies occurring between these two positions, the article analyses as paradigmatic cases the anti-sceptical argument *ex communi sciendi desiderio*, proposed by Pierre de Villemandy, and Cicero's more sceptical and purely anthropological reading of the characterization of man as a knowledge-seeker.

Floucat, Yves. Chronique de philosophie. *Rev Thomiste*, 94(2), 285-319, Ap-Je 94.

Floucat, Yves. Étienne Gilson et la métaphysique de l'acte d'être. *Rev Thomiste*, 94(3), 360-395, Jl-S 94.

Flüeler, Christoph. Ontologie und Politik: Quod racio principantes et subiecti sumitur ex racione actus et potencie. *Frei Z Phil Theol*, 41(3), 445-462, 1994.

Fluri, Philippe. New Trends in Russian Philosophy. *Philosophia (Athens)*, 23-24, 292-296, 1993-94.

In this study the new trends in contemporary Russian philosophy are examined and emphasis is mainly given to that of Russian personalism, represented by famous thinkers as they are Solovjov, Berdjajev, Schestov, Bulgakov, Frank, Losskij. Russian personalism not only rejects Marxism but also capitalism. Its objective is to challenge Western individualism at least on three levels: 1) To give history an aim, 2) To give dignity to the human person, and 3) To favor solidarity as the necessary condition for human survival and, at the same time, as the condition for the possibility of becoming one-self.

Flusser, Vilém. *Ende der Geschichte, Ende der Stadt?*. Vienna, Picus, 1992.

Flynn, Thomas R. "Inauthentic and Authentic Love in Sartrean Existentialism" in *The Nature and Pursuit of Love, Goicoechea, David (ed)*, 208-220. Buffalo, Prometheus, 1995.

After rehearsing the better known passages in Sartre's phenomenological ontology that militate against even the most basic concept of love as mutual well wishing (*amor benevolentiae*), I consider other passages, especially from his *Notebooks for an Ethics*, that defend a concept of love which contradicts the one usually associated with his work. I conclude with thoughts on the significance of this paradox for Sartrean existentialism as well as with observations about what theorists like Irving Singer might learn from Sartre's phenomenology, his politico-economic philosophy, his aesthetics, and his social ontology regarding a more adequate account of the phenomenon of love.

Flynn, Thomas R. The Future Perfect and the Perfect Future: History has its Reasons. *Amer Cath Phil Quart*, 68(Supp), 1-15, 1994.

History is a practical discipline whose formal object, in classical terms, is the "good" more than the "true." But the recalcitrance of the event resists linguistic reductionism. If the focus of history as history remains the future perfect (the "not yet" of the "already was"), the focus of human history as human (as poietic act) rests on the *ideal* future, the future as value or ought-to-be. One's "choice" of history is a function of one's choice or rejection of a projected end-terminus of history. So if each generation has the science it inherits, it has the history it deserves.

Flynn, Thomas R. Truth Is a Thing of This World. Review of *Michel Foucault's Force of Flight: Toward an Ethics for Thought* by James W Bernauer. *Res Phenomenol*, 23, 193-201, 1993.

Foucault's work, whether archaeology, genealogy, or "problematization," aims not simply to render the familiar strange and the strange familiar, but to face us with the *Other* that questions our certainties and counters our projects, the other that we have excluded by the truths and other forms of normalization prevalent in our society. No promises are made, not even the *als ob* of a practical ideal. Bernauer captures this spirit in his excellent study as he defends the thesis of Foucault's "vision of thought as an essentially ethical activity" and goes on to describe his "ecstatic" thinking as a "worldly mysticism."

Flynn, Thomas W. Rekindling Humanity's Love Affair with Science and Technology. *Free Inq*, 14(4), 14-17, Fall 94.

Flynn, Thomas W and Madigan, Timothy J. Francis Crick on the Workings of the Brain. *Free Inq*, 14(4), 18-21, Fall 94.

An interview with Crick on his book *The Astonishing Hypothesis*, wherein he discusses his views on why the search for "The Soul" is futile.

Fodor, Jerry A. "*Déjá vu* All Over Again: How Danto's Aesthetics Recapitulates the Philosophy of Mind" in *Danto and his Critics, Rollins, Mark (ed)*, 41-54. Cambridge, Blackwell, 1993.

Fodor, Jerry A. "The Mind-Body Problem" in *The Mind-Body Problem: A Guide to the Current Debate, Warner, Richard (ed)*, 24-40. Cambridge, Blackwell, 1994.

Fodor, Jerry A and Lepore, Ernest. "Is Intentional Ascription Intrinsically Normative?" in *Dennett and his Critics, Dahlbom, Bo (ed)*, 70-82. Cambridge, Blackwell, 1995.

Fodor, Jerry A and Lepore, Ernie. What *Is* The Connection Principle?. *Phil Phenomenol Res*, 54(4), 837-845, D 94.

Fodor, Jerry A and LePore, Ernest. "Replies" in *Holism: A Consumer Update, Fodor, Jerry (ed)*, 303-322. Amsterdam, Rodopi, 1993.

Fodor, Jerry A (ed) and LePore, Ernest (ed). *Holism: A Consumer Update*. Amsterdam, Rodopi, 1993.

Fodor, Jerry A and McLaughlin, Brian P. "Connectionism and the Problem of Systematicity" in *Connectionism: Debates on Psychological Explanation, Macdonald, Cynthia (ed)*, 199-222. Cambridge, Blackwell, 1995.

Fodor, Jerry A and Pylyshyn, Zenon W. "Connectionism and Cognitive Architecture: A Critical Analysis" in *Connectionism: Debates on Psychological Explanation, Macdonald, Cynthia (ed)*, 90-163. Cambridge, Blackwell, 1995.

Fogarty, Timothy J. Accountant Ethics: A Brief Examination of Neglected Sociological Dimensions. *J Bus Ethics*, 14(2), 103-115, F 95.

Traditional treatments of accountant ethics make implicit assumptions inconsistent with a sociological perspective. This paper identifies the ways in which accountant ethics have been approached both in literature pertaining to practice and the classroom. The boundaries of the topic, when its definitions are left tacit, systematically preclude many important features of ethics. Included in these are sociological treatments of the accounting profession as a group extra-personal aspects of decision making, the stratification of accounting practice, and a sense of ethical action. The paper concludes with an illustration of how institutional theory has the potential to create a systematic sociological interpretation of accountant ethics.

Fogelin, Robert. "Pierre, Saul, Ruth, and Bob and a Puzzle about Belief" in *Modality, Morality, and Belief, Sinnott-Armstrong, Walter (ed)*, 201-214. New York, Cambridge Univ Pr, 1994.

This essay examines Ruth Marcus's treatment of Kripke's "A Puzzle about Belief". It shows that the puzzle lacks depth, simply turning on a failure to distinguish having a coherent world picture from having a coherent picture of the world. Given this distinction, the puzzle is easily solved. Thus Marcus does not need much of the heavy weaponry she brings against it. Her claim—that it is not possible to have a belief whose content is self-contradictory—is not needed to deal with Kripke's puzzle. It is, however, an important idea which she develops in an innovative and persuasive way.

Foley, Richard. "Egoism in Epistemology" in *Socializing Epistemology: The Social Dimensions of Knowledge, Schmitt, Frederick (ed)*, 53-73. Lanham, Rowman & Littlefield, 1994.

The article is an examination of egoism and nonegoism epistemology. Epistemic egoists grant no fundamental authority to the opinions of others. They are prepared to accept the testimony of others only if they have independent reasons for thinking the testimony is reliable. Nonegoists, by contrast, grant fundamental authority to at least some people. The danger of egoism is that it threatens not to do justice to the fact that intellectually, as in other matters, we are thoroughly social beings; the danger of nonegoism is that it threatens not to do justice to the temptations of group-think and the values of independent opinions. The author sketches a position that gives due recognition to the fact that as intellectual beings we are both social and autonomous.

Foley, Richard. "Pragmatic Reasons for Belief" in *Gambling on God: Essays on Pascal's Wager, Jordan, Jeffrey (ed)*, 31-46. Lanham, Rowman & Littlefield, 1994.

In our deliberations and discussions about what to believe, we rarely consider the practical benefits of belief. This can seem puzzling, since what we believe has consequences for the quality of our lives and the lives of those around us. The author proposes a general theory of rationality and then within that theory shows how the practical consequences of a belief can affect its rationality. But within the context of the general theory, it is also possible to defend our practice of generally not taking the practical benefits of a belief into account in our deliberations about what to believe.

Foley, Richard. How Should Future Opinion Affect Current Opinion?. *Phil Phenomenol Res*, 54(4), 747-766, D 94.

If I discover that in one year I will believe P, how should this affect my current attitude towards P? The author argues, against van Fraassen and others, that except in a few highly unusual situations, there is no reason to make our own future opinions a significant factor in deliberations about what now to believe.

Foley, Richard. Probabilism. *Midwest Stud Phil*, 15, 114-129, 1990.

According to probabilists, the central normative requirement governing our degrees of belief is that they be coherent. The author argues that probabilists are mistaken in claiming that incoherence is always symptomatic of irrationality. The discovery of incoherence does tell us that it is not possible for all of our opinions to be accurate, and it thus puts us on guard about them. The mistake of probabilists is one of oversimplifying this role. They make the avoidance of incoherence into an epistemic categorical imperative.

Folina, Janet. Putnam, Realism, and Truth. *Synthese*, 103(2), 141-152, My 95.

There are several distinct components of the realist antirealist debate. Since each side in the debate has its disadvantages, it is tempting to try to combine realist theses with antirealist theses in order to obtain a better, more moderate position. Putnam attempts to hold a realist concept of truth, yet he rejects realist metaphysics and realist semantics. He calls this view "internal realism". Truth is realist on this picture for it is objective, rather than merely intersubjective, and eternal. Putnam introduces a concept of epistemic idealization—epistemically ideal conditions, or idealized justification—to try to ground the strong objectivity of truth without sliding into metaphysical realism. I argue that the concept of ideal conditions to which Putnam appeals does not cohere with his (antirealist) commitment to an assertability conditions account of meaning.

Follari, Roberta A. Sobre la construcción histórica de la razón occidental. *Rev Filosof (Costa Rica)*, 31(75-76), 193-201, D 93.

From Plato, Logos was assumed as possibility for superation of disorder and evil in the world. This implicates an imaginary subordination of sensitiveness and body to reason and spirit. The history of philosophy—a part of social history—sustained that position in different ways, beginning with Greek philosophers until modernity.

Folscheid, Dominique. The Status of the Embryo from a Christian Point of View. *Ethics Med*, 10(3), 57-59, Autumn 94.

The Christian point of view about the embryo is paradoxical, because it is not a matter for faith. Christian principles appeal for the use of reason. But scientific reason cannot pronounce itself upon the ontological status of the embryo. So the Christian has to become a philosopher. However, philosophical reason needs the experience of the recognition of the 'more-than-neighbor', which is a Christian experience.

Foltz, Bruce V. *Inhabiting the Earth: Heidegger, Environmental Ethics, and the Metaphysics of Nature*. Atlantic Highlands, Humanities Pr, 1995.

Fonnesu, Luca. Der Optimismus und seine Kritiker im Zeitalter der Aufklärung. *Stud Leibniz*, 26(2), 131-162, 1994.

This paper examines the terminological history and the conceptual ambiguity of "optimism" in the philosophical discussion of the European Enlightenment. "Optimism" is in fact a neologism of the XIIIth century which arises in the discussion on the concept of the best possible world and spreads rapidly from France to all the European countries. The concept of "optimism" has not a unique meaning. Several forms of optimism can be isolated in connection with the crisis of the philosophical theodicy, i.e., with the discussion about the sense of the universe, the value of human life, the ethical disposition of human nature.

Fonnesu, Luca. La Società Concreta: Considerazioni su Fichte e Hegel. *Daimon Rev Filosof*, 9, 231-248, 1994.

This study suggests a comparison between the social and political philosophy of Fichte and Hegel, with special attention to the problem of the existence of classes or ranks, the *Stände*. Both Fichte and Hegel think that the determination of the abstract juridical subject in a concrete social figure can avoid the social and ethical disorder caused by the new industrial world. Nevertheless, Fichte and Hegel give different interpretation of the concept of *Stand*, and of its significance for a theory of society and of State. A further important common feature—the search for a "universal class"—reveals a different conception of the relationship between State and society.

Font, Josep Maria and Rodríquez, Gonzalo. Algebraic Study of Two Deductive Systems of Relevance Logic. *Notre Dame J Form Log*, 35(3), 369-397, Sum 94.

In this paper two deductive systems (i.e., two consequence relations) associated with relevance logic are studied from an algebraic point of view. One is defined by the familiar, Hilbert-style, formalization of R; the other one is a weak version of it, called WR, which appears as the semantic entailment of the Meyer-Routley-Fine semantics, and which has already been suggested by Wójcicki for other reasons. This weaker consequence is first defined indirectly, using R, but we prove that the first one turns out to be an axiomatic extension of WR. Moreover we provide WR with a natural Gentzen calculus (of a classical kind). It is proved that both deductive systems have the same associated class of algebras but different classes of models on these algebras.

Fontán, Manuel. La Estética de Kant como Filosofía de la Cultura. *Themata*, 13, 157-174, 1995.

In his *Critique of Judgment* (KrU) Kant put forth his aesthetics as the crowning achievement of a transcendental system, in order to present a solution to a question whose problematic nature he considered to be gnoseological (transcendental). The thesis of this paper is to present Kant's aesthetics as a philosophy of culture, given the fact that the question he tried to solve was much more vexing in the realm of the philosophy of culture than in the realm of gnoseology.

Fontana, Andrea (ed) and Dickens, David R (ed). *Postmodernism and Social Inquiry*. New York, Guilford, 1994.

Fontanille, Jacques. Modalisations et modulations passionnelles. *Rev Int Phil*, 48(189), 341-362, 1994.

Foot, Philippa. "Moral Dilemmas Revisited" in *Modality, Morality, and Belief, Sinnott-Armstrong, Walter (ed)*, 117-128. New York, Cambridge Univ Pr, 1994.

Foot, Philippa. Utilitarianism and the Virtues. *Proc Amer Phil Ass*, 57(2), 273-283, N 83.

Foppa, Carlo. L'analyse philosophique jonassienne de la théorie de l'évolution: aspects problématiques. *Laval Theol Phil*, 50(3), 575-593, O 94.

Le *Principe Responsabilité* est certainement l'oeuvre la plus connue de Hans Jonas; toutefois son système est fondé, pour une bonne partie, sur la philosophie de la biologie exposée essentiellement dans *The Phenomenon of Life*. Dans le quatrième essai de cet ouvrage, Jonas propose une analyse critique de la théorie de l'évolution qui nécessite un approfondissement. En particulier il s'agit d'analyser la conviction de Jonas selon laquelle le darwinisme serait une sorte d'ancêtre de l'existentialisme et du nihilisme. De plus il faut se demander si Jonas avait vraiment besoin d'une hypothèse scientifique pour fonder sa métaphysique surtout à la lumière du fait que la science moderne n'a aucune référence métaphysique.

Forbes, Alexander M. Ultimate Reality and Ethical Meaning: Theological Utilitarianism in Eighteenth Century England. *Ultim Real Mean*, 18(2), 119-138, Je 95.

The conjunction of utilitarian ethics with Christian theology had an impact upon the thought of eighteenth-century England that has been underestimated. Reexamination of what is usually considered the first utilitarian treatise, Richard Cumberland's *De legibus naturae* (1672), provides new evidence that the earliest utilitarianism was, specifically, "theological"—and, furthermore, that this utilitarianism reshaped natural law theory in ways that have been overlooked. In later writers such as Samuel Johnson and Sarah Fielding, additional evidence is to be found which suggests that "theological utilitarianism" had a much wider impact upon eighteenth-century social thought than has been assumed.

Forbes, Graeme R. Realism and Scepticism: Brains in a Vat Revisited. *J Phil*, 92(4), 205-222, Ap 95.

I argue that Putnam's proof that we are not brains in a vat is technically successful but does not refute scepticism.

Ford, Ann and Yeo, Michael. "Integrity" in *Concepts and Cases in Nursing Ethics, Yeo, Michael (& others)*, 184-218. Peterborough, Broadview Pr, 1991.

Ford, Lewis S. The Creation of 'Eternal' Objects. *Mod Sch*, 71(3), 191-222, Mr 94.

Uncreated eternal objects may be reconceived as repeatable atemporal objects, provided their function in explaining novelty can be accounted for. The initial subjective aim needs to be considered as an unobjectifiable divine subjective form. By its guidance we can construct novel final forms by means of conceptual reproduction from past actualities. The forms are "fixed" by the physical prehensions these forms unify. Successor occasions then pretend and abstract these forms as atemporal forms. Once abstracted, these objects appear to be 'eternal', having no temporal traces.

Ford, Lewis S. The Riddle of *Religion in the Making*. *Process Stud*, 22(1), 42-50, Spr 93.

Many interpret the final vision of God in Whitehead's *Process and Reality* as already largely anticipated in his earlier book. Compositional analysis reveals, however, that there are two layers of insertions portraying two distinct, unanticipated conceptions of God. The final layer presents the familiar God of process theism. The other layer portrays "the primordial actuality" as purely nontemporal but concrescent. If we put these insertions to one side, the original text of *Process and Reality* (over 200 pages) mentions God only as nontemporal and nonconcrescent. What led to this apparent impoverishment? Why did Whitehead draw back from the magnificent portrayal he had just proclaimed?

Forest, F and Siksou, M. Concept Development and Computation of Meaning Thought and Language by Vygotsky. *Commun Cog—AI*, 11(1-2), 181-199, 1994.

Vygotsky's approach to the construction of concepts contrasts with the models which are commonly used in artificial intelligence. We shall present the main ideas of Vygotsky's work on the relations between thought and language, and the main steps of concept building in a child's mind. We shall outline what makes this approach so modern and into a potential basis for computing systems for the representation of meaning linked to learning and adaptation. We propose some architectural and structural choices for such a system. We hope this attempt will allow the testing of some hypotheses.

Forgie, J William. The Cosmological and Ontological Arguments: How Saint Thomas Solved the Kantian Problem. *Relig Stud*, 31(1), 89-100, Mr 95.

Let us call the Dependency Theses (DT) the view, first stated by Kant, that certain versions of the cosmological argument depend on the ontological argument. At least two different reasons have been given for the supposed dependence. Given the DT, some of Aquinas' views about God's essence, and about our knowledge of God's existence, can seem, at least at first, to be inconsistent. I consider two different ways of defending Aquinas against this suspicion of inconsistency. On the first defense, based on a widespread understanding of his notion of 'necessary being', Aquinas' views fall outside the scope of the DT. The success of this defense is doubtful. There is, however, another defense to be found in Aquinas' work, one directed not to avoiding, but actually to rejecting, the DT. In this second defense, the DT is not a correct assessment even of those views that *do* fall within its scope. It success means that Aquinas had available a principled refutation of the DT some five hundred years before it was first formulated.

Forhan, Kate Langdon (ed & trans) and De Pizan, Christine. *The Book of the Body Politic*. New York, Cambridge Univ Pr, 1994.

Forment, Eudaldo. El Ente Como Objeto Formal de la Metafísica. *Analogia*, 4(2), 37-68, 1990.

Formigari, Lia. La Sémiotique Empiriste Face au Kantisme. Bruxelles, Pierre Mardaga, 1994.

This book aims at retracing a semiotic trend in German late 18th-and early 19th-century philosophy, which has been largely overlooked by historians of the *deutsche Bewegung*. Kant's and Hegel's contemporaries have variously contributed to delineate such a trend, by attempts to approach epistemology from the standpoint of a general theory of signs, by their use of linguistic argumentation in the refutation of Kant's transcendental philosophy and Hegel's metaphysics, by the studies of linguistic behaviors in empirical psychology, and by practising a philosophy generally conceived as analysis of language.

Fornari, Aníbal. Dialéctica y Política. *Stromata*, 50(1-2), 57-103, Ja-Je 94.

Forrest, Peter. Inherited Responsibility, Karma and Original Sin. *Sophia (Australia)*, 33(3), 1-13, N 94.

My aim of this paper is to show how it is possible that we can: 1) inherit responsibility for what our culture ancestors have done; 2) pass on karma to others who will live in the future; and 3) be born in a state of original sin. My method will be to sketch how these three doctrines can be explained using the reincarnation thesis which I reject, and then to offer a speculation in which X's being a reincarnation of person Y is replaced by X's being partly constituted by participation in a collective entity which contains Y as an earlier stage. The result will then provide speculative reconstructions of the three doctrines.

Forrest, Peter. Māya and the Pluralist Predicament. *Austl J Phil*, 73(1), 31-48, Mr 95.

In this paper the māyā thesis and the atman thesis are used to discuss the *pluralist predicament*, namely the difficulty in jointly satisfying the following requirements: i) We should be able to have genuine respect for those with whom we disagree. ii) We should be faithful to the transcendence of reality. iii) We should not be forced to suspend judgment out of respect for those with whom we disagree. The proposed way out of the pluralist predicament is based on the Ideal Knower Theory. As a first approximation this states that the truth is what God believes.

Forrester, James William. Conflicts of Obligation. *Amer Phil Quart*, 32(1), 31-44, Ja 95.

Forsberg, Ralph P. Rationality and Allocating Scarce Medical Resources. *J Med Phil*, 20(1), 25-42, F 95.

In an article titled, "Who Shall Live When Not All Can?", James Childress proposes a system for allocating scarce lifesaving medical resources based on random selection procedures. Childress writes of random selection procedures, (They) "cannot be dismissed as a 'nonrational' and 'nonhuman' ... without an inquiry into the reasons, including human values which might justify it". My thesis is that once we concentrate on determining the rationality of random selection procedures, we will see that Childress's claim that we cannot dismiss such procedures as 'nonrational' is open to question. My claim will be that while both random selection and social worth procedures are rationally defensible systems, random selection procedures easily lead to specific choices that are objectively irrational, apart from the limited perspective of the random selection process itself.

Forster, Malcolm and Saidel, Eric. Connectionism and the Fate of Folk Psychology: A Reply to Ramsey, Stich and Garon. *Phil Psych*, 7(4), 437-452, 1994.

Ramsey, Stich and Garon (1991) argue that if the correct theory of mind is some parallel distributed processing theory, then folk psychology must be false. Their idea is that if the nodes and connections that encode one representation are causally active then all representations encoded by the same set of nodes and connections are also causally active. We present a clear, and concrete, counterexample to RSG's argument. In conclusion, we suggest that folk psychology and connectionism are best understood as complementary theories. Each has different limitations, yet each will co-evolve with the other in an overlapping domain of 'normal' psychology.

Forster, Malcolm R. Non-Bayesian Foundations for Statistical Estimation, prediction, and the Ravens Example. *Erkenntnis*, 40(3), 357-376, My 94.

The paper provides a formal proof that efficient estimates of parameters, which vary as little as possible when measurements are repeated, may be expected to provide more accurate predictions. The definition of predictive accuracy is motivated by the work of Akaike (1973). Surprisingly, the same explanation provides a novel solution for a well known problem for standard theories of scientific confirmation—the Ravens Paradox. This is significant in light of the fact that standard Bayesian analyses of the paradox fail to account for the predictive utility of universal laws like "All ravens are black".

Forster, Paul D. The Limits of Pragmatic Realism. *Phil Today*, 38(3-4), 243-258, Fall 94.

Hilary Putnam and Nicholas Jardine defend a Peircean, or, limit theory of truth largely because it provides a middle-ground between metaphysical realism and relativism by reconciling an antinomy involving intuitions about the immanence and the transcendence of reason. I argue that Peirce's original solution to this antinomy fails *by its own lights*. Moreover, neither Putnam's nor Jardine's revisions of Peirce's limit theory is immune from these problems. In fact the problems with the limit theory get worse once Peirce's contentions about the history of science are corrected.

Fort, Andrew O. Going on Knowing? The Development of the Idea of Living Liberation in the Upanisads. *J Indian Phil*, 22(4), 379-390, D 94.

My article looks at the development of the idea of living liberation (*jivanmukti*), so significant in Advaita Vedanta, in the early *Upanisads*. There we see both the notion that one gains eternal life in a blissful heavenly realm only after leaving the body ("going") and the idea of desireless liberation while living by realizing *atman/brahman* identity ("knowing"). This latter, increasingly important, sense of liberation takes one beyond both the birth-and-death cycles of *samsara* and any "physical" or material heavenly realm. The paper also considers related conceptions of immortality in the *Upanisads*.

Fortin, Ernest L. "Nietzsche and the Crisis of Nihilism" in *Meaning, Truth, and God, Rouner, Leroy S (ed)*, 195-215. Notre Dame, Univ Notre Dame Pr, 1982.

Fortman, Bas de Gaay. Conceptualizing Democracy in an African Context. *Quest*, 8(1), 60-75, Je 94.

A partir d'une définition générale de la démocratie comme "gouvernement pour et par le peuple" l'article offre une analyse de trois dimensions des processus de démocratisation. Chacunes de ces dimensions peut être abordées à patir de questions concrètes; les expériences africaines concernant ces questions sont ici analysées. En conclusion il sera débattu de toute une séries de problèmes liés aux processus de démocratisation.

Foss, Jeffrey. On the Evolution of Intentionality as Seen from the Intentional Stance. *Inquiry*, 37(3), 287-310, S 94.

Like everyone with a scientific bent of mind, Dennett thinks our capacity for meaningful language and states of mind is the product of *evolution* (Dennett (1987, chapter VIII)). But unlike many of this bent, he sees virtue in viewing evolution itself from the *intentional stance*. From this stance, 'Mother Nature', or the process of evolution by natural selection, bestows intentionality upon us, hence we are not unmeant meaners. Thus, our intentionality is extrinsic, and Dennett dismisses the theories of meaning of Dretske, Fodor, Burge, Putnam, and Kripke on the grounds that each requires that our mental states, unlike those of artifacts, have meaning intrinsically. I argue that we *are* unmeant meaners, incidentally defending Dretske *et al.*, though my goal is to test the explanatory virtue of the intentional stance as applied to the evolution of intentionality.

Foss, Jeffrey E. Materialism, Reduction, Replacement, and the Place of Consciousness in Science. *J Phil*, 92(8), 401-429, Ag 95.

The central problem in the philosophy of mind is the place of consciousness in science. Contemporary materialisms misconceive the place of consciousness in science because of their shared misconception of the structure and development of science, which in turn stems from their use of the concepts of theory reduction and theory replacement. Instead of the reduction-replacement contrast, an account is proposed of the information-economy of science which more accurately captures the relationships among particular scientific theories, various scientific disciplines, and science as a whole. This done, the place of consciousness in science is more readily outlined.

Foss, Laurence. Putting the Mind Back into the Body: A Successor Scientific Medical Model. *Theor Med*, 15(3), 291-313, S 94.

This paper examines today's received scientific medical model with respect to its ability to satisfy two conditions: 1) its explanatory adequacy relative to the full range of findings in the medical literature, including those indicating a correlation between psychosocial variables and disease susceptibility; and 2) the fit between its physicalist patient and disease concepts and what today's basic sciences, so-called

sciences of complexity, tell us about the way matter, notably complex systems (e.g., patients), behave and the nature of scientific explanation. I conclude that the received (biomedical) model falls short on both counts and to satisfy these conditions is to articulate a formal successor model. This successor must be guided by premises consistent with the findings and methods of today's basic sciences on which an applied science like medicine depends for its validity. Additionally, the successor model must be able to explain (and predict) the full range of clinical findings, both those that its predecessors explains and at least some of those that it does not. The aim of the paper is to identify such a model.

Fossa, John and Erickson, Glenn. O Número Nupcial no Livro VIII da República. *Cad Hist Filosof Cie*, 4(1), 9-23, Ja-Je 94.

A new interpretation of Plato's nuptial number (geometrical number), which is described in Book VIII of the Republic, is described herein. The geometric figure corresponding to the nuptial number is reconstructed. The figure is a Pythagorean triangle, that is, a triangle whose sides are in the proportion 3:4:5; the triangle is partioned into various similar triangles. The perimeters of the triangle determine those periods in which human reproduction will result in a man of gold, a man of silver, or a man of bronze and iron.

Foster, John. "The Token-Identity Thesis" in *The Mind-Body Problem: A Guide to the Current Debate, Warner, Richard (ed)*, 299-310. Cambridge, Blackwell, 1994.

Foster, Stephen P. Edward Gibbon and the Anti-Miracle Man: Hume's 'Of Miracles' at Work in the *Decline and Fall of the Roman Empire*. *Mod Sch*, 71(3), 223-245, Mr 94.

This article examines the influence of the philosophy of David Hume on Edward Gibbon's critique of Christianity in his *Decline and Fall of the Roman Empire*. The article shows the influence of Hume's essay "Of Miracles" on Gibbon's account of the history of Christianity in the *Decline and Fall* with a particular focus on the notorious chapter fifteen where Gibbon examines the "progress of Christianity" and applies the argumentation of "Of Miracles" to the apostolic accounts. Like Hume, Gibbon takes a naturalistic approach to the study of religion.

Foster, Thomas R and Fetzer, James H and Davies, Paul Sheldon. Logical Reasoning and Domain Specificity: A Critique of the Social Exchange Theory of Reasoning. *Biol Phil*, 10(1), 1-37, Ja 95.

The social exchange theory of reasoning, which is championed by Leda Cosmides and John Tooby, falls under the general rubric "evolutionary psychology" and asserts that human reasoning is governed by content-dependent, domain-specific, evolutionarily-derived algorithms. According to Cosmides and Tooby, the presumptive existence of what they call "cheater-detection" algorithms disconfirms the claim that we reason via general-purpose mechanisms or via inductively acquired principles. We contend that the Cosmides/Tooby arguments in favor of domain-specific algorithms or evolutionarily-derived mechanisms fail and that the notion of a social exchange rule, which is central to their theory, is not correctly characterized. As a consequence, whether or not their conclusion is true cannot be established on the basis of the arguments they have presented.

Foucault, Michel. Qué es la Ilustración?. *Rev Filosof (Daimon)*, 7, 5-18, 1993.

Foucault, Michel and Stastny, Peter (trans) and Sengel, Deniz (trans). Madness, the Absence of Work. *Crit Inquiry*, 21(2), 290-298, Wint 95.

Fournier, Christian (trans) and Bouveresse, Jacques and Laugier, Sandra (trans). Philosophy from an Antiphilosopher: Paul Valéry. *Crit Inquiry*, 21(2), 354-381, Wint 95.

Fowl, Stephen E (ed) and Jones, L Gregory (ed). *Rethinking Metaphysics*. Cambridge, Blackwell, 1995.

Here is a series of important essays which re-think the place of metaphysics in theological and philosophical inquiry. This book ranges across a variety of philosophical and theological traditions, engaging such figures as Plato and Augustine as well as Gillian Rose, Jacques Derrida, Donald Davidson, C S Peirce, and Jean Luc Marion. The authors of these essays confront a variety of post-modern critiques of metaphysical speculation while, nonetheless, arguing that there is still a significant future for reflection on metaphysical questions. Unified by an agreement about the urgent need to re-think metaphysics, these essays should provoke a wide-ranging and lively discussion among philosophers and theologians.

Fowler, Bridget. The Hegemonic Work of Art in the Age of Electronic Reproduction: An Assessment of Pierre Bourdieu. *Theor Cult Soc*, 11(1), 129-154, F 94.

Bourdieu has developed sociology as a science which demystifies culture. Artistic knowledge has come to serve the ancient purpose of ideology in justifying social inequality and domination. This article explores the fields of literature and art as they are depicted by Bourdieu, especially the specific forms of power and prestige generated in the competition for consecration in anomic art-worlds. It is argued that Bourdieu's work possesses certain lacunae, however, especially in his failure to analyze in any depth forms of art in which the producers are drawn from the dominated class, and a failure to reveal the permeable nature of the boundaries between art and entertainment.

Fowler, Sarah B and Fisher, David H. Reimaging Moral Leadership in Business. *Bus Ethics Quart*, 5(1), 29-42, Ja 95.

In this paper we explore challenges facing leadership in a culture of "all consuming images" from a perspective which claims that images have a moral or normative dimension. The cumulative effect of contemporary image saturation is increased resistance to the normative power of an image. We also suggest that in a culturally diverse global economy, it is necessary to expand the moral aspects of good business leadership beyond providing a basis for productive, coherent group identity within a firm at the expense of seeing outsiders as "others". We also explore what imagining leadership in business might be like in a world in which visual images shape our understandings of individual and group identity. While our focus is on leadership in business, we also use examples from the political arena. We also suggest that imagining business leadership in the ways we propose may be helpful to women, providing them with an image of business leadership more closely reflective of their experience of corporate culture, its limits, and possibilities.

Fox, Michael Allen. Environmental Ethics and the Ideology of Meat Eating. *Between Species*, 9(3), 121-132, Sum 93.

Many proponents of holistic environmental ethics are not vegetarians. It would seem that they ought to be, but as theorists whose special commitment is to extending our ethical horizons and making new conceptual connections. After examining the moral case for vegetarianism, I argue that this discrepancy is not just a logical inconsistency but also a form of ethical and epistemological self-neglect. I then explore the ideology of meat eating and demonstrate its power to shape our attitudes and thoughts with respect to dietary choices, suggesting that environmental ethicists may be no more immune to this influence than others in the population. I conclude that environmental ethicists need to learn from animal rights theorists, and to move in the direction of analyzing connections between forms of oppression which ecofeminists have indicated.

Fox, Michael W. Ahimsa (Noninjury) Revisited. *Between Species*, 9(3), 156-159, Sum 93.

Fox, Michael W. Bioethics; Its Scope and Purpose. *Between Species*, 10(1-2), 61-63, Win-Spr 94.

Fox, Richard Wightman (ed) and Kloppenberg, James T (ed). *A Companion to American Thought*. Cambridge, Blackwell, 1995.

Fox, Robin. Moral Sense and Utopian Sensibility. *Crim Just Ethics*, 13(2), 19-23, Sum-Fall 94.

Fox, Warwick. Education, the Interpretive Agenda of Science, and the Obligation of Scientists to Promote this Agenda. *Environ Values*, 4(2), 109-114, May 95.

This paper presents an argument that emphasises the following points: 1) the importance of public education; 2) the essential difficulty facing all involved in public education that is aimed at sustaining a biologically and culturally rich world; 3) the recognition of science as having both a technical agenda and an interpretive agenda; 4) the scientific interpretation of the universe: an evolutionary and ecological world-view; and 5) the importance of the interpretive agenda of science for the public education and the obligation of scientists to promote this agenda.

Fraedrich, John and Thorne, Debbie M and Ferrell, O C. Assessing the Application of Cognitive Moral Development Theory to Business Ethics. *J Bus Ethics*, 13(10), 829-838, O 94.

Cognitive moral development (CMD) theory has been accepted as a construct to help explain business ethics, social responsibility and other organizational phenomena. This article critically assesses CMD as a construct in business ethics by presenting the history and criticisms of CMD. The value of CMD is evaluated and problems with using CMD as one predictor of ethical decisions are addressed. Researchers are made aware of the major criticisms of CMD theory including disguised value judgments, invariance of stages, and gender bias in the initial scale development. Implications for business ethics research are discussed and opportunities for future research delineated.

Fraley, Lawrence E. Uncertainty About Determinism: A Critical Review of Challenges to the Determinism of Modern Science. *Behavior Phil*, 22(2), 71-83, Fall-Wint 94.

Contemporary scientific determinism is a grand induction from scientific experience. Limitations on measurement of the kind represented by the *Heisenberg uncertainty principle* have thrown doubt on deterministic philosophy. But the case against determinism does not stand examination. Scientific support for deterministic philosophy continues to be justified.

Francescotti, Robert M. Even: The Conventional Implicature Approach Reconsidered. *Ling Phil*, 18(2), 153-173, Ap 95.

Analyses of the meaning of "even" have traditionally assumed that 1) "even" does not affect truth-conditions but, instead, makes a difference only in conventional implicature, and that 2) what "even" conventionally implicates is some type of unexpectedness or surprise. Lycan (*L&P*, 1991) rejects 1) by claiming that "even" is a quantifier, and Kay (*L&P*, 1990) rejects 2), arguing that "even" may be used appropriately without implying surprise. I defend 2) against Kay's objections, and I defend 1) by refining Bennett's (*L&P*, 1982) account of "even". I show how my new analysis of "even" avoids difficulties facing quantificational accounts, and can also handle various other problem cases presented in the recent literature.

Francescotti, Robert M. Qualitative Beliefs, Wide Content, and Wide Behavior. *Nous*, 28(3), 396-404, S 94.

Francez, Nissim and Lappin, Shalom. E-Type Pronouns, 1-Sums, and Donkey Anaphora. *Ling Phil*, 17(4), 391-428, Ag 94.

We propose an E-type account of donkey pronouns which interprets these pronouns as denoting functions to i-sums of individuals. Our account provides a single representation for donkey sentences from which it is possible to obtain both universal and existential readings. It also permits us to explain the distribution of these readings in a straightforward way, on the basis of a parameterized maximality condition on the i-sums selected by E-type pronoun functions. We suggest that quantificational adverbs be interpreted as generalized quantifiers on sets of situations. When our i-sum based E-type account of donkey pronouns is integrated into this framework, we are able to derive the observed readings of conditional donkey sentences.

Franchella, Miriam. Heyting's Contribution to the Change in Research into the Foundations of Mathematics. *Hist Phil Log*, 15(2), 149-172, 1994.

After the 1930s, the research into the foundations of mathematics changed. None of its main directions (logicism, formalism and intuitionism) had any longer the pretension to be the only true mathematics. Usually, the determining factor in the change is considered to be Gödel's work, while Heyting's role is neglected. In contrast, in this paper I first describe how Heyting directly suggested the abandonment of the big foundational questions and the putting forward of a new kind of foundational research consisting in the isolation of formal, intuitive, logical and platonistic elements within classical mathematics. Furthermore, I describe how Heyting indirectly influenced the abandonment of the old directions of foundational research by making out some lists of degrees of evidence that exist within intuitionism.

Franchi, Alfredo. Osservazioni sul Problema del Male in Filosofia. *Sapienza*, 48(1), 3-30, 1995.

Francks, Richard and Woolhouse, Roger S. Leibniz, Lamy, and 'The Way of Pre-Established Harmony'. *Stud Leibniz*, 26(1), 76-90, 1994.

Die Kontroverse mit François Lamy ist unter denen von Leibniz' *Système nouveau* (1695) hervorgerufenen eine der am wenigsten diskutierten. Die wenigen neueren Quellen sind schlecht dokumentiert und in wichtigen Details nicht korrekt. Wir versuchen hier, die Bibliographie richtigzustellen. Da Lamys Arbeit äusserst selten ist, fügen wir englische Übersetzungen der relevanten Stellen bei. Nach Pierre Bayle war eher Lamy als Leibniz der erste, der den Begriff 'prästabilierte Harmonie' verwendete. Es stellt sich heraus, dass dem nicht so ist.

Frangiotti, Marco Antonio. Is the Skeptic Defeated by Putnam's "Transcendental Argument"?. *Dialogos*, 30(66), 79-92, Jl 95.

My aim in this article is to show that transcendental arguments are not effective to defeat the skeptic. In this way, I argue at first that skepticism is intrinsic to metaphysical realism. Secondly, I show that metaphysical realism is inadequate as a philosophical background against which skeptical doubts can be defused. Finally, I analyse Putnam's transcendental argument that we are not brains in a vat. I try to show that his argument does not prevent the skeptic from seeking refuge in a metaphysical realist picture and therefore from continuing to doubt about our epistemological credentials.

Frangiotti, Marco Antonio. Refuting Kant's "Refutation of Idealism". *Ideal Stud*, 25(1), 93-106, Wint 95.

My aim in this paper is to show that Kant's "Refutation of Idealism" falls short of a proper response to the sceptic. This is accomplished by pointing out that, while it is dependent upon transcendental idealism, the Refutation is inconsistent with it. I argue that the notion of the permanent as a prerequisite for empirical self-consciousness cannot be properly interpreted in transcendental idealist terms unless we embrace a picture of the external world that is, according to Kant's own stand-point, quite objectionable, to wit, transcendental realism. Since the notion of the permanent lies at the very heart of the Refutation, Kant's overall strategy therein is deprived of any anti-sceptical import.

Frangiotti, Marco Antonio. The Ideality of Time. *Manuscrito*, 17(2), 135-158, O 94.

In this article I show that the thesis of the ideality of space and time is the hallmark of Kant's transcendental idealism. It is a thesis we cannot deny without destroying the whole system of Kant's theoretical philosophy. This being the case, I reject Strawson's view that the thesis of the apriority of space and time does not, and cannot, imply the ideality thesis. At the same time, I defend the view that Kant's claim that space and time are subjective forms of sensible intuition is the most adequate philosophical account of space and time. I analyze McTaggart's argument that time is not real. I show that, since he lacked the ideality thesis, McTaggart based his account of time on the assumption of a reality constituted independently of our epistemic resources. A solution to McTaggart's puzzle is then proposed by inserting the ideality thesis into his approach.

Frangiotti, Marco Antonio. Transcendental Idealism and Phenomenalism. *Critica*, 26(78), 73-95, D 94.

El idealismo trascendental de Kant a menudo es considerado una forma de fenomenalismo. De esta forma, algunos comentadores de Kant han equiparado su doctrina con la de Berkeley. Los defensores de este punto de vista han argumentado en forma general que, limitando el campo del conocimiento a objetos asequibles a los sentidos, Kant habría restablecido la principal fuerza propulsora del idealismo de Berkeley y reducido los elementos del mundo externo a simples representaciones o ideas. Aunque algunos de los pasajes de la *Crítica de la razón pura* apoyan este punto de vista, creo que el intento de clasificar a Kant como berkeleyano es equivocado. Por tanto, mi propósito en este artículo es demostrar en qué apectos sus filosofías pueden distinguirse una de la otra. Para hacerlo, establezco una línea de pensamiento según la cual Kant puede evitar ser acusado de fenomenalista.

Frank, Garry L and Cooper, Robert W and Heaston, Patrick H. Helps for CPAs in Dealing with Ethical Issues. *Bus Prof Ethics J*, 13(1-2), 165-183, Spr-Sum 94.

The paper reports the findings of a study of CPAs designed to determine whether they tend to find factors related to their professional environment (especially the guides to professional conduct of the American Institute of Certified Public Accountants) to be more helpful than factors related to their business environment when faced with ethics problems. Like internal auditors surveyed earlier, the CPAs tend to view a number of factors in their business environment to be even more helpful than factors related to their professional environment in dealing with ethical dilemmas. Implications for CPAs as individuals and for their professional associations are discussed.

Frank, Martin. Transformation oder Verteidigung: Zu Will Kymlickas liberaler politischer Philosophie. *Deut Z Phil*, 43(3), 549-564, 1995.

The essay examines two recent publications of W Kymlicka. It argues that there is a certain conception of liberal equality that underlies these writings. Kymlicka's discussions of various theories in political philosophy (Marxism, libertarianism, feminism and communitarianism) that seem to be introductions, are actually intended as a comprehensive defense of Kymlicka's modified liberal political theory. The essay argues also that this defense of liberalism amounts to a far-reaching transformation of current liberal positions. It criticizes Kymlicka for not having drawn these conceptual consequences adequately.

Frankenberry, Nancy. Introduction: Prolegomenon to Future Feminist Philosophies of Religions. *Hypatia*, 9(4), 1-14, Fall 94.

Frankfurt, Harry G. The Faintest Passion. *Proc Amer Phil Ass*, 66(3), 5-16, N 92.

Franklin, Betty and Townsend, Lucy. Relational Ethics in Writing a Woman's Life. *J Thought*, 30(1), 71-83, Spr 95.

The authors address relational ethics as developed and practiced in scholarly work. The piece documents the unfolding consciousness of the relation between collaborators, and includes an example of work which embodies ethical concerns in biographical research and writing. The authors also track the mentoring relationship which supports this delicate work of reframing the conventions of research and writing to move beyond positivist practice and an assumed static relation between participants in scholarly work.

Franklin, J. The Formal Sciences Discover the Philosophers' Stone. *Stud Hist Phil Sci*, 25(4), 513-533, Ag 94.

The last 50 years have seen the creation of a number of new 'formal' or 'mathematical' sciences, or 'sciences of complexity'. Examples are operations research, theoretical computer science, information theory, descriptive statistics, mathematical ecology, control theory,... Theorists of science have almost ignored them, despite the remarkable fact that (from the way that practitioners speak) they seem to have come upon the 'philosophers' stone': a way of converting knowledge about the real world into certainty, merely by thinking. The paper illustrates the mode of thought in the formal sciences with some picturesque examples, and defends the thesis that they do indeed achieve certain knowledge about the actual world.

Franklin, James. Scepticism's Health Buoyant. *Philosophy*, 69(270), 503-504, O 94.

My article 'Healthy scepticism' (*Philosophy* 66 (1991): 305-324) defended the 'symmetry' argument for global scepticism—that there is no reason to prefer the realist scenario over alternatives such as vat or demon worlds. The present note defends the argument against the criticism of Eswald Hanfling (*Philosophy* 68 (1993): 91-3), who argued that symmetry arguments ignore the possibility of interaction with the world. It is replied that the Deceitful Cray can create a virtual reality alternative world with which one can interact in a way indistinguishable from one's interaction with the real world.

Franssen, Maarten. Constrained Maximization Reconsidered—An Elaboration and Critique of Gauthier's Modelling of Rational Cooperation in a Single Prisoner's Dilemma. *Synthese*, 101(2), 249-272, N 94.

Gauthier's argument for constrained maximization, presented in *Morals by Agreement*, is perfected by taking into account the possibility of accidental exploitation and discussing the limitations on the values of the parameters which measure the translucency of the actors. Gauthier's argument is nevertheless shown to be defective concerning the rationality of constrained maximization as a strategic choice. It can be argued that it applies only to a single actor entering a population of individuals who are themselves not rational actors but simple rule-followers. A proper analysis of the strategic choice situation involving two rational actors who confront each other shows that constrained maximization as the choice of both actors can only result under very demanding assumptions.

Frápolli, María José. Lógica y Ontología: Verdad, Existencia e Identidad como Funciones de Segundo Nivel. *Rev Filosof (Spain)*, 7(11), 265-274, 1994.

This paper is devoted to argue for Williams's theses about truth, existence, and identity as they are presented in his last book *Being, Identity and Truth* (Oxford, Clarendon Press, 1992). Williams follows Frege in treating existence as a second order function. Identity and truth are also second order functions. Identity is an operator that converts n-place predicables into n-1-place predicables. Truth is explained as a case of identity: the case in which the involved predicables have sentences as arguments. Williams's theory of truth is a deeply worked-out prosentential theory, developed independently from Grover's account. In this paper, the details and merits of Williams's approach to existence, identity, and truth are presented and explained.

Fraser, Nancy. "Pragmatism, Feminism, and the Linguistic Turn" in *Feminist Contentions, Benhabib, Seyla (& others)*, 157-171. New York, Routledge, 1994.

Recasting recent disagreements among feminist theorists as disputes over the most fruitful way to make the linguistic turn, I assess the relative strengths and weaknesses of three "pure" approaches: 1) Seyla Benhabib's Habermassian approach, 2) Judith Butler's Foucauldian approach, and 3) Drucilla Cornell's Lacanian-Derridean approach. I argue that none of the three, taken alone, can handle the full range of feminist-theoretical tasks. In the eclectic spirit of pragmatism, therefore, I propose a fourth "impure" alternative, which incorporates useful elements from Benhabib and Butler, in particular, while avoiding the false antitheses of sectarian metaphysics.

Fraser, Nancy. After the Family Wage: Gender Equity and the Welfare State. *Polit Theory*, 22(4), 591-618, N 94.

I evaluate two alternative feminist models of a postindustrial welfare state: a *Universal Breadwinner* model centered on promoting women's employment, and a *Caregiver Parity* model aiming to "make difference costless via caregiver allowances. Defining gender equity as a compound of several normative principles (anti-poverty, anti-exploitation; equality of income, leisure time, and respect; anti-marginalization, and anti-androcentrism), I show that neither model can possibly achieve it. Universal Breadwinner fails to promote equality of leisure time and to combat androcentrism, while Caregiver Parity fails to promote income equality and to prevent women's marginalization. I conclude that only a third—*Universal Caregiver*—model can deliver gender equity in a postindustrial welfare state. The key is to discourage male free-riding on women's informal carework.

Frede, Michael. Los dos tipos de asentimiento del escéptico y el problema de la posibilidad del conocimiento. *An Seminar Metaf*, 27, 247-271, 1993.

Fredenhagen, Klaus. "The Mathematical Frame of Quantum Field Theory" in *Philosophy, Mathematics and Modern Physics, Rudolph, Enno (ed)*, 200-204. New York, Springer-Verlag, 1994.

The deep interrelation between the physics of quantum fields, and the mathematics used for their description is illustrated on three examples: the topology of the state space of a C*-algebra explains the emergence of classical structure in a quantum system as it occurs in a measurement process; the concept of subsystems corresponding to subregions of spacetime and realized by subalgebras of the algebras of observables leads to a description of configurations of scattered particles; and finally, the modular symmetry of von Neumann algebras of local observables is the mathematical counter part of the Hawking radiation of black holes.

Freedman, Benjamin. Bioethics and the Old-Time Religion: Response to Dena Davis. *J Clin Ethics*, 5(4), 353-355, Wint 94.

Freedman, Joseph S. Classifications of Philosophy, the Sciences, and the Arts in Sixteenth- and Seventeeth-Century Europe. *Mod Sch*, 72(1), 37-66, N 94.

Freeman, Mark and Locurto, Charles. Radical Behaviorism and the Problem of Nonshared Development. *Behavior Phil*, 22(1), 1-21, Spr-Sum 94.

New findings emerging from developmental behavior genetics indicate that individuals living in the same family develop in ways that make them remarkably different from each other despite the commonalities of shared genes and shared environments. These findings suggest that there are important factors residing within families that are not shared by family members that are nevertheless influential in development. The most discussed of these influences has been called "nonshared environment", meaning environmental influences that operate within families and that are uniquely experienced by particular family members. In this paper we explore the nature of nonshared influences on development, develop a set of criteria that any theoretical approach must incorporate to deal effectively with the development of individuality in light of these new findings, and offer an analysis of the extent to which these criteria can be incorporated by an established theory of environmental influence: radical behaviorism.

Freeman, Michael. The Holocaust and Philosophy. *J Applied Phil*, 12(2), 125-128, 1995.

This is an introduction to three papers on the Holocaust and philosophy. It argues that, although the Holocaust has had a considerable impact on several academic disciplines, it has had little direct influence on moral and political philosophy. Epistemological and moral arguments for the silence of philosophy about the Holocaust are considered and rejected. It is argued that most traditions of Western philosophy are inadequate for the analysis of the Holocaust, but that the best-suited is a rights-oriented neo-Kantian liberalism. The relation of postmodernism to the Holocaust is briefly considered.

Freeman, Samuel. Utilitarianism, Deontology, and the Priority of Right. *Phil Pub Affairs*, 23(4), 313-349, Fall 94.

Frege, Gottlob. Begriff und Gegenstand. *Wittgenstein Stud*, n.a., 1994.

Frege, Gottlob. Die Verneinung. *Wittgenstein Stud*, n.a., 1994.

Frege, Gottlob. Sinn und Bedeutung. *Wittgenstein Stud*, n.a., 1994.

Frege, Gottlob. Tagebuch. *Deut Z Phil*, 42(6), 1067-1098, 1994.

French, Peter A. Ethics and Agency Theory. *Bus Ethics Quart*, 5(3), 621-627, Jl 95.

One of the most popular of the "transposed" versions of atomistic contract theory is agency theory. The basic tenets of agency theory amount to explicit denials of the foundations of any robust theory of corporate moral/social responsibility. In fact, in agency theory corporations (and all other corporate-like organizations and institutions) virtually disappear as social entities. Rather than players in the "social game," organizations are treated as something like the field of play. This paper is an attack on agency theory as developed through a critical review of some of the papers in a volume edited by Bowie and Freeman called *Ethics and Agency Theory* in the Ruffin Series in Business Ethics (Oxford University Press, 1992).

French, Peter A. The Practical and Ethical Costs of Corporate Reengineering. *Bus Prof Ethics J*, 13(3), 3-18, Fall 94.

French, Robert M. Refocusing the Debate on the Turing Test: A Reply to Jacquette. *Behavior Phil*, 23(1), 59-60, Spr-Sum 95.

French, Steven and Krause, Décio. A Formal Framework for Quantum Non-Individuality. *Synthese*, 102(1), 195-214, Ja 95.

H Post's conception of quantal particles as 'nonindividuals' is set in a formal logico-mathematical framework. By means of this approach certain metaphysical implications of quantum mechanics can be further explored.

French, Steven and Krause, Décio. Vague Identity and Quantum Non-Individuality. *Analysis*, 55(1), 20-26, Ja 95.

Lowe has recently argued that quantum particles offer examples of vague objects. While accepting the premise of the argument that such particles can be regarded as individuals, we point out that there is a lacuna here, to be filled by a detailed analysis of the nature of the entangled states which they enter into. We then elaborate the alternative view, according to which such particles should be regarded as 'nonindividuals' and situate it in the context of recent developments of a logic of nonindividuality. Our conclusion is that it is here that one encounters genuine ontic vagueness.

French, Warren A and Chang, Linda and Sheng, Peihua. Business's Environmental Responsibility in Taiwan—Moral, Legal or Negotiated. *J Bus Ethics*, 13(11), 887-897, N 94.

This study explores both the negotiating styles and moral reasoning processes of business people and governmental officials in Taiwan, so as to provide a footing for "outsiders" when negotiating with Taiwanese over environmental concerns. Findings imply that Taiwanese business people and governmental officials can and will reason both at the conventional level and at the postconventional level of moral judgment. But, results of this study also indicate that Taiwanese negotiating styles do not necessarily match their levels of moral reasoning. With respect to pollution concerns, Taiwanese seem unwillingly to accept responsibility as autonomous individuals. Instead, responsibility is accepted when mandated by the law.

French, William C. Against Biospherical Egalitarianism. *Environ Ethics*, 17(1), 39-58, Spr 95.

Arne Naess and Paul Taylor are two of the most forceful proponents of the principle of species equality. Problematically, both, when adjudicating conflict of interest cases, resort to employing explicit or implicit species-ranking arguments. I examine how Lawrence Johnson's critical, species-ranking approach helpfully avoids the normative inconsistencies of "biospherical egalitarianism". Many assume species-ranking schemes are rooted in arrogant, ontological claims about human, primate, or mammalian superiority. Species ranking, I believe, is best viewed as a justified articulation of moral priorities in response to individuals' or entities' relative ranges of vulnerability and need, rooted in their relative ranges of capacities and interests.

Frewer, Lynn J and Shepherd, Richard. Ethical Concerns and Risk Perceptions Associated with Different Applications of Genetic Engineering. *Agr Human Values*, 12(1), 48-57, Winter 95.

Questions were directed at either perceived risk or ethical objections. The applications of genetic engineering were seen as riskier and less beneficial when applied to food production than medicine, although perceived control was independent of application. Optimistic bias was observed. Ethical and risk related objections were greater for applications to food than to medicine, and again dependent of the type of organism manipulated. The transfer of genetic material between "dissimilar" types of organism (for example, between plants and animals) were not associated with greater risk or ethical concern than transfers between "similar" types of organism (for example, between animals and animals). The public requirement for legislative control was also dissociated into risk or ethical objections to the technology, and found to be greater for risk-related concerns, although ethical considerations were also important.

Frey, Gerhard. *Anthropologie der Künste*. Freiburg, Alber, 1994.

The main problem discussed in this book is the question of why the different arts necessary for all human beings. Artistic abilities and activities are a constitutive element of human evolution. It seems that in the historical development arts and performances are as old as verbal languages. There are different preconditions for art: biological, cultural, sociological, anthropolical, technical and material. Such preconditions are to be found constantly in all forms of art. The most important functions of Arts are: 1) the shading of the world in which we live, 2) the identity of our civilization, 3) the promotion of creativity, 4) the nonverbal communication. The analysis of these different functions shows us the importance of Art. There is no common definition of Art. But the anthropological constants and functions show us why Art and artistic performances are constitutive for being human.

Freydberg, Bernard D. Kant and the Irrational. *Hist Euro Ideas*, 20(4-6), 945-949, F 95.

The paper seeks to locate Kant within the contemporary discussion of rationalism and its competitors and to contribute to a side of Kant scholarship which is not often emphasized, namely his treatment of the irrational. The role of imagination in synthesis generally and in the schematism bears witness to an irrational element at the heart of synthetic judgment in the first critique; desire provides the battleground for the problem of morality in the second; aesthetical ideas, which no language can express but which empower the creation of beautiful art, testify to the place of the irrational in the third.

Freytag, Matthew. Genus/Diferentia, Matter/Form, and Levels of Complexity. *Dialogos*, 30(66), 31-42, Jl 95.

Both differentia and form represent, in discussions of living things, a level of organic or systematic complexity, and both genus and matter represent a lower level or organic or systematic complexity. On this principle, gleaned from Aristotle's biological works, problems concerning the unity of genus and differentia in definition and concerning the unity of matter and form in the essences of living things can be solved—both are the unity of a schema and its articulation. This principle guides Aristotle's construction of taxonomies of living things, and suggests that an Aristotelian taxonomy might be more fluid than Aristotle's own.

Freytag, Matthew. MacIntyre's Conservatism and Its Cure: The Formal Structure of Traditions. *Phil Cont World*, 1(2), 1-10, Sum 94.

Conservative communitarian Alasdair MacIntyre makes a fundamental claim about the formal conditions for rationality, personhood, and intelligible valuation, and a detachable, less fundamental empirical claim that these formal conditions can be met only in a hierarchically organized social tradition. Having suggested a formal account of narrative tradition which relies on the schematic notion of systematic complexity, MacIntyre retreats to an account in terms of canon and authority. He thus obscures the structures that underlie his own metaphysics of morals, the *structures* of the practices, narrative unities, and traditions which on his account are both identity-constituting and value-creating. Once these structures are discerned, the possibility of good lives will no longer seem linked to preservation of the forms of the existing *polis*.

Frias, Marcelo F and Baum, Gabriel A and Haeberer, Armando M. Fork Algebras are Representable. *Bull Sec Log*, 24(2), 64-75, Je 95.

Fork algebras are extensions of relation algebras by a new binary operator, *fork*. The expressiveness of fork algebras is known to encompass that of first order logic with equality, i.e., in any proper fork algebra (a standard model) every binary relation that is first-order definable is also denoted by a fork term. Here we complement this result by a representation theorem: every atomic abstract fork algebra is isomorphic to a proper one. This gives a framework specially adequate for program specification and development within relational calculi.

Fricker, Elizabeth. Telling and Trusting: Reductionism and Anti-Reductionism in the Epistemology of Testimony. *Mind*, 104(414), 393-411, Ap 95.

Reviews Coady's book *Testimony*, and sketches my own account of the epistemology of "testimony"—i.e., how users of a common language can share their knowledge through telling each other things. The issue of epistemological "reductionism" about testimony is explained as: whether the status as knowledge of beliefs gained through testimony can be explained without appeal to a primitive epistemic principle pertaining to testimony, a presumptive right to believe what one is told just as such—i.e., without evidence of sincerity and competence concerning her subject matter of the speaker. A key distinction between "global" versus "local" reduction of a hearer's right to trust her audience is made, and the main arguments on each side concerning this central epistemological issue about testimony are reviewed.

Fricker, Miranda. Intuition and Reason. *Phil Quart*, 45(179), 181-189, Ap 95.

The discussion concerns the relation between intuition and reason. Far from standing in a relation of opposition to reason, as one might suppose, it is argued that intuition plays an essential role within human reasoning broadly construed. This view has two implications: firstly, that *intuition* is not well understood if it is sharply contrasted with reason; and, secondly, that a conception of *reason* which is sharply contrasted with intuition is an unduly technical or 'thin' conception. Intuition is characterized as a mode of hypothesis formation crucial to rational inquiry, for it is suggested—with certain qualifications—that intuition and reason may be characterized respectively as a 'generator' and a 'tester' of new hypotheses.

Fried, Michael. Between Realisms: From Derrida to Manet. *Crit Inquiry*, 21(1), 1-36, Autumn 94.

Fried, Terri and Gillick, Muriel R. The Limits of Proxy Decision Making: Undertreatment. *Cambridge Quart Healthcare Ethics*, 4(2), 172-177, Spr 95.

With the passage by virtually every state legislature of healthcare proxy laws, the medical profession increasingly can expect to rely on the participation of surrogates in making decisions on behalf of incompetent patients. Several concerns about the legitimacy of proxy decision making have been discussed in the ethical and general medical literature: the lack of concordance between the views of patients and their surrogates have been documented on multiple occasions, and cases of abuse by proxies or potential conflict of interest have been reported. Another dilemma that deserves discussion arises when proxies demand withdrawal of treatment that physicians and nurses regard as essential to the well-being of the patient. The following case highlights this dilemma.

Friedlander, Albert H. "Leo Baeck: New Dimensions and Explorations" in *Thinkers and Teachers of Modern Judaism, Goldsmith, Emanuel S (ed)*, 83-101. New York, Paragon House, 1994.

Friedlander, Judith (trans) and Finkielkraut, Alain. *The Defeat of the Mind*. New York, Columbia Univ Pr, 1995.

Friedman, David D. Law as a Private Good: A Response to Tyler Cowen on the Economics of Anarchy. *Econ Phil*, 10(2), 319-327, O 94.

Tyler Cowen argues that a system of competing law enforcement agencies of the sort I have described elsewhere is unstable because the network of contracts by which each pair of agencies agree on legal rules and an arbitrator makes the entire industry into the equivalent of a single firm, able to set prices, exclude new entrants, and in other ways pursue its common interest. I argue that this is mistaken. Common legal rules and the network of contracts are an equilibrium, not a constraint, and provide no mechanism to coordinate firms and prevent an ordinary competitive outcome.

Friedman, Harvey and Sheard, Michael. Elementary Descent Recursion and Proof Theory. *Annals Pure Applied Log*, 71(1), 1-45, Ja 95.

We define a class of functions, the *descent recursive* functions, relative to an arbitrary elementary recursive system of ordinal notations. By means of these functions, we provide a general technique for measuring the proof-theoretic strength of a variety of systems of first-order arithmetic. We characterize the provable well-orderings and provably recursive functions of these systems, and derive various conservation and equiconsistency results.

Friedman, Jeffrey. Economic Consequentialism and Beyond. *Crit Rev*, 8(4), 493-502, Fall 94.

Libertarian thought suffers from a tension between consequentialist arguments for the benefits of free markets, and deontological claims for the intrinsic value of private property. "Postlibertarians" resolve this conflict in favor of consequentialism. Freed of deontological commitments to capitalism, postlibertarians face the question originally implied by the Enlightenment tradition from which economic consequentialism springs: What social institutions are conducive to human happiness? Economistic answers tend to assume that material prosperity is coextensive with happiness, but this assumption is contestible. Reviving the Enlightenment concern with happiness will require empirical research into all the prerequisites of happiness, economic and otherwise.

Friedman, Jeffrey. On Libertarian Anti-Intellectualism: Rejoinder to Shaw and Anderson and Leal. *Crit Rev*, 8(3), 483-492, Sum 94.

Against my claim that free-market environmentalism (FME) cannot solve major environmental problems, my critics deny that such problems exist. Against my contention that FME depends on the democratic policymaking it decries, they retreat from FME to libertarian environmentalism (LE). Against my argument that LE is incoherent, they resort to anti-intellectualism. These responses stem from demonstrable precommitments to libertarian ideology, suggesting that the debate over FME and LE has profound implications, not only for their practitioners, but for all libertarians and many free-market social scientists.

Friedman, Jeffrey. The Politics of Communitarianism. *Crit Rev*, 8(2), 297-340, Spr 94.

Taylor, Sandel, Walzer and MacIntyre waver between granting the community authority over the individual and limiting this authority so severely that communitarianism becomes a dead letter. The reason for this vacillation can be found in the aspiration of each theorist to base liberal values—equality and liberty—on particularism. Communitarians compound liberal formalism by adding to the liberal goal, individual autonomy, the equally abstract aim of grounding autonomy in a communally shared identity. Far from returning political theory to substantive considerations of the good, communitarianism legitimizes really existing liberal politics—the politics of the nation-state.

Friedman, Joel I. Towards an Adequate Definition of Distribution for First-Order Logic. *J Phil Log*, 24(2), 161-192, Ap 95.

The main purpose of this paper is to revive a standard entailment notion of distribution generalized to first-order logic, meeting several criteria of adequacy, including avoiding Geach's counterexamples. The definition is: predicate F is SQL-determined in sentence A if and only if for some formula B, C(1) A entails every F satisfies B, C(2) A does not entail everything satisfies B, C(3) B is 1-place, not containing F. SQL-distribution is invariant under logical equivalence, and satisfies the traditional distribution table for the categoricals. It thus satisfies the Law of Valid process restricted to syllogistic arguments (LVPs), but fails to satisfy unrestricted LVP. An open problem is to find a variation additionally satisfying LVP.

Friedman, Jonathan (ed) and Lash, Scott (ed). *Modernity and Identity*. Cambridge, Blackwell, 1992.

Friedman, Marilyn. Multicultural Education and Feminist Ethics. *Hypatia*, 10(2), 56-68, Spr 95.

Feminist ethics supports the contemporary educational trend toward increased multiculturalism and a diminished emphasis on the Western canon. First, I outline a feminist ethical justification for this development. Second, I argue that Western canon studies should not be altogether abandoned in a multicultural curriculum. Third, I suggest that multicultural education should help combat oppression in addition to simply promoting awareness of diversity. Fourth, I caution against an arrogant moralism in the teaching of multiculturalism.

Friedman, Sy D. A Simpler Proof of Jensen's Coding Theorem. *Annals Pure Applied Log*, 70(1), 1-16, N 94.

Friedman, Sy D. Jensen's Σ^* Theory and the Combinatorial Content of $V = L$. *J Sym Log*, 59(3), 1096-1104, S 94.

Friedrich, Clemens. Bachtins Polyphonie der Stimmen: Ein Dialogkonzept zwischen Moderne und Postmoderne. *Deut Z Phil*, 43(1), 93-102, 1995.

Bakhtin's philosophy of difference delivers a mediating position between modern and postmodern thinking. The idea of general dialogicity of human utterances is supposed to protect the single individual from pretended generalities and universalities. Already his conception of individuation and truth within language utterances shows how he reacts to the events of the political history of the whole century. Bakhtin criticizes the pretended universality of an obligatory system of reason and wants to replace it by the affirmation of unsurmountable conflicts and a plurality of single rationalities.

Friend, Stacie. Constructionalism in Dewey's Theory of Knowing. *Dialogue (PST)*, 37(2-3), 41-47, Ap 95.

The article attempts a compromise between radical and trivial interpretations of Dewey's apparent constructionalism, the view that the act of knowing changes its object. For Dewey, knowing is an activity within experience, modifying antecedent reality. An examination of his claims reveals that the transformation is from ordinary, brute experience to quantified, scientific objects of knowledge. This change gives events meaning; it does not make them different events.

Frisby, David. Introduction to the Simmel Texts. *Theor Cult Soc*, 11(1), 1-3, F 94.

Frisina, Warren G. Heaven's Partners or Nietzschean Free Spirits?. *Phil East West*, 45(1), 29-60, Ja 95.

This paper develops a comparison between the Neo-Confucian struggle with Taoism and the contemporary struggles between Deweyan pragmatists and post-modern pragmatists like Richard Rorty. Specifically, I argue that Deweyan pragmatists can learn from Rorty just as Neo-Confucians like Wang Yang-ming learned from Taoists. It is addressed to scholars interested in John Dewey, Richard Rorty, Confucianism, Neo-Confucianism and Taoism.

Fritsche, Johannes. On Brinks and Bridges in Heidegger. *Grad Fac Phil J*, 18(1), 111-186, 1995.

With regard to examples taken from *Being and Time* and writings up to the fifties, it is shown that English translations cannot convey connotations of Heidegger's vocabulary, which are ridiculous, shameless, and/or politically extremely conservative. In addition, Heidegger was not silent about Auschwitz. Rather, in conformity with his logic of submission and decision he actively silenced the Jews in Auschwitz silently.

Frohman, Larry. Neo-Stoicism and the Transition to Modernity in Wilhelm Dilthey's Philosophy of History. *J Hist Ideas*, 56(2), 263-287, Ap 95.

Froment-Meurice, Marc and Walsh, Peter (trans). *Solitudes: From Rimbaud to Heidegger*. Albany, SUNY Pr, 1995.

Fromm, Erich and Funk, Rainer (ed). *The Erich Fromm Reader*. Atlantic Highlands, Humanities Pr, 1994.

Fronterotta, Francesco. L'Ambiguità del non Essere e l'Inganno del Sofista: Una Nuova Edizione Francese del *Sofista* di Platone. *Teoria*, 14(2), 127-134, 1994.

Frost, Frederick A. The Use of Stakeholder Analysis to Understand Ethical and Moral Issues in the Primary Resource Sector. *J Bus Ethics*, 14(8), 653-661, Ag 95.

The mineral resources sector is critical to Australia's economic and social well-being. Minerals and energy have a value of $30 billion in export revenues, providing 50 percent of Australia's merchandise exports. The industry is characterized by substantial capital investment and very long lead times for project developments and a very competitive international market. The future direction and location of the industry is inextricably linked to long term exploration activities. The industry is faced with a far more complex set of environments than most. The paper identifies the range of complex issues and the wide variety of players using a stakeholder analysis. By monitoring such interactions, and knowing the objective set of the parties, a guide could be established to define moral and ethical frameworks for each interaction.

Fry, Iris. Evolution in Thermodynamic Perspective: A Historical and Philosophical Angle. *Zygon*, 30(2), 227-248, Je 95.

The recently suggested reformulation of Darwinian evolutionary theory, based on the thermodynamics of self-organizing processes, has strong philosophical implications. My claim is that the main philosophical merit of the thermodynamic approach, made especially clear in J S Wicken's work, is its insistence on the law-governed, continuous nature of evolution. I attempt to substantiate this claim following a historical analysis of beginning-of-the-century ideas on evolution and matter-life relationship, in particular, the fitness-of-the-environment-for-life theory of the Harvard physiologist L J Henderson. In addition, I point to an epistemological common ground underlying the studies of the "thermodynamics school" and other currently active research groups focusing on the emergence and evolution of biological organization.

Fu, Daiwei. On the Competitive Structure of Problem-Solving. *Phil Hist Sci*, 1(1), 59-110, O 92.

This essay begins by introducing and criticizing Laudan's "logic of anomalous problems". Through these criticisms, a new thesis, (Thesis G) in terms of the "*bottleneck problem*", emerges: a thesis that on the one hand captures the intuition concerning the challenges of anomaly among rival theories and, on the other hand, covers the concrete historical and sociological situations of problem-solving capacity—an anomalous problem poses no threat to a rival theory unless it is a bottleneck problem. Once the historical and sociological situations of scientific competition and development are open for philosophical considerations, we thereby enter the controversial intersected areas of history, philosophy and sociology of science. A further step of this paper is taken in the second half of this essay by considering the debates of *ad hocness*. In order to have a thesis of *ad hocness* (thesis AD) sensitive to historical-sociological situations, arguments and contentions almost identical to those of bottleneck problem are again envoked and developed. (edited)

Fuchs, Erich. Fichtes Einfluss auf seine Studenten en Berlin zum Beginn der Befreiungskriege. *Fichte-Studien*, 2, 178-192, 1990.

Fuchs, Erich. Fichtes Stellung zum Judentum. *Fichte-Studien*, 2, 160-177, 1990.

Fuchs, Wolfgang W. Does a Good Market Make a Good European?. *Hist Euro Ideas*, 19(1-3), 385-389, Jl 94.

Fuchs, Yuval. Philosophy of Methodology in Heidegger's *Die Idee der Philosophie und das Weltanschuungsproblem* (1919). *J Brit Soc Phenomenol*, 25(3), 229-240, O 94.

Fürst, Maria. Art as a Means of Understanding in the Teaching of Philosophy. *Filozof Cas*, 42(6), 1037-1045, 1994.

Fuertes, José Félix. Ernesto Sábato: Físico Antes que Escritor. *El Basilisco*, 17, 67-74, Ju-De 94.

Some aspects and defects of scientific creativity are reviewed following the work of E Sábato, both as an essayist and novelist. Human being becomes a mere thing if the real contribution of science to civilization is only based on economic and technological payoffs. Searching the enrichment of human spirit must be also emphasized. Since the 40's, E Sábato has been quite a voice crying in wilderness. Now, fortunately, this is rather a common fact.

Fuhrmann, André and Levi, Isaac. Undercutting and the Ramsey Test for Conditionals. *Synthese*, 101(2), 157-169, N 94.

There is an important class of conditionals whose assertibility conditions are not given by the Ramsey test but by an inductive extension of that test. Such inductive Ramsey conditionals fail to satisfy some of the core properties of plain conditionals. Associated principles of nonmonotonic inference should not be assumed to hold generally if interpretations in terms of induction or appeals to total evidence are not to be ruled out.

Fukuyama, Francis. The End of History, Five Years Later. *Hist Theor*, 34(2), 27-43, 1995.

The argument contained in the *The End of History and the Last Man* (New York, 1992) consists of an empirical part and a normative part: critics have confused the two and their proper relationship. The assertion that we have reached the "end of history" is not a statement about the empirical condition of the world, but a normative argument concerning the justice or adequacy of liberal democratic political institutions. The normative judgment is critically dependent on empirical evidence concerning, for example, the workability of capitalist and socialist economic systems, but ultimately rests on supra-empirical grounds. The empirical part queries whether there is something like the Hegelian-Marxist concept of history as a coherent, directional evolution of human societies taken as a whole. The answer to this is yes, and lies in the phenomenon of economic modernization based on the directional unfolding of modern natural science. The latter has unified mankind to an unprecedented degree, and gives us a basis for believing that there will be a gradual spread of democratic capitalist institutions over time. This empirical conclusion, however, does no more than give us *hope* that there is a progressive character to world history, and does not prove the normative case. The normative grounding of modern liberal democracy has indeed been put in jeopardy by the philosophical "crisis of modernity" inaugurated by Nietzsche and Heidegger. Contemporary postmodernist critiques of the possibility of such a grounding have not, however, adequately come to terms with the destructive consequences of their views for liberal democratic societies. This *aporia*, discussed most seriously in the Strauss-Kojève debate, is the central intellectual issue of our age.

Fulford, K W M. "Medical Education: Knowledge and Know-How" in *Ethics and the Professions, Chadwick, Ruth (ed)*, 14-26. Brookfield, Avebury, 1994.

In concentrating on the basic and clinical sciences, medical education has tended to neglect the skills necessary for the successful *application* of medical knowledge in practice. A new course for medical students in Oxford is described in which ethics, law and communication skills (collectively "practice skills") are taught alongside traditional clinical sciences. This approach reflects a model of the concept of disease, described by the author in detail elsewhere, in which its descriptive and evaluative logical elements are fully reconciled. This model in turn shows the importance of values in the constitutive as well as regulative aspects of the nature of medicine as a profession.

Fulford, K W M. "Psychiatry, Compulsory Treatment, and the Value-Based Model of Mental Illness" in *Introducing Applied Ethics, Almond, Brenda (ed)*, 148-165. Cambridge, Blackwell, 1995.

This chapter examines the ways in which bioethics, analytical ethical theory and general philosophy respectively contribute to the theory and practice of psychiatry. Taking involuntary psychiatric treatment as a case in point (illustrated with a series of clinical vignettes), it is shown that: 1) Bioethics seek to define the relevant ethical principles; 2) Analytical ethical theory helps to clarify the proper scope of such treatment; and 3) General philosophy (e.g., in areas such as rationality and causation) is required for its justification, notably in the paradigm case of delusion. It is concluded that in psychiatry there is no real distinction between applied and general philosophy.

Fulford, K W M. "Value, Illness, and Failure of Action" in *Philosophical Psychopathology, Graham, George (ed)*, 205-233. Cambridge, MIT Pr, 1993.

Traditional psychopathology—based on supposedly value-free facts about mental functioning—fails to explain important features of the actual symptoms of mental illness, notably those of the paradigmatic symptom of delusion. This occurs in a remarkable range of logical forms: true as well as false factual beliefs; positive or negative value judgments; and the paradoxical delusion of mental illness. It is argued that a psychopathology which is capable of encompassing these and other important features of mental illness will have to be placed within a richer conception of mind, one which acknowledges practical reasoning as well as cognitive functioning, and the significance of values as well as facts in the structure of rational action.

Fulford, K W M. Mind and Madness: New Directions in the Philosophy of Psychiatry. *Philosophy*, 37(Supp), 5-24, 1994.

The links between Descartes logito and the schizophrenic symptom of "inserted thoughts" are used to illustrate the potential for two-way exchange between philosophy and psychiatry. Patients suffering thought insertion have thoughts in their heads, which *they* are thinking, but which they experience as the thoughts of someone else: "I think therefore someone else is". Philosophical work on personal identity helps to clarify the remarkable phenomenological features of thought insertion: conversely, thought insertion challenges philosophical theories of personal identity. More generally, future cross-disciplinary work will require a strong academic infrastructure, including training and research.

Fulford, K W M (ed) and Gillett, Grant (ed) and Soskice, Janet Martin (ed). *Medicine and Moral Reasoning*. New York, Cambridge Univ Pr, 1994.

The unifying theme of this edited collection is that moral reasoning in medicine should draw on a wide variety of sources, both philosophical and empirical articles include: Midgley on Darwinism; Soskice on creation and relation; Hare on embryo experimentation; Brandton on genetic testing; Lockwood on identity; William May on the suicide; Gillett on children; Oddie on moral uncertainty; Urmson on invention and discovery in morality; Crisp on quality of life; Campbell on dependency; and Fulford on involuntary psychiatric treatment.

Fulford, K W M and Hope, Tony and Moore, Andrew. Mild Mania and Well-Being. *Phil Psychiat Psych*, 1(3), 165-177, S 94.

This paper explores the relationship between mania, or pathologically elevated mood, and philosophical theories of well-being. A patient, Mr M, is described who oscillated between periods when he refused medication and periods when he was willing to accept it, and whose desires and life objectives were radically different in his medicated and unmedicated states. The practical dilemmas this raised are explored in terms of the three principal philosophical theories of well-being: hedonism, the desire fulfillment theory, and objectivism. (edited)

Fulford, K William M. "Not More Medical Ethics" in *Medicine and Moral Reasoning*, Fulford, K W M (ed), 193-205. New York, Cambridge Univ Pr, 1994.

This chapter is a contribution to an edited collection illustrating the way in which moral reasoning in medicine should draw on a wide variety of both philosophical and empirical perspectives. The value of linguistic (or ordinary language) philosophy, and of work in this tradition on the fact-value divide, is illustrated for the case of involuntary psychiatric treatment. It is argued from this example that although ordinary language philosophy is nowadays widely considered somewhat unproductive, it could nonetheless make an important contribution to the development of a new medical ethics, at once theoretically richer and with sharper practical teeth than traditional bioethics.

Fulford, Robert. "Irving Singer on Love in the Twentieth Century" in *The Nature and Pursuit of Love*, Goicoechea, David (ed), 23-32. Buffalo, Prometheus, 1995.

Fulford, Robert. "Irving Singer on the History of Love" in *The Nature and Pursuit of Love*, Goicoechea, David (ed), 11-22. Buffalo, Prometheus, 1995.

Fullbrook, Edward and Fullbrook, Kate. "Sartre's Secret Key" in *Feminist Interpretations of Simone de Beauvoir*, Simons, Margaret A (ed), 97-111. University Park, Penn St Univ Pr, 1995.

In this essay the Fullbrooks describe the complex process of writing their landmark book, *Simone de Beauvoir and Jean-Paul Sartre: The Remaking of a Twentieth-Century Legend*. The essay is structured through an analogy between the stories and legends which shape biography, and the hypotheses and theories of science as devices for selecting and ordering facts. The Fullbrooks began research for their biography under the influence of the conventional account of the Sartre/Beauvoir partnership: Sartre was the original philosopher, Beauvoir his interpreter. This essay traces the process by which this account was found to be fallacious, with the result that many of Beauvoir's ideas wrongly have been ascribed to Sartre.

Fullbrook, Kate and Fullbrook, Edward. "Sartre's Secret Key" in *Feminist Interpretations of Simone de Beauvoir*, Simons, Margaret A (ed), 97-111. University Park, Penn St Univ Pr, 1995.

In this essay the Fullbrooks describe the complex process of writing their landmark book, *Simone de Beauvoir and Jean-Paul Sartre: The Remaking of a Twentieth-Century Legend*. The essay is structured through an analogy between the stories and legends which shape biography, and the hypotheses and theories of science as devices for selecting and ordering facts. The Fullbrooks began research for their biography under the influence of the conventional account of the Sartre/Beauvoir partnership: Sartre was the original philosopher, Beauvoir his interpreter. This essay traces the process by which this account was found to be fallacious, with the result that many of Beauvoir's ideas wrongly have been ascribed to Sartre.

Fuller, Steve. A Tale of Two Cultures and Other Higher Superstitions. *Hist Human Sci*, 8(1), 115-125, F 95.

This article critically reviews *Higher Superstition* by Paul Gross and Norman Levitt, the first booklength critique by practicing scientists of postmodern, feminist, multiculturalist and social constructivist accounts of science. Theirs is the latest installment of the "Two Cultures" problem first identified by C P Snow, which was concerned partly with the compatibility of scientific expertise and democracy, something that Gross and Levitt deny. I specifically counter their dismissal of "standpoint epistemology" by showing that the natural sciences were themselves originally marginal in Western culture, but came to cultural prominence only after

non-Westerners, especially Japan, achieved world-class stature as a result of adopting science. This suggests that the attitudes of "The Other" may be integral to the value attributed to one's own cultural products.

Fuller, Steve. On the Motives for the New Sociology of Science. *Hist Human Sci*, 8(2), 117-124, My 95.

The sociology of science is increasingly regarded as antiscientific, though it was important in normalizing the role of science in society during a time (the Cold War) when many wanted greater public control of science. Since then, sociologists have shown that science is much more fallible and prosaic than philosophers or scientists have previously maintained. Still, the question remains how ordinary people with little or no exposure to science continue to attribute extraordinary powers to it. One hypothesis worth exploring is that people are taught to value aspects of science that would not be so highly valued in the conduct of other social activities. The implications of this hypothesis are presented for Robert Merton's famous four norms of science: universalism, communalism, disinterestedness, and organized skepticism.

Fuller, Steve. Retrieving the Point of the Realism-Instrumentalism Debate: Mach vs Planck on Science Education Policy. *Proc Phil Sci Ass*, 1, 200-208, 1994.

I aim to recover some of the original cultural significance that was attached to the realism-instrumentalism debate.(RID) when it was hotly contested by professional scientists in the decades before World War I. Focusing on the highly visible Mach-Planck exchange of 1908-13, I show that arguments about the nature of scientific progress were used to justify alternative visions of science education. Among the many issues revealed in the exchange are realist worries that instrumentalism would subserve science entirely to human interests, as well as instrumentalist worries that realism could become the basis of a science-based religion. I conclude by addressing some issues relating to RID that are now occluded because of Planck's triumph over Mach.

Fuller, Steve. The Governance of Big Science: On the Wisdom of Solomon. *Inform Log*, 16(1), 59-60, Wint 94.

This article is written in response to Miriam Solomon's critique of my 'The sphere of critical thinking in the post-epistemic world' (*Informal Logic* XVI, no 1 (1994) pp 39-54). Whereas Solomon thinks that my criticisms of 'Big Science' are more moral than epistemic, I argue that the epistemic is distinct from the moral only when inquiry is of such a size and shape that it can proceed in relative autonomy from other social activities. Because this is not the case today, I conclude that we live in a 'post-epistemic' world.

Fuller, Steve. The Reflexive Politics of Constructivism. *Hist Human Sci*, 7(1), 87-93, F 94.

Is it possible to conduct research in a 'business as usual' fashion once one admits that all knowledge (including one's own) is socially constructed? I answer no. Interestingly, this seems to be a minority position in the sociology of knowledge. I argue that an implication of accepting the socially constructed character of one's own epistemic practices is the opening up of questions as to the intended contributors and beneficiaries of the knowledge one produces, which, in turn, moves epistemology into issues traditionally identified with rhetoric.

Fuller, Steve. The Sphere of Critical Thinking in a Post-Epistemic World. *Inform Log*, 16(1), 39-53, Wint 94.

Just as political theorists have long argued that democracy is viable only in communities of certain sizes and shapes, perhaps epistemologists should also entertain the idea that knowledge is possible only within certain social parameters—ones which today's world may have exceeded. This is what I mean by the "post-epistemic" society. I understand an "epistemic society" in Popperian terms as an environment that fosters the spirit of conjectures and refutations. After castigating analytic philosophers for their failure to see this point, I show how Rousseau and Feyerabend occupy analogous positions as critics of, respectively, the nation-state and Big Science. Rather than endorsing the disestablishment of the state, however, I offer a proposal for reinjecting the critical attitude into Big Science. It involves heightening the sporting character of scientific disputes, perhaps even to the point of enabling the public to bet on their outcomes.

Fullinwider, Robert K. Citizenship, Individualism, and Democratic Politics. *Ethics*, 105(3), 497-515, Ap 95.

Fumerton, Richard. Group Action and Act Consequentialism. *Midwest Stud Phil*, 15, 296-310, 1990.

I examine the charge that an act consequentialist cannot account for the rightness and/or rationality of certain actions when the consequences of an individual's action are insignificant but the consequences of the group's action are momentous. In doing so, I critically examine methodological assumptions underlying certain sorts of objections to act consequentialism.

Fumerton, Richard. The Incoherence of Coherence Theories. *J Phil Res*, 19, 89-102, 1994.

In this paper I am primarily interested in establishing that a coherence theory of truth is conceptually incoherent. Although my primary concern is with the coherence theory of truth, I shall point out that the problem I raise has a striking parallel in a now well-known objection to coherence theories of justification (an objection that, ironically, was brought to the fore by a proponent of a coherence theory of justification, Laurence Bonjour).

Funda, Otakar A. The Philosophy of Nature and European Ontology. *Filozof Cas*, 42(4), 651-660, 1994.

The author rejects a tendency in European ontology which prefers dealing with being in the abstract to a concrete existence. Such ontology, the author says, creates an artificial antithesis between a subject as perceiving being from a perspective of anthropocentric categories and nature. The usual schemes: theory-praxis, subject-object, matter-spirit, content-form, induction-deduction, do not do justice to a reality which is complementary. In the area of ethics, such anthropocentrism leads to an exaggerated moral pathos, to a glorification of martyrdom and a messianic complex. The author proposes to take for an ethical foundation a life as such, which does not need any further justification, instead of partial ideas or religious certainties. Thus, he says, one can avoid scientism—without becoming an irrationalist and without enforcing rational explanations of ethical-existential decisions.

Funk, Rainer (ed) and Fromm, Erich. *The Erich Fromm Reader*. Atlantic Highlands, Humanities Pr, 1994.

Funke, Gerhard. Volver a Kant Significa Avanzar. *An Seminar Hist Filosof*, 9, 13-37, 1992.

La clave de la gran influencia y autoridad de la figura de Kant en su época no está sólo en su tesis del primado de la razón práctica, tal como aparece en sus obras "esotéricas" (de carácter crítico o sistemático-doctrinal), sino también en la atención que dedicó, en sus escritos "exotéricos", a las cuestiones fácticas de la realización de la razón práctica. Desde esta perspectiva, Kant enfoca las tareas públicas o privadas que considera urgente que el individuo emancipado emprenda. Estas no han perdido su vigencia en la actualidad. Más bien se las ha "olvidado" en su significado práxico fundamental. Recordar el giro radical, la "revolución en el modo de pensar" que en ellas se propugna y realiza, "volver a Kant" en ese sentido significa avanzar.

Furley, David. Some Points About Stoic Dynamics. *Proc Boston Colloq Anc Phil*, 9, 57-75, 1993.

Fynsk, Christopher. Reading the *Poetics* after the *Remarks*. *Res Phenomenol*, 24, 57-68, 1994.

Gabaude, Jean-Marc. La Théologie Apophatique de Denys et la Théodicée de Leibniz. *Diotima*, 23, 133-142, 1995.

Le Pseudo-Denys l'Aréopagite subordonne le *cataphatique* à l'*apophatique* et élabore une théologie mystique, Dieu étant inconnaissable. En revanche, Leibniz estime qu'un avocat de la *Cause de Dieu* a le devoir de justifier Dieu. Il opère démonstrativement des distinctions dans la nature divine afin de rendre compte du calcul existentialisant le monde. Cependant Denys et Leibniz considèrent que la dissemblance ne va pas sans quelque ressemblance. D'où, sur fond d'opposition, des convergences à propos des essences *intradivines*, de l'unité de toute multiplicité, de l'harmonie dans la proportion et dans l'ordre, de l'échelle des êtres et du problème du mal.

Gabaude, Jean-Marc. Le Romantisme de M de Guérin et la Grèce. *Diotima*, 22, 122-131, 1994.

Maurice de Guérin (1810-1839) a vécu le premier romantisme dans l'amour de la nature, avant tout de sa terre natale (château du Cayla, sud-ouest de la France) imaginée à travers les arts et lettres de la Grèce antique. Ainsi ses deux poèmes en prose (*Le Centaure, La Bacchante*) et ses poésies en vers (par exemple *Glaucus*) sont-ils imprégnés de mythologie et de réminiscences antiques. Guérin ressent et exprime son existence à l'unisson des rythmes et variations de la nature. Indissociablement romantique et hellène, il retient une charge émotionnelle grâce à une sobriété classique.

Gabbard, Glen O. Teetering on the Precipice: A Commentary on Lazarus's "How Certain Boundaries and Ethics Diminish Therapeutic Effectiveness". *Ethics Behavior*, 4(3), 283-286, 1994.

Gabbay, Dov M and Reyle, Uwe. Direct Deductive Computation on Discourse Representation Structures. *Ling Phil*, 17(4), 343-390, Ag 94.

We present a deductive component for discourse representation theory. The computation procedures are described for both, intuitionistic and classical logic. They are based on the notion of run time skolemisation, i.e., Skolem functions are introduced at run time and not at the beginning of the proof. Therefore each proof stage is meaningful and has a natural relation to the original query. Finally we show how the Skolem dependencies can be expressed by the hierarchical structure of the DRS's, i.e., by the accessibility relation. This serves to avoid computational problems connected with the treatment of equality. (edited)

Gabhart, Mitchell. Freedom, Understanding, and Therapy in Spinoza's Moral Psychology. *Int J Applied Phil*, 9(1), 1-9, Sum-Fall 94.

Gabriel, Gottfried and Kienzler, Wolfgang. Gottlob Freges politisches Tagebuch. *Deut Z Phil*, 42(6), 1057-1066, 1994.

The text composes the introduction to Frege's diary of 1924 which follows (pp 1067-1098), now published for the first time. It attempts to exhibit the conflict between Frege's political rhetoric and his philosophical logic. The commentary explains the historical references of the diary and essays a critical evaluation of Frege's extreme right-wing political convictions against the background of the First World War lost by Germany.

Gadamer, Hans-Georg. "Die Viefalt Europas—Erbe und Zukunft" in *Das geistige Erbe Europas, Buhr, Manfred (ed)*, 50-68. Napoli, Vivarium, 1994.

Gadamer, Hans-Georg. "Europa und die Oikoumene" in *Europa und die Philosophie, Gander, Hans-Helmuth (ed)*, 67-86. Frankfurt/M, Klostermann, 1993.

Gadamer, Hans-Georg. "Truth in the Human Sciences" in *Hermeneutics and Truth, Wachterhauser, Brice (ed)*, 25-32. Evanston, Northwestern Univ Pr, 1994.

Gadamer, Hans-Georg. "What Is Truth?" in *Hermeneutics and Truth, Wachterhauser, Brice (ed)*, 33-46. Evanston, Northwestern Univ Pr, 1994.

Gärdenfors, Peter. The Social Stance. *Protosoz*, 6, 90-94, 1994.

I argue that it is necessary to go beyond Dennett's notion of the "intentional stance" and adopt a social stance to certain phenomena. I introduce the notion of a social intention, which is an intention that cannot be replaced by individual intentions. The assumption of such intentions are helpful for understanding language and other social conventions. At the end of the article, I also discuss the relation between social intentions and social values.

Gaeta, Rodolfo. "Qué Necesidad Hay?" in *Temas Actuales de Filosofía, Palacios, María Julia (ed)*, 233-240. Buenos Aires, Univ Nacional Salta, 1993.

In this paper several kinds of necessity (logical, natural and metaphysical) are under consideration. It is held that any non-trivial use of the concept of logical necessity implies the admission of logical truths that are not necessary. The author considers that modal notions do not have complete justification by either empirical science or pure formal logic. Consequently, the use of such notions shows the persistence of an irreducible metaphysical rest.

Gaffney, James. Patriotism: Virtue or Vice?. *Phil Theol*, 8(2), 129-148, Wint 93.

The term "patriotism" has had different meanings, deriving from different historical circumstances. In its predominant modern sense it has been condemned as vicious, extolled as virtuous, and judged to be a quality potentially virtuous, but only in moderation. It is argued that, as most commonly understood by writers in this century, neither unrestricted patriotism, nor even moderate patriotism, is a virtue, but it is a socially pernicious vice, the more virulent for being associated with virtue.

Gaffney, Paul. The Morality of legal Retribution. *Cont Phil*, 16(5), 11-17, S-O 94.

Gage, N L. The Scientific Status of Research on Teaching. *Educ Theor*, 44(4), 371-384, Fall 94.

The scientific status of process-product research on teaching has been disparaged as a) not theory-driven and b) not theory-productive. Criticism *a* ignores the implicit theories guiding the research, the flexibility of philosophers on scientific method, the role of serendipity in science, and the history of theory in the criticized research. Criticism *b* disregards the qualifier "systematic" in characterizations of the theory already produced and the distinction between theory as summum bonum (accepted) and theory as sine qua non (rejected) in viewing theory as product.

Gagnebin, Jeanne-Marie. Histoire, mémorie et oubli chez Walter Benjamin. *Rev Metaph Morale*, 99(3), 365-389, Jl-S 94.

Gagnon, Eric. Sur la photographie sociale. *Horiz Phil*, 5(1), 74-83, Autumn 94.

Gagnon, Martin. La phénoménologie à la limite. *Eidos*, 11(1-2), 111-130, Je-D 93.

In *Réduction et donation*, Marion intends to explore the possibilities of phenomenological investigation. His critic of the Husserlian and Heideggerian conceptions of phenomenology leads him to propose a somewhat more radical model of the phenomenological reduction. The reduction to the pure form of the call is thus presented not only as more radical than the Husserlian reduction to the transcendental ego, but also as more radical than the Heideggerian reduction to the *Dasein*. The article examines the phenomenological relevance of Marion's model, and tries to show at what conditions it could in fact resists to some objections it already received in the realm of French philosophy.

Gagnon, Martin. Ricoeur et la fiction de l'autonomie. *Eidos*, 11(1-2), 45-54, Je-D 93.

In his recent work, *Soi-même comme un autre*, Ricoeur intends to redefine the relation between ethics and morals. Considered from a teleological point of view, ethics should be understood as something more fundamental than the deontological perspective of morals. But at the same time, morals is defined so as to keep his critical autonomy against certain goals of the ethical life. The situation of morals is his relation to ethics is thus presented as something like a situation of subordination without submission. This article examines the implications of such a situation.

Gaidenko, P P. Under the Badge of Moderation: The Liberal Conservatism of P B Struve. *Russian Stud Phil*, 33(2), 27-45, Fall 94.

Gaines, Jane. Feminist Heterosexuality and Its Politically Incorrect Pleasures. *Crit Inquiry*, 21(2), 382-410, Wint 95.

Gajano, Alberto. Enseigner et Apprendre chez Descartes. *Rev Phil Fr*, 2, 165-190, Ap-Je 95.

The article attempts to show, following the hypothesis that the Recherche de la vérité has been written not long after the Regulae ad directionem ingenii, that the theory of the principles of the science, as it has been outlined on the Recherche, gives a contribution to the understanding of the way in which the science is conceived in the Regulae. The article reaches the conclusion that Descartes in both works conceives of science as a whole of certain and evident judgements founded on a preexistent knowledge. He considers the principles of science to be as first judgements which are intuitively known, and the truth of which depends upon the truth of notions in themselves implicitly contained (the naturae simplices of the Regulae).

Gal, Ofer. Hesse and Rorty on Metaphor: Rhetoric in Contemporary Philosophy. *J Speculative Phil*, 9(2), 125-146, 1995.

Galán Vélez, Francisco V. La estructura del conocimiento humano segun Lonergan y la analogia trinitaria de Beck. *Rev Filosof (Mexico)*, 27(81), 448-468, S-D 94.

Galasso, Giuseppe. Il Debutto Politico di Gentile: Introduzione agli Scritti sulla Prima Guerra Mondiale. *G Crit Filosof Ital*, 73(2-3), 401-413, My-D 94.

Galbraith, Sharon and Stephenson, Harriet Buckman and Grimm, Robert B. Ethical Congruency of Constituent Groups. *J Bus Ethics*, 14(2), 145-158, F 95.

This research investigates the perceptions of five constituent groups of an accredited business school—their perceptions of others' ethics, of their own ethics and ideal values, and of how business ethics can be improved. Self-described behavior from the constituent groups is quite similar, yet is decidedly different from that which respondents felt others would do. (edited)

Gale, Richard. Why Alston's Mystical Doxastic Practice Is Subjective. *Phil Phenomenol Res*, 54(4), 869-875, D 94.

William Alston argues in his *Perceiving God* that the doxastic practice of taking experiential inputs of apparent direct perceptions of God as giving prima facie justification, subject to defeat by overriders, for belief outputs that God exists and is as he presents himself is a reliable, cognitive practice. This paper argues that the practice is not cognitive, because its experiential inputs have cognate accusatives.

Gale, Richard M. James on Self Identity Over Time. *Mod Sch*, 71(3), 165-189, Mr 94.

James's psychological continuity account of personal identity, like Parfit's, is based on what we take to be important about self-identity. It gives rise to two unresolved aporias: a person's identity is both made and discovered; and introspectively based claims of identity are supposed to be subject to overriders but James provides no place for third person criteria of identity. The latter is symptomatic of James's insider approach to understanding the nature of reality.

Galeotti, Anna Elisabetta. A Problem with Theory: A Rejoinder to Moruzzi. *Polit Theory*, 22(4), 673-677, N 94.

Galewicz, Wlodzimierz. "Das Problem des Seinsstatus der gegenständlichen Sinne und Ingardens Ontologie..." in *Kunst und Ontologie, Wlodzimierz, Galewicz (ed)*, 5-19. Amsterdam, Rodopi, 1994.

Galin, David. The Structure of Awareness: Contemporary Applications of William James' Forgotten Concept of "The Fringe". *J Mind Behav*, 15(4), 375-401, Autumn 94.

Modern psychology does not address the great variety of elements constituting subjective experience or the relations among them. This essay examines ideas on the fine structure of awareness and suggests a more precisely characterized set of variables, useful to all psychologists interested in awareness, whether their focus is on computer simulation, neuroscience, or clinical intervention. This view builds on William James' insight into the qualitative differences among the parts of subjective experience, a concept nearly forgotten until recently reinterpreted in contemporary cognitive terms by Mangan. I review, revise, and expand these ideas, and suggest their application to self-monitoring in several domains, including metacognition, action, and emotion. Sharpening and extending the distinctions James drew among key descriptive aspects of awareness gives us a more differentiated vocabulary for research and theory.

Galison, Peter. The Ontology of the Enemy: Norbert Wiener and the Cybernetic Vision. *Crit Inquiry*, 21(1), 228-266, Autumn 94.

Gallagher, David M. Person and Ethics in Thomas Aquinas. *Acta Phil*, 4(1), 51-71, 1995.

L'articolo indica la centralità della persona nell'etica di Tommaso d'Aquino, attraverso l'analisi della comprensione tommasiana dell'amore. L'amore è il movimento affettivo più basilare, sia al livello dello passioni (appetiti sensibili) che a quello della volontà. L'amore che si trova nella volontà, la *dilectio*, ha due componenti: un amore indirizzato verso una persona, chiamato amore di amicizia (*amor amicitiae*), e un amore indirizzato verso ciò che è buono per la persona, l'amore di concupiscenza (*amor concupiscentiae*). L'amore di amicizia è più basilare dell'amore di concupiscenza, e ne è il presupposto; di conseguenza, l'affetto più basilare della volontà è l'amore per una persona. L'intera vita morale gira intorno alle persone e le loro perfezioni, e, infatti, i fini principali di tutte le scelte morali sono persone. In seguito, si parla della centralità della persona nelle dottrine di Tommaso sulle virtù e sulla legge. L'articolo conclude mettendo la nozione di persona in rapporto con un'altra nozione centrale, quella di teleologia.

Gallagher, David M. Tomás de Aquino, la voluntad y la Ética a Nicómaco. *Topicos*, 4(6), 59-70, 1994.

This article points to several ethical themes in which Thomas Aquinas' analysis employs the notion of *will* while Aristotle's does not. It argues that Aquinas' explanations are more complete precisely because he introduces the will into the discussion. This introduction of the will represents a greater emphasis on the *freedom* of moral acts.

Galleni, Lodovico. How Does the Teilhardian Vision of Evolution Compare with Contemporary Theories?. *Zygon*, 30(1), 25-45, Mr 95.

Teilhard de Chardin's ideas about the mechanisms of biological evolution are revised and their connections with contemporary theories are reported. Teilhard de Chardin's main contribution is the proposal of a new scientific discipline, geobiology—the science of the biosphere evolving as a whole. The main fields of interest of geobiology are reported, and its relationships with contemporary hypotheses, such as Lovelock's Gaia, are discussed. The consequences of this kind of approach are the parallel evolution described as orthogenesis and the presence of canalization phenomena. These Teilhardian hypotheses are discussd in relation to those of the process structuralists and to the novelties of the molecular evolution of the genome. Conclusions are that the mechanisms discussed by Teilhard are presently taken into consideration by contemporary evolutionists in order to construct a new theory of biological evolution.

Gallichio, Santiago. "El Marxismo Analítico y el Problema Moral del Trabajo" in *Temas Actuales de Filosofía, Palacios, María Julia (ed)*, 241-246. Buenos Aires, Univ Nacional Salta, 1993.

Gallichio, Santiago. La alienación del trabajo según la perspectiva del marxismo analítico. *Rev Filosof (Argentina)*, 8(1-2), 19-46, N 93.

The purpose of this paper is to discuss one of the central concepts of Marxian philosophy: alienation under capitalism. First, we ponder whether it is plausible to approach Marxian philosophy from an ethical perspective. Secondly, we examine the concept of *alienation*. Thirdly, we focus on the concept of *work* and we consider it to be a specifically economic human action. Afterwards, we offer a scheme of universalist formulation of the respective scopes of ethics and economics regarding the economical organization of the society. We think that this amounts to justification of criterion used by Marxian philosophy to criticize capitalism.

Gallino, Guglielmo. Kierkegaard e l'ironia socratica. *Filosofia*, 45(2), 143-161, My-Ag 94.

Gallino, Guglielmo. Kierkegaard: La Seduzione, l'Interiorità, l'Ironia. *Filosofia*, 45(3), 291-328, S-D 94.

Gallino, Guglielmo. Lo spirito di serietà e l'ironia. *Filosofia*, 44(3), 393-432, S-D 93.

Gallois, André. Asymmetry in Attitudes and the Nature of Time. *Phil Stud*, 76(1), 51-69, O 94.

Gallois, Cynthia. Group Membership, Social Rules, and Power: A Social-Psychological Perspective on Emotional Communication. *J Prag*, 22(3-4), 301-324, O 94.

This paper reviews research on the language and communication of emotion in interpersonal situations between people in different social groups. Three main areas are reviewed: self-disclosures between people of different ages or different social status, conflict in close relationships, including the tendency of men to withdraw and women to engage conflict; and assertive communication. All these contexts are highly rule-governed, and power is also a highly salient variable in all of them. Overall, the literature suggests that people communicate their emotions in such difficult contexts using strategies that maximize their own comfort and sense of power. These strategies are closely tied to sociostructural power differences.

Galston, William A. Two Concepts of Liberalism. *Ethics*, 105(3), 516-534, Ap 95.

Galton, Antony and Partridge, Derek. The Specification of "Specification". *Mind Mach*, 5(2), 243-255, My 95.

The notion of "specification" plays a key role in the developing science of computing. It is typically considered to be the keystone in the software development process. However, there is no single, generally agreed meaning of "specification" that bears close scrutiny. Instead there is a variety of different, although partially interlocking and overlapping interpretations of the term. We catalogue this varietal profusion and attempt to lay bare both the sources and consequences of each major alternative. We attempt to present the full range of possibilities, and the biases inherent in each style of interpretation. We believe that there is a pressing need for clarification of the meaning of "specification" (and several other important terms), especially in view of the fact that so many practitioners and theoreticians assume, erroneously, that a clear meaning already exists (even though they might disagree as to what it is). In particular, we feel that a more general awareness of the difficulties that currently attach to this key concept may go some way towards bridging (if not actually healing) the rift that currently exists between the engineering and scientific aspects of computing.

Gálvez, Jesús Padilla. Presupuestos de una Teoría de la Verdad. *Manuscrito*, 17(1), 65-89, Ap 94.

In this paper we will show some of the difficulties raised by a theory of truth based on the structure of language as proposed by Tarski's orthodox interpretation and by Kripke's divergent version. We will present the basic elements on which the predicate 'true' depends, and then describe the elementary differences between the term 'proof' and the expression 'truth' by means of results attained by Gödel in 1931. After this, we shall review the divergent proposal with the aim of investigating the conditions on which it depends and then finish this article presenting certain conclusions.

Galy, Jean-Michel. Le Romantisme des Premiers Lyriques Grecs. *Diotima*, 22, 28-36, 1994.

Gamarra, Daniel. J G Fichte: l'affermazione dell'Assoluto. *Acta Phil*, 2(3), 247-270, 1994.

The problem of God, or of the Absolute, in the transcendental philosophy has not a classical metaphysical character; the position of the problem has a subjective origin, and in Fichte's philosophy God appears as a certain last point in the way of the *Wissenschaftslehre*. The "doctrine of the science" is the theory of foundation of the philosophy and of the totality of sciences: Fichte finds its first principle in a subjective and last act of the mind. But on a latter period of his thought, but in continuity with its former philosophy, Fichte maintains that the Absolute appears as an imagine in the conscience: this thesis constitutes the possibility of an affirmation of God from an indirect point of view, perhaps the only possible point of view in transcendental philosophy.

Gander, Hans-Helmuth. "Europa und die Philosophie" in *Europa und die Philosophie, Gander, Hans-Helmuth (ed)*, 9-29. Frankfurt/M, Klostermann, 1993.

Gander, Hans-Helmuth (ed). *Europa und die Philosophie*. Frankfurt/M, Klostermann, 1993.

Ganeri, Jonardon. Vyadi and The Realist Theory of Meaning. *J Indian Phil*, 23(4), 403-428, D 95.

Vyadi, a celebrated Indian linguist, endorses a version of the realist theory of meaning, that the meaning of a word is the object for which it stands. As applied to generic nominals like "(the) cow", Vyadi's thesis faced two much rehearsed objections: 1) if, for each token utterance, a separate meaning rule must be given, then the number of such rules will be *limitless*, and the word will be radically homonymous; 2) if only some finite set is given, use of the word to refer outside this set will be *aberrant*. These arguments significantly resemble certain Davidsonian constraints on a theory of meaning. The application of Vyadi's theory to proper names is also examined.

Ganssle, Gregory E. Reply to Hasker: Does the B-Theory of Time Imply Fatalism?. *Int Phil Quart*, 35(2), 217-218, Ju 95.

Hasker suggests that the B-theory of time is fatalistic. I propose an argument to show this and I explain the flaws in the argument. I then explain why we are tempted to agree with Hasker. Finally, I show the flaws in that reasoning and how we know the B-theory does not prohibit libertarian free will.

Ganzini, Linda and Lee, Melinda A and Heintz, Ronald T. The Capacity to Make Decisions in Advance and Borderline Personality Disorder. *J Clin Ethics*, 5(4), 360-363, Wint 94.

Garber, Daniel. "Leibniz: Physics and Philosophy" in *The Cambridge Companion to Leibniz, Jolley, Nicholas (ed)*, 270-352. New York, Cambridge Univ Pr, 1994.

This essay is a survey of Leibniz's views on the physical world, particularly those that are connected with his philosophical work. Topics discussed include Leibniz's early physical system, his rejection of the Cartesian conception of body, his conception of force and its relation to substance, his views on space and void, his views on motion, and the laws of motion, his critique of atomism and views on the elasticity of all bodies, his critique of Newton and the theory of universal gravitation, and his views on the role of God and final causes in physics.

Garcia, Jorge L A and Nelson, M T. The Problem of Endless Joy: Is Infinite Utility Too Much for Utilitarianism?. *Utilitas*, 6(2), 183-192, N 94.

Traditional utilitarianism stumbles on cases of infinite utility, since its ability to discriminate morally between actions typically requires that the utility value of those actions be finite. Recently, Peter Vallentyne has tried to defend utilitarianism from this objection by stipulating a new definition of "...produces more utility..." that enables the utilitarian to discriminate morally between actions even in cases of infinite utility, while remaining faithful to the spirit of traditional utilitarianism. We argue that Vallentyne's solution is unsatisfactory for various reasons, notably because its distribution-sensitive character deviates from traditional utilitarianism's commitment to sumranking principles.

García, Francisco Vázquez. Ambivalencias de Bentham en la lectura de Foucault. *Telos (Spain)*, 1(2), 81-90, Je 92.

According the Benthamites, Foucault might have deformed the image of Bentham; thought identified with the ideological embryo of modern totalitarisms. Confronted with this simplification of the clash between Foucault and Bentham, this paper intends to show: a) that the French philosopher is not a historian of philosophy, he does not try to work out Bentham's true thought; he just points out the conditions of possibility of a utopia materialized in the panoptical machinery; b) that Foucault's reading is ambivalent; Bentham appears as one of the pioneers of the modern social engineering, but also as one of the most significant critics of punishment and the techniques of state control in the Ancien Régime. (edited)

García, Pablo Sebastián and Brunsteins, Patricia C. Acciones básicas y teoría del conocimiento: una tesis de P Ricoeur sobre de la teoría de A Danto. *Rev Filosof (Argentina)*, 8(1-2), 79-84, N 93.

In this paper, we have tried to present the main lines of Danto's theory of basic actions alone with the criticisms of that theory advanced by Ricoeur. We also put forward some objections to Ricoeur's criticisms, without meaning thereby a full-blooded defense of Danto's theory. Moreover, we point out some difficulties in the theory of basic actions.

García Añón, José. Una aproximación al concepto de derecho a la intimidad en John Stuart Mill. *Telos (Spain)*, 2(1), 17-30, Je 93.

The object of this paper is an examination of different interpretations of the role of legal and moral norms in Mill's utilitarianism. The article starts with the distinction between act and rule consequentialism, and considers the problems of interpretating J S Mill's idea of rights in relation to this distinction. The article concludes with a selected bibliography of secondary sources concerning this issue.

García Bacca, Juan David. "Science, Technology, History, and Philosophy..." in *Philosophy of Technology in Spanish Speaking Countries, Mitcham, Carl (ed)*, 229-247. Dordrecht, Kluwer, 1994.

Garcia Bazán, Francisco. Le Dieu Transcendant dans le Néoplatonisme et chez Denys. *Diotima*, 23, 36-42, 1995.

El fin del artículo es mostrar la originalidad dionisiana de su concepción del Dios desconocido y la *Thearchía* divina, más allá de las semejanzas que ofrece con las ideas del neoplatonismo ateniense, filosófico y teúrgico. La intermediación de los *Oráculos Caldeos* ha sido fundamental para este logro, pero Dionisio recibe en ambos aspectos influjos del gnosticismo como lo prueban textos de la biblioteca de Nag Hammadi (*Eugnosto el Bendito, Tratado tripartito*, los que asimismo han influido en su concepción esotérica del símbolo y de los ritos sacramentales (*Pensamiento trimorfo, Evangelio de Felipe, Testimonio Verdadero).*

García Casanova, Juan Francisco. El Hegelianismo de la Inédita *Filosofía Lógica* de Unamuno. *An Seminar Metaf*, 27, 157-180, 1993.

Unamuno's "Filosofía Lógica" can be regarded as an outline of his future philosophy, because it contains some of its most important ideas. It also helps us to reconstruct the Spanish philosophy at the end the XIX century. In this paper Unamuno is not only investigating the limits of positivism, but he is also dealing with different aspects of humanism. This is also the place where we have to start in order to understand his religious crisis in 1897. The question about the relation between Hegelianism, which is regarded as the most important philosophical position, Spencer's evolutionism and Hartman's synthesis introduces us into the above mentioned problematics. Here, still in the Hegelian context, appears the category of the existence exposed in "Del Sentimiento Trágico de la vida".

García de la Huerta, Marcos. "Technology and Politics: Toward Artificial History?" in *Philosophy of Technology in Spanish Speaking Countries, Mitcham, Carl (ed)*, 3-14. Dordrecht, Kluwer, 1994.

This article intends to demonstrate the internal relation between technology and politics. Two main aspects are explored. Firstly, the platonic denontiation of the *doxa* and the Greek background of the technocratic conception of politics, that is, the technical legitimation of politics. The Greeks, specially Plato and Aristotle, always understood the *politeia* as a special kind of *techné*. Technology for them never came to include the kind of theoretical science required by *politeia*. By contrast, the modern determination of reason allows an extension of the technical to spheres intially deemed non-technical such as society and politics. Secondly, politics understood as the application of the sciences of administration is equivalent to characterizing technology as the application of science to dominate nature, and is directly derived therefrom. This approach tends to stress a verticalist, authoritarian form of power, taking for granted the neutrality of technology, while underlining solely the relation of technology to knowledge. The ethical and political invalidation of manual laborers in Greek thought established at an early stage the dominance of theoretical knowledge, which in turn provides the conceptual basis for this modern "technical abolition of politics".

García de la Sienra, Adolfo. "Idealization and Empirical Adequacy in Economic Theory" in *Idealization VI: Idealization in Economics, Hamminga, Bert (ed)*, 117-133. Amsterdam, Rodopi, 1994.

The problem of idealization itself can be formulated thus: *Important economic theories are defined by axioms ("assumptions") that are clearly false of the objects they avowedly intend to theorize about.* Does this fact make of economic theories pseudo-sciences? Why? At any rate, what usefulness can such theories have to know economic phenomena? The aim of the present paper is to deal with these questions by means of a real-life example Musgrave's threefold distinction between negligibility, domain, and heuristic assumptions is examined in a formal and detailed way. The problem of the usefulness of formal economic theory is approached through the idea of empirical relevance, understood in terms of statistical goodness of fit.

García del Campo, Juan Pedro. La Consideración de las ideas Innatas en Descartes y la Problemática del Conocimiento de lo Físico. *An Seminar Hist Filosof*, 11, 77-94, 1994.

Tras un análisis de las modificaciones que se producen en los textos de Descartes a propósito de las ideas innatas, de una primera visión que las considera contenidos innatos en la mente a otra que considera innata la facultad de pensar y, así, a todas las ideas por ella formadas, se señala que esta modificación está unida a un abandono de la identificación idea-imagen, y se sugiere que esta transformación sólo es explicable desde la problemática suscitada por la fundamentación de la nueva Física.

García García, Javier. A Bowie: Estética y Subjetividad. *An Seminar Metaf*, 28, 337-345, 1994.

It is a critical comment of the book by Andrew Bowie *Aesthetics and Subjectivity: from Kant to Nietzsche* (Manchester/New York: Manchester Univ. Press, 1993, 248 p.). Bowie maintains convincingly that the German philosophy of the 18th and 19th centuries in aesthetical reflections foresees many of the arguments put forward by the contemporary philosophy—not only by the analytic one but also and especially by the hermeneutic and poststructuralist ones—in its criticism of the "subject". In consequence, he claims the need of knowing that fertile period of aesthetical reflection in depth in order to avoid the sterility of many current debates.

García Leal, José. Sociedad Real y Comunidad Ideal Según K-O Apel. *Rev Filosof (Spain)*, 7(11), 199-218, 1994.

The author analyzes the normative ethical principles that Apel calls "Principles of Conservation and Complementation". On this basis, he discusses the status of the ideal community in Apel. Opposing those who understand the ideal community as having some determinate contents in theoretical and political spheres, the author maintains that community has only a formal nature and just requires the fulfillment of those conditions that make the full rational communication among the human beings possible. Finally, this is related to the Utopian perspectives.

García Moriyón, Félix. Ciencia, tecnología y sociedad. *Dialogo Filosof*, 10(2), 255-260, My-Ag 94.

El nuevo Bachillerato ofrece algunas posibilidades de presencia filosófica cuya puesta en práctica requiere el compromiso de los profesores de Filosofía. Una de esas posibilidades es la nueva asignatura *Ciencia, tecnología y Sociedad*, por cuya asignación al Seminario de Filosofía se define con claridad el autor de este artículo.

García Norro, Juan José. Consideraciones en Torno a la Esencia del Formalismo Ético. *Rev Filosof (Spain)*, 7(11), 305-315, 1994.

García Norro, Juan José. La respuesta Husserliana en las Investigaciones Lógicas a la aporía del antropologismo. *An Seminar Metaf*, 27, 127-135, 1993.

García Norro, Juan José. Lo Obligatorio, lo Meritorio y Otras Nociones Deónticas en la Ética Formal de Kant. *An Seminar Hist Filosof*, 9, 127-136, 1992.

Tras caracterizar brevemente el formalismo ético que constituye el núcleo de la ético de Kant y recordar la convicción kantiana de que el imperativo categórico no es sino la aclaración del principio moral que la razón vulgar prefilosófica posee, se intenta mostrar cómo algunas tesis que se siguen del sistema moral de Kant entran en contradicción con certezas de ese saber moral vulgar. Estas tesis son cuatro: la no existencia de voliciones indiferentes, la carencia de auténticos preceptos postivos que expresen deberes y no sólo prohibiciones, la equivalente gravedad de todo acto indebido y la no aceptación de lo meritorio, pero no obligado.

García Prada, Ovidio. La Fundamentación de la Matemática y la Génesis de la Metódica Fenomenológico-Reductiva. *An Seminar Hist Filosof*, 6, 47-78, 1986-89.

García-Bárcena, Rafael. Friedrich Nietzsche: His Christian Spirit. *Int Stud Phil*, 26(3), 93-105, 1994.

García-Baró, Miguel. Introducción a un tratado de filosofía primera. *Rev Filosof (Spain)*, 4(6), 247-269, 1991.

García-Baró, Miguel. Realismo fenomenológico y Metafísica. *Rev Filosof (Spain)*, 4(5), 207-217, 1991.

García-Carpintero, Manuel. Dretske on the Causal Efficacy of Meaning. *Mind Lang*, 9(2), 181-202, Ju 94.

The paper presents a way of interpreting Dretske's "structuring causes" such that this apparently peculiar kind of explanation can be easily fitted in the traditional way of looking at explanations. Traditionally, it is contemplated just two sorts of explanations: "horizontal" explanations of particular events in terms of causally preceding events (which corresponds well to Dretske's "triggering causes") and "vertical" explanations of macro-types in terms of lower-level types. The second variety of explanation serves to justify the causal efficacy of the macro-types, according to orthodox views. The paper contends that what Dretske calls 'structuring causes' are explanations of the second kind, appropriate when the macro-type is a teleo-functional property. It is in this way that structuring causes establish the causal efficacy of meaning.

García-Clavel, Manuel and d'Ors, Angel. Sobre las *Obligationes* de Robert Fland: Antiqua et Nova Responsio. *Rev Filosof (Spain)*, 7(11), 51-88, 1994.

García-Cuadrado, José Angel. Aspectos Gnoseológicos de la *Suppositio Naturalis* de San Vicente Ferrer. *Analogia*, 7(2), 153-167, 1993.

The comparison between *suppositio naturalis* by Pedro Hispano and Vincent Ferrer, clearly shows us the gnoseological differences underlining the theory of one supposition from the other. Vincent Ferrer speaks of a "moderate realism" as seen by Thomas Aquinas; Ferrer proposes a new notion and classification of the *suppositio naturalis* which helps to solve some of the logical-semantic problems raised by the theory of supposition by Pedro Hispano.

García-Cuadrado, José Angel. Los Tratados Filosóficos de S Vicente Ferrer: Nota Histórica y Bibliográfica. *Rev Espan Filosof Med*, 1, 61-73, 1994.

The philosophical treatises by Vincent Ferrer (*Questio de Unitate Universalis* and *Tractatus de Suppositionibus*) were discovered in 1909 thanks to a publication by Fages O.P. These treatises have been studied by various historians, specialists in the field of logic and medieval semiotics; their discoveries show that the treatises display a notable degree of originality. There is also an ample range of bibliography on these topics.

García-Huidobro, Joaquín. Derecho Natural o Derecho Racional?. *Analogia*, 7(1), 143-156, 1993.

García-Merita, María Luisa. "Technology and Human Nature" in *Philosophy of Technology in Spanish Speaking Countries, Mitcham, Carl (ed)*, 145-151. Dordrecht, Kluwer, 1994.

The author of this chapter presents a critical reflection on the impact that technology is having on the human being, on society and on nature itself. The author proposes that far from the happy world that technology promised us, it has in reality favoured the creation of a hostile, alienating and dangerous world in which it becomes necessary to take control of our own development. The article analyzes that psychological repercussions of this technological society as well as their causes.

Gardies, Jean-Louis. I Preliminari Logici. *Riv Int Filosof Diritto*, 71(4), 569-582, 1994.

The article first explains in which conditions there appeared, throughout the evolution of the Western philosophy, a gap more and more pronounced between knowledge on one side and normativity on the other. Now, contrary to what this evolution could suggest, the normative reasoning lets itself be analyzed in terms of truth-functions. Indeed such truth-functions, proper to the normative order, are entirely original relative to those proper to the theoretical order. Nevertheless there are a few truth-functional transitions between both, in such a manner that moral and legal reasoning can directly base itself on certain forms of natural knowledge.

Gardner, Martin R. Self-Defense Theory. *Crim Just Ethics*, 14(1), 72-79, Wint-Spr 95.

Gardner, Sebastian. Wallace Stevens and Metaphysics: The Plain Sense of Things. *Euro J Phil*, 2(3), 322-344, D 94.

This paper is an attempt to make out, and express in philosophical terms, a pattern of metaphysical thought in the poetry and prose writings of Wallace Stevens.

Gardner, William. Can Human Genetic Enhancement be Prohibited?. *J Med Phil*, 20(1), 65-84, F 95.

This article seeks to reframe the ethical discussion of genetic enhancement, which is the use of genetic engineering to supply a characteristic that a parent might want in a child that does not involve the treatment or prevention of disease. I consider whether it is likely that enhancement can be successfully prohibited. If genetic enhancement if feasible, it is likely that there will be demand for it because parents compete to produce able children and nations compete to accumulate human capital in skilled workers. If some parents or nations begin using genetic enhancement, this will change these competitions in ways that increase the incentives for others to use it. Therefore, a ban on genetic enhancement would be unstable, because once the ban was breached by defectors the motivation of others to uphold it would weaken, making the ban liable to collapse. The argument provides a new perspective on slippery slopes to dangerous technology.

Gare, Arran E. Understanding Oriental Cultures. *Phil East West*, 45(3), 309-328, Jl 95.

If the arguments of Edwards Said's *Orientalism* are valid, Joseph Needham's *Science and Civilisation in China* stands condemned. The opposition between Foucault, Said's main source of inspiration, and both Marxism and hermeneutics is highlighted. Utilizing the work of MacIntyre, recent hermeneutic philosophy is defended against Foucault, and through this, Needham's work is defended as a form of Marxist hermeneutics.

Garguilo, René. D'Atala à Athéna: L'Itinéraire Poétique et Politique de Chateaubriand. *Diotima*, 22, 79-86, 1994.

Garin, Eugenio. Attualità di Bruno. *G Crit Filosof Ital*, 72(3), 394-404, S-D 93.

Garin, Eugenio. Filosofi a Bologna fra Ottocento e Novecento. *G Crit Filosof Ital*, 73(1), 1-15, Ja-Ap 94.

Garin, Eugenio. Ricordando Giovanni e Gianfrancesco Pico della Mirandola. *G Crit Filosof Ital*, 74(1), 5-19, Ja-Ap 95.

Garnett, George (ed). *Vindiciae, Contra Tyrannos: Or, Concerning the Legitimate Power of a Prince Over the People, and of the People Over a Prince*. New York, Cambridge Univ Pr, 1994.

The *Vindiciae, Contra Tyrannos* was the most infamous of the monarchomach treatises produced during the French wars of religion, and continued to be revered (or execrated) as a key part of the radical canon for well over a century after its publication. It is one of the first attempts to advance a systematic justification, with interlocking secular and religious arguments, or resistance against legitimately constituted political authority. This edition presents the first complete and accurate English translation of the work, a comprehensive apparatus, and an introduction which provides the first detailed analysis of the argument and also reconsiders the much-disputed question of authorship.

Garns, Rudy. Journal Writing in an Introductory Philosophy Course. *Teach Phil*, 17(1), 57-68, Mr 94.

Garon, Joseph and Stich, Stephen and Ramsey, William. "Connectionism, Eliminativism, and the Future of Folk Psychology" in *Connectionism: Debates on Psychological Explanation, Macdonald, Cynthia (ed)*, 311-338. Cambridge, Blackwell, 1995.

Garrett, Brian. Vagueness, Identity, and the World. *Log Anal*, 34, 349-358, S-D 91.

Garrett, Brian J. Anscombe and the First Person. *Critica*, 26(78), 97-113, D 94.

Garrett, Brian J. Non-Reductionism and John Searle's *The Rediscovery of the Mind*. *Phil Phenomenol Res*, 55(1), 209-215, Mr 95.

Garrett, Don. The Representation of Causation and Hume's Two Definitions of 'Cause'. *Nous*, 27(2), 167-190, Je 93.

Hume offers two distinct definitions of 'cause', one appealing to constant conjunction and the other to association and inference. First, I explain why it has been so difficult to determine Hume's attitude towards the two definitions. Next, I examine the problem that the definition of causation poses within Hume's own theory of mental representation and the argument that leads him to the definitions. I then develop an analogy between Hume's definitions of 'cause' and his definitions of 'virtue', explain why he offers two definitions of 'cause', and argue that he regards both definitions of 'cause' as correct.

Garrett, Richard. "The Problem of Despair" in *Philosophical Psychopathology, Graham, George (ed)*, 73-89. Cambridge, MIT Pr, 1993.

Garrido, Julián Garrido. Circularidades en la contrastación experimental. *Critica*, 26(78), 3-26, D 94.

The experimental test of scientific laws has two essential characteristics: a) the holism of predictious generation (the predication are deduced from sets of laws and not from individual laws) and b) the theoretical weight of measurements (the measurements are based on laws). The former aspect brings about "Duhem's problem": if a prediction is refuted, it is necessary to decide which of its different premises must be modified. Point b) above implies circularities in experimental test that can be extreme: the same laws may be part of the deduction of a prediction and, simultaneously, of the fundaments of the prediction that allows to verify it. The analysis of one of such cases, the Venturi effect, reveals that circularity does not protect the theories of experimentation and, furthermore, that its methodological effects reduce to reinforce holism, thus increasing "Duhem's problem".

Garrido-Maturano, Angel E. Los Modos de Manifestación de la Alteridad y su Articulación en el Pensamiento de Emmanuel Levinas. *Analogia*, 8(2), 73-95, 1994.

Garrison, James W and Macmillan, C J B. Process-Product Research on Teaching: Ten Years Later. *Educ Theor*, 44(4), 385-398, Fall 94.

Garrison, Jim and Kimball, Stephanie. "Hermeneutic Listening: An Approach to Understanding in Multicultural Conversations" in *Identity, Culture, and Education, Smeyers, Paul (ed)*, 171-183. Leuven, Leuven Univ Pr, 1994.

Garrn, Heino. "Wertproblematik und Begründungsstruktur im Recht" in *Mythos Wertfreiheit?, Apel, Karl Otto (ed)*, 213-233. Frankfurt, Campus Verlag, 1994.

Garson, James W. Cognition Without Classical Architecture. *Synthese*, 100(2), 291-305, Ag 94.

Fodor and Pylyshyn (1988) argue that any successful model of cognition must use classical architecture; it must depend upon rule-based processing sensitive to constituent structure. This claim is central to their defense of classical AI against the recent enthusiasm for connectionism. Connectionist nets, they contend, may serve as theories of the implementation of cognition, but never as proper theories of psychology. Connectionist models are doomed to describing the brain at the wrong level, leaving the classical view to account for the mind. This paper considers whether recent results in connectionist research weigh against Fodor and Pylyshyn's thesis. (edited)

Garver, Eugene. *Aristotle's Rhetoric: An Art of Character*. Chicago, Univ of Chicago Pr, 1994.

Garver, Newton. "In Defense of the French" in *European Philosophy and the American Academy, Smith, Barry (ed)*, 123-141. Peru, Open Court, 1994.

French philosophical works tend to differ from Anglo-American ones in two significant respects. One is the search for an encyclopedic synthesis, as in the work of Montaigne, Descartes, Diderot, Poincaré, and Serres. The other is the quality of writing, which often leads to French philosophical works being read as literature, as in the case of Montaigne, Descartes, Rousseau, Voltaire, and Sartre. These differences are illustrated through special attention to Sartre, Foucault, Serres, Weil, and Monet. By paying attention to these and other differences of style, we can avoid misunderstandings that are otherwise likely to arise.

Garver, Newton. "Naturalism and Transcendentality: The Case of 'Form of Life'" in *Wittgenstein and Contemporary Philosophy, Teghrarian, Souren (ed)*, 41-69. Bristol, Thoemmes, 1994.

Wittgenstein's conception of forms of life as part of natural history challenges familiar conceptions of both naturalism and the transcendental. His naturalism ("natural history") is what Strawson calls the "liberal or catholic" variety, sharply distinguished from the "strict or reductive" variety (scientism). What is "transcended" by Wittgenstein's natural history is therefore not nature but scientific accounts of nature. In these respects Wittgenstein's philosophy includes elements of both Aristotle and Kant and is sharply contrary to Dewey and Quine.

Gasarch, William and Downey, Rod and Moses, Michael. The Structure of the Honest Polynomial m-Degrees. *Annals Pure Applied Log*, 70(2), 113-139, D 94.

A language *A* is said to be honest polynomial time *m*-reducible to a language *B* iff there is a polynomial *p* and a polynomial time computable function *f* such that $f \varepsilon A$ iff $f(x)\ \alpha\ B$ and $|f(x)|$ is less than or equal to $P(|x|)$. The paper at hand explores the structure of the recursive sets partitioned by the ordering induced by honest polynomial time reductions.

Gaskin, Richard. Bradley's Regress, the Copula and the Unity of the Proposition. *Phil Quart*, 45(179), 161-180, Ap 95.

If we make the basic assumption that the components of a proposition have reference on the model of proper name and bearer, we face the problem of distinguishing the proposition from a 'mere list' of names. We neutralize the problem posed by that assumption of we first of all follow Wiggins and distinguish, in every predicate, a strictly predicative element (the copula), and a strictly nonpredicative conceptual component (available to be quantified over). If we further allow the copula itself to conform to the basic assumption, a regress ('Bradley's regress') arises: the referent of the copula will be instantiation, the instantiation of instantiation etc. To avert the regress, Wiggins simply legislates that the basic assumption is to fail for the copula. But we are entitled to regard the regress as constitution not a difficulty, but the solution: the infinitism it imports (capturable in a finitistic theory of meaning) is just what the unity of the proposition *is*. (edited)

Gaskin, Richard. Molina on Divine Foreknowledge and the Principle of Bivalence. *J Hist Phil*, 32(4), 551-571, O 94.

Molina has two different approaches to the metaphysics of the future: in his commentary on Aristotle's *De Interpretatione* 9 he follows Aristotle in seeking to restrict the "Principle of Bivalence" with respect to future contingencies, but in his *Concordia* he offers an account of foreknowledge and middle knowledge which presupposes that Bivalence remains unrestricted. These two approaches are in conflict. Furthermore, the conflict is imported by Molina into the *Concordia* itself. The article engages in detail with the interpretations of Craig and Freddoso, who seek to reconcile Molina's various pronouncements on foreknowledge and future contingency. Molina's best course, if he wishes to restrict Bivalence, would be to embrace a Thomistic approach to future contingency; his objections to this approach are spurious.

Gaskin, Richard. *The Sea Battle and the Master Argument: Aristotle and Diodorus Cronus on the Metaphysics of the Future*. Hawthorne, de Gruyter, 1995.

The book provides a detailed historical analysis of Aristotle's discussion of future contingency in *De Interpretatione* 9, as well as a reconstruction of Diodorus Cronus's master argument. It is argued that Aristotle adhered to an antirealist view of statements about the future, along the lines of the view attributed to him by his earliest extant commentators, Ammonius and Boethius. The master argument is reconstructed without adducing extra premisses, but with the help of the Aristotelian principle that any contingency may be assumed to be actual without incoherence. The connections between Diodorus and Aristotle, as well as other pertinent Aristotelian texts, are examined. Appendices consider relevant Peripatetic sources, as well as the medieval commentaries on *De Interpretatione* 9.

Gaskin, Richard and Harrison, Bernard. Symposium: Truth, Meaning and Literature. *Brit J Aes*, 34(4), 376-388, O 94.

Gasparski, Wojciech W (ed) and Collen, Arne (ed). *Design & Systems: General Applications of Methodology*. New Brunswick, Transaction Books, 1995.

This third volume in a series consists of a set of contributions to the methodological study of design from a wide representation of disciplines and professions. Informed by general systems theory and praxiological-systemic perspectives, the contributors of this collection convey a variety of applications of theoretical and generic import, but with special concern for the effectiveness, purposive action, efficiency, and efficiency of methodology for design and systems.

Gatens, Moira. "Between the Sexes: Care or Justice?" in *Introducing Applied Ethics*, Almond, Brenda (ed), 42-57. Cambridge, Blackwell, 1995.

This paper considers present and historical accounts of the ethical relations between the sexes. It offers a critical reading of the "care/justice" debate (Gilligan vs. Rawls) in contemporary moral theory and argues against the hypothesis that men's and women's reasoning in moral matters takes two distinct forms. The paper considers "maternalist" views in recent feminist moral theory (Held) and rejects these as capable of providing an adequate basis for morality. The impact of "care"-based moral theories on the law are criticised. (Mackinnon) The paper concludes by arguing that feminist theorists need to think beyond the dualism of either a "masculinised" private sphere or a "maternalised" public sphere.

Gatens-Robinson, Eugenie. Finding Our Feminist Ways in Natural Philosophy and Religious Thought. *Hypatia*, 9(4), 207-228, Fall 94.

The essay explores the connection between ecological wisdom and feminist spirituality. It takes a careful look at the difficulties that feminist thinkers have had in establishing such wisdom through a tradition of ethics focused on intrinsic value, a tradition of scientific thinking in which the knower is distanced from nature, and Western religious thinking in which both the feminine and nature are taken as profane. The suggestion is made that the resources of American Naturalism may provide a truly spiritual means to the needed transformation.

Gatter Jr, Robert A and Moskop, John C. From Futility to Triage. *J Med Phil*, 20(2), 191-205, Ap 95.

Basic disagreements about what makes human life valuable hinder use of the concept of futility to decide whether it is appropriate to continue life support for one in a permanent state of unconsciousness, or to provide intensive medical care to one in the last stages of a terminal illness (the "paradigm cases"). Triage planning (the process of establishing criteria for health care prioritization) is an attractive alternative framework for addressing the paradigm cases. Triage planning permits society to see the cases in the context of diverse moral perspectives, limited resources, and competing health care demands. Furthermore, at least one essential question posed by the paradigm cases is whether treatment is wasteful, and triage planning is a useful model for identifying and eliminating wasteful medical care. The authors describe how triage planning can be implemented to address the paradigm cases, and conclude that it offers one way of moving debate about these cases beyond futility.

Gatzemeier, Matthias. "Die Verantwortung des Wissenschaftlers" in *Freiheit, Verantwortung und Folgen in der Wissenschaft*, Sandkühler, Hans Jörg (ed), 9-35. New York, Lang, 1994.

Gaukroger, Stephen. The Arts and Scientism: A Comment on 'Wittgenstein and Aesthetics'. *Lit Aes*, 4, 117-120, O 94.

Gaul, Marek. "Statistical Dependencies, Statements and the Idealizational Theory of Science" in *Probability in Theory-Building*, Brzezinski, Jerzy (ed), 9-43. Amsterdam, Rodopi, 1994.

Gault, Richard. In and Out of Time. *Environ Values*, 4(2), 149-166, May 95.

This paper explores the nature of time and its relation to our concerns for the future. It is shown how a new sense of time, chronological time, emerged with the rise of science and modernity. This now familiar time is rarely questioned. Yet, it is argued, this time is intimately bound up with our contemporary problems and our failure to effect solutions. In analysing chronological time it is revealed that the future explains our careless despoiling of the environment. To save our environment we need to resurrect a real sense for the future: only then can the future be truly valued. This means rediscovering another sense of time. This other time is named *kairological time*. In kairological time there is a more vivid awareness of the future. In this time, too, new ways of acting for the future are opened up. Possibilities for a wiser way to the future in part stem from a revaluation of the past. So the sense of being out of time to save ourselves and our planet can be overcome by a living in this other, kairological time.

Gaus, Gerald F. Sentiments, Evaluations, and Claims. *Crim Just Ethics*, 13(2), 7-15, Sum-Fall 94.

This essay is a contribution to a symposium on James Q Wilson's *The Moral Sense*. In his book Wilson ascribes a central role to feelings in moral judgments. In this essay I question whether feelings have the dominating role in morality that Wilson ascribes to them. Our feelings often diverge. Nothing, I argue is quite so common as reasonable people having different feelings, leading them to different evaluations of the same object. This basic affective diversity of our natures, I believe, renders our feelings unsuitable as the focus of a public, shared, morality in a diverse society. That, at least, is what I argue in this essay.

Gaus, Gerald F. Taking Drugs and Rights Seriously. *Crim Just Ethics*, 14(1), 63-71, Wint-Spr 95.

Gaut, Berys. Rawls and the Claims of Liberal Legitimacy. *Phil Papers*, 24(1), 1-22, Ap 95.

The liberal ideal of legitimacy is that the basic laws of the state should be justifiable to all citizens. In his recent work *Political Liberalism*, Rawls gives an interpretation of this ideal as the liberal principle of legitimacy, in terms of what all reasonable citizens can agree to. It is argued that this interpretation cannot justify liberalism. By setting the standards of what is reasonable too low, the standard of the agreement of all reasonable citizens becomes too demanding. An alternative interpretation of the liberal ideal in terms of what all maximally reasonable citizens would endorse is proposed, and its implications explored.

Gaut, Berys. The Enjoyment Theory of Horror: A Response to Carroll. *Brit J Aes*, 35(3), 284-289, Jl 95.

In his paper "Enjoying Horror Fictions: A Reply to Gaut" (The British Journal of Aesthetics, 35 (1), January 1995), Noël Carroll criticizes several claims made in my paper "The Paradox of Horror" .(The British Journal of Aesthetics, 33 (4), October 1993). The current paper responds to Carroll's reply. I raise objections to the points he makes in reply to my earlier criticisms of his own theory about how we can enjoy horror fictions. I also respond to his criticisms of my own view, the enjoyment theory of horror, which holds that it is possible to enjoy horror fictions, since it is possible to enjoy being afraid.

Gauthier, David. Breaking Up: An Essay on Secession. *Can J Phil*, 24(3), 357-371, S 94.

The paper examines the right of secession from existing legitimate political orders. I argue solely in terms of individual rights, defending on contraction grounds a weak right to enter into and continue political association with those with whom she wishes to associate and who wish to associate with her, and to avoid or exit from association with those with whom she wishes not to associate. I limit this weak right by the requirement that one must justify unilaterally imposing costs on or worsening the position of another, in relation to a background that includes existing normative relationships. I discuss briefly the situation of northern Ireland, and at greater length, that of Québec.

Gauthier, Yvon. Construction et Structure Dynamique des Théories Physiques. *Horiz Phil*, 2(2), 51-63, Spring 92.

The paper is devoted to a constructivist conception of physical theories which emphasizes the analytical apparatus (Hilbert's) "Analytischer Apparatus" in contrast to a model-theoretic approach. The concept is elaborated in the author's book *La logique interne des théories physiques*, Bellarmin-Vrin: Montreal-Paris, 1992.

Gauthier, Yvon. Hilbert and the Internal Logic of Mathematics. *Synthese*, 101(1), 1-14, O 94.

Hilbert's program is shown to have been inspired in part by what we can call Kronecker's program in the foundations of an arithmetic theory of algebraic quantities. While finitism stays within the bounds of intuitive finite arithmetic, metamathematics goes beyond in the hope of recovering classical logic. The leap into the transfinite proved to be hazardous, not only from the perspective of Gödel's results, but also from a Kroneckerian point of view. Hilbert's rare admission of a Kroneckerian influence does not constitute the basis of such a reconstruction; it is rather Kronecker's mathematical practice which is seen as a forerunner of Hilbert's endeavour in the foundations of mathematics.

Gay, Hannah. Wilderness Philosophy. *Dialogue (Canada)*, 33(4), 661-675, Fall 94.

An essay review of, Max Oeschlaeger, *The Idea of Wilderness from Prehistory to the Age of Ecology*.

Gay, William C. From Wittgenstein to Applied Philosophy. *Int J Applied Phil*, 9(1), 15-20, Sum-Fall 94.

For Wittgenstein, meaning is understood in the context of use. Ranjit Chatterjee has noted the meaning of a philosopher varies according to the use of that philosopher in society. Wittgenstein's endeavor can be used as a critique of language becoming an idol and also idle in linguistic and metalinguistic theory. Furthermore, Wittgenstein's philosophy can be used as a facilitator of applied philosophy. This interpretation of Wittgenstein's anti-theoretical posture also draws on Ferruccio Rossi-Landi to argue that an applied Wittgenstein approach seeks to expose and them remove linguistic alienation and increases the involvement of philosophers in addressing everyday problems.

Gay, William C. Ricoeur on Metaphor and Ideology. *Darshana Int*, 32(1/125), 59-70, Ja 92.

I argue that metaphor and ideology, which Paul Ricoeur treats separately, should be considered jointly to understand linguistic creativity. Phenomenologists like Maurice Merleau-Ponty view metaphors as creative and positive. They applaud them as authentic expressions of autonomous subjects. Marxists like V N Volosinov view Ideology as distortive and negative. They condemn them as class-based expressions of false consciousness. I argue both metaphors and ideology are creative and distortive and can be positive or negative. I use 'creative distortions' to refer to positive formulations which expand perception and 'distortive creations' to refer to the negative formulations which constrict perception.

Gecas, Viktor and Weigert, Andrew J. Multiplicity and Dialogue in Social Psychology: An Essay in Metatheorizing. *J Theor Soc Behav*, 25(2), 141-174, Je 95.

This paper suggests moving the premise of dialogue among social psychologists from the historical "fact" of different social psychological traditions to metatheoretical constructs in the service of further theorizing. Based on the writings of George H Mead, a metatheoretical space is presented for the symbolic realm and similarities and differences are noted for selected illustrations. The discussion leads to the illuminating power of works that bridge previously separated domains. Reference is made to the importance of developments in the physical realm and their links to the symbolic, e.g., dialectic of a neural and symbolic self. The fruitfulness of the schema is portrayed in clarifying the idea of "risk". Continual metatheorizing is needed, since shared metatheoretical constructs make productive dialogue possible even among theoretically diverse traditions.

Gedő, András. "Der philosophische Aufstieg des faustischen Menschen" in *Das geistige Erbe Europas, Buhr, Manfred (ed)*, 595-623. Napoli, Vivarium, 1994.

Gehron, Christiane and Rée, Jonathan. Interview: Hans-Georg Gadamer. *Rad Phil*, 69, 27-35, Ja-F 95.

In this interview, conducted in October 1993, Gadamer reflects on his life and work in general: how he feels about writing, about teaching and the future of philosophy; Husserl, Heidegger, Nietzsche, Derrida, de Man, and Freud; intellectual life in the Nazi time; analytic philosophy, traditionality and the history of philosophy; Marxism, Christianity, the position of women, the unification of Germany and the prospects for peace in the world.

Geiger, Gebhard. Why are There No Objective Values? A Critique of Ethical Intuitionism from an Epistemological Point of View. *J Gen Phil Sci*, 26(1), 35-62, 1995.

Geis, Gilbert. Moral Innatism, Connatural Ideas, and Impuissance in Daily Affairs: James Q Wilson's Acrobatic Dive into an Empty Pool. *Crim Just Ethics*, 13(2), 77-82, Sum-Fall 94.

The paper maintains that in *The Moral Sense*, James Q Wilson fails utterly to demonstrate that human beings possess an innate moral sense. The argument is made that the issue is not demonstrable and that Wilson fails to pay heed to alternative plausible explanations when he sets out what he maintains are illustrations of his theme. Further, Wilson continuously qualifies his statement by the use of words such as "most", and "many" so that his theme is never susceptible to either proof or rebuttal.

Geisdorfer Feal, Rosemary and Feal, Carlos. *Painting on the Page: Interartistic Approaches to Modern Hispanic Texts*. Albany, SUNY Pr, 1995.

Painting on the Page devises critical strategies that combine psychoanalysis, feminism, semiotics, and philosophy to examine late 19th- and 20th-century Spanish and Spanish-American literature in relation to painting and to larger questions of art and literary history. The authors widen the theoretical lines to Hispanism, where approaches of this kind are rare. The book raises crucial concerns that relocate the art works and texts in question beyond the historical or aesthetic framework in which they have been traditionally placed.

Geisler, Jacek and Nowak, Marek. Conditional Negation on the Positive Logic. *Bull Sec Log*, 23(3), 130-136, O 94.

In the paper a paraconsistent logic is considered, representative of a class of sentential logics which, taking into account their features, can be called the class of classical paraconsistent logics. The truth conditions for negation in the frame-semantics adequate for that logic are expressed in a conditional way.

Geismann, Georg. Fichtes *Aufhebung* des Rechtsstaates. *Fichte-Studien*, 3, 86-117, 1991.

Gélinas, Gérard. Qu'est-ce Qu'Apprendre en Philosophie?. *Philosopher*, 15, 163-170, 1994.

Gemes, Kenneth. A New Theory of Content I: Basic Content. *J Phil Log*, 23(6), 595-620, D 94.

Philosophers of science, for instance, Carnap and Popper, take the (logical) content of a proposition to be given by its consequence class. This notion of content is inappropriate for many of the formal needs of philosophers of science. The basic problem is that given this notion of content any arbitrary α and β share common content namely $(\alpha \vee \beta)$. This notion of content has disastrous effects on, for instance, Carnap's attempts to explicate the notion of confirmation in terms of probabilistic favorable relevance, and Popper's attempts to define verisimilitude. After reviewing some of the problems of the traditional notion of content I present an alternative notion of (basic) content which better fits our intuitions about content and better serves the formal needs of philosophers of science.

Gemes, Kenneth. Schurz on Hypothetico-Deductivism. *Erkenntnis*, 41(2), 171-181, S 94.

Schurz has demonstrated two derivations of unacceptable conclusions drawn from a standard version of hypothetico-deductivism (H-D1). The first derivation proceeds via recourse to a principle (P1) proposed by Schurz. The second proceeds via a principle (P2) proposed by Hempel. To avoid these conclusions Schurz suggests that we reject (H-D1) in favor of an alternative version of Hypthetico-deductivism (H-D2). I show 1) Schurz's (P1) and (P2) are questionable; 2) Schurz's (H-D2), combined with (P1) and (P2) also has unacceptable consequences; 3) (H-D2) can only avoid the type of tacking problem Glymour presses against (H-D1) at the price of denying a canonical equivalence principle; 4) Schurz's (H-D2) by itself has counter-intuitive consequences.

Gendin, Sidney. Am I Wicked?. *Teach Phil*, 18(2), 167-168, Je 95.

People enter the profession of philosophy because they find philosophy very interesting. Almost nobody enjoys teaching very much. They enjoy the lifestyle of teachers. No one would refuse a teaching load of one course every other semester although he would be deprived of much contact with students.

Gendlin, E T. Response. *Human Stud*, 17(3), 381-400, Jl 94.

Gendron, Diane. Autopsie de l'approche par Compétences. *Philosopher*, 17, 205-227, 1995.

Gendron, Pierre. La philosophie de Spinoza, l'éthique et la vérité. *Horiz Phil*, 5(1), 116-132, Autumn 94.

Comment savoir si l'éthique n'est pas un stratagème? En amour comme à la guerre, toute ruse est bonne. La question de la vérité de l'éthique, comme le montre la problématique particulièr du signe dans la philosophie de Spinoza, est inéluctable, Il ne fait aucun doute que l'existence de ce genre de question est caractéristique du domaine de l'éthique; mais non moins caractéristique est l'absence de solution. Cela est indécidable.

Gendron, Pierre. Les comités d'éthique comme mécanisme de contrôle des activités de recherche: Le point de vue de la philosophie. *Horiz Phil*, 5(2), 109-131, 1995.

Genosko, Gary. "The Drama of Theory: Vengeful Objects and Wily Props" in *Baudrillard: A Critical Reader, Kellner, Douglas (ed)*, 292-312. Cambridge, Blackwell, 1994.

Genova, Judith. Response to Anderson and Keith. *Soc Epistem*, 8(4), 341-343, O-D 94.

Genova, Judith. Turing's Sexual Guessing Game. *Soc Epistem*, 8(4), 313-326, O-D 94.

Gentile, Nélida. "Acerca de la Distinción entre Reglas Constitutivas y Reglas Regulativas" in *Temas Actuales de Filosofía, Palacios, María Julia (ed)*, 271-274. Buenos Aires, Univ Nacional Salta, 1993.

In "Speech Acts", J Searle draws a distinction between constitutive rules and regulative rules: the former ones regulate preexisting forms of behavior, while the last ones not only regulate but also, and basically, "create and define new forms of behavior". In addition to this characterization, Searle offers some other criterions to favor such distinction. It is my purpose to show that these criterions are ambiguous and, besides, that regulating behavior rules are always constitutive of the action itself.

Geoghegan, Vincent. National Past, Socialist Future. *Hist Euro Ideas*, 19(1-3), 293-299, Jl 94.

The article addresses the question of the 'end of socialism' by looking at the early historical experience of the ideology. In particular it discusses a cluster of problems associated with the relationship between socialism and national identities. It uses two historical case studies: the attempt to introduce socialism into Ireland in the first half of the nineteenth century, and the conflict between two socialist utopian works, those of William Morris and Edward Bellamy. Its conclusion is a slightly tongue in cheek alternative question—did socialism ever begin?

George, Alexander. Intuitionism and the Poverty of the Inference Argument. *Topoi*, 13(2), 79-82, S 94.

Intuitionism is occasionally advanced on the grounds that a classical understanding of mathematical discourse could not be acquired, given limitations of the experience available to the language learner. In this note, focusing on the acquisition of the universal quantifier, I argue that this route of attack against a classical construal results, at best, in a Pyrrhic victory. The conditions under which it is successful are such as to redound upon the tenability of intuitionism itself. Adjudication will not follow merely from attending to the learner's experience. The nature of the agent's ability to engage in conceptual extrapolation from the experience must be considered as well. (And divergent views regarding this are likely to recapitulate the original disagreement.)

George, Marie I. Wonder as Source of Philosophy and of Science: A Comparison. *Phil Sci (Tucson)*, 6, 97-128, 1995.

This paper investigates the similarities and differences between the wonder which stimulates the scientist and that which goads the philosopher. We conclude that while the two kinds of wonder both result from an effort to shape naive wonder into a more intellectual form, they differ in three ways: 1) scientific wonder bears on less general matters; 2) it involves the imagination more than philosophical wonder does; 3) scientific wonder is a motivation not only to seeking the solution of particular problems, but also takes the form of a desire to see the mathematical harmony of the world for its own beauty.

Georgiadis, Constantine. Aristotle's Theology and Its Influence on the Philosophers of Islam, Judaism and Christianity. *Dialogue Hum*, 3(1), 11-23, 1993.

Aristotle's theology, of a noncreationist character, was meant historically to have a unifying influence in the middle ages on the philosophers of Islam, Judaism, and Christianity. The paper discusses the poetic nature of Aristotle's God who is responsible for the eternity of the celestial movement and the unity of order in the universe simply as a final cause. The reception of Aristotle's theology from the perspective of three different religious traditions is discussed with reference to Averroes, Maimonides and Thomas Aquinas, with regard to the problem of creation and the question of the knowledge that God may have of things other than Himself.

Georgiadis, Constantine. Sophocles' *Oedipus the King*: Art and the Mystery of Human Existence. *Dialogue Hum*, 4(2-3), 41-64, 1994.

Georgieff, Andrey. Death and the Radical Smile. *Hist Euro Ideas*, 19(1-3), 391-397, Jl 94.

This article offers a philosophical investigation into the Gulf War as an example of the end of history. In the modern age war was political: its fundamental basis was the limitation of violence. But the technological ecstasy of pure war and death used as a weapon in holy war has destroyed the illusion of a just political war. America conducted the Gulf War like a nuclear war by shifting the explosive power of "conventional" weapons into nuclear spheres. It was a war like a nuclear war. The deterrent of the nuclear bomb has become a farce. With each future war the (third) world is left no other choice but to make the nuclear first strike. (edited)

Geraets, Theodore F and Harris, H S. On Translating Hegel's *Encyclopedia Logic*: A Response. *Owl Minerva*, 26(1), 95-96, Fall 94.

Geras, Norman. Richard Rorty and the Righteous Among the Nations. *J Applied Phil*, 12(2), 151-173, 1995.

Richard Rorty has proposed the hypothesis that those who came to the rescue of Jews in Nazi Europe are more likely to have been moved to help by parochialist sorts of consideration—sympathy for a colleague, fellow national, and the like—than they are by universalist motives having to do with the proper treatment of *human beings*. Although inconclusive on many other points, the research on rescuer behavior during the Holocaust embodies a consensus contrary to Rorty's hypothesis; and extensive reference to the rescuers' own testimony supports that consensus.

Gerber, William. *Nuggets of Wisdom from Great Jewish Thinkers: From Biblical Times to the Present*. Amsterdam, Rodopi, 1994.

This book offers a copious selection of insights about the world and life, crafted in engaging language by Jewish sages, scholars, rabbis, and literary luminaries, from ancient to modern times. These remarkable explanations, queries, and proposals are connected by expository comments and comparisons by the author. The passionate care for human values which underlies much of Jewish thinking is made accessible in this comprehensive work. In it the reader may find counsel on how to achieve a good and satisfying life while responding to the joys and sorrows that touch us all.

Gergen, Kenneth. Metaphor and Monophony in the 20th-Century Psychology of Emotions. *Hist Human Sci*, 8(2), 1-23, My 95.

Given the dilemma of linking psychological terms to specific internal conditions, we are freed to consider the discourse of emotion in terms of socio-rhetorical processes. Psychological science has struggled unsuccessfully for over a century to determine the nature of emotions. The continuing conflict can be understood first, in terms of the differing metaphors available to the field from its inception, and second, the ways in which these discourses were variously utilized to position the field politically. Attempts toward monophonic reductionism are continuously unsettled by the polyphonic resources of the field. Social constructionist accounts of emotion now raise new and significant questions.

Gergen, Kenneth J. "The Limits of Pure Critique" in *After Postmodernism*, Simons, Herbert W (ed), 58-78. Newbury Park, Sage, 1994.

Gerhardt, Volker. "Kunst und Leben" in *Naturzweckmässigkeit und ästhetische Kultur*, Schwabe, Karl-Heinz (ed), 77-94. Sankt Augustin, Academia, 1993.

Gerhart, Mary. "The Live Metaphor" in *The Philosophy of Paul Ricoeur*, Hahn, Lewis Edwin (ed), 215-232. Peru, Open Court, 1994.

Ricoeur's theory of metaphor is firmly integrated within his other work, particularly that pertaining to the problem of multiple interpretations of probable human behavior. Metaphor in this context is primarily linguistic although metaphor exceeds language in two senses. Ricoeur draws from the theory of nominal deviance and of predicative deviance, but surpasses them in showing how the creative imagination redescribes, as well as describes, the real. The author shows how Ricoeur's understanding of metaphor differs from Husserl's, Heidegger's, Derrida's and Wittgenstein's treatment of metaphor and related issues.

Gerhart, Mary and Russell, Allan Melvin. A Scientist and a Theologian See the World: Compromise or Synthesis?. *Zygon*, 29(4), 619-638, D 94.

A scientist (for whom the world is the universe) and a theologian (for whom the world is planet Earth) engage in dialogue, not contrived Platonic or Galilean dialogue, but true bidisciplinary dialogue that strives for higher viewpoint. S: Is the preservation of the human species a primary human responsibility? T: It may be a responsibility we share with God. S: The human species has a limited future if confined to the planet Earth. We must diversify our habitat by colonizing space. T: We are responsible for other life on the planet as well. The discussants conclude that besides protecting Earth ecologies, we should create new ecologies in space.

Gerken, John D. *An American Ethic: A Philosophy of Freedom Applied to Contemporary Issues*. Middletown, Caslon Co, 1995.

Gerlich, Siegfried. *Sinn, Unsinn, Sein: Philosophische Studien über Psychoanalyse, Dekonstruktion und Genealogie*. Vienna, Passagen, 1992.

Psychoananalyse als Philosophie und vice versa—unter den Auspizien poststrukturalistischen Denkens eine paranoische Verschlingung ohne Ende? Tatsächlich führen diese paralacanschen Studien auf dem Wege einer philosophischen Transformation der Psychoanalyse hinein in ein hoffnungslos immanenzverstricktes Denkdickicht um dem rationalitätskonstitutiven Ordnungsbegehren selber dessen unauflösliche Verdrängungsknoten in blutiger Mimikry vorzuhalten. (edited)

Germain, Gilbert G. "The Revenge of the Sacred: Technology and Re-enchantment" in *The Barbarism of Reason*, Horowitz, Asher (ed), 248-266. Toronto, Univ of Toronto Pr, 1994.

This essay explores a central tension in the thought of Max Weber, namely, that between his depiction of modern society in terms of an "iron cage", and his belief that the future remains open-ended. This tension, it is argued, is a reflection of the categorical distinction Weber draws between means (technical reasoning) and ends (subjective valuing). The systems theory analyst, Jacques Ellul, is introduced into the discussion to illustrate the potential weaknesses of the Weberian dichotomy, especially given the trajectory of modernity since Weber's time. The essay ends by suggesting that Weber's guarded optimism regarding the future may be misguided.

Gerratana, Federico and Brusotti, Marco. "Dappertutto e in Nessun Luogo": Volontà e Potenza di un'edizione Nietzscheana. *G Crit Filosof Ital*, 72(3), 513-529, S-D 93.

Gerson, L. Why Ethics is Political Science for Aristotle. *Amer Cath Phil Quart*, 68(Supp), 93-107, 1994.

An examination of the meaning of *epistēmē* as applied to ethics for Aristotle. The universal and necessary truths which are the objects of any science are considered. Finally, it is argued that ethics provides the theoretical basis for the practical science of politics.

Gerstenkorn, Tadeusz and Manko, Jacek. The Philosophy of Fuzziness and the Mathematics of Randomness. *Stud Phil Christ*, 30(2), 83-97, 1994.

In the article we present various conceptions of the probability of fuzzy events as well as their evolution from the beginnings of fuzzy set theory. We want to call one's attention to their great variety and, with that, show the contribution of Polish mathematicians to the solving of this problem. The large number of ideas presented here witnesses the fact that the question of the connecting of fuzziness with randomness is still vivid, and that the search for an optimal solution is being continued without cease. We wish to convince the reader of the dissimilarity of the ideas of fuzziness and randomness as well as to stress the role of M Lubanski in the propagation of "fuzziness" in Poland at the very early stage of existence of this theory.

Gert, Bernard and Bernat, James L and Mogielnicki, R Peter. Distinguishing between Patients' Refusals and Requests. *Hastings Center Rep*, 24(4), 13-15, Jl-Ag 94.

Not distinguishing between patient requests and patient refusals, but referring to them both as choices or decisions and then talking of patient autonomy, has resulted in both theoretical and practical confusion. Patient refusals must be honored when they represent the rational decisions of competent patients even when physicians know death will result. Honoring such refusals is not killing; it is, at most, allowing to die. In contrast, there is no moral requirement to honor patient requests when physicians know death will result.

Gert, Heather. Viability. *Int J Phil Stud*, 3(1), 133-142, Mr 95.

In seeking a compromise on abortion, many have suggested that the woman's rights supersede the fetus's until the fetus becomes viable, at which point the fetus's right to life becomes paramount. Others have objected that this is arbitrary. Nevertheless, we can make principled use of viability. Once viability is achieved it is possible to respect both values: a woman may choose to have the fetus removed from her body, and the fetus can be kept alive. Thus, if it is *the State's* duty, or interest, to protect the life of the fetus, there should be no "problem of abortion" after viability.

Gért, Heather. Alternative Analyses. *S J Phil*, 33(1), 31-37, Spr 95.

Classical analyses in terms of necessary and sufficient conditions have been out of favor for quite some time, and many philosophers have attempted to offer alternatives. This paper argues that many of these alleged alternatives are, in fact, specific types of classical analyses. For instance, cluster concept analysis offers analyses in terms of disjunctive necessary and sufficient conditions. Even the more sophisticated prototype theory offered by Eleanor Rosch can be similarly reduced to a classical account. A true alternative will have to be more radically distinct from the alternatives offered thus far.

Gervais, Richard. Difficulté de l'hégélianisme. Apropos de l'ouvrage de Jean-François Kervégan: *Hegel, Carl Schmitt: le politique entre spéculation et positivité*. *Laval Theol Phil*, 51(2), 405-420, Je 95.

Les travaux de Jean-Francois Kervégan sont à inscrire dans le renouveau hégélien actuel. Son récent livre, *Hegel, Carl Schmitt: le politique entre spéculation et positivité*, constitue en effet une véritable défence et illustration de l'hégélianisme, tant des idées politiques de Hegel contre les soupcons de totalitarisme qui pèsent sur elles que du mode de pensée *spéculatif* et de l'unité du système souvent mise à mal par la postérité hégélienne. Mais cette défense et illustration ne se présente pas telle, en tout cas pas directement: elle s'effectue à la faveur de l'interprétation de la pensée d'un tiers, celle du constitutionnaliste allemand Carl Schmitt, ce qui donne lieu à un chassé-croisé où Schmitt s'éclaire par Hegel et réciproquement, et qui confère à l'étude un double caractère, à la fois interprétation du schmittisme et actualisation de l'hégélianisme.

Gesang, Bernward. *Wahrheitskriterien im Kritischen Rationalismus*. Amsterdam, Rodopi, 1995.

Das Buch enthält einen Versuch, *Wahrheitskriterien* für empirische Theorien aufzustellen. Diese Kriterien sollen fallibel aber doch leistungsfähig sein. Um Theorien prüfen zu können, erweist es sich als notwendig, Kriterien fur die Wahrheit von *Beobachtungssätzen* zu entwickeln, ohne in einen neuen Fundamentalismus zu fallen. Nur so können die Probleme der Kohärenztheorie überwunden werden. Probleme der empirischen Basis werden folglich ausführlich erörtert, wobei auch der kausale Ursprung der Beobachtungssätze thematisiert wird. Das führt zu einer Analyse der *Evolutionären Erkenninistheorie*. Nachem ein Wahrheitskriterium für Beobachtungssätze formuliert wurde, wird untersucht, wie man Theorien mit wahren Beobachtungssätzen prüfen kann. Dazu werden Strukturelemente des *kritischen Rationalismus* aufgegriffen, der sich auch als ein Verifikationismus begreifen lässt, den man allerdings nicht induktivistisch interpretieren darf.

Geuijen, Karin (ed) and Raven, Diederick (ed) and De Wolf, Jan (ed). *Post-Modernism and Anthropology: Theory and Practice*. Assen, Gorcum, 1995.

During the nineteen eighties the term *post-modern* started to be applied to tendencies within the field of cultural and social anthropology. To many post-modernism appeared not merely as another theoretical paradigm but as an ill conceived attempt to put the whole discipline on its head. In this volume the contributors want to consider two important questions which are crucial to a reasoned assessment of the ensuing debates. First, to what extent and in which way does post-modernism in anthropology differ from existing, 'modern' approaches? Secondly, what consequences does post-modernism have for the presentation of that quintessential anthropological experience: participant-observation in field work?

Geuss, Raymond. Auffassungen der Freiheit. *Z Phil Forsch*, 49(1), 1-14, Ja-Mr 95.

Geuss, Raymond. Nietzsche and Genealogy. *Euro J Phil*, 2(3), 274-292, D 94.

Geva, Nehemia and Mintz, Alex and Derouen Jr, Karl. Mathematical Models of Foreign Policy Decision-Making: Compensatory vs Noncompensatory. *Synthese*, 100(3), 441-460, S 94.

There are presently two leading foreign policy decision-making paradigms in vogue. The first is based on the classical or rational model originally posited by von Neumann and Morgenstern to explain microeconomic decisions. The second is based on the cybernetic perspective whose groundwork was laid by Herbert Simon in his early research on bounded rationality. In this paper we introduce a third perspective—the *poliheuristic* theory of decision-making—as an alternative to the rational actor and cybernetic paradigms in international relations. This theory is drawn in large part from research on heuristics done in experimental cognitive psychology. According to the poliheuristic theory, policy makers use poly (many) heuristics while focusing on a very narrow range of options and dimensions when making decisions. Among them, the political dimension is noncompensatory. The paper also delineates the mathematical formulations of the three decision-making models.

Gevers, Sjef. Physician Assisted Suicide: New Developments in the Netherlands. *Bioethics*, 9(3-4), 309-312, Jl 95.

Until recently, physician assisted suicide was dealt with on the same basis as active voluntary euthanasia in the Netherlands. Over the last years, several cases relating to assistance in suicide of mental patients did raise specific issues, not addressed so far in the debate on euthanasia. One of these cases resulted in a Supreme Court decision. The paper summarized this decision and comments on it from a legal point of view.

Gewirth, Alan. Replies to Comments. *Stud Phil Educ*, 13(2), 139-140, 1993-94.

Gewirth, Alan. The Immoral Sense. *Crim Just Ethics*, 13(2), 4-6, Sum-Fall 94.

James Q Wilson bases his explication and justification of morality on various empirical considerations. I show that on the basis of similar considerations about history and human relations, he would be logically committed to holding that there is an immoral sense as well as a moral one. His argument fails the test of determinacy.

Gewirth, Alan. The Moral Basis of Liberal Education. *Stud Phil Educ*, 13(2), 111-124, 1993-94.

The moral right to liberal education involves issues of distribution and of content. The former issue bears on the distribution of educational resources. The latter issue bears on the issue of multiculturalism. Both issues are discussed from the standpoint of equal rights.

Ghilardi, Silvio. An Algebraic Theory of Normal Forms. *Annals Pure Applied Log*, 71(3), 189-245, F 95.

Normal forms for some basic propositional calculi of modal type are investigated from an algebraic point of view. General category-theoretic techniques for free monoids are used. Some applications to duality for finitely generated free algebras and to definability of higher-order quantifiers are given.

Ghiraldelli Júnior, Paulo. Contribuiçao par as Discussoes ao Projeto de Implantaçao do Curso de Pedagogia na Fac de Ciências da Univ Estadual Paulista "Júlio de Mesquita Filho". *Educ Filosof*, 8(16), 247-284, Jl-D 94.

Ghiselin, Michael T. Darwin's Language May Seem Teleological, But His Thinking is Another Matter. *Biol Phil*, 9(4), 489-492, O 94.

Darwin's biology was "teleological" only if the term "teleology" is defined in a manner that fails to recognize his contribution to the metaphysics and epistemology of modern science. His use of teleological metaphors in a strictly teleonomic context if irrelevant to the meaning of his discourse. The myth of Darwin's alleged teleology is partly due to misinterpretations of discussions about whether morphology should be a purely formal science. Merely rejecting such notions as special creation and vitalism does not prevent the pernicious effects of teleological reasoning, even at the present time.

Ghiselin, Michael T. Ostensive Definitions of the Names of Species and Clades. *Biol Phil*, 10(2), 219-222, Ap 95.

Ghiselin, Michael T. The Origin of Vertebrates and the Principle of Succession of Functions: Genealogical Sketches by Anton Dohrm, 1875—An English Translation. *Hist Phil Life Sci*, 16(1), 3-96, Ja 94.

Ghosh, Dipankar and Crain, Terry L. Ethical Standards, Attitudes Toward Risk, and Intentional Noncompliance: An Experimental Investigation. *J Bus Ethics*, 14(5), 353-365, My 95.

Prior research has investigated the influence of decision maker characteristics on decision choice. This research examines the effect two personality traits of taxpayers, attitude towards risk and ethical standards, on intentional noncompliance. A taxpayer who is more (less) ethical will have lower (greater) intentional noncompliance, while a taxpayer who is more (less) risk averse will have lower (greater) intentional noncompliance. However, this study also found significant correlation between risk attitudes and ethical standards. This is because tax evasion is not just a gamble which can be explained by merely considering the risk variable. To understand tax evasive behavior better requires incorporation of noneconomic factors in the analysis, such as ethical standards, although risk attitudes may be an important explanatory factor. The current research suggests that individuals with lower ethical standards will have more intentional noncompliance. However, since ethical standards are correlated with attitude toward risk, the Internal Revenue Service (IRS) can partially overcome the influence of ethics by making the tax audit environment more uncertain. Thus, the research results justify the decision of the IRS no to release all its audit parameters because it makes the audit environment less uncertain.

Ghosh, Raghunath. Can There Be Ontological Argument in Nyaya-Vaisesika?. *Indian Phil Quart*, 21(2), 119-127, Ap 94.

The ontological argument for Divine existence is quite a prestigious one is Western philosophical literature. No argument of such sort is found to be offered in Indian philosophical tradition. What may be the reasons for the difference? One might think that such an argument is not possible in Indian Philosophy. In this paper an effort will be made to show that an argument of the ontological sort should be made possible for proving the Divine existence in Indian Philosophy, particularly in *Nyaya-Vaisesika* system, if the relevant theories are reviewed carefully. To this effect I have presented a comparative study in order to show that there could be a fruitful dialogue between the East and the West. So far as this argument is concerned, I add thereupon some critical remarks.

Ghosh, Raghunath. The Concept of Rasa According to Abhinavgupta. *Darshana Int*, 32(3/127), 22-27, Jl 92.

The main objective of the paper is to consider the nature of aesthetic experience with special reference to Abhinavagupta. In aesthetic experience there is some sort of identity between audience, creator and art-object. This identity is possible through self-involvement. That is why a real appreciator of the literary form of art is called *sahrdaya*. Aesthetic pleasure is qualitatively same but quantitatively different from the pleasure of Brahman. Though these are mentioned in the context of literary forms of art the same can be applicable to other forms of art also, e.g., dance, music, etc. The properties of *sahrdayatva*, universalisation etc. are also essential in the aesthetic experience arising from music, dance, etc.

Giacalone, Robert A (& others). The Impact of Ethical Ideology on Modifiers of Ethical Decisions and Suggested Punishment for Ethical Infractions. *J Bus Ethics*, 14(7), 497-510, Jl 95.

The present study sought to determine the extent to which individuals' ethical ideologies, as measured by Forsyth's (1980) Ethics Position Questionnaire (EPQ), impacted the degree of punishment they advocated for differing ethical infractions, as well as their selection of nonethics related variables that might be used to modify judgments of disciplinary action. The data revealed that individual ideology does impact both advocated punishment and choice of nonethics related variables, but only in some measures. The data are discussed in terms of potential moderating variables that could be examined in future studies.

Giacalone, Robert A and Payne, Stephen L. Evaluation of Employee Rule Violations: The Impact of Impression Management Effects in Historical Context. *J Bus Ethics*, 14(6), 477-487, Je 95.

The study sought to determine whether impression management tactics by an employee could effectively lessen the recommended punishment for an ethical rule infraction by this individual. Subjects read a vignette in which an employee violated the confidentiality of personnel records. The employee was presented as either having had a history of previous infractions or not such historical information was provided. Additionally, the employee was described as using either no impression management tactics, an apology, or a justification for his behavior. Results show that in the case of a history of multiple offenses, the employee's use of justifications effectively mitigated others' judgments of the wrongfulness of the employee's action, while apologies did not. Similarly, the justification appeared to lessen respondent recommendations for punishment, prevention of promotion, and demotion/firing, but only when there is a history of multiple offenses. In most cases, apologies tended to exacerbate the problem when previous offenses had been committed. The data are discussed in terms of their implications for the study of employee use of impression management tactics.

Giacalone, Robert A and Ralston, David A and Terpstra, Robert H. Ethical Perceptions of Organizational Politics: A Comparative Evaluation of American and Hong Kong Managers. *J Bus Ethics*, 13(12), 989-999, D 94.

This paper presents a cross-cultural analysis of ethics with US and Hong Kong Chinese managers as subjects. These managers were given the Strategies of Upward Influence instrument and asked to evaluate the ethics of using various political strategies to attain influence within their organizations. Differences were found between Hong Kong and US managers on a variety of dimensions, indicating important differences between these two groups on their perceptions of ethical behavior. In the paper, we identify potential reasons for the findings, and suggest directions for future work in this area.

Giaquinto, Marcus. Epistemology of Visual Thinking in Elementary Real Analysis. *Brit J Phil Sci*, 45(3), 789-813, S 94.

Can visual thinking be a means of discovery in elementary analysis, as well as a means of illustration and a stimulus to discovery? The answer to the corresponding question for geometry and arithmetic seems to be 'yes' and so a positive answer might be expected for elementary analysis too. But I argue here that only in a severely restricted range of cases can visual thinking be a means of discovery in analysis. Examination of persuasive visual routes to two simple theorems (Rolle, Bolzano) shows that they are not ways of discovering the theorems; the type of visual thinking involved can never be used to discover analytic theorems of a certain generality. (edited)

Giardini, F. Dalla nostalgia di patria alla nostalgia del paradiso. *Sapienza*, 47(2), 147-171, 1994.

Gibbard, Allan F. Why Theorize How to Live with Each Other?. *Phil Phenomenol Res*, 55(2), 323-342, Je 95.

Gibbons, Sarah. *Kant's Theory of Imagination: Bridging Gaps in Judgement and Experience*. New York, Clarendon/Oxford Pr, 1994.

This book departs from much of the scholarship on Kant by demonstrating the centrality of imagination to Kant's philosophy as a whole. For Kant, cognition and experience are simultaneously passive and active, thought and sensed, free and unfree. These dualisms are often considered unfortunate byproducts of his system. Sarah Gibbons, however, shows that imagination performs vital function in 'bridging gaps' between the different elements of cognition and experience. Thus, the role imagination plays in Kant's works expresses his fundamental insight into the complexity of cognition for finite rational beings such as ourselves. (edited)

Gibson, Diane. User Rights and the Frail Aged. *J Applied Phil*, 12(1), 1-11, 1995.

There is a growing acceptance of user rights models with regard to dependent populations such as nursing home residents, but classic theories of rights presuppose levels of human rationality and human agency often lacking in the case of highly dependent populations. While user rights models have strong advantages at a rhetorical level, the reduced capacity for dependent groups to assert their rights constitutes a significant structural limitation. Policies, practices and regulatory strategies developed on the assumption that very dependent groups can indeed assert such rights thus proceed on a premise which is fatally flawed.

Gibson, Martha I. Reference and Unity in Kant's Theory of Judgement. *Can J Phil*, 25(2), 229-256, Je 95.

Gibson, Roger (ed) and Barrett, Robert (ed). *Perspectives on Quine*. Cambridge, Blackwell, 1993.

Gibson, Roger F. Quine and Davidson: Two Naturalized Epistemologists. *Inquiry*, 37(4), 449-463, D 94.

I juxtapose Quine's and Davidson's approaches to naturalized epistemology and assess Davidson's reasons for rejecting Quine's account of the nature of knowledge. Davidson argues that Quine's account of the nature of knowledge is Cartesian in spirit and consequence, i.e., it is essentially first person and invites global skepticism. I survey Quine's response to Davidson's criticisms and suggest that the view that Davidson criticizes may not be Quine's after all. I conclude by raising some questions about Quine's definition of 'observation sentence'.

Gick, Mary L and Lockhart, Robert S. "Cognitive and Affective Components of Insight" in *The Nature of Insight, Sternberg, Robert J (ed)*, 197-228. Cambridge, MIT Pr, 1995.

The cognitive and affective properties and processes of insight are discussed within a theoretical framework of problem solving in cognitive psychology. Insight involves properties of a period of incomprehension, often frustrating and perplexing, that is followed by a sudden transition to a state of understanding. The initial incomprehension is often the result of a failure to retrieve a concept from memory, or construct a new concept, needed to solve the problem. Once successfully accessed or constructed, the concept yields very rapid comprehension. Applications to the understanding of jokes, the solving of riddles and puzzles, and scientific discoveries are discussed.

Gier, Nicholas F. *Ahimsa*, the Self, and Postmodernism: Jain, Vedantist, and Buddhist Perspectives. *Int Phil Quart*, 35(1), 71-86, Mr 95.

This essay begins with the assumption that one's view of self must affect one's social practices. If individual agency is ultimately unreal, as Advaita Vedanta maintains, then it is difficult to see how a dynamic and engaged practice of *ahimsa* (nonviolence) can be possible. On the other hand, if the self is real but exhorted to detach itself from other selves and from an unredeemable nature (the Jain and Sankhya-Yoga view), then it is uncertain how either real dialogue with others or ecological values can be supported. If we say that the primordial unity of the Upanishads offers a premodern view of the self, and recognize the Jain-Sankhya-Yoga philosophies as anticipating modern selfhood, then Buddhist thought has the potential of a postmodern interpretation. Following a "constructive" postmodernism rather than French deconstruction, this essay argues that an early Buddhist concept of self is the best model for the practice of *ahimsa*.

Gier, Nicholas F. Hindu Titanism. *Phil East West*, 45(1), 73-96, Ja 95.

In his classic work *The Philosophies of India*, Heinrich Zimmer has called the preemption of divine perogatives and confusion of human and divine attributes the "heresy of Titanism". Titanism is a form of radical humanism whose extreme anthropomorphism and anthropocentrism has distorted the human place in the cosmos. Following Zimmer's lead, I have identified five types of Indian Titanism: Asura Titanism, in which the *asuras* (antigods or Titans) constantly battle the Hindu gods; Brahmin Titanism, in which the priests take over the divine power of the sacrifice; Yoga Titanism, in which yogis are empowered by the practice of austerities; Gnostic Titanism, in which humans contend that they have perfect knowledge; and Bhakti Titanism, in which humans such as Krishna are bestowed with powers of universal redemption. I argue that Asura Titanism is the weakest form of Indian superhumanism and Yoga Titanism is the most disturbing form.

Gier, Nicholas F. Xunzi and the Confucian Answer to Titanism. *J Chin Phil*, 22(2), 129-151, Je 95.

Titanism is a form of radical humanism whose extreme anthropomorphism and anthropocentrism have distorted the human place in the cosmos. The spiritual Titan takes over divine prerogatives and attributes and claims independence from and superiority over other people, the gods, and nature. The Confucian concept of a cosmic trinity of Heaven, Earth, and humans—with each in harmony and of equal value—appears to be the best answer to Titanism. In this paper I analyze Xunzi's view of the cosmic triad, drawing on the recent contributions of Edward Machle. As deification of the human being is a typical feature of Titanism, I critique Machle's view that the sage is deified.

Gifford, Fred. Community-Equipoise and the Ethics of Randomized Clinical Trials. *Bioethics*, 9(2), 127-148, Ap 95.

This paper critically examines a particular strategy for resolving the central ethical dilemma associated with randomized clinical trials (RCT's)—the "community equipoise" strategy (CE). The dilemma is that RCT's appear to violate a physician's duty to choose that therapy which there is most reason to believe is in the patient's best interest, randomizing patients even once evidence begins to favor one treatment. The community equipoise strategy involves the suggestion that our judgment that neither treatment is to be preferred is to be assessed according to a *community* rather than an *individual* standard. Thus, though a physician may personally believe that there is some reason to prefer one treatment, patients can legitimately be randomized if there remains disagreement in the community of medical professionals. I argue that even if use of CE was justified, it would not justify carrying out RCT's anywhere near long enough to discharge our duty to gain reliable knowledge on which to base safe and effective medical practice. (edited)

Gigante, Mario. Neotomismo a Salerno: L'Ambiente Culturale in cui visse ed Operò Pasquale Naddeo. *Sapienza*, 48(1), 87-103, 1995.

Gil, Marta Lopez. Pensar después de Nietzsche y Heidegger. *Cuad Etica*, 14, 53-63, D 92.

This paper is structured by three tematic axis: 1) nihilism as epochal or historico-cultural "destiny"; 2) nihilism as the assertion of an ontology of contemporary present or "we"; 3) the controversy between hermeneutic ethics, on the one side, and ethics of the communication's community, on the other. In addition, a "de-centralization" of philosophy as discipline is suggested.

Gil Ruiz, Juana María. Una visión de mujer en el pensamiento de John Stuart Mill. *Telos (Spain)*, 2(1), 31-42, Je 93.

The object of this article is to appreciate the life and work of Harriet Taylor, the wife of J S Mill. This brief exposition of her life and work considers the range of her ideas as well as her influence on J S Mill, especially on his understanding of freedom and equality.

Gilbert, Christopher. A Lonerganian Critique of the Pragmatic Method of Education. *Method*, 11(2), 199-214, Fall 93.

This paper surveys the educational theory presented in Dewey's *Democracy and Education*, paying particular attention to the model on which Dewey bases his theory and the aim of education as Dewey conceives it. On the basis of Bernard Lonergan's cognitional theory, I endeavor to show that Dewey's account of knowing and learning contains what Lonergan calls a 'counter-position'—i.e., it is derived from an implicit cognitional theory that is inconsistent with verifiable facts about cognition. Dewey's ideas about the human good, and about the role of education in achieving that good, suffer as a result.

Gilbert, Margaret. "Remarks on Collective Belief" in *Socializing Epistemology: The Social Dimensions of Knowledge, Schmitt, Frederick F (ed)*, 235-256. Lanham, Rowman & Littlefield, 1994.

The author develops and elaborates on her account of "collective belief", something standardly referred to, in her view, when we speak of what "we" believe. This paper focuses on a special response hearers may experience in the context of expressions of belief, a response that may issue in offended rebukes to the speaker. It is argued that this response would be appropriate if both speakers and hearers were parties to what the authors calls a "joint commitment" to believe a certain proposition as a body. This joint commitment puts speakers under an obligation to refrain from speaking in certain ways, and gives hearers a correlative right to such refraining, and hence a basis for offended rebukes.

Gilbert, Margaret. Sociality as a Philosophically Significant Category. *J Soc Phil*, 25(3), 5-25, Wint 94.

Different accounts of what it is for something to have a social nature have been given. Sociality does not appear to be a category worthy of philosophical focus, given some of these accounts. If sociality is construed as plural subjecthood, it emerges as a category crucial for our understanding of the human condition. Plural subjects are constituted by a joint commitment of two or more persons to do something as a body. Such commitments generate rights and obligations of a special type, and underlie such phenomena as social conventions, agreements, shared action and social groups on one standard understanding of what these are.

Gilbert, Margaret. Walking Together: A Paradigmatic Social Phenomenon. *Midwest Stud Phil*, 15, 1-14, 1990.

The everyday concept of a social group is approached by examining the concept of going for a walk together, an example of doing something together, or "shared action". Two analyses requiring shared personal goals are rejected, since they fail to explain how people walking together have obligations and rights to appropriate behavior, and corresponding rights of rebuke. An alternative account is proposed: those who walk together must constitute the *plural subject* of a goal (roughly, their walking alongside each other). The nature of plural subjecthood, the thesis that social groups are plural subjects, and the relation of these ideas to Rousseau's and Hobbes's, are briefly explored.

Gilbert, Michael A. Arguments and Arguers. *Teach Phil*, 18(2), 125-138, Je 95.

I argue that there are three basic problems in critical reasoning. The first is the use of fallacies as a fundamental mode of analysis; the second is the essentially negative outlook as expressed in the very title "Critical Reasoning"; and the third is the lack of focus on the people who are arguing or who have made the argument under examination. I see all three of these problems as instances of a larger issue, viz., the almost total emphasis critical reasoning puts on the argument as an artifact, as opposed to the process of arguing as it occurs between two or more people who are in disagreement. Critical reasoning needs to be expanded and modified to embrace arguers, and not just arguments.

Gilbert, Paul. Expérience et métaphysique. *G Metaf*, 16(1-2), 211-237, Ja-Ag 94.

In *L'enigma dell'essere (The Enigma of Being 1990)*, Angelo Crescini, scientist and philosopher, elucidates Heidegger's "ontological difference" with the help of science. The article discusses Crescini's work in three parts. First, it describes *ordinary experience*, which, when grasping a particular substance, seeks a knowledge of the whole in all its reality. Second, it presents *scientific experience*, which takes such implicit knowledge and makes it explicit. Third, it articulates *metaphysical experience*, demonstrating that particular substances combine so that each might be revealed: this is the basis of the "*esse commune*."

Gilead, Amihud. *The Platonic Odyssey: A Philosophical-Literary Inquiry into the "Phaedo"*. Amsterdam, Rodopi, 1994.

This book argues that Plato fails in solving the philosophical problem of the separation of the Ideas from sensible things. Thus, he turns to poetical, dramatic attempt in challenging the separation problem. Gilead demonstrates in detail how Plato constructs one of his seminal philosophical dialogues, the *Phaedo*, as a unique tragedy, a poetical masterpiece whose structure is organic and symmetrical. The dramatic structure and details of the *Phaedo* fulfill, so to speak, most of the Aristotelian requirements of tragedy. Poetically speaking, there is no separation between the Platonic philosophy and its dramatic depiction. Remaining faithfully Platonic in philosophy, Plato's art of writing in practice implements the Aristotelian demand to bring the Ideas from "heaven" down to earth. The analysis of the internal drama of the *Phaedo* traces the Platonic turn concerning the mental Odyssey, rival to that of Homer. Gilead analyzes the sources of the idea of the mental Odyssey and its various literary and philosophical offspring.

Giles, James. A Theory of Love and Sexual Desire. *J Theor Soc Behav*, 24(4), 339-358, D 94.

The experience of being in love involves a longing for union with the other, where an important part of this longing is sexual desire. But what is the relation between being in love and sexual desire? A phenomenological theory is put forward which suggests that the experience of being in love involves a complex of desires for reciprocal vulnerability in order to care and be cared for. Sexual desire is then seen to involve the physical expression of these desires in the form of desires for mutual caring in order to caress and be caressed. It is concluded that other desires which often appear in instances of being in love are not basic to the experience of being in love. (edited)

Gilkey, Langdon. "Biology and Theology on Human Nature" in *Biology, Ethics, and the Origins of Life, Rolston III, Holmes (ed)*, 163-190. Boston, Jones & Bartlett, 1995.

Gilkey, Langdon. Evolution, Culture, and Sin: Responding to Philip Hefner's Proposal. *Zygon*, 30(2), 293-308, Je 95.

In his recent book, *The Human Factor*, Philip Hefner proposes to deepen theological understanding of the natural world and the place of humans within it. He describes humans as products of converging streams of genes and culture, and as possessors of freedom that requires them to be "created cocreators." In accordance with the requirements of "the way things really are" (God), humans are to become divine agents in enlarging the realm of freedom in the world through self-sacrificing altruism. While Hefner's insights are admirable, his work could be viewed, in part, as a covert expression of nineteenth century liberal beliefs in progress. In fact, human culture and freedom are more ambiguous products of both good and evil, and hence we must take more cognizance of the pervasiveness of what theology has termed sin.

Gilkey, Langdon. Nature as the Image of God: Reflections on the Signs of the Sacred. *Zygon*, 29(4), 489-505, D 94.

This is a brief survey of aspects of the modern scientific view of nature to see if implied therein are signs or traces of the sacred—as early religious apprehension surely supposed. Nature's power and order are discussed as is the strange dialectic of death and life, evident in modern biology as it also is in all early religion.

Gill, Jerry H. Langer, Language, and Art. *Int Phil Quart*, 34(4), 419-432, D 94.

While appreciating Suzanne Langer's efforts to combat a narrow, positivist view of art, I argue that her own position is predicated on a rigid dichotomy between fact and value. Thus her understanding of both language and art is itself too narrow to do the job. What is needed is a more polysignificant theory of language in general and of metaphor in particular.

Gill, Mary Louise. Commentary on Charles's "Aristotle on Substance, Essence and Biological Kinds". *Proc Boston Colloq Anc Phil*, 7, 262-269, 1991.

Gillespie, Michael Allen. *Nihilism Before Nietzsche*. Chicago, Univ of Chicago Pr, 1994.

Gillespie reconstructs the development of nihilism from Ickham and the nominalist revolution to Descartes, Fichte, the German Romantics, the Russian nihilists, and Nietzsche himself. Nihilism, he argues, is not the result of the death of God, as Nietzsche believed, but the consequence of a new idea of a God of will who overturns all eternal standards of truth and justice. To understand nihilism, one has to understand how this notion of God came to inform a new notion of man and nature, one that puts will in the place of reason, and freedom in the place of necessity and order.

Gillett, Grant. "Women and Children First" in *Medicine and Moral Reasoning, Fulford, K W M (ed)*, 131-143. New York, Cambridge Univ Pr, 1994.

Gillett, Grant. Commentary on "Puppetmasters and Personality Disorders". *Phil Psychiat Psych*, 1(2), 101-103, Je 94.

I comment on Elliot's paper regarding Wittgenstein's views on compulsive behaviour by highlighting the difference between attitudes and factual opinions in our view of what is the case. I also comment on the difference between laws and rules. I note that disorders of intention are assessed using reactive attitudes and moral assessments of others and make a remark on the nature of psychopathy.

Gillett, Grant. Insight, Delusion, and Belief. *Phil Psychiat Psych*, 1(4), 227-236, D 94.

The concepts of insight and delusion present philosophical problems even though they remain clinically useful. However, these concepts are usually defined against the background of traditional empiricism or rationalism, which have difficulties in accounting for normal human thought. I outline a Wittgensteinian approach that puts knowledge in an interpersonal and practical framework. The resulting account accommodates a number of the phenomenological features of self-knowledge in mental disorder. It also gives an entrée into the vulnerabilities of thought to social and interpersonal influences, even though it does not suggest a "social construct" view of mental disorders.

Gillett, Grant. Virtue and Truth in Clinical Science. *J Med Phil*, 20(3), 285-298, Je 95.

Since the time of Hippocrates, medical science sought to develop a practice based on "knowledge rather than opinion". However, in the light of recent alternative approaches to healing and a philosophy of science that, through thinkers like Kuhn, Rorty, and Foucault, is critical of claims to objective truth, we must reappraise the way in which medical interventions can be based on proven pathophysiological knowledge rather than opinion. Developing insights in Foucault, Lacan, and Wittgenstein, this essay argues for a recovery of the Aristotelian idea of techne, where there is a dynamic interplay between praxis and conceptualization. The result is a post-Kuhnian epistemology for medical science that recognizes the evaluative dimension of knowledge, but that also looks to a Platonic conception of the good as the ultimate constraint on human thought.

Gillett, Grant (ed) and Fulford, K W M (ed) and Soskice, Janet Martin (ed). *Medicine and Moral Reasoning*. New York, Cambridge Univ Pr, 1994.

The unifying theme of this edited collection is that moral reasoning in medicine should draw on a wide variety of sources, both philosophical and empirical articles include: Midgley on Darwinism; Soskice on creation and relation; Hare on embryo experimentation; Brandton on genetic testing; Lockwood on identity; William May on the suicide; Gillett on children; Oddie on moral uncertainty; Urmson on invention and discovery in morality; Crisp on quality of life; Campbell on dependency; and Fulford on involuntary psychiatric treatment.

Gillick, Muriel R. An Algorithm for Determining Best Interest?. *J Clin Ethics*, 6(1), 82-85, Spr 95.

Gillick, Muriel R and Fried, Terri. The Limits of Proxy Decision Making: Undertreatment. *Cambridge Quart Healthcare Ethics*, 4(2), 172-177, Spr 95.

With the passage by virtually every state legislature of healthcare proxy laws, the medical profession increasingly can expect to rely on the participation of surrogates in making decisions on behalf of incompetent patients. Several concerns about the legitimacy of proxy decision making have been discussed in the ethical and general medical literature: the lack of concordance between the views of patients and their surrogates have been documented on multiple occasions, and cases of abuse by proxies or potential conflict of interest have been reported. Another dilemma that deserves discussion arises when proxies demand withdrawal of treatment that physicians and nurses regard as essential to the well-being of the patient. The following case highlights this dilemma.

Gillies, Donald. *Philosophy of Science in the Twentieth Century: Four Central Themes*. Cambridge, Blackwell, 1993.

This book traces the development during the 20th century of four central themes in the Philosophy of Science: inductivism, conventionalism, the nature of observation, and the demarcation between science and metaphysics. The movement of ideas is placed against the background of the lives of the philosophers and of contemporary developments in science. The four themes have been chosen because of their central importance, and are expounded in a way which does not presuppose any previous knowledge of Philosophy of Science. The book could thus be used as an introduction to the Philosophy of Science.

Gilligan, Carol. Hearing the Difference: Theorizing Connection. *Hypatia*, 10(2), 120-127, Spr 95.

Hearing the difference between a patriarchal voice and a relational voice defines a paradigm shift: a change in the conception of the human world. Theorizing connection as primary and fundamental in human life leads to a new psychology, which shifts the grounds for philosophy and political theory. A crucial distinction is made between a feminine ethic of care and a feminist ethic of care. Voice, relationship, resistance, and women become central rather than peripheral in this reframing of the human world.

Gilman, Daniel. Simplicity, Cognition and Adaptation: Some Remarks on Marr's Theory of Vision. *Proc Phil Sci Ass*, 1, 454-464, 1994.

A large body of research in computational vision science stems from the pioneering work of David Marr. Recently, Patricia Kitcher and others have criticized this work as depending upon optimizing assumptions, assumptions which are held to be inappropriate for evolved cognitive mechanisms just as anti-adaptationists (e.g., Lewontin and Gould) have argued they are inappropriate for other evolved physiological mechanisms. The paper discussed the criticism and suggests that it is, in part, misdirected. It is further suggested that the criticism leads to interesting questions about how one formulates constraints—across "levels of organization" and disciplinary boundaries—on one's models of complex systems, such as human vision.

Gilmore, Jonathan. David Carrier's Art History. *J Aes Art Crit*, 53(1), 39-47, Wint 95.

Ginebra i Molins, M P. El control experimental y la construcción del objeto científico. *Dialogo Filosof*, 10(2), 225-232, My-Ag 94.

A partir de un análisis "a posteriori" de los objetivos de las ciencias experimentales, es posible establecer el papel que en su método desempeña el control experimental. Aunque las formas concretas que adopta en las diversas ciencias y en las distintas etapas del trabajo científico varían, la función determinante que asume en la construcción del objeto científico es común a todas ellas, y permite deducir una serie de características acerca de la naturaleza y alcance del método científico-experimental, como su irreductibilidad tanto a categorías lógicas como empíricas, y su peculiar fiabilidad.

Ginev, Dimitri. On the Existential Interpretation of Human Sciences. *Man World*, 27(4), 349-359, O 94.

The paper explores the idea of an analytic of the "ontological genesis" of the sciences concerned with human beings. It brings to focus those aspects of hermeneutico-phenomenological investigation of human sciences which are inaccessible to any other program in philosophy of science. A special attention is paid to the critique of Gadamer's anti-methodological position. The existential-ontological interpretation of science is considered as a special kind of "critique of epistemological reason".

Ginsberg, Robert. "Aesthetics in Hiroshima: The Architecture of Remembrance" in *Philosophy and Architecture, Mitias, Michael H (ed)*, 221-234. Amsterdam, Rodopi, 1994.

This illustrated case study explores the interrelationship of architecture, philosophy, and peace studies as experienced in the first city to be atom-bombed. Four sites/sights in Hiroshima are analyzed as architecture: the Dome (a ruin of the bombing), the memorial Cenotaph, the Art Museum, and the Chinese Bridge in a notable garden. The four works address one another—and we human beings—in striking dialogue. In grappling with ultimate horror, human beings respond with aesthetic powers. Experiencing Hiroshima ultimately is humanizing.

Ginsberg, Robert. National Justice, International Justice, World Justice: Dialogues. *Dialogue Hum*, 2(3-4), 139-154, 1992.

This set of dialogues highlights paradox as well as passion in exploring the formation and the limits of justice in the three interlocked realms of the state, the international order of states, and the emergent world community. While a social contract account of the state lays a foundation for justice among citizens, it leaves a multiplicity of independent states which by warfare may destroy people, indeed, the whole world. The effort to extend social contract terms to those states so that a world government is instituted to protect everybody is countered by the argument that states cannot renounce their sovereignty.

Ginzburg, Carlo. Killing a Chinese Mandarin: The Moral Implications of Distance. *Crit Inquiry*, 21(1), 46-60, Autumn 94.

Ginzo, Arsenio. En torno a la nueva edición de Schleiermacher. *Rev Filosof (Spain)*, 4(6), 441-455, 1991.

Giolito, Christophe. Les Raisons du Coeur: Lectures de la Relation de Comte à Clotilde. *Philosopher*, 14, 131-153, 1993.

Giovagnoli, Raffaela. Unità e molteplicità in Juergen Habermas. *Aquinas*, 37(1), 197-208, Ja-Ap 94.

Giralt, Pau. Cómo Volver a dar un Sentido a la Palabra "Humanismo"?. *Rev Filosof (Mexico)*, 28(82), 1-35, Ja-Ap 95.

Girard, Louis and Berlinger, Rudolph (ed) and Schrader, Wiebke (ed). *Elementa: L'argument Ontologique chez Saint Anselme et chez Hegel (Band 60)*. Amsterdam, Rodopi, 1995.

L'exposé cartésien de l'argument ontologique s'écarte radicalement de l'esprit originaire de la preuve, chez Saint Anselme. Le Dieu de Descartes, parfait parce que tout-puissant, est bien différent du Dieu de *Proslogion*, "Celui qui est tel que rien de plus grande ne puisse être pensé", fin de la pensée et du désir humains. La preuve d' Anselme conceptualise une expérience humaine qui se pense comme l'expérience chrétienne orthodoxe, décrivant, de ce fait, l'homme en sa vérité. Mais on n'entrera pleinement dans la pensée spéculative que si l'aspiration à Dieu en l'homme est considérée comme l'envers dialectique de l'amour, créateur de l'homme, en Dieu. Chez Hegel, ce n'est pas l'esprit fini qui accomplit la preuve ontologique, mais l'Esprit dans sa totalité. Ce mouvement de l'Esprit vers soi à travers sa division d'avec soi n'est pas un simple processus logique; en sa profondeur, il est le mouvement de réconciliation de la liberté humaine avec la liberté divine, créatrice et rédemptrice. La vérité de la Totalité, et donc, aussi, de l'histoire, dans le Concept, dit également la libre unification de l'homme et de Dieu dans et par la figure historique du Christ. Hegel pense le christianisme sans le réduire, parce qu'il le pense à partir de l'acte préalable de la foi, par lequel la liberté humaine s'ouvre à l'amour divin, posant ainsi l'unité dialectique du Tout. Que la foi puisse être rationnellement exposée ne l'empêche pas d'être la foi, c'est-à-dire la vie en union au Christ, Logos éternel et homme crucifié. On a dit: "Un Dieu compris n'est plus un Dieu". Cela n'est vrai que des faux dieux.

Giraud, Raymond. Ethical Considerations in the Use of Transgenic Animals. *Between Species*, 10(1-2), 55-60, Win-Spr 94.

Girndt, Helmut. Die fünffache Sicht der Natur im Denken Fichtes. *Fichte-Studien*, 1, 108-120, 1990.

Fichte's dominant and best known conception of nature is that of a "material of duty". But this moralistic idea of nature is the expression of only one of five possible stands towards nature as Fichte systematically demonstrated in his *Wissenschaftslehre* of 1804 (2). Nature can be considered from a "natural", as well as from a "legal", a "poetic" point of view of "hight morality" as well as from a religious one. The fifth point of view is that of the Wissenschaftslehre itself. These views are the expression of the viewer's basic existential choice or the expression of his dominant attitude towards reality.

Giroux, Laurent. Dialogue sur un dialogue: A propos du *Dialgoue* d'Ernest Joós *avec Heidegger sur les valeurs*. *Laval Theol Phil*, 50(3), 629-636, O 94.

Gitlin, Andrew and Thompson, Audrey. Creating Spaces for Reconstructing Knowledge in Feminist Pedagogy. *Educ Theor*, 45(2), 125-150, Spr 95.

This paper argues for a feminist pedagogy in which classroom relationships are foregrounded and problematized. Changing relations of power within spaces created for inquiry makes it possible to call into question assumptions regarding relevance, appropriateness, and legitimacy—assumptions that usually dictate what counts as knowledge. To move away from those framings, knowledge must be reconstructed through power shifts within relationships. We argue that intentional shifts within pedagogical power relations can at once reveal and alter prevailing local relations of power. Such a pedagogy does not escape institutional power relations but rather addresses them as sites of experimental and emergent inquiry.

Giusti, Miguel. Topische Paradoxien der kommunitaristischen Argumentation. *Deut Z Phil*, 42(5), 759-781, 1994.

This paper is a balance of the communitarian stance. The main is that, as a moral view, communitarianism undergoes a categorical deficiency which consists in not being able to solve the problems communitarianism itself detects or originates. When taken to its last consequences, the communitarian argumentation drives to some paradoxes that acquire a paradigmatical or topical character. This claim is developed via an analysis of three of the main notions in the communitarian view: the starting point of moral argumentation, the notion of "community", and the notion of "tradition".

Givant, Steven and Shelah, Saharon. Universal Theories Categorical in Power and κ-Generated Models. *Annals Pure Applied Log*, 69(1), 27-51, S 94.

We investigate a notion called *uniqueness in power* κ that is akin to categoricity in power κ, but is based on the cardinality of the generating sets of models instead of on the cardinality of their universes. The notion is quite useful for formulating categoricity-like questions regarding powers below the cardinality of a theory. We prove, for (uncountable) universal theories T, that if T is κ-unique for one uncountable κ, then it is κ-unique for every uncountable κ; in particular, it is categorical in powers greater than the cardinality of T.

Glannon, Walter. Omnipotence and the Transfer of Power. *Int J Phil Relig*, 36(2), 81-103, O 94.

There is a class of paradoxes that seem to threaten the coherence of the doctrine of omnipotence. These all involve the notion of God creating things that he cannot control once he has created them, which suggests that God can act in such a way as to render himself less than omnipotent. I argue that these paradoxes can be resolved by employing what I call the Transfer of Power Principle. This Principle says that God's power transfers from his timeless intellect and will to the temporal effects of his will, without implying any reduction in that power. The coherence of omnipotence is thus preserved.

Glannon, Walter. Responsibility and the Principle of Possible Action. *J Phil*, 92(5), 261-274, My 95.

The Principle of Possible Action (PPA) says that a person is morally responsible for failing to perform a given act only if he could have performed that act. This article argues that PPA is false. For there are cases in which persons may be morally responsible for omissions and refrainings, even when they lack the physical ability to perform actions that would have prevented the obtaining of harmful states of affairs.

Glas, Eduard. Post-positivisme en de ontwikkeling van wiskunde. *Kennis Methode*, 18(4), 291-314, 1994.

In this paper I explore possibilities of bringing post-positivist philosophies of science to bear on the dynamics of mathematical development. This is done by way of a convergent accommodation of the (reconstructed) mathematical version of Lakatos's methodology of research programmes, and a version of Kuhn's approach in terms of paradigm-guided practices, made applicable to mathematics by cleansing it from all references to the psychology of perception. The resulting view is argued in the light of two case-histories of crucial conceptual innovations.

Glass, Arthur. The Author of Common Law Texts. *Ratio Juris*, 8(1), 91-103, Mr 95.

Legal texts not only have as a fact a particular kind of author and a certain sort of reader but they assume and prescribe many of the norms associated with these social roles. The writer considers the authorship of common law texts (statutes and case reports) and the way in which the notion of authorship helps to determine the meaning of these texts. What emerges are the differences between different types of texts as to how the author figure is understood and the role which it plays in interpretation.

Glass, Ronald J and Flage, Daniel E. Hume's Problem and the Possibility of Normative Ethics. *J Value Inq*, 29(2), 231-239, Je 95.

The essay shows that if the covering law model of moral justification is correct, Hume's "is"-"ought" paragraph calls the possibility of a justifiable theory of moral obligation into doubt. The doubts are delineated through a careful examination of the "is"-"ought" paragraph, and a skeptical solution to the doubts is presented.

Glauser, Richard. Philosophie, Raison, Histoire. *Rev Theol Phil*, 127(2), 113-125, 1995.

L'auteur expose et défend l'idée suivant laquelle une partie significative de la connaissance de l'histoire de la philosophie, conçue comme discipline à la fois descriptive, interprétative et évaluative, est indispensable à un type précis de connaissance philosophique: la connaissance des raisons pour lesquelles les problèmes philosophiques fondamentaux, qui apparaissent actuellement, apparaissent précisément avec telle structure ou forme théorique déterminée. Cette connaissance est philosophique parce qu'elle fait partie de la compréhension des problèmes eux-mêmes.

Glausier, Richard. Substance et attribut chez Spinoza. *Stud Phil (Switzerland)*, 53, 225-247, 1994.

Against the background of Descartes' theory of distinctions with which Spinoza was quite familiar, the author proposes an interpretation of the relationship between substance and attribute in Part I of Spinoza's *Ethics*. He argues that although the Spinozistic attributes are really distinct from one another, Gueroult's identification of each attribute with a (simple) substance is both useless and mistaken. He defends the conclusion that Spinoza emphasizes Descartes' tendency to identify a substance with its essence, but what this means is that Spinoza's unique substance is nothing over and above a mere complex of attributes, this complex being the infinitely infinite essence.

Gleeson, G P. The Linguistic and Personal Meaning of Metaphorical Speech. *Lit Aes*, 1, 60-81, Spr 91.

This article explores the relationship between linguistic meaning and that nonlinguistic or "significant" meaning experienced in cultural, aesthetic and religious contexts. Metaphorical speech is shown to involve both forms of meaning. Metaphor requires no new linguistic meaning (Davidson), but presupposes, and evokes, an appreciation of significance which speaker and audience share, and which thereby constrains interpretation. The use of metaphor involves the reciprocity of personal speech in which significance is "suspended" between utterance and the "faithful, but striking" response it seeks. As with symbol and gesture, significance is not governed by semantic content. Rather speakers find themselves united by their mutual attachment to expressions which are inherently vulnerable to loss of meaning. As ritual transcends utility, so metaphor transcends the language-game of information.

Gleeson, Gerald. The Value of Reading Fiction. *Lit Aes*, 2, 67-81, Spr 92.

The "meaning" evoked by a work of literature is best explained in terms of an experience of significance and relevance which goes beyond its literal linguistic meaning. This significance is analogous to that experienced in cultural, ritual and aesthetic contexts. Yet all experiences of "significance" are deceptive, insofar as they conceal their inherent vulnerability to loss of meaning. Literary works discipline the imagination, and so "contain" and protect this vulnerability. The work of art is a "limited whole" (Wittgenstein). Fiction is valuable because it allows the deceptiveness of significant meaning to come indirectly, but lucidly, to consciousness. Fiction reveals not a new reality, but our inescapably vulnerable relationship to the significance of all reality.

Glendon, Mary Ann. Comparative Law as Shock Treatment. *Method*, 11(2), 137-153, Fall 93.

Glenn, Gary D. Speculations on Strauss' Political Intentions Suggested by *On Tyranny*. *Hist Euro Ideas*, 19(1-3), 171-177, Jl 94.

The explicit purpose of Strauss's commentary on Xenophon's *Hiero* is scholarly: to enable modern political science to "grasp tyranny as what it really is". This purpose cultivates recognition of tyrannical elements within collectivized human thought, a perpetual threat from which Western liberal democracies are not immune. Modern liberalism's theoretical defects and practical weakness intensifies democratic society's pressure to force conformity in thought. Yet liberalism also encourages considerable tolerance and generosity. Strauss's political intentions seem to be preventing destruction of the latter liberal virtues by the former democratic vices thus forestalling emergence of full fledged tyranny out of only incipiently tyrannical liberal regimes.

Glennan, Stuart S. Why There Can't Be a Logic of Induction. *Proc Phil Sci Ass*, 1, 78-86, 1994.

In this paper I offer a criticism of Carnap's inductive logic which also applies to other formal methods of inductive inference. Criticisms of Carnap's views have typically centered upon the justification of his particular choice of inductive method. I argue that the real problem is not that there is an agreed upon method for which no justification can be found, but that different methods are justified in different circumstances.

Glock, Hans-Johann. "Wittgenstein Vs Quine on Logical Necessity" in *Wittgenstein and Contemporary Philosophy, Teghrarian, Souren (ed)*, 185-221. Bristol, Thoemmes, 1994.

The paper argues that the similarities between Wittgenstein's and Quine's discussions of logical necessity hide fundamental differences. Wittgenstein's distinction between empirical and grammatical propositions does not fall prey to Quine's attack on the analytical synthetics distinction, but undermines Quine's assimilation of the necessary and the contingent. He shares Quine's holism and hostility to the positivist's "truth by virtue of meaning", but this is compatible with a distinction between those propositions which are up for grabs, and those which we, at any given time, treat as norms for the meaningful use of words. Without implicit linguistic norms, linguistic behaviour would reduce to a meaningless phonetic babble (the "deep need for the convention"). This normative conception of linguistic behaviour allows Wittgenstein to make sense of, rather than to reject, the notion of logical necessity.

Glock, Hans-Johann. A Radical Interpretation of Davidson: Reply to Alvarez. *Phil Quart*, 45(179), 206-212, Ap 95.

The paper is a reply to the accusation (*Philosophical Quarterly*, 44, 1994) that my 'The Indispensability of Translation' (*Philosophical Quartrely*, 43, 1993) misrepresents Davidson's account of radical interpretation. It defends my claim that Davidson assimilates everyday understanding to the interpretation of an alien language, and discusses the ways in which he identifies interpretation with translation. I admit that Davidson has recently acknowledged first person authority concerning speaker's meaning, but show that this is a change of his views. Davidson's position is inconsistent both diachronically and synchronically. One cannot subscribe to most of Quine's paradoxes and still do semantic business as usual.

Glock, Hans-Johann. The Euthanasia Debate in Germany—What's the Fuss?. *J Applied Phil*, 11(2), 213-224, 1994.

Both opponents and proponents of Singer's right to speak about euthanasia have concentrated on the tenability of his claims. They have ignored the question of what legitimate grounds there are for suppressing academic discussion, and have failed to take into account the discussion of freedom of speech in recent legal theory. To do this is the aim of my paper. Section 1 claims that Singer's position is immoral. Section 2 turns to the question of whether it is protected by freedom of speech, irrespective of its merits. I reject two lines of defense for Singer's opponents, that they had no opportunity to present *their* case, and the Kantian idea of the primacy of practical reason. Section 3 turns to a defense from legal theory. It argues that Singer's views do not pose the kind of threat to other legal and moral values which would license a suspension of his freedom of expression. I conclude that it is illegitimate to silence Singer, since he does not deny the right to live of his disabled opponents, but legitimate to protest against him, since he denies that some of their lives are worth living, in disregard of their own preferences.

Glombik, Czeslaw. The Philosophy and the History of Philosophy in the Neoscholastic Interpretation of Josef Kratochvil. *Filozof Cas*, 42(5), 762-778, 1994.

The article presents Josef Kratochvil (1882-1940) as one of the most outstanding Czech Catholic philosophers. A prolific writer throughout the first four decades of the 20th century, his creativity flourished during the 25 years between the outbreaks of the two world wars. His philosophical position was expounded in his conception of Neoidealism ("nonoidealismus"), which was meant to transgress both the program frames of Neoscholasticism and the pursuits of the Neothomistic movement. Neoidealism, the expression of Kratochvil's metaphysical beliefs, was primarily to unify these intellectual orientations, which referred to the philosophical tradition of the Christian Middle Ages on the one hand, and the ontological conceptions and the noblest ethical values of Greek antiquity on the other. (edited)

Glouberman, Mark. P F Strawson and the Ghost of F H Bradley. *Iyyun*, 43, 243-263, Jl 94.

Despite stated reliance on Frege, P F Strawson's views on subjects and predicates do not fit into the philosophy of language mainstream. Attention to *Individuals* reveals the dominating influence on Strawson of F H Bradley's ontological treatment of predication as a relational tie. Indeed, Strawson is not only reacting to Bradley's thesis, but he also fails to supply an answer to Bradley's charge that predicative discourse is incoherent. For Strawson effectively to meet Bradley, he would have to espouse an idealism not unlike the Kantian one he himself harshly criticizes. The ghostly presence of yet another figure, Cook Wilson, serves to explain Strawson's complacency in this regard.

Glouberman, Mark. The Palinode of the Analyst Rationality and Self in the *Euthyphro*. *Phil Inq*, 16(3-4), 38-55, Sum-Fall 94.

Against an 'analytic' reading of the *Euthyphro* which the author on earlier occasions endorse, it is argued that the dialogue's thesis is better comprehended by reference to the Homeric picture of human agency. Plato is defending a certain (Pythagorean) view of rationality not simply to combat an insouciant and blameworthy ignorance on Euthyphro's part, but as part of a wider attempt to meet a need for coherence in human agency which cannot be satisfied by appealing, as we moderns might appeal, to a 'core' self whose deliberations precede action. Euthyphro's violation of the imperative 'Know Thyself' reflects his failure to be integrated as an actor in the world. The need to be able to come up with a definition is thus strictly correlative with a need for definiteness which the self-contained self cannot independently supply. 'Know Thyself' is not, then, a principle of proto-Cartesian consciousness.

Glover, Kelly D. A Prototype View of Context and Linguistic Behavior: Context Prototypes and Talk. *J Prag*, 23(2), 137-156, F 95.

This paper discusses how and why the interface between talk and activity types departs from prototypical realization. A 'context prototype' model is proposed in which lexical choice and propositional content is determined by the interactants' perception of a prototypical norm. Intersubjectivity between the participants in a speech event is not an assumed notion. Instead there are gradient properties which may be realized along a continuum. The model uses the analogue of a 'sliding scale' to refer to a system by which one aspect (linguistic behavior) automatically varies according to the fluctuations of another aspect (context). (edited)

Gloy, Karen. Die Naturauffassung bei Kant, Fichte, und Schelling. *Fichte-Studien*, 6, 253-275, 1994.

A comparison of the concept of nature between Kant, Fichte, and Schelling on the basis of the status of the thing in itself. 1) Kant's concept of nature is a nonnatural, nonusual one, but a concept of systematical experience with the following difficulties: a) The categories are only valid for the appearance, not for the thing in itself, b) It is undecided whether the thing in itself is transcendent to experience or is the self. 2) In his early position Fichte identifies the thing in itself with the self, in his later position (since 1807) it seems to be the absolute beyond the self. 3) For Schelling the thing in itself is the usual nature in its autonomy, out of which the self will develop. In his philosophy of identity nature and self are based on the absolute, that means the absolute identity.

Gloy, Karen. Selbstbewusstsein als Prinzip des neuzeitlichen Selbstverständnisses: Seine Grundstruktur und seine Schwierigkeiten. *Fichte-Studien*, 1, 41-72, 1990.

Self consciousness is the main subject in contemporary philosophy since Descartes. It appears in different variants, none is free of difficulties. The traditional model of Kant, the reflection mode which is analog to light reflection, collapses on two difficulties: 1) The regress, 2) The nonidentification. In the case that the self has some knowledge of itself, it is redundant, because it presupposes what it has to withdraw, in the case that there is not any knowledge, identification between subject and object of the self is impossible, as we know from psychology or Romans, where someone can live in his own field without knowing it. The production model of Fichte has other difficulties: 1) The stealing in of moments of the reflection theory, 2) The contradiction between the different kinds of dependence and interdependence, and 3) The failure of explication of the unity of self-production and self-consciousness. Also Fichtes latest theory after 1800, which tries to solve the third point, is insufficient.

Glymour, Clark. On the Methods of Cognitive Neuropsychology. *Brit J Phil Sci*, 45(3), 815-835, S 94.

Contemporary cognitive neuropsychology attempts to infer unobserved features of normal human cognition, or 'cognitive architecture', from experiments with normals and with brain-damaged subjects in whom certain normal cognitive capacities are altered, diminished, or absent. Fundamental methodological issues about the enterprise of cognitive neuropsychology concern the characterization of methods by which features of normal cognitive architecture can be identified from such data, the assumptions upon which the reliability of such methods are premised, and the limits of such methods—even granting their assumptions—in resolving their uncertainties about that architecture. With some idealization, the question of the capacities of various experimental designs in cognitive neuropsychology to uncover cognitive architecture can be reduced to comparatively simple questions about the prior assumptions investigators are willing to make. This paper presents some of simplest of those reductions.

Glymour, Clark and Juhl, Cory and Kelly, Kevin. "Reliability, Realism, and Relativism" in *Reading Putnam, Clark, Peter (ed)*, 98-160. Cambridge, Blackwell, 1995.

Glymour, Clark and Meek, Christopher. Conditioning and Intervening. *Brit J Phil Sci*, 45(4), 1001-1021, D 94.

We consider the dispute between causal decision theorists and evidential decision theorists over Newcomb-like problems. We introduce a framework relating causation and directed graphs developed by Spirtes *et al* (1993) and evaluate several arguments in this context. We argue that much of the debate between the two camps is misplaced; the disputes turn on the distinction between conditioning on an event E as against conditioning on an event I which is an action to bring about E. We give the essential machinery for calculating the effect of an intervention and consider recent work which extends the basic account given here to the case where causal knowledge is incomplete.

Glynn, Simon V. Reply to Wil Coleman's "Simon Glynn on a Unified Epistemology of the Natural Human/Sciences". *J Brit Soc Phenomenol*, 26(1), 96-98, Ja 95.

Taking issue with Coleman's suggestion that we apply the term "interpretation" to our attempt to make sense of literary texts, I affirm that hermeneutics, being nothing other than the science or method of interpretation, may be legitimately applied to human experience and behavior, as well as to the behavior of certain objects and events in the physical sciences, and indeed to anything, including "existence" itself, which *could* be regarded as meaningful. Like literary texts then, the meaning of which may be understood differently in different contexts, the meaning or significance of physical observations may also be contextually dependent of Kuhn, the Gestaltists and others have demonstrated. Consequently the understanding of such meanings is as central to the physical sciences as understanding or *Verstehen* is to the human and social sciences.

Gnanagbe, Gogoua. L'absolutisme dans la Philosophie: Politique de Thomas Hobbes. *Philosopher*, 17, 161-174, 1995.

Gobry, Ivan. La Ténèbre chez Denys: Sources du Chapître I de la *Théologie Mystique*. *Diotima*, 23, 64-68, 1995.

Godfrey-Smith, Peter. A Modern History Theory of Function. *Nous*, 28(3), 344-362, S 94.

Godfrey-Smith, Peter. Of Nulls and Norms. *Proc Phil Sci Ass*, 1, 280-290, 1994.

Neyman-Pearson methods in statistics distinguish between Type I and Type II errors. Through rigid control of Type I error, the "null" hypothesis typically receives the benefit of the doubt. I compare philosophers' interpretations of this feature of Neyman-Pearson tests with interpretations given in statistics textbooks. The pragmatic view of the tests advocated by Neyman, largely rejected by philosophers, lives on in many textbooks. Birnbaum thought the pragmatic view had a useful "heuristic" role in understanding testing. I suggest that it may have the opposite effect.

Godlove Jr, Terry F. "Ricoeur, Kant, and the Permanence of Time" in *The Philosophy of Paul Ricoeur, Hahn, Lewis Edwin (ed)*, 399-415. Peru, Open Court, 1994.

In *Temps et récit*, v III (1985), Paul Ricoeur argues against one of the premises of Kant's First Analogy of Experience, namely, that time must be "permanent" (*beharrlich*) if human experience is to be possible. In particular, he argues that the

Analogy undermines a central result of the Transcendental Aesthetic, that the parts of time are successive. The present article offers an interpretation of Ricoeur's criticism and then opposes to it a reading of Kant on which time can be permanent yet successive. Ricoeur has elsewhere urged respect for elements of Kant's theoretical philosophy; yet there is good reason to think that little remains of Kant's enterprise when stripped of the permanence of time.

Godlovitch, Stan. Ontology, Epistemic Access, and the Sublime. *Iyyun*, 44, 55-71, Ja 95.

Gödel, Kurt and Fagnot, Dominique (trans) and Heinzmann, Gerhard (trans). Les Mathématiques Sont-Elles une Syntaxe du Langage?. *Dialogue (Canada)*, 34(1), 3-34, Wint 95.

Goenner, Hubert F M. "What Kind of Science is Cosmology?" in *Philosophy, Mathematics and Modern Physics, Rudolph, Enno (ed)*, 144-167. New York, Springer-Verlag, 1994.

Cosmology shows features of descriptive astronomy, palaeontology, history mathematics, and natural philosophy. The article discusses, from the point of view of a theoretical physicist with an interest in philosophy, the position of cosmology within physics. To what extent is it supported empirically; what are its epistemological and methodological problems (definition as a physical system, predictive power of model, testing of theory etc.)? Three phases of cosmological modeling, i.e., the standard model, early universe and quantum cosmology are distinguished and classified as useful, marginally helpful and just speculative. The introduction of a new interdisciplinary science called extrapolative physics is suggested.

Goetschel, Willi. *Kant als Schriftsteller*. Vienna, Passagen, 1990.

Selbstbewusst setzt mit Kants erster Schrift seine Laufbahn als Schriftsteller ein. Diese Bestimmung hat für ihn als Philosophen grundlegende Bedeutung. Das schrfitstellerische Experimentieren mit verschiedenen literarischen Formen und Ausdrucksweisen, aus denen nach einer langen Reihe von *Versuchen* die neue Literaturgattung der Kritik entwickelt wurde, bezeichnet Kants Suche nach der theorieadäquaten Form seines kritischen Philosophierens. Das bedeutet aber, dass Kant neu und auf neue Art kritisch gelesen werden muss. (edited)

Goetschel, Willi (ed). *Perspektiven der Dialogik: Zürcher Kolloquium zum 80. Geburtstag von Hermann Levin Goldschmidt*. Vienna, Passagen, 1994.

Zum Schlagwort geworden, scheint der Dialog längst zum Konsensus geronnen zu sein. Die Beiträge dieses Bandes zeigen, inwiefern die von Goldschmidt so geprägte Philosophie als Dialogik gegen eine solche Vereinnahmung Widerstand bietet. (edited)

Goetz, Stewart C. The Choice-Intention Principle. *Amer Phil Quart*, 32(2), 177-185, Ap 95.

Götz, Ignacio L. On Teaching as a Profession. *J Thought*, 30(3), 7-17, Fall 95.

This paper advances the notion that the question whether or not teaching is/should be a profession is misplaced. Five reasons are given: that the term "profession" is inadequate since it refers to all kinds of occupations; that "profession" defines by way of exclusion and therefore means nothing; that professionalism thwarts that personalization of teaching; that professionalism is based on views of the self which are primarily masculine; and that "profession" defines activities which have tended to exclude women. A suggestion is then made that, to achieve what professionalism sought, one should insist on the notion of vocation with all that it entails.

Goicoechea, David. "Appraising-Bestowing-Growing-Adoring" in *The Nature and Pursuit of Love, Goicoechea, David (ed)*, 61-72. Buffalo, Prometheus, 1995.

Irving Singer throughout his three volume work on the nature and history of love thinks of love in the classical terms of appraisal (eros) and bestowal (agape). By thinking of Singer in terms of Nietzsche this paper asks if the essential traits of love must not also include "Growing in Love" and "Adoring". The paper suggests that Singer is moving in the direction of Nietzsche with notions of love's metamorphoses and Dionysian adoration.

Goicoechea, David (ed). *The Nature and Pursuit of Love*. Buffalo, Prometheus, 1995.

This text is the beginning of a discussion about love between Irving Singer and his critics and friendly commentators. It begins with two interviews of Irving Singer about love. Twenty papers discuss his theory and treatment of love. The introduction discusses each of the papers from the focal point of Singer's major categories appraisal (eros) and bestowal (agape). Singer concludes the text with a forty page reply to the papers.

Goisis, Giuseppe L. "Il sogno di un'alt(r)a morale: Considerazioni su *Les deux sources* di Henri Bergson" in *L'etica e il suo Altro, Vigna, Carmelo (ed)*, 189-215. Milano, FrancoAngeli, 1994.

Gokhale, Pradeep P. Is There a Moral Perspective in Patañjali's Yogasutras?. *Indian Phil Quart*, 22(1), 41-53, Ja 95.

Describing moral perspective as the one in which universal human values rather than context-specific values are central, the author makes a case for the presence of a moral perspective in Patanjali's *Yogasutra*. By criticising Prof. V K Bharadwaja's argument he tries to show that the direct aim of *Yamas* (abstentions) like non-injury prescribed by Patanjali is universalistic though the indirect aims like *Samadhi* (Meditative Trance) or *Kaivalya* (Emancipation) are egoistic. Patanjali's perspective is not a case of self-inconsistent ethical egoism, because the egoistic goal, for him, does not serve as an essential condition of morality though perfection in moral conduct serves as a necessary condition of the egoistic goal.

Gokhale, Pradeep P. Language and World: Some Classical Indian Approaches *vis-a-vis* Analytical Western Approaches. *Indian Phil Quart*, 21(4), 317-328, O 94.

In this paper four classical Indian approaches to language and world have been compared with some Western analytical approaches. The Vaisesika approach according to which the realms of real, knowables and nameables are co-extensive is found similar to Meinong's approach. The Buddhist approach according to which the basic particulars constituting reality cannot be captured by language, is found comparable with, though different from the views of Russell and Wittgenstein. The

Jaina approach according to which language is essentially imprecise and relative is found comparable with the view of Gilbert Ryle. The two models of the Carvaka approach 1) that of empirical testability 2) that of conformity to common sense, are found similar to the views of logical positivists and G E Moore respectively.

Golash, Deirdre. Pluralism, Integrity, and the Interpretive Model of Law. *Phil Cont World*, 1(3), 15-21, Fall 94.

In *Law's Empire*, Ronald Dworkin argues that the choice between conflicting interpretations of law is, and should be, influenced by the aspiration to "integrity," that is, the construction of law as a coherent whole, as though it were the product of a single author. I argue that, particularly under conditions where opinion on relevant issues is significantly divided, the search for a single coherent explanation of law may be seriously misleading. The idea of integrity is a principled basis for legal interpretation only where there is an underlying unity, rather than an underlying plurality. Dworkin suggests that there is a basis for striving toward such unity, and for an obligation to obey the law, in our "associative" obligations to fellow members of our political community. I argue that such obligations, to the extent that they exist, are too weak to provide an adequate basis for a moral obligation to obey the law.

Golash, Deirdre. Review of "The Community Reconstructs: The Meaning of Pragmatic Social Thought" by James Campbell. *J Value Inq*, 29(2), 284-288, Je 95.

Campbell's argument for a radical reconstruction of the ideas of democracy, freedom, and individualism without regard to historical meanings is premised on a timely and appealing view of the appropriate relationship between the individual and the community, but may overemphasize his opponents' reliance on historical meanings. Campbell persuasively argues for a reconception of rights and freedom that will ameliorate the tension between individual rights and social welfare, but slights the key issue of the role of government in securing the good life for its citizens. Campbell's discussion of the special role of philosophers in achieving social change is of particular interest.

Golash, Deirdre. The Retributive Paradox. *Analysis*, 54(2), 72-78, Ap 94.

Retributivists must show that the aggressive act of punishment is right although the aggressive act of crime is wrong. Hampton suggests that the crime represents a false claim of superiority over the victim; punishment refutes that claim. But if A's theft from B says that A is more valuable than B, punishment by fine must say that B is more valuable than A. I argue that the statement made by punishment is that A has low value. Thus Hampton's theory conflicts with the equal value of persons and with the retributivist aim of restoring the status quo ante.

Golcher, Cristián. Bioética y derechos humanos II: Aspectos formales y sustanciales para una normativa biomédica en un mundo biotecnológico. *Rev Filosof (Costa Rica)*, 31(75-76), 217-225, D 93.

The reader must place himself in the perspective of a world where the inedited biological technification of desire confronts us with unexpected unknowns. Afterwards the reader must observe the determination that looks for the establishment of criteria of liberty, which are necessary in order for development and conjugation of standards which express diverse ethical requirements of human action. He must relate the importance of freedom with an existence seen as a destiny. He must go through the importance of corporeal reality in problems of biomedical ethics, and he must conclude this with a reading that attempts to think over the foundation of the ethical requirement that subordinates the human existence to the internal life of sense and meaning, which project human existence as a destiny. The reader must appreciate the study of a criticism of the judgment that guides the preference of criteria that establish the foundation of actions and standards implicated in dialectical advances of an uncertain and powerful biomedicine.

Gold, Jay A. Global Budgeting in the Real World. *J Clin Ethics*, 5(4), 342-343, Wint 94.

The article critiques an article by Robert Veatch in the same issue on ethical aspects of global budgeting in healthcare. Dr Veatch astutely spells out a very important problem. However, the way he deals with that problem is based upon assumptions that violate the way such decisions actually are made: funds never are unlimited; relevant factors cannot be reduced to harms vs. benefits; some treatments objectively are better than others; metaethical theories have dubious relevance to clinical decisionmaking; and one must take into account the pervasive discrimination that exists against the poor in this arena.

Gold, Steven Jay. "The Analytic Defense of Functional Marxism and Law" in *Radical Philosophy of Law, Caudill, David S (ed)*, 32-37. Atlantic Highlands, Humanities Pr, 1995.

Gold, Steven Jay (ed) and Caudill, David S (ed). *Radical Philosophy of Law*. Atlantic Highlands, Humanities Pr, 1995.

This volume is a collection of essays by scholars from various disciplines engaged in the critical evaluation of contemporary legal processes and institutions. Part I includes examples of radical theories, such as Marxism, critical psychoanalytic social theory, radical feminism, and postmodern literary theory, while Part II includes exemplary analyses of criminal law, tort law, contract law, Native American rights, Gay Rights, and Hate Speech.

Goldberg, David Theo. *Multiculturalism: A Critical Reader*. Cambridge, Blackwell, 1994.

Multiculturalism: A Reader delineates the prevailing concerns and considerations, principles and practices, concepts and categories that fall under the rubric of "multiculturalism." Contributors spell out what they take multiculturalism to be committed to as much as against, what vision of education and knowledge and social relations form its fabric, what metaphors structure its representations in and across and beyond traditional definitions of the disciplines, what practices are encouraged by its articulations and expressions, and how these differ from and are opposed to and undertake to overthrow or go beyond those that are given and presumed, that constitute the tradition and prevailing forms of common sense.

Goldberg, David Theo. *Racist Culture: Philosophy and the Politics of Meaning*. Cambridge, Blackwell, 1993.

Goldberg, David Theo. Racist Exclusions. *Phil Forum*, 26(1), 1-32, Fall 94.

The standard philosophical and social scientific conception of racism views it as irrational personal prejudiced upon the arbitrary and so morally irrelevant category of 'race'. Racism is supposed to make necessarily false claims about biologically based differences between racial groups, or about hierarchical evaluations of inferiority and superiority. This view, I argue, fails to capture critical features of racism, and what we should find wrong with it. There is no single generic racism, only a set of racist manifestations—of racisms—commonly identifiable in terms of the racially identifiable exclusions effected. Conceiving racisms nonessentially in this way avoids the philosophical and practical shortcomings of insisting that racist expressions necessitate the presence of racist intentions (in the case of individuals) or racist rules or principles (in the case of institutions). Racist exclusions likewise identify the wrongs involved as significantly more severe than simply appealing to an arbitrary category. On the basis of this reformulation of racism, I assess some of the more usual explanations and rationalizations for racism, suggesting in either case that no single paradigmatic account can be offered. I conclude by offering a defense of preferential treatment programs that avoids the charge of racism or reverse discrimination.

Goldberg, David W. Nietzschean Recurrence: The Science and the Moment. *Auslegung*, 20(1), 1-10, Wint 95.

Nietzsche's concept of eternal recurrence has traditionally been understood according to two primary interpretations: the cosmological and hypothetical. Those who opt for the cosmological suggest that recurrence is a factual, almost scientific, account of the circularity of both time and events. In opposition, Magnus, and those who accept the hypothetical position, offer circularity as an attitudinal approach to existence. This article argues that both understandings are suspect when confronted with the remainder of Nietzschean thought. As an alternative I will suggest that recurrence can only be grasped in the remainder can only be grasped in the recognition of the 'Moment' as the 'what' of the return.

Goldberg, Laura and Greenberg, Michael. A Survey of Ethical Conduct in Risk Management: Environmental Economists. *Ethics Behavior*, 4(4), 331-343, 1994.

A sample survey of members of the Association of Environmental and Resource Economists (AERE) found relatively low rates of obvious ethical misconduct, such as data fabrication and falsification, and higher rates of dubious behaviors, such as deliberate overstatement of positive and understatement of negative results. AERE members reported that job-related pressures—including competition with peers, pressure due to professional implication and on-the-job pressure—were the most important causes. The most effective preventive measures, according to respondents, were discussion of ethics in existing classes, codes of ethics, and short courses at professional meetings. The vast majority of AERE members were against government audits and regulations.

Goldberg, Sandy. An Intuition About Self-Knowledge: A Challenge to Fodor. *Conference*, 4(1), 50-63, Spr 93.

Goldblatt, David. Power, Modernity and Morality in the Long Nineteenth Century. *Theor Cult Soc*, 12(1), 157-173, F 95.

Goldbort, Robert C. "How Dare You Sport Thus with Life?": Frankensteinian Fictions as Case Studies in Scientific Ethics. *J Med Human*, 16(2), 79-91, Sum 95.

Fictional scenarios involving "hard" science offer what are in effect case studies of scientific ethics. From his analysis of Shelley's novel, biologist Leonard Isaacs constructed a model of a "Frankenstein scenario," applicable to the dilemmas posed by the advancement of science in our time, as well as to fiction about science by such contemporary writers as Robin Cook and Michael Crichton. The special contribution of fiction to the study of ethics is that it both reflects and evaluates reality's infinite permutations. In reflecting and judging, the fictional scenarios engage our moral imagination and compel us to confront our personal ethos in relation to the evolving ethos of science.

Goldie, Mark. The New 'Everyman' Edition of Locke's *Two Treatises*. *Locke News*, 25, 87-88, 1994.

This note draws attention to a new edition of Locke's *Two Treatises of Government* which provides the first modernised edition of that work based on Locke's own corrected text as he left it for posterity at his death. The edition includes a glossary identifying all Locke's citations, and a key word index which identifies all his usages of certain words and phrases.

Goldman, Alan. Emotions in Music (A Postscript). *J Aes Art Crit*, 53(1), 59-69, Wint 95.

Peter Kivy is right that arousing emotions is neither necessary nor sufficient for expressing them in music. But it is a necessary part of the explanation of the value of such expression. This paper offers explanations of how music arouses emotions, of what sort of emotions these are, and of the value of musical expression. It takes a middle ground between cognitivists, who deny that music arouses ordinary emotions, and emotivists, who analyze expression in terms of arousal. It also addresses the problem of how negative emotions of art contribute to its enjoyment.

Goldman, Alan H. The Aesthetic Value of Representation in Painting. *Phil Phenomenol Res*, 55(2), 297-310, Je 95.

Plato's criterion of pictorial representation is defended against contemporary objections. Several answers to his question about the value of representation are considered and rejected as incomplete, and a more complex answer in terms of the interaction of representation with other sources of aesthetic value is provided.

Goldman, Alvin. Empathy, Mind, and Morals. *Proc Amer Phil Ass*, 66(3), 17-41, N 92.

This paper illustrates how empirical research in cognitive science can affect philosophical inquiry by concentrating on one phenomenon, empathy, which may have applications both to philosophy of mind and to moral theory. In philosophy of mind, an empathy or "simulation" theory might explain how people ascribe mental states to others, namely, by taking their perspective. In moral theory, empathy might help explain altruism, for example. The plausibility of these ideas can only be sustained through psychological research. The paper reviews some suggestive and encouraging work in this vein, especially in the area of developmental psychology.

Goldman, Alvin I. Simulation and Interpersonal Utility. *Ethics*, 105(4), 709-726, Jl 95.

Interpersonal utility (IU) comparisons are important to ethical theory, but their legitimacy depends on philosophy of mind, epistemology, and cognitive science. The meaningfulness of IU comparisons depends on the meaning of mental language in general. It is argued that experientialism offers better prospects for the meaning of such comparisons than functionalism. Empathy, or the simulation heuristic, could explain how IU comparisons are actually made. Such judgments could be knowable if reliabilism is a correct epistemology and the simulation heuristic is reliable. The prospects for such reliability could be confirmed or disconfirmed with the help of cognitive science.

Goldman, Alvin I and Cox, James C. "Accuracy in Journalism: An Economic Approach" in *Socializing Epistemology: The Social Dimensions of Knowledge*, Schmitt, Frederick F (ed), 189-215. Lanham, Rowman & Littlefield, 1994.

Goldman, Michael. Why?. *Teach Phil*, 17(4), 285-292, D 94.

I consider various interpretations of the locution "Why does S do A?" and show how each probes a different way of understanding human action. I explore a variety of ways in which the distinctions made manifest by these interpretations can be used in teaching several issues that are commonly encountered in philosophy courses at all levels. I also suggest some worthwhile problems that emerge in comparing these different modes of explanation.

Goldman, René. Moral Leadership in Society: Some Parallels between the Confucian "Noble Man" and the Jewish *Zaddik*. *Phil East West*, 45(3), 329-365, Jl 95.

Beyond the empressionistic similarities Chinese and Jews sometimes detect in each other, a study of the scriptual texts of the two traditions reveals surprising parallels. Eleven such parallels in ideas and values are examined and it is suggested that the comparative study of cultural traditions developed independently of each other is a worthwhile undertaking. This serves to apprehend that which is genuinely universal beyond the diversity of expression.

Goldman, Robert and Papson, Steven. "The Postmodernism That Failed" in *Postmodernism and Social Inquiry*, Dickens, David R (ed), 224-253. New York, Guilford, 1994.

Goldring, Noa. Measures: Back and Forth Between Point Sets and Large Sets. *Bull Sym Log*, 1(2), 170-188, Je 95.

Goldschmidt, Hermann Levin. *Das Vermächtnis des deutschen Judentums: Werke 2*. Vienna, Passagen, 1994.

Zuerst 1957 erschienen und seit der dritten Auflage (1965) vergriffen, bietet *Das Vermächtnis des deutschen Judentums* noch immer die einzige Darstellung des deutschen Judentums aus philosophischer Sicht. Im Durchgang durch die Geschichte wird nicht nur die kulturelle Eigenständigkeit verständlich, sondern darüber hinaus auch die paradigmatische Rolle, die das Judentum bei der Entstehung der Moderne spielt. Deshalb handelt es sich, wo es um sein Vermächtnis geht, nicht um etwas Vergangenes, sondern, wie Goldschmidt deutlich macht, um Zukunftweisendes.

Goldschmidt, Hermann Levin. *Die Botschaft des Judentums: Werke 3*. Vienna, Passagen, 1994.

Zuerst 1960 erschienen, gibt Goldschmidt in der *Botschaft des Judentums* eine Interpretation der Grundbegriffe und der Geschichte des Judentums, und zwar vom Standpunkt einer kritischen "Philosophie aus den Quellen des Judentums", wie der Autor in Anlehnung an Hermann Cohen formuliert. Die Bedeutung des Judentums besteht dabei nicht nur in seiner Vergangenheit. Vielmehr verweist diese auf die ungebrochene Geschichtsmächtigkeit der gesellschaftskritischen prophetischen Forderungen, welche die Botschaft des Judentums solange als zukunftsverheissend bestätigt, wie es jene Botschaft menschheitlicher Forderungen noch zu verwirklichen gilt.

Goldschmidt, Hermann Levin. *Freiheit für den Widerspruch: Werke 6*. Vienna, Passagen, 1993.

Philosohieren heisst für Goldschmidt, den Widerspruch ernst nehmen: "Wo ein Widerspruch laut wird, dort, meint man, sei etwas falsch, statt zu begreifen, dass dort, wo kein Widerspruch vorliegt, etwas falsch sein muss." So lautet der Kernsatz der *Freiheit für den Widerspruch*. In Weiterentwicklung der *Philosophie als Dialogik* (1944/48) und *Dialogik. Philosophie auf dem Boden der Neuzeit* (1964) formuliert der Verfasser in diesem Werk seine Losung kritischen Denkens und Lebens. (edited)

Goldschmidt, Hermann Levin. *Philosophie als Dialogik: Frühe Schriften Werke 1*. Vienna, Passagen, 1992.

"Wo ein Widerspruch laut wird, dort, meint man, sei etwas falsch, statt zu begreifen, dass dort, wo kein Widerspruch vorliegt, etwas falsch sein muss." In diesem Satz spricht sich Goldschmidts Kernthese aus. Wird die wissenschaftlich notwendige Widerspruchsfreiheit verabsolutiert, so wird sie zur jeden Widerspruch totalisierend ausschliessender Ideologie und damit zur Unfreiheit selbst. Die Dialogik formuliert in wissenschafts- wie gesellschaftskritischer Absicht die Forderung der "Freiheit für den Widerspruch". (edited)

Goldsmith, Emanuel S. Salvational Zionism and Religious Naturalism in the Thought of Mordecai M Kaplan. *Process Stud*, 22(4), 204-210, Winter 93.

Goldsmith, Emanuel S (ed) and Patai, Raphael (ed). *Thinkers and Teachers of Modern Judaism*. New York, Paragon House, 1994.

Goldstein, Jan (ed). *Foucault and the Writing of History*. Cambridge, Blackwell, 1994.

Goldstein, Laurence. A Yabloesque Paradox in Set Theory. *Analysis*, 54(4), 223-227, O 94.

Stephen Yablo recently discovered a paradox which, although in the Liar family, is not self-referential. I devise a set-theoretic counterpart to Yablo's paradox: Consider an infinite sequence K of classes such that an object is a member of any given class in K if and only if it is not a member of any subsequent class in K. This generates a contradiction. I first solve that paradox, and this leads to a solution of Yablo's original along lines which I have already suggested for the Strengthened Liar. A solution so all-embracing must be true!

Goldstein, Laurence. Fallacious Reasoning. *Teach Phil*, 18(2), 139-146, Je 95.

Humans are imperfectly rational animals. Our fallacious reasoning springs from psychological sources which underlie not just reasoning but much of our other behavior—our biases, survival strategies, our moral failings, the way we learn our native language. Principles of correct reasoning, adherence to which would help us overcome our argumentative imperfections, are different in nature from the rules of logic. Taxonomizing fallacies is not a particularly useful end in itself, but studying the sources of fallacious reasoning is very revealing of the kind of creature humans are—how they differ from communities of interacting Turing machines.

Goldstick, D. Are There Theories?. *Log Anal*, 34, 345-348, S-D 91.

When people theorize, it is not (standardly) their theorizing they are thinking of, but rather their theorizing's subject-matter. A theory, though, is supposed to be an object of thought if anything is; and yet, the heliocentric theory, for example, is *said* to have been brought into existence (unlike the facts which form its subject-matter) by the commencement historically of heliocentristic theorizing. How *could* there be something like that, whose *esse* was *cogitari*.

Goldstick, D. Justified Belief. *Dialogue (Canada)*, 34(1), 99-111, Wint 95.

A belief can sometimes constitute "knowledge"—on pure reliabilist grounds—without being "justified"—because the account of "justification" offered here adds internalist "accessibility" elements. However, a strict, unconditional epistemic "obligation" to embrace (any) correct rational first principles is affirmed. So is the logical impossibility of consciously believing something without considering the belief "justified", and therefore also the logical impossibility of any consistent self-aware scepticism without opinionlessness. But "justified" does not entail "rationally justified". And the special sense of "justification" paralleling credibility "probability" concerns an ideal reasoner's confidence level. Rebuttals are offered to Bonjour, Ginet, Pollock, and Jacobson.

Goldstick, D. Marxism on Dialectical and Logical Contradiction. *Austl J Phil*, 73(1), 102-113, Mr 95.

The claim is defended that Engels and his friend Marx never doubted the unreality of all logical impossibilities. A dialectical "contradiction" occurs wherever two processes or tendencies in nature causally depend on each other while militating against each other's effects. Inconsistency in someone's thinking is thus an example of the phenomenon. The lesson of the "lottery paradox" is that sometimes even clearly inconsistent thinking is rational, because of being (for certain or probably) truer, overall, than any alternative thinking which suggests itself.

Golomb, Jacob. Camus's Ideal of Authentic Life. *Phil Today*, 38(3-4), 268-277, Fall 94.

Camus's three literary works demonstrate that already at the level of fiction his literature has a vital philosophical import. Though, like Kierkegaard and Nietzsche, not a philosopher in the technical, his literary fiction is intimately related to the ideal of authenticity. Camus's early notion of authentic life is found in *The Outsider*; that of his transitional period in *Caligula*, and his later perspective in "The Guest". Camus understood that since the ideal of authenticity goes beyond rational discourse it is best evoked by literature rather than exposition. By generating in us deep existential anguish, Camus offers us a chance to overcome it by being true to ourselves.

Golomb, Jacob. *In Search of Authenticity: From Kierkegaard to Camus*. New York, Routledge, 1995.

The first chapters: "Authenticity, sincerity and honesty", "Authenticity, literature and irony" examine problems inherent in an attempt to write about this ideal and the ways used to overcome them. Kierkegaard, Nietzsche, Heidegger, Sartre and Camus dealt also with the ethical viability of this ideal. Their fictional heroes wished to become faithful to scripts they have written for themselves; to transcend the ethos of objectivity and embrace an 'aesthetic' (as opposed to 'biological') model of authenticity. The suppression of individuality invigorates the quest for authenticity as a corrective ideal if not an objectively viable norm. As there is no proof of the impossibility of authenticity, the search for a personal pathos of authenticity, that can prevent the betrayal of our own selfhood, will continue.

Gomberg, Paul. Autonomy and Free Expression. *J Soc Phil*, 25(2), 97-104, Fall 94.

Gómez, Francisco Navarro (trans) and Vico, G. Oración II Pronunciada el 18 de Octubre de 1700. *Cuad Vico*, 3, 211-218, 1993.

Gómez, Francisco Navarro (trans) and Vico, G. Oración III Pronunciada el 18 de Octubre de 1701. *Cuad Vico*, 4, 191-198, 1994.

Gómez, Francisco Navarro (trans) and Vico, G. Oración IV Pronunciada el 18 de Octubre de 1704. *Cuad Vico*, 4, 201-208, 1994.

Gómez Ibáñez, Vicente. La liquidación de la Filosofía: Notas sobre la disputa entre R Rorty y J Habermas. *Convivium*, 6, 104-128, 1994.

On prosecuting one of the traditions in modern philosophy, the Hegelian-Marxist one, J Habermas states again the problem of relation between sciences and philosophy, in order to save in opposing to R Rorty the pretension of reason for philosophical thought. But the discussion remains undecided, if not occurs rather that, considering the pragmatist assumptions that both share, it is perhaps Rorty's position the more consistent. Habermas has obviated very theoretical elements of the critical tradition, that he pretends to continue, that are decisive for the success of this claim. T W Adorno's philosophy conserves even these elements. Not every epistemological reflection involves necessarily the confusion of the "Mirror of Nature" that Rorty ascribes to the whole modern philosophy. Dialectical critic of traditional epistemology, that dialectics, completes without abandoning, doesn't involve such a confusion.

Gómez Robledo, Antonio. "La Ley en el Pensamiento Platónico" in *Platón: Los Diálogos Tardíos, Lan, Conrado Eggers (ed)*, 151-160. Sankt Augustin, Academia, 1986.

Gomez-Lobo, Alfonso. "Autopredicación" in *Platón: Los Diálogos Tardíos, Lan, Conrado Eggers (ed)*, 103-123. Sankt Augustin, Academia, 1986.

Gómez-Lobo, A and Rowe, C J. "Discusión: La Autenticidad de la Carta VII" in *Platón: Los Diálogos Tardíos, Lan, Conrado Eggers (ed)*, 161-168. Sankt Augustin, Academia, 1986.

Gómez-Lobo, Alfonso. Sócrates: Filósofo en el Límite?. *Rev Latin de Filosof*, 21(1), 159-165, Fall 95.

In reply to O Nudler's note, these remarks try to provide a precise framework for the discussion of Socratic irony and show that the early Platonic dialogues attribute to Socrates positive claims in moral philosophy. Since his achievements are not purely negative, Socrates cannot be considered "a philosopher at the limit" in Nudler's sense.

Gonda, Joseph. On Jacob Klein's *Greek Mathematical Thought and the Origin of Algebra*. *Interpretation*, 22(1), 111-128, Fall 94.

Jacob Klein's *Greek Mathematical Thought and the Origin of Algebra*—is characterized by Leo Strauss as possessing an intrinsic worth unique among contemporary histories of ideas. This essay explicates the central theses of Klein's book. First, ancient and modern mathematics differ in their modes of conceptualization and each yields a different ontology. Second symbolic mathematics, is not merely a more general or abstract form of mathematics, but involves a new understanding of abstraction, "symbol generating abstraction." Third, modern mathematical physics and science in general bypass rather than answer the fundamental ontological questions. For Klein the proper study of the origins of algebra and mathematical physics reopens these questions.

Gonza, Guillermo. "La Filsofía va al Taller" in *Temas Actuales de Filosofía, Palacios, María Julia (ed)*, 247-253. Buenos Aires, Univ Nacional Salta, 1993.

The teaching of philosophy at secondary level has always been proposed as a finished knowledge, conspiring against the espirit of philosophy itself and against the principles of constructivism. The aim of the present work is to attract the possibility of a philosophy based on the constructivistic didactics. Steps to be followed: 1) To characterize the traditional pedagogy of constructivism and projectwork, taking the students, the teacher, philosophy and cultural backgound, as variables. 2) An experience is related. Arriving at the conclusion that our proposal is possible, nidding is a pleasant way of learning that implies the teacher as an investigator of his practice.

Gonzáles, Juliana. "Psique y Eros en el *Fedro*" in *Platón: Los Diálogos Tardíos, Lan, Conrado Eggers (ed)*, 139-150. Sankt Augustin, Academia, 1986.

Gonzáles R, Edgar. La Teoria de la Argumentacion y el Circulo de Viena. *Topicos*, 1(1), 59-78, 1991.

Gonzalez, Orestes J. The Apprehension of the Act of Being in Aquinas. *Amer Cath Phil Quart*, 68(4), 475-500, Autumn 94.

Gonzalez, Wenceslao J. Economic Prediction and Human Activity: An Analysis of Prediction in Economics from Action Theory. *Epistemologia*, 17(2), 253-294, Ju-De 94.

To clarify what economic prediction is and ought to be, the character of human activity in economic bearing should be considered. This requires, firstly, taking into account the relation between prediction and scientific status of economics (section 1). Secondly, the problem of prediction in economics should be seen from the perspective of action theory (section 2). We need to study the complexity of economic reality condensed in the duality "economic activity" and "economics as activity". Thus, thirdly, both are considered in order to clarify the subject-matter of economics and its nexus with prediction (section 3). An alternative to the main conceptions of economic prediction (predictivist thesis, quasi-scientific option, dualist posture and cautious attitude) is proposed, which finds its basis in the nature of the economic activity.

González, Esther Romero. Metáfora Literaria y Conocimiento. *Daimon Rev Filosof*, 8, 109-118, 1994.

In this article it is shown that metaphorical utterances in literature have, among others, a cognitive end. This proposal is drawn from the more general thesis that metaphorical utterances have a cognitive value independently from the field they are produced. Such value depends on the fact that metaphor is a mechanism that allows producing, in a systematic way, non-conventional meanings (metaphorical provisional meanings) that were not available in the linguistic competence of the speakers of the same linguistic community in that moment of the language. In addition, it is pointed out that, although the type of knowledge produced by metaphorical utterances in the literary field is the same as the one yielded by the rest of metaphorical utterances, metaphorical utterances in literature have several specific characteristics.

González, M and Sanmartín, J and López Cerezo, J A. Filosofía actual de la ciencia. *Dialogo Filosof*, 10(2), 164-208, My-Ag 94.

Después de 30 años tras la revolución kuhniana en filosofía de la ciencia es clara la necesidad de un estudio interdisciplinar de la ciencia. pero no se ve que sea posible el que la filosofía tenga algo que decir en tal marco interdisciplinar de análisis empírico. La tendencia general a la naturalización parece dejar fuera de juego a una disciplina, la filosofía, cuyo tradicional estilo normativo es muy difícil de asimilar. Con todo, la polémica continúa. En estas páginas se recoge, entre algunos otros problemas, el enfrentamiento contemporáneo entre el racionalismo filosófico y el relativismo en la comprensión de la naturaleza de la ciencia.

González, María Cristina. "Es la Psicología del Sentido Común (Folk Psychology) una Teoría?" in *Temas Actuales de Filosofía, Palacios, María Julia (ed)*, 255-261. Buenos Aires, Univ Nacional Salta, 1993.

Churchland thesis about folk psychology is revised. Concepts like theoretical terms, lawlike statements, explanation, prediction, research programs, etc. used with regard to scientific theories, are applied by Churchland to folk psychology. These applications are argued. It is intended that his arguments for folk psychology as an empirical theory are not conclusive. Instead, folk psychology as a system of convictions capable of changes is suggested.

González, María Cristina and Stigol, Nora and Rabossi, Eduardo A. "Los Seminarios en la Enseñanza de la Filosofía" in *Temas Actuales de Filosofía, Palacios, María Julia (ed)*, 521-524. Buenos Aires, Univ Nacional Salta, 1993.

Seminars as successful learning situations for philosophical goals are considered. It is mentioned some special features in our university classrooms that hinder teachers from getting the main aim: to learn to philosophize. Strategies used during a seminar are described: a preparatory stage and a discussion stage. The experience is evaluated.

González Altable, M Pilar. El contractualismo libero de D Gauthier: Contratualismo vs Utilitarismo. *Telos (Spain)*, 1(2), 111-125, Je 92.

In these pages we shall try to describe the thought of D Gauthier in one of his last works: "Why Contractualism?", although we shall also keep in views his central work, *Morals by Agreement*. We shall start from Gauthier's statement to the effect that contractualism is the only plausible solution to overcome the crisis of foundation of today's ethics. We shall go on to examine his statement that utilitarianism enables us to present any basic principle to rational cooperation. We shall conclude that Gauthier's ethics presents a morality of justified restrictions, in which the model of the economic individual is replaced by the idea of a liberal individual, for whom to act rationally is to behave morally.

González Fernández, Martín. Medievo y Renacimiento, Ruptura o Continuidad?. *Rev Espan Filosof Med*, 1, 9-26, 1994.

González Miguel, Jesús Graciliano. La filosofía, el método y el hombre en el pensamiento de Adolfo Muñoz Alonso. *Logos (Mexico)*, 22(66), 11-61, S-D 94.

E pensamiento de Adolfo Muñoz Alonso está centrado en tres puntos: 1) el concepto de filosofía como búsqueda y aspiración personal a la verdad y, fundamentalmente, como búsqueda de lo que es y hay en el hombre; 2) el método filosófico, que es el idealismorealista o método ontológico-sicológico: ontológico, en cuanto que se basa en la experiencia, y sicológico, en cuanto que dota de significación a la experiencia; 3) el hombre como ser personal (espíritu encarnado), como ser esencialmente relacionado con los demás (ser social), y como ser abierto a la trascendencia de Dios (ser immortal destinado a completarse en Dios).

González Recio, José Luis. El programa reduccionista en las Ciencias de la vida (1910-1944). *An Seminar Metaf*, 27, 111-125, 1993.

The ontological rupture produced by the appearance and development of quantum mechanics is probably the most revolutionary aspect of contemporary science. That ontological break has affected along the century to the project of a reductionist foundation of biology. Before the fifties, the key question was to know which was to be the conceptual support and the ontological horizon of future biology. This paper describes how the approach between physics and biology adopted three basic models: the philosophy of biology of Jacques Loeb, the biochemical interpretation of general physiology that Otto Warburg undertook, and the intent of looking for a point of connection between quantum physics and molecular biology carried out by Erwin Schrödinger.

Gonzalo de Aguirre, Adriana. "Holismo y el Problema de la Validación de las Teorías Científicas en la Perspectiva s Need-Stegmüller" in *Temas Actuales de Filosofía, Palacios, María Julia (ed)*, 263-270. Buenos Aires, Univ Nacional Salta, 1993.

Gonzalo I Carbó, Antoni. La mirada errante: de la "Spaltung" en Lacan, al "caos-cosmos" de Deleuze. *Convivium*, 6, 29-52, 1994.

In psychoanalysis, *Spaltung* is represented as a schism or division between the subject "I" or the most intimate psychism of the conscious speech of the subject. The distance which separates subconscious language of the spoken articulation is shown as an abysm in the depth of which the writer or artist are lost. In contemporaneous artistic experience there is evidence of this form of feedback between the "I" of the enunciated and the psychic reality it represents: its oscillating look doesn't find any other reflection that that of the opaque mirror of its subjectivity. Only the announcement of the fragmented speech by the *crack*, in the sacrifice of one self, and that which the body crystallizes as *chaos-cosmos*, can liberate the resources which in the forgetting of the eternal return represents, the only possibility of the wandering look.

Gooch, Paul W. "A Mind to Love: Friends and Lovers in Ancient Greek Philosophy" in *The Nature and Pursuit of Love, Goicoechea, David (ed)*, 83-97. Buffalo, Prometheus, 1995.

A study of Plato and Aristotle on love with reference to Irving Singer's interpretation, the paper first deals with Aristotle's careful analysis. Aristotle captures much of friendship, but in restricting its perfect form to the morally excellent, he does not appreciate the importance of intimacy in relationships. The paper's second part examines Plato's characterization of Socrates and Socratic relationships, finding Socrates too divinized to exemplify Aristotelian friendship with another self. Socratic love of the immortal forms is distinguished from Platonic love, which permits intimacy between two like-minded lovers, although for the sake of transformation and ascent to the Beautiful.

Gooch, Paul W. Sovereignty, Soft Determinism and Responsibility. *Sophia (Australia)*, 33(3), 89-100, N 94.

It is part of Christian faith to affirm God's sovereignty over all events, and also to affirm human responsibility for at least some of those events. How these affirmations fit together is a question treated differently in different theological traditions. This paper concerns one answer which bears close resemblance to the philosophical doctrine of soft determinism. It argues that such an answer is available neither for believers nor for skeptics who have used it to attack divine goodness.

Goode, R and Griffiths, P E. The Misuse of Sober's Selection for/Selection of Distinction. *Biol Phil*, 10(1), 99-108, Ja 95.

Elliott Sober's selection for/selection of distinction has been widely used to clarify the idea that some properties of organisms are side-effects of selection processes. It has also been used, however, to choose between different descriptions of an evolutionary product when assigning biological functions to that product. We suggest that there is a characteristic error in these uses of the distinction. Complementary descriptions of function are misrepresented as mutually excluding one another. This error arises from a failure to appreciate that selection processes can be described at several different theoretical levels.

Goodenough, Ursula W. The Religious Dimensions of the Biological Narrative. *Zygon*, 29(4), 603-618, D 94.

A cell/molecular biologist challenges the thesis that science and religion are two ways of experiencing and interpreting the world and explores instead the possible ways that the modern biological worldview might serve as a resource for religious perspectives. Three concepts—meaning, valuation, and purpose—are argued to be central to the entire biological enterprise, and the continuation of this enterprise is regarded as a sacred religious trust.

Gooderham, David. Towards Discourse in the Public Domain: Adolescent Fictions in Moral and Political Education. *J Moral Educ*, 23(4), 439-450, 1994.

The article argues the value of contemporary adolescent fictions in Moral Education, on grounds not of content but of their treatments of moral and political issues. Two contrasting models, based on the literary concepts of "realistic" and "modern" forms of narrative, are used to highlight the stylistic and structural distinctiveness of these contemporary texts—and to make clear their appropriateness for a Moral Education which involves not only induction into public life, but also into the discourse of the public domain. Four contemporary texts, dealing with aspects of public life, and exemplifying a broad range of sub-genres and treatments, are then examined in the light of this perspective, and a summary statement of their particular features is made to justify their appropriateness for a critical Moral Education.

Goodin, Susanna. Tertiary Qualities in Locke's 'Essay'. *Locke News*, 23, 59-81, 1992.

The article provides a detailed account of how tertiary qualities, qualities of "the third sort," are to be understood in Locke's *Essay concerning Human Understanding* and then discusses the relevance of this fleshed-out account of tertiary qualities for Locke's skepticism concerning scientific knowledge of bodies. Tertiary qualities are powers of a body's corpuscularian configuration to cause changes in the corpuscularian configurations of other bodies. An *idea* of a tertiary quality is a complex idea consisting of the state of the first body, the state of the second body (before and after the interaction), and the relationship between the two bodies.

Gooding, David. Imaginary Science. *Brit J Phil Sci*, 45(4), 1029-1045, D 94.

Goodman, Nelson. *Ways of Worldmaking*. Indianapolis, Hackett, 1978.

Goodman, Nelson and Elgin, Catherine Z and Cometti, Jean-Pierre (trans). *Reconceptions en philosophie*. Paris, Pr Univ France, 1994.

Goodman, Robert F. William James: Rationality as a Pragmatic Choice. *Hist Euro Ideas*, 20(4-6), 951-955, F 95.

This paper analyzes William James's pragmatic account of rationality. James was opposed to those versions of rationality that posit a transcendental or *a priori* logic or a rational world of nature. Yet, he strongly favors rationality as a general orientation to the problems of human existence. The paper argues that the roots of James's rationality, like other aspects of his philosophy, are to be found in his concern that philosophical positions must be analyzed in terms of their suitability to human needs. Jamesian rationality is at the core of his effort to give a philosophical account of the constructive life. It is argued that as opposed to a rationality of fixed standards or methods, James's rationality is tenuous and threatened by the irrational forces of life.

Goodpaster, Jeffery R and Kirby, Gary R. *Thinking*. Englewood Cliffs, Prentice Hall, 1995.

This book exercises the most important part of your body: your brain. It is designed to challenge your mind and to strengthen your thinking ability. Spanning the disciplines, the authors offer a classical well-spring of thought, drawing on ideas from every period of history, from philosophy, literature, the natural sciences, and psychology. The authors organize the material into interrelated thinking bases that include sensing, feeling, language, creativity, organization, logical thought, judgment, decision making, and action. And to actively engage, enlarge, and enrich your thinking and to help you adapt and personalize the chapter concepts, they include numerous thinking challenges throughout the book.

Goodrich, R A. Intention and Representation: Searle's 'Internal' Thesis. *Lit Aes*, 2, 53-66, Spr 92.

Through Searle's provocative analysis of intentionality, this article begins by disclosing the complexities underpinning our common references to the role intention plays in artistic representation. Using the test-case of Verdi's *Otello* and Boito's libretto, it is argued that Searle's 'internalising' approach to intention and definition of representation proves not merely stipulative, circular, and incomplete, but also unable to overturn 'external' accounts of both concepts. Indeed, 'external', Wittgensteinian accounts enable us not only to separate intention from introspection generally and motivation particularly, but also to re-connect aspect perception ('seeing as') with intention when examining representation in the literary-based arts.

Goranko, Valentin. A Note on Derivation Rules in Modal Logic. *Bull Sec Log*, 24(2), 98-104, Je 95.

Gorayska, Barbara. How to Lose the Soul of Language. *J Prag*, 22(5), 536-547, N 94.

This paper expresses the view that formal pragmatics, which captures pragmatic behavior, both linguistic and nonlinguistic, strictly in terms of rule sets is an oxymoron. The critical reasons for this position are: a) an infinite regression of autonomous agents and contexts that are required to put formal models to use, and b) a lack of consideration of sensory inputs, in particular the intuition and the physical touch, that complement, and are important for the proper utilization of, symbols when these symbols are used in their natural organic settings. Implications for modern information technology and human computer interaction are considered.

Gorayska, Barbara and Lindsay, R O. On Putting Necessity in Its Place. *J Prag*, 23(3), 343-346, Mr 95.

A response to Mey's (J Prag, 23(3) 341-342) critique of the proposal that objects are relevant when they form part of a plan which is sufficient to achieve a goal, and irrelevant when they do not. Mey argues that an object is irrelevant when it fails to figure in a *necessary* plan. It is replied that the term "necessary plan" has no useful application. Necessity applies to sets of plan elements not plans themselves. Redundant plan elements are not relevant to the goal of a plan, but usually plans require any member of a functional equivalence set, not some particular element.

Gorbett, Jason. AIDS, Confidentiality, and Ethical Models. *De Phil*, 10, 71-84, 1993.

What ethical models best provide means of arriving at solutions to problems in biomedical ethics? Using a case study that involves the issue of AIDS and doctor-patient confidentiality, the author argues that models which involve appeals to higher levels of justification are ineffective. A "bottom-up" model that refrains from such appeals is developed and defended.

Gordeev, L. A Modified Sentence Unprovable in "PA". *J Sym Log*, 59(4), 1154-1157, D 94.

Gordley, James and Cooter, Robert D. "The Cultural Justification of Unearned Income" in *Profits and Morality, Cowan, Robin (ed)*, 150-175. Chicago, Univ of Chicago Pr, 1995.

Gordon, Anna M and Perkins, Henry S. Should Hospital Policy Require Consent for Practicing Invasive Procedures on Cadavers?. *J Clin Ethics*, 5(3), 204-210, Fall 94.

Gordon, Avery and Newfield, Christopher. White Philosophy. *Crit Inquiry*, 20(4), 737-757, Sum 94.

Gordon, Dane R. Philosophy in Post-Communist Europe. *Metaphilosophy*, 25(2-3), 214-223, Ap-Jl 94.

Considerable attention has been given to the political and economic conditions of the countries of post-communist Europe. Little attention has been given to the ethical, philosophic and religious issues which these countries face. This paper attempts to address these issues and reflect upon them in light of a conference, Philosophy in Post-Communist Europe, held at Rochester Institute of Technology, Rochester, New York, in January, 1994.

Gordon, Haim and Gordon, Rivca. *Sartre and Evil: Guidelines for a Struggle*. Westport, Greenwood Pr, 1995.

The book presents and examines many of the discussions and portrayals of evil in a large number of Sartre's philosophical and literary works. It suggests how these discussions and portrayals can guide us to fight evil here and now. To help make Sartre's wisdom vivid, the authors draw on their own experience in struggling for human rights.

Gordon, Jill. By Any Means Necessary: John Locke and Malcolm X on the Right to Revolution. *J Soc Phil*, 26(1), 53-85, Spr 95.

After laying out Locke's theory of legitimate rebellion, the paper looks at the circumstances of the lives, liberty, and property of black Americans showing that the conditions under which they lived justify legitimate rebellion by Locke's criteria. The paper then examines Malcolm's speeches, demonstrating that his reasoning about the legitimacy of rebellion concurs with Locke's ideas. The paper then compares the two thinkers on the necessity of the use of force during extreme political discord. The paper concludes that both Locke and Malcolm X justify rebellion and force under the same circumstances, even though history has judged them differently.

Gordon, Lewis R. *Bad Faith and Antiblack Racism*. Atlantic Highlands, Humanities Pr, 1995.

This book is the first systematic discussion of antiblack racism as a form of Sartrean bad faith. The text includes discussions of the body in bad faith; bad faith and the evasion of evidence; the errors of the intrinsic-extrinsic motif in race theory; a defense of Fanonian sociodiagnostics and theory of phobogenesis; an existential-phenomenological treatment of "an antiblack world"; the homoerotic dimensions of antiblack racism; the misogynous dimensions of antiblack racism; the theodician dimensions of an antiblack world; the relationship between bad faith/antiblack racism and misanthropy.

Gordon, Rivca and Gordon, Haim. *Sartre and Evil: Guidelines for a Struggle*. Westport, Greenwood Pr, 1995.

The book presents and examines many of the discussions and portrayals of evil in a large number of Sartre's philosophical and literary works. It suggests how these discussions and portrayals can guide us to fight evil here and now. To help make Sartre's wisdom vivid, the authors draw on their own experience in struggling for human rights.

Gordon, Robert M. Sympathy, Simulation, and the Impartial Spectator. *Ethics*, 105(4), 727-742, Jl 95.

The paper sketches a theoretical framework for an empirically based moral psychology that gives central importance to empathy. It begins with Hume's insight that our minds are sympathetic "mirrors" to one another, updated in the light of recent psychological research. The mirroring is more pervasive that even Hume had thought, according to the simulation account of commonsense psychological competence. In moral assessment, however, it is important to hold back from the all-out identification that may be required when we want to predict another's behavior —a point suggested by Adam Smith's criticism of Hume's treatment of sympathy.

Gordon, Robert M and Barker, John A. "Autism and the 'Theory of Mind' Debate" in *Philosophical Psychopathology, Graham, George (ed)*, 163-181. Cambridge, MIT Pr, 1993.

Gorevan, Patrick. The 'Passions of the Soul': Descartes' Shadow on Theories of the Emotions. *Amer Cath Phil Quart*, 68(4), 515-528, Autumn 94.

Gorman, Jonathan. *Understanding History: An Introduction to Analytical Philosophy of History*. Ottawa, Univ of Ottawa Pr, 1992.

The debate in analytical philosophy of history about whether historians can provide knowledge about reality is developed. The book concentrates on examples from econometric history, and analyzes the metaphysical presuppositions of the contributors to the debate. Knowledge is analyzed in an elementary manner suitable for those not familiar with philosophy. A new contribution is made through the philosophical analysis of narrative history in comparison with econometric history. The empathetic understanding of human action is explained in terms of cost-benefit analysis. The justification of the rational economic man assumptions, and of rival theories of human nature used in historical writing, is analyzed in terms of holistic empiricism. The input of historical and economic research to our overall philosophical understanding is explained in the light of this approach.

Gorovitz, Samuel. Whose Patient Am I, Anyway?. *Phil Exch*, 24-25, 29-36, 1993-94.

Gosepath, Stefan. Eine einheitliche Konzeption von Rationalität. *Protosoz*, 6, 104-119, 1994.

This article argues for the thesis that there is only one basic form of rationality, which is applied in different areas. First of all, there is one meaning of the term "rational" which applies to all situations in which the term is used: "justified." If "rational" means simply "justified", then rationality can be broken down into as many types as there are kinds of justification. Two distinctions between kinds of justification seem particularly plausible: 1) Relative vs. absolute justifications and 2) Theoretical justifications of opinions vs. practical justifications of actions. Taken together, these two distinctions yield a division into four types of rationality. I maintain, however, that these two distinctions collapse upon more careful examination. In this article I will simply assume that no form of ultimate justification is convincing; thus, the first distinction does not apply. Against the second distinction I try to argue in this paper that theoretical rationality represents a form of practical rationality. The idea of an optimal choice of aims, actions, and opinions, which nonetheless differs from the orthodox model of practical rationality, thus proves to be the comprehensive central ingredient of the concept of rationality.

Gosepath, Stefan. The Place of Equality in Habermas' and Dworkin's Theories of Justice. *Euro J Phil*, 3(1), 21-35, Ap 95.

This article concerns the role played by the idea of equality in the political theories of justice of Jürgen Habermas and Ronald Dworkin. Their theories represent alternative ways of specifying the fundamental egalitarian idea of treating people as equals, accepted by most as the kernel of any plausible political morality. Habermas (in the tradition of Kant) claims that liberal justice is primarily concerned with rights to basic liberties and to participation. Consequently, his theory has little to say about distributive justice. For Dworkin, on the other hand, the primary liberal ideal is equality, which he sees embodied in equality of resources; all other principles of liberalism are supposed to follow from this primary ideal. After a critical examination of Habermas's and Dworkin's theories, another alternative is very briefly sketched that might be able to avoid the disadvantages of both theories while preserving their advantages.

Goshorn, A Keith. "Valorizing 'the Feminine' while Rejecting Feminism? —Baudrillard's Feminist Provocations" in *Baudrillard: A Critical Reader, Kellner, Douglas (ed)*, 257-291. Cambridge, Blackwell, 1994.

Goswami, Amit. Monistic Idealism May Provide Better Ontology for Cognitive Science: A Reply to Dyer. *J Mind Behav*, 16(2), 135-150, Spr 95.

This is a response to Michael Dyer's (1994) *Commentary on Goswami's Quantum-Based Theory of Consciousness and Free Will*, a theory that I will call idealist science—a science based on the primacy of consciousness rather than matter. First, I review Dyer's main points: 1) There is no need for idealist science since cognitive science can explain whatever human phenomena idealist science purports to explain; and 2) idealist science offers nothing new, such as, new methodology or experimental prediction. I then review some of the inadequacies of the cognitive science model of consciousness stemming in part from its impoverished ontology of physical realism. It is shown that cognitive science follows from the new idealist science (as classical physics follows from quantum physics) in the limit of a correspondence principle. In this way, idealist science is seen to support cognitive science (rather than replace it) while generalizing the scope of science itself to include the subjective aspects of reality. Next, I point out what idealist science gains for us: 1) Treatment within science of the subjective aspects of creativity, ethics, free will, and spirituality (without the need to explain these away as epiphenomena); and 2) Integration of all the forces of psychology, and also of physics and biology. Finally, I discuss possible experiments to distinguish between realist and idealist models of reality.

Gottdiener, M. "Semiotics and Postmodernism" in *Postmodernism and Social Inquiry, Dickens, David R (ed)*, 155-181. New York, Guilford, 1994.

Gottdiener, Mark. "The System of Objects and the Commodification of Everyday Life: The Early Baudrillard" in *Baudrillard: A Critical Reader, Kellner, Douglas M (ed)*, 25-40. Cambridge, Blackwell, 1994.

Gottlieb, Lawrence and Zucker, Mark J. Organs for Undocumented Aliens? A Transplantation Dilemma. *Cambridge Quart Healthcare Ethics*, 4(2), 229-232, Spr 95.

Undocumented aliens may appear in United States transplantation programs without any mechanism to pay for their treatment. Our institution, Newark Beth Israel Medical Center, Newark, New Jersey, faced the decision and developed a policy in order to try to approach the problem fairly and in compliance with all appropriate unos policies.

Gottlieb, Michael C. Ethical Decision Making, Boundaries, and Treatment Effectiveness: A Reprise. *Ethics Behavior*, 4(3), 287-293, 1994.

The article is a response to Lazarus (same issue) who argues that contemporary ethical principles and risk management procedures in psychology may compromise treatment effectiveness and even be inhumane. A brief literature review is followed by a critical evaluation of examples cited by Lazarus. The article concludes that recent literature on risk management and ethical guidelines represent a significant advance in the quality of professional practice which benefit consumers and practitioners. Emphasis is placed on the fact that clinical judgment and ethical decision-making must be made in conjunction with one another.

Gottlieb, Michael C. Family Violence and Family Systems: Who Is the Patient?. *Ethics Behavior*, 5(3), 273-277, 1995.

Bourne presents a case that raises provocative and difficult questions for all those in clinical practice. In responding to his article, I have made three assumptions. First, my remarks are based on a family systems perspective, a theoretical approach that emphasizes that understanding human behavior requires an appreciation of the context in which it occurs (Hoffman, 1981). Second, there are numerous issues raised in the article regarding legal matters, institutional policy, and clinical issues. I restrict myself to a discussion of some of the more salient ethical issues. Third, Bourne's article is written from the perspective of the institution's attorney. Mine is written from the perspective of a mental health professional.

Gottlieb, Paula. Aristotle on Dividing the Soul and Uniting the Virtues. *Phronesis*, 39(3), 275-290, 1994.

Gotz, Gerhard. *Letztbegründung und systematische Einheit: Kants Denken bis 1772*. Vienna, Passagen, 1993.

Das auch für Spezialisten oft kryptische Material der handschriftlichen Reflexionen Kants aus der vorkritischen Zeit verlangt schon lange nach einer grundlegenden Systematisierung. Gerhard Gotz entwickelt in der vorliegenden Arbeit mit grosser Präzision einen solchen Raster. Dank seiner einfühlsamen und kontextbedachten Lektüre eröffnet der Autor ein in seiner Bedeutung für die Forschung kaum abschätzbares Potential neuer Ansätze und Perspektivierungen Kants. Dennoch richtet sich dieses wichtige Werk nicht nur an Kant-Experten; durch seine klare Gliederung ermöglicht das Buch auch jenen Lesern eine gründliche Ein- und Hinführung zu Kant, die sich bisher nicht oder kaum mit der Materie befasst haben. Das grundlegende Wissen dieser Arbeit liefert ein solides Fundament für eine eigenständige Kant-Lektüre.

Goula-Mitacou, Xéni. Flaubert en Grèce. *Diotima*, 22, 132-138, 1994.

Gould, Carol C. Between Discrimination and Differentiation: Introductory Reflections. *Hypatia*, 9(3), 183-187, Sum 94.

A panel titled Feminist Philosophy after Twenty Years was organized by Carol C Gould for the session sponsored by the Committee on the Status of Women at the American Philosophical Association's 1993 Eastern Division Meeting, December 30, 1993 in Atlanta, GA. The remarks of the three panelists, Linda Lopez McAlister, Ann Ferguson and Kathy Addelson are included in this issue.

Gould, Elizabeth S. Getting the Whole Picture: The View From Here. *Phil Music Educ Rev*, 2(2), 92-97, Fall 94.

As a music educator with teaching experience in a variety of settings, I have had a unique opportunity to view the landscape of music education from several vantage points. Each standpoint framed my perspective, disclosing features that are invisible except in the more comprehensive and inclusive panoramas revealed from marginalized positionalities. Grounded in postmodern decentering, these newly visible contours of the landscape are outlined in my reflections regarding transformative possibilities of the concept of music educator in the context of unequal social relations and the role(s) of women in music. The final picture, of course, is never complete.

Gould, James A. Sex, Sin and Immortality. *Int J Applied Phil*, 9(1), 11-13, Sum-Fall 94.

Gould, James B. Discussing Divorce in Introductory Ethics. *Teach Phil*, 18(2), 101-113, Je 95.

By discussing divorce in ethics courses instructors can 1) bridge the gap between abstract ethical theory and our students' daily lives (divorce is an everyday issue almost everyone faces sooner or later, unlike social policy questions like fetal-tissue research), and 2) illustrate important points in ethical theory and moral reasoning: egoism vs the ethical point of view, the importance of facts and consequences in moral reasoning, and the nature of self-realization.

Gould, Stephen J. The Buddhist Perspective on Business Ethics: Experiential Exercises for Exploration and Practice. *J Bus Ethics*, 14(1), 63-70, Ja 95.

While Buddhism focuses on the same ethical concerns as Western ethical traditions, it provides a distinct perspective and method for dealing with them. This paper outlines the basic Buddhist perspective and then provides some experiential exercises which offer insight for self-understanding and ethical practices in business. Implications for business and ethics research are provided.

Goulet, Denis. "Biological Diversity and Ethical Development" in *Ethics, Religion and Biodiversity, Hamilton, Lawrence S (ed)*, 17-40. Cambridge, White Horse, 1994.

Govier, Trudy. Is It a Jungle Out There? Trust, Distrust and the Construction of Social Reality. *Dialogue (Canada)*, 33(2), 237-252, Spr 94.

I offer an account of trust and distrust, and explore the significance of the attitude of trust in our construction of beliefs about the social world. Trust is an attitude based on beliefs and feelings and implying dispositions as to the interpretation and evaluation of other people's behavior. Both trust and distrust are relative to context and evidence. Nevertheless we can distinguish between those inclined to be more trusting and those inclined to be less trusting. I explore a recent account by Alex Michalos arguing that to a considerable extent we construct social relativity and should construct it in a more trusting way than we do. There are significant objections to his arguments. An alternative account, emphasizing trustworthiness, is suggested.

Goyard-Fabre, Simone. L'inspiration nietzschéenne de Leo Strauss et ses limites. *Dialogue (Canada)*, 33(3), 391-413, Sum 94.

Gozzano, Simone. Mental Images and their Ontology. *Epistemologia*, 17(2), 225-252, Ju-De 94.

This paper is divided in three parts. In the first part, I summarize the main points of the debate among Descartes, Locke and Berkeley on the general problem of ideas and mental imagery. In particular I focus both on the question whether it is possible to form general ideas and on the relationship between imagery and conception. In the second part, I describe the more important empirical results on the subject, in particular the effect of "confusion" between perception and imagery, the relationship between language and imagery and the main general theories proposed by Pylyshyn and Kosslyn. Moreover, the descriptionalist vs pictorialist controversy is described. In the final part, I develop a philosophical argument to show how the problems of mental imagery can be treated and unified under the more general problem of their ontology.

Grabinska, Teresa. Mathematical Conceptual Apparatus of Physical Theory and Special Metaphysics. *Stud Phil Christ*, 30(2), 99-113, 1994.

The Schlick's concept of meaning related to empirical verification is discussed and the Ajdukiewicz's concept of meaning is set against it. Ajdukiewicz associates with a conceptual apparatus of scientific theory—a scientific perspective of world. This perspective is compared with a special metaphysics corresponding to a mathematical conceptual apparatus. Types and functions of such a metaphysics are considered and a need of hermeneutic meaning directive in empirical science is argued.

Gracia, Diego. Hard Times, Hard Choices: Founding Bioethics Today. *Bioethics*, 9(3-4), 192-206, Jl 95.

The discussions of these past twenty years have significantly improved our knowledge about the foundation of bioethics and the meaning of the four bioethical principles with concern to at least three different points: that they are organised hierarchically, and therefore not "prima facie" of the same level; that they have exceptions, and consequently lack of absolute character; and that they are neither strictly deontological nor purely teleological. The only absolute principle of moral life can be the abstract and unconcrete respect of human beings. But when determining the material content of this respect, principles become contingent and relative. Therefore, moral reasoning must have necessarily no less than three moments, one absolute but merely formal, namely respect for all human beings, and the other two relative and material. The first material moment is comprised of the four bioethical principles, divided into two levels, one private, including the principles of autonomy and beneficence, and the other one public, including those of nonmaleficence and justice. The second material moment deals with specific cases, and requires analysis of their context, including their circumstances and consequences. Only when following these steps, and therefore balancing principlism and contextualism, can moral reasoning be correct and complete.

Gracia, Jorge J E. "Can There Be Definitive Interpretations?" in *European Philosophy and the American Academy, Smith, Barry (ed)*, 43-53. Peru, Open Court, 1994.

This article considers the widespread thesis that definitive interpretations are impossible. It argues, first that both those who adopt this idea and those who reject if fail to understand two important distinctions concerning interpretations. It argues, second, that if one understands those distinctions, the claim that there can be no definitive interpretations loses its shocking character, and thus can find a place within a sensible hermeneutic theory. The distinctions in question are between textual and nontextual interpretations, and among three different functions of textual interpretations: historical, meaning, and implicative functions.

Gracia, Jorge J E. *A Theory of Textuality: The Logic and Epistemology*. Albany, SUNY Pr, 1995.

This book presents a comprehensive and systematic theory of textuality that takes into account the relevant views of both analytic and Continental thinkers and also of major historical figures. It claims that most of the confusion surrounding textuality is the result of three factors: a too-narrow understanding of the category; a lack of a proper distinction among logical epistemological and metaphysical issues; and a lack of proper grounding of epistemological and metaphysical questions on logic analyses.

Gracia, Jorge J E. Author and Repression. *Cont Phil*, 16(4), 23-29, Jl-Ag 94.

This article argues against the view that the author of a text always functions repressively, forcing readers to understand a text in ways consonant with the ways he or she understood the text. The argument is based on an analysis of the identity of the author and the aims pursued by audiences when they seek to understand texts. In some cases the author functions repressively, but in other cases it does not.

Graczynska, Ewa. On Some Operators on Pseudovarieties II. *Bull Sec Log*, 24(2), 80-88, Je 95.

This is a continuation of my paper *On some operators on pseudovarieties* [6]. We adopt the HSP Theorem of G Birkoff [1] and the Theorem of H Lakser, R Padmanabhan, C R Platt [11], for pseudovarieties. Some of the results were presented at the 48 Workshop on General Algebra, in Linz (Austria), 2-5 June, 1994. An extended version of the paper will be published separately.

Grady, Christine. HIV Preventive Vaccine Research: Selected Ethical Issues. *J Med Phil*, 19(6), 595-612, D 94.

This paper explores three selected issues which present ethical challenges unique to the development and testing of preventive HIV vaccines. The issues are: when to move forward with large scale efficacy testing of vaccines, how to incorporate behavioral interventions into the study of vaccine efficacy, and how to plan for and mitigate social harms associated with participation in an HIV vaccine trail. Careful and ongoing consideration must be given to the ethical implications of these decisions. Proposed solutions include planning for a more complex prevention trial which would integrate the evaluation of behavioral interventions and vaccine efficacy; scrupulous attention to the process of individual informed consent and community participation; and serious and deliberate attempts to plan for, educate about, and minimize the social harms.

Graeser, Andreas. *Philosophie in Sein und Zeit*: Kritische Erwägungen zu Heidegger. Sankt Augustin, Academia, 1994.

This study focusses on a number of passages in *Being and Time* central to the argument of the book. Upon a close examination of the text, including passages from other publications, it turns out that Heidegger's ideas do not stand scrutiny.

Graeser, Andreas. Substanz und Mensch: Spinozas Auffassung der Wirklichkeit. *Frei Z Phil Theol*, 41(1-2), 91-115, 1994.

Graf, Georg. "Reine Rechtslehre und schmutzige Verfassungstricks" in *Der geistige Anschluss, Fischer, Kurt R (ed)*, 59-68. Wien, WUV Univ, 1993.

Graham, George and Stephens, G Lynn. "An Introduction to Philosophical Psychopathology: Its Nature, Scope, and Emergence" in *Philosophical Psychopathology, Graham, George (ed)*, 1-23. Cambridge, MIT Pr, 1993.

Surveys the topics and literature of the field of philosophical psychopathology with emphasis upon the field's most recent areas of activity.

Graham, George and Stephens, G Lynn. "Mind and Mine" in *Philosophical Psychopathology, Graham, George (ed)*, 91-109. Cambridge, MIT Pr, 1993.

Examine introspective alienation as this phenomenon occurs in a variety of different psychopathological states or conditions. Distinguishes between two aspects of self-consciousness operative in such states or conditions. One is being conscious of one's own stream of consciousness; the other is being conscious of one's own mental agency.

Graham, George and Stephens, G Lynn. Commentary on "Kant, Thought Insertion, and Mental Unity". *Phil Psychiat Psych*, 1(2), 115-116, Je 94.

Graham, George (ed) and Stephens, G Lynn (ed). *Philosophical Psychopathology*. Cambridge, MIT Pr, 1993.

Collection of mostly original papers by more than a dozen philosophers and psychopathologists on topics at the intersection of philosophy of mind and psychopathology.

Graham, George and Stephens, G Lynn. Self-Consciousness, Mental Agency, and the Clinical Psychopathology of Thought-Insertion. *Phil Psychiat Psych*, 1(1), 1-10, Mr 94.

This paper shows that self-consciousness actually contains two distinct experiences: the sense of being the subject of consciousness, and the sense of being the agent of mental events within one's psychological history. This claim is based mainly on an analysis of psychopathological data concerning thought insertion, or thought alienation. These data may also seem to support the separability of self-consciousness from introspection. It is shown, however, that the data do not support separability. The experience of thought insertion requires the sense of being the subject of consciousness.

Graham, Gordon. Art, Pleasure, and Play. *J Value Inq*, 28(2), 217-232, Je 94.

Graham, Gordon. Learning from Art. *Brit J Aes*, 35(1), 26-37, Ja 95.

The essay argues in defense of aesthetic cognitivism, the view that the value of art lies in its ability to teach us. Its main purpose is to show that some of the traditional objections to this view can be answered if we observe a distinction between an increase in knowledge and an increase in understanding, and if we see that art enhances our understanding by supplying images which we can bring to our experience.

Graham, Gordon. Liberal vs Radical Feminism Revisited. *J Applied Phil*, 11(2), 155-170, 1994.

This essay considers the movement away from a feminism based upon liberal political principles, such as John Stuart Mill espoused, and towards a radical feminism which seeks to build upon more recent explorations of psychology, biology and sexuality. It argues that some of these moves are philosophically suspect and that liberal feminism can accommodate the more substantial elements in these radical lines of thought.

Graham, Gordon. The Value of Music. *J Aes Art Crit*, 53(2), 139-153, Spr 95.

This paper examines possible explanations for attributing intrinsic value to music. It argues against both expressionism and representation as applied to music and in favor of a conception of music as an exploration of aural experience.

Graham, Gordon. Toleration in Politics. *Filozof Istraz*, 14(2-3), 333-342, 1994.

The author offers an argument for toleration in politics which will appeal not only to the liberal, but also to the fundamentalist, i.e., a person who is fully confident that his or her belief is the true one and doubts the value of toleration. The author's strategy is one that draws on one of the main arguments in favor for religious toleration and expands it to apply to politics as well. (edited)

Graham, Jill W. Leadership, Moral Development, and Citizenship Behavior. *Bus Ethics Quart*, 5(1), 43-54, Ja 95.

This paper suggests that different styles of leadership arouse different sorts of normative motivation among followers, and these diverse motivational sources in turn are associated with different forms of participant contribution to organizational success. Three interrelated clusters of leadership styles, normative motivation of followers, and organizational citizenship behavior are described. Leadership that appeals exclusively to followers' self-interests is associated with preconventional moral development and dependable task performance. Leadership styles focusing on interpersonal relationships and social networks are associated with followers' conventional moral development and work group collaboration. Transforming leadership that both models and nurtures servant leadership abilities is associated with post-conventional moral development and responsible participation in organizational governance.

Grainger, Arthur D. Flat Sets. *J Sym Log*, 59(3), 1012-1021, S 94.

Gramsci, Antonio and Boothman, Derek (ed & trans). *Further Selections from the Prison Notebooks*. Minneapolis, Univ of Minn Pr, 1995.

Granada, Miquel A. Agostino Steuco y la *Perennis Philosophia*. *Daimon Rev Filosof*, 8, 23-38, 1994.

El presente ensayo examina la obra fundamental de Agostino Steuco, *De perenni philosophia* publicada en 1540, como un desarrollo del programa de Ficino tendente a mostrar la concordia doctrinal entre *prisca theologia* y cristianismo. Se estudia la concepción de la historia de la humanidad como una común y universal "tradición" doctrinal desde Adán, en la cual los diferentes y sucesivos pueblos participan en una serie de verdades fundamentales: Tri-unidad divina, creación del mundo, inmortalidad del alma humana individual, fin del mundo creado y renovación escatológica. En esta perspectiva, en la que desaparecen los reconocimientos de Ficino y Pico a la "novedad" del cristianismo, la religión de Cristo posee más bien el carácter de una renovación magisterial de la universal verdad filosófico-religiosa, a la que el curso del tiempo amenazaba con oscurecer de manera irremediable.

Grandjean, Fabien. David Hume: la révolution praxologique du matérialisme. *Rev Phil Fr*, 1, 19-32, Ja-Mr 95.

Hume demonstrated that materialistic reductionism is mere nonsense. However he also described an entirely new meaning of matter itself, neither a speculative nor a gnosiologic meaning, but a pragmatic and praxological one. The author aims to show how Hume's sensualist atomism had to result in the recognition of the "industry" as historical principle, particularly after 1740. Before Marx, Hume was the first to understand that the essence of materialism, as Heidegger said, does not consist in asserting that all is but matter; it consists rather in a metaphysical determination according to which all being appears as the matter of a work.

Grange, Joseph. Whitehead and Heidegger on Technological Goodness. *Res Phil Technol*, 14, 161-173, 1994.

This essay compares Heidegger's and Whitehead's concepts of technology. Where Heidegger sees technology as the culmination of Western metaphysics, Whitehead sees it as one more development in the creative urge that characterizes process as reality. Heidegger envisions technology as the cultural manifestation of the will to power. It is the final result of the forgetfulness of being that began when Plato created metaphysics. On the other hand, for Whitehead, technology is a propositional lure that beckons human beings into different ways of creativity. It can be either good or bad. Finally, where Heidegger sees unredeemed power and arrogance, Whitehead sees the opportunity for significant cultural transformation. I use the thought of Borgmann and Dewey to develop these notions further. My essay concludes with a defense of Whitehead's position and a rejection of types of Heideggerean postmodernism.

Granier, Jean. L'exigence morale. *Rev Phil Fr*, 4, 401-420, O-D 94.

Grant, Brian. Wittgenstein's Elephant and Closet Tortoise. *Philosophy*, 70(272), 191-215, Ap 95.

Arguments are offered for two conclusions. The first conclusion is in the form of a dilemma: We must either be sceptics or beg the sceptic's question. The second is that we should grasp the latter horn of the dilemma and not be sceptics. The argument for this second conclusion is, as should be expected given its content, not of your nice tight Euclidean variety. Those who might see this as a flaw are reminded of the first conclusion. The argument there is quite straightforward—and the other horn of the dilemma is so much worse. Hume's sort of choice.

Grant, Robert. Hirsch on Education and National Culture: A Critique. *Hist Euro Ideas*, 19(1-3), 357-367, Jl 94.

Grant, Robert. Must New Worlds Also be Good?. *Inquiry*, 38(1-2), 123-141, Je 95.

The activities analysed by Spinosa *et al.*, viz entrepreneurship, citizen action, and cultural leadership, are all central to the American experience. They have a common phenomenological structure and a common purpose, which is to "disclose new worlds", i.e., so to reconfigure the collective perceptions as to bring about "large-scale cultural and historical changes". Each, more or less unself-consciously, is an exercise of skill, an expression of freedom, and a building of solidarity through the recovery or discovery of human meanings. I argue that unless we know the ends to which skill and freedom tend, and in which meaning is found, all three (which the authors treat rather as ends in themselves) are underdescribed, and impossible to see as possessing or conferring value simply *per se*. The same goes for the original three activities. Cultural leadership, citizen action, and entrepreneurship can work as easily towards bad ends as good. To see them as virtual ends in themselves, then, is premature, and a kind of formalism.

Grant, Simon. A Strong (Ross) Characterization of Multivariate Risk Aversion. *Theor Decis*, 38(2), 131-152, Mr 95.

Using the 'addition of uncorrelated noise' as a natural definition of increasing risk for multivariate lotteries, I interpret risk aversion as the willingness to pay a (possibly random) vector premium in exchange for a reduction in mutivariate risk. If no restriction is placed on the sign of any co-ordinate of the vector premium then (as was the case in Kihlstrom and Mirman's (1974) analysis) only pairs of expected utility maximizers with the *same* ordinal preferences for outcomes can be ranked in terms of their aversion to increasing risk. However, if we restrict the premium to be a nonnegative random variable then comparisons of aversion to increasing risk may be possible between expected utility maximizers with *distinct* ordinal preferences for outcomes. The relationship between their utility functions is precisely the multi-dimensional analog of Ross's (1981) *global* condition for *strongly more risk averse*.

Grassi, Ernesto. La Rehabilitacíon del Humanismo Retórico: Considerando el Antihumanismo de Heidegger. *Cuad Vico*, 2, 21-34, 1992.

The dilemma of Heidegger's anti-humanism is clarified in the light of the real and proper value of humanism itself, whose principal themes reach through Vico their highest significance and expression. This work debates the problem generated by the identification of humanism with a traditional metaphysical attitude of ontological indifferentation; when elucidating *rhetorical humanism* it is understood that humanist thought does not begin with the problem of the beings but with the preeminence of the word, especially the metaphoric word, giving rise to a rhetorical philosophizing. In such a way, the anti-humanism of Heidegger is strengthened by an indirect knowledge of humanism with the prejudices of modern interpretations, and not in the knowledge of its own specific and original value. The rehabilitation of the rhetorical humanism show us more over, that the Heideggerian thesis of the priority of the poetic and metaphoric words brings us to the most important point for us: the specificity of humanistic thought that does not—in its particular and new philosophizing—begin with the problem of beings, but with that of the word, namely poetic, metaphorical, and rhetorical word. Thus, the question dealt with, goes beyond a discussion of Heidegger, to confront important historical and theoretical problems.

Graves, David and Alon, Ilai. A Language for the Description of God, Part I: A Unique Language for a Unique Object. *Int J Phil Relig*, 36(3), 169-186, D 94.

Gray, Christopher Berry. Alice in Wittgenstein: Inside the Great Mirror. *J Value Inq*, 29(1), 77-88, Mr 95.

Wittgenstein developed successively more mature understandings of how to rescue human intelligence from the flybottle of language. Alice's maturation throughout her several discussions improves her dealing with the world while exiting the mirror of imagination. The stages of each recovery are compared in order that each can help the appreciation of the other.

Gray, Vivienne. Herodotus and the Rhetoric of Otherness. *Amer J Philo*, 116(2), 185-211, Sum 95.

This paper investigates the validity of current readings of the portrayal of women in Herodotus in terms of the rhetoric of male/female otherness as defined by Hartog. The stories examined include the murder of Candaules (1.1.8-12), the exposure of Cyrus (1.107-129) and the murder of the wife of Masistes (9,108-113). The conclusion is that features currently identified as characteristic of women are also attributed to men in these and other stories. The significant otherness both for men and women depends not on gender but on status, and is particularly conveyed through the polarity of master and subject.

Graybosch, A J. *Two Concepts of Utopia*. *J Value Inq*, 29(2), 167-180, Je 95.

The priority of the good and the right reflected in utopian writing is mirrored in contemporary approaches to liberalism. The priority of the right and the good is the major area of discussion in contemporary Anglo-American political philosophy. The presence of the same difference in emphasis in utopian writing suggests that different utopian visions underlie and animate contemporary approaches to liberalism. If this perception is correct, the argument over the priority of the right and the good can be seen as one over the nature of the good life.

Greco, John. A Second Paradox Concerning Responsibility and Luck. *Metaphilosophy*, 26(1-2), 81-96, Ja-Ap 95.

A paradox arises because agents who are in certain respects similar seem deserving of similar moral evaluations. But given any agent who is a candidate for moral praise or blame, we can describe a second agent who is similar in relevant respects, but who is clearly not responsible for the event in question. It is argued that to resolve the paradox we should recognize a distinction between moral responsibility and moral worth. We can then admit that luck infects responsibility, but save the intuition that worth is isolated from the effects of luck.

Greco, John. Reid's Critique of Berkeley and Hume: What's the Big Idea?. *Phil Phenomenol Res*, 55(2), 279-296, Je 95.

Reid thought that the linchpin of his response to skepticism was his rejection of the theory of ideas. I argue that Reid's assessment of his own work is incorrect; the theory of ideas plays no important role in at least one of Berkeley's and Hume's arguments for skepticism, and rejecting the theory is therefore neither necessary nor sufficient as a reply to that argument. Reid does in fact answer the argument, but with his theory of evidence rather than his rejection of the theory of ideas.

Greeley, Roger E. *Thomas Jefferson's Freethought Legacy: A Saying Per Day by the Sage of Monticello*. Buffalo, Prometheus, 1995.

This delightful collection of quotes from Jefferson establishes, beyond dispute, his enormous contributions to rationalism, freethought and science. Often, what historians (and especially politicians) have done is to select those quotes that reflect conventional religiosity and beliefs. Here great care has been taken to exclude those quotes and to present, instead, Jefferson's freethought legacy. Readers are invited to meander through these pages enjoying the diverse and wide-ranging views of one of America's early intellectuals. Or, savor one quote each day and delight in Jefferson's well-reasoned thoughts for 365 days, and for years to come. Roger E Greeley (Kalamazoo, MI) is consultant to the North American Committee for Humanism and a retired Unitarian minister.

Green, Judith M. The Diverse Community or the Unoppressive City: Which Ideal for a Transformative Politics of Difference?. *J Soc Phil*, 26(1), 86-102, Spr 95.

Green, Lucy. Gender, Musical Meaning, and Education. *Phil Music Educ Rev*, 2(2), 99-105, Fall 94.

Green, Michele. Conflicting Principles or Completing Counterparts? J S Mill on Political Economy and the Equality of Women. *Utilitas*, 6(2), 267-285, N 94.

Green, Mitchell S. Quantity, Volubility, and Some Varieties of Discourse. *Ling Phil*, 18(1), 83-112, F 95.

Grice's quantity maxims have been widely misinterpreted as enjoining a speaker to make the strongest claim that she can, while respecting the other conversational maxims. Although many writers on the topic of conversational implicature interpret the quantity maxims as enjoining such volubility, so construed the quantity maxims are unreasonable norms for conversation. Appreciating this calls for attending more closely to the notion of what a conversation requires. When we do so, we see that eschewing an injunction to maximal informativeness need not deprive us of any ability to predict or explain genuine cases of implicature. Crucial to this explanation is an appreciation of how what a conversation, or a given stage of a conversation, requires, depends upon what kind of conversation is taking place. I close with an outline of this dependence relation that distinguishes among three importantly distinct types of conversation.

Green, Philip (ed). *Democracy*. Atlantic Highlands, Humanities Pr, 1994.

Green, Ronald M. At the Vortex of Controversy: Developing Guidelines for Human Embryo Research. *Kennedy Inst Ethics J*, 4(4), 345-356, D 94.

The author reviews the year of controversy surrounding the work of the Human Embryo Research Panel of the National Institutes of Health, on which he served. He outlines the specific recommendations of the Panel, and develops the moral arguments behind them. Particular attention is given to the Panel's most controversial recommendation: that the Federal government be allowed to fund research involving the deliberate creation of embryos for research purposes only.

Green, Stephen A. Annette Baier and the Context of Risk. *Int J Applied Phil*, 9(1), 59-65, Sum-Fall 94.

The author analyzes the ethical underpinnings of quantitative risk analysis (QRA) as a means of identifying potential health risks and distributing their consequences across society. He argues that risk-cost-benefit analysis (RCBA), based in utilitarian calculations and hypothetical contractarian agreements, can too readily impose unacceptable moral harms on individuals while attempting to maximize benefits to society as a whole. He concludes that Baier's method of contextual analysis is the most appropriate means of determining the moral acceptability of public policies that convey significant dangers of illness and death.

Green, Steven. Vigilantism and the Common Good. *Cont Phil*, 16(4), 17-22, Jl-Ag 94.

Though vigilantism and the common good may seem incompatible, I argue that this is not always so. I conclude that when it corrects the imbalance of burdens and benefits between those who abide by the law, and those who use the law's complexity to pursue their own interest at the expense of the common good, vigilantism serves that good. It meets the human needs force serves, and reminds us of the principles of practical reason which underlie a legal system and their place in securing a communal form of life where the demands of the common good may be met.

Green, William. Periodizing World History. *Hist Theor*, 34(2), 99-111, 1995.

Although the article attempts to demonstrate how comprehensive theories of change can facilitate the formulation of world history periodization, it does not minimize the difficulty of developing a universally operative organic theory of change. It examines several theoretical orientations, but principal attention is given to world-systems analysis, the most fully refined and well articulated body of theory currently commended as a vehicle for structuring world history. Acknowledging that no body of theory currently achieves a satisfactory universal integration of world history and that this situation may prevail in the future, the author recommends, for the present, an eclectic periodization of four epochs divided at roughly 1000 BCE, 400-600 CE, and *circa* 1492.

Greenawalt, Kent. *Private Consciences and Public Reasons*. New York, Oxford Univ Pr, 1995.

This book asks what kinds of grounds officials and citizens should employ in reaching and justifying political positions. Examining the views of a number of theorists, it argues that much depends on historical and cultural contexts. It rejects claims that citizens and officials should in all respects limit themselves to "public reasons" and claims that all reasons should enjoy an equal status. The intermediate position that it defends for the United States proposes greater self-limitation for judges and legislators than for citizens and greater self-limitation as to advocacy than judgment.

Greenberg, Ira and Kantor, Jeffrey and David, Jeanne M. Possible Ethical Issues and Their Impact on The Firm: Perceptions Held by Public Accountants. *J Bus Ethics*, 13(12), 919-937, D 94.

The accounting profession is concerned with the ethical beliefs of its members. To this end, the authors surveyed public accountants, questioning them about the AICPA's "Code of Professional Conduct" and their perceptions of how potentially unethical behaviors impact the firm. The paper focuses on respondents' perceptions of the impact on the firm's practice, image and degree of concern. (edited)

Greenberg, Michael and Goldberg, Laura. A Survey of Ethical Conduct in Risk Management: Environmental Economists. *Ethics Behavior*, 4(4), 331-343, 1994.

A sample survey of members of the Association of Environmental and Resource Economists (AERE) found relatively low rates of obvious ethical misconduct, such as data fabrication and falsification, and higher rates of dubious behaviors, such as deliberate overstatement of positive and understatement of negative results. AERE members reported that job-related pressures—including competition with peers, pressure due to professional implication and on-the-job pressure—were the most important causes. The most effective preventive measures, according to respondents, were discussion of ethics in existing classes, codes of ethics, and short courses at professional meetings. The vast majority of AERE members were against government audits and regulations.

Greenberg, Robert S. The Content of Kant's Logical Functions of Judgment. *Hist Phil Quart*, 11(4), 375-392, O 94.

Commentators of Kant's *Critique of Pure Reason* hold that the logical *functions* of judgment in the Table of Judgments are logical *forms* of judgment, and hence belong to formal logic. Since formal logic abstracts from all content of knowledge in general, these functions have no content. Consequently, it is incoherent for Kant to argue that the categories are identified with or are even grounded in them. The paper tries to save Kant from that incoherence by arguing that and how the functions *do* have content and that the discussion of them in the Analytic of Concepts belongs to transcendental, not formal, logic.

Greenberg, William M. Commentary on "The Alzheimer's Disease Sufferer as Semiotic Subject". *Phil Psychiat Psych*, 1(3), 163-164, S 94.

Commentary is provided on Sabat and Harré's paper, "The Alzheimer's Disease Sufferer as Semiotic Subject". Sabat and Harré sensitively recognize their Alzheimer's Disease subjects' needs for dignity, self-respect and meaning, and appropriately warn of psychometric tests' limited ability to demonstrate such individuals' best performances. However, their focus on recognizing such individuals as "semiotic subjects" (per Shweder and Sullivan) has particular limitations. "Semiotic subjecthood" is not a strong enough notion to protect against the frequent infantilization or dehumanization of these afflicted persons, and more accurately should be appreciated clinically as a (multi)dimensional rather than a categorical judgment.

Greenberg, Yudit Kornberg. Martin Heidegger and Franz Rosenzweig on the Limits of Language as Poetry. *Hist Euro Ideas*, 20(4-6), 791-800, F 95.

Greenspan, P S. *Practical Guilt: Moral Dilemmas, Emotions, and Social Norms*. New York, Oxford Univ Pr, 1994.

Moral dilemmas may be regarded as possible consequences of a set of social rules simple enough to be teachable. Their problematic motivational force can be explained by reference to the moral role of emotion. This book defends guilt in the face of dilemmas on the basis of a "nonjudgmentalist" account of emotions that accepts guilt as appropriate even in some cases of unavoidable wrongdoing. In its treatment of the role of emotion in ethics the argument of the book outlines a new way of packing motivational force into moral meaning that allows for a socially based version of moral realism.

Greenspan, Patricia. "Perspectival Guilt" in *Modality, Morality, and Belief*, Sinnott-Armstrong, Walter (ed), 129-151. New York, Cambridge Univ Pr, 1994.

I use Ruth Marcus' comments on moral dilemmas and my own treatment of guilt and emotional appropriateness in connection with dilemmas—in *Practical Guilt* (New York: Oxford, 1995)—to argue that the notion of appropriate emotional guilt can serve as the basis for a semi-objective notion of "perspectival guilt" strong enough to yield a notion of wrong suitable for dilemmas.

Gregor, Mary J. Leslie Mulholland on Kant's *Rechtslehre*. *Dialogue (Canada)*, 33(4), 693-700, Fall 94.

Gregory, Paul. "Love and Personal Relationships" in *Introducing Applied Ethics*, Almond, Brenda (ed), 33-41. Cambridge, Blackwell, 1995.

Greinacher, Norbert and Kotowski, Mathias. End of Utopia? Religion, Rationality and Art as Elements of Transcendence. *Hermathena*, 150, 45-56, Wint 93.

Grelot, Pierre. Le Combat de Kierkegaard. *Rev Thomiste*, 95(2), 195-216, Ap-Je 95.

L'aspect philosophique de l'oeuvre de Kierkegaard n'est pas examiné ici directement. Une allusion à son opposition à Hegel et à son détachement de Shelling n'interviennent qu'occasionnellement. L'essentiel concerne son combat pour la lecture "existentielle" de la Bible et du regard porté sur le Christ dans la foi. Ce souci l'a amené à combattre les théologiens et les exégètes influencés par Hegel et finalement à se séparer de l'Eglise luthérienne du Danemark. Sa névrose personnelle a malheureusement pesé sur ce combat du croyant sincère et profond: elle en explique pour une part la violence. Sa pensée reste stimulante, mais il faut tenir compte de son expression paradoxale.

Grene, Marjorie. *A Philosophical Testament*. Peru, Open Court, 1995.

The author considers a number of figures and themes in the history of philosophy and in other disciplines that have influenced her reflections. Her chief concerns have been with the problem of knowledge and the nature of the person.

Grene, Marjorie and Ariew, Roger. Ideas, In and Before Descartes. *J Hist Ideas*, 56(1), 87-106, Ja 95.

We ask how the term "idea" was used in the seventeenth century before Descartes and consider in the light of this evidence both the possible sources for Descartes's usage and the true originality in his conception. Descartes appears to be drawing on a current literary usage, in which ideas are not just exemplars in God's mind, but actual psychological events in our minds, while at the same time refusing the identification of idea and image that the new literary sense suggests. So we ask, further, where did the current image-oriented use appear in the philosophical as against the literary works of the period, and on the other hand, how does the conceptual (nonimage) use Descartes was to devise relate to the philosophical use of "idea" in general? We suggest answers to such questions by referring to a number of early seventeenth century philosophical writers: Eustachius a Sancto Paulo, Jean Crassot, Charles François d'Abra de Raconis, and Rudolph Goclenius.

Grewendorf, Günther. Interview with Noam Chomsky On Linguistics and Politics. *Protosoz*, 6, 293-303, 1994.

In this interview, MIT professor Noam Chomsky comments on what is known as the Chomskyan Turn within the recent history of modern linguistics, the major goals of generative grammar as a theory explaining the human language faculty, and its position within the fields of the cognitive sciences. He outlines the architecture of the latest model of linguistic theorizing, the *Minimalist Program*, which is committed to reducing its assumptions to cognitive principles of economy. The interview closes with some notes on Chomsky's second field of interest, the structure of political power, with Middle Eastern politics serving as an example.

Griener, Glenn G. Moral Integrity of Professions. *Prof Ethics*, 2(3-4), 15-38, Fall-Wint 93.

Griener, Glenn G. The Physician's Authority to Withhold Futile Treatment. *J Med Phil*, 20(2), 207-224, Ap 95.

The debate over futility is driven, in part, by physicians' desire to recover some measure of decision-making authority from their patients. The standard approach begins by noting that certain interventions are futile for certain patients and then asserts that doctors have no obligation to provide futile treatment. The concept of futility is a complex one, and many commentators find it useful to distinguish 'physiological futility' and 'qualitative futility'. The assertion that physicians can decide to withhold physiologically futile treatment generates little controversy. The claim that they can withhold qualitatively futile treatment runs afoul of standard objections to medical paternalism. There is reason to believe that the conceptual distinction will not be maintained in clinical practice. This paper contends that the scientific data which would support a physician's unilateral decision to withhold physiologically futile treatment also provide support for an institutional policy restricting access to the treatment. The data the doctor uses to take decision-making power out of the hands of the patient can be used by the administrator to take power out of the hands of the doctor. While this loss of power is unproblematic, there is reason to believe that the ambiguity in the term 'futility' will allow a much greater loss of physicians' power.

Griffin, Drew E. Nietzsche on Tragedy and Parody. *Phil Lit*, 18(2), 339-347, O 94.

Griffin, James. Contra la sistetización en ética. *Telos (Spain)*, 1(1), 99-128, F 92.

"Against System in Ethics" is an attempt to advance a new qualified approach to consequentialism. Human flourishing and personal committments play an important role here, so that considerations of general benevolence can never be moral "trumps". The author strengthens the link between the prudential and the moral, the "can" and the "must", in order not to make ethics too demanding. General benevolence, and general well-being, are only at the background in moral theory, as the "animating aim", but never as a first principle, as classic utilitarianism required, never within a system in ethics.

Griffin, James. Ética y Bienestar. *Telos (Spain)*, 2(2), 11-29, D 93.

How are human rights grounded in well-being? In this paper, the author tries to give an answer to the crucial question, focusing on a current—and practical—clash between Europe and Islam concerning the freedom of expression: "The Rushdie Affair". This is achieved by two ways: first through the delineation of a substantive theory of rights; and secondly, by way of an argument that tries to arrive at a solution for conflicts with liberty, namely, liberty of cult vs liberty of expression. An answer to the question about Rushdie's apparent exceeding the limits of liberty is proposed by means of the author's original concepts of personhood and practicalities. Finally, the diversity of conceptions about the "holy" is pointed out as one of the origins of the conflict. A clear defense of the primacy of liberty of expression is argued: In the future, Muslim children, Christian children, all children will grow up spontaneously questioning their way of life. The only defense is, not suppressing the questions, but having some answers.

Griffin, James. The Distinction Between Criterion and Decision Procedure: A Reply to Madison Powers. *Utilitas*, 6(2), 177-182, N 94.

This note is a reply to an article by Madison Powers in the same issue. It explores the distinction between criterion and decision procedure as it applies to utilitarianism, arguing that some of the knowledge constraints that apply to the latter must also apply to the former.

Griffin, Miriam. "Roman Suicide" in *Medicine and Moral Reasoning, Fulford, K W M (ed)*, 106-130. New York, Cambridge Univ Pr, 1994.

The purpose of this historical chapter is to explain the sophisticated type of argumentation that was developed in classical antiquity to help with making moral decisions and moral assessments in the difficult area of suicide. The current renewal of interest in practical ethics among English-speaking philosophers, as well as changing social attitudes to suicide, make it possible for us to learn from the ancient philosophical approach, which was based on the belief that suicide could be a rational act. The period particularly studied is roughly 100 BC-100 AD when many acts of suicide are given detailed treatment in classical literature.

Griffioen, Sander (ed) and Klapwijk, Jacob (ed) and Groenewoud, Gerben (ed). *Bringing into Captivity Every Thought: Capita Selecta* in the History of Christian Evaluations of Non-Christian Philosophy. Lanham, Univ Pr of America, 1991.

Griffioen, Sander (ed) and Verhoogt, Jan (ed). *Norm and Context in the Social Sciences*. Lanham, Univ Pr of America, 1990.

Griffiths, P E and Goode, R. The Misuse of Sober's Selection for/Selection of Distinction. *Biol Phil*, 10(1), 99-108, Ja 95.

Elliott Sober's selection for/selection of distinction has been widely used to clarify the idea that some properties of organisms are side-effects of selection processes. It has also been used, however, to choose between different descriptions of an evolutionary product when assigning biological functions to that product. We suggest that there is a characteristic error in these uses of the distinction. Complementary descriptions of function are misrepresented as mutually excluding one another. This error arises from a failure to appreciate that selection processes can be described at several different theoretical levels.

Griffiths, Paul E. The Cronin Controversy. *Brit J Phil Sci*, 46(1), 122-137, Mr 95.

The controversy over Helena Cronin's book 'the Ant and the Peacock', involving figures such as S J Gould, D C Dennett, J Maynard-Smith, E Sober and D Sloan-Wilson, reflects fundamental divisions in current biology and philosophy of biology. Cronin argues that a 'modern Darwinism' based on adaptationist reasoning and gene selection has replaced earlier forms of Darwinism. In fact, Cronin's 'modern Darwinism' is the view of only one school of thought in modern biology. I review the issues that divide this school from the others, and describe some recent progress on these issues.

Griffiths, Paul J. CODA. *Faith Phil*, 11(2), 286-289, Ap 94.

In "Blindingly Obvious Christian Anti-Semitism" Eleonore Stump and Norman Kretzmann further defend their claim that Christianity is not responsible for antisemitism by drawing a sharp distinction between a doctrinal account of Christianity and (what they call) a sociological one. I argue in response that the distinction they make between these two kinds of account cannot, on pain of incoherence, be drawn as sharply as they wish; that in making it they have misread my argument about the kinds of connection that obtain between Christianity and antisemitism in two important ways; and that there are good Christian doctrinal reasons for expecting that any culturally significant body of belief—including Christian doctrine itself—will be implicated with moral (as well as other kinds of) failure, and that it therefore ought not to be surprising to find a case in point.

Grim, Patrick. Tomberlin's *Philosophical perspectives, 5, Philosophy of Religion, 1991*. *Nous*, 28(3), 405-413, S 94.

This piece attempts to offer both 1) a glowing review of an excellent collection, and 2) some brief philosophical notes on a general issue underlying different arguments by different authors in the volume. It is suggested that as yet unresolved problems of several sorts arise regarding the role of counterfactuals in the standard picture of divine rationality.

Grimaldi, Nicolas. Dieu dans la philosophie de Descartes. *Acta Phil*, 2(3), 201-226, 1994.

L'idea di Dio è un concetto centrale di tutta la filosofia cartesiana, anzi si tratta di una questione che ne costituisce il fondamento. La ricerca di Dio secondo Cartesio non è comunque un movimento dimostrativo che faccia a meno del primo principio della sua filosofia: Cartesio non abbandona la dimensione definita dal *cogito* per proporre delle prove dell'esistenza di Dio. L'articolo esamina non solo le prove proposte da Cartesio per dimostrare l'esistenza di Dio, ma anche si sofferma a considerare il bisogno interno alla filosofia cartesiana, e perciò al *cogito* stesso, costituito appunto dall'esistenza di Dio come questione basilare sul piano dell'evidenza; infatti l'evidenza del primo principio cartesiano non è sufficiente per fondare tutte le istanze filosofiche che lo stesso *cogito* solleva.

Grimaltos, Tobies and Hookway, Christopher. When Deduction Leads to Belief. *Ratio*, 8(1), 24-41, Ap 95.

The paper questions the common assumption that rational individuals believe all propositions which they know to be logical consequences of their other beliefs: although we must acknowledge the truth of a proposition which is a deductive consequence of our beliefs, we may not genuinely *believe* it. This conclusion is defended by arguing that some familiar counterexamples to the claim that knowledge is justified true belief fail because they involve propositions which are not really believed. Beliefs guide conduct or issue in assertion by answering questions which arise in the course of deliberation and conversation, but the troublesome cases present propositions which do not present the agent's answer to any question. The paper concludes by sketching the conditions, under which the deductive consequences of our beliefs can be believed.

Grimm, Robert B and Galbraith, Sharon and Stephenson, Harriet Buckman. Ethical Congruency of Constituent Groups. *J Bus Ethics*, 14(2), 145-158, F 95.

This research investigates the perceptions of five constituent groups of an accredited business school—their perceptions of others' ethics, of their own ethics and ideal values, and of how business ethics can be improved. Self-described behavior from the constituent groups is quite similar, yet is decidedly different from that which respondents felt others would do. (edited)

Grint, Keith and Woolgar, Steve. On Some Failures of Nerve in Constructivist and Feminist Analyses of Technology. *Sci Tech Human Values*, 20(3), 286-310, Sum 95.

Whereas many constructivist and feminist approaches to the social study of technology share an antipathy to technological determinism, they offer an insufficiently radical critique of technology. Three main problems in "anti-essentialist" critiques of technological determinism are identified, all of which mean that such critiques remain committed to a form of essentialism. These characteristics recur in many recent feminist arguments about technology, illustrated by the example of reproductive technologies. To overcome weaknesses in political radicalism based on anti-essentialism, it is necessary to move to a "post-essentialist" approach. The unwillingness to do so is shown to be based on unfounded objections to "excessive" relativism.

Griswold, Charles. Commentary on Sayre's "Why Plato Never Had a Theory of Forms". *Proc Boston Colloq Anc Phil*, 9, 200-212, 1993.

The central issue in my exchange with Sayre (the exchange includes a reply by Sayre to my commentary on his essay) concerns the meaning of and evidence for his thesis that Plato had no theory of forms (or indeed of any other important topic). I discuss a number of points, including the meaning of the words "theory" and "form"; the problem of interpreting a Platonic dialogue; the issue of esotericism; and the problematic role of the *Epistles* in Sayre's argument. By way of illustration, I conclude with a brief discussion of the reasons for which the promised dialogue *Philosopher* was never written.

Grodin, Michael. Commentary on "Helping Ken and Marie Pines". *J Clin Ethics*, 5(2), 127-128, Sum 94.

Groenewold, Hip. Field or Print. *Synthese*, 102(1), 1-59, Ja 95.

Hard-nosed physicists are content with elementary quantum mechanics as it is. Deep searchers desire a deeper comprehension of the theory or rather of reality. Observable internal correlations in micro-systems and external correlations between widely separated parts can be calculated to the office. But how can for that purpose indispensable information be observed, coded and stored and transmitted in the real systems? A spectacular example is Einstein-Podalsky-Rosen entanglement. 'How can one part know what has been or will be happening at the other distant part?'.

Groenewoud, Gerben (ed) and Griffioen, Sander (ed) and Klapwijk, Jacob (ed). *Bringing into Captivity Every Thought: Capita Selecta in the History of Christian Evaluations of Non-Christian Philosophy*. Lanham, Univ Pr of America, 1991.

Grohe, Martin. Complete Problems for Fixed-Point Logics. *J Sym Log*, 60(2), 517-527, Je 95.

Gromow, Ivan G and Kuvakina, Olga D. Noospheric Synarchy: From an Ancient Hellenic Democracy to the Aristocracy of Spirit. *Philosophia (Athens)*, 23-24, 15-24, 1993-94.

Grondin, Jean. "Gadamer and Augustine: On the Origin of the Hermeneutical Claim to Universality" in *Hermeneutics and Truth*, Wachterhauser, Brice (ed), 137-147. Evanston, Northwestern Univ Pr, 1994.

Drawing on Gadamer's suggestion that the Augustinian and Christian idea of the incarnation of the word represents the only exception to the forgetfulness of language in Western thought, this paper stresses the hermeneutical fecundity of the notion of the inner word which highlights the imbeddedness of every expression in a previous dialogue, of context, which can never be fully stated.

Grondin, Jean. *Sources of Hermeneutics*. Albany, SUNY Pr, 1995.

This book provides an introduction to the historical sources of philosophical hermeneutics as it has come to fruition in the work of Heidegger and Gadamer. Among the sources investigated are the roots of hermeneutics in ancient thought, in Plato, Augustine, Humanism, and Husserlian phenomenology.

Grootendorst, Rob and van Eemeren, Frans H. Frans H van Eemeren and Rob Grootendorst Perelman and the Fallacies. *Phil Rhet*, 28(2), 122-133, 1995.

The authors argue that in Perelman and Olbrechts-Tyteca's New Rhetoric no critical analysis of fallacies is to be found, due to its extremely relativistic concept of reasonableness. They discuss a pragma-dialectical alternative approach to argumentation in which a critical-rationalist concept of reasonableness is adopted. Fallacies are pragma-dialectically analysed as incorrect discussion moves because they violate one or more of the rules of a critical discussion aimed at resolving a dispute. The authors argue for the integration of the New Rhetoric and Pragma-Dialectics as a result of which Perelman and Olbrechts-Tyteca's lengthy and detailed discussion of argumentation schemes and techniques is used as a rich source for the analysis of fallacies.

Groothuis, D. Wagering Belief: Examining Two Objections to Pascal's Wager. *Relig Stud*, 30(4), 479-486, D 94.

This paper concerns two objections to Pascal's wager. The first claims that Pascal's recommendation to habituate oneself to believe in God is tantamount to religious brainwashing. I argue that this construal misses important aspects of what Pascal had in mind, which may render the habituation process a legitimate means to acquire new understanding. The second objection is based on the idea that a key assumption of the wager—that theistic belief is required for eternal felicity—is morally absurd. I argue that theistic belief. as Pascal understands it, is a necessary aspect for spiritual restoration. Not merely an isolated belief in an imperious deity.

Groothuis, Douglas. Bacon and Pascal on Mastery Over Nature. *Res Phil Technol*, 14, 191-203, 1994.

Francis Bacon's vision of mastery over nature, while bold and prophetic, was flawed by hubris. Blaise Pascal accurately diagnosed the areas of hubris that Bacon never squarely faced. Pascal, born three years before Bacon's death, was a practicing scientist and an apologist for Christianity in an age of rapid scientific discovery. Bacon can be understood as an apologist for a new scientific methodology and technology. Yet despite their differences, both were pivotal figures whose reflections on humanity's place in nature remain worthy of scrutiny. I appeal to several of Pascal's insights into cosmology and human nature in order to chasten Bacon's optimism without rejecting his insights.

Gross, Alan G. Is a Science of Language Possible? The Derrida-Searle Debate. *Soc Epistem*, 8(4), 345-359, O-D 94.

Gross, Alan G. On Not Taking Sides. *Soc Epistem*, 8(4), 373-381, O-D 94.

Gross, Barry R. What Could a *Feminist* Science Be?. *Monist*, 77(4), 434-444, O 94.

Gross, Hyman. "Benign and Malign Morality" in *In Harm's Way, Coleman, Jules L (ed)*, 344-350. New York, Cambridge Univ Pr, 1994.

Groszek, Marcia. ω_1^* as an Initial Segment of the c-Degrees. *J Sym Log*, 59(3), 956-976, S 94.

By an "inverse iteration" of Sacks forcing over a model of $V = L$ we produce a model in which the degrees of constructibility of nonconstructible reals have order type ω_1^*.

Grube, Dirk-Martin. Religious Experience After the Demise of Foundationalism. *Relig Stud*, 31(1), 37-52, Mr 95.

In this article, I argue that foundationalist reconstructions of religious experience lose on all counts: First, philosophical defenses of foundationalism are untenable. Second, the theological benefits that can be reaped from foundationalism come at too high a price. I show that both William Alston's and Alvin Plantinga's foundationalism leads to sceptical conclusions. Third, I argue that the epistemic implications of foundationalist reconstructions of religious experience are incompatible with Christian ontology. Criticizing the account Plantinga develops in his books on warrant, I suggest that it is preferable to reconstruct religious experience in antifoundationalist, i.e., coherentist, terms and develop the model of a mobile for these purposes.

Gruber, Howard E. "Insight and Affect in the History of Science" in *The Nature of Insight, Sternberg, Robert J (ed)*, 397-431. Cambridge, MIT Pr, 1995.

Grünbaum, Adolf. Freud's Theory: The Perspective of a Philosopher of Science. *Proc Amer Phil Ass*, 57(1), 5-31, S 83.

This is the author's December 1982 Presidential Address to the Eastern Division of the American Philosophical Association in Baltimore, MD. Beginning with an account of Freud's own notion of the scientificity of a theory, the paper takes detailed issue with the charge of Ricoeur, Habermas and Jaspers that Freud misunderstood his own psychoanalytic enterprise "scientistically". This compliant, and its proposed alternative "hermeneutic" reconstruction of psychoanalysis are shown to rest on mythic, untutored conceptions of the natural sciences, as does Gadamer's view of science. In the second part, the author gives a highly critical appraisal of Freud's cornerstone theory of repression, comprising his accounts of psychopathology, dream-production, slip-generation and psychotherapy.

Grünberg, Ludwig. De la Justification de la Démocratie: Une Approche Universaliste. *Philosopher*, 15, 81-86, 1994.

Grünberg, Ludwig. The Future of Art and the Theory of Post-Philosophical Culture. *J Value Inq*, 28(2), 273-280, Je 94.

Grünberg, Ludwig. Universal Metaphilosophy of Life and Universalist Ethics: An Axiological Approach. *Dialogue·Hum*, 4(2-3), 67-79, 1994.

Grünewald, Bernward. "Zur moralphilosophischen Funktion des Prinzips vom höchsten Gut" in *Naturzweckmässigkeit und ästhetische Kultur, Schwabe, Karl-Heinz (ed)*, 133-139. Sankt Augustin, Academia, 1993.

Grugan, Arthur A. Heidegger on Hölderlin's *Der Rhein*: Some External Considerations. *Phil Today*, 39(1), 16-24, Spr 95.

Grugan, Arthur A. The Instress of Being and the Coronach of Dasein in Hölderlin's *Germanien*. *Heidegger Stud*, 9, 77-95, 1993.

Grumet, Madeleine R. Somewhere Under the Rainbow: The Postmodern Politics of Art Education. *Educ Theor*, 45(1), 35-42, Wint 95.

Grumley, John. Fukuyama's Hegelianism—Historical Exhaustion or Philosophical Closure. *Hist Euro Ideas*, 21(3), 379-392, My 95.

Gruzalski, Bart. Healing the Ills of Unemployment, Societal Breakdown, and Ecological Degradation: Gandhi's Vision for a Sustainable Society. *Phil Cont World*, 1(3), 22-27, Fall 94.

In this paper I describe Gandhi's vision for a way of life that would be an essential part of any sustainable solution to worldwide problems of unemployment, societal breakdown and ecological degradation. Gandhi's vision included a communitarian lifestyle of simplicity and nonaccumulation in which agriculture would be supported by cottage industries using appropriate technologies (e.g., spinning). Assuming obligations to future generations, Gandhi's proposal highlights the degree to which our First-World lifestyle is morally impermissible. One objection to this criticism of our First-World lifestyles is that we can solve the problem of ecological degradation by exporting only appropriate technologies to the Third World and supplementing our use of consumptive technologies with technological cleanups. This suggestion is not only irresponsible and unjust, but also hopeless, for our resource consumptive standards are already the model for development worldwide. To counteract this destructive model we must begin to recreate, in the First World, sustainable lifestyles that others will want to emulate. Part of this task involves the inner work that has been a casualty of the ideologies of modernity, and Gandhi's vision is a blueprint for both the outer and inner work that are essential to recreate a sustainable society.

Grzegorczyk, Andrzej. God's Action in the Human World: Our Intellectual Humility and Dialogue between Religions. *Dialogue Hum*, 3(3), 73-84, 1993.

Christianity, Islam and Judaism proclaim God's dialogue with humans. God reveals truths, summons and challenges us, also intellectually for self-criticism. If we do not undertake His challenge He hands upon another one and often repairs what was destroyed by us. The teaching of God should inspire us also to critical view on historical activities of these three religion communities. It should be a common act of humility, the necessary condition for intellectual reconciliation between Abrahamic religions.

Guagliardo, Vincent. Being-as-First-Known in Poinsot: A Priori or Aporia?. *Amer Cath Phil Quart*, 68(3), 363-393, Sum 94.

For John Poinsot (1589-1644) being-as-first-known is given primordially in the human experience of things. This experience of being, however, is not tied to the entitative order. It expresses the intentional life of the human, relating not to human intelligence as such but to the basis of intelligibility for the human knower. It indicates otherness, in which both daseinal and nondaseinal being alike are understood, constituting the "between", relatable to Heidegger's "Being". From the viewpoint of semiotics, being-as-first-known constitutes the basis of anthroposemiosis, in which the "pre-apprehension of being" demarcates human semiosic activity from that of other beings, such as animals.

Guariglia, Osvaldo. "Se debe", entonces "yo debo": implicación?. *Rev Latin de Filosof*, 20(2), 303-310, 1994.

In this paper I examine the metaethical thesis of R M Hare that "if a person says 'I ought to act in a certain way, but nobody else ought to act in that way in relevantly similar circumstances', then he is implicitly contradicting himself". P Winch has argued against Hare that when somebody says 'This is what I ought to do', there is nothing in the meaning of 'ought' which logically commits him to accepting as a corollary: 'And anyone else in a situation like this ought to do the same', because the meaning of 'ought' in this sentence is primary 'expressive'. As a proof of his contention Winch exposes the story of the well known tale of H Melville, "Billy Budd, Foretopman", and places himself in the shoes of captain Vere. With the aid of another story, "Emma Zuntz", of J L Borges, I demonstrate that the difference between the prescriptive and the expressive meaning of 'ought' lies in the difference of the grammatical person: in the first person, it is expressive; in the third, impersonal, universalizable and prescriptive.

Guariglia, Osvaldo. "Universalismo y Particularismo en la Etica Contemporánca" in *Temas Actuales de Filosofía, Palacios, María Julia (ed)*, 13-33. Buenos Aires, Univ Nacional Salta, 1993.

Guariglia, Osvaldo. Respuesta a algunas objectiones. *Rev Latin de Filosof*, 20(2), 327-332, 1994.

Guariglia, Osvaldo. Universalismo y Particularismo en la Ética Contemporánea. *Rev Filosof (Spain)*, 7(11), 177-198, 1994.

Guarino, Thomas G. Rahner, Popper and Kuhn: A Note on Some Critical Parallels in Science and Theology. *Phil Theol*, 8(1), 83-89, Autumn 93.

The article discusses some parallels between *Weltanschauung* analysis in contemporary philosophy of science and Rahner's criticism of the context/content approach to theological pluralism.

Guattari, Félix and Bains, Paul (trans) and Pefanis, Julian (trans). *Chaosmosis: An Ethico-Aesthetic Paradigm*. Bloomington, Indiana Univ Pr, 1995.

Gubar, Susan. Feminist Misogyny: Mary Wollstonecraft and the Paradox of "It Takes One to Know One". *Fem Stud*, 20(3), 453-473, Fall 94.

Gubman, Boris L. The Horizons of the Organic Vision of the Universe and Humanity: Vladimir Solovyev Revisited in the Light of Process Theology. *Process Stud*, 22(4), 211-214, Winter 93.

Günther, Klaus. Legal Adjudication and Democracy: Some Remarks on Dworkin and Habermas. *Euro J Phil*, 3(1), 36-54, Ap 95.

Günzler, Claus. Späte Begegnung: Ernst Cassirer und Albert Schweitzer: Biographische Anmerkungen zur deutschen Kulturphilosophie. *Z Phil Forsch*, 49(2), 312-320, Ap Jo 95.

The article elucidates the biographical circumstances and the philosophical consequences of the encounter, in Oxford, between E Cassirer and A Schweitzer on the 18th October 1934. Against the backdrop of the Nazi rise to power, Cassirer adopted Schweitzer's analysis of culture and particularly his criticism of purely academically oriented philosophy, views Schweitzer had published as early as 1923. From then on Cassirer saw it as his role to represent philosophy as the guardian of public culture and as the unambiguous advocate of reason and freedom.

Guerrero M, Luis. La Claridad en el Pensamiento. *Topicos*, 1(1), 89-97, 1991.

Guéry, François. Leibniz et les Langues. *Rev Phil Fr*, 2, 239-250, Ap-Je 95.

Guglielmina, Pierre (trans) and Hartje, Hans (trans) and Strauss, Leo. Le problème de la connaissance dans la doctrine philosophique de Fr H Jacobi (II). *Rev Metaph Morale*, 99(4), 505-532, O-D 94.

Guichardet, Jeannine. Edgar Quinet, Chantre de "La Grèce Moderne". *Diotima*, 22, 111-121, 1994.

Guidelli, Chiara. Estetica e storia dell'estetica: una questione ancora aperta in Italia. *Teoria*, 14(1), 109-128, 1994.

Guignon, Charles (ed) and Pereboom, Derk (ed). *Existentialism: Basic Writings—Kierkegaard, Nietzsche, Heidegger, Sartre*. Indianapolis, Hackett, 1995.

This collection of readings from the four most influential existentialists features extensive introductions by the volume's editors. The general introduction, "The Legacy of Existentialism," sets existentialism in the context of modern thought, and examines the enduring relevance of its discussions of freedom, commitment, agency, authenticity, human nature, moral obligation, faith, and perspectivism. The editors also present original scholarly interpretations of each of the philosophers whose works appear in the book. The volume includes long, continuous selections from *Fear and Trembling, The Gay Science, Being and Time, Being and Nothingness*, and other works.

Guillemot, Jean-Louis. L'évolution de la critique de l'hermenéutique chez Habermas. *Eidos*, 11(1-2), 55-75, Je-D 93.

This paper gives a critical account of the evolution of Habermas's position towards hermeneutics. During the 70's, he refutes hermeneutics claim's to universality at two levels: i) Hermeneutics is unable to reconstruct the monological linguistics system of formal sciences; ii) The critique of Ideology is the only critical theory able to restore the linguistic agreement (*Verständigung*) when the meaning of our discourse is systematically distorted. *Moral and Communication* (1983) and the ethics of discussion mark a shift in the Habermassian conception of hermeneutics: The hermeneutics of tradition is revalorised in the process of choosing valid norms for practical discussions.

Guillermo Pissinis, C. Dato e interpretación: el problema de la base empírica del psicoanálisis. *Rev Filosof (Argentina)*, 9(1-2), 3-27, N 94.

The aim of this paper is to analyze the epistemological problem about the validity of psychoanalytic hypotheses tested "on the couch". In order to assess it, two issues are considered. An examination of the structure of this theory so as to be able to reject the Popperian criticism concerning the untestability of Freudian hypotheses. On the contrary, the demarcation criterion, as it was set by Popper, is met by psychoanalysis. Nonetheless, one important question remains: where can psychoanalytic theory be tested? I consider three difficulties regarding the appropriateness of clinical method as the way to do it. Because of this, it ought to be recognized by psychoanalysts that their confidence on the data given by patients under treatment is unavailing. (edited)

Guindon, André. Pour une éthique du vêtement ou de la nudité?. *Laval Theol Phil*, 50(3), 555-574, O 94.

Au moment où les questions sur la nudité refont surface, et que s'imposent de nouveaux discernements éthiques, il importe de revoir là-dessus le sens de la "preuve patristique", telle qu'établie par Erik Peterson. Sa thèse sera ici contestée sur deux points fondamentaux: le sens de la nudité mythique d'Adam et ave, et de celle des néophytes au baptême.

Guisán, Esperanza. A favor de la sistematización en Ética: Una réplica a James Griffin. *Telos (Spain)*, 1(1), 129-146, F 92.

This reply to "Against System in Ethics" stresses both agreement and disagreement between the author and Griffin's point of view. There is an argument for a strong link between the prudential and the moral, as well as for the relevance of personal excellence and personal flourishing. However there is a proposal here to make personal, individual, flourishing dependent on *sympathetic* feelings and a broad frame of mind so to embrace individual and personal flourishing for everybody else. Griffin's aminating aim, is brought from the background to the front now, as the author believes that general benevolence *frees* every single person from petty feelings and misery (moral and otherwise).

Gulick, Walter B. The Creativity of Intellect: From Ontology to Meaning—The Transmutation of the Sensible and Intelligible Worlds in Kant's Critical Work. *Ultim Real Mean*, 17(2), 99-1, Ju 94.

Gulick, Walter B and Ess, Charles M. Kant and Analogy: Categories as Analogical Equivocals. *Ultim Real Mean*, 17(2), 89-99, Ju 94.

Kant's critical philosophy is hobbled by a charge of contradiction regarding his central notion of the thing-in-itself. Textual analysis shows, however, that Kant's use of the categories—including the fundamental category of causality—intentionally takes up analogical predication to allow for a primary meaning of the category to refer phenomena, while a secondary meaning refers to the relationship between things-in-themselves and phenomena. This use of analogical predication preempts the familiar charge of contradiction and allows Kant to speak coherently of the things-in-themselves, including human freedom and (the idea of) God.

Gumpel, Liselotte. "Language as Bearer of Meaning: The Phenomenology of Roman Ingarden" in *Kunst und Ontologie, Wlodzimierz, Galewicz (ed)*, 21-57. Amsterdam, Rodopi, 1994.

Ingarden's "Phenomenology" is well suited to analyzing the reciprocity between "pure-intentional object" and "intending act"—between world content and speaker intent—which generates the sphere of "ontic heteronomy", signitively induced. Only after the sentence has formed in the "correlation" of "meaning" and "signifying" (Meinen/Vermeinen), may it become functionally literal or literary: either it undergoes "adequation" with an objective referent or it creates worlds from words, minus a reality-nexus, with every semantic aspect determining the identity of the fictional "object". Ingarden enabled me to develop a non-Aristotelian theory of semantics that treats meaning and metaphor—reference and transference—in language functionally by assessing deployment rather than denomination of content.

Gunderson, Keith. Movements, Actions, the Internal, and *Hauser Robots*. *Behavior Phil*, 22(1), 29-33, Spr-Sum 94.

Gunderson, Martin and Mayo, David J. "Privacy and the Ethics of Outing" in *Gay Ethics, Murphy, Timothy F (ed)*, 47-65. New York, Haworth Pr, 1994.

This essay argues that, in the absence of a compelling justification, outing is immoral as a violation of privacy. Reasons for respecting privacy involve fundamental interests which encompass information about gay and lesbian sexual orientation. Utilitarian defenses of outing are criticized, as is Richard Mohr's analysis of privacy and defense of outing in the name of dignity. Mohr's claim that gay or lesbian sexual orientation does not fall within the scope of the right to privacy is rejected.

Gunn, Giles. "Pragmatism, Democracy, and the Imagination: Rethinking the Deweyan Legacy" in *Pragmatism: From Progressivism to Postmodernism, Hollinger, Robert (ed)*, 298-313. Westport, Praeger, 1995.

Gunter, Pete A Y. "Coherence Lost": Education, Modernity, and Fractured Meaning. *Humanist*, 55(3), 25-30, My-Je 95.

This essay is a critique of hierarchical and analytical (atomistic) assumptions behind both modern thought and modern education. In their place, the author proposes the Whiteheadian notions of creativity and internal relation. Analytical-hierarchical approaches lead both to the ignoring of wholeness in knowledge and to over-reliance on merely technical solution to the problems of education. The author stresses Whitehead's insistence that all education should have both a strict, technical component *and* a broad humanist side. Even the technical side of education should not lose sight of "grounded knowing": of context, concrete realities, and their interrelations.

Gupta, Narendra Nath. On Wittgenstein's Way of Doing Philosophy. *Darshana Int*, 32(4/128), 60-66, O 92.

This paper aims at providing a philosophical account of the phenomenon of arising a philosophical problem. This account differs from Wittgensteinian one which maintains that philosophical problems arise when language is misused. In the light of the account, provided by this paper, it seems reasonable to believe that Wittgenstein's way of doing philosophy is not entirely opposed to the traditional way of doing philosophy, for the both ways of doing philosophy share a common phase, which consists in perceiving clearly a philosophical problem.

Gupta, R K. A Look at the Ethics of the *Gītā*. *J Indian Counc Phil Res*, 11(2), 122-125, Ja-Ap 94.

Gupta, R K. Mirror of Consciousness. *Indian Phil Quart*, 21(3), 249-255, Jl 94.

The article supports the view that the correspondence or Mirror theory of truth cannot avoid infinite regress. But although this is so ultimately, nonultimately steps can be taken to make our consciousness as mirror-like as possible. These steps include intellectual clarity, exactness and discrimination and moral impartiality. The article adds that, from the point of view of what is given, it does not matter whether one is an epistemological realist or epistemological idealist. This does not, however, mean that the distinction between the two disappears.

Gustafson, James M. Explaining and Valuing: An Exchange between Theology and the Human Sciences. *Zygon*, 30(2), 159-175, Je 95.

A comparison of E O Wilson's *On Human Nature* and Abraham Heschel's *Who Is Man?* introduces a discussion of how descriptions and explanations of the human are related to valuations of the human. More intense comparative analysis focuses on Melvin Konner, *The Tangled Wing*, and Reinhold Niebuhr, *The Nature and Destiny of Man*. Similarities of outlook toward life in the world are noted, although the supporting information, concepts, and arguments are radically different. The article illustrates how a subject matter, here the human, that is addressed by different disciplines and methods can yield fruitful interdisciplinary analysis.

Gustafson, James M. Response to Rottschaefer, Beckley, and Konner. *Zygon*, 30(2), 221-226, Je 95.

All three articles properly locate my work as interactive between the sciences on the one hand and theology and ethics on the other. They disagree on whether tradition, science, or experience "trumps" the others when they conflict; Beckley shows the importance of tradition, which is slighted by the other two. Comments on each article indicate where further discussion is needed and where I have learned from the authors or agree with them.

Gustafson, James M. Tracing a Trajectory. *Zygon*, 30(2), 177-190, Je 95.

Theology and ethics intersect with sciences at different points depending upon whether the scholars involved are interested in, for example, general epistemological issues or practical moral judgments. The intersection affects theology and ethics in different ways, depending upon various commitments or resistances on the part of theologians. The author surveys his own writings to show how openness to the sciences has had an impact on various phases of his work and what issues remain somewhat unresolved.

Gustafsson, Barbro and Pörn, Ingmar. A Motivational Approach to Confirmation: An Interpretation of Dysphagic Patients' Experiences. *Theor Med*, 15(4), 409-430, D 94.

In this paper we articulate confirmation and disconfirmation as components in human motivation. We develop a theory of motivation on the basis of a model of human action and we explore aspects of confirmation and disconfirmation in the context of the meeting of dysphagic patients with their physicians. We distinguish four central elements in confirmation and disconfirmation and use these and the relations between them for the purpose of constructing a typology. Finally, on the basis of the results obtained we interpret a small volume of remarks reflecting the meaning field of some dysphagic patients in relation to the physicians. The underlying motive is to develop tools for understanding health care processes. The "SAUC-Confirmation-Model" and the theoretical framework in which it is embedded should be seen from that point of view.

Gutenberg, Norbert and Johnstone Jr, Henry W. On the Category of the Controversial: An Approach through Schleiermacher's Dialectic. *Phil Rhet*, 27(4), 347-358, 1994.

All theories of argumentation and all rhetorical concepts have to do, either implicitly or explicitly, with the category of the controversial.' In this article I shall attempt to approach the Category of the Controversial from the point of view of philosophical dialectic. My project presupposes the recovery of the unity of the epistemic and communicative aspects of dialectic and rhetoric. In Friedrich Schleiermacher's "Dialectic" both the communicative basis of knowledge and the epistemic aspect of communication become evident. The Category of the Controversial can be defined on this basis through the occurrence together of communicative and epistemic differences, which, in the process of communication, become oppositions that are seen as in need of resolution. (edited)

Gutheil, Thomas G. Discussion of Lazarus's "How Certain Boundaries and Ethics Diminish Therapeutic Effectiveness". *Ethics Behavior*, 4(3), 295-298, 1994.

Discussion centers on three rubrics. First, intent vs impact: Dr Lazarus describes benign intent in his interventions, but scants the impact on the patient, who may perceive the intervention differently. Second, boundary crossing vs boundary violation: the former represents a mere deviation from standard role functions which advances the therapy and does not harm the patient; the latter represents an exploitative, harmful deviation that may render therapy invalid. Third, the development of our field: many archaic practices in our field (e.g., nude marathons in hot tubs) are now eschewed. Understanding these distinctions is important to clinicians.

Gutiérrez, Gilberto and Salcedo, Damián and Lara, Francisco. Observaciones y respuesta. *Rev Filosof (Spain)*, 4(6), 429-436, 1991.

Gutiérrez, Ramón Mandado. La Estética del Estado en la Polis Clásica. *An Seminar Hist Filosof*, 11, 53-75, 1994.

The political experience which the classical 'Polis' was based on seemed unavoidable and even natural to those who philosophically reflected on it; besides, it can be considered, for the view of the contemporary philosophy, 'existenciary' and 'aporetic'. In V b.C. Athenes, we can find political formulae which show the strength which, connected to the expression of the public matters, is held by aesthetic experience, myth and metaphor. Something that attracts our attention about then is the wish to make perfect the human ways of living on, living together and belonging according to the patterns related to life experience (physical, corporeal, family related...).

Gutiérrez Esturo, José Luis. El Espejismo Feminista. *El Basilisco*, 17, 51-66, Ju-De 94.

The Feminist Mirage is an examination of a wide variety of topics (from philosophy of science, history and archaeology, and theory of art to literature and even Christian theology), all of them labelled as "the feminist approach" against the so-called patriarchal science and culture. The author asks himself in perplexity how such a methodology "ad hoc" so flawed, using dubious scientific data and without any respect for evidence and argument, has become accepted by most of the public (through the mass media), and what is more dangerous by scholars. Furthermore, an ideology so coercive and devoid of sound thinking is acclaimed as the height of "the progressiveness"! What is hidden behind such a cowardly attitude?

Gutman, Amy. Civic Education and Social Diversity. *Ethics*, 105(3), 557-579, Ap 95.

Gutmann, Amy. Das Problem des Multikulturalismus in der politischen Ethik. *Deut Z Phil*, 43(2), 273-305, 1995.

Guttenplan, Samuel (ed). *A Companion to the Philosophy of Mind*. Cambridge, Blackwell, 1994.

Guttenplan, Samuel. Belief, Knowledge and the Origins of Content. *Dialectica*, 48(3-4), 287-305, 1994.

Virtually all discussions of the propositional attitudes center around belief. I suggest that, when one takes a broad look at the kinds of constraint which affect our attributions of attitude, this is a mistake. Not only is belief not properly representative of the propositional attitudes generally, but, more seriously, taking it to be representative can be positively distorting. In this paper I offer reasons why we should give knowledge a more central role in discussions of the propositional attitudes and suggest that its almost complete neglect in current philosophy of mind is unjustified. In essence, I argue that we should consider knowledge to be the central attitude and think of belief as a later and special development of the attitude scheme. In place of the usual explanation of knowledge as belief plus something, we should think of belief as knowledge minus something. The final sections choose Kripke's puzzle about belief as an example of where the conventional wisdom leads us astray.

Gutterman, David S. "Postmodernism and the Interrogation of Masculinity" in *Theorizing Masculinities, Brod, Harry (ed)*, 219-238. Newbury Park, Sage, 1994.

This paper examines the implications of postmodern conceptions of subjectivity on theoretical and political challenges to normative masculinity. I discuss the ways in which gay male gender identity and the deconstructive efforts of pro-feminist men illustrate the contingency of masculinity and inform potential strategies for social change.

Gutting, Gary. Foucault's Genealogical Method. *Midwest Stud Phil*, 15, 327-343, 1990.

Guyer, Paul. "Locke's Philosophy of Language" in *The Cambridge Companion to Locke, Chappell, Vere (ed)*, 115-145. New York, Cambridge Univ Pr, 1994.

Guyer, Paul. Beauty, Sublimity, and Expression: Reply to Wicks and Cantrick. *J Aes Art Crit*, 53(2), 194-195, Spr 95.

Gyekye, Kwame. "An Essay on African Philosophical Thought—The Akan Conceptual Scheme" in *African Philosophy: Selected Readings, Mosley, Albert G (ed)*, 339-349. Englewood Cliffs, Prentice Hall, 1995.

Haac, Oscar A (ed & trans). *The Correspondence of John Stuart Mill and Auguste Comte*. New Brunswick, Transaction Books, 1995.

Haack, Susan. *Evidence and Inquiry: Towards Reconstruction in Epistemology*. Cambridge, Blackwell, 1995.

The chief purposes of the book are to articulate a new theory of empirical justification, "foundherentism"; to show that it can withstand the objections fatal to more familiar theories; and to defend the legitimacy of epistemology. The book includes detailed explication of the foundherentist criteria of good evidence; arguments that satisfaction of those criteria is truth-indicative if any truth-indication is possible; case studies of C I Lewis's foundationalism, BonJour's and Davidson's coherentism, Popper's "epistemology without a knowing subject," and Goldman's reliabilism; a disambiguation of Quine's "epistemology naturalized" and defense of a modest naturalism; and detailed critiques of Rorty's, Stich's, and the Churchlands' arguments against epistemology.

Haag, Louis J. "The Abortion Dilemma" in *The 1994 Annual of Hermeneutics and Social Concern, Lawler, Justus George (ed)*, 224-259. New York, Continuum, 1994.

Haar, Michel. Nietzsche and Van Gogh: Representing the Tragic. *Res Phenomenol*, 24, 15-24, 1994.

Haber, Joram G (ed) and Cahn, Steven M (ed). *Twentieth Century Ethical Theory*. Englewood Cliffs, Prentice Hall, 1995.

Twentieth Century Ethical Theory is a compilation of the complete texts of many of the most influential or provocative papers in twentieth-century, Anglo-American ethical theory beginning with G E Moore's "The Subject-Matter of Ethics" and concluding with Judith Thomson's Presidential Address for the 89th Annual Eastern Division Meeting of the American Philosophical Association. Selections from some major books of the period also have been included. The readings are presented chronologically in order to clarify and emphasize their historical sequence. The book also contains an overview of twentieth century ethical theory written by James Rachels exclusively for this volume.

Haberman, Bonna Devora. What is the Content of Education in a Democratic Society?. *J Phil Educ*, 28(2), 183-189, Wint 94.

Democratic theory values diversity and pluralism, a market-place of visions and experiences of the good life. Presently conceived, education in democratic societies, because of the assumed requirement of neutrality concerning life choices, deters the flourishing of valuable versions of the good life which are the *sine qua non* of democratic society. A proposal is made about education which, on the one hand, upholds the relationships of democratic society, but at the same time fosters co-existence with dignity of a plethora of cultural, ideological, ethnic and religious life options.

Habermas, Jürgen. "Peirce and Communication" in *Peirce and Contemporary Thought: Philosophical Inquiries, Ketner, Kenneth Laine (ed)*, 243-266. New York, Fordham Univ Pr, 1995.

Habermas, Jürgen. On the Internal Relation Between the Rule of Law and Democracy. *Euro J Phil*, 3(1), 12-20, Ap 95.

Habermas, Jürgen. Reconciliation through the Public Use of Reason: Remarks on John Rawls' Political Liberalism. *J Phil*, 92(3), 109-131, Mr 95.

Habermas, Jürgen. Three Normative Models of Democracy. *Constellations*, 1(1), 1-10, Ap 94.

I would like to sketch a proceduralist view of democracy and deliberative politics which differs in relevant aspects from both the liberal and the republican paradigm. Let me 1) remind you the opposite features of these two established models. I will then 2) introduce a new proceduralist conception by way of a critique of the "ethical overload" of the republican view. The last part of the paper further elaborates 3) the three normative models of democracy by comparing their corresponding images of state and society.

Habermas, Jürgen and Haller, Michael (ed). *Vergangenheit als Zukunft*. Vienna, Piper, 1993.

Habermehl, Lawrence. *The Counterfeit Wisdom of Shallow Minds: A Critique of Some Leading Offenders of the 1980's*. New York, Lang, 1995.

During the 1980s American popular opinion was heavily influenced by the ideas of several highly-visible public figures whose misguided views continue to command the respect and endorsement of millions. This book systematically exposes the distortions and misunderstandings that permeate four of these positions: the "metaphysical" speculations of Shirley MacLaine, the Nicaraguan policy of Ronald Reagan, the Rocky and Rambo films of Sylvester Stallone, and the electronic evangelism of Jim and Tammy Bakker. Through vigorous and sustained critiques, the author shows that all of them, though posturing as wise approaches to important problems, are so severely flawed as to constitute prime examples of shallow-minded thought.

Hacker, P M S. *Appearance and Reality: A Philosophical Investigation into Perception and Perceptual Qualities*. Cambridge, Blackwell, 1991.

The subject is the claim that secondary qualities are mind-dependent or relative, rather than objective features of reality. The origins and development of this conception of appearance and reality from Galileo onwards are sketched. An analysis of sensation and perception leads to a critical examination of 4 theses: 1) that such perceptual qualities, as we perceive them, are sensations; 2) that as they are in objects, they are dispositions to cause sensations; 3) that concepts of such qualities are explained by reference to how things appear to a normal observer under normal conditions; 4) that secondary qualities, though not subjective, are relative. The concepts of the senses are anatomized and the concepts of various perceptual qualities (colour, sound, smell, etc.) are analyzed. An analytic account of the notions of the apparent and the real, and of the distinctions between appearances and perceptual experience is given.

Hacking, I. "The Logic Of Pascal's Wager" in *Gambling on God: Essays on Pascal's Wager, Jordan, Jeffrey (ed)*, 21-29. Lanham, Rowman & Littlefield, 1994.

A reprint of American Philosophy Quarterly 9 (No 2) April 1972, 186-192.

Hacking, Ian. Memoro-Politics, Trauma and the Soul. *Hist Human Sci*, 7(2), 29-52, My 94.

Three new sciences of memory arise during the nineteenth century. One is anatomical, located in the brain, one, which started in the physicological model, became statistical. The other is pathological. All three, but especially the last, represent positivist ways of studying the soul. During the same time frame of late nineteenth century trauma turns from being physical lesion to psychological pain, and is used as an explanation of amnesia. All these events provide a "memoro-politics", analogous to Foucault's biopolitics and anatomo-politics which provides the ground for contemporary debates about memory as science, standing as surrogate for spiritual debates about the soul.

Haddox, Bruce. Meditations On the Shared Life. *Tradition Discovery*, 21(1), 12-19, 1994-95.

This paper examines the dominant Western image of Being as presence. It then explores William Poteat's alternative picture of our mindbodily inherence in a world and its relevance for a more adequate understanding of our lived existence.

Hadley, Robert F. Systematicity Revisited: Reply to Chater and Christiansen and Niklasson and Van Gelder. *Mind Lang*, 9(4), 431-444, D 94.

Hadley, Robert F. The "Explicit-Implicit" Distinction. *Mind Mach*, 5(2), 219-242, My 95.

Much of traditional AI exemplifies the "explicit representation" paradigm, and during the late 1980's a heated debate arose between the classical and connectionist camps as to whether beliefs and rules receive an explicit or implicit representation in human cognition. In a recent paper, Kirsh (1990) questions the coherence of the fundamental distinction underlying this debate. He argues that our basic intuitions concerning "explicit" and "implicit" representations are not only confused but inconsistent. Ultimately, Kirsh proposes a new formulation of the distinction, based upon the criterion of *constant time processing*. The present paper examines Kirsh's claims. It is argued that Kirsh fails to demonstrate that our usage of "explicit" and "implicit" is seriously confused or inconsistent. Furthermore, it is argued that Kirsh's new formulation of the explicit-implicit distinction is excessively stringent, in that it banishes virtually all sentences of natural language from the realm of explicit representation. By contrast, the present paper proposes definitions for "explicit" and "implicit" which preserve most of our strong intuitions concerning straightforward uses of those terms. It is also argued that the distinction delineated here sustains the meaningfulness of the above-mentioned debate between classicists and connectionists.

Hadot, Pierre and Davidson, Arnold I (ed) and Chase, Michael (trans). *Philosophy as a Way of Life: Spiritual Exercises from Socrates to Foucault*. Cambridge, Blackwell, 1995.

Haeberer, Armando M and Baum, Gabriel A and Frias, Marcelo F. Fork Algebras are Representable. *Bull Sec Log*, 24(2), 64-75, Je 95.

Fork algebras are extensions of relation algebras by a new binary operator, *fork*. The expressiveness of fork algebras is known to encompass that of first order logic with equality, i.e., in any proper fork algebra (a standard model) every binary relation that is first-order definable is also denoted by a fork term. Here we complement this result by a representation theorem: every atomic abstract fork algebra is isomorphic to a proper one. This gives a framework specially adequate for program specification and development within relational calculi.

Haefliger, Gregor. "Ens multipliciter dicitur: The Ingardian Variant of an Old Thesis" in *Kunst und Ontologie, Wlodzimierz, Galewicz (ed)*, 59-77. Amsterdam, Rodopi, 1994.

Häfner, Ansgar. *Sehnsucht—Affekt und Antrieb: Begriff, Struktur und praktische Bedeutung*. Freiburg, Alber, 1993.

Häyry, Heta and Häyry, Matti. "The Nature and Role of Professional Codes in Modern Society" in *Ethics and the Professions, Chadwick, Ruth (ed)*, 136-144. Brookfield, Avebury, 1994.

It is argued in this article that the role of professional codes is twofold. On the one hand, they should ensure that professionals know how to satisfy people's needs. Professional codes should thus include a nonmoral element, which defies the technical skills that doctors, lawyers, journalists or business executives must possess in order to be true professionals. On the other hand, since professional activities produce undesirable as well as desirable consequences, the codes must also determine the ethical rules that professionals ought to follow in order to avoid the condemnation of public opinions, laws and ethical theories.

Häyry, Heta and Häyry, Matti. Obedience to Rules and Berkeley's Theological Utilitarianism. *Utilitas*, 6(2), 233-242, N 94.

In this paper the ethical theory of George Berkeley as expressed in his sermon *Passive Obedience* is studied. Two conclusions are reached. First, Berkeley's theory can most probably be classified as a form of 'ideal rule-utilitarianism', as this doctrine is understood in contemporary literature. Second, however, Berkeley's theological views forced him to demand, against his own initial commitment to utilitarianism, obedience to rules which do not in the real world promote the greatest happiness of humankind.

Häyry, Matti and Häyry, Heta. "The Nature and Role of Professional Codes in Modern Society" in *Ethics and the Professions, Chadwick, Ruth (ed)*, 136-144. Brookfield, Avebury, 1994.

It is argued in this article that the role of professional codes is twofold. On the one hand, they should ensure that professionals know how to satisfy people's needs. Professional codes should thus include a nonmoral element, which defies the technical skills that doctors, lawyers, journalists or business executives must possess in order to be true professionals. On the other hand, since professional activities produce undesirable as well as desirable consequences, the codes must also determine the ethical rules that professionals ought to follow in order to avoid the condemnation of public opinions, laws and ethical theories.

Häyry, Matti and Häyry, Heta. Obedience to Rules and Berkeley's Theological Utilitarianism. *Utilitas*, 6(2), 233-242, N 94.

In this paper the ethical theory of George Berkeley as expressed in his sermon *Passive Obedience* is studied. Two conclusions are reached. First, Berkeley's theory can most probably be classified as a form of 'ideal rule-utilitarianism', as this doctrine is understood in contemporary literature. Second, however, Berkeley's theological views forced him to demand, against his own initial commitment to utilitarianism, obedience to rules which do not in the real world promote the greatest happiness of humankind.

Hagengruber, Ruth. *Tommaso Campanella: Eine Philosophie der Ähnlichkeit*. Sankt Augustin, Academia, 1994.

Nach Michel Foucault ist die Ähnlichkeitsepisteme der Renaissance eine vorwissenschaftliche Erkenntnisform. Diese Auffassung wird widerlegt durch die Philosophie Campanellas, die gerade in der Ähnlichkeitswahrnehmung das wissenschaftliche Messen und Erkennen begründet. Zum ersten Mal wird in diesem Buch Campanellas eigenständige Ähnlichkeitslehre nachgezeichnet. Campanella definiert Ähnlichkeit nicht als Merkmalsübereinstimmung, sondern leitet sie aus dem *Primalitätenmotiv* und seiner Gegensatzlehre ab. Sein philosophisches Schaffen fasst er unter dem programmatischen Titel einer *Instauratio scientarum* zusammen. Die Begründung der Wissenschaften zeigt ihn als Zeitgenossen von Galilei und Descartes, aber auch als Kritiker eines mathematischen Wissenschaftverständnisses.

Hager, Paul J. *Continuity and Change in the Development of Russell's Philosophy*. Dordrecht, Kluwer, 1994.

Russell has had a reputation amongst philosophers for repeatedly and erratically changing his philosophical position. Recently there have been signs of a growing awareness that the extent of these changes may have been greatly exaggerated. Based on a general account of Russellian analysis, this book provides a detailed elucidation of the fundamental unity that lies within all of Russell's philosophical work, as well as of the reasons for those limited orderly changes that did, in fact, occur within it. Russellian analysis turns out to have a highly organized structure, which he consistently applied throughout all of his post-idealist philosophizing.

Hahn, Karl. "Fichtes und Prodhons Begriff des Eigentums als Recht auf Arbeit" in *Das geistige Erbe Europas, Buhr, Manfred (ed)*, 548-557. Napoli, Vivarium, 1994.

Western economic order is regarded incompatible with the right to work as realized in Socialist systems. Fichte elaborates this right as elementary though and as key issue of proprietary right. He also emphasizes the universal and international dimension of the right to work. According to Fichte, people out of work living in underprivileged countries may demand work from the propertied classes in privileged nations. Working on this theory and our economic constitution Karl Hahn gives evidence of the lasting actuality of the philosopher.

Hahn, Karl. Die Idee der Nation als Implikat der Interpersonalitäts- und Geschichtstheorie. *Fichte-Studien*, 2, 20-26, 1990.

In this essay, Karl Hahn tries to point out the dialectical coherence between interpersonality, language, time, history and nationality. Especially the very significance of the concept of interpersonality in this context will be illustrated. By interpreting and reflecting on quotations, the reader will gain a new understanding of the phenomenology of the national, which allows to comprehend a great variety of phenomenons concerning the national subject. What a gain not only for the political science, but also for many other sciences like ethnology, anthropology or sociology!

Hahn, Lewis Edwin (ed). *The Philosophy of Paul Ricoeur*. Chicago, Open Court, 1995.

The volume follows the standard format of the Library of Living Philosophers with Ricoeur's Intellectual Autobiography, critical essays by twenty-five highly diverse, able natives of seven different countries with his replies, and an exceptionally extensive bibliography compiled by Frans D Vansina and Ricoeur. His autobiography and dialogues with his critics shed fresh light both on the development of his own views and the intellectual climate of our time. The extraordinarily broad range of his writings from history of philosophy, literary criticism, and aesthetics to metaphysics, ethics and morals, religion and theology, semiotics, psychoanalysis, Marxism, and conflict of interpretations makes for a rich volume.

Hahn, Susan. Hegel on Saying and Showing. *J Value Inq*, 28(2), 151-168, Je 94.

Hegel's most interesting and controversial claims about nonconceptual knowledge arise in contexts of value. This paper examines the relation between nonconceptual and conceptual knowledge in Hegel's Phenomenology, specifically in connection with early Greek aesthetics. I take up Hegel's claim that the ancient Greeks expressed in their myths, religious narratives, sculpture, and artistic materials certain high powered philosophical truths which they shouldn't express in words. I raise a paradox about his claims and show how his claims about ineffable knowledge clash with his general propositional criterion of knowledge, namely, that for something to count as knowledge it must be expressible in words. However I argue that Hegel's thoughts about the matter were coherent and I solve the paradox.

Haight, Catherine and Whitman, Jeffrey P and Tipton, Paul. Citizens and Soldiers: Teaching Just War Theory. *Teach Phil*, 17(1), 29-39, Mr 94.

Using the core curriculum course on ethics and just war theory taught at the US Military Academy as an example, this paper offers some guidelines on how to incorporate instruction in just war theory into similar ethics courses at other colleges and universities. Furthermore, arguing that there is a real need for the public to understand just war concepts, this paper presents an overview and prescription for informed citizenship in the post-cold war age.

Haines, Victor Yelverton. Aesthetic Order. *J Value Inq*, 28(2), 193-215, Je 94.

Aesthetic order is the integral order an individual has as itself *ipse*, and when appreciated is the realm of beauty. Aesthetics defines an individual object's appeal for appreciation; beauty is the actual response to that appeal. The value of this appeal lies in the apprehension of its integrity. Since only an integer can truly be integral, the primary symptom of the aesthetic is world-making, for the only truly integral integer is a world. The object of aesthetic appreciation is not part but all of an individual and, hence, of its indivisible, integral order—an everything.

Haines, Victor Yelverton. Without Guilt, What's the Matter? How Tragedy Matters: Response to Richard Eldridge's "How Can Tragedy Matter For Us?". *J Aes Art Crit*, 53(2), 187-188, Spr 95.

If, as Eldridge argues, tragedy is not bad luck or punishment but results from the hero's virtue, then the audience and the hero both are implicated in a collective and unconscious guilt as members of a culture in which the practice of its virtues leads to tragedy.

Hajdin, Mane. Sexual Harassment in the Law: The Demarcation Problem. *J Soc Phil*, 25(3), 102-122, Wint 94.

This paper argues that the present law about sexual harassment is incapable of providing workable criterion of demarcation between sexual harassment and those forms of sexual interaction between people who work together that do not constitute sexual harassment, without leaving the latter class empty or almost empty. The argument of the paper is based on the examination of the role that the notions of unwelcomeness and offensiveness play in the law.

Hajdin, Mane. *The Boundaries of Moral Discourse*. Chicago, Loyola Univ Pr, 1994.

This book offers an account of what distinguishes moral discourse from other types of prescriptive discourse, by appealing to the role that is played in it by terms for moral agents and terms for moral "patients." That account leads to treating questions about membership in the "moral community," as importantly different and relatively independent from questions about the content of moral rules. The impact of R M Hare's refutation of moral relativism is seen to be limited to relativism about the content of moral rules: it leaves open the possibility of relativism about membership in the moral community.

Hajduk, Zygmunt. Gegenwärtige Diskussionen über eine Konzeption der Naturphilosophie. *Stud Phil Christ*, 30(2), 115-134, 1994.

In diesem Artikel, der aus drei Teilen besteht, stellen wir ein Paradigmawechsel in der Metaphilosophie der Natur vor. Als ein Paradigmawechsel bezeichnen wir ein übergang von einer theoretischen zu einer praktischen Philosophie der Natur. Auch die bisherige Naturphilosophie, wenngleich nicht immer explizit, ein jeweils spezifisches Verhältnis von Mensch und Natur zum Ausdruck gebracht und zugleich normiert hat. Dies gilt für das natürphilosophische Paradigma der Antike und des Mittelalters ebenso wie für seinen neuzeitlichen Nachfolger. Die Naturphilosophie der Gegenwart muss zwei Postulate erfüllen. Erstens, die neue Naturphilosophie muss neben der theoretischen Aneignung von Natur vor allem den praktischen Umgang mit ihr thematisieren, sie muss generell mit dem menschlichen Handeln in der Natur zu tun haben. (edited)

Hájek, Alan. "Triviality on the Cheap?" in *Probability and Conditionals, Eells, Ellery (ed)*, 113-140. New York, Cambridge Univ Pr, 1994.

I show that an attractive hypothesis concerning probabilities of conditionals is untenable. Said simply, the hypothesis is that the probability of the conditional "if A, then B", equals the conditional probability of B, given A. I sharpen various negative results in the literature, including Lewis' famous 'triviality results', and I refute certain reformulations of the hypothesis (ones which restrict the domain of propositions to which the hypothesis is supposed to apply). I provide a recipe for generating counterexamples to the hypothesis based on the notion of 'perturbation'. Very roughly, a perturbation of a probability function agrees with that function over certain regions of logical space, and disagrees with it elsewhere. If a given function conforms to the hypothesis, then any perturbation of it does not.

Hájek, Alan. In Defense of Hume's Balancing of Probabilities in the Miracles Argument. *SW Phil Rev*, 11(1), 111-118, Ja 95.

I vindicate Hume's argument against belief in miracle reports against a prevalent objection. Hume has us balance the probability of a miracle's occurrence against the probability of its being falsely attested to, and argues that the latter must inevitably be the greater; thus, reason requires us to reject any miracle report. The "flaw" in this reasoning, according to Butler and many others, is that it proves too much—it counsels us to never believe historians, newspaper reports of lottery results, and so on; and this is clearly absurd. I show that this objection is misguided: far from providing counterexamples to Hume's *balancing principle*, as I call it, these cases actually confirm it, as some simple calculations of probabilities show.

Hájek, Alan and Hall, Ned. "The Hypothesis of the Conditional Construal of Conditional Probability" in *Probability and Conditionals, Eells, Ellery (ed)*, 75-111. New York, Cambridge Univ Pr, 1994.

Very roughly, the *conditional construal of conditional probability* is the hypothesis that the conditional probability P(B|A) equals the probability of the conditional 'if A, then B'. We hone this rough statement down to various precise versions of *the Hypothesis*, as we call it. We discuss reasons for caring about the Hypothesis, and reasons for believing it. We then offer an opinionated survey of the various negative results in the literature, sharpening several of them along the way, and argue against certain strategies for resuscitating the Hypothesis. We conclude that the Hypothesis is untenable; however, we suggest some open questions as avenues for future research.

Haji, Ishtiyaque. A Deadly Delight: Feldman on the Nature and Value of Death. *Dialogue (Canada)*, 33(4), 677-684, Fall 94.

I first present an overview of Fred Feldman's *Confrontations with the Reaper*. I then turn to some critical discussion. I focus attention, initially, on Feldman's principle that necessarily nothing dies at a time unless it was alive at some earlier time. I conclude by commenting on Feldman's views regarding the connection between intrinsic and extrinsic evils.

Haji, Ishtiyaque. Autonomy and Blameworthiness. *Can J Phil*, 24(4), 593-612, D 94.

Various cases—for example, those involving covert manipulation—appear to show that autonomy is a necessary condition of moral blameworthiness. Others—some involving akratic action, for instance—seem to show that there is no such connection between autonomy and being to blame. After critically examining various accounts of autonomy and tracing their implications for whether blameworthiness presupposes autonomy, I sketch an account of autonomy which distinguishes between autonomous decisions and autonomous actions. It implies that (given certain conditions) an agent can be blameworthy for performing an action without being autonomous relative to that action.

Haji, Ishtiyaque. Critical Notice Alfred R Mele *Springs of Action: Understanding Intentional Behavior*. *Can J Phil*, 24(3), 511-524, S 94.

After providing an overview of *Springs of Action*, I examine Mele's notion of irresistible desire, tracing its relevance for issues pertaining to moral responsibility. I then show that Mele's rejection of the principle that preponderant motivation is an essential feature of intending motivates rejection of the view that a person is blameworthy for performing an action only if she intentionally performed that action. Finally, I indicate how Mele's views on intentional action point to inroads in developing an account of individual autonomy.

Haken, Hermann. "Are Synergetic Systems (Including Brains) Machines?" in *The Machine as Metaphor and Tool, Haken, Hermann (ed)*, 123-137. New York, Springer-Verlag, 1993.

Haken, Hermann (ed) and Karlqvist, Anders (ed) and Svedin, Uno (ed). *The Machine as Metaphor and Tool*. New York, Springer-Verlag, 1993.

Halaczek, Bernard. Das Gemeinsame von Ökologie und Bioethik. *Stud Phil Christ*, 30(2), 135-150, 1994.

Im Hauptteil dieser Arbeit wird der Versuch unternommen, das Gemeinsame von Oekologie und Bioethik darzulegen. Dieses hängt vor allem mit der Aehnlichkeit der Probleme zusammen, die der wissenschaftlich-technische Fortschritt unnerhalb der beiden Disziplinen hervorruft. So deckt beispielsweise die Geschichte von Seveso ebenso wie die der hirntoten Schwangeren von Erlangen eine ähnliche Unfähigkeit des Menschen auf, mit all seinen Möglichkeiten richtig umzugehen. Viel drastischer kommt dasselbe in der Ambivalenz des DDT einerseits und der künstlichen Befruchtung anderseits zum Ausdruck. Will der Mensch einigermassen Herr der eigenen Errungenschaften bleiben bzw. werden, hat sowohl der Oekologe wie der Bioethiker an ein Dreifaches zu denken. (edited)

Halbach, Volker. A System of Complete and Consistent Truth. *Notre Dame J Form Log*, 35(3), 311-327, Sum 94.

Haldane, John. "Education: Conserving Tradition" in *Introducing Applied Ethics, Almond, Brenda (ed)*, 73-88. Cambridge, Blackwell, 1995.

Education involves the authoritative transmission of beliefs, attitudes and abilities from those who possess them to those who lack them. In some sense, therefore, education is necessarily conservative, for it seeks to inculcate understanding of, and respect for, certain cognitive and social values. The present essay elaborates these considerations in relation to relent philosophy of education, arguing the need for this to take full account of contemporary concerns in social and political philosophy.

Haldane, John. Algunas presuposiciones metafísicas de la acción humana. *Anu Filosof*, 27(3), 923-938, 1994.

In opposition to compatibilism, it is argued that the thesis of universal causal determinism is at odds with the idea of free action. Free agency involves liberty of indifference—that is to say the nondetermination of action by antecedent events. Action issues from habitual behavioral tendencies; but this relation is neither deterministic nor random: it is one of propensity, in this case conditioned by practical rationality. In general, specifying reasons for action is not identifying antecedent causes but describing the intentional content of action—saying what kind of behavior it is. Practical reasons directs the agent's behavior towards ends conceived of as good; it is further questioned whether, as Plato suggests, the end of action, standardly, is a, or the, good.

Haldane, John. Reason, Truth, and Sacred History?. *Amer Cath Phil Quart*, 68(Supp), 173-185, 1994.

This essay attempts to defend the idea of non-reductive pluralistic realism by examining the common assumptions of two opposing positions: those of Hilary Putnam and Ernest Gellner as presented in *Reason, Truth, and History* (1981) and *Postmodernism, Reason, and Religion* (1992) respectively. The anti-realism of the former and the rationalist realism of the latter both assume that knowledge requires a systematic account of justification. This assumption is queried.

Haldane, John. Religious Toleration. *Filozof Istraz*, 14(2-3), 263-267, 1994.

The author discusses some arguments for religious tolerance, searching for an argument that might be offered to the true believer. Such a believer is not likely to be impressed by the liberal view that the state should remain neutral between competing conceptions of good and should be organized on the basis of a *modus vivendi*; he will see it as an invitation to indifference. The intolerant true believer has to meet the challenge of *demonstrating* the virtue of intolerance to those he/she would intolerantly suppress. By proving the independent merit of an initially implausible doctrine—advanced by the faith in question—he/she will have advanced the cause of his/her religion; and the more extensively this is done, the more likely it is that false (and non) believers will become true believers. As a result, intolerance will no longer be necessary. (edited)

Haldane, John. Some Metaphysical Presuppositions of Agency. *Heythrop J*, 35(3), 296-303, Jl 94.

In opposition to compatibilism it is argued that the thesis of universal causal determinism is at odds with the idea of free action. Free agency involves liberty of indifference presupposing the nondetermination of action by antecedent events. Action issued from habitual behavioral tendencies; but this relation is neither deterministic nor random: it is one of propensity conditioned by practical rationality. In general, specifying reasons for action is not identifying antecedent causes but describing the intentional content of action; saying what kind of behavior it is. Practical reasons direct the agent's behavior towards ends conceived of as good; it is a further question whether, as Plato suggests, the end of action is standardly a, or the, good.

Haldane, John J. "Analytical Philosophy and the Nature of Mind" in *The Mind-Body Problem: A Guide to the Current Debate*, Warner, Richard (ed), 195-203. Cambridge, Blackwell, 1994.

This essay begins with a survey and assessment of current positions in analytical philosophy on the question of the relationship between mental states and processes and physical ones. It is argued that eliminative materialism, anomalous monism and neo-dualism are inadequate and the subject stands in need of new possibilities—or the recovery of old ones. In the latter connection the merits of Aristotelian-Thomistic approaches are briefly outlined and it is argued that there is a confusion between two senses of "matter"—one philosophical, the other empirical-cum-scientific.

Hale, Bob. A Desperate Fix. *Analysis*, 55(2), 74-81, Ap 95.

This paper continues the debate between Rosen and Hale over the tenability of modal fictionalism—the thesis that the advantages of construing ordinary modal statements as quantifications over possible worlds can be had without ontological and epistemological cost, by prefixing them with a fictional operator 'According to possible worlds theory...' It argues that Rosen's attempts to disarm the dilemma presented in Hale's 'Modal fictionalism—a simple dilemma' (both in *Analysis 55.2*) is ineffective.

Hale, Bob. Modal Fictionalism—a Simple Dilemma. *Analysis*, 55(2), 63-67, Ap 95.

Modal fictionalism, as propounded by Gideon Rosen (in Mind 99), claims to secure the advantages of quantifying over possible worlds at no ontological and epistemological cost by prefixing such quantifications with a nonfactive operator 'According to possible worlds theory...', understood on analogy with fictional operators like 'In Conan Doyle's stories...'. This paper argues that the fictionalist confronts a potentially lethal dilemma turning on the question whether he views possible worlds theory as merely contingently false or as necessarily so.

Hale, Bob (ed) and Clark, Peter (ed). *Reading Putnam*. Cambridge, Blackwell, 1995.

The volume contains nine essays on major themes of Putnam's thought with a tenth chapter containing replies and comments by Putnam. The essays comprise: Simon Blackburn on internal realism; George Boolos on Peirce, Dedekind and Boole; Michael Dummett on Wittgenstein on Necessity; Michael Hallett on the model theoretic argument; Kevin Kelly, Cory Juhl and Clark Glymour on reliabilism; Michael Redhead on the Quantum Logic programme; Thomas Ricketts on Carnap and The Principle of Tolerance; David Wiggins on Natural Kinds and Crispin Wright on Putnam's Proof that we are not brains in a vat.

Hales, Steven D. Epistemic Closure Principles. *S J Phil*, 33(2), 185-201, Sum 95.

This paper evaluates a number of closure principles (for both knowledge and justification) that have appeared in the literature. Counterexamples are presented to all but one of these principles, which is conceded to be true but trivially so. It is argued that a consequence of the failure of these closure principles is that certain projects of doxastic logic are doomed, and that doxastic logic is of dubious merit for epistemologists interested in actual knowers in the actual world.

Hales, Steven D. Self-Deception and Belief Attribution. *Synthese*, 101(2), 273-289, N 94.

One of the most common views about self-deception ascribes contradictory beliefs to the self-deceiver. In this paper it is argued that this view (the contradiction strategy)

is inconsistent with plausible common-sense principles of belief attribution. Other dubious assumptions made by contradiction strategists are also examined. It is concluded that the contradiction strategy is an inadequate account of self-deception. Two other well-known views—those of Robert Audi and Alfred Mele—are investigated and found wanting. A new theory of self-deception relying on an extension of Mark Johnston's subintentional mental tropisms is proposed and defended.

Hales, Steven D. Was Nietzsche a Consequentialist?. *Int Stud Phil*, 27(3), 25-34, 1995.

In this paper I argue that Nietzsche is a consequentialist, and that his acceptance of the distinction between intrinsic and instrumental value underwrites his investigations into the value of truth and the value of morality. His famous criticisms of utilitarianism are criticisms not of the structure of the theory, but of happiness as the *summon bonum*. Nietzsche offers instead that it is life that has intrinsic value. The relationships among his consequentialism and his thoughts on virtue and the experimental life are also explored, and found to form a coherent whole.

Halevy, Amir and Brody, Baruch A. Is Futility a Futile Concept?. *J Med Phil*, 20(2), 123-144, Ap 95.

This paper distinguishes four major types of futility (physiological, imminent demise, lethal condition, and qualitative) that have been advocated in the literature either in a patient dependent or a patient independent fashion. It proposes five criteria (precision, prospective, social acceptability, significant number, and non-agreement) that any definition of futility must satisfy if it is to serve as the basis for unilaterally limiting futile care. It then argues that none of the definitions that have been advocated meet the criteria, primarily because their proponents have not paid sufficient attention to the problematic nature of the data supporting the use of their definitions.

Halfwassen, Jens. Sur la Limitation du Principe de Contradiction chez Denys. *Diotima*, 23, 46-50, 1995.

Denys the Areopagite violences in his theology the principle of contradiction, when he argues, that affirmation and negation related to the One are at the same time right and not right; this paradox indicates the transcendence of the One, which is ineffable. The sources of Denys in this are Plato's Parmenides and his interpretation by the Neoplatonists. For Plotinus and Proclus the first One is beyond both affirmation and negation; for Plotinus, but not for Proclus, the second One, the Nus, can be described in conjunction of opposite terms as unity and plurality. Denys combines in his concept of God Plotinus' first and second One.

Hall, Joan Krakover (trans) and Carabelli, Giancarlo. *On Hume and Eighteenth-Century Aesthetics: The Philosopher on a Swing*. New York, Lang, 1995.

This study is an original approach to the notion of "golden mean" in eighteenth-century culture. It bravely combines intellectual history and material history, spanning the field so philosophy, aesthetics, painting, sociology, optics, music, theater and garden history in an effort to cross the borders of academic writing, in the stylistic treatment of the subject. Giancarlo Carabelli examines the "golden mean" both in one of the highlights of Enlightenment philosophy—David Hume's essays and his discussion of the middle station of life and of the standard of taste—and in a modest artifact, "intermediate structure" par excellence: the invisible fence of the ha-ha, that magical "middle", that "simple enchantment", as Walpole called it, that was typical of eighteenth-century "modern garden".

Hall, Jon. Persuasive Design in Cicero's *De oratore*. *Phoenix*, 48(3), 210-225, Autumn 94.

This article examines the devices that Cicero employs in books two and three of the *De Oratore* in order to encourage the reader to accepts Crassus' arguments concerning the education of the ideal orator. This persuasive goal, however, only emerges once Cicero has examined the issue in a more objective way in book one, according to the precepts of the Academy.

Hall, Mark A. The Problems with Rule-Based Rationing. *J Med Phil*, 19(4), 315-332, Ag 94.

Centralized, democratic rules are often asserted as a superior basis for rationing than individualized physician discretion. This article counters this prevailing wisdom by exploring the deficiencies of rule-based rationing. Rules are too imprecise to accurately reflect all the nuances of physical and mental impairment and the complexity of medical science, particularly considering the widely varying personal values that different patients attach to medical risk and benefit. Rule-based rationing also suffers from the biasing effects of interest group pressure on political processes and the tendency to absolve physicians from any moral responsibility for the rationing decision they implement. Internalizing cost constraints is a more socially and professionally acceptable means of rationing. (edited)

Hall, Ned. "Back in the CCCP" in *Probability and Conditionals*, Eells, Ellery (ed), 141-160. New York, Cambridge Univ Pr, 1994.

Hall, Ned and Hájek, Alan. "The Hypothesis of the Conditional Construal of Conditional Probability" in *Probability and Conditionals*, Eells, Ellery (ed), 75-111. New York, Cambridge Univ Pr, 1994.

Very roughly, the *conditional construal of conditional probability* is the hypothesis that the conditional probability P(B|A) equals the probability of the conditional 'if A, then B'. We hone this rough statement down to various precise versions of *the Hypothesis*, as we call it. We discuss reasons for caring about the Hypothesis, and reasons for believing it. We then offer an opinionated survey of the various negative results in the literature, sharpening several of them along the way, and argue against certain strategies for resuscitating the Hypothesis. We conclude that the Hypothesis is untenable; however, we suggest some open questions as avenues for future research.

Hall, Pamela M. *Narrative and the Natural Law: An Interpretation of Thomistic Ethics*. Notre Dame, Univ Notre Dame Pr, 1994.

This book examines Aquinas's understanding of natural law in the *Summa Theologiae*, discussing the natural law's connections to the virtues, especially prudence and charity, and its relationships to the other kinds of law Aquinas discusses: eternal, human, and divine. Thomistic natural law requires the work of prudence for the natural law's discovery and for its application in practice. Learning the natural law is for Aquinas an historical, "narrative" process, manifested in communal reflection about the human good and how best to achieve it. The book also addresses the issue of tragedy in relation to the natural law.

Hall, Roland. Recent Publications on Locke. *Locke News*, 21, 3-8, 1990.

Hall, Roland. Recent Publications on Locke. *Locke News*, 22, 3-16, 1991.

Hall, Roland. Recent Publications on Locke. *Locke News*, 23, 3-9, 1992.

This list of articles, chapters, and books dealing with Locke continues a regular series in *The Locke Newsletter*, and will be valuable to all students of Locke. These collections supplement with recent material the standard bibliographical guide by Hall and Woolhouse, Eighty Years of Locke Scholarship (Edinburgh University Press, 1983). Authors of any piece on Locke can ensure inclusion in future listings by sending an offprint or copy to the Editor of *The Locke Newsletter*.

Hall, Roland. Recent Publications on Locke. *Locke News*, 24, 3-18, 1993.

Hall, Roland. Recent Publications on Locke. *Locke News*, 25, 3-11, 1994.

Hall, Roland. The Nature of the Will and its Place in Schopenhauer's Philosophy. *Schopenhauer Jahr*, 76, 73-90, 1995.

The aim is to clarify the notion of the will in Schopenhauer. Misunderstandings by some commentators are criticised, and Schopenhauer's actual new vision of the world and the will is examined. His fresh insight, and the way in which he supports it, as well as some apparent difficulties, and a possible solution are presented. The inner dissension of the will, and its other characteristics, are documented. Finally, the function of the will in Schopenhauer's world-view, and its connection with his personal experience, are filled out, and related to his metaphysical pessimism.

Hall, Roland. The Place of Reason in Locke's *Essay*. *Locke News*, 23, 11-24, 1992.

The place of reason in Locke's *Essay* has been almost entirely neglected. The important and fundamental role it has for Locke is examined here: it is not merely the capacity for reasoning, but a God-given faculty that is the ultimate judge of revelation, and of the meaning of religious claims. Book IV, chapter xvii is devoted to the nature of reason, and chapter xviii to the relation between reason and faith. The well-known criticism of the syllogism in chapter xvii, as not being 'the proper instrument' of reason, is shown not to be an attack on Aristotle, nor even a denial of the adequacy of syllogistic reasoning, but a claim that, despite the usefulness of syllogism in philosophical argument, those unfamiliar with logic should not be deterred from reasoning.

Hall, Roland. 'Idea' in Locke's Works. *Locke News*, 21, 9-26, 1990.

Hallaq, John H and Steinhorst, Kirk. Business Intelligence Methods—How Ethical. *J Bus Ethics*, 13(10), 787-794, O 94.

An empirical study was conducted during Spring and Summer of 1991 about information gathering methods by businesses regarding operations of competitors. Respondents were employed in a variety of different industries. A convenience sample was administered in two adjoining states, with one group residing in an urban city and the other in smaller predominantly rural communities. Analysis of perceptions held by these two groups supports the hypothesis that rural residents tend to be more conservative and less approving of questionable methods of information gathering. Similarly, within each group and in the sample as a whole, differences in condoning or disapproving information gathering methods were discovered on the basis of demographic characteristics of respondents. (edited)

Hallen, Barry. Indeterminacy, Ethnophilosophy, Linguistic Philosophy, African Philosophy. *Philosophy*, 70(273), 377-393, Jl 95.

A variety of analytic techniques adapted from orthodox philosophy of language may be profitably applied to African discourse. Paradigm cases and demonstrations of correct and incorrect usage can help illumine underlying semantic networks that, for example, then can be used to provide alternative perspectives on traditional epistemological problems and topics. This provides one credible methodological basis with which academic philosophy can meaningfully assess the philosophical prepossessions of nonWestern cultures generally. W V O Quine's persistent skepticism about the universality of meanings and the facility of precise inter-cultural translations between languages that are not cognates provide a healthy propaedeutic to such undertakings.

Hallen, Barry and Sodipo, J O. "Excerpts from Knowledge, Belief, and Witchcraft" in *African Philosophy: Selected Readings, Mosley, Albert G (ed)*, 350-356. Englewood Cliffs, Prentice Hall, 1995.

Hallen, Barry and Sodipo, Olubi. The House of the "INU": Keys to the Structure of a Yoruba Theory of the Self. *Quest*, 8(1), 2-23, Je 94.

La méthode utilisée parles auteurs pour rechercher l'explication du concept de la "personne" formulée par un médecin (onísègùn) Yoruba est imprunteé à la tradition analytique en philosophie. Le concept Yoruba de "inú" est supposé être l'équivalent du "self" en Anglais. Il est identifi comme la source de l'intellect (opolo), de la sagesse (ogbón)—ici interprété comme incluant la tradition orale—de la moralité personnelle (iwà), et de la patience (sùúrù). Les auteurs analysent aussi la possibilité de corrélations physiques, organiques, avec les aptitudes psychologiques. La théorie du moi, comme il est expliquée par l'onísègùn, semble être plus compatible avec la théorie "double-aspect" qu'avec le "dualism". Le concept de la personne deviendrait plus fondamental, capable d'avoir des attributs soit mentaux, soit physiques. (edited)

Haller, Michael (ed) and Habermas, Jürgen. *Vergangenheit als Zukunft*. Vienna, Piper, 1993.

Haller, Rudolf. "Heinrich Gomperz und die Österreichische Philosophie" in *Heinrich Gomperz, Karl Popper und die österreichische Philosophie, Seiler, Martin (ed)*, 47-67. Amsterdam, Rodopi, 1994.

Haller, Rudolf and Henrichs, Norbert and Roser, Andreas. Wittgenstein Bibliographie 1992-93. *Wittgenstein Stud*, n.a., 1994.

Hallett, Michael. "Putnam and the Skolem Paradox" in *Reading Putnam, Clark, Peter (ed)*, 66-97. Cambridge, Blackwell, 1995.

Halliday, Robert. The Quality of Life. *J Value Inq*, 29(2), 269-278, Je 95.

A review essay of *The Quality of Life*, edited by Martha Nussbaum and Amartya Sen (Oxford: Clarendon Press, 1993). The essay focuses on three questions: 1) When we are measuring the quality of life, what are we measuring? 2) How are we to measure that quality? and, 3) Can the evaluation of quality of life based on these measurements have any cross-cultural value?

Hallyn, Fernand. "La machine de l'exemple ou la comparison chez Descartes" in *Rhétoriques de la science, De Coorebyter, Vincent (ed)*, 33-52. Paris, Pr Univ France, 1994.

Halper, Edward C. "The Substance of Aristotle's Ethics" in *The Crossroads of Norm and Nature, Sim, May (ed)*, 3-28. Lanham, Rowman & Littlefield, 1995.

This paper argues that Aristotle treats happiness and the good state as if they were substances. He defines each as an actuality or function of parts, and many of the features he ascribes to them follow from their quasi-substantial natures. In particular, his insistence on harmony in the soul and his critique of faction in the state are consequences of his requirement that substances be one. The lives and states he regards as the best are most one and, thus, most substantial. This analysis shows not only how Aristotle's functional accounts have moral import but also that his practical philosophy is grounded more in metaphysics than in empirical observation.

Halpern, Jodi and Wenger, Neil S. Can A Patient Refuse a Psychiatric Consultation to Evaluate Decision-Making Capacity?. *J Clin Ethics*, 5(3), 230-234, Fall 94.

Halpern, Jodi and Wenger, Neil S. The Physician's Role in Completing Advance Directives: Ensuring Patients' Capacity to Make Healthcare Decisions in Advance. *J Clin Ethics*, 5(4), 320-323, Wint 94.

Halpin, John F. Legitimizing Chance: The Best-System Approach to Probabilistic Laws in Physical Theory. *Austl J Phil*, 72(3), 317-338, S 94.

Contemporary physical theory proposes laws involving ineliminable probabilities for micro events. But the postulation of fundamental, objective probability may seem metaphysically extravagant; one would like to know how a cautious empiricist might construe such probability. One empiricist answer equates the set of laws of nature with the deductive closure of the "best system" for axiomitizing particular facts and then equates objective probability with the probabilities ascribed by these laws. However, David Lewis has recently argued that such a proposal faces significant difficulties. In this paper, I attempt to reformulate the best system account to circumvent the Lewis arguments. This results in context dependent notions of law and chance. These "perspectival" laws and chances, I argue, are appropriate from the empiricist point of view.

Hamacher-Hermes, Adelheid. *Inhalts- oder Umfangslogik? Die Kontroverse zwischen E Husserl und A H Voigt*. Freiburg, Alber, 1994.

In the early 1890's an argument took place between Edmund Husserl and Andreas Heinrich Voigt in the pages of the *Vierteljahrsschrift für wissenschaftliche Philosophie*. It concerned the relative merits of a logic of content (*Inhaltslogik*) and of a logic of extension (*Umfangslogik*). In this book an analysis and evaluation is given of this hitherto disregarded debate. It is complemented by a short biography of Voigt whose work and significance as a logician is almost unknown today. Acquaintance with the controversy is indispensable for a deeper understanding of Husserl's attitude towards mathematical theories of logic, in particular the algebra of logic.

Hamilton, Andy. A New Look at Personal Identity. *Phil Quart*, 45(180), 332-349, Jl 95.

Hamilton, Lawrence S (ed). *Ethics, Religion and Biodiversity*. Cambridge, White Horse, 1994.

Hamilton, Paul. "The Romanticism of Contemporary Ideology" in *Intersections: Nineteenth-Century Philosophy and Contemporary Theory, Rajan, Tilottama (ed)*, 302-321. Albany, SUNY Pr, 1995.

Hamilton III, J Brooke and Strutton, David. Two Practical Guidelines for Resolving Truth-Telling Problems. *J Bus Ethics*, 13(11), 899-912, N 94.

The news reminds us almost daily that the "truth" is apparently not highly valued by many in business. This paper develops two prescriptive standards—the expectation and reputation guidelines—that may help businesspeople avoid violating clearly accepted truth standards. The guidelines also assist in determining whether truth is required in circumstances where honesty seems in conflict with the practical demands of business. A discussion of why, when and how these guidelines may be applied to facilitate truth-telling by business organizations follows, along with illustrative examples.

Hammacher, Klaus. Fichte und die Freimaurerie. *Fichte-Studien*, 2, 138-159, 1990.

Hammacher, Klaus. Fichtes praxologische Dialektik. *Fichte-Studien*, 1, 25-40, 1990.

Hamme, Nancy Steele and English, Parker. "Morality, Art, and African Philosophy: A Response to Wiredu" in *African Philosophy: Selected Readings, Mosley, Albert G (ed)*, 407-420. Englewood Cliffs, Prentice Hall, 1995.

This work discusses Kwasi Wiredu's claim that traditional Akan moral thought is less supernaturalistically authoritarian than is contemporary Western moral thought. We recognize that no written records of the traditional Akan exist with which to examine this claim. Instead, we focus on the preserved record found in the art artifacts and associated legends produced by traditional Akan societies, and then demonstrated that these societies were substantially authoritarian because of their supernaturalistic beliefs. We also endorse Wiredu's more general suggestion that traditional African moral thought be compared with traditional Western moral thought while contemporary African moral thought be compared with contemporary Western moral thought.

Hamminga, Bert and Cools, Kees and Kuipers, Theo A F. "Truth Approximation by Concretization in Capital Structure Theory" in *Idealization VI: Idealization in Economics, Hamminga, Bert (ed)*, 205-228. Amsterdam, Rodopi, 1994.

This paper supplies a structuralist reconstruction of the Modigliani-Miller theory and shows that the economic literature following their results reports on research with an implicit strategy to come "closer-to-the-truth" in the modern technical sense in philosophy of science.

Hamminga, Bert and De Marchi, Neil. "Idealization and the Defence of Economics" in *Idealization VI: Idealization in Economics, Hamminga, Bert (ed)*, 11-40. Amsterdam, Rodopi, 1994.

Illustrates and compares the opinions of the economists J R McCulloch (1825), J S Mill (1836), K Marx (1864), L Robbins (1932) and M Friedman (1953) on the problem of idealization in economics, both from a logical point of view (the structure of economic theories) and from a social point of view (idealizational methodology as a defense of theory against sceptical outsiders).

Hamminga, Bert (ed) and De Marchi, Neil B (ed). *Idealization VI: Idealization in Economics*. Amsterdam, Rodopi, 1994.

This book explores the different ways in which economic theories can be viewed as idealizations, and the consequences of these views for the methodology of economics and econometrics as well as for the nature of the epistemic claims of its theories. It starts with an inspection and comparison of the explicit views on the subject by some important authors in the history of economics. The contributors to the volume use their expertise in both economics, econometrics and philosophy of science.

Hammond, Peter J. "The Moral Status of Profits and Other Rewards: A Perspective from Modern Welfare Economics" in *Profits and Morality, Cowan, Robin (ed)*, 88-123. Chicago, Univ of Chicago Pr, 1995.

Standard neoclassical welfare economics justifies competitive profit maximization by firms. But when lump-sum transfers are used to achieve distributive justice, a firm's owners and managers are entitled only to "normal" profits paid for services rendered. Yet with private information about effort or technology, not even efficient production is always desirable, let alone profit maximization. Furthermore, some profits should then be distributed specifically to the firm's managers as incentive payments. In intertemporal economies these conclusions are reinforced, and profits harder even to define. Finally, it is argued that valuing freedom for its own sake may make profits more acceptable than otherwise.

Hampsher-Monk, Iain. *A History of Modern Political Thought: Major Political Thinkers from Hobbes to Marx*. Cambridge, Blackwell, 1993.

Hampshire, Stuart. Justice is Strife. *Proc Amer Phil Ass*, 65(3), 19-27, N 91.

Hampton, Jean. "Liberalism, Retribution and Criminality" in *In Harm's Way, Coleman, Jules L (ed)*, 159-182. New York, Cambridge Univ Pr, 1994.

Joel Feinberg's work on the criminal law never directly addresses the issue of the difference between criminal law and tort law. This paper considers how to make that distinction, using the notion of retribution, and considers whether doing so is consistent with Feinberg's over-all theory of the nature of the criminal law. It also considers, more generally, the way in which a Feinbergian theory of the criminal law, coupled with a retributive justification of criminal sanctions, can be considered consistent with the liberal conception of the state.

Hampton, Jean. The Common Faith of Liberalism. *Pac Phil Quart*, 75(3-4), 186-216, S-D 94.

Is Rawl's political liberalism, which he defends in his book *Political Liberalism*, really different from the enlightenment form of liberalism that he criticizes in that book? Has he really succeeded in formulating a kind of liberalism that is "less" than a comprehensive moral view and genuinely non-sectarian, or has he subtly built into it the reason-based moral commitments that have always been the hallmark of enlightenment liberals from Jefferson, to Mill, to liberals of our time? This paper argues that a thorough explication of his views reveals that his political liberalism is little different from anything that would count as enlightenment liberalism. Thus I will be extending the argument I have made in two earlier papers, that Rawl's attempt to build a neutral form of liberalism, that is more than a modus vivendi for a democratic society but less than a comprehensive moral conception, ultimately fails. If, as seems to be the case in his new book, Rawls rejects a conception of political stability that is based on a politically expedient (and likely temporary) consensus, he must endorse a conception of liberalism little different from the Enlightenment liberalism he claims to reject.

Hampton, Jean. The Contractarian Explanation of the State. *Midwest Stud Phil*, 15, 344-371, 1990.

The contractarian theory of the state can be used not only to justify political authority, but also to explain the structure and origin of political society by providing a model of state creation and maintenance. This paper sets out that model, with an effort to locating the kind of consent that, whether or not it justifies the authority of any ruler, at least explains why the ruler has political authority.

Hampton, Jean. The Failure of Expected-Utility Theory as a Theory of Reason. *Econ Phil*, 10(2), 195-242, O 94.

Can expected-utility (EU) theory be used to portray reason? The paper argues that EU theory fails as portrayal of reason, no matter whether it is interpreted normatively or descriptively, and no matter whether it is understood as an instrumental theory or as a noninstrumental theory, because it is too consequentialist in character. Counter-examples developed by theorists such as Allais, Ellsberg, Kahenman and Tversky, and Loomes and Sugden are used to justify this conclusion.

Hamrick, William S. Merleau-Ponty's View of Creativity and Its Philosophical Consequences. *Int Phil Quart*, 34(4), 401-412, D 94.

This essay discusses the role that creativity played in Maurice Merleau-Ponty's phenomenology of perception and the lived-body as well as in his phenomenology of the social world—mainly through language. The author identifies three main examples of the philosophical importance that creativity had for Merleau-Ponty: 1) the origin of meaning, 2) the rejection of the Cartesian mind-body dualism, and 3) necessary conditions for human dignity in the relationship of culture and nature. Finally, the last of these examples and the significance of creativity are considered in the light of Merleau-Ponty's last, unfinished work, *The Visible and the Invisible*.

Hancock, Curtis L. Cicero Versus Machiavelli: Does the End Justify the Means. *Cont Phil*, 16(6), 14-18, N-D 94.

Philosophers since ancient times have asked whether political leaders may with some justification make decisions that conflict with personal conscience and customary morality. Cicero's *On Duties* and Machiavelli's *The Prince* seem to give contrary answers to this question. The former argues that political decisions ought never to compromise what is right. To think that vicious actions are permissible for the sake of expediency is to suffer confusion about the proper relationship between leadership and morality. Machiavelli, on the other hand, appears to regard Cicero's alternative as naive, holding that such a view will inevitably bring ruin to a prince, given the harsh dimensions of *realpolitik*. There is a much overlooked irony in the contrasting positions between these two thinkers, however, in that Cicero, writing sixteen centuries before the Florentine, anticipated his many arguments and convincingly criticized them. This article presents the essential outlines of the two thinkers' positions, and afterward defends the Stoic's moral vision of politics against Machiavelli.

Hand, Seán. *The Levinas Reader*. Cambridge, Blackwell, 1994.

Handelsman, Mitchell M (& others). Does Legally Mandated Consent to Psychotherapy Ensure Ethical Appropriateness?: The Colorado Experience. *Ethics Behavior*, 5(2), 119-129, 1995.

We analyzed a sample of 356 forms containing information that Colorado law legally requires both licensed and unlicensed therapists to disclose to clients. The majority of forms contained the legally mandated information; fewer forms contained ethically desirable information. The average readability grade level was 15.74, corresponding to upper-level college, and 63.9% of the forms reached the highest (most difficult) readability grade of 17+. Therapists are obeying the law, but do not appear to be taking advantage of the opportunity to provide their clients useful information in an accessible way.

Handley, W G and Wainer, S S. Equational Derivation vs Computation. *Annals Pure Applied Log*, 70(1), 17-49, N 94.

Subrecursive hierarchy classifications are used to compare the complexities of recursive functions according to 1) their derivations in a version of Kleen's equation calculus, and 2) their computations by term-rewriting. In each case ordinal bounds are assigned, and it turns out that the respective complexity measures are given by 1) a version of the Fast Growing Hierarchy, and 2) the Slow Growing Hierarchy. Known comparisons between the two hierarchies then provide ordinal trade-offs between 1) derivation and 2) computation. Characteristics of some well-known subrecursive classes are also read off.

Hands, D Wade. Blurred Boundaries: Recent Changes in the Relationship Between Economics and the Philosophy of Natural Science. *Stud Hist Phil Sci*, 25(5), 751-772, O 94.

This paper argues that there is a new relationship between economics and the philosophy of natural science. Instead of the previous one-way relationship where economists simply took ideas off the shelf of scientific philosophy, there is now a two-way relationship where philosophers are actually using economics in their work on scientific knowledge. The argument is supported by three examples from the recent philosophical literature: evolutionary epistemology, Cartwright's work on capacities, and Laudan's normative naturalism.

Hands, D Wade. Restabilizing Dynamics: Construction and Constraint in the History of Walrasian Stability Theory. *Econ Phil*, 10(2), 243-283, O 94.

The paper provides an alternative reconstruction of the history of Walrasian dynamics in the 1940s and 1950s general equilibrium theory. The study starts from the same constructivist positions as Roy Weintraub's 1991 book *Stabilizing Dynamics*, but puts more emphasis on the constraints faced by the economic theorists who developed Walrasian dynamics. The paper shows how this alternative reading contributes to a better understanding of later developments in Walrasian economics.

Haney, Frank. Alternativen der Wissenschaftsgeschichte. *J Gen Phil Sci*, 25(2), 207-222, 1994.

The paper deals with the function of the scientist's subjective activity in the research process. This will be discussed at the background of the discourse between distant action and narrow action theories of electromagnetism in nineteenth century physics. The analysis shows in which high degree the protagonists of these theories (Weber, Maxwell) regarded this situation consciously as a bifurcation (alternative) in the development of their science. This article describes then how the history of science values the case. The results of this valuation is dependent on the different philosophical points of view. Finally we point out some desiderata for the further discussion on methodology of science that would be the consequence of the acknowledgment of real bifurcations in scientific thought.

Haney, Mitchell R. Hard Rules, Soft Rules, and Moral Vision: Models of Ethical Rationality. *Kinesis*, 21(2), 13-30, Fall 94.

This essay focuses upon the role of moral rules and principles, as well as, nonrule based moral judgment in ethical rationality. The aim of the essay is to provide a taxonomy of various models of ethical rationality. The essay progresses from articulating a position which holds that competent moral reasoning ought to be understood strictly in terms of subsuming cases under exceptionless rules to a position which holds that competent moral reasoning is analogous to moral perception; hence, moral rules are useless.

Hanfling, Oswald. Art, Artifact and Function. *Phil Invest*, 18(1), 31-48, Ja 95.

I argue that works of art, like other artifacts, can be defined in terms of their function, which is to provide aesthetic satisfaction. Having given my definition, I explain that it is a 'paradigmatic' one, enabling me to accommodate various cases as being more or less close to the paradigm. I then consider a) the question of defining 'aesthetic' in a noncircular way, and b) the status of my definition versus examples such as ready-mades, which are excluded by it.

Hanfling, Oswald. Changing the Subject. *Philosophy*, 70(273), 448-452, Jl 95.

Hankinson, Jennifer. The Normative Nature of Coercion. *SW Phil Rev*, 11(1), 49-57, Ja 95.

I argue that as a result of ambiguity at the fundamental level of definition, use of the term coercion is both controversial and open to blatant misuse. I examine both descriptive and normative uses of the term as applied to cases of alleged coercion by institutional bodies (rather than individuals), and argue that unless the term is used in its normative sense, we are unable to distinguish coercive acts from those which are merely undesirable because of other (legitimate) reasons. I conclude that the term "coercion" must be reserved for those cases in which the victim suffers a rights violation.

Hankinson, R J. "Philosophy of Science" in *The Cambridge Companion to Aristotle, Barnes, Jonathan (ed)*, 109-139. New York, Cambridge Univ Pr, 1995.

Hankinson, R J. "Science" in *The Cambridge Companion to Aristotle, Barnes, Jonathan (ed)*, 140-167. New York, Cambridge Univ Pr, 1995.

Hankinson, R J. Pollution and Infection: An Hypothesis Still-born. *Apeiron*, 28(1), 25-65, Mr 95.

Hanks, Donald K. Statistical Victims and Their Rights. *Cont Phil*, 16(5), 1-4, S-O 94.

Hanna, Patricia. The Vanishing Tortoise. *Philosophia (Israel)*, 24(1-2), 211-223, D 94.

Hannan, Barbara. *Subjectivity and Reduction: An Introduction to the Mind-Body Problem.* Boulder, Westview Pr, 1994.

This work provides a concise, clear account of contemporary debate on the mind-body problem. The book is accessible to beginning students, but is sufficiently sophisticated to be of use to graduate students and professionals who want an accurate overview of the field. A special effort is made to explain the jargon endemic to philosophy of mind. Substance dualism, property dualism, eliminative materialism, and other theories are discussed. Contemporary philosophers who subscribe to these views are mentioned; their individual theories are presented and criticized. A nonreductive materialist view of mental states is defended, as well as an internalist view of mental content.

Hannay, Alastair. Two Ways of Coming Back to Reality: Kierkegaard and Lukács. *Hist Euro Ideas*, 20(1-3), 161-166, Ja 95.

Lukács, along with many other influential thinkers early in the twentieth century, was both influenced and provoked by what he knew of Kierkegaard's writings. Later, Lukács held Kierkegaard partly responsible for the existentialist cult of a "fetishised inwardness". I argue that there is an important feature of Kierkegaard's treatment of subjectivity—a dialectical aspect which as a Hegelian Lukács should have been appreciated—which, had he noted it, might have saved him from a fate as tragic as that which he imputes to Kierkegaard.

Hans, James S. *The Site of Our Lives: The Self and the Subject from Emerson to Foucault.* Albany, SUNY Pr, 1995.

This book addresses the question of human uniqueness at a time when academic discourse has all but abandoned its long-held commitment to the value of individuality. Through an appraisal of Emerson, Nietzsche, Heidegger, Derrida, and Foucault, the author establishes the ways in which the current critique of the self has grossly distorted the nature of the debate by reducing it to a simple choice between essential or constructed selves. The book demonstrates how the tradition that emerges from Emerson's work is based on a relational sense of the individual that has its equivalent in all of the major thinkers of our time.

Hansbauer, Severin. *Augen.Blick: Eine Skizze zu Bildern Arnold Schönbergs und Texten Theodor W Adornos.* Vienna, Passagen, 1994.

Im *Augen.Blick* liegen Wesenszüge geborgen, die von Künstlern und Denkern des 20. Jahrhunderts eigens zum Vorschein gebracht worden sind. Hier geht es um Arnold Schönberg und die "Blicke", die er in der Zeit um 1910 gemalt hat. Schönberg drängt sich dabei ein eher leiblicher Zug des *Augen.Blicks* auf, den er in ganz bestimmter Weise ins Bild bringt. Doch geraten seine "Blicke" zunehmend in Gefahr sie sind im Verschwinden begriffen. So werden die Bilder zur Auseinandersetzung mit einem weiteren Zug des *Augen.Blicks*—dem zeitlichen. Diese Skizze versucht, übereinanderliegende Schichten vorichtig abzutragen und neu zu ordnen. Der plastische Charakter, der behutsam ertastet werden will, kann sich so der oder dem Lesenden erschliessen. (edited)

Hansberg, Olbeth. Miedo e Incertidumbre. *Critica*, 26(76-77), 155-184, Ap-Ag 94.

Fear and Uncertainty discusses Robert Gordon's thesis according to which fear is an epistemic. Hansberg argues against both parts of this thesis, which purports to offer part of the structure of the emotion of fear. Now, what about the uncertainty, whatever its form, condition? Hansberg finds several examples in which someone fears *p* even though he actually is certain that *p*. She also argues against Gordon's distinction between propositional fears and mere 'states of fear' with no semantic content. Finally, Hansberg claims that all fears do have a propositional structure, even though some fears have it in a concealed way. Thus it is always possible to find propositional contents for fears which apparently have none, although in some cases this might be a difficult task. (edited)

Hansen, Chad. "Qing (Emotions) in Pre-Buddhist Chinese Thought" in *Emotions in Asian Thought, Marks, Joel (ed)*, 181-211. Albany, SUNY Pr, 1995.

Translators render *qing* as 'emotions' and 'reality'. I argue that Chinese philosophers viewed heart-mind as internalizing guidance (a social *dao*) and then *executing* it. It identifies items using the names in the social discourse. We internalize conventional action-guiding attitudes. *Qing* fits into this scheme as the input from the world to the action processor. The heart-mind categorizes the input using social distinctions. So *qing* is 'reality inputs' in contrast to the 'social-conventional' inputs. Later Conventional Confucianism treats *qing* as disruptive of inherited social order and evil. Buddhism, then adapted *qing* to its belief-desire psychology as its "origin of suffering" (evil).

Hansen, Forest. Philosophy of Music Education in a Slightly New Key. *Phil Music Educ Rev*, 1(1), 61-74, Spr 93.

Sound objections can be made to Susanne K Langer's central thesis that music articulates feelings, and thus to Bennett Reimer's philosophy of music education built on her theory. However, Langer often seems to argue for a claim that is in some respects narrower, in some broader: that (good) music presents an illusion of organic life. This alternate position withstands the objections to her primary thesis. It also seems more relevant both to the judgment of aesthetic merit of musical compositions and performances and to the rationale and method of music education.

Hansen, Forest. Values in Music Education. *Phil Music Educ Rev*, 2(1), 3-13, Spr 94.

Music education should be largely exempt from debate about multi-cultural values, because unlike other humanities its most relevant value is intrinsic. While this challenges the dominant philosophy of music education, it probably reflects and justifies what most music teachers practice. Although culture-bound in a way that mathematics is not, music similarly transcends linguistic cultures, partly because it is essentially nonrepresentational. Leonard Meyer's theory of music and musical listening explains and illustrates this intrinsic value—its meaning primarily as organized sound. His theory is applied to music education. David Elliot's recent discussion of intrinsic value is criticized.

Hansen, Kaj B. An Inverse of Bell's Theorem. *J Gen Phil Sci*, 26(1), 63-74, 1995.

Hansson, Sven Ove. A Note on Anti-Cyclic Properties of Complete Binary Relations. *Rep Math Log*, 27, 41-44, 1993.

A simplified notation is introduced for transitivity and related properties of binary relations. Interrelations of such properties can be proved in a facilitated way with manipulation-rules that the new notation makes possible.

Hansson, Sven Ove. Changes in Preference. *Theor Decis*, 38(1), 1-28, Ja 95.

A basic framework for studies of changes in preference is introduced, and four types of changes in preference are identified. *Revision* by a sentence such as '*A* is better than *B*' means that a preference for *A* over *B* is acquired. The result of *contraction* by '*A* is better than *B*' is that the subject no longer holds *A* to be better than *B*. In *addition* and *subtraction*, an alternative is added to, or subtracted from, respectively, the set of alternatives that are under consideration. Formal models of these four types of change are introduced, and they are shown to satisfy plausible postulates for rational changes in preferences.

Hansson, Sven Ove (ed). *Idéer om Ägande.* Stockholm, Tiden, 1994.

Sven Ove Hansson (ed) *Idéer om ägande* (Ideas on property) Tidens förlag, Stockholm, 1994. In Swedish. 297 pp. The book contains major texts on the philosophy of property by Felix Cohen, Tony Honoré, Gerald Cohen, Robert Goodin, Peter Karlen, Edwin Hettinger, Mark Suchman, and Thomas Grey. Each of these texts is preceded by an introduction by the editor.

Hansson, Sven Ove. *Idéer om Arbete.* Stockholm, Tiden, 1992.

Sven Ove Hansson (ed) *Idéer om arbete* (Ideas on work), Tidens förlag, Stockholm, 1992. In Swedish. 234 pp. The book contains major texts on the philosophy and sociology of work by Richard Edwards, Michael Burawoy, Marie Jahoda, and Jon Elster. Each of these texts is preceded by an introduction by the editor.

Hansson, Sven Ove. John Stuart Mill och socialismen. Stockholm, Tiden, 1995.

This essay on the political philosophy of John Stuart Mill puts much emphasis on Mill's views on socialism and on the connections between his epistemological and political views.

Hansson, Sven Ove. Kernel Contraction. *J Sym Log*, 59(3), 845-859, S 94.

Kernel contraction is a natural nonrelational generalization of safe contraction. All partial meet contractions are kernel contractions, but the converse relationship does not hold. Kernel contraction is axiomatically characterized. It is shown to be better suited than partial meet contraction for formal treatments of iterated belief change.

Hansson, Sven Ove. Philosophical Craftsmanship. *Metaphilosophy*, 25(4), 316-325, O 94.

Three skills are pointed out as central parts of philosophical craftsmanship: thought-experimenting, linguistic analysis, and idealization. These skills are to a large extent learnt by practice and apprenticeship. By paying close attention to the nature of these skills we can better understand some of the characteristics of philosophy, such as the lack of "progress", the increasing role of formalization, and philosophy's relationships to science, to literature and to pre-philosophical standpoints in world-view issues.

Hansson, Sven Ove (ed) and Hermansson, Jörgen. *Idéer om Demokrati.* Stockholm, Tiden, 1992.

Sven Ove Hansson and Jörgen Hermansson (eds) *Idéer om demokrati* (Ideas on democracy), Tidens förlag, Stockholm, 1992. In Swedish. 316 pp. The book contains major texts on the philosophy of democracy by Brian Barry, Norberto Bobbio, Robert Dahl, Jon Elster, David Miller, and Adam Przeworski. The editors have contributed three introductions, that center on the three issues; What is democracy?, Why democracy?, and The problems of democracy.

Hanzawa, Takamaro. The Political Thought of John Dunn and the Cambridge School. *Hist Euro Ideas*, 19(1-3), 179-183, Jl 94.

Hanzel, I and Cernik, V and Vicenik, J. What is a Category?. *Metaphilosophy*, 25(2-3), 181-193, Ap-Jl 94.

The task of this paper is to analyze the problems connected with philosophical categories as well as with systems of philosophical categories. We begin with some meta-reflections on the internal structure of philosophy. We then scrutinize the logical categories of cognition. Finally we explicate the concepts "philosophical category" and "system of philosophical categories", as well as the relation of categories to the history of human thinking.

Harak, G Simon. Child Abuse and Embodiment from a Thomistic Perspective. *Mod Theol*, 11(3), 315-340, Jl 95.

This article uses current research to present the principal and lasting effects of child abuse upon the person, concentrating on physical abuse and its influence upon the self as embodied. It then seeks to understand such abuse and its long-term impact theologically, using the theology of embodiment in Thomas Aquinas's *Summa theologiae*, and especially in his "Treatise on the Passions." The article thus presents Thomas's theology in a new yet authentic way, reveals a "classical" analysis of child abuse that agrees with and furthers current analysis, and indicates pathways to recovery for survivors of abuse.

Harbers, Hans. Constructivisme, Epistemologie en Maatschappijtheorie: Een Reactie op Blom. *Kennis Methode*, 19(2), 181-188, 1995.

Hardcastle, Gary L. S S Stevens and the Origins of Operationism. *Phil Sci*, 62(3), 404-424, S 95.

Despite influencing the social sciences since the 1930s, S S Stevens's "operationist" philosophy of science has yet to be adequately understood. I reconstruct Stevens's operationism from his early work and assess the influence of various views (logical positivism, behaviorism and the "operational viewpoint" of P W Bridgman, among others) on Stevens. Stevens's operationism emerges, on my reconstruction, as a naturalistic methodological directive aimed at agreement, founded in turn on the belief that agreement is constitutive of science, the scientific community, and objectivity. Further, I show that operationism is historically and philosophically independent of the views mentioned above.

Hardcastle, Valerie Gray. A Critique of Information Processing Theories of Consciousness. *Mind Mach*, 5(1), 89-107, F 95.

Information processing theories in psychology give rise to "executive" theories of consciousness. Roughly speaking, these theories maintain that consciousness is a centralized processor that we use when processing novel or complex stimuli. The computational assumptions driving the executive theories are closely tied to the computer metaphor. However, those who take the metaphor serious—as I believe psychologists who advocate the executive theories do—end up accepting too particular a notion of a computing device. In this essay, I examine the arguments from theoretical computational considerations that cognitive psychologists use to support their general approach in order to show that they make unwarranted assumptions about the processing attributes of consciousness. I then go on to examine the assumptions behind executive theories which grow out of the computer metaphor of cognitive psychology and conclude that we may not be the sort of computational machine cognitive psychology assumes and that cognitive's approach in itself does not buy us anything in developing theories of consciousness. Hence, the state space in which we may locate consciousness is vast, even within an information processing framework.

Hardcastle, Valerie Gray. Indicator Semantics and Dretske's Function. *Phil Psych*, 7(3), 367-382, 1994.

In his *Explaining Behavior*, Fred Dretske uses a reliabilist theory of representation to try to vindicate the use of intentional explanation for behavior against latter-day eliminativism. Although Dretske's indicator semantics turns on the notion of function, he himself never explicitly defines what function means. Dretske's reticence in discussing function may ultimately be an error, for, as I argue, his implicit understanding of what a function amounts to does not fit with data from operant conditioning. Still, this need not be a deep flaw in Dretske and I offer one way in which we may patch up the notion of function via the changes known to occur with learning in the brain. Ultimately, I conclude that the only facts needed to explain behavior are 1) the conditions in the world that are paired with neuronal circuit activation (as picked out by goals in some circumstances); and 2) what motor output that condition triggers.

Hardin, Tim and Walters, Bruce and Schick, James. Top Executive Compensation: Equity or Excess? Implications for Regaining American Competitiveness. *J Bus Ethics*, 14(3), 227-234, Mr 95.

The debate over compensation packages for top executives is discussed. Particular emphasis is placed on the decoupling of CEO pay and organizational performance. A contrast is drawn between firms that are owner-controlled and those that are manager-controlled. Owner-controlled firms tend to be more market-driven. In manager-controlled firms, however, ownership can become diluted to the point where decisions may not always be in the best interest of shareholders. The process of determining CEO compensation packages is examined, and special attention is given to the handling of stock options. In order to stem the threat of increased government intervention, suggestions are made for increasing the leverage of compensation committees and of shareholders in general.

Hardt, Michael. "Spinoza's Democracy: The Passions of Social Assemblages" in *Marxism in the Postmodern Age, Callari, Antonio (ed)*, 24-32. New York, Guilford, 1994.

This essay considers Spinoza's notion of democracy and attempts to place it within the context of modern democratic thinking. Spinoza's direct discussion of democracy in the political treatise is unfinished, but the groundwork is laid in the logics of association and assemblage developed in the ethics. Gilles Deleuze's work on Spinoza is praticularly useful for highlighting that a Spinozian notion of democracy must rely heavily on the constitutive powers of the body, affect, and passion.

Hare, John. Puffing Up the Capacity. *J Phil Res*, 19, 75-88, 1994.

This paper is about the failure of a particular strategy to overcome the problem of the gap between the moral demand and natural human capacities to meet that demand. The strategy is that of the optimist, who thinks that humans do in fact have the resources to empower themselves to live by the moral demand. A conspicuous optimist of this sort is Shelly Kagan, in his book *The Limits of Morality*. The optimist makes a counterfactual claim about morality: If all our beliefs were vivid, including especially our beliefs about the interests of others, we would tend to conform to the impartial standpoint (to what the utilitarian principle requires). This paper argues that the counterfactual claim is false.

Hare, Richard M. "Embryo Experimentation: Public Policy in a Pluralist Society" in *Medicine and Moral Reasoning, Fulford, K W M (ed)*, 29-40. New York, Cambridge Univ Pr, 1994.

Hare, William. Content and Criticism: The Aims of Schooling. *J Phil Educ*, 29(1), 47-60, March 95.

A number of recent writers have urged that schools not try to foster critical thinking in students, and this attack on what had lately emerged as very widely held to be a central aim of schooling is examined and found wanting. The debate is placed in the context of the evolving discussion in twentieth-century philosophy of education of critical thinking as an educational aim, and it is argued that the distinctions and arguments which are needed to rebut the attack on critical thinking can in large measure be found in the literature from Dewey on.

Hark, Michael. Electric Brain Fields and Memory Traces: Wittgenstein and Gestalt Psychology. *Phil Invest*, 18(2), 113-138, Ap 95.

The goal of this article is to show that the purport of Wittgenstein's much discussed remarks about mind and brain in *Zettel*, par 608 ff. is not radical anti-physicalistic. Evidence is provided that the intended target of Wittgenstein's remarks is Köhler's metaphysical thesis of psychophysical isomorphism and his theory of electrical brainfields. It is argued that Wittgenstein is especially critical of Köhler's idea that memory traces isomorphically related to what they are traces of *must* be postulated in order to bridge the gap between a causally inefficacious part event and present recall. It is argued that Wittgenstein's Jottings analogy has to be seen in this light. The point of this analogy is that just as the connection between the jottings and the text is not made before the text is actually cited, but is made by us in the act of reciting the text, the fact that I am able to, e.g., resume the thread is evidence that a memory trace was a memory trace, rather than the trace being a standard for correct recall already present ahead of time. The article concludes with a critical discussion of earlier interpretations of these remarks by M Budd, C McGinn and R Donough. The upshot of this discussion is that Wittgenstein not a radical anti-physicalist as these authors have pictured him.

Harkavy, Allan Abraham. *Human Will: The Search for Its Physical Basis*. New York, Lang, 1995.

This book presents a speculative philosophy, based on physics and neurophysiology, which offers explanations of how will is possible in a world described by physical laws. There is a history of similar attempts by scientists and philosophers that are also reviewed in this book. All of the proposals have to do with how quantum mechanics and in particular the uncertainty principle might operate in the human brain to provide a physical basis for human will.

Harle, Vilho. On the Concepts of the 'Other' and the 'Enemy'. *Hist Euro Ideas*, 19(1-3), 27-34, Jl 94.

Harman, Gilbert. "Meaning Holism Defended" in *Holism: A Consumer Update, Fodor, Jerry A (ed)*, 163-171. Amsterdam, Rodopi, 1993.

The meaning of a symbol is determined by its use, but the canonical way of specifying meaning is in a statement of the form "S means ...." To be able to provide such a specification is equivalent to being able to translate the symbol S into one's own terms. A change in usage of terms involves a change of meaning if and only if the correct translation between earlier usage and later usage takes a term into a different expression. Such translation is holistic, a matter of finding the best mapping. Sameness of meaning is a similarity relation, as is sameness of concept. The meaning of a larger expression is derived from the meaning of its parts if and only if the translation of the whole is derived from the translation of its parts.

Harnad, Stevan. Computation Is Just Interpretable Symbol Manipulation; Cognition Isn't. *Mind Mach*, 4(4), 379-390, N 94.

Computation is interpretable symbol manipulation. Symbols are objects that are manipulated on the basis of rules operating only on their *shapes*, which are arbitrary in relation to what they can be interpreted as meaning. Even if one accepts the Church/Turing Thesis that computation is unique, universal and very near omnipotent, not everything is a computer, because not everything can be given a systematic interpretation; and certainly everything can't be given *every* systematic interpretation. But even after computers and computation have been successfully distinguished from other kinds of things, mental states will not just be the implementations of the right symbol systems, because of the symbol grounding problem: The interpretation of a symbol system is not intrinsic to the system; it is projected onto it by the interpreter. This is not true of our thoughts. We must accordingly be more than just computers. My guess is that the meanings of our symbols are grounded in the substrate of our robotic capacity to interact with that real world of objects, events and states of affairs that our symbols are systematically interpretable as being about.

Harnad, Steven. L'Ancrage des Symboles dans le Monde *Analogique* à l'Aide de Réseaux Neuronaux: Un Modèle Hybride. *Lekton*, 4(2), 65-83, 1994.

The predominant approach to cognitive modelling is still what has come to be called "computationalism," the hypothèsis that cognition is computation. The more recent rival approach is "connectionism," the hypothesis that cognition is a dynamic pattern of connections and activations in a "neural net." Are computationalism and connectionism really deeply different from one another, and if so, should they compete for cognitive hegemony, or should they collaborate? These questions will be addressed here, in the context of an obstacle that is faced by computationalism (as well as by connectionism if it is either computational or seeks cognitive hegemony on its own): the symbol grounding problem.

Haroutunian-Gordon, Sophie. The Selection of Texts: Response to Professor Alan Gewirth. *Stud Phil Educ*, 13(2), 125-129, 1993-94.

Harper, William. On Calling God 'Mother'. *Faith Phil*, 11(2), 290-297, Ap 94.

Patricia Altenbernd Johnson argues that referring to God in female terms is desirable in that it would help overcome patriarchy, bring to our image of God positive qualities missing when God is referred to in male terms, and would be more inclusive. I find that Johnson's notion of patriarchy is such that overcoming it involves introducing pantheistic elements into Christian belief. Also, Johnson's arguments assume an objectionable stereotype of maleness. The argument from inclusiveness is not supported by observation. Concluding that Johnson's arguments fail, I suggest that biblical example is sufficient permission for referring to God exclusively in male terms.

Harpine, William D. The Appeal to Tradition: Cultural Evolution and Logical Soundness. *Inform Log*, 15(3), 209-219, Fall 93.

The Appeal of Tradition, often considered to be unsound, frequently reflects sophisticated adaptations to the environment. Once developed, these adaptations are often transmitted culturally rather than as reasoned argument, so that people may or may not be aware of why their traditions are wise. Tradition is more likely to be valid is a stable environment in which a wide range of variations have been available for past testing; however, traditions tend to become obsolete in a rapidly changing environment.

Harré, Rom. Emotion and Memory: The Second Cognitive Revolution. *Philosophy*, 37(Supp), 25-40, 1994.

Psychology has moved through positivism (behaviorism) to hypothetico-deductivism (cognitive science) to a new general theory of cognition as mediated by discourse, public and private. By examining an imaginary research program the functional duality between physiological processes structured by causality and intentional acts structured by meaning rules is demonstrated. Language appears in psychological research both as a topic and as a model. This is illustrated by the treatment of emotional displays as discursive acts, and memory as socially negotiated. On this view individual psychology is the study of the acquisition and application of skills.

Harré, Rom. Vigotsky and Artificial Intelligence: What Could Cognitive Psychology Possibly Be About?. *Midwest Stud Phil*, 15, 389-399, 1990.

The project of cognitive science (CS) has been to build a theory of human cognition and perception, while that of artificial intelligence (AI) has been to design and test machines capable of simulating human performances. As a psychology AI has been used to develop CS. A key set of problems for the project has emerged in the AI/CS treatment of language use, discussed in this paper in five critical theses: 1) AI/CS picks out only those patterns of cognition that it fits apriori; 2) Cognition in both origin and practice is collective; 3) All uses of language are indeterminate and indexical; 4) Discourse tolerates contradiction; 5) Cognition is an activity of persons, not their parts. These theses can be found in Vygotsky and other authors. I conclude that AI/CS is best interpreted as a set of models interpretable either as discourse grammars or as schematic neurophysiology.

Harré, Rom and Aronson, Jerrold L and Way, Eileen Cornell. *Realism Rescued: How Scientific Progress Is Possible*. Peru, Open Court, 1995.

A full-blown version of convergent realism is defined and defended by replacing the logicist technique for analyzing scientific theories with one found in knowledge representation, the dynamic type hierarchy. The authors use these hierarchies to provide an analysis of models that displays their indispensable role in science. They go on to use this analysis to develop a semantics for verisimilitude, truth and modalities. An inductive justification for convergent realism is then presented, one which, the authors contend, is not open to the objections that anti-realists have made against the inference to the best explanation defense.

Harré, Rom and Sabat, Steven R. The Alzheimer's Disease Sufferer as a Semiotic Subject. *Phil Psychiat Psych*, 1(3), 145-160, S 94.

The discourse of Alzheimer's disease sufferers, studied in depth, is found to reveal the afflicted as being semiotic subjects, that is, persons for whom meaning is the driving force behind their behavior. This is despite the fact that the subjects are categorized, on the basis of standard psychometric measures, as being in moderate to severe stages of the disease. The research presented herein is meant to suggest the possibility that such disparities may be more common than is presently acknowledged, and that if so, such semiotic behavior as can be found in Alzheimer's sufferers may be used to help facilitate interactions between the afflicted and the healthy, and to inform further our understanding of cognition and intention by suggesting a complementary approach to assessing cognitive function. In keeping with the discursive approach to psychology, this study is based on the principle that meanings are jointly constituted by the participants to a conversation.

Harré, Rom and Van Langenhove, Luk. Cultural Stereotypes and Positioning Theory. *J Theor Soc Behav*, 24(4), 359-372, D 94.

This paper addresses the application of *positioning theory*, a new emerging theoretical scheme on the issue of cultural stereotyping. First, a critical conceptual analysis of the words 'cultural stereotype' is presented. Secondly, the basic tenets of positioning theory are outlined. Finally, it will be demonstrated how the framework of positioning theory can be used to analytically refine the concept of cultural stereotype. The main upshot of the article is that within social psychology, the concept of cultural stereotype is used in a conceptually vague and blurred way and that, with the necessary conceptual refinements, other research-agendas on stereotypes will have to be tackled if social psychologists want to contribute anything to the societal efforts of changing stereotypes.

Harriott, Howard. On the Rationality of Irrational Ideals. *Cont Phil*, 16(4), 1-6, Jl-Ag 94.

The concept of rationality is often couched in a way that rejects as "irrational" the cultivation of actions and goals that have little chance of realization given the way the world actually is. In this paper it is claimed that the human habit of creating impossible goals and ideals, can sometimes be defended as reasonable, and even essential for human flourishing. Three areas of human endeavour are examined; the striving for a perpetual peace, the commitment to transcendental values where rationality might suggest skepticism, and the attempt to excel in the moral virtues.

Harris, Errol E. Dialectic and the Advance of Science. *Ideal Stud*, 24(3), 227-239, Fall 94.

Prompted by Christiansen's admonition to address McMullin's criticism of "Dialectic and Scientific Method" (*Idealistic Studies*, III, 1973), the nature of dialectic is restated and the distinction is clarified between the dialectic of nature and that of scientific thinking. The inadequacy of the current critique of inductive theory of scientific method, based on Hume, is shown to be due to its failure to detect the dialectical structure of science. The distinction of the context of discovery from that of justification is reconsidered and McMullin's strictures rebutted. Historical examples of continuous development are discussed. Hegel's procedure in the *Naturphilosophie* is defended and differentiated from the author's account of dialectic in scientific advance. Contemporary evidence of dialectical procedure in science is cited.

Harris, H S. *Hegel: Phenomenology and System*. Indianapolis, Hackett, 1995.

This little book aims to do two things: to provide a reliable skeleton key to the argument of the phenomenology of spirit; and to show how the "science of experience" which it contains is the *necessary* "first part" of "Hegel's System". The position defended is that the science of experience (or of appearance) is *coordinate* with the logical of "what truly is" (or of reality). Hegel's system can only be defended against Kantian critical objections if it is interpreted in this light.

Harris, H S and Geraets, Theodore F. On Translating Hegel's *Encyclopedia Logic*: A Response. *Owl Minerva*, 26(1), 95-96, Fall 94.

Harris, Henry S. "Fichtes Verdienst". *Rev Int Phil*, 49(191), 79-91, 1995.

This essay shows how the comment on *Fichtes Verdienst* in Hegel's *Wastebook* of 1804-6—that it is only after the history of consciousness that we know what we have in "these abstractions"—is reflected in the actual execution of the *Phenomenology of Spirit*. Fichte is thus the presiding genius of Hegel's "Science of the Experience of Consciousness".

Harris, Henry S. How Philosophy *Instructs the World*. *Laval Theol Phil*, 51(2), 311-322, Je 95.

This essay examines the Preface of Hegel's *Philosophy of Right* in its relation to the work itself. It is shown that, in spite of the explicit declaration that "philosophy always comes too late to instruct the world how to be", the rational structure that systematic philosophy uncovers in the world is an ideal that is not perfectly realized anywhere. Thus philosophy is in fact, "instructive" (or action-guiding and attitude-directing) in certain important ways.

Harris, Ian. "The Politics of Christianity" in *Locke's Philosophy, Rogers, G A J (ed)*, 197-215. New York, Oxford Univ Pr, 1994.

Argues that Locke's *Two Treatises* has a hitherto unsuspected relation to revealed theology. Firstly, its view of representation in politics is diametrically opposed to the theological conception of representation involved in both the Augustinian view of the Fall and in Filmer's political theory. Secondly, the positions Locke assumed in *Two Treatises* have a consequent bearing on the positions he would assume in revealed theology.

Harris, James. Reasons, Desires, Actions. *Conference*, 5(2), 79-90, Wint 94-95.

Harris, Nigel G E. "Professional Codes and Kantian Duties" in *Ethics and the Professions, Chadwick, Ruth (ed)*, 104-115. Brookfield, Avebury, 1994.

Harris, R Baine. Can We Have a Common Humanity?. *Dialogue Hum*, 3(2), 88-95, 1993.

Harris, R Baine. Neoplatonism in Christianity, Judaism and Islam. *Dialogue Hum*, 3(1), 31-40, 1993.

Harris, Sandra. Pragmatics and Power. *J Prag*, 23(2), 117-135, F 95.

This paper sets out to ascertain on the basis of actual language behavior whether 'universal pragmatics', especially Grice's maxims and Habermas's validity claims, can provide a sustainable conceptual framework for understanding the relationship between pragmatics and power. On the basis of a data base of magistrate/defendant and police/suspect discourse, it examines the nature of strategic discourse in settings where participants have conflicting goals. The paper concludes with an assessment of the usefulness of the work of Grice and Habermas in relationship to strategic discourse and proposes a possible model for future work. (edited)

Harris, Wendell V. Late-Marxist, Post-Poststructuralist Critical Nebulosity. *Phil Lit*, 19(1), 127-135, Ap 95.

Much of what has gone awry in contemporary literary and cultural criticism is nicely illustrated in J Hillis Miller's *Illustrations*. The cultural criticism offered in the first portion proceeds according to the unargued assumptions of a kind of diluted Marxism while the "empowerment" there celebrated turns out to stand for a laudable goal the means of achieving which are ignored. In the second portion, Miller works hard to find the paradoxes and undecidabilities fashionable among poststructuralists in the relations between words and images, but what his commentary most seems to reveal is that the author is just beginning to try to think about art.

Harrison, Bernard and Gaskin, Richard. Symposium: Truth, Meaning and Literature. *Brit J Aes*, 34(4), 376-388, O 94.

Harrison, Charles (ed) and Wood, Paul (ed). *Art in Theory 1900-1990: An Anthology of Changing Ideas*. Cambridge, Blackwell, 1994.

Current debates about the status of Modernism have led to an increasing interest in critical and aesthetic theories, and to a questioning of some of the traditional assumptions and limits of art history. The aims of this substantial anthology is to equip the student, teacher and interested general reader with the materials for an up-to-date understanding of twentieth-century art. Beside the writings of the century's major artists, *Art in Theory* includes relevant texts by critics, philosophers, politicians and literary figures. It is organized into eight sections, from the legacy of Symbolism at the turn of the century to contemporary debates about the postmodern. Each section is prefaced by a brief essay. There are introductions for all of the 300-plus texts, so that theories and critical approaches are placed in context. The volume also includes an extensive bibliography. The result is both a comprehensive collection of documents on twentieth-century art and an encyclopedic history of relevant theory.

Harrison, Christine, (& others). Should People Do unto Others as They Would Not Want Done unto Themselves:. *J Clin Ethics*, 6(1), 14-19, Spr 95.

This paper reports on a study, the purpose of which was to test two hypotheses: that people systematically choose more extensive care for their family members than they would want for themselves; and that they provide even more aggressive treatment for unknown patients when they assume the role of physicians. This treatment is often unwanted, and provides little, if any, benefit. The survey results support the hypotheses; we suggest some advantages and disadvantages of using special public opinion polls as part of the decision making process of choosing treatment for others, and recommend the use of advance directives.

Harriss-White, Barbara (ed) and Hoffenberg, Raymond (ed). *Food: Multidisciplinary Perspectives*. Cambridge, Blackwell, 1994.

At the core of this collection are the Wolfson College, Oxford, public lectures of 1992. These examine, in accessible language, the frontiers of research on food from the following disciplinary perspectives: medicine, nutrition, food science, anthropology, gender studies, development economics and political sociology. To these have been added specially commissioned papers from nutritional biochemistry, law and ethics. An introduction summarises the contributions, develops certain themes, and draws out the varied implications for public action.

Hart, B and Starchenko, S. Superstable Quasi-Varieties. *Annals Pure Applied Log*, 69(1), 53-71, S 94.

We present a structure theorem for superstable quasi-varieties without DOP. We show that every algebra in such a quasi-variety weakly decomposes as the product of an affine algebra and a combinatorial algebra, that is, it is bi-interpretable with a two sorted structure where one sort is an affine algebra, the other sort is a combinatorial algebra and the only nontrivial polynomials between the two sorts are certain actions of the affine sort on the combinatorial sort.

Hart, Hendrick. Liberalism, Pluralism, and Lived Faith. *Phil Theol*, 8(2), 149-165, Wint 93.

Liberalism is no longer defensible as a strategy for coping with conflicts in a pluralistic society, but is itself one of the pluralities in conflict. Hence its strategy for coping with plurality—tolerant suspension or privatization of the deep commitments that are the roots of conflict, coupled with rational discussion to form a public consensus not connected to the plurality of commitments—can no longer serve as a *common* sense approach for *all* citizens. In this paper I explore as a solution the continuation of discussion toward shared public policy, but now discussion openly tied to underlying commitments. Truth in this context is pursued not as a matter of argument, but as fruitful consequences of action.

Hart, Hendrik. *Understanding Our World: An Integral Ontology*. Lanham, Univ Pr of America, 1984.

Hart, Hendrik and Nielsen, Kai. *Search for Community in a Withering Tradition: Conversations between a Marxian Atheist and a Calvinian Christian*. Lanham, Univ Pr of America, 1990.

Hartje, Hans (trans) and Strauss, Leo and Guglielmina, Pierre (trans). Le problème de la connaissance dans la doctrine philosophique de Fr H Jacobi (II). *Rev Metaph Morale*, 99(4), 505-532, O-D 94.

Hartl, Daniel L and Orel, Vitezslav. Controversies in the Interpretation of Mendel's Discovery. *Hist Phil Life Sci*, 16(3), 423-464, D 94.

For twenty years there has been controversy over the level at which Gregor Mendel understood the implications of his experiments for heredity. We argue that he was a hybridist in the tradition of the nineteenth century who 1) designed innovative experiments in plant hybridization and 2) formulated a fundamental new theory for the transmission of traits from parents to offspring based on hypothetical determinants present in germ cells. His own summary, that '...pea hybrids form germinal and pollen cells that in their composition correspond in equal numbers to all the constant forms resulting from the combination of traits united through fertilization', is tantamount to the discovery of what are now called the 'laws' of segregation and independent assortment. Mendel is therefore rightly credited with formulating a new theory of heredity.

Hartley, Troy W. Environmental Justice: An Environmental Civil Rights Value Acceptable to All World Views. *Environ Ethics*, 17(3), 277-289, Fall 95.

In accordance with environmental injustice, sometimes called environmental racism, minority communities are disproportionately subjected to a higher level of environmental risk than other segments of society. Growing concern over unequal environmental risk and mounting evidence of both racial and economic injustices have led to a grass-roots civil rights campaign called the environmental justice movement. The environmental ethics aspects of environmental injustice challenge narrow utilitarian views and promote Kantian rights and obligations. Nevertheless, an environmental justice value exists in all ethical world views, although it involves a concept of equitable distribution of environmental protection that has been lacking in environmental ethics discussion.

Hartmann, Bruno. *Logik und Arbeit*. Sankt Augustin, Academia, 1994.

Der Autor hebt (in Teil I) mit einer philosophisch-logischen Erklärung und Kritik der FREGEschen Logik (= Logistik) an und unternimmt sodann (in Teil II) den *Versuch der ökonomisch-praktischen Fundierung von Logik und logischer Fundierung ökonomishcer Theorie*. Indem er das MARXsche Arbeits-Konzept für dieses methodologische Vorhaben mobilisiert, zeigt er im Ausgang von der Arbeits-Wirklichkeit, wie das *Vergleichen und Unterscheiden* über die *materiellen* Vorstellungen zur *Inhaltslogik* führt, die auch Inhaltsverhältnisse (I_x/I_y) einschliesst. So wird der Anschluss an das absolute Masssystem von *Gauss* und *Weber* realisiert und eine Logik der Masse (der Physik oder Ökonomie) möglich.

Hartmann, Frank. "Geistiger Anschluss? Das Wiener Philosophische Institut und der Nationalsozialismus" in *Der geistige Anschluss, Fischer, Kurt R (ed)*, 170-178. Wien, WUV Univ, 1993.

Hartmann, Frank. "Philosophie und Drittes Reich" in *Der geistige Anschluss, Fischer, Kurt R (ed)*, 101-122. Wien, WUV Univ, 1993.

Hartmann, Frank. "Wider Natur: Die Biologisierung sozialer Praxis im 'naturwissenschaftlichen Monismus'" in *Nationalsozialismus und Moderne, Welzer, Harald (ed)*, 150-165. Tübingen, Ed Diskord, 1993.

Hartmann, Frank. *Denker Denken Geschichte Erkundungen zu Philosophie und Nationalsozialismus*. Vienna, Passagen, 1994.

Die Ignoranz politischer Implikationen schien eine Wesensbestimmung besonders der deutschen Philosophie zu sein, bis sich dies 1933 schlagartig änderte. Während die kritischen *Intellektuellen* das Schicksal der Emigration traf, exerzierten die verbleibenden *Denker* bald als *Soldaten des Geistes* für die neuen Machthaber. Die Zäsur von 1945 und die ebenso verspätete wie verfehlte Debatte über die Folgen jenes politischen Engagements der "Philosophen" bedeutet letztlich die Verabschiedung von der Vorstellung, dass "Philosophie" als die Subkultur einiger Textinterpreten ein unangefochtenes gesellschaftliches Reflexionsmonopol besitzt. (edited)

Hartshorne, Charles. "Grounds for Believing in God's Existence" in *Meaning, Truth, and God, Rouner, Leroy (ed)*, 17-33. Notre Dame, Univ Notre Dame Pr, 1982.

Hartshorne, Charles. "Peirce and Religion: Between Two Forms of Religious Belief" in *Peirce and Contemporary Thought: Philosophical Inquiries, Ketner, Kenneth Laine (ed)*, 339-355. New York, Fordham Univ Pr, 1995.

Hartshorne, Charles. Hartshorne's Response to Haugen and Keeling: "Hartshorne's Process Theism and Big Bang Cosmology". *Process Stud*, 22(3), 172, Fall 93.

Hartwig, Michael J. Parenting Ethics and Reproductive Technologies. *J Soc Phil*, 26(1), 183-202, Spr 95.

Reproductive technologies make some alternative family and parenting arrangements easier to bring about. This essay concludes that family structure (the immediate and specific configuration of persons in a family unit) is not the morally salient feature of ethical parenting. A paradigm of "life-long covenantal advocacy" is proposed as a criterion that would encompass both traditional family systems and contemporary alternatives (including, for example, gay and lesbian families). Some general ethical evaluations of reproductive technologies are carried out, considering several deontological concerns.

Harvey, Charles and Press, Jon. John Ruskin and the Ethical Foundations of Morris and Company, 1861-96. *J Bus Ethics*, 14(3), 181-194, Mr 95.

In *Unto this Last*, John Ruskin argued that Britain's industrial society was morally degenerate and pernicious in that it drove the laboring class into cultural and material poverty. Ruskin's writings are in essence an appeal to the business leader to behave in a socially responsible, paternalistic fashion according to his own moral prescriptions. This article examines the ways in which William Morris sought to give practical expression to these ideas. There is no perfect correspondence between the business notions of John Ruskin and the practice of William Morris. Yet it is evident that Morris stuck to many of his mentor's ideas with remarkable tenacity. (edited)

Harvey, J. Forgiving as an Obligation of the Moral Life. *Int J Moral Soc Stud*, 8(3), 211-222, Autumn 93.

The main focus in literature so far has been on forgiveness as the letting go of resentment. No contribution from the wrongdoer is strictly necessary here. But there are limits to the degree of voluntary control the victim has over forgiveness, since it involves a change in emotional state. I argue that there is something more under control which can fairly be described as forgiving: giving permission for the wrongdoer to make a 'fresh start' with respect to her 'public moral status'. This requires contributions from both victim and wrongdoer. Furthermore, sometimes we have an obligation to forgive in this sense, since we should be committed to a life of moral endeavour in spite of failures and setbacks, and should also support this commitment in others.

Harvey, J. Humor as Social Act: Ethical Issues. *J Value Inq*, 29(1), 19-30, Mr 95.

The paper examines the value and uses of humor. Accounts of the desirability of humor often embody two major problems. First, the "individual-based approach" assesses the value of humor via its role in the individual's approach to life (e.g., "humor enables a person to handle failure well"). But it is important to articulate the social dimensions of acts of humor, and in particular, the relevance of non-peer relationships. Secondly, the usual focus is on socially privileged people while drawing moral issues which are explored in an examination of put-down humor with its various social structures.

Harvey, J. The Emerging Practice of Institutional Apologies. *Int J Applied Phil*, 9(2), 57-65, Wint-Spr 95.

The paper examines the moral grounds for offering public apologies for institutional wrongs. Types and degrees of institutional involvement in wrongs are set out, since the more "institutional" (less individual) the wrong, the more appropriate that apologies be offered. For institutional wrongs where the agents are not morally culpable, there are still grounds for public expressions of regret. Finally, some conclusions are drawn about what counts as "sincere" institutional apologies.

Harvey, Robert (ed) and Lyotard, Jean-François and Roberts, Mark S (ed). *Toward the Post-Modern*. Atlantic Highlands, Humanities Pr, 1995.

Hasker, William. Can Philosophy Defend Theology? A Response to James Keller. *Faith Phil*, 11(2), 272-278, Ap 94.

James Keller has recently defended Gordon Kaufman from the criticisms leveled against him by Eleonore Stump and Norman Kretzmann. I point out that, while Keller does resolve some of the problems with Kaufman's article, in the process he reveals and/or creates some deep tensions in the resulting "Kaufman-Keller view"—tensions which, I maintain, cast serious doubt on the viability of Keller's defense. In closing, I offer some thoughts concerning the difference between contemporary Christian theologians and philosophers.

Hasker, William. Gale on God: The Return of Philo?. *Dialogue (Canada)*, 33(4), 685-691, Fall 94.

In his *On The Nature and Existence of God* (Cambridge, 1991), Richard Gale reviews a number of arguments for and against the existence of the God of traditional theism. He finds none of the arguments compelling, though some of the anti-theistic arguments force revisions in the conception of certain divine attributes. His treatment is insightful, usually accurate, and often remarkably humorous. His most serious challenge to theism is found in his contention that religious experience is not cognitive and could not provide warrant for theistic belief.

Haslanger, Sally. Humean Supervenience and Enduring Things. *Austl J Phil*, 72(3), 339-359, S 94.

It is plausible that what happens across time depends on what is the case at each moment, i.e., that a world's nonoccurrent properties supervene on the occurrent. David Lewis suggests that it follows from this that there are no enduring particulars; instead actual particulars persist by perduring. I argue that depending on one's choice of background principles—concerning synchronic/diachronic unity, part/whole, and predication—there are parallel strategies to guarantee that both perduring and enduring things supervene on occurrent qualities. A careful selection of principles allows a sparse theory of enduring things compatible with desired supervenience.

Hasselberg, Erwin (ed) and Radtke, Frank (ed). *Hegels "Wissenschaft der Logik": Eine internationale Bibliographie ihrer Rezeption im XX Jahrhundert*. Vienna, Passagen, 1993.

Die Rezeption der Philosophie G W F Hegels hat sich besonders in unserem Jahrhundert immer wieder als ein Prisma der geistigen Hauptströmungen ausgewiesen. Mit der bisher umfangreichsten Bibliographie zur Rezeption der *logischen Begrifflichkeit* Hegels wurde eine Möglichkeit geschaffen, die auftretenden Defizite im internationalen Forschungsvergleich weiter zu beseitigen. Neben dem Vorteil eines breiten, nach Ländern geordneten Überblicks—China, Deutschland (Band 1), Frankreich, Grossbritannien und USA, Israel, Italien, Japan, Jugoslawien, Polen, Portugal (Band 2), Russland, Spanien, Ungarn und weitere Länder (Band 3)—sind dem überwiegenden Teil der 2600 Titel kurze bis ausführliche Inhaltsangaben beigegeben, basierend auf umfangreichen Recherchen und Übersetzungen.

Hastedt, Heiner. Enlightenment and Technology: Outline for a General Ethics of Technology. *Res Phil Technol*, 14, 205-217, 1994.

Hatab, Lawrence J. Human Nature in a Postmodern World: Reflections on the Work of Eugene Gendlin. *Human Stud*, 17(3), 363-371, Jl 94.

The essay confronts the question of human nature in the wake of the postmodern critique of traditional universals and essences. It discusses how ontological "negativity" might work against both universalistic and particularistic forms of closure and exclusion. Eugene Gendlin's objections to both traditional notions of fixed form and postmodern notions of formlessness are then considered. Gendlin argues that a kind of cross-cultural human nature can be read out of human experience and practice, avoiding a false choice between ground and groundlessness. The essay concludes with a response to Gendlin and an appeal not to forget the tragic dimension of human existence.

Hattingh, Herselman and van Veuren, Pieter. Identity and the Narrative Structure of Life. *S Afr J Phil*, 14(2), 60-71, My 95.

In this essay the relationship between narrative structure and identity formation is explored. Starting with a discussion of the notion on narratives as MacIntyre uses it in an attempt to provide a more solid basis for moral discussion and meaningful identity formation, the argument progresses to the work of Ricoeur, in an attempt to undermine the usefulness of the teleological narrative (advanced by MacIntyre) and finally to support the idea that much value is to be derived from the nontelelogical narrative, especially in view of our situatedness in a postmodern era.

Haucke, Kai. Behutsamkeit, Mimesis, und Aisthetisierung: Zur Differenz Ästhetisch Inspirierter Freiheitsvorstellungen. *Deut Z Phil*, 43(2), 233-257, 1995.

The work tries to translate sociological and aesthetical vocabularies. Central issues of social philosophy (interaction between strangers, double contingency, liberty) are described with aesthetical concepts (autoreflexivity, mimesis, aisthesis), that a reciprocal broadening will be possible. This procedure of translation is shown at the case of interaction between strangers, which includes a paradox of liberty. Three possible reactions to this situation are distinguished: 1) Autoreflective opening up of opportunities, which exceed the own horizon of certainty (Behutsamkeit). 2) Rationalistic disregarding of strangeness by decontextualized universals, supported by a special sort of mimesis. 3) Orientation at events, in which strangeness vanishes into pure sensation (aisthesis).

Hauerwas, Stanley. How Christian Ethics Became Medical Ethics: The Case of Paul Ramsey. *Christian Bioethics*, 1(1), 11-28, Mr 95.

Over the last century Christian ethics has moved from an attempt to Christianize the social order to a quandary over whether being Christian unduly biases how medical ethics is done. This movement can be viewed as the internal development of protestant liberalism to its logical conclusion, and Paul Ramsey can be taken as one of the last great representatives of that tradition. By reducing the Christian message to the 'ethical upshot' of neighbor love, Ramsey did not have the resources to show how Christian practice might make a difference for understanding or forming the practice of medicine. Instead, medicine became the practice that exemplified the moral commitments of Christian civilization, and the goal of the ethicist was to identify the values that were constitutive of medicine. Ramsey thus prepared the way for the Christian ethicist to become a medical ethicist with a difference, and the difference simply involved vague theological presumptions that do no serious intellectual work other than explaining, perhaps, the motivations of the ethicist.

Haug, Wolfgang Fritz. Allgemeine Arbeit. *Das Argument*, 207, 897-909, N-D 94.

This text, a sketch of an article for the *Historical-Critical Dictionary of Marxism*, makes a new attempt to learn from the questions of the "housework debate" of the seventies and early eighties. The author examines what Marx and Engels really said about this complex of issues, which sets of problems they thus opened up, and which they were unable to address. The logic of one sphere (housework) should not be forced into the logic of another (wage labor); rather, the development of political strategies should follow from an analysis of the differences and connections between the two spheres.

Haugeland, John. "Pattern and Being" in *Dennett and his Critics, Dahlbom, Bo (ed)*, 53-69. Cambridge, Blackwell, 1995.

Haugen, David and Keeling, L Bryant. Hartshorne's Process Theism and Big Bang Cosmology. *Process Stud*, 22(3), 163-171, Fall 93.

We attempt to establish a dilemma for Charles Hartshorne's process theism. We argue that if the general picture of the universe presented by the big bang theory is accepted, then Harshorne must abandon either the concept of God as perfectly preserving the past (divine memory) or he must abandon the attempt to explain God's relation to the world in terms of psychicalism.

Haught, Christine and Downey, Rod. Embedding Lattices into the *wtt*-Degrees Below 0'. *J Sym Log*, 59(4), 1360-1382, D 94.

The authors prove that every finite lattice can be embedded into the weak truth table degrees below 0' preserving 0 and 1.

Hauser, Larry. Acting, Intending, and Artificial Intelligence. *Behavior Phil*, 22(1), 23-28, Spr-Sum 94.

The difference between agents' acts and mere bodily movement, on John Searle's account, is the causal involvement of intention in acts. Yet we distinguish similar differences between robots' acts and *their* bodily movements. Either robots are rightly credited with intentions, which Searle denies; or else it's not intention that

distinguishes action from mere movement. In any case, full-blooded acts under "aspects" are truly attributable to robots and computers. Since the truth of such attributions depends crucially on intrinsic features of the things, not on the attributor's "intentional stance," these are no merely figurative "as if" attributions.

Hauser, Larry. Propositional Actitudes: Reply to Gunderson. *Behavior Phil*, 22(1), 35-40, Spr-Sum 94.

Keith Gunderson allows that robots and computers genuinely *do* act under "aspects" but denies such machines the mentalities their acts seems to bespeak: given our intuitive conviction that such machines lack "consciousness," Gunderson contends, their performances show, instead, the dementalizability of whatever acts (of calculation, detection, etc.) they perform. Against Gunderson, I contend such performances provide *prima facie* empirical warrant for attributions of mental properties; warrant that appeals to (lack of) consciousness are empirically too vexed and theoretically too ill-connected to override. Indeed, acts of calculation, detection, etc., *themselves* (considered as types) *are* mental properties.

Hausman, Carl R and Anderson, Douglas R. The Telos of Peirce's Realism. *Trans Peirce Soc*, 30(4), 825-838, Fall 94.

The paper is intended to show how Joseph Margolis's critique of Charles Peirce's unique kind of realism treats Peirce's "reality" as static rather than dynamic and evolutionary. This overlooking of the unique features of Peirce's realism seems to be the product of assuming the ultimacy of analytic presuppositions, especially a Cartesian notion of reason that Peirce argued against.

Hausman, Daniel M. "Paul Samuelson as Dr Frankenstein: When an Idealization Runs Amuck" in *Idealization VI: Idealization in Economics, Hamminga, Bert (ed)*, 229-242. Amsterdam, Rodopi, 1994.

This paper is concerned with relations between highly unrealistic or idealized models and the world, with how such models can be informative, with how they can be criticized, and with how their constituents can be incorporated into other models. It will focus on only one case, and its conclusions will be skeptical and suggestive.

Hausman, Daniel M. Rational Choice and Social Theory: A Comment. *J Phil*, 92(2), 96-101, F 95.

Hausman, Daniel M. The Deductive Method. *Midwest Stud Phil*, 15, 372-388, 1990.

Hausman, Daniel M. The Impossibility of Interpersonal Utility Comparisons. *Mind*, 104(415), 473-490, Jl 95.

This essay argues that if well-being is the satisfaction of preference, then an interpersonal comparison of well-being must be a comparison of the extent to which preferences are satisfied. Such comparisons are not generally possible unless preferences are cardinally representable, in which case the zero-one rule is the right way to make interpersonal comparisons. Since the zero-one rule is unacceptable, so is the identification of well-being with the satisfaction of preferences.

Havas, Randall. *Nietzsche's Genealogy: Nihilism and the Will to Knowledge*. Ithaca, Cornell Univ Pr, 1995.

By means of an interpretation of the relationship of nihilism to the modern commitment to truthfulness, *Nietzsche's Genealogy* explores the role the notions of community and individual play in Nietzsche's defense of individualism. Nihilism is, for Nietzsche, a form of skepticism that is combated neither by replacing nor by augmenting truthfulness with some other virtue, but rather by taking responsibility for that very commitment. Because such responsibility is always an individual matter, overcoming nihilism is a task for each person alone. Havas's chief interpretative aim is to show how the concepts of obedience and authority underwrite Nietzsche's understanding of responsibility.

Hawk, Stephen R. The Effects of Computerized Performance Monitoring: An Ethical Perspective. *J Bus Ethics*, 13(12), 949-957, D 94.

Considerable controversy has surrounded the use of computerized performance monitoring (CPM) by employers. Critics of this technology contend that CPM usage raises serious ethical concerns. Beliefs that the use of computerized performance monitors results in unfair performance evaluation, stress and health problems underlie much of the current concern over this technology. A field study was undertaken to provide empirical evidence that could be used to guide the design and use of computerized performance monitors to minimize these problems. One hundred forty three members of the Communication Workers of America participated in a cross sectional field study. The study examined the relationship between various monitoring system characteristics and employees' health problems, stress and satisfaction with the performance evaluation process. The ethical implications of the results are discussed.

Hawkins, Anne Hunsaker. Literature, Medical Ethics, and "Epiphanic Knowledge". *J Clin Ethics*, 5(4), 283-290, Wint 94.

Hawthorne, James. On the Nature of Bayesian Convergence. *Proc Phil Sci Ass*, 1, 241-249, 1994.

The objectivity of Bayesian induction relies on the ability of evidence to produce a *convergence to agreement* among agents who initially disagree about the plausibilities of hypotheses. I will describe three sorts of Bayesian convergence. The first reduces the objectivity of inductions about simple "occurrent events" to the objectivity of posterior probabilities for theoretical hypotheses. The second reveals that evidence will generally induce *convergence to agreement* among agents on the posterior probabilities of theories *only if* the convergence is 0 or 1. The third establishes conditions under which evidence will *very probably* compel posterior probabilities of theories to converge to 0 or 1.

Hawthorne, James and Silberstein, Michael. For Whom the Bell Arguments Toll. *Synthese*, 102(1), 99-138, Ja 95.

We will formulate two Bell arguments. Together they show that if the probabilities given by quantum mechanics are approximately correct, then the properties exhibited by certain physical systems must be nontrivially dependent on the *types* of measurements performed *and* either *nonlocally* connected or *holistically* related to distant events. Although a number of related arguments have appeared since John Bell's original paper (1964), they tend to be either highly technical or to lack full generality. The following arguments depend on the weakest of premises, and the structure of the arguments is simpler than most (without any loss of rigor or generality). The technical simplicity is due in part to a novel version of the generalized Bell inequality. The arguments are self contained and presuppose no knowledge of quantum mechanics. We will also offer a Dutch Book argument for measurement type dependence.

Hayden, Patrick. From Relations to Practice in the Empiricism of Gilles Deleuze. *Man World*, 28(3), 283-302, Jl 95.

This paper addresses the issue of relations in Deleuze's philosohpy. I argue that Deleuze's take on relations is based on his early reading of Hume and that a focus on relations is a central aspect of Deleuze's own version of empiricism. In particular, I contend that Deleuze's claim that relations are external or exterior to their terms is to be understood as an empiricist critique of essentialism and the view that relations are internal to their terms. The paper concludes by demonstrating the importance of the exteriority of relations in some of Deleuze's later writings.

Haydon, Graham. Thick or Thin? The Cognitive Content of Moral Education in a Plural Democracy. *J Moral Educ*, 24(1), 53-64, 1995.

It is sometimes thought that in a society in which a plurality of moral traditions and points of view are represented, the cognitive content of moral education must be thin, being confined to a recognition of a few shared values. It is argued here, to the contrary, that citizenship in a plural democracy demands a cognitively substantial form of moral education. The argument for a shared, and cognitively demanding, form of moral education to some extent parallels the argument in a plural society for political liberalism—where the strongest argument may be a pragmatic one. Both democratic participation and the pragmatic demands of toleration demand a level of moral understanding which can only be achieved through a cognitively rich moral education.

Haye, Thomas. Divisio Scientiarum: Ein bisher unveröffentlichtes Wissenschaftsmodell in der Clavis Compendii des Johannes von Garlandia. *Vivarium*, 32(1), 51-61, My 94.

Hayes, Gregory J. Issues of Consent: The Use of the Recently Deceased for Endotracheal Intubation Training. *J Clin Ethics*, 5(3), 211-216, Fall 94.

The bodies of recently deceased patients are often used for training health professionals in endotracheal intubation and other invasive techniques without the permission of the patient or patient representative. Consumers are rarely informed that this is the norm in most American hospitals, believing instead that informed consent is always required. To justify this situation, a variety of arguments have been articulated, arguments the author examines and finds scientifically and ethically wanting. The author instead suggests the need for alternatives which avoid deception and honor patient autonomy, while meeting the training needs of health professionals. One such potential alternative is explored.

Hayes, Richard P. Nagarjuna's Appeal. *J Indian Phil*, 22(4), 299-378, D 94.

Haynes-Curtis, Carole. Sartre and the Drug Connection. *Philosophy*, 70(271), 87-106, Ja 95.

Hayward, Tim. "Kant and the Moral Considerability of Non-Rational Beings" in *Philosophy and the Natural Environment, Attfield, Robin (ed)*, 129-142. New York, Cambridge Univ Pr, 1994.

Hazen, A P. Is Even Minimal Negation Constructive?. *Analysis*, 55(2), 105-107, Ap 95.

From a certain constructive standpoint it is possible to motivate a propositional logic weaker than Johansson's.

Hazen, A P. On Quantifying Out. *J Phil Log*, 24(3), 291-319, Je 95.

A semantics of "Russellian" propositions, which is arguably at least an approximation to what Russell believed in in the first decade of this century, is equivalent to ordinary possible-worlds semantics for modalities and attitudes with an additional constraint of "actualism." A variety of examples, many of them previously discussed in the literature, suggest that neither Russellian semantics nor possible-worlds semantics in general can give a straightforward account of the semantics of natural language.

Hazera, Alejandro. A Comparison of Japanese and U S Corporate Financial Accountability and its Impact on the Responsibilties of Corporate Managers. *Bus Ethics Quart*, 5(3), 479-497, Jl 95.

This paper addresses whether the adoption of Japanese financial practices by US corporations can be used as a basis for encouraging US managers to promote the interests of their (human) organizations over those of stockholders. A historical overview is provided of how the corporate organization in each country evolved and the corresponding development of managers' responsibilities to the corporate organization versus shareholders. These concepts are then examined within the context of each country's contemporary corporate financial structure and the corresponding financial responsibilities of managers to the corporate organization versus shareholders. A discussion is then provided of whether the values embodied in each system would affect the ability of the United States to encourage a more "corporate-oriented" ethic in its managers by adopting Japanese financial practices.

Heal, Jane. "Simulation vs Theory Theory: What is at Issue?" in *Objectivity, Simulation and the Unity of Consciousness, Peacocke, Christopher (ed)*, 129-144. New York, Oxford Univ Pr, 1994.

The dispute between 'simulation' and 'theory' as approached to understanding other minds collapses if it is taken to concern the subpersonal machinery underpinning abilities with psychological concepts. A better conceptualization of the dispute takes it to concern the relations between cognitive abilities. The theory theorist supposes that we can handle thoughts, have knowledge of their effects in others' minds etc. without ourselves thinking about the subject matter of those thoughts. The simulationist, by contrast, claims that ability to think about others' thoughts is necessarily an extension and redeployment of the ability to think about the subject matter of those thoughts.

Healey, Richard. Dissipating the Quantum Measurement Problem. *Topoi*, 14(1), 55-65, Mr 95.

The integration of recent work on decoherence into a so-called "modal" interpretation offers a promising new approach to the measurement problem in quantum mechanics. In this paper I explain and develop this approach in the context of the interactive interpretation presented in Healey (1989). I begin by questioning a number of assumptions which are standardly made in setting up the measurement problem, and I conclude that no satisfactory solution can afford to ignore the influence of the environment. Further, I argue that there are good reasons to believe that on a "modal" interpretation environmental interactions rapidly ensure that a quantum-mechanically describable apparatus indeed records a definite result following a measurement interaction.

Healey, Richard. Substance, Modality, and Spacetime. *Erkenntnis*, 42(3), 287-316, My 95.

The "hole argument" attempts to refute spacetime substantivalism by tying it to the absurd conclusion that classical spacetime theories are radically indeterministic. By taking seriously the claim that spacetime is a substance, I offer a new response to this argument. A serious substantivalism involves modal claims which go beyond a mere realism about spacetime: these require clarification and defense. The key idea is to recognize that a substantial spacetime may be composed of much less substantial parts. This leaves several positions immune to the hole argument, between which the spacetime substantivalist may choose to suit her particular metaphysical tastes.

Healy, Paul. Rationality, Judgment, and Argument Assessment. *Inform Log*, 16(1), 31-38, Wint 94.

In contrast to approaches to critical thinking which emphasize the importance of rules, strategies and criteria for the analysis and evaluation of arguments, this paper seeks to vindicate the central role which judgment plays in the assessment process. To counteract charges of arbitrariness of subjectivism in the exercise of judgment, individual and intersubjective constraints are outlined which can ensure its reliable exercise. The contextuality of argumentation, as it affects judgment, is discussed, and some conclusions are drawn about how acknowledgment of the role of judgment in argumentation can influence our conception of the reasoning process.

Healy, Seán D. Teaching Foundations...or Foundationalizing Teaching. *J Thought*, 30(3), 71-85, Fall 95.

Heaston, Patrick H and Frank, Garry L and Cooper, Robert W. Helps for CPAs in Dealing with Ethical Issues. *Bus Prof Ethics J*, 13(1-2), 165-183, Spr-Sum 94.

The paper reports the findings of a study of CPAs designed to determine whether they tend to find factors related to their professional environment (especially the guides to professional conduct of the American Institute of Certified Public Accountants) to be more helpful than factors related to their business environment when faced with ethics problems. Like internal auditors surveyed earlier, the CPAs tend to view a number of factors in their business environment to be even more helpful than factors related to their professional environment in dealing with ethical dilemmas. Implications for CPAs as individuals and for their professional associations are discussed.

Hébert, Robert. *L'homme Spéculaire. Philosopher*, 13, 235-248, 1992.

Heck Jr, Richard G. The Sense of Communication. *Mind*, 104(413), 79-106, Ja 95.

According to the "Hybrid View", Frege was half right. The notion of sense is needed in an account of *belief*, but the *meaning* of a proper name is just its reference. This view is unstable. The Hybrid View implies that understanding an utterance of a proper name requires only preservation of its reference. But understanding must be all that is required for successful communication, which in turn must 'enable' the transmission of knowledge: if S says and knows that *p*, and if H, understanding and accepting what S says, comes to believe that *p*, this belief typically constitutes knowledge. However, examples show that preservation of reference does not enable the transmission of knowledge; knowledge that reference is preserved is necessary. It follows that a proper account of communication's capacity to transmit knowledge requires re-introducing at least a weak notion of sense.

Hedwig, Klaus. "Edith Stein und die analogia entis" in *Studien zur Philosophie von Edith Stein, Fetz, Reto Luzius (ed)*, 320-352. Freiburg, Alber, 1993.

Heffernan, George (trans) and Simon, Josef. *Philosophy of the Sign*. Albany, SUNY Pr, 1995.

This book considers the concept "sign" to be a fundamental concept of philosophy. According to Kant, we have no access to "things-in-themselves"—we "have" only representations; according to the philosophy of the sign—which transcends the "subjectivity" of representations—we are left with only signs. "Cognition" is understood as operating sign variations. With reference to classical and, especially, to ontological positions, prominent philosophical problems are reconstructed and discussed from the vantage point of this sign philosophy. The issue is not "semiotics" in a strict sense; rather, the book deals with the most important questions of philosophy based upon an universally understood philosophy of the sign.

Hegmann, Horst. *Politischer Individualismus: Die Rekonstruktion einer Sozialtheorie unter Bezugnahme auf Machiavelli, Bodin, und Hobbes*. Berlin, Duncker Humblot, 1994.

Modern social theorists have much to learn from Machiavelli, Bodin and Hobbes. A viable design for the "good order" must reduce violence and deception as much as possible, must rely primarily on interests rather than on morals, and must keep society as a whole independent of fluctuations in public opinion. The "night watchman state" of the classical liberal period was a first, albeit insufficient, step towards solving this problem. Based on constitutional rights and duties, it reduced need for consensual collective action, while police or military actions increased the price of uncooperative behavior. Last but not least, the liberal order restricted the legitimate use of violence to the enforcement of contracts. In a society in which there are strong and weak, the strong may profit from changing the rules of the game in their own favor. If the weak are unable to resist this, they will eventually reject the social institutions, and conflict will necessarily follow. Hence, a limited degree of material equality is necessary for lasting social stability; should this balance not establish itself spontaneously, then any minimal state responsible for organizing lasting, acceptable community life must guarantee it constitutionally. (edited)

Heidbrink, Ludger. Grenzen der Verantwortung. *Phil Rundsch*, 41(4), 277-299, D 94.

Heidegger, Martin. "Europa und die deutsche Philosophie" in *Europa und die Philosophie, Gander, Hans-Helmuth (ed)*, 31-41. Frankfurt/M, Klostermann, 1993.

Heidegger, Martin. "Kant's Doctrine of the Beautiful: Its Misinterpretation by Schopenhauer and Nietzsche" in *Nietzsche: A Critical Reader, Sedgwick, Peter R (ed)*, 104-110. Cambridge, Blackwell, 1995.

Heidegger, Martin. "Only a God Can Save Us Now". *Filozof Cas*, 43(1), 3-34, 1995.

Heidegger, Martin. Die nachgelassenen Klee-Notizen (Zusammengestellt von Günter Seubold). *Heidegger Stud*, 9, 5-12, 1993.

Heidegger, Martin. *Gesamtausgabe (III Abteilung): Unveröffentlichte Abhandlungen*. Frankfurt/M, Klostermann, 1995.

Heidegger, Martin and Brogan, Walter (trans) and Warnek, Peter (trans). *Aristotle's Metaphysics* Theta 1-3: On the Essence and Actuality of Force. Bloomington, Indiana Univ Pr, 1995.

Heidelberger, Michael. "Fechners Verhältnis zur Naturphilosophie Schellings" in *Schelling und die Selbstorganisation, Heuser-Kessler, Marie-Luise (ed)*, 201-218. Berlin, Duncker Humblot, 1994.

Heil, John. "Going to Pieces" in *Philosophical Psychopathology, Graham, George (ed)*, 111-133. Cambridge, MIT Pr, 1993.

In an effort to cope with puzzles associated with the ascription of certain sorts of irrational thoughts and deeds, some theorists—most notable Donald Davidson and David Pears—have suggested that we regard the mind as *divided* or *partitioned*. I examine a line of reasoning that might be taken to motivate such a notion, and argue that there are, in fact, simpler, more plausible and attractive explanations of the species of irrationality for which the model of the divided mind seems most apt.

Heil, John. "Minds and Bodies" in *The Mind-Body Problem: A Guide to the Current Debate, Warner, Richard (ed)*, 156-164. Cambridge, Blackwell, 1994.

The mind-body problem, long thought to stem from metaphysical dualism, nowadays appears in new guises. First, if mental properties supervene on nonmental, physical properties, how can the former be implicated in causal relations that seem entirely explicable by reference to the latter? Second, if contentful states of mind (beliefs, for instance) depend on agents' relational properties, how could such states of mind cause bodily motions? These questions are discussed and their implications assessed.

Heilless, Hellem. Les Éterneis Galilées. *Philosopher*, 14, 87-100, 1993.

Heimes, Klaus F. Interdisciplinary and Intercultural Aspects of Music. *S Afr J Phil*, 14(1), 24-28, F 95.

Stock is taken of the structural impediments to interdisciplinary interests in South African musicology, such as its colonial history, perceived function and place value in tertiary education, and its doubt in the legitimacy of all but musico-technical concerns. An assessment is made of the cost of professional insularity in terms of its default *vis-a-vis* politico-cultural developments within the country and the ever-widening interdisciplinary horizons without. It is shown that compelling practical and scholastic reasons exist for musicology to join dialogical communities in the physical and human sciences, not least because the phenomenon of music cannot be understood from within its phenomenology.

Hein, Hilde. Value Inquiry—Aesthetic Value. *J Value Inq*, 28(2), 141-149, Je 94.

Heine, Steven. 'Critical Buddhism' and the Question of Philosophical Syncretism. *Asian Phil*, 4(2), 175-177, 1994.

This article was written as a response to a panel on Asian Philosophy in which the papers dealt with syncretisms between Buddhist thought and indigenous East Asian ideologies, especially Taoism, Confucianism and Shinto. From the standpoint of a recent methodology in Japanese Buddhist studies known as "Critical Buddhism" (*hihan bukkyô*) it raises questions about how to identify the integrity and independence of the respective philosophical traditions. It also argues that explanations of East Asian philosophical syncretism at times have a reductionalist basis.

Heinrichs, Johannes. Nationalsprache und Sprachnation: Zur Gegenwartsbedeutung von Fichtes *Reden an die deutsche Nation*. *Fichte-Studien*, 2, 51-73, 1990.

Heinrichs, Thomas. Die Ehe als Ort gleichberechtigter Lust. *Kantstudien*, 86(1), 41-53, 1995.

This essay presents a critical survey of Kant's concept of marriage in feminist literature. The emanzipatori aspects of this Enlightenment concept are examined in juxtaposition to the legal constrictions made on woman at the time and are compared with later concepts of marriage in German Idealism. The historical limitations of Kant's marriage concept are shown and necessity of a concept of "marriage", that is not based on contractual thought, is postulate.

Heintel, Erich. Gewissheit und Wahrheit bei Fichte. *Fichte-Studien*, 6, 157-177, 1994.

Heintz, Ronald T and Lee, Melinda A and Ganzini, Linda. The Capacity to Make Decisions in Advance and Borderline Personality Disorder. *J Clin Ethics*, 5(4), 360-363, Wint 94.

Heinze, Martin. Commentary on "Moralist or Therapist?". *Phil Psychiat Psych*, 2(1), 31-32, Mr 95.

Foucault's oeuvre offers important tools for analyzing psychiatric institutions and the antipsychiatry movement. His epistemology shows the field of mental health shaped by history. He prompts us to recognize how much psychiatrists influence patients' decisions and reminds us that psychiatry is a political arena. Matthews's distinction between moralist and therapist does not do full justice either to Foucault or antipsychiatry. Therapy should not be seen as wholly objective. Therapy is practical and its question, therefore, are moral ones. Thus, how can we achieve objectivity? The discussion of Foucault challenges us to a critique of our own standards.

Heinzmann, Gerhard. On the Controversy between Poincaré and Russell about the Status of Complete Induction. *Epistemologia*, 17(1), 35-52, Ja-Je 94.

L'induzione completa è un principio sintetico a priori—come sosteneva Poincaré—o una conseguenza di definizioni logiche—come sosteneva Russell? A condizione di allargare il concetto di logica in modo da includere un certa definizione di numero finito, Russell sembra essere riuscito a ridurre analiticamente l'induzione completa a definizioni logiche. D'altro lato Poincaré considera l'induzione completa come una *conferma* della capacità mentale di afferrare l'indefinita ripetizione della stessa azione. Questa abilità deve consistere nel poter addizionare 1 a un qualsiasi numero. Di qui si può espimere la ripetizione indefinita con la definizione induttiva dei numerali. Se questa è corretta, Poincaré pone l'accento sul fatto che le clausole dirette della definizione induttiva dei numerali non possono implicare analiticamente le clausole estreme o il principio di induzione. L'induzione è un'asserzione sulla construzione induttiva dei numerali e in quanto tale sintetica.

Heinzmann, Gerhard (trans) and Fagnot, Dominique (trans) and Gödel, Kurt. Les Mathématiques Sont-Elles une Syntaxe du Langage?. *Dialogue (Canada)*, 34(1), 3-34, Wint 95.

Heischmidt, Kenneth A and Crain, Karen A. Implementing Business Ethics: Sexual Harassment. *J Bus Ethics*, 14(4), 299-308, Ap 95.

Sexual harassment is a problem for many organizations. Organizations must understand that sexual harassment lies within the broader context of sex discrimination and inequality of opportunity in the workplace. Sexual harassment is both an illegal and unethical practice. Companies need to implement a policy which respects the rights of individual employees by prohibiting sexual harassment. This policy needs to be clearly stated in the company Code of Ethics and enforced rigorously.

Heiss, Gernot. "...wirkliche Möglichkeiten für eine nationalsozialistische Philosophie?" in *Der geistige Anschluss, Fischer, Kurt R (ed)*, 130-169. Wien, WUV Univ, 1993.

Hekman, Susan. "Max Weber and Post-Positivist Social Theory" in *The Barbarism of Reason, Horowitz, Asher (ed)*, 267-286. Toronto, Univ of Toronto Pr, 1994.

This article presents a postmodern, specifically Foucaultian reading of Weber's methodology. It argues that the principal elements of Weber's approach—the ideal type, objectivity, causality, and logic—challenge the fundamental violates the neat dichotomies on which modernist thought and scientific method rest. Finally, with his conception of the relationship between ethics and science, Weber anticipates Foucault in his belief that we must take responsibility for our value choices in a world devoid of intrinsic meaning. The conclusion is that although Weber saw the limitations of modernist discourse, unlike the postmoderns, he ultimately refused to abandon it.

Hekman, Susan J. *Moral Voices, Moral Selves: Carol Gilligan and Feminist Moral Theory*. University Park, Penn St Univ Pr, 1995.

This book argues that the approach to morality suggested by Carol Gilligan's work constitutes a radically different approach to moral theory. Gilligan's emphasis on the different moral voice of women entails an approach to morality that defines moral voice as the product of relationships with others. It suggests that there are many different moral voices, voices constituted by race, class and culture as well as gender. This approach constitutes a sharp departure from contemporary moral theory that is defined in universal, abstract terms and rests on a conception of the subject that is disembodied and autonomous. This book outlines the parameters of this new approach to morality and its implications for feminism and contemporary moral theory.

Held, Carsten. The Meaning of Complementarity. *Stud Hist Phil Sci*, 25(6), 871-894, D 95.

Held, Dirk T D. Bernard Williams, *Shame and Necessity*. *Int J Phil Stud*, 3(1), 173-178, Mr 95.

Williams believes that Greek ethical concepts better describe the facts of moral life than does modern moral philosophy. This article highlights Williams's analysis of agency, noting that he overlooks complexities in the Greek view, particularly the paratactic nature of Greek thought. Parataxis enables a logic of shared responsibility between human and divine, and structures causality with parameters of agency and responsibility incompatible with modern practice. Further difficulties in Williams's projects to fit Greek concepts to modern practices arise from the semantic complexity of the Greek term for intentionality or voluntariness (Ihekousia) its consequently poor fit with modern notions.

Held, Klaus. "Europa und die interkulturelle Verständigung" in *Europa und die Philosophie, Gander, Hans-Helmuth (ed)*, 87-103. Frankfurt/M, Klostermann, 1993.

Held, Klaus. Intercultural Understanding and the Role of Europe. *Monist*, 78(1), 5-17, Ja 95.

Held, Virginia. The Meshing of Care and Justice. *Hypatia*, 10(2), 128-132, Spr 95.

This essay attempts to work out how justice and care and their related concerns fit together. I suggest that as a basic moral value, care should be the wider moral framework into which justice should be fitted.

Heldring, Ottho G. Wetenschap, Filosofische Hermeneutiek, Metafysica. *Tijdschr Filosof*, 57(2), 250-266, Je 95.

How can we intellectually come to grips with empirical science? The logical analysis of science abstracts from its social and historical character, whereas the sociological and historical investigation of science cannot give an adequate account of its rationality. We have to understand the internal relationship of the rationality and the factuality of science by way of philosophical hermeneutics. Hermenuetics interprets various historical shapes of science as examples of the striving for rationality. The sociological and methodological role of Max Weber is due to elucidate this thesis. The question of the roots of the perspectivity of science, is, however, not a hermeneutical but a metaphysical one. The intuitions that guide the concept formation and the ordering of data are the intellectual roots of the rationality of empirical science. This is a metaphysical reflection on transcendence in human existence. Metaphysics clarifies in this way our freedom in relation to the scientific analysis of our existence. The intellectual grip on science demonstrates its existential thing. (edited)

Helleman, Wendy E (ed). *Christianity and the Classics: The Acceptance of a Heritage.* Lanham, Univ Pr of America, 1990.

Heller, Agnes. *A Philosophy of History in Fragments.* Cambridge, Blackwell, 1993.

Heller, Mark. Might-counterfactuals and Gratuitous Differences. *Austl J Phil*, 73(1), 91-101, Mr 95.

It is tempting to associate the *most similar worlds* approach to counterfactuals with the principle of No Gratuitous Differences: the worlds relevant for evaluating a counterfactual should be no more different from the actual world than they have to be in order to accommodate the truth of the antecedent. I present three arguments to show that this principle is not an appropriate restriction on the evaluation of might-counterfactuals and to raise doubts about its even being an appropriate restriction for would-counterfactuals. The first is an argument by counterexamples, the second is based on the relationship between nonconditional mights and might-counterfactuals, and the third is grounded in the differing characters of might- and would-counterfactuals.

Heller, Mark and Krasner, Daniel. The Miracle of Counterfactuals: Counterexamples to Lewis's World Ordering. *Phil Stud*, 76(1), 27-43, O 94.

Heller, Michael. Teilhard's Vision of the World and Modern Cosmology. *Zygon*, 30(1), 11-23, Mr 95.

Some physical aspects of Teilhard's synthesis are focused upon and confronted with the recent achievements of physics and cosmology. The stuff of the universe, according to modern physical theories, has become something more similar to a structure or form than to inert pieces of material substratum. Directedness of time and history no longer seems to be an ontological *a priori* of any existence, but rather an outcome of finely tuned initial conditions. And the growth of complexity is now regarded as a process of emerging out of physical laws rather than a foreign element in the body of physics. The question is considered of how these results affect Teilhard de Chardin's vision of the world.

Heller, Michal. John Bell's Philosophy of Quantum Mechanics. *Stud Phil Christ*, 30(2), 151-161, 1994.

The proof of John Bell's Inequality is briefly reviewed, and its connection with the hidden parameter theory is emphasized. Bell's assessment of various interpretations of quantum mechanics allows us to reconstruct his own philosophical predilections. It turns out that he fostered rather traditional views (he favored de Broglie-Bohm interpretation) and only under the pressure of the theorem proved by himself switched to more revolutionary standpoint. Some critical remarks are made. It is argued that quantum mechanics is a nonlocal theory from the very beginning: vectors of Hilbert space do not live in the physical space-time; they naturally contain all physical information available about a quantum object even if this object consists of space-like separated "parts".

Hellman, Geoffrey and Feferman, Solomon. Predicative Foundations of Arithmetic. *J Phil Log*, 24(1), 1-17, F 95.

Helm, Bennett W. The Significance of Emotions. *Amer Phil Quart*, 31(4), 319-331, O 94.

Desires must be distinguished from mere goal-directedness in that desires normally say something in favor of the relevant course of action because of its significance: Objects of desires are normally)worth pursuing. Accounts of desire are typically given in terms of instrumental rationality, but this cannot by itself capture significance. I argue that significance can only be understood in terms of a pattern of noninstrumental rationality in a creature's emotions. Consequently, rationality encompasses more than instrumental and epistemic rationality, and so the capacities for belief and desire are not intelligible apart from the capacity for emotions.

Helm, Paul. Calvin and Bernard on Freedom and Necessity: A Reply to Brümmer. *Relig Stud*, 30(4), 457-465, D 94.

It is argued that Calvin does not veer between two incompatible accounts of grace, freedom and necessity in *Institutes II. 2*, but presents a consistent position. The consistency is evident once it is seen that Calvin carefully distinguished between *necessity* and *compulsion*. For him not all necessitated acts are compelled, but all human acts which are the outcome of efficacious divine grace are necessitated by that grace. Because Calvin is consistent, there is no need to suppose that he has mistaken the causal sufficiency of divine saving grace for its causal importance.

Hemmo, Meir and Bacciagaluppi, Guido. Making Sense of Approximate Decoherence. *Proc Phil Sci Ass*, 1, 345-354, 1994.

In realistic situations where a macroscopic system interacts with an external environment, decoherence of the quantum state, as derived in the decoherence approach, is only approximate. We argue that this can still give rise to facts, provided that during the decoherence process states that are, respectively, always close to eigenvectors of pointer position and record observable are correlated. We show in a model that this is always the case.

Henderson, David K. Account for Macro-level Causation. *Synthese*, 101(2), 129-156, N 94.

By a macro-level feature, I understand any feature that supervenes on, and is thus realized in, lower-level features. Recent discussions by Kim have suggested that such features cannot be causally relevant insofar as they are not classically reducible to lower-level features. This seems to render macro-level features causally irrelevant. I defend the causal relevance of some such features. Such features have been thought causally relevant in many examples that have underpinned philosophical work on causality. Additionally, in certain typical biological cases, we conceive of causally relevant features at various compatible levels of analysis. When elaborated, these points make a strong prima facie case for macro-level causal relevance.

However, we might abandon both the philosophical guideposts and the corresponding explanatory practice in the special sciences were we convinced that no reflective philosophical account could provide for the causal relevance there supposed. I show that such drastic measures are not necessary, for we can make sense of macro-level causal relevance by drawing on Paul Humphreys' recent work in ways suggested by the concrete examples considered here.

Henderson, David K. Epistemic Competence. *Phil Papers*, 23(3), 139-167, N 94.

The author develops a notion of epistemic competence that is intended as a model for the appropriate naturalizing of epistemology. Models of epistemic competence are ideal models with a normative force, as befits the motivations for naturalized epistemology. The composition and construction of such models is discussed.

Henderson, David K. Epistemic Competence and Contextualist Epistemology: Why Contextualism Is Not Just the Poor Person's Coherentism. *J Phil*, 91(12), 627-649, D 94.

This paper provides one argument for a contextualist epistemology of empirical knowledge. Contextualism is a underdeveloped alternative to the more familiar epistemic approaches of foundationalism and coherentism. Reflecting on the naturalizing of epistemology leads to certain constraints on the sorts of ideal models that can serve as proper epistemic standards or norms. This provides the basis for a criticism of Bonjour's coherentist model of empirical knowledge. Further, when combined with emerging results in connectionist work on perception, these constraints lead to a normative model of epistemic competence that can properly be called contextualist.

Hendin, Herbert. Selling Death and Dignity. *Hastings Center Rep*, 25(3), 19-23, My-Je 95.

Hendley, Steven. Putting Ourselves Up for the Question: A Postmodern Critique of Richard Rorty's Postmodernist Bourgeois Liberalism. *J Value Inq*, 29(2), 241-253, Je 95.

Richard Rorty's "postmodernist bourgeois liberalism" fails to think through what Jean-Francois Lyotard has dubbed our "postmodern condition." Lacking any universal standpoint from which to justify liberal democracy, Rorty falls back on the ethnocentric standpoint of "our" culture, assuming it is possible to specify something like a common sense of who "we" are within a postmodern framework. This assumption is challenged in the paper which suggests an alternative approach in the work of Lyotard and Claude Lefort which understands democracy as the construction of a public space which places our sense of who "we" are in question.

Hendriks, Ruud and Benschop, Ruth and Nelis, Annemiek. De Winst van Tranen: Over de Aarzeling als Methode. *Kennis Methode*, 19(2), 220-227, 1995.

Hendry, David and Cook, Steven. "The Theory of Reduction in Econometrics" in *Idealization VI: Idealization in Economics, Hamminga, Bert (ed)*, 71-100. Amsterdam, Rodopi, 1994.

Analysis of a number of types of reduction to be used in 'general to specific' modelling in econometric methodology. Specification of measures for the loss of information resulting from every type of reduction. Based upon this analysis, the formulation of criteria for model design in econometrics.

Hengehold, Laura. An Immodest Proposal: Foucault, Hysterization, and the "Second Rape". *Hypatia*, 9(3), 88-107, Sum 94.

This article places Foucault's 1977 suggestions regarding the reform of French rape law in the context of ongoing feminist debates as to whether rape should be considered a sex crime or a species of assault. When viewed as a disciplinary matrix with both physical and discursive effects, rape and the rape trial clearly contribute to the "hysterization" of women by cultivating complainants' confessions in order to demonstrate their supposed lack of self-knowledge.

Henley, Tracy B. More Theoretical Risks. *J Theor Phil Psych*, 13(1), 40-41, Spr 93.

Hennessy, Rosemary. "Incorporating Queer Theory on the Left" in *Marxism in the Postmodern Age, Callari, Antonio (ed)*, 266-275. New York, Guilford, 1994.

The essay offers a critique of post-structuralist queer theory by situating it in relation to other "strategies of incorporation" whereby homosexuals are being assimilated into a postmodern culture. In so doing it puts forth an argument for a systemic materialist critique that connects more flexible sexual identities to unequal divisions of labor in capital's global economy.

Hennigfeld, Jochem. Fichte und Humboldt—Zur Frage der Nationalsprache. *Fichte-Studien*, 2, 37-50, 1990.

"*Sprache*, im weitesten Sinne des Wortes, ist der *Ausdruck unserer Gedanken durch willkürliche Zeichen*" (SW VIII, 302). Das ist die traditionelle Definition der Sprache, die Fichte in seinem Journal-Aufsatz *Von der Sprachfähigkeit und dem Ursprunge der Sprache* aus dem Jahr 1795 anführt. Die Unzulänglichkeit dieser Wesensbestimmung weist Fichte selbst auf, ohne sie expressis verbis zurückzunehmen. Zwar gibt bereits der frühe Aufsatz eine eigenwillige Interpretation dieser Formel; aber erst die *Reden an die deutsche Nation* (1807/08) brechen vollends mit dieser traditionellen Sprachauffassung. Dabei stehen Fichtes Thesen über die Sprache (vierte und fünfte Rede) in auffälliger Nähe zu Humboldts spätem Sprachdenken. Diesem Zusammenhang soll im folgenden nachgegangen werden. Es geht mir allerdings nicht darum, eine einseitige oder wechselseitige Abhängigkeit von Denkern nachzuweisen. Vielmehr soll nach den spezifischen Möglichkeiten gefragt werden, wie eine neuzeitlich-idealistische Philosophie das Wesen der Sprache bestimmen und ergründen kann.

Henrichs, Norbert and Haller, Rudolf and Roser, Andreas. Wittgenstein Bibliographie 1992-93. *Wittgenstein Stud*, n.a., 1994.

Henrique, Luiz and Dutra, Araújo. Van Fraassen e os Limites da Observabilidade. *Cad Hist Filosof Cie*, 3(1-2), 133-150, Ja-D 93.

This paper discusses the difference between the classical empiricist view on the limits of observability, such as exposed in Locke's work, and the contemporary naturalist view on this topic, which is defended by van Fraassen's constructive empiricism. According to van Fraassen, the problem of the limits of observability is to be answered not by philosophy, but by empirical science, which can furnish a simpler answer; but this doesn't seem to be the case if we consider the different scientific solutions to the problem.

Henry, Christine. "Professional Behaviour and the Organisation" in *Ethics and the Professions, Chadwick, Ruth (ed)*, 145-155. Brookfield, Avebury, 1994.

The chapter introduces the concept of a research based ethics and values audit. It briefly identifies the value of charters, codes and mission statements. This discussion is followed by a detailed synopsis of the ethics and values audit, abbreviated to Eva, as an ethical management tool. The chapter concludes by stating that ethical issues are central to management practice within organizations.

Henry, Granville C and Valenza, Robert J. Whitehead's Early Philosophy of Mathematics. *Process Stud*, 22(1), 21-36, Spr 93.

This article examines Whitehead's philosophy of mathematics as revealed by his early works, especially *An Introduction to Mathematics* (1911), *Universal Algebra* (1898), and the first volume of *Principia Mathematica* (1910). The authors argue that Whitehead was mainly an empiricist, perhaps tainted with Platonism, and indicate how his approaches to mathematical generality failed to anticipate the direction of twentieth century mathematics, although—surprisingly—his mature philosophy did.

Henry, Michel. *Die Barbarei: Eine phänomenologische Kulturkritik*. Freiburg, Alber, 1994.

Henry, Paul. "Mathematical Machines" in *The Machine as Metaphor and Tool, Haken, Hermann (ed)*, 101-122. New York, Springer-Verlag, 1993.

Henthorne, Tony L and La Tour, Michael S. A Model to Explore the Ethics of Erotic Stimuli in Print Advertising. *J Bus Ethics*, 14(7), 561-569, Jl 95.

This paper discusses a test of a hypothetical model of the role of perceived ethical feelings about the use of female nudity/erotic stimuli in print advertising. Specifically, the linkages between perceived ethicalness of the use of the print ad (as measured by the Reidenbach and Robin ethics scale) and attitude toward the ad, brand, and purchase intention are explored.

Herbert, Robert T. The Nonrationality and Noncognivity of the Belief in God's Existence. *Phil Invest*, 18(3), 281-288, Jl 95.

Herman, Arthur L. Materials for an Analysis of a Just Universe. *Asian Phil*, 5(1), 3-22, 1995.

There is one assumption that is shared by practically all popular religious and philosophic systems, ancient and modern, Eastern and Western. In truth it may well be that it is this single assumption which makes such 'systems' possible. That shared assumption is the belief in a 'just universe', i.e., 'just' in the sense of morally ordered, morally predictable and morally explainable. This assumption rests, as most assumptions must, on pragmatic grounds; that is to say, the assumption is retained or used because it gets the users where they want to go, i.e., the assumption works. But if it could be shown that this assumption, aside from being useful, leads to insuperable logical or empirical problems, then this might be *prima facie* grounds for rejecting the assumption. Part I examines the historical roots of the assumption of a just universe. Part II examines three implications that would seem to follow from the assumption that the universe, the world, is a just place in which to live. Part III explores the unacceptable consequences that are found in and that follow from these three implications and that necessitate the rejection of the assumption of the just universe of Part I.

Herman, Judith Lewis. Reply to Daniel's "Exclusion and Emphasis Reframed as a Matter of Ethics". *Ethics Behavior*, 4(3), 237, 1994.

Hermansson, Jörgen and Hansson, Sven Ove (ed). *Idéer om Demokrati*. Stockholm, Tiden, 1992.

Sven Ove Hansson and Jörgen Hermansson (eds) *Idéer om demokrati* (Ideas on democracy), Tidens förlag, Stockholm, 1992. In Swedish. 316 pp. The book contains major texts on the philosophy of democracy by Brian Barry, Norberto Bobbio, Robert Dahl, Jon Elster, David Miller, and Adam Przeworski. The editors have contributed three introductions, that center on the three issues; What is democracy?, Why democracy?, and The problems of democracy.

Hermerén, Göran. Art and Life: Models for Understanding Music. *Austl J Phil*, 73(2), 280-292, Je 95.

Hernández, Héctor H. La Obligación en el Positivismo: El Caso de H L A Hart. *Analogia*, 7(1), 3-29, 1993.

Herra, Rafael Angel. Crítica de la filosofía global quinientos años después. *Rev Filosof (Costa Rica)*, 31(75-76), 173-179, D 93.

When the questions of philosophy ask about the relationship between Europe and non-Western cultures, they are also conditioned. Philosophy is an instrument of the globalization of Europe. On the other hand, critical philosophy, even though it remains Western, can become a position against global philosophy as a criticism of the fundamentals of power, violence and self-deception ethics. The legitimation of normative ethical systems and artifices of moral reason have been and still are useful to the Western history of teleologically produced violence. It is possible to pose these questions in our Latin American countries 500 years after Columbus' voyages... Is it possible?

Herremans, Irene and Falkenberg, Loren. Ethical Behaviours in Organizations: Directed by the Formal or Informal Systems?. *J Bus Ethics*, 14(2), 133-143, F 95.

Past research has focused on individual culpability with the assumption that individuals will further their own self interest over that of the organization, given an appropriate opportunity. In contrast this research shifts the focus from individual motivation to the influence of the formal and informal control systems of organizations on ethical behaviors. An open-ended interview approach was used to collect data. It was found that pressures within the informal system were the dominant influence in the resolution of ethical issues. The dominance of the informal system, however, varies according to the economic position of the organization.

Herrera, Christopher D. Civil Disobedience and Plato's *Crito*. *S J Phil*, 33(1), 39-55, Spr 95.

The theme of civil disobedience is often discussed in the context of the Crito. Yet an examination of that dialogue and the nature and objectives of civil disobedience

reveals that there is probably little gained in linking the two. Socrates' options, and Plato's apparent philosophical intentions, in the Crito will support even a loose interpretation of would-be civil disobedience. Where the dialogue touches on legal and political obligation it does not do so in a way that makes an obvious connection with modern civil disobedience.

Herrera Ibáñez, Alejandro. La Aproximación a la Verdad en Peirce. *Analogia*, 5(2), 143-154, 1991.

From his criticism to Cartesian scepticism, Peirce adopts his doctrine of *fallibilism*, which shouldn't be considered as a form of scepticism. Fallibilism is closely related to another doctrine of Peirce's, namely, Sinechism. From both fallibilism and sinechism it turns out that 1) Any temporal state of a body of knowledge is only an *approximation* to truth, and 2) Truth is only and ideal postulate whose existence we don't know. After briefing Peirce's ideas on this respect, I examine some objections that have been advanced.

Herrero, Libia. David Bohm, físico y filósofo: In Memoriam. *Rev Filosof (Costa Rica)*, 31(75-76), 263-267, D 93.

David Bohm was one of the most distinguished theoretical physicists of his generation. He offered the Causal Interpretation of the Quantum Theory which is the basis of his theory of the Implicate Order and the Indivisible Wholeness. He proposed the existence of a quantum potential which guides the motion of particles by providing "active information" about the whole environment creating a quantum interconnectedness. His basic idea of order was that, beyond the visible tangible, unfolded or explicated order lies a deeper, implicated or enfolded order of undivided wholeness. His interests and influence extended far beyond physics and philosophy, embracing biology, psychology, art, religion and others.

Herring, Herbert. The Reception of German Philosophy in Contemporary Indian Thought. *J Indian Counc Phil Res*, 11(3), 81-97, My-Ag 94.

This survey shows how the direct encounter of contemporary Indian philosophers with German philosophy and some of its eminent representatives has much contributed to a more genuine understanding of the mainstreams of modern German thought in India, from Kant and Hegel *via* Husserl to N Hartmann, Heidegger and Jaspers. As to those Indian scholars of philosophy who had spent some time in German universities, as students and/or teachers, detailed mention is made of N V Banerjee (1897-1982), Poola T Raju (born 1903) and Syed Vahiduddin (born 1909), and the younger generation is represented by the brilliant Heidegger scholar J L Mehta (1912-88), the erudite Husserl interpreter J N Mohanty (born 1928), and N S S Raman (born 1928) and R K Gupta (born 1930) are mentioned mainly for their contributions to Comparative Philosophy. The survey is completed with a list of more recent Indian investigations into German thought.

Herron, Timothy and Seidenfeld, Teddy and Wasserman, Larry. The Extent of Dilation of Sets of Probabilities and the Asymptotics of Robust Bayesian Inference. *Proc Phil Sci Ass*, 1, 250-259, 1994.

We experience the phenomenon of dilation, where updating using sets of Bayesian conditional probabilities always causes the upper (and lower) probability of an event to increase (and decrease), thereby causing more uncertainty with regards to the event's truth. First, we contrast short-run dilation with standard long-run convergence of opinion results. Second, we note when dilation occurs and how dilation is connected to the independence of the conditioned and conditioning events. Third, we use sets of probabilities and asymptotic (increasing sample size) dilation to provide an interpretation of the difference between standard Neyman-Pearson hypothesis testing and Harold Jeffrey's Bayesian hypothesis testing.

Hersch, Jeanne. Le poids du pouvoir et la liberté. *Philosophica*, 52(2), 45-48, 1993.

The paper states that in human condition, no real freedom can exist without any use of power. Whatever change can happen in reality, it has to use the means of power. There is no law without police, but any police has to be submitted to law by means of force. That is because man's body has to be nourished and defended. Nobody can offer a shelter to the prosecuted when he has no house which he is ready to protect by force.

Hershenov, David B. The Limits of Liberal Tolerance: The Rights of Gays and Lesbians to Adopt. *Int J Applied Phil*, 9(2), 27-34, Wint-Spr 95.

Hershock, Peter D. Person as Narration: The Dissolution of 'Self' and 'Other' in Ch'an Buddhism. *Phil East West*, 44(4), 685-710, O 94.

Hertzberg, Lars. On Being Moved by Desire. *Phil Invest*, 18(3), 250-263, Jl 95.

Some problems connected with Harry Frankfurt's suggestion that free will is to be analyzed in terms of second order desires are pointed out. It is argued that his account of the relation between second and first order volitions is not satisfactory, that free will as he defines it has little connection with the notion as traditionally understood, that the notion of an action's being someone's doing is not to be spelled out in terms of desires, and that the problem his theory was designed to solve can be dissolved simply by taking note of the difference between the concepts of desire and intention.

Herwig, Bernhard. Weight w in Stable Theories with Few Types. *J Sym Log*, 60(2), 353-373, Je 95.

We construct a type p with preweight w with respect to itself in a theory with few types. A type with this property must be present in a stable theory with finitely many (but more than one) countable models. The construction is a modification of Hrushovski's important pseudoplane construction.

Herwitz, Daniel A. "John Cage's Approach to the Global" in *John Cage: Composed in America, Perloff, Marjorie (ed)*, 188-205. Chicago, Univ of Chicago Pr, 1994.

Herwitz, Daniel A. "The Beginning of the End: Danto on Postmodernism" in *Danto and his Critics, Rollins, Mark (ed)*, 142-158. Cambridge, Blackwell, 1993.

Herzog, Ivo and Eklof, Paul C. Model Theory of Modules Over a Serial Ring. *Annals Pure Applied Log*, 72(2), 145-176, Mr 95.

We use the Drozd-Warfield structure theorem for finitely presented modules over a serial ring to investigate the model theory of modules over a serial ring, in particular, to give a simple description of pp-formulas and to classify the pure-injective indecomposable modules. We also study the question of whether every pure-injective indecomposable module over a valuation ring is the hull of a uniserial module.

Herzog, Max. *Weltentwürfe: Ludwig Binswangers phänomenologische Psychologie*. Hawthorne, de Gruyter, 1994.

Herzog, Max. William James and the Development of Phenomenological Psychology in Europe. *Hist Human Sci*, 8(1), 29-46, F 95.

It is put forward that William James has influenced the development of phenomenological psychology in Europe in three ways: 1) The "principles of psychology" prepared the phenomenological turn in the sciences around 1900. 2) Edmund Husserl's early conception of descriptive psychology was in central aspects stimulated by James. 3) James became the link between Husserl's "pure" phenomenology and the "mundane" or "empirical" phenomenological psychology as developed by followers of Husserl. Central conceptions are investigated to show that the phenomenological concept of intentionality was in its essence anticipated by James and that his psychology was more advanced at that time than Husserl's insofar as it allowed to encompass an objective psychology into descriptive psychology.

Herzog, Maximilian. Entwicklungsdenken bei Piaget und Merleau-Ponty. *Phil Rundsch*, 41(4), 321-327, D 94.

Herzog, Patricia. Music Criticism and Musical Meaning. *J Aes Art Crit*, 53(3), 299-312, Sum 95.

Heschel, Susannah. "Konfigurationen des Patriarchats, des Judentums und des Nazismus im deutschen feministischen Denken" in *Der feministische "Sündenfall"?, Kohn-Ley, Charlotte (ed)*, 160-184. Vienna, Picus, 1994.

Hesse, Mary. Habermas and the Force of Dialectical Argument. *Hist Euro Ideas*, 21(3), 367-378, My 95.

In his theory of rational discourse, Habermas has made essential use of the concept of 'force of the better argument'. He does not explicitly discuss the theories of meaning and of inference that must underpin this concept, but usually construes it in terms of univocal meaning and propositional inference. These assumptions are challenged by means of examples from the use of metaphor and analogical argument in science, and it is suggested that a generalization of such arguments applies to philosophical discourse also. Habermas's conception of modes of argument as monotonically directed towards truth should therefore be replaced by dialogue and dialectics, but it does not follow from this that argument is without rational rules.

Hesse, Mary. How to Be Postmodern Without Being a Feminist. *Monist*, 77(4), 445-461, O 94.

The postmodernist revolution in epistemology of science emerges from post-empiricist emphases on social and cultural factors in theory-making, resulting in debates about rationality versus ideology and relativism in science. The radical program of an alternative feminist science is part of this debate, but is rejected here as both unscientific and undemocratic. A proposal is made for an epistemology of science incorporating less extreme feminist virtues. Emphasis is put on creative theory-languages rather than logical method, and on the human sciences rather than physics as normative for science in general.

Hestevold, H Scott and Carter, William S. On Passage and Persistence. *Amer Phil Quart*, 31(4), 269-283, O 94.

Hetherington, Stephen Cade. Sceptical Insulation and Sceptical Objectivity. *Austl J Phil*, 72(4), 411-425, D 94.

Epistemic sceptics assume that their knowledge-denials are made from a particularly *objective* perspective. I identify that sense of objectivity—and I argue that sceptical perspectives are no more objective than are any other perspectives.

Heuser-Kessler, Marie-Luise (ed) and Jacobs, Wilhelm G (ed). *Schelling und die Selbstorganisation*. Berlin, Duncker Humblot, 1994.

The reference-point for the contributions in this anthology is the discovery that the naturphilosoph F W J Schelling had developed a complete theory of self organization as early as around 1800. This theory exerted considerable influence on the development of science in the nineteenth century, a development that took place not only in the Romantic movement, but also, for example, in crystallography, mathematics or nonequilibrium chemistry. In their contributions Hermann Haken, the founder of synergetics, and René Thom, the father of catastrophe theory, science historians and authority on Schelling, attempt to answer the question: "Of what historical and contemporary significance could Schelling's Naturphilosophie be for the nonlinear natural sciences of today?" The answer is that Schelling's dynamic constructivism can still provide us with important impulses for a philosophy of mathematics, for a theory of emergence and for the analysis of the cultural significance of the idea of self-organization.

Hewa, Soma. Medical Technology: A Pandora's Box?. *J Med Human*, 15(3), 171-181, Fall 94.

This paper examines the development of medical technology in terms of Max Weber's theory of rationalization. It argues that medical technology is a part of the general process of social, political and economic changes in modern Western societies. Medical technology today keeps many people alive who, in the past, would have died from their illness. In reent years, burgeoning technological achievements in medicine have been regarded as a threat to the individual's freedom to die. Many people believe that the prolongation of life only adds to the suffering of the patient and to the emotional distress of the family. They argue that a quiet death is preferable to the indignities inflicted by mechanical life support. This paper addresses these issues in light of Weber's theoretical arguments.

Heyd, David. Supererogation and Ethical Methodology: A Reply to Mellema. *Philosophia (Israel)*, 24(1-2), 183-189, D 94.

The article attempts to criticize Mellema's solution to the so-called "paradox of supererogation" (how can one be permitted not to do what is overall the best?). Mellema's solution is based on the distraction between supererogatory acts and acts which lie beyond duty though one ought to do, thus creating an intermediate category between the supererogatory and the obligatory. The particular difficulty in Mellema's strategy lies in the vagueness of his concept of "ought" and its deontic status. The article criticizes Mellema's analysis of both forgiveness and friendship which for two different reasons do not fall under Mellema's intermediate category.

Heyd, Thomas. Locke's Arguments for the Resemblance Thesis Revisited. *Locke News*, 25, 13-28, 1994.

Until relatively recently *Essay* II. viii. 15-22 has been assumed to contain arguments, based on differences apparent on observational grounds, for Locke's distinction between primary and secondary qualities. Mostly these arguments have been considered rather poor. In this paper I argue that the text in question is really intended to undermine the scholastic doctrine of the transmission of substantial forms, and that, as such, it is successful. I first briefly indicate the arguments that Locke is generally credited with in II. viii. 15-22, and some of the objections that are raised to them, and point out in a general way how my alternative reading makes sense of the text in question. Second, I note Locke's rendering of the scholastic doctrine of the transmission of substantial forms and his reaction to it, and why I claim that Locke is arguing against this doctrine at II. viii. 15-22 rather than earlier in the *Essay*. Third, I proceed through II. viii. 15-22 indicating how Locke's argumentation works.

Heyde, L. Wat is metafysica?. *Tijdschr Filosof*, 56(4), 739-751, D 94.

The article contains a presentation, analysis and critical appraisal of a recently published book from the Dutch philosopher Herman Berger on Metaphysics: *Wat is metafysica? een studie over transcendentie*, Assen/Maastricht, Van Gorcum, 1993, VI-174 p (What is Metaphysics? An inquiry concerning transcendence). In opposition to the thesis of Heidegger Berger argues that metaphysics is not at its end. The most important condition of the new future for metaphysics is to eliminate every rest of essentialistic and dualistic thinking. The criticism which is given in the article concerns mainly the tendency to identification Berger makes of one form of metaphysics (namely the Aristotalian-Thomistic type) with metaphysics as such.

Heyer, Dieter and Mausfeld, Rainer. "A Theoretical and Experimental Inquiry Into the Relation of Theoretical Concepts..." in *Probability in Theory-Building, Brzezinski, Jerzy (ed)*, 75-97. Amsterdam, Rodopi, 1994.

Heyes, Cecilia and Chater, Nick. Animal Concepts: Content and Discontent. *Mind Lang*, 9(3), 209-246, S 94.

We argue that the notion of concept that is used in research on animal concepts research has no analog in human concepts research. Animal concepts researchers study discriminative abilities, whereas human concepts research focuses on internal mental structures. We also argue that discrimination data alone leaves the category that the animal has learned underdetermined.

Hickey, Lance P. Kant's View of the Transcendental Imagination in the First *Critique*. *Conference*, 4(2), 68-76, Fall 93.

Hickman, Larry A. "Pragmatism, Technology, and Scientism" in *Pragmatism: From Progressivism to Postmodernism, Hollinger, Robert (ed)*, 72-87. Westport, Praeger, 1995.

I argue against a common charge that John Dewey's instrumentalism was a variety of scientism. Dewey did not think the methods of the sciences paradigmatic for other forms of inquiry. He did think that the methods of the scientific-technical disciplines, together with the methods of the arts, law, historiography, and others, nourish and are in turn refined by an overarching pattern of inquiry. This general pattern of inquiry serves as "liason officer" for the various disciplines, allowing them to communicate with one nother. Dewey thought of philosophy as uniquely involved with analysis of this general pattern of inquiry.

Hickman, Larry A. John Dewey: Philosopher of Technology. *Free Inq*, 14(4), 41-43, Fall 94.

John Dewey was the first American philosopher to develop a systematic critique of technology. His version of pragmatism, which he called "instrumentalism," defined technology so broadly that it included not only tangible tools and artifacts such as machines, but intangible ones such as mathematical and logical objects as well. He thought that the number two was no less a constructed artifact than a telephone. Dewey proposed instrumentalism as an antidote to the split between facts and values that has plagued human societies, and he argued that the experimental method should be applied wherever social problems are experienced.

Hickman, Larry A. Remodelling Nature: The Roots of Pragmatic Theory. *SW Phil Rev*, 11(Supp), 5-16, Mr 95.

This essay was presented as a part of a celebration of the 65th birthday of Douglas Browning. It seeks to demonstrate some of the ways in which Browning's work both draws on the insights of classical American pragmatism and advances its program. One element that Browning's work shares with that of the earlier pragmatists is the notion that nature is continually "remodelled" as criteria of judgment are criticized and reformulated. Another is that the development of productive skills clears the way for the construction of the various "stances" by means of which our experiences are refined and rendered more meaningful.

Hickman, Larry A. Science Education for a Life Curriculum. *Stud Phil Educ*, 13(3-4), 379-391, 1994-95.

Despite the successes of scientific technology, ignorance of its outcomes and attacks on its methods are increasing. False economy threatens public health. Scientific presentations of evolution and sex education in the schools are under increasing attack. Public support for scientific technology is in decline. The work of John Dewey offers a three pronged program to address this situation. First, the religious mainstream should examine its relation to fundamentalisms. Second, scientists and engineers should devote more time to public education. Third, educators should redouble their efforts to teach more scientific technology as a necessary (but not sufficient) condition of social intelligence.

Hidalgo-Serna, Emilio. Víves, Calderón y Vico: Lenguaje Metafórico y Filosofar Ingenioso. *Cuad Vico*, 2, 75-88, 1992.

Considering Vico's definition of *ingenium*, the relationship between necessity, *ingenium*, metaphor, and religious poetry is analysed in the ingenious Spanish rhetoric of before Vico. The primordial capacity of metaphor is raised again, along with the real value of the ingenious filosophizing in the face of rational and deductive knowledge, interpreting *ingenium* through the humanist appreciation of original function in the make-up of the human world and history, of language and rhetorical-philosophical knowledge.

Higginbotham, Jim. Mass and Count Quantifiers. *Ling Phil*, 17(5), 447-480, O 94.

Higgins, Ann. Teaching as a Moral Activity: Listening to Teachers in Russia and the United States. *J Moral Educ*, 24(2), 143-158, 1995.

In 1992, I conducted a study in two schools, the Scarsdale High Alternative School (SAS) in New York, a Kohlbergian Just Community Program for 16 years, headed by Tony Arenella; and Public School No. 825, a kindergarten to senior high school on the outskirts of Moscow, Russia, an experimental school in Developmental Education following the ideas of Lev Vygotsky, headed by Vladimir Karakovsky. This article presents a narrative comparison of the philosophies and practices of the secondary teachers in each school. The teachers' philosophies seemed to be like Janus, facing in two directions—outward toward the school culture, reflecting each school's shared norms and values, and inward, expressing each person's own values and ways of thinking. It was the influence of each school's culture that created the most striking philosophical differences. Teachers from Russia and the US held only one value in common: community. Other particular norms and values differed almost completely and seem to reflect the larger cultures of the US and Russia: affection and harmony rooted in love of Motherland for the Russians, and for the Americans, a sense of self and responsibility expressing the value of individualism. The paper first focuses on how teachers in each school conceived of the morality of teaching and of the moral authority of teachers. The focus then moves to a discussion of both the common and unique norms and values the teachers desired to transmit to their students, the practices they use and the moral conflicts they face. The article concludes with remarks about what we can learn from these schools for moral education.

Higgins, Kathleen M and Solomon, Robert C. "Atomism, Art, and Arthur: Danto's Hegelian Turn" in *Danto and his Critics, Rollins, Mark (ed)*, 107-126. Cambridge, Blackwell, 1993.

In this chapter, we discuss Arthur Danto's transformation from epistemological atomist and "analytic" philosopher into one of this country's premier art critics and theorists. What is perhaps most surprising is the "Hegelian" structure of his recent philosophy, including, notoriously, his speculations about "the end of art." We suggest, however, that Danto's criticism is taking and should take a further turn, more in the model of a philosopher he helped bring into the American philosophical mainstream, namely Nietzsche.

Higgs, Philip. The Nature of Philosophy of Education Reconsidered. *S Afr J Phil*, 14(2), 41-47, My 95.

In this article it is argued that the role of philosophy of education has been subjected to the idiosyncratic stranglehold and abuse of ideological and cultural considerations. This it is claimed can be attributed to the fact that philosophy of education has been mislocated in the social science tradition rather than being authentically located as one of the *studia humanitatis* in the tradition of the human sciences. As a human science, philosophy of education focuses its attention on the nature of education as a distinctively human act that transcends the bounds of particular social and cultural definitions which characterize the present debate in education.

Hilbert, David. Is Seeing Believing?. *Proc Phil Sci Ass*, 1, 446-453, 1994.

One of the traditional problems of philosophy is the nature of the connection between perceptual experience and empirical knowledge. That there is an intimate connection between the two is rarely doubted. Three case studies of visual deficits due to brain damage are used to motivate the claim that perceptual experience is neither necessary nor sufficient for perceptual knowledge. Acceptance of this claim leaves a mystery as to the epistemic role, if any, of perceptual experience. It is argued that one function of perceptual experience is to provide information about the sources of beliefs, both as to which perceptual modality and within a given modality. This information is useful in assessing the reliability of perceptual beliefs.

Hilbert, David and Byrne, Alex. Perception and Causation. *J Phil*, 92(6), 323-329, Je 95.

A defence of the causal analysis of perception, rebutting the arguments against it given by John Hyman [in "Vison and Power", Journal of Philosophy, XCI, 5 (May 1994): 236-52].

Hildebrand, David L. Kimball on Whitehead and Perception. *Process Stud*, 22(1), 13-20, Spr 93.

A response to Robert H Kimball's charge that A N Whitehead's account of perception is incoherent. Kimball argued that Whitehead's account failed to reconcile two traditional theories of perception: phenomenological (sense-data) theory and causal (physiological) theory. Kimball's charge results from a misguided attempt to place Whitehead's theory within the parameters of a debate between two traditional theories. Instead, Whitehead supersedes that debate by offering a more comprehensive picture.

Hiley, B J and Bohm, David. *The Undivided Universe: An Ontological Interpretation of Quantum Theory*. New York, Routledge, 1995.

Hilhorst, Medard. "The Ethical Assessment of New Technologies: Some Methodological Considerations" in *Ecology, Technology, and Culture*, Zweers, Wim (ed), 262-271. Cambridge, White Horse, 1994.

Hill, Christopher. Two Cheers for Process Reliabilism. *Pac Phil Quart*, 75(1), 12-28, Mr 94.

Hill, Claire Ortiz. Frege's Attack on Husserl and Cantor. *Monist*, 77(3), 345-357, Jl 94.

Hill, John. Can We Talk About Ethics Anymore?. *J Bus Ethics*, 14(8), 585-592, Ag 95.

It is difficult to talk about ethics in Australia these days, because 1) The different metamoral languages make it difficult for people to communicate on moral matters; 2) There are no generally accepted criteria for assessing the meaning and truth of

moral propositions; and 3) Witness talks larger in these matters than theoretical expertise, and the ideals that favour the acceptance of credible role models are no longer generally accepted. We should not assume that we can say anything meaningful about "business ethics".

Hill, Susanne. "Two Perspectives on the Ultimate End" in *The Crossroads of Norm and Nature, Sim, May (ed)*, 99-114. Lanham, Rowman & Littlefield, 1995.

This paper considers Aristotle's conception of the good in the physical and metaphysical works, on the one hand, and the ethical works on the other. It concludes that the conception of the good in the latter is dependent on that in the former.

Hill, T Patrick and Teno, Joan M and O'Connor, Mary Ann. Advance Care Planning: Priorities for Ethical and Empirical Research. *Hastings Center Rep*, 24(6), Supp 1-36, N-D 94.

Federal statute endorses advance directives as one means for patients to control medical decisions in advance of incompetence. We invited investigators from multiple disciplines to develop priorities for conceptual and empirical research. Conference participants noted research should focus on the merits of a process of communication which we titled "advance care planning". Priorities for conceptual research included: 1) the moral weight of autonomy; 2) what preferences should be voiced in advance (considering importance, authenticity and stability); and 3) appropriate safeguards. Multidisciplinary empirical research utilizing both quantitative and qualitative research methodologies should describe the current process and outcomes of decision-making generally.

Hill Jr, Thomas E. The Stability Problem in *Political Liberalism*. *Pac Phil Quart*, 75(3-4), 333-352, S-D 94.

John Rawls says that most innovations in *Political Liberalism* were needed because his treatment of stability in *A Theory of Justice* failed to take account of "the fact of reasonable pluralism." In *Political Liberalism* Rawls argues that a just pluralistic society can be stable by winning an overlapping consensus of reasonable doctrines on a *political* conception of justice as fairness. This claim is implausible if the task regarding stability is to show why a just society is likely to endure. The claim, however, is more plausible on the better understanding of that task as the attempt to satisfy liberal constraints on the legitimate use of coercive power.

Hillar, Marian. "The Problem of the Soul in Aristotle's *De anima*" in *Contributors to the Philosophy of Humanism, Hillar, Marian (ed)*, 51-81. Pasadena, Humanists Houston, 1994.

The essay analyzes Aristotle's understanding of the soul and compares it with verious previous and religious concepts. Aristotelian concept of the soul is fundamentally functional of the psychomatic entity and fits into his larger ontological scheme of reality as composed of matter and form. The soul, being a form of the living organism, perishes with the organism at death. Still, in the Aristotelian ontology the *nous* of the rational living organism requires a transcendental First Rational Cause, Cosmic *Nous*, that sets in motion the intellectual process. The concept of the First Cause is based on erroneous law of motion and anthropomorphic transposition of the relationship between the cause and effect from the sphere of human activity to the Universe.

Hillar, Marian (ed) and Prahl, Frank (ed). *Contributors to the Philosophy of Humanism*. Pasadena, Humanists Houston, 1994.

The book is as collection of 12 essays on the various contributors to the philosophy of Humanism: Robert W Burch, "The Contribution to Humanism of Konstantin Kolenda"; Ellen K Suchiel, "Radiance and Religious Belief" (on Kolenda); Jacquelyn A K Kegley, "Too Thin a Self, too Small a Human" (on Kolenda); Robert D Finch, "Aristotle's Ethics"; Marian Hillar, "The Problem of the Soul in Aristotle's *De anima*"; Sheila A Finch, "Fracois Rabelais as Humanist"; Frank Prahl, "The Contributions to Humanism of Mark Twain"; Alice Leuchtag "Elizabeth Cady Stanton: Free Thinker and Radical Revisionist"; Frank Prahl "Haldeman-Julius: Publisher, Freethinker, Humanist"; George Lattie, "The Philosophy of Corliss Lamont"; Carl Veley, "Isaac Asimov's Contribution to Humanism"; Robert D Finch, "The Philosophy of Sir Karl Popper."

Hilpinen, Risto. "Peirce on Language and Reference" in *Peirce and Contemporary Thought: Philosophical Inquiries, Ketner, Kenneth Laine (ed)*, 272-303. New York, Fordham Univ Pr, 1995.

This paper discusses C S Peirce's analysis of speech acts and propositions and his account of different forms of determinate and indeterminate reference. Peirce explained the meaning of speech acts and propositions by means of semantical games played by an utterer and an interpreter of a proposition, and this made it possible for him to give a game-theoretical account of indeterminate reference (quantifier phrases and modalities). He distinguished proper names from descriptions: even if the referent of a proper name is determined by means of a description, the latter is not part of the significance (meaning) of the name.

Hilpinen, Risto. Belief Systems as Artifacts. *Monist*, 78(2), 136-155, Ap 95.

This paper studies belief systems as artifacts, as instruments which have been intentionally created for certain purposes. The evaluation principles of artifacts are discussed, and the evaluation of a belief system is considered as a special case of the evaluation of an artifact. The concept of knowledge is analysed in the light of the instrumentalist analysis of belief systems. It is argued that epistemology and philosophy of science can be regarded as "sciences of the artificial" in Herbert Simon's sense.

Hilpinen, Risto. On Artifacts and Works of Art. *Theoria*, 58(1), 58-82, 1992.

Artists and authors create works by making artifacts. This paper discusses the nature of artifacts and the relationship between works and the artifacts made by the authors of the works. It is suggested that the ontology of works of art can be best understood by studying this relationship.

Hiltebeitel, Kenneth M and Jones, Scott K. Organizational Influence in a Model of the Moral Decision Process of Accountants. *J Bus Ethics*, 14(6), 417-431, Je 95.

This paper reports on a survey that investigated the moral decision processes of accountants. A formal belief revision model is adapted and hypotheses based on theorizations from the cognitive-developmental school are tested. The moral decision processes of accountants are hypothesized to be influenced by professional expectations, organizational expectations and internalized expectations. Subjects provided specific demographic data and were asked to access the appropriateness of fourteen principles for making moral decisions in business. Subjects were also asked to indicate which of the fourteen approaches would be most appropriate for resolving each of five ethical situations that are representative of common ethical dilemmas in accounting. Subjects' responses to the appropriateness of the fourteen principles are reduced to two dimensions using factor analysis. The factors are consistent and representative of important underlying dimensions of the stages of moral development. Demographic variables are correlated with the extracted factors using analysis of variance. The results show that subjects consider interpersonal expectations and conformity to be more appropriate than approaches that are self-serving. These findings suggest that ethical decision processes of accountants are influenced by organizational support. Age, gender, and education were also found to influence the moral decision process. Overall, the findings are consistent with the expectations hypothesized from the cognitive-developmental school and suggest that the moral development of accountants is ongoing.

Hiltscher, Reinhard. Stellt Fichtes Theorie vom "Ich" in der WL von 1794/95 eine Produktionstheorie des "Ich" dar?. *Fichte-Studien*, 5, 107-116, 1993.

Fichtes Lehre vom Selbstbewusstsein resp. vom Ich wird in der Fichte-forschung oftmals als Produktionstheorie des Ich verstanden. Ob Fichte jedoch in der Wissenschaftslehre von 1794/95 wirklich dezidiert eine Produktionstheorie des Ich ins Auge gefasst hat, lässt sich aus systematischen Gründen bezweifeln. Dieter Henrich hat in seiner Studie "Fichtes ursprüngliche Einsicht" Fichtes Produktionstheorie des Ich als Antwort auf die Aporien der Reflexionstheorie des Ich gerühmt.

Himschoot, Robert A and Rappaport, Allen. Ethics Perceptions of American Farmers: An Empirical Analysis. *J Bus Ethics*, 13(10), 795-802, O 94.

A 123 item survey of ethics perceptions of farmers had 796 respondents. Of these, 517 (64.9%) felt that farm ethics had gotten worse. A discriminant analysis employed to offer insight into the extent and nature of group differences produced 22 independent variables along with an adequate increase in classification results above expectations due to chance. These variables reflect a division between the outside business and political world and the concerns of farmers. The responses suggest an appreciation by the respondents of the interdependence of their business actions with their neighbors. The results are also suggestive of both an absolute and a relative ethics component. Further research on the relevance of communitarian ethics is suggested.

Hinckfuss, Ian. B, A Buridan-Style Propositional Logic. *Log Anal*, 34, 333-344, S-D 91.

This paper presents a natural deduction system, B, which is a Buridan-style of propositional logic, extended to include a truth predicate for locutions, and with a metatheoretic model. It is shown that the system is sound and complete with respect to that model. An attempt to re-introduce the liar paradox within an extension to B of its own metatheory, by allowing a locution to assert that its own content in not true, is shown to fail.

Hindess, Barry. Socialism and Democracy: Elaborations of the Idea of a Self-Governing Community. *Hist Euro Ideas*, 19(1-3), 309-315, Jl 94.

The end of socialism has been seen as the triumph of democracy. In fact, socialism and democracy have more in common than their counterposition might seem to indicate. Both suggest that significant features of the life of a community should be brought under community control and they have understood that control as working mainly through the state. The major problems for socialism and for democracy concern their idealizations of government. The contrary idealizations of their opponents are equally problematic. An overemphasis on government by the state involves a correlative neglect of alternative modes of governing the behavior of others.

Hine, Christine. Representations of Information Technology in Disciplinary Development: Disappearing Plants and Invisible Networks. *Sci Tech Human Values*, 20(1), 65-85, Wint 95.

This article describes developments in the use of information technology (IT) in the biological discipline of taxonomy, using both a historical overview and a detailed case study of a particular information systems project. Taxonomy has experienced problems with both its scientific legitimacy and its utility to other biologists. IT has been introduced into the discipline in response to these perceived problems. The information systems project described here served as a means of managing the tensions between scientific legitimacy and utility. It is argued that this project represents an example of the use of a technological development in an attempt to re-engineer a discipline. The development of the information system is analyzed as an attempt to develop a scientific instrument that will embody a particular model of the discipline. The concerns of taxonomy with status and legitimacy make it appropriate that this new technology should be introduced at the interface between the discipline and the rest of biology as a means of disseminating results, and thus come to represent the discipline and the plants described to outsiders, just as the system represents outsiders to taxonomists.

Hinkle, Gisela J. Postmodern Feminist Reflections on Reading Wolff. *Human Stud*, 17(4), 433-448, 1994-95.

Hinrichs, Bruce. Chaos and Cosmos: The Search for Meaning in Modern Art. *Humanist*, 55(2), 22-28, Mr-Ap 95.

Do aesthetic works within the Modernist Zeitgeist reflect alienation and disillusionment, or help reveal meaning and order? The oeuvres of Modernist painters and filmmakers are critically examined with respect to chaos and cosmos. Examples of paintings and films illustrate how Modern artists used abstraction either to deconstruct cosmos (e.g., Mondrian, Duchamp, Antonioni) or manipulate chaos (e.g., Kandinsky, Buñuel, Resnais). Modern and Postmodern art are contrasted. Paintings (e.g., Warhol, Johns, Bartlett), films (e.g., "Through a Glass Darkly", "Wings of Desire", "Naked"), and genres (e.g., Surrealism, Dada, punk rock, Cubism, Pointillism) illustrate the artistic ethos. Implications for a philosophy of aesthetics are suggested.

Hinrichs, C Clare. Off the Treadmill? Technology and Tourism in the North American Maple Syrup Industry. *Agr Human Values*, 12(1), 39-47, Winter 95.

The contrast between the nostalgic pictures on maple syrup packaging and sophisticated technologies actually used in the sugarbush and sugarhouse suggests disjunctures between image and practice in the contemporary North American maple syrup industry. This paper argues that although evidence of a "technological treadmill" exists within the maple syrup industry, as it does in other rural production sectors, such a trend is incomplete due to the increasing importance of consumption-based activities and concerns in the countryside. In response to the interests of tourists, second home owners and other increasingly influential nonproducer groups, "traditional" maple enterprises persist, demonstrating a logic and appeal unaccounted for by treadmill theory. By addressing growing consumer concern about the appearance of the rural landscape, the health of the environment, and the quality of food, these "traditional" maple practices can provide distinct advantages from producers over technological modernization. The tension between technology use and tourism in the maple syrup industry offers insights about the role of small-scale specialty agriculture for sustainability in rural areas of advanced industrial countries undergoing social and economic change.

Hinsch, Bret. Harmony (He) and Gender in Early Chinese Thought. *J Chin Phil*, 22(2), 109-128, Je 95.

Hintikka, Jaakko. "The Phenomenological Dimension" in *The Cambridge Companion to Husserl, Smith, Barry (ed)*, 78-105. New York, Cambridge Univ Pr, 1995.

Husserlian intentionality operates via what is immediately given in experience. Phenomenological reductions are calculated to uncover these given elements in experience and the constitution of our world from them. What is given are not phenomena, but part of the reality. Husserl's term for the medium of immediate givenness is *Anschauung*. Husserl's transcendental reduction can be compared with Russell's reduction to acquaintance. A major difference is that for Russell the unedited given is already categorically structured into objects of different logical types, whereas for Husserl empirical experience yields in the first place only unstructured *hyle* on which we impose forms.

Hintikka, Jaakko. "'Die Wende der Philosophie': Wittgenstein's New Logic of 1928" in *Wittgenstein and Contemporary Philosophy, Teghrarian, Souren (ed)*, 1-40. Bristol, Thoemmes, 1994.

Around 1928 Wittgenstein abandoned his belief that truth-function theory is complete. Accordingly, language-world comparisons could not be immediate, but required human operations on the propositions in question. Initially, this meant that atomic propositions contained numerical parameters and that the operations needed were arithmetical calculations. Hence mathematics was now more fundamental for Wittgenstein than logic, a view he also found in Brouwer. Since language belongs to the physical world, those calculations involve temporally persistent physical objects. In October 1929 these ideas led Wittgenstein to think that language can directly represent only the world of physical objects.

Hintikka, Jaakko. Commentary on Smith's "What Use is Aristotle's *Organon*?". *Proc Boston Colloq Anc Phil*, 9, 286-296, 1993.

Smith construes Aristotle's *Organon* as a characterization of epistemic virtue, not as a methodological treatise. But for Aristotle the obvious model of the induction of epistemic virtue is the Socratic *elenchus*. Hence Smith's view implies that Aristotle's methodology was an interrogative (dialectical) one. This agrees with the *Topics*, and there also is a hidden dialectical ingredient in the *Analytics*. This interrogative character of Aristotle's methodology provides also a perspective on Aristotle's anti-regress argument Smith discusses: Since atomic premises are the best answers to what-questions, a regress would mean that we do not know what we are talking about.

Hintikka, Jaakko and Sandu, Gabriel. Uses and Misuses of Frege's Ideas. *Monist*, 77(3), 278-293, Jl 94.

Frege's achievement as the creator of contemporary logic should not blind us to the limitations of his approach to logic, language and mathematics. Frege accepted the universality of language and its corollaries, the ineffability of semantics, the one-world view of meaning, and the hypostatization of meanings into meaning entities (Sinne). He assumed compositionality and hence overlooked informationally independent quantifiers. His thesis of the ambiguity of words like "is" is unacceptable in the semantics of natural languages. In higher-order logic, he assumed a nonstandard interpretation, which made it impossible for him to handle the important idea of arbitrary function.

Hiraga, Masako K. Diagrams and Metaphors: Iconic Aspects in Language. *J Prag*, 22(1), 5-21, Jl 94.

The problem of iconicity has been a recurring theme in linguistic inquiry into the nature of the linguistic sign. The property of iconicity includes not only the narrow category of sound symbolism, but also the broad categories of isomorphism and metaphor. This paper surveys recent research, and offers a classification of diagrammatic and metaphorical iconicity in language. Problems of structural diagram, relational diagram, grammatical metaphor, conventional metaphor and poetic metaphor are discussed, with a few illustrative examples. This review shows that an evaluation of the property of iconicity in language has implications for the general theory of language as a 'natural' phenomenon.

Hirschauer, Stefan and Mol, Annemarie. Shifting Sexes, Moving Stories: Feminist/Constructivist Dialogues. *Sci Tech Human Values*, 20(3), 368-385, Sum 95.

How can constructivism and feminism inform and strengthen one another? The author of this text is a constructivist-feminist hermaphrodite, and so s/he addresses this question in the form of an inner dialogue. Instead of taking sex as a characteristic of individuals, s/he analyzes it as something performed locally in ways that vary from one situation to another. Investigating these performances offers constructivism an interesting theoretical opportunity and a chance to turn away from a sterile anti-epistemological stance. For feminism, a radicalized notion of the construction of sexes opens up new political spaces and strategies. Constructivist texts, moreover, have the potential to "do" both the contingency and the necessity of our forms of life in their very style.

Hirsh, Elizabeth and Olson, Gary A. "Je—Luce Irigaray": A Meeting with Luce Irigaray. *Hypatia*, 10(2), 93-114, Spr 95.

The authors conducted this interview with Luce Irigaray in her home in Paris in May, 1994.

Hirtler, Eva. *Die Musik als scientia mathematica von der Spätantike bis zum Barock*. Frankfurt am Main, Lang, 1995.

The book describes the development of the idea of music as 'scientia mathematica'. Although already conceived by the Pythagoreans it obtained its definite form not until the late antiquity and has been handed down through the centuries from then on. Together with the idea of numbers creating harmony this concept often includes cosmological aspects. Aristotle was the first to criticize it systematically. On this basis a new interpretation has come up since the late Middle Ages. Many theorists of music, however, have continued to retain the cosmological idea of music; then it gains the function to justify aesthetic rules. The resultant inconsistencies finally caused its disappearance.

Hitchcock, Christopher Read. Discussion: Salmon on Explanatory Relevance. *Phil Sci*, 62(2), 304-320, Je 95.

One of the motivations for Salmon's (1984) causal theory of explanation was the explanatory *irrelevance* exhibited by many arguments conforming to Hempel's covering-law models of explanation. However, the nexus of causal processes and interactions characterized by Salmon is not rich enough to supply the necessary conception of explanatory relevance. Salmon's (1994) revised theory, which is briefly criticized on independent grounds, fares no better. There is some possibility that the two-tiered structure of explanation described by Salmon (1984) may be pressed into service, but more work would have to be done. Ironically, Salmon's difficulties are similar to those suffered by his seventeenth-century predecessors.

Hitchcock, Christopher Read. The Mishap at Reichenbach Fall: Singular vs General Causation. *Phil Stud*, 78(3), 257-291, Je 95.

This paper explores the relationship between singular causal claims, which describe relations between particular events, and general causal claims, which describe relations between event types. Authors such as Good, Sober, and Eells have argued that there is no such relationship: singular and general causal claims describe distinct species of causal relations. With the aid of a probabilistic theory of causation that I have defended elsewhere, I diagnose a flaw in their arguments. I then show how the resources of probability theory may be used to provide a positive account of the relationship between singular and general causal claims.

Hitchcock, Christopher Read. Wittgenstein on Private Language: Exorcising the Ghost from the Machine. *Philosophia (Israel)*, 24(1-2), 127-147, D 94.

Saul Kripke and Crispin Wright have published influential interpretations of Wittgenstein's Private Language Argument. I diagnose their strengths and weaknesses. I then present my own interpretation, which, I argue, combines the strengths of the other two arguments. My interpretation is based on broadly verificationist principles, but I argue that normal objections to verficationism can not gain a purchase in this context.

Hix, H L. *Spirits Hovering Over the Ashes: Legacies of Postmodern Theory*. Albany, SUNY Pr, 1995.

In a series of topical explorations structured like a sonata, *Spirits Hovering Over the Ashes* follows the consequences of postmodern theory through such issues as grief, freedom, beauty, obscenity, love, and sex to its axiological results. A basic motif, postmodernism's distribution of meaning over space rather than time, recurs throughout the chapters, each of which in some way amplifies the book's underlying theme, virtue. The "exposition" of the theme in the first ten chapters receives its "development" in the chapter "Postmodern Virtue" and its "recapitulation" in the aphorisms of the final chapter.

Hjorth, Greg. Pi^1_1 Wellfounded Relations. *Notre Dame J Form Log*, 35(4), 542-549, Fall 94.

If there is a good $delta_3^1$ well-ordering of the reals, then there is a Pi_1^1 well-founded relation for which the comparison relation is not projective. (edited)

Hjorth, Greg and Rosado Haddock, Guillermo E and Spinas, Otmar. El Frege Kantiano. *Dialogos*, 30(65), 189-212, Ja 95.

Ho, David Y F. Selfhood and Identity in Confucianism, Taoism, Buddhism, and Hinduism: Contrasts With the West. *J Theor Soc Behav*, 25(2), 115-139, Je 95.

This article explores conceptions of selfhood and identity originating from four intellectual traditions: the relational self in Confucianism, selflessness in Taoism, self-renunciation in Buddhism, and Atman-Brahman identity in Hinduism. These conceptions are compared with one another and with the core of prevailing Eastern conceptions pertaining to: 1) subject-object distinction, 2) self-other demarcation and individual identity, and 3) the centrality and sovereignity of the self. Psychological decentering is identified as a unifying theme underlying the Eastern conceptions. A reconstruction of selfhood informed by these conceptions promises to enlarge our horizons about the self and its place in society, nature, and the cosmos.

Hobart, Ann (trans) and Canguilhem, Georges. Introduction to *Penser la folie: Essais sur Michel Foucault*. *Crit Inquiry*, 21(2), 287-289, Wint 95.

Hobart, Ann (trans) and Canguilhem, Georges. On *Histoire de la folie* as an Event. *Crit Inquiry*, 21(2), 282-286, Wint 95.

Hobart, Ann (trans) and Canguilhem, Georges. Report from Mr Canguilhem on the Manuscript Filed by Mr Michel Foucault, Director of the Institut Français of Hamburg.... *Crit Inquiry*, 21(2), 277-281, Wint 95.

Hochberg, Herbert. Particulars *as* Universals: Russell's Ontological Assay of Particularity and Phenomenological Space-Time. *J Phil Res*, 20, 83-111, 1995.

Russell's elimination of basic particulars, in *An Inquiry into meaning and Truth* and *Human Knowledge: Its Scope and Limits*, by purportedly construing them as "bundles" or "complexes" of universal qualities has been attacked over the years by A J Ayer, M Black, D M Armstrong, M Loux, and others. These criticisms of Russell's ontological essay of "particularity" have been based on misconstruals of his analysis. The present paper interprets Russell's analysis, rebuts arguments of his critics, and sets out a different criticism of "bundle" analyses of particulars of the Russellian kind.

Hochkeppel, Willy. "Wider den Modernismus in der Kunst" in *Heinrich Gomperz, Karl Popper und die österreichische Philosophie, Seiler, Martin (ed)*, 163-180. Amsterdam, Rodopi, 1994.

Popper exemplifies his thoughts about art on music. He rejects the interpretation of art as self-expression and confronts Beethoven's "expressionism" against Bach's "objective music". In the genuine work of art, the artist's personality steps back behind his work. Dangerous is the longing for novelty as such or the greed for "being ahead of his time". Those modern ideas of Wagner or Schönberg lead to the formation of cliques or pressure groups. Popper regards development in art (music) by way of a dialectic of dogma and criticism. So being creative in art means the same as in science: problem-solving.

Hocutt, Max. Relativism and Moral Judgements: A Reply to Sullivan. *Philosophia (Israel)*, 24(1-2), 203-209, D 94.

Hocutt, Max. Some Truths About Truth. *Behavior Phil*, 22(2), 1-5, Fall-Wint 94.

There is no such thing as Truth, but there are such things as truths, and behavior science is a search for them. Saying so is not dogmatic, because to claim that there are truths is not the claim to know them. Early in this century, much dispute about "theories of truth" confused definitions with criteria. Tarski's semantic account of truth clarifies it. Pace William James, a change in opinions does not constitute a change in truth, which is independent of opinions.

Hodge, Joanna. Heidegger, Early and late: The Vanishing of the Subject. *J Brit Soc Phenomenol*, 25(3), 288-301, O 94.

Hodge, Roger D. On Neitzsche's Enigmatic Anti-Kantian Categorical Imperative. *Conference*, 4(1), 36-49, Spr 93.

Hodges, Michael. The Status of Ethical Judgments in the *Philosophical Investigations*. *Phil Invest*, 18(2), 99-112, Ap 95.

Hodgson, Peter E (ed) and De La Peña, Luis (ed) and Brody, Thomas A. *The Philosophy Behind Physics*. New York, Springer-Verlag, 1993.

In this work, Thomas Brody was concerned to remove the barriers between physics and philosophy by discovering the philosophy implicit in the actual process of scientific research. He developed the theory of 'active epistemic cycles' to explain how we come to know things. This theory does justice to the richness and complexity of scientific research, in contrast to the superficial and bloodless accounts current among philosophers of science who have no experience of scientific research. He applied his ideas to a wide range of problems in the philosophy of physics, especially probability theory and quantum mechanics, giving special attention to the Bell inequalities and the ensemble interpretation.

Hodkinson, Ian. Finite H-Dimension Does Not Imply Expressive Completeness. *J Phil Log*, 23(5), 535-573, O 94.

A conjecture of Gabbay (1981) states that any class of flows of time having the property known as finite H-dimension admits a finite set of expressively complete one-dimensional temporal connectives. Here we show that the class of 'circular' structures refutes the generalization of this conjecture to Kripke frames. We then construct from this class, by a general method, a new class of irreflexive transitive flows of time that refutes that original conjecture. Our paper includes full descriptions of a method for establishing finite H-dimension for a class of structures and of the technique for extending finite H-dimension to other classes, and an introduction surveying the area of expressive completeness.

Hoefer, Carl and Rosenberg, Alexander. Empirical Equivalence, Underdetermination, and Systems of the World. *Phil Sci*, 61(4), 592-607, D 94.

The underdetermination of theory by evidence must be distinguished from holism. The latter is a doctrine about the testing of scientific hypotheses; the former is a thesis about empirically adequate logically incompatible global theories or "systems of the world". The distinction is crucial for an adequate assessment of the underdetermination thesis. The paper shows how some treatments of underdetermination are vitiated by failure to observe this distinction, and identifies some necessary conditions for the existence of multiple empirically equivalent global theories. We consider how empiricists should respond to the possibility of such systems of the world.

Höffe, Otfried. Aristoteles' "Politik" kommentieren. *Z Phil Forsch*, 48(3), 455-459, Jl-S 94.

Professor Höffe reviews the first two volumes of Eckard Schütrump's German translating of Aristotle's "Politics". (The whole translation is calculated for four volumes. It is part of the "Works of Aristotle in German Language" in which all works of Aristotle are edited in new translations with detailed commentaries). Professor Höffe gives a recommendation, but takes the publication as an occasion for some critical considerations about the edition in general, especially about the disproportionately growing size of the commentary.

Höffe, Otfried. Una Conversione della Teoria Critica? Sulla Teoria del Diritto e dello Stato di Habermas. *Riv Int Filosof Diritto*, 71(4), 270-290, 1994.

The "Critical Theory" of Adorno, Horkheimer and Marcuse has a serious philosophical lack: it does not accept any political claim to power, not even that of democracy. In his second "opus magnus", *Faktizität und Geltung* (1992), Jürgen Habermas tries to rectify this lack by accepting the importance of political power. Without it laws cannot be in force. Habermas's central concepts of "integration", "overtaxing" (Überforderung), and "differentiation" (Ausdifferenzierung), however, do not achieve their purpose: they characterize the function of law in modern societies in an insufficient way. Other deficiencies of the book are its theoretical abandonment of human rights, its confusion of obligatory and supererogative parts of ethics, and its misrepresentation of modern theories in natural law.

Höft, Harmut and Howard, Paul. Well Ordered Subsets of Linearly Ordered Sets. *Notre Dame J Form Log*, 35(3), 413-425, Sum 94.

The deductive relationships between six statements are examined in set theory without the axiom of choice. Each of these statements follows from the axiom of choice and involves linear orderings in some way.

AUTHOR INDEX WITH ABSTRACTS 573 **Hollander, Edwin P**

Hoenen, Maarten. Johannes Tauler in den Niederlanden: Grundzüge eines philosophie- und rezeptionsgeschichtlichen Forschungsrogramms. *Frei Z Phil Theol*, 41(3), 389-444, 1994.

This article, which is the presentation of a historico-philosophical research program, examines the impact of the German mystic Johannes Tauler on the spiritual culture of the Netherlands in the period 1400-1647. First the philosophical significance of Tauler is delineated, especially Tauler's role as conveyer of academic knowledge (Albertism) to nonacademics. Next the three most important stages of his impact on the spiritual culture of the Netherlands are investigated: 1) his influence on Gerlach Peters (before 1403), which establishes his first appearance in the Netherlands, 2) the reaction to his (pseudo-)writings in the 16th century, with emphasis on Louis de Blois, 3) the Protestant and the Catholic translations of his writings (1588-1647) and their difference, adding a synopsis of relevant passages. The article closes with a short description of the projects that are part of this research program.

Hoff, Paul. Der Begriff der psychischen Krankheit aus der Sicht der Fichteschen Transzendentalphilosophie. *Daimon Rev Filosof*, 9, 173-191, 1994.

Psychiatry's relationship with philosophy is much closer than one might think if applying a narrow dichotomy between natural sciences and the humanities. In a first step, the paper discusses this relationship with regard to Karl Jaspers's critical arguments in this general Psychopatology (1913). Then, in its main part, I try to develop the fundamental principles of transcendental philosophy as proposed by Kant and Fichte and to prove their importance for basic psychiatric questions. It can be shown that psychiatry is specially at risk to follow dogmatical empiricism as well as dogmatical idealism. Both are clearly rejected the transcendental philosophy, which provides an adequate theoretical link between the three necessary levels of empirical and teleological finding and the individual person. Two concepts that are of central importance for any psychiatric application, are highly typical for Fichte's philosophy, the idea of freedom and the crucial role of interpersonality.

Hoffenberg, Raymond (ed) and Harriss-White, Barbara (ed). *Food: Multidisciplinary Perspectives*. Cambridge, Blackwell, 1994.

At the core of this collection are the Wolfson College, Oxford, public lectures of 1992. These examine, in accessible language, the frontiers of research on food from the following disciplinary perspectives: medicine, nutrition, food science, anthropology, gender studies, development economics and political sociology. To these have been added specially commissioned papers from nutritional biochemistry, law and ethics. An introduction summarises the contributions, develops certain themes, and draws out the varied implications for public action.

Hoffman, Joshua and Rosenkrantz, Gary S. *Substance Among Other Categories*. New York, Cambridge Univ Pr, 1994.

Hoffman, Paul. Freedom and Strength of Will: Descartes and Albritton. *Phil Stud*, 77(2-3), 241-260, Mr 95.

Hoffman, Paul. Responses to Chappell and Watson. *Phil Stud*, 77(2-3), 283-292, Mr 95.

Hoffmann, Michael. The "Realization of the Due-Measure" as Structural Principle in Plato's *Statesman*. *Polis*, 12(1-2), 77-98, 1993.

The key for understanding Plato's *Statesman* is the proposition that an indispensable prerequisite of all arts should be the "measuring in the realization of the due-measure". Plato, by emphasizing the process of "realizing" a measure, which at the same time should orient the processes of the arts, shows that besides having a knowledge of the "ideas" and the methods used in every art, we need the knowledge of how to put both into practice, a knowledge we can acquire only by training. This reasoning determines not only Plato's definition of the art of statesmanship, but the course of the dialogue as well: defining statesmanship is young Socrates' training program to become a better dialectician. Thus the entire dialogue can be reconstructed as a well-ordered diairesis.

Hofman-Veselinovic, Mijana. Les aspects mythologieques de la musique (le passage du modernisme au post-modernisme). *Horiz Phil*, 5(1), 20-30, Autumn 94.

Hofmann, Alexander. On the Nature of Meaning and Its Indeterminacy: Davidson's View in Perspective. *Erkenntnis*, 42(1), 15-40, Ja 95.

In order to illustrate the nature of the indeterminacy of meaning. Donald Davidson sometimes compares it to the fact that we can measure length or temperature on different scales. In the following paper I try to explain first why we are supposed to expect such an analogy, given the semantics of the word 'meaning' and of the word 'length' or 'temperature'. In the second part I examine how close the analogy is by distinguishing different forms of indeterminacy of meaning (viz., the indeterminacy of reference and the indeterminacy of truth) and ask whether both forms have an equivalent in a theory of measurement. I shall conclude that this is indeed the case.

Hofmann, T R. Let Bachelors and Lacking Wives Rest! (In Reaction to Edwards, 1994). *J Prag*, 23(4), 449-450, Ap 95.

Hogan, Melinda. What is Wrong with an Atomistic Account of Mental Representation?. *Synthese*, 100(2), 307-327, Ag 94.

Hogan, Patrick Colm. The Possibility of Aesthetics. *Brit J Aes*, 34(4), 337-349, O 94.

The argument is that: 1) There are no principles of taste. 2) Singular judgments of taste can be true if and only if there are normative principles of taste or a *sensus communis*. 3) There is no *sensus communis*; thus singular judgments of taste are neither true nor false. However, 4) judgments of taste are open to rational debate in terms of idiosyncrasy, though such debate is valid only relative to shared general preferences of the disputants. And 5) the systematic study of beauty is viable because there are laws of taste or, equivalently, aesthetic universals (in the broad, linguistic sense of "universals").

Hogarth, Mark. Non-Turing Computers and Non-Turing Computability. *Proc Phil Sci Ass*, 1, 126-138, 1994.

A true Turing machine (TM) requires an infinitely long paper tape. Thus a TM can be housed in the infinite world of Newtonian spacetime, but not necessarily in our world, because our world—at least according to our best spacetime theory, general relativity—may be finite. One can argue for the "existence" of a TM on the basis that there is no such housing problem in some other relativist worlds that are similar to our world. But curiously enough—and this is the main point of this paper—some of these close worlds have a special spacetime structure that allows TMs to perform certain Turing unsolvable tasks. For example, in one kind of spacetime a TM can be used to solve first-order predicate logic and the halting problem. And in a more complicated spacetime, TMs can be used to decide arithmetic. These new computers serve to show that Church's thesis is a thoroughly contingent claim. Moreover, since these new computers share the fundamental properties of a TM in ordinary operation, a computability theory based on these non-Turing computers is no less worthy of investigation than orthodox computability theory. Some ideas about this new mathematical theory are given.

Hogervorst, S. *Staat en Welzijn: Het belang van een vernieuwde conceptie van de Minimale Staat*. Assen, Van Gorcum, 1995.

Hogervorst, S. *Welzijn Arbeid en Zekerheid*. Assen, Gorcum, 1986.

Hogervorst, S. *Welzijn-Zeggenschap en Eigendom*. Assen, Gorcum, 1989.

Holcomb III, Harmon R. To Bet the Impossible Bet. *Int J Phil Relig*, 36(2), 65-79, O 94.

The problem of how to defend or critique Pascal's infamous Wager argument should not be solved; instead, it would be dissolved. There is no genuine Wager argument because the wager is not a possible bet, and so debate over whether it makes belief in God prudent is moot. The missing insight is that the relation of the payoff matrix to the act of betting undermines the practical rationality of the wager itself. This point is sharpened through formalization into an impossibility proof; the wager violates the preconditions of rational betting, and so is not a rationally conceivable bet.

Holder Jr, John J. An Epistemological Foundation for Thinking: A Deweyian Approach. *Stud Phil Educ*, 13(3-4), 175-192, 1994-95.

In this article, I argue that Dewey's naturalistic theory of experience provides a philosophically appropriate basis for understanding thinking both as a rational and a creative process. Many of the prevalent theories of thinking assume a "cognitivist" epistemology that opposes rational and creative processes. On a cognitivist model, therefore, creative thinking is an oxymoron. Dewey's naturalistic theory of experience, supplemented by the recent work of Mark Johnson on imagination, solves this problem by giving much greater consideration to the structural features of the noncognitive levels of experience—here rational and creative processes are not in opposition. I conclude the article by considering some of the implications of the Deweyan model for teaching thinking.

Holdsworth, Dick. "Accountability: The Obligation to Lay Oneself Open to Criticism" in *Ethics and the Professions, Chadwick, Ruth (ed)*, 42-57. Brookfield, Avebury, 1994.

Holdsworth, Dick. "Ethical Decision-Making in Science and Technology" in *Introducing Applied Ethics, Almond, Brenda (ed)*, 130-147. Cambridge, Blackwell, 1995.

Holenstein, Elmar. Human Equality and Intra- as well as Intercultural Diversity. *Monist*, 78(1), 65-79, Ja 95.

According to a classic Platonic thesis, cultural universals are to be found in the deep structure of essential ideas, but not in the surface structure of contingent expressions. According to a Romantic antithesis, content and form, meaning and expression as well as text and context are interdependent: Ideas change along with their expression from one culture to another. A present-day synthesis accepts the interdependence of text and context. Thus, contingent universals can be found at the level of both content and expression.

Holenstein, Elmar. Worin unterscheiden sich die Gesellschaftsverträge der Schweizer-von jenen der Philosophiegeschichte?. *Stud Phil (Switzerland)*, 53, 143-176, 1994.

Four aspects are elaborated that distinguish Swiss 'social contracts' from the 'social contracts' developed by philosophers: 1) Swiss 'social contracts' are contracts not only between individuals, but also between communities. 2) They guarantee the particular laws of the particular communities and do not tend to uniform law. 3) Informal mediation is preferred over formal sanctions as a means to resolve conflicts. 4) Equity and 'good faith' are as important as 'strict law'.

Holguín, Magdalena. Sobre la certeza. *Rev Latin de Filosof*, 20(2), 347-356, 1994.

Holland, Alan. "Natural Capital" in *Philosophy and the Natural Environment, Attfield, Robin (ed)*, 169-182. New York, Cambridge Univ Pr, 1994.

Holland, Michael (ed). *The Blanchot Reader*. Cambridge, Blackwell, 1995.

Hollander, Dana. Franz Rosenzweig on Nation, Translation, and Judaism. *Phil Today*, 38(4), 380-389, Wint 94.

Reading sections from Rosenzweig's central philosophical work, *The Star of Redemption* (1921), as well as some of his essays on translation and on Judaism, I trace the interconnections between questions of nation, language, and translation in Rosenzweig's analyses. In examining the role of Rosenzweig's notions of translation and language in his larger understanding of Judaism, we find that language is more than an example for a more general 'national' problematic. Rather, it is a privileged field in which the features of the Jewish situation are preeminently visible—a situation for which translation is constitutive.

Hollander, Edwin P. Ethical Challenges in the Leader-Follower Relationship. *Bus Ethics Quart*, 5(1), 55-65, Ja 95.

Leadership and followership are unified in an interdependent relationship exemplified by the idea of teamwork. Ethical concerns are among the valuational elements essential to developing loyalty and trust in this relationship. However, because of their need to maintain power and distance, self-serving leaders may become detached from how their actions are perceived and reacted to by followers. This pattern can be especially damaging to teamwork when leaders continue to receive disproportionate rewards despite their poor performance, especially when coupled with organizational downsizing and layoffs. Implications are drawn regarding the ethics of equity, responsibility, and accountability in the exercise of authority and power.

Hollander, Eric and Stein, Dan J. A Neural Network Approach to Obsessive-Compulsive Disorder. *J Mind Behav*, 15(3), 223-237, Sum 94.

A central methodological innovation in cognitive science has been the development of connectionist or neural network models of psychological phenomena. These models may also comprise a theoretically integrative and methodologically rigourous approach to psychiatric phenomena. In this paper we employ connectionist theory to conceptualize obsessive-compulsive disorder (OCD). We discuss salient phenomenological and neurobiological findings of the illness, and then reformulate these using neural network models. Several features and mechanisms of OCD may be explicated in terms of disordered networks. Neural network modeling appears to constitute a novel and potentially fertile approach to psychiatric disorders such as OCD.

Holleman, Warren L (& others). Obligations of Physicians to Patients and Third-Party Payers. *J Clin Ethics*, 5(2), 113-120, Sum 94.

The increasing presence of third-party payers has created a need to redefine the physician-patient relationship in triadic rather than dyadic terms. Third parties have legitimate interests in the physician-patient encounter. However, as third-party demands for information and control increase, physicians must reassert their own moral authority and that of their patients, and they should consider limiting the amount and type of information transmitted to employers, insurance companies, and government agencies. Although physicians and patients no longer enjoy an exclusive relationship, physicians must strive to preserve trust and communication, along with basic standards of care and respect for the confidentiality and autonomy of the patient.

Hollingdale, R J. "Theories and Innovations in Nietzsche: Logic, Theory of Knowledge, and Metaphysics" in *Nietzsche: A Critical Reader*, Sedgwick, Peter R (ed), 111-122. Cambridge, Blackwell, 1995.

Hollinger, David A. "The Problem of Pragmatism in American History" in *Pragmatism: From Progressivism to Postmodernism*, Hollinger, Robert (ed), 19-37. Westport, Praeger, 1995.

This historical study first published in 1980, and now reprinted, interprets pragmatism as an episode in the articulation of a general program for "scientific" culture. It treats the leading pragmatist philosophers and their popularizers in the context of their own times. It narrates the constructing, by John Dewey and his followers, of a "pragmatist tradition" which retroactively claimed writings by Peirce, James, and eventually Holmes and Emerson. It argues against historians who have "flattened" pragmatism by making it co-terminus with "America", and philosophers who have found its historical significance exhausted by its most enduring theories of meaning, truth, and goodness.

Hollinger, Robert (ed) and Depew, David (ed). *Pragmatism: From Progressivism to Postmodernism*. Westport, Praeger, 1995.

This collection of essays examines American pragmatism in cultural and historical context, beginning with Progressivism and running through the era of Post-World War II positivism up to contemporary postmodernism. A main thesis of the essays is that Dewey's evolutionary metaphysics is a necessary ingredient of his vision of a democratic culture.

Hollis, Martin. The Gingerbread Game. *Analysis*, 54(4), 196-200, O 94.

Wherein Hansel and Gretl recall their ordeal at the gingerbread cottage and how the wicked witch snared them with a paradox of backward induction. They reflect that, if rationality is to be a Good Thing, joint decisions need to be distinguished from a sum of strategic choices by separately rational individuals, and reciprocity from mutual self-interest. There are more reasons for action than are dreamt of in game theory.

Hollis, Martin. *The Philosophy of Social Science: An Introduction*. New York, Cambridge Univ Pr, 1994.

The book takes explanation and understanding as its major theme, holism and individualism as its minor one. Should we relate social action to laws of behaviour or to webs of meaning? Are social actors makers of rational choices or followers of normative rules? Such questions are fertile for philosophers and social scientists alike, when posed by connecting, for instance, problems of reasons for action, personal identity and Other Minds with those of game theory, role-playing and Other Cultures. This introduction makes such connections in simple and lucid prose, while exploring the tensions between naturalism and hermeneutics.

Hollis, Martin and Bellamy, Richard. Liberal Justice: Political and Metaphysical. *Phil Quart*, 45(178), 1-19, Ja 95.

Metaphysics is necessary to determine those minimum standards of just conduct which liberals insist are owed to all human beings. Politics enables us both to appreciate these basic obligations by bringing us into communication with our fellow citizens and makes possible practical agreements that go beyond this bare minimum by providing the extensive public services necessary to the functioning of a well-ordered modern state. Liberal justice needs to be both metaphysical and political.

Hollywood, Amy M. Beauvoir, Irigaray, and the Mystical. *Hypatia*, 9(4), 158-185, Fall 94.

By reading the analyses of mysticism found in Beauvoir and Irigaray with and against some medieval women's mystical texts, the paper articulates a possible space for the divine within feminist thought.

Holmes, Jeremy. Meaning and Mechanism in Psychotherapy and General Psychiatry. *Philosophy*, 37(Supp), 41-53, 1994.

Holmes, Robert L. Pacifism and Wartime Innocence: A Response. *Soc Theor Pract*, 20(2), 193-202, Sum 94.

Holmström-Hintikka, Ghita. Evidence, Experts, and Legal Reasoning. *Commun Cog*, 28(1), 7-36, 1995.

Holstein, Martha. Ethics in an Aging Society. *J Med Human*, 15(3), 185-193, Fall 94.

Holton, Gerald. "La métaphore dans l'histoire de la physique" in *Rhétoriques de la science*, De Coorebyter, Vincent (ed), 149-169. Paris, Pr Univ France, 1994.

Holton, Richard. Sources and Leapfrogging: Reply to Pickles. *Mind*, 104(415), 583-584, Jl 95.

Holveck, Eleanore. "Can a Woman Be a Philosopher? Reflections of a Beauvoirian Housemaid" in *Feminist Interpretations of Simone de Beauvoir*, Simons, Margaret A (ed), 67-78. University Park, Penn St Univ Pr, 1995.

Holway, Richard. Achilles, Socrates, and Democracy. *Polit Theory*, 22(4), 561-590, N 94.

Plato's account of Socrates' life, trial, and death is modeled on the epic tale of an evanescent "public" Achilles who pays the price for speaking truth to power in the *Iliad*. Socrates' philosophic initiation by Diotima in the *Symposium* draws on myths in which divine mothers such as Achilles' attempt to burn away their sons' mortal parts. These narratives—Homeric and Platonic alike—are rooted in a culturally pervasive psychology in which quasi-incentuous liaisons between mothers and sons and fathers and daughters undermine marital bonds, responsible parental care, and children's maturation. This same psychology informs Platonic political philosophy, particularly its skewed vision of democracy.

Holyer, Robert. Capital Punishment and the Sanctity of Life. *Int Phil Quart*, 34(4), 485-498, D 94.

It is often commonly asserted that capital punishment violates the sanctity of life. In this paper, I examine the role of appeals to the sanctity of life in arguments for and against capital punishment, focusing mainly on the version of the principle that assigns to human life the highest or infinite value. While I argue that several important arguments commonly invoked by abolitionists that appeal to this version of the sanctity of life are without promise, my larger conclusion is that the sanctity of life is of little value in deciding the issue of capital punishment.

Holyer, Robert. Justice and Mercy: A Reply to Thomas Talbott. *Relig Stud*, 30(3), 287-294, S 94.

In this article I take exception to the claim, advanced by Thomas Talbott in his recent article in *Religious Studies* (1993), that for God justice and mercy are the same thing. I argue first, contrary to Talbott, that justice and mercy are not conceptually identical. Second, I argue that Talbott does not adequately defend the weaker claim that justice and mercy serve the same end. Finally, I argue that, though he has options to pursue, Talbott has not adequately developed or defended the claim that for God the requirements of mercy and justice are identical.

Holz, Hans Heinz. "Die nachmetaphysischen Wurzeln der Politik in der europäischen Moderne" in *Das geistige Erbe Europas*, Buhr, Manfred (ed), 236-249. Napoli, Vivarium, 1994.

Honderich, Ted. "Functionalism, Identity Theories, the Union Theory" in *The Mind-Body Problem: A Guide to the Current Debate*, Warner, Richard (ed), 215-235. Cambridge, Blackwell, 1994.

Strict functionalism, despite its idea of variable realization, is not more swallowable that eliminative materialism. It is also incoherent, in that it depends on a conception of mental events which it disallows. Given a realist conception of mental events, certain identity theories mentalize the brain or else are epiphenomenalist. The union theory, involving nomic correlation between mental and neural facts, is the correct account of the mind-brain relation. It is not more dualistic than some identity theories.

Honderich, Ted (ed). *The Oxford Companion to Philosophy*. New York, Oxford Univ Pr, 1995.

This is an encyclopedia of philosophy, of 1009 pp or about 820,000 words, with about 2000 entries by 249 philosophers, mostly American and British. It is in effect a history of all the philosophy that has entered into the English language and a survey of contemporary philosophy mainly in that language but to some extent in others. The longest entries are over 3000 words, on the principal parts of philosophy and on the greatest philosophers. The shortest entries, of 70 words, provide definitions of terms. There are entries on selected contemporary philosophers. A secondary aim of the book is to divert. It contains small entries on such things as the famous lines of poetry having to do with philosophy.

Honeycutt, Earl D and Siguaw, Judy A and Hunt, Tammy G. Business Ethics and Job-Related Constructs: A Cross-Cultural Comparison of Automotive Salespeople. *J Bus Ethics*, 14(3), 235-248, Mr 95.

Although a number of articles have addressed ethical perceptions and behaviors, few studies have examined ethics across cultures. This research focuses on measuring the job satisfaction, customer orientation, ethics, and ethical training of automotive salespersons in the U S and Taiwan. The relationships of these variables to salesperson performance were also investigated. Ethics training was found to be negatively related to perceived levels of ethicalness and performance. High performance U S salespeople reported high ethical behavior, while the opposite was true in Taiwan. Customer orientation in both countries was influenced by ethics training. Managers should evaluate current ethics training programs to insure correct ethical behavior is taught and rewarded.

Honig, Bonnie (ed). *Feminist Interpretations of Hannah Arendt*. University Park, Penn St Univ Pr, 1995.

This volume explores the significance of Hannah Arendt's political thought for feminist theory and politics. By considering Arendt's treatments for the pariah, salon society, public and private, nature, violence, revolution, nationalism, race, childhood, friendship, forgiving, promising, and the politics of identity, thirteen contributors advance contemporary debates within feminism about women's identity; the intersection of gender with other axes of difference such as race, class, and sexuality; and the possibilities, limits, and preconditions of feminist political action. The volume concludes with a comprehensive annotated bibliography of feminist engagements with Arendt in English, German, French, and Italian. The Hannah Arendt who emerges from this volume, while not herself a feminist, is a vital and reinvigorating thinker for feminists to engage.

Honneth, Axel. "The Other of Justice: Habermas and the Ethical Challenge of Postmodernism" in *The Cambridge Companion to Habermas*, White, Stephen K (ed), 289-323. New York, Cambridge Univ Pr, 1995.

Honneth, Axel. The Social Dynamics of Disrespect: On the Location of Critical Theory Today. *Constellation*, 1(2), 255-269, O 94.

Honneth, Axel and Wright, Charles W (ed). *The Fragmented World of the Social: Essays in Social and Political Philosophy*. Albany, SUNY Pr, 1995.

The essays in this volume weave together arguments and insights drawn from German critical theory, diverse traditions of French philosophy and social theory, and recent Anglo-American moral and political theory. Pursuing the problem of sources of normative insight that emerges through his analysis of classical Marxism and early critical theory, Honneth canvasses these other traditions in an effort to identify more refined conceptual tools by which it might fruitfully be addressed. Ending the volume with careful discussions of modernism and postmodernism as well as of liberalism and communitarianism, the author points toward a conception of human sociability that promises to evade the familiar entrapments of contemporary social and ethical thought.

Hont, Istvan. "Commercial Society and Political Theory in the Eighteenth Century" in *Main Trends in Cultural History, Melching, Willem (ed)*, 54-94. Amsterdam, Rodopi, 1994.

Hoogland, J. Die uitdrukkingskracht van de transcendentale denkkritiek. *Phil Reform*, 59(2), 114-136, 1994.

Antinomies play an important role in contemporary (post-modern) philosophy. In his *transcendental critique of theoretical thought* the Dutch philosopher Herman Dooyeweerd (1894-1977) has developed an original view on the origin of antinomies in theoretical thought. If some usual misinterpretations are removed, this view is highly relevant to the problem of antinomies or reflexive paradoxes in contemporary philosophy. In his transcendental critique Dooyeweerd tries to show that antinomies are the result of dogmatizing the autonomy of theoretical thought.

Hook, Sidney. *John Dewey: An Intellectual Portrait*. Amherst, Prometheus, 1995.

Hooker, Brad. Compromising with Convention. *Amer Phil Quart*, 31(4), 311-317, O 94.

When norms conventionally accepted in our society as morally binding could be replaced by better ones, which should we obey? This paper starts by attacking the view (here called "unrestricted conventionalism") that complying with the norms conventionally accepted as morally binding is always morally required. The paper then attacks the actutilitarian view that maximizing utility is always right whether or not the act that maximizes utility happens to accord with any conventional or ideal social norms. It also attacks the view ("satisficing conventionalism") that complying with the norms conventionally accepted as morally binding is always morally required as long as these norms are "good enough". As against all those views, the paper defends the rule-consequentialist view that we should follow the norms whose inculcation would produce the best results, even if the norms don't match existing conventions.

Hooker, Brad. Is Rule-Consequentialism a Rubber Duck?. *Analysis*, 54(2), 92-97, Ap 94.

Some things aren't what their names suggest. This is true of rubber ducks, stool pigeons, clay pigeons, hot dogs, and clothes horses. Frances Howard-Snyder's "Rule Consequentialism is a Rubber Duck" (*APQ*, 30 (1993) 271-78) argues that the answer is Yes. Howard-Snyder thinks rule-consequentialism is a form of deontology, not a form of consequentialism. This thought is understandable: many recent definitions of consequentialism are such as to invite it. Thinking rule-consequentialism inferior to act-consequentialism, many philosophers, when discussing consequentialism, have had act-consequentialism in mind. Having just one kind of consequentialism in mind has led them to offer definitions of consequentialism that are really definitions of just act-consequentialism. My paper discusses three different possible definitions of consequentialism and defends one that does justice to rule-consequentialism's family membership.

Hooker, Brad. Rule-Consequentialism, Incoherence, Fairness. *Proc Aris Soc*, 95, 19-35, 1994-95.

One important objection to rule-consequentialism is that the theory could require rule-following even when disaster would result. Another important objection is that the theory collapses into extensional equivalence with act-consequentialism. This paper briefly mentions Richard Brandt's replies to these objections and then goes on to sketch a new reply to the objection that rule-consequentialism can escape collapse into act-consequentialism only by becoming incoherent. The incoherence is supposed to consist in rule-consequentialists' having maximising the good as their ultimate moral goal and yet simultaneously believing that in certain situations it is wrong to do what would maximize the good. But rule-consequentialism need not be incoherent in this way. As the paper explains someone could be a rule-consequentialist without having maximizing the good as an overarching moral goal. The paper ends by defending rule-consequentialism against the objection that it doesn't supply an account of fairness.

Hooker, C A. *Reason, Regulation, and Realism: Toward a Regulatory Systems Theory of Reason and Evolutionary Epistemology*. Albany, SUNY Pr, 1995.

Hookway, Christopher. "Metaphysics, Science, and Self-Control: A Response to Apel" in *Peirce and Contemporary Thought: Philosophical Inquiries, Ketner, Kenneth Laine (ed)*, 398-415. New York, Fordham Univ Pr, 1995.

Hookway, Christopher. Naturalized Epistemology and Epistemic Evaluation. *Inquiry*, 37(4), 465-485, D 94.

The paper explores Quine's 'naturalized epistemology', investigating whether its adoption would prevent the description or vindication of normative standards standardly employed in regulating beliefs and inquiries. Quine's defense of naturalized epistemology rejects traditional epistemological questions rather than using psychology to answer them. Although one could persuade those sensitive to the force of traditional epistemological problems only by employing the kind of argument whose philosophical relevance Quine is committed to denying, Quine can support his view by *showing* how scientific inquiry need not confront any evaluative issues which cannot be addressed in naturalistic terms. A survey of Quine's own epistemological writings supports this account of his position: naturalized epistemology it is argued, requires acceptance of the shallowness of epistemic reflection, and traditional epistemology employs general epistemic norms and principles which Quine endeavours to show that we can do without. The closing sections of the paper argue that Quine can consistently resist recent criticisms by Alvin Plantinga in spite of the fact that an unsympathetic reader could reasonably be unimpressed by this resistance. Finally, an attempt is made to understand the normative role of Quine's empiricism and of his claim that prediction is the checkpoint of inquiry.

Hookway, Christopher and Grimaltos, Tobies. When Deduction Leads to Belief. *Ratio*, 8(1), 24-41, Ap 95.

The paper questions the common assumption that rational individuals believe all propositions which they know to be logical consequences of their other beliefs: although we must acknowledge the truth of a proposition which is a deductive consequence of our beliefs, we may not genuinely *believe* it. This conclusion is defended by arguing that some familiar counterexamples to the claim that knowledge is justified true belief fail because they involve propositions which are not really believed. Beliefs guide conduct or issue in assertion by answering questions which arise in the course of deliberation and conversation, but the troublesome cases present propositions which do not present the agent's answer to any question. The paper concludes by sketching the conditions, under which the deductive consequences of our beliefs can be believed.

Hooper, J Leon (ed) and Murray, John Courtney. *Bridging the Sacred and the Secular*. Washington, Georgetown Univ Pr, 1994.

This collection highlights Murray's 1940s and 1960s writings on various public and ecclesial issues and is meant to supplement the 1950s essays in his *We Hold These Truth*. Its ordering and introductions focus on the relationship of philosophical and theological knowledge. Whereas *WHTT* presumes a sharp distinction (if not dichotomy) between philosophy and theology, these essays explore common grounds between them—the earlier within the methods of canonical Scholasticism, the later in terms of common social environments and cognitional operations. At issue is the ethics of bringing specific religious beliefs to the determination of public policy.

Hoover, Kevin D. "Six Queries about Idealization in an Empirical Context" in *Idealization VI: Idealization in Economics, Hamminga, Bert (ed)*, 43-53. Amsterdam, Rodopi, 1994.

Inventarization of the main questions for research into the idealizational character of economic theories, focusing on the new classical macroeconomic research programme. It suggests a method to discriminate between rival idealized models.

Hope, Tony. Commentary on "The Alzheimer's Disease Sufferer as Semiotic Subject". *Phil Psychiat Psych*, 1(3), 161-162, S 94.

This paper comments on a paper by Sabat and Harre: "The Alzheimer's Disease Sufferer as Semiotic Subject". This commentary agrees that it is important for the carers of those with Alzheimer's disease to try and understand patient's meanings and not focus simply on cognitive deficits. It takes issue with Sabat and Harre over their analogy that the sufferer from Alzheimer's condition is like someone trying to play tennis with a damaged racquet. This inner mental life itself, as well as the expression of that inner life can be affected by the disease process.

Hope, Tony. Personal Identity and Psychiatric Illness. *Philosophy*, 37(Supp), 131-143, 1994.

This article centers around two somewhat contrasting case histories: one involving a person with dementia; the other a person with mild mania. These two cases are interesting because they are real examples from psychiatric practice, and what made them clinically difficult was that they were conceptually, or philosophically, puzzling. (edited)

Hope, Tony and Moore, Andrew and Fulford, K W M. Mild Mania and Well-Being. *Phil Psychiat Psych*, 1(3), 165-177, S 94.

This paper explores the relationship between mania, or pathologically elevated mood, and philosophical theories of well-being. A patient, Mr M, is described who oscillated between periods when he refused medication and periods when he was willing to accept it, and whose desires and life objectives were radically different in his medicated and unmedicated states. The practical dilemmas this raised are explored in terms of the three principal philosophical theories of well-being: hedonism, the desire fulfillment theory, and objectivism. (edited)

Hoping, Helmut. Time, Eternity, and the Visual Moment (Augenblick): Heidegger and the Problem of a Theology of Time. *Amer Cath Phil Quart*, 68(Supp), 187-202, 1994.

Hoping, Helmut. Understanding the Difference of Being: On the Relationship between Metaphysics and Theology. *Thomist*, 59(2), 189-221, Ap 95.

Hopkins, James. "Introduction to *Philosophical Essays on Freud*" in *Philosophy of Psychology: Debates on Psychological Explanation, Macdonald, Cynthia (ed)*, 409-432. Cambridge, Blackwell, 1995.

Hopkins, James. "Reply: Irrationality, Interpretation, and Division" in *Philosophy of Psychology: Debates on Psychological Explanation, Macdonald, Cynthia (ed)*, 461-484. Cambridge, Blackwell, 1995.

Hopkins, Patrick D. Simulation and the Reproduction of Injustice: A Reply. *Hypatia*, 10(2), 162-170, Spr 95.

Melinda Vadas rejects my claim that there are morally relevant differences between simulations of unjust events and actual unjust events on the ground that I overlook the connection between simulations and that which they simulate. I argue that this purported moral connection can only be understood as either the result of a necessary psychological disposition or as a "magical," metaphysical attachment, neither of which is defensible or satisfactory.

Horák, Petr. On the Anniversary of the First World War. *Filozof Cas*, 42(4), 609-621, 1994.

The Great War 1914-1918 and the philosophers: for Hermann Cohen (an address to the German Kant's Society, October 14, 1914) the war was the expression of the German nation's will to defend the highest, i.e., the German culture against its enemies—the British and the French in the first place. Henri Bergson expressed (an address to the French Academy of the Moral and Political Sciences, December 12, 1914) his conviction that this war was a legitimate defense against Prussian militarism and barbarism. Three brief letters by Ludwig Wittgenstein to Bertrand Russell and John Maynard Keynes, from the battlefield (1914 and 1915), demonstrate W resolution to continue his philosophical work and his relationship with his British friends in spite of the war which has separated them.

Hord, Fred Lee (ed) and Lee, Jonathan Scott (ed). *I Am Because We Are: Readings in Black Philosophy*. Amherst, Univ of Mass Pr, 1995.

Horenstein, Norma. "Modelos de Procesos Justificatorios" in *Temas Actuales de Filosofía, Palacios, María Julia (ed)*, 275-280. Buenos Aires, Univ Nacional Salta, 1993.

The difficulty in obtaining agreement upon guidelines to identify legitimate scientific knowledge leads to the development of a taxonomy of positions in relation to the justification and linkage of relevant epistemological views. The analysis is centered around three models of the justification process and then the problem is considered, to a certain extent, as the *trilemma of justification*. The principles and criteria exposed refer to the externalist, the internal realist and the consensus positions. These accounts are next confronted with the thesis we name *weak foundationalism*.

Horgan, Terence. "Nonreductive Materialism" in *The Mind-Body Problem: A Guide to the Current Debate, Warner, Richard (ed)*, 236-241. Cambridge, Blackwell, 1994.

Nonreductive materialism makes three main claims. First, the mental and the neurobiological explanatory frameworks are compatible, rather than excluding each other. Second, although their compatibility does require that certain inter-level constraints be satisfied, it does not require that mentalistic psychology be reducible to neurobiology; and psychology probably is not so reducible. Third, mentalistic causal explanations have an important kind of autonomy vis-a-vis neurobiological causal explanations. I briefly summarize my own proposed explication of these three claims.

Horgan, Terence. Naturalism and Intentionality. *Phil Stud*, 76(2-3), 301-326, D 94.

I argue for three principle claims. First, philosophers who seek to integrate the semantic and the intentional into a naturalistic metaphysical worldview need to address a task that they have thus far largely failed even to notice: explaining into-level connections between the physical and the intentional in a naturalistically acceptable way. Second, there are serious reasons to think that this task cannot be carried out in a way that would vindicate realism about intentionality. Third, there is much to be said for an irrealist, noneliminativist, naturalistic approach to intentionality that I call *preservative irrealism*.

Horgan, Terence. Reply to Egan's "A WORLD without MIND". *Phil Stud*, 76(2-3), 339-347, D 94.

Frances Egan's paper, a commentary on my "Naturalism and Intentionality," poses important challenges both for the general approach to language/world relations I call contextual semantics, and for the philosophical treatment of intentionality I propose to wed to contextual semantics-preservative irrealism. I address various of her concerns, taking up points about 1) contextual semantics and ontological commitment; 2) the irrealist accommodation of common sense presumptions about intentionality, 3) my analogy between irrealist positions in meta-ethics and preservative irrealism about intentionality; and 4) naturalism and the explanation of supervenience.

Horgan, Terence. Transvaluationism: A Dionysian Approach to Vagueness. *S J Phil*, 33(Supp), 97-126, 1995.

Transvaluationism asserts 1) that vagueness is logically incoherent, but 2) that vagueness is also an essential feature of human language and thought. I situate transvaluationism within a general approach to language/world relations I call contextual semantics, which asserts 1) that truth is semantically-correct assertibility, and 2) that often our statements are rendered true (correctly assertible) by virtue of indirect, not direct, language/world correspondences. Although vague predictions are often true under contextually operative semantic standards, they are never true under maximally strict standards involving genuine ontological commitment. There is no vagueness in the world itself, but only in language and thought.

Horgan, Terence. Wright's *Truth and Objectivity*. *Nous*, 29(1), 127-138, Mr 95.

In this critical study I first summarize Crispin Wright's *Truth and Objectivity*. Wright maintains 1) that truth-aptness of a given discourse is neutral about questions of realism and anti-realism concerning the discourse, but also 2) that such metaphysical questions largely turn on discourse-specific constraints governing the truth-predicate. I urge a distinction between i) Wright's general approach to truth and objectivity, and ii) his apparent inclination to implement and the approach by construing truth as a fundamentally epistemic notion. I argue against an epistemically reductive implementation, and I briefly sketch an alternative way to implement the book's core ideas.

Horgan, Terence and Tienson, John. A Nonclassical Framework for Cognitive Science. *Synthese*, 101(3), 305-345, D 94.

David Marr provided a useful framework for theorizing about cognition within classical, AI-style cognitive science, in terms of three levels of description: the levels of i) cognitive function, ii) algorithm and iii) physical implementation. We generalize this framework: i) cognitive state transitions, ii) mathematical/functional design and iii) physical implementation or realization. Specifying the middle, design level to be the theory of dynamical systems yields a nonclassical, alternative framework that suits (but is not committed to) connectionism. We consider how a brain's (or a network's) being a dynamical system might be the key both to its realizing various essential features of cognition—productivity, systematicity, structure-sensitive processing, syntax—and also to a nonclassical solution of (frame-type) problems plaguing classical cognitive science.

Horgan, Terence and Tienson, John. Soft Laws. *Midwest Stud Phil*, 15, 256-279, 1990.

According to the standard philosophical conception of scienctific law, proper laws permit no exceptions within their own domain. We argue, to the contrary, that proper laws in intentional psychology virtually always have exceptions within their own domain—psychological exceptions, as opposed to "had a stroke" or "hit by a bus" exceptions. These soft laws, as we call them, have ineliminable *ceteris paribus* clauses. The argument draws on a critique of classical cognitive science, which embodies the standard conception of law. We also argue that, given the proper understanding of law, psychological explanation requires laws.

Hori, Ryuichi and Ono, Hiroakira and Schellinx, Harold. Extending Intuitionistic Linear Logic with Knotted Structural Rules. *Notre Dame J Form Log*, 35(2), 219-242, Spr 94.

In this paper, extensions of the intuitionistic linear logic with knotted structural rules are discussed. Each knotted structural rule is a rule of inference of the following form; from X, A, ..., A (n times)...C infer X, A, ..., A (k times)...C. This rule is called the (n,k)-rule, which is a restricted form of the weakening when n k and of the contraction when n k. It is shown that when either n=1 or k=1, strong similarities hold between logics with the (n,k)-rule and the logics with the weakening or the contraction, as for the cut elimination, decision problems and the finite model property.

Horn, Joachim Christian. "Die nachkantische Wende als Vollendung der Transzendentalphilosophie" in *Das geistige Erbe Europas, Buhr, Manfred (ed)*, 250-271. Napoli, Vivarium, 1994.

1) Der sogenannte Deutsche Idealismus ist in Wahrheit *nicht* idealistisch. 2) Die Denker Leibniz-Fichte-Schelling-Hegel schufen eine *neue* Ontologie. 3) Die neue Ontologie begründet den universalen Zusammenhang: von den einfachen Dingen zu den Lebewesen, zu den Menschen,—bis zu Gott, dem Absoluten. 4) Die neue Ontologie überschreitet die Neuzeit, weil die Vermittlung des Endlichen mit dem Unendlichen nicht dem Menschen Zufällt, wie bei Kant, sondern der Seele, dem Selbst und dessen Bewusstsein. 5) Das Selbst ist die Quelle der Rationalität. Es verbindet den Menschen mit allen Lebewesen und mit Gott. 6) Diese 5 Europäischen Denker besitzen Weltformat, weil sie den Westen mit dem Osten verbinden.

Horne, Janet S. "Changing the Subject: Rorty and Contemporary Rhetorical Theory" in *Recovering Pragmatism's Voice, Langsdorf, Lenore (ed)*, 235-249. Albany, SUNY Pr, 1995.

This article reviews the issues raised by writers involved in the debate over the relationship between rhetoric and epistemology. The essay argues that the debate itself is an example of the kind of fruitless philosophical argumentation that Rorty suggests should be set aside in favor of more pragmatic concerns.

Horne, Thomas A. Liberalism and the Problem of Poverty: Reply to Ashcraft. *Crit Rev*, 8(3), 427-434, Sum 94.

In *Property Rights and Poverty*, I argued that seventeenth to mid-nineteenth-century liberal theories of the natural right to property included both the ability to exclude others from resources lawfully acquired and the ability to claim as property the resources necessary for life and livelihood. Virtually every defense of the right to exclude written during this period carried limits which allowed and even required the government to enforce the rights of those without resources to the property of others. But although Locke, among others, was a theorist of welfare rights, it is a mistake to describe him as a radical, as Richard Ashcraft does, which identifies Locke's purposes too closely with the legitimately radical theorists of the early nineteenth century who were deeply influenced by his work.

Hornsby, Jennifer. Reasons for Trying. *J Phil Res*, 20, 525-539, 1995.

The purpose is to demonstrate that both *volitionalist* and *purely instrumentalist* accounts of *trying to* are misconceived, by showing how to take proper account of the fact that a person may have a reason to try to do something which is not a reason to do the thing. The picture painted is one in which agents try to do something when moved by reasons. Reasons operate in a world in which a) one may not actually do everything one tries to do, and in which b) one cannot try to do everything that one might actually do.

Horowitz, Amir. A Note on the Intentionality of Fear. *Philosophica*, 53(1), 73-80, 1994.

Searle (in *Intentionality*) and Wittgenstein (in *Philosophical Investigations*) take fear to be intentional. The paper argues that fear is never intentional. First, an alternative to the intentionalistic view of fear is sketched. According to this alternative, fear is *a sensation* that lacks content and intentional objects, and its alleged intentional objects are its *causes*. Then, in the light of this alternative, the paper tries to show the inadequacy of the intentionalistic view of fear.

Horowitz, Amir. Content and Sensitivity. *Iyyun*, 44, 3-30, Ja 95.

The paper discusses the principles of correlational psychosemantics, criticizes Fodor's and Dretske's correlational theories of content, and suggests a different version of correlational theory. According to the suggested theory, a representation of type R that is tokened in a representational system RS represents the property the instantiations of which covary with tokens of R under circumstances that are optimal for RS's sensitivity to environmental parameters. It is argued that only mental representations of some types are correlational, while the content of others is derived from the content of the correlational ones by virtue of causal relation that prevail among them.

Horowitz, Amir. Functional Role and Intentionality. *Theoria*, 58(2-3), 197-218, 1992.

The purpose of the paper is to present and criticize various versions of functional role theories of mental content. The holistic character functional approach and the ways it deals with intentionality are discussed. It is argued that both solipsistic functional role theories (supplemented with a referential role theory) and non-solipsistic ones are basically inadequate as accounts of mental content.

Horowitz, Asher. "The Comedy of Enlightenment: Weber, Habermas, and the Critique of Reification" in *The Barbarism of Reason, Horowitz, Asher (ed)*, 195-222. Toronto, Univ of Toronto Pr, 1994.

Horowitz, Asher (ed) and Maley, Terry (ed). *The Barbarism of Reason*. Toronto, Univ of Toronto Pr, 1994.

Horowitz, Gregg. Daniel Herwitz, *Making Theory/Constructing Art: On the Authority of the Avant-Garde*. *J Aes Art Crit*, 53(2), 203-209, Spr 95.

Horsten, Leon. Modal-Epistemic Variants of Shapiro's System of Epistemic Arithmetic. *Notre Dame J Form Log*, 35(2), 284-291, Spr 94.

This paper presents formalizations of classical first-order arithmetic which contain a modal and an epistemic operator. The embedding under variants of Gödel's translation of intuitionistic arithmetic in such systems is discussed, and for one modal-epistemic system of arithmetic a possible worlds semantics is given.

Horsten, Leon. The Church-Turing Thesis and Effective Mundane Procedures. *Mind Mach*, 5(1), 1-8, F 95.

We critically discuss Cleland's analysis of effective procedures as 'mundane effective procedures'. She argues that Turing machines cannot carry out mundane procedures, since Turing machines are abstract entities and therefore cannot generate the causal proceses that are generated by mundane procedures. We argue that if Turing machines cannot enter the physical world, then it is hard to see how Cleland's "mundane procedures" can enter the world of numbers. Hence her arguments against versions of the Chruch-Turing thesis for number theoretic functions miss the mark.

Horstman, Rolf-Peter. Zur Aktualität des Deutschen Idealismus. *Neue Hefte Phil*, 35, 3-17, 1995.

Horton, John. Three (Apparent) Paradoxes of Toleration. *Filozof Istraz*, 14(2-3), 249-261, 1994.

The paper deals with some conceptual and theoretical questions concerning toleration, together with some apparent paradoxes involved in the concept of toleration. The first paradox of toleration is concerned with the moral status of what is tolerated: how can it be right to tolerate something wrong? A second paradox of toleration has been suggested by Sir Karl Popper, who claims that unlimited tolerance must lead to the disappearance of tolerance. The third paradox consists in the apparent implication of the concept of toleration that the wider the range of a person's negative attitudes, the wider the scope for practicing toleration. All three paradoxes are the result of concentrating on an excessively narrow understanding of the conceptual structure of toleration, while not enough attention is awarded to the moral context in which the employment of the concept is given coherence and point. (edited)

Horton, Robin. "African Traditional Thought and Western Science" in *African Philosophy: Selected Readings, Appiah, Kwame Anthony*, 301-338. Englewood Cliffs, Prentice Hall, 1995.

Horvath, Charles M. Excellence V Effectiveness: Macintyre's Critique of Business. *Bus Ethics Quart*, 5(3), 499-532, Jl 95.

Alasdair MacIntyre (1984) asserts that the ethical systems of the Enlightenment (formalism and utilitarianism) have failed to provide a meaningful definition of "good." Lacking such a definition, business managers have no internal standards by which they can morally evaluate their roles or acts. MacIntyre goes on to claim that managers have substituted external measures of "winning" or "effectiveness" for any internal concept of good. He supports a return to the Aristotelian notion of virtue or "excellence." Such a system of virtue ethics depends on an interrelationship of the community, one's roles in that community, and the virtues one needs to perform that role well. This article develops MacIntyre's concept of virtue ethics and shows how this paradigm fits well with existing theories about organizational behavior.

Horvath, Charles M. The Social Equation: Freedom and its Limits. *Bus Ethics Quart*, 5(2), 329-352, Ap 95.

Western business philosophy is rooted in the concepts of free enterprise, free markets, free choice. Yet freedom has its limits. Nature itself imposes constraints. In the state of nature each business must try to accomplish everything autonomously and ward off the attacks of rivals. These activities cost the business a great deal of freedom. The social contract emerges from such anarchy to increase the limits on individual freedom available within the system. The Social Equation presents a relational model of this contract to show how overall freedom is increased in a state of society. In so doing, the obligations which society places on businesses to produce beneficial goods and services is developed. Next, the complex relationship between socially enforced constraints and social moral constraints is examined, showing that social moral constraints increase freedom more than do enforced constraints. This work concludes with proposed uses of the Social Equation as a heuristic for business ethics.

Horwich, Paul. Meaning, Use and Truth. *Mind*, 104(414), 355-368, Ap 95.

It is argued (against Kripke) that a use-theory of meaning is *not* precluded by the requirement that whatever constitutes the meaning of a predicate be capable of determining the set of things of which the predicate is true and to which it ought to be applied.

Horwitz, Steven. Systemic Rationality and the Effects of Financial Regulation: Rejoinder to Kindleberger. *Crit Rev*, 8(4), 615-621, Fall 94.

In his reply, Kindleberger falsely ascribes to me the views that political actors are utterly incompetent, while market actors are completely rational; and that political processes are pure chaos, while market processes are perfectly efficient. My point was that the relatively better performance of the market is a result of systemic factors, not the rationality of individuals. Kindleberger fails to address the historical evidence indicating the comparatively poor performance of government intervention in the monetary order. "Market manias" are, in fact, largely the product of ill-conceived government regulations.

Horwitz, Wendy A. Characteristics of Environmental Ethics: Environmental Activists' Accounts. *Ethics Behavior*, 4(4), 345-367, 1994.

This article describes a qualitative investigation of environmental ethics as construed by environmental activists. Twenty-nine participants responded in writing to open-ended questions on their definitions of an environmental ethic, how they expressed and experienced this moral orientation in their lives, and what sustained it. Four major themes emerged. First, ethical consideration of the natural environment pervaded morality, values, and private and public life. Second, emotional or spiritual experiences, or personal fulfillment, were important for many. Third, there was disagreement on the relationships among environmental principles, intentions, and behaviors, as well as the necessity of prescribing specific behaviors. Finally, there were diverse views on the role of humanitarian concerns in an environmental ethic. These themes are discussed in terms of parallels to religious experience, motivations for an environmental ethic, and implications for nonenvironmental realms of ethics and justice.

Hoshino, Kazusama. HIV +/AIDS Related Bioethical Issues in Japan. *Bioethics*, 9(3-4), 303-308, Jl 95.

Annual and cumulative incidences of HIV+ and AIDS in patients reported by the AIDS Surveillance Committee of the Ministry of Health and Welfare are cited to illustrate some characteristics in Japan: nearly 59% of either HIV+ or AIDS patients were infected through injection of blood products or by blood transfusion. A number of plaintiffs have sued the Japanese government and pharmaceutical companies since 1989, but no judicial decisions have yet been made. The incidence of HIV decreases for each of the following routes of infection: the second highest route of transmission being heterosexual, followed by bisexual and unconfirmed or unknown cases, and less frequently homosexual, drug use and lastly via vertical transmission. The most serious bioethical problems with HIV+ and AIDS patients in Japan is the social segregation of these patients. There are many emotional fears among the general public and medical personnel about AIDS because of their inadequate scientific knowledge of this disease. The Japan Hospital Association is doing The Stop AIDS Campaign and made several surveys. Japan has become increasingly aware of the importance of AIDS education and a great deal of effort is being made to enhance bioethical considerations.

Hosmer, LaRue Tone and Masten, Scott E. Ethics vs Economics: The Issue of Free Trade with Mexico. *J Bus Ethics*, 14(4), 287-298, Ap 95.

The authors, one an ethicist and the other an economist, look at the issue of free trade with Mexico and other low wage rate countries from the viewpoints of their disciplines differ on their priorities and analytical methods, not on their objectives.

Hostetler, Karl. Getting Serious About the Questions of Democracy. *Educ Theor*, 45(1), 101-118, Wint 95.

Houben, Jan E M. Bhartrhari's Solution to The Liar and Some Other Paradoxes. *J Indian Phil*, 23(4), 381-401, D 95.

In a passage in the Vakyapadiya which should be of special interest to logicians and semanticists, the grammarian-philosopher Bhartrhari (India, 5th century CE) deals with paradoxes of negation, self-reference and truth (including the so-called 'Liar paradox'). The strategy of Russell and others attempting to establish a perfect formal language was to try to preclude their occurrence. The more recent trend to accept them as paradoxes has stimulated interesting developments in semantics, formal logic and related areas. Bhartrhari, however, presents the key to a solution based on the way intention, reference, and negation 'work' in everyday language and communication.

Houghton, David. Reasonable Doubts about Rational Choice. *Philosophy*, 70(271), 53-67, Ja 95.

Houle, K. Wes Jackson, Wendell Berry, and Bruce Colman (eds): *Meeting the Expectations of the Land: Essays in Sustainable Agriculture and Stewardship*. *J Agr Environ Ethics*, 8(1), 85-92, 1995.

This review revisits an older text, making apparent the deep tension which persists in the broader discourse: the proper way to conceptualize the "Man/Nature" relation and the proper course of action to pursue. Contributers agree that a "truly radical vision" is necessary, but propose radically different remedies, both theoretical and practical. Coleman props up the inside/outside Nature rift and berates human arrogance as the key to Nature's demise, directing us to attend to the needs of the Earth. Other essays locate the human agent and human needs as central to responsible action.

Houlgate, Stephen. "Hegel, Kant, and the Formal Distinctions of Reflective Understanding" in *Hegel on the Modern World, Collins, Ardis B (ed)*, 125-141. Albany, SUNY Pr, 1995.

In the first part of this paper, I examine certain criticisms which have been made of Hegel's reading of Kant by commentators such as Karl Ameriks (in particular that Hegel misinterprets Kant as a "subjective idealist") and I conclude that many of these criticisms are justified. In the second part, I then examine Hegel's charge that Kant fails to criticize the categories of reflective understanding in the manner suggested by Hegel himself in the *Science of Logic* and I conclude that, despite some evident shortcomings in his interpretation of Kant, Hegel is right to see Kant as an abstractly formalist thinker.

Houlgate, Stephen. Hegel and Fichte: Recognition, Otherness, and Absolute Knowing. *Owl Minerva*, 26(1), 3-19, Fall 94.

This article contains a discussion of Robert Williams' book, *Recognition. Fichte and Hegel on the Other* (Albany: SUNY Press, 1992). In it I argue that Williams is right to understand Hegel's "spirit" to be constituted by relations of mutual recognition between human beings, but wrong to understand there to be any such relation between philosophical thought (or "absolute knowing") and *truth*. Truth, for Hegel, is not something to which thought *relates* but is unfolded *in* thought itself. In conclusion, I compare Hegelian absolute knowing with Fichtean subjectivity and point to the quasi-Spinozan and quasi-Kantian elements in Hegelian absolute knowing.

Houlgate, Stephen. The Unity of Theoretical and Practical Spirit in Hegel's Concept of Freedom. *Rev Metaph*, 48(4), 859-881, Je 95.

This essay examines the unity of theoretical and practical spirit in Hegel's *Philosophy of Right*. In it I analyze Hegel's accounts of right, crime, morality and ethical life and conclude that the will or practical spirit gains in freedom as it is educated into a proper *theoretical* understanding of what freedom entails. Accordingly, whereas the moral (or abstractly free) will claims the right to judge for itself what is right and true, the ethical (or truly free) will allows its activity to be guided by the laws and institutions which it knows actually secure freedom.

Hountondji, Paulin. "The Particular and the Universal" in *African Philosophy: Selected Readings, Mosley, Albert G (ed)*, 172-198. Englewood Cliffs, Prentice Hall, 1995.

House, I W O. Flew on Anti-Social Determinism. *Philosophy*, 70(271), 111-113, Ja 95.

Houser, R Edward. *Chronos* and *Logos*: Rhetoric and the Rise of Philosophy. *Amer Cath Phil Quart*, 68(Supp), 247-258, 1994.

Based on a case study of the connection between rhetoric and philosophy in the 4C debate about the nature of rhetoric, moving from Gorgias to Aristotle, I draw the following conclusions: Aristotle rightly understood rhetoric (against Plato and the sophists) because he thought philosophy a synthetic discipline. To be synthetic, philosophy must be intrinsically historical. Philosophers use its history for the central images which are within the proper domain of rhetoric. Therefore, philosophy is intrinsically and essentially both historical and rhetorical.

Howard, Dick. "Revolution as Foundation of Political Philosophy" in *Hegel Reconsidered, Engelhardt Jr, H Tristram (ed)*, 187-209. Dordrecht, Kluwer, 1994.

The essay reflects with a re-examination of Klaus Hartmann's attempt to translate his categorial ontology and his reading of Hegel into the arena of politics and political theory. After an expression of personal debt to Hartmann, a re-reading of Hegel's concept of Objective Spirit on the basis of an interpretation of the American Revolution and of the French Revolution suggests the need for what the author has called an "originary transformation of ontology." Its results is a theory of democracy as both revolutionary and as the foundation of the structure that Hegel called Objective Spirit.

Howard, Dick. Between Culture, Politics and Philosophy. *Theor Cult Soc*, 11(2), 123-128, My 94.

Originally published in a special issue of a French journal (*Politiques*), this article asks what is unique about French intellectuals. It suggests that a crucial factor is the role of the teaching of philosophy in high school (the "classe terminale"). This, not the principles of 1789, or the Marxist theory of revolution is the crucial variable in the formation of the "intellectual". Which, in turn, points to the crucial place of the Republic in the creation of a democracy.

Howard, Dick. Hermeneutics and Critical Theory: Enlightenment as Political (in Portuguese). *Trans/Form/Acao*, 17, 51-61, 1994.

This paper analyses Gadamer's hermeneutics and the critical theory of Horkheimer and Marcuse. It tries to show that, if modern society is conceived as political, then it is possible to elaborate a theory of modernity where hermeneutics and critical theory, instead of opposing, complement each other.

Howard, Dick. Towards a Politics of Judgement. *Constellation*, 1(2), 286-305, O 94.

The essay begins with a consideration of the new political challenges facing the post-1989, post-communist world. It suggests that the new situation can be compared with that which emerged with the French Revolution, in 1789. Analysis of that revolution, and then of the Marxian project that attempted to realize the "merely formal" freedom won in the French Revolution then shows the nature and the dangers of a *politics of the will*. An analysis of the phenomenon of totalitarianism, making use of the work of Claude Lefort and that of Hannah Arendt, then suggests the need to develop a *politics of judgment*. The outline of such a politics is presented by means of a return to Kant's *Critique of Judgment*. Finally, some practical implications are suggested.

Howard, George S. When Psychology Looks Like a "Soft" Science, It's for Good Reason!. *J Theor Phil Psych*, 13(1), 42-47, Spr 93.

The natural (or physical) sciences are sometimes called "hard" sciences in contrast to the social sciences (and sometimes the life sciences also) which are thought to represent "soft" sciences. Hedges (1987) made an important effort to determine the empirical cumulativeness of various research programs, with an eye toward assessing if this criterion is related to a discipline's "hardness" or "softness". This article discusses another criterion, a research program's predictive accuracy, that might also be considered along with a program's empirical cumulativeness. Finally, recent improvements in the predictive accuracy of multifaceted psychological theories are discussed.

Howard, Paul and Höft, Harmut. Well Ordered Subsets of Linearly Ordered Sets. *Notre Dame J Form Log*, 35(3), 413-425, Sum 94.

The deductive relationships between six statements are examined in set theory without the axiom of choice. Each of these statements follows from the axiom of choice and involves linear orderings in some way.

Howard, V A and Scheffler, Israel. *Work, Education, and Leadership: Essays in the Philosophy of Education*. New York, Lang, 1995.

This book examines the relations among work, education and leadership in philosophical and practical perspective. Among the topics included are the concepts of education and training, the nature of vocational education, the relations of art and utility in schooling, and the roles of leadership in education and work. This book draws together influences from the American Pragmatist, John Dewey, and the British Idealist R G Collingwood.

Howard-Snyder, Daniel. Theism, the Hypothesis of Indifference, and the Biological Role of Pain and Pleasure. *Faith Phil*, 11(3), 452-466, Jl 94.

Following Hume's lead, Paul Draper argues that, given the biological role played by both pain and pleasure in goal-directed organic systems, the observed facts about pain and pleasure in the world are antecedently much more likely on the Hypothesis of Indifference than on theism. I examine one by one Draper's arguments for this claim and how they miss the mark.

Howard-Snyder, Daniel and Howard-Snyder, Frances. How an Unsurpassable Being Can Create a Surpassable World. *Faith Phil*, 11(2), 260-268, Ap 94.

This seems coherent: a morally unsurpassable and omnipotent being (Jove) is faced with a choice of which world to actualize where for any he might actualize there is a better. He creates a device that randomly selects from amongst the worlds he can actualize. The world that is chosen is, of course, surpassable, and yet, he seems not. We defend this conclusion against three versions of the claim that since someone could produce a world which surpassed Jove's, that being could morally surpass Jove. The first is that a superior being confronted with Jove's choice would not create at all; the second is that he would use Jove's device and it would select a superior world; the third is that he would create a superior world without using Jove's device. We argue that none of these ways of behaving would show that he was morally superior to Jove.

Howard-Snyder, Frances. The Heart of Consequentialism. *Phil Stud*, 76(1), 107-129, O 94.

Howard-Snyder, Frances and Howard-Snyder, Daniel. How an Unsurpassable Being Can Create a Surpassable World. *Faith Phil*, 11(2), 260-268, Ap 94.

This seems coherent: a morally unsurpassable and omnipotent being (Jove) is faced with a choice of which world to actualize where for any he might actualize there is a better. He creates a device that randomly selects from amongst the worlds he can actualize. The world that is chosen is, of course, surpassable, and yet, he seems not. We defend this conclusion against three versions of the claim that since someone could produce a world which surpassed Jove's, that being could morally surpass Jove. The first is that a superior being confronted with Jove's choice would not create at all; the second is that he would use Jove's device and it would select a superior world; the third is that he would create a superior world without using Jove's device. We argue that none of these ways of behaving would show that he was morally superior to Jove.

Howarth, J M. Nature's Moods. *Brit J Aes*, 35(2), 108-120, Ap 95.

Standard accounts of emotion make it obscure how we can intelligibly apply emotion terms to the natural world. I propose a revised account, applicable specifically to the ascription of moods to nature. I suggest that this sort of account might help make sense of the claim that we depend on our environment in conceptual and not merely practical ways, and that our encironment is a 'field of meaning'. It emerges, however, that the orthodox interpretation of such claims may not adequately recognise that dependence or those meanings. The phenomenological interpretation, in contrast, offers a more adequate recognition.

Howarth, J M. The Crisis of Ecology: A Phenomenological Perspective. *Environ Values*, 4(1), 17-30, F 95.

If we are to act properly with regard to the natural world, to protect, preserve, conserve, manage or leave it alone, we need both appropriate knowledge of that world, and a sound foundation for value to guide our actions. The thesis of this paper is that scientific ecology, though some of its interpreters claim it as a 'post-modern' eco-friendly science, in fact, while perhaps not as guilty as other of its post-modern interpreters might claim of the worst excesses of 'modernism', nonetheless does retain the underlying assumptions of modernism. (The 'jargon' will be further explained.) The thesis will be supported by methods drawn from phenomenology. Phenomenological enquiry can reveal and criticize the modernist assumptions, while traditional phenomenological notions, in particular Heidegger's notion of Dwelling and Merleau-Ponty's notion of the body-subject, I shall suggest, might form a more eco-friendly framework for enquiring into the character of interactions within the natural world and the basis of values in those interactions.

Howe, Edmund G. Approaches (and Possible Contraindications) to Enhancing Patients' Autonomy. *J Clin Ethics*, 5(3), 179-188, Fall 94.

This article explores how negative emotions such as apprehension of medical procedures may adversely affect patients' capacity for self-determination. Patients' capacity to respond under these circumstances is analyzed in light of current brain research to which chaos theory has been applied. Based on the above considerations, optimal clinical approaches are considered in several clinical contexts. These include obtaining informed consent, deciding whether to perform psychosurgery, and discussing with patients their advance directives. The author suggests that current approaches to several clinical situations such as those discussed in the paper, in the light of recent research, may be based on unrealistic presuppositions. Since there may be greater differences in patients' capacity to exercise autonomy that previously have been appreciated, careproviders optimally might take into account these differences and act more paternalistically when making clinical interventions.

Howe, Edmund G. Deciding Whether to Intervene. *J Clin Ethics*, 5(2), 129-131, Sum 94.

This article discusses when, if ever, ethics committees and ethics consultants should take positions on patients' behalf against their careproviders in a research setting. Two cases in which ethics committees were faced with this same conflict in a clinical setting are presented as grounds for comparison. Related issues, such as the need for patients to have time to determine their genuine wishes and to have other persons with them for support are raised and discussed. The author argues that, in general, ethics committees and consultants should be innovative and attempt to find ways in which the patient/careprovider relationship can be preserved since this relationship is of overriding importance not only to careproviders but to patients.

Howe, Edmund G. Impossible Choices: When Patients and Careproviders Face Impossible Decisions. *J Clin Ethics*, 6(1), 3-13, Spr 95.

This article explores the different reactions patients have when they face decisions which are exceptionally difficult or impossible to decide. The author discusses the work of Daniel C Dennett in considering the possibility that patients making such decisions may lack their normal capacity for self-determination. The author suggests that it may be desirable for careproviders to make more paternalistic choices in these instances than normally they would. A possible harmful effect on careproviders, themselves, of facing and making decisions which are exceptionally difficult or impossible, finally, is considered.

Howe, Leslie A. Kierkegaard and the Feminine Self. *Hypatia*, 9(4), 131-157, Fall 94.

Kierkegaard shows two contrary attitudes to woman and the feminine: misogyny and celebration. The Kierkegaardian structure of selfhood, because combined with a hierarchical assumption about the relative value of certain human characteristics, and their identification as male or female, argues that woman is a lesser self. Consequently, the claim that the Kierkegaardian ideal of selfhood is androgynist is rejected, though it is the latter assumptions alone that force this conclusion.

Howe, Norma. Peer Pressure and Children's Religious Belief. *Free Inq*, 14(3), 37-39, Sum 94.

Howell, Joseph H (ed) and Sale, William Frederick (ed). *Life Choices: A Hastings Center Introduction to Bioethics*. Washington, Georgetown Univ Pr, 1995.

Howie, John. Human-Centered or Ecocentric Environmental Ethics?. *Dialogue Hum*, 3(4), 127-137, 1993.

This essay explores some proposed answers to questions of this sort: Is human-centered or ecocentric environmental ethics the most readily defensible view? Are ethical principles that guide our behavior in human relations suitable for the burgeoning array of complex new environmental problems? Are the principles of humanistic ethics compatible with the principles of environmental ethics? In situations where the two sets of principles are incompatible are there ways the conflicts can be resolved or at least ameliorated?

Howland, Jacob A. Aristotle on Tragedy: Rediscovering the *Poetics*. *Interpretation*, 22(3), 359-403, Spr 95.

This article focuses on Aristotle's account of the philosophical and political significance of tragedy. It takes the form of a critical discussion of the scholarly literature, including five recent books on the *Poetics*. I try to show that Aristotle manages to do justice to three distinctive dimensions of tragedy: its profound beauty, its philosophically significant tensions and ambiguities, and its educative role within the Greek *polis*.

Howland, Jacob A. The Eleatic Stranger's Socratic Condemnation of Socrates. *Polis*, 12(1-2), 15-36, 1993.

Is Socrates a philosopher or a sophist? The Stranger's answer is ambiguous: Socrates, the most perfect available instance of the *eidos* or *genos* "philosopher", turns out to be a sophist just to the extent that he embodies pure philosophical zeal in the pursuit of *phronesis*. Conversely, the genuine philosopher forgoes the full acquisition of *phronesis* in the name of *phronesis* itself. The philosopher is thus a radically paradoxical being: he is the being whose proper understanding of his own nature leads him to retreat from his own nature, or who becomes what he is only in being less than what he is.

Howson, Colin. Theories of Probability. *Brit J Phil Sci*, 46(1), 1-32, Mr 95.

My title is intended to recall Terence Fine's excellent survey, *Theories of Probability* (1973). I shall consider some developments that have occurred in the intervening years, and try to place some of the theories he discussed in what is now a slightly longer perspective. Completeness is not something one can reasonably hope to achieve in a journal article, and any selection is bound to reflect a view of what is salient. In a subject as prone to dispute as this, there will inevitably be many who will disagree with any author's views, and I take the opportunity to apologize in advance to all such people for what they will see as the narrowness and distortion of mine.

Hoy, David Couzens. Skillful Solidarity. *Inquiry*, 38(1-2), 65-74, Je 95.

This discussion of "Disclosing New Worlds" by Charles Spinosa, Fernando Flores, and Hubert Dreyfus raises four groups of questions. First, do *skills*, which are largely unreflective, need to be distinguished more sharply from *strategies* for social action, which are more reflective and deliberative? Second, is there a tension between the article's emphasis on the importance of background practices, which are collective and nonindividual, and its frequent appeal to examples of single individuals (the entrepreneur, the cultural hero) who are able to transform these practices? Third, why does the appeal to solidarity not undermine democratic action, since solidarities compete and conflict with one another, and are often formed by *excluding* others? Or are the ideas of solidarity and universality not necessarily inconsistent with each other? Fourth, without universalistic values how will a theory of pluralistic solidarities explain social resistance to perceived oppression? Is the authors' notion of being willing to die for the group's commitments too extreme a test for social solidarity? Even if it were offered as only a limiting case, is it an adequate test for the value or justice of the commitments themselves?

Hoy, David Couzens and McCarthy, Thomas. *Critical Theory*. Cambridge, Blackwell, 1994.

Philosophical controversies within contemporary critical social theory arise largely from questions about the nature, scope, and limits of human reason. In this book David Hoy and Thomas McCarthy bring those disagreements into focus around a familiar set of philosophical issues concerning reason and the rational subject, truth and representation, knowledge and objectivity, identity and difference, relativism and universalism, the right and the good. These perennial problems are resituated within the context of critical theory as it has developed from the work of the Frankfurt School in the 1930s and 1940s to the multiplicity of contemporary approaches: genealogical, hermeneutic, neopragmatist, deconstructive, and reconstructive.

Hoy, Ronald C. Parmenides' Complete Rejection of Time. *J Phil*, 91(11), 573-598, N 94.

How should Parmenides' rejection of time be understood? It is common (amongst thinkers as different as Russell and Heidegger) to try to explain this rejection in terms of his alleged semantic aversion to "what is not". I argue such semantic interpretations do not do justice to Parmenides' worries, and more justice can be done by reading him as proscribing the *contradictions* which infect becoming. Indeed, these problems are more basic than his alleged cosmogonic aversion to genesis from nothing. The contradictions stem from needing to talk about temporal entities as both what is and what is not. I propose and discuss an interpretation in terms of the current debate between "tensed" and "tenseless" theories of time. Though I urge that the tenseless view (but not the tensed view) can avoid these contradictions, one can find other reasons why Parmenides would reject tenseless time. One can also find reasons for avoiding interpretations which view Parmenides as advancing some concept of an "eternal present" or "timeless present".

Hoyer, Ulrich. "Das Naturverständnis Johannes Keplers" in *Naturauffassungen in Philosophie, Wissenschaft, Technik: Band II*, Schäfer, Lothar (ed), 101-138. Freiburg, Alber, 1994.

Hoyos Jaramillo, Luis Eduardo. La filosofía trascendental bajo la óptica de la teoría evolucionista del conocimiento. *Rev Latin de Filosof*, 20(2), 195-219, 1994.

A programatical aspect of the evolutionary epistemology is its critical relationship with Kant's transcendental philosophy. In this paper I discuss two important topics of this critical relationship: The interpretation that evolutionary epistemology has given of the Kantian concept of the *a priori* in order to complete the project of the Kantian epistemology, and the criticism of the distinction between the objects understood as *appearances* and as *things in themselves*. With respect to the first topic I attempt to point that the defective interpretation of the issue about the *a priori* by the evolutionary epistemology puts into question its status as *epistemology* or as a *second-order theory*. Concerning the second topic, I argue that the evolutionary epistemology falls into a metaphysical realism by formulating of its programatical thesis of the hypothetical realism against the Kantian concept of *a thing in itself*.

Hoyt-O'Connor, Paul E. Lonergan and Bellah: Social Science as Public Philosophy. *Amer Cath Phil Quart*, 68(Supp), 259-270, 1994.

Hrachovec, Herbert. Deutsche Positionen zur Informationstechnologie. *Phil Rundsch*, 41(4), 300-314, D 94.

Hrachovec, Herbert. Fotogene Enttäuschungen. *Deut Z Phil*, 43(3), 455-463, 1995.

Hrachovec, Herbert. Vorzukunft. *Wittgenstein Stud*, n.a., 1994.

Niemand kann von vornherein, abgesehen von empirischen Untersuchungen, die chemische Zusammensetzung von Wasser oder die physikalische Erklaerung der Waerme kennen. Andererseits ist ein Satz wie "Wasser ist H2O" schwerlich eine Aussage ueber etwas, das auch ganz anders sein koennte. S Kripke hat in Naming and Necessity daran erinnert, dass solche Saetze Wahrheiten enthalten, die zwar empirisch herausgefunden werdern muessen, dann aber unter allen Umstaenden gelten. Wenn wir die chemische Zusammensetzung von Wasser festgestellt haben, steht die Beschaffenheit dieses unseres Wassers nicht mehr in Frage. Hinsichtlich der Newtonschen Physik hat N R Hanson dasselbe Thema bereits zur Zeit der Hochbluete analytischer Wissenschaftstheorie angeschnitten. Er bemerkt zum logischen Status der klassischen Mechanik: "Sie (sc. die Mechanik) entsteht aus empirischen Behauptungen, deren Widerlegung man sich nicht immer vorstellen kann. Eine Widerlegung wuerde nicht zu Entwuerfen fuehren, welche jene der Gesetzesaussagen negieren, sondern zu ueberhaupt keinen verstaendlichen Entwuerfen. (edited)

Hrachovec, Herbert and Turner, Charles (ed). Blumenberg: Truly Memorable Memories. *Hist Human Sci*, 7(4), 61-72, N 94.

An investigation of Hans Blumenberg's "dynamic Platonism" is attempted. It is situated in relation to Husserl's "Mistiftung" and to Wittgenstein's considerations concerning rule-following.

Hrushovski, Ehud. Finitely Axiomatizable $\aleph_1$ Categorical Theories. *J Sym Log*, 59(3), 838-844, S 94.

Finitely axiomatizable $\aleph_1$ categorical theories are locally modular.

Hua, Shiping. *Scientism and Humanism: Two Cultures in Post-Mao China (1978-1989)*. Albany, SUNY Pr, 1995.

This book is a study of the transformation of Chinese political consciousness during the post-Mao era. Departing from the common wisdom of the day that Deng Xiaping's pragmatic-oriented reform has made ideological discussions irrelevant, this book holds that while it is probably true that no single, fixed ideology has existed during the period, the ideological dimensions not only have persisted, but also can be analyzed systematically.

Huang, Frederick Y and Emanuel, Linda L. Physician Aid in Dying and the Relief of Patients' Suffering: Physicians' Attitudes Regarding Patients' Suffering and End-of-Life Decisions. *J Clin Ethics*, 6(1), 62-67, Spr 95.

Huang, Yong. Religious Beliefs after Foundationalism: Wittgenstein between Nielsen and Phillips. *Relig Stud*, 31(2), 251-267, Je 95.

Religious beliefs have often been taken either as absolutely foundational to all others or as ultimately founded on something else. This essay starts with an endorsement of the contemporary critique of foundationalism but sets its task as to search for the foundation(s) of religious belief after foundationalism. In its third and main part, it argues for a Wittgensteinian reflective equilibrium (within a belief system, between believing and acting and among people with different ways of believing and acting) as such a foundation. In this reflective equilibrium, religious beliefs are no more and no less foundational to, or founded by, other beliefs and practices. To appreciate this perspective better, I argue, in the first part, the Kai Neilsen's charge of Wittgenstein as a fideist is not accurate, and, in the second part, that D Z Phillip's fideistic contentions are unWittgensteinian.

Huang, Yong. Religious Pluralism and Interfaith Dialogue: Beyond Universalism and Particularism. *Int J Phil Relig*, 37(3), 127-144, Je 95.

Against exclusivism and inclusivism, religious pluralism maintains equality of all religions but in two different ways. Universalists affirm the common essence of all religions and aspire a world religion through interfaith dialogue. Particularists emphasize the uniqueness of each religion and see interfaith dialogue as the best way to recognize this uniqueness. This article criticizes this too and proposes an alternative model of religious pluralism: religions are all interconnected but have no common essence and are all unique but not isolated from each other. Interfaith dialogue is thus significant primarily for their self-transformations through mutual learning and teaching.

Huber, Gerhard. Remarques sur l'histoire de la notion philosophique d'absolu. *Rev Theol Phil*, 126(4), 333-344, 1994.

Adoptante le point de vue de l'histoire des notions philosophiques (Begriffsgeschichte), le présent article décrit quelques étapes majeures du développement de la notion d'absolu, ses antécédents en grec, et ses transformations dans la philosophie moderne. Au courant de cette évolution, cinq éléments de signification se font jour, à savoir les caractères métaphysiques d'"être en soi" (et non "relatif"), "détaché" (ou "séparé"), "parfait" et par là "divin", ainsi que le caractère "inconditionnel" de l'éthique en tant que tel. Cette notion d'absolu dialectiquement nuancée pourrait être d'un grand intérêt pour la philosophie systématique.

Hubert, Bernard. La perception du mouvement chez Aristote. *Rev Thomiste*, 94(2), 211-240, Ap-Je 94.

Hubert, Jerzy Z. In Quest of Inner and Outer Coherence: Synergetic Approach to Ecumenism. *Dialogue Hum*, 3(1), 41-51, 1993.

Is there something common to different religions and spiritual traditions, something that could transcend—go beyond—the existing among them contradictions and conflicts? This presentation offers a new approach to this problem: instead of looking for common beliefs, traditions or structural similarities it tries to look for common dynamic, synergetic effects (both of individual and social character) of religious and/or spiritual in general, practices. A view is offered of an ecumenism—named *positive* ecumenism—which does not seek to allay the existing differences but rather to show the ways in which they could be used to enhance these dynamical effects. (edited)

Hubert, Jerzy Z. Positive Universalism: The Universal Language of Science Used to Construct a Universal Metatheory. *Dialogue Hum*, 3(3), 139-146, 1993.

Hubin, Donald C. The Moral Justification of Benefit/ Cost Analysis. *Econ Phil*, 10(2), 169-194, O 94.

Some have attempted to justify benefit/cost analysis by appealing to a moral theory that appears to directly ground the technique. This approach is unsuccessful because the moral theory in question is wildly implausible and, even if it were correct, it would probably not endorse the unrestricted use of benefit/cost analysis. Nevertheless, there is reason to think that a carefully restricted use of benefit/cost analysis will be justifiable from a wide variety of plausible moral perspectives. From this, it is reasonable to conclude that such use of the technique is probably morally justified and should be acceptable to most people.

Hudson, James. Individual and Community: Charles Murray's Political Philosophy. *Crit Rev*, 8(2), 175-216, Spr 94.

Charles Murray's political philosophy is utilitarian, individualist, and communitarian. The basis for his success in making these components cohere is his account of happiness, inspired by the motivation theory of Abraham Maslow. Murray claims that belonging to a community and self-respect (which on his analysis require a certain social commitment) are constituents of happiness. Hence utilitarians should attribute special value to community. He also argues that active national governments are inimical to the formation and functioning of communities, and that communities are fostered by governments that observe the constraints of liberal individualism.

Hudson, Robert G. Background Independence and the Causation of Observations. *Stud Hist Phil Sci*, 25(4), 595-612, Ag 94.

It is now commonplace to accept the theory-ladenness of observation. With this acceptance, though, we have introduced the problem of empirical relativism. Some philosophers have argued that one can avoid this potential relativism by insuring that the theory under test does not inform the experiment that generated the observations. This view I entitle 'background independence'. In this paper I argue that there is no need in rebutting relativism to require the background independence of observations so long as the experimental methods used to generate observations are fixed and unchanging.

Hülsz Piccone, Enrique. "Aporía y Dialéctica en el *Teeteto*" in *Platón: Los Diálogos Tardíos, Lan, Conrado Eggers (ed)*, 77-102. Sankt Augustin, Academia, 1986.

This article is an exploration of a fundamental and complex connection (*aporia* and dialectics) in this paradigmatic work of Plato's. The aporetic nature of philosophical method proper is shown to be much farther-reaching than usually acknowledged: Plato's many-sided concept of *aporia* appears as something essential to the epistemic dynamics of *logos*. Analysis stresses the euporetic side of dialectics as maieutics, an image that compliments the dialogue's arguments through recognizing (and probing) the fertility of philosophic *logos* and the uniqueness of man's being. Conclusions point to the need of not neglecting this joining of things ontological, epistemological, methodological, and ethical when interpreting Plato.

Hufnagel, Cordula. *Die kultische Gebärde: Kunst, Politik, Religion im Denken Franz Rosenzweigs*. Freiburg, Alber, 1994.

This book attempts to interpret and examine Franz Rosenzweig's philosophy in connection with trends of thought contemporary to him. Here it concentrates mainly on developments in aesthetics before 1933. Rosenzweig is a key figure among the mythogenic tendencies of that time. His ambition was to stimulate a radical renewal of thought from its very foundations, a "new philosophy". Guided by his vision that the third or Johannic age had begun, Rosenzweig developed not only a theological but also an applied aesthetic. This must be understood both within the context of its time and also in relation to its ultimate aim of counteracting the disintegration of traditional norms and values with the aid of aesthetics.

Hufnagel, Erwin. Platons Vermächtnis: Eine bildungstheoretische Reflexion. *Filozof Istraz*, 13(4), 825-842, 1993.

In diesem Text untersucht der Autor, in bildungstheoretischer Absicht, Platons Erkenntnis- und Bildungs- bzw. Erziehungslehre, um ihre paradigmatische bildungstheoretische Geltung für die heutige Bildungstheorie wie auch die Bildungspraxis zu zeigen. Zuerst distanziert sich der Autor von jenen Missverständnissen, wonach die Staats- und Bildungslehre Platons (vor allem in seinem Werk *Politeia*) als Grundlage für totalitaristische politisch-pädagogische Konzepte und Praktiken gedeutet wurde. Der Autor bemüht sich, den positiven, konstruktiven und immer noch verpflichtenden Sinn der Platonschen Lehre aufzuzeigen. Leitmotiv und zentrales hermeneutisches Feld dieses Textes ist das Platonsche 'Höhlengleichnis', das der Verfasser als Ausgangspunkt für seinen umfassenden Versuch nimmt, die Strukturierung von Wirklichkeit, Erkenntnis und menschlichem Wertsystem bei Platon als hochaktuell und verpflichtend darzustellen. (edited)

Huggett, Nick and Weingard, Robert. Interpretations of Quantum Field Theory. *Phil Sci*, 61(3), 370-388, S 94.

In this paper we critically review the various attempts that have been made to understand quantum field theory. We focus of Teller's (1990) harmonic oscillator interpretation, and Bohm et al.'s (1987) causal interpretation. The former unabashedly aims to be a purely heuristic account, but we show that it is only interestingly applicable to the free bosonic field. Along the way we suggest alternative models. Bohm's interpretation provides an ontology for the theory—a classical field, with a quantum equation of motion. This too has problems; it is not Lorentz invariant.

Huggett, Nick and Weingard, Robert. On the Field Aspect of Quantum Fields. *Erkenntnis*, 40(3), 293-301, My 94.

In this paper we contrast the idea of a field as a system with an infinite number of degrees of freedom with a recent alternative proposed by Paul Teller in Teller (1990). We show that, although our characterization lacks the immediate appeal of Teller's it has more success producing agreement with intuitive categorizations than his does. We go on to extend the distinction to quantum mechanics, explaining the important role that it plays there. Finally, we take some time to investigate the way in which strings are to be considered fields, and the important differences with scalar fields. Overall, we aim to show that many types of systems may be viewed as fields, and to point out significant distinctions amongst them, thereby expanding our understanding of what it is to fall in this category.

Huggett, Nick and Weingard, Robert. The Renormalisation Group and Effective Field Theories. *Synthese*, 102(1), 171-194, Ja 95.

Much apprehension has been expressed by philosophers about the method of renormalisation in quantum field theory, as it apparently requires illegitimate procedure of infinite cancellation. This has lead to various speculations, in particular in Teller (1989). We examine Teller's discussion of perturbative renormalisation of quantum fields, and show why it is inadequate. To really approach the matter one needs to understand the ideas and results of the 'renormalisation group', so we give a simple but comprehensive account of this topic. With this in hand, we explain how renormalisation can and should be understood. One thing that is revealed is that apparently very successful theories such as quantum electro-dynamics cannot be universally true; resolving the tension between success and falsity leads to a picture in which any theory may be viewed as irreducibly phenomenological. We explain how, and argue that the support for this view is tenuous at best.

Hughes, Edward J. How Subjectivity is Truth in the *Concluding Unscientific Postscript*. *Relig Stud*, 31(2), 197-208, Je 95.

The present article returns to Soren Kierkegaard's *Concluding Unscientific Postscript* in order to delineate the complex relations that obtain between his concepts of subjectivity, inwardness and passion. Supporting concepts, such as appropriation, existence, and interest, are also referred to as aids in tracing these relationships. I argue that the entire gestalt of terms in the *Concluding Unscientific Postscript* is coherent, consistently used, and that Kierkegaard, despite the poetic format of his style, has constructed a rigorous philosophical anthropology that is neither objectivist, nor subjectivist in its ultimate statement. This is the basis for the name of the article, 'How Subjectivity is Truth in the *Concluding Unscientific Postscript*'. *Subjectivity* can be *truth* in Kierkegaard's work because his use of the term transcends the normal denotation of both *subjectivity* and *objectivity* in religious philosophical discourse and refers to a state of existence with a unique ontological status.

Hughes, Judith and Midgley, Mary. "Trouble with Families?" in *Introducing Applied Ethics, Almond, Brenda (ed)*, 17-32. Cambridge, Blackwell, 1995.

Many philosophers, form Plato to Marx and Nietzche, have attacked "the family" as a corrupting institution. More lately, various psychologists, sociologists and feminists, along with the designers of the Israeli Kibbutzim, have also denounced its influence. Yet, today, its apparent breakdown causes widespread alarm. The main cause of that breakdown is probably just increased social mobility. But individualist theories have also contributed, calling for a quite unrealistic degree of autonomy and contempt for interpersonal dependence. Humans it seems, can reach wider loyalties only through a gradual, careful expansion which has to start from vigorous personal and local bonds.

Hughes, Paul M. Moral Anger, Forgiving, and Condoning. *J Soc Phil*, 26(1), 103-118, Spr 95.

Forms of anger (e.g., indignation, contempt) count as personal moral anger just in case they involve the belief that you have been wronged. Since forgiving and condoning may involve neutralizing personal moral anger, they appear to be indistinguishable. I resolve this paradox by suggesting that renouncing personal moral anger may be neither forgiving nor condoning wrongdoing, but some third manner of overcoming moral anger. Moreover, of the various ways of condoning wrongdoing, the only sort similar to forgiving is tantamount to unvirtuous forgiving. Consequently, forgiving wrongdoing and condoning it are synonymous only when one should *not* renounce one's personal moral anger toward a wrongdoer.

Hughes, Paul M. On Forgiving Oneself: A Reply to Snow. *J Value Inq*, 28(4), 557-560, D 94.

In this reply to N E Snow's "Self-forgiveness" (*Journal of Value Inquiry*, 27(1), 75-81), I argue that forgiving oneself is not merely a first step to full interpersonal forgiveness, or a way of enabling wrongdoers to get on with their lives. Rather, self-forgiving can occur in cases of purely self-directed wrongs, or in cases of minor interpersonal wrongs where no issue of restoring oneself to full moral agency is in question. Moreover, until forgiveness is adequately distinguished from cognate moral phenomena like pardons, condoning, and mercy, *self* forgiving will continue to remain morally obscure.

Hughes, Paul M. Revolutionary Rationality and the Good Life. *Int J Applied Phil*, 9(1), 27-34, Sum-Fall 94.

It is argued here that contrary to the usual Marxist view, it is rational for proletarians to refrain from engaging in the revolutionary struggle to overthrow capitalism, thereby taking a "free ride" to communism. It is further argued that adopting collective (class) interests as one's primary orientation in life (a strategy that appears to render participation in revolutionary activity "rational") yields the unexpected conclusion that engaging in revolutionary activity is *morally* undesirable. Hence, participating in the Marxist revolutionary struggle is either irrational or immoral.

Hugly, Philip and Sayward, Charles. Quantifying Over the Reals. *Synthese*, 101(1), 53-64, O 94.

Peter Geach proposed a substitutional construal of quantification over thirty years ago. It is not standardly substitutional since it is not tied to those substitution instances currently available to us; rather, it is pegged to possible substitution instances. We argue that i) quantification over the real numbers can be construed substitutionally following Geach's idea; ii) a price to be paid, if it is that, is intuitionism; iii) quantification, thus conceived, does not in itself relieve us of ontological commitment to real numbers.

Huhn, Thomas. The Kantian Sublime and the Nostalgia for Violence. *J Aes Art Crit*, 53(3), 269-275, Sum 95.

The essay poses the sublime as central, constitutive aesthetics judgment because it avoids objective subreption, Kant's term for the mistaken gesture that attributes aesthetic qualities to an *object*—mistaken because aesthetic judgment is a *subjective* harmony of faculties. Beauty evidences this mistake. The sublime thwarts this mistakenness insofar as it fails to present anything objective—Kant characterizes the sublime as the failure of presentation. The sublime rather than beauty is more central to Kant's aesthetics because it prolongs and problematizes the project of generating a self-subsistent and unified subject, whereas beauty merely (but pleasurably) confirms subjectivity's self-misrecognition.

Huijer, Marli. Verontrustende vriendschappen: Foucault, Nietzsche en de bestaansesthetiek. *Alg Ned Tijdschr Wijs*, 87(2), 69-83, Ap 95.

Foucault's Instrument of an aesthetics of being is presented as a possibility to practise ethical and political thinking without the presupposition of an autonomous subject. Elements of this instrument are 1) a critical diagnostic attitude towards the present, 2) self-chosen guidelines adapted to the specific situation, 3) an active working on oneself and openness to transformation, 4) a focus on making one's life a work of art. The relation to intimate others, shaped as friendship, is crucial in this ethical-aesthetic approach. The implications of Foucault's aesthetics of being for political and ethical thought are traced to the works of Nietzsche.

Hull, Robert. Distributive Justice and the Minnesota Health Access Initiative. *J Med Human*, 16(2), 93-103, Sum 95.

Hull, Robert. Styling Nietzsche: A Note on the Genealogy of Derridean Deconstruction. *Man World*, 27(3), 325-333, Jl 94.

Hulse, James W. *The Reputations of Socrates: The Afterlife of a Gadfly*. New York, Lang, 1995.

The Reputations of Socrates examines the uses and misuses of the name of that Athenian philosopher through the centuries. James W Hulse argues that the central ethical message of Socrates as expresed in the *Apology* and *Crito* was distorted by generations of admirers and detractors from the time of Plato through the Enlightenment. Beginning in the eighteenth century, the process generating the central ideas of the paradigmatic gadfly began, and the development has continued to our time.

Humberstone, I L. Hempel Meets Wason. *Erkenntnis*, 41(3), 391-402, N 94.

The adverse reaction to Hempel's 'ravens paradox' embodied in giving it that description is compared with the usual reaction (universally regarded as incorrect) of experimental subjects to the Wason selection task.

Hume, David and Fieser, James (ed). *Natural History of Religion*. New York, Macmillan, 1992.

This annotated edition of Hume's *Natural History of Religion* follows the posthumous 1777 edition which includes Hume's final alterations; spelling and punctuation have not been modernized. The text restores two controversial passages which originally appeared in the unpublished edition of *Five Dissertations* (1756). The editor's introduction discusses the intellectual background of the *Natural History*, the problems of censorship which Hume faced, and 18th century reactions to the work.

Hummel, Tamara Lakins. Effective Versions of Ramsey's Theorem: Avoiding the Cone Above 0'. *J Sym Log*, 59(4), 1301-1325, D 94.

Humphreys, Glyn W (ed). *Understanding Vision: An Interdisciplinary Perspective*. Cambridge, Blackwell, 1992.

The work takes an inter-disciplinary approach to the understanding of consciousness, with chapters contributed by experimental psychologists, neuropsychologists, and philosophers. Recent empirical work on consciousness is integrated with accounts of consciousness in the philosophy literature.

Humphreys, Paul. Abstract and Concrete. *Phil Phenomenol Res*, 55(1), 157-161, Mr 95.

I argue that Nancy Cartwright's account of abstraction in her *Nature Capacities and their Measurement* is incoherent and cannot provide, as she claims, an argument for capacities.

Hund, John. A Case of Affirming the Consequent in International Law: UN Security Council Resolution 232 (1966)—Southern Rhodesia. *Hist Phil Log*, 15(2), 201-210, 1994.

In this note I examine a case of teleological reasoning in international law and find it to be the fallacy of affirming the consequent. I then show that and how the basis of this fallacy is a manipulation (or juxtaposition) of "necessary" and "sufficient" conditions. I conclude by giving reasons for thinking that this kind of reasoning is a regular feature of international law.

Hund, William B. Paul Crowther and the Experience of the Sublime. *Kantstudien*, 85(3), 337-340, 1994.

In Paul Crowther's recent book, *The Kantian Sublime, From Morality to Art*, he claimed that the idea of infinity need not be an essential element in the experience of the sublime. My article evaluates Crowther's claim and defends Kant's view that infinity is an essential element in the experience.

Hundert, Edward M. Autonomy, Informed Consent, and Psychosurgery. *J Clin Ethics*, 5(3), 264-266, Fall 94.

Hunt, Alan and Wickham, Gary. *Foucault and Law: Towards a Sociology of Law as Governance*. Boulder, Westview Pr, 1994.

This book explores what Foucault had to say about law and then goes on to use in the construction of a new framework for the sociology of law. It does not set out to construct a 'Foucaultian theory of law'. But it does contend that an exploration of his work can contribute to the construction of new and fruitful approach to the exploration of legal phenomena. This book has three parts. Part 1 provides a general introduction Foucault's thought to a readership which is familiar with law as a significant focus on inquiry, but is not familiar with Foucault's writing. Part 2 provides an exposition of the treatment of law in his texts. Rather it offers a critical commentary and evaluation of Foucault's treatment of legal themes. The argument advanced is that Foucault's equation of law with absolutism and sovereignty seriously undermines his capacity to engage with the role of law in modernity. In Part 3 a new framework for the sociology of law is advanced in which law is treated as a form of governance. Four principles of governance and some methodological rules for such a project.

Hunt, David P. Does Theological Fatalism Rest on an Equivocation?. *Amer Phil Quart*, 32(2), 153-165, Ap 95.

A well-known objection to "theological fatalism" is that God's past beliefs about what is yet future amount to no more than "soft" facts about the past. One cost of this approach is that it makes divine beliefs mysteriously different from human beliefs. The present paper avoids such special pleading by charging the fatalist instead with an equivocation between two ordinary and unmysterious senses of 'belief': *occurrent* and*dispositional*. While arguing that dispositional foreknowledge can be conceived in such a way that the fatalistic implications of occurrent foreknowledge are avoided, the paper nevertheless identifies a residual problem which remains impervious to the dispositional approach.

Hunt, Geoffrey. Death, Medicine and Bioethics. *Theor Med*, 15(4), 431-447, D 94.

The assumptions of philosophy need scrutiny as much the assumptions of medicine do. Scrutiny shows that the philosophical method of bioethics is compromised, for it shares certain fundamental assumptions with medicine itself. To show this requires an unorthodox style of philosophy—a literary one. To show the compromised status of bioethics the paper discusses some seminal utilitarian discussions of the definition of death of whether it is a bad thing, and of when it ought to occur.

Hunt, Harry T. Some Developmental Issues in Transpersonal Experience. *J Mind Behav*, 16(2), 115-134, Spr 95.

Developmental understanding of transpersonal experience and its diverse impact on human life has been bedeviled by the opposed, monolithic extremes of Freud's regression to infant "narcissism," on the one hand, and more recent views of the transpersonal as the sole endpoint for any "higher" or "postformal operations" development of human intelligence, on the other. Here it is shown that "higher states of consciousness" can be more specifically understood as developments of a "presentational" intelligence, thereby constituting one line of adult development among the several open to our symbolic capacity. The demonstrated but relatively infrequent occurrence of transpersonal states in early childhood then becomes understandable as a developmental precocity akin to that shown in mathematical and musical prodigies. The overlap of this developmental line with some to the thematics and regressive states of psychoanalytic object relations theories of infancy follows from the experiential nature of presentation intelligence. Early emotional traumata and deficits must reappear in transpersonal experience to the extent that they were internalized as part of the mother-infant dyad whose structure underlies our symbolic, dialogic consciousness.

Hunt, Lester H. An Argument Against a Legal Duty to Rescue. *J Soc Phil*, 26(1), 16-38, Spr 95.

Our legal system contains no general duty to render aid to those in need, nor should it. Such a duty would make it obligatory to pursue a certain end—namely, the security of others. As such, it is necessary that the actions it encourages us to take be rational, in that the end pursued is more important than the ends that are sacrificed to it. However, such actions would not tend to be rational. The problem that such a duty would purport to solve is of a sort that is better suited to treatment by morality than by the law.

Hunt, Morton. The 'Soul': Modern Psychological Interpretations. *Free Inq*, 14(4), 22-25, Fall 94.

Hunt, Tammy G and Siguaw, Judy A and Honeycutt, Earl D. Business Ethics and Job-Related Constructs: A Cross-Cultural Comparison of Automotive Salespeople. *J Bus Ethics*, 14(3), 235-248, Mr 95.

Although a number of articles have addressed ethical perceptions and behaviors, few studies have examined ethics across cultures. This research focuses on measuring the job satisfaction, customer orientation, ethics, and ethical training of automotive salespersons in the U S and Taiwan. The relationships of these variables to salesperson performance were also investigated. Ethics training was found to be negatively related to perceived levels of ethicalness and performance. High performance U S salespeople reported high ethical behavior, while the opposite was true in Taiwan. Customer orientation in both countries was influenced by ethics training. Managers should evaluate current ethics training programs to insure correct ethical behavior is taught and rewarded.

Hunter, Geoffrey. The Churchlands' Eliminative Materialism. *Phil Invest*, 18(1), 13-30, Ja 95.

This paper demolishes the Churchlands' arguments for their Eliminative Materialism and casts doubt on the logical possibility of their thesis. In passing, the paper draws attention to a mistake in history of science made in one of the arguments.

Hunter, J F M. "Wittgenstein on Grammar and Essence" in *Wittgenstein and Contemporary Philosophy, Teghrarian, Souren (ed)*, 71-88. Bristol, Thoemmes, 1994.

Hunter, Nan D. "Marriage, Law, and Gender: A Feminist Inquiry" in *Radical Philosophy of Law, Caudill, David S (ed)*, 221-233. Atlantic Highlands, Humanities Pr, 1995.

Professor Hunter recasts the question of legalizing the lesbian and gay marriage from one of whether a minority should be granted equal rights to an inquiry into whether such a change has the much broader potential to dismantle the structure of gender at the heart of marriage law. She argues that same-sex marriage would move beyond the formalistic equality in marriage law that has been achieved to date, and would radically denaturalize the social construction of male/female differentness, once expressed as authority/dependence relationships, that courts have deemed essential to the definition of marriage. Issues of power and equality within intimate relationships frame the discussion of legalizing same-sex marriage, and, she argues, need to be incorporated into analyses of proposals for domestic partnership, constructive marriage, and other strategies for the pluralization of family law. Because of the culturally complex issues involved, Professor Hunter argues for the use of concepts such as "gender dissent" to augment the "rights talk" of litigation.

Hunyadi, Mark. Défendre Rawls contre Rawls. *Stud Phil (Switzerland)*, 53, 57-74, 1994.

Hunyadi, Mark. La Règle d'Or: l'effet-radar. *Rev Theol Phil*, 126(3), 215-222, 1994.

Paul Ricoeur voit dans la Règle d'Or l'expression la plus achevée de la norme morale, en ce qu'elle exprime l'idée même de réciprocité. Mais telle qu'elle est formulée, il est douteux qu'elle puisse rendre justice de l'altérité véritable. Les présupposés phénoménologiques qui président à son établissement sont tels qu'elle produit un "effet-radar": autrui est une réverbération de moi. C'est pourquoi une autre formulation en sera proposée.

Hurley, Paul E. Getting Our Options Clear: A Closer Look at Agent-Centered Options. *Phil Stud*, 78(2), 163-188, My 95.

Hurley, S L. A New Take from Nozick on Newcomb's Problem and Prisoner's Dilemma. *Analysis*, 54(2), 65-72, Ap 94.

Hurley, Susan. "Unity and Objectivity" in *Objectivity, Simulation and the Unity of Consciousness, Peacocke, Christopher (ed)*, 49-77. New York, Oxford Univ Pr, 1994.

Hurtado, Guillermo. Subjetividad y Privacidad. *Critica*, 26(76-77), 185-203, Ap-Ag 94.

The traditional doctrine of the privacy of the mental describes our mental lives as corridors without doors or windows. According to this view a mental state is private if: 1) One and only one person has direct access to that mental state, and 2) That person is the authority with respect to the content and character of such a mental state (*i.e.*, has an incorrigible and infallible knowledge of it). 2) has been rejected on the basis of externalist arguments concerning the nature of mental content. However, very few have put 1) into doubt. The purpose of this essay is to claim that 1) is not a necessary feature of our mental lives. (edited)

Hurtubise, Denis. The Original Version of Process and Reality, Part V: A Tentative Reconstruction. *Process Stud*, 22(1), 1-12, Spr 93.

In *Emergence of Whitehead's Metaphysics* (1984), Lewis S Ford argues that Whitehead's thought evolved on many topics throughout his career as a metaphysician, and that such evolutions can be traced even in individual books through the recovery of corrective insertions made by Whitehead to his original text. This article proposes a reconstruction of what may have been the original version of the fifth and last part of Whitehead's magnum opus, that is *Process and Reality*.

Husain, Martha. Cognition and Human Actualization in Plotinus and Aristotle. *J Neoplatonic Stud*, 1(1), 111-123, Fall 92.

Husted, Bryan W. Honor Among Thieves: A Transaction-Cost Interpretation of Corruption in Third World Countries. *Bus Ethics Quart*, 4(1), 17-27, Ja 94.

This paper views corruption as a form of contracting amenable to analysis from the viewpoint of transaction-cost economics. Concepts such as transaction, bounded rationality, opportunism, and asset specificity are shown to apply to cases of corruption. Both market and parochial corruption are hypothesized to vary in accordance with changes in the specificity of assets invested to support the corruption transaction. Evidence from a number of different studies tends to support the hypothesized relation. The implications of the transaction-cost perspective are developed for policy makers and directions for future research are suggested.

Hutcheon, Pat Duffy. "Through a Glass Darkly: Freud's Concept of Love" in *The Nature and Pursuit of Love, Goicoechea, David (ed)*, 183-195. Buffalo, Prometheus, 1995.

Hutchings, Patrick. Flowers as 'Free Beauties of Nature'. *Lit Aes*, 4, 17-30, O 94.

Robert Mapplethorpe's and Larianne Fonseca's flower photographs, by implicit reference to human sexuality, draw attention to flowers as "the reproductive organs of plants." This would seem to negate, here, Kant's idea of flowers as "free beauties". Generally, *pulchritudo vaga* appears blocked by our knowledge of a teleology: this entails that *pulchritudo adhaerens* is the "real" beauty of flowers. Or: In aesthetic judgements we must prescend from our knowledge of flowers' purposes? The paper's literary references are to: Angelus Silesius, Auden, Eric Gill, Lorca, David Malouf, Marvell, Milton and Edward Saavedra. There are two illustrations, Mapplethorpe and Fonseca. Botanical reference: *Dendrobium speciosum*.

Hutchings, Patrick. The Old and the New Sublimes: Do They Signify? God?. *Sophia (Australia)*, 34(1), 49-64, Mr-Ap 95.

Kant's "old" sublime concerns what lies at the edge of the transcendental epistemological field. God and immortality, 1) lie there; 2) are topically sublime; 3) God, even for believers, is a *Deus absconditus*. Current intellectual fashions create a "new" sublime: 1) By severing the nexus word/refrent, making refrents things-absconded; 2) By defining word-meaning by differential position on a Saussurean grid: meaning thus becomes, indeteminate, deferred; unattainable? 3) The possible grid-array is itself so vast as to constitute an, atopical, sublime. One objects: the grid is not authentically sublime; absconded refrents were never God, nor are, absconded or not.

Hutchinson, D S. "Ethics" in *The Cambridge Companion to Aristotle, Barnes, Jonathan (ed)*, 195-232. New York, Cambridge Univ Pr, 1995.

An exposition in clear language of Aristotle's ethical theory and views. The sources on which the chapter draws are: *Nicomachean Ethics, Eudemian Ethics, Protrepticus (= Exhortation to Philosophy)*, and Aristotle's last will and testament, with some passages from other works. The whole purpose of the chapter is to present the main elements and the overall shape of Aristotle's thinking, rather than to engage in scholarly discussion of disputed passages, where the precise interpretation is, or might be, controversial. The chapter rests directly on the primary sources named above, and is not a survey of recent scholarship on the topic.

Hutchison, Keith. Temporal Asymmetry in Classical Mechanics. *Brit J Phil Sci*, 46(2), 219-234, Je 95.

This paper argues against a standard view that all deterministic and conservative classical mechanical systems are time-reversible, by asking how the temporal evolution of a system modulates parametric imprecision (either ontological or epistemic). It notes that well-behaved systems (e.g., inertial motion) can possess a dynamics which is unstable enough to fail at reversing uncertainties—even though exact values are reliably reversed. A limited (but significant) source of irreversibility is thus displayed in classical mechanics, closely analogous the lack of predictability revealed by unstable chaotic systems.

Hutter, Axel. Schellings Neuanfang von 1827. *Z Phil Forsch*, 49(1), 131-137, Ja-Mr 95.

Schelling wird 1827 auf den philosophischen Lehrstuhl der neugegründeten Universität München berufen. Seine erste Vorlesung im Wintersemester 1827/28 bedeutet, wie Schelling selbst betont hat, eine wichtige Zäsur in der Entwicklung seines philosophischen Denkens. Deshalb stellen die in letzter Zeit erfolgten Editionen von Mitschriften der Münchener Vorlesungen von 1827/28, 1830, 1831/32 und 1832/33 die Deutung der Schellingschen Spätphilosophie auf eine neue Grundlage. Erstmals wird jetzt eine bislang kaum bekannte Periode des Schellingschen Denkens anhand einer breiten Textgrundlage zugänglich, wodurch sich das Bild der Gesamtentwicklung seiner Philosophie, insbesondere aber das Verständnis des ursprünglichen Programms der Spätphilosophie grundlegend verändert.

Hyde, Dominic. Commentary: Proliferating Conceptions of Truth: Comments on McGee and McLaughlin. *S J Phil*, 33(Supp), 253-261, 1995.

The sorites problem arises, according to McGee and McLaughlin, because we confuse two distinct notions, which they take to be two conceptions of "truth". However, rather than the problem being, as McGee and McLaughlin seem to suggest, all solved when we recognise the equivocal nature of "truth", it is more plausibly seen as providing a test-case upon which to base a choice of univocal "truth". The recalcitrant nature of the sorites paradox is insufficient reason for proliferating conceptions of truth and thus their theory collapses into either one of the two familiar (and problematic) theories from which it appears hybridised.

Hyde, Michael J. The Call of Conscience: Heidegger and the Question of Rhetoric. *Phil Rhet*, 27(4), 374-396, 1994.

Hyland, Drew A. *Finitude and Transcendence in the Platonic Dialogues*. Albany, SUNY Pr, 1995.

Hyttinen, Tapani and Shelah, Saharon. Constructing Strongly Equivalent Nonisomorphic Models for Unsuperstable Theories, Part A. *J Sym Log*, 59(3), 984-996, S 94.

We study how equivalent nonisomorphic models an unsuperstable theory can have. We measure the equivalence by Ehrenfeucht-Fraisse games. This paper continues the work started in (HT).

Iannuzzo, Rebecca and Sieber, Joan E and Rodriguez, Beverly. Deception Methods in Psychology: Have They Changed in 23 Years?. *Ethics Behavior*, 5(1), 67-85, 1995.

To learn whether criticism and regulation of research practices have been followed by a reduction of deception or use of more acceptable approaches to deception, the contents of all 1969, 1978, 1986, and 1992 issues of the *Journal of Personality and Social Psychology* were examined. Deception research was coded according to type of (non)informing (e.g., false informing, consent to deception, no informing), possible harmfulness of deception employed (e.g., powerfulness of induction, morality of the behavior induced, privacy of behavior), method of deception (e.g., bogus device or role, false purpose of study, false feedback), and debriefing employed. Use of confederates has been partly replaced by uses of computers. "Consent" with false informing declined after 1969, then rose in 1992. Changes in the topics studied (e.g., attribution, socialization, personality) largely accounted for the decline in deception in 1978 and 1986. More attention needs to be given to ways of respecting subjects' autonomy, to appropriate debriefing and desensitizing, and to selecting the most valid and least objectionable deception methods.

Ibáñez, Alfonso. El Conflicto de los Proyectos Históricos en la Perspectiva de Leopoldo Zea. *Analogia*, 7(1), 65-89, 1993.

Ibañez-Noé, Javier A. Synopsis of a Theory of Modernity. *Man World*, 27(4), 361-381, O 94.

This paper outlines a theory of modernity, taking as the key concept the freedom of the nontranscending self. The main thesis is that all central modern phenomena (this is shown in particular for modern science) are to be ultimately explained as manifestations of the project to institute this freedom both by liberating the subject from all heteronomous sources of determination and by transforming the world into its instrument (technology). The paper shows finally that all attempts to legitimize the modern age presuppose unreflectively the validity of the project of instituting the freedom of the subject in its immanence.

Ibáñez-Noé, Javier A. Heidegger, Nietzsche, Jünger, and the Interpretation of the Contemporary Age. *S J Phil*, 33(1), 57-81, Spr 95.

The theses are: Heidegger's interpretation of the contemporary age is 1) largely based on his reading of Nietzsche; 2) this reading is mediated in decisive respects by Ernst Jünger's work. This mediation explains, or helps to explain, Heidegger's theses that a) the truth of the culminating stage of the modern age is marked by the dominance of the will to power manifested in the technological mobilization of the world; b) that all movements which negate this truth are condemned to historical impotence; and c) that the task of the age is the correspondence in thought and action to this truth.

AUTHOR INDEX WITH ABSTRACTS 583 **Ingravalle, Francesco**

Ibarra, Andoni and Diederich, Werner and Mormann, Thomas. Bibliography of Structuralism II (1989-1994 and Additions). *Erkenntnis*, 41(3), 403-418, N 94.

Five years have passed since our "Bibliography of Structuralism" has been published in this journal (*Erkenntnis*, 30, 1989). The aim of the present bibliography is twofold: First, we list a number of titles up to 1989 which we regretfully failed to include five years ago. Second, we augment the bibliography by titles which have appeared since 1989.

Ibarra, Andoni and Mormann, Thomas. Simetrías versus leyes? Apostilla a Van Fraassen sobre la representación. *Pensamiento*, 198(50), 383-406, S-D 94.

Se analiza la reciente tesis de van Fraassen acerca del carácter no explicitable del concepto de ley natural y su consiguiente inadecuación en el estudio de la ciencia. Alternativamente, él propone acercarse a ésta tomándola en sí misma, esto es, como una actividad dirigida hacia la construcción de modelos y regulada por la noción de simetría. Esta, sin embargo, es de naturaleza esencialmente distinta a la de la ley. En el artículo, por el contrario, sostenemos, desde una perspectiva representacionalista de la ciencia, que la noción de simetría debe conservar algo del espíritu original atribuible al concepto de ley.

Iervolino, Domenico. Sull'Ermeneutica della Secolarizzazione. *Stud Filosofici*, 267-276, 1991-92.

Iggers, Georg G. Historicism: The History and Meaning of the Term. *J Hist Ideas*, 56(1), 129-152, Ja 95.

A history of the term "historicism" (Historismus) since its first uses in the late 18th-century and its changing meanings. Particular space is given to recent literature on historicism.

Iglesias, Mercedes. La alteridad en el Sofista de Platón. *Rev Filosof (Venezuela)*, 19, 1-19, 1994.

The present work is on the concept of participation in Plato's Sophist. His main purpose was epistemological but this touches the ontological dimension. There are three types of participation: 1) Ideas between themselves, 2) from the soul to the Ideas, 3) from the sensitive things to the Ideas. Participation becomes possible because Being is no more Absolute. Being is and is not; Not-Being is not and is. Not-Being or Diversity will be another way of being of the Not-Being. Identity and Diversity will participate with *all* the rest of the Forms.

Ihde, Don. "Paul Ricoeur's Place in the Hermeneutic Tradition" in *The Philosophy of Paul Ricoeur, Hahn, Lewis Edwin (ed)*, 59-70. Peru, Open Court, 1994.

This essay gives an overview on the place and development of Paul Ricoeur's approach to a hermeneutical philosophy, particularly in comparison to the works of Martin Heidegger and Hans Georg Gadamer who occupy similar positions. Ricoeur is seen to remain closer to the textual and particularly biblical traditions than either of the other two prominent hermeneuts, but he is also the philosopher who most seriously enters into interdisciplinary investigations and arguments of the present. The article also traces some of the developments through Ricoeur's long publishing history and the diversity of interests he has investigated.

Imbach, Ruedi. "Natur bei Wilhelm von Ockham" in *Naturauffassungen in Philosophie, Wissenschaft, Technik: Band I, Schäfer, Lothar (ed)*, 185-208. Freiburg, Alber, 1993.

Imbach, Ruedi. Notabilia IV: Hinweise auf wichtige Neuerscheinungen aus dem Bereich der mittelalterlichen Philosophie. *Frei Z Phil Theol*, 41(1-2), 229-251, 1994.

The "Notabilia" gives a survey and evaluation of the most important new publishings (1992-1995) in the field of middleage philosophy.

Imbach, Ruedi. Notabilia V. *Frei Z Phil Theol*, 42(1-2), 186-212, 1995.

Imber, Jonathan B (ed) and Woolfolk, Alan (ed) and Masaryk, Thomas G. *Constructive Sociological Theory*. New Brunswick, Transaction Books, 1994.

This volume is a selection of major writings by Thomas G Masaryk (1850-1937), first president of the state of Czechoslovakia and a forgotten but distinguished founder of the discipline of sociology in central Europe. These writings and the introduction reveal the intertwining of politics and social theory that is characteristic of Masaryk's philosophical sociology—with chapters on modern suicide, Comte, religion, the problems of Marxism, nationalism, democracy, and other topics. The volume aims to introduce students and teachers of sociology to Masaryk's unified theory, which opposed the separation of facts and values, knowledge and belief, feeling and reason, and theory and practice that became dominant in sociological theory.

Imbert, Claude. Stanley Cavell: Au-delà du scepticisme. *Arch Phil*, 57(4), 633-644, O-D 94.

A red thread runs through Cavell's work: a skepticism too self-evident to be amenable to any Cartesian argument. It is less our knowledge of the outside world that it affects than our relation to ourselves and others and our confidence in an essentially tragic world. In Cavell's reading, this "habitual" doubt links the *Philosophical Investigations*, to ordinary philosophy. He finds it prophetically illustrated in Shakespeare's plays, discovers its menacing presence at work in Emerson perfectionism and his political judgment, and traces its subsequent effects in American art and contemporary democratic thought.

Imbrosciano, Anthony. Inevitable Martrydom: The Connection Between Faith and Suffering in Kierkegaard's Later Writings. *Int J Phil Relig*, 36(2), 105-116, O 94.

Imielinski, Christian. The Ideas of Contemporary Universalim and Medicine. *Dialogue Hum*, 4(2-3), 183-196, 1994.

Imlay, Robert A. Descartes und der Traumskeptizismus. *Stud Leibniz*, 25(2), 189-200, 1993.

Descartes' dream hypothesis, despite what he sometimes says himself, is supposed to inspire genuine existential doubt regarding the material world. Furthermore the hypothesis resists the criterion of coherence by means of which Descartes finally distinguishes dreaming from waking. The dream hypothesis turns out, nonetheless, to be untenable. What is more its untenability is apparent from a close analysis of the very example of a dream described in the first Meditation.

Inada, Kenneth K. The Buddhist Aesthetic Nature: A Challenge to Rationalism and Empiricism. *Asian Phil*, 4(2), 139-150, 1994.

The challenge is focused on developing a new perspective in perception based on a more intimate examination of experiential reality within the becomingness of things. Western perception based by and large on empiricism and/or rationalism is truncated and does not cover the fullness of reality. Buddhist perception, on the other hand, touches the very depths of experience by including the unique nature of emptiness (sunyata) or nonbeing to round out ordinary perception of things. The function of being-in-nonbeing and the balance derived thereof is the source of the aesthetic nature.

Incardona, Nunzio. Breviarium Principii: Prosènanchos Archèten. *G Metaf*, 16(3), 293-297, S-D 94.

Lately from the principle enigmatically subsists the foundation of a metaphoric *exàifnes*, shut up in an aorgic bond where any beginning conforms itself to know something. This is the origin of what by chorismòs shall result as act and is itself an advanced resulting to the act that shall result *after*, i.e., *in the end*, the termination itself of the beginning: the nonbeing of every start and the fulfillment of every started being up to the liberation of the *exàifnes*. These outlines want just to draw the contours of a radical abbreviation that has concept in the act and term in the start of every start. Almost is determined a radical gloss of thinking that compels every start to the principle up to the start.

Inciarte, Fernando. Bien común y mal común. *Anu Filosof*, 27(3), 939-948, 1994.

The paper deals with the tension between morality and efficacy both from the point of view of economics (and politics) on the one hand and ethics (and politics) on the other.

Indrzejczak, Andrzej. Natural Deduction System for Tense Logics. *Bull Sec Log*, 23(4), 173-179, D 94.

Infante, Giancarlo. Il mondo "Pesante" di Newton. *Sapienza*, 47(3), 357-362, 1994.

Ingenkamp, Heinz Gerd. Shopenhauers Ästhetik bei Wieland. *Schopenhauer Jahr*, 76, 203-209, 1995.

Ingensiep, Hans Werner. Die biologischen Analogien und die erkenntnistheoretischen Alternativen in Kants Kritik der reinen Vernunft B 27. *Kantstudien*, 85(4), 381-393, 1994.

The purpose of this work is to explain the meaning of the biological terms "generatio aequivoca, Epigenesis, Präformation" in Kant's "Critique of Pure Reason", Chapter 27, within the historical context, and to show Kant's intentions by using them. Kant used these terms as biological analogies to illustrate the different epistemological positions of Locke, Leibniz and Hume (sensualism, rational dogmatism, scepticism) to form a contrast to his own point of view: "Epigenesis" stands for apodicticity, apriority, spontaneity and productivity of the categories of the intellect. This biological term allowed a dynamic imagination of knowledge as a product of pure intellect (form) and sensuality (matter). Kant defined the basic terms in his critique of the judgment (Chapter 81).

Ingram, David. "Legitimation Crisis in Contract Law: A Test Case for Critical Legal Studies and Its Critics" in *Radical Philosophy of Law, Caudill, David S (ed)*, 140-161. Atlantic Highlands, Humanities Pr, 1995.

One of the chief tensions in liberal theory criticized by exponents of the Critical Legal Studies Movement is an ambivalence with respect to distinctions between objective facts and subjective values, abstract rights and concrete goods, formal procedures and substantive outcomes, individual liberties and collective utilities, public concerns and private interests. I argue that these tensions are symptomatic of contradictions inherent in the democratic institutions of the welfare state. These institutions manifest a profound ambivalence with respect to the priority of conflict over consensus. Since opposed groups within the private sector cannot be counted on to resolve their differences, compromises must be manufactured in closed legislative chambers by leaders of the various parties or worked out by functionaries within the judicial establishment.

Ingram, David. *Reason, History, and Politics: The Communitarian Grounds of Legitimation in the Modern Age*. Albany, SUNY Pr, 1995.

Reason, History, and Politics shows that certain conceptions of rationality in current theories of science, technology, and law can account for neither the legitimacy of paradigm shifts nor the communitarian integrity of rational decision and learning internal to paradigms generally. Ingram proposes an alternative conception of rationality that does. Drawing on a rich literature that encompasses classical German Idealism, pragmatism, poststructuralism, and hermeneutics, Ingram shows how a specific model of art criticism and aesthetic judgment illuminates the kind of discursive rationality found in all domains of rational undertaking. The book synthesizes debates in law, political science, philosophy of science and history, and social philosophy, and covers Anglo-American, French, and German schools of philosophy, discussing topics such as critical legal studies, the logic of scientific discovery and explanation, and subjectivity, hegemony, and totalitarianism.

Ingram, Virginia. Grounding Benefit in Responsibility. *Kinesis*, 21(2), 4-12, Fall 94.

I argue that in some cases benefiting from an oppression or social injustice is a ground for assigning responsibility for that oppression or injustice. I do not claim that benefiting always results in responsibility. In some cases, however, where X benefits from Y, X is responsible for Y. While much attention has focused on the ways women are harmed by oppression, little attention has been paid to the ways men may benefit from that harm. I focus on the ways men benefit from the oppression of women and, in certain cases, ought to feel responsible for that oppression.

Ingravalle, Francesco. L'iper-razionalismo di Oswald Spengler e l'interpretazione di Otto Neurath del Tramonto dell'Occidente. *Filosofia*, 45(2), 163-176, My-Ag 94.

Innerarity, Daniel 584 **AUTHOR INDEX WITH ABSTRACTS**

Innerarity, Daniel. Estética del límite: Transformaciones en la configuración literaria del horizonte. *Pensamiento*, 198(50), 353-382, S-D 94.

La representación estética del horizonte puede tomarse como registro de las transformaciones culturales. En este artículo se recogen aquellos cambios más significativos de la idea de límite, desde el universo antiguo al pluralismo postmoderno, la infinitud racionalista y la trasgresión romántica, que configura el escenario espacial de la autocomprensión humana.

Innerarity, Daniel. Filosofía como arte y experiencia de la vida. *Acta Phil*, 2(3), 327-338, 1994.

Innerarity, Daniel. Tras la postmodernidad. *Anu Filosof*, 27(3), 949-968, 1994.

If we understand modernity as the construction of a distinction—i.e., subjectivity vs objectivity—postmodernity can be considered the abolition of that distinction, after the experience of its apories. In this paper the interest points towards a non disjunctive direction, towards a kind of thought that may embrace both ambiguity and the relative indiscernibility of the opposites.

Innes, David C. Bacon's *New Atlantis*: The Christian Hope and the Modern Hope. *Interpretation*, 22(1), 3-37, Fall 94.

There is a hope which underlies and animates modern civilization. This is the promise of modern science. Francis Bacon takes what had been a feature solely of Biblical religion, hope of heavenly rest on God's presence, secularizes it, and links it with his scientific project to conquer nature, even human nature, for "the relief of our estate." Bacon's *New Atlantis* presents this hope, reconciles it with a subtly transformed Christianity, and quietly intimates the frightening, though to Bacon acceptable, moral and political price that must be paid. The *New Atlantis* shows us the uniqueness and ambiguity of the modern hope.

Innis, Robert E. *Consciousness and the Play of Signs*. Bloomington, Indiana Univ Pr, 1994.

Do signs and the play of signification define our fundamental modes of being-in-the-world and of giving structure to our experience? Is the 'play' of signs without an anchor? Or must sign-based accounts of consciousness and of world making be grounded in nonsemiotic theories of consciousness, perception, and meaning? Relying primarily on conceptual tools derived from Peirce, Polanyi, Dewey, Bühler, Husserl, and Cassirer I explore the variety of contexts—including the motoric, the perceptual, the aesthetic, the linguistic, and the theoretical—in which semiotic and nonsemiotic factors in consciousness and world building can be related and distinguished.

Inoué, Takao. Hintikka Formulas as Axioms of Refutation Calculus, a Case Study. *Bull Sec Log*, 24(2), 105-114, Je 95.

In this paper, we shall propose an elegant Hilbert-style axiomatic rejection (that is, refutation calculus) for Ishimoto's propositional fragment L_1 of Lesniewski's ontology with Hintikka formulas as axioms. In this framework, we shall prove, among other things, that the L-decidability of Hilbert-style system for L_1 is equivalent to the cut elimination theorem for its corresponding tableau system TL_1 for L_1. In addition, we shall introduce the notion of the name variable property, which is weaker than that of the atomic formula property, and show that TL_1 has the proposed property. Every argument in this paper is syntactical.

Inoué, Takao. On the Atomic Formula Property of Härtig's Refutation Calculus. *Bull Sec Log*, 23(4), 146-150, D 94.

Gentzen's sequent calculus LK enjoys the so-called subformula property: that is, a proof without cut in LK contains only subformulas of the formula occurring in the end-sequent. In this paper, we shall propose a similar property, namely the atomic formula property, and we shall show that for every formula provable in Härtig's refutation calculus HC for classical propositional logic, there is a proof of it in HC with the proposed property. Some comments and open problems will be given.

Inoué, Takao. The Single Axiom-Schema of March 8th. *Bull Sec Log*, 24(2), 115, Je 95.

In this paper, we shall give a nontrivial single axiom-schema for the three characteristic axiom-schemata of Ishimoto's propositional fragment L_1 o f Lesniewski's ontology (for L_1, see Takao Inoué, Hintikka formulas as axioms of refutation calculus, a case study, Bulletin of the Section of Logic (Lódz), vol 24 (1995), pp 105-114).

Insua, Elda and Sardisco, Ana M. "Enseñanga, Políticae Institución" in *Temas Actuales de Filosofía, Palacios, María Julia (ed)*, 281-288. Buenos Aires, Univ Nacional Salta, 1993.

The goal of this work is to make relations between the philosophy teaching, the national policy and the university institutions created for invertigate these subjects, and the professional shape in Argentina. It is interesting to point up some modalities and strategies in order to intent to make up a periodization that remarks the intellectual production conditions together with the political event during democratic periods and during the constitutional break, expliciting the weave that articulates knowledge and power.

Intrigila, Benedetto. Some Results on Numeral Systems in Lambda-Calculus. *Notre Dame J Form Log*, 35(4), 523-541, Fall 94.

In this paper we study numeral systems in the lambda-beta-eta-calculus. With one exception, we assume that all numerals have normal form. We study the independence of the conditions of adequacy of numeral systems. We find that, to a great extent, they are mutually independent. We then consider particular examples of numeral systems, some of which display paradoxical properties. One of these systems furnishes a counterexample to a conjecture of Böhm. Next, we turn to the approach of Curry, Hindley, and Seldin. We dwell with the general problem of obtaining their results with the additional requirement of nonconvertibility of numerals. In particular we solve a problem that they left open. Finally, we give the first example of an adequate unsolvable numeral system without a test for zero in the usual sense, thus solving a problem of Barendregt and Barendsen. (edited)

Ippolito, Maria F and Tweney, Ryan D. "The Inception of Insight" in *The Nature of Insight, Sternberg, Robert J (ed)*, 433-462. Cambridge, MIT Pr, 1995.

Insightful discoveries are characterized as emerging from a dynamic blend of context and behavior and this discussion of insight centers on the unfolding of individual process in context. Specifically, the focus is on the resolution of a specific class of optical deceptions by the physicist Michael Faraday. The primary features of the proposed model of insight which emerges include repeated observation of key perceptual events, the generation and selection of inceptions (reconstructed perceptions which operate in ways veridical to reality that can be manipulated independently of the physical world), and the active construction of a workable mental model.

Iranzo, Valeriano. Epistemic Values in Science. *Sorites*, 81-95, Ap 95.

The paper is a critical examination of some aspects of Laudan's views in his book *Science and Values*. Not only do the aims of science change; there are axiological disputes in science as well. Scientific disagreements are not solely theoretical or methodological. Progress in science consists not only in developing new theories more suitable for implementing certain epistemic values than earlier ones but also in reaching a deeper understanding of those values. The paper considers whether there are principles to guide axiological choices in science, whether the task of assessing the legitimacy of goals makes any sense. Larry Laudan's criteria to settle questions concerning the aims of science are critically canvassed. According to Laudan, axiological choices are on the same footing as the theoretical and methodological ones: all of them may be objectively grounded. The generality of the principles and their naturalistic flavour are the most remarkable merits of Laudan's account but the results are rather meagre. His principle of coherence may be, in the end, a mere *a posteriori* justification of changes in axiological directions carried out by the scientific community. The rejection of a demonstrable utopian goal, granting naturalistic assumptions, is completely sound but it has a very limited scope. The paper suggests that science could not *demonstrate* much about goals. From the rejection of semantic utopianism we can draw a need for a previous clarification rather than sustantive criticisms and, finally, Laudan's charge of epistemic utopianism is very controversial.

Irele, Abiola. "Contemporary Thought in French Speaking Africa" in *African Philosophy: Selected Readings, Appiah, Kwame Anthony*, 263-296. Englewood Cliffs, Prentice Hall, 1995.

The study provides an account of the origins and evolution in French-speaking Africa of a coherent discourse centered of the nature and destiny of the African in the modern world, as well as a critical appraisal of this discourse in relation both to the general context of African self-reflection and to significant developments in Western thought in modern times.

Irele, Dipo. Rorty's Critique of Philosophy: The Implications for the Search for a Method in Contemporary African Philosophy. *Quest*, 8(2), 83-94, D 94.

Dans cet article l'auteur rappelle les principaux points de la critique de la philosophie par Rorty. Ensuite il analyse les conséquences de cette critique pour le dédat sur le caractère de la philosophie africaine. L'opinion de Rorty, qu'il ni a pas de forme privilégiée de rationalité pouvant prétendre à un fondement rationel indépendant, devrait avoir pour résultat une attitude de tolérance envers les divers variantes de la philosophie africaine: "Laissez éclore les fleurs par centaines".

Iribarne, Julia V. *Husserls Theorie der Intersubjektivität*. Freiburg, Alber, 1994.

Irie, Yukio. Dialektik und Entschluss bei Fichte. *Fichte-Studien*, 5, 93-106, 1993.

Die meisten Aufsätze, die den dialektischen Charakter der Fichteschen Philosophie klarzumachen versuchen, erörtern die drei Grundsätze in der *Grundlage der gesammten Wissenschaftslehre*. Das beruht vielleicht darauf, dass wir die drei Grundsätze verhältnismässig einfach mit der Triade von These, Antithese und Synthese vergleichen können, die bisher als Schema der Hegelschen Dialektik verstanden worden ist. Demgegenüber versuche ich hier, die Fichtesche Dialektik im Vergleich zur Kantschen Dialektik zu bestimmen. Dadurch können wir ein Diskussionsthema kenntlich machen, das bisher übersehen worden ist, nämlich "Dialektik und Entschluss". Im folgenden möchte ich meine Ansicht über das Verhältnis zwischen Kant, Fichte und Hegel bezüglich dieses Diskussionsthemas darlegen. Zunächst machen wir den Zusammenhang zwischen Dialektik und Entschluss bei Fichte klar und suchen dann in der Fischteschen Theorie vom Entschluss die zwei Möglichkeiten, den Dezisionismus zu überwinden.

Iris, Madelyn Anne. The Ethics of Decision Making for the Critically Ill Elderly. *Cambridge Quart Healthcare Ethics*, 4(2), 135-141, Spr 95.

Irvine, Andrew D. What Was Plato's Real Name?. *Teach Phil*, 17(2), 97-140, Je 94.

This article consists of a collection of anecdotes concerning famous (and infamous!) philosophers. It was designed to help make otherwise scattered biographical material accessible for classroom use. The collection is arranged in the form of a quiz. It consists of 101 of the most archaic, perplexing, infuriating and useless questions concerning philosophers and their accomplishments from antiquity to the present. The questions are divided into six historical categories: the Ancients, the First Millennium, the Mediaevals, the Early Moderns, the Later Moderns, and the 20th Century. Professional philosophers are to be warned that the intersection between this quiz and all known doctoral comprehensive examinations is the null set.

Irwin, T H. Prudence and Morality in Greek Ethics. *Ethics*, 105(2), 284-295, Ja 95.

Irwin, T H. 'Say What You Believe'. *Apeiron*, 26(3-4), 1-16, S-D 93.

Irwin, Terence. *Plato's Ethics*. New York, Oxford Univ Pr, 1994.

Irwin, Terence (trans) and Fine, Gail (trans). *Aristotle: Selections*. Indianapolis, Hackett, 1995.

Irwin, William. Sartre, Freedom, and the Gambler. *Cont Phil*, 16(6), 9-13, N-D 94.

In this paper I defend the Sartrean conception of freedom against charges that it is absolute and absurd. I demonstrate that Sartre did in fact accept significant restrictions on freedom. Still, for Sartre, we do have great freedom even in cases in which freedom appears to be quite restricted. I take up the example of a gambler to develop Sartre's existential psychoanalytic conception of the fundamental project. It is because of the fundamental project that we often seem to be subject to determinism. Sartre tells us, though we have the freedom to change even the fundamental project. Through such a deep seated change the gambler is free to quit gambling.

AUTHOR INDEX WITH ABSTRACTS 585 Jacobs, Michael

Isaak, Matthew I and Just, Marcel Adam. "Constraints on Thinking in Insight and Invention" in *The Nature of Insight, Sternberg, Robert J (ed)*, 281-325. Cambridge, MIT Pr, 1995.

Iserson, Kenneth V. Life Versus Death: Exposing a Misapplication of Ethical Reasoning. *J Clin Ethics*, 5(3), 261-264, Fall 94.

Ishay, Micheline R (ed) and Dahbour, Omar (ed). *The Nationalism Reader*. Atlantic Highlands, Humanities Pr, 1995.

The National Reader provides a wide selection of important writings on nationalism for the Enlightenment to the present, with emphasis on key figures, both nationalist and internationalist, from the history of thought. Thinkers from various ideologies—liberal, conservative, socialist, fascist, and anticolonial—and from different cultures—European, American, Asian, Islamic, and African—are represented. Many selections—including those by Mazzini, Acton, Renan, Ranke, Bauer, and Bourne—are out-of-print or hard to find and several are reproduced in their entirety. The volume concludes with some recent assessments of the revival of nationalism at the end of the twentieth century.

Ishigaki, Toshio. A Formal System for Classical Particle Mechanics, Its Model-Theoretic Applications and Space-Time Structure. *Synthese*, 102(2), 267-292, F 95.

In the history of Newtonian mechanics physicists and astronomers did not rely on so-called inertial frames, indeed they were not able to identify such frames. So the usual neo-Newtonian formalism of Newtonian mechanics contains some superfluous components. In the present paper I will formulate a formal system for classical particle mechanics in Leibnizian space-time, where a relation, a counterpart of the second law of motion, between force on bodies and derivative of their momentum will be defined relative to every, inertial or not, reference frame. And I will present a view that in the research process under Newtonian mechanics the accumulation of those models of the relation that satisfied some realistic conditions determined an additional structure of non-rotating frames to Leibnizian space-time.

Ishmuratov, Anatoliy. Quest Schemes in Analytical Models of Discourse. *Synthese*, 100(1), 29-38, Jl 94.

In this article a discourse (sequence of sentences) is regarded as a verbalization of some interactive cognitive process (discussion) which may be represented in form of a logical-cognitive scheme as a model of this discourse. Such model is elaborated on the ground of logical-cognitive theory of practical reasoning (Ishmuratov, 1987) by using the definitions of analytical rules for construing model sets (Smullyan, 1968). The discourse's formal language is defined and takes into account the significance of quest intensional (forms of questionable propositions) which are included in different kinds of intensional (intentional, cognitive) contexts of discourse expressions. The discourse model is described in terms of cognitive interpretations which determine conditions of the actualization of cognitive events as elements of the discourse semantic. The peculiarities of this model are explained by deciding one cognitive riddle.

Itkonen, Esa. Iconicity, Analogy, and Universal Grammar. *J Prag*, 22(1), 37-53, Jl 94.

In this paper I shall consider the notion of structural iconicity (or isomorphism) as it is used to explain putative universals of language. Iconicity turns out to be a special case of the more comprehensive notion of analogy. The type of universal grammar based on analogy is contrasted with the one based on modularity.

Itxaso, María Elósegui. Utilidad, arte, virtud y riqueza en la Ilustración Escocesa. *Telos (Spain)*, 1(2), 51-59, Je 92.

This paper deals with some of the relations between art, utility, wealth and virtue stated during the Scottish enlightenment. Philosophers as David Hume and Adam Smith turned the interest from aesthetics as a science of beauty to aesthetics as a science of taste (objectivity to subjectivity), with two main theses: 1) there is a straight relation between ethics and aesthetics, that is, between moral and aesthetical standards, and 2) there is not an opposition between arts and utility, so that wealth could be a general condition for the improvement of all arts.

Ivaldo, Marco. Das Problem des Bösen bei Fichte. *Fichte-Studien*, 3, 154-169, 1991.

Ivaldo, Marco. Il Livello Religioso Dell'intersoggettività nel Pensiero di Fichte. *Daimon Rev Filosof*, 9, 193-209, 1994.

The essay treats the religious level of the intersubjectivity in Fichte's transcendental philosophy. The first section explains the idea of "world of reason" as ground of the individuality. The second moment illustrates the relation between divine and human will in the *Bestimmung des Menshen*. Love as radical bond between absolute and relative being is a distinctive theme in Fichte's religious doctrine (third section). The fourth part treats the interesting development of Fichte's religious thought in the *Staatslehre* 1813 and particularly the notion of "kingdom of heaven". The intersubjectivity has in Fichte's philosophy not only a juridical and moral level but also a radical religious sense.

Ivaldo, Marco. Zur Geschichtserkenntnis nach der Transzendentalphilosophie. *Fichte-Studien*, 6, 303-319, 1994.

Ivanhoe, Philip J. On the Metaphysical Foundations of Neo- and New Confucianism: Reflections on Lauren Pfister's Essay on Religious Confucianism. *J Chin Phil*, 22(1), 81-89, Mr 95.

Iwano, Takuji. Philosophie et technique autour de l'université. *Horiz Phil*, 5(2), 49-73, 1995.

Iwinski, Tadeusz B. "Rough Set Methods in Psychology" in *Probability in Theory-Building, Brzezinski, Jerzy (ed)*, 101-133. Amsterdam, Rodopi, 1994.

Jack, Andrew. Materialism and Supervenience. *Austl J Phil*, 72(4), 426-444, D 94.

I argue that no version of the claim that the mental supervenes upon the physical helps clarify what materialism is. I begin by attempting to formulate materialism and then distiguish various versions of the claim that the mental supervenes upon the physical. I then argue that materialism does not require that physical indiscernibles are mentally indiscernible across, or even within, every metaphysically possible world. I further argue that no version of the claim that the mental supervenes on the physical suffices for materialism, even in conjunction with the claim that every mental particular is physical.

Jackson, Frank. Essentialism, Mental Properties, and Causation. *Proc Aris Soc*, 95, 253-268, 1994-95.

This paper is about how a type-type identity theory of mind (for intentional states) set within a commonsense, 'arms length' style or wide style of functionalism, can give us a theory of mental causation that does two things together: it has content as a causally efficacious property of the right sort of behavior, and has the content causing the right sort of behavior in virtue of the content that it is.

Jackson, Frank and Pettit, Philip. Moral Functionalism and Moral Motivation. *Phil Quart*, 45(178), 20-40, Ja 95.

The contents of moral judgments about decisions, assuming the cognitivist view that moral judgments are beliefs, have to be such as rationally to justify certain conclusions about what should be done; and the judgments have to be such that assenting to them generally goes with desiring the action justified. This paper offers a functionalist account of the contents of moral judgments—an account that loosely parallels the functionalist account of the contents of psychological judgments—and shows that such an account can solve both of these challenges.

Jackson, Jennifer. "Common Codes: Divergent Practices" in *Ethics and the Professions, Chadwick, Ruth (ed)*, 116-124. Brookfield, Avebury, 1994.

How realistic is it to expect professional codes of practice to establish agreed ways of handling cases—shared practice? Is divergent practice morally objectionable? It is argued that variation in how rules are applied is inevitable but innocuous whereas variation in interpretation of rules is harmful but avoidable. In order to avoid variation in interpretation it is necessary to sustain on-going dialogue both among professionals and involving their clients.

Jackson, Jennifer. "Reconciling Business Imperatives and Moral Virtues" in *Introducing Applied Ethics, Almond, Brenda (ed)*, 104-117. Cambridge, Blackwell, 1995.

Why might it be especially difficult to live virtuously while pursuing a career in business? Three problematic aspects of business life are examined. 1) In business you aim to succeed in competition against others. Yet justice includes protecting the weak, not taking advantage of them. 2) Compassion suggests offering a helping hand to those who are in difficulty. 3) Commercial activity seems to thrive on worldliness. But those who are temperate have a low opinion of worldly pursuits. It is argued here that justice, compassion and temperateness, properly conceived, present no real obstacle to successful lives in business.

Jackson, Myles W. Artisanal Knowledge and Experimental Natural Philosophers: The British Response to J Fraunhofer and the Bavarian Usurpation of Their Optical Empire. *Stud Hist Phil Sci*, 25(4), 549-575, Ag 94.

This essay discusses why supremacy in optical technology shifted from Britain to Bavaria during the early nineteenth century. The central theme of this essay is Joseph Fraunhofer's artisanal knowledge and the responses to it by leading British experimental natural philosophers including John Herschel, David Brewster and Michael Faraday. The skills and labor of artisanal practices provide a heurestic tool for analysing how these philosophers formulated a new scientific discipline, physics, and a new reformed society. This paper investigates what experimental natural philosophers thought of artisanal knowledge and how such knowledge could be replicated and transmitted throughout the scientific enterprise.

Jackson, Philip W. If We Took Dewey's Aesthetics Seriously, How Would the Arts Be Taught?. *Stud Phil Educ*, 13(3-4), 193-202, 1994-95.

Jacob, Pierre. Consciousness, Intentionality and Function: What Is the Right Order of Explanation?. *Phil Phenomenol Res*, 55(1), 195-200, Mr 95.

Jacobs, Bart. Semantics of Weakening and Contraction. *Annals Pure Applied Log*, 69(1), 73-106, S 94.

Jacobs, Frans. "Can Liberal Democracy Help us to Survive the Environmental Crisis?" in *Ecology, Technology, and Culture,* Zweers, Wim (ed), 158-163. Cambridge, White Horse, 1994.

Jacobs, Jo Ellen. "The Lot of Gifted Ladies Is Hard": A Study of Harriet Taylor Mill Criticism. *Hypatia*, 9(3), 132-162, Sum 94.

The question, "Why has Harriet Taylor Mill appeared in the history of philosophy as she has?" has several answers. The answers intertwine the personality and politics of Harriet, the sexism of those who wrote of her (which was a reflection of the overall status of women during the period the commentator wrote), misunderstandings of the means and meaning of her collaboration with John Stuart Mill, and the disturbing challenge of her questioning.

Jacobs, Jonathan. *Practical Realism and Moral Psychology*. Washington, Georgetown Univ Pr, 1995.

The book develops a realist metaethic, according to which there is a comprehension of the ethical significance of facts by practical reason. The aim is to show that there is practical cognition, cognition prescriptive for action. There is not an ontologically distinct set of moral facts but the moral significance of factual considerations is to be interpreted realistically. Different versions of realism and antirealism are discussed, and the merits of the account defended are exhibited through exploration of central topics in moral psychology. Accounts of self-love, friendship, and moral respect are developed on the basis of practical realism.

Jacobs, Jonathan. Values, Naturalism, and Teaching the Nature of Values. *Teach Phil*, 17(1), 17-28, Mr 94.

Jacobs, Michael. Sustainable Development, Capital Substitution and Economic Humility: A Response to Beckerman. *Environ Values*, 4(1), 57-68, F 95.

Wilfred Beckerman accepts two of the premises of the environmentalist argument: that long-term environmental impacts may have serious effects on future generations, and that these future generations should be the object of ethical concern. However he rejects the conclusion that is widely claimed to follow: namely that 'sustainability' should be a principal objective of economic policy. For him, the proper (and ultimately the only) objective of economic policy remains optimality, the maximization of benefits over costs—even when environmental concerns are taken into account. His argument has five elements: a redefinition, a positive proposition, two negative ones, and a very large assumption. I shall take each in turn.

Jacobs, Struan. Laws of Nature, Corpuscles, and Concourse: Non-Occasionalist Tendencies in the Natural Philosophy of Robert Boyle. *J Phil Res*, 19, 373-393, 1994.

It has been said that Robert Boyle gave in the century of The Scientific Revolution the "fullest expression" of the view that laws of nature are continually impressed by God ("occasionalism"). So regarded, the universe is anything but an autonomous machine, its ordered operation depending on God's continuous imposition of lawful, patterned relations between phenomena and his continuous provision of motion for them to actually enter relations. The present paper contests this treatment of Boyle. Evidence is elicited to show that, for Boyle, most physical relations issue from *intrinsic* dispositions of phenomena, not divine impositions, dispositions determined by corpuscular textures. Members of classes of phenomena have capacities to make specific changes which members of other classes have capacities to receive, these correlative capacities being *necessarily* connected, subjects in principle of *a priori* synthetic necessary knowledge. The same view is found in John Locke's *Essay Concerning Human Understanding*. It is additionally argued that Boyle's God, the quintessentially active being, imparted motion at the creation, whereafter the motion (at least of most) natural phenomena has derived from *natural*, not supernatural impulsion.

Jacobs, Wilhelm G (ed) and Heuser-Kessler, Marie-Luise (ed). *Schelling und die Selbstorganisation*. Berlin, Duncker Humblot, 1994.

The reference-point for the contributions in this anthology is the discovery that the naturphilosoph F W J Schelling had developed a complete theory of self organization as early as around 1800. This theory exerted considerable influence on the development of science in the nineteenth century, a development that took place not only in the Romantic movement, but also, for example, in crystallography, mathematics or nonequilibrium chemistry. In their contributions Hermann Haken, the founder of synergetics, and René Thom, the father of catastrophe theory, science historians and authority on Schelling, attempt to answer the question: "Of what historical and contemporary significance could Schelling's Naturphilosophie be for the nonlinear natural sciences of today?" The answer is that Schelling's dynamic constructivism can still provide us with important impulses for a philosophy of mathematics, for a theory of emergence and for the analysis of the cultural significance of the idea of self-organization.

Jacobson, Jay A. Informed Consent: Pondering a New Piece of the Puzzle. *J Clin Ethics*, 5(3), 244-246, Fall 94.

Jacquet, Chantal. La Spécificité de la Conception Spinoziste de l'Eternité de l'Esprit. *Rev Phil Fr*, 2, 229-237, Ap-Je 95.

Jacquette, Dale. Formalization in Philosophical Logic. *Monist*, 77(3), 358-375, Jl 94.

The formalization of logic is justified when it contributes to the clear expression of the formal structures of thought, or to the systematization of logic as an inference mechanism. Thetic abuse of logic occurs whenever the formalist fallacy is committed, in which attempts are made to deduce the substantive content of science, metaphysics, or normative theory from the purely formal structures of logic. Examples of the thetic abuse of logic are critically examined in Russell's proposal to substitute a logically perfect notation for thought (in the Introduction to Wittgenstein's *Tractatus*), Carnap's reductively inferentialist semantics, Quine's interpretation of the 'existential' quantifier in his extensionalist criterion of ontic commitment, and the application of Gödel's first incompleteness theorem in distinguishing between minds and machines.

Jacquette, Dale. Hume's Aesthetic Psychology of Distance, Greatness and the Sublime. *Brit J Hist Phil*, 3(1), 89-112, F 95.

Hume distinguishes in the *Treatise* between the effect on conception and the passions of great distance, distance in space as opposed to time, and past as opposed to future time, with precisely opposite results in the case of subjective aesthetic judgments of admiration and esteem for great distance in space and time. Hume's efforts to provide an explanation of the aesthetic impact of distance via Locke's associationist psychology is critically examined in historical context as part of the Enlightenment's interest in aesthetic categories of the beautiful and the sublime. The conflict in Hume's pronouncements about the effect of distance on conception and the passions as opposed to that of aesthetic judgment is resolved by the hypothesis that for Hume aesthetic response belongs essentially to the mind's faculty of reason and reflection rather than exclusively to emotion and the passions.

Jacquette, Dale. Intentionality and the Myth of Pure Syntax. *Protosoz*, 6, 76-89, 1994.

The assumption that it is possible to distinguish pure syntax from any semantic interpretation is common to contemporary extensionalist approaches to philosophy of language, mind, cognitive science, and artificial intelligence. The origin of the term "pure syntax" is traced to Carnap's distinction between pure and applied syntax and semantics, and to formalist analyses of mathematical systems as uninterpreted token manipulating games. It is argued in opposition to this trend that syntax can never be purified entirely of semantics, that there can be no such thing as meaningless syntactical tokens or uninterpreted symbols, but that tokens must always be token and symbols always symbolize something. The implications of the myth of pure syntax in rule-structured and connectionist artificial intelligence, semantic network processing, and their philosophical-psychological rationales, are explored. The fact that rule-structured artificial intelligence in principle can simulate any connectionist model, and that rule-structured artificial intelligence presupposes the myth of pure syntax links the myth to traditional approaches and new paradigms in cognitive engineering.

Jacquette, Dale. On the Designated Student and Related Induction Paradoxes. *Can J Phil*, 24(4), 583-592, D 94.

The designated student paradox is Roy A Sorensen's spatial variation of the prediction or surprise event paradox. A teacher places stars on each of five students'

backs, standing in such a way that each can only see the backs of students in line before them. The teacher announces that one student is to be designated by receiving a gold star where the others receive silver, and that it will come as a surprise to the student at the end when they are given an opportunity to look at their backs. By an exclusionary induction, similar to that in the surprise event paradox, it appears that no student can be designated, contrary to experience. Several solutions to the paradox are considered and rejected, and two directions for resolving the paradox are defended and compared. One adapts W V O Quine's solution to the standard surprise event paradox, and the other is a deflationary resolution, according to which the designation scenario, upon examination of its assumptions, is technically nonparadoxical.

Jacquette, Dale. Tarski's Quantificational Semantics and Meinongian Object Theory Domains. *Pac Phil Quart*, 75(2), 88-107, Je 94.

Tarski's model set theoretical analysis of logical truth presupposes a reduction principle, by which, if a universally quantified sentence is true, then all of its instances are logically true. John Etchemendy, in a recent critique, rejects the reduction principle on the basis of intuitive counterexamples. Etchemendy's objections to the reduction principle on the basis of intuitive counterexamples. Etchemendy's objections to the reduction principle are avoided when Tarski's quantificational criterion of logical truth is applied to a Meinongian domain of existent and nonexistent objects, rather than to an extensional domain of existent objects only. The conclusion is not that Tarski intended a Meinongian object theory domain for his analysis of logical truth, but that Etchemendy's criticisms inadvertently show this to be its proper semantic application.

Jacquette, Dale. Wittgenstein on Private Language and Private Mental Objects. *Wittgenstein Stud*, n.a., 1994.

Wittgenstein's private language argument in his *Philosophical Investigations* is explained and critically evaluated. The implications of Wittgenstein's conclusion that there can be no private sensation language are examined, in light of claims that Wittgenstein by the private language argument also proves that there can also be no private mental objects. The concept of a criterion of correctnessed is discussed as the key to Wittgenstein's reflections, and counterexamples are considered that raise doubts about the soundness of the private language argument. Difficulties identified in standard interpretations of Wittgenstein's argument indicate that the rejection of private sensation languages does not automatically imply a third-person hard psychological theory, such as logical behaviorism, nor does the argument effectively support reductivist or anti-intentionalist philosophy of mind.

Jadacki, Jacek Juliusz. Change, Action and Causality. *Dialogue Hum*, 2(3-4), 87-99, 1992.

Having at his disposal the notions of object, identity (of objects), residing (of properties in object), belonging (of a part to an object), persistence (of an object over a period of time), anteriority (of a period relative to a period), locality (of an object in an area), and equality (of periods or areas), the author successively determines such important philosophical notions, like the notion of change, action, and causality (as well as many derivative notions). Using this conceptual apparatus, the author reformulates the traditional ontological theses of variabilism, statism, finalism, monocausalism, causalism, effectualism, accidentalism, tychism, fatalism, and regularism.

Jaki, Stanley. Consistent Bioethics and Christian Consistency. *Ethics Med*, 11(1), 17-20, Spr 95.

Jakobsen, Janet R. Agency and Alliance in Public Discourses About Sexualities. *Hypatia*, 10(1), 133-154, Wint 95.

Alliance politics is not always an easy proposition. In public discourses about sexualities, unexpected alliances and splits occur even as accomplished alliances fail to achieve their political goals. By considering the models of agency enacted in a series of these alliances, I question how lesbian and feminist and queer actors can more effectively pursue alliance politics in relation to US public policy.

Jalbert, Paul L. Structures of the 'Unsaid'. *Theor Cult Soc*, 11(4), 127-160, N 94.

Jalihal, Govind A. Gender Study as a New Branch or Aspect of Social Philosophy. *J Dharma*, 20(1), 47-50, Ja-Mr 95.

Although social philosophy has been studying man and woman as the two basic pillars of the human family and of the human society, in general, and also the structure and function of their interrelationship within the family set up, a separate and specialized philosophical study of the gender-aspect in the familial relationship and in the social relationship, at large, has not yet been undertaken in a systematic and sustained manner by social philosophers in general. From this fact the paper proceeds to make out a case for the incorporation of gender-study as a separate branch or aspect of social philosophy now, after making a brief historical survey of the philosophical writings on women, from the earliest times onwards, in India and in the West. Such an incorporation, it is argued, has become all the more necessary and expedient with the present coming of age of democracy in our world, in general, and with the gaining in strength of the movement of Feminism today throughout the world.

James, David. "'The Instruction of Any' and Moral Philosophy" in *African Philosophy: Selected Readings, Mosley, Albert G (ed)*, 147-155. Englewood Cliffs, Prentice Hall, 1995.

James, Joy. "Racism, Genocide, and Resistance: The Politics of Language and International Law" in *Marxism in the Postmodern Age, Callari, Antonio (ed)*, 115-125. New York, Guilford, 1994.

James I and James VI and Sommerville, Johann P (ed). *Political Writings: King James VI and I*. New York, Cambridge Univ Pr, 1994.

James VI and Sommerville, Johann P (ed) and James I. *Political Writings: King James VI and I*. New York, Cambridge Univ Pr, 1994.

Jamieson, Dale. "Global Environmental Justice" in *Philosophy and the Natural Environment, Attfield, Robin (ed)*, 199-210. New York, Cambridge Univ Pr, 1994.

This paper argues that once the concept of global environmental justice is analyzed, it breaks apart into several different concerns. Some of these concerns cannot be adequately addressed by "big picture" theories of justice such as those of Rawls and

Nozick. In the end, concerns about global environmental justice lead us away from a preoccupation with justice between nations, towards greater concern with nongovernmental forms of organization and the relationships between them.

Jamison, David (trans) and Meyer, Michel. *Of Problematology: Philosophy, Science, and Language*. Chicago, Univ of Chicago Pr, 1995.

Problematology is a new way of doing philosophy and conceiving thought, language and reason at large. Instead of considering propositions as self-sufficient, problematology sees them as answers, i.e. as situated in reference to underlying questions. Questioning has unfortunately never been questioned as such, in spite of Socrates or Descartes' doubt. Meyer's views aims at explaining why questioning has been repressd at the thematic level of philosophy throughout its history. But the author also wants to show why and where questioning is so important for a new and enlarged view of Reason. *Problematology* is itself the response to the *deconstructivist* approach in virtue of its positive and constructivist outlook on the problematical.

Jamros, Daniel P. *The Human Shape of God: Religion in Hegel's "Phenomenology of Spirit"*. New York, Paragon House, 1994.

A detailed explanation of all the *Phenomenology*'s texts on religion shows Hegel developing the concept of spirit as divine essence in human shape—a concept which leads to the Christian "Manifest Religion" of God incarnate. The same concept of spirit also appears in Hegel's later system as well as in an earlier Jena manuscript. It makes Hegel a philosophical theist, for whom divine essence is world-essence differentiating itself into human subjectivity. Divine essence completes itself by human thinking on earth, and contains no life beyond this one.

Janát, Bohumir. Saunterring as a Great Symbol of Philosophy. *Filozof Cas*, 42(5), 779-803, 1994.

Saunterring—written with two "r"s in order to indicate the authentic meaning of this word, a pilgrimage towards Sancta Terra, a journey to the Holy Land—is a term used by H D Thoreau in his late essay *Walking*; it is used as a metaphor of the sense of philosophy and human life itself. This study takes up this symbol in order to elaborate a way of philosophy which is and should be an alternative to prevalent stream of modern thinking. The movement of the modern secularisation, desacration of the world and setting of man as autonomous is here confronted with a challenge and perspective of transcendency, faith and empathy. Some ideas of the Czech philosopher Jan Patocka from his *Heretical Essays on the Philosophy of History* are broadly used in this study. In order to establish saunterring as a great symbol of philosophy, a historical philosophical triptych is drawn up which consists of three spiritual portraits: 1) Thoreau's Knighthood of Solitude and Civil Disobedience, 2) The Don Quijotean Catholicism of Miguel de Unamuno, 3) John S Dunne—Gilgamesean Pilgrim towards Homing Horizon of Christianity. The study, written in the form of an essay, is intended as a contribution to the challenging and urging ethos of philosophy.

Jané, Ignacio. The Role of the Absolute Infinite in Cantor's Conception of Set. *Erkenntnis*, 42(3), 375-402, My 95.

The main purpose of the paper is to elucidate Cantor's distinction between consistent and inconsistent multiplicities, which essentially amounts to the distinction between the transfinite and the absolute infinite, epitomized in the ordinal sequence. It is argued on the basis of textual evidence that Cantor had two successive conceptions of the absolute. According to the earlier conception, Cantor conceived the absolute infinite as actually existing although not an object of mathematics, while later he viewed it as existing only potentially. This difference of conception has effects on the possibility to appeal to the absolute in mathematical arguments.

Janicaud, Dominique and Birmingham, Peg (trans) and Birmingham, Elizabeth (trans). *Powers of the Rational: Science, Technology, and the Future of Thought*. Bloomington, Indiana Univ Pr, 1994.

Janke, Wolfgang. Amor Dei Intellectualis: Vernunft—und Gottesliebe in Gipfelsätzen neuzeitlicher Systembildungen (Spinoza, Hegel, Schelling, Fichte). *Daimon Rev Filosof*, 9, 101-114, 1994.

There is a remarkable fact concerning the history of modern philosophy. The axiom since Spinoza runs: Love ("amor Dei intellectualis", "absolute Liebe", "Wille der Liebe"), not reason ("Vernunft", "Geist", "Reflexion") is the first principle, which unifies all beings. The first division of our inquiry explains this principle within of the systems from Spinoza to Schelling in a critical way. The second part resumes the same axiom among Fichte's philosophy of religion and reintroduces it as the real principle of human speculation.

Janke, Wolfgang. *Entgegensetzungen: Studien zu Fichte-Konfrontationen von Rousseau bis Kierkegaard*. Amsterdam, Rodopi, 1994.

Janke, Wolfgang. Intellektuelle Anschauung und Gewissen: Aufriss eines Begründngsproblems. *Fichte-Studien*, 5, 21-55, 1993.

Janke, Wolfgang. Limitative Dialektik: Überlegungen im Anschluss an die Methodenreflexion in Fichtes *Grundlage* 1794/95. *Fichte-Studien*, 1, 9-24, 1990.

Janko, Richard. Philodemus Resartus: Progress in Reconstructing the Philosophical Papyri from Herculaneum. *Proc Boston Colloq Anc Phil*, 7, 271-308, 1991.

A breakthrough in reconstructing the fragmentary papyri from Herculaneum, achieved independently by D Obbink and D Delattre, will enable us to reconstitute many philosophical texts. The outer layers of the papyrus-rolls can be reconstructed by reversing the sequences of the sets of the nineteenth-century drawings which are often all that survives of them. The method is tested on Philodemus's *On Poems* Treatise B. The restored sequence of 64 columns is confirmed by an extensive series of parallels in Treatise A. Philodemus's opponent turns out to be the euphonist *kritikos* Pausimachus; Treatise B is probably Book I, and Treatise A Book II.

Janmohamed, Abdul. "Refiguring Values, Power, Knowledge: Or Foucault's Disavowal of Marx" in *Whither Marxism?, Magnus, Bernd (ed)*, 31-64. New York, Routledge, 1994.

Janney, Richard W and Caffi, Claudia. Toward a Pragmatics of Emotive Communication. *J Prag*, 22(3-4), 325-373, O 94.

The task of developing a unified pragmatics of emotive communication poses many interesting challenges for future research. This paper outlines some areas in which more work could be done to help coordinate present linguistic research. After briefly reviewing some pioneering historical work on language and affect, the paper discusses the following concepts, all of which seem to be in need of further clarification: 'emotive meaning', 'involvement', 'emotive markedness', 'degree of emotive divergence', 'objects of emotive choice', '*loci* of emotive choice', and 'outer vs. inner deixis'. Competing categories of emotive devices in current studies of language and affect are reviewed, and a simplified framework is proposed, consisting of: 1) evaluation devices, 2) proximity devices, 3) specificity devices, 4) evidentiality devices, 5) volitionality devices, and 6) quantity devices. (edited)

Janovic, Tomislav. Adaptationism or the Theory of Optimization. *Filozof Istraz*, 13(4), 917-938, 1993.

"Adaptationist program" represents an "approach to evolutionary studies which assumes without further proof that all aspects of the morphology, physiology and behavior of organisms are adaptive optimal solutions to problems" (Lewontin 1978: 6). Since adaptation and optimality can be viewed as a priori assumptions, rather than testable hypotheses, this program of explanation and understanding of various kinds of evolutionary phenomena (including those related to human studies) has come under severe attack in the late seventies. This, in turn, animated an extensive and fruitful debate during the eighties among biologists, philosophers of biology and social and human scientists, centered around the issues of adaptationist and optimalist methodology, and the possibility of extending such methodology to the human sciences, especially those of sociology, psychology and anthropology. The aim of the present paper is to give a review of the objections to adaptationism given by R C Lewontin and S J Gould (1979), and to examine whether and to what degree this criticism can be warranted against the adaptationist counter-arguments and in regard to the alleged explanatory and research achievements of the modern (neo-Darwinian) evolutionary theory. The most important issues here concern the role and relative importance of *natural selection* versus internal and ecological *constraints* and alternative, nonselective forces (e.g., random genetic drift, cultural influences, etc.) for the evolution of various properties (*traits*) of organisms and populations.

Jansen, Henry. *Relationality and the Concept of God*. Amsterdam, Rodopi, 1995.

In this book the author investigates the questions of whether one can conceive of God apart from the metaphysical attributes and whether reflection on the biblical depiction of God leads necessarily to a relational concept of God. The author explores the questions by examining the relational concepts of God found in two contemporary German theologians, Jürgen Moltmann and Wolfhart Pannenberg, and uses the divine attribute of immutability as a focus for the discussion. He argues that the relational concept of God presupposes another metaphysical conception of God, which raises problems as serious as those in classical theism, and that the Bible itself is ambiguous in many respects as far as God is concerned. (edited)

Janssen, H C I M. Relativity, Absoluteness and Observation. *Method Sci*, 27(3), 149-160, 1994.

Janssen, Maarten C W. "Economic Models and Their Applications" in *Idealization VI: Idealization in Economics, Hamminga, Bort (ed)*, 101-116. Amsterdam, Rodopi, 1994.

Discussion of idealization and concretization in economics. Fully concretized economic models are claimed to be principally beyond reach. Observed phenomena can, however, be explained on the basis of tendency laws, provided that the assumptions made in those models are consistent with the information we have about the economy or, if not, that replacing these assumptions by others that are consistent with our information should not make a significant difference for the results of the analysis under investigation.

Jansz, Jeroen and Fischer, Agneta H. Reconciling Emotions with Western Personhood. *J Theor Soc Behav*, 25(1), 59-80, Mr 95.

It has often been taken for granted that Western everyday conceptions characterize emotions as irrational, involuntary, primitive bodily forces. This view of emotions is at odds with the main features of the cultural ideal of a person, here referred to as Western personhood. In this article we focus on the question of whether Western personhood really clashes with everyday conceptions of emotions. We will argue that this is not the case. Our claim will be supported by illustrating how Western persons make sense of their emotions, and more specifically how they reconcile their emotional experiences and expressions with Western personhood. People account for their feelings by telling a narrative in which emotions are presented as normal, intentional and appropriate reactions. Drawing from interviews about anger and fear, we show that people generally do not see their emotions as irrational and primitive forces, but as rational and functional responses in a particular situation. Thus, Western persons often hold a rationalized view on emotions. This bounded emotionality does not clash with the dominant form of Western personhood.

Jantzen, Grace M. Feminists, Philosophers, and Mystics. *Hypatia*, 9(4), 186-206, Fall 94.

This article challenges the widely held view that mysticism is essentially characterized by intense, ineffable, subjective experiences. Instead, I show that mysticism has undergone a series of social constructions, which were never innocent of gendered struggles for power. When philosophers of religion and popular writers on mysticism ignore these gendered constructions, as they regularly do, they are in turn perpetuating a post-Jamesian understanding of mysticism which removes mysticism and women from involvement with political and social justice.

Japaridze, Giorgi. A Simple Proof of Arithmetical Completeness for -conservativity Logic. *Notre Dame J Form Log*, 35(3), 346 354, Sum 94.

Jarczyk, Gwendoline and Labarrière, Pierre-Jean. Absolu/Sujet. *Laval Theol Phil*, 51(2), 239-250, Je 95.

Hegel, de son propre aveu, a transcrit l'héritage de l'ontologie métaphysique (dont il n'excepte pas le transcendantalisme kantien) dans les canons d'une logique dont il a profondément bouleversé l'intelligence. Avec le mouvement réflexif, qui s'impose alors à la base de son système, sont récusées d'un même mouvement l'abstraction d'un universel formel et vide et l'attention à une immédiateté seulement donnée qui ne serait pas saisie comme le corps d'effectivité de l'idée. D'où la clef de cet univers: la conviction de ce que le sujet (ou l'esprit) est structuré en lui-même de telle sorte que son effectuation historique, à même la contingence, fasse partie de son essence. Une < totalité-mouvement > qui, sans achèvement possible, identifie processuellement logique et histoire, absolu et contingence.

Jaroszynski, Piotr. Kalokagathia. *Dialogue Hum*, 4(5), 79-87, 1994.

To understand the meaning of *kalokagathia* one must take into account not the contemporary but the Greek theories of beauty and the good. Beauty in the Greek tradition had at least three significations: as an end in itself, as harmony and what pleases as seen. The so conceived beauty comes to a very close relation with the moral goodness, especially with *bonum honestum*. *Bonum honestum* is also an end in itself, and , when other moral values are properly related to it, there is a harmony on the personal as well as on the social level. And finally, the moral goodness is something to be admired (it pleases as seen). The concept of *kalokagathia*, then, was at the core of morality, education and culture. It is too precious a pearl to be forgotten.

Jarrold, Chris (& others). Pretend Play: Is It Metarepresentational?. *Mind Lang*, 9(4), 445-, D 94.

Jasper, David. Violence and Post-Modernism. *Hist Euro Ideas*, 20(4-6), 801-806, F 95.

The postmodern text exposes and enacts a violence which is visionary in the tradition of biblical apocalypse. Disintegrating the order of time and space, it abandons also the mimetic tradition of art and the principles of correlation between the images of our world and their reference. Taking examples from postmodern fiction (J G Ballard) and film (Francis Ford Coppola) as well as thinkers like Jean Baudrillard, this article argues that the literature of postmodernity exhibits the absolutism of our so-called moral preoccupations, unveiling them for our own final judgment.

Jauch, Ursula Pia. *Damenphilosophie und Männermoral: Von Abbé de Gérard bis Marquis de Sade Ein Versuch über die lächelnde Vernunft*. Vienna, Passagen, 1990.

In Emilie du Châtelet, eigenwillige Leibniz-Schülerin und prominente Newton-Übersetzerin, findet sich die erste, brilliante *Damenphilosophin*. Und schon bald kommen die männlichen Nachahmer. Auf die Damenphilosophie folgt die *Männermoral*: Francesco Algarotti übersetzt Newton *für die Damen*, ein Herr LaLande schreibt eine *Damenastronomie*, und selbst Immanuel Kant gibt seinen Kommentar. Schliesslich schickt ein Marquis d'Argens die Philosophie definitiv ins erotomane Boudoir, wo sie der Marquis de Sade als Geschichte über die Männermoral weitertraktiert. (edited)

Jauch, Ursula Pia. *Immanuel Kant zur Geschlechterdifferenz: Aufklärerische Vorurteilskritik und bürgerliche Geschlechtsvormundschaft*. Vienna, Passagen, 1989.

Abseits der Kantlektüren ihrer männlichen Kollegen geht die Autorin Kants verstreuten Reflexionen zur Geschlecterdifferenz nach. Dabei kann sie überzeugend zeigen, dass Kant mehr war, als der "galante Magister", oder, wie der alte Feminismus will, ein patriarachalischer Frauenverächter. Kant entlaravte auch mit überraschend scharfem Blick den Warencharakter der weiblichen Sexualität. Philosophiehistorisch gut abgesichert zeigt uns die Autorin einen ganz neuen Kant: Einen Feministen "avant la lettre", etwa mit seinem bisher unbemerkten Versuch einer "Grundlegung zur Ethik der intersexuellen Egalität". (edited)

Jauregui, Claudia. "Autoafección y Juicios de Percepción en la Filosofía Kantiana" in *Temas Actuales de Filosofía, Palacios, María Julia (ed)*, 289-295. Buenos Aires, Univ Nacional Salta, 1993.

The Kantian doctrine of judgments of perception in the *Prolegomena* (Sections 18-20) has often been considered as contrary to the principles of the transcendental idealism. In this paper, I try to demonstrate that this problem is apparent and has its origin in a literal interpretation of the passage in which Kant says that every judgment is first a judgment of perception and then becomes a judgment of experience. Against this view, I present a different possible interpretation of the doctrine, taking account of some texts added in the second edition of the KrV., especially those that speak about the self-affection.

Javeau, Claude. "De l'homme moyen à la moyenne des hommes" in *Rhétoriques de la science, De Coorebyter, Vincent (ed)*, 53-67. Paris, Pr Univ France, 1994.

Jayashanmukham, N. Author's Response to the Comments by A Rama Murty. *J Indian Counc Phil Res*, 11(3), 112-114, My-Ag 94.

Professor Rama Murthy has raised three objections: i) the term *mrtyu* in the mantra is wrongly taken to mean natural death; ii) nor can it give the sense of unnatural death; iii) Sayana is right in interpreting it as signifying bondage. In the author's response these objections are dismissed on the ground that they are not related to the text of the original article.

Jayashanmukham, N. The Tryambaka Mantra: Its Meaning and Significance. *J Indian Counc Phil Res*, 11(3), 101-110, My-Ag 94.

The article critically examines the interpretations of the mantra by Sayana and Raimundo Panikkar and concludes that neither of them brings out its true sense. An alternate interpretation is developed by the author. He points out that the mantra is concerned with two things: i) freedom from ultimately death; ii) attainment of immortality. Apart from this, he shows how the ideas of Vasishtha proceed very clearly on a logical basis, as also how the Vedic poet anticipates the Ishavasya Upanisad.

Jeauneau, Édouard. Néant Divin et Théophanie: Erigène Disciple de Denys. *Diotima*, 23, 121-127, 1995.

Jecker, Nancy S. Calling It Quits: Stopping Futile Treatment and Caring for Patients. *J Clin Ethics*, 5(2), 138-142, Sum 94.

This paper defends the concept of medical futility against opponents. I argue first that studies showing empirical differences of opinion about the meaning of medical futility among physicians do not suffice to show that the use of medical futility should be abandoned. After pointing out that variations in medical judgment and practice occur in many areas, the paper emphasizes the importance of continued discussion and clarification of futility's meaning and ethical implications. While opponents of medical futility seek to purge medicine of ethical components, this paper urges greater recognition of ethics as integral to medicine.

Jecker, Nancy S (& others). Caring for Patients in Cross-Cultural Settings. *Hastings Center Rep*, 25(1), 6-14, Jan-Feb 95.

This paper proposes an ethical framework for resolving cross-cultural conflicts between patients and health care providers. Health professionals first identify both their and the patient's goals; then locate alternative strategies to meet these goals. Finally providers evaluate alternative means of realizing goals. Ethical guidance in this process derives from the standard of ethical integrity which requires acting in accordance with ethical convictions that are one's own, scrutinizing values and regarding them as open to revision, and adjudicating through a procedure sensitive to inequalities in the provider-patient relationship.

Jecker, Nancy S and Jonsen, Albert R. Healthcare as a Commons. *Cambridge Quart Healthcare Ethics*, 4(2), 207-216, Spr 95.

Jecker, Nancy S and Schneiderman, Lawrence J. Judging Medical Futility: An Ethical Analysis of Medical Power and Responsibility. *Cambridge Quart Healthcare Ethics*, 4(1), 23-35, Wint 95.

This essay rejects the criterion of potential benefit, which holds that medical treatments are appropriate if they might have some benefit for the patient. We argue instead for granting physicians the power to establish and apply standards of medical futility. Rather than assigning individual physicians the power to define medical futility, we propose that this power rests with the medical profession as a group, and is part of the profession's more general responsibility to define general standards of medical care.

Jecker, Nancy S and Schneiderman, Lawrence J. When Families Request That 'Everything Possible' Be Done. *J Med Phil*, 20(2), 145-163, Ap 95.

The paper explores the ethical and psychological issues that arise when family members request that "everything possible" be done for a particular patient. The paper first illustrates this phenomenon by reviewing the well known case of Helga Wanglie. We proceed to argue that in Wanglie and similar cases family members may request futile treatments as a means of conveying that (1) the loss of the patient is tantamount to losing a part of themselves; (2) the patient should not be abandoned or disvalued in any way; or (3) the patient is owed special obligations by virtue of the special relationship in which the family and the patient stand. We maintain that families can best express these important messages by caring for patients, rather than by making requests for futile interventions. Likewise, when life-sustaining measures are futile, health providers can best fulfill their professional obligations by assuring patients' dignity and comfort, rather than by applying futile interventions.

Jeffrey, Richard. A Brief Guide to the Work of Carl Gustav Hempel. *Erkenntnis*, 42(1), 3-7, Ja 95.

Jeffrey, Richard. Probability Reparation: The Problem of New Explanation. *Phil Stud*, 77(1), 97-101, Ja 95.

Jeffrey, Richard. The Works of Carl Gustav Hempel. *Erkenntnis*, 42(1), 9-14, Ja 95.

Jeffrey, Richard (trans) and Kolmogorov, A N. Complete Metric Boolean Algebras. *Phil Stud*, 77(1), 57-66, Ja 95.

Jeffrey, Richard and Stalnaker, Robert. "Conditionals as Random Variables" in *Probability and Conditionals, Eells, Ellery (ed)*, 31-46. New York, Cambridge Univ Pr, 1994.

Jegstrup, Elsebet. A Questioning of Justice: Kierkegaard, the Postmodern Critique, and Political Theory. *Polit Theory*, 23(3), 425-451, Ag 95.

The article presents Kierkegaard in a postmodern mood and demonstrates that his text is the originary source of the postmodern critique. It especially focuses on his deconstruction of justice as law (*droit*) and on his suggestion that there is another justice whose source is radically other and whose call addresses singularity. The call of this other justice commands the single self (*den Enkelte*) to love the other as self, and the meaning of this injunction is found to have a particularly contemporary meaning that resembles Heidegger's concept of *Gelassenheit*, that one loves the other by letting the other be.

Jenkins, J L. The Possibility of Communist Altruism. *Hist Phil Quart*, 12(1), 95-109, Ja 95.

Philosophical opinion is heavily weighted against the notion that members of a large community can care about one another except in cases of extreme emergency, such as war or natural disaster. Marx disagrees. Relations between unalienated citizens incorporate features usually thought of as characteristic of personal relations such as friendships. How can the type of motivation now reserved for friends and family be extended to all of the members of a large community? An account of what the mechanisms are that might make it possible is given. The discussion relies, in part, on Aristotle's views about the nature of friendship.

Jervolino, Domenico. "The Depth and Breadth of Paul Ricoeur's Philosophy" in *The Philosophy of Paul Ricoeur, Hahn, Lewis Edwin (ed)*, 533-543. Peru, Open Court, 1994.

Jervolino, Domenico. *Logica del Concreto ed Ermeneutica della Vita Morale: Newman, Blondel, Piovani*. Napoli, Morano, 1994.

All the three of the thinkers dealt with in my book—Newman, Blondel, Piovani—are engaged in a search for what has been called a "living logic". This logic can be seen as a sort of hermeneutics of concrete, moral and historical, existence. If so, we can speak of a second current of hermeneutics in the 19th and 20th centuries, in addition to the current, centered on text, that starts with Schleiermacher.

Jesson, Nicholas. Comments on Peter Staples' 'Ultimates as Paradoxical Limits'. *Ultim Real Mean*, 18(2), 151-154, Je 95.

This work provides brief comments on the preceding work by Peter Staples. While supporting the general direction of Staples' article, Jesson questions the paradoxes as outlined by Staples. He suggests that careful ecumenical dialogue will lead to union or covenant proposals which avoid the Three-from-Two Paradox. Jesson further suggests that the "Ultimate" Paradox as outlined by Staples is too strict. Jesson's comments provide an optimistic counterpoint to Staples' article.

Jimenez, Jose D. Kant: La Religión como *Veneración Moral Pura de Dios*. *Pensamiento*, 199(51), 69-88, Ja-Ap 95.

Fue Kant un hombre religioso? Qué piensa de la religión? Cuál es su crítica? Se pretende en este estudio una exposición de la crítica kantiana de la religión y una valoración, tanto de las aportaciones positivas como de las carencias y enfoques a mi entender parcial o totalmente desenfocados. El hombre tiende a la felicidad, y se hace digno de ella mediante la práctica de la virtud moral. Por el recurso a la religión es como podemos esperar participar en esa felicidad: la inmortalidad del alma y la existencia de un garante supremo de la justicia—piensa Kant—lo posibilitan.

Jiménez, Jorge. Leviatán en los confines de la modernidad: Una crítica anarquista de la sociedad civil y el Estado. *Rev Filosof (Costa Rica)*, 32(77), 27-40, Jl 94.

Working from the hub of criticism directed against civil society and State, the author analyzes some of the more notable moments of anarchistic thought, in particular its passage from the 19th century Promethean spirit toward contemporary formulations, enriched by Marxism and Psicolanalysis, and by the profound sense of defeat that May 1968 left in our generation.

Jimenez Glez, J E and Del Rosario, M. Phonological Awareness in Learning Literacy. *Commun Cog—AI*, 11(1-2), 127-152, 1994.

The present research examines accessibility to different levels of phonological awareness and their relationship to the mastery of the alphabetic code in Spanish language. The results obtained suggest that the pre-reader subjects are more sensitive to syllabic units than to intra-syllabic and phonemic units. Similarly, a greater mastery of the alphabetic code is associated with higher levels of intra-syllabic and phonemic awareness. (edited)

Jin, Renling and Shelah, Saharon. Essential Kurepa Trees Versus Essential Jech-Kunen Trees. *Annals Pure Applied Log*, 69(1), 107-131, S 94.

Joblin, Joseph. Ingérence des États en temps de guerre: Action humanitaire des organisations bénévoles chrétiennes et témoignage de l'évangile. *Gregorianum*, 76(1), 95-123, 1995.

Humanitarian action is understood by voluntary organizations in a specific sense. Its primary motivation is to witness to human solidarity by meeting basic human needs without any political, religious or ideological considerations, in situations where States are too easily moved by concerns of national interest in exercising the so-called right of ingerence. These differences of perspective may make it impossible for voluntary organizations to be associated with some humanitarian operations. Christian voluntary action also has it own specificity, and Christian organizations will sometimes have to ask themselves whether participation in a particular operation retains its Christian value and meaning. (edited)

Jockusch Jr, Carl G and Soare, Robert I. Boolean Algebras, Stone Spaces, and the Iterated Turing Jump. *J Sym Log*, 59(4), 1121-1138, D 94.

Johann, Patricia. Normal Forms in Combinatory Logic. *Notre Dame J Form Log*, 35(4), 573-594, Fall 94.

Let *R* be a convergent term rewriting system, and let *CR*-equality on (simply typed) combinatory logic terms be the equality induced by *Beta Eta R*-equality on terms of the (simply typed) lambda calculus under any of the standard translations between these two frameworks for higher-order reasoning. We generalize the classical notion of strong reduction to a reduction relation which generates *CR*-equality and whose irreducibles are exactly the translations of long *Beta R*-normal forms. The classical notion of strong normal form in combinatory logic is also generalized, yielding yet another description of these translations. Their resulting tripartite characterization extends to the combined first-order algebraic and higher-order setting the classical combinatory logic descriptions of the translations of long *Beta*-normal forms in the lambda calculus. As a consequence, the translations of long *Beta R*-normal forms are easily seen to serve as canonical representatives for *CR*-equivalence classes of combinatory logic terms for nonempty, as well as for empty, *R*.

Johansson, S Ryan. "The Brain's Software: The Natural Languages and Poetic Information Processing" in *The Machine as Metaphor and Tool, Haken, Hermann (ed)*, 9-43. New York, Springer-Verlag, 1993.

Computer metaphors for the human brain (i.e., the brain is a computer) identify a machine which is "engineered" by nature, and still basically unfamiliar, with one engineered by people, and therefore familiar. But computers respond to instructions coded in precise signs. Human brains respond to signs which have multiple meanings, and are therefore inherently vague. The pervasive vagueness of the natural programming languages is treated as a barrier to successful communication by philosophers; whereas poets capitalize on the freedom of interpretation it permits. But in complex social situations the vague signs force people to agree upon their meaning in specific contexts, thereby facilitating the continual social construction of reality based on shared perceptions.

Johnson, David E and Moss, Lawrence S. Grammar Formalisms Viewed as Evolving Algebras. *Ling Phil*, 17(6), 537-560, D 94.

We consider the use of *evolving algebra* methods of specifying grammars for natural languages. We are especially interested in distributed evolving algebras. We proved the motivation for doing this, and we give a reconstruction of some classic grammar formalisms in directly dynamic terms. Finally, we consider some technical questions arising from the use of direct dynamism in grammar formalisms.

Johnson, Deborah G (ed) and Nissenbaum, Helen (ed). *Computers, Ethics and Social Values*. Englewood Cliffs, Prentice Hall, 1995.

The pervasive use of computers and the emergence of new, highly sophisticated information technologies have raised many social concerns. This anthology of readings addresses the ethical issues arising from the development and deployment of computers in society. Selections represent a range of diverse opinions and perspectives, offering a balance between theoretical analysis and description of real-life cases. The volume is broken into seven chapters: What is Computer Ethics?; Crime, Abuse, and Hacker Ethics; Ownership of Computer Software; Privacy and Databases; The Risks of Computing; Responsibility, Liability, and Professional Codes; and The Networked World.

Johnson, Jeffery L. Constitutional Privacy. *Law Phil*, 13(2), 161-193, My 94.

This paper defends the view that constitutional privacy should be understood as certain socially defined areas of their lives in which citizens can expect immunity from the judgment of the state. It argues that such a liberal view of constitutional privacy can be defended on jurisprudential grounds. It further argues that careful analysis of the Supreme Court's reasoning in privacy cases in the past half century, in both Fourth Amendment and Fourteenth Amendment contexts, clearly legitimates a robust right to constitutional privacy.

Johnson, Julia A. Comments on Smolarski's 'Finding Meaning in Mathematics'. *Ultim Real Mean*, 17(4), 321-322, D 94.

Smolarski's thesis is that '...meaning and reality in mathematics is that which is experienced by someone who actually does mathematics.' It follows from Smolarski's thesis that a computer does not do mathematics like a mathematician does. This review provides additional evidence for the view that '...it will be a number of years before the human race needs to fear self-powered computers that become neurotic' (Smolarski 1994). I also comment on how the field of artificial intelligence relates to modern mathematics.

Johnson, Julia A. Disambiguation of Language: The Ultimate Reality and Meaning of Computer Studies. *Ultim Real Mean*, 17(4), 277-294, D 94.

We review the fundamental ideas in the field of computer studies culminating with the halting problem which sets ultimate limits on what can be computed on a computer. Limits on what can be computed are imposed by natural language which permits ambiguous specification. We examine characteristics of computer sublanguages of natural language with respect to the notions of inauthentic and authentic language use as Heidegger defines them. A semantic relatedness heuristic for disambiguation in a sublanguage of natural language is presented by example.

Johnson, Lawrence E. From the Chariot: The Katha and the Phaedrus. *Darshana Int*, 32(2/126), 42-57, Ap 92.

Johnson, M L. Stages and Transitions in Cognitive Development. *J Thought*, 30(3), 45-69, Fall 95.

Johnson, Oliver A. *The Mind of David Hume: A Companion to Book I of 'A Treatise of Human Nature'*. Chicago, Univ of Illinois Pr, 1995.

The Mind of David Hume is a companion to Book I of *A Treatise of Human Nature*. In it the author does two things: 1) He follows Hume's argument step by step from the beginning to the end of the Book, clarifying, interpreting, and analyzing it. 2) He evaluates that argument, to determine whether Hume's thought constitutes a viable system of philosophy. The book is written for practicing philosophers, as well as for graduate students and undergraduates majoring in philosophy.

Johnson, Phillip E. *Reason in the Balance: The Case Against Naturalism in Science, Law, and Education*. Downers Grove, InterVarsity Pr, 1995.

Phillip Johnson, Professor of Law at Berkeley, identifies metaphysical naturalism as "the established religious philosophy of America." Naturalism asserts that nature is all there is, and that God is therefore no more than a subjective entity in the human mind. Much of the cultural power of naturalism comes from the mistaken assumption that science has shown that a Darwinian evolutionary process is our true creator. Johnson argues that theistic realism provides a better foundation for rational thought than scientific naturalism, and documents the extent to which naturalistic thinking has led to relativism and nihilism in the domain of values.

Johnston, Mark. "Self-Deception and the Nature of Mind" in *Philosophy of Psychology: Debates on Psychological Explanation, Macdonald, Cynthia (ed)*, 433-460. Cambridge, Blackwell, 1995.

Johnstone, D J and Lindley, D V. Bayesian Inference Given Data 'Significant at α': Tests of Point Hypothesis. *Theor Decis*, 38(1), 51-60, Ja 95.

In empirical research in the social sciences expressions of statistical significance are meant to capture and summarize the evidence implied by data. To evaluate the evidential content of statements such as 'the difference between means in significant at $\alpha = 5\%$', we consider the Bayesian probability of the hypotheses tested, where the conditioning event is an announcement of general form *significant at* α. By proceeding as if neither observed effects nor their exact *P*-values are reported, the meaning of such descriptions *of themselves* is revealed. It is demonstrated, for large samples particularly, that a report merely that data are *significant at* α has no objective meaning, and under some conditions should be interpreted not as evidence against the null hypothesis, as is usually supposed, but as strong evidence in its favor. This conclusion is supported by both algebraic arguments and example calculations for the special, but important case of the normal mean. It is also found that significance at one level tends to imply significance at much lower levels, the more strongly the larger the sample.

Johnstone Jr, Henry W and Gutenberg, Norbert. On the Category of the Controversial: An Approach through Schleiermacher's Dialectic. *Phil Rhet*, 27(4), 347-358, 1994.

All theories of argumentation and all rhetorical concepts have to do, either implicitly or explicitly, with the category of the controversial.' In this article I shall attempt to approach the Category of the Controversial from the point of view of philosophical dialectic. My project presupposes the recovery of the unity of the epistemic and communicative aspects of dialectic and rhetoric. In Friedrich Schleiermacher's "Dialectic" both the communicative basis of knowledge and the epistemic aspect of communication become evident. The Category of the Controversial can be defined on this basis through the occurrence together of communicative and epistemic differences, which, in the process of communication, become oppositions that are seen as in need of resolution. (edited)

Jolley, Kelly D and Perry, Clifton B. Contraposition and Existential Import. *Phil Sci (Tucson)*, 6, 153-157, 1995.

Jolley, Nicholas. "Introduction" in *The Cambridge Companion to Leibniz, Jolley, Nicholas (ed)*, 1-17. New York, Cambridge Univ Pr, 1994.

Jolley, Nicholas (ed). *The Cambridge Companion to Leibniz*. New York, Cambridge Univ Pr, 1994.

This volume provides systematic and comprehensive account of the full range of Leibniz's thought, exploring the metaphysics in detail and showing its subtle and complex relationship to his views on logic, language, physics, and theology. Other chapters examine the intellectual context of this thought and its reception in the eighteenth century. The volume is intended to be of interest to both the specialist and the general reader.

Joly, Jacques. Spontanéité et nature: le cas d'Andô Shôeki: Comparatisme et récupération. *Rev Phil Louvain*, 92(4), 546-569, N 94.

By concentrating on the case of Andô Shôeki, a Confucianist thinker of the middle of the Tokugawa period, himself inseparable from the interpretation of his thought in a Marxist or ecologist sense, this article attempts to explain how two words with very different meanings and from such different intellectual traditions as are *shizen* and "nature" (the idea of spontaneity is their only common denominator), became, due to their identical ideological role, identical in meaning at the *Meiji* period. The article then seeks to emphasize certain difficulties that a comparative problematic centered on the idea of nature may encounter.

Jonathan, Ruth. Liberal Philosophy of Education: A Paradigm Under Strain. *J Phil Educ*, 29(1), 93-107, March 95.

This paper suggests that liberal philosophy of education, which shares the implicit commitments of modern neutralist liberalism, also exhibits that political philosophy's theoretical inadequacies and inability to guide practice. It argues that neither theoretical perspective can redeem its claims to equally respect the demands of liberty and equity, when those claims rely only on arguments of procedural value. Consequent implications, for both educational theory and educational aims, are discussed.

Jones, Anne Hudson. Literature as Mirror or Lamp? Commentary on "Literature, Medical Ethics, and 'Epiphanic Knowledge'". *J Clin Ethics*, 5(4), 340-341, Wint 94.

Jones, D Gareth and Telfer, Barbara. Before I Was an Embryo, I Was a Pre-Embryo: Or Was I?. *Bioethics*, 9(1), 32-49, Ja 95.

In this paper we look critically at the term 'pre-embryo', and we shall present the case for an alternative set of terms, namely, embryo-placenta and embryo-fetus. We consider this latter to be biologically-based terminology, that does not have any connotation of restricted moral value as the term pre-embryo does for some. (edited)

Jones, James M. A Perpetrator-Less Crime?. *Ethics Behavior*, 4(4), 395-397, 1994.

Jones, John D. Multiculturalism and Welfare Reform. *Phil Cont World*, 1(2), 11-18, Sum 94.

The paper considers the relation between welfare reform and multiculturalism. Three defects of welfare reform, and their relation to multiculturalism, are discussed. First, welfare reform emphasizes welfare-to-work programs. Yet, necessary, political and economic support has rarely been forthcoming. Second, welfare reform fails to provide a comprehensive framework for alleviating poverty since many poor receive no significant assistance. Third, welfare policy is driven by stigmatizing distinctions between the disreputable and reputable poor. Thus, the paper argues that people of color will continue to bear the brunt of economic and symbolic marginalization despite the apparent gains of multiculturalism.

Jones, Kath Renark. "Modernity, Ethics and Irony: The Return of the Subject in the Later Works of Foucault" in *Reconstructing Foucault, Miguel-Alfonso, Ricardo (ed)*, 201-215. Amsterdam, Rodopi, 1994.

This paper was written in response to recent claims that in Foucault's later work there is proposed a return to an ethics of subjectivity. By way of a reading of Foucault's work on Kant, and his notion of an "ontology of the present", it is argued that interpreting the Foucauldian subject in metaphysical terms (as is required in the positing of an Enlightenment subject) is clearly mistaken. For Foucault, the subject is not the focus of a re-born humanism, but the configuration of forces that can make possible new ways of thinking and expanding what might be called an "ethics of existence".

Jones, L Gregory (ed) and Fowl, Stephen E (ed). *Rethinking Metaphysics*. Cambridge, Blackwell, 1995.

Here is a series of important essays which re-think the place of metaphysics in theological and philosophical inquiry. This book ranges across a variety of philosophical and theological traditions, engaging such figures as Plato and Augustine as well as Gillian Rose, Jacques Derrida, Donald Davidson, C S Peirce, and Jean Luc Marion. The authors of these essays confront a variety of post-modern critiques of metaphysical speculation while, nonetheless, arguing that there is still a significant future for reflection on metaphysical questions. Unified by an agreement about the urgent need to re-think metaphysics, these essays should provoke a wide-ranging and lively discussion among philosophers and theologians.

Jones, Michael Ponder. Remembering My Own Madness: A Hermeneutics of That Which is Prior to Rationality. *Kinesis*, 21(2), 50-64, Fall 94.

Jones, Peter. Toleration, the Rushdie Affair, and the Perils of Identity. *Filozof Istraz*, 14(2-3), 269-281, 1994.

The author examines how the issue of toleration is affected by a particular way of evaluating religious beliefs: the conception of belief as an expression of identity. The paper discusses the example of the reception of Salman Rushdie's *Satanic Verses*, since the Rushdie affair has brought questions of toleration, belief and identity in sharp focus. It concentrates on the charge that the book amounts to an assault on the very identity of Muslims. The author examines the implications of this critique. He tries to show that its restrictive potential is far greater than those who advance it seem to appreciate. On the other hand, he also argues that this particular way of construing the Rushdie affair is very problematic not only for Rushdie himself, but also for his Muslim critics. The price of this translation of beliefs into indentities turns out to be so high for all concerned, that the whole enterprise is best abandoned. (edited)

Jones, Scott K and Hiltebeitel, Kenneth M. Organizational Influence in a Model of the Moral Decision Process of Accountants. *J Bus Ethics*, 14(6), 417-431, Je 95.

This paper reports on a survey that investigated the moral decision processes of accountants. A formal belief revision model is adapted and hypotheses based on theorizations from the cognitive-developmental school are tested. The moral decision processes of accountants are hypothesized to be influenced by professional expectations, organizational expectations and internalized expectations. Subjects provided specific demographic data and were asked to access the appropriateness of fourteen principles for making moral decisions in business. Subjects were also asked to indicate which of the fourteen approaches would be most appropriate for resolving each of five ethical situations that are representative of common ethical dilemmas in accounting. Subjects' responses to the appropriateness of the fourteen principles are reduced to two dimensions using factor analysis. The factors are consistent and representative of important underlying dimensions of the stages of moral development. Demographic variables are correlated with the extracted factors using analysis of variance. The results show that subjects consider interpersonal expectations and conformity to be more appropriate than approaches that are self-serving. These findings suggest that ethical decision processes of accountants are influenced by organizational support. Age, gender, and education were also found to influence the moral decision process. Overall, the findings are consistent with the expectations hypothesized from the cognitive-developmental school and suggest that the moral development of accountants is ongoing.

Jones, Todd. Reductionism and the Unification Theory of Explanation. *Phil Sci*, 62(1), 21-30, Mr 95.

P Kitcher's unification theory of explanation appears to endorse a reductionistic view of scientific explanation that is inconsistent with scientific practice. In this paper, I argue that this appearance is illusory. The existence of multiply realizable generalizations enable the unification theory to also count many high-level accounts as explanatory.

Jonkers, P. Immanence and Transcendence in Modern Philosophy: Some Questions with Reference to Fichte's 'Dispute on Atheism' (in Dutch). *Tijdschr Filosof*, 56(4), 667-692, D 94.

The aim of this article is to analyze and evaluate Fichte's criticism of traditional theism and his attempt to develop a 'post-theistic' philosophy of religion. For Fichte it is evident that God as a supersensible being cannot be thought if one starts from the sensual world; there is an absolute incommensurability between the two. Therefore, not only the traditional proofs of God's existence lose their validity, but also any conceptual knowledge of God in general becomes impossible. (edited)

Jonkers, Peter. Metafysica in Leuven. *Tijdschr Filosof*, 57(2), 331-343, Je 95.

Jonsen, Albert R and Jecker, Nancy S. Healthcare as a Commons. *Cambridge Quart Healthcare Ethics*, 4(2), 207-216, Spr 95.

Joós, Ernest. La fin de l'histoire serait-elle le commencement de la sagesse? L'aliénation de l'esprit dans la *Phénoménologie* de Hegel. *Laval Theol Phil*, 51(2), 271-292, Je 95.

L'auteur propose une lecture de la *Phénoménologie de l'esprit* qui attribue une importance primordiale à la manifestation qui a lieu au niveau de la conscience (*im Bewusstsein*) et qui est donc entièrement libre face aux vicissitudes de l'histoire. Il essaie ainsi de ramener la *Phénoménologie* à un point de vue individuel et à une sagesse, dont la condition est un devenir qui met l'accent sur l'intériorisation des problèmes comme problèmes existentiels.

Jordan, Jeff. Is it Wrong to Discriminate on the Basis of Homosexuality?. *J Soc Phil*, 26(1), 39-52, Spr 95.

Jordan, Jeffrey (ed). *"Introduction" Gambling on God: Essays on Pascal's Wager*, 1-10. Lanham, Rowman & Littlefield, 1994.

Jordan, Jeffrey. "The Many-Gods Objection" in *Gambling on God: Essays on Pascal's Wager, Jordan, Jeffrey (ed)*, 101-113. Lanham, Rowman & Littlefield, 1994.

Jordan, Jeffrey (ed). *Gambling on God: Essays on Pascal's Wager*. Lanham, Rowman & Littlefield, 1994.

This is a collection of ten essays concerning various aspects of Pascal's Wager. Among the topics discussed are: the relation of pragmatic reasoning to rationality, the propriety of the concept of an infinite payoff, moral objections to Pascalians, wagering, and the soundness of the many-gods objection. There are original essays by Richard Foley, Thomas Morris, Philip Quinn, George Schlesinger, Jeff Jordan, Edward McClennen, and Roy Sorenson.

Jori, Mario. Uberto Scarpelli, Giurista e Filosofo. *Riv Int Filosof Diritto*, 71(4), 181-199, 1994.

Jorion, Paul. L'Intelligence Artificielle: Au Confluent des Neurosciences et de l'Informatique. *Lekton*, 4(2), 85-114, 1994.

Jorland, Gérard. "Idealization and Transformation" in *Idealization VI: Idealization in Economics, Hamminga, Bert (ed)*, 265-275. Amsterdam, Rodopi, 1994.

A critical evaluation of Nowak's application of the model of concretization to Marx's model of theory development in 'Capital'. It focuses on Nowak's account of transformation and of Marx's methods, and discusses the status of Nowak's method.

José, Elena Teresa. "Perspectivas Epistemológicas para un Modelo Macrosocial" in *Temas Actuales de Filosofía, Palacios, María Julia (ed)*, 297-305. Buenos Aires, Univ Nacional Salta, 1993.

El trabajo pretende esbozar pautas metodológicas para la construcción de un modelo macrosocial. En la primera parte se aclara el sentido de los "términos" usados. En la segunda, se elabora un marco teórico, a partir de la categorización que hace Oscar Varsavsky de los distintos tipos de enfoques que podría haber en lo que él llama "Una filosofía para politicos y planificadores". En la tercera se esbozan las distintas etapas e items a tenerse en cuenta al delinear y poner en marcha el modelo. En la cuarta parte se establecen algunos criterios y requisitos epistemológicos que debe cumplir el modelo.

AUTHOR INDEX WITH ABSTRACTS 591 Jutronic-Tihomirovic, Dunja

José Acero, Juan. Sintáxis Lógica, Fisicalismo y la Unidad de la Ciencia. *Rev Filosof (Spain)*, 7(12), 421-436, 1994.

José Frápolli, María. Extensionalidad, Opacidad y Estructura Intensional: Un Análysis de las Falacias en Contextos Epistémicos. *Rev Filosof (Spain)*, 7(12), 355-367, 1994.

Josipovic, Marko. Begriff und Abriss der Entwicklung der Neuscholastik. *Filozof Istraz*, 14(2-3), 437-452, 1994.

Im Artikel wird die Spezifität der neuscholastischen Philosophie definiert und auf die wichtigsten und einflussreichsten Förderer, auf ihre Werke und eigenen Beiträge zur Erneuerungsbewegung des traditionellen Denkens hingewiesen—von den Anfängen, die mit dem Philosophiestudium am Collegio Alberoni in Piacenza (gegründet im Jahr 1751) in Verbindung gebracht werden, bis auf die heutigen Tage. Dies gilt sowohl für das philosophische Denken auf Weltebene als auch bei den Kroaten, in den gegebenen Umständen und im kritischen Betrachten der modernen und gegenwärtigen philosophisch-wissenschaftlichen Errungenschaften. Die Neuscholastik ist Anerkennung und Bestätigung der dauernden Gültigkeit des Erbes christlichen Denkens, das die Philosophen auf eine dem Verlangen der modernen Zeit angepasste Weise darzulegen sich bemüht haben. Der flüchtige und fragmentarische Abriss ihrer Entwicklung zeigt, dass die Neuscholastik ein wichtiges Kapitel der Geschichte der Philosophie überhaupt und insbesondere der christlichen Philosophie der letzten zwei Jahrhunderte darstellt.

Jovchelovitch, Sandra. Social Representations In and Of the Public Sphere: Towards a Theoretical Articulation. *J Theor Soc Behav*, 25(1), 81-102, Mr 95.

The relationship between social representations and the public sphere is explored through the processes whereby the subject develops a self, creates symbols and opens up to a 'not-me' world. This is done at two levels. The first concerns the *logic of production* of social representations, or social representations *in* the public sphere. The second level examines the problem of social representations *of* the public sphere. I discuss how something like a "public" becomes representable and how the transformations which public life undergoes, institute individualism as expression of personal life. I argue that understanding symbolic representations of public life is crucial to assess both contemporary experiences of selfhood and the possibilities of preserving a *sensus communis*.

Jowett, Benjamin (trans) and Plato. *Plato's Gorgias*. Millis, Agora Pub, 1995.

Joyal, A and Moerdijk, I. A Completeness Theorem for Open Maps. *Annals Pure Applied Log*, 70(1), 51-86, N 94.

This paper provides a partial solution to the completeness problem for Joyal's axiomatization of open and etale maps, under the additional assumption that a collection axiom (related to the set-theoretical axiom with the same name) holds.

Juárez, Federico Augusto. "Teoría de la Acción Comunicativa: Entre la Reconstruccion de la Critica y la Justificacion Reconstruida" in *Temas Actuales de Filosofía, Palacios, María Julia (ed)*, 307-313. Buenos Aires, Univ Nacional Salta, 1993.

Juchler, Jakob. The Formation Approach and the Crisis of "Real Socialism". *Dialogue Hum*, 2(1), 109-122, 1992.

The actual development in Eastern Europe has shown that the kind of social system, which was labelled "socialism" or "real socialism", has practically no future. What about Marxism and its formation approach, one of the ideological cornerstones of the "socialist" system? Is this theory now falsified and senseless, too? In what follows, an unconventional conception is sketched out which allows a new interpretation of the "socialist" societies and their astonishing transformation phase.

Juchler, Jakob. The Post-Socialist Change in Eastern Europe: Specific Development or Universal Trend of Global History? A Formation Approach. *Dialogue Hum*, 4(2-3), 269-289, 1994.

The paper analyzes the transformation in Eastern Europe in the perspective of global history and compares it to actual world-wide developments. The theoretical frame of reference is a strongly modified formation theory which allows for a truly comparative and interdisciplinary perspective. The main topic is the presentation of basic aspects of the fundamental changes in postsocialist societies in comparison with global tendencies: the economic process with its deep crisis, the political process with its instabilities, the changes in social consciousness with their complicated contradictions and some social features such as rising intolerance and violent conflicts. Finally future options are discussed.

Jucker, Andreas H. The Feasibility of Historical Pragmatics. *J Prag*, 22(5), 533-536, N 94.

While contrastive pragmatics compares the realization of linguistic units in different cultures or in different languages, historical pragmatics studies the realization of these units at different stages in the development of one language. As a new field of study historical pragmatics will have to suggest answers to at least the following questions: 1) Are some pragmatic frameworks more suitable for historical pragmatics than others? 2) What kind of topics may profitably be tackled in historical pragmatics? 3) What is the *tertium comparationis* for historical pragmatics? 4) What kind of data may be used for historical pragmatics?

Judah, Haim and Roslanowski, Andrzej. Martin's Axiom and the Continuum. *J Sym Log*, 60(2), 374-391, Je 95.

Jürgensen, Sven. Die Unterscheidung der Realität in Fichtes *Wissenschaftslehre* von 1794. *Fichte-Studien*, 6, 45-70, 1994.

Obwohl Fichte in den Grundsätzen der *Wissenschaftslehre von 1794* an die Qualitätskategorien der *Kritik der reinen Vernunft* Kants erinnert, wird gezeigt, dass sie als Verstandes-Kategorien erst im theoretischen Teil abgeleitet werden. Daraufhin wird deutlich, dass die Realität des absoluten Ich sich als Idee, die Negation des Nicht-Ich sich als Ideal und die Limitation sich als Streben im praktischen Teil konkretisieren. Es zeigt sich, dass das absolute Ich nicht Selbstbewusstsein ist, welches erst im praktischen Teil deduziert wird. Der zeitlose Moment klärt die konstitutive Bedeutung des 11. Paragraphen, mit dem die *Wissenschaftslehre* in ihren Anfang zurückkehrt und sich als System vollendet.

Juhl, Cory. Is Gold-Putnam Diagonalization Complete?. *J Phil Log*, 24(2), 117-138, Ap 95.

Diagonalization is a proof technique that formal learning theorists use to show that inductive problems are unsolvable. The technique intuitively requires the construction of the mathematical equivalent of a "Cartesian demon" that fools the scientist no matter how he proceeds. A natural question that arises is whether diagonalization is *complete*. The answer to that question turns out to depend upon what axioms of set theory we adopt. The two main results of the paper show that if we assume Zermelo-Fraenkel set theory plus AC and CH, there exist undetermined inductive games. The existence of such games entails that diagonalization is incomplete. On the other hand, if we assume the Axiom of Determinacy, or even a weaker axiom known as Wadge Determinacy, then diagonalization is complete. (edited)

Juhl, Cory and Kelly, Kevin and Glymour, Clark. "Reliability, Realism, and Relativism" in *Reading Putnam, Clark, Peter (ed)*, 98-160. Cambridge, Blackwell, 1995.

Juhl, Cory and Kelly, Kevin T. Realism, Convergence, and Additivity. *Proc Phil Sci Ass*, 1, 181-189, 1994.

In this paper, we argue for the centrality of countable additivity to realist claims about the convergence of science to the truth. In particular, we show how classical sceptical arguments can be revived when countable additivity is dropped.

Juhl, Cory F. The Speed-Optimality of Reichenbach's Straight Rule of Induction. *Brit J Phil Sci*, 45(3), 857-863, S 94.

In his *Theory of Probability*, Hans Reichenbach attempted to 'vindicate' induction with his 'straight rule' of induction. A central problem facing his attempt to vindicate the straight rule is that too many other rules are just as good as the straight rule if our only constraint on what counts as 'success' for an inductive rule is that is 'asymptotic', i.e., that it converges in the limit to the true limiting frequency (of some type of outcome O in a sequence of events) whenever such a limiting frequency exists. In this paper I consider the consequences of requiring speed-optimality of asymptotic methods, that is, requiring that inductive methods must get to the truth *as quickly as possible*. Two main results are proved: 1) the straight rule is speed-optimal; 2) there are (uncountably) many nonspeed-optimal asymptotic methods. (edited)

Juji, Azuma. The Formation of New *Lixue*: Feng Youlan and New Realism. *J Chin Phil*, 21(3-4), 303-335, S-D 94.

Jung, Hwa Yol. The *Tao* of Transversality as a Global Approach to Truth: A Metacommentary on Calvin O Schrag. *Man World*, 28(1), 11-31, Ja 95.

Junkerman, Charles (ed) and Perloff, Marjorie (ed). *John Cage: Composed in America*. Chicago, Univ of Chicago Pr, 1994.

Juranville, Alain. L'écriture. *Rev Phil Fr*, 2, 167-180, Ap-Je 94.

Juristo, N and Maté, J L and Pazos, J. Expert Systems Evaluation. *Commun Cog—AI*, 11(3), 225-255, 1994.

The six honest servants of human kind that Kipling pointed out: what, when, where, who, why and how, are studied for knowledge-based systems evaluation. We place special emphasis on the procedural aspect of evaluation which is reflected by how. In this sense, Jain's methodology for computer systems performance evaluation is made suitable for KBS evaluation. Practical guidelines on how to proceed with KBS evaluation are provided.

Just, Marcel Adam and Isaak, Matthew I. "Constraints on Thinking in Insight and Invention" in *The Nature of Insight, Sternberg, Robert J (ed)*, 281-325. Cambridge, MIT Pr, 1995.

Jutronic-Tihomirovic, Dunja. Language and Determinism: A Contribution to the Cognitivist Critique of Chomsky's Innateness Hypothesis. *Filozof Istraz*, 14(1), 99-104, 1994.

Chomsky believes that there are highly abstract determinate structures which constrain the acquisition of language. Language develops like any other organ or system in the body so that in some way fundamental way we do not learn the language but language grows in our mind. Connectionistic mode as a new model of the workings of the mind, and thus of language, goes against such rigid generic determinism. More recently, psychological investigations of thought and language (see S Gelman & J P Byrnes eds 1991) stress the influence of speech community as an important factor in the acquisition of lexical units, on equal footing with the genetic dispositions. It seems that the experimental investigations show that rigid determinism is becoming less plausible and that the time has come for the theorists to reconsider its premises.

Jutronic-Tihomirovic, Dunja. New Trends in Analytical Philosophy in Croatia. *Filozof Istraz*, 14(2-3), 585-591, 1994.

In the first part of the article the author gives some facts about the development of the analytical philosophy in Croatia. The section for the analytical philosophy was created at the end of the seventies within the philosophy department in Zadar and later in Rijeka, too. The main instigators were professor doctor Heda Festini i professor doctor Nenad Miscevic. With the arrival of professor doctor Georges Rey from the States regular meetings were introduced at both places. In the second part of the article the author concentrates more on the philosophy of language and philosophy of mind within the following framework: philosophy searches and gives answers taking into account respective scientific achievements, the new cognitive-psychological picture views human mind as a kind of a complex computer. In this respect language and mind are studied as natural phenomena. (edited)

Jutronic-Tihomirovic, Dunja. The Language of Thought and Connectionism. *Filozof Istraz*, 13(4), 783-791, 1993.

How does the connectionist model of cognition relate to the sentential explanation of cognition? These theses are considered. *Radical* which says: Connectionist models are going to replace the language of thought model of the mind. *Implementational* which takes connectionist models as mere implementations of the representational theory of the mind. There is a third option. We call it the *division of labor thesis*. It might be that pattern recognition and some low-level processings are in the domain of connectionist models while problem solving, language processing and behavior planning are in the domain of the sentential description. It is plausible, the author tries to argue, that there exist different levels and kinds of information processing. (edited)

Kaalikoski, Katri and Airaksinen, Timo. Instrumental Rationality. *Protosoz*, 6, 151-159, 1994.

The standard view of rationality distinguishes between instrumental rationality and the rationality of ends. We discuss this conception briefly before introducing an alternative theory. According to it, means and ends are interconnected so that the means will produce the ends. In other words, the means are used to shape our ends. We describe and discuss this view, asking whether it can be called rationality. It is clear that this alternative view has many irrational features. But at the same time it is clear that much of our technological culture is based on this view so that also it is hampered by the emerging irrationality. We conclude by discussing the case of genetic engineering as a technology we cannot possibly accept. Its characteristic ends may be of a wrong type.

Kadarkay, Arpad (ed). *The Lukács Reader*. Cambridge, Blackwell, 1995.

The Lukacs Reader includes, in original translations, and with introductory essays, Lukacs on: Kierkegaard, Shakespeare, Ford, Strindberg, Ibsen, Wilde, Shaw, Gauiguin, Dostoevsky, Nietzsche and Heidegger. Also collected are: the autobiographical essay 'On Poverty of Spirit', material from Lukac's diary, and such key articles as: 'Aesthetic Culture', 'The Ideology of Modernism', 'Bolshevism as an Ethical Problem', and 'Class Consciousness'. What emerges is a figure very much at the center of European thought whose value to modern culture and philosophy is of seminal importance.

Kadish, Sanford H. "Letting Patients Die: Legal and Moral Reflections" in *In Harm's Way, Coleman, Jules L (ed)*, 290-323. New York, Cambridge Univ Pr, 1994.

Fifty years of medical advances have challenged some of our most deeply held moral beliefs about life and death. Doctors and hospitals that once would have prolonged life now routinely discontinue life-sustaining treatment. Professor Kadish examines the legal and moral aspects of these decisions. He then considers advance directives and the doctrine courts use when there has been no advance directive, the doctrine of substituted judgment. Finally, he concludes that courts have gone astray by invoking the principle of autonomy in substituted judgment situations, because autonomy cannot be at issue when the patient has made no choice. (edited)

Kaelin, Eugene F. "Paul Ricoeur's Aesthetics: On How to Read a Metaphor" in *The Philosophy of Paul Ricoeur, Hahn, Lewis Edwin (ed)*, 237-255. Peru, Open Court, 1994.

The purpose of this chapter is to evaluate the aesthetic theory of Paul Ricoeur in phenomenological terms. The phenomenon is called 'the surplus of meaning,' which was treated differently by the author in the three phases of his philosophical development. Within that development, the earlier theory of tragedy was replaced by the metaphorical reading of three "Fables of Time" in the novels of V Woolf, T Mann, and M Proust. The theory is expounded in the first three sections of the chapter, and evaluated in the fourth. Ricoeur appended his reply in following pages.

Kafatos, Menas and Nadeau, Robert. *The Conscious Universe: Part and Whole in Modern Physical Theory*. New York, Springer-Verlag, 1990.

This work builds on Bohr's principle of complementarity to show that it forms a generalized framework to understand the universe. The authors build the thesis that complementarity can be involved in cosmological theories of the universe and in constructions of all human realities. Moreover, the book concludes by making the case that consciousness can no longer be divorced from the way science operates and that this realization entails a new way of understanding the universe.

Kafkoulis, George. The Consistency Strength of an Infinitary Ramsey Property. *J Sym Log*, 59(4), 1158-1195, D 94.

The purpose of this paper is to prove that assuming the consistency of a certain large cardinal axiom with the usual axioms of Zermelo Fraenkel Set Theory with the axiom of choice then it is consistent with Zermelo Fraenkel Set Theory with the axiom of choice that a certain Infinitary Ramsey Property holds at some strong limit cardinal of countable confinality. The large cardinal hypothesis is that of the existence of a supercombat cardinal and an inaccessible cardinal above it. The Infinitary Ramsey partition property at a given cardinal is of the following form: For every ordinal below the cardinal and for every ordinal definable coloring of countable sequences from the cardinal into colors taken from the sets of rank less than the ordinal, there exists a homogeneous countable sequence, i.e., a countable sequence whose every subsequence is colored by the same color. The techniques involve forcing construction using the supercombat prikry forcing, certain absoluteness arguments and a careful analysis of a symmetric model of the main forcing extension model.

Kagan, Shelly. "The Argument from Liberty" in *In Harm's Way, Coleman, Jules L (ed)*, 16-41. New York, Cambridge Univ Pr, 1994.

It is often argued that libertarianism is the moral system that most fully reflects the value of (negative) freedom. There is, of course, a dispute as to whether other values should be recognized *besides* negative freedom, but critics and friends of libertarianism alike typically accept the claim that libertarianism is indeed the system that provides the greatest (negative) freedom to everyone. I argue, however, that if we are careful to distinguish different possible concepts of negative freedom, we find there is no good reason to believe this commonly accepted claim. Libertarianism can find no support in an "argument from liberty."

Kahan, Alan. Defining Opportunism: The Writings of Eugène Spuller. *Hist Polit Thought*, 15(3), 423-445, Autumn 94.

Kahn, Jeffrey and Elliott, Carl. Docs on the Box: Or, How We Learned to Stop Worrying and Love the Tube. *Hastings Center Rep*, 24(6), 22-23, N-D 94.

Kahn, Victoria. Reading Machiavelli: Innocent Gentillet's Discourse on Method. *Polit Theory*, 22(4), 539-560, N 94.

Kahn Jr, Peter H. Resolving Environmental Disputes: Litigation, Mediation, and the Courting of Ethical Community. *Environ Values*, 3(3), 211-228, Autumn 94.

Litigation and mediation offer substantive and important approaches toward resolving environmental disputes. Yet as currently practiced both approaches have shortcomings. For example, litigation often promotes divisive, adversarial relationships. Mediation often yields untenable ground given the seriousness of many environmental problems. This paper offers a reconception of both approaches. It is argued that both litigation and mediation need to be embedded within a more ethically comprehensive context, one of 'courting ethical community'. Discussion focuses on what it means in this sense to court, on what defines and bounds the ethical, and how courting depends on understanding not only differences but commonalities in people's environmental views and values.

Kain, Philip J. Niccolò Machiavelli-Adviser of Princes. *Can J Phil*, 25(1), 33-56, Mr 95.

Machiavelli's advice to the prince is to avoid self-interest and to work for the good of the state. This is not to say, however, that Machiavelli does not counsel evil. To achieve the good, one must do evil. It is necessary. But it is still evil. Machiavelli is not a utilitarian or a moral consequentialist in ethics. If an action has certain desirable consequences, it may be politically necessary to perform that action. But that does not make the action moral. If it is evil, it remains evil. Yet it is necessary to do it to achieve the good.

Kainz, Howard P. Hegel on the Bacchanalian Revel of Truth. *Phil Rhet*, 28(2), 146-152, 1995.

This article is an interpretation of the extended metaphor in the Preface to Hegel's *Phenomenology*, in which the truth is compared to a "Bacchanalian revel in which every member is intoxicated...." I show that this metaphor, when unpacked, offers us an excellent introduction to the non-epistemological Hegelian concept of truth, according to which various philosophical positions in their very one-sidedness lead out of themselves and instigate the continual advancement of truth.

Kainz, Howard P. The Definition of Philosophy, Revisited. *Epistemologia*, 17(2), 197-204, Ju-De 94.

"Philosophy" is a complex subject/object, like "democracy" or "theology," and thus hard to define. Linguistic philosophy's "discourse about discourse," scholasticism's "study of first principles," phenomenology's "bracketing of the natural world," etc., all lead to question-begging impasses. Socrates' project of reexamining meanings and values seems to offer the best overall definition.

Kaipayil, Joseph. *The Epistemology of Comparative Philosophy: A Critique with Reference to P T Raju's Views*. Rome, Ctr Ind & Int-Rel St, 1995.

The book seeks to identify and examine the theoretical and methodological problems involved in doing comparative philosophy, by analysing the views and ideas of the noted comparativist P T Raju. The book argues that comparative philosophy is theoretically unsound and practically unsuccessful and calls for a paradigm shift in East-West studies in philosophy. In the place of comparative philosophy the author suggests the ideal of what he calls an "open philosophizing."

Kal, Victor. Het monisme van Herman Berger. *Alg Ned Tijdschr Wijs*, 86(3), 207-223, Jl 94.

Kal, Victor. Van Participatie tot Zelflimitatie; Over Thomas' Filosofie van de Schepping. *Tijdschr Filosof*, 57(2), 308-325, Je 95.

Kalsi, Marie-Luise Schubert. Apriori Concepts. *SW Phil Rev*, 11(1), 1-14, Ja 95.

The central questions of the paper are whether there are a priori concepts and whether there is a priori theorizing not making any claim on being knowledge. In the discussion of the first question three classes of concepts are studied, namely those gained by abstraction, those created by definition, and those which are neither gained abstraction nor definition. They are called "naturally a priori". Examples of these are: similar, dissimilar, one, identity, cause, reason. Additionally it is found that abstraction in presupposing perception contains a priori elements. The second question deals with story telling, scientific and philosophical hypotheses, musical compositions, and natural applications of rules of logic.

Kambayashi, Tsunemichi. Über das Malerische oder Pittoreske. *Aesthetics*, 3, 59-74, Mr 88.

Kamenka, Eugene. "Nationalism: Ambiguous Legacies and Contingent Futures" in *The End of "Isms"?, Shtromas, Alexsandras (ed)*, 127-141. Cambridge, Blackwell, 1994.

Kamenka, Eugene. Reflections on Art, Culture and Universalism. *Lit Aes*, 3, 67-79, Spr 93.

Kamenka, Eugene. Universalism and Evil. *Dialogue Hum*, 3(2), 156-164, 1993.

Kamm, Frances M. To Whom?. *Hastings Center Rep*, 24(4), 29-32, Jl-Ag 94.

Kanai, Yasuo. On a Generalization of Distributivity. *J Sym Log*, 59(3), 1055-1067, S 94.

Kandulski, Maciej. Axiomatizations of Commutative and Non-Associative Ajdukiewicz Calculus. *Bull Sec Log*, 23(4), 151-157, D 94.

Lambek syntactic calculi, when enriched by a structural rule of permutation, can be equivalently formalized as bidirectional and as unidirectional systems. In the latter case the rule of permutation is not indispensable in the system. A similar result, however, is not generally valid in the Ajdukiewicz calculus with permutation. It is shown in the paper that the equivalence of bidirectional and unidirectional axiomatizations is valid only for formulas consisting of types of order less than 2, with a right-hand type (succedent) being a primitive type.

Kane, Michael T. Heidegger and Aristotle's Treatise on Time. *Amer Cath Phil Quart*, 69(2), 295-309, Spr 95.

Heidegger's 1927 lecture course, *The Basic Problems of Phenomenology*, fulfills *Being and Time*'s promise of a reading of Aristotle *Physics* 4.10-14. This article examines Heidegger's reading of the treatise on time and considers his ambivalent relationship towards Aristotle. The paper sets out Heidegger's interpretation itself and shows how Heidegger forces Aristotle into a series of *aporiai*, which only his doctrine of original time can resolve. The article concludes by suggesting the ways in which Heidegger uses this appropriation of Aristotle for his project of fundamental ontology.

Kaneda, Chiaki. The *focus imaginarius* of Kantian Theory of Aesthetical Judgement. *Bigaku*, 45(4), 1-11, Spr 95.

The aim of this paper is to answer the following question about the first part of Immanuel Kant's "Critique of Judgment". Is it possible to understand the three successive paragraphs, the 16th, 17th and the 18th, as working as a unit? In other words, is it possible for us to discover a right viewpoint, from which these three paragraphs are regarded as controlled by a common theoretical motivation? I do answer in the affirmative. The Ideal of Beauty (17), in my opinion, is no more and no less than an a-priori condition, on which the truth or falsity of an aesthetical judgment is (ideally) *determined*. This a-priori condition has two aspects, just as determination in general does. On the other hand this condition makes it possible for us to *negate* (ideally) the opponent judgment (16). On the other it affords us a right to make a statement of taste in the mode of *postulation*, that is, in the mode of necessity (18). In this way those three paragraphs are coordinated.

Kaneko, Mamoru. Axiomatic Considerations of Nash Equilibrium. *Bull Sec Log*, 24(1), 6-12, Mr 95.

Kang, Beom-Mo. On the Treatment of Complex Predicates in Categorial Grammar. *Ling Phil*, 18(1), 61-81, F 95.

Kannonier-Finster, Waltraud and Ziegler, Meinrad. "Erinnern ohne Gedenken" in *Nationalsozialismus und Moderne, Welzer, Harald (ed)*, 61-104. Tübingen, Ed Diskord, 1993.

Kansara, N M. Dr Kansara's Comments. *J Indian Counc Phil Res*, 12(1), 135-156, S-D 94.

The Vajasaneyi Samhita in the text is inferior in originality to the text of the Krsna Yajurveda; the former was reduced to its present form when the influence of the Rgveda was more and more predominating, as is evident from the traditional connection of Yajñavalkya with the Rgveda too. The difference between their ritual lies in the tilt towards the divine aspect in the Sukla Yajurveda. The point stressed by Heesterman has nothing to do with the distinction between the Sukla and the Krsna Yajurveda. His assumption about patron-brahmana pair being "two opposed groups", is but a matter of subjective conjecture, based on his second-hand evidence of Kulper.

Kanthamani, A. Are Quine's Two Dogmas Still Dogmas. *Indian Phil Quart*, 21(3), 195-213, Jl 94.

The above question has a positive answer. Quine's repudiation stands in the face of many onslaughts. Contrary to belief, Quine has a theory about meaning and it is an extended theory about meaning and translation. Within his work, there is a *modus vivendi* between meaning and translation. In a Dummettian vein, it is argued that Quine's critique stands on stronger grounds, and premised on the primacy of translation. The dogmas have identical roots *contra* Gochet. With this, Quine has already turned post-analytical.

Kantor, Jeffrey and David, Jeanne M and Greenberg, Ira. Possible Ethical Issues and Their Impact on The Firm: Perceptions Held by Public Accountants. *J Bus Ethics*, 13(12), 919-937, D 94.

The accounting profession is concerned with the ethical beliefs of its members. To this end, the authors surveyed public accountants, questioning them about the AICPA's "Code of Professional Conduct" and their perceptions of how potentially unethical behaviors impact the firm. The paper focuses on respondents' perceptions of the impact on the firm's practice, image and degree of concern. (edited)

Kapferer, Norbert. *Das Feindbild der marxistisch-leninistischen Philosophie in der DDR 1945-1988*. Darmstadt, Wiss Buchgesell, 1990.

The history of the rise and fall of Marxist-Leninist philosophy in the "Soviet zone" (1945-1948) and in the "German Democratic Republic" (1949-1988) including the main ideological controversies about the philosophical enemy (Feindbild) like "Romantic Philosophy", "Philosophy of Life" (Friedrich Nietzsche) "Hermeneutic Philosophy" (Dilthey) "Phenomenology", Existentialism (Heidegger-Jaspers-Sartre), Positivism and Critical Rationalism (Popper), Psychoanalyse (Freud) and the "Revisionism" (Bloch, Lukacs, Havemann, Harich). Also documented are the "Stalinist campaignes" against modern art, literature and experimental theatre (Brecht) from 1948/49 till 1956.

Kapitan, Tomis. Double's *The Non-Reality of Free Will*. *Nous*, 28(1), 90-95, Mr 94.

In the *Non-Reality of Free Will* (Oxford 1991) Richard Double provides a number of considerations designed to cast doubt upon the coherence and applicability of the concepts of moral responsibility and free will. I argue that Double's argumentation is insufficient, that both libertarians and compatibilists have the resources for replying to his points, and, consequently, that he has not done enough to justify the skeptical position he advances.

Kaplan, Andrew. Conversing With Other Minds: A Symposium of Themes. *Phil Rhet*, 28(2), 105-121, 1995.

The conversation we enter in order to understand and participate in the modern world is polyphonic: we form our identity in a community of cultures. Yet the vast amounts of information that the modern world makes available seem to frustrate our best efforts to grasp what is essential. We wouldn't enhance conversation even if we could master all the subjects that the rage for specialization has multiplied so fervently. But if we turn our attention to themes, we seek the connections of subjects that illuminate culture as a shared continuity. The modern symposium concerns not drinking together but living together.

Kaplan, Bonnie. The Computer Prescription: Medical Computing, Public Policy, and Views of History. *Sci Tech Human Values*, 20(1), 5-38, Wint 95.

This article traces past trends and current developments in medical computing in the United States. It suggests a link between shifts in emphases in medical computing and in federal government policy toward health care delivery. The development of medical computing was not driven solely by the internal imperatives of science and technology, but by dreams and visions of how computers could revolutionize medicine. Such dreams and visions constitute a mythical charter similar to ideologies and rhetoric used to mobilize support by other computerization movements. This mythical charter influenced development of medical computing by tying computing in medicine to policy goals. This charter also affected historical accounts in medical computing, which are characterized by technological determinism and evidence of cognitive dissonance due to failure to achieve policy goals.

Kaplan, David. From Ontology to Text in *Being and Time*. *Conference*, 3(2), 76-88, Fall 92.

Heidegger's claim in *Being and Time* that the locus of truth cannot be in an assertion, which is derivative of discourse, privileges speech over writing. Because writing is derivative of discourse it hinders the project of fundamental ontology, and leads to inauthentic understanding. Ricouer's conception of discourse in *Interpretation Theory* includes both speech and writing. There he shows how written discourse extends and includes both speech and writing. There he shows how written discourse extends and preserves communication in ways that spoken discourse cannot. The issue is the relationship between experience and its inscription in writing. The thesis of this paper is that the two imply one another, that fundamental ontology completes itself in Ricoeur's conception of discourse, while discourse presupposes and emerges out from Dasein's disclosure of being. Early Kaplan.

Kaplan, David B. "A Problem in Possible-World Semantics" in *Modality, Morality, and Belief, Sinnott-Armstrong, Walter (ed)*, 41-52. New York, Cambridge Univ Pr, 1994.

Kaplan, Laura Duhan. Teaching as Applied Philosophy. *Teach Phil*, 17(1), 5-16, Mr 94.

Ernest L Boyer has defined "scholarship" as the discovery, integration, application, and teaching of knowledge. I suggest that the teaching of philosophy provides us with opportunities to advance the scholarships of discovery, integration and application. An argument by example shows that the teaching of philosophy provides opportunities to advance the three types of scholarship in the fields of political philosophy, epistemology, and feminist theory. Conversely, the argument also shows that research in these three areas of philosophy provides resources for the evaluation and improvement of teaching.

Kaplan, Mark. Believing the Improbable. *Phil Stud*, 77(1), 117-146, Ja 95.

Can I reasonably believe the claim that everything I believe is true? Most think not, on the grounds that the claim is manifestly improbable. But is it really the case that, once I acknowledge that a claim is highly improbable, I cannot rationally believe it true? Only on an entirely untenable conception of belief—or so I argue. I offer in its place another account of belief and its rational pursuit that shows, within a broadly Bayesian framework, how (among other things) believing the truth of ambitious (and, hence, improbable) theories can be entirely rational.

Kaplan, Morris B. Philosophy, Sex and Gender: Mutual Interrogations. *Metaphilosophy*, 25(4), 293-303, O 94.

Kapus, Jerry. The Liar and the Prosentential Theory of Truth. *Log Anal*, 34, 283-291, S-D 91.

According to the prosentential theory of truth, the Liar paradox can be resolved by treating 'true' as a constituent of a prosentence rather than as a property ascribing predicate. In the first half of this article, I briefly explicate the proposed prosentential resolution of the Liar paradox. In the second half, I present an example which shows that the prosentential treatment of the Liar is open to the objection that the paradox has not been resolved, but rather relocated.

Karakostas, Vassilios and Dickson, Michael. Decoherence in Unorthodox Formulations of Quantum Mechanics. *Synthese*, 102(1), 61-96, Ja 95.

The conceptual structure of orthodox quantum mechanics has not provided a fully satisfactory and coherent description of natural phenomena. With particular attention to the measurement problem, we review and investigate two unorthodox formulations. First, there is the model advanced by GRWP, a stochastic modification of the standard Schrödinger dynamics admitting statevector reduction as a real physical process. Second, there is the ontological interpretation of Bohm, a causal reformulation of the usual theory admitting no collapse of the statevector. Within these two seemingly quite different approaches, we discuss in a comparative manner, several points: The meaning of the state vector, the status of quantum probability, the legitimacy of attributing macro objective properties to physical systems, and the possibility of retrieving the classical limit. Finally, we consider aspects on non-locality and relevant difficulties with formulating a relativistic generalization of the two approaches.

Karger, Élizabeth. Théories de la pensée, de ses objets et de son discours chez Guillaume d'Occam. *Dialogue (Canada)*, 33(3), 437-456, Sum 94.

Karkama, Pertti. "Friedrich Schiller als Ästhetiker der (Post)Moderne" in *Das geistige Erbe Europas, Buhr, Manfred (ed)*, 321-333. Napoli, Vivarium, 1994.

The purpose of the article is to show that the aesthetic problems discussed in the postmodern theory have their theoretical roots in the idealistic German aesthetics. Especially Friedrich Schiller's notion of the *aesthetic space* ("der ästhetische Zustand") seems to be worth noticing. The aesthetic space, purified from all previous ideological meanings, is in reality a process of inner speech in which new meanings and new concepts take shape. It shows up the dialectical dynamic relation between space and time. Schiller's theories, interpreted in a new way, could serve the re-evaluation of the problems in the seemingly unistorical postmodern cultural situation.

Karl, Gregory and Robinson, Jenefer. Levinson on Hope in *The Hebrides*. *J Aes Art Crit*, 53(2), 195-199, Spr 95.

Karlqvist, Anders (ed) and Haken, Hermann (ed) and Svedin, Uno (ed). *The Machine as Metaphor and Tool*. New York, Springer-Verlag, 1993.

Karni, Edi. The Impossibility of Experimental Elicitation of Subjective Probabilities. *Theor Decis*, 38(3), 313-320, My 95.

We show that if decision makers may have stakes in certain events then the experimental elicitation of their subjective probabilities of these events is impossible.

Karpenko, Alexander S. Sheffer's Stroke for Prime Numbers. *Bull Sec Log*, 23(3), 126-129, O 94.

From results of V K Finn (1970), H E Hendry (1983) and A Urquhart (1986) it follows that Lukasiewicz's many-valued logic L_{n+1} has the pure number theoretical nature, that is, L_{n+1} is functionally precomplete if and only if n is a prime number. Given paper the author discovers Sheffer's stroke for precomplete Lukasiewicz logics, that is, some function f is Sheffer's stroke for Ln+1 if and only if L_{n+1} is precomplete logic. Given sense this function f is Sheffer's stroke for prime numbers. From Lemma 2 under some assumptions it is possible to obtain the interesting result: the iteration of formula (6) produces the law of prime numbers generating. The detailed proof of Lemmas and Theorems has been published in: Logical Investigations, vol 3 (1995). Moscow (Russian).

Karu, George. Epistemic Justification and the Possibility of Empirical Evidence. *J Indian Counc Phil Res*, 12(1), 29-48, S-D 94.

This paper is an attempt to clarify certain fundamental confusions that bedevil the concept of epistemological justification. I argue that if the epistemic goal is to settle cognitive disputes, then the object of justification must be propositional and the process intersubjective. While the former rules out considerations related to the person of the believer from the domain of epistemology, the latter rules out phenomenal considerations as evidence. Can we have such evidence which is experiential and yet nonphenomenal? After an initial exploration, this question is tentatively answered in the affirmative.

Karvalics, László Z. The Peace of the Soul...(Harmonizing Techniques in the World-religions). *Magyar Filozof Szemle*, 5-6, 591-616, 1994.

The author investigates the fundamental (internal) teachings of the selected world religions as techniques of harmony-creating. He shows that the structure and logic of Hinduism, Buddhism, Confucianism, Taoism, Christianity and Islam are more different than the traditional typologies described that, and than they seem from their formal and external features. These religions have really original solutions: the paper emphasizes this originality, and also tries to find some relevant new aspects of connections and similarities among them.

Kasachkoff, Tziporah. Toleration and Moral Compromise. *Filozof Istraz*, 14(2-3), 295-323, 1994.

The paper aims at coming to an understanding of tolerance and moral compromise and the relationship between the two, and in particular at answering the following questions: Why is acting tolerantly and making compromises each regarded sometimes as a virtue, sometimes as a moral failing? What is the relationship betweeen being tolerant and intolerant and being willing and unwilling to make moral compromises? When does acting tolerantly amount to making a morally illegitimate compromise? (edited)

Kasprisin, Lorraine. "Ideas of Self and Community" in *Identity, Culture, and Education, Smeyers, Paul (ed)*, 161-170. Leuven, Leuven Univ Pr, 1994.

Kastin, Jonathan. The Logic of Fictional Descriptions. *Conference*, 4(2), 16-30, Fall 93.

This paper presents a theory of truth in fiction. Three other such theories—due to John Searle, David Lewis, and Steven Ross—are considered, but found inadequate. The present author draws on Arnold Koslow's structuralist theory of logic, presenting an account according to which each fictional work provides a recipe for the construction of an implication structure—the 'world of the novel'. Truth in a fiction f is then just the appropriate truth operator, relativized to the implication structure generated by f.

Kasulis, Thomas P. Sushi, Science, and Spirituality: Modern Japanese Philosophy and Its Views of Western Science. *Phil East West*, 45(2), 227-248, Ap 95.

Kato, Motoaki. Plato on Self-Predication of "the fine"—*Hippias Major* 292, e6-7. *Bigaku*, 45(4), 12-22, Spr 95.

In Plato's *Hippias Major* 292e6-7, we can find a self-predication sentence; "The fine is always fine." (We have similar expressions in *Protagoras* 330c4-6, 330d8-el, *Lysis* 220b6-7.) How should we interpret this sentence? We cannot give it any metaphysical meaning drawn from Plato's own theory of Form, which is explicit in his middle dialogues. "The fine" here should be the logical cause, not the one of the metaphysical essentials (cf. Paul Woodruff's *Plateo Hippias Major*, p. 150). So taking a sentence like "parthenos kalê kalon" (287e4), we can safely paraphrase it in Woodruff's manner: "a fine girl is a fine thing." This can avoid reading the metaphysical meaning into the text. And I would like to make a new proposal for reading of 292e6-7: "the fine thing is what is to be called fine." This is to emphasize the unique character of the self-predication sentences in the early dialogues. In the Socratic way of discourse, Socrates and his partner get involved into "trial and error" during their pursuit of the knowledge. What they can do then is to give their opinions which seem to them true (so-called " alêthês doxa", cf. *Meno* 85c), and to get close examinations of them. And in this way they are getting closer to the knowledge. My interpretation well describes these activities.

Kattago, Siobhan. Judgement and Intersubjectivity in Kant and Habermas's Ethics. *Conference*, 5(2), 43-58, Wint 94-95.

In a narrow interpretation, Habermas's discourse ethics results in a necessary idealization, leaving little room for conflict and moral judgement because the ideal speech situation is unable to represent a differentiated moral point of view which both reasons in abstract situations and is reasonable in concrete political situations. In an expansive interpretation, Habermas's discourse ethics is examined in light of the enlarged mentality found in Hannah Arendt's interpretation of Kant's Third Critique. It is my claim that Arendt's interpretation of the *sensus communis* suggests a modest yet worldy intersubjectivity which is compatible with an expansive interpretation of Habermas's communicative ethics.

Katz, Bernard D. Making Comparisons. *Mind*, 104(414), 369-392, Ap 95.

This paper sets out an account of the logical form of comparatives, such as "taller" and "as tall as". The paper argues that the standard representation in quantification theory of the comparative form of an attributive adjective like "tall" as an unstructured two-place predicate is unsatisfactory and proposes an analysis that takes as basic the relative form displayed in a sentence such as "Alfred is 6 feet tall". It is argued—against Quine and Davidson—that a term such as "6 feet" in "Alfred is 6 feet tall" must be taken as referring to a particular height, rather than simply a number, and accordingly, that the range of the relation underlying the analysis of "taller" and "as tall as" should be taken as a domain of quantities, rather than numbers.

Katz, Claire Elise. The Neglected Alternative in Kant's Philosophy Revisited. *SW Phil Rev*, 11(1), 91-100, Ja 95.

The neglected alternative is the view that appearances as spatio-temporal, do not preclude the possibility that things in themselves are also spatio-temporal. Kant stated that space and time are forms of intuition and as such can only apply to appearances. Lorne Falkenstein, who agrees with Kant's conclusion, offers a more comprehensive account than past arguments (e.g., Henry Allison's) against the possibility of space and time applying to things in themselves. My paper explores Allison's and Falkenstein's arguments and questions Falkenstein's charge that the previous arguments, in particular Allison's and Kant's own argument, are insufficient.

Katz, Claudio. The Greek Matrix of Marx's Critique of Political Economy. *Hist Polit Thought*, 15(2), 229-248, Sum 94.

Katz, Jerrold J. What Mathematical Knowledge Could Be. *Mind*, 104(415), 491-522, Jl 95.

Katzoff, Charlotte and Widerker, David. Zimmerman on Moral Responsibility, Obligation and Alternate Possibilities. *Analysis*, 54(4), 285-287, O 94.

In "Obligation, Responsibility and Alternate Possibilities", (*Analysis*, 53, 1993, 51-53) Michael Zimmerman rejects the alleged link between the Kantian principle that "ought" implies "can" and the Principle of Alternate Possibilities as applied to moral blame, argued for by Widerker in 'Frankfurt on "Ought Implies Can" and Alternative Possibilities', (*Analysis*, 51, 1991, 222-224). We show that the principle upon which Zimmerman bases his argument—that one's blameworthiness for an action is a function of what one believes one's obligations to be—is false.

Kaufman, Frederik. An Answer to Lucretius' Symmetry Argument Against the Fear of Death. *J Value Inq*, 29(1), 57-64, Mr 95.

A plausible response to Epicurus' claim that death is no evil is to suggest that it is an evil of deprivation. Death deprives a person of the goods of life that person otherwise would have. But a supporter of this position must confront Lucretius' symmetry argument. The symmetry argument purports to show that if death deprives a person of time that person otherwise would have, then so does birth; for the time prior to birth is also time which, had a person not been born as late as he or she was, that person would have lived. I defend the view that while it is possible for someone to live longer than he or she actually does, it is impossible for that person to be born earlier than he or she was. This entails that death can be deprivation but birth cannot.

Kaufman, Michael (ed) and Brod, Harry (ed). *Theorizing Masculinities*. Newbury Park, Sage, 1994.

Kaufmann, Walter. "Nietzsche's Attitude toward Socrates" in *Nietzsche: A Critical Reader, Sedgwick, Peter R (ed)*, 123-143. Cambridge, Blackwell, 1995.

Kaufmann, Walter Arnold. *The Future of the Humanities: Teaching Art, Religion, Philosophy, Literature, and History (New Edition)*. New Brunswick, Transaction Books, 1995.

Kavka, Gregory S. Some Social Benefits of Uncertainty. *Midwest Stud Phil*, 15, 311-326, 1990.

Kavka, Gregory S. The Rationality of Rule-Following: Hobbes's Dispute with the Foole. *Law Phil*, 14(1), 5-34, F 95.

Kaye, Lawrence J. A Scientific Psychologistic Foundation for Theories of Meaning. *Mind Mach*, 5(2), 187-206, My 95.

I propose, develop and defend the view that theories of meaning—for instance, a theory specifying the logical form or truth conditions of natural language sentences—should be naturalized to scientific psychological inquiry. This involves both psychologism—the claim that semantics characterizes psychological states—and scientific naturalism—the claim that semantics will depend on the data and theories of scientific psychology. I argue that scientific psychologism is more plausible than the traditional alternative, the view that a theory of meaning is a priori. After defending scientific psychologism against several objections, I offer a speculative proposal that shows how a theory of meaning can be integrated into scientific psychology.

Kaye, Lawrence J. The Languages of Thought. *Phil Sci*, 62(1), 92-110, Mr 95.

I critically explore various forms of the language of thought (LOT) hypothesis. Many considerations, including the complexity of representational content and the systematicity of language understanding, support the view that some, but not all, of our mental representations occur in language. I examine several arguments concerning sententialism and the propositional attitudes, Fodor's arguments concerning infant and animal thought, and Fodor's argument for radical concept nativism and show that none of these considerations require us to postulate a LOT that is innate or otherwise distinct from spoken languages. Instead, I suggest that we maintain the more conservative hypothesis, supported by introspection, that some of our thoughts occur in the languages that we speak.

Kazez, Jean. Can Counterfactuals Save Mental Causation?. *Austl J Phil*, 73(1), 71-90, Mr 95.

The "counterfactual strategy" has been employed by a number of philosophers (e.g., Heil and Mele, Lepore and Loewer, and Horgan) to defend the causal efficacy of content. I argue that the promise this strategy appears to hold is illusory. First, the pivotal counterfactuals simply aren't true. Second, the counterfactual analysis of causal-explanatory relevance conflicts with common sense and scientific conceptions of explanation. I argue that Mill's method of differences provides an alternative test for the explanatory relevance of content—a test that content fails.

Keagy, Tom and Drozdek, Adam. A Case for Realism in Mathematics. *Monist*, 77(3), 329-344, Jl 94.

The paper takes issue with anti-realist position in philosophy of mathematics, which denies an existence of mathematical entities independent of the cognitive subject. Anti-realism has appeared in various forms, and some of the arguments are discussed (Brouwer, Kitcher, Machover). The paper opts for realism and gives both philosophical arguments substantiating this position and an example of mathematical proof which was possible only due to the realist view (the proof concerns a transform of Levin to be used in approximating the limit of a sequence).

Kearney, Richard. *Poetics of Modernity: Toward a Hermeneutic Imagination*. Atlantic Highlands, Humanities Pr, 1995.

Poetics of Modernity addresses one of the central issues of modern European thought—how the crisis of values (ethics) relates to the crisis of imagination (poetics). Through a series of in-depth studies of thinkers such as Kierkegaard, Husserl, Heidegger, Levinas, Ricoeur, Derrida and others, the author explores the ways in which continental philosophy, in both its modern and postmodern guises, has endeavoured to respond to these twin crises. Some studies focus on the dilemma of individual imagination faced with the fragmentation of inherited concepts of truth, God, and the good. Others concentrate on conflicts internal to the social imagination of our times—e.g., ideology versus utopia, myth versus critique, tradition versus reason, modernity versus postmodernity. The author also applies these philosophical disputes to literature and painting.

Kearns, Paul. The Opening up of Natural Law. *Vera Lex*, 13(1-2), 43-45, 1993.

Keat, Russell. Citizens, Consumers and the Environment: Reflections on *The Economy of the Earth*. *Environ Values*, 3(4), 333-349, Wint 94.

This paper presents a critical evaluation of Mark Sagoff's critique of economistic approaches to environmental decision-making in *The Economy of the Earth*. Whilst endorsing many of Sagoff's specific arguments against the use of extended versions of cost-benefit analysis in making such decisions, it criticizes the conceptual framework within which these arguments are developed. In particular, it suggests that what Sagoff represents as a tension between consumers and their public roles as citizens is better understood as one between culturally shared values concerning both the protection of nature and the pursuit of consumption; and that this conflict has itself to be resolved by them as citizens.

Keating, Bernard. Éthique de la mort et droit à la mort: A propos d'un livre récent. *Laval Theol Phil*, 50(3), 651-656, O 94.

Kebede, Messay. *Meaning and Development*. Amsterdam, Rodopi, 1994.

This book is a learned yet passionate critique of alternative theories of development as addressed to traditional societies. It offers a forceful argument for sacrifice to be made in the name of moral faith. The metaphysical grounds and the scientific verification for such a faith are explored. An eloquent and original case for pursuing economic development in accordance with democracy and human dignity.

Kedourie, Elie. *Hegel and Marx: Introductory Lectures*. Cambridge, Blackwell, 1995.

Kedourie, Elie. *Nationalism (Fourth, Expanded Edition)*. Cambridge, Blackwell, 1993.

Kee, Howard Clark. "Weber Revisited" in *Meaning, Truth, and God, Rouner, Leroy (ed)*, 112-134. Notre Dame, Univ Notre Dame Pr, 1982.

Keeley, Michael. Continuing the Social Contract Tradition. *Bus Ethics Quart*, 5(2), 241-255, Ap 95.

Social contract theory has a rich history. It originated among the ancients with recognition that social arrangements were not products of nature but convention. It developed through the centuries as theorists sought ethical criteria for distinguishing good conventions from bad. The search for such ethical criteria continues in recent attempts to apply social contract theory to organizations. In this paper, I question the concept of consent as a viable ethical criterion, and I argue for an alternate principle of impartiality as a more appropriate moral norm in a social contract theory of organizations.

Keeley, Michael. The Trouble with Transformational Leadership: Toward a Federalist Ethic for Organizations. *Bus Ethics Quart*, 5(1), 67-96, Ja 95.

Popular media, communitarian writings, and recent management literature suggest that communities and organizations are rent by factional mischief: by individuals and groups who pursue their own selfish interests without regard for the common good. An emerging solution to this problem is "transformational" leadership, which seeks to refocus individuals' attention on higher visions and collective goals. The dangers of such a solution were identified by James Madison at the Constitutional Convention of 1787; and mechanisms to thwart it were designed into the framers' system of government. This article examines Madison's objections and the implications of his political theory for the leadership of modern organizations.

Keeling, L Bryant and Haugen, David. Hartshorne's Process Theism and Big Bang Cosmology. *Process Stud*, 22(3), 163-171, Fall 93.

We attempt to establish a dilemma for Charles Hartshorne's process theism. We argue that if the general picture of the universe presented by the big bang theory is accepted, then Harshorne must abandon either the concept of God as perfectly preserving the past (divine memory) or he must abandon the attempt to explain God's relation to the world in terms of psychicalism.

Kegley, Jacquelyn A K. "Too Thin a Self, Too Small a Human" in *Contributors to the Philosophy of Humanism, Hillar, Marian (ed)*, 31-42. Pasadena, Humanists Houston, 1994.

This argues that philosophy has operated too long with thin and reductionistic views of self and human person, views inadequate to deal with the complex issues of selfhood and personhood raised by technological advances in genetics and psycho-technologies as well as those quandries posed by increased acts of physical/mental/social violence against persons. A view of "self" and "person" is explored which emphasizes creative and crucial interactions between self and nature, self and body, self and others, and individual self and communal self.

Keita, Lansana. "La Vraie Face de la Démocratie": A Note. *Quest*, 8(1), 97-103, Je 94.

Keith, William. Artificial Intelligence, Feminist and Otherwise. *Soc Epistem*, 8(4), 333-340, O-D 94.

After critiquing J Genova's gender analysis of the Turing test, this paper advances an original argument for understanding the material and cultural role of gender in artificial intelligence.

Kélessidou, Anna. Du Parfait et de l'Un. Connexions Entre les Pensées Plotinienne et Dionysienne. *Diotima*, 23, 31-35, 1995.

While the Neoplatonism of Dionysius was not that of Plotinus, some assertions, about the first and supreme principle, the Divine One, included in Pionysius' chapter XIII of the *Divine Names*, recall—directly or indirectly—Plotinus' teaching about the One. It is possible to make a parallelism concerning the connections between the One and the many, the One and the Being, the One and the number, the One and the Logos.

Kélessidou, Anna. Du Parfait et de l'Un. Sur Quelques Connexions de la Pensée Plotinienne et de la Théologie de Denys. *Philosophia (Athens)*, 23-24, 326-332, 1993-94.

Les interprètes du chapitre 13 "Du parfait et de l'Un" de l'Oeuvre de Denis l'Aréopagite, *Desnoms divins*, renvoient de manière implicite ou explicite à la pensée du maître du néoplatonisme. Le rapport entre Denis et Plotin ne porte pas sur l'influence directe entre les deux penseurs, mais sur ceraines orientations philosophiques parallèles. Les rapports ici en question sont: 1) Rapport de l'un et du multiple; 2) De l'un et de l'être; 3) De l'un et du nombre; 4) De l'un et du nom.

Kélessidou, Anna. La vie et la Mort Selon Platon et Plotin. *Philosophia (Athens)*, 23-24, 164-171, 1993-94.

L'étude de la doctrine platonicienne et de mystique plotinienne concernant la vie et la mort est un travail infini. Certains passages des *Dialogues* et des *Ennéades*, permettent l'accès à l'enseignément du "divin" Platon et de son "exegète" Plotin, et ils manifestent l'optimisme platonicien—qui consiste à une dynamique et axiologie ontologique—, et l'idéal de conversion à l'Un selon la mystique plotinienne.

Kélessidou, Anna. Plotin et la Thèse de L'incorruptibilité du Monde. *Philosophia (Athens)*, 23-24, 320-324, 1993-94.

Selon Plotin l'avenir du monde est tracé par son passé: le monde n'a jamais commencé, en conséquence, il ne finira jamais. Plotin met l'accent sur la cosmogénèse du *Timée* platonicien ainsi que sur l'enseignément aristotélicien du monde, qu'il interprète sans les déformer. La thèse plotinienne de l'incorruptibilité du monde n'est pas en corrélation avec la nature de celui-ci, mais avec l'âme immortelle qui gouverne l'univers.

Kelkar, Ashok R. Language as Empowerment. *Indian Phil Quart*, 22(1), 25-40, Ja 95.

Language has power (Latin *potentia*) to mediate understanding so long as the bond between words and meanings is secure. Language faculty manifests as language learning and language learning as interior monologue, addressed monologue, or dialogue. Language always conveys power (Latin *auctoritas*) in communicating meanings within power space and, with moral acceptance, polity. Access to language (or its lack) can affect power relationships of authority and subjection. Better control of language means better power play. Stagnation or inauthenticity, mystification or demystification, diversity and uniformity, monologic or dialogic use could variously affect power play at shallower or even deeper levels.

Kellenberger, J. *Relationship Morality*. University Park, Penn St Univ Pr, 1995.

Relationship morality develops the thesis that all of morality, from obligations to virtues, rests upon relationships between persons, including the person/person relationship, which persons have to persons by virtue of being persons. It also argues that among morality types—such as guilt and shame morality—relationship morality better accommodates our moral experience. How relationship morality can respect the strengths of a feminist ethic of care is brought out, as is the continuity between a human relationship morality and a religious relationship-to-God morality, and as are the implications of relationship morality for an intuitively acceptable account of animal rights.

Keller, Evelyn Fox. "Der Diskurs über Gen-Tätigkeit" in *Mythos Wertfreiheit?, Apel, Karl-Otto (ed)*, 301-318. Frankfurt, Campus Verlag, 1994.

Keller, James A. The Hiddenness of God and the Problem of Evil. *Int J Phil Relig*, 37(1), 13-24, F 95.

Most people, including most theists, admit that the existence, nature, and will of God are not clear to them. In light of other things theists say about God, this unclarity, which I refer to as the *hiddenness of God*, constitutes a problem which has close relations to the problem of evil. In this paper I discuss and assess variations on three sorts of explanations which theists propose for the hiddenness of God: divine transcendence, human defectiveness, and the appropriateness of divine hiddenness. I argue that none of them are adequate, and I suggest another explanation.

Kellerwessel, Wulf. *Referenztheorien in der analytischen Philosophie*. Stuttgart, Frommann-Holzboog, 1995.

The study describes the analytical theories of reference as completely as possible. It examines them critically and tries to develop a new theory of reference on the basis of the obtained results. It contains chapters dealing with the theories of G Frege, B Russell, P T Geach, G Ryle, P F Strawson, J R Searle, L Wittgenstein, P Ziff, W V O Quine, K S Donnellan, S A Kripke, H Putnam and J J Katz. The critical judgment of these theories leads to the conclusion that one could raise arguments against each of them. Therefore, the author proposes a new semantic *and* pragmatic approach.

Kellner, Douglas and Antonio, Robert J. "The Future of Social Theory and the Limits of Postmodern Critique" in *Postmodernism and Social Inquiry, Dickens, David R (ed)*, 127-152. New York, Guilford, 1994.

This essay addresses postmodern criticism of modern social theory, and especially its relevance for later nineteenth and early twentieth century theories with a sociological and historical thrust. We explore "critical" and "dogmatic" features of these approaches and argue that some of their most central critical themes anticipated postmodern criticism. We contend that postmodernists contribute to advancing a critique of enlightenment that began in modern theory, but, in their effort to shed the tradition's dogmatic elements, they also abandon its critical "social" resources stressing interdependence, cooperation, and solidarity. We conclude with a discussion of postmodernism and critical theory.

Kellner, Douglas M. "The End of Orthodox Marxism" in *Marxism in the Postmodern Age, Callari, Antonio (ed)*, 33-41. New York, Guilford, 1994.

I argue that the collapse of communism portends the end of orthodox Marxism, but *not* the obsolescence of the Marxian theory. I indicate the differences between classical Marxian theory and Marxism-Leninism and argue that Marx's ideas continue to be relevant for the critique of capitalism and democratization of contemporary societies.

Kellner, Douglas M. "The Obsolescence of Marxism?" in *Whither Marxism?, Magnus, Bernd (ed)*, 3-30. New York, Routledge, 1994.

Against theories which claim that the collapse of communism portend the bankruptcy and obsolescence of Marxism, I argue that these events primarily point to the obsolescence of a version of orthodox Marxism, known as Marxism-Leninism or Stalinism. I argue that classical Marxism provides resources for explaining precisely the failure of communism in the Soviet Union and Soviet bloc and that Marxism also provides resources for critiques of Western so-called capitalist democracies. Thus, I claim that Marxism is not obsolete but continues to contain resources for theory and politics in the present age.

Kellner, Douglas M (ed). *Baudrillard: A Critical Reader*. Cambridge, Blackwell, 1994.

Baudrillard: A Critical Reader contains a series of original studies of the significance of one of the most important theorist's and cultural critics of the contemporary era. Douglas Kellner's introduction makes a case for considering Baudrillard as one of the foremost theorists of the postmodern turn and other contributors connect Baudrillard's thought to Marxism, Debord and French situationism, Habermas, Simmel, McLuhan, and other forms of critical theory. Studies also interrogate Baudrillard's investigations of commodities, media, advertising, fashion, cybernetics, war, and modernist and postmodernist art. The collections closes with some philosophical explorations of Baudrillard's thought.

Kelly, Andrew. Reciprocity and the Height of God: A Defence of Buber Against Levinas. *Sophia (Australia)*, 34(1), 65-73, Mr-Ap 95.

Kelly, Charles J. Circularity and Amphiboly in Some Anselmian Ontological Proofs: A Syllogistic Inquiry. *Nous*, 28(4), 482-504, D 94.

Kelly, John C. Wittgenstein, the Self, and Ethics. *Rev Metaph*, 48(3), 567-590, Mr 95.

Kelly, Kevin and Juhl, Cory and Glymour, Clark. "Reliability, Realism, and Relativism" in *Reading Putnam, Clark, Peter (ed)*, 98-160. Cambridge, Blackwell, 1995.

Kelly, Kevin T and Juhl, Cory. Realism, Convergence, and Additivity. *Proc Phil Sci Ass*, 1, 181-189, 1994.

In this paper, we argue for the centrality of countable additivity to realist claims about the convergence of science to the truth. In particular, we show how classical sceptical arguments can be revived when countable additivity is dropped.

Kelly, Michael. Humanism and Unity. *Hist Euro Ideas*, 20(4-6), 923-928, F 95.

Kelly, Michaeleen J. Rights and Power: A Feminist Rethinking of Liberal Rights. *J Soc Phil*, 25(2), 73-88, Fall 94.

Kemp, Gary. Salmon on Fregean Approaches to the Paradox of Analysis. *Phil Stud*, 78(2), 153-162, My 95.

Frege's anti-psychologism and related Context Principle suggest a certain view of what it is to think *about* a thought, which in turn suggests a certain compositional treatment of the operation of forming thought-names. This treatment is used to show that, in opposition to Nathan Salmon, Frege does have a consistent (and cogent) solution to the paradox of analysis.

Kemp, Gary. The Status of Expressive Content. *Brit J Aes*, 35(2), 121-133, Ap 95.

The starting point is Nelson Goodman's claim that an artwork expresses X only if X metaphorically denotes it. This is detached from Goodman's general aesthetics, independently supported and clarified, and shown to imply that the ascription of expressive properties is based upon aspect-perception, or seeing-as. This leads to the claim that ascriptions of expressive properties can be held to acquire truth-values only if an appeal is made to the artist's intention. A brief comparison is made with an argument due to Phillip Petit on this point.

Kemp, Peter. "Ethics and Narrativity" in *The Philosophy of Paul Ricoeur, Hahn, Lewis Edwin (ed)*, 371-394. Peru, Open Court, 1994.

Selon l'ouvrage de Paul Ricoeur: *Temps et récit* le temps ne devient pensable que comme raconté. Alors se pose la question suivante: quel est l'enqeu *éthique* de la narrativité du temps. L'auteur cherche à dépister le rôle de l'éthique dans la poétique du temps que développe Ricoeur lorsqu'il décrit l'activité mimétique qui fait mettre en intrigue le récit et qui implique son rapport au temps par sa préfiguration (précompréhension), sa configuration (formation du texte) et sa réfiguration (effet du texte).

Kemp, Peter. La crainte pour autrui. *Philosophica*, 52(2), 49-61, 1993.

Following the original greek signification of the word ethos, ethics means the home where we live together. Thus the moral rule is established to protect the good life and not to create it. The fundamental feeling founding this protection is considered: it cannot be the anxiety as it has been analyzed by Heidegger to whom anxiety only concerns my own existence, but must be the worrying about the other as Levinas has described it.

Kendall, Timothy J G. Commentary on "Beyond Liberation". *Phil Psychiat Psych*, 2(1), 15-17, Mr 95.

This work is a commentary on a paper outlining Michel Foucault's critique of Psychiatry and 'Anti-Psychiatry'. Foucault's philosophy is outlined succinctly and its relevance for a critical understanding of involuntary *and* voluntary patients is described.

Kendeffy, Gábor. Diaphonia: A Sceptical Argument at the Fathers of Church in the 2-3rd Centuries. *Magyar Filozof Szemle*, 1-2, 47-70, 1994.

Au sens plus restreint, l'argument de *diaphonie* est basé sur les contradictions entre les opinions des philosophes particuliers, au sens plus large sur la diversité extréme entre les façons de vivre, moeurs, lois, croyances mythiques et, enfin, opinions philosophiques différentes. Même dans le sens restreint, l'argument a deux présentations fondamentales. L'une, disons, dynamique, laquelle se trouve dans les *Académiques* de Cicéron, est inserée dans une situation dramaturgique, celle du choix entre les écoles différentes, présentée du point de vue du commençant, bien confus en face du désaccord extréme. Manque d'un critère valide de choix,—dit Cicéron—c'est à l'autorité de quelq' un, soit à la foi, qu'on peut s'appuyer. L'autre présentation de l'argument, purement descriptive et statique, se trouve plutôt dans les sources néopyrrhoniennes, fréquemment comme un des tropes sceptiques. (edited)

Kennaway, Richard (& others). From Finite to Infinite Lambda Calculi. *Bull Sec Log*, 24(1), 13-20, Mr 95.

In a previous paper we have established the theory of transfinite reduction for orthogonal term rewriting systems. In this paper we perform the same task for the lambda calculus. This results in several new Böhm models of the lambda calculus, and new unifying descriptions of existing models.

Kenny, Anthony (ed) and Wittgenstein, Ludwig. *The Wittgenstein Reader*. Cambridge, Blackwell, 1994.

Kent, Bonnie. Moral Provincialism. *Relig Stud*, 30(3), 269-285, S 94.

Kent, Theodore C. *Mapping the Human Genome: Reality, Morality, and Deity*. Lanham, Univ Pr of America, 1995.

This book examines the new field of genetic engineering and addresses the troubling questions about nature and morality that it brings. Kent warns that while gene technology offers great opportunities, it also raises questions that science cannot and should not answer alone. (edited)

Keown, John. Euthanasia in the Netherlands: Sliding Down the Slippery Slope?. *Notre Dame J Law Ethics*, 9(2), 407-448, 1995.

Kerfoot, Deborah and Knights, David. "Into the Realm of the Fearful: Power, Identity and the Gender Problematic" in *Power/Gender, Radtke, H Lorraine (ed)*, 67-88. Newbury Park, Sage, 1994.

This chapter is concerned to explore 'gender differentiation', defined as the social construction of sexual difference: how sex-based specificities come to be maintained rather than from what point of origin women's oppression emanates. Our purpose is twofold; to offer an account of how the division of labor has remained so stable, within the context of a discussion of gender and sexuality; and, following Game (1991:36) a second purpose is to begin to address the question 'how are we constituted now, and how might we be otherwise, *now*?." Informed by a reading of Foucault, it is our contention that a conception of power and its operation provides as escape from what we regard as the dualistic thinking of many radicals and Marxist feminists, and may lead us toward an understanding of how sex inequality and male dominance are perpetuated.

Kern, Iso. The Foundation of Ethics in Late Confucianism. *Tijdschr Filosof*, 57(1), 51-66, Mr 95.

Concerning the foundation of ethics, three different types of theories may be distinguished inside the Confucian tradition. A first type considers ethical rules as necessary for a harmonious social life and the welfare of man as a social being. A second type sees the foundation of ethics in its correspondence with the cosmical order. For a third type, the original tendencies and demands of the human heart or mind are the roots of ethics. The ethical theory more closely discussed in this paper, and which belongs to the third type, is that of Wang Yangming (1472-1529). In his ethical theory, Wang endorsed first the position of Menicus (fourth and third cent. B.C.) and based ethics on original human tendencies and feelings such as love, sympathy, shame, indignation against injustice, etc. However later he was faced with the problem, of how we are able to distinguish these original good tendencies form egoistic (bad) intentions which also belong to our heart. Wang solves this problem by his new theory of *liang zhi* ("original knowing"). According to this theory, "original knowing" is a kind of immediate consciousness of awareness present in every intention: In every intention we are more or less aware of the ethical quality of this intention, and in acting according to this awareness, this awareness becomes more and more clear and may attain full enlightenment.

Kernohan, Andrew. Rights Against Polluters. *Environ Ethics*, 17(3), 245-257, Fall 95.

When there is only one source of pollution, the language of rights is adequate for justifying solutions to pollution problems. However, pollution is often both a public and an accumulative harm. According to Feinberg, an accumulative harm is a harm to some person brought about by the actions of many people when the action of no single person is sufficient, by itself, to cause the harm. For example, although no single car emits enough exhaust to do any harm, the emissions from many cars can accumulate to an unhealthy level. In this paper, I argue that rights, understood in terms of the will theory of Hart and the interest theories of Lyons and Raz, cannot justify protecting people from public, accumulative harms. I conclude that pollution regulation should focus not on protecting people's rights, but on preventing harm to people's interests.

Kerr, Dale and Stake, Robert. René Magritte, Constructivism, and the Researcher as Interpreter. *Educ Theor*, 45(1), 55-62, Wint 95.

In this brief illustrated paper, we reflect upon the increasing legitimacy of direct interpretation in educational research. We draw upon the paintings of René Magritte, the Belgian surrealist of middle century, to cast the qualitative researcher also as bricoleur and provocateur, providing ingredients and stimulus to personal construction of knowledge by the reader. The responsibility of research becomes less the representation and explanation of phenomena and more the drawing of attention to what is worth pondering. This science is robust not because it can predict and prescribe but because it can develop a gallery of alternative perspectives.

Kerr-Lawson, Angus. Pragmatism and Santayana's Realms. *Bull Santayana Soc*, 12, 17-21, Fall 94.

A partial response to Henry Levinson's claim that Santayana should be read, by and large, as a member of the pragmatist school. It is argued only that Santayana's broad ontological treatment of philosophy in his later years, and his delineation of realms of truth, essence, and spirit, are strongly antithetic to the speculatively narrow focus found in pragmatism.

Kersh, Rogan. Explaining Old Worlds. *Inquiry*, 38(1-2), 83-97, Je 95.

This comment treats each of Spinosa, Flores, and Dreyfus's three subjects—entrepreneurship, democratic activity, and cultivation of solidarity—in turn. Though marred by inattention to moral consequences and an accordingly unjustified meliorism, the authors' insights reaffirm and strengthen a number of convictions obscured in current political-theory debates. In particular, their account of the virtuous citizen, and of a variant of solidarity which grows out of such citizens's activity, deserves recognition. The basic contention that humans are "at their best" when self-consciously engaged in transformative activities is accepted, with the essential *caveat* that such activity can only be sustained for relatively short periods of time by individuals and politics alike.

Kerstetter, Wayne and Tyler, Tom R. Moral Authority in Law and Criminal Justice: Some Reflections on Wilson's *The Moral Sense*. *Crim Just Ethics*, 13(2), 44-53, Sum-Fall 94.

Kersting, Wolfgang. Die Wiederkehr der Tugend: Zur gegenwärtigen Diskussion der politischen Theorie über die moralischen. *Stud Phil (Switzerland)*, 53, 35-56, 1994.

Kersting, Wolfgang. Egalitärer Liberalismus und Unparteilichkeitsethik: Die politische Philosophie Thomas Nagels. *Deut Z Phil*, 43(1), 143-164, 1995.

Kersting, Wolfgang. Probleme der Wirtschaftsethik. *Z Phil Forsch*, 48(3), 350-371, Jl-S 94.

Kervégan, Jean-François. La vie éthique perdue dans ses extrêmes... Scission et réconciliation dans la théorie hégélienne de la *Sittlichkeit*. *Laval Theol Phil*, 51(2), 371-388, Je 95.

Au sein du système hégélien, la doctrine de l'esprit objectif, notamment l'analyse de la *Sittlichkeit*, a connu des remaniements particulièrement importants. Au delà des motifs conjoncturels, ce fait exprime la difficulté qu'il y a à penser les médiations qui organisent cette sphère. La question que pose l'analyse des pathologies de la société civile est celle de la possibilité et des formes d'une réconciliation effective en son sein. Cette réconciliation est présentée comme étant de nature politique: c'est l'État rationnel qui veille à la réconciliation avec elle-même d'une vie éthique < perdue dans ses extrêmes >. Son effectivité suppose néanmoins une garantie méta-politique tacite, celle du *Weltgeist*, voire celle de l'esprit absolu. Ainsi, la philosophie politique hégélienne n'accède à sa signification plénière qu'à la condition de reconnaître son incomplétude.

Kesselring, Thomas. A Comparison between Evolutionary and Genetic Epistemology or: Jean Piaget's Contribution to a Post-Darwinian Epistemology. *J Gen Phil Sci*, 25(2), 293-325, 1994.

The viewpoint of evolutionary epistemology (EE) and of genetic epistemology (GE) on classical epistemological questions is strikingly different: EE starts with evolutionary biology, the subject of which is populations dynamics. GE, however, starts with developmental psychology and thus focusses the development of individuals. By EE knowledge is seen as portraying or copying process, and truth is interpreted as a product of adaptation, whereas for GE knowledge is due to a construction process in which the production of true insights is only one possibility among others. Like falsity, error and deception, true knowledge goes back to a free relationship to reality. The difference between scientific and common knowledge is hard to be checked by EE, since both result ultimately from human hereditary structures. The study of how scientific knowledge emerges from everyday cognition is rather the task of GE.

Kessidis, Theoharis. Le Probléme du "Miracle Grec". *Philosophia (Athens)*, 23-24, 308-318, 1993-94.

L'esprit compétitif des Grecs constitue non seulement un principe créatif, mais aussi un principe destructif, qui les a menés à la guerre du Péloponnèse, dont les conséquences ont marqué le déclin de la Grèce antique. La "vie théorique" a conduit les Hellènes à l'échec, par opposition à l'esprit pratique" des Romains. Ainsi, les dons exceptionnels des Hellènes à l'humanité n'a pas assuré leur destinée historique. La cause pour laquelle les scientistes n'ont pas traité du "miracle hellénique" consiste au fait qu'il est associé à un nombre de questions idéologiques (eurocentrisme et autres).

Kessler, Andreas. Tertullian und das Vergnügen in *De spectaculis*. *Frei Z Phil Theol*, 41(3), 313-353, 1994.

The article offers an examination of Tertullian's discussion about pleasure (voluptas) in his De spectaculis. Special attention is given to the Christian pleasures proposed by Tertullian to replace the pagan ones. Thereby it can be shown that these pleasures are not—as commonly held—only pure artificial rhetoric or unrealistic wishful thinking, but offer on different levels real alternatives of a Christian pleasure culture: awareness of salvation, status of inner freedom and contempt of the world, power to exorcise, to cure, to ask for revelations and to destroy pagan idols, martyrdom, chastity and visionary anticipation of the last judgment.

Kessler, Eckhard. "Naturverständnisse im 15 und 16 Jahrhundert" in *Naturauffassungen in Philosophie, Wissenschaft, Technik: Band II, Schäfer, Lothar (ed)*, 13-57. Freiburg, Alber, 1994.

Ketner, Kenneth Laine (ed). *Peirce and Contemporary Thought: Philosophical Inquiries*. New York, Fordham Univ Pr, 1995.

The plenary addresses and responses of the Charles S Peirce Sesquicentennial International Congress held at Harvard University 5-10 September 1989, organized by Harvard and Texas Tech University, convened by the Charles S Peirce Society.

Kettle, David. Michael Polanyi and Human Identity. *Tradition Discovery*, 21(3), 5-18, 1994-95.

This paper conceives the distinction between human and animal identity in terms (drawn from theological anthropology) of distinctively human "habitation of a world." It develops models for this using Polanyi's account of the figure-ground polarity of acts of knowing in general. It identifies three distinct forms taken by this polarity, each offering its own model for human identity in its engagement with the world. Two of these models prove fatally one-sided. The third discloses the character of human identity in its relatedness and openness, its continuity and discontinuity with animal identity. This characterisation of human identity resonates with ideas found in Christian theological anthropology.

Kettner, Matthias. "Ideologiekritik und Psychoanalyse: Awei Seiten einer hermeneutischen Medaille?" in *Mythos Wertfreiheit?, Apel, Karl Otto (ed)*, 49-76. Frankfurt, Campus Verlag, 1994.

This is a critique of ideology and psychoanalytic therapy that both deal with relations of symbolic meanings and forms of power. Starting from this long recognized similarity, I probe the analogy between both interpretative practical enterprises by introducing a framework of hermeneutic theory which highlights the distinctive profile each. Drawing on Habermasian discourse ethics I criticize the received Marxian view of ideology and define ideology in terms of systematic impoverishment of chances for thematizations in discourse. I amend R Geuss's concept of ideology in terms of systematic impoverishment of chances for thematizations in discourse. I amend R Geuss's concept of ideology and discuss its structural similarity to the psychoanalytic theory of defense mechanisms. The upshot is that the communicative action of the therapist and that of the ideology critic both presuppose backgounds of legitimizing values. In therapy, such values are provided by consensus about the patient-therapist relationship. In critique of ideology, however, they must be drawn from other contexts, e.g., from consensus about moral concerns.

Kettner, Matthias (ed) and Apel, Karl Otto (ed). *Mythos Wertfreiheit?*. Frankfurt, Campus Verlag, 1994.

Ketzer, Hans-Jürgen. "'Die Aktualität der Kantischen Ästhetik'" in *Naturzweckmässigkeit und ästhetische Kultur, Schwabe, Karl-Heinz (ed)*, 141-149. Sankt Augustin, Academia, 1993.

Keuzenkamp, Hugo A. "What If an Idealization is Problematic?" in *Idealization VI: Idealization in Economics, Hamminga, Bert (ed)*, 243-254. Amsterdam, Rodopi, 1994.

Discusses the econometric literature on testing the *a priori* plausible condition of homogeneity in consumer demand. Such usually disconfirming test did not lead to a rejection of this particular conditions, but to the rejections of other idealizations needed to perform the test. It is possible, but not necessary to describe this process in terms of idealization and concretization.

Keyt, David and Miller, Fred D. *A Companion to Aristotle's Politics*. Cambridge, Blackwell, 1991.

Khamara, Edward J. Mackie's Paradox and the Free Will Defence. *Sophia (Australia)*, 34(1), 42-48, Mr-Ap 95.

Khan, Abrahim H. Kierkegaard on Authority and Leadership: Political Logic in Religious Thought. *Sophia (Australia)*, 33(3), 74-88, N 94.

This paper examines a political theory implicit in Kierkegaard's critique of the novel Two Ages. To achieve that aim, it views Kierkegaard as a political radical relative to modern liberalism and aristocratic conservatism of the 1840's in Denmark, by juxtaposing him to Locke. Basic to the theory is a notion of individuality which relies on three interlocking concepts: will, equality, and autonomy. That notion in turn supports ideas of authority and leadership that throw further light on Kierkegaard's understanding of the relation between religion and politics and suggests what is central to the political logic operative in the critique in his publication Literary Review.

Khushf, George. "The Meta-Ontological Option: On Taking the Existential Turn" in *Hegel Reconsidered, Engelhardt Jr, H Tristram (ed)*, 119-141. Dordrecht, Kluwer, 1994.

Khushf, George. Grammacentrism and the Transformation of Rhetoric. *Phil Rhet*, 28(1), 30-44, Ja 95.

Khushf, George. Illness, the Problem of Evil, and the Analogical Structure of Healing: On the Difference Christianity Makes in Bioethics. *Christian Bioethics*, 1(1), 102-120, Mr 95.

A Christian bioethic needs to place the medical approach to sickness, suffering, and death within the context of redemption and the renewal of humanity in the image of God. This can be done by accounting for the way in which the disruptions of the human life-world that attend the illness experience manifest the structure of the problem of evil and point toward an answer that transcends the individual and the medical community. Further, the disease-oriented approach to medicine, when understood in the context of the *analogia entis*, can be taken as an analogy for a deeper spiritual healing, and can thus become a vehicle through which one can minister to the disruptions of a patient's life-world. An appreciation of the analogical structure of healing provides the basis for a Christian ethic of care.

Kidd, James W. Investigative Interviewing: A Phenomenological Approach to a Universal Method. *Dialogue Hum*, 3(2), 165-169, 1993.

Kidd, James W and Kidd, Sunnie D. *Person to Person Inspiration*. New York, Lang, 1994.

Kidd, James W and Kidd, Sunnie D. The Dynamic Aspects of Inspiration: An Essay on the Phenomenon of Authentically Being Inspired. *Philosophia (Athens)*, 23-24, 26-54, 1993-94.

This article is the heart of our text, *Person to Person Inspiration*. It explores the meaning of inspiration and finds that inspiring experiences arise in a time of questioning and searching. Henri Bergson once said "always follow your inspiration." Bergson's conception of the human being as a "measureless virtuality" displays the height, depth and breadth of inspiration. Inspiration is the human being's most creative act. It is direct and seen only when enacted by the person who has been inspired. Inspiration comes from beyond one's self, lighting up something within the inspired person and disclosing personal meaning in a new way. This is an *inspiration/aspiration dialectic*, the occasion for a mutual interflow. Three aspects describe the dynamics of this experience: *Aspiring, Authentic Moments and Breaking Through Boundaries*.

Kidd, James W and Zonneveld, Leo W. The Energetics of Spirituality and Human Sexuality. *Dialogue Hum*, 3(2), 147-155, 1993.

Kidd, Sunnie D and Kidd, James W. *Person to Person Inspiration*. New York, Lang, 1994.

Kidd, Sunnie D and Kidd, James W. The Dynamic Aspects of Inspiration: An Essay on the Phenomenon of Authentically Being Inspired. *Philosophia (Athens)*, 23-24, 26-54, 1993-94.

This article is the heart of our text, *Person to Person Inspiration*. It explores the meaning of inspiration and finds that inspiring experiences arise in a time of questioning and searching. Henri Bergson once said "always follow your inspiration." Bergson's conception of the human being as a "measureless virtuality" displays the height, depth and breadth of inspiration. Inspiration is the human being's most creative act. It is direct and seen only when enacted by the person who has been inspired. Inspiration comes from beyond one's self, lighting up something within the inspired person and disclosing personal meaning in a new way. This is an *inspiration/aspiration dialectic*, the occasion for a mutual interflow. Three aspects describe the dynamics of this experience: *Aspiring, Authentic Moments and Breaking Through Boundaries*.

Kidder, Paulette. Gadamer and the Platonic *Eidos*. *Phil Today*, 39(1), 83-92, Spr 95.

This paper presents Hans-Georg Gadamer's reading of the Platonic theory of *eide*. According to Gadamer, the central point of the theory of forms is to express the way meanings inherited in language guide the inquirer to distinguish the essential from the inessential. Many commentators have rightly noted Gadamer's debt to the open-ended, "dialogical" character of Plato's thought. The paper argues that Gadamer has also appropriated into hermeneutic theory the Platonic concern for the *eidos*.

Kidner, David W. Why Psychology Is Mute about the Environmental Crisis. *Environ Ethics*, 16(4), 359-376, Wint 94.

Psychology, often defined as the science of human behavior, has so far had little to say about the environmental destruction which is currently occurring as the result of human behavior. I consider the reasons why it has not and suggest that the ideological preconceptions that underpin the discipline are similar to those of the technological-economic system that is largely responsible for degradation of the environment. Psychology, by normalizing the behavioral, life-style, and personality configurations associated with environmental destruction, and lacking a historical perspective on changes in consciousness and technology, is unable to contribute effectively to the ecological debate. I conclude that the discipline needs to locate itself historically and ideologically before it can offer an adequate analysis of environmental destruction.

Kiefer, Claus. "Quantum Cosmology and the Emergence of a Classical World" in *Philosophy, Mathematics and Modern Physics, Rudolph, Enno (ed)*, 104-119. New York, Springer-Verlag, 1994.

Quantum cosmology is a branch of modern physics, where quantum theory is applied to the Universe as a whole. It is shown here on a nontechnical level how the observed classical world can be recovered as an approximate notion within this framework. This involves in particular a careful investigation into the conceptual role of time in quantum cosmology. It is also outlined how a simple boundary condition for the wave function of the Universe can lead to the observed time asymmetry of the world.

Kielkopf, Charles F. 'Surveyability' Should not be Formalized. *Phil Math*, 3(2), 175-178, My 95.

These invited comments on an immediately preceding paper by Mark Addis review how Mark Addis has made a case that it would require great effort for scant philosophical profit to formalize a notion of surveyability as a metamathematical predicate demarcating strict finitistic mathematics. It is then suggested how the notion of surveyability is useful in informal philosophizing about mathematics.

Kienzler, Wolfgang and Gabriel, Gottfried. Gottlob Freges politisches Tagebuch. *Deut Z Phil*, 42(6), 1057-1066, 1994.

The text composes the introduction to Frege's diary of 1924 which follows (pp 1067-1098), now published for the first time. It attempts to exhibit the conflict between Frege's political rhetoric and his philosophical logic. The commentary explains the historical references of the diary and essays a critical evaluation of Frege's extreme right-wing political convictions against the background of the First World War lost by Germany.

Kieran, Matthew. Applied Philosophy and Business Ethics. *J Applied Phil*, 12(2), 175-187, 1995.

Given the socio-economic incentives for academic relevance, the sceptic may well challenge the academic integrity of the evolving discipline of business ethics. For, the question is, how could such an emerging field of enquiry constitute applied philosophy? I critically examine certain arguments, principally advanced by Michael Oakeshott and Stephen Clark, which might be thought to underwrite such scepticism, via a wholesale suspicion of applied ethics. Yet, I argue, philosophy can be and is properly concerned with our practical experience and actions. The significance of more general, abstract ethical questions derives, in great part, from their bearing upon our practical deliberations and actions. Moreover, reflection about the nature and role of ethical principles need not deny a role for moral judgment. Although for contingent reasons we may be right to be worried, I present an argument to show that, as a matter of principle, the sceptical challenge regarding business ethics can be refuted.

Kieran, Matthew. The Impoverishment of Art. *Brit J Aes*, 35(1), 15-25, Ja 95.

The dominant paradigms applied to questions concerning the nature or evaluation of art are linguistic. Traditionally, art's meaning and thus truth is considered trivial or, more radically, art is falsely conflated with other forms of discourse and reduced to mere theory. I argue that the application of pictures of meaning, from the philosophy of language, have proved inadequate to a sound appreciation of art and its significance. What is primary is our experiential engagement as spectators with an artwork. Once we appreciate this, we may recognize art's potential profundity through the kind of imaginative experience afforded.

Kikuchi, Makoto and Tanaka, Kazuyuki. On Formalization of Model-Theoretic Proofs of Gödel's Theorems. *Notre Dame J Form Log*, 35(3), 403-412, Sum 94.

Kikyo, Hirotaka and Tsuboi, Akito. On Reduction Properties. *J Sym Log*, 59(3), 900-911, S 94.

Kilgour, D M and Zagare, F C. Uncertainty and the Role of the Pawn in Extended Deterrence. *Synthese*, 100(3), 379-412, S 94.

This paper develops an incomplete information model of extended deterrence relationships. It postulates layers who are fully informed about the costs of war and all other relevant variables, save for the values their opponents place on the issues at stake, i.e., the pawn. We provide consistent and intuitively satisfying parallel definitions for two types of players, Hard and Soft, in terms of the parameters of our model. We also answer several particular questions about the strategy choices of players in an extended deterrence relationship and, by identifying all the Perfect Bayesian Equilibria of the game model we construct, specify typical behavior patterns. Our most general finding is that an extended deterrence game always has a unique perfect Bayesian equilibrium with a rather simple form. (edited)

Kililis, George. Beyond Representationalism: Ontological Alternatives in Heidegger and Lonergan. *Conference*, 5(2), 29-42, Wint 94-95.

Killoran, John. Conscience and the Moral Law: A Critical Review of Antonio Rosmini's Moral Thought. *Vera Lex*, 13(1-2), 13-15, 1993.

Kim, Jaegwon. "Explanatory Exclusion and the Problem of Mental Causation" in *Philosophy of Psychology: Debates on Psychological Explanation, Macdonald, Cynthia (ed)*, 121-141. Cambridge, Blackwell, 1995.

Explanatory exclusion, or causal/explanatory exclusion, is the principle that there can be at most one *complete* and *independent* explanation (in particular, causal explanation) for any single event. I try to motivate this principle, and then apply it to consider some recent proposals concerning mental causation—those made by Davidson, LePore and Loewer, Dretske, and others. I then discuss how the problem of exclusion should be approached in the context of mental causation.

Kim, Jaegwon. Mental Causation in Searle's "Biological Naturalism". *Phil Phenomenol Res*, 55(1), 189-194, Mr 95.

In this short discussion of John Searle's *The Rediscovery of the Mind* (Cambridge: The MIT Press, 1992), I express agreement and sympathy with Searle's stance against the prevailing views concerning the status of "cognitive science"—in particular, the view that there is a class of special "computational" or abstract "cognitive" properties investigated by psychology—but I draw what appear to be some very peculiar and unacceptable consequences concerning mental causation, from Searle's claim that mental phenomena are "caused" by their underlying neural processes. It is doubtful that a viable account of mental causation could be developed within the framework of Searle's "biological naturalism".

Kim, Jaegwon (ed) and Sosa, Ernest (ed). *A Companion to Metaphysics*. Cambridge, Blackwell, 1995.

This reference work provides exhaustive coverage of main topics and areas, positions, movements, concepts, distinctions, arguments, and historical and contemporary figures in metaphysics and related fields. It includes more than 260 entries ranging from brief definitions of common terms to major discursive essays and reflects the most recent and sophisticated treatment of metaphysics. Alphabetically arranged with a comprehensive index and extensive and up-to-date bibliographical information, the *Companion* should be a highly useful reference source relevant to all fields of philosophy.

Kim, Kihyeon. The Deontological Conception of Epistemic Justification and Doxastic Voluntarism. *Analysis*, 54(4), 282-284, O 94.

Kim, S M. ω-Consistency and Löb's Theorem. *Bull Sec Log*, 23(4), 158-162, D 94.

Despite the provable equivalence between Löb's Theorem and Gödel's Second Incompleteness Theorem, the former and its proof do not explicitly involve any assumption of consistency, while the latter and its proof do. This paper establishes some logico-mathematical relationship between Löb's Theorem and ω-consistency.

Kim, Sangmun. Absolute Forms of Gödel's Incompleteness Theorem. *Epistemologia*, 17(2), 329-338, Ju-De 94.

If one accepts the contentious assumption that knowledge is limited to recursively enumerable sets of sentences, then Gödel's Incompleteness Theorem shows that there exist unknowable noncontingent truths. I examine this assumption concerning the limits of human knowledge, which has been disseminated in literature on philosophy of logic, and show via counter-examples that it is not defendable, in fact, completely groundless. Furthermore, I conclude that Gödel's Theorem gives us no reason to claim that there are unknowable noncontingent truths of arithmetic. The paper then proceeds to an investigation of the following questions: 1) What is the epistemological significance of absolute forms of Gödel's Incompleteness Theorem? Do we have any grounds to suppose that all unknown sentences are ultimately knowable? 2) Determine the epistemological consistency/relevance of Gödel's Incompleteness to Wittgenstein's unsayability in Tractatus.

Kimball, Stephanie and Garrison, Jim. "Hermeneutic Listening: An Approach to Understanding in Multicultural Conversations" in *Identity, Culture, and Education, Smeyers, Paul (ed)*, 171-183. Leuven, Leuven Univ Pr, 1994.

Kincaid-Smith, Priscilla. Opening Address: The Fifth Freedom. *Bioethics*, 9(3-4), 183-191, Jl 95.

Women in developing countries suffer considerable moribidity and mortality due to inability to control their own fertility and lack of access to family planning services. Over 500,000 deaths each year are related to pregnancy. Two thirds of these maternal deaths could be prevented by providing contraception to those women who wish to use it in developing countries. There is no tenable ethical defence of cultural and religious behaviour which denies a woman a choice as to whether she will undertake a pregnancy or not. Inplementation of the principles of the programme of action from the 1994 Cairo Population Conference would, through empowering women to control their own fertility, have a huge impact on maternal health in the developing world.

Kindi, Vassiliki. Incommensurability, Incomparability, Irrationality. *Method Sci*, 27(1), 41-55, 1994.

In this paper it is argued that the use of the term *incommensurable* in its original context of ancient Greek mathematics does not have the connotations of incomparability and irrationality. The use of the Greek word (incommensurable), (ineffable), (irrational), which are all employed to refer to incommensurable magnitudes are investigated in order to contend that: 1) The lack of a common measure in the case of incommensurable magnitudes does not preclude an overall evaluation at a pre-theoretical level. 2) The contemporary identification of incommensurable and irrational should be attributed to the ambiguity of the Greek word λογοσ and to the word *ratio* that translated λογοσ into Latin. (edited)

Kindi, Vasso P. Kuhn's *The Structure of Scientific Revolutions* Revisited. *J Gen Phil Sci*, 26(1), 75-92, 1995.

The present paper argues that there is an affinity between Kuhn's *The Structure of Scientific Revolutions* and Wittgensteing's philosophy. It is maintained, in particular, that Kuhn's notion of paradigm draws on such Wittgensteinian concepts as language games, family resemblance, rules, forms of life. It is also claimed that Kuhn's incommensurability thesis is a sequal of the theory of meaning supplied by Wittgenstein's later philosophy. As such its assessment is not fallacious, since it is not an empirical hypothesis and it does not have the relativistic implications Kuhn's critics repeatedly indicated. Although concepts are indeed relative to a language game or paradigm, interparadigmatic intelligibility is preserved through the standard techniques of translation or praxis. The impossibility of radical translation which is captured by the claim of incommensurability lies with that which cannot be said but only shown.

Kindleberger, Charles P. Theory vs History: Reply to Horwitz. *Crit Rev*, 8(4), 609-614, Fall 94.

Analysts such as Steven Horwitz, with strong prior beliefs, are seldom impressed by mere fact, and tend to explain away deviations from their theories. The belief that markets are moved only by fundamentals and not by occasional faddism and overshooting rests on the assumption that market participants form their opinions independently, when in fact they are driven from time to time by emulation. The belief that markets are rational and well-informed but government officials and central bankers incompetent is implausible on its face. The period since 1970 has seen bubble after bubble, some of which seemed likely to lead to finacial crisis had it not been for the Federal Reserve.

King, Jonathan and Acklin, David. Creating Common Ground: A Lesson from the Past. *J Bus Ethics*, 14(1), 1-16, Ja 95.

Orthodox business ethics, conventional management theory, and a great deal of higher education embody the overriding emphasis accorded to "analysis" by yesteryear's science. An alternative strategy, exemplified by the war stories told by a Confederate General, is more consistent with late twentieth century science in general and soft systems methodology in particular.

King, Paul John. Reconciling Austinian and Russellian Accounts of the Liar Paradox. *J Phil Log*, 23(5), 451-494, O 94.

King, Peter (trans). *Augustine: Against the Academicians* and *The Teacher*. Indianapolis, Hackett, 1995.

King, Preston. Historical Contextualism: The New Historicism?. *Hist Euro Ideas*, 21(2), 209-234, Mr 95.

The career of Professor John Pocock is distinguished both by industry and insight. A new collection of essays, edited by Phillipson and Skinner, has been produced in his honour. Two features mark this book, impose an unusual coherence and reflect the recipient's style and interests. First, virtually all of the essays are to do with 17th-18th century thinkers and movements. Second, all are exercises in small-scale, historical reconstruction—being more concerned to describe than to exemplify political or philosophical discourse.

King, Richard. Early Yogacara and Its Relationship with the Madhyamaka School. *Phil East West*, 44(4), 659-683, O 94.

It has often been assumed that the Madhyamaka and Yogacara schools of Buddhism represent distinctive philosophical positions. Early Yogacara clearly reformulates key Buddhist themes, notably the Mahayana concept of emptiness (sunyata). It is argued that philosophical discussion in the early Yogacara works of Asanga and Vasubandhu concerns itself primarily with the question of the ineffability of emptiness in an attempt to circumvent the problems perceived in traditional Madhyamaka exposition. Finally, evidence is discussed which suggests that early Yogacara is ambivalent in regard to its apparently "idealistic" ontology and in its attitude to the Madhyamaka.

King, Thomas M. An Explosion of Dazzling Flashes: Teilhard's Unity of Faith and Science. *Zygon*, 30(1), 105-115, Mr 95.

Science and revelation have been presented as two books with the same "author," their reconciliation being called "concordism." Teilhard opposed concordism, insisting that supposed "revelations" be treated as scientific hypotheses to be verified or not in experience. Applying his criterion for truth (Does it bring "coherence and fecundity" to the phenomena?) to Christian revelation, he told of finding "an explosion of dazzling flashes." So Teilhard spoke of the hypothesis as the supreme spiritual act wherein the dust of experience takes on form and is kindled at the fire of knowledge.

King, Thomas M and Salmon, James F. Works on Teilhard, 1980-1994: An Annotated Bibliography. *Zygon*, 30(1), 131-142, Mr 95.

King, Ursula. Teilhard's Reflections on Eastern Religions Revisited. *Zygon*, 30(1), 47-72, Mr 95.

References to Eastern religions are found throughout Teilhard's work. Often considered to be mainly negative, these need to be critically reassessed within the wider context of Teilhard's experience and thought. Primarily interested in the renewal of Christianity (criticized more sharply than Eastern religions), he emphasized the living branches of religion and the need for a gradual convergence toward a religion of action in order to bring about a global transformation of life and thought. He spoke of the "road of the West" or a "new mysticism" which, however, cannot come into existence without the contribution of Eastern religions.

Kingsley, Peter. Empedocles and his Interpreters: The Four-Element Doxography. *Phronesis*, 39(3), 235-254, 1994.

Kinna, Ruth. William Morris and Anti-Parliamentarism. *Hist Polit Thought*, 15(4), 593-613, Wint 94.

This paper examines Morris's commitment to anti-parliamentarism. His withdrawal from this position in 1890 is often seen as a result of his shifting political affiliations. But by examining his reasons for rejecting parliamentary activity it appears that this withdrawal was a consequence of his disillusion with the prospect of revolution and his abiding commitment to an idea of political education. Morris's ideas about education are central to his observed 'utopianism'. But whilst his utopianism is interpreted as part of an educational project, it can also be seen to have been constructed on an understanding of political reality.

Kirby, Gary R and Goodpaster, Jeffery R. *Thinking*. Englewood Cliffs, Prentice Hall, 1995.

This book exercises the most important part of your body: your brain. It is designed to challenge your mind and to strengthen your thinking ability. Spanning the disciplines, the authors offer a classical well-spring of thought, drawing on ideas from every period of history, from philosophy, literature, the natural sciences, and psychology. The authors organize the material into interrelated thinking bases that include sensing, feeling, language, creativity, organization, logical thought, judgment, decision making, and action. And to actively engage, enlarge, and enrich your thinking and to help you adapt and personalize the chapter concepts, they include numerous thinking challenges throughout the book.

Kirmmse, Bruce H. Kierkegaard and 1848. *Hist Euro Ideas*, 20(1-3), 167-175, Ja 95.

As is well-known, the year 1848 was one of revolutionary unrest in much of Europe, Denmark included. A careful reading of Kierkegaard's *Papirer* and his published writings shows that he considered the revolutionary year 1848 to be pivotal in several respects: in world history, in the history of Christianity, and in his own personal development as an author. There can be no doubt, first of all, that the *events* of 1848 made Kierkegaard's final understanding of Christianity and his assault on the Church *possible*, and secondly, that Kierkegaard's *interpretation* of the events of 1848 made his final assault *inevitable*.

Kiros, Teodros. A Practical Idea of Blackness. *Quest*, 8(1), 24-43, Je 94.

Kirschenmann, P P. Tautology, Methodological Warning or Explanatory Make-Shift? (in Dutch). *Tijdschr Filosof*, 56(3), 469-493, S 94.

The Anthropic Principle (AP), in its many versions, has received diverging assessments. I mainly examine the less speculative weak (WAP) and strong (SAP) versions and their assessments. I argue, among others, the following points. The construal of the WAP as a consistency requirement of a truth of (Bayesian) confirmation theory, while correct, does not quite capture its spirit. The charge of its being a tautology, which occasions comparisons with the Principle of Natural Selection (PNS), is overstated. Still, in contrast with PNS's role, it is never substantially involved in "anthropic explanations". "Many worlds" hypotheses, joined to the SAP, can yield (rather speculative) explanation. Friends of the AP roughly accept common scientific standards, which make the AP appear—even to some of them—as a temporary stop-gap.

Kirzner, Israel M. "The Nature of Profits: Some Economic Insights and Their Ethical Implications" in *Profits and Morality, Cowan, Robin (ed)*, 22-47. Chicago, Univ of Chicago Pr, 1995.

Kis, János. Between Reform and Revolution: Three Hypotheses about the Nature of the Regime Change. *Constellations*, 1(3), 399-421, Jan 95.

Kishani, Bongasu Tanla. Language Problems in Anglophone Cameroon: Present Writers and Future Readers. *Quest*, 8(2), 101-129, D 94.

En choisissant officiellement l'écriture en anglais, l'écrivain camerounais d'expression anglaise se trouve en face d'un défi historique important. Au niveau pratique comme théorique, on constate que l'écrivain anglophone camerounais ne fait montre ni de l'écriture ni de l'élocution de l'anglais des anglais. Et chose curieuse, l'usage d'origine coloniale d'une telle langue européenne empêche les camerounais de maîtriser véritablement les langues camerounaises. Il sagit d'une crise chez l'écrivain d'expression anglophone au Cameroun à travers laquelle l'anglais triomphe officiellement et officieusement des langues camerounaises. Pourtant la pratique de l'écriture anglophone chez les camerounais révèle la vitalité des langues camerounaises comme on peut le constater à travers les multiples structures sous-jacentes ainsi qu'à travers certaines structures de surface. (edited)

Kisiel, Theodore. The Genetic Difference in Reading *Being and Time*. *Amer Cath Phil Quart*, 69(2), 171-187, Spr 95.

The genetic perspective upon *Being and Time* reveals Heidegger's governing question to be really the question of the language *of* Be-ing, understood methodologically as the formal indication of life's facticity, and linguistically as a grammatology of the indexical expressions converging in Da-sein: here, now, I. The formal indication guiding *Being and Time*, ex-sistence, seeks to indicate the most immediate dimension of human experience, which at once proves to be its most "formal" dimension: time. This formal ontology of the intentionally directed self-motion of experience accordingly would have culminated in a grammaontology of time's tenses, aspects, moods, and "voices".

Kisiel, Theodore. Why Students of Heidegger Will Have to Read Emil Lask. *Man World*, 28(3), 197-240, Jl 95.

Heidegger's lifelong expression of a debt of gratitude to Emil Lask's philosophical logic receives detailed substantiation through explication of the Scotus dissertation (1915) on the grammar and concepts of being. Lask's proclivity to phenomenology's matter of intentionality manifests itself especially in the "material determination of form" used in the dissertation as a principle to differentiate categorial regions. Lask's distinction between constitutive and reflexive categories applied to the analogy of being guides Heidegger in 1919 to his method of concept formation through "formal indication." Heideggerian heterology and the dispersion of equiprimordiality, the play on *es gibt*, terms like ontological difference, *Bewandtnis*, world and our absorption in it, facticity, and lived truth likewise stem from Lask's logic of concept formation.

Kisiel, Theodore J. Heidegger's *Gesamtausgabe*: An International Scandal of Scholarship. *Phil Today*, 39(1), 3-15, Spr 95.

Kisner, Wendell. *Erinnerung, Retrait*, Absolute Reflection: Hegel and Derrida. *Owl Minerva*, 26(2), 171-186, Spr 95.

In this essay I will attempt to show that Derrida not only mistakenly reads the Hegelian text in terms of reflection, but that his own way of thinking could be characterized from a Hegelian perspective as itself reflective. I will focus upon one of Derrida's texts which indicates his own contribution to the field of thinking and writing and the directions for inquiry initiated in his work, as well as his engagement with Hegel. Such a text is his masterful essay, *White Mythology: Metaphor in the Text of Philosophy*, a writing overtly concerned with the difficulties posed by metaphoricity in the text of philosophy and the attempt in the latter to domesticate and "interiorize" its tropic reserve or condition of possibility within the concept of metaphor itself, which turns out to be a philosopheme. Derrida will indicate what he takes to be the conditions of the impossibility of such an account, but it is precisely his reasons for this impossibility that I find problematic in terms of reflection. (edited)

Kiss, Endre. The Notion of Enlightenment in Friedrich Nietzsche's Philosophy. *Magyar Filozof Szemle*, 5-6, 671-683, 1994.

Nietzsches Aufklaerung geht von dem Faktum eines Endes der Religion. bzw. des Mythos aus, artikuliert jedoch die ganze neue 'condition humaine' des streng ökumenisch aufgefassten Menschheit. Diese neue 'condition humaine' erscheint für Nietzsche in der Gestalt von zwei gleichzeitigen und einander reflexiv bedingenden Gefahren. Die eine Gefahr ist das 'falsche' Bewusstsein, in der Form der mentalen Beharrung von überholten gedanklichen Inhalten. Die andere Gefahr ist—im Falle einer schockartigen Veraenderung der mentalen Konditionen—der Verlust der individuellen und der menschheitlichen Identitaet. Nietzsches ganze Aufklaerungskonzeption bewegt sich auf einer Bahn, die diesen beiden Gefahren ökumenisch entgehen will. Dadurch kommt er nicht nur der grossen Aufklaerung des achtzehnten Jahrhunderts nahe (kein Zufall, dass er ein wichtiges Werk an Voltaire widmet), sondern thematisiert zum ersten Mal das neue gesamtmenschliche Schicksal zwischen der Notwendigkeit des Abschieds von den Mythen und der ebenfalls strengen Notwendigkeit einer neu durchdachten emanzipativen Praxis.

Kiss, Endre. Zwischen Apriorismus und Empirismus im Kontext der Isomorphie zweier Apriorismen: Zur Rekonstruktion von Fichtes philosophischer Konzeption. *Fichte-Studien*, 6, 149-154, 1994.

Die Dynamik der neuzeitlichen Philosophie war in grossem Ausmass von der Konkurrenz des Apriorismus und des Empirismus abhaengig. Eine gemeinsame philosophische Kritik der beiden Richtungen erfolgte im philosophischen Werk Kants. Fichte teilte die allgemeine Auffassung, dass das von Kant theoretisch neu definierte philosophische Feld im Zeichen eines umfassenden neuen Prinzips neu vereinigt werden muss. Er verbindet aber diese Forderung nach einem umfassenden Prinzip mit den ursprünglichen überlegungen über die Problematik von Apriorismus und Empirismus. Seine Hauptidee dabei ist der Begriff der "Setzung", der selber schon eine Synthese zwischen Apriorismus und Empirismus darstellt. In der Auffassung dieses gesuchten umfassenden Prinzips mischen sich Elemente einer traditionell-vorkantischen und einer qualitativ neuen, pragmatischen Auffassung. Sein Schwanken zwischen diesen beiden Auffassungen bleibt in vielen Perioden seiner Philosophie erhalten, wobei es auch angenommen werden soll, dass er Kant nicht immer als einen Denker ansieht, der die Humehsche Skepsis ganz beseitigt hatte.

Kiss, Róbert Szemán. Jan Patocka: Negative Platonism. *Magyar Filozof Szemle*, 5-6, 759-790, 1994.

Kissack, Michael. Nietzsche and Foucault: An Interpretation of Influence. *S Afr J Phil*, 14(1), 29-33, F 95.

This article presents a particular interpretation of Nietzsche's influence on the work of Foucault, arguing that Foucault's study of French institutions and the nature of modern society is a concrete consideration of Nietzsche's view that knowledge is an imposition of 'being' on the flux of 'becoming'. The 'normalizing practices', which constitute a particular institutional or social order contain distinctions and discriminations which are mutable but indispensable. These constraints significantly complicate contemporary aspirations towards freedom or emancipation.

Kistner, Wietske. "Presuppositions in Science" in *Life, World and Meaning, Roux, A P J (ed)*, 56-68. Pretoria, Univ of S Africa, 1990.

Kitamura, Kiyohiko. De la connaissance esthétique (in Japanese). *Bigaku*, 45(3), 12-22, Wint 94.

D'abord alors que l'oeuvre d'art n'est pas dans l'espace et le temps abstraits, il faut considérer le champ cosmologique propre à chaque oeuvre. Ensuite, elle est polysémique comme un symbole. Et finalement, on doit la comprendre avec l'imagination en tant qu'intropathie (P Ricouer) qui fonctionne par l'intermédiaire de nos corps. La connaissance pour éclaircir cette oeuvre comme telle, nous l'appelons 'la connaissance esthétique', qui est différente de la connaissance scientifique moderne. Mais ces deux connaissances ne sont pas laternative, celle-ci doit finalement être comportée dans celle-là. S'il en est ainsi, nous pourrait obtenir la nouvelle possibilité de la connaissance qui saisit affirmativement le monde en tant que tel.

Kitamura, Kiyohiko. De la Distance Esthétique. *Aesthetics*, 5, 53-64, Mr 92.

What new aspects of art will turn up, when we reconsider the problems belonging to the aesthetics from the point of view of the 'distance'? I describe three phases of distance of art; creation, artwork and appreciation. Then investigating the concept 'psychical distance' of Edward Bullough (1880-1934), I maintain that the concept which functions in the artistic phenomena is not psychological but ontological. And according to the hermeneutics of Paul Ricoeur (1913-), it becomes clear that such distance makes not only our aesthetic experience possible but also our aesthetic conscience matured in the ceaseless activity of interpretation. In order to distinguish it from the scientific one, I call it "aesthetic distance".

Kitcher, Philip. "Contrasting Conceptions of Social Epistemology" in *Socializing Epistemology: The Social Dimensions of Knowledge, Schmitt, Frederick F (ed)*, 111-134. Lanham, Rowman & Littlefield, 1994.

Kitcher, Philip. Author's Response. *Phil Phenomenol Res*, 55(3), 653-673, S 95.

Kitcher, Philip. Précis of *The Advancement of Science*. *Phil Phenomenol Res*, 55(3), 611-617, S 95.

Kitromilides, Paschalis M. "John Locke and the Greek Intellectual Tradition" in *Locke's Philosophy, Rogers, G A J (ed)*, 217-235. New York, Oxford Univ Pr, 1994.

This essay examines primarily the reception of Locke's philosophical and pedagogical ideas in Greek culture in the course of the eighteenth century as a particular instance of the broader intellectual phenomenon of the dissemination of his thought in the Age of the Enlightenment. Secondly the essay looks into one particular aspect of this process of intellectual reception, graphically illustrated by the Greek evidence, the restricted audience of Locke's political thought on the European continent in the eighteenth and its eclipse during the nineteenth century. The appraisal of pertinent evidence suggests the methodological need for a reconsideration of conventional historiographical views concerning the pattern of transmission, the media of transmission and the selective reception of Locke's thought in continental Europe.

Kittay, Eva Feder. Taking Dependency Seriously: The Family and Medical Leave Act Considered in Light of the Social Organization of Dependency Work and Gender Equality. *Hypatia*, 10(1), 8-29, Wint 95.

Contemporary industrialized societies have been confronted with the fact and consequences of women's increased participation in paid employment. Whether this increase has resulted from women's desire for equality or from changing economic circumstances, women and men have been faced with a crisis in the organization of work that concerns dependents, that is, those unable to care for themselves. This is labor that has been largely unpaid, often unrecognized, and yet is indispensable to human society.

Kittrie, Nicholas. "'Wanted' and 'Unwanted' Life" in *Ethics on the Frontiers of Human Existence, Badham, Paul (ed)*, 137-151. New York, Paragon House, 1992.

Kitzinger, Celia. "Problematizing Pleasure: Radical Feminist Deconstructions of Sexuality and Power" in *Power/Gender, Radtke, H Lorraine (ed)*, 194-209. Newbury Park, Sage, 1994.

Radical feminism has depicted heterosexuality as a compulsory institution into which women are coerced against their will. This chapter seeks to develop radical feminist theory around women's *pleasure* in heterosexual sex, incorporating into our politics (some) women's claim that they voluntarily choose to engage in sexual intercourse, enjoy it and have orgasms through it. It is argued that power does not simply deny and repress women's sexuality; it also constructs it. Accounts of heterosexual and lesbian desire are used to explore the ways in which power is implicated in the very "doing" of sex and the experience of sexual pleasure.

Kivy, Peter. *Authenticities: Philosophical Reflections on Musical Performance*. Ithaca, Cornell Univ Pr, 1995.

The present book is a philosophical inquiry into the desirability of using or re-creating historical practices in performance. In the first part of the book, four concepts are examined of what it might mean to be an "authentic" performance. In the second part, these four kinds of authenticity are evaluated.

Kjonstad, Bjorn and Willmott, Hugh. Business Ethics: Restrictive or Empowering?. *J Bus Ethics*, 14(6), 445-464, Je 95.

There is a tendency in the business ethics literature to think of ethics in restrictive terms: what one should not do, and how to control this. Drawing on Lawrence Kohlberg's theory of moral development, the paper focuses on, and draws attention to, another more positive aspect of ethics: the capacity of ethics to inspire and empower individuals, as well as groups. To understand and facilitate such empowerment, it is argued that it is necessary to move beyond Kohlberg's justice reasoning so as to appreciate the value and importance of feeling and care. Accordingly, we draw upon case study material to review the meaning of Kohlberg's higher stages—5, 6 and 7—to question the meaning of ethical "reasoning". With such deeper understanding of particular ethical codes or practices, it is thought that members of organisations may come closer to the *spirit*, as opposed to the letter, of ethical conduct in organisations. This, we argue, is consistent with the degree of trust and integrity demanded by leaner, post-bureaucratic ways of organizing and conducting business as well as being personally beneficial to the people involved.

Klapwijk, J. Pluralism of Norms and Values: On the Claim and Reception of the Universal. *Phil Reform*, 59(2), 158-192, 1994.

Klapwijk, Jacob (ed) and Griffioen, Sander (ed) and Groenewoud, Gerben (ed). *Bringing into Captivity Every Thought: Capita Selecta* in the History of Christian Evaluations of Non-Christian Philosophy. Lanham, Univ Pr of America, 1991.

Klaw, Barbara. "Sexuality in Beauvoir's *Les Mandarins*" in *Feminist Interpretations of Simone de Beauvoir, Simons, Margaret A (ed)*, 193-221. University Park, Penn St Univ Pr, 1995.

This study responds to critics who fault Beauvoir for perpetuating patriarchal stereotypes of female sexuality throughout her life. I argue that her fourth novel, *Les Mandarins*, honestly portrays the originality of her eroticism in fictional guise. Showing that women do experience physical pleasure from fleeing sexual encounters, Beauvoir foregrounds the greater intensity of their delectation in situations involving commitment from the head and heart of both parties. She illustrates how patriarchal commonplaces and myths discourage woman from maximizing her erotic joys and implies ways to subvert these detrimental discourses. She depicts bisexual relationships as an acceptable possibility and redefines rape.

Klein, Anne C. Presence with a Difference: Buddhists and Feminists on Subjectivity. *Hypatia*, 9(4), 112-130, Fall 94.

Essentialist and postmodern feminisms are often regarded as incompatible. I propose that Buddhist theories of subjectivity change the nature of the tension between them as presently construed because Buddhist traditions describe a mind not wholly governed by language, and a subjective mental dimension that is entirely integrated with the body and its sensations. A corollary is the compatibility Buddhists perceive between conditioned subjective states (akin to postmodern feminisms) and the unconditioned (akin to essentialist feminisms).

Klein, Ellen R. Nomad, Come Home. *Free Inq*, 15(2), 31-32, Spr 95.

In Braidotti's hysterical desire to run away from home—classical epistemology—she has, like all feminists of her tribe, landed herself in the relativist's muck. From an analytic standpoint her criticisms fail. Looking out from a more continental view the metaphors are, at best, hackneyed, at worst dangerous. Braidotti demonstrates, once again, that feminism's desire to undo rationality will ultimately harm women.

Klein, Gudrun. Philosophizing Crossdressers; or, Who Does What Things with Which Words?. *Hypatia*, 9(3), 163-182, Sum 94.

The purpose of the essay is to point to the limits of argumentation between pragmatist philosophers laying claim to feminism of a certain kind and feminists claiming their own space and discourses, by playfully enacting argument and counterargument visually represented as a continuous moving back and forth, rarely meeting on common ground while using a common language. The mode of the essay is an expression of hope for a creative subversion of the traditions which have informed the discourses evoked.

Klein, Hans-Dieter. "Dialog der Religionen und Eurozentrismus" in *Das geistige Erbe Europas, Buhr, Manfred (ed)*, 436-441. Napoli, Vivarium, 1994.

Klein, Hans-Dieter. "Philosophischer Idealismus und Nationalsozialismus" in *Der geistige Anschluss, Fischer, Kurt R (ed)*, 36-52. Wien, WUV Univ, 1993.

Klein, Sherwin. Drucker's Knowledge Society and Socratic *Sophrosyne*. *Bus Prof Ethics J*, 12(4), 51-71, Wint 93.

In his latest book, *Post-Capitalist Society*, Peter Drucker presents his vision of a society of organizations dominated by the knowledge of specialists. I argue that a basic fault in his vision is the neglect of Socratic *sophrosyne*. Socratic *sophrosyne*, which implies self-knowledge or knowledge of the human soul, is impossible without Socratic inquiry, and this inquiry aims at gaining knowledge of the human good and the dialectical skills which are necessary for such a search. I argue that this quest, which defines the goal of Socratic, *sophrosyne*, should provide the guiding light for Drucker's vision.

Klein, Ted. "The Idea of a Hermeneutical Ethics" in *The Philosophy of Paul Ricoeur, Hahn, Lewis Edwin (ed)*, 349-366. Peru, Open Court, 1994.

Klein, Wayne. Truth and Illusion in *The Birth of Tragedy*. *Int Stud Phil*, 26(3), 137-144, 1994.

Kleinberg, Stanley S. Teichman, Freedom of Expression, and the Public Platform. *J Applied Phil*, 12(1), 95-100, 1995.

In the course of her defense of German protesters against Peter Singer's lectures, Jenny Teichman claims that the right to make use of a public platform is not covered by the principle of freedom of expression. I argue that this view is mistaken, and that she is also wrong to focus on whether Singer deserved a public platform. Instead I suggest that what matters is whether there was an attempt to prevent communication between a speaker and willing hearers. But I agree with Teichman that there are some relevant differences between speaking from a public platform and speaking privately. In particular I argue that protesters have a right, though not one based on freedom of expression, to interrupt a public speaker. Such a right is on a par with the speaker's freedom to draw public attention to the fact that she has opinions which she thinks worthy of a hearing, and in exercising it a protester must not prevent those who wish to hear the speech from doing so. Finally I offer an argument against the view that disrupting Singer's lectures could be seen as a justified interference with freedom of expression.

Kleinig, John. "Ethical Questions Facing Law Enforcement Agents" in *Introducing Applied Ethics, Almond, Brenda (ed)*, 212-226. Cambridge, Blackwell, 1995.

Several problems in police ethics are introduced and discussed: police discretionary authority; the use of force, intermediate and deadly; the use of deception during the investigative, interrogatory and testimonial phases of police work; the acceptance of gratuities and corruption; police loyalty and "the blue wall of silence."

Klibansky, Raymond. Jan Patocka. *Magyar Filozof Szemle*, 5-6, 791-807, 1994.

Klibansky, Raymond. The German University in the 1930's. *Filozof Cas*, 42(4), 543-559, 1994.

Kline, Goerge L. La posible contribución de la filosofía clásica rusa a la construcción de una sociedad humanista. *Dialogo Filosof*, 11(1), 77-90, Ja-Ap 95.

Una importante causa filosófica e ideológica de la inhumanidad de la sociedad rusa durante las décadas del marxismo-leninismo fue la obsesiva orientación de los marxistas-leninistas hacia el futuro histórico (futuro comunismo) en aras de lo cual, comunidades, culturas y personas podían ser reducidas a medios para alcanzar ese fin histórico. El autor de los debates apoyándose en los propios pensadores rusos de la "tradición clásica", como por ejemplo Herzen, Dostoievsky, Tolstoy, Leontiev y Berdiaev. No se opone a cualquier tipo de orientación de futuro, pero recalca la importancia de las personas actuales.

Klinger, Gerwin. "Schopenhauer als Ahnherr einer faschistischen Anthropologie" in *Die besten Geister der Nation, Korotin, Ilse (ed)*, 87-114. Vienna, Picus, 1994.

Klink, William H. Ecology and Eschatology: Science and Theological Modeling. *Zygon*, 29(4), 529-545, D 94.

The possibility of in-breakings of God in science is discussed. A realist philosophy of science is used as a framework in which new paradigms are seen as providing ever better approximations to the true underlying structure of nature, which will be revealed in the eschaton. It is argued that ecology—the study of the earth as a whole—cannot be treated as a natural science because there can be no paradigms for understanding the earth as a whole. Instead technology is used as a means for interacting with God through nature.

Klippel, Diethelm. Johann August Schlettwein and the Economic Faculty and the University of Giessen. *Hist Polit Thought*, 15(2), 203-227, Sum 94.

Kloppenberg, James T (ed) and Fox, Richard Wightman (ed). *A Companion to American Thought*. Cambridge, Blackwell, 1995.

Klosko, George. Political Obligation and the Natural Duties of Justice. *Phil Pub Affairs*, 23(3), 251-270, Sum 94.

Examination of John Rawls's influential attempts to justify political obligations through the natural duties of justice indicates that the political duties will be either not "natural" in the appropriate sense or not sufficiently strong to function as political obligations. In addition, Rawls's reasons for rejecting political obligations based on the principle of fairness in favor of the natural duties of justice do not withstand critical scrutiny, if examined from the standpoint of representative individuals in the original position.

Kloskowska, Antonina. National Identification and the Transgression of National Boundaries: The Steps Toward Universalization. *Dialogue Hum*, 3(4), 5-17, 1993.

Kloskowski, Kazimierz. The Chance and the Prebiotic Evolution. *Stud Phil Christ*, 30(2), 163-169, 1994.

Klotz, Christian. Schritte auf dornichten Pfaden: Zu neuerer Kantliteratur. *Phil Rundsch*, 42(1), 11-34, Mr 95.

Klotzko, Arlene Judith. CQ *Interview*: Dr Boudewijn Chabot on Assisted Suicide in the Absence of Somatic Illness. *Cambridge Quart Healthcare Ethics*, 4(2), 239-249, Spr 95.

Kluxen, Wolfgang. "Europas Identität und seine pilosophische Erbschaft" in *Das geistige Erbe Europas, Buhr, Manfred (ed)*, 177-192. Napoli, Vivarium, 1994.

Knabenschuh de Porta, Sabine. Signo, Texto y Contexto: Alcance y conexiones filosóficas de las Teoría Semiótica. *Rev Filosof (Venezuela)*, 19, 59-80, 1994.

One of the most outstanding characteristics of Semiotic Theory is that it manages to transcend the boundaries of Linguistical Semantics, coming into contact with, among others, two philosophical disciplines: Logic and Philosophy of Language. Concretely, a comparison between the Greima's Semiotics, Frege's Logic of Language and Merleau-Ponty's Phenomenology of Language demonstrates that these three theories work with the same basic notions of *structure, context* and *veridiction*, presenting in this regard only differences in degree. Thus, Semiotic Theory proves to be a *logic of the subject* and a *phenomenology of speech*, and as such it provides the necessary conditions to serve as a point of departure in the development of an authentic *general theory of language*. (edited)

Knapp, Gudrun-Axell. "Frauen und Rechtsextremismus: 'Kampfgefährtin' oder 'Heimchen am Herd'?" in *Nationalsozialismus und Moderne, Welzer, Harald (ed)*, 208-239. Tübingen, Ed Diskord, 1993.

The article focuses on tensions existing between gender ideology and gender relations in militant Neo-Nazi organizations in contemporary Germany. Based on an analysis of the newsletter of the "Deutsche Frauenfront", "Die Kampfgefaehrtin", the article sketches the divergent views which women of the extreme Right express in criticizing their male "comrades" traditional approach to gender roles and femininity. Women's claims to equal rights are articulated within a racist framework of difference. In a symptomatic conflict they argue against being excluded from street-fighting by their male group members. They attempt to justify their right to participate in militant action by referring to NS discourses on gender relations, a critique of patriarchal gender hierarchies and "voelkisch" notions of the heroic Nordic woman.

Knappik, Georg J. Der Schöpfer als Wirklichkeit—Gegenüber dem Atheismus als nichtwissenschaftlicher Ideologie. *Stud Phil Christ*, 30(2), 171-184, 1994.

Knasas, John F X. Intellectual Dynamism in Transcendental Thomism: A Metaphysical Assessment. *Amer Cath Phil Quart*, 69(1), 15-28, Wint 95.

By focusing on Marechal, Rahner, and Lonergan, I extract a common conception of intellectual dynamism. In sum, all three understand the dynamism of the intellect to be an a priori mediating factor of human consciousness for the appearance of things as beings. My paper argues the incompatibility of this conception with classical metaphysical claims. Given what we can observe to be sometimes true of less encompassing mediating contexts, one can acquaint oneself with the ideas of something standing outside a context and the context placing the thing in a different light. These ideas can be used to wonder if the a priori intellectual dynamism is revealing things for what they truly are.

Knebel, Sven K. Necessitas moralis ad optimum (IV): Repertorium zur Optimismusdiskussion im 17 Jahrhundert. *Stud Leibniz*, 25(2), 201-208, 1993.

Knebel, Sven K. Vom Ursprung der Soziologie aus der posttridentinischen Theologie. *Frei Z Phil Theol*, 41(3), 463-490, 1994.

I challenge the view which has recently been given further support in I Hacking's "Taming of Chance" that not till the nineteenth century probabilistic laws have been conceived. When the seventeenth century-Molinists tried to make sense of the Tridentine dogma that sinning cannot be avoided during man's lifetime, they took this dogma to be equivalent to the proposition "Referring to 1,000 people, there must be a sin". Aside from a logical account by means of merely confused supposition, they employed an aleatory account of why such a "moral necessity" does not destroy the contingency of each single case.

Kneepkens, C H. From Eternal to Perpetual Truths: A Note on the Mediaeval History of Aristotle, *De interpretatione*, Ch 1, 16a18. *Vivarium*, 32(2), 161-185, N 94.

Knetsch, Jack L. Environmental Valuation: Some Problems of Wrong Questions and Misleading Answers. *Environ Values*, 3(4), 351-368, Wint 94.

Contingent valuation of people's willingness to pay has rapidly become the method of choice to value all manner of environmental damages. The correct measure is, however, the sum people require to compensate them for such losses, an amount which will normally be far larger than their willingness to pay. And on present evidence, responses to contingent valuation questions are not likely to represent any measure of economic values. The results of these valuation practices will, therefore, bias environmental policies and distort incentives.

Knight, Christopher. Structure Not Substance: Theological Realism for a Pluralistic Age. *Int J Phil Relig*, 37(3), 167-180, Je 95.

The adoption of a critical realism in theology, on the basis of an apparently similar realism in the sciences, is examined. The work of Rom HarrÉ and Mary Hesse on scientific realism, when applied to theology, suggests the importance of a structural, rather than substantial, understanding of realism. This is related to the traditional theological concept of apophaticism, and has important implications for interfaith dialogue. Richard Boyd's concept of epistemic access may shed further light on these.

Knight, Deborah. Selves, Interpreters, Narrators. *Phil Lit*, 18(2), 274-286, O 94.

Knight, J F and Ash, C J. Mixed Systems. *J Sym Log*, 59(4), 1383-1399, D 94.

This paper gives a metatheorem designed to handle priority constructions with infinitely many requirements at different levels. The new metatheorem extends results of Ash in which either all of the requirements were at one (top) level, or, in the special case where the top level was a limit ordinal, there was one requirement at each level in a recursive sequence converging to the top.

Knight, J F and Ash, C J. Ramified Systems. *Annals Pure Applied Log*, 70(3), 205-221, D 94.

This paper extends a metatheorem of Ash for nested priority constructions (see Ash, C J, "Recursive labelling systems and stability of recursive structures in hyperarithmetical degrees," *Trans of the Amer Math Soc*, 1986, pp 497-514; corrections, ib, 1988, p 851). The new result involves enumerating sets at various levels, while the original result involved enumerating a set at the recursive level only. The paper includes sample problems where the new metatheorem yields results, and the original metatheorem, and other variants, do not apply.

Knight, Margaret (ed). *Humanist Anthology: From Confucius to Attenborough*. Buffalo, Prometheus, 1995.

Knights, David and Kerfoot, Deborah. "Into the Realm of the Fearful: Power, Identity and the Gender Problematic" in *Power/Gender, Radtke, H Lorraine (ed)*, 67-88. Newbury Park, Sage, 1994.

This chapter is concerned to explore 'gender differentiation', defined as the social construction of sexual difference: how sex-based specificities come to be maintained rather than from what point of origin women's oppression emanates. Our purpose is twofold; to offer an account of how the division of labor has remained so stable, within the context of a discussion of gender and sexuality; and, following Game (1991:36) a second purpose is to begin to address the question 'how are we constituted now, and how might we be otherwise, *now*?." Informed by a reading of Foucault, it is our contention that a conception of power and its operation provides as escape from what we regard as the dualistic thinking of many radicals and Marxist feminists, and may lead us toward an understanding of how sex inequality and male dominance are perpetuated.

Knitter, Paul F. Pitfalls and Promises for a Global Ethics. *J Dharma*, 19(3), 248-259, Jl-S 94.

This essay examines recent widespread calls for a "Global Ethics", such as the "Declaration of a Global Ethic" approved at the World Parliament of Religions in Chicago 1991. It points out that such efforts are as dangerous as they are necessary. Their danger is rooted in the facility with which such efforts can be coopted or manipulated, perhaps unconsciously, by the dominant powers which are in control of both international economics and discourse. To offset such manipulation, all efforts toward a global ethics must be sure to hear and honor *all* voices, especially the voices of those who have been marginalized or exploited by the dominant economic powers.

Knoell, Dieter Rudolf. *Zur gesellschaftlichen Stellung der Kunst zwischen Natur und Technik (Band 2)*. Hildesheim, Olms, 1994.

Subject of this work is the relationship between art and aesthetics and the 'technical progress' as well as the 'retarded nature'. By means of socio-cultural methods and the theories of literature and fine arts the author analyses the neopositivist attempts orientated towards the natural sciences to 'demystify art', which are correlated with a remystification of politics; furthermore attempts inspired by the philosophy of history and social criticisms to 'politicize art' and to demystify politics. The different answers to the fascist aesthetisation of politics acknowledged by Walter Benjamin are followed up to the current production of art and the theories reflecting them.

Knox Jr, John. Pre-Existence, Survival, and Sufficient Reason. *Amer Phil Quart*, 32(2), 167-176, Ap 95.

Every self-conscious being ("person") exists, I claim, for all earlier time, and not improbably survives the death of its current body, if it has one. For, first, no being enters the temporal stream at some given point for absolutely no reason at all. The smallest reason for why a given person should do so turns out, however, to be lacking. So a person who exists at any time exists, also, at all earlier times—and may be expected to survive the death of any physical body that it may currently possess.

Koana, Akiko. Le Rôle de la Notion de Caractère. *Horiz Phil*, 4(1), 15-29, Autumn 93.

The purpose of this article is to consider the role of "character" in the history of aesthetics. In the eighteenth century in France, the "imitation of nature" was considered to be the authoritative principle of art. We can interpret the appearance of "character" especially in the writings about music and architecture as a result of the conflict between this principle and the recognition of the importance of nonrepresentative approaches in these arts. This theory provides us with a good example to manifest the turning point of the history of aesthetics from objectivism to subjectivism under the influence of "sensationalism" in the field of philosophy.

Koch, Anton Friedrich. Wozu noch Erste Philosophie? Über das Wechselverhältnis von Subjektivität und raumzeitlicher Einzelnheit. *Z Phil Forsch*, 48(4), 497-517, 1994.

This paper argues a version of internal or Kant-like realism from the nature of space and time: Our universe, being spatiotemporal, 1) necessarily grows knowing subjects somewhere and somewhen and 2) could not, in principle, be exhaustively known aperspectivally (i.e., from no particular point of view within it). 3) Subjectivity is essentially embodied in space and time, as persons among other things, to whom it is internally related (as witness their phenomenal, secondary qualities). First philosophy has to study these and related issues.

Koch, Gertrud. Nachstellungen—Film und historischer Moment. *Deut Z Phil*, 43(3), 497-506, 1995.

The article is based on the assumption that there are cases where the genetic argument of photography as referent becomes crucial, e.g., for film genres like historical documents and documentaries. In fiction film the interplay between the 'real' as photographical references and the montage as hidden center of derealization is exemplified in surrealist aesthetics, namely Bunuel and Adorno. Film is based on these twofolded practices has affinities to surrealism in the sense of navigating the artificial recognition of concrete objects into a surface reality.

Koch, Gertrud. Schwerpunkt: Philosophie und Film—ein hundertjähriges Verhältnis. *Deut Z Phil*, 43(3), 453-454, 1995.

The introductory remark gives a short overview to a collection of articles on philosophical problems of film theory. The reference problem for the introduction to the special section on philosophy and film emphasizes the troubled relationship between philosophy and film compared to other aesthetic media. The problem of concepts and notions of realism in philosophy and film/photography theory is the focus for the special section, which includes articles on Peirce (H Pape), name theory and photography (M Seel), fiction and psychoanalysis (R Allen), the audio-visual and Lacan (S Zizek), time, history and the 'real' (G Koch).

Koch, Günter. *Kausalität Determinismus und Zufall in der wissenschaftlichen Naturbeschreibung*. Berlin, Duncker Humblot, 1994.

Koch, Lutz. "Common Sense as an Ingredient of the Self and the Community" in *Identity, Culture, and Education, Smeyers, Paul (ed)*, 185-193. Leuven, Leuven Univ Pr, 1994.

The new situation in Europe, as exemplified in Germany, calls for a common consciousness, one traditionally characterized as *sensus communis* or common sense. Kant organized his ruminations on common sense—specifically, the logical common sense—around three maxims: enlightenment, the extended way of thinking and the consistent way of thinking. These are here described with eye to their consequences for the issues of identity, community and pedagogy.

Koch, Tom. The Gulf Between: Surrogate Choices, Physician Instructions, and Informal Network Responses. *Cambridge Quart Healthcare Ethics*, 4(2), 185-192, Spr 95.

Health care providers have been criticized for too often providing inadequate information to patient surrogates who make critical care decisions for critically ill patients. They also have been accused of a general failure to adequately consider the needs and perspectives of patient caregivers, surrogates, and family members, involved in ethical decision making on behalf of severely ill patients. What is not well understood, however, is the basis on which those patient representatives make ethical decisions concerning medical treatment in bioethical contexts. Do they share the same decision making criteria as medical officials? If medical information is limited, to whom do they turn for support and information? This paper describes the decision making process of a surrogate faced with deciding on whether or not to approve continued life support for a comatose parent. Report data is drawn from an electronic dialog between the patient surrogate and other members of an online computer forum, and the surrogate's response to an author questionnaire submitted after the decision process was completed. The information received illustrates a set of criteria used by patient surrogates which differs markedly from that used by medical professionals in critical care contexts. The increasing use of telecommunication technology by patient representatives faced with critical care decisions offers, it is argued, an invaluable window onto the distance separating the perspectives of both medical personnel and patient representatives involved in bioethical dilemmas.

Kochunny, C M and Rogers, Hudson. Head-Heart Disparity Among Future Managers: Implications for Ethical Conduct. *J Bus Ethics*, 13(9), 719-729, S 94.

An examination of the ethical perceptions of business students using Macobby's head/heart traits and a comparison to earlier studies of managers, accountants, and business students is made. The data were collected at three universities that are similar in size, enrollment and degree programs within the College of Business. Results indicate that present day business students are no less ethically inclined than are their business counterparts in previous eras. In general head traits dominated over heart traits, an indication that business schools continued to do a good job emphasizing and developing analytical skills but a poor job of developing the qualities of the heart that are generally associated with ethical behavior. The implications of these findings are discussed.

Kockelkoren, Petran. "The Mouse in the Cat's Claws: A Framework for a Hermeneutics of Nature" in *Ecology, Technology, and Culture,* Zweers, Wim (ed), 99-117. Cambridge, White Horse, 1994.

Koczanowicz, Leszek. G H Mead and L S Vygotsky on Meaning and the Self. *J Speculative Phil*, 8(4), 262-276, 1994.

An examination of the relation between meaning and the self in the thought of George Herbert Mead and L S Vygotsky. For both Mead and Vygotsky meaning is neither thought nor idea existing in mind; instead, meaning is constituted in action and in human interaction. Vygotsky pays attention to two factors constituting meaning: it is both a means of communication and presentation of the essence of things or natural laws. For Mead, meaning is constituted in the process of interaction, especially in carrying out social acts. Both try to answer the behaviouristic Challenge proving that such concepts as "self" or "consciousness" can be preserved in the body of science even if an objective point of view would be accepted. For Vygotsky, the main point in the process of self-formation is to assimilate the cultural heritage of mankind included in meanings. For Mead, becoming a self means the ability to take the role of others on increasingly generalized levels. It is argued that their assumption that the ability to enter the world of meanings is the indispensable part of the process of self-formation is crucial for overcoming the restrictions of behaviouristic social sciences.

Koehn, Daryl. A Role for Virtue Ethics in the Analysis of Business Practice. *Bus Ethics Quart*, 5(3), 533-539, Jl 95.

This article explores differences in the ways in which utilitarian, deontological, and virtue/aretic ethics treat of act, outcome, and agent. I argue that virtue ethics offers important and distinctive insights into business practice, insights overlooked by utilitarian and deontological ethics.

Koen, Avraam. *Atoms, Pleasure, Virtue: The Philosophy of Epicurus*. New York, Lang, 1995.

This book offers a reconstruction, reinterpretation and reevaluation of the philosophy of Epicurus. It aims to show that his thought represents the most significant and systematic contribution of the Hellenistic age; and speaks with special clarity and urgency to us who find ourselves in a similar predicament. The book opens with a sketch of the Hellenistic world and proceeds to consider in detail the principal ontological, epistemological and ethical tenets of Epicurus' philosophy.

König, Josef and Kümmel, Friedrich (ed). *Der logische Unterschied theoretischer und praktischer Sätze und seine philosophische Bedeutung.* Freiburg, Alber, 1994.

This book is a collection of highly sophisticated lectures by Josef König (1893-1974). They concern the formal or radical distinction between "theoretical sentences" and "practical sentences", which marks essential differences in the forms of knowledge and behavior concerned. König reformulates the *ontological* difference as well as the *transcendental* difference in terms of a *logical* difference. He gives a new explication of the epistemological function of *singular sentences* (these to be distinguished from the Vienna Circle's "Basissätz"!). This could not be rendered adequately within the framework of traditional logic.

König, Siegfried. *Zur Begründung der Menschenrechte: Hobbes-Locke-Kant.* Freiburg, Alber, 1994.

Koenis, Sjaak. Laat honderd bloemen bloeien. *Kennis Methode*, 18(2-3), 169-172, 1994.

Koeppl, Peter M and Bersoff, Donald N. The Relation Between Ethical Codes and Moral Principles. *Ethics Behavior*, 3(3-4), 345-357, 1993.

We describe the application of fundamental moral principles, with particular emphasis on prima facie duties, to formal codes of ethics that regulate the conduct of forensic psychologists who act as expert witnesses. Then we discuss the American Psychological Association's (1992) "Ethical Principles of Psychologists and Code of Conduct" and the Committee on Ethical Guidelines for Forensic Psychologist's "Specialty Guidelines for Forensic Psychologists" (1991) and critically appraise how these documents translate basic moral principles. We conclude that, in many ways, the documents exemplify ethical obligations such as nonmaleficence, beneficence, and justice, but they fall short in many other ways, particularly with regard to autonomy and fidelity.

Koetsier, Teun and Allis, Victor. One Some Paradoxes of the Infinite II. *Brit J Phil Sci*, 46(2), 235-247, Je 95.

In an earlier paper the authors discussed some super-tasks by means of a kinematical interpretation. In the present paper we show a semi-formal way that a more abstract treatment is possible. The core idea of our approach is simple: if a super-task can be considered as a union of (finite) tasks, it is natural to define the effect of the super-task as the union of the effects of the finite tasks it consists of. We show that this approach enables us to handle two of the three super-tasks that we discussed earlier. We also argue that recent objections against our original kinematical interpretation do not hold water. One of our arguments is based on the construction of an elegant correspondence between the first of those three super-tasks and Zeno's *Achilles and the Tortoise*.

Köveker, Dietmar. Zwischen "objektiver Gültigkeit" und "subjektiv-notwendigem Probierstein" der Wahrheit. *Z Phil Forsch*, 49(2), 274-293, Ap-Je 95.

The purpose of the article is to clarify the systematic function and epistemological significance of consensus theory of truth as contained in Kant's work in three steps: 1) A sketch of the various truth-theoretical accounts in Kant's work; 2) An outline of the consensus-oriented deliberations of his political philosophy; 3) The confrontation of these accounts with the truth-conception underlying crucial parts of his "Critique of Pure Reason". This leads to the conclusion that Kant was unable to develop a convincing model of how to integrate the contended "objective validity" of theoretical statements with the intersubjective validity of practical statements.

Kofman, Sarah. "Accessories (*Ecce Homo*, 'Why I Write Such Good Books', 'The Untimelies', 3)" in *Nietzsche: A Critical Reader*, Sedgwick, Peter R (ed), 144-157. Cambridge, Blackwell, 1995.

Kohák, Erazim. Being Human, More or Less. *Human Stud*, 17(3), 287-305, Jl 94.

Author surveys conceptions of human summum bonum through Western intellectual history, Egyptian ideal of permanence, Greek ideal of goodness and beauty, Hebraic idea of righteousness, mediaeval, conception of salvation, contemporary ideal of expanding consumption, suggesting that the last is both decadent and self-destructive. Rejecting ideas of "return to nature" as an option, author offers a latter day version of a Puritan ideal—acceptance of moral responsibility and self-transcendence in service of nature and neighbor—as a viable option.

Kohan, Walter O. "Lo Apeiron de Anaximandro y lo Inconsciente Freudiano" in *Temas Actuales de Filosofía, Palacios, María Julia (ed)*, 315-319. Buenos Aires, Univ Nacional Salta, 1993.

The purpose of this article is to draw some connections between the "Unlimited", set by Anaximander as the principle that governs the whole universe and the "Unconscious" that according to Freud governs human conduct. Linguistically, both are nouns constructed with a negative prefix that modifies an adjective of negative connotations; as a result of this double negation, both imply an absolute affirmation. From their linguistic similarity, I analyze their similar impersonal character, relationship to causality, necessity and time, and their like function and legality.

Kohl, Marvin. "Caring Love and Liberty: Some Questions" in *The Nature and Pursuit of Love, Goicoechea, David (ed)*, 221-228. Buffalo, Prometheus, 1995.

There is something about the nature of caring love that justifies moderate paternalistic behavior. Given the constituents of this kind of affection, X is required to help Y in certain circumstances (given the usual caveats about the limits of reasonable action) if that help proves necessary, even if it involves unwanted intervention.

Kohl, Marvin. "Singer's Idealization of Love: A Postscript" in *The Nature and Pursuit of Love, Goicoechea, David (ed)*, 229-235. Buffalo, Prometheus, 1995.

Irving Singer purports to be describing a neutral naturalism. Yet libertarian preferences appear as self-evident truths. One of his claims is that the bestowal of love does not seek to alter the object in ways that are alien or contrary to the beloved's own inclinations and desires. This appears to be a mistake, since appreciating and having respect for the autonomy of a beloved is not necessarily the same as never intervening in their behalf unless one has consent.

Kohler, Georg. Vorrang der Demokratie vor der Philosophie? Über den Sinn von Politischer Philosophie. *Stud Phil (Switzerland)*, 53, 201-224, 1994.

Kohlmann, Ulrich. Überwindung des Anthropozentrismus durch Gleichheit alles Lebendigen?. *Z Phil Forsch*, 49(1), 15-35, Ja-Mr 95.

Some philosophers maintain that an excessive anthropocentrism has caused the ecological crisis. Drawing consequences from this opinion, they try to develop nonanthropocentric ethics which attribute equal moral status to man and nature. This paper attacks these endeavours both in general and through a critique of Tom Regan's ethics in particular: 1) Although Regan provides sound arguments for an equal moral status of man and animals he fails in resolving moral conflicts without falling back to an anthropocentric argumentation. 2) The basic normative structure of nonanthropocentric "quality-ethics" confronts all of these ethics with similar problems as those weakening Regan's position. 3) Nature *and* man suffer under the same destructive process which is *not* governed by anthropocentric principles: the laws of world economy. The article thus concludes by arguing that it is not within the field of nonanthropocentric ethics but rather within critical social philosophy that philosophers should face environmental devastation and cruelty to animals.

Kohn-Ley, Charlotte (ed) and Korotin, Ilse (ed). *Der feministische "Sündenfall"?*. Vienna, Picus, 1994.

Koizumi, Takashi. Fukuzawa Yukichi and Religion. *Asian Phil*, 4(2), 109-118, 1994.

When the Meiji government allowed Christianity to be proclaimed in Japan in 1873, there aroused heated controversy about how to deal with religion including Christianity. Fukuzawa Yukichi, the most influential thinker and opinion-leader among Japanese intellectuals in those days, participated in the controversy and wrote more than 80 articles concerning religion. At first, he took a critical standpoint against Christianity from the Utilitarian viewpoint. Then he changed his viewpoint of religion and came to admit a Unitarian Christianity for a little while. But he gradually came to be familiar with Pure Land Buddhism and developed his original philosophy of religion in his later years. In this article I trace the process of change in Fukuzawa's religious viewpoint and clarify his philosophy of religion in his later years, by examining his writings in chronological order.

Kolaitis, Phokion G. Generalized Quantifiers and Pebble Games on Finite Structures. *Annals Pure Applied Log*, 74(1), 23-75, Je 95.

Kolakowski, Leszak. Ethics. *Dialogue Hum*, 4(4), 5-44, 1994.

Kolakowski, Leszek. Even When the Devil Says He Is Telling the Truth, He Is Lying. *Dialogue Hum*, 2(3-4), 11-17, 1992.

Kolany, Adam. Hypergraphs and the Intuitionistic Propositional Calculus. *Rep Math Log*, 27, 55-66, 1993.

Every compact and locally finite hypergraph, determines a free distributive lattice with 0 and 1 generated by vertices of that hypergraph. In the paper *Hypergraphs and the Intuitionistic Propositional Calculus*, it is shown that the considered lattice is a Heyting algebra, even if the hypergraph is infinite. What seems be important, the connective of intuitionistic implication, and from which follows of the negation, have clear interpretations in the lattices generated by hypergraphs. It is also proved that the logic of the class of all (finite) hypergraphs is the Intuitionistic Propositional Calculus. In other words, a propositional formula is intuitionistically provable if it is true in every Heyting algebra obtained in the way described above.

Kolár, Petr. The Speech of Facts and Logic. *Filozof Cas*, 42(6), 1000-1011, 1994.

The notion of fact has a long philosophical pedigree, the highlights of which being later Moore's, Russell's, and the young Wittgenstein's conceptions of facts as truth-makers of beliefs or propositions. In this paper, I concentrate on facts understood as the subject matter of 'fact' *talk*—as something that can be communicated, known, sought for, etc., rather than supposed to do the truth-making job. A fact taken as a 'linguistic' fact is an abstract complex that is mirrored by the syntactic structure of a sentence and represents a particular way to arrive at, or *construct* a proposition expressed by the sentence, provided the proposition is actually true (true in the actual world). 'Linguistic' facts are more like Fregean true thoughts than Russellian truth-makers, and don't serve as the entities required in constructing a correspondence theory of truth based on the concept of fact. They can, however, help in making our 'fact' *talk* more transparent, meaningful independently of a particular theory of truth one professes, and, hopefully, socially correct. The main goals of the papers are as follows: to submit a local analysis of 'fact'-talk in terms of intensional logic, and propose alternative solutions to some of the traditional quandaries about facts, like the question of what forms of ('linguistic') fact there are, and how the distinction between genuine and derivative facts can be drawn and understood.

Kolcaba, Katharine and Kolcaba, Raymond. Health Maintenance as Responsibility for Self. *Phil Cont World*, 1(2), 19-24, Sum 94.

Many kinds of health compromising norms, habits, and beliefs are highly resistant to change thereby preventing new knowledge about health maintenance from advancing widespread better health. Persons would be more responsive if they used a health ethic to harmonize personal behavior with health-maintaining practices. We argue that common sense morality includes a portion of a health ethic in the guise of responsibilities to maintain health as well as avoid self destruction. We discuss an example in which its application can retard decline in older age that results from a sedentary lifestyle.

Kolcaba, Raymond and Kolcaba, Katharine. Health Maintenance as Responsibility for Self. *Phil Cont World*, 1(2), 19-24, Sum 94.

Many kinds of health compromising norms, habits, and beliefs are highly resistant to change thereby preventing new knowledge about health maintenance from advancing widespread better health. Persons would be more responsive if they used a health ethic to harmonize personal behavior with health-maintaining practices. We argue that common sense morality includes a portion of a health ethic in the guise of responsibilities to maintain health as well as avoid self destruction. We discuss an example in which its application can retard decline in older age that results from a sedentary lifestyle.

Kolek, Leszek S and Seidler, Leopold G. Rotarians in a Changing World. *Dialogue Hum*, 4(2-3), 167-176, 1994.

Kolenda, Konstantin. "American Pragmatism and the Humanist Tradition" in *Pragmatism: From Progressivism to Postmodernism, Hollinger, Robert (ed)*, 238-255. Westport, Praeger, 1995.

Kolenda, Pauline. "Konstantin Kolenda: His Life and Times" in *Contributors to the Philosophy of Humanism, Hillar, Marian (ed)*, 1-5. Pasadena, Humanists Houston, 1994.

Konstantin Kolenda, Professor of Philosophy at Rice University, holding the Fred and Carolyn McManis Chair, died December 5, 1991. In this personal remembrance, his wife, Pauline Kolenda, traces his life from his birth in eastern Poland May 17, 1923, through a youth preceding and during World War II when he was a captive laborer in Germany, to migration to the United States after liberation, then education and life as a philosopher. The account was given at an even honoring the appearance of a posthumous work by Kolenda, entitled *The Heart of the Matter*.

Kolmogorov, A N and Jeffrey, Richard (trans). Complete Metric Boolean Algebras. *Phil Stud*, 77(1), 57-66, Ja 95.

Konaté, Yacouba. Le Syndrome Hampâté Bâ ou Comment Naissent les Proverbes. *Quest*, 8(2), 23-45, D 94.

Syndrome is understood here as meaning cross-roads. Hampâté Bâ's personality, his life and experiences can equally be considered as a meeting place, a locus where things come together. In his thought the theme of cross-roads is of central importance. The thought of Hampâté's Bâ is little known, apart from his famous saying expressed at a UNESCO meeting in 1962 "In Africa, when an old man dies a library is burnt down". Even so, this sentence is not well understood, some even consider it be a proverb. What is the meaning of this thought? What is his life-story?

Konner, Melvin. Following a Trajectory: On "Tracing a Trajectory" and "Explaining and Valuing" by James M Gustafson. *Zygon*, 30(2), 191-200, Je 95.

The roots of religious faith—and the provenance of ethical thought—may be sought in the human sciences, the physical sciences, literature, religious traditions, and deep human intuitions. Gustafson's religious stance and the author's, while different on their face, in common reflect a mingling—and tangling—of skepticism, understanding, and transcendence. Let all of us hope and believe what we can.

Kono, Shigemi. "Birth Control and the Value of Human Life" in *Ethics on the Frontiers of Human Existence, Badham, Paul (ed)*, 81-99. New York, Paragon House, 1992.

Kontos, Alkis. "The World Disenchanted, and the Return of Gods and Demons" in *The Barbarism of Reason, Horowitz, Asher (ed)*, 223-247. Toronto, Univ of Toronto Pr, 1994.

This is an interpretation of enchantment, disenchantment and reenchantment. Religion, science, and the rationalization of the world are the primary forces of disenchantment. They create the structures of the iron cage of modernity and cause the loss of nature as our normative axis. It is within the structures of the disenchanted world that the once again enchanted human beings, awakened to the reality of the "polytheism" of ultimate values, must realize their essential being in making ultimate choices. Weber hostile to both moral dogmatism and relativism, articulates the difficult and challenging status of responsible action in the denatured world of modernity.

Koons, Robert C. Gauthier and the Rationality of Justice. *Phil Stud*, 76(1), 1-26, O 94.

In Gauthier's *Morals by Agreement*, game theory is applied to the ancient question of the rationality of justice. I propose a friendly amendment to Gauthier's definition of justice that resolves problems discovered by Kraus and Coleman. I also point out that the defining of fairness can be seen as a coordination problem, thereby undermining Gauthier's choice of a Lockean baseline. Finally, I uncover a new problem for Gauthier's theory: the generalization of two-person bargains to the n-person case. I argue that the possibility of coalition-building substantially restricts the range of cases in which justice can be rational.

Kopelman, Loretta M. Conceptual and Moral Disputes about Futile and Useful Treatments. *J Med Phil*, 20(2), 109-121, Ap 95.

A series of cases have crystallized disputes about when medical treatments are useful or futile, and consequently about the doctor-patient relationship, resource allocation, communication, empathy, relief of suffering, autonomy, undertreatment, overtreatment, paternalism and palliative care. It is helpful to understand that utility and futility are complimentary concepts and that judgements about whether treatments are useful or futile in the contested cases have common features. They are: (1) grounded in medical science, (2) value laden, (3) at or near the threshold of utility, and (4) burdensome. No schema for line-drawing escapes borderline cases and we should focus upon justification of the empirical, ethical and evaluative components underlying these judgements, rather than make an arbitrary decision about whether doctors, patients or societal consensus should be the final arbiter.

Kopelman, Loretta M. Informed Consent and Anonymous Tissue Samples: The Case of HIV Seroprevalence Studies. *J Med Phil*, 19(6), 525-552, D 94.

Human Immonodeficiency Virus (HIV) seroprevalence studies use anonymous tissue samples obtained in hospitals and clinics without donor consent. This can be justified as a response to a public health emergency, but should not be seen as setting a precedent for waiving consent whenever samples are anonymous. (edited)

Kopelman, Loretta M. Normal Grief: Good or Bad? Health or Disease?. *Phil Psychiat Psych*, 1(4), 209-220, D 94.

Darwin, Freud, and Pollock considered normal grief an adaptive emotion, associating grieving with empathy, creativity, and the capacity to overcome loss and form new attachments. In contrast, Engel, Bowlby, and Hofer, building upon the work of Lindemann, argued that both normal and pathological grief are diseases. Determining whether normal grief is adaptive or a disease depends in part upon whether it is bad, because a necessary condition of something being a disease is that it is bad. Psychiatrists holding that normal grief is a disease (whether adopting a biomedical or biopsychosocial model) suggested that it is bad for nonmoral rather than moral reasons. The question of whether grief is bad is interesting in its own right. It turns out to be harder than one might expect to say just how and why normal grief is bad, a surprising conclusion given its association with increased pain, distress, morbidity, mortality, and dysfunction. Nonmoral badness may be instrumental, extrinsic, inherent, intrinsic, or contributory. Systematically considered, there is no basis for concluding that normal grief is, all things considered, nonmorally bad, and thus for claiming that it is a disease.

Kopelman, Loretta M. Rejoinder: If Grief Is Not Bad, Is It Good?. *Phil Psychiat Psych*, 1(4), 225-226, D 94.

The case cannot be made that the capacity for grief is nonmorally bad. Accordingly there is more support for the view, held by Darwin and Freud, that normal grief is nonmorally good than for a competing psychiatric theory that it is a disease. Normal grief cannot be shown nonmorally bad, a necessary condition of something being a disease. As for moral categories, grief is neither morally bad nor good in itself but may play a role in our moral lives, for example, by causing reflection upon the nature of what we value or upon whether grief distracts us from pursuing a more virtuous life. The author uses Dicken's characters to illustrate this.

Kopper, Joachim. Die Signatur der Zeit—Zum 80, Geburstag von Gerhard Funke. *Z Phil Forsch*, 48(3), 460-466, Jl-S 94.

Koprek, Ivan. Freedom for the Good: Thomistic Philosophy on Freedom in the Context of Linguistic-Analytic Reception. *Filozof Istraz*, 14(1), 33-39, 1994.

The phenomenon from which linguistic-analytic discussions on freedom is being characterized by the said pageant statement "X could have acted differently". Action, therefore, depends on the agent. The question is only how should this be interpeted. Should it be understood as: "X could have acted differently in the case the he *decided* differently"? It would appear that the decision of the agent is primarily, as was held by P H Nowell-Smith, the determined *character* of the agent who freely and willfully desired, intended, a certain act. In this context, the author examines the Thomistic concept of freedom of will as the rational aspiration or ability of man to be induced *according to reasons* to act (see *Summa Theologia* I II 6, 2), and which A J P Kenny introduced in analytical philosophy and attempted to interpret in his book *Will, Freedom, and Power*.

Kopton, K. 'The Unnatural Desire for More than one Needs': An Objection to James Tully's View. *Locke News*, 25, 75-78, 1994.

Kopytko, Roman. Against Rationalistic Pragmatics. *J Prag*, 23(5), 475-491, My 95.

Is it rational to accept the claims of "rationalistic pragmatics"-(RP) such as 1) the postulate of the "rationality of human behavior", 2) the deterministic approach, 3) the principle of methodological reductionism? Is there a deductive relationship between the theoretical assumptions of RP and the descriptive analyses based on them? Are concepts of RP such as "rationality" and "face" predictable? What is the function of context in RP? What are the basic pragmatic paradoxes in RP? Is there any reasonable alternative to RP? These and related questions will be addressed in this paper.

Korab-Karpowicz, Wlodzimierz J. Freedom and Tradition. *Dialogue Hum*, 2(2), 79-84, 1992.

Kordic, Ivan. Denken, Sprechen und Verstehen bei Matthias Flacius Illyricus. *Filozof Istraz*, 13(4), 755-781, 1993.

Denken als spekulativer Zugang zur Wirklichkeit nimmt immer auch eine sprachliche Form an, gleich ob diese Form ausdrücklich oder unausdrücklich artikuliert wird. Diese sprachliche Form will in ihrer Geschichte und in ihrer Aktualität verstanden werden. So sind Denken und Sprechen immer wieder Gegenstand einer verstehenden, hermeneutischen Reflexion. Dieser Sachverhalt wurde von vielen Denkern in Geschichte und Gegenwart thematisiert. Einer dieser Denker war auch Matthias Flacius Illyricus, der sich in seiner Zeit besonders der Frage nach dem Verstehen der Heiligen Schrift gegenübersah. Für dieses Verstehen nahm er das ganze denkerische und sprachliche Instrumentarium der Tradition und seiner Zeit in Anspruch. Auf den ersten Blick kann seine diesbezügliche Reflexion als fixiert und dogmatisch aussehen. Der tiefere Einblick in seine Denkart lässt ihn aber als einen Denker erscheinen, der die Vielschichtigkeit und Vielseitigkeit seiner Problematik durchaus kannte und sie in ihrer geschichtlichen und systematischen Dimension zu meistern suchte, und zwar auf die Art, dass moderne Denker wie zB Dilthey und Gadamer ihre Erörterung als beispielhaft und zukunftsweisend betrachteten. Denken, Sprechen und Verstehen zeigten sich in ihrem Verhältnis zueinander auch bei ihm als unerschöpflicher Bereich des Gedankenspiels, der die Tiefen und Breiten des menschlichen Geistes auszuloten versucht.

Korfiatis, K J and Stamou, G P. Emergence of New Fields in Ecology: The Case of Life History Studies. *Hist Phil Life Sci*, 16(1), 97-116, Ja 94.

We examine the emergence of the field of life-history strategies during the 1950s. (We consider a 'field' an area of scientific activity consisting of a theoretical core, a subject of research, a vocabulary and research tools). During the late 1940s and early 1950s, population ecology faced many problems, concerning its conceptual framework, its mathematical models, experimental deficiencies, etc. Research on life-history characteristics remained descriptive, lacking explanations about the causes and significance of phenomena. This was due to the deficiencies of the theoretical framework of population ecology up to the 1950s. The catalyzing factor for the emergence of the new field was the interdisciplinary impacts, and especially the impact of neo-Darwinism. The elaboration of a new theoretical core, invoking also methodological shifts, was the triggering factor, conditioning the emergence of the new field.

Korn, James H and McGaha, Annette Christy. The Emergence of Interest in the Ethics of Psychological Research with Humans. *Ethics Behavior*, 5(2), 147-159, 1995.

We describe the growth of interest in the ethics of research with human participants based on articles abstracted in *Psychological Abstracts* and *PsycLIT*. Interest was low and variable until 1974, after which there was a marked increase in the number of articles published. We explain this emergence of ethical interest on terms of the social climate of concern for human rights in 1960s and 1970s, the 1973 revision of the American Psychological Association's ethical principles, and the developments of federal regulation of research with human participants.

Kornblith, Hilary. "A Conservative Approach to Social Epistemology" in *Socializing Epistemology: The Social Dimensions of Knowledge*, Schmitt, Frederick (ed), 93-110. Lanham, Rowman & Littlefield, 1994.

Those who favor a naturalistic approach to epistemology have long argued that work in psychology is relevant to epistemological problems. Similar considerations show the relevance of work in sociology, and thus militate in favor of a socialized epistemology. At the same time, the kind of socialized epistemology which is thereby motivated is far more conservative than many theorists now favor. The present paper defends this more conservative account of the role which social factors should play in a proper understanding of knowledge.

Kornblith, Hilary. In Defense of Deductive Inference. *Phil Stud*, 76(2-3), 247-257, D 94.

Korotin, Ilse. "Die mythische Wirklichkeit eines Volkes " in *Der feministische "Sündenfall"?*, Kohn-Ley, Charlotte (ed), 84-130. Vienna, Picus, 1994.

Korotin, Ilse. "Nach Verschiedenen Zwischenfällen ist die Arbeit Schliesslich bei mir Gelandet" in *Die besten Geister der Nation*, Korotin, Ilse (ed), 240-290. Vienna, Picus, 1994.

Korotin, Ilse (ed). *Die besten Geister der Nation*. Vienna, Picus, 1994.

Korotin, Ilse (ed) and Kohn-Ley, Charlotte (ed). *Der feministische "Sündenfall"?*. Vienna, Picus, 1994.

Korotin, Ilse Erika. *"Am Muttergeist soll die Welt genesen": Philosophische Dispositionen zum Frauenbild im Nationalsozialismus*. Vienna, Boehlau, 1992.

Korthals, Michiel. Filosofie en wetenschapsonderzoek als meervoudig gestoorde persoonlijkheden. *Kennis Methode*, 18(2-3), 192-197, 1994.

Kortooms, Toine. Following Edmund Husserl on One of the Paths Leading to the Transcendental Reduction. *Husserl Stud*, 10(3), 163-180, 1993-94.

In the first book of his *Ideas Pertaining to a Pure Phenomenology and to a Phenomenological Philosophy* Husserl sketches out a way that leads to the disclosure of the transcendental domain. The purpose of this article is to explain why Husserl in the 1920s called this way a psychological one whereas in the 1930s he considered it to be a Cartesian way. The main reason for this change is that the psychological analysis in *Ideas* is introduced as a means, while later on Husserl developed a way via psychology in which the foundation of a pure psychology is a goal in itself and the discovery of the transcendental domain only happens by chance.

Koselleck, Reinhart. "Some Reflections on the Temporal Structure of Conceptual Change" in *Main Trends in Cultural History*, Melching, Willem (ed), 7-16. Amsterdam, Rodopi, 1994.

Koslowski, Peter. Razón e historia: La modernidad del postmodernismo. *Anu Filosof*, 27(3), 969-989, 1994.

The paper distinguishes between a free form of modernity and an ideological form of modernity, whereby the latter can also be called modernism. Free modernity aims at realising the modern, i.e., that which responds to the needs to the present and realises what corresponds to the state-of-the-art. Modernism as an ideology, however, believes in "the" ultimate modernism, in one final modern age of reason. The modernist Hegelian and Marxist philosophies of history and of dialectical metaphysics have come to an end. It demonstrates that we are living in a post-modern age that gives a new freedom for the Christian interpretation of history and for the theological and personalist form of metaphysics.

Kosolapov, N A. An Integrative Ideology for Russia. *Russian Stud Phil*, 33(4), 6-40, Spr 95.

Ideology is an objective phenomenon; scholarly understanding of its nature presents substantial psychological, political, and other difficulties. The purpose of the article was twofold: first, to stress the need for a scientific general theory of ideology, covering both religion and ideologies of the modernity. And second, to speculate as to the kind of ideology that might be stimulating, objectively constructive and psychologically acceptable for Russia which presently lives ideologically in the Communist or pre-Communist past. Proposed "integrative" ideology is expected to be a development rather than negation of essentially socialist (as contrary to Marxist-Leninist) ethics, methodology and world view.

Kossler, Matthias. Empirischer und intelligibler Charakter: Von Kant über Fries und Schelling zu Schopenhauer. *Schopenhauer Jahr*, 76, 195-201, 1995.

Kostyrko, Teresa. "Remarks on 'Aesthetization' in Science on the Basis of History" in *Historiography Between Modernism and Postmodernism*, Topolski, Jerzy (ed), 213-221. Amsterdam, Rodopi, 1994.

The paper attempts to arrange different ways of understanding the notion aesthetization present in the contemporary culture and to show that reasons for the career of this notion in the contemporary humanities. The author focuses on one of the distinguished senses of aesthetization—on aesthetization of the professional cognitive practice and considers the case of this practice on the basis of a discussion on historiography from F R Ankersmit's text "Narrative as Representation". The author concludes that Ankersmit's main thesis, that there is an analogy between art and historiography, and his postulate, that philosophy of history should listen to lessons taught by aesthetics, both "raise essential doubts". This is so because Ankersmit based them on arbitrarily chosen aesthetic conceptions which do not form the basis for any generalizations. Therefore—in the author's view—aesthetization justified in such a way can hardly have reasonance in the domain of history discussed here.

Koszmider, Piotr. Semimorasses and Nonreflection at Singular Cardinals. *Annals Pure Applied Log*, 72(1), 1-24, Mr 95.

Kotarbinska, Janina. Tadeusz Kotarbinski's Independent Ethics. *Dialogue Hum*, 2(3-4), 5-10, 1992.

Kotlarski, Henryk. On the Incompleteness Theorems. *J Sym Log*, 59(4), 1414-1419, D 94.

We give new proofs of both incompleteness theorems. We do not use the diagonalization lemma, but work with some quickly growing functions instead.

Kotowski, Mathias and Greinacher, Norbert. End of Utopia? Religion, Rationality and Art as Elements of Transcendence. *Hermathena*, 150, 45-56, Wint 93.

Koutlouka, Maria. La Problématique de Denys sur Dieu: Théologie ou Philosophie?. *Diotima*, 23, 92-94, 1995.

Koutras, D N. Le Beau chez Denys. *Diotima*, 23, 99-105, 1995.

Koutstaal, Wilma and Rosenthal, Robert. "Contrast Analysis in Behavioral Research" in *Probability in Theory-Building*, Brzezinski, Jerzy (ed), 135-173. Amsterdam, Rodopi, 1994.

Several methods of computing contrasts are reviewed and compared. Approaches to contrast analysis in both between-subjects and repeated-measures designs are demonstrated. The versatility, precision, and enhanced statistical power achieved through contrast analysis are emphasized.

Kovacs, George. The Way to Ultimate Meaning in Meister Eckhart's Mysticism. *Ultim Real Mean*, 18(1), 34-53, Mr 95.

The basic question guiding this study may be expressed as: What can one learn, especially for today, from Eckhart's speculative mysticism on the search for ultimate meaning, on understanding ultimate reality? The following reflections, in responding to this question, 1) indicate the significance of Eckhart's mysticism for the question of ultimate meaning, 2) describe his life as a teacher and thinker, 3) examine the nature of his thought and its background and impact, 4) unearth and assess his main teachings on ultimate meaning, 5) and identify some final conclusions and insights in evaluating and for appropriating his thought.

Kovel, Joel. "Marxism and Spirituality" in *Marxism in the Postmodern Age*, Callari, Antonio (ed), 42-50. New York, Guilford, 1994.

It is argued that "spirit", properly understood, is a category integral to Marxism. Spirit, as the transformational motion of being, is anterior to religions, which are particular historical manifestations of spirit. Marxism is another such manifestation; indeed, Marx criticized religion in the name of spirit. Marxism also insists that the notion of spirit be given material content, i.e., it calls for a "historical materialism of spirit". In practice, Marxist appropriation of spirituality is tenuous at best, owing largely to the intolerance of Marxists for subjective reflection. Marxism's defeats may signal a change of direction, however.

Kovel, Joel. Commentary on "Beyond Liberation" and "Moralist or Therapist?". *Phil Psychiat Psych*, 2(1), 33-34, Mr 95.

Kowalczyk, Stanislaw. Buber's Dialogic Personalism. *Dialogue Hum*, 3(1), 115-126, 1993.

Buber's dialogic personalism should be employed in the Judaistic-Christian dialogue. We can distinguish two aspects of this dialogue: formal-methological and thematic-substantial. Characterizing the formal-methodological requirements of dialogue, Buber distinguished the attitude of real dialogue (partnership) and the attitude of monologue (an attempt to subordinate another man). An authenting dialogue is a relation of reciprocity and equality. Interhuman dialogue should have detemined aims: theoretical-cognitive and practical, existential and social, Buber concentrates also on the thematic-substantial aspect of the Judaistic-Christian dialogue. The basis of such dialogue should be—existential personalism, affirmation of community, the ethos of love, theism and religious faith. The idea of personal God, common to Judaism and Christianity, can become an impulse for brotherly dialogue whose foundations should include truth, benevolence and existential solidarity.

Kowalczyk, Stanislaw. Personalist and Universalistic Aspects of the Idea of Development in the Encyclical *Sollicitudo rei socialis* by John Paul II. *Dialogue Hum*, 4(2-3), 93-105, 1994.

The purpose of the article is to prove that according to John Paul II an adequate conception of development becomes possible when it is formulated on the basis of the theory of personalism. Idea of development is connected with the category of liberation: economic, political and internal-moral. Moral evil constitutes an opposition to development. Social-economic development should take into account the psychic-spiritual dimension of human person. The Pope concentrates on the axiology of development, namely the ideas of truth, good, freedom , solidarity and peace. Integral development signifies an authentic participation in social common good. The common good of the society is a consequence of its logos and freedom. Development is an effect of co-responsibility and co-participation in tasks undertaken for the whole society.

Koza, Julia Eklund. Aesthetic Music Education Revisited: Discourses of Exclusion and Oppression. *Phil Music Educ Rev*, 2(2), 75-91, Fall 94.

In a critical feminist analysis of Bennett Reimer's second edition of *A Philosophy of Music Education*, Koza argues that aesthetic music education, the philosophy advocated by Reimer, adheres to exclusionary philosophical discourses and that it evades history, politics, and context. These discourses, Koza contends, are integrally connected to power relations that have tended to perpetuate the oppression of women and other marginalized groups.

Kozhamthadam, Job. Creation Without a Creator: Reflections on Contemporary Scientific Cosmologies. *Phil Sci (Tucson)*, 6, 9-46, 1995.

The scientific study of the creation of the universe has become a very fascinating area in recent times, especially with the outstanding work of Stephen Hawking. A study of this kind is beset with three fundamental issues: the problem of singularity, the problem of boundary conditions, and the problem of creator/creation. The "no boundary" theory of Hawking attempts to circumvent these difficulties. This paper is a critical study of this theory (without going into its mathematical complexities). The criticism of several scholars are discussed. I conclude that although Hawking's ideas are an outstanding contribution to scientific cosmology, the various conclusions he draws from the theory are highly questionable.

Krabbe, Erik C W and Walton, Douglas N. *Commitment in Dialogue: Basic Concepts of Interpersonal Reasoning*. Albany, SUNY Pr, 1995.

This book develops a logical analysis of dialogue in which two or more parties attempt to advance their own arguments. It includes a classification of the major types of dialogues and a discussion of several important informal fallacies. The authors define the concept of commitment in a way that makes it useful in evaluating arguments. In traditional logic, a proposition is either true or false, and that is the end of it. In this new framework, an arguer can be held to his or her commitments in some cases, but in other cases, he or she can retract them without violating any rule of the dialogue. "Commitment in Dialogue" studies the conditions under which commitments should be held or may be retracted within an argument.

Kraege, Jean-Denis. Logique théologique et logique systémique: Dialogue avec Edgar Morin. *Rev Theol Phil*, 126(3), 223-242, 1994.

La théologie ne peut plus, aujourd'hui, ignorer la nébuleuse systématique. Parmi les adeptes de la réflexion systématique, Edgar Morin représente un interlocuteur exceptionnel pour le théologien. Il est l'un des seuls à avoir tenté de développer systémiquement une "pensée globale" et pourtant non totalitaire. Il répond ainsi à deux exigences auxquelles la pensée théologique doit également satisfaire. De plus, sa recherche d'une théorie générale du système ne peut qu'interpeller le systématicien. Ces raisons et quelques autres incitent à un dialogue avec E. Morin sur la question des logiques qui, fondamentalement, régulent tant la méthode morinienne que la théologie dialectique.

Krämer, Felix. *Der Zusammenhang der Wirklichkeit*. Amsterdam, Rodopi, 1994.

Whitehead ignorierte Fichte, und beider Denk—und Darstellungsweisen sind auf den ersten Blick vollkommen verschieden. Dennoch bestätigen sie einander in der für beide zentralen Lehre von der untrennbaren Verbundenheit von Erkennen, Handeln, Fühlen und Selbstbewusstsein. Versucht man aber diese Lehre konsequent als schlechthin apriorische Einsicht zu verstehen, so löst sie such unweigerlich in leere Redewendungen auf. Die tiefe Bedeutung, um die es durchaus bereits bei Fichte geht, kommt der Einsicht in die Einheit des Menschen in Erkennen, Handeln, Fühlen und Selbstbewusstsein eigentlich erst dann zu, wenn man wie Whitehead die Last des rein aprioristischen Denkens abwirft.

Krämer, Felix. Maimons Versuch über Transzendentalphilosophie: Eine interpretierende Skizze der Grundgedanken. *Fichte-Studien*, 1, 178-197, 1990.

Krämer, Felix. Realität und Tätigkeit im ersten Teil von Fichtes *Grundlage*, beurteilt aus der Sicht Whiteheads. *Fichte-Studien*, 5, 83-92, 1993.

Krämer, Hans. Zur Rekonstruktion der Philosophischen Hermeneutik. *J Gen Phil Sci*, 26(1), 169-185, 1995.

Towards a reconstruction of philosophical hermeneutics. Following Nietzsche, Heidegger and, on the other hand, Cassirer and Wittgenstein, a philosophy of interpretation, i.e., a relativism of world-views, is at present increasing in continental as well as in analytical philosophy. From the basis of a critical fallibilism the shortcomings of the new epistemological antirealism are pointed out in general, and, hence, consequences are drawn for the more specialized case of metahermeneutics (hermeneutics being defined as a sort of pragmatical semiotics). A combination of realistic and antirealistic elements is recommended as unevitable. According to this, firstly, the key-concepts of hermeneutics must be differentiated, and, secondly, a fundamental set of criteria can be established that bridges the gap between metahermeneutics and hermeneutical practice.

Krämer, Sybille. Melancholie—Sizze zur epistemologischen Deutung eines Topos. *Z Phil Forsch*, 48(3), 397-419, Jl-S 94.

Krahn, Irene and Yeo, Michael. "Confidentiality" in *Concepts and Cases in Nursing Ethics, Yeo, Michael (& others)*, 117-146. Peterborough, Broadview Pr, 1991.

Krajewski, Stanislaw. Judaism, Christianity, Islam and Universalism. *Dialogue Hum*, 3(3), 99-101, 1993.

Science cannot prove the universalist thesis that all humans are brothers. The Bible, as understood by the Jewish tradition, does. The same is true about many other religions. The problem is that each revelation must be particularistic. If religious universalism is sought in a rational common core or the common denominator of all religions, or even all Biblical religions, it is their enemy because it is not faithful to the specific revelations. If universalism is seen as an imperative to include all humans as equal, it must be based on non-universalistic foundations. This is the paradox of religious universalism.

Krajewski, Wladyslaw. Philosophy of Science in Poland. *Stud Phil Christ*, 30(2), 185-192, 1994.

Krajewski, Wladyslaw. The Scientific Community as the Ideal of the Universal Human Community. *Dialogue Hum*, 3(2), 58-62, 1993.

Krajewski, Wladyslaw. The Universal Scientific Methods. *Dialogue Hum*, 2(3-4), 57-61, 1992.

Each science has its own peculiar methods. However, there are general methodological postulates which ought to be shared by all sciences, including humanities: intersubjective communicability and testability, logical coherence, agreement with facts, empirical honesty and reliability, critical attitude including self-criticism, etc.

Krajewski, Wladyslaw. Two Logical Patterns of the Reduction of Theories: Comments on Józef Werle's Paper "How the Physical Sciences Discovered the Unity of Nature". *Dialogue Hum*, 3(3), 121-123, 1993.

Kramer, Matthew H. *Critical Legal Theory and the Challenge of Feminism: A Philosophical Reconception*. Lanham, Rowman & Littlefield, 1994.

Both a systematic critique and an extension of ideas that underlie the critical legal studies movement, this book provides a comprehensive philosophical framework for political and legal theory. The book's first chapter explores the tenuous relations between metaphysics and politics. Chapter Two attempts to transform critical legal scholarship by laying out a framework of five general themes—contradictions, contingency, patterning, perspective, and ideology. Chapter Three addresses some controversies in feminist theory, with the aid of analyses that the earlier chapters have developed; it joins the earlier chapters in arguing that theories can greatly profit by taking account of inescapable paradoxes.

Krans, H M J. The Communication of Cells Within the Body. *Method Sci*, 27(2), 57-71, 1994.

In a short overview modern knowledge about the transfer of information from outside the cell into the cell is discussed. The units involve and do not act for the transfer of information only, but they have also modulating and potentiating functions. Systems like the G-proteins, the tyrosine-kinase, proteïnkinase C and the nuclear receptor are described. The external messages are integrated in the existing intracellular information system, which is for a major part determined by programmed genetic background. The cell contains also its own desintegration programme (apoptosis). This limits the lifetime of a cell and makes that death is already programmed as soon as life starts.

Krapiec, Mieczyslaw Albert. Monism and Pluralism. *Dialogue Hum*, 3(3), 5-48, 1993.

Krasevac, Edward L. Aquinas, *Vertitatis Splendor*, and Contemporary Moral Theology. *Listening*, 30(1), 50-63, Wint 95.

Krasner, Daniel and Heller, Mark. The Miracle of Counterfactuals: Counterexamples to Lewis's World Ordering. *Phil Stud*, 76(1), 27-43, O 94.

Krasser, Helmut. Dharmottara's Theory of Knowledge in His *Laghupramanyapariksa*. *J Indian Phil*, 23(2), 247-271, Je 95.

Kratzer, Angelika. "Stage-Level and Individual-Level Predicates" in *The Generic Book, Carlson, Gregory N (ed)*, 125-175. Chicago, Univ of Chicago Pr, 1995.

Krause, Bodo. "Modeling Cognitive Learning Steps" in *Probability in Theory-Building, Brzezinski, Jerzy (ed)*, 61-73. Amsterdam, Rodopi, 1994.

Cognitive learning is characterized by forming generalized knowledge structures which include potential advantages for further behavioral activities. This can be experimentally investigated by learning invariances and transferring this knowledge to new instances. Then the learning result and the transfer effect should depend on the content of invariances and the learning level. The learning content was varied by using feature-based and relation-based invariances. The main findings show that a stronger learning criterion results in more confirmed decision structures and a more efficient transfer effect. Regarding the learning content, it is shown that feature-based invariances will be learned faster than relation-based invariances. Moreover, we can show that there are remarkable differences in learning processes by humans and neuronal networks. While in the case of an one-feature invariance humans and networks are producing similar results, we see a growing difference for more feature invariances and relation-based invariances. These differences are higher for Boltzmann machines than for error back propagation networks.

Krause, Décio and French, Steven. A Formal Framework for Quantum Non-Individuality. *Synthese*, 102(1), 195-214, Ja 95.

H Post's conception of quantal particles as 'nonindividuals' is set in a formal logico-mathematical framework. By means of this approach certain metaphysical implications of quantum mechanics can be further explored.

Krause, Décio and French, Steven. Vague Identity and Quantum Non-Individuality. *Analysis*, 55(1), 20-26, Ja 95.

Lowe has recently argued that quantum particles offer examples of vague objects. While accepting the premise of the argument that such particles can be regarded as individuals, we point out that there is a lacuna here, to be filled by a detailed analysis of the nature of the entangled states which they enter into. We then elaborate the alternative view, according to which such particles should be regarded as 'nonindividuals' and situate it in the context of recent developments of a logic of nonindividuality. Our conclusion is that it is here that one encounters genuine ontic vagueness.

Kraut, Richard. Return to the Cave: *Republic* 519-521. *Proc Boston Colloq Anc Phil*, 7, 43-62, 1991.

In the *Republic* Socrates holds that it is just to require the philosophers to return to the cave, even though they would prefer to continue their philosophical studies. Does this show that justice conflicts with the good of the philosophers? No, because the good for humans consists in replicating, within the political community, the harmonious relationships that exist among the forms. Plato assumes that justice requires reciprocity and that this relationship is good for us because it is analogous to the balanced proportions of the ideal world.

Kraut, Richard H. "Reply to Professor Roche" in *The Crossroads of Norm and Nature, Sim, May (ed)*, 139-148. Lanham, Rowman & Littlefield, 1995.

Timothy Roche argues against my thesis that according to Aristotle contemplation is the ultimate end of the best human life. He claims that in Book I of the *Nicomachean Ethics* Aristotle is principally concerned with defeating Platonism, and is not searching for some substantive goal that is to serve as our ultimate end. I argue that there are texts that undermine Roche's interpretation. Even after Aristotle has completed his attack on Platonism, he is still searching for the final end, and this search is not completed until he defends the contemplative life in Book X.

Kraut, Richard H. Desire and the Human Good. *Proc Amer Phil Ass*, 68(2), 39-54, N 94.

Modern conceptions of human well-being equate it with the satisfaction of rational desire. Some of the main objections to such theories are discussed. The underlying problem is that they do not provide adequate resources for the evaluation of our desires; they are excessively conservative in that they are too accepting of desires as we happen to find them. Older conceptions of the human good, found throughout the ancient and medieval periods, are in this respect on stronger ground-although they seem overly narrow. A successful theory of the good must possess a critical element that enables us to evaluate the worthiness of desires to be fulfilled.

Kraut, Richard H. Gregory Vlastos on Justice and Equality. *Apeiron*, 26(3-4), 99-109, S-D 93.

This paper is an appreciation and critique of a 1962 paper of Gregory Vlastos, "Justice and Equality." Vlastos tries to respond to Plato's critique of democracy by spelling out the underlying basis of egalitarianism. For Vlastos, egalitarianism consists in the thesis that regardless of one's merits (moral or otherwise), one's well-being is as valuable as anyone else's. The main problem for Vlastos's thesis is that it conflicts with an objective conception of happiness, for on any such conception some lives are more worth leading than others.

Kraut, Richard H. Soul Doctors. *Ethics*, 105(3), 613-625, Ap 95.

A review of Martha Nussbaum's interpretation of Hellenistic ethics in her book, *The Therapy of Desire*.

Krawczyk, Zbigniew. Categories of the Ethics of Sport. *Dialogue Hum*, 4(2-3), 17-182, 1994.

Krecz, Charles A. Browning and Two Traditions. *SW Phil Rev*, 11(Supp), 117-129, Mr 95.

This paper is an exploration of a number of ontological themes in Douglas Browning's work with respect to two great traditions, the substance tradition and the process tradition. The paper shows how Browning's view is defended, a question is raised with regard to the extent to which Browning is able to accommodate the correct and significant features of the traditions Browning attacks, particularly the process tradition. The paper concludes with a suggestion of the means by which this may be done.

Kreiner, Anna. The Ethics of the Pharmaceutical Industry and the Need for a Dual Market System. *J Med Human*, 16(1), 55-68, Spr 95.

In an era of increasing medical costs and cries for health care reform in the United States, the pharmaceutical industry has come under intense scrutiny. Ethical issues are inherent in the pharmaceutical marketplace, and there is a need to address the moral rights and responsibilities of drug manufacturers, consumers, health care professionals, and governmental agents in the production, distribution, regulation, and use of these products. A dual market system protecting individual rights to access and autonomy without placing an undue strain on societal resources would provide an adequate and equitable framework for an ethical pharmaceutical industry.

Kremer, Elmar J. The Hume-Plantinga Objection to the Argument from Design. *Amer Cath Phil Quart*, 68(Supp), 85-92, 1994.

The paper discusses an objection raised by Hume and Plantinga against the argument from design: that it does not prove enough to prove the existence of God as He is conceived in the Hebrew-Christian tradition. If the argument is taken as an attempt to prove *de dicto* that the Hebrew-Christian God exists, then it is refuted by the objection; but if it is taken as an attempt to prove *de re*, about the Hebrew-Christian God, that He exists, it is not so refuted. But it falls before a related objection.

Kremer, Klaus. "Vernunft im abendländischen Denken: Wandel und Konstanz" in *Das geistige Erbe Europas, Buhr, Manfred (ed)*, 291-299. Napoli, Vivarium, 1994.

For all their differences, Plato, Plotinus, Boethius, Cusanus, and Leibniz preserve a common basic tendency in their understanding of Reason (Intellectus-Nus). Reason is the faculty ranking above the discursively operating Mind (Ratio-Dianoia). It is no longer subsumed under the concept of opposition; it is independent of sense-perception, but requires the impetus of the latter. Reason, although capable of grasping everything, can only perceive in proportion as it is found extant in itself. Reason is therefore autonomous, has complete spontaneity, and yet remains an instance as meted out by its divine basis. Reason is both a "loving" and "tasting" power of knowledge/cognition.

Kremer-Marietti, Angèle. "Le figuré et le littóral dans le langage scientifique" in *Rhétoriques de la science, De Coorebyter, Vincent (ed)*, 133-148. Paris, Pr Univ France, 1994.

What means an expression is supposed to exist, but there is a fallacy: the illusion about the literal. Concrete ontology draws back for the benefit of scientific ontology. The literal language of sciences is the result of the abstract processes of the mind. The question is: does the figural part of scientific concepts completely disappear? The new problem is to know the punctual relations between figural and literal in the scientific language, or the relation between expression and signification, which is the heuristic opposition. The essential in sciences is to change what was probable into an expression of certainty.

Kremer-Marietti, Angèle. De la passionnalité. *Rev Int Phil*, 48(189), 275-285, 1994.

Krettek, Tom. Introducing Philosophy Through Concepts of Ultimate Reality and Meaning. *Teach Phil*, 17(2), 141-150, Je 94.

The paper proposes a way that the study of concepts of ultimate reality and meaning can help introduce students to philosophy. It supplements proposals that appeared previously in *Teaching Philosophy*, which presented ways to establish student rapport with philosophy and to take seriously cultural diversity.

Kretzmann, Norman. St Teresa, William Alston, and the Broadminded Atheist. *J Phil Res*, 20, 45-66, 1995.

Alston includes St Teresa's vision among paradigms of "experiential awareness of God" in his book *Perceiving God*. An atheist might agree that experiences like St Theresa's *would* justify someone in believing that she had experienced God if he accepted what Alston calls a "deontological" account of justification, which Alston rejects in favor of a "truth-conductive" account, leading to his arguing along these lines: Putative experiences of God provide justification for beliefs about God, but putative experiences of X provide justification for belief about X only if many of those experiences are veridical; therefore, many putative experiences of God are veridical. Alston's line of reasoning undermines his project of addressing readers who do not antecedently believe "that people are sometimes genuinely aware of God and do genuinely perceive God".

Kretzmann, Norman and Stump, Eleonore. Blindingly Obvious Christian Anti-Semitism. *Faith Phil*, 11(2), 279-285, Ap 94.

This article is part of an on-going public discussion between philosophers and theologians, prompted by Gordon Kaufman's "Evidentialism: A Theologian's Response", which tried to explain and defend the neglect of philosophy on the part of theologians. Part of what is at issue is the degree to which a religion is responsible for the evils committed in its name by its adherents. We make a distinction between sociological and doctrinal understandings of religion and religious claims. If a religion is defined only sociologically, then (if, in fact, any determination can be made) every major worldview is responsible for serious evil. This conclusion does not hold, however, if religion is taken doctrinally.

Krichmar, Fernando Gabriel and Feldman, Susana B. "La Enseñanza de la Epistemología en la Carrera de Psicología o Técnicas Para Desvestir a una Invitada Molesta" in *Temas Actuales de Filosofía, Palacios, María Julia (ed)*, 179-185. Buenos Aires, Univ Nacional Salta, 1993.

Krieger, Gerhard. "Die Entdeckung des Primats der Methode in der Metaphysik.." in *Naturauffassungen in Philosophie, Wissenschaft, Technik: Band I, Schäfer, Lothar (ed)*, 209-249. Freiburg, Alber, 1993.

Krieger, Martin H. Corruption and the Culture of Real Estate Development. *Bus Prof Ethics J*, 13(3), 19-32, Fall 94.

Market disequilibrium, speculation, fantasy, transaction-richness, and nonlinear stochasticity contribute to the entrepreneurial aspects of real estate development. Yet, these features are just what makes the industry particularly subject to corruption. Here corruption is defined by an "impairment of itegrity, virtue, or moral principle," generally perceived as dishonest and unfair behavior. In particular, corruption is evidenced by rent-seeking behavior and windfall profits, deliberate bankruptcy and welshing on contracts, false advertising, graft, and influence peddling. None of this, of course, demands that real estate development be intrinsically corrupt; perhaps any corruption derives from the governmental and financial institutions it deals with. If in fact real estate development proved to be no more corrupt than other enterprises, one might conclude from these arguments that its participants are remarkably immune to temptation.

Krieger, Martin H. Could the Probability of Doom Be Zero or One?. *J Phil*, 92(7), 382-387, Jl 95.

The probability of doom may be shown to be 0 or 1, by applying the Kolmogorov zero-or-one law of probability theory to a model of the path to doom. Loosening the model's restriction, so as to avoid this conclusion, will indicate the significance of planning, finite decision horizons, probabilistic estimates of risk, and scientific vs theological perspectives.

Krieglstein, Werner. Chaos Theory Can Close the Gap Between the Sciences and the Humanities. *Dialogue Hum*, 3(2), 96-99, 1993.

Krifka, Manfred. "Common Nouns: A Contrastive Analysis of Chinese and English" in *The Generic Book, Carlson, Gregory N (ed)*, 398-411. Chicago, Univ of Chicago Pr, 1995.

Krifka, Manfred. "Focus and the Interpretation of Generic Sentences" in *The Generic Book, Carlson, Gregory N (ed)*, 238-264. Chicago, Univ of Chicago Pr, 1995.

This article treats the influence of focus (accent) on the interpretation of generic sentences, arguing that de-accented expressions determine the restrictor of a generic quantifier. The analysis is couched within a framework that models the contribution of focus by structured meanings.

Krifka, Manfred (& others). "Genericity: An Introduction" in *The Generic Book, Carlson, Gregory N (ed)*, 1-124. Chicago, Univ of Chicago Pr, 1995.

This essay is a detailed overview of recent research in linguistics and philosophy on generic sentences. It differentiates between reference to kinds and characterizing sentences, and includes a discussion of proposals for the semantics of the latter type (modal theories, nonmonotonic logics, prototypes, etc.). Also, a wide range of uses of reference to kinds is discussed.

Krishna, Daya. Is Nyaya Realist or Idealist?. *J Indian Counc Phil Res*, 12(1), 161-163, S-D 94.

Krishna, Daya. Kant's Doctrine of the Categories: Some Problems. *J Indian Counc Phil Res*, 11(3), 143-144, My-Ag 94.

The discussion raises the following fundamental questions regarding Kant's Doctrine of the Categories: 1) Are all the twelve categories involved in each judgment, or only one each out of the four sub-sets of quantity, quality, relation and modality in any individual judgment? In case it is the latter, what shall be the ground of the choice between the categories under each sub-set? 2) The categories under "relation" and "modality" are dual in nature, while those under quantity and quality are singular in nature. Why is it so? 3) The categories under "modality" are opposed to each other in the sense that if one obtains, the other cannot; while those under "relation" do not seem to have such a character. What is its significance? 4) The category of reality under "quality" and the category of "existence" under modality seem to be the same. Why has Kant repeated the categories under two different headings if they are the same?

Krishna, Daya. On the Radical Distinction between the *Krsna* and the *Sukla Yajurveda* and *Professor Heesterman's Remarks Thereon. J Indian Counc Phil Res*, 12(1), 133-135, S-D 94.

Krishna, Daya. Some Comments on Professor R Sundararajan's Book Entitled *Towards a Critique of Cultural Reason*. *J Indian Counc Phil Res*, 11(3), 99-101, My-Ag 94.

The discussion note raises some fundamental objections against the distinctions between "signification" and "symbolization", on the one hand and between "determinative" and "reflective" judgment, on the other. The former is based on the presumed distinction between that which is "context-bound" and that which is "context-free", while the latter depends on the notion that there are perceptual objects which are completely described by the concept under which they are subsumed, as distinct from those which can never be exhausted, in principle, by any set of concepts, however large they may be. Sundararajan has taken these distinctions from Ricouer and Kant and used them in his new attempt at understanding culture. Their critique is, thus, also a critique of Ricouer and Kant respectively. There is also a discussion of the notion of "disinterested feeling" which Sundararajan has used for elucidation the apprehension fo aesthetic objects and cultures, thus assimilitating the latter to the former in an important sense.

Krishnaiah, V Gopala. Self and Ontology in Descartes and Upanishads. *Darshana Int*, 32(3/127), 68-70, Jl 92.

Kristiansen, Roald E. Ecology and Globalism: Response to Professor E H Cadwallader's Paper 'Ultimate Meaning and Reality in the Battle Between Globalism and Anti-Globalism. *Ultim Real Mean*, 17(4), 317-321, D 94.

Krob, Josef. Time. *Filozof Cas*, 42(4), 635-645, 1994.

Author's attempt to work out the conception of classical ontological category with regard to contemporary physical knowledge and with employing of topical notions in modern physics. In four parts—The history of concept, Fundamental properties of time, Time and universe, Nonphysical conceptions of time—he attempts to expose in what way the question of time has always been connected with the problems of natural sciences and in what way the contemporary solutions are immediately linked with the knowledge in modern physics and cosmology. The last part of this essay indicates that it is possible to apply the above-mentioned attitude even in the branch of nonphysical sciences.

Krob, Josef. What is Ontology?. *Filozof Cas*, 42(6), 1031-1033, 1994.

The short essay is the component of discussions concerning the theme "The End of Ontology", in which there were put several questions. The author answers three of them: 1) What is ontology? 2) Is ontology possible today? 3) What ought the new ontology be like? 1) The author points out to the conflict of objectivist tendencies in ontology and the knowledge of modern science going on as far as to the beginning of twentieth century and he also refers to the the danger arising from anthropocentric attitude to given problems. 2) He proposes not to trust all the statements such as "this is really the case", to work consciously with subjective contribution to the things being recognized, but everything must be based on rationality, and not on its refusal. 3) The new ontology is arising. The end of purposeless intellectual exercises, the necessity of overworking the fundamental categories with respect to science.

Kroeck, K Galen and Sims, Randi L. The Influence of Ethical Fit on Employee Satisfaction, Commitment and Turnover. *J Bus Ethics*, 13(12), 939-947, D 94.

This study examines the influence of ethical fit on employee attitudes and intentions to turnover. The results of this investigation provides support for the conjecture that ethical work climate is an important variable in the study of person-organization fit. Ethical fit was found to be significantly related to turnover intentions, continuance commitment, and affective commitment, but not to job satisfaction. Results are discussed in regard to some of the affective and cognitive distinctions among satisfaction, commitment, and behavioral intentions.

Kroeger-Mappes, Joy. The Ethic of Care vis-à-vis the Ethic of Rights: A Problem for Contemporary Moral Theory. *Hypatia*, 9(3), 108-131, Sum 94.

Carol Gilligan has delineated two ethics, the ethic of rights and the ethic of care. In this article I argue that the two ethics are part of one overall system, the ethics of care functioning as a necessary base for the ethic of rights. I also argue that the system is seriously flawed. Because women are held accountable to both ethics and because the two ethics frequently conflict, women recurrently find themselves in a moral double bind.

Krohn, Wolfgang. "Die Natur als Labyrinth, die Erkenntnis als Inquisition.. " in *Naturauffassungen in Philosophie, Wissenschaft, Technik: Band II, Schäfer, Lothar (ed)*, 59-100. Freiburg, Alber, 1994.

Krois, John Michael (trans) and Apel, Karl Otto. *Charles S Peirce: From Pragmatism to Pragmaticism*. Atlantic Highlands, Humanities Pr, 1995.

Kronen, John D. The Substantial Unity of Material Substances According to John Poinsot. *Thomist*, 58(4), 599-615, O 94.

In recent years there has been a revival of interest in essentialism and in substance metaphysics. This has produced a great deal of work on questions concerning the difference between the necessary and contingent properties of things, and on questions concerning the differences between substances and their properties. But there is a problem concerning composite substances that has been much neglected by recent essentialist philosophers; that is the problem of how a composite can be unified so as to constitute a single substance. John Poinsot devoted an entire chapter to this question in his great work on the philosophy of nature. In this paper I present the arguments Poinsot uses to show that the unifier of a substance cannot be a relational structure but must instead be a thing-like entity (a *res*), which he calls "substantial form." I further give Poinsot's arguments against a reductive materialist philosophy of material substances. My conclusions is that Poinsot has a least shown that neither structuralism nor reductive materialism are viable ways of explaining the nature of material substances.

Kruks, Sonia. "Simone de Beauvoir: Teaching Sartre About Freedom" in *Feminist Interpretations of Simone de Beauvoir, Simons, Margaret A (ed)*, 79-95. University Park, Penn St Univ Pr, 1995.

This paper argues that during the 1940s Beauvoir developed an account of freedom that was (contrary to commonly held views about Beauvoir's relationship to Sartre) both original and distinct from Sartre's. Against Sartre's radically individualistic account of freedom, Beauvoir developed an account of freedom as situated and always socially interdependent. In some ways her account was similar to that of Merleau-Ponty, whose work she knew well. The paper concludes by suggesting there is evidence that Sartre's later shift towards a less individualistic conception of freedom, in the *Critique of Dialectical Reason*, was due in part to the influence of Beauvoir.

Kruks, Sonia. Identity Politics and Dialectical Reason: Beyond an Epistemology of Provenance. *Hypatia*, 10(2), 1-22, Spr 95.

Identity politics is important within feminism. However, if often presupposes an overly subjectivist theory of knowledge that I term an epistemology of provenance. I explore some works of feminist standpoint theory that begin to address the difficulties of such an epistemology. I then bring Sartre's account of knowledge in the *Critique of Dialectical Reason* to bear on these difficulties, arguing that his work offers tools for addressing them more adequately.

Krummel, J. Truth and Control in Being and Language. *Auslegung*, 20(1), 25-34, Wint 95.

This paper examines possible converging points between Heidegger and Foucault on being and language. Both are concerned with the temporal movement of a transient event which, whether "presencing" as a thing-present or erupting-forth out of conflicting forces as a discursive configuration, becomes preserved as a subsistent "thing"—as a mode of being for Heidegger, as a mode of knowledge in relation to techniques of power for Foucault. This is accompanied with the claim to persist throughout its coming-to-be, transformations, and disappearing—an artificial preservation accomplished in relation to language which names "that-which-cannot-be-named".

Kruse, Felicia. A Critical Discussion of John E Smith's Communitarian Vision. *Trans Peirce Soc*, 31(1), 41-51, Wint 95.

Kruse, Felicia. An Ordinal Context for Ecofeminism. *J Speculative Phil*, 9(1), 14-35, 1995.

Kryspin, Jan and Phillips, Heather. "The Appropriate Medical Care of the Terminally Ill" in *Ethics on the Frontiers of Human Existence, Badham, Paul (ed)*, 179-207. New York, Paragon House, 1992.

Krzemien-Ojak, Slaw. The Paradox of Levi-Strauss or Cultural Time Yesterday and Today. *Dialogue Hum*, 4(1), 159-162, 1994.

Kucera, T and Chartrand, R. Deissler Rank Complexity of Powers of Indecomposable Injective Modules. *Notre Dame J Form Log*, 35(3), 398-402, Sum 94.

Minimality ranks in the style of Deissler are one way of measuring the structural complexity of minimal extensions of first-order structures. In particular, *positive Deissler rank* measures the complexity of the injective envelope of a module as an extension of that module. In this paper we solve a problem of the second author by showing that certain injective envelopes have the maximum possible Deissler rank complexity. The proof shows that this complexity naturally reflects the internal structure of the injective extension in the form of the levels of the Matlis hierarchy.

Kuczewski, Mark (& others). Make My Case: Ethics Teaching and Case Presentations. *J Clin Ethics*, 5(4), 310-315, Wint 94.

The authors briefly consider the role and importance of using real cases in the teaching of medical ethics. They note reasons that it is better to have the seminar participants bring their own cases then for the instructor to supply them. The authors analyze different difficulties that medical students have in identifying and presenting an ethics case and contrast them with those of health care professionals in a continuing education program. The appendix contains teaching materials designed to meet the differing educational needs each of these seminar populations has in presenting medical ethics cases.

Kuczynski, Alicja. The Work of Art as a Model of "The Open Whole". *Dialogue Hum*, 3(2), 32-38, 1993.

Kuczynski, Janusz. Diversity and Unity of Sciences as the Foundation of Universalism. *Dialogue Hum*, 4(4), 143-175, 1994.

Kuczynski, Janusz. John Paul II's Manifesto on Labor and Vision of a Universal Society. *Dialogue Hum*, 4(2-3), 107-117, 1994.

Kuczynski, Janusz. Postmodern Business, Complexity and Universal Society. *Dialogue Hum*, 4(5), 99-110, 1994.

Kuczynski, Janusz. Universalism as the Vision and Proclamation of a New Covenant: Thinking—Wisdom—Love. *Dialogue Hum*, 3(2), 21-31, 1993.

Kuczynski, Janusz. What Is Universalism?. *Dialogue Hum*, 2(3-4), 165-177, 1992.

Küchler, T. From a Restricted to a General Economy of Play: Heidegger's Critique of Metaphysics. *Phil Inq*, 16(1-2), 55-80, Wint-Spr 94.

Kügler, Peter. Die Zurückführung des Möglichen auf das Wirkliche. *J Gen Phil Sci*, 25(2), 223-240, 1994.

Modern philosophy cannot avoid dealing with possible worlds—neither in the field of intensional logic nor in other fields not directly connected with logical investigations. This paper attempts to develop a method to substitute possible worlds by the real world, referring to the works of Stig Kanger and Nino B Cocchiarella. This is done by investigating the metaphorical and dynamical functions of natural languages. As an example a language is constructed, which is based on the Aristotelian view of universal concepts.

Kuehn, Manfred. "Kant's Critique of Hume's Theory of Faith" in *Hume and Hume's Connexions, Stewart, M A (ed)*, 239-255. University Park, Penn St Univ Pr, 1995.

Kühn, Rolf. Bedürfen und Vorstellungsdestrucktion. *Gregorianum*, 76(2), 323-342, 1995.

Si la phénoménologie consiste à analyser le *comment* de l'auto-apparaître de l'apparaître, le Besoin offre une certitude immédiate et absolue qui n'est pas la <présence> anonyme de l'Etre, mais donation absolue de la Vie par elle-même et en elle-même. Pour une telle révision de l'ontologie chez Heidegger, Claude Bruaire avait déjà proposé la métaphysique d'une onto-*do*-logie qui est assumée ici par une phénoménalisation de toute ontologie à partir du besoin autoaffectif. Enfin, Simone Weil loge le désir du Bien absolu dans notre sensibilité charnelle même, ce qui corrobore notre analyse du besoin en tant que possibilité de la révélation de l'Absolu, sans soumettre cette Révélation à une exigence anthropoligique préalable. Le besoin, dans sa chair phénoménologique pure même, est *l'entrée de la Vie absolue dans son Oubli représentatif absolu même*, ce qui sauve entièrement le <mystère> de cet Absolu sans se défaire pour autant de notre être le plus vrai hors de toute théorie ou de toutes nos représentations. Leur <destruction> phénoménologique est réalisée à tout moment par le besoin même, si on confère à sa <naissance> la dignité <onto-do-logique> d'une donation pure égale à notre subjectivité absolu, comme il convient pour une phénoménologie radicale.

Kühne-Bertram, Gudrun (ed) and Misch, Georg (ed) and Rodi, Frithjof (ed). *Der Aufbau der Logik auf dem Boden der Philosophie des Lebens*. Freiburg, Alber, 1994.

This book presents for the first time Georg Misch's lectures on logic and epistemology. On the basis of Dilthey's philosophy of life and the latest linguistic, anthropological discoveries of the period, as well as in response to the positions of Heidegger and Husserl, Misch attempts to offer an extension of and at the same time a new foundation for traditional logic. As a hermeneutic logic which is not restricted to discursive cogitation, this extends *all* types of thinking. The author tries to derive logical phenomena from everyday life and ordinary language, in order to make evident the original unity of life and thought.

Kümmel, Friedrich (ed) and König, Josef. *Der logische Unterschied theoretischer und praktischer Sätze und seine philosophische Bedeutung*. Freiburg, Alber, 1994.

This book is a collection of highly sophisticated lectures by Josef König (1893-1974). They concern the formal or radical distinction between "theoretical sentences" and "practical sentences", which marks essential differences in the forms of knowledge and behavior concerned. König reformulates the *ontological* difference as well as the *transcendental* difference in terms of a *logical* difference. He gives a new explication of the epistemological function of *singular sentences* (these to be distinguished from the Vienna Circle's "Basissätz"!). This could not be rendered adequately within the framework of traditional logic.

Kuhn, Wilfried. "Eine wissenschaftstheor. Analyse d. histor. Entwicklung d. Chaos-Forschung" in *Schelling und die Selbstorganisation, Heuser-Kessler, Marie-Luise (ed)*, 161-181. Berlin, Duncker Humblot, 1994.

Kuhse, Helga. Clinical Ethics and Nursing: "Yes" to Caring, But "No" to a Female Ethics of Care. *Bioethics*, 9(3-4), 207-219, Jl 95.

According to a contemporary school of thought there is a specific female approach to ethics which is based not on abstract "male" ethical principles or rules, but on "care". Nurses have taken a keen interest in these female approaches to ethics. Drawing on the views expounded by Carol Gilligan and Nel Noddings, nurses claim that a female "ethics of care" better captures their moral experiences than a traditional male "ethics of justice". This paper argues that "care" is best understood in a dispositional sense, that is, as sensitivity and responsiveness to the particularities of a situation and the needs of "concrete" others. While "care", in this sense, is necessary for ethics, it is not sufficient. Ethics needs "justice" as well as "care". If women and nurses excessively devalue principles and norms, they will be left without the theoretical tools to condemn some actions or practices, and to defend others. They will, like generations of nurses before them, be condemned to silence.

Kuhse, Helga and Singer, Peter. "Hard Choices: Ethical Questions Raised by the Birth of Handicapped Infants" in *Ethics on the Frontiers of Human Existence, Badham, Paul (ed)*, 153-177. New York, Paragon House, 1992.

Modern medical technology allows us to sustain the lives of many seriously disabled newborn infants. Should we do this? Our answer is "no". In drawing a distinction between infants and "persons", and rejecting the argument that decision-making should be based on the infant's potential to become a person, we argue that there are occasions when it is in an infant's best interest to be allowed, or helped, to die.

Kuhse, Helga and Singer, Peter. *Individuals, Humans, Persons: Questions of Life and Death*. Sankt Augustin, Academia, 1994.

This is a collection of eight previously published (and one formerly unpublished) essays by Helga Kuhse and Peter Singer of the Centre for Human Bioethics at Monash University in Australia, with an introduction by Edgar Morscher, Professor of Philosophy at the University of Salzburg in Austria. After some initial reflections on the nature of bioethics, the articles raise questions about the nature of individuality, humanhood and personhood, in the context of contemporary debates about in vitro fertilization, embryo experimentation, contraception, abortion and euthanasia. The authors argue that early human embryos are not individuals, that not every human individual has a "right to life", and that some forms of euthanasia are morally justified.

Kuipers, Theo A F. Falsificationisme versus efficiënte waarheidsbenadering. *Alg Ned Tijdschr Wijs*, 86(4), 270-290, O 94.

It is argued that Kuhnian and Lakatosian justifications and explanations of nonfalsificationist behaviour are essentially redundant from the viewpoint of truth approximation, for the truth or falsity of a theory is rather irrelevant for its distance to the truth. More precisely, the irony of the cunning of reason is that the instrumentalist methodology, which may keep a falsified theory in the game, or replace it with a better but also already falsified theory, e.g., essential for idealization and concretization (Nowak), is (much) more efficient for truth approximation than a falsificationist methodology. Some consequences for the empirical studies of science are drawn.

Kuipers, Theo A F. Observationele referentiële en theoretische waarheidsbenadering. *Alg Ned Tijdschr Wijs*, 87(1), 33-49, Ja 95.

In response to a critical challenge by Ton Derksen it is argued that the rule of success, i.e., preferring a theory if it is convincingly more successful than another, is functional for approaching the observationally true theory as well as for approaching the theoretically true theory. The latter, however, with the proviso that the preferred theory is referentially at least as close to the truth. Though it is conceded that it has not yet been demonstrated that the rule of success is also functional for referential truth approximation, some optimism in this respect is also motivated.

Kuipers, Theo A F and Hamminga, Bert and Cools, Kees. "Truth Approximation by Concretization in Capital Structure Theory" in *Idealization VI: Idealization in Economics, Hamminga, Bert (ed)*, 205-228. Amsterdam, Rodopi, 1994.

This paper supplies a structuralist reconstruction of the Modigliani-Miller theory and shows that the economic literature following their results reports on research with an implicit strategy to come "closer-to-the-truth" in the modern technical sense in philosophy of science.

Kuipers, Theo A F and Wisniewski, Andrzej. An Erotetic Approach to Explanation by Specification. *Erkenntnis*, 40(3), 377-402, My 94.

In the present paper it is shown that four kinds of erotetic argumentative steps occurring in the train of thought of explanation by specification are valid arguments in the sense of inferential erotetic logic. Hence, in view of the fact that other argumentative steps were already shown to be valid, it may be concluded that the logical structure of explanation by specification can be as well-established as that of explanation by nomological subsumption. Moreover, explanation by specification provides some illustrations of the applicability of erotetic logic in everyday life and some empirical sciences. (edited)

Kujundzic, Nebojsa. Thought Experiments: Architecture and Economy of Thought. *J Brit Soc Phenomenol*, 26(1), 86-93, Ja 95.

This paper takes a historical approach to philosophy of science. It suggests two accounts of thought experiments offered in the early twentieth century by Ernst Mach and Edmund Husserl. Ernst Mach's understanding of variation of thought was very close to the idea of experimentation as practiced in science. Edmund Husserl's understanding of variation of thought was close to the way we imagine the work of an architect. Following the presentation of Mach's and Husserl's concept of thought experiments, this paper suggests that these two concepts give rise to a need to form an exclusive dichotomy between empiric and formal accounts of human understanding. However, contemporary cognitive science, in giving a complete picture of thought experimentation, may find *both* Machian and Husserlian accounts useful.

Kujundzic, Nebojsa and Buschert, William. Instruments and the Body: Sartre and Merleau-Ponty. *Res Phenomenol*, 24, 206-215, 1994.

We argue that no sharp boundary can be drawn between the "authentic" human body and its instruments. In contrast to some other theorists of the continental canon—notably Heidegger and the Frankfurt school—Sartre and Merleau-Ponty can be read as asserting that the body (transitively) *lives* its instruments, weaving with them an intricate web of habitual actions and experiences. For Merleau-Ponty especially, the human body and its instruments are capable of complementing, supplementing, and melting into one another.

Kukla, André. Forster and Sober on the Curve-Fitting Problem. *Brit J Phil Sci*, 46(2), 248-252, Je 95.

Forster and Sober present a solution to the curve-fitting problem based on Akaike's Theorem. Their analysis shows that the curve with the best epistemic credentials need not always be the curve that most closely fits the data. However, their solution does not, without further argument, avoid the two difficulties that are traditionally associated with the curve-fitting problem: 1) that there are infinitely many equally good candidate-curves relative to any given set of data, and 2) that these best candidates include curves with indefinitely many bumps.

Kukla, André. Medium AI and Experimental Science. *Phil Psych*, 7(4), 493-502, 1994.

It has been claimed that a great deal of AI research is an attempt to discover the empirical laws describing a new type of entity in the world—the artificial computing system. I call this enterprise 'medium AI', since it is in some respects stronger than Searle's 'weak AI', and in other respects weaker than 'strong AI'. Bruce Buchanan, among others, conceives of medium AI as an empirical science entirely on a par with psychology or chemistry. I argue that medium AI is not an empirical science at all. Depending on how artificial computing systems are categorized, it is either an *a priori* science like mathematics, or a branch of engineering.

Kukla, André. Non-Empirical Theoretical Virtues and the Argument from Underdetermination. *Erkenntnis*, 41(2), 157-170, S 94.

The antirealist argument from the underdetermination of theories by data relies on the premise that the empirical content of a theory is the only determinant of its belief-worthiness (premise NN). Several authors have claimed that the antirealist cannot endorse NN, on pain of internal inconsistency. I concede this point. Nevertheless, this refutation of the underdetermination argument fails because there are weaker substitutes for NN that will serve just as well as a premise to the argument. On the other hand, antirealists have not made a convincing case *for* NN (or its weaker substitutes) either. In particular, I criticize van Fraassen's recent claim that all ampliative rules in epistemology must be rejected on the grounds that they lead to incoherence. The status of the underdetermination argument remains unsettled.

Kukla, André. Scientific Realism, Scientific Practice, and the Natural Ontological Attitude. *Brit J Phil Sci*, 45(4), 955-975, D 94.

Both sides in the debate about scientific realism have argued that their view provides a better account of actual scientific practice. For example, it has been claimed that the practice of theory conjunction presupposes realism, and that scientists' use of multiple and incompatible models presupposes some form of instrumentalism. Assuming that the practices of science are rational, these conclusions cannot both be right. I argue that neither of them is right, and that, in fact, all scientific practices are compatible with both realism and instrumentalism. I also repudiate van Fraassen's argument to the effect that the instrumentalist account of scientific practice is logically weaker, hence better, than the realist account. In the end, there are no scientific practice arguments on the table that support either side of the debate. It is also noted that the deficiencies of van Fraassen's argument are recapitulated in Putnam's miracle argument for realism. My pessimistic assessment of the state of the debate is reminiscent of Arthur Fine's. However, Fine's argument for the 'natural ontological attitude' once again repeats the problems of van Fraassen's and Putnam's arguments.

Kuklick, Bruce. "American Philosophy and Its Lost Public" in *Pragmatism: From Progressivism to Postmodernism, Hollinger, Robert (ed)*, 142-152. Westport, Praeger, 1995.

Kukoc, Mislav. Die Aufhebung der Ethik in der kroatischen Praxisphilosophie. *Filozof Istraz*, 14(1), 143-151, 1994.

Die Intention, das Problem von Moralität und Ethik als Moraltheorie abzuschaffen, tritt in der kroatischen Praxisphilosophie im Rahmen des marxistischen revolutionären Konzepts der "Aufhebung" auf, da als Instrument der revolutionären Umwandlung der Welt zum Zweck der Verwirklichung des Eschatons der neuen Geschichte promoviert wurde. Aufgrund einer kritischen Analyse werden zwei Einwände gegen besagte Position vorgebracht. Erstens: In den Werken der Praxisphilosophen Milan Kangrga und Gajo Petrovic geht die Kritik der Moralität von einem Standpunkt aus, der einem gewissen Typus von ethischem Normativismus sehr nahe liegt. Zweitens: Die Aufhebung moralischen Handelns bzw. seine Ersetzung durch geschichtliche, revolutionäre Praxis birgt, mit Rücksicht auf das komplexe Wesen des Menschen, die reale Gefahr von Nihilismus und Voluntarismus. Daher ergibt sich moralisches Handeln als notwendiges und ewiges Verhaltensregulativ eines unvollkommenen Wesens, als wirkliches, unerreichbares Vorbild. In der notwendigen Diskrepanz von Sein und Sollen bleibt es stets unvollendet und unvollendbar, so wie auch die Welt de Menschen ewig unvollendbar bleibt. Hierbei geht es jedoch nicht um "schlechte", sondern um "gute Unendlichkeit"!

Kukoc, Mislav. Die philosophische und literarische Rezeption des Kommunismus. *Filozof Istraz*, 13(4), 793-802, 1993.

In seinem Text argumentiert der Verfasser die These, dass die Destruktion der kommunistischen Ideologie auf literarischer Ebene viel erfolgreicher verlief als auf philosophischer. In den Verhältnissen der Dominanz der totalitären kommunistischen Ideologie werden sämtliche Aspekte der ihr entgegengesetzten bürgerlichen Kultur als ideelle Instrumente eines unversöhnlichen Klassenfeindes verworfen. Die Repression des totalitären kommunistischen Bewusstseins ist auf philosophischer Ebene, wo Diskussionen innerhalb des vorgezeichneten marxistischen Paradigmas geführt werden, sehr viel ausgeprägter. Obwohl auch im literarisch-künstlerischen Bereich ein ideologischer Rahmen in Form des sog. sozialistischen Realismus vorgegeben ist, ist der heterodoxe Widerstand dort sehr viel ausgeprägter und wirksamer. Beweis dafür sind zahlreiche Vertreter der Dissidentenliteratur, von Pasternak, Bulgakow und Solschenizyn bis zu mitteleuropäischen Autoren wie Kundera, Skvorecky und Hrabal. Auch in der kroatischen Kulturtradition tolerierte das totalitäre kommunistische Bewusstsein Abweichungen von der Orthodoxie auf literarisch-ästhetischer Ebene eher als auf wissenschaftlich-philosophischer, wozu sicherlich auch die unbestrittene Autorität Miroslav Krlezas beigetragen hat. (edited)

Kulp, Christopher B. Rejoinder to Scott L Pratt. *Mod Sch*, 72(1), 77-80, N 94.

Kultgen, John. *Autonomy and Intervention: Parentalism in the Caring Life*. New York, Oxford Univ Pr, 1994.

An exploration of modes of intervention in the lives of others that may reasonably be categorized as paternalistic (here re-labeled as "parentalistic") and the ways they encroach on the autonomy of the recipient. They are interpreted as forms of care and intrinsic to the caring life. Issues are examined in relation to both personal and public forms of intervention. A form of soft anti-paternalism is proposed according to which paternalism is prima facie objectionable, but can be justified when other values are more important than autonomy. Criticisms are leveled against sterner forms of anti-paternalism for absolutizing the value of autonomy.

Kumamoto, Chukei. "Vernunft und Selbstbewusstsein—Zur Fichte-Rezeption in Japan" in *Das geistige Erbe Europas, Buhr, Manfred (ed)*, 378-386. Napoli, Vivarium, 1994.

Shin'ichiro Nishi (1873-1943), der an der Univesität Hiroshima als Professor tätig war, entwickelte durch eine Synthese von europäischem und chinesisch-japanischem Denken ein eigentliches System der Philsophie. Er hat vor allem durch Fichtes Philsophie gefunden, dass Philsophie nichts anderes als die Darstellung des jeweiligen Philosophen sei, und dass sich die Wahrheit im Menschen individuarisieren solle. Nach ihm ist so die Vernunft nicht nur ein Prinzip der Welt, sondern auch ein Prinzip des Menschen, der eigentlich als Individuum eine Person ist, in der sich die Wahrheit verwirklicht, und die den Geist der Schöpfung der Welt durch Gott einsieht.

Kumamoto, Chukei. Die transzendentale Freiheit bei Fichte. *Fichte-Studien*, 1, 99-107, 1990.

Fichte, der schon zu Beginn seines Philosophierens gegen den Widerstreit von Freiheit und Notwendigkeit, der Ordnung des Herzens und des Kopfs angekämpft hatte, fand in Kants Freiheitslehre die Grundlage seines eigenen Systems der Philosophie. Im Jahr 1800 schrieb er Jacobi, sein System sei von Anfang bis zu Ende nur eine Analyse des Begriffs der Freiheit. Und in den *Einleitungsvorlesungen in die Wissenschaftslehre* von 1813 behauptete er, das allgemein mangelnde Verständnis Kants sowie seines eigenen Denkens beklagend, um die Wissenschaftslehre zu verstehen, müsse der ganze Mensch vom natürlichen Sein zum freien sein erweitert werden. Auf diese Weise scheint die Frage der Freiheit immer den Kernpunkt der Fichteschen Philosophie gebildet zu haben. (edited)

Kumamoto, Yasuhiro. Die methodologische Funktion des Verhältnisses von "Herr und Knecht" in der Philosophie Hegels. *Fichte-Studien*, 3, 51-67, 1991.

Im vierten Kapitel sind die verschiedenen Aspekte des Verhältnisses von Herr und Knecht und dessen Bedeutung dargestellt worden. Damit ist die Schlussfolgerung erlaubt, dass die im dritten Kapitel durch die Untersuchung des Kapitels "Herrschaft und Knechtschaft" gefundene Einsicht für alle Aspekte des "Herr-Knecht"-Verhältnisses gilt: das Verhältnis von "Herr und Knecht" lässt durch die Einheit der zwei Verdoppelungen des Selbstbewusstseins, d.h. die Übereinstimmung seiner inneren Doppelheit und seiner äusseren Doppelheit, den Geist sich von seiner Naturhaftigkeit zur Freiheit entwickeln. Indem der Geist in seinem Inneren das Verhältnis von "Herr und Knecht"—wo er sich dem Herrn, der Naturhaftigkeit, unterordnet—überwindet, überwindet er zugleich das äussere Verhältnis von "Herr und Knecht". Dadurch entsteht das freie allgemeine Selbstbewusstsein in der Welt, d.h. in Geschichte, Staat, Volk, dem Einzelnen und in der Religion. Das Herr-Knecht-Verhältnis hat die methodologische Funktion, den Geist aus seiner Natürlichkeit zum allgemeinen Selbstbewusstsein, zur Freiheit des Denkens zu bringen. (edited)

Kumamoto, Yasuhiro. Fichtes Erziehungslehre als erste logische Begründung der Vorbilderziehung. *Daimon Rev Filosof*, 9, 249-257, 1994.

Therefore, the task of this paper is set on fixing Fichte's philosophy and pedagogy as unified one. And by means of performing this consideration we can bring out a new reading of Fichte's pedagogy which has never been reached by clinging to the nationalistic explanation of his pedagogy. We take the fundamental point of Fichte's philosophical theory is the freedom and the education is the most important method for realization of the freedom. In addition, we make the essence of Fichte's educational theory clear depending upon the elucidation of the meaning of the concept *freedom*. Fichte's true historic achievement in pedagogy is to found *the ideal education* by the precise logic. If we grasp Fichte's educational theory in this context, we can also understand the meaning of *national education* and *isolating education* more clearly and exactly than over. (edited)

Kummert, Michael. Ökonomisches Handeln. *Protosoz*, 1, 100-106, Ap 91.

This research is the attempt to introduce economic acting as a relevance of Protosociology. In the first step I will try to describe economic acting in terms of speech/act/theory. It will take us from illocutionary and perlocutionary acts to a useful understanding of strategic acting. It will be shown that the assumption that economy has to deal with perfect markets cannot be made in a context of strategic acting.

Kuo, Lenore and Anechiarico, Frank. The Justified Scoundrel: The Structural Genesis of Corruption. *J Soc Phil*, 26(1), 147-161, Spr 95.

Kuokkanen, Martti and Tuomivaara, Timo. The Threshold Model of Scientific Change and the Continuity of Scientific Knowledge. *J Gen Phil Sci*, 25(2), 327-335, 1994.

The continuity thesis of the Poznan school threshold model of the growth of scientific knowledge is considered in the light of the example of Van der Waals' and Boyle-Mariotte's laws. It is argued—using both traditional logical means and the structuralist reconstruction of the example—that the continuity thesis does not hold. (edited)

Kupperman, Joel J. "The Emotions of Altruism, East and West" in *Emotions in Asian Thought, Marks, Joel (ed)*, 123-138. Albany, SUNY Pr, 1995.

Altruism, as a policy of giving equal weight to the interests of every sentient being, is a feature of much Asian thought, notably in the Buddhist tradition, and also of utilitarianism. This East-West parallel, though, masks some important differences. Buddhism points toward a life of compassion, as an all-pervasive mild emotion. Western altruism is usually applied within a limited sphere, roughly that of public life: this points toward a split emotional life, with one part likely to seem impersonal and even cold and the other part incorporating the partiality normal in the culture.

Kurland, Nancy B. Ethics, Incentives, and Conflicts of Interest: A Practical Solution. *J Bus Ethics*, 14(6), 465-475, Je 95.

Couched in positive agency theory, it is shown that the straight-commission compensation system (SCCS) creates a conflict of interest between the agent's and the client's self-interests. Based on this, it is hypothesized that the SCCS will encourage agents to intend to act unethically towards their clients. Two hundred and forty five insurance agents in the U.S. were surveyed, with 59% responding. The results suggest that the SCCS does not significantly affect agents' ethical intentions, positively or negatively. This lack of empirical evidence may be due to the unique nature of the sample. Indeed, the company which enabled this sample appears to have found a practical solution to temper the potential negative effects of the SCCS in its commitment to selective hiring and marketing products which benefit both the client and the agent.

Kurthen, Martin. Ahistorical Intentional Content. *J Gen Phil Sci*, 25(2), 241-259, 1994.

One of the main problems of current theory of intentionality concerns the possibility of ahistorical intentional content, that is, content in the absence of any developmental history of the respective item. Biosemanticists like Millikan (1984) argue that content is essentially historical, while computationalists like Cummins (1989) hold that a system's current ahistorical state alone determines content. In the present paper, this problem is discussed in terms of some popular 'cosmic accident' thought experiments, and the conceptual framework of these experiments is enriched by some new versions like accidental 'duplicates' without any preexisting original. As a result of these evaluations, it is argued that for an item to bear intentional content it is necessary to have a 'function' in the forward-looking sense introduced by Bigelow and Pargetter (1987). Since historicity is not necessary for functionality, ahistorical states can be intentional as long as they have functions. This result does not support computationalism, since functionality cannot be determined in terms of current ahistorical state alone, but only with reference to the present and future environmental context of the cognitive system that harbours these states.

Kurucz, H Andréka and Németi, I. Connections Between Axioms of Set Theory and Basic Theorems of Universal Algebra. *J Sym Log*, 59(3), 912-923, S 94.

One of the basic theorems in universal algebra is Birkhoff's variety theorem: the smallest equationally axiomatizable class containing a class *K* of algebras coincides with the class obtained by taking homomorphic images of subalgebras of direct products of elements of *K*. G Grätzer asked whether the variety theorem is equivalent to the Axiom of Choice. In 1980, two of the present authors proved that Birkhoff's theorem can already be derived in *ZF*. Surprisingly, the Axiom of Foundation plays a crucial role here: we show that Birkhoff's theorem cannot be derived in *ZF + AC*/(Foundation), even if we add Foundation for Finite Sets. We also prove that the variety theorem is equivalent to a purely set-theoretical statement, the Collection Principle. This principle is independent of *ZF*/(Foundation). The second part of the paper deals with further connections between axioms of *ZF*-set theory and theorems of universal algebra.

Kurzon, Dennis. The Case of a Broken Cohesive Chain. *J Prag*, 22(2), 213-215, Ag 94.

The usual cohesive chain in a text moves from the unknown to the known, from an indefinite noun phrase at first mention to definite noun phrases. However, in newspaper reports of a crime and its perpetrator, after the alleged criminal and his (or her) activities have already been described in the form of definite noun phrases, the indefinite noun phrase is used to refer to the arrested person, since he is considered innocent until proven guilty. Hence, the cohesive chain seems to be broken.

Kurzon, Dennis. The Right of Silence: A Socio-Pragmatic Model of Interpretation. *J Prag*, 23(1), 55-69, Ja 95.

Firstly, a sociopragmatic model of the interpretation of the silent answer is set up, with focus on the suspect in custody who is being asked questions by the police or by a lawyer in court. It is claimed that there are two types of silence—unintentional and intentional. Unintentional silence is psychological in nature, usually occurring because of personal inhibitions on the part of the addressee. Intentional silence, on the other hand, is a deliberate attempt by the addressee not to be cooperative with the addresser. A schema is then put forward that shows the process by which the questioner (the police or the court) interprets the silence of the suspect. In normal conversation, such silence is interpreted to the detriment of the silent person. However, because of the so-called right of silence, the suspect's refusal to speak may not usually be brought to the attention of the court adjudicating in the case.

Kushner, Thomasine. Jessica Mitford Discusses Attitudes on Aging. *Cambridge Quart Healthcare Ethics*, 4(2), 133-134, Spr 95.

Kusukawa, Sachiko. *The Transformation of Natural Philosophy: The Case of Philip Melanchthon*. New York, Cambridge Univ Pr, 1995.

I propose in this work that Philip Melanchthon was responsible for transforming natural philosophy into a specifically Lutheran one. Motivated by the desire to check civil disobedience and promote Lutheran orthodoxy, he created a natural philosophy based on Aristotle, Galen, Plato, Copernicus and Vesalius. The fields of astrology, anatomy, botany, and mathematics all constituted a natural philosophy in which Melanchthon wished to demonstrate God's providential design in the physical world. Rather than dichotomizing or synthesizing the two distinct areas of 'science and religion', I argue the need to look at 'natural philosophy' as a discipline *sui generis*.

Kuteva, Tania. Iconicity and Auxiliation. *J Prag*, 22(1), 71-81, Jl 94.

In this paper the notion of iconicity is considered in relation to a particular language change phenomenon, namely the development of regular, lexical verb structures into grammaticalized auxiliary constructions. It is argued that depending on the subtype of iconicity, auxiliary constructions exhibit behavior ranging from violation of iconic encoding to a clear case of iconicity. More precisely, the claims it made that of all verb grammatical morphemes, i.e., prefixes, suffixes, infixes, stem change, reduplication, auxiliaries, etc., it is auxiliary grams that present the clearest case of what is here regarded as metaphoric-metonymic iconicity.

Kuvakin, V A. Russian Philosophy as an Area of Study and as a Spiritual Value. *Metaphilosophy*, 25(2-3), 132-137, Ap-Jl 94.

Kuvakina, Olga D and Gromow, Ivan G. Noospheric Synarchy: From an Ancient Hellenic Democracy to the Aristocracy of Spirit. *Philosophia (Athens)*, 23-24, 15-24, 1993-94.

Kuznetsov, Vladimir and Burgin, Mark. Scientific Problems and Questions from a Logical Point of View. *Synthese*, 100(1), 1-28, Jl 94.

Scientific knowledge systems function as effective and specialized apparatus for formulating, analyzing and solving scientific problems. In science, problems become internal parts of the knowledge systems; thus they acquire new forms and properties in comparison with common-sense problems. Definite theoretical structures connected with problems and questions appear in the theory. Among them are erotetic expressions and languages, calculi and algebras of problems. On the basis of the structure-nominative reconstruction of a theory, the unified treatment of these structures is given. Methods of the theory of named sets are used in the logical analysis of problems and their systems. As a consequence a new formalized model of the problem part of theory is constructed.

Kuznicki, Leszek. Integration of Sciences—Theory and Practice. *Dialogue Hum*, 4(4), 137-141, 1994.

Kvanvig, Jonathan L. Coherentism: Misconstrual and Misapprehension. *SW Phil Rev*, 11(1), 159-168, Ja 95.

Kvart, Igal. Counterfactuals: Ambiguities, True Premises, and Knowledge. *Synthese*, 100(1), 133-164, Jl 94.

In this paper I explore the ambiguity that arises between two readings of the counterfactual construction, the *n-d* and the *l-p*, analyzed in my book *A Theory of Counterfactuals*. I then extend the analysis I offered there to counterfactuals with true antecedents, and offer a more precise formulation of the conception of temporal divergence points used in the *l-p* interpretation. Finally, I discuss some ramifications of these issues for counterfactual analyses of knowledge.

Kvart, Igal. Seeing That and Seeing As. *Nous*, 27(3), 279-302, S 93.

In this paper I propose an analysis of a variety of perceptual constructions. I will take as the basic construction the seeing-that construction, analyzing it in terms of visual images and the concepts of knowledge and being a cause. I will then propose a reduction of the seeing-x, the seeing-as and the seeing-x-F constructions to the seeing-that construction.

Kvart, Igal. Stich and the *De Dicto-De Re* Ambiguity. *Iyyun*, 44, 31-45, Ja 95.

Kverndokk, Snorre. Tradeable CO_2 Emission Permits: Initial Distribution as a Justice Problem. *Environ Values*, 4(2), 129-148, May 95.

One characteristic of tradeable emission permits is that efficiency and justice considerations can be separated. While Pareto optimality is an accepted efficiency principle, there is not a consensus on a 'best' equity principle. In this article, conventional justice principles are used to evaluate alternative allocation rules for tradeable CO_2 permits, and a distribution proportional to population is recommended. Arguments against the population rule are discussed, especially those pertaining to political feasibility. While justice and political feasibility may indeed contrast, it still may be possible to emphasise the population rule in the future.

Kwa, Chung Lin. "Models and Modernism: Between Anxiety and Hubris" in *Ecology, Technology, and Culture*, Zweers, Wim (ed), 89-93. Cambridge, White Horse, 1994.

Kwame, Safro (ed). *Readings in African Philosophy: An Akan Collection*. Lanham, Univ Pr of America, 1995.

Unlike most of the texts in the field, this anthology includes classics as well as contemporary writings; it deals extensively with philosophical as well as metaphilosophical issues; it covers both traditional and current areas of philosophical research, and presents material at both the introductory and advanced levels. In it, Appiah defines philosophy, Abraham characterizes the Akan worldview, Oguah and Gyekye compare Akan and Western theories; Danquah and Wiredu provide Akan conceptions of God, mind and truth, and Amo critiques Descartes. Also, Nkrumah and Busia debate socialism while Dolphyne and Kwame deal with feminism and business ethics.

Kymlicka, Will. Communitarianism, Liberalism, and Superliberalism. *Crit Rev*, 8(2), 263-284, Spr 94.

Although Roberto Unger is sometimes described as a communitarian critic of liberalism, his recent three-volume work on *Politics* disavows the major tenets of contemporary communitarianism. Unger's aim is to criticize liberalism from a perspective which takes the original liberal desire to emancipate individuals from the chains of social custom and hierarchy and rids it of the stultifying economic and political institutions within which liberals have sought to contain it. Three main

components of Unger's theory are analyzed: the idea of "negative capability," the idea of an "empowered democracy," and the idea of "immunity rights." I argue that all three underestimate the risks to individual liberty of the over-politicization of social life. (edited)

L Prades, Josep. Antirrealismo y Verdad: La Realidad del Pasado. *An Seminar Metaf*, 28, 39-55, 1994.

L'Etang, Jacquie. Ethical Corporate Social Resonsibility: A Framework for Managers. *J Bus Ethics*, 14(2), 125-132, F 95.

Managers encounter difficulties in developing corporate social responsibility programs. This paper attempts to highlight problem areas for managers and to develop a pragmatic framework of analysis which will help identify and clarify corporate social responsibilities. The paper, which is written from a UK perspective, discusses the contribution of stakeholder models and highlights limitations of this approach. (edited)

La Guardia, Giovanni. Faust e Lust. *Stud Filosofici*, 277-288, 1991-92.

La Torre, Massimo. Citizenship: A European Wager. *Ratio Juris*, 8(1), 113-123, Mr 95.

La Tour, Michael S and Henthorne, Tony L. A Model to Explore the Ethics of Erotic Stimuli in Print Advertising. *J Bus Ethics*, 14(7), 561-569, Jl 95.

This paper discusses a test of a hypothetical model of the role of perceived ethical feelings about the use of female nudity/erotic stimuli in print advertising. Specifically, the linkages between perceived ethicalness of the use of the print ad (as measured by the Reidenbach and Robin ethics scale) and attitude toward the ad, brand, and purchase intention are explored.

Labarrière, Pierre-Jean and Jarczyk, Gwendoline. Absolu/Sujet. *Laval Theol Phil*, 51(2), 239-250, Je 95.

Hegel, de son propre aveu, a transcrit l'héritage de l'ontologie métaphysique (dont il n'excepte pas le transcendantalisme kantien) dans les canons d'une logique dont il a profondément bouleversé l'intelligence. Avec le mouvement réflexif, qui s'impose alors à la base de son système, sont récusées d'un même mouvement l'abstraction d'un universel formel et vide et l'attention à une immédiateté seulement donnée qui ne serait pas saisie comme le corps d'effectivité de l'idée. D'où la clef de cet univers: la conviction de ce que le sujet (ou l'esprit) est structuré en lui-même de telle sorte que son effectuation historique, à même la contingence, fasse partie de son essence. Une < totalité-mouvement > qui, sans achèvement possible, identifie processuellement logique et histoire, absolu et contingence.

Labedzki, Grzegorz and Repicky, Miroslav. Hechler Reals. *J Sym Log*, 60(2), 444-458, Je 95.

Labica, Georges. "Die verlorene Wette—Versuch über die Krisen des 'realen' Sozialismus" in *Das geistige Erbe Europas*, Buhr, Manfred (ed), 809-825. Napoli, Vivarium, 1994.

LaBossiere, Michael. Body and Environment. *Environ Ethics*, 16(4), 411-418, Wint 94.

My thesis is the biconditional that it is morally wrong to pollute human bodies if and only if it is morally wrong to pollute the environment. The argument for each conditional is by analogy: pollution of one type is analogous to pollution of the other type in morally relevant respects. I argue that the truth of the biconditional makes it difficult to maintain that it is morally wrong to pollute human bodies without maintaining that it is morally wrong to pollute the environment and conversely.

LaBossiere, Michael C. Substances and Substrata. *Austl J Phil*, 72(3), 360-369, S 94.

In this work, the focus is on the issue of deciding between a trope-substrata view and a bundle of tropes view. It is concluded that the trope-substrata view is superior. The paper itself is divided into three main sections. The first involves a discussion of tropes, substances, and substrata. The second focuses on three arguments for substrata. The third is dedicated to defending substrata from historical and modern attacks. Other issues discussed include the distinction between tropes and universals, individuation, minimal entities, and the problem of bare particulars.

Labrada, María Antonia. A Proposito de la Critica del Juicio. *Topicos*, 1(1), 183-196, 1991.

This essay tries to explain, from Kant's Critique of Judgment, the deep reasons which have given rise to the prevailing malaise in today's culture. The division between nature and freedom which had been started at the heart of modern philosophy, was the subject of Kant's third Critique. He established a new unity within subjectivity. As a result, the sphere of objectivity was kept under the characteristic mechanical rationality of the determining and objective use of reason. The division between nature and freedom became a division between culture and creativity. This approach tries to answer whether a negative interpretation of today's culture sense of unease is correct whether this type of interpretation also belongs to modern premises.

Labriola, Albert C. *Christus Patiens* and *Christus Victor*: John Donne's Ultimate Reality and Meaning. *Ultim Real Mean*, 18(2), 92-101, Je 95.

John Donne's religious metaphysical poetry centers upon two interrelated concepts: *Christus Patiens* (the suffering Christ) and *Christus Victor* (the triumphant Christ). These concepts are essential constituents of so-called Paschal mystery, whereby the humiliation of the Lord is followed by his exaltation. To undergo the Lord's triumph or exaltation, Donne through his devotional poetry urges humankind to withstand adversity and to endure suffering with faith, patience, and fortitude. As such, humankind will bring about the necessary though not sufficient conditions of salvation. The Lord while recognizing humankind's readiness to be saved may effectuate that process by an infusion of grace.

Labude, Joachim. Formalisierungsversuch der Sprechakttheorie. *Protosoz*, 2, 71-75, Ja 92.

In their book *Foundation of Illocutionary Logic* the authors attempt to formalize the theory of speech acts. In set theoretical terms they describe their basic notions of illocutionary forces and points, define new 'illocutionary' symbols and operations and formulate some axioms and postulates, which should explicitly describe their theory, but their creativity of introducing new functional symbols and connectives conjoint with an unsystematic representation opposes this purpose.

LaCasse, Chantale and Ross, Don. The Microeconomic Interpretation of Games. *Proc Phil Sci Ass*, 1, 379-387, 1994.

This paper is part of a larger project defending of the foundations of microeconomics against recent criticisms by philosophers. Here, we undermine one source of these criticisms, arising from philosophers' disappointment with the performance of microecomonic tools, in particular game theory, when these are applied to normative decision theory. Hollis and Sugden have recently articulated such disappointment in a sophisticated way, and have argued on the basis of it that the economic conception of rationality is inadequate. We argue, however, that their claim rests upon a misunderstanding of the concept of a game as it is used in microeconomics.

Lacharité, Normand. Le Problème de l'Architecture dans le Débat entre l'Approche Connexionniste et les Approches "Classiques" de la Représentation. *Lekton*, 4(2), 37-64, 1994.

Lachlan, Alistair H and Soare, Robert I. Models of Arithmetic and Upper Bounds for Arithmetic Sets. *J Sym Log*, 59(3), 977-983, S 94.

We settle on a question in the literature about degrees of models of true arithmetic and upper bounds for the arithmetic sets. We prove that there is a model of true arithmetic whose degree is not a uniform upper bound for the arithmetic sets. The proof involves two forcing constructions.

Lachmann, Rolf. *Ethik und Identität: Der ethische Ansatz in der Prozessphilosophie A N Whiteheads und seine Bedeutung für die gegenwärtige Ethik*. Freiburg, Alber, 1994.

This book works out an ethical theory adumbrated in Whitehead's philosophy, an ethics opposed to basic conceptions in modern metaphysics of substance and moral philosophy. The author interprets this new ethics as a particular form of the production of identity, and relates this position to a discussion of contemporary approaches to ethics (G Pfafferott, E Tugendhat, A Wellmer, J Rawls, H Jonas, a MacIntyre, O Schwemmer, M Nussbaum, H S Richardson). The author shows that an ethics of identity admits the existence of different ethical identities without leading to relativistic consequences.

Lachs, John. Moral Truth or Empirical Truth about Morality. *Bull Santayana Soc*, 12, 13-16, Fall 94.

Lackey, Douglas. Time and Value from Aristippus to Plotinus. *J Neoplatonic Stud*, 1(1), 91-110, Fall 92.

Lackman, Conway and Sisaye, Seleshi. Ethics in Undergraduate Accounting Education: An Empirical Study. *Bus Prof Ethics J*, 13(1-2), 79-87, Spr-Sum 94.

The extent to which ethics education has been incorporated in the business program, particularly in the accounting curriculum, has received substantial attention among accounting educators and administrators. This paper discusses the results of a case study of a business undergraduate program on the integration of ethics in the accounting curriculum. The study revealed that ethics and social issues are the least integrated subject areas in accounting courses when compared to other business courses. While ethics has been slightly more covered in the upper than the lower level accounting courses, the most commonly methods of ethics integration primarily included short problems and individual projects or case assignments.

Lad, Lawrence J and Calton, Jerry M. Social Contracting as a Trust-Building Process of Network Governance. *Bus Ethics Quart*, 5(2), 271-295, Ap 95.

Social contracting has a long and important place in the history of political philosophy (Hardin, 1991; Waldron, 1989) and as a theory of justice (Baynes, 1989; Rawls, 1971). More recently, it has been developed into an individual rights based-theory of organizations (Keeley, 1980, 1988), and as a way to integrate ethics and moral legitimacy into corporate strategy and action (Donaldson, 1982; Freeman and Gilbert, 1988). Currently, it is being proposed as an integrative theory of economic ethics (Donaldson and Dunfee, forthcoming). This paper will extend the Donaldson and Dunfee approach by arguing that *social contracting can best be understood and applied in organizational settings if it is perceived and treated as a network governance process*. This insight can benefit management scholars and practitioners alike, since it calls attention to the processes by which trust is created and sustained in on-going contractual relationships. It also strongly suggests that a new approach to applying managerial discretion, as *moral agency*, is needed to realize the full competitive and ethical potential of emerging network forms.

Laffond, Gilbert and Laine, Jean. Weak Covering Relations. *Theor Decis*, 37(3), 245-265, N 94.

This paper proposes and justifies a natural way to weaken the concept of covering relation defined on a finite tournament. Various weak covering relations, called *k*-covering relations, are introduced. To each *k*-covering relation corresponds a strong uncovered set containing all non *k*-covered outcomes. It is proved that those strong uncovered sets may be empty. Moreover, the set of all tournaments having an empty strong uncovered set is characterized within two rather large classes of tournaments. Finally, we offer a complete study of the cases where the directed graph defined by a *k*-covering relation coincides with the initial tournament.

Laffranchi, M. Verità ed etica nella *Dialectica* di Lorenzo Valla. *Riv Filosof Neo-Scolas*, 86(1), 44-109, Ja-Mr 94.

LaFollette, Hugh and Shanks, Niall. Chaos Theory: Analogical Reasoning in Biomedical Research. *Ideal Stud*, 24(3), 241-254, Fall 94.

In this article we discuss two divergent accounts of nonhuman animals an analog models of human biomedical phenomena. Using a classical account of analogical reasoning, toxicologists and teratologists claim that if the model and subject modeled are substantially similar, then test results in nonhuman animals are likely applicable to humans. However, the same toxicologists report that different species often react very differently to the same chemical stimuli. The best way to understand their findings is to abandon the classical view of analogical—i.e., linear—reasoning, and replace it with a version informed by chaos theory. We briefly outline the current understanding of chaos, and trace its implications for toxicology and teratology.

LaFollette, Hugh and Shanks, Niall. Two Models of Models in Biomedical Research. *Phil Quart*, 45(179), 141-160, Ap 95.

Most biomedical researchers construe animal models as *causal* models designed to uncover underlying mechanisms of biomedical phenomenon. There is a competing view of animal experimentation which, although not entrenched in biomedical theory, is alive and well in biomedical practice. On this view animal models are *heuristic devices*. Although these do not reveal causal mechanisms, they may prompt scientific inquiry which leads indirectly to biomedical discoveries. We argue that there are compelling theoretical, historical, and pragmatic reasons for construing animal experiments as heuristic divides rather than causal models.

LaFollette, Hugh and Shanks, Niall. Util-izing Animals. *J Applied Phil*, 12(1), 13-25, 1995.

Biomedical experimentation on animals is justified, researchers say, because of its enormous benefits to human beings. Sure, animals suffer and die, but that is morally insignificant since the benefits of research *incalculably* outweigh the evils. Although this utilitarian claim appears straightforward and relatively uncontroversial, it is neither straightforward nor uncontroversial. This defence of animal experimentation is likely to succeed only by rejecting three widely held moral presumptions. We identify these assumptions and explain their relevance to the justification of animal experimentation. We argue that, even if nonhuman animals have considerably less moral worth than humans, experimentation is justified only if the benefits are overwhelming. By building on and expanding on arguments offered in earlier papers, we show that researchers cannot substantiate their claims on behalf of animal research. We conclude that there is currently no acceptable utilitarian defence of animal experimentation. Moreover, it is unlikely that there could be one. Since most apologists of animal experimentation rely on utilitarian justifications of their practice, it appears that biomedical experimentation on animals is not morally justified.

Lafont, Cristina. Spannungen im Wahrheitsbegriff. *Deut Z Phil*, 42(6), 1007-1023, 1994.

This article examines the discursive theory of truth (truth as rational acceptability under ideal conditions) developed by J Habermas. The main thrust of the article is to bring out the inevitable antifallibilist consequences stemming from epistemic conceptions of truth. On the basis of this analysis it is argued that the only viable way to reconcile as much the epistemic as the realist intuition connected with the concept of truth seems to be to adopt a genuinely pragmatic viewpoint that might help to explain the central role of his concept within our fallibilistic procedures of belief revision due to its internal connection with the concept of reality, avoiding however at the same time the bad alternative of either antifallibilism rooted in an epistemic conception of truth or metaphysical realism.

Lafont, Cristina. Truth, Knowledge, and Reality. *Sorites*, 100-114, Ap 95.

The main argument of this article is that the concept of truth is as much internally linked to the concept of knowledge as to the concept of reality. As a consequence it is affirmed that all attempts to explain its structure which are either exclusively biased in an epistemic point of view (that is, which connect only truth and knowledge) or in a purely realist metaphysics (which only connect truth and reality) are bound to fail. Instead this article proposes the adoption of a pragmatic standpoint which would permit to reconstruct the fallibilistic role displayed by the concept of truth in the epistemic practices of belief-revision, which must in turn be reconstructed precisely taking in account the connection of truth and reality. In that way both intuitions as to the concept of truth, the epistemic and the realist one, can be reconciled. Moreover this strategy provides as such, if correct, a strong argument in favor of an essential function of the concept of truth against contemporary deflationist tendencies.

Lafrance, Yvon. *Dictionnaire des philosophes antiques*, publié sous la direction de Richard Goulet, t.II *Babélyca d'Argos á Dyscolius*. *Apeiron*, 28(1), 67-73, Mr 95.

This essay is a critical review of the *Dictionnaire des philosophes antiques*.

Lagrée, Jacquline. Spinoza "athée & épicurien". *Arch Phil*, 57(3), 541-558, Jl-S 94.

Lahav, Ran. A New Challenge for the Physicalist: Indistinguishability. *Philosophia (Israel)*, 24(1-2), 77-104, D 94.

I present a new argument against the physicalist approach to the mind. The argument is related to Nagel's and Jackson's Argument from Knowledge, but instead of focusing on knowledge of phenomenal qualities, whose obscurity allows for various physicalist interpretations, focuses on mental events which are phenomenally indistinguishable from one another. I argue that under certain conditions physical information is insufficient to determine which mental events are phenomenally indistinguishable from each other, and that the physicalist cannot explain this fact. I also show that this argument is immune to the physicalist responses standard Argument from Knowledge.

Lai, Chen. "New *Lixue*" Metaphysics: Examination and Critique. *J Chin Phil*, 21(3-4), 363-396, S-D 94.

Lai, Karyn L. Confucian Moral Thinking. *Phil East West*, 45(2), 249-272, Ap 95.

By examining fundamental Confucian concepts—*cheng ming, jen, li, hsiao, shu* and *tao*—the essay demonstrates that Confucian ways of thinking do not always fit neatly into categories such as 'moral' or 'rights'. The author provides a positive interpretation of certain Confucian ideas including: the concept of a person as a self-in-relation; the notion of responsibility as particularistic and dependent upon the kinds of relationships one has and the social positions one occupies; and the view of the moral community as comprised by selves-in-relation who are reciprocally connected and who share similar ideals and forms of life.

Lai, Whalen. White Horse not Horse: Making Sense of a Negative Logic. *Asian Phil*, 5(1), 59-74, 1995.

Kung-sun Lung's thesis on 'White Horse [is] not Horse' has been solved by A C Graham on the basis of a part/whole logic and by Chad Hansen on that and a 'mass-noun' hypothesis. We present it as a case of reducing White Horse to its two most telling marks and then, on the basis of the good Sense (instead of Reference) in a Negative Logic—the pragmatics of locating X as the remainder left over when all non-Xs have been removed—show how a stable hand, receiving an order for White Horse would scan first for Horse by removing all non-horse shapes and then for White by removing all colours except White. This way we can prove how indeed "A request for White Horse cannot be satisfied by Black and Brown that fills an order for

Horse...(because) to exclude some colour [in the second scan] is not the same as to exclude yet no colour [in the first scan]." No part/whole or mass-sum is presumed. The whole discussion is set in the context of shifting criteria for judging name from Confucius to Hsun-tzu.

Laine, Jean and Laffond, Gilbert. Weak Covering Relations. *Theor Decis*, 37(3), 245-265, N 94.

This paper proposes and justifies a natural way to weaken the concept of covering relation defined on a finite tournament. Various weak covering relations, called *k*-covering relations, are introduced. To each *k*-covering relation corresponds a strong uncovered set containing all non *k*-covered outcomes. It is proved that those strong uncovered sets may be empty. Moreover, the set of all tournaments having an empty strong uncovered set is characterized within two rather large classes of tournaments. Finally, we offer a complete study of the cases where the directed graph defined by a *k*-covering relation coincides with the initial tournament.

Laird, Michael. Political Correctness Commentary. *Ethics Behavior*, 4(4), 390-394, 1994.

Laliga, Rensoli. El Ideal de la Vida Filosófica Según Leibniz. *Rev Filosof (Spain)*, 7(11), 115-137, 1994.

Lamacchia, Ada (ed & trans) and Ponzio, Paolo (ed & trans) and Campanella, Tommaso. *Metafisica: Universalis Philosophiae SEU Metaphysicarum Rerum Iuxta Propria Dogmata, Liber I*. Bari, Levante Ed, 1994.

"Mirifica nondum promulgata doctrina, nisi in nostris Metaphysicis". Thus, Tommaso Campanella (1568-1639) denotes his *Philosophia Universalis*, the monumental text published, now, in critical edition, with parallel Italian translation. The *Metaphysics*, in fact, published in 1638, is never more edited in integral form or in critical edition. With the present text, the first of eighteen books that constitute the opera omnia, we hope to take part in the knowledge of metaphysics arguments of Tommaso Campanella in his profundity and entirety.

Lamadrid, Lucas. Anonymous or Analogous Christians? Rahner and von Balthasar on Naming the Non-Christian. *Mod Theol*, 11(3), 363-384, Jl 95.

This essay compares the thought of Karl Rahner and Hans Urs von Balthasar, concentrating on an analysis of each thinker's approach to the status of the non-Christian within their respective theologies. The article analyzes the role which language and the symbolic plays in both theologians, as well as the ways they construe the relationship between nature and grace. What the essay shows is that Rahner tends to stress identity in his concept of anonymous christianity to the detriment of difference and that van Balthasar is sensitive to difference, but can become inward looking in Christianity's posture toward non-Christians.

Lamarque, Peter. Tragedy and Moral Value. *Austl J Phil*, 73(2), 239-249, Je 95.

Lamb, Roberta. Feminism as Critique in Philosophy of Music Education. *Phil Music Educ Rev*, 2(2), 59-74, Fall 94.

Lambert, Karel and Schurz, Gerhard. Outline of a Theory of Scientific Understanding. *Synthese*, 101(1), 65-120, O 94.

The basic theory of scientific understanding presented in Sections 1-2 exploits three main ideas. *First*, that to understand a phenomenon *P* (for a given agent) is to be able to fit *P* into the cognitive background corpus *C* (of the agent). *Second*, that to fit *P* into *C* is to connect *P* with parts of *C* (via "arguments" in a very broad sense) such that the unification of *C* increases. *Third*, that the cognitive changes involved in unification can be treated as sequences of shifts of phenomena in *C*. How the theory fits typical examples of understanding and how it excludes suprious unifications is explained in detail. Section 3 gives a formal description of the structure of cognitive corpuses which contain descriptive as well as inferential components. The theory of unification is then refined in the light of so-called "puzzling phenomena", to enable important distinctions, such as that between consonant and dissonant understanding. In Section 4, the refined theory is applied to several examples, among them a case study of the development of the atomic model. The final part contains a classification of kinds of understanding and a discussion of the relation between understanding and explanation.

Lambert, Karel and Simons, Peter. Characterizing Classifying: Explicating a Biological Distinction. *Monist*, 77(3), 315-328, Jl 94.

This paper formally explicates the biological distinction between classifying and characterizing in a free first order logic. It shows, via a translation theorem, that the explication is language neutral.

Lamm, Richard D. The Ethics of Excess. *Hastings Center Rep*, 24(6), 14, N-D 94.

Lamont, John R T. An Argument for an Uncaused Cause. *Thomist*, 59(2), 261-277, Ap 95.

Lamont, Julian. Pareto Efficiency, Egalitarianism, and Difference Principles. *Soc Theor Pract*, 20(3), 311-325, Fall 94.

In this paper I consider a new version of John Rawls' difference principle proposed by Rex Martin. Instead of appealing to the maximization of the position of the least advantaged, this new version appeals to pareto efficiency and egalitarianism. This new difference principle is an interesting improvement over Rawls' original version. I critically consider Martin's innovative argument for this new principle. Although I show that his argument, in the end, fails to select uniquely the new difference principle, the precise identification of where it fails should facilitate further arguments in support of it.

Lampe, James C and Finn, Don W. Teaching Ethics in Accounting Curricula. *Bus Prof Ethics J*, 13(1-2), 89-128, Spr-Sum 94.

The purpose of this study has been to determine the impact on auditors if educational interventions were successfully implemented to raise students' levels of post-conventional principled reasoning as measured by the Defining Issues Test (DIT). Data concerning attitudes, decision responses to auditor dilemmas, and DIT responses were collected from over 300 auditing students, recent graduates, and experienced audit practitioners. Conclusions are that: 1) differing interventions lead to different levels of moral development, 2) differing levels of moral development generate different decisions, and 3) students' levels of moral reasoning and decisions are different from those of both staff and experienced auditors.

Lampert, Jay. Hegel and Ancient Egypt: History and Beocming. *Int Phil Quart*, 35(1), 43-58, Mr 95.

Lan, Conrado Eggers (ed). *Platón: Los Diálogos Tardíos*. Sankt Augustin, Academia, 1986.

Lanasa, John and Fawcett, Jeffrey K and Burns, David J. Business Students' Ethical Perceptions of Retail Situations: A Microcultural Comparison. *J Bus Ethics*, 13(9), 667-679, S 94.

Due in part to a growing realization of the importance of the role that retailing plays in the marketing channel, and to the increasing numbers of college graduates being employed by retailers, growing attention is being placed on business students' ethical perceptions of retailing practices. This study continues this focus by examining the ethical perceptions of collegiate business students attending two different universities which likely represent two different microcultures—conservative evangelical Protestant and secular. The results suggest that ethical perceptions may vary between the students attending two universities which likely represent differing microcultures. (edited)

Lance, Charles E and Mallard, Alison G and Michalos, Alex C. Tests of the Causal Directions of Global-Life Facet Satisfaction Relationships. *Soc Indic Res*, 34(1), 69-92, Ja 95.

Previous research generally has supported multiple discrepancies theory (MDT) of the processes by which individuals arrive at judgments of satisfaction with various aspects of their lives as well as with life overall. However, the nature of possible causal relationships between overall and life facet satisfaction has been ignored. The purpose of this study was to extend MDT by testing alternative theoretical models which specified bottom-up, top-down, and bidirectional relationships between overall life satisfaction and satisfaction with eleven life facets in a sample of 1354 US college students. Results most strongly favored the bidirectional model in which the overall—life facet satisfaction relationship varied across life domains. The need to identify boundary conditions which determine the direction of the overall—life facet satisfaction relationship is discussed.

Lance, Mark. Two Concepts of Entailment. *J Phil Res*, 20, 113-137, 1995.

The latter half of the twentieth century has seen, for even the simplest languages, a proliferation of distinct formal entailment systems, each having those willing to defend its status as the answer. Among those defenders, and among the most adamant and mutually critical, are the champions of strict implication and relevance logic. I argue that the defenders of the two systems are right to suggest that something deeper is at issue between them than mere usefulness in particular applied contexts. Once we see what this is, however, we will see that they are, after all, talking past one another. When we succeed in clarifying the crucial underlying issue, we can then succeed in clarifying the crucial distinction between two dimensions of the underlying concept. (edited)

Lance, Mark Norris. Subjective Probability and Acceptance. *Phil Stud*, 77(1), 147-179, Ja 95.

Recently a number of philosophers have argued that Bayesian decision theory and epistemology vitiate the status of belief or, in their semi-technical terminology, "acceptance". I argue against such positions and show that Bayesian decision theory is itself conceptually dependent upon a notion of acceptance. I show further how to integrate such acceptance into a modest Bayesianism, and how to understand Bayesian probabilities themselves within a theory of acceptance. In short, Bayesianism not only must presuppose the concept of acceptance, but Bayesian assignments of subjective probability to a proposition are best understood as themselves a special case of acceptance of a (different) proposition.

Land, Nick. "Shamanic Nietzsche" in *Nietzsche: A Critical Reader, Sedgwick, Peter R (ed)*, 158-170. Cambridge, Blackwell, 1995.

Landau, Iddo. Should There Be Separatist Epistemologies?. *Monist*, 77(4), 462-471, O 94.

Works which support the idea of feminist epistemologies tend to avoid a thematic, detailed consideration of the question whether such epistemologies should be constructed and used only by women, or whether they should be seen as universal. However, some feminist writers do support, even if not always explicitly, feminist epistemological separatism. Possible arguments in favor of this cognitive separatism are identified and rebutted: that bodily differences influence women and men to think differently; that constancy in the differences between men's and women's behaviors through history and across cultures proves that these differences are inherent; that there are social conditions that affect women only and not men; and that women need what may be called an "epistemic room of their own".

Landesman, Cliff. When to Terminate a Charitable Trust?. *Analysis*, 55(1), 12-13, Ja 95.

The prospect of infinite investment growth presents the utilitarian donor to a charitable trust with a problem: when should the trust stop growing and start helping?

Landman, Willem A. Educated Folly About Animal Minds and Animal Suffering. *Between Species*, 9(3), 143-155, Sum 93.

Landman, Willem A. Moral Standing, Value, and Environmental Ethics. *S Afr J Phil*, 14(1), 9-18, F 95.

The question I address is the following: how should an environmental ethic be philosophically grounded? An answer to this question involves a commitment to a criterion of moral standing and its application and a wider commitment to a taxonomy of the senses of 'value' that inform our relationship with nature. I address this question and these two commitments in the following way. I begin by mapping the different environmental philosophies in order to contextualize my argument. Second, after an analysis of the concept of moral standing, I analyse why being a person is a sufficient condition of moral standing. Third, I defend sentience as a condition of moral standing that is not only sufficient but also necessary and I set out the taxonomy of the senses of 'value' that informs a sentience-based environmental ethic. I end with some concluding remarks about the concern that a sentience-based environmental ethic might be inadequate if we should lose our aesthetic and spiritual sense.

Landry, Cécile 614 AUTHOR INDEX WITH ABSTRACTS

Landry, Cécile. Etretien Avec Michel Salomon. *Philosopher*, 15, 27-37, 1994.

Landry, Cécile. L'approche par Compétences (Entretien avec Michel Jean). *Philosopher*, 17, 191-204, 1995.

Landry, Cécile. La Culture Amérindienne: Cette Inconnue (Entretien avec Robert Vachon). *Philosopher*, 17, 7-26, 1995.

Lane, Gilles. La Science Contemporaine Connaît-elle Vraiment le Monde?. *Horiz Phil*, 2(2), 185-203, Spring 92.

Lane, J C. Ethics of Business Students: Some Marketing Perspectives. *J Bus Ethics*, 14(7), 571-580, Jl 95.

This study explores the reactions of 412 business students to a range of ethical marketing dilemmas. Reviewing some of the comparable Australian and U S research in the field, the study examines the ethical judgements for potential demographic differences. The findings suggest that a majority of students are prepared to act unethically in order to gain some competitive or personal advantage. Yielding the highest ethical response are situations of potential and significant social impact. The results support some previous research that shows the existence of gender and age differences in ethical response and likely behaviour. This (gender) difference was most divergent on the issue of portrayal of women in advertising. In particular, females and older students respond more ethically in a majority of situations. The research concludes a number of opportunities for new directions in education, public policy making, and future research.

Lane, Robert E. The Road Not Taken: Friendship, Consumerism, and Happiness. *Crit Rev*, 8(4), 521-554, Fall 94.

Since the mid 1960s in advanced and rapidly advancing economics there has been a rising tide of clinical depression, dysphoria, and decline in mutual trust. Above the poverty level, income is irrelevant to subjective well-being but friendship is crucial to it. The cause of our growing dysphoria, therefore, seems to lie in the measured loosening of family and friendship bonds apparent also since the mid-1960s. In specified respects, the market is partly responsible for this loss of friendship. An advanced society that maximizes friendship instead of income and commodities will increase its "utility" more than one that focuses on greater GNP.

Lang, André. Le Pessimisme Romantique et le Pessimisme Dionysiaque des Hellènes Selon Nietzsche. *Diotima*, 22, 62-65, 1994.

Lang, André. Transcendance et Inconnaissance chez Plotin et Denys. *Diotima*, 23, 51-54, 1995.

Lang, Berel. Forgiveness. *Amer Phil Quart*, 31(2), 105-117, Ap 94.

In contrast to views of forgiveness as superogatory—or as having no moral weight at all—the conception of forgiveness argued here views it as the outcome of a 'normal' moral judgment. This means that there are times when to forgive is obligatory—and other when to forgive would be wrong. Apart from the domain of the unforgivable, the factors involved in determining whether forgiveness should be granted to include the acknowledgement of wrongdoing (and request for forgiveness) and a willingness to make good on the wrong so far as possible—and the injured party's acceptance. The moral and social functions of forgiveness as a phenomenon are further discussed.

Lang, Berel. Is It Possible to Misrepresent the Holocaust?. *Hist Theor*, 34(1), 84-89, 1995.

The essays by Hans Kellner, Wulf Kansteiner, and Robert Braun in the Forum, "Representing the Holocaust" (*History and Theory*, May 1994) attack historical realism as a legitimate form of such representation. Like any other part of narrative, "facts" do not speak for themselves in respect to the Holocaust or any other historical "event"; they are context-dependent and thus speak only in the voice of their interpreters. The symposiasts adopt this view on the assumption that an alternative to historical realism will yet reaffirm the primary data of the Holocaust: the number of deaths, identities, places, dates. But I argue to the contrary: that ontologically there is but one alternative to historical realism, and that this alternative offers no ground even in principle for acknowledging a contradiction between an assertion and a denial that, for example, "On January 20th, 1942, Nazi officials at Wannsee formulated a protocol for the 'Final Solution of the Jewish Question.'" Thus, at least in respect to items of chronicle, historical realism (and the principle of contradiction) must be granted—unless one is ready to affirm, as the symposiasts apparently are not, a radical epistemic and moral (and of course historical) skepticism.

Lang, Berel. *Mind's Bodies: Thought in the Act*. Albany, SUNY Pr, 1995.

The book attempts both to mark and subvert the boundary between philosophy and literature. On the analogy of the body-mind relation, it argues for the textual—bodily—character of philosophical writing and ideas, suggesting also a connection between theoretical and practical judgment. Of the distinction between friction and non-fiction, the question is posed whether that distinction itself is fiction or non-fiction. The answer given is in the writing.

Lang, Démètre. Le Discours de la Théologie Face à L'Indicible chez Denys. *Diotima*, 23, 81-85, 1995.

Lang, Helen S. "Why the Elements Imitate the Heavens: *Metaphysics* IX.8 1050b28-34" in *The Crossroads of Norm and Nature, Sim, May (ed)*, 305-324. Lanham, Rowman & Littlefield, 1995.

Lang, Helen S. Why the Elements Imitate the Heaven: *Metaphysics* i x 8.1050b28-34. *Ancient Phil*, 14(2), 335-354, Fall 94.

Metaphysics IX 8.1050b28-34 presents three problems: 1) the claim that the elements 'imitate' the heavens, 2) the association of the four elements with continuous activity, and, finally, 3) the assertion that they have their motion in virtue of themselves and in themselves. Their solution, I argue, lies both in the larger context of *Metaphysics* IX and in the background of the *Physics*. Ultimately I conclude that Aristotle gives the notion of 'imitation' entirely his own meaning: when there is only one potency (and nothing intervenes) to be moved is another way of being ever active.

Lang, Wieslaw. Universalism in Morality, Ethics and Law. *Dialogue Hum*, 4(2-3), 139-155, 1994.

Lange, Marc. Are There Natural Laws Concerning Particular Biological Species?. *J Phil*, 92(8), 430-451, Ag 95.

Familiar arguments that no natural laws concern particular biological species mistakenly presuppose that a law-statement refers to no particular location or object, or that law involves an exceptionless regularity. I argue that "*The* human being has exactly 46 chromosomes" states a law (although some human beings have 47 chromosomes) because for certain purposes, it is best for us to take a human being to have 46 chromosomes unless we have information to the contrary, and because this inferential rule results from pursuit of the best "inductive strategies." I discuss the nature of biological species, derivative laws, and how laws support counterfactuals.

Lange, Marc. Dispositions and Scientific Explanation. *Pac Phil Quart*, 75(2), 108-132, Je 94.

Some have held that dispositional claims play no role in scientific explanations of the manifestations of those dispositions, save as placeholders for categorical claims. Others have contended that explanations can appeal to dispositional claims and even that all properties science discusses are dispositional. I adjudicate this dispute. I criticize the standard means of distinguishing dispositional from categorical claims by their relation to counterfactuals. I then refine this approach by exploiting the relation of dispositions to natural laws. This proposal, combined with a counterfactual account of scientific explanation (which I explore), suggests *why* dispositional claims are otiose in certain scientific explanations.

Lange, Marc. Earman on the Projectibility of Grue. *Proc Phil Sci Ass*, 1, 87-95, 1994.

In *Bayes or Bust?*, John Earman attempts to express in Bayesian terms a sense of "projectibility" in which it is logically impossible for "All emeralds are green" and "All emeralds are grue" simultaneously to be projectible. I argue that Earman overlooks an important sense in which these two hypotheses cannot both be projectible. This sense is important because it allows projectibility to be connected to lawlikeness, as Goodman intended. Whether this connection suggests a way to resolve Goodman's famous riddle remains unsettled, awaiting an account of lawlikeness. I explore one line of thought that might prove illuminating.

Lange, Marc. Lawlikeness. *Nous*, 27(1), 1-21, Mr 93.

It is argued that only generalizations believed "lawlike" (i.e., believed, if true, to state natural laws) can be confirmed "inductively"; induction is distinguished from other ways to confirm a generalization's truth. Evidence for a generalization's truth is contrasted with evidence for its lawlikeness. A generalization following logically from lawlike claims need not be lawlike; examples are provided. An analysis of lawlikeness is proposed to save these phenomena: To believe "All F's are G" lawlike is to hold that were it true and one believed "... is F", then "... is F" would be an optimal way for one to justify "... is G".

Langford, Peter E and Lovegrove, Hildegard and Lovegrove, Malcolm N. Do Senior Secondary Students Possess the Moral Maturity to Negotiate Class Rules?. *J Moral Educ*, 23(4), 387-407, 1994.

Two studies are reported using written question sheets to assess attitudes to and moral reasoning about class rules among a total of 117 senior secondary school students and 87 trainee teachers. The studies confirmed the prediction of the multidimensional control model of the development of moral reasoning of Langford 1991a, b; 1992a, b) that the moral reasoning of such students about this topic is much more mature than predicted by Kohlbergian theory, their most important source of information for making moral decisions in this area being the general welfare of students and teachers. (edited)

Langlois, Luc. Éthique et fondation ultime de la raison: Considérations sur un ouvrage de V Hösle. *Laval Theol Phil*, 50(3), 637-650, O 94.

Langsam, Harold. Why Pains Are Mental Objects. *J Phil*, 92(6), 303-312, Je 95.

Langsdorf, Lenore. "Philosophy of Language and Philosophy of Communication" in *Recovering Pragmatism's Voice, Langsdorf, Lenore (ed)*, 195-208. Albany, SUNY Pr, 1995.

Langsdorf, Lenore and Smith, Andrew R. "The Voice of Pragmatism in Contemporary Philosophy of Communication" in *Recovering Pragmatism's Voice, Langsdorf, Lenore (ed)*, 1-19. Albany, SUNY Pr, 1995.

Langsdorf, Lenore (ed) and Smith, Andrew R (ed). *Recovering Pragmatism's Voice*. Albany, SUNY Pr, 1995.

Langtry, Bruce. Reply to Chrzan's Comments. *Sophia (Australia)*, 34(1), 74-78, Mr-Ap 95.

This paper continues a discussion of Alvin Plantinga's treatment, in *The Nature of Necessity*, to the probabilistic argument from evil.

Lanigan, Richard L. "A Good Rhetoric Is Possible" in *The Philosophy of Paul Ricoeur, Hahn, Lewis Edwin (ed)*, 309-326. Peru, Open Court, 1994.

The article is subtitled: "Ricoeur's Philosophy of Language as a Phenomenology of Discourse in the Human Sciences." Many of Ricoeur's essays on rhetoric are analyzed according to the model of rhetoric that he has drawn from Aristotle's *Rhetoric*. Connections to Husserl's phenomenology, Merleau-Ponty's phenomenology and semiotics, and C S Peirce's semiotics are drawn. The postmodern notion of discourse is also explored. A reply to the article, by Ricoeur, follows immediately in the text.

Lanigan, Richard L. "From Enthymeme to Abduction" in *Recovering Pragmatism's Voice, Langsdorf, Lenore (ed)*, 49-70. Albany, SUNY Pr, 1995.

The essay reviews Aristotle's conditions for constructing an enthymeme, Peirce's use and formulation of those concepts to distinguish deduction, induction, abduction, and adduction. Examples are given of this "argument cycle" among the logics. A connection is made to the modern notion of argument and a tropic logic that uses the Foucault concept of "le meme et l'autre" (self, other; same, different) to specify the discourse conditions in logic for synecdoche, metaphor, metonymy, and irony. The contextual argument for the chapter appears in Lanigan, *The Human Science of Communicology* (Duquesne UP, 1992).

Lanteigne, Josette. Le bien suprême est-il virtuellement réalisé dans le monde? Le jugement politique chez Jacques Poulain. *Horiz Phil*, 5(2), 74-83, 1995.

The primacy of practical reason over theoretical reason advocated by Kant and all his followers (including Habermas) has not conducted to the realization of the *summum bonum*. On the contrary, all is becoming political and political relations are based on force only. Poulain proposes to reverse the hierarchy and to place in first rank judgments and statements instead of action. As a result, do we virtually live in a free world? No, for judgement cannot be anticipated.

Lantéri-Laura, Georges. La matière illusoire de la médecine mentale au XIXe siècle. *Rev Phil Fr*, 1, 33-42, Ja-Mr 95.

The author describes the evolution of the notion of matter in the XIX century, especially in the world of mental medicine. He explores the waning of living matter, the triumph of organic chemistry and the important part of the neuro-histology. He studies the importance of this evolution upon the conception of the role of brain in the psychiatry of this time.

Lantin, Robert. Individualism, Physicalism, and Spinoza on Minds and Bodies. *Manuscrito*, 17(1), 35-64, Ap 94.

In this paper, I first try to show that Spinoza's philosophy of mind—whether interpreted along the lines of a type- or token-identity theory or that of what may be termed propositional functionalism—is committed to the doctrine of individualism. Then, I propose a general characterization of individualism that departs somewhat from the currently accepted view, and show that (some) type- and token-identity versions of physicalism, as well as (some) narrow and wide versions of functionalism, fall under its heading. Finally, based on a thought experiment construed in a way such that both the internal and external physical environments of two molecular twins are fixed, I show that they may nevertheless entertain distinct mental contents, and conclude that the structures of individualism, as characterized, fail to provide sufficient conditions in order to individuate some intentional mental states, thus stressing individualism's—and, by extension, Spinoza's view's—inability at solving the mind-body problem.

Lapoujade, María Noel. El misterio construido. *Rev Filosof (Costa Rica)*, 32(77), 103-107, Jl 94.

Thinking is fecundated in dialogue. The plot of texts, in their various meetings and separations, weaves beautiful shaping of mystery with the delicate thread of language. This is the paradox of the presence that involves the ultimate absence, which is mystery. If we think, with Novalis, that "every word is an invocation", the sign of plea is to invoke mystery. The appeal that I propose here, flows in three registers of human reality that Plato legated the West: the search for truth, good and beautiful. This is an indissoluble ontological plot in which the zeal of knowledge that defines human being is combined with unreachable aims of fullness in fundamental-ethical and aesthetic-truth. So, in the following pages I propose an epistemic, ontological and aesthetic construction of mystery.

Lappin, Shalom and Francez, Nissim. E-Type Pronouns, I-Sums, and Donkey Anaphora. *Ling Phil*, 17(4), 391-428, Ag 94.

We propose an E-type account of donkey pronouns which interprets these pronouns as denoting functions to i-sums of individuals. Our account provides a single representation for donkey sentences from which it is possible to obtain both universal and existential readings. It also permits us to explain the distribution of these readings in a straightforward way, on the basis of a parameterized maximality condition on the i-sums selected by E-type pronoun functions. We suggest that quantificational adverbs be interpreted as generalized quantifiers on sets of situations. When our i-sum based E-type account of donkey pronouns is integrated into this framework, we are able to derive the observed readings of conditional donkey sentences.

Lara, Francisco and Salcedo, Damián and Gutiérrez, Gilberto. Observaciones y respuesta. *Rev Filosof (Spain)*, 4(6), 429-436, 1991.

Lara Sánchez, Francisco Damián. La justificación consecuencialista de las lealtades. *Telos (Spain)*, 1(2), 37-47, Je 92.

The objective of the ethical theories to integrate moral intuitions to the maximum degree is as usual as its failure to achieve this aim. This is especially evident where we believe ourselves obliged to fulfill our personal duties even when it means going against principles of justice or well-being. Neither the goals nor the finding of outcomes ethics are exceptions to this generalization. After a critical examination of the important neoconsequentialist attempts to morally justify the fulfilling of personal loyalties, I intend to argue that the best way to achieve this goal is not by revising the normative postulate of consequentialism, but by re-examining the most widely accepted interpretation of evaluative implications of such postulates.

Lardic, Jean-Marie. Hegel et Schelling: critique du formalisme et prise en charge de la contingence. *Arch Phil*, 57(4), 683-691, O-D 94.

The acceptance of contingency reveals the difference between the dialectic and the formalism of Schelling's "construction". It shows Hegel's distancing from Schelling at Iena and makes us glimpse at the ideas that only the *Science of Logic* will later develop which will allow the dialectic distinction between the infinite spirit and the finite nature.

Largeault, Jean. La logique hier, les logiques aujourd'hui. *Arch Phil*, 58(1), 55-72, Ja-Mr 95.

Among the ancient Greeks, logic grew out of the critiques of various arguments (of Sophists, rhetoricians, philosophers, geometricians) and from the admission of a permanent Being, the condition for intelligibility; critique here seen as movement against a back drop of Being, the immovable. Today, in accord with the idealistic tendencies of philosophy and the sciences, the search for intelligibility and the art of critique tend to merge. Is it possible to disregard completely the element of permanency? Is discussion possible without a common ground of independent reality? These two questions would be "too metaphysical" for most contemporary mathematical logicians.

Largeault, Jean. Quine, le continuisme et la fin de l'épistémologie néo-positiviste. *Rev Phil Fr*, 3, 317-336, Jl-S 94.

Larmore, Charles. The Foundations of Modern Democracy: Reflections on Jürgen Habermas. *Euro J Phil*, 3(1), 55-68, Ap 95.

Larose, Pascal. De la Morale d'aujourd'hui. *Philosopher*, 17, 251-260, 1995.

Larrabee, M J. Inside Time-Consciousness: Diagramming the Flux. *Husserl Stud*, 10(3), 181-210, 1993-94.

Husserl's theory of inner time-consciousness incorporates both serialized and decentering aspects. The theory requires a new metaphor, a re-mapping from serialistic diagrams to more dynamic ones. Achieving this re-mapping is a challenge, but so too is showing the relation of dynamic diagrams to the serialistic ones still vital to complete description of inner time-consciousness. I use as an organizing device the diagrams of time-consciousness Husserl sprinkled throughout *Husserliana* X. I first look at the three levels of constituted temporality and constituting consciousness in connection with the diagrams. Next I give a reading of time-apprehendings which interweaves descriptions of two Togethers (*Zusammen*) that provide nontemporal consecutiveness and simultaneity, with an analysis of time-constituting intentionalities. I end by suggesting diagrams to supplement Husserl's, models that reflect the dynamism of intentionalities grounded on time-constitution—genetic interconnections, the Living Present, and the transcendental historicity of subjectivity.

Larre, Olga L. El Método de la Simulación: Ocaso del Método Experimental?. *Analogia*, 8(2), 175-185, 1994.

Larre, Olga L and Bolzán, Juan Enrique. Orden, Desorden, Azar. *Sapientia*, 49(193-4), 327-336, 1994.

Larrosa, Jorge. "Identity, Education, and the Experience of Language" in *Identity, Culture, and Education, Smeyers, Paul (ed)*, 195-203. Leuven, Leuven Univ Pr, 1994.

Larson, Erica. Needs versus Desires. *Dialogue (PST)*, 37(1), 1-10, O 94.

Usually it is assumed that needs claims carry more moral weight than desires. The central question in this article is whether needs really deserve moral priority over desires. The question is explored by first defining the terms "need" and "desire". Needs claims are then broken up into three types, and conditions for prioritizing the claims are discussed. Finally, the author concludes that needs and wants claims ought to be given priority based on the value of the ends toward which they strive.

Lash, Scott (ed) and Friedman, Jonathan (ed). *Modernity and Identity*. Cambridge, Blackwell, 1992.

Latawiec, Anna and Lemanska, Anna and Slaga, Szczepan W. Mieczyslaw Lubanskis Leben und Werk. *Stud Phil Christ*, 30(2), 5-64, 1994.

Zum Anlass des siebzigsten Geburstages wird das wissenschaftliche Wirken und das wissenschaftliche Werk von Professor Mieczyslaw Lubanski dargelegt und besprochen. 1924 geboren, hat er in den Jahren 1945-50 zuerst Mathematik an der Universität Warschau, dann 1955-58 Theologie im Warschauer Priesterseminar und 1959-62 Naturphilosophie an der Katholischen Universität in Lublin studiert. An dieser Hochschule erwarb Er 1965 das Doktorat. Seine Habilitationsschrift verteidigte Er 1973 an der Akademie für Katholische Theologie zur Warschau, wo Er 1982 zum Professor ernannt wurde und bis heute den Lehrstuhl für Methodologie der System und Informationslehre inne hat. Gleichzeitigg doziert Er seit 1965 Philosophie an der Päpstliche Theologischen Fakultät in Warschau, sowie an der Philosophischen Fakultät der Katholischen Universität in Lublin. Die wissenschaftliche Forschung Professors Lubanski lässt sich den folgenden thematischen einzuordnen: Geschichte und Philosophie der Wissenschaft, Philosophie der Mathematik, Informations- und Simulationstheorie, allgemeine Systemtheorie, Naturwissenschafts- und Natur-Philosophie, Systemanthropologie, Philosophie der Kybernetik. Einige Seiner Veröffentlichungen befassen sich zudem mit aktuellen weltanschaulichen Problemen.

Latham, Noa. Causally Irrelevant Reasons and Action Solely from the Motive of Duty. *J Phil*, 91(11), 599-618, N 94.

It is argued that no sense can be made of the popular view that when one has several reasons for an action one performs, some of those reasons may be causally irrelevant to the action. From this it follows that when one has reason both of duty and inclination for an action, the action cannot be motivated solely by duty. This undermines the view, attributed to Kant by such writers as Barbara Herman, that an action may have moral worth when there are reasons of inclination for it so long as those reasons are nonmotivating. It is argued, finally, that Kant did not hold such a view of moral worth.

Lathe, Robert F (trans) and Steiner, Rudolf and Whittaker, Nancy Parsons (trans). *The Spirit of the Waldorf School*. Hudson, Anthroposophic Pr, 1995.

Lather, Patti. "Staying Dumb? Feminist Research and Pedagogy With/in the Postmodern" in *After Postmodernism, Simons, Herbert W (ed)*, 101-132. Newbury Park, Sage, 1994.

This paper deconstructs my three year empirical study of student resistance to liberatory curriculum in an introductory women's studies course in order to illustrate how poststructuralist debates are restructuring approaches to knowledge production and legitimation across the disciplines. By addressing a series of methodological questions raised by poststructuralism, I use the data amassed in this study to explore the parameters of what might be called deconstructive empirical work. In such work, questions of interpretive strategy, narrative authority and critical perspective go far toward blurring the lines between "the humanities" and "the social sciences".

LaTour, Michael S and Tsalikis, John. Bribery and Extortion in International Business: Ethical Perceptions of Greeks Compared to Americans. *J Bus Ethics*, 14(4), 249-264, Ap 95.

This study investigates the differences in the way bribery and extortion is perceived by two different cultures—American and Greek. Two hundred and forty American business students and two hundred and four Greek business students were presented with three scenarios describing a businessmen offering a bribe to a government official and three scenarios describing a businessman being forced to pay a bribe to an official in order to do business. The Reidenbach-Robin instrument was used to measure the ethical reactions of the two samples to these scenarios. Results indicate that ethical reactions to bribery and extortion vary by (a) the nationality of the person offering the bribe, and (b) the country where the bribe is offered. In addition, Greeks perceived some of the scenarios as being less unethical than did Americans.

Lattie, George. "The Philosophy of Corliss Lamont" in *Contributors to the Philosophy of Humanism, Hillar, Marian (ed)*, 125-128. Pasadena, Humanists Houston, 1994.

The essay describes and summarizes the basic philosophical tenets of Corliss Lamont. His philosophy constitutes a whole system based on reason and human experience. But the wisest tenet of Lamont's philosophy, in author's view, is that all aspects of Humanism should be re-evaluated and questioned continuously. The philosophy should evolve as men and societies evolve.

Laube, Johannes. Sur la personne et l'oeuvre de Hajime Tanabe. *Rev Phil Louvain*, 92(4), 423-429, N 94.

The author seeks to introduce to the European reader the thought of Tanabe, the second pillar of the school of Kyoto—whose links with Husserl's phenomenology had not yet been very closely examined.

Lauder, George V and Amundson, Ron. Function without Purpose: The Uses of Causal Role Function in Evolutionary Biology. *Biol Phil*, 9(4), 443-469, O 94.

Philosophers of evolutionary biology favor the so-called "etiological concept" of function according to which the function of trait is its evolutionary purpose, defined as the effect for which that trait was favored by natural selection. We term this the selected effect (SE) analysis of function. An alternative account of function was introduced by Robert Cummins in a nonevolutionary and nonpurposive context. Cummins's account has received attention but little support from philosophers of biology. This paper will show that a similar nonpurposive concept of function, which we term causal role (CR) function, is crucial to certain research programs in evolutionary biology, and that philosophical criticisms of Cummins's concept are ineffective in this scientific context. (edited)

Laugier, Sandra. Une ou deux indéterminations. *Arch Phil*, 58(1), 73-96, Ja-Mr 95.

The author means to reinterpret Quine's indeterminacy thesis as to show that what is at stake in this thesis is not merely (as *Word and Object* more or less claims) a critique of the idea of meaning but a general reformulation of the ontological problem of "what there is". Beyond Quine's many explanations and denials, his indeterminacy thesis *can* have a strong *epistemological* meaning, not only as a particular case of theoretical underdetermination, but as showing the nature of ontological change in the evolution of knowledge.

Laugier, Sandra (trans) and Fournier, Christian (trans) and Bouveresse, Jacques. Philosophy from an Antiphilosopher: Paul Valéry. *Crit Inquiry*, 21(2), 354-381, Wint 95.

Laugstien, Thomas. *Philosophieverhältnisse im deutschen Faschismus*. Hamburg, Argument Verlag, 1990.

Laurier, Daniel. Pangloss, L'Erreur et la Divergence. *J Phil Res*, 19, 345-372, 1994.

The theory of radical interpretation, as based on the principle of charity, sets a priori limits on the possibility that different agents have different beliefs, and on the possibility that one has false beliefs. David Papineau put forward a teleological approach to intentional states which, he claims, doesn't have these unacceptable consequences. Having distinguished half a dozen of different forms that the problem of radical interpretation might take, I show that Papineau's approach is not radically different from those based on the principle of charity. Finally, I suggest that the consequences of the principle of charity with respect to the problems of error and divergence are in fact both unavoidable and acceptable.

Lauth, Reinhard. "Zur derzeitigen weltgeschichtlichen Situation im Lichte transzendentaler Erkenntnisse" in *Das geistige Erbe Europas, Buhr, Manfred (ed)*, 79-88. Napoli, Vivarium, 1994.

Lauth, Reinhard. Kann Schellings Philosophie von 1804 als System bestehen?. *Kantstudien*, 85(1), 48-77, 1994.

Lauth, Reinhard. Transzendentale Basis, Materialismus, und Religion. *Fichte-Studien*, 1, 132-144, 1990.

Lautier, Nicole. "At the Crossroads of Epistemology and Psychology" in *Historiography Between Modernism and Postmodernism, Topolski, Jerzy (ed)*, 201-212. Amsterdam, Rodopi, 1994.

The various ways of teaching and learning history to be found in practice are listed. It is postulated that the didactic of history should be dedicated to an analysis of the results of the clash of these methods at schools. It means that such an analysis should be situated at the meeting point of epistemology and psychology (cognitive and social). The problem consists in the identification of events by learners, on the one hand, and historians and epistemologists, on the other. The texts of history is identified with the help of two large categories: change and stability but always conforming to the reception schemes. The teachers are hardly prepared to recognize this cognitive plurality. It is suggested that a distinction should be made between four models of didactic practice: the exemplarity of history to assure the function of education, the education by the training of behavioral and cognitive capacities, a classical (chronological) transmission of knowledge and the model in which the specificities of scholarly history and of a taught history are clearly distinguished and its educative function is not particularly tied to the contents of teaching.

Lavallée, Alain. Penser l'Autonomie, Penser la Connaissance: l'Évolution d'un Centre de Recherche en Épistémologie. *Horiz Phil*, 2(2), 109-130, Spring 92.

We present here the notion of "self-organisation" through the works of the CREA which is a research center in epistemology located in Paris, France. This center has dedicated four years of research to the historical, scientific and epistemological aspects of the notion of self-organization and how this notion has migrated from natural sciences to social sciences. Their works also show how the limits of the notion of program, in biology and cybernetics, has opened the way for the notion of "self-organized system", and to the notion of complexity. Self-organization is a dynamic process. It refers to the complexity of social systems and living systems. But this notion of complexity refers to knowledge and even to the knowledge of knowledge. So in recent years, the works of the CREA has evolved from epistemology to cognitive sciences and philosophy of mind.

Lavelle, Pierre. Nishida Kitarô, l'école de Kyôto et l'ultra-nationalisme. *Rev Phil Louvain*, 92(4), 430-458, N 94.

Nishida Kitaro and his direct disciples in the Kyoto school, Tanabe Hajime, Kosaka Masaaki, Nishitani Keiji and Koyama Iwao adopted an attitude of collaboration towards the ultra-nationalist regime and of resistance to its extremist wings: the ultra-orthodox shintoists and the partisans of military rule. They belonged to the enlightened wing of ultra-nationalism, being at the same time convinced of Japanese superiority of the need for its world hegemony, and of the compatibility of the imperial doctrine—a religious traditionalism—with the academic objectivity and advanced culture.

Lavin, Michael. Who Should be Committable?. *Phil Psychiat Psych*, 2(1), 35-47, Mr 95.

The paper criticizes the prevailing, danger-based involuntary commitment criteria that have characterized U S law since the U S Supreme Court's 1975 *O'Connor v. Donaldson* decision. Numerous medical and moral inadequacies are identified in *O'Connor*-style commitment criteria. It is argued that a treatment-based criterion—derived from the American Psychiatric Association's Model Commitment Law, but a version that disdains reliance on dangerousness to self or others as a ground for commitment—is medically and morally preferable to the prevailing U S commitment standard. This treatment-based approach respects competent treatment refusals, but does permit treatable, incompetent individuals to be involuntarily hospitalized for treatment. This approach is defended against possible objections and some of its advantages are identified.

Lavine, Thelma Z. "Paul Ricoeur and the Conflict of Interpretations" in *The Philosophy of Paul Ricoeur, Hahn, Lewis Edwin (ed)*, 169-188. Peru, Open Court, 1994.

Lavoisier, Antoine-Laurent. Memórias sobre a Natureza do Princípio que Encontra com os Metais Durante sua Calcinaçao e que Aumenta seu Peso. *Cad Hist Filosof Cie*, 4(1), 109-115, Ja-Je 94.

Lawatsch, Hans-Helmut. Fichte und die hermetische Demokratie der Frlemaurer. *Fichte-Studien*, 3, 204-218, 1991.

Das angeschlagene Thema ist nicht neu. Es wurde im Grunde bereits von Klaus Hammacher erschöpfend behandelt. Wir beziehen uns ausdrücklich auf Hammachers Studie; was wir hinzufügen können, sind allenfalls Ergänzungen und kleinere Korrekturen. Immerhin, der Teufel steckt im Detail, dieses wollen wir ernstnehmen. Andererseits sind Korrekturen und Vermutungen erlaubt, wo Text- oder Sachzeugnisse fehlen.

Lawler, James M. The University of Liberal Capitalism and the Possibility of Renewed Socialism: Reflections on the Soviet Coup of August 1991. *Dialogue Hum*, 3(2), 43-57, 1993.

Lawler, Justus George (ed). *The 1994 Annual of Hermeneutics and Social Concern*. New York, Continuum, 1994.

Lawlor, Robert. "Ancient Temple Architecture" in *Homage to Pythagoras, Bamford, Christopher (ed)*, 35-132. Hudson, Lindisfarne Pr, 1994.

Lawlor, Robert. "Pythagorean Number as Form, Color, and Light" in *Homage to Pythagoras, Bamford, Christopher (ed)*, 187-209. Hudson, Lindisfarne Pr, 1994.

Lawrence, Joseph P. Commentary on Patterson's "The Ascent in Plato's *Symposium*. *Proc Boston Colloq Anc Phil*, 7, 215-225, 1991.

In this paper I argue that the "ascent" passage in Plato's *Symposium* must be read in the context of a prior "descent". Diotima seeks to transform Socrates' abstract intellectualism by focusing his erotic energy first on beautiful bodies. The consequence of this move is that thinking is imbued with a passionate character that transcends logic and method. Thinking is not the autonomous activity of a self-transparent subject, but the gift of understanding that is granted to a soul ecstatically elevated toward the beautiful. The condition of such illumination is the recognition of the poverty of that human understanding that knows only that it does not know.

Lawson, Craig. Research Participation as a Contract. *Ethics Behavior*, 5(3), 205-215, 1995.

In this article, I present a contractualist conception of human-participant research ethics, arguing that the most appropriate source of the rights and responsibilities of researcher and participant is the contractual understanding between them. This conception appears to explain many of the more fundamental ethical incidents of human-participant research. I argue that a system of contractual rights and responsibilities would allow a great deal of research that has often been felt to be ethically problematic, such as research involving deception, concealed research, and research on dependent populations. However, in defining the conditions under which such research should be permissable, my contractualist theory also makes it clear that there are limits—and explains what thoses limits are—to the propriety of such research.

Laymon, Ronald E. Experimentation and the Legitimacy of Idealization. *Phil Stud*, 77(2-3), 353-375, Mr 95.

Layson, Rita T (& others). Discussions about the Use of Life-Sustaining Treatments: A Literature Review of Physicians' and Patients' Attitudes and Practices. *J Clin Ethics*, 5(3), 195-203, Fall 94.

Laywine, Alison. *Kant's Early Metaphysics and the Origins of the Critical Philosophy*. Atascadero, Ridgeview, 1993.

Lazari-Pawlowska, Ija. Die Tugend der Toleranz in Polen nach dem Zerfall des Kommunismus. *Filozof Istraz*, 14(2-3), 393-401, 1994.

Die Autorin geht davon aus, dass die Idee der Toleranz eine hochkomplexe Idee ist, besonders wenn man sie im Kontext der realen Gesellschaftsverhältnisse betrachtet. Am Beispiel der neuesten politischen Veränderungen in Polen versucht die Autorin zu zeigen, in welchem Masse der Toleranzanspruch notwendig ist, gleichzeitig aber auch, welche realen Geschehnisse und realen, für Polen spezifischen Voraussetzungen die Frage der Toleranz bestimmen, d.h. die Toleranz fördern oder einschränken. Ihre Darstellung der Toleranzfrage in Polen heute beginnt die Autorin mit einem Entwurf des Toleranzbegriffs. Zunächst einmal sind der Gegenstand der Toleranz "Bezeugungen" und "Taten" die in den menschlichen Interaktionen "toleriert" oder "nicht toleriert" werden. In diesem Sinne sollte die Toleranz immer komplementär mit Intoleranz betrachtet werden. (edited)

Lazarus, Arnold A. How Certain Boundaries and Ethics Diminish Therapeutic Effectiveness. *Ethics Behavior*, 4(3), 255-261, 1994.

This paper underscored how rigid roles and codified rules of conduct between a psychotherapist and his or her patient only undermines clinical effectiveness. One of the worst ethical violations, in my view, is to permit risk-management principles to take precedence over humane interventions. The field of psychotherapy has become obsessed with needless boundaries that try to convert innovative clinicians into anxious conformists. Many actual clinical examples are cited. They show precisely how adherence to certain rules of conduct makes patients into infants and insults their intelligence while undermining their autonomy.

Lazarus, Arnold A. The Illusion of the Therapist's Power and the Patient's Fragility: My Rejoinder. *Ethics Behavior*, 4(3), 299-306, 1994.

Le Doeuff, Michèle. "Simone de Beauvoir: Falling into (Ambiguous) Line" in *Feminist Interpretations of Simone de Beauvoir, Simons, Margaret A (ed)*, 59-65. University Park, Penn St Univ Pr, 1995.

Le Doeuff, Michèle. *Hipparchia's Choice: An Essay Concerning Women, Philosophy, etc.* Cambridge, Blackwell, 1990.

Le Guern, Michel. Arnauld et Pascal. *Rev Int Phil*, 48(190), 463-480, 1994.

Le Moigne, Jean-Louis. Joyeuse Méditation Épistémologique sur la Modélisation Symbolisante de l'Intelligence. *Lekton*, 4(2), 115-138, 1994.

Le Poidevin, Robin. Worlds within Worlds? The Paradoxes of Embedded Fiction. *Brit J Aes*, 35(3), 227-238, Jl 95.

An embedded fiction is a fiction within a fiction. A novel, for example, may contain scenes which are explicitly presented in the novel as fictional. The relation between an embedded fiction and the fiction in which it is embedded might seem to be analogous to the relation between fiction and reality. However, some authors deliberately break the rules and allow the boundary between an embedded fiction and the fiction in which it is embedded to dissolve. This article explores the difficulties such cases pose for philosophical accounts of fiction, in particular Lewis's possible worlds account of fictional truth.

Leach, Joan. Let the Audience De-Side: Possibilities for Postmodern Discourse Ethics. *Soc Epistem*, 8(4), 383-387, O-D 94.

The occasion for this essay is a Symposium on the Ethics of Postmodern Debate. The essay considers the possibility of ethics and postmodern debate and suggests that ethical postmodern debate will proceed along anti-foundationalist lines. Most importantly, the essay places the audience to debate at the center of any consideration of discourse ethics.

Leach, Joan. Taking Sides: Science, Language, and Debate after Derrida, Searle, and Alan Gross. *Soc Epistem*, 8(4), 361-372, O-D 94.

The occasion for this essay is a Symposium on the Ethics of Postmodern Debate. The essay considers the proposition that a science of language is possible and ultimately discerns that not only is it unlikely, but also undesirable. To arrive at this conclusion, the discussion evolves around several key thinkers to contemporary philosophy of language and philosophy of science.

Leach, Mary. (Re)searching Dewey for Feminist Imaginaries: Linguistic Continuity, Discourse and Gossip. *Stud Phil Educ*, 13(3-4), 291-306, 1994-95.

Leahey, Thomas H. Waiting for Newton. *J Mind Behav*, 16(1), 9-19, Wint 95.

Argues that Newton's influence on psychology has been broad and profound, if not always acknowledged. From the Enlightenment onward, most philosophers and psychologists have tried to be "Newtons of the Mind," trying to do psychology as Newton did physics, stressing mathematics and mechanism. No Newton has arrived in psychology, but we go on waiting nonetheless. But Newton's influence has been deeper than this, because he defined the modern style in science and ushered in a revolutionary concept of the universe and humans' relation to it. Newton's great influence has tended, especially in English-speaking psychology, to crowd out or depreciate other visions of psychology such as Wittgenstein and hermeneutics that do not conform to the Newtonian ideal of science. It is suggested that Newton, like Beckett's Godot, may never arrive.

Leahy, Robert. Authenticity: From Philosophic Concept to Literary Character. *Educ Theor*, 44(4), 447-462, Fall 94.

This article sketches authenticity historically from Rousseau to Charles Taylor, with reference to philosophic works and literary characters. Authenticity as an ethical perspective implies recognition of reciprocal relationships within the context of democratic principles. Authenticity is compared to Nel Nodding's feminine ethic of care grounded in the mother child relationship, and the historically male ethic of autonomy grounded by universalizable moral principles outlined by Ken Strike. Discussion of literary characters' movement toward authenticity suggests that authenticity may be a useful bridge between the ethic of care and autonomy, and that to develop authenticity is a worthwhile goal for educators.

Leal, Donald R and Anderson, Terry L. Freedom and the Environment: Reply to Critics. *Crit Rev*, 8(3), 461-465, Sum 94.

Two fundamental principles are overlooked by critics. First, environmental quality is a good that is increasingly demanded as incomes rise, and incomes rise as a result of market forces. Second, environmental quality is more likely to be supplied in cases where well-specified property rights provide positive incentives for the human actors. Free market environmentalism, which focuses on voluntary action, is the only sure way of accounting for subject values, material or aesthetic. For the environmentalist who is not libertarian, it is a pragmatic way of improving resource stewardship. For the libertarian who is not an environmentalist, it maximizes freedom.

Leal, José García. La expresión en el arte. *Rev Filosof (Spain)*, 4(6), 351-375, 1991.

This paper deals in the first place with the notion of expression that is usually employed in the artworld, insists on its ambiguities and comments on the problems it creates. Secondly, the most important trend of expression analysis, what it might be called the "classical theory", arised from Croce and Collingwood, is analyzed in order to show that most of nowadays attitudes towards art expression clusters around the classical theory either developing it or refecting it. Finally, the paper offers an alternative point of view inspired in Nelson Goodman's influential work.

Leaman, George. "Deutsche Philosophen und das 'Amt Rosenberg'" in *Die besten Geister der Nation, Korotin, Ilse (ed)*, 41-65. Vienna, Picus, 1994.

This article provides an account of the efforts of German philosophers to interpret the philosophical tradition from a specifically National Socialist perspective. These efforts

culminated in 1939 at a philosophy conference organized and sponsored by an office of the Nazi Party. Alfred Rosenberg invited a group of promising and politically sympathetic young philosophers to participate in this event, whose declared purpose was to secure the philosophical foundations of a world view built on National Socialist thought. Conference participants included such philosophers as Alfred Baeumler, Karl Schlechta, Joachim Ritter, and Eduard Baumgarten. The article quotes from transcripts of this conference, which was the only philosophy conference ever organized by the Nazi Party.

Leaman, George. *Heidegger im Kontext: Gesamtüberblick zum NS-Engagement der Universitätsphilosophen*. Hamburg, Argument Verlag, 1993.

This book presents an overview of the development of philosophy in Germany from 1933 to 1945, and provides an account of the professional and political activities of each of the philosophers who held university positions during this time. This information is used to provide a context for an examination of Heidegger's political thought. It is shown that Heidegger, like many other German philosophers, was committed to his own particular interpretation of the Nazi assertion of innate German superiority. Heidegger's chauvinism in this regard was based on beliefs about the nature of the German language, rather than a belief in the biological superiority of the German *Volk*. After the war, Heidegger, like many other German philosophers, intentionally obscured the nature of his past commitment to Nazism by suppressing politically revealing texts and by manipulating post-war editions of his earlier work.

Leaman, George and Simon, Gerd. Die Kant-Studien im Dritten Reich. *Kantstudien*, 85(4), 443-469, 1994.

This extensively documented article examines the publishing history of *Kant-Studien* during the years of the Nazi dictatorship. The article provides a detailed account of the work of the German philosophers who transformed the journal into a sophisticated instrument of Nazi cultural propaganda, and situates their efforts within the larger context of pro-Nazi philosophical activities in Germany. The article also presents a hitherto unknown volume of *Kant-Studien* (Band 42, Heft 1, Jg 1941/42) and provides a brief account of the journal's post-war resurrection.

Lear, Jonathan. Plato's Politic of Narcissism. *Apeiron*, 26(3-4), 137-159, S-D 93.

Leary, Christopher C. The Structure of Pleasant Ideals. *Notre Dame J Form Log*, 35(2), 292-297, Spr 94.

Continuing the work begun in Pleasant Ideals (*Notre Dame Journal of Formal Logic* vol 32 (1991) pp 612-617), we investigate the relationships among selective, normal and pleasant ideals. Our major result is that any selective ideal extending NS_k is normal.

Leary, David E. William James, the Psychologist's Dilemma and the Historiography of Psychology: Cautionary Tales. *Hist Human Sci*, 8(1), 91-106, F 95.

This article reviews William James's thoughts about science vs self, and individual vs society, particularly as they are relevant to the historiography of psychology. On the one hand, if science vs objective, how is the self to be understood and treated? On the other hand, if the self is subjective, how is the objectivity of science to be understood and treated? And relatedly, does the individual make a difference in history, or is the individual merely a corollary of social factors? In sum how is the historian to understand and treat science, self, individual, and society? The author believes that James's thoughts bear consideration.

Lebowitz, Michael A. "Situating the Capitalist State" in *Marxism in the Postmodern Age, Callari, Antonio (ed)*, 198-207. New York, Guilford, 1994.

Lebrun, Richard A (ed & trans) and De Maistre, Joseph. *Considerations on France: Joseph de Maistre*. New York, Cambridge Univ Pr, 19ed.

Lecaldano, Eugenio. Las reflexiones sobre la moral en Italia entre la Ética teórica y la Ética aplicada. *Telos (Spain)*, 3(1), 87-106, Je 94.

The article starts with an examination of the consequences of the public discussion in Italy on bioethical cases. The hypothesis developed and argued in these pages are that in contemporary culture in Italy there are the conditions for the diffusion of the empirical approach to the morality. The new questions in individual ethical life favor a growing attention for noncognitivist meta-ethics, utilitarianism and empirical analysis of the motivational role of emotions and reason. For the first time in Italy, perhaps, there are the cultural basis for a confrontation between different conceptions of human nature and then for the surpassing of the monopoly and supremacy of the spiritualistic philosophy.

Leclerc, Bruno. La Bioéthique, une Interface entre Théorie et Pratique?. *Philosopher*, 16, 157-170, 1994.

Leddy, Thomas. Everyday Surface Aesthetic Qualities: "Neat," "Messy," "Clean," "Dirty". *J Aes Art Crit*, 53(3), 259-268, Sum 95.

Aesthetics has traditionally neglected an entire category of aesthetic qualities. These include neat, messy, clean, dirty, ordered, cluttered, cleared, blemished and a number of others. I call these everyday surface aesthetic qualities. Although they do not refer primarily to art, these terms serve a number of purposes in artistic discourse. I show how they can be taken to be aesthetic concepts in Sibley's and Beardsley's senses. I end by suggesting that they might best be seen as proto-aesthetic qualities which provide a basis for such more complex qualities as elegance, beauty, and sublimity.

Leddy, Thomas W. A Pragmatist Theory of Artistic Creativity. *J Value Inq*, 28(2), 169-180, Je 94.

Analytic theorists of creativity have long insisted that product is prior to process to a creative (that is, novel and valuable) product. Although we cannot determine creativity of a work simply by looking at artist's psychology, it is wrong to assume that processes of evaluation and creation may be completely separated. Drawing from Dewey's pragmatism, I argue that examination of the creative process *is* relevant to evaluation of the product precisely because evaluation, including the very evaluation that determines that a work is creative, is *part* of the creative process.

Leddy, Tom. "Dialogical Architecture" in *Philosophy and Architecture, Mitias, Michael H (ed)*, 183-202. Amsterdam, Rodopi, 1994.

The Socratic/Platonic conception of wisdom through dialogue has been attacked in the recent deconstructionist literature on architecture by Jacques Derrida, Christopher Norris and Andrew Benjamin. I suggest modification of the Socratic approach to philosophy and architecture which rejects eternal, unchanging and absolute essences but retains essences as the objects of philosophical dialogue. Returning to Plato's *Seventh Letter* and the *Phaedrus*, I show that the deconstructionists have misinterpreted Plato. I then apply this to architecture, sketching a theory of "dialogical architecture". I conclude with an example of a recent house designed according to these principles.

Leder, Matthias. Willensfreiheit: Zwei gute Argumente und eine schlechtes. *Z Phil Forsch*, 49(1), 76-83, Ja-Mr 95.

Three arguments are examined. The first leads to the conclusion that it is impossible to predict one's own actions and also the actions of people who might be influenced by us. Our future, therefore, is in principle open to us. The second argument, called "Stehaufmännchen-Argument", is the well known argument that we are not free if determinism is true. It is shown to be unsound. Its suggestive power rests on our inability to imagine metamorphoses where the result of a developmental process is essentially different from its starting-point (e.g., a rose out of a seed, a baby out of fertilized egg). The third argument ends up with the conclusion that an undetermined being has no advantage over a determined one. It is argued that compatabilism is a very weak relation and doesn't yet tell us very much about freedom.

Leduc-Fayette, Denise. La "clef" de Job—Pascal: la liberté/le mal. *Rev Phil Fr*, 2, 181-194, Ap-Je 94.

Leduc-Fayette, Denise. La Catégorie Pascalienne de l'Hérésie. *Rev Phil Fr*, 2, 211-228, Ap-Je 95.

Lee, Jonathan Scott (ed) and Hord, Fred Lee (ed). *I Am Because We Are: Readings in Black Philosophy*. Amherst, Univ of Mass Pr, 1995.

Lee, Keekok. "Awe and Humility: Intrinsic Value in Nature" in *Philosophy and the Natural Environment, Attfield, Robin (ed)*, 89-101. New York, Cambridge Univ Pr, 1994.

This paper argues for conception of intrinsic value which tries to do justice to the following issues: a) that Nature need not and should not be understood to refer only to what exists on this planet, Earth; b) that an environment ethic informed by features unique to Earth may be misleading and prove inadequate as technology increasingly threatens to invade and colonize other planets in the Solar system; c) that a comprehensive environmental ethic must encompass not only our attitude to Earth, but to other planets as well—in other words, it must not simply be an earthbound but virtually an astronomically bounded ethic.

Lee, Melinda A and Ganzini, Linda and Heintz, Ronald T. The Capacity to Make Decisions in Advance and Borderline Personality Disorder. *J Clin Ethics*, 5(4), 360-363, Wint 94.

Lee, Peter H. Does Kant's Categorical Imperative Allow for a Concept of Mercy?. *Dialogue (PST)*, 37(2-3), 73-85, Ap 95.

Does Kant's Categorical Imperative allow for a concept of mercy? I answer this question in the negative, arguing that the Categorical Imperative's rigid adherence to an a priori ethical system that is not bound to any particular system prevents it from taking into account mercy. Moreover, I argue that the Categorical Imperative not only disallows mercy, but views it as a vice to be avoided. Therefore, I demonstrate that since the Categorical Imperative does not allow for mercy, Kant's ethical theory is undesirable and inconsistent with our basic human sensibilities.

Lee, S C and Muncaster, R G and Zinnes, D A. 'The Friend of My Enemy is My Enemy': Modeling Triadic Internation Relationships. *Synthese*, 100(3), 333-358, S 94.

The evolution of internation relationships is studied by means of a mathematical model based on a popular rule of triadic interaction: "the friend of my friend is my friend, the friend of my enemy is my enemy, the enemy of my enemy is my friend, the enemy of my friend is my enemy". The rule is shown to lead to the formation and preservation of unipolar and bipolar configurations of nations, with the strengths of relationships, both friendly and conflictual, intensifying through time. These results confirm speculations originally made in static, graph theoretic studies of the balancing of relationships within individuals, small groups and systems of nations.

Lee, Thomas H C. Las ideas chinas en la conceptualización transcultural: La relevancia de la historia intelectual. *Rev Filosof (Costa Rica)*, 31(75-76), 269-280, D 93.

This paper is about translation of Chinese words, ideas and intellectual orientations into Western languages. Nevertheless, this is no more than the background of a reflection on the translation's process. According to the author, the first is intellectual history of the ideas that are going to be expressed in another language. Second is translation itself. Finally, third is communication, which is obtained insofar as introduction and interpretation of key concepts become part of the common human heritage. The previous implies that every true communication involves the interlocutors' transformation.

Lee, Vicki L. Organisms, Things Done, and the Fragmentation of Psychology. *Behavior Phil*, 22(2), 7-48, Fall-Wint 94.

Attempts to sanitize psychology's fragmentation will postpone the inevitable task of identifying and conceptualizing the particular represented by psychological data. Psychological data represent things done, changes brought about by one or more organisms. Things done comprise a vast, densely populated, and always changing domain of events. Things done depend on organisms but are conceivable apart from organisms. The domain of things done contains particulars (i.e., content) and universals (i.e., patterns). Developing a compelling linkage between psychological theory and psychological data will require psychologists to abandon the assumption that the organism is the psychological unit.

Lee-Lampshire, Wendy. Women-Animals-Machines: A Grammar for a Wittgensteinian Ecofeminism. *J Value Inq*, 29(1), 89-101, Mr 95.

While a number of feminists have raised important political objections to the notion of an emancipatory standpoint, I argue that recent work in philosophy of mind, particularly eliminativism, raises serious philosophical questions about whether it makes sense to refer to "the subject" of any standpoint—emancipatory or otherwise. The remarks of later Wittgenstein, however, offer an alternative way of conceiving the subject, particularly his remarks concerning the use of psychological/anthoropomorphizing terms to describe behavior. I argue on the basis of these remarks it is possible to construct not only a viable conception of subject or subjecthood, but a feminist and emancipatory standpoint as well.

Leeds, Stephen. Constructive Empiricism. *Synthese*, 101(2), 187-221, N 94.

Leeds, Stephen. Holes and Determinism: Another Look. *Phil Sci*, 62(3), 425-437, S 95.

I argue that Earman and Norton's familiar "hole argument" raises questions as to whether GTR is a deterministic theory only given a certain assumption about determinism: namely, that to ask whether a theory is deterministic is to ask about the physical situations described by the theory. I think this is a mistake: whether a theory is deterministic is a question about what sentences can be proved within the theory. I show what these sentences look like: for interesting theories, a harmless bit of infinitary logic puts in an appearance.

Leeds, Stephen. Qualia, Awareness, Sellars. *Nous*, 27(3), 303-330, S 93.

I discuss the plausibility of the so-called "argument of the manifestation of linguistic knowledge," advanced by Dummett and his followers against the realistic approach. I focus on the defense of the argument set forth by Javier Legris. According to Dummett, if we admit that i) explaining the meaning of linguistic expressions is explaining our knowledge of these expressions and that ii) our knowledge is manifested in the way we use those expressions, then—if we accept the principle of bivalence—we have to conclude that iii) our knowledge of the truth-conditions of undecidable statements is not communicable. Legris' position is that this argument is plausible. My view is rather different. I think that Dummett's argument is plausible only on the assumption that his particular conception of truth and its relation to linguistic knowledge is true. But this is just what the realism-antirealism dispute is all about.

Leeds, Stephen. Truth, Correspondence, and Success. *Phil Stud*, 79(1), 1-36, Jl 95.

Lefebvre, Henri and Nicholson-Smith, Donald (trans). *The Production of Space*. Cambridge, Blackwell, 1991.

Leftow, Brian. Anselm on the Necessity of the Incarnation. *Relig Stud*, 31(2), 167-185, Je 95.

Anselm's *Cur Deus Homo* argues that only by the Incarnation can God save humanity. This seems to sit with the claim that God is omnipotent and absolutely free, for this entails that God could save humanity in other ways. I show that features of Anselm's concept of God and treatment of necessity make the claim that the Incarnation is a necessary means of salvation problematic. I then show that for Anselm, all conditions which make the Incarnation necessary for human salvation stem from God's nature and prior choices. If so, the Incarnation's necessity restricts neither God's freedom nor His power. For that the Incarnation is necessary given God's actual choices does not entail that it would have been necessary had God made other choices, or that God could not have made choices which would have made the Incarnation non-necessary.

Legault, Georges A. De la Croyance Morale à la Parole Éthique. *Philosopher*, 16, 29-37, 1994.

Legris, Javier. "Aspectos Epistémicos de la Lógica" in *Temas Actuales de Filosofía, Palacios, María Julia (ed)*, 321-326. Buenos Aires, Univ Nacional Salta, 1993.

In this paper some epistemic aspects of intuitionistic logic are brought out. The discussion is based on an embedding of intuitionistic logic in an epistemic system, where knowledge is to be understood as justified true belief. The main consequence to be drawn is the interpretation of intuitionistic atomic sentences as "epistemic assertions", that is, as statements of the form "It's known that...", so that the whole intuitionistic language is viewed as referring to mathematical knowledge.

Legris, Javier. La Lógica Intuicionista Como una Lógica del Conocimiento Matemático. *Dialogos*, 30(66), 21-29, Jl 95.

Legris, Javier. Nota sobre las críticas al realismo semántico: el caso de los enunciados indecidibles. *Rev Filosof (Argentina)*, 9(1-2), 79-85, N 94.

This note focuses on the argument from semantic anti-realism against the principle of bivalence based on the existence of undecidable sentences in mathematics. Some obscure statements in it are elucidated and a new formulation is presented, so that it can be argued for its plausibility and it can be shown how this argument provides a solution to problems old verificationism had in relation with the meaning of undecidable sentences.

Legris, Javier. Repuesta a E Barrio acerca de su defensa del realismo semántico. *Rev Filosof (Argentina)*, 9(1-2), 95-98, N 94.

Lehmann, N Joachim. Neue Erfahrungen zur Funktionsfähigkeit von Leibniz' Rechenmaschine. *Stud Leibniz*, 25(2), 174-188, 1993.

A new and thorough investigation of Leibniz's calculator has been carried out. When Burkhardt investigated the calculating machine between 1894 and 1896 he concluded that it could never have functioned since the multiple decimal carrying mechanism was defective. Burkhardt overlooked, however, the fact that the two phases of the adding process are to a great extent independent of each other. By means of a reconstruction it has now been proved that Leibniz's calculator was completely functional.

Lehmann, Scott. *Privatizing Public Lands*. New York, Oxford Univ Pr, 1995.

This study critically examines the thesis that public lands, such as national forests, would be more productive if they were private (or, failing that, managed as if they were private). It concludes that there is no sense of "productivity" for which it is true that greater productivity is both desirable and a likely consequence of privatizing public lands (or "marketizing" their management). The discussion is self-contained, with background chapters on United States federal lands and management agencies, economics, and ethics.

Lehning, Percy B. The Idea of Public Reason: Can It Fulfill Its Task?. *Ratio Juris*, 8(1), 30-39, Mr 95.

Lehrer, Keith. Knowledge and the Trustworthiness of Instruments. *Monist*, 78(2), 156-170, Ap 95.

The primary feature of an instrument of knowledge is that it be a trustworthy source of information. To obtain knowledge from an instrument, however, we must evaluate the trustworthiness of the instrument. The *evaluation* model of our knowledge from instruments contrasts causal or reliabilist model. This model enables us to explicate the distinction between observation statements and theoretical statements by construing theories as instruments of knowledge. To be trustworthy in what we accept we must accept what is worth accepting which takes us beyond the naturalistic domain of success to the realm of value and what is worth believing.

Leibniz, G W. *Primae veritates*. *Rev Metaph Morale*, 98(1), 7-30, Ja-Mr 95.

Leighton, Stephen. The Value of Passions in Plato and Aristotle. *SW Phil Rev*, 11(Supp), 41-56, Mr 95.

Whereas Plato is shown to argue for passions' elimination and limitation, idealizing a dispassionate self in which virtue involves intellect mastering passion, Aristotle is shown to reject the elimination or limitation of passion, endorsing a passionate self as virtuous. These and other differences in evaluation are discussed, then traced to differences in the psychological models used. More particularly, whereas Plato's evaluation stems from a psychology of parts, oppositionally defined, exclusive and separate, Aristotle orders the soul hierarchically in terms of distinctions without separations or exclusivity, therein allowing for unity throughout the soul and a value to passion that Plato cannot countenance.

Leiser, Burton M. On the Intolerable. *Filozof Istraz*, 14(2-3), 427-435, 1994.

The author discusses the concept of the 'intolerable' in the context of civil society and its institutions, but also in other contexts. Like so many other words, *tolerable* and its derivatives originally refer to concrete phenomena or qualities that can be observed in ordinary ways. It was subsequently extended to human experiences and purely psychological phenomena. Finally, the intolerable took on a normative sense of that which can, but ought not, to be tolerated. The term is also used in legal contexts. (edited)

Leisey, Robert G and Post, Stephen G. Analogy, Evaluation, and Moral Disagreement. *J Value Inq*, 29(1), 45-55, Mr 95.

This article examines the role of two distinct forms of analogy in moral discourse. The use of analogy in moral discourse. The use of analogy in abortion debates in used as an example of the dominance of analogy in applied ethics.

Leist, Anton. "Metaethischer Nonkognitivismus und moralische Aufmerksamkeit" in *Mythos Wertfreiheit?, Apel, Karl Otto (ed)*, 175-195. Frankfurt, Campus Verlag, 1994.

The article analyses noncognitivist metaethics, in both its linguistic and psychologic (Humean) form. Noncognitivism is shown to be deficient—in contrast to its empirico-analytical force—under the aspect of a justificatory attitude towards values and duties. To provide some alternative principally within the range of noncognitivism the concept of moral attention is suggested. Moral attention could perhaps explain what seems cognitive within our moral attitudes, without making use of a cognitive and objectivist theory of morals.

Leiter, Brian. Morality in the Pejorative Sense: On the Logic of Nietzsche's Critique of Morality. *Brit J Hist Phil*, 3(1), 113-145, F 95.

Does Nietzsche have a unified target in mind in criticizing "morality" (in his pejorative sense of that term)? This essay argues that he does. Nietzsche is a critic of morality in the sense of any values that 1) presuppose for their intelligible application the truth of certain descriptive claims about human agency (e.g., that agents have free will) ("the Descriptive Component"); and 2) embody norms that are harmful to the flourishing of those Nietzsche calls "the highest men" ("the Normative Component"). The essay concentrates on setting out the logic of the Normative Component of "morality" as it figures in Nietzsche's critique. The essay should be of interest to philosophically-minded Nietzsche scholars and analytic moral philosophers.

Lelouche, R and Doublait, S. Proposal for a Multi-Agent Model with a Human-Assisted Adaptation and Learning Mechanism. *Commun Cog—AI*, 11(1-2), 91-125, 1994.

Very few attempts have been made to address the problem of modeling and adapting complex mental attitudes in multi-agent environments. In this paper, we introduce the tile concept of scene static description and propose a categorization of actors' mental and physical attitudes, based on the concepts of role, status, and behaviour. We also model background knowledge of a scene through spatial and temporal statements. (edited)

Leloup, G. Elimination des Quantificateurs dans des Paires de Corps. *J Sym Log*, 60(2), 548-562, Je 95.

We show it's possible to eliminate quantifiers for some theories of pairs of fields in a given language. In case of pairs of algebraically closed fields, this language is obtained from the usual one by adding predicates saying: "for two given algebraic sets, there exist points of the sub-field that are rational over the first one but not over the second one". Extending the definition of an algebraic set to all predicates of a language, we have the same result with pairs of real closed fields and of valued fields of residual characteristic zero in dense and separate case.

Lemanska, Anna and Latawiec, Anna and Slaga, Szczepan W. Mieczyslaw Lubanskis Leben und Werk. *Stud Phil Christ*, 30(2), 5-64, 1994.

Zum Anlass des siebzigsten Geburstages wird das wissenschaftliche Wirken und das wissenschaftliche Werk von Professor Mieczyslaw Lubanski dargelegt und besprochen. 1924 geboren, hat er in den Jahren 1945-50 zuerst Mathematik an der Universität Warschau, dann 1955-58 Theologie im Warschauer Priesterseminar und 1959-62 Naturphilosophie an der Katholischen Universität in Lublin studiert. An dieser Hochschule erwarb Er 1965 das Doktorat. Seine Habilitationsschrift verteidigte Er 1973 an der Akademie für Katholische Theologie zur Warschau, wo Er 1982 zum Professor ernannt wurde und bis heute den Lehrstuhl für Methodologie der System und Informationslehre inne hat. Gleichzeitigg doziert Er seit 1965 Philosophie an der Päpstliche Theologischen Fakultät in Warschau, sowie an der Philosophischen Fakultät der Katholischen Universität in Lublin. Die wissenschaftliche Forschung Professors Lubanski lässt sich den folgenden thematischen einzuordnen: Geschichte und Philosophie der Wissenschaft, Philosophie der Mathematik, Informations- und Simulationstheorie, allgemeine Systemtheorie, Naturwissenschafts- und Natur-Philosophie, Systemanthropologie, Philosophie der Kybernetik. Einige Seiner Veröffentlichungen befassen sich zudem mit aktuellen weltanschaulichen Problemen.

Lembcke, V L. Locke's Educational Theories (and) the Woman Question. *Locke News*, 21, 141-164, 1990.

Lembeck, Karl-Heinz. "Von der Kritik zur Mystik: Edith Stein und der Marburger Neukantianismus" in *Studien zur Philosophie von Edith Stein, Fetz, Reto Luzius (ed)*, 170-196. Freiburg, Alber, 1993.

Lembeck, Karl-Heinz. Sollen, Wollen, Tun. *Phil Rundsch*, 41(3), 256-264, Je 94.

Under consideration of new publications about the idea and problem of volition the following questions are in discussion: If you know about our moral duty, does that directly mean, that it is your will that this duty also will be done by you? What kinds of criteria decides on the accountability (Zurechenbarkeit) of human actions in general? From what kind of presupposition volition develops essential? The answering of those questions allows a discussion of the ethical problems of obligation as well as the theory-of-rights problem of accountability.

Lemos, Noah M. *Intrinsic Value: Concept and Warrant*. New York, Cambridge Univ Pr, 1994.

This book attempts to answer some basic questions about intrinsic value. The first six chapters address the explication of intrinsic value, the bearers of value, value and part-whole relations, pluralism and hedonism. I defend the existence of a plurality of intrinsic goods, the thesis of organic unities, the view that some goods are "higher" than others, and the view that intrinsic value can be explicated in terms of "fitting" or "required" emotional attitudes. The final three chapters focus on moral epistemology and ontology. I defend a species of nonnaturalistic cognitivism and the view that some value beliefs enjoy "modest" *a priori* justification. I reject pure coherence accounts and the view that some value beliefs are warranted on the basis of emotional experience.

Lemos, Noah M. Neutrals. *SW Phil Rev*, 11(Supp), 27-40, Mr 95.

I distinguish four different types of neutral states of affairs, and discuss the value of taking pleasure of displeasure in these different kinds and what should be our attitudes toward them.

Lempert, Wolfgang. Moral Development in the Biographies of Skilled Industrial Workers. *J Moral Educ*, 23(4), 451-468, 1994.

This article is based on a longitudinal study of relations between biographical conditions and the personality development of 21 young workers ranging from 23 to 30 years of age who had passed through an apprenticeship in large plants of the metal industry in West Berlin. The biographical analyses focuses mainly on occupational conditions; the personality analyses, on such socio-cognitive variables as patterns of control awareness and structures of moral judgement. Occupational experiences appeared to have contributed considerably to moral development in most respondents. (edited)

Lempp, Steffen and Lerman, Manuel. A General Framework for Priority Arguments. *Bull Sym Log*, 1(2), 189-201, Je 95.

The paper outlines a new framework for priority arguments in classical computability theory, reminiscent of the way forcing is used in modern set theory. This framework is based on previous work of Harrington, Ash and Knight, and others. It was used in the authors' proof of the decidability of the existential theory of the enumerable Turing degrees with jump reducibility predicates and is applicable to all known priority arguments.

Lence, Sergio H and Babcock, Bruce A. Flexibility, Endogenous Risk, and the Protection Premium. *Theor Decis*, 38(1), 29-49, Ja 95.

We introduce two types of protection premia. The unconstrained protection premium, π^u, is the individual's willingness to pay for certain protection efficiency given flexibility to adjust optimally the investment in protection. The constrained protection premium, π^c, measures willingness to pay for certain protection efficiency given no flexibility to adjust the investment in protection. π^u depends on tastes and wealth as well as protection technology whereas π^c depends only on technology. We show that π^c cannot exceed π^u and develop necessary conditions for $\pi^c = \pi^u$. Optimal protection for an individual with decision flexibility may be larger or smaller than that desired under no flexibility.

Lengers, Frank P. The Idea of the Absurd and the Moral Decision: Possibilities and Limits of a Physician's Actions in the View of the Absurd. *Theor Med*, 15(3), 243-251, S 94.

In reference to two central concepts of Albert Camus' philosophy, that is, the absurd and the rebellion, this article examines to what extent his *The Plague* is of interest to medical ethics. The interpretation of this novel put forward in this article focuses on the main character of the novel, the physician Dr Rieux. For Rieux, the plague epidemic, as it is described in the novel, implies an unquestioning commitment to his patients and fellow men. According to Camus this epidemic has to be understood as a symbol of the absurd. Unable to base his actions on a Christian, metaphysical value system, Rieux sees his commitment as a continuous rebellion against the fact of the absurd, which opposes him in the form of evil, suffering and death. As a physician, Rieux is therefore forced to adjust his actions to life in its immediacy, that is, the suffering of his patients. In this article, it will be shown that Rieux's attention to the "immediate" is of particular interest to medical ethics: The *other* person in need, rather than *my* moral convictions, sets the norm.

Lenhardt, Christian. "Max Weber and the Legacy of Critical Idealism" in *The Barbarism of Reason, Horowitz, Asher (ed)*, 21-48. Toronto, Univ of Toronto Pr, 1994.

Lenka, Laxminarayan. An Understanding of Contemporary Foundationalism. *Indian Phil Quart*, 21/4(Supp), 13-25, O 94.

This paper aims at an exposition of how temporary foundationalism (of Alston, Audi and Chisholm, etc.) presupposes the structure-content distinction of beliefs.

Lenman, James. Finding Beauty. *J Value Inq*, 28(2), 245-256, Je 94.

It is argued that finding something beautiful is a matter of responding to some aspect of our experience and that any more general notion of thinking something beautiful relies for its contentfulness on the prior notion of finding beautiful. It is only thus indirectly that things other than aspects of experiences can be objects of aesthetic evaluation. Attention to this distinction, it is suggested, may help to highlight both the appeal of and the limitations to a cognitivist understanding of our imputations of beauty—as well as of our imputations of goodness, a concept to which beauty is extensively compared.

Lennox, James G. Aristotelian Problems. *Ancient Phil*, 14, 53-77, 1994.

The concept of a 'problem' plays central, but distinct, roles in Aristotle's *Topics, Prior Analytics*, and *Posterior Analytics*, and is known to have played an important role in Greek mathematics. In this paper, Aristotle's use of this concept is argued to shift from referring to a topic for dialectical debate in the *Topics*, to a proposition to be proved in the *Prior Analytics* and finally to a proposition appropriate for explanation in the *Posterior Analytics*. In all cases, however, a problem is an object of inquiry: once it is proved or explained, it is no longer a problem. This provides a means of connecting Aristotle's 'problems' with those of Greek mathematics.

Lennox, James G. Aristotle's Biology: Plain, But Not Simple. *Stud Hist Phil Sci*, 25(5), 817-823, O 94.

The occasion for this critical review is the publication of a second, revised edition of David M Balme's translation, with introduction and notes, of Aristotle's *De Partimus Animalium I* and *De Generatione Animalium I* in the Clarendon Aristotle series. The second edition includes an appendix by Allan Gotthelf with a selective bibliography and a guide to the philosophical literature occasioned by Balme's notes. This critical review discusses Balme's unique style of translation and commentary, analyzing in detail a number of key passages in both.

Lennox, James G. Teleology by Another Name: A Reply to Ghiselin. *Biol Phil*, 9(4), 493-495, O 94.

A paper by the author entitled "Darwin *was* a Teleologist" was published in *Biology and Philosophy* (Vol 8 1993). This brief note is a reply to a critical response to that paper written by Michael Ghiselin. It is argued that Ghiselin continues to ignore the textual evidence for Darwin's use of teleological explanations, and that he is completely wrong in his view that these *apparently* teleological explanations aren't *really* such.

Leonardi de Herran, Teresa and Simesen de Bielke, Ana. "La Filosofía en Tiempos del Cólera" in *Temas Actuales de Filosofía, Palacios, María Julia (ed)*, 577-581. Buenos Aires, Univ Nacional Salta, 1993.

Our aim is to present a diffuse panorama of Philosophy at the end of the millenium. Universalisms, with their advantages and disadvantages, have been legitimated. It is not believed any more that Philosophy can systematize the sense and the progress of the world. It is not believed that Philosophy can legitimate the scientific discourse. It is argued in favour of Wittgenstein's games. In social terms, we witness the "end of representation." In social terms, we witness the "end of representation." Which will the task of Philosophy be after the "end of universalisms?"

LePore, Ernest and Fodor, Jerry A. "Is Intentional Ascription Intrinsically Normative?" in *Dennett and his Critics, Dahlbom, Bo (ed)*, 70-82. Cambridge, Blackwell, 1995.

LePore, Ernest and Fodor, Jerry A. What *Is* The Connection Principle?. *Phil Phenomenol Res*, 54(4), 837-845, D 94.

LePore, Ernest and Fodor, Jerry A. "Replies" in *Holism: A Consumer Update, Fodor, Jerry (ed)*, 303-322. Amsterdam, Rodopi, 1993.

LePore, Ernest (ed) and Fodor, Jerry A (ed). *Holism: A Consumer Update*. Amsterdam, Rodopi, 1993.

Lerman, Manuel and Lempp, Steffen. A General Framework for Priority Arguments. *Bull Sym Log*, 1(2), 189-201, Je 95.

The paper outlines a new framework for priority arguments in classical computability theory, reminiscent of the way forcing is used in modern set theory. This framework is based on previous work of Harrington, Ash and Knight, and others. It was used in the authors' proof of the decidability of the existential theory of the enumerable Turing degrees with jump reducibility predicates and is applicable to all known priority arguments.

Leroux, François. Démocratie et expérience: introduction à la démocratie créatrice de John Dewey. *Horiz Phil*, 5(2), 20-40, 1995.

Leroux, Georges. Protreptique et Dialectique. *Philosopher*, 16, 249-257, 1994.

The reasons brought forward to justify the teaching of moral philosophy to college students are most often limited to the dialectical aspect of teaching philosophy in general. The history of ethics is indeed full of interesting arguments on the nature of virtue and the essence of the good. But this dialectical aspect, most important in the apprenticeship of democratic discussion, is not only one. There is also a protreptic aspect: teaching ethics to students is a unique possibility to offer them the opportunity to discuss the variety of models of life, as represented in the history of philosophy from Socrates to contemporary philosophers.

Leroux, Jean. L'Épistémologie de Helmholtz et la Question du Réalisme Scientifique. *Horiz Phil*, 2(2), 83-107, Spring 92.

In this paper, we indicate first how Helmholtz, through his physiological investigations, came to consider sensations as signs. We then expose this semiotic approach in order to exhibit its epistemological implications. More specifically, our intent is to trace back the development of Helmhotz's views on scientific realism and to exhibit increasingly strong antirealist aspects in his theory of science. It is argued that this feature can be explained by Helmhotz's progressively (but never fully: he always upheld a transcendental, Kantian version of nomological realism) integrating his views on scientific explanation into insights on language.

Lértora Mendoza, Celina A. Vico y Sarmiento. *Cuad Vico*, 3, 143-156, 1993.

Sarmiento and the '37 Generation were not Vichians, but they carried out a historic and civilizing piece of work, in accord with the ideals of Vico, who lived and thought in a very different context. The influence of Vico on Sarmiento is a matter of debate, and requires a methodological purification and the theoretical clarification of possible connections. The issues that demand this present study refer to the possiblility of such an influence on the Argentine thinker. The two lines pursued in this study are: if there are indeed, objectively, theses parallel to the principles of Vico in the work of Sarmiento; and what subjective connection could have existed.

Léry, Nicole. Vers une Éthique de Responsabilité en Milieu Médical. *Philosopher*, 14, 35-49, 1993.

Leske, Monika. *Philosophen im "Dritten Reich": Studie zu Hochschul- und Philosophiebetrieb im faschistischen Deutschland*. Berlin, Dietz, 1990.

Leslie, John. Cosmology: A Philosophical Survey. *Philosophia (Israel)*, 24(1-2), 3-27, D 94.

The article discusses competing answers to philosophically interesting problems raised by modern cosmology. These include whether space is a substance, and time just one dimension of a four-dimensional reality; how our universe came into existence; whether there exist many more or less separate universes; whether readily understandable mechanisms could give such universes very varied sets of properties; and whether (as an application of the anthropic principle) observational selection could then explain why ours has properties so apparently fine tuned to permit the evolution of observers, an alternative perhaps being divine selection of those properties.

Lessa, Sergio. Reproduction and Ontology in Lukács (in Portuguese). *Trans/Form/Acao*, 17, 63-79, 1994.

This article aims to discuss the most fundamental nexus of the social category of reproduction, as outlined in Lukács posthumous work *Per una ontologia dell'essere sociale*.

Lessa da Fonseca, Thelma Silveira Mota. Nietzsche: A Origem da Linguagem. *Educ Filosof*, 8(16), 107-118, Jl-D 94.

O presente texto consiste em parte de um estudo maior voltado para a compreensao da gênese da preocupaçao de Nietzsche com a linguagem. Será aqui abordado um escrito do período de juventude do autor, que poderia ser classificado como "filológico". No entanto, reconhece-se aí algumas consideraçoes de teor propriamente filosófico e que ganharao densidade na obra posterior do autor. Buscarse-á mostrar que as primeiras que, justamente neste grande passo em direçao à filosofia, o autor defrontou-se com problemas e impasses que somente uma reflexao especificamente filosófica poderia resolver.

Lesser, A H. The Holocaust: Moral and Political Lessons. *J Applied Phil*, 12(2), 143-150, 1995.

In many discussions, whether general or academic, the Holocaust is used as a warning of how initially small corruptions can lead to terrible consequences. In particular, it has been seen as illustrating the "slippery slope" from euthanasia to murder, as showing the consequences of an exaggerated respect for law, and as showing the effects of a corrupt ideology. It is argued that these three points are all somewhat inaccurate, and that 1) the "slippery slope" occurred much earlier, the so-called "euthanasia" programme being already murder; 2) it was power rather than law that was excessively respected; and 3) it was the corruption of the sense of moral responsibility that did the real harm, rather than the establishment of any coherent ideology.

Lestienne, Rémy and Neher, E C (trans). *The Children of Time: Causality, Entropy, Becoming*. Champaign, Univ of Illinois Pr, 1995.

Leuchtag, Alice. "Elizabeth Cady Stanton: Free Thinker and Radical Revisionist" in *Contributors to the Philosophy of Humanism, Hillar, Marian (ed)*, 105-113. Pasadena, Humanists Houston, 1994.

Elizabeth Cady Stanton (1815-1902), who taught that orthodox religion was the prime oppressor of women, advocated free thought and the separation of church and state. Married to abolitionist organizer Henry Stanton, she gave birth to seven children. Susan B Anthony became her comrade in the struggle for equality for women. Stanton organized the first women's rights convention and, with Anthony, founded a newspaper and the National Woman Suffrage Association. She led an international committee to revise the Bible. In *The Woman's Bible* Stanton exposed the hateful images and treatment of women that abound in the Old and New Testaments.

Levering, Bas. "How Much 'Heimat' does a Human Being Need?" in *Identity, Culture, and Education, Smeyers, Paul (ed)*, 205-211. Leuven, Leuven Univ Pr, 1994.

The problem of nationalism is our topic, and the existential roots of nationalism are our main research interest. "How much 'Heimat' does a human being need?" is the question that guides our research into the existential roots of the problem of nationalism. Before we start analysing the concept of 'home' in modern Dutch poetry, we line up the results of a first attempt to answer the question, a critical analysis of O F Bollnows *Neue Geborgenheit* (A New Sense Of Security). Preceeding that a short fundamental philosophical issue must be looked at concerning the relationship between 'needs' and 'rights'.

Lévesque, Claude. Portrait du Philosophe en Poète. *Philosopher*, 13, 169-178, 1992.

Lévesque, Gérard. La Formation Générale au Niveau Collégial. Sa Qualité Passe d'Abord par la Consolidation de la Formation de Base. *Philosopher*, 14, 189-203, 1993.

Levi, Albert William and Verene, Donald Phillip (ed) and Verene, Molly Black (ed). *The High Road of Humanity: The Seven Ethical Ages of Western Man*. Amsterdam, Rodopi, 1995.

Levi, Don S. The Gettier Problem and the Parable of the Ten Coins. *Philosophy*, 70(271), 5-25, Ja 95.

Gettier's argument is puzzling because when his much too sketchy examples are filled in they are not what the Gettier Problem requires. If there are not more details to supply or they should not be supplied by thinking in terms of actual discourse, then the question arises as to how they could admit of truth or falsity or be believed. It is suggested that Gettier's answer is based on the assumption that examples devised in the context in which he is operating can be understood as proxies for actual discourse. The paper concludes by criticizing this assumption.

Levi, Honor (trans) and Pascal, Blaise. *Pensées and Other Writings: A New Translation by Honor Levi*. New York, Oxford Univ Pr, 1995.

Levi, Isaac. "Closure and Consistency" in *Modality, Morality, and Belief, Sinnott-Armstrong, Walter (ed)*, 215-234. New York, Cambridge Univ Pr, 1994.

Levi, Isaac. "Induction According to Peirce" in *Peirce and Contemporary Thought: Philosophical Inquiries, Ketner, Kenneth Laine (ed)*, 59-93. New York, Fordham Univ Pr, 1995.

Levi, Isaac. Cognitive Value and the Advancement of Science. *Phil Phenomenol Res*, 55(3), 619-628, S 95.

This essay participates in a symposium on Philip Kitcher's important book *The Advancement of Science*. It considers critically the way in which Kitcher identifies autonomous goals for scientific inquiry that characterize scientific progress and worries, in particular, about Kitcher's emphasis on these values as goals of scientific institutions to whose interest the aims of individual inquirers appear to be subordinated.

Levi, Isaac and Collins, John and Costa, Horacio Arló. Desire-as-Belief Implies Opinionation or Indifference. *Analysis*, 55(1), 2-5, Ja 95.

The anti-Humean proposal of constructing desire as belief about what would be good must be abandoned on pain of triviality. Our central result shows that if an agent's belief-desire state is represented by Jeffrey's expected value theory enriched with the Desire as Belief Thesis (DAB), then, provided that three pairwise inconsistent propositions receive nonzero probability, the agent must view with indifference any proposition whose probability is greater than zero. Unlike previous results against DAB our Opinionation or Indifference Theorem is a purely synchronic one that depends in no way of the properties of Jeffrey conditionalization.

Levi, Isaac and Fuhrmann, André. Undercutting and the Ramsey Test for Conditionals. *Synthese*, 101(2), 157-169, N 94.

There is an important class of conditionals whose assertibility conditions are not given by the Ramsey test but by an inductive extension of that test. Such inductive Ramsey conditionals fail to satisfy some of the core properties of plain conditionals. Associated principles of nonmonotonic inference should not be assumed to hold generally if interpretations in terms of induction or appeals to total evidence are not to be ruled out.

Levin, David Michael. Making Sense: The Work of Eugene Gendlin. *Human Stud*, 17(3), 343-353, Jl 94.

This article discusses Gendlin's radically innovative philosophy of language, showing some connections between his approach to language and the approaches of Heidegger, Adorno, and Merleau-Ponty. Gendlin's primary interest is in how experience and concepts interact, i.e., how the body of experience generates concepts and how these concepts function, in turn, to change this experience. Gendlin argues that our uses of words—and the philosophical accounts intended to interpret them—conceal their rootedness in the body of felt experience. His hermeneutical phenomenology sheds crucial light on this embodiment of language, showing a multiplicity of concept-forming processes in their intricate detail. Gendlin's theory and practice has profound implications for ethics, moral education, and politics.

Levin, Michael. "Tolerance" as an Excuse for Censorship on Campus. *Filozof Istraz*, 14(2-3), 403-416, 1994.

The author argues that the *new censorship* is not only brought about by feminism and the racial civil rights movement, but also that it is a reaction to the growing evidence that these movements rest on errors. Having gotten what they said they wanted—the right to compete by the rules that govern competition among white males—blacks and feminists in higher education found themselves unhappy with the results. They insisted, still in the name of equality, that the rules be changed. New rules were then imposed to satisfy these demands, including the restrictions on free speech on the campus. The promise implicit in the initial demand for an even playing field was thus broken. As a result, racial and gender tolerance comes to mean forbidding speech that blacks and feminists cannot tolerate. By an Orwellian inversion, tolerance and diversity amount to intolerance for certain opinions. (edited)

Levin, Michael. A Formal Treatment of Gene Identity, Genetic Causation, and Related Notions. *Behavior Phil*, 22(2), 49-58, Fall-Wint 94.

A gene is identified with its range of reaction—that is, a gene is defined as a function from environments to phenotypes. This analysis is shown to permit the explication of a number of disputed such concepts as "genetic identity," and to allow a natural explication of gene/environment correlation and interaction. Some arguments against the heritability concept are shown to be groundless.

Levin, Michael. Tortuous Dualism. *J Phil*, 92(6), 313-322, Je 95.

This note criticizes Bealer's recent restatement of Kripke's modal argument against dualism. Bealer bypasses the question of the kinds of designators used to name mental states, and asserts directly that pain can be imagined without any one kind of accompanying physical state. The materialist replies that Bealer is confused about what he thinks he is imagining or intuiting in such cases. I conclude with some speculation as to why the modal argument is so appealing. Kripkenstein's virtual solipsism is criticized passim.

Levin, Michael E. Reply to Adler's "More on Race and Crime: Levin's Reply". *J Soc Phil*, 25(2), 115-118, Fall 94.

It is pointed out that Adler appears to concede the principle that the state may use race-consciousness in a way burdensome to blacks to oppose crime.

Levinas, Emmanuel. Time is the Breath of the Spirit (in Hebrew). *Iyyun*, 43, 441-444, O 94.

Levinas, Emmanuel and Billings, Blake (trans). The Primacy of Pure Practical Reason. *Man World*, 27(4), 445-453, O 94.

Levine, Joseph. "Intentional Chemistry" in *Holism: A Consumer Update, Fodor, Jerry A (ed)*, 103-134. Amsterdam, Rodopi, 1993.

This paper discusses the debate between atomists and molecularists regarding the nature of mental content. A molecularist believes that some, but not all, of a mental symbol's inferential connections to other mental symbols, are at least partly constitutive of that symbol's intentional content. An atomist believes that none of the symbol's inferential connections play such a constitutive role. The paper is divided into two principal parts. First, attempts by Michael Devitt and Georges Rey to defend molecularism against traditional Quinean arguments are evaluated. The conclusion is that their attempts fall short of providing an adequate defense. Second, the prospects for an atomistic theory are investigated, building on the various remarks of Fodor and LePore in their book, *Holism: A Shopper's Guide*. It is argued that the prospects are better than at first they appear.

Levine, Joseph M. R G Collingwood, *The Idea of History*. *Clio*, 24(1), 85-90, Fall 94.

Levine, Peter. *Lolita* and Aristotle's Ethics. *Phil Lit*, 19(1), 32-47, Ap 95.

Aristotle claims that narrative can depict virtue and vice in particular cases, and that literature's moral meanings are not subject to philosophical paraphrase. He distrusts generalization in ethics, asserting that valid judgments rest on the perception of particulars. But this position is itself an unprovable generalization. If philosophy cannot prove the superiority of narrative over moral theory, perhaps literature can show it. In *Lolita*, Nabokov reveals the moral hazards of theory while depicting one man's profound evil. Thus *Lolita* is an illuminating example of pure Aristotelian fiction that serves a moral function without recourse to theory.

Levins, Richard. "Beyond Democracy: The Politics of Empowerment" in *Marxism in the Postmodern Age, Callari, Antonio (ed)*, 208-217. New York, Guilford, 1994.

Levinski, Jean-Pierre. Filters and Large Cardinals. *Annals Pure Applied Log*, 72(2), 177-212, Mr 95.

Levinson, Henry Samuel. Santayana and Making Claims on the Spiritual Truth about Matters of Fact. *Bull Santayana Soc*, 12, 1-12, Fall 94.

Levinson, Jerrold. Messages in Art. *Austl J Phil*, 73(2), 184-198, Je 95.

This paper is primarily concerned with what it means to say an artwork conveys a message, and relatedly, with how one determines what the message, if any, is. An analysis is proposed, in light of some examples of traditional art (by Ibsen, Goya, Browning), and then is applied to and tested against two recent, nontraditional examples, a feminist performance artwork and a hard rap song. The paper also discusses, toward the end, the issues of who, if anyone, is responsible, in various ways, for a work's message, and how art can remain artistic even though containing and communicating a detachable message.

Levinson, Jerrold. Still Hopeful: Reply to Karl and Robinson. *J Aes Art Crit*, 53(2), 199-201, Spr 95.

Levinson, Sanford. Is Liberal Nationalism an Oxymoron? An Essay for Judith Shklar. *Ethics*, 105(3), 626-645, Ap 95.

Levy, Sanford S. The Coherence of Two-Level Utilitarianism: Hare vs Williams. *Utilitas*, 6(2), 301-309, N 94.

According to R M Hare, we ought to teach two levels of moral thought, an act utilitarian "critical" level and a deontological "intuitive" level. Bernard Williams objects that the act-utilitarian level conflicts with the intuitive level. Thus, the two-level system is incoherent and unstable. However, I argue that there is an interpretation of the system that is free of incoherence or instability. It all depends on what we mean by "intuitions." When they are understood as "moral commitments," the intuitive levels rests comfortably with the critical level.

Levy-Bruhl, Lucien. "How Natives Think" in *African Philosophy: Selected Readings, Mosley, Albert G (ed)*, 40-61. Englewood Cliffs, Prentice Hall, 1995.

Lewis, David. *Parts of Classes*. Cambridge, Blackwell, 1991.

The parts of a class are exactly its (nonempty) subclasses; thus a class is the mereological fusion of its singleton subclasses. If we axiomatize set theory with "singleton" as primitive (added to an ontologically innocent framework of plural quantification and mereology) our axioms for "singleton" resemble the Peano axioms for "successor": set theory is mereologized arithmetic. But the primitive notion of singleton was never properly explained. But, using methods due to Burgess and Hazen, we can in effect quantify over relations; then we can go structuralist, dump the primitive member-singleton relation, and instead treat set theory as the general theory of relations having a suitable structure.

Lewis, David. Should a Materialist Believe in Qualia?. *Austl J Phil*, 73(1), 140-144, Mr 95.

The answer is yes and no. A materialist should believe in imperfect occupants of the role, and imperfect deservers of the name, of qualia: in properties of experiences that are causally responsible for the power of experiences to impart mental abilities to recognize and imagine experiences of the same kind. But he should not believe in perfect occupants of the role and deservers of the name. For part of our folk-psychological concept of qualia is that we can *identify* them: just by having an experience you can know exactly which property is the qualia of the experience you are having. If materialism is true, nothing satisfies this part of our concept of qualia.

Lewis, Eric. The Stoics on Identity and Individuation. *Phronesis*, 40(1), 89-108, 1995.

Lewis, Peter. Art, the Community's Medicine. *Brit J Aes*, 35(3), 205-216, Jl 95.

Numerous philosophers have compared art to medicine as a way of explaining why art matters. The acute problems raised by this analogy are diagnosed by R C Collingwood in *The Principles of Art*. And yet, at the end of that book, he suggests art is the community's medicine for the worst disease of mind, the corruption of consciousness. The aim of this paper is to 1) To show that Collingwood is not guilty of careless inconsistency and 2) To argue that his understanding of art as the community's medicine helps illuminate the place of art in society.

Lewis, Peter. GRW and the Tails Problem. *Topoi*, 14(1), 23-33, Mr 95.

The GRW theory is a recent attempt to solve the measurement problem in quantum mechanics, and the tails problem is a well-known and potentially fatal criticism of the GRW theory. The first half of the paper is an exposition of the measurement problem, the GRW theory, and the tails problem. In the remainder of the paper, two methods of dealing with the tails problem are considered: first, altering the GRW theory so as to avoid the tails problem; and second, denying that the tails problem is more than a novel aspect of a universal vagueness in the way scientific theories relate to everyday language.

Ley, Michael. "Prolegomena zu einer National-Sozialistischen Rechtsphilosophie" in *Die besten Geister der Nation, Korotin, Ilse (ed)*, 115-140. Vienna, Picus, 1994.

Hegel's law philosophy can be interpreted as the predecessor to nationalsocialistic law philosophy and the perversion of the state under the rule of law. Hegel alters Christian ideas concerning Eschatology for his own historical philosophy. He defines the "Weltgeist" as the bearer of the divine World plan. Every nation incarating the "Weltgeist" becomes the bearer of absolute right, to which all other nations must subordinate themselves. He developed the theory of an absolute "Power State" which became the model for modern Totalitarianism. According the Hegel, the ultimate historical empire was the Germanic Reich. The Germans are therefore the chosen accomplishers of historical salvation. Seen historically, Hegel's theory and the political theology of national socialism coincide with each other.

Ley, Michael. *Genozid und Heilserwartung: zum nationalsozialistischen Mord am europäischen Judentum*. Vienna, Picus, 1993.

Leydet, Dominique. L'Enseignement de l'Histoire de l'Éthique. *Philosopher*, 16, 259-263, 1994.

Leyra, Ana María and Mataix, Carmen. *Arte y Ciencia: Una Visión Especular*. Madrid, Ed La Palma, 1992.

This book is rooted in the crisis of thought in the 19th and 20th centuries and confronts two domains apparently so distant as the field of art and of science—through its development one can discover parallel situations in both matters and draw the conclusion that the same cultural trends govern both the art expression and the theories of science. Representation, truth, "logocentrism", "supplement" are philosophical terms that can be applied as well to the field of aesthetics as to that of reflexion about science.

Li, Chenyang. Mind-Body Identity Revised. *Philosophia (Israel)*, 24(1-2), 105-114, D 94.

The identity theorist should step back from the type-type identity position but move forward from the token-token identity position, and take as the first step to overcome their main difficulty by proposing that there is a genus-species relation between pain and C-fiber stimulation. This claim is stronger than the token-token identity thesis, because it deals with pain and C-fiber stimulation as kinds, but it is weaker than the type-type identity, because it does not claim the two kinds are identical kinds. After the identity theorist demonstrates this position is consistent, the burden of disproving this position is on those who try to invalidate this position.

Li, Hon-Lam. On Nietzsche's Perspectivism. *Phil Hist Sci*, 3(1), 71-83, Ap 94.

This paper is a critical exposition of Nietzsche's perspectivism, the doctrine that there are "no facts", "only interpretations". In the course of expounding perspectivism, I compare and contrast it with Kant's position on "privileged perspective", Derek Parfit's reductionism of personal unity, and Hume's view on secondary qualities. I also examine the relation of perspectivism to Nietzsche's views on will-to-power and on truth. In the end, I argue 1) that perspectivism seems both implausible and self-refuting, 2) that the "hypothesis" of will-to-power is probably best seen as a collorary rather than a premise—of perspectivism, and 3) that Nietzsche's claim that truth is for self-preservation seems to conflict with perspectivism. However, I suggest that perspectivism, with suitable modification, could be saved from the charge of self-refutation. But it is evident that Nietzsche is not tempted by such a move. And this in turn shows that Nietzsche's position is more radical than some suppose.

Libbrecht, Ulrich. *Inleiding Comparatieve Filosofie*. Assen, Gorcum, 1995.

Libbrecht, Ulrich J. Fundamentals of Taoist Thinking. *Tijdschr Filosof*, 57(1), 3-35, Mr 95.

Tao, the "Way", the dynamic principle of the universe, can only operate within a *ch'i*-space, i.e., and energetic space, or a universe of becoming. This becoming is a nonchaotic process—fact that is expressed in the tao-metaphor. Tao is not an automonous transcendent principle, but is immanent to the universe, which is by itself creative. In this organic cosmos, time can only be cyclical—expressed in the yin-yang polarity; motion is transformation; causality is reticular. The process of becoming emanates the "ten thousand things", i.e., the phenomena, which have their individual form (*hsing*), itself coded in the "seed-essence" (*ching*). Man has some free energy, and hence his energetic personality (*te*). Happiness in life depends on the attuning of the individual *te* to the universal *tao*. This requires going back to natural spontaneity. Hence the great principle of practical life: *wu-wei*, no-action, i.e., no transcendent action in civilisation; and a direct approach to the mystery of tao in natural meditation.

Liberman, Kenneth. A Case for Convergence in Tibetan and Vedāntin Meditative Practices. *J Indian Counc Phil Res*, 11(2), 55-67, Ja-Ap 94.

Buddhist and Hindu philosophers have been engaging in serious philosophical debates for more than fifteen centuries,and there are irreconcilable differences between them regarding the existence of a soul, whether external objects have inherent essences, and belief in a Creator, among others: however, despite these philosophical differences they share in common many meditative practices. This article explores the question of whether these common practices extend to the core of the spiritual experiences of Tibetan and Vedantin meditators.

Liberman, Kenneth. Knowing and Being: Eugene Gendlin's Experience. *Human Stud*, 17(3), 355-362, Jl 94.

The essay reviews the phenomenological method developed and applied by Eugene Gendlin. While phenomenologists accept that existence precedes essence, the ease with which phenomenological thinkers have given themselves over to theorizing can render them impotent to carry out phenomenological research. Gendlin's inquiries into language and conceptualization, social relationships, reflexivity and therapy retain always the heart of the phenomenological epoche, which is to articulate experience as actually had, rather than as theorized. This leads Gendlin to an instructive confrontation with post-phenomenological critics.

Liberman, Kenneth. The Hermeneutics of Formal Analytics: The Case of Tibetan Philosophical Criticism. *Int Phil Quart*, 35(2), 129-140, Ju 95.

Liccione, Michael. Mystery and Explanation in Aquinas's Account of Creation. *Thomist*, 59(2), 223-245, Ap 95.

Kretzmann and Lovejoy argue that Aquinas' explanation of God's creating is inconsistent with his account of God's freedom in creating. Defending Aquinas, I argue that for him, the world's existence is both *fully explicable* and *essentially mysterious*. It is fully explicable in that God wills it effectively and with sufficient reason: by manifesting and communicating his goodness, creation befits God. It is essentially mysterious in that God wills it freely and his goodness would be complete and absolute without it: thus there is *no* reason to create *rather than* not. This result is of general philosophical interest.

Lichtblau, Klaus. Sociology and the Diagnosis of the Times or: The Reflexivity of Modernity. *Theor Cult Soc*, 12(1), 25-52, F 95.

Starting with the thesis that the classical sociological discourse on modernity has been profoundly challenged by the contemporary philosophical, literary and aesthetic proclamations of the age of "postmodernity" the article discusses some specific contributions of modern sociology to a genuine "diagnosis of the times". First, Georg Simmel's philosophy of culture is compared with Charles Baudelaire's aesthetics of modernity and Karl Mannheim's sociology of knowledge. Then Arnold Gehlen's notion of "posthistorie" is contrasted with Niklas Luhmanns's description of the "paradox of time" and Ulrich Beck's analysis of the reflexivity of "postindustrial" society.

Lichtenstein, Benyamin M and Smith, Beverly A and Torbert, William R. Leadership and Ethical Development: Balancing Light and Shadow. *Bus Ethics Quart*, 5(1), 97-116, Ja 95.

What makes a leader ethical? This paper critically examines the answer given by developmental theory, which argues that individuals can develop through cumulative stages of ethical orientation and behavior (e.g., Hobbesian, Kantian, Rawlsian), such that leaders at later developmental stages (of whom there are empirically very few today) are more ethical. By contrast to a simple progressive model of ethical development, this paper shows that each developmental stage has both positive (light) and negative (shadow) aspects, which affect the ethical behaviors of leaders at that stage. It also explores an unexpected result: later stage leaders can have more significantly negative effects than earlier stage leadership.

Lie, Merete and Berg, Anne-Jorunn. Feminism and Constructivism: Do Artifacts Have Gender?. *Sci Tech Human Values*, 20(3), 332-351, Sum 95.

This article explores possibilities for establishing dialogues between feminism and constructivism in the field of technology studies. Based on an overview of Norwegian feminist debates about technology, it indicates several points where feminism and constructivism meet and can mutually benefit from each other. The article critically examines feminist studies questioning the problems of technological determinism, social determinism, and essentialism. It criticizes constructivism for a lack of concern for gender and politics but holds that it is still possible to use theoretical tools from constructivism in feminist analyses. Fruitful dialogues require the application of the principle of symmetry to the dialogues and sharing some common ground and mutual recognition of each other's strengths and weaknesses.

Liebowitz, Jay and Mata-Toledo, Ramon A. Expert System Evaluation: A Review and Integrative Model. *Commun Cog—AI*, 11(3), 297-321, 1994.

As expert systems become more commonplace worldwide and as mission critical applications of expert systems increase in number, the importance of performing verification and validation (V&V) of the expert system is paramount. The expert system V&V community worldwide is fairly small. More careful attention needs to be placed on expert system V&V methodologies and practices. The expert system V&V community needs to be much larger than its current size. More resources have to be put into testing and evaluation of expert systems. Management needs to be less ignorant of the need for proper testing of expert systems. This paper will review some of the leading work in verification and validation of conventional and expert system software, and will discuss an integrative model that may be useful in evaluating expert systems.

Liendo, María Cristina. "Para Pensar Latinoaméerica" in *Temas Actuales de Filosofía, Palacios, María Julia (ed)*, 327-332. Buenos Aires, Univ Nacional Salta, 1993.

I want to state some questions with reference to the matter about the philosophy in Latin América understood as an existential function: 1) Which patterns could rule the Latin American thought in its formal expression to reach the category of original philosophy? 2) How should we include the American ethnic diversities taken as a social basis to the philosophical task? Postulating the preeminence of the action above the rule for the former, and the desontologization of the Indian for the latter, these answers spread themselves as a project of philosophical action and as critic of the postulates around which that action is developed.

Liessmann, Konrad Paul. *Ohne Mitleid: Zum Begriff der Distanz als ästhetische Kategorie mit ständiger Rücksicht auf Theodor W Adorno*. Vienna, Passagen, 1991.

Lange Zeit galten Kunst und Ästhetik als der aufklärerischen Humanitätsidee verschwistert—vor allem in der deutschen Philosophie. Noch bei Adorno soll Kunst Erscheinungsform von Wahrheit sein, die Utopie eines besseren Lebens offen halten. Die Arbeit von Konrad Liessmann stellt solche Affinitäten zwischen Kunst, Gesellschaft und Philosophie radikal in Frage. Das Schöne, so seine These, ist asozial und erbarmungslos—weil es ihm nur um das Schöne geht. Die eigentlichen Zentralbegriffe aller Ästhetik sind deshalb: *Distanz, Kälte, Schweigen*. (edited)

Lievers, Menno. Individu, identiteit, soort. *Alg Ned Tijdschr Wijs*, 86(4), 306-320, O 94.

This article is an extensive critical discussion of J van Leeuwen's work *Individuals and Sortal Concepts*. The main positive claim of the review article is that identity is a central issue in the debate between realists like Michael Ayers and linguistic idealists like Dummett. The article contains a brief outline of that debate and the main positions taken in that debate. It also recommends to distinguish carefully between a criterium of identity and a principle of individuation.

Light, Steve. Philosophical Disappointment: Introduction. *Int Stud Phil*, 26(4), 101-104, 1994.

Lijmbach, Susanne. "Potter's Bull and Castrated Pigs: Considering the Impossibility of a Hermeneutic Natural Science" in *Ecology, Technology, and Culture,* Zweers, Wim (ed), 127-134. Cambridge, White Horse, 1994.

The idea is criticized that a hermeneutical understanding of the intrinsic value of nature is opposed to technological knowledge of the instrumental value of nature. Hermeneutical knowledge is not knowledge of the intrinsic value of other beings, but knowledge within a common horizon of understanding, which is problematic with regard to nonhumans. The conclusion of this article is, that, in order to understand hermeneutically nonhuman nature, we have to clarify our own experiences and treatments of nature, for instance of laboratory animals as instruments as well as beings who are able to be in pain.

Lima, Joseph. Hannah Arendt and the Question of Mass Society. *Conference*, 3(2), 89-105, Fall 92.

Lima, María Herrera. Los ejemplos literario en la filosofia moral: Comentario al trabajo de Osvaldo Guariglia. *Rev Latin de Filosof*, 20(2), 319-326, 1994.

Limper, Peter. Albert Bormann and John Dewey on Everyday Technology. *Res Phil Technol*, 14, 27-43, 1994.

A comparison of John Dewey's discussion of technology with that in Albert Borgmann's *Technology and the Character of Contemporary Life* reveals interesting similarities. Like Borgmann, Dewey holds that modern technological society is deeply flawed by a separation of means and ends, which reveals itself in everyday activities such as work and leisure. However, Dewey's methodology for the criticism and reform of technology and his underlying social and metaphysical assumptions differ from Borgmann's in a number of ways. Dewey's anticipation of key aspects of Borgmann's influential analysis suggests the continuing relevance of Dewey's thought for the critique of technological society.

Lind, Douglas. Kant on Capital Punishment. *J Phil Res*, 19, 61-74, 1994.

Kant maintains that retribution is the only morally sound justification for criminal punishment. He claims that all just criminal punishment must conform to the "principle of equality," an inflexible juridical rule which takes the form of a categorical imperative. Focusing on his further claim that the principle of equality establishes that capital punishment is the only suitable punishment for murder, I question Kant's contention that the principle of equality is a categorical imperative. Following two lines of inquiry drawing upon the nature of a categorical imperative, I suggest that the principle of equality is a principle conditioned by experience, a hypothetical imperative which Kant only shows to be consistent with, not necessarily mandated by, the idea of a just civil state.

Lindemann, Kate. Philosophy of Liberation in the North American Context: Transforming Oppressor Consciousness. *Phil Cont World*, 1(2), 25-32, Sum 94.

This paper utilizes concepts from the works of Paulo Freire and other Latin American philosophers of liberation to formulate a philosophy of liberation in a North American context. Since many North Americans experience a double consciousness, that is, both oppressor and oppressed consciousness, our liberating task is quite complex. This study offers both a philosophical framework and an example of the process of demythologizing one aspect of North American consciousness, the consciousness of privilege.

Lindenfeld, Jacqueline. Cognitive Processes and Social Norms in Natural Discourse at the Marketplace. *J Prag*, 22(5), 465-476, N 94.

This study constitutes a preliminary attempt to begin answering the following question: how can we hope to reconcile two seemingly opposite views of natural discourse, namely one which focuses on cognitive processes and underlying knowledge structures, and another which focuses on the participants' 'social construction of reality' through ongoing interactive processes? The focus in this paper is on one particular dimension of communicative competence which relates to both models, namely the interactants' ability to deal with changeable goals during a conversation. (edited)

Lindley, D V and Johnstone, D J. Bayesian Inference Given Data 'Significant at α': Tests of Point Hypothesis. *Theor Decis*, 38(1), 51-60, Ja 95.

In empirical research in the social sciences expressions of statistical significance are meant to capture and summarize the evidence implied by data. To evaluate the evidential content of statements such as 'the difference between means in significant at $\alpha = 5\%$', we consider the Bayesian probability of the hypotheses tested, where the conditioning event is an announcement of general form *significant at* α. By proceeding as if neither observed effects nor their exact *P*-values are reported, the meaning of such descriptions *of themselves* is revealed. It is demonstrated, for large samples particularly, that a report merely that data are *significant at* α has no objective meaning, and under some conditions should be interpreted not as evidence against the null hypothesis, as is usually supposed, but as strong evidence in its favor. This conclusion is supported by both algebraic arguments and example calculations for the special, but important case of the normal mean. It is also found that significance at one level tends to imply significance at much lower levels, the more strongly the larger the sample.

Lindner, Konrad. "Auf der Suche nach einer 'Metaphysik der Natur'" in *Naturzweckmässigkeit und ästhetische Kultur, Schwabe, Karl-Heinz (ed)*, 151-165. Sankt Augustin, Academia, 1993.

Lindner, Konrad. Pölitz und Schelling: Ein unbekannter Brief aus dem Stadtgeschichtlichen Museum Leipzig. *Fichte-Studien*, 5, 175-188, 1993.

Im Stadtgeschichtlichen Museum Leipzig wird ein Brief aufbewahrt, der über die regionalgeschichtliche Bedeutung hinaus die Aufmerksamkeit der Spezialisten für die Wirkungsgeschicte Fichtes und Schellings verdient. Es handelt sich um ein Schreiben von Karl Heinrich Ludwig Pölitz (1772-1838) an den Buchhändler Gottfried Christoph Härtel (1756-1827) vom 7. August 1804. Insbesondere der Schelling-Forschung werden mit diesem Dokument einige unerwartete Fragen gestellt, zumal die Kommunikation des jungen Schelling mit kursächsischen Partnern noch immer eine terra incognita in den archivalischen Nachforschungen zur deutschen Geistesgeschichte ist. Der Dokumentation des Briefes von Pölitz stellen wir einige ausführlichere Bemerkungen voran. Vor allem wollen wir die geistige Persönlichkeit von Pölitz etwas beleuchten. Dabei lassen wir uns von der folgenden Hypothese leiten: Die Universitäts- und Buchstadt Leipzig gehörte in den beiden Jahrzehnten nach dem Erscheinen von Kants *Kritik der reinen Vernunft* (1781) zu jenen Regionen, von denen in Deutschland für den Diskurs über die kritische Philosophie wichtige Anregungen ausgingen.

Lindsay, R O and Gorayska, Barbara. On Putting Necessity in Its Place. *J Prag*, 23(3), 343-346, Mr 95.

A response to Mey's (J Prag, 23(3) 341-342) critique of the proposal that objects are relevant when they form part of a plan which is sufficient to achieve a goal, and irrelevant when they do not. Mey argues that an object is irrelevant when it fails to figure in a *necessary* plan. It is replied that the term "necessary plan" has no useful application. Necessity applies to sets of plan elements not plans themselves. Redundant plan elements are not relevant to the goal of a plan, but usually plans require any member of a functional equivalence set, not some particular element.

Lindström, Sten and Rabinowicz, Wlodzimierz. The Ramsey Test Revisited. *Theoria*, 58(2-3), 131-182, 1992.

Lingis, Alphonso F. Death Drive. *J Value Inq*, 29(2), 217-229, Je 95.

Contemporary culture, making all things present in images, and engendering images that are images of images, engenders a body of pure appearance to inhabit it, a Nietzschean body made entirely of veils, surfaces, masks, and masquerade, a body made of femininity and seduction. But our bodies, which experience themselves as simulacra, now need and use the touch of death compulsively as the sole means of making contact with reality. In this body a death drive functions to connect it with reality. Not simply annihilation, but overkill is the new characteristic of all the destructive machines of our time.

Lingis, Alphonso F. In Orbit. *J Soc Phil*, 25(3), 165-180, Wint 94.

In advanced postindustrial postindustrious societies today, citizens are required not as producers but as consumers. A new material culture now exists, in which individuals construct their identity and worth, and form associations with others, with personal collections of mass-produced consumer goods. But does the mass-production of consumer goods alone satisfy an ever-growing world population? What kind of sense of identity and worth can be constructed in material culture?

Link, Godehard. "Generic Information and Dependent Generics" in *The Generic Book, Carlson, Gregory N (ed)*, 358-382. Chicago, Univ of Chicago Pr, 1995.

Linker, Damon. Machiavelli, Harrington, and the Character of Modern Utopia. *Conference*, 3(2), 15-28, Fall 92.

Liske, Michael-Thomas. Ist eine reine Inhaltslogik möglich? Zu Leibniz' Begriffstheorie. *Stud Leibniz*, 26(1), 31-55, 1994.

If every concept is not, in trivial terms, to have a content, then the content of a concept has to be understood as the set of all concepts that it contains, the concept itself and the tautological concept being expected. Since a negated concept can only include, in terms of content, the negations of the special concepts, the negated individual concepts are consequently without content (and therefore also the negate general concepts that have these individual concepts as content). The individual concept whose content is the sufficient condition for establishing a possible individual as extension, is indispensable if Leibniz's theses are to be upheld: equality of extent is also always equality of content. The intensional conceptual estimation can also be extensionally interpreted. Conceptual negations are however indispensable if a Spinozistic monism is to be avoided and a multitude of the most general (but not lacking content) elementary concepts obtained.

Liske, Michael-Thomas. Veranlasste die Universalienlehre Ockham, die Prädikation zuletzt ohne ein intentionales Moment zu verstehen?. *Theol Phil*, 69(4), 511-536, 1994.

Ockham first regarded mental universals as entities of their own right, formed by the intellect as a likeness of reality (fictum), which exist as objects of thinking (esse obiectivum), afterwards he took them for acts of intellection. Does this change also mean, that predication is now considered in a pure extensional way? Is the genuine universal, which must be understood intensionally as a universal content of mind, entirely eliminated? Are there remaining only general rules, how to operate with signs for and with classes of similar individuals (class: mereologically understood as a concrete whole).

List, Peter C. "Some Philosophical Assessments of Environmental Disobedience" in *Philosophy and the Natural Environment, Attfield, Robin (ed)*, 183-198. New York, Cambridge Univ Pr, 1994.

The purpose of this essay is to consider how well two well-known philosophical theories about the nature and justifications of civil disobedience apply to the ethical reasoning underlying the use of more uncompromising ecotactics. The theories of John Rawls and Carl Cohen are matched up against two examples of environmental disobedience, specifically logging protests in an old-growth forest and ramming drift-net boats on the ocean, and found to be only partially illuminating. In brief, Rawls' account fails to adequately consider the environmental ethics of disobedients in generating conclusions about the political morality of their actions; Cohen's theory establishes too strict an intellectual standard for justifying those actions. It is suggested that ecological moralities make better sense of the factual circumstances and the important ethical considerations in these cases.

Little, Miles. *Humane Medicine: A Leading Surgeon Examines What Doctors Do, What Their Patients Expect from Them, and How the Expectations of Both Are Not Being Met*. New York, Cambridge Univ Pr, 1995.

There is increasing public distrust of medicine. The reasons for this lie partly in the structure of medical epistemology. Science underpins most of medicine's progress in physical treatment, but much medical practice is based on inductive inference. This book examines the clinical encounter (using a Popperean model), the impact of authority in medicine and medical research and the difficulties of probabilism in medicine. Neither more science nor better ethics can solve medicine's problems. Hermeneutics promises more than either. Medical education can be restructured to preserve the science, while radically emphasising the value-laden aspects of medicine.

Liu, Chuang. The Aharonov-Bohm Effect and the Reality of Wave Packets. *Brit J Phil Sci*, 45(4), 977-1000, D 94.

The objective of this paper is to show that, instead of quantum probabilities, wave packets are physically real. First, Cartwright's recent argument for the reality of quantum probabilities is criticized. Then, the notion of 'physically real' is precisely defined and the difference between wave functions and quantum probabilities clarified. Being thus prepared, some strong reasons are discussed for considering the wave packet to be physically real. Finding the reasons inconclusive, I explain how the Aharonov-Bohm effect delivers the final punch. I conclude that wave packets are the quantum objects that underlie the indeterministic quantum processes and have the propensity of displaying probabilistic (or indeterministic) behavior.

Liu, Shu-Hsien. Reflections on World Peace through Peace among Religions—A Confucian Perspective. *J Chin Phil*, 22(2), 193-213, Je 95.

A symposium on world religions and human rights was held in Paris, 1989. Hans Küng presented his views on the theme from a Christian perspective, his article was entitled: "Kein Weltfriede ohne Religionsfriede" (no world peace without peace among religions). Scholars from other religious traditions such as Islamism, Judaism, Confucianism, Buddhism, and Hinduism were asked to give their response to his views. I had responded from a Confucian perspective. The world situation has changed a great deal since then, further reflections on the problem are certainly needed. I firmly believe that creative interpretation of the Neo-Confucian idea *li-i-fen-shu* (one principle, many manifestations) can shed some light on possible solution of the difficult problem we have to face today.

Liubomirova, Nataly. Identificational Recruit: Between the Temptation of Nihilism and a Tie-In with the Body. *Hist Euro Ideas*, 20(1-3), 537-544, Ja 95.

Livingston, Paisley. What is Mimetic Desire?. *Phil Psych*, 7(3), 291-305, 1994.

This essay provides a conceptual analysis and reconstruction of the notion of mimetic desire, first proposed in Girard (1961). The basic idea behind the idea of mimetic desire is that imitation can play a key role in human motivational processes. Yet mimetic desire is distinguished from related notions such as social modelling and imitation. In episodes of mimetic desire, the process in which the imitative agent's desires are formed is oriented by a particular species of belief about the model or mediator whose desire is copied. These 'tutelary beliefs' essential to mimetic desire are distinguished from the 'thin' and purely instrumental beliefs about the model central to Bandura's (1986) social cognitive theory and similar models of observational learning. The problem of the identity of the objects of desire in episodes of social modelling motivates a distinction between internal and external forms of interpersonal mediation. Girard's claims about cognitive constraints associated with mimetic desire are examined, and scenarios of reciprocal mimetic modelling are analyzed.

Liwen, Zhang. Reflections on Song-Ming *Lixue* and the Philosophy of Harmony and Integration. *J Chin Phil*, 21(3-4), 453-470, S-D 94.

Song-Ming Lixue can be divided into three schools: namely Cheng-Zhu Lixue, Lu-Wang Xinxue, and Qixue (ZhangZai to WangFuzhi). Modern New Confucians connected with and succeeded Song Ming Lixue, creating three new doctrines: New Lixue (Feng Youlan), New Xinxue (HeLin), and New Qixue (Zhang Dainian). Now, the "new doctrines" have become out-of-date. Chinese philosophy shouts to new patterns. Confronted with five large conflicts between man and nature, man, society, mind, and civilization, the writer advances a new theory—philosophy of harmony and integration (Hehexue). Harmony and integration (Hehe) is the quintessence of Chinese humanism. Philosophy of harmony and integration is believed to be the best alternative for humanity in the 21st century.

Liz, Manuel. Meaning, Realism, and the Rejection of Analyticity. *Sorites*, 51-80, Ap 95.

There is a widespread view in philosophy of language and in philosophy of mind according to which the <quinean> rejection of analyticity can be made compatible with some sort of realism about meaning. Against such compatibilist claim, Paul Boghossian (1993) has recently held the thesis that one cannot coherently reject the analytical/synthetical distinction maintaining at the same time a meaning realism. His arguments are very pervasive, but they can be replied. The main objective of this paper is to show that in fact it is possible to reject analyticity being at the same time a meaning realist, even a meaning realist of a non-holist kind. The prevailing view is basically right. Moreover, it is possible to go on maintaining the compatibilist claim in its most radical form. In short, even if we adopt a non-holist meaning realism, we must reject analyticity because language is always conceptually motivated and engaged with reality. There is no linguistic arbitratiness. That forces us to go far from classical conceptions of meaning and to have a much more pluralistic one. With respect to it, for instance, to say that some statements are true once their meanings are fixed would not entail the theory are true by virtue of meanings. The problem to get such a conception of meaning remains open. However, the reasons against analyticity do not force us to any irreductible meaning holism.

Lizalde, Carlos Lorenza. Nota Sobre la Poesía Algorítmica de Ramón Llull. *Rev Espan Filosof Med*, 0, 95-103, 1993.

Llano, Alejandro. "Being as True" According to Aquinas. *Acta Phil*, 4(1), 73-82, 1995.

Una corrente forte della filosofia contemporanea propone l'analisi linguistica come la nuova "*philosophia prima*". Questa proposta si basa sulle tesi che il senso principale di *ens* sia *verum*, e che lo studio proprio della verità sia l'analisi formale delle proposizioni. Nella filosofia realista di Aristotele e Tommaso d'Aquino, il *verum* è un senso *distinto* di *ens*, senza però esserne il senso principale. La dottrina tommasiana sulla verità concorda con la filosofia analitica nel situare la verità nel giudizio. Ma per Tommaso la verità del giudizio non si può trovare, né spiegare, a livello dell'analisi formale; il giudizio vero e il giudizio falso sono ugualmente giudizi, ma non ugualmente veri. E soltanto la nozione della verità come corrispondenza con la cosa —che non è affatto una *somiglianza* alla cosa—che spiega perché la verità appartiene propriamente al giudizio. Ciò vuol dire che fare del *verum* il senso principale di *ens* è fraintendere la natura della verità stessa.

Llano, Carlos. Cuatro conceptos para un pensamiento no ilustrado (analogía, otredad, empatía y epimeleia). *Topicos*, 4(6), 117-155, 1994.

The author shows how the multiform (and nevertheless, articulated) richness of reality, which has been forgotten by univocalist thinking of Enlightenment, was a central theme in Aristotelian philosophy by the noetic concept of *analogy*, and it also appears under the name of *analogy* and *otherness* in the poetical thinking of Octavio Paz and Antonio Machado; in the anthropological phenomenon of *empatia*, as it is conceived by Edith Stein; and under the Greek concept of *epimeleia* in social science.

Llewelyn, John (ed). *Emmanuel Levinas: The Genealogy of Ethics*. New York, Routledge, 1995.

Against the background of Nietzsche's genealogy of morals and "the death of God" Levinas's writings are analyzed in more or less chronological order. Their topics are treated as moments of a turn from ontological claustrophobia to ethical agoraphobia, repeating the catastrophic history of the passion of Israel from captivity in Egypt through its puberty at Auschwitz.

Llosa-Vasquez, Vincenzo. L'Etre et les Sciences. *Philosopher*, 14, 75-85, 1993.

Lloyd, Dan. Connectionist Hysteria: Reducing a Freudian Case Study to a Network Model. *Phil Psychiat Psych*, 1(2), 69-88, Je 94.

Connectionism—also known as parallel distributed processing, or neural network modeling—offers promise as a framework to unite clinical and cognitive psychology, and as a tool for studying conscious and unconscious mental activity. This paper describes a neural network model of the case study of Lucy R, from Freud and Breuer's *Studies on Hysteria*. Though very simple in architecture, the network spontaneously displays analogues of repression and hallucination, corresponding to Lucy R's symptoms. In the case of Lucy R, Freud's theoretical inference regarding active but unconscious thought is not required by his data. Instead, the unconscious can be understood as a set of complex dispositions embodied in connections between elements of conscious experience. (edited)

Lloyd, Dan. Consciousness: A Connectionist Manifesto. *Mind Mach*, 5(2), 161-185, My 95.

Connectionism and phenomenology can mutually inform and mutually constrain each other. In this manifesto I outline an approach to consciousness based on distinctions developed by connectionists. Two core identities are central to a connectionist theory of consciousness: conscious states of mind are identical to occurrent activation patterns of processing units; and the variable dispositional strengths on connections between units store latent and unconscious information. Within this broad framework, a connectionist model of consciousness succeeds according to the degree of correspondence between the content of human consciousness (the world as it is experienced) and the interpreted content of the network. Constitutive self-awareness and reflective self-awareness can be captured in a model through its ability to respond to self-reflexive information, identify self-referential categories, and process information in the absence of simultaneous input. The qualitative "feel" of sensation appears in a model as states of activation that are not fully discriminated by later processing. Connectionism also uniquely explains several specific features of experience. The most important of these is the superposition of information in consciousness—our ability to perceive more than meets the eye, and to apprehend complex categorical and temporal information in a single highly-cognized glance. This superposition in experience matches a superposition of representational content in distributed representations.

Lluch-Baixauli, Miguel. Razón e Intelecto en Boecio. *Rev Espan Filosof Med*, 0, 105-110, 1993.

Lobato, Abelardo. Fenomenología y metafísica. *Aquinas*, 37(2), 335-352, My-Ag 94.

Professor A Lobato, after an analysis of the content and significance in the totality of Edith Stein's Thought, of her work entitled "The Search of the Truth: From Phenomenology to Christian Philosophy", published in Italian by Città Nuova, 1993, proposes two problems for discussion: the philosophical validity of the itinerary of Stein's towards Christian philosophy something which Husserl rejected, and the possibility of the passage from phenomenology to metaphysics, from immanence to transcendence. This is a crucial problem which Stein resolves positively. Lobato proposes the hypothesis of a possible inspiration Stein could have found in Thomas Aquinas, Disputed Questions, On Truth, q. 1, 9; q, 10, 8.

Lochhead, Judy. Hearing New Music: Pedagogy from a Phenomenological Perspective. *Phil Music Educ Rev*, 3(1), 34-42, Spr 95.

Lockhart, Robert S and Gick, Mary L. "Cognitive and Affective Components of Insight" in *The Nature of Insight, Sternberg, Robert J (ed)*, 197-228. Cambridge, MIT Pr, 1995.

The cognitive and affective properties and processes of insight are discussed within a theoretical framework of problem solving in cognitive psychology. Insight involves properties of a period of incomprehension, often frustrating and perplexing, that is followed by a sudden transition to a state of understanding. The initial incomprehension is often the result of a failure to retrieve a concept from memory, or construct a new concept, needed to solve the problem. Once successfully accessed or constructed, the concept yields very rapid comprehension. Applications to the understanding of jokes, the solving of riddles and puzzles, and scientific discoveries are discussed.

Lockwood, Michael. "Identity Matters" in *Medicine and Moral Reasoning, Fulford, K W M (ed)*, 60-74. New York, Cambridge Univ Pr, 1994.

Lockwood, Michael. "Issues of Unity and Objectivity" in *Objectivity, Simulation and the Unity of Consciousness*, Peacocke, Christopher (ed), 89-95. New York, Oxford Univ Pr, 1994.

Lockwood, Michael. Human Identity and the Primitive Streak. *Hastings Center Rep*, 25(1), 45, Jan-Feb 95.

Locurto, Charles and Freeman, Mark. Radical Behaviorism and the Problem of Nonshared Development. *Behavior Phil*, 22(1), 1-21, Spr-Sum 94.

New findings emerging from developmental behavior genetics indicate that individuals living in the same family develop in ways that make them remarkably different from each other despite the commonalities of shared genes and shared environments. These findings suggest that there are important factors residing within families that are not shared by family members that are nevertheless influential in development. The most discussed of these influences has been called "nonshared environment", meaning environmental influences that operate within families and that are uniquely experienced by particular family members. In this paper we explore the nature of nonshared influences on development, develop a set of criteria that any theoretical approach must incorporate to deal effectively with the development of individuality in light of these new findings, and offer an analysis of the extent to which these criteria can be incorporated by an established theory of environmental influence: radical behaviorism.

Lodzinski, Don. Empty Time and the Eternality of God. *Relig Stud*, 31(2), 187-195, Je 95.

The present paper defends Augustine's claim that time is ontologically dependent on the world. My proof is accomplished by establishing two sub-proofs. First, I argue that time requires change by criticizing Shoemaker's argument for the counterclaim that time does not require change. Second, I go on the show that there is no source of change apart from the created universe. I conclude that if we grant the traditional theistic assumption that the created universe has a beginning and an end, then since time is ontologically dependent on the world, time cannot extend from the infinite past into the infinite future, then a temporal God has a beginning and endures for only a finite period of time. This implausible consequence gives us reason to believe that God is eternal.

Lodzinski, Don. Leibnizian Freedom and Superessentialism. *Stud Leibniz*, 26(2), 163-186, 1994.

The present paper consists of three basic components. First, since Mondadori and others have argued that Leibniz was a superessentialist, a brief sketch will be given of the doctrine of superessentialism in the context of Leibniz's overall theory. Second, I will examine the basic features of Leibniz's notion of freedom, especially as it is developed in Leibniz's mature work, the *Théodicée*. Finally, I will argue that this notion of freedom and the doctrine of superessentialism are incompatible. This conclusion lends some support to the view that Leibniz was not a superessentialist.

Loeb, Don. Full-Information Theories of Individual Good. *Soc Theor Pract*, 21(1), 1-30, Spr 95.

Full-information theories of individual good appeal to us because of the way they seem to accommodate two powerful intuitions, one motivational and the other epistemic. The motivational intuition is a version of *internalism*. Full-information theories typically characterize a person's good in terms of her actual or potential motivations. The epistemic intuition is that our informed motivations are improvements over our uniformed ones. I examine two contrasting and highly sophisticated full-information theories, those of Richard Brandt and Peter Railton, arguing that such theories are untenable because they fail to accommodate the two intuitions, and because the intuitions themselves are suspect.

Loeb, Paul S. Is There a Genetic Fallacy in Nietzsche's Genealogy of Morals?. *Int Stud Phil*, 27(3), 125-141, 1995.

This paper criticizes the following three-part strategy, employed by Alexander Nehamas and others, for rebutting the charge of a genetic fallacy: In fact, 1) Nietzsche does not claim that his genealogical results prove the disvalue of moral values; of course, 2) If Nietzsche had claimed this, he would have to admit to committing the genetic fallacy; but 3) Nietzsche himself exposes the unacceptability of such an argument. As an alternative rebuttal, this paper suggests that the genetic-fallacy charge begs Nietzsche's question of the value of moral values.

Loeb, Stephen E. Ethics and Accounting Doctoral Education. *J Bus Ethics*, 13(10), 817-828, O 94.

This paper expands the literature on accounting ethics education by considering the teaching of ethics in accounting doctoral education. Some of the ethical issues that might be addressed in accounting doctoral education are reviewed. A number of matters relating to teaching ethics to accounting doctoral students are considered. The paper concludes with a summary and some final remarks.

Löhr, Gebbhard. *Das Problem des Einen und Vielen in Platons "Philebos"*. Göttingen, Vandenhoeck, 1990.

The purpose of the book is to find an explanation for the first of the metaphysical passages in Plato's dialogue *Philebos*. The problem Plato seems to be dealing with is how general terms, understood as *units*, can nevertheless be used for *many* particulars. Obviously Plato's solution makes use of the dihairesis-method. But in order to understand his solution it is necessary to find a new interpretation of this method itself. The second part of the book discusses the perennial problem of the status of the ideas in Plato's later philosophy and attempts an explanation for the fact that Plato seems not to make use of technical dihairesis in the classification of pleasures and forms of knowledge in the body of the dialogue.

Löhr, Gebbhard. *Gott—Gebote—Ideale: Analytische Philosophie und theologische Ethik*. Göttingen, Vandenhoeck, 1991.

Can morality be derived from the will of God? The author develops his own model for the relationship between morality and theistic belief. His idea is to understand morality not primarily as a matter of commandments and interdictions but as having to do with one's self-ideal. Self-ideals can be informed by religious belief; in this way it seems possible to combine autonomous morality with belief in God. The book provides an overview of important issues in current debates between theology and

ethical theory. Fundamental concepts of contemporary ethics are examined such as forgiveness, supererogation and moral luck. The author stresses the necessity of rational justification also for seemingly "good" deeds such as an act of forgiveness or supererogation.

Lönne, Karl-Egon. Storia e Politica nel Pensiero di Benedetto Croce. *G Crit Filosof Ital*, 73(2-3), 226-237, My-D 94.

Löw-Beer, Martin. Sind wir einzigartig? Zum Verhältnis von Selbstbewusstsein und Individualität. *Deut Z Phil*, 42(1), 121-139, 1994.

Löwith, Karl. *Mein Leben in Deutschland vor und nach 1933*. Frankfurt, Fischer Taschenbuch, 1989.

Löwith, Karl and Wolin, Richard (ed) and Steiner, Gary (trans). *Martin Heidegger and European Nihilism*. New York, Columbia Univ Pr, 1995.

Loewy, Erich H. Care Ethics: A Concept in Search of a Framework. *Cambridge Quart Healthcare Ethics*, 4(1), 56-63, Wint 95.

Löwy, Michael. Walter Benjamin and Marxism (in Portuguese). *Trans/Form/Acao*, 17, 7-13, 1994.

This article analyses the relationship between Benjamin and Marxism, without however failing to recognize that the philosophers' thought has at the same time two sides: one Marxist and another messianic.

Löwy, Michael and Varikas, Eleni. 'The World Spirit on the Fins of a Rocket': Adorno's Critique of Progress. *Rad Phil*, 70, 9-15, Mr-Ap 95.

Apart from a lecture given in 1962, Adorno never offered a "systematic" or detailed account of his views on progress. Nonetheless, the critique of "progressivist" illusions runs right through his work. It is central to his historical vision and decisively important in the development of his ideas in art, literature and culture. His writings are marked not so much by a vacillation between positive and negative judgments as by a true "dialectic of progress" which both draws upon and participates in the dialectic of Enlightenment. In spite of his melancholy and pessimism, he does not give up the hope in a future humankind emancipated from the fateful magic of interlocking "progress" and "regression".

Lofts, Steve. Husserl, Heidegger, Cassirer: Trois philosophies de crise. *Rev Phil Louvain*, 92(4), 570-584, N 94.

The philosophy of Husserl, Heidegger, and Cassirer is considered in the light of their interpretation of, and response to the "crisis". Each sees the "crisis" as in terms of a crisis in and of reason, logos. However, whereas Husserl is content to restore a traditional concept of reason, and whereas Heidegger only furnishes an essentially negative critique of "logo-centricism", it is Cassirer's philosophy of symbolic forms which, as the *media via* position, goes the furthest in addressing the crisis by its redefining our understanding of reason as *logos*. Cassirer shows that reason should be understood not as a monolithic unity, but rather as being comprised of a multiplicity of, what Foucault has called *épistémai* within the interior of reason itself.

Logan, George M (& other eds) and More, Thomas. *Utopia: Latin Text and English Translation*. New York, Cambridge Univ Pr, 1995.

Logsdon, Jeanne M. Software Piracy: Is It Related to Level of Moral Judgment?. *J Bus Ethics*, 13(11), 849-857, N 94.

The possible relationship between widespread unauthorized copying of microcomputer software (also known as software piracy) and level of moral judgment is examined through analysis of over 350 survey questionnaires that included the Defining Issues Test as a measure of moral development. It is hypothesized that the higher one's level of moral judgment, the less likely that one will approve of or engage in unauthorized copying. Analysis of the data indicate a high level of tolerance toward unauthorized copying and limited support for the hypothesis.

Logue, Gerald and Wear, Stephen. A Desperate Solution: Individual Autonomy and the Double-Blind Controlled Experiment. *J Med Phil*, 20(1), 57-64, F 95.

The randomization ingredient in double-blind controlled experiments may be objectionable to patients who, in their desperation, come to such trials seeking a last chance of cure. Minogue *et al*, who view such a situation as inherently exploitive and undermining of patient autonomy, propose that such "desperate volunteers" instead be enrolled in the active arm, while other patients, less desperate and more committed to medical progress, continue to be randomized. Their view is critiqued as destructive of medical progress, inappropriate in its lack of clinical response to such patients, and fatally flawed by unrealistic notions of autonomy and voluntariness.

Logue, James. *Projective Probability*. New York, Oxford Univ Pr, 1995.

Lohmann, Georg. Faktizität und "liberale Gemeinschaften". *Stud Phil (Switzerland)*, 53, 75-94, 1994.

Der Aufsatz untersucht die Frage, ob mit den Konzeptionen einer "liberal community" (z B, von Dworkin und Feinberg) die Probleme gelöst werden können, für die die Communitarians auf der Notwendigkeit von community bestehen. Dabei wird 1) der Begriff "community" relativ zu den sozialen Beziehungstypen von Interaktion, Organisation und Gesellschaft genauer definiert, und dann gezeigt, 2) dass auch für eine liberale Position es nicht sinnvoll ist, alle Gemeinschaftsbildungen zu liberalisieren, und 3) dass die Förderung bedrohter Gemeinschaften nicht mit Bezug auf eine "liberal community", sondern als verfassungsmässige, gerechte Regelung subjektiver Rechte angemessen begründet werden kann.

Loizzo, Joseph. Commentary on "Insight, Delusion, and Belief". *Phil Psychiat Psych*, 1(4), 241-242, D 94.

This commentary presents Gillett's view of insight as a partial Wittgensteinian solution to dualism in psychiatry. It reviews his argument that our problems accounting for insight stem from Kant and Descartes's views of knowledge as founded on independent subjects and objects. Gillett's model of insight as a learned social skill is then traced to Wittgenstein's account of language-learning. Its Wittgensteinian virtues are stressed: by basing self-knowledge on human interaction and the interaction of neural hardware with cultural software it avoids the dualistic pitfalls of constructivism and relativism. The commentary closes with a critique of Gillett's "holistic" reading of Wittgenstein, showing the Wittgenstein introduces a nondualistic psychology by reducing axioms of independent subjects and objects to absurdity with the definitive linguistic conventions of reason.

Lombraña, Julián Velarde. Filosofía del conocimiento y sistemas expertos. *El Basilisco*, 16, 51-64, Ap-Je 94.

London, Herb. The *Fin De Siècle* Redux. *Cont Phil*, 17(1), 2-3, Ja-F 95.

This paper argues that the *fin de sièle* of a century ago bears a striking resemblance to the current one, and that perhaps the only difference between them is the more extreme and therefore frightening character of the latter.

Lonergan, Bernard J F. Analytic Concept of History. *Method*, 11(1), 1-35, Spr 93.

Lonergan, Bernard J F. Method in Catholic Theology. *Method*, 10(1), 3-26, Spr 92.

Lonergan, Bernard J F. Philosophy and the Religious Phenomenon. *Method*, 12(2), 125-146, Fall 94.

Long, Ann. A Response to David Cockburn. *Philosophy*, 70(271), 119-121, Ja 95.

Long, Christopher Philip. Reluctant Transcendence: The Face to Face in Levinas' *Totality and Infinity*. *Conference*, 5(1), 19-34, Spr 94.

Long, Steven A. Yves Simon's Approach to Natural Law. *Thomist*, 59(1), 125-135, Ja 95.

Longino, Helen E. "The Fate of Knowledge in Social Theories of Science" in *Socializing Epistemology: The Social Dimensions of Knowledge, Schmitt, Frederick F (ed)*, 135-157. Lanham, Rowman & Littlefield, 1994.

While many of the claims about the philosophical implications of recent work in social studies of science are exaggerated, the empirical studies of laboratory interactions do challenge individualist biases in standard philosophical construals of scientific knowledge. This paper integrates results of the empirical sociological work with conceptual analysis to argue for the social character of observation and reasoning—cornerstones of philosophical accounts of justification. The new understanding of scientific knowledge that results is compared with traditional accounts of accounts of knowledge. On the social account, scientific knowledge is neither absolute and certain nor relative, but provisional, plural, and partial.

Longino, Helen E. Gender, Sexuality Research, and the Flight from Complexity. *Metaphilosophy*, 25(4), 285-292, O 94.

This essay briefly reviews the conceptual foundations of some recent attempts to demonstrate a biological etiology of sexual orientation. Apart from empirical shortcomings, these essays are notable for their assimilation of sexual orientation to sexual difference. Thus, homoeroticism is understood as possessing anatomical or physiological traits typical of the opposite sex. This is a symptom of the reductionism running throughout these studies which can be read as a collective refusal of the complexity of sexual life. This reductionism has parallel in the narrowness of philosophical discussions of human desire.

Longino, Helen E. In Search of Feminist Epistemology. *Monist*, 77(4), 472-485, O 94.

This paper rejects the view that claims about hypothesized "women's ways of knowing" would constitute a feminist epistemology, and urges that one think of feminist epistemology not as a particular content but as a kind of practice: "doing epistemology as a feminist". It offers as an example of such a practice the examination of normative claims made or implied in feminist critical analyses of science. Here one finds a set of theoretical virtues advanced that constitute an alternative to mainstream theoretical virtues. The elevation of these virtues as criteria of theoretical appraisal raises philosophical questions about their status and role. The discussion of such questions is one of a complex of activities that would constitute doing epistemology as a feminist.

Longuenesse, Béatrice. Logique et métaphysique dans le système critique: L'exemple de la causalité. *Bull Soc Fr Phil*, 88(2), 65-105, Jl-S 94.

The purpose of the paper is to show the importance of Kant's conception of logic in his exposition of the *problem* of causality, his formulation of the *principle* of causality, and his *proof* for this principle. The analysis of these points yields some striking results concerning the relation between synthetic a priori and analytic judgments, and concerning the relation between logic, psychology, and transcendental philosophy.

Longxi, Zhang. "Marxism: From Scientific to Utopian" in *Whither Marxism?, Magnus, Bernd (ed)*, 65-77. New York, Routledge, 1994.

Reversing Engels' *Socialism: From Utopian to Scientific*, this essay examines and rejects the claim of Marxism as the theory of scientific socialism. The limitations of Marxist political economy were noticed in the late 1960's by Western Marxists like Adorno, but it is the collapse of communism in the East since 1989 that has discredited Marxism as repressive social practice in China and the former Soviet Union, and destroyed the symbol of an alternative good society for the Left in the West. It is now Marx's utopian vision for an authentically human society that may yet sustain our interest in Marxism.

Lopes, Dominic. Pictorial Realism. *J Aes Art Crit*, 53(3), 277-285, Sum 95.

This paper examines a form of pictorial realism that has epistemic import. Gombrich and Schier claim that some pictures are realistic because they convey accurate information. The difficulty is that judgments of realism vary across cultural and historical contexts. Goodman counters that pictures belong to different systems and realistic pictures belong to familiar systems. However, this does not explain the 'revelatory realism' of pictures in novel systems. I propose that two views can be combined: a realistic picture is one which belongs to a system that conveys the kind of information that suits the needs of users in a context.

López Cerezo, J A and Sanmartín, J and González, M. Filosofía actual de la ciencia. *Dialogo Filosof*, 10(2), 164-208, My-Ag 94.

Después de 30 años tras la revolución kuhniana en filosofía de la ciencia es clara la necesidad de un estudio interdisciplinar de la ciencia. pero no se ve que sea posible el que la filosofía tenga algo que decir en tal marco interdisciplinar de análisis empírico. La tendencia general a la naturalización parece dejar fuera de juego a una disciplina, la filosofía, cuyo tradicional estilo normativo es muy difícil de asimilar. Con todo, la polémica continúa. En estas páginas se recoge, entre algunos otros

problemas, el enfrentamiento contemporáneo entre el racionalismo filosófico y el relativismo en la comprensión de la naturaleza de la ciencia.

López Fernández, Alvaro. Anticipación de la naturaleza y giro copernicano: La naturaleza de la explicación científica en Bacon y en Kant. *Dialogos*, 30(65), 49-73, Ja 95.

Notwithstanding its differences, Bacon's and Kant's philosophies of science are part of what can be called a logic of objective observation. Such a logic has, in Bacon, the name of *interpretation of nature* and is a methodology of objective observation of facts and description of forms. It is, in Kantian terminology, a propedeutic of the reflective judgement. Kant's logic, which does not represent any concrete proposal of scientific methodology, moves on a different level. It is a reflection about the transcendental conditions of possibility a priori of objective observation. These conditions pertain to Kant's famous *Copernican turn*.

López Frías, Francisco. La recepción del Utilitarismo en el mundo hispánico: El caso de Ortega y Gasset. *Telos (Spain)*, 1(3), 111-144, O 92.

López Molina, Antonio M. Trabajo e Interacción como Intereses Rectores del Conocimiento. *An Seminar Metaf*, 28, 103-120, 1994.

López Ruiz, Francisco. Fuentes del Derecho y del sistema jurídico. *El Basilisco*, 16, 65-68, Ap-Je 94.

López Ruiz, Isabel. Definición del Hombre en Términos de lo que Quiere Ser. *Analogia*, 7(1), 131-142, 1993.

López Vázquez, J Ramón. Fr Benito J Feijóo, profesor de filosofía escolástica. *Pensamiento*, 198(50), 457-469, S-D 94.

El análisis de un manuscrito inédito de Fr Benito J Feijóo sirve para rellenar un hueco dentro de la trayectoria vital y académica del benedictino. A su luz, se entienden mejor los arrepentimientos por haber sido y profesado como escolástico y, a la vez, se apuntan levísimos balbuceos de purturas e innovaciones, que serán los que definan su obra madura. Dar luz a un espacio oscuro, entender la necesidad de romper con la escolástica barroca y detectar los primeros síntomas de tal necesidad, precisamente en el manuscrito donde se profesa la escolástica, son las tres ideas de este breve apunte.

López Vázquez, J Ramón. La Función de la Intuición Ockhamista. *Rev Espan Filosof Med*, 0, 89-93, 1993.

The universal lacks of every kind of nature 'Physis'. Its being, amounts to nothing more than pure convention 'nomos'. The intuition ockhamista is a sensitive anthropological reality and, at the same time, intellectual. It serves to put in direct contact the singular subjects with the singular objects. To feel 'the sensitive seeing' and the intelligible, 'the mental seeing', are psychological activities respectively necessary; they constitute a sole and unique process of human knowledge and they offer a sole and unique known object. The function of the intuition ockhamista consists in eliminate and psychological and ontological duality as much in the subject that knows, as in the known object.

López-Domínguez, Virginia. Individuo y Comunidad: Reflexiones Sobre el Eterno Círculo Fichteano. *Daimon Rev Filosof*, 9, 211-227, 1994.

This article shows that Fichte's defense of individuality (the most radical among the idealists) descend from the illustrated problematic which, after Kantian framing, changes to the question of how to maintain the individual freedom opposite to the absolute. Fichte resolves this trouble in the GWL: 1) Admitting the indeducibility and irrationality of second principle and accepting it from the practice point of view; 2) Avoiding to turn the absolute I into metaphysic hypothesis, and this is the reason of his refusal to use the term "intellectual intuition"; 3) Converting the beginning of the particular human life (Anstoss) in a factum which doesn't admit further explanation. As a result of this, the representation genesis will be expressed in solipsistic terms, though the faith which Fichte refers to is a moral one, that goes in first place to the intelligible other intersubjective world. Also, after this monodism continues necessarily the socialization of the I by means of the material community that appears in GNR, where the body is considered as meeting point of human being.

López-Domínguez, Virginia. Muerte y Nihilismo en el Pensamiento de J G Fichte. *An Seminar Hist Filosof*, 11, 139-154, 1994.

This article analyses the accusation of nihilism that F H Jacobi made against Fichte in a letter of mars. 1799, imputation that lays on the personal conception of Jacobi about the reason as a negative capacity which only can destroy its objects. The letter in question implicates two different types of nihilism: 1) The cosmological one, accepted by Fichte and named acosmism by him. It is only a reformulation of the sensible world from practical principles, but doesn't suppose an annihilation or scorn of this world. On the contrary, the religious view, for example, shows the world as a manifestation of godlife and, based on moral exigencies, doesn't admit the existence of death. Of course, the immortality isn't for a particular soul but for the order of moral actions (=God). 2) The radical one, which doesn't exist in Fichte and lays on a bad interpretation of his intellectual intuition assumed from a point of view next to Schelling.

Loptson, Peter. Anne Conway, Henry More, and their World. *Dialogue (Canada)*, 34(1), 139-146, Wint 95.

This article is a critical notice of the second (revised) edition of Marjorie Hope Nicolson, ed., *The Conway Letters*. Nicolson collected, and joined with philosophically-informed narrative, letters of Anne Conway, Henry More, and their circle 1640-1676. The book, long out of print, appeared in 1930. Sarah Hutton has reedited the work, adding new letters, passages omitted in the earlier edition, and other texts, together with her own introduction. This is an important volume, historically and philosophically. Hutton's work involves some scholarly blemishes, mostly minor, but is otherwise useful and impressive. The present article also briefly assesses Conway and More philosophically.

Lorand, Ruth. The Concept of Order. *Iyyun*, 43, 305-327, Jl 94.

Order enters every aspect of life. Philosophy and science examine its various forms. Nevertheless, the concept itself has been neglected in the literature. This paper, which is a part of a larger project, offers an analysis of 'order', 'disorder' and their related concepts. Order expresses heterogeneity and it is quantitative, although not always measurable. Disorder is a state of homogeneity in probabilities which can take different forms: randomness, chaos, clash of orders, symmetry and atomism. The extreme poles: perfect order and perfect disorder, raise logical and practical problems. Notwithstanding, these poles serve as essential markers for understanding and evaluating experience.

Lorca, Andres Martinez. *Communitas Liberorum*: En Torno a *Sententia Libri Politicorum* de Tomás de Aquino. *Pensamiento*, 199(51), 89-100, Ja-Ap 95.

La *Política* de Aristóteles, de la que no se ha conservado ningún comentario griego y que no llegaron a concocer los filósofos árabes medievales, se difunde en Occidente gracias al comentario de Tomás de Aquino *Sententia libri Politicorum*. Por vez primera, los pensadores cristianos tuvieron que enfrentarse solos a una teoría política radicalmente opuesta a las doctrinas teocráticas hasta entonces imperantes. Fruto de esa apasionante lectura fue no sólo la creación de un lenguaje político que seguimos usando todavía, sino también la afirmación de una serie de principios que contienen el germen del moderno Estado democrático.

Lorca, Daniel. A Critique of Quentin Smith's Atheistic Argument from Big Bang Cosmology. *Philosophy*, 70(271), 39-51, Ja 95.

Lorenz, Chris. Historical Knowledge and Historical Reality: A Plea for "Internal Realism". *Hist Theor*, 33(3), 297-327, 1994.

In this article I argue that it is the task of philosophy of history to elucidate the *practice* of history. Therefore philosophy of history must stick to the analysis of the debates of *historians* and neither literary theory nor aesthetics can function as "models" for philosophy of history. This is so because historians present reconstructions of a past reality on the basis of factual adequacy. The fact that these discussions seldom lead to a consensus constitutes a basic feature of "doing history" to be analyzed by its philosophy. (edited)

Lorenz Daiber, Dietrich. Actualidad Bibliográfica de la Analogía y de sus Diversas Aplicaciones (I). *Analogia*, 5(2), 169-203, 1991.

Lorite Mena, J. Movimiento y acto en Aristóteles. *Pensamiento*, 197(50), 177-195, My-Ag 94.

La coherencia textual de la *Física* de Aristóteles parece imponer una simetría epistémica entre movimiento y acto, una equivalencia significativa que marcaría el recinto de comprensión de la *physis*. Y sin embargo, el acto desborda al movimiento fundativamente: tanto a nivel ontológico como a nivel cosmológico. Sólo un análisis de la ontología del movimiento permitiría comprender los diferentes niveles conceptuales que Aristóteles hace intervenir en su definición *física* del movimiento.

Lorite Mena, José. Es negociable la diferencia?. *Dialogo Filosof*, 11(1), 31-41, Ja-Ap 95.

Plantearse la realidad de la mujer en el marco del problema antropológico no se reduce a una cuestión reivindicativa de resonancias meramente política o ética, sino que, cuando se piensa a fondo, es todo el universo de la realidad, la historia, los parámetros de la "normalidad" humana lo que se pone en cuestión.

Lorraine, Tamsin. Nietzsche and Feminism: Transvaluing Women in *Thus Spoke Zarathustra*. *Int Stud Phil*, 26(3), 13-21, 1994.

Losito, William F. "Philosophizing about Education in a Postmodern Society" in *Identity, Culture, and Education, Smeyers, Paul (ed)*, 213-222. Leuven, Leuven Univ Pr, 1994.

Losonsky, Michael. "Locke on Meaning and Signification" in *Locke's Philosophy, Rogers, G A J (ed)*, 123-141. New York, Oxford Univ Pr, 1994.

The author argues against the view that Locke's theory of signification was not a theory of linguistic meaning and defends the traditional view that Locke is offering a semantic theory in his discussion of the signification of words.

Losonsky, Michael. Reasoned Freedom: John Locke and Enlightenment. *Can J Phil*, 25(2), 293-314, Je 95.

Losskij, Nikolaj O. Wesensmerkmale der russischen Philosophie. *Deut Z Phil*, 43(1), 55-62, 1995.

Losurdo, Domenico. "Selbstbewusstsein, falsches Bewusstsein, Selbstkritik des Abendlandes" in *Das geistige Erbe Europas, Buhr, Manfred (ed)*, 733-770. Napoli, Vivarium, 1994.

Celebrating Western Europe as a small island of liberty in the middle of an unbounded ocean of slavery, A Smith overlooks the trade in negro slaves carried on by the West itself, above all by liberal England. We are faced with an essential document of the false consciousness which characterizes the history of the West. It is not a matter of a posing picture of subdued colors in the traditional rosy historiography. The best page of the West have been written by those who have known how to achieve a self-critical consciousness. This self-critical consciousness has had an important role in the great revolutions which have heralded the birth of the contemporary world.

Lotito, Leonardo. Le radici romantiche della simbolica di Otto Weininger. *Filosofia*, 44(3), 433-455, S-D 93.

Lottenbach, Hans and Tenenbaum, Sergio. Hegel's Critique of Kant in the Philosophy of Right. *Kantstudien*, 86(2), 211-230, 1995.

There is general agreement among commentators that in the *Philosophy of Right* Hegel misunderstands important aspects of Kant's practical philosophy. It is often claimed that Hegel entirely misses the point of Kant's universal law test and the mode of its application. We argue that these charges rest on misreadings of the *Philosophy of Right* in which Hegel's conception of the will is not taken into account. We show that Hegel's critique of Kant can be defended if it is interpreted as arising in response to Kant's own question of how the self-determination of a rational will can have determinate content.

Louden, Robert B. On Pincoffs' Conception of Ethics. *J Phil Res*, 19, 9-22, 1994.

This essay focuses on Edmund Pincoffs's arguments in defense of virtue ethics and against ethical theory. His advocacy of virtue ethics hinges on the claims that: 1) the virtues are central to ancient ethics, modern ethics representing an unjustifiable change in orientation; 2) modern ethics is overly legalistic, construing morality merely as a set of universalistic action-guiding rules; 3) modern ethics is objectionably reductivistic, reducing morality to conscientiousness. Pincoffs's opposition to ethical theory is based on the claims that: 4) ethical theories are objectionably reductivistic (in numerous ways); 5) they exhibit an individualist bias which results in an indefensible abstractness; 6) they mistakenly assume that moral experts exist; 7) they lack justificatory power; 8) they are a modern invention toward which we should be skeptical. In my critical remarks concerning Pincoffs's positions, I argue (with numerous qualifications) against each of the above claims.

Loughran, Thomas. Freedom and Good in the Thomistic Tradition. *Faith Phil*, 11(3), 414-436, Jl 94.

Alasdair MacIntyre has presented an interpretation of the Thomistic tradition according to which moral principles are grounded in tradition-gathered wisdom concerning the good for human beings. In this essay I sketch a route to MacIntyre's conclusions departing from the kind of informed-desire analysis of good to which utilitarian moral philosophers have recently drawn attention. On the way, I identify two relativist challenges regarding the good so conceived—arising respectively from human cognitive limitations and from human freedom—and show how the Thomistic tradition has the resources to overcome them.

Louw, Dirk J. The Soteriocentrism of John Hick. *S Afr J Phil*, 14(1), 19-23, F 95.

John Hick claims that religious traditions can (at least in principle) be graded *objectively* according to their soteriological efficiency. For Hick this means that a religious tradition must be judged 'true' in so far as it promotes salvific transformation, that is in so far as it adheres to the so-called *Golden Rule*: grant another what you grant yourself. By applying this rule, Hick seeks to evade the 'absolutism' and 'imperialism' of exclusivism and inclusivism. However, a comparative study of the soteriologies of religious traditions shows that Hick's soteriological criterion does not respect the self-understanding of (at least some) religious traditions. He is therefore guilty of the very same absolutism and imperialism for which he criticizes.

Loux, Michael. "Composition and Unity: An Examination of *Metaphysics* H.6" in *The Crossroads of Norm and Nature, Sim, May (ed)*, 247-279. Lanham, Rowman & Littlefield, 1995.

Loux, Michael. "Understanding Process: Reflections on *Physics* III.1" in *The Crossroads of Norm and Nature, Sim, May (ed)*, 281-303. Lanham, Rowman & Littlefield, 1995.

Love, Nancy S. "What's Left of Marx?" in *The Cambridge Companion to Habermas, White, Stephen K (ed)*, 46-66. New York, Cambridge Univ Pr, 1995.

This article assesses Marx(ist) residues in Habermas's concept of "socialism-as-critique." I argue that, despite Habermas's increasingly liberal emphases, his concept of communicative rationality retains socialist intuitions and impulses. Habermas employs Marx(ist) concepts of alienation and reification to identify crisis potentials in late capitalism. He also continues to affirm a humanity that makes its history with conscious will. For Habermas, socialism persists as a "discourse-in-exile," as an affirmation of value(s) beyond equivalence. I conclude that what Habermas—with tragic irony—ultimately retains of Marx(ism) originates in Jewish mysticism.

Lovegrove, Hildegard and Langford, Peter E and Lovegrove, Malcolm N. Do Senior Secondary Students Possess the Moral Maturity to Negotiate Class Rules?. *J Moral Educ*, 23(4), 387-407, 1994.

Two studies are reported using written question sheets to assess attitudes to and moral reasoning about class rules among a total of 117 senior secondary school students and 87 trainee teachers. The studies confirmed the prediction of the multidimensional control model of the development of moral reasoning of Langford 1991a, b; 1992a, b) that the moral reasoning of such students about this topic is much more mature than predicted by Kohlbergian theory, their most important source of information for making moral decisions in this area being the general welfare of students and teachers. (edited)

Lovegrove, Malcolm N and Lovegrove, Hildegard and Langford, Peter E. Do Senior Secondary Students Possess the Moral Maturity to Negotiate Class Rules?. *J Moral Educ*, 23(4), 387-407, 1994.

Two studies are reported using written question sheets to assess attitudes to and moral reasoning about class rules among a total of 117 senior secondary school students and 87 trainee teachers. The studies confirmed the prediction of the multidimensional control model of the development of moral reasoning of Langford 1991a, b; 1992a, b) that the moral reasoning of such students about this topic is much more mature than predicted by Kohlbergian theory, their most important source of information for making moral decisions in this area being the general welfare of students and teachers. (edited)

Lovell, David W. Propositions on 'The End of Socialism?'. *Hist Euro Ideas*, 19(1-3), 271-277, Jl 94.

The current crisis of socialism was preceded by a protracted decline of confidence among socialists in their own analyses and solutions. Socialists can no longer rely on Marxism as a theoretical resource; socialism, it is argued here, must reevaluate more sympathetically its other currents. Three areas are surveyed: the market, democracy and identity. Each area represents an aspect of the socialist quest for human control over social and natural environments, the single-minded pursuit of which is self-defeating. If socialism is to be revived, it must be specific about the institutions it proposes and the values they are meant to serve.

Lovisolo, Jorge. "La Epistemología de las Ciencias Sociales: Sus Políticas Inexpresas" in *Temas Actuales de Filosofía, Palacios, María Julia (ed)*, 333-341. Buenos Aires, Univ Nacional Salta, 1993.

Lovitt, Harriet Brundage and Lovitt, William. *Modern Technology in the Heideggerian Perspective, Volume I*. Lewiston, Mellen Pr, 1994.

This study, drawing upon Heidegger's writings from *Being and Time* to the late works, has as its underlying intention the evidencing of a continuity of outlook in Heidegger's thinking as a whole. Heidegger's work is also seen here to evince pervasively a protrayal of reality according to a particular structuring, the authors show how the latter lends to that work throughout a discernibly systematic character.

Pursuance of the book's major theme, Heidegger's understanding of modern technology, entails inquiry into the full range of Heideggerian thinking. An orienting prologue is provided. The ensuing primary presentation comprises five main parts. The book closes with a critical appraisal, both positive and negative, of salient elements of Heidegger's thought as set forth in the preceding discussions. A topical summary opens and glossaries and an extensive index close the work. Copius cross references are given in numerous footnotes.

Lovitt, Harriet Brundage and Lovitt, William. *Modern Technology in the Heideggerian Perspective, Volume II*. Lewiston, Mellen Pr, 1995.

Lovitt, William and Lovitt, Harriet Brundage. *Modern Technology in the Heideggerian Perspective, Volume I*. Lewiston, Mellen Pr, 1994.

This study, drawing upon Heidegger's writings from *Being and Time* to the late works, has as its underlying intention the evidencing of a continuity of outlook in Heidegger's thinking as a whole. Heidegger's work is also seen here to evince pervasively a protrayal of reality according to a particular structuring, the authors show how the latter lends to that work throughout a discernibly systematic character. Pursuance of the book's major theme, Heidegger's understanding of modern technology, entails inquiry into the full range of Heideggerian thinking. An orienting prologue is provided. The ensuing primary presentation comprises five main parts. The book closes with a critical appraisal, both positive and negative, of salient elements of Heidegger's thought as set forth in the preceding discussions. A topical summary opens and glossaries and an extensive index close the work. Copius cross references are given in numerous footnotes.

Lovitt, William and Lovitt, Harriet Brundage. *Modern Technology in the Heideggerian Perspective, Volume II*. Lewiston, Mellen Pr, 1995.

Low, Douglas. Merleau-Ponty's Concept of Reason. *J Phil Res*, 19, 109-125, 1994.

In this paper I will provide a brief summary of Merleau-Ponty's philosophy as it is relevant to the concept of reason. Merleau-Ponty's position comes between the two now dominant views of reason: the traditional view that relies on principles of rationality(identity and noncontradiction) that are supposedly preexistent, either in a realm of ideas or in nature in itself, and the postmodern/deconstructionist view that claims that language is a system of differences with no positive terms, that the concepts of identity and presence are simply a creation of "deferring" language. For Merleau-Ponty the principle of identity (presence) is neither pregiven nor an arbitrary creation of language but has its roots in a bodily blending of lived perceptual perspectives, of the individual's within his or her own body and of the individual's with the perspectives of others. Merleau-Ponty's thesis thus allows us to escape the traditional error of accepting principles of reason as absolute and pregiven, for the blending of perspectives always remains to be accomplished, and it allows us to avoid the postmodernist claim that the principles of rationality are simply a creation of language, for in Merleau-Ponty's philosophy, language is a sublimation of the body's openness unto the world and others.

Low-Beer, F H. *Questions of Judgment: Determining What's Right*. Amherst, Prometheus, 1995.

The book examines the concept of judgment as *exercise*, an aspect that had received little attention since Aristotle. Under this aspect the author considers the use of "judgment" in the language as well as the judgmental function itself. The author distinguishes the exercise of judgment from related propositional attitudes. Within judgment he locates as ingredients the concepts of importance and appropriateness and concludes these subsidiary concepts are themselves central to cognition. In an interdisciplinary way, the book also discusses the critical role the exercise of judgment plays in the professions and other foundational social institutions.

Lowe, E J. The Truth about Counterfactuals. *Phil Quart*, 45(178), 41-59, Ja 95.

'If' is not ambiguous. The subjunctive/indicative distinction, as applied to conditionals, is of no logical importance. There is a single, unified logic of conditionals, and conditionals do, in general, have truth values. Conditionals of all types submit to a uniform analysis in modal terms, and such differences of interpretation as do arise can be attributed to differences in the species of modality invoked or to differing types of context-sensitivity.

Lowe, E J. Vague Identity and Quantum Indeterminacy. *Analysis*, 54(2), 110-114, Ap 94.

Standard quantum theory suggests that we can intelligibly countenance ontically indeterminate identity statements, contrary to the widespread philosophical opinion that vagueness must reside in our representations rather than in the world. Gareth Evans' supposed proof that no identity statement of the form *'a + b'* can be of indeterminate truth value contains a fallacious step violating a formal restriction which needs to be placed on the operation of property-abstraction.

Lowe, Scott. Teaching the Liberal-Communitarian Debate. *Teach Phil*, 18(1), 31-37, Mr 95.

An important topic in contemporary political philosophy is the challenge of communitarian critics to the dominant political philosophy of liberalism. Critics such as Sandel, MacIntyre and Taylor argue that liberalism misconstrues the relationship between the individual and society and emphasizes individual rights to the neglect of community interests. Many articles and books have appeared exploring this debate, and present important criticisms of liberalism that illuminate some of its deepest assumptions. In this paper I explain how I have incorporated the liberal-communitarian debate into my political philosophy course, and offer some suggestions about readings with which to approach this topic.

Lowen, Jeanette. How Can We Live in a World of the Absurd? The Humanism of Albert Camus. *Free Inq*, 14(4), 50-54, Fall 94.

Lowry, Atherton C. A Contemporary Challenge to Religion: The Question of Eternity. *Amer Cath Phil Quart*, 68(4), 529-543, Autumn 94.

Loy, David. Preparing For Something That Never Happens: The Means/ Ends Problem in Modern Culture. *Int Stud Phil*, 26(4), 47-68, 1994.

This paper reflects on the way contemporary culture has become so preoccupied with means that it loses ends—or rather they become inverted, in that end-less means have come to constitute our ends. It looks first at what Weber wrote about the rationalization and desenchantment of the modern world, and our reactive flights into innerworldly subjectivity. Simmel's *The Philosophy of Money* contains the most profound reflections on the means-ends split in modern culture. It also challenges our distinction between them. The conclusion considers how the Buddhist deconstruction of subject-object duality responds to this problem.

Lucas, Ramón Lucas. Cuerpo humano y visión integral del hombre. *Gregorianum*, 76(1), 125-146, 1995.

This essay explains in brief synthesis the most salient aspects of the philosophical anthropology of José Ortega y Gasset on the theme of corporality. Based on this, a reflection, is proposed on how to insert a theory of the body within an integral theory of man. The vision of man as an incarnate spirit leads to the philosophical foundation of those human values related to corporality, and to the conviction that the ethical aspects involved do not come from something extrinsic to man. The essay concludes with a reference to the positive evaluation of the body within Catholic Christianity.

Lucas Jr, George R. *Is* Hermeneutics 'Philosophy'? Interpretation and Overinterpretation of the Past. *Hist Euro Ideas*, 21(2), 177-194, Mr 95.

The title of this paper deliberately transforms Hans-Georg Gadamer's bold and well-known assertion that "hermeneutics *is* philosophy" into a question about the relationship of hermeneutics and philosophy. After the manner of G E Moore's "refutation" of idealism (1903), I propose to show that at many important junctures hermeneutics and philosophy are distinct, and that the mad rush of philosophers of all methodological persuasions into the hermeneutics camp is untenable.

Lucash, Frank. Essence and Existence in Part 3 of Spinoza's "Ethics". *Manuscrito*, 17(2), 11-29, O 94.

A number of difficulties arise in reading Book 3 of Spinoza's "Ethics". There appears to be a lack of a specific meaning of "power of activity". There is ambiguity concerning the meanings of the words "adequate" and "inadequate". The following questions need answering: How can the mind strive both in so far as it has adequate and inadequate ideas, being that the nature of the mind is to strive to preserve itself and increase in power? Is the essence of the mind really the idea of an actually existing body? Why would we want to change a passive emotion into an active emotion if there is nothing defective in nature? I propose to examine each of these difficulties by using the distinction between essence and existence given in Parts 1 and 2 of the "Ethics" and applying it to Part 3, which Spinoza did not always do or did not always do clearly.

Lucero, Susana. "Sobre la 'Falsación' del Falsacionismo" in *Temas Actuales de Filosofía, Palacios, María Julia (ed)*, 343-348. Buenos Aires, Univ Nacional Salta, 1993.

Luchte, James. Between Terrestriality and Aquacity: Miller's 'Limit Experience'. *Conference*, 4(1), 93-102, Spr 93.

Luckhardt, C Grant. Lion Talk. *Phil Invest*, 18(1), 1-12, Ja 95.

The standard interpretation of Wittgenstein's claim that humans couldn't understand a talking lion takes the animal to be speaking English (or another natural human language), and posits its unintelligibility as resulting from its radically strange form of life. Using various textual sources, I argue that these are misunderstandings, and that the remark has a very different and much more limited meaning that is closely linked to what Wittgenstein calls "find shades of behavior".

Ludlow, Peter. Externalism, Self-Knowledge, and the Prevalence of Slow Switching. *Analysis*, 55(1), 45-49, Ja 95.

Ludlow, Peter. Logical Form and the Hidden-Indexical Theory: A Reply to Schiffer. *J Phil*, 92(2), 102-107, F 95.

Ludlow, Peter. The Logical Form of Determiners. *J Phil Log*, 24(1), 47-69, F 95.

Ludwig, Kirk A. "Is Content Holism Incoherent?" in *Holism: A Consumer Update, Fodor, Jerry A (ed)*, 173-195. Amsterdam, Rodopi, 1993.

The doctrine of content holism is made precise, and distinguished from related doctrines, such as anatomism and molecularism about content, and meaning holism. While content holism entails both anatomism with respect to the property of having content, and meaning holism, neither of the latter doctrines entails content holism. Content holism, which holds that everyone must have a large number of psychological attitudes of any given type whose content are essentially interrelated, is shown to be self-contradictory in the light of our ordinary criterion for individuating attitude contents. The argument against content holism is defended against objections that its intended force or content has been incorrectly characterized.

Ludwig, Kirk A. Blueprint for a Science of Mind: A Critical Notice of Christopher Peacocke's *A Study of Concepts*. *Mind Lang*, 9(4), 469-491, D 94.

This article discusses Peacocke's program in *A Study of Concepts* for giving accounts of concepts in terms of their possession conditions, the application of the program to the systematicity of thought and the concept of belief, and its reconciliation with naturalism. Two main conclusions are reached: first, Peacocke has provided little reason to think that the program can be successfully carried out; second, the use of the notion of primitive compellingness in explaining how the account is naturalistically acceptable is incompatible with the motivation for introducing it to play a central in capturing what it is to possess a concept.

Ludwig, Kirk A. Trying the Impossible: Reply to Adams. *J Phil Res*, 20, 563-570, 1995.

This paper defends the autonomy thesis, which holds that one can intend to do something even though one believes it to be impossible, against attacks by Fred Adams. Adams denies the autonomy thesis on the grounds that it cannot, but must, explain what makes a particular trying, a trying for the aim it has a view. If the autonomy thesis were true, it seems that I could try to fly across the Atlantic ocean merely by typing out this abstract, a palpable absurdity. If we deny the autonomy thesis, we have an easy explanation: one simply cannot try to do something which one believes to be impossible. In response, I argue, first, by means of examples, that one clearly can try and intend to do what one believes to be impossible; and then I show how we can provide an answer to Adams's challenge even so.

Luebke, Neil R. Response to Michael Davis. *Bus Prof Ethics J*, 12(4), 47-50, Wint 93.

Lüdtke, Karlheinz. Interdisziplinarität und Wissensentwicklung: Wie Phänomene in interdisziplinärer Kommunikation wissenschaftlich bedeutsam werden. *J Gen Phil Sci*, 26(1), 93-117, 1995.

The author is engaged in the question how to explain the development of scientific meanings of facts which does not coincide with producing them rather with processes of the scientists' public communication. So long as the facts are adjustable to the conventional theories of those disciplines which the researcher belongs to this connection does not reveal perfectly clear. More instructive is a consideration of so-called 'anomalies'. The author demonstrates with an example of the history of science that researchers in case of new phenomena use to borrow concepts from other disciplines for resoving the interpretative problems. It emerges a loose net-work of concepts. In this way the researchers are producing a disciplinary mixed public at the same time. This process is seen as an important phase of the development of new theories and, complementary, new disciples.

Lütterfelds, Wilhelm. Fichtes Konzept absoluter Einheit (1804)—Ein performativer Selbstwiderspruch?. *Fichte-Studien*, 6, 401-421, 1994.

Das Thema der Wissenschaftslehre (1804) ist die Möglichkeit, die Mannigfaltigkeit der empirischen Welt mit unserem kategorialen Denken zu einer absoluten Einheit zu verbinden und so Wissen von der Welt zu begründen. Diese absolute Einheit, von Fichte "Sein" bzw. "Wissen" oder ach "Gott" genannt, ist weder idealistisch oder realistisch zu erreichen, noch über ein begriffliches Synthese-Programm. Auch andere Einheitsmodelle wie das der Bezeichnung, der Abbildung, der Identität oder der genetischen Spaltung sind unzureichend. Die absolute Einheit ist theoretisch nicht begreifbar, sondern nur praktisch als absoluter Zweck zu postulieren. Und dies vor allem deshalb, weil die Struktur unserer prädikativen, propositionalen Behauptungen über die absolute Einheit diese relativiert, sodass die Aussageform der Aussagenreferenz, dem absoluten Sein, performativ widerspricht.

Luhmann, Niklas. Observing Re-Entries. *Protosoz*, 6, 4-13, 1994.

Rationality can be defined as a reentry of a distinction in itself and in particular as a reentry of the distinction between system and environment in the system. This is a paradoxical and, for practical matters, utopian concept. It has the advantage that one can show that different "unfoldments" of the paradox are possible and that choosing one of them depends upon historical conditions of plausibility.

Luhmann, Niklas. Politicians, Honesty and the Higher Amorality of Politics. *Theor Cult Soc*, 11(2), 25-36, My 94.

Luizzi, Vincent. Human Nature and Universalism. *Dialogue Hum*, 4(2-3), 5-10, 1994.

In this essay I review recent thinking about human nature by members of the International Society of Universalism and offer my own theory as a foundation for universalism without upsetting the thinking of my colleagues. Regardless of whether one endorses my view as the best way of grounding universalism, it at least assists us in developing our thinking about universalism; for my theory of human nature leads naturally to our inquiring into an environment which is important for establishing a universal society, namely, the environment of transition.

Lujun, Yin. From Montague to Neo-Confucianism: Feng Youlan's "New *Lixue*" and Logical Analysis. *J Chin Phil*, 21(3-4), 337-361, S-D 94.

Lukacher, Ned. "The Ring of Being" in *Intersections: Nineteenth-Century Philosophy and Contemporary Theory, Rajan, Tilottama (ed)*, 197-221. Albany, SUNY Pr, 1995.

Luke, Timothy W. "Aesthetic Production and Cultural Politics: Baudrillard and Contemporary Art" in *Baudrillard: A Critical Reader, Kellner, Douglas M (ed)*, 209-226. Cambridge, Blackwell, 1994.

Lukes, Steven. Reply to Van Parijs. *Ratio Juris*, 8(1), 64-67, Mr 95.

Lummerding, Susanne. *"Weibliche" Ästhetik? Möglichkeiten und Grenzen einer Subversion von Codes*. Vienna, Passagen, 1994.

Die Autorin untersucht künstlerischer Arbeiten, die sich kritisch mit kulturellen Praktiken auseinandersetzen, durch welche "Weiblichkeiten" (und "Männlichkeiten") produziert werden, und veranschaulicht exemplarisch, auf welche Weise Geschlecht als semiotische Kategorie die "Frau" als funktionalen Bezugswert innerhalb eines Systems von Differenzen setzt, welche Rolle Repräsentationsprozesse in der Konstituierung sexuell differenzierter Subjekte spielen und welche Möglichkeiten der Analyse von Signifikations- bzw. Repräsentationsprozessen sich im ästhetischen Diskurs eröffnen lassen. (edited)

Lun, A W C and Crossley, J N. The Logic of Liu Hui and Euclid as Exemplified in Their Proofs of the Volume of a Pyramid. *Phil Hist Sci*, 3(1), 11-27, Ap 94.

We present a comparison of the logic employed in Euclid's *Elements* in the West and the *Jiu Zhang Suan Shu* in China. Previously it has been said that Chinese mathematics was algorithmic and practical, as opposed to the logical and theoretical Euclidean mathematics. We point out that Euclid uses logic which either is, or could be, as constructive as that of Liu Hui and has a number of points of contact even though the traditions are very different.

Luna, Florencia. Paternalism and the Argument from Illiteracy. *Bioethics*, 9(3-4), 283-290, Jl 95.

Throughout this essay, I will consider an argument frequently used to justify paternalistic behavior toward a specific class of persons: illiterate people. The argument states that illiterate people are uneducated, lack information and understanding, and are thus unable to make decisions. Therefore, it is argued, paternalism in their case is justified. The conclusion is that illiterate persons cannot be autonomous. The justification for this view is based on an a priori attitude: since it is impossible to communicate, physicians should decide which kind of treatment the illiterate patient should receive. This argument is frequently used even though its proponents may not be aware of its implications. Given the important and uncritical acceptance of this argument has in Argentina, and also in other Latin American countries, I think it is relevant to analyze carefully what it means. I propose a thorough analysis of this argument, of its implications and an evaluation of whether it is acceptable.

Luna, Florencia. Sida y confidencialidad: un problema complejo. *Rev Filosof (Argentina)*, 9(1-2), 55-64, N 94.

In this paper I am going to examine a difficult issue in the medical setting: does a doctor confronted by a patient with AIDS have a duty to maintain absolute confidentiality or could that doctor be considered to have some overriding duty to the sexual contacts of the AIDS sufferer? I will outline some of the responses classic and contemporary philosophers have given. And I will suggest that these proposals cannot show any relevant difference between the two paradigmatic cases I present. Finally, I will propose to reconsider the moral agent, the person and its character. By doing this I am recovering some of the ideas of Aristotle's ethics.

Lundmark, Lennart. "The Mechanization of Time" in *The Machine as Metaphor and Tool, Haken, Hermann (ed)*, 45-65. New York, Springer-Verlag, 1993.

The basic argument of the paper is that clocks and other technical devices have molded our concept of time to a much greater extent than we are generally aware of. Mechanical clocks started to push the conception of time in an absolute direction as early as the mid-14th century when hours of equal length were introduced. With the arrival of pendulum clocks in the late 17th century the irregularities of the apparent motion of the sun became a problem and true solar time was changed to mean solar time (i.e., clock time) in civilian life. This led to absolute time being conceived of as "natural". The technical innovation sin the communications sector then made standard time necessary and finally the need to conserve energy by utilizing more daylight has led to the introduction of summertime. All these interventions have made everyday time a self-contradictory mixture of absolute and conventionalist concepts.

Lundquist, Lita. Indefinite Noun Phrases in Legal Texts: Use, Function and Construction of Mental Spaces. *J Prag*, 23(1), 7-29, Ja 95.

As a counterpart to the many studies on definite noun phrases, the present article sets out to study the functions of indefinite noun phrases in texts, represented by four types of legal texts in French (textbooks, judgments, laws and legal articles). The study brings out characteristic features of the different text types, indefinite noun phrases being used mainly in a nonreferential, predicative function in laws and textbooks, and in a referential; specific function in judgments. In legal articles, indefinite noun phrases fill a more evenly distributed set of functions. Though the study is mainly empirical, theoretical questions are also raised as to how to describe the textual function of indefinite noun phrases, and an answer is given in terms of the theory of mental spaces.

Luque Alcaide, Elisa. Santo Tomás y el Progreso Histórico en el Conocimiento de la Verdad. *Rev Espan Filosof Med*, 1, 99-107, 1994.

The philosophy of immanance has proposed that the philosophical investigation is actually an ahistoric enterprise in which each philosopher must initiate his work from ground-zero, "a radice". Thomas Aquinas proceeds in another fashion: In his work "De substantiis separatis" or "De angelis", he undertakes a study of the philosophers of antiquity in order to establish his arguments of the theme in question. In this mature Thomistic work, Aquinas exhibits the harmony of the positions of Plato and Aristotle.

Lurbe, Pierre. John Toland et l'épicurisme. *Arch Phil*, 57(3), 559-573, Jl-S 94.

Lurçat, François. "Space and Time" in *Philosophy, Mathematics and Modern Physics, Rudolph, Enno (ed)*, 48-66. New York, Springer-Verlag, 1994.

The Einstein-Bergson discussion can remind us of the connection between (usual) time and earth. Husserl's reflections on Copernicanism show how physics can be understood by leaning on everyday experience. Bohr's interpretation of quantum mechanics, although it seems at first sight to prohibit such notions as virtual particles, can in fact help to understand the real nature of the quantum vacuum and its fluctuations. Furthermore, Husserl's identification of the thing studied by the physicist with the perceived physical thing is closely connected with Bohr's quantum postulate. These examples suggest how fruitful could be relations between physics and general philosophy.

Luri, Gregorio. A la sombra de Artemis: Reflexión sobre los espacios mítico e histórico de "La República". *Convivium*, 6, 72-90, 1994.

Plato thought it appropriate that the action of *The Republic* took place in the Piraeus, in the course of a summer's night when the goddess Bendis was worshipped for the first time. This is well-known. However, the significance of his choice has not been looked into very often. Why did Plato pick out the most critical spot in the whole Greek territory to locate a discussion of justice and why to devote the discussion to a newly arrived goddess, the Thracian Bendis? Moreover, why does it take the form of a banquet? There is no doubt that Plato is presenting us the scene of a drama (of a tragedy perhaps?). What does he want to suggest with this choice? What is he hinting at? This paper aims to place *The Republic* in relation to the context that Plato has given us in the initial scene of the discussion. Something elementary? Yes, as elementary as the conclusion one may draw from this attempt: Plato is not a typical Platonist!

Luterbacher, Urs. International Cooperation: The Problem of the Commons and the Special Case of the Antarctic Region. *Synthese*, 100(3), 413-440, S 94.

Lutterbach, Hubertus. 'Auf die Kräfte des Leibes achten': Die Bedeutung der Gesundheit im Leben und Wirken des Ignatius von Loyola. *Theol Phil*, 69(4), 556-569, 1994.

Lutz, Catherine. "Need, Nurturance, and the Emotions on a Pacific Atoll" in *Emotions in Asian Thought, Marks, Joel (ed)*, 235-252. Albany, SUNY Pr, 1995.

Lyas, Colin. Renewing Philosophy. *Phil Books*, 36(1), 26-33, Ja 95.

Putnam's *Renewing Philosophy* speaks in highly critical terms of certain methods in philosophy, notably certain analytic methods. I show Putnam to be committed to the very methods he criticizes.

Lycan, William G. Conditional Reasoning and Conditional Logic. *Phil Stud*, 76(2-3), 223-245, D 94.

This paper surveys Psychologistic views of deductive validity, with emphasis on conditional reasoning, and argues that not even the weakest and most plausible of those views is acceptable in the face of both philosophical objections and recent empirical research on reasoning. In particular, the "competence"/"performance" distinction offers little help to the champion of Psychologism. In passing, the "Deduction System Hypothesis" or "Mental Logic" theory proposed by psychologists such as Lance Rips and John Macnamara is subjected to criticism.

Lycan, William G (ed). *Mind and Cognition: A Reader*. Cambridge, Blackwell, 1992.

Lycan, William G. Reply to Hilary Kornblith's "In Defense of Deductive Inference". *Phil Stud*, 76(2-3), 259-261, D 94.

Lynch, Joseph J. Harrison and Hick on God and Animal Pain. *Sophia (Australia)*, 33(3), 62-73, N 94.

Animal pain constitutes a distinct challenge to theism. It has been suggested that there are significant differences between animal and human pain and that these differences are important for theodicy. Peter Harrison has argued that animal pain is nonconscious, while John Hick has contended that only human beings are capable of genuine suffering. In either case, animal pain is alleged not to threaten seriously the goodness or the power of God. I argue that both Harrison's and Hick's theodicies deny the obvious reality of animal pain and that animal suffering should be acknowledged by Theists.

Lynch, Joseph J. Is Animal Pain Conscious?. *Between Species*, 10(1-2), 1-7, Win-Spr 94.

Peter Carruthers and Peter Harrison have in separate articles resurrected a Cartesian attitude toward animal pain. If their positions are sound, we are mistaken in thinking that animals can feel their pains; and consequently we are also mistaken in thinking that animals could possibly be the appropriate objects of our moral sympathies. I contend that both arguments fail. We have compelling, if not conclusive, evidence for holding that animals feel their pains, and therefore have little reason to accept the skeptical and less plausible conclusions of either Carruthers or Harrison.

Lynch, Michael and Bogen, David. Harvey Sacks's Primitive Natural Science. *Theor Cult Soc*, 11(4), 65-104, N 94.

Starting in the 1960's, Harvey Sacks developed a unique approach to the analysis of natural language use, which later became known as conversation analysis. Unlike most innovators in the social sciences, Sacks did not try to emulate the natural sciences; instead, he argued that an incipient 'natural observational science of human behavior' was already part of successful sciences. Scientists describe how to do observations as well as features of the things they observe, and the adequacy of such descriptions demonstrates the possibility of making replicable descriptions of human actions. Sacks aimed to expand this program of scientific description to cover a full range of ordinary communicative 'methods'. This paper is a critical appreciation of conversation analysis which tries to account for how Sacks's practical philosophy of science was turned into an empiricist research program.

Lyons, David. "Critical Analysis and Constructive Interpretation" in *In Harm's Way, Coleman, Jules L (ed)*, 76-91. New York, Cambridge Univ Pr, 1994.

This paper examines Dworkin's "constructive" interpretation and mode of critical analysis suggested by critical legal scholars. The paper suggests that an aim of theory should be to guide legal interpretation so as to maximize the likelihood that judicial decisions and what is done to people in the name of the law are morally justifiable. Each of the approaches attributes a deep value structure to the law though one does it generously and the other ungenerously. Neither can insure that judicial decisions are justifiable either directly or indirectly because nothing can make a silk purse out of a sow's ear.

Lyotard, Jean-François and Harvey, Robert (ed) and Roberts, Mark S (ed). *Toward the Post-Modern*. Atlantic Highlands, Humanities Pr, 1995.

Lysaker, John T. Heidegger After the Fall. Review of *Heidegger and the Poets* by Véronique M Fóti. *Res Phenomenol*, 23, 201-211, 1993.

M Rosales, J. Los argumentos del individualismo: En torno a la primera identidad liberal. *Pensamiento*, 197(50), 197-211, My-Ag 94.

La defensa de lo que desde C B Macpherson se conoce como individualismo posesivo ha representado una de las claves para el desarrollo de la moralidad y el pensamiento político liberales. Sin embargo, la interpretación del sentido de la libertad individual, desglosada en los momentos de la autonomía moral y la libertad política, no ha descrito justamente una trayectoria homogénea. Entre las primeras formulaciones de Hobbes y Locke y las posteriores de Mill y Tocqueville, psasando por las traducciones de Rousseau, Kant y Hegel, el individualismo originario, aferrado a la idea de propiedad, ha dado pie a una nueva forma de individualismo racional que trata de conjugar la defensa de la libertad con las propuestas de igualdad y solidaridad.

Maar, Wolfgang Leo. Galileu e a Dialética: Síntese pelo Experimento e Natureza como Domínio dos Objectos. *Cad Hist Filosof Cie*, 3(1-2), 11-65, Ja-D 93.

The objective of this article is to discuss Galileo's work by criticizing its 'objectivist' interpretations—nowadays predominant—from the standpoint of a dialectic reading, based mainly on the works of Koyré, Mondolfo, and other German recent works on natural sciences. The aim is to replace the philosophical dimension of the problem of the relations between concept and reality and the subject matter of knowledge. This is done following the development of the problem from the theoretical Aristotelian synthesis to his Galilean practical reformulation by the experiment. By doing this Galileo develops a new conception of theory which is able to overcome the paradox characteristics of the antique sciences—the exclusion of the empiric realm from that of the natural law. (edited)

Maat, Harro and Baggen, Peter. De Disciplinering van het Hoger Onderwijs: Aantekeningen bij de Massa-Universiteit. *Kennis Methode*, 19(2), 194-219, 1995.

Few attempts have been made to connect social studies of sciences with related areas of investigation, such as higher education studies. Discussing the work of Wittrock and Elzinga, 1985, the authors focus on the rise and possible decline of 'disciplines' within Dutch higher education. Disciplines are usually seen as the constituting element of universities because of the education-research junction they provide. Furthermore, most analyses emphasize the epistemic characteristics of disciplines. In this article it is argued that disciplines are primarily structures for the educational function of the university. For a proper analysis of disciplines, besides the epistemic component, attention must be paid to the educational and pedagogical features. Applying such analysis to the Dutch universities shows that the importance of disciplines in higher education is much more contingent than generally assumed.

Mabbett, Ian W. Nāgārjuna and Deconstruction. *Phil East West*, 45(2), 203-225, Ap 95.

A comparison of deconstruction (on the authority of some of the writings of J Derrida especially, alongside others) with the philosophy of Nagarjuna (on the authority of an independent interpretation of the *Mulamadhyamakakarikas*, used here without detailed defense against variant interpretations) shows that, despite underlying major differences of purpose and context, the two programmes share many substantial features—more than commonly recognized. Both avoid claims about determinate reality, attribute only relative reality to things, criticize the logic of binary oppositions, celebrate emptiness, use 'four-cornered logic', dismantle the concept of the self, and recognize both conventional and higher truths.

Macbeth, Danielle. Names, Natural Kind Terms, and Rigid Designation. *Phil Stud*, 79(3), 259-281, S 95.

Kripke argues that natural kind terms are rigid designators much as names are, and also that theoretical statements purportedly expressing what it is to be a kind of thing are necessary (if true) by virtue of being identities involving two rigid designators. Both claims, it is argued, are false. Rather, on the account outlined, predications involving natural kind terms are (sometimes) "epistemically rigid", at least in the context of scientific investigation. Through such predications, objects acquire the status of paradigm instances of (natural) kinds and play a critical role in the discovery of truths about the kinds they instantiate.

Macbeth, Danielle. Pragmatism and the Philosophy of Language. *Phil Phenomenol Res*, 55(3), 501-523, S 95.

After sketching familiar pragmatist arguments that seem to show that relations of reference and meaning shed no light on the role of language in our claims to knowledge, an alternative conception (inspired by Kripke's work on proper names and Sellars' conception of concepts and causal laws) is outlined. Neither relations of reference nor meanings are given; instead both essentially involve commitments that are different in kind from the sorts of propositional commitments made in judgment. If so, the pragmatist is mistaken in concluding that meaning is a philosopher's fiction and reference nothing more than a technical notion of formal semantics.

Macbeth, Danielle. The Logic of Relations and the Ideality of Space. *J Phil Res*, 20, 367-379, 1995.

As Friedman has argued, Kant's argument for the ideality of space turns on the nondeductive character of geometrical reasoning in Euclid's system. Since geometry can be axiomatized, this argument fails. But (*pace* Russell) Leibniz's argument based on the unreality of constitutive relations is not thereby answered as well. I argue that what is needed in response to Leibniz is a properly post-Kantian conception of concepts as inferentially articulated. This conception, I suggest, is based on the same fundamental insight that underlies the axiomatization of geometry.

MacCallum Jr, Gerald C. "Competition and Moral Philosophy (1975)" in *Legislative Intent and Other Essays on Law, Politics, and Morality, Singer, Marcus G (ed)*, 203-223. Madison, Univ of Wisconsin Pr, 1993.

MacCallum Jr, Gerald C. "Justice and Adversary Proceedings (1977)" in *Legislative Intent and Other Essays on Law, Politics, and Morality, Singer, Marcus G (ed)*, 224-234. Madison, Univ of Wisconsin Pr, 1993.

MacCallum Jr, Gerald C. "Violence and Appeals to Conscience (1974)" in *Legislative Intent and Other Essays on Law, Politics, and Morality, Singer, Marcus G (ed)*, 178-202. Madison, Univ of Wisconsin Pr, 1993.

MacCallum Jr, Gerald C. "What Is Wrong with Violence? (1970)" in *Legislative Intent and Other Essays on Law, Politics, and Morality, Singer, Marcus G (ed)*, 235-256. Madison, Univ of Wisconsin Pr, 1993.

MacCallum Jr, Gerald C and Singer, Marcus G (ed) and Martin, Rex (ed). *Legislative Intent and Other Essays on Law, Politics, and Morality*. Madison, Univ of Wisconsin Pr, 1993.

This book contains fourteen papers by the late Gerald MacCallum, five not previously published. In addition to the author's corrected version of "Legislative Intent and Negative and Positive Freedom," it contains papers that link with them, such as "On Applying Rules" and "Some Truths and Untruths about Civil Disobedience." There are also interrelated papers on such themes as conscience, law, violence, personal integrity, and representation, and a little known paper on "Censorship in the Arts." The previously unpublished writings include groundbreaking papers on "Competition and Moral Philosophy" and "Justice and Adversary Proceedings," discussions of violence and conscience, and "Dworkin and Judicial Discretion." The editors have provided a preface, an introduction, a memoir of the author, a bibliography of his writings, and explanatory comments when needed.

MacCormick, Neil. The Relative Heteronomy of Law. *Euro J Phil*, 3(1), 69-85, Ap 95.

Macdonald, Cynthia. "Anti-Individualism and Psychological Explanation" in *Philosophy of Psychology: Debates on Psychological Explanation, Macdonald, Cynthia (ed)*, 156-172. Cambridge, Blackwell, 1995.

Macdonald, Cynthia. "Classicism v Connectionism" in *Connectionism: Debates on Psychological Explanation, Macdonald, Cynthia (ed)*, 3-27. Cambridge, Blackwell, 1995.

Macdonald, Cynthia. "Connectionism and Eliminativism" in *Connectionism: Debates on Psychological Explanation, Macdonald, Cynthia (ed)*, 293-310. Cambridge, Blackwell, 1995.

Macdonald, Cynthia and Macdonald, Graham. "Causal Relevance and Explanatory Exclusion" in *Philosophy of Psychology: Debates on Psychological Explanation, Macdonald, Cynthia (ed)*, 86-106. Cambridge, Blackwell, 1995.

Macdonald, Cynthia and Macdonald, Graham. "How to be Psychologically Relevant" in *Philosophy of Psychology: Debates on Psychological Explanation, Macdonald, Cynthia (ed)*, 60-77. Cambridge, Blackwell, 1995.

Macdonald, Cynthia and Macdonald, Graham. "Supervenient Causation" in *Philosophy of Psychology: Debates on Psychological Explanation, Macdonald, Cynthia (ed)*, 4-28. Cambridge, Blackwell, 1995.

Macdonald, Cynthia (ed) and Macdonald, Graham (ed). *Connectionism: Debates on Psychological Explanation*. Cambridge, Blackwell, 1995.

Macdonald, Cynthia (ed) and Macdonald, Graham (ed). *Philosophy of Psychology: Debates on Psychological Explanation*. Cambridge, Blackwell, 1995.

Macdonald, Graham. "Psychoanalytic Explanation" in *Philosophy of Psychology: Debates on Psychological Explanation, Macdonald, Cynthia (ed)*, 394-408. Cambridge, Blackwell, 1995.

Macdonald, Graham. "Tacit Knowledge" in *Philosophy of Psychology: Debates on Psychological Explanation, Macdonald, Cynthia (ed)*, 296-308. Cambridge, Blackwell, 1995.

Macdonald, Graham. "The Biological Turn" in *Philosophy of Psychology: Debates on Psychological Explanation, Macdonald, Cynthia (ed)*, 238-252. Cambridge, Blackwell, 1995.

Macdonald, Graham and Macdonald, Cynthia. "Causal Relevance and Explanatory Exclusion" in *Philosophy of Psychology: Debates on Psychological Explanation, Macdonald, Cynthia (ed)*, 86-106. Cambridge, Blackwell, 1995.

Macdonald, Graham and Macdonald, Cynthia. "How to be Psychologically Relevant" in *Philosophy of Psychology: Debates on Psychological Explanation, Macdonald, Cynthia (ed)*, 60-77. Cambridge, Blackwell, 1995.

Macdonald, Graham and Macdonald, Cynthia. "Supervenient Causation" in *Philosophy of Psychology: Debates on Psychological Explanation, Macdonald, Cynthia (ed)*, 4-28. Cambridge, Blackwell, 1995.

Macdonald, Graham (ed) and Macdonald, Cynthia (ed). *Connectionism: Debates on Psychological Explanation*. Cambridge, Blackwell, 1995.

Macdonald, Graham (ed) and Macdonald, Cynthia (ed). *Philosophy of Psychology: Debates on Psychological Explanation*. Cambridge, Blackwell, 1995.

MacDonald, James E and Beck-Dudley, Caryn L. Are Deontology and Teleology Mutually Exclusive?. *J Bus Ethics*, 13(8), 615-623, Ag 94.

Current discussions of business ethics usually only consider deontological and utilitarian approaches. What is missing is a discussion of traditional teleology, often referred to as "virtue ethics". While deontology and teleology are useful, they both suffer insufficiencies. Traditional teleology, while deontological in many respects, does not object to utilitarian style calculations as long as they are contained within a moral framework that is not utilitarian in its origin. It contains the best of both approaches and can be used to focus on the individual's role within an organization. More work is needed in exposing students and faculty to traditional teleology and its place in business ethic's discussions.

Macedo, Stephen. Liberal Civic Education and Religious Fundamentalism: The Case of God v. John Rawls?. *Ethics*, 105(3), 468-496, Ap 95.

Machamer, Peter. Kitcher and the Achievement of Science. *Phil Phenomenol Res*, 55(3), 629-636, S 95.

Machan, Tibor R. "A Defence of Property Rights and Capitalism" in *Introducing Applied Ethics, Almond, Brenda (ed)*, 260-271. Cambridge, Blackwell, 1995.

Capitalism rests on the principle of the individual's right to private property ownership, which is a basic social norm to be upheld in law. This essay argues there are two reasons for upholding this principle: 1) Private property is a precondition for sovereignty and moral responsibility (it prevents the moral tragedy of the commons), and 2) ownership is the result of practicing the virtue of prudence (productivity, industry, etc.). A society that provides people with 1 and 2 is superior to one in which these are missing.

Machan, Tibor R. Human Rights Reaffirmed. *Philosophy*, 69(270), 479-490, O 94.

Three types of skeptical arguments against human rights are addressed, one which claims utilitarianism secures our liberties better in the face of the metaethical failings of natural rights theory; the other which is skeptical of the universalism, individualism and (more recently) neo-Aristotelianism advanced in various defenses of human rights, and one which disputes the possibility of arriving at a consistent conception of human nature. Each of these—van den Haag, John N Gray, and John O Nelson—is discussed, with the conclusion offered that despite their criticism, human rights stand reaffirmed.

Machan, Tibor R. Professional Responsibilities of Corporate Managers. *Bus Prof Ethics J*, 13(3), 57-69, Fall 94.

Against M Friedman, this paper argues that corporations ought to be managed in line with several moral principles or virtues, even though prudence—making profit—will be a priority or the dominant standard. Against others (e.g., Nader, Galbraith) the paper holds that no justification exists to subject corporations to regimentation for the public interest. Generally, it is contended that a robust type of ethical egoism gives support to these considerations, on that may be seen to underlie business ethics in general.

Macherey, Pierre. *Ethique* IV propositions 70-71. *Rev Metaph Morale*, 99(4), 459-474, O-D 94.

Machiedo, Mladen. In the Philosophical Key: The Questionable Characteristics of Italian Literature. *Filozof Istraz*, 14(1), 167-195, 1994.

The approximate, though not altogether wrong, belief that Italian writers are mainly not inclined towards philosophy (and this is confirmed by the span from Aretino to Quasimodo) is opposed by the author with a series of thinkers who, throughout the centuries, were indebted to and constantly endorsed literature (Machiavelli, Leonardo da Vinci, Galilei, Bruno, Campanella and Vico). In a particular way, the main section of the text belongs to three poets, between whom is established an unusual intelligible intertextuality (they are Dante, Leopardi and Montale). Elsewhere, philosophy *yields* itself in alternative binaries: now towards religion (Manzoni), now towards aesthetics, or history (the areas of Croce's dominant interests). Further prejudice relates to the allegedly anti-Germanic orientation in Italian literature. This is refuted, however, by the Heideggerian openness of two Florentine poets (Luzio and Bigongiario, the latter also as a critic of *reflexive explosion*). (edited)

Machina, Mark J. The Two Errors: A Summary. *Theor Decis*, 38(3), 301-307, My 95.

This paper summarizes the debate between Allais and Machina over the validity of an assertion about nonexpected utility preferences for risky prospects. Allais has asserted that the notion of "local utility" cannot be defined for any outcome that does not currently have positive probability. Machina's response gives the formal procedure for doing so, and identifies two separate mathematical mistakes in Allais's proposed proof: an invalid assertion of when two utility functions should be linear transformations of each other, and the use of a moment-based representation function on a domain where it is shown to be mathematically invalid.

Machina, Mark J. Two Errors in the 'Allais Impossibility Theorem'. *Theor Decis*, 38(3), 231-250, My 95.

In his so-called 'Allais Impossibility Theorem', Allais (1988) asserts that the technique of 'generalized expected utility analysis' from Machina (1982) is invalid, on the grounds that its key tool, the 'local utility function', cannot be well-defined for preferences over finite-outcome lotteries. This paper presents a brief description of the local utility function and a summary of Allais's argument, and points out two separate errors in the latter. The first error consists of believing that two local utility functions should be affinely equivalent even when their outcome variables differ by a nonlinear transformation. The second error consists of an incorrect derivation of the local utility function, resulting from extending a moment representation function beyond its valid domain, and/or invoking the chain rule at a point where this function is not differentiable.

Machovec, Milan. Egon Bondy's Place in the History of Metaphysics. *Filozof Cas*, 42(5), 823-837, 1994.

Egon Bondy (born 1930), original name Zbynek Fiser, published his philosophical chef d'oeuvre "Utecha z Ontologie" ("The Consolation of Ontology") as early as 1967 (publishing house Aademia, Prague), to continue with his work during the two following decades but not being allowed to publish officially a single line of his further works until 1990. The essential contribution of his work is found in his convincing eradication of the so-called "substantial model of reality", i.e., any model of the universe in which a certain "substance" (being intelligible—a god, or nonintelligible—a matter) would occupy a privileged position, thus making anything else only an epiphenomenon. Bondy underlines the absurdities rising from any "substantial model", especially as far as axiologic approaches are concerned; on the other hand he makes up a "nonsubstantial model of reality" in which no being is privileged and axiologic values (especially ethics) prevail. M Machovec interprets Bondy's work as a logical continuation of theories of the greatest thinkers of the past, especially Aristotle and I Kant.

Machover, Moshé and Felsenthal, Dan S. Postulates and Paradoxes of Relative Voting Power—A Critical Re-Appraisal. *Theor Decis*, 38(2), 195-229, Mr 95.

This paper re-evaluates the problem of measuring the *a priori* relative voting power of a voter in an assembly. We propose several new intuitively compelling postulates that any reasonable index of voting power ought to satisfy. At the same time we argue that most of the paradoxes of voting power discussed in the literature are paradoxical only in a weak sense, if at all. This leaves three crippling paradoxes—the well-known paradox of *weighted voting*, and two new ones presented here: the *bloc* and *donation* paradoxes. We evaluate the four main relative power indices discussed in the literature with respect to these three severe paradoxes. The Shapley-Shubik index is seen to be immune to all three paradoxes, while the Deegan-Packel index is vulnerable to all three. The Banzhaf and the Johnston indices are demonstrably immune to the paradox of weighted voting. However, they are shown to suffer from both the bloc and the donation paradoxes. We argue that this seriously undermines these indices in a hitherto unsuspected way. Several other theoretical issues relating to voting power are discussed.

MacIntosh, J J. Belief-In Revisited: A Reply to Williams. *Relig Stud*, 30(4), 487-503, D 94.

In 'Belief-In and Belief in God' (*Religious Studies, 28, 1992*), J N Williams suggests that belief in God cannot be rational unless one has rational beliefs *that* God exists. While agreeing with his conclusion (though not with his statement of it), I disagree at almost every step with his method of arriving at it. In particular I suggest that Williams goes astray concerning the dual aspect of *belief in*, the nature of performatives, the arousal of belief states, and the correct account of belief in God.

MacIntosh, J J. Sleigh's *Leibniz and Arnauld*. *Dialogue (Canada)*, 33(3), 473-516, Sum 94.

This critical notice deals with two aspects of Sleigh's *Leibniz and Arnauld*: 1) The question of how the history of philosophy ought to be tackled; and 2) the host of problems which arise when we consider Leibniz's interlocking notions of individual concepts, identity, miracles, and laws, including laws of nature. If we allow all relational properties as part of an individual's concept Leibniz's claim that every monad mirrors the universe becomes trivial; if we allow no relational properties it becomes self-evidently false. I consider, among other aspects of Sleigh's fascinating book, his attempted rescue of Leibniz's position.

MacIntyre, Alasdair. "Truthfulness, Lies, and Moral Philosophers" in *The Tanner Lectures on Human Values, Volume 16, Peterson, Grethe B (ed)*, 307-361. Salt Lake City, Univ of Utah Pr, 1995.

This is a discussion of contemporary attitudes to and disagreements about truthtelling and lying in North America and also of the philosophical issues dividing those for whom lying is primarily an offense against truth from those for whom it is primarily an offense against trust. Particular attention is paid to the treatment of lying by Mill and by Kant. An exceptionless, nonconsequentialist rule prohibiting almost, but not quite all lying is defended.

MacIntyre, Alasdair. My Station and Its Virtues. *J Phil Res*, 19, 1-8, 1994.

This paper compares the central theses of Edmund M Pincoff's *Quandries and Virtues* with those of F H Bradley's *Ethical Studies*. Both Pincoffs and Bradley understand virtues as functional in respect of the common good of the social order. Both reflect the individualism of Kantian and utilitarian theories. Both believe that ordinary moral agents do not appeal to and do not need to appeal to the kinds of justification for action defended by such theories. It is argued that the importance of these resemblances is partly disguised by the differences between Pincoffs's and Bradley's view. Pincoffs and Bradley are among those who, in the debates of modern moral philosophy, have recurrently defended an antitheoretical account against a variety of theorists. It is claimed that this debate is and must be inconclusive.

MacIntyre, Alasdair. Relativism, Power and Philosophy. *Proc Amer Phil Ass*, 59(1), 5-22, S 85.

The central claim is that there are rival conceptual schemes and the inability to translate from the language of one into that of another does not preclude understanding. The strength of the case for relativism is emphasized, but the final conclusion is antirelativist.

MacIntyre, Alasdair and Corral, Carmen (trans) and Román, Begoña (trans). Persona corriente y filosofía moral: reglas, virtudes y bienes. *Convivium*, 5, 63-80, 1993.

Mack, Eric. "Rights to Natural Talents and Pure Profits: A Critique of Gauthier on Rights and Economic Rent" in *Profits and Morality, Cowan, Robin (ed)*, 124-149. Chicago, Univ of Chicago Pr, 1995.

Mackay, Peta and Prenzler, Tim. Police Gratuities: What the Public Think. *Crim Just Ethics*, 14(1), 15-25, Wint-Spr 95.

This paper reports on a survey of residents of Brisbane, Australia. The research found that the majority of respondents opposed all gratuities other than very small incidental gifts. The main sources of concern were the appearance of compromise and the potential for unequal treatment of users of police services. Overall, the study showed that public expectations of police conduct are quite exacting and that conformity to those standards is essential for public confidence in the police. The survey also indicated that the practice of police accepting gratuities is still occurring in Australia. In light of this, some strategies are suggested for implementing policy more effectively.

Macke, Frank J. "Pragmatism Reconsidered: John Dewey and Michel Foucault on the Consequences of Inquiry" in *Recovering Pragmatism's Voice, Langsdorf, Lenore (ed)*, 155-176. Albany, SUNY Pr, 1995.

Macklin, Ruth. Cloning without Prior Approval: A Response to Recent Disclosures of Noncompliance. *Kennedy Inst Ethics J*, 5(1), 57-60, Mr 95.

Macklin, Ruth. Reproductive Technologies in Developing Countries. *Bioethics*, 9(3-4), 276-282, Jl 95.

Are there any ethical concerns about reproductive technologies that are specific or unique to developing countries? Three ethical concerns often mentioned specifically in regard to developing countries are 1) The "overpopulation argument"; 2) The limited resources argument; and 3) The ethical problem of poorly trained practitioners offering their services to unsuspecting and uninformed infertile individuals or couples. Each argument is explored in some detail, with the conclusion that ethical problems do, in fact, exist but are not unique to developing countries. Nevertheless, the difficulties relating to reproductive technologies are likely to be greater in developing countries than in developed ones because of limited resources and a larger number of poor people residing there.

Macklin, Ruth. Splitting Embryos on the Slippery Slope: Ethics and Public Policy. *Kennedy Inst Ethics J*, 4(3), 209-225, S 94.

Neither the George Washington University embryo splitting experiment nor the technique of embryo splitting itself has ethical flaws. The experiment harmed or wronged no one, and the investigators followed intramural review procedures for the experiment, although some might fault them for failing to seek extramural consultation or for not waiting until national guidelines for research on preembryos were developed. Ethical objections to such cloning on the basis of possible loss of individuality, possible lessening of individual worth, and concern about potential harm to the resulting children are discussed and challenged, as are objections to the creation of embyros for the purpose of genetic diagnosis. Many of the ethical questions raised by the George Washington experiment are similar to those posed by existing reproductive technologies that allow the simultaneous production of several embryos. A multidisciplinary group should consider whether regulation of cloning is needed, and laws should be enacted to prohibit a commercial market for all frozen embryos.

MacLennan, Bruce J. "Words Lie in Our Way". *Mind Mach*, 4(4), 421-437, N 94.

The central claim of computationalism is generally taken to be that the brain is a computer, and that any computer implementing the appropriate program would ipso facto have a mind. In this paper I argue for the following propositions: (1) The central claim of computationalism is not about computers, a concept too imprecise for a scientific claim of this sort, but is about physical calculi (instantiated discrete formal systems). (2) In matters of formality, interpretability, and so forth, analog computation and digital computation are not essentially different, and so arguments such as Searle's hold or not as well for one as for the other. (3) Whether or not a biological system (such as the brain) is computational is a scientific matter of fact. (4) A substantive scientific question for cognitive science is whether cognition is better modeled by discrete representations or by continuous representations. (5) Cognitive science and AI need a theoretical construct that is the continuous analog of a calculus. The discussion of these propositions will illuminate several terminology traps, in which it's all too easy to become ensnared.

Macmillan, C J B and Garrison, James W. Process-Product Research on Teaching: Ten Years Later. *Educ Theor*, 44(4), 385-398, Fall 94.

MacMillan, C J B. "Is Community Necessary: Quasi-Philosophical Ruminations" in *Identity, Culture, and Education, Smeyers, Paul (ed)*, 21-48. Leuven, Leuven Univ Pr, 1994.

In responding to and examining Mary Anne Raywid's (1989) adoption of community-building as an aim for schools, I survey a number of types of communities, including natural, intentional, professional and language communities. In considering all of these, I try to show both the power of communities in our personal lives and some idea of why we might be of two minds about promoting community as an ideal in the modern world and in schools in particular.

Macnamara, John. "The Mind-Body Problem and Contemporary Psychology" in *The Mind-Body Problem: A Guide to the Current Debate, Warner, Richard (ed)*, 165-170. Cambridge, Blackwell, 1994.

Macnamara, Michael and Ferreira-Ross, Jeanette. "Drama and the Notion of Scheme-Role Meaning" in *Life, World and Meaning, Roux, A P J (ed)*, 121-157. Pretoria, Univ of S Africa, 1990.

Maddux, Roger D and Andréka, Hajnal. Representations for Small Relation Algebras. *Notre Dame J Form Log*, 35(4), 550-562, Fall 94.

There are eighteen isomorphism types of finite relation algebras with eight or fewer elements, and all of them are representable. We determine all the cardinalities of sets on which these algebras have representations.

Madigan, Timothy J. "Pursuing Love with the Proper Map" in *The Nature and Pursuit of Love, Goicoechea, David (ed)*, 312-321. Buffalo, Prometheus, 1995.

An examination of the relevance of Santayana's works to Irving Singer's exploration of the nature of love, focusing in particular on the formation of idealized love objects.

Madigan, Timothy J. *FI* Interview: Camille Paglia on Freethought, Feminism, and Iconoclasm. *Free Inq*, 15(2), 5-8, Spr 95.

A freewheeling discussion on the collapse of liberalism and the need for a new "spirituality" to unite the Western world.

Madigan, Timothy J. The Open Society and the Open Mind. *Free Inq*, 15(1), 12-13, Wint 94-95.

A brief comparison between Popper's notion of "The Open Society", and the sociological concept of "Total Institutions" developed by Erving Goffman and explored by filmmaker Frederick Wiseman.

Madigan, Timothy J and Flynn, Thomas W. Francis Crick on the Workings of the Brain. *Free Inq*, 14(4), 18-21, Fall 94.

An interview with Crick on his book *The Astonishing Hypothesis*, wherein he discusses his views on why the search for "The Soul" is futile.

Madison, G B. "Ricoeur and the Hermeneutics of the Subject" in *The Philosophy of Paul Ricoeur, Hahn, Lewis Edwin (ed)*, 75-92. Peru, Open Court, 1994.

Madsen, Peter. A Theoretical Ground for the Practice of Business Ethics. *Bus Ethics Quart*, 5(3), 451-462, Jl 95.

This article offers two things: 1) a commentary on John Dienhart's paper titled "Rationality, Ethical Codes and an Egalitarian Justification of Ethical Expertise: Implications for Professions and Organizations" that appears in the same volume of Business Ethics Quarterly and 2) a contribution to the growing issues around business ethics consulting or the practice of business ethics. Borrowing Dienhart's concept of rationality and ethical expertise, this article demonstrates the importance of business ethics understood as a practice rather than just a theoretical concern.

Mäki, Uskali. "Isolation, Idealization and Truth in Economics" in *Idealization VI: Idealization in Economics, Hamminga, Bert (ed)*, 147-168. Amsterdam, Rodopi, 1994.

Challenges the widely held view that good models must necessarily be simplifications and hence cannot be true. This is done by distinguishing between whole truth (complete description) and truth (essential description, attained by the method of isolation).

Maffia, Diana Elena. "La Filosofía Sexista, la Epistemología Feminista y Otras Vicisitudes de la Razón" in *Temas Actuales de Filosofía, Palacios, María Julia (ed)*, 349-357. Buenos Aires, Univ Nacional Salta, 1993.

In what sense, if any, can we say that philosophy is "male"? In this paper, I explore this and other problems of feminist metaphilosophy, like the critic of traditional philosophers, the exclusion of women in some conceptions about rationality, and different positions on feminist epistemology and its limits.

Maffie, James. Towards an Anthropology of Epistemology. *Phil Forum*, 26(3), 218-241, Spr 95.

Naturalists seek continuity between epistemology and the sciences. Most implement continuity by employing the findings of science in substantive level epistemic tasks such as determining the limits, sources, and scope of justified belief and knowledge. I urge naturalists to expand continuity by adopting a broadly anthropological, *a posteriori* approach to meta-level epistemic tasks such identifying the correct ends, norms, and concepts of epistemology's axiological, evaluative, and normative independence from science, and without reducing epistemology to or replacing it by successor subjects such as psychology, cognitive sociology, or metascience.

Magdziak, Marek. Truth as an Object. *Bull Sec Log*, 23(3), 113-117, O 94.

By semantic theory of truth is meant an approach in which the notion of truth is characterized by means of an expression chosen from a given language of interpretation. The most influential contemporary theories concern themselves with the truth predicate. These approaches assume that truth is a property of sentences. Alternatively, the work considers truth as an individual object as an extension of an individual name from the language. It is also assumed that a valuation can be partly rendered in the language. It is studied some families of such valuations and its properties especially connected with the liar paradox.

Magee, John. The Text of Boethius' *De divisione*. *Vivarium*, 32(1), 1-50, My 94.

The textual tradition of Boethius' *De divisione* reaches back to an edition made in Constantinople in the mid-520s. An archetype made at Vivarium in the later sixth century stands at the head of the extrant tradition, which is highly contaminated. Terms for the proof that the tradition is contaminated are set forth and then followed up in light of what the manuscripts report.

Maggi de Gandolfi, María Celestina D. El *Index Thomisticus* y la Semántica lingüística. *Analogia*, 7(1), 199-203, 1993.

Magill, Kevin. Epicurus, Determinism, and the Security of Knowledge. *Theoria*, 58(2-3), 183-196, 1992.

The article criticises various interpretations of Epicurus's claim that belief in determinism is self-invalidating; especially Ted Honderich's argument that the real force of the Epicurean claim is that if belief acquisition is causally necessitated, we have produced new knowledge and shown some of what we take to be undetermined inquirers might fail to make discoveries that determined inquirers could not fail to make. Determinism would not, therefore, put us in a worse position as seekers of knowledge than indeterminism.

Magnell, Thomas. Moral Theory, Its Scope and Limits: Bernard Gert and Richard T De George. *J Value Inq*, 28(4), 541-556, D 94.

This is the second of two dialogues between Richard De George, Bernard Gert, and Thomas Magnell. It addresses issues having to do with the nature of moral theory, and the principles and procedures we may use in dealing with moral problems. De George, Gert, and Magnell focus on conditions of rationality, impartiality, and publicity. They also consider how meta-ethics fits within value inquiry, how a decision procedure may set limits on the extent of moral disagreement, and how theoretical and applied ethics are allied to one another.

Magnell, Thomas. Present Concerns and Future Interests. *Dialogue Hum*, 3(4), 67-73, 1993.

Future interests may be divided into fairly near-term interests that belong to the politically enfranchised future and more distant interests that lie in the politically unenfranchised future. The former receive serious political consideration in the present; the latter do not. Our neglect of interests that range into the politically unenfranchised future is an insidious moral failing that reflects *temporal bigotry*. Those interests demand that we particularly pay heed to the preconditions of civilization—matters concerning the management of nonrenewable resources, the protection of the environment, the control of population growth, the elimination of extreme poverty, and the reduction of nationalistic passions that fan the flames of war.

Magnus, Bernd. "Postmodern Pragmatism: Nietzsche, Heidegger, Derrida, and Rorty" in *Pragmatism: From Progressivism to Postmodernism, Hollinger, Robert (ed)*, 256-283. Westport, Praeger, 1995.

It is argued that postmodernism in philosophy, can best be understood through a genealogical account of the changed self-image of philosophy that emerges from selected works of Nietzsche, Heidegger, Derrida, and Rorty. Nietzsche's works may usefully be construed as establishing a quasi-narrative for themes, plot, and filial connection among authors. It is also argued that Rorty's postmodern pragmatism is the end of the road whose starting point began with the inscription "God is dead." An attempt is made, following Wittgenstein, to create a thought experiment to isolate and identify the defining postmodern disposition.

Magnus, Bernd (ed) and Cullenberg, Stephen (ed). *Whither Marxism?*. New York, Routledge, 1994.

What is living and what is dead in Marxism? Has the collapse of communism also spelled the death of Marxism, and of Marx as an important political thinker? Have we reached "the end of history" as Fukayama has argued, where pluralistic democracies and capitalist economies reign supreme? Is the future now a choice between Scandinavian style social democracy and unrestrained free market capitalism? Given the plight of the homeless, the lack of adequate health care, environmental degradation, racism, enormous national debt burdens, what sort of model for the future do we have? What is one to make of the violent nationalisms, ethnocentrism and xenophobia perhaps not seen since Hitler's Germany? What is the status of Marxist social goals such as the egalitarian distribution of income, increased workplace democracy, the end of economic exploitation and the eradication of class differences? Does the "end of history" also portend the end of Marxist theory? The *Whither Marxism* volumes raise these and related questions in an international and interdisciplinary context. (edited)

Maher, Patrick. Probabilities for New Theories. *Phil Stud*, 77(1), 103-115, Ja 95.

Mahoney, Daniel J. Modern Man and Man *Tout Court*: The Flight from Nature and the Modern Difference, Review Essay on *La Cité de l'homme*, by Pierre Manent. *Interpretation*, 22(3), 417-438, Spr 95.

Mahoney, Deirdre M (trans) and Clément, Catherine and O'Driscoll, Sally (trans). *Syncope: The Philosophy of Rapture*. Minneapolis, Univ of Minn Pr, 1994.

Mahowald, Mary Briody (ed). *Philosophy of Woman: An Anthology of Classic to Current Concepts (Third Edition)*. Indianapolis, Hackett, 1994.

Maia Neto, José R and Popkin, Richard H. Bishop Pierre-Daniel Huet's Remarks on Pascal. *Brit J Hist Phil*, 3(1), 147-160, F 95.

Bishop Pierre-Daniel Huet is an early modern sceptic who owned one of the largest private libraries in the period. Many of Huet's books are now preserved at the Bibliothèque Nationale in Paris, most of which contain marginal notes written by the Bishop. In the article, we examine Huet's remarks on the Port-Royal edition of Pascal's *Pensées*. Most of Huet's notes are very critical. Although both thinkers were critics of Descartes and inclined to scepticism, they construe scepticism quite differently. These differences are pointed out and traced to Pascal's and Huet's conflicting theological views.

Maidana, Susana H and de Medici, Cristina B. "La Posmodernidad en la Encrucijada Argentina" in *Temas Actuales de Filosofía, Palacios, María Julia (ed)*, 359-365. Buenos Aires, Univ Nacional Salta, 1993.

The presence of postmodernism and its contradictions in Latin American countries is shown in this work. While in central countries it is necessary to pay attention to consumerism and high technology, we are struggling against illiteracy, infant mortality and unemployment. The Latin American man has to face a hard choice: either his "belonging" to a rich culture, full of mysteries and myths, or his "alienation" in view of the speed of changes. His true challenge will be to root himself into the mythological universe which is his by nature, and at the same time venture the new paths of present culture.

Maillard, Chantal. Poétique de la Perception. *Horiz Phil*, 4(1), 1-14, Autumn 93.

An instant is always something that occurs and an occurence is a sheaf of relationships. How to talk about an occurence without the concept fitting it into portions of "reality"? How is an instant to be expressed? The author of this work tries to show the way to express this describing what she names "phenomenological poetry: a way to capture the fugacity & immediateness in the trajectory of the unifying gesture. The world, in this way, could be conceived as aesthetic object.

Mainberger, Gonsalv K. *Rhetorische Vernunft Oder: Das Design in der Philosophie*. Vienna, Passagen, 1994.

Rhetorik ist seit den griechischen Anfängen umstritten, ihr theoretischer Status und ihre praktische Anwendung provozieren zwiespältige Reaktionen. Mainbergers Studien besetzen genau den Ort dieses Zwiespalts—im Übergang von der Moderne zur Postmoderne und zurück. Hier ist rhetorisches Reden vernünftiges Reden, der Vernunftgebrauch umgekehrt ein rhetorischer. Vernunft-Wasser, so zeigen die Lektüren von Lévi-Strauss, Ricouer oder Derrida, speist die Quellen des Mythos und der Symbole, zerfliesst in sie, behält nur noch kryptische Präsenz. Der mit allen Wassern der kirchlichen und weltlichen Rhetorik-Tradition gewaschene Autor entziffert zuletzt noch das moderne Design als Transformation der rhetorischen Vernunft unter der Gestalt der *technē* in der Technik.

Mainzer, Klaus. *Computer-Neue Flügel des Geistes?*. Hawthorne, de Gruyter, 1994.

Computer and information technologies are the new 'wings' of modern culture in the sense of the Daidalos' myth. The book describes the foundation and development of these technologies (e.g., program-controlled computers, AI, knowledge-based systems, neural networks, cellular automata). It analyzes epistemic questions of computer-assisted mathematics, natural and social sciences, arts, virtual reality, and science fiction (e.g., computer experiments, simulations). It aims at a new approach to epistemology considering the possibilities and limits of a computer-assisted philosophy of language, science, and mind. Special emphasis is given to the ethical consequences of the new computer and information technologies.

Mainzer, Klaus. *Thinking in Complexity: The Complex Dynamics of Matter, Mind, and Mankind*. New York, Springer-Verlag, 1994.

The theory of nonlinear complex systems has become a successful and widely used problem solving approach in the natural sciences. It also has been recognized that many of the social, ecological, economic, and political problems of mankind are of a global, complex, and nonlinear nature. Even the human mind and brain seem to be governed largely by the nonlinear dynamics of complex systems, leading to the new perspectives of neural computers. Special emphasis is given to the ethical consequences of complex systems in the natural and cultural evolution. Thus the new integrative approach of complexity theory overcomes traditional reductionistic methods.

Maiocchi, Roberto. Fisica e Filosofia nella Cultura Italiana dei Primi due Decenni del Novecento. *G Crit Filosof Ital*, 72(3), 489-507, S-D 93.

Maiza Ozcoidi, Idoia. El Problema de la Causalidad en el *Tahafut* de Averroes. *Rev Espan Filosof Med*, 1, 75-97, 1994.

El Tahagut al-Tahagut de Averroes supuso la restauración del aristotelismo en toda su pureza. Escrito para defender la filosofía de los ataques de Algazel, polemiza con el teólogo persa sobre todas las grandes cuestiones filosóficas, entre otras, sobre el problema de la causalidad. Como el resto de los teólogos musulmanes, Algazel niega la eficacia de las causas segundas y atribuye a Dios la creacion de todos los movimientos y todos los accidentes. Averroes no pudo aceptar esta doctrina tan contraria a la experiencia. El presente articulo recoge los argumentos con los que el filósofo cordobés defendi la existencia de las causas segundas y examina las implicaciones metafísicas y epistemológica de ese ocasionalismo, tan pernicioso para el ejercicio de la autentica filosofía.

Maker, William. Reason *as* Revolution. *Phil Forum*, 26(1), 49-62, Fall 94.

This essay outlines out a defense of Hegel's claims to have completed philosophy with a system of freedom which provides a legitimation of modernity. The crucial Hegelian move is to show that coincidence of the self-legitimation required for philosophy with the self-determination basic to freedom. A revolutionary rejection of the authority of the given provides the key to that move by indicating how conceptual and practical normativity have a common source. This then makes possible a legitimation of modernity by overcoming relativism and postmodern nihilism.

Makin, Gideon. Making Sense of 'On Denoting'. *Synthese*, 102(3), 383-412, Ma 95.

The widely held assumption about what motivated "On Denoting" is irreconcilable with Russell's position shortly beforehand; but discarding it leaves one with a carefully worked out solution whose problem is missing. The real motivation is to be found in a notoriously obscure passage in OD, in which Russell exposes a decisive (though easily overlooked) flaw in his former theory of denoting; a flaw which also cripples Frege's theory of sense and reference. A comprehensive account of this passage is the chief concern of the present paper. Recognizing the critical role of this argument of Russell's leads to a more credible account of his argumentation in that essay. It also suggests that the fundamental standpoint underlying *The Principles of Mathematics* remains intact. In this light, the appropriation of OD to the philosophy of language may be misguided.

Makkai, M. Completeness Results for Intuitionistic and Modal Logic in a Categorical Setting. *Annals Pure Applied Log*, 72(1), 25-101, Mr 95.

Versions and extensions of intuitionistic and modal logic involving biHeyting and bimodal operators, the axiom of constant domains and Barcan's Formula, are formulated as structured categories. Representation theorems for the resulting concepts are proved. Essentially stronger versions, requiring new methods of proof, of known completeness theorems are consequences. A new type of completeness result, with a topos theoretic character, is given for theories satisfying a condition considered by Lawvere (1992). The completeness theorems are used to conclude results asserting that certain logics are conservatively interpretable in others.

Makropoulos, Michael. Moderne, Modernisierung, Modernität. *Phil Rundsch*, 41(3), 235-244, Je 94.

Maksimova, Larisa. On Variable Separation in Modal Logics. *Bull Sec Log*, 24(1), 21-25, Mr 95.

Malachov, Vladimir. Ist Philosophie auf Russisch möglich?. *Deut Z Phil*, 43(1), 63-73, 1995.

Malcolm, Norman and von Wright, Georg Henrik (ed). *Wittgensteinian Themes: Essays 1978-1989*. Ithaca, Cornell Univ Pr, 1995.

These are essays by the late Norman Malcolm (1911-1990) from the last twelve years of his life, a companion volume to his two earlier collections of essays *Knowledge and Certainty* and *Thought and Knowledge*. Some essays deal directly with aspects of Wittgenstein's thought—defending Wittgenstein's position against what the author considers misunderstandings or distortions. Others deal in what may be called a Wittgensteinian spirit with topics in the writings of Anscombe and Kripke—the last one, published posthumously, treats of Moore's Paradox. The essays are of high quality and stylistic elegance and testify to the originality and forcefulness of Malcolm's mind.

Maley, Terry. "The Politics of Time: Subjectivity and Modernity in Max Weber" in *The Barbarism of Reason, Horowitz, Asher (ed)*, 139-168. Toronto, Univ of Toronto Pr, 1994.

Maley, Terry (ed) and Horowitz, Asher (ed). *The Barbarism of Reason*. Toronto, Univ of Toronto Pr, 1994.

Maley, Yon. From Adjudication to Mediation: Third Party Discourse in Conflict Resolution. *J Prag*, 23(1), 93-110, Ja 95.

In Western societies, a range of institutional third party roles are employed in conflict or dispute resolution. This paper examines two of these: the traditional legal role of adjudicator and the newer, 'alternative' role of mediator. It is argued that they can best be described and explained in terms of institutional activity types, constituted by their linguistic and discoursal practices, and distinguished in terms of their relative degree of control over the process, substance and outcome of the dispute. Texts taken from Australian courts and divorce mediation sessions show how the third party's intervention and control is affected by the contextual purpose of the interaction, the job being done. Judges do more than adjudicate, and mediators do more than facilitate. Their jobs constitute a range of functional or rhetorical modes. Typically, their interventions can also be distinguished by the degree of authoritative intervention, and the kinds of directness and indirectness expressed.

Malherbe, Jean-François. Chemins et Impasses de l'Éthique à l'Hôpital. *Philosopher*, 16, 171-178, 1994.

Malherbe, Jean-François. Y a-t-il un Droit de Mourir?. *Philosopher*, 13, 69-91, 1992.

Malherbe, Jean-François and Rocchetti, Loretta and Boire-Lavigne, Anne-Marie. Validité et limites du consensus en éthique clinique. *Laval Theol Phil*, 50(3), 531-543, O 94.

Le caractère multiculturel qui marque profondément nos systèmes de valeurs rend difficile la référence à des normes reconnues par tous lorsqu'il est nécessaire de prendre une décision qui engage de multiples acteurs sociaux. Cette difficulté est particulèrement sensible lorsqu'il s'agit de prendre des décisions à l'égard de la mise en oeuvre des techniques biomédicales. Face à cette difficulté bien réelle, une tendance est apparue de fonder de telles décisions sur le consensus des personnes les plus directement concernées. L'objet de la présente discussion est d'évaluer la validité et les limites d'un tel recours au consensus. Le consensus auguel vise la discussion rationnelle entre les sujets éthiques à propos de la critique des normes particulières comme de l'application des normes universelles et particulières aux situations singulières, constitue une indispensable garantie à l'encontre de bien des arbitraires qui tendraient à s'emparer du pouvoir. Mais le refus inconditionnel de reconnaître l'existence de *dissensus avérés* aurait pour conséquence immédiate de restaurer subrepticement une forme d'arbitraire particulièrement subtile puisqu'elle se cacherait derrière le masque de la rationalité.

Malherbe, Jeanette. "Empirical Justification" in *Life, World and Meaning, Roux, A P J (ed)*, 79-92. Pretoria, Univ of S Africa, 1990.

This article develops an argument concerning the character of *empirical* justification as opposed to other possible kinds of justification. If it is sound, the argument provides support for foundationalism and poses a problem for coherentist accounts of empirical justification. It is shown that the general assumption that *empirical justification* is simply *the justification of an empirical belief* is mistaken by showing that there are at least three distinct kinds of reasons (semantic, probabilifying and empirical) that can be offered in justifying an empirical belief. They are distinguished by reference to the different relations they bear to the belief to be justified. The first two kinds of justification may apply to any sort of belief, while the last is peculiar to empirical beliefs.

Malherbe, Michel. "Hume and the Art of Dialogue" in *Hume and Hume's Connexions, Stewart, M A (ed)*, 201-223. University Park, Penn St Univ Pr, 1995.

Mali, Joseph. On Giambattista Vico. *Hist Euro Ideas*, 21(2), 287-290, Mr 95.

Maliandi, Ricardo. Convergencia ética. *Cuad Etica*, 14, 65-82, D 92.

Metaphysical theories have always considered conflictivity, whether to sustain that it makes the core of the real world, or, on the contrary, to reduce it to mere illusion, behind which some armony reigns. These two positions are related to (though do not identify with) metaphysical "dualisms" and "monisms" respectively. Although ethics may not find itself on metaphysics any more, it shares with the latter that concern about conflict, and may accept important suggestions from those theories that, as the Heraclitean, present ambiguity about their own positions. Ethics, understood as reason considering praxis, combines its tendency to solve conflicts with the acknowledgement of conflictivity, even at the level of moral principles. The moral convergence represented by that combination excludes both rigorism and relativism.

Malinowski, Jacek. Some Theorems on Equivalential Tense Logic. *Bull Sec Log*, 23(3), 98-103, O 94.

Mall, Ram Adhar. *Philosophie im Vergleich der Kulturen*. Darmstadt, Wiss Buchgesell, 1995.

The meeting of different cultures, philosophies and religions points to a de facto hermeneutic situation which calls for a new intercultural philosophical orientation. The book introduces a concept of intercultural philosophy which is not syncretism of different cultures and philosophies but represents a philosophical conviction that the one "philosophia perennis" is the exclusive possession of no one philosophical tradition. The theory and practice of intercultural philosophy serve the cause of such a conviction.

Mall, Ram Adhar. Wie indisch ist das Indienbild Schopenhauers?. *Schopenhauer Jahr*, 76, 151-172, 1995.

Malla, N. *Karma*, Causality and Freedom. *Indian Phil Quart*, 21(3), 237-248, Jl 94.

Malla, N. Value Neutrality of Social Sciences. *Indian Phil Quart*, 21(4), 297-306, O 94.

Mallard, Alison G and Lance, Charles E and Michalos, Alex C. Tests of the Causal Directions of Global-Life Facet Satisfaction Relationships. *Soc Indic Res*, 34(1), 69-92, Ja 95.

Previous research generally has supported multiple discrepancies theory (MDT) of the processes by which individuals arrive at judgments of satisfaction with various aspects of their lives as well as with life overall. However, the nature of possible causal relationships between overall and life facet satisfaction has been ignored. The purpose of this study was to extend MDT by testing alternative theoretical models which specified bottom-up, top-down, and bidirectional relationships between overall life satisfaction and satisfaction with eleven life facets in a sample of 1354 US college students. Results most strongly favored the bidirectional model in which the overall—life facet satisfaction relationship varied across life domains. The need to identify boundary conditions which determine the direction of the overall—life facet satisfaction relationship is discussed.

Malo, Antonio. Tre teorie sulle emozione: cognitiva, fenomenologica e comportamentistica (seconda parte). *Acta Phil*, 2(3), 339-352, 1994.

The second part of this article synthesizes the two other theories on emotions (phenomenological and behaviorist). After analyzing the main suggestions and problems which they contain, the author concludes that the connection between internal and external experiences seems to be necessary for the constitution of the emotion. However this connection can be explained neither in terms of efficient causality (as the modern cognitivism suggests) nor in terms of identity between emotion and behavior (as the behaviorism sustains), but in terms of a particular intention which corresponds to the vital relation between the person's tendencies and the reality.

Malone, David and Roberts, Robin W. An Analysis of Public Interest Reporting: The Case of General Motors in South Africa. *Bus Prof Ethics J*, 13(3), 71-92, Fall 94.

Malone, Patricia and Benson, Norman. Liberal Universalism and Multicultural Curricular Reform in the Social Studies: Issues to Consider. *J Thought*, 30(2), 9-20, Sum 95.

Liberal universalism's doctrine of political equality as an effective limitation on multicultural presentations of American history is linked to debates over the social studies curriculum. The liberal refusal to recognize cultural maintenance as a primary good in a liberal society and pluralists' objections to it are clarified. Modifications of liberal universalism are discussed. Teachers of American history are urged to emphasize the historical struggle between social groups to define the public culture as a unifying theme, to foster an understanding of the society as a whole and to allow minorities to be seen as active contestants in producing mainstream culture.

Maloney, J Christopher. Content: Covariation, Control and Contingency. *Synthese*, 100(2), 241-290, Ag 94.

The Representational Theory of the Mind allows for psychological explanations couched in terms of the contents of propositional attitudes. Propositional attitudes themselves are taken to be relations to mental representations. These representations (partially) determine the contents of the attitudes in which they figure. Thus, Representationalism owes an explanation of the contents of mental representations. This essay constitutes an atomistic theory of the content of formally or syntactically simple mental representation, proposing that the content of such a representation is determined by the intersection of the representation's correlational and control properties. The theory is distinguished from standard information-based accounts of mental content in allowing that the relevant correlations be contingent while insisting on an efferent aspect to mental content. The theory on offer allows for a natural explanation of misrepresentation, finds a niche for the notion of *narrow* content, welcomes radical first person fallibility with respect to questions of content, admits of mental ambiguity and recognizes that the future of a psychological agent is a factor in determining the content of the agent's present psychological states.

Malpas, J E (ed) and Donagan, Alan. *The Philosophical Papers of Alan Donagan: Volume I, Historical Understanding and the History of Philosophy*. Chicago, Univ of Chicago Pr, 1994.

This volume contains papers from 1957-1993 (two previously unpublished) on the methodology of historical research, the problems of historical understanding, and topics in the history of philosophy including a number of papers on Descartes, Spinoza, Collingwood and Wittgenstein. The volume contains an editorial introduction and a foreword by Stephen Toulmin.

Malpas, J E (ed) and Donagan, Alan. *The Philosophical Papers of Alan Donagan: Volume II, Action, Reason, and Value*. Chicago, Univ of Chicago Pr, 1994.

This volume contains papers from 1974-1991 (one previously unpublished) on the philosophy of action and moral philosophy. With papers on Kant, Von Wright, Sellars and Chisholm, the volume also addresses a range of issues in applied ethics from just war theory to the nature of legal practice. The volume includes a complete bibliography of Alan Donagan's published work as well as an editorial introduction and a foreword by Donald Davidson.

Malpas, Jeff. A Taste of Madeleine: Notes Toward a Philosophy of Place. *Int Phil Quart*, 34(4), 433-451, D 94.

This paper uses Proust's *A la recherche du temps perdu* as the starting point for an exploration of the nature and significance of the idea of place. The aim is thus to mark out some of the themes and ideas that indicate the direction the philosophical inquiry into place might take and, at the same time, to elaborate some of the ideas and images of place that are so central to Proust's search for lost time. The paper draws, not only on Proust, and the work of Proust scholars such as Georges Poulet, but also on the work of Martin Heidegger.

Malpas, R M P. An Electronic Text of Locke's *Essay*. *Locke News*, 21, 57-110, 1990.

Malpas, R M P. Locke and Hume Contrasted. *Locke News*, 22, 71-72, 1991.

Malter, Rudolf. Kant-Bibliographie 1992. *Kantstudien*, 85(4), 485-508, 1994.

Maltese Guerra, Luis F. "Aspectos Semióticos del Tractatus" in *Temas Actuales de Filosofía, Palacios, María Julia (ed)*, 367-378. Buenos Aires, Univ Nacional Salta, 1993.

Malusa, Luciano. Filosofia e Religione nelle Pagine del Giovane Gentile. *Riv Filosof Neo-Scolas*, 87(1), 83-118, Ja-Mr 95.

The young Giovanni Gentile makes his academic debut with a dissertation thesis on Rosmini and Gioberti. We find in this early work some interpretive themes which, subsequently, will remain at the core of his speculation in the period 1899-1915. The author of the present article claims that the aforementioned early work does not allow one to find the elements justifying Gentile's pro-Fascist political and ideological choice of 1923. On the contrary—the author argues—Gentile's reconstruction of Italian thought shows the attempt of reconciling idealism with the Catholic religious tradition of the Italian nation.

Malvern, S B. Inventing 'Child Art': Franz Cizek and Modernism. *Brit J Aes*, 35(3), 262-272, Jl 95.

The article examines the invention of 'child art' in modernism through a case study of the work of Frank Cizek, a Viennese art teacher who was well known in Britain, Europe and America in the 20s and 30s. In particular, the article sets the study within a wider framework of theories of modernism referring to writers such as Herbert Read and Jurgen Habermas, and ending with remarks about Gombrich and Popper. It examines some taken-for-granted assumptions about modernism, 'primitivism' and the child concluding that theories of 'child art' are no longer relevant but need to be considered within their historical context.

Mamzer, Henryk and Ostoja-Zagorski, Janusz. "Deconstruction of the Evolutionist Paradigm in Archaeology" in *Historiography Between Modernism and Postmodernism, Topolski, Jerzy (ed)*, 191-199. Amsterdam, Rodopi, 1994.

It is demonstrated that the claims of the evolutionary schema to universality are groundless. That schema reflects the specific point of view developed in the sphere of West European culture. Treating is as a modern conception projected onto the past tantamounts to questioning the causal order as the order of history. It means the decomposition of the linear concept of time as a mild continuum: the past- the present- the future. The pictures of the reality studies appear then as functionally determined relational systems whose functioning is not determined by the preceding situation. The teleological nature of history turns out to be a Utopia.

Mancini, Antonella and Montagna, Franco. A Minimal Predicative Set Theory. *Notre Dame J Form Log*, 35(2), 186-203, Spr 94.

Mandel, Ernest. "The Relevance of Marxist Theory for Understanding the Present World Crisis" in *Marxism in the Postmodern Age, Callari, Antonio (ed)*, 438-447. New York, Guilford, 1994.

Mandle, Jon. Having It Both Ways: Justification and Application in Justice as Fairness. *Pac Phil Quart*, 75(3-4), 295-317, S-D 94.

Mandrioni, Héctor D. Pulsión y Símbolo. *Stromata*, 50(1-2), 135-141, Ja-Je 94.

Manfreda, Luigi Antonio. *Aporie del Simbolo: Saggio su Otto Weininger*. Napoli, Liguori Ed, 1995.

The book deals with Otto Weininger's philosophical work which is put in relation with the Viennese cultural environment at the beginning of the 20th century. Weininger's work, which became famous for the theme of "sexes struggle", expresses, in Manfreda's view, a metaphysical conception based upon the scansion spirit/matter and the radicalization of Kantian ethical principle. Weininger leads the latter to the ultimate, aporethical consequences: the moral obligation, which is assumed in order to exclude the contingent from the quotidian, turns into the negation of life itself, proposing again the problem of an ontological foundation of moral itself.

Mangiagalli, Maurizio. Aristotle nel Novecento. *Aquinas*, 36(3), 613-641, S-D 93.

Manicas, Peter T. Nature and Culture. *Proc Amer Phil Ass*, 66(3), 59-76, N 92.

Manimala, Varghese. Economic Disparity: A Philosophic Response. *J Dharma*, 20(1), 94-103, Ja-Mr 95.

Man is a being unto himself. A human person is a project in the process of making himself or herself. Since man is a being-in-the-world, he has a responsibility to the whole world especially to all the human beings. Ours is a 'we-existence', a pro-existence (an existence for others). We complete our communitarian existence in the process of creating more just and human structures. The more just our structures are, the more human they become, and they help the human beings to reach that state of growth in which there is an experience of existing-for-one-another. The process of humanisation calls for the end of those structures which promotes dehumanisation. In the world of daily experience men are made use of for purposes which hardly befits them as human beings. In this paper our effort will be to analyze the proper response of philosophers towards economic inequality.

Manko, Jacek and Gerstenkorn, Tadeusz. The Philosophy of Fuzziness and the Mathematics of Randomness. *Stud Phil Christ*, 30(2), 83-97, 1994.

In the article we present various conceptions of the probability of fuzzy events as well as their evolution from the beginnings of fuzzy set theory. We want to call one's attention to their great variety and, with that, show the contribution of Polish mathematicians to the solving of this problem. The large number of ideas presented here witnesses the fact that the question of the connecting of fuzziness with randomness is still vivid, and that the search for an optimal solution is being continued without cease. We wish to convince the reader of the dissimilarity of the ideas of fuzziness and randomness as well as to stress the role of M Lubanski in the propagation of "fuzziness" in Poland at the very early stage of existence of this theory.

Mann, Doug. Collingwood's Hermeneutic of Acts and Events in Historical Explanation. *Eidos*, 11(1-2), 19-43, Je-D 93.

In this essay I first sketch out the act/event distinction that Collingwood makes in his theory of historical understanding in *The Idea of History*, and then go on the critique this distinction as excluding from historical explanation unintended consequences, botched plans, and moral evaluation, along with physiological and unconscious drives as causal factors in human action. I conclude that with these "amendments", Collingwood's hermeneutic of acts and events can be reconstructed as a serviceable historiographical principle.

Mann, Jesse D. William of Ockham, Juan de Segovia, and Heretical Pertinacity. *Med Stud*, 56, 67-88, 1994.

Mann, Patricia S. "Hate Speech, Freedom, and Discourse Ethics in the Academy" in *Radical Philosophy of Law, Caudill, David S (ed)*, 255-271. Atlantic Highlands, Humanities Pr, 1995.

The hate speech controversy cannot be satisfactorily resolved until two fundamental questions are fully explored: 1) Should sanctions against hate speech be deemed an important instrument for combatting racism, sexism, and homophobia on college campuses? 2) Can hate speech restrictions be formulated and theoretically justified in such a way as to forestall either capricious or repressive applications? I believe both questions can be answered affirmatively, and in this article I attempt to demonstrate that restrictions on campus hate speech are socially and politically warranted at this time.

Mannath, Joe. Gender Discrimination Today: A Philosophical Response. *J Dharma*, 20(1), 51-62, Ja-Mr 95.

Manninezhath, Thomas. A Vedantic Response to the Ecological Crisis. *J Dharma*, 20(1), 26-33, Ja-Mr 95.

At the very outset let us ask two significant questions: Is there an ecological crisis which decisively threatens our existence on earth, this beautiful planet? Should philosophers be concerned with the impending ecological crises which adversely affect our peaceful and authentic co-existence on this earth? I shall briefly discuss these two questions in this paper.

Manning, Rita C. Toward a Thick Theory of Moral Agency. *Soc Theor Pract*, 20(2), 203-220, Sum 94.

Manns, James W. *Reid and His French Disciples: Aesthetics and Metaphysics*. Leiden, Brill, 1994.

The book traces the spread of Thomas Reid's expressionist aesthetic theory through nineteenth-century France. It begins with an in-depth analysis of Reid's aesthetics, placing it in the framework of his metaphilosophy and epistemology. This is followed by chapters on Victor Cousin and Théodore Jouffroy. Cousin was France's most influential philosopher of the post-Napoleonic era, and his dependence on Reid in his epistemological and aesthetic thinking is demonstrated. Jouffroy was Cousin's student, then colleague. He thoroughly absorbed Reid's philosophical approach, and developed and enriched his aesthetic theory considerably. The influence these two individuals exerted on succeeding generations of academia and intellectuals is shown, with special attention given to Charles Lévêque and René Sully-Prudhomme.

Manos, Andreas. The Neoplatonic Interpretation as to the Teaching of Divine Love in Dionysius. *Diotima*, 23, 55-59, 1995.

Mans, Dieter. Argumentation im Kontext. *Protosoz*, 6, 160-183, 1994.

Some principles of logic-oriented theories of argumentation are discussed. A sharp distinction is drawn between arguments in formal contexts and arguments in nonformal contexts. It is argued, that the analysis of colloquial arguments cannot be based on the logic-oriented theories of argumentation. The outline of a more realistic theory of argumentation is given, by using defeasible inferences as a starting point. The model is applied to some everyday arguments.

Mansbach, A. Heidegger on the Work of Art and Human Existence (in Hebrew). *Iyyun*, 43, 427-440, O 94.

Mansbridge, Jane. Using Power, Fighting Power. *Constellations*, 1(1), 53-73, Ap 94.

Against theorists who associate democratic coercion with "violence": To act justly, democracies must practice some forms of more or less legitimate coercion ("power"), that legitimacy is partly independent of deliberative processes. Against theorists who accept the procedural fairness of majority rule: All forms of coercion can be correctly accused of procedural unfairness. Because democracies must use coercion to act justly, and because no coercion can be perfectly fair (indeed, most actual coercion embodies great unfairness), citizens must find ways of fighting coercion while using it (e.g., through the deliberative enclaves or "sequestered spaces" of identity politics).

Mansfeld, Jaap. Critical Note: Empedocles and his Interpreters. *Phronesis*, 40(1), 109-115, 1995.

Mansfeld, Jaap. The Idea of the Will in Chrysippus, Posidonius, and Galen. *Proc Boston Colloq Anc Phil*, 7, 107-145, 1991.

Mansfield, Harvey C. Self-Interest Rightly Understood. *Polit Theory*, 23(1), 48-66, F 95.

Mansilla, H C F. Las ambigüedades de la democracia y los enfoques postmodernistas. *Rev Filosof (Costa Rica)*, 31(75-76), 181-192, D 93.

Postmodernist approaches can supply a contribution in order to understand problems of actual political sciences, for they can relieve the rigours of the more classical theories. Those approaches help us to perceive more positively all phenomena of social and political heteregeneity; they provide us with a sceptical view of the grand systems and discourses; they allow a critique of modernity and thus a critique of material progress and development (as the most important normative goals of historical evolution); they favor the autonomy of different fields of action and thinking. Postmodernist approaches may help us to understand the ambiguities of modernization processes, but they also tend to dilute the conception of any public welfare and thus to justify the given situation of a society only because it is the actual one.

Mansini, Guy. Understanding St Thomas on Christ's Immediate Knowledge of God. *Thomist*, 59(1), 91-124, Ja 95.

This article argues, first, that the grounds on which St Thomas imputes an immediate vision of the essence of God to the human mind of the earthly Jesus have not been well understood. This vision is not deduced from the metaphysics of the hypostatic union, but invoked to explain the actual teaching of Jesus. It is argued, second, that the teaching of Jesus, even critically assessed, still requires St Thomas's explanation. B Lonergan's treatment of this issue is appealed to throughout.

Manson, Aaron. The Fate of Idealism in Modern Medicine. *J Med Human*, 15(3), 153-162, Fall 94.

William Osler's description of the ideal physician remains the dominant character-ideal for modern physicians. He believed that the personality traits that resulted from a belief in ascetic Protestantism, what has been called the Puritan temper, were essential in the practice of medicine. However, this idealism has been weakened by modern psychological theories which view idealism as an illness. In a culture oriented to health, rather than virtue, as an ultimate ideal, physicians can help develop a science of limits.

Manstetten, Reiner. *Esse est Deus: Meister Eckharts christologische Versöhnung von Philosophie und Religion und ihre Ursprünge in der Tradition des Abendlandes*. Freiburg, Alber, 1993.

Mantsivoda, Andrei. The Semantics of Flang. *Bull Sec Log*, 24(1), 26-30, Mr 95.

Mara, Gerald. The Near Made Far Away: The Role of Cultural Criticism in Aristotle's Political Theory. *Polit Theory*, 23(2), 280-303, My 95.

Within the postmodern liberalism of (say) Richard Rorty, cultural sources such as literature and ethnography play the largely reassuring role of confirming the adequacy of liberalism's public commitments. Yet this limited use of cultural sources may deprive public liberalism of an important and enriching kind of self criticism. I suggest that part of Aristotle's educational strategy in both the *Ethics* and the *Politics* is to reexamine cultural expressions (epic poetry, tragedy, history, ethnography) with a view to encouraging critical reflection on public priorities. This strategy signals a commitment to a discursive political philosophy which stands as an alternative to the possibilities envisaged within postmodernism.

Maraguianou, E. Le juste Politique est-il selon Platon Supérior aux Lois?. *Philosophia (Athens)*, 23-24, 145-153, 1993-94.

Platon dans le *Politique* déclare que le juste politique est supérieur aux lois, car la seule règle de la cité platonicienne est l'Idée du Bien contemplée par lui, Idée que le gouverneur doit imposer aux citoyens soit par la persuasion soit par la force, puisque son application sur la vie quotidienne rendra tout le monde vertueux et heureux. Il s'agit en réalité de la véritable science politique que possède l'homme d'Etat et qui crée une légitimité supérieure aux lois, une vie fondée sur la justice. En outre, les lois ont plusieurs défauts, i.e., elles sont trop générales en ce qui concerne les divers détails des cas particuliers; en plus elles n'ont pas la condescendence et la tolérance nécessaires du roi-philosophe, ni l'exactitude de la science politique. (edited)

Marcel, Anthony. "What is Relevant to the Unity of Consciousness?" in *Objectivity, Simulation and the Unity of Consciousness, Peacocke, Christopher (ed)*, 79-88. New York, Oxford Univ Pr, 1994.

Marchese, Francis T (ed). *Understanding Images: Finding Meaning in Digital Imagery*. New York, Springer-Verlag, 1995.

Marchildon, Louis. Causalité et Physique Moderne. *Horiz Phil*, 2(2), 65-82, Spring 92.

Quantum mechanics and the theory of relativity have brought forth a significant reexamination of the notion of causality. More recently, spin correlation measurements have cast doubt on the impossibility of sending faster-than-light signals. We review arguments showing that, on closer look, this impossibility is maintained. It appears, however, that systematic correlations between two event types cannot always be explained by a common cause.

Marchland, Suzanne L. The Rhetoric of Artifacts and the Decline of Classical Humanism: The Case of Josef Strzygowski. *Hist Theor*, 33(4), 106-130, 1994.

This essay argues that in overlooking the assault on the autonomy, unity, and tenacity of the classical world (and especially Rome) underway in Europe after 1880, historians have failed to appreciate an important element of historiographical reorientation at the fin de siècle. This second "revolution" in humanistic scholarship challenged the conviction of the educated elite that European culture was rooted exclusively in classical antiquity. The essay focuses on a relatively obscure Austrian art historian, Josef Strzygowski, whose insistence upon Europe's dependence on Oriental forms and upon the superior historical value of material, over textual, evidence provided critics of philologically-based humanism with two important argumentative avenues. (edited)

Marcil, Louise. Enseigner l'Éthique par l'Histoire. *Philosopher*, 16, 265-273, 1994.

Marcondes Cesar, Constança. La Pensée Comme Rédemption. *Diotima*, 23, 95-98, 1995.

Marconi, Diego. An Algebraic Characterization of Thomason's System Δ. *Rep Math Log*, 27, 3-18, 1993.

I show that S K Thomason's system Delta of paraconsistent logic is complete with respect to a class of structures called "Delta-algebras" (distributive lattices with nonstandard complementation). I try to make algebraic sense of the idea that Delta is a modal logic in disguise. Finally, I bring out certain relations between Delta, the classic propositional calculus, and Jaskowski's discussive logic.

Marconi, Diego. On the Structure of Lexical Competence. *Proc Aris Soc*, 95, 131-150, 1994-95.

In an intuitively motivated picture, to be competent in the use of words is, partly, to be able to manage a network of connections among words (*inferential* competence), and partly to be able to map the lexical items onto the world (*referential* competence). The two sides of competence are to some extent independent of and irreducible to each other. Command of either aspect may vary widely among individual speakers and, for each speaker, among different classes of words. Neuropsychological research on brain damaged patients appears to provide some evidence for a partial separation of two subsystems of lexical competence, one in charge of inferential performances such as definition, paraphase etc., the other involved in application (finding objects or pictures corresponding to a given word) and naming (finding the word appropriate to a given object or picture). However, the picture must be complicated: application and naming turn out to involve separate abilities; on the other hand, both referential and inferential performances appear to share a set of data—the semantic lexicon—whose units cannot be taken to coincide with mental representations of written or spoken words.

Marcuse, Herbert and Neumann, Franz. The Theory of Social Change with Introduction by Bill Scheuerman. *Constellations*, 1(1), 113-143, Ap 94.

Mares, Edwin D. A Star-Free Semantics for R. *J Sym Log*, 60(2), 579-590, Je 95.

The purpose of this paper is to show that semantics for relevance logic, based on the Routley-Meyer semantics, can be given without using the Routley star operator to treat negation. In the resulting semantics, negation is treated implicationally. It is shown that, by the use of restrictions on the ternary accessibility relation, simplified by the use of some definitions, a semantics can be stipulated over which *R* is complete.

Mares, Edwin D. Andersonian Deontic Logic. *Theoria*, 58(1), 3-20, 1992.

Marga, Andrei. "The Modern World and the Individual: From the Metamorphosis of Eastern European Marxism to Marx's Errors" in *Whither Marxism?, Magnus, Bernd (ed)*, 79-107. New York, Routledge, 1994.

Margolis, Eric. A Reckoning of Sorts on the Prospects of Moral Philosophy. *Phil Exch*, 24-25, 63-78, 1993-94.

Margolis, Joseph. "Deferring to Derrida's Difference" in *European Philosophy and the American Academy, Smith, Barry (ed)*, 195-226. Peru, Open Court, 1994.

Margolis, Joseph. "Vs (Wittgenstein, Derrida)" in *Wittgenstein and Contemporary Philosophy, Teghrarian, Souren (ed)*, 161-184. Bristol, Thoemmes, 1994.

Margolis, Joseph. A Biopsy of Recent Analytic Philosophy. *Phil Forum*, 26(3), 161-188, Spr 95.

Margolis, Joseph. Plain Talk About Interpretation on a Relativistic Model. *J Aes Art Crit*, 53(1), 1-7, Wint 95.

Margolis, Joseph. The Methodological and Metaphysical Peculiarities of the Human Sciences. *Midwest Stud Phil*, 15, 167-182, 1990.

Margolis, Joseph. *The Truth About Relativism*. Cambridge, Blackwell, 1991.

Margulis, Lynn and Sagan, Dorion. "Facing Nature" in *Biology, Ethics, and the Origins of Life, Rolston III, Holmes (ed)*, 39-62. Boston, Jones & Bartlett, 1995.

"Facing the Earth" is a study from the combined vantage point of evolutionary biology and continental philosophy of ethical frontiers and responsibilities with regard to humanities relationship to Earth. Alluding to work of E Levinas, G Bataille and J Derrida as well as H Spencer, C Darwin, M Ruse and E O Wilson it comes to the unsettling conclusion that no guard rails exist for an evolutionary ethic. Discussions include our predilection for ethical face-to-face relationships (i.e., with organisms that have faces and the fact that Earth now has nearly gained a face), Michael Ruse's literally adaptive morality, E O Wilson's ethical dilemma of biophilia, Derrida's possible solutions to the monstrosity of an infinite ethical abyss, Harold Bloom's interpretation of the ethnocentric behavior of nations as the ethically suspect history of superorganisms (acts necessary to the survival or expansion of larger biological entities) and the changing boundary of self, or "in-group" and of "out-group" as we move and remove the ethical line to include fewer or more of our planetmates.

Mari, Enrique E. "La Epistemología de Emile Zola" in *Temas Actuales de Filosofía, Palacios, María Julia (ed)*, 379-393. Buenos Aires, Univ Nacional Salta, 1993.

Marín, Vicente Serrano. Reflexiones Acerca del Papel de las *Eigne Meditationen* para la Formación del Sistema Transcendental de Fichte. *Daimon Rev Filosof*, 9, 39-49, 1994.

The article contrasts the transcendental treatment upon which Fichte attempts to establish theoretical-praxis unity in the bosom of Kant's philosophy, and the "precritical" nature of Reinhold project, aimed at basing this same philosophy on a principle. After making this distinction, the article considers that Reinhold's philosophy supposed, in part, a deviation for Fichte's original project. This deviation, moreover, would be echoed in the treatment, somewhat equivocal, that was given the notion of first principle in *Grundlage* in 1794. On the contrary, the essay *Eigne Meditationen* proved to be much more in line with Fichte's original intention; here, the notion of first principle appears in unquestionably transcendental terms.

Marín Casanova, José A. Ilustración y Romanticismo en la *Scienza Nuova*: La Racionalidad del Mito y el Mito de la Racionalidad. *Cuad Vico*, 2, 35-50, 1992.

Philosophy and History slept in the uterine peace of myth, where perhaps the fact of the beginning was the beginning of fact, where it was not conscious of the distinction between chronological origin and logical origin. But Philosophy and History woke up and, not remembering their maternal marriage, they mutually agreed to divorce. Probably the struggle between Enlightenment and Romanticism was the "ideal" expression of this effective scission between the rational and historical. However, this historical knowledge of the separation itself contributed to the very possibility of its being overcoming: the very conscience of history itself. This was the necessary requisite for a "Philosophy of History". The *Scienza Nuova* fullfills this as, in effectively reuniting Philosophy and Philology, it ideally relates the suppression of the Enlightenment-Romanticism dichotomy. Vico contributes a historical conscience which tells of a new logic, a modification of the Mind which, in making history of reason and reason of history, returns to myth its historical and rational condition, just as Philosophy and History regain their mythical originality.

Marinelli, Vincenzo. Giuridicità e durata. *Riv Int Filosof Diritto*, 71(3), 438-451, 1994.

Tratti caratteristici della regola sono la durata e la 'paradigmaticità—riduzione o uniformazione a un tipo, e più specificamente rapportarsi a una classe di azioni od omissioni omologhe—, non la generalità—nel comune significato che la riferisce a tutti i consociati o comunque ad una vasta pluralità di soggetti—, e non l'astrattezza—il volgersi esclusivamente a fatti futuri e magari incerti nell'*an o/e* nel *quando*—. La regola giudiziara è un riflesso della 'ricorsività' della regola legislativa o consuetudinaria, nella quale si riflette a sua volta l'esperienza della ricorsività dei fatti, nel loro risalto giuridico. (edited)

Marinho Sampaio, Tânia Maria. O Método Paulo Freire: A Inter-Relaçao da Teoria do Conhecimento com a Teoria da Sociedade. *Educ Filosof*, 8(16), 151-158, Jl-D 94.

Marini, Giuliano. Aspetti Sistematici della "Filosofia del Diritto" di Gentile. *G Crit Filosof Ital*, 73(2-3), 462-483, My-D 94.

Marinoff, Louis. Hobbes, Spinoza, Kant, Highway Robbery and Game Theory. *Austl J Phil*, 72(4), 445-462, D 94.

You are abducted by a highway robber, who intends to ransom you. In return for your release, you promise to deliver the ransom yourself. Should you subsequently keep your promise? Conflicting prescriptions by Hobbes, Spinoza, Kant and Kan (a hypothetical philosopher) are compared axiologically and assessed game-theoretically. Hobbes's strategy appears most robust. The problem itself is identified as a member of a class of games against nurture—as opposed to nature. And while constrained maximizers in this context are rational because they are moral, one cannot conclude (*pace* Gauthier) that they are moral because they are rational.

Marinov, Marin. The Case Against Connectionism: Productivity and Systematicity. *Eidos*, 12(1), 59-85, Je 94.

Marion, Jean-Luc. "Aporie ed origini della teoria spinoziana dell'idea adequata" in *L'etica e il suo Altro, Vigna, Carmelo (ed)*, 240-267. Milano, FrancoAngeli, 1994.

Marion, Jean-Luc and Carlson, Thomas A (trans). Metaphysics and Phenomenology: A Relief for Theology. *Crit Inquiry*, 20(4), 572-591, Sum 94.

Markakis, Manolis. Epistemology of the Value-Judgements. *Philosophia (Athens)*, 23-24, 88-103, 1993-94.

In this paper an attempt is being made to examine the epistemology of the value judgements and propositions of the social sciences in particular in comparison to that of the sciences of nature. In the degree to which the value element is a substantive and constitutive part of social action and of social institutions, such an element definitely enters into the formulation of social action propositions, the tendency to challenge the objectivity of such propositions and to consider them as wrong ones is erroneous. In addition, in the degree to which the value judgement in social science's propositions is indispensable, there also emerged the impossibility for their definitely classification as either false or true. (edited)

Market, Oswaldo. Aproximación al Morfema: Romanticismo Alemán. *An Seminar Hist Filosof*, 6, 155-175, 1986-89.

The aim of this article is to charactize the german "Frühromantik" by putting together the manifold outlines of his creative scopes and achievements. The Author defends that this movement is a "global movement"—not only a literary one—that shares with German Idealism and Classicism the leading role in the "revolution of the spirit" accomplished at the time. Its printing mark is to change the ideal of praxis into one of poiesis, to convert destiny into freedom and to assume the tragic creative split, by which the "progressive" and "interesting" opposes itself to the "objective" of Classicism.

Market, Oswaldo. Etica y Racionalidad en Kant. *An Seminar Hist Filosof*, 9, 59-75, 1992.

El gran edificio de la Moral kantiana, construido sobre una sólida concepción de la naturaleza de lo ético, deja con todo un margen a la perplejidad: No acaba de convencer. Estudiadas las líneas maestras de su arquitectónica, la investigación que busca hallar la raíz de esta insatisfacción, termina por centrarse en el concepto kantiano de "razón práctica". En él se descubre el uso del modelo jurídico, que tiene como consecuencia una concepción de la ley moral que encaja más en el orden del derecho que en el ético.

Market, Oswaldo. La Exigencia Ontológica Radical en Fichte y su Necesaria Ruptura con el Criticismo. *An Seminar Hist Filosof*, 11, 155-170, 1994.

Der Verfasser versucht zu erklären, inwiefern schon bei der ursprünglichen Standpunkt Fichtes einen unabsichtigen aber nicht desto weniger unvermeidlichen Bruch mit dem Kritizismus Kants sich *in nuce* versteckt. Zuerst weist der V darauf hin, dass schon die frühesten Abweichungen von wichtigen Thesen Kants, die mit der Abzielung Fichtes zum Ich—nicht zum *Ich denke*—unvereinbar sind, das Problem des Zugangs zum Sein des Ich herausstellen. Von solchem Zugang wird dann vom V eine transzendentale ontologische Deduktion unternommen, die die spätere Darstellungen Fichtes (besonders in der *WL* 1805) erhellen soll. Zum Schluss wird die Aufgabe Fichtes als einen grundlegenden Versuch interpretiert, der das Problem des Seins in seinem einzigen möglichen Form (die des Ich) einbringt.

Markosian, Ned. The 3D/4D Controversy and Non-Present Objects. *Phil Papers*, 23(3), 243-249, N 94.

The "endurance versus perdurance", or "3D versus 4D", controversy has been much-discussed in recent philosophy. But on the standard way of formulating the 3D and 4D views, both views have unwanted consequences. For on the standard formulations, both views entail presentism, the view that only present objects exist. The aim of this paper is to show that this is so, and to propose improved formulations of the views at issue in the 3D/4D controversy.

Markosian, Ned. The Open Past. *Phil Stud*, 79(1), 95-105, Jl 95.

I first spell out the open future response to fatalistic arguments. Then I formulate what I take to be the only plausible, nonquestion-begging defense of the open future response. This defense involves both 1) The claim that the laws of nature are indeterministic and 2) A certain version of the correspondence theory of truth. Finally, I argue that there is a very surprising consequence of justifying the open future response by making the defense in question, namely, that the past is sometimes open.

Markovic, Mihailo. "Political Rights Versus Social Rights" in *Human Rights and the World's Religions, Rouner, Leroy (ed)*, 46-60. Notre Dame, Univ Notre Dame Pr, 1988.

Marks, Joel. "Dispassion and the Ethical Life" in *Emotions in Asian Thought, Marks, Joel (ed)*, 139-159. Albany, SUNY Pr, 1995.

The dominant ideology among contemporary emotion theorists, cognitivism, undercuts the traditional philosophic view of emotion as irrational or even as simply nonrational. Furthermore, feminists have championed the value of emotion as a way of knowing. In this essay a virtue of dispassion is defended by reference to a particular analysis of emotion. Emotion is argued to involve not only belief, but also desire, and in particular strong desire. It is then possible to defend dispassion as the absence of emotion, while yet retaining, indeed enhancing, the sorts of feelings, attitudes, and motivations one would prize in an ethical life.

Marks, Joel. "Emotions in Western Thought: Some Background for a Comparative Dialogue" in *Emotions in Asian Thought, Marks, Joel (ed)*, 1-38. Albany, SUNY Pr, 1995.

This is the introductory essay to a volume that addresses the nature and ethics of emotions from both Asian and comparative perspectives. This introduction prepares the way with some background on the contemporary debate in the West, beginning with the "New View" of emotions as complex intentional structures, as opposed to mere feelings, and proceeding to the "Newer View," whose roots lie in feminism and social theory, that emotions are essentially cultural. Originally appearing in an issue of *Philosophy East and West*, the essay has been revised and contains an extensive bibliography updated for this volume.

Marks, Joel (ed) and Ames, Roger T (ed). *Emotions in Asian Thought*. Albany, SUNY Pr, 1995.

In recent years emotion has become the focus of intensive theoretical work among philosophers of the West, but what is striking to a comparative philosopher is the almost total lack of references to non-Western thought. This book redresses that situation. Beginning with an overview of recent work in the West, the inquiry preceeds to the main business of scrutinizing various relevant issues from both Asian and comparative perspectives, including original essays by June McDaniel, Purushottama Bilimoria, Leroy Rouner, Joel Kupperman, Joel Marks, Mary Bockover, Chad Hansen, and Graham Parkes. The book concludes with an extensive overview by Robert Solomon.

Markus, György. The Ends of Metaphysics. *Grad Fac Phil J*, 18(1), 249-270, 1995.

The history of metaphysics—evoked through reminders of its conceptualisation by Aristotle, Descartes, Kant and Hegel—represents a continuous effort to unify some cognitive interests and ends; the onto-logical, the cosmo-theological and the anthropological, that in the course of this history repeated fall apart but simultaneously manifested a particular affinity. Today this cohesion and even the striving for it seems to have disappeared. Particular and isolated problems that can directly be traced back to the heritage of metaphysics may well live on as matters of genuine philosophical interest, but they are no longer thought to be encompassable by a single conceptual framework and thereby lost precisely their metaphysical significance. It is argued that the animating motive and intention of metaphysics today is present only in those "narrative" philosophies which renounce its claim to explanatory knowledge.

Marlin, Randal. Public Relations Ethics: Ivy Lee, Hill and Knowlton, and the Gulf War. *Int J Moral Soc Stud*, 8(3), 237-256, Autumn 93.

The public relations firm of Hill and Knowlton has received severe criticism for the methods it used on behalf of its client, Citizens for a Free Kuwait, to persuade the US Congress and the American people to wage war on Iraq. In particular, a widely circulated story about Iraqis removing 312 babies from incubators and leaving them to die on the floor fuelled anger against the Iraqis. The story was later discredited, though other atrocities have been documented. A major factor in public acceptance of the story was endorsement by Amnesty International and emotional testimony by a girl identified only as 'Nayirah'. The incident underscores the importance of the most central ethical concern expressed by the highly successful early practitioner and theorist of public relations, Ivy Lee; namely, that the source of persuasive materials presented to the public should never be disguised. The factual record of the incubator story and Lee's ethical writings are both examined with a view to exploring the ethics of the case.

Marquand, David. "After Socialism" in *The End of "Isms"?, Shtromas, Alexsandras (ed)*, 45-58. Cambridge, Blackwell, 1994.

Marques, António. Schopenhauer, Kant y las Aporías de la Voluntad Incondicionada. *An Seminar Hist Filosof*, 9, 169-179, 1992.

Schopenhauer's argument against Kantian morals defines for contemporary thought a model of that radical critique of reason, which our century in many ways has developed. More or less explicitly, the Schopenhauerian critique will be present in the work of figures such as Nietzsche, Freud, Adorno or Foucault. The modern self-assertion founded on unconditional laws of reason begins to be considered as a fictional creation of a "formalistic", "instrumental", or "provocative" reason. Still it is important to come back to the genesis of this critical thought be a new evaluation of the Schopenhauerian argumentation. Our conclusion: such an argument doesn't destroy the basic presuppositions of the Kantian ethics, but appears as a challenge in order to a more comprehensive understanding of the dialectical process between freedom and nature, developed by Kant in his first two *Critiques*.

Marquet, Jean-François. Subjectivité et absolu dans les premiers écrits de Schelling (1794-1801). *Rev Int Phil*, 49(191), 39-58, 1995.

Marquéz, Gustavo. Actitud crítica y racionalidad en Popper. *Rev Filosof (Argentina)*, 9(1-2), 43-54, N 94.

This paper deals with two conceptions about Popper's rationality, one of them belonging properly to the negative, eliminatory tradition, and the other one the positive and creative attitude to the development of knowledge. To examine the differences between both approaches to rationality I will compare Popper's conceptions with Mill's. Finally, I will defend the position that both notions are important and should be preserved and integrated in a broader and richer conception of rationality.

Marqueze, Jorge R. Es la uniformidad semántica una condición de corrección formal de una teoría del modo oracional?. *Rev Filosof (Spain)*, 4(6), 285-310, 1991.

Is there a condition of semantic uniformity that any adequate theory of sentential mood should meet? I examine the relevance of this condition for the construction of a (preferably Davidsonian) truth-conditional theory of mood. I review several notions of semantic uniformity but focus my attention mainly on Dummett's notion of *key concept of semantics*. In particular, I criticize a thesis suggested by Dummett: the idea that a strong notion of semantic uniformity is a necessary condition for accepting the basic, Fregean sense/force distinction. I conclude that the condition of uniformity admits formulations of different strength. In its stronger versions, the alleged condition is not a genuine condition. In its weaker versions it is acceptable, but (largely) trivial.

Marquinez Argote, Germán. Existe en Zubiri una protopolítica?. *Dialogo Filosof*, 10(3), 377-390, S-D 94.

Pese a la ausencia de una filosofía formalmente política en Zubiri, descubrimos en su pensamiento el esbozo de una protopolítica a partir de una protofilosofía del poder. Los dinamismos más propios de la historia no son potencias ni poderes naturalmente emergentes, sinno poderes opcionalmente posibilitantes. Este poder de las posibilidades es un concepto arraigado en la metafísica zubiriana que, en sus diversas vertientes, permite comprender también el dinamismo político como potestativo.

Marquínez Argote, Germán. Reflexiones Zubirianas Sobre la Fruición y el Amor. *Analogia*, 8(2), 3-35, 1994.

Marquis, Don. Justifying the Rights of Pregnancy: The Interest View. *Crim Just Ethics*, 13(1), 67-81, Wint-Spr 94.

Bonnie Steinbock in *Life Before Birth* claims that her interest view provides a better defense of pregnancy rights than a personhood strategy or Thomson's view. I argue that, contrary to Steinbock, the interest view does not entail that insentient fetuses lack moral standing. Even if it did, Steinbock's actual personhood defense of abortion rights renders the interest view redundant. In addition, the interest view fits poorly with her treatment of maternal-fetal conflicts. Steinbock's theory also leaves one without a plausible account of the wrongness of infanticide.

Marra, Michele. Japanese Aesthetics: The Construction of Meaning. *Phil East West*, 45(3), 367-386, Jl 95.

Two major hermeneutical practices in the history of interpretation in premodern Japan are located. The first—a deconstructive practice followed by medieval thinkers (Dogen) and poets (Fujiwara Shunzei and Fujiwara Teika)—interprets reality by deferring and dispersing it in its representations. The analogies of this methodology are highlighted with what the Italian philosopher Gianni Vattimo has called "*pensiero debole*" (weak thought). The latter recuperates the centrality of the concept of presence whose disclosure becomes the major task of the interpreter. Examples of this solidification of meaning are taken from works of the Nativist scholars Motoori Norinaga (1730-1801) and Fujitani Mitsue (1768-1822).

Marras, Ausonio. Nonreductive Materialism and Mental Causation. *Can J Phil*, 24(3), 465-493, S 94.

The aim of this paper is to defend a version of nonreductive materialism against the epiphenomenalist objection to which Davidson's anomalous monism has often been held to be vulnerable. After considering a number of options for dealing with the objection, I argue that an appeal to the notion of strong supervenience (properly explicated) can both rebut a common form of the *property* (*type*) epiphenomenalist objection and provide a grounding for the causal relevance ("efficacy") of mental properties.

Marrone, Pierpaolo. Rorty, Rawls, e il relativismo. *G Metaf*, 16(1-2), 239-248, Ja-Ag 94.

Marsh, James. *Critique, Action, and Liberation*. Albany, SUNY Pr, 1995.

Marsh, James L. Post-Modernism: A Lonerganian Retrieval and Critique. *Int Phil Quart*, 35(2), 159-173, Ju 95.

Marshall, Bruce D. 'We Shall Bear the Image of the Man of Heaven': Theology and the Concept of Truth. *Mod Theol*, 11(1), 93-117, Ja 95.

This essay proposes a theological account of the notion of truth in light of the widespread assumption that realism is dead. It argues that Davidson's conception of truth is a plausible alternative to both realism and anti-realism, and as such the best currently available philosophical treatment of the notion of truth. But an adequate theological account of truth needs to discipline the best available philosophical treatment by lodging the whole debate about what truth is in reflection on the triune being and action of God; that is what the concluding sections of this essay attempt to do.

Marshall, James. "The Autonomous Chooser and 'Reforms' in Education" in *Identity, Culture, and Education, Smeyers, Paul (ed)*, 223-231. Leuven, Leuven Univ Pr, 1994.

Underlying recent reform literatures in Western educational systems have been notions of freedom, autonomy, choice, and quality, with the notion of the autonomous chooser paramount. It is claimed that the quality of educational choices, the quality of the community, and the relations between learning institutions are enhanced by the consumer driven activities of autonomous choosers. But are these reforms, or merely *changes* in the forms that governmentality takes? It is argued, against a Foucauldean background, that choice, needs, interests, and quality are constituted in such ways that personal autonomy is problematic at the least and politically dangerous at the worst.

Marshall, James. Michel Foucault: Governmentality and Liberal Education. *Stud Phil Educ*, 14(1), 23-34, 1995.

Educational philosophers in the liberal tradition write as if power is at best a necessary evil, and something which is contrary to the interests of the young. In this liberal paradigm it is rational authority exercised in the interests—the "real" interests of the child—which carries the conceptual, theoretical and practical weight, and which produces the autonomous individual. Foucault believed this was a myth, which obscured the ways in which our notions of ourselves as free and autonomous choosers were themselves social constructions, and which permitted us to be *governed* both individually and collectively. According to Foucault governmentality has touched us all, so that we are not the free autonomous individuals that liberal education would make us out to be.

Marshall, James D. On What We May Hope: Rorty on Dewey and Foucault. *Stud Phil Educ*, 13(3-4), 307-323, 1994-95.

Rorty (1982) argues that there is little essential difference between Dewey and Foucault. If we accept Rorty's general line of argument, that the lines between novels and the human sciences become blurred and are drawn only pragmatically then, there are still two ways to go. Essentially, these are the optimistic and pessimistic paths taken by Dewey and Foucault respectively. The paths do not differ theoretically, he claims, but only over what we may hope. It is argued that this is not only a gross simplification of the positions of Dewey and Foucalt, but that also the central claim is mistaken.

Marshall, Paul (ed) and Chaplin, Jonathan (ed). *Political Theory and Christian Vision: Essays in Memory of Bernard Zylstra*. Lanham, Univ Pr of America, 1994.

This is a compilation of articles in political theory written from a Christian perspective and published in memory of Bernard Zylstra, who taught at the Institute for Christian Studies in Toronto. Its aim is to illustrate the fruitfulness of Christian political theorizing across a range of contemporary subjects. The first part deals with foundational themes including law and grace, the basis of rights, and the link between normative and empirical theory. The second explores a Christian conception of the state with special reference to its implications for cultural pluralism and inter-state relations. The final part addresses themes in political economy.

Marshall, Paul A (ed) and Vandervennen, Robert E (ed). *Social Science in Christian Perspective*. Lanham, Univ Pr of America, 1988.

Marsolais, Arthur. Quelques Pistes de Réflexion sur l'Avenir de l'Enseignement Collégial de la Philosophie. *Philosopher*, 14, 181-188, 1993.

Marsonet, Michele. *Science, Reality, and Language*. Albany, SUNY Pr, 1995.

This book criticizes the antirealist stance currently flourishing in philosophy of science and maintains that many contemporary philosophers of science, although they define themselves empiricists, have in fact evolved into "linguistic idealists". After underlining that most practicing scientists find the linguistically oriented philosophy of science useless, the conclusion is that a naturalistic philosophy of science is needed, in which language is no longer taken to be the whole of reality, but just a human product created for practical and social purposes. The book means to transform the current debate between realism and antirealism, and to reestablish some form of naturalism. It also contains a reevaluation of the contributions of American pragmatism to the philosophy of science and the philosophy of language.

Marten, Rainer. *Heidegger Lesen*. München, Wilhelm Fink, 1991.

Reading Heidegger means bringing him back from mythical and mystical claims to the test of truth. Crucial point is the review of the relationship between philosophical existence and the "phenomenon" ("appropriation") of "being's" being "illuminated" at all; the dramatization of "human" existence as being devoted to the very Being ("Being 'itself'"). An extended analysis of Heidegger's rather free treatment of Greek philosophers demonstrates his effort to legitimize and immunize his own philosophy.

Martens, David. Demonstratives, Descriptions, and Knowledge: A Critical Study of Three Recent Books. *Phil Phenomenol Res*, 54(4), 947-963, D 94.

Marti, Genoveva. Do Modal Distinctions Collapse in Carnap's System?. *J Phil Log*, 23(6), 575-593, D 94.

Marti, Genoveva. The Essence of Genuine Reference. *J Phil Log*, 24(3), 275-289, Je 95.

A discussion of two characterizations of the notion of genuine reference: first, a purely Millian characterization, according to which a genuinely referential term is one whose connection to an object is essentially unmediated. Second, the characterization of Direct Reference theory, according to which a genuinely referential term is one that contributes its referent to the propositions expressed by sentences containing it. It is claimed that both conceptions of genuine reference do not capture the same underlying notion. They rely on different intuitions, they use different tools and they do not even coincide in their classifications of terms as genuinely referential.

Martin, Bill. *Humanism and its Aftermath: The Shared Fate of Deconstruction and Politics*. Atlantic Highlands, Humanities Pr, 1995.

Martin, Christopher. An Ingenuous Account of the Doctrine of the Mean. *Topicos*, 4(6), 31-57, 1994.

Aristotle admits the possibility of many vices opposed to one virtue, but insists that there are always at least two, related as deficiency and excess. The doctrine that "virtue is in a mean" is thus both true and useful.

Martin, Christopher. Libertad y revocabilidad. *Anu Filosof*, 27(3), 991-1005, 1994.

The article treats with the voluntary action (in which we can include the free human action) and non voluntary causality. The author wants to give some aclarations over the actual controversy, from Aquinas thought.

Martin, Christopher. On a Mistake Commonly Made in Accounts of Sixteenth-Century Discussions of the Immortality of the Soul. *Amer Cath Phil Quart*, 69(1), 29-37, Wint 95.

Martin, Michael. Scepticism About Legal Reasoning. *Commun Cog*, 28(1), 55-76, 1995.

Legal reasoning is supposed to provide an objective rationale for legal decisions. Without such reasoning, it has been said, legal decisions would be arbitrary, capricious and subjective. Judges justify their decisions by appealing to rules, principles, precedents, and other legal standards. Reasoning from these by deductive logic, analogy, and other forms of inference they draw conclusions and make their decisions. In this paper I will consider five arguments purporting to show that legal reasoning lacks objectivity: the arguments from a class bias in the ability of legal reasoners, from rationalization, from conflicting conclusions, from legal gaps, from the meaningless nature of legal concepts. After saying how these can be challenged, I will maintain that the skepticism about legal reasoning embodied in them can be formulated into a useful research program. (edited)

Martin, Michael R. Ritual Action (*Li*) in Confucius and Hsun Tzu. *Austl J Phil*, 73(1), 13-30, Mr 95.

Confucian conceptions of the self and of morality more generally are criticized against the backdrop of current discussions of autonomy and individualism. While Hsun Tzu saw better than Confucius some of the epistemological difficulties in justifying the central Confucian notion of ritual action (*li*), the article suggests why Hsun Tzu failed to liberate Confucianism from its more authoritarian flourishes.

Martin, Mike W. Adultery and Fidelity. *J Soc Phil*, 25(3), 76-91, Wint 94.

The ethics of adultery is more complex than obeying rules against promise breaking, deception, and avoiding harm. With regard to traditional relationships, the moral status of adultery centers on commitments to love, where love is understood in terms of moral ideals such as lifelong caring, trust, and honesty—ideals which make love a special way to value persons. Complicating matters, however, are changing commitments, lost love, new loves, and the relevance of self-esteem and luck. These complexities bear upon evaluating the reported adultery of public officials.

Martin, Mike W. Religion Ethics and Professionalism. *Prof Ethics*, 3(2), 17-35, Sum 94.

Religion ethics is the study of the moral implications of religious organizations and practices, whereas clergy ethics is the narrower ethical study of norms of professional clergy. Margaret Battin's pioneering book *Ethics in the Sanctuary* is best viewed as a work on religion ethics. She would do better, however, to sharply distinguish professional and nonprofessional religious practitioners, and to bear in mind the moral relevance of voluntary membership in religious organizations. Also objectionable is her way of precluding fundamental religious doctrines from scrutiny by applied ethicists.

Martin, Mike W. Rethinking Reverence for Life. *Between Species*, 9(4), 204-213, Fall 93.

Albert Schweitzer's ethics of reverence for life is more complex than first appears. It contains themes relevant to contemporary environmental ethics, including a virtue-ethics approach, personal responsibility and tolerance, the fundamental unity of life, and empathy for all living things. Schweitzer's metaphysics blurred his elaboration of these themes, but the metaphysics can be set aside without substantial loss.

Martin, Mike W. Teaching Philanthropy Ethics. *Teach Phil*, 17(3), 245-260, S 94.

Philanthropy Ethics—that is, moral inquiry into voluntary giving (of time, money, or things) for public purposes—is a neglected area of philosophical study and teaching. Courses on philanthropy ethics might focus on social and political issues about the overall impact of philanthropy on society, the professional ethics of fund raisers and executives in nonprofit organizations, or (as with my course) personal ethics concerning responsibilities to help, duties to respect autonomy (of givers and receivers), virtues in helping, motives in giving, and the claim that giving is self-fulfilling. I discuss teaching strategies, texts, and interdisciplinary approaches.

Martin, Nicholas. 'We Good Europeans': Nietzsche's New Europe in *Beyond Good and Evil*. *Hist Euro Ideas*, 20(1-3), 141-144, Ja 95.

Martin, Rex (ed) and MacCallum Jr, Gerald C and Singer, Marcus G (ed). *Legislative Intent and Other Essays on Law, Politics, and Morality*. Madison, Univ of Wisconsin Pr, 1993.

This book contains fourteen papers by the late Gerald MacCallum, five not previously published. In addition to the author's corrected version of "Legislative Intent and Negative and Positive Freedom," it contains papers that link with them, such as "On Applying Rules" and "Some Truths and Untruths about Civil Disobedience." There are also interrelated papers on such themes as conscience, law, violence, personal integrity, and representation, and a little known paper on "Censorship in the Arts." The previously unpublished writings include groundbreaking papers on "Competition and Moral Philosophy" and "Justice and Adversary Proceedings," discussions of violence and conscience, and "Dworkin and Judicial Discretion." The editors have provided a preface, an introduction, a memoir of the author, a bibliography of his writings, and explanatory comments when needed.

Martin, Robert M. *There are Two Errors In the the Title of This Book: A Sourcebook of Philosophical Puzzles, Problems, and Paradoxes*. Peterborough, Broadview Pr, 1992.

This book is a collection of puzzles, paradoxes, thought-experiments, jokes, fables, etc., with brief discussions of the philosophical questions each one raises, and possible answers.

Martin, Shirley Davis. Differences in the Ethical Decision-Making of Nursing Faculty and Nursing Staff. *Prof Ethics*, 2(3-4), 173-186, Fall-Wint 93.

Ethical decision making is an integral part of nursing practice. However, substantive content related to ethics is applied inconsistently in nursing curricula and models of decision making for nurses are in a developing state. This study was conducted to compare differences between nursing staff and nursing faculty responses to selected ethical dilemmas. Fifty-two staff and thirty-three faculty completed Crisham's Nursing Dilemma Test. The group were distinctly different in age and educational level, the factors reported to enhance ethical decision making most consistently. However, no significant differences were found between the groups. This demonstrates a continuing need for nurses to receive education in bioethics and ethical decision making.

Martin, Tony and Brant, Renée and Wyatt, Gail Elizabeth. Child Abuse or Acceptable Cultural Norms. *Ethics Behavior*, 5(3), 283-292, 1995.

Martineau, Emmanuel. L'ontologie de la spécificité. *Rev Phil Fr*, 3, 337-349, Jl-S 94.

Martineau, Jean-François. La Réforme et le Rôle de la Philosophie dans la Formation Collégiale. *Philosopher*, 15, 155-161, 1994.

Martineau, Jean-François. Pour un Enseignement Relativiste de l'Éthique. *Philosopher*, 16, 181-187, 1994.

Martinez, Roy. Pedagogy, Philosophy, and African-American Students. *Teach Phil*, 17(4), 351-358, D 94.

The aim of this essay is twofold: 1) to report a dramatic turn of events at Spelman College concerning attitudes towards philosophy among students, and 2) to explain how it might have occurred. The reason for writing it is to respond to several chairs who have approached me inquiring about pedagogic methods and curricula they could adopt in order to attract African-American students to philosophy. I will address that question by offering some practical suggestions.

Martínez, José A. Filosofía e Historia Según I. Ellacuría. *Pensamiento*, 199(51), 149-153, Ja-Ap 95.

I. Ellacuría, en su obra póstuma *Filosofía de la realidad histórica*, realiza la fundamentación de la filosofía de la historia basándose nuclearmente en la metafísica de X. Zubiri, entendiendo que la "realidad histórica" es el "objeto último" de la filosofía. A esta tesis llega Ellacuría, tras años de labor filosófica, a partir inicialmente de los textos y cursos principales de Zubiri y de trabajos que sobre la historia escribiera desde 1935, de los que Ellacuría comenzó a dar cuenta hacia 1966 en un artículo titulado "La historicidad del hombre en Xavier Zubiri". El comentario se refiere al contenido de las partes de la obra de Ellacuría, en las que se incluye tanto la definición real de la historia cuanto los elementos y componentes de la misma que es preciso analizar para la cabal comprensión y exposición de su consistencia y desarrollo, sin rechazar la apertura a la trascendencia del mundo y la historia, de la que Ellacuría se ha ocupado en trabajos que también póstumamente han aparecido en *Mysterium liberationis*.

Martinez Bisbal, Josep. Vico in Spagna: Per Introdurre. *Boll Centro Stud Vichiani*, 24-25, 205-209, 1994-95.

This paper was the introduction to a debate on "Vico in Spanish Culture" held in 1991 at the University of Valencia, Spain. It offered a general view of Spanish Vichism from the eighteenth century to the present that would serve as a background to the contributions of the participants in the round table. The paper states that Vico's philosophy has had little influence on Spanish philosophy, although, in recent years, a remarkable increase in studies concerning Vico and his thought has been observed.

Martínez de Velasco, Jesús. El Cambio Científico y el Modelo de Solución de Problemas de L Laudan. *Themata*, 13, 199-210, 1995.

In this article we compare and contrast the points of view of Kuhn and Laudan about their respective models in considering rational change in science. If Kuhn insists, above all, on the external history of science as the motor of scientific change, Laudan bases his argument on cognitive history which, by means of questions and answers, as in whichever other cognitive activity, has progressed in clarifying unknown factors, solving mysteries, eliminating anomalities, explaining facts, clarifying concepts and, in short, solving problems. We see how Laudan—starting from his reticulated model of rationality, in which methods, theories and objectives can change in a partial and gradual way—allows us to continue referring to progressive scientific change, simply when a theory or set of the theories of a research tradition are more efficient than its rivals at solving problems. Although it's impossible to establish a valid criteria of rationality for all eras, Laudan believes that science, globally considered, continues to be a rational enterprise which change progressively, although, at the local level, non-rational elements can be encountered when choosing a theory or research tradition.

Martínez Esteruelas, Cruz. El Humanismo de Santo Tomás Moro y sus Obras Desde la Torre. *Analogia*, 7(1), 191-197, 1993.

Martínez Porcell, Juan. Metafísica de la Persona y Análisis Existencial. *Sapientia*, 49(193-4), 364-371, 1994.

Martínez Sendra, María Carmen. El Concepto de Complexión y Alma en Tomás de Aquino y Galena. *Rev Espan Filosof Med*, 0, 111-118, 1993.

Martini, Simone and Masini, Andrea. A Modal View of Linear Logic. *J Sym Log*, 59(3), 888-899, S 94.

We present a sequent calculus for the modal logic *S4* and building on some relevant features of this system (the absence of contraction rules and the confinement of weakenings into axioms and modal rules) we show how *S4* can easily be translated into full propositional linear logic, extending the Grishim-Ono translations of classical logic into linear logic. The translation introduces linear modalities (exponentials) only in correspondence with *S4* modalities. We discuss the complexity of the decision problem for several classes of linear formulas naturally arising from the proposed translations.

Martinich, A P. *A Hobbes Dictionary*. Cambridge, Blackwell, 1995.

A Hobbe's Dictionary contains almost 130 entries, from the entire spectrum of his thought; they cover his most important and most difficult concepts. There are also entries devoted to all of his major works and several of his minor ones. Also included is a biography that situates his life within his cultural context, a detailed chronology of his life and important events in Stuart England, and a descriptive bibliography of first editions of his works and the most important secondary sources.

Martino, Enrico and Usberti, Gabriele. Temporal and Atemporal Truth in Intuitionistic Mathematics. *Topoi*, 13(2), 83-92, S 94.

In section 1 we argue that the adoption of a tenseless notion of truth entails a realistic view of propositions and provability. This view, in turn, opens the way to the intelligibility of the *classical* meaning of the logical constants, and consequently is incompatible with the antirealism of orthodox intuitionism. In section 2 we show how what we call the "potential" intuitionistic meaning of the logical constants can be defined, on the one hand, by means of the notion of atemporal provability and, on the other, by means of the operator K of epistemic logic. Intuitionistic logic, as reconstructed within this perspective, turns out to be a part of epistemic logic, so that it loses its traditional foundational role, antithetic to that of classical logic. In section 3 we uphold the view that certain consequences of the adoption of a *temporal* notion of truth, despite their apparent oddity, are quite acceptable from an antirealist point of view.

Martinovic, Ivica. Quantitas Inassignabilis: Language and Knowledge in Boskovic's Approach to Infinitesimals. *Filozof Istraz*, 13(4), 745-754, 1993.

At the beginning of his mathematical career, Boskovic understood the infinitesimal as an *indefinitely small quantity* (*quantitas indefinite parva*), moreover as an indeterminable quantity. From the gnoseological point of view, Boskovic understood the infinitesimal as *inassignable quantity* (*quantitas inassignabilitis*), i.e., as a quantity whose magnitude could not be distinctly observed with selected measures. This conclusion led Boskovic to relativism of mathematical cognition: *that which could not be given or assigned regarding one finite intellect, could be from another intellect.* The methodological approach of the young professor in 1740, and the gnoseological approach of the experienced professor in 1754, were focused on the foundations of infinitesimal calculus. According to Boskovic, the meaning of the infinitesimal, both as *indefinitely small quantity* and later as *inassignable quantity*, is an open problem in the mid 18th century. (edited)

Masaryk, Thomas G and Woolfolk, Alan (ed) and Imber, Jonathan B (ed). *Constructive Sociological Theory*. New Brunswick, Transaction Books, 1994.

This volume is a selection of major writings by Thomas G Masaryk (1850-1937), first president of the state of Czechoslovakia and a forgotten but distinguished founder of the discipline of sociology in central Europe. These writings and the introduction reveal the intertwining of politics and social theory that is characteristic of Masaryk's philosophical sociology—with chapters on modern suicide, Comte, religion, the problems of Marxism, nationalism, democracy, and other topics. The volume aims to introduce students and teachers of sociology to Masaryk's unified theory, which opposed the separation of facts and values, knowledge and belief, feeling and reason, and theory and practice that became dominant in sociological theory.

Masciarelli, Pasqualino. Il Primo Hegel in Traduzione Italiana. *G Crit Filosof Ital*, 74(1), 99-107, Ja-Ap 95.

Masi, Giuseppe. Lo spiritualismo indiano antico: Echi egizi nelle Upanisad. *G Metaf*, 16(1-2), 83-153, Ja-Ag 94.

Masini, Andrea and Martini, Simone. A Modal View of Linear Logic. *J Sym Log*, 59(3), 888-899, S 94.

We present a sequent calculus for the modal logic *S4* and building on some relevant features of this system (the absence of contraction rules and the confinement of weakenings into axioms and modal rules) we show how *S4* can easily be translated into full propositional linear logic, extending the Grishim-Ono translations of classical logic into linear logic. The translation introduces linear modalities (exponentials) only in correspondence with *S4* modalities. We discuss the complexity of the decision problem for several classes of linear formulas naturally arising from the proposed translations.

Maso, I (& other eds). *Openness in Research: The Tension Between Self and Other*. Assen, Gorcum, 1995.

Openness in qualitative research is often taken for granted: qualitative researchers have to be open to the research situation, to the research and to themselves. At the same time however, there is a realization that to a certain extent researchers cannot be open-minded or open-hearted. The question how open-minded and open-hearted one can be and how this openness can be obtained, is addressed in the three successive parts of this volume. Firstly, the more general statements about the possibility of openness are discussed. Secondly, the possibility of open-heartedness is addressed. Thirdly, the possibility of openness in concrete situations is presented.

Mason, Jeff. Rhetoric and the Perlocutionary Field. *Phil Rhet*, 27(4), 410-414, 1994.

This work extends the Austinian notion of 'perlocutionary force' to the human communication situation in general. The 'perlocutionary field' is the contingent unpredictable background to all communicative acts. This field and the effects of speech within it are the subjects of rhetoric. Austin did not develop the idea of a perlocutionary field because of his need for illocutionary order. I argue that an unstable perlocutionary field surrounds all communicative action, though it often appears to be stable in straightforward (serious and literal) linguistic communication. Nevertheless, the perlocutionary force of any utterance never can be wholly a matter of convention.

Masschelein, Jan. "Individualization, Singularization, and E-Ducation (Between Indifference and Responsibility)" in *Identity, Culture, and Education*, Smeyers, Paul (ed), 233-240. Leuven, Leuven Univ Pr, 1994.

Individualization as the loss of common norms/values is often considered to be at the basis of indifference as absence of responsibility. Referring to H Arendt attention is drawn to another condition: thinking as a response to the address of others. Thinking as dialogical praxis between me and myself testifies the receipt of the address, which singularizes 'me', asks 'me' to respond. Individualization destroys this space of responsibility, not by depriving of norms/values, but by levelling out singularization, by destroying the intimate distance between me and myself. E-ducation provokes this 'inner' space through problematization, leading out of oneself.

Massey, Susan R and Mehlman, Maxwell J. The Patient-Physician Relationship and the Allocation of Scarce Resources: A Law and Economics Approach. *Kennedy Inst Ethics J*, 4(4), 291-308, D 94.

Patients with insufficient financial resources place physicians in a conflict of interest between the patients' needs and the financial interests of the physician, other patients, and society. Not only must physicians act ethically, but they must avoid liability for violating their legal duties to their patients. The traditional rules of contract and malpractice law that govern the patient-physician relationship do not provide satisfactory guidelines. Better answers are found in the rules of fiduciary law, but only with regard to direct conflicts between patients and physicians and only at the risk of reducing patient access to care. Certain types of legislative action can resolve these conflicts by altering the traditional legal rules, but care must be taken to preserve patient-physician trust, which the legal rules were designed to enhance.

Massini, Carlos Ignacio. La Inevitabilidad del Objetivismo Etico. *Analogia*, 4(2), 189-194, 1990.

Massini Correas, Carlos I. El Primer Principio del Conocimiento Práctico: Objeciones y Respuestas. *Analogia*, 5(2), 75-87, 1991.

Masten, Scott E and Hosmer, LaRue Tone. Ethics vs Economics: The Issue of Free Trade with Mexico. *J Bus Ethics*, 14(4), 287-298, Ap 95.

The authors, one an ethicist and the other an economist, look at the issue of free trade with Mexico and other low wage rate countries from the viewpoints of their disciplines differ on their priorities and analytical methods, not on their objectives.

Mastroianni, Giovanni. Positivismo e Metafisica in Russia in uno Scritto di Vladimir Solov'ev. *G Crit Filosof Ital*, 72(3), 508-512, S-D 93.

Mastroianni, Giovanni. Tre Improbabili Nani Sulle Spalle dei Giganti. *G Crit Filosof Ital*, 74(1), 108-111, Ja-Ap 95.

Mastroianni, Giovanni. Una Polemica su Gentile alle Origini dello Stalinismo Filosofico. *G Crit Filosof Ital*, 73(2-3), 484-488, My-D 94.

Mata-Toledo, Ramon A and Liebowitz, Jay. Expert System Evaluation: A Review and Integrative Model. *Commun Cog—AI*, 11(3), 297-321, 1994.

As expert systems become more commonplace worldwide and as mission critical applications of expert systems increase in number, the importance of performing verification and validation (V&V) of the expert system is paramount. The expert system V&V community worldwide is fairly small. More careful attention needs to be placed on expert system V&V methodologies and practices. The expert system V&V community needs to be much larger than its current size. More resources have to be put into testing and evaluation of expert systems. Management needs to be less ignorant of the need for proper testing of expert systems. This paper will review some of the leading work in verification and validation of conventional and expert system software, and will discuss an integrative model that may be useful in evaluating expert systems.

Mataix, Carmen. El buen relojero. *An Seminar Metaf*, 27, 11-23, 1993.

The subject of my works "The Good Watchmaker" deals with the autonomy of the classical mechanics universe which is based on its internal logics (Leibniz) to which God has had to submit in order to create it by making a perfect machine (watch) not needing His intervention. But a new concept of time, introduced by the second principle of thermodynamics in the nineteenth century, has produced a new and different conception of universe. Thus introducing the need of a God capable of reversing the process of "entropy" instead of turning his back on the universe.

Mataix, Carmen. El Giro de la Nueva Ciencia: De Platón a Aristóteles. *Rev Filosof (Spain)*, 7(12), 436-453, 1994.

The aim of this article is to show that science (physics and biology) are evolving to a aristotelic model. Wholeness (D Bohm, Prigogine), anti-reductionism, and a less rationalistic position, conform a new paradigm whose features remind more Aristotle than Plato, even though science continue to get the platonist model (mathematic structure) as an ideal to represent reality.

Mataix, Carmen. Tautologías y circularidad en la Mecánica clásica. *Rev Filosof (Spain)*, 4(5), 45-52, 1991.

The article emphasizes the underlying tautologies of classical mechanics. Three of the fundamental topics: 1) The tautology of inertia, since Newton's principle of inertia only explains what is already implicit in all the concepts of the mechanical universe: the matter, the mass, is indifferent to movement and to rest. 2) Universe is conceived as given in a whole "in its initial conditions". 3) Mechanics resorts fundamentally to explaining macrocosmos through the movement of invisible particles whose model precisely comes from macroscopic movements.

Mataix, Carmen and Leyra, Ana María. Arte y Ciencia: Una Visión Especular. Madrid, Ed La Palma, 1992.

This book is rooted in the crisis of thought in the 19th and 20th centuries and confronts two domains apparently so distant as the field of art and of science —through its development one can discover parallel situations in both matters and draw the conclusion that the same cultural trends govern both the art expression and the theories of science. Representation, truth, "logocentrism", "supplement" are philosophical terms that can be applied as well to the field of aesthetics as to that of reflexion about science.

Mate, Reyes. La Historia de los Vencidos (Un Ensayo de Filosofía de la Historia Contra las Ontologías del Presente). *Analogia*, 4(1), 33-58, 1990.

Maté, J L and Juristo, N and Pazos, J. Expert Systems Evaluation. *Commun Cog—AI*, 11(3), 225-255, 1994.

The six honest servants of human kind that Kipling pointed out: what, when, where, who, why and how, are studied for knowledge-based systems evaluation. We place special emphasis on the procedural aspect of evaluation which is reflected by how. In this sense, Jain's methodology for computer systems performance evaluation is made suitable for KBS evaluation. Practical guidelines on how to proceed with KBS evaluation are provided.

Matheron, Alexandre. Les fondements d'une éthique de la similitude. *Rev Metaph Morale*, 99(4), 475-491, O-D 94.

Mathews, M R. Social and Environmental Accounting: A Practical Demonstration of Ethical Concern?. *J Bus Ethics*, 14(8), 663-671, Ag 95.

The accounting profession has regarded itself as ethical ever since the first modern professional accounting body was founded in the second half of the 19th Century. However, the code by which members have bound themselves have been professional ethics codes, which are more concerned with the relationship between professional and professional, or professional and client, than that of the professional and society as a whole. Recently, a number of educational programmes have been developed which attempt to go beyond the limited view of professional ethics, and into the field of ethics and professionalism. These programmes are based on an application of the work of Kohlberg and that of Rest. In the opinion of the author these aspects of ethics and professionalism are important developments, which need to be followed up by the development of social accounting, which would be a practical demonstration of ethical concerns by members of the accounting profession. This aspect of business ethics is outlined in the chapter.

Mathieu, Vittorio. La Prospettiva Religiosa di Augusto Guzzo. *Filosofia*, 45(1), 81-96, Ja-Ap 94.

Mathur, Durga Lal. Baudelaire and 'Philosophy'. *J Indian Counc Phil Res*, 11(2), 89-96, Ja-Ap 94.

Mathy, Jean-Philippe. The End of Philosophy and the Pragmatisation of French Thought, Culture, and Society. *Hist Euro Ideas*, 20(1-3), 545-551, Ja 95.

Matilal, Bimal K. The Problem of Inter-Faith Studies. *Sophia (Australia)*, 34(1), 167-172, Mr-Ap 95.

Matravers, Derek. Beliefs and Fictional Narrators. *Analysis*, 55(2), 121-122, Ap 95.

Greg Currie has suggested the content of a given fiction is equivalent to what would be reasonable to suppose the narrator believed were the story to have been narrated as true. I suggest an alternative, namely, that it is equivalent to what it would be reasonable for an audience to believe were the story to be narrated as true. This avoids some of the problems Currie encounters, although it raises others.

Matsuno, Koichiro and Salthe, Stanley N. Global Idealism/Local Materialism. *Biol Phil*, 10(3), 309-337, July 95.

We are concerned with two modes of describing the dynamics of natural systems. Global descriptions require simultaneous global coordination of all dynamical operations. Global dynamics, including mechanics, remain invariant in the absence of external perturbation. But, failing impossible global coordination, dynamical operations could actually become coordinated only locally. In local records, as in global ones, the law of the excluded middle would be strictly observed, but without global coordination it could only be fulfilled sequentially by passing causative factors forward onto subsequent contiguous operations. The local dynamics of sequential operations would be indefinite with regard to how commitments will be made which will avoid violating the law of the excluded middle, but any resulting record will be as definite as if there had been global coordination.

Matsuo, Hiroshi. Der Begriff der ästhetischen Kategorie bei Baumgarten. *Aesthetics*, 5, 15-25, Mr 92.

Matthews, Eric. Moralist or Therapist? Foucault and the Critique of Psychiatry. *Phil Psychiat Psych*, 2(1), 19-30, Mr 95.

"Anti-psychiatrists" have criticized psychiatric practice on the grounds that it represents not genuine therapy, but a moralistic form of social control. One argument used in support of this critique consists of showing that the concept of "mental illness" is not eternal or self-evident but has a history of particular culture, and that this history reveals that it always had a moralistic role. Foucault's account of the history of madness in the "Age of Reason" is considered from this point of view. A counter-critique of anti-psychiatry then is proposed, in which the philosophical value of such a historical account is called into question. Modern concepts of "mental illness," it is argued, are significantly different from older concepts of "madness" in that they include reference to harm suffered by the patient, which justifies the assimilation of mental to bodily illness. The anti-psychiatry movement, however, offers a salutary warning against the temptation to confuse mental illness with social deviancy.

Matthews, Gareth B. Commentary on Caston's "Toward a History of the Problem of Intentionality Among the Greeks". *Proc Boston Colloq Anc Phil*, 9, 246-260, 1993.

Matthews, Robert J. Three-Concept Monte: Explanation, Implementation and Systematicity. *Synthese*, 101(3), 347-363, D 94.

Fodor and Pylyshyn (1988), Fodor and McLaughlin (1990) and McLaughlin (1993) challenge connectionists to explain systematicity without simply implementing a classical architecture. In this paper I argue that what makes the challenge difficult for connectionists to meet has less to do with what is to be explained than with what is to count as an explanation. Fodor et al are prepared to admit as explanatory, accounts of a sort that only classical models can provide. If connectionists are to meet the challenge, they are going to have to insist on the propriety of changing what counts as an explanation of systematicity. Once that is done, there would seem to be as yet no reason to suppose that connectionists are unable to explain systematicity.

Matthis, Michael J. Kierkegaard and the Problem of the Social Other. *Phil Today*, 38(4), 419-439, Wint 94.

The question is to what extent is SK's emphasis on freedom of self consistent with the acceptance of a social dimension of self, or a religious emphasis. Later existentialists may stress the incompatibility of individual freedom and a relation of self to God. SK develops the position that only in relation to God is the self fully free. At the same time, the self cannot undertake similar relations to other humans without logically undermining this freedom. Such a view disturbs many thinkers and critics, but SK has good reasons, both logically and morally (e.g., the autonomy of conscience), for insisting on this apparently rigid position. SK does have a theory of community, but it is not one that allows an encounter with the reality of the other self (as it does with the reality of God): rather it incorporates the other self as an equal in worth and reality merely as an idea within the self.

Matustik, Martin J. Democratic Multicultures and Cosmopolis: Beyond the Aporias of the Politics of Identity and Difference. *Method*, 12(1), 63-89, Spr 94.

If Francis Fukuyama were right that the revolutionary changes of 1989 signify "the end of history and the last man," then we would not have to worry about the crisis of identity and community in the wake of the New World Order. This essay takes up these types of crises and examines them through Jürgen *Habermas's* critical social perspectives and Bernard *Lonergan's* existential critique of the social surd. Both approaches not only complement each other—insofar as they present two aspects of ideology critique—but they represent those types of suspicion of the present age that require one another in order to sustain that critique.

Matustík, Martin J. Derrida and Habermas on the Aporia of the Politics of Identity and Difference: Towards Radical Democratic Multiculturalism. *Constellations*, 1(3), 383-398, Jan 95.

Can we envision a critical theory that would join Habermas's fallibilist self-limitation of the Enlightenment project with Derrida's intensification of this same promise in his resistance to the identity-logic of cultural and ecomonic hegemony? The essay moves beyond the self-involved modernist/postmodernist impasse. Habermas locates the overcoming of the politics of hatred in the procedural institutionalization of postnational identity. Derrida unmasks the binary logics of Eurocentrism and anti-Eurocentrism and proposes its transgression by attacking both the idea of the hegemonic centre and techno-culture. In his attack on technocapital, not so popular a move now after the demise of totalitarianism in the East, Derrida joins his hope, fear and trembling to Marx's critique of market dogmatism. From this encounter emerges a composite figure of critical social theory that would learn from both thinkers.

Maudlin, Tim. Discussion: Why Bohm's Theory Solves the Measurement Problem. *Phil Sci*, 62(3), 479-483, S 95.

Abraham Stone recently has published an argument purporting to show that David Bohm's interpretation of quantum mechanics fails to solve the measurement problem. Stone's analysis is not correct, as he has failed to take account to the conditions under which the theorems he cites are proven. An explicit presentation of a Bohmian measurement illustrates the flaw in his reasoning.

Maudlin, Tim. Three Measurement Problems. *Topoi*, 14(1), 7-15, Mr 95.

The aim of this essay is to distinguish and analyze several difficulties confronting attempts to reconcile the fundamental quantum mechanical dynamics with Born's rule. It is shown that many of the proposed accounts of measurement fail at least one of the problems. In particular, only collapse theories and hidden variables theories have a chance of succeeding, and, of the latter, the modal interpretations fail. Any real solution demands new physics.

Maund, Barry. *Colours: Their Nature and Representation*. New York, Cambridge Univ Pr, 1995.

Colours as they are represented in experience are intrinsic, nonrelational, manifest qualities of physical objects, qualities which have a causal role to play and which have a rich phenomenological character. It turns out, the author argues, that no physical object has the colours they are represented as having. Colour is a virtual property in the way phlogiston and caloric are virtual natural kinds. In the case of colour, however, there is an important dispositional property: the power to appear a certain distinctive way. The author develops a pluralist framework of colour, one which includes both concepts: colour as a virtual property, and colour as a dispositional property.

Mauri, Margarita. Akrasia. *Philosophia (Athens)*, 23-24, 181-188, 1993-94.

Mauri, Margarita. El tema de la virtud: recientes debates. *Rev Filosof (Spain)*, 4(5), 219-227, 1991.

This is an introduction to virtue considering new contributions to its analysis such as MacIntyre, Foot, Wallace or Trianosky. This article specially deals with the confrontation between Virtue Ethics and Duty Ethics. Its main purpose is to present recent works in the field of virtue.

Mauro, Letterio. Bedeutung der Philosophiegeschichte: W Weischedel als Philosophie-Historiker. *Frei Z Phil Theol*, 41(3), 546-559, 1994.

Mausfeld, Rainer and Heyer, Dieter. "A Theoretical and Experimental Inquiry Into the Relation of Theoretical Concepts..." in *Probability in Theory-Building, Brzezinski, Jerzy (ed)*, 75-97. Amsterdam, Rodopi, 1994.

Mautner, Thomas. Locke's Own. *Locke News*, 22, 73-80, 1991.

Some writers, among them J Tully, ascribe to Locke the view that a person can equally be said to be the owner of his possessions and of his actions. This, it is argued, is a misinterpretation, due to a failure to recognize that in the relevant passages in Locke, "to own" is not used in the possessive sense, but means to admit, to acknowledge.

Mautner, Thomas. Two Dualisms. *J Value Inq*, 29(2), 181-185, Je 95.

A brief discussion and refutation of an argument which infers that factual statements can imply a value-judgment from two premisses: 1) that there are value-judgments which imply a factual statement, and 2) that if value-judgments can imply a factual statement, then factual statements can imply a value-judgment. The main objection raised against this argument (which is proposed by Anthony Kenny) concerns the second premiss.

Maxcy, David J. Meaning in Nature: Rhetoric, Phenomenology, and the Question of Environmental Value. *Phil Rhet*, 27(4), 330-346, 1994.

Maxwell Jr, Michael P. A Critique of Jerome Miller's Interpretation of Lonergan on Knowing and Being. *Method*, 11(2), 229-241, Fall 93.

Maxwell Jr, Michael P. Deconstruction or Genuineness: A Response to Jerome Miller. *Method*, 13(1), 83-87, Spr 95.

May, Larry. Challenging Medical Authority: The Refusal of Treatment by Christian Scientists. *Hastings Center Rep*, 25(1), 15-21, Jan-Feb 95.

I presented two contrasting cases of Christian Scientists who have refused medical treatment for their children. I rehearsed some of the main doctrines and arguments espoused by Christian Scientists who refuse medical treatment, and contrasted these with arguments advanced by the American Pediatric Association and others in the medical profession who have tried to get courts to override the decisions of Christian Science parents. I discussed the conflict between Christian Scientists and medical scientists as a conflict of belief and authority in a pluralistic society. At the end, I briefly proposed how this controversy might be resolved in a way which is respectful of both medical and Christian Science communities.

May, Larry and Strikwerda, Robert. Reply to Victoria Davion's Comments on May and Strikwerda. *Hypatia*, 10(2), 157-158, Spr 95.

This is a very brief response to a largely positive review of our paper "Men in Groups: Collective Responsibility for Rape" Hypatia 9/2 (Spring 1994).

May, Thomas. The Concept of Autonomy. *Amer Phil Quart*, 31(2), 133-144, Ap 94.

May, Todd G. The Limits of the Mental and the Limits of Philosophy: From Burge to Foucault and Beyond. *J Speculative Phil*, 9(1), 36-47, 1995.

In different ways, Tyler Burge and Michel Foucault undermine the closure of the mental that has formed the basis of much epistemological foundationalism. Burge's undermining is conceptual, while Foucault's is causal. This paper argues that, seen in their complementarity, Burge and Foucault also undermine two current conceptions of philosophy: that philosophy is aloof from politics and that we have reached the end of philosophy.

May, William F. "The Virtues in a Professional Setting" in *Medicine and Moral Reasoning, Fulford, K W M (ed)*, 75-90. New York, Cambridge Univ Pr, 1994.

Mayer, Ann Elizabeth. "The Dilemmas of Islamic Identity" in *Human Rights and the World's Religions, Rouner, Leroy (ed)*, 94-110. Notre Dame, Univ Notre Dame Pr, 1988.

This chapter contrasts the relatively unconstrained development of culture in premodern Islamic civilization with the constraints placed on culture in contemporary Muslim countries, where regimes seek to subordinate culture to serve ideological functions and to enhance state control over society. The stultifying impact of Islamization programs on culture is attributed to the reactive, anti-Western character of current programs for forging a new "Islamic" cultural identity. In this hostile climate, in which Islam is converted into a criterion for censorship and deprivation of freedom, the progress of Islamic thought itself is being blocked, but this is in turn prompting resistance by Muslims who want their religion to be something other than a system of repression.

Mayer, Don and Cava, Anita. Social Contract Theory and Gender Discrimination: Some Reflections on the Donaldson/Dunfee Model. *Bus Ethics Quart*, 5(2), 257-270, Ap 95.

This paper relates Donaldson and Dunfee's Integrative Social Contracts Theory to the problem of gender discrimination. We make the assumption that multinational managers might seek some guidance from ISCT to resolve ethical issues of gender discrimination in countries indifferent or hostile to gender equality. The role of Donaldson and Dunfee's "hypernorms" seems especially crucial, and we find that, under their writings thus far, no "hypernorms" exist to make unethical the most blatant acts of sex discrimination in a host country whose local norms tolerate such discrimination. The genesis of "hypernorms" as "global moral minimums" is recounted, and specific application of ISCT to a familiar ethics case ("A Foreign Assignment") is provided.

Mayer, Günter. Visionen für das 21 Jahrhundert?. *Das Argument*, 207, 917-927, N-D 94.

The aesthetics of the media developed by radical constructivists leads to a totalization of a perspective which claims that reality is generally understood aesthetically (Welsch) or that the primary perspective of Western society is a mediated reality whose basic structure is no longer liable to essential change (Bolz). A critical examination of such positions makes the need for precise social analysis clear, as well as the need for an ecological transformation of aesthetics and its development into an aesthetics of resistance.

Mayer, J R A. Jens Jacobsen's Conception of Wisdom. *Dialogue Hum*, 2(3-4), 101-103, 1992.

Mayer, J R A. Reaction to Marek Siemek's "Critique of 'Non-Instrumental Reason'". *Dialogue Hum*, 3(4), 95-96, 1993.

Mayer, John R A. "The Marriage of Love and Reason" in *The Nature and Pursuit of Love, Goicoechea, David (ed)*, 142-148. Buffalo, Prometheus, 1995.

Mayer, Richard E. "The Search for Insight: Grappling with Gestalt Psychology's Unanswered Questions" in *The Nature of Insight, Sternberg, Robert J (ed)*, 3-32. Cambridge, MIT Pr, 1995.

Creative thinking occurs when a problem solver invents a novel solution to a problem. The term insight has been used to name the process by which a problem solver suddenly moves from a state of not knowing how to solve a problem to a state of knowing how to solve it. Yet providing a name for this process does not substitute for providing an explanation. The goal of this chapter is to explore several paths that have been taken in the search for insight, including viewing insight as 1) Completing a schema, 2) Reorganizing visual information, 3) Reformulating a problem, 4) Overcoming a mental block, and 5) Finding a problem analog.

Mayer, Robert. Lenin, Kautsky and Working-Class Consciousness. *Hist Euro Ideas*, 18(5), 673-681, S 94.

This article contrasts the theory of working-class consciousness set forth by V I Lenin in the second chapter of *What It To Be Done?* with the views of Karl Kautsky. Although Lenin quoted a long passage from one of Kautsky's articles in support of his position, I demonstrate that Lenin misunderstood Kautsky's theory and garbled it in his famous pamphlet. Lenin's view was significantly more pessimistic than Kautsky's, and it was inconsistent with the orthodoxy of both Russian and German Social-Democratic theory.

Mayo, David J and Gunderson, Martin. "Privacy and the Ethics of Outing" in *Gay Ethics, Murphy, Timothy F (ed)*, 47-65. New York, Haworth Pr, 1994.

This essay argues that, in the absence of a compelling justification, outing is immoral as a violation of privacy. Reasons for respecting privacy involve fundamental interests which encompass information about gay and lesbian sexual orientation. Utilitarian defenses of outing are criticized, as is Richard Mohr's analysis of privacy and defense of outing in the name of dignity. Mohr's claim that gay or lesbian sexual orientation does not fall within the scope of the right to privacy is rejected.

Mayo, Deborah G. The New Experimentalism, Topical Hypotheses, and Learning from Error. *Proc Phil Sci Ass*, 1, 270-279, 1994.

An important theme to have emerged from the new experimentalist movement is that much of actual scientific practice deals not with appraising full-blown theories but with the mainfold local task required to arrive at data, distinguish fact from artifact, and estimate backgrounds. Still, no program for working out a philosophy of experiment based on this recognition has been demarcated. I suggest why the new experimentalism has come up short, and propose a remedy appealing to the practice of standard error statistics. I illustrate a portion of my proposal using Galison's (1987) experimental narrative on neutral currents.

Mayos, Gonça. De Sade o la subversión de/en la Ilustración. *Rev Filosof (Daimon)*, 7, 89-102, 1993.

To study De Sade's theory exclusively with no thought about Marquis De Sade's biography is to analyze the question of the nature of radical subversion he sets forth. This is referred to as the traditional Christian moral as well as the values he clearly illustrates. Nevertheless De Sade does not surpan the conceptual frame of the illustration—we argue the difference from romanticism—however much he leads, in a parasitical way to the extreme of his phantoms, contradictions and essential components (that we compare with Hegelian dialectic of master and slave).

Mayr, Ernst. Reasons for the Failure of Theories. *Phil Sci*, 61(4), 529-533, D 94.

A theory may be invalid, not owing to erroneous observations or the invocation of an inappropriate law, but because of the use of equivocal terms. This is demonstrated for Darwin's failed model of sympatric speciation through the principle of divergence.

Mazis, Glen. *Emotion and Embodiment: Fragile Ontology*. New York, Lang, 1993.

Merleau-Ponty's ontology of the body is expanded to reconsider the traditionally undervalued epistemological role of emotion. A phenomenological analysis of the "world" of emotion uncovers notions of "phenomenality," "magic," "interpersonal valence," "faces of others," and "open embodiment"; as well as characteristic of the emotionally known, such as "nuance," "complexification," "vortical identity," "compersonality," etc. Also the dangers of emotion (and Romanticism and Kitsch) are explored, as well as the domain of "fragile ontology." Literary works are used extensively (especially Woolf, Duras, Melville) and other philosophies of emotion examined (Descartes, Plato, James, Darwin, Sartre, Heidegger, Levinas, Solomon, Daly, Iragaray, Trungpa, etc.)

Mazzara, Giuseppe. "Teeteto. 201e-208b. Totalità (Holon) e Insieme (Pan): Un Problema di non Facile Soluzione" in *Platón: Los Diálogos Tardíos, Lan, Conrado Eggers (ed)*, 67-76. Sankt Augustin, Academia, 1986.

Mazzarella, Eugenio. L'Istanza Cosmologica tra Scienzatecnica e Filosofia. *Stud Filosofici*, 289-298, 1991-92.

Mazzola, Roberto. I Giganti in Vico. *Boll Centro Stud Vichiani*, 24-25, 49-78, 1994-95.

Mbiti, John. "African Religions and Philosophy" in *African Philosophy: Selected Readings, Mosley, Albert G (ed)*, 87-115. Englewood Cliffs, Prentice Hall, 1995.

McAleer, Graham. Old and New: The Body, Subjectivity, and Ethics. *Phil Today*, 38(3-4), 259-267, Fall 94.

McAlister, Linda Lopez. On the Possibility of Feminist Philosophy. *Hypatia*, 9(3), 188-196, Sum 94.

This paper was originally presented as part of a panel entitled "Feminist Philosophy After Twenty Years" at the 1993 meeting of the Eastern Division of the American Philosophical Association (APA). It is a discussion of the conditions that needed to be—and were—present in the United States in the 1970s in order for feminist philosophy to take root and flourish.

McBride, James. *War, Battering, and Other Sports: The Gulf Between American Men and Women*. Atlantic Highlands, Humanities Pr, 1995.

Activists in the battered women's movement have argued that Superbowl Sunday is the day on which the highest number of battering incidents is reported and that domestic violence rose during the Gulf War. This book explores these contentions, concluding that football, war, and battering are related neurotic symptoms of a masculinist psychic economy. Using the theories of Theodor Adorno, René Girard, Georges Bataille and Luce Irigaray, the author demonstrates how castration and phallic penetration rhetoric depicts the enemy as woman, even in ostensibly male-dominated activities like war and football, and why the men's movement holds little promise for change.

McBride, William L. The Pathos of European Political Philosophy After Marxism. *J Phil Res*, 19, 331-343, 1994.

The paper begins by raising some doubts concerning the appropriateness of the phrase, "after Marxism," despite current sociological realities which point to its accuracy. It then discusses a certain "pathology" that may be *intrinsic* to the combined theory and practice of political philosophy; some examples are offered. Next, it is suggested that the discourse of contemporary European political philosophy suffers from the absence of certain Marxian notions, especially that of ideology. Some current trends—postmodernism, nationalism, critical theory, and religious theory—are then briefly explored. It is contended that none of them by itself is adequate for developing the kind of global worldview which, *malgre tout*, seems needed to counteract the increasing hegemony of the "Coca-Cola culture" of the present day. The paper concludes by raising questions about the possible role, at best an awkward one, of American philosophers in this enterprise.

McBride, William L. The Progress of Technology and the Philosophical Myth of Progress. *Phil Hist Sci*, 1(1), 31-58, O 92.

Horace's ode to Vergil setting out on a sea voyage to Greece serves as a starting-point: Horace inveighs against the invention of "impious vessels" and other technological advances. The paper surveys, first, the current conditions of increased dependence on technology, especially military technology; then Mill's and Rousseau's opposed views of progress (with criticism of both); then Hegel's simultaneous critique of superficial enlightenment optimism and enormous confidence in spiritual progress; and finally Marx's thought, which is found, through textual analyses, to be more ambiguous about playing the role of cheerleader for technological progress than is often believed. Similar ambiguity prevails here.

McCabe, David. Liberal Education *Is* Moral Education. *Soc Theor Pract*, 21(1), 83-96, Spr 95.

In this article I take up the question of what sort of education the liberal state should provide its citizens. After suggesting that the liberal endorsement of state neutrality derives from the ideals of equality and autonomy, I argue that a liberal education should promote students' capacities for autonomous choice. I then discuss the implications of this position with respect to public school curricula and argue against the ideas that public schools should inculcate only the civic virtues and should not get involved in the area of morality.

McCabe, Donald L and Dukerich, Janet M and Dutton, Jane E. The Effects of Professional Education on Values and the Resolution of Ethical Dilemmas: Business School versus Law School Students. *J Bus Ethics*, 13(9), 693-700, S 94.

Prior research on the impact of ethics education within the business curriculum has yielded mixed results. Although the impact is often found to be positive, it appears to be both small and short-lived. Interpretation of these results, however, is subject to important methodological limitations. The present research employed a longitudinal methodology to evaluate the impact of an MBA program versus a law program on the values and ethical decision making behavior of a cohort of students at two major universities in the northeast. The results suggest that the MBA curriculum remains a value-neutral experience for most students. In contrast, the law school program had a significant impact on both values and ethical decision making.

McCann, Edwin. "Locke's Philosophy of Body" in *The Cambridge Companion to Locke, Chappell, Vere (ed)*, 56-88. New York, Cambridge Univ Pr, 1994.

McCann, Hugh. Intention and Motivational Strength. *J Phil Res*, 20, 571-584, 1995.

The tension between reductivist view of intention and views which credit intention with a distinctive functional role in the genesis of action is what I explore in this paper. The first two sections are devoted to showing how that conflict arises. In sections II and IV I shall consider two ways of trying to resolve the conflict, neither of which seems to me adequate. Finally, I shall urge briefly that if the conflict cannot be resolved, we should favor a theory which maintains a nonreductive view of intention. (edited)

McCarrick, Pat Milmoe. Gender Issues in Health Care. *Kennedy Inst Ethics J*, 5(1), 61-82, Mr 95.

A brief background essay is followed by an annotated bibliography of documents referring to differences between the treatment of women and men in the health care setting and the omission or underrepresentation of women in clinical research. Government reports, association statements, books and journal articles are included.

McCarrick, Pat Milmoe and Coutts, Mary Carrington. Eugenics. *Kennedy Inst Ethics J*, 5(2), 163-178, Je 95.

Eugenics, Scope Note 28 in the National Reference Center for Bioethics Literature, Kennedy Institute of Ethics series, offers a source to recent literature about eugenics as well as a brief background history of this controversial topic which has been both praised and scorned in the twentieth century. The series provides overviews to topics in biomedical ethics and includes annotated citations to books, journal articles, and government documents.

McCarthy, Charles R. To Be or Not to Be: Waiving Informed Consent in Emergency Research. *Kennedy Inst Ethics J*, 5(2), 155-162, Je 95.

McCarthy, Charles R. When OPRR Comes Calling: Enforcing Federal Research Regulations. *Kennedy Inst Ethics J*, 5(1), 51-56, Mr 95.

McCarthy, J C. Some Preliminary Remarks on "Cognitive Interest" in Husserlian Phenomenology. *Husserl Stud*, 11(3), 135-152, 1994-95.

Human "interests" are commonly said to deform experience, putting us at a distance from things as they are. Remedy has sometimes been sought in an epistemological asceticism, whereby the knower's every purpose is held in abeyance. When this is recognized as impossible, the goal of science in the ancient sense is usually abandoned. Refuge is then sought in some form of pragmatism. Husserl's teaching on cognitive interest, a feature of "genetic phenomenology," offers a way through this impasse. Husserl articulates our knowing desire to let things be, and, correlatively, the drawing power of the real *qua* intelligible.

McCarthy, J C. The Being of the Maybe: Husserl on Doubting. *Man World*, 28(3), 261-281, Jl 95.

Husserl's account of doubt is rich with promise. Drawing from several Husserlian texts, this article proposes an overcoming of the legacy of the "Cartesian" understanding of the dubitable. The article shows how doubt is not principally an "epistemological" concern. Doubt is, rather, a "mode of presentation." As Husserl describes it, doubt turns on the dyad same/other, and on the structure of temporality. The article concludes that the act of doubt is never a cognitive defeat. Doubt always leads from certainty to greater certainty; it both depends upon and promises a vigorous engagement with the world in its self-display.

McCarthy, Jeremiah. "The Closet and the Ethics of Outing" in *Gay Ethics, Murphy, Timothy F (ed)*, 27-45. New York, Haworth Pr, 1994.

Because social circumstances have changed, the question of outing has assumed an importance unknown in a time when homsexuality was a guarded secret. This essay describes the evils of the closet in terms of its affronts to the worth of gay men and lesbians. While outing might appear as a repudiation of the closet, this essay argues that not all outing is justified. On the other hand, the article also rejects those arguments that criticize outing as a violation of privacy as well as arguments that defend outing as no violation of others' rights.

McCarthy, John C. Pascal on Certainty and Utility. *Interpretation*, 22(2), 247-269, Wint 94-95.

Pascal's celebrated gibe, "Descartes: inutile et incertain," plainly targets the watchwords of Descartes' most programmatic writing, the *Discourse on Method*. Commentators upon Pascal have not reflected adequately on the implications of the purpose driving Cartesian utility, namely, the mastery of nature, nor on the presuppositions of the method describing Cartesian certainty, especially the renunciation of "first principles" in the traditional sense. Consequently they have not appreciated the extent to which Pascal rejects Descartes' philosophical foundations. This essay proposes that Pascal considers Descartes useless because Descartes' view of the good is uncertain, and uncertain because his understanding of the true is useless.

McCarthy, Michael. The Critique of Reason. *Method*, 10(2), 89-125, Fall 92.

McCarthy, Thomas. Legitimacy and Diversity: Dialectical Reflections on Analytical Distinctions. *Protosoz*, 6, 199-228, 1994.

In general, Habermas has more readily accommodated conflicts of interest in his discourse theory of democracy than he has conflicts of values, ways of life, and worldviews. Though he has continuously elaborated upon notions of "ethical-political" discourse, culture, and identity since 1988, his treatments of diversity, pluralism, multiculturalism, and multinationalism have left agreement at the center and disagreement in the margins of his conception of legitimacy. This essay

examines the development of that conception from the early 1970s to the present and argues that "the consent of the governed" cannot be given so cognitive an interpretation as Habermas gives it.

McCarthy, Thomas and Hoy, David Couzens. *Critical Theory*. Cambridge, Blackwell, 1994.

Philosophical controversies within contemporary critical social theory arise largely from questions about the nature, scope, and limits of human reason. In this book David Hoy and Thomas McCarthy bring those disagreements into focus around a familiar set of philosophical issues concerning reason and the rational subject, truth and representation, knowledge and objectivity, identity and difference, relativism and universalism, the right and the good. These perennial problems are resituated within the context of critical theory as it has developed from the work of the Frankfurt School in the 1930s and 1940s to the multiplicity of contemporary approaches: genealogical, hermeneutic, neopragmatist, deconstructive, and reconstructive.

McCarthy, Thomas A. "Philosophical Foundations of Political Theology" in *Civil Religion and Political Theology, Rouner, Leroy S (ed)*, 23-40. Notre Dame, Univ Notre Dame Pr, 1986.

McCarty, Luise Prior. Bodies of Knowledge. *Stud Phil Educ*, 14(1), 35-48, 1995.

McCarty, Richard. Are There "Cont-Moral Virtues?". *Metaphilosophy*, 25(4), 362-375, O 94.

Michael Glote's conception of admirable immorality ("contra-moral virtue") is defended against critical challenges; also considered is a related problem posed by unadmirable moral sainthood ("super-moral virtue"). Both seem to pose puzzles for traditional moral philosophy respecting morality's overridingness. A wider view of the scope of morality is proposed, which seems to accommodate both the puzzling cases and the overridingness thesis: the suggestion is that morality may also encourage the pursuit of nonmoral values, thus giving rise to the puzzling cases.

McCarty, Richard. Motivation and Moral Choice in Kant's Theory of Rational Agency. *Kantstudien*, 85(1), 15-31, 1994.

This paper develops the apparent implication by many of Kant's comments on respect for the moral law that respect is a moral feeling and a motivational incentive (*Triebfeder*) for action *from duty*. It shows Kantian moral judgments to be always comparative, in contrast to views like Hutcheson's, because of Kantian morality's overridingness and distinguishes Kant's and Hutcheson's views of moral motivation as *elective* and *desiderative*, respectively. It defends a "conflict-of-forces" conception of motivation and moral choice, where the strongest incentive determines the choice and it attempts to coordinate Kant's view of moral weakness of will (frailty) with his theory of freedom.

McClamrock, Ron. Kim on Multiple Realizability and Causal Types. *Analysis*, 54(4), 248-252, O 94.

McClamrock, Ron. Screening-Off and the Levels of Selection. *Erkenntnis*, 42(1), 107-112, Ja 95.

In "The Levels of Selection" (Brandon, 1984), Robert Brandon provides a suggestive but ultimately unsuccessful attempt to use the probabilistic notion of *screening off* in providing a schema for dealing with an aspect of the "units of selection" question in the philosophy of biology. I characterize that failure, and suggest a revision and expansion of Brandon's account which addresses its key shortcoming.

McClamrock, Ron and Steinbock, Bonnie. When Is Birth Unfair to the Child?. *Hastings Center Rep*, 24(6), 15-21, N-D 94.

We argue that having children under extremely adverse conditions may be unfair to the children, even if their lives are not so bad as to qualify as "wrongful." Instead, we appeal to a principle of parental responsibility to show how the child is wronged.

McCleary, Richard C. Against Ethics. *Phil Today*, 38(4), 440-446, Wint 94.

No philosophizing (moral or otherwise) that ignores the relationship between the work professional philosophers do in pursuit of their careers and the political economy whose orthodoxies they uncritically accept, whose structures and functions they help reproduce, and whose dominant-class hegemony they help sustain can avoid distorting ideologically the world it claims to reveal, or avoid impeding the advent of the world it professes to advocate. No philosophizing can justifiably hope to advance Western philosophy's traditional goal of helping establish "the reign of universal reason" unless it makes integral to its mode of life and understanding a critical analysis of their concrete historical foundations and functions.

McClennen, Edward. "Pascal's Wager and Finite Decision Theory" in *Gambling on God: Essays on Pascal's Wager, Jordan, Jeffrey (ed)*, 115-137. Lanham, Rowman & Littlefield, 1994.

McClintock, Alexander. *The Convergence of Machine and Human Nature: A Critique of the Computer Metaphor of Mind and Artificial Intelligence*. Brookfield, Avebury, 1995.

McCloskey, Donald N. "La rhétorique de l'expertise économique" in *Rhétoriques de la science, De Coorebyter, Vincent (ed)*, 171-188. Paris, Pr Univ France, 1994.

McCloskey, Elizabeth Leibold and Cohen, Cynthia B. Private Bioethics Forums: Counterpoint to Government Bodies. *Kennedy Inst Ethics J*, 4(3), 283-289, S 94.

McClung, John Arthur. Time and Language in Bioethics: When Patient and Proxy Appear to Disagree. *J Clin Ethics*, 6(1), 39-43, Spr 95.

Time and the context in which events occur can completely alter the apparent literal meaning of advance directives. A clinical example of this phenomenon is presented in which ethical analysis is facilitated by asking four procedural questions: 1) What is the contextual meaning of the patient's requests? 2) Does the patient's current condition render the contemplated treatment medically appropriate? 3) Are the patient's requests, the surrogate's requests' and the appropriateness of the therapy in genuine conflict? 4) How can the patient's wishes be best respected? Use of this process enhances comprehension and assures that the intent of a statement is carefully researched.

McColm, Gregory L. The Dimension of the Negation of Transitive Closure. *J Sym Log*, 60(2), 392-414, Je 95.

We prove that any positive elementary (least fixed point) induction expressing the negation of transitive closure on finite nondirected graphs requires at least two recursion variables.

McCormick, John P. Fear, Technology, and the State: Carl Schmitt, Leo Strauss, and the Revival of Hobbes in Weimar and National Socialist Germany. *Polit Theory*, 22(4), 619-652, N 94.

McCormick, Richard A. Does Christianity Make a Difference?. *Christian Bioethics*, 1(1), 97-101, Mr 95.

The human person makes great demands on the physician and calls for unique attention. Hence the doctor-patient relationship calls for the highest ideals of kindness, patience, trustworthiness, generosity and skill. The Catholic physician brings these demands a specific meaning: ministering to the sick is to see Christ in them and to show Him to them.

McCracken, Janet and Shaw, Bill. Virtue Ethics and Contractarianism: Towards a Reconciliation. *Bus Ethics Quart*, 5(2), 297-312, Ap 95.

The notion of rationality underlying contemporary business and business ethics, or the "rational actor" model of moral decision-making in business, links a roughly utilitarian notion of the good to a contractarian notion of human agency. The "C-U model" provides inadequate means for explaining how business people do or ought to behave or think about their behavior, because the notion of rationality upon which it relies is far too narrow a picture or business people's character. An alternative to these assumptions and to the Contractarian-Utilitarian model, is offered in an ethics of virtue. Despite the traditional apparent conflict between these divergent models, the C-U model, if founded in a notion of rationality consistent with Aristotelian ethics, is recognized as a useful instrument in business ethics and business decision-making. Hence, a reconciliation is effected between the C-U model and virtue ethics.

McCulloch, Gregory. Not Much Trouble for Ultra-Externalism. *Analysis*, 54(4), 265-269, O 94.

McCullough, Laurence B. Preventive Ethics, Professional Integrity, and Boundary Setting: The Clinical Management of Moral Uncertainty. *J Med Phil*, 20(1), 1-11, F 95.

This paper introduces the 1995 "clinical ethics" number of the *Journal of Medicine and Philosophy*. Preventive ethics strategies—informed consent, negotiation, respectful persuasion, the use of ethics committees, and institutional policy—can be used to manage morally the clinical uncertainty that is inevitable in medical practice. Integrity sets of boundary condition on what is ethically justifiable and preventive ethics should aim to prevent violations of professional and individual integrity. The role of integrity in preventive ethics is described in the papers in this number of the *Journal* on the topics of physician-assisted suicide, the allocation of scarce medical resources, the response to patient desperate to bypass experimental protocols, and genetic enhancement.

McCullough, Laurence B. Psychosocial and Citizenship Status of Patients Needing Transplant. *Cambridge Quart Healthcare Ethics*, 4(2), 236-238, Spr 95.

This case study addresses transplantation for foreign nationals on the basis of a Lockean account of ownership of a national economy. Those who contribute to the national economy, including undocumented foreign nationals, should not be excluded from transplantation. Newly arrived foreign nationals may be justifiably excluded.

McDaniel, June. "Emotion in Bengali Religious Thought: Substance and Metaphor" in *Emotions in Asian Thought, Marks, Joel (ed)*, 39-63. Albany, SUNY Pr, 1995.

This article explores some understandings of emotion in Indian philosophy and religion. It shows how various Indian traditions value and devalue emotion, understanding it differently due to their differing constructions of self and mind. The perspectives of yoga, vedanta, ayurveda, alamkarasastra and bhakti are explored. Both the language of religious emotion and folk ideas about emotion are described. The article shows that emotion is used in many Indian traditions to aid concentration, structure aesthetic experience, increase spirituality, generate new personalities ("building a soul") and gain insight into the self.

McDermott, John J. All We Seem To Get Is Life Implicitness: The Practical As Ontological. *SW Phil Rev*, 11(Supp), 17-26, Mr 95.

McDermott, John J. The Confrontation Between Royce and Howison. *Trans Peirce Soc*, 30(4), 779-790, Fall 94.

McDermott, John M. Dialectical Analogy: The Oscillating Center of Rahner's Thought. *Gregorianum*, 75(4), 675-703, 1994.

Rahner's analogy attempts to mediate between Barth and Przywara. An objective analogy of emanation and return corresponds to a subjective analogy of sensation, abstraction, and judgment. The juncture depends on the complex relations among *esse commune* known in judgment, the concept of *esse*, the concept of *ens commune*, and *esse absolutum*, God, who transcends the horizon of *esse commune* and fills it. A *Schwebe*, or dialectical oscillation, joins dynamically while distinguishing conceptually matter and spirit, nonbeing and being, objectivity and subjectivity, concept and judgment, world and man, man and God.

McDermott, Michael. Lewis on Causal Dependence. *Austl J Phil*, 73(1), 129-139, Mr 95.

McDonough, Kevin. The Importance of Examples for Moral Education: An Aristotelian Perspective. *Stud Phil Educ*, 14(1), 77-103, 1995.

The paper develops and contrasts two views about the role of examples in moral education—one based on R M Hare's recent "two-level" conception of moral reasoning and one based on Aristotle's conception of *phronesis*. It concludes that a Harean view leads to a harmful and impoverished form of moral education by encouraging children to ignore or distort the complexity of particular moral judgments. It also concludes that an Aristotelian view, by emphasizing the importance of rich examples such as those found in literature, enables children to develop and exercise a capacity for moral judgment that is sensitive to the complexities of particular moral judgments. Finally, the role of examples in public moral education in liberal pluralist societies is examined.

McDonough, Richard. A Note on Frege's and Russell's Influence on Wittgenstein's *Tractatus*. *Russell*, 14(1), 39-45, Sum 94.

McDonough, Richard. Kant's "Historicist" Alternative to Cognitive Science. *S J Phil*, 33(2), 203-219, Sum 95.

McFee, Graham. Back to the Future: A Reply to Sharpe. *Brit J Aes*, 35(3), 278-283, Jl 95.

McGaha, Annette Christy and Korn, James H. The Emergence of Interest in the Ethics of Psychological Research with Humans. *Ethics Behavior*, 5(2), 147-159, 1995.

We describe the growth of interest in the ethics of research with human participants based on articles abstracted in *Psychological Abstracts* and *PsycLIT*. Interest was low and variable until 1974, after which there was a marked increase in the number of articles published. We explain this emergence of ethical interest on terms of the social climate of concern for human rights in 1960s and 1970s, the 1973 revision of the American Psychological Association's ethical principles, and the developments of federal regulation of research with human participants.

McGandy, Michael. Communion and its Limits: Expression and Communication in Susanne Langer's Aesthetics. *Conference*, 4(1), 21-35, Spr 93.

An exposition of Langer's aesthetics is provided in terms of her ontology of primordial "forms of feeling" which highlights the neo-Kantian roots of her aesthetics. This account of art, founded on the ability to strictly separate these primordial forms from the historical accidents of our association and communication, is subsequently considered from a Wittgensteinian perspective. The critical claim is that Langer is unable to clearly separate the level of ontological expression from the level of historical communication as her aesthetics requires. Further, it is claimed that this blindness to the historical dimension of art runs counter to Langer's own commitment to provide a phenomenology, and not a priori metaphysics, of art.

McGee, Glenn. The Relevance of Foucault to Whiteheadian Environmental Ethics. *Environ Ethics*, 16(4), 419-424, Wint 94.

Although he devotes little explicit analysis to ethics, Whitehead's understanding of the human moral life immerses both human moral agency and environmental ethics in the natural world, judging *good* actions in the context of complex and interdependent histories of value present in *societies* of what he calls *actual occasions*. In this sense, Whiteheadian environmental ethics draws on the most interesting features of Michel Foucault's genealogies of values that suffuse institutions. Nevertheless, a Whiteheadian notion of environmental ethics exceeds Foucault's work in that Whitehead acknowledges the possibility of responsible human values and actions with regard to the environment.

McGee, Vann. "Learning the Impossible" in *Probability and Conditionals, Eells, Ellery (ed)*, 179-199. New York, Cambridge Univ Pr, 1994.

How do we extend the doctrine that one's subjective probability of Q upon learning P should be one's prior probability of Q given P to encompass cases in which Pr(P) = 0? Lewis and Skyrms recommend letting Pr(P) be nonzero but infinitesimal. Popper proposes taking conditional probability as primitive, rather than defining it in terms of absolute probability. These proposals come to the same thing: a standard-real-valued function satisfies Popper's axioms just in case it is the standard part of a function defining conditional probabilities from nonstandard absolute probabilities. A dynamic Dutch book argument is given. Also applications to Adams's and Stalnaker's theories of conditionals.

McGee, Vann and McLaughlin, Brian. Distinctions Without a Difference. *S J Phil*, 33(Supp), 203-251, 1995.

The sorites paradox is blamed on a conflict between two ideas about truth: the (T)-sentences; and the thesis that, if a sentence is true, the thoughts and practices of speakers of the language, together with the nonlinguistic facts, make it true. Distinguishing the notion of truth (defined by the (T)-sentences) from definite truth, it is definitely truth that, for some n, there is a bald man with n hairs but no bald man with n+1 hairs; whereas there is no n such that it is definitely true that there is a bald man with n hairs but none with n+1. The supervaluational metatheory treats "true" and "definitely true" both as vague terms.

McGhee, Michael. The Turn Towards Buddhism. *Relig Stud*, 31(1), 69-87, Mr 95.

The paper draws on the Heideggerian distinction between *Bildung* and *Besinnung* to locate a discussion of theological strategies in the face of Nietzsche's pronouncement that God is dead, and sketches what should be an epistemologically vigilant (and thus properly sceptical) Buddhist response to that pronouncement. The theological options that are mentioned or discussed include naive and critical theological realism, anti-realism and a nontheistic 'spiritual realism'. Buddhism is discussed in terms of its naturalistic sources and their development in the expression of states of mind rather than in terms of belief.

McGilvray, James A. Constant Colors in the Head. *Synthese*, 100(2), 197-239, Ag 94.

I defend a version of color subjectivism—that colors are sortals for certain neural events—by arguing against a sophisticated form of color objectivism and by showing how a subjectivist can legitimately explain the phenomenal fact that colors seem to be properties of external objects.

McGinn, Colin. "Logic, Mind, and Mathematics" in *Dennett and his Critics, Dahlbom, Bo (ed)*, 83-96. Cambridge, Blackwell, 1995.

McGinn, Colin. *Mental Content*. Cambridge, Blackwell, 1991.

McGinn, Colin. Reply to Carol Rovane's "Comment on McGinn's 'The Problem of Philosophy'". *Phil Stud*, 76(2-3), 169-174, D 94.

McGinn, Colin. *The Problem of Consciousness: Essays Towards a Resolution*. Cambridge, Blackwell, 1991.

McGinn, Colin. The Problem of Philosophy. *Phil Stud*, 76(2-3), 133-156, D 94.

McGinnis, Michael V. Myth, Nature, and the Bureaucratic Experience. *Environ Ethics*, 16(4), 425-436, Wint 94.

From the "deep" ecological perspective, there is a dualism between an ecocentric and an anthropocentric perspective, and this dualism is reflected in the ideal of the bureaucratic experience. The bureaucrat lives by the myth of the human ability to control nature. An eco-myth is evolving that can offer one means of transcending the dominant bureaucratic mythic experience. This eco-myth moves toward a positive and sensitive human relationship with nature—a collective experience that values nature on its own terms and not as standing reserve. This position is no less mythic than the one it is replacing, but it is a better myth, because, being non-dualist, it offers the prospect of a political society in harmony with nature.

McGrath, Alister E. *Reformation Thought: An Introduction (Second Edition)*. Cambridge, Blackwell, 1993.

McGrath, P J. Does the Ontological Argument Beg the Question?. *Relig Stud*, 30(3), 305-310, S 94.

This article is a defense of my claim that the modal version of the ontological argument begs the question. Since a necessary being exists in all possible worlds or in none, one cannot assume that it is possible that a greatest conceivable being exists without assuming that it actually exists, which is the conclusion of the argument. However, William Valicella has replied by claiming that if the concept an *x* is internally coherent, then an *x* exists in some possible world. But this is true only of contingent beings. If a necessary being does not exist in the real world, then it does not exist in any possible world.

McGraw, John G. Loneliness, Its Nature and Forms: An Existential Perspective. *Man World*, 28(1), 43-64, Ja 95.

Loneliness is a pedestrian phenomenon whose sheer ubiquity and familiarity have camouflaged its capacity for individual and communal affliction and disruption. However, this ancient nemesis incorporates but surpasses, to use the language of Kant and Marcel, the phenomenal and problematic (the mundane) and, in so doing, approaches the realm of the noumenal and mysterious (the arcane), the domain of the person in its distinctive sociality and intersubjectivity. This interdisciplinary essay examines the nature of loneliness and develops a taxonomy which entails the following ten types: metaphysical, epistemological, communicative, ontological, existential, ethical, emotional (eros-loneliness), social (friendship-loneliness), cultural and cosmic.

McGraw, John G. Love: Its Universe and Universality. *Dialogue Hum*, 4(2-3), 11-21, 1994.

This article sketches the kinds of universality predicated of love in terms of philosophy and the sciences. It considers the universe of love with respect to its meaning, properties and its unique logic and language. It indicates some contrasts between unconditional and conditional love, existence- and essence-love as well as between benevolence and self-benevolence. The essay concludes that love is both the most subjective and "transobjective" of phenomena, one that personalizes nature and naturalizes the person and that, of all phenomena, it is the best qualified to justify its own universality and universe, other universals and the entire universe itself.

McGregor, Joan L. "Force, Consent, and the Reasonable Woman" in *In Harm's Way, Coleman, Jules L (ed)*, 231-254. New York, Cambridge Univ Pr, 1994.

In this paper, I argue that in the current laws of rape are assumptions and standards about rape, consent, force, resistance, and reasonable belief which not only fail to account for the perspective of women but work to their detriment. This paper analyzes the nature of the moral wrong of rape, supposing that the law should reflect, whenever possible, the moral proscription. I consider the current rape laws and show how those fail to capture the variety of contexts in which women are wronged. Finally, I argue for changes in the rape statutes, specifically that the rules should include explicit consent, and the rules of evidence for prosecuting rape should rely upon a reasonable woman standard.

McGrew, Tim. Two Cheers for Bayes's Theorem. *Analysis*, 55(2), 123-125, Ap 95.

In his recent book *Particles and Waves*, Peter Achinstein offers an argument which purports to demonstrate that inductive confirmation does not accrue to a successful theory in the absence of information regarding that theory's rivals. His proof, however, does not establish this conclusion; his premises violate the conditions which make inductive confirmation an interesting prospect.

McGuire Jr, Charles and Strong, Kelly C and Solberg, Joseph. Living (Not Learning) Ethics. *J Bus Ethics*, 14(1), 71-81, Ja 95.

The results of our survey of AACSB member schools confirm prior reports of similar surveys: The teaching of business ethics is indiscriminate, unorganized, and undisciplined in most North American schools of business. If universities are to be taken seriously in their efforts to create more ethical awareness and better moral decision-making skills among their graduates, they must provide a rigorous and well-developed system in which students can "live ethics" instead of merely learn ethics. (edited)

McHenry, Leemon. Quine's Pragmatic Ontology. *J Speculative Phil*, 9(2), 147-158, 1995.

Quine has often been interpreted as a contemporary adaption of the American pragmatist movement that originated with Peirce, James, and Dewey. In this paper I examine the extent of Quine's commitment to pragmatism by investigating his views on ontology and his criteria for theory selection. I conclude that while Quine accepts an element of pragmatism at the heart of his naturalism, this is not sufficient to connect him with the classical pragmatists or with recent movements. Quine's realism about posits and his rejection of the pragmatic theory of truth result in important differences.

McHoul, Alec. Towards a Critical Ethnomethodology. *Theor Cult Soc*, 11(4), 105-126, N 94.

This is not a philosophical paper. It attempts to rethink Garfinkel's concept of indexicality in a slightly different way from standard ethnomethodological versions,

using (vaguely) Derridean ideas about undecidability. At the end, this slightly altered (critical) version of indexicality is used to read a cinephilic account of the musical film *Singin' in the Rain*. Not much use to philosophers—except for the odd lapsed phenomenologist who has turned to matters empirical, concrete, actual.

McIntyre, Alison. Compatibilists Could Have Done Otherwise: Responsibility and Negative Agency. *Phil Rev*, 103(3), 453-488, Jl 94.

McKee, Patrick L and Quinn, Carol. Temporal Gestalt: A Concept for Quantum Theory. *Method Sci*, 27(4), 235-243, 1994.

McKenna, Erin. Feminism and Vegetarianism: A Critique of Peter Singer. *Phil Cont World*, 1(3), 28-35, Fall 94.

To challenge Singer I use views of the individual proposed by socialist feminist and radical feminist theories. Both of these theories (in all their variety) propose a substantial revisioning of the individual and thereby shift the focus form rights talk to issues of responsibility and care. While there are clear dangers in these approaches as well, I believe there is a fruitful combination of Singer's argument with these feminist approaches that will help us see the deep nature of our connectedness to nonhuman animals and make us realize that the eating of meat is really a form of cannibalism.

McKenny, Gerald P. Whose Tradition? Which Enlightenment? What Content? Engelhardt, Hauerwas, Capaldi, and the Future of Christian Bioethics. *Christian Bioethics*, 1(1), 84-96, Mr 95.

The development of a content-full Christian bioethics requires an analysis of the particular contents and traditions which different Christians bring to morality. For Hauerwas, the content of Christian ethics is the speech and practices of the community. For Engelhardt, only a content-full tradition, such as the Orthodox tradition, will be able to arrive at closure on the moral issues presented by the contemporary practice of medicine. Capaldi calls, in contrast, for a Kantian society of autonomous self-legislators whose responsible freedom is grounded in a cosmic order that must be explicated and retrieved in particular practices. The manner in which we view our own traditions and the shortcomings of modernity determine the content that Christianity brings to bioethics.

McKeon, Richard and Owen, David B (ed) and McKeon, Zahava K (ed). *On Knowing—The Natural Sciences*. Chicago, Univ of Chicago Pr, 1994.

McKeon outlines the history of Western thinking on the sciences into the twentieth century. Treating the central concepts of motion, space, time, and cause, he traces modern intellectual debates back to the ancient Greeks, notably Plato, Aristotle, Democritus, and the Sophists. As he brings the story of Western science up to the twentieth century, he uses his fabled semantic schema (reproduced here for the first time with extended commentary) to uncover new ideas and observations about cosmology, mechanics, dynamics, and other aspects of physical science. Illustrating the broad historical sweep of the lectures are a series of discussions, which give detail to the course's intellectual framework. These discussions of Plato, Aristotle, Galileo, Newton, and Maxwell are perhaps the first published rendition of a philosopher in literal dialogue with his students. (edited)

McKeon, Zahava K (ed) and Owen, David B (ed) and McKeon, Richard. *On Knowing—The Natural Sciences*. Chicago, Univ of Chicago Pr, 1994.

McKeon outlines the history of Western thinking on the sciences into the twentieth century. Treating the central concepts of motion, space, time, and cause, he traces modern intellectual debates back to the ancient Greeks, notably Plato, Aristotle, Democritus, and the Sophists. As he brings the story of Western science up to the twentieth century, he uses his fabled semantic schema (reproduced here for the first time with extended commentary) to uncover new ideas and observations about cosmology, mechanics, dynamics, and other aspects of physical science. Illustrating the broad historical sweep of the lectures are a series of discussions, which give detail to the course's intellectual framework. These discussions of Plato, Aristotle, Galileo, Newton, and Maxwell are perhaps the first published rendition of a philosopher in literal dialogue with his students. (edited)

Mckie, John R. Linguistic Competence and Moral Development: Some Parallels. *Phil Inq*, 16(1-2), 20-31, Wint-Spr 94.

The author argues that moral maturity is a skill or an ability and does not consist in the possession of a complex fund of propositional knowledge. Just as it is possible to achieve a high level of proficiency in riding a bicycle without having acquired the sophisticated concepts physical theory uses to describe the activity, or knowing the relevant mechanical laws, so one can attain a high degree of moral maturity without having acquired such concepts as *right, duty, desert, obligation, responsibility, justice,* or knowing moral rules or principles couched in terms of them. Moral knowledge does not consist in knowledge-that, but in knowledge-how.

McKinsey, Michael. Accepting the Consequences of Anti-Individualism. *Analysis*, 54(2), 124-128, Ap 94.

McKinzie, Bruce Wayne. *Objectivity, Communication, and the Foundation of Understanding*. Lanham, Univ Pr of America, 1994.

McKinzie interrogates lay and scholarly arguments to answer this question and finds that objectivism endures because of practical necessity. Objectivism and related presumptions form a backdrop for understandings that appear to be indispensable in everyday living. McKinzie explores and attempts to reconcile relativism and absolutism and in so doing, searches for common ground between the hermeneutic world of unending interpretation and the world of concrete meanings that are evidently necessitated by the exigencies of day-to-day life. The findings of the study also suggest a theory that unites human understanding and human communication.

McKirahan, Voula Tsouna. "The Socratic Origins of the Cynics and Cyrenaics" in *The Socratic Movement, Vander Waerdt, Paul A (ed)*, 367-391. Ithaca, Cornell Univ Pr, 1994.

McLarty, Colin. Numbers Can Be Just What They Have To. *Nous*, 27(4), 487-498, D 93.

An allegory of two girls who learn arithmetic with foundations in a simple categorical set theory (CS) aims to make CS at least as intuitive as Zermelo Frankel set theory (ZF). The girls prove all models of arithmetic in CS are indistinguishable. One girl meets 'Ernie' from Benacerraf "What numbers could not be" (*Philosophical Review*, 74, 1965, 47-73) and argues with him that the numbers form a set, and also meet structuralist scruples, if we use CS sets rather than ZF.

McLaughlin, B P and Warfield, Ted A. The Allure of Connectionism Reexamined. *Synthese*, 101(3), 365-400, D 94.

There is currently a debate over whether cognitive architecture is classical or connectionist in nature. One finds the following three comparisons between classical architecture and connectionist architecture made in the pro-connectionist literature in this debate: 1) connectionist architecture is neurally plausible and classical architecture is not; 2) connectionist architecture is far better suited to model pattern recognition capacities than is classical architecture; and 3) connectionist architecture is far better suited to model the acquisition of pattern recognition capacities by learning than is classical architecture. If true, 1)-3) would yield a compelling case against the view that cognitive architecture is classical, and would offer some reason to think that cognitive architecture may be connectionist. We first present the case for 1)-3) in the very works of connectionist enthusiasts. We then argue that the currently available evidence fails to support any of 1)-3).

McLaughlin, Brian and McGee, Vann. Distinctions Without a Difference. *S J Phil*, 33(Supp), 203-251, 1995.

The sorites paradox is blamed on a conflict between two ideas about truth: the (T)-sentences; and the thesis that, if a sentence is true, the thoughts and practices of speakers of the language, together with the nonlinguistic facts, make it true. Distinguishing the notion of truth (defined by the (T)-sentences) from definite truth, it is definitely truth that, for some n, there is a bald man with n hairs but no bald man with n+1 hairs; whereas there is no n such that it is definitely true that there is a bald man with n hairs but none with n+1. The supervaluational metatheory treats "true" and "definitely true" both as vague terms.

McLaughlin, Brian P and Fodor, Jerry A. "Connectionism and the Problem of Systematicity" in *Connectionism: Debates on Psychological Explanation, Macdonald, Cynthia (ed)*, 199-222. Cambridge, Blackwell, 1995.

McLean, Edward B. Natural Law as the Defense for Human Life. *Vera Lex*, 13(1-2), 23-25, 1993.

McLean, George F. The Plurality of Philosophical and Religious Traditions and Principles of Freedom and Peace. *Magyar Filozof Szemle*, 5-6, 617-632, 1994.

In the most recent years and even months, we have found that authentic liberation is not merely a matter of establishing new ecomonic systems—though that cannot be low on the long list of things to be done. More directly, it is the task of living freedom, that is, of understanding the new sense of identity on the part of the peoples and finding ways to promote this identity and to interrelate it with other peoples in a new fusion of strengths, rather than of destructive confrontation. Toward this end the present paper will look first to the nature and formation of cultural traditions as works of human freedom. Second, in order to locate the proper mode of operation of freedom in matters of cultural self-affirmation and interchange it will examine the different levels at which freedom operates. Finally, it will look to that level of freedom for the foundations not only of passive tolerance, but of positive cooperation between peoples of different cultures. (edited)

McLeod, Mark S. Religious Plurality and Realist Christianity: Idolatry and the Testing of One's Faith. *Faith Phil*, 11(2), 224-241, Ap 94.

The descriptive realist Christian, as portrayed here, is one who holds both that there is only one true description of salvific reality, and no other description, save the Christian one, is true and that those who do not come to faith in Christ are not among the redeemed. I argue that there is an existential problem of religious plurality that descriptive realist Christians face. I analyze it in terms of sin and idolatry, explicating it in terms of the problem of evil, and suggest how the descriptive realist Christian is called to respond to the problem within the framework of descriptive realist Christian commitment.

McLeod, Owen. Aristotle's Method. *Hist Phil Quart*, 12(1), 1-18, Ja 95.

Prior to explaining his own views on a given topic, Aristotle is apt to review the preexisting opinions or *endoxa* on that topic. Why? Several scholars (Martha Nussbaum, Jonathan Barnes and Terence Irwin) have advanced a striking answer: Aristotle's reviews of *endoxa* are the first step in a philosophical method based on the assumption that the truth on a given subject is more or less immanent in and restricted to *endoxa*. I argue that neither Aristotle's remarks nor his practice commit him to this conservative philosophical method. I conclude by noting several reasons for Aristotle's interest in *endoxa*.

McMahan, Jeff. Revising the Doctrine of Double Effect. *J Applied Phil*, 11(2), 201-212, 1994.

The Doctrine of Double Effect has been challenged by the claim that what an agent intends as a means may be limited to those effects that are precisely characterized by the descriptions under which the agent believes that they are minimally causally necessary for the production of other effects that the agent seeks to bring about. If based on so narrow a conception of an intended means, the traditional Doctrine of Double Effect becomes limitlessly permissive. In this paper I examine and criticize Warren Quinn's attempt to reformulate the Doctrine in such a way that it retains its force and plausibility even if we accept the narrow conception of an intended means. Building on Quinn's insights, I conclude by offering a further version of the Doctrine that retains the virtues of Quinn's account but avoids the objections to it.

McMahan, Jeff. The Metaphysics of Brain Death. *Bioethics*, 9(2), 91-126, Ap 95.

The dominant conception of brain death as the death of the whole brain constitutes an unstable compromise between the view that a person ceases to exist when she irreversibly loses the capacity for consciousness and the view that a human organism dies only when it ceases to function in an integrated way. I argue that no single criterion of death captures the importance we attribute both to the loss of the capacity for consciousness and to the loss of functioning of the organism as a whole. This is because the person of self is one thing and the human organism is another. We require a separate account of death for each. Only if we systematically distinguish between persons and human organisms will we be able to provide plausible accounts both of the conditions of our ceasing to exist and of when it is that we begin to exist. This paper, in short, argues for a form of mind-body dualism and draws out some of its implications for various practical moral problems.

McMahon, Christopher. The Ontological and Moral Status of Organizations. *Bus Ethics Quart*, 5(3), 541-554, Jl 95.

The paper has two parts. The first considers the debate about whether social entities should be regarded as objects distinct from their members and concludes that we should let the answer to this question be determined by the theories that social science finds to have the most explanatory power. The second part argues that even if the theory with the most explanatory power regards social entities such as organizations as persons in their own right, we should not accord them citizenship in the moral realm. Rather we should accept moral individualism, the thesis that only individual humans can have rights and duties. The moral status of corporations and other organizations is often thought to depend on their ontological status. In particular, it is thought to depend on whether they can be said to exist as distinct entities, and especially as persons distinct from the individuals who are their members. In this article I argue that the two questions are actually independent of each other. No matter what the ontological status of organizations, they should not be accorded citizenship in the moral realm in their own right.

McManus, Denis. Sympathy for the Devil: Edwards and Heidegger. *Philosophy*, 70(272), 263-272, Ap 95.

Certain unrecognized expectations support the mutual incomprehension of Edwards and Janusz and Webster in their debate in *Philosophy* over the worth of the works of Heidegger. For example, presenting Heidegger as using language playfully is no defense in the eyes of someone like Edwards without an account of the legitimacy of such use. Edwards, on the other hand, fails to appreciate Heidegger's involvement in the Kantian enterprise of exploring the presuppositions of philosophical reflection. Whether such a radical philosophical conscientiousness is genuinely possible or not, it's pursuit shapes Heidegger's later, often mystifying reflections of metaphor and the relationship between Being and beings.

McMullin, Ernan. Underdetermination. *J Med Phil*, 20(3), 233-251, Je 95.

When trying to assess the implications of recent deep shifts in the philosophy of science for the broader arena of medicine, the theme that most readily comes to mind is *underdetermination*. In scientific research one always hopes for determination: that the world should *determine* the observations we make of it; that evidence should *determine* the theories we adopt; that the practice of science should *determine* results independent of the sort of society in which that practice takes place. In this essay, doubts cast on each of these ideas by recent work in philosophy of science will be discussed and the consequences for philosophy of medicine will be indicated.

McMurtry, John. "Evaluating Sexual Love: A Prolegomenon to Postromantic Inquiry" in *The Nature and Pursuit of Love, Goicoechea, David (ed)*, 265-283. Buffalo, Prometheus, 1995.

This discussion of Irving Singer's three-volume study, *The Nature of Love*, locates love within the larger social and ethical questions overlooked by Singer and the 2500-year philosophical tradition he explores—the private-property structures of sexual love's exploitation, the problematic of physical and psychological health, and the reproduction and care of future children. Rejecting the "selfishness *à deux*" perspective within which commentary has been traditionally confined, the chapter proposes a universal principle of value to guide oral imagination and action in sex love, and shows the way in which it can resolve the most vexing and dangerous problems of sexual conflict and desire.

McNally, Ruth and Wheale, Peter. "Environmental and Medical Bioethics in Late Modernity" in *Philosophy and the Natural Environment, Attfield, Robin (ed)*, 211-225. New York, Cambridge Univ Pr, 1994.

McNamara, Peter. Popular Government and Effective Government. *Interpretation*, 22(3), 439-448, Spr 95.

McNeill, Will. "Traces of Discordance: Heidegger-Nietzsche" in *Nietzsche: A Critical Reader, Sedgwick, Peter R (ed)*, 171-202. Cambridge, Blackwell, 1995.

McNeill, William H. The Changing Shape of World History. *Hist Theor*, 34(2), 8-26, 1995.

After surveying the development of world-historical views from Herodotus and Ssu-ma Chen to Spengler and Toynbee, the author sketches his own current understanding of the best approach to the subject. The organizing concept is hard to name, being the geographically largest circle of effective interaction among peoples of diverse cultures and circumstances. In recent times interaction has become literally world-wide; but before 1500 several different communications nets co-existed, each with a dynamic of its own, though the largest was always situated in Eurasia and now embraces the globe. Competing terms exist: "interactive zone," "world system," and "ecumene," but none is completely satisfactory or generally accepted by world historians. Nonetheless, the author asserts that a perceptible drift towards recognizing the reality and centrality of this large structure in the human past has begun to show up among practicing world historians; and the balance of the essay sketches how key alterations in patterns of Eurasian communication mark the principal stages in the expansion and intensification of interaction within the Eurasian ecumene.

McPherran, Mark L. Commentary on Morgan's "Philosophy in Plato's *Sophist*". *Proc Boston Colloq Anc Phil*, 9, 112-129, 1993.

This paper consists of three parts. The first part summarizes and critiques Michael Morgan's account of the characterization of philosophy he finds in the *Sophist*; the second attempts to extend fruitfully Morgan's observations concerning the elements of Platonic religion he discovers in the *Sophist*, showing how Plato uses the dialogue to contrast his own understanding of piety and religion with that of Socrates; the third presents a brief, interpretive account of the major differences between Socratic and Platonic religion.

McPherran, Mark L. Socrates on Teleological and Moral Theology. *Ancient Phil*, 14(2), 245-262, Fall 94.

In the *Memorabilia* (*Mem*. 1.4.1-19; 4.3.1-18) we find Socrates arguing for the existence of an omniscient, omnipresent God: the Creator of a universe especially suited to satisfying our needs and who now governs it in a fashion analogous to the way in which *our* minds govern *our* bodies. However, many scholars have found Xenophon's ascription a spurious one, holding that he has clearly misrepresented Socrates, who was in fact no such 'dabbler in teleological cosmology'. This paper assesses Xenophon's teleological argument, and then argues that there are better reasons than not for accepting Xenophon's ascription.

McQuade, Thomas J. From Syllogism to Predicate Calculus. *Teach Phil*, 17(4), 293-309, D 94.

A simple calculus is developed which, when applied to categorical syllogisms, enables conclusions to be calculated from premises. It replaces the traditional notation (Aristotle's four forms augmented with Venn or Euler diagrams) with one more suited to algebraic manipulation. This notation can be progressively generalized to encompass hypothetical syllogisms, Boolean calculus, and first-order predicate calculus so that a student can be led from syllogism to predicate calculus without any obvious break in notation or technique. Emphasis is placed on the use of logic as a tool for constructing concise and elegant arguments at a level appropriate to the problem.

McRae, Robert. "The Theory of Knowledge" in *The Cambridge Companion to Leibniz*, Jolley, Nicholas (ed), 176-198. New York, Cambridge Univ Pr, 1994.

The determining factor in Leibniz's theory of knowledge is his solution to the problem of the labyrinth of the continuum. The solution lies in the distinction between phenomena and substances. This in turn gives rise to three levels of concepts. 1) The sensible, 2) the imaginable as abstractions from sensible continua and as such are the objects of mathematics, and 3) the intelligible objects of metaphysics resulting from consciousness of the self. Physics combines the imaginable or mathematics and the purely intelligible concept of force. Physics also employs fictions which are unimaginable because involving a contradiction, like infinitely small motion, but which are highly useful.

McRobert, Laurie. On Fractal Thought: Derrida, Hegel, and Chaos Science. *Hist Euro Ideas*, 20(4-6), 815-821, F 95.

The purpose of the paper is threefold: 1) to see whether or not Derrida's model for thought which seems so uncannily related to the dynamics of chaos science can indeed be analogically related to some of the latter's mathematical/physical formulas; 2) to see whether or not we can superimpose Derrida's dynamics of deconstruction onto a phase space grid and thus open new windows of logic with his "formula" *différance*; 3) to see whether Derridian dynamics can help us establish a new structure for thought—what I am calling *fractal thought*. Since deconstructionism takes off from Hegel's *Aufhebung*, Hegel's dynamics become a natural sparring partner for Derrida's.

McShane, Philip. General Method. *Method*, 13(1), 35-52, Spr 95.

McWhorter, Ladelle. Is There Sexual Difference in the Work of Georges Bataille?. *Int Stud Phil*, 27(1), 33-41, 1995.

Irigaray claims that sexual difference is "the burning issue" of our time and thus that the work of a philosopher can be judged by whether (or how) he or she addresses that issue. This essay argues that, though Bataille does not directly address sexual difference, he does resist phallic subjectivity—total individualism, indentificational statis—and therefore his work is valuable by Irigarayan standards. In fact, in many ways his work parallels Irigaray's own, although this point will always be missed if we misread Irigaray's "sexual difference" as itself some specific, static difference rather than as radical differing.

Mead, Walter B. William Poteat's Anthropology: "Mindbody In the World". *Tradition Discovery*, 21(1), 33-44, 1994-95.

Using the metaphor of a circle with its center, periphery, and radius, this essay explores William Poteat's understanding of the self, or "mindbody", in its dynamic and creative relation to the larger world, or cosmos, identifying the mindbody's prereflective radix with the "center", its boundary or point of interface with the larger world with the "periphery", and its dialectical evolution and articulation of a sense of coherence and meaning in terms of a pretensive and retrotensive "radius".

Meaney, Mark E. Money, Monetary Crisis, and the Doctrine of Being. *Owl Minerva*, 26(2), 149-169, Spr 95.

Scholars who consider the relationship between Marx's and Hegel's scientific method often make a critical mistake. In the exposition of the manner in which Marx had made use of Hegel's logic, they fail to consider the relationship between form and content in the logical progression of categories. They fail to comprehend the circular nature of scientific method, with its attending concepts of "dialectic" and *Aufhebung*. In this paper, I briefly consider the nature of this mistake and a response to it to establish the thesis that the doctrinal content of Marx's *Grundrisse der Kritik der politischen Ökonomie (Rohentwurf 1857/58)* is indebted for its logical form to Hegel's exposition of logical categories as found in the *Wissenschaft der Logic* to an extent not recognized in prior scholarly literature. (edited)

Meara, Naomi M and Punzo, Vincent A. The Virtues of a Psychology of Personal Morality. *J Theor Phil Psych*, 13(1), 25-39, Spr 93.

The field of moral psychology has been confined to the study of social morality; resulting in a nearly exclusive focus on the primary other-regarding virtue of justice. An understanding of personal morality, with its concern with self-regarding virtues and the dynamics of intimate relationships, is needed to complement this approach. The importance of personal morality issues to moral psychology is foreshadowed in Gilligan's caring ethic. This paper expands on Gilligan's schematic portrayal in order to provide a more complete theoretical understanding of personal morality. Social and personal morality are contrasted on five salient issues to highlight their differences and interrelatedness.

Medina, Manuel. "Philosophy, Technology, and Society" in *Philosophy of Technology in Spanish Speaking Countries*, Mitcham, Carl (ed), 153-166. Dordrecht, Kluwer, 1994.

Medina F, Nelson. Leyendo a Rudolf Carnap. *Analogia*, 9(1), 101-124, 1995.

The Neopositivism had between its goals to reach a unified language, on the basis of a self-coherent set of propositions that should be logically derivable from the Russell's *Principia Mathematica*, or strictly an exhibition of verifiable *data*. It was expected that in this way science was finally founded as a consistent and self-contained body of understanding that, in fact, would progressively contain every valid knowledge. This vision would exclude every religious or metaphysical statement. However, the article offers a detailed analysis of some Carnap's central propositions that shows that they have their own kind of nonscientific, faithful character.

Medrano, Concepción. A Model of Intervention for Improving Moral Reasoning: An Experiment in the Basque Country. *J Moral Educ*, 23(4), 427-437, 1994.

The experiment presented falls within Kohlberg's constructivist model, and attempts to respond to the need for work on those interpersonal values which may be called ethical or moral, in practical education. The intervention took place in a state school in Vizcaya (Basque Country), with a sample of 97 subjects between the ages of 9 and 14 years. A pre-test—post-test design was used in order to check for the achievement of more mature states of moral development. The main working strategy was the discussion of hypothetical and real values dilemmas in class discussion groups. The results show that many advances were made. The data indicate that discussing dilemmas leads to higher levels of moral reasoning in students.

Medushevskii, A N. Democracy and Tyranny in Modern and Recent Times. *Russian Stud Phil*, 33(3), 62-96, Wint 94-95.

Meehan, Johanna. Autonomy, Recognition and Respect: Habermas, Benjamin, Honneth. *Constellation*, 1(2), 270-285, O 94.

It has been argued that deontological ethical theories like Jürgen Habermas's discourse ethics reproduce a formal, abstract Cartesian subject and defend a problematic Kantian derived notion of autonomy. Jessica Benjamin condemns such rationalized notions of the subject as based on a model of subjectivity rooted in male domination and female submission. In this essay I argue that the intersubjective constitution of the Habermasian subject lends itself to exactly the object relations theoretical model Benjamin embraces. I suggest that Benjamin's and Habermas's notions of subjectivity, recognition, and normativity complement each other and can be bridged by Axel Honneth's concept of respect.

Meek, Christopher and Glymour, Clark. Conditioning and Intervening. *Brit J Phil Sci*, 45(4), 1001-1021, D 94.

We consider the dispute between causal decision theorists and evidential decision theorists over Newcomb-like problems. We introduce a framework relating causation and directed graphs developed by Spirtes *et al* (1993) and evaluate several arguments in this context. We argue that much of the debate between the two camps is misplaced; the disputes turn on the distinction between conditioning on an event E as against conditioning on an event I which is an action to bring about E. We give the essential machinery for calculating the effect of an intervention and consider recent work which extends the basic account given here to the case where causal knowledge is incomplete.

Meggle, Georg. Das Universalisierungsproblem in der Moralphilosophie. *Protosoz*, 6, 184-198, 1994.

Moral judgments have to be universalizable. There are many problems with this thesis (U). The problems to be dealt with here, are: 1) What is the connection between U and justifiability? 2) Is U a logical thesis? 3) Is U analytically true? 4) Is U adequate? 5) Is utilitarianism a logical consequence of U?

Meggle, Georg and Ulkan, Maria. Grices Doppelfehler: Ein Nachtrag zum Griceschen Modell. *Protosoz*, 2, 16-23, Ja 92.

This paper takes up again Grice's Basic Model (GBM) for analysing communicative acts. We draw attention to a 'new' fault in GBM, i.e., a fault not yet noticed in the literature: Grice's definiens for CA (=communicative attempt) is not only too weak (as it is not satisfying the reflexivity-condition according to which any CA implies the speaker's intention of CA's being understood by the hearer); it is also too strong—and just for the same reason.

Mehlman, Maxwell J (& others). Informed Consent to Amnestics, or: What Sound Does a Tree Make in the Forest When It Falls on Your Head?. *J Clin Ethics*, 5(2), 105-108, Sum 94.

Mehlman, Maxwell J and Massey, Susan R. The Patient-Physician Relationship and the Allocation of Scarce Resources: A Law and Economics Approach. *Kennedy Inst Ethics J*, 4(4), 291-308, D 94.

Patients with insufficient financial resources place physicians in a conflict of interest between the patients' needs and the financial interests of the physician, other patients, and society. Not only must physicians act ethically, but they must avoid liability for violating their legal duties to their patients. The traditional rules of contract and malpractice law that govern the patient-physician relationship do not provide satisfactory guidelines. Better answers are found in the rules of fiduciary law, but only with regard to direct conflicts between patients and physicians and only at the risk of reducing patient access to care. Certain types of legislative action can resolve these conflicts by altering the traditional legal rules, but care must be taken to preserve patient-physician trust, which the legal rules were designed to enhance.

Mehuron, Kate. Flesh Memory/Skin Practice. *Res Phenomenol*, 23, 73-91, 1993.

This essay addresses the depiction of the friendship between the philosopher Michel Foucault and the French novelist Herve Guibert, in Guibert's fictional autobiography *To the Friend Who Did Not Save My Life*. Critical reception of this book tends to interpret Guibert's thinly-veiled depiction of his friendship with Foucault as a betrayal of the friendship and a violation of the discretion surrounding the HIV positive status of both Guibert and Foucault. The essay argues that this critical reception trivializes Guibert's contribution to sketching the ethical and political significance of the AIDS pandemic. Guibert's novel signals the need for genealogies of the institutional bases of AIDS-related knowledge.

Mehuron, Kate (ed) and Percesepe, Gary (ed). *Free Spirits: Feminist Philosophers on Culture*. Englewood Cliffs, Prentice Hall, 1995.

This is a multicultural anthology of feminist essays designed for undergraduate and graduate classroom use in courses such as social and political philosophy, women's studies, and gender studies. The selections by well-known feminist thinkers address themes from popular culture: cultural images, communities, urban spaces, body politics, ecofeminism, sexualities, masculinities, and the politics of hope. Each essay is followed by reading questions, a suggested bibliography, and recommended audiovisual materials. The editor's introduction provides an overview of the organization of the book, and brief summaries of the contents of individual essays.

Meijer, Wilna. "General Education, Cultural Diversity, and Identity" in *Identity, Culture, and Education, Smeyers, Paul (ed)*, 241-250. Leuven, Leuven Univ Pr, 1994.

The paper discusses cultural diversity as a problem for general education and for personal identity. 'Cultural diversity' and 'cultural pluralism' are distinguished and it is argued that open pluralism can only be maintained if there is a basic common culture. Therefore, there yet is an indispensable role for general education. Finally, a concept of identity that is not in sheer opposition to diversity is added.

Meister, Robert. Is Moderation a Virtue? Gregory Vlastos and the Toxins of Eudaemonism. *Apeiron*, 26(3-4), 111-135, S-D 93.

Meister, Robert. *Political Identity: Thinking Through Marx*. Cambridge, Blackwell, 1991.

Mélançon, Marcel J. La Bioéthique: d'Une Révolution à l'Autre. *Philosopher*, 16, 145-156, 1994.

Melaney, William D. Vattimo and Literary Understanding: An Essay on Recent Hermeneutics. *Int Stud Phil*, 27(1), 51-62, 1995.

The paper centers around Vattimo's 1985 publication, *The End of Modernity*, a philosophical work that develops the hermeneutical approach to modern history and culture. First, Descartes's *ego cogito* is interpreted as a metaphysical construct that generally conceals the modern crisis of the self. Modernity is then related to Arendt's attempt to view history as an unstable process, and also to Heidegger's effort to "overcome" metaphysics through art and poetry. Vattimo's anti-Hegelian readings of Heidegger and Nietzsche are subsequently identified with postmodern hermeneutics. On this basis, Goethe's *Elective Affinities* is discussed as a postmodern document rather than as a Romantic novel.

Melchin, Kenneth R. Moral Decision-Making and the Role of the Moral Question. *Method*, 11(2), 215-228, Fall 93.

Melching, Willem (ed) and Velema, Wyger (ed). *Main Trends in Cultural History*. Amsterdam, Rodopi, 1994.

Mele, Alfred R. *Autonomous Agents: From Self-Control to Autonomy*. New York, Oxford Univ Pr, 1995.

Part I develops an account of an ideally self-controlled agent (self-control being construed as the contrary of akrasia) and shows that even such an agent may fall short of autonomy or free will. Part 2 asks what can be added to such an agent to generate a free or autonomous individual and offers a pair of overlapping answers—one for compatibilists and one for incompatibilists. The result is a pair of overlapping sets of sufficient conditions for autonomy that are argued to be satisfiable by real human agents, for all that is known about human psychology and the world.

Mele, Alfred R. Desiring to Try: Reply to Adams. *Can J Phil*, 24(4), 627-636, D 94.

In an earlier paper, the author argued that it is conceptually possible for an agent, in the absence of a desire to *A*, to want to *try* to *A* and to act on that want. This paper responds to Frederick Adams's attempt to undermine this thesis in "Trying, Desire, and Desiring to Try" (*Canadian Journal of Philosophy* 24, 1994). It is argued that Adams's attempt fails; and some problems are developed for Adams's positive view.

Mele, Alfred R. Effective Deliberation about What to Intend: Or Striking it Rich in a Toxin-Free Environment. *Phil Stud*, 79(1), 85-93, Jl 95.

This paper attacks three theses: reasons for intending to A do not extend beyond reasons for A-ing; deliberation, by its very nature, is never (even in part) about what to intend; reasons for intending to A that are not also reasons for A-ing cannot play a deliberative role in the formation of an intention to A. The third thesis is the paper's primary focus.

Mele, Alfred R. Self-Control and Belief. *Phil Psych*, 7(4), 419-435, 1994.

Although the extent to which motivational factors are involved in the production and sustaining of biased or 'irrational' beliefs continues to be a controversial issue in social psychology, even those who urge that such beliefs are often explained by nonmotivational tendencies admit that biased beliefs sometimes have motivational sources. Sometimes we are influenced by motivational pressures in ways proscribed by principles that we accept for belief-acquisition or belief-revision ('doxastic' principles). Many garden-variety instances of self-deception are cases in point. We are not always helpless victims of those pressures, however. This paper examines the nature of doxastic self-control (roughly, a capacity to counteract motivational pressures that incline us to acquire or retain beliefs that would violate our doxastic principles) and explores our prospects for avoiding motivationally biased believing by exercising self-control.

Mele, Alfred R and Moser, Paul K. Intentional Action. *Nous*, 28(1), 39-68, Mr 94.

This paper formulates an analysis of the ordinary notion of intentional action that clarifies a commonsense distinction between intentional and nonintentional action. The analysis builds on some typically neglected considerations about relations between lucky action and intentional action. The paper also explains why some vagueness is indispensable in a characterization of intentional action as ordinarily understood.

Melehy, Hassan (trans) and Rancière, Jacques. *The Names of History: On the Poetics of Knowledge*. Minneapolis, Univ of Minn Pr, 1994.

Melle, Ullrich. De zaak van de dieren. *Tijdschr Filosof*, 56(4), 752-763, D 94.

Melle, Ullrich. Selbstverwirklichung und Gemeinschaft in Husserls Ethik, Politik und Theologie. *Tijdschr Filosof*, 57(1), 111-128, Mr 95.

Mellema, Gregory. Supererogation, Blame, and the Limits of Obligation. *Philosophia (Israel)*, 24(1-2), 171-182, D 94.

Two theses about moral blame have held a wide appeal. One is that acts of supererogation are sometimes morally blameworthy to omit, and the other is that it is never permissible to do that which is morally blameworthy. I argue that these two theses are incompatible. However, they can be reconciled by distilling their intuitively appealing features from elements of each which are dubious or controversial. Nevertheless, the real concern of this article is not these two principles as such. Out of the process of reconciling them emerge some important conclusions about the limits of moral obligation.

Mellor, D H. Cambridge Philosophers I: F P Ramsey. *Philosophy*, 70(272), 243-262, Ap 95.

The article is the text of a public lecture on the life and work of F P Ramsey, it incorporates material from a 1978 broadcast including contributions by I A Richards, R B Braithwaite, A J Ayer, R C Jeffrey, and Ramsey's widow and brother.

Mellor, D H. *The Facts of Causation*. New York, Routledge, 1995.

The book presents a complete theory of causation. It covers all kinds of causing and affecting, of both events and facts: deterministic and undeterministic, mental and physical, transparent and opaque. It shows what makes a cause explain, be evidence for, and be a means of bringing about, its effects, and why causation entails the laws of nature that determine the kinds of facts our world contains. It also shows how causation distinguishes time from space, makes time linear, gives it its direction and enables us to perceive it.

Mellor, David Hugh. Nothing Like Experience. *Filozof Cas*, 42(6), 985-999, 1994.

This is a translation of my article of the same title published in English in the proceedings of the Aristotelian Society, Volume 93 (1993), 1-16.

Mellos, Koula. The Post-Modern Challenge to Community. *Hist Euro Ideas*, 19(1-3), 131-136, Jl 94.

Melnyk, Andrew. Inference to the Best Explanation and Other Minds. *Austl J Phil*, 72(4), 482-491, D 94.

Argues against the view that we are justified in believing that other humans have mental states by an inference to the best explanation from evidence consisting solely of their gross behavior. Criticizing Pargetter's account (*Australasian Journal of Philosophy*, 1984), it argues that this view probably misrepresents the way folk *actually* reason, and that in any case it fails to justify the belief that others have qualitative mental states. My remedy is an old idea: to make facts about one's own case play an evidential role in the inference to other minds, facts apparently playing no such role in the criticized view.

Melnyk, Andrew. Physicalism, Ordinary Objects, and Identity. *J Phil Res*, 20, 221-235, 1995.

Any philosopher sympathetic to physicalism (or materialism) will allow that there is *some* sense in which ordinary objects—tables and chairs, etc.—are physical. But what sense, exactly? John Post holds a view implying that every ordinary object is identical with some or other *spatio-temporal sum* of fundamental entities. I begin by deploying a modal argument intended to show that ordinary objects, for example elephants, are *not* identical with spatio-temporal sums of such entities. Then I claim that appeal to David Lewis's counterpart theory, even if acceptable in principle, would not permit post to make a plausible reply to this argument. Finally, I sketch an alternative account of ordinary objects, which does not require identity with spatio-temporal sums of fundamental physical entities, and argue that, despite Post's protestations, this account is acceptably physicalist: his identity claims are not required for physicalism.

Melnyk, Andrew. Two Cheers for Reductionism: Or, the Dim Prospects for Non-Reductive Materialism. *Phil Sci*, 62(3), 370-388, S 95.

I argue that a certain version of physicalism, which is viewed by both its admirers and its detractors as nonreductionist, in fact entails two claims which, though not reductionist in the currently most popular sense of 'reductionist', conform to the spirit of reductionism sufficiently closely to compromise its claim to be a *comprehensively* nonreductionist version of physicalism. Putatively nonreductionist versions of physicalism in general, I suggest, are likely to be nonreductionist only in some senses, but not in others, and hence to disappoint those who wish to be physicalists but still to remain soft and cuddly nonreductionists.

Melrose, Robin. The Seduction of Abduction: Peirce's Theory of Signs and Indeterminacy in Language. *J Prag*, 23(5), 493-507, My 95.

Charles Sanders Peirce's theory of signs is well known, but less well known is his notion of *abduction*, cited by Chomsky as a principle in first language acquisition. The paper sums up Peirce's three triads (firstness, secondness, thirdness: icon, index, symbol; abduction, induction, deduction), then goes on to link them with what Peirce calls the *law of mind*. The law of mind is then shown to have remarkable similarities with what Douglas Hofstadter, a researcher into artificial intelligence, calls *subcognition*, in that both involve abduction (icon-feelings attaching themselves to indices with a certain "arbitrary spontaneity"; patterns of neural firings triggering other patterns of neural firings, sometimes in "apparently random ways"). Abduction is seen as crucial to Jacques Derrida's principles of *differance* and *dehiscence*, and to the linguist Michael Halliday's view of language as *particle*, *wave* and *field*; and it may well prove to be a key concept in developing a linguistics of indeterminacy.

Mendell, Mark. The Problem of the Origin of Pragmatism. *Hist Phil Quart*, 12(1), 111-131, Ja 95.

This paper reinterprets the early relationship between philosophical and legal pragmatism. It takes a new look at the problem of the origin of pragmatism from both historical and philosophical perspectives, and it offers a critique of the separate studies of Fisch and Wiener, whose influence was such that later scholars simply repeated their conclusions and assumptions. The analysis invites two conclusions: 1) despite their fundamental kinship, the two pragmatisms do not depend upon each other nearly as much as has been supposed; 2) despite functioning as an attractive framework for interpreting the origins of pragmatism, the Metaphysical Club's importance has been much exaggerated.

Mendez, Julio R. "La Teoría de los Géneros en San Agustín y S Tomás de Aquino" in *Temas Actuales de Filosofía, Palacios, María Julia (ed)*, 395-402. Buenos Aires, Univ Nacional Salta, 1993.

The author studies Augustin's and Thomas Aquina's texts within their historical context. The concepts found out show discordant aspects concerning the general thought of the period with regard to women. These medieval authors' doctrinal novelty has its source in Metaphysics and in Christian Theology. Méndez claims that Augustin's and Thomas's theses in relation to women are more comprehensible and assimilable in the contemporary context.

Méndez Baiges, Víctor. Qué Locke? Tradición y Cambio en la Historia del Liberalismo. *Convivium*, 7, 64-80, 1995.

This paper refers to the change which has undergone within the hermeneutics of Locke's political philosophy in the last thirty years, and the way the introduction and the study of the so-called *language of the Classical Republicanism* has meant an important turn in the history of the relations between John Locke and liberalism. The paper is, then, an interpretation of interpretations. It follows the birth and development of what is called "traditional interpretation", and the way it arrives to its climax with C B Macpherson's *possessive individualism* it reviews later the works of his critics, making a relation between three items: the *Second Treatise*, the republican tradition and the British Enlightment. As it could be expected, it ends with an invitation to read the original works, the only thing interpretations do have in common.

Mendieta, Eduardo. G H Mead: Linguistically Constituted Intersubjectivity and Ethics. *Trans Peirce Soc*, 30(4), 959-1000, Fall 94.

Through a reconstruction of Mead's writings, the author argues for the centrality of ethics in his overall social psychology. Mead's theory of ethics is also demonstrated to be a major influence in the development of discourse ethics. The friendly and appropriative criticisms of Jürgen Habermas and Ernst Tugendhat are closely analyzed and shown to elucidate strengths and weakness in Mead's ethical theory. The essay concludes by arguing that Mead's moral theory, in conjunction with Apel's and Habermas's discourse ethics, can be said to answer the criteria and challenges, as Benhabib has delineated them, a post-metaphysical, post-Hegelian, and post-Kantian ethics must meet.

Mendieta, Eduardo (ed). *Karl-Otto Apel: Selected Essays (Volume 1)*. Atlantic Highlands, Humanities Pr, 1994.

Mendilow, Jonathan. Nathaniel Hawthorne and Conservatism's "Night of Ambiguity". *Polit Theory*, 23(1), 128-146, F 95.

The importance of Hawthorne's early work for political theorists lies in his insufficiently appreciated attempt to formulate a conservative response to the threats to liberty posed by the spread of egalitarianism in the emerging mass society of the early 1830's. The significance of his approach is best understood when compared with that of contemporary European conservatives who wrestled with similar problems, not particularly Tocqueville who was touring the USA at the time. A major focus of the paper is on the implications of Hawthorne's enigmatic "My Kinsman, Major Molineux" and other early works and the contribution of the ideas they reveal to the understanding of conservatism both in his time and in ours.

Mendonça, Cristina Diniz. Sarte's *L'Etre et le Néant*: A Philosophical Discovery of "Modern Times" (in Portuguese). *Trans/Form/Acao*, 17, 105-112, 1994.

This article defends the view that Sartre's "phenomenological ontology essay", *L'Etre et le Néant*, could be understood as a philosophical re-creation of a crucial historical experience.

Mendus, Susan. Feminism and Toleration. *Filozof Istraz*, 14(2-3), 361-374, 1994.

Feminists (and in particular radical feminists) have combined forces with moral conservatives on important political issues such as pornography or speech codes. The author finds this alliance questionable. There is something particularly unpleasant about intolerance displayed by a group which itself claims to be (or have been) oppressed, and sees itself as working for liberation. Secondly, the feminist-conservative alliance is predicated upon, and tends to promote, a problematic view of woman's nature and an unattractive moral vision. Women are presented as sexually pure or passive and morally superior to men (women's "different voice"); and the solution to moral, social and political problems is sought in legal restraint of male sexuality, rather than in assertion of female sexuality. Thus law becomes the main tool by means of which people (particularly men) are to be "forced to be moral". And feminism is ineluctabley drawn into practices of intolerance which keep women in a state of oppression and condone the oppression of men. Drawing on Michael Walzer's account of messianic thinking, the author argues that feminism should distance itself from moral conservatism. (edited)

Mendus, Susan. John Stuart Mill and Harriet Taylor on Women and Marriage. *Utilitas*, 6(2), 287-299, N 94.

The aim of this paper is to suggest that John Stuart Mill's *Subjection of Women* and Harriet Taylor's *Enfranchisement of Women* are far more radical texts than is usually believed. Both Mill and Taylor argue for the equality of women as necessary for moral improvement, and their arguments anticipate modern radical feminism in two important respects. Firstly, they emphasize the position of women as sexual slaves. Secondly, they argue that emotion should be re-valued and recognized as an important complement to reason. The two works are, therefore, more than merely remedies for legal disability. They are moral and radical texts.

Menne, Albert. *Einführung in die Logik*. Tubingen, Francke, 1993.

Mensch, James R. Husserl and Sartre: A Question of Reason. *J Phil Res*, 19, 147-184, 1994.

Husserl's defenders generally ooppose Sartre's demand that the ego fall to the reduction, arguing that the ego, because of its functions, cannot be reduced. But the

C manuscripts show that Husserl does perform the reduction on the ego. They indicate that Sartre and Husserl differ, not with regard to the reducibility of the ego, but with regard to the consequences of this reduction. For Sartre, the reduction of the ego implies the contingency of reason. For Husserl it does not. I explain this opposition in terms of the difference between the two philosophers' views on the openness of consciousness.

Mensching, Günther. "Metaphysik und Naturbeherrschung im Denken Roger Bacons" in *Naturauffassungen in Philosophie, Wissenschaft, Technik: Band I, Schäfer, Lothar (ed)*, 161-184. Freiburg, Alber, 1993.

The purpose of my contribution is to demonstrate the intimate relation between Bacon's modifications of Aristotelian metaphysics and his amazing ideas of a technological development. A traditional Neoplatonic conception of the theological foundations of science is in Bacon's philosophy curiously connected with a medieval anticipation of modern theories of energy to which Bacon wants to applicate mathematical methods. His plan of a reform of the whole science which he presented to Pope Clement IV. in 1268, outlines a Christian universalism based on social domination of nature and on the progress of civilization.

Menser, Michael K. Exploring the Possibility of Dasein's Original Multiplicity in *Being and Time*. *Conference*, 4(2), 54-67, Fall 93.

Menssen, Sandra L. The Existential Problem of Evil: Reflections on the Analogy Between Creation and Procreation. *Amer Cath Phil Quart*, 68(Supp), 229-246, 1994.

Menuge, Angus. The Scope of Observation. *Phil Quart*, 45(178), 60-69, Ja 95.

A dialogue occurs between a constructive empiricist and a realist. The empiricist maintains that evidence of detectability by the naked eye is especially good reason to believe that an object is observable. The realist attacks the assumption that instruments generally decrease the reliability of the sensory system. He also shows that any principled reason to doubt the deliverances of instruments is also a reason to doubt the unaided senses. The dialogue concludes that instruments often provide just as good reason to think that an entity is observable as does evidence that it can be seen with the naked eye.

Mercado Pacheco, Pedro. Análisis Económico del Derecho y Utilitarismo: Concordancias y Divergencias. *Telos (Spain)*, 3(2), 99-123, D 94.

The bulk of the article is devoted to an analysis of the relations between the *Law and Economics* movement and utilitarianism. *Among the most* severe critics of the economic approach to law are those who attack it as a version of utilitarianism in contemporary legal theory, but R Posner, the leading scholar in this movement, rejects this classification. This article shows that Posner's proposal is flawed by arguing that economic anathesis of law is utilitarian in two central tenets: the human action theory—the self—interestedness of human motivation—and the consequentialist character of economic theory of law. (edited)

Mercer, Christia and Sleigh Jr, R C. "Metaphysics: The Early Period to the *Discourse on Metaphysics*" in *The Cambridge Companion to Leibniz, Jolley, Nicholas (ed)*, 67-123. New York, Cambridge Univ Pr, 1994.

The authors trace the development of Leibniz's mature metaphysics. They present the intellectual context in which his youthful metaphysics is most easily understood and summarize both his original metaphysical principles and his first conception of substance. They argue that his concept of substance, combined with certain theological commitments, led Leibniz to develop most of the central doctrines of his mature thought. For example, they claim that by April 1676, Leibniz had arrived at his doctrine of preestablished harmony.

Merchant, Betty. Current Educational Reform: "Shape-shifting" or Genuine Improvement in the Quality of Teaching and Learning?. *Educ Theor*, 45(2), 251-268, Spr 95.

This essay examines three books on educational change and explores the following themes: the role of external forces in school change, philosophy and goals of schools, school governance and decision making, organization of schools for teaching and learning, and potential consequences of school change efforts for participants. The American Indian concept of "shape-shifting" reflects the author's skepticism, not so much about the merits of specific educational change efforts detailed in these books, as about the level of commitment of key actors within these reform movements towards improving the schooling experiences of students traditionally marginalized within mainstream public education.

Merchant, Carolyn (ed). *Ecology*. Atlantic Highlands, Humanities Pr, 1994.

Mercier, Adèle. Consumerism and Language Acquisition. *Ling Phil*, 17(5), 499-519, O 94.

Consumerism—the view that "words come to us pre-packaged with their semantic value" (Kaplan 1989)—is implicitly presupposed by popular current conceptions of language which individuate idiolects by reference to communal norms. Consumerism implies a tacit account of language transmission which conflicts essentially with Chomskyan assumptions about acquisition and which faces principled difficulties in accounting for language change. The paper argues that consumerism about semantic rules, if motivated at all, applies in the same way and for like reasons to syntactic rules. A thought-experiment then presents a learned language countchancing no sentence in common with its source language, thereby suggesting that "pre-packaging" is no essential component of language acquisition.

Merelo, J J and Exteberria, A and Moreno, A. Studying Organisms with Basic Cognitive Capacities in Artificial Worlds. *Commun Cog—AI*, 11(1-2), 31-53, 1994.

In this paper we pose the problem of how to study basic cognitive processes in the frame of simulations of artificial worlds of the style of Artificial Life. The main difficulty of simulating biologically grounded cognitive processes lies in the search for forms of organisms suitable to establish functional relationships with their environments and co-evolve with them. In order to attempt this, we study the properties of autonomous systems at different degrees of complexity and the origin of cognitive processes as a sophistication of primitive sensori-motor loops of living systems. (edited)

Merkel, Reinhard. "Ärztliche Entscheidungsprobleme zwischen Leben und Tod" in *Freiheit, Verantwortung und Folgen in der Wissenschaft, Sandkühler, Hans Jörg (ed)*, 167-188. New York, Lang, 1994.

Merker, Nicolao. "Zum Gebrauch von Traditionen" in *Das geistige Erbe Europas, Buhr, Manfred (ed)*, 209-220. Napoli, Vivarium, 1994.

Two distinct and opposed traditions coexist in German culture since the Reformation: the one embodied in democratic action in view of politically and socially progressive aims, the other bound to authoritarian theory and practice. The author investigates some of the turning points of German modern history to retrace this twofold heritage and evaluate how it can still be relevant for our future.

Merle, Jean-Christophe. Fichte's Economic Philosophy and the Current Debate Concerning Distributive Justice. *Daimon Rev Filosof*, 9, 259-273, 1994.

It is nevertheless true that Fichte is the first to have introduced the double synthesis I have emphasized, that is to say, the synthesis of right and progress and that of the individual and the community. In this he was innovative both compared to the egalitarian currents of his period and in comparison with a long, later tradition. He defends an egalitarianism that neither rejects efficiency and progress nor, on the other hand, private property, the liberty of the individual and the differences demanded by progress. Lastly and above all, his is not a moral finality of the economy, perfect in the Rawlsian sense. (edited)

Merleau-Ponty, Jacques. La cosmologie contemporaine doit-elle intéresser les philosophes?. *Rev Phil Fr*, 3, 273-294, Jl-S 94.

Merrell-Wolff, Franklin. *Transformations in Consciousness: The Metaphysics and Epistemology*. Albany, SUNY Pr, 1995.

Merricks, Trenton. On the Incompatability of Enduring and Perduring Entities. *Mind*, 104(415), 523-531, Jl 95.

I argue that if one view of the present (presentism) is true, then there cannot be perduring entities (four-dimensional entities composed of temporal parts). If another view of the present (indexicalism) is true, then there cannot be enduring entities (three-dimensional entities wholly present at each time at which they exist). Either presentism or indexicalism is true, so it is not possible that *both* perduring entities *and* enduring entities exist. One upshot of this conclusion is that it is not possible that there be both three-dimensional enduring objects and four-dimensional perduring events.

Mertens, F. Should Franciscus van den Enden's Role in the Outset of Spinozism Be Reconsidered? (in Dutch). *Tijdschr Filosof*, 56(4), 717-738, D 94.

By elaborating the existing criticism on Klever's thesis about Van den Enden, I try to show that not only Klever's statements, but also the traditional view on Spinoza's teacher, must be corrected in many ways. Too often speculation was built upon speculation, which made it become increasingly difficult to tell fact from fiction. The only way this problem can be solved, is by renewed and thorough examination of the relevant sources. In my opinion such an examination does not only prove many of Klever's specific assertions to be false, it is equally devastating for his main thesis.

Mertens, Thomas. Zweckmässigkeit der Natur und politische Philosophie bei Kant. *Z Phil Forsch*, 49(2), 220-240, Ap-Je 95.

Kant's treatise "Toward Perpetual Peace" presents the legal conditions for making peace, and a teleological conception of nature which attests them. In this article is claimed that the above conception is compatible with Kant's concept of teleology as established in his Critique of (teleological) Judgment. This Critique not only accepts the possibility of the so-called intrinsic purposiveness, but the one of extrinsic purposiveness, too. Consequently it contains (in sections 82-4) a succinct account of Kant's Philosophy of History wherein human culture is presented as the preparation of morality. The teleology of Kant is an "ethicotheology".

Merttens, Ruth. Adolescents, Post-Structuralism, and "Playing It Cool!". *J Thought*, 29(4), 47-54, Wint 94.

Mesch, Walter. Kontinuität oder Bruch? Zum Verhältnis von sokratischer und platonischer Dialektik. *Phil Rundsch*, 41(3), 212-221, Je 94.

The two books reviewed in the article are Gregory Vlastos' *Socrates: Ironist and Moral Philosopher* (Cambridge 1991), and Peter Stemmer's *Platons Dialektik: Die frühen und mittleren Dialoge* (Berlin 1992). Vlastos' book is called to task because the stress Vlastos lays on the difference between Plato's portrayal of Socrates in the early and middle dialogues obstructs understanding how the Platonic dialectic could have evolved out of the Socratic. In contrast, Stemmer's inquiry makes this transition far more plausible by showing how the complicated dialectic of the middle dialogues developed out of the Socratic *elenchus*.

Meschiari, Alberto. La Filosofia Tedesca del Secondo Ottocento tra Scienze dello Spirito e Scienze della Natura. *G Crit Filosof Ital*, 73(1), 139-148, Ja-Ap 94.

Meslin, Eric M and Sutherland, Heather J and Till, James E. What's Missing from Current Clinical Trial Guidelines? A Framework for Integrating Science, Ethics, and the Community Context. *J Clin Ethics*, 5(4), 297-303, Wint 94.

The purpose of the work was to produce a framework to guide the development of meritorious clinical trial proposals. The framework consists of essential features of rigourous methodology, ethical acceptability, and a component referred to as "community context". These three domains were woven together in a checklist format under the headings of general, scientific and ethical considerations. Since texts concerning clinical trial methodology do not integrate ethics criteria and ethics guidelines do not provide detailed scientific criteria in obvious and practical ways, we outline a more contemporary and comprehensive set of guidelines.

Messinese, Leonardo. Kant, Heidegger e la logica filosofica. *Aquinas*, 37(1), 89-122, Ja-Ap 94.

Messinese, Leonardo. Nota sulla "creazione". *Aquinas*, 37(1), 225-228, Ja-Ap 94.

Messuti de Zabala, Ana. La victima y el "No-sujeto de derecho". *Riv Int Filosof Diritto*, 71(3), 493-498, 1994.

Mester, Fiore. Saint Ignatius of Loyola's Search for Ultimate Reality and Meaning. *Ultim Real Mean*, 18(2), 75-91, Je 95.

Mestre, Antonio. Boturini e la Diffusione di Vico in Spagna. *Boll Centro Stud Vichiani*, 24-25, 209-230, 1994-95.

Metz, Johann Baptist and Ashley, J Matthew (trans). Suffering unto God. *Crit Inquiry*, 20(4), 611-622, Sum 94.

Metz, Wilhelm. Die Weltgeschichte beim späten Fichte. *Fichte-Studien*, 1, 121-131, 1990.

Das erste grosse Werk der Fichteschen Geschichtsphilosophie, nämlich die *Grundzüge des gegenwärtigen Zeitalters*, ist auf Basis zweier unterschiedlicher Schemata errichtet. Ich möchte zuerst diese beiden Schemata und ihre spannungsreiche Synthesis aufweisen. In einem zweiten Teil soll gezeigt werden, dass die *Reden an die deutsche Nation* nur die erste Geschichtskonzeption der *Grundzüge* weiterführen, während sich in der *Staatslehre* von 1813 die zweite Konzeption und mit ihr die religiöse Betrachtung der Weltgeschichte endgültig durchsetzt.

Metz, Wilhelm. Fichtes genetische Deduktion von Raum und Zeit in Differenz zu Kant. *Fichte-Studien*, 6, 71-94, 1994.

The originally-synthetical unity of apperception refers in Kant to space and time, and determines them a priori as "unities"; but space and time do not result as forms of the receptivity from the self-consciousness. The productive "I" thought by Fichte is yet, as the one principle of theoretical and practical reason, *pure* activity; the "I" itself produces the matter of the sensation as much as the pure forms of the intuition, space and time, who render possible the "ideal object". Finally Fichte's genetical construction of space and time from the "I" makes *Freedom* visible as theoretical principle.

Metz, Wilhelm. La genesi della coscienza reale nella "Grundlage der gesamten Wissenschaftslehre" di Fichte. *Teoria*, 14(1), 21-53, 1994.

The central thesis of the article is that the *productive reflection* thought by Fichte is the principle of the real consciousness. In its theoretical function the reflection transforms the pre-conscious positions of the "I" into the real consciousness and self-consciousness. In its practical function the reflection transports the consciousness within the most interior of the "I", through which Impulse and Action, or more exactly, their Harmony or Disharmony become conscious to the "I". Only with the consciousness of the "Moral Law" the real consciousness in its totality originates in the "I".

Meuter, Günter. *Der Katechon: Zu Carl Schmitts fundamentalistischer Kritik der Zeit*. Berlin, Duncker Humblot, 1994.

Mey, Jacob L. On Gorayska and Lindsay's Definition of Relevance. *J Prag*, 23(3), 341-342, Mr 95.

Meyer, Albert R and Seiferas, Joel I. Characterization of Realizable Space Complexities. *Annals Pure Applied Log*, 73(2), 171-190, Je 95.

Meyer, Eric. "Reconstructing Aesthetic Education" in *Intersections: Nineteenth-Century Philosophy and Contemporary Theory, Rajan, Tilottama (ed)*, 286-301. Albany, SUNY Pr, 1995.

Meyer, Eva. "Im Gestell der Sprache" in *Macht Geschlechter Differenz, Müller-Funk, Wolfgang (ed)*, 112-127. Vienna, Picus, 1994.

Meyer, Michael J. Dignity, Death and Modern Virtue. *Amer Phil Quart*, 32(1), 45-55, Ja 95.

The much touted phrase "death with dignity"—figuring prominently in public discussion and private deliberations about dying—makes conspicuous use of two ideas that are less than clear, since the concepts of dignity and death are both quite complex. The paper helps clarify the concept "death with dignity" by examining in turn: 1) dignity, 2) death, 3) death with dignity, and 4) dying with dignity. Just what sense of "dignity" is employed in 3 and 4? And what is the role of the Kantian moral tradition, touting *human* dignity, in understanding the idea—and the virtue—of dying with dignity?

Meyer, Michel. Introduction: De l'importance et de la résurgence des passions. *Rev Int Phil*, 48(189), 269-273, 1994.

Meyer, Michel. Les problèmes des passions chez Saint Thomas d'Aquin. *Rev Int Phil*, 48(189), 363-374, 1994.

Meyer, Michel and Jamison, David (trans). *Of Problematology: Philosophy, Science, and Language*. Chicago, Univ of Chicago Pr, 1995.

Problematology is a new way of doing philosophy and conceiving thought, language and reason at large. Instead of considering propositions as self-sufficient, problematology sees them as answers, i.e. as situated in reference to underlying questions. Questioning has unfortunately never been questioned as such, in spite of Socrates or Descartes' doubt. Meyer's views aims at explaining why questioning has been repressd at the thematic level of philosophy throughout its history. But the author also wants to show why and where questioning is so important for a new and enlarged view of Reason. *Problematology* is itself the response to the *deconstructivist* approach in virtue of its positive and constructivist outlook on the problematical.

Meyer, Robert K. Rationalizing Relevant Primitives, of Course!. *Bull Sec Log*, 24(2), 76-79, Je 95.

Meyers, Diana Tietjens. Rights in Collision: A Non-Punitive, Compensatory Remedy for Abusive Speech. *Law Phil*, 14(2), 203-243, My 95.

In this paper, I shall examine some recent work by critical race theorists on the problem of hate speech. Their discussions of this issue suggest two key elements of a nonideal rights theory. First, rights that address real-world injustice are best grounded in empathic understanding of diverse right-holders. Second, empathy-based rights may conflict with established rights, and, where this is the case, we must avoid lapsing into orthodox approaches to resolving the conflict and must instead be resourceful in envisaging ways to respect everyone's rights. I shall defend these claims by attempting to show that embracing them leads to fruitful results with respect to the vexing problem of hate speech on United States college and university campuses. (edited)

Meyers, Kurt and Murray, Michael J. Ask and It Will Be Given to You. *Relig Stud*, 30(3), 311-330, S 94.

The practice of petitionary prayer raises a number of philosophical problems for the Christian theistic tradition. This paper addresses two of those problems. First, why is it that God would choose to make the distribution of earthly blessings contingent on the believer's recognition of her needs and her requests that God make provision for them? Second, why would God, as the Christian tradition holds, command human creatures to pray for the needs of others? It is argued that the first can be justified by the fact that petitionary prayer can act as a powerful deterrent against idolatry for the believer. In addition, individual petitionary prayer allows the believer to learn more about divine purposes and the divine will. The second, corporate prayer, can be justified by the fact that it serves to foster an essential interdependence among the members of the community of praying believers.

Meyerstein, F Walter and Brisson, Luc. *Inventing the Universe: Plato's Timaeus*, The Big Bang, and the Problem of Scientific Knowledge. Albany, SUNY Pr, 1995.

The "extra-logical gap" between perception and scientific explanation can be appraised historically. Three stages are to be distinguished. 1) Plato's *Timaeus* furnishes the first example of a scientific cosmology dealing with a realm of ideality which cannot be derived from immediate sensible perception. A list of presuppositions or axioms is first set down, then their consequences are expressed mathematically, and finally the degree of correspondence between this theoretical construction and the data of observation is established. But Plato refuses a naively operational interpretation of this correspondence, according to which a scientific explanation would be exhausted when predictions based on a theorem turn out to be appropriate. 2) Just as the world-order fashioned by the demiurge according to Plato manifests itself as symmetry, the Big Bang model is also mainly constituted on the basis of the geometrical notion of symmetry. Furthermore, the two cosmologies, whose overall parallelism is shown to be striking, take simplicity for granted. The list of axioms of Big Bang cosmology begins with metrical considerations. The Friedmann-Robertson-Walker metric for a homogeneous and isotropic universe is derived, and the various problems (theoretical and observational) associated with it are discussed. 3) In the more recent Algorithmic Information Theory, the analysis of the purely symbolic language expressing physical reality reveals the level of complexity of any given theory formulated in this language. The result is that the probability that the universe is actually in conformity with simple mathematics is zero.

Meynell, Guy. Locke as Author of *Anatomia* and *De Arte Medica*. *Locke News*, 25, 65-73, 1994.

Meynell, Guy. Locke's Medical Notebook, 'Adversaria 3'. *Locke News*, 25, 85-86, 1994.

Meynell, Hugo. Archdeconstruction and Postpostmodernism. *Heythrop J*, 36(2), 125-139, Ap 95.

Deconstruction and postmodernism are often, reasonably, supposed to lead to nihilism. But the basic norms of cognition and evaluation may be established by advertence to the fact that some statements are self-destructive—'I never speak the truth', 'I never judge for good reason', 'I never make a responsible decision, even to speak truly for good reason.' The required norms are derivable from the contradictories of these self-destructive statements. Once established, the norms may be corroborated, clarified and amplified by attitudes and techniques analagous to deconstruction and postmodernism; these are designated by the barbarous neologisms of the title.

Meynell, Hugo. Post-Analytic Philosophy: Its Causes and Its Cure. *Method*, 10(2), 77-88, Fall 92.

The cause of post-analytic philosophy is the apparent collapse of foundations of knowledge, both of fact and value; this has led to pervasive scepticism and relativism. Its cure is advertence to the real foundations, which are the attentiveness to experience, intelligence in envisaging possibilities, and reasonableness in affirming the possibility best confirmed by the evidence, of the authentic human subject. It is self-destructive to deny that these are the sovereign means to truth, since any such denial could only be justified on the grounds that it was intelligent and reasonable to make it on the basis of experience.

Miccolis, Stefano. Frammenti Politici di Antonio Labriola con una Postilla Bibliografica. *G Crit Filosof Ital*, 72(3), 473-488, S-D 93.

Miccolis, Stefano. Rassegne Crociane: I. I Carteggi dell'Ultimo Decennio. II. Una Bibliografia "Ragionata". *G Crit Filosof Ital*, 73(2-3), 326-352, My-D 94.

Michael, Michaelis. The Dialectics of Scepticism: Comments on Gallois. *Austl J Phil*, 73(1), 123-128, Mr 95.

Gallois has explored the dialectical relationship between the "global sceptic" and his opponents, suggesting that a cogent argument for scepticism can never be forced on the opponents of scepticism. The idea is that global scepticism is self-defeating because it is self-refuting. I argue that first, the incoherence of the global sceptic's conclusion is not at all established by Gallois' line of thought and that second, the purported incoherence, even if it could be established, would have no effect on the effectiveness of the sceptic's arguments against the nonsceptic.

Michaels, Walter Benn. Critical Response II: The No-Drop Rule. *Crit Inquiry*, 20(4), 758-769, Sum 94.

Michalos, Alex C and Mallard, Alison G and Lance, Charles E. Tests of the Causal Directions of Global-Life Facet Satisfaction Relationships. *Soc Indic Res*, 34(1), 69-92, Ja 95.

Previous research generally has supported multiple discrepancies theory (MDT) of the processes by which individuals arrive at judgments of satisfaction with various aspects of their lives as well as with life overall. However, the nature of possible causal relationships between overall and life facet satisfaction has been ignored. The purpose of this study was to extend MDT by testing alternative theoretical models which specified bottom-up, top-down, and bidirectional relationships between overall life satisfaction and satisfaction with eleven life facets in a sample of 1354 US college students. Results most strongly favored the bidirectional model in which the overall—life facet satisfaction relationship varied across life domains. The need to identify boundary conditions which determine the direction of the overall—life facet satisfaction relationship is discussed.

Michelsen, John Magnus. The Place of Buddhism in Santayana's Moral Philosophy. *Asian Phil*, 5(1), 39-46, 1995.

Within the moral philosophy of the Spanish-American philosoper George Santayana (1863-1952), reference to Buddhism becomes an essential feature in his formulation of the notion of *post-rational morality*, which is that "phase" of morality which involves an effort to subordinate all precepts to one that points to some single eventual good. Post-rational morality is synonymous with the *spirit life*, an essential feature of which is *detachment*; and this is why the Buddhists can be said to be the "true masters" of the subject. Santayana's claim that Buddhism "suffers from a fundamental contradiction" can also be seen as an opportunity for us to deepen our own understanding of that philosophy.

Michnowski, Leslaw. Holistic Approach to Development. *Dialogue Hum*, 4(2-3), 247-253, 1994.

Middeldorp, Aart and Zantema, Hans. Simple Termination of Rewrite Systems. *Bull Sec Log*, 24(1), 31-36, Mr 95.

In this paper we investigate the concept of simple termination. A term rewriting system (TRS for short) is called simply terminating if its termination can be proved by means of a simplification order. We propose a new definition of simplification order and we investigate the properties of the resulting class of simply terminating systems.

Middleton, Darren J N. David Pailin's Theology of Divine Action. *Process Stud*, 22(4), 215-226, Winter 93.

Midgley, Mary. "Darwinism and Ethics" in *Medicine and Moral Reasoning, Fulford, K W M (ed)6-18*. New York, Cambridge Univ Pr, 1994.

Midgley, Mary. "The End of Anthropocentrism?" in *Philosophy and the Natural Environment, Attfield, Robin (ed)*, 103-112. New York, Cambridge Univ Pr, 1994.

Midgley, Mary. *Beast and Man: The Roots of Human Nature*. New York, Routledge, 1995.

Midgley, Mary. *The Ethical Primate: Humans, Freedom and Morality*. New York, Routledge, 1994.

This book deals with the paradox that each human being is a living part of the natural world, yet is also free and free *as a whole*—not just by having one component, the will, placed outside a world which is itself mechanical, alien and dead. What matters for freedom is not unpredictability but genuine agency, which we have. Our uniqueness does not lie in suppressing our inner conflicts but in our power, which is slight but real, to grasp and arbitrate them. Thus, our continuity with the biosphere is not an imprisonment. It is an opportunity.

Midgley, Mary and Hughes, Judith. "Trouble with Families?" in *Introducing Applied Ethics, Almond, Brenda (ed)*, 17-32. Cambridge, Blackwell, 1995.

Many philosophers, form Plato to Marx and Nietzche, have attacked "the family" as a corrupting institution. More lately, various psychologists, sociologists and feminists, along with the designers of the Israeli Kibbutzim, have also denounced its influence. Yet, today, its apparent breakdown causes widespread alarm. The main cause of that breakdown is probably just increased social mobility. But individualist theories have also contributed, calling for a quite unrealistic degree of autonomy and contempt for interpersonal dependence. Humans it seems, can reach wider loyalties only through a gradual, careful expansion which has to start from vigorous personal and local bonds.

Miedema, Siebren. The Beyond in the Midst: The Relevance of Dewey's Philosophy of Religion for Education. *Stud Phil Educ*, 13(3-4), 229-241, 1994-95.

Dewey's philosophy of religion and its connection to his philosophy of education is examined. The contribution begins by emphasizing the 'intersubjectivist turn' in critical-pragmatism and critical-theory. Using recent studies on Dewey's philosophy of religion and Hans Joas's Deweyan critique of Habermas, it is argued that, unlike the critical theorist, the Deweyan pragmatist has valuable things to say to those interested in religious education. Joas's critique with its focus on creativity is connected to Thomas A Alexander's work on Dewey's aesthetics and its relation to the creation of the ideals of action that for Dewey had religious significance.

Miedema, Siebren and de Ruyter, Doret J. "Schools, Identity, and the Conception of the Good" in *Identity, Culture, and Education, Smeyers, Paul (ed)*, 145-156. Leuven, Leuven Univ Pr, 1994.

Schools have an important contribution to the formation of a child's identity. Identity can be divided into three aspects, namely those characteristics, values, and ideals a person describes to herself that she has derived from 1) her person; 2) the communities she is part of; 3) the society she lives in. In denominational schools frictions can arise regarding the contribution to the development of the child's societal identity and of her communital identity. Regarding this friction we take the stance that as the schools are fully subsidized by the state that makes freedom and diversity in (religious) identity possible, the state has the right to make freedom of choice for children possible as well. Thus, the balance tips to the societal identity.

Mier y Terán, Rocío. Algunas consideraciones sobre "lo sensible" en *De Anima*. *Topicos*, 4(7), 67-74, 1994.

Here I argue that there can be found three different meanings of "sensible" in Aristotle's *De Anima*. These meanings suppose that it is better to understand sensation as activity more than as a passion.

Mier y Terán, Rocío. Principialidad de las Facultades en el Orden del Ser. *Topicos*, 1(1), 137-157, 1991.

Miessgang, Thomas. *X-Sample: Gespräche am Rande der Zeit*. Vienna, Passagen, 1993.

Das Buch will das konvulsivische Zucken der Gedankenfiguren in einem unausgemessenen gesellschaftlichen Raum durch Interviews von KRS-One bis Slavoj Zizek, von Camille Paglia bis Boris Groys dokumentieren. (edited)

Mieth, Dietmar. The Model of an Ethics of Being in Meister Eckhart and in the Structural Philosophy of Heinrich Rombach. *Listening*, 29(3), 186-198, Fall 94.

Migotti, Mark. Peirce's First Rule of Reason and the Bad Faith of Rortian Post-Philosophy. *Trans Peirce Soc*, 31(1), 89-136, Wint 95.

This paper argues that Richard Rorty's attempts to overcome traditional philosophy in the interest of heralding a "post-philosophical culture" suffer from an instability that mirrors that of Sartrean bad faith. I claim that Rorty cannot escape the following dilemma: either he tries to give *good reasons* for welcoming a post-philosophical world—but giving good reasons is central to traditional philosophy; or he promotes his hopes without concern for evidence and argument—and then it is unclear what heed the unpersuaded should pay him. Rorty's vacillations between these two unappealing alternatives prompts the diagnosis of bad faith.

Miguel-Alfonso, Ricardo (ed) and Caporale-Bizzini, Silvia (ed). *Reconstructing Foucault*. Amsterdam, Rodopi, 1994.

Mihayara, Isamu. Communicative Universals. *Monist*, 78(1), 30-40, Ja 95.

Mikel, Anton. A Problem with the Minimalist Theory of Truth. *Phil Papers*, 23(2), 137-138, Ag 94.

I criticize in this paper Paul Horwich's minimalist theory, his recent attempt at reviving the redundancy theory of truth. I argue that there is at least one substantial and intuitively legitimate truth claim that his theory fails to account for.

Mikkelsen, Jon Mark. The Dialectic of System and Critique in Recent Interpretations of Kant's Critical Philosophy. *Ultim Real Mean*, 17(2), 136-149, Ju 94.

This paper offers a defense of the "systematic" interpretation of the critical philosophy developed in the period since the 1924 Marburg Kant congress and still commonly employed in German scholarship. This view is presented as an alternative to interpretative methods common in Anglo-analytic scholarship since the publication of Strawson's *The Bound of Sense* (London, 1966) and defended on the grounds that it can better explain the development of Kant's project from the pre-critical period through the works of the late 1790's, with special emphasis placed upon the *Critique of Judgment*. I concede, however, that contemporary Kant research can learn from both of these views.

Milbank, John. "Can a Gift be Given? Prolegomena to a Future Trinitarian Metaphysic" in *Rethinking Metaphysics, Jones, L Gregory (ed)*, 119-161. Cambridge, Blackwell, 1995.

The article claimed: 1) That a gift *can* expect a return. 2) That only a reciprocal gift can occur at all. 3) That the mark of a gift is non-identical repetition rather than unconditional freedom. 4) That Christianity thinks unlimited gift-exchange free of fetishization it objects. 5) That Christian *agape* is more like an exchanged gift than a free gift. 6) That the true, exchanged gift is not "before" being.

Milbank, John. Can a Gift Be Given? Prolegomena to a Future Trinitarian Metaphysic. *Mod Theol*, 11(1), 119-161, Ja 95.

Derrida's deconstruction of the notion of gift remains confined by the modern contrast of gift and contract. A gift *may* be exchangist, rather than unilateral, but remains a gift by virtue of nonidentical repetition. Such a genuine gift is anticipated by archaic societies, but only fully arises with Christian *agape*. A nonidentical repetition within a circulation of exchange implies that the gift is not beyond Being, although Being is gift. Trinitarian theology articulated such a revised metaphysics.

Miles, M L. Leibniz on Apperception and Animal Souls. *Dialogue (Canada)*, 33(4), 701-724, Fall 94.

Leibniz holds three apparently inconsistent views: Animals sense; sensation involves apperception; animals cannot apperceive (McRae). One solution (cf. Belaval, Naërt, and Parkinson) distinguishes nonreflexive apperception. The former is necessary for sensation and ascribable to animals. A different solution (cf. Jalalbert and Kulstad) distinguishes two types of reflection. Leibniz denied only apperception involving focused reflection to beasts. This is obviously not the same as denying beasts the capacity for apperception *tout court*, or the capacity for apperception involving reflection *tout court*. The paper argues against Kulstad and McRae for a form of the second view.

Miles, Steven H. Physician-Assisted Suicide and the Profession's Gyrocompass. *Hastings Center Rep*, 25(3), 17-19, My-Je 95.

This paper distinguishes the legalization of physician-assisted suicide from accepting or understanding personal decisions to commit suicide. It considers how a public policy legalizing physician assisted suicide would change suicide from a personal and interpersonal event into a biological and patient-centered event. The safeguards requiring physician control over suicidal choices by "depressed," but competent, persons would give physicians a new kind of authority over controversial personal decisions that has troubling implications for the current consensus on privacy and freedom with regard to choices in reproduction and end of life medical care.

Milet, Jean-Philippe. La technique et le temps (sur le livre de Bernard Stiegler). *Rev Phil Fr*, 4, 439-448, O-D 94.

Mileur, Jean-Pierre. "The Return of the Romantic" in *Intersections: Nineteenth-Century Philosophy and Contemporary Theory, Rajan, Tilottama (ed)*, 325-348. Albany, SUNY Pr, 1995.

Milhau, Jacques. "Menschenrechte und Menschheit des Rechts" in *Das geistige Erbe Europas, Buhr, Manfred (ed)*, 506-516. Napoli, Vivarium, 1994.

Mondialement reconnus depuis 1948, les Droits de l'homme n'en sont pas moins le fruit déune histoire. S'ils ont érigé dès 1789 l'homme en sujet libre et à égalité de droits civils et politiques, longtemps la femme, l'enfant, le vieillard, l'immigré, le paria mais aussi le non-propriétaire, le prolétaire ou le colonisé en furent exclus. Deux siècles ont pourtant fait des droits de l'homme une création continue élargie à l'économique, au social, au culturel. Evoluant des droits-libertés aux droits-besoins, ils attendent de devenir les droits-pouvoirs d'une authentique démocratie, d'un développement durable profitable à tous. Inégalement acceptés et appliqués, trop souvent bafoués et violés, ces droits indivisibles sont un enjeu planétaire. Leur avenir est dans les mains des citoyens, des peuples, dépend de leur volonté de construire un monde plus humain, d'assurer l'émancipation universelle, sans exclusive.

Milidoni, Carmen Beatriz. Some Considerations on the Status of the Psychic in "Freudian" Project (in Portuguese). *Trans/Form/Acao*, 17, 151-166, 1994.

Although Freud's "Project" does not contain overt formulations concerning the nature of the psychic, we think that it is possible to sketch some of its essential traits. To do so, we shall interpret the model of the mind constructed in the "Project". From this, we shall proceed to put the "Project" views on the nature of the psychic in connection with the classic mind-body problem. Our account will rest especially on a distinction we shall make between "representing", seen as an intentional act, and "the representation", seen as a memorytrace. We shall consider the behavior of the quantitative-energetic factor in both the psychological and neuro-physiological process orders.

Millar, Terrence. Model Completions and Omitting Types. *J Sym Log*, 60(2), 654-672, Je 95.

Universal theories with model completions are characterized. A new omitting types theorem is proved. These two results are used to prove the existence of a universal Aleph sub zero-categorical partial order with an interesting embedding property. Other aspects of these results also are considered.

Miller, Alex and Divers, John. Platitudes and Attitudes: A Minimalist Conception of Belief. *Analysis*, 55(1), 37-44, Ja 95.

The claim that minimalism about truth-aptitude successfully undercuts traditional expressivism about value has been resisted on the grounds that: 1) a conception of truth-aptitude can be adequate and minimalist only if there is a supporting conception of belief which is adequate and minimalist; and 2) no minimalist conception of belief is adequate, since none can account for all of the nonsemantic platitudes about belief. We accept 1) but reject 2), arguing that a minimalist conception of belief can account for what is platitudinous about belief, and that what the minimalist conception can't account for isn't platitudinous.

Miller, Alexander. Truth, Permanence, and the Regulation of Belief. *Ratio*, 7(2), 111-121, D 94.

In this paper I outline an argument which Louis Loeb attributes to Descartes, which attempts to ground the epistemic priority of reason over sense-perception in the brute psychological irresistibility of the former. I claim that the position thus ascribed to Descartes collapses into a crude form of idealism, and attempt to pinpoint precisely the flaw in the argument which gives rise to this collapse. I finish by suggesting that the same flaw might be apparent in Philip Pettit's recent development of the notion of response-dependent concepts.

Miller, Arthur I and Bullock, Frederick W. Neutral Currents and the History of Scientific Ideas. *Stud Hist Phil Sci*, 25(6), 895-932, D 95.

Miller, Barry. On "Divine Simplicity: A New Defense". *Faith Phil*, 11(3), 474-477, Jl 94.

I have two criticisms of Vallicella's "Divine Simplicity: A New Defense." One is that its argument for property self-exemplification fails because it ignores the distinction between "what" clauses employing first-level quantification and those employing second-level quantification. The second criticism is that his refection of logically simple propositions stems from a failure to see that the argument for those propositions is based on a logical premiss, not a grammatical one.

Miller, Cecilia. Review Essay: Leon Pompa's *Vico: A Study of the 'New Science'*. *Hist Theor*, 34(1), 132-138, 1995.

Miller, David (& other eds). *The Blackwell Encyclopaedia of Political Thought*. Cambridge, Blackwell, 1995.

Miller, Franklin G and Brody, Howard. Professional Integrity and Physician-Assisted Death. *Hastings Center Rep*, 25(3), 8-17, My-Je 95.

This article discusses physician-assisted death from the perspective of professional integrity. After introducing the concept of personal integrity, we develop an account of the professional integrity of physicians, which is tied to ethically appropriate ends and means of medicine. We identify three goals of medicine—healing, promoting health, and helping patients die peacefully—and four basic duties constraining medical practice—competence, avoiding harm, refraining from fraudulent misrepresentation, and fidelity. In the light of this account we conclude that the practice of voluntary physician-assisted death as a last resort is morally problematic but does not necessarily violate professional integrity.

Miller, Fred D and Keyt, David. *A Companion to Aristotle's Politics*. Cambridge, Blackwell, 1991.

Miller, Harlan B. Science, Ethics, and Moral Status. *Between Species*, 10(1-2), 10-18, Win-Spr 94.

There is no fundamental gap between science and ethics. Ethics is, like the natural and social sciences, an organized and rational inquiry into an aspect of the world. Any ethical theory includes or presumes some theory of moral status. A rational reconstruction of widespread moral beliefs reveals (at least) three sharply demarcated levels of moral status, with all humans granted a status assigned to no nonhuman animals. This radical separation is inconsistent with our biological knowledge and many of our other moral beliefs, and must be abandoned.

Miller, James (& others). A Debate on *The Passion of Michel Foucault*. *Conference*, 4(1), 77-92, Spr 93.

In an extended interview, James Miller answers questions about his interpretive methodology, his approach to philosophical biography, and his use of Nietzsche in his book *The Passion of Michel Foucault*. He also briefly responds to some of his critics, among them David Halperin and James Luchte. In an essay that accompanies the interview, Luchte charges Miller with a "project of teleological orchestration" that illegitimately turns Foucault into a "self-aware actor"—a fictive illusion that serious readers would do well to reject.

Miller, Jerome A. "All Love is Self-Surrender". *Method*, 13(1), 53-81, Spr 95.

This article argues that Bernard Lonergan's *Insight* and *Method in Theology* are not, as they are often interpreted, "modernist" works but rather efforts to free thinking from its modernist fetters. By developing a distinction (largely implicit in Lonergan) between possessive desire and passionate self-abandonment, and rethinking Lonergan's cognitional theory in terms of it, I argue that knowing, as Lonergan explains it, is not to be understood as a totalizing project; on the contrary, it requires a whole-hearted surrender to exigencies that we neither invent nor control.

Miller, Jerome A. A Reply to Michael Maxwell. *Method*, 12(1), 109-119, Spr 94.

This is a response to Maxwell's criticism of *In the Throe of Wonder* (State University of New York Press, 1992), a book in which I explore a path that leads beyond the aporia of post-modernism, with the help of Bernard Lonergan's *Insight*. I argue that, contrary to Maxwell's claims, I do not turn Lonergan himself into a post-modernist who despairs of knowing being. But our knowledge of being is made possible not by our standing on an unshakable foundation but by our being caught "in the throe of being". I interpret Lonergan's thought as moving in this direction.

Miller, Jim and Weinert, Regina. The Function of LIKE in Dialogue. *J Prag*, 23(4), 365-393, Ap 95.

Two bodies of Scottish English data are analyzed. There are two major constructions with LIKE. The one with clause-final LIKE is used to (anticipate and) counter (possible) objections and assumptions; the second one, with LIKE in other positions, is analyzed as noncontrastive focus, a highlighting devise. The structures are not verbal tics but follow regular patterns with regular functions. They are not associated with hesitations and poor syntactic planning. There are far more frequent than clefts, possibly because they do not disrupt the syntax of a given construction. The structure is far from new but previous accounts either limit themselves to one particular function absent from the Scottish English data (see Romaine and Lange, 1991) or operate with a rather vague analytical concept (see Schourup, 1985).

Miller, Mitchell. "Unwritten Teachings" in the *Parmenides*. *Rev Metaph*, 48(3), 591-633, Mr 95.

I examine together the hypotheses in the *Parmenides* and Aristotle's account of Plato's teachings in *Metaphysics* A6 in order to find, in the hypotheses, a basis for interpreting that account. The essay focuses on the status of "the One" and the work, in the *Parmenides*, which the notion of unity does in distinguishing sensibles, forms, and principles of forms; on the development in hypotheses II and V of the dyad of greatness and smallness; and on the ways in which the seminal account of participation in hypthesis III presupposes—and, so, provides an exhibition of—the interplay of the One and the dyad that Aristotle reports.

Miller, Peter and Rose, Nikolas. On Therapeutic Authority: Psychoanalytical Expertise Under Advanced Liberalism. *Hist Human Sci*, 7(3), 29-64, Ag 94.

In contemporary European and North American societies, there has occurred a transformation in authority, a reshaping of the ethical warranting for the exercise of authority over the conduct of conduct. We term this "therapeutic authority". This transformation of authority relations has brought about a shift in modes of governing life in locales as varied as the family, the factory, the school, the hospital and the office. In this article, we investigate the formation of this new species of authority through one particular set of events: the ideas and actions associated with the Tavistock Clinic and the Tavistock Institute of Human Relations.

Miller, Richard W. The Advancement of Realism. *Phil Phenomenol Res*, 55(3), 637-645, S 95.

Miller, Seumas. Intentions, Ends, and Joint Action. *Phil Papers*, 24(1), 51-66, Ap 95.

I argue: 1) Joint actions are acting directed to the realisation of a collective end. 2) Collective ends are a species of individual ends. I argue against the rival accounts of joint action of Tuomela, Bratman, Cohen and Levesque, Searle and Silbert.

Miller, Thomas G. Developing Philosophical Literacy. *Teach Phil*, 18(1), 39-58, Mr 95.

This paper criticizes a private model of students' philosophical experience in teaching—the model of Descartes—and defends a public model in its place—the model of Socrates. The latter sees students as apprentices and emphasizes the development of their performance skills through publicly monitored practice. The aim of undergraduate teaching in philosophy is to develop philosophical literacy: the working mastery of the fundamental concepts of philosophical discourse, as displayed through the five basic philosophical activities of thinking, reading, writing, listening, and speaking. Ways in which a public model might be implemented in teaching are discussed.

Miller, William Ian. Upward Contempt. *Polit Theory*, 23(3), 476-499, Ag 95.

The essay argues for the crucial role of contempt in the creation and maintenance of rank and hierarchy. It identifies and describes the peculiar style of "upward contempt," the contempt the low have for the high. The particular style of contempt depends on the political and moral regime in which it operates. Contempt can range from complacent indifference to revulsion and loathing. The claim here, developed by historical examples, is that the styles of the usual downward contempt as well as upward contempt change with the advent of democratic ideals. Where once the contempt of indifference had only been available to the master, democracy allows for the low to find the high as disattendable as the high have always found the low. The high in return find their contempt for the low shifting from indifference to horror and disgust. One of democracy's achievements is to expand access to contempt, not diminish it.

Miller-Frank, Felicia. Lyotard's Homeopathic Indeterminacy: The Medicinal Sublime. *Hist Euro Ideas*, 20(4-6), 823-827, F 95.

Millgram, Elijah. An Apprentice Argument. *Phil Phenomenol Res*, 54(4), 913-916, D 94.

Millican, Peter. Statements and Modality: Strawson, Quine and Wolfram. *Int J Moral Soc Stud*, 8(3), 315-326, Autumn 93.

Sybil Wolfram extended the Strawsonian tradition in Philosophical Logic, applying the sentence-statement distinction to a range of important issues. 1) One of her major concerns is to oppose Quine's 'Necessity Argument', which seems to show that statements cannot coherently be assigned a modal status based on the analyticity of the sentences which express them. 2) She does so by defining a necessary statement as one which *can be* expressed by an analytic sentence. 3) Unfortunately this encounters problems with Kripke's 'weak' notion of necessity ('true whenever the relevant objects exist'), and 4) can be refuted by sentences which are guaranteed to express a truth (i.e., which are analytic), even though the statement expressed is manifestly contingent. 5) However this new category of the *contingent analytic* can be accommodated within a Strawsonian framework, by simply defining a necessary statement as one necessarily true of the relevant objects. It even provides an argument in favor of some such multi-level framework of analysis.

Millikan, Ruth Garrett. "On Mentalese Orthography" in *Dennett and his Critics, Dahlbom, Bo (ed)*, 97-123. Cambridge, Blackwell, 1995.

Part One contains a clarification of Millikan's notions "tacit representation," "intentional icon," "representation" and "mental sentence," as these relate to notions that Dennett himself has used, and a request for clarification and discussion of disagreements that we may have in this area. Part two is a critique of the Fodorian notion of a mental sentence. The analogy implied between language and thought by this notion cannot be carried through.

Millikan, Ruth Garrett. "Reply: A Bet with Peacocke" in *Philosophy of Psychology: Debates on Psychological Explanation, Macdonald, Cynthia (ed)*, 285-292. Cambridge, Blackwell, 1995.

Contains clarification of the notion that entirely novel biological items can have proper functions, especially, that quite new beliefs and desires can. "Normal explanations" of such functions are discussed and also the role of "mapping" or "picturing" in biosemantics. Peacocke's claim that Millikan's biosemantic has a problem with thoughts about the past and with thoughts of universal propositions is the springboard.

Mills, Andrew. Unsettled Problems with Vague Truth. *Can J Phil*, 25(1), 103-118, Mr 95.

Mills, Charles. Non-Cartesian *Sums*: Philosophy and the African-American Experience. *Teach Phil*, 17(3), 223-243, S 94.

I argue that the essential feature of the experience of people of African descent in the "New World" is that they were not seen as full persons; rather, they were categorized as *Untermenschen*, racial sub-persons. Correspondingly, their *sum* is differentiated from the Cartesian *sum* in being an assertion of personhood against the intellectual universe of white supremacy. On this basis, I outline how a course in African-American Philosophy was taught, structured around this central theme; the African-American existential condition, racism, identity, personhood and sub-personhood, carnal alienation, sexuality, black feminism, the underclass, black liberation.

Mills, Charles W. Marxism, 'Ideology,' and Moral Objectivism. *Can J Phil*, 24(3), 373-393, S 94.

The theoretical commitments of Marxism are standardly taken to be difficult or impossible to reconcile with objectivism in ethics. Pro-objectivist commentators must grapple with the argument (among others) that Marx's categorizing of morality as illusory "ideology" shows he was clearly an anti-objectivist. Drawing on a revisionary interpretation of what "ideology" really meant for Marx, I argue that what he actually meant by this was that morality is typically "idealist" in its assumptions about how society works. Thus the "illusions" involved are illusions about causal efficaciousness rather than cognitive content, and a conceptual space is opened for the objectivist interpretation.

Mills, Claudia. Politics and Manipulation. *Soc Theor Pract*, 21(1), 97-112, Spr 95.

Manipulation is influence that deliberately falls short of the ideal of persuasion; in manipulation, A purports to be offering B good reasons for doing x, when in fact she is not. I argue that while A need not present B with all the relevant reasons for and against doing x, she should not intentionally offer B bad reasons for doing x. This can be condemned as a species of lying; however, I argue that manipulation does *not* wrongfully violate its victims' autonomy. I conclude by examining a variety of possibly problematic campaign strategies to determine which are manipulative.

Milne, Peter. Classical Harmony: Rules of Inference and the Meaning of the Logical Constants. *Synthese*, 100(1), 49-94, Jl 94.

The thesis that, in a system of natural deduction, the meaning of a logical constant is given by some or all of its introduction and elimination rules has been developed recently in the work of Dummett, Prawitz, Tennant, and others, by the addition of harmony constraints. Introduction and elimination rules for a logical constant must be in harmony. By deploying harmony constraints, these authors have arrived at logics no stronger than intuitionist propositional logic. Classical logic, they maintain, cannot be justified from this proof-theoretic perspective. This paper argues that, while classical logic can be formulated so as to satisfy a number of harmony constraints, the meanings of the standard logical constants cannot all be given by their introduction and/or elimination rules; negation, in particular, comes under close scrutiny.

Milner, Andrew. Cultural Materialism, Cultural and Post-Culturalism: The Legacy of Raymond Williams. *Theor Cult Soc*, 11(1), 43-73, F 94.

Milo, Ronald D. Contractarian Constructivism. *J Phil*, 92(4), 181-204, Ap 95.

Milovanovic, Dragan. "Postmodern Law and Subjectivity: Lacan and the Linguistic Turn" in *Radical Philosophy of Law, Caudill, David S (ed)*, 38-44. Atlantic Highlands, Humanities Pr, 1995.

Milton, J R. "Locke at Oxford" in *Locke's Philosophy, Rogers, G A J (ed)*, 29-47. New York, Oxford Univ Pr, 1994.

Milton, J R. "Locke's Life and Times" in *The Cambridge Companion to Locke, Chappell, Vere (ed)*, 5-25. New York, Cambridge Univ Pr, 1994.

Milton, J R. John Locke and the Fundamental Constitutions of Carolina. *Locke News*, 21, 111-133, 1990.

Milton, J R. Locke and Gilles de Launay. *Locke News*, 23, 115-130, 1992.

Milton, J R. Locke's Early Political Reading. *Locke News*, 24, 81-93, 1993.

Milton, J R. Manservant as Amanuensis: Sylvester Brounower. *Locke News*, 25, 79-83, 1994.

Milton, J R. Review Article on Ayers, 'Locke'. *Locke News*, 24, 115-141, 1993.

Milton, J R. Review of *Drafts for the Essay Concerning Human Understanding, and Other Philosophical Writings*, Volume 1: Drafts A and B. *Locke News*, 22, 125-139, 1991.

Milward, David. Dynamic Dependency Grammar. *Ling Phil*, 17(6), 561-605, D 94.

Minar, Edward H. Feeling at Home in Language (What Makes Reading *Philosophical Investigations* Possible?). *Synthese*, 102(3), 413-452, Ma 95.

What do we learn about language from reading Wittgenstein's *Philosophical Investigations?* This question gains urgency from Wittgenstein's alleged animus against philosophical theorizing and his indirectness. Section 1 argues that

Wittgenstein's goal is to prevent philosophical questioning about the foundations of language from the beginning. This conception of his aim is not in tension with Wittgenstein's use of the notion of community; "community interpretations" of his views betray a misguided commitment to the coherence of the idea that language might need grounding. Wittgenstein's goal is not to enjoin us not to step "outside of language-games", but to show that we have a insufficiently clear grasp of the terms we try to use to express the limits of intelligibility. Section 2 suggests that appreciating Wittgenstein's moral concerning the relation between language and philosophizing about it involves allowing him to teach us how to read his book. What makes reading *Philosophical Investigations* possible is openness to learning how not to forget our lives in language.

Minassian, Marie-José. Freud: d'une *tension* autobiographique. *Horiz Phil*, 5(1), 105-115, Autumn 94.

What is the meaning of Freud's refusal to acknowledge his tribute to philosophical tradition and his desire to be recognized as the one origin of psychoanalysis? In particular, why did he avoid referring to Nietzsche's ideas concerning science? Freud's denials constitute an interesting case whereby the disillusory power of science is destroyed by his own illusion of its power. Harold Bloom's *Anxiety of Influence* offers a valuable tool with which to analyze the problem in terms of discontinuity as a liberating factor. However in acknowledging his position in tradition Freud would have provided his theory with a dialectical, permanently creative, possibility.

Mineau, André. Basic Values of Western Industrial Society: Feedback Effect of Rationality. *Hist Euro Ideas*, 20(4-6), 957-961, F 95.

Miner, Earl. Armistice in the Recent Battle of the Books: Paul de Man, Claudio Guillén, and History. *Clio*, 24(1), 1-20, Fall 94.

Minghua, Li and Tongqi, Lin. Subjectivity: Marxism and "The Spiritual" in China Since Mao. *Phil East West*, 44(4), 609-646, O 94.

Minkes, A L. Business Policy, Ethics, and Society. *J Bus Ethics*, 14(8), 593-601, Ag 95.

The paper will first explain the meaning of the phrase "business policy" and will briefly outline the kinds of strategic decision which have to be made in business enterprises. It will go on to consider whether there are things a business "ought" or "ought not" to do even if they are within the law. The section will illustrate these problems with examples in the light of changing attitudes towards business policy and market behaviour in the 1980's and 1990's. It will take into account some recent cases of corporate crime in Australia and elsewhere and also of behaviour which while neither against the law or outside the power of the board, might be thought "inappropriate".

Minkevicius, Jokubas. Universalism: Humanistic Principles and Antipodes. *Dialogue Hum*, 3(2), 39-42, 1993.

Minkevicius, Jokubas. Universalistic Aspects of Jewish Culture and Religion. *Dialogue Hum*, 3(1), 71-78, 1993.

Minogue, Brendan. *Bioethics: A Committee Approach*. Boston, Jones & Bartlett, 1996.

Minogue, Brendan P (& others). Individual Autonomy and the Double-Blind Controlled Experiment: The Case of Desperate Volunteers. *J Med Phil*, 20(1), 43-55, F 95.

This essay explores some concerns about the quality of informed consent in patients whose autonomy is diminished by fatal illness. It argues that patients with diminished autonomy cannot give free and voluntary consent, and that recruitment of such patients as subjects in human experimentation exploits their vulnerability in a morally objectionable way. Two options are given to overcome this objection: i) recruit only those patients who desire to contribute to medical knowledge, rather than gain access to experimental treatment, or ii) provide prospective subjects the choice to participate in standard double-blind study or receive the experimental treatment. Either option would guarantee that patients in desperate conditions are given a more meaningful choice and a richer freedom, and thus a higher quality of informed consent, than under standard randomized trials.

Minogue, Kenneth. "Ideology after the Collapse of Communism" in *The End of "Isms"?, Shtromas, Alexsandras (ed)*, 5-21. Cambridge, Blackwell, 1994.

The collapse of communism has not, as might be expected, led to the end of ideologies. Instead of the grand revolutionary projects of the past, however, we now have a set of overlapping fragments of revelation which cooperate with each other in social transformation. These fragments exhibit an 'identity monism' which can tell us something about the character of ideology in general. This form of monism is the necessary condition of turning a modern state into a managed enterprise for the satisfaction of human needs—a project which happens also to be adumbrated in much normative political philosophy. A managed civil state responds to opinion rather than interest, and the opinions on which the project rests commend themselves by some version on self-evidence.

Mintz, Alex and Geva, Nehemia and Derouen Jr, Karl. Mathematical Models of Foreign Policy Decision-Making: Compensatory vs Noncompensatory. *Synthese*, 100(3), 441-460, S 94.

There are presently two leading foreign policy decision-making paradigms in vogue. The first is based on the classical or rational model originally posited by von Neumann and Morgenstern to explain microeconomic decisions. The second is based on the cybernetic perspective whose groundwork was laid by Herbert Simon in his early research on bounded rationality. In this paper we introduce a third perspective—the *poliheuristic* theory of decision-making—as an alternative to the rational actor and cybernetic paradigms in international relations. This theory is drawn in large part from research on heuristics done in experimental cognitive psychology. According to the poliheuristic theory, policy makers use poly (many) heuristics while focusing on a very narrow range of options and dimensions when making decisions. Among them, the political dimension is noncompensatory. The paper also delineates the mathematical formulations of the three decision-making models.

Mintz, Steven M and Moffeit, Katherine S. Ethics and the Law: US Supreme Court Rulings on the Solicitation of Clients. *Prof Ethics*, 3(1), 47-70, Spr 94.

This paper explores the implications for the professions of U S Supreme Court ruling on advertising and solicitation practices of lawyers and CPAs. Generally, the Court's position is that the free commercial speech rights of the CPAs and attorneys, and the consuming public's needs for comparative information about the price, quality and nature of services, provide the basis of support so long as such practices are not false, misleading, deceptive, or coercive. The investing public's reliance on the auditor's opinion on a client's financial statements imposes a burden on CPAs to solicit clients in a manner that doesn't create any impairments to objectivity and independence.

Misak, Cheryl. Pragmatism and the Transcendental Turn in Truth and Ethics. *Trans Peirce Soc*, 30(4), 739-775, Fall 94.

The argument of this paper is that the justification of the pragmatic account of truth must remain resolutely naturalist. Habermas' transcendental justification is criticized and a Peircean naturalist view of truth in ethics is put forward.

Misch, Georg (ed) and Kühne-Bertram, Gudrun (ed) and Rodi, Frithjof (ed). *Der Aufbau der Logik auf dem Boden der Philosophie des Lebens*. Freiburg, Alber, 1994.

This book presents for the first time Georg Misch's lectures on logic and epistemology. On the basis of Dilthey's philosophy of life and the latest linguistic, anthropological discoveries of the period, as well as in response to the positions of Heidegger and Husserl, Misch attempts to offer an extension of and at the same time a new foundation for traditional logic. As a hermeneutic logic which is not restricted to discursive cogitation, this extends *all* types of thinking. The author tries to derive logical phenomena from everyday life and ordinary language, in order to make evident the original unity of life and thought.

Miskiewicz, Wioleta. Le sphinx de la connaissance: Husserl et l'énigme de l'*a priori* corrélationnel. *Rev Metaph Morale*, 99(3), 345-364, Jl-S 94.

This study explains the principal figures of Husserl's correlational *a priori (Korrelationsgedanke)* in a perspective introduced in his courses on the theory of meaning in 1908. Due to the concept of *Triftigkeit*, which replaced that of adequacy, the criticism of naif philosophical objectism found an original form of expression.

Misra, Nilima. Other Minds—the Sartrean Solution. *Indian Phil Quart*, 21/3 (Supp), 1-10, Jl 94.

Missa, Jean-Noël. Matérialisme et neuro-sciences: la question des localisations cérébrales. *Rev Phil Fr*, 1, 43-53, Ja-Mr 95.

Mitcham, Carl (ed). *Philosophy of Technology in Spanish Speaking Countries*. Dordrecht, Kluwer, 1994.

Twenty five mostly original reflections on technology primarily from Chile, Costa Rica, Mexico, Spain, and Venezuela. Mitcham's general introduction is followed by Marcos Garcia de la Huerta on politics and technology, Luis Camacho on the philosophy of technology in Costa Rica, Enrique Dussel's neo-Marxist interpretation of technology, classic Mexican studies of technology by Jose Gaos, Hugo Padilla, and Leopoldo Zea, Miguel Angel Quintanilla on the theory of technological design, Jose Sanmartin on genethics, Juan David Garcia Bacca's philosophy of the history of technology, Ernesto Mayz Vallenilla's phenomenology of instrumentation, Judith Sutz on the social implications of computers, and others.

Mitchell, C Ben. Comment: Genetic Engineering—Bane or Blessing?. *Ethics Med*, 10(3), 50-55, Autumn 94.

Mitchell, Helen Buss. *Roots of Wisdom: Speaking the Language of Philosophy*. Belmont, Wadsworth, 1995.

Roots of Wisdom: Speaking the Language of Philosophy is an introductory text that blends the Western discourse with wisdom from a multicultural world. Its ten chapters are framed by thought-provoking issues representing major topics in philosophy, beginning with metaphysics (reality, human nature, philosophy and God), moving to epistemology (knowledge sources, truth tests, aesthetic experience), and concluding with axiology (political philosophy, social philosophy, ethics). The chapters move historically, following the Western canon and including women and both Asian and African thought in every chapter. A mini course in logic, using arguments from the text, is integrated throughout the book.

Mitchell, Sam. Toward a Defensible Bootstrapping. *Phil Sci*, 62(2), 241-260, Je 95.

An amended bootstrapping can avoid Christensen's counterexamples. Earman and Edidin argue that Christensen's examples to bootstrapping rely on his failure to analyze background knowledge. I add an additional condition to bootstrapping that is motivated by Glymour's remarks on variety of evidence. I argue that it avoids the problems that the examples raise. I defend the modification against the charge that it is holistic, and that it collapses into Bayesianism.

Mitchell, Sandra and Yeo, Michael. "Truthfulness" in *Concepts and Cases in Nursing Ethics, Yeo, Michael (& others)*, 86-116. Peterborough, Broadview Pr, 1991.

Mitchell, Sandra D. Function, Fitness and Disposition. *Biol Phil*, 10(1), 39-54, Ja 95.

In this paper I discuss recent debates concerning etiological theories of functions. I defend an etiological theory against two criticisms, namely the ability to account for malfunction, and the problem of structural "doubles". I then consider the argument provided by Bigelow and Pargetter (1987) for a more "forward looking" account of function as propensities or dispositions. I argue that their approach fails to address the explanatory problematic for which etiological theories were developed.

Mitchell, Sandra D and Mulder, Monique Borgerhoff. Rough Waters between Genes and Culture: An Anthropological and Philosophical Views on Coevolution. *Biol Phil*, 9(4), 471-487, O 94.

Mitias, Michael H. "Expression in Architecture" in *Philosophy and Architecture, Mitias, Michael H (ed)*, 87-107. Amsterdam, Rodopi, 1994.

Nelson Goodman has argued that a building means by exemplifying the qualities which belong to it. This paper presents a critique of Goodman's concept of exemplification. It tries to show that a building "means" by expressing the aesthetic qualities which we attribute to it. These qualities exist in the building as potentialities awaiting realization in the aesthetic experience.

Mitias, Michael H. "Is Meaning in Architecture a Myth? A Response to Ralf Weber" in *Philosophy and Architecture, Mitias, Michael H (ed)*, 121-138. Amsterdam, Rodopi, 1994.

Ralf Weber holds that the meaning which we attribute to an architectural work is extrinsic to the work. In this paper I argue that meaning is intrinsic to the artwork. I also argue that the relation which holds between the architectural work and the properties which belong to it is one of expression. These properties originate from the work itself and come to life in the aesthetic experience.

Mitias, Michael H (ed). *Philosophy and Architecture*. Amsterdam, Rodopi, 1994.

This book is a critical examination of three main questions: 1) Is Architecture art? 2) How does a building express meaning? 3) What is the nature of the aesthetic experience in architecture? A number of distinguished scholars such as F H Sparshott, A Berleant, S Davies, D Novitz, B Tilghman, A Carlson, R Ginsberg, have made important contributions toward the clarification of these questions. The book should generate a lively dialogue on basic issues in the philosophy of architecture.

Mitias, Michael H. Toward a Concept of Universal Justice. *Dialogue Hum*, 2(3-4), 105-122, 1992.

Mitias, Michael H. Universalism and the Meaning of History. *Dialogue Hum*, 4(5), 27-38, 1994.

This paper is a universalist conception of the meaning of human history. It first argues that history has a meaning and that this meaning does not lie outside the historical process; it lies within this process, in the creative vision and action of the people who cooperatively participate in the construction and management of the basic institutions which give structure to human life. A basic premise of this paper is that human history is the history of humankind as such.

Mitias, Michael H. Universalism and World Peace. *Dialogue Hum*, 3(1), 103-113, 1993.

Mitsis, Phillip T and DeFilippo, Joseph G. "Socrates and Stoic Natural Law" in *The Socratic Movement, Vander Waerdt, Paul A (ed)*, 252-271. Ithaca, Cornell Univ Pr, 1994.

Mittelstrass, Jürgen. "Die Zukunft der Antike" in *Das geistige Erbe Europas, Buhr, Manfred (ed)*, 635-655. Napoli, Vivarium, 1994.

Mittelstrass, Jürgen. Rationalität und Reproduzierbarkeit. *Protosoz*, 6, 28-37, 1994.

The unity of scientific rationality once written into the program of modern philosophy of science has disintegrated into a collection of differing models of rationality. The present contribution 1) Describes this development, 2) Presents an analysis of one representative criteria of rationality (reproducibility), 3) Distinguishes between a rationality tied to theories and a rationality of research, and 4) Argues for a conception of rationality that transcends particular paradigmata.

Mitterer, John. "Male and Female in the Modern World" in *The Nature and Pursuit of Love, Goicoechea, David (ed)*, 248-264. Buffalo, Prometheus, 1995.

Mitterer, Josef and Engelmann, Peter (ed). *Das Jenseits der Philosophie: Wider das dualistische Erkenntnisprinzip*. Vienna, Passagen, 1992.

Der Autor kritisiert das dualistische Erkenntnisprinzip im Rahmen einer nichtdualisierenden Argumentationsweise, die ein Jenseits des Diskurses als Diskursregulativ und Erkenntnisziel weder voraussetzt noch hervorbringt. (edited)

Mixie, Joseph. *The Atheist Trap*. Lanham, Univ Pr of America, 1994.

The purpose of this work is to analyze the most recent literature and scientific date and their philosophical implications for the argument from design. The work also provides as concise historical summary of the classical statements and critiques of the argument.

Mixie, Joseph. The Teleological Argument. *Thomist*, 58(4), 635-654, O 94.

The purpose of this work is to formulate the teleological argument as an empirical scientific theory according to the school of scientific falsificationism as stated by Karl Popper. Once stated in this form, it is then argued that according to the criteria of "Inference to the Best Explanation", the teleological argument provides the best explanation for the existence of natural order in the universe.

Mizraji, Eduardo. Modalities in Vector Logic. *Notre Dame J Form Log*, 35(2), 272-283, Spr 94.

Vector logic is a mathematical model of logic in which the truth values mapped on elements of a vector space. The binary logical functions are performed by rectangular matrices operating on the Kronecker product of their vectorial arguments. The binary operators acting on vectors representing ambiguous (fuzzy) truth values, generate many-valued logics. In this article we show that, within the formalism of vector logic, it becomes possible to obtain truth-functional definitions of the modalities "possibility" and "necessity". These definitions are based on the matrix operators that represent disjunction and conjunction respectively, and each modality emerges by means of an iterative process. (edited)

Mizzoni, John. Moral Realism, Objective Values, and J L Mackie. *Auslegung*, 20(1), 11-24, Wint 95.

The arguments levelled by J L Mackie against objective values and moral realism still have sway over many philosophers. In this paper I carefully analyze these arguments. My analysis covers the following areas: 1) his (rather narrow) notion of objective value, 2) his metaethical methodology, 3) his attempt at outlining a normative ethics in light of his metaethical skepticism, and 4) his understanding of the concept "institution". I conclude that a version of moral realism can be maintained in the face of Mackie's arguments. I offer a moral realist rejoinder to each of the four above areas and the rebuttals culminate into a thesis I call contextual moral realism.

Modell, Stephen M. Concepts of Chaos: The Analysis of Self-Similarity and the Relevance of the Ethical Dimension. *Ultim Real Mean*, 17(4), 310-315, D 94.

Modell, Stephen M. Using the Human Body as a Paradigm for the Structure of Time: Some Reflections on Time's URAM. *Ultim Real Mean*, 17(3), 197-221, S 94.

Modrak, Deborah. "Theories of Meaning and Ontology in Aristotle's *Metaphysics*" in *The Crossroads of Norm and Nature, Sim, May (ed)*, 221-234. Lanham, Rowman & Littlefield, 1995.

This paper is an examination of Aristotle's attempt in the *Metaphysics* to develop an ontology that will meet the needs of his epistemology. Aristotle's program has several parts: first, to arrive at an epistemically perspicuous conception of substance, essence and definition; second, to argue for the identity of the formula expressed in a real definition and the formula embodies in a particular object; third, to explicate the relation betweeen form and matter; and fourth, to differentiate between forms and ordinary universals. Aristotle's handling of each of these topics is analyzed.

Möckel, Christian. Die Phänomenologie in Russland: Ein Nachwort. *Deut Z Phil*, 43(1), 89-91, 1995.

Die russischen Philosophen wenden sich seit Ende der 80er Jahre auf drei Wegen verstärkt wieder der Phänomenologie zu. 1) Es werden wichtige Texte Husserls und anderer Phänomenologen erstmals ins Russische übertragen. Dabei haben sich die Moskauer Zeitschriften "Voprosy filosofii" und "Logos" hervorgetan. 2) Man druckt Texte vaterländischer Autoren neu oder erstmals ab, in denen vor 1917 oder danach in der Emigration die Phänomenologie rezipiert, kritisiert und zu ihrer Entwicklung beigetragen wurde. (Spet, Schestov, Losskij) 3) Die wichtigste Form des phänomenologischen Philosophierens bilden aktuelle Studien und Auseinandersetzungen mit der Phänomenologie in den oben genannten Zeitschriften. (Gaidenko, Moltschanov, Chestanov)

Moerdijk, I. A Model for Intuitionistic Non-standard Arithmetic. *Annals Pure Applied Log*, 73(1), 37-52, May 95.

This paper provides an explicit description of a model for intuitionistic non-standard arithmetic, which can be formalized in a constructive metatheory without the axiom of choice.

Moerdijk, I and Joyal, A. A Completeness Theorem for Open Maps. *Annals Pure Applied Log*, 70(1), 51-86, N 94.

This paper provides a partial solution to the completeness problem for Joyal's axiomatization of open and etale maps, under the additional assumption that a collection axiom (related to the set-theoretical axiom with the same name) holds.

Moffeit, Katherine S and Mintz, Steven M. Ethics and the Law: US Supreme Court Rulings on the Solicitation of Clients. *Prof Ethics*, 3(1), 47-70, Spr 94.

This paper explores the implications for the professions of U S Supreme Court ruling on advertising and solicitation practices of lawyers and CPAs. Generally, the Court's position is that the free commercial speech rights of the CPAs and attorneys, and the consuming public's needs for comparative information about the price, quality and nature of services, provide the basis of support so long as such practices are not false, misleading, deceptive, or coercive. The investing public's reliance on the auditor's opinion on a client's financial statements imposes a burden on CPAs to solicit clients in a manner that doesn't create any impairments to objectivity and independence.

Moggach, Douglas. Marx and German Idealism: Labour and the Transcendental Synthesis. *Hist Euro Ideas*, 19(1-3), 137-143, Jl 94.

This paper disputes Habermas' accounts of labor as monological expressivist-aesthetic or instrumental action. It shows how tensions in Kant's account of experience, as developed by Fichte and Hegel, enable Marx to formulate two distinct intersubjective models of labor, teleological and structural. Marx elaborates the former in the 1844 Manuscripts, and the latter in the German Ideology. He combines the two models the two models in Capital. Each model has normative implications for theories of intersubjectivity and democracy.

Mogielnicki, R Peter and Bernat, James L and Gert, Bernard. Distinguishing between Patients' Refusals and Requests. *Hastings Center Rep*, 24(4), 13-15, Jl-Ag 94.

Not distinguishing between patient requests and patient refusals, but referring to them both as choices or decisions and then talking of patient autonomy, has resulted in both theoretical and practical confusion. Patient refusals must be honored when they represent the rational decisions of competent patients even when physicians know death will result. Honoring such refusals is not killing; it is, at most, allowing to die. In contrast, there is no moral requirement to honor patient requests when physicians know death will result.

Mohanty, J N. "The Development of Husserl's Thought" in *The Cambridge Companion to Husserl, Smith, Barry (ed)*, 45-77. New York, Cambridge Univ Pr, 1995.

Mohanty, J N. Theory and Practice in Indian Philosophy. *Austl J Phil*, 73(1), 1-12, Mr 95.

Mohr, Richard D. Prejudice and Homosexuality: America's Experience. *Filozof Istraz*, 14(2-3), 417-426, 1994.

This article deals with the treatment of homosexuality in contemporary American society. The overall view of homosexuality is burdened with manifold prejudices. These prejudices have been encouraged and propagated by American judicial and legal practices. In effect, they tacitly tolerate violent actions against individuals and groups of people who are considered to be homosexuals. Stereotypes about 'gays' as being gender-confused persons reinforce existing and powerful gender roles in American society. Society at large is unaware, through the maintenance of accepted stereotypes, of the many ways in which 'gays' are subjected to discrimination resulting from widespread fear and hatred. (edited)

Moi, Toril. *Simone de Beauvoir: The Making of an Intellectual Woman*. Cambridge, Blackwell, 1994.

This book is a "personal genealogy" of Simone de Beauvoir that focuses on what it meant for her as an intellectual and as a writing woman to train as a philosopher in France in the 1920s, as well as on her relationship to Sartre and to other women. The book also offers readings of a wide range of her works, particularly *L'invitée* and *The Second Sex*. What factors determined Beauvoir's personal and professional trajectory? How do her conflicts and contradictions illuminate the situation of intellectual women today? To answer these questions, the book draws on philosophical and literary analysis, psychoanalytic theory, reception studies, and the sociology of intellectual institutions and of literary taste in France.

Moiso, Francesco. "Formbildung, Zufall und Notwendigkeit" in *Schelling und die Selbstorganisation, Heuser-Kessler, Marie-Luise (ed)*, 73-112. Berlin, Duncker Humblot, 1994.

Moiso, Francesco. "Wille" e "Willkür" in Fichte. *Rev Int Phil*, 49(191), 5-38, 1995.

Mol, Annemarie and Hirschauer, Stefan. Shifting Sexes, Moving Stories: Feminist/Constructivist Dialogues. *Sci Tech Human Values*, 20(3), 368-385, Sum 95.

How can constructivism and feminism inform and strengthen one another? The author of this text is a constructivist-feminist hermaphrodite, and so s/he addresses this question in the form of an inner dialogue. Instead of taking sex as a characteristic of individuals, s/he analyzes it as something performed locally in ways that vary from one situation to another. Investigating these performances offers constructivism an interesting theoretical opportunity and a chance to turn away from a sterile anti-epistemological stance. For feminism, a radicalized notion of the construction of sexes opens up new political spaces and strategies. Constructivist texts, moreover, have the potential to "do" both the contingency and the necessity of our forms of life in their very style.

Molina, Francisco. Los límites de una teoría del progreso. *Anu Filosof*, 27(3), 1007-1021, 1994.

L Laudan proposes a rational method in order to properly analyse the development of sciences. He also proposes an epistemology model. Both have been criticized because of their weak ground and their foreseeable results.

Molina, Jorge Alberto. Observaçoes sobre a Concepçao Kantiana do Espaço. *Cad Hist Filosof Cie*, 3(1-2), 117-132, Ja-D 93.

The goal of the present paper is to show the independence of the Kantian thesis of ideality of space from the changes in the scientific conception of space. Kantian arguments of the metaphysical and transcendental expositions are examined. It is attempted to show that some of the arguments of the metaphysical exposition do prove that space is an "a-priori" intuition, whereas the arguments of the transcendental exposition are not satisfactory.

Molina, Leopoldo. "Education for Freedom versus Socio-Technical Control..." in *Philosophy of Technology in Spanish Speaking Countries, Mitcham, Carl (ed)*, 259-268. Dordrecht, Kluwer, 1994.

Molinaro, Aniceto. Edith Stein-fenomenologia e/ o metafisica. *Aquinas*, 37(2), 395-401, My-Ag 94.

Molinuevo, José Luis. Fichte y Ortega (II). Héroes o Ciudadanos. El Mito de Don Quijote. *Daimon Rev Filosof*, 9, 341-358, 1994.

En mi trabajo anterior sobre el diálogo entre Ortega y Fichte hacía los planteamientos metodológicos del mismo y recorría un trecho del camino hasta 1914. Ese año emblemático para Ortega era examinado parcialmente, a propósito de teorías referidas a la Estética y la Fenomenología, remitiéndome a la Ética y la Política para un avance posterior. He intentado antes mostrar la importancia de Fichte en el proyecto orteguiano de la construcción de la identidad española. Ahora quisiera hacer lo mismo en el momento de su crisis y redefinición. Parto de un texto clave, que es puro contexto. La metodología me obliga, esta vez, no al cotejo de textos de ambos autores, sino al examen del problema de fondo. Se trata, pues, de mostrar cómo Ortega *recibe* a Fichte, no de cómo lo interpreta.

Molke, Trudy and Yeo, Michael. "Beneficence" in *Concepts and Cases in Nursing Ethics, Yeo, Michael (& others)*, 25-53. Peterborough, Broadview Pr, 1991.

Molland, George. "The Limited Lure of Arabic Mathematics" in *The 'Arabick' Interest of the Natural Philosophers in Seventeenth-Century England, Russell, G A (ed)*, 215-223. Leiden, Brill, 1994.

Mollenhauer, B. Plato and the Scientific Spirit. *Darshana Int*, 32(2/126), 31-32, Ap 92.

Molnar, Thomas. Authority and Its Enemies (New Edition). New Brunswick, Transaction Books, 1995.

Molnár, Tamás. The Palace, the Temple, and the Civil Society. *Magyar Filozof Szemle*, 3-4, 365-376, 1994.

There are now roughly two modern theories about the early structuralization of political society in the West. Both are merely groping in the darkness of prehistory, but both are plausible and conform to what is known with a reasonable certainty. One hypothesis holds that in "early times" the function of the king and high priest is found in a state of fusion: the king (or tribal chief, etc.) was an absolutely sacred figure, directly communicating with the deity or the pantheon of gods, at times even as god himself. There are many signs or such a state of affairs in the annals of mankind, from China to the Malabar coastal region of India and to the position of the Inca in ancient Peru. The other hypothesis, rather ill-received in scholarly circles but gaining ground, was proposed and documented in this century by Georges Dumezil who took Indo-European documents (archaeology, sagas, linguistics) to show that political structure in this basic "tribe" of the present day European peoples was tri-partite: the king and the warriors, the priestly class, and the artisans/peasants/tradesmen, what we call today civil society.

Momeyer, Richard. Does Physician Assisted Suicide Violate the Integrity of Medicine?. *J Med Phil*, 20(1), 13-24, F 95.

This paper evaluates the arguments against physician assisted suicide which contend that it violates the integrity of medicine and the physician-patient relation; i.e., that it contradicts the goal of seeking health and healing, violates an absolute prohibition against killing, and undermines the patient's trust in the physician. These arguments against physician assisted suicide 1) misuse notions of teleology and teleological explanation; 2) rely on inappropriate notions of "ideal medicine", for which death is a defeat; 3) turn on a highly selective reading for the Hippocratic tradition; and 4) are unacceptably paternalistic.

Monahan, Michael J. Nietzsche's Laughter; Plato's Beard. *Dialogue (PST)*, 37(2-3), 57-61, Ap 95.

Nietzsche is arguably the first philosopher to engage in what we would now call a

"postmodern" discourse. Primarily through an exploration of the myth of Silenus found in *The Birth of Tragedy*, this article attempts to explicate Nietzsche's problematic in terms of its critique of metaphysics, its philosophical and psychological implications, and its relevance in the scope of contemporary thought. Ultimately, this exploration of the myth of Silenus leads to inescapable ignorance of mankind. In the end, this article espouses laughter as the only effective way to grapple with the Apollonian aspects of the world in which we live.

Moncada, Jesús Salvador. Naturaleza del principio de la debida discreción de juicio en el consentimiento matrimonial (segunda y última parte). *Logos (Mexico)*, 22(66), 71-94, S-D 94.

Moncho, Josep. Moral y Derecho en Bentham. *Rev Filosof (Venezuela)*, 19, 35-40, 1994.

Mondadori, Fabrizio. On Some Disputed Questions in Leibniz's Metaphysics. *Stud Leibniz*, 25(2), 153-173, 1993.

Mondal, Sunil Baran. An Evaluation of Karl Popper's Criticism of Sociology of Knowledge. *Indian Phil Quart*, 22/1(Supp), 1-4, Ja 95.

Mondin, Battista. Filosofia cristiana, fenomenologia e metafisica secondo E Stein. *Aquinas*, 37(2), 377-386, My-Ag 94.

During the years of the hot discussion concerning the possibility and the nature of "Christian philosophy" (1927-1936). E Stein wrote two important essays on this subject. She explains that there are two types of Christian philosophy: 1) *natural philosophy*, where the dependence from faith and revelation is merely extrinsic; 2) *supernatural philosophy*, where the dependence is intrinsic. But the same E Stein recognizes that the second type coincides with theology and that, consequently, cannot be properly called philosophy. *Phenomenology* can be certainly applied to metaphysics as Stein brilliantly does in her main work, *Finite being and eternal being*, but what one actually obtains in this way is a metaphysics of essences, not a metaphysics of actual beings: not the metaphysics of the *actus essendi* of St Thomas, but the metaphysics of the possibles of Avicenna.

Mondin, Battista. Originalità del pensiero filosofico di S Tommaso. *Sapienza*, 47(2), 129-146, 1994.

The greatness and originality of St Thomas Aquinas's philosophical thought has been the extraordinary discovery of Neothomism. Through the accurate studies of Gilson, Masnozo, Fabro, Maritain, De Finance etc. it has been shown that St Thomas's philosophy certainly includes many Aristotelian elements but that it cannot be reduced to Aristotle. St Thomas has a new concept of being (*actualitas omnium actuum*) which inspires his entire vision of reality. Such principle provides him with new proofs of the existence of God (based on participation, real distinction and degrees of being) a new concept of god (*Ipsum esse subsistens*) a new definition of the nature of angels and of human soul, a new proof of the immortality of the soul, a new foundation for the transcendentals (unity, truth, goodness, and beauty) etc.

Mongin, Philippe. L'optimisation est-elle un critère de rationalité individuelle?. *Dialogue (Canada)*, 33(2), 191-222, Spr 94.

The paper discusses several objections against the view that optimization is a criterion of individual rationality: 1) Intransitive choice behavior does not always involve irrationality. 2) Revealed preference theory suggests that some of the conditions imposed on choice functions by optimizing behavior are implausibly strong. 3) Since optimization implies nonnegligible computation costs, the optimizing model leads to an infinite regression. The paper concludes that none of these objections is compelling but their conjunction casts a doubt on the received view that the optimizing model of decision is a model of rationality.

Monserrat, Javier. Lectura Epistemológica de la Teoría Unificada de la Cognición en Allen Newell. *Pensamiento*, 199(51), 3-42, Ja-Ap 95.

El moderno desarrollo de la ingeniería y lógica del ordenador ha conducido al nacimiento de una disciplina científica conocida como *ciencia cognitiva* y a la *ingeniería del conocimiento*. Por ello, el estudio actual del conocimiento el la *epistemología* no puede olvidar las aportaciones de estas disciplinas científicas. Tanto más cuanto que desde ellas se pretende construir una teoría unificada del conocimiento que abarca tanto la inteligencia artificial como la inteligencia y conocimiento natural, incluido el humano. La obra de Allen Newell *Unified Theories of Cognition* puede ser una ocasión apropiada para plantearse las aportaciones de la ciencia cognitiva a la psicología cognitiva y a la teoría del conocimiento en general. El artículo presenta analíticamente la obra de Newell y discute seguidamente su argumentación epistemológica.

Montag, Warren. "A Process Without a Subject or Goal(s)" in *Marxism in the Postmodern Age, Callari, Antonio (ed)*, 51-58. New York, Guilford, 1994.

Montagna, Franco and Artëmov, Sergei. Our First-Order Theories with Provability Operator. *J Sym Log*, 59(4), 1139-1153, D 94.

In this paper the modal operator "X is provable in Peano Arithmetic" is incorporated into first-order theories. A provability extension of a theory is defined. Presburger Arithmetic of addition, Skolem Arithmetic of multiplication, and some first order theories of partial consistency statements are shown to remain decidable after natural provability extensions. It is also shown that natural provability extensions of a decidable theory may be undecidable.

Montagna, Franco and Mancini, Antonella. A Minimal Predicative Set Theory. *Notre Dame J Form Log*, 35(2), 186-203, Spr 94.

Montague, Phillip. Forced Choices and Self-Defence. *J Applied Phil*, 12(1), 89-93, 1995.

This paper is a reply to three objections raised by Seumas Miller against a "forced-choice" account of the morality of self-defence. It is argued that Miller's first objection rests on a misconception of how the forced-choice account is supposed to work; that his second objection is simply mistaken; and that his third objection overlooks how the forced-choice account explicitly accommodates the moral difference between self-defence and "other-defence." Finally, it is suggested that Miller's entire approach is defective in its failure to examine the principle of justice which underlies the forced-choice account, and whether it applies to standard self-defence situations.

AUTHOR INDEX WITH ABSTRACTS 657 Moravcsik, Julius

Montague, Phillip. Patriotism and Political Obligation. *J Soc Phil*, 25(2), 44-56, Fall 94.

This paper proposes an approach to the problem of political obligation which centers on these two propositions: that the question of whether there are political obligations is related to the question of whether there are political *virtues*—whether, in particular, loyalty to one's own country is a virtue; and that addressing this latter question yields valuable insights into how the former should be answered.

Montanari, Bruno. La Legge e il Diritto. *Riv Int Filosof Diritto*, 71(4), 583-619, 1994.

Montau, Robert. "Höss lesen" in *Nationalsozialismus und Moderne, Welzer, Harald (ed)*, 128-149. Tübingen, Ed Diskord, 1993.

Rudolf Höss, the commander of the Concentration Camp at Auschwitz, describes in his autobiography his childhood, his socialization during his military service, the SS and what he was doing at Auschwitz. In a hermeneutic analysis Montau tries to examine the historical and biographical facts which finally made Höss culprit. Montaus reflections on the autobiography is that of a member of the 'grand-children' generation and so he approaches to Höss's reasons and justifications. This analysis is disturbed by the effort necessary to understand Höss's biological decisions and actions, instead of only seeing the brutish way he treats his victims.

Monteiro, Joao Paulo. Induçao, Acaso e Racionalidade. *Manuscrito*, 17(1), 11-33, Ap 94.

Inductive inference cannot be justified, only explained. Nondemonstrative inference, however, should not be reduced to induction. Causal inferences derived from repeated experience consist, first, in elimination of conjectures of causality—hypotheses attributing observed conjunctions to chance. These conjectures of fortuity imply a kind of phenomenon that excludes repetition, and consequently observed repetition discredits and excludes any hypothesis of chance. Chance conjunctions are those derived from two or more causal chains, the only alternative being that they be derived from only one of such chains. Rejection of a conjecture of causality thus leads to choice of the alternative hypothesis, the resulting causal inference being thus, in a sense, confirmed. Causal inference in this sense may refrain from any inductive, universal conclusion, induction being "bracketed". It thus escapes the trap of invalid generalization. Causal inference, derived from "refutation of chance", is the work of a kind of reason where conjecture is supplemented by a few deductive steps—provided we accept "Cournotean" causal chains as a starting point.

Montero Moliner, Fernando. El "Averroísmo" en la Filosofía Moral de Kant. *An Seminar Hist Filosof*, 9, 39-58, 1992.

Siguiendo el precedente de Herder, con el término "averroísmo" se alude a una preponderancia de lo universal (y a la correspondiente subordinación de la individualidad) en la filosofía moral de Kant. Ciertamente, éste hizo de la universalidad la condición necesaria de la eticidad. Ello colocó a las inclinaciones individuales, incluso a la misma felicidad, dentro de un egoísmo incompatible con la moralidad. La individualidad del hombre parecía eliminada del campo de la Etica. Sin embargo, ese "averroísmo" debe ser mitigado desde dos puntos de vista: 1) De acuerdo con el "uso regulador" que Kant atribuye a la idea de *libertad*, las inclinaciones pasionales forman una experiencia exigida por la actividad racional libre. No son el fundamento de la moralidad, pero peuden secundarla postivamente como "sentimientos morales", originado una felicidad que, junto con la virtud, constituye el "sumo bien". O, de modo negativo, las inclinaciones pasionales son exigidas por el mismo deber, en la medida en que las domine y someta a la moralidad. De ambas formas, constituyen una experiencia emotiva individual que integra el mismo *factum* moral. 2) La libertad y la razón práctica brotan de la *mente (Gemüt)*, que significa la "identidad oculta" y la "facultad radical" absolutamente individual que origina toda actividad racional.

Montgomery, Richard. Explanation and Evaluation in Cognitive Science. *Phil Sci*, 62(2), 261-282, Je 95.

With some regularity, cognitive scientists seem to introduce cognitive *values* into their explanations. After identifying examples of this practice, I sketch an account of psychological explanation that, under certain conditions, legitimizes value-laden cognitive explanations in which evaluative claims appear in the explanandum. I then present and discuss two applications of the proposed account in order to show its viability and explore its consequences.

Montgomery, Richard. Non-Cartesian Explanations Meet the Problem of Mental Causation. *S J Phil*, 33(2), 221-241, Sum 95.

Montinari, Mazzino (ed) and Colli, Giorgio (ed) and Nietzsche, Friedrich. *The Complete Works of Friedrich Nietzsche: Volume 2: Unfashionable Observations*. Stanford, Stanford Univ Pr, 1995.

Montoya, Isaac D and Richard, Alan J. A Comparative Study of Codes of Ethics in Health Care Facilities and Energy Companies. *J Bus Ethics*, 13(9), 713-717, S 94.

Though written corporate codes of ethics have been touted as a panacea for the embarrassments and uncertainties of the past two decades, the absence of clear evaluation procedures severely compromises their usefulness. An ethnographic study comparing development processes and compliance outcomes in large health care facilities and energy companies shows that neither of the two industries has encountered much success with a codes of ethics program. (edited)

Montoya, José. D Gauthier o Hobbes sin Leviatán. *Rev Filosof (Spain)*, 4(5), 199-205, 1991.

The purpose of the work is to present the main ideas of Gauthier's *Moral by Agreement* and make a global evaluation of them. It underlines specially the novelty of an attempt to build up a moral theory that doesn't need (like Kant's) to lean on a mysterious transcendental rationality, nor (like Hume's) rest on a generalized benevolence. The judgment of the writer is generally in favor of this attempt, although some difficulties are tentatively raised in the end.

Moody, Harry R. Commentary on "The Forgetful Mourner". *Hastings Center Rep*, 25(1), 33, Jan-Feb 95.

Mooij, Anton. Towards an Anthropological Psychiatry. *Theor Med*, 16(1), 73-91, Mr 94.

The situation of present day psychiatry is described as being dominated by an empiricist perspective. The limitations of this perspective are analyzed and a rough sketch of the hermeneutical approach in psychiatry is offered. It is argued that a fully developed hermeneutical psychiatry implies a reference towards anthropological themes. Three of them, time, historicity and corporality, are investigated.

Moon, J Donald. "Practical Discourse and Communicative Ethics" in *The Cambridge Companion to Habermas, White, Stephen K (ed)*, 143-164. New York, Cambridge Univ Pr, 1995.

Moor, James H. Is Ethics Computable?. *Metaphilosophy*, 26(1-2), 1-21, Ja-Ap 95.

Although there may be no one ethically correct decision in every situation, good ethical decisions may nonetheless be computable. A thought experiment is considered in which we are asked to give advice to a robot manufacturer about what decision making should be programmed into an epistemologically sophisticated robot to make it behave ethically. Various suggestions are made and rejected until a more plausible hypothesis emerges. This approach to modelling ethics can have a theoretical impact on our understanding of ethical theories themselves as well as a potentially practical impact on the construction of ethical agents with artificial intelligence.

Moore, Andrew and Hope, Tony and Fulford, K W M. Mild Mania and Well-Being. *Phil Psychiat Psych*, 1(3), 165-177, S 94.

This paper explores the relationship between mania, or pathologically elevated mood, and philosophical theories of well-being. A patient, Mr M, is described who oscillated between periods when he refused medication and periods when he was willing to accept it, and whose desires and life objectives were radically different in his medicated and unmedicated states. The practical dilemmas this raised are explored in terms of the three principal philosophical theories of well-being: hedonism, the desire fulfillment theory, and objectivism. (edited)

Moore, Gareth. Sexual Needs and Sexual Pleasures. *Int Phil Quart*, 35(2), 193-204, Ju 95.

Moore, James. "Hume and Hutcheson" in *Hume and Hume's Connexions, Stewart, M A (ed)*, 23-57. University Park, Penn St Univ Pr, 1995.

The moral philosophies of David Hume and Francis Hutcheson were very different in origin and inspiration. These differences are apparent in Hutcheson's initial reactions to Book III of Hume's *Treatise*, and in Hume's rejoinders. Hume attempted to bring his moral ideas closer to those of Hutcheson by altering or revising the early sections of Book III. Those alterations have generated the misleading impression that Hume was a follower of Hutcheson's in moral philosophy. A close examination of the opening sections of Book III and the Conclusion is designed to illustrate the profound and lasting disagreements between the two philosophers.

Moore, Robert C. *Logic and Representation*. Stanford, CSLI, 1995.

Moosa, Imtiaz. Formalism of Kant's A Priori Versus Scheler's Material A Priori. *Int Stud Phil*, 27(2), 33-47, 1995.

The objective of the paper is to compare and contrast Kant's "formal" and Scheler's "material" apriori. To accomplish this, it will examine 1) Why *for Scheler* Kant's apriori is formal, 2) Scheler's reasons for rejecting Kant's formalism, and his reasons for positing a material apriori, and 3) The points of agreement and differences between their notions of the apriori. It will be shown that, notwithstanding Scheler's assertion to the contrary, their apriorism are not totally at odds. They differ regarding the origin of apriori knowledge. (For Scheler it is grounded in "phenomenological intuition" while for Kant it is entirely nonempirical.) But they agree on the nature and function of apriori knowledge.

Morales, Fabio. Relational Attributes in Aristotle. *Phronesis*, 39(3), 255-274, 1994.

Aristotle's theory of relations involves serious difficulties of interpretation. By attempting to solve some of the problems posed by J L Ackrill in his famous commentary on the *Categories* (Ackrill, 1963), I hope to contribute to a better understanding of Aristotle's statements on the nature and status of relational attributes. In general, my procedure has been to analyze the criteria by which entities are supposed to fall under the category of "the relative". The following topics will be considered: i) Aristotle's two definitions of relatives in *Categories* 7, ii) the pseudo-relational character of the parts of substances, and iii) the threefold classification of relatives in *Metaphysics* chapter 15. A corollary of these discussions will be that relations may have played for Aristotle a far more conspicuous role in the *definition* of substances and attributes than has been hitherto acknowledged.

Moran, Richard. Arthur Collins's *The Nature of Mental Things*. *Phil Phenomenol Res*, 54(4), 917-920, D 94.

Morán y C, Jorge. Tomas de Aquino: Los Proemios a Aristoteles. Introduccion, Traduccion y Notas. *Topicos*, 1(1), 197-206, 1991.

Morán y Castellanos, Jorge. Evidencia de la naturaleza en Aristóteles. *Topicos*, 4(6), 71-87, 1994.

The concept of *Evidence* in Aristotle's work does not imply the passive perception of reality, but the gradual process of its discovery: we shall start from *that which is more evident and certain for us to the things most evident and certain in nature.*

Moravcsik, Julius. "The Philosophic Background of Aristotle's *Aitia*" in *The Crossroads of Norm and Nature, Sim, May (ed)*, 237-246. Lanham, Rowman & Littlefield, 1995.

The paper takes up recent claims that interpreting Aristotle's theory of four "causes" as explanatory factors arises only out of dissatisfaction with trying to squeeze the Aristotelian account into some form of a causal theory, and offers the alternative as a "what else?" option. My paper shows that the Aristotelian theory is the outcome of Aristotle's contribution to a long Greek tradition of "explanations" in the sense of trying to "make sense" of reality, and that such efforts have a "logic" of their own. Then in detail an interpretation is presented that construes the Aristotelian account as anything but a "what else" theory of what renders elements of reality intelligible.

Moravia, Sergio and Staton, Scott (trans). *The Enigma of the Mind: The Mind-Body Problem in Contemporary Thought*. New York, Cambridge Univ Pr, 1995.

The author analyzes the debate on the mind-body problem in the last 50 years. His approach is essentially theoretical: it examines the interpretations of the mental offered by the main contemporary philosophies of mind. Moravia's central theses are that both materialism and mentalism are untenable and that the true "subject" of the psychophysical experiences is the concrete person in-the-world. As to the mental, it should be viewed as a peculiar language which gives voice to some aspects (subjective, existential) of human being and human acting that no other language could express adequately.

Morawetz, Thomas. "Liberalism and the New Skeptics" in *In Harm's Way, Coleman, Jules L (ed)*, 122-138. New York, Cambridge Univ Pr, 1994.

This essay examines the challenge to liberal theory offered by critical legal theory. It describes that challenge as an antifoundationalist attack on the foundationalist aspects of liberalism. It distinguishes two forms of the challenge, forms that rest respectively on skeptical and nonskeptical premises. Finally it attacks the skeptical form of the challenge as incomplete and unpersuasive. The nonskeptical form of the challenge draws its strength from communitarian arguments. The article considers the role of the concepts of autonomy and individualism within the debates between liberals and communitarians.

Morawiec, Edmund. Die Metaphisik als die eigentliche Ontotheologie. *Stud Phil Christ*, 30(2), 193-201, 1994.

Morawski, Stefan. On Leszek Kolakowski's Philosophizing. *Dialogue Hum*, 2(2), 11-18, 1992.

Kolakowski is a many-sided thinker and as well an exceedingly talented historian of philosophy as an original philosopher of culture. This text is focused on his philosophizing present in the writings concerned with the nature of philosophy, religion, culture in general and especially at the actual moment of civilisational turn-over. Kolakowski's thinking rests on the dialectic tension between scepticism supported by critical reason and mysticism accepting the indespensibility of transcendent values (calling for no proof because such would be out of point or simply ridiculous). Kolakowski brilliantly argues that the world matters and primarily the existential problems are of dramatic and aporetic character. We look for solving them by a definite conception which always somewhat fails. We cannot escape assuming some absolute standards but realize that they are shaky. We know that sciences provide only instrumental answers and thus we need metaphysics but no metaphysical decree is able to convince those who think in another manner. Thus good and evil are always mixed up. We have to be mytho-poetic but as well distinguish between positive and negative mythology. The author finds Kolakowski's philosophizing very persuasive and one of the most intriguing as much as promising against the troubles of our civilisation and culture.

Morawski, Stefan. On Various Faces of Postmodernist Philosophical Thinking. *Dialogue Hum*, 3(4), 39-65, 1993.

The article consists of six fragments, in which the author argues that postmodernism (in any domain) is part of a bigger problem called postmodernity—related to a striking change of cultural and civilizational phenomena.

More, Thomas and Logan, George M (& other eds). *Utopia: Latin Text and English Translation*. New York, Cambridge Univ Pr, 1995.

Moreau, Pierre-François. Épicure et Spinoza: la physique. *Arch Phil*, 57(3), 459-469, Jl-S 94.

Malgré la divergence sur le vide, la physique d'Epicure et celle de Spinoza sont proches par leur but, leurméthode et leur place dans l'ensemble du système.

Morelli, Elizabeth. Post-Hegelian Elements in Lonergan's Philosophy of Religion. *Method*, 12(2), 215-238, Fall 94.

This article examines in what sense Lonergan's philosophic approach to religious studies is post-Hegelian. It explores how Lonergan repudiates certain fundamental features of Hegel's philosophy yet appropriates others. The specific topics examined are logic vs method, including discussion of dialectical necessity and the ideal of comprehensiveness; and the issue of the sublation of religion by philosophy.

Morelli, Elizabeth. The Existence of the Self Before God in Kierkegaard's *The Sickness Unto Death*. *Heythrop J*, 36(1), 15-29, Ja 95.

This article presents a compact and detailed exposition of Kierkegaard's notion of existence as found in his *The Sickness Unto Death*, specifically, the notion of the existence of the self in its relation to God. First, it contains analysis of the background issues of repetition and anxiety, the definition of the self, and despair versus faith, as elaborated in Part I of *SUD*. Secondly, it explores the unique nature of the relation of the self to God, as elaborated in Part II of *SUD*, focussing on the ontological constitution of the self as relation, and the transparency of the relation.

Moreno, A and Merelo, J J and Exteberria, A. Studying Organisms with Basic Cognitive Capacities in Artificial Worlds. *Commun Cog—AI*, 11(1-2), 31-53, 1994.

In this paper we pose the problem of how to study basic cognitive processes in the frame of simulations of artificial worlds of the style of Artificial Life. The main difficulty of simulating biologically grounded cognitive processes lies in the search for forms of organisms suitable to establish functional relationships with their environments and co-evolve with them. In order to attempt this, we study the properties of autonomous systems at different degrees of complexity and the origin of cognitive processes as a sophistication of primitive sensori-motor loops of living systems. (edited)

Moreno Márquez, César. Proximidad, Trascendencia y Subjetividad en la Metafenomenología de E Levinas. *An Seminar Hist Filosof*, 6, 37-45, 1986-89.

Moreno Villa, Mariano. Filosofia e Pedagógica da Libertaçao Latinoamericana. *Educ Filosof*, 8(16), 183-205, Jl-D 94.

Moretti, Giampiero. La Perduta Prossimità del dio: Mito e Poesia in Walter Otto. *Stud Filosofici*, 299-306, 1991-92.

Morey, Patricia S. "Teoría Social y Pluralidad Teórica" in *Temas Actuales de Filosofía, Palacios, María Julia (ed)*, 403-407. Buenos Aires, Univ Nacional Salta, 1993.

Morgan, Michael. Philosophy in Plato's *Sophist*. *Proc Boston Colloq Anc Phil*, 9, 83-111, 1993.

Morgan, Thomas D and Rotunda, Ronald D. *Problems and Materials on Professional Responsibility (Sixth Edition)*. Westbury, Foundation Pr, 1995.

Morgan, Vance G. Foreknowledge and Human Freedom in Augustine. *J Phil Res*, 19, 223-242, 1994.

In this paper, I consider Augustine's attempted solution of the problem of divine foreknowledge and free will. I will focus on two distinct notions of God's relationship to time as they relate to this problem. In *Confessions* XI, Augustine develops an understanding of time and foreknowledge that clearly offers a possible solution to the foreknowledge/free will problem. I then turn to *On Free Will* 3.1-4, where Augustine conspicuously declines to use a solution similar to the one in the *Confessions*, rather developing a response that demands a very different conception of foreknowledge. I subsequently argue that in *On Free Will*, Augustine's argument requires that God's foreknowledge, when considered in light of events involving human freedom, must be in a real sense dependent on the results of free choice.

Mori, Gianluca. Spinozismo e Libertinismo: A Proposito di due Recenti Libri su Boulainviller. *G Crit Filosof Ital*, 73(1), 124-138, Ja-Ap 94.

Moriconi, Enrico. All'inizio è il linguaggio. *Teoria*, 14(1), 55-68, 1994.

The paper focusses on W W Tait's attempt to exploit a *modified* version of the "proposition-as-type" notion of constructivity in order to preserve the "good" core of Platonism (i.e., the independence of truth from provability), while abandoning any idea of an original *nonpropositional* knowledge of, for instance, the properties of the natural numbers system. Because the *modification* amounts to a distinction between "to be" an object of a certain type, and "to construct" or present such an object, the paper argues for a tight connection between this renewed Platonism and formalism.

Morikawa, Isao. Patients' Rights in Japan: Progress and Resistance. *Kennedy Inst Ethics J*, 4(4), 337-343, D 94.

The discussion of patients' rights in Japan began in 1968 when a surgeon was accused of violating a potential organ donor's right to life by arbitrarily employing brain-based criteria in the determination of his death. A proliferation of documents that articulate and endorse patients' rights occurred in the 1980s and early 1990s. The doctrine of informed consent, which has been a central aspect of the movement toward patients' rights, is increasingly recognized in Japan, although importance rarely has been attached to the element of the patient's "appreciation" of the information disclosed by the physician, much less to the "voluntariness" of the patient's decision. Nevertheless, recent court decisions indicate progress both in the acceptance and the understanding of the doctrine in Japan.

Morissette, Jacques. Le Monde de l'éthique et l'essence de la Morale. *Philosopher*, 17, 63-72, 1995.

Morito, Bruce. Value, Metaphysics, and Anthropocentrism. *Environ Values*, 4(1), 31-47, F 95.

The paper attempts to show that our inclusion as members of the ecological community makes our valuational activity an integral and transformational element within more comprehensive ecological processes. As such, our moral commitment to the environment must be radically reshaped in order adequately to incorporate this renewed understanding. (edited)

Mormann, Thomas. A Representational Reconstruction of Carnap's Quasianalysis. *Proc Phil Sci Ass*, 1, 96-104, 1994.

According to general wisdom, Carnap's quasianalysis is an ingenious but definitively flawed approach to epistemology and philosophy of science. I argue that this assessment is mistaken. Rather, Carnapian quasianalysis can be reconstructed as a special case of a general theory of structural representation. This enables us to exploit some interesting analogies of quasianalysis with the representational theory of measurement. It is shown how Goodman's well-known objections against the quasianalytical approach may be defused in the new framework. As an application, I sketch how the thesis of empirical underdetermination of theories may be elucidated in the framework of quasianalysis.

Mormann, Thomas. Accessibility, Kinds, and Laws: A Structural Explication. *Phil Sci*, 61(3), 389-406, S 94.

"Accessibility" is a crucial concept of possible worlds semantics. The simplest approach to accessibility is the "magical theory" that construes this relation as analogous to spatial or temporal relations. In this paper I give a nonmagical structural account of the accessibility relation that can be used to give a necessitarian account of kinds an laws. Laws are characterized in a structural way as stable invariants of the world's gestalt. Finally, I point out how the structural approach can be embedded in a general representational theory of modality.

Mormann, Thomas. Incompatible Empirically Equivalent Theories: A Structural Explication. *Synthese*, 103(2), 203-249, My 95.

The thesis of the empirical underdetermination of theories (U-thesis) maintains that there are incompatible theories which are empirically equivalent. Whether this is an interesting thesis depends on how the term 'incompatible' is understood. In this paper a structural explication is proposed. More precisely, the U-thesis is studied in the framework of the 'model theoretic' or 'semantic' approach according to which theories are not to be taken as linguistic entities, but rather as families of mathematical structures. Theories of similarity structures are studied as a paradigmatic case. The structural approach further reveals that the U-thesis is related to problems of uniqueness in the representational theory of measurement, questions of geometric conventionalism, and problems of structural underdetermination in mathematics.

Mormann, Thomas. Space Curvature and Repeatable Properties, Almost No Problems With a Peaceful Coexistence. *Austl J Phil*, 73(1), 114-122, Mr 95.

Recently, Peter Forrest has maintained that there are no repeatable vector-valued properties if we assume that space is curved. Allegedly, this is due to the fact that the vector-valued properties of an item depend on its geometrical history, i.e., on the paths it has been travelling. It is argued that Forrest's thesis is mistaken. The general format of the argument is that in most cases there is a geometrically motivated way of singling out a unique special path that can be used to identify the item's vector-valued properties.

Mormann, Thomas and Ibarra, Andoni. Simetrías versus leyes? Apostilla a Van Fraassen sobre la representación. *Pensamiento*, 198(50), 383-406, S-D 94.

Se analiza la reciente tesis de van Fraassen acerca del carácter no explicitable del concepto de ley natural y su consiguiente inadecuación en el estudio de la ciencia. Alternativamente, él propone acercarse a ésta tomándola en sí misma, esto es, como una actividad dirigida hacia la construcción de modelos y regulada por la noción de simetría. Esta, sin embargo, es de naturaleza esencialmente distinta a la de la ley. En el artículo, por el contrario, sostenemos, desde una perspectiva representacionalista de la ciencia, que la noción de simetría debe conservar algo del espíritu original atribuible al concepto de ley.

Mormann, Thomas and Ibarra, Andoni and Diederich, Werner. Bibliography of Structuralism II (1989-1994 and Additions). *Erkenntnis*, 41(3), 403-418, N 94.

Five years have passed since our "Bibliography of Structuralism" has been published in this journal (*Erkenntnis*, 30, 1989). The aim of the present bibliography is twofold: First, we list a number of titles up to 1989 which we regretfully failed to include five years ago. Second, we augment the bibliography by titles which have appeared since 1989.

Morpurgo-Tagliabue, Guido. Ambiguità e Semiosi. *Filosofia*, 44(3), 457-480, S-D 93.

Morreau, Michael and Asher, Nicholas. "What Some Generic Sentences Mean" in *The Generic Book, Carlson, Gregory N (ed)*, 300-338. Chicago, Univ of Chicago Pr, 1995.

Morrill, Glyn. Discontinuity in Categorical Grammar. *Ling Phil*, 18(2), 175-219, Ap 95.

Discontinuity refers to the character of many natural language constructions wherein signs differ markedly in their prosodic and semantic forms. As such it presents interesting demands on monostratal computational formalisms which aspire to descriptive adequacy. Pied piping, in particular, is argued by Pollard (1988) to motivate phrase structure-style feature percolation. In the context of categorial grammar, Bach (1981, 1984), Moortgat (1988, 1990, 1991) and others have sought to provide categorial operators suited to discontinuity. These attempts encounter certain difficulties with respect to model theory and/or proof theory, difficulties which the current proposals are intended to resolve. Lambek calculus is complete for interpretation by *residuation* with respect to the adjunction operation of groupoid algebras (Bruszkowski 1986). In Moortgat and Morrill (1991) it is shown how to give calculi for families of categorial operators, each defined by residuation with respect to an operation of prosodic adjunction (associative, nonassociative, or with interactive axioms). The present paper treats discontinuity in this way, by residuation with respect to three adjunctions: + (associative), (.,.) (split-point marking), and *W* (wrapping) related by the equation $s_1+s_2+s_3=(s_1,s_3)Ws_2$. We show how the resulting methods apply to discontinuous functors, quantifier scope and quantifier scope ambiguity, pied piping, and subject and object antecedent reflexivisation.

Morris, Brian. Taoism, Confucianism and the Chinese Self. *Int J Moral Soc Stud*, 8(3), 273-296, Autumn 93.

The present paper examines conceptions of the self in the classical traditions of Chinese philosophy and indicates the contrasting conceptions of self that are evident in the Taoist and Confusian traditions. The first part of the paper outlines the three basic cultural concepts that both traditions share—the concept of Tao, the theory of the Yin/Yang polarity, and the symbolic construct of five phases or elements. The underlying differences in the social and political values of Taoism and Confucianism are emphasized. The second part of the paper explores the contrasting self-conceptions that these two traditions imply, the Taoist conception suggesting a mystical naturalism where self-realization entails spontaneously identifying with the processes on nature, the Confucian conception, an ethical humanism, a sociocentric notion of subjectivity, where self-realization is an ethical task, involving conformity to the dictates of social status and the development of the 'humanity' within in each person.

Morris, Nancy A. The Authenticity of the Attribution to St Thomas Aquinas of *De natura materiae et dimensionibus interminatis/ De principio individuationis*. *Aquinas*, 37(1), 151-176, Ja-Ap 94.

Morris, Susan. Articulating the Aesthetic in the Ethical: Aesthetics and the Ethics of Care. *Kinesis*, 21(2), 31-40, Fall 94.

In a critique of the work of Carol Gilligan regarding the ethical issue of *care*, the article attempts to show that the scientific arena of inquiry is not fully appropriate to the treatment of the issue. Since *care* is not a simple, empirical item, but rather a multiplicitous, complex experience, it is suggested that the arena of aesthetics is more appropriate to the examination of ethical issues regarding *care*. A critique of rule-governed ethics is included in the analysis.

Morris, Thomas V. "Wagering and the Evidence" in *Gambling on God: Essays on Pascal's Wager, Jordan, Jeffrey (ed)*, 47-60. Lanham, Rowman & Littlefield, 1994.

Morrisey, Will. Strengthening Social Contract Theory: *Justice and Modern Moral Philosophy*, by Jeffrey Reiman. *Interpretation*, 22(2), 271-281, Wint 94-95.

In his book Jeffrey Reiman undertakes to restate modern rationalist-contractarian political philosophy. He locates the origin of this philosophy in the thought of Descartes, with its intent to view all existing opinions and social conventions as doubtful and changeable, and to find a method whereby political societies may be reconstructed on a rational foundation. The review article argues that Marx and Nietzsche are right about modernity; that the Cartesian enterprise begins and must end in a Machiavellian quest for power. Modern rationalism and irrationalism alike are finally exercises of the will, not plausibly moralized by thinkers in the vein of Kant and Rawls.

Morrison, Donald R. "Xenophon's Socrates as Teacher" in *The Socratic Movement, Vander Waerdt, Paul A (ed)*, 181-208. Ithaca, Cornell Univ Pr, 1994.

Morrison, Donald R. The Place of Unity in Aristotle's Metaphysical Project. *Proc Boston Colloq Anc Phil*, 9, 131-156, 1993.

Morrison, James C. Merleau-Ponty and Literary Language. *Int Stud Phil*, 26(4), 69-83, 1994.

Morrison, James V. A Key Topos in Thucydides: The Comparison of Cities and Individuals. *Amer J Philo*, 115(4), 525-541, Wint 94.

Morrison, Margaret. Capacities, Tendencies and the Problem of Singular Causes. *Phil Phenomenol Res*, 55(1), 163-168, Mr 95.

The paper, part of a book symposium on Nancy Cartwright's *Nature's Capacities and Their Measurement*, discusses some of the difficulties with Cartwright's account of capacities as she relates it to Mill's notion of tendencies. I claim that the two cannot be linked in the way that Cartwright suggests and that her attempt to do so leaves unresolved the tension between the singular and universal aspects of capacities. This tension is also discussed as it arises on the context of the gyro experiment used to test GTR, an example Cartwright uses to argue for the importance of capacities for science. I claim that capacities are not required for understanding this experiment and its relation to GTR; a simple causal account will suffice.

Morrow, Raymond. "Mannheim and the Early Frankfurt School" in *The Barbarism of Reason, Horowitz, Asher (ed)*, 169-194. Toronto, Univ of Toronto Pr, 1994.

Morscher, Edgar. Die Gottesbeweise als vermeintliche Stütze von Religion und Theologie. *Frei Z Phil Theol*, 42(1-2), 101-117, 1995.

Morse, Stephen J. The "New Syndrome Excuse Syndrome". *Crim Just Ethics*, 14(1), 3-15, Wint-Spr 95.

This paper addresses the relevance of alleged new psychiatric and psychological abnormalities to criminal culpability. The general thesis is that extant criminal law doctrines are sufficient fairly to adjudicate legitimate claims for justification and excuse and that new defenses tailored to new syndromes should not be created. It argues that causes are not excuses, that the distinction between justifications and excuses is theoretically and practically important, and that in appropriate cases mental abnormality is an excusing condition and not a proper ground for broadening justifications by subjectivizing the criteria for right action.

Mortensen, Preben. Francis Hutcheson and the Problem of Conspicuous Consumption. *J Aes Art Crit*, 53(2), 155-165, Spr 95.

In this essay I suggest a cultural historical or social historical framework wherein the emergence of aesthetics in the early eighteenth century can be understood. On this basis aspects of Francis Hutcheson's *Inquiry into the Original of our Ideas of Beauty and Virtue* are interpreted. Most interpretations of the emergence of aesthetics proceed from the assumption that early theoreticians, such as Shaftesbury and Hutcheson, carved out an independent, "aesthetic" realm for art, which became the domain of their theoretical efforts. The interpretation in this essay shows that, on the contrary, Hutcheson (as his predecessor Shaftesbury) wanted to give moral legitimacy to the contemplation of art.

Mortier, Freddy. De Piaget á Habermas et Rawls: les Problèmes de la Reconstruction Rationnelle du Jugement Moral chez Kohlberg. *Philosophica*, 53(1), 5-37, 1994.

The author examines Kohlberg's arguments for his claim that his theory of moral development is inevitably normative because it is an instance of what Habermas has called "hermeneutic objectivism". It is argued that two different approaches are involved in Kohlberg's characterisation of the stages. The first derives from the earlier Piaget's psychological interest in morality as a cybernetics of the affective life, the second from the philosophy of moral language. These approaches, however, imply respectively a "strong" and a "weak" conception of the developmental stages, although Kohlberg constantly treats them as one. It is further argued that the "strong" conception" can be dispensed with in Kohlberg's methodology. The corresponding theory would be both neutral, hermeneutical and compatible with a large range of moral theories.

Morton, Charlene. Feminist Theory and the Displaced Music Curriculum: Beyond the "Add and Stir" Projects. *Phil Music Educ Rev*, 2(2), 106-121, Fall 94.

This paper argues that, notwithstanding their benefits, pedagogical projects to eliminate elitism in the musical canon and to restore a more inclusive musical practice are not enough to secure music programs a place in school curricula. Also required are philosophical inquiries into the relationship between the displaced music curriculum and the feminized location of music. Using Sandra Harding's critical analysis of similar projects in feminist research, the paper concludes that music educator's experience as crusaders for their "frill subject" is a catalyst and untapped theoretical resource for inquiries into the weak epistemological status of music education.

Moruzzi, Norma Claire. A Problem with Headscarves: Contemporary Complexities of Political and Social Identity. *Polit Theory*, 22(4), 653-672, N 94.

Moruzzi, Norma Claire. A Response to Galeotti's "A Problem with Theory". *Polit Theory*, 22(4), 678-679, N 94.

Moschovakis, Joan Rand. More About Relatively Lawless Sequences. *J Sym Log*, 59(3), 813-829, S 94.

In the author's *Relative lawlessness in intuitionistic analysis* (J Sym Log, vol 52, (1987) pp 68-88) and *An intuitionistic theory of lawlike, choice and lawless sequences (Logic Colloquium '90.* Springer-Verlag. Berlin. 1993. pp 191-209) a notion of lawlessness relative to a countable information base was developed for classical and intuitionistic analysis. Here we simplify the predictability property characterizing relatively lawless sequences and derive it from the new axiom of closed data (classically equivalent to open data) together with a natural principle of invariance under finite translation. We characterize relative lawlessness in terms of a notion of forcing. Finally, we study relative lawlessness on an arbitrary fan and show that the collection of lawless binary sequences (which is comeager in the sense of Baire) has probability measure zero. The reasoning is predominantly constructive.

Moser, Paul K and Mele, Alfred R. Intentional Action. *Nous*, 28(1), 39-68, Mr 94.

This paper formulates an analysis of the ordinary notion of intentional action that clarifies a commonsense distinction between intentional and nonintentional action. The analysis builds on some typically neglected considerations about relations between lucky action and intentional action. The paper also explains why some vagueness is indispensable in a characterization of intentional action as ordinarily understood.

Moser, Paul K and Mulder, D Hudson. Probability in Rational Decision-Making. *Phil Papers*, 23(2), 109-128, Ag 94.

This paper argues that it is not universally true that the rationally preferable action in a suitable long run of repetitions of a particular decision-situation is likewise rationally preferable in an isolated individual case of that decision-situation. The paper distinguishes between statistical and epistemic probability, and identifies some common fallacies in statistical reasoning. It uses the 'Monty Hall' problem to illustrate its points.

Moses, Michael and Gasarch, William and Downey, Rod. The Structure of the Honest Polynomial m-Degrees. *Annals Pure Applied Log*, 70(2), 113-139, D 94.

A language *A* is said to be honest polynomial time *m*-reducible to a language *B* iff there is a polynomial *p* and a polynomial time computable function *f* such that $f \varepsilon A$ iff $f(x)\ \alpha\ B$ and $|f(x)|$ is less than or equal to $P(|x|)$. The paper at hand explores the structure of the recursive sets partitioned by the ordering induced by honest polynomial time reductions.

Moshier, M Andrew and Pollard, Carl J. The Domain of Set-Valued Feature Structures. *Ling Phil*, 17(6), 607-631, D 94.

Mosini, Valeria. Some Considerations on the Reducibility of Chemistry to Physics. *Epistemologia*, 17(2), 205-223, Ju-De 94.

The paper discusses two aspects of the relationships between chemistry and physics which are relevant to the question of reduction: the application of Schroedinger's equation to the solution of problems of chemical interest and the concept of electronegativity. The conclusions reached are: that chemistry and physics *share the same theoretical body* which needs modifying according to the *same approximations* when applied to many-body systems; that electrochemistry, one of the key-concepts of chemistry, has been reduced to physical concepts. The paper is in favour of reductionism, yet it challenges the primacy of physics by showing that this is as approximate a discipline as chemistry.

Moskop, John C and Gatter Jr, Robert A. From Futility to Triage. *J Med Phil*, 20(2), 191-205, Ap 95.

Basic disagreements about what makes human life valuable hinder use of the concept of futility to decide whether it is appropriate to continue life support for one in a permanent state of unconsciousness, or to provide intensive medical care to one in the last stages of a terminal illness (the "paradigm cases"). Triage planning (the process of establishing criteria for health care prioritization) is an attractive alternative framework for addressing the paradigm cases. Triage planning permits society to see the cases in the context of diverse moral perspectives, limited resources, and competing health care demands. Furthermore, at least one essential question posed by the paradigm cases is whether treatment is wasteful, and triage planning is a useful model for identifying and eliminating wasteful medical care. The authors describe how triage planning can be implemented to address the paradigm cases, and conclude that it offers one way of moving debate about these cases beyond futility.

Moskowitz, Ellen H. Long-Acting Contraceptives: Ethical Guidance for Policymakers and Health Care Providers. *Hastings Center Rep*, 25(1), S1-S8, Jan-Feb 95.

The introduction of Norplant and other long-acting contraceptives into the United States expanded options, but also raised moral questions, particularly with respect to how government might incorporate the methods into programs that target poor women. It is insufficient to distinguish appropriate from inappropriate practices based on notions of freedom and coercion. A richer perspective is needed that rests on a case-by-case analysis attentive to the social dimension and consequences of contraceptive decisionmaking, that takes special note of the need for access to long-acting contraceptives, the possibility for mistaken nonuse as well as mistaken use, and the United State's past and present biases and power imbalances.

Mosley, Albert G. "Negritude, Nationalism, and Nativism: Racists or Racialists?" in *African Philosophy: Selected Readings, Appiah, Kwame Anthony*, 216-235. Englewood Cliffs, Prentice Hall, 1995.

Mosley, Albert G (ed). *African Philosophy: Selected Readings*. Englewood Cliffs, Prentice Hall, 1995.

Mosolova, S V. Sophiology: A Human Reading of the Book of God. *Russian Stud Phil*, 33(4), 49-65, Spr 95.

The author addresses the controversial doctrine of Sophia, or Divine Wisdom, as a fourth divine hypostasis, that was developed by philosophers, such as Pavel Florenskii and Sergei Bulgakov, who were active in the Russian religious and philosophical renaissance of the early twentieth century. Although she believes that the doctrine is philosophically fruitful and helps to resolve certain theological problems, she argues that it is internally contradictory, conflicts with the Christian doctrine of creation *ex nihilo*, and leads inescapably to pantheism.

Moss, Lawrence S. Power Set Recursion. *Annals Pure Applied Log*, 71(3), 247-306, F 95.

Moss, Lawrence S and Johnson, David E. Grammar Formalisms Viewed as Evolving Algebras. *Ling Phil*, 17(6), 537-560, D 94.

We consider the use of *evolving algebra* methods of specifying grammars for natural languages. We are especially interested in distributed evolving algebras. We proved the motivation for doing this, and we give a reconstruction of some classic grammar formalisms in directly dynamic terms. Finally, we consider some technical questions arising from the use of direct dynamism in grammar formalisms.

Mosser, Kurt. Kants's Critical Model of the Experiencing Subject. *Ideal Stud*, 25(1), 1-24, Wint 95.

Mott, Peter. On the Intuitionistic Solution of the Sorites Paradox. *Pac Phil Quart*, 75(2), 133-150, Je 94.

Intuitionistically the Sorites Paradox is just a fallacy. The intuitionistic treatment, probably first proposed by Putnam, has not been much discussed. This paper articulates and defends it.

Mott, Peter. Towards a Winograd/Flores Semantics. *Mind Mach*, 5(1), 69-87, F 95.

A basic theme of Winograd and Flores (1986) is that the principal function of language is to co-ordinate social activity. It is, they claim, from this function that meaning itself arises. They criticise approaches that try to understand meaning through the mechanisms of reference, the Rationalist Tradition as they call it. To seek to ground meaning in social practice is not new, but the approach is presently attractive because of difficulties encountered with the notion of reference. Without taking a view on whether these are insuperable, the present paper accepts Winograd and Flores's challenge and attempts to lay aside reference and to base a conception of meaning directly in terms of co-ordination and consensus within a linguistic community.

Mottolese, Maurizio. Mito, tragedia, reivelazione: Sulla presenza di Franz Rosenzweig nell'opera di Benjamin. *Teoria*, 14(1), 93-108, 1994.

Mouffe, Chantal. Political Liberalism: Neutrality and the Political. *Ratio Juris*, 7(3), 314-324, D 94.

The paper examines the current discussion in liberalism around the issue of the "neutrality" of the state. It scrutinizes the "political liberalism" defended by John Rawls and Charles Larmore and shows that the consequence of their approach is to evacuate the dimension of "the political" from the idea of a well-ordered society. By presenting the exclusions existing in their model of liberal society as the product of free agreement resulting from rational procedures, "political liberals" offer us a picture in which antagonism, violence and power have only disappeared because they have been made invisible. The consequence is to leave liberalism unable to conceptualize power and antagonism. The paper concludes that there cannot be such a thing as "neutral justification of the neutrality of the state" (Larmore 1987) and that a pluralist perfectionist perspective like the one proposed by Joseph Raz offers a more adequate way to envisage the specificity of modern pluralist democracy.

Mouffe, Chantal. Politics, Democratic Action, and Solidarity. *Inquiry*, 38(1-2), 99-108, Je 95.

I agree with the critique of rationalism proposed by Spinosa, Flores, and Dreyfus in "Disclosing New Worlds." Today the defence of democracy requires us to understand that allegiance to democratic institutions can only rest on identification with the practices, the language-games, and the discourses which are constitutive of the democratic "form of life," and that it is not a question of providing them with a *rational* justification. My comments are developed in two directions. First, as a development of their thesis concerning the centrality of practices. I suggest that in order to grasp the present crisis of democratic forms of individuality we can learn a lot from Nietzsche's analysis of "nihilism." Second, I point to a dimension which I consider to be missing in the perspective put forward in the article. It fails to take account of the fact that the constitution of a "we" always requires the determination of a "them." This, in my view, has important consequences for the relation between solidarity and politics. I conclude by arguing for the need to introduce an *agonistic* element in the view of solidarity, and for the crucial role of the category of the *adversary* in a pluralist democracy whose aim is to transform *antagonism* into *agonism*.

Mougin, Gregory and Sober, Elliott. Betting Against Pascal's Wager. *Nous*, 28(3), 382-395, S 94.

Only one traditional objection to Pascal's wager is telling: Pascal assumes a particular theology, but without justification. We produce two new objections that go deeper. We show that even if Pascal's theology is assumed to be probable, Pascal's argument does not go through. In addition, we describe a wager that Pascal never considered, which leads away from Pascal's conclusion. We then consider the impact of these considerations on other prudential arguments concerning what one should believe, and on the more general question of when and why belief formation ought to be based solely on the evidence.

Moutsopoulos, Evanghélos. Considérations Rétrospectives. *Diotima*, 22, 147-148, 1994.

Moutsopoulos, Evanghélos. Fuite et Nostalgie Romantiques de la Grèce. *Diotima*, 22, 9-13, 1994.

A movement of liberal inspiration extended to the whole European West, romanticism seems to have been a real philhellenic trend. Nostalgia of classical Greece appears to have been cured through the approach of modern Greece and the recognition of their continuity not only in the works of scholars like Fustel de Coulanges, but also in those of thinkers of the caliber of Renan in those of important philosophers like Nietzsche.

Moutsopoulos, Evanghélos. La Fonction Catalytique de l'Echaiphnes chez Denys. *Diotima*, 23, 9-16, 1995.

The catalytic function of what suddenly occurs is, at an ontological level, as much dramatic as a demarcation of the ontological quasi-continuity that Dionysius Areopagite initially imposes by multiplying the number of the intermediate beings and by minimalizing the intervals which separate them. However, the suppression of such a quasi-continuity through the insertation of what suddenly occurs cannot be assimilated to a *kairic* (from: *kairos*, seasonability) moment. The latter supposes an intentional preparation, whereas the sudden is the effect of a blant intrusion within a given course. Besides, for Dionysius, the sudden is invested with a transcendent character which differentiates it even more from the immanent *kairic* process.

Moutsopoulos, Evanghélos. Recherches Épistémologiques Platoniciennes. *Diotima*, 23, 143-156, 1995.

This threefold research deals with the following problems: *1) The Notion of Creed in Plato*. The author namely examines its semantic and methodological aspects and proceeds to the distinction between creed and opinion *doxa* envisages under its two aspects: the irrational and the rational one which leads to science. *2) The Ontological, Epistemological and Methodological aspects of the Platonic Anamnesis*. It is shown that the two first of these aspects are inseparable, unless one accepts to schematize the problem. Maieutics and modern psychoanalysis have recourse to parallel methods and means in order to clarify certain noetic data, but that all similarities stop here. Maieutics then, may be considered as a cathartic method. *3) Artistic Rhetoric and Sophistic*. Sophistic is, for Plato, an art of illusions his contemporary artists have. According to him, adopted sophistic methods in order to provide illusory works. Arts that have adopted depreciating illusory, impure, fluid and acrobatic devices are indebted to sophistics and aim at flattering the lowest layers of the Athenian population.

Moutsopoulos, Evanghélos A. L'idée de Finalité dans l'esthétique de Giovanni Gentile. *Philosophia (Athens)*, 23-24, 252-266, 1993-94.

Le formalisme artistique qui domine l'esthétique de Gentile n'a rien de commun avec l'idéalisme esthétique kantien ou avec le dialectisme fonctionnaliste de Hegel. Il dérive directement de la tradition ontologique réaliste d'inspiration aristotélicienne, corroborée à l'occasion par le dynamisme ontologique leibnizien. Aux termes de cette tradition, la forme est elle-même contenu dans la mesure où elle constitue et contient son propre programme de réalisation, qui en exprime la finalité laquelle, de son côté, s'affirme comme postulat créationnel et comme exigence de l'être; exigence qui ne saurait toutefois trouver satisfaction que dans son adoption de la part du génie créateur. L'analyse rigoureuse des textes gentiliens relatifs à la question rendent compte de la complexité déroutante du cheminement suivi par leur auteur. Mitigé, relativisé, le formalisme esthétique de Gentile, une fois mis en lumière, n'en apparaît pas moins original, pertinent et valable autant que séduisant.

Movia, Giancarlo. Finito e infinito e l'idealismo della filosofia: La logica hegeliana dell'essere determinato: Parte Prima. *Riv Filosof Neo-Scolas*, 86(1), 110-133, Ja-Mr 94.

Movia, Giancarlo. Finito e infinito e l'idealismo della filosofia: La logica hegeliana dell'essere determinato: Parte Seconda. *Riv Filosof Neo-Scolas*, 86(2), 323-357, Ap-Je 94.

This paper offers an essay of running commentary on the Hegelian logic of Determinate Being (Dasein) from the point of view of classical logic and metaphysics. Hegel show particularly that the intrinsic contradiction of the finite implies the existence of the true infinite. The author of this paper maintains, however, that if the true infinite cannot be either the infinite of rationalistic metaphysics, or the infinite of Kantian or Fichtean philosophy, it, therefore, cannot be either the Hegelian infinite, which contains, as his ideal moment, the finite. In order to resolve completely the contradiction of the finite and the problematical character of the experience in general, it must be supposed or better demonstrated the infinite as actus purus according to Aristotelean tradition.

Moya, Carlos J. Las Emociones y la Naturalización de la Intencionalidad. *An Seminar Metaf*, 28, 227-255, 1994.

Moya, Eugenio. Inconmensuralbilidad Empírica: Un Enfoque Macrológico. *Daimon Rev Filosof*, 8, 119-130, 1994.

According to Professor Kuhn, the theories do not evolve piecemeal to fit facts that were there all the time; rather, they emerge together with facts. The scientific revolutions are, in this way, genuine "ontological changes". Just, because it is a transition between incommensurables, the transition between competing paradigms cannot be seen forced by neutral experience. In accordance with the structuralist program, the difficulty lies in knowing if pairs of incompatible theories—for example, classical and relativistic mechanics—are connected by nontrivial links, that can restore the commensurability.

Mozur, Gerald. Half-Hearted Pragmatism. *J Speculative Phil*, 8(4), 247-261, 1994.

This paper examines Richard Rorty's "neo-pragmatism" and its claim that there are no beliefs, or justifications of belief, which hold good independently of their linguistic and historical circumstances. I examine Rorty's historicism and linguisticism and argue that these doctrines do not exclude either trans-historical truths or a nonlinguistic criterion for the warrantability of beliefs. On the contrary, acceptance of both historicism and linguisticism leads to a more *robust* pragmatism than the *half-hearted* version offered by Rorty.

Mrozek-Dumanowska, Anna. Does Courtly Love Have an Arabic Background?. *Dialogue Hum*, 3(3), 107-113, 1993.

The topic of investigations is the possible influence of Arab literature and philosophy on the conception of pure love, represented in the poetry and songs of troubadours in XII-XIII century. The courtly love expressed in the songs of troubadours, could be influenced by Muslim Spain. The neoplatonic trend predominating in Arabic philosophy, accentuating the importance of pure love in approach to God, introduced also the genre of fin amors to earthly beauty. In authors' opinion, the treatises of Arabic philosophy, translated into Latin as early as XI-XII century, influenced also the Western conception of courtly love.

Mudrack, Peter E. Are the Elderly Really Machiavellian? A Reinterpretation of an Unexpected Finding. *J Bus Ethics*, 13(9), 757-758, S 94.

In an article published recently in the *Journal of Business Ethics*, Vitell *et al.* (1991) found that elderly respondents scored surprisingly high on a measure of Machiavellianism. This paper offers an alternative explanation for this unexpected result—it may be an artifact of the survey format employed—and recommends additional research to help clarify the issues raised by Vitell and his colleagues.

Mudrovcic, María Inés. "La Verdad de la Historia y la Verdad en la Historia" in *Temas Actuales de Filosofía*, Palacios, María Julia (ed), 409-413. Buenos Aires, Univ Nacional Salta, 1993.

When we talk of truth and apply it to history, we can distinguish two meanings of truth, one epistemological and one metaphysical. After discussing the extent of both meanings, this work concludes that: 1) In its metaphysical sense, truth and history are incompatible, 2) This incompatibility is due to the atemporal conception of truth, 3) This temporality of truth also has paradoxical consequences on theories of truth in its epistemological meaning, and 4) The metaphysical and the epistemological are two incompatible meanings of truth.

Mudrovcic, María Inés. Voltaire y la Enciclopedia: La Génesis del Nuevo Campo Epistémico de la Historia. *Rev Latin de Filosof*, 21(1), 53-65, Fall 95.

The Enlightenment gave birth to our modern understanding of history. This discloses a rupture with the "traditional orthodoxy". This article aims to show one of the features of this change in connection with history. In the first part of the paper, the role of history in the *Encyclopédie* is examined. Finally, I try to show how the rupture with the old conceptual view and the birth of the new epistemic domain of history is located within the *Encyclopédie*: in the article "histoire" written by Voltaire.

Mühlhölzer, Felix. "On the Assumption That Our Concepts 'Structure the Material of Our Experience'" in *Philosophy, Mathematics and Modern Physics, Rudolph, Enno (ed)*, 170-185. New York, Springer-Verlag, 1994.

The paper argues, in accordance with Donald Davidson, but in the context of the philosophy of science and not in the Davidsonian context of a theory of meaning, that the idea of a fundamental dualism of some material given to us and waiting to be organized, on the one hand, and some conceptual scheme doing the organization, on the other, should be rejected.

Mueller, Axel. Natural Kinds and Projectible Predicates. *Sorites*, 13-45, Ap 95.

The focus of this article is on the pragmatic presuppositions involved in the use of general terms in inductive practices. The main thesis is that the problem of characterizing the assumptions underlying the projection of predicates in inductive practices and the ones underlying the classification of certain general terms as *natural kind terms* coincide to a good extent. The reason for this, it is argued, is that both classifications, *projectibility* and *natural kind term*, are attempts to answer to the same semantico-epistemological phenomenon, viz. underdetermination. It is proposed a *deflationary* (i.e., non-essentialist) reading of the so-called *theory of direct reference* as to enable an evaluation of its contribution to epistemological problems associated with this kind of phenomena, as well as it is argued that a purely de facto account of projectibility (i.e., entrenchment) is not viable. The resulting hypothesis is that the conception of *natural kind terms* is only interesting insofar as they are seen as a kind of projectible general terms and thus parts of classifications used in natural science, more generally, in inductive practices, and that this is a perspective that makes undue metaphysical readings avoidable.

Müller, Andreas Uwe. *Grundzüge der Religionsphilosophie Edith Steins*. Freiburg, Alber, 1993.

Müller, Denis. Rationalité des traditions et possibilité d'une éthique universelle: discussion de la position de MacIntyre. *Laval Theol Phil*, 50(3), 499-509, O 94.

La conception de la tradition proposée par Alasdair MacIntyre dans "Quelle justice? Quelle rationalité?" souffre d'une opposition excessive entre tradition et raison, qui résulte d'une prise en compte insuffisante de la modernité. D'autre part, la tendance à confondre tradition et croyance (ou religion) est l'indice d'une sacralisation de la tradition. Il importe donc de mieux articuler le problème 1) (tradition et raison) et le problème 2) (tradition et croyance), si l'on veut saisir comment, en assumant de façon critique la modernité, peut naître une nouvelle relation entre l'éthique laïque et l'éthique religieuse.

Müller, Klaus. Subjektivität und Theologie: Eine hartnäckige Rückfrage. *Theol Phil*, 70(2), 161-186, 1995.

Contemporary theology (protestant and catholic) tends to abandon definitively the concept of subject. The recourse to postmodern inspirations seems to grant a more adequate base for conceptualizing the foundations of the essentials of Christian tradition. But this attitude not only neglects the intrinsic problems of postmodernity. At the same time the multiple rehabilitation of subjectivity on the part of analytic philosophy is omitted. The surprising coincidence of these philosophies with present continental interpretations of classical statements about subjectivity challenges the experiment of a critical redintegration of the subject in philosophy and theology. A first draft of this project is presented.

Müller, Max. "Macht und Gewalt" in *Europa und die Philosophie, Gander, Hans-Helmuth (ed)*, 225-244. Frankfurt/M, Klostermann, 1993.

Müller, Ulrich. Philosophie und Struktur: Über die Notwendigkeit strukturtheoretischer Reflexionen in den hermeneutischen Wissenschaften. *J Gen Phil Sci*, 25(2), 261-277, 1994.

In this essay I give reasons for the thesis that hermeneutic philosophy has to adopt considerations on structural theory in order to avoid the paradox of historism. Concepts of structure like 'criticism', 'centralism', 'creativity' etc. possess both a metaphilosophical and an empirical status which enables us to compare and to combine different and opposed philosophies by means of common structures. Such a hermeneutic reflection on philosophical structures requires the methodical work of fiction and selection. Otherwise relativism concerning the evaluation of philosophical traditions would be the result.

Müller-Funk, Wolfgang. "Von den Differenzen von Differenzen" in *Macht Geschlechter Differenz, Müller-Funk, Wolfgang (ed)*, 152-173. Vienna, Picus, 1994.

Müller-Funk, Wolfgang (ed). *Die berechnende Vernunft: Über das Ökonomische in allen Lebenslagen*. Vienna, Picus, 1993.

Müller-Funk, Wolfgang (ed). *Macht Geschlechter Differenz*. Vienna, Picus, 1994.

Müller-Hohagen, Jürgen. "Komplizenschaft über Generationen" in *Nationalsozialismus und Moderne, Welzer, Harald (ed)*, 26-60. Tübingen, Ed Diskord, 1993.

Münster, Gernot. "The Role of Mathematics in Contemporary Theoretical Physics" in *Philosophy, Mathematics and Modern Physics, Rudolph, Enno (ed)*, 205-212. New York, Springer-Verlag, 1994.

The relation between mathematics and physics is considered in a historical and conceptual context. The view that many objects and concepts of modern mathematics have their origin in physics is exemplified. The close relation between mathematics and physics started to break off in the last century, when mathematics and physics started to break off in the last century, when mathematics began to undertake abstractions as a major element of its development. After a discussion of Wigner's thesis on the "unreasonable effectiveness of mathematics in the natural sciences", the recently observed new convergence and increasing overlap between mathematics and physics is considered in view of that thesis.

Münster, Reinhold. Gleichzeitigkeit des Ungleichzeitigen: zur Frühen Lessingrezeption bei Friedrich Schlegel. *Rev Filosof (Daimon)*, 7, 55-71, 1993.

Die Rezeption Lessings durch Friedrich Schlegel wird als spezifische Aneignung des 18 Jahrhunderts betrachtet. Diese verfährt diachron/historisch und synchron/systematisch. Rezipiert werden daher nicht nur vergangene Kontexte, sondern auch die Diskurse der Epoche der Frühromantik. Unter den Stichworten der Paradoxie, des Choquanten und des Zynismus, besonders aber des Gemütes werden von Schlegel der Schriftsteller Lessing, dessen Wirkungsgeschichte und rezente Wirkung angeeignet. Der Prozess selbst stellt sich als kritische Wechselwirkung dar. In ihr findet Schlegel einen Weg zur Lösung der Krise der Modernität.

Mues, Albert. Der Grund der Dualität der Materie und des Indeterminismus in der physikalischen Natur: Die Lösung eines quantenphysikalischen Rätsels. *Fichte-Studien*, 6, 277-301, 1994.

Mulaik, Stanley A. The Metaphoric Origins of Objectivity, Subjectivity, and Consciousness in the Direct Perception of Reality. *Phil Sci*, 62(2), 283-303, Je 95.

This paper utilizes the theories of metaphor of George Lakoff, Mark Johnson and Julian Jaynes to extend Jaynes's metaphor theory of consciousness by treating consciousness as an operator that works with "covert behavior" so that humans can integrate temporally discontinuous percepts with concepts based on metaphoric extensions of the embodied schemas of direct and immediate perception and thereby transcend the limitations of direct perception. A theory of firstperson expressions and convert behavior to account for self-conscious awareness as language-based is advanced. Subjectivity and objectivity are metaphors based on schemas of perception.

Mulder, D Hudson and Moser, Paul K. Probability in Rational Decision-Making. *Phil Papers*, 23(2), 109-128, Ag 94.

This paper argues that it is not universally true that the rationally preferable action in a suitable long run of repetitions of a particular decision-situation is likewise rationally preferable in an isolated individual case of that decision-situation. The paper distinguishes between statistical and epistemic probability, and identifies some common fallacies in statistical reasoning. It uses the 'Monty Hall' problem to illustrate its points.

Mulder, Monique Borgerhoff and Mitchell, Sandra D. Rough Waters between Genes and Culture: An Anthropological and Philosophical Views on Coevolution. *Biol Phil*, 9(4), 471-487, O 94.

Mulgan, Richard. Aristotle and the Political Role of Women. *Hist Polit Thought*, 15(2), 179-202, Sum 94.

In his attitude to women, Aristotle has been interpreted in three ways, as a humane family man (the old orthodoxy), as an ideologue of sexism (the new orthodoxy) and as a female sympathizer and crypto-feminist (the new Straussian revisionism). These interpretations are discussed in relation to Aristotle's views on the value of political activity, the relation of husband and wife within the household and the female psyche. Though the sexist critique of Aristotle overstates the supposed value of political life and the corresponding inferiority of the household, Aristotle cannot be plausibly seen as a champion of women's equality.

Mulhall, Stephen. Re-monstrations: Heidegger, Derrida and Wittgenstein's Hand. *J Brit Soc Phenomenol*, 26(1), 65-85, Ja 95.

This article has two aims: 1) to contest Derrida's reading of the role of the hand in Heidegger's early and late philosophy; 2) to extend Cavell's treatment of the hand in Emerson's writings in the direction of a reading of Wittgenstein's later philosophy. The implication of linking these tasks is that this issue provides a further reason for detecting family resemblances between Wittgenstein and Heidegger.

Mulhall, Stephen. Reply to Alain Boyer on "Democracy and Disagreement". *Ratio Juris*, 8(1), 9-14, Mr 95.

This reply criticizes Boyer's paper as follows: 1) The inapplicability of Popperian models of scientific theorising to moral and political philosophy, particularly that of Rawls. 2) The inaccuracy of Boyer's interpretation of political liberalism's commitment to a perpetually self-challenging democracy. 3) The inaccuracy of Boyer's interpretation of Rawl's communitarian critics as advocating forms of community which would or should stifle political disagreement.

Mulhall, Stephen and Swift, Adam. *Liberals and Communitarians*. Cambridge, Blackwell, 1992.

This book provides an overview of recent and contemporary debates between liberal political theorists and their communitarian critics. Structured by an agenda of five key themes, it examines the work of Sandel, MacIntyre, Taylor and Walzer, and evaluates their criticisms of Rawls (both early and late), Rorty and Raz.

Mulhauser, Gregory R. Materialism and the "Problem" of Quantum Measurement. *Mind Mach*, 5(2), 207-217, My 95.

For nearly six decades, the conscious observer has played a central and essential rôle in quantum measurement theory. I outline some difficulties which the traditional account of measurement presents for material theories of mind before introducing a new development which promises to exorcise the ghost of consciousness from physics and relieve the cognitive scientist of the burden of explaining why certain material structures reduce wavefunctions by virtue of being conscious while others do not. The interactive decoherence of complex quantum systems reveals that the oddities and complexities of linear superposition and state vector reduction are irrelevant to computational aspects of the philosophy of mind and that many conclusions in related fields are ill founded.

Mullarkey, John C. Duplicity in the Flesh: Bergson and Current Philosophy of the Body. *Phil Today*, 38(4), 339-355, Wint 94.

This essay examines the conflict between the 'modernist' and 'postmodernist' conceptions of the body. The former privileges the body as a constant in a world of flux, the latter views it as the epitome of flux. My purpose is to see if this division might not be overcome by looking at Bergson and the influence his philosophy has had on Merleau-Ponty and Deleuze, the two thinkers who can be regarded as respectively paradigmatic of the modern and postmodern interpretations of the body. In Bergson's conception of corporeality, one can see both Merleau-Ponty's 'lived-body' and Deleuze's 'body without organs'. The difference, however, is that in their nascent, Bergsonian form, these conceptions of carnality coexist to the extent that each is actually the other's condition of possibility.

Mullen, John D. *Hard Thinking: The Reintroduction of Logic to Everyday Life*. Lanham, Rowman & Littlefield, 1995.

Muller, F A and Butterfield, Jeremy. Is Algebraic Lorentz-Covariant Quantum Field Theory Stochastic Einstein Local?. *Phil Sci*, 61(3), 457-474, S 94.

The general context of this paper is the locality problem in quantum theory. In a recent issue of this journal, Rédei (1991) offered a proof of the proposition that algebraic Lorentz-covariant quantum field theory is past stochastic Einstein local. We show that Rédei's proof is either spurious or circular, and that it contains two deductive fallacies. Furthermore, we prove that the mentioned theory meets the *stronger* condition of stochastic Haag locality.

Muller, Philippe. Profils d'Ernesto Grassi. *Rev Theol Phil*, 126(4), 345-352, 1994.

Ernesto Grassi, disparu en décembre 1991, s'est révélé à l'auteur par profils successifs. Tout d'abord en directeur d'une collection de poche aux éditions Rowohlt (rde) visant à mettre à disposition de l'homme moderne les grands thèmes actuels par l'exposé d'une recherche type en chaque domaine. Puis comme homme multiple, formé en Italie du début de ce siècle, se colletant aux penseurs les plus éminents, Blondel, Scheler, Jaspers, Heidegger. Ensuite comme l'avocat de l'humanisme italien, notamment de Vico, qu'il présente comme protagoniste principale du cartésianisme d'abord, du marxisme surtout. Enfin comme le découvreur d'un continent nouveau, celui d'une philosophie à hauteur d'homme centrée sur la création littéraire et artistique.

Mullet, Sheila Mason. Enseigner l'Éthique Selon le Paradigme du "Moi Moralement Relié". *Philosopher*, 16, 73-86, 1994.

The purpose of this article is to demonstrate some of the approaches to teaching ethics that can be derived from the picture of the self as essentially constituted by its relations with others. This involves a description of the 'morally connected self' and a set of strategies to elicit reflection on personal experiences of connection with others. The conclusion resides in the plausibility of the teaching techniques as a way of facilitating a greater appreciation of this interpretation of the self.

Mulligan, Kevin. "Perception" in *The Cambridge Companion to Husserl, Smith, Barry (ed)*, 168-238. New York, Cambridge Univ Pr, 1995.

This paper presents and analyzes the account of visual perception developed by Husserl. Husserl's views on nonconceptual perceptual content, perceptual objects and the primacy of dynamic perception are presented and briefly compared with views familiar from recent analytic philosophy.

Mullin, Amy. The Safeguarded Self. *Dialogue (Canada)*, 34(1), 45-59, Wint 95.

Hegel's account of the development of self-consciousness in the *Phenomenology of Spirit* is understood in terms of self-consciousness' struggle with confusion between transcendental empirical egos. In analyzing Hegel's account, Adorno's charge that Hegel is insufficiently Hegelian in remaining a "partisan of unity" is investigated.

Mulsow, Martin. Appunti sulla Fortuna di Gabriel Naudé nella Germania del Primo Illuminismo. *Stud Filosofici*, 145-156, 1991-92.

Mulvihill, James. 'Essence' and 'Accident' in Lamb's Elia Essays. *Clio*, 24(1), 37-54, Fall 94.

Mumford, Stephen. Dispositions, Bases, Overdetermination and Identities. *Ratio*, 8(1), 42-61, Ap 95.

In this paper I aim to make sense of our pre-theoretic intuitions about dispositions by presenting an argument for the identity of a disposition with its putative categorical base. The various possible ontologies for dispositions are outlined. The possibility of an empirical proof of identity is dismissed. Instead an *a priori* argument for identity is adapted from arguments in the philosophy of mind. I argue that dispositions occupy, by analytic necessity, the same causal roles that categorical bases occupy contingently and that properties with identical causal roles are identical. The validity of the argument depends upon the possibility of overdetermination of disposition manifestations being rejected. 'Ungrounded dispositions' are dismissed as not genuine dispositions. Identity conditions for dispositions and categorical bases are outlined.

Muncaster, R G and Lee, S C and Zinnes, D A. 'The Friend of My Enemy is My Enemy': Modeling Triadic Internation Relationships. *Synthese*, 100(3), 333-358, S 94.

The evolution of internation relationships is studied by means of a mathematical model based on a popular rule of triadic interaction: "the friend of my friend is my friend, the friend of my enemy is my enemy, the enemy of my enemy is my friend, the enemy of my friend is my enemy". The rule is shown to lead to the formation and preservation of unipolar and bipolar configurations of nations, with the strengths of relationships, both friendly and conflictual, intensifying through time. These results confirm speculations originally made in static, graph theoretic studies of the balancing of relationships within individuals, small groups and systems of nations.

Mundici, Daniele and Sieg, Wilfried. Paper Machines. *Phil Math*, 3(1), 5-30, Ja 95.

Machines were introduced as calculating devices to simulate operations carried out by human computers following fixed algorithms. The mathematical study of (paper) machines is the topic of our essay. The first three sections provide necessary logical background, examine the analyzes of effective calculability given in the thirties, and describe results that are central to recursion theory, reinforcing the conceptual analyses. In the final section we pursue our investigation in a quite different way and focus on principles that govern the operations of physically realizable machines.

Muñiz, Joaquín R T. Utilidad y autonomía de la dogmática jurídica. *Telos (Spain)*, 3(1), 29-47, Je 94.

This paper argues that utilitarianism has resources to understand the role of legal reasoning in backing judgments autonomously from moral reasoning. It replies a lecture Joseph Raz previously published in *Telos*, which suggested that since some options are incommensurate in value judges sometimes cannot decide on moral grounds, so that the role of legal reasoning to rule out personal preferences in those decisions cannot be recognized by utilitarianism. The paper debates some of Raz's assumptions, even confronting them with ideas expressed elsewhere by Raz himself about incommensurability, law's authority and institutional systems. It points out that avoiding arbitrariness is itself a value, so that the options favored by legal doctrine are also the ones an utilitarian judge should chose if no other can be assessed as better. Moreover, utilitarianism are not necessarily blind when examining legal justification from an internal point of view.

Munk, Linda. What Does Hegel Make of the Jews?: A Scato-Logical Reading of Kafka's *Die Verwandlung*. *Hist Euro Ideas*, 18(6), 913-925, N 94.

Munnichs, Geert. "Demokratie, Macht und Legitimität" in *Mythos Wertfreiheit?, Apel, Karl Otto (ed)*, 199-212. Frankfurt, Campus Verlag, 1994.

Muñoz Delgado, Mercedes. De cómo "el ser" devino época. *An Seminar Metaf*, 27, 181-193, 1993.

Muñoz Delgado, Vicente. El "Tractatus Consequentiarum" (1518) en la Lógica de Juan de Oria. *Rev Espan Filosof Med*, 1, 49-60, 1994.

Muñoz García, Angel. La "Confusa" Suposición Sólo Confusa. *Analogia*, 4(2), 113-141, 1990.

Partiendo de la tradicional dificultad en distinguir entre suposicion determinada y suposicion solo confusa, se estudia el problema a partir de la nocion de "descensus" para establecer sus diferencias. Se estudia asimismo las dos teorias de los semanticos medievales sobre el "descensus" de la suposicion solo confusa, al establecer unos un "descensus" disyunto, y otros copulado; teniendo en cuenta la diferencia que hay entre que un termino suponga en lugar de algo y que el termino se verifique en lugar de ello.

Muñoz García, Angel. La Partícula Medieval "Vel": Excluyente o no Excluyente?. *Analogia*, 8(1), 103-121, 1994.

Es frecuente entre los autores modernos sostener que el signo de disyuncion no excluyente "v" tiene su origen en que los autores medievales habrian habrian utilizado la particula "vel" exclusivamente para tal disyuncion, y para la excluyente otras particulas. En este trabajo se hace un recorrido por algunos medievales principales para llegar a la conclusion de que tal tesis de los modernos es insostenible. Ello es tambien ocasion para ver como entendieron los medievales la disyuncion.

Muñoz García, Angel. Proposiciones con Términos Negativos. *Rev Espan Filosof Med*, 0, 119-127, 1993.

Estudio de la negacion desde el punto de vista de la semantica medieval. Se estudian los distintos tipos de negacion-negativa, infinitante, privativay los distintos terminos a que dan origen, para pasar al estudio de las proposiciones a que dan lugar dichos terminos utilizados como Predicado de tales proposiciones, y concluir con la pregunta de si "S no es P" es equivalente o no a "S es no-P".

Muñoz Veiga, Jacobo. Más Problemas con el Realismo. *An Seminar Metaf*, 28, 27-38, 1994.

Muñoz-Alonso López, Gemma. La Crítica de Vico a Descartes. *Cuad Vico*, 2, 51-63, 1992.

Vico's references to Descartes and the Cartesians are kept constant along his work. Regardless of their opposition and also Vico's arguments against the philosophy of Descartes we think that the influence of the Cartesianism in Vico is greater than what this author would have admitted. We are trying to show in a broad approach, the position of both Vico and Descartes regarding the mathematical knowledge. This analysis will allow us a better understanding of their philosophical positions.

Munson, Ronald (ed). *Intervention and Reflection: Basic Issues in Medical Ethics (Fifth Edition)*. Belmont, Wadsworth, 1995.

Muquim, M. Rawls' Conception of a Person. *Darshana Int*, 32(1/125), 71-80, Ja 92.

This paper shows how the notion of person progresses, gets refined and how it has been woven into the network of Rawls' theory of justice. Moreover, the notion of a moral person developed in *A Theory of Justice* is based on weaker grounds as compared to Rawl's later phase, in which two moral powers are driven by two higher ordered interests. For this reason, it is plausible to hold that the later account of basic liberties and primary goods in terms of moral persons is definitely an improvement in the Rawlsian system.

Muray, Leslie A. Introduction: Thinking Seriously About Issues of Importance as Jews and Christians. *Process Stud*, 22(4), 191-193, Winter 93.

Murdock, Nancy L and Baer, Barbara E. Nonerotic Dual Relationships Between Therapists and Clients: The Effects of Sex, Theoretical Orientation, and Interpersonal Boundaries. *Ethics Behavior*, 5(2), 131-145, 1995.

We surveyed 223 APA members to investigate the roles of therapists' sex, theoretical orientation, interpersonal boundaries, and clients' sex in predicting therapists' assessments of the ethicality of nonerotic dual relationships with their clients. Results indicated that therapists' sex, interpersonal boundaries, and theoretical orientation influenced ethical judgments of these relationships. Theoretical and practical implications of our findings are discussed.

Murillo, Ildefonso. El Lenguaje Sobre Dios en Juan Escoto Eriúgena. *Rev Espan Filosof Med*, 0, 129-142, 1993.

John Scotus Eriugena succeeded in posing with rigor and depth the question about the language on God. After making a short mention to some assumptions that strongly condition his point of view, this article limits itself to present an overall view of his manner of posing and solving the question.

Murphree, Wallace A. The Irrelevance of Distribution for the Syllogism. *Notre Dame J Form Log*, 35(3), 433-449, Sum 94.

While accepting that distribution is a coherent notion, I argue that it is nevertheless irrelevant to the working of the syllogism. Instead, I propose: 1) that a term's being distributed or undistributed in a proposition is its capacity to be replaced in a truth-preserving substitution with a narrower or a wider term; 2) that which capacity the term has is determined by whether it occurs as the predicate of a negative or of an affirmative statement of the proposition; and 3) that it is only the term's occurrence as the predicate of a negative or an affirmative statement—rather than its distribution value—that is relevant to syllogistic entailment.

Murphy, Frank J. The Problem of Evil and a Plausible Defence. *Relig Stud*, 31(2), 243-250, Je 95.

This paper argues that God may create and exist in any possible world, no matter how much suffering of any sort that world includes. It combines the traditional free will defense with the notion of an 'occasion' for good or evil action and limits God's responsibility to the creation of these occasions. Since no possible world contains occasions for more evil than good action, God is morally permitted to create any possible world. With regard to suffering that is not due to free will, namely the suffering of beings who are not moral agents, the paper questions the idea that the relief of such suffering is a moral problem.

Murphy, James B. Language, Communication, and Representation in the Semiotic of John Poinsot. *Thomist*, 58(4), 569-598, O 94.

Language may be viewed either as a medium of communication, as in pragmatics, or as a system of representations, as in semantics. After exploring each of these models of language, I try to locate language within the larger domain of sign-systems. By examining the *Treatise on Signs* of John Poinsot, I show that whereas all sign-systems are representational, only a few serve as media of communication. Representation is logically prior to communication.

Murphy, Jeffrie G. "Some Ruminations on Women, Violence, and the Criminal Law" in *In Harm's Way, Coleman, Jules L (ed)*, 209-230. New York, Cambridge Univ Pr, 1994.

Murphy, John W and Callaghan, Karen A and Choi, Jung Min. *The Politics of Culture: Race, Violence, and Democracy*. Westport, Praeger, 1995.

The protests in Los Angeles during the spring of 1992 signaled that the United States is a troubled society. Specifically, although American society is becoming increasingly diverse, many people are not close to experiencing democracy. Certain powerful interests constrict the American policy in very important ways. Clearly stated, conservatives have manipulated symbols and other cultural factors to maintain social control. Postmodernism exposes the limitations of the conservative project while introducing a new mode of order conducive to sustaining a democratic society.

Murphy, Julien. "Beauvoir and the Algerian War: Toward a Postcolonial Ethics" in *Feminist Interpretations of Simone de Beauvoir, Simons, Margaret A (ed)*, 263-297. University Park, Penn St Univ Pr, 1995.

Beauvoir's coauthored book, Djamila *Boupacha*, though relatively obscure, calls attention to her writings about the Algerian war. I argue three points: that the war was catalytic for her political consciousness; that the theme of decolonization in Algeria is often missing from scholarly accounts on Beauvoir, and its absence alters how her work is read and understood; and that a radical notion of freedom and a deconstruction of identities is implicit in her Algerian writings. The sense of freedom that emerges is more nuanced that the discussions in *The Ethics of Ambiguity* and better able to address the complexities of postcolonialism.

Murphy, Julien S. *The Constructed Body: AIDS, Reproductive Technology, and Ethics*. Albany, SUNY Pr, 1995.

This collection of essays contributes to new directions in medical ethics by using recent philosophical theories, such as phenomenology, deconstruction, and post-structuralism, to allow for the influences of politics, cultural difference, and history on ethics. Four chapters are on the AIDS epidemic and address issues of AIDS phobia, ethical issues for women with AIDS, society's responsiblity toward children with AIDS, and the penalization of the body with AIDS. Three chapters address controversial issues in reproductive technology, such as: sustaining pregnancy in brain-dead women, feminist arguments on ectogenesis, and the search for a feminist health care ethics.

Murphy, Mark C. Acceptance of Authority and the Duty to Comply with Just Institutions: A Comment on Waldron. *Phil Pub Affairs*, 23(3), 271-277, Sum 94.

Jeremy Waldron has recently defended a natural duty account of political obligation, on which the authoritativeness of institutions derives from their being necessary for implementation of the demands of justice. I argue against Waldron's view that it is unclear whether natural duty accounts show that justice requires that we comply with our governing institutions, or that justice requires that we bind ourselves to such compliance.

Murphy, Mark C. Philosophical Anarchism and Legal Indifference. *Amer Phil Quart*, 32(2), 195-198, Ap 95.

Philosophical anarchism is the thesis that there is no reason to obey the law as such. *Legal indifference* is the thesis that obedience to law is as much in need of justification as disobedience to law is. It is sometimes held that the legal indifference thesis is a consequence of the philosophical anarchism thesis. The aim of this paper is to show that the most straightforward and plausible way of establishing an implication from philosophical anarchism to legal indifference does not succeed. Indeed, there are grounds for believing that even if philosophical anarchism is true, disobedience to law is more in need of justification than obedience to law is.

Murphy, Mark C. Was Hobbes a Legal Positivist?. *Ethics*, 105(4), 846-873, Jl 95.

In this paper I challenge the prevailing consensus that Hobbes's account of civil law in *Leviathan* is a variety of legal positivism rather than a natural law account. Hobbes endorses the distinctive natural law thesis that there can be no conflict between natural and civil law, and he explains the necessary consistency of natural and civil law in the same way that Aquinas does, disagreeing with Aquinas only with respect to their accounts of goods. If Hobbes's account of goods does not preclude his theory of law from being a genuine natural law theory—and I argue that it does not—then Hobbes's jurisprudential view should be classified as a variety of natural law theory rather than a version of legal positivism.

Murphy, Patrick E and Enderle, Georges. Managerial Ethical Leadership: Examples Do Matter. *Bus Ethics Quart*, 5(1), 117-128, Ja 95.

The central role of corporate leaders in setting the ethical tone for their organization is widely accepted. Four well known former CEOs are profiled to illustrate how their managerial ethical leadership not only influenced their firms but also the practice of business. Insights are drawn from their writings and speeches as well as other sources which examine demonstrated leadership abilities. Their behavior not only provides examples of leadership but also is exemplary from an ethical point of view. The article concludes with five common themes that describe these individuals and the essence of managerial ethical leadership.

Murphy, Timothy F. "Homosex/Ethics" in *Gay Ethics, Murphy, Timothy F (ed)*, 9-25. New York, Haworth Pr, 1994.

Against the view that homoeroticism requires any special justification or consideration, this essay argues that homoeroticism is morally unproblematic in itself and that its genuine moral significance resides in illuminating the nature and meaning of human relations. Seen as a form of language, homosex shares common moral justification with heterosex as a bearer of human meanings and intentions. Thus understood, homosex is an important moral good as a language that expresses human meanings in ways that are not otherwise possible.

Murphy, Timothy F (ed). *Gay Ethics*. New York, Haworth Pr, 1994.

Murphy, Timothy F. Health Care Workers with HIV and a Patient's Right To Know. *J Med Phil*, 19(6), 553-569, D 94.

Accidental human immunodeficiency virus (HIV) infection of patients in health care settings raises the question about whether patients have a right to expect disclosure of HIV/AIDS diagnoses by their health workers. Although such a right—and the correlative duty to disclose—might appear justified by reason of standards of informed consent, I argue that such standards should only apply to questions of risks of and barriers to HIV infection involved in a particular medical treatment, not to disclosure of personal diagnoses. Because the degree of risk of HIV infection is low and disclosure would also have damaging consequences for health workers, and because patient protection is available in other ways, it is argued that no such generalized right should be recognized.

Murphy, Timothy F and Walters, LeRoy. The Moral Significance of AIDS. *J Med Phil*, 19(6), 519-524, D 94.

Murray, James Stuart. Interpreting Plato on Sophistic Claims and the Provenance of the "Socratic Method". *Phoenix*, 48(2), 115-134, Sum 94.

This paper seeks to demonstrate that recent trends in scholarship dealing with sophistic methodology and pedagogy are incorrect and misleading when they present Plato's portrayal of sophistic claims to be able to "answer any question" and to "speak more briefly than anyone" as evidence that the sophists "invented" the "Socratic method". An analysis of the Platonic testimony shows clearly that, for Plato at least, there exists no confusion between the work of Socrates and the methods of his sophistic contemporaries.

Murray, John Courtney and Hooper, J Leon (ed). *Bridging the Sacred and the Secular*. Washington, Georgetown Univ Pr, 1994.

This collection highlights Murray's 1940s and 1960s writings on various public and ecclesial issues and is meant to supplement the 1950s essays in his *We Hold These Truth*. Its ordering and introductions focus on the relationship of philosophical and theological knowledge. Whereas *WHTT* presumes a sharp distinction (if not dichotomy) between philosophy and theology, these essays explore common grounds between them—the earlier within the methods of canonical Scholasticism, the later in terms of common social environments and cognitional operations. At issue is the ethics of bringing specific religious beliefs to the determination of public policy.

Murray, Michael J. Leibniz on Divine Foreknowledge of Future Contingents and Human Freedom. *Phil Phenomenol Res*, 55(1), 75-108, Mr 95.

This essay examines Leibniz's views on divine providence and human freedom against the background of the competing views of his day. It is argued that Leibniz develops a unique position according to which a sufficient reason for free acts is found in dispositions of the intellect and will. It is these dispositions which account for the choice and also provide the means by which God can foreknow the free choices of a creature. Nonetheless, Leibniz argues that these dispositions neither metaphysically nor physically necessitate choice but only necessitate them "morally", a modality he borrows from seventeenth century scholasticism.

Murray, Michael J and Dudrick, David F. Are Coerced Acts Free?. *Amer Phil Quart*, 32(2), 109-123, Ap 95.

This article begins by describing a conception of coercion that differs from other accounts in the literature. The account offered is, it is argued, indifferent between libertarian and compatibilist accounts of freedom. The article then discusses the way in which the libertarian rendering of "could have done otherwise" applies to coerced act as characterized, concluding that such acts should be counted as free. The final section of the article contains a discussion of how such a libertarian might address the objection that, on this account, one should be held morally responsible for all acts performed under coercion.

Murray, Michael J and Meyers, Kurt. Ask and It Will Be Given to You. *Relig Stud*, 30(3), 311-330, S 94.

The practice of petitionary prayer raises a number of philosophical problems for the Christian theistic tradition. This paper addresses two of those problems. First, why is it that God would choose to make the distribution of earthly blessings contingent on the believer's recognition of her needs and her requests that God make provision for them? Second, why would God, as the Christian tradition holds, command human creatures to pray for the needs of others? It is argued that the first can be justified by the fact that petitionary prayer can act as a powerful deterrent against idolatry for the believer. In addition, individual petitionary prayer allows the believer to learn more about divine purposes and the divine will. The second, corporate prayer, can be justified by the fact that it serves to foster an essential interdependence among the members of the community of praying believers.

Murray, Patrick T. *The Development of German Aesthetic Theory from Kant to Schiller: A Philosophical Commentary on Schiller's Aesthetic Education of Man (1795)*. Lewiston, Mellen Pr, 1994.

Murray, Thomas H. "Medical Ethics, Moral Philosophy and Moral Tradition" in *Medicine and Moral Reasoning, Fulford, K W M (ed)*, 91-105. New York, Cambridge Univ Pr, 1994.

This article describes difficulties encountered by theory-driven models of moral reasoning (deductivist models) for practical moral reasoning. It examines an alternative-reasoning about cases of conscience (casuistry). Contemporary discussions about casuistry often fail to distinguish between two meanings of the term: 1) as immersion in the particularity of specific cases or problems coupled with the inescapable need for interpretation, and 2) as a claim about the relation between moral judgment and moral theory as sources of moral knowledge. Attentiveness to particulars and careful interpretation are indispensable elements of practical moral analysis. The second meaning of casuistry—moral judgments as sources of moral knowledge—suggest a more nuanced understanding of the role of moral traditions in practical moral reasoning.

Murthy, Viren. Universals and Infinite Modes in the Thought of Spinoza. *Dialogue (PST)*, 37(2-3), 48-56, Ap 95.

Murty, A Rama. Comments on Jayashanmukham's "The Tryambaka Mantra: Its Meaning and Significance". *J Indian Counc Phil Res*, 11(3), 111-112, My-Ag 94.

Muscari, Paul G. The Depersonalization of Creativity. *J Mind Behav*, 15(4), 311-322, Autumn 94.

Since much of modern discourse, extending from cognitivism to connectionism has been greatly inclined to look at human behavior in relation to processes where the subjective factor plays little if any causal role, it would not be inaccurate to say that the person has been left with but a trivial part to play in the overall script. The intent of this paper is to address this theoretical disproportionality by offering a more symmetrical account of creativity—one that reconsiders the reconstructive nature and generative capabilities of the person while not ignoring the contributions of technical and scientific thought.

Musschenga, A W. Identity and Quality of Life (in Dutch). *Tijdschr Filosof*, 56(4), 643-666, D 94.

In several publications Charles Taylor makes a distinction between 'strong' and 'weak' evaluations. Strong evaluations are qualitative distinctions—in terms of 'noble', 'demeaning', etc. Weak evaluators evaluate desires only on the basis of their strength and intensity. The ethical theory par excellence that is not capable of making qualitative distinctions, is for Taylor utilitarianism. After having explored the meaning of the concept of strong evaluations, I analyze Taylor's argument for that critique on utilitarianism. I argue that qualitative distinctions cannot be built into a utilitarian theory. However, not all utilitarians are weak evaluators. More sophisticated utilitarians evaluate desires by their contribution to a rational life-plan. They do have an identity, but it is not a moral one. My conclusion is that what Taylor really means is that utilitarians are not able to articulate their identity. (edited)

Musschenga, Bert. "Liberal Neutrality and the Justification of Environmental Conservation" in *Ecology, Technology, and Culture,* Zweers, Wim (ed), 164-174. Cambridge, White Horse, 1994.

In this contribution I discuss whether a neutral, nonperfectionistic, liberal justification of environmental preservation is possible. In justifying the preservation of species which are of no direct interest for human beings, one cannot do without the concept of intrinsic value. That nonhuman natural entities can have intrinsic value is a metaphysical belief. Justifications using that concept are perfectionistic: they conflict with the principle of political neutrality conceived as neutrality of aim. The core of the liberal idea of neutrality however is not neutrality of aim but fundamental or constitutional neutrality. Political neutrality, however, is not implied by constitutional neutrality.

Musse, Ricardo. The Heirs of German Idealism (in Portuguese). *Trans/Form/Acao*, 17, 31-37, 1994.

This article evaluates the pertinence of Engel's lemma according to which Marxism is the "heir of German idealism" in Lukác's, Horkheimer's and Adorno's theories. While Lukács considers the Marxist method as springing from the Hegelian philosophy and Horkheimer explicitly assumes the Kantian legacy, Adorno does not intend to be himself the heir, but the critic of the German idealism.

Muthoo, Abhinay. A Bargaining Model with Players' Perceptions on the Retractability of Offers. *Theor Decis*, 38(1), 85-98, Ja 95.

This paper studies a generalization of Rubinstein's bargaining model with retractable offers. The model incorporates and parameterizes the bargainers' perceptions on the retractability of offers. Our key result characterizes the limiting set of perfect equilibria as the time interval between two consecutive offers tends to zero. In this limit, for any possible players' perceptions on the retractability of offers such that at least one of the players perceives that there is at least a small chance that offers may be retractable, the bargaining game possesses a continuum of perfect equilibria.

Myers, Peter C. Equality, Property, and the Problem of Partisanship: The Lockean Constitution as Mixed Regime. *Interpretation*, 22(1), 39-64, Fall 94.

Myers, Richard. Montesquieu on the Causes of Roman Greatness. *Hist Polit Thought*, 16(1), 37-47, Spr 95.

This article examines Montesquieu's account of the causes of Rome's "greatness" in the first chapter of the *Considerations sur la grandeur et decadence des romains*. The article focuses on Montesquieu's discussion of the "principle" of the Roman regime. In *The Spirit of the Laws*, Montesquieu would subsequently argue that every regime has a unique principle or spirit that is of decisive importance for everything it does. Here in the *Considerations*, Montesquieu argues that as a result of a number of historical particularities, the Roman regime was based on the principle of "war." It is the emergence of this principle that accounts for Rome's ultimate greatness. This article considers the implications of Montesquieu's discussion of the principle of war. It is argued that Montesquieu finds here a response to the Machiavellian argument that founders must strive to imitate Rome in order to avoid imitating Rome's victims. If Rome's greatness was based on a highly idiosyncratic principle, future Romes are unlikely. We are therefore free to build liberal regimes devoted to freedom and commerce.

Myers, Robert H. On the Explanation, the Justification, and the Interpretation of Action. *Nous*, 29(2), 212-231, Je 95.

I begin by arguing that, given the internalist thesis about reasons for action and a dispositional analysis of goals and desires, the only way to avoid the instrumentalist conclusion that people's reasons depend on their desires is to adopt a Davidsonian conception of what desires are. I then go on to consider whether the Davidsonian conception of desire offers any particular support to moralism, the view that people's

AUTHOR INDEX WITH ABSTRACTS 665 Narveson, Jan

reasons for action are primarily determined by the demands that morality directs at them. I conclude that it does not because, while it shows that some values must be both objective and universal, it does not show that any must be agent-neutral.

Myers, William. Toward a Universalist Ethics. *Dialogue Hum*, 3(2), 125-137, 1993.

Myro, George. "On the Distinctness of the Mental and the Physical" in *The Mind-Body Problem: A Guide to the Current Debate, Warner, Richard (ed)*, 329-342. Cambridge, Blackwell, 1994.

NABER Report. Report on Human Cloning through Embryo Splitting: An Amber Light. *Kennedy Inst Ethics J*, 4(3), 251-282, S 94.

Naddaf, Gerard. Mind and Progress in Plato. *Polis*, 12(1-2), 122-133, 1993.

In this paper I examine Plato's position on the origin of the universe from a perspective that few commentators discuss, that is, his position on the subject of investigation and discovery, on humanity's development or progress to use a more current term. I show that Plato's position on the subject is one of ambivalence and perplexity, one of a philosopher torn in two directions due to his difficulty in coming to terms with how human *nous* (intelligence), and *techne* (art and/or science) originate and develop. This helps explain why his position on the origin of the universe is so difficult, if not impossible, to determine.

Naddaf, Gerard. The Atlantis Myth: An Introduction to Plato's Later Philosophy of History. *Phoenix*, 48(3), 189-209, Autumn 94.

This paper aims to show that although the Atlantis story is purely Plato's invention, he intends it to be taken quite seriously. The story may be considered a sort of preamble to the foundation of a new constitution—the one proposed for the future city of Magnesia in the *Laws*. Although "second best" if one were to compare it to the *ariste politeia* of the *Republic* (or to the constitution of the Primeval Athens of the Atlantis story which amounts to the same thing), is nevertheless the best possible constitution when one takes into consideration the conditions of existence here on earth. I demonstrate that Plato's philosophy of history is not negative but positive, for it contains the solution to humanity's future well-being both on earth and the afterlife.

Nadeau, Robert and Kafatos, Menas. *The Conscious Universe: Part and Whole in Modern Physical Theory*. New York, Springer-Verlag, 1990.

This work builds on Bohr's principle of complementarity to show that it forms a generalized framework to understand the universe. The authors build the thesis that complementarity can be involved in cosmological theories of the universe and in constructions of all human realities. Moreover, the book concludes by making the case that consciousness can no longer be divorced from the way science operates and that this realization entails a new way of understanding the universe.

Nadel, Mark E. Scott Heights of Abelian Groups. *J Sym Log*, 59(4), 1351-1359, D 94.

Nadler, Steven. Choosing a Theodicy: The Leibniz-Malebranche-Arnauld Connection. *J Hist Ideas*, 55(4), 573-589, O 94.

A comparison of Malebranche and Leibniz on the theodicy issue in the light of Arnauld's critique of Malebranche. The main question concerns the preservation of divine omnipotence.

Nadler, Steven. Dualism and Occasionalism. *Rev Int Phil*, 48(190), 421-439, 1994.

An examination of the way in which Arnauld uses occasionalism to resolve what he takes to be a mind-body problem facing Cartesian dualism; and how this represents an important stage in the development of the 17th century Cartesianism.

Nagasawa, Kunihiko. Intellektuelle Anschauung und Dialektik. *Fichte-Studien*, 6, 35-44, 1994.

Dieser Aufsatz analysiert zunächst Fichtes Begriff der intellektuellen Anschauung vor allem anhand der *zweiten Einleitung* und des ersten Paragraphs der *Grundlage der gesamten Wissenschaftslehre*, erörtert dann die Besonderheit des transzendentalen Denkens in der Wissenschaftslehre (WL) und zeigt anschliessend, dass Fichtes WL mit Hegels dialektischer Spekulation nicht vereinbar ist.

Nagel, Chris. Sexualities: Merleau-Ponty and Foucault on the Meaning of Sex. *Int Stud Phil*, 27(1), 63-71, 1995.

This essay argues that Merleau-Ponty's phenomenology of sexual transcendence may be too easily opposed to Foucault's discovery of the discourse of sexuality produced by power-knowledge. The ordinary, impoverished interpretations of their views open each to criticism which miss the point of their views. Instead of opposing phenomenology to post-structuralism, Merleau-Ponty and Foucault lead us back to renewed articulations of the meaning of sexuality.

Nagel, Thomas. "Consciousness and Objective Reality" in *The Mind-Body Problem: A Guide to the Current Debate, Warner, Richard (ed)*, 63-68. Cambridge, Blackwell, 1994.

Nagel, Thomas. *Other Minds: Critical Essays 1969-1994*. New York, Oxford Univ Pr, 1995.

Nagl-Docekal, Herta. "Das Institut für Philosophie der Universität Wien: Der Status quo und seine Genese" in *Der geistige Anschluss, Fischer, Kurt R (ed)*, 206-220. Wien, WUV Univ, 1993.

Nagl-Docekal, Herta. Ist Fürsorglichkeit mit Gleichbehandlung unvereinbar?. *Deut Z Phil*, 42(6), 1045-1050, 1994.

The paper discusses Axel Honneth's thesis that "equal treatment" and "care" are mutually exclusive moral principles. Objecting to both reasons given for this thesis, the paper argues 1) that care does not necessarily jeopardize autonomy, and 2) that the ideal of "symmetry" does not adequately represent our common understanding of "morality": we see it as our duty to respect and provide, as far as possible, aid to others even if they fail to treat us in the same manner. Drawing upon the concept of "duties of love" as formulated in Kant's *Groundwork*, the paper explains that care is an indispensable element rather than "the other" of equal treatment.

Naik, A D. Springe's Argument for Absolute Idealism. *Darshana Int*, 32(4/128), 36-44, O 92.

On the basis of a number of possibly effective objections it is concluded that the argument does not seem to work. To the temporal, spatial and experiential relations offered as examples of strongly holistic relations which may suggest that reality is a comprehensive experiential whole counter examples are offered. Other nonholistic logical and ontological relations are also offered as counter examples. It is argued that what is required is a general argument that all relations are strongly holistic, or that one special one is. It is also concluded that the argument is not independent of that for panpsychism.

Nakasone, Ronald Y. A Buddhist Reflection on the Task of Elders. *Cambridge Quart Healthcare Ethics*, 4(2), 167-171, Spr 95.

The Japanese Buddhists revere in elders the spiritual quality of *Kyogai* "one's station in life." Kyogai suggests a fullness of life that comes from living in a transient and interdependent world. The task for elders is to integrate the countless causes and conditions of the past and present that impacted their lives and to discover new dimensions for spiritual explorations in the circumstances they find themselves. The presence of ease and equanimity characterizes such elders who manifest an authentic kyogai. Elders have a responsibility to cultivate their kyogai and be mentors for the young.

Nandy, Ashis. History's Forgotten Doubles. *Hist Theor*, 34(2), 44-66, 1995.

The historical mode may be the dominant mode of constructing the past in most parts of the globe but it is certainly not the most popular mode of doing so. The dominance is derived from the links the idea of history has established with the modern nation-state, the secular worldview, the Baconian concept of scientific rationality, nineteenth-century theories of progress, and, in recent decades, development. This dominance has also been strengthened by the absence of any radical critique of the idea of history within the modern world and for that matter, within the discipline of history itself. As a result, once exported to the nonmodern world, historical consciousness has not only tended to absolutize the past in cultures that have lived with open-ended concepts of the past or depended on myths, legends, and epics to define their cultural selves, it has also made the historical worldview complicit with many new forms of violence, exploitation, and satanism in our times and helped rigidify civilizational, cultural, and national boundaries.

Napoli, Ernesto. (Direct) Reference. *J Phil Log*, 24(3), 321-339, Je 95.

Narayan, Uma. "Male-Order" Brides: Immigrant Women, Domestic Violence, and Immigration Law. *Hypatia*, 10(1), 104-119, Wint 95.

This essay analyzes why women whose immigration status is dependent on their marriage face higher risks of domestic violence than women who are citizens and explores the factors that collude to prevent acknowledgment of their greater susceptibility to battering. It criticizes elements of current US immigration policy that are detrimental to the welfare of battered immigrant women, and argues for changes that would make immigration policy more sensitive to their plight.

Narayan, Uma. Colonialism and Its Others: Considerations On Rights and Care Discourses. *Hypatia*, 10(2), 133-140, Spr 95.

I point to a colonial care discourse that enabled colonizers to define themselves in relationship to "inferior" colonized subjects. The colonized, however, had very different accounts of this relationship. While contemporary care discourse correctly insists on acknowledging human needs and relationships, it needs to worry about who defines these often contested terms. I conclude that improvements along dimensions of care and of justice provide "enabling conditions" for each other.

Narayana, Sampat. Does Mimamsa Treat the Theory of *Karma* as a *Purvapaksa*?: Two Responses to the Query. *J Indian Counc Phil Res*, 12(1), 163-164, S-D 94.

In the Mimamsa Sutras as well as in the Bhasya a question was raised as to whom the result of an action goes to—the agent who actually performs it or to the person who orders the performance on his behalf. The karma theory posits that the result of an action always goes to the performer. In Purvamimamsa the performer invariably is a Rtvik who is bought by the sacrificer for doing the act. In that school the result of actions go to—1) the sacrificer, 2) the sacrificer and the performer, and 3) the performer. There is an apparent contradiction here and hence clarification was sought. Answer given in the article is that karma theory is not opposed to the Purvamimamsa, and that intention and desire are the deciding factors for the accrual of results of actions.

Narbonne, Jean-Marc. La notion de puissance dans son rapport à la *causa sui* chez les stoïciens et dans la philosophie de Spinoza. *Arch Phil*, 58(1), 35-53, Ja-Mr 95.

The Stoics and Spinoza developing a concept of similar power that may be called an active power, opposed to Aristotelian potentiality, are led to conceive their God according to a similar schema of immanence where the first principle, by acting on itself, simultaneously acts upon the world. This action on self, improperly called *causa sui*, is required in all immanentist systems, and appears to be incompatible with individual *causa sui*, that is to say, with human liberty.

Narveson, Jan. "Deserving Profits" in *Profits and Morality, Cowan, Robin (ed)*, 48-87. Chicago, Univ of Chicago Pr, 1995.

Desert is distinguished from entitlement, and the latter defended in the case of market exchanges. The claims that profits are not deserved, or at least that large ones aren't, are founded mainly on Rawlsian or Marxian arguments; both are shown to be entirely mistaken. Desert is determined by the interests of those who control what is to be distributed; thus not only hard work, but natural talent, etc., are perfectly capable of counting as merits toward desert. Investments come under the same analysis, and profits from them can reasonably be said, sometimes, to be deserved.

Narveson, Jan. Resources and Environmental Policy. *Phil Exch*, 24-25, 39-61, 1993-94.

This paper is a partly empirical and partly conceptual inquiry into the notion of resources. Current "Environmentalists" evidently think of resources as *natural*, identifying them with quantities of *stuff*—oil, say, or land. And they suppose that such resources must be finite in amount and therefore scarce, so that when we use any of these we leave less left—less for others. This way of thinking is, I argue, *entirely wrong*. Resources for people are not finite; they expand with human thought and effort, without upper limit. There are no global shortages of anything that we have to worry about, nothing requiring the imposition of extra-market controls on our use of the stuff of the world. All environmental policies based on such premises are consequently ill-conceived, and bound to work only harm.

Narveson, Jan. The Agreement to Keep Our Agreements: Hume, Prichard, and Searle. *Phil Papers*, 23(2), 75-87, Ag 94.

The idea that there is a sort of "general agreement" (say, "social contract") to keep our particular agreements is supported against important criticisms by Hume; a suggestion by Prichard along this line is taken up and proposed to be meaningful; and Searle's famed argument that promising gets us from "is" to "ought" is rebutted. The paper argues that a general agreement to keep particular agreements should be understood as community support for local promising transactions.

Natadecha-Sponsel, Poranee and Sponsel, Leslie E. "The Potential Contribution of Buddhism in Developing an Environmental Ethic..." in *Ethics, Religion and Biodiversity, Hamilton, Lawrence S (ed)*, 75-97. Cambridge, White Horse, 1994.

The environmental ideas, actions, and consequences of Buddhism in Thailand are explored. While environmental ethics for a sustainable society are inherent in Buddhism, Westernization has weakened Thai adherence to Buddhism. Only when the actions of the populace adhere more closely to the ideals of Buddhism is the environmental crisis likely to be resolved or at least reduced in Thailand. Some hope is offered by forest monks who have applied Buddhist principles as environmental activitists. In recent years they have provided leadership among villagers to try to conserve some of the remaining forest and restore some of the deforested areas.

Natale, Samuel M (ed) and Rothschild, Brian M (ed). *Values, Work, Education: The Meanings of Work*. Amsterdam, Rodopi, 1995.

Natali, Carlo. "Azioni ed eventi in Aristotele" in *L'etica e il suo Altro, Vigna, Carmelo (ed)*, 93-125. Milano, FrancoAngeli, 1994.

Natali, Monica. Tra stoicismo e platonismo: concezione della filosofia e del fine ultimo dell'uomo in Seneca. *Riv Filosof Neo-Scolas*, 86(3), 427-447, Jl-S 94.

Nathan, N M L. The Multiplication of Utility. *Utilitas*, 6(2), 217-218, N 94.

Nathanson, Stephen. Nationalism, Patriotism, and Toleration. *Filozof Istraz*, 14(2-3), 375-391, 1994.

The thesis of the author is that nationalism and patriotism (which are treated as equivalent for the purposes of the paper) can only be morally legitimate if they are constrained by a commitment to the ideal of toleration. The author points out that there are degrees of nationalist commitment. He discusses and rejects the views of nationalism which make it fanatical and immoral by definition. Nationalism as such is allowed by morality; the question—which parallels the questions about self-interest and family loyalty—is how, by what means, one goes about promoting it. There are certain moral constraints on all such pursuits. (edited)

Nathanson, Stephen. *The Ideal of Rationality: A Defense, within Reason (Revised Edition)*. Peru, Open Court, 1994.

Naticchia, Chris. Kant on the Third Antinomy, Is Freedom Possible in a World of Natural Necessity?. *Hist Phil Quart*, 11(4), 393-403, O 94.

I argue that, despite impressions to the contrary, Kant defends the claim that freedom is conceptually possible, that there is no contradiction between it and nature, not that it is ontologically possible. Freedom is conceptually possible, according to Kant, because it and nature are predicates of different grammatical subjects, noumena and phenomena, respectively. I then defend an explanation of why Kant offers more argumentation than strictly necessary for establishing this conclusion: our ability to endorse rules of conduct provides evidential weight for believing transcendental subjects likelier than transcendental objects to possess transcendental freedom. I reject Beck's speculation that Kant would otherwise be committed to the absurd view that, in order to conceive of freedom anywhere, he must conceive of its possibility everywhere. He is still committed to this view, I argue, but it is not as absurd as Beck supposes.

Natsoulas, Thomas. An Introduction to Reflective Seeing: Part II. *J Mind Behav*, 15(4), 351-374, Autumn 94.

After two sections of background information regarding a) some views of inner (second-order consciousness, ancient, modern, and present-day, and b) some recent deployments of James J Gibson's ecological approach to visual perception relevant to our understanding of reflective seeing, I present my own view of reflective seeing for the remainder of the present article. Although I include detailed references to Edmund Husserl's conception of straightforward perceptual consciousness and reflective perceptual consciousness, the present article is not about Husserl. Rather, I use quotations from and about Husserl to add resonance and depth to my own conception of the complex psychological process that is reflective seeing—particularly, the stream of perceptual consciousness that is a product and a part of it, that flows at the heart of reflective seeing. It will be evident that I very largely agree with the Husserl material which I use. And I do not take that space to bring out any disagreements that I might have with him. Thus, this article has as its main purpose making known, in an introductory way, just one, my own, view of reflective seeing.

Natsoulas, Thomas. Consciousness and Commissurotomy: VI Evidence for Normal Dual Consciousness?. *J Mind Behav*, 16(2), 181-205, Spr 95.

This article addresses the problem of evidence for Puccetti's hypothesis of normal dual consciousness, i.e., the hypothesis that a stream of consciousness flows in each cerebral hemisphere when both are functioning normally in intact, healthy people. Evidence counts as supportive only if it is not explainable by a certain close alternative hypothesis that holds consciousness to proceed in the nondominant hemisphere only when the dominant hemisphere is unable to inhibit it (e.g., complete commissurotomy, dominant hemispherectomy, dominant anesthesia). From this perspective, I discuss 1) Two experiments involving anesthesia of the dominant hemisphere that were proposed, respectively, by Wilson and Puccetti, 2) An actual experiment on normal, unanesthetized subjects reported by Landis, Graves, and Goodglass, as well as 3) A further kind of experiment which, I suggest, may discriminate between the hypotheses. Assuming Puccetti is right, this experiment

should yield a distinct pattern of reports from the dominant hemisphere about its experiences of acting as the individual deals with different kinds of tasks ("nondominant" vs "dominant"). Also considered is the stream, never two distinct experiences at the same time. I argue, in support of Puccetti, that this is as it should be because introspection-at-a-distance is impossible; privileged access is internal to a stream, never occurs between streams.

Natsoulas, Thomas. On the Distinction Between the Object and Content of Consciousness. *J Mind Behav*, 15(3), 239-264, Sum 94.

This article treats of the distinction between objects and contents of pulses of consciousness—those minimal temporal sections of James's stream that give veridical or nonveridical consciousness of, or as though of, something, which can be anything perceivable, feelable, imaginable, thinkable, or internally apprehensible. I argue *inter alia* 1) that not all pulses of consciousness have objects, though James holds that they all possess cognitive content; 2) that centaurs can be neither objects nor contents of consciousness, since they do not, have not, and will not exist; and 3) that some hallucinations whose objects are not physically present have objects anyway, such as a long lost relative or a historical figure. (edited)

Natsoulas, Thomas. The Concept of Consciousness$_4$: The Reflective Meaning. *J Theor Soc Behav*, 24(4), 373-400, D 94.

In this article, which is fourth in a series of six articles, I address the fourth concept of consciousness that the *Oxford English Dictionary* ("the OED") defines in its six main entries under the word *consciousness*. I first introduce this fourth concept, the concept of consciousness$_4$, by a) identifying the previous three OED concepts of consciousness, which I have already discussed in this series of articles, and b) by indicating how that to which we make reference, respectively, by means of those three concepts is related to the referents of the concept of consciousness$_4$. I then address the latter concept more directly by pursuing for the remainder of the article where the OED's fourth entry leads. Among other things, I am led to consider two competing accounts of consciousness$_4$ that figure prominently in the OED entry, namely the intrinsic, self-intimational account of William Hamilton and the inner-eye, perceptionlike account of John Locke. Both kinds of account are very much with us today.

Natsoulas, Thomas. The Concept of Consciousness$_5$: The Unitive Meaning. *J Theor Soc Behav*, 24(4), 401-424, D 94.

This is the fifth of a series of six articles examining respectively the six concepts of consciousness identified in the main entries of the *Oxford English Dictionary* under the word. I call the concept of consciousness$_5$ the unitive meaning because it is said to refer to the totality of mental-occurrence instances that constitute a person's conscious being. The present article consists mainly of an effort to answer the question of which totality of mental-occurrence instances it is to which the fifth concept refers. Four possible answers are considered, and the fourth, derived from Locke, is found to capture best the dictionary's meaning. (edited)

Naumann-Beyer, Waltraud. Annäherung an Derrida oder: Wer spät kommt, den belohnt das Lesen. *Deut Z Phil*, 42(1), 15-33, 1994.

The aim of the paper is to show that postmetaphysical thinking in a wider, transdiscursive sense is not necessarily relevant for the decision between either Derrida or Habermas, either deconstruction or communication of the "heterogeneous". The paper indicates the applicability of Derrida's approach not only to poetic texts but also the philosophical and political topics: it points out the fertility of the "logic of supplement" for an understanding of the other without identification. The point in question here is, how the incommensurability of modern philosophical issues and languages can be connected with one's own "self". One of the most revealing approaches is Derrida's method. That means: not to reduce the variability, but to get a sensibility for the strange and unknown.

Navamuel de Figueroa, Leonor. "Posmodernidad y Arte desde América" in *Temas Actuales de Filosofía, Palacios, María Julia (ed)*, 217-224. Buenos Aires, Univ Nacional Salta, 1993.

Navia, Luis E. *The Philosophy of Cynicism: An Annotated Bibliography*. Westport, Greenwood Pr, 1995.

A detailed research work for the study of the origins, development, and significance of the cynical movement among the Greeks and Romans. The purpose of this volume is to provide bibliographical information on over 650 books and articles dealing with various aspects of cynicism. These works were written as early as the 16th century and as recently as 1994 in a variety of languages. This volume includes numerous revealing quotations from the annotated works.

Nayak, Abhaya C. Foundational Belief Change. *J Phil Log*, 23(5), 495-533, O 94.

This paper is concerned with the construction of a base contraction (revision) operation such that the theory contraction (revision) operation generated by it will be fully AGM-rational. It is shown that the theory contraction operation generated by Fuhrmann's *minimal base contraction operation*, even under quite strong restrictions, fails to satisfy the "supplementary postulates" of belief contraction. Finally Fuhrmann's construction is appropriately modified so as to yield the desired properties. The new construction may be described as involving a modification of safe (base) contraction so as to make it maxichoice.

Nayak, Abhaya C. Iterated Belief Change Based on Epistemic Entrenchment. *Erkenntnis*, 41(3), 353-390, N 94.

In this paper, it is argued that, in order to solve the problem of iterated belief change, both the belief state and its input should be represented as epistemic entrenchment (EE) relations. A belief revision operation is constructed that updates a given EE relation to a new one in light of an evidential EE relation. It is shown that the operation in question satisfies generalized versions of the Gärdenfors revision postulates. The account offered is motivated by Spohn's ordinal conditionalization functions, and can be seen as the Jeffrization of a proposal considered by Rott.

Nayak, Abhaya C and Sotnak, Eric. Kant on the Impossibility of the "Soft Sciences". *Phil Phenomenol Res*, 55(1), 133-151, Mr 95.

In the *Metaphysical Foundations* Kant declares that every discipline is a science only to the extent that it can be mathematized and he refuses the status of science to chemistry and psychology. In the *First Critique* he suggests that qualities can be mathematized. Since chemistry and psychology are traditionally taken to be the study of certain qualities, Kant's claims seem to be conflicting. We resolve this conflict by suggesting that although mathematics can be applied to chemistry or psychology in some measure, it cannot be applied enough or in the right manner.

Ndiaye, Aloyse-Raymond. La philosophie d'Antoine Arnauld. *Rev Int Phil*, 48(190), 391-419, 1994.

Neander, Karen. Pruning the Tree of Life. *Brit J Phil Sci*, 46(1), 59-80, Mr 95.

Some (e.g., Elliott Sober) argue that natural selection does not explain the genotypic and phenotypic properties of individuals. On this view, natural selection explains the adaptedness of individuals, not by explaining why the individuals that exist have the adaptations they do, but rather by explaining why the individuals that exist are the ones with those adaptations. This paper argues that this 'Negative' view of natural selection ignores the fact that natural selection is a culmulative selection process. So understood, it explains how the genetic sequences that individuals inherit and that are responsible for their complex (and co-adapted) adaptations first arose in the gene-pool.

Near, Janet P and Burton, Brian K. Estimating the Incidence of Wrongdoing and Whistle-Blowing: Results of a Study Using Randomized Response Technique. *J Bus Ethics*, 14(1), 17-30, Ja 95.

Student cheating and reporting of that cheating represents one form of organizational wrongdoing and subsequent whistle-blowing, in the context of an academic organization. An innovative method, the Randomized Response Technique (RRT), was used here to assess the validity of reported incidences of wrongdoing and whistle-blowing. Surprisingly, our findings show that estimates of these incidences did not vary significantly when RRT questionnaire results were compared to those obtained from standard surveys. (edited)

Neblett, William. Mysticism and Phenomenology. *Darshana Int*, 32(4/128), 67-84, O 92.

Nebreda, J J. Para una historia de las "muertes de Dios": De Newton a Wittgenstein. *Pensamiento*, 198(50), 471-488, S-D 94.

Neckel, Sighard and Wolf, Jürgen. The Fascination of Amorality: Luhmann's Theory of Morality and its Resonances among German Intellectuals. *Theor Cult Soc*, 11(2), 69-99, My 94.

Nedo, Michael (ed). *Ludwig Wittgenstein: Wiener Ausgabe/Vienna Edition—Introduction*. New York, Springer-Verlag, 1993.

The 'Wiener Ausgabe', edited by Michael Nedo, presents for the first time the manuscripts of Wittgenstein in complete form, faithfully reproduced, and so arranged by content and chronology that it is possible to study the process of this thought, 'which developed in the course of these long and complex wanderings'. This bilingual volume is an introduction to the 'Wiener Ausgabe' of the works of Ludwig Wittgenstein (1889-1951). It not only explains the editorial methods used in the new edition to unravel and make readable the complex structure of Wittgenstein's work, but also serves as a practical tool for the study of his writings.

Nedo, Michael (ed) and Wittgenstein, Ludwig. *Ludwig Wittgenstein: Wiener Ausgabe/Vienna Edition—Band 1: Philosophische Bemerkungen*. New York, Springer-Verlag, 1994.

Nedo, Michael (ed) and Wittgenstein, Ludwig. *Ludwig Wittgenstein: Wiener Ausgabe/Vienna Edition—Band 2: Philosophische Betrachtungen, Philosophische Bemerkungen*. New York, Springer-Verlag, 1994.

Neeley, G Steven. Dworkin, Vague Constitutional Clauses, and the Eighth Amendment's Admonition Against "Cruel and Unusual Punishment". *Cont Phil*, 16(5), 18-27, S-O 94.

Ronald Dworkin has argued that vague constitutional provisions should be interpreted as statements which appeal to general moral concepts rather than as edicts which articulate specific conceptions of law. Recent capital punishment decisions reveal that the Supreme Court has applied a Dworkin-style analysis to the Eighth Amendment's admonition against "cruel and unusual" punishment. The upshot of this analysis suggests that capital punishment is constitutionally permissible *if* it is moral. But since the morality of the death penalty has been decided neither by the judiciary nor the populous, the constitutionality of capital punishment effectively remains an open question.

Neeley, Kathryn A and Soudek, Ingrid H. The Match and Other Agents of Liberation: The Role of Technology in the Social Thought of Louise Otto. *Res Phil Technol*, 14, 119-137, 1994.

In *The Life of Women in the German Empire* (1876), the German feminist Louise Otto (1819-95) assesses the impact of the match and other technological developments on the lives of middle-class German women of her day. Through her very detailed and concrete treatments, Otto shows us that technology has great impact not so much because of its inherent power or incorporation into large systems but because it thoroughly permeates our everyday lives. Otto's work demonstrates the value of an approach that is simultaneously material, social, and emotional and uses the lived experience of individuals to expand our understanding of technological change.

Negri, Antonio and Wolf, Charles (trans). On Gilles Deleuze and Félix Guattari, *A Thousand Plateaus*. *Grad Fac Phil J*, 18(1), 93-109, 1995.

Nehamas, Alexander (trans) and Woodruff, Paul (trans) and Plato. *Phaedrus*. Indianapolis, Hackett, 1994.

Neher, E C (trans) and Lestienne, Rémy. *The Children of Time: Causality, Entropy, Becoming*. Champaign, Univ of Illinois Pr, 1995.

Neill, Alex. Emotional Responses to Fiction: Reply to Radford. *J Aes Art Crit*, 53(1), 75-78, Wint 95.

Neill, Alex. Fear and Belief. *Phil Lit*, 19(1), 94-101, Ap 95.

Neiman, Alven M. "Rorty's Dewey: Pragmatism, Education, and the Public Sphere" in *Identity, Culture, and Education, Smeyers, Paul (ed)*, 251-270. Leuven, Leuven Univ Pr, 1994.

In a chapter of their recent book *The Good Society* Robert Bellah and his associates argue that a pragmatist inspired epistemology can help solve the ongoing "crisis of education" in America. My paper is meant to examine this claim. I begin by asking: Whose pragmatism? Cornel West's prophetic pragmatism, Nancy Fraser's pragmatic feminism, Robert Westbrook's Aristotelian version of Dewey's philosophy, etc.? There are so many pragmatisms! The major portion of the paper is meant to argue what may seem at first to be a paradox: Richard Rorty's ironic antiepistemology and related deconstruction of the public-private distinction in political and social philosophy provides the best possible specification of pragmatism given Bellah's overall program, concerns, etc.

Neiman, Alven Michael. Rationality, Oppression and Excellence: A Response to Professor Gewirth. *Stud Phil Educ*, 13(2), 131-137, 1993-94.

This article is a response to a paper by Alan Gewirth, published in the same issue of *Studies*, concerning recent debates over the canon, or content of the liberal arts curriculum. In theory I agree with Gerwirth's ideas, including his use of "the oppression thesis", a maxim often used to support the inclusion of nonstandard texts in college general education programs. My concern, as a philosopher and director of a core program, is to see how Gewirth's ideas would work in practice; my question is: do Gewirth's ideas work? In the end I myself say something general, or theoretical, about politics and liberal education while noting, in a somewhat Rortyian vein, the limitations of theory, even good theory, in this regard.

Neisser, Philip T. The Will to Harmony and the Pursuit of Family. *Soc Theor Pract*, 20(3), 253-277, Fall 94.

The Western ideal of family finds sustenance in a will to harmony. The "will to harmony" is the aim to deny and overcome the inevitable ambiguity of worth of human creations and the inherent uncertainty of human knowledge. The modern faith in family is a crucial expression of this rejection of the politics. We need ways and to recognize the ambiguity of worth of any organization of relations structured along lines of kin; this can perhaps tame the powers of normalization now involved in the politicization of family.

Nelis, Annemiek and Hendriks, Ruud and Benschop, Ruth. De Winst van Tranen: Over de Aarzeling als Methode. *Kennis Methode*, 19(2), 220-227, 1995.

Nelkin, Norton. Reconsidering Pain. *Phil Psych*, 7(3), 325-343, 1994.

Previously, I argued that phenomenal states only accompany pains, that pains are essentially a combination of cognitive, affective, and behavioral/motivational states. I now wish to argue that phenomenal states *are* necessary for pains, though not sufficient. A cognitive state involving an *evaluation* of the phenomenon is also necessary. The evaluation is a *de re* belief, regarding the phenomenon as itself representing harm to the body. Besides admitting that phenomenal states are necessary for pains, I now claim that other belief, affective, and behavioral/motivational states are *unnecessary* for pain, but normal *consequences* of pain.

Nelson, Alan. How *Could* Scientific Facts Be Socially Constructed?. *Stud Hist Phil Sci*, 25(4), 535-547, Ag 94.

An analysis of what is at issue between constructivists and realists about science. Both approaches are shown to depend on interpretations of crucial counterfactuals.

Nelson, Alan. Micro-Chaos and Idealization in Cartesian Physics. *Phil Stud*, 77(2-3), 377-391, Mr 95.

Descartes' metaphysics entails that extension is micro-chaotic. This means that the laws of physics cannot be used to calculate the behavior of bodies, not even in idealized situations. The laws are, nevertheless, not hypothetical, but absolutely true.

Nelson, Alan J. Social Science and the Mental. *Midwest Stud Phil*, 15, 194-209, 1990.

It is sometimes thought that Davidsonian arguments against the possibility of intentional psychology also count as arguments against the possibility of social science couched in intentional terms. This article shows how social science can be immunized against this kind of attack by providing a refined understanding of the doctrine of Methodological Individualism.

Nelson, Beatrice K. Susanne K Langer's Conception of 'Symbol'—Making Connections through Ambiguity. *J Speculative Phil*, 8(4), 277-296, 1994.

Nelson, Hilde Lindemann. Resistance and Insubordination. *Hypatia*, 10(2), 23-40, Spr 95.

I introduce the notion of the counterstory: a story that contributes to the moral self-definition of its teller by undermining a dominant story, undoing it and retelling it in such a way as to invite new interpretations and conclusions. Counterstories can be told anywhere, but particularly when told within chosen communities, they permit their tellers to reenter, as full citizens, the communities of place whose goods have been only imperfectly available to its marginalized members.

Nelson, Hilde Lindemann and Nelson, James Lindemann. Feminism, Social Policy, and Long-Acting Contraception. *Hastings Center Rep*, 25(1), S30-S32, Jan-Feb 95.

Begetters as well as birthgivers bear responsibility for nurturing their children, but men do far less to fulfill this obligation than women—a state of affairs that has resulted in women's being denied full participation in business, the professions, and other valued social endeavors. A feminist test for whether social policy regarding the use of long-acting contraceptives is ethical, then, is to note where birthgiving is unfairly aggregated to bearing the brunt of childrearing responsibilities, and to disaggregate wherever possible. We apply this test to the use of Norplant as a condition of probation and as a solution to the problem of teenage pregnancy.

Nelson, Jack and Nelson, Lynn Hankinson. No Rush to Judgment. *Monist*, 77(4), 486-508, O 94.

Nelson, James Lindemann. Commentary on "But Is It Assisted Suicide?". *Hastings Center Rep*, 25(3), 25, My-Je 95.

In this brief case study discussion, I argue that honoring a refusal of potentially life-sustaining therapy by a person attempting to kill herself is not tantamount to assisting in her suicide. I also suggest that respecting her wishes is not incumbent on only those who accept the "canonical" (and now widely assailed) preeminent status that the principle of respect for autonomy has had among bioethicists.

Nelson, James Lindemann. Publicity and Pricelessness: Grassroots Decisionmaking and Justice in Rationing. *J Med Phil*, 19(4), 333-342, Ag 94.

The "grassroots turn" in bioethical discussions about justice in allocation of health care resources has attracted a great deal of support; in the absence of a convincing theory of justice in rationing, democratic decisionmaking concerning priority setting emerges with a kind of inevitability. Yet there remain suspicions about this approach—most importantly, worries about the socially corrosive impact of explicit, public decisionmaking that in effect sets a price on the lives of persons. These worries have been quieted, particularly by the work of Leonard Fleck, but not altogether stilled. I explore more sympathetically the ideals to which concerns about public rationing somewhat dimly respond, and suggest constraints on priority setting discussions which might accommodate those ideals rather better.

Nelson, James Lindemann. Two Essays in Public Philosophy: Callahan's *The Troubled Dream of Life* and Dworkin's *Life's Dominion*. *Theor Med*, 16(1), 115-123, Mr 94.

The criteria for assessing quality in philosophical as opposed to more popular writing would seem to be not only distinct but incompatible. In this review essay, I examine Callahan's and Dworkin's recent books as efforts to make substantive contributions to our philosophical understanding of the highly complex and contested issues of euthanasia and abortion in ways that are, at the same time, broadly accessible and vividly presented. Despite reservations about particular features of their arguments, I conclude that both serve as models of how public philosophy can avoid becoming philosophy manqué.

Nelson, James Lindemann and Nelson, Hilde Lindemann. Feminism, Social Policy, and Long-Acting Contraception. *Hastings Center Rep*, 25(1), S30-S32, Jan-Feb 95.

Begetters as well as birthgivers bear responsibility for nurturing their children, but men do far less to fulfill this obligation than women—a state of affairs that has resulted in women's being denied full participation in business, the professions, and other valued social endeavors. A feminist test for whether social policy regarding the use of long-acting contraceptives is ethical, then, is to note where birthgiving is unfairly aggregated to bearing the brunt of childrearing responsibilities, and to disaggregate wherever possible. We apply this test to the use of Norplant as a condition of probation and as a solution to the problem of teenage pregnancy.

Nelson, James S. Divine Action: Is It Credible?. *Zygon*, 30(2), 267-280, Je 95.

The concept of God's acting in the world has been seen to be problematic in light of the claims of scientific knowledge that the regularity of a lawlike universe rules out divine action. There are resources in both scientific knowledge and religion that can render meaningful and credible divine action. The new physics, chaos theory, cognitive psychology, and the concept of top-down causation are used to understand how God acts in the world. God's action is not an intervention, but is understood on the model of how the mind influences the brain in a downward causative manner. Suggestions for imagining God's actions are discussed.

Nelson, John O. Pragmatism According to Rorty: A Disaster Area. *J Phil Res*, 20, 349-366, 1995.

The limited objectives of this paper are to show that A), what seem to be merely superficial incoherencies in Rorty's preferred pragmatism (according to which, "the only constraints on inquiry are conversational ones") really are not but B), along with every assertion of Rorty's defining his system and its consequences, belie an intrinsic incoherency resulting from that system's intended conflation of "correspondence truth" and "pragmatic truth." Then C), I shall argue that should we ask of a philosophy that denies to its own statements of purported fact correspondence truth what use it is, the answer has to be, "Worse than no use at all"—at least, if like Rorty's preferred pragmatism it demonstrably concludes in the conceptual annihilation of all inquiry.

Nelson, John O. That a Worker's Labour Cannot be a Commodity. *Philosophy*, 70(272), 156-166, Ap 95.

"That a Worker's Labour Cannot be a Commodity" argues in the first place that in so conceiving his labour one illicitly coverts the capitalist's wage system into the literal enslavement of the worker. It is then argued that a proper conception entails that persons, and not their labour or other factors, are the basic causes in the realm of economics and that, hence, the sciences of psychology and sociology should be called on in economics to play a much more determinant and rigorous role than has been the case.

Nelson, Julianne. Business Ethics in a Competitive Market. *J Bus Ethics*, 13(9), 663-666, S 94.

Consequentialist reasoning and neoclassical assumptions about perfectly competitive markets encourage business school faculty and students to overlook the role of ethics in a market system. In a perfectly competitive economy, self-interest suffices to bring about a desirable outcome. However, discrepancies between an economist's assumptions and the realities of a market economy establish a need for business ethics. This essay, written as a lecture for MBA students, first reviews Pareto optimality as an argument in favor of market allocations. It then uses the discrepancies between actual and hypothetical markets to derive a Rawlsian duty of civility. This neoclassical case for business ethics requires individuals to avoid exploiting the defects that are inevitable in any social structure.

Nelson, Lynn Hankinson and Nelson, Jack. No Rush to Judgment. *Monist*, 77(4), 486-508, O 94.

Nelson, M T and Garcia, Jorge L A. The Problem of Endless Joy: Is Infinite Utility Too Much for Utilitarianism?. *Utilitas*, 6(2), 183-192, N 94.

Traditional utilitarianism stumbles on cases of infinite utility, since its ability to discriminate morally between actions typically requires that the utility value of those actions be finite. Recently, Peter Vallentyne has tried to defend utilitarianism from this objection by stipulating a new definition of "...produces more utility..." that enables the utilitarian to discriminate morally between actions even in cases of infinite utility, while remaining faithful to the spirit of traditional utilitarianism. We argue that Vallentyne's solution is unsatisfactory for various reasons, notably because its distribution-sensitive character deviates from traditional utilitarianism's commitment to sumranking principles.

Nemeth, Elisabeth. "Zwischen Orthodoxie und gesellschaftlicher Sichtbarkeit" in *Der geistige Anschluss, Fischer, Kurt R (ed)*, 221-235. Wien, WUV Univ, 1993.

Németi, I and Kurucz, H Andréka. Connections Between Axioms of Set Theory and Basic Theorems of Universal Algebra. *J Sym Log*, 59(3), 912-923, S 94.

One of the basic theorems in universal algebra is Birkhoff's variety theorem: the smallest equationally axiomatizable class containing a class K of algebras coincides with the class obtained by taking homomorphic images of subalgebras of direct products of elements of K. G Grätzer asked whether the variety theorem is equivalent to the Axiom of Choice. In 1980, two of the present authors proved that Birkhoff's theorem can already be derived in *ZF*. Surprisingly, the Axiom of Foundation plays a crucial role here: we show that Birkhoff's theorem cannot be derived in *ZF + AC*/(Foundation), even if we add Foundation for Finite Sets. We also prove that the variety theorem is equivalent to a purely set-theoretical statement, the Collection Principle. This principle is independent of *ZF*/(Foundation). The second part of the paper deals with further connections between axioms of *ZF*-set theory and theorems of universal algebra.

Nemirow, Laurence E. Understanding Rules. *J Phil*, 92(1), 28-43, Ja 95.

Nerlich, Brigitte and Clarke, David D. Language, Action and Context: Linguistic Pragmatics in Europe and America. *J Prag*, 22(5), 439-463, N 94.

Pragmatics is considered to be a fairly recent addition to the sciences of language, dating back to the works of Austin, Searle and Grice. However, this apparently new approach to language has its roots in the philosophical, psychological and linguistic traditions of the past. This is true of all four approaches to pragmatics which one can distinguish in Europe and America: the Anglo-Saxon one which emerged from Ordinary Language Philosophy and which has dominated the field until the present; the French one which is based on the theory of enunciation elaborated by Benveniste; the German one which wants to study pragmatics as part of a general theory of action; and the American one of pragmatism. To varying degrees all these strands of thought are blind to their own history, and have cut themselves off from a wealth of ideas, developed during the 19th century, of how language and the mind work. In this article we want to give an overview of the evolution of these traditions and stimulate discussion among colleagues in all fields and disciplines which are based in one way or another on linguistic pragmatics.

Nerlich, Graham. *The Shape of Space (Second Edition)*. New York, Cambridge Univ Pr, 1994.

Nesbitt, Winston. Is Killing No Worse than Letting Die?. *J Applied Phil*, 12(1), 101-106, 1995.

Those who wish to refute the view that it is worse to kill than to let die sometimes produce examples of cases in which an agent lets someone die but would be generally agreed to be no less reprehensible than if he had killed. It is argued that the examples produced typically possess a feature which makes their use in this context illegitimate, and that when modified to remove this feature, they provide support for the view which they were designed to undermine.

Nesteruk, Alexei V. The Idea of Eternal Life in Modern Cosmology: Its Ultimate Reality and Metaethical Meaning. *Ultim Real Mean*, 17(3), 222-231, S 94.

Nesteruk, Jeffrey. Law and the Virtues: Developing a Legal Theory for Business Ethics. *Bus Ethics Quart*, 5(2), 361-369, Ap 95.

This article puts forth a new conception of law for the field of business ethics. In particular, it examines the ways in which legal doctrines and principles contribute to fostering virtue in the corporate setting. The article looks at how changes in legal rules affect both the roles and character development of individuals in the corporate hierarchy.

Neuhaus, Richard John. "From Civil Religion to Public Philosophy" in *Civil Religion and Political Theology, Rouner, Leroy S (ed)*, 98-110. Notre Dame, Univ Notre Dame Pr, 1986.

Neujahr, Philip J. *Kant's Idealism*. Macon, Mercer Univ Pr, 1995.

This work addresses the question of what sort of idealism is contained in Kant's critical philosophy. Neujahr argues that Kant's doctrines of perception (intuition) and thought (judgment) pull Kant's philosophy in different directions regarding both the nature of the knowing subject and the relation of this subject to the object of its awareness. Because of the competing demands of the accounts of perception and thought, Neujahr argues, there is not a single Kantian view of the status of the space-time world ("empirically real and transcendentally ideal") or a single kind of idealism ("transcendental") which is contained in the critical philosophy.

Neumaier, Otto (ed). *Angewandte Ethik im Spannungsfeld von Ökologie und Ökonomie*. Sankt Augustin, Academia, 1994.

This volume contains three contributions that deal with moral problems connected with the environmental consequences of modern-day economic enterprises. Gerhard Schurz attempts at clarifying the possibilities of justification for norms in environmental ethics. Otto Neumaier analyses the notion of collective responsibility in order to show in which sense it is justified to ascribe moral responsibility to collective entities. Alfons Süssbauer gives an account of the conditions that are necessary for calling corporations to account for the consequences of their actions.

Neumann, Franz and Marcuse, Herbert. The Theory of Social Change with Introduction by Bill Scheuerman. *Constellations*, 1(1), 113-143, Ap 94.

Neville, Robert Cummings. *Creativity and God: A Challenge to Process Theology*. Albany, SUNY Pr, 1995.

Neville, Robert Cummings. *Normative Cultures*. Albany, SUNY Pr, 1995.

Normative cultures present theories of theoretical and practical reasoning addressing the fact that high cultures are different from one another, recognize themselves as conventional, and are normative ways of being human. A nonreductive approach to theory is offered developing Peirce's analysis of the criticism of descriptive categories. Practical reason is developed using a Confucian theory of ritual. This volume completes the author's trilogy, *Axiology of Thinking*, treating imagination, interpretation, theory, and responsibility.

Neville, Robert Cummings. *The Cosmology of Freedom (New Edition)*. Albany, SUNY Pr, 1995.

Nevo, Isaac. "James, Quine, and Analytic Pragmatism" in *Pragmatism: From Progressivism to Postmodernism, Hollinger, Robert (ed)*, 153-169. Westport, Praeger, 1995.

Nevo, Isaac. "Richard Rorty's Romantic Pragmatism" in *Pragmatism: From Progressivism to Postmodernism, Hollinger, Robert (ed)*, 284-297. Westport, Praeger, 1995.

Nevo, Isaac. Reason and Utopia: Richard Bernstein and the Rage against Reason. *Iyyun*, 43, 265-287, Jl 94.

New, Caroline. Structure, Agency and Social Transformation. *J Theor Soc Behav*, 24(3), 187-205, S 94.

Revisiting the structure/agency debate, the article puts forward the broad position shared by Giddens' structuration theory and Bhaskar's transformational model. It defends Giddens' concept of structure as 'rules and resources' against charges of idealism, arguing that its strength is its focus on the interface of structure and agency. But both Giddens and Bhaskar emphasize social reproduction as an *unintended* consequence of social action. Taking issue with postmodern pessimism, the article goes on to consider the conditions of possibility, and requisite forms of knowledgeability, for *deliberate* social transformation.

New, Christopher. Punishing Times: Reply to Smilansky. *Analysis*, 55(1), 60-62, Ja 95.

I argue that Sand Smilansky's attempt (*Analysis* 54, 1994, 50-53) to refute my argument (*Analysis* 52, 1992, 35-40) that under certain conditions we might be justified in punishing someone for a crime he has not yet committed fails. Smilansky's claim that much pre-punishment could fail to respect the agent's moral personality and choice is rebutted, and it is argued that on the contrary we might fail to respect them is we refused to pre-punish the agent.

Newcombe, Hanna. Federalist Theory and World Peace. *Dialogue Hum*, 3(2), 138-144, 1993.

Newelski, Ludomir. A Model and Its Subset: The Uncountable Case. *Annals Pure Applied Log*, 71(2), 107-129, F 95.

Assume Q is a definable subset of a model of T. We define a notion of Q-isolated type, generalizing an earlier definition for countable Q. This notion is absolute. For superstable T, we give some sufficient conditions for the existence of Q-atomic models. We apply this to prove some results on weak categoricity over a predicate.

Newelski, Ludomir. Meager Forking. *Annals Pure Applied Log*, 70(2), 141-175, D 94.

A small superstable theory is either w-stable or some type in it has infinite multiplicity. We investigate the topological shape of the set of stationavizations of such a type. We define the notion of meager forking and meager type, and prove that a meager type is locally modular. This improves results of Buechler, Pillay, and is related to results of Hvushovshi and Shelah. Using this notion we prove conjecture of vanishing multiplicities and other conjectures of ours regarding theories with few countable models. We prove a counterpart of Saffe's condition. This condition was crucial in the proof of Vaught's conjecture for weakly minimal theories.

Newfield, Christopher and Gordon, Avery. White Philosophy. *Crit Inquiry*, 20(4), 737-757, Sum 94.

Newman, Amy. Feminist Social Criticism and Marx's Theory of Religion. *Hypatia*, 9(4), 15-37, Fall 94.

Feminist philosophers and social theorists have engaged in an extensive critique of the project of modernity during the past three decades. However, many feminists seem to assume that the critique of religion essential to this project remains valid. Radical criticism of religion in the European traditions presupposes a theory of religion that is highly ethnocentric, and Marx's theory of religion serves as a case in point.

Newman, Andrew. Cartwright's *Nature's Capacities and their Measurement*. *Nous*, 29(2), 274-283, Je 95.

Newman, Geoffrey. Adrian Stokes and Venice. *Brit J Aes*, 35(3), 254-261, Jl 95.

This article considers the work of the British art critic and theorist Adrian Stokes (1902-72), specifically his writings on the city of Venice. The author relates these to Stokes's psychoanalytical approach to art as symbolic of the integrated ego, and in this context Venice can be seen as a paradigm of the whole, good external object. Stokes's writings on buildings and sculptures in the city, and his essay on Giorgione's *Tempesta*, are discussed, exemplifying the unique character of his sensibility. It is concluded that what is developed in Stokes's work is less a psychoanalytic theory than a aesthetic philosophy.

Newman, Jay. Fanaticism and Integrity. *Filozof Istraz*, 14(2-3), 325-331, 1994.

Fanaticism is often viewed as a deeper, more complete noncompromising form of commitment. This view neglects the serious moral flaws inherent in fanaticism, suggests the identification of fanaticism with commitment as such, and provides fanatics and extremists with a totally undeserved glamor associated with integrity and steadfastness. It thus functions as a propaganda weapon in the hands of extremists and apologists of extremism. According to the alternative account, offered in this paper, fanaticism is excessive commitment and a vice. The excessive dimension of the fanatic's commitment does not relate to the degree of commitment, but rather to certain specific conditions of the commitment. Integrity, on the other hand, is construed as proper or sound commitment and thus a virtue. Accordingly, it represents a mean between two extremes: the vice of fanaticism which, in Aristotelian language, "depends on excess", and a general vice which "depends on defect", and takes such forms as hyprocrisy, irresoluteness, and weakness of will. In this sense, integrity parallels tolerance itself.

Newman, Lex. Descartes on Unknown Faculties and Our Knowledge of the External World. *Phil Rev*, 103(3), 489-531, Jl 94.

In this paper, it is argued that Descartes' treatment of our knowledge of the existence of the external, corporeal world centers on a sceptical worry that the cause of our sensory experiences may be an unknown, internal (mental) faculty rather than external (corporeal) objects. This sceptical hypothesis—one that originates with the

Academic sceptics—is distinct from the standard Dreaming Argument, and it foreshadows Descartes' theory of innate ideas. To refute this unknown faculty worry, Descartes appeals to his famous transparency doctrine of the mind in the Sixth Meditation passage intended to restore our knowledge of the external world.

Newman, M E and Chittleborough, P. Defining the Term "Argument". *Inform Log*, 15(3), 189-207, Fall 93.

Informal logic has expanded the concept of an 'argument' beyond that presented traditionally by formal logicians—to include arguments as encountered in 'real-life'. Existent definitions of argument structure are argued to be inadequate by failing to fully recognize that, ultimately, arguments have a human source. Accordingly, a new definition is proposed which appeals to relevant cognitive and behavioral factors. The definition retains some traditional concepts, but introduces the term 'supportive' as a modification to 'premiss'. The concept of a 'persuader' is also developed. The definition is argued to capture more fully the intricacies, subtleties and rich diversity of informal arguments.

Newman, Michael. Derrida and the Scene of Drawing: A Discussion of *Mémoires D'aveugle. L'Autoportrait et autres ruines* by Jacques Derrida. *Res Phenomenol*, 24, 218-234, 1994.

Newton, Adam Zachary. Narrative Ethics. Cambridge, Harvard Univ Pr, 1995.

Neymeyr, Barbara. Die Kunstskepsis des Ästhetikers: Anmerkungen zu einer singulären Parabel in Schopenhauers "Parerga und Paralipomena". *Schopenhauer Jahr*, 76, 91-102, 1995.

Ng, Yew-Kwang. Towards Welfare Biology: Evolutionary Economics of Animal Consciousness and Suffering. *Biol Phil*, 10(3), 255-285, July 95.

Welfare biology is the study of living things and their environment with respect to their welfare (defined as net happiness, or enjoyment minus suffering). Despite difficulties of ascertaining and measuring welfare and relevancy to normative issues, welfare biology is a positive science. Evolutionary economics and population dynamics are used to help answer basic questions in welfare biology: Which species are affective sentients capable of welfare? Do they enjoy positive or negative welfare? Can their welfare be dramatically increased? Under plausible axioms, all conscious species are plastic and all plastic species are conscious (and, with a stronger axiom, capable of welfare). More complex niches favour the evolution of more rational species.

Nguyen, Vinh-De. La Politique du Développement Durable: Voie ou Impasse. *Philosopher*, 13, 143-165, 1992.

Niarchos, C G. Good, Beauty, and Eros in Dionysius' Doctrine of Divine Causality. *Diotima*, 23, 106-108, 1995.

Nicholls, Moira. Schopenhauer, Feeling and the Noumenon. *Schopenhauer Jahr*, 76, 53-71, 1995.

The purpose of this paper is to show that feeling plays a much more significant role in Schopenhauer's philosophy than has generally been recognised. I argue that for Schopenhauer feeling has the epistemological status of knowledge, that it is a nonconceptual awareness and that it is the immediate means by which we become aware of reality. I consider the importance of feeling in Schopenhauer's discussion of aesthetics, music, eternal justice and compassion and discuss his claim that it is through feeling that we become aware of our inner nature, the will that is the thing-in-itself.

Nicholls, Moira. The Kantian Inheritance and Schopenhauer's Doctrine of Will. *Kantstudien*, 85(3), 257-279, 1994.

Schopenhauer asserts numerous times throughout his writings that the thing-in-itself is will, and the traditional interpretation accepts that he intends this assertion to be a straightforward claim of identity. However, I argue that his claim has at least six possible interpretations. I assess the relative importance of each, both to Schopenhauer himself and to the commentator attempting to construct the most consistent account of Schopenhauer's central doctrines. I also suggest that the pervasive influence of both Kant and Eastern thought on Schopenhauer's metaphysics, epistemology and conceptual doctrines is important in explaining how the possibility of multiple interpretations arises.

Nicholson, Graeme. "Love and Knowledge in the Bible" in *The Nature and Pursuit of Love, Goicoechea, David (ed)*, 98-112. Buffalo, Prometheus, 1995.

Nicholson, Graeme. Hermeneutics and Critical Theory in Canada. *Eidos*, 11(1-2), 131-141, Je-D 93.

Nicholson, Nigel. Ethics in Organizations: A Framework for Theory and Research. *J Bus Ethics*, 13(8), 581-596, Ag 94.

In a climate of increasing interest and activity within the field of business ethics, as yet there exists no coherent conceptual framework for organizational theory and research. From a review of current thinking and previous writings a framework of concepts is suggested to help set an agenda for empirical research. The elements of this are, first, a taxonomy of "ethical domains": the foci of organizations' and their agents' ethical concerns and conduct. Second, it is considered how "ethical functioning" might be analyzed in terms of causal relationships between expressive forms, voluntary action and instituted forms. Third is discussed "ethical process", the means by which ethical awareness is aroused. Fourth and last, the paper examines how normative evaluations might apply to the "ethical condition" of organizations and their agents, meaning change or stability in reputation and integrity. At each stage of the argument possible objects for research are developed.

Nicholson, Peter. T H Green's Doubts About Hegel's Political Philosophy. *Bull Hegel Soc Gt Brit*, 31, 61-72, Spr-Sum 95.

How Hegelian is Green in his political philosophy? After discussing the possible extent of Green's knowledge of Hegel, the article asks where Green sets the limit to his agreement with Hegel. It is suggested that this is not as easy to establish as is often supposed, because in his key comments on Hegel, Green is not analysing him in any precise academic manner but expressing his own repudiation of conservatism—and of Hegel's views so far as they are misread as conservative.

Nicholson-Smith, Donald (trans) and Lefebvre, Henri. *The Production of Space*. Cambridge, Blackwell, 1991.

Nickel, James. The Value of Cultural Belonging: Expanding Kymlicka's Theory. *Dialogue (Canada)*, 33(4), 635-642, Fall 94.

This paper criticizes Will Kymlicka's account (in *Liberalism, Community, and Culture*) of the value of secure cultural belonging, and attempts to provide an alternative or expanded account. The main criticism is that Kymlicka's two arguments cannot work in tandem. The Options for Choice argument is only plausible when applied to children's ability to make intelligent choices, but the Harm for Cultural Transplantation argument is not generally sound when applied to children. The alternative account of the value of secure cultural belonging denies that it is a primary good in the Rawlsian sense, but identifies a number of interests in secure belonging that most people have.

Nickel, James W. What's Wrong with Ethnic Cleansing?. *J Soc Phil*, 26(1), 5-15, Spr 95.

This paper analyzes the concept of ethnic cleansing, attempts to deepen our understanding of why it generally merits harsh condemnation, and considers whether its milder forms are sometimes permissible. A framework is proposed that evaluates ethnic cleansing in terms of: 1) the legitimacy or illegitimacy of its goal; 2) the mass killing and violence that are usually used to destroy the group or force it to move; 3) the lost territory and property; 4) the hazards of the process of relocation; and 5) where the group ends up and whether it can create a successful life there.

Nicoloff, Franck. MAY and Meaning$_{SN}$. *J Prag*, 22(5), 529-533, N 94.

The formulaic utterance-type *modal "may" + proposition (May the best man win!)* is shown to have a peculiar syntactic and semantic structure. This is described as the unconventional grammatical encoding of the optative function of language, the tentative shaping of future events by means of the magical power of prayer.

Nicolosi, Salvatore. Metafisica ed Esistenza di Dio nel Periodo Precritico di Kant. *Aquinas*, 37(3), 501-521, S-D 94.

Nida-Rümelin, Julian. Die Vielfalt guter Gründe und die Theorie praktischer Rationalität. *Protosoz*, 6, 95-103, 1994.

There is a plurality of good reasons for action. An adequate theory of practical rationality has to be compatible with it even if it requires certain modifications of our everyday practices of reasoning. Usual theories of practical rationality do not pass this test. It is envisaged how to revise adequately our understanding of practical rationality.

Nida-Rümelin, Julian. Rational Choice: Extensions and Revisions. *Ratio*, 7(2), 122-144, D 94.

The rational choice paradigm has proved to be a fruitful means of analysis and explanation in various disciplines concerned with questions of practical rationality, but in various attempts to extend its fields of application the deficiencies of the original account of rational choice have become evident. This paper tries to give a systematic overview of ways in which the rational choice paradigm can be extended and modified.

Nida-Rümelin, Martine. *Farben und Phänomenales Wissen*. Wien, VWGÖ, 1993.

Niedersen, Uwe. "Prozessstrukturen" in *Schelling und die Selbstorganisation, Heuser-Kessler, Marie-Luise (ed)*, 183-199. Berlin, Duncker Humblot, 1994.

Nielsen, Kai. Is "True Philosophy" Like "True Art"?. *Phil Exch*, 24-25, 107-123, 1993-94.

Nielsen, Kai. Justice as a Kind of Impartiality. *Laval Theol Phil*, 50(3), 511-529, O 94.

Kantian conceptions of justice construe justice as impartiality, Hobbesian ones construe justice as mutual advantage. It is argued that these are not rival conceptions, but that justice has become the equal consideration of the legitimate interests of everyone alike: where all persons are treated as equals, as persons of equal moral standing. That is what justice as impartiality comes to. Mutual advantage theories, by contrast, do not tell us what justice is, or has become, but give us prudential reasons for being just by showing that, generally speaking, doing what just people do pays.

Nielsen, Kai. Methods of Ethics: Wide Reflective Equilibrium and a Kind of Consequentialism. *J Soc Phil*, 25(2), 57-72, Fall 94.

Nielsen, Kai. *On Transforming Philosophy: A Metaphilosophical Inquiry*. Boulder, Westview Pr, 1995.

Nielsen, Kai and Hart, Hendrik. *Search for Community in a Withering Tradition: Conversations between a Marxian Atheist and a Calvinian Christian*. Lanham, Univ Pr of America, 1990.

Niesen, Peter. Gemeinschaft, Normativität, Praxis: Debatte zu L Wittgenstein's Regelbegriff. *Protosoz*, 1, 87-99, Ap 91.

This article surveys recent literature on Wittgenstein's "Rule-following considerations", most notably S Kripke's, C McGinn's, and G P Baker's and P M S Hacker's contributions. I argue that the normativity requirements in rule-following is to be located not in transtemporal but interpersonal sameness of meaning, and that the community-view is false when viewed as a condition on correct rule-following, but true when viewed as providing criteria for the possibility of rule-following.

Niestroj, Brigitte H E. Women as Mothers and the Making of the European Mind: A Contribution to the History of Developmental Psychology and Primary Socialization. *J Theor Soc Behav*, 24(3), 281-303, S 94.

A major purpose of this essay is to show that our assumptions regarding human development in general, and in particular, the mother and child have their roots in a Christian-humanistic tradition. I also wish to locate the origins of the discourse on the mother and child within a critical historical review of notions of a changing anthropology of the human subject. The working hypothesis is as follows: A changing view of the human being is associated with a changing approach to child care and child development. This changing approach to child is accompanied by a 'new woman'. Women are newly constructed when children, and thus a future person and a future society is defined.

Nietzsche, Friedrich and Colli, Giorgio (ed) and Montinari, Mazzino (ed). *The Complete Works of Friedrich Nietzsche: Volume 2: Unfashionable Observations*. Stanford, Stanford Univ Pr, 1995.

Niiniluoto, Ilkka. Truthlikeness Misapplied: A Reply to Ernest W Adams. *Synthese*, 101(2), 291-300, N 94.

Nijenhuis, John. Existence vs Being: An All-important Matter of Terminology. *Amer Cath Phil Quart*, 69(1), 89-95, Wint 95.

This is a Reply to objections to a previous article: For ontological purposes, dictionaries, which regard "be" and "exist" as synonyms, cannot be trusted. Aquinas uses *existere* some 4,000 times, but not necessarily in the sense of today's English "exist": it has the original etymological sense of "come out of"; it has a "quasi-copulative" use, when joined with a noun or verb. Replacing the Latin verb *esse* in the *essentia-esse* phrase with the English noun "existence" radically contorts its intent. "Existents," in today's sense, are composed of a quantity of "being" (esse) measured by their *ESSE*nce.

Nikiforov, Aleksandr and Borodaj, Jurij. East and West: Russian Renewal and the Future. *Stud East Euro Thought*, 47(1-2), 61-116, Je 95.

Two philosophers and prominent public figures explore the spiritual and cultural framework within which Russia's crisis and prospects for social renewal must be understood. Their discussion ranges over several main areas of concern in Russia today: the nature of the person and her capacities as social actor, the forms of sociality Russia has known as seen against the background of Orthodoxy and Communism, and Russia's tragedy during the seventy-five years of Communism. A "third path" is envisaged for Russian renewal based on geopolitical, cultural, and spiritual constants in the history of the nation.

Nikkel, David H. The Postmodern Spirit and The Status of God. *Sophia (Australia)*, 33(3), 46-61, N 94.

The postmodern spirit has challenged modern standards of truth and selfhood. This paper overviews possible responses to this postmodern spirit regarding the concept of God (including rejection of any such concept). It argues that a fairly traditional concept of God can be consistent with the postmodern spirit, especially when this concept is modified to include panentheistic immanence. Finally, given the postmodern rejection of absolute or unmediated knowledge, a model of our knowing God through God's embodiment in the world is developed.

Nimtz, Christian H. Parfit und die Theorie C. *Z Phil Forsch*, 48(3), 435-447, Jl-S 94.

Derek Parfit argues that the theory C which is the core of consequentialism i) is self-defeating, ii) that if it was not self-defeating, it would not evaluate actions in an intuitively correct way, and iii) that one cannot consistently act upon it. Parfit concludes that this is true of most consequentialist theories. This is shown to be false. For simple (logical) reasons, Parfit cannot establish any of his claims. Parfit's generalistic method of dealing with consequentialism is thus shown to be inadequate. It is moreover argued that no plausible consequentialist theory is flawed the way Parfit envisages.

Ninnes, L E. Hegel, Marx and Idealistic Vapourizing. *Dialogue Hum*, 3(4), 97-111, 1993.

Nino, Carlos Santiago. Consecuencialismo: debate ético y jurídico. *Telos (Spain)*, 1(1), 73-96, F 92.

The bulk of the article is devoted to analyze three problems that are confronted by consequentialism in the broadest sense, which implies to take into account the causal effects of the actions when undertaking their moral appraisal. As a conclusion, there seems to be an unsolvable tension between the consideration of actual and ideal effects in undertaking the morally right conduct. Insofar as ideal effect must be taken into account, a radical departure from the broadest form of consequentialism has to be accepted. In sum, even the minimum sense of "consequentialism" does not seem to denote a plausible moral outlook without important qualifications.

Nissani, Moti. An Experiential Component in Teaching Philosophy of Science. *Teach Phil*, 18(2), 147-154, Je 95.

This note argues that introductory nature-of-science classes can be best taught through a mix of 1) lectures on the philosophy of science, 2) hands-on experiences which mimic one or another aspect of the process of scientific discovery, and 3) brief, self-contained, readily intelligible, historical case studies. This non-traditional instructional approach is then illustrated through a few exercises and historical case studies.

Nissenbaum, Helen (ed) and Johnson, Deborah G (ed). *Computers, Ethics and Social Values*. Englewood Cliffs, Prentice Hall, 1995.

The pervasive use of computers and the emergence of new, highly sophisticated information technologies have raised many social concerns. This anthology of readings addresses the ethical issues arising from the development and deployment of computers in society. Selections represent a range of diverse opinions and perspectives, offering a balance between theoretical analysis and description of real-life cases. The volume is broken into seven chapters: What is Computer Ethics?; Crime, Abuse, and Hacker Ethics; Ownership of Computer Software; Privacy and Databases; The Risks of Computing; Responsibility, Liability, and Professional Codes; and The Networked World.

Nitta, Hiroë. On Artistic Process: Eye, Hand, Language. *Aesthetics*, 3, 1-21, Mr 88.

Niznik, Jozef. The Ideological Involvement of Philosophy. *Metaphilosophy*, 25(2-3), 194-204, Ap-Jl 94.

The author discusses relations between philosophy, religion and political ideology. Established definition of ideology known from the Marx—Mannheim tradition has been here reserved for political ideology. An additional definition of ideology, as elevation of an idea to the position of absolute, is proposed in order to stress affinities of philosophy, religion and political ideology. The failure of political ideology—which was observed in communist countries—exhibits the weakness of political coercion in the realm of ideas.

Noble, Mary Thomas (trans) and Pinckaers, Servais. *The Sources of Christian Ethics*. Washington, Cath Univ Amer Pr, 1995.

Noble, Paul R. Hermeneutics and Postmodernism: Can We Have a Radical Reader-Response Theory? Part I. *Relig Stud*, 30(4), 419-436, D 94.

This paper argues that if Stanley Fish's postmodernist hermeneutics is correct then it has far-reaching consequences for Biblical Studies, because it licenses radical reinterpretations that traditional approaches would consider inadmissible. The theory is then tested out by examining Fish's own attempts at radical reinterpretation. Following a methodological discussion of the criteria by which his exegesis should be assessed, a wide-ranging survey of Fish's examples shows that they consistently fail to support his claims, and that the nature of their failure suggests that his hermeneutical theory is seriously flawed. This is further proved by showing that Fish's theory entails an extreme form of solipsism.

Noble, Paul R. Hermeneutics and Postmodernism: Can We Have a Radical Reader-Response Theory? Part II. *Relig Stud*, 31(1), 1-22, Mr 95.

The flaws in Fish's hermeneutics that were diagnosed in Part I (it is now argued) are consequences of his underlying epistemology. This is a version of anti-foundationalism which claims that facts are the product of interpretation; but a careful study of how this issue is handled by N R Hanson and Thomas Kuhn shows that Fish's epistemology is fundamentally unsound. An alternative account of the fact-interpretation relationship is then proposed, and the outline of an objectivist, reader-independent hermeneutics are sketched. This is further developed by showing how a common argument against objectivism (based on the historical situatedness of reason and knowledge) may be refuted.

Noé, Keiichi. Cultural Universals as Endless Tasks: Phenomenology, Relativism, and Ethnocentrism. *Monist*, 78(1), 41-51, Ja 95.

The purpose of this paper is to find a narrow path between universalism and relativism through examining the development of Husserlian phenomenology. In the early stage, Husserl aimed at "philosophy as rigorous science" and severely criticized naturalism and historicism. But, in the later stage, his universalism paradoxically amounted to a kind of Eurocentrism. To escape from such a predicament, the cultural universals should not be substatialized in the form of "European reason," but be functionalized as working hypotheses. This paper tried to overcome both cultural imperialism and relativism in terms of reinterpreting concepts of "the historical *a priori*" and "ethnocentrism."

Noel, Jana. "Evolving Conceptions of Self through Community or The Development and Overcoming of Prejudice" in *Identity, Culture, and Education*, Smeyers, Paul (ed), 271-281. Leuven, Leuven Univ Pr, 1994.

Using discussion from Gadamer, Burbules and Rice, and Banks, and practical examples from a multicultural teacher education classroom, this paper examines the effects of community on the construction of identities and the development and overcoming of prejudice.

Noggle, Robert. Autonomy, Value, and Conditioned Desire. *Amer Phil Quart*, 32(1), 57 69, Ja 95.

Conditioning can produce desires that are "alien" to the self. Desire-based theories of welfare claim that the satisfaction of desires creates value. But the satisfaction of alien desires seems *not* to create value. I suggest that alien desires *would* be rational *if* the person believed something that *in fact* she believes is false. Such desires could be produced by mental representations—or "quasi-beliefs"—with contents that conflict with the contents of one's beliefs. The postulation of quasi-beliefs is plausible, for they explain important empirical facts about our behavior. This theory explains the moral status of alien desires.

Nola, Robert. There are More Things in Heaven and Earth, Horatio, Than are Dreamt of in Your Philosophy: A Dialogue on Realism and Constructivism. *Stud Hist Phil Sci*, 25(5), 689-727, O 94.

Many sociological studies of science are embedded in a metaphysics of constructivism, or social constructivism. This position is contrasted, in the form of a dialogue, with a realist view of science. In sections II and III there is a discussion of some of the different things 'social' and 'constructivism' might mean. In IV an account is given of the construction of material objects that accords with an account of scientific realism set out in V. Section VI is devoted to a discussion of some remarks of Karen Knorr Cetina on constructivism and the way it differs from scientific realism. Section VII contains a discussion of some remarks of Karen Knorr Cetina on constructivism and the way it differs from scientific realism. Section VII contains a discussion of Pickering's constructivism, and VIII that of Latour and Woolgar. It is argued that science studies ought to be pursued independently of the strong version of neo-Kantian constructivism that these authors endorse. It is also argued that such constructivism faces two philosophical difficulties of its own. Each science construct its own objects in such a way that the distinction between theories with correct and incorrect ontological commitments is lost; in addition it cannot account for how a theory can have correct ontological commitments yet make false claims about what exists.

Nolt, John and Bennett, James. A Venn-Euler Test for Categorical Syllogisms. *Teach Phil*, 17(1), 41-55, Mr 94.

We present a method for testing the validity of standard form categorical syllogisms, which differs from the Venn diagram test in two basic respects: it uses Euler's way of representing universal statements, although it retains Venn's way of representing particular ones, and it seeks a counter-example to the argument, by attempting to represent the antilogism. After presenting the test, we discuss its advantages over the Venn diagram test and two other, alternative methods.

Noonan, Harold W. E J Lowe on Vague Identity and Quantum Indeterminacy. *Analysis*, 55(1), 14-19, Ja 95.

The paper defends Gareth Evan's argument against vague identity *de re* from a criticism that quantum mechanics provides actual counter-examples to its validity. A more general version of Evans's argument is stated in which identity involving properties are not essential and it is claimed that the scientific facts as so far known are consistent with the Evansian thesis that indeterminacy in truth-value must always be due to semantic indecision.

Norbert, Bilbeny. Como Pensar los Valores Morales a Partir de Kant?. *An Seminar Hist Filosof*, 9, 181-186, 1992.

El autor expone las sucesivas concepciones del valor de la moralidad en Kant a través de la primera *Crítica*, de la *Fundamentación de la metafísica de las costumbres* y de la *Crítica de la razón práctica*. Kant identifica el valor moral con la moralidad misma, en el sentido de legalidad—"ley moral"—, lo que hará que asuma explícitamente como valores morales de la "humanidad", la "dignidad", la "sabiduría" y la "santidad". Con todo, interesa destacar en Kant la separación entre el valor y el ser, sin desligar al primero del hecho de la moralidad: el valor como "idea" y a la vez "ideal" de la razón práctica, supuesto retomable para una ética de hoy.

Norcross, Alastair. Should Utilitarianism Accommodate Moral Dilemmas?. *Phil Stud*, 79(1), 59-83, Jl 95.

It is clear that classical utilitarianism does not allow for moral dilemmas. Michael Slote has suggested modifying maximizing utilitarianism to accommodate dilemmas by adding the requirement that a right act must have consequences that are, on balance, good. I examine two interpretations of this suggestion. Each involves giving moral weight to the distinction between doing and allowing, that is unacceptable to utilitarians. Furthermore, ordinary benevolence, in which utilitarianism is based, is not sensitive to the distinction. I conclude that it is at best highly unlikely that utilitarianism can accommodate moral dilemmas without incorporating a distinction that violates the spirit of the theory.

Nordenfelt, Lennart. Mild Mania and the Theory of Health: A Response to "Mild Mania and Well-Being". *Phil Psychiat Psych*, 1(3), 179-184, S 94.

In this response to "Mild Mania and Well-Being" I propose a different analytic strategy and scrutinize the presented case of mild mania within the framework of a holistic theory of health. I distinguish between the following fundamental questions: 1) is mild mania a disease or illness? 2) does the mild mania of Mr M reduce his health significantly? and 3) should Mr M be recommended treatment with lithium or not? I answer the first question in the affirmative. I propose some theoretical tools for resolving the second one. A complete resolution of it, however, requires a deeper analysis of Mr M's state of mind and general situation. Finally, I hold that an affirmative answer to the third, namely that Mr M should be recommended treatment with lithium. Other considerations, in particular ethical ones, should play a role.

Norman, Richard. *Ethics, Killing and War*. New York, Cambridge Univ Pr, 1995.

The first half of the book examines philosophical accounts of the wrongness of killing, rejecting utilitarian and consequentialist accounts and defending a strong principle of respect for human life. This position is brought to bear on the ethics of war, arguing that attempts to justify killing in war from within the 'just war' tradition cannot be sustained. The book concludes with an attempt to show how further rational debate is possible between pacifists and those who argue that war is sometimes an unavoidable and necessary evil.

Norman, Wayne. La Philosophie Politique et la Formation du Citoyen. *Philosopher*, 16, 235-240, 1994.

This article makes a case for philosophy as a required component in higher education—e.g., as it is in the colleges of Quebec. Suggestions are made for a philosophical training that sharpens the critical abilities necessary for good citizenship.

Norrick, Neal R. Involvement and Joking in Conversation. *J Prag*, 22(3-4), 409-430, O 94.

This paper seeks to relate involvement and joking in conversation through close investigation of passages from everyday talk. Conversationalists maintain involvement—or the coherent give and take of talk in interaction—by signaling their understanding of and attitudes toward their jointly constructed discourse. Joking impinges on involvement in various ways, affecting coherence at the micro-level, expressing both rapport and aggression, and reframing the interaction as play. Thus world play tends to disrupt topical turn-by-turn coherence, though it signals rapport overall, just as exchanging personal anecdotes enhances positive affect. Sarcasm and mocking seem to signal negative affect, but even these aggressive forms of joking reframe the interaction as play like the other joking strategies, so they end up conveying solidarity and modulating involvement, especially among conversationalists who maintain a customary joking relationship.

Norris, Christopher. "The 'Apocalyptic Tone' in Philosophy" in *European Philosophy and the American Academy*, Smith, Barry (ed), 145-193. Peru, Open Court, 1994.

This article examines Jacques Derrida's complex and ambivalent dealings with the so-called 'apocalyptic tone'. Starting out from his essay on Kant's polemic against Hamann, Jacobi and suchlike claimants to an order of intuitive wisdom beyond mere critical reason, it then seeks to show how similar issues arise at many points in Derrida's work, especially his writings on Plato, Husserl and Levinas. What is involved here is the idea of language as somehow always exceeding the limit of any possible construction that can be placed upon it by systematizing theorists and philosophers. However we shall be wrong if we think of Derrida as allied to the mystagogues or irrationalists and hence as opposed to the tradition of Enlightenment critique from Kant to Habermas. Rather, he is raising some important speculative questions with regard to the fraught but curiously close (even mutually dependent) relationship between these rival parties.

Norris, Stephen P. Sustaining and Responding to Charges of Bias in Critical Thinking. *Educ Theor*, 45(2), 199-211, Spr 95.

The paper deals with three issues. First, bias in critical thinking increases in importance as critical thinking includes more of our educational aspirations. Second, charges of bias in critical thinking require empirical evidence of a high standard. Such evidence is difficult to find and to produce, but social-psychological, anthropological, and cognitive science research are possible sources. An example of evidence from each of these sources is provided. Third, the nature of the response of the critical thinking field to charges of bias is very important, and has often been inappropriate. The narrative genre, rather than the argumentative, is suggested as an appropriate initial response. This suggestion does not rule out other genres of response being used subsequently, but, if adopted, would facilitate the engagement necessary to treat the charges fairly and honestly and to learn what they have to offer.

Norton, Bruce. "Late Capitalism and Postmodernism: Jameson/Mandel" in *Marxism in the Postmodern Age, Callari, Antonio (ed)*, 59-70. New York, Guilford, 1994.

The paper criticizes Frederic Jameson's conception of postmodernism for relying on a modernist, teleological theory of the economic. In situating cultural phenomena as the product of a capitalist epoch—Ernest Mandel's third expansionary long wave—Jameson adapts a particular Marxian falling rate of profit framework. The fit is problematic. As the paper argues, Jameson's argument (stressing the expansive and subject-transforming power of capital) is incompatible with Mandel's own (in which capitalism is marked by an eventually explosive essential contradiction). Nevertheless the two share certain general characteristics, particularly the view that an abstract logic of capital ultimately shapes social life.

Norton, Bryan G. Economists' Preferences and the Preferences of Economists. *Environ Values*, 3(4), 311-332, Wint 94.

Economists, who adopt the principle of consumer sovereignty, treat preferences as unquestioned for the purposes of their analysis. They also represent preferences for future outcomes as having value in the present. It is shown that these two characteristics of neoclassical modelling rest on similar reasoning and are essential to achieve high aggregatability of preferences and values. But the meaning and broader implications of these characteristics vary according to the arguments given to support these methodological choices. The resulting ambiguities raise questions regarding economists' attitudes toward the study (by other disciplines) of preference formation and reformation. Under a strong, positivist interpretation (which is philosophically problematic), consumer sovereignty represents a rejection of any meaningful study of these subjects; under a weaker, methodological understanding, consumer sovereignty merely draws a boundary between economics and other disciplines. The weaker version is argued to be more defensible, and economists are urged to engage in interdisciplinary work that will clarify how preferences are formed, criticized and reformed.

Norton, John D. The Theory of Random Propositions. *Erkenntnis*, 41(3), 325-352, N 94.

The theory of random propositions is a theory of confirmation that contains the Bayesian and Shafer-Dempster theories as special cases, while extending both in ways that resolve many of their outstanding problems. The theory resolves the Bayesian "problem of the priors" and provides an extension of Dempster's rule of combination for partially dependent evidence. The standard probability calculus can be generated from the calculus of frequencies among infinite sequences of outcomes. The theory of random propositions is generated analogously from the calculus of frequencies among pairs of infinite sequences of suitably generalized outcomes and in a way that precludes the inclusion of contrived or *ad hoc* elements. The theory is also formulated as an uninterpreted calculus.

Norton, M Scott. Department Reorganization and Faculty Status in Educational Administration. *J Thought*, 30(3), 87-96, Fall 95.

Norton, Robert E. *The Beautiful Soul: Aesthetic Morality in the Eighteenth Century*. Ithaca, Cornell Univ Pr, 1995.

In the eighteenth century the "beautiful soul" was for many the symbol of enlightened humanity, representing the possibility of fusing aesthetic beauty and moral goodness in a new, indivisible unity. I trace the history of this cultural icon, exploring the reasons for its initial popularity and its subsequent decline as a cultural ideal during the enlightenment. The book shows that the attempt to combine the good and the beautiful was a response to the rise of secular authority at the end of the seventeenth and beginning of the eighteenth centuries. It draws on English, French, and German sources to demonstrate how philosophical, theological, and cultural themes were united in the elaboration of the beautiful soul.

Norwood, Rick. The Evolution of the Will. *Phil Sci (Tucson)*, 6, 143-151, 1995.

Action by an effort of will exists. The proof is that in the absence of such action, no correlation would exist between subjective feelings and objective fitness to survive and reproduce.

Nota, John. "Love's Moral and Religious Implications: Irving Singer's Trilogy" in *The Nature and Pursuit of Love, Goicoechea, David (ed)*, 196-207. Buffalo, Prometheus, 1995.

Notturno, M A (ed) and Popper, Karl R. *Knowledge and the Body-Mind Problem: In Defence of Interaction*. New York, Routledge, 1994.

Knowledge and the Body-Mind Problem is based on lectures given in 1969 at Emory University which raised problems connected with human freedom, creativity, rationality, and the relationship between human beings and their actions. Popper defends the existence of an interaction between mental states (such as hopes, needs, plans, pains, dogmatically held ideologies, or tentatively held scientific hypotheses) and physical states of our brain and their physical consequences (such as the writing of a letter, a visit to the dentist or to a friend). (edited)

Notturno, M A (ed) and Popper, Karl R. *The Myth of the Framework: In Defence of Science and Rationality*. New York, Routledge, 1994.

Novgorodtsev, P I. On the Tasks of the Contemporary Philosophy of Law. *Russian Stud Phil*, 33(3), 43-48, Wint 94-95.

Novgorodtsev, P I. The Idea of Law in the Philosophy of V S Solov'ev. *Russian Stud Phil*, 33(3), 49-61, Wint 94-95.

Novick, Alvin. Some Thoughts on AIDS and Death. *J Clin Ethics*, 6(1), 91-92, Spr 95.

The developing dialogue on physician assisted death has almost entirely involved physicians and ethicists. The voices of dying persons are not being heard. We have failed to encourage research on what has actually been happening in our nation, what the obstacles have been, and what costs and benefits have been perceived. Serious concerns have been expressed about authorizing assisted death, yet no systematic studies have developed to enlighten us. We focus instead on "establishment values", some of which, the perceived benefit of suffering or the sanctity of life are currently imposed, like sentences, on those seeking help.

Novikova, L and Sizemskaia, I. Liberal Tradition in the Cultural-Historical Experience of Russia. *Russian Stud Phil*, 33(3), 6-25, Wint 94-95.

The article provides a history of liberal political thinking in Russia. It points up both its original Western inspiration and the particular coloration assumed in Russia by such liberal concepts as the rule of law and the absolute value of the individual. The authors develop the concept of "new liberalism", relevant to Russian mentality. It made by greater emphasis on constitutionalism and active role of the state in providing social benefits and promoting cultural values. Since 1860 the social development of Russia followed this way, but this process was broken by revolutions of 1917.

Novitz, David. "Architectural Brilliance and the Constraints of Time" in *Philosophy and Architecture, Mitias, Michael H (ed)*, 67-85. Amsterdam, Rodopi, 1994.

The idea that architecture is generated in response to practical needs, prevailing values, interests, and concerns is not at all new. One of its more recent, very influential, appearances has been in the work of the architectural historian Sigfried Giedion. Over the last fifteen years, however, Giedion's work has been subjected to extensive criticism in the work of John Watkin and Roger Scruton. In the process his central claim that architecture is produced in response to, and in terms of, the values, needs, achievements, and interest of an age has either been ignored or else dismissed. It is this thesis, and the attack on it, that is examined.

Novitz, David. Messages 'In' and Messages 'Through' Art. *Austl J Phil*, 73(2), 199-203, Je 95.

An attempt to distinguish two different ways in which works of art may make assertions about the real world.

Nowak, Leszek. "The Idealization Methodology and Economics" in *Idealization VI: Idealization in Economics, Hamminga, Bert (ed)*, 303-336. Amsterdam, Rodopi, 1994.

A reply to the papers by Kevin D Hoover, Maarten C W Janssen, Werner Diederich, Gerard Jorland, Uskali Mäki, all in the present volume. It contains some additional explanations of various elements of the idealizational methodology and more detailed extensions and developments. Some of these extensions are available only in the Polish writings of various authors from the Poznan milieu. However, there still remain some objections that challenge the conception as, even in its most developed forms, it does not contain a ready answer to them. These require new findings in the idealizational approach to science and in certain cases some conjectures are proposed.

Nowak, Leszek and Nowakowa, Izabella. "On Correspondence between Economic Theories" in *Idealization VI: Idealization in Economics, Hamminga, Bert (ed)*, 135-146. Amsterdam, Rodopi, 1994.

An analysis of the relationships between theories in terms of 'dialectical correspondence' in the sense of the idealizational theory of science. Such correspondence can be observed in the history of economic theory, though somewhat less clearly than in physics, due to the secondary influence of ideology.

Nowak, Marek and Geisler, Jacek. Conditional Negation on the Positive Logic. *Bull Sec Log*, 23(3), 130-136, O 94.

In the paper a paraconsistent logic is considered, representative of a class of sentential logics which, taking into account their features, can be called the class of classical paraconsistent logics. The truth conditions for negation in the frame-semantics adequate for that logic are expressed in a conditional way.

Nowakowa, Izabella and Nowak, Leszek. "On Correspondence between Economic Theories" in *Idealization VI: Idealization in Economics, Hamminga, Bert (ed)*, 135-146. Amsterdam, Rodopi, 1994.

An analysis of the relationships between theories in terms of 'dialectical correspondence' in the sense of the idealizational theory of science. Such correspondence can be observed in the history of economic theory, though somewhat less clearly than in physics, due to the secondary influence of ideology.

Nowicki, Andrzej. A Voice in Discussion About Mr Tsung-I Dow's Report. *Dialogue Hum*, 4(2-3), 231-232, 1994.

We should aim at such a unity of the world in which is respected and appreciated the variety of cultures and their reciprocal complement and enrichment. The beauty of signs of the Chinese written language and the possibility of different pronounciation of them by each nation in its own language—should incline the world to accept it as one of international languages. The principle objection to the report: wrongful for Chinese culture and damaging the great wealth of its internal differentiation is identification of the Chinese culture with Confucianism. The similar harm does identification of the wealth of Arabic countries with Islam or of the Polish culture with Christianism, ignoring the wealth and variety of its secular components.

Nubiola, Jaime. *La Renovación Pragmatista de la Filosofía Analítica: Una Introducción a la Filosofía Contemporánea del Lenguaje*. Pamplona, EUNSA, 1994.

Contrary to what is often stated about the end of analytic philosophy, in this book is suggested that the views of the later Wittgenstein and the rediscovery of Charles S Peirce have been key elements for a renewal of analytic tradition. Following mainly the lines suggested by H Putnam, this renewal has a strong pragmatist flavour, which encourages the unity of philosophy and the responsibility of philosophical work. In contemporary philosophical reflection a multilateral approach to the understanding of language and of our communicative practices has taken the old central place of logic.

Nuchelmans, Gabriel. Walter Burleigh on the Conclusion that You Are an Ass. *Vivarium*, 32(1), 90-101, My 94.

Nudler, Oscar. Sócrates: Filósofo Dogmático? Una Réplica a Alfonso Gómez-Lobo. *Rev Latin de Filosof*, 21(1), 167-172, Fall 95.

In order to reply to A Gómez-Lobo's criticisms of my paper "Socrates, Philosopher at the Limit", it is argued that they miss the point for not taking duly into account the distinction between expert and nonexpert knowledge. At the same time, it is shown that Gomez-Lobo's reading of Socrates' philosophy as involving claims to expert knowledge of ethical principles is not supported by textual evidence. Reasons are provided for preferring an interpretation which, instead of abusing of the attribution of irony to Socrates' disavowals of knowledge, takes them as evidence of his critical, nondogmatic and nonskeptical approach to philosophical questions.

Nudler, Oscar. Sócrates: Filósofo en el Límite. *Rev Latin de Filosof*, 21(1), 145-157, Fall 95.

Several interpretations of the main purposes that would have inspired Socrates' thought and action—religious, political, moral—are reviewed and found not fully satisfactory. An alternative epistemological interpretation, based on a model of Western epistemic history, and more particularly on its notion of philosophy as a critical activity with some self-imposed limits, is offered. In the light of that model, Socrates is seen as a paradigmatic case of such critical approach to philosophy.

Nunan, Richard. Militant Gayes, Gayes in the Military, and Privacy as Social Freedom. *Law Phil*, 13(4), 481-492, N 94.

Núñez Cea, Victoria Martha. Qué es Poesía?. *Logos (Mexico)*, 23(67), 65-72, Ja-Ap 95.

Considerando a la poesía como una vía de conocimiento alternativa, afiliada con el mito y la reflexión filosófica se plantea una de las interrogantes esenciales: la immortalidad. Pero la inmoratlidad se ha transformado en soberbia y fama a la que se inmola el espíritu; la ironía de esta dudosa posterdad radica en la memoria ingrata que el hombre tiene de sí mismo. Ante esto la filosofía y la poesía continúan dialogando, el sabio medita y el poeta crea variaciones; de modo que donde la Razón y el entendimiento no alcanzan, la imagen poética tiende un puente.

Nurmi, Hannu. On the Difficulty of Making Social Choices. *Theor Decis*, 38(1), 99-119, Ja 95.

The difficulty of making social choices seems to take on two forms: one that is related to both preferences and the method used in aggregating them and one which is related to the preferences only. In the former type the difficulty has to do with the discrepancies of outcomes resulting from various preference aggregation methods and the computation of winners in elections. Some approaches and results which take their motivation from the computability theory are discussed. The latter 'institution-free' type of difficulty pertains to solution theory of the voting games. We discuss the relationships between various solution concepts, e.g., uncovered set, Banks set, Copeland winners. Finally rough sets are utilized in an effort to measure the difficulty of making social choices.

Nussbaum, Charles. The Birth of Cadential-Harmonic Music from the Spirit of Modern Idealism. *Ideal Stud*, 25(1), 69-91, Wint 95.

The years 1750-1900 saw a sudden and remarkable efflorescence of musical creativity in the German-speaking countries. But these years also bore witness to another, similarly localized cultural flowering that was hardly less significant: the waxing and waning of German idealism. These occurrences are not unrelated, for they can be interpreted historically as culminations of two signal cultural posits of the 17th century which are themselves related: the system of cadential harmony of the Baroque and the Cartesian philosophy of the subject. This paper traces this set of relations and explores their ramifications.

Nussbaum, Martha C. Beatrice's 'Dante': Loving the Individual?. *Apeiron*, 26(3-4), 161-178, S-D 93.

Nussbaum, Martha C. Feministinnen und Philosophie. *Deut Z Phil*, 43(2), 375-387, 1995.

Nussbaum, Martha C. The Transfiguration of Everyday Life. *Metaphilosophy*, 25(4), 238-261, O 94.

Nuyen, A T. Critique of Ideology: Hermeneutics or Critical Theory?. *Human Stud*, 17(4), 419-432, 1994-95.

Habermas criticizes Gadamer for failing to provide a critique of ideology. For Habermas, such a critique has to be grounded in some universal principle of reason. For Gadamer, there is no transcendental principle which is beyond interpretation. Strictly speaking, hermeneutics is quite capable of providing a critique of ideology provided that we give a flexible interpretation of the hermeneutic appeal to tradition. On the other hand, insofar as Habermas has in mind a universal principle which is itself beyond critique, he is in danger of turning the autonomy of reason into a dictatorship of reason.

Nuyen, A T. Interpretation and Understanding in Hermeneutics and Deconstruction. *Phil Soc Sci*, 24(4), 426-438, D 94.

It seems that Derrida objects to Gadamer's hermeneutics on the grounds that it is, as Gadamer puts it, "a discipline that guarantees truth", taking it as something that partakes in the "metaphysics of presence". However, this criticism is based on a misunderstanding of the nature of hermeneutic truth. It would be on target if hermeneutic truth were some kind of universal condition of correspondence. Gadamer has tried to correct this conception of hermeneutic truth in his various attempts at opening a dialogue with deconstructionism. In this article, the author argues that in a possible debate between hermeneutics and deconstructionism, there are good reasons to judge in favor of the former.

Nuyen, A T. Power and Knowledge: Some Educational Implications of Foucault's Epistemology. *J Thought*, 30(2), 75-91, Sum 95.

The principle lesson from Foucault is that knowledge is manufactured. It is thus important to learn about conditions under which knowledge is produced, its conditions of possibility. For Foucault, they are embedded in the underlying discourse of the epoch. Contrary to Foucault, it is possible to gain access to the underlying discourse. If so then it is possible to alter one's cognitive viewpoint by switching to a different set of conditions of possibility. It is possible to see the world differently. It is important to learn to do so.

Nuyen, A T. Straining the Quality of Mercy. *Phil Papers*, 23(2), 61-74, Ag 94.

It is often assumed that there is a moral requirement to be merciful in the context of punishment. The paper argues that mercy is often confused with equity. To take into account circumstances pertaining to the offender is not to be merciful but to be equitable in the Aristotelian sense. Strained of what is properly equity, mercy amounts to responding to one's own feelings about the offender, and as such it is not clear that it is a virtue in the context of punishment even though it could be a personal virtue.

Nuyen, A T. The Heart of the Kantian Moral Agent. *Amer Cath Phil Quart*, 69(1), 51-62, Wint 95.

It is often supposed that the Kantian agent may not take into account his or her inclinations toward the outcome of an act if the act is to have moral worth. This view follows from the interpretation of Kant according to which the sensuous side of the agent has no moral significance. I argue that, following Allison's two-aspect account, sensuous inclinations do have a role to play in Kant's ethics. An act that does not have moral worth in the strict Kantian sense (because inclinations are mixed up in the motive) may still be meritorious.

Nuyen, A T. The Rhetoric of Feminist Writings. *Phil Rhet*, 28(1), 69-82, Ja 95.

Lyotard has pointed out that the feminist who wishes to speak against marginalization faces a problem (called *différend*): either the complaint will not be taken seriously, or if it is then what is being complained about (i.e., marginalization, or not being taken seriously) is not true. I argue that the unusual styles found in some feminist writings may be regarded as a way of overcoming Lyotard's *différend*. However, for Lyotard, such stylistic devices are "non-cognitive regimens". Against Lyotard, I argue that they have a cognitive function.

Nuzzo, Enrico. Natura Umana e Conoscenza Storica in Vico: Sulle Recenti 'Riletture' Vichiane di Leon Pompa. *Boll Centro Stud Vichiani*, 24-25, 163-182, 1994-95.

This paper examines Pompa's two most recent volumes on Vico, trying to point out how the theoretical interests and the analytical basic methods supporting them be at the same time the basis of their assets, but also of many interpretative limits. More particularly, if the critical perspective on Vico is valid regarding the necessity to highlight Vico's claim that he founded a science of the historical world, it should be rectified over a number of other fundamental points: the characteristics of the human culture, the relationship between reason and fantasy, a conception of history which is not thoroughly deterministic. Besides, Pompa's theoretical perspective on the question of the conditions of the possibility of historical knowledge would benefit from a reflection on neohistorical and humanistic points of view.

Nyikos, Peter and Piatkiewicz, Leszek. On the Equivalence of Certain Consequences of the Proper Forcing Axiom. *J Sym Log*, 60(2), 431-443, Je 95.

O'Brien, Lucy. Evans on Self-Identification. *Nous*, 29(2), 232-247, Je 95.

Gareth Evans in his *The Varieties of Reference* seems to try to explain first person reference using a model based upon that he develops to explain the reference of perceptual demonstratives. This paper argues that this account cannot give a satisfactory account of first person reference even in Evans's own terms. It also suggests that we should in general be wary of taking any sort of perceptual or quasi-perceptual relation as the basis of our capacity to self-refer.

O'Brien, Lucy F. Anscombe and the Self-Reference Rule. *Analysis*, 54(4), 277-281, O 94.

Anscombe has argued that an account of 'I' as a device of reflexive reference will be either insufficient or circular. The article argues that Anscombe has made a mistake but has also pointed towards an important insight. Given that speakers know that they are using a term when they are, if they use 'I' as a device of self-reference, they will succeed in referring to themselves in the first person way. The insight Anscombe has lead us to is that there remains as a problem with accounting for the knowledge I have that I am using the term 'I'.

O'Brien, Lucy F. The Problem of Self-Identification. *Proc Aris Soc*, 95, 235-251, 1994-95.

The paper gives a brief overview of current approaches to the problem of self-identification. It identifies two main approaches to the problem—the perceptual and the self-reference. It argues that despite problems with both, the self-reference approach is more promising. A discussion of problems faced by this approach and a suggestion that goes some way to meeting them is offered. Central to the positive suggestion is the idea that we have—even when we have no observational awareness of ourselves—an awareness of ourselves through participation (in our actions) which can be exploited by the self-reference approach.

O'Connor, David K. "The Erotic Self-Sufficiency of Socrates" in *The Socratic Movement, Vander Waerdt, Paul A (ed)*, 151-180. Ithaca, Cornell Univ Pr, 1994.

In the *Memorabilia*, Xenophon gives a complex account of why Socrates was attractive to and attracted by so many different sorts of people, from politically ambitious men like Alcibiades to apolitical intellectuals like Aristippus and Aristodemus. Xenophon makes the key to these various erotic relationships the attempts of Socrates' admirers to imitate his self-sufficiency. But Xenophon also shows indirectly that all of these imitations run up against one essential problem: Socrates' divine sign (*daimonion*) gives him a unique access to the knowledge necessary to guarantee success, so that in the end he cannot be successfully imitated.

O'Connor, Martin and Vadnjal, Dan. What is the Value of Rangitoto Island?. *Environ Values*, 3(4), 369-380, Wint 94.

Contingent valuation has been promoted as a catch-all approach to environmental valuation. While there have been numerous attempts in recent years to place monetary values on environmental amenities, studies have often reported a high frequency of protest, zero or inordinately large dollar-value responses. This paper reports on the results of a survey designed to obtain information on how people actually interpret questions of paying to avoid changes in their views of Rangitoto Island. Evidence suggests that the meaning respondents attach to the actual dollar values they offer or bid are inconsistent with the conventional logic that underlies contingent valuation. Instead, respondents might be seen to be expressing views about how things ought to be in society, and that it is simply not right to develop Rangitoto Island.

O'Connor, Mary Ann and Hill, T Patrick and Teno, Joan M. Advance Care Planning: Priorities for Ethical and Empirical Research. *Hastings Center Rep*, 24(6), Supp 1-36, N-D 94.

Federal statute endorses advance directives as one means for patients to control medical decisions in advance of incompetence. We invited investigators from multiple disciplines to develop priorities for conceptual and empirical research.

Conference participants noted research should focus on the merits of a process of communication which we titled "advance care planning". Priorities for conceptual research included: 1) the moral weight of autonomy; 2) what preferences should be voiced in advance (considering importance, authenticity and stability); and 3) appropriate safeguards. Multidisciplinary empirical research utilizing both quantitative and qualitative research methodologies should describe the current process and outcomes of decision-making generally.

O'Connor, Peg. Locke's Challenge to Innate Practical Principles Revisited. *Locke News*, 25, 41-51, 1994.

O'Connor, Timothy. An Evolutionary Argument Against Naturalism?. *Can J Phil*, 24(4), 527-539, D 94.

Alvin Plantinga has recently argued that belief in evolutionary naturalism is self-defeating. He contends that reflection on certain features of this view should undermine the naturalist's confidence in the basic reliability of human cognitive faculties, and consequently lead her to refrain from belief in their reliability. But if she does withhold such belief, she must likewise refrain from believing propositions that are the output of her cognitive faculties. And, for evolutionary naturalists, one such output is belief in evolutionary naturalism itself. However, reflection on the place of the reliability belief in one's noetic structure shows that Plantinga's argument is mistaken.

O'Connor, Timothy. Emergent Properties. *Amer Phil Quart*, 31(2), 91-104, Ap 94.

The notion that a natural phenomenon might be at once *grounded in* and yet *emergent from* its underlying material basis has received renewed attention, with the focus of application being biological consciousness. But how such claims are to be interpreted remains controversial. This paper criticizes a few formulations of the concept of property emergence, and then defends an alternative account as better suited for the purposes of philosophical and scientific theory. Finally, the neurophysiologist R W Sperry's theory of emergent consciousness is presented and clarified.

O'Connor, Timothy. On the Transfer of Necessity. *Nous*, 27(2), 204-218, Je 93.

O'Connor, Timothy. Thomas Reid on Free Agency. *J Hist Phil*, 32(4), 605-622, O 94.

Reid takes it to be part of our commonsense view of ourselves that *we—qua* enduring substances, not merely *qua* subjects of efficacious mental states—are often the immediate causes of our own volitions. Only if this conviction is veridical, Reid thinks, may we be properly held to be responsible for our actions (indeed, may we truly be said to *act* at all). This paper offers an interpretation of Reid's account of such agency (taking account of Rowe's recent commentary), with particular attention to the issue of the causation of and responsibility for an agent's *causing* of his volition.

O'Dea, Jane W. Authenticity in Musical Performance: Personal or Historical?. *Brit J Aes*, 34(4), 363-375, O 94.

The proliferation of articles dealing with historical authenticity in musical and philosophical journals of the last ten years affirms its central influence in contemporary performance practice. Recognizing its significance, yet mindful also of its tendency to polarize creative imagination and historical scholarship this paper asks: are historical research and personal convictions on the part of the performer really so incompatible? It is suggested that they are not. But the answer lies in performers cultivating and exercising not "historical" authenticity but rather "personal" authenticity. The ramifications for music performance of this later notion of authenticity are posited and explored.

O'Dea, Jane W. Pursuing Truth in Narrative Research. *J Phil Educ*, 28(2), 161-171, Wint 94.

In substituting aesthetic criteria for the time-honored yardsticks of reliability, validity and generalization, narrative researchers are sometimes criticized for devaluing the notion of truth. This paper suggests that what is an issue here is not so much empirical quantitative truth as rather artistic literary truth. The latter notion of truth is characterized in terms of 'authenticity' and the ramifications of authentic truth for narrative research are posited and explored. Only such an understanding of truth and the resolve seriously to apply it will garner narrative researchers the epistemic respectability they seek.

O'Donnell, John. The Trinitarian Panentheism of Sergej Bulgakov. *Gregorianum*, 76(1), 31-45, 1995.

Le théologien russe du 20ème siècle, Bulgakov, a influencé certains théologiens contemporains importants, tels Moltmann et Balthasar. Sa synthèse théologique confronte le problème central du rapport entre Dieu et le monde. Pour lui la clé du problème est la "sophia" éternelle qui n'est pas une hypostase en Dieu mais un principe médiateur entre Dieu et la création. Pour Bulgakov c'est en dernière analyse ce principe qui rend pensable l'incarnation de Dieu en Jésus-Christ. Bulgakov parle également dans la Trinité d'une kénose qui l'ouvere au monde: cette kénose trouve son expression suprême dans la croix. Bulgakov comprend Dieu comme décidant éternellement de créer le monde, de telle sorte que la créatione st temporelle en son être mais éternelle en son fondement. Il prolonge la tradition d'Origène en enseignant la victoire finale du Christ sur toutes choses, même le démon. Sa vision trinitaire de la relation Dieu-monde fait impression. On peut cependant se demander si le cadre de la "sophiologie" russe est nécessaire a communiquer ses intuitions les plus profondes.

O'Driscoll, Sally (trans) and Clément, Catherine and Mahoney, Deirdre M (trans). *Syncope: The Philosophy of Rapture*. Minneapolis, Univ of Minn Pr, 1994.

O'Grady, Paul and Rigby, Paul and Van Den Hengel, John. Must a Hermeneutical Psychoanalysis Exclude Science?. *Man World*, 28(2), 115-128, Ap 95.

O'Hagan, Timothy. Bad Faith and Gestalt. *J Brit Soc Phenomenol*, 25(3), 302-304, O 94.

O'Hara, Daniel T. "Why Foucault No Longer Matters" in *Reconstructing Foucault, Miguel-Alfonso, Ricardo (ed)*, 139-158. Amsterdam, Rodopi, 1994.

O'Hara, Mary L. The Vanishing Person: A Century of the *Encyclopaedia Britannica* on the Meaning of "Person". *Int Stud Phil*, 27(2), 101-107, 1995.

A study of successive editions of the *Encyclopedia Britannica* during its first century of existence shows that a shift in the definition of 'person' took place between 1771 and 1859, reflecting a change in the intellectual climate of the time, and in particular the influence of extra-philosophical (religious) considerations. From the more structural (Aristotelian) definition of Boethius, incoherently explained in the first edition, the word tended toward a more functional one, under the influence of Locke and Kant. Except for writers like Gordon Allport, few twentieth-century thinkers refer to the Boethian definition which held sway for 1500 years.

O'Keefe, John. "Cognitive Maps, Time and Causality" in *Objectivity, Simulation and the Unity of Consciousness, Peacocke, Christopher (ed)*, 35-45. New York, Oxford Univ Pr, 1994.

O'Leary, Paul. A Critical Review of Allen Pearson, *The Teacher: Theory and Practice in Teacher Education*. *Stud Phil Educ*, 13(2), 157-162, 1993-94.

In his book *The Teacher*, Allen Pearson examines the relationship between educational theory and practice. Unlike other approaches, Pearson considers this relationship in terms of how belief and action are connected by way of a teacher's practical reasoning. In developing certain principles of practical reasoning, Pearson utilizes McIntyre's notion of "a practice" and applies it to teaching. My article raises several objections to Pearson's approach, the general upshot of which is that it gives the current practices of teaching far too much normative force over the educational beliefs of teachers.

O'Leary-Hawthorne, Diane. Theaetetan Epistemology as Platonic Epistemology. *Austl J Phil*, 73(1), 49-70, Mr 95.

In the dialogue bearing his name Theaetetus suggests that "knowledge is nothing but perception", a suggestion construed by Socrates as "knowledge and sense perception are the same thing". I argue that Plato's contemporaries might likely have construed Theaetetus' point as "to come to know is to come to notice or to understand", and that while readers will be tempted to passively accept Socrates' construal, Plato expects the good reader to resist. In spite of his misconstrual Socrates' discussion with Theaetetus serves to develop Theaetetus' original point in a way that unifies not only this dialogue, but also apparently conflicting views about knowledge offered in others.

O'Leary-Hawthorne, John. A Corrective to the Ramsey-Lewis Account of Theoretical Terms. *Analysis*, 54(2), 105-110, Ap 94.

O'Loughlin, Marjorie. "Ways of Thinking and Being: Explorations in Ontologies" in *Identity, Culture, and Education, Smeyers, Paul (ed)*, 283-293. Leuven, Leuven Univ Pr, 1994.

O'Meara, Thomas F. "Christianity is the Future of Paganism: Schelling's Philosophy of Religion, 1826-1854" in *Meaning, Truth, and God, Rouner, Leroy S (ed)*, 216-235. Notre Dame, Univ Notre Dame Pr, 1982.

O'Meara, Thomas F. The History of Being and the History of Doctrine: An Influence of Heidegger on Theology. *Amer Cath Phil Quart*, 69(2), 351-374, Spr 95.

O'Meley, Serena. Otto's Idea of the 'Numinous': A Crosscultural Reappraisal. *Sophia (Australia)*, 34(1), 241-258, Mr-Ap 95.

O'Neill, John. Essentialism and the Market. *Phil Forum*, 26(2), 87-100, Wint 94.

O'Neill, John. Intrinsic Evil, Truth, and Authority. *Relig Stud*, 31(2), 209-219, Je 95.

This paper responds to Pope John Paul's *Veritatis Splendor*. It defends one of its claims, that some human acts are intrinsically evil, and relates it to another, that one should live in truth. It outlines two versions of the idea of living in truth and argues that the Thomist position defended in the encyclical is to be preferred. However, the paper rejects the encyclical's authoritarianism. It criticizes not the concept of 'authoritative teaching' as such—all teaching presupposes epistemological authority—but the way in which the encyclical's characterization of such authority is incompatible with one of its preconditions—reasoned dialogue.

O'Neill, John. Should Communitarians be Nationalists?. *J Applied Phil*, 11(2), 135-143, 1994.

It is widely supposed by both its proponents and critics that communitarianism is committed to the defense of ties of nationhood: the nation forms a surviving communal attachment in a world in which the individual is otherwise denuded of ties of community. I argue in this paper that this assumption is mistaken. It depends on a romantic image of the nation which was constructed in the eighteenth and nineteenth centuries. That image hides the recent historical origins of the nation and its foundation in the suppression of older allegiances or their later privatization; it continues to disguise the illusory nature of the national community. The nation is not a surviving pre-modern community to which individuals are attached as a bulwark against the impersonality of public life in modern society. Rather the nation is one of the main vehicles for the construction of the modern unencumbered self. Communitarians need not be committed to the defense of the specifically modern forms of public irrationality and immorality that nationalism embodies.

O'Neill, John. 'The Same Thing Therefore Ought To Be and Ought Not To Be': Anselm on Conflicting Oughts. *Heythrop J*, 35(3), 312-314, Jl 94.

This paper shows that Anselm's assertion of the possibility of ethical conflicts is consistent with Aquinas's later denial of moral dilemmas. That Anselm consistently both asserts the possibility of ethical conflicts and denies the possibility of moral dilemmas is instructive for recent debates on ethical dilemmas. It shows that the existence of ethical conflict does not necessarily entail the existence of moral dilemmas. And it highlights the importance in the denial of moral dilemmas of a strong interpretation of the Pauline principle, that it is impermissible to do evil that good may come of it.

O'Neill, Onora. Practical Reason and Possible Community: A Reply to Jean-Marc Ferry. *Ratio Juris*, 7(3), 308-313, D 94.

Various conceptions of practical reason are used in contemporary positions in political philosophy. Communitarians appeal to the actual standards of existing communities; Rawls to ideals (which he now identifies with those of actual liberal communities). Habermas has variously appealed to actual and to ideal standards of conducting dialogue within communities, but has recently taken a more Kantian turn in appealing to the necessary conditions of possible community. Since appeals to the conditions for dialogue in actual or in idealized communities do not provide a convincing account of practical reason, it is important to take strictly Kantian conceptions of practical reason seriously.

O'Neill, Shane. Morality, Ethical Life and the Persistence of Universalism. *Theor Cult Soc*, 11(2), 129-149, My 94.

This article assesses Jürgen Habermas's discourse ethics as a version of moral universalism. Habermas's contextualist critics, inspired by Hegel's critique of Kant, reject his distinction between moral and ethical questions. They maintain that no moral norms could be justified without reference to some substantive ethical commitment. The article reviews recent contributions of Seyla Benhabib, Georgia Warnke and Charles Taylor to this debate. While discourse ethics is defended in general, it is argued that Habermas needs to develop further his thinking on the relationship between moral and ethical uses of practical reason if his defense of universalism is to convince.

O'Neill, William. The Ethics of Our Climate: Hermeneutics and Ethical Theory. Washington, Georgetown Univ Pr, 1994.

The Ethics of Our Climate charts a via media between the abstract formalism of neo-Kantian morality and relativist interpretations of neo-Aristotelian ethics. The three parts of the book treat of the eclipse of the Aristotelian conception of practical reason (*phronesis*), the Kantian heritage in the modern moral theories of John Rawls and R M Hare, and a critical retrieval of a moral interpretation of the world in light of Hans-Georg Gadamer's philosophical hermeneutics, analytical criticism, and Jürgen Habermas' discourse ethics. The final chapter applies the preceding hermeneutical critique to the question of the distinctiveness of religious ethics.

O'Regan, Cyril. "The Religious and Theological Relevance of the French Revolution" in *Hegel on the Modern World, Collins, Ardis B (ed)*, 29-52. Albany, SUNY Pr, 1995.

O'Shaughnessy, Brian. "The Mind-Body Problem" in *The Mind-Body Problem: A Guide to the Current Debate, Warner, Richard (ed)*, 204-214. Cambridge, Blackwell, 1994.

O'Sullivan, Noël. "Political Integration, the Limited State, and the Philosophy of Postmodernism" in *The End of "Isms"?, Shtromas, Alexsandras (ed)*, 23-44. Cambridge, Blackwell, 1994.

O'Sullivan, Noël. Nietzsche and the Agenda of Post-Modernity. *Hist Euro Ideas*, 20(1-3), 145-151, Ja 95.

Oaigen, Edson Roberto. A Educaçao e a Autonomia do Profesor: Caminhos para a Emancipaçao. *Educ Filosof*, 8(16), 159-172, Jl-D 94.

A Educaçao e a Autonomia do Professor: Caminhos para a Emancipaçao. A instituiçao escolar, num trabalho integrado entre os diferentes segmentos da comunidade e dos respectivos níveis de ensino, atuando concomitantemente, com certeza possibilitara a preparaçao adequada do cidadao, autônomo, responsável e emancipado. Convém destacar o conceito que atribuo ao cidadao: homem capaz de intervir em seu mundo sócio cultural, por meio do exercício da co-participaçao, principalmente em realidades subdesenvolvidas. O objetivo do trabalho possibilita um momento de reflexao crítica, dinâmica e participativa, através da mudança e do esforço dos professores, das comunidades escolares e de todos os segmentos sociais no encontro de uma nova educaçao crítica e autônoma, construindo um cidadao inteligente e capaz de vencer os obstáculos do cotidiano.

Oaklander, L Nathan. Bigelow, Possible Worlds and The Passage of Time. *Analysis*, 54(4), 244-248, O 94.

In his article, "Worlds Enough for Time," *Nous* (March, 1991), John Bigelow argues that the tensed theory of time can be defended against McTaggart's paradox by an appeal to the notion of possible worlds. In this paper I argue that and why Bigelow's attempts to vindicate the tensed theory is unsuccessful.

Oaklander, L Nathan. Time and Foreknowledge: A Critique of Zagzebski. *Relig Stud*, 31(1), 101-103, Mr 95.

One problem facing those who attempt to reconcile divine foreknowledge with human freedom is to explain how a temporal God can have knowledge of the future, if the future does not exist. In her recent book, *The Dilemma of Freedom and Foreknowledge*, Linda Zagzebski attempts to provide an explanation by making use of a four-dimensional model in which the past, present and future exist. In this note I argue that the model Zagzebski offers to support the coplausibility of divine foreknowledge and human freedom is inconsistent with the A-theory of time she propounds.

Oaklander, L Nathan and Smith, Quentin. *Time, Change, and Freedom: An Introduction to Metaphysics*. New York, Routledge, 1995.

Oakley, Francis. Nederman, Gerson, Conciliar Theory, and Constitutionalism: Sed Contra. *Hist Polit Thought*, 16(1), 1-19, Spr 95.

Oakley, Justin. Consequentialis, Moral Responsibility, and the Intention/Foresight Distinction. *Utilitas*, 6(2), 201-216, N 94.

A standard consequentialist argument against the moral relevance of the intention/foresight distinction is based on the claim that there is no asymmetry in moral responsibility between intending and foreseeing evil. We argue that even if this claim is correct, it does not entail that there is no moral asymmetry between acts of intended and foreseen evil. Similarly, consequentialists cannot plausibly base their rejection of such asymmetry by appealing to an equivalence in an agent's blameworthiness in both cases. Consequentialist moves to allow this asymmetry only at the level of agent evaluations are also rejected, since they unacceptably sever important connections between act and agent evaluations.

Obenchain, Diane B. Continuity—Guo Xiang, Chan, Cheng-Zhu *Lixue*, New Realism, and Marxism—Feng's Discernment of the Way. *J Chin Phil*, 21(3-4), 481-519, S-D 94.

Oberdiek, Hans F. Just the Facts. *Int J Moral Soc Stud*, 8(3), 191-195, Autumn 93.

We contrast facts with fiction, forecasts, opinion, conjectures, theories, and values. Unlike them, facts seem solid, objective, and grounded in reality. These features of facts lead us to attribute to them an ontological status—a 'thinghood'—they do not have. Instead, reference to facts belongs to discourse *about* the world. When a scientist, e.g., says he wants 'just the facts' about something, he means that he wants to hear only what is *beyond controversy* about it. This analysis is fully

compatible with the view that there is a changing but structured world that exists independently of our talk about it (contrary to the views of some radical social constructivists). This account should also make us suspicious of claims that an unbridgeable chasm separates facts and values. For neither facts nor values are the sort of thing that *could* exist on either side of a chasm, bridgeable or not.

Obiols, Guillermo A. "Un Modelo Formal para la Enseñanza Filosófica en la Escuela Secundaria y un Ejemplo de Aplicacion del Mismo" in *Temas Actuales de Filosofía, Palacios, María Julia (ed)*, 415-422. Buenos Aires, Univ Nacional Salta, 1993.

Obuchowski, Kazimierz. The Psychological Aspects of Temporal Orientation. *Dialogue Hum*, 4(1), 31-35, 1994.

Ocaña, Enrique. Meta-Química, Estética e Iluminación. *Daimon Rev Filosof*, 8, 155-166, 1994.

Ocaña García, Marcelino. Actualidad de un Filósofo del Siglo XVI: Francisco de Vitoria. *An Seminar Hist Filosof*, 11, 191-219, 1994.

Francisco de Vitoria, in spite of being a theologian, is also an excellent philosopher. Although he lived in the 16th century, the topics he writes about are still relevant. Even though he was a priest and lived under an imperialist and inquisitorial regime, he didn't share those ideals. On some topics he was even more advanced than we are today. In any case as James Brown Scott says, "the modern school of international law came into being because there was somebody who determined the guidelines". And this was *Francisco de Vitoria*.

Ocaña García, Marcelino. El Sujeto Tridimensional. *An Seminar Hist Filosof*, 6, 79-88, 1986-89.

That the human being is tridimensional means that he cannot develop himself if it is not in the triple direction of experience, living together (with others) and transcendency. That is the reason why it is not necessary to have a reflected knowledge about this reality. Through experience we capture a tensional "I" without backgound, in which we always have some options of election. Living together appeals to the intersubjectivity, unavoidable, of course, but only with the fringe of possibilities which go from the pure living together (with others) to the profound living together of an "I" and a "thou" united in an "ourselves". Transcendency aims to the perpetuation of the "I", which is neither explicitly looked for nor accepted.

Ochs, Peter. "Scriptural Logic: Diagrams for a Postcritical Metaphysics" in *Rethinking Metaphysics, Jones, L Gregory (ed)*, 65-92. Cambridge, Blackwell, 1995.

A postcritical metaphysics is based on rules for repairing failed rules of reasoning, rather than on propositions about the world or conditions for knowing it. These rules of repair are what Charles Peirce called the irremediably vague and indubitable reasonings that we use everyday to correct our definable and fallible rules of behavior. Within the formal system of Peirce's "Existential Graphs," these vague rules are identified through the *performance* of diagramming them formally, rather than through the product of any single diagramming. Peirce calls this performance "scripture." This essay explores the logic that results when scripture is identified with Scripture.

Ochs, Peter. Scriptural Logic: Diagrams for a Postcritical Metaphysics. *Mod Theol*, 11(1), 65-92, Ja 95.

A postcritical metaphysics is grounded in rules for repairing failed rules of reasoning, rather than in propositions about the world or conditions for knowing it. Such rules function as what Charles Peirce considered the irremediably vague and indubitable reasonings that we, in fact, use to correct our definable and fallible rules of everyday conduct. According to Peirce's Existential Graphs, these vague rules may be identified through the *performance* of diagramming them formally, although not through the product of any single diagramming. Peirce calls this performance "scripture". This essay explores the logic that results when scripture is identified with Scripture.

Oddie, Graham. "Moral Uncertainty and Human Embryo Experimentation" in *Medicine and Moral Reasoning, Fulford, K W M (ed)*, 144-161. New York, Cambridge Univ Pr, 1994.

Moral dilemmas can arise from uncertainty, including uncertainty of the real values involved. Human embryo experimentation is a case in point. The moral status of such experimentation depends on the moral weight of the embryo, but that is hotly disputed and some of us are uncertain as to what its real moral weight is. Decision-theoretic consequentialism can help us here. I show that those who are uncertain are morally justified in experimenting only if the goods that would be obtained are comparable in value to those that would morally justify lethal experimentation on nonconsenting human persons.

Odegard, Douglas. Descartes and the Dream Argument. *Hist Phil Quart*, 12(2), 155-164, Ap 95.

One form of the dream argument is that we lack knowledge of the world because a) we have it only if we know we are not dreaming and b) we do not know that we are not dreaming. Recent discussion has tended to focus on whether a) is sound and, if it is, whether the dream argument can be consistently accepted. A case can be made for a) that preserves consistency. But b) does not survive close scrutiny.

Odegard, Douglas. Locke and the Preface Paradox. *Locke News*, 25, 29-40, 1994.

Locke probably would not like the conclusion that we are justified in believing that at least one of our justified beliefs is false. But the combination of his fallibilism and his thoughts on probability seem to make the conclusion unavoidable. We can help him out by distinguishing different concepts of knowledge and probability latent in his position and using them to argue that we are simply not justified in believing the conjunction of our individually justified beliefs.

Oehler, Klaus. "A Response to Habermas" in *Peirce and Contemporary Thought: Philosophical Inquiries, Ketner, Kenneth Laine (ed)*, 267-271. New York, Fordham Univ Pr, 1995.

Habermas' paper "Peirce and Communication" contains four major claims, of which the response is a critical consideration. The main thesis of the reply is the statement that Habermas' "Peirce" is not the historical Peirce.

Oehler, Klaus. *Sachen und Zeichen: Zur Philosophie des Pragmatismus*. Frankfurt/M, Klostermann, 1995.

At the end of this century philosophy of pragmatism for the first time has reached a firm position within the spectrum of philosophical theories in Germany. The decline of political doctrines, which had been dominant in Europe such a long time, decomposed prejudices and resentiments against American pragmatism. This volume presents a series of contributions about the philosophy of pragmatism from the perspective of Europe today.

Oehrle, Richard T. Term-Labeled Categorial Type Systems. *Ling Phil*, 17(6), 633-678, D 94.

Oelkers, Jürgen. Influence and Development: Two Basic Paradigms of Education. *Stud Phil Educ*, 13(2), 91-109, 1993-94.

The article discusses two basic paradigms of Western educational theory, namely the concept of "influence" and the concept of "development". Two historical contexts are analyzed, John Locke's theory of human learning and Jean-Jacques Rousseau's theory of natural development. Both theories are rejected in favor of a position beyond "influence" and "development". This position of a theory of education (*Erziehung*) is marked with the term "moral communication".

Oelschlaeger, Max (ed). *Postmodern Environmental Ethics*. Albany, SUNY Pr, 1995.

Oelschlaeger, Max and Bruner, Michael. Rhetoric, Environmentalism, and Environmental Ethics. *Environ Ethics*, 16(4), 377-396, Wint 94.

The growth of environmental ethics as an academic discipline has not been accompanied by any cultural movement toward sustainability. Indices of ecological degradation steadily increase, and many of the legislative gains made during the 1970s have been lost during the Reagan-Bush anti-environmental revolution. This situation gives rise to questions about the efficacy of ecophilosophical discourse. We argue 1) that these setbacks reflect, on the one hand, the skillful use of rhetorical tools by anti-environmental factions and, on the other, the indifference (even hostility) of the ecophilosophical community toward rhetoric, 2) that since the linguistic turn in philosophy, no rigid line of demarcation can be maintained between rhetoric and philosophy, and 3) that rhetoric offers resources to the ecophilosophical community that increase its potential to effect change in society.

Oesterle, Jean (trans). *Saint Thomas Aquinas: On Evil*. Notre Dame, Univ Notre Dame Pr, 1995.

Oesterreich, Peter L. Die Naturgeschichte des menschlichen Geistes: Schellings *Ideen zu einer Philosophie der Natur* als Entwurf konnaturaler Vernunft. *Fichte-Studien*, 5, 159-170, 1993.

My article focuses on the foundations of Schellings connatural style of thinking, which can be found in his famous introduction "Ideen zu einer Philosophie der Natur" from 1797. It deals with the central topics of this programmatical text as the history of nature, the postulate of the absolute identity and the organological phenomenology. This thematical pluralism corresponds to a philosophical rhetoric, which includes as well narration as transcendental or empirical argumentation, in order to convince to the new connatural paradigm.

Oesterreich, Peter L. Politische Philosophie oder Demagogie? Zur rhetorischen Metakritik von Fichtes *Reden an die deutsche Nation*. *Fichte-Studien*, 2, 74-88, 1990.

The article is a contribution to the history of political thinking, especially to the theory of nation. It gives a rhetorical criticism of Fichtes's famous "Reden an deutsche Nation" from 1807/8, which are not only examples of political—and partly demagogical—speeches, they also imply a hitherto ignored philosophical theory of language, which anticipates the present 'rhetorical turn'.

Ofsti, Audun. Das Metasprachenproblem und die Bedingungen einer welterschliessenden, formal selbständigen Sprache. *Deut Z Phil*, 42(5), 801-818, 1994.

Against Wittgenstein it is contended that a notion of "complete" language is needed. Completeness turns on a specific (linguistic) unity of use and mention—on language being its own meta-language. It is maintained a) that Wittgenstein's verdict against meta-language in the *Tractatus* should be retained in the sense of Tugendhat (1976) but rejected in the sense that world-pictures must be ascribable if solipspism is to be avoided (cf. Castañeda); b) that a complete language must comprise two deictic systems: a "horizontal" system to constitute the possibility of index free propositions and a "vertical" system to make "responsible" acts possible.

Ogawa, Nobuko. Der Begriff der Ironie und die Kunsttheorie des frühen Friedrich Schlegels (in Japanese). *Bigaku*, 45(3), 23-33, Wint 94.

Dieser Aufsatz versucht den Terminus 'Ironie' Friedrich Schlegels auf einen klaren Begriff zu bringen. Die eigene Problematik, die die Ironie enthält, scheint aus seinen Betrachtungen über den Wesenszug der modernen Poesie zu entstehen, den er mit Berufung der Fichteschen Philosophie begründet. Der Wesenszug ist nämlich die Reflexion. Die Ironie ist eine 'poetische Reflexion' d h die durch steten Wechsel von 'Selbstschöpfung und Selbstvernichtung' sich fortzeugende Bewegung. Mit dieser Formulierung überträgt er die dynamische aber abstrakte Bestimmung des transzendentalen Ich Fichtes auf konkrete Tätigkeiten des Künstlers, der ein Kunstwerk als ein eine 'inner Einheit' erhaltendes Ganzes bildet. Seine Welt-Philosophie, die Fichtes Bewusstseinsphilosophie ontologisch konkretisiert, betrachtet die Welt als ein nie vollendbar, unendlich werdendes Ich. Die unendliche 'Realität' der Welt, die für Schlegel die 'Bedeutung' des Banzen ist, kann mit einem abgeschlossenen System nie aufgefasst werden; sie kann durch die Kunst nur geahnt werden. Die innere Einheit des Werkes wird dadurch ermöglicht, dass die Ironie über einzelne Darstellungen und endliche Illusionen hinausgeht und diese zu dem Mittelpunkt des Werkes d h der Ahnung der unendlichen Bedeutung des Ganzen führt. Dabei betrachtet er Goethes "Meister" als eine Realizierung solcher Ironie.

Ogawa, Tadashi. Translation as a Cultural-Philosophical Problem: Towards a Phenomenology of Culture. *Monist*, 78(1), 18-29, Ja 95.

Ohashi, Ryôsuke. "Iki" and "Kire"—als Frage nach der Kunst im Zeitalter der Moderne. *Aesthetics*, 5, 105-116, Mr 92.

In his famous essay "The structure of iki" Shûzô Kuki proposed a hermeneutic explanation of the aesthetic phenomena of "iki" which he thought would at the same time be the hermeneutics of the Japanese culture. In order to appreciate his work, we should look at the most fundamental element of these phenomena, "kire" ("cutting"). Through "kire" in the ikebana-art, for example, a flower is cut, not to be annihilated but to be a flower which reveals the beauty of a flower. The background of the art of "kire", the religious tradition in Japan, is to be examined.

Ohayon, Elan Liss. Connectionism and the Mind: An Introduction to Parallel Processing in Networks. *Eidos*, 12(1), 161-168, Je 94.

Oisermann, Teodor I. "Entstehen und Werden allgemeinenschlicher Kulturuniversalien" in *Das geistige Erbe Europas, Buhr, Manfred (ed)*, 334-345. Napoli, Vivarium, 1994.

Okabayashi, Hiroshi. Das Paradox des Schweigens: Über den Begriff der Kunst Sören Kierkegaards seit seiner Kritik der romantischen Ironie. *Aesthetics*, 5, 39-51, Mr 92.

Okè, Moses. Towards an African (Yoruba) Perspective on Empirical Knowledge: A Critique of Hallen and Sodipo. *Int Phil Quart*, 35(2), 205-216, Ju 95.

Okin, Susan Moller. Response to Jane Flax. *Polit Theory*, 23(3), 511-516, Ag 95.

Okruhlik, M Kathleen. Catherine Wilson on Leibniz's Metaphysics. *Dialogue (Canada)*, 33(4), 725-732, Fall 94.

Olábarri, Ignacio. "New" New History: A *Longue Durée* Structure. *Hist Theor*, 34(1), 1-29, 1995.

Historians of historiography have paid more attention to differences and innovations than to similarities and constants. This article investigates the importance of "longue durée structures" in nineteeth- and twentieth-century historiography. The first part shows the extent of the common philosophical ideas shared by the "new histories" on the rise from the 1920s to the 1970s. From the postmodern point of view, all "new histories" are also "modern histories"; since the 1970s various types of history have come to be regarded as postmodern and, therefore, radically different. The second part of the article brings to light major continuities running from modern to postmodern thought. The article ends with some ideas on how to "reconstruct" a plural historiographical community. (edited)

Olafson, Frederick A. *Human Sciences* or *Humanities*: The Case of Literature. *Midwest Stud Phil*, 15, 183-193, 1990.

I explore the implications of substituting the term "human sciences" for "humanities" and show that these center in the difference between conceiving classic texts as sources of insight into human fact *for us* and treating them as discursive artifacts of a certain social order that stand in need of deflationary analysis. Such analyses are typically in the service of a political orientation that has effectively prejudged the issue of any validity that may be claimed for these texts. Against these tendencies in contemporary academic life, I offer a defense of the older humanistic conception of the studies in question.

Olafson, Frederick A. Individualism, Subjectivity, and Presence: A Response to Taylor Carman. *Inquiry*, 37(3), 331-337, S 94.

This is a reply to an article in the preceding issue. I show that Carman's attempt (*Inquiry*, 37, 1994, pp 203-23) to meet my critique of Dreyfus's interpretation of Heidegger is itself open to criticism on several important points. He imputes an 'anti-individualistic' attitude to Heidegger and denies that the concept of *Dasein* is in any sense the concept of a subject; but both these claims are refuted by appealing to express statements by Heidegger. Carman also denies that the concept of presence plays any significant role in Heidegger's early thought; and against this I show that it is *centrally involved* in several of the lecture series from the period of *Being and Time*. A number of other criticisms are taken up among them those having to do with the concept of a clearing (*Lichtung*), the role of perception in Heidegger's account of *Dasein*, and the anonymous public kind of selfhood that Heidegger calls *Das Man*. In the case of this last, I argue that the case of regarding it as a necessary condition of the intelligibility of the world to us is extremely weak.

Olafson, Frederick A. *What is a Human Being? A Heideggerian View*. New York, Cambridge Univ Pr, 1995.

This book draws on the thought of Martin Heidegger to present an alternative to both dualism and materialism in the philosophy of mind. Beginning with a critique of the conception of mind as our inner reality, it argues that human beings are not compound entities—body and mind—but unitary entities that are distinguished by "having a world". The central constructive concept of the book is that of "presence"—the being-there for us, in the several temporal and modal forms of our "ek-sistence", of the entities that make up the world. The final chapter offers a sustained critique of physicalism, the currently popular version of a unitary theory of human nature.

Oldfield, Kenneth. An Impolite View of the Graduate Record Examination: Some Practical Reasons Why Most Studies Find This Test Has Low Predictive Validity. *J Thought*, 30(2), 61-73, Sum 95.

Most research has shown that GRE (Graduate Record Examination) scores do not forecast academic achievement very well. Past explanations for this outcome have identified methodological and procedural shortcomings associated with the test's administration. The present product propounds several, more practical, reasons for the GRE's predictive shortcomings. In particular, the paper argues that the test's low predictive validity derives mostly from its (the GRE's) inability to replicate the philosophy and practices of the real world of graduate study.

Oldrini, Guido. La "Rinascita dell'Idealismo" e il suo Retroterra Napoletano. *G Crit Filosof Ital*, 73(2-3), 205-225, My-D 94.

Benedetto Croce and Giovanni Gentile are known for their own philosophies; more and more they now are studied as "European philosophers". However their philosophical making is connected with a Neapolitan background: Croce's especially with De Sanctis's tradition, Gentile's with Bertrando Spaventa and the developments of Neapolitan Hegelianism. Out of this background—here reconstructed in a tentative way—the "idealistic Renaissance" of the first years of the twentieth century is absolutely unintelligible.

Olejnik, Roman M. Attualità nelle leggi logiche in Giovanni Duns Scoto. *Aquinas*, 36(3), 575-591, S-D 93.

Olejnik, Roman M. Il Programma e il Metodo dell'Insegnamento della Logica nei Seminari Maggiori. *Aquinas*, 37(3), 665-672, S-D 94.

Olender, Maurice. Europe, or How to Escape Babel. *Hist Theor*, 33(4), 5-25, 1994.

Since William Jones announced the kinship of Sanskrit and the European languages, a massive body of scholarship has illuminated the development of the so-called "Indo-European" language group. A new history of the European languages developed, one which traced them back to the language of the barbarian Scythians and emphasized the connections between Persian and European languages. It came to seem implausible that the European languages derived from Hebrew. By the eighteenth century, in short, all the preconditions were present for discovery that the ancestors of the Europeans, like the common ancestor of their languages, had been independent of Semitic influence. A modern scholarly thesis whose political and intellectual consequences are still working themselves out reveals the continuing impact of a millennial tradition of speculation about language and history. (edited)

Oléron, Pierre. "Révolutions scientifiques et paradigmes: le cas des sciences cognitives" in *Rhétoriques de la science, De Coorebyter, Vincent (ed)*, 69-89. Paris, Pr Univ France, 1994.

Olin, John C. *Erasmus, Utopia, and the Jesuits: Essays on the Outreach of Humanism*. Bronx, Fordham Univ Pr, 1994.

This work consists of six essays, each treating an aspect of Renaissance humanism and serving to highlight the broad range of that movement and underscore the close connection between humanism and reform in the early sixteenth century. They deal with Erasmus's patristic scholarship, his collaboration with the Venetian printer Aldus Manutius, and his *Adagia*, with Thomas More's *Utopia* and other utopian projections, and with the influence of humanism on the early Jesuits and their vast educational enterprise.

Oliveira, Maurício Pietrocola. O Éter Luminoso como Espaço Absoluto. *Cad Hist Filosof Cie*, 3(1-2), 163-182, Ja-D 93.

Until the last century, wave optics was based on the luminous aether, which was first seen as a mechanical concept and after Maxwell, as a electromagnetic one. Although it had been introduced in optics to explain the luminous waves, aether was an important concept to many works in astronomy, mainly in the celest mechanics. The aim of the present work is to analyze, in the scientific context of XIX century, the aether's role as a way to determine the absolute motion, replacing Newton's absolute space.

Olivelle, Patrick. Food in India. *J Indian Phil*, 23(3), 367-380, S 95.

This paper analyses the recent scholarly literature on food habits of India. Issues relating to food—what one is permitted to eat, how one should prepare it, when and how much one should eat, from whom one can accept it, with whom one can eat—are central questions both in the legal literature in India and in the minds of ordinary people. The cultural construction of food transforms it from a nutritional necessity to a medium of thought and communication. Food habits encode social structures and relationships, and the study of food is an important key to understanding a society.

Oliver, Alex. Are Subclasses Parts of Classes?. *Analysis*, 54(4), 215-223, O 94.

The fundamental thesis of David Lewis's *Parts of Classes* is that the nonempty subsets of a set are mereological parts of it. This paper shows that Lewis's considerations in favor of this thesis are unpersuasive. First, common speech provides no support. Second, the formal analogy between mereology and the boolean algebra of sets can be explained without accepting the thesis. Third, it is very doubtful that the thesis is fruitful. Certainly, Lewis's claim that it helps us understand set theory is unwarranted.

Oliver, Alex. Dummett and Frege on the Philosophy of Mathematics (Michael Dummett, *Frege: Philosophy of Mathematics*). *Inquiry*, 37(3), 349-392, S 94.

I take issue with Dummett's interpretation of Frege's philosophy of mathematics in his recent book. Dummett mistakenly attributes to Frege a distinction between analytic truths and those which are expressed in purely logical terms. He is also wrong about the role of cardinal and ordinal numbers in Frege's work. His criticism of alternative semantics for numerical sentences is spoiled by a misinterpretation of Frege's semantics for plural subjects. In the final section I show how Dummett's diagnosis of the inconsistency in Frege's system is faulty, I question whether he is right to think that concepts such as 'natural number' and 'real number' are indefinitely extensible and I expose problems in Dummett's revision of Frege's project.

Oliver, David. *The Shaggy Steed of Physics: Mathematical Beauty in the Physical World*. New York, Springer-Verlag, 1994.

The *two-body problem*—the motion of two bodies bound by the inverse-square force of gravity and electricity—is the Shaggy Steed of Physics, guiding the reader to an understanding of the unifying themes of symmetry and topology in physics. On the scale of the solar system this motion generates the Kepler ellipse—the fundamental orbit of celestial mechanics. On the scale of the quantum it generates the hydrogen atom—the primal element. This remarkable unity of the heavens and the elements rests upon hidden symmetry which also contains the symmetry of the relativistic space-time of Einstein and is the paradigm for the unitary symmetries of the elementary particles.

Olivier, Bert. Why a Philosophy of Architecture? The Importance of Harries's Contribution. *S Afr J Phil*, 13(4), 167-174, N 94.

In this article the author focuses mainly, although not exclusively on the work of the American philosopher, Karsten Harries, in an attempt to ascertain whether and how philosophy can make a distinctive contribution to architectural education and reflection. The specific contribution of the social sciences is examined in the light of the architectural implications of 'community' and 'communication', before turning to Harries's reflections on the distinctiveness of a philosophical approach. He locates this in the first place in what he terms the 'ethical' task of architecture, which he distinguishes from an aesthetic task. Architecture's articulation of an *ethos* is further linked to the 'language' of architecture which Harries clarifies by means of the concepts 'representation' and 're-presentation' in architecture. (edited)

Olkowski, Dorothea. Nietzsche-Deleuze: The Aesthetics and Ethics of Chance. *J Brit Soc Phenomenol*, 26(1), 27-42, Ja 95.

Oller, Carlos A. "Acciones Complejas e Indiferencias Adverbiales" in *Temas Actuales de Filosofía, Palacios, María Julia (ed)*, 423-427. Buenos Aires, Univ Nacional Salta, 1993.

Davidson's analysis of the logical form of action sentences fails to validate certain intuitively valid inferences. The introduction of complex actions in an analysis of this kind is proposed as a solution to this problem. This solution is illustrated by the explanation of why adverbial modifiers are not always distributive in the context of action sentences.

Ollero Tassara, Andrés. Giudicare o Decidere: Il Senso della Funzione Giudiziaria. *Riv Int Filosof Diritto*, 71(4), 679-703, 1994.

Olson, Ellen and Chichin, Eileen R. An Ethics Consult Team in Geriatric Long-Term Care. *Cambridge Quart Healthcare Ethics*, 4(2), 178-185, Spr 95.

Olson, Gary A and Hirsh, Elizabeth. "Je—Luce Irigaray": A Meeting with Luce Irigaray. *Hypatia*, 10(2), 93-114, Spr 95.

The authors conducted this interview with Luce Irigaray in her home in Paris in May, 1994.

Olson, Kathryn M. The Role of Dissociation in Redeeming Knowledge Claims: Nineteenth-Century Shakers' Epistemological Resistance to Decline. *Phil Rhet*, 28(1), 45-68, Ja 95.

Every system of thought relies on both knowledge claims expressing what is known and knowledge criteria, or evidence rules, establishing whether one knows by determining what "counts" as adequate evidence. This essay argues that dissociation at the level of knowledge criteria offers a unique way to redeem knowledge claims discredited by formerly acceptable evidence. Using the rhetoric of American Shakers at the end of the nineteenth century to illustrate, it explicates dissociation at the level of knowledge criteria as simultaneously a transformative and conservative approach to defending a thought system, whether that system is religious, scientific, or of another type.

Olson, Steven. Old Guards, Young Turks, and the $64,000 Question: What is Business Ethics?. *Bus Ethics Quart*, 5(2), 371-379, Ap 95.

Traditional business ethics textbooks employ abstract philosophical, and socially individualistic, methods of analysis which offer little practical help in resolving real business issues. This review essay discusses some strengths and weaknesses of Robert Solomon's alternative approach in his revised textbook *Above the Bottom Line*. Solomon's neo-Aristotelian/Hegelian approach distinguishes between philosophical ethics (Moralitat) and reflection on the nature and shared moral meanings of business activities and their place in personal, social, and cultural life (Sittlichkeit). By explicating the personal, organizational and cultural stakes and meanings of business issues, Solomon creates "thick descriptions" to inform intersubjectively negotiable and philosophically valid ethical judgments.

Olsovsky, Jirí. Concrete Logic—The Lifelong Subject of T G Masaryk. *Filozof Cas*, 43(1), 50-62, 1995.

The article considers the appearance of Masaryk's concrete logic and its subsequent development in Masaryk's thought. For Masaryk, concrete logic was a possibility to clarify what is not only logic but also philosophy and science in their mutual relations. The longing to orient himself in philosophy led Masaryk to write *The Foundations of Concrete Logic*. This was followed by further moves in the direction of concrete logic. Masaryk worked on his concept of concrete logic up until 1932 and prepared a second corrected and extended edition of *Concrete Logic*. He constantly followed the development of knowledge and the article traces his incorporation of this into in his concept of concrete of knowledge. The sixth section of the article follows the idea of Masaryk's concrete logic itself. It attempts to construct a single system of all learning. From 1928 he began to call concrete logic and thus sought to draw closer to (and at the same time to create a distinction from) Bolzano. His orientation towards a single scientific view of the world brought Masaryk to form a so-called scientific philosophy and so to a link with Bacon, Comenius and Comte. The critiques of this concept by Patocka and Fischer are also considered.

Olszewski, Stanislaw. Can Time be a Discrete Parameter?. *Stud Phil Christ*, 30(2), 203-208, 1994.

We stressed in this paper that time can be considered as a subjective parameter, the characteristic of which depends both on the physical properties of a given system and the observing ability of an observer. For a perfectly periodic system the time scale consistent with the system is topologically a circle, having a finite circumference, the length of which does not exceed the system's period. If an atom is considered a perfectly periodic system, then the discrete time parameters can be ascribed to the individual atomic states having different energies. The discrete character of time parameters is similar to the discrete character of energies of the atomic states. We assumed that the differences between the time parameters characteristic for the atomic states are proportional to some time quanta which can be used in the calculation of the energy intensity dispensed by an atom in the course of an emission process. A comparison with the data checked by experiment supports this view.

Oluwole, Sophie. "On the Existence of Witches" in *African Philosophy: Selected Readings, Mosley, Albert G (ed)*, 357-370. Englewood Cliffs, Prentice Hall, 1995.

Omine, Akira. Intellektuelle Anschauung und Mystik. *Fichte-Studien*, 3, 184-203, 1991.

Omundson, Bruce. Philosophy and General Education: "World Civilizations" as Virtue Ethics. *Teach Phil*, 18(2), 155-164, Je 95.

Philosophers teaching interdisciplinary general education courses should use their training to achieve conceptual coherence rather than merely importing substantive material. This may require a more Rorty-like view of themselves as philosophers. The first quarter of a World Civilizations course taught as virtue ethics is offered as a model. The goals, methods, and techniques are explained. Paradigm figures, both historical and literary, are analyzed as ideal representatives of each culture.

Oñate, Luis Romera. Libertad y verdad en Heidegger: Una visión unilateral?. *Aquinas*, 36(3), 539-560, S-D 93.

Oncina, Faustino. *Para la Paz Perpetua* de Kant y el *Fundamento del Derecho Natural* de Fichte: Encuentros y Desencuentros. *Daimon Rev Filosof*, 9, 323-339, 1994.

In the *Foundation of Natural Right* Fichte showed that his three sources of inspiration were S Maimon, J B Erhard and Kant's *The Perpetual Peace*. In 1796 Fichte wrote a review of Kant's work, in which he anticipated some of the ideas of this book. This paper analyses the following three aspects that are common to this review and the *Foundation of Natural Right*: 1) The emancipation of right with respect to moral. 2) The relation between right and history. 3) The role of publicity in the concept of republican democracy. It is precisely his misunderstanding of the Kantian spirit what propiciates the transition from Enlightenment to Romanticism.

Oncina Coves, Faustino. Geheimnis und Öffentlichkeit bei Fichte. *Fichte-Studien*, 6, 321-344, 1994.

The purpose of this paper is to examine the different changes that the concepts of secret and publicity undergo in three stages, biographically and thematically connected, in the J G Fichte's writings and their importance in the argumentation about the intersubjectivity. First it analyses the rejection of the distinction between esoteric truths and exoteric truths in the *Revolutionsschriften* (1793-1794) and his vindication about a dynamic, dialectical and public concept of truth. In second place, it studies the double concept of democracy, direct and representative, from the time of Jena (1795-1799) and the role of the ephors, sometimes as an institutional mediation organ between publics (community) and government, sometimes as potential usurpers of the publicity. In third place it underlines (over all after on 1799) the function of the philosophy of freemasonry (of a secret society or hermetic democracy) as a critical watchtower from which can be observed and corrected the evils of modernity.

Ono, Hiroakira and Aoto, Takahito. Non-Uniqueness of Normal Proofs for Minimal Formulas in Implication-Conjunction Fragment of BCK. *Bull Sec Log*, 23(3), 104-112, O 94.

Y Komori asked whether normal proofs of minimal formulas are unique in the implicational fragments of natural deduction systems for the intuitionistic logic and the logic BCK. It was already shown that the answer is positive for BCK, while it is negative for the intuitionistic logic. We show normal proofs for minimal formulas are not necessarily unique for the implication-conjunction fragment of BCK. This result contrasts sharply with the uniqueness of normal proofs of balanced formulas for the implication-conjunction fragment of the intuitionistic logic.

Ono, Hiroakira and Hori, Ryuichi and Schellinx, Harold. Extending Intuitionistic Linear Logic with Knotted Structural Rules. *Notre Dame J Form Log*, 35(2), 219-242, Spr 94.

In this paper, extensions of the intuitionistic linear logic with knotted structural rules are discussed. Each knotted structural rule is a rule of inference of the following form; from X, A, ..., A (n times)...C infer X, A, ..., A (k times)...C. This rule is called the (n,k)-rule, which is a restricted form of the weakening when n k and of the contraction when n k. It is shown that when either n=1 or k=1, strong similarities hold between logics with the (n,k)-rule and the logics with the weakening or the contraction, as for the cut elimination, decision problems and the finite model property.

Oppenheim, Frank. Four Practical Challenges of the Mature Royce to Californians and Others. *Trans Peirce Soc*, 30(4), 803-824, Fall 94.

Treating a bit of Josiah Royce's mature thought (1912-1916), this article focuses on these four challenges: 1) With fitting affective and existential bases, adopt the "third attitude of will", since it is the indispensable condition for genuine loyalty. 2) So purify your ideal of the human person that you receive the gift of integrating your masculine and feminine energies. 3) In the interpersonal relations found in family, business, and elsewhere, emphasize *non*-forensic mediation as more basic and unifying than forensic mediation. 4) In the face of the intensifying problem of evil, let your "prayer to interpret" and your "cult of the dead" help anchor your bold well-grounded hope for the eventual coming of the Great Community.

Oppy, Graham. A Note about a Quinean Argument against Direct Reference. *Philosophia (Israel)*, 24(1-2), 157-170, D 94.

In "California Semantics Meets the Great Fact", Wagner claims that an argument of Quine's about definite descriptions can be adapted to reduce direct reference theories to absurdity. I reply 1) that Wagner's argument is invalid; and 2) that, for the same kinds of reasons, Quine's original argument is also seen to fail.

Oppy, Graham. On an Argument about Reference to Future Individuals. *Phil Quart*, 45(178), 84-87, Ja 95.

Some philosophers have supposed that there are good arguments against four-dimensionalist (tenseless) theories of time which proceed from premises concerning alleged difficulties about reference to entirely future individuals. I argue that there is no reason to suppose that any such argument will succeed; in particular, I argue: i) that it is at best unclear whether four-dimensionalist (tenseless) theories of time require a (damaging) commitment to reference to entirely future individuals; and ii) that there is a sense in which even three-dimensionalist (tensed) theories of time can allow the use of descriptions to fix the reference of names which refer to entirely future individuals.

Oppy, Graham. Reply to Craig: Inverse Operations with Transfinite Numbers and the *Kalam* Cosmological Argument. *Int Phil Quart*, 35(2), 219-221, Ju 95.

Craig claims that (ordinal and/or cardinal) infinities should be rejected because inverse arithmetical operations—subtraction and division—are not defined for them. I reply 1) that John Conway, among others, has shown how these operations can be defined for the ordinals; and 2) that even the standard arithmetical operations—addition and multiplication—are not defined over the cardinals (though certain set-theoretical surrogates are).

Oppy, Graham. Weak Agnosticism Defended. *Int J Phil Relig*, 36(3), 147-167, D 94.

Strong agnosticism is the view that agnosticism is rationally required, weak agnosticism the view that agnositicism is rationally permitted, all things considered. Strong agnosticism is too strong; but—contra the view of many recent philosophers—weak agnositicism is defensible. One plausible defense—essayed here—draws upon considerations of doxastic conservatism.

Opschoor, Hans. "Market Forces as Causes of Environmental Degredation" in *Ecology, Technology, and Culture,* Zweers, Wim (ed), 175-197. Cambridge, White Horse, 1994.

The essay links the phenomenon of environmental change (pollution, resource exhaustion, ecosystems degradation) to driving forces (population growth, economic growth) and structural causes at the ideological and institutional levels. It focuses on institutional aspects, especially the role of the market mechanism, in the context of a liberalizing and globalizing economy. It puts the latter tendency in an historical context by describing the transitions to it, via the 'commercial society' (Adam Smith) and the 'social market economy' (post-war Europe and USA). The market mechanism is seen to enhance economic growth which is directed by signals derived from market forces that fail to adequately reflect effects taking place at a distance in space and time, and at scales beyond that of the individual decision makers. The result is a practice of 'cost shifting' of environmental costs in the economic process and neglect of the social percussions of current decisions in the political process. A plea is made to base environmental policies on this more profound understanding of the underlying causes of environmental degradation, rather than on the more current analysis of technological and legislative failure. Environmental concerns are—and will increasingly be—politically discriminating issues.

Orayen, Raúl. Un Esbozo de Solución a un Enigma de Kripke. *Critica*, 26(76-77), 93-127, Ap-Ag 94.

The principle of substitutivity of identical yields well-known paradoxes, when applied to epistemic contexts. In "A Puzzle about Belief", Kripke has tried to show that similar paradoxes arise without any use of the above mentioned principle. This paper analyzes the main paradox involved in Kripke's article and tries to give a solution to it based on Kripke's theory of proper names as presented in *Naming and Necessity*.

Orel, Vitezslav and Hartl, Daniel L. Controversies in the Interpretation of Mendel's Discovery. *Hist Phil Life Sci*, 16(3), 423-464, D 94.

For twenty years there has been controversy over the level at which Gregor Mendel understood the implications of his experiments for heredity. We argue that he was a hybridist in the tradition of the nineteenth century who 1) designed innovative experiments in plant hybridization and 2) formulated a fundamental new theory for the transmission of traits from parents to offspring based on hypothetical determinants present in germ cells. His own summary, that '...pea hybrids form germinal and pollen cells that in their composition correspond in equal numbers to all the constant forms resulting from the combination of traits united through fertilization', is tantamount to the discovery of what are now called the 'laws' of segregation and independent assortment. Mendel is therefore rightly credited with formulating a new theory of heredity.

Orenstein, Alex. How to get Something from Nothing. *Proc Aris Soc*, 95, 93-112, 1994-95.

Oreskovic, Kreso. The Rainbow Theory of Art. *Brit J Aes*, 35(2), 154-159, Ap 95.

It is proposed that in the idea of art there is a core that does not change with its use: 1) the borders; 2) the entities inside those borders—16 kinds in the spectrum, from natural objects to thought not included in some kinds of mental states; 3) a harmony, or a disharmony, or their combinations. It is reminded that ontology is immersed in man's ontos, that both ontoses are equal categories, because we cannot look at anything but as men. Also, that we cannot live in any other way but by creating, because when we conceive—we create.

Orio, Bernardino. Leibniz y la Tradición Neoplatónica: Estado Actual de la Cuestión. *Rev Filosof (Spain)*, 7(12), 493-517, 1994.

Orlando, Teodosio. Husserl in discussione. *Teoria*, 14(1), 129-140, 1994.

Orlowski, James P. Politically Correct Ethical Thinking and Intubation Practice on Cadavers. *J Clin Ethics*, 5(3), 256-260, Fall 94.

Orlowski, James P and Vinicky, Janicemarie K. The Quantifiability of Medical Futility. *J Clin Ethics*, 5(2), 147-149, Sum 94.

Oroz Ezcurra, Javier. Función de la Creatividad en la Filosofía de A N Whitehead. *Convivium*, 7, 50-63, 1995.

A N Whitehead is usually considered an obscure odd philosopher because of his terminology, categories and plans. But his problems are really similar to those of the great metaphysicians. The question of creativity is basic in his philosophy. Creativity is the ultimate principle which creates and moves the world. God is also a creature of creativity. But creativity is not subsistent by itself. It lies in the actualities which it creates. Only in this way is a world conceivable in process of autocreation. Audacious position and difficult to be metaphysically explained. In this project I want to consider the nature and function of creativity and to judge its coherence in this system.

Orozco, Teresa. "Die Platon-Rezeption in Deutschland um 1933" in *Die besten Geister der Nation, Korotin, Ilse (ed)*, 141-185. Vienna, Picus, 1994.

Orr, Robert D and Perkin, Ronald M. Clinical Ethics Consultations with Children. *J Clin Ethics*, 5(4), 323-328, Wint 94.

This retrospective review of 64 ethics consultations done on children (birth to 18 years of age) assessed demographic data, previous health of the child, reasons for the consultation request, and survival data. The children were critically ill (94% in ICU; 73% technology dependent; 61% died) and 84% of them were also chronically ill. Questions about limitation of treatment were present in 91% of cases and conflicts about further management were found in 59%. Management conflicts were significantly more common in children who had been healthy prior to admission (90%) than in those who had been chronically ill (54%).

Orser, Mari E. Pornography and the Justifiability of Restricting Freedom of Expression. *J Soc Phil*, 25(3), 40-64, Wint 94.

Orsolic, Marco. El Cristianismo como *A Priori* de la Revolución en la Filosofía de Ernst Bloch. *Analogia*, 5(2), 37-47, 1991.

Orth, E W. Zu Husserls Wahrnehmungsbegriff. *Husserl Stud*, 11(3), 153-168, 1994-95.

Orth, Ernst Wolfgang. "Hönigswalds Neukant. u. Husserls Phänomenol. als Hintergrund d. Denkens von Stein" in *Studien zur Philosophie von Edith Stein, Fetz, Reto Luzius (ed)*, 16-52. Freiburg, Alber, 1993.

Ortiz, Gustavo. Lenguaje religioso y racionalidad argumentativa. *Stromata*, 50(3-4), 189-220, Jl-D 94.

Ortiz de Landázuri, Carlos. "Positivismusstreit", 30 años después: A través del giro semiótico de Apel. *Anu Filosof*, 27(3), 1041-1061, 1994.

The controversy on positivism is very important because of its influence on human sciences and comprehensive sociology. Karl-Otto Apel is the central philosopher in this controversy that moves a transformation of contemporary philosophy.

Oruka, H Odera. Las preguntas básicas sobre la filosofía-de-los sabios en Africa. *Rev Filosof (Costa Rica)*, 32(77), 7-17, Jl 94.

This paper is about one of the main trends in african philosophy: the sage-philosophy. The author examines the characteristics that constitute its peculiarity. Three characteristics stand out amongst them: in first place, the fact that the sage can distinguish the opinions of his own from communal beliefs, realized in sayings and representation of popular wisdom. A second characteristic is that the sage answers with creativeness to intellectual challenges proceeding from another conceptions of the world, either replacing the points of view of his own or elaborating answers that are consistent with those points of view. Finally, the sage's disposition towards application in the practical order of everything that he praises in theory.

Osborne, Catherine. Perceiving Particulars and Recollecting the Forms in the *Phaedo*. *Proc Aris Soc*, 95, 211-233, 1994-95.

Osborne asks whether the recollection argument commits Plato to the view that the Forms are known only through sense perception. She argues that Plato does not confine knowledge to empirically-based recollection, but does hold that our explicit awareness of the Forms is *first* prompted by puzzles involving sense-perception. However, once critical awareness of the Forms is established, reflection at a conceptual level leads to continued recollection (learning) without further sensory input; hence the detachment practised by the philosopher 'in training for death' can, after all, be reconciled with the positive role of sense perception in the recollection argument.

Osborne, Peter. Cornel West: American Radicalism. *Rad Phil*, 71, 27-38, My-Je 95.

Osborne, Peter. Tactics, Ethics, or Temporality? Heidegger's Politics Reviewed. *Rad Phil*, 70, 16-28, Mr-Ap 95.

Osborne, Peter. The Politics of Time. *Rad Phil*, 68, 3-9, Autumn 94.

This article advocates a revival of the philosophy of history after the critique of Hegelianism as a philosophy of historical time. Historical time, it argues, drawing upon Ricoeur and Heidegger, is the unity of the process of temporalization as such. As the fundamental category of a hermeneutics of historical existence, it constitutes 'the political' as the condition of the social production of possibility.

Osbrun, Jerry R and Thomson, Ernie. Discussion: Just Another Simi Valley Jury: The Supreme Court and the Death Penalty. *Phil Forum*, 26(1), 78-83, Fall 94.

This paper challenges an argument by C Meyers that the Supreme Court ruling in *McCleskey v. Kemp* (1987) was "just" despite clear evidence of death sentencing discrimination in Georgia. Meyers argues that McCleskey deserved his sentence and the fact that others similarly situated were not so sentenced did not change that fact. We argue that the evidence of racial discrimination was clear, and that the conservative Court majority distorted this evidence in reaching a blatantly *unjust* decision. *McCleskey* (1987) is clearly in the racist tradition of Dred Scott (1857) and *Plessey v. Ferguson* (1896) and represents a reversal of the attempt to remove racial discrimination from our legal system.

Osherson, Daniel and Weinstein, Scott. On the Danger of Half-Truths. *J Phil Log*, 24(1), 85-115, F 95.

Criteria of approximate scientific success are defined within a formal paradigm of empirical inquiry. One consequence of aiming for less than perfect truth is examined.

Osorio, Carlos Rojas. El Positivismo en el Caribe Hispano. *Dialogos*, 30(66), 153-171, Jl 95.

Ossipow, William. Droits individuels, bien commun et vertu civique dans la querelle des libéraux et des communautariens. *Stud Phil (Switzerland)*, 53, 109-142, 1994.

Ostoja-Zagorski, Janusz and Mamzer, Henryk. "Deconstruction of the Evolutionist Paradigm in Archaeology" in *Historiography Between Modernism and Postmodernism, Topolski, Jerzy (ed)*, 191-199. Amsterdam, Rodopi, 1994.

It is demonstrated that the claims of the evolutionary schema to universality are groundless. That schema reflects the specific point of view developed in the sphere of West European culture. Treating is as a modern conception projected onto the past tantamounts to questioning the causal order as the order of history. It means the decomposition of the linear concept of time as a mild continuum: the past- the present- the future. The pictures of the reality studies appear then as functionally determined relational systems whose functioning is not determined by the preceding situation. The teleological nature of history turns out to be a Utopia.

Otabe, Tanehisa. Moses Mendelssohn and the *End of Illusion Theory*: An Inquiry into Innovation in Aesthetics in the Middle of the Eighteenth-Century. *Bigaku*, 45(4), 23-33, Spr 95.

In European aesthetics in the first half of the eighteenth century "illusion theory" was predominant. This was founded on two basic postulates: 1) the copy, namely the work of art, should be "transparent" in its representation of the original, 2) the "address (i.e., skill) of the artist" arouses less interest as compared with "original". The

purpose of this paper is to show how Moses Mendelssohn, who had once accepted illusion theory in the *Über die Empfindungen* (1755) and the *Betrachtungen über die Quellen...* (1757), came to deny it, and what theoretical innovation he thence enabled. Lessing's explanation of the "vermischte Empfindungen" (see the *Briefwechsel über das Trauerspiel* in 1757) made Mendelssohn aware of the insufficiency of the first postulate, and his own reflection on the sublime, especially on the "subjective sublime" in the *Über das Erhabene...* (1757) led him to deny the second postulate. The late Mendelssohn insisted: 1) the postulate of the transparency of representation is ill-founded because it does not take account of the representing subject, i.e., the recipient, 2) the work of art is a "stamp of the abilities of the artist". In conclusion: The traditional dualism "original—copy" was about to transform itself into the modern scheme "artist—work of art—recipient".

Otakpor, Nkeonye. Cultural Relativism: Some Comments. *Philosophica*, 53(1), 57-80, 1994.

Ott, Hugo. "Die Randnotizen Martin Honeckers zur Habilitationsschrift 'Potenz und Akt'" in *Studien zur Philosophie von Edith Stein, Fetz, Reto Luzius (ed)*, 140-145. Freiburg, Alber, 1993.

Ott, Hugo. "Edith Stein und Freiburg" in *Studien zur Philosophie von Edith Stein, Fetz, Reto Luzius (ed)*, 107-139. Freiburg, Alber, 1993.

Ott, Hugo. Martin Heidegger's Catholic Origins. *Amer Cath Phil Quart*, 69(2), 137-156, Spr 95.

Otto, Dirk. *Das utopische Staatsmodell von Platons "Politeia" aus der Sicht von Orwells "Nineteen Eighty-Four"*. Berlin, Duncker Humblot, 1994.

In the polarized dispute about totalitarianism in Plato's Republic, this study offers a differentiated view. The analysis of the political institutions of the Republic shows that Plato never designed it as a political program, but as an abstract harmony model, a *utopia*. Thus, major misunderstandings of Plato's critics concerning the *author's intentions* can be refuted. But on a different methodical level, some criticism remains. The comparison of Plato's Republic and Orwell's Nineteen Eighty-Four reveals far-reaching analogies. Orwell's anti-utopian criticism shows a totalitarian potential of the *Republic itself*. Consequently, this utopian harmony model is unsuitable for the legitimation of political systems.

Otto, Stephan. Semiótica y Metafísica: El Subtexto Transcendental de los Textos Sígnicos de Vico. *Cuad Vico*, 4, 39-51, 1994.

The writing of *Scienza Nuova* is an encoded text. It might perhaps be deciphered not only that very text but the whole Vico's work as well by using the connected game of two distincts hermeneutic cleves: one is metaphysical, the other semiotic. Both maintain a mutual relationship and both also are conditioned by the "geometrical syntax", a textualization of which seems to rest in a nonwritten text. This subtext which makes possible to carry a complete synthesis of both metaphysics and semiotic in Vico, is nothing but his particular way of transcendental thinking, which has little to do with the Kantian tradition and is fully rooted in the contemporary thinking.

Otto, Walter F and Palmer, Robert B (trans). *Dionysius: Myth and Cult*. Bloomington, Indiana Univ Pr, 1965.

Ouattara, Ibrahim. L'interprétation de la position originelle et la question de la fondation. *De Phil*, 10, 43-58, 1993.

What is the theoretical function of Rawls' original position? Through an analysis of the reception of Rawls' theory, the author argues that 1) despite the anti-foundationalist tendencies noted by the "Methodological Rawlsians", there is a residual foundationalism to Rawls' original position, 2) what divides the commentators on Rawls is precisely the question of philosophical justification, 3) on this last question, a foundationalist point of view is to be preferred to that of the anti-foundationalists.

Outhwaite, William. "Nietzsche and Critical Theory" in *Nietzsche: A Critical Reader, Sedgwick, Peter R (ed)*, 203-221. Cambridge, Blackwell, 1995.

Nietzsche's pervasive yet ambiguous influence on twentieth-century thought is nowhere more striking than in neomarxist critical theory. Whereas Lukács, one of the main sources of critical theory, moved from an early adulation of Nietzsche to an intemperate attack on his contribution to the 'destruction of reason' in Germany, the key theorists of what came to be called the Frankfurt School—Adorno, Horkheimer, Marcuse, and Benjamin, and more recently Habermas—adopted from the beginning a more nuanced and sympathetic approach to his work. This article aims to show that critical theory is largely defined by its relationship to Nietzsche.

Outhwaite, William. *Habermas: A Critical Introduction*. Stanford, Stanford Univ Pr, 1994.

A comprehensive introduction to Habermas's work, from his early book on the public sphere to this most recent study of law and the state. The book traces the ways in which Habermas's theories have developed, while stressing the continuity of his underlying concerns.

Owen, David. "Hume's Doubts about Probable Reasoning: Was Locke the Target?" in *Hume and Hume's Connexions, Stewart, M A (ed)*, 140-159. University Park, Penn St Univ Pr, 1995.

Although "the problem of induction" has taken on a life of its own as a central problem in philosophy, there is no doubt its origins lie in Hume's doubts about probable reasoning. I try to show that whatever the merits of couching the modern problem in terms of deductive reasoning, that can't have been Hume's framework. Locke's nonformal account of reasoning in terms of chains of ideas provides a better perspective of Hume's text, and Hume's problem.

Owen, David. Locke on Reason, Probable Reasoning, and Opinion. *Locke News*, 24, 35-79, 1993.

Owen, David B (ed) and McKeon, Richard and McKeon, Zahava K (ed). *On Knowing—The Natural Sciences*. Chicago, Univ of Chicago Pr, 1994.

McKeon outlines the history of Western thinking on the sciences into the twentieth century. Treating the central concepts of motion, space, time, and cause, he traces modern intellectual debates back to the ancient Greeks, notably Plato, Aristotle, Democritus, and the Sophists. As he brings the story of Western science up to the twentieth century, he uses his fabled semantic schema (reproduced here for the first time with extended commentary) to uncover new ideas and observations about cosmology, mechanics, dynamics, and other aspects of physical science. Illustrating the broad historical sweep of the lectures are a series of discussions, which give detail to the course's intellectual framework. These discussions of Plato, Aristotle, Galileo, Newton, and Maxwell are perhaps the first published rendition of a philosopher in literal dialogue with his students. (edited)

Owens, Joseph. "Psychological Externalism" in *The Mind-Body Problem: A Guide to the Current Debate, Warner, Richard (ed)*, 137-155. Cambridge, Blackwell, 1994.

Owens, Joseph. Psychological Externalism and Psychological Explanation. *Phil Phenomenol Res*, 54(4), 921-928, D 94.

Owens, Joseph. The Need for Christian Philosophy. *Faith Phil*, 11(2), 167-183, Ap 94.

With its probative force drawn solely from premises accessible to the human mind's own inherent powers, Christian philosophy probes the divinely revealed truths under their naturally knowable aspects. From the apologetic or defensive angle, this type of philosophy is needed to meet rational queries—one's own or those of others—arising from religious doctrines, for instance from the tenets of creation, divine providence, immortality of the spiritual soul, or human destiny. On the positive side, Christian philosophy deepens the attraction of revealed doctrines in a way comparable to the enhancement given them by architecture, music art and poetry in actual Christian life.

Owens, Joseph J. The Keystone of the Aristotelian *Metaphysics*. *J Neoplatonic Stud*, 1(1), 125-131, Fall 92.

In the construction of the old-fashioned stone arch, each block was supported by external means until finally the keystone was set in place at the crown of the structure. When that wedge-shaped block was dropped into position, the whole arch became self-supporting. In comparable fashion, the Aristotelian *Metaphysics* has been regarded by modern critics as replete with inconsistencies, incoherences and even downright contradictions. This charge would be true if the detailed teachings of the *Metaphysics* depended upon the external support of later philosophies instead of upon Epsilon's explanation of being qua being as the being of the separate forms.

Owensby, Jacob. *Dilthey and the Narrative of History*. Ithaca, Cornell Univ Pr, 1994.

Owolabi, Kolawole. Edmund Husserl's Rehabilitation of Cartesian Foundationalism: A Critical Analysis. *Indian Phil Quart*, 22(1), 13-24, Ja 95.

Owomoyela, Oyekan. "Africa and the Imperative of Philosophy: A Skeptical Consideration" in *African Philosophy: Selected Readings, Appiah, Kwame Anthony*, 236-262. Englewood Cliffs, Prentice Hall, 1995.

Western-trained African philosophers challenge the philosophical claims of certain works their authors describe as African philosophy, but which the challengers dismiss as "ethnophilosophy." The latter claim that they are intuitive rather than analytic, and distilled from communal beliefs and oral traditions rather than the thoughts of known individuals. The critics, who espouse the superiority of Western thought and institutions to African ones, ascribe Africa's technological backwardness and historical vulnerability to European exploitation to the continent's failure to embrace Western-type philosophy. This article argues that philosophy, as defined by these critics (or Western thought), and institutions are not cultural or developmental necessities.

Ozawa, Masanao. Forcing in Nonstandard Analysis. *Annals Pure Applied Log*, 68(3), 263-297, Ag 94.

A nonstandard universe is constructed from a superstructure in a Boolean-valued model of set theory. This provides a new framework of nonstandard analysis with which methods of forcing are incorporated naturally. Various new principles in this framework are provided together with the following applications: 1) An example of an $\aleph_0$-saturated Boolean ultrapower of the real number field which is not Scott complete is constructed. 2) Infinitesimal analysis based on the generic extension of the hyperreal numbers is provided, and the hull completeness theorem and the Loeb measure construction are extended to objects in the generic extension of the internal universe. 3) The reduction theory of the Boolean-valued complex numbers are developed as a prototype of the applications to the topological reduction theory of Boolean sheaves or operator algebras.

Pacherie, Elisabeth. Do We See with Microscopes?. *Monist*, 78(2), 171-188, Ap 95.

The contribution of microscopes to our quest for reliable knowledge is compared with that of visual systems: Do the relations that hold either between the distal stimulus and the image or between the image and the cognitive end-product of the process show differences important enough to justify denying that we see with microscopes? The discussion focuses on whether, assuming that the main purpose is to inform us on distal spatial layouts, there remain fundamental enough differences as to the means employed for reaching this goal to justify such a denial.

Pacho G, J. El Programa del Naturalismo Epistémico Evolucionista: Alcance y Límites. *An Seminar Metaf*, 28, 171-195, 1994.

What does Evolutionary Epistemology mean? To research the human knowledge, specially related to the origin of the elementary structures, as another element in the natural world. Then it's a naturalized epistemology. *What does it state?* Basically that these elementary structures are the product of the phylogenetic evolution, so they are valid a priori (or determinants) of the individual experience. *What does it get?* To solve the "Meno paradox" in a naturalistic way. However it does not explain the 'cognitive excess' of a system which (is said that it) has arisen to survive, not to know.

Packman, Wendy L and Cabot, Mithran G and Bongar, Bruce. Malpractice Arising From Negligent Psychotherapy: Ethical, Legal, and Clinical Implications of *Osheroff vs Chestnut Lodge*. *Ethics Behavior*, 4(3), 175-197, 1994.

Traditionally, there have been few legal actions brought against psychotherapists that allege negligent psychotherapy and negligent treatment of psychiatric disorders. However, in the case of *Osheroff v Chestnut Lodge*, a patient-physician (Dr Osheroff) sued Chestnut Lodge, a private psychiatric facility, for negligence based on the staff's decision to apply a psychodynamic model of treatment (through psychotherapy) and not a biological model. The case sparked a heated debate between adherents of the psychodynamic model and those of the biological model. This article explores the implications of the *Osheroff* litigation for mental health professionals. It is proposed that an interactive informed consent process be used to protect psychotherapists against *Osheroff*-type litigation.

Padilla Rodríguez, J Teresa. Presente eterno y dolor: La tematización unamuniana de la estructura temporal de la existencia y el problema de la intersubjectividad. *An Seminar Metaf*, 27, 137-156, 1993.

Padilla-Gálvez, Jesús. Was leister die semantische Interpretation der Wahrheit. *Z Phil Forsch*, 48(3), 420-434, Jl-S 94.

Paetzold, Heinz. *Ernst Cassirer—Von Marburg nach New York: Eine philosophische Biographie*. Darmstadt, Wiss Buchgesell, 1995.

Paetzold, Ramona L. A Postmodern Feminist View of "Reasonableness" in Hostile Environment Sexual Harassment. *J Bus Ethics*, 13(9), 681-691, S 94.

In the following "dialogue", we address the issue of the "reasonable woman" standard in hostile environment sexual harassment, revealing two quite disparate points of view. It is our desire that the dialogue that we open here will lead to further efforts to eliminate the male-bias that pervades both the workplace and the legal system.

Páez, Alicia. "R Rorty: Pragmatismo, Horizonte Postfilosófico y Conversación" in *Temas Actuales de Filosofía, Palacios, María Julia (ed)*, 429-437. Buenos Aires, Univ Nacional Salta, 1993.

Pagallo, Ugo. An Introduction to the Philosophy of Giuseppe Capograssi. *Riv Int Filosof Diritto*, 71(3), 452-461, 1994.

This introduction to the Capograssi's thought aims at showing the main themes and problems which represent the fundamental structure of one of the most important philosophies of law in the mid of the twentieth century in Italy. The essay follows the same chronological order of the capograssian tests for they present a theoretical cadence of identity and difference which corresponds with the historical questions that were emerging in this work between the 1920s and the 1950s. And just because unity does not exist without multiplicity as well as identity without difference, that explains why it remains as crucial the concept of mediation.

Paganini, Gianni. *Analisi della Fede e Critica della Ragione nella Filosofia di Pierre Bayle*. Firenze, La Nuova Ital Ed, 1980.

Paganini, Gianni. *Scepsi Moderna: Interpretazioni dello Scetticismo da Charron a Hume*. Cosenza, Ed Busento, 1991.

Paganini, Gianni (ed) and Canziani, Guido (ed). *Theophrastus Redivivus, Volumes 1 and 2*. Firenze, La Nuova Ital Ed, 1981.

Page, Benjamin B (ed). *Marxism and Spirituality: An International Anthology*. Westport, Bergin & Garvey, 1993.

Pagin, Peter. Knowledge of Proofs. *Topoi*, 13(2), 93-100, S 94.

If proofs are nothing more than truth makers, then there is no force in the standard argument against classical logic. The standard intuitionistic conception of a mathematical proof is stronger: there are epistemic constraints on proofs. But the idea that proofs must be recognizable as such by us, with our actual capacities, is incompatible with the standard intuitionistic explanations of the meanings of the logical constants. Proofs are to be recognizable in principle, not necessarily in practice, as shown in section 1. Section 2 considers unknowable propositions of the kind involved in Fitch's paradox. The third section considers one attempt to save intuitionism while partly giving up verification. It is argued that this move will have the effect that some standard reasons against classical semantics will be effective also against intuitionism. (edited)

Pakaluk, Michael. Commentary on Morrison's "The Place of Unity in Aristotle's Metaphysical Project". *Proc Boston Colloq Anc Phil*, 9, 157-166, 1993.

Pakszys, Elzbieta. The Philosophy of Science and Women's Issues in Poland: Possibilities and Obstacles Today (A Personal Account). *Metaphilosophy*, 25(2-3), 156-162, Ap-Jl 94.

The article is a testimony and reflection of the time witness. The author's short curriculum vitae serves for presenting various aspects of climbing the steps of the education system in post-WW2 Poland. Continued at post-graduate studies her juvenile fascination of science and philosophy sketches the Poznan School at its heyday in the 1970s. Social-political perturbations in Poland during the 1980s and their impact on society and individuals resulted in differentiation of the author's interests, expanding philosophy of life sciences into broader humanist reflection of religion and women's issues. In conclusion the author discusses her paths in the 1990s as possible reflections of Polish transformation from totalitarianism to democracy. However application of the new system creates problems, it is considered to be the most promising direction and context for society and philosophy development.

Pal, Santosh Kumar. The Existential Perspective of Language and Meaning. *Darshana Int*, 32(2/126), 33-41, Ap 92.

Palacios, Juan Miguel. Brentano contra Kant: Sobre el imperativo categórico. *Pensamiento*, 197(50), 213-234, My-Ag 94.

Enmarcándola en el singular discurso de Brentano sobre la naturaleza y el conocimiento de lo éticamente correcto, se expone y discute en este trabajo su crítica del imperativo categórico de Kant como criterio del conocimiento de la ley moral.

Palacios, Juan Miguel. La esencia del formalismo ético. *Rev Filosof (Spain)*, 4(6), 335-349, 1991.

Criticando algunos falsos modos habituales de interpretar el formalismo ético, el autor lo presenta como la respuesta ofrecida por Kant al problema del conocimiento de la ley moral. Esta respuesta estriba en sostener que es la forma de la ley lo que permite descubrir la materia o contenido de la misma. Y, como la universalidad es lo que constituye la forma característica de las leyes morales, el formalismo ético sostiene qu el carácter universal de un principio moral es el criterio que permite establecer su materia, es decir, determinar el contenido que inevitablemente tal principio ha de tener.

Palacios, Juan Miguel. Zubiri ante el problema del valor. *Dialogo Filosof*, 10(3), 407-410, S-D 94.

En su obra *Sobre el Sentimiento y la Volición*, Zubiri advierte que la relación entre una cualidad de valor y aquello que la ostenta es intrínseca. Ello le lleva a sostener que el acto de estimar no recae, como pretende Scheler, sobre el valor, sino sobre la realidad en cuanto "bien". Esta tesis plantea, sin embargo, el problema de la estimabilidad de lo qúe no es real ni posible.

Palacios, María Julia. "Filosofia, para qué?" in *Temas Actuales de Filosofía, Palacios, María Julia (ed)*, 7-12. Buenos Aires, Univ Nacional Salta, 1993.

En al trabajo se intenta defender la idea de cierto progreso en Filosofía a partir de mostrar que no es un mero re-pensar lo mismo o una simple "adecuación" a los tiempos, pues analiza y discute nuevos problemas; ha elaborado nuevas formas de abordaje a viejos problemas y, fundamentalments, ha logrado acrecentar y refinar su aparato conceptual y crítico. Por otra parte, se sostiene que no es un saber desconectado de la realidad sino que presta servicio a la sociedad aportando reflexiones que ayudan a distinguir problemas y a la mayor conciencia de ellos.

Palacios, María Julia (ed). *Temas Actuales de Filosofía*. Buenos Aires, Univ Nacional Salta, 1993.

Palamiotou, Constantina. Lumière et Ténèbre chez Denys. *Diotima*, 23, 68-70, 1995.

Palau, Gladys. "Los Grados de la Necesidad Lógica" in *Temas Actuales de Filosofía, Palacios, María Julia (ed)*, 439-455. Buenos Aires, Univ Nacional Salta, 1993.

Palau, Gladys. El significado de las constantes lógicas. *Rev Filosof (Argentina)*, 9(1-2), 65-77, N 94.

There are two standard ways to assign the meaning of logical constants. In the first, the meaning of logical constants is determined by *truth conditions*, and in the second, by specifing the *rules* that govern their use. In this paper we analyze the objections made for both alternatives and we propose to define the meaning of logical constants by means of *axiomatic deductive basis*. Nevertheless, the last way rest without solve the relation problem between logical constant and logical expressions of natural language for the logician is free to introduce as many logical constants as he wishes and to change the meaning of those already in use. So, the existence of logical constants in only a necessary condition for the existence of natural logical expressions. But, since each selection of logical constants corresponds to an idea of logical truth and logical consequence, this position maybe lead to rather different conceptions of classical ones.

Palladini, Fiammetta. Translating Samuel Pufendorf: On Two English Editions. *Hist Polit Thought*, 16(1), 121-132, Spr 95.

Pallarés Gonzalez, José Luis. La intimidad como valor antropológico y social. *Dialogo Filosof*, 10(3), 391-406, S-D 94.

El presente artículo es la aportación del autor al VI Congreso Internacional de Filosofia Personalista Insistencial sobre Axiología: Valores personales y ética del hombre de hoy. Se limita a una reflexión sobre la "*intimidad*", valor ético fuertemente erosionado en nuestros días.

Pallavidini, Renato. Estetica e politica in Rousseau: Il sentimento come movente di critica al modello sociale del "Bourgeois". *Filosofia*, 44(3), 481-515, S-D 93.

Pallotini, Michele. Ideas sobre Ortega y Gasset y el ocaso del marxismo. *El Basilisco*, 16, 69-78, Ap-Je 94.

Palmer, Anthony. Direct Reference, Mental Causation and Consciousness: Old Wine in New Bottles. *Phil Invest*, 18(1), 65-73, Ja 95.

Palmer, Anthony J. Toward an Integrated Aesthetic and the Implications for Music Education. *Phil Music Educ Rev*, 2(1), 37-46, Spr 94.

Traditional Western aesthetics bifurcates subject and object, distrusting values generating from the subject's point of view, necessarily relying on the object to carry the full aesthetic stimulus and information. Western aesthetics can be made more effective by integrating the theories of Zeami and Nō theater, which synthesizes both subject and object in the sacred Nō space. After comparisons are made between east and west, three implications for music education are drawn: 1) a premium on direct experience; 2) how the personal world of the subject's experiences, feelings, thoughts, perceptions and responses can be brought to bear on the aesthetic event; and 3) understanding the artistic experience as a holistic, here and now experience, dispensing with all extraneous considerations other than that which exists in the space of the event. These three propositions are then given specific examples of how they might work in music education in the classroom.

Palmer, Robert B (trans) and Otto, Walter F. *Dionysius: Myth and Cult*. Bloomington, Indiana Univ Pr, 1965.

Palmer-Fernandez, Gabriel. A Note on the Relation of Pacifism and Just-War Theory: Is There a Thomistic Convergence?. *Thomist*, 59(2), 247-259, Ap 95.

This paper examines a recent Catholic view on the relation of pacifism and just-war theory that says both of these approaches to the morality of war converge in an important respect—namely, they share a presumption against war. This view was first advanced in the Catholic bishop's letter on war and peace, and then given a theoretical articulation by David Hollenbach and J Bryan Hehir, both of who appeal to Aquinas' writings on the problem of war. I argue, however, that there is nothing Aquinas says that suggest such a convergence; on the contrary, that if there is a presumption in Aquinas' writings on war is that justice be done for the sake of the common good. I therefore reject the bishops', Hollenbach's and Hehir's contention that, following Aquinas, we should presume war to be morally unacceptable and incompatible with a fundamental Christian orientation.

Palmgren, E. A Constructive Approach to Nonstandard Analysis. *Annals Pure Applied Log*, 73(3), 297-325, Je 95.

In the present paper we introduce a constructive theory of nonstandard arithmetic in higher types. The theory is intended as a framework for developing elementary nonstandard analysis constructively. More specifically, the theory introduced is a conservative extension of HA^{W} + AC. A predicate for distinguishing standard objects is added as in Nelson's internal set theory. Weak transfer and idealisation principles are proved from the axioms. Finally, the use of the theory is illustrated by extending Bishop's constructive analysis with infinitesimals.

Palmquist, Stephen. "The Kingdom of God is at Hand!" (Did *Kant* Really Say *That*?). *Hist Phil Quart*, 11(4), 421-437, O 94.

This article sets Kant's political philosophy into the wider context of his views on religion and human history. His references to God's Kingdom reveal a dual emphasis: in some respects Kant's religion is anthropocentric, while in other, it is theocentric. His view of the inevitable progress of human history towards a rational goal turns out to be integrally connected with an individually-legislated politic verging on theocracy. Kant's defense of an apparently egalitarian liberalism in some writings must therefore by qualified by his insistence elsewhere that such systems are only temporary measures: eventually they will give way to a higher end.

Palmquist, Stephen. Triangulating God. *Faith Phil*, 11(2), 302-310, Ap 94.

After describing the basic structure of Kant's System of Perspectives, I respond to Anthony Perovich's claim that my interpretation misconstrues Kant's true intentions concerning religion. Perovich assumes the "perspectives" require unsystematic "openness," accommodating numerous conflicting ways of interpreting religious phenomena. Yet Kant has in mind a fixed relationship between three specific perspectives (or "standpoints"): the practical, theoretical and judicial. The first and third can be used to construct a theology even though the theoretical standpoint alone cannot. Perovich's suggested *revision* of Kant along these lines therefore turns out to reflect a position which a perspectival interpretation shows to be Kant's own.

Palubicki, Wladyslaw. Human Life as a Value in Anthropology of Old Judaism. *Dialogue Hum*, 3(3), 91-98, 1993.

Biblical texts provide a number of reasons for the high evaluation of human life in the anthropology of old Judaism. Both quality (joyful life) and quantity (long life as a reward for good life) were seen as essential for the success in life. This traditional appreciation of human life is also present in contemporary Judaism. The paper presents many examples and reasons explaining this axiological phenomena.

Pande, G C. Culture and Cultures. *J Indian Counc Phil Res*, 11(3), 41-61, My-Ag 94.

Pandey, Indu. Hume's View on External Object: A Critical Analysis. *Darshana Int*, 32(1/125), 15-21, Ja 92.

Pandit, G L. Deconstructing the Driving Forces of Human Knowledge: D P Chattopadhyaya's *Induction, Probability and Scepticism*. *J Indian Counc Phil Res*, 11(3), 132-136, My-Ag 94.

Pandolfi, Carmelo. Il Prologo al Commento a Giobbe di San Tommaso d'Aquino. *Aquinas*, 37(3), 597-620, S-D 94.

Pandurangi, K T. A Note on the Concepts of *Nitya-karma, Naimittika-karma* and *Kamya-karma*. *J Indian Counc Phil Res*, 11(2), 118-122, Ja-Ap 94.

Pangle, Thomas L. "Socrates in the Context of Xenophon's Political Writings" in *The Socratic Movement, Vander Waerdt, Paul A (ed)*, 127-150. Ithaca, Cornell Univ Pr, 1994.

This essay attempts to situate Xenophon's *Sokratikoi logoi* within his corpus taken as a whole and viewed as a "system", as suggested by Shaftesbury's discussion of Xenophon's manner of writing. The relation between politics and philosophy is the guiding thread of the discussion. Among the Socratic writings, particular attention is paid to the contrast developed in the *Oeconomicus* between Socrates and the gentleman Ischomachus, a contrast that clarifies the relation between the conventional and the Socratic standard of *kalokagathia*, or gentlemanliness. Among the political writings, the greatest attention is paid to the *Cyropaedia*, considered in light of Machiavelli's esteem and pointers toward a radical interpretation.

Pannenberg, Wolfhart. Breaking a Taboo: Frank Tipler's *Physics of Immortality*. *Zygon*, 30(2), 309-314, Je 95.

In his book *The Physics of Immortality*, Frank Tipler has broken a longstanding intellectual taboo by dealing as a physicist with the theological themes of God and immortality, as well by arguing that theology can provide material for concept formation in the field of physics. His work on the anthropic principle convinced Tipler that, since the emergence of intelligent life is of the essence of the universe as a whole, the future of life is of fundamental significance. His Omega Point theory takes theological theories of the future's significance seriously from a scientific point of view. Theories of computers play a central role in Tipler's theory of immortality, and even though many critics have misunderstood his thrust in these theories, they are worthy of further exploration. Perhaps Tipler's most important contribution is his insistence that the world as described by physics is more open to interaction with biblical and theological perspectives than is often believed.

Pannier, Russell. Being, Existence, and the Future of Thomistic Studies: A Reply to Professor Nijenhuis. *Amer Cath Phil Quart*, 69(1), 83-88, Wint 95.

In criticism of our "Aquinas on *Exists*" John Nijenhuis argues that use of "the usual existence-terminology" leads to a flawed understanding of St. Thomas; Aquinas has a philosophy of being, not of existence. We argue 1) that this view of the matter is incorrect and 2) that rigid insistence on favored terminology hinders Thomistic studies, needlessly blocking dialogue with those who choose to express themselves in slightly different terms.

Pannier, Russell and Sullivan, Thomas D. Aquinas's Solution to the Problem of Universals in *De Ente et Essentia*.... *Amer Cath Phil Quart*, 68(Supp), 159-172, 1994.

It is sometimes said that in *De Ente et Essentia* Aquinas dissolves the problem of universals. We agree that the Aquinas attempts a dissolution, but argue that the attempt fails. Aquinas's argument is set out in detail.

Panova, Elena. About the Philosophical Style of Thinking. *Metaphilosophy*, 25(2-3), 163-180, Ap-Jl 94.

Panthanmackel, George. The Roots of Economic Disparity and Poverty. *J Dharma*, 20(1), 89-93, Ja-Mr 95.

The purpose of the work is to make a philosophical response to the problems of "Economic Disparity and Poverty" in India. In the work the author is of the opinion that the phenomenal situation of economic disparity and poverty has noumenal roots that require a deeper philosophical analysis revealing their philosophical causes: ontological, epistemological, psychological, cosmological and ethical. Ontology calls for a rediscovery of the "ontological difference" between Being and beings; epistemology, for critical examination of one's own knowledge; psychology, for a renewed emphasis on man who is single, unitary being; cosmology, for a reconstruction of a beautiful world; and ethics, for focusing on honesty and sincerity. Such a philosophical response is to reduce much of economic disparity and poverty.

Panti, Giovanni. A Geometric Proof of the Completeness of the Lukasiewicz Calculus. *J Sym Log*, 60(2), 563-578, Je 95.

We give a self-contained geometric proof of the completeness theorem for the infinite-valued sentential calculus of Lukasiewicz.

Paoletti, Giovanni. Credere all Cose e Credere Agli Dei: Teorie della Credenza da Renouvier a Durkheim. *Teoria*, 14(2), 87-110, 1994.

Paoli, Francesco. Semantics for First Degree Relatedness Logic. *Rep Math Log*, 27, 81-94, 1993.

In this paper, we axiomatize the first-degree entailments of relatedness logic, and introduce both tabular and algebraic semantics for such a fragment. Thereby, we partly answer the problems referred to as P1 and P28 in the Problem Section of this journal.

Paolicchi, Piero. Narratives of Volunteering. *J Moral Educ*, 24(2), 159-173, 1995.

The specific features and complexity of volunteerism are outlined with respect to other forms of helping behaviour, and a narrative perspective is stressed as the best way of describing and explaining decisions to join a volunteer group and persevering in it. Interviews from 12 members of a volunteer group in a small Italian town are analysed in the light of respondents' personal life histories in a shared social and historical milieu. Search for meaning at the individual level and co-construction of meanings and goals at the collective level are hypothesised as the core psycho-social constructs by which volunteering can be understood. Volunteers are defined not by a common set of personality traits or motivations, nor by some common values articulated explicitly in a principled way, but by the way they live the network of their concrete relationships: a shared lived world in which feeling close to others stands as a significant feature of everyday life.

Papamichalopoulos, Andreas. The Transcendence of the Pythagorean Arithmetical Ontology in the Areopagitic Writings. *Diotima*, 23, 26-30, 1995.

Pape, Helmut. Der Gedanke als Überblendung in der Folge der Bilder: Peirces visuelles Modell geistiger Prozesse. *Deut Z Phil*, 43(3), 479-496, 1995.

This essay deals with the importance of visual notions in Peirce's semiotical account of thought and experience. I argue that Peirce provided the key elements for a cognitive account of the structure of propositional consciousness that is using the idea of blending over or into one another, into one "composite photograph" the visual forms and contents of experiential situations with the same or with different objects. This yields an account of the logic and semiotics of propositional consciousness related to operations of perception and imagination which assigns to Qualia and qualitative consciousness the role of providing the content manipulated by different semiotical forms of judgmental representation. The ultimate success of Peirce's visual account of thought was his graphical logic, the Existential Graphs, which allow to express the whole of first order predicate calculus and some weak modal logics in two-dimensional format.

Papineau, David. Mental Disorder, Illness and Biological Disfunction. *Philosophy*, 37(Supp), 73-82, 1994.

This paper is about the relationship between mental disorder and physical disorder. It is also concerned with the connection between these notions and the notion of "illness". The paper considers the "anti-psychiatry" view that the lack of a physical basis excludes many familiar mental disorders from the category of "illness". It argues that anti-psychiatrists are probably right to hold that most mental disorders do not involve any physical disorder (in any strict sense of physical), but that they are wrong to conclude from this that these mental disorders are not illnesses.

Papineau, David. *Philosophical Naturalism*. Cambridge, Blackwell, 1993.

This book defends naturalism in metaphysics and epistemology. Part I (Physicalism) shows that physical supervenience and realization follow from simple premises. It also argues for the type reducibility to physics of any special laws that are not products of selection processes. Part II (Mind) elaborates the teleological theory of representation, highlighting its connections with "success semantics", and argues that consciousness is physical, attributing contrary intuitions to an "antipathetic fallacy" fostered by the special structure of thoughts about experience. Part III (Knowledge) shows how a principled defence of reliabilism blocks sceptical challenges, and offers a detailed defence of mathematical fictionalism.

Pappas, George S. Perception and Mystical Experience. *Phil Phenomenol Res*, 54(4), 877-883, D 94.

Pappas, Gregory. A Reexamination of Browning's View of Experience. *SW Phil Rev*, 11(Supp), 97-108, Mr 95.

Paprzycka, Katarzyna. A Note on Von Bretzel's Solution to an Alleged Problem with Reichenbach's Definition of Time Direction. *Epistemologia*, 17(1), 3-11, Ja-Je 94.

In his paper "Concerning a Probabilistic Theory of Causation Adequate for the Causal Theory of Time", Philip von Bretzel makes an interesting but subtle point. He endorses the first and the third stage of one of Hans Reichenbach's (1956) ways of introducing time direction in terms of macrostatistical relations only while rejecting the second stage of the construction on account of its circularity. In this note, we shall show, first, that Reichenbach is not guilty of the crime and, second, that there are problems with von Bretzel's solution to the alleged problem.

Paprzycka, Katarzyna. How Carnap Should Bite Goodman's Bullet. *Philosophia (Israel)*, 24(1-2), 149-156, D 94.

Goodman's famous objection to Carnap's *Aufbau* is that the method of construction Carnap relies on, quasi-analysis, fails on logical grounds. It does indeed. We counter the force of this objection by showing that it relies on a fundamental misunderstanding of the enterprise Carnap engages in. Far from seeing the logical failures of quasi-analysis as fatal to that enterprise, one may actually see them as having the potential of enriching it.

Papson, Steven and Goldman, Robert. "The Postmodernism That Failed" in *Postmodernism and Social Inquiry, Dickens, David R (ed)*, 224-253. New York, Guilford, 1994.

Paquette, Michel. Relativisme Éthique et Rationalité. *Philosopher*, 16, 197-206, 1994.

Pardey, Ulrich. In welchem Sinne ist die Identität eine Äquivalenzrelation?. *Z Phil Forsch*, 48(4), 543-557, 1994.

Äquivalenzrelationen sind in der klassischen Logik symmetrisch, transitiv und also uaf ihrem Bereich reflexiv. In der *Umgangssprache* sind die angeblichen Äquivalenzrelationen aber nicht reflexiv, folglich auch nicht *symmetrisch und transitiv*. Diese heiden Begriffe sollten *enger* gefasst werden: eine symmetrische Relation kann es sinnvoll *nur* zwischen jeweils *zwei* Dingen, eine transitive Relation *nur* zwischen jeweils *drei* Dingen geben. Aus diesen *engeren* Begriffen der Symmetrie und Transitivität folgt nicht mehr die Reflexivität. Dennoch lassen sichdie Äquivalenzklassen der klassischen Logik rekonstruieren: (x/x ist *genauso gross* wie a) = die Vereinigungsmenge von (a) und (x/x ist *genauso gross* wie a), wobei "*genauso gross*" als reflexiv, aber "*genauso gross*" als nicht-reflexiv zu verstehen ist. Analog ist (x/x = a) = (a). Lässt sich dann noch der Identitätsbegriff der Umgangssprache als Äquivalenzrelation explizieren?

Pardo Bazán, Emilia. Stuart Mill. *Telos (Spain)*, 1(3), 145-158, O 92.

Parekh, Bhikhu. "Decolonizing Liberalism" in *The End of "Isms"?, Shtromas, Alexsandras (ed)*, 85-103. Cambridge, Blackwell, 1994.

In nineteenth-century Europe liberalism and colonialism developed alongside each other. With rare exceptions liberals approved of colonialism and provided it with a legitimizing ideology. Although the liberal and even the nonliberal accounts of the history of liberalism ignore the fact, the colonial experience deeply shaped the nineteenth-century liberal thought and introduced elements that are either absent in or at best marginal to its predecessors. Liberalism became missionary, ethnocentric and narrow, dismissing nonliberal ways of life and thought as primitive and in need of the liberal civilizing mission. (edited)

Parekh, Bhikhu. "The Concept of Fundamentalism" in *The End of "Isms"?, Shtromas, Alexsandras (ed)*, 105-126. Cambridge, Blackwell, 1994.

The rise of what is called religious fundamentalism has caused and continues to cause enormous havoc in many societies. Hundreds of thousands of people have died as a result of it, the development of many societies has been deeply distorted by it, and there is no end in sight to this tragedy. The phenomenon is not confined to the developing, especially the Muslim, countries, although they have suffered the most from it. Even in the stable and secular West where they have no real chance of coming to power, the fundamentalists have sometimes exercised a considerable influence. In America, for example, they helped Presidents Reagan and Bush come to power and contributed to fostering a climate of intolerance toward secular humanist and liberal ideas. This paper examines the nature, logic and historical specificity of fundamentalism.

Parekh, Bhikhu (ed) and Pieterse, Jan Nederveen (ed). *The Decolonization of Imagination: Culture, Knowledge, and Power*. London, Zed Books, 1995.

Parellada, Ricardo (trans) and Burnyeat, M. El escéptico en su lugar y su tiempo. *An Seminar Metaf*, 27, 273-306, 1993.

Parens, Erik. The Goodness of Fragility: On the Prospect of Genetic Technologies Aimed at the Enhancement of Human Capacities. *Kennedy Inst Ethics J*, 5(2), 141-153, Je 95.

Beginning with the assumptions that genetic technology will make possible the enhancement of some significant human capacities and that our society will have self-evident reasons to pursue such enhancements, this essay suggests less evident reasons to proceed with extreme caution. The essay asks: Will we, in our attempts to enhance humans by reducing their subjection to chance and change, inadvertently impoverish them? It explores how technologies aimed at enhancement might affect the good that is our experience of some forms of the beautiful and the excellent, the good that is relationships of care, and the good that is diversity across the life span. In the end, it speculates about the fundamental philosophical difference that underlies the disagreement between those who would tend to embrace a project to enhance human capacities and those who would tend to criticize such a project.

Parens, Erik. The Pluralist Constellation. *Cambridge Quart Healthcare Ethics*, 4(2), 197-206, Spr 95.

After surveying a significant swath of the pluralism literature, I attempt to describe three commitments that seem to be shared by an exceptionally heterogeneous group of thinkers. Those intimately related commitments are to 1) epistemological humility, 2) self-criticism, and 3) conversation.

Parfitt, Barbara and Williams, Stephen. Models of Nursing and Theories of Humanity: A Christian Perspective. *Ethics Med*, 11(1), 12-17, Spr 95.

Parikh, Rohit. Vagueness and Utility: The Semantics of Common Nouns. *Ling Phil*, 17(6), 521-535, D 94.

The problem of semantics for vagueness is examined. A hitherto unnoticed problem is that different people use—and must use for theoretical reasons—such predicates differently and even the same person at different times. Any semantics must explain why people can still communicate. Two frameworks, fuzzy logic and super-valuations are examined critically. Since neither of these two tackles the problem, the suggestion is made that we use vague predicates because they result in an increase in utility—i.e., make our lives easier. Some examples are given of how this can happen despite a lack of a common social meaning.

Paris, Claude. Réflexions sur l'Enseignement de l'Éthique. *Philosopher*, 16, 63-71, 1994.

Paris, J B and Vencovská, A and Wilmers, G M. A Natural Prior Probability Distribution Derived from the Propositional Calculus. *Annals Pure Applied Log*, 70(3), 243-285, D 94.

A σ-additive probability measure on the real interval [0, 1] is defined by considering the expected values of "randomly chosen" large formulae of the propositional calculus, where the propositional variables are treated as independent random variables on {0, 1} with expected value 1/2. Although arising naturally from logical and/or cognitive considerations, this measure is extremely complex and displays certain formally pathological features, including infinite density at all points of a certain dense subset of [0, 1]. Certain variants of the construction are also considered. The introduction includes an account of motivation for the study of such measures arising from a fundamental problem in inexact reasoning.

Paris, Jeffrey. Interrogating Whiteness: Dialogue as a Pragmatist Tool for Postmodern Identity-Formation *or* Breaking Bread with Bell Hooks and Cornel West. *Int Stud Phil*, 27(1), 73-84, 1995.

Parizeau, Marie-Hélène. Éthique et Éthiques Appliquées. *Philosopher*, 16, 133-143, 1994.

Park, S B G and Young, A H. Connectionism and Psychiatry: A Brief Review. *Phil Psychiat Psych*, 1(1), 51-58, Mr 94.

Connectionist models have been developed in diverse areas of psychiatric inquiry. Their span is from low-level biologically inspired models of the effects of synaptic pathology and drug action on mental function to attempts to implement higher levels of description such as psychodynamic psychopathology within a brainlike framework. This article reviews a number of the models relevant to psychiatry and argues that the connectionist approach, particularly because of its ability to model failures in psychological function, offers a powerful new tool in the exploration of the substrate of mental disorder.

Parker, James. The Protection Laboratory Animals: A Response to Stephenson. *J Med Phil*, 19(4), 389-394, Ag 94.

This paper clarifies certain issues raised by Wendell Stephenson (*The Journal of Medicine and Philosophy* 18: 375-388, 1993) about research programs and animal care practices at the Oregon Regional Primate Research Center. It also responds to Stephenson's critique of the National Institute of Health's *Guide for the Care and Use of Laboratory Animals*. It identifies utilitarianism as the ethical theory underlying Stephenson's critique. Arguing that such an ethical theory is unworkable in addressing concerns about biomedical research and the use of animals the paper defends the *Guide's* reliance on a wider tradition of ethical theories.

Parker, Jenneth. "Moral Philosophy—Another 'Disabling Profession?'" In *Ethics and the Professions, Chadwick, Ruth (ed)*, 27-41. Brookfield, Avebury, 1994.

Parker, Lisa S. Beauty and Breast Implantation: How Candidate Selection Affects Autonomy and Informed Consent. *Hypatia*, 10(1), 183-201, Wint 95.

Candidate evaluation for breast implantation presents a more important obstacle to the fulfillment of the normative requirements of informed consent than do the social roles of women or cultural norms governing female beauty. I argue that women's decisions to receive breast implants may indeed be informed, competently made, and substantially voluntary, but that the cultural construction of beauty may undermine women's autonomy by influencing the evaluation of surgical candidates and risk disclosure during informed consent.

Parker, Lisa S. Breast Cancer Genetic Screening and Critical Bioethics' Gaze. *J Med Phil*, 20(3), 313-337, Je 95.

This paper illustrates a role that bioethics should play in developing and criticizing protocols for breast cancer genetic screening. It demonstrates how a critical bioethics, using approaches and reflecting concerns of contemporary philosophy of science and science studies, may critically interrogate the normative and conceptual schemes within which ethical considerations about such screening protocols are framed. One of the frequently neglected worldviews in traditional bioethics' treatment of protocols concerning breast care is constituted by women's own views of their breasts and breast cancer, both within the technologically-oriented social practice of American medicine and in light of the social construction of their breasted experience in American society. This paper attempts to redress and critically assess this neglect on the part of traditional bioethics.

Parker, Michael. "Children Who Run: Ethics and Homelessness" in *Introducing Applied Ethics, Almond, Brenda (ed)*, 58-70. Cambridge, Blackwell, 1995.

The number of homeless children in Europe and the United States presents a range of ethical and social problems. This chapter goes beyond the usual individualist-communitarian debate, arguing that the interaction between society and the individual is worked out or negotiated in the lives of real people. It argues that youth homelessness will continue as long as we fail to reconstruct the nature of family life and life in our community in general in such a way that children feel themselves to be participating fully in the development of their own and their community's way of life.

Parkes, Graham R. "Nietzsche and Zen Master Hakuin on the Roles of Emotion and Passion" in *Emotions in Asian Thought, Marks, Joel (ed)*, 213-233. Albany, SUNY Pr, 1995.

A comparison of the views of emotion of the eighteenth-century Zen master Hakuin Ekaku with those of Friedrich Nietzsche reveals remarkable similarities, which serve to show the inadequacy of received understandings of both figures. Hakuin's notion of harnessing the energies of the emotions in order to break through to "realizing one's true nature" is paralleled by Nietzsche's concern to effect a "great economy of the passions" that will discipline unruly psychical forces and direct them toward creative ends. They also share similar understandings of the cognitive role of the emotions and the potentially valuable features of sickness and suffering.

Parkinson, G H R. "Philosophy and Logic" in *The Cambridge Companion to Leibniz, Jolley, Nicholas (ed)*, 199-223. New York, Cambridge Univ Pr, 1994.

Parks, Ward. "Textual Imperialism" in *European Philosophy and the American Academy, Smith, Barry (ed)*, 67-79. Peru, Open Court, 1994.

Parret, Herman. Le timbre de l'affect et les tonalités affectives. *Rev Int Phil*, 48(189), 287-302, 1994.

Parry, David M. Holiness as Service: *Therapeia* and *Hyperetike* in Plato's *Euthyphro*. *J Value Inq*, 28(4), 529-539, D 94.

This article constructs a Socratic conception of holiness as service that is both unrefuted in the *Euthyphro* and consistent with Socrates's claims in the *Apology*.

Parsons, Charles. "Structuralism and the Concept of Set" in *Modality, Morality, and Belief, Sinnott-Armstrong, Walter (ed)*, 74-92. New York, Cambridge Univ Pr, 1994.

Parsons, Charles. Platonism and Mathematical Intuition in Kurt Gödel's Thought. *Bull Sym Log*, 1(1), 44-74, Mr 95.

Gödel is well known as a defender both of platonism or realism about mathematical objects and knowledge and of a strong conception of mathematical intuition. The paper attempts to characterize these views and discusses their development. Gödel claimed late in life to have been a "conceptual realist" since 1925, but some earlier remarks raise questions about his views in the 1930's. But a robust form of realism is avowed very forcefully in "Russell's Mathematical Logic" (1944) and other writings up to 1951. These hardly mention intuition and do not give it a role in defending Gödel's position. In Gödel's published writings, the strong conception of intuition appears clearly only in the 1964 supplement to "What is Cantor's continuum problem?" Intuition is discussed in an unfinished paper from the 1950's. The remarks of 1964 are cryptic and an attempt is made to explicate them. In assessing Gödel's position, I suggest that Gödel's conception of intuition belongs to what other philosophers might call a theory of reason.

Parsons, Howard L. Preparing for the 21st Century: A Philosophy for New Thinking. *Darshana Int*, 32(1/125), 8-14, Ja 92.

The world's state today indicates and requires a formulation of philosophical beliefs about it and certain imperatives for action, such as: Consider our common estate and its implications; discover the meaning of individual mortality; take time seriously; renounce and induce others to renounce all claims for absolute rule; practice the virtues of social action and struggle; cherish the earth; uphold the people's right of revolution. On the broad scale of humanity, poverty and injustice in the undeveloped countries call for new thinking, a new economic order, and a widespread "moral mutation".

Parsons, Terence. "Ruth Barcan Marcus and the Barcan Formula" in *Modality, Morality, and Belief, Sinnott-Armstrong, Walter (ed)*, 3-11. New York, Cambridge Univ Pr, 1994.

Parsons, Terence. Anaphoric Pronouns in Very Late Medieval Supposition Theory. *Ling Phil*, 17(5), 429-445, O 94.

Parsons, Terence and Woodruff, Peter. Worldly Indeterminacy of Identity. *Proc Aris Soc*, 95, 171-191, 1994-95.

Parthasarthy, Malini. Violation of Social Contract with Kashmiri People. *Phil Soc Act*, 20(3-4), 7-10, Jl-D 94.

There is understandably considerable elation in New Delhi, that an eleventh hour intervention by Iran and China resulted in the withdrawal of Pakistan's resolution indicting India's record on human rights in Kashmir. That Pakistan has been forced into another tactical defeat after a high-pitched campaign in the international arena as it had been in the United Nations General Assembly last year, certainly dilutes its credibility on the world stage. Islamabad's strategic move to put Kashmir on the map to the world's "danger zones requiring International intervention" backfired badly but the sense of satisfaction as a result of this should not entrench itself as complacence.

Partridge, Derek and Galton, Antony. The Specification of "Specification". *Mind Mach*, 5(2), 243-255, My 95.

The notion of "specification" plays a key role in the developing science of computing. It is typically considered to be the keystone in the software development process. However, there is no single, generally agreed meaning of "specification" that bears close scrutiny. Instead there is a variety of different, although partially interlocking and overlapping interpretations of the term. We catalogue this varietal profusion and attempt to lay bare both the sources and consequences of each major alternative. We attempt to present the full range of possibilities, and the biases inherent in each style of interpretation. We believe that there is a pressing need for clarification of the meaning of "specification" (and several other important terms), especially in view of the fact that so many practitioners and theoreticians assume, erroneously, that a clear meaning already exists (even though they might disagree as to what it is). In particular, we feel that a more general awareness of the difficulties that currently attach to this key concept may go some way towards bridging (if not actually healing) the rift that currently exists between the engineering and scientific aspects of computing.

Parush, Adi. Nietzsche on Guilt, Responsibility, and the Concept of the Subject. *Iyyun*, 44, 123-148, Ap 95.

Nietzsche considered guilt feelings to be both harmful and groundless. In claiming that no one is guilty of anything, he relies not only on his criticism of the common moral distinctions between good and bad actions, but also upon his view that no one is responsible—accountable—for the actions attributed to him. This view of Nietzsche is derived from his metaphysical picture of a flowing, everchanging, holistic world, a picture which leaves no room for the idea of the self as an enduring source of successive, distinct actions. The purpose of this article is to clarify and reconstruct Nietzsche's position on this issue.

Pascal, Blaise and Levi, Honor (trans). *Pensées and Other Writings: A New Translation by Honor Levi*. New York, Oxford Univ Pr, 1995.

Paskow, Alan. Phenomenological Reflections on the Self and the Other—As Real, As Fictional. *Man World*, 27(3), 309-323, Jl 94.

Who are the people of literary fiction? How do they fit into our overall scheme of what is real? In what ways are they both like and unlike "real" people? I respond to these questions by building upon Heidegger's concepts of being-in-the-world and being-with (*Mitsein*). His ontological categories enable him to claim that a fictional being is never a mere entity in a person's *head*; instead it should be viewed as a being whom we feel and believe to be part of *our* world, thus, in an important sense, identical to a "real" being. If I am right, then we are in a better position to say what the function of literature most basically is.

Passell, Dan. Natural Fact, Moral Reason. *J Phil Res*, 20, 463-480, 1995.

In his book *Ethics* J L Mackie says that moral facts would have to be queer facts. I argue that an act's hurting somebody is necessarily a reason, though not necessarily a conclusive reason, not to do that act; and that such hurting is a natural fact, not a queer fact. I try to defend this externalist position about this particular reason against internalists such as Mackie, and in particular against the position of Stephen Darwall in *Impartial Reason*.

Passos Videira, Antonio Augusto. Ciência, Técnica e Filosofia da Ciência. *Cad Hist Filosof Cie*, 4(1), 93-108, Ja-Je 94.

It is frequently considered that the issues connected with the subject of technique do not belong to the proper problems of the realm of philosophy of science. However, since the birth of the so-called modern science—the period of which is taken here as an example—the interrelation between science and technique has been quite more complex than admitted up to now by the philosophers of science.

Pastor Pérez, Miguel A. Arteaga y Vico. Génesis del Arte Total: La Opera. *Cuad Vico*, 1, 43-53, 1991.

The artistic relevance of the modern opera has its roots on a philosophical-aesthetic system which goes back into the eighteenth-century. One of the main scholars who studied this theme was E de Arteaga, who indebted to Vico in many aspects. The difference between the Neapolitan and the Spanish Abbot is useful to determine his role in the composition of this fundamental and founder system. His evolution from Viquian positions to Lockian ones constitutes the essence of his aesthetic and philosophical expositions, and in addition his idea of the opera as a total *Art*.

Pastor Pérez, Miguel A. Vico o la Metafísica como Método de Fundamentación de la Naturaleza Humana. *Cuad Vico*, 2, 193-206, 1992.

An account of Josè M Sevilla's book *G Vico: Metafísica de la Mente e Historicismo Antropológico* (Sevilla, 1989) in which the author analyzes professor's Sevilla main thesis and endeavors to show the originality of the historical "metaphysics" (where man is regarded as an historical being) rooted in the "new science": man is born within the frame of history through which is capable to develop the elements involved with his own science.

Patai, Raphael (ed) and Goldsmith, Emanuel S (ed). *Thinkers and Teachers of Modern Judaism*. New York, Paragon House, 1994.

Paté-Cornell, M Elisabeth and Davis, Donald B. A Challenge to the Compound Lottery Axiom: A Two-Stage Normative Structure and Comparison to Other Theories. *Theor Decis*, 37(3), 267-309, N 94.

This paper examines references among uncertain prospects when the decision maker is uneasy about his assignment of subjective probabilities. It proposes a two-stage lottery framework for the analysis of such prospects, where the first stage represents an assessment of the vagueness (ambiguity) in defining the problem's randomness and the second stage represents an assessment of the problem for each hypothesized randomness condition. Standard axioms of rationality are prescribed for each stage, including weak ordering, continuity, and strong independence. The 'Reduction of Compound Lotteries' axiom is weakened, however, so that the two lottery stages have consistent, but not collapsible, preference structures. (edited)

Patel, Kartikeya C. Women, Earth, and the Goddess: A Shākta-Hindu Interpretation of Embodied Religion. *Hypatia*, 9(4), 69-87, Fall 94.

This essay explores the notion of female embodiment and its relation to the phenomenon of religion. It explains religious beliefs, acts, and events in terms of the worship of the female body. By elucidating this standpoint, this essay hopes to reclaim the centrality of the female body and its importance in the study of philosophy of religion.

Patfoort, Albert. De quelques emplois médiévaux du verbe "convincere" au sens moderne du mot. *Rev Thomiste*, 94(2), 273-284, Ap-Je 94.

Pathiraj R. The Sphota Doctrine of Bhartrhari. *Indian Phil Quart*, 22(1), 67-74, Ja 95.

The article tries to understand the ancient theory of Sphota, expounded by Bhartrhari (c.450-510 A.D.), an indian philosopher grammarian, as an answer to the linguistic problem of grasping the unified meaning from a physically distinct sequential sound stretch. Bhartrhari holds that the sequential sound stretch reveals an indivisible unit, Sphota, which, by its self-revelatory nature, manifests the meaning to the hearer. At which point is the sphota revealed? If at the first/last the rest of the sound units become redundant! However, Bhartrhari explains that all the units are necessary for its manifestation.

Patnaik, Tandra. Purusarthas in Aesthetics. *Indian Phil Quart*, 22(1), 55-66, Ja 95.

The paper deals with the Indian conception of the fourfold values of life, i.e., physical, psychic, moral, and spiritual, and the art forms. According to the ancient Indian aestheticians art represents not an immitation of life but a form of life. Therefore art can raise the spectator/reader from mere mundane enjoyment to the level of pure spiritual bliss. The paper discusses the view of two eminent aestheticians Bharata and Abhinava-Gupta in the context of their theories of rase (aesthetic relish). The paper also contests the charges of "subjectivism" and "mysticism" raised by modern critics against this ancient theory.

Patterson, John. Maori Environmental Virtues. *Environ Ethics*, 16(4), 397-409, Wint 94.

The standard sources for Maori ethics are the traditional narratives. These depict all things in the environment as sharing a common ancestry, and as thereby required, ideally, to exhibit certain virtues of respect and responsibility for each other. These environmental virtues are expressed in terms of distinctively Maori concepts: respect for *mauri* and *tapu, kaitiakitanga, whanaungatanga, manaakitanga*, and environmental balance. I briefly explore these Maori environmental virtues, and draw from them some messages for the world at large.

Patterson, Richard. *Aristotle's Modal Logic: Essence and Entailment in the Organon*. New York, Cambridge Univ Pr, 1995.

Patterson, Richard. The Ascent in Plato's *Symposium*. *Proc Boston Colloq Anc Phil*, 7, 193-214, 1991.

Diotima's description of the ascent from eros for bodily beauty, through a series of intermediate erotic attachments, to eros of beauty itself, does not say how the lover is supposed to achieve any of these steps upward. I suggest that the lover is stimulated by the erotic object to produce logoi saying why the beloved is so beautiful; that this logos (directed in part by a "guide" in ways illustrated in various dialogues) reveals that the supposed beauty of the beloved is actually a beauty of a higher kind—that what one desired all along was really a higher kind of beauty; and that this same pattern is repeated with each new beauty until one reaches beauty itself, whose beauty is not the beauty of anything other than itself.

Pattery, George. Justice: An Inter-Faith Task. *J Dharma*, 19(3), 260-274, Jl-S 94.

The article aims at articulating the pedagogical role of cultures and religions in defining human progress. Three ideologies of modernization, nationalism and secularism are at work in the present Indian (S Asian) social situation. They presuppose that scientific technological rationality is the only valid way of knowing and relating to realities, and that self-identity of peoples is defined in terms of 'modernity' as proposed by the west. Calling these presuppositions into question, the present work argues for an integral approach. Cultures and development, religions and justice are interrelated issues and have to be addressed together. Justice is an inter-cultural, inter-religious and inter-disciplinary task. Perspectives of the ancient and living cultures and religions should be taken into account in evolving a methodology to achieve justice.

Pattin, Adriaan. Autour du *Liber de causis*: Quelques réflexions sur la récente littérature. *Frei Z Phil Theol*, 41(3), 354-388, 1994.

Patton, Paul (trans) and Deleuze, Gilles. *Difference and Repetition*. New York, Columbia Univ Pr, 1994.

This brilliant exposition of the critique of identity is a classic in contemporary philosophy and one of Deleuze's most important words. Of fundamental importance to literary critics and philosophers, the book develops two central concepts—pure difference and complex repetition—and shows how the two concepts are related. While difference implies divergence and decentering, repetition is associated with displacement and disguising. Central in initiating the shift in French thought away from Hegel and Marx and toward Nietzsche and Freud, the book moves deftly to establish a fundamental critique of Western metaphysics.

Pauen, Michael. Die Wissenschaft vom Schönen: Kunstpsychologie und die Ästhetik der Moderne. *Z Phil Forsch*, 49(1), 54-75, Ja-Mr 95.

This paper focuses on the development of aesthetics in late 19th century Germany; authors are Herbart, Fechner, Vischer, and Lipps. In an effort to meet the standards of natural science, these authors dismiss the metaphysical speculations of Hegelian philosophy and try to establish aesthetics as a psychological science. Fechner even runs experiments in order to find the laws of beauty; the results of this approach, however, turned out to be quite unsatisfactory. This might be one of the reasons why metaphysical aesthetics were revived after the turn of the century. Nevertheless, psychological aesthetics exerted an influence even on well known authors like Ernst Bloch or Theodor W Adorno.

Pauer-Studer, Herlinde. Bioethik und Feminismus. *Deut Z Phil*, 42(1), 155-166, 1994.

In this critical review of recent feminist literature on bioethics it is argued that certain methodological assumptions that underlie a large part of feminist analysis of bioethics (e.g., the strong emphasis on particularism and contextualism) seem doubtful. There are also incoherences pointed out in the way that some feminist philosophers deal with the problem of abortion on the one hand and the issue of IVF on the other.

Paul, Karen (& others). The Ethics of International Trade: Use of Deviation from Average World Price to Indicate Possible Wrongdoing. *Bus Ethics Quart*, 4(1), 29-41, Ja 94.

The measure proposed here, the ratio of the price reported in a given trade to the average world price for that commodity, is based on the average world price for a given commodity reported for all trades between the U S and all other countries for a given period. This new measure can be used to enable government agencies to identify trades between U S firms or individuals and their counterparts in other countries which are designed to further prohibit activities such as money laundering or tax avoidance. This measure would also enable the U S government to monitor trade flows more accurately, facilitating more analysis of trade imbalances between countries and tracking trade in strategic materials, for example, weapons. Use of this new measure could enable naive buyers and sellers of goods, for example, those situated in remote or underdeveloped markets, to know what their counterparts in more central and informed countries are paying or being paid for comparable goods, and hence to become more informed as trading partners.

Paulson, Stanley L. Lon L Fuller, Gustav Radbruch, and the "Positivist" Theses. *Law Phil*, 13(3), 313-359, Ag 94.

Pavic, Zeljko. Die *Philosophia fundamentalis* von Josip Stadler. *Filozof Istraz*, 14(2-3), 473-491, 1994.

In diesem Aufsatz untersucht der Verfasser das philosophische System des bosnischen Erzbischofs Josip Stadler (1843-1918), um dessen Beitrag zur Entwicklung der Neuscholastik in Bosnien, aber ebenso auch der Neuscholastik im allgemeinen aufzuzeigen. Stadler fragte nach den letzten Gründen alles Seienden (in der Tradition von Aristoteles und Thomas von Aquin) vom Standpunkt der Ontologie, Logik, Kosmologie, Psychologie und natürlichen Theologie aus. Zwar geht Stadler nicht über den Rahmen der neuscholastischen Fragestellung hinaus, doch hat er dem Verständnis der nach ihm folgenden philosophischen Probleme weit die Tore geöffnet. (edited)

Pavlík, Ján. Bernard Bolzano and German Classical Philosophy. *Filozof Cas*, 42(6), 1013-1029, 1994.

The work of the Prague-based philosopher Bernard Bolzano gave rise to a very significant European cultural phenomenon which is generally referred to as the

Austrian philosophical tradition. A fundamental feature of this tradition is its critical opposition to the philosophy of the other German-speaking countries, and to German classical philosophy in particular. In Bolzano's writings, the debate between the Austrian and the German philosophical traditions (that is with Kantian transcendental subjectivism and its implications) became a revival of the celebrated polemic between Socrates and Plato on the one hand and the sophists on the other. Instead of Kantian intuition, Bolzano supported the strictly conceptual character of mathematics, and this places him among the leaders in the attempt to emancipate it from all extraneous (metaphysical and especially objective) elements which disrupt the inner logical coherency of its structure. (edited)

Pavlov, Dejan. Philosophy and the Self-Determination of Nation and Person Today. *Darshana Int*, 32(3/127), 4-7, Jl 92.

Pawelzik, Markus. "Krankheit als Tat-Sache" in *Mythos Wertfreiheit?, Apel, Karl-Otto (ed)*, 275-299. Frankfurt, Campus Verlag, 1994.

Pawlowska, Ija Lazari. The Concept of Morality. *Darshana Int*, 32(3/127), 28-39, Jl 92.

Payette, Daniel and Rialle, Vincent. Richesse, Tensions et Diversité des Sciences de la Cognition. *Lekton*, 4(2), 5-20, 1994.

Payne, E F J (trans) and Schopenhauer, Arthur. *On the Basis of Morality*. Providence, Berghahn, 1995.

This work is one of the most significant nineteenth-century treatises on ethics. It is also Schopenhauer's most extended discussion of traditional themes in ethics and presents a descriptive ethics radically at odds with rationally based, prescriptive ethical theories. Schopenhauer begins this book with a wide-ranging critique of Kant's ethics. Schopenhauer argues that compassion is the basis of morality, and in so doing presents a virtue ethics in which passion and desire are viewed as the keys for explaining different moral characters, behaviors, and world views. In the concluding part of his essay, Schopenhauer sketches his metaphysics of moral, using Kant's transcendental idealism as a ground for stressing both the interconnectiveness of being and the affinity of his ethics to Eastern thought. (edited)

Payne, Michael. *Reading Theory: An Introduction to Lacan, Derrida, and Kristeva*. Cambridge, Blackwell, 1993.

The two aims of this book are suggested in the ambiguity of its title: to provide a reading of major texts by Lacan, Derrida, and Kristeva and to trace the outlines of the reading theories they propose. Lacan heralds a return to the writings of Freud in order to hear in his texts the voice of the unconscious; Derrida proposes to examine so carefully the structures of the texts he reads as to discover the deconstructive openings in those texts to structures of thought that are outside or beyond them; Kristeva extends the methods of semanalysis, a psychoanalytically enhanced semiotics, to an examination of the speaking subject and the signifying structures of social practice.

Payne, Stephen L. Epistemological and Ethical Development for Human Resource Professionals. *Bus Prof Ethics J*, 13(3), 33-56, Fall 94.

Paradigmatic or epistemological assumptions underlying the theory and practice of human resource management (HRM) are often taken for granted or merely implied in published work on ethics in the field. The lack of ethics-related dialogues involving HRM practitioners with other organizational stakeholders, especially those exploring their contrasting epistemological assumptions, may help explain why larger-scale ethics reform within work organizations has been slow or has not occurred. Expanded ethics training and development activities are suggested for HRM practitioners that would examine how a wide range of epistemological and values assumptions affect ethical positions of those in work organizations.

Payne, Stephen L and Giacalone, Robert A. Evaluation of Employee Rule Violations: The Impact of Impression Management Effects in Historical Context. *J Bus Ethics*, 14(6), 477-487, Je 95.

The study sought to determine whether impression management tactics by an employee could effectively lessen the recommended punishment for an ethical rule infraction by this individual. Subjects read a vignette in which an employee violated the confidentiality of personnel records. The employee was presented as either having had a history of previous infractions or not such historical information was provided. Additionally, the employee was described as using either no impression management tactics, an apology, or a justification for his behavior. Results show that in the case of a history of multiple offenses, the employee's use of justifications effectively mitigated others' judgments of the wrongfulness of the employee's action, while apologies did not. Similarly, the justification appeared to lessen respondent recommendations for punishment, prevention of promotion, and demotion/firing, but only when there is a history of multiple offenses. In most cases, apologies tended to exacerbate the problem when previous offenses had been committed. The data are discussed in terms of their implications for the study of employee use of impression management tactics.

Pazanin, Ante. Bosnjaks *Geschichte der Philosophie* und das geschichtliche Denken. *Filozof Istraz*, 14(2-3), 493-498, 1994.

Im Sinne einer möglichen Einführung in ein Gespräch über Bosnjaks *Povijest filozofije* (Geschichte der Philosophie) geht vorliegende Arbeit von der Tatsache aus, dass Branko Bosnjak all jenen Generationen Philosophiegeschichte lehrte, die in der zweiten Hälfte des 20. Jahrhunderts an der Philosophischen Fakultät der Universität Zagreb Philosophie studierten. Unter verschiedenen Zugängen in Erforschung und Schreibung der Geschichte der Philosophie folgt Bosnjak dem Gedanken der Einheit von Philosophie und Philosophiegeschichte, denn ohne ein Studium der Philosophiegeschichte sind weder die Philosophie noch deren Studium denkbar. (edited)

Pazanin, Ante. Ethik und Freundschaft. *Filozof Istraz*, 14(1), 5-25, 1994.

Um die Bedeutung der Freundschaft für das ethische Handeln und für das politische Leben des Menschen zu zeigen, wird hier zunächst der Sinn der praktischen Philosophie als Einheit von Ethik und Politik bei Aristoteles erörtet. Die aristotelischen Auslegungen über die Freundschaft in der *Nikomachischen Ethik* zeigen sich dabei als das Beste, was zu dieser Problematik in der ganzen Geschichte der Philosophie überhaupt gesagt wurde. (edited)

Pazdyka, Pawel. The First-Order Coding of Models in Models with a Single Binary Relation. *Rep Math Log*, 27, 45-54, 1993.

Pazos, J and Maté, J L and Juristo, N. Expert Systems Evaluation. *Commun Cog—AI*, 11(3), 225-255, 1994.

The six honest servants of human kind that Kipling pointed out: what, when, where, who, why and how, are studied for knowledge-based systems evaluation. We place special emphasis on the procedural aspect of evaluation which is reflected by how. In this sense, Jain's methodology for computer systems performance evaluation is made suitable for KBS evaluation. Practical guidelines on how to proceed with KBS evaluation are provided.

Peach, W Bernard (ed) and Price, Richard. *The Correspondence of Richard Price, Volume III: February 1786-February 1791*. Durham, Duke Univ Pr, 1994.

Peachment, Allan (& others). Means or Ends? Ethical Decision Frameworks in the Western Australian Public Service. *J Bus Ethics*, 14(8), 629-641, Ag 95.

The paper analyses results from a questionnaire-based survey of "ethical behavior" of members of the Western Australian Senior Executive Service. Relating to definitions of deontology (duty) and teleology (ends over means) the study examines the validity of three hypotheses on ethical behavior/decision making frameworks. Longitudinal data is related to the 1983-90 *WA Inc* period. The study establishes that SES managers apply ethical frameworks in order to understand the meaning of: "ethical behaviour" and that there are groups of managers with distinct understandings of what constitutes ethical behavior which is reflective of particular ethics theories. Three groups of managers are identified: 1) emphasises teleology 2) focuses on external influences (rules, standards and codes) and 3) encompasses both teleology and external influences and, to a lesser extent deontology. Only this latter group is regarded as having an appropriate repertoire of potential responses to any given ethical dilemma. There is no support for the view that those beginning employment in the public service post 1984 adversely affected the ethical decision making frameworks of other senior managers.

Peacocke, Arthur. The Religion of a Scientist: Explorations into Reality (*Religio philosophi naturalis*). *Zygon*, 29(4), 639-659, D 94.

Sir Thomas Browne's reflection on the synthesis between his Christian religion and his practice as a medical doctor, made over three centuries ago, leads into reflections on the present relation between religion and science in the personal experience of the writer. An account is given of how the actual practice of scientific investigation led the author to theistic inferences and how the study of DNA provoked questions concerning reductionism and emergence. This evoked the need for a map of knowledge, and an attempt is presented in a figure which also serves to clarify what kind of realistic reference is involved in both scientific and humanistic contexts. Theological investigations thereby receive at least provisional legitimization and, with this encouragement, the article pursues the questions of the nature of the divine Source ("God") of the world's being and becoming, and of God's interaction and communication with the world. (edited)

Peacocke, Christopher. "Concepts and Norms in a Natural World" in *Philosophy of Psychology: Debates on Psychological Explanation, Macdonald, Cynthia (ed)*, 277-284. Cambridge, Blackwell, 1995.

Peacocke, Christopher. Nonconceptual Content: Kinds, Rationales and Relations. *Mind Lang*, 9(4), 419-430, D 94.

Peacocke, Christopher (ed). *Objectivity, Simulation and the Unity of Consciousness*. New York, Oxford Univ Pr, 1994.

Peacocke, Christopher. Rationality, Norms and the Primitively Compelling: A Reply to Kirk Ludwig. *Mind Lang*, 9(4), 492-498, D 94.

Pearl, Judea. "From Adams' Conditionals to Default Expressions, Causal Conditionals, and Counterfactuals" in *Probability and Conditionals, Eells, Ellery (ed)*, 47-74. New York, Cambridge Univ Pr, 1994.

We describe several investigations into establishing a sound probabilistic semantics for a variety of conditional sentences. A semantics based on infinitesimal conditional probabilities is shown to be capable of serving as a universal core for defaults expressions. Extensions using ranked models, maximum entropy, and conditional entailment are described and compared. We then show how an account based on conditioning can serve to unify indicative and subjunctive conditionals, by conditioning the former on observations and the latter on actions. Finally, we show that adding a qualitative causal theory (in the form of a graph) as part of an epistemic state is sufficient to facilitate the analysis of action sequences, their consequences, their interaction with observations, and, hence, the assertability of causal and counterfactual conditionals.

Pearl, Leon. God Had to Create the World. *Relig Stud*, 30(3), 331-333, S 94.

Pearson, Allen T. Teaching as a Practice: A Rejoinder. *Stud Phil Educ*, 13(2), 163-168, 1993-94.

Paul O'Leary has provided an excellent review of *The Teacher: Theory and Practice in Teacher Education*. By this I mean that he has identified issues that are crucial in the development of the book's arguments and that raise difficult questions. An excellent review makes the author's rejoinder a challenging task. One might have hoped for the review to focus on issues that are peripheral to the book's purpose or to raise questions that can be answered easily. Both of these can be handled by the author with dispatch. Unfortunately for me, O'Leary has done neither. There are three issues O'Leary raises that I would like to comment on: my conception of the practice of teaching, the possible result of my argument that teachers can hold some pretty bizarre beliefs, and the fact that my argument does not recognize the domain specific nature of evidence. I will try to clarify the meaning of these objections and to provide a response to them.

Peetz, Siegbert. *Die Freiheit im Wissen: Eine Untersuchung zu Schellings Konzept der Rationalität*. Frankfurt/M, Klostermann, 1995.

The central claim of this study concerns Schelling's concept of rationality. Schelling develops freedom as the possibility of a modifiable relation, which is a constitutive epistemic mode for the constitution of knowledge. The center of the study is constituted by Schelling's 'On Human Freedom' (1809). In opposition to traditional scholarship which emphasized the issue of evil as the real agenda it is argued that Schelling's thought should be understood from the perspective of Schelling's response to Jacobi's criticism of the idealistic concept of subjectivity. Schelling's response is the flawed attempt to reformulate his system of identity in practical terms. This attempt led to difficulties which Schelling was incapable of solving in his 'Ages of the World'. Indeed, the later philosophy of Schelling did not attain the conceptual richness of the possibilities afforded by the basic sketch in 'On Human Freedom'.

Pefanis, Julian (trans) and Bains, Paul (trans) and Guattari, Félix. *Chaosmosis: An Ethico-Aesthetic Paradigm*. Bloomington, Indiana Univ Pr, 1995.

Peffer, Rodney G. Towards a More Adequate Rawlsian Theory of Social Justice. *Pac Phil Quart*, 75(3-4), 251-271, S-D 94.

In *Marxism, Morality, and Social Justice* (Princeton University Press, 1990), I put forward and defend a modified version of Rawl's substantive theory of social justice which I claim is superior to the original. In *Political Liberalism* (pp 7-8), Rawls has agreed that all of the modifications I have made are justified, save one. Here I review these modifications (and my arguments as to why they're justified); examine Rawls's reasons for rejecting my proposed modification in favor of social and economic (in addition to political) democracy; and offer what I take to be an improved version of my theory.

Peijnenburg, Jeanne. Formal Proof or Linguistic Process? Beth and Hintikka on Kant's Use of 'Analytic'. *Kantstudien*, 85(2), 160-178, 1994.

In 1973 Hintikka published his famous studies on Kant's distinction between the analytic and the synthetic. Professor Hintikka never kept it a secret that his astute and highly original interpretation of Kant is taken from the work of E W Beth, a Dutch logician and philosopher who died in 1964. Consequently, one often speaks of *the Beth-Hintikka theory*. In the present paper it is argued that this linkage is inappropriate: a fundamental difference exists between Hintikka's and Beth's Kant interpretations. The essence of this difference is explained, as also the reason that it has so far remained unnoticed.

Pejovic, Danilo. Bosnjaks Geschichte der Philosophie. *Filozof Istraz*, 14(2-3), 499-502, 1994.

Bosnjaks *Geschichte der Philosophie* in 3 Bänden, Zagreb 1993, ist die bisher umfangreichste Darstellung (1654 S.) des philosophischen Denkens in kroatischer Sprache, nach den Werken der bekannten Vorgänger Albert Bazala (1906-1912) und Franjo Sanc (1942-1943). In diesem Buch versucht der Verfasser, einen Dialog mit den grossen Denkern der Vergangenheit von Thales bis Heidegger herzustellen und dabei auch die eigene Position zum Verständnis zu bringen. Im geschichtlichen Kontext des europäischen Denkens findet bei Bosnjak auch die kroatische Philosophie ihren Ort, von M Vlacic (Flacius) und F Petric (Patricius) in der Renaissance und R Boskovic in der neuzeitlichen Naturphilosophie bis zu A Bazala und V Filipovic im 20 Jahrhundert.

Peled, Yoav and Brunner, José. Staatsbürgerliche Identität und Selbstachtung im jüdischen Staat: Eine Rawls'che Perspektive. *Deut Z Phil*, 43(2), 329-348, 1995.

This essay examines the Israeli-Palestinian conflict from the vantage point of John Rawls's notions of respect and self-respect. 1) It provides a critical analysis of the pivotal role of these notions in Rawls's theorizing. 2) It considers the extent to which aspects of Israeli-Palestinian relations are compatible with—or even corroborate—Rawls's empirical hypotheses and normative claims concerning the interdependence of respect and self-respect. 3) It establishes where the values entailed in Rawls's perspective on respect and self-respect would place a Rawlsian vis-a-vis some issues of the Israeli-Palestinian question.

Pellauer, David. "The Symbol Gave Rise to Thought" in *The Philosophy of Paul Ricoeur*, Hahn, Lewis Edwin (ed), 99-122. Peru, Open Court, 1994.

Pellecchia, Pasquale. I principi matematici kantiani del mondo fisico. *Aquinas*, 36(3), 499-526, S-D 93.

The Kantian formalism is such that could not, should not be analytically determined. The denotation of space and time, of quantity, quality, relation and method, are critically placed only by virtue of the contemporary or even Aristotelian problems. Consequently the intelligence, that is a natural gift, the reason that can't be trained, the imagination, that is blind and root unknown to us, the schematism, that is art hidden in the spirit's depth, the scheme, that is vermittelnde Vorstellung, the categories, that are blindly taken from Aristotle, can't have rational power to set up any science, any mathematics.

Pellecchia, Pasquale. I principi matematici kantiani del mondo fisico, II. *Aquinas*, 37(1), 3-34, Ja-Ap 94.

Intuition's axioms and perception's advances are misled in Kant, owing to the empty formalism I talked about in the previous abstract. Having placed in intuitions' axioms in a-priori way: 1) supposes a self-comprehension of the I-think; 2) supposes that the I-think can't produce anything except the Heuclidean axioms. Now the 1) requires and intellectual intuition that Kant has himself refused; the 2) was historically disproved by the series of non-Heuclidean geometries. Kant thinks to be able to place axioms and advances, intending sensation and perception only as an act and not also as contents. We can prove that this method is incomplete and misleading, and so it makes not legitimate every form of philosophic, mathematic, and empiriological (Kantian and post-Kantian) apriorism.

Pellecchia, Pasquale. Kant, la razza e la storia. *Aquinas*, 37(2), 263-298, My-Ag 94.

Kant deals with the races' question precisely in two essays, the first one in 1775 and the other one in 1785, and generically in "useful anthropology" and somewhere else. The race is one of the most considerable evidence of the human species' difference. But Kant wishes to be the purity's philosopher: the philosopher of the pure theoretical reason, of the pure practical reason, of the pure judgment; and, consequently, of the pure man, of the man whose race has not any "moral-historical" sense. For this reason his position, inherited from the Age of Enlightenment, appears aristocratic, "split": he "respects" the man, the reason, but doesn't respect the races, doesn't love the races, doesn't "love" the man in the flesh.

Pellecchia, Pasquale. L'Esilio Ou-topico dell'Etica: L Wittgenstein. *Aquinas*, 37(3), 523-545, S-D 94.

Pellegrino, Edmund D. Allocation of Resources at the Bedside: The Intersection of Economics, Law, and Ethics. *Kennedy Inst Ethics J*, 4(4), 309-317, D 94.

In the preceding article, Mehlman and Massey examine possible legal responses to the issues that confront physicians faced with treating patients who have insufficient financial resources. This commentary explores the same issues from the perspective of ethics, including a comparison of the way law and ethics interpret the physician-patient relationship, the ethical obligations of physicians that are inherent in that relationship, and the propriety of Mehlman and Massey's legal and ethical proposals to ameliorate physicians' conflicting obligations in providing or withholding care on grounds of conservation of society's resources.

Pellegrino, Edmund D. To Save the Logic, the Facts Must Fit. *J Clin Ethics*, 5(2), 158-159, Sum 94.

Pelletier, Francis Jeffry (ed) and Carlson, Gregory N (ed). *The Generic Book*. Chicago, Univ of Chicago Pr, 1995.

Two types of linguistic phenomena have been called "generics": reference to a kind (or genus) and the attribution of a general property (which might admit exceptions) to an individual or to a kind. An example of the former type is "The horse was introduced to North America by the conquistadors", where 'the horse' clearly does not refer to any particular horse; an example of the latter type is "The horse has four legs and stands between 10 and 22 hands tall", which is true despite the existence of three-legged horses and horses that are not in this height range—it is only that the typical, or normal, or important horses have the properties ascribed. This book addresses the many problems surrounding these types of statements. The seven-authored, 125 page introductory chapter surveys the history and state of the field, and presents various directions for further research. The remaining chapters are by individual researchers, and take one or another of these topics further than has been done before. The book ends with a comprehensive bibliography of work done on generics, especially from the philosophical, linguistic, and computational realms. The book is available in hard and soft cover. (edited)

Pelton, Lou and Strutton, David and Rawwas, Mohammed Y A. Ethical Attitudes of Mental Health Practitioners: Balancing Therapeutic Practices and Treatments. *J Bus Ethics*, 13(8), 597-608, Ag 94.

This paper reports the responses of 251 mental health care practitioners to a mail survey examining their views concerning ethical conflicts and practices within their work environments. Besides identifying the sources and types of conflicts they experience, respondents were asked how ethical standards have changed over the last 10 years as well as the factors influencing these changes. Conclusions and implications are outlined and future research needs are described.

Peña, Angel Bustillos. El concepto de propiedad privada en el Derecho Constitucional Venezolano. *Rev Filosof (Venezuela)*, 19, 81-90, 1994.

This paper is an edited version of an earlier, much longer work of the same title, in which the thesis is maintained that property rights, in particular rights concerning private property, are limited and contrained by Venezuelan legislation, from which arises the social function that property rights serve in Venezuela. This study is historic, jurisprudential, political, economical and philosophical—all facets which are pertinent, due to the complex character of property rights. The fields of history, economy and philosophy are called upon in order to lay a foundation for the thesis in question. (edited)

Peña, Lorenzo. El Pluscuamracionalismo de Nicolás de Cusa: Las Contradicciones Allende la Contradicción. *Rev Espan Filosof Med*, 0, 143-158, 1993.

Within Nicholas de Cusa's philosophical approach, there is bound to be a level of unity lower than the one pertaining to God as such but higher than those of common creatures. That intermediate level belongs to the intellect and is characterized by an affirmative coincidence of opposites hinging around universal equality. Such intellectual equality among all things, as they are in the intellect, constitutes the root of number and multiplicity.

Peña, Vidal. Algunas preguntas acerca de la Idea de Progreso. *El Basilisco*, 15, 3-14, Ja-Mr 94.

Peña Aguado, María Isabel. *Ästhetik des Erhabenen: Burke, Kant, Adorno, Lyotard*. Vienna, Passagen, 1994.

Die spektakuläre Renaissance der Ästhetik des Erhabenen im philosophischen Diskurs der letzten Jahre verlangt eine Revision des Erhabenen. Weshalb gerät gerade dieser beinahe vergessene Begriff in den Mittelpunkt des gegenwärtigen Philosophierens? Welche Bedeutung hat er für das Denken am Ende des 20. Jahrhunderts? Diesen Fragen geht die Autorin in einer Auseinandersetzung mit der Philosophiegeschichte nach, wobei sie im 18 Jahrhundert bei Burke, der das Phänomen des Erhabenen stark von dem Schönen unterscheidet, und Kant, der massgeblich ist für die Etablierung des Erhabenen als philosophischer Begriff, ansetzt. (edited)

Peñafort, Juan J E. "La Identidad del Discurso Estético y la Crítica Ideológica en la Etapa Post-Estructuralista de Roland Barthes" in *Temas Actuales de Filosofía*, Palacios, María Julia (ed), 457-467. Buenos Aires, Univ Nacional Salta, 1993.

Peñalver, Patricio. "Archaeology, History, Deconstruction" in *Reconstructing Foucault*, Miguel-Alfonso, Ricardo (ed), 3-33. Amsterdam, Rodopi, 1994.

Penati, Giancarlo. Archè come Fondamento e Origine in Martin Heidegger. *G Metaf*, 16(3), 341-351, S-D 94.

This study points out the importance of the thought concerning the "Principle" as *Arché*, absolute Origin dominating not only as first condition, but as permanent and absolutely free meaning and cause of the whole. The history of philosophy is (according to Heidegger) a misunderstanding and oblivion of this original conception of the *Arché* as *Physis* in Presocratic fragments. The "Onto-theology" of Western thought has logically naturalized and humanized the events of history in order to human aims of power. The true freedom and humanity of Man requires a radical return to the original conception of principle as one and indeterminable Word, principle of all events, and to a "humble" humanity as "guardian" or "sheperd (*Berger*) of Being, replaced in his "sacred" dignity of absolutely free principle of things, life and human "destinations".

Penati, Giancarlo. Modernità e post-modernità dell'agostinismo. *G Metaf*, 16(1-2), 31-44, Ja-Ag 94.

This study gives the main elements for a judgment concerning the actuality of Augustin's thought. It points out the interiority of Augustinian way to fundamental philosophical truth, but also the ontological and not only subjective or merely "consciential" nature of this truth, so not merely "modern" and immanent in man, but transcendent and finally divine. This position accepts the exigences of criticism in modern philosophical inquiry, but avoids the subsequent "nihilism" of subject or individual and historical perspectives of truth and other human values. A presence of Augustinian thought is also noted in some important passages of Heidegger's main works, and so in postmodernism.

Pencak, William. *The Conflict of Law and Justice in the Icelandic Sagas*. Cambridge, Blackwell, 1995.

This work examines legal and political conflicts within the major medieval sagas (*Njal's, Grettir's, Eyrbyggja, Laxdaela, Egil's*). It takes a semiotic approach to questions of freedom, justice, violence, and legal codes as they pose tragic choices to heroic figures. It centers on the issue what are the values, virtues, and flaws of republican governments of free people such as in Iceland. While the imaginary and historical worlds of medieval Iceland reside in the distant past, the conflicts of the great sagas spring to life in present-day philosophical reflection on the persistence and decay of republics.

Pence, Greg. Dr Kevorkian and the Struggle for Physician-Assisted Dying. *Bioethics*, 9(1), 62-71, Ja 95.

This article summarizes the controversy surrounding Dr. Jack Kevorkian's first 20 cases of physician-assisted dying. It discusses major ethical arguments on both sides of the morality of physician-assisted dying for terminal adult patients. It defends Dr. Kevorkian and notes that he enjoys the support of most ordinary Americans but that he is condemned by most physicians and medical ethicists.

Pence, Gregory. Case Study in the Ethics of Teaching Philosophy. *Teach Phil*, 18(2), 165-166, Je 95.

The piece describes a fictional, but representative, case of the exploitation of part-time faculty in departments of Philosophy. Some would see such a practice as paradoxical when the same department is exhorting students about virtues and moral principles in courses on ethics.

Pence, Gregory and Stephens, G Lynn. *Seven Dilemmas in World Religions*. New York, Paragon House, 1994.

Pence, Gregory E. *Classic Cases in Medical Ethics (Second Edition)*. New York, McGraw-Hill, 1995.

Penco, Carlo. *Vie della scrittura: Frege e la svolta linguistica*. Milan, Angeli, 1994.

The aim of the book is introductory. Frege's philosophy of language and logic is presented through an examination of similarities and differences from classical logic, Aristotle, Kant and Boolean Calculus. The main themes of Frege's philosophy and logic from the chapters of the book: Judgement, Deduction, Function, Quantification, Content (Sense and Reference). Many references are given to Wittgenstein's discussion of Fregean arguments. Dummett's interpretation is accepted and refined; some hints are given towards contemporary discussion, giving stress to the porceural themes which can be found in Frege's analysis of sense. Fregean analysis of assertion is considered as a starting point for a new formal pragmatics which would enclose classical and intuitionistic logic.

Pendlebury, Michael. Content and Causation in Perception. *Phil Phenomenol Res*, 54(4), 767-785, D 94.

To perceive something is to have a sense experience with a content which fits it to an appropriate degree (which varies in a specified way between state of affairs, events and thing perception), providing that the item concerned causes the experience through a mechanism which is reliable in the sense that in relevant circumstances it is generally apt to connect facts with experiences which fit those facts. I elaborate and defend this account, showing how it solves a number of problems in the philosophy of perception and avoids the main weaknesses of its rivals.

Penelhum, Terence. Ateismo, scetticismo e fideismo. *Riv Filosof Neo-Scolas*, 86(1), 134-153, Ja-Mr 94.

This is an Italian translation of a paper, "Atheism, Scepticism and Fideism" published in *Ateismo e Societa* ed Albino Babolin, Editrice Benucci, Perugia, 1992. The essay attempts to explain how some Christian apologists have tried to use classical scepticism in opposition to atheism, emphasizing particularly the views of Bayle, Pascal and Kierkegaard. It also tries to show how Hume makes use of the language of sceptical fideism to serve anti-Christian purposes, and how recent forms of Christian apologetic show some likenesses to that tradition.

Peñalver Gómez, Patricio. Éticas del don: Aporías y negociaciones. *Rev Filosof (Daimon)*, 7, 179-184, 1993.

Pennock, Robert T. Moral Darwinism: Ethical Evidence for the Descent of Man. *Biol Phil*, 10(3), 287-307, July 95.

Could an ethical theory ever play a substantial evidential role in a scientific argument for an empirical hypothesis? In *The Descent of Man*, Darwin includes an extended discussion of the nature of human morality, and the ethical theory which he sketches is not simply developed as an interesting ramification of his theory of evolution, but is used as a key part of his evidence for human descent from animal ancestors. Darwin must rebut the argument that, because of our moral nature, humans are essentially different in kind from other animals and so had to have had a different origin. I trace his causal story of how the moral sense could develop out of social instincts by evolutionary mechanisms of group selection, and show that the form of Utilitarianism he proposes involves a radical reduction of the standard of value to the concept of biological fitness. I argue that this causal analysis, although a weakness from a normative standpoint, is a strength when judged for its intended purpose as part of an evidential argument to confirm the hypothesis of human descent.

Penrose, Roger. "Is Conscious Awareness Consistent with Space-Time Descriptions?" in *Philosophy, Mathematics and Modern Physics, Rudolph, Enno (ed)*, 34-47. New York, Springer-Verlag, 1994.

Pensky, Max. "Universalism and the Situated Critic" in *The Cambridge Companion to Habermas, White, Stephen K (ed)*, 67-94. New York, Cambridge Univ Pr, 1995.

Pentz, Rebecca D. Veatch and Brain Death: A Plea for Soul. *J Clin Ethics*, 5(2), 132-135, Sum 94.

In this article, I argue that the higher brain definition of death recommended by Robert Veatch relies on a dualistic view of human anthropology that divides humans into minds and bodies. I suggest that such a dualism is inconsistent with the Judeo-Christian unitary view of the person and with the feminist emphasis on women as bodies. I describe the Hebraic notion of soul that is the foundation of the Judeo-Christian view.

Pentzopoulou-Valalas, Thérèse. Fichte et Husserl: A la recherche de l'intententionnalité. *Fichte-Studien*, 1, 153-166, 1990.

Penzo, Giorgio. Nietzsche e il nichilismo. *Sapienza*, 47(4), 377-386, O-D 94.

Peperzak, Adriaan. "Hegel and Hobbes Revised" in *Hegel on the Modern World, Collins, Ardis B (ed)*, 199-217. Albany, SUNY Pr, 1995.

Against Leo Strauss and Jacques Taminiaux, this article shows how independent and different Hegel's political philosophy is from that of Hobbes.

Peperzak, Adriaan. Life, Science, and Wisdom According to Descartes. *Hist Phil Quart*, 12(2), 133-153, Ap 95.

How does Descartes see the relations between the search for wisdom, philosophy and the praxis of human life? His view of philosophy as most certain guide on the path that leads to happiness, invites a comparison of his method with other spiritual journeys. To what extent does Descartes succeed in his renewal of Graeco-Christian spirituality?

Pera, Marcello and Botsford, Clarissa (trans). *The Discourses of Science*. Chicago, Univ of Chicago Pr, 1994.

The book suggests a remedy for the "Cartesian syndrome"—the fixation on method shared by both the "standard" and "new" philosophy of science. Examining Galileo's *Dialogue*, Darwin's *Origin*, and the Big Bang-Steady State controversy, it develops a general picture according to which scientific research is not just an interchange between nature and the inquiring mind, but a dialogical game with *three* players, nature, the inquiring mind, and a community which, through the process of attack and defense determines what scientific knowledge is. Rhetoric, then, taken as the practice of argumentation, is an essential element of science; and dialectics, taken as the logic of scientific rhetoric, is the organon of science.

Percesepe, Gary. *Introduction to Ethics: Personal and Social Responsibility in a Diverse World*. Englewood Cliffs, Prentice Hall, 1995.

This comprehensive reader in general ethics blends classical philosophical selections with writings of such diverse "nonphilosophical" writers as Czech President Vaclav Havel, the Reverend Martin Luther King, Jr., and poet Adrienne Rich. Throughout the text, questions are raised to provide stimulus for discussion or writing. Preceded by an original essay on ethical theory, and including the voices of women throughout, the readings are grouped into these chapters: Ethical Theories, Ethics of Community, Ethics of Friendship, Love and Caring, Ethics of Truth, Power, and Lying, Ethics of War, Violence, and Peace, Ethics of Hunger and Welfare, Ethics of Race and Power, Ethics of Sex and Power, Ethics of Abortion, Ethics of Animals and the Nonhuman Environment.

Percesepe, Gary (ed) and Mehuron, Kate (ed). *Free Spirits: Feminist Philosophers on Culture*. Englewood Cliffs, Prentice Hall, 1995.

This is a multicultural anthology of feminist essays designed for undergraduate and graduate classroom use in courses such as social and political philosophy, women's studies, and gender studies. The selections by well-known feminist thinkers address themes from popular culture: cultural images, communities, urban spaces, body politics, ecofeminism, sexualities, masculinities, and the politics of hope. Each essay is followed by reading questions, a suggested bibliography, and recommended audiovisual materials. The editor's introduction provides an overview of the organization of the book, and brief summaries of the contents of individual essays.

Perczel, István. Denys et les Hénades de Proclus. *Diotima*, 23, 71-76, 1995.

Pereboom, Derk. Determinism *Al Dente*. *Nous*, 29(1), 21-45, Mr 95.

Pereboom, Derk. Self-Understanding in Kant's Transcendental Deduction. *Synthese*, 103(1), 1-42, Ap 95.

I argue that sections 15-20 of the B-Deduction contain two independent arguments for the applicability of a priori concepts, the first an argument from above, the second an argument from below. The core of the first argument is section 16's explanation of our consciousness of subject-identity across self-attributions, while the focus of the second is section 18's account of universality and necessity in our experience. I conclude that the B-Deduction comprises powerful strategies for establishing its intended conclusion, and that some assistance from empirical psychology might well have produced a completely successful argument.

Pereboom, Derk. Stoic Psychotherapy in Descartes and Spinoza. *Faith Phil*, 11(4), 592-625, Oct 94.

The psychotherapeutic theories of Descartes and Spinoza are heavily influenced by Stoicism. Stoic psychotherapy has two central features. First, we have a remarkable degree of voluntary control over our passions, and we can and should exercise this control to keep ourselves from having any irrational passions at all. Second, the universe is determined by the providential divine will, and in any situation we can and should align ourselves with this divine will in order to achieve equanimity. Whereas Descartes largely endorses the Stoic picture, Spinoza develops a distinctive, intellectualized version of this view.

Pereboom, Derk (ed) and Guignon, Charles (ed). *Existentialism: Basic Writings —Kierkegaard, Nietzsche, Heidegger, Sartre*. Indianapolis, Hackett, 1995.

This collection of readings from the four most influential existentialists features extensive introductions by the volume's editors. The general introduction, "The

Pereda, Carlos 688 AUTHOR INDEX WITH ABSTRACTS

Legacy of Existentialism," sets existentialism in the context of modern thought, and examines the enduring relevance of its discussions of freedom, commitment, agency, authenticity, human nature, moral obligation, faith, and perspectivism. The editors also present original scholarly interpretations of each of the philosophers whose works appear in the book. The volume includes long, continuous selections from *Fear and Trembling, The Gay Science, Being and Time, Being and Nothingness*, and other works.

Pereda, Carlos. Rigor se Dice de muchas Maneras. *Analogia*, 7(2), 73-99, 1993.

Pereda, Carlos. *Vértigos argumentales: Una ética de la disputa*. Barcelona, Anthropos, 1994.

Pereda F, Carlos. Vicisitudes de los Topicos. *Topicos*, 1(1), 25-58, 1991.

Pereira Jr, Alfredo. Um Comentário sobre a Filosofia da Natureza na Enciclopédia de Hegel. *Cad Hist Filosof Cie*, 4(1), 25-50, Ja-Je 94.

An interpretation of Hegel's philosophy of nature is done, bringing it near to "Self-organization" concepts, which are used in many areas of scientific research nowadays. The comments begin with the Aristotelian tradition, studied by Hegel, and focus on the science of logic and philosophy of nature, in his "Encyclopedia of Philosophical Sciences". Two major themes discussed in this context are the Hegelian concept of theleology, and the relationship between philosophical reflection and scientific work.

Péres Antia, Jesús A. Lógica en Razonamiento Ordinário: Razonamiento Práctico. *Manuscrito*, 17(2), 31-64, O 94.

The aim of this paper is to discuss the role of logic as a real tool for commonsense reasoning. First, we present a general overview of the limitations of the so-called logicist approach to using logic as a representation language for commonsense theories. Then, we point out a sharp distinction between theoretical and practical reasoning, in such a way that we can criticize not only the idealistic reasoners but also reasoning grounded on minimal rationality. Finally, we sketch the main lines of what must be understood by practical reasoning.

Pérez, Berta E. Reverence for the Earth is Animal Rights Ethics. *Between Species*, 9(4), 181-192, Fall 93.

This article presents a historical overview of the animal rights movement (ARM), discussing its emergence, growth, and changes through time. The discussion examines the key issues that have proven to be a rallying point for its members and reviews the main intellectual contributions of the seminal figures who have defined the moral philosophy on which many of these issues are based. In providing a historical perspective, this article aims to show that the development of the ethical underpinnings of the animal rights movement go beyond mere animal rights, that animal liberation is human and environmental liberation, too.

Pérez, Diana Inés. "Hechos, Eventos, Tropos y el Análisis de la Causalidad" in *Temas Actuales de Filosofía, Palacios, María Julia (ed)*, 477-484. Buenos Aires, Univ Nacional Salta, 1993.

Pérez, Diana Inés. Davidson, la relación causal y los eventos particulares. *Rev Filosof (Argentina)*, 9(1-2), 29-42, N 94.

This paper deals with Davidson's claim that the causal relation is a relation holding between two particular events. First, a few intuitive arguments trying to show that the causal relation is not a relation between concrete particular events are developed. Second, after describing Davidson's account of the causal relation and causal laws, two different interpretations are offered, one of which is compatible with the claim that the causal relation cannot be a relation between concrete events, as Davidson proposes.

Pérez, Diana Inés. Leyes Causales Intencionales? Sobre los Argumentos de Fodor en Favor de las Leyes Intencionales. *Rev Latin de Filosof*, 21(1), 67-81, Fall 95.

This paper deals with Fodor's arguments concerning the existence of intentional laws. It is divided in three parts. Firstly, Fodor's claim that there are folk psychological intentional laws is examined. Secondly, the paper considers Fodor's defense of the causal power of intentional properties invoking intentional laws. Finally, Fodor's account of special sciences laws (*ceteris paribus* laws) is analysed. None of the arguments is found conclusive.

Pérez, Gilles. La Relación Esencia-existencia en la Segunda de las Meditaciones Metafísicas de Descartes. *Rev Filosof (Spain)*, 7(11), 89-113, 1994.

Pérez, Jorge Navarro. El Individuo y la Nación: El Sujeto y lo Absoluto en las Filosofías del Lenguaje de Humboldt y Fichte. *Daimon Rev Filosof*, 9, 51-62, 1994.

This paper sketches an analysis of W v Humboldt's reaction to Fichte's philosophy of language in the essay "On the Speech Faculty and the Origin of Language" (1795) and in the "Discourses to the German Nation" (1808). By using the idea of the individual, it tries to provide an alternative to the interpretations of Humboldt's writings that underline the idea of the absolute.

Pérez Camacho, Juan José and Sols Lucía, Ignacio. Domingo de Soto en el Origen de la Ciencia Moderna. *Rev Filosof (Spain)*, 7(12), 455-475, 1994.

Pérez de Laborda, Miguel. El "Unum Argumentum" de San Anselmo: Un Intento de Demonstrar lo Que la fe Enseña Sobre Dios. *Acta Phil*, 4(1), 95-103, 1995.

Pérez de Tudela, Jorge. Regular, Ambiguo, Disposicional. *An Seminar Metaf*, 28, 121-138, 1994.

The aim of this paper is to suggest that the discussion about the nature of the (so-called) "dispositional properties" may be attacked drawing a parallel between the "ontological" and the "juridical" sides of the problem of the "dispositions". This leads to the suggestion that the "dispositional properties" of the objective realities are as reducible to the laws of science as the "legal capacities" or "rights" of the human beings are reducible, according to certain interpretation to the rules of law. That opens the field of an enlarged investigation about the next question: what is exactly the nature of a "rule"?.

Pérez Herranz, Fernando. La Teoría de las Catástrofes de René Thom, nuevo contexto determinante para las ciencias morfológicas. *El Basilisco*, 16, 22-42, Ap-Je 94.

Pérez Luño, Antonio-Enrique. Jeremy Bentham y la educación jurídica en la Universidad de Salamanca durante el siglo XIX. *Telos (Spain)*, 1(3), 69-94, O 92.

Pérez Zavala, Carlos. "Integración Cultural y Económica de América Latina: El Caso Argentina—Brasil" in *Temas Actuales de Filosofía, Palacios, María Julia (ed)*, 469-476. Buenos Aires, Univ Nacional Salta, 1993.

Perez-Estevez, Antonio. Hegel y América. *Analogia*, 8(2), 119-137, 1994.

This paper tries to do a critical reading of Hegel's text on America in the *Vorlesungen über die Philosophie der Geschichte*. The discovery of America is a product of the analytical spirit of the period and is, with the improvement of arts and sciences, the main feature of modernity. If European spirit is almighty, the Indian culture is impotent. The natural culture of Indians vanishes as soon as it gets in contact with the Europeans what makes possible the beginning of true history, made by the spirit. All that happens in America, since its discovery, is just a repetition of Europe. Nevertheless America is the land of future, where the spirit will move from old Europe. Hegel foresees the confrontation between Protestant Nord-America and Catholic Sud-America.

Perissinotto, Luigi. Wittgenstein, ill Linguaggio e l'Interpretazione. *Teoria*, 14(2), 29-61, 1994.

Perkin, Ronald M and Orr, Robert D. Clinical Ethics Consultations with Children. *J Clin Ethics*, 5(4), 323-328, Wint 94.

This retrospective review of 64 ethics consultations done on children (birth to 18 years of age) assessed demographic data, previous health of the child, reasons for the consultation request, and survival data. The children were critically ill (94% in ICU; 73% technology dependent; 61% died) and 84% of them were also chronically ill. Questions about limitation of treatment were present in 91% of cases and conflicts about further management were found in 59%. Management conflicts were significantly more common in children who had been healthy prior to admission (90%) than in those who had been chronically ill (54%).

Perkins, David N. "Insight in Minds and Genes" in *The Nature of Insight, Sternberg, Robert J (ed)*, 495-533. Cambridge, MIT Pr, 1995.

Perkins, Henry S. Commentary on "Organs for Undocumented Aliens?" Distributing American Hearts for Transplantation: The Predicament of Living in the Global Village. *Cambridge Quart Healthcare Ethics*, 4(2), 232-236, Spr 95.

Perkins, Henry S and Gordon, Anna M. Should Hospital Policy Require Consent for Practicing Invasive Procedures on Cadavers?. *J Clin Ethics*, 5(3), 204-210, Fall 94.

Perkins, Mary Anne. Coleridge and the Limits of Speculation: A Response to Douglas Hedley's Criticism. *Heythrop J*, 36(2), 202-203, Ap 95.

An answer to a critical review by Douglas Hedley of three articles entitled "Logic and Logos: The Search for Unity in Hegel and Coleridge" (Heythrop Journal, 1991).

Perkins, Mary Anne. Coleridge's "Ideal Realism": An Alternative to the "Doctors of the Absolute"?. *Bull Hegel Soc Gt Brit*, 31, 1-16, Spr-Sum 95.

A comparison of the philosophies of G W Hegel and S T Coleridge, this study gives particular attention to differences in their understanding of 'ideas' and suggests the relative strengths of Coleridge's position.

Perkins, Pheme. Commentary on Attridge's "Gnostic Platonism". *Proc Boston Colloq Anc Phil*, 7, 30-41, 1991.

Perkins, Robert L. "Three Critiques of Schlegel's *Lucinde*" in *The Nature and Pursuit of Love, Goicoechea, David (ed)*, 149-166. Buffalo, Prometheus, 1995.

The article focuses the three most important critiques of Schlegel's *Lucinde* that appeared in the nineteenth century: those of Schleiermacher, Hegel, and Kierkegaard. Each of these argue from an ethical perspective, though by no means from the same one. The real surprise in this article is that when one just reads Schleiermacher's *Confidential Letters*, forgetting his friendship with Schlegel and his immature infatuation with the romantic circle, one finds that there are important differences between the ethical views of the two. Schleiermacher's effort, usually thought of as a defense or apology for *Lucinde*, is highly qualified. Schleiermacher's critique shows interesting connections between his own thought and that of Hegel and Kierkegaard.

Perkins, Robert L. 'What a Hegelian Fool I was'. *Hist Euro Ideas*, 20(1-3), 177-181, Ja 95.

This article attempts to determine the depth and significance of Kierkegaard's rather Hegelian reading of the nature of the established order and the character of Socrates in his dissertation, *The Concept of Irony with Continual Reference to Socrates*. Unraveling all this is made difficult by the manifest irony of the book, the use of many Hegelian categories and insights with apparent, and sometimes real, approval, and the developing hostility to Hegel in the development of some major concepts: his own account of subjectivity, which he opposes both to romantic subjectivism and the idealist absolute ego, and his version of ethical universalism.

Perkins, Sylvia Walsh. "Kierkegaard's Philosophy of Love" in *The Nature and Pursuit of Love, Goicoechea, David (ed)*, 167-179. Buffalo, Prometheus, 1995.

Perkins Jr, Raymond K. *Logic and Mr Limbaugh: A Dittohead's Guide to Fallacious Reasoning*. Peru, Open Court, 1995.

This book provides an elementary account of logic and informal fallacy in the context of Rush Limbaugh's written material on the environment, animal rights, etc. Many of Limbaugh's arguments are found to be fallacious.

Perler, Dominik. Descartes in der angelsächsischen Diskussion. *Phil Rundsch*, 41(3), 193-203, Je 94.

Perler, Dominik. Spiegeln Ideen die Natur? Zum Begriff der Repräsentation bei Descartes. *Stud Leibniz*, 26(2), 187-209, 1994.

Several commentators, among them R Rorty, argue that Cartesian ideas are to be understood as internal objects or pictures that are presented to the mind on an 'inner arena'. In this paper I intend to show that such an interpretation is flawed if one takes into account Descartes's definition of ideas as mental acts having a representational content. I analyze this definition, paying particular attention to three crucial theses: 1) intentionality is an intrinsic feature of all mental acts; 2) mental acts primarily represent the essence of an object, not the existing object; 3) the object, insofar as it is presented to the mind, determines the so-called 'objective reality' of an idea. I reach the conclusion that one ought to be careful in attributing a representational theory to Descartes. His theory may be called representational only if it is understood as a theory about representing mental acts that are immediately directed towards external objects.

Perler, Dominik. What Am I Thinking About? John Duns Scotus and Peter Aureol on Intentional Objects. *Vivarium*, 32(1), 72-89, My 94.

Perloff, Marjorie (ed) and Junkerman, Charles (ed). *John Cage: Composed in America*. Chicago, Univ of Chicago Pr, 1994.

Perloff, Michael. Stit and the Imperative. *Amer Phil Quart*, 32(1), 71-81, Ja 95.

Stit theory (a logic of agents seeing-to-it-that) is used to explore some facets of imperative constructions. First, there is a brief introduction to Hofstadter and McKinsey's theory of fiats and to Ross's paradox. Before explaining the stit proposals concerning that paradox, a short introduction to the stit sentence and its semantics is presented. Next, Ross's paradox is reconsidered with the help of stit. After that, some of Chella's suggestions about imperatives are discussed. Subsequently, stit normal forms are used to explore three topics previously treated by Hamblin: the nature of agentive constructions, the negations of imperatives, and the varieties of imperatives. Finally, we look at further examples of clarification by stit normal forms, specifically some constructions in which imperatives embed.

Perner, Josef. "The Necessity and Impossibility of Simulation" in *Objectivity, Simulation and the Unity of Consciousness, Peacocke, Christopher (ed)*, 145-154. New York, Oxford Univ Pr, 1994.

In this commentary I indicate an emerging consensus about how to distinguish simulation from the theory. I add an update on our own empirical evidence against children using simulation to typical theory-of-mind tasks and end by distinguishing two types of simulation: *content simulation* and *attitude simulation*, which is to capture another emerging consensus that simulation is in some cases virtually necessary while in other cases contested if not impossible.

Peroli, E (trans) and Rist, John M. Plotino, Ficino e noi stessi: alcuni riflessi etici. *Riv Filosof Neo-Scolas*, 86(3), 448-467, Jl-S 94.

Perricone, Christopher. The Layers of Artistic Illusion. *J Value Inq*, 28(2), 233-243, Je 94.

In this essay I examine the marriage of Apollo and Dionysis, as it is expressed in Nietzsche's *Birth of Tragedy*. I show how we learn much about the nature of art and art experience from this homosexual couple and its offspring (the wild illusion underlying art), whose nature, says Nietzsche, is of Antigone/Cassandra.

Perrinjaquet, Alain. "Wirkliche" und "philosophische" Anschauung: Formen der intellektuellen Anschauung in Fichtes *System der Sittenlehre* (1798). *Fichte-Studien*, 5, 57-81, 1993.

The "intellectual intuition of the I" is one of the essential notions of Fichte's fundamental philosophy, especially in the years 1796-1801. Fichte says it is the starting point of the philosophical reflection, but he also stresses the close connection between this intuition and the consciousness of moral law, which everybody experiences and which, according to Fichte, is also an intellectual intuition, the "real" one he says. The paper examines (especially in the beginning of the *Science of ethics*) the relation between both intellectual intuition itself and shows how moral intuition is according to Fichte a condition of philosophical reflexion.

Perrinjaquet, Alain. Individuum und Gemeinschaft in der WL zwischen 1796 und 1800. *Fichte-Studien*, 3, 7-28, 1991.

Fichte was sometimes held a solipsist, or a "speculative egoist", and other times a "universalist" (indeed even a totalitarian) who denies the individual any worth and affirms the community is all worth. This paper should show that both interpretations are wrong. It analyses the complex relation between the individual I and the universal I (transcendental I) in Fichte's *fundamental* philosophy in the Jena time, within the practical sphere as well as within the theoretical. It comes to the conclusion that the principles of Fichte's philosophy lead to a well balanced synthesis, which avoids as well individualistic atomism as authoritarian universalism.

Perrinjaquet, Alain and Colbois, Sylvie. "Recht zur Aufklärung und Sozialrechte—Zu J B Erhards Theorie der Menschenrechte" in *Das geistige Erbe Europas, Buhr, Manfred (ed)*, 558-572. Napoli, Vivarium, 1994.

Perry, Clifton B and Jolley, Kelly D. Contraposition and Existential Import. *Phil Sci (Tucson)*, 6, 153-157, 1995.

Perry, John. Davidson's Sentences and Wittgenstein's Builders. *Proc Amer Phil Ass*, 68(2), 23-37, N 94.

I argue that Davidson's arguments for sentence holism in "Reality Without Reference" do not work. I claim that the Builders language game in Wittgenstein's *Philosophical Investigations* can help us see how the meaning of words can be based on their role in *expressing propositions* without being based on their role as being *parts of sentences*. These ideas suffice to counter Davidson's arguments, even if we adhere to an austere, propositionless, Tarshi-style approach to semantics.

Persson, Ingmar. Genetic Therapy, Identity and Person-Regarding Reasons. *Bioethics*, 9(1), 16-31, Ja 95.

It has been argued that there can be no person-regarding reasons for practicing genetic therapy, since it affects identity and causes to exist an individual who would not otherwise have existed. And there can be no such reasons for causing somebody to exist because existing cannot be better for an individual than never existing. In the present paper, both of these claims are denied. It is contended, first, that in practically all significant cases genetic therapy will not affect the identity of beings of our kind. This is so irrespective of whether, essentially, we are beings with minds or beings of certain biological species, the human one. Second, it is contended that, even if genetic therapy were to affect our identity, there could be person-regarding reasons for conducting it, for existence can be better than nonexistence for the individual.

Persson, Ingmar. Van Inwagen's *Material Beings*. *Nous*, 27(4), 512-517, D 93.

This critical notice chiefly examines Peter van Inwagen's claim in *Material Beings* that 'every physical thing is either a living organism or a simple', that the simples of physics compose a larger object if and only if their activity constitutes *a life*. It questions both that being alive is a necessary condition for being a composite object and that composite objects that are alive are so *in virtue of* being alive.

Peruzzi, Alberto. "Holism: The Polarized Spectrum" in *Holism: A Consumer Update, Fodor, Jerry (ed)*, 231-282. Amsterdam, Rodopi, 1993.

The paper deals with three sources of holistic arguments: confirmation of scientific theories, translation between languages, and the relationships of meaning with belief. Certain difficulties of each of the involved versions of holism are pointed out: such difficulties concern the lack of evidence in support of holistic theses, as well as the presence of slippery slope arguments, and finally inconsistencies, in holism. We argue that the dualism of atomism and holism is just a polarization of a much richer spectrum of cohesiveness levels, and that their consideration is needed in order to provide explanatory power to naturalistic epistemology. In the end, the features of a "local" alternative to holism are sketched, taking into account the role of gestaltic schemata in making stable reference possible.

Pessin, Andrew. In Defense of Conceptual Holism: Reply to Fodor and Lepore. *J Phil Res*, 20, 269-280, 1995.

In their recent book *Holism*, Jerry Fodor and Ernest Lepore (F&L) argue that various species of content holism face insuperable difficulties. In this paper I reply to their claims. After describing the version of holism to which I subscribe, I follow them in addressing, in turn, its implications for these related topics: interpersonal understanding, false belief and reference, psychological explanation, content similarity and identity, the analytic-synthetic distinction, and empirical evidence. The most prominent theme in my response to F&L is that while holism does suffer from the problems they note in principle, it's able to avoid them in practice. Holism's implications, in short, are not only not fatal, but not even so bad—and very possibly desirable.

Pessin, Andrew. Mentalese Syntax: Between a Rock and Two Hard Places. *Phil Stud*, 78(1), 33-53, Ap 95.

Pestieau, Joseph. En Deçà de la Souveraineté. *Philosopher*, 16, 229-234, 1994.

Public administrations faces three problems whose effects are intermingled. 1) The people, who are sovereign and can vote, are unable to speak with one voice, and are increasingly divided by the claims of new and competing identities. This situation is the result of liberal democracy, but could undermine democracy. 2) Regions are thus less a part of national economy. National solidarities, cultures and identities are also in jeopardy, as a result of economic liberalism and globalization. 3) In an information society, the consistency of policies can no longer be guaranteed. Information that is well dissiminated makes people equal, but could lead to chaos.

Péter, László. Montesquieu's Paradox on Freedom and Hungary's Constitutions 1790-1990. *Hist Polit Thought*, 16(1), 77-104, Spr 95.

Peters, Rik. Collingwood's Reform of Hegelian Dialectic. *Bull Hegel Soc Gt Brit*, 31, 90-105, Spr-Sum 95.

Petersen, Karl Thomas. *Pathognostica: Aufsätze zur Theorie und Anwendung genealogischer Philosophie*. Vienna, Passagen, 1994.

Seit Freuds Konzeption der Psychoanalyse beherrscht die Rede von der "Dezentrierung des Subjekts" die philosophische Diskussion. Gerade deswegen aber gilt es, den Subjektbegriff einer kritischen Prüfung zu unterziehen. Die vorliegende Aufsatzsammlung ist einer Theoriebildung verpflichtet, die der Psychoanalyse das nachzuweisen imstande ist, ws diese zu überwinden trachtete: einen nach wie vor reüssierenden *Subjekt-Zentrismus*, dem es bis heute verwehrt ist, hinreichende Erklärungen der Verfasstheit kultureller Wirklichkeit bereitstellen zu können. Das vermag die *Pathognostik*—so der Name dieses innovativen Unternehmens—auf dem Wege einer *Objektivitätswende der Psychoanalyse*. (edited)

Peterson, Grethe B (ed). *The Tanner Lectures on Human Values, Volume 16*. Salt Lake City, Univ of Utah Pr, 1995.

Peterson, Michel. De la Nature au Social. *Horiz Phil*, 4(1), 31-52, Autumn 93.

Peterson, Philip. Are Some *Propositions* Empirically Necessary?. *Phil Phenomenol Res*, 55(2), 251-277, Je 95.

Kripke and Putnam hold that certain identity statements are necessarily true but only empirically justifiable. Is their position compatible with the non-Putnam, anti-Kripke view that non-linguistic propositions (rather than sentence types, sentence tokens, statements, or sentence meanings) are the proper objects of belief and justification, and the bearers of truth values? Yes. Propositionalizing the Kripke-Putnam view reveals that although a single proposition cannot (or need not) be both intuitive and demonstrative, still one and the same proposition can be empirically justified *and* justified *a priori*. Propositionalizing Kripke and Putnam does not remove all the mysteries about identity statements, but it does replace the issues about questionable phenomena like individual concepts and reference-in-thought with those concerning identities between (and alternative cognitive approaches to) propositions themselves. It is not clear, however, that any identity statement about propositions can be as empirical as some identity statements about concrete objects.

Peterson, Philip. Which Universals are Laws?. *Austl J Phil*, 72(4), 492-496, D 94.

Armstrong's dilemma is the tension between taking a natural law to be a relation between universals (and thereby second-order) and holding that the law is first-order, instantiated by things or actualities themselves. To improve on his unsatisfactory resolution, the article develops the concept of event (situation, etc.) *kinds*, so that R-ing by an F-ing of a G-ing is what a law, N(F,G), is. Two alternatives arise for an instance of the law: Armstrong's apparent choice that a concrete pair, <la,b (where *a* is an F-ing and *b* a G-ing), is the instance; and the proposal that a complex event of *a* R-ing *b* is the instance (the law taken to be the complex event *kind* of something's being an R-ing by an F-ing of a G-ing).

Peterson, Philip L. Contraries and the Cubes and Disks of Opposition. *Metaphilosophy*, 26(1-2), 107-137, Ja-Ap 95.

Prior, Sommers, and McIntosh hold that propositional contrariety is derivative, based on term contrariety. I argue that propositional contrariety is basic. In a proper

Aristotelian square, one proposition is contrary to another if and only if the one properly entails the denial of the other. Term contrariness produces a *cube* of opposition. Contrariety can be further elaborated on "bare" cubes and disks. Geach's analyses involving multiple quantifiers give no support for term-contrariness-as-basic, and there is little hope for developing H W B Joseph's vague idea about "furtherest apart" on a quantitative scale.

Peterson, Philip L. Distribution and Proportion. *J Phil Log*, 24(2), 193-225, Ap 95.

My aim is to defend the Aristotelian concept of distribution by expanding Robert Carnes' application of it (cf Carnes & Peterson 1991, Peterson & Carnes ms and 1983). In Section I, I apply distribution to *k*-quantity "fractional" syllogistic systems. In Section II, I consider unrestricted "proportional" syllogisms and sorites. Proportional systems with an infinite number of quantities are described in Section III. Finally, in Section IV, I show how the new understanding of distribution survives Geach's criticisms.

Peterson, Roland and Terwee, Sybe. Can Functionalism Provide the Proper Basis for a Core Theory of Psychoanalysis?. *Phil Psych*, 7(4), 463-469, 1994.

Before embarking upon the project of reformulating psychoanalysis in the 'scientific' terminology of cognitive science, we should first clearly define what psychoanalysis is about and what it is not about. Cognitive science is based upon a functionalistic philosophy of the mind. As a consequence such a project would require a functionalistic core theory of psychoanalysis. But Freud's claim of the therapeutic effect of psychoanalysis, attained through the rendering conscious of what is unconscious or the making personal of what is experienced by the neurotic patient as impersonal, cannot be explained by a functionalistic theory of the mind. We examine Freud's claim and conclude that there ought to be a philosophy of qualia at the core of psychoanalysis.

Petho, Bertalan. On Derrida's Confrontation with Husserl. *Magyar Filozof Szemle*, 5-6, 685-710, 1994.

In dieser Arbeit, welche ein Teil einer Reihe von verschiedenen/post/modernen Konfrontationen ist, diskutiert der Autor einige wichtigen Termini der Grammatologie im Verhältnis von Husserls im Bann der neuzeitlichen Ontologie stehenden Phänomenologie. Nach der Erhebung der von Husserl fallweise erwähnten zweiten Epoche, und nach der Unterscheidung einer in der phänomenologischen Philosophie sich steckenden dritten Epoche, die Differänz (französische "differance" mit "a") ist begriffen als Mobilisiert-Werden "hinter" der dritten Epoche. Neben dem Fortreissen der die (i. s. von Heidegger genommene) ontologische Differenz rücktransferierenden Differenzen, ist in diesem Mobilisiert-Werden auch die Leiblichkeit aufs Spiel gesetzt. Die hauptsächlich anhand des Ursprungs der Sprache, der Entstehung des Sprachlauts und der Zeitlichkeit thematisierte Auto-Affektion ist der Prozess, welcher für das Konstituieren und zugleich für das Destitutieren der Leiblichkeit—nicht nur in transzendentalem Sinn—verantwortlich ist. In dem Namen der die Auto-Affektion energisierende Differänz rivalisiert Derrida mit Husserl, als ein Gegenspieler derselben Sache, des diskursiven Absolutismus. Aber bei Husserl ist das Subjektt der Sinn dieses Absolutismus, dagegen bei Derrida das Subjekt ist der Gefahr ausgesetzt, verlorenzugehen. Diese Kontroverse und die Zugehörigkeit der Differenz wird nach der vom Verfasser früher formulierte Peratologie interpretiert, als ein Moment der sich später anmeldenden Postmoderne-Diskussion.

Petit Sullá, José María. El Nivel Epistemológico de las Ciencias Medias en el Pensamiento de Tomás de Aquino. *Rev Espan Filosof Med*, 0, 159-163, 1993.

Petkovic, Tomislav. *Timaeus* and Modern Cosmology. *Filozof Istraz*, 13(4), 851-877, 1993.

This paper is the first (Croatian) attempt to reconcile Plato's thought and various elements and concepts of his cosmology with the modern cosmological models/scenarios describing the birth, early evolution and structure formation of the universe as the wholeness. Since Timaeus and philosophers before Plato's time have taught about the four elements; water, earth, air and fire, as the material constituents of the universe, we reviewed in our opinion three main cosmological models—Standard Hot Big Bang Model, viable Inflation Models and Cosmic String Picture—emphasizing the basic points, phenomenological consequences and current problems. Today, the big hopes are connected with the theory of superstrings especially on the way from the basic principles of the theory towards their phenomenological consequences on energy scale not far below the Planck scale. In this work we discussed distinguished gnoseological and ontological questions just opened as the new deep problems by modern cosmoparticle physics, such as the possibility of mini-universes, baby universes, a nature of space and time at the Planck scale,...etc. A philosophical overview reveals many unsolved problems inside and between the cosmological models. (edited)

Petrone, Giuseppe Landolfi. Un Inedito di Bertrando Spaventa sul Concetto di Filosofia. *Stud Filosofici*, 195-212, 1991-92.

Petrus, Helke. "Beschrieene Dunkelheit" und "Seichtigkeit". *Kantstudien*, 85(3), 280-302, 1994.

Petry, Michael John. "Die Philosophielehre im neuen Europa—Bemerkungen zur niederländischen Perspektive" in *Das geistige Erbe Europas, Buhr, Manfred (ed)*, 121-136. Napoli, Vivarium, 1994.

The article gives an account of the way in which, over the last twenty years, the History of Philosophy in the Netherlands has been developed as a research topic in its own right, and as a sub-discipline within the Honours Course in Philosophy, at the Erasmus University Rotterdam. The philosophical tradition itself is presented as a microcosm of mainstream European developments,—the break with the mediaeval logical tradition (Agricola), the philosophical foundations of international law (Grotius), the logical-positivist criticism of Spinozism (Nieuwentijt), the Platonizing of Newtonianism (Hemsterhuis) etc. The national and international significance of offering courses on the subject is discussed in some detail, special emphasis being laid on the importance of thinking in terms of cultural federalism in the new Europe.

Pettit, Philip. Microphysicalism without Contingent Micro-Macro Laws. *Analysis*, 54(4), 253-257, O 94.

The contingent supervenience of the macro-configuration of the world on the microphysical realm, such as (micro) physicalists defend, does not require contingent micro-macro laws: this, pace Tim Crane. Consider a two-dimensional world in which certain dots constitute shapes of various kinds, and in which no other shape-makers appear. The shape-configuration of the world in question supervenes on the dot-configuration and does so contingently: duplicate the dot-configuration and, under the contingency that no continuous lines make an appearance, for example, you will duplicate the shape-configuration too. Yet this contingent supervenience does not involve any contingent dot-shape laws.

Pettit, Philip and Brennan, Geoffrey. Consecuencialismo Restrictivo. *Telos (Spain)*, 3(2), 73-97, D 94.

While it might be appropriate to evaluate options by the criterion of maximizing probable value, it need not be sensible to select them on that basis. To satisfy the criterion of evaluation may often be to restrict or forswear its application, relying rather on some other criterion of choice. Consequentialists must be restrictive in choosing actions, avoiding the calculative evaluation of options, whenever calculation undermines maximazation of objectively probable value. Restrictive consequentialism is a real possibility when the pursued benefit is *calculatively elusive* and *calculatively vulnerable*. The disposition to satisfice is a more interesting case, since it may be extrapolated to three derived cases where the consequence of deliberation, not the deliberation itself, is what undermines the benefit. (edited)

Pettit, Philip and Jackson, Frank. Moral Functionalism and Moral Motivation. *Phil Quart*, 45(178), 20-40, Ja 95.

The contents of moral judgments about decisions, assuming the cognitivist view that moral judgments are beliefs, have to be such as rationally to justify certain conclusions about what should be done; and the judgments have to be such that assenting to them generally goes with desiring the action justified. This paper offers a functionalist account of the contents of moral judgments—an account that loosely parallels the functionalist account of the contents of psychological judgments—and shows that such an account can solve both of these challenges.

Pezzella, Anna Maria. Edith Stein fenomenologa. *Aquinas*, 37(2), 353-376, My-Ag 94.

Pezzella, Anna Maria. Edith Stein: l'Apprendistato Fenomenologico. *Aquinas*, 37(3), 547-579, S-D 94.

In this brief article we want to show how the phenomenological training was fundamental to E Stein, since this philosophical apprenticeship will emerge strengthly even after she entered a convent, in works as "Endliches und Ewigessein" and "Scientia Crucis". Here we consider all works written before 1922, from "Zum Problem der Einfühlung" to "Beitragezur Philosophischen Begründung der Psychologie und Geisteswissenschaften" and "Eine Untersuchung über den staat". We seeked particularly to point out the passages of agreement/disagreement regarding E Stein's thought compared with her master's thought, E Husserl.

Pezzillo, Lelia. Rôle et fonction des valeurs à l'origine des sociétés. *Rev Metaph Morale*, 99(4), 449-458, O-D 94.

Pfau, Thomas. "Immediacy and Dissolution" in *Intersections: Nineteenth-Century Philosophy and Contemporary Theory, Rajan, Tilottama (ed)*, 222-242. Albany, SUNY Pr, 1995.

Pfeifer, Jeffrey E and Brigham, John C. Ethical Concerns of Nonclinical Forensic Witnesses and Consultants. *Ethics Behavior*, 3(3-4), 329-343, 1993.

Current research suggests that nonclinical forensic psychologists are appearing increasingly more often in the legal arena. We argue that many of the ethical dilemmas that face these psychologists differ from those encountered by clinical forensic psychologists. To test the accuracy of this assertion, 37 nonclinical forensic psychologists were surveyed to identify some of the ethical issues and dilemmas they have encountered while engaging in expert testimony or pretrial consulting. Respondents were asked also about how they have resolved these ethical issues and whether they were aware of the "Specialty Guidelines for Forensic Psychologists" (Committee on Ethical Guidelines for Forensic Psychologists, 1991). Results of the survey are discussed in terms of the need for additional regulatory guidelines or professional standards that speak directly to the ethical issues confronting nonclinical, forensic expert witnesses and consultants.

Pfeiffer, María Luisa. Cuerpo e intencionalidad. *Rev Filosof (Mexico)*, 27(81), 514-520, S-D 94.

Pfersmann, Otto. "Philosophie in Wien zwischen "Anschluss" und Befreiung, Mythos, Affekt und Praktischer Vernunft" in *Der geistige Anschluss, Fischer, Kurt R (ed)*, 69-100. Wien, WUV Univ, 1993.

Pfersmann, Otto. "Rechts- und Sozialphilosophie bei Heinrich Gomperz" in *Heinrich Gomperz, Karl Popper und die österreichische Philosophie, Seiler, Martin (ed)*, 95-118. Amsterdam, Rodopi, 1994.

The contributions of Heinrich Gomperz to political philosophy are much less known than his work in ancient Greek philosophy. There is indeed no systematic and comprehensive approach. Instead, he elaborates his thought while reflecting on actual events. One can therefore distinguish two periods: the first ("Austrian") is mainly concerned with the First World War and the following peace settlements (relativistic and pessimistic approach, war being regrettable but "necessary" for democratic progress), the second ("American") deals with problems of international wealth distribution (critique of utilitarianism, necessity of higher incomes and property in order to promote civil liberties and social justice) and the question of collective responsibility.

Pfister, Lauren. The Different Faces of Contemporary Religious Confucianism. *J Chin Phil*, 22(1), 5-79, Mr 95.

The metaphysical openness of Confucian traditions, especially after their precipitous fall from governmentally supported prestige after 1911, left it with an ambivalent religious heritage. Religious renewal of one kind began with the 1958 Confucian Manifesto. Its claims are placed against five different religio-metaphysical systems advocated by five major Chinese Confucian scholars who flourished after the Manifesto's publication. These include the evolving pantheistic Confucianism of Fang Tung-mei, the phenomenological Confucianism of T'ang Chün-i, the transcendental Confucianism of Mou Tsung-san, the pragmatic and progressive Confucianism of Cheng Chung-ying, and the dialogic Confucianism of Tu Weiming.

Phemister, Pauline. Real Essences in Particular. *Locke News*, 21, 27-55, 1990.

Philibert, Michel. "Philosophical Imagination: Paul Ricoeur as the Singer of Ruins" in *The Philosophy of Paul Ricoeur, Hahn, Lewis Edwin (ed)*, 127-137. Peru, Open Court, 1994.

Philipse, Herman. "Heidegger's *Question of Being*: A Critical Interpretation" in *European Philosophy and the American Academy, Smith, Barry (ed)*, 99-122. Peru, Open Court, 1994.

The central thesis of this paper is that Heidegger's celebrated "Question of Being" is in fact not one coherent question at all. Rather, there are five different strands in the question, which are like the leitmotifs in a Wagnerian overture. These five themes are developed, their interconnections are discussed, and their philosophical merits are assessed. The paper ends with a short study of Heidegger's rhetoric.

Philipse, Herman. "Transcendental Idealism" in *The Cambridge Companion to Husserl, Smith, Barry (ed)*, 239-322. New York, Cambridge Univ Pr, 1995.

This very long (83 pp.) paper contains a rational reconstruction and an interpretation of Husserl's transcendental idealism. It is argued that transcendental idealism was a solution to problems which were due to the theory of perception Husserl adhered to in his *Logical Investigations* and, finally, to assumptions inherent in the scientific revolution. An attempt is made to specify Husserl's relation to Descartes, Berkeley, and Kant, and to determine Husserl's place in the history of modern philosophy. There are sections on, i.a., naturalism, the natural attitude, *Ideal I*, Husserl's notions of epistemology and metaphysics, his philosophy of science, the thing in itself, the paradox of human subjectivity, and on the life world.

Phillips, Anne. Dealing with Difference. *Constellations*, 1(1), 74-91, Ap 94.

Phillips, D C. Art as Research, Research as Art. *Educ Theor*, 45(1), 71-84, Wint 95.

This paper comments upon a symposium on the relation between the arts and research in education centered upon the work of Elliot Eisner. Eisner holds that art is closely related to research. The present paper points to important differences: research aims to produce warranted belief, and researchers can be wrong—both of which do not apply to the work of artists. Furthermore, Eisner miscasts the aim of research as being descriptive, as conveying a sense of "being there". He also fails to recognize that beliefs, no matter how fervently held, can be false.

Phillips, D Z. Glaucon's Challenges. *Phil Invest*, 17(3), 536-551, Jl 94.

Phillips, D Z. On Giving Practice Its Due—A Reply. *Relig Stud*, 31(1), 121-127, Mr 95.

Phillips, D Z. Reply: Can Which Good Man Know Himself?. *Phil Invest*, 18(2), 156-161, Ap 95.

Phillips, D Z. The World and 'I'. *Phil Invest*, 18(3), 235-249, Jl 95.

Phillips, David. On Moral Relativism. *SW Phil Rev*, 11(1), 69-78, Ja 95.

Phillips, Heather and Kryspin, Jan. "The Appropriate Medical Care of the Terminally Ill" in *Ethics on the Frontiers of Human Existence, Badham, Paul (ed)*, 179-207. New York, Paragon House, 1992.

Phillips, Hollibert E. *Vicissitudes of the I: An Introduction to the Philosophy of Mind*. Englewood Cliffs, Prentice Hall, 1995.

Primarily an undergraduate text, *Vicissitudes of the I* presents a highly accessible introduction to the philosophy of mind, thorough theoretical coverage, topical currency, and a lively, clear, and engaging writing style that holds the interest of the reader throughout. Among content highlights: Engages readers with primary texts and sources; devotes considerable attention to the concept of identity and to the issue of personal identity; brings readers face to face with issues and questions of strong contemporary interest, debate, and research activity; singles out notions or considerations that have proven pivotal in the ongoing debate over the nature of mind.

Phillips, James and Woody, J Melvin. Commentary on "Connectionist Hysteria". *Phil Psychiat Psych*, 1(2), 89-90, Je 94.

Phillips, Michael J. Corporate Moral Responsibility: When It Might Matter. *Bus Ethics Quart*, 5(3), 555-576, Jl 95.

The debate over corporate moral responsibility has become a fixture in business ethics research and teaching. Only rarely, however, does the sizable literature on that question consider whether the debate has important practical implications. This article examines that question from a corporate control perspective. After assuming corporate moral responsibility's existence for purposes of argument, the article concludes that such responsibility makes a difference in cases where it is present but personal responsibility is absent. Then the article tries to identify the forces that diminish personal responsibility when corporate responsibility exists. The most important such forces, it concludes, spring from the socialization processes people undergo when they enter groups. One example is the well-known phenomenon of groupthink, which can exculpate individuals by rendering them justifiably ignorant of foreseeable risks of harm.

Philpott, Daniel. In Defense of Self-Determination. *Ethics*, 105(2), 352-385, Ja 95.

Piacenza, Eduardo. Formas Gramaticales, Formas Lógicas y Frases Denotativas: Sorpresas en la Historia de la Semántica. *Analogia*, 4(1), 131-147, 1990.

Piacenza, Eduardo. Suppositio Personalis y Cuantificación Múltiple. *Analogia*, 4(2), 101-111, 1990.

Piatkiewicz, Leszek and Nyikos, Peter. On the Equivalence of Certain Consequences of the Proper Forcing Axiom. *J Sym Log*, 60(2), 431-443, Je 95.

Piazza, Mario. A Comparison between Two Different Tarski-Style Semantics for Linear Logic. *Epistemologia*, 17(1), 101-116, Ja-Je 94.

In recent years the "resource-sensitive" linear logic, introduced by Girard in 1986, has represented a new approach to proof theory. We analyze the Tarskian semantics for linear logic and we compare two forms of this semantics, both from a methodological and a logical viewpoint: *phase semantics* and *quantale semantics*. We show that phase semantics is not free from certain drawbacks, and so that our preference for quantale semantics can be entirely justified. More generally, the Tarksian semantics for linear logic is a case study for a methodological axiom always valid: *a genuine semantics must not be a "rewrite-system"*.

Piché, Claude. Max Weber et le néo-Kantisme: Pour une politique de la modernité. *Rev Metaph Morale*, 99(3), 327-344, Jl-S 94.

While the great ideological narratives are crumbling, Max Weber's ethics of politics reminds us that the power of conviction is as essential a component of human conduct as the sense of responsibility. In this regard the neo-Kantian philosophy of values, notwithstanding its formalism, not only provides Weber with a theoretical framework which proves fruitful for his sociology, but it also confirms in his eyes that role of an utopian dimension in history.

Pichot, André. Pour une Approche Naturaliste de la Connaissance. *Lekton*, 4(2), 199-241, 1994.

Picken, Stuart D B. *Essentials of Shinto: An Analytical Guide to Principal Teachings*. Westport, Greenwood Pr, 1994.

Shinto is finally receiving the attention it deserves as a fundamental component of Japanese culture. Nevertheless, it remains a remarkably complex and elusive phenomenon to which Western categories of religion do not readily apply. A knowledge of Shinto can only proceed from an understanding of Japanese shrines and civilization, for it is closely intermingled with the Japanese way of life and continues to be a vital natural religion. This book is a convenient guide.

Pickering, John. Buddhism and Cognitivism: A Postmodern Appraisal. *Asian Phil*, 5(1), 23-38, 1995.

Cognitivism, presently the major paradigm of psychology, presents a scientific account of mental life. Buddhism also presents an account of mental life, but one which is integral with its wider ethical and transcendental concerns. The postmodern appraisal of science provides a framework within which these two accounts may be compared without inheriting many of the assumed oppositions between science and religion. It is concluded that cognitivism and Buddhism will have complementary roles in the development of a more pluralist psychological science. In this development it will be necessary to address what values are implicit in science.

Pickering, W S F. Durkheim and Moral Education for Children: A Recently Discovered Lecture. *J Moral Educ*, 24(1), 19-36, 1995.

Emile Durkheim (1858-1917) is rightly called the father of the sociology of education. Although he saw his major task to be the establishment of sociology as an academic discipline which would be taught in French universities, he was obliged to spend much of his time lecturing on education. This was required by the wording of his university appointments; first in Bordeaux, then in Paris. His interests in education covered large areas, including the purpose of education, the social qualities of the group who were taught in the classroom, punishment and the history of higher education. What, however, concerned him most was moral education which he saw as the key to education as a whole. With him, as with all of France at the time, the burning issue was the teaching of secular morality to the young. This was the subject he coverd in *L'Education morale* (1925). A lecture, recently discovered and translated here, reflects in a sharper way than in the book the issue of secular, moral education. The questions he raises can be seen to be relevant to the teaching of morality in schools today.

Pickles, David. Holton on Attitude Ascriptions and Intermediate Scope. *Mind*, 104(415), 577-582, Jl 95.

Piekarczyk, Stanislaw. Time in Medieval Man's Model of the World. *Dialogue Hum*, 4(1), 110-124, 1994.

Pierson, Christopher. *Socialism After Communism: The New Market Socialism*. University Park, Penn St Univ Pr, 1995.

Pierson, Robert. The Epistemic Authority of Expertise. *Proc Phil Sci Ass*, 1, 398-405, 1994.

When is it more rational to think for oneself or to defer to the relevant expert? Expertise is either closed-system oriented or lay-person oriented. The first sort is concerned primarily with controlling and manipulating a discipline's defining set of variables as a closed or relatively closed system. The second sort is simply in the business of "advising" clients. I argue that when expert claims are of the first sort, the layperson must defer to the experts; but when experts either extrapolate from their closed-systems, or if they are of the second sort, then the layperson should think for herself.

Pierson, Robert and Reiner, Richard. Hacking's Experimental Realism: An Untenable Middle Ground. *Phil Sci*, 62(1), 60-69, Mr 95.

As Laudan and Fine show, and Boyd concedes, the attempt to infer the truth of scientific realism from the fact that it putatively provides the best explanation of the instrumental success of science is circular, since what is to be *shown* is precisely the legitimacy of such abductive inferences. Hacking's "experimental argument for scientific realism about entities" is one of the few arguments for scientific realism that purports to avoid this circularity. We argue that Hacking's argument is as dependent on inference to the best explanation (IBE), and therefore as weak, as the other realist arguments.

Pieters, Toine. In het land der doven is éénoog nog geen koning. *Kennis Methode*, 18(2-3), 185-191, 1994.

Pieterse, Jan Nederveen (ed) and Parekh, Bhikhu (ed). *The Decolonization of Imagination: Culture, Knowledge, and Power*. London, Zed Books, 1995.

Pietroski, Paul. Un Dérangement Modulaire de la Compétence Linguistique. *Lekton*, 4(2), 163-198, 1994.

Pietroski, Paul and Rey, Georges. When Other Things Aren't Equal: Savings *Ceteris Paribus* Laws from Vacuity. *Brit J Phil Sci*, 46(1), 81-110, Mr 95.

A common view is that *ceteris paribus* clauses render lawlike statements vacuous, unless such clauses can be explicitly reformulated as antecedents of 'real' laws that face no counterinstances. But such reformulations are rare; and they are not, we argue, to be expected in general. So we defend an alternative sufficient condition for the nonvacuity of *ceteris paribus* laws: roughly, any counterinstance of the law must be independently explicable, in a sense we make explicit. *Ceteris paribus* laws will carry a plethora of explanatory commitments; and claims that such commitments are satisfied will be as (dis)confirmable as other empirical claims.

Pietroski, Paul M. Executing the Second Best Option. *Analysis*, 54(4), 201-207, O 94.

There is an interesting connection between (i) the question of whether there are moral dilemmas—situations in which an agent cannot do all he ought to do—and (ii) a class of puzzling cases in which an agent *ought* to take the morally second best course of action simply because he *won't* take the best course of action. Brink argues that a plausible means-end principle excludes dilemmas; this principle supports the diagnosis of the puzzle cases defended by Jackson and Pargetter; and their proposed solution to the puzzle helps defend Brink's principle from a possible objection.

Pietroski, Paul M. Mental Causation for Dualists. *Mind Lang*, 9(3), 336-366, S 94.

I defend a form of (non-Cartesian) event dualism, thus providing an alternative to token (and hence type) physicalism: human mental events are in some sense constituted by, but not identical with, neural events (or any events specifiable in the language of any nonintentional science). Overdetermination objections to this view are handled by rejecting a familiar "bump" conception of causation (which, I contend, leads to type physicalism), in favor of a covering-law conception according to which causal laws are *ceteris paribus* laws. The resulting account of mental causation borrows features of "anomalous monism," but differs significantly from Davidson's view.

Pietruska-Madej, Elzbieta. Unification and the History of Science: Comments on Józef Werle's Paper "How the Physical Sciences Discovered the Unity of Nature". *Dialogue Hum*, 3(3), 125-132, 1993.

Pigden, Charles. Popper Revisited, or What Is Wrong With Conspiracy Theories?. *Phil Soc Sci*, 25(1), 3-34, Mr 95.

Conspiracy theories are widely deemed to be superstitious. Yet history appears to be littered with conspiracies successful and otherwise. (For this reason, "cock-up" theories cannot in general replace conspiracy theories, since in many cases the cock-ups are simply failed conspiracies.) Why then is it silly to suppose that historical events are sometimes due to conspiracy? The only argument available to this author is drawn from the work of the late Sir Karl Popper, who criticizes what he calls "the conspiracy theory in society" in *The Open Society* and elsewhere. His critique of the conspiracy theory is indeed sound, but it is a theory no sane person maintains. Moreover, its falsehood is compatible with the prevalence of conspiracies. Nor do his arguments create any presumption against conspiracy theories of this or that. Thus the belief that it is superstitious to posit conspiracies is itself a superstition. The article concludes with some speculations as to why this superstition is so widely believed.

Pigler-Rogers, Agnès. La *Penthésilée* de Kleist. *Diotima*, 22, 37-45, 1994.

Piguet, J Claude. Esthétique musicale et éthique humaine. *Rev Theol Phil*, 127(1), 63-70, 1995.

Les *Carnets* de Furtwängler ne sont qu'un recueil de notes prises au hasard des loisirs de l'illustre chef d'orchestre. La traduction proposée en a retenu l'essentiel. Le contenu pose le problème de l'interprétation. De là découlent quelques règles esthétiques: primat de l'intériorité, sens des grandes formes, primat de la vérité sur la perfection technique, refus du mythe progressiste. Toutefois cette esthétique débouche sur l'éthique: refus de l'intellectualisme, et supériorité de la clarté. Cette éthique—proprement humaine—trouve sa source profonde moins dans la philosophie académique que dans les oeuvres de la culture—et dans la musique.

Pillay, Anand. Definability of Types, and Pairs of 0-Minimal Structures. *J Sym Log*, 59(4), 1400-1409, D 94.

Pillay, Anand and Chowdhury, Ambar. On the Number of Models of Uncountable Theories. *J Sym Log*, 59(4), 1285-1300, D 94.

The main result established in this paper is that if T is a complete first-order theory which is uncountable, then T has infinitely many pairwise nonisomorphic models having the same cardinality as T.

Pillay, Anand and Poizat, Bruno. Corps et Chirurgie. *J Sym Log*, 60(2), 528-533, Je 95.

Les corps algébriquement clos, réels clos et pseudo-finis n'ont, pour chaque entier *n*, qu'un nombre fini d'extensions de degré *n*; nous montrons qu'ils partagent cette propriété avec tous les corps qui, comme eux, satisfont une propriété très rudimentaire de préservation de la dimension, de nature modèle-théorique. Ce résultat est atteint en montrant qu'une certaine action du groupe GL_n d'un tel corps n'a qu'un nombre fini d'orbites.

Pimentel, David. Amounts of Pesticides Reaching Target Pests: Environmental Impacts and Ethics. *J Agr Environ Ethics*, 8(1), 17-29, 1995.

Less than 0.1% of pesticides applied for pest control reach their target pests. Thus, more than 99.9% of pesticides used move into the environment where they adversely affect public health and beneficial biota, and contaminate soil, water, and the atmosphere of the ecosystem. Improved pesticide application technologies can improve pesticide use efficiency and protect public health and the environment.

Pinckaers, Servais and Noble, Mary Thomas (trans). *The Sources of Christian Ethics*. Washington, Cath Univ Amer Pr, 1995.

Pinkard, Terry (ed) and Engelhardt Jr, H Tristram (ed). *Hegel Reconsidered*. Dordrecht, Kluwer, 1994.

Hegel's thought influenced much of contemporary political theory, social thought and philosophy. Described as both a metaphysician and a narrator whose irony anticipated philosophy after metaphysics, Hegel has been characterized as both a defender of freedom and an enemy of the liberal state. This volume reassesses Hegel's work, building on the thought of Klaus Hartmann, and goes beyond considerations of metaphysics and the authoritarian state. It explores a nonmetaphysical reading of Hegel's philosophy and shows how Hegel's thought supports a liberal democratic state. This volume provides a basis for utilizing Hegel's work in the reassessment of ontology, aesthetics and revolution.

Pinkard, Terry P. "Constitutionalism, Politics, and the Common Life" in *Hegel Reconsidered, Engelhardt Jr, H Tristram (ed)*, 163-186. Dordrecht, Kluwer, 1994.

Pinkard, Terry P. Historicism, Social Practice, and Sustainability: Some Themes in Hegelian Ethical Theory. *Neue Hefte Phil*, 35, 56-94, 1995.

Pinkas, Daniel. Suivre une règle: Wittgenstein et les sciences cognitives. *Rev Theol Phil*, 127(1), 1-25, 1995.

Les sciences cognitives devraient-elles tenir compte des remarques de Wittgenstein sur la notion de règle? J'aborde çette question par le biais d'un examen du paradoxe sceptique que Kripke attribue à Wittgenstein. Les principales solutions à ce paradoxe sont passées en revue et crtiquées. Une attention particulière est accordée aux solutions de type téléologique et computationnaliste que l'on peut tirer de postulats en vigueur dans les sciences cognitives. Après avoir contesté l'interprétation de Kripke, je m'efforce de caractériser la conception de la <force de la règle> que Wittgenstein propose. Cette conception a des conséquences antithéoriques.

Pinnick, Cassandra L. Feminist Epistemology: Implications for Philosophy of Science. *Phil Sci*, 61(4), 646-657, D 94.

This article examines the best contemporary arguments for a feminist epistemology of scientific knowledge as found in recent works by S Harding. I argue that no *feminist* epistemology of science is worthy of name, because such an epistemology fails to escape well-known vicissitudes of epistemic relativism. But feminist epistemology merits attention from philosophers of science because it is part of a larger relativist turn in the social sciences and humanities that now aims to extend its critique to science, and Harding's "standpoint feminism" is the best-developed case. She attempts to make new use of discredited philosophical ideas concerning underdetermination, Planck's Hypothesis, and the role of counterfactuals in historical studies of science.

Pintor Ramos, A. Carta abierta al Dr Wessell. *Dialogo Filosof*, 11(1), 73-76, Ja-Ap 95.

Pippin, Robert B. Hegel on the Rationality and Priority of Ethical Life. *Neue Hefte Phil*, 35, 95-126, 1995.

Pirruccello, Ann. Interpreting Simone Weil: Presence and Absence in Attention. *Phil East West*, 45(1), 61-72, Ja 95.

This article examines Simone Weil's concept of attention and relates it to Hase Shoto's work on the structure of authentic faith. Attention in both its "natural" and "supernatural" forms is discussed, with special emphasis on attention as something which reveals what is absent or nonexistent. Weil's ideas about attention as it is realized in intellectual, moral, aesthetic and spiritual practices are discussed.

Pittenger, David J. The Cross-Disciplinary Ethical Responsibilities of Psychology Faculty. *Ethics Behavior*, 4(3), 199-208, 1994.

This article discusses the ethical responsibilities that psychology faculty have when psychological information is seriously misrepresented or psychological techniques are misused by nonpsychology faculty. General values derived from the American Psychological Association's (APA) ethical principles are identified and reviewed. The APA ethical code recommends that psychologists limit the misrepresentation of psychological information and protect students from the misuse of psychological techniques. Examples from my experience are presented to illustrate these ethical principles and responsibilities.

Pizzi, Laura Cristina V. Escola Pública: Trabalho Produtivo ou Improdutivo. *Educ Filosof*, 8(16), 77-86, Jl-D 94.

This research starts with the concepts of productive and unproductive work developed by Karl Marx and Harry Bravermann in order to reveal that the unproductive work in fact is just the one not contributing directly to the richness production. In Brazil, a mechanical adaptation of concepts like factory work to the public school has generated some ambiguous and reductionist results concerning the organization of work at the school. This work intends to produce a better understanding of the practice and nature of the teaching work as well its relation with the civil society and the government.

Pizzorini, Reginaldo M. Giustizia e carità nella dottrina dei padri, II. *Sapienza*, 47(3), 249-311, 1994.

Plant, Raymond. *Modern Political Thought*. Cambridge, Blackwell, 1992.

Plantinga, Alvin. How to Be an Anti-Realist. *Proc Amer Phil Ass*, 56(1), 47-70, S 82.

Plantinga, Alvin. What's the Question?. *J Phil Res*, 20, 19-43, 1995.

Two kinds of critical questions have been asked about the propriety or rightness of Christian beliefs. The first is the de facto question: is Christian belief true? The second is the de jure question: is it rational, or reasonable, or intellectually acceptable, or rationally justifiable? This second question is much harder to locate than you'd guess from looking at the literature. In "Perceiving God" William Alston suggests that the (or a) right question here is the question of "the practical rationality", construed as he construes it. I argue that the question is ambiguous: and one of the disambiguees is too easy to answer, while the other is such that its answer is really irrelevant to any sensible version of the de jure question. I conclude by venturing a suggestion as to what a sensible de jure question might be.

Plantinga, Alvin. Why We Need Proper Function. *Nous*, 27(1), 66-82, Mr 93.

Plato and Annas, Julia (& other eds) and Waterfield, Robin (trans). *Statesman*. New York, Cambridge Univ Pr, 1995.

Plato and Jowett, Benjamin (trans). *Plato's Gorgias*. Millis, Agora Pub, 1995.

Plato and Woodruff, Paul (trans) and Nehamas, Alexander (trans). *Phaedrus*. Indianapolis, Hackett, 1994.

Platts, Mark. Deseos Distinguidos. *Critica*, 26(76-77), 129-154, Ap-Ag 94.

In the paper "Distinguished Desires", Mark Platts examines three basic, widely spread opinions about desires: 1) Desires are not susceptible of a reasonable evaluation no can be a product of reason. 2) Desires are active powers, internal forces which prompt the agents to act. 3) Desires are not propositional attitudes. Platts does not conclude, as Kenny does, that Hume denies the propositional character of desires. Rather, in Hume's theory, the object of the *attitude* of desire shall be, indeed, some "idea" or proposition, whereas the objective of the *state* of desire shall never be some "real existence". It may now be inferred (although not in a straightforward way) that Hume should agree with the thesis that desires are isolated from reason. The last philosopher that Platts takes into consideration is the Bertrand Russell of *The Analysis of Mind*, who does maintain a nonpropositional theory of desires. (edited)

Plaut, W Gunther. *Asylum: A Moral Dilemma*. Westport, Praeger, 1995.

Plaza Müller, Elsa. "Sobre Picasso y Algunos Retratos Femeninos" in *Temas Actuales de Filosofía, Palacios, María Julia (ed)*, 485-490. Buenos Aires, Univ Nacional Salta, 1993.

Plotnikov, Nikolaj. Phänomenologische Erschliessung der russischen Philosophie. *Phil Rundsch*, 41(4), 328-337, D 94.

Plotnitsky, Arkady. "Complementarity, History, and the Unconscious" in *Intersections: Nineteenth-Century Philosophy and Contemporary Theory, Rajan, Tilottama (ed)*, 263-285. Albany, SUNY Pr, 1995.

Pluzanski, Tadeusz. Time and the Tragic. *Dialogue Hum*, 4(1), 149-158, 1994.

Pochelú, Alicia G. "La Primacía de la Percepción y del mundo Vivido" in *Temas Actuales de Filosofía, Palacios, María Julia (ed)*, 491-496. Buenos Aires, Univ Nacional Salta, 1993.

This article deals with the primacy of the perception and the life's world above the intellectual reflection and the objective world in the adult and children's life. The body's orgatination permits the perceptive experience and the subject can captive and comprise the meaning of the world in the perception. The conclusion of Merleau-Ponty is: a unit exists before all judgment.

Podgorski, Frank R. Paths to Perfection: Yoga and Confucian. *Asian Phil*, 4(2), 151-164, 1994.

The classical Yoga tradition is pictured in four moments: 1) human awareness, 2) psychic awareness, 3) intuitive wisdom, 4) liberating consciousness. The Confucian tradition is pictured as pointing to a unique cross-fertilizing oneness of "jen, ti, and t'ien". The conclusion suggests that an in-depth conversation between these two apparently diverse spiritualities would be mutually enriching.

Pöltner, Günther. The Importance of Dionysius for St Thomas Aquinas' Comprehension of Being. *Diotima*, 23, 128-132, 1995.

Pörn, Ingmar and Gustafsson, Barbro. A Motivational Approach to Confirmation: An Interpretation of Dysphagic Patients' Experiences. *Theor Med*, 15(4), 409-430, D 94.

In this paper we articulate confirmation and disconfirmation as components in human motivation. We develop a theory of motivation on the basis of a model of human action and we explore aspects of confirmation and disconfirmation in the context of the meeting of dysphagic patients with their physicians. We distinguish four central elements in confirmation and disconfirmation and use these and the relations between them for the purpose of constructing a typology. Finally, on the basis of the results obtained we interpret a small volume of remarks reflecting the meaning field of some dysphagic patients in relation to the physicians. The underlying motive is to develop tools for understanding health care processes. The "SAUC-Confirmation-Model" and the theoretical framework in which it is embedded should be seen from that point of view.

Pogge, Thomas W. An Egalitarian Law of Peoples. *Phil Pub Affairs*, 23(3), 195-224, Sum 94.

In his recent Amnesty International Lecture, Rawls claims that the parties to an international original position would adopt a "law of peoples" that does not limit international economic inequalities. He reaches this result by describing these parties as representatives of peoples who care only about the justice of domestic institutions. This description is implausible, because such parties should be presumed to care at least a little about the affluence of the peoples they represent. And even granting Rawls's description, his conclusion does not follow, because the institutions of a country that is very poor relative to others are much more vulnerable to corruption from abroad. Radical international inequalities can plausibly be mitigated through a Global Resources Tax (or Dividend). Such a GRT can be supported not only on Rawlsian grounds. It can also be presented as a way of mitigating the effects of historical wrongs, and again as a novel Lockean proviso to deal with the externalities of unilateral appropriation.

Pohlenz, Gerd. *Phänomenale Realität und Erkenntnis: Umrisse einer Theorie im Ausgang von der eigentümlichen Natur des Qualia-Begriffs*. Freiburg, Alber, 1994.

This book justifies our naive, realistic view of the qualia, especially the phenomenal colours. It explicates our intuition of their theoretical irreducibility by a nontrivial circular (tautological) definition and its contrast with physical thinking. A *philosophical* qualia theory, which integrates physical thinking is therefore required. Such a theory may also interpret the *empirical* qualia as primarily and irreducibly bound to *objects*. Kant's and Husserl's theories are analyzable in this fashion, but clearly reproduce the structure of empirical thought. That alternative outlined here works instead with "*theoretical border concepts*". Some resulting theses: methodological privacy and direct cognitive grasps are ruled out; the qualia—as the material essence of empirical reality—are neither inside nor outside consciousness; consciousness is an aspect of metaphysical appearance of the world as well as the metaphysical aspect of bodily perception.

Poirier, Jean-Louis. Commémoration du Centenaire de la Mort de Jules Lagneau: "Jules Lagneau, Professeur: L'Obscure Clarté de la Philosophie". *Bull Soc Fr Phil*, 88(4), 111-120, O-D 94.

Poizat, Bruno and Pillay, Anand. Corps et Chirurgie. *J Sym Log*, 60(2), 528-533, Je 95.

Les corps algébriquement clos, réels clos et pseudo-finis n'ont, pour chaque entier *n*, qu'un nombre fini d'extensions de degré *n*; nous montrons qu'ils partagent cette propriété avec tous les corps qui, comme eux, satisfont une propriété très rudimentaire de préservation de la dimension, de nature modèle-théorique. Ce résultat est atteint en montrant qu'une certaine action du groupe GL_n d'un tel corps n'a qu'un nombre fini d'orbites.

Pojman, Paul. Are Beliefs and Experiences Candidates for Elimination?. *Dialogue (PST)*, 37(1), 11-14, O 94.

This paper argues against Paul Churchland's philosophy of eliminative materialism as set forth in *A Neurocomputational Perspective*. First, I undermine Churchland's defense against the reductio by showing that it contains a doubtful premise. Then I discuss Churchland's response to Frank Jackson's 'knowledge' argument, concluding that Jackson's attack upon physicalism is reasonable.

Polacik, Tomasz. Operators Defined by Propositional Quantification and Their Interpretation Over Cantor Space. *Rep Math Log*, 27, 67-79, 1993.

The paper concerns intuitionistic propositional logic and its topological interpretation. In particular, it contains a study of a class of nonstandard operators defined by propositional quantification in Heyting calculus. It is proved that the operators in question are definable in Cantor space by means of the standard propositional connectives (negation, disjunction, conjunction, implication), although this fact is not generally true in topological models. A restricted coincidence of Pitts' interpretation (via interpolants) and the topological interpretation of propositional quantification in intuitionistic logic is obtained as a corollary.

Polakovic, Stefan. *Pensando la nación*. Buenos Aires, GEL, 1994.

After assassination of King, French Revolution rose "nation" to symbolize sovereignty, identifying thus "nation" with "political society" (State). Due to political interests this identification spread all over the world rapidly. Historically "nation" signified "spiritual family" (viz Jewish and Greek history). These "spiritual families" form a special genus among world's beings and deserve to be object of anthropological discipline whose name should be "nationology". In this work ontological, sociological, political, juridical, cultural and human aspects of nations are treated. The very essence of nations consists in their culture which as product of spiritual activity has got universal character and represents human message intelligible to all men independently of its ethnic origin.

Polan, Dana. Art, Society and 'Contrapuntal Criticism': A Review of Edward Said's *Culture and Imperialism*. *Clio*, 24(1), 69-79, Fall 94.

Poland, Jeffrey and Von Eckardt, Barbara and Spaulding, Will. "Problems with the *DSM* Approach to Classifying Psychopathology" in *Philosophical Psychopathology, Graham, George (ed)*, 235-260. Cambridge, MIT Pr, 1993.

Polemis, Michael. *Zum Begriff der Trinität*. Vienna, Passagen, 1993.

Zentrales Anliegen dieser Studie ist es, das erste grosse christliche Reich der Weltgeschichte, das oströmische Reich, in seinen strukturellen Unterschieden vom weströmischen Reich zu erfassen und unter Einbeziehung der Konsequenzen dieser Spannung zwischen Ost und West für die europäische Zivilisation bis heute auf den Begriff zu bringen—zum Beispiel anhand einer Gegenüberstellung des augustinischen und des byzantinischen Zeitbegriffs. (edited)

Pollard, Carl J and Moshier, M Andrew. The Domain of Set-Valued Feature Structures. *Ling Phil*, 17(6), 607-631, D 94.

Pollock-Ellwand, Nancy. Cultural Landscapes and Environmental Ethics: The Case of Puslinch Township's Historic Roadside Trees. *J Agr Environ Ethics*, 7(2), 189-203, 1994.

The manner in which cultural landscapes develop is fundamentally influenced by the ethical perspective its human inhabitants have towards their environment. The roadscape in Puslinch Township, Ontario, is an excellent example of how environmental ethics influence the form given to a particular cultural landscape. As the ethic shifts through time so too does the landscape's disposition. Trends are changing again in the Township of Puslinch and a new environmental ethic is beginning to emerge. This attitudinal change, is once again influencing Puslinch's roadscape. (edited)

Poltawski, Andrzej. "Painting and the Structure of Consciousness: Remarks on Roman Ingarden's Theory of Painting" in *Kunst und Ontologie, Wlodzimierz, Galewicz (ed)*, 79-95. Amsterdam, Rodopi, 1994.

Poltier, Hugues. Le pragmatisme: Solution au problème moral de la modernité?. *Rev Theol Phil*, 126(4), 353-39, 1994.

Etude critique de *Morale et Modernité*, cet article présente et discute le projet de son auteur de défendre l'idée d'une morale pragmatiste et intuitionniste. Restituant la pensée de l'auteur, il expose les arguments en faveur d'une conception pragmatiste de la vérité morale et ceux en faveur du recours à l'intuition pour découvrir le contenu de nos obligations morales. Dans une brève note critique, enfin, il suggère que le pragmatisme semble incapable d'échapper tout à fait au reproche de relativisme.

Poltier, Hugues. Qu'est-ce que la pensée du politique? Une introduction au projet philosophique de Claude Lefort. *Rev Theol Phil*, 126(2), 119-141, 1994.

L'article se donne pour tâche d'introduire à la "pensée du politique" du philosophe français Claude Lefort, et surtout de marquer l'originalité de ce projet philosophique par rapport à la philosophie politique classique. Opposée au présupposé du réalisme normatif qui fonde la pensée classique, et basée au contraire sur la conviction que la signification est constitutive du social, la pensée du politique de Lefort prend la forme d'une interrogation de la diversité des formes de société. Ce biais interprétatif permet seul de retrouver une dimension normative. En préliminaire, l'article donne une brève biographie, et en conclusion, une bibliographie sélective.

Ponferrada, Gustavo Eloy. Rehabilitación de Galileo?. *Sapientia*, 49(193-4), 241-272, 1994.

Ponton, Lionel. L'opposition de Hegel au conservatisme de Charles-Louis de Haller. *Laval Theol Phil*, 51(2), 323-334, Je 95.

En préconisant une science politique <expérimentale> fondée sur la loi naturelle, Charles-Louis de Haller tente énergiquement, dans les années 1816-1820, de contrer toute forme de modernisation de l'Etat. Hegel, dans une note au 258 des *Principes de la philosophie du droit*, lui reproche de manquer de pénétration, de mépriser la loi et la juridiction, de sous-estimer les libertés nationales et de confondre l'Etat moderne avec l'Etat révolutionnaire. Axée sur le rapport *nature-raison*, cette polémique éclaire d'un jour nouveau l'orientation maîtresse de la philosophie politique de Hegel.

Ponzio, Paolo 694 **AUTHOR INDEX WITH ABSTRACTS**

Ponzio, Paolo (ed & trans) and Lamacchia, Ada (ed & trans) and Campanella, Tommaso. *Metafisica: Universalis Philosophiae SEU Metaphysicarum Rerum Iuxta Propria Dogmata, Liber I*. Bari, Levante Ed, 1994.

"Mirifica nondum promulgata doctrina, nisi in nostris Metaphysicis". Thus, Tommaso Campanella (1568-1639) denotes his *Philosophia Universalis*, the monumental text published, now, in critical edition, with parallel Italian translation. The *Metaphysics*, in fact, published in 1638, is never more edited in integral form or in critical edition. With the present text, the first of eighteen books that constitute the opera omnia, we hope to take part in the knowledge of metaphysics arguments of Tommaso Campanella in his profundity and entirety.

Pope, Kenneth S and Butcher, James N. Seven Issues in Conducting Forensic Assessments: Ethical Responsibilities in Light of New Standards and New Tests. *Ethics Behavior*, 3(3-4), 267-288, 1993.

The publication of a new ethics code for the American Psychological Association (1992), new guidelines (Committee on Ethical Guidelines for Forensic Psychologists, 1991), and two new versions of the Minnesota Multiphasic Personality Inventory (the MMPI-2, Butcher, Dahlstrom, Graham, Tellegen, and Kaemmer, 1989; and the MMPI-A, Butcher et al., 1992) provide an opportunity to review ethical aspects of forensic assessment. Seven major issues—appropriate graduate training, competence in the use of standardized tests, using tests that fit the task, using tests that fit the individual, administering tests correctly, using computers appropriately in forensic assessment, and assessing and reporting factors that may affect the meaning of test findings—are discussed. The revision of the MMPI is used to illustrate some of these issues.

Pope, Kenneth S and Tabachnick, Barbara G and Bernsen, Ann. National Survey of Social Workers' Sexual Attraction to Their Clients: Results, Implications, and Comparison to Psychologists. *Ethics Behavior*, 4(4), 369-388, 1994.

A survey form sent to psychologists (Pope, Keith-Spiegel, and Tabachnick, 1986) was adapted and sent to 1,000 clinical social workers (return rate = 45%). Most participants reported sexual attraction to a client, causing (for most) guilt, anxiety, or confusion. Some reported having sexual fantasies about a client while engaging in sex with someone other than a client. Relatively few (3.6% men; 0.5% women) reported sex with a client; training was related to likelihood of offending, though the effect is small and complex. An analysis of eight national studies (data from 5,148 therapists) found significant effects for gender (more male offenders) and year of study (about 10% annual decrease in reported offenses since 1977) but not profession (i.e., no difference among psychiatrists, psychologists, and social workers). Most social workers reported no graduate training whatsoever about sexual attraction; only 10% reported adequate training.

Popkin, Richard H and Maia Neto, José R. Bishop Pierre-Daniel Huet's Remarks on Pascal. *Brit J Hist Phil*, 3(1), 147-160, F 95.

Bishop Pierre-Daniel Huet is an early modern sceptic who owned one of the largest private libraries in the period. Many of Huet's books are now preserved at the Bibliothèque Nationale in Paris, most of which contain marginal notes written by the Bishop. In the article, we examine Huet's remarks on the Port-Royal edition of Pascal's *Pensées*. Most of Huet's notes are very critical. Although both thinkers were critics of Descartes and inclined to scepticism, they construe scepticism quite differently. These differences are pointed out and traced to Pascal's and Huet's conflicting theological views.

Poppendieck, Janet E. Dilemmas of Emergency Food: A Guide for the Perplexed. *Agr Human Values*, 11(4), 69-76, Fall 94.

The proliferation of emergency food programs in the United States over the past decade and a half has created a dilemma for advocates and others who approach issues of social provision from the standpoint of a commitment to social justice. While the soup kitchens, food pantries, food banks, and food rescue programs that comprise the emergency food system may be able to meet some of the urgent, immediate needs of poor people, they do so in ways that may further undermine rights and entitlements and erode the cultural basis of support for the welfare state. Should advocates of distributive justice work to improve such emergency programs, ignore them, or call for their abolition? This paper explores the history of advocates' involvement with emergency food, assesses the strengths and weaknesses of emergency food programs from a social justice standpoint, and offers some guidelines for action.

Popper, Karl R. Los dos significados de *falsabilidad*. *Rev Filosof (Spain)*, 4(5), 3-11, 1991.

Popper, Karl R and Notturno, M A (ed). *Knowledge and the Body-Mind Problem: In Defence of Interaction*. New York, Routledge, 1994.

Knowledge and the Body-Mind Problem is based on lectures given in 1969 at Emory University which raised problems connected with human freedom, creativity, rationality, and the relationship between human beings and their actions. Popper defends the existence of an interaction between mental states (such as hopes, needs, plans, pains, dogmatically held ideologies, or tentatively held scientific hypotheses) and physical states of our brain and their physical consequences (such as the writing of a letter, a visit to the dentist or to a friend). (edited)

Popper, Karl R and Notturno, M A (ed). *The Myth of the Framework: In Defence of Science and Rationality*. New York, Routledge, 1994.

Portalupi, Enzo. L'uso dell'*Index Thomisticus* nello studio delle fonti di Tommaso d'Aquino: considerazoni generali e questioni di metodo. *Riv Filosof Neo-Scolas*, 86(3), 573-585, Jl-S 94.

Porter, Elisabeth. Abortion Ethics: Rights and Responsibilities. *Hypatia*, 9(3), 66-87, Sum 94.

Abortion considerations require deep reflection on law, convention, social mores, religious norms, family contexts, emotions, and relationships. I have three arguments. First, a liberal "right to choose" framework is inadequate because it is based on individualist notions of rights. Second, reproductive freedoms should be extended to all women. Third, abortion ethics involves a dialectical interplay between rights and responsibilities, and between social, cultural, and particular contexts, and is best understood in terms of moral praxis.

Porter, Roosevelt. Some Peculiarities about Musical Aesthetic Qualities. *Rev Metaph*, 48(3), 483-509, Mr 95.

Posavac, Zlatko. Die kroatische Ästhetik des 17 Jahrhunderts: Die Epoche der Gegenreformation, des Rationalismus und des Empirismus. Barock und Klassizismus. *Filozof Istraz*, 14(2-3), 507-541, 1994.

Der im hier vorliegenden ersten Teil des Textes enthaltene Versuch, die kroatische Ästhetik des gesamten 17. Jahrhunderts zusammenfassend darzustellen—ein Versuch, der den derzeitigen Forschungsstand belegt—, stellt ausser einer positiven Explikation auch eine Hilfestellung zur Erfassung von "Leerstellen" dar. Er vermittelt so klare Richtlinien und verweist auf all das, was es in Zukunft, und zwar so schnell wie möglich, zu erforschen gilt. Trotz der klar deklarierten Qualifikation, dass es sich hier tatsächlich um einen Abriss handelt, beschränkt sich dieser Text nicht einfach auf blosses Referieren, und dies nicht nur, weil darin viele vom Verfasser für diese Gelegenheit selbst erarbeitete Forschungserkenntnisse enthalten sind, sondern auch deshalb, weil er als ein Ganzes heuristisch-historiographische Bedeutung hat. (edited)

Posavac, Zlatko. Sprache und ästhetische Terminologie: Kunst und Sprachwissenschaft in der Funktion der Zerstörung von Leben und Geistigkeit. *Filozof Istraz*, 13(4), 893-909, 1993.

Die Möglichkeit bzw. Unmöglichkeit der Herstellung von zwischenmenschlicher Kommunikation, wobei der Sprache eine erstrangige, wenn nicht gar ausschliessliche Bedeutung zukommt, ist etwas Reales. Daher gilt es Betrachtungen über Sprache als existentiell, als existentielles Problem, als Problem des Existierens, der Existenz der Individualität sei es des einzelnen oder der Nation zu nehmen. Aus dem Horizont der Existenzphilosophie bedarf das Sprachproblem also einer ernsthaften Hermeneutik, um ausser einer blossen Identifizierung die Wirklichkeit der Ideologisierung bzw. ein ideologisierendes Manipulieren mit Sprache zu übertreffen. Daher auch die Erläuterung des Postulats, wonach die Frage der Sprache nicht einfach nur der Philologie überlassen werden kann, denn—die Sprache ist ein existentielles Problem. Genausowenig kann sie aber irgendeiner Wissenschaft überhaupt überlassen werden, da die Wissenschaft selbst bereits ideologisiert, operationalisiert, pragmatisiert ist, da mit ihr manipuliert wird, statt sie am Prinzip oder zumindest am Ideal der Wahrheit zu orientieren. (edited)

Possenti, Vittorio. "Dio e il male" in *L'etica e il suo Altro, Vigna, Carmelo (ed)*, 41-68. Milano, FrancoAngeli, 1994.

Possenti, Vittorio. Ateismo, filosofia e cristianesimo in Del Noce. *G Metaf*, 16(1-2), 179-198, Ja-Ag 94.

Possenti, Vittorio. Human Rights and Human Nature. *Cont Phil*, 17(1), 4-10, Ja-F 95.

This paper examines critically the validity of the claim that human rights are universal. It argues that the Christian tradition of human rights, by relying on the doctrine that natural law is the participation of the eternal law in man, is both original and universal.

Post, Robert C. *Constitutional Domains: Democracy, Community, Management*. Cambridge, Harvard Univ Pr, 1995.

Constitutional rights function to create forms of social structure that embody distinct values. American constitutional law uses rights to divide structures of democracy, in which individual and collective autonomy are reconciled through public discourse, from structures of community, in which individual and collective identity are mutually defined and enforced through intersubjective norms, and also from structures of management, in which social life is arranged for the instrumental achievement of given ends.

Post, Stephen G. Dementia in Our Midst: The Moral Community. *Cambridge Quart Healthcare Ethics*, 4(2), 142-147, Spr 95.

This article focuses on the elderly patient with a progressive and irreversible dementia, most often of the Alzheimer type. However dementia, the decline in mental function from a previous state, can occur in all ages. For example, if Alzheimer's disease (AD) is the dementia of the elderly, increasingly AIDS is the dementia of many who are relatively young. I will not present the major ethical issues relating to dementia care following the progression of disease from the mild to the severe stages, for I have done this elsewhere. Among the issues included are: presymptomatic testing, both psychological and genetic; responsible diagnostic disclosure and use of support groups; restrictions on driving and other activities; preemptive assisted suicide; advanced directives for research and treatment; quality of life in relation to the use of life-extending technologies; and euthanasia.

Post, Stephen G and Leisey, Robert G. Analogy, Evaluation, and Moral Disagreement. *J Value Inq*, 29(1), 45-55, Mr 95.

This article examines the role of two distinct forms of analogy in moral discourse. The use of analogy in moral discourse. The use of analogy in abortion debates in used as an example of the dominance of analogy in applied ethics.

Postema, Gerald J. Implicit Law. *Law Phil*, 13(3), 361-387, Ag 94.

According to Lon Fuller, law's central task is to provide baselines for self-directed interaction among citizens. This, rather than authority, is the central organizing idea of a distinctively legal order. Thus, he argues, "made law" depends for its existence and value on a vast network of informal understandings rooted in social interaction. His argument for this implicit dimension of law rests on two theses drawn from the above premise. The *vertical interaction thesis* holds that the meaning and practical force of legal norms depends on reciprocity between citizens and law-making and law-applying officials. The *congruence thesis* holds that self-directed social interaction is possible only if legal norms are broadly congruent with informal social practices and conventions.

Postema, Gerald J. Morality in the First Person Plural. *Law Phil*, 14(1), 35-64, F 95.

Moral judgment is made from a common standpoint. First person plural judgment (and deliberation) is characterized, not by the content or ownership of ends, nor by the value agents place on cooperation, but rather by its orientation towards others as partners in deliberation and action. Plural deliberators first consider the question, What are we to do, then ask What is my part in the cooperative scheme? From this view, group actions are considered holistically, and individual component actions are regarded as related mereologically and teleologically. Since the structural features of plural deliberation are analogous to those of intertemporal deliberation, the former is no less intelligible than the latter.

Poster, Carol. Persuasion in an Empty Ontology: The Eleatic Synthesis of Philosophy, Poetry, and Rhetoric. *Phil Rhet*, 27(4), 277-299, 1994.

This article shows how the radical ontological and epistemological notions of the Eleatic philosophers resulted in 1) the necessity for deceptive and persuasive discourse and 2) verse and poetic (Gorgiastic) prose as rhetorical strategies in the writings of Xenophanes, Parmenides, Empedocles, and Gorgias. Once philosophical speculation undermines the possibility of absolute knowledge, two paths are possible: rehabilitation of epistemology (Plato's form, Aristotle's logic) or discourse that attempts to assert ambiguity and unknowability. This article shows how the latter path, in sixth and fifth century B C Sicily, has two distinct but inter-related results, philosophic discourse in poetic form and Gorgiastic rhetoric.

Poster, Mark. "Critical Theory and Technoculture: Habermas and Baudrillard" in *Baudrillard: A Critical Reader, Kellner, Douglas M (ed)*, 68-88. Cambridge, Blackwell, 1994.

The critical comparison of the concepts of culture and technology in the work of Jürgen Habermas and Jean Baudrillard.

Postma-de Beer, Zach. "A Rethink in Political Philosophy" in *Life, World and Meaning, Roux, A P J (ed)*, 108-120. Pretoria, Univ of S Africa, 1990.

Potter, Jonathan and Ashmore, Malcolm and Edwards, Derek. Death and Furniture: The Rhetoric, Politics, and Theology of Bottom Line Arguments against Relativism. *Hist Human Sci*, 8(2), 25-49, My 95.

Potter, Nancy. The Severed Head and Existential Dread: The Classroom as Epistemic Community and Student Survivors of Incest. *Hypatia*, 10(2), 69-92, Spr 95.

I discuss pedagogical issues that concern incest survivors. As teachers, we need to understand the ways in which the legacy of incest variously affects survivors' educational experiences and to be aware that the interplay of trust, knowledge, and power may be particularly complex for survivors. I emphasize the responsibility teachers have to create classrooms that are inclusive of survivors, while raising concerns about the practice of personal disclosure and assumptions about trust and safety in the classroom.

Potter, R Dennis. Wong on Davidson. *Phil Papers*, 24(1), 75-81, Ap 95.

In his paper 'To Interpret, Or To Be Omniscient' (*Phil Papers* 22(3), 189-198, 1993) Wai-hung Wong wants to defeat Davidson's omniscient interpreter argument by arguing that the very conception of an omniscient interpreter is inconsistent. This paper examines the arguments for this claim, showing that they do not establish the desired conclusion. Instead, it shows that Wong's considerations only establish that the omniscient interpreter argument rests on more controversial assumptions than might be supposed.

Potter, Robert Lyman. The Hermeneutical Project and Clinical Ethics. *J Clin Ethics*, 6(1), 88-91, Spr 95.

Potter, Vincent G. "A Response to Hartshorne" in *Peirce and Contemporary Thought: Philosophical Inquiries, Ketner, Kenneth Laine (ed)*, 356-365. New York, Fordham Univ Pr, 1995.

Potter, Vincent G. Objective Chance: Lonergan and Peirce on Scientific Generalization. *Method*, 12(1), 91-107, Spr 94.

Potts, Michael. Hopkins and the Theory of Metaphor. *Amer Cath Phil Quart*, 68(4), 501-513, Autumn 94.

In this paper I explore some of the philosophical implications for metaphor and poetry found in Gerard Manley Hopkins' theory of parallelism. I first summarize the interaction theory of metaphor, emphasizing the particular contributions made to the theory by Paul Ricoeur. I next summarize Hopkins' theory of parallelism. Then I defend the thesis that Hopkins' theory of parallelism has a great deal in common with an interaction theory of metaphor. Finally, I suggest that Hopkins' theory of parallelism can be used to expand the role of the interaction theory of metaphor to poetry as a whole.

Potts, Michael. The Spatio-Temporal Theory of Individuation. *Thomist*, 59(1), 59-68, Ja 95.

I begin by tracing the spatio-temporal theory of individuation back to its roots in Plato's "receptacle", through Aristotle's theory of individuation by matter, and through Aquinas' modification of Aristotle which holds that the principle of individuation is "matter considered under determinate dimensions". After identifying the key issue in individuation as incommunicability, not numerical diversity, I argue that any spatio-temporal theory fails as an adequate account of individuation since spatio-temporal locations, relations, or histories already *presuppose* the prior existence of individuals.

Povar, Gail J. "How Do You Catch a Cloud and Pin It Down?" (With Apologies to Rogers and Hammerstein): A Commentary on Layson and Colleagues. *J Clin Ethics*, 5(3), 253-256, Fall 94.

Povelones Jr, Arthur A. When the Majority Says You May Die: Aid-in-Dying Initiatives. *Notre Dame J Law Ethics*, 9(2), 537-564, 1995.

Proposals to legalize physician aid-in-dying (assisted suicide and/or euthanasia) have been the subject of legislative debate and ballot initiatives. These efforts are evaluated in order to analyze the advantages and disadvantages of the legislative and initiative processes. The conclusion proposes a lawmaking approach more conducive to resolving aid-in-dying and similar issues by combining aspects of the two systems.

Powderly, Kathleen E. Contraceptive Policy and Ethics: Illustrations from American History. *Hastings Center Rep*, 25(1), S9-S11, Jan-Feb 95.

Power, William L. Divine Poiesis and Abstract Entities. *Relig Stud*, 30(3), 335-341, S 94.

In this paper, I attempt to give an informal explication of the notion of Divine Poiesis or God's productive perfection, with special attention to the issue of God's relation to abstract entities such as classes, properties, relations propositions, numbers and their like. I argue that abstract entities are neither ontologically independent and necessary (Platonism) or ontologically dependent as created and necessary (Morris and Menzel) but rather ontologically dependent as generated and necessary (Power).

Powers, Madison. Repugnant Desires and the Two-Tier Conception of Utility. *Utilitas*, 6(2), 171-176, N 94.

A problem for utilitarianism is that it may count as morally relevant contributions to individual well-being items which are morally or rationally suspect. A potential solution lies in James Griffin's suggestion that the account of utility needed by a moral theory may be more restrictive than the one needed by a theory of prudence. However, a principle restricting utilitarianism's theory of the good, if made applicable to its fundamental criterion of rightness (and not just its decision procedure), yields neither a single principle moral theory nor a utility maximizing theory that one expects of utilitarianism.

Pozaic, Valentin. Personal Freedom and Responsibility for the Environment. *Filozof Istraz*, 14(1), 47-58, 1994.

The author discusses the dimensions of personal freedom and responsibility for the environment, particularly in light of the biblical injunction, *dominium terrae*, as well as that of cultivating and protecting the earth, the garden of man's existence. It has become obvious that man's survival and development includes the drama of the manipulation of the world. The biblical model of the world is anthropocentric, but relativised in theocentrism. *Dominium terrae*, understood correctly, is based upon *amor terrae* and achieved through *servitium terrae*. The solution to the present state of environmental crisis is not a flight from reality and responsibility, but rather a return to the authentic biblical message of the world and man's role within it.

Pozo, Antonio Gutierrez. Razón Vital y Fenomenología (Génesis del Raciovitalismo Orteguiano). *Pensamiento*, 199(51), 129-147, Ja-Ap 95.

No es injusto calificar la razón vital orteguiana de fenomenológica. Ahora bien, la necesidad de medirse con todos los parámetros vitales para poder "salvar a España", motivo determinante de su origen y desarrollo, exigen a la razón vital, además de superar el subjetivismo, renunciar a la orientación trascendental que Husserl imprimió a su pensamiento. Esta supeditación a la circunstancia española no rebaja las aspiraciones intelectuales y liberadoras de la razón: únicamente inclinándose sobre la vida tiene sentido, y puede servirla sólo penetrando en la verdad.

Prada Oropeza, Renato. Semiosis y Objetos: Los Objetos Naturales. *Analogia*, 9(1), 157-172, 1995.

This essay is a reduced version of another one which will integrate the book *Literatura y realidad* (Reality and Literature) actually in process of writing. It is based on Marx's intuition (Economic-philosofics Papers of 1844); The man *humanize* all "object" when he converts it in a social object, created by man and destinated to the man. The hominization (Latin hommo) of the man, like his being-in-the-world (Heidegger) is the product of human *praxis*. This *praxis* that founds and creates the world is the *culture*. For the man, social being and cultural being are practically the same. In this way, properly, we can't talk about objects on themselves, out of the social-cultural scope: the natural objects do not exist, or at least, do not make sense to the being-in-the-world of man.

Pradhan, R C. Transcendental Subjectivity Meets Transcendental Grammar. *Indian Phil Quart*, 21(2), 173-177, Ap 94.

That transcendental subjectivity meets transcendental grammar is the central theme of Wittgenstein's philosophy. To allow a gap between the two is to go back to the Ego-centric framework of Descartes and Kant. Wittgenstein has abolished the thinking Ego without dissolving the transcendental subjectivity which is presupposed by the transcendental grammar. Without the transcendental subjectivity grammar itself would lose its transcendental character. So there would be no standpoint from which grammar can be studied. In that case philosophy of language would not be possible. On this issue there is a marked continuity between Wittgenstein's early and later philosophy.

Pradhan, R C. Wittgenstein on Forms of Life: Towards a Transcendental lperspective. *J Indian Counc Phil Res*, 11(3), 63-79, My-Ag 94.

The paper intends to highlight the fact that Wittgenstein's concept of forms of life is not an anthropological one. That is, forms of life, according to Wittgenstein, are not the anthropological phenomena that can be studied naturalistically. They can be taken as the constitutive grounds of our language and thought. So there is a grammatical way of representing them. This way of bringing out their grammatical significance can be called transcendental because it leads us to overcome the limitations of the naturalist taxomony of the forms of life. According to this interpretation, forms of life constitute the transcendental horizon of language and the world.

Prado, C G. *Starting with Foucault: An Introduction to Genealogy*. Boulder, Westview Pr, 1995.

The book is an introduction to Foucault's historicization of truth and knowledge and is written for those with an analytic background. The focus on "genealogy" is intended to be of greatest interest to those whose main philosophical concerns are epistemological. The aim is to present Foucault's views, as developed primarily in *Discipline and Punish* and *The History of Sexuality* (Vol.I), in as clear and concise a manner as possible and one allowing for a lack of background in European or "Continental" philosophy. Also included is a chapter with a novel classification of Foucault's various uses of "true" and "truth."

Prado, José Hernández. Max Weber y la racionalización, desmagificación y remagificación del mundo. *Topicos*, 4(7), 7-17, 1994.

Max Weber wrote about a rationalization process of the human and social world, and he thought that this very process led towards a situation of world's disenchantment. Nowadays, it is possible to refer a re-enchantment of the social world as a consequence of the same process of rationalization; a philosophical index of this cultural change can be found in Wittgenstein's ideas on religious language.

Prado, José Julián. "Sobre las Explicaciones Evolucionistas de la Razón" in *Temas Actuales de Filosofía, Palacios, María Julia (ed)*, 497-504. Buenos Aires, Univ Nacional Salta, 1993.

Prahl, Frank. "Haldeman-Julius: Publisher, Freethinker, Humanist" in *Contributors to the Philosophy of Humanism, Hillar, Marian (ed)*, 115-124. Pasadena, Humanists Houston, 1994.

E Haldeman-Julius was one of the most significant publishers in the US this century, perhaps saving and inspiring the Freethought and Humanist movements in the 1920's and 30's, but few people today have even heard of him. He published over 3000 Little Blue Books & Big Blue Books, about a third of which were Freethought literature. Unfortunately, because they were pamphlets instead of books, they were not carried by the Library of Congress—the primary cataloger of literature. As copyrights run out soon, expect much of his literature to reappear. This essay reintroduces E Haldeman-Julius as a publisher whose works need to be sought after and to demonstrate how difficult it is for alternative views to overcome religious intolerance.

Prahl, Frank. "The Contributions to Humanism of Mark Twain" in *Contributors to the Philosophy of Humanism, Hillar, Marian (ed)*, 91-103. Pasadena, Humanists Houston, 1994.

Mark Twain's writings have been critiqued many times, but seldom by a Secular Humanism or Freethinker. This essay tracks Twain's evolution to Humanism using excerpts from some of his published writings, letters and comments from authors who have written about him. Much of his philosophy was woven into his novels, but the messages were often lost in his dazeling stories. During the last ten years of his life Twain attacked religion openly, but allowed little of these writings to be published until long after his death. Now that they are being published, it is easy to understand the increased efforts of the Radical Religious Right to purge Twain's books from our public schools.

Prahl, Frank (ed) and Hillar, Marian (ed). *Contributors to the Philosophy of Humanism*. Pasadena, Humanists Houston, 1994.

The book is as collection of 12 essays on the various contributors to the philosophy of Humanism: Robert W Burch, "The Contribution to Humanism of Konstantin Kolenda"; Ellen K Suchiel, "Radiance and Religious Belief" (on Kolenda); Jacquelyn A K Kegley, "Too Thin a Self, too Small a Human" (on Kolenda); Robert D Finch, "Aristotle's Ethics"; Marian Hillar, "The Problem of the Soul in Aristotle's *De anima*"; Sheila A Finch, "Fracois Rabelais as Humanist"; Frank Prahl, "The Contributions to Humanism of Mark Twain"; Alice Leuchtag "Elizabeth Cady Stanton: Free Thinker and Radical Revisionist"; Frank Prahl "Haldeman-Julius: Publisher, Freethinker, Humanist"; George Lattie, "The Philosophy of Corliss Lamont"; Carl Veley, "Isaac Asimov's Contribution to Humanism"; Robert D Finch, "The Philosophy of Sir Karl Popper."

Prakash, Madhu Suri. Ecological Literacy for Moral Virtue: Orr on (Moral) education for postmodern sustainability. *J Moral Educ*, 24(1), 3-18, 1995.

David Orr's postmodern philosophical investigations begin with the recognition that our modern culture is not ecologically sustainable; and therefore threatens all life on earth in the long term, even as it continues to destroy sustainable cultures in the short term. Hopeful of redirecting our civic culture or morality, as well as our technologies towards postmodern sustainability, Orr proposes an education for ecological literacy. This paper examines Orr's account of ecological literacy. Following his attempts to take us beyond modern literacy, it analyses Orr's conception of moral virtue. It concludes with some reflections on Orr's deconstruction of professional academic boundaries, including those that continue to separate ecological literacy from moral education.

Prasad, M. Religious Belief and Philosophical Inquiry. *Darshana Int*, 32(2/126), 24-30, Ap 92.

The object of the present paper is to show the relevance of philosophical inquiry for religious belief. Religion and religious beliefs are generally considered to be based on faith and as such they are not amenable to reason. The present study will also try to clear the mist behind such a view. To show the relevance of philosophical inquiry for religious beliefs, we must have a clear notion of what philosophical inquiry is and what exactly is signified by religious belief.

Prasad, Rajendra. Philosophy, Education and the Quality of Life. *Indian Phil Quart*, 21(2), 99-117, Ap 94.

Prasad, Rajendra. The Paradox of Obligation. *J Indian Counc Phil Res*, 11(2), 1-27, Ja-Ap 94.

Prasad, Ranjendra. Universal Values: An Indian Perspective. *Dialogue Hum*, 4(4), 45-50, 1994.

Prati, N. A Partial Model of "NF" with E. *J Sym Log*, 59(4), 1245-1253, D 94.

Partial models of the theory New Foundations (NF) introduced by Quine have already appeared in the literature, but in every model the membership set of NF is missing. On the other hand, Jensen showed that "NF + Urelements" is consistent with respect to ZF and, in the model built there, the membership set of the theory exists. Here we build a partial model of NF from the one of Jensen in which the membership set exists.

Pratt, Scott L. A Reply to Christopher Kulp's "Dewey, Indeterminacy, and the Spectator Theory of Knowledge". *Mod Sch*, 72(1), 67-76, N 94.

Prauss, Gerold. "Kant and the Straight Biangle" in *Philosophy, Mathematics and Modern Physics, Rudolph, Enno (ed)*, 226-234. New York, Springer-Verlag, 1994.

Prawitz, Dag. Quine and Verificationism. *Inquiry*, 37(4), 487-494, D 94.

The theme of these notes is the relation between verificationism and Quine's approach to philosophy of language. The main thesis is that a tenable theory of meaning along verificationist lines must distinguish between canonical and indirect verification and that this distinction is related to observable features of language use. It is argued that a theory of meaning along such lines is not vulnerable to Quine's arguments against verificationism, and suggested that, on the whole, a verificationism of this kind is compatible with Quine's basic approach to philosophy of language.

Preece, Rod and Chamberlain, Lorna. *Animal Welfare and Human Values*. Waterloo, Wilfrid Laurier U Pr, 1995.

Grounding their ideas in Wordsworth's 'primal sympathy' and Jung's 'unconscious identity' with animals, the authors discuss the most contentious issues in animal welfare disputes—animal experimentation, fur-farming and trapping, the use of animals for human entertainment, and the conditions under which animals are raised for human consumption. The authors argue that 'community' and 'belonging' rather than 'individuality' and the pleasure-pain continuum are the appropriate categories through which to understand our relationships to other species. They conclude that common sense and compromise are the surest paths to the goals of respect and consideration which must underlie a sound conception of animal welfare.

Prenzler, Tim and Mackay, Peta. Police Gratuities: What the Public Think. *Crim Just Ethics*, 14(1), 15-25, Wint-Spr 95.

This paper reports on a survey of residents of Brisbane, Australia. The research found that the majority of respondents opposed all gratuities other than very small incidental gifts. The main sources of concern were the appearance of compromise and the potential for unequal treatment of users of police services. Overall, the study showed that public expectations of police conduct are quite exacting and that conformity to those standards is essential for public confidence in the police. The survey also indicated that the practice of police accepting gratuities is still occurring in Australia. In light of this, some strategies are suggested for implementing policy more effectively.

Presnell, Mick. "Icons, Fragments, and Ironists" in *Recovering Pragmatism's Voice, Langsdorf, Lenore (ed)*, 251-269. Albany, SUNY Pr, 1995.

Press, Jon and Harvey, Charles. John Ruskin and the Ethical Foundations of Morris and Company, 1861-96. *J Bus Ethics*, 14(3), 181-194, Mr 95.

In *Unto this Last*, John Ruskin argued that Britain's industrial society was morally degenerate and pernicious in that it drove the laboring class into cultural and material poverty. Ruskin's writings are in essence an appeal to the business leader to behave in a socially responsible, paternalistic fashion according to his own moral prescriptions. This article examines the ways in which William Morris sought to give practical expression to these ideas. There is no perfect correspondence between the business notions of John Ruskin and the practice of William Morris. Yet it is evident that Morris stuck to many of his mentor's ideas with remarkable tenacity. (edited)

Press, Nancy and Browner, C H. Risk, Autonomy, and Responsibility: Informed Consent for Prenatal Testing. *Hastings Center Rep*, 25(3), S9-S12, My-Je 95.

Why is informed consent required for noninvasive prenatal screening, such as maternal serum alphafetoprotein (MSAFP) testing? Consent is routinely sought, but examination of its implementation suggests a need to reconceptualize both the risks and responsibilities involved in offering and accepting prenatal testing. This work traces the history of informed consent and the different, sometimes contradictory logics of ethics and law driving it. It concludes with a consideration of how to conceptualize informed consent in the face of a patient's desire *not to know* and asks whether informed consent for prenatal testing might imply patient obligations as well as rights.

Preston, Beth. Behaviorism and Mentalism: Is There a Third Alternative?. *Synthese*, 100(2), 167-196, Ag 94.

Behaviorism and mentalism are commonly considered to be mutually exclusive and conjunctively exhaustive options for the psychological explanation of behavior. Behaviorism and mentalism do differ in their characterization of inner causes of behavior. However, I argue that they are not mutually exclusive on the grounds that they share important foundational assumptions, two of which are the notion of an inner-outer split and notion of control. I go on to argue that mentalism and behaviorism are not conjunctively exhaustive either, on the grounds that dropping these common foundational assumptions results in a distinctively different framework for the explanation of behavior. This third alternative, which is briefly described, is a version of nonindividualism.

Preston, John. Frictionless Philosophy: Paul Feyerabend and Relativism. *Hist Euro Ideas*, 20(4-6), 963-968, F 95.

The version of moral relativism that Paul Feyerabend discusses in his 1991 book *Three Dialogues on Knowledge* is evaluated. It is shown to be in conflict with an essential feature of appraisal vocabulary known as supervenience. This is enough to render this version of relativism untenable. But the way in which Feyerabend defends his relativist principle against the Platonic objection that relativist is self-refuting also involves that might be called 'semantic nihilism', the idea that nothing can be said to logically follow from our beliefs and utterances. The roots of semantic nihilism in Feyerabend's philosophy are traced, and semantic nihilism is shown to be untenable in virtue of being dialectically self-refuting.

Preston, John. Methodology, Epistemology and Conventions: Popper's Bad Start. *Proc Phil Sci Ass*, 1, 314-322, 1994.

Popper's conception of methodology and its relationship to epistemology is examined, and found wanting. Popper argues that positivist criteria of demarcation fail because they are attempts to discover a difference in the natures of empirical science and metaphysics. His alternative to naturalism is that a plausible criterion of demarcation is a proposal for an agreement, or convention. But this conventionalism about methodology is misplaced. Methodological rules are conventions, but which methodological rules are followed by scientists it is not itself a matter of convention. This casts doubt upon the status of Popper's famous criterion of demarcation.

Preti, Consuelo. Externalism and Analyticity. *Phil Stud*, 79(3), 213-236, S 95.

Semantic externalism is the view that meaning is at least partly determined by reference. This suggests that the classic philosophical distinction between truth in virtue of meaning alone and truth in virtue of the world may need reconsideration. If all sentences are true in virtue of reference it is difficult to see how we can distinguish some sentences from others as true in virtue of the world-independent, purely semantic entities that their truth-conditions involve. I argue, to the contrary, that semantic externalism instead exposes significant problems with the orthodox view about meaning that underlies the orthodox view about analytic truth, and I offer an account of analyticity from the perspective of semantic externalism. On this view, the truth-value of analytic sentences will not be distinguished from those of synthetic sentences. The truth-conditions of an analytic sentence are, however, to be distinguished from what makes it *analytic*. This account is one that revokes the customary world-independence of analytic sentences, but does not sacrifice their unique modal and epistemic features.

Preyer, Gerhard. Die Rationalitätsbegriffe des Handelns: Eine Grundlegung zu einer Typologie sozialen Handelns. *Protosoz*, 6, 120-150, 1994.

For understanding human action rationality is a fundamental point of view. A prototheory of social science elaborates the types of social action under the conceptualization of rationalization and human freedom in societies. On this way it must be distinguished too—not interchangable—concepts of rationalization: the rationality of purpose, e.g., the rational choice of means (Zweckrationalität) and the rationality of understanding (Verständigungsrationalität). Language behaviour has for this conceptualization the status of the frametheory. But actions are not identical with language behaviour and are based on language external resources. The conceptualizations of concepts of rationality are basic-assumptions for the construction of a structure-model of societal rationalization.

Preyer, Gerhard. Protosoziologie: Problemebenen, Foki, Rekonstruktionshypothesen. *Protosoz*, 1, 2-49, Ap 91.

The basic-principle of Protosociology is that all creatures who have propositional attitudes and the ability to act intentionally (voluntarily) are examples of application of the standard (norm) of rationality. This level is the basis for methodical construction and reconstruction of Protosociology and the Frankfurt version of action (speech act) theory. This version starts from cognition, that the concept of meaning cannot be understood completely, independent of propositional truth, propositional structure of language (saying that...) are fundamental features of the basic knowledge of this approach. But Protosociology does not claim that understanding social reality is committed to a sociologism or linguistic community semantic as overall viewpoint of agency, reasoning, and understanding. (edited)

Preyer, Gerhard. Sprachpragmatik. *Protosoz*, 2, 24-46, Ja 92.

The domain of pragmatics is to arrange in the architectonic of competences. Competences are to discriminate on the base of distinction between rule-following behavior and action-rules. This can be understood as a critic of L Wittgenstein's conception of following a rule. The Frankfurter version of speech/act/theory has argued—following partial K Bühler—that three fundamental properties (functions) of language can be identified: the representation of state of affairs, the generation of interpersonal relationship and the expression of Intentional make happen someone (Erlebnisse). Further dimensions and explications for concerning these properties shall be elaborated. Steps to constructive pragmatics can be gone.

Price, B B. *Medieval Thought: An Introduction*. Cambridge, Blackwell, 1992.

Medieval Thought studies the course of medieval intellectualization, analyzing how tension between the religious and non-religious components of medieval culture resulted in its sophisticated development. The most influential vehicle for medieval intellectualization was philosophy. Philosophy became the mode of expression in religion, providing religious thinkers with a unifying vocabulary and means of reasoning. In turn, philosophers found in religion fertile ground for metaphysical discussion. The initial alliance between philosophy and religion did not hold, however, for Christianity's need for theological strength through uniformity inevitably clashed with the dissenting questioning of philosophy. This marriage and separation are analyzed chronologically in light of the foundations and developments of: medieval religious thought; medieval education and classical philosophy; Latin and vernacular languages; the evolution of medieval philosophical ideas in scholasticism; and the tensions between the Church and the intellectuals in the late Middle Ages.

Price, Colin and Artigas, Mariano. Evolution: Science and Metaphysics—A Commentary on Michel Delsol's Article. *Laval Theol Phil*, 50(3), 595-600, O 94.

Neo-Darwinism does appear like an island between on the one hand physics and on the other metaphysics. The purpose of this article is to help fill out the anomalies from both sides.

Price, Huw. *The Common Mind: An Essay on Psychology, Society, and Politics* by Philip Pettit. *Phil Phenomenol Res*, 55(3), 689-699, S 95.

Price, Huw. Reinterpreting the Wheeler-Feynman Absorber Theory: Reply to Leeds. *Brit J Phil Sci*, 45(4), 1023-1028, D 94.

Price, Kingsley. Philosophy in a New Key: An Interpretation. *Phil Music Educ Rev*, 1(1), 33-43, Spr 93.

Price, Richard and Peach, W Bernard (ed). *The Correspondence of Richard Price, Volume III: February 1786-February 1791*. Durham, Duke Univ Pr, 1994.

Priest, Graham. *Beyond the Limits of Thought*. New York, Cambridge Univ Pr, 1995.

The book is an investigation of the nature of the limits of thought. Drawing on techniques from paraconsistent logic, it shows that the descriptions of such limits are contradictory, and argues that these contradictions are veridical. After an analysis of the way these limits occur in pre-Kantian philosophy, it discusses how they were theorized by Kant and Hegel. The book offers novel interpretations of Berkeley's master argument for idealism, and Kant on the antinomies. Next, the book discusses the paradoxes of self-reference, and provides a unified account of such paradoxes. In its final part, it looks at the role played by the limits of thought in modern philosophy of language, including discussions of Wittgenstein and Derrida.

Priest, Graham. Etchemendy and Logical Consequence. *Can J Phil*, 25(2), 283-292, Je 95.

The paper is a commentary on J Etchemendy, *The Concept of Logical Consequence* (Harvard University Press, 1990). It defends the orthodox (Tarskian) account of logical consequence against Etchemendy's objections whilst noting the possibility of others.

Priest, Graham. Gaps and Gluts: Reply to Parsons. *Can J Phil*, 25(1), 57-66, Mr 95.

The paper is a reply to T Parsons, "True Contradictions", *Canadian Journal of Philosophy* 20 (1990), 335-53. It argues that "gap" solutions and "glut" solutions to the semantic paradoxes are not entirely dual; and where the duality breaks down, this is to the advantage of glut solutions.

Priest, Graham. Sorites and Identity. *Log Anal*, 34, 293-296, S-D 91.

Standard Sorites paradoxes can be put in a canonical form which uses only the inference of *Modus Ponens*. The paper shows that there is a structurally similar, but different, kind of Sorites paradox that uses only the inference of Transitivity of Identity. The consequences of the existence of this kind of paradox for general solutions to the Sorites paradox are briefly discussed.

Prijatelj, Andreja. Reflections on "Difficult" Embeddings. *J Phil Log*, 24(1), 71-84, F 95.

The main purpose of this note is to present "difficult" embeddings of minimal and full intuitionistic logic into classical linear logic, and to prove their soundness and faithfulness. Moreover, it is also pointed out that Girard's translation of intuitionistic logic into classical linear logic is provably equivalent to one of the translations considered in this paper.

Primoratz, Igor. The Word 'Liberty' on the Chains of Galley-Slaves: Bosanquet's Theory of the General Will. *Hist Polit Thought*, 15(2), 249-267, Sum 94.

An examination of the most elaborate statement of the general will theory. Drawing on Rousseau and Hegel, Bosanquet tries to show that the individual's 'real' will is the internalized 'general will' of the community, which makes up his/her 'higher', 'better' self. This is meant to solve the problem of political obligation: when obeying the law, I am obeying myself, and my freedom is affirmed rather than curtailed. It is argued that Bosanquet's theory fails at both main steps: it does not succeed in contrasting our 'actual' and our 'real' will in the required way, nor in identifying the latter with the 'general will' of the community. The individual will is not embedded in the community in the way Bosanquet makes it out to be, and if I have a moral obligation to obey the law, it is not grounded in the 'general will' of the community as my own 'true', 'real' will.

Principe, Walter H. "Loving Friendship According to Thomas Aquinas" in *The Nature and Pursuit of Love, Goicoechea, David (ed)*, 128-141. Buffalo, Prometheus, 1995.

Pringle, Helen. Locke's Political Sympathies. *Locke News*, 21, 135-140, 1990.

Prins, Baukje. The Ethics of Hybrid Subjects: Feminist Constructivism According to Donna Haraway. *Sci Tech Human Values*, 20(3), 352-367, Sum 95.

This article discusses the viability of a feminist constructivist approach of knowledge through the careful reading of the work of the feminist scholar and historian of science and technology, Donna Haraway. Haraway proposes an interpretation of objectivity in terms of "situated knowledges." Both the subject and the object of knowledge are endowed with the status of material-semiotic actors. By blurring the epistemological boundary between subject and object, Haraway's narratives about scientific discourse become populated with hybrid subjects/objects. The author argues that the ethics of these hybrid subjects consists of an uneasy mixture of a Nietzchean and a socialist-Christian ethic. The article concludes by setting out why Haraway's project constitutes an interesting effort to fuse postmodern insights and feminist commitments.

Prinsloo, E D. "The Relevance of Philosophy in the Quest for the Meaning of Life" in *Life, World and Meaning, Roux, A P J (ed)*, 9-29. Pretoria, Univ of S Africa, 1990.

Prior Olmos, Angel. Habermas y el universalismo moral. *Rev Filosof (Daimon)*, 7, 145-155, 1993.

The article states the relations between the discourse ethics of Habermas and the moral universalism, specially in its Kantian form. The logic of the practical discourse and the formulation of a principle of universalization interpreting as nucleus of the moral point of view constitutes the principle pieces of the intention to reformulate the Kantian ethics. The controversy between Habermas and Agnes Heller about the range of the cognitivism shows the complex and difficult relation between morality and legality. During the last years Habermas has given space to objections proceeding from the Hegelian tradition, that reduce the force of their initial pretensions and reiterate the necessity to turn back to a planning of critical theory.

Procesi, Lidia. La Funzione Terapeutica del Mito: Un Problema di Psicologia Analitica. *Stud Filosofici*, 307-320, 1991-92.

Protevi, John. *Time and Exteriority: Aristotle, Heidegger, Derrida*. Lewisburg, Bucknell Univ Pr, 1995.

Time and Exteriority examines two contemporary responses to Aristotle's time treatise. The author first develops a conceptual scheme implicit in Derrida's reading of Husserl that shows the irreducible link of time and exteriority in general. The exteriority of time is not simply space, but neither is it without relation to space; rather, an "economy of exteriority" is to be thought. The second chapter examines exteriority in Aristotle, while the third shows exteriority at work in Derrida's reading of Aristotle. The fourth and fifth examine Heidegger's readings of Aristotle. The conclusion advances a notion of generation as a field for future study of time and exteriority.

Protopapas, Maria. La Méditation Philosophique et la Logocratie Médicale chez Hippocrate. *Philosophia (Athens)*, 23-24, 155-162, 1993-94.

L'homme, depuis son apparition jusqu'à nos jours, a parcouru des differentes étapes concernant le diagnostic et le traitement des maladies. Au début, il se soigne par instinct, ensuite par dévotion et conviction aux capacités thérapeutiques des sorciers, par sa foi aux divinités, pour finir avec Hippocrate, à travers l'expérience et la méditation philosophiques, à la logocratie médicale, laquelle se forme en s'appuyant à la philosophie naturaliste et anthropocentrique. Grace à Hippocrate, la médecine devient scientifique, son aspect pourtant, s'accomplit à travers l'expérience et l'Anatomie pendant le Moyen Age, et, surtout, pendant la Renaissance. Hippocrate a été le premier à saisir le sens de l'utilité de la théorie des humeurs, selon laquelle l'être humain est composé d'âme et de corps se trouvant tout les deux en perpétuel mouvement. L'instabilité d'équilibre de ces composants provoque la maladie, tandis que leur équilibre garantie la santé. Cette théorie, en principe exprimée par Platon et universellement acceptée jusqu'à nos jours, met en question celle cartesienne, selon laquelle il y a une séparation entre l'âme et le corps. (edited)

Protopapas, Maria. Montaigne et la Valeur de la Voix (Sur Une Influence Stoïcienne dans l'écriture des Essais). *Philosophia (Athens)*, 23-24, 334-339, 1993-94.

La voix, moyen de transmission de la pensée, est pour les Stoïciens clasée parmi les vertus, et, caracerisée "fleur de la beaute". Montaigne s'appuie au modèle stoïcien du discours tout en admettant la valeur de la voix. Il fonde ainsi, sa propre théorie du langage sur celle des Stoïciens, pour lesquels les choses prennent leur nom par nature. Car, il n'y a pas d'obscénité dans le langage. Les mots sont innocents. Ils ont toujours, chez Montaigne, le dernier mot, et comme, vehicules de la pensée, leur énoncé s'accorde avec le contenu du discours qu'ils prononcent.

Proudfoot, Diane and Copeland, B Jack. Turing, Wittgenstein and the Science of the Mind. *Austl J Phil*, 72(4), 497-519, D 94.

Proulx, Robert. Le Traitement Symbolique et non Symbolique dans les Réseaux Neuronaux: Un Problème de Catégorisation. *Lekton*, 4(2), 21-35, 1994.

Proust, Joëlle. Descripteurs distaux et externalisme. *Dialectica*, 48(3-4), 249-265, 1994.

Cet article s'attaque au problème de l'indétermination fonctionnelle dans l'un de ses aspects, dit intensif, celui où un indicateur intrene peut répondre soit au stimulus proximal occasionné sur les récepteurs sensoriels par une propriété extérieure, soit au stimulus correspondant—cette propriété elle-même. Après avoir montré pourquoi la solution de Dretske ne permet pas de rendre compte principiellement de ce qui distingue les deux types de fonction rerpérsentationnelle d'un indicateur, cet article procèdè à une analyse de ce qui distingue un descripteur de stimulus proximal d'un descripteur de stimulus distal. Deux critères sont utilisés: 1) le graphe des fonctions de traitement de l'information d'entrée (soit un vecteur d'action neuronale dans l'aire cérébrale correspondante) est différent s'il s'agit d'un stimulus proximal-covariant ou distal-covariant; 2) en cas de conflit entre les informations proximales, des capacités de recalibration de l'information par le recours à une modalité sensorielle dominante sont mises en oeuvre quand le système est capable de former des descripteurs distaux. La capacité de rectifier l'information proximale pour maintenir la covariation avec la source distale de l'information constitue ainsi une condition nécessaire et suffisante de l'existence d'une représentation distale contrôlant le comportement. Plusieurs conséquences de cette définition de la distalité sont examinées du point de vue de l'approache externaliste de l'intentionnalité.

Prouvost, Géry. Les relations entre philosophie et théologie chez É Gilson et les thomistes contemporains. *Rev Thomiste*, 94(3), 413-430, Jl-S 94.

Prouvost, Géry. Lettres d'Étienne Gilson à Henri Gouhier. *Rev Thomiste*, 94(3), 460-478, Jl-S 94.

Prozesky, Martin. The Philosophical Anthropology of Alfred North Whitehead. *S Afr J Phil*, 14(2), 54-59, My 95.

The main contention in this article is that Whitehead offers important ideas about what it means to be human for a country like South Africa in a world where liberal capitalism, failed socialism and confused religious beliefs are all problematic. The first section summarizes the main ideas in Whitehead's metaphysics, especially the prominence he gives to creativity in his account of the process of the cosmos. This is followed by a second section where the ideas about what it means to be human that are implicit in his metaphysics are identified, while the third part of the article explains some important further ideas in the social philosophy contained in his main later writings. While there are problems about aspects of his work, its fertility as a liberation philosophy is nonetheless defended.

Prudovsky, Gad. Arguments from Conceivability. *Ratio*, 8(1), 63-69, Ap 95.

What can be inferred from the fact that something is, or is not, conceivable? In this paper I argue, contrary to some deflationary remarks in recent literature, that arguments which use such facts as their starting point may have significant philosophical import. I use Strawson's results from the first chapter of *Individuals* in order to show that Galileo's arguments in favor of the distinction between primary and secondary qualities, which are based on premises concerning conceivability, should not be dismissed: they are the first step towards recognizing an important conceptual truth.

Przelecki, Marian. Meanings and Ways of Reconciliation. *Dialogue Hum*, 3(3), 49-57, 1993.

Przelecki, Marian. On Some Forms of Illogic in Political Argumentation. *Dialogue Hum*, 2(1), 123-131, 1992.

I shall concentrate on two forms of "political illogic". One of them consists, roughly speaking, in improper logical structure of the argument, the other—in improper epistemic attitude of the arguer. In both cases we have to do with an attempt to arrive at an unduly strong conclusion in political debate. Logic is what provides some means for discrediting such unwarranted claims. (edited)

Przelecki, Marian. Platonism as a Common Element of Different Religious Axiologies. *Dialogue Hum*, 2(2), 27-31, 1992.

Pu, Pang. Recollecting Professor Feng's 1957 Lectures in the Spring. *J Chin Phil*, 21(3-4), 399-405, S-D 94.

Under the "open out" (*kaifang*) policy of 1957 in China, the celebrated Chinese philosopher Feng Youlan returned to the lecture hall in Beijing University. As responding to "*kaifang*," Feng selected several core sections from *Zhuang Zi* and elaborated from the "carefree realm," the "neither absolute nor relative realm" to the ultimate Daoist standing—spontaneity (*ziran*). Feng also lectured on Mencius's "nourishing the flood-like energy-matter" (*yang haoran zhi qi*), for it fills space between Heaven and Earth and all things are complete in oneself. The implication of the lectures assumes that Feng's universal concern (*Tian Di*) transcends the moral one (*daode*). Ironically, after five lectures, Feng no longer had the Daoist-like ease and the technical ways in speaking.

Puhl, Klaus. State of the Art. *Protosoz*, 6, 304-313, 1994.

Puligandla, Ramakrishna. The Relativity of Scientific Views of Reality. *Darshana Int*, 32(1/125), 22-31, Ja 92.

Pullen, J M. Malthus on Colonization and Economic Development: A Comparison with Adam Smith. *Utilitas*, 6(2), 243-266, N 94.

Pullman, Daryl. Can Virtue Be Bought?. *Teach Phil*, 17(4), 321-333, D 94.

This paper likens the teaching of applied ethics and the related field of ethics consultation, to a production model in which a specific commodity is produced and sold. In this case the commodity is virtue, and the teachers and consultants are the entrepreneurs of values. It is argued that the political, economic and educational structures in which we live and work often force us to "market our product" in this manner. However, values are not commodities to be bought; rather they emerge out of the growth process by which we come to understand ourselves both individually and corporately. If ethicists are to retain a vital role in this process, the production model under which we currently operate will need to give way to one more conducive to growth.

Puló de Ortiz, Mercedes. "Acerca de la Filosofía en Latinoamérica" in *Temas Actuales de Filosofía, Palacios, María Julia (ed)*, 505-512. Buenos Aires, Univ Nacional Salta, 1993.

For Francisco Miró Quesada the Latin American philosophy borns by artificial insemination, that means the philosophers are mentally steriles and should get "imported semen" in order to procreate. It's about an "inferiority complex", created and fed from the academic structures by different reasons. So those who here called themselves "philosophers" were resigned to be receivers and transmisors of theories an foreing speculations. Where the Latin Americans were prolific is in the "thought", there is where we must recuperate that belongs to us without having care to borrow ideas that annul our half freed identity, being careful in sclerossig regionalisms.

Punzo, Vincent A and Meara, Naomi M. The Virtues of a Psychology of Personal Morality. *J Theor Phil Psych*, 13(1), 25-39, Spr 93.

The field of moral psychology has been confined to the study of social morality; resulting in a nearly exclusive focus on the primary other-regarding virtue of justice. An understanding of personal morality, with its concern with self-regarding virtues and the dynamics of intimate relationships, is needed to complement this approach. The importance of personal morality issues to moral psychology is foreshadowed in Gilligan's caring ethic. This paper expands on Gilligan's schematic portrayal in order to provide a more complete theoretical understanding of personal morality. Social and personal morality are contrasted on five salient issues to highlight their differences and interrelatedness.

Purviance, Susan M. Infertility Treatment for Postmenopausal Patients: An Equity-Based Approach. *Ethics Behavior*, 5(1), 15-24, 1995.

This article examines two questions pertaining to the extension of infertility treatment to postmenopausal women. First, what concepts and principles of infertility practice apply to assisted reproduction for the postmenopausal patient? Second, what role should these concepts play in the development of an ethical justification for extending women's reproductive lives past the menopausal boundary? The argument offered here supports their claim to infertility services on the basis of the formal principle of justice, which requires that similar cases be treated similarly. The cases of many postmenopausal patients are argued to be relevantly similar to classes of patients who already receive assistance in reproduction.

Putallaz, François-Xavier. Pourquoi penser au Moyen Age?. *Rev Theol Phil*, 126(3), 243-252, 1994.

Cette étude du livre d'André de Muralt, *L'enjeu de la philosophie médiévale*, met en évidence les idées centrales de la thèse: l'intuition historiographique majeure consiste en la découverte de structures de pensée qui charpentent la totalité de l'histoire des doctrines. Quant à l'idée philosophique qui sert de fil conducteur, elle réside dans le concept d'*esse objectivum*. L'étude des divers modes de causalité (Duns Scot, Thomas d'Aquin, Occam) montre les divergences irréductibles existant entre ces pensées. Cette manière de pratiquer la philosophie médiévale, aux antipodes des projets historicistes contemporains, ne se présente pas comme une histoire de la philosophie; c'en est l'intérêt et la limite.

Putman, Daniel. In Defence of Aristotelian Honour. *Philosophy*, 70(272), 286-288, Ap 95.

In response to a recent article by Christopher Cordner this paper argues that the appearance of the virtuous person before others is a critical part of virtue. In defending this, the paper also argues that Aristotle's concept of honor for virtue is as significant today as it was in ancient Athens.

Putman, Daniel. The Primacy of Virtue in Children's Moral Development. *J Moral Educ*, 24(2), 175-183, 1995.

The concept of levels of moral maturity in psychology focuses on character formation in children's development. Virtue theory in ethics, with its concern for character, can be helpful in pointing out the ethical implications of much of the current work with children. This paper ties together several concepts in virtue theory with the current information on children's moral development. The paper argues for the usefulness of some very ancient ethical concepts.

Putnam, Hilary. "Comments and Replies" in *Reading Putnam, Clark, Peter (ed)*, 242-295. Cambridge, Blackwell, 1995.

Putnam, Hilary. "Peirce's Continuum" in *Peirce and Contemporary Thought: Philosophical Inquiries, Ketner, Kenneth Laine (ed)*, 1-22. New York, Fordham Univ Pr, 1995.

Putnam, Hilary. "Select Bibliography of the Publications of Hilary Putnam" in *Reading Putnam, Clark, Peter (ed)*, 296-299. Cambridge, Blackwell, 1995.

Putnam, Hilary. Pragmatism. *Proc Aris Soc*, 95, 291-306, 1994-95.

Putnam, Hilary. *Pragmatism: An Open Question*. Cambridge, Blackwell, 1995.

Putnam, Hilary. Pragmatismus und Verifikationismus. *Deut Z Phil*, 43(2), 219-231, 1995.

Putnam, Hilary. The Idea of Science. *Midwest Stud Phil*, 15, 57-64, 1990.

This essay analyzes the difficulties which arise when we try to treat the notion of a "science" as if it were a precise one. Some of them arise from the informality of the "scientific method" itself, others from disputes as to what counts as "observation" (can *Intentional* notions be used in an observation report?), while still others arise because we are divided as to what we want science to be. The indeterminacy issue is used as an illustration. (This essay has been collected in the author's *Words and Life*.)

Putnam, Hilary and Albert, David Z. Further Adventures of Wigner's Friend. *Topoi*, 14(1), 17-22, Mr 95.

Pycior, Helena M. "Peirce at the Intersection of Mathematics and Philosophy" in *Peirce and Contemporary Thought: Philosophical Inquiries, Ketner, Kenneth Laine (ed)*, 132-145. New York, Fordham Univ Pr, 1995.

Pylyshyn, Zenon W and Fodor, Jerry A. "Connectionism and Cognitive Architecture: A Critical Analysis" in *Connectionism: Debates on Psychological Explanation, Macdonald, Cynthia (ed)*, 90-163. Cambridge, Blackwell, 1995.

Quante, Michael. "Wann ist ein Mensch tot?" Bemerkungen zum Streit um den menschlichen Tod. *Z Phil Forsch*, 49(2), 167-193, Ap-Je 95.

While in Anglo-American bioethics defenders of "higher-brain-death" criteria criticize the "whole-brain-death" criterion as conceptually and ethically inadequate in Germany the general conception of "brain-death" is hotly discussed by critics of organ transplantation. In this paper a general definition of "death" is suggested and its main features are explicated. Then it is argued that for human beings the "whole-brain" criterion is adequate. Accounts which regard "death" as a moral concept are criticized (Veatch, Hoffman). Lamb's biological theory and Gervais's ontological solution also are criticized as inadequate. It is argued that there is no alternative between death of the human being and death of the person. The main argument is that 1)"Person" is no natural-kind-term and 2) Person-making characteristics are biological features of human beings, too.

Quante, Michael. Die Identität der Person: Facetten eines Problems. *Phil Rundsch*, 42(1), 35-59, Mr 95.

The main aim of this paper is threefold: 1) the main strands in the post-Parfitian discussion about personal identity are analyzed; 2) the relation between the ontological and the practical dimension of personal identity are discussed; and 3) the relation between personal identity and authenticity or individuality is discussed. It is argued that in ontological accounts elements of the practical category "person" are always present. The ontological basis is captured best by the natural-kind-term "human being" which gives causal constrains for diachronic identity. This basis underdetermines our practical notion of personhood with its ethical, social and aesthetical aspects.

Quartim de Moraes, Joao. A Investigaçao sobre o Tempo na "Física" de Aristóteles. *Manuscrito*, 17(2), 97-134, O 94.

The investigation of time in Aristotle's *Physics* begins by asking whether it is a being or a nonbeing. The focus of the problem is "now", the only part of time which exists. However, to conceive of it as a *part* of time implies attributing to its continuity, and hence a decomposition into the "before" (which no longer exists) and the "after" (which does not yet exist). Conceiving of "now" as an *atom* of *duration* implies negating time considered as a *successive* continuum. Both hypotheses lead to *aporías*. The question, 'what is time?' already leads to a result which, although it is negative (since we cannot accept either of the current conceptions of the nature of time), opens the way to an understanding of the essence of time. It is neither movement, not without movement. The assertion of an essential connection between time and movement marks the step from negative dialectic (the identification of a theoretical impasse) to dialectic (the discovery of the conditions and principles of analytic definition).

Quay, Paul M. Final Causality in Contemporary Physics. *Ultim Real Mean*, 18(1), 3-19, Mr 95.

Final causality, understood as the purpose of something or someone to achieve a goal, is a philosophical category rarely used in contemporary physics. And yet the phenomena of randomness, and entanglement in quantum interactions as well as the experiments of A Aspect and P Grangier (1987. Hyperfine Interactions 37.3) point to final causality and to quantum theory as reality description rather than merely a useful instrument.

Queraltó Moreno, Ramón. "Does Technology 'Construct' Scientific Reality?" in *Philosophy of Technology in Spanish Speaking Countries, Mitcham, Carl (ed)*, 167-172. Dordrecht, Kluwer, 1994.

This work raises whether the technification of scientific procedures implies nowadays an artificial construction of scientific object: to what extent technification becomes a means of scientific objectivity? The question is analyzed by explaining the specific traits of scientific knowledge at the end of modernity. To elucidate the quest, the technical factor is considered as a condition of the possibility of scientific knowledge. So, this notion is especially developed in a new sense according to the present situation of science. This perspective makes possible to harmonize the necessity of scientific technification and the epistemological exigence of objectivity.

Queraltó Moreno, Ramón. Teoría metafísica de las propensiones y universo abierto en la filosofía de Popper. *Pensamiento*, 197(50), 235-252, My-Ag 94.

Se analiza en este aticulo el contenido y orígenes científicos y filosóficos de la teoría de las propensiones de Popper, mostrando cómo se constituye en base fundamental de la concepción cosmológica del "universo abierto". En la primera parte se desarrolian los fundamentos de la teoría propensivista, muy en especial la génesis de la noción de propensión física. De esta forma se obtienen en la segunda parte, la explicación de algunos caracteres estructurales de la imagen del mundo físico. Finalmente, la tercera parte expone la teoría del universo abierto con referencia a su vez a la teoría de los tres mundos de Popper.

Quesada, Daniel. Es la Matemática un lenguaje?. *Rev Filosof (Spain)*, 4(5), 31-43, 1991.

Quiggin, John. Economic Choice in Generalized Expected Utility Theory. *Theor Decis*, 38(2), 153-171, Mr 95.

Generalized expected utility models have enjoyed considerable success in explaining observed choices under uncertainty. However, there has been only limited progress in deriving comparative static results. This paper presents a general framework which permits the incorporation of a wide range of generalized expected utility models, but is sufficiently powerful to permit the derivation of comparative static results. The central idea is to represent preferences by the expected utility of a transformed probability distribution.

Quijano, Francisco. Sobre la Experiencia y el Conocimiento del Alma. *Analogia*, 4(1), 105-129, 1990.

Quillian, M Ross. A Content-Independent Explanation of Science's Effectiveness. *Phil Sci*, 61(3), 429-448, S 94.

This paper proposes an explanation in terms of three kinds of freedom, first for the special efficacy of science in general and then for why such efficacy has been more impressive in the natural than the social sciences. This explanation thus complements "post-positivist" interpretations of science which argue that science's effectiveness cannot be accounted for by fundamental epistemic differences from other kinds of discourse. My explanation tries to say what *is* responsible for science's effectiveness, in purely nonepistemic, sociological terms. All of the three kinds of freedom have so far been denied to most other forums, including in particular nations' populations taken overall. And one of these freedoms, while now allowed to the natural sciences, it still denied to the social sciences.

Quine, W V. "Peirce's Logic" in *Peirce and Contemporary Thought: Philosophical Inquiries, Ketner, Kenneth Laine (ed)*, 23-31. New York, Fordham Univ Pr, 1995.

Quine, W V. Responses. *Inquiry*, 37(4), 495-505, D 94.

Quine, W V. *Selected Logic Papers: Enlarged Edition*. Cambridge, Harvard Univ Pr, 1995.

Quinn, Andrew. Rationalisme et Éthique Naturalisée. *Philosopher*, 16, 101-121, 1994.

Quinn, Carol and McKee, Patrick L. Temporal Gestalt: A Concept for Quantum Theory. *Method Sci*, 27(4), 235-243, 1994.

Quinn, Philip. "Moral Objections to Pascalian Wagering" in *Gambling on God: Essays on Pascal's Wager, Jordan, Jeffrey (ed)*, 61-81. Lanham, Rowman & Littlefield, 1994.

This paper discusses three moral objections to Pascal's Wager. They are that one corrupts oneself, fails in one's duty to others by contributing to rendering them credulous, and makes oneself complicit in a wicked system of religious practice if one argues in Pascalian Wagering. A defense of Pascalian Wagering against these objections is offered. It involves specifying epistemic and theological conditions in which one could make Pascal's Wager without corrupting oneself, acting contrary to a duty to others, or becoming complicit in a wicked system of practice.

Quinn, Philip L. Ecclesioethics: Theologically Neutral But Morally Toothless. *Prof Ethics*, 3(2), 57-70, Sum 94.

This paper is a critical examination of the methodology proposed in Margaret P Battin's *Ethics in the Sanctuary* for the ethical analysis of the practices of organized religion. It argues that her insistence on theological neutrality in such analysis has the consequence that it can at most show that religious practices are morally problematic and cannot show that they are morally unacceptable or wrong to engage in. It concludes with the suggestion that theological neutrality be abandoned because it renders the ethical critique of religious practices morally toothless.

Quinney, Laura. Weiskel's Sublime and the Impasse of Knowledge. *Phil Lit*, 18(2), 309-319, O 94.

Thomas Weiskel's *The Romantic Sublime* (1976) helped to inaugurate the demystifying analysis of the sublime in contemporary literary theory. His tendentious readings of Kant, Wordsworth and Shelley, who are said to be "naive", betray the limitations of demystifying analysis, in which creativity is equated with innocence and insight with disillusion. This equation results in a bias toward skepticism and a covert attraction to tragic sense.

Quintanilla Navarro, Ignacio. Ortega y la importancia de meditar la técnica. *Dialogo Filosof*, 10(2), 209-223, My-Ag 94.

Tradicionalmente el discurso filosófico sobre la técnica se presenta como corolario de un discurso ético, político o epistemológico más general. El análisis de la doctrina orteguiana de la técnica, además de destacar su extraordinario vigor y originalidad, nos invita a contemplar el evento técnico desde un mayor nivel de radicalidad. La noción de téchne no sólo no es subsidiaria de las de *physis, polis o episteme* ni subsumible en las de *trabajo, instrumento o interés*, sino que es, en cierto sentido, mucho más básica que todas ellas al conformar junto con la *theoría*—como correlato eminente e ineludible de la misma—el fundamento original de la razón. Será, así, precisamente desde una meditación de la técnica, desde donde habrá que recobrar y esclarecer hoy el sentido primordial de la *theoría*.

Quinton, Anthony. Homosexuality. *Philosophy*, 37(Supp), 197-211, 1994.

Quirk, Michael J. Just War in the Balkans?. *Int J Applied Phil*, 9(1), 21-26, Sum-Fall 94.

Rabinowicz, Wlodek and Segerberg, Krister. Actual Truth, Possible Knowledge. *Topoi*, 13(2), 101-115, S 94.

D Edgington has suggested that Fitch's paradox of verificationism can be avoided if we formulate verificationism using the actuality operator: $A\theta \rightarrow \Diamond KA\theta$. However, as long as actuality and knowledge are interpreted in terms of a fixed actual world and an epistemic accessibility relation between worlds, respectively, this proposal still yields an absurd conclusion that all actual truths are known. To avoid this problem, we develop a two-dimensional semantics, in which each formula is evaluated at a world with respect to another world chosen as a perspective. The knowledge operator is then interpreted in terms of an accessibility relation between pairs of worlds, modeling two sources of epistemic uncertainty: one concerning the world being described and the other the world constituting the perspective.

Rabinowicz, Wlodzimierz and Lindström, Sten. The Ramsey Test Revisited. *Theoria*, 58(2-3), 131-182, 1992.

Rabossi, Eduardo. "Esquemas Conceptuales: Relativismo y Ontología" in *Temas Actuales de Filosofía, Palacios, Maria Julia (ed)*, 35-46. Buenos Aires, Univ Nacional Salta, 1993.

The aim of my paper is to relativize recent discussions on metaphysical and internal realism, conceptual relativism and incommensurability: there is no "fact of the matter" but just tactical decisions about how to connect the cognitive, linguistic and ontological levels, where to place objectivity and what to say about truth. I describe and compare four "theoretical patterns" that, curiously enough, supersede each other in a sort of circular way. The first pattern has a Whorfian origin, the second a metaphysical realistic bent, the third a Kantian look and the fourth a sort of Hegelian flavor. The final section is devoted to a discussion of Davidson's argument concerning conceptual schemes and conceptual relativism.

Rabossi, Eduardo A and Stigol, Nora and González, María Cristina. "Los Seminarios en la Enseñanza de la Filosofía" in *Temas Actuales de Filosofía, Palacios, María Julia (ed)*, 521-524. Buenos Aires, Univ Nacional Salta, 1993.

Seminars as successful learning situations for philosophical goals are considered. It is mentioned some special features in our university classrooms that hinder teachers from getting the main aim: to learn to philosophize. Strategies used during a seminar are described: a preparatory stage and a discussion stage. The experience is evaluated.

Rachkov, P A. "The End of History" as a Sociosophical Problem. *Russian Stud Phil*, 33(2), 9-26, Fall 94.

Racionero, Quintín. "Politische Aufklärung und Staatstheorie bei Leibniz" in *Das geistige Erbe Europas, Buhr, Manfred (ed)*, 517-539. Napoli, Vivarium, 1994.

Racionero, Quintín. Heidegger urbanizado (Notas para una crítica de la hermenéutica). *Rev Filosof (Spain)*, 4(5), 65-131, 1991.

Racionero, Quintín. Ilustración política y teoría del estado en Leibniz (Materiales para una reflexión contemporánea). *G Metaf*, 16(1-2), 155-178, Ja-Ag 94.

Radbruch, Knut. "Was kann die heutige Mathematik von Schelling lernen?" in *Schelling und die Selbstorganisation, Heuser-Kessler, Marie-Luise (ed)*, 55-72. Berlin, Duncker Humblot, 1994.

There has been a renaissance of the philosophy of mathematics during the last years. Consequently the writings of the standard philosophers of the 18th and 19th century have to be studied again, since they had included mathematics in their thinking. Schelling's opinion of the identity of universals and particulars in mathematical entities is an ingenious alternative to Kant's position. This article is to prove Schelling's idea is a promising approach to the late 20th century philosophy of mathematics.

Radcliffe, Dana M. Hanfling on Neighbour Love. *Philosophy*, 69(270), 497-502, O 94.

Oswald Hanfling claims that the precept, "Love your neighbor as yourself," is both central to morality and logically incapable of guiding conduct. Its moral importance, he argues, must derive from nonprescriptive uses, such as reminding us of the value of love in motivating benevolent acts and as a component of happiness. I show that Hanfling's interpretation fails to account for the moral significance he says we generally take the injunction to have. Further, I point out that the alleged logical difficulties vanish when we see how the principle is interpreted in the moral traditions in which it typically functions.

Radcliffe, Dana M. Nondoxastic Faith: Audi on Religious Commitment. *Int J Phil Relig*, 37(2), 73-86, Ap 95.

In several recent articles, Robert Audi argues that there are important kinds of theistic religious faith—including possibly a kind of Christian faith—which do not entail substantive theistic beliefs. Such "nondoxastic" faith, he says, can make one a "person of faith" even if one's cognitive attitude toward God's existence is weaker than belief. Audi identifies three sorts of nondoxastic faith, and I argue 1) that he fails to show that two of them (propositional and attitudinal) are in fact nondoxastic and 2) that the third (volitional) does not qualify as Christian faith.

Radden, Jennifer. Recent Criticism of Psyhicatric Nosology: A Review. *Phil Psychiat Psych*, 1(3), 193-199, S 94.

The advent of DSM-IV has stimulated renewed discussion of psychiatric classification. Such discussion is philosophically sophisticated and far-ranging, responsive to post-Kuhnian philosophy of science, to feminist critiques of mental health norms, and to multicultural perspectives. As "weak normativists" (Agich), today's critics are committed to understanding the interplay between descriptive and evaluative elements, clinical facts and cultural constructs, in psychiatric norms and categories, and are alert to the question of what purposes and whose interests are and should be served by such systems. They offer alternative taxonomic principles as well as analyses and revisions of traditional classificatory concepts and systems.

Radden, Jennifer. Second Thoughts: Revoking Decisions Over One's Own Future. *Phil Phenomenol Res*, 54(4), 787-801, D 94.

We are invited by a standard alignment; advance directives are morally binding while traditional identity notions prevail, not when we adopt a parfitian metaphysics. But exotic metaphysics aside, there are more reasons to question the authority of advance directives than are customarily recognized. Overemphasis on a central expression of autonomy (our ability to plan for the future and adhere to that plan) and on easy cases, have led theorists to neglect an equally central expression of autonomy in our ability to change our minds. The tension between these aspects of autonomy is regularly and vividly illustrated where marginally competent mental patients struggle to revoke earlier decisions.

Radden, Jennifer. Shame and Blame: The Self through Time and Change. *Dialogue (Canada)*, 34(1), 61-74, Wint 95.

Radder, Hans. Repliek. *Kennis Methode*, 18(2-3), 198-201, 1994.

Radder, Hans. Wetenschapsfilosofie en wetenschapsonderzoek: op weg naar een vruchtbare lat-relatie?. *Kennis Methode*, 18(2-3), 157-168, 1994.

Radford, Colin. Fiction, Pity, Fear, and Jealousy. *J Aes Art Crit*, 53(1), 71-75, Wint 95.

Radford, Colin. MacColl, Russell, the Existential Import of Propositions, and the Null-Class. *Phil Quart*, 45(180), 316-331, Jl 95.

Radrizzani, Ives. Der Übergang von der *Grundlage* zur *Wissenschaftslehre nova methodo*. *Fichte-Studien*, 6, 355-365, 1994.

The *Wissenschaftslehre nova methodo*, second version of the Fichtean foundation of transcendental philosophy, goes further in the development of the principles by bringing the conditions of possibility of the first presentation. The main innovation is the introduction of the theory of intersubjectivity, in Fichte's eye the key not only to this work, but to all the critical idealism. Although this innovation is perfectly compatible with the transcendental philosophy practiced in the *Grundlage der gesammten Wissenschaftslehre*, it introduces a metaphysical point of view, which could explain the transition to the philosophy of the Absolute.

Radrizzani, Ives. Ist Fichtes Modell des Kosmopolitismus pluralistisch?. *Fichte-Studien*, 2, 7-19, 1990.

Radtke, Frank (ed) and Hasselberg, Erwin (ed). *Hegels "Wissenschaft der Logik": Eine internationale Bibliographie ihrer Rezeption im XX Jahrhundert*. Vienna, Passagen, 1993.

Die Rezeption der Philosophie G W F Hegels hat sich besonders in unserem Jahrhundert immer wieder als ein Prisma der geistigen Hauptströmungen ausgewiesen. Mit der bisher umfangreichsten Bibliographie zur Rezeption der *logischen Begrifflichkeit* Hegels wurde eine Möglichkeit geschaffen, die auftretenden Defizite im internationalen Forschungsvergleich weiter zu beseitigen. Neben dem Vorteil eines breiten, nach Ländern geordneten Überblicks—China, Deutschland (Band 1), Frankreich, Grossbritannien und USA, Israel, Italien, Japan, Jugoslawien, Polen, Portugal (Band 2), Russland, Spanien, Ungarn und weitere Länder (Band 3)—sind dem überwiegenden Teil der 2600 Titel kurze bis ausführliche Inhaltsangaben beigegeben, basierend auf umfangreichen Recherchen und Übersetzungen.

Radtke, H Lorraine (ed) and Stam, Henderikus J (ed). *Power/Gender*. Newbury Park, Sage, 1994.

This is a multidisciplinary collection focussed on the interrelations of power and gender. Some chapters explicate the gendered nature of power, while others analyze how the social construction of gender reflects the workings of power. Both micro- and macro-processes are discussed. The central thesis is that gender and power are inextricably connected such that a full understanding of one can only be achieved through consideration of the other. Drawing from a variety of theoretical frameworks and definitions of power, the contributors include R Connell, Marilyn French, Wendy Hollway, and Jean Lipman-Blumen.

Radwanska-Williams, Joanna. The Problem of Iconicity. *J Prag*, 22(1), 23-36, Jl 94.

The problem of iconicity involves a critique of de Saussure's principle of the arbitrariness of the linguistic sign. De Saussure himself admitted that the linguistic system is relatively motivated or limited in its arbitrariness. The salient question for iconicity is similarity: both the similarity between the signifier and the signified, and similarity within the context of the linguistic system. The iconic nature of metaphor involves a latent similarity or parallelism toward which the metaphor points, which can be interpreted, and which is beheld as an image in the mind's eye. Thus, metaphor is both the most abstract and the most concrete instance of iconicity, and is a bridge between language and the world. (edited)

Rae, Murray A. Kierkegaard and the Historians. *Int J Phil Relig*, 37(2), 87-102, Ap 95.

Rafalko, Robert J. Remaking the Corporation: The 1991 US Sentencing Guidelines. *J Bus Ethics*, 13(8), 625-636, Ag 94.

This is an essay about the philosophical and practical problems associated with the concept of punishment for corporations that have grievously broken the law. It is specifically an essay about the special incentives that the US Governments has put in place to encourage American corporations to create comprehensive ethics programs and observe them faithfully. First, I will look at the sorts of obstacles to effective punishment of recalcitrant corporations that eventually prompted extraordinary measures by the US Government. Then I will present a detailed description of the Federal Sentencing Guidelines which took effect on November 1, 1991, describe what they entail, examine what purposes for which they were intended and question how likely they will be to accomplish their objectives. Finally, we will raise the question whether such policies will help further corporate social responsibility and ethical conduct in the workplace.

Raffel, Stanley. Identity, Self-Reflection and the Problem of Validating Standards. *Hist Human Sci*, 7(2), 65-81, My 94.

Raffelt, Albert. Blaise Pascals "Discours sur la religion": Zu einer neueren Ausgabe der "Pensées". *Theol Phil*, 69(3), 402-410, 1994.

The article gives a critical evaluation of the editorial principles applied by Emmanuel Martineau in his edition of the >Pensées< by Blaise Pascal (B Pascal: Discours sur la religion... Paris 1992).

Raffman, Diana. Commentary: Transvaluationism: Comments on Horgan. *S J Phil*, 33(Supp), 127-132, 1995.

Raftopoulos, Athanasse. Was Cartesian Science Ever Meant to Be A Priori? A Comment on Hatfield. *Phil Sci*, 62(1), 150-160, Mr 95.

In a recent article G Hatfield claims that Descartes for a certain time thought a purely a priori science to be possible. Hatfield's evidence consists of his reading of the Cartesian method in the *Regulae* and of a letter to Mersenne, written in May 1632. I argue that Hatfield misinterprets the Cartesian method and Descartes's claim in the letter to Mersenne. I first show that the latter does not argue for an a priori science. Then, I show that the method of the *Regulae* is not a priori. Finally, I propose a reading of Descartes's letter.

Ragghianti, Renzo. Spigolature Crociane: Il Centenario della "Revue de Métaphysique". Con Lettere di Croce ed Altri e una Pagina Crociana Dimenticata. *G Crit Filosof Ital*, 74(1), 65-98, Ja-Ap 95.

Rahman, Lutfor. Act-Utilitarianism and Coordination: A Critique of Allan Gibbard's View. *Indian Phil Quart*, 21(4), 307-315, O 94.

Rai, A K. Paksata in Navya-Nyaya. *J Indian Phil*, 23(1), 1-8, Mr 95.

Rai, Chhaya. A Debate on African Philosophy. *Darshana Int*, 32(3/127), 71-81, Jl 92.

The need to debate is felt due to the dilemma in which most of the contemporary African philosophers—professionals as well as nonacademics—find themselves. On the one hand, they accept western concept of philosophy as the paradigm and on the other hand, they feel that Africa, has always had a popular and mythical philosophy, and that such a philosophy needs to be peeled off from the African cultural tradition, proverbs, past linguistic structures. Hountondji represents the first view while E A Ruch and N Otakpor represent the second. The paper attracts attention towards some of the arguments, presented in support of their views by Hountondji, Ruch and Otakpor and concludes that to end the debate interapreters of African Philosophy must differentiate various usages and senses of the term 'Philosophy', i.e., as a discipline, as system, as living philosophy or as philosophyizing. They must accept that philosophizing is basic to philosophy and it essentially comprises intuitive insights, contemplation, speculation, rational procedures such as criticism and reflections and also creative imagination.

Rainbow, Bernarr. The Challenge of History. *Phil Music Educ Rev*, 3(1), 43-51, Spr 95.

Current disenchantment with historically based studies is being replaced by realisation that knowledge of the past is useful when we come to think about the present. This essay seeks to pursue that concept by selecting two strategic periods when music education was vigorously developed in the past and then posing two questions; *How* and *Why* was music taught at this particular time? The exercise exposes inadequacy in the provision of basic music training at primary/elementary level as a current international defect and emphasises the need for teachers and policy-makers alike to develop historical awareness.

Rajan, Tilottama. "Language, Music, and the Body" in *Intersections: Nineteenth-Century Philosophy and Contemporary Theory, Rajan, Tilottama (ed)*, 147-169. Albany, SUNY Pr, 1995.

This essay looks at the relationship between Nietzsche and Julie Kristwa in terms of the role played by the figures of music and the body in their work. It locates in Kristwa's work a demonstration that intersects with phenomenology, and traces its genealogy back to Nietzsche so as to delynonymise "deconstruction" and "post-structuralism".

Rajan, Tilottama (ed) and Clark, David L (ed). *Intersections: Nineteenth-Century Philosophy and Contemporary Theory*. Albany, SUNY Pr, 1995.

This collection of essays defines "theory" as a field that emerges after Kant, and attempts to reconceive nineteenth-century and contemporary theory through each other. The collection thus looks at intersections between contemporary theory and a number of nineteenth-century thinkers: Hegel, Schelling, Nietzsche, Schopenhauer, Kierkegaard. Contributors include Tilottama Rajan, David Clark, John Sallis, Christopher Noris, Stanley Corngold, Judith Butler and others.

Ralston, David A and Giacalone, Robert A and Terpstra, Robert H. Ethical Perceptions of Organizational Politics: A Comparative Evaluation of American and Hong Kong Managers. *J Bus Ethics*, 13(12), 989-999, D 94.

This paper presents a cross-cultural analysis of ethics with US and Hong Kong Chinese managers as subjects. These managers were given the Strategies of Upward Influence instrument and asked to evaluate the ethics of using various political strategies to attain influence within their organizations. Differences were found between Hong Kong and US managers on a variety of dimensions, indicating important differences between these two groups on their perceptions of ethical behavior. In the paper, we identify potential reasons for the findings, and suggest directions for future work in this area.

Ram Sharma, Sri. Does Mimamsa Treat the Theory of *Karma* as a *Purvapaksa*?: Two Responses to the Query. *J Indian Counc Phil Res*, 12(1), 164-167, S-D 94.

Ram-Prasad, C. Is the Experienced World a Determinate Totality? Vācaspati on *Anyathakhyativada* and *Anirvacaniyakhyativada*. *J Indian Counc Phil Res*, 12(1), 107-132, S-D 94.

This paper looks at the examination of erroneous cognition in the work "Bhamati" of the 9th century Indian, Vacaspati. The analysis of error is for the purpose of establishing the relationship between subject and object, and eventually an ontology, by asking the question: what is the metaphysical status and the nature of the object of an erroneous cognition? Vacaspati gives a critical analysis of a realist theory of independent objects, and argues that a logical analysis of error suggests a nonrealist metaphysics of indeterminate objects.

Ram-Prasad, C. The Provisional World: Existenthood, Causal Efficiency, and Sri Harsa. *J Indian Phil*, 23(2), 179-221, Je 95.

By analyzing the concept of 'existenthood' (satta) as a generic state, the realist metaphysics of the Indian Nyaya school is reconstructed. This state is equated with causal efficiency; objects of a realist ontology are essentially causal objects so construed. The Advaita philosopher, Sri Harsa (12th century), discerns two senses of the notion of 'existenthood' and explores the tensions between them and the consequent problems. Sri Harsa's own reinterpretation of the realist account of objects and causal efficiency is developed and the crucial cognitive constrains he places on this account is presented as the exemplification of a nonrealist metaphysics.

Ramachandran, Murali. Methodological Reflections on Two Kripkean Strategies. *Proc Aris Soc*, 95, 67-81, 1994-95.

I explore Kripke's defense of Russell's theory of descriptions against the charge that the existence of referential and attributive uses of descriptions reflects a *semantic* ambiguity. I argue that Kripke's argument is not so forceful if we appeal to the *prevalence* (rather than merely the existence) of referential uses to back-up the ambiguity thesis. I then consider Kripke's use of a similar strategy to argue *against* a semantic theory (his 'schmidentity' argument); I argue that this offensive line of reasoning is unsound and attempt to locate its error. Finally I draw a moral regarding the semantic/pragmatics distinction.

Ramachandran, V S and Churchland, P S. "Filling In: Why Dennett is Wrong" in *Dennett and his Critics, Dahlbom, Bo (ed)*, 28-52. Cambridge, Blackwell, 1995.

Ramaley, Kenneth. Preventing Tonkitis: A Defense of Belnap. *Conference*, 3(2), 29-37, Fall 92.

Rambachan, Anantanand. Response to Professor Arvind Sharma. *Phil East West*, 44(4), 721-725, O 94.

In his feature review of my book, *Accomplishing the Accomplished: The Vedas as a Source of Valid Knowledge in Sankara*, in "Philosophy East and West" 43 (4) (October 1993), Prof A Sharma contends that Sankara treats personal experience, like the scripture, as a means of valid knowledge for the attainment of the absolute. This article questions Prof Sharma's conclusion by arguing that he overlooks the context of Sankara's discussion on *Brahma-sutra* I.i.2 and mistakenly equates an opponent's arguments with Sankara in *Brahma-sutra* II.i.4.

Rametta, Gaetano. Quintuplicatà e Individualità: La Construzione dell'io in WL 1807. *Daimon Rev Filosof*, 9, 115-134, 1994.

The main topic in Rametta's essay is the transcendental notion of individuality as it appears in Fichte's doctrine of science in 1807. In WL strictu sensu Fichte sets the problem of individuality within his twofold concept of quintuplicity. On the one hand, quintuplicity is seen as the fundamental structure of intuition, i.e., as the necessary law to which life is submitted in his appearing. On the other hand, quintuplicity is opened by the free act through which the thinking I project itself on that appearance. Fichte sets the institution of individuality in connection to these five possible kinds of vision (Einsicht). Thus he indicates five worlds constituting the original projections of the I and, at the same time, the shapes through which life collects itself as concrete image of its actual becoming. In this perspective, the Fichtean doctrine of Einsicht takes an ontological meaning and not a merely existential one. The possibility for the I of constituting itself as individuality is the condition without the absolute couldn't appear as life.

Ramírez, Edgar Roy. Tecnología y calidad según Robert M Pirsig. *Rev Filosof (Costa Rica)*, 32(77), 51-59, Jl 94.

Robert M Pirsig falls within the literary tradition of philosophy of technology initiated by Samuel Butler. This paper explores some interrelationships among the concepts of "technology", "rationality" and "quality" and some of the conceptual tensions as present in his book *Zen and the Art of Motorcycle Maintenance*.

Ramírez Luque, Isabel. La Reivindicación de la Sabiduría Poética en G B Vico y A Machado. *Cuad Vico*, 1, 69-80, 1991.

Nevertheless the differences between Vico's fantastic universals and Machado's universals of sentiments, both of them are two ways to vindicate the universality (claimed by rationalism as an exclusive sphere of rationality of concepts) in order to get other ways of human thinking as fantasy or imagination. In such a way it is possible to blaze a trail in order to achieve a kind of poetical wisdom whose foundation is a free manner of reflective thought such a thing is not tied to the discipline of any sort of abstract logic.

Ramón, Rafael. Al-Fârâbî: El Concepto del Ser. *Rev Filosof (Spain)*, 7(11), 27-49, 1994.

In this article I present a Spanish translation of the paragraphs on the being, which can be found in al-Fârâbî's *Kitâb al-hurûf*, in order to help further the understanding of the al-Fârâbî's metaphysical thought.

Ramón Guerrero, Rafael. Los "Articulos de Necesario Conocimiento Para Quien se Inicie en el Arte de la Lógica" de ABU NASR AL-FARABI. *An Seminar Hist Filosof*, 6, 143-153, 1986-89.

To continue with a task which I formerly undertook, in this article I present the Spanish translation of the al-Fârâbî's text entitled *Fusûl tashtamil 'alà jamî 'fî sinâ 'at al-mantiq*. This translation can help further the understanding of Farabian thought for the Spanish reader.

Ramos, Alice. Karol Wojtyla—John Paul II's Idea of Ultimate Reality and Meaning. *Ultim Real Mean*, 18(2), 102-118, Je 95.

Ramos, Francisco José. El Espacio Público de la Filosofía. *Dialogos*, 30(66), 117-136, Jl 95.

Ramos, Pedro. El Enigma de Kripke: Una Solución Formal-Intensional. *Critica*, 26(76-77), 51-92, Ap-Ag 94.

In this article, as its title says, I present a formal solution in the intensional line to Kripke's paradoxes on belief. I analize and formalize the main three cases he expounds, about Tully-Cicero, Paderewski and *Londres*-London, according to his principles and presuppositions in one version, I think, developing my solution to each case in another. My idea is that if Kripke's principles and presuppositions lead to paradoxical ascriptions of belief in these cases, that is enough to suspect that they cannot have the nonrestrictive application Kripke thinks they have. My solution to those paradoxes fundamentally presupposes the following facts (or at least I think it does): 1) The existence of idiolects; 2) The existence of dispositions to substitution of expressions inside the sentences that subjects assent to, which are able to show the idiosyncratic understanding of certain expressions possessed by some subjects in some cases; and 3) With respect to the "meaning" of proper names, that it is only necessary to take into account their idiosyncratic reference and the mentioned dispositions. One through three allow us to see a solution to the paradoxes intermediate between Fregean solutions and Russellian ones, as it does not presuppose so much as the Fregean notion of sense nor so little as the Kripkean thesis that the meaning of names is just their reference.

Ramos, Pedro. Significado Pragmático en Peirce. *Analogia*, 5(2), 101-141, 1991.

Ramose, M B. Violence, Peaceful Human Coexistence and Universalism. *Dialogue Hum*, 3(1), 89-101, 1993.

Rampley, Matthew. Meaning and Language in Early Heidegger: From Duns Scotus to *Being and Time*. *J Brit Soc Phenomenol*, 25(3), 209-228, O 94.

Ramsey, Jeffry L. Construction by Reduction. *Phil Sci*, 62(1), 1-20, Mr 95.

Scientists employ a variety of procedures to eliminate degrees of freedom from computationally and/or analytically intractable equations. In the process, they often construct new models and discover new concepts, laws and functionally relations. I argue these procedures embody a central notion of reduction, namely, the containment of one structure within another. However, their inclusion in the philosophical concept of reduction necessitates a reevaluation of many standard assumptions about the ontological, epistemological and functional features of a reduction. On the basis of the reevaluation, I advocate a continuum of reduction which proceeds from the eliminative to the constructive. The metaphysical aspects of theory use in constructive reductions are sketched.

Ramsey, Jeffry L. Ideal Reaction Types and the Reactions of Real Alloys. *Proc Phil Sci Ass*, 1, 149-159, 1994.

Research on the oxidation of alloys supports the claim that natural scientists can and do use ideal type concepts when confronted with analytical or computational intractability. In opposition to those who collapse ideal types into 'standard' theoretical concepts, I argue ideal types possess a unique structure, function and axiology. In phenomenologically complex situations, scientists use these features to articulate experiment with theory generally and in particular to discover new boundary conditions. This conceptual articulation is achieved using models rather than objective perceptual attributes alone. The analysis supports a claim of local rather than global identities of methodology.

Ramsey, Ramsey Eric. The Earth Might be Round, But the World is Flat: The Groundwork for an Ethics of Relief. *Kinesis*, 21(2), 41-49, Fall 94.

In this essay the author reads Heidegger's reflection on technology in such a way as to make the reading a groundwork for an ethical position based in communicative praxis. The ethical position developed here is one that seeks to bring relief to an ethical world flattened in dangerous ways by what Heidegger calls the essence of technology and in other works calls calculative thinking. By moving beyond what many take to be Heidegger's quietism, the author suggests an interpretation of *Gelassenheit* that takes active shape against the backdrop of concerns inspired by ethical struggles within the texture of communicative praxis.

Ramsey, William. Distributed Representation and Causal Modularity: A Rejoinder to Forster and Saidel. *Phil Psych*, 7(4), 453-461, 1994.

In "Connectionism and the fats of folk psychology", Forster and Saidel argue that the central claim of Ramsey, Stich and Garon (1991)—that distributed connectionist models are incompatible with the causal discreteness of folk psychology—is mistaken. To establish their claim, they offer an intriguing model which allegedly shows how distributed representations can function in a causally discrete manner. They also challenge our position regarding projectibility of folk psychology. In this essay, I offer a response to their account and show how their model fails to demonstrate that our original argument was mistaken. While I will discuss several difficulties with their model, my primary criticism will be that the features of their model that are causally discrete are not truly distributed, while the features that are distributed are not really discrete. Concerning the issue of projectibility, I am more inclined to agree with Forster and Saidel and I offer a revised account of what we should have said originally.

Ramsey, William and Stich, Stephen and Garon, Joseph. "Connectionism, Eliminativism, and the Future of Folk Psychology" in *Connectionism: Debates on Psychological Explanation, Macdonald, Cynthia (ed)*, 311-338. Cambridge, Blackwell, 1995.

Rancière, Jacques and Melehy, Hassan (trans). *The Names of History: On the Poetics of Knowledge*. Minneapolis, Univ of Minn Pr, 1994.

Rand, Nicholas T (ed) and Torok, Maria (ed). *Rhythms: On the Work, Translation, and Psychoanalysis of Nicolas Abraham*. Stanford, Stanford Univ Pr, 1995.

Rhythms outlines in four essays a phenomenology of poetic consciousness; the creation of temporality through poetic rhythm; a literary esthetics based on psychoanalytic and phenomenological principles; a field of research concerned at once with literary criticism, translation, and psychoanalysis. The essays offer a new approach to the problem of literary creation an psychoanalytic definition of temporality, both seen in terms of a dynamic interplay between expectation and surprise, between unforeseen incidents and the modes of their integration. *Rhythms* forms a sequel to Abraham's previous work in *The Wolf Man's Magic Word* and *The Shell and the Kernel*.

Ranea, Alberto Guillermo. From Galileo to Leibniz: Motion, Qualities and Experience at the Foundation of Natural Science. *Rev Int Phil*, 48(188), 161-174, 1994.

This paper tries to find a connection between Galileo's science of motion and Leibniz's justification of his principles of dynamics. I would like to support the thesis according the which the a priori foundation Leibniz proposed for his dynamics purported to protect Galileo's mechanics from the attacks it suffered during the second half of the seventeenth century. The paper focuses on the way Leibniz rejected the a posteriori arguments advanced by Francois Blondel and Denis Papin in defense of the trustworthiness of Galileo's definition of acceleration, the scientific status of which had been challenged by ballistic studies of the time.

Range, Lillian M and Cotton, C Randy. Reports of Assent and Permission in Research With Children: Illustrations and Suggestions. *Ethics Behavior*, 5(1), 49-66, 1995.

This study ascertained reports of assent (affirmative agreement) and permission (agreement by an adult fully capable of being informed) in 114 children's research articles in 1990 in *Child Development (CD), Journal of Consulting and Clinical Psychology (JCCP), Journal of Pediatric Psychology*, and *Journal of Clinical Child Psychology*. Of the research projects, 43% failed to specify permission, and 68.5% failed to specify assent. *JCCP* reported assent significantly more than *CD*. Assent was reported significantly more in research with older children than with younger children. This lack of sensitivity to assent and permission suggests that many authors, reviewers, and editors consider reporting assent and permission unessential. We recommend specifying assent and permission in all manuscripts, highlighting children's research issues in graduate training, and using specific safeguards when conducting research with children.

Rao, P Srinivasa. The Place of Morality in Karma Yoga. *Darshana Int*, 32(4/128), 45-50, O 92.

Rao, S N. Encounter of Hindus with the Ancient Thomas Christians in Kerala. *J Dharma*, 19(2), 138-159, Ap-Je 94.

Raphael, Melissa. Feminism, Constructivism and Numinous Experience. *Relig Stud*, 30(4), 511-526, D 94.

This article brings together constructivist epistemology and feminist study of religion to provide phenomenological evidence that numinous consciousness is not the immediate, *sui generis* essence of religious experience that Rudolf Otto believed it to be. Whilst there are certain peculiarities in the Ottonian scheme that might make numinous consciousness unusually resistant to conceptual and ideological mediation, it can be shown that androcentric epistemological and axiological structures make the experience intelligible and worthy of accommodation within a given patriarchal religious tradition. By contrast, contemporary gynocentric spiritualities in which women celebrate their psychobiological difference as itself a necessary medium of religious experience, have no interest in protecting the holy from the limitations of its immanence.

Raposa, Michael. Poinsot on the Semiotics of Awareness. *Amer Cath Phil Quart*, 68(3), 395-408, Sum 94.

Rapp, Christof. Die Moralität des antiken Menschen: Über Bernhard Williams Buch "Shame and Necessity". *Z Phil Forsch*, 49(2), 259-273, Ap-Je 95.

Rappaport, Allen and Himschoot, Robert A. Ethics Perceptions of American Farmers: An Empirical Analysis. *J Bus Ethics*, 13(10), 795-802, O 94.

A 123 item survey of ethics perceptions of farmers had 796 respondents. Of these, 517 (64.9%) felt that farm ethics had gotten worse. A discriminant analysis employed to offer insight into the extent and nature of group differences produced 22 independent variables along with an adequate increase in classification results above expectations due to chance. These variables reflect a division between the outside business and political world and the concerns of farmers. The responses suggest an appreciation by the respondents of the interdependence of their business actions with their neighbors. The results are also suggestive of both an absolute and a relative ethics component. Further research on the relevance of communitarian ethics is suggested.

Rappaport, Steven. Is Economics Empirical Knowledge?. *Econ Phil*, 11(1), 137-158, Ap 95.

Alexander Rosenberg has affirmed that (C) economics does not count as empirical scientific knowledge. He asserts (C) on the basis of the following pair of premises: P1) A necessary condition for a theory or discipline being scientific knowledge is that it exhibit predictive improvement over time; and P2) Economics has failed to show the requisite predictive improvement. I argue that the predictive empiricism expressed by (P1) is false. Also, I show that considerations Rosenberg advances to justify (P2) fail to justify it. Thus, Rosenberg does not establish the skepticism about economic knowledge expressed by (C).

Rappe, Sara L. Socrates and Self-Knowledge. *Apeiron*, 28(1), 1-24, Mr 95.

Rascaglia, Maria. Croce e Gentile nell'Epistolario di Fausto Nicolini. *G Crit Filosof Ital*, 73(2-3), 306-325, My-D 94.

Raschini, Maria-Adelaide and Rocher, Emmanuel (trans). *Rosmini et l'Idée de Progrès*. Bordeaux, Biere, 1995.

Rashid, Harun. Critical Thinking and Reasoning. *Indian Phil Quart*, 21(3), 215-236, Jl 94.

Rasmussen, Douglas B. The Significance for Cognitive Realism of the Thought of John Poinsot. *Amer Cath Phil Quart*, 68(3), 409-424, Sum 94.

Rastier, François. Sémantique Interprétative et Compréhension du Langage. *Lekton*, 4(2), 139-161, 1994.

Les traitements automatiques du langage sont en crise parce qu'ils ne tiennent pas compte de la diversité et de la complexité des langues. A l'objectif maximaliste de compréhension, il faut substituer un objectif minimaliste d'interprétation. Cela suppose, pour la sémantique, de nouer des liens avec l'interprétation philologique et critique, et de reconnaître, outre l'ordre référentiel, un ordre herméneutique qui laisse toute leur place au contexte et au texte. Pour cela, le niveau sémantique doit être soigneusement distingué du niveau des représentations mentales.

Ratcliffe, Derek. More Thoughts on Nature Conservation and the Voluntary Principle. *Environ Values*, 4(1), 71-72, F 95.

Rath, Matthias. "Die Stellung Edith Steins im Psychologismusstreit" in *Studien zur Philosophie von Edith Stein, Fetz, Reto Luzius (ed)*, 197-225. Freiburg, Alber, 1993.

Rath, Matthias (ed) and Fetz, Reto Luzius (ed) and Schulz, Peter (ed). *Studien zur Philosophie von Edith Stein*. Freiburg, Alber, 1993.

Ratner, Carl. The Unconscious: A Perspective from Sociohistorical Psychology. *J Mind Behav*, 15(4), 323-342, Autumn 94.

This article extends concepts from Vygotsky's sociohistorical psychology to explain unconsciousness. Freud's conception of the unconscious is criticized for minimizing the importance of social and cognitive aspects of unconsciousness. In contrast, sociohistorical psychology explains unconsciousness as emanating from social values. These social values organize the manner in which we perceive people, and therefore account for oversights and distortions in our perception of self and others. Implications for overcoming unconsciousness are also discussed according to sociohistorical psychological principles.

Raulet, Gérard. L'équivoque de l'histoire: Ontologie ou philosophie des formes symboliques—Bloch et Merleau-Ponty. *Man World*, 28(1), 33-42, Ja 95.

Rauth, Eric (trans) and Debray, Régis. The Three Ages of Looking. *Crit Inquiry*, 21(3), 529-555, Spr 95.

This essay translates chapter 8 in Debray's *Vie et mort de l'image*. It marks the first appearance in English of "mediology," since *Teachers, Writers, Celebrities*. Mediological history of the Western eye explores social groups of producers, theologians, critics, viewing subjects, and technologies that "mediate" representation and viewing of visual forms. Successive horizons of ocular expectation have linked practices of looking with belief. Idols (="indices") overcome death with eternity and miracle; icons (="Art") cultivate aesthetics and taste; the "visual" divinizes novelty, economy, influence. Their relation to inscription technologies (writing, print, computer-graphics) clarifies understanding of images *and* signs in culture and modernity.

Rauzy, Jean-Baptiste. *Quid sit natura prius?* La conception leibnizienne de l'ordre. *Rev Metaph Morale*, 98(1), 31-48, Ja-Mr 95.

It is well known that Leibniz's logic is grounded in the inherence of the predicate in the subject and in the compossibility of notions. It naturally stresses, therefore, relations of equivalence, rather than of order. Nevertheless, Leibniz provided a logical analysis of order, i.e., an account of the meaning of "prior", "subsequent", "concomitant". His account comprises three points: 1) Given two beings, the one that is more simple (i.e., the one whose analysis requires less operations of the mind) is prior by nature (*natura prius*); hence, concomitant (*simul*) being. 2) The degree of composition of being corresponds to its degree of perfection. Hence, prior beings being simpler, subsequent beings are more perfect. 3) Given two beings such that one is simpler and the other more perfect, they differ temporally if they also contradict each other; conversely, two compossible beings contradict each other if, and only if, they are not simultaneous (i.e., if they do not belong to the same "state of the universe"). It will be shown that this relation makes it possible to characterize the axiomatic order of incomplete notions (in the field of the *mathesis universalis*). But the attempt to explain the terms prius, posterius and simul in a metaphysical manner, i.e., by laying the stress on the order among substances, raises grave philosophical problems.

Raven, Diederick. Incommensurabel, incompatibel, onvergelijkbaar. *Alg Ned Tijdschr Wijs*, 86(3), 183-206, Jl 94.

This paper makes a defense for the integrity of the notion of 'incommensurability'. The strategy used is twofold. Firstly, it is argued that the notion of 'incommensurability' should not be taken as a synonym for 'incompatibility' or 'incomparability'. Secondly, two fashionable interpretations of the notion of 'incommensurability' are rejected. They are 1) that the choice between incommensurable theories cannot be a rational one, and 2) that incommensurability implies the impossibility of translation, and hence the impossibility of understanding. In response to the first interpretation it is argued that the problem only arises because rationality is understood as a rule-governed activity. If however, rationality is understood as a judgmental process than the issue automatically dissolves. In response to 2) it is argued that the problem is an artifact of the wrong model of understanding and translation. If the two are not identified and if understanding is construed not as a decoding process but instead as an inferential process then impossibility in translation does not imply impossibility of understanding.

Raven, Diederick (ed) and Geuijen, Karin (ed) and De Wolf, Jan (ed). *Post-Modernism and Anthropology: Theory and Practice*. Assen, Gorcum, 1995.

During the nineteen eighties the term *post-modern* started to be applied to tendencies within the field of cultural and social anthropology. To many post-modernism appeared not merely as another theoretical paradigm but as an ill conceived attempt to put the whole discipline on its head. In this volume the contributors want to consider two important questions which are crucial to a reasoned assessment of the ensuing debates. First, to what extent and in which way does post-modernism in anthropology differ from existing, 'modern' approaches? Secondly, what consequences does post-modernism have for the presentation of that quintessential anthropological experience: participant-observation in field work?

Ravizza, Mark and Fischer, John Martin. "Responsibility for Consequences" in *In Harm's Way, Coleman, Jules L (ed)*, 183-208. New York, Cambridge Univ Pr, 1994.

We seek to give the conditions for moral responsibility for the consequences of one's actions. We employ the notion of control in a certain way. An agent can be held morally responsible for a consequence (on our approach), even though he could not have prevented it from obtaining.

Ravizza, Mark and Fischer, John Martin. Ducking Harm and Sacrificing Others. *J Soc Phil*, 25(3), 135-144, Wint 94.

There is a descriptive distinction between ducking harm and sacrificing others. But does this distinction have normative force? We suggest not; at least it is unclear that the distinction has the sort of moral consequences sometimes attributed to it.

Rawling, Piers. Psychology and Newtonian Methodology. *J Mind Behav*, 16(1), 35-43, Wint 95.

According to Newton, the goals of natural philosophy comprise quantitative generalizations and causal knowledge, the latter being paramount. Quantitative generalizations are sometimes explanatory, in psychology as elsewhere (the role of the Gaussian model in explaining the shape of the ROC curve in signal detection is discussed). However, in psychology, they are not explanatory when the human subject is considered qua bearer of psychological states (beliefs, desires, and their ilk), but only when she is considered qua physical system. In the former case quantitative generalizations are, rather, *to be causally explained*. In this sense, psychology may be closer to the Newtonian methodological mark than contemporary physics.

Rawls, John. Reply to Habermas's "Reconciliation through the Public Use of Reason". *J Phil*, 92(3), 132-180, Mr 95.

Rawls, John. The Priority of Right and Ideas of the Good. *Filozof Cas*, 42(6), 938-965, 1994.

Rawwas, Mohammed Y A and Strutton, David and Pelton, Lou. Ethical Attitudes of Mental Health Practitioners: Balancing Therapeutic Practices and Treatments. *J Bus Ethics*, 13(8), 597-608, Ag 94.

This paper reports the responses of 251 mental health care practitioners to a mail survey examining their views concerning ethical conflicts and practices within their work environments. Besides identifying the sources and types of conflicts they experience, respondents were asked how ethical standards have changed over the last 10 years as well as the factors influencing these changes. Conclusions and implications are outlined and future research needs are described.

Ray, G Thomas. "Some Moral Contradictions in the Conservative Educational Reform Discourse in the US" in *Identity, Culture, and Education, Smeyers, Paul (ed)*, 295-304. Leuven, Leuven Univ Pr, 1994.

This paper examines claims of educational critics such as William Bennett, Diane Ravitch, Chester Finn Jr, and William Kilpatrick that much of this nation's cultural and

moral deterioration is a result of public schooling's lack of attention to traditional curricula, and that a return to such a canon of civic verities and virtues would restore national unity and moral commitment. I argue that the events, personalities, and literature that provide the substance of their recommendations are framed within a modernistic epistemology that privileges a view of humans as rational, autonomous, and individualistic, and puts out of focus ways of thinking that involve an integrated sense of community and obligation. Thus, what is problematic is that the metaphors embedded within their curricula contain the seeds of precisely that social dissolution that they inveigh against.

Ray, G Thomas. On the Language of Consciousness: Propositional Discourse and Moral Sensibility. *J Thought*, 29(4), 65-76, Wint 94.

This paper develops the argument that language patterns of classroom and text restrict moral learning. By using Gregory Bateson's work as a conceptual lens, discourse that is characteristic of schooling can be seen as reinforcing linear, sequential, and rational ways of apprehending the world, and putting out of focus a view of phenomena as embedded in an ecology of relationship and requiring ethical reciprocity. In this way, language of schooling—critical discourse, propositional discourse, or essayist text—contributes to students' sense of isolation and detachment, and limits their potential for acting competently as adults against significant social problems—poverty, racism, and environmental abuse, for example.

Raymond, Elfie. The Remains of the Night. *Cont Phil*, 16(5), 5-10, S-O 94.

In the essay *The Remains of the Night* the question is raised under which circumstances the authority of conscience legitimizes, as well as enjoins, resistance to and defiance of powers external to the individual. How does one know when compliance with orders is unconscionable, constituting complicity and collusion rather than obedience? The essay's main argument holds in favor of the twin proposition that in the absence of a constitutive object the subject cannot constitute itself; yet only a fully constituted subject is capable of acting on the authority of conscience. Examples from scripture and history, backed by arguments from reformed theology, show the subject-object connection indispensable for the effective operations of conscience, voiding possibilities to use the notions of autonomy and/or autexousia as sufficient explanation for actions based on conscience's generative authority.

Raymond, François. Marcel Duchamp, la musique et les machines. *Horiz Phil*, 5(1), 1-19, Autumn 94.

This is a survey of Duchamp's thoughts and things about sounds, music and reorganizing sensory inputs. Being a play on and against synaesthesia in his notes concerning the Large Glass. It explores his "irrational serialism" and his notion of non-oriented time. The 2 Musical Erratum (1914) are machines which choose notes in decreasing random order out of a given set. Duchamp explores the "beauty of indifference" by devising something that writes random music, without the use of the hand, by dry machine effect, away from virtuoso and against the formation of taste. Also some thought experiences on hearing sounds.

Raz, Joseph. Inconmensurabilidad y razonamiento jurídico. *Telos (Spain)*, 2(1), 85-98, Je 93.

This paper considers the implications for the relations between legal and moral reasoning of correcting one major defect of standard utilitarianism. The feature of standard utilitarianism, the rejection of which is the subject of this paper, is the assumption that all options are commensurate in value. The author suggests, on the contrary, that many options are incommensurate in value. Although he rejects the strong thesis of the autonomy of legal reasoning he asserts that when morality runs out there is a place for legal doctrine independent of moral considerations.

Raz, Joseph. Multikulturalismus: eine liberale Perspektive. *Deut Z Phil*, 43(2), 307-327, 1995.

Read, James H. "Our Complicated System": James Madison on Power and Liberty. *Polit Theory*, 23(3), 452-475, Ag 95.

How is it possible to make government *more powerful* without making citizens *less free*? The essay explores the complicated relation between liberty and power in Madison's writings, especially in the crucial period when Madison appears to change from advocate to opponent of powerful government. Madison's shifts reflect an underlying consistency. Protecting liberty from governmental power does not depend upon *how much* power is vested in government; but upon the existence of *clear boundaries* to whatever degree of power is established. Liberty can be threatened by either too much or too little governmental power, a conclusion still relevant today.

Read, Rupert. The Unstatability of Kripkean Scepticisms. *Phil Papers*, 24(1), 67-74, Ap 95.

Against Sartorelli, Brueckner, and Van Cleve, I argue that 'concept-scepticism' cannot even get as far as being intelligibly stated. (Thus it cannot even get as far as refuting *itself*!) I then extend the argument to (linguistic) meaning-scepticism, and show that "It is a deep mistake to think that Kripkean scepticisms are statable. That *this* is a hand and that *that* is an addition sum are, normally, completely unproblematically *presumed*."

Read, Stephen. *Thinking About Logic: An Introduction to the Philosophy of Logic*. New York, Oxford Univ Pr, 1994.

The purpose is to introduce students to the philosophical ideas underlying formal logic, and help them understand the aim of logic, and why it proceeds as it does. Topics treated include: the correspondence theory of truth and Tarski's work; logical consequence, compactness and the notion of logical form; theories of conditionals-truth-functional, probabilistic, similarity-theories and relevance theories; the metaphysics of possible worlds; empty names and free logic; the semantic paradoxes and various solutions including Kripke's; the sorites paradox, fuzzy logic and the theory of rough sets; and constructivism and intuition. There is a full index, bibliography and glossary.

Reagan, Charles E. "Words and Deeds: The Semantics of Actions" in *The Philosophy of Paul Ricoeur, Hahn, Lewis Edwin (ed)*, 331-345. Peru, Open Court, 1994.

Reale, Miguel. Axiological Invariants. *J Value Inq*, 29(1), 65-75, Mr 95.

The author, after a brief history of the meaning of the term "value" since the ancient philosophy, points that the central problem of the axiology is the existence or not of axiological invariants. In his opinion, the objectivity of values must be placed on historical value, which acquire a superlative meaning, with the force of a transcendental entity. They are as if (als ob) are innate, in contrast with the relativity of other values. The axiological invariants are always resultants of the value of human being, which the author presents as the "value-source" of all the axiological questions.

Reath, Andrews. Legislating the Moral Law. *Nous*, 28(4), 435-464, D 94.

This paper interprets Kant's thesis that the moral law is the law which the rational will gives to itself through the following claims: a) The fundamental law regulating moral deliberation is a principle derived from the nature of rational volition. b) It leads to a procedure which assesses uses of practical reason by asking whether all can regard as them valid, rather than by testing them against a rule. c) This law invests rational agents with authority to enact their maxims as universal law, i.e., to enact law through their wills. d) Substantive moral principles are those arrived at by carrying out this deliberative procedure, and they apply to individuals in such a way that they may be regarded as their legislators. That is, they apply in a way that collapses the distinction between subject and legislator.

Recanati, François. How Narrow is Narrow Content?. *Dialectica*, 48(3-4), 209-229, 1994.

In this paper I discuss two influential views in the philosophy of mind: the *two-component picture* draws a distinction between 'narrow content' and 'broad content', while *radical externalism* denies that there is such a thing as narrow content. I argue that 'narrow content' is ambiguous, and that the two views can be reconciled. Instead of considering that there is only one question ('Are mental contents internal to the individual?') and three possible answers ('Yes', 'Yes and No', and 'No') corresponding to Cartesian internalism, the two-component picture, and radical externalism respectively, I show that there are two distinct questions: 'Are mental contents internal to the individual?' and, 'Are mental contents analysable in two-components?'. In the last section of the paper, I deal with internal representation which *seems* to be independent even of the normal environment. I show that such contents are themselves independent of the normal environment only in a relative sense: they are *locally* independent of the normal environment, yet still depend on it via the concepts to which they are connected in the concept system.

Recas Bayón, Javier. Hacia un Nuevo Concepto de Trascendentalismo?. *An Seminar Metaf*, 28, 139-167, 1994.

Rechach, Carmen Alicia. "Para una Relectura Posible de la Epistemología Kantiana" in *Temas Actuales de Filosofía, Palacios, María Julia (ed)*, 513-520. Buenos Aires, Univ Nacional Salta, 1993.

How could be read the transcendental aesthetic? Which is the relation between geometry and the natural science? Are other spaces possible and in what sense? Is it possible to epistemologically revalidate the hypothesis of the Critics of Pure Reason without contradicting with the no-Euclidean geometrics and the contemporary physics? Could the Kantian categories be rescued? Considering that: 1) The spontaneity of pure knowledge not only generates the objects of mathematics, but those of the natural sciences and 2) The thesis that transcendents ideality of space and time supports this proposal, I will try to base a return to a framed Kant.

Recki, Birgit. "Die promesse de bonheur in Kants *Kritik der Urteilskraft*" in *Naturzweckmässigkeit und ästhetische Kultur, Schwabe, Karl-Heinz (ed)*, 95-115. Sankt Augustin, Academia, 1993.

Redding, Paul. Philosophical Republicanism and Monarchism—and Republican and Monarchical Philosophy—in Kant and Hegel. *Owl Minerva*, 26(1), 35-46, Fall 94.

Hegel's relation to Kant is examined by drawing general implication from a specific difference within their political philosophies. By extending the conception of Kant's "republicanism" to his epistemology, it can be seen that Hegel's objections there parallel his monarchical critique of republicanism. In the realm of knowledge, the philosopher plays a role parallel to that played by the monarch in politics. Looking at these issues in this way reveals how the traditional account of what Hegel has in mind by both the nature of philosophical knowledge and the nature of such a knowing subject has been greatly misunderstood.

Redhead, Michael. "Logic, Quanta, and the Two-slit Experiment" in *Reading Putnam, Clark, Peter (ed)*, 161-175. Cambridge, Blackwell, 1995.

Redman, Barbara K. Clinical Practice Guidelines as Tools of Public Policy: Conflicts among Purpose, Issues of Autonomy, and Justice. *J Clin Ethics*, 5(4), 303-309, Wint 94.

The purpose is to address ethical issues inherent in clinical practice guidelines. Conflicts of purpose occur when guidelines are used to advise patients and providers and at the same time are used to ration care or foreclose treatment options by denying reimbursement. With strong emphasis on their being research based, practice guidelines will reflect the biases inherent in individual bodies of research and in the questions scientists have chosen to address, leaving problems of vulnerable groups unaddressed. Patient values must be incorporated into guidelines and should support their autonomous decision making.

Redmond, Walter. Friar Alonso on the Logic of God. *Vivarium*, 32(2), 227-260, N 94.

Redmond, Walter. Una Lógica del Compromiso Social. *Analogia*, 8(1), 3-39, 1994.

Redpath, Peter A. The New World Disorder: A Crisis of Philosophical Identity. *Cont Phil*, 16(6), 19-24, N-D 94.

This paper is a development of two lectures which were given several years at Loras College in Dubuque, Iowa and an international congress at the Institute International "Jacques Maritain" in Treviso, Italy. In it I argue that the current political upheavals occurring both within Europe and the United States are not rooted either in politics or in economics but that they are ultimately grounded upon philosophy and upon the fact that, by and large, philosophy in our culture today is principally neosophistry and that, unless and until, leaders in the East and the West begin to realize this fact they have no hope of identifying their main problems, much less to come to grips with them.

Rée, Jonathan (trans). The Deconstruction of Actuality: An Interview with Jacques Derrida. *Rad Phil*, 68, 28-41, Autumn 94.

This is a full translation of the French text of an interview Derrida gave in August 1993, first published in *Passages* the following month. It begins with a discussion of how philosophy can be "in touch with the moment," where Derrida problematises the very idea of actuality, and develops a conception of "the event" as essentially unforeseeable. Then it turns to more concrete issues of Immigration, Nationality, Justice, Marxism and Algeria.

Rée, Jonathan and Gehron, Christiane. Interview: Hans-Georg Gadamer. *Rad Phil*, 69, 27-35, Ja-F 95.

In this interview, conducted in October 1993, Gadamer reflects on his life and work in general: how he feels about writing, about teaching and the future of philosophy; Husserl, Heidegger, Nietzsche, Derrida, de Man, and Freud; intellectual life in the Nazi time; analytic philosophy, traditionality and the history of philosophy; Marxism, Christianity, the position of women, the unification of Germany and the prospects for peace in the world.

Reed, Edward. The Psychologist's Fallacy as a Persistent Framework in William James's Psychological Theorizing. *Hist Human Sci*, 8(1), 61-72, F 95.

Reed, Gay Garland. Moral/Political Education in the People's Republic of China: Learning Through Role Models. *J Moral Educ*, 24(2), 99-111, 1995.

This paper discusses the use of role models as a means for political socialization and moral education in the People's Republic of China. It looks at the use of role models in historical context and shows the ways in which children were encouraged to learn from the socialist role model, Lei Feng. In answer to the question, "What are the children *really* learning from Comrade Lei Feng?" the paper suggests that Chinese children in post-Liberation China were actually learning a set of core virtues that have their roots in the Confucian tradition and that individual Chinese constructed their own versions of the role model in accordance with their own beliefs. Finally, the paper suggests that although the socialist role model, Lei Feng, may disappear as China becomes increasingly capitalistic, the use of role models as a pedagogical tool will not. Indeed, the excesses of "commodity socialism" may call for new role models who perpetuate certain values like benevolence which are rooted in Confucian and communist thought.

Reeder, Nick. Are Physical Properties Dispositions?. *Phil Sci*, 62(1), 141-149, Mr 95.

Averill (1990) argues that not every property is a disposition. I claim here that his reasoning is faulty, suffering at one point from a logical error and at other points from an inadequate account of counterfactuals.

Reedy, W Jay. The Traditionalist Critique of Individualism in Post-Revolutionary France: The Case of Louis de Bonald. *Hist Polit Thought*, 16(1), 49-75, Spr 95.

Louis de Bonald (1754-1840) was a French noblemen and the leading theorist of the Counter-Revolution. A theocrat (Catholic and royalist), Bonald produced a wide-ranging "traditionalism" that valued holistic, hierarchical community over modern individualism in its myriad manifestations—religious, cultural, sociopolitical, and economic. The bane of individualism had roots in the Renaissance and Reformation; its culmination was the Enlightenment and the French Revolution. For Bonald, republican politics and capitalist economics work in tandem; both spur not only instability but also divisiveness, amorality, and insecurity as well. Moreover, democracy is always a sham since some sort of elite inevitable dominates in every nation regardless of its type of government. Bonald wrote historical and rationalistic defenses of the corporatist social order of the Old Regime in hopes of aiding its full restoration. However, he also assaulted the "deracinated," atomized and alienating society he saw emerging at the beginning of the 1800's. In these analyses, Bonald anticipates the structural-functional sociologists (especially Le Play and Durkheim). What is more, his reactionary criticisms of the bourgeoisie presage the Social Catholicism of Lamennais, on the one hand, and the attacks of the utopian socialists and Karl Marx, on the other.

Reeve, C D C. Platonic Politics and the Good. *Polit Theory*, 23(3), 411-424, Ag 95.

What is platonic politics? What do the philosopher-kings know? What are forms? What is the good itself? How are forms related to the good itself? New answers are proposed to these formidable questions.

Reeve, C D C (ed) and Curd, Patricia (ed) and Cohen, S Marc (ed). *Readings in Ancient Greek Philosophy: From Thales to Aristotle*. Indianapolis, Hackett, 1995.

Extensive selections from the most important philosophical texts of ancient Greece from the Presocratics through Aristotle. Includes introductions, headnotes, maps, a concordance to the Presocratic fragments, an Aristotle glossary, and many new translations. 1) Presocratics and Sophists: Thales, Anaximander, Anaximenes, Pythagoras, Philolaus, Xenophanes, Heraclitus, Parmenides, Anaxagoras, Empedocles, Zeno, Leucippus, Democritus, Melissus, Protagoras, Gorgias, Antiphon, Critias. 2) Plato's dialogues: Euthyphro, Apology, Crito, Protagoras, Gorgias, Meno, Phaedo, Symposium, Republic, Parmenides, Timaeus. 3) Aristotle's treatises: Categories, De Interpretatione, Topics, Posterior Analytics, Physics, Generation and Corruption, On the Heavens, Meteorologica, Parts of Animals, Metaphysics, De Anima, Nicomachean Ethics, Politics.

Reeves, Hubert. L'Origine de l'Univers. *Horiz Phil*, 2(2), 1-25, Spring 92.

Reeves, M Francis. The Gadfly Business Ethics Project. *J Bus Ethics*, 13(8), 609-614, Ag 94.

This article provides a brief description of the origin and development, results, and future plans of the "Gadfly Business Ethics Project" at Bentley College. A business ethics gadfly in the context of our Gadfly Project, is a catalyst who motivates and strengthens an ethics dimension in functional business courses. (edited)

Reginster, Bernard. *Ressentiment*, Evaluation, and Integrity. *Int Stud Phil*, 27(3), 117-124, 1995.

The article offers a brief analysis of Nietzsche's notion of *ressentiment* and of its impact upon evaluation. It also attempts to determine the status and the source of the normative force of a critique of value judgments in terms of *ressentiment*. On the interpretation proposed here, such a psychological critique concerns not the values themselves but their place in the agent's psychological economy, and it consists in showing that values held out of *ressentiment* undermine the agent's integrity.

Reheis, Fritz. Ökologische Blindheit: Die Aporie der herrschenden Wirtschaftswissenschaft. *Das Argument*, 208, 79-90, Ja-F 95.

The dominant contemporary model of economics, which understands itself as "neoclassical", has not properly understood the issue of "ecology". A largely immanent argumentation shows that standard attempts to integrate "nature" into neoclassical theoretical paradigms are unconvincing. Only a fundamental paradigm shift in economic theory will be able to overcome contemporary theory's incapacity to address the challenge of ecological problems.

Reich, Warren Thomas. The Word "Bioethics": Its Birth and the Legacies of Those Who Shaped Its Meaning. *Kennedy Inst Ethics J*, 4(4), 319-335, D 94.

Extensive historical sleuthing reveals that the word "bioethics" and the field of study it names experienced, in 1970/1971, a "bilocated birth" in Madison, Wisconsin, and in Washington, DC. Van Rensselaer Potter, at the University of Wisconsin first coined the term; and André Hellegers, at Georgetown University, at the very least, latched onto the already-existing word "bioethics" and first used it in an institutional way to designate the focused area of inquiry that became an academic field of learning and a movement regarding public policy and the life sciences. A further comparison of the Potter and the Hellegers/Georgetown understandings of bioethics and the relative acceptance of the two views will appear in the March 1995 issue of this journal.

Reich, Warren Thomas. The Word "Bioethics": The Struggle Over Its Earliest Meanings. *Kennedy Inst Ethics J*, 5(1), 19-34, Mr 95.

An article by Warren Reich in the December 1994 issue of this journal concludes that the word "bioethics" and the field of study it names experienced a "bilocated birth" in 1970/1971 under Van Rensselaer Potter, at the University of Wisconsin, and André Hellegers, at Georgetown University. Further historical inquiry confirms 1) that there were, from the start, some major differences—even clashes—between the Potter and the Hellegers/Georgetown understandings of bioethics; and 2) that the Hellegers/Georgetown approach came to be the more widely accepted meaning of the term, while Potter's idea of bioethics remained largely marginalized. However, this inquiry also results in a third, unanticipated, conclusion: that Hellegers (in contrast to the dominant model offered by the Georgetown scholars) actually proposed a global approach to bioethics, bringing his vision much closer to Potter's evolving view than previously has been acknowledged.

Reichling, Mary J. Susanne Langer's Theory of Symbolism: An Analysis and Extension. *Phil Music Educ Rev*, 1(1), 3-17, Spr 93.

Susanne Langer's theory of symbols follows the tradition of Cassirer and Kant and presages the work of contemporary semioticians. Langer's theory in application to music suggests both ontological and functional characteristics of the symbol. Ontological characteristics divide into syntactical and semantic considerations while the functional address literal and/or metaphorical reference as well as expression and/or representation. Langer's thesis can be extended to include aspects of Peter Kivy's typology of representation, Nelson Goodman's notion of reference, and Israel Scheffler's concepts of ambiguity and reenactment. For Langer, music is not only a symbol but also a symbol complex.

Reid, Jeffrey. L'université d'état et ses contradictions philosophiques: Hegel et la création de l'université de Berlin. *Horiz Phil*, 5(2), 1-19, 1995.

The philosophical contradictions inherent in the relationship between the state and the university were already apparent at the coming-into-being of what was arguably the first state university: the University of Berlin, in 1810. Absolute versus relative academic freedom, research versus teaching are two contemporary dilemma that have their sources in contradictions embodied by the romantic (Herdier, Fichte, Schleiermacher) versus Hegelian notions of "Bildung", freedom and the state itself.

Reidenbach, R Eric and Robin, Donald P. A Response to "On Measuring Ethical Judgements". *J Bus Ethics*, 14(2), 159-162, F 95.

This article discusses the major criticisms posed in "On Measuring Ethical Judgments" concerning our ethics scale development work. We agree that the authors of the criticism do engage in what they accurately refer to as "armchair theorizing". We point out the errors in their comments.

Reifarth, G T. Sprachebenen und Sprachliche Einheiten in Ludwig Wittgenstein's Tractatus Logico-Philosophicus. *Wittgenstein Stud*, n.a., 1994.

Meine Arbeit fragt: Was ist, nach *Wittgensteins Tractatus Logico-Philosophicus*, Sprache und wie setzt sie sich zusammen? Diese Frage wird unter semantischen und pragmatischen Gesichtspunkten zu beantworten versucht. Im Mittelpunkt steht das Verhaeltnis zweier Sprachebenen, der Zeichensprache und der Umgangssprache, das am Ende als ein Doppelverhaeltnis—ein Verhaeltnis von Analyse und Generierung—klassifiziert wird, von dem allerdings nur eine Seite funktionstuechtig ist: die analytische Seite. Zu dieser Erkenntnis fuehrt die Analyse der Einheiten der beiden Systeme "Zeichensprache" und "Umgangssprache". Die atomare Ebene der Zeichensprache und ihr ontologisches Gegenstueck erweisen sich bei dieser Analyse als fuer Sprachbetrachtung untaugliche logische Konstruckte. Die Sprachdarstellung des *Tractatus* wird weitgehend verworfen, da sie meiner pragmatisch-semantisch angelegten Pruefung nicht standhalten kann.

Reigadas, Maria Cristina. Etica y política en la encrucijada posmoderna: Una interpretación de Daniel Bell. *Cuad Etica*, 14, 83-123, D 92.

Daniel Bell, an American contemporary sociologist, is basically known due to his thesis about the end of ideologies, his sociological theory of the forthcoming of postindustrial society and his interpretation about modernity's double link, which constitutes, together with his postmodernity's analysis, the central core of the cultural contradictions of capitalism. Although Bell has not elaborated any political theory in a strict sense, in this paper I maintain that *the political*—re-defined in terms of *public home*, and re-centered around the notion of *justice*—constitutes the

articulating dimension of his thought, and that the ethical-religious problem is his horizontal and his fundamental intention.

Reill, Peter Hanns. Science and the Construction of the Cultural Sciences in Late Enlightenment Germany: The Case of Wilhelm von Humboldt. *Hist Theor*, 33(3), 345-366, 1994.

One of the master narratives in the history of the cultural sciences recounts how the modern *Geisteswissenschaften* were constructed in opposition to Enlightenment "scientism." It is assumed that a radical split between natural science and the descriptive historical sciences occurred, enabling the cultural sciences to develop their own unique methods, epistemology, and explanatory procedures. In this article I analyze Wilhelm von Humboldt's concepts of history and linguistics as a test case to question this master narrative, arguing that Humboldt consciously constructed his version of historical and linguistic science upon a model of science formulated in and by Enlightenment thinkers. (edited)

Reiman, Jeffrey. "The Marxian Critique of Criminal Justice" in *Radical Philosophy of Law*, Caudill, David S (ed), 111-139. Atlantic Highlands, Humanities Pr, 1995.

Reimer, Bennett. Langer on the Arts as Cognitive. *Phil Music Educ Rev*, 1(1), 44-60, Spr 93.

Reinders, Johannes S. "Human Rights from the Perspective of..Religious Morality" in *Human Rights and Religious Values*, An-Na'im, Abdullahi A (& other eds), 3-23. Grand Rapids, Eerdmans, 1995.

Reiner, Richard and Pierson, Robert. Hacking's Experimental Realism: An Untenable Middle Ground. *Phil Sci*, 62(1), 60-69, Mr 95.

As Laudan and Fine show, and Boyd concedes, the attempt to infer the truth of scientific realism from the fact that it putatively provides the best explanation of the instrumental success of science is circular, since what is to be *shown* is precisely the legitimacy of such abductive inferences. Hacking's "experimental argument for scientific realism about entities" is one of the few arguments for scientific realism that purports to avoid this circularity. We argue that Hacking's argument is as dependent on inference to the best explanation (IBE), and therefore as weak, as the other realist arguments.

Reinhardt, Lloyd. Aesthetic Realism. *Lit Aes*, 1, 28-37, Spr 91.

This paper is a brief exploration of the face and implications of the fact that we do not, on pain of a kind of misuse of language, pass on evaluative judgments of others in our own voice, but always insist on oratio recta or oratio obliqua. This is deemed to be some sort of support for the fact-value dichotomy in that factual information that we do not doubt is normally happily passed on in our own voice. But even aesthetic judgment we trust we pass on not in our own voice. A possible explanation is that aesthetic response is of the nature of the awareness of aspects rather than of objective properties. The thought no doubt traces back to Kant, who spoke of the importance of seeing for yourself.

Reisberg, Daniel. Equipotential Recipes for Unambiguous Images: A Reply to Rollins. *Phil Psych*, 7(3), 359-366, 1994.

Several authors have alleged that mental images are inherently unambiguous, obligatorily accompanied by descriptive information, specifying how the depiction is to be understood. Rollins argues, however, that images are neutral with regard to interpretation, and that prior results, suggesting unambiguity, simply indicate an interpretive bias, manifest in how subjects read their (ambiguous) images. I argue that Rollins' claims are unpersuasive, resting on a confusion between information contained within the image itself, and other information, supplied from long-term memory, about a depicted form.

Reisch, George. Scientism without Tears: A Reply to Roth and Ryckman. *Hist Theor*, 34(1), 45-58, 1995.

In response to Roth and Ryckman, I explain in more detail why narratives fashioned with ideal, quantitative covering laws cannot be combined into large-scale covering-law explanations and specify further reasons for supposing that history can be conceived as dynamically nonlinear. I also appeal to an episode in the history of science to examine the idea that dynamical complexity is local in historical space and time and to suggest that such complexity does not pose a unique problem for historical narration. Finally, I suggest that Roth and Ryckman's critique of the use of nonlinear dynamical concepts in historical explanation must extend to explanations employing concepts from linear science. I conclude that their warning against the incoherence of scientism is not convincing.

Reiser, Stanley Joel. The Ethical Life of Health Care Organizations. *Hastings Center Rep*, 24(6), 28-36, N-D 94.

Reisner, Ann and Walter, Gerry. Journalists' Views of Advertiser Pressures on Agricultural News. *J Agr Environ Ethics*, 7(2), 157-172, 1994.

All major journalism ethical codes explicitly state that journalists should protect editorial copy from undue influence by outside sources. A study of newspaper reporters who cover agricultural news found that the most pressing ethical concern is the effect of advertiser (agri-business) pressure on editorial copy, and that their concerns in general parallel those of farm magazine writers and editors. The majority reported being in situations in which they might be exposed to advertiser pressure, including pressures to change or withhold editorial copy. The newspaper reporters who cover agricultural beats showed slightly more resistance to advertiser pressure than did farm magazine editors in a parallel study. (edited)

Reitan, Eric. The Irreconcilability of Pacifism and Just War Theory: A Response to Sterba (1992). *Soc Theor Pract*, 20(2), 117-134, Sum 94.

Renard, Philip. Historical Bibliography of Upanisads in Translation. *J Indian Phil*, 23(2), 223-246, Je 95.

Renaut, Alain. L'Éthique Aujourd'hui: Entre Fondation et Application. *Philosopher*, 16, 277-296, 1994.

Rendón Rojas, Miguel Angel. La Estética del Romanticismo y su Análisis Dentro de la Filosofía Existencial (Kierkegaard y Dostoievsky). *Analogia*, 8(2), 139-157, 1994.

This article analyzes the aesthetic theory of the romanticism. We understand the romanticism like the conception that places the Beauty in the center of its system, and the Kindness and the Truth are subordinated to Beauty. But Kierkegaard and Dostoyevsky warned the existential contradictions of this conception: The Beauty is outside of the moral sphere, the experimentation of it is subjective and the condition of its creation is the freedom, for what if somebody applies those principles in the practice, he could become the free absolute spirit: the Demon, that sees the Beauty in the delight of the Evil. For an aesthete, whose moral conscience is not silent, this produces crisis like in the case of Tolstoy or Briuvel.

Rendtorff, Trutz. "Christian Concepts of the Responsible Self" in *Human Rights and the World's Religions, Rouner, Leroy (ed)*, 33-45. Notre Dame, Univ Notre Dame Pr, 1988.

Facing the question of the status of human rights the author asks whether they can be seen as originally given with the individual person or as being derived from the persons' existence within society. By viewing the theoretical debate over the religious foundations of modern Western society (G Jellinek, M Weber, E Troeltsch), it is pointed out, that one might well speak of a Christian concept of freedom and responsibility. This also allows the justification of the importance of civil rights for shaping society, although the author stresses upon the fact, that human rights in this form will not bring the ultimate fulfillment which the religious believer finds in relation to God.

Rengger, N J. *Political Theory, Modernity, and Postmodernity: Beyond Enlightenment and Critique*. Cambridge, Blackwell, 1995.

Rennie, B S. The Religious Creativity of Modern Humanity: Some Observations on Eliade's Unfinished Thought. *Relig Stud*, 31(2), 221-235, Je 95.

Eliade proposed to 'undertake to analyze the religious creativity of modern societies' in his *History of Religious Ideas* but never did so. In this paper I have attempted to suggest the general direction that this analysis would have taken—the identification of the real with the actual is a religious valorization of contemporary humanity. This is not a generic shift from religion to non-religion but a belief of a religious nature which constitutes a novel departure from the traditional operations of the religious mind. It is accompanied by a refusal to countenance our creative involvement in the construction of reality. This Eliade labels 'modern' and 'historical'.

Repetto Milán, Guillermo. Réquiem por la Filosofía?. *Analogia*, 7(2), 189-195, 1993.

Repicky, Miroslav and Labedzki, Grzegorz. Hechler Reals. *J Sym Log*, 60(2), 444-458, Je 95.

Requate, Angela. Was R G Collingwood an Undercover Pragmatist?. *Dialogos*, 30(66), 93-115, Jl 95.

Rescher, Nicholas. "Chisholm's Ontology of Things" in *American Philosophy Today and Other Philosophical Studies, Rescher, Nicholas*, 137-151. Lanham, Rowman & Littlefield, 1994.

Rescher, Nicholas. "Concretization Quandaries and Pragmatic Anomalies" in *American Philosophy Today and Other Philosophical Studies, Rescher, Nicholas*, 113-128. Lanham, Rowman & Littlefield, 1994.

Rescher, Nicholas. "Obligation Dynamics and Deontic Metamorphosis" in *American Philosophy Today and Other Philosophical Studies, Rescher, Nicholas*, 81-90. Lanham, Rowman & Littlefield, 1994.

Rescher, Nicholas. "On Writing Philosophy" in *American Philosophy Today and Other Philosophical Studies, Rescher, Nicholas*, 43-80. Lanham, Rowman & Littlefield, 1994.

Rescher, Nicholas. "Peirce on the Validation of Science" in *Peirce and Contemporary Thought: Philosophical Inquiries, Ketner, Kenneth Laine (ed)*, 103-112. New York, Fordham Univ Pr, 1995.

Rescher, Nicholas. "Reichenbach Falls (Or Only Stumbles?)" in *American Philosophy Today and Other Philosophical Studies, Rescher, Nicholas*, 129-136. Lanham, Rowman & Littlefield, 1994.

Rescher, Nicholas. "Religious Belief and Scientific Method" in *American Philosophy Today and Other Philosophical Studies, Rescher, Nicholas*, 153-172. Lanham, Rowman & Littlefield, 1994.

Rescher, Nicholas. "The Rise and Fall of Analytic Philosophy" in *American Philosophy Today and Other Philosophical Studies, Rescher, Nicholas*, 31-42. Lanham, Rowman & Littlefield, 1994.

Rescher, Nicholas. *American Philosophy Today and Other Philosophical Studies*. Lanham, Rowman & Littlefield, 1994.

A series of studies of logical issues in philosophy and in the history of philosophy. The aim is to show how philosophical inquiry can at once enliven and illuminate topics of widely current interest for philosophers.

Rescher, Nicholas. Luck and the Enigmas of Fate. *Phil Exch*, 24-25, 95-105, 1993-94.

Rescher, Nicholas. Pragmatischer Idealismus oder idealistischer Pragmatismus?. *Deut Z Phil*, 42(5), 883-904, 1994.

Rescher, Nicholas. Reason and Reality. *Protosoz*, 6, 14-27, 1994.

The project of inquiry into the nature's *modus operandi* faces extensive and deep-rooted difficulties. In particular there are four major problems: 1) Data undetermine theories, 2) Theories undetermine facts, 3) Reality transcendes the *descriptive* resources of language, and 4) Reality transcendens the *explanatory* resources of language. The lesson of these delierations is not a sceptical despair but a healthy dose of cognitive humility. In pursuing the aims of science we can expect improvement but not completion; however, deeply we push our inquiries into nature, we cannot get to the bottom of things.

Resnick, Stephen and Wolff, Richard. "Lessons from the USSR: Taking Marxian Theory the Next Step" in *Whither Marxism?, Magnus, Bernd (ed)*, 207-234. New York, Routledge, 1994.

A surplus labor rather than a power or property definition of class is deployed to ask what was the class structure of the USSR. Individuals other than the workers in state enterprises were always the appropriators and distributors of the surplus produced by those workers. The former used the appropriated surplus to secure a specific kind of property, power, cultural, and economic structure that kept them in their class position in the Soviet state. This distinctive surplus labor approach suggests that what collapsed in the Soviet Union was not socialism, but rather state capitalism, now being replaced by private capitalism.

Resnik, David. Repairing the Reticulated Model of Scientific Rationality. *Erkenntnis*, 40(3), 343-355, My 94.

In *Science and Values* (1984) and other, more recent, works, e.g., (1987a, 1987b, 1989a, 1989b, 1990), Larry Laudan proposes a theory of scientific debate he dubs the "reticulated model of scientific rationality" (Laudan, 1984, pp 50-66). The model stands in sharp contrast to hierarchical approaches to rationality exemplified by Popper (1959), Hempel (1965), and Reichenbach (1938), as well as the conventionalist views of rationality defended by Carnap (1950), Popper (1959), Kuhn (1962), and Lakatos (1978). Ironically, the model commits some of the same errors Laudan finds in hierarchicalist and conventionalists approaches to scientific rationality. This paper will show that the model can be fixed by recognizing that criteria of goal assessment have no privileged status. These rules are best viewed as simply rules of rationality (or rules of scientific method) by another name.

Resnik, David B. Epistemic Value: Truth or Explanation?. *Metaphilosophy*, 25(4), 348-361, O 94.

This paper summarizes and criticizes a dispute about the nature of epistemic value. Reliabilists hold that truth is our highest epistemic aim, while explanationists hold that explanatory coherence is our highest aim. I argue that both aims should be treated as ultimate, epistemic values and that we should accept a pluralistic account of epistemic value.

Resnik, David B. Functional Language and Biological Discovery. *J Gen Phil Sci*, 26(1), 119-134, 1995.

This paper provides an explication and defense of a view that many philosophers and biologists have accepted though few have understood, the idea that functional language can play an important role in biological discovery. I defend four theses in support of this view: 1) functional statements can serve as background assumptions that produce research problems; 2) functional questions can be important parts of research problems; 3) functional concepts can provide a framework for developing general theories; 4) functional statements can serve as heuristics for generating hypotheses. I develop and defend these four claims by describing a taxonomy of functional discourse, providing an account of scientific discovery, and by applying this framework to some cases of successful research in biology.

Resnik, David B. Hacking's Experimental Realism. *Can J Phil*, 24(3), 395-411, S 94.

This paper provides a critical analysis of Ian Hacking's experimental realism and argues that Hacking does not succeed in shifting the defense of realism away from questions about representation to questions about intervention.

Resnik, Michael D. Scientific versus Mathematical Realism: The Indispensability Argument. *Phil Math*, 3(2), 166-174, My 95.

Penelope Maddy and Elliott Sober recently attacked the confirmational indispensability argument for mathematical realism. We cannot count on science to provide evidence for the truth of mathematics, they say, because either scientific testing fails to confirm mathematics (Sober) or too much mathematics occurs in false scientific theories (Maddy). I present a pragmatic indispensability argument immune to these objections, and show that this argument supports mathematical realism independently of scientific realism. Mathematical realism it turns out, may be even more firmly established than scientific realism.

Restall, Greg. Four-Valued Semantics for Relevant Logics (and Some of Their Rivals). *J Phil Log*, 24(2), 139-160, Ap 95.

This paper gives an outline of three different approaches to the four-valued semantics for relevant logics (and other nonclassical logics in their vicinity). The first approach borrows from the 'Australian Plan' semantics, which uses a unary operator '*' for the evaluation of negation. This approach can model anything that the two-valued account can, but at the cost of relying on insights from the Australian Plan. The second approach is natural, well motivated, independent of the Australian Plan, and it provides a semantics for the contraction-free relevant logic *C* (or *RW*). Unfortunately, its approach seems to model little else. The third approach seems to capture a wide range of formal systems, but at the time of writing, lacks a completeness proof.

Rethy, Robert A. Nietzsche: *Das religiöse Wesen*. *Int Stud Phil*, 26(3), 67-91, 1994.

Alongside his resounding proclamation of the "death of God" is Nietzsche's announcement of the return of a "new" god, Dionysus. The complications of the relation of Nietzsche, the pastor's son, to religion as well as that of religion and philosophy are examined through an interpretation of *Beyond Good and Evil*, Chapter III as well as a portion of *The Antichrist*. Of particular concern is the nature of the teaching of Nietzsche's "new god" and its relation to that of the "old". The paper concludes by offering a new perspective on the phrase with which *Ecce Homo*, and Nietzsche's publications as a whole, ends: "Have I been understood? Dionysus against the Crucified..."

Reverter Bañón, Sonia. J L Austin: un análisis de la percepción desde la fenomenología lingüística. *Dialogo Filosof*, 10(2), 233-238, My-Ag 94.

La explicación, defensa y justificación de la teoría de los datos sensibles ha absorbido grandes energías dentro de la filosofía de la percepción. Con todo se nos presenta hoy en día como una teoría tan derruida como el edificio epistemológico al cual pretendía sustentar: el fundamentalismo. Muchas, y desde muy diferentes Flancos, han sido las críticas que han sausado su caído. Precisamente aquí se expone la que considero una de las más agudas: la que realiza J L Austin desde la postura teórica que él llama "fenomenología lingüística".

Revonsuo, Antti. Consciousness, Dreams, and Virtual Realities. *Phil Psych*, 8(1), 35-58, 1995.

In this paper I develop the thesis that dreams are essential to an understanding of waking consciousness. In the first part I argue in opposition to the philosophers

AUTHOR INDEX WITH ABSTRACTS 707 Richardson, Robert C

Malcolm and Dennett that empirical evidence now shows dreams to be real conscious experiences. In the second part, three questions concerning consciousness research are addressed. 1) How do we isolate the system to be explained (consciousness) from other systems? 2) How do we describe the system thus isolated? 3) How do we reveal the mechanisms on which this system is based? I suggest that empirical dream research combined with other empirical approaches can help us to sketch answers to all of these questions. I argue that the subjective form of dreams reveals the subjective, macro-level form of consciousness in general and that both dreams and the everyday phenomenal world may be thought of as constructed "virtual realities". A major task for empirical consciousness research is to find out the mechanisms which bind this experienced world into a coherent whole.

Rey, Georges. "The Unavailability of What We Mean: A Reply to Quine, Fodor and LePore" in *Holism: A Consumer Update, Fodor, Jerry A (ed)*, 61-101. Amsterdam, Rodopi, 1993.

Fodor and LePore's attack on conceptual role semantics relies on Quine's attack on the traditional analytic/synthetic and a priori/a posteriori distinctions, which in turn consists of four arguments: an attack on truth by convention; an appeal to revisability; a claim of confirmation holism; and a charge of explanatory vacuity. Once the different merits of these arguments are sorted out, their proper target can be seen to be not the traditional distinctions, but an implicit assumption about their superficial availability that we have abundant reason to reject. Once we reject it, we can see how issues of the absorption of conventions, the revisability of belief, and confirmation holism are compatible with the traditional distinctions, and that Quine's discussion only serves to camouflage the question of whether some confirmation relations are constitutive of meaning and knowable a priori.

Rey, Georges and Pietroski, Paul. When Other Things Aren't Equal: Savings *Ceteris Paribus* Laws from Vacuity. *Brit J Phil Sci*, 46(1), 81-110, Mr 95.

A common view is that *ceteris paribus* clauses render lawlike statements vacuous, unless such clauses can be explicitly reformulated as antecedents of 'real' laws that face no counterinstances. But such reformulations are rare; and they are not, we argue, to be expected in general. So we defend an alternative sufficient condition for the nonvacuity of *ceteris paribus* laws: roughly, any counterinstance of the law must be independently explicable, in a sense we make explicit. *Ceteris paribus* laws will carry a plethora of explanatory commitments; and claims that such commitments are satisfied will be as (dis)confirmable as other empirical claims.

Reyle, Uwe and Gabbay, Dov M. Direct Deductive Computation on Discourse Representation Structures. *Ling Phil*, 17(4), 343-390, Ag 94.

We present a deductive component for discourse representation theory. The computation procedures are described for both, intuitionistic and classical logic. They are based on the notion of run time skolemisation, i.e., Skolem functions are introduced at run time and not at the beginning of the proof. Therefore each proof stage is meaningful and has a natural relation to the original query. Finally we show how the Skolem dependencies can be expressed by the hierarchical structure of the DRS's, i.e., by the accessibility relation. This serves to avoid computational problems connected with the treatment of equality. (edited)

Reynolds, Steven L. Proxy Functions and Inscrutability of Reference. *Analysis*, 54(4), 228-235, O 94.

Quine's proxy function argument for the inscrutability of reference fails, for proxy function reinterpretations do not in fact have either the same connections to sensory stimuli or the same logical interconnections as do the standard interpretations. This is so in spite of the guarantee of sameness of truth value.

Reynolds, Terrence. Two McFagues: Meaning, Truth, and Justification in *Models of God*. *Mod Theol*, 11(3), 289-313, Jl 95.

The purpose of this essay is to assess the nature of theological meaning, truth, and justification at work in Sallie McFague's *Models of God*. I suggest that McFague is methodologically ambiguous at times, and thereby weakens the force of her argument. I then attempt to re-state what I take to be her position as clearly as possible and locate her work within contemporary discussions of historicism, alethiology, epistemology, and ontology. I argue that her approach represents a theological adaptation of Jeffrey Stout's neopragmatism, and that understanding her project in that light bring its signficance into bold relief.

Rheinberger, Hans-Jörg. Representation(s). *Stud Hist Phil Sci*, 25(4), 647-654, Ag 94.

The article is an essay review. It argues that, as a result of the developments in 20th century sciences, especially in physics and semiotics, the positivisitic notion of representation has gone. Representation and reference have entered into an inextricable interconnection. This interconnection is followed through an essay collection of M Lynch and S Woolgar (eds) concerning *Representation in Scientific Practice*, and a collection of papers on art and literature by W J T Mitchell, *Iconology: Image, Text, Ideology*. As a consequence, the perspective of a pragmatogony of representation is sketched, in which the relation between representation and reality is reversed.

Rhonheimer, Martin. Intentional Actions and the Meaning of Object: A Reply to Richard McCormick. *Thomist*, 59(2), 279-311, Ap 95.

In defence of the encylical *Veritatis splendor*, the article points out the erroneous action theory underlying proportionalism and consequentialism, mainly their lack of an adequate concept of intentional action. For proportionalists, action itself remains a physical event that realizes the state of affairs one has a "proportionate reason" to bring about. This leads to unacceptable consequences, mainly an "expanded notion of object" which falsely allows to redescribe, according to ones preferences, any concrete action, rendering it impossible that there exist universal moral norms referring to intrinsically evil types of action. Thus, on principle any action can be morally justified. Instead of offering a virtue centered approach, proportionalism shows itself to be a late product of casuistic methodology.

Rhook, Graeme and Zangari, Mark. Should We Believe in the Big Bang?: A Critique of the Integrity of Modern Cosmology. *Proc Phil Sci Ass*, 1, 228-237, 1994.

We analyze aspects of the Big Bang program in modern cosmology, with special focus on the strategies employed by its adherents both in defending the theory against anomalous data and in dismissing rival accounts. We illustrate this by critically examining four aspects of Big Bang cosmology: the interpretation of the cosmic red-shift, the explanation of the cosmic background radiation, the inflation hypothesis and the search for dark matter. We conclude that the Big Bang's dominance of contemporary cosmology is not justified by the degree of experimental support it receives relative to rival theories.

Rialle, Vincent and Payette, Daniel. Richesse, Tensions et Diversité des Sciences de la Cognition. *Lekton*, 4(2), 5-20, 1994.

Ribeiro dos Santos, Leonel. La Vivencia de lo Sublime y la Experiencia Moral en Kant. *An Seminar Hist Filosof*, 9, 115-126, 1992.

Partiendo del recononcimiento del papel que Kant atribuye al sentimiento, incluso en el ámbito de la ética crítica, se pretende mostrar la íntima solidaridad existente entre el sentimiento moral y el sentimiento de lo sublime y encarar la posibilidad de considerar a este último no sólo en tanto que manifestación y expresión estéticas de la moralidad, sino también en tanto que vivencia matriz de la condición moral humana. Desde la "Analítica de lo sublime" de la *Crítica del Juicio*, el llamado "formalismo ético" kantiano asume otro sentido, y expresiones como las de "santidad", "majestad", "pureza" y "sublimidad" de la ley moral se nos revelan en toda su intención.

Ribeiro Silva, Idalice. Natureza e História: Os Sentidos da Liberdade e da Igualdade. *Educ Filosof*, 8(16), 35-76, Jl-D 94.

Ricci, Saverio. Un'idea alla Ricerca di un Partito: L'eredità di Silvio Spaventa nel Liberalismo di Fine Ottocento. *G Crit Filosof Ital*, 72(3), 453-472, S-D 93.

Rice, Lee and Barbone, Steven. "Coming Out, Being Out, and Acts of Virtue" in *Gay Ethics, Murphy, Timothy F (ed)*, 91-110. New York, Haworth Pr, 1994.

We examine three philosophical models for (gay) self-identity: utilitarianism (exemplified by Eichberg), deontologism (Mohr), and individualism (Spinoza). The first two, we argue, overlook the personal and multi-faceted nature of social relations. We argue that the framework of methodological individualism is better suited to deal with the issues of self-identity as they affect questions of whether, when, and how to come out, and being out. This framework suggests that there is no moral principle which could apply universally in regard to being out and that there are common situations in which it is not morally appropriate to come out or to be out at all.

Rich, John Martin. Students and Legal Obedience. *J Thought*, 29(4), 55-63, Wint 94.

Richard, Alan J and Montoya, Isaac D. A Comparative Study of Codes of Ethics in Health Care Facilities and Energy Companies. *J Bus Ethics*, 13(9), 713-717, S 94.

Though written corporate codes of ethics have been touted as a panacea for the embarrassments and uncertainties of the past two decades, the absence of clear evaluation procedures severely compromises their usefulness. An ethnographic study comparing development processes and compliance outcomes in large health care facilities and energy companies shows that neither of the two industries has encountered much success with a codes of ethics program. (edited)

Richard, Mark E. Boër and Lycan's *Knowing Who*. *Nous*, 27(2), 235-242, Je 93.

Richards, David A J. Review Essay: Perfectionist Moral Theory, the Criminal Law, and the Liberal State—*Making Men Moral* by Robert P George. *Crim Just Ethics*, 13(2), 93-101, Sum-Fall 94.

Richards, Norvin W. Innocence. *Amer Phil Quart*, 31(2), 157-167, Ap 94.

This paper concerns the quality of innocence which we associate with young children and think of them as losing, gradually and unevenly with the passage of time. I offer analyses of what this quality is as it occurs in children, and of what it is as it (sometimes) occurs in adults, and of how these are related. The analyses are meant to explain why the innocence of a child excuses it so completely from culpability as to rendor a trial wholly inappropriate and why an adult's innocence about some matter does not have that same effect.

Richardson, Bill and Curwen, Peter. Do Free-Market Governments Create Crisis-Ridden Societies?. *J Bus Ethics*, 14(7), 551-560, Jl 95.

The paper is concerned with the potential or actual impact that free-market governmental principles and policies might have, or might have had, in helping to create a more crisis-prone world. It is concerned with organizationally-induced crises where organizations and their environment interact to create disasters. The nature of the crisis-prone organization is discussed in the context of the relevant management literature. It is argued that the disastrous interaction of such an organization with its environment is promoted by a laisser-faire attitude on the part of the authorities. This is illustrated in the context of two recent British disasters involving the King's Cross Underground fire and the sinking of the Herald of Free Enterprise.

Richardson, Henry S. *Practical Reasoning about Final Ends*. New York, Cambridge Univ Pr, 1994.

Richardson, Kurt Anders. The Naturalness of Creation and Redemptive Interests in Theology, Science, and Technology. *Zygon*, 30(2), 281-291, Je 95.

This paper advances ways in which the understandings of "nature" and "creation" can be seen to overlap through specialized relations between humans and their environment. The hope of redemption of nature, united with evidences of grace in the advancements of science, can become helpful guides toward a theological interpretation of technology and the emerging character of human relations with nature.

Richardson, Robert C. Optimization in Evolutionary Ecology. *Proc Phil Sci Ass*, 1, 13-21, 1994.

Optimization models treat natural selection as a process tending to produce maximal adaptedness to the environment, measured on some "criterion scale" defining the optimal phenotype. These models are descriptively adequate if they describe the outcomes of evolutionary processes. They are dynamically adequate if the variables which describe the outcomes also are responsible for those evolutionary outcomes. Optimality models can be descriptively adequate, but dynamically unrealistic. Relying on cases from evolutionary ecology, I provide reasons to question the dynamic adequacy of optimality models, and offer reasons for distinguishing, at least at a theoretical level, between satisficing and optimizing.

Richardson, William J. Dasein and the Ground of Negativity: A Note on the Fourth Movement in the *Beiträge*-Symphony. *Heidegger Stud*, 9, 35-52, 1993.

Richardson, William J. Heidegger's Fall. *Amer Cath Phil Quart*, 69(2), 229-253, Spr 95.

Richardson, William J. Lacan and the Enlightenment: Antigone's Choice. *Res Phenomenol*, 24, 25-41, 1994.

Richer, Renée. Le Romantisme Grec. *Diotima*, 22, 139-146, 1994.

Richli, Urs. "Ich aber fordere Sie auf, absolute Genesis ins Auge zu fassen!". *Fichte-Studien*, 6, 423-433, 1994.

Mediation and immediacy are the fundamental principles in the representation of absolute knowledge by Hegel and Fichte. Both thinkers take mediation as a negative relation, whose links are reduced to moments by negativity and thus in the same respect are related positively. While Hegel determines immediacy as the identity of the negative unity, that is to say as a self-referential negation, Fichte conceives nonmediatable essence, invading the diverging negativity and focusing it. Both Hegel and Fichte insist in introducing immediacy without imputting it on the negativity by an external reflexion. Against Hegel's pretension of a total mediation we are to consider that the operation of self-referential negation implies an immediacy absolutely immediatable.

Richter, Dirk. Existentialism and Postmodernism: Continuities, Breaks, and Some Consequences for Medical Theory. *Theor Med*, 15(3), 253-265, S 94.

Since existentialism lost its influence in philosophy in the 1960s, postmodern theory has taken over criticizing basic concepts of Western thought. From a postmodern point of view, the main shortcomings of existentialism is that is criticizes traditional unitarian concepts, while re-inventing new unitarian models. Against these unitarian approaches postmodernism holds that the world can only be described in terms of difference. In this article the postmodern program and its differences from existentialism are explained in reference to three concepts of Western philosophy: subject, truth, and ethics. Applying these concepts, the relevance of postmodernism for medical theory is illustrated.

Richter, Duncan. The Incoherence of the Moral 'Ought'. *Philosophy*, 70(271), 69-85, Ja 95.

The purpose of the paper is to explain and evaluate Elizabeth's Anscombe's thesis, in "Modern Moral Philosophy", that special 'moral' uses of terms such as 'obligation', 'ought', 'right' and 'wrong' are often or always incoherent. This thesis is examined in the light of criticisms by Kurt Baier, Paul Johnston and Peter Winch, and a defense by Cora Diamond. The conclusions reached are that Anscombe is largely right, that her critics have generally failed to understand her argument, and that there is probably little awareness of the dangers to which she has drawn our attention. Moral philosophers should beware.

Rickard, Maurice. Liberalism, Multiculturalism, and Minority Protection. *Soc Theor Pract*, 20(2), 143-170, Sum 94.

The article explores the idea of minority protection for both aboriginal and immigrant minorities. The basic claim is that ethnocultural minorities in liberal multicultures are in danger of disadvantaged access to their cultural communities, disadvantage that can only be redressed if it is viewed as an injustice. Accordingly, the article does some groundwork toward a liberal egalitarian theory of minority rights. In particular, the discussion seeks to reduce the force of the following four common reservations about ethnic minority rights. 1) disadvantaged access to one's cultural community doesn't seem objectionable enough to warrant political redress; 2) even if aboriginal culture warrants protection, it's a completely different matter with immigrants; 3) ethnic minority rights are destabilizing and require an absurd pluralism, where different laws and institutions apply to different groups in the one society; and 4) differential cultural rights are inegalitarian in the eyes of difference-blind liberal principles of justice.

Ricken, Friedo. Tradition und Natur: Über Vorgaben und Grenzen der praktischen Rationalität. *Theol Phil*, 70(1), 62-77, 1995.

R. discusses four issues of the Liberitarian-Communitarian debate. 1) He distinguishes between the moral identity of a person which cannot be conceived without tradition and the political identity for which you need Rawls' concept of a person. 2) Not all rationality is tradition-immanent; nevertheless a tradition has the positive function of transmitting morally relevant experiences. 3) There are objective, tradition-independent basic goods which are differently interpreted in different traditions. 4) The priority of the right to the good is defended; nonetheless life needs a teleological dimension.

Ricketts, Thomas. "Carnap's Principle of Tolerance, Empiricism, and Conventionalism" in *Reading Putnam, Clark, Peter (ed)*, 176-200. Cambridge, Blackwell, 1995.

Rickman, H P. From Hermeneutics to Deconstruction: The Epistemology of Interpretation. *Int Stud Phil*, 27(2), 65-80, 1995.

Deconstruction—represented by such authors as Derrida, de Man, Barthes and Hillis Miller—offers a challenging nihilism which undermines our notions of truth, meaning and knowledge. Considering its origin and ways of combatting it, this article offers—documented in brief outline—a threefold thesis. 1) Deconstruction is rooted in an epistemological development embracing both hermeneutics and Kant's "Copernican Revolution." 2) It supports its negative claims by intellectually questionable strategies such as abolishing the author or rejecting contrasts between center and periphery. 3) To reject its radical skepticism we need to reexamine some crucial turning point in nineteenth century epistemology.

Ricoeur, Paul. "Etica e morale" in *L'etica e il suo Altro, Vigna, Carmelo (ed)*, 217-227. Milano, FrancoAngeli, 1994.

Ricoeur, Paul. "Intellectual Autobiography of Paul Ricoeur" in *The Philosophy of Paul Ricoeur, Hahn, Lewis Edwin (ed)*, 3-53. Peru, Open Court, 1994.

Ricoeur, Paul. "The Status of *Vorstellung* in Hegel's Philosophy of Religion" in *Meaning, Truth, and God, Rouner, Leroy (ed)*, 70-88. Notre Dame, Univ Notre Dame Pr, 1982.

Ricoeur, Paul. Commémoration du Centenaire de la Mort de Jules Lagneau: "Le jugement et la Méthode Réflexive selon Jules Lagneau". *Bull Soc Fr Phil*, 88(4), 120-138, O-D 94.

Ricoeur, Paul. El escándalo del mal. *Rev Filosof (Spain)*, 4(5), 191-197, 1991.

Ricoeur, Paul. Homage to Jan Patocka. *Magyar Filozof Szemle*, 5-6, 809-815, 1994.

Ricoeur, Paul. Multiple Foreigness. *Filozof Cas*, 43(1), 37-49, 1995.

Ricoeur, Paul. The Plurality of Sources of Law. *Ratio Juris*, 7(3), 272-286, D 94.

In this paper, the author contends with the problem of an infra-state differentiation of sources of law. He examines two accounts of a juridical pluralism, that of Walzer (1983) and that of Boltanski and Thévenot (1991). Both these works reveal a similar inability to account for the political dimension. The author identifies this inability as the result of the paradox of the political. He goes on to discuss this paradox in terms of a need to reconcile indivisible popular sovereignty with the proliferation of a multitude of sources of legality.

Ricoeur, Paul and Vansina, Frans D. "Bibliography of Paul Ricoeur" in *The Philosophy of Paul Ricoeur, Hahn, Lewis Edwin (ed)*, 605-815. Peru, Open Court, 1994.

The bibliography opens with the list of Paul Ricoeur's Honorary Degrees, Awards and memberships in Learned Societies (p 609). Then the primary bibliography offers a quasi exhaustive listing of the books and articles written by Paul Ricoeur and published in fifteen different languages from 1947 up to 1994 (pp 611-735). The secondary bibliography lists the books and only the main articles on Paul Ricoeur's writing published in sixteen languages and covering years 1947 up to 1993 (pp 735-815). Both bibliographies retake and complete an early bibliographical publication: *A Primary and Secondary Systematic Bibliography of Paul Ricoeur 1935-1948* by Faus D Vansina (Louvain-la-Neuve Editions Peeters, 1985). This bibliographical work could only be achieved thanks to the substantial and precious help of Paul Ricoeur himself.

Ridley, Aaron. *Music, Value, and the Passions*. Ithaca, Cornell Univ Pr, 1995.

This book is about musical expression. I attempt to offer an account that does justice both to the resemblances between musical gestures and human expressive behaviour and to the affective character of the experience of expressive music. In the course of setting out this account, approaches are offered to the problems of musical understanding and of music and negative emotion. The book concludes with a reappraisal of the work of the great Beethoven critic, J W N Sullivan.

Ridley, Aaron. Musical Sympathies: The Experience of Expressive Music. *J Aes Art Crit*, 53(1), 49-58, Wint 95.

Riedel, Manfred. "Heideggers europäische Wendung" in *Das geistige Erbe Europas, Buhr, Manfred (ed)*, 411-423. Napoli, Vivarium, 1994.

Riedel, Manfred. "Heideggers europäische Wendung" in *Europa und die Philosophie, Gander, Hans-Helmuth (ed)*, 43-66. Frankfurt/M, Klostermann, 1993.

Riedel, Sharon L and Adelman, Leonard. Using the Multitrait-Multimethod Matrix to Evaluate Knowledge-Based Systems. *Commun Cog—AI*, 11(3), 277-297, 1994.

This paper presents empirical data illustrating how the multitrait-multimethod matrix can be applied to assess the adequacy of knowledge-based systems in difficult but common evaluation settings, where there is only one problem scenario, experts who disagree, and no accuracy measures.

Ries, Wiebrecht. Schopenhauer im Spiegel der europäischen Literatur des 19 und 20 Jarhunderts. *Schopenhauer Jahr*, 76, 173-193, 1995.

Rigby, Paul and O'Grady, Paul and Van Den Hengel, John. Must a Hermeneutical Psychoanalysis Exclude Science?. *Man World*, 28(2), 115-128, Ap 95.

Riggsby, Andrew M. Pliny on Cicero and Oratory: Self-Fashioning in the Public Eye. *Amer J Philo*, 116(1), 123-135, Spr 95.

In letter 1.20, on the basis of minimal evidence, Pliny claims that Cicero published his speeches in abridged form. Pliny's inferences are motivated by his close association with Cicero. He chooses to form this association because the interpretive instability created by contemporary tyranny made an identity from the past safer. Even this strategy, however, cannot guarantee a stable identity. Hence the need to defend a particular version of "Cicero".

Rigobello, Armando. Dio nella modernità: Husserl. *Acta Phil*, 2(3), 271-286, 1994.

In Husserl, God is identified as cause of the teleological order of the world, absolute and transcendent; but the divine being falls outside the scope of phenomenological study and must be "bracketed". Husserl insists on a radical distinction between God's transcendence and that of consciousness. However, the nature of the difference is unclear. The analysis of transcendental subjectivity manifests a priori grounds or functions which possess a seemingly divine absoluteness: the logos of all possible beings, at once universal and concrete, reminiscent of the Spinozian and Kantian conceptions of the divine mind; the guarantee of intersubjectivity analogous to God's role as the guarantee of truth in Descartes; and a tension toward omni-comprehension, with religious connotations comparable to those of Kant's "ideal of reason". As in the case of the transcendental subject's role as "constitutive" of meaning, a role which is ambivalent between "creativity" and mere "dynamic discovery", the limits of the phenomenological method proclude a definitive resolution of the ambiguity. The question requires a positive confrontation between phenomenology and classical metaphysics.

Rigotti, Francesca. The Influence of the Rhetoric on the Ethics. *Z Phil Forsch*, 49(2), 241-258, Ap-Je 95.

In this paper we ask whether and, if so, how rhetoric interferes with the world of norms and action. The answer is affirmative, and shows that rhetoric, with its appeal to the passions and the imagination, to the unsaid and the unsayable, is linken in various ways to the field of ethics. Ethics and rhetoric both have to do with values accepted as preferable not because they are evident, but because they are not questioned by reasonable people. Metaphors of the ethical theory are here also examined because they are an essential form for the understanding the rhetorical moment of the invention of an original moral theory.

AUTHOR INDEX WITH ABSTRACTS 709 Rizzacasa, Aurelio

Rigsby, Roberta K. "Jungians, Archetypalists, and Fear of Feminism" in *The 1994 Annual of Hermeneutics and Social Concern, Lawler, Justus George (ed)*, 35-58. New York, Continuum, 1994.

Riley, Patrick (ed & trans) and Fénelon, François. *Telemachus, Son of Ulysses*. New York, Cambridge Univ Pr, 1994.

Riley II, Charles A. *Color Codes: Modern Theories of Color in Philosophy, Painting and Architecture, Literature, Music, and Psychology*. Hanover, Univ Pr New England, 1995.

Color Codes is an interdisciplinary study of the theory and practice of color that examines seminal texts by Kant, Goethe, Hegel, Wittgenstein, Spengler, Adorno, Barthes, Derrida, Hardin, Westphal and Hacker. It also examines the parallels between philosophical texts on color and the studio practice of artists (including Cezanne, Matisse, Kandinsky, Albers and contemporary artists including Frank Stella, Roy Lichtenstein and Peter Halley among others), composers, poets and novelists (including Stevens, Joyce, Pynchon and Proust), and psychologists (including Jung, Arnheim and Oliver Sacks). In a series of interviews with artists, composers, philosophers, psychologists, architects, designers and other contemporary thinkers on color, the variety of approaches to the problem of color is emphasized.

Rinderle, Peter. Liberale Integrität. *Deut Z Phil*, 42(1), 73-95, 1994.

Rip, Arie and de Jong, Hidde. Ontdekkingspraktijk in Plaats van Logica: Wetenschappelijk Ontdekken in Computer-Ondersteunde Ontdekkingsomgevingen. *Kennis Methode*, 19(2), 131-159, 1995.

The idea that computer programs might be able to make scientific discoveries provides a challenging perspective for both computer scientists and philosophers. Discussions on discovery programs often depart from the assumption that these programs should be seen as autonomous super scientists in which a certain logic of discovery has been embodied. In this article an alternative view will be elaborated, namely a view in which discovery programs are understood as supporting tools in a scientific practice. These supporting discovery programs are integrated with other computer tools and conventional tools in a computer-supported discovery environment. In order to illustrate the power of such a discovery environment, a realistic scenario is sketched describing the route to a discovery in molecular biology. In conclusion, the consequences of the introduction of a computer-supported discovery environment for scientific practices are discussed.

Ripperger, Chad. The Species and Unity of the Moral Act. *Thomist*, 59(1), 69-90, Ja 95.

In an article written by Gerard Casey in the *New Scholasticism*, the problem of a lack of unity among the constituents of the moral act in St Thomas's action theory is posed. The question he asks is a valid one: where does the moral act receive its unity? I believe St Thomas answers that question, but before we take a look at his answer, it is necessary first to discuss what the constituents of the moral act are. This in itself is not without its complications, for what the constituents of the moral act are for Aquinas is likewise open to debate. In order to answer Casey's question, the article will take the following form: first, we will consider what the constituents of the moral act are; then, we shall try to answer Casey's question: "Where does the moral act receive its unity?"

Ripstein, Arthur. Questionable Objectivity. *Nous*, 27(3), 355-372, S 93.

Riser, John J. Democracy as a Reflection of Principles of Universalism. *Dialogue Hum*, 4(2-3), 119-126, 1994.

Risser, James C. "The Remembrance of Truth: The Truth of Remembrance" in *Hermeneutics and Truth, Wachterhauser, Brice (ed)*, 123-136. Evanston, Northwestern Univ Pr, 1994.

This paper claims that the experience of truth in philosophical hermeneutics is determined from the analysis of the beautiful that is presented at the end of *Truth and Method*. The consequence of this determination is a renewed understanding of the nature of "image". I conclude that this experience of truth is not simply, as Richard Bernstein claims, that which can be argumentatively validated by a community of interpreters, nor is it simply the event of truth as described by Heidegger in his retrieval of the Greek word "*aletheia*". Rather, the experience of truth pertains to the continual reacquisition of insight found in the "veritable image".

Risser, James C. Poetic Dwelling in Gadamer's Hermeneutics. *Phil Today*, 38(4), 369-379, Wint 94.

This paper claims that there is a notion of poetic dwellings in Gadamer's philosophical hermeneutics that properly understood not only describes the experience with art and poetry, but more importantly expresses the character of the theoretical as such as this came to be understood by the hermeneutics of facticity developed in the 1920s. In this context poetic dwelling is understood in terms of an enactment of sense within the temporal dimension of *Verweilen*. The paper concludes by arguing that poetic dwelling is directly related to the task of philosophy itself.

Rist, John M and Peroli, E (trans). Plotino, Ficino e noi stessi: alcuni riflessi etici. *Riv Filosof Neo-Scolas*, 86(3), 448-467, Jl-S 94.

Ritchie, Gisela F. Contributors to the Genesis of Europe: Gotthold Ephraim Lessing and His Followers. *Hist Euro Ideas*, 19(1-3), 425-430, Jl 94.

Ritter, Mark (trans) and Simmel, Georg. Bridge and Door. *Theor Cult Soc*, 11(1), 5-10, F 94.

Ritter, Mark (trans) and Simmel, Georg. The Picture Frame: An Aesthetic Study. *Theor Cult Soc*, 11(1), 11-17, F 94.

Ritter, Mark A (trans) and Beck, Ulrich. *Ecological Enlightenment: Essays on the Politics of the Risk Society*. Atlantic Highlands, Humanities Pr, 1995.

Ecological Enlightenment examines the politics of the risk society. The book considers the ecological issue—viewed both politically and sociologically—as a systematic, legalized violation of fundamental civil rights and argues that the ecological conflict is the successor to the industrial conflict. It concludes with the plaidoyer for the unfinished democracy: Can we survive in freedom? This may be the most significant question before us. Democracy has to be rethought and rebuilt towards a global ecological citizenship.

Riva, Franco. L'analogia dell'ente in Domenico di Fiandra. *Riv Filosof Neo-Scolas*, 86(2), 287-322, Ap-Je 94.

The Domenico's Flanders (d 1479) doctrine of analogy is very important for the history of problem before Cajetan. In *Metaphysics* IV, II, he is inspired by Thomas of Aquinas, discusses with the School of Scotus and mentions many discussions and different authors of XIV and XV centuries: it results that the problem of analogy was discussed among the Thomists, who gave different solutions to different questions. According to Domenico, analogy of attribution is able to answer the problems of abstraction, distinction and comparation of concept of being. The analogy differs from equivocity and univocity: it is a predication of the common concept about priority and posteriority.

Rivera, José. Fundamentos Filosóficos del Concepto Muñocista de la Libertad. *Dialogos*, 30(66), 137-151, Jl 95.

The parallel between the philosophy of Yves R Simon (1903-1961), and the political thought of Luis Muñoz Marín (1898-1980), founding father of the Commonwealth of Puerto Rico, is explored. Simon's philosophy is seen to found and articulate Muñoz's politics, while Muñoz's politics confirms the value of Simon's philosophy. Both view liberty not as mere undetermination, but as autonomy. The concept of "autonomy" is the keystone of Simon's theory of government. Democracy is considered a superior form of government precisely because it maximizes autonomy. Muñoz thought that Puerto Rico should cultivate as much autonomy as is compatible with American citizenship.

Rivera de Rosales, Jacinto. Cuestiones Metodológicas en la Investigación Filosófica. *An Seminar Hist Filosof*, 11, 9-52, 1994.

Se reflexiona aquí sobre las estrategias básicas de una investigación filosófica en base a la estructura de la subjetividad y de la comprensión: su originariedad, su finitud y la intersubjetividad. Por ello el estudioso ha de partir de su propio interés, delimitar el tema según sus capacidades, pensar por sí mismo y dialogar. En esto ha de tener en cuenta la originariedad y temporalidad característica del diálogo filosófico, la tarea interpretativa de los textos, las deficiencias de todo lenguaje y la situación personal. Por último se hacen algunas observaciones sobre la redacción.

Rivera de Rosales, Jacinto. De Philosophia. *An Seminar Hist Filosof*, 6, 89-109, 1986-89.

This article provides a systematic presentation of the tasks, purpose and method that in general terms characterise philosophical thought. It is based on the Platonic dialectic as its first complete programme and, making a fundamental comparison of this dialectic and modern science, currently the form of knowledge most revered, asks what is left of that primitive reasoning.

Rivera de Rosales, Jacinto. La Universalidad de la ley Moral. *An Seminar Hist Filosof*, 9, 99-106, 1992.

La reflexión de este artículo no se dirige a dirimir qué máximas serían o no universalizables, sino a estudiar qué significa la universalidad de la ley moral. En primer lugar, expresa la exigencia racional de salir del mundo particular de cada uno y vivir en la realidad real. Quiere decir también que la autonomía del sujeto ha de determinar en última instancia *todos* sus actos. Y, finalmente, la universalidad hace relación a la intersujetividad o reino de fines, que constituye el mundo moral. De este modo, la universalidad de la ley moral se presenta como la forma básica de la relación de la libertad consigo misma, el ámbito donde ha de realizarse el acto individual libre.

Rivera de Rosales, Jacinto. Sujeto y Realidad: Del Yo Analítico Substante al Yo Sintétoco Transcendental. *Daimon Rev Filosof*, 9, 9-38, 1994.

The inevitable intervention of subjectivity in the knowledge process already lead to scepticism in Greece, when philosophical reflection was centred on the empiric aspects of same. Coming out of that isolation or enclosure as things are in which the subject is considered (even in the present criticisms of the notion) is only possible by discovering the most basic moments of subjectivity through which it is necessarily open to the other reality (to the world and to others) since this opening or acceptance of its finitude constitutes a condition of possibility for it. This was something which Descartes with his analytical method was unable to achieve, but which Kant and Fichte did achieve through synthetic transcendental reflection.

Rivier, Dominique. Une réflexion sur les rapports entre science et foi. *Rev Theol Phil*, 127(1), 55-61, 1995.

Après une présentation de l'ouvrage *Science et foi font système*[1], contenant une demi-douzaine d'exposés indépendants mais utilisant tous l'approche herméneutique, l'étude critique signale un certain nombre d'écueils attachés à la vision systémique généralement adoptée par les auteurs: abstraction des représentations, <symétrisation> des interlocuteurs. Est mise en question notamment l'opportunité de limiter le dialogue entre science et foi à la problématique *dogmatique*.

Rivoli, Pietra. Ethical Aspects of Investor Behavior. *J Bus Ethics*, 14(4), 265-277, Ap 95.

The neoclassical paradigm assumes that shareholders' utility is solely a function of their wealth, and prescribes that management should act in a manner consistent with share price maximization. The stakeholder view also assumes that shareholders' utility derives from wealth, but prescribes that managers must balance the shareholder wealth maximization objective against the rights of other constituencies. Thus, while neoclassicists and stakeholder theorists have different prescriptives for management behavior, their definitions of the shareholders' interest are consistent—shareholders are self-interested economic agents whose utility is best served by share price maximization. However, if shareholders are "other-interested," and attack importance to ethical and moral values, then both the neoclassical and stakeholder view derive from invalid assumptions. In this paper, I present evidence that much shareholder behavior is ethically motivated. As a result, the basis for both the neoclassical and the stakeholder view is weakened.

Rizzacasa, Aurelio. La persona nell'itinerario filosofico ermeneutico di P Ricoeur. *Aquinas*, 36(3), 561-574, S-D 93.

Ricoeur, whilst elaborating upon his conclusions on the theory of subjectivity proposes a hermeneutic itinerary in which the revival of the individual is affected by overcoming individualism. In this framework the investigations compare the doubts emerging from the philosophical theory of individualism with those contained in the hermeneutics of subjectivity putting in evidence the renewed method which is available in modern anthropological philosophy. This also applies in the recovery of ontological applications present in traditional, western philosophy. This means that human individualism can be found in an existential context which is able to realize its uniqueness.

Rizzacasa, Aurelio. La riappropriazione di Aristotele nell'ultimo Ricoeur. *Aquinas*, 37(1), 35-57, Ja-Ap 94.

The investigations are based on Ricoeur's presumptions. The conclusion of his recent studies on subjectivity proved, through hermeneutics, the recovery of the ontologic applications present, either in anthropological philosophy, or in the analysis of ethical-political issues. In this framework the explanation results in an objective theme in social reality focusing on the problem of the movement. The above demonstrates the recovery of the Aristotelian concepts of power and action, and even "dinamis" and "energheia" which became particularly significant for the Ricoeurian philosophical attempt, which is also directed towards the revival of the traditional concept.

Rizzacasa, Aurelio. Per una riconsiderazione del rapporto tra etica e politica. *Convivium*, 5, 5-21, 1993.

The main purpose of this paper is recovering the theoretical significance of the notions: "ethics" and "politics", in a deeper sense than an analytic approach. The author thinks the autonomy of these notions and, at the same time, their common issues; first from an historical perspective and, then, from the personal author's view. The author explains an anthropological standard as a possibility to understand these notions and their connections.

Rizzi, Dominick A. Causal Reasoning and the Diagnostic Process. *Theor Med*, 15(3), 315-333, S 94.

The purpose of this paper is to analyze aspects of causation relevant for discussing causal reasoning in a diagnostic context. Causal reasoning and diagnosis go well in hand, especially if both concepts are widened. The theory of causes as nonredundant components in effective causal complexes, modulated by what is referred to as the stop problem and causal fields, is valuable for explaining the many aspects of causal reasoning in medical diagnosis. (edited)

Rizzo, Mario J and Cowan, Robin. "Fundamental Issues in the Justification of Profits" in *Profits and Morality, Cowan, Robin (ed)*, 1-21. Chicago, Univ of Chicago Pr, 1995.

This paper discusses some of the more prominent arguments for and against the justification of profits. Early in the paper several different types of profit are distinguished to set the stage for normative evaluation. Then arguments like utilitarianism and Pareto-efficiency, evolutionism, rights and free exchange, fair exchange, "sweat-of-the-brow", and discovery are analyzed. The paper raises the important issues with which any normative theory of profits must deal.

Rizzo, Mario J (ed) and Cowan, Robin (ed). *Profits and Morality*. Chicago, Univ of Chicago Pr, 1995.

This book of papers addresses the issue of the moral justification of profits. Presenting arguments for and against the morality of profit-making, the contributors examine the nature of profits and the ethical theories that can support them. Two essays address economic aspects of profits: one explores entrepreneurship as a legitimate source of profits; the other argues that recent advances in welfare economics weaken the case for the morality of profits. The other chapters focus on ethical theory, covering the right to profit from economic rent; the morality of how profits are used; and whether or not profits are deserved.

Robbins, J Wesley. Is Naturalism Irrational?. *Faith Phil*, 11(2), 255-259, Ap 94.

Alvin Plantinga's epistemological argument in the last chapter of *Warrant and Proper Function*, to the effect that it is self-defeatingly irrational to believe the combination of naturalism and evolutionary theory, is seriously flawed. It presupposes that beliefs are subjective states intrinsically specifiable without reference to what is going on in the world around their holders. Evolutionary naturalists, most notably pragmatists, who reject that conception of beliefs in favor of a holistic one, are untouched by Plantinga's argument.

Robert, Serge. Réflexion Épistémologique sur l'Intelligence Artificielle et les Sciences Cognitives: à Quelles Conditions une Machine Pourrait-elle Connaître?. *Horiz Phil*, 2(2), 167-184, Spring 92.

The debate about the possibility for a computer to have knowledge is a contemporary version of the old philosophical debate between the materialist and dualist accounts of the mind. The paper holds that the most fruitful philosophical position in cognitive science is emergentism while in artificial intelligence it is rather reductivist materialism. So, one has not to choose between Searle and Churchland in their famous controversy: each standpoint having its fruitfulness and its limits. The paper holds that the main difference between the knowing mind and our actual nonknowing computers is the human capability of correction relative to its environment.

Roberts, David D. La Fortuna di Croce e Gentile negli Stati Uniti. *G Crit Filosof Ital*, 73(2-3), 253-281, My-D 94.

Roberts, Julian. Suchen, sich Verständigen, Kämpfen: das Umfeld der Sprache. *Deut Z Phil*, 42(5), 841-860, 1994.

Roberts, Mark S (ed) and Harvey, Robert (ed) and Lyotard, Jean-François. *Toward the Post-Modern*. Atlantic Highlands, Humanities Pr, 1995.

Roberts, Robert C. Feeling One's Emotions and Knowing Onself. *Phil Stud*, 77(2-3), 319-338, Mr 95.

In the context of the construal account of emotion, emotions are distinguished from the feelings or consciousness of them. Just as an emotion can err (getting the object or its importance wrong), so a feeling can err (getting the emotion wrong, either as to its type or as to its object). Emotions are states of awareness of situations, including the self as part of the situation; feelings, in the presently discussed sense, are states of awareness of the self as in an emotional state. Six criteria are offered for the truth of feelings.

Roberts, Robin W and Malone, David. An Analysis of Public Interest Reporting: The Case of General Motors in South Africa. *Bus Prof Ethics J*, 13(3), 71-92, Fall 94.

Robertson, Diana C and Ross Jr, William T. Decision-Making Processes on Ethical Issues: The Impact of a Social Contract Perspective. *Bus Ethics Quart*, 5(2), 213-240, Ap 95.

This paper develops a framework for examining decision making about ethical issues and tests the applicability of a social contract perspective. Using two separate samples of students and salespeople, we determine that community members (salespeople) tend to judge a potentially unethical act to constitute a violation of an implicit social contract and noncommunity members (students) do not. Also, consistent with the emphasis on context specificity of integrative social contracts theory, situational variables influence perceptions of ethicality for the community members, but do not affect the perceptions of individuals outside the community. The study finds considerable support for the use of a social contractarian perspective in the study of decision-making processes about ethical issues.

Robertson, John A. Norplant and Irresponsible Reproduction. *Hastings Center Rep*, 25(1), S23-S26, Jan-Feb 95.

Robertson, John A. Symbolic Issues in Embryo Research. *Hastings Center Rep*, 25(1), 37-38, Jan-Feb 95.

Robin, Donald P and Reidenbach, R Eric. A Response to "On Measuring Ethical Judgements". *J Bus Ethics*, 14(2), 159-162, F 95.

This article discusses the major criticisms posed in "On Measuring Ethical Judgments" concerning our ethics scale development work. We agree that the authors of the criticism do engage in what they accurately refer to as "armchair theorizing". We point out the errors in their comments.

Robinet, André. "Leibniz, die Gelehrtenrepublik und Italien" in *Das geistige Erbe Europas, Buhr, Manfred (ed)*, 137-148. Napoli, Vivarium, 1994.

Robinson, Daniel N. Wild Beasts and Idle Humours: Legal Insanity and the Finding of Fault. *Philosophy*, 37(Supp), 159-177, 1994.

A reaction of a book-length study of the history of the legal concept of insanity this essay reviews the different conceptions mental competence framed within juridical, scientific and psychological contexts. There are signal incompatibilities between foundational assumptions of law (e.g., moral autonomy, rational prowess, *mens rea*) and certain deterministic elements in scientific and psychological conceptions of human nature. The plausibility of insulating the former from the latter is explored and defended.

Robinson, Jenefer. *L'Éducation Sentimentale*. *Austl J Phil*, 73(2), 212-226, Je 95.

Robinson, Jenefer and Karl, Gregory. Levinson on Hope in *The Hebrides*. *J Aes Art Crit*, 53(2), 195-199, Spr 95.

Robinson, Jenefer M. Startle. *J Phil*, 92(2), 53-74, F 95.

There are reasons for thinking that the startle mechanism is a primitive emotional response. A theory of emotional response in general is developed using startle as a model. It is claimed that this model solves conceptual problems about emotional response that cannot be solved by theories which make cognitive evaluation an essential feature of emotional response.

Robinson, John H. Physician Assisted Suicide: Its Challenge to the Prevailing Constitutional Paradigm. *Notre Dame J Law Ethics*, 9(2), 345-366, 1995.

In this article I argue first that dying, as a social construct, has undergone a significant restructuring during the course of the present century. I then argue that dying occupies a precarious place in the current substantive due process jurisprudence of the United States Supreme Court. Finally I argue that dying and the diminishment that is ordinarily incident to it ought to be of special interest to Christian communities just insofar as that diminishment has the potential to reveal certain basic truths about the human condition.

Robinson, Michael D. *Eternity and Freedom: A Critical Analysis of Divine Timelessness as a Solution to the Foreknowledge/Free Will Debate*. Lanham, Univ Pr of America, 1995.

"In this work, Robinson explores whether appeal to divine timelessness is a viable solution to the conflict that exists between the notions that God knows the future and that humans are free. While divine timelessness formally provides a resolution to this dilemma, it is often argued that divine timelessness generates its own set of difficulties; namely, it is an unintelligible concept, it conflicts with the idea that God is personal, and it produces its own form of determinism. Robinson engages each of these complications that is intelligible, does not conflict with the idea of a personal deity, and does not imply its own form of determinism."

Robinson, Peter. A Reply to Antony Flew's Discussion of "E O Wilson After 20 Years". *Phil Soc Sci*, 25(2), 216-218, Je 95.

Robinson, T M. "Sobre la Fecha de Composición del *Timeo*" in *Platón: Los Diálogos Tardíos, Lan, Conrado Eggers (ed)*, 57-65. Sankt Augustin, Academia, 1986.

Robinson, Timothy A. *Aristotle in Outline*. Indianapolis, Hackett, 1995.

A survey designed for beginners in philosophy, intended either to accompany Aristotle's texts or to provide background for studying philosophers influenced by Aristotle. I try to show the reasoning behind Aristotle's doctrines and to illustrate how concepts and principles that emerge in one field are deployed to good effect in others. The first part treats the four causes, demonstration, scientific principles, dialectic, the soul, and the unmoved movers. I then attempt to make Aristotle's conception of virtue intelligible to contemporary students. The final chapter revolves around the sense in which the political association can be called "natural."

Robinson, Viviane M J. Dialogue Needs a Point and Purpose. *Educ Theor*, 45(2), 235-249, Spr 95.

Robinson, William S. Brain Symbols and Computationalist Explanation. *Mind Mach*, 5(1), 25-44, F 95.

Computationalist theories of mind require brain symbols, that is, neural events that represent kinds or instances of kinds. Standard models of computation require multiple inscriptions of symbols with the same representational content. The satisfaction of two conditions makes it easy to see how this requirement is met in computers, but we have no reason to think that these conditions are satisfied in the brain. Thus, if we wish to give computationalist explanations of human cognition, without committing ourselves *a priori* to a strong and unsupported claim in neuroscience, we must first either explain how we can provide multiple brain symbols with the same content, or explain how we can abandon standard models of computation. It is argued that both of these alternatives require us to explain the execution of complex tasks that have a cognition-like structure.

Robinson, William S. Commentary on "Contractarianism Gone Wild: Carruthers and the Moral Status of Animals". *Between Species*, 10(1-2), 49-52, Win-Spr 94.

Peter Carruthers has claimed that his version of contractarianism can support certain distinctions that his theory of ethics regarding animals requires. Boonin-Vail's paper disputes this, holding that the required distinctions cannot be maintained in a principled way within Carruthers's contractarian framework. I defend Carruthers's ability to make the needed distinctions. One key point turns on being careful to exclude certain obvious *moral* judgments from behind the veil of ignorance, where they cannot legitimately enter because they depend on *results* of contracting. Another requires careful separation of *intrinsic* (noninstrumental) possession of moral rights from possession of *full* moral rights.

Robinson, William S. Orwell, Stalin, and Determinate Qualia. *Pac Phil Quart*, 75(2), 151-164, Je 94.

In *Consciousness Explained*, Dennett holds that at very short intervals the distinction between Orwellian and Stalinesque revisions of experience fails to have sense. I explain how this view seems to imply a denial of determinate causes for qualia, and thus a denial of qualia. This is a devastating argument against qualia if it works, but I show that it does not. I cite evidence that Dennett believes that qualia, and therefore their causes, can be temporally point-like. But qualia theorists are committed to no such view; and without this commitment, the argument from Orwellian/Stalinesque indeterminacy does not succeed against qualia.

Roccaro, Giuseppe. Il soggetto della scienza prima. *G Metaf*, 16(1-2), 45-82, Ja-Ag 94.

Roccaro, Giuseppe. L'Élenchos del Principio nella Metafisica di Averroé. *G Metaf*, 16(3), 353-382, S-D 94.

Averroes considers the question of the demonstration of the first principles of the knowledge in the light of IV book of Aristotelian *Metaphysics*. Averroes's 9th commentary specifies the principle essence and comes to the conclusion that the demonstration of the first principle by difference is the demonstration of the impossibility in the error direction. So this possibility of demonstrating is bound to the eventuality of saying by radical necessity: every *ex principiis* demonstration of the first principle is impossible. But Averroes's commentary shows the radical indifference of the simple demonstration and the one by error, because the possibility of the error is given only by the acknowledgement of the foundation.

Rocchetti, Loretta and Malherbe, Jean-François and Boiro-Lavigne, Anne-Marie. Validité et limites du consensus en éthique clinique. *Laval Theol Phil*, 50(3), 531-543, O 94.

Le caractère multiculturel qui marque profondément nos systèmes de valeurs rend difficile la référence à des normes reconnues par tous lorsqu'il est nécessaire de prendre une décision qui engage de multiples acteurs sociaux. Cette difficulté est particulièrement sensible lorsqu'il s'agit de prendre des décisions à l'égard de la mise en oeuvre des techniques biomédicales. Face à cette difficulté bien réelle, une tendance est apparue de fonder de telles décisions sur le consensus des personnes les plus directement concernées. L'objet de la présente discussion est d'évaluer la validité et les limites d'un tel recours au consensus. Le consensus auguel vise la discussion rationnelle entre les sujets éthiques à propos de la critique des normes particulières comme de l'application des normes universelles et particulières aux situations singulières, constitue une indispensable garantie à l'encontre de bien des arbitraires qui tendraient à s'emparer du pouvoir. Mais le refus inconditionnel de reconnaître l'existence de *dissensus avérés* aurait pour conséquence immédiate de restaurer subrepticement une forme d'arbitraire particulièrement subtile puisqu'elle se cacherait derrière le masque de la rationalité.

Roche, Timothy. "The Ultimate End of Action: A Critique of Richard Kraut's *Aristotle on the Human Good*" in *The Crossroads of Norm and Nature, Sim, May (ed)*, 115-138. Lanham, Rowman & Littlefield, 1995.

Rocher, Emmanuel (trans) and Raschini, Maria-Adelaide. *Rosmini et l'Idée de Progrès*. Bordeaux, Biere, 1995.

Rocher, Guy. Le Défi Éthique dans un Contexte Social et Cuturel en Mutation. *Philosopher*, 16, 11-26, 1994.

This article was the keynote speech opening a conference on "The Ethical Challenge: Issues and Perspectives". The approach is sociological, based on several years of research on health, medicine, and bioethics. Four dimensions of modernity are developed, and the ethical issues they create. The dominance of the middle class raises the issues of individualism and consumerism. With the disenchantment of the world and history appears the problem of truth and uncertainty. The new social relationhips raise the ethical matter of human difference. The fragmentation of the spheres of life puts into question the status of ethics and of the new ethicians.

Rochon, François. Notes pour une archéologie du postmodernisme. *Horiz Phil*, 5(1), 56-73, Autumn 94.

This paper considers the genesis of the notion of postmodernism, particularly in literary studies, as it was theoretically defined during the 1970's and the first half of the 1980's. Taking into account Fredric Jameson's and Jean-François Lyotard's different conceptions of postmodernism, one can argue that postmodernism related to literature consists in three types of mutation in comparison with literary modernism: psychological, narratological and epistemological. However, these mutations are rather a question of degrees and variations than of ruptures and contrasts. In fact, it seems that what is called postmodernism is a means for literary modernism to resist the regressive movement of history and to ensure its own duration and its own renewal.

Rockmore, Tom. "Hegel's Metaphysics, or the Categorial Approach to Knowledge of Experience" in *Hegel Reconsidered, Engelhardt Jr, H Tristram (ed)*, 43-56. Dordrecht, Kluwer, 1994.

Rockmore, Tom. "Zur Relevanz der Vernunft im Bewusstsein der Gegenwart" in *Das geistige Erbe Europas, Buhr, Manfred (ed)*, 277-290. Napoli, Vivarium, 1994.

Rockmore, Tom. Fichtean Circularity, Antifoundationalism, and Groundless System. *Ideal Stud*, 25(1), 107-124, Wint 95.

Rockmore, Tom. Hegel and the Hermeneutics of German Idealism. *Int J Phil Stud*, 3(1), 111-131, Mr 95.

Rockwell, W Teed. Beyond Determinism and Indignity: A Reinterpretation of Operant Conditioning. *Behavior Phil*, 22(1), 53-66, Spr-Sum 94.

B F Skinner's writing on the free will issue has received much attention because it was assumed that his dismissal of free will was based on his scientific discoveries. In this article, I show that when we look at Skinner's place in the history of psychology, and his own descriptions of his laboratory procedures, we find that Skinner's scientific work offers no evidence for determinism. In fact, it could be argued that it offers partial evidence (although not proof) for the existence of free will. The concept of free choice, although difficult to define or justify, is seen to be fully compatible with the effectiveness and validity of operant conditioning. We must therefore conclude that Skinner has not resolved the free will question, with either scientific facts or philosophical arguments.

Rockwell, W Teed. On What the Mind is Identical With. *Phil Psych*, 7(3), 307-323, 1994.

The unity of mind and *body* need not imply accepting the unity of mind and *brain*, because the mind-brain identity is something that science has presupposed, not discovered. I cite evidence from modern neuroscience that cognitive activities are distributed throughout the human nervous system, which challenges the 'scientific' assumption (believed by Descartes, among others) that the brain is the seat of the soul, and the rest of the nerves are mere message cables to the brain. Dennett comes close to accepting this point when he criticizes 'Cartesian materialism', and yet he still claims that 'the head is headquarters'. Accepting that the mind is the entire nervous system solves some philosophical problems, for Dennett and others. There is also some evidence that indicates that some cognitive activities may be hormonal rather than neural, which raises some challenging problems for the once obvious distinction between *causing* a mental state and *embodying* that state.

Rocque, André. L'éthique des Affaires: Un Concept Problématique. *Philosopher*, 17, 45-61, 1995.

The concept of business ethics is basically antinomic. In this paper, the four basic antinomies of business ethics are presented and discussed. The relationship of these antinomies to one another is then debated. Three questions are then raised and discussed: moral responsibility when following orders; the degree of loyalty to one's employer in ethical matters; and the conditions of collective responsibility. Finally, some thoughts are offered on how we think about business ethics, specifically on the gap between entrepreneurial behaviour and community expectations, and on the very concept of immoral acts in business.

Roddy, Bernard. The Problem of Generality (on Alan Millar's *Reasons and Experience*). *Ratio*, 7(2), 183-190, D 94.

In *Reasons and Experience* Alan Millar proposes that empirical beliefs are justified by sensory experience only if the experience is of the right type. I think that the idea is subject to an objection that has been raised against some reliabilist theories of epistemic justification. This objection is that reliabilism does not have any clear implications about the justificatory status of beliefs until further details are provided, and that no such details can avoid The Problem of Generality. After a brief discussion of this problem for reliabilists, I explain why Millar's view suffers from a similar difficulty.

Rodi, Frithjof (ed) and Misch, Georg (ed) and Kühne-Bertram, Gudrun (ed). *Der Aufbau der Logik auf dem Boden der Philosophie des Lebens*. Freiburg, Alber, 1994.

This book presents for the first time Georg Misch's lectures on logic and epistemology. On the basis of Dilthey's philosophy of life and the latest linguistic, anthropological discoveries of the period, as well as in response to the positions of Heidegger and Husserl, Misch attempts to offer an extension of and at the same time a new foundation for traditional logic. As a hermeneutic logic which is not restricted to discursive cogitation, this extends *all* types of thinking. The author tries to derive logical phenomena from everyday life and ordinary language, in order to make evident the original unity of life and thought.

Rodón, Eulalia. Variaciones Isidorianas. *Rev Espan Filosof Med*, 1, 159-165, 1994.

The paradoxical character of Isidere of Seville, the contradictions and undeniable incoherences in his work are to be understood in the light of the social culture of Visigethie, Spain. Nevertheless the studies in this line of research have always been restricted to culture in the sense of literary or scholarly learning, a written production. But all along these centuries where a great part of people were unable to read an important bulk of social culture was communicated through oral transmission and images or figurative illustration, an amalgam of pagan symbols and myths and Christian legends or beliefs. This was the original source to which most of Isidere's blamed incongruities or absurd statements can be traced back.

Rodrigo, Lidia Maria. Entre a Sabedoria Silenciosa e a Fala sem Fim. *Educ Filosof*, 8(16), 207-227, Jl-D 94.

This article focuses Parmenides and Heraclitus's thought as two different possibilities of articulation of philosophical discourse in ancient Greece. It examines critically Alexandre Kojève's interpretation, for whom Parmenides's thesis about Being results in a "silent wisdom" while Heraclitean conception constitutes an "endless talk".

Rodrigues, Alcione. Pedagogia Pelo e Para o Trabalho: Açao Disciplinadora da Burguesia e a Resistência dos trabalhadores. *Educ Filosof*, 8(16), 87-105, Jl-D 94.

Rodriguez, Beverly and Iannuzzo, Rebecca and Sieber, Joan E. Deception Methods in Psychology: Have They Changed in 23 Years?. *Ethics Behavior*, 5(1), 67-85, 1995.

To learn whether criticism and regulation of research practices have been followed by a reduction of deception or use of more acceptable approaches to deception, the contents of all 1969, 1978, 1986, and 1992 issues of the *Journal of Personality and Social Psychology* were examined. Deception research was coded according to type of (non)informing (e.g., false informing, consent to deception, no informing), possible harmfulness of deception employed (e.g., powerfulness of induction, morality of the behavior induced, privacy of behavior), method of deception (e.g., bogus device or role, false purpose of study, false feedback), and debriefing employed. Use of confederates has been partly replaced by uses of computers. "Consent" with false informing declined after 1969, then rose in 1992. Changes in the topics studied (e.g., attribution, socialization, personality) largely accounted for the decline in deception in 1978 and 1986. More attention needs to be given to ways of respecting subjects' autonomy, to appropriate debriefing and desensitizing, and to selecting the most valid and least objectionable deception methods.

Rodriguez, Victor. Comentarios Sobre la Teoría de las Cantidades Conservadas. *Rev Latin de Filosof*, 21(1), 23-35, Fall 95.

This paper is an exposition and critical view of the theory of conserved quantity from the basic definitions to its version of causal asymmetry. The theory is exhibited through the examples given by the author. At the end it is proposed an extension of the concept of conserved quantity related to the concepts of invariants, conservation laws and physical constants. In particular, causality in this physicalist approach is seen as strongly dependent on physical constants.

Rodríguez, Amán Rosales. Heidegger, lector de Nietzsche. *Rev Filosof (Costa Rica)*, 32(77), 93-101, Jl 94.

Nietzsche plays a crucial role in the philosophy of Martin Heidegger. Nietzsche is, according to Heidegger, the last speaker for Western metaphysics after Plato, Aristotle, Descartes and Hegel. This means, for Heidegger, that Nietzsche's ideas announce the end of philosophy: the culmination in our days of the scientific-technological rationality, as well as the possibility of a new beginning for thinking (das Denken) at the end of history.

Rodríguez, Mariano. Introducción a la Filosofía de las Emociones. *An Seminar Metaf*, 28, 287-296, 1994.

It is the aim of this paper to attain a general view of the present reflexion about emotions. In the first place something is said about two preludial questions, the legitimacy of the so-called common-sense psychology, and the relevance we could nowadays recognize to introspection. In order to discuss the concept of emotion we decide to defend the evaluative view thus resolving the problems of the emotional intentionality and the motivational function of emotions. The final conclusion consists of questioning the passivity our philosophical tradition attributes to emotion.

Rodríguez, Rosa M. "The Female Subject after the Death of Man" in *Reconstructing Foucault, Miguel-Alfonso, Ricardo (ed)*, 245-266. Amsterdam, Rodopi, 1994.

Rodríguez Alcázar, Javier. Cientificismo, Kanitsmo y Esencialismo. *Rev Filosof (Spain)*, 7(12), 519-522, 1994.

Rodríguez Braun, C and Schwartz, P. Las relaciones entre Jeremías Bentham y S Bolívar. *Telos (Spain)*, 1(3), 45-68, O 92.

Rodríguez Braun, Carlos. Ilustración y Utilitarismo en Iberoamérica. *Telos (Spain)*, 1(3), 95-109, O 92.

Rodríguez Donís, Marcelino. G Vico: Oración I (1669). *Cuad Vico*, 2, 253-259, 1992.

Rodriguez Gonzalez, M. Metafísica de la finalidad natural: Su metamorfosis en la línea Kant-Schopenhauer-Nietzsche. *Pensamiento*, 198(50), 435-455, S-D 94.

En el concepto de "adecuación a un fin" se condensan los esquemas fundamentales de la metafísica occidental. Desde la audaz aproximación aristotélica de finalidad natural y técnica humana hasta la especificación kantiana de aquélla como principio subjetivo o heurístico, asistimos a un proceso de paulatina clarificación de este concepto paradigmático. En las obras de Schopenhauer y Nietzsche, por otro lade, la finalidad accede a su más elevade significación, ya sea en sentido positivo o negativo. Todo vendría a concluir en la ruptura del enlace entre naturaleza y metafísica dogmática: quedan empero abiertos otros cominos para la finalidad.

Rodríguez Larreta, Juan. "Espacio, Tiempo y Particulares" in *Temas Actuales de Filosofía, Palacios, María Julia (ed)*, 525-531. Buenos Aires, Univ Nacional Salta, 1993.

Rodríguez Pereyra, Gonzalo. La anotación de las Investigaciones Filosóficas de Wittgenstein. *An Seminar Metaf*, 27, 25-37, 1993.

Rodríguez Piñeiro, Hipólito. "El Proyecto Moderno de la Razón el Pensamiento de la Diferencia" in *Temas Actuales de Filosofía, Palacios, María Julia (ed)*, 533-545. Buenos Aires, Univ Nacional Salta, 1993.

The project of the modernity, represented by Husserl, and that of postmodern thought, that Derrida exemplifies in Joyce, they are relative one to the other: Joyce notes to master the multiplicity in a sincronic sought, Husserl struggles against the equivocity knowing however that, since an experience is carried to the word enters in nets of significance and extralinguistic situations in (those) which the meanings are substantially occasional.

Rodríguez-Bachiller, Angel. El Eclipse de la Verdad. *Rev Espan Filosof Med*, 0, 169-175, 1993.

A vital philosophy is the result of an empirical metaphysics by real-life experience. Nonvalid human philosophy can be based on negation and nothingness. Being and the principles of being constitute the basis of real philosophy. The problem of truth and life is formed by consciousness and action, ideas and behavior. The "international cultured-conscience" makes humanity coexist. Philosophy requires tradition and progress, past an evolution. The truth is impersonal, it has to be seen in itself. The Thomism which was "guiding light", in crisis will eclipse the truth.

Rodríquez, Gonzalo and Font, Josep Maria. Algebraic Study of Two Deductive Systems of Relevance Logic. *Notre Dame J Form Log*, 35(3), 369-397, Sum 94.

In this paper two deductive systems (i.e., two consequence relations) associated with relevance logic are studied from an algebraic point of view. One is defined by the familiar, Hilbert-style, formalization of R; the other one is a weak version of it, called WR, which appears as the semantic entailment of the Meyer-Routley-Fine semantics, and which has already been suggested by Wójcicki for other reasons. This weaker consequence is first defined indirectly, using R, but we prove that the first one turns out to be an axiomatic extension of WR. Moreover we provide WR with a natural Gentzen calculus (of a classical kind). It is proved that both deductive systems have the same associated class of algebras but different classes of models on these algebras.

Rodwin, Marc A. *Medicine, Money, and Morals: Physicians' Conflicts of Interest*. New York, Oxford Univ Pr, 1993.

Roe, John H. Revisionary Materialism: A Critique of Stich. *Conference*, 3(2), 67-75, Fall 92.

I defend the plausibility of there being an intermediate position between eliminative and the full retention of the folk-psychological conception of belief in a future science of behavior. Future cognitive scientists might posit states which we would find difficult to categorize as beliefs or to dismiss as clearly not being beliefs. Whether or not they are properly construed as beliefs might turn out to be an indeterminate matter.

Roebben, Bert. Catching a Glimpse of the Palace of Reason: The Education of Moral Emotions. *J Moral Educ*, 24(2), 185-197, 1995.

The main issue of this paper concerns how the education of emotions can contribute to moral education. This reflection starts from the intuition that a mere cognitive-developmental approach is insufficient to understand the phenomenon of moral growth as a whole. Moral education can be cold and ineffective without any real commitment to the emotional stratum of the human person. Therefore, a theory on the appropriateness and reasonableness of emotions is presented from which conclusions are drawn on the educability of emotions. A distinction is then made between altruistic and rule-emotions, and the development from the first to the second is described. Children learn to care for others and through this process they learn the relevant rules for this praxis of care. Some results from research in developmental psychology are helpful here. Finally, the necessity of an ongoing education of emotions, even within an analytical approach to ethical formation at school, is argued. Communication on values and norms implies principally the emotional involvement and existential readiness to share the *communio* of dialogue partners.

Röd, Wolfgang. "Descartes' Auffassung der Natur zw. Physik und Metaphysik" in *Naturauffassungen in Philosophie, Wissenschaft, Technik: Band II, Schäfer, Lothar (ed)*, 185-216. Freiburg, Alber, 1994.

Roelcke, Volker. Jewish Mysticism in Romantic Medicine? Indirect Incorporation of Kabbalistic Elements in the Work of Gotthilf Heinrich Schubert. *Hist Phil Life Sci*, 16(1), 117-140, Ja 94.

This paper attempts a first outline of an analysis of the connection between the Kabbalah, the tradition of Jewish mysticism, and medicine in the Romantic age. The physician and natural philosopher Gotthilf Heinrich Schubert (1780-1860), a friend and pupil of the philosopher Freidrich Wilhelm Joseph Schelling, is chosen as a representative of the era. The political, institutional, and philosophical background at the beginning of the nineteenth century is outlined to make intelligible the contemporary disposition for mystical ideas. The historical lines of connection between the Kabbalistic tradition and Romantic medical thought as represented by Schubert are investigated, and examples are given for some correspondences of ideas and topics. The specific combination of these topoi, and a multitude of historical lines of connection, primarily through the work of Schelling and the theologian Friedrich Christoph Oetinger, support the hypothesis that Schubert was indirectly influenced by ideas from the Kabbalah. Finally, the history of the reception of Romantic medicine is sketched, with special regard to those strands that are likely to have incorporated elements from the Jewish mystical tradition.

Römelt, Johannes. "Merke auf dich selbst" Das Verhältnis des Philosophen zu seinem Gegenstand nach dem *Versuch einer neuen Darstellung der Wissenschaftslehre*. *Fichte-Studien*, 1, 73-98, 1990.

Römelt, Josef. Von der Autonomie zur Authentizität der Freiheit: Die "Studie zur theologischen Ethik" als kaleidoskop gegenwärtiger Fundamentalmoral. *Frei Z Phil Theol*, 41(3), 560-573, 1994.

"Autonome Moral im christlichen Kontext" versucht, den neuzeitlichen Freiheitsbegriff als Pfeiler aufzunehmen. Eine starke diskursethische Rezeption geht heute über die moraltheologische Autonomiediskussion hinaus. Es geht um konsenstheoretische Öffnung der ethischen Reflexion der Kirche. Darüberhinaus wird in erfahrungsbezogenen Ansätzen die bloss rationale Wirklichkeitsbewältigung prozessualer Diskursethik verlassen. Ist die Frage moderner Kultur noch, ob die Rechte einer 'starken' Freiheit anerkannt werden, deren rationale Autonomie gewahrt werden muss? Ist die Frage nicht vielmehr, ob die Freiheit in ihrer Pluralisierten Schwäche und ihren technisch-zivilisatorischen Grenzerfahrungen wahrgenommen wird? Die Frage der Autonomie wandelt sich in die Frage der Authentizität der Freiheit in ihren neuen Grenzerfahrungen.

Roemer, John E (ed). *Foundations of Analytical Marxism (Volume I)*. Aldershot, Elgar, 1994.

Reprints of thirteen major papers in the analytical Marxist tradition, on class, exploitation, power, and domination.

Römpp, Georg. Kant's Ethics as a Philosophy of Happiness: Reflections on the *Reflexionen*. *Mod Sch*, 71(4), 271-284, My 94.

Röska-Hardy, Louise. Denken, Handeln, und Erklärung durch Gründe: Ein Diskussionsbeitrag. *Deut Z Phil*, 43(2), 259-270, 1995.

Röska-Hardy, Louise. Sprechen, Sprache, Handeln. *Protosoz*, 1, 72-86, Ap 91.

The idea that saying it are doings is a platitude among speech act theorists. In the following I argue that the assimilations of the speakers intentions, beliefs and desires

AUTHOR INDEX WITH ABSTRACTS 713 Romera, Luis

to the linguistic meaning of expression types in J R Searles influential speech act theory precludes or explaining, saying, truely as doings, i.e., specifically as linguistic actions. An adequate explanation of speech acts must treat linguistic meaning of expression type and the speakers intentions, beliefs and desires as separate, but coordinate factors in the performance and understanding of linguistic acts.

Rössler, Beate. Gültigkeit und Vielfalt: Einige Bemerkungen über das Verstehen philosophischer Texte. *Deut Z Phil*, 43(1), 31-51, 1995.

The article defends a thesis on the relation between (methods of) understanding a philosophical text and a conception of philosophy itself. The author first differentiates four methods of understanding: (hermeneutic) understanding of intentions, (analytic) rational reconstruction, (French) neostructuralism and (generally used) 'quarry'-method. She explains these methods by citing examples from Schleiermacher's Plato to Kripke's Wittgenstein and demonstrates the relation to accompanying conceptions of philosophy. Finally, in pointing out the analogy of interpretating philosophical texts and philosophically interpreting the work, she develops a conception of philosophy allowing for the 'diversity' of methods of understanding while holding to the claim to 'validity' of interpretation.

Rogers, G A J (ed). *Locke's Philosophy*. New York, Oxford Univ Pr, 1994.

A collection of original papers by well-known Locke scholars, with a substantial Introduction that places Locke's philosophy in its context and shows ways in which his epistemology and political thought were interrelated. The topics covered are Locke's early intellectual biography, the structure of his general philosophy, the Molyneux Problem, Locke on the will, Locke on meaning, solidity and elasticity in the seventeenth century. Locke and aboriginal rights, the politics of Christianity, and Locke's reception and influence in Greece and in Poland.

Rogers, Hudson and Kochunny, C M. Head-Heart Disparity Among Future Managers: Implications for Ethical Conduct. *J Bus Ethics*, 13(9), 719-729, S 94.

An examination of the ethical perceptions of business students using Macobby's head/heart traits and a comparison to earlier studies of managers, accountants, and business students is made. The data were collected at three universities that are similar in size, enrollment and degree programs within the College of Business. Results indicate that present day business students are no less ethically inclined than are their business counterparts in previous eras. In general head traits dominated over heart traits, an indication that business schools continued to do a good job emphasizing and developing analytical skills but a poor job of developing the qualities of the heart that are generally associated with ethical behavior. The implications of these findings are discussed.

Rogers, Kelly. Aristotle on Loving Another for His Own Sake. *Phronesis*, 39(3), 291-302, 1994.

One often hears it said that, despite his eudaimonism, Aristotle endorses altruism or disinterest in some form—for which perhaps the key piece of evidence is his description of the virtuous agent as loving and benefiting his friend "for his own sake". There does seem to be reason to interpret the "for the sake of" proviso nonegoistically, but since both "altruism" and "disinterest" are complex, even "loaded" concepts, for which no equivalents exist in Aristotelian Greek, we have a real need to clarify what we mean in applying them to Aristotle's proviso, and what precisely they commit him to. Finding altruism unhelpful and misleading in interpreting Aristotle, this paper focuses on the idea of disinterest. Elucidated in terms of Aristotle's doctrine of the noble (*to kalon*), disinterest proves to be a more fruitful and instructive concept for understanding the proviso, as well as Aristotelian virtue generally.

Rogler, Erwin. Ist Carnaps Philosophie Reflexionslos?. *Protosoz*, 6, 61-75, 1994.

According to some critics Carnap's philosophy is "reflectioness", i.e., without epistemic content. In contrast to this assertion this essay will show that in the writings of Carnap's semantical period, especially in "Empiricism, Semantics, and Ontology", the fundamentals of an epistemology are developed. It may be called linguistic internalism. The exposition of frameworks are interpreted as an epistemological foundation of semantics. Several problems within this project are discussed, e.g., the determination of domains of frameworks, ontological existence sentences, the relation between theories and frameworks and limits of rationality.

Rohrlich, Fritz. Scientific Explanation: From Covering Law to Covering Theory. *Proc Phil Sci Ass*, 1, 69-77, 1994.

A new model of scientific explanation is proposed: the covering *theory* model. Its goal is understanding. One chooses the appropriate scientific theory and a model within it. From these follows the functioning of the explanandum, i.e., the way in which the model portrays it on one particular cognitive level. It requires an ontology and knowledge of the causal processes, probabilities, or potentialities (propensities) according to which it functions. This knowledge yields understanding. Explanations across cognitive levels demand pluralistic ontologies. An explanation is believed or only accepted depending on the credibility of the theory and the idealizations in the model.

Rohs, Peter. Der materiale Gehalt des Sittengesetzes nach Fichtes Sittenlehre. *Fichte-Studien*, 3, 170-183, 1991.

Rohs, Peter. Lenzen vs Castañeda. *Z Phil Forsch*, 48(4), 572-584, 1994.

Rohs, Peter. Neuhousers Fichte-Deutung. *Z Phil Forsch*, 48(4), 614-619, 1994.

Rohs, Peter. Über die Zeit als das Mittelglied zwischen dem Intelligiblen und dem Sinnlichen. *Fichte-Studien*, 6, 95-116, 1994.

Roic, Sanja. Giulio Bajamonti, un Vichiano Dalmata. *Boll Centro Stud Vichiani*, 24-25, 195-203, 1994-95.

Rollins, Mark (ed). *Danto and his Critics*. Cambridge, Blackwell, 1993.

The purpose of the work is to provide a critical assessment by leading philosophers of the work of Arthur Danto, organized in a way that provides an integrated view of some of his writings on aesthetics, philosophy of history, theory of knowledge, and action theory. The concept of representation and the method of indescernibles are taken as central, unifying themes in this work. Various interpretations are offered of Danto's use of these themes, to which he replies. An analytic introduction to the arguments contained in the articles is included.

Rollins, Mark. Perception and Proper Explanatory Width. *Proc Phil Sci Ass*, 1, 437-445, 1994.

Marr's theory of vision is often said to exemplify wide psychology. The claim rests primarily on Marr's appeal to a high level theory of computational functions. I agree that Marr's theory embodies an exemplary form of wide psychology; what is exemplary about it is the appeal to perceptual tasks. But I argue that the result of invoking task considerations is that we should not adhere to Marr's own conception of proper explanatory width. There is no one conception of width that has a privileged place in explanation.

Rollins, Mark. Re: Reinterpreting Images. *Phil Psych*, 7(3), 345-358, 1994.

The questions addressed in research on mental imagery have become more refined as experimental techniques have become more exact. One issue that has emerged in current work is whether, or in what ways, imaging is like perceiving. Daniel Reisberg and Deborah Chambers have devised a series of experiments that put that question to the test by asking whether images can be reinterpreted in the same ways that perceptual objects can be reinterpreted. They argue that the evidence points to a negative conclusion. Other psychologists have responded, and a debate has ensued. The debate intersects with philosophy in two ways: i) philosophers have appropriated the empirical results in defense of their views on imagery; and ii) psychologists on both sides have argued about the role of 'philosophical considerations' in evaluating the results. My aim is to clarify the issues at stake, to dispel certain confusions apparent in the literature, and to show that recent research does not support the claim that imaging is unlike perceiving in specific respects.

Rolston III, Holmes. "Biology, Ethics and the Origins of Life: An Introduction" in *Biology, Ethics, and the Origins of Life, Rolston III, Holmes (ed)*, 1-14. Boston, Jones & Bartlett, 1995.

Two critical points are of intense biological and philosophical interest: the origin of life, and of human life. With the first biology began, with the second ethics began. In the history of life on Earth, the chemical evolution of life is the opening chapter, the evolution of human life the latest chapter, but one that opens up a whole new drama. We today stand at a crossroads; the Earth history is at that junction with us. The chapters in the anthology here introduced try to understand ethics in its interaction with biology, evaluating origins to discover the nature in, the nature of human duties.

Rolston III, Holmes. "God and Endangered Species" in *Ethics, Religion and Biodiversity, Hamilton, Lawrence S (ed)*, 40-64. Cambridge, White Horse, 1994.

Species have evolved from an evolutionary point of view, but translated into contemporary religious conviction, species exist with a divinely authorized claim to life, which life ought to be respected by humans, who are the overseers of creation. Life is sacred. Human-caused extinctions shut down the creative processes. Human dominion over the Earth is constrained by the inherent goodness in and value of creation. This insight is revealed in the nickname of the "the God committee", authorized to permit extinctions under the Endangered Species Act. "Playing God" is sacreligious. Extinction of species is ungodly. Such religious convictions can be an effective force in conservation biology.

Rolston III, Holmes. "Value in Nature and the Nature of Value" in *Philosophy and the Natural Environment, Attfield, Robin (ed)*, 13-30. New York, Cambridge Univ Pr, 1994.

In nature, animals are able to value their lives, and, although nothing matters to organisms such as plants, matters can be vital for them. Species are historical forms of life defended over generations, and ecosystems are valuable, where this means, "able to generate value", such as occurs with the evolution and ecological support of organisms, animals, and humans. Earth, taken as earth, dirt, seems of little intrinsic value; but Earth, the home planet, is systemically valuable, and importantly the ground of all value. Socrates said that the unexamined life is not worth living; life in an unexamined world is not worthy living either.

Rolston III, Holmes (ed). *Biology, Ethics, and the Origins of Life*. Boston, Jones & Bartlett, 1995.

Eight contributors ask about the nature and origins of life, of ethics, and the relations between biology, ethics, and human values. Contains: Thomas R Cech, "The Origin of Life and the Value of Life"; Dorion Sagan and Lynn Margulis, "Facing Nature"; Niles Eldredge, "Mass Extinction and Human Responsibility"; Michael Ruse, "Evolutionary Ethics"; Francisco J Ayala, "The Difference of Being Human"; Elliott Sober, "When Natural Section and Culture Conflict"; Langdon Gilkey, "Biology and Theology on Human Nature"; and Charles Birch, "Darwinism and Postmodern Theism".

Román, Begoña (trans) and Corral, Carmen (trans) and MacIntyre, Alasdair. Persona corriente y filosofía moral: reglas, virtudes y bienes. *Convivium*, 5, 63-80, 1993.

Romano, Carlin. "Looking Beyond the Visible: The Case of Arthur C Danto" in *Danto and his Critics, Rollins, Mark (ed)*, 175-190. Cambridge, Blackwell, 1993.

Rombach, Heinrich. L'ontologie structurale et le dialogue des mondes. *Rev Phil Louvain*, 92(4), 459-473, N 94.

Structural ontology is opposed to the substantialist or essentialist (or again systematic) ontology of metaphysical tradition and assigns to each cultural grouping a structure of its own that cannot be translated into the categories of another. This implies the abandonment of the abstract universality proper to classical philosophical anthropology in favor of a "dialogue of worlds", i.e., an attempt to establish, in an attitude of listening that respects all cultures, a concrete anthropology that forms the basis of a many-sided ontology to which the various traditions will find themselves to be related. The author sees the elucidation of this structural ontology in particular in a mutual fertilization of European phenomenology and of the thought of nothingness inherent in the school of Kyoto. Thus Rombach perceives a via media equidistant from "Western" and "Eastern" thought and seeks to map it out.

Romera, Luis. Dio e la questione dell'essere in Heidegger. *Acta Phil*, 2(3), 287-314, 1994.

The problem of God is profoundly present in Heidegger's thought. It has been the object of frequent discussion in the attempt to determine both the modality of Heidegger's God and the attitude of thought that according to Heidegger is capable of perceiving God's gesture. The question of God is developed in four moments: the analysis of the absence of God in our age, the lack of God as fruit of onto-theology, the thought of being as the first stage towards the sacred, towards the divinity, and therefore towards God, and the final result of Heidegger's thought (regarding God). This study concludes with a question regarding the ambiguity or problematic of a transcendent God in Heidegger's thought.

Romera Oñate, Luis. El Estatuto Noético del Primum Cognitum: Una Aproximación desde Tomás de Aquino. *Rev Espan Filosof Med*, 0, 177-184, 1993.

Starting from the Aristotelic distinction about the different operativities of the reason, St Thomas of Aquinas appoints that the "ens" sets in the "intellectus", which is statim perceived, remains as a habit and is a principle on which the other kinds of knowledge rest.

Romero, Esther and Soria, Belén. Metáforas y Convención. *Rev Filosof (Spain)*, 7(12), 383-402, 1994.

Romero Baró, José. Elementos para una crítica del positivismo científico. *Convivium*, 6, 15-28, 1994.

The net scientific value of the basic principles of modern sciences (physics, chemistry, and biology) is analyzed in order to identify their debatable elements, and to conclude the nonvalidity of a strict positivism in which the building of purely rational knowledge and cosmovision is still possible on the basis of merely empirical facts. The different interpretation of the principles of quantum mechanics, the difficulties of an atomism strictly considered, and the postulates of the evolution of life, give enough arguments to legitimate the doubt in our scientific points of view as a coherent and acceptable philosophy of the nature.

Romero Baró, José María. Líneas de Pensamiento Positivista y Antipositista en América. *Analogia*, 4(1), 169-176, 1990.

Some of the lines of the postivist thought more representatives in Latin America (the scientific spirit of Argentinians F Ameghino and J Ingenieros, the postivist education of G Barreda in Mexico, and the human religion of M Lemos in Brazil) are exposed. Immediately after, the points of view opposing to the former are presented by A Korn in Argentina and by A Caso in Mexico. Finally, the work of the Uruguaian C Vaz Ferreira is also included as an example of the inner criticism that is possible to be realized through the criticism of the science.

Romero Baró, José María. Santo Tomás de Aquino como Inspirador de Francisco de Vitoria. *Analogia*, 7(1), 157-166, 1993.

The basis of the natural law defending the properties of the Indians from the greediness of conquerors was presented by Vitoria immediately after the discovery of America. Vitoria inspired most of his treatise, *De Indis*, in the *Summa Theologiae* of Thomas Aquinas, especially in the idea that the Indians had full right to possess their properties even in their natural state, that is, even if they were very distant from Christian faith. In consequence, removing anything of theirs had to be considered as proper robbery as if the Indians were Christian owners.

Romero Baró, José María. The Epistemology of the Uruguayan Philosopher Carlos Vaz Ferreira. *Dialogue Hum*, 2(1), 79-86, 1992.

Vaz Ferreira abandoned scientific positivism as being a theory of knowledge which eliminated all metaphysical conjecture. His reservation over the application of reason and logic in interpreting reality as well as the application of mathematics as an expression of the physical world meant a return to a philosophical approach. Thus science is always to be interpreted as philosophy (or metaphysics) and philosophy should be seen as the unit of knowledge which denies the dualism propounded by scientific positivism.

Roncaglia, H Gino. Smiglecius on *Entia Rationis*. *Vivarium*, 33(1), 27-49, My 95.

The paper deals with the discussion of impossible entities in the *Logica* written by the Polish Jesuit Martinus Smiglecius (1564-1618). Two preliminary sections give some information on Smiglecius's life and works, and on the general structure of his *Logica*. A third section offers some historical background on the logical status of impossible entities, and their inclusion in the class of *entia rationis*. The fourth and main section presents Smiglecius's ideas on this topic in some detail.

Ronnow-Rasmussen, Toni. *Logic, Facts, and Representation: An Examination of R M Hare's Moral Philosophy*. Lund, Lund Univ Pr, 1993.

This work examines R M Hare's theory of moral thinking. The two central questions are: How does Hare defend his metaethical theses—that moral judgments in their typical uses are 1) universalizable and 2) have prescriptive meaning—and how does he use them to arrive at a utilitarian position? Attention is focused on Hare's argument that certain uses of 'ought' must be understood as having prescriptive meaning, as well as on his speech act theory of meaning. It is maintained that Hare's argument rests on an unsubstantiated premiss, and that the theory of prescriptive meaning is in need of a revision to cope with notably first- and third-person 'ought'-judgments. A central question that is raised with regard to the universalizability-thesis is whether we are logically committed to universalize our singular 'ought'-judgments. It is argued that it is logically conceivable that a speaker can have nonuniversalizable reasons for his 'ought'-judgments. In order to understand Hare's argument for utilitarianism, his views on especially moral relevance, prudence, and interpersonal comparisons are considered. Regarding the latter issue, Hare attempts to show in his later works that interpersonal reference conflicts can be turned into intrapersonal ones. A crucial idea here, which is examined in detail, is Hare's claim that the term 'I' has prescriptive meaning. It is maintained, among other things, that this idea appears inconsistent with what Hare elsewhere has to say about word meaning. It is concluded that Hare's argument for utilitarianism is not convincing: the logical ground on which Hare founds his theory of moral thinking is less firm than he seems to think.

Roochnik, David L. Counting on Number: Plato on the Goodness of *Arithmos*. *Amer J Philo*, 115(4), 543-563, Wint 94.

Rooney, Paul. Divine Commands and Arbitrariness. *Relig Stud*, 31(2), 149-165, Je 95.

According to the divine command theory of morality, what is right or wrong, good or bad, is entirely dependent on the will and command of God: what He commands is right and what He forbids is wrong just because He commands or forbids it. It is argued here that the principal religious objection to this theory—that if it were true, moral precepts would be arbitrary—is rendered ineffective when due consideration is given to the consequences of God's omnipotence, and in particular, to His rationality and to His responsibility for deciding, in creation, what the characteristics of human nature are to be.

Rooney, Phyllis A. Rationality and the Politics of Gender Difference. *Metaphilosophy*, 26(1-2), 22-45, Ja-Ap 95.

This paper explores the philosophical impact of the *literal* exclusion of women from ideals of reason, the historically persistent claim that women are in some literal sense less rational than men. It is maintained that such an examination of the constitutive role of gender difference claims in philosophical conceptions of reason and rationality is best undertaken within a more "expansive" understanding of the development of such conceptions (more expansive that many contemporary accounts entertain). Such an examination, it is argued, has important implications for contemporary discussions of rationality, for recent developments in feminist epistemology, and for work in naturalized epistemology that seeks to take into account scientific findings about cognition that draw in part from gender and cognition studies.

Rooth, Mats. "Indefinites, Adverbs of Quantification, and Focus Semantics" in *The Generic Book, Carlson, Gregory N (ed)*, 265-299. Chicago, Univ of Chicago Pr, 1995.

Rorty, Richard. "Consciousness, Intentionality, and the Philosophy of Mind" in *The Mind-Body Problem: A Guide to the Current Debate, Warner, Richard (ed)*, 121-127. Cambridge, Blackwell, 1994.

Rorty, Richard. "Holism, Intrinsicality, and the Ambition of Transcendence" in *Dennett and his Critics, Dahlbom, Bo (ed)*, 184-202. Cambridge, Blackwell, 1995.

Rorty, Richard. Is Truth a Goal of Enquiry? Davidson versus Wright. *Phil Quart*, 45(180), 281-300, Jl 95.

Rorty, Richard. Philosophy and Future. *Magyar Filozof Szemle*, 5-6, 877-884, 1994.

Rorty, Richard. Sind Aussagen universelle Geltungsansprüche?. *Deut Z Phil*, 42(6), 975-988, 1994.

Rosa, Hartmut. Goods and Life Forms: Relativism in Charles Taylor's Political Philosophy. *Rad Phil*, 71, 20-26, My-Je 95.

Rosado, Juan. Dialéctica de Casiciaco. *G Metaf*, 16(1-2), 3-23, Ja-Ag 94.

Rosado Haddock, Guillermo E and Hjorth, Greg and Spinas, Otmar. El Frege Kantiano. *Dialogos*, 30(65), 189-212, Ja 95.

Rosales, Amán. Enfoques contemporáneos de la regularidad causal. *Rev Filosof (Costa Rica)*, 31(75-76); 245-254, D 93.

Here the principal ideas of the so called theory of the causal regularity are presented. These ideas were presented by Hume and developed by the following contemporary philosophers: Braithwaite, Nagel, Hempel and Scheffler. These authors represent, in their analysis of the structure of scientific explanation, what some people called the 'orthodox' position in theory of science. At the end, it is suggested the possibility of accepting another alternative than that presented by those philosophers.

Rosati, Connie. Naturalism, Normativity, and the Open Question Argument. *Nous*, 29(1), 46-70, Mr 95.

Many would contend that the phenomenal influence of G E Moore's "open question" argument is undeserved. But certain "new naturalists" acknowledge that Moore's argument exposed a genuine problem about how an account of good can be simultaneously descriptive and normative. They believe, however, that this problem can be answered by formulating an account with the right descriptive content. I argue that Moore's argument can be raised just as meaningfully against the new naturalism as against analytic naturalism, because neither form of naturalism adequately accounts for our character as creatures who construct and guide ourselves by ideals of the person.

Rosati, Connie. Persons, Perspetives, and Full Information Accounts of the Good. *Ethics*, 105(2), 296-325, Ja 95.

Rose, Gillian. *Hegel: Contra Sociology*. London, Athlone, 1995.

Rose, Gillian. *Judaism and Modernity: Philosophical Essays*. Cambridge, Blackwell, 1993.

Rose, Gillian. *The Broken Middle: Out of our Ancient Society*. Cambridge, Blackwell, 1992.

Rose, Nikolas and Miller, Peter. On Therapeutic Authority: Psychoanalytical Expertise Under Advanced Liberalism. *Hist Human Sci*, 7(3), 29-64, Ag 94.

In contemporary European and North American societies, there has occurred a transformation in authority, a reshaping of the ethical warranting for the exercise of authority over the conduct of conduct. We term this "therapeutic authority". This transformation of authority relations has brought about a shift in modes of governing life in locales as varied as the family, the factory, the school, the hospital and the office. In this article, we investigate the formation of this new species of authority through one particular set of events: the ideas and actions associated with the Tavistock Clinic and the Tavistock Institute of Human Relations.

Rosemont Jr, Henry. "Why Take Rights Seriously? A Confucian Critique" in *Human Rights and the World's Religions, Rouner, Leroy (ed)*, 167-182. Notre Dame, Univ Notre Dame Pr, 1988.

After sketching the role-based moral theory of early Confucianism, this paper employs that theory to challenge the concept of human rights, especially the assumption of human beings on which it rests, namely, the autonomous, freely-choosing, self-interested individual.

Rosen, Aviva. Adam, Eve and the Controversial Rib: Gender, Technology, Conflict and Universalism. *Dialogue Hum*, 4(2-3), 23-30, 1994.

The segregation of the labor market stands in antagonism to universalistic and humanistic ideas. Although women constitute approximately half of every population, they are often regarded as a sociological minority. Universal equality cannot be reached until we cease taking Eve out of Adam's rib. The small proportion of women in the engineering professions is usually explained in two ways: Women's lack of motivation and interest, and in various barriers they encounter before entering those professions, and in different stages of their careers. The article deals mainly with explanations of the second sort. The conclusion of this paper is, that one way to achieve a more egaliterian society is by implementing "affirmative action" as a national policy.

Rosen, Edward. The Scientific Revolution in the Renaissance—A Unique Phenomenon in the History of Mankind. *Dialogue Hum*, 2(3-4), 48-56, 1992.

Rosen, Fred. Es Bentham utilitarista?. *Telos (Spain)*, 3(1), 11-26, Je 94.

The object of this paper is to examine the extent to which Bentham's thought measures up to the sort of utilitarianism which is usually ascribed to him in modern philosophical literature. The starting point is the fact that Bentham was neither the first utilitarian nor did his conclusions about morals and politics coincide with those of other utilitarians writing at the same time. To understand why his position differed from other utilitarians has led to a reassessment of the material which is commonly used now to depict Bentham's utilitarianism, i.e., the first chapters of the *Introduction to the Principles of Morals and Legislation*. It is argued that this material does less to establish Bentham as a utilitarian, or as a philosopher with a specific utilitarian doctrine, and more to display his commitment to rationality in the resolution of moral and political questions. The paper then considers why Bentham's own doctrine seems different from those of his utilitarian contemporaries and pays special attention to the role of liberty in his system.

Rosen, Fred. Libertad constitucional y democracia reprsentativa. *Telos (Spain)*, 1(2), 93-109, Je 92.

The main argument in this paper is that the emergence of democratic ideas within utilitarian thought takes place within the framework of a theory of constitutional liberty. One of the most important contentions is that, for Bentham, representative democracy was not seen as one form of government to be opposed to another, but as one means to achieve liberty. Although this paper focuses on Bentham whose thought the conjunction of liberty and democracy takes place, the starting point is Montesquieu who is the source of some of Bentham's ideas and important terms. From this historical perspective the utilitarian account of representative democracy is thus considerably different from what has been widely believed.

Rosen, Gideon. Modal Fictionalism Fixed. *Analysis*, 55(2), 67-73, Ap 95.

Bob Hale ("Modal Fictionalism: A Simple Dilemma", Analysis 55 (2), 63-7) has suggested that Modal Fictionalism cannot coherently assign a modal status to the proposition that there exist many non-actual possible worlds. The present note argues that Modal Fictionalism is committed to regarding the proposition as a necessary falsehood. Hale's objection to this solution—that it implies, given the fictionalist's account of modal discourse, that all modal statements are vacuously true—turns on the mistaken supposition that the fictionalist's operator "According to the many-worlds hypothesis..." is equivalent to "If the many-worlds hypothesis were true, then...".

Rosen, Gideon. The Shoals of Language: Michael Dummett: *The Seas of Language*. *Mind*, 104(415), 599-609, Jl 95.

A critical study of Michael Dummett's collection *The Seas of Language* (Oxford: Clarendon Press, 1993). The review discusses the structure of the Dummetian case for antirealism, focusing on the suggestion that a commitment to classical two valued semantics is a necessary component of any realist view. Against this I urge the familiar point that failures of bivalence due to vagueness, failure of reference, and the like, are not incompatible with realism as it is normally understood. The review concludes with a discussion of Dummett's claim that Fregean Platonism (the view that abstract singular terms introduced by means of contextual definitions refer to genuine abstract entities) amounts to something less than a full-blooded realism about the abstract.

Rosen, Henryk Zvi. Hermann Cohen's Concept of Judaic Universalism. *Dialogue Hum*, 3(1), 25-30, 1993.

Rosen, Robert. "Bionics Revisited" in *The Machine as Metaphor and Tool, Haken, Hermann (ed)*, 87-100. New York, Springer-Verlag, 1993.

The present work briefly reviews the history, ambitions and philosophy of a scientific initiative once called "bionics". It was intended to explore the interfaces between biology and technology. A number of circumstances caused it to be largely abandoned around 1970; all that remains of it today is "artificial intelligence", and that in a much mutated form. It is argued that the abandonment of bionics was premature, and that biology comprises an enormous encyclopedia on how to solve (and how not to solve) complex problems.

Rosenau, Hartmut. Der "consensus gentium"—fundamentaltheologische Erwägungen zu einem vernachlässigten Gottesbeweis. *Theol Phil*, 69(4), 481-492, 1994.

As far as the arguments to prove the existence of God in contemporary philosophy of religion are discussed, the argument "e consensu gentium" (Cicero) is—in comparison with the so called ontological or cosmological arguments—not very much reputed. But if we put this argument into a weaker form—not referring to a universal but to a particular acceptance of the existence of God—it implies a meaningful challenge for modern philosophy of religion, namely to explain the view of reality believers have within a consense-theory of truth.

Rosenau, Hartmut. Self-Reflection and Autobiography—Kierkegaard's Writings about Himself. *Hist Euro Ideas*, 20(1-3), 183-188, Ja 95.

Rosenbaum, Stuart E (ed) and Baird, Robert M (ed). *Punishment and the Death Penalty: The Current Debate*. Buffalo, Prometheus, 1995.

These essays raise two questions: What justifies punishment in general? What justifies capital punishment? Essays by Mabbot, Rawls, Menninger, Wasserstrom, Morris, and Dagger consider such questions as: Should we distinguish between justifying the institution of punishment and justifying punishment of particular individuals? Can punishment be best justified by retributive or utilitarian arguments? Should punishment be replaced by therapy? Essays by Bedau, van den Haag, Nathanson, Justices Blackmun and Scalia, and others focus on capital punishment. This debate too pits retributivists against utilitarians, the former tending to support capital punishment and the latter frequently opposing it. Additional issues are involved, however, and the essays capture many of these.

Rosenberg, Alexander. *Instrumental Biology or the Disunity of Science*. Chicago, Univ of Chicago Pr, 1994.

This book argues that the character of theories and laws in biology is much more contingent on cognitive and computational powers of *homo sapiens* than either chemistry of physics. The argument proceeds by examining intertheoretical relations, drift, the levels-of-selection controversy and the role of models in the life sciences. The nature of biological science turns on the evolutionary causes of supervenience.

Rosenberg, Alexander. Moral Realism and Social Science. *Midwest Stud Phil*, 15, 150-166, 1990.

The paper argues that attempts to ground a naturalistic account of moral goodness on theoretical claims by social scientists about the functions of social institutions are not warranted. Making particular reference to Railton's "Moral Realism", I identify theoretical claims by social scientists sharply contrary to those Railton cites.

Rosenberg, Alexander and Hoefer, Carl. Empirical Equivalence, Underdetermination, and Systems of the World. *Phil Sci*, 61(4), 592-607, D 94.

The underdetermination of theory by evidence must be distinguished from holism. The latter is a doctrine about the testing of scientific hypotheses; the former is a thesis about empirically adequate logically incompatible global theories or "systems of the world". The distinction is crucial for an adequate assessment of the underdetermination thesis. The paper shows how some treatments of underdetermination are vitiated by failure to observe this distinction, and identifies some necessary conditions for the existence of multiple empirically equivalent global theories. We consider how empiricists should respond to the possibility of such systems of the world.

Rosenberg, Paul. Liberal Neutralism and the Social-Democratic Project. *Crit Rev*, 8(2), 217-234, Spr 94.

Liberalism is either nonneutral toward, or unfair about, ways of life that fail to produce goods that are instrumental to social purposes. Nonredistributive, Nozickian liberalism is neutral toward such ways of life, but it unfairly fails to make them accessible to those who lack the means to pursue them at their leisure. Social-democratic liberalism attempts to universalize access to all ways of life, but in practice it violates neutrality by drawing everyone into the production of redistributable primary goods. This is why the notoriously noninstrumentalist humanities have been marginalized; challenging the belief in liberal neutrality may therefore be essential to their survival.

Rosenfeld, Robert P. Parsimony, Evolution, and Animal Pain. *Between Species*, 9(3), 133-137, Sum 93.

Peter Harrison appeals to the notion of parsimony to argue that mental pain states could not have evolved in animals. I argue that Harrison misuses the notion of parsimony and assumes an excessively adaptationist view of evolutionary theory. Appeals to parsimony can just as easily show that we *should* attribute mental pain states to animals. In addition, the process of evolution itself is not strictly parsimonious. Mental pain could still have arisen even if it were not the only or the best adaptive response to danger or harm. Harrison's evolutionary parsimony case against animal pain is thus unconvincing.

Rosenfeld, Robert P. Reply to Boonin-Vail's "Response—Parsimony Made Simple". *Between Species*, 9(3), 141-142, Sum 93.

I agree with Boonin-Vail (and Sober) that parsimony is a complex notion, whose proper use depends on a context of inquiry in which empirical assumptions may play a crucial role. After distinguishing several types of parsimony, I argue that Boonin-Vail's possible "Harrisonian" objection to my position commits the fallacy of composition. I agree with Boonin-Vail that the notion of parsimony, unconstrained by empirical considerations, could allow Harrison to "hide behind" other aprioristic parsimony objections, but conclude that it would be irresponsible for Harrison to do so.

Rosenkrantz, Gary S and Hoffman, Joshua. *Substance Among Other Categories*. New York, Cambridge Univ Pr, 1994.

Rosenstock, Bruce. Socrates as Revenant: A Reading of the *Menexenus*. *Phoenix*, 48(4), 331-347, Wint 94.

R argues that the anachronism of the dialogue can be explained as part of Plato's representation of a post-mortem Socrates whose praise of Athens is really its indictment. The dialogue is seen as a careful reversal of the rhetoric and staging of the *Apology*. R concludes with remarks about the implications of this analysis for dating a dialogue as early, middle, or late.

Rosenthal, David M. Self-Knowledge and Moore's Paradox. *Phil Stud*, 77(2-3), 195-209, Mr 95.

Rosenthal, Robert and Koutstaal, Wilma. "Contrast Analysis in Behavioral Research" in *Probability in Theory-Building, Brzezinski, Jerzy (ed)*, 135-173. Amsterdam, Rodopi, 1994.

Several methods of computing contrasts are reviewed and compared. Approaches to contrast analysis in both between-subjects and repeated-measures designs are demonstrated. The versatility, precision, and enhanced statistical power achieved through contrast analysis are emphasized.

Rosenthal, Sandra B. *Charles Peirce's Pragmatic Pluralism*. Albany, SUNY Pr, 1994.

This work runs counter to the traditional interpretations of Peirce's philosophy by eliciting an inherent strand of pragmatic pluralism that is embedded in the very core of this thought and that weaves his various doctrines into a systematic pattern of pluralism. It gives a new design to the seeming bedrock of Peirce's position: convergence toward the final ultimate opinion of the community of interpreters in the idealized long run. It further shows the way in which Peirce's position provides needed epistemic and metaphysical underpinnings for a Kuhnsian interpretation of science.

Rosenthal, Sandra B and Bourgeois, Patrick. Deconstruction or Reconstruction of The Living Present: Derrida or Merleau-Ponty and Mead. *Int Stud Phil*, 26(4), 1-17, 1994.

Rosenzweig, Kenneth and Fischer, Marilyn. Attitudes of Students and Accounting Practitioners Concerning the Ethical Acceptability of Earnings Management. *J Bus Ethics*, 14(6), 433-444, Je 95.

There are many ways that accountants and managers can influence the reported accounting results of their organizational units. When such influence is directed at changing the amount of reported earnings, it is known as earnings management. The purpose of this paper is to present the results of surveys of undergraduate students, MBA students, and practicing accountants concerning their attitudes on the ethical acceptability of earnings management. Analysis of the survey results reveals how the attitudes of the three groups differ and what variables are associated with these differences. Based on the analysis, the authors suggest changes in accounting education curriculum and ethics awareness programs in business which might increase students' and practitioner's sensitivity to the ethical ramifications of earnings management.

Roser, Andreas and Henrichs, Norbert and Haller, Rudolf. Wittgenstein Bibliographie 1992-93. *Wittgenstein Stud*, n.a., 1994.

Roser, Andreas and Schulten, Holger. Ein Brief Johann Gottlieb Fichtes. *Fichte-Studien*, 5, 171-174, 1993.

In diesem Brief—vemutlich an Gottlieb Hufeland—schreibt Fichte unter anderem: "(...) verschaffen Sie mir ein MagisterDiplom von Leipzig oder Wittenberg, oder woher es sey. Leisten kann ich JETZT weiter nichts als GELD GEBEN (...)". Diese Bitte Fichtes, ihm ein Magisterdiplom "zu verschaffen", steht in einem engen Zusammenhang mit Fichtes Absicht eine Anstellung als Professor an der Universtiät Jena zu finden.

Rosicka, Janina. "John Locke and the Polish Enlightenment" in *Locke's Philosophy, Rogers, G A J (ed)*, 237-252. New York, Oxford Univ Pr, 1994.

Rosinski, Franciszek M. Das Aggressionsverhalten der subhumanan Primaten. *Stud Phil Christ*, 30(2), 209-226, 1994.

Das Aggresionsverhalten, das die Verdrängung anderer Individuen bezweckt, ist zwar bei den subhumanen Primaten genetisch bedingt und arttypisch, doch in seinem Zustandekommen und Erscheinungsbild weit vielgestaltiger und komplizierter als bei anderen Arten, bei denen es festgestellt werden konnte. Es bestehen hierbei beträchtliche Unterschiede hinsichtlich der Frequenz, Auslösemechanismen und Intensivität der Aggression zwischen Tieren, die in freier Wildbahn oder in Gefangenschaft sich befindern. Die Ausdrucksformen der Aggressivität sind bei Affen viel differenzierter als bei anderen Tieren, dagegen ihre Ursachen sind meist dieselben wie bei diesen. Auch der Mensch trägt dieses phylogenetische Erbe als Antriebskraft, Schicksal und zu bewältigende Desruktivität mit sich durchs Leben, mit dem er sich auseinandersetzen muss. Dank seiner Einbindung in Kultur und ins Sozialnetz, auf Grund der Entfaltung seiner Persönlichkeit, Erziehung zum Humaniszmus und typisch menschlichem Altruismus, Liebe und Barmherzigkeit, lernt er jedoch seine Aggressivität zu überwinden.

Roslanowski, Andrzej and Judah, Haim. Martin's Axiom and the Continuum. *J Sym Log*, 60(2), 374-391, Je 95.

Rosmini, Antonio. Human Good does not Consist in Isolated Pleasures, but in Contentment. *Vera Lex*, 13(1-2), 11-12, 1993.

Rosner, Fred. Setting Up a Straw Man: Commentary on Dena Davis. *J Clin Ethics*, 5(4), 355-357, Wint 94.

Rosnow, Ralph L and Strohmetz, David B. "A Mediational Model of Research Artifacts" in *Probability in Theory-Building, Brzezinski, Jerzy (ed)*, 177-196. Amsterdam, Rodopi, 1994.

Because humans are sentient and active participants in behavioral research, they present unique problems of researchers. This chapter focuses on these systematic, uncontrolled biases (i.e., research artifacts). A model is proposed to conceptualize how artifacts can be introduced at different stages in the research process. By identifying potential sources of artifacts, researchers can employ strategies to circumvent these threats, thereby increasing confidence in the validity of the study's outcomes and implications. The chapter elaborates on each part of the model, focusing on these potential artifacts as well as making suggestions on how to minimize these potential biases.

Ross, Don. Dennett's Conceptual Reform. *Behavior Phil*, 22(1), 41-52, Spr-Sum 94.

This paper is a response to the first wave of criticism of Daniel C Dennett's *Consciousness Explained* (1991). I argue that some of Dennett's critics have missed the main point of the book, which is to argue not for an empirical theory of consciousness—as Dennett himself somewhat rashly claims—but instead for a radical philosophical reconceptualization of consciousness. I defend the coherence of this reconceptualization in the context of Dennett's life's work (to date), which, I argue, can be summarized as an attempt to clearly separate three central concepts in the philosophy of cognitive science: agency, consciousness and self.

Ross, Don. Instrumental Realism and the Idea of Embodied Knowledge. *Res Phil Technol*, 14, 251-269, 1994.

Philosophers of science show increasing interest in scientific experiment. Motivations for this include the belief that scientists' ontological commitments are reflected in the entities they seek to physically manipulate and the apparatus they design. This reasoning can lead to fallacious inferences if applied crudely, since choices of apparatus and method are limited by factors external to domains of application. One such set of factors are cognitive constraints reflected in the sorts of physical manipulations that the human organism finds natural. In the paper, I review preliminary concepts of such constraints, and suggest that episodes in the history of commercial design engineering are a fruitful source of data about them.

Ross, Don. Minimal Strong Functionalism. *J Phil Res*, 20, 237-268, 1995.

This paper is motivated by the concern that increasingly fewer philosophers of mind seem prepared to call themselves 'functionalists' these days. I suggest that this has less to do with explicit arguments presented against functionalism than with a gradual decay in the clarity of the term's reference. This decay has two sources: functionalism has involved several different, logically independent research commitments, and it has become tightly associated, to an unnecessary degree, with classical computationalism, a program which is now under severe pressure from connectionist and other bottom-up methodologies in AI. After diagnosing the causes of this drift, I seek to arrest it by sketching a version of functionalism—minimal strong functionalism—that is strong enough to have ontological and methodological bite, but that is sufficiently minimal in its empirical commitments so as to not be hostage to the outcome of the current dispute in AI between connectionists and classicists.

Ross, Don. Real Patterns and the Ontological Foundations of Microeconomics. *Econ Phil*, 11(1), 113-136, Ap 95.

This paper proposes that microeconomics is best interpreted as the empirical study of real, though abstract, empirical phenomena, namely, games. This view is motivated by way of a detailed critical analysis of Alexander Rosenberg's recent (1992) book on economics. I argue that Rosenberg's instrumentalist account of is unsuccessful, but that it exposes the constraints that a defense of microeconomics as empirical inquiry must satisfy. My own view, which owes much to Dennett's recent work on 'Real Patterns', is then offered as an account which captures the best of Rosenberg's insights without surrendering microeconomists' conviction that they are engaged in sound empirical science.

Ross, Don and LaCasse, Chantale. The Microeconomic Interpretation of Games. *Proc Phil Sci Ass*, 1, 379-387, 1994.

This paper is part of a larger project defending of the foundations of microeconomics against recent criticisms by philosophers. Here, we undermine one source of these criticisms, arising from philosophers' disappointment with the performance of microecomonic tools, in particular game theory, when these are applied to normative decision theory. Hollis and Sugden have recently articulated such disappointment in a sophisticated way, and have argued on the basis of it that the economic conception of rationality is inadequate. We argue, however, that their claim rests upon a misunderstanding of the concept of a game as it is used in microeconomics.

Ross, Don and Zawidzski Jr, Tad. Information and Teleosemantics. *S J Phil*, 32(4), 393-419, Wint 94.

This essay seeks to reconcile the information-based account of representation due to Dretske and Lloyd with the position of the 'teleosemanticists' (Dennett, Millikan, etc.) who analyze intentionality in terms of 'proper function' determined by natural selection. We argue that the analysis of intentionality in terms of information flow, if properly understood in the context of thermodynamics, is not only compatible with appealing to adaptations in fixing representational content, but actually helps to explain the utility of doing so in psychology and ethology.

Ross, Martin Michael. "'Die Staatgründende Tat'—Alfred Baeumler und die Politisierung der Ästhetik" in *Die besten Geister der Nation, Korotin, Ilse (ed)*, 66-86. Vienna, Picus, 1994.

Ross, Philip J. Utility, Subjectivism and Moral Ontology. *J Applied Phil*, 11(2), 189-199, 1994.

The paper seeks to show that underlying Bentham's concept of utility is a commitment to a criterion or principle of moral status distinguishing morally relevant beings from the morally irrelevant. Further, that the notion of moral status is ultimately inconsistent with Bentham's utility; that it implies something like a Kantian ethic barring the use of morally relevant beings as mere means to some other's satisfaction, an ethic which suitably interpreted may be more useful in defense of some concerns for which Bentham has traditionally been cited, animal rights for example. The paper concludes by noting the history and politics of moral status and argues that the concept involves a fusion of fact and value, the empirical and the evaluative, undermining assumptions of a rigid separation of the two and the consequent essential subjectivity of the latter.

Ross, Stephen David. *Locality and Practical Judgment: Charity and Sacrifice*. Bronx, Fordham Univ Pr, 1994.

Development of a theory of practical judgment based on the ideas of locality and inexhaustibility, leading to a theory of valor (not value) based on charity and sacrifice. Third volume of a trilogy whose other works are *Inexhaustibility and Human Being: An Essay on Locality* and *The Limits of Language*. Topics discussed are: judgment, practice, valor, charity and sacrifice, politics, technology, query, and wisdom.

Ross, Stephen David. *Plenishment in the Earth*. Albany, SUNY Pr, 1995.

This book develops an ethic of inclusion leading from gender and sexual difference through the social work of race and culture, to the natural world, to multiple and heterogeneous natural kinds. This thought of two genders joined with the immeasurable heterogeneity of the natural and social world leads to animals and other natural creatures and things, to ecological feminism and other ecologies and feminisms, then to thoughts of multiple kinds emerging from other cultures and subcultures.

Ross Jr, William T and Robertson, Diana C. Decision-Making Processes on Ethical Issues: The Impact of a Social Contract Perspective. *Bus Ethics Quart*, 5(2), 213-240, Ap 95.

This paper develops a framework for examining decision making about ethical issues and tests the applicability of a social contract perspective. Using two separate samples of students and salespeople, we determine that community members (salespeople) tend to judge a potentially unethical act to constitute a violation of an implicit social contract and noncommunity members (students) do not. Also, consistent with the emphasis on context specificity of integrative social contracts theory, situational variables influence perceptions of ethicality for the community members, but do not affect the perceptions of individuals outside the community. The study finds considerable support for the use of a social contractarian perspective in the study of decision-making processes about ethical issues.

Rossetti, Andrea. Performativi in Jean-Louis Gardies: verità, verificabilità, vero-funzionalità. *Riv Int Filosof Diritto*, 71(3), 462-492, 1994.

The article is divided into two parts. The first one describes the evolution of Gardies' studies on performativity and exposes the three principle thesis defended by Gardies on performativity the first thesis regards the truth of the "performative propositions": the performatives are either true or false; the second thesis regards the verifiability of the "performative propositions". Only some performatives are essentially true; the third thesis regards the truth-functionality of performative propositions. Some performatives are susceptible to truth-functional treatment. In the second part of the article, the three thesis are examined in the prospects of the concepts of apophanticity (the property of the propositions of being either true or false) and self-referentiability.

Rossetti, Livio. "Sui Rischi di un'Attitudine Troppo Benevola dell'Interprete verso il Testo" in *Platón: Los Diálogos Tardíos, Lan, Conrado Eggers (ed)*, 9-34. Sankt Augustin, Academia, 1986.

Apart of being an attitude actually (and often wisely) encouraged by their authors—and Plato is no exception—charitable interpretation is a well-established attitude among most commentators, who therefore risk to exceed in stressing the coherence and conclusiveness of a text. Whence a certain need of reconsidering Plato's dialogues with less enthusiastic an attitude. In this paper I made a preliminary attempt to re-read Plato's *Statesman*, and argued that towards the beginnings Plato was covertly retractating the political utopia of his *Republic*.

Rossi, Pietro. Max Weber und das Problem der Weltanschauung. *Rev Int Phil*, 49(192), 155-186, 1995.

Rossi, Pietro (& others). Tavola Rotonda. *Filosofia*, 45(1), 97-129, Ja-Ap 94.

Rossouw, Gedeon J. Business Ethics in Developing Countries. *Bus Ethics Quart*, 4(1), 43-51, Ja 94.

Underlying this paper is the conviction that it is of utmost importance that business ethics should indeed become an integral part of business culture in all, and therefore also in developing countries. It is not to be denied that business ethics has to a much larger extent become part of the business culture in developed countries than in developing countries. In this paper, I first of all wish to provide an explanation for the fact that business culture in developing countries. Secondly I want to give a thumbnail sketch of the preconditions that have to be fulfilled in order to stimulate the development of a moral business culture in developing countries. In order to achieve these goals I will focus mainly on Africa, and more specifically on South Africa.

Rost, Joseph C. Leadership: A Discussion About Ethics. *Bus Ethics Quart*, 5(1), 129-142, Ja 95.

In this article, the author lists three problems that make any serious discussion about the ethics of leadership a very difficult undertaking. He then proposes a new, postindustrial paradigm of leadership. Using that understanding of leadership, two different sets of ethical analyses of leadership are possible: 1) those concerned with the process of leadership and 2) those concerned with the content of leadership (the changes proposed by the leaders and collaborators). In the end, the author suggests that the industrial paradigm of ethics (the 18th century liberal philosophy) is inadequate to deal with the ethical decision making that leaders and collaborators must do in the 21st century. Thus, a postindustrial paradigm of ethics must be developed to enable leaders and collaborators to make the tough ethical choices that will be demanded in the new millennium.

Rotenstreich, Nathan. Needs and Essence. *Kantstudien*, 85(1), 32-47, 1994.

Roth, Michael S. *The Ironist's Cage: Memory, Trauma, and the Construction of History*. New York, Columbia Univ Pr, 1995.

Roth, Paul A. Can Post-Newtonian Psychologists Find Happiness in a Pre-Paradigm Science?. *J Mind Behav*, 16(1), 87-97, Wint 95.

This paper is a commentary on the essays by Faulconer (1995), Leahey (1995), Rawling (1995), Slife (1995a, 1995b), Vandenberg (1995), and Williams (1995). Whatever the differences among these essays, they nonetheless share a common concern with the image of science which Newton promulgated. What might be termed the Newtonian meta-paradigm is positivistic, in the contemporary sense. This meta-paradigm has survived the demise of the Newtonian paradigm in physics. Each of the authors in this volume, in turn, is concerned with how to expose, and so liberate, psychology from the grip of this meta-paradigm. I comment briefly on their respective strategies and relative success in doing so.

Roth, Paul A. What Does the Sociology of Scientific Knowledge Explain?: Or, When Epistemological Chickens Come Home to Roost. *Hist Human Sci*, 7(1), 95-108, F 94.

What has been explained about the evolution of beliefs in scientific communities since Kuhn? I approach this question by examining two key methodological assumptions animating Sociology of Scientific Knowledge (SSK) case studies, a) the symmetry principle, and b) the alleged naturalism of the SSK method. It is these tenets that are to distinguish the new, sociological explainers of science from the old, philosophical ones. However, I detail how the professed naturalism of the SSK is at odds with their favored interpretation of the symmetry principle, i.e., intercepted as a claim to provide causal explanations for all beliefs. The article argues that the symmetry principle (causality interpreted) and naturalism are not reconcilable within SSK practice.

Roth, Paul A and Ryckman, Thomas A. Chaos, Clio, and Scientific Illusions of Understanding. *Hist Theor*, 34(1), 30-44, 1995.

A number of authors have recently argued that the mathematical insights of "chaos theory" offer a promising formal model or significant analogy for understanding at least some historical events. We examine a representative claim of each kind regarding the application of chaos theory to problems of historical explanation. We identify two lines of argument. One we term the Causal Thesis, which states that chaos theory may be used to plausibly model, and so explain, historical events. The other we term the Convergence Thesis, which holds that, once the analogy between history and chaos theory is properly appreciated, any temptation to divide history from the rest of science should be greatly lessened. We argue that the proffered analogy between chaos theory and history falls apart upon closer analysis. The promised benefits of chaos theory *vis-à-vis* history are either fantastic or, at best, an extremely loose heuristic which, while retaining nothing of the considerable intrinsic interest of nonlinear dynamics, easily seduces the unwary into taking at face value terms and concepts that have a specifically precise meaning only within the confines of mathematical theory.

Rothbart, Daniel. Discovering Natural Kinds Through Inter-Theoretic Prototypes. *Method Sci*, 26(4), 171-189, 1993.

Frequently, scientific progress is generated by the interaction of scientific ideas across distinct theories. Such inter-theoretic relations assume analogical comparisons between parallel theoretical structures. Certain variables, relations, and structures are projected from one (donor) theory to a distinct (target) theory. This paper focuses on the epistemic value of inter-theoretic analogies. In many cases the intelligibility of a physical property rests on such analogical projections of structures. Such analogies support an experimental realism of a specimen's natural kinds. These themes are illustrated by the case of the 19th century unification of organic and inorganic chemistries.

Rothbart, Daniel. Spectrometers as Analogues of Nature. *Proc Phil Sci Ass*, 1, 141-148, 1994.

The success of chemistry is directly credited to the capacity of instruments to provide human contact to the structures of physical reality. Empiricist philosophers have given scant attention to instruments as a separate topic of inquiry on the grounds that reliability of instruments is reducible to the epistemology of common sense experience. I argue that the reliability of many modern instruments is based on their design as analogical replication of natural systems. Scientists designed absorption spectrometers as artificial technological replicas of familiar physical systems. Such designs are generated by analogical projections of theoretical insights from known physical systems to unknown terrain. Instrumentation enables scientists to extend theoretical understanding to previously hidden domains. After exploring this analogical function of instruments, the nature of instrumental data is discussed, followed by an explicit rejection of both skepticism and naive realism. In the end I argue for an experimental realism which lacks any theory-neutral access to the fundamental analogies of nature.

Rothermel, Peter. Semantische Implikaturen. *Protosoz*, 2, 76-88, Ja 92.

Semantic implicatures are features for understanding the use of sentences. The status of these implementations of meaning is a quasi-logical relation as a "weak implication". They are determinated through types of lexical units and expressions in grammatical positions. But both are only necessary conditions for semantic implicatures. Further assumption for meaningful use of sentences are presupposed e.g. existence presuppositions, evidences, customs, etc. So, the delimination to pragmatic (presuppositions) is indicated.

Rothschild, Brian M (ed) and Natale, Samuel M (ed). *Values, Work, Education: The Meanings of Work*. Amsterdam, Rodopi, 1995.

Rotoli, Daniela. Cinque Esemplari Postillati della *Scienza Nuova*. *Boll Centro Stud Vichiani*, 24-25, 11 47, 1994-95.

Rott, Hans. Modellings for Belief Change: Prioritization and Entrenchment. *Theoria*, 58(1), 21-57, 1992.

We distinguish the set of explicit beliefs of a reasoner, his "belief base", from the beliefs that are merely implicit. Syntax-based belief change governed by the structure of the belief base and the ranking ("prioritization") of its elements is reconstructed with the help of an epistemic entrenchment relation in the style of Gärdenfors and Makinson. Though priorities are essentially different from entrenchments, distinguished relations of epistemic entrenchment may be obtained from prioritized belief bases by a number of different constructions. An approximate reconstruction of syntax-based belief change is possible, which can be strengthened to a strict identity in some important special cases. A competitive interpretation and a minimal change interpretation of the basic idea of entrenchment are discussed. It is argued that entrenchment essentially involves multiple belief changes, i.e., changes by sets of sentences.

Rottschaefer, William A. Gustafson's Theocentrism and Scientific Naturalistic Philosophy: A Marriage Made in Heaven?. *Zygon*, 30(2), 211-220, Je 95.

Examining James M Gustafson's views on the relationships between the sciences, theology, and ethics from a scientifically based naturalistic philosophical perspective, I concur with his rejection of separatist and antagonistic interactionist positions and his adherence to a mutually supportive interactionist position with both descriptive and normative features. I next explore three aspects of this interactionism: religious empiricism, the connections between facts and values, and the centering of objective values in the divine. Here I find much accord between Gustafson's theocentrism and a scientifically based naturalistic philosophical account of the relationships between the sciences, theology, and ethics.

Rotunda, Ronald D and Morgan, Thomas D. *Problems and Materials on Professional Responsibility (Sixth Edition)*. Westbury, Foundation Pr, 1995.

Rougemont, Jean-Daniel. Spinoza et le Totalitarisme: Fiction et Réalité. *Rev Theol Phil*, 127(2), 127-141, 1995.

Spinoza propose une hypothèse et nie qu'elle puisse devenir réalité: l'hypothèse du totalitarisme. Nous rappelons ce qu'est le totalitarisme, comme projet et come réalité (section 1), et nous expliquons ce qu'en dit Spinoza (section 2). Nous indiquons ensuite les limites qu'il fixe à un pouvoir politique quel qu'il soit: l'intégrité de la nature humaine et la liberté de la pensée (sections 3,4). Nous montrons que les violations de ces limites, qu'il juge impensables, sont précisément celles que les nazis et les communistes ont testées et appliquées (sections 5,6). Enfin nous mentionnons la question essentielle du rôle de la violence et de son "extinction" dans l'Etat totalitaire, en d'autres termes la question du "dépérissement de l'Etat" (section 7).

Roumanes, Jacques Bernard. Le Paradigme Esthétique. *Horiz Phil*, 4(1), 53-76, Autumn 93.

Rouner, Leroy (ed). *Human Rights and the World's Religions*. Notre Dame, Univ Notre Dame Pr, 1988.

Various perspectives on religious attitudes toward human rights, and the debate between individual rights and the needs of a community.

Rouner, Leroy (ed). *Meaning, Truth, and God*. Notre Dame, Univ Notre Dame Pr, 1982.

Collection of essays on the distinction between meaning and truth in the question about the reality of God.

Rouner, Leroy S. "Ecstasy and Epistemology" in *Emotions in Asian Thought*, Marks, Joel (ed), 91-107. Albany, SUNY Pr, 1995.

On the question of how we know that the *archai* of any science are true. Aristotle and Tillich compared to Sri Aurobinds on the role of *ananda* (bliss) in knowledge.

Rouner, Leroy S. "To Be at Home: Civil Religion as Common Bond" in *Civil Religion and Political Theology*, Rouner, Leroy S (ed), 125-137. Notre Dame, Univ Notre Dame Pr, 1986.

Rouner, Leroy S (ed). *Civil Religion and Political Theology*. Notre Dame, Univ Notre Dame Pr, 1986.

Rousset, Bernard. Spinoza, lecteur des *Objections* de Gassendi à Descartes. *Arch Phil*, 57(3), 485-502, Jl-S 94.

Comme le montrent le *Traité de la réforme de l'entendement* et déjà le *Court traité*, Spinoza, élaborant sa philosophie, était un lecteur attentif des *Objections et Réponses* aux *Méditations* de Descartes, et tout spécialement des *Objections* de Gassendi; malgré son opposition à l'empirisme et au scepticisme, il y a trouvé des formules, des arguments et même des idées qui ont enrichi sa réflexion et ses analyses: notamment dans la mise en place progressive de sa doctrine de l'imagination et surtout avec la déduction de la conservation de son être qu'est le *conatus* du mode fini, clé de voûte de l'*Ethique*.

Roux, A J P (ed). *Life, World and Meaning*. Pretoria, Univ of S Africa, 1990.

This is a Festschrift containing ten essays in honor of the South African philosopher, Michael Macnamara. With the exception of one (Brian Farrell) the authors are all South African academics, mainly philosophers. The central theme is the problem of existential meaning and themes such as work and meaning, understanding an ancient society, scheme-role meaning and the point of the question about the meaning of life, are discussed. Other themes discussed are: Presuppositions in science, empirical justification, emotion and fiction and the present re-think in political philosophy.

Roux, Yvon. *La Décadence*. *Philosopher*, 13, 249-258, 1992.

Rovane, Carol. Comment on McGinn's "The Problem of Philosophy". *Phil Stud*, 76(2-3), 157-168, D 94.

McGinn offers a naturalistic hypothesis about why philosophical problems, such as the mind-body problem, are insoluble by human beings, viz., the solutions lie beyond our cognitive capacities. This comment offers three reservations: 1) cognitive capacities can be extended by cognitive aids (e.g., computers); 2) distinct cognitive capacities can conspire to yield new cognitive possibilities; 3) it is our current theoretical outlook, rather than our absolute cognitive limitations, that makes the mind-body problem seem so intractable.

Rovira, Rogelio. Las Divisiones de la Filosofía Práctica de Kant. *An Seminar Hist Filosof*, 9, 79-87, 1992.

Kant divides practical philosophy into three disciplines: the critique of practical reason, the metaphysics of morals and the practical or moral anthropology. The first one is equivalent to the whole system of the critique of practical reason (propaedeutic); the two last-named constitute the system of the practical science (metaphysics). The aim of this paper is to distinguish the three mentioned disciplines attending, firstly, to their diverse object of knowledge; secondly, to the use of reason (theoretical or practical) from each of them are originated; and, finally, to the origin (rational or empirical) of their respective judgments.

Rowbotham, Sheila. "Retrieval and Renewal" in *Marxism in the Postmodern Age*, Callari, Antonio (ed), 71-78. New York, Guilford, 1994.

Rowe, C J and Gómez-Lobo, A. "Discusión: La Autenticidad de la Carta VII" in *Platón: Los Diálogos Tardíos, Lan, Conrado Eggers (ed)*, 161-168. Sankt Augustin, Academia, 1986.

Rowe, Christopher. "Public and Private Speaking in Plato's Later Dialogues" in *Platón: Los Diálogos Tardíos, Lan, Conrado Eggers (ed)*, 125-137. Sankt Augustin, Academia, 1986.

The paper traces in outline form the rehabilitation of rhetoric in the course of the Platonic dialogues. *Gorgias* is dismissive of any 'art of speaking' which extends beyond telling the truth, and *Republic* too is reluctant to grant any positive role to oratory, although it does find a role for story-telling, and in general for the purveying of fictions/falsehoods in the public interest. This prepares for the installation of rhetoric as one of the central *technai* underpinning the model city of *Politicus*, and by implication in *Laws*. The theoretical justification for this shift is provided by *Phaedrus*.

Rowe, Christopher. Philosophy and Literature: The Arguments of Plato's *Phaedo*. *Proc Boston Colloq Anc Phil*, 7, 159-181, 1991.

The central arguments of the *Phaedo* are frequently analyzed in isolation both from each other and from their context, with the result that attention is centered on their weaknesses. However, examination of the relationships between them, and of the responses to them by the main characters, demonstrates that they form a carefully articulated series, in which each successive argument attempts to make good the acknowledged flaws and gaps in what has preceded it. The work as a whole is a singular illustration of philosophy as cooperative dialogue, in which Simmias and Cebes—both good Socratics, rather than Pythagoreans—show themselves almost as expert as Socrates himself.

Rowe, William L. The Problem of No Best World. *Faith Phil*, 11(2), 269-271, Ap 94.

Professors Daniel and Frances Howard-Snyder hold that there is no reason to believe that it is *logically impossible* for an essentially omnipotent, omniscient, morally unsurpassable being to create a world that is morally inferior to some other world he, or some other possible being, could have created. They try to show this by imagining an omnipotent, omniscient good being, Jove, who creates a good world by using a randomizing device. They then argue that there is no reason to think that Juno and Thor (other omnipotent beings who happen to create better worlds) would be morally

superior to Jove. I argue that in the case of Thor, once we explicitly acknowledge his omniscience as well as his omnipotence, we do have a reason to think that he is morally superior to Jove. Hence, I conclude they have failed to show how an unsurpassable being can create a surpassable world.

Rowlands, Mark. Against Methodological Solipsism: The Ecological Approach. *Phil Psych*, 8(1), 5-24, 1995.

This paper argues that an ecological approach to psychology of the sort advanced by J J Gibson provides a coherent and powerful alternative to the computational, information-processing, paradigm. The paper argues for two principles. Firstly, one cannot begin to understand what internal information processing an organism must accomplish until one understands what information is available to the organism in its environment. Secondly, an organism can process information by acting on or manipulating physical structures in its environment. An attempt is made to show how these principles can be extended to cognition as a whole. It is suggested that these principles may have a foundation in evolutionary biology.

Roy, Jean. L'art de se diviser et la tentation du bien. *Laval Theol Phil*, 51(1), 77-110, F 95.

Dans son sens usuel le terme "démocratie", universellement revendiqué, réfère à la démocratie libérale ou "constitutionnelle-pluraliste" (R Aron) qui s'est constituée en Occident à l'époque moderne. Il reste que la démocratie n'est pas nécessairement libérale et que la forme actuellement dominante n'est pas la seule légitime. Le long combat pour la tolérance qui fut au coeur de la tradition libérale constitue une histoire pleine d'enseignements en ce qui touche au sens authentique de cette notion Les pirncipes acquis au long de ce processus pouvaient être transposés à la critique des "religions séculières". Peuvent-ils être également transposés tels quels sur le front de l'intolérance ethnique ou nationalitaire qui mine parfois les "sociétés ouvertes"? Sauf de très rares exceptions, les rapports minorité-majorité dans les démocraties hétérogènes n'ont nulle part trouvé une solution satisfaisante. A cet égard, le type de libéralisme auquel on associe souvent les noms de Rawls et de Dworkin semble disposer de ressources théoriques trop étroites pour intégrer adéquatement la dimension collective et conflictuelle de la dynamique politique.

Roy, Tirthankar. A Concept of Indian Music. *J Indian Counc Phil Res*, 11(2), 69-75, Ja-Ap 94.

Ruben, David-Hillel. A Counterfactual Theory of Causal Explanation. *Nous*, 28(4), 465-481, D 94.

Even if the causal relation is extensional, the causal explanatory relation is not. Why are some descriptions of a thing explanatory, and other descriptions of the same thing not? This is a perplexing difficulty, especially in these cases in which the explanatory descriptions do not figure in laws of nature. The article develops an account of causal explanatoriness, in terms of counterfactuals about causation (*not* in terms of a counterfactual account of causation itself). The account is developed by dealing with several apparent counter examples.

Ruben, David-Hillel. Mental Overpopulation and the Problem of Action. *J Phil Res*, 20, 511-524, 1995.

The causal theory of actions holds that an action just *is* an event caused by a rationalising mental state. On one version of this theory, the rationalising mental state is a belief and desire pair. Assuming that we engage in a great deal of action, the theory overpopulates the mind with beliefs and desires (or, on another version, with intentional states). The article examines numerous strategies that the theory has at its disposal, and concludes that all of them fail in the case of skilled activity, like swimming or speaking.

Ruben, David-Hillel. Singular Explanation and the Social Sciences. *Midwest Stud Phil*, 15, 130-149, 1990.

Rubio Carracedo, José. Democracia y racionalidad: Una relación conflictiva. *Dialogo Filosof*, 10(3), 324-362, S-D 94.

Las dos columnas sobre las que se asienta la democracia liberal, la libertad individual y los mecanismos de decisión pública, no se dejan conciliar fácilmente. Buena parte de la reflexión moderna sobre la vida pública se orienta a tratar de solucionar esa tensión. El presente artículo plantea el problema en sus términos precisos y repasa los principales intentos recientes de solución.

Ruccio, David F and Amariglio, Jack. "Postmodernism, Marxism, and the Critique of Modern Economic Thought" in *Marxism in the Postmodern Age*, Callari, Antonio (ed), 13-23. New York, Guilford, 1994.

The essay discusses the effects of modernist notions of cognition, behavior, subjectivity, and social determination on Marxian economic theory, such as capitalism vs. socialism, present capitalism as disordered, alienating, socially fragmented, and mystifying, and socialism as socially ordered, organically unified, and subjectively whole. The essay teases out the postmodern notions of disorder, decentering, and uncertainty that are implicit in the oppositions of classical Marxism and contends that the modernist faith in the inherent rationality of socialist economy be replaced by the recognition that capitalism has no unique purchase on disorder, decentering, and uncertainty.

Rudinow, Joel. Reply to Taylor. *J Aes Art Crit*, 53(3), 316-317, Sum 95.

A rejoinder to Paul Taylor's criticism of my earlier argument that White Blues need not be dismissed as inauthentic. Taylor's "Black Blues Authenticity" thesis posits listeners for whom the performer's racial identity is aesthetically relevant, i.e., racist listeners. Taylor's criticisms are grounded in "Racial Formation Theory" which posits "race" and "racism" as fluid historically determined concepts, which leaves the question of the authenticity of White Blues open.

Rudnick, Hans H. "Naive and Sentimental Hermeneutics: Keeping Language Open" in *The Philosophy of Paul Ricoeur*, Hahn, Lewis Edwin (ed), 141-145. Peru, Open Court, 1994.

To characterize the tension between the phenomenologist's experiencing the "lived" world, and the hermeneut's intentioning "creative" human activity, Friedrich Schiller's understanding of "naïve" and "sentimental" is used to draw (from the perspective of literary theory) attention to Ricoeur's consistent odyssey to mediate between the poetic and the scientific use of language by thematizing openness of mind and prioritization of the imagination.

Rudolph, Enno. "Substance as Function" in *Philosophy, Mathematics and Modern Physics, Rudolph, Enno (ed)*, 235-242. New York, Springer-Verlag, 1994.

Cassirer's former program of the philosophy of science to replace the traditional concept of substance—as established by the classical natural science—by the modern concept of function was not only confirmed by the consequent result of his critical and in its effect anti-Kantian interpretation of Leibniz. The following text is to systematize and to evaluate Cassirer's arguments in favor of the present relevance of the Leibnizian function concept by means of a synopsis of the publications relative to this subject.

Rudolph, Enno and Stamatescu, I O. "On the Dialogue Between Physics and Philosophy" in *Philosophy, Mathematics and Modern Physics, Rudolph, Enno (ed)*, 2-17. New York, Springer-Verlag, 1994.

Rudolph, Enno (ed) and Stamatescu, I O (ed). *Philosophy, Mathematics and Modern Physics*. New York, Springer-Verlag, 1994.

Rueda, Luis Sáez. Acerca del Conflicto Entre los Discursos "Metafísico", "Postmetafísico", y "Teológico". *Daimon Rev Filosof*, 8, 63-82, 1994.

This article analyzes the principal aspects of the contemporary dispute between the three "ways of thinking" mentioned in the title. It tries to reconstruct, at the same time, different uses of the said watchwords. The article, in particular, deals with the arguments of Habermas and Apel in favor of a "postmetaphysical thought", and the reaction in the area of theology. Those arguments are brought into confrontation with Heidegger's and Nietzsche's criticism of the "Occidental Metaphysics". In this context, the author argues against a theological basis of the theory of rationality, and maintains that the present German Enlightenment involves, against its own conviction, a theological system of thought in the Platonist sense. Finally, it proposes possible meanings of a nontheological, but hypothetical and sceptic metaphysics from a 'tragic' conception of meaning of rationality.

Rueger, Alexander. Brain Water, the Ether, and the Art of Constructing Systems. *Kantstudien*, 86(1), 26-40, 1995.

The paper explores the status of the ether in Kant's *Opus Postumum* by considering some probable sources of Kant's views. By comparing Kant's model of the ether from the late 1790's with his speculations of 1795 about the constitution and role of the recently discovered 'brain water' I argue 1) that there are striking similarities between the ether and Kant's views about the ventricular fluid which can be traced back to Kant's reception of contemporary chemical theories; and 2) that the comparison shows that the ether does have a different status than the empirical brain water, that is, a regulative status.

Rühle, Volker. Zur Situation der Philosophie in Spanien. *Z Phil Forsch*, 49(1), 124-130, Ja-Mr 95.

Twenty years after the end of the Franco-dictatorship Spanish philosophers no longer perceive their partly suspicious, partly broken history as a mere lack of tradition. Since the Counter-reformation, under the oppression of the inquisition and in the shadow of the Neoscholastic the philosophy of the European Enlightenment constantly had difficulties to establish a consistent academic tradition in Spain, where tradition often showed her ambiguity. Especially this lack of a firm traditional academic establishment keeps alive the sensitiveness of the dialectic of Enlightenment in view of the spreading doubts about an unbroken continuity of enlightened optimism. This offers possibilities for discussions transgressing academic borders.

Rüsen, Jörg. Historical Studies between Modernity and Postmodernity. *S Afr J Phil*, 13(4), 183-189, N 94.

Modernity in historical studies means rationalism; postmodernity is an attempt to overcome the hitherto developed standards of rationality in historical thinking. The modern concept of 'the history' as an entire subject matter of historical thinking is closely related to the methods of historical research which constitute history as an academic discipline. Postmodernism denies this concept and replaces it by a plurality of histories, and at the same time brings about a change in the framework of historical interpretation: away from macro-historical developments towards micro-historical phenomena. The established dichotomy between modernist and postmodernist attitudes towards history should be overcome in favor of a synthesis. This synthesis is described in respect to the concept of history, and to the methodology of historical research. (edited)

Ruesga, G Albert. Selective Conscientious Objection and the Right Not to Kill. *Soc Theor Pract*, 21(1), 61-81, Spr 95.

Ruhleder, Karen. Reconstructing Artifacts, Reconstructing Work: From Textual Edition to On-Line Databank. *Sci Tech Human Values*, 20(1), 39-64, Wint 95.

New media can change the way that artifacts are constructed and used. Changes in these artifacts, in turn, will be reflected in work practices and processes. This article draws on an empirical investigation of the impact of computer-based technologies on classical scholarship to discuss some of the ramifications that a switch in medium may have for work. The article defines both traditional and computer-based data tools as "packages" that consist of artifacts, skill sets, data, beliefs about the work process, and organizational infrastructures, and applies the package metaphor to understand the multiple levels of changes taking place within classics as the use of textual databanks (and other forms of computing) becomes more prevalent.

Ruhs, August (ed) and Seitter, Walter (ed). *Auflösen, Untersuchen, Aufwecken: Psychoanalyse und andere Analysen*. Vienna, Passagen, 1995.

Die Themenstellung des Sammelbandes ergibt sich aus der logischen Analyse des Wortes "Psychoanalyse", die nahelegt, dass die Psychoanalyse eine besondere Art von Analyse—neben anderen—ist, welch es etwa in den Naturwissenschaften, in der Mathematik, in der Philosophie, vielleicht in der Kunst gibt. Einige der verschiedenen Analysen—sozusagen entfernte Kollegen—werden miteinander konfrontiert und es stellt sich heraus, dass es zwischen ihnen auch Einflüsse und Gemeinsamkeitien gibt. Die wichtigste Gemeinsamkeit ist vielleicht die, dass Analysen Erkenntnis-Aktionen sind (sein können), die das Erkannte (und vielleicht sogar das Erkennende) nicht unverändert lassen.

Ruiz Moreno, Luisa. El Mundo y el Arbol, Tareas de la Mirada. *Analogia*, 5(2), 89-100, 1991.

Ruiz Rodríguez, Virgilio. La Vida Humana, La Etica y la Ley. *Rev Filosof (Mexico)*, 28(82), 36-60, Ja-Ap 95.

Rule, Paul. The Rushdie Affair: Tolerance, Pluralism, or Secularism?. *Sophia (Australia)*, 34(1), 226-232, Mr-Ap 95.

Rumfitt, Ian. Frege's Theory of Predication: An Elaboration and Defense, with Some New Applications. *Phil Rev*, 103(4), 599-637, O 94.

I explain the merits of Frege's "functional" theory of predication, develop this in the face of certain basic objections, and use what results to extend Frege's notion of sameness of sense so that applies between predicates. This leads me to a novel semantical theory for attributions of intention, which is deployed in support of Peter Geach in his dispute with Gareth Evans about the character of reflexive pronouns. I conclude by showing how my results refute a key argument in Anscombe's article, "The First Person".

Rumfitt, Ian. Truth Wronged (on Crispin Wright, *Truth and Objectivity*). *Ratio*, 8(1), 100-107, Ap 95.

This piece is a critical notice of Crispin Wright's 1992 book, *Truth and Objectivity*. After a brief summary of the book, I focus upon Wright's arguments for what he calls "minimalism" about truth, whereby the ascription of truth or falsity to a sentence is invested with little metaphysical weight. I criticise those arguments as resting upon an inadequate account of assertion.

Ruprecht Jr, Louis A. "After Virtue? On Distorted Philosophical Narratives" in *The 1994 Annual of Hermeneutics and Social Concern, Lawler, Justus George (ed)*, 9-34. New York, Continuum, 1994.

In the past decade a great deal of attention has been paid to the rehabilitation of the Aristotelian account of the moral life which we find in Alasdair MacIntyre's groundbreaking *After Virtue*. Indeed, a collection of essays has recently been published with the title *After MacIntyre*. We find much that we should expect in this collection of criticisms: that he is wrong about Aristotle, wrong about Aquinas, wrong about utilitarianism, wrong about Kant, wrong about enlightenment. No one has taken issue with the most essential claim of the book however, in my judgment. In a book which argues for the centrality of *narrative* in the construction of moral arguments and moral selves, no one has taken issue with the fundamental structure of *MacIntyre's* narrative. It is a seductive tale of harmonious origins (Homeric and pre-Classic Greece) giving way to the Fall (industrial capitalism and bourgeois society) and culminating in a moral apocalypse ("modern times"). What I argue is that if MacIntyre's beginning is wrong, then so is his conclusion. I perform a close reading of one of the central scenes in the *Iliad* to demonstrate that the heroic world of the poem is neither so harmonious nor so morally seamless as MacIntyre alleges. The individual of emotive and private appeals is no modern invention. And if our beginnings were not so harmonious, then it stands to follow that we are not living at the end.

Ruse, Michael E. "Evolutionary Ethics: A Defense" in *Biology, Ethics, and the Origins of Life, Rolston III, Holmes (ed)*, 89-112. Boston, Jones & Bartlett, 1995.

I argue that sociobiology offers not only normative guides for moral action, but points one in the direction of some sort of ethical scepticism at the metaethical level. That is to say one sees that through evolution that ethics is no more than an adaptation of use to humans in the struggle for existence and reproduction.

Russell, Allan Melvin and Gerhart, Mary. A Scientist and a Theologian See the World: Compromise or Synthesis?. *Zygon*, 29(4), 619-638, D 94.

A scientist (for whom the world is the universe) and a theologian (for whom the world is planet Earth) engage in dialogue, not contrived Platonic or Galilean dialogue, but true bidisciplinary dialogue that strives for higher viewpoint. S: Is the preservation of the human species a primary human responsibility? T: It may be a responsibility we share with God. S: The human species has a limited future if confined to the planet Earth. We must diversify our habitat by colonizing space. T: We are responsible for other life on the planet as well. The discussants conclude that besides protecting Earth ecologies, we should create new ecologies in space.

Russell, G A. "The Impact of the *Philosophus Autodidactus*" in *The 'Arabick' Interest of the Natural Philosophers..., Russell, G A (ed)*, 224-265. Leiden, Brill, 1994.

In 1671, shortly before Locke started on the first drafts of his *Essay on Human Understanding*, a bi-lingual text in Arabic and Latin was published at Oxford, entitled the 'Philosophus autodidactus', which depicted the emergence of the mind of a child, in complete isolation from society, by means of sensory experience and reasoning, without innate ideas. It is argued that this unique work had a formative influence on Locke. Locke was not only acquainted with the 'Philosophus autodidactus', but during the period of its translation, he was also intimately involved with the translators, Dr Pococke (the Laudian Professor of Arabic and the Canon of Christ Church) and his son, Edward Pococke. This close relationship provides, for the first time, a concrete explanation for the dramatic shift in Locke's thought from his previous concerns to epistemological questions and specifically to the nature and development of mind.

Russell, G A (ed). *The 'Arabick' Interest of the Natural Philosophers in Seventeenth-Century England*. Leiden, Brill, 1994.

Contrary to all expectation, the seventeenth century is characterized by an astonishing 'second wave' of Arabic influence (as distinct from the medieval transmission). Focusing on England, historians in fourteen essays examine, for the first time, the nature and sources of its pervasive impact in areas ranging from Biblical scholarship and theology, to alchemy, astronomy, botany, education, mathematics, medicine, philology, and philosophy as well as diplomacy and trade. This 'second wave' of Arabic interest was rooted in the Protestant Reformation, the humanist classical revival, and the 'expansion' and emergence of Europe as a center of world trade. It led to the institutionalization of Arabic studies at Oxford and Cambridge, where Arabic became a requirement for the Arts degree, and after 1660's features substantially in the concerns of the Fellows of the Royal Society. Arabic is shown to have been a significant component of the rise of Protestant intellectual tradition and the evolution of secular scholarship at universities. This volume casts a new light on the period and reveals a crucial aspect of seventeenth-century thought which has been neglected.

Russell, Robert John. Cosmology from Alpha to Omega. *Zygon*, 29(4), 557-577, D 94.

This paper focuses on four passages in the journey of the universe from beginning to end: its origin in the Big Bang, the production of heavy elements in first generation stars, the buzzing symphony of life on earth, and the distant future of the cosmos. As a physicist and a Christian theologian, I will ask how each of these passages casts light on the deepest questions of existence and our relation to God, and in turn how these questions are being explored through ongoing research into the interaction between Christian theology and the natural sciences.

Russo, Francesco. Contemplazione e Interpretazione: L'Estetica Kantiana Nell'Analisi di Luigi Pareyson. *Acta Phil*, 4(1), 105-110, 1995.

La teoria estetica di Luigi Pareyson ha evidenti punti di contatto con la concezione kantiana dell'arte. Il concetto kantiano di contemplazione pura viene ripreso da Pareyson per parlare del risultato della interpretazione artistica, nella quale sono uniti il movimento della ricerca e il godimento della scoperta.

Russon, John. Embodiment and Responsibility: Merleau-Ponty and the Ontology of Nature. *Man World*, 27(3), 291-308, Jl 94.

Rutecki, Gregory W. Blurring Distinctions between the Dying and the Dead: A Call for Discernment in Organ Donation. *Ethics Med*, 10(3), 60-67, Autumn 94.

Rutecki, Gregory W. Liver Transplantation and Alcoholic Patients: When is it Justified to Just Say No?. *Ethics Med*, 11(2), 36-43, 1995.

Access to liver transplantation is unique. Since 50% or more of end-stage liver disease is alcohol-mediated and donor livers remain scarce, alcoholic patients could theoretically utilize all livers donated leaving none for other varieties of liver disease. The ethical guidelines designed for access have evolved from exclusion of alcoholic persons (NIH 1983) to limited access at selected centers. Historical perspective suggests that the early period excluding alcoholic persons was based on social value criteria. This paper reframes the issue of alcoholic persons access to liver transplantation from a Christian-Hippocratic perspective. Two syntheses for access are proposed (equal access for alcohol persons vs unequal access). Since outright exclusion relies on social value criteria, it appears that alcoholic persons must be permitted access to liver transplantation with abstinence.

Ruthenberg, Klaus. "Das Verständnis von Auslösung und Beschleunigung.." in *Naturauffassungen in Philosophie, Wissenschaft, Technik: Band III, Schäfer, Lothar (ed)*, 41-69. Freiburg, Alber, 1995.

Rutherford, Donald. "Metaphysics: The Late Period" in *The Cambridge Companion to Leibniz, Jolley, Nicholas (ed)*, 124-175. New York, Cambridge Univ Pr, 1994.

Rutherford, Donald. "Philosophy and Language in Leibniz" in *The Cambridge Companion to Leibniz, Jolley, Nicholas (ed)*, 224-269. New York, Cambridge Univ Pr, 1994.

Rutherford, Donald. *Leibniz and the Rational Order of Nature*. New York, Cambridge Univ Pr, 1995.

This book aims to demonstrate the systematic unity of Leibniz's thought, in which theodicy, ethics, metaphysics, and natural philosophy contribute to a single vision of the best of all possible worlds. The key idea underlying the system is a conception of nature as a harmonious order designed by God to maximize opportunities for the exercise of reason. From this emerges an ethical ideal in which the virtued and happiness of human beings are promoted through the gradual extension of intellectual enlightenment. The book includes extended analyses of Leibniz's accounts of substance and of the relationship between monads and bodies.

Rutowski, Tadeusz. Versuche die ersten Prinzipien in Frage zu stellen. *Stud Phil Christ*, 30(2), 227-243, 1994.

Thomistische Philosophen behaupten, dass die Hauptgesetze der Ontologie, wie etwa das Prinzip der Identität, das Gesetz vom ausgeschlossenen Widerspruch und das Gesetz vom ausgeschlossnene Dritten notwendige, gewisse und adäquate Sätze sind. Im Ramen der Physik ist aber heutzutage die Meinung vebrietet, dass man alle wissen—schaftlichen Sätze bezweifeln darf. Es geht also darum, mit welchem Erfolg die erwähnten Prinzipien im Frage gstellt wurden? Man wird da gezeigt, dass es keine hinreichenden Gründe bis jetzt untergebracht worden sind, die uns zur Ablehnung der ersten Prinzipien führen dürfen. Es ist meistens zu bemerken, dass der Zweifel an die Gültigkeit der ersten Prinzipien von den Definitionen der Wahrheit (bzw. der Falschheit) der Sätze abhängig. Es entsteht auch das problem: gemiesst Priorität die ontologische oder die metalogische Version der prinzipien, oder sind die beiden versionen äquivalent.

Rutte, Heiner. "Zu Heinrich Gomperz: *Die Wissenschaft und die Tat*" in *Heinrich Gomperz, Karl Popper und die österreichische Philosophie, Seiler, Martin (ed)*, 119-145. Amsterdam, Rodopi, 1994.

Rutten, Christian. Moralité privée et moralité publique chez Aristote. *Philosophica*, 52(2), 63-74, 1993.

Ryan, John K. "The Wager in Pascal and Others" in *Gambling on God: Essays on Pascal's Wager, Jordan, Jeffrey (ed)*, 11-19. Lanham, Rowman & Littlefield, 1994.

Ryan, Maura A. Clinical Ethics and Intervention in Domestic Violence. *Ethics Behavior*, 5(3), 279-282, 1995.

Ryan, Michael. "Foucault's Fallacy" in *Reconstructing Foucault, Miguel-Alfonso, Ricardo (ed)*, 159-181. Amsterdam, Rodopi, 1994.

Ryan, William F. The Incompatibility of Intuition and Constitution in Husserl's *The Idea of Phenomenology* (1907). *Method*, 10(2), 147-181, Fall 92.

The purpose of this article is to identify and then to contrast the two key notions of intuition and constitution in Edmund Husserl's pivotal lectures *The Idea of Phenomenology* (1907). The conclusion of the article is that, since the notions of intuition and of constitution are irreconcilably opposed to each other in their very meaning, Husserl's use of them as if they were superficially interchangeable concepts leads to incoherent positions in *The Idea of Phenomenology*.

Rybakov, Vladimir V. Even Tabular Modal Logics Sometimes do not have Independent Base for Admissible Rules. *Bull Sec Log*, 24(1), 37-40, Mr 95.

Ryckman, Thomas A. Weyl, Reichenbach and the Epistemology of Geometry. *Stud Hist Phil Sci*, 25(6), 831-870, D 95.

Hermann Weyl's early attempt (1918-1923) to "broaden" Einstein's theory of gravitation by incorporating the electromagnetic field into the metric of spacetime was the initial example of a "unified field theory". Though criticized by Einstein and Pauli as empirically inadequate, it played a decisive role in spurring other unification schemes, including those of Einstein himself. But it also provides a powerful challenge of principle to Reichenbach's proposal for empirical determination of the metric after conventionally setting "universal forces" equal to zero. Yet Reichenbach's treatment became orthodoxy in philosophy of science, establishing a paradigm for the analysis of physical theories in terms of "coordinative definitions".

Ryckman, Thomas A and Roth, Paul A. Chaos, Clio, and Scientific Illusions of Understanding. *Hist Theor*, 34(1), 30-44, 1995.

A number of authors have recently argued that the mathematical insights of "chaos theory" offer a promising formal model or significant analogy for understanding at least some historical events. We examine a representative claim of each kind regarding the application of chaos theory to problems of historical explanation. We identify two lines of argument. One we term the Causal Thesis, which states that chaos theory may be used to plausibly model, and so explain, historical events. The other we term the Convergence Thesis, which holds that, once the analogy between history and chaos theory is properly appreciated, any temptation to divide history from the rest of science should be greatly lessened. We argue that the proffered analogy between chaos theory and history falls apart upon closer analysis. The promised benefits of chaos theory *vis-à-vis* history are either fantastic or, at best, an extremely loose heuristic which, while retaining nothing of the considerable intrinsic interest of nonlinear dynamics, easily seduces the unwary into taking at face value terms and concepts that have a specifically precise meaning only within the confines of mathematical theory.

Ryder, John. Introduction: Reconstructing Philosophy in Eastern Europe. *Metaphilosophy*, 25(2-3), 111-116, Ap-Jl 94.

This is an Introduction to a collection of articles by contemporary Eastern European philosophers from 5 countries: Russia, Latvia, Poland, Slovakia and Bulgaria. The contributors are all working philosophers in Academies or Universities, and their current work represents ways Eastern European philosophers are dealing with the profound changes in their societies. The dominant themes include the flaws of Marxist philosophy in the socialist period; the re-emergence of traditional Russian philosophy; the philosophy of science in Eastern Europe; the impact of current critical approaches to philosophy in the West, especially feminist and generally post-modernist criticism; and finally the role of philosophy in Eastern Europe's future.

Ryle, Martin. Reply to Easthope. *Rad Phil*, 70, 32-33, Mr-Ap 95.

In response to Antony Easthope's criticisms of an earlier article (Ryle, 'Long Live Literature', *Radical Philosophy* 67), it is acknowledged that a purely aesthetic criticism of literary texts is inadequate, and is increasingly superseded by the analysis and evaluations of 'cultural studies'. Nonetheless, critics and cultural historians need to develop terms in which distinctions of kind and quality can be drawn between texts: undifferentiated notions of 'cultural production' are unsatisfactory. The interaction between formal properties and intertextual/social settings must be analyzed. We must grant the integrity of the text, which remains the foundation of the various 'readings' derived from it.

Rynasiewicz, Robert. Absolute vs Relational Theories of Space and Time: A Review of *World Enough and Space-Time* by John Earman. *Phil Phenomenol Res*, 55(3), 675-687, S 95.

This review not only explains why Earman's monography counts as a landmark contribution to the traditional absolute-relational debate, but goes on to explore a number of key issues: 1) What is the distinction between absolute and relative motion supposed to be? 2) Does the program of Leibniz algebras offer an alternative to substantivalism? 3) What should be concluded from the whole argument regarding the substantival-relational debate? 4) Does that debate remain meaningful in the context of modern field theory?

S-Christofelli, M. From Logos to Style. *Philosophia (Athens)*, 23-24, 56-60, 1993-94.

Human language in all its achievements is a sensuous and an intellectual form of expression. Even in highly developed languages, there is a language of emotions side by side with conceptual language. Reason alone is a very inadequate mean to express human culture in all its richness. This inherent feature of language becomes a starting point for style: the two sources of language—emotional and conceptual—have an unlimited variety in their connection, which serves the variation and originality of linguistic forms. (edited)

Saab, Salma. Una Posición Intermedia Entre el Fisicalismo y el Intencionalismo: Dennett. *Critica*, 26(76-77), 205-227, Ap-Ag 94.

This article assesses Dennett's position with respect to mental states, intermediate between the extremes of physicalism and intentionalism. Dennett concentrates most of his theses with respect to our attribution of mental states to others, or to other systems, on what he calls the intentional stance. It is suggested that one can make certain analogies between Dennett's proposal and Wittgenstein's use of the term "seeing as". The analogy with "seeing as" has the advantage of preserving Dennett's main claims, while eliminating the use of "abstracta", thus avoiding the discomfort that some philosophers have felt with regard to "abstracta". The identification of characteristics common to mental discourse and "seeing as" allows that author to make sense of the claim that there are certain aspects of things or of situations, such as patterns, which while they properly belong to the things or situations themselves, nevertheless depend for their recognition on the skills of the observer. (edited)

Saari, David J. *Too Much Liberty?: Perspectives on Freedom and the American Dream*. New York, Praeger, 1995.

David Saari provides an extended essay on the nature of freedom in contemporary America, its historical roots, and its present-day manifestations. Drawing on the fields of history, law, politics, business, and philosophy, this wide-ranging study examines three facets of freedom—national freedom, freedom from the state, and freedom within the state—as they have developed in American law, politics, and society. Each of these facets is carefully defined and then applied to such contemporary issues as authority, property, equality, justice, and privacy.

Sabat, Steven R and Harré, Rom. The Alzheimer's Disease Sufferer as a Semiotic Subject. *Phil Psychiat Psych*, 1(3), 145-160, S 94.

The discourse of Alzheimer's disease sufferers, studied in depth, is found to reveal the afflicted as being semiotic subjects, that is, persons for whom meaning is the driving force behind their behavior. This is despite the fact that the subjects are categorized, on the basis of standard psychometric measures, as being in moderate to severe stages of the disease. The research presented herein is meant to suggest the possibility that such disparities may be more common than is presently acknowledged, and that if so, such semiotic behavior as can be found in Alzheimer's sufferers may be used to help facilitate interactions between the afflicted and the healthy, and to inform further our understanding of cognition and intention by suggesting a complementary approach to assessing cognitive function. In keeping with the discursive approach to psychology, this study is based on the principle that meanings are jointly constituted by the participants to a conversation.

Sabatés, Marcelo. "Esencilaismo y Conjuntivismo Mereológico" in *Temas Actuales de Filosofía, Palacios, María Julia (ed)*, 555-562. Buenos Aires, Univ Nacional Salta, 1993.

Mereological essentialism asserts that a whole ceases to be itself when there is some change in its parts. Mereological conjunctivism claims that any two objects constitute a third object that contains them as parts. Both theses come in various strengths. In this paper 1) I discuss and reject two arguments for unrestricted conjunctivism offered by James Van Cleve, one from our everyday acceptance of scattered objects and the other from the acceptance of a plausible moderate essentialism; and 2) I explore a combination of radical essentialism and extreme anticonjunctivism.

Sabini, John and Schulkin, Jay. Biological Realism and Social Constructivism. *J Theor Soc Behav*, 24(3), 207-217, S 94.

In this paper we attempt to reconcile two important, current intellectual traditions: Darwinism and social constructionism. We believe that these two schools have important points of contact that have been obscured because each school has feared that the other wanted to put it out of business. We try to show that both traditions have much to offer psychology, a discipline that has often been too individualistic, too concerned with the private and the subjective. The spirit of American pragmatism can be found in both camps; like the social constructivists, pragmatists focused on social transaction rather than internal happening, and like the Darwinian they were rooted in functionalism and the biological.

Sacchi, Mario Enrique. El Significado de la Contrariedad. *Sapientia*, 49(193-4), 337-356, 1994.

Sacchi, Mario Enrique. La presencia virtual de los elementos en la combinación química según Santo Tomás de Aquino. *Aquinas*, 37(1), 123-149, Ja-Ap 94.

Sacks, Mark. Wittgenstein, transzendentale Gründzüge und transzendentale Einschränkungen. *Deut Z Phil*, 42(5), 819-839, 1994.

Sadakane, Keiji. The Genesis of Buddhist Painting in Ancient India and Its Early Development. *Aesthetics*, 5, 89-103, Mr 92.

This paper aims to elucidate the genesis and development of Buddhist painting in early India as evidenced by the few extant works and early literary references. Buddhist painting seems to have first evolved in the form of cloth paintings for recitation. Such cloth paintings may have encouraged not only the development and diffusion of Buddhist narratives but also the appearance of Buddhist relief sculpture. In following stages, cloth paintings for recitation are thought to have influenced the subjects and functions of secular wall paintings, resulting in the new genre of Buddhist wall painting.

Sadler, Ted. *Nietzsche: Truth and Redemption*. London, Athlone, 1995.

Sadovskii, V N. Philosophy in Moscow in the Fifties and Sixties. *Russian Stud Phil*, 33(2), 46-72, Fall 94.

Sadurski, Wojciech. The Moral Neutrality of the Liberal State. *Filozof Istraz*, 14(2-3), 343-354, 1994.

The paper discusses some of the basic characteristics of moral neutrality of the liberal state. The idea of neutrality is already at home in some legal contexts: in the doctrine of nonestablishment of religion, or in the provision of *viewpoint neutrality* of the state in matters of free speech. Mill's *harm to others* principle is often considered the defining principle of liberalism; the idea of moral neutrality of the state could be seen as a way of construing this principle that helps avoid some of the difficulties that plague it. (edited)

Saez Rueda, L. Fundamentación última y factidad: (Un intento de argumentar "con Apel contra Apel"). *Pensamiento*, 197(50), 267-292, My-Ag 94.

Dirige el presente trabajo la intención de confrontar el actual proyecto apeliano de una *fundamentación última filosófica* con sus límites internos, mediante el análisis de la *teoria de la racionalidad* que lo sustenta. Se *interpreta la meta* de dicho proyecto como la de aprehender autorreflexivamente un ámbito de "*facticidad racional*", que está estructurado en las dimensiones polares "normativa" y "hermenéutica", interpretación que conduce a negar, contra Apel, tanto la posibilidad de una fundamentación definitiva, como una concepción dialéctica de la relación entre los polos mencionados, relación que el autor propone, finalmente, entender en términos de *tensión irreductible*.

Saffrey, Henri Dominique. Florence, 1492: Réapparaît Plotin. *Frei Z Phil Theol*, 42(1-2), 134-151, 1995.

Sagan, Dorion and Margulis, Lynn. "Facing Nature" in *Biology, Ethics, and the Origins of Life, Rolston III, Holmes (ed)*, 39-62. Boston, Jones & Bartlett, 1995.

"Facing the Earth" is a study from the combined vantage point of evolutionary biology and continental philosophy of ethical frontiers and responsibilities with regard to humanities relationship to Earth. Alluding to work of E Levinas, G Bataille and J Derrida as well as H Spencer, C Darwin, M Ruse and E O Wilson it comes to the unsettling conclusion that no guard rails exist for an evolutionary ethic. Discussions include our predilection for ethical face-to-face relationships (i.e., with organisms that have faces and the fact that Earth now has nearly gained a face), Michael Ruse's literally adaptive morality, E O Wilson's ethical dilemma of biophilia, Derrida's possible solutions to the monstrosity of an infinite ethical abyss, Harold Bloom's interpretation of the ethnocentric behavior of nations as the ethically suspect history of superorganisms (acts necessary to the survival or expansion of larger biological entities) and the changing boundary of self, or "in-group" and of "out-group" as we move and remove the ethical line to include fewer or more of our planetmates.

Sagi, Avi. Is the Absurd the Problem or the Solution? *The Myth of Sisyphus* Reconsidered. *Phil Today*, 38(3-4), 278-284, Fall 94.

Sagi (Schweitzer), Avi. Tolerance and the Possibility of Pluralism in Judaism. *Iyyun*, 44, 175-200, Ap 95.

This article analyzes the conceptual possibility in Judaism of tolerance and pluralism vis-à-vis religiously nonobservant individuals. First, a distinction is drawn between tolerance and pluralism. A tolerant person is one who assumes that s/he knows the truth, and denies the truth-value of other positions, yet for reasons outlines in the paper, s/he permits others to hold and advocate their (mistaken) positions. A pluralist, however, assigns equal status to positions other than his own. Two types of pluralism are defined: *weak* pluralism recognizes the fallibility of all positions, *strong* pluralism recognizes the coexistence of multiple goods. Following these distinctions, it becomes apparent that several modes of tolerance are possible within Judaism. (edited)

Sagoff, Mark. Environmentalism vs Value Subjectivism: Rejoinder to Anderson and Leal. *Crit Rev*, 8(3), 467-473, Sum 94.

This essay takes up the old refrain the either *liberty* or *utility* may justify free markets. If Free Market Environmentalists cite liberty, they must rule out all pollution and many other "externalities" as instances of coercion. If they cite utility, then they must endorse all sorts of regulation—indeed, centralized planning—to cope with costs and benefits markets fail to price. Anderson and Leal, being unaware of the distinction between utility and liberty, are caught upon the horns of the dilemma.

Sagoff, Mark. Four Dogmas of Environmental Economics. *Environ Values*, 3(4), 285-310, Wint 94.

Four dogmas have shaped modern neoclassical economics. The first proposes that markets may fail to allocate resources efficiently, that is, to those willing to pay the most for them. The second asserts that choices, particularly within markets, reveal preferences. The third is the assumption that people always make the choices they expect will benefit them or enhance their welfare. The fourth dogma holds that perfectly competitive markets will allocate resources to their most beneficial uses. This is the doctrine of the invisible hand. I argue that these dogmas of applied welfare economics should be abandoned. One consequence of doing so will be an increased interest in the institutional context of production. A second will be a turn toward empiricism.

Saidel, Eric. Content and Causal Powers. *Phil Sci*, 61(4), 658-665, D 94.

Owens (1993) argues that a tension exists between our commonsense view of mental states and the scientific view that psychological explanations not contradict supervenience. He suggests that one cannot accept the anti-individualistic conclusions of Twin-Earth thought experiments and continue to use folk psychological states to explain behavior. I argue that his conclusions are based on individuating content widely and causal powers narrowly, and that such individuation violates consistency assumptions about the terms of his discussion. Thus, I argue, the tension he points to evaporates when we adopt either a consistently wide view or a consistently narrow view.

Saidel, Eric and Forster, Malcolm. Connectionism and the Fate of Folk Psychology: A Reply to Ramsey, Stich and Garon. *Phil Psych*, 7(4), 437-452, 1994.

Ramsey, Stich and Garon (1991) argue that if the correct theory of mind is some parallel distributed processing theory, then folk psychology must be false. Their idea is that if the nodes and connections that encode one representation are causally active then all representations encoded by the same set of nodes and connections are also causally active. We present a clear, and concrete, counterexample to RSG's argument. In conclusion, we suggest that folk psychology and connectionism are best understood as complementary theories. Each has different limitations, yet each will co-evolve with the other in an overlapping domain of 'normal' psychology.

Sainati, Vittorio. Gentile e Gödel. *Teoria*, 14(1), 5-19, 1994.

Sainati, Vittorio. Il Ritorno dell'Identità nel "Sistema di Logica" di G Gentile. *G Crit Filosof Ital*, 73(2-3), 414-427, My-D 94.

Sainsbury, Mark. Why the World Cannot be Vague. *S J Phil*, 33(Supp), 63-81, 1995.

In this article I look for, but do not find, a substantive thesis of ontic vagueness. Everyone can agree that some objects are borderline cases for vague expressions (including expressions specifying spatio-temporal and parthood relations); so the existence of such objects cannot do justice to a substantive claim that the world is vague. I also consider whether it is easier to find a substantive thesis to the effect that there are vague properties. My conclusion is that there is more hope in this direction, but that it requires some supplementary, and in my opinion implausible, views about properties in general.

Sainsbury, R M. *Paradoxes (Second Edition)*. New York, Cambridge Univ Pr, 1995.

Saint-Arnaud, Jocelyne. Trois discours de Pie XII et le débat sur l'euthanasie. *Laval Theol Phil*, 50(3), 545-553, O 94.

Trois discours de Pie XII portant sur le soulagement de la douleur et la cessation de traitement sont analysés dans le but d'examiner la pensée de Pie XII sur ce que Joseph Fletcher a nommé euthanasies directe et indirecte, terminologie qui est à l'origine de la distinction entre euthanasies active et passive. Il est démontré que non seulement Pie XII n'identifie pas le soulagement de la douleur et la cessation de traitement à des actes d'euthanasie, ne seraitelle qu'indirecte ou passive, mais encore que de tels actes sont moralement bons, même s'ils accélèrent le processus de la mort, pour autant qu'ils respectent certaines conditions énoncées sous le principe du double effet. Dans cette perspective, le caractère passif ou actif de l'action n'est pas pertinent pour juger de la moralité de l'acte.

Saint-Germain, Christian. Groupe et idéologie: A propos de *Fonctionnaires de Dieu* d'Eugen Drewermann. *Laval Theol Phil*, 51(1), 183-189, F 95.

Dans son important ouvrage intitulé *Fonctionnaires de Dieu*, Eugen Drewermann pose le problème du statut psychologique de clerc moderne. Il s'emploie à décrire les impasses, à soulever les contradictions inhérentes à cette fonction dans la tradition catholique. Ce bref article en prend acte touten questionnant les limites de cette analyse. Le propos de cet article consiste dans la réception des griefs adressés par Drewermann à l'égard de la structure ecclésiale mais porte une question supplémentaire: peut-il en être autrement? N'y a-t-il pas dans la démarche de Drewermann des présupposés angéliques à l'endroit de ceux qui occupent une fonction, fûtelle religieuse? Enfin, le portrait du prêtre recèle bien davantage que des contradictions d'ordre psychologique, il préfigure le contexte bureaucratique à travers lequel les démocraties libérales se donnent à penser. La "somme" de Drewermann s'avère fort stimulante pour réfléchir autour du portrait des acteur d'un système mais pourrait s'appliquer éventuellement à tout ceux qui représentent les institutions.

Saint-Pierre, Gaston. Le Juste Milieu, le Trop et le pas Assez. *Horiz Phil*, 4(1), 109-116, Autumn 93.

Sakai, Kiyoshi. Zum Wandel der Leibniz-Rezeption im Denken Heideggers. *Heidegger Stud*, 9, 97-124, 1993.

Sala, Giovanni B. Kant and Lonergan on Insight Into the Sensible. *Method*, 13(1), 89-97, Spr 95.

Kant denies in human beings an intellectual intuition in the sense that our thinking (concept and judging) is not able to "see" and therefore to know reality. All our intuitions are sensible. But if we take intuition as "insight into the sensible" from which concepts arise, then we must say that Kant simply ignores this act and consequently postulates a priori concepts. Nevertheless Kant comes closest to "insight into the sensible" when he, towards the end of his *Critique of Pure Reason*, discusses how the mathematician constructs his concepts in the sensible intuition and so arrives at new knowledge.

Sala, J F A. La falsedad en el pensamiento y en el discurso: Comentarios al *Sofista* 259b al 265e. *Rev Filosof (Mexico)*, 27(81), 432-4, S-D 94.

Salazar, Ignacio. En Torno a la Noción de Pobreza Voluntaria. *Rev Espan Filosof Med*, 0, 185-192, 1993.

Salbu, Steven R. Insider Trading and the Social Contract. *Bus Ethics Quart*, 5(2), 313-328, Ap 95.

The law of insider trading has progressed from an expansive approach, according to which all trading on nonpublic information was considered illegal, to a constricted approach, under which corporate outsiders are permitted to trade on nonpublic information provided such trading does not breach a fiduciary duty. This article analyzes both the former, expansive theory and the currently utilized constricted theory, within a framework of basic tenets of the American capitalist social contract regarding legitimacy of property claims.

Salcedo, Damián. Consecuencialismo e imparcialidad. *Rev Filosof (Spain)*, 4(5), 163-190, 1991.

Salcedo, Damián and Lara, Francisco and Gutiérrez, Gilberto. Observaciones y respuesta. *Rev Filosof (Spain)*, 4(6), 429-436, 1991.

Sale, William Frederick (ed) and Howell, Joseph H (ed). *Life Choices: A Hastings Center Introduction to Bioethics*. Washington, Georgetown Univ Pr, 1995.

Saleem, Mohammad Anwar. Ibn Sina's Contribution to Philosophy. *Darshana Int*, 32(1/125), 52-58, Ja 92.

The contribution of the West to the various fields of knowledge is no doubt laudable but the remarkable addition to the treasury of the world knowledge made by the East is also commendable. Ibn Sina or Avecenna is regarded as one of the important celebrities of the East in the galaxy of world intellectuals. He was born in Isfahan in 980 A D and educated in Bukhara. Unfortunately, Avecenna as a systematic philosopher and a physician of the first order has not been properly introduced in the Western countries. His famous book *Al-Shifa*, "a book of healing," covers almost all doctrines on the subject of medicine. Another important book "Qanun", a canon of medicine, encompasses his own useful observations with regard to human body and its functioning process. In the field of metaphysics, Avecenna's thoughts revolve around the system of originality and its transformation into the essence for which he was honored with the title of "Philosopher of Being". In brief, it can be fairly concluded that most of the researches and discoveries in modern medicine owe much to Avecenna's achievements in 10th Century.

Sales, Bruce D and Simon, Leonore. Institutional Constraints on the Ethics of Expert Testimony. *Ethics Behavior*, 3(3-4), 231-249, 1993.

We examined the dilemmas posed by the involvement of expert witnesses in court cases and the institutional constraints on the ethics of expert testimony. The causes for the incorporation of bad science into legal decisions, potential solutions to this dilemma, and the limitations of these solutions are considered. We concluded that law, science, and experts must respond to the problems posed by expert witnessing.

Salinas Espinosa, Concepción. De Vicios y Virtudes en Algunos Textos Castellanos del Siglo XV. *Rev Espan Filosof Med*, 1, 149-157, 1994.

Salles, Eduardo and Barra, Oliveira. Newton sobre Movimento, Espaço e Tempo. *Cad Hist Filosof Cie*, 3(1-2), 85-115, Ja-D 93.

Analysis of the origins of the Newtonian doctrine about the absolute movement, space and time, in which is shown that this doctrine originates in the consolidation of the first ideas of Newton about the dynamics of circular movements. This analysis emphasizes both the meaning of the criticism to the Cartesian relativism present in the texts in which Newton exposes his doctrine and the possibility of interpreting these texts having as a starting point the exigencies of the Newtonian system of the "rational mechanics".

Sallis, John. "Mimesis and the End of Art" in *Intersections: Nineteenth-Century Philosophy and Contemporary Theory*, Rajan, Tilottama (ed), 60-78. Albany, SUNY Pr, 1995.

Against the background of the Platonic and Aristotelian discussions of mimesis, this paper shows that Hegel's critique of mimesis applies only to an inferior, reductive form and that his rejection of this form of mimesis is for the sake of affirming a more fundamental sense of mimesis. The resulting conception of art as the sensible presentation of spirit is explored in relation to Hegel's thesis that art is at an end.

Sallis, John. *Delimitations: Phenomenology and the End of Metaphysics (Second, Expanded Edition)*. Bloomington, Indiana Univ Pr, 1995.

Delimitations characterizes the end of metaphysics as a limit, or horizon, both enclosing metaphysical thought and opening the field of thinking beyond it. It explores the bearing of phenomenology, of the question of imagination, and of certain key texts by Heidegger on the end of metaphysics thus conceived. This second, expanded edition adds an entirely new part on nonidentity, with chapters dealing with Gadamer, with Derrida, and with Schelling.

Sallusti, Marina. Eric Voegelin: Le Ragioni e il Metodo della Conscienza. *Riv Int Filosof Diritto*, 71(4), 762-775, 1994.

Salmeri, Giovanni. Un Unico Heidegger? Note sul *Systematischer Index* di Eduard Landolt. *Teoria*, 14(2), 111-126, 1994.

Salmon, James F and King, Thomas M. Works on Teilhard, 1980-1994: An Annotated Bibliography. *Zygon*, 30(1), 131-142, Mr 95.

Salmon, Nathan. A Problem in the Frege-Church Theory of Sense and Denotation. *Nous*, 27(2), 158-166, Je 93.

There is an inconsistency among claims made by Alonzo Church concerning Frege's distinction between sense and denotation, taken together with plausible assertions by Frege concerning his notion of indirect sense (*ungerade Sinn*). It is argued that the most plausible resolution, in light of Church's own arguments, is to reject Church's Fregean solution to the Paradox of Analysis. Yet adopting an alternative solution involves abandoning the theory of sense and denotation, in the form in which it has been staunchly advocated by Frege and Church. The inconsistency in the Frege-Church theory thus goes to the heart of that theory.

Salmon, Nathan. Being of Two Minds: Belief with Doubt. *Nous*, 29(1), 1-20, Mr 95.

It is argued that our common-sense theory of belief does not correctly accommodate the possibility, emphasized by Kripke's famous example of Pierre, of combining belief of proposition with doubt (either in the form of disbelief or in the form of suspension of judgment) concerning that same proposition. An alternative theory is proposed and defended. The theory incorporates elements of Frege's notion of indirect sense, but is neutral between Fregeanism and Millianism. The so-called hidden-indexical theory of Stephen Schiffer and Crimmins-and-Perry is refuted. It is shown moreover that Schiffer's version of the theory is inconsistent.

Salmon, W. La Comprensión Científica en el Siglo Veinte. *Rev Latin de Filosof*, 21(1), 3-21, Fall 95.

During the last millenium a huge evolution has taken place with respect to scientific knowledge and in the last century with respect to the acceptance of scientific understanding as well. This paper concerns the intellectual value of scientific explanation, not the practical one. Two forms of scientific understanding are examined: explanation as unification and causal-mechanical explanation. They are not opposed to one another and both are compatible with scientific rigor. The term "understanding" is broad and ambiguous. The main focus here is on the understanding of natural phenomena—as studied by the empirical sciences—by way of both forms of scientific explanation. Afterward, historical examples of world-pictures, related to explanation as unification, and historical examples of causal-mechanical explanations, related also to the possibility of accepting the existence of theoretical entities, are given. Finally, an example is used to show the compatibility of both forms of explanation. The superiority of understanding in the scientific sense to the mere sense of psychological satisfaction is emphasized.

Salthe, Stanley N and Matsuno, Koichiro. Global Idealism/Local Materialism. *Biol Phil*, 10(3), 309-337, July 95.

We are concerned with two modes of describing the dynamics of natural systems. Global descriptions require simultaneous global coordination of all dynamical operations. Global dynamics, including mechanics, remain invariant in the absence of external perturbation. But, failing impossible global coordination, dynamical operations could actually become coordinated only locally. In local records, as in global ones, the law of the excluded middle would be strictly observed, but without global coordination it could only be fulfilled sequentially by passing causative factors forward onto subsequent contiguous operations. The local dynamics of sequential operations would be indefinite with regard to how commitments will be made which will avoid violating the law of the excluded middle, but any resulting record will be as definite as if there had been global coordination.

Samar, Vincent J. "A Moral Justification for Gay and Lesbian Civil Rights Legislation" in *Gay Ethics*, Murphy, Timothy F (ed), 147-178. New York, Haworth Pr, 1994.

This essay explores, in two parts, the problems of justifying civil rights legislation for gays, lesbians, and bisexuals. Part I shows that discrimination against gays and lesbians at least in respect to employment, housing, and public accommodations is an evil unsupported by ethical traditions in utilitarianism, rights theory, ad communitarianism. It also shows that two theories, Kantian theory and natural law theory, which do support such discrimination on the claim that homoerotic behavior is universally or objectively immoral only do so because of a failure to make precise the concept of "natural" which underlies those theories. Part II argues that antidiscrimination legislation is both an appropriate and effective means to promote the idea that discrimination against lesbians and gays in respect to most employment, housing, and public accommodations is sufficiently injurious to both individuals and society that it should not be tolerated. The section also explains how such legislation might succeed practically in eliminating discrimination in these areas.

AUTHOR INDEX WITH ABSTRACTS 723 **Sandkühler, Hans Jörg**

Samar, Vincent J. Just Society: A Review of John Rawls, *Political Liberalism*. *Bus Ethics Quart*, 5(3), 629-645, Jl 95.

Samberg, Mark. Law and Politics in Plato's *Statesman*. *Polis*, 12(1-2), 204-212, 1993.

Sample, Ruth. Lacan, Kant, and Sade. *J Brit Soc Phenomenol*, 26(1), 5-16, Ja 95.

The author argues that Kant, Lacan, and Sade all are concerned with the issue of freedom. Each writer had tried to solve the problem of a life experienced as constrained by forces beyond one's control. Lacan recognized this common theme in Kant and Sade, and used their failed attempts to illuminate certain problems central to psychoanalysis.

Samuelson, Norbert M. "Franz Rosenzweig's Doctrine of Creation" in *Thinkers and Teachers of Modern Judaism, Goldsmith, Emanuel S (ed)*, 27-41. New York, Paragon House, 1994.

San, Debra. Thinking Mortal Thoughts. *Phil Lit*, 19(1), 16-31, Ap 95.

In Book II of the *Nicomachean Ethics*, Aristotle advises us not to think mortal thoughts, but to attempt to make ourselves immortal (1177b31-33). This is startling advice for someone who advocates the temperate virtue of *sophrosune* and a doctrine of the mean. The advice is not, however, an aberration in Aristotle's thinking. It reflects a recurring, conflicted dimension of the *Ethics* that can be traced throughout the treatise, as well as in many other major works of Western literature.

Sanabria, Carolina. Rebelión y goce: aproximación a la estética de Camus. *Rev Filosof (Costa Rica)*, 32(77), 123-129, Jl 94.

This article approaches the humanist thought of Albert Camus, in from *The rebel man*. It analyzes the role of rebellion in artistic creation of contemporary occidental society, taking into consideration the view of other authors that may enrich what was intended to be, to some extent, an intertextual dialogue.

Sanabria, José Rubén. Etica y filosofia primera en E Levinas. *Rev Filosof (Mexico)*, 27(81), 469-4, S-D 94.

El artículo se propone dar a conocer uno de los temas fundamentales del pensamiento de E Levinas: le ética tiene que ocupar el lugar de la antigua metafísica; la ética es la filosofía primera. Aquí ya no hay ser ni esencia ni persona, solamente la ética, donde "el otro" es más importante que el yo: yo soy rehén del otro. El prójimo, que me obsesiona, es rostro único, visible, en la preocupación por la justicia. el otro tiene supremacía sobre el yo. Por lo que no se trata de pensar el ser, sino de escuchar al otro. Yo soy siervo del otro; él tiene derecho a todo. Por eso reconocer al otro es darle, pero es dar al maestro, al amo, al que se debe abordar en una dimensión de grandeza. La ética, para Levinas, es la filosofía primera.

Sanabria, José Rubén. Hay una Filosofía Latinoamericana?. *Analogia*, 7(1), 31-64, 1993.

Hace tiempo se discute si hay o no una filosofía latinoamericana. Con ocasión del quinto centenario del descubrimiento de América la polémica continuó con mayor vigor. Y no desaparecieron las dos opinines opuestas: hispanista e indigenista. Para la primera, el descubrimiento fue una hazaña extraordinaria y gloriosa; para la segunda, fue el mayor genocidio de la historia humana. Para algunos de los conquistadores los indios no eran hombres sino "bestezuelas" hasta que Paulo III en 1537 con la Bula Sublimis Deus declaró que los indios eran verdaderos hombres. Qué es América Latina? se preguntan todavía algunos. Aquí va el problema de la cultura y el de la filosofía. Y a pesar de que no hay una sola opinión, la mayor parte de pensadores de nuestra América defiende la existencia de una filosofía latinoamericana. Que no tiene la misma calidad que la filosofía europea, por ejemplo, es claro, pero ahí está en el ámbito de la historia.

Sanchez, J Martin and Self, Donnie J. Gender Bias and Moral Decision Making: The Moral Orientations of Justice and Care. *J Med Human*, 16(1), 39-53, Spr 95.

This study investigated gender related moral reasoning in student essays containing arguments on moral issues. Undergraduate students in a medical ethics course viewed two films on morally controversial issues. The students wrote brief essays about the films on morally controversial issues. The students wrote brief essays about the films which were transcribed and numerically coded to conceal the author's gender from the evaluator. Using a coding scheme originated by Lyons, the evaluator classified each essay as a justice/right essay or a care/response essay or an equal response essay. Subsequently, calculations were made to determine the percentage of male authored essays that were justice/rights essays or care/response essays and the percentage of female authored essays that were justice/rights or care/response essays. The males (87.7%) tended to exhibit the justice/rights moral orientation, and the females (69.4%) exhibited the care/response moral orientation. (edited)

Sánchez de la Torre, D Angel. *La Tirania en la Grecia Antigua*. Madrid, Hispagraphis, 1994.

Sánchez del Río, Carlos. La Percepción Jeráquica de la Realidad. *Rev Filosof (Spain)*, 7(12), 319-354, 1994.

Sánchez Meca, Diego. El concepto de Bildung en el primer romanticismo alemán. *Rev Filosof (Daimon)*, 7, 73-88, 1993.

The fame of romanticism arises from the fact that it yields to a demand for absoluteness, inherent to human nature, while rejecting ontological transcendence, as abhorrent to our modern positive mind. There is no being beyond space and time, nothing absolute if not the realizations of mind in experience and history. The notion of *Bildung*, which progressive realization some reflections are suggested in this text about, is to be found in the heart of a finite-infinite dialectic which do not come together at the conclusive synthesis.

Sánchez Sorondo, Marcello. Per un Servizio Sapienziale della Filosofia nella Chiesa. *Aquinas*, 37(3), 483-499, S-D 94.

Sánchez-Gay Venegas, Juana. La Filosofía de los Poetas en la Fundación Fernando Rielo. *Analogia*, 9(1), 205-207, 1995.

Sánchez-Gey Venegas, Juana. Mujer y filosofía. *Dialogo Filosof*, 11(1), 4-30, Ja-Ap 95.

Un estudio sobre mujer y filosofía debe dar cuenta del feminismo como la primera reflexión que se ha realizado acerca de la condición humana de la mujer. Tras detenernos en ello hemos visto otras propuestas que, sin ser feministas, reflexionan desde la conciencia y la sensibilidad de expresar una nueva mirada sobre el mundo. Por último, se expone brevemente la trayectoria intelectual de tres filósofas, reconocidas internacionalmente, en las que se percibe su creatividad y su compromiso religioso, ético y político.

Sánchez-Romate, María José Gómez. La Dialéctica en el Cancionero de Baena. *Rev Espan Filosof Med*, 0, 83-88, 1993.

Sanday, Peggy Reeves. Trapped in a Metaphor. *Crim Just Ethics*, 13(2), 32-38, Sum-Fall 94.

Sandelands, Lloyd E. The Idea of Social Life. *Phil Soc Sci*, 25(2), 147-179, Je 95.

This paper reclaims the idea that human society is a form of life, an idea once vibrant in the work of Toennies, Durkheim, Simmel, Le Bon, Kroeber, Freud, Bion, and Follett but moribund today. Despite current disparagements, this idea remains the only and best answer to our primary experience of society as vital feeling. The main obstacle to conceiving society as a life is linguistic; the logical form of life is incommensurate with the logical form of language. However, it is possible to extend our conceptual reach by appealing to alternative symbolisms more congenial to living form such as, and especially, art.

Sandelands, Lloyd E. The Sense of Society. *J Theor Soc Behav*, 24(4), 305-338, D 94.

Human society is unique in the animal kingdom in the degree to which it depends upon its members reflective awareness of self and society. Whereas much has been learned about the sense of self, little is known about the sense of society. This paper develops three points about the human sense of society. Having registered these three points, the paper concludes with a brief summary and discussion of implications for expanding the scope of inquiry in social science. (edited)

Sanders, John T. Assessing Responsibility: Fixing Blame versus Fixing Problems. *Bus Prof Ethics J*, 12(4), 73-86, Wint 93.

In the midst of even the most tragic circumstances attending the aftermath of disaster arises a practical consideration: how might similar tragedies be prevented in the future? In this paper, I offer some reasons for being concerned that efforts directed toward insuring that similar tragedies do not occur in the future can easily be *obstructed* by attempts to fix blame—that is, efforts directed toward determining which agent among those involved is guilty of wrong-doing.

Sanders, John T. Honor Among Thieves: Some Reflections on Professional Codes of Ethics. *Prof Ethics*, 2(3-4), 83-103, Fall-Wint 93.

In this paper, I argue that as important as service to the community and the interests of professionals may be in the full understanding of the multiple role that "codes of ethics" play in many or most professions, it is equally important to see them as expressive of the *romance* of a profession. Professional codes should be understood not only in terms of their utility to the community, or in terms of their utility to practitioners, but as expressions of callings.

Sanders, Theresa. "A Postmodern Trinity?" in *The 1994 Annual of Hermeneutics and Social Concern, Lawler, Justus George (ed)*, 138-151. New York, Continuum, 1994.

Mark C Taylor and Jacques Derrida challenge Christianity's supposition of unity in God. In response, Robert Magliola points to the Trinity as Christianity's recognition of difference within the Godhead. This article reviews Taylor's and Derrida's critiques, shows why I believe Magliola's response is flawed, and concludes with a sketch of what a Trinitarian theology that takes full account of postmodern critiques might look like. I suggest we think of the Trinity not as a trio of bonded persons but as the meaning, mystery, and desire evident in human experience.

Sandilands, Catriona. From Natural Identity to Radical Democracy. *Environ Ethics*, 17(1), 75-92, Spr 95.

Environmentalism is traversed by a dilemma between a movement toward identity politics and the impossibility of a speaking natural subject; this dilemma calls into question both the relevance of identity politics for ecological struggle and dominant classical constructions of the subject itself. Using Lacanian-inspired insights on subjectivity, and the works of Ernesto Laclau and Chantal Mouffe on radical democracy, I investigate the alternative versions of the subject implicit in ecological discourses and suggest that it is through these alternatives that environmentalism can forge necessary alliances with other movements oriented toward human liberation. In particular, the very impossibility of a natural speaking subject suggests that the ecological project of redefining humanity's relationships to nonhuman nature(s) is always contingent on reorienting human subjectivity itself; this fact highlights the centrality of political coalition between ecological and other social movements.

Sandkühler, Hans Jörg. "Die Krise der Urteilsfähigkeit und die Verantwortbarkeit des Handelns" in *Freiheit, Verantwortung und Folgen in der Wissenschaft, Sandkühler, Hans Jörg (ed)*, 51-78. New York, Lang, 1994.

Sandkühler, Hans Jörg. Crítica y Defensa de lo Existente. Referencias de la Filosofía a la Realidad. Estudio Sobre la Filosofía Hegeliana del Derecho. *An Seminar Hist Filosof*, 6, 11-35, 1986-89.

Diese Studie zur Rechts- und Staatsphilosophie GWF Hegels untersucht in ihrem ersten Teil, auf welche Weise Hegel seine idee der "Vernüftigkeit des Wirklichen" begründet. Die These lautet, dass Hegels seine Argumentation weniger auf die spekulative Idee der "Vernunft" stützt als vielmehr auf ein *normatives* Konzept der "Kritik des Bestehenden", das er in der "Idee des Rechts" entfaltet: die Aufgabe der Philosophie besteht nicht in der Anerkennung des Faktischen, sondern in der *Kritik* der Wirklichkeit der bürgerlicher Gesellschaft (des "Systems der Bedürfnisse") und in der *Konstruktion* eines Rechtsstaates als Korrektiv der bürgerlichen Gesellschaft. Im zweiten Teil wird die Auseinandersetzung um die Hegelsche Rechtsphilosophie in Preussen dargestellt.

Sandkühler, Hans Jörg (ed). *Freiheit, Verantwortung und Folgen in der Wissenschaft*. New York, Lang, 1994.

Sandkühler, Hans Jörg (& others). Le livre de la nature dans l'écrit de la culture: Cassirer et le Nouvel esprit scientifique. *Bull Soc Fr Phil*, 88(1), 1-38, Ja-Mr 94.

Philosophy and the sciences have been confronted since the second tertial of the nineteenth century with three discoveries: 1) Science translates "reality" into signs and symbols; 2) Its "facts" are essentially theory-laden; and 3) Its data are the result of interpretation. They have discovered by degree that science in general has to do with possible worlds and that natural science deals with "natures", the "facts" of which derive their significance as "facts in logical space" within the context of models. Summarizing developments in the theory of science since Helmholtz and basing his argumentation on the philosophy of E Cassirer, the author puts forward the thesis that, from the perspective offered by contemporary physics, we have left nature and entered a "factory of phenomena". This implies that natural science forms part of the humanities.

Sandler, Blair and Diskin, Jonathan. "Post-Marxism and Class" in *Marxism in the Postmodern Age, Callari, Antonio (ed)*, 178-187. New York, Guilford, 1994.

Sandu, Gabriel and Hintikka, Jaakko. Uses and Misuses of Frege's Ideas. *Monist*, 77(3), 278-293, Jl 94.

Frege's achievement as the creator of contemporary logic should not blind us to the limitations of his approach to logic, language and mathematics. Frege accepted the universality of language and its corollaries, the ineffability of semantics, the one-world view of meaning, and the hypostatization of meanings into meaning entities (Sinne). He assumed compositionality and hence overlooked informationally independent quantifiers. His thesis of the ambiguity of words like "is" is unacceptable in the semantics of natural languages. In higher-order logic, he assumed a nonstandard interpretation, which made it impossible for him to handle the important idea of arbitrary function.

Sanfélix, Vicente. Las Personas y su Identidad. *An Seminar Metaf*, 28, 257-285, 1994.

Identity of a Cartesian disembodied subject either a Lockean stream of consciousness is different from identity that pretheoretically we attribute to persons. This last identity is similar to identity that we attribute to organisms. Persons are organisms. But not simple organisms. They have self-consciousness. And self-consciousness is a linguistic and social product. That is the reason because—criteria of personality vary historically and culturally.

Sanford, David H. The Problem of the Many, Many Composition Questions, and Naive Mereology. *Nous*, 27(2), 219-228, Je 93.

Naive mereology studies ordinary, common-sense beliefs about part and whole. Some of the speculations in this article on naive mereology do not bear directly on Peter van Inwagen's *Material Beings*. The other topics, 1) and 2), both do. 1) Here is an example of Peter Unger's "Problem of the Many". How can a table be a collection of atoms when many collections of atoms have equally strong claims to be that table? Van Inwagen invokes fuzzy sets to solve this problem. I claim that an alternative treatment of vagueness, supervaluations over many-value valuations, provides a better solution. 2) The Special Composition Question asks how parts compose a whole. One who rejects van Inwagen's answer in terms of constituting a life need not provide some alternative answer. Even if all answers to the Special Question fail, there are a multitude of less general composition questions that are not so difficult.

Sanjeev, M P. For a Better Understanding of Philosophy, For a Better Philosophical Method. *Darshana Int*, 32(3/127), 44-52, Jl 92.

Today academic philosophy is being alienated from social practice. This paper is intended as a correction to this deviation. Following Hegel, Marxist thinkers like Engels and Lenin tried for new definition, for logic. According to him logic is the sum total of the history of knowledge of the world. Science without philosophy and philosophy without science are absurd. Both are complementary. Propositions in science are based on philosophical propositions. All men are philosophers to a good extent. But a man who is more philosophical generalises his knowledge and goes to the root of its innerconnections. Surely this will bring greater depth to thinking mind and will be helpful to humanity. Study of philosophy can't be limited to certain journals or books or theories of certain well-known philosophers, but everything that exists before us should be considered in proper manner for such a study.

Sankey, Howard. Judgement and Rational Theory-Choice. *Method Sci*, 27(3), 167-182, 1994.

Recent work in the philosophy of scientific theory-choice suggests that there is no fixed, universally applicable algorithm capable of determining choice between theories. However, the nature of rational choice in the absence of an algorithm remains unclear. In this article, it is argued, by means of a justificatory regress and the multi-criterial nature of theory evaluation, that a role must necessarily be played by deliberative judgment in choosing between theories. The paper also discusses the model of rational judgment due to Harold I Brown, and defends judgment against an objection of subjectivity.

Sanmartín, J and López Cerezo, J A and González, M. Filosofía actual de la ciencia. *Dialogo Filosof*, 10(2), 164-208, My-Ag 94.

Después de 30 años tras la revolución kuhniana en filosofía de la ciencia es clara la necesidad de un estudio interdisciplinar de la ciencia. pero no se ve que sea posible el que la filosofía tenga algo que decir en tal marco interdisciplinar de análisis empírico. La tendencia general a la naturalización parece dejar fuera de juego a una disciplina, la filosofía, cuyo tradicional estilo normativo es muy difícil de asimilar. Con todo, la polémica continúa. En estas páginas se recoge, entre algunos otros problemas, el enfrentamiento contemporáneo entre el racionalismo filosófico y el relativismo en la comprensión de la naturaleza de la ciencia.

Sanmartín, José. "From World3 to the Social Assessment of Technology" in *Philosophy of Technology in Spanish Speaking Countries, Mitcham, Carl (ed)*, 197-209. Dordrecht, Kluwer, 1994.

Sanmartín, José. "Genethics" in *Philosophy of Technology in Spanish Speaking Countries, Mitcham, Carl (ed)*, 211-225. Dordrecht, Kluwer, 1994.

Sanna, Manuela. Le Epistole Vichiane e la Nascita dell'idea di Scienza Nuova. *Boll Centro Stud Vichiani*, 24-25, 119-129, 1994-95.

Sannino, Antonella. Metafisica Teologica e Filosofia Naturale in Roberto Grossatesta. *Stud Filosofici*, 125-143, 1991-92.

Santa, Angels. Stendhal et la Grèce. *Diotima*, 22, 87-94, 1994.

Santa Cruz, María Isabel (& others). "Aportes para una Crítica de la Teoría del Género" in *Temas Actuales de Filosofía, Palacios, María Julia (ed)*, 625-634. Buenos Aires, Univ Nacional Salta, 1993.

In the first part, this paper aims at suggesting a comprehensive concept of "gender" as positional, relational and historical. In this sense, gender is defined as form of possible modes of ascription to human beings in dual, familial or social relationships of properties and functions depending on sex in an imaginary way. In the second part, it points out some problems that arise in ontology, epistemology and history of philosophy when gender is introduced. Finally, it makes some remarks about the incidence of taking account of gender in teaching philosophy.

Santa Cruz, María Isabel. Actualidad del tema del hombre: los estudios de la mujer. *Rev Latin de Filosof*, 20(2), 337-346, 1994.

This paper presents some important issues in feminist theory, a main line among the contemporary currents of thought. It starts with a brief consideration of the nature of women's studies, with a special reference to the recent research in our country. The category of gender is examined and defined. As a result of this approach the name "Gender Studies" is preferred. The final section suggests that the use of gender as an analysis category can only be justified if the utopian dimension of feminism as a social theory is maintained.

Santaniello, Carlo. Noterelle in Margine a due Convegni su Plutarco. *Stud Filosofici*, 177-182, 1991-92.

Santas, Gerasimos. Socratic Goods and Socratic Happiness. *Apeiron*, 26(3-4), 37-52, S-D 93.

Santayana, George. *Dominations and Powers: Reflections on Liberty, Society, and Government*. New Brunswick, Transaction Books, 1995.

Santayana, George and Cory, Daniel (ed). *The Birth of Reason and Other Essays*. New York, Columbia Univ Pr, 1995.

Santillán, Miguel Angel and del Valle Manzur, Analía. "Verdad y Validez" in *Temas Actuales de Filosofía, Palacios, María Julia (ed)*, 563-569. Buenos Aires, Univ Nacional Salta, 1993.

Santoni, Ronald E. On the Existential Meaning of Violence. *Dialogue Hum*, 3(4), 139-150, 1993.

In this paper, I explore the existential/ontological implications of violence—what violence does to us as human beings and to our condition. Pursuing insights of Sergio Cotta and Jean-Paul Sartre, I contend that violence violates the ontological status of the other, separates us from the other and ourselves, destroys co-existence, community, and communication with the other, and debases our human condition. In addition, I suggest an extension of my thesis to other "living beings" and "nature". Doing violence to them is also *anti-existential*: it violates their ontological status and natural "rights", and ruptures co-existence and communication both *with* them and *within* the biotic community of our planet.

Sanvisens Herreros, Alejandro. Defensa de la Causalidad. *Convivium*, 7, 31-49, 1995.

The microphysical indetermination to the effect that is given by the Copenhague interpretation, find insolubles paradoxes. Only a causal version of the quantic indeterminism of the measure is capable to resolve the problems. On the other hand, the validity and reaching of the causality "principle", questionated by Hume, Kant and the positivist authors, is revised again from a realistic point of view. At last, the denominated principle of enough reason of being, is demonstrated, to setting the principle of causality about safe anyone impugnation.

Sanz, Víctor. Historia de la Filosofía e Historia: Notas Para un Debate. *Acta Phil*, 4(1), 111-122, 1995.

The article raises the question of whether the character of the history of philosophy is mainly historical or philosophical, dealing with that question in a dialogue with some philosophers (Hegel, Jaspers, Ortega, Zubiri) and some historians (Febvre, Braudel). The fact that new specialized branches have arisen in the field of history (intellectual history, Begriffsgeschichte, cultural history, Histoire des mentalités) is understood as the necessity of filling the gap left by history of philosophy because of its exclusively intraphilosophical character. That fact shows the lack of relationship between philosophers and historians, whose cause is to be found in the negative sense bearing on the expression "Philosophy of History", in Hegelian way understood, which is rejected by historians.

Saperstein, Alvin M. Mathematical Modeling of the Effects of 'Capability' and 'Intent' on the Stability of a Competitive International System. *Synthese*, 100(3), 359-378, S 94.

In international relations theory, there is a long history of Richardsonlike modeling of the evolution of military capability. Usually, such models are deterministic and predictive and do not allow for the representation of the transition from competitive peace to shooting war. More recently, models have been developed which attempt to represent the evolution of 'relationship' between nations. The 'relationship' between nations, varying from friendship to hostility, is taken to be synonymous with the 'intent' of nations towards each other, varying from good will to malice. Generally, these relationship models do not include 'capability' though common sense would indicate that capability and mutual intent should profoundly influence each other. A model is presented here which combines these two fundamental attributes of international relations and attempts to represent the outbreak of war in the world system by the onset of deterministic chaos in the extended model.

Sapp, Vicki J. The Philosopher's Seduction: Hume and the Fair Sex. *Phil Lit*, 19(1), 1-15, Ap 95.

David Hume's essays apparently targeting a female readership have been almost universally deemed "frivolous and finical," mercenary and essentially unphilosophical. Feminist readers of the 1970s and '80s failed as well to assign any merit to the eight woman-appeal essays. A closer, more non-"factional" reading of these texts featuring discussions of marriage, female education, polite social intercourse and other domestic topics reveals substantive links with Hume's undisputedly philosophical writing. Hume did not deviate from philosophical practice in these texts; rather, he packaged his moral philosophy in a form more readily available to a new reader economy—one including and even perhaps dependent upon the polite female reader. The woman-appeal essays provide us an ideal study of Hume's experiments with the conflicts and collusions of philosophy and commerce.

Sarachek, Bernard. Images of Corporate Executives in Recent Fiction. *J Bus Ethics*, 14(3), 195-205, Mr 95.

While post-World War II business fiction writers viewed the modern corporation as a threat to individualism, the author makes the point that modern fiction writers do not share that concern. However, modern fiction does describe the business world as being heavily populated by amoral or immoral valueless people, especially among those businessmen engrossed in financial manipulations. The author also observes that the world of business fiction remains an essentially white male dominated one.

Saravia Sacchelli, Hugo O. "Reflexiones Sobre la Propuesta Epistém. Formulada por Quine en 'Dos Dogmas d. Empirismo'" in *Temas Actuales de Filosofía, Palacios, María Julia (ed)*, 547-553. Buenos Aires, Univ Nacional Salta, 1993.

The purpose of this work is to show and analyze some implications of the epistemic theory that Quine advances in *Two Dogmas of Empiricism*—particularly the assertion "No statement is immune to revision"—in relation to mentalistic statements such as "*I believe* that smoking is unhealthy", "*I intend* to buy a new car", "*I feel* a pain", and so on. The conclusion reached is that Quine's theory presents problems that are difficult to solve.

Sardisco, Ana M and Insua, Elda. "Enseñanga, Políticae Institución" in *Temas Actuales de Filosofía, Palacios, María Julia (ed)*, 281-288. Buenos Aires, Univ Nacional Salta, 1993.

The goal of this work is to make relations between the philosophy teaching, the national policy and the university institutions created for invertigate these subjects, and the professional shape in Argentina. It is interesting to point up some modalities and strategies in order to intent to make up a periodization that remarks the intellectual production conditions together with the political event during democratic periods and during the constitutional break, expliciting the weave that articulates knowledge and power.

Sargent, Rose-Mary. *The Diffident Naturalist: Robert Boyle and the Philosophy of Experiment*. Chicago, Univ of Chicago Pr, 1995.

This reassessment of Boyle's philosophy begins with a discussion of how his epistemological views were in part shaped by his study of various philosophical, legal, experimental and religious traditions and then shows how the insights that he gained from his own extensive laboratory practice led him to transform those original ideas and to develop sophisticated methodological strategies as well as a complex justification of experimental activity. The study concludes with an examination of how Boyle's dynamic conception of knowledge acquisition remains relevant for issues discussed today in history, philosophy, and sociology of science.

Sarin, Indu. Knowledge of Value. *Indian Phil Quart*, 21(4), 329-335, O 94.

The present paper elucidates the concept of value showing that creation of value and knowing a value are internally related. Any value-concept fixes an ideal of praxis and its role in the hierarchy of intrinsic values. While 'knowing that' and 'knowing how' could be the basis of 'knowing a value' but former's objects are external to the knower. Value is one's own being formulated as an imperative. Forming a value-concept transforms the person who forms it. The paper calls for a serious review of interdependence of self (shorn of metaphysics) with intrinsic values that a person holds.

Sarkar, Anil K. Personal Identity: In Buddhist and Whiteheadian Thought (An Exercise with an Intercultural Experience). *Darshana Int*, 32(2/126), 25-23, Ap 92.

The general ideas of my published paper in 'Darahana International' with a title, have been taken from my book 'Buddhism And Whitehead's Process Philosophy'. The main purpose of my book was to probe deep into the positions of the advanced currents of the emergent post-intellectual aspects of Buddhist and Whiteheadian deliberations, in contrast to the abstract intellectual processes of their respective early cultural processes. The insightful deliberations of both, in their respective post-intellectual meditative contexts, open up varied advanced alternative philosophical prospects, considered by nine American, and American-Asian thinkers, of a book, 'Buddhism and American Thinkers', edited by Inada Jacobson.

Sarkar, Sahotra. The Selection of Alleles and the Additivity of Variance. *Proc Phil Sci Ass*, 1, 3-12, 1994.

It is shown that, for technical reasons, the additivity of variance criterion employed by Lloyd (1988) to define a unit of selection is, in almost all models of selection, inconsistent with the possibility that genes are sometimes not the unit of selection. A case when the latter view is particularly attractive is that of heterosis, and the additivity criterion is inadequate in even such an extreme case. The connection between that criterion and the so-called "fundamental theorem of natural selection" is briefly explored. Skepticism is expressed about the value of measures such as variance in efforts to resolve any of the disputes about the "units of selection".

Sarkowicz, Ryszard. Levels of Interpretation of a Legal Text. *Ratio Juris*, 8(1), 104-112, Mr 95.

The role played in literary, biblical and legal interpretation by the concepts of "objective" or "right" interpretation is briefly examined. It is shown that nowadays the concepts "objective" or "right" interpretation are frequently perceived as Kantian *regulative ideas*, and as such they have proved to be very useful concepts in current theories of interpretation.

Sarre, Philip. Towards Global Environmental Values: Lessons from Western and Eastern Experience. *Environ Values*, 4(2), 115-127, May 95.

The paper argues that new environmental values are needed as the advanced industrial economy becomes global. Reviewing a range of values from hunter-

gatherer, agricultural and industrial societies, the paper suggests that environmental value systems should ideally satisfy three criteria. They should be consistent with scientific understanding of natural systems, they should lead to practical ethical and political proposals and, crucially, they should inspire aesthetic responses and pleasure and awe. Current global value systems fall short of this ideal: Gaia had the potential to combine science and awe, but lacks humane decision criteria, while sustainable development is pragmatic but environmentally minimalist and lacks aesthetic inspiration. The short term need is to integrate different strands of current positions as Hinduism combined pre-existing views. A sequence of priorities is suggested: eliminating irreversible environmental change; stabilising population change through more equitable trade; and reconsidering the boundaries, practical and aesthetic, between society and nature.

Sartorelli, Joseph. "Gay Rights and Affirmative Action" in *Gay Ethics, Murphy, Timothy F (ed)*, 179-222. New York, Haworth Pr, 1994.

While affirmative action programs exist for a number of groups, little serious consideration has been given to the establishment of such programs for gay men and lesbians. This essay argues that many of the conditions that justify current affirmative action programs would also justify their extension to gay people, both in terms of compensation for injuries suffered and in terms of benefit to both individuals and society generally. It is argued that antidiscrimination policies are hard to enforce and in any case would be inadequate to redress many of the wrongs suffered by gays and lesbians. It is concluded that programs favoring gay visibility are morally justified.

Sartorelli, Joseph J. Avoiding Mistakes in Reasoning about Naturalness: A Reply to Dalcourt. *Int J Applied Phil*, 9(1), 67-71, Sum-Fall 94.

In the most recent issue of this journal (Volume 8, Number 2, 1994), I criticized Gerard J Dalcourt's views on naturalness and homosexuality expressed in an earlier piece of his. He gave a reply in the same issue. Dalcourt's attempts to salvage his criticisms of Gould against my objections fail. His approach is often to claim that he has been misinterpreted when, in fact, what he now claims is the correct interpretation of his views does not accord well with his earlier text. Ironically, too, he sometimes misinterprets the objections made against him. And sometimes he just fails to grasp their point or their impact on his position.

Sartorelli, Joseph J. Ruse on Gay Rights and Affirmative Action. *Analysis*, 54(2), 84-91, Ap 94.

In his book *Homosexuality*, Michael Ruse argues that the state has no obligation to provide affirmative action benefits for gay people. I argue that Ruse's stated reasons do not justify this conclusion; that the conception of affirmative action he deals with is far too narrow to guarantee that if there is no obligation to provide affirmative action benefits (on that narrow conception) then there is no obligation to provide positive benefits not provided to all; and that the attempt to use the narrower rather than the wider conception in this case severely underestimates the plight of gay people in the present social contact.

Sartorelli, Joseph J. Spikes on Kripke. *Phil Lit*, 18(2), 348-353, O 94.

Sartwell, Crispin. Appropriation and Interpretation. *J Value Inq*, 28(2), 327-338, Je 94.

This paper is an attack on formalism: the view that the aesthetic aspects of a work of art are a matter of the form of the work (line and color in the case of painting, e.g.). It discusses the work of "appropriation artists" Elaine Sturtevant and Sherrie Levine.

Sartwell, Crispin. Radical Externalism Concerning Experience. *Phil Stud*, 78(1), 55-70, Ap 95.

This paper formulates and defends a radical version of externalism in philosophy of mind. It contends that the mind is not strictly, contained in the body, but is a *situation* of a body in an environment.

Sartwell, Crispin. *The Art of Living: Aesthetics of the Ordinary in World Spiritual Traditions*. Albany, SUNY Pr, 1995.

The Art of Living: Aesthetics of the Ordinary in World Spiritual Traditions is the first truly multicultural philosophy of art. It develops a new theory of what art is, and discusses it in relation to Zen Buddhism, Taoism, and Hinduism, as well as Native American, African, and African-American traditions.

Sas, Peter. Transcendentaal-Pragmatiek en Semantiek. *Alg Ned Tijdschr Wijs*, 87(2), 84-96, Ap 95.

Some semantical implications of Karl-Otto Apel's transcendental pragmatics are developed by confronting Apel's philosophy with Quine's thesis of the indeterminacy of the meaning and reference of terms. First, I deal with the question whether the idea of an ideal consensus, which according to Apel is a condition of the possibility of argumentation, is rendered obsolete by Quine's thesis of indeterminacy. I argue that this is not the case. Secondly, I deal with the question whether our knowledge of the reference and objective meaning (i.e., propositions) of sentences can be justified by Apel's transcendental pragmatics. I argue that we can know the reference and objective meaning of sentences unambiguously in a cognitive ideal situation, which—as Apel has pointed out—is a condition of the possibility of argumentation. Third and last, we have to ascertain whether Quine's thesis of indeterminacy can be refuted on the basis of Apel's transcendental pragmatics—whether our knowledge of the reference and meaning of terms can be justified in terms of Apel's philosophy. Apel's philosophy cannot do the trick on its own. Only when Apel's philosophy is combined with the rigid designator-theory of Kripke and Putnam it can be shown that in the case of names Quine's thesis of indeterminacy is false.

Sasaki, Ken-ichi. Fiction et Vérité. *Aesthetics*, 3, 33-46, Mr 88.

Sass, Louis A. Civilized Madness: Schizophrenia, Self-Consciousness and the Modern Mind. *Hist Human Sci*, 7(2), 83-120, My 94.

The paper describes affinities between schizophrenic psychosis and modern consciousness, and addresses modernity's possible role in schizophrenia's etiology. Characteristic paradoxes or dualities of schizophrenic selfhood are discussed: namely, an alternation or coexistence of a sense of omnipotence and solipsistic centrality with a diminished sense of identifying with or controlling one's experiences. These dualities are compared with the modern post-Kantian self or subject, characterized by Foucault as an "empirico-transcendental doublet." Cross-cultural and trans-historical data concerning the nature and incidence of schizophrenia and related conditions are reviewed. Finally, features of modern society that might mold or produce schizophrenic symptoms are considered.

Sasso, Gennaro. La Questione dell'Astratto e del Concreto fra il 1912 e il 1917. *G Crit Filosof Ital*, 73(2-3), 353-400, My-D 94.

Sasso, Javier. Sobre el 'Pensamiento Latinoamericano' y su Historiografía. *Analogia*, 4(1), 61-81, 1990.

The historians in whose hands the narrative of Latin America's intellectual history fell were convinced that philosophy is the total priviledged reflection of each era, thereby formulating the first scientific reconstruction of this past. However, it was distorted, creating a narrative in which different actors were included or excluded of their roles re-described in a rather unconvincing fashion. This paper attempts to show the need to abandon this approach in order to permit the emergence of a history in which more attention is paid to the purposes of the figures of the past, as well as the pre-discursive forms of collective thought.

Sastre, Gerardo López. Por qué son necesariamente inútiles las virtudes específicamente religiosas?. *Telos (Spain)*, 1(1), 15-19, F 92.

The moral value of religion could be doubtful from an utilitarian evaluative standpoint. J S Mill's analysis about that question in *Utility of Religion* is well-known. However Hume's similar study in his *Enquiry Concerning the Principles of Morals* is not known in the same degree. There Hume writes that we consider something a virtue when 1) it is useful to others; 2) it is useful to the subject himself; 3) it is immediately agreeble to others; or 4) it is immediately agreeable to the person himself. But, if everything which is useful or agreeable must be considered a virtue, on the contrary everything useless or disagreeable must be a vice. That is the case with Christian, Monkish, or religious virtues, or *virtues*?, in general terms.

Sauer, James. Discourse and Narrative: Ethics after the Linguistics Turn. *SW Phil Rev*, 11(1), 119-134, Ja 95.

Saunders, Simon. Time, Quantum Mechanics, and Decoherence. *Synthese*, 102(2), 235-266, F 95.

State-reduction and the notion of "actuality" are compared to "passage" through time and the notion of "the present"; already in classical relativity the latter give rise to difficulties. The solution proposed here is to treat both tense and value-definiteness as relational properties or "facts as relations"; likewise the notions of change and probability. In both cases "essential" characteristics are absent: temporal relations are tenselessly true; probabilistic relations are deterministically true. The basic ideas go back to Everett, although the technical development makes use of the decoherent histories theory of Griffiths, Omnes, and Gell-Mann and Hartle. Alternative interpretations of the decoherent histories framework are also considered.

Saura, Emilio. En la confluencia de filosofía y esoterismo: Jean D'Encausse y la doctrina del "despertar". *Rev Filosof (Daimon)*, 7, 185-194, 1993.

The dilemma between philosophy and initiation posed by D'Encausse is not completely pertinent: in its original form initiation does not imply extinction of human being in the absolute. Nevertheless, confrontation with esoteric ambit is today an undeniable philosophical problem.

Saurer, Edith. "Über die Beziehung von Schamhaftigkeit, Öffentlichkeit und Geschlecht" in *Macht Geschlechter Differenz, Müller-Funk, Wolfgang (ed)*, 63-90. Vienna, Picus, 1994.

This essay focuses on the discourse on shame around 1800. It also contributes to current sociological, anthropological and historiographical discussions on this topic. Special attention is paid on the growing discussion on shame and the legal concept of "public shame". The discussion starts analyzing popular books for private female devotion taking blushing and female chastity as sign of shame. The essay focuses then on legal aspects by discussing the theological concept of the public sphere and the legal concept of "encitement of public nuisance" as a criminal misdemeanor with special reference to Austria. An analysis of the legal practice of the Austrian Supreme Court reveals a shift of focus. A slow change was affected from a concept to "protect female eyes" toward the protection of an imagined intact social panorama.

Sauvé, Kevin. Gauthier, Property Rights, and Future Generations. *Can J Phil*, 25(2), 163-176, Je 95.

In *Morals by Agreement*, Gauthier admits that his Lockean Proviso and his assumption of mutual unconcern both motivate social contractors toward highly depletionary rates of natural-resource exploitation. He then presents three arguments toward showing that rational social contractors will nonetheless implement sustainable resource exploitation practices. I show that these arguments, individually and in concert, fail to motivate efficient long-term resource use. Adequate and efficient provision for future generations can be achieved only if we weaken the assumption of mutual unconcern, and if we employ a conception of malleable, community-centered property rights that differs radically from Gauthier's.

Savan, David. "Peirce and Idealism" in *Peirce and Contemporary Thought: Philosophical Inquiries, Ketner, Kenneth Laine (ed)*, 315-327. New York, Fordham Univ Pr, 1995.

The aim of this paper is to suggest a resolution of the problem of the antithesis between idealist and realist tendencies that are found in Peirce's thought. The thesis of the paper is that semiotics is the center from which most of Peirce's philosophy radiates and that to appreciate the problem of the proposition one must relate it to Peirce's theory of scientific knowledge, inquiry and truth. It is especially in the latter area that one can find realist/idealist tendencies, for which semeiotic can offer the grounds for their clarification and reconciliation.

Savi, Cristina. *Husserl e lo scetticismo*. Milano, Guerini, 1995.

Savignano, Armando. Il problema della filosofia spagnola. *Aquinas*, 36(3), 655-665, S-D 93.

Savignano, Armando. La dimensione teologale dell'uomo e la teologia fondamentale in Xavier Zubiri. *Aquinas*, 37(1), 59-87, Ja-Ap 94.

Savitt, Steven F. Is Classical Mechanics Time Reversal Invariant?. *Brit J Phil Sci*, 45(3), 907-913, S 94.

In a recent paper Keith Hutchison argued that, contrary to received opinion, classical mechanics is really not time reversal invariant. In this paper I distinguish three senses of time reversal invariance and claim that Hutchison's argument does not establish the time asymmetry of classical mechanics in the most important of the three senses.

Savitt, Steven F. The Replacement of Time. *Austl J Phil*, 72(4), 463-474, D 94.

Part I of this paper, inspired by Kurt Gödel's paper, "A Remark About the Relationship between Relativity Theory and Idealisitic Philosophy", argues that, given certain peculiar but undeniably possible features of general relativistic spacetimes, there is no reason to suppose that there is an objective lapse of time in our world. Part II then compares responses that this argument might evoke to objections to claims by eliminative materialists that the mental is not real and finds them lacking for similar reasons.

Savorelli, Alessandro. Gentile e Jaja. *G Crit Filosof Ital*, 74(1), 42-64, Ja-Ap 95.

Savorelli, Alessandro. Neoidealismo ed Hegelismo Ortodosso nel Carteggio Croce-Mariano. *G Crit Filosof Ital*, 73(2-3), 282-305, My-D 94.

Sawaf, Ayman. The Virgin Paradigm. *Darshana Int*, 32(3/127), 53-67, Jl 92.

Sawchuk, Kim. "Semiotics, Cybernetics, and the Ecstasy of Marketing Communications" in *Baudrillard: A Critical Reader, Kellner, Douglas M (ed)*, 89-116. Cambridge, Blackwell, 1994.

This paper explores the pertinence of Jean Baudrillard's theories on advertising and communication in the context of marketing research. Particular attention is paid to his understanding of cybernetics, the concept of the code, and his championing of seduction as an explanation of the efficacy of an image. Central to this is a consideration of Baudrillard's critique of Michel Foucault. It is argued that Baudrillard's understanding of the process of the circulation of presentations in neo-cybernetic capitalist culture, in fact, needs to be supplemented with a more profound Foucauldian analysis of the marketing process.

Sawyer, Keith and Csikszentmihalyi, Mihaly. "Creative Insight: The Social Dimension of a Solitary Moment" in *The Nature of Insight, Sternberg, Robert J (ed)*, 329-363. Cambridge, MIT Pr, 1995.

Saxonhouse, Arlene W. The Moral Sense: Ancient and Modern. *Crim Just Ethics*, 13(2), 39-44, Sum-Fall 94.

James Q Wilson's *The Moral Sense* asks why we do not consistently take advantage of others even when there may be no laws to enforce that care, why we act heroically when there are not obvious rewards. His questions are similar to ones that confronted the interlocutors of Socrates in Plato's *Republic* and that Aristotle addressed in his works. Wilson, like Aristotle, ties our "moral sense" to our natures, but while Aristotelian nature is teleological, Wilson's nature is evolutionary. The difference between these two approaches is captured by the difficulty (which Wilson acknowledges) of giving content to the moral sense. Plato, whose works try to identify the content of virtue, help us understand some of the differences between the ancient and the modern moral sense.

Sayers, Dorothy L. Aristotle on Detective Fiction. *Interpretation*, 22(3), 405-415, Spr 95.

Sayre, Kenneth. Why Plato Never Had a Theory of Forms. *Proc Boston Colloq Anc Phil*, 9, 167-199, 1993.

By 'theory' in this context is meant a set of general propositions (principles, axioms, etc.) capable of yielding explanations by deductive inference. The paper argues, against Cherniss and others, 1) that no theory of forms of this sort can be found in the dialogues, and 2) that Plato himself never thought of the forms as suitable subjects for such a theory. Evidence for 1) comes from an examination of relevant passages, most notably *Phaedo* 100A-107B. Evidence for 2) comes from an analysis of Plato's testimony in the Seventh Letter concerning the unsuitability of (propositional) language for the expression of philosophic knowledge.

Sayward, Charles and Hugly, Philip. Quantifying Over the Reals. *Synthese*, 101(1), 53-64, O 94.

Peter Geach proposed a substitutional construal of quantification over thirty years ago. It is not standardly substitutional since it is not tied to those substitution instances currently available to us; rather, it is pegged to possible substitution instances. We argue that i) quantification over the real numbers can be construed substitutionally following Geach's idea; ii) a price to be paid, if it is that, is intuitionism; iii) quantification, thus conceived, does not in itself relieve us of ontological commitment to real numbers.

Sazbon, J. De Angelis Difusor de Vico. *Cuad Vico*, 3, 157-186, 1993.

The author tries to determinate if the reception of G Vico in the context of the River Plate Culture of the nineteenth century was due directly to De Angelis, or to Michelet, apparently influenced in turn by De Angelis. If the first idea is plausible, through the stay of the Italian himself in the Argentine, then the conclusion seems clear: the true rôle of De Angelis in the spread of Vico in the nineteenth century is an unknown, and not a fact. However, the fact that something is not shown by documentary evidence does not prevent it being fictionally supposed.

Scanlan, James P. A F Losev and Mysticism in Russian Philosophy. *Stud East Euro Thought*, 46(4), 263-286, D 94.

The Russian philosopher Aleksei Losev (1893-1988), although known primarily as an authority on classical antiquity, also devoted considerable attention to Russian philosophy and its relation to mysticism. From an early conviction that mysticism was virtually a universal characteristic of Russian philosophy, Losev later moderated his views on the subject. His study of the history of philosophy, especially that of the Russian thinker Vladimir Solovyov (1853-1900), convinced him that, although mystical experience is one possible avenue of access to reality, all philosophy, Russian as well as Western, requires the rational conversion of experience into conceptual knowledge.

Scanlan, Michael. Wittgenstein, Truth-Functions and Generality. *J Phil Res*, 20, 175-193, 1995.

Although it is common to attribute to Wittgenstein in the *Tractatus* a treatment of general propositions as equivalent to conjunctions and disjunctions of instance propositions, the evidence for this is not perfectly clear. This article considers Wittgenstein's comments in 5.521, which can be read as rejecting such a treatment.

It argues that properly situating the *Tractatus* historically allows for a revised reading of 5.521 and other parts of the *Tractatus* relevant to Wittgenstein's theory of generality. The result is that 5.521 does not conflict with the view that general propositions are truth-functions of instance propositions. Common problems with such a view are to some extent obviated by the fact that Wittgenstein, following Russell and Moore, was not concerned with a syntactically defined language, but with propositions conceived as independent of a fixed language.

Scanlon, Thomas M. Moral Theory: Understanding and Disagreement. *Phil Phenomenol Res*, 55(2), 343-356, Je 95.

Aims of moral theory include clarification of the substantive content of morality and explanation of the kinds of claims moral judgments make and the reasons we have for taking them seriously. Inquiry into these reasons may disclose that each of us uses the term "morality" to refer to requirements supported by diverse reasons, and that as used by different people this term may express requirements that have quite different sources. Some moral disagreement may therefore be better understood as disagreement about what reasons are to be taken seriously than as disagreement about a single subject matter, "morality".

Scannone, J C. Aportes Filosóficos para una Teoría y Práctica de Instituciones Justas. *Stromata*, 50(3-4), 157-173, Jl-D 94.

El artículo expone primeramente elementos para una teoría filosófica de las instituciones y su eticidad propia. Luego trata de la mediación ético-histórica para lograr instituciones más justas a partir de situaciones institucionales injustas como las latinoamericanas. Para ello plantea una dialéctica abierta o "anadialéctica". Por último indica algunas "estrategias de humanidad", que ayuden a transformar éticamente las actuales instituciones (económicas, políticas, culturales) latinoamericanas. Para hacerlo reflexiona filosóficamente experiencias ya en curso.

Scarre, Geoffrey. Epicurus as a Forerunner of Utilitarianism. *Utilitas*, 6(2), 219-231, N 94.

Scerri, Eric R. Has Chemistry Been at Least Approximately Reduced to Quantum Mechanics?. *Proc Phil Sci Ass*, 1, 160-170, 1994.

Differing views on reduction are briefly reviewed and a suggestion is made for a working definition of 'approximate reduction'. Ab initio studies in quantum chemistry are then considered, including the issues of convergence and error bounds. This includes an examination of the classic studies on CH2 and the recent work on the Si2C molecule. I conclude that chemistry has not even been approximately reduced.

Scerri, Eric R. The Exclusion Principle, Chemistry and Hidden Variables. *Synthese*, 102(1), 165-169, Ja 95.

The Pauli Exclusion Principle and the reduction of chemistry have been the subject of considerable philosophical debate. The present article considers the view that the lack of derivability of the Exclusion Principle represents a problem for physics and denies the reduction of chemistry to quantum mechanics. The possible connections between the Exclusion Principle and the hidden variable debate are also briefly criticized.

Schacht, Richard. "Zarathustra/Zarathustra as Educator" in *Nietzsche: A Critical Reader*, Sedgwick, Peter R (ed), 222-249. Cambridge, Blackwell, 1995.

Schacht, Richard. *Making Sense of Nietzsche: Reflections Timely and Untimely*. Champaign, Univ of Illinois Pr, 1995.

Schacht, Richard. *The Future of Alienation*. Champaign, Univ of Illinois Pr, 1994.

Schäfer, Lothar. "Herrschaft der Vernunft und Naturord in Platons 'Timaios'" in *Naturauffassungen in Philosophie, Wissenschaft, Technik: Band I*, Schäfer, Lothar (ed), 49-83. Freiburg, Alber, 1993.

Schäfer, Lothar (ed) and Ströker, Elisabeth (ed). *Naturauffassungen in Philosophie, Wissenschaft, Technik: Band I*. Freiburg, Alber, 1993.

Schäfer, Lothar (ed) and Ströker, Elisabeth (ed). *Naturauffassungen in Philosophie, Wissenschaft, Technik: Band II*. Freiburg, Alber, 1994.

Schäfer, Lothar (ed) and Ströker, Elisabeth (ed). *Naturauffassungen in Philosophie, Wissenschaft, Technik: Band III*. Freiburg, Alber, 1995.

Schaffer, Simon. Babbage's Intelligence: Calculating Engines and the Factory System. *Crit Inquiry*, 21(1), 203-227, Autumn 94.

Schalkwyk, David. Fiction as "Grammatical" Investigation: A Wittgensteinian Account. *J Aes Art Crit*, 53(3), 287-298, Sum 95.

Schall, James V. On the Uniqueness of Socrates. *Gregorianum*, 76(2), 343-362, 1995.

La philosophie politique a son origine dans les oeuvres de Platon. La cité telle qu'elle est conçue dans *La république* est elle à mettre en pratique: cela reste une question disputée. Des auteurs modernes, tel Leo Strauss, ont pensé que *La république* était un document anti-utopie, et voulait prévenir contre l'enthousiasme moral et politique. Des auteurs récents ont repensé les raisons qui soutiennent les propositions faites par Platon. Leur fin thérapeutique continue de fasciner, spécialement à la lumière de la pensée chrétienne classique sur le corps.

Schall, James V. The Role of Christian Philosophy in Politics. *Amer Cath Phil Quart*, 69(1), 1-14, Wint 95.

Philosophy and philosophical systems by themselves come to inconclusive positions about man and his place in the world. The modern project has even made man an object of science itself so that man's higher purposes and his physical integrity itself are reduced to objects of a science that recognizes no unique or normative human being as given from nature. The role of Christian philosophy in politics is itself philosophical. That is, it is in the area of politics in which the conditions of human being have become most controverted. Philosophy by itself seems evidently unable to protect the human being to remain what he is. Christian philosophy recognizes that part of the problem arises because philosophy remains unable to decide about the being of man to such a degree that no guidance to what is human can follow in the practical order from philosophy. A philosophy that recognizes the possibility of a certain definiteness to man can provide a grounding to political things and this, in experience, requires a philosophy open to matters open to revelation.

Schalow, Frank. Language and the Etymological Turn of Thought. *Grad Fac Phil J*, 18(1), 187-203, 1995.

This paper explores the relation between thinking and language from a Heideggerian perspective. It is argued that Heidegger's turn to language seeks to cultivate a greater responsiveness to the modes of expression which govern the attempt to articulate the most ancient philosophical concepts. Heidegger's controversial way of deriving etymologies, then, illustrates how thought depends upon being to reveal itself within the finite parameters of language. In this way, the subtlety of etymological translation provides a hinge in the turn of thought to its other beginning.

Schalow, Frank. Language and the Tragic Side of Ethics. *Int Stud Phil*, 27(2), 49-63, 1995.

This paper develops Heidegger's attempt to outline a postmetaphysical ethics by addressing the tragic side of humanity's historical situatedness. Human history includes the constellation of a conflict which can be understood by appealing to the Greek sense of tragedy. Conversely, the tragic vision of life also provides a clue to the weightedness of human decision and to the need to cultivate a more original relation to language. As we transpose our relation to language and become listeners as well as speakers, we take from our experience of tragedy a new sense of stewardship over existence. This stewardship constitutes the beginning of a postmetaphysical ethics.

Schalow, Frank. The *Gesamtausgabe* Nietzsche: An Exercise in Translation and Thought. *Heidegger Stud*, 9, 139-152, 1993.

Schalow, Frank. The Topography of Heidegger's Concept of Conscience. *Amer Cath Phil Quart*, 69(2), 255-273, Spr 95.

This paper attempts to cast new light on Heidegger's analysis of conscience by showing the role that it plays in unbuilding the Cartesian view of the self as pure presence. It is argued that through this "destruction" Heidegger executes a step back from a theoretical approach to being in terms of the *cogito* to a practical orientation which is prefigured in Aristotle's *Ethics*. By retracing this path, we discover that the call of conscience arises first and foremost as a catalyst of self-transformation (authenticity), which in turn can only be explicated by considering a unique linkage between doing and knowing, praxis and *logos*, as found in "primal Christianity." Heidegger's formal, ontological analysis of conscience depends on integrating this practical context; for only in this manner can hermeneutics break the shackles of representationalism and find its way granted through the radically singular event of the "there is".

Schalow, Frank. Why Evil? Heidegger, Schelling, and the Tragic View of Being. *Ideal Stud*, 25(1), 51-67, Wint 95.

This paper outlines the basic strategies by which Heidegger retrieves Schelling's positive philosophy. It is argued that Heidegger employs Schelling's treatment of evil as the backdrop against which to address the clash between the light and darkness of being, the conflict between unconcealment and revealment. The paper concludes by showing that Heidegger's dialogue with Schelling is crucial for transforming a narrower, volitional concept of freedom into the more ontologically primary sense of freedom as "letting be."

Scharfstein, Ben-Ami. *Amoral Politics: The Persistent Truth of Machiavellism*. Albany, SUNY Pr, 1995.

Amoral Politics deals with the justification of deceit and force in politics. It shows in detail that this justification was given and acted on in ancient China and India no less than in Europe. It is therefore clear that the theories and practices of amorality are inseparable from political life—as evidence from anthropology and ethology also shows. So whatever position it takes, a philosophy that ignores the near universal persistence of amorality is unlikely to be of much relevance to actual political life. The individual and social reasons for the persistence of political amorality are explored and evaluated.

Scharfstein, Ben-Ami. On Individual Amorality as the Background to Machiavellism. *Iyyun*, 43, 289-303, Jl 94.

The explicit contention is made that people accept the Machiavellism of their leaders because they themselves are rather Machiavellian to begin with. The implicit moral drawn is that philosophical arguments on ethics and politics should be based on an accurate understanding of how and why people act. Just as no philosopher worth the name would philosophize about physics or biology without learning a good deal about these sciences, so a philosopher ought not to deal with ethics or politics without studying them seriously on an empirical level, with the help of psychology, anthropology, sociology, or any other relevant discipline.

Schatzki, Theodore R. Aerobics as Political Model and Schooling. *J Soc Phil*, 25(2), 29-43, Fall 94.

This paper examines a new phase of the "decline of the individual" ushered in by the political schooling aerobics provides in the United States. In two earlier phases of this decline, individuals were either negated through absorption into the political-economic system (fascism) or trimmed to the system's needs by conformity to stereotyping norms (the culture industry à la Horkheimer and Adorno). In the aerobics model, by contrast, individuals receive real autonomy over what Foucault called "the care of the self". This circumscribed autonomy, however, is irrelevant to and unthreatening to the system. So the system solidifies itself to the extent that individuals, in applying themselves to the cultivation of the self, renounce claims to autonomy elsewhere. In addition to making the above argument, the paper opens by examining the intelligibilities animating fitness activities, and concludes by considering the genuine happiness and possible emancipatory moment embedded in the aerobic experience.

Schatzki, Theodore R. Do Social Structures Govern Action?. *Midwest Stud Phil*, 15, 280-295, 1990.

The paper examines the relations between action and structure that are postulated by a group of theorists dubbed the "New Structuralists". The bulk of the paper considers the specific accounts of these relations offered by Roy Bhaskar and Anthony Giddens, criticizing 1) Bhaskar's conception of social mechanisms and their goverance of action and 2) Gidden's distinction between rules and resources and the adequacy of his notion of rules. In conclusion, the paper outlines an alternative picture of social structures and how they determine action.

Schauer, Frederick. Acts, Omissions, and Constitutionalism. *Ethics*, 105(4), 916-926, Jl 95.

Schauer, Frederick. Critical Notice of Roger Shiner *Norm and Nature: The Movements of Legal Thought*. *Can J Phil*, 24(3), 495-509, S 94.

Schauer, Frederick. Fuller's Internal Point of View. *Law Phil*, 13(3), 285-312, Ag 94.

The legal philosopher Lon Fuller has achieved prominence in part because of his procedural version of a natural law theory, a theory pursuant to which satisfaction of procedural norms such as generality and prospectivity are necessary conditions for the existence of valid law in all possible legal systems. As exemplified in Fuller's debate with H L A Hart, it is assumed that legal positivism and Fuller's natural law are mutually exclusive. Yet it can be seen that Fuller's natural law approach is a function of his own perspective from inside the legal system. As someone who saw himself as a lawyer training other lawyers to operate within the legal system, Fuller's approach can lead to morally enriching the tasks of lawyers and the legal system. From outside the legal system, however, moral evaluation or condemnation of a legal system is often just as important, and from that external perspective the legal positivism that Fuller rejected has decided moral advantages.

Scheffler, Israel and Howard, V A. *Work, Education, and Leadership: Essays in the Philosophy of Education*. New York, Lang, 1995.

This book examines the relations among work, education and leadership in philosophical and practical perspective. Among the topics included are the concepts of education and training, the nature of vocational education, the relations of art and utility in schooling, and the roles of leadership in education and work. This book draws together influences from the American Pragmatist, John Dewey, and the British Idealist R G Collingwood.

Scheibe, Erhard. "A Most General Principle of Invariance" in *Philosophy, Mathematics and Modern Physics, Rudolph, Enno (ed)*, 213-225. New York, Springer-Verlag, 1994.

During the last two or three decades symmetries seem to have become the hallmark of physics. However, we have to remember that according to Wigner "if we knew all the laws of nature ... the invariance properties of these laws would not furnish us new information". Indeed, not all, but many physical invariances can be retraced to an exceedingly general principle of invariance according to which any structure isomorphic to a model of a theory is itself a model of that theory. Among the cases that cannot be subsumed under this principle there seem to be all the gauge invariances of elementary particle physics.

Scheibe, Erhard. "On the Mathematical Overdetermination of Physics" in *Philosophy, Mathematics and Modern Physics, Rudolph, Enno (ed)*, 186-199. New York, Springer-Verlag, 1994.

It is usually assumed that the axioms of a theory have to be and actually can be formulated in the language of that theory. This, however, is not always the case in physics. There the axioms are often formulated in purely mathematical terms much stronger than the proper physical terms. This mathematical overdetermination gives rise to an elimination program whose realization in general is by no means evident. It is this fact which may help us in explaining Wigner's "unreasonable effectiveness of mathematics in the natural sciences".

Schellinx, Harold and Ono, Hiroakira and Hori, Ryuichi. Extending Intuitionistic Linear Logic with Knotted Structural Rules. *Notre Dame J Form Log*, 35(2), 219-242, Spr 94.

In this paper, extensions of the intuitionistic linear logic with knotted structural rules are discussed. Each knotted structural rule is a rule of inference of the following form; from X, A, ..., A (n times)...C infer X, A, ..., A (k times)...C. This rule is called the (n,k)-rule, which is a restricted form of the weakening when n k and of the contraction when n k. It is shown that when either n=1 or k=1, strong similarities hold between logics with the (n,k)-rule and the logics with the weakening or the contraction, as for the cut elimination, decision problems and the finite model property.

Scheltens, D. Mensenrechten: Enkele reflecties naar aanleiding van de studie van Ph Van Haute. *Alg Ned Tijdschr Wijs*, 86(3), 242-245, Jl 94.

Schenk, Richard. Discretely Metaphysical: Refracting Metaphysical Light in Post-Metaphysical Prisms. *Listening*, 30(1), 15-34, Wint 95.

After confronting older philosophies of identity with newer philosophies of difference, the article shows the basis in Thomas Aquinas' anthropology for nonunitive metaphysics (discretio or diakrisis as opposed to unitio). In the three key areas of anthropology (epistemology, morality, eschatology), Thomas develops a philosophy of relational human finitude between an indicative metaphysics of fact and a subjective metaphysics of possibility: metaphysics in the optative mood based on the uncertain hope for what is not evident or certain, but needfully desired. This refraction of metaphysical light reveals in its discretion darker colors of existence and an optative basis for justice.

Schenk, Richard. Interpretación de K Rahner Sobre Tomás de Aquino. *Analogia*, 4(2), 143-157, 1990.

Schick, Friedrike. *Hegels Wissenschaft der Logik—metaphysische Letztbegründung oder Theorie logischer Formen?*. Freiburg, Alber, 1994.

Schick, James and Hardin, Tim and Walters, Bruce. Top Executive Compensation: Equity or Excess? Implications for Regaining American Competitiveness. *J Bus Ethics*, 14(3), 227-234, Mr 95.

The debate over compensation packages for top executives is discussed. Particular emphasis is placed on the decoupling of CEO pay and organizational performance. A contrast is drawn between firms that are owner-controlled and those that are manager-controlled. Owner-controlled firms tend to be more market-driven. In manager-controlled firms, however, ownership can become diluted to the point where decisions may not always be in the best interest of shareholders. The process of determining CEO compensation packages is examined, and special attention is given to the handling of stock options. In order to stem the threat of increased government intervention, suggestions are made for increasing the leverage of compensation committees and of shareholders in general.

Schiffer, Stephen. A Paradox of Meaning. *Nous*, 28(3), 279-324, S 94.

Schiffer, Stephen. Descriptions, Indexicals, and Belief Reports: Some Dilemmas (But Not the Ones You Expect). *Mind*, 104(413), 107-131, Ja 95.

Schiffer, Stephen. Meanings and their Nature. *Filozof Cas*, 42(5), 725-744, 1994.

Mym tématem je stará, ale dosud nezodpovezená otázka teorie vyznamu: existují takové *veci* jako vyznamy, a pokud ano, jakou mají povahu? Na tuto otázku nabídnu cástecnou odpoved', která ovsem nebude originální. Originalita, kterou mohu nabídnout, je prinejlepsím spekulativní a vztahuje se k tomu, jak by ona cástecná odpoved' mela byt doplnena. Budu povazovat za úspech, podarí-li se mi vyjasnit problémy obklopující uvedenou otázku a uvést hledání odpovedi na slibnou cestu.

Schiffer, Stephen. Reply to Yagisawa's "Thinking in Neurons". *Phil Stud*, 76(2-3), 297-300, D 94.

Schiffer, Stephen. The Language-of-Thought Relation and Its Implications. *Phil Stud*, 76(2-3), 263-285, D 94.

Schiffler, Ljerka. Philosophy as Destiny?. *Filozof Istraz*, 13(4), 735-743, 1993.

In a historical-philosophical perspective, and through the important dates of Croatian history of philosophy—Cres 1529-1979—the authoress searches for the present (Cres 1993) meaning of the message of Frane Petric, a classic of Croatian, European and world philosophy, considering some of the perpetual issues and dilemmas of thought (life/thought, essence/the apparent, tradition/the novum etc.) that are focused on the essence of the question concerning the place, the meaning and the destiny of philosophy—the destiny of thought—through the same question concerning the thinker who dares to live an authentic life, a life of thought.

Schindler, Ralf-Dieter. A Dilemma in the Philosophy of Set Theory. *Notre Dame J Form Log*, 35(3), 458-463, Sum 94.

Schirn, Matthias. Axiom V and Hume's Principle in Frege's Foundational Project. *Dialogos*, 30(66), 7-20, Jl 95.

Schlabach, Gerald W (& other trans) and Arnaldez, Roger. *Three Messengers for One God*. Notre Dame, Univ Notre Dame Pr, 1994.

Roger Arnaldez's *Three Messengers for One God* summarizes a lifetime of scholarship into matter Islamic to offer a comparative approach to the three religions which espouse an active revelation of God. His doctoral studies included a second dissertation on Philo, so that he is better qualified than most Islamicists to incorporate Jewish thought as well. Without seeking a common denominator, he rather emphasizes differences, finding in the respective mystical traditions a kind of rapprochement which is never reductive yet can be seen to be mutually illuminating for each tradition's search for the face of God.

Schlag, Martin. The Revolution of Human Dignity. *Vera Lex*, 13(1-2), 19-22, 1993.

Schlagel, Richard H. *From Myth to Modern Mind: A Study of the Origins and Growth of Scientific Thought, Volume I*. New York, Lang, 1995.

More than any other discipline, science has shaped the modern view of the world. The purpose of this two volume study is to recount how this came to be. Beginning with a depiction of primitive forms of mentality, Volume I, *Theogony through Ptolemy*, traces the contributions of the Presocratics and Plato to the sustained growth of scientific rationalism, culminating in Aristotle's organismic cosmology. This is followed by a description of the research of the Hellenistic precursors of modern science from Euclid and Archimedes through Ptolemy and Galen, comparing their mental outlook with that of the early church fathers.

Schlegelová, Jaroslava. How to Teach Philosophy in High Schools. *Filozof Cas*, 43(1), 127-136, 1995.

The aim of the article is to inform a philosophical and pedagogical public about possibilities of teaching philosophy in high schools in the Czech republic. In the first part the author thinks of reasons of putting the subject philosophy into the system of secondary education. She doesn't see the main sense of teaching in telling about philosophers and their ideas, but finds the most important philosophical debates with students. The teacher should be in close contact with students, lead a lively dialogue with them and teach them to understand themselves and their situation in the contemporary world and to take a responsible attitude towards life and perspectives of the future development of mankind. In the second part the author shows concrete of preparing possibilities the seminar of social science on a philosophical basis. She has in mind such a seminar which would stimulate students to finish their studies in high schools to go on studying different subjects at the university.

Schlesinger, George. "A Central Theistic Argument" in *Gambling on God: Essays on Pascal's Wager, Jordan, Jeffrey (ed)*, 83-99. Lanham, Rowman & Littlefield, 1994.

Schluchter, Wolfgang. Individuelle Freiheit und soziale Bindung: Vom Nutzen und Nachteil der Institutionen für den Menschen. *Rev Int Phil*, 49(192), 241-262, 1995.

Schluchter, Wolfgang. Zeitgemässe Unzeitgemässe: Von Friedrich Nietzsche über Georg Simmel zu Max Weber. *Rev Int Phil*, 49(192), 107-126, 1995.

The alleged influence of Friedrich Nietzsche on Max Weber is scrutinized. It is shown that Weber appropriated only one aspect of Nietzsche's work seriously, the theory of resentment. Even this aspect is altered in a telling way. Weber's theory of personality, however, which is very often related to Nietzsche's, is much more indebted to Kant and the Christian tradition. Those aspects of Nietzsche's work which have some similarity to Weber's approach in this regard were mediated by Georg Simmel's work on Schopenhauer and Nietzsche. Here again it is rather the Christian and Kantian interpretation of personality that informs the line of reasoning.

Schmal, Dániel. St Augustine on Just War. *Magyar Filozof Szemle*, 1-2, 11-32, 1994.

The author's aim is to investigate the so-called 'bellum justum' (just-war) theory in St Augustine's works. St Augustine never wrote a systematic treatise on war, so we can find only tentative approaches and texts sometimes incoherent. Being this so, the paper wants to improve that incoherency is not only due to the troublesome times of

AUTHOR INDEX WITH ABSTRACTS 729 Schneider, Martin

the 4-5th centuries. During the interpretation of the theory we are not entitled to make the ideas more coherent, supposing a remote and sufficient theory of which—unfortunately—only fragments are available. After making some critical points of this endeavour common both to most of the medieval and modern commentators we argue that the tensions of the just-war theory are explicable by the very fact that the moral questions of killing in a Christian state and society are essentially insoluble and this fact is one of the most excellent features of this earthly being after the original sin. The responsibility of the soldier, the question of obedience and freedom of the Christian personality, while induce the Christian living in a state to find the solution of the problem, cannot be reduced in a compact and watertight system. This lack of consistency compel Christian people to be in quest of another world where this consistency in regard to the social problems can be attained by the aid of divine grace. So the insufficient character of this worldly obedience helps us to find the real meaning of such conceptions effectually in their own theological connotations.

Schmaltz, Tad M. Malebranche on Descartes on Mind-Body Distinctness. *J Hist Phil*, 32(4), 573-603, O 94.

This article considers Descartes's famous claim that mind and body are distinct substances from the unusual perspective of Nicolas Malebranche. In particular, it focuses on Malebranche's argument that since Cartesians feel compelled to support such a claim by appealing to their clear idea of body, they must lack access to a clear idea of soul. The main conclusion is that while such an argument does not apply directly to Descartes's discussion in the *Meditations* of mind-body distinctness, this discussion nonetheless renders Descartes vulnerable to Malebranche's central charge that the nature of body is for Cartesians better known than the nature of the soul.

Schmerl, James H. The Isomorphism Property for Nonstandard Universes. *J Sym Log*, 60(2), 512-516, Je 95.

Schmidt, Dennis. On the Memory of Last Things. *Res Phenomenol*, 23, 92-104, 1993.

An interpretation of the notion of "the Last God" in Martin Heidegger's text *Beiträge zur Philosophie*.

Schmidt, Dennis J. Why I am so Happy. *Res Phenomenol*, 24, 3-14, 1994.

A discussion of the notion of sacrifice in Heidegger and Greek tragedy.

Schmidt, William C. Intentionality in Artificial Life. *Eidos*, 12(1), 25-45, Je 94.

Schmidt Andrade, Ciro E. La Belleza como Camino Hacia Dios (Santo Tomás de Aquino). *Sapientia*, 49(193-4), 217-228, 1994.

Schmidt Andrade, Ciro E. Santo Tomás y el *De Amina* (Comentario a los Caps. 4 y 5 del Libro III del *De Anima* de Aristóteles). *Analogia*, 8(1), 123-136, 1994.

Schmidt Andrade, Ciro E. Sentido del Tiempo y la Historia desde Santo Tomás de Aquino. *Analogia*, 9(1), 125-156, 1995.

Schmidt Osmanczik, Ute. "Epichereîn..Katà Pólin Therapeían Téchnei Gnorízein" in *Platón: Los Diálogos Tardíos, Lan, Conrado Eggers (ed)*, 35-47. Sankt Augustin, Academia, 1986.

The aim of this article is to show some implications of the term *Therapeia*. The real, good statesman must be able not only to conserve the physical health and the material goods of the people he governs, but also their "moral health", that means, their moral melioration. In order to do that, he possesses the political art, which is considered to be a *therapeutic* art. For this reason, the statesman must be a *therapeut* looking for the entire welfare of the *polis*. This art is unfolded in the *Statesman*, in a very complicated way, through a lot of therapeutic arts.

Schmit, Roger. A propos de l'analyse des jugements universels dans la *Logique de Port-Royal*. *Rev Int Phil*, 48(190), 481-484, 1994.

Schmitt, Annette (& other trans) and Bulygin, Eugenio and Alchourrón, Carlos E. *Normative Systeme*. Freiburg, Alber, 1994.

Schmitt, Frederick F. "Socializing Epistemology" in *Socializing Epistemology: The Social Dimensions of Knowledge, Schmitt, Frederick (ed)*, 1-27. Lanham, Rowman & Littlefield, 1994.

This is an introduction to the field of social epistemology, the normative and conceptual study of the relevance of social relations to knowledge. I divide the field into the topics of individual knowledge, the organization of cognitive labor, and collective knowledge. I focus on two issues: whether human knowledge depends ineliminably on testimony, and whether knowledge is in any sense socially constructed. I argue that there are currently no good reasons to affirm or deny that knowledge depends ineliminably on testimony. I also cast doubt on all but one claim to the social construction of knowledge.

Schmitt, Frederick F. "The Justification of Group Beliefs" in *Socializing Epistemology: The Social Dimensions of Knowledge, Schmitt, Frederick F (ed)*, 257-287. Lanham, Rowman & Littlefield, 1994.

This paper canvases various ways in which group justification might be social, over and above the trivial point that it is justification possessed by a group of individuals. I argue in favor of a joint rather than a summative account of group justification, analogous to Margaret Gilbert's joint account of group belief. I argue that several prominent views of individual justification—perspectivism, accessibility internalism, and coherentism—cannot carry over to group justification. I critically discuss claims to the primacy of group justification over individual justification, suggesting one claim that might be defensible.

Schmitt, Frederick F (ed). *Socializing Epistemology: The Social Dimensions of Knowledge*. Lanham, Rowman & Littlefield, 1994.

This is a collection of previously unpublished articles on social epistemology, the study of the relevance of social relations to knowledge. It includes articles on individual knowledge, the organization of cognitive labor, and group knowledge. There are articles by William Alston, Richard Foley, C A J Coady, Richard Feldman, Hilary Kornblith, Philip Kitcher, Helen Longino, Alvin Goldman and James Cox, Miriam Solomon, Margaret Gilbert, and Frederick F Schmitt. There is a comprehensive bibliography of social epistemology.

Schmitt, Frederick F. *Truth: A Primer*. Boulder, Westview Pr, 1995.

Schmitt, Frederick F and Spellman, James. "Socializing Epistemology: A Bibliography" in *Socializing Epistemology: The Social Dimensions of Knowledge, Schmitt, Frederick F (ed)*, 289-310. Lanham, Rowman & Littlefield, 1994.

This is a comprehensive bibliography of books and articles on social epistemology by philosophers. It includes classical writings as well as contemporary writings.

Schmitter, Amy Morgan. Representation, Self-Representation, and the Passions in Descartes. *Rev Metaph*, 48(2), 331-357, D 94.

This discussion addresses what Descartes means by "representation" by looking at particular issues of self-representation. I suggest that representations in general are complicated structures in which an object is represented to a "subject position", i.e., the first-person for whom the representation is a representation. Self-representation is properly the representation *of* this subject-position. I argue that the possibility of self-representation is best realized in certain higher-order representations—representations of representations, complete with their subject-positions—and that such higher-order representations are illustrated in the passions of love and joy, which establish a joyful and representative union of mind and body.

Schmitz, Hermann. Immanenz als Falle des Lebens. *Phil Rundsch*, 42(1), 69-75, Mr 95.

The subject of this review is the work of the French phenomenologist Michel Henry, based on his vision of a pure immanence of life without evidence by seeing and its intellectual derivatives. Such evidence is the lode-star of an over-objectivation in the leading intellectual tradition in Europe since Democritus, whereby the world as experienced is reduced to some classes of well-identifiable qualities. The seamy side of this reduction is the introjection by which the world-stuff peeled off by reduction is dumped into the inward world of the individual. Henry is right in his protest against reductionism, but inconsequently holds the course of introjection, whereby his immanence results in monadism without dialogue.

Schmitz, Kenneth L. What Happens to Tradition When History Overtakes It. *Amer Cath Phil Quart*, 68(Supp), 59-72, 1994.

Schmitz-Moormann, Karl. The Future of Teilhardian Theology. *Zygon*, 30(1), 117-129, Mr 95.

The impossibility of predicting the future allows us only to indicate which theological developments seem to be needed. These developments concern our changing perception of the world, which requires a reversal in our understanding of God's Creation, from its most imperfect beginnings to its unforeseeable future. The passing of evolution from the biological to the human level has opened moral dimensions that must be explored. Rather than return to the beginnings of the church, theology needs to try to understand Christian faith within evolution, to reinterpret the past in the light of the new. In evolution, no final doctrine is possible. The necessity for doctrine creates a constant tension with the necessity of its revision. New truth must be paid for by suffering. The need is for a coherent theological vision of Creation, Redemption, and God's action in the world. Teilhard's metaphysics of union may be the key to it. In this view love becomes the central force of creation, which Teilhard's view opens into an eternal future in God: in its final stage, evolution becomes Christogenesis.

Schmitz-Moormann, Nicole. New Perspectives on Teilhard Publications. *Zygon*, 30(1), 91-104, Mr 95.

Teilhard's texts were published in two complementary publications, the more philosophical-theological ones in the *Oeuvres* (OV), the scientific ones in the *L'Oeuvre Scientifique* (OS). His letters were published in a nonsystematic way. The publication of the *Oeuvres* presented thematic compilations. The papers had their own production history, creating different versions. Scientific texts were published by Teilhard in widely dispersed journals and have been collected into *L'Oeuvre Scientifique*. The scientific status of Teilhard is related to his positions in the scientific world and the continued use of his publications. The influences causing different versions of theological and philosophical papers are analyzed. The present accessibility of the diaries and their importance for a full understanding of Teilhard is elaborated.

Schnabel, Jim. Puck in the Laboratory: The Construction and Deconstruction of Hoaxlike Deception in Science. *Sci Tech Human Values*, 19(4), 459-492, Autumn 94.

One of the most dramatic techniques for constructing accounts of "undiscovery" or incompetence in science involves the manipulative deception—in some accounts, the "hoaxing"—of the putatively incompetent researcher, ostensibly as an experiment to evaluate his or her methodology and the soundness of his or her knowledge claims. In this article, the author examines five cases in which such deceptions have been employed, noting the patterns of argument that typically follow these deceptions and the factors that seem to determine the power of these arguments. The author suggests that the "hoaxer" in such cases is most likely to be successful when his or her views about the targeted researcher's methodology and knowledge claims are orthodox with respect to his or her intended audience.

Schnädelbach, Herbert. Morbus Hermeneuticus: Theses on a Philosophical Sickness. *Magyar Filozof Szemle*, 5-6, 849-854, 1994.

Schneewind, J B. "Locke's Moral Philosophy" in *The Cambridge Companion to Locke, Chappell, Vere (ed)*, 199-225. New York, Cambridge Univ Pr, 1994.

Schneider, Carl E. Bioethics in the Language of the Law. *Hastings Center Rep*, 24(4), 16-22, Jl-Ag 94.

Schneider, Helmuth. "Anmerkungen zu einem möglichen Dialog Schellings mit der modernen Biologie" in *Schelling und die Selbstorganisation, Heuser-Kessler, Marie-Luise (ed)*, 135-148. Berlin, Duncker Humblot, 1994.

Schneider, Helmuth. "Natur und technisches Handeln im antiken Griechenland" in *Naturauffassungen in Philosophie, Wissenschaft, Technik: Band I, Schäfer, Lothar (ed)*, 107-160. Freiburg, Alber, 1993.

Schneider, Martin. Leibniz Konzeption der "characteristica universalis" zwischen 1677 und 1690. *Rev Int Phil*, 48(188), 213-236, 1994.

Schneiderman, Lawrence J (& others). Attitudes of Seriously Ill Patients toward Treatment that Involves High Costs and Burdens on Others. *J Clin Ethics*, 5(2), 109-112, Sum 94.

Rationale: An argument that appears in almost every critique of physician-assisted suicide and euthanasia is that these procedures may induce seriously ill patients to "begin to feel an obligation to get out of the way" to avoid creating costs and burdens on others. Purpose of study: To determine the responses of seriously ill patients who are asked how long they would want to live and what percentage of their life-savings they would be willing to spend if their treatment left them totally dependent on family and friends for daily care. Conclusions: Most seriously ill patients already consider reducing costs and burdens they might place on others when contemplating their own terminal care.

Schneiderman, Lawrence J and Jecker, Nancy S. Judging Medical Futility: An Ethical Analysis of Medical Power and Responsibility. *Cambridge Quart Healthcare Ethics*, 4(1), 23-35, Wint 95.

This essay rejects the criterion of potential benefit, which holds that medical treatments are appropriate if they might have some benefit for the patient. We argue instead for granting physicians the power to establish and apply standards of medical futility. Rather than assigning individual physicians the power to define medical futility, we propose that this power rests with the medical profession as a group, and is part of the profession's more general responsibility to define general standards of medical care.

Schneiderman, Lawrence J and Jecker, Nancy S. When Families Request That 'Everything Possible' Be Done. *J Med Phil*, 20(2), 145-163, Ap 95.

The paper explores the ethical and psychological issues that arise when family members request that "everything possible" be done for a particular patient. The paper first illustrates this phenomenon by reviewing the well known case of Helga Wanglie. We proceed to argue that in Wanglie and similar cases family members may request futile treatments as a means of conveying that (1) the loss of the patient is tantamount to losing a part of themselves; (2) the patient should not be abandoned or disvalued in any way; or (3) the patient is owed special obligations by virtue of the special relationship in which the family and the patient stand. We maintain that families can best express these important messages by caring for patients, rather than by making requests for futile interventions. Likewise, when life-sustaining measures are futile, health providers can best fulfill their professional obligations by assuring patients' dignity and comfort, rather than by applying futile interventions.

Schneiders, Werner. Descartes' Cogito als Prinzip. *Stud Leibniz*, 26(1), 91-107, 1994.

The philosophy of Descartes is the classical example of a philosophy as a system intending to found itself on an absolute point of view or to come from an absolute starting point. However, the cogito being regarded by Descartes as the first principle, actually is neither a first nor a definite nor a sufficient principle, leading to further conclusions. Above all Descartes himself, thus becoming the first anti-Cartesian, compromises this so-called first and greatest evidence by stating that God is the most evident principle, from which everything has to be deduced. The myth of clarity conceals the true, uncertain and inquiring Descartes.

Schockenhoff, Eberhard. Brauchen wir ein neues Weltethos? Universale Ethik in einer geschichtlichen Welt. *Theol Phil*, 70(2), 224-244, 1995.

The article delineates the strategies of the philosophical debate with ethical relativism, then asks about a possible intercultural basis for a future "world-ethos". The second part examines the systematical place of such a project of "world-ethos" between the ethics of human rights on the one side and global religious meaning on the other. The structural dilemma is shown: the common basis of a future "world-ethos" threatens to be too noncommital regarding the at least initially possible legal action concerning human rights; on the other hand, regarding the orientation of the person, which the ethical exemplariness of the world religions richly provides, this common basis seems to lack a distinct image. A model of parliamentary consent, which subordinates the specific contribution of each world religion toward ethical dialogue to a higher criterion of truth seems to provide—by reason of this inner structural defect—no sufficient basis for the dialogue of world religions of the ethical problems concerning the future of the human race.

Schöffski, Oliver. "Lebensqualitätsbewertung im Gesundheitswesen als Problem der Medizin und der Ökonomie" in *Mythos Wertfreiheit?, Apel, Karl-Otto (ed)*, 259-273. Frankfurt, Campus Verlag, 1994.

Schoen, Edward L. The Methodological Isolation of Religious Belief. *Phil Cont World*, 1(2), 33-40, Sum 94.

According to Langdon Gilkey, both religion and science are cognitive enterprises, but they are separated methodologically. As a result, science and religion are concerned with different, though related levels of truth. Against these claims, historical examples are used to argue that scientific and religious explanations cannot be so neatly separated. To the contrary, both fields frequently treat overlapping ranges of data in methodologically opportunistic ways.

Schöndorf, Harald. Setzt Kants Philosophie die Existenz Gottes voraus?. *Kantstudien*, 86(2), 175-195, 1995.

Kant's critical philosophy presupposes God's existence. The thing-in-itself would be self-contradictory without an absolute subject. The intellectus "ectypus" presupposes an "intellectus archetypus". The "fact" of reason needs a cause, the intelligible world. Founding the respect for every person, it must be ruled by a God. The transcendental ideal is part of the ideas of reason. Their determination is unknown, but not their existence: Kant recognizes the existence of me and the world. Moreover, the twofold division of the objective synthesis of totality shows that Kant already presupposes God's existence.

Schönherr, Hans-Martin. Die Technik und die Schwäche: Ökologie nach Nietzsche, Heidegger und dem "schwachen" Denken. Vienna, Passagen, 1994.

Nach zehn Jahren hitzig geführter Debatte ist die Ökologie heute in einer Sackgasse. Die Alternativen heissen technische Modernisierung oder ganzheitliche Rückkehr zur Natur. Beide Modelle sind jedoch nur willkürliche Verständnisformen von Natur und setzen die destruktive Naturbeherrschung fort. Am schwachen Denken Gianni

Vattimos orientiert schlägt der Autor einen enuen Weg vor: Ökologie als einen vagen rhetorischen Entwurf der Welt, dessen Objektivität schwach geworden ist. Das Buch schliesst zum ersten Mal die bisher getrennt verlaufenden Debatten um Postmoderne und Ökologie zusammen und eröffnet damit neue Perspektiven für beide. (edited)

Schönherr, Ulrich. Das unendliche Altern der Moderne: Untersuchungen zur Romantrilogie Gert Jonkes. Vienna, Passagen, 1994.

Mit diesem Buch wird zum ersten Mal eine umfassende Studie zu Gert Jonke vorgelegt—eine der singulärsten Erscheinungen der deutschsprachigen Gegenwartsliteratur—, dessen Erzählwerk von der Literaturwissenschaft bislang weitgehend unerforscht geblieben ist. Am Leitfaden zentraler Fragestellungen zum Geschichts- und Wirklichkeitsbegriff, zur Konstitution literarischer Subjektivität sowie zur intertextuellen Erzählpraxis und Funktion der Musik versucht die Arbeit exemplarisch die ästhetische Besonderheit der Romantrilogie Schule der Geläufigkeit, Der Ferne Klang und Erwachen zum grossen Schlafkrieg aufzuzeigen. Dabei wurde nicht nur die Interdependenz des Werks mit der Tradition der Moderne untersucht, sondern auch dessen spezifischer historischer Ort im Hinblick auf eine ästhetische Gegenwart am Schnittpunkt von Moderne/Postmoderne konturiert.

Schönherr-Mann, Hans-Maring. Ein Anfang der Gerechtigkeit: Postmoderne Theorien des Politischen. *Z Phil Forsch*, 49(1), 36-53, Ja-Mr 95.

Schönherr-Mann, Hans-Martin. Politik der Technik: Heidegger und die Frage der Gerechtigkeit. Vienna, Passagen, 1992.

Was heisst Gerechtigkeit im technischen Zeitalter? Die Frage stellt sich technikphilosophisch aus dem Spätwerk Heideggers und aus dessen Konfrontation mit aktuellen Philosophien heraus. Sie weist die Politische Wissenschaft aus ihrer ethisch leitenden Position und stellt ihr die Aufgabe, das Fragen zu lernen. Gerechtigkeit transformiert sich politisch von der historischen und porspektiven Idee zu einer Frage nach dem eksistenziellen Verhältnis zwischen dem Menschen und den sich technisch schwächenden Konturen des Seins. (edited)

Schollmeier, Paul. Simian Virtue. *Between Species*, 10(1-2), 19-25, Win-Spr 94.

Despite current interest in animal ethics and in ethology, we have yet to ask whether animals other than humans exhibit moral virtue. One might think that other animals do not, for they do not appear to have a practical intellect, nor do they appear able to develop moral habits. But a recent study of wild primates suggests that chimpanzees possess a practical intellect enabling them to perform actions which are better than others and to acquire habits better than others. Though they do not have ideal human virtue, these animals possess habits which come rather close to our quotidian virtues.

Schooler, Jonathan W (& others). "Putting Insight into Perspective" in *The Nature of Insight, Sternberg, Robert J (ed)*, 559-587. Cambridge, MIT Pr, 1995.

Schoonmaker, Sara. "Capitalism and the Code: A Critique of Baudrillard's Third Order Simulacrum" in *Baudrillard: A Critical Reader, Kellner, Douglas M (ed)*, 168-188. Cambridge, Blackwell, 1994.

Schopenhauer, Arthur and Payne, E F J (trans). On the Basis of Morality. Providence, Berghahn, 1995.

This work is one of the most significant nineteenth-century treatises on ethics. It is also Schopenhauer's most extended discussion of traditional themes in ethics and presents a descriptive ethics radically at odds with rationally based, prescriptive ethical theories. Schopenhauer begins this book with a wide-ranging critique of Kant's ethics. Schopenhauer argues that compassion is the basis of morality, and in so doing presents a virtue ethics in which passion and desire are viewed as the keys for explaining different moral characters, behaviors, and world views. In the concluding part of his essay, Schopenhauer sketches his metaphysics of moral, using Kant's transcendental idealism as a ground for stressing both the interconnectiveness of being and the affinity of his ethics to Eastern thought. (edited)

Schopman, Joop. Chaos Theory, the End of Physicalism?. *J Gen Phil Sci*, 26(1), 135-142, 1995.

Recent challenges of the mechanistic world picture seem only to have strengthened the position of mathematics. So it continues to guarantee perfect predictability, the dream of physicalism. During recent decades, however, computer simulations have shown mathematicians that even simple sets of eqations may have, not an exact, but a whole range of solutions. With some of their examples we demonstrate the unpredictable begavior of simple systems. As a result, the dream is over. On the other hand, mathematicians also discovered that previously 'chaotic' phenomena could be represented by relatively simple formules. This leads to a dramatic increase in the explanatory power of mathematics. This change of the scientific scenery will have a profound methodological impact on the relationship between the natural and the other sciences.

Schopp, Robert F. "Self-Defense" in *In Harm's Way, Coleman, Jules L (ed)*, 255-289. New York, Cambridge Univ Pr, 1994.

This paper advances and defends a theory of self-defense as morally justified individual action and as morally justified law. It derives the theory of self-defense from the more abstract principles of liberal political philosophy represented by the American legal system. The theory authorizes any force necessary to defend against a culpable aggressor, with no requirements of retreat or proportionality. The individual exercising defensive force must consider the interests of innocent aggressors, bystanders or shields.

Schorcht, Claudia. "Gescheitert—Der Versuch zur etablierung Nationalsozialistischer Philosophen an der Un. München" in *Die besten Geister der Nation, Korotin, Ilse (ed)*, 291-327. Vienna, Picus, 1994.

Schorcht, Claudia. Philosophie an den bayerischen Universitäten 1933-1945. Erlangen, Harald Fischer, 1990.

Schottky, Richard. Das Problem der Gewaltenteilung bei Rousseau und Fichte. *Daimon Rev Filosof*, 9, 289-322, 1994.

This study deals with the problem of the separation of powers in the writings of Rousseau and Fichte on the theory of the state. Rousseau concentrates all power in the sovereign will of the people, the volonté générale, which is indivisible and inalienable and exercised directly by the people's assembly. After his ultraliberal early years, Fichte, like Rousseau, calls for an infallible volonté générale that derives from the will of the sovereign, the citizens as a whole (*Das Naturrecht*, 1796). This study concludes that Rousseaus's and Fichte's rejection of the separation of powers does not lead to an institutionalizable theory of constitutional law. (edited)

Schottky, Richard. Fichtes Nationalstaatsgedanke auf der Grundlage unveröffentlichter Manuskripte von 1807. *Fichte-Studien*, 2, 111-137, 1990.

Schottky, Richard. Rechtsstaat und Kulturstaat bei Fichte: Eine Erwiderung. *Fichte-Studien*, 3, 118-153, 1991.

Schrader, Wiebke (ed) and Berlinger, Rudolph (ed) and Girard, Louis. *Elementa: L'argument Ontologique chez Saint Anselme et chez Hegel (Band 60)*. Amsterdam, Rodopi, 1995.

L'exposé cartésien de l'argument ontologique s'écarte radicalement de l'esprit originaire de la preuve, chez Saint Anselme. Le Dieu de Descartes, parfait parce que tout-puissant, est bien différent du Dieu de *Proslogion*, "Celui qui est tel que rien de plus grande ne puisse être pensé", fin de la pensée et du désir humains. La preuve d' Anselme conceptualise une expérience humaine qui se pense comme l'expérience chrétienne orthodoxe, décrivant, de ce fait, l'homme en sa vérité. Mais on n'entrera pleinement dans la pensée spéculative que si l'aspiration à Dieu en l'homme est considérée comme l'envers dialectique de l'amour, créateur de l'homme, en Dieu. Chez Hegel, ce n'est pas l'esprit fini qui accomplit la preuve ontologique, mais l'Esprit dans sa totalité. Ce mouvement de l'Esprit vers soi à travers sa division d'avec soi n'est pas un simple processus logique; en sa profondeur, il est le mouvement de réconciliation de la liberté humaine avec la liberté divine, créatrice et rédemptrice. La vérité de la Totalité, et donc, aussi, de l'histoire, dans le Concept, dit également la libre unification de l'homme et de Dieu dans et par la figure historique du Christ. Hegel pense le christianisme sans le réduire, parce qu'il le pense à partir de l'acte préalable de la foi, par lequel la liberté humaine s'ouvre à l'amour divin, posant ainsi l'unité dialectique du Tout. Que la foi puisse être rationnellement exposée ne l'empêche pas d'être la foi, c'est-à-dire la vie en union au Christ, Logos éternel et homme crucifié. On a dit: "Un Dieu compris n'est plus un Dieu". Cela n'est vrai que des faux dieux.

Schrader, Wolfgang H. "Rechtsfrieden als Grundlage der Einheit Europas —Überlegungen zu Kant und Fichte" in *Das geistige Erbe Europas, Buhr, Manfred (ed)*, 540-547. Napoli, Vivarium, 1994.

Schrader, Wolfgang H. J G Fichte und das postmoderne Denken (Jean-François Lyotard). *Fichte-Studien*, 1, 167-177, 1990.

Schrader, Wolfgang H. Nation, Weltbürgertum, und Synthesis der Geisterwelt. *Fichte-Studien*, 2, 27-36, 1990.

Schrama, Martijn. Blondel and the Tradition of the Innate Longing for God (in Dutch). *Bijdragen*, 55(4), 412-434, 1994.

An intensive discussion concerning the relation between mankind and its divinization, concerning the unbreakable bond between man and God, and using the expression of the innate longing for God, has continued for many centuries. Undeniably one can see in this discussion the influence of Saint Augustine: in the Middle Ages, in the 16th century of the Reformation, in the 17th century of Jansenism. Within the discussion too little attention was paid to what had been voiced by some of the *Schola Augustiniana* theologians. The main activity of the *Schola Augustiniana* shifted from Salamanca (16th century) to Louvain (17th century) and from there to Italy (18th century). Later, French Catholic philosophers appealed to the theologians of the *Schola Augustiniana* to take up the discussion again, this time in a 19th century framework, and finally, the *Nouvelle Théologie* is a 20th century presentation of the centuries old discussion.

Schrenk, Lawrence. Cicero on Rhetoric and Philosophy: *Tusculan Disputations* i. *Ancient Phil*, 14(2), 355-360, Fall 94.

Schrift, Alan D. "Putting Nietzsche to Work: The Case of Gilles Deleuze" in *Nietzsche: A Critical Reader, Sedgwick, Peter R (ed)*, 250-275. Cambridge, Blackwell, 1995.

This essay examines briefly Deleuze's interpretation of Nietzsche vis-á-vis Hegel in *Nietzsche and Philosophy* by comparing it with Derrida's reading of Nietzsche vis-á-vis Heidegger in *Spurs: Nietzsche's Styles*. It then examines Deleuze's discussion of desire as an appropriation of Nietzschean will to power and explores how Deleuze's notion of becoming might figure in an interpretation of the *Übermensch*. It concludes with an extended analysis of how Nietzsche's genealogical critique of Christian morality and the origin of the modern state in *On the Genealogy of Morals* serves as a model for Deleuze and Guattari's critique of psychoanalysis in *Anti-Oedipus*.

Schrift, Alan D. "Reconfiguring the Subject: Foucault's Analytics of Power" in *Reconstructing Foucault, Miguel-Alfonso, Ricardo (ed)*, 185-199. Amsterdam, Rodopi, 1994.

This essay argues that Foucault's analysis of power follows Nietzsche's example by focusing not on the subjects of power but on power relations, the relations of force that operate within social practices and social systems. I argue that by developing the Nietzschean linkage between power and knowledge, Foucault is able to develop a critique of the substantive subject. I conclude by suggesting that although Foucault does not fully resolve the problem of agency, the recent work of Judith Butler and Ernesto Laclau and Chantal Mouffe show what a Foucaultian solution might look like.

Schrift, Alan D. On the Gift-Giving Virtue: Nietzsche's Unacknowledged Feminine Economy. *Int Stud Phil*, 26(3), 33-44, 1994.

This paper examines Nietzsche's reflections on economy, exchange and the giving of gifts. While not specifically connected to gender in Nietzsche, a comparison with Hélène Cixous's comments on gifts, giving, and feminine libidinal and political economies reveals an unacknowledged "feminine" side to Nietzsche's economic discourse. By examining the exchange model and the definition of subjectivity in terms of property acquisition that accompanies this model, another model of what intersubjective relations, one grounded on practices of generosity rather than the reciprocal exchange of private property, comes to the fore.

Schroeder, Severin. Is Thinking a Kind of Speaking?. *Phil Invest*, 18(2), 139-150, Ap 95.

Taking its cue from a remark by Wittgenstein, the article puts forward that in some crucial respects thinking is neither a process nor an activity. The author argues that even where thinking takes the form of an internal monologue, the two should still not be viewed as identical.

Schröder, Hannelore. "Der Antifeminismus und Antisemitismus Otto Weiningers" in *Der feministische "Sündenfall"?, Kohn-Ley, Charlotte (ed)*, 60-83. Vienna, Picus, 1994.

The purpose of this article is twofold: to convincingly demonstrate the likeness of mind between Weininger and Hitler; to show that republication of Weininger's "Sex and Character" (1903) should therefore be subject to the same law that prohibits reprints of *Mein Kampf*. The republication of Weininger's book has to be seen as part of a revival of fascist anti-semitism and anti-feminism. The publication of Weininger and the like should be legally prohibited and morally rejected to protect human dignity and the lives of women and Jewish people. (edited)

Schroeter, Francois. Tugend und Moraltheorie. *Z Phil Forsch*, 49(1), 104-123, Ja-Mr 95.

This paper surveys some of the most recent developments in virtue ethics. Virtue theorists claim that the evaluation of character traits takes precedent over judgments about the rightness of actions in ethical theory. The paper challenges arguments offered in support of this claim. Special emphasis is also placed on the potential of traditional moral theories (viz. utilitarianism and Kantianism) to account for the importance of the virtues.

Schroeter, François. Une approche déflationniste de la liberté de la volonté: un autre visage de Kant. *Frei Z Phil Theol*, 41(1-2), 116-136, 1994.

Schroevers, Pieter. "Science: A Modest Hope" in *Ecology, Technology, and Culture*, Zweers, Wim (ed), 94-98. Cambridge, White Horse, 1994.

"Pronouncements concerning future events are not possible, so restrict yourself to ad-hoc-solutions for daily problems, and forget the big lines in global development" says Tenekes in his article in the same book, on which this article serves as a reaction. Such a statement denies the explicit meaning of science, whose task, it is, to look better into the future with the help of experience of the past. Mistakes are to be found everywhere in history, also in its large lines, and it belongs to the task of science to make them clear. Arguments for this point of view are given.

Schueler, G F. *Desire: Its Role in Practical Reason and the Explanation of Action*. Cambridge, MIT Pr, 1995.

Desire examines a fundamental issue in philosophy of mind, the nature of desires and how, if at all, they motivate and justify actions. At least since Hume said that reason "is and of right ought to be the slave of the passions", many philosophers have held that desires play an essential role both in practical reason and in the explanation of intentional action. Schueler looks at accounts of both roles in Williams, Dretske, Schiffer, Dennett, Davidson, Nagel and others, arguing that once two different senses of "desire" are clearly distinguished, the usual belief—desire accounts need to be replaced.

Schuhmann, Karl. "Edith Stein und Adolf Reinach" in *Studien zur Philosophie von Edith Stein, Fetz, Reto Luzius (ed)*, 53-88. Freiburg, Alber, 1993.

Schulkin, Jay and Sabini, John. Biological Realism and Social Constructivism. *J Theor Soc Behav*, 24(3), 207-217, S 94.

In this paper we attempt to reconcile two important, current intellectual traditions: Darwinism and social constructionism. We believe that these two schools have important points of contact that have been obscured because each school has feared that the other wanted to put it out of business. We try to show that both traditions have much to offer psychology, a discipline that has often been too individualistic, too concerned with the private and the subjective. The spirit of American pragmatism can be found in both camps; like the social constructivists, pragmatists focused on social transaction rather than internal happening, and like the Darwinian they were rooted in functionalism and the biological.

Schulten, Holger and Roser, Andreas. Ein Brief Johann Gottlieb Fichtes. *Fichte-Studien*, 5, 171-174, 1993.

In diesem Brief—vemutlich an Gottlieb Hufeland—schreibt Fichte unter anderem: "(...) verschaffen Sie mir ein MagisterDiplom von Leipzig oder Wittenberg, oder woher es sey. Leisten kann ich JETZT weiter nichts als GELD GEBEN (...)". Diese Bitte Fichtes, ihm ein Magisterdiplom "zu verschaffen", steht in einem engen Zusammenhang mit Fichtes Absicht eine Anstellung als Professor an der Universtiät Jena zu finden.

Schultz, Norm and Collins, Allison. A Critical Examination of the AICPA Code of Professional Conduct. *J Bus Ethics*, 14(1), 31-41, Ja 95.

The American Institute of Certified Public Accountants (AICPA) is responsible for the Code of Professional Conduct that governs the actions of CPAs. In 1988, the Code was revised by the AICPA, but a number of issues still remain unresolved. These issues are examined in light of the profession's stated commitment to the public good. (edited)

Schulz, Ortrun. Schopenhauers Ethik—die Konsequenz. *Schopenhauer Jahr*, 76, 133-149, 1995.

Schulz, Peter. "Die Schrift 'Einführung in die Philosophie'" in *Studien zur Philosophie von Edith Stein, Fetz, Reto Luzius (ed)*, 228-255. Freiburg, Alber, 1993.

Schulz, Peter (ed) and Rath, Matthias (ed) and Fetz, Reto Luzius (ed). *Studien zur Philosophie von Edith Stein*. Freiburg, Alber, 1993.

Schulz, Wolfgang. Multiple-Discrepancies Theory Versus Resource Theory. *Soc Indic Res*, 34(1), 153-169, Ja 95.

The explanatory value of two theories expounding the quality of life are compared and discussed. To make this comparison possible, it is necessary to distinguish between rather clear theoretical assumptions and avoid a mix of theories: the variance explained by comparisons (multiple discrepancies) is compared with the variance explained by resource. Data obtained from the Vienna Student Survey (n = 350) are presented. Although multiple-discrepancies theory (MDT) does explain far more variance than the resource approach, critical comments and proposals complete the study.

Schurr, Adolf. "Das Prinzip der Geschichte—Zur Geschichtlichkeit und Ungeschichtlichkeit des Menschen" in *Das geistige Erbe Europas, Buhr, Manfred (ed)*, 400-410. Napoli, Vivarium, 1994.

Schurz, Gerhard. "Karl Popper und das Induktionsproblem" in *Heinrich Gomperz, Karl Popper und die österreichische Philosophie, Seiler, Martin (ed)*, 147-161. Amsterdam, Rodopi, 1994.

In this paper three different kinds of principles of induction are distinguished: empirical induction, logical induction and pragmatical induction. All three principles are the object of criticism in Karl Poppers writings. It is argued, first, that Poppers refutation of empirical induction was shared also by inductivists like Carnap, and hence nothing really new. Second, Poppers arguments against logical induction are his most important theoretical achievement. Third, Poppers' argument against pragmatic induction are inconsistent with his own account of theory corroboration.

Schurz, Gerhard. Admissible Versus Valid Rules: A Case Study of the Modal Fallacy. *Monist*, 77(3), 376-388, Jl 94.

The modal fallacy is the invalid argument from the two premises "Necessarily: if A then B" and "A" to "Necessarily: B". This paper discusses an attempt of Jerzy Perzanowski to rehabilitate this invalid argument pattern by showing it to be a derivable rule of modal logics. It is argued that Perzanowski confuses two logical properties of rules which have to be carefully distinguished: the *validity* of a rule as opposed to its *admissibility*. Roughly speaking, in order to be *admissible* a rule need to preserve only *logical truth*, while in order to be valid the rule has to preserve (contingent) truth—which is a much stronger requirement. The final section discusses the general logical relations between the validity, derivability and admissibility of rules.

Schurz, Gerhard. Relevant Deduction and Hypothetico-Deductivism: A Reply to Gemes. *Erkenntnis*, 41(2), 183-188, S 94.

In this paper I defend my account of hypothetico-deductive theory confirmation based on my theory of relevant deduction (*Erkenntnis* 1991) against some objections of Gemes (*Erkenntnis* 1994). I show that if one requires that both confirmans and confirmandum are represented as conjunctions of their relevant consequence elements, then all problems raised by Gemes can be solved. Finally I discuss similarities as well as differences between my concept of "relevant consequence element" and Gemes' concept of "content part".

Schurz, Gerhard and Lambert, Karel. Outline of a Theory of Scientific Understanding. *Synthese*, 101(1), 65-120, O 94.

The basic theory of scientific understanding presented in Sections 1-2 exploits three main ideas. *First*, that to understand a phenomenon *P* (for a given agent) is to be able to fit *P* into the cognitive background corpus *C* (of the agent). *Second*, that to fit *P* into *C* is to connect *P* with parts of *C* (via "arguments" in a very broad sense) such that the unification of *C* increases. *Third*, that the cognitive changes involved in unification can be treated as sequences of shifts of phenomena in *C*. How the theory fits typical examples of understanding and how it excludes suprious unifications is explained in detail. Section 3 gives a formal description of the structure of cognitive corpuses which contain descriptive as well as inferential components. The theory of unification is then refined in the light of so-called "puzzling phenomena", to enable important distinctions, such as that between consonant and dissonant understanding. In Section 4, the refined theory is applied to several examples, among them a case study of the development of the atomic model. The final part contains a classification of kinds of understanding and a discussion of the relation between understanding and explanation.

Schuster, Eleanor A (ed) and Brown, Carolyn L (ed). *Exploring Our Environmental Connections*. New York, NLN Pr, 1994.

This is a collection of peer reviewed papers which, for the first time, expresses what the discipline of professional nursing has to say about health, healing, environment and wholeness. It represents a paradigm shift toward an expanded awareness of environment and prevention of illness. The common thread throughout is the issue of the nature of our relationships: with self, with one another, with earth and with all other inhabitants of the planet. Perspectives of twenty-four international nurse scholars are presented. The forward, by the futurist Hazel Henderson, places the work in the contexts of the present and the future.

Schuster, Shlomit C. Report on Applying Philosophy in Philosophical Counseling. *Int J Applied Phil*, 9(2), 51-55, Wint-Spr 95.

In philosophical counseling theoretical and practical matters of life are questioned in an ongoing way. The difference between applied philosophy, psychotherapy, and philosophical counseling is in a personal "tone" and the "accent" on equal relations between dialogue partners. A case story shows how discussing topics as optimism, "false" needs, and Russell's happiness helped a desperate woman. Depression, alcoholism, unemployment, and child abuse were discussed as human, meta-clinical problems that have philosophical connotations. The author describes her private philosophy practice during 1989-92. Part of the practice is a nonprofit first-aid telephone service for existential problems and ethical dilemmas.

Schuster, Shlomit C. The Practice of Sartre's Philosophy in Philosophical Counseling and Existential Psychotherapy. *Iyyun*, 44, 99-114, Ja 95.

A brief introduction to the new profession of philosophical counseling is followed by a description of Sartre's philosophy in different counseling settings. By comparing a Sartrean perspective in philosophical counseling with Existential psychotherapy, essential differences in method, aim and content are found to exist. The incompatibility of Sartre's philosophy with Freudian psychoanalytic theory necessitates a radical conception of Existential psychotherapy. Philosophical counseling does not contradict applying Sartre's basic assumptions. The practice of Sartre's thought in philosophical counseling is illustrated by a case-story.

Schuster-Stein, Paul. Kants Philosophie in Rumänien. *Kantstudien*, 86(1), 70-86, 1995.

Schwab, Georg. Contextualising Carl Schmitt's Concept of *Grossraum*. *Hist Euro Ideas*, 19(1-3), 185-190, Jl 94.

Schwab, Richard N (trans) and D'Alembert, Jean Le Rond. *Preliminary Discourse to the Encyclopedia of Diderot*. Chicago, Univ of Chicago Pr, 1995.

Schwabe, Karl-Heinz. "Kants Ästhetik und die Moderne" in *Naturzweckmässigkeit und ästhetische Kultur, Schwabe, Karl-Heinz (ed)*, 31-61. Sankt Augustin, Academia, 1993.

Schwabe, Karl-Heinz (ed) and Thom, Martina (ed). *Naturzweckmässigkeit und ästhetische Kultur*. Sankt Augustin, Academia, 1993.

For the present discussion on the relationship between man and nature and on the matters of mental acquisition of the "world" Kant's philosophical approaches are not renouncable. The authors of the studies to the "Kritik der Urteilskraft" collected in this volume turn to Kant's problems and their reception from different points of view. In this connection they pursue both the problems of reasoning in modern aesthetics in connection with reflections on anthropology and philosophy of life and epistemological questions of modern science, e.g., physics, which were paid less attention to in the literature to Kant's third Critique. This volume makes a contribution to the current discussion on enlightening and modernity.

Schwartz, Barry. On Morals and Markets. *Crim Just Ethics*, 13(2), 61-69, Sum-Fall 94.

Schwartz, Justin K. What's Wrong with Exploitation?. *Nous*, 29(2), 158-188, Je 95.

Schwartz, P and Rodríguez Braun, C. Las relaciones entre Jeremías Bentham y S Bolívar. *Telos (Spain)*, 1(3), 45-68, O 92.

Schwartz, Pedro and Braun, Carlos Rodríguez. Entrevista: Carlos R Braun dialoga con Pedro Schwartz. *Telos (Spain)*, 1(1), 167-182, F 92.

En la presente entrevista Carlos Rodríguez Braun, socio fundador de la SIEU, destacado profesor de economía, Subdirector de Cambio 16, y uno de los más importantes investigadores del utilitarismo en el ámbito iberoamericano entrevista a Pedro Schwartz, presidente honorario de la SIEU, pionero de los estudios utilitaristas en el mundo iberoamericano en el presente siglo, una de las mentes más lúcidas de nuestro panorama intelectual que analiza con rigor las aportaciones del utilitarismo, y sus relaciones con el pensamiento liberal y socialista. La lúcida acidez de Pedro Schwartz es un magnífico estimulante para comenzar nuestra andadura como investigadores y críticos del utilitrismo. *Telos* agradece al entrevistador y el entrevistado sus punzantes e inteligentes preguntas y respuestas.

Schwartz, Robert. Is Mathematical Competence Innate?. *Phil Sci*, 62(2), 227-240, Je 95.

Despite a vast philosophical literature on the epistemology of mathematics and much speculation about how, in principle, knowledge of this domain is possible, little attention has been paid to the psychological findings and theories concerning the acquisition, comprehension and use of mathematical knowledge. This contrasts sharply with recent philosophical work on language where comparable issues and problems arise. One topic that is the center of debate in the study of mathematical cognition is the question of innateness. This paper critically examines the controversy.

Schwartz, Robert. *Vision: Variations on Some Berkeleian Themes*. Cambridge, Blackwell, 1994.

The book consists of four essays examining longstanding problems in the theory of vision. Each chapter begins by looking at the issues as raised in Berkeley's *New Theory of Vision*. Based on this historical background, along with analyses of current psychological research, new solutions are explored. Chapter 1, on distance perception, is the most historical and helps set the stage. Chapter 2, examines a prominent theory of size perception and challenges its widely accepted presuppositions. Chapter 3 questions the empirical significance of the continuing controversy over perceptual inference. Chapter 4 discusses the status of J J Gibson's "direct-perception" approach to these issues.

Schwarzkopf, Friedemann-Eckart. *The Metamorphosis of the Given: Toward an Ecology of Consciousness*. New York, Lang, 1995.

The Metamorphosis of the Given leads us to experience reality as a product of what is given and not-given. Given are the perceptual world and all organizing systems of the mind. Not-given is the act of the human spirit of giving attention and *new meaning*; these are not given, because only the human being can give them. The *conversation* of humanity reflects this interaction between the human spirit and the world. In this process the feeling of reality changes and gives birth to possibilities for a new, emerging shared paradigm.

Schweizer, Paul. Intentionality, Qualia, and Mind/Brain Identity. *Mind Mach*, 4(3), 259-282, Ag 94.

The paper examines the status of conscious presentation with regard to mental content and intentional states. I argue that conscious presentation of mental content should be viewed on the model of a secondary quality, as a subjective *effect* of the microstructure of an underlying brain state. The brain state is in turn viewed as the instantiation of an abstract computational state, with the result that introspectively accessible content is interpreted as a presentation of the associated computational state realized by the brain. However, if the relation between consciousness and representational content is construed in this manner, then conscious presentation does not provide an adequate foundation for the claim that human mental states are *intrinsically* intentional. On this model, I argue that functionalism is able to account for (nonintrinsic) intentionality, but not for consciousness, which has implications for the computational paradigm, as well as for Searle's Chinese room thought experiment.

Schwengel, Hermann. Beyond the Philosophy of the Subject and Beyond the Economics of Choice: Sociology in a Changed World. *Theor Cult Soc*, 11(3), 77-100, Ag 94.

Schwinn, Thomas. Wieviel Subjekt benötigt die Handlungstheorie? Zur Weber-Rezeption von Alfred Schütz und Talcott Parsons. *Rev Int Phil*, 49(192), 187-220, 1995.

AUTHOR INDEX WITH ABSTRACTS 733 Sedgwick, Peter R

Schwoerer, Catherine E (& others). Organizational Characteristics and HRM Policies on Rights: Exploring the Patterns of Connections. *J Bus Ethics*, 14(7), 531-549, Jl 95.

The protection of employee rights in the workplace is one of the fundamental ethical questions facing organizations today. Organizations differ in the extent to which they protect the rights of both employees and themselves as employers, yet little research has examined the types of organizations that have rights protection policies. Instead of the classic normative approach to ethical issues, this study took a contextual approach to the management of rights in the workplace through human resource policies. Associations were found between the organizational characteristics of size, industry, unionization, business condition, and the existence of employee and employer rights policies. Additional analyses revealed underlying dimensions in right policies and the relationship of organizational characteristics to these aspects of rights management were examined. The results are discussed in terms of understanding human resource rights management within an organizational context.

Schwyzer, Hubert. "Wittgenstein and 'Mainstream' Contemporary Philosophy" in *Wittgenstein and Contemporary Philosophy, Teghrarian, Souren (ed)*, 261-285. Bristol, Thoemmes, 1994.

Sciabarra, Chris Matthew. *Ayn Rand: The Russian Radical*. University Park, Penn St Univ Pr, 1995.

This book provides the first comprehensive analysis of the intellectual roots and thought of novelist-philosopher, Ayn Rand. Sciabarra views Rand's "objectivism" as a rejection—and affirmation—of key elements in the Russian tradition. Born in Russia during the Silver Age, Rand was educated at Leningrad University and studied with the neo-Idealist, N O Lossky. She absorbed a dialectical method of inquiry that profoundly influenced her literary and philosophic project. Her distinctive libertarian synthesis is presented as a major contribution to radical social theory. Ultimately, Sciabarra challenges Rand's followers and critics to reassess her thought and its place in intellectual history.

Scilironi, Carlo. La "Filosofia Positiva" di Bruno Forte. *Sapienza*, 48(1), 75-85, 1995.

Scilironi, Carlo. La Filosofia Cristiana nei Secoli XIX e XX. *Aquinas*, 37(3), 647-654, S-D 94.

Scillitani, Lorenzo. Dimensione Transculturale dei Fenomeni Giuridici nella Ricerca Antropologica. *Riv Int Filosof Diritto*, 71(4), 291-313, 1994.

Sciulli, David. An Interview with Niklas Luhmann. *Theor Cult Soc*, 11(2), 37-68, My 94.

Sciuto, Italo. "Sinderesi, desidereio naturale e fondamento dell'agire morale nel pensiero medieval" in *L'etica e il suo Altro, Vigna, Carmelo (ed)*, 126-149. Milano, FrancoAngeli, 1994.

Il saggio è uno studio storico-critico del concetto di "Synderesis", dalla sua formazione in età patristica alla sua trasformazione medievale. Esaminato in vari autori (da Agostino a Meister Eckhart attraverso i mistici e gli scolastici dei secoli XII e XIII), questo concetto è importante perché assume il significato di fondamento e senso dell'agire morale. E quindi riassuntivo dei concetti di natura, desiderio, fine. Ma non viene inteso da tutti i filosofi medievali allo stesso modo. Le due posizioni più rilevanti, e opposte, si possono vedere in Tommaso d'Aquino e Meister Eckhart: nel primo serve a fondare un'etica delle *potenze* o delle *virtù*, nel secondo un'etica dell'*immagine* e del *distacco*. Come conclusione, il saggio mostra l'attualità della prospettiva di Eckhart in un tempo, come il nostro, dominato dall'assoluto potere della tecnica.

Sciuto, Italo. Ermeneutica, Metafisica e Nichilismo in Heidegger. *Riv Filosof Neo-Scolas*, 87(1), 119-136, Ja-Mr 95.

Scofield, Giles R. Ethics Consultation: The *Most* Dangerous Profession: A Reply to Critics (CQ Vol 2, No 4). *Cambridge Quart Healthcare Ethics*, 4(2), 225-228, Spr 95.

Scolnicov, Samuel. Socrates, Plato and the Development of Reason: A Rejoinder to Professor Sichel. *Stud Phil Educ*, 13(2), 149-156, 1993-94.

This is a rejoinder to Sichel's review of my *Plato's Philosophy of Education*, Stud Phil Educ, 13, 2, 141-148, 1993-94). For Socrates, the focus of the moral personality was in an integrated perspective of one's whole experience. He has to let the person reach the conclusions for himself; but knowledge in the strict sense is also true. Method is not enough. Socrates objects to Protagoras that for him reason plays in education an ancillary role. Plato ultimately rejects Protagoras' *techne*. It is not escaping *tuche* that counts, but *why* one escapes it. Human life is not self-sufficient, and reason has its own interests.

Scott, Alwyn. *Stairway to the Mind: The Controversial New Science of Consciousness*. New York, Springer-Verlag, 1995.

The aim of this book is to provide a context for considerations of life and consciousness that emphasizes the hierarchical nature of biological reality. From the peculiar nonlinear dynamics that obtain at each level of this heirarchy, newly minted objects emerge to provide bases for dynamical descriptions at higher levels. Since each level has its own dynamical laws—determined largely by happenstance—reductive materialism is seen to be untenable. Nested between reductionism and vitalism, *emergent dualism* finds a home in natural science, where the phenomena of life and consciousness arise from several layers of the biological hierarchy.

Scott, Michael. Time and Change. *Phil Quart*, 45(179), 213-218, Ap 95.

Scotto, Silvia C. "El Lenguaje como Límite en el 2do. Wittgenstein" in *Temas Actuales de Filosofía, Palacios, María Julia (ed)*, 571-576. Buenos Aires, Univ Nacional Salta, 1993.

My purpose is to argue that the main problem of Wittgenstein's *Tractatus*, "the limits of language", was the central topic of Wittgenstein's later thought too, as a doctrine with a critical and positive direction. The treatment and solution of that question was more profound and less schematic than of the *Tractatus*'s, and viewed from the perspective of the "language as a limit", it links different problems into a strong unity, without a trascendental perspective. To show this, I pursue some thesis about the conception of philosophy and specially about "grammar", related to the new conception of language as "language games".

Scoville, Judith N. Value Theory and Ecology in Environmental Ethics: A Comparison of Rolston and Niebuhr. *Environ Ethics*, 17(2), 115-133, Sum 95.

The objective of Holmes Rolston, III's writings has been the development of an "ecologically formed" environmental ethics based both on environmental values and ecological description. I show how recasting Rolston's value theory in terms of H. Richard Niebuhr's relational value theory can clarify and strengthen this project. Niebuhr developed a theory of value in which value is found in relationships and value systems are constructed in relation to centers of value. Niebuhr's contextual method, with which Rolston's methodology has substantial affinity, is particularly open to use of such sciences as ecology. I conclude that this recasting of Rolston's important work in terms of relational value and contextual method can clarify the use of ecology in ethics (including the *is/ought* dichotomy) and can contribute to ethical reflection on such difficult problems as the spotted owl controversy.

Scruton, Roger. Oikophobia and Xenophilia. *Filozof Istraz*, 14(2-3), 355-360, 1994.

This article deals with the circumstances in which oikophobia (hatred of home) emerges as a result of 'multiculturalism' in an 'inclusive' society. A new stereotype of American society derives from a philosophy which can be summarized as follows: American society, morality and law express a 'culture'—in the anthropologist's sense—which is distinguished by imperialism, its desire to absorb, override or extinguish every possible rival. But, in reality, American society is not a 'culture' in the anthropologist's sense, but rather a part of Western civilization. It was formed by legal rather than cultural forces, and has absorbed culture after culture without undergoing a change in its fundamental structure. Tolerance has been a cornerstone of American society. (edited)

Scruton, Roger. Upon Nothing. *Phil Invest*, 17(3), 481-506, Jl 94.

A critical survey of deconstruction and the writings of Derrida, which sets the texts in the context of French intellectual life since 1968, and diagnoses the spiritual calamity exemplified in them.

Scudder Jr, John R and Bishop, Anne H. *Nursing Ethics: Therapeutic Caring Presence*. Boston, Jones & Bartlett, 1996.

The authors challenge the applied approach to nursing ethics by contending that nursing ethics articulates the moral sense inherent in nursing practice and assesses its fulfillment, appraises its adequacy, and explores new possibilities for fulfilling and expanding its moral sense. Through interpreting exemplars of nursing excellence, they disclose the integral relationship of care as practice with care a motive in good nursing practice and develop an ethics of therapeutic caring presence. The goal of their ethics is to help practicing nurses fulfill the moral sense of nursing by making ethics integral to nursing practice rather than applying detached expertise to it.

Scult, Allen. Heidegger's Hermeneutics and the Rhetoric of Biblical Theology. *Phil Rhet*, 27(4), 397-409, 1994.

Seager, William. Dretske on HOT Theories of Consciousness. *Analysis*, 54(4), 270-276, O 94.

Higher-order thought theories of consciousness identify S's mental state being conscious with S believing that he is in that state. Recently Fred Dretske has proposed an objection which depends upon a distinction between an experience's *being conscious* and someone's being conscious of that experience ("state" versus "creature consciousness"). Dretske's challenge requires that there is a kind of consciousness devoid of any conceptual articulation. I argue that Dretske's makes no persuasive case for this sort of consciousness while the opposing thesis is intrinsically plausible. Thus, HOT theories can accommodate what is right in Dretske's attack within their own account of consciousness.

Seager, William. Ground Truth and Virtual Reality: Hacking vs van Fraassen. *Phil Sci*, 62(3), 459-478, S 95.

Hacking argues against van Fraassen's *constructive empiricism* by appeal to features of microscopic imaging. Hacking relies on both our practices involving imaging instruments and the structure of the images produced by these micropractices. Van Fraassen's reply is formally correct yet fundamentally unsatisfying. I aim to strengthen van Fraassen's reply, but must then extend constructive empiricism, specifically the central notion of "theoretical immersion." I argue that immersion is more analogous to entering a virtual reality than to learning a language. This metaphor assimilates instrument-based practice as well as theoretical debate and explanation, and can provide an anti-realist view of our micro-practices consonant with constructive empiricism.

Searle, John R. "Consciousness, Explanatory Inversion, & Cognitive Science" in *Philosophy of Psychology: Debates on Psychological Explanation, Macdonald, Cynthia (ed)*, 331-355. Cambridge, Blackwell, 1995.

Searle, John R. Consciousness, the Brain and the Connection Principle: A Reply. *Phil Phenomenol Res*, 55(1), 217-232, Mr 95.

Searle, John R. The Connection Principle and the Ontology of the Unconscious: A Reply to Fodor and Lepore. *Phil Phenomenol Res*, 54(4), 847-855, D 94.

Sebeok, Thomas A. "Indexicality" in *Peirce and Contemporary Thought: Philosophical Inquiries, Ketner, Kenneth Laine (ed)*, 222-242. New York, Fordham Univ Pr, 1995.

Secretan, Philibert. Tentations et tentatives hégéliennes. *Frei Z Phil Theol*, 41(1-2), 252-258, 1994.

Secrétan, Philibert. "Individuum, Individualität und Individuation nach Edith Stein und Wilhelm Dilthey" in *Studien zur Philosophie von Edith Stein, Fetz, Reto Luzius (ed)*, 148-169. Freiburg, Alber, 1993.

Sedghi, Darjosh. "Dopplung als Leugnung: Zur Theorie von Robert J Lifton" in *Nationalsozialismus und Moderne, Welzer, Harald (ed)*, 184-207. Tübingen, Ed Diskord, 1993.

Sedgwick, Peter R (ed). *Nietzsche: A Critical Reader*. Cambridge, Blackwell, 1995.

This volume collects together key readings from the Anglo-American, German and American traditions of Nietzsche interpretation. In doing so it seeks to provide a guide to central aspects of Nietzsche's influence as they have been addressed within these scholarly traditions. The book's aim is thus to present a critical appreciation of both the interpretative divergences and similarities which exist within these traditions. The editor's Introduction to the volume assists in the reader gaining an understanding of this by specificly addressing the question of these different approaches to Nietzsche's work.

Sedley, David. Commentary on Mansfeld's "The Idea of the Will in Chrysippus, Posidonius, and Galen". *Proc Boston Colloq Anc Phil*, 7, 146-157, 1991.

Seedhouse, David. The Trouble with Well-Being: A Response to "Mild Mania and Well-Being". *Phil Psychiat Psych*, 1(3), 185-191, S 94.

Moore, Hope and Fulford have argued that the study of theories of well-being may help to make clinicians more sensitive to patients' perspectives. This claim is disputed, and it is further argued that no theory of well-being can give definitive, nonpaternalistic guidance to clinicians who seek to assist third parties. A theory of health, not well-being, is required. One such theory is briefly summarized and is applied to offer a solution to the apparently perplexing "case of Mr M."

Seel, Martin. Fotografien sind wie Namen. *Deut Z Phil*, 43(3), 465-478, 1995.

Die Betrachtung gilt dem kognitiven Status fotografischer Bilder. Die leitende Frage lautet, ob es einen Wirklichkeitsbezug gibt, der Fotos als Fotos zukommt und der sie möglicherweise von allen anderen Bildmedien unterscheidet. Die Antwort lautet, dass es diese besondere Referenz fotografischer Bilder tatsächlich gibt. Fotografien benennen momentane Dingkonfigurationen, die in allen bezeichnenden Verwendungsweisen mitpräsentiert beliben.

Segal, Lynne. Hiding Out or Moving On?. *Rad Phil*, 68, 1-2, Autumn 94.

Segerberg, Krister and Rabinowicz, Wlodek. Actual Truth, Possible Knowledge. *Topoi*, 13(2), 101-115, S 94.

D Edgington has suggested that Fitch's paradox of verificationism can be avoided if we formulate verificationism using the actuality operator: $A\theta \rightarrow \Diamond KA\theta$. However, as long as actuality and knowledge are interpreted in terms of a fixed actual world and an epistemic accessibility relation between worlds, respectively, this proposal still yields an absurd conclusion that all actual truths are known. To avoid this problem, we develop a two-dimensional semantics, in which each formula is evaluated at a world with respect to another world chosen as a perspective. The knowledge operator is then interpreted in terms of an accessibility relation between pairs of worlds, modeling two sources of epistemic uncertainty: one concerning the world being described and the other the world constituting the perspective.

Segerdahl, Pär. Critique of Pure Capacity. *Phil Invest*, 17(3), 507-535, Jl 94.

A common reaction to a philosophical problem is to suggest a theory. This work investigates one such theory, John R Searle's hypothesis about 'the Background', as an example or the theoretical approach to philosophical problems. The purport is not that Searle's hypothesis might be untenable in certain respects, nor that it is a fundamentally incorrect hypothesis: a number of problems about Searle's concept seem to arise simply because it is a hypothesis. What is being criticized is ultimately the theoretical approach itself: the very idea of constructing theories in philosophy.

Seguin, Eve. A Modest Reason. *Theor Cult Soc*, 11(3), 55-75, Ag 94.

Segura, Armando. *Identidad y Relación en Kant* Los Juicios Sintéticos a Priori como Principios. *Pensamiento*, 199(51), 43-68, Ja-Ap 95.

Desde el principio de la Crítica, Kant se sitúa en el centro de gravedad de toda filosofía: la aporética cuestión de la Identidad y la Diferencia. El juicio establece, en la medida en que sea juicio, la diferencia del sujeto respecto del predicado, esa diferencia, implicada inmanentemente en el sujeto, obliga a Kant, si quiere fundamentar la experiencia científica, a elaborar una nueva lógica—la lógica trascendental—en la que el predicado sea de experiencia. Se produce la ruptura de la lógica racionalista. Emerge una nueva lógica. El principio de identidad, es sustituido por el principio de relación.

Segura, Carmen. El ser de la verdad en la *Metafísica* de Aristóteles. *Topicos*, 4(6), 89-115, 1994.

Taking as its starting point the Aristotelian consideration of the *different senses of being*, this paper concentrates on being as true (*ens ut verum*) analyzing and commenting on the text of *Metaphysics* in which this concept appears, in order to delimit, as far as possible, its authentic meaning and to resolve the apparent contradictions that may be observed in these texts. The analysis is made using the commentaries by St Thomas Aquinas. The conclusions reached are that *being as true* is properly one of the *senses of being* that must not be mistaken with *ontological truth*. It is also determined in this article in what *being as truth* consists, and there is a final remark on the essence of the truth of the simple.

Segura Peraita, Carmen. La Formación del Juicio en Santo Tomás de Aquino. *Rev Espan Filosof Med*, 0, 193-199, 1993.

Seidel, Bradley. Critical Concept of Nothing. *Ideal Stud*, 24(3), 255-268, Fall 94.

Kant's "Table of the Concept of Nothing", given in the last section of the Transcendental Analytic of the *First Critique*, is discussed. When nothing rather than something is taken as the object of consciousness, it must be taken problematically as a noumenon. On this basis, the "Table of Concepts of Nothing" is filled out as to all twelve categories, and the necessity of the noumenon to the system of critical philosophy is demonstrated.

Seidel, George J. A Key to Heidegger's *Beiträge*. *Gregorianum*, 76(2), 363-372, 1995.

The article suggests a different reading of Martin Heidegger's 1936-1938 work entitled *Beiträge zur Philosophie* subtitled: *Vom Ereignis* (Contributions to Philosophy: Concerning the Event), published as volume 65 in the collected edition of his works. Recent books and articles on the work have tended to interpret it in the light of the political and personal events in Heidegger's life at the time, or in terms of his overall philosophical concerns. The author suggests that this strange work should be read as containing Heidegger's Christology. The article then goes on the describe the sort of Christology represented and the problems associated with a Christology of any sort in Heidegger.

Seidel, George J. Minded Body/Embodied Mind. *Man World*, 27(4), 399-413, O 94.

Seidenfeld, Teddy and Herron, Timothy and Wasserman, Larry. The Extent of Dilation of Sets of Probabilities and the Asymptotics of Robust Bayesian Inference. *Proc Phil Sci Ass*, 1, 250-259, 1994.

We experience the phenomenon of dilation, where updating using sets of Bayesian conditional probabilities always causes the upper (and lower) probability of an event to increase (and decrease), thereby causing more uncertainty with regards to the event's truth. First, we contrast short-run dilation with standard long-run convergence of opinion results. Second, we note when dilation occurs and how dilation is connected to the independence of the conditioned and conditioning events. Third, we use sets of probabilities and asymptotic (increasing sample size) dilation to provide an interpretation of the difference between standard Neyman-Pearson hypothesis testing and Harold Jeffrey's Bayesian hypothesis testing.

Seidl, Horst. *Beiträge zu Aristoteles' Naturphilosophie*. Amsterdam, Rodopi, 1995.

Seidler, Leopold G and Kolek, Leszek S. Rotarians in a Changing World. *Dialogue Hum*, 4(2-3), 167-176, 1994.

Seidman, Steven. *Contested Knowledge: Social Theory in the Postmodern Era*. Cambridge, Blackwell, 1994.

Seiferas, Joel I and Meyer, Albert R. Characterization of Realizable Space Complexities. *Annals Pure Applied Log*, 73(2), 171-190, Je 95.

Seifert, Colleen M (& others). "Demystification of Cognitive Insight" in *The Nature of Insight, Sternberg, Robert J (ed)*, 65-124. Cambridge, MIT Pr, 1995.

Seifert, Josef. Qué es filosofía? La respuesta de la fenomenología realista. *Anu Filosof*, 28(1), 91-108, 1995.

What is philosophy? This question (in this case, a philosophical question) deals with the problem of philosophy as a science. The philosophy origin is the 'admiration at universal'. Husserl's phenomenology wants to resolve this question searching an 'a priori' sintetic. This is not the Kantian answer, nor a subjective answer. It is a new consideration of experience as the author wants to show.

Seifert, Josef. Was ist Philosophie? Die Antwort der realistischen Phänomenologie. *Z Phil Forsch*, 49(1), 92-103, Ja-Mr 95.

Phenomenological realism has shown that the philosophical method is grounded in a peculiar nature of the objects of philosophical knowledge: highly intelligible and essentially necessary essences and states of affairs grounded in them. Adolf Reinach and particularly Dietrich von Hildebrand have developed this notion. It requires a special type of necessary essences, which are clearly distinct from contingent such-being unities. The intrinsic and absolute necessity of essences proves that they are totally independent from any human subjectivity. Another cornerstone of realist phenomenology is the rediscovery of real existence in its radical distinction from essence. This development is continued today at the International Academy of Philosophy in the Principality of Liechtenstein.

Seifert, Joseph and Smith, Barry. "The Truth about Fiction" in *Kunst und Ontologie, Wlodzimierz, Galewicz (ed)*, 97-118. Amsterdam, Rodopi, 1994.

The paper undertakes the attempt to unfold an important contribution Roman Ingarden made to the theory of the literary work of art and to uncover a deficiency contained in his theory. Apart from the stratification of the literary work of art, Ingarden discovers a special logical entity which he calls the quasi-judgment. He shows that this type of logical entity is not truly a judgment, it does not affirm a state of affairs that would be asserted as independently existing but rather builds up the fiction-world. It makes only an "as if" claim to truth. Therefore the meaning units expressed in such quasi-judgments cannot be true or false. While the authors agree fully with this signification discovery of Ingarden, they seek to show that Ingarden's thesis is mistaken. (edited)

Seigfried, Charlene Haddock. "Devising Ends Worth Striving For: William James and the Reconstruction of Philosophy" in *Recovering Pragmatism's Voice, Langsdorf, Lenore (ed)*, 115-128. Albany, SUNY Pr, 1995.

This essay explores how pragmatists justify their claims after denying that one can just look and see how things are. In appealing to experience instead of reality, they also bring out its ambiguous status as both objectively undergone and shared and subjectively apprehended through perspectival interpretations and valuations. Rather than denying either aspect, pragmatists determine objectivity by focusing on beliefs as rules of action and inquire into what distinguishes satisfactory from unsatisfactory beliefs or assertions. Using William James's model of knowing as it exists concretely, I develop the claim that only through recognizing and evaluating the purposes that structure beliefs can they become rationally justified.

Seigfried, Hans. Art as Fetish in Nietzsche and Heidegger?. *Int Stud Phil*, 27(3), 95-103, 1995.

I dismiss inflated postmodern expectations about the magical role that the arts should play in the management of human affairs under the conditions of advanced technology. I argue that we can avoid metaphysical entrapment only by maintaining our "artists' sovereignty" and coming to realize that the order and beauty we bring out in the world, and on which our lives depend, are strictly functions of the sophisticated design of our research programs and experimental promptings. And I show that we can survive our demanding modern technology only by cultivating our "artist' piousness" and accepting nature's answers and respecting its resistances to our promptings. Consequently, nothing is worth more today than art in the broadest and profoundest sense.

Seiler, Martin. "Epistemologie, Sprachanalyse und Semiotik bei H Gomperz" in *Heinrich Gomperz, Karl Popper und die österreichische Philosophie, Seiler, Martin (ed)*, 31-46. Amsterdam; Rodopi, 1994.

Seiler, Martin (ed) and Stadler, Friedrich (ed). *Heinrich Gomperz, Karl Popper und die österreichische Philosophie*. Amsterdam, Rodopi, 1994.

Seitter, Walter. "Das Denken des Politischen in der mittelalterlichen Epik und in der modernen Forschung" in *Das geistige Erbe Europas, Buhr, Manfred (ed)*, 300-308. Napoli, Vivarium, 1994.

In post-war-age there were different approaches regarding the medieval epic poetry in the German countries. In West Germany the mainstream-approach historized and depolitized the epic texts as pure literature. In East Germany on the contrary the scholars included their hostility to "feudalism" into their interpretations. Only in the last decades some women scholars in Austria and in West Germany began to uncover the political and critical sense in the medieval texts. The author is referring to his three works "Das politische Wissen im Nibelungenlied" (Berlin 1987), "Versprechen, versagen" (Berlin 1990), "Distante Siegfried-Paraphrasen" (Berlin 1993).

Seitter, Walter (ed) and Ruhs, August (ed). *Auflösen, Untersuchen, Aufwecken: Psychoanalyse und andere Analysen*. Vienna, Passagen, 1995.

Die Themenstellung des Sammelbandes ergibt sich aus der logischen Analyse des Wortes "Psychoanalyse", die nahelegt, dass die Psychoanalyse eine besondere Art von Analyse—neben anderen—ist, welch es etwa in den Naturwissenschaften, in der Mathematik, in der Philosophie, vielleicht in der Kunst gibt. Einige der verschiedenen Analysen—sozusagen entfernte Kollegen—werden miteinander konfrontiert und es stellt sich heraus, dass es zwischen ihnen auch Einflüsse und Gemeinsamkeitien gibt. Die wichtigste Gemeinsamkeit ist vielleicht die, dass Analysen Erkenntnis-Aktionen sind (sein können), die das Erkannte (und vielleicht sogar das Erkennende) nicht unverändert lassen.

Seitz, Brian. *The Trace of Political Representation*. Albany, SUNY Pr, 1995.

Seitz, Steven Thomas. Apollo's Oracle: Strategizing for Peace. *Synthese*, 100(3), 461-495, S 94.

This paper examines the role of power structures and strategic decisions in trajectories toward war and peace. Part I introduces a fuzzy inference engine for computationally simulating "balance of power". Part II compares simulation results from hegemonic, bi-polar, and multi-polar system structures, each with three actors. Part III explores strategies for maximizing peace under each of these system structures. Part IV applies these lessons to real-world event chronologies.

Self, Donnie J and Sanchez, J Martin. Gender Bias and Moral Decision Making: The Moral Orientations of Justice and Care. *J Med Human*, 16(1), 39-53, Spr 95.

This study investigated gender related moral reasoning in student essays containing arguments on moral issues. Undergraduate students in a medical ethics course viewed two films on morally controversial issues. The students wrote brief essays about the films on morally controversial issues. The students wrote brief essays about the films which were transcribed and numerically coded to conceal the author's gender from the evaluator. Using a coding scheme originated by Lyons, the evaluator classified each essay as a justice/right essay or a care/response essay or an equal response essay. Subsequently, calculations were made to determine the percentage of male authored essays that were justice/rights essays or care/response essays and the percentage of female authored essays that were justice/rights or care/response essays. The males (87.7%) tended to exhibit the justice/rights moral orientation, and the females (69.4%) exhibited the care/response moral orientation. (edited)

Seligman, David B. A Threat or a Promise. *S J Phil*, 33(1), 83-96, Spr 95.

Promising is a more complex linguistic and social undertaking than has been recognized by Searle, Ardahl, Downie and others. Misled by the apparent symmetry between threats and promises, some have been inclined to view threats as "unwelcome promises," and to see them both as creating similar moral commitments. As a consequence it has been difficult to explain how those commitments could be sustained or defeated under various conditions. By contrasting threats and promises, we are able to sort out three types of obligations incurred in promising—nonmoral or *institutional obligations*, external or *weak moral obligations*, and internal or *strong moral obligations*—and to explicate the conditions that sustain or defeat each of them. We may then void the temptation to view promissory obligations as somehow preeminent or foundational among obligations and come to understand the relationship of the moral dimensions of promising to intended benefit and potential harm, and thus to be no different from the bulk of our moral obligations.

Sellmann, James D. A Belated Response to Hu Shih and D T Suzuki. *Phil East West*, 45(1), 97-104, Ja 95.

In this review I reopen the discussion between Hu Shih and D T Suzuki to show that their respective positions have serious shortcomings. I propose the Hu and Suzuki equivocate on the meaning of Ch'an/Zen. I argue that Zen is not irrational but irrational, and yet one can give a rational description of it. I distinguish living history from the academic study of historiography to show that Suzuki's criticism of Hu is incorrect. Finally, I agree with Suzuki's criticism that Hu has mistranslated *chih* as "knowledge" when it means "*prajña-intuition*."

Sells, Michael. Emanation and Mysticism in the Writings of Meister Eckhart. *Listening*, 29(3), 174-185, Fall 94.

This article locates Eckhart's mystical concepts (birth-of-the-son-in-the-soul, the self-birth of the deity, and the breakthrough to the ground of being) in the emanation paradigm. It is also in the emanation paradox (that the procession is the return) that Eckhart achieves the most radical apophatic language. At issue is the transformation of "in-the-soul" from the notion of locus and receptacle to the principal notion of "in" established in Eckhart's Latin works. The article builds upon the analysis of Eckhart in M Sells, *Mystical Languages of Unsaying* (University of Chicago Press, 1994).

Selting, Margret. Emphatic Speech Style—With Special Focus on the Prosodic Signalling of Heightened Emotive Involvement in Conversation. *J Prag*, 22(3-4), 375-408, O 94.

After a review of previous work on the prosody of emotional involvement, data extracts from natural conversations are analyzed in order to argue for the constitution of an 'emphatic (speech) style', which linguistic devices are used to signal heightened emotive involvement. Participants use prosodic cues, in co-occurrence with syntactic and lexical cues, to contextualize turn-constructional units as 'emphatic'. Only realizations of prosodic categories that are marked in relation to surrounding uses of these categories have the power to contextualize units as displaying 'more-than-normal involvement'. In the appropriate context, and in co-occurrence with syntactic and lexical cues and sequential position, the context-sensitive interpretation of this involvement is 'emphasis'. (edited)

Semane, Tatjana. The Image of Wisdom and the Wise Man in the History of European Philosophy. *Hist Euro Ideas*, 20(4-6), 969-972, F 95.

Sen, Amartya. Entrevista con Amartya Sen. *Telos (Spain)*, 3(2), 127-132, D 94.

Sen, Amit Kumar. Nyaya Inference-Deductive-Inductive Pattern. *Indian Phil Quart*, 21(2), 179-183, Ap 94.

On the one hand, the Nyaya valid inference is deductive because its premises and conclusion always stand in the relationship of entailment, though it does not have to do with abstract relation among terms, and the assessment of the validity of it is not a matter comparing it with abstract models to see if it instantiates one of the valid forms of inference. On the other hand, a Nyaya valid inference is inductive because it seeks material truth of the conclusion by introducing Udaharana Vakya as one of the premises which is established by inductive methods and the assessment of validity of it is a matter of trying to detect errors in the adducing of evidence for the constituent judgment.

Sena, Marylou. Dionysos as Antidote: The Veils of Maya. *Res Phenomenol*, 24, 189-205, 1994.

Senanayake, Ranil. "The Religious and Ethical Tradition of Ancient and Contemporary Australia" in *Ethics, Religion and Biodiversity, Hamilton, Lawrence S (ed)*, 98-117. Cambridge, White Horse, 1994.

Sencerz, Stefan. Personal Goodness and Moral Facts. *J Phil Res*, 20, 481-498, 1995.

Peter Railton argues that *normative* realism is justified because the *non-moral goodness* of an individual has explanatory uses. After having equated *moral rightness* with a kind of impersonal social rationality, he argues that rightness, so defined, helps to explain various social phenomena. If he is right, then *moral* realism would be justified, too. Railton's argument fails, however, on both counts. Several crucial steps in his reasoning are unsupported and are likely to be false. The explanations he proposes may be dismissed in favor of better explanations that do not use any normative or moral terms. Some of us may share Railton's moral standards. There is no reason, however, to embrace his metaethical position as well. His arguments do not support either normative or moral facts.

Seneca, L Annaeus and Brok, M F A (ed & trans). *Naturwissenschaftliche Untersuchungen*. Darmstadt, Wiss Buchgesell, 1995.

Sengel, Deniz (trans) and Stastny, Peter (trans) and Foucault, Michel. Madness, the Absence of Work. *Crit Inquiry*, 21(2), 290-298, Wint 95.

Senghor, Leopold S. "On Negrohood: Psychology of the African Negro" in *African Philosophy: Selected Readings, Mosley, Albert G (ed)*, 116-127. Englewood Cliffs, Prentice Hall, 1995.

Sennett, James F. Is God Essentially God?. *Relig Stud*, 30(3), 295-303, S 94.

In this paper I argue that there may be properties essential to Godhood, but not essential to the being that is God (call it 'Yahweh'). I first consider the claim that the greatness of a being in a given world is dependent on the properties it bears in other worlds, and argue that his claim is false. Next I consider the claim that Yahweh does not bear his Godhood adventitiously or accidentally. I agree with this claim, but argue that it is not equivalent to the claim that Yahweh bears his Godhood *contingently*—the position whose cogency I defend here.

Sennett, James F. *Modality, Probability, and Rationality*. New York, Lang, 1992.

This work examines several major projects in Plantinga's career, particularly as they relate to his defense of the rationality of theistic belief. Chapters are dedicated to his modal ontological argument, his free will defense, his attacks on inductive arguments from evil, and his "Reformed epistemology" program, in which he argues that theistic belief can be rational without reliance on propositional evidence. Along the way the book deals with important issues in possible worlds semantics, probability theory, and the theory of knowledge, demonstrating the richness and provocativeness of Plantinga's philosophical endeavors.

Senofonte, Ciro. Arnauld et Malebranche. *Rev Int Phil*, 48(190), 441-461, 1994.

Sepp, Hans-Rainer. Teleogía y ética en la obra tardía de Edmund Husserl. *Anu Filosof*, 28(1), 19-39, 1995.

In his later writings, Husserl treats ethics as discipline wherein he transforms it step by step and connects it with a teleological concept. In this process the ethical enquiry into the strivings of the 'Vernuft' get integrated into metaphysics. This metaphysics is an ontological teleology to be founded on a transcendental phenomenology which thematizes the absolute factity of the transcendental subject.

Serrano, Agustín. Actos básicos y actos fundados. *Anu Filosof*, 28(1), 61-89, 1995.

Phenomenology is supposed to provide an intrinsic account of the possible types of conscious acts and of their relationship to each other. Husserl's enduring frame on this subject rests on the distinction between "objectifying acts" (representations) and "non-objectifying acts" (emotions and volitions). But the sense of the dependence of every act on representations, suffered a deep change from *Logical Investigations* (intentional reference of non-objectifying act proceeds completely from cognitive reference) to *Ideas* (the peculiar emotional reference to values needs preferably a doxic-objectifying modality). Both theories remain, in the end, problematic.

Serrano, Manuel G. Racionalidad Común. *Analogia*, 7(2), 39-71, 1993.

Serrano, Vicente. Las Tres Reseñas de Fichte del Otoño de 1793. *An Seminar Hist Filosof*, 11, 171-187, 1994.

El artículo aborda la evolución de Fichte a lo largo del año 1793, y en particular se enfrenta a la clásica consideración de la *Reseña de Enesidemo* como momento de ruptura con Reinhold y punto de partido de la *WL*. Se afirma en este sentido que la distancia frente a Reinhold estaba ya dada en la lectura práctica que Fichte hace de Kant, encontrando ésta una primera manifestación en la 2ª edición del VeKaO, respecto de la que muestran una perfecta continuidad todos los escritos del 93. A la luz de todo ello, la lectura de *Enesidemo* no habría sido el detonante del descubrimiento de la *WL*, sino más bien el pretexto para elevar a un nivel sistemático y fundamental las ideas ya elaboradas por Fichte, lo que se traduce en la afirmación de un primer principio alternativo.

Serrano de Haro, Agustín. Recepción de *La Verdad y el Tiempo*. *Rev Filosof (Spain)*, 7(12), 523-529, 1994.

Serres, Michel (ed). *A History of Scientific Thought: Elements of a History of Science*. Cambridge, Blackwell, 1995.

Sesé Sanz, Juan Carlos. La Tradición de los Disticha Catonis, Entre la Auctoritas Medieval y la Renovatio Humanística. *Rev Espan Filosof Med*, 0, 201-211, 1993.

La finalidad del presente estudio es apreciar en qué medida una tradición literaria que permanece desde la latinidad tardía hasta el Renacimiento es tributaria de cada época.

Sethi, S Prakash. Imperfect Markets: Business Ethics as an Easy Virtue. *J Bus Ethics*, 13(10), 803-815, O 94.

This paper marks a radical diversion from the large body of prevailing literature in business ethics which primarily views the issue in individual-personal terms. While this approach has strong intellectual roots in moral philosophy and religion, it fails in explaining the persistence of unethical and illegal behavior among corporations of all sizes, financial health, competitive market conditions, and, level of individual executive compensation. This paper argues for a fundamentally different approach to understanding ethical behavior, or lack thereof, among corporations and their executives. It is only under conditions of imperfect markets that individual executives can play an important role in guiding their corporations toward greater ethical norms. (edited)

Sève, Lucien. "Bioethik und Geld: Kommt ein Europa der Werte?" in *Das geistige Erbe Europas, Buhr, Manfred (ed)*, 695-705. Napoli, Vivarium, 1994.

Les logiques financières envahissent aujourd'hui la recherche biomédicale (refus de payer le coût de l'éthique, accélération aveugle de l'innovation, subordination des fins aux moyens). Au souci kantien de la dignité de l'homme s'oppose partout la frénésie utilitariste de la rentabilité. Le débat est vif et les législations sont contradictoires selon les pays sur des questions comme la vénalité ou non du corps humain, la brevetabilité ou non des gènes. Une "Europe des valeurs" ne doit-elle pas réaffirmer le primat éthique de la personne sur la chose et rétablir la subordination des moyens financiers aux finalités sanitaires démocratiquement évaluées?

Sevilla, José M. De la crisis de la racionalidad a la racionalidad de la crisis: Una nota sobre G Vico. *Rev Filosof (Daimon)*, 7, 157-168, 1993.

This paper intends to sketch a few guidelines in order to understand modernity within its problematic and critical framework, the starting point of which seemed to contain already the rationality's of the original crisis' elements. In this very crisis there are some aspects which, embodied in Vico's ideals, might eventually allow us to think again in *vichian* terms the own modernity's challenging condition as a post-cursory-modern condition from the contemporary rationality's view which has come about from the crisis; an issue which has proven to be crucial in current discussions.

Sevilla, José M. En Torno al *Postcursorismo* Viquiano de la Modernidad Problemática. *Cuad Vico*, 4, 53-72, 1994.

Vico allows us to *re-think* the *problematic* condition of the very modernity when regarded it as a condition of "verosimile" (likely) and consequently how we may arrange Vichian elements in order to offer a wilder and manifold view of this very modernity. We try to supply in this way another element to understand modernity in its *problematic background*, seeing also within it how soon we can observe the elements of the *crises of racionality*: a dimension in which there are some aspects which, embodied in Vico's ideas, allow us in Viquian terms and from the stand point of the racionality springing out of the crisis, that very same *problematic condition of modernity* in this "postcursor" modern attitude (Vico "postcursor" and "postcursive").

Sevilla, José M. Universales Poéticos, Fantasía y Racionalidad. *Cuad Vico*, 3, 67-113, 1993.

Vico confers on 'fantasia' a double rôle: creating and expressing (historical dimension—*modifications of the human mind*) and recognizing and reconstructing (epistemological dimension-human faculty), which has its Vichian significance in the 'poetic characters' (*universali fantastici*) and in the consideration of the 'poetic nature' of primitive man, and furthermore, in a second sense, in the characteristics that imagination possesses as a 'Key' to the *Scienza nuova* itself. Concrete aspects of this question have been already developed by the author in earlier published works, emphasizing its importance as much for Vichian thought as for the Human Sciences. In this present work the question of 'fantasia' is considered, bringing together the most interesting perspectives through which this topic has been re-evaluated, especially those of the three significant scholars and Vico interpreters: D P Verene, I Berlin and E Grassi.

Sevilla, José M. Vico en Italia y en USA. *Cuad Vico*, 4, 173-184, 1994.

Sevilla Fernández, José M. Bibliografía Viquiana en Español. *Cuad Vico*, 1, 179-196, 1991.

The bibliography of Vico in Spanish, elaborated upon the basis of previous contributions of the Author and highly increased with new evidences that have been brought forward, appears as a useful tool for the specialist on Vico. The bibliographic index (catalogue of 266 entries) constitutes the basis to elaborate continuously a wide investigation directed to the critical commentary of the works and to the realization of a compiling activity, opening for which a call from the pages of this contribution is made.

Sevilla Fernández, José M. Consolación Mediante la Historia: Cuatro *visiones* de la Historia Universal. *Cuad Vico*, 2, 207-212, 1992.

An historical-bibliographical study and critical survey of Ferrater Mora's Vico's review focused on the "renaissancing" vision on history which Ferrater Mora claims for Vico.

Sevilla Fernández, José M. Giambattista Vico en la Cultura Española: Estudio y Tratamiento en la Década de los Ochenta. *Cuad Vico*, 2, 89-170, 1992.

This historiographic study and critical review, following those two previous ("La presencia de G Vico en la cultura española. 1) Notas sobre su tratamiento y estudio en los siglos XVIII y XIX" y "2) Notas sobre su tratamiento y estudio durante el siglo XX hasta la década de los 70"; both in *Cuadernos sobre Vico*, 1, 1991, pp. 11-42 and 97-132), attends to the studies and publications of Vico's work in Spanish from 1980 to 1991.

Sevilla Fernández, José M. La Presencia de Giambattista Vico en la Cultura Española (I). *Cuad Vico*, 1, 11-42, 1991.

It has been frequently admitted that there was a lack of references to Vico in the Spanish culture. Even though, this prejudgment is cleared by means of a double viewpoint study—historiographic and critical outline—therefore, Vico's presence is registered throughout two and a half centuries; from 1735 with Luzán to our time. A historiographical study about the way in which Vico's ideas have gone into the Spanish culture and have developed and envolved is achieved by means of a simple scheme: contact stage, introduction-diffusion stage, and stage of study. Coherently the study is presented divided in two essential parts (also separated in its edition): 1) The treatment in the XVIII and XIX Centuries; and 2) The study in the XX Century to the beginning of '80. Therefore, it constitutes a reasonable review of texts and a denoted critical apparatus in the marginal notes with a dense information.

Sevilla Fernández, José M. La Presencia de Giambattista Vico en la Cultura Española (II). *Cuad Vico*, 1, 97-132, 1991.

Sevilla Fernández, José M. Verdad Acrítica y Verdad Crítica: Viquianismo Diádico. *Cuad Vico*, 2, 213-228, 1992.

A critical discussion of Vico's "diadic" interpretation. The author purports this kind of reading as a new assessment of the classical Catholic line of interpretation (F Amerio, L Bellofiore, etc.), normally opposing the immanent one (B Groce). The author uses two Spanish monographies which both agree precisely with this very own "diadic" and transcendentalist interpretation: that of Juan Cruz Cruz's (*Hombre e Historia en Vico*) and Montserrat Negre Rigol's (*Poiésis y Verdad en G Vico*).

Sextus Empiricus and Barnes, Jonathan (trans) and Annas, Julia (trans). *Outlines of Scepticism*. New York, Cambridge Univ Pr, 1994.

Sfendoni-Mentzou, Demetra. "A Response to Savan" in *Peirce and Contemporary Thought: Philosophical Inquiries, Ketner, Kenneth Laine (ed)*, 329-337. New York, Fordham Univ Pr, 1995.

The purpose of this paper is to suggest another key, than the one chosen by D Savan, for the resolution of the problem of idealism/realism in Peirce. Thus, the position put forward is that there is a peculiar type of idealism in Peirce's philosophy—namely 'pragmatistic idealism'—which should not be viewed in opposition to this realism, since it is not an expression of the identity of reality with thought. On the contrary, the claim of this paper is that both realism and idealism can be combined into an integral whole, since both are grounded on the Aristotelean idea of potentiality.

Shafer, Ingrid H. From the Senses to Sense: The Hermeneutics of Love. *Zygon*, 29(4), 579-602, D 94.

Drawing on philosophy, theology, comparative religion, spirituality, Holocaust studies, physics, biology, psychology, and personal experience, I argue that continued human existence depends on our willingness to reject nihilism—not as an expedient "noble lie" but because faith in a meaningful cosmos and the power of love is at least as validly grounded in human experience as insistence on cosmic indifference and ultimate futility. I maintain that hope will free us to develop nonimperialistic methods of bridging cultural differences by forming a mutually intelligible vocabulary that celebrates diversity, enters the worlds of others in respectful dialogue, and fosters a postmechanistic, organic, ecological, holistic, dynamic, interactive, open-ended model of reality. I lay the foundation for a "hermeneutics of love" to complement Paul Ricoeur's "hermeneutics of suspicion" and invite speculation on the ways science, technology, and society would be transformed if those "glasses of friendship" were widely applied.

Shafer-Landau, Russ. Supervenience and Moral Realism. *Ratio*, 7(2), 145-152, D 94.

Simon Blackburn has developed an interesting challenge to moral realism based on its alleged inability to account for supervenience relations between the moral and nonmoral. I offer three responses on behalf of the moral realist. The first rejects the need for explanation, arguing that supervenience should be understood as closely analogous to Leibniz's law, which, I argue, needs no defense. I next argue that ethical naturalism may be right, and if so, would provide an adequate response to Blackburn. Lastly, I show that the success of Blackburn's arguments implies a global antirealism, and so does not, as he claims, amount to a special problem for realism in ethics. (edited)

Shafer-Landau, Russ. Vagueness, Borderline Cases and Moral Realism. *Amer Phil Quart*, 32(1), 83-96, Ja 95.

Vague properties are those that generate borderline cases. Most metaphysicians, and many ethicists, have thought that real properties must have precisely determinate extensions. This has led philosophers to one of two conclusions: i) realism is true, and therefore all borderline moral cases are resolvable, or ii) some borderline cases are irresolvable, and hence the implicated properties cannot be construed realistically. By analyzing the sources of moral vagueness, I try to show that both alternatives are mistaken. Vague moral properties can have a place in a realistic ontology. The existence of irresolvable borderline cases in ethics is compatible with moral realism.

Shafiquil Alam, M. Bentham's Social and Political Thoughts: A Brief Account. *Indian Phil Quart*, 22/1(Supp), 5-15, Ja 95.

The purpose of the work is to show Bentham's contribution in the field of social and political thoughts for modernizing Britain. Through his great ethical principle "the greatest happiness for the greatest number" he devoted to the production of a complete, rational code of law for a state engaged in promoting the general happiness. He predominantly worked for reforms and a more humanitarian standard of jurisprudence. Bentham is the founder of British utilitarianism and the recognized leader of the "Philosophical radicals" out of which British Liberal Party later developed. He applied his utility concept to legal, social, political and ethical spheres. In conclusion, it can be said that Bentham may be counted as one of the great teachers and permanent intellectual ornaments of the human race. Credit owes to him in diffusing utilitarian social thought and political ideas in nineteenth century Bengal.

AUTHOR INDEX WITH ABSTRACTS 737 Sharma, Jyotirmaya

Shalkowski, Scott A. Semantic Realism. *Rev Metaph*, 48(3), 511-538, Mr 95.

Semantic Realism is the combination of the semantic doctrine that statement meanings are truth conditions and the metaphysical doctrine that truth conditions are robust worldly structures. Four major theses are defended. First, a truth-conditional theory of meaning is compatible with a verificationist theory of linguistic competence. Second, a verificationist theory of understanding warrants truth conditional semantics. Third, metaphysics is prior to semantics in a way that foils Michael Dummett's attempt to re-cast traditional metaphysical disputes as disputes over a proper theory of meaning. Fourth, skeptical objections to robust truth conditions create equal problems for plausible verificationist alternatives.

Shalkowski, Scott A. The Ontological Ground of the Alethic Modality. *Phil Rev*, 103(4), 669-688, O 94.

This paper is concerned with the wholly metaphysical question of whether necessity and possibility rest on nonmodal foundations—whether the truth conditions for modal statements are, in the final analysis, nommodal. It is argued that Lewis's modal realism is either arbitrary and stipulative or else it is circular. Even if there were Lewisean possible worlds, they could not provide the grounds for modality. D M Armstrong's combinatorial approach to possibility suffers from similar defects. Since more traditional reductions to cognitive or linguistic facts suffer similar fates, the conclusion that the alethic modality is primitive and incapable of reduction is offered.

Shanker, Stuart. Turing and the Origins of AI. *Phil Math*, 3(1), 52-85, Ja 95.

Reading through *Mechanical Intelligence*, volume III of Alan Turing's *Collected Works*, one begins to appreciate just how propitious Turing's timing was. If Turing's major accomplishment in 'On Computable Numbers' was to expose the epistemological premises built into formalism, his main achievement in the 1940s was to recognize the extent to which this outlook both harmonized with and extended contemporary psychological thought. Turing sought to synthesize these diverse mathematical and psychological elements so as to forge a union between 'embodied rules' and 'learning programs'. Through their joint service in the Mechanist Thesis each would validate the other; and the frameworks from whence each derived. In this paper I will try to show how Turing's psychological thesis forces us to reassess the consequences of establishing AI on the epistemological foundation that underlies behaviorism.

Shanks, Andrew. *Civil Society, Civil Religion*. Cambridge, Blackwell, 1995.

Civil Society, Civil Religion is an attempt to pioneer an essentially new genre: a philosophically systematic form of "civil theology". That is, a study of history-as-revelation; but in relation to civil identities rather than confessional ones. The nearest precedent would be Hegel. The Hegelian system, however, remains a confessional one. And in the late twentieth century context the need is no longer, as in Hegel's day, for a civil religious sensibility tied to the interest of the secular state. The emergence—for the first time—of a coherently and pluralistically organized international civil society changes everything.

Shanks, Niall. Minds, Brains, and Quantum Mechanics. *S J Phil*, 33(2), 243-260, Sum 95.

The central concern of this essay is with the role of consciousness in orthodox accounts of quantum theory. von Neumann and others make consciousness play a special role in the account of the reduction of the wave packet, but they do so in a decidedly Cartesian spirit which physicalists find objectionable. I explore the possibility that consciousness may be given an appropriate physicalist analysis and explanation, and then explore its implications for quantum mechanics. I consider both reductive and non-reductive physicalist analyses of consciousness, and conclude that both physicalist strategies render quantum phenomena quite mysterious. The consciousness of the observer, introduced to enable orthodox quantum mechanics to evade measurement paradoxes, does not leave orthodox quantum mechanics paradox-free.

Shanks, Niall and LaFollette, Hugh. Chaos Theory: Analogical Reasoning in Biomedical Research. *Ideal Stud*, 24(3), 241-254, Fall 94.

In this article we discuss two divergent accounts of nonhuman animals an analog models of human biomedical phenomena. Using a classical account of analogical reasoning, toxicologists and teratologists claim that if the model and subject modeled are substantially similar, then test results in nonhuman animals are likely applicable to humans. However, the same toxicologists report that different species often react very differently to the same chemical stimuli. The best way to understand their findings is to abandon the classical view of analogical—i.e., linear—reasoning, and replace it with a version informed by chaos theory. We briefly outline the current understanding of chaos, and trace its implications for toxicology and teratology.

Shanks, Niall and LaFollette, Hugh. Two Models of Models in Biomedical Research. *Phil Quart*, 45(179), 141-160, Ap 95.

Most biomedical researchers construe animal models as *causal* models designed to uncover underlying mechanisms of biomedical phenomenon. There is a competing view of animal experimentation which, although not entrenched in biomedical theory, is alive and well in biomedical practice. On this view animal models are *heuristic devices*. Although these do not reveal causal mechanisms, they may prompt scientific inquiry which leads indirectly to biomedical discoveries. We argue that there are compelling theoretical, historical, and pragmatic reasons for construing animal experiments as heuristic divides rather than causal models.

Shanks, Niall and LaFollette, Hugh. Util-izing Animals. *J Applied Phil*, 12(1), 13-25, 1995.

Biomedical experimentation on animals is justified, researchers say, because of its enormous benefits to human beings. Sure, animals suffer and die, but that is morally insignificant since the benefits of research *incalculably* outweigh the evils. Although this utilitarian claim appears straightforward and relatively uncontroversial, it is neither straightforward nor uncontroversial. This defence of animal experimentation is likely to succeed only by rejecting three widely held moral presumptions. We identify these assumptions and explain their relevance to the justification of animal experimentation. We argue that, even if nonhuman animals have considerably less moral worth than humans, experimentation is justified only if the benefits are overwhelming. By building on and expanding on arguments offered in earlier papers, we show that researchers cannot substantiate their claims on behalf of animal research. We conclude that there is currently no acceptable utilitarian defence of animal experimentation. Moreover, it is unlikely that there could be one. Since most apologists of animal experimentation rely on utilitarian justifications of their practice, it appears that biomedical experimentation on animals is not morally justified.

Shanley, Mary L. Fathers' Rights, Mothers' Wrongs? Reflections on Unwed Fathers' Rights and Sex Equality. *Hypatia*, 10(1), 74-103, Wint 95.

This article examines arguments concerning the right of an unwed biological father to consent to the adoption of his offspring, and to take custody of the child even against the mother's wishes. The understanding of gender-neutrality that supposedly supports many such arguments is false, and risks diminishing women's decision-making authority under the guise of sex equality. Laws governing unwed parent's rights must emphasize the centrality of parental responsibility in establishing parental rights.

Shapere, Dudley. Kitcher on Advancing Science. *Phil Phenomenol Res*, 55(3), 647-651, S 95.

Shapiro, Daniel. Recent Work on Liberalism and Communitarianism. *Phil Books*, 36(3), 145-155, Jl 95.

I summarize common themes in the liberalism-communitarianism controversy, and discuss whether eight recent books have advanced that debate. The books are Daniel Bell, *Communitarianism and Its Critics*; Jack Crittenden, *Beyond Individualism*, Amitai Etzioni, *Antiliberalism*, Stephen Mulhall and Adam Swift, *Liberals and Communitarians*, J Donald Moon, *Constructing Community*, Margaret Moore, *The Foundations of Liberalism*, and Derek Phillips, *Looking Backwards*. I conclude that these books do advance our understanding of liberalism's view of the self and community, the possibility of liberal neutrality, and the political content of communitarianism.

Shapiro, Gary. "Art and its Doubles: Danto, Foucault, and their Simulacra" in *Danto and his Critics, Rollins, Mark (ed)*, 129-141. Cambridge, Blackwell, 1993.

I contrast Danto's and Foucault's understanding of Andy Warhol, who is perhaps the foundational artist for Danto's aesthetics. Danto, emphasizing the supposed singularity of Warhol's *Brillo Box* etc. sees him as showing that even this can be art; Foucault, stressing the indefinitely repeated nature of such images (boxes, Marilyns, etc.) argues that the multiplication of Simulacra empties the "original" image of its meaning.

Shapiro, Gary. Go Figure! Refiguring *Disfuguring*. *Phil Today*, 38(3-4), 326-333, Fall 94.

The essay explores the practice of de-centering in art and aesthetics by way of a reading of Mark Taylor's *Disfiguring*.

Shapiro, Joel B. Heidegger's Virtue is Knowledge: Being-With and Solicitude in Chapter 26 of *Being and Time*. *Phil Today*, 38(4), 400-418, Wint 94.

Heidegger argues that being-with is equiprimordial with being-in-the-world. This implies that being-with would have to be read alongside every structure analyzed in *Being and Time*, even though Heidegger himself failed to do this. Further, Heidegger not only shows that Dasein's understanding of itself determines its comportment toward others, but that its comportment also determines its understanding of itself and of being. Thus, Dasein's ontical affairs, its socio political practices, are conditions of the possibility of fundamental ontology. The intimate connection between disclosure and comportment, finally, suggests a link to Plato's notion that virtue is knowledge.

Shapiro, Lionel Stefan. 'Coordinative Definition' and Reichenbach's Semantic Framework: A Reassessment. *Erkenntnis*, 41(3), 287-323, N 94.

Focusing on his notion of 'coordinative definition', it is argued that Hans Reichenbach's *Philosophy of Space and Time* (1928) avoids most of the logical positivist pitfalls this book is nearly unanimously held to exemplify, notably both conventionalism and verificationism. While Reichenbach proposes a flawed reductionist interpretation of the relations that figure in theories of physical geometry, he retains here a thoroughly holistic understanding of empirical confirmation. Establishing this involves reexamining this notorious discussion of 'universal forces'. Some attention is paid to historical context (Schlick, Carnap, the evolution of Reichenbach's views).

Shapiro, Michael. "History as Theory: One Linguist's View" in *Peirce and Contemporary Thought: Philosophical Inquiries, Ketner, Kenneth Laine (ed)*, 304-311. New York, Fordham Univ Pr, 1995.

Shapiro, Stewart. Reasoning, Logic and Computation. *Phil Math*, 3(1), 31-51, Ja 95.

The idea that logic and reasoning are somehow related goes back to antiquity. It clearly underlies much of the work in logic, as witnessed by the development of computability, and formal and mechanical deductive systems, for example. On the other hand, a platitude is that logic is the study of correct reasoning; and reasoning is cognitive if anything is. Thus, the relationship between logic, computation, and correct reasoning makes an interesting and historically central case study for mechanism. The purpose of this article is to begin the articulation of this relationship pointing out its sources and its limitations.

Sharma, Arvind. A Reply to Anantanand Rambachan. *Phil East West*, 45(1), 105-113, Ja 95.

The paper further investigates the claim that, according to Sankara, the Vedas constitute the sole means of knowledge about *Brahman*.

Sharma, Arvind. *The Philosophy of Religion and Advaita Vedānta*: A Comparative Study in Religion and Reason. University Park, Penn St Univ Pr, 1995.

This book is an attempt to address the defining issues of the philosophy of religion as a field (e.g., arguments for and against the existence of God, theodicy, nature and religious language etc.) from the perspective of Advaita Vedānta.

Sharma, Jyotirmaya. The Philosophy of Nicolas Berdyaev. *Indian Phil Quart*, 21(4), 337-345, O 94.

Sharma, R S and Conrath, D W. The Post-Implementation Evaluation of Expert Systems: Enlightenment after Five Years in the Trenches. *Commun Cog—AI*, 11(3), 257-275, 1994.

We present a retrospective analysis of a five-year project on investigating methodologies for determining the quality of expert systems. More specifically, a multiple-criteria and multiple-stakeholder based subjective assessment technique is proposed as a sound and viable alternative to current practices. In short, the proposed approach elicits from users, developers and managers, their evaluations of an operational expert system along thirty-nine dimensions of quality spanning the various aspects of task, technology, people and organization. The underlying framework of the evaluation is based on a socio-technical model of quality. The intended contribution of our research efforts was to provide an assessment tool for knowledge engineers in the development of expert systems. Such a potential has been field-tested and confirmed.

Sharp, James D. Combinatorics on Ideals and Axiom A. *J Sym Log*, 59(3), 997-1000, S 94.

Sharp, James D and Thomas, Simon. Uniformization Problems and the Cofinality of the Infinite Symmetric Group. *Notre Dame J Form Log*, 35(3), 328-345, Sum 94.

Assuming Martin's Axiom, we compute the value of the cofinality of the symmetric group on the natural numbers. We also show that Martin's Axiom does not decide the value of the covering number of a related Mycielski ideal.

Sharpe, Eric J. 'Do You Understand What You are Reading?'. *Lit Aes*, 1, 3-14, Spr 91.

This is an essay in intercultural hermeneutics, that is, the interpretative possibilities which arise when holy scripture is read by those to whom it is not "holy". Scripture serves the needs of a community of faith, and in traditional societies is made fully available only to initiates, under the guidance of authorized interpreters. Now most scriptures are universally available. The central illustrations here are those of the Muslim Qur'an and the Hindu Bhagavadgita, as read by the Christian and secular West in the 19th and 20th centuries. It urges that this hermeneutical enterprise, despite being difficult and open to absolute, is an imperative necessity in today's world.

Sharpe, R A. Music, Platonism and Performance: Some Ontological Strains. *Brit J Aes*, 35(1), 38-48, Ja 95.

The program which endeavors to produce a generally acceptable analysis of the concept of a work of music is doomed because there is no pre-analytic agreement on the central issue of whether the work is transmitted to the audience by a performance (roughly the Platonic approach) or recreated in performance (approximately the nominalist). Musical practice is divided.

Sharples, Bob. Aristotle and Hellenistic Philosophy. *Phronesis*, 39(3), 338-346, 1994.

Sharples, R W (trans). *Alexander of Aphrodisias: Quaestiones 2.16-3.15*. Ithaca, Cornell Univ Pr, 1994.

Shaub, Michael K. Limits to the Effectiveness of Accounting Ethics Education. *Bus Prof Ethics J*, 13(1-2), 129-145, Spr-Sum 94.

This paper addresses several potential weaknesses in the primary approach taken to implementing accounting ethics education in the classroom. Specifically, the Socratic method of repeated questioning endorsed by Kohlberg (1980) that represents the most widely discussed approach to accounting ethics education may be limited in its effectiveness because of 1) the failure to take into account students' ethics education backgrounds; 2) overreliance on a single paradigm; 3) overreliance on dilemma ethics to shape reasoning and behavior; and 4) the potential of the method to unintentionally undermine restraints on individual behavior. This paper's purpose is to motivate accounting educators to develop more effective ethics teaching models.

Shavrukov, V Y. A Smart Child of Peano's. *Notre Dame J Form Log*, 35(2), 161-185, Spr 94.

Shaw, Bill and McCracken, Janet. Virtue Ethics and Contractarianism: Towards a Reconciliation. *Bus Ethics Quart*, 5(2), 297-312, Ap 95.

The notion of rationality underlying contemporary business and business ethics, or the "rational actor" model of moral decision-making in business, links a roughly utilitarian notion of the good to a contractarian notion of human agency. The "C-U model" provides inadequate means for explaining how business people do or ought to behave or think about their behavior, because the notion of rationality upon which it relies is far too narrow a picture or business people's character. An alternative to these assumptions and to the Contractarian-Utilitarian model, is offered in an ethics of virtue. Despite the traditional apparent conflict between these divergent models, the C-U model, if founded in a notion of rationality consistent with Aristotelian ethics, is recognized as a useful instrument in business ethics and business decision-making. Hence, a reconciliation is effected between the C-U model and virtue ethics.

Shaw, Jane S. Real People Prefer Free-Market Environmentalism: Reply to Friedman. *Crit Rev*, 8(3), 475-482, Sum 94.

Responding to an earlier critique of free market environmentalism by Jeffrey Freidman, Jane S Shaw argues that this approach offers a realistic alternative that is neither utopian or statist. Free market environmentalism recognizes that people respond to incentives and information, and that institutions frame people's incentives and filter their information. Research confirms the harmful environmental effects of coercion and the benefits of private property. Shaw disputes Friedman's claim that free market environmentalists deny the existence of global environmental problems. She also argues that advancing technology may bring solutions that are currently infeasible.

Shaw, William H and Barry, Vincent. *Moral Issues In Business (Sixth Edition)*. Belmont, Wadsworth, 1995.

Moral Issues in Business is a textbook for use in business ethics classes. There are chapters on the nature of morality, normative theories of ethics, justice and economic distribution, the nature of capitalism, corporations, issues in the workplace, moral choices facing employees, job discrimination, consumers, and the environment. Forty-three case studies and thirty-three readings by other authors supplement the main text.

Sheard, Michael. A Guide to Truth Predicates in the Modern Era. *J Sym Log*, 59(3), 1032-1054, S 94.

This paper provides a survey of recent research on languages which contain their own truth predicates, with emphasis on technical results about formal systems. It suggests a classification scheme for viewing varied semantic and axiomatic approaches as parts of a unified subject.

Sheard, Michael and Friedman, Harvey. Elementary Descent Recursion and Proof Theory. *Annals Pure Applied Log*, 71(1), 1-45, Ja 95.

We define a class of functions, the *descent recursive* functions, relative to an arbitrary elementary recursive system of ordinal notations. By means of these functions, we provide a general technique for measuring the proof-theoretic strength of a variety of systems of first-order arithmetic. We characterize the provable well-orderings and provably recursive functions of these systems, and derive various conservation and equiconsistency results.

Sheehan, Thomas. How (Not) to Read Heidegger. *Amer Cath Phil Quart*, 69(2), 275-294, Spr 95.

Heidegger's analysis of temporality is skewed by the usual translation of *das Gewesen* as "what is as having been." The paper addresses this problem by providing a close reading of *Metaphysics* IX, 6 and 8, with attention to Aristotle's ideosyncratic use of the present perfect tense ("Aristotelian aspect") in his delineation of the kinds of *praxis*. On that basis the paper offers a five-part reinterpretation of Heidegger's work as a whole—with a focus on discursiveness, distention, and dispensation—and provides references to relevant texts in Thomas Aquinas.

Shelah, Saharon and Givant, Steven. Universal Theories Categorical in Power and κ-Generated Models. *Annals Pure Applied Log*, 69(1), 27-51, S 94.

We investigate a notion called *uniqueness in power* κ that is akin to categoricity in power κ, but is based on the cardinality of the generating sets of models instead of on the cardinality of their universes. The notion is quite useful for formulating categoricity-like questions regarding powers below the cardinality of a theory. We prove, for (uncountable) universal theories T, that if T is κ-unique for one uncountable κ, then it is κ-unique for every uncountable κ; in particular, it is categorical in powers greater than the cardinality of T.

Shelah, Saharon and Hyttinen, Tapani. Constructing Strongly Equivalent Nonisomorphic Models for Unsuperstable Theories, Part A. *J Sym Log*, 59(3), 984-996, S 94.

We study how equivalent nonisomorphic models an unsuperstable theory can have. We measure the equivalence by Ehrenfeucht-Fraisse games. This paper continues the work started in (HT).

Shelah, Saharon and Jin, Renling. Essential Kurepa Trees Versus Essential Jech-Kunen Trees. *Annals Pure Applied Log*, 69(1), 107-131, S 94.

Sheldrake, Rupert. *A New Science of Life: The Hypothesis of Morphic Resonance*. Rochester, Park St Pr, 1995.

Sheldrake, Rupert. *The Presence of the Past: Morphic Resonance and the Habits of Nature*. Rochester, Park St Pr, 1995.

Shelley, James. Hume's Double Standard of Taste. *J Aes Art Crit*, 52(4), 437-445, Fall 94.

In all the literature on Hume's "Of the Standard of Taste", virtually no attention has been given to Hume's enigmatic definition of the standard as "a rule, by which the various sentiments of men may be reconciled; at least a decision, afforded, confirming one sentiment, and condemning another". This is a costly omission, I argue, since unless we understand Hume's definition, we simply do not understand what Hume's standard is. My central aim, consequently, is to elucidate this definition and provide a reading of Hume's essay in which it makes sense.

Shelley, James. Rule and Verdict. *J Aes Art Crit*, 53(3), 319-320, Sum 95.

Shelton, Jim. Seeing and Paradigms in the Chemical Revolution. *Phil Sci (Tucson)*, 6, 129-141, 1995.

The primary objective in this paper is to show that Kuhn was misled by his metaphor of "seeing" in his evaluation of the phlogiston-chemistry debate in the revolution in chemical theory, I show how that use of the Gestalt notion resulted in confusion about the nature of a paradigm and about Lavoisier's role in the chemical revolution.

Sheng, C L. A Suggested Solution to the Trolley Problem. *J Soc Phil*, 26(1), 203-217, Spr 95.

This paper suggests a solution to the Trolley Problem, based on my unified utilitarian theory. I distinguish between the case where the agent is a bystander and the case where the agent is a participant, by introducing the "Driver" case where the agent is the driver of the trolley. When the agent is a participant, I further distinguish between the "Driver" case and the "Transplant" case. (edited)

Sheng, C L. On the Nature of Moral Principles. *J Value Inq*, 28(4), 503-518, D 94.

Sheng, Peihua and Chang, Linda and French, Warren A. Business's Environmental Responsibility in Taiwan—Moral, Legal or Negotiated. *J Bus Ethics*, 13(11), 887-897, N 94.

This study explores both the negotiating styles and moral reasoning processes of business people and governmental officials in Taiwan, so as to provide a footing for "outsiders" when negotiating with Taiwanese over environmental concerns. Findings imply that Taiwanese business people and governmental officials can and will reason both at the conventional level and at the postconventional level of moral judgment. But, results of this study also indicate that Taiwanese negotiating styles do not necessarily match their levels of moral reasoning. With respect to pollution concerns, Taiwanese seem unwillingly to accept responsibility as autonomous individuals. Instead, responsibility is accepted when mandated by the law.

Shenk, Ian. Patients' Perceptions of Consent. *J Clin Ethics*, 5(3), 243-244, Fall 94.

Shepard, Jon M (& others). The Place of Ethics in Business: Shifting Paradigms?. *Bus Ethics Quart*, 5(3), 577-601, Jl 95.

This article uses concepts from sociology, history, and philosophy to explore the shifting relationship between moral values and business in the Western world. We examine the historical roots and intellectual underpinnings of two major business-society paradigms in ideal-type terms. In pre-industrial Western society, we argue that business activity was linked to society's values of morality (the moral unity paradigm)—for good or for ill. With the rise of industrialism, we contend that business was freed from moral constraints by the alleged "invisible hand" of efficient markets (the amoral theory of business). Armed with this understanding of the intellectual history of the moral unity and amoral business-society paradigms, we suggest that some variant of the moral unity paradigm may be recurring in post-industrial society.

Shepard, Jon M and Wimbush, James C. Toward an Understanding of Ethical Climate: Its Relationship to Ethical Behavior and Supervisory Influence. *J Bus Ethics*, 13(8), 637-647, Ag 94.

In recent years, theoretical and empirical developments in the area of organizational climate has provided the impetus for research concerning ethical climate. According to this latter research, ethical climate is a multi-dimensional construct which is manifested in organizations. Studies, however, have not focused on the relationship between ethical climate and ethical behavior. Furthermore, an enhanced understanding of the multi-dimensionality of ethical climate will likely advance what we know about organizational climate and culture in general. We propose further examination of ethical climate by: 1) showing the conceptual relationship between ethical climate and ethical (or unethical) behavior in organizations; and 2) examining supervision as one of the principle influences on ethical climate and concomitant subordinate behavior. Finally, we explore the implications for future research on ethical climate.

Shepherd, Richard and Frewer, Lynn J. Ethical Concerns and Risk Perceptions Associated with Different Applications of Genetic Engineering. *Agr Human Values*, 12(1), 48-57, Winter 95.

Questions were directed at either perceived risk or ethical objections. The applications of genetic engineering were seen as riskier and less beneficial when applied to food production than medicine, although perceived control was independent of application. Optimistic bias was observed. Ethical and risk related objections were greater for applications to food than to medicine, and again dependent of the type of organism manipulated. The transfer of genetic material between "dissimilar" types of organism (for example, between plants and animals) were not associated with greater risk or ethical concern than transfers between "similar" types of organism (for example, between animals and animals). The public requirement for legislative control was also dissociated into risk or ethical objections to the technology, and found to be greater for risk-related concerns, although ethical considerations were also important.

Shepherdson, Charles. Vital Signs: The *Place* of Memory in Psychoanalysis. *Res Phenomenol*, 23, 22-72, 1993.

This article focuses on Freud and Lacan, showing how the concept of memory is related to the imaginary, symbolic and real. It discusses memory as the retention of an image or perception, and moves to memory as a symbolic phenomenon, structured by language, exploring the difference between these two conceptions, and their consequences for the concept of the body. The primary argument, however, concerns the insufficiency of the "symbolic" conception—unconscious memory revealed in free association, the dream, lapsus, and negation. The symptom and "sexuality" lead Lacan from an initial linguistic orientation, evident in "the Rome Discourse" (the Other), to the category of "real" in Seminar XI (the "object a"). Lacan's discussion of "Anna O" is explored.

Sher, George. Rights, Neutrality, and the Oppressive Power of the State. *Law Phil*, 14(2), 185-201, My 95.

The idea that the sheer magnitude of the state's power is a threat to its citizens, and that this threat must somehow be tamed, has long been a prominent theme of liberal thought. More recently, many liberals have advanced the further thesis that the state should not favor any particular conception of the good, but should remain strictly neutral toward all such conceptions. In this paper, I shall explore the relations between these familiar claims, and in particular the prospects for grounding the latter in the former. That is, I want to discuss the argument that we ought to adopt the neutrality principle precisely in order to curb the state's oppressive power. Although this argument has achieved some currency, and although it is very much in the air, I shall argue that it does not succeed.

Sherline, Edward. Heteronomy and Spurious Principles of Morality in Kant's Groundwork. *Pac Phil Quart*, 76(1), 32-46, Mr 95.

In this paper I explain Kant's rejection of all heteronomous principles as spurious in *Foundations* 440-444. I do this through the idea that Kant is a practical foundationalist. In the process I clarify Kant's notion of heteronomy.

Sherman, David. Camus's Meursault and Sartrian Irresponsibility. *Phil Lit*, 19(1), 60-77, Ap 95.

Camus's Meursault can best be understood within the context of Sartre's psychoanalytic framework. Based upon Meursault's own narration, I show that his is in "radical" bad faith. It is not merely that his conception of Self is distorted; rather, he has rejected (at least for him) the very concept of selfhood. This extreme rejection of "self-responsibility," and all that it entails, is at the root of Meursault's strangeness.

Sherman, Nancy. The Role of Emotions in Aristotelian Virtue. *Proc Boston Colloq Anc Phil*, 9, 1-33, 1993.

On an Aristotelian account, virtue is expressed not merely in fine action, but in fine emotions; both are morally praiseworthy aspects of character. This essay explores an Aristotelian cognitivist account of the emotions and the bearing of such an account on Aristotle's general views about the habituation of moral character. The general question is raised as to how stable and reliable virtue is when rooted in the emotions.

Shermer, Michael. Exorcising Laplace's Demon: Chaos and Antichaos, History and Metahistory. *Hist Theor*, 34(1), 59-83, 1995.

This essay: I) reviews the precedents for integrating chaos and history; II) gives a brief history of this integration including an evaluation of a critique of Reisch and McCloskey by Roth and Ryckman, and presents a metahistory of how chaos theory explains its own development; III) defends a chaotic model of historical sequences; IV) gives a specific historical example of nonlinear history; V) explores the latest trends in the field of self-organization, antichaos, simplexity, and feedback mechanisms, providing data to show that modern and historical social movements change in a parallel fashion; and VI) exorcises Laplace's demon by showing it was always a chimera. (edited)

Sherwin, Susan. The Ethics of Babymaking. *Hastings Center Rep*, 25(2), 34-37, Mr-Ap 95.

A critical review of three works on the ethics of new reproductive technologies. The works covered are *Human Reproduction: Principles, Practices, Policies*, by Christine Overall (Toronto: Oxford University Press, 1993). *Children of Choice: Freedom and the New Reproductive Technologies*, by John A Robertson (Princeton: Princeton University Press, 1994), and *Proceed with Care: Final Report of the Royal Commission on New Reproductive Technologies* (Ottawa: Minister of Supply and Services, 1993). This article examines and contrasts the very different ethical assumptions behind these three radically different proposals for managing reproductive technologies.

Shibles, Warren. Anxiety: A Pseudo-Concept. *Int J Applied Phil*, 9(1), 43-52, Sum-Fall 94.

Anxiety is not a clear or precise concept. It reduces to a wide range of concepts as shown by the analysis of its word-field. An analysis of anxiety by the cognitive theory of emotion shows that it reduces to assessments plus bodily feelings, and from that a number of characteristics may be deduced. The specific assessments are typically negative and fallacious. A clarification of these assessments requires a careful concrete, interdisciplinary, critical and accountable analysis of a sort which is not now being given.

Shibles, Warren. Humanistic Art. *Crit Rev*, 8(3), 371-392, Sum 94.

The cognitive theory of emotion (also called the rational-emotive theory) clarifies the notion of aesthetic emotion and evaluation, and when combined with Dewey's humanism and a naturalistic theory of valuation provides a basis for a holistic theory of aesthetics. From the holistic perspective, no act is moral unless it is also aesthetic. On this view, the aesthetic is no longer reduced to atomistic or quantitative perspectives, but becomes a part of our total purposive life experience. It expresses itself in gentleness and *joie de vivre*.

Shibles, Warren. The Meaning of *Express* in Aesthetics: The Reconstruction of Literature. *J Thought*, 30(2), 21-41, Sum 95.

It is unclear what, if anything, the word *express* means in aesthetics. This is because there has not been an acceptable theory of emotion. The cognitive-emotive theory is here used to clarify such concepts as the "expression of emotion." Croce's view of "intuition is expression," is also explicated in these terms. In addition, a theory of meaning is briefly presented upon which to ground such phrases as "the expression of meaning." On these bases, the word-field of "express" is analyzed and its various meanings clarified.

Shibles, Warren A. Hanslick on Hearing Beauty. *Iyyun*, 44, 73-90, Ja 95.

The Cognitive Theory of Emotion has been used to help clarify Hanslick's formalist theory of aesthetics. Hanslick attempted to show how much nonmusical cognition and emotion can be regarded a extraneous and superfluous to the musically beautiful, how much they can be subtracted from music, but in so doing he subtracts music from music itself. He attempts to objectify music to the extent that we can even hear beauty as we hear sounds themselves. An analysis of the value assessments involved in the examination of aesthetic emotion showed that objective music is a fiction, and that sounds are silent in regard to beauty.

Shibles, Warren A. The Cognitive-Emotive Theory of Desire. *J Indian Counc Phil Res*, 11(3), 25-40, My-Ag 94.

Desire is still a controversial term. Its analysis depends on a sound theory of emotion. The majority of recent philosophical work on emotion has supported the cognitive theory of emotion. This theory comes together, for mutual support, with the rational-emotive theory in the area of therapy. Using this theory, a number of characteristics of desire are discovered. It is also used as a tool by which to give insight into, and to evaluate, a number of classical and contemporary theories: Stoics, Buddhism, Hume, Schopenhauer, Dewey. The concept of metadesire is introduced which is seen to solve some of the problems and paradoxes regarding desire.

Shields, Christopher. An Ontology of Art. *Austl J Phil*, 73(2), 293-300, Je 95.

Shields, Christopher J. "Socrates Among the Skeptics" in *The Socratic Movement*, Vander Waerdt, Paul A (ed), 341-366. Ithaca, Cornell Univ Pr, 1994.

Arcesilaus identifies Socrates as the source of his own extreme skepticism. This rings hollow to many, given that Socrates is not a skeptic, or at least not the radical sort of skeptic Arcesilaus advertises himself to be. The suggestion consequently lies near that Arcesilaus relies on Socrates only disingenuously, that he misrepresents the historical Socrates in an effort to forge a false philosophical lineage. Still, it would be incorrect to convict Arcesilaus too hastily. Rather, by developing selected strands of Socratic dialectic into the modal tropes necessary for generating a commitment to Arcesilaus can claim to be an heir of Socrates.

Shimura, Tatsuya. On Completeness of Intermediate Predicate Logics with Respect to Kripke Semantics. *Bull Sec Log*, 24(1), 41-45, Mr 95.

In spite of the existence of many examples of incomplete logics, it is an important problem to find intermediate predicate logics complete with respect to Kripke frame (or Kripke sheaf) semantics because they are closed under substitution. But, most of known completeness proofs of finitely axiomatizable logics are difficult to apply to other logics since they are highly dependent on the specific properties of given logics. So, it is preferable to find a general methods of completeness proof. We give some results on this problem using canonical formulas of *propositional* logics [8,2].

Shin, Un-Chol. The Role of Imagination in Integrative Knowledge: A Polanyian View. *Tradition Discovery*, 21(2), 16-28, 1994-95.

How do we know the degree of imagination involved in knowing a reality? This is essentially an epistemological question. This essay discusses first the role of imagination in Polanyi's epistemology since it is used here as the basis of integrative reality. The essay then discusses the degree of imagination involved in three types of integrative reality that are found respectively in technology, science, and humanities. It concludes with a discussion on the role of imagination in education.

Shiner, Roger A. Accounting Ethics: The General Part. *Bus Prof Ethics J*, 13(1-2), 9-23, Spr-Sum 94.

The paper lays out some general background issues for the consideration of substantive problems in accounting ethics. I define applied ethics as a branch of philosophy. I distinguish outcome-oriented and action-oriented reasoning in ethical deliberation. I sketch how the divergence between these approaches underlies problems of professional ethics generally, and especially in the case of accountancy. I consider Nagel's idea that public institutions may properly exhibit a bias towards outcome-oriented reasoning. I discuss the special stringency of the requirement for impartiality in accountancy in view of the explicitly public utility of the audit function.

Shirley, Edward S. Marquis' Argument Against Abortion: A Critique. *SW Phil Rev*, 11(1), 79-89, Ja 95.

Shlapentokh, Alexandra. Diophantine Equivalence and Countable Rings. *J Sym Log*, 59(3), 1068-1095, S 94.

We show that Diophantine equivalence of two suitably presented countable rings implies that the existential polynomial languages of the two rings have the same "expressive power" and that their Diophantine sets are in some sense the same. We also show that a Diophantine class of countable rings is contained completely within a relative enumeration class and demonstrate that one consequence of this fact is the existence of infinitely many Diophantine classes containing holomorphy rings of "Q".

Shlapentokh, Alexandra. Diophantine Undecidability in Some Rings of Algebraic Numbers of Totally Real Infinite Extensions.... *Annals Pure Applied Log*, 68(3), 299-325, Ag 94.

This paper describes examples of subrings of some totally real infinite extensions of rationals where Diophantine problem is undecidable.

Sho'ala, Abdulnabi Al. Islam and the Concept of Tolerance and Co-Existence. *J Dharma*, 19(4), 350-357, O-D 94.

Shoemaker, Sydney. "The Mind-Body Problem" in *The Mind-Body Problem: A Guide to the Current Debate*, Warner, Richard (ed), 55-60. Cambridge, Blackwell, 1994.

Shoemaker, Sydney. Moore's Paradox and Self-Knowledge. *Phil Stud*, 77(2-3), 211-228, Mr 95.

Shoemaker, Sydney. Phenomenal Character. *Nous*, 28(1), 21-38, Mr 94.

Shoemaker, Sydney. The First-Person Perspective. *Proc Amer Phil Ass*, 68(2), 7-22, N 94.

Shogenji, Tomoji. The Problem of Rule-Following in Compositional Semantics. *S J Phil*, 33(1), 97-108, Spr 95.

One of the central issues in the recent discussion of rule-following has been the apparent gap between the finitude of any facts about the rule-follower and the infinitude of possible applications of rules. In this paper the author argues that the combination of the rule-follower's disposition and explicit directions can fill this gap with respect to the interpretation of individual words, but that the problem of finitude remains a serious threat to compositional semantics for natural language because there are no explicit directions we can rely on in learning its rules.

Shotter, John. Making Sense on the Boundaries: On Moving Between Philosophy and Psychotherapy. *Philosophy*, 37(Supp), 55-72, 1994.

Shouchang, Wang. Feng Youlan and the Vienna Circle (A Synopsis). *J Chin Phil*, 21(3-4), 263-267, S-D 94.

Shrader-Frechette, Kristin. Ecological Explanation and the Population-Growth Thesis. *Proc Phil Sci Ass*, 1, 34-45, 1994.

Many ecologists have dismissed alleged ecological laws as tautological or trivial. This essay investigates the epistemological status of one prominent such "law", the population-growth thesis, and argues for four claims: 1) Once interpreted, the thesis cannot be denied the status of empirical law on the grounds that it is always and everywhere untestable. 2) Contrary to Peters' (1991) claim, some interpretations of the thesis have significant heuristic power. 3) One can use the reasoning of Brandon (1990), Lloyd (1987), and Sober (1984) to show that some interpretations of the thesis are not *a priori*. 4) Even if the thesis is *a priori*, it has explanatory power as a "schematic law".

Shrader-Frechette, Kristin. Environmental Risk Assessment and Nuclear Waste Disposal. *Epistemologia*, 17(1), 53-72, Ja-Je 94.

Permanent disposal of nuclear waste may be unworkable. Despite billions of dollars being spent to evaluate the proposed yucca mountain high-level radioactive waste facility for permanent disposal of nuclear waste, the environmental risk assessments of the site are flawed by ethical and epistemological errors. Two central errors occurring throughout the assessment are the appeal to ignorance and begging the question.

Shrader-Frechette, Kristin. Equity and Nuclear Waste Disposal. *J Agr Environ Ethics*, 7(2), 133-156, 1994.

The US Department of Energy has proposed Yucca Mountain, Nevada as the site of the world's first permanent repository for high-level nuclear waste. The main justification for permanent underground disposal is that it guarantees safety by means of waste isolation. This essay argues, however, that considerations of equity undercut the safety rationale. The article surveys some prima facie arguments for equity in the distribution of radwaste risks and then evaluates four objections. The conclusion is that permanent waste disposal is highly questionable, in part, because it fails to distribute risk equitably or to compensate, in full, for this inequity.

Shrader-Frechette, Kristin. *Ethics of Scientific Research*. Lanham, Rowman & Littlefield, 1994.

Challenging long-held theories of scientific rationality and remoteness, Kristin Shrader-Frechette argues that research cannot be "value free". Rather, any research will raise important moral issues for those involved, issues not only of truthfulness but of risk to research subjects, third parties, and the general public. *Ethics of Scientific Research* gives researchers in medicine, engineering, science, and other fields principles and practices to ensure ethical research. The book concludes with three chapters by other authors, addressing specific problems in scientific, engineering, and public health research.

Shtromas, Aleksandras (ed). *The End of "Isms"?*. Cambridge, Blackwell, 1994.

The subject of this book is the state of ideological politics in the postcommunist world. After examining first the world's ideological situation, the book considers the influence Marxist and other socialist ideologies continue today to exert and, in that context, analyzes the potential impact the socialist ideological orientation may have on politics in the twenty-first century. Liberalism, religious fundamentalism and nationalism are analyzed in the same perspective next. Then, in two consecutive chapters, the ideological situation in the USA and contemporary Russia is scrutinized with the view of establishing ideology's role in both present day and future politics of these two dominant world powers. The book is concluded by a chapter summarizing the ideological spectrum of the contemporary world, assessing the political potential of various current world ideologies and trying to define the place ideology is likely to occupy in postmodern politics generally. Throughout the book due attention is paid to the discussion of the concept of ideology and other theoretical problems related to the phenomenon of ideology and its influence on practical politics.

Shukla, Dipti. Freedom and Faith in Kierkegaard's Philosophy. *Darshana Int*, 32(1/125), 81-84, Ja 92.

Shukla, Sanjay Kumar. An Enquiry into Kant's Conceptual Revolution. *Indian Phil Quart*, 21/2(Supp), 11-20, Ap 94.

The purpose of the article is to investigate the nature of Kant's conceptual revolution in the realm of philosophy as Copernicus did in the field of astronomy. The heliocentric hypothesis of Copernicus altered old geocentric model of Ptolemy. The nature of Kant's conceptual revolution is highly debatable as some interpreted as Copernican and others anticopernican. Kant establishes egocentric view of knowledge against cosmocentric (empiricist) and theocentric (rationalist) view. His revolutionary zeal is not confined to epistemology but in other fields of metaphysics and morality. There is no genuine similarity between two but mere analogy.

Shusterman, Richard. "Art in a Box" in *Danto and his Critics*, Rollins, Mark (ed), 161-174. Cambridge, Blackwell, 1993.

Shusterman, Richard. Art Infraction: Goodman, Rap, Pragmatism. *Austl J Phil*, 73(2), 269-279, Je 95.

This paper compares pragmatist themes from Goodman's philosophy and rap's aesthetic practice to illustrate each other and show the value of pragmatist aesthetics as developed in my book of that title.

Shusterman, Richard. Dewey on Experience: Foundation or Reconstruction?. *Phil Forum*, 26(2), 127-148, Wint 94.

Shusterman, Richard. On Analysing Analytic Aesthetics. *Brit J Aes*, 34(4), 389-394, O 94.

This paper responds to various criticisms of my account of analytic aesthetics (published in a 1989 book with that title). In dealing with these criticisms, I explain two different but potentially complementary strategies for clarifying the concept of analytic aesthetics that are also applicable to other historical concepts: range analysis and genealogical analysis. The paper also distinguishes three forms of anti-essentialism and discusses the relationship of pragmatist and analytic aesthetics.

Shusterman, Richard. Popular Art and Education. *Stud Phil Educ*, 13(3-4), 203-212, 1994-95.

Shusterman, Richard. *Pragmatist Aesthetics: Living Beauty, Rethinking Art*. Cambridge, Blackwell, 1992.

After situating pragmatist aesthetics through a comparative analysis of its Deweyan themes with analytic aesthetics and continental theory, this book develops new pragmatist positions of the following topics: aesthetic experience, the definition of art, organic unity, the nature, aims, and limits of interpretation, the educational potential and ideological dangers of art, its social functions and abuses, the aesthetics of popular art (which is exemplified by a separate chapter on the art of rap music). The book closes with a study of postmodern ethics as an art of living. It exists in French (Minuit, 1992) and German translation (Fischer, 1994).

Shusterman, Ronald. In Defense of "Elitism". *Phil Lit*, 18(2), 242-252, O 94.

One recent trend in criticism has suggested that literary theory is either useless, harmful or both. This pragmatist argument corresponds to contemporary attacks on the distinction between high and low art. My purpose is to show that theory is indeed useful, and that "classical" criteria of depth and clarity do establish a pertinent distinction between art and entertainment. These criteria limit the role of the purely somatic. Theory is a necessary part of our heritage.

Shweder, Richard A. Are Moral Intuitions Self-Evident Truths?. *Crim Just Ethics*, 13(2), 24-31, Sum-Fall 94.

Shyles, Leonard and Smith, Andrew R. "On Ethnocentric Truth and Pragmatic Justice" in *Recovering Pragmatism's Voice*, Langsdorf, Lenore (ed), 71-94. Albany, SUNY Pr, 1995.

Smith and Shyles take up the issue of "ethnocentric truth and pragmatic justice" as a way of examining how the classical pragmatism of Peirce (pragmaticism) and Dewey (instrumentalism) contribute to the modern-postmodern debate on the impossibility of truth and justice. They address the semiotics of consequence in both Peirce and Dewey by first reviewing how this logic has been appropriated by Rorty in philosophy and Schweder in cultural psychology. The authors side with Shweder against Rorty and argue that the imaginative dimensions of "abductive" communication are crucial for any sense of intercultural "truth" or "justice." Dewey's critique of custom is advanced and the Peircian notion of "ends" is reconceptualized, not as a way of invoking some determinate judgment, but organizing conditionally and fallibly an "evolutionary" axiology through communication practice.

Siassos, Lambros. Le Champ Ontologique de l'Apparition du Mal chez Proclus et Denys. *Diotima*, 23, 43-45, 1995.

Sichel, Betty A. A Review of Samuel Scolnicov's *Plato's Metaphysics of Education*. *Stud Phil Educ*, 13(2), 141-148, 1993-94.

Sider, David. Commentary on Asmis's "Epicurean Poetics". *Proc Boston Colloq Anc Phil*, 7, 94-105, 1991.

Epicurus's discouragement of the writing of poetry by the wise man (AKA the Epicurean) was not absolute. Provided that it gave pleasure, it allows for Lucretius' poem (which could win converts to the cause). Philodemos, composing for the already converted, could argue that his epigrams, touching upon erotic and philosophical topoi (not exclusively Epicurean) produce harmless, albeit not necessary, pleasures. Viewed in this light, his epigrams are entirely in accord with his own Epicurean theories on the nature of poetry.

Sidorov, Igor. The Philosophy of Pavel Florenskii and the Future of Russian Culture. *Russian Stud Phil*, 33(4), 41-48, Spr 95.

Siebelt, Frank. Zweierlei Holismus: Überlegungen zur Interpretationstheorie D Davidsons. *Protosoz*, 1, 60-71, Ap 91.

What makes utterances and beliefs of other persons on the base of behavior intelligible? D Davidson gives us a possible answer in his analysis of the holistic nature of beliefs from the view point of radical interpretation. D Davidson's argument is, that having propositional attitudes is a necessary condition for the understanding of (personal) utterances. In the context of his theory of radical interpretation he will give an explication and a refutation of critics of the still not enough recipated thesis of D Davidson.

Sieber, Joan E and Iannuzzo, Rebecca and Rodriguez, Beverly. Deception Methods in Psychology: Have They Changed in 23 Years?. *Ethics Behavior*, 5(1), 67-85, 1995.

To learn whether criticism and regulation of research practices have been followed by a reduction of deception or use of more acceptable approaches to deception, the contents of all 1969, 1978, 1986, and 1992 issues of the *Journal of Personality and Social Psychology* were examined. Deception research was coded according to type of (non)informing (e.g., false informing, consent to deception, no informing), possible harmfulness of deception employed (e.g., powerfulness of induction, morality of the behavior induced, privacy of behavior), method of deception (e.g., bogus device or role, false purpose of study, false feedback), and debriefing employed. Use of confederates has been partly replaced by uses of computers. "Consent" with false informing declined after 1969, then rose in 1992. Changes in the topics studied (e.g., attribution, socialization, personality) largely accounted for the decline in deception in 1978 and 1986. More attention needs to be given to ways of respecting subjects' autonomy, to appropriate debriefing and desensitizing, and to selecting the most valid and least objectionable deception methods.

Siebert, Rudolf J. Kant and Hegel on War and Peace. *Filozof Istraz*, 14(2-3), 543-584, 1994.

The purpose of this essay is to explore Immanuel Kant's and Georg W F Hegel's positions on the issue of war and peace. The intention of this text is to show the development of the concepts of and the attitude toward war and peace from Kant to Hegel. This study is produced in the context of the Gulf War, the conflicts in Ireland, Lebanon, Israel, Somalia, Rwanda, Haiti, and particularly the wars in former Yugoslavia, and in other parts of Eastern Europe. It is the goal of this essay, with the help of Kant and Hegel to deepen the theory of war in all its forms, in order to make possible a more adequate peace-keeping or, if necessary, peace-making activity in war zones, wherever they may open up around the globe: in the framework of the third new world order in this century.

Sieg, Wilfried and Mundici, Daniele. Paper Machines. *Phil Math*, 3(1), 5-30, Ja 95.

Machines were introduced as calculating devices to simulate operations carried out by human computers following fixed algorithms. The mathematical study of (paper) machines is the topic of our essay. The first three sections provide necessary logical background, examine the analyzes of effective calculability given in the thirties, and describe results that are central to recursion theory, reinforcing the conceptual analyses. In the final section we pursue our investigation in a quite different way and focus on principles that govern the operations of physically realizable machines.

Siegel, Harvey. Naturalized Epistemology and 'First Philosophy'. *Metaphilosophy*, 26(1-2), 46-62, Ja-Ap 95.

Recent calls for the naturalizing of epistemology typically take for granted that Quine's arguments against 'first philosophy' have undermined any such approach to epistemology, and so have paved the way for that naturalization. In this paper I examine arguments for rejecting 'first philosophy' or 'traditional epistemology', and for naturalizing epistemology, offered by Quine and by Roger F Gibson. I argue here that those arguments fail. In light of this failure, I urge that epistemologists enthusiastic about the naturalization of their subject reconsider their enthusiasm.

Siegel, Harvey. Not by Skill Alone: The Centrality of Character to Critical Thinking. *Inform Log*, 15(3), 163-177, Fall 93.

Connie Missimer (1990) challenges what she calls the Character View, according to which critical thinking involves both skill and character, and argues for a rival conception—the Skill View—according to which critical thinking is a matter of skill alone. In this paper I criticize the Skill View and defend the Character View from Missimer's critical arguments.

Siegel, Harvey. 'Radical' Pedagogy Requires 'Conservative' Epistemology. *J Phil Educ*, 29(1), 33-46, March 95.

Many defences of multiculturalist educational initiatives conjoin a "liberal" or "radical" moral/political view—that education should endeavour to treat students with respect, and that respecting nondominant, "marginalised" students requires

protecting them from the hegemonic domination of the dominant culture—with what appears to be an equally radical epistemological view, according to which respecting minority students and cultures requires respecting their culturally specific epistemologies, which in turn requires refraining form imposing upon them a dominating hegemonic epistemology concerning the nature of truth, rational justification, and so on. In this paper I argue 1) that this "radical" epistemological position is fatally flawed; and 2) that, if true, it would undermine, rather than undergird, the favoured moral/political view. I argue, that is, that proponents of "radical" pedagogy would do better to reject the associated "radical" epistemological view in favour of a more traditional, "conservative" one.

Siegel, Muffy E A. Such: Binding and the Pro-Adjective. *Ling Phil*, 17(5), 481-497, O 94.

This article argues that *such* is syntactically a simple adjective, but that it translates as a variable corresponding to a pro-common noun. Further, *such* and some other nonargument pro-forms (as well as a wide variety of argument pro-forms, such as pro-VPs and pro-sentences) actually obey Chomsky's binding conditions, although these were formulated to account only for arguments, particularly pronouns. This evidence leads to the conclusion that any form translated as a variable is a pro-form, and that pro-forms very generally obey binding conditions requiring them to be free within their governing categories.

Siemek, Marek J. "Drei Standpunkte der Philosophie zur modernen Wissenschaft" in *Das geistige Erbe Europas, Buhr, Manfred (ed)*, 624-634. Napoli, Vivarium, 1994.

Siemek, Marek J. A Critique of "Non-Instrumental Reason". *Dialogue Hum*, 3(4), 87-94, 1993.

Siemek, Marek J. Husserl und das Erbe der Tranzendentalphilosophie. *Fichte-Studien*, 1, 145-152, 1990.

Siena, R M. Giuseppe Rensi e la lettura antimetafisica della teologia di Spinoza. *Sapienza*, 47(4), 469-476, O-D 94.

Sierra, Pelayo García. La evolución filosófica e ideológica de la Asociación Española para el Progreso de las Ciencias (1908-1979). *El Basilisco*, 15, 49-81, Ja-Mr 94.

Sigad, Ran. God as Final Cause in Spinoza (in Hebrew). *Iyyun*, 43, 375-398, O 94.

Siguaw, Judy A and Honeycutt, Earl D and Hunt, Tammy G. Business Ethics and Job-Related Constructs: A Cross-Cultural Comparison of Automotive Salespeople. *J Bus Ethics*, 14(3), 235-248, Mr 95.

Although a number of articles have addressed ethical perceptions and behaviors, few studies have examined ethics across cultures. This research focuses on measuring the job satisfaction, customer orientation, ethics, and ethical training of automotive salespersons in the U S and Taiwan. The relationships of these variables to salesperson performance were also investigated. Ethics training was found to be negatively related to perceived levels of ethicalness and performance. High performance U S salespeople reported high ethical behavior, while the opposite was true in Taiwan. Customer orientation in both countries was influenced by ethics training. Managers should evaluate current ethics training programs to insure correct ethical behavior is taught and rewarded.

Siguret, Pierre. La Nausée de Jean-Paul Sartre: Un Roman Phénoménologique. *Philosopher*, 14, 103-129, 1993.

Sikka, Sonya. Heidegger's Appropriation of Schelling. *S J Phil*, 32(4), 421-448, Wint 94.

In its examination of the relation between Heidegger's thought and that of F W J Schelling, this essay first gives an overview of Schelling's treatise, *On the Essence of Human Freedom*, drawing both on the original text and Heidegger's two commentaries. It then looks at parallels between Schelling's thought as presented in this text and themes in a number of Heidegger's own works, from *Being and Time* to "The Turning". It argues that Heidegger's debt to Schelling is much deeper than his explicit appraisals of Schelling's place in the history of metaphysics might lead one to believe, while making some broader points about Heidegger's relation to the metaphysical tradition in general and about the positive possibilities available within that tradition.

Sikka, Sonya. Heidegger's Concept of *Volk*. *Phil Forum*, 26(2), 101-126, Wint 94.

This article examines Heidegger's concept of *Volk*, of 'people' or 'nation', against the background of a certain line of German political thought which includes Herder, Fichte, Schleiermacher, Nietzsche, Carl Schmitt and Spengler. It especially examines the basic ideas about ethnic identity and nationhood which Heidegger shares with the German political Romantics. It points out the flaws inherent in many of these ideas, but also emphasizes how, in spite of these flaws, Heidegger's writings still contain some valuable insights concerning the constitution of an ethnic identity. The essay is divided into four main sections: 1) "*Volk* in the *Rektoratsrede* and other Addresses", 2) "*Volk* and Language", 3) "*Volk* and Destiny" and 4) "*Volk* and *Voelker*".

Sikka, Sonya. The Philosophical Bases of Heidegger's Politics: A Response to Wolin. *J Brit Soc Phenomenol*, 25(3), 241-262, O 94.

This essay responds to the various criticisms levelled against Heidegger by Richard Wolin in his book, *The Politics of Being*. Its analysis, which proceeds by reference to Heidegger's philosophical and theological background, revolves around three crucial themes in Heidegger's writings: 1) the question of decision, 2) collective identity and destiny, and 3) the concept of truth. It concludes that, in spite of Wolin's stated intention to establish a link between Heidegger's philosophy and his politics through a cautious and restrained analysis, he actually fails to engage at any deep level with the genuine philosophical issues at stake.

Siksou, M and Forest, F. Concept Development and Computation of Meaning Thought and Language by Vygotsky. *Commun Cog—AI*, 11(1-2), 181-199, 1994.

Vygotsky's approach to the construction of concepts contrasts with the models which are commonly used in artificial intelligence. We shall present the main ideas of Vygotsky's work on the relations between thought and language, and the main steps of concept building in a child's mind. We shall outline what makes this approach so modern and into a potential basis for computing systems for the representation of meaning linked to learning and adaptation. We propose some architectural and structural choices for such a system. We hope this attempt will allow the testing of some hypotheses.

Sikula Sr, Andrew and Costa, Adelmiro D. Are Women More Ethical than Men?. *J Bus Ethics*, 13(11), 859-871, N 94.

This article reports that the idea that women are more ethical than men is not supported by the empirical data of this particular study of a large sample of California State University college-aged students. This study uses four different value measures and four different nonparametric statistical tests of probability and significance to conclude that women are *not* more ethical than men. They may have historically been so inclined, and perhaps even today may still be when fully matured. But among today's youth of normal college age, there are no significant differences between the ethical values of male and female students (in this sample of Northern California university enrollees).

Silberstein, Michael and Hawthorne, James. For Whom the Bell Arguments Toll. *Synthese*, 102(1), 99-138, Ja 95.

We will formulate two Bell arguments. Together they show that if the probabilities given by quantum mechanics are approximately correct, then the properties exhibited by certain physical systems must be nontrivially dependent on the *types* of measurements performed *and* either *nonlocally* connected or *holistically* related to distant events. Although a number of related arguments have appeared since John Bell's original paper (1964), they tend to be either highly technical or to lack full generality. The following arguments depend on the weakest of premises, and the structure of the arguments is simpler than most (without any loss of rigor or generality). The technical simplicity is due in part to a novel version of the generalized Bell inequality. The arguments are self contained and presuppose no knowledge of quantum mechanics. We will also offer a Dutch Book argument for measurement type dependence.

Silverberg, Arnold. Meaning Holism and Intentional Content. *Pac Phil Quart*, 75(1), 29-53, Mr 94.

In this essay I defend meaning holism against certain criticisms that Jerry Fodor has presented against it. In *Psychosemantics* he argued that meaning holism is incompatible with the development of scientific psychology given the ways in which scientific psychology adverts to intentional content. In his recent book *Holism* (co-authored with Ernest Lepore) he indicates that he still upholds this argument. I argue that Fodor's argument fails, and argue in favor of the compatibility of meaning holism with scientific psychology. I also argue positively in favor of meaning holism, arguing in part that, contrary to Fodor's claims, psychofunctionalism provides a strong basis for defending meaning holism. As part of this argument, I contend, contrary to Fodor, that narrow content, as derived from psychofunctionalism, should be construed as semantic.

Silverberg, Arnold. Narrow Content: A Defence. *S J Phil*, 33(1), 109-127, Spr 95.

Silverman, Hugh J. Postmodernism and Contemporary Italian Philosophy. *Man World*, 27(4), 343-348, O 94.

Silverman, Paul H. Commerce and Genetic Diagnostics. *Hastings Center Rep*, 25(3), S15-S18, My-Je 95.

Techniques for determining genetic mutations are rapidly moving from the academic research laboratory to the commerical arena. DNA diagnostics (genetic anaylsis) has the potential for potent impact on society because of its predictive capacities. The ability to predict late-onset diseases, both common (e.g., cancer) and unusual (e.g., Huntington's) can result in dramatic changes in life-style. Premarital genetic analysis can affect the selection of prospective marriage partners, or even whether one will choose to marry. Genetic analysis is already being used for decisions on childbearing or adoption. And in prenatal genetic analysis the prospect of pregnancy termination is confronted directly. The impact of genetic analysis on health and life insurance is the cause of much concern. It does not appear that these social issues will alter or impede the rate at which commercial development of DNA diagnostics will occur.

Silverman, Sam. Process and Detection in Fraud and Deceit. *Ethics Behavior*, 4(3), 219-228, 1994.

There has been considerable interest recently in scientific misconduct. Although much has been written and discussed about specific cases, very little, if any, research has been carried out on the process of fraud. An understanding of this aspect can contribute much to methods of detection and lead to recommendations for preventing misconduct and for implementation of appropriate sanctions where fraud has been detected and proved. In this article I initiate a study of the process of fraud using a series of case studies. Hypotheses are generated by methods pioneered by Peirce and most recently developed and thoroughly discussed by Galser and Strauss under the name of grounded theory. Some illustrations of what can be learned from such studies are included.

Silvers, Anita. Reconciling Equality to Difference: Caring (F)or Justice For People With Disabilities. *Hypatia*, 10(1), 30-55, Wint 95.

A feminist ethics that bases morality on dependence or vulnerability challenges the moral priority of uniform over disparate treatment. Persons with disabilities resist equality's homogenization of moral personhood. But displacing equality in favor of caring or trust reprises the repression of those already marginalized. The ethics of difference proves an ineffective remedy for the negative consequences attendant on how historically marginalized groups are different. An historical conception of equality resolves the dilemma.

Sim, May (Mui Hwa). "Senses of Being in Aristotle's *Nicomachean Ethics*" in *The Crossroads of Norm and Nature, Sim, May (ed)*, 51-77. Lanham, Rowman & Littlefield, 1995.

I propose a solution to the apparent disunity between the lives of practical wisdom and contemplation in the *Nicomachean Ethics* by comparing Aristotle's three senses of substance in his *Metaphysics* with his understanding of the activities that correspond to the human substance in the *Nicomachean Ethics*. Focus on the most

challenging issues in the *Metaphysics* and the *Nichomachean Ethics* sheds light on these works because the problems and solutions in both rest upon the question of what primary substance is. Since the *Metaphysics* investigates and solves the questions about primary substance, which solution in turn will illuminate the human substance and subsequently its ultimate well-being in the *Nichomachean Ethics*, the *Nichomachean Ethics* relies on or presupposes the *Metaphysics* for its solution. By showing that Aristotle's understanding of substance in the *Nichomachean Ethics* rests upon that of his *Metaphysics*, the unity as well as consistency of the highest human activity will become evident, for it reflects the consistency and hierarchical ordering of the various senses of substance in the *Metaphysics*.

Sim, May (Mui Hwa). The Becoming of Aristotelian Virtues. *SW Phil Rev*, 11(1), 101-109, Ja 95.

It is common knowledge to any student of Aristotle's *Ethics* that one becomes virtuous or acquires a certain virtue by performing the right action in the right way and right context repeatedly. However, what is the thing that 'becomes' virtuous? and what are the kinds of changes one undergoes in 'becoming' virtuous? are two questions that are often ignored. These are significant questions because it is also common knowledge that Aristotelian substances do not change (viz. *Met* 1044a 9-10). If so, then how do such Aristotelian substances change to become virtuous? The purpose of this essay is to investigate the becoming of Aristotelian substances and show that the becoming of virtues in such substances are to be understood along the model of the becoming of substances rather than qualitative changes as is commonly taken for granted (e.g., viz. *Categories* 8).

Sim, May (Mui Hwa) (ed). The Crossroads of Norm and Nature. Lanham, Rowman & Littlefield, 1995.

This collection of essays explores the relations between Aristotle's *Ethics and Metaphysics*. Core essays argue for the intimate connection between the *Ethics and Metaphysics* so that the one cannot be understood apart from the other. The collection also contains close analyses of change, potency, and act, and Aristotle's *stoicheia* and *aitiai* which provide indispensible background material for both texts and their intersection.

Sim, Stuart. *Georg Lukács*. Hertfordshire, Harvester-Wheatsheaf, 1994.

Lukacs's oeuvre is examined to see whether it can survive the collapse of Marxism as a political force and the advent of postmodernism. The survey ranges from the early pre-Marxist writings to the late studies on materialist ontology. Chapters are devoted to Lukacs's major works on realism as well as his contributions to Marxist philosophy and political theory. It is concluded that Lukacs still has considerable relevance to contemporary cultural debates and that his work transcends the Marxist moment, the contention being that postmodernism's problematization of the modernist enterprise has given his antimodernism a new topicality.

Simesen de Bielke, Ana and Leonardi de Herran, Teresa. "La Filosofía en Tiempos del Cólera" in *Temas Actuales de Filosofía, Palacios, María Julia (ed)*, 577-581. Buenos Aires, Univ Nacional Salta, 1993.

Our aim is to present a diffuse panorama of Philosophy at the end of the millenium. Universalisms, with their advantages and disadvantages, have been legitimated. It is not believed any more that Philosophy can systematize the sense and the progress of the world. It is not believed that Philosophy can legitimate the scientific discourse. It is argued in favour of Wittgenstein's games. In social terms, we witness the "end of representation." In social terms, we witness the "end of representation." Which will the task of Philosophy be after the "end of universalisms?"

Simmel, Georg and Ritter, Mark (trans). Bridge and Door. *Theor Cult Soc*, 11(1), 5-10, F 94.

Simmel, Georg and Ritter, Mark (trans). The Picture Frame: An Aesthetic Study. *Theor Cult Soc*, 11(1), 11-17, F 94.

Simmons, A John. Historical Rights and Fair Shares. *Law Phil*, 14(2), 149-184, My 95.

My aim of this paper is to clarify, and in a certain very limited way to defend, historical theories of property rights (and their associated theories of social or distributive justice). It is important, I think, to better understand historical rights for several reasons: first, because of the extent to which historical theories capture commonsense, unphilosophical views about property and justice; then, because historical theories have fallen out of philosophical fashion, and are consequently not much scrutinized anymore; and finally, because of (what I see as) the continuing need to better understand the historical components of our society's responsibilities to the descendants of victims of systematic injustice in our own past. The case I will have in mind throughout is that of the property claims of Native American tribes, claims based on their historical standing as the original owners of certain lands and resources. And while I will concentrate here only on the question of rectifying past violations of property rights, this will constitute at least a start to answering more general questions about just rectification, which includes the more serious and less compensable wrongs of violence against persons.

Simmons, A John. Locke on the Death Penalty. *Philosophy*, 69(270), 471-477, O 94.

Brian Calvert has offered us a clear and careful analysis of Locke's views on punishment and capital punishment. The primary goal of his paper—that of correcting the misperception of Locke as a wholehearted proponent of capital punishment for a wide range of offenses—must be allowed to be both laudable and largely achieved in his discussion. But Calvert's analysis also encourages, I think, a number of serious misunderstandings of Locke's true position.

Simmons, Keith. On an Argument Against Omniscience. *Nous*, 27(1), 22-33, Mr 93.

Simmons, Keith. Paradoxes of Denotation. *Phil Stud*, 76(1), 71-106, O 94.

Simmons, Lance. Three Kinds of Incommensurability Thesis. *Amer Phil Quart*, 31(2), 119-131, Ap 94.

Three kinds of incommensurability theses have been advanced in ethics and the philosophy of science. "Global" theses concern rival scientific or moral thought-styles regarded as total conceptual systems. "Thin" and "thick" theses concern the relationships between particular elements of rival thought-styles. Thin elements perform functions which must be discharged in every thought-style, whereas the functions of thick elements are adequately characterizable only in terms internal to particular thought-styles. This article distinguishes among these three kinds of theses, distinguishes incommensurability theses from relativity theses, and proposes initial analyses of all the claims discussed.

Simon, Caroline J. Just Friends, Friends and Lovers, or...?. *Phil Theol*, 8(2), 113-128, Wint 93.

This paper explores the question of whether there is a conceptual distinction between romantic love and friendship and whether such a distinction would support the normative conclusion that friends should not be lovers. Laurence Thomas has argued that, given an egalitarian conception of romantic love, there is no such distinction between romantic love and friendship. This paper shows that equally egalitarian alternatives to Thomas's conceptions of love and friendship do suggest that friends should not be lovers. Moreover, the alternative view of romantic love defended in the paper supports a link between romantic love and sexual exclusivity.

Simon, Gerd and Leaman, George. Die Kant-Studien im Dritten Reich. *Kantstudien*, 85(4), 443-469, 1994.

This extensively documented article examines the publishing history of *Kant-Studien* during the years of the Nazi dictatorship. The article provides a detailed account of the work of the German philosophers who transformed the journal into a sophisticated instrument of Nazi cultural propaganda, and situates their efforts within the larger context of pro-Nazi philosophical activities in Germany. The article also presents a hitherto unknown volume of *Kant-Studien* (Band 42, Heft 1, Jg 1941/42) and provides a brief account of the journal's post-war resurrection.

Simon, Josef. "World-Picture and Conscience" in *Hermeneutics and Truth, Wachterhauser, Brice (ed)*, 190-205. Evanston, Northwestern Univ Pr, 1994.

Words can only come to have a meaning when explicated and used *in concreto* within the framework of a "world-picture". This process of explication is characterized by two important properties: 1) It serves to redefine this world-picture, which gives the individual a large degree of responsibility for it, and 2) it can never reach a final conclusion; there is always some room for slippage between the "particular" and the "general" or between the interpretations of the different individuals in a linguistic community. Due to structural similarities, the uncertainty resulting from this possible slippage is present in both the epistemological and ethical realms—yet, we often are forced to act upon this "incomplete" knowledge. These reflections concerning the uncertainty of our "knowledge" lead to the only possible conclusion that we should use it "conscientiously"—for the outcome of our actions is just as uncertain as the knowledge upon which they are based, an outcome which unforgivably determines the *value* of our world-picture.

Simon, Josef and Heffernan, George (trans). *Philosophy of the Sign*. Albany, SUNY Pr, 1995.

This book considers the concept "sign" to be a fundamental concept of philosophy. According to Kant, we have no access to "things-in-themselves"—we "have" only representations; according to the philosophy of the sign—which transcends the "subjectivity" of representations—we are left with only signs. "Cognition" is understood as operating sign variations. With reference to classical and, especially, to ontological positions, prominent philosophical problems are reconstructed and discussed from the vantage point of this sign philosophy. The issue is not "semiotics" in a strict sense; rather, the book deals with the most important questions of philosophy based upon an universally understood philosophy of the sign.

Simon, Julia. *Mass Enlightenment: Critical Studies in Rousseau and Diderot*. Albany, SUNY Pr, 1995.

Mass Enlightenment uncovers the tensions and contradictions associated with the rise of capitalism and mass culture as they were already making themselves felt during the second half of the eighteenth century and shows that the works of Rousseau and Diderot display a manifest awareness of the negative side of "enlightenment" and "progress." Using the insights of the Frankfurt School, the themes of individual freedom and moral autonomy, the growth of a consumer market, alienated social relations, the split between the public and private spheres, and the appearance of commodification are explored in the writings of Rousseau and Diderot.

Simon, Julia. Natural Freedom and Moral Autonomy: Emile as Parent, Teacher, and Citizen. *Hist Polit Thought*, 16(1), 21-36, Spr 95.

The development of Emile's sense of natural freedom and independence is purchased at the expense of his moral autonomy. Rousseau's project for educational reform provides only a well-developed conception of individuality for his student, but never fosters the sense of connection or commitment to other human beings requisite for moral personhood. Echoing the shortcomings of liberalism, Rousseaus's *Emile* neglects a positive conception of freedom in favor of negative conceptions of freedom, rights and education itself. Ironically, Rousseau's education for Emile produces an adult without the moral autonomy necessary to fulfill the roles of parent, teacher, and citizen.

Simon, Lawrence H. Rationality and Alien Cultures. *Midwest Stud Phil*, 15, 15-43, 1990.

How are we to understand the practices and beliefs of alien cultures? Can we judge the practices and associated beliefs of alien cultures, in particular, those we find puzzling, inconsistent or bizarre, to be rationally deficient? The essay argues that we must avoid the opposing errors of ethnocentrism and relativism as well as the temptation to discount questions about the rationality of the agents we are attempting to understand, and that we can do so in a way that still allows us to criticize alien cultures from the point of view of rationality.

Simon, Leonore and Sales, Bruce D. Institutional Constraints on the Ethics of Expert Testimony. *Ethics Behavior*, 3(3-4), 231-249, 1993.

We examined the dilemmas posed by the involvement of expert witnesses in court cases and the institutional constraints on the ethics of expert testimony. The causes for the incorporation of bad science into legal decisions, potential solutions to this dilemma, and the limitations of these solutions are considered. We concluded that law, science, and experts must respond to the problems posed by expert witnessing.

Simon, Thomas W. "A Theory of Social Injustice" in *Radical Philosophy of Law, Caudill, David S (ed)*, 54-72. Atlantic Highlands, Humanities Pr, 1995.

This paper answers the challenge of providing means of determining whether a social group qualifies as disadvantaged so as to qualify for judicial protection. A case for disadvantaged status would include the following elements: it would pinpoint a social cause, substantiate a group harm, and recount the group's relative powerlessness. Most importantly, the case would uncover the negative aspects of group identity that lie behind the harm. Applying these criteria, the following characteristics define disadvantaged groups: race and ethnicity, gender and sexual orientation, poverty, infirmity, and age. The analysis is defended as not only consistent with radical democratic theory but also as integral to any democracy.

Simon, Thomas W. *Democracy and Social Injustice: Law, Politics, and Philosophy*. Lanham, Rowman & Littlefield, 1995.

Using perspectives drawn from law, political science, philosophy, and policy studies, the author argues that democratic theory must address the injustices inflicted upon disadvantaged groups. By shifting theoretical sights from justice to injustice, Simon recasts the nature of democracy and provides a new perspective on social problems. He examines the causes and effects of injustice, victims' responses to injustice and historical theories of disadvantage, revealing that those theories have important repercussions for contemporary policy debates. Finally, Simon considers which institutions and practices come within the grasp of democracy and discusses the concept of "Negative Utopia," or, a future without injustice.

Simonds, Roger T. *Rational Individualism: The Perennial Philosophy of Legal Interpretation*. Amsterdam, Rodopi, 1995.

Traditional Western methods for interpretating legal instruments (e.g. statutes, wills, contracts) embody some definite commitments as to the nature of human thought and expression that imply a teleological, rational, and interactively dualistic model of human personality called "rational individualism" by the author. Although this model of personality has been largely rejected in modern philosophy and social science, there has been no comparable revolution in interpretive jurisprudence. The author demonstrates here that the traditional principles of jurisprudence are logically self-sustaining; therefore, the modern philosophical rejection of "rational individualism" must be mistaken. The concluding chapter discusses constitutional and literary hermeneutics.

Simons, Herbert W. "Teaching the Pedagogies: A Dialectical Approach to an Ideological Dilemma" in *After Postmodernism, Simons, Herbert W (ed)*, 133-149. Newbury Park, Sage, 1994.

Simons, Herbert W (ed) and Billig, Michael (ed). *After Postmodernism*. Newbury Park, Sage, 1994.

Simons, Margaret A. "The Second Sex: From Marxism to Radical Feminism" in *Feminist Interpretations of Simone de Beauvoir, Simons, Margaret A (ed)*, 243-262. University Park, Penn St Univ Pr, 1995.

In response to dismissive readings of *The Second Sex* as historically insignificant, I draw on Alice Echol's recent historical study of radical feminism to argue that Beauvoir's text laid the philosophical foundation for radical feminism and defined many of the points differentiating contemporary socialist feminism from traditional Marxist analysis. Beauvoir was a social constructionist who relied on an analogy with racism and developed a critique of Freudian psychoanalysis as did radical feminists in the 1960s. Her methodology privileges women's experience and rejects essentialist definitions of women's identity.

Simons, Margaret A (ed). *Feminist Interpretations of Simone de Beauvoir*. University Park, Penn St Univ Pr, 1995.

The essays in this volume use a variety of methodological approaches to challenge dismissive interpretations of Beauvoir's philosophy: placing her within the Husserlean phenomenological tradition; focusing on her posthumously published letters and notebooks; using little-known texts such as "Literature and Metaphysics" in rereadings of texts such as *Ethics of Ambiguity;* analyzing her concept of the body in *The Second Sex* as the foundation of radical feminism and her Algerian War writings as a historical antecedent of postmodern deconstruction.

Simons, Peter. "Meaning and Language" in *The Cambridge Companion to Husserl, Smith, Barry (ed)*, 106-137. New York, Cambridge Univ Pr, 1995.

Husserl's theory of meaning is examined from his early works to *Experience and Judgment*, in particular the details of his position in the *Logical Investigations*. Topics covered include the general theory of signs and meaning, the nature of indexicals and the theory of meaning categories. By examining the transitional view of the 1908 *Lectures on the Theory of Meaning* it is shown how and why Husserl's view changed between the 1901 *Investigations* and the 1913 *Ideas*.

Simons, Peter. "Strata in Ingarden's Ontology" in *Kunst und Ontologie, Wlodzimierz, Galewicz (ed)*, 119-140. Amsterdam, Rodopi, 1994.

According to Ingarden, language, literary works and other artworks are ontologically structured into strata. This paper examines Ingarden's conception and concludes that while suggestive it is not unobjectionably founded.

Simons, Peter. Discovering Lesniewski: *Collected Works*. *Hist Phil Log*, 15(2), 227-235, 1994.

This discussion review examines the English edition of Lesniewski's collected works. Points emphasized include: the early (pre-symbolic) period, the quality of translation and typesettings, and the scandalously outdated bibliography.

Simons, Peter. Multivalence and Vagueness: A Reply to Copeland. *Proc Aris Soc*, 95, 201-209, 1994-95.

I rebut a claim by B J Copeland that using a four-valued logic to illustrate some aspects of vagueness is a mere formal game without significance. Firstly, it is acknowledged that the logic only partly captures vagueness; secondly, the logic is motivated by using Meinong's conception of factuality and shown to be semantically serious and not just a game.

Simons, Peter and Lambert, Karel. Characterizing Classifying: Explicating a Biological Distinction. *Monist*, 77(3), 315-328, Jl 94.

This paper formally explicates the biological distinction between classifying and characterizing in a free first order logic. It shows, via a translation theorem, that the explication is language neutral.

Simonton, Dean Keith. "Foresight in Insight? A Darwinian Answer" in *The Nature of Insight, Sternberg, Robert J (ed)*, 465-494. Cambridge, MIT Pr, 1995.

The article develops further a Darwinian (variation-selection) model of the creative process. After providing introspective and anecdotal evidence for the theory, two key questions are addressed. First, what is the role of chance in the creative process? Second, how aware are creators of the processes underlying their insights? The article then treats the problem of whether creative insights can display any foresight according to the Darwinian model. The discussion begins with the role of prior preparation, both in the long-term and in the short-term. It then ends with an examination of whether the ultimate fate of insights can be predicted at either personal or social levels.

Simpson, Evan and Williams, Mark. The Ideal of Social Disillusionment. *Phil Forum*, 26(1), 63-77, Fall 94.

In this paper we argue that individuals in modern societies can share a general appreciation of the contingency of moral and political engagement without endangering these purposeful attachments. Depending upon the acceptance of various cognitive conventions, social practices and institutions cannot be sustained by appeals to advantage alone, but these conventions do not demand ontological commitment. Transparent fictions rather than ideological illusions can suffice to sustain valued forms of life. In contrast to Rorty's ironic society in which "only the intellectuals would be ironists", we suggest the benign disillusionment can characterize the public generally.

Simpson, Peter. Liberalism, State, and Community. *Crit Rev*, 8(2), 159-173, Spr 94.

Arguments for and against liberalism are vitiated by failing to distinguish between states (which have millions of citizens) and communities (which have only a few thousand citizens). The state should be liberal or minimal, but the community should not. The state is an alliance of communities for mutual defense and is concerned with matters of defense alone. Two reasons are given for this conclusion, one from Aristotle and one from Hobbes (though Hobbes's argument has to be corrected in two important respects). The community, by contrast, is a moral community and should not be liberal. Two arguments are also given for this conclusion, one from the naturalness of the family and one from the need for moral education. Once state and community have been thus distinguished and described, standard arguments both for and against the liberal state are seen to be correct but misdirected.

Simpson, Peter. Political Authority and Moral Education. *Pub Affairs Quart*, 9(1), 47-62, Ja 95.

It is a principle of liberalism that political authority may use coercion to prevent harm and ensure a fair distribution of primary goods but not to impose a moral code. I argue that no arguments for this conclusion are sound, including the arguments from the subjective character of happiness and from autonomy. Virtue is more of a primary good with respect to attaining happiness than other such goods even if happiness is subjective (which, however, it is not), and autonomy is part of, but not a means to, happiness and is, like virtue, not given but acquired through enforced subjection to good laws.

Sims, Jesse. Justice and Moral Conflict. *Dialogue (PST)*, 37(2-3), 62-72, Ap 95.

This paper attacks MacIntyre's position that the practice of justice as a *virtue* is impossible for a society characterized by pluralism and individualism. Rule-based theories of justice are not incompatible with justice understood as giving to each her proper desert; rather, they constitute different *standards* for its application. This application is possible in a complex society only if the standards conflict. The liberal state thus provides a means by which justice is made possible.

Sims, Randi L and Kroeck, K Galen. The Influence of Ethical Fit on Employee Satisfaction, Commitment and Turnover. *J Bus Ethics*, 13(12), 939-947, D 94.

This study examines the influence of ethical fit on employee attitudes and intentions to turnover. The results of this investigation provides support for the conjecture that ethical work climate is an important variable in the study of person-organization fit. Ethical fit was found to be significantly related to turnover intentions, continuance commitment, and affective commitment, but not to job satisfaction. Results are discussed in regard to some of the affective and cognitive distinctions among satisfaction, commitment, and behavioral intentions.

Sinclair, Melinda. Fitting Pragmatics into the Mind: Some Issues in Mentalist Pragmatics. *J Prag*, 23(5), 509-539, My 95.

This article presents a comparative analysis of two recent theories on the representation of pragmatics in the mind, namely Kasher's and Sperber and Wilson's. The main focus of the analysis is their respective claims on what the mental entities are that should be postulated in order to account for pragmatic phenomena. At the more specific level, major similarities and differences between Kasher's and Sperber and Wilson's claims are highlighted. At the more general level, the analysis is aimed at locating Kasher's and Sperber and Wilson's theories in the wider domain of mentalist linguistics, and at clarifying the conceptual foundations of mentalist pragmatics.

Sindhu, L. Sartrean Concept of Intersubjectivity. *Indian Phil Quart*, 21/4(Supp), 1-12, O 94.

The article attempts to analyse the nature of interpersonal relationships which is inevitable to build up a stable society. Also exposes the inadequacies of the contributions of Jean-Paul Sartre to the treatment of intersubjectivity in his phenomenological essay on ontology *Being and Nothingness* which comes 'alive' in two of his well acclaimed literary works, *The Wall* and *No Exit*. The Sartrian assertion of conflict as the essence of human relationships is questioned with the support of mundane evidences. Finally it concludes that this assertion is only the universalisation of a partial existential experience.

Singer, Beth J. Basing 'Ought' On 'Is'. *Metaphilosophy*, 25(4), 304-315, O 94.

After criticizing several classic attempts to solve or reinterpret the "is-ought problem," I propose a nondeductive model of prescriptive argumentation in terms of which an "ought" judgment is an appraisal of a factual one. I then discuss what it might mean for the conclusion of such an argument to be justified.

Singer, Irving. "A Reply to My Critics and Friendly Commentators" in *The Nature and Pursuit of Love, Goicoechea, David (ed)*, 323-361. Buffalo, Prometheus, 1995.

In this essay, written after his book *The Pursuit of Love*, Irving Singer traces the development of his philosophy in the last 35 years and presents his current thinking about the nature of love. Addressing the various papers on his views, he reformulates his distinction between appraisal and bestowal, refines his ideas about love as acceptance of another's autonomy, and clarifies his affiliation to Nietzsche, Freud, Santayana, Dewey, and Sartre while also specifying the differences between his approach and theirs. More comprehensively than ever before, Singer discusses his methodology and locates his writings in relation to contemporary naturalism, pluralism, and humanism.

Singer, Marcus G (ed) and MacCallum Jr, Gerald C and Martin, Rex (ed). *Legislative Intent and Other Essays on Law, Politics, and Morality*. Madison, Univ of Wisconsin Pr, 1993.

This book contains fourteen papers by the late Gerald MacCallum, five not previously published. In addition to the author's corrected version of "Legislative Intent and Negative and Positive Freedom," it contains papers that link with them, such as "On Applying Rules" and "Some Truths and Untruths about Civil Disobedience." There are also interrelated papers on such themes as conscience, law, violence, personal integrity, and representation, and a little known paper on "Censorship in the Arts." The previously unpublished writings include groundbreaking papers on "Competition and Moral Philosophy" and "Justice and Adversary Proceedings," discussions of violence and conscience, and "Dworkin and Judicial Discretion." The editors have provided a preface, an introduction, a memoir of the author, a bibliography of his writings, and explanatory comments when needed.

Singer, Peter. Feminism and Vegetarianism: A Response. *Phil Cont World*, 1(3), 36-38, Fall 94.

Erin McKenna is correct to question the relative weight that I give to emotions and reason in *Animal Liberation*. In 1975 when the first edition was published, emotion played a key role in the campaigns of animal societies, and I wished to make an appeal to reason that would have ethical and political impact. I disagree with McKenna's conclusion that an impartial, objective stance is either impossible or undesirable. I argue that we should not abandon the attempt to reach an impartial position. Admittedly, in some disputes, giving equal weight to all interests will be extremely difficult, and a decision must be made regarding which course is better on the whole. This difficulty gives no reason to abandon impartiality.

Singer, Peter. *How Are We to Live? Ethics in an Age of Self-Interest*. Buffalo, Prometheus, 1995.

How Are We To Live? explores the way in which standard contemporary assumptions about human nature and self-interest have led to a world that is fraught with social and environmental problems. Peter Singer asks whether selfishness is in our genes, and concludes that we do not have to accept the bleak view of human nature sometimes believed to be inevitable, given our evolutionary origins.

Singer, Peter. Presidential Address: Is the Sanctity of Life Terminally Ill?. *Bioethics*, 9(3-4), 327-343, Jl 95.

Our growing technical capacity to keep human beings alive has brought the sanctity of life ethic to the point of collapse. The shift to a concept of brain death was already an implicit abandonment of the traditional ethic, though this has only recently become apparent. The 1993 decision of the British House of Lords in the case of Anthony Bland is an even more decisive shift towards an ethic that does not ask or seek to preserve human life as such, but only a life that is worth living. Once this shift has been completed and assimilated, we will no longer need the concept of brain death. Instead we can face directly the real ethical issue: when may doctors intentionally end the life of a patient?

Singer, Peter and Kuhse, Helga. "Hard Choices: Ethical Questions Raised by the Birth of Handicapped Infants" in *Ethics on the Frontiers of Human Existence, Badham, Paul (ed)*, 153-177. New York, Paragon House, 1992.

Modern medical technology allows us to sustain the lives of many seriously disabled newborn infants. Should we do this? Our answer is "no". In drawing a distinction between infants and "persons", and rejecting the argument that decision-making should be based on the infant's potential to become a person, we argue that there are occasions when it is in an infant's best interest to be allowed, or helped, to die.

Singer, Peter and Kuhse, Helga. *Individuals, Humans, Persons: Questions of Life and Death*. Sankt Augustin, Academia, 1994.

This is a collection of eight previously published (and one formerly unpublished) essays by Helga Kuhse and Peter Singer of the Centre for Human Bioethics at Monash University in Australia, with an introduction by Edgar Morscher, Professor of Philosophy at the University of Salzburg in Austria. After some initial reflections on the nature of bioethics, the articles raise questions about the nature of individuality, humanhood and personhood, in the context of contemporary debates about in vitro fertilization, embryo experimentation, contraception, abortion and euthanasia. The authors argue that early human embryos are not individuals, that not every human individual has a "right to life", and that some forms of euthanasia are morally justified.

Singh, D and Choudhary, A K. A Note on the Relevance of Relevance Implication. *J Indian Counc Phil Res*, 11(2), 113-118, Ja-Ap 94.

The paper attempts to counteract a number of explications presented in defense of material implication. It argues that opinions like 'inferentially harmless', 'pernicious' and the like do not apply to material implication. It advances the argument that exploiting the intentional dimension would remain an undiminable premise underlying any genuine attempt at comprehending the relation of implication. The seminal idea of the paper is, relevance requires that as disjunctions and negated conjunctions are instinctively intentional, they need to be represented by intentional connectives.

Singh, Fateh. 'Brahmin, Ritual and Renouncer' A Comment by Dr Fateh Singh. *J Indian Counc Phil Res*, 12(1), 156-159, S-D 94.

The work contradicts the view that the Vedic Brahamin, with reference to the ritual performed by him, becomes a queer mixture of opposites, as he poses to be a renouncer and a worldly man at one and the same time. The fact is that the ritual is only a symbol of spiritual training, meant for the harmonious development of his inward and the outward simultaneously. Inwardly he has to acquire divine power through Yogie concentration, whereas outwardly he has to use that power in the best possible selfless human behavior.

Singh, R P. Spirit, Estrangement and Unification: Hegel's Philosophico-Religious Quest. *Indian Phil Quart*, 21(2), 161-172, Ap 94.

The objective of this paper is to formulate Hegel's philosophico-religious quest by developing its key concepts—Spirit, Estrangement and Unification. It is proposed to be achieved in the following manner: Part I: Hegel's exposition of Spirit as the central concept of his philiosophico-religious quest, and at the same time, as the locus of both estrangement and unification. I shall basically dwell upon Hegel's early work which hitherto been neglected. Part II: A critical assessment of the basic charges levelled by Ludwig Feuerbach on the one hand and Charles Taylor on the other against Hegel's doctrine of Spirit.

Singh, Ravindra M. Is There a Break in Sartre's Thought?. *Indian Phil Quart*, 21(4), 279-296, O 94.

Sinha, Shyam Deo Kumar. The Philosophy of Samuel Frederick Hahnemann—A Perspective. *Darshana Int*, 32(4/128), 29-35, O 92.

Sinigaglia, Corrado. Neuere Interpretationen der Phänomenologie Husserls in Italien (1986-1992). *Phil Rundsch*, 42(1), 76-90, Mr 95.

Sinisi, John. "Marxism in the Shadow of Hobbes" in *Marxism in the Postmodern Age, Callari, Antonio (ed)*, 79-88. New York, Guilford, 1994.

Sinnott-Armstrong, Walter (ed). *Modality, Morality, and Belief*. New York, Cambridge Univ Pr, 1994.

These essays are inspired by the groundbreaking work of Ruth Barcan Marcus. Their authors try to live up to her high standards of rigor, clarity, originality, and insight. The Barcan Formula and other issues about modality, such as possible-world semantics and essentialism, are explored by Terence Parsons, Robert Stalnaker, Maxwell Cressell, David Kaplan, Kit Fine, Charles Parsons, and David Wiggins. Moral dilemmas and deontic modalities are examined by Philippa Foot, Patricia Greenspan, Joel Feinberg, and Nuel Belnap and Paul Bartha. Marcus's work on belief and related topics are discussed by Robert Fogelin, Isaac Levi, Ernest Sosa, and Scott Soames.

Sirgy, M Joseph (& others). A Life Satisfaction Measure: Additional Validational Data for the Congruity Life Satisfaction Measure. *Soc Indic Res*, 34(2), 237-259, F 95.

Meadow *et al.* (1992) have developed a measure of life satisfaction based on judgment theory, referred to as Congruity Life Satisfaction (CLS). This paper, by M Joseph Sirgy, Dennis Cole, Rustan Kosenko, H Lee Meadow, Don Rahtz, Muris Cicic, Guang Xi Jin, Duygun Yarsuvat, David L Blenkhorn and Natasha Nagpal, reports the results of a major study involving six samples from different countries testing the construct validity of the CLS measure. The results of these studies provide additional validational support for the CLS measure.

Sisaye, Seleshi and Lackman, Conway. Ethics in Undergraduate Accounting Education: An Empirical Study. *Bus Prof Ethics J*, 13(1-2), 79-87, Spr-Sum 94.

The extent to which ethics education has been incorporated in the business program, particularly in the accounting curriculum, has received substantial attention among accounting educators and administrators. This paper discusses the results of a case study of a business undergraduate program on the integration of ethics in the accounting curriculum. The study revealed that ethics and social issues are the least integrated subject areas in accounting courses when compared to other business courses. While ethics has been slightly more covered in the upper than the lower level accounting courses, the most commonly methods of ethics integration primarily included short problems and individual projects or case assignments.

Sistare, Christine T. In the Land of Omissions: An Opinionated Guide. *Crim Just Ethics*, 14(1), 26-48, Wint-Spr 95.

Liability for omissions has long been a controversial subject in Anglo-American legal theory. Nonetheless, the debate as to the nature of omissive conduct and the propriety of liability for omissions continues with little movement towards a generally satisfactory resolution or, apparently, improved understanding among theoretical adversaries. This article provides an admittedly idiosyncratic tour of selected matters that contribute to this controversy, offered to help others traverse what the author takes to be the more boggy areas. Among these are: the relation of various levels of discourse, the ontological status of omissions as a form of conduct, the function of the requirement of *actus reus* for criminal liability, and the persistence of liberal fears of extended liability.

Sitter-Liver, Beat. Skepsis und Praxis: Zur Grundlegung der praktischen Philosophie. *Z Phil Forsch*, 48(3), 372-396, Jl-S 94.

Scepticism is the adequate attitude under conditions of ethical pluralism. Yet consequently investigated, sceptical self-reflection yields a number of general principles permitting moral strangers to cooperate for mutual benefit. The transcendental argument is developed through discussing Sextus Empiricus, Descartes, Marquard, and others. Sceptical rationality is not a contradiction in itself, and there is no scepticism without any principle. Freedom is the first, respect of others' liberty the second principle necessarily supporting scepticism. Equality, impartiality, and tolerance ensue. They lead to a contractarian theory including theory of political ethics and politics. Scepticism thus becomes the foundation of a timely and universal practical philosophy.

Sizemskaia, I and Novikova, L. Liberal Tradition in the Cultural-Historical Experience of Russia. *Russian Stud Phil*, 33(3), 6-25, Wint 94-95.

The article provides a history of liberal political thinking in Russia. It points up both its original Western inspiration and the particular coloration assumed in Russia by such liberal concepts as the rule of law and the absolute value of the individual. The authors develop the concept of "new liberalism", relevant to Russian mentality. It made by greater emphasis on constitutionalism and active role of the state in providing social benefits and promoting cultural values. Since 1860 the social development of Russia followed this way, but this process was broken by revolutions of 1917.

Skagestad, Peter. "Discussion: Peirce and the History of Science" in *Peirce and Contemporary Thought: Philosophical Inquiries, Ketner, Kenneth Laine (ed)*, 196-201. New York, Fordham Univ Pr, 1995.

Charles Peirce's account of the evolution of science gives a clear statement of the incommensurability doctrine later made famous by Thomas Kuhn. However, since in Peirce's view all concepts are vague, mere incommensurability of meaning does not exclude progress towards truth through increased verisimilitude, made possible by increased precision.

Skawran, Karin M. "The Cultural Boycott: An Act of Censorship or a Tool of Liberation?" in *Life, World and Meaning, Roux, A P J (ed)*, 69-78. Pretoria, Univ of S Africa, 1990.

This essay examines the effectiveness of a cultural boycott as a means to dismantle apartheid in South Africa. The cultural boycott, arbitrarily implemented by the Anti-Apartheid Movement in England, merely served to retard the process of liberation because it hurt mainly those artists who themselves were opposed to apartheid. The revolutionary power of art is not being questioned here, while the demand for art as a weapon in the struggle for liberation is. By its very nature, such art is one-dimensional and transitory. Any interference with artistic expression, whether it be in the form of internal or external censorship, strikes at the very heart of civilization.

Skidelsky, Liza D. "Acerca de la Dificultad para Identificar Personas como Particulares Básicos en Strawson" in *Temas Actuales de Filosofía, Palacios, María Julia (ed)*, 583-590. Buenos Aires, Univ Nacional Salta, 1993.

Strawson claims that there are two categories of basic particulars the fundamental features of which constitute our conceptual/ontological scheme: material bodies and persons. First, I show that the fundamental features are physical. Second, I intend to show the difficulty to identify persons (as different from mere bodies). Finally, I suggest that the way to preserve the concept of person consists in the enlargement of the features that constitute our conceptual/ontological scheme to include those that respond to a behavioral criterion.

Skillen, Anthony. Can a Good Man Know Himself?. *Phil Invest*, 18(2), 151-155, Ap 95.

I extract from D Z Phillips' *Interventions in Ethics* a general view that there is an asymmetry between self-description and "spectators" descriptions of virtuous acts—especially acts of generosity, courage and humility. Phillips argues, for example, that to think of oneself as pure or humble or generous is (at least sometimes) self-refuting. I criticize this view, developing situations where the virtuous cannot, without radical self-ignorance, deny their virtue. I argue that Phillips conflates egotistical self-consciousness and self-knowledge.

Skinner, Quentin. "The Study of Rhetoric as an Approach to Cultural History: The Case of Hobbes" in *Main Trends in Cultural History, Melching, Willem (ed)*, 17-53. Amsterdam, Rodopi, 1994.

Skirbekk, Gunnar. Ethischer Gradualismus: Jenseits von Anthropozentrismus und Biozentrismus?. *Deut Z Phil*, 43(3), 419-434, 1995.

In the article—ethical gradualism, beyond anthropocentrism and biocentrism—I look into arguments in favour of the view that all human beings and only human beings have ethical status and arguments in favour of the view that there is an ethical gradualism between human beings and other mammals (and thus between man and nature). Cases from biomedical ethics are discussed and compared with cases from animal life, and in so doing I discuss these cases in relation to different theoretical positions, such utilitarianism, the deontological position(s), and discourse ethics. While defending the view that persons (possibly defined in different theoretical perspectives) have a paradigmatic ethical status, I conclude by defending an ethical gradualism between persons and other moral subjects (who are not moral agents, nor moral discussants)—the crucial point being that moral status is seen in relation to actual and potential characteristics (which are defined differently in different theoretical perspectives) and not as a metaphysical property of the human race (and the human race alone).

Skledar, Nikola. Platons und Plotins Zugang zur transzendenten Wesenheit. *Filozof Istraz*, 13(4), 843-850, 1993.

Plato und Plotin sind herausragende Vertreter zweier gründlich verschiedener Typen des erkenntnismässigen Zugangs zur transzendenten Wesenheit: des Rationalismus (der das Erkenntnisverhältnis in den Bereich der Vernunft stellt) und des A-Rationalismus (der dieses Verhältnis dem Bereich des Glaubensbekenntisses und der Ekstase zuordnet). Der vorliegende Text erörtert Platos und Plotins Zugang zur Idee des Guten bzw. des Einen im besonderen.

Skokowski, Paul G. Can Computers Carry Content 'Inexplicitly'?. *Mind Mach*, 4(3), 333-344, Ag 94.

I examine whether it is possible for content relevant to a computer's behavior to be carried without an explicit internal representation. I consider three approaches. First, an example of a chess playing computer carrying 'emergent' content is offered from Dennett. Next I examine Cummins' response to this example. Cummins says Dennett's computer executes a rule which is inexplicitly represented. Cummins describes a process wherein a computer interprets explicit rules in its program, implements them to form a chess-playing device, then this device executes the rules in a way that exhibits them inexplicitly. Though this approach is intriguing, I argue that the chess-playing device cannot exist as imagined. The processes of interpretation and implementation produce explicit representations of the content claimed to be inexplicit. Finally, the Chinese Room argument is examined and shown not to save the notion of inexplicit information. This means the strategy of attributing inexplicit content to a computer which is executing a rule, fails.

Skolimowski, Henryk. Eco-Ethics—The Key to Survival. *Dialogue Hum*, 4(4), 73-82, 1994.

Skolimowski, Henryk. In Defence of Sustainable Development. *Environ Values*, 4(1), 69-70, F 95.

Our intellectual honesty requires that we recognize economic theories as normative, at least as containing the normative substratum. If there is a clash between our intellectual honesty and our intellectual respectability, we must choose the former, for intellectual respectability so often is a euphemism standing for institutional commitment and servitude to the old, while our intellectual honesty is a new moral stance through which we attempt to help the threatened life on the whole planet. The idea of sustainable development tries to combine what needs to be combined: the economic and the moral, the idea of justice with the appropriate economic tools which should serve the idea of justice—particularly with regard to the poor and the underprivileged. Some admonish us that we use vague concepts as a vehicle leading to the amelioration of the environment and of human life. Yes, we do. It is better to muddle through to salvation than to go crisply to damnation.

Skorobogatov-Gray, Yevgenia. Bakhtin, Rabelais, and Utopia. *Int Stud Phil*, 27(1), 85-96, 1995.

The paper is an attempt to both deepen the significance of the notion of utopia and to provide an analysis of the particular kind of utopianism that emerges in Bakhtin's *Rabelais and His World*. The paper draws on the connection between Bakhtin's German predecessors, Kant, Schelling, Hegel, and Nietzsche.

Skorupski, John. Possessed by Concepts: Christopher Peacocke's *A Study of Concepts*. *Int J Phil Stud*, 3(1), 143-163, Mr 95.

In this book and elsewhere Christopher Peacocke offers a general theory of concepts which he uses to provide a new account of a priori knowledge. The review concentrates on this aspect of the theory. It argues 1) That Peacocke's theory is inadequate because it gives no account of the apriocity of the principle that concepts determine semantic values, though it needs to assume it, 2) That a theory which in contrast took concepts to be constituted by epistemic norms would not require an account of 'a priori knowledge' at all.

Skrupskelis, Ignas K. James's Conception of Psychology as a Natural Science. *Hist Human Sci*, 8(1), 73-90, F 95.

My aim is to arrange various texts in order to elucidate James's conception of psychology as a natural science, independent of metaphysics. I argue that 1) he seeks to eliminate metaphysical explanations from psychology; 2) that he thinks that psychology can proceed on the basis of common sense assumptions, thereby postponing metaphysical wrangling; 3) that over the years he wavered about the possibility of metaphysically neutral descriptions of mental states, sometimes thinking that metaphysical biases could be eliminated entirely, at other times, that they could be reduced to a harmless minimum.

Skrupskelis, Ignas K. The Royce-Howison Debate on the Conception of God. *Trans Peirce Soc*, 30(4), 791-802, Fall 94.

In examining some aspects of the 1895 debate between George Holmes Howison and Josiah Royce, I argue that Howison throughout the dispute places Christianity in a privileged position and claims that Royce's conception of the absolute is mistaken because it is incompatible with Christian beliefs. Royce, on the other hand, is interested in formal conceptions of individuality and in the course of the debate realizes that he must rework his metaphysics to make room for human moral agency.

Skubik, Daniel W. Ethics and Australian International Business: Which Way to Asia?. *J Bus Ethics*, 14(8), 643-652, Ag 95.

In an era of domestic and economic reform wherein deregulation/privatisation becomes a priority, short shift has too often been given to evaluative analyses of business activities. Evaluative monitoring and oversight are especially needful in highly competitive international business environments, where the temptations are very strong to adjudge individual effectiveness by the sole criterion of the bottom line. But what additional or alternative criteria should be administered, and by whom, is less clear. That any but the most vague Judeo-Christian or secular ethical standards are applicable (e.g., notions of fairness) is widely contested. The debated is significantly only widened when doing business across national borders involving peoples from different cultures and languages. This section is devoted to explicating the normative role of international codes of conduct for guiding the decision making of managers involved in multinational operations, and clarifying what ethical frameworks are available to the international manager for taking decisions which require selecting actions inconsistent with either home or host country demands.

Skura, Tomasz. Syntactic Refutations against Finite Models in Modal Logic. *Notre Dame J Form Log*, 35(4), 595-605, Fall 94.

The purpose of the paper is to study syntactic refutation systems as a way of characterizing normal modal propositional logics. In particular it is shown that there is a decidable modal logic without the finite model property that has a simple finite refutation system.

Skutch, Alexander F. Responsabilidad y castigo. *Rev Filosof (Costa Rica)*, 32(77), 19-25, Jl 94.

The author, avoiding determinism and the side of free will, chooses the voluntary assumption of a radical responsibility for all our acts and words. He thinks that we chiefly need a wide dissemination of responsibility for the consequences of our own behaviors, so that some of our major problems become manageable problems.

Skyrms, Brian. "Adams Conditionals" in *Probability and Conditionals, Eells, Ellery (ed)*, 13-26. New York, Cambridge Univ Pr, 1994.

This discusses Adams's conditional probability approach to conditionals under subject and objective interpretations of the probability. The objective probability conditional is related to decision making and extended to a general Bayesian theory of conditional. It is shown how other theories of subjunctive conditionals are special cases.

Skyrms, Brian. Darwin Meets *The Logic of Decision*: Correlation in Evolutionary Game Theory. *Phil Sci*, 61(4), 503-528, D 94.

The proper treatment of correlation in evolutionary game theory has unexpected connections with recent philosophical discussions of the theory of rational decision. *The Logic of Decision* (Jeffrey 1983) provides the correct framework for correlated evolutionary game theory and a variant of "ratifiability" is the appropriate generalization of "evolutionarily stable strategy". The resulting theory unifies the treatment of correlation due to kin, population viscosity, detection, signaling, reciprocal altruism, and behavior-dependent contexts. It is shown that 1) a strictly dominated strategy may be selected, and 2) under conditions of perfect correlation a strictly efficient strategy *must* be selected.

Skyrms, Brian. Ratifiability and the Logic of Decision. *Midwest Stud Phil*, 15, 44-56, 1990.

This paper dicusses the concept of ratifiability in decision theory and game theory. Two theorems relating ratifiability to choice worthiness are proved.

Skyrms, Brian. Strict Coherence, Sigma Coherence and the Metaphysics of Quantity. *Phil Stud*, 77(1), 39-55, Ja 95.

This paper discusses the interplay between various kinds of coherence in standard, infinitesimal and measure algebra frameworks.

Skyrms, Brian (ed) and Eells, Ellery (ed). *Probability and Conditionals*. New York, Cambridge Univ Pr, 1994.

This is a collection of essays on the relation between conditional probabilities and probabilities of conditionals. Many of the essays provide new negative results concerning the natural idea that the probability of a conditional coincides with the corresponding conditional probability (i.e., concerning the relation between the probability of a statement of the form "if X, then Y" and the corresponding probability of Y given X). The essays in this volume elaborate on, advance, and evaluate the theories of Ernest Adams, a founder of this field of philosophical and logical investigation, whose important work in these areas is the main focus of the essays.

Slaga, Szczepan W and Lemanska, Anna and Latawiec, Anna. Mieczyslaw Lubanskis Leben und Werk. *Stud Phil Christ*, 30(2), 5-64, 1994.

Zum Anlass des siebzigsten Geburstages wird das wissenschaftliche Wirken und das wissenschaftliche Werk von Professor Mieczyslaw Lubanski dargelegt und besprochen. 1924 geboren, hat er in den Jahren 1945-50 zuerst Mathematik an der Universität Warschau, dann 1955-58 Theologie im Warschauer Priesterseminar und 1959-62 Naturphilosophie an der Katholischen Universität in Lublin studiert. An dieser Hochschule erwarb Er 1965 das Doktorat. Seine Habilitationsschrift verteidigte Er 1973 an der Akademie für Katholische Theologie zur Warschau, wo Er 1982 zum Professor ernannt wurde und bis heute den Lehrstuhl für Methodologie der System und Informationslehre inne hat. Gleichzeitigg doziert Er seit 1965 Philosophie an der Päpstliche Theologischen Fakultät in Warschau, sowie an der Philosophischen Fakultät der Katholischen Universität in Lublin. Die wissenschaftliche Forschung Professors Lubanski lässt sich den folgenden thematischen einzuordnen: Geschichte und Philosophie der Wissenschaft, Philosophie der Mathematik, Informations- und Simulationstheorie, allgemeine Systemtheorie, Naturwissenschafts- und Natur-Philosophie, Systemanthropologie, Philosophie der Kybernetik. Einige Seiner Veröffentlichungen befassen sich zudem mit aktuellen weltanschaulichen Problemen.

Slater, B H. Paraconsistent Logics. *J Phil Log*, 24(4), 451-454, Ag 95.

In this article, I point out a basic mistake in writings on 'paraconsistent logic': taking a subcontrariety functor to be a contradiction functor. Thus, against Graham Priest, in many places, there are no 'true contradictions' merely 'true subcontraries'. The point is also made that, in this context, 'Australian', or 'ontic' truth values must give way to 'American' or 'epistemic' truth values. And consequences such as the invalidity of Tarski's T-scheme are drawn out. Truth is not a predicate of sentences, but the identity modality, to be formulated as an operator.

Slater, B H. The Epsilon Calculus' Problematic. *Phil Papers*, 23(3), 217-242, N 94.

The Second Epsilon Theorem states that the epsilon calculus is a conservative extension of standard predicate logic. Theorems in the epsilon calculus, not formalizable in predicate logic's language, may therefore relate to further forms of speech and argument. Here I show that they do indeed do so. Referential terms, and cross referencing personal pronouns, both in extensional and intensional contexts, can be symbolized. A number of other attempts to do this are commented on; notably those of Russell, Evans, Cooper, Gawron Nerbonne and Peters, Lewis, Edelberg, Saarinen, and King.

Slater, Carol. Discrimination Without Indication: Why Dretske Can't Lean on Learning. *Mind Lang*, 9(2), 163-180, Ju 94.

Slater, Hartley. Scare Quoted "Seeing". *Amer Phil Quart*, 32(1), 97-103, Ja 95.

In this paper it is argued that Ryle's account of images in terms of scare quoted sensory verbs is complete, and also correct. It is complete since, although the subject's words are not endorsed, because nothing is experienced, still an experience is reported by the subject. It is correct because images are intensional, and so they are limited by the descriptions given of them. These points are made in the context of similar discussions by Tye, Dennett, Ishiguro and Hannay. Sartre's definition of imagining proves useful in making a crucial distinction between visualization and misperception.

Slater, J G. *Bertrand Russell*. Bristol, Thoemmes, 1994.

Sleeper, Ralph W. "Vanishing Frontiers in American Philosophy: Two Dogmas of Idealism" in *Pragmatism: From Progressivism to Postmodernism, Hollinger, Robert (ed)*, 170-179. Westport, Praeger, 1995.

Sleigh, Robert. Leibniz on Divine Foreknowledge. *Faith Phil*, 11(4), 547-571, Oct 94.

Leibniz believed that his metaphysical system provided a structure acceptable to all Christian intellectuals of good will and sound reason, within which the leading issues of philosophical theology could be given a sharp formulation, and, at least in some cases, adequately resolved. In this paper, I discuss Leibniz's treatment of one such issue—God's foreknowledge of contingent truths, especially contingent truths concerning free actions of creatures. Leibniz aimed to provide an account of divine foreknowledge without recourse to middle knowledge, as espoused by Molina, or premotion, as espoused by Banez. I aim to provide an account of his account.

Sleigh Jr, R C and Mercer, Christia. "Metaphysics: The Early Period to the *Discourse on Metaphysics*" in *The Cambridge Companion to Leibniz, Jolley, Nicholas (ed)*, 67-123. New York, Cambridge Univ Pr, 1994.

The authors trace the development of Leibniz's mature metaphysics. They present the intellectual context in which his youthful metaphysics is most easily understood and summarize both his original metaphysical principles and his first conception of substance. They argue that his concept of substance, combined with certain theological commitments, led Leibniz to develop most of the central doctrines of his mature thought. For example, they claim that by April 1676, Leibniz had arrived at his doctrine of preestablished harmony.

Sleinis, E E. *Nietzsche's Revaluation of Values: A Study in Strategies*. Champaign, Univ of Illinois Pr, 1994.

Nietzsche's project of revaluing all values and of revaluing the highest values is both inherently important and theoretically intriguing. It immediately raises the issue of the means available to revalue all values, especially the highest values. This book focuses on the overall intelligibility of Nietzsche's project and the strategies he employs in it. It analyses key attempts at revaluation in the areas of knowledge, morality, art and religion and assesses their effectiveness. The work seeks to characterize Nietzsche's positive contributions to thinking about values and singles out Nietzsche's theory of value, his conception of higher-order values, and his conception of the maximally affirmative attitude as creations of enduring importance.

Slicer, Deborah. Is There an Ecofeminism-Deep Ecology "Debate"?. *Environ Ethics*, 17(2), 151-169, Sum 95.

I discuss six problem's with Warwick Fox's "The Deep Ecology-Ecofeminism Debate and Its Parallels" and conclude that until Fox and some other deep ecologists take the time to study feminism and ecofeminist analyses, only disputes—not genuine debate—will occur between these two parties. An understanding of the six issues that I discuss is a precondition for such a debate.

Slife, Brent D. Introduction to "Newton's Legacy for Psychology". *J Mind Behav*, 16(1), 1-7, Wint 95.

This first article (of the group that follows) is intended as a brief introduction to the general philosophical assumptions of Newton: namely, his mathematicism, empiricism, positivism, reductionism, and dualism. These five "isms" provide an important background to the main articles that are also briefly described.

Slife, Brent D. Newtonian Time and Psychological Explanation. *J Mind Behav*, 16(1), 45-62, Wint 95.

Newton's conception of time has had a profound influence upon science, particularly psychology. Five characteristics of explanation have devolved from Newton's temporal framework: objectivity, continuity, linearity, universality, and reductivity. These characteristics are outlined in the present essay and shown to be central to psychological theories and methods. Indeed, Newton's temporal framework is so central that it often goes unexamined in psychology. Examination is important, however, because recent critics of Newton's framework—including both scientists and philosophers—have questioned its validity and usefulness.

Sloboda, Myron. Intuition, Involvement, Interrogation: The Meaning of Self-Making. *Amer Cath Phil Quart*, 68(Supp), 215-227, 1994.

Slors, Marc. Realisme zonder representatie. *Alg Ned Tijdschr Wijs*, 87(1), 15-32, Ja 95.

In this article it is argued that in order to explain the meaning of 'realism' we do not need the notion of 'accurate representation', by defending a particular aspect of Richard Rorty's antirepresentationalism. We have to distinguish between a 'practical' and a conceptual argument for antirepresentationalism. The conceptual argument, which can only be rejected by means of a petitio principii, can be subject to two different interpretations. Against Rorty, I argue that a realistic reading of the argument is the most plausible one, defending Charles Taylor's common sense realism.

Slote, Michael. Law in Virtue Ethics. *Law Phil*, 14(1), 91-113, F 95.

It is often said that virtue ethics is either incapable of dealing with larger issues of social morality or profoundly and irrelevantly anti-democratic in its treatment of such questions (as with Plato and Aristotle). But a form of virtue ethics that grounds all moral judgment in aretaic characterizations of motives can evaluate the justice of societies in terms of the motives of its members and evaluate laws as expressions of such motives, and do so compatibly with present-day democratic and egalitarian ideals.

Sluga, Hans. "Der Nationalsozialismus und die Idee der Welthistorischen Krise" in *Die besten Geister der Nation, Korotin, Ilse (ed)*, 18-40. Vienna, Picus, 1994.

Sluga, Hans. "Die verfehlte Sendung: Die Philosophie und der Nationalsozialismus" in *Der geistige Anschluss, Fischer, Kurt R (ed)*, 9-35. Wien, WUV Univ, 1993.

Smajs, Josef. Evolutionary Ontology. *Filozof Cas*, 42(4), 623-635, 1994.

Small, Michael W. Business Ethics and Commercial Morality in Western Australia. *J Bus Ethics*, 14(4), 279-285, Ap 95.

Recent events in Western Australia culminating in the 'Royal Commission into Commercial Activities of Government and Other Matters 1992', and the subsequent publication of the Report, highlighted the fact that the commercial activities of the State Government in Western Australia had been in disarray for some time. However, in spite of some early interest in the outcomes of the Report, the general reaction by the public was largely one of disinterest. This paper traces some of the events which took place after the main hearings. A number of leading citizens felt that some action was warranted. In brief, a series of lectures on different aspects of business ethics were planned and given to business students at Curtin Business School. This paper highlights some of the observations made during this series of lectures.

Small, Michael W. Business Ethics and Commercial Morality: Report of the Royal Commission into Commercial Activities. *J Bus Ethics*, 14(8), 613-628, Ag 95.

This section is focused on some areas of concern which were identified in "The Report of the Royal Commission into Commercial Activities of Government and Other Matters (1990-1992)". In the report a number of situations were examined in which some individuals acted without recourse to any ethical guidelines. Most of the people mentioned in the report held responsible positions in either Government or the private sector, and all were very well known in the community. The report of the Royal Commission made a number of findings of "serious impropriety" on the part of several individuals, although there was comparatively little evidence of illegal or corrupt conduct. This section shows what happened to a governmental system in an Australian state when a number of Ministers and their advisors placed their personal or party advantage over their constitutional obligation to act in the community's interests.

Smart, J J C. "Mind and Brain" in *The Mind-Body Problem: A Guide to the Current Debate, Warner, Richard (ed)*, 19-23. Cambridge, Blackwell, 1994.

A defense of the mind-brain identity theory accessible to the general reader. There is a comparison with functionalism and it is suggested that the difference between functionalism and identity theory has commonly been much exaggerated. There is also a discussion of the distinction between 'wide' and 'narrow' belief and its relevance to identity theory.

Smart, J J C. A Form of Metaphysical Realism. *Phil Quart*, 45(180), 301-315, Jl 95.

This essay defends a view which is near enough to Putnam's characterization of metaphysical realism for it to be called by the same name. Indeterminacy of reference is conceded, in the sense that there may be multiple reference relations, but it is denied that this implied belief in unknowable noumena. It is enough for metaphysical realism as conceived here, that there be at least one reference relation. The essay also argues against defining truth epistemically. Even a Peircean ideal theory might be false, in a contextual sense of 'might' stronger than that of the logically possible.

Smart, Ninian. Theravada Buddhism and the Definition of Religion. *Sophia (Australia)*, 34(1), 161-166, Mr-Ap 95.

Smeyers, Paul. Education and the Educational Project I: The Atmosphere of Post-modernism. *J Phil Educ*, 29(1), 109-119, March 95.

The paper deals with the way postmodernism has been discussed within philosophy of education and argued for by some authors within this context, and with what this kind of postmodernism can offer to education and to philosophy of education. Particular attention is paid to one of the basic presuppositions, namely the requirement to break with the cultural heritage and look for radical alternatives. A second paper will develop a different view of human action, following the later Wittgenstein, and draw on Frankfurt's ideas on "the importance of what we care about" to revitalise the conception of the educational project.

Smeyers, Paul (ed). *Identity, Culture, and Education*. Leuven, Leuven Univ Pr, 1994.

The contemporary political situation, fraught with struggles between ethnic identity and national unity, between cultural isolation and the globalization of culture, requires us to refigure and aid attitudes and answers. Questions of identity and the self in relation of community and culture—perennial philosophical issues—are taken up by postmodern and feminist scholars. They speak of fractures, discomforts and multiple standpoints. The philosophers of education contributing to this collection. Take up an extra challenge: to rethink the contributions—conceptual, social and political—of philosophy to education in the new era of uncertainty.

Smeyers, Paul. On the Unavoidability of Power in Child-rearing: Is the Language of Rights Educationally Appropriate?. *Stud Phil Educ*, 14(1), 9-21, 1995.

It is argued that all educational situations, including those within the context of the family as well as within the context of the school, can in one way or another be conceived in terms of the powerlessness children find themselves in. The paper starts from an analysis of this (and related concepts), indicates some historical antecedents within the philosophy of education and illustrates how power is always present in an educational context. Next a structuralist interpretation is scrutinized and finally, it is elaborated, how, if rightly conceived, "power" thus reveals in an educational situation something of the human condition.

Smilansky, Saul. Fortunate Misfortune. *Ratio*, 7(2), 153-163, D 94.

Sometimes people are unfortunate in ways which facilitate their success—and happiness. This creates the perplexity whether someone can be said to have been unfortunate, if an apparent misfortune has been, overall, beneficial to his or her life. I argue that whether something is a misfortune cannot be determined in itself, even in seemingly obvious cases. It depends also upon what one makes of it, what it makes of one. In short, it depends upon what happens later. People cannot claim to have suffered a misfortune for which they are to be pitied or compensated, when this 'misfortune' is crucial in having made them what they are, what they are happy to be. Hard determinism aside, the notion of 'fortunate misfortune' lacks, however, as easy parallel in 'unfortunate good-fortune'.

Smilansky, Saul. Is There a Moral Obligation to Have Children?. *J Applied Phil*, 12(1), 41-53, 1995.

I argue, counter-intuitively, that under certain conditions many people are under some moral requirement to attempt to bring children into being (in order to raise them). There is only rarely a strict obligation to have children, but more moderate, inclining moral considerations in favour of having children, have a place in our moral world. I begin by considering a large number of arguments of favour and against the possibility of an obligation to have children. Then I examine when the weight of one set of arguments is greater. And I conclude by pointing out some general lessons from the discussion.

Smilansky, Saul. May We Stop Worrying About Blackmail?. *Analysis*, 55(2), 116-120, Ap 95.

The serious moral condemnation and legal penalization of blackmail has often been considered paradoxical. This practice, after all, often simply combines two fairly innocuous elements; asking for money or other favors, and threatening to do something which one is *allowed* to do. Michael Clark has recently argued that previous discussions of this issue were fundamentally mistaken, and that there is no paradox about blackmail. The relation between the two elements, Clark argues, brings forth something new, and thus there is nothing paradoxical about the fact that *in themselves* the elements which make up the practice of blackmail are permissible.

I argue for the paradoxality of blackmail in a different way, which considers the practice as a whole, and is not based only on the permissibility of the elements of ordinary blackmail when taken separately.

Smilansky, Saul. Methodological Cynicism in Ethics. *Int J Applied Phil*, 9(1), 53-58, Sum-Fall 94.

Cynicism has a bad reputation. The cynic is not only after teaching us something new about morality, but seeks to unmask it, claiming that it derives from illicit and undeclared motivations. I explore whether there is anything we can learn from cynicism about morality, particularly about the content of morality. I distinguish between three basic forms of skepticism and the parallel forms of cynicism. I then examine four examples of suggestive ethical cynicism. Finally, I try to see in which areas ethical cynicism is likely to be more enlightening.

Smilansky, Saul. Nagel on the Grounds for Compensation. *Pub Affairs Quart*, 9(1), 63-73, Ja 95.

I consider Thomas Nagel's treatment of the issue of the grounds for compensation, i.e., of what counts as a basis for the obligation to compensate people in a (more or less ideal) political system, in his recent *Equality and Impartiality*. I argue that on the issue of compensation Nagel is unconvincing, and that he reflects here much of liberal thinking. It emerges that a consistent egalitarianism must see the grounds for compensation in very wide way, and this radically affects the acceptability of such a position.

Smilansky, Saul. Who Should a Utilitarian Be?. *Iyyun*, 44, 91-98, Ja 95.

I argue that utilitarianism has serious difficulties in accommodating the central human need of maintaining one's identity, over a long period of time. There is no clear reason in utilitarian terms for remaining oneself, and there might well be good reason for transforming oneself into someone else. If my arguments are convincing being a utilitarian becomes, if not incoherent, then at least very unattractive for most human beings.

Smiley, Timothy. Aristotle's Completeness Proof. *Ancient Phil*, 14, 25-38, 1994.

In Prior Analytics i 23 Aristotle presents a completeness proof for syllogistic logic, or so I maintain. I reconstruct the crucial step, which I take to be his highly condensed argument that every syllogistic-style deduction with more than two premises can be reduced to a series of syllogisms proper. I detect two big holes in the argument, but show that they can be filled without recourse to anachronistically modern methods. I end with a principle about the ordering of terms, and discuss the connections between it, Platonic division and Aristotle's exclusion of the fourth figure.

Smit, Harry. Are Animal Displays Bodily Movements or Manifestations of the Animal's Mind. *Behavior Phil*, 23(1), 13-19, Spr-Sum 95.

Smith, Andrew R and Langsdorf, Lenore. "The Voice of Pragmatism in Contemporary Philosophy of Communication" in *Recovering Pragmatism's Voice, Langsdorf, Lenore (ed)*, 1-19. Albany, SUNY Pr, 1995.

Smith, Andrew R (ed) and Langsdorf, Lenore (ed). *Recovering Pragmatism's Voice*. Albany, SUNY Pr, 1995.

Smith, Andrew R and Shyles, Leonard. "On Ethnocentric Truth and Pragmatic Justice" in *Recovering Pragmatism's Voice, Langsdorf, Lenore (ed)*, 71-94. Albany, SUNY Pr, 1995.

Smith and Shyles take up the issue of "ethnocentric truth and pragmatic justice" as a way of examining how the classical pragmatism of Peirce (pragmaticism) and Dewey (instrumentalism) contribute to the modern-postmodern debate on the impossibility of truth and justice. They address the semiotics of consequence in both Peirce and Dewey by first reviewing how this logic has been appropriated by Rorty in philosophy and Schweder in cultural psychology. The authors side with Shweder against Rorty and argue that the imaginative dimensions of "abductive" communication are crucial for any sense of intercultural "truth" or "justice." Dewey's critique of custom is advanced and the Peircian notion of "ends" is reconceptualized, not as a way of invoking some determinate judgment, but organizing conditionally and fallibly an "evolutionary" axiology through communication practice.

Smith, Barry. "Common Sense" in *The Cambridge Companion to Husserl, Smith, Barry (ed)*, 394-437. New York, Cambridge Univ Pr, 1995.

Can there be a theory-free experience? And what would be the object of such an experience. Drawing on ideas set out by Husserl in the *Crisis* and in the second book of his *Ideas*, the paper presents answers to these questions in such a way as to provide a systematic survey of the content and ontology of common sense. In the second part of the paper Husserl's ideas on the relationship between the common-sense world (what he called the 'life-world') and the world of physical theory are subjected to a critical evaluation. The relation of Husserl's ideas to current work in folk psychology and naive physics and to the direct realism of J J Gibson are also treated.

Smith, Barry (ed). *European Philosophy and the American Academy*. Peru, Open Court, 1994.

Many current developments in American academic life—multiculturalism, 'political correctness', the growth of critical theory, rhetoric and hermeneutics—have been closely associated with, and indeed in part inspired by, the ideas of European philosophers such as Foucault, Derrida, Lyotard, and others. This volume contains the principal papers from the Second Monist Colloquium, which addressed the work of the so-called 'advanced continental philosophers' from a critical, scholarly perspective, paying special attention to their influence in the United States. Contributions are included by Dallas Willard, Pascal Engel, Jorge J E Gracia, David Detmer, Ward Parks, J Claude Evans, Herman Philipse, Newton Garver, Christopher Norris and Joseph Margolis.

Smith, Barry. On Feminist Nomadism. *Free Inq*, 15(2), 30-31, Spr 95.

This article is a commentary on a piece by Rosi Braidotti (*Free Inquiry*, 15, 2, 23-29), proposing a new "nomadic style" of thinking that is to replace Western science. This "more daring, more risky form of intelligence", we are told by Ms Braidotti, belongs to that "great space of female theoretical creativity... where repetitive chores are made, especially doing the dishes or ironing the clothes." Ms Braidotti's claims on behalf of this new style of thinking and its "beautiful", "ethical" (but not further specified) outcomes are criticized.

Smith, Barry and Seifert, Joseph. "The Truth about Fiction" in *Kunst und Ontologie, Wlodzimierz, Galewicz (ed)*, 97-118. Amsterdam, Rodopi, 1994.

The paper undertakes the attempt to unfold an important contribution Roman Ingarden made to the theory of the literary work of art and to uncover a deficiency contained in his theory. Apart from the stratification of the literary work of art, Ingarden discovers a special logical entity which he calls the quasi-judgment. He shows that this type of logical entity is not truly a judgment, it does not affirm a state of affairs that would be asserted as independently existing but rather builds up the fiction-world. It makes only an "as if" claim to truth. Therefore the meaning units expressed in such quasi-judgments cannot be true or false. While the authors agree fully with this signification discovery of Ingarden, they seek to show that Ingarden's thesis is mistaken. (edited)

Smith, Barry (ed) and Smith, David Woodruff (ed). *The Cambridge Companion to Husserl*. New York, Cambridge Univ Pr, 1995.

A collection of original papers on the philosophy of Edmund Husserl, paying particular attention to those of Husserl's contributions which are of particular relevance to current debates in analytic philosophy. The volume contains papers on Husserl's theory of part and whole, on mathematics, on the mind-body problem, on the life-world and the ontology of common sense, on perception, on knowledge and on the nature of Husserl's phenomenology. It is supplemented by an extensive biography of primary and secondary literature.

Smith, Beverly A and Lichtenstein, Benyamin M and Torbert, William R. Leadership and Ethical Development: Balancing Light and Shadow. *Bus Ethics Quart*, 5(1), 97-116, Ja 95.

What makes a leader ethical? This paper critically examines the answer given by developmental theory, which argues that individuals can develop through cumulative stages of ethical orientation and behavior (e.g., Hobbesian, Kantian, Rawlsian), such that leaders at later developmental stages (of whom there are empirically very few today) are more ethical. By contrast to a simple progressive model of ethical development, this paper shows that each developmental stage has both positive (light) and negative (shadow) aspects, which affect the ethical behaviors of leaders at that stage. It also explores an unexpected result: later stage leaders can have more significantly negative effects than earlier stage leadership.

Smith, David Woodruff. "Mind and Body" in *The Cambridge Companion to Husserl, Smith, Barry (ed)*, 323-393. New York, Cambridge Univ Pr, 1995.

Husserl fashioned an intricate ontology of mind and body, coordinated with a rich phenomenology of our awareness of body and mind, as well as an epistemology of the kinds of evidence we have about body and mind. This essay reconstructs Husserl's ontology cum phenomenology, focussing on the essences called nature, culture or spirit, and consciousness, and the correlative levels of noematic sense. The result is a monism of substrata (individuals or events) and a pluralism of essences as well as senses of body and mind (which may apply to the same individuals or events). Husserl's position is distinguished from those of Descartes, Berkeley, and Kant as well as contemporary philosophers of mind such as Davidson, Fodor, and Dennett.

Smith, David Woodruff (ed) and Smith, Barry (ed). *The Cambridge Companion to Husserl*. New York, Cambridge Univ Pr, 1995.

A collection of original papers on the philosophy of Edmund Husserl, paying particular attention to those of Husserl's contributions which are of particular relevance to current debates in analytic philosophy. The volume contains papers on Husserl's theory of part and whole, on mathematics, on the mind-body problem, on the life-world and the ontology of common sense, on perception, on knowledge and on the nature of Husserl's phenomenology. It is supplemented by an extensive biography of primary and secondary literature.

Smith, F Joseph. Toward a Phenomenology of Music: A Musician's Composition Journal. *Phil Music Educ Rev*, 3(1), 21-33, Spr 95.

Smith, Gregory Bruce. The Post-Modern Leo Strauss?. *Hist Euro Ideas*, 19(1-3), 191-197, Jl 94.

Smith, Holly M. "Fetal-Maternal Conflicts" in *In Harm's Way, Coleman, Jules L (ed)*, 324-343. New York, Cambridge Univ Pr, 1994.

Smith, Joel R. Nishitani and Nietzsche on the Selfless Self. *Asian Phil*, 4(2), 165-172, 1994.

Keiji Nishitani, perhaps the leading figure of the Kyoto school after Nishida, offers a striking appreciation and critique of Nietzsche in *Religion and Nothingness*. Nishitani argues that Nietzsche develops the idea of nothingness better than most Western thinkers but retains vestiges of being, attaining a deep notion of the selfless self but not the full selfless self of Mahayana Buddhism. After developing Nishitani's critique, I argue that while each moves toward a mature view of the selfless self, both Nishitani and Nietzsche retain vestiges of the self as 'other'. Each displays a subtle ontological bias, and there is no philosophical reason to prefer Nishitani's bias over Nietzsche's bias.

Smith, John E. "Freud, Philosophy, and Interpretation" in *The Philosophy of Paul Ricoeur, Hahn, Lewis Edwin (ed)*, 147-164. Peru, Open Court, 1994.

Ricoeur is taken to hold a "realistic" view of symbolism in his insistence on a *nonarbitrary* connection between the material of a symbol and what it means. One of Ricoeur's main contributions is his original account of what he calls the hermeneutic of suspicion, represented by Marx, Nietzsche and Freud, which aims at the unmasking of false consciousness. It is his great merit to go beyond destruction in an effort to arrive at a purified form of reason and faith. The aim is well illustrated in this "dialectic of truth" version of *Oedipus Rex* as a counterbalance to Freud's account.

Smith, John E. "Royce: The Absolute and the Beloved Community Revisited" in *Meaning, Truth, and God, Rouner, Leroy (ed)*, 135-153. Notre Dame, Univ Notre Dame Pr, 1982.

Smith, John E. Response. *Trans Peirce Soc*, 31(1), 53-87, Wint 95.

This is my response to four papers written for a symposium on my book, *America's Philosophical Vision*. The papers are: John J Stuhr, "Philosophical Night Vision"; Kathleen Wallace, John Smith's *America's Philosophical Vision*"; Vincent M

AUTHOR INDEX WITH ABSTRACTS 749 Smythies, John R

Colapietro, "Toward a Fuller Recovery of Living Reason"; Felicia E Kruse, "A Critical Discussion of John E Smith's Communitarian Vision". Among the topics discussed are the difference between "American philosophy" and "philosophy in America"; philosophy as discipline and as cultural activity; the future of philosophy; the conceptions of experience and reason in the pragmatists, Whitehead and others; the current relevance of Royce's and Dewey's ideas of community.

Smith, John E. The New Need for a Recovery of Philosophy. *Proc Amer Phil Ass*, 56(1), 5-18, S 82.

Smith, John Milton. Ethics as Excellence: A Strategic Management Perspective. *J Bus Ethics*, 14(8), 683-693, Ag 95.

Confidence in Australian business was severely shaken by the corporate scandals and collapses of the 1980s. Many commentators called for more emphasis on ethics education. This paper surveys the initiatives of Australian business schools and professional bodies and finds them superficial and ineffective. It then presents a case study in "Quality Improvement" which highlights the need to take a strategic and integrated approach to the development of core values such as quality, trust, ethics and social responsibility. In exploring the process of cultural change, the paper identifies a number of key leadership roles, responsibilities and competencies which are distinguished from the more traditional management functions.

Smith, Joseph Wayne. The Beginning of Sorrows: The Ecological Crisis and the Prospects of Human Survival. *Darshana Int*, 32(4/128), 51-59, O 92.

Smith, Michael. Internal Reasons. *Phil Phenomenol Res*, 55(1), 109-131, Mr 95.

According to internalism, an agent has a reason to do something just in case she would desire to do that thing if she were fully rational. The 'advice' model of internalism is distinguished from the 'example' model. Though Korsgard accepts the 'example' model, the 'advice' model is argued to be superior. Williams argues that internalism entails that reasons are relative to the desires agents actually have. But once different kinds of relativism about reasons are distinguished, this claim is seen to be false. Internalism is consistent with rationalism, and so with nonrelativism about reasons.

Smith, Michael. *The Moral Problem*. Cambridge, Blackwell, 1994.

The "moral problem" is the apparent impossibility of reconciling the objectivity of morality, the action-guiding character of moral judgment, and the Humean theory of motivation. This is the central organizing problem in contemporary meta-ethics, as theories are shaped by which doctrine they reject. Since all three should be accepted, contemporary theories are largely mistaken. But is reconciliation possible? It is if we properly interpret moral facts as facts about our reasons for action. Topics discussed include: cognitivism vs expressivism; internalism vs externalism; Humean vs anti-Humean theories of motivation; and hypothetical vs categorical imperative accounts of practical rationality.

Smith, Michael A. Common Advantage and Common Good. *Laval Theol Phil*, 51(1), 111-125, F 95.

The author draws upon the Aristotelian-Thomistic tradition to address the question of the relationship of the political common good to other goods, especially the private good of the individual. In both Aristotle and Thomas Aquinas, the discussion is framed, not as an opposition of the common good to that of individual citizens, but rather as an opposition of the common good to the private interests of rulers.

Smith, Michael A. *Human Dignity and the Common Good in the Aristotelian-Thomistic Tradition*. Lewiston, Mellen Pr, 1995.

There are two fundamental themes in the social teaching of the Catholic Church: the dignity of the human person, and the common good. Through an analysis of texts of Aristotle, Thomas Aquinas, Jacques Maritain, and Charles De Koninck, the author deals with the relationship between these two fundamental principles. He seeks to show that the recognition of rights, far from being threatened by the common good, depends in fact on the common good so that persons can live well. In the final chapter, the author formulates a synthesis, and applies this synthesis to human rights in general, to the "three generations" of rights, and to the relationship between individual and collective rights.

Smith, Nicholas D and Brickhouse, Thomas C. HE MANTIKE TECHNE: *Statesman* 260e1 and 290c4-6. *Polis*, 12(1-2), 37-51, 1993.

In this paper, we shall consider what Plato's view of divination. We shall argue that, recent interpretations to the contrary, Plato is consistent throughout the dialogues in portraying the diviner as possessing a genuine, though relatively meager, form of knowledge. We shall approach our topic anachronistically—beginning with what Plato's Stranger has to say in the *Politicus* about the diviner's craft, and then comparing that to the pronouncements of Plato's Socrates in the earlier dialogues.

Smith, Nick. Charles Taylor, Strong Hermeneutics and the Politics of Difference. *Rad Phil*, 68, 19-27, Autumn 94.

The article situates the central claims of Taylor's *Ethics of Authenticity* and *The Politics of Recognition* in the broader context of recent hermeneutic philosophy. The term 'strong hermeneutics' is coined for Taylor's position, which is distinguished from the 'weak hermeneutics' of Rorty and postmodernism and the 'deep hermeneutics' of Habermas. These three kinds of hermeneutics show different levels of scepticism to the claim that ideals are accountable to reason. The defensibility of this claim is explored with a focus on the ideal of authenticity and the political conditions of this instantiation.

Smith, Patricia. "Feminist Legal Critics: The Reluctant Radicals" in *Radical Philosophy of Law, Caudill, David S (ed)*, 73-87. Atlantic Highlands, Humanities Pr, 1995.

Feminist legal criticism began not as radical critique, but as liberal argument for the universal application of traditional legal categories or norms. Employing a contradiction between liberal rhetoric and practice, feminists argued effectively for the inclusion of women. This strategy successfully removed formal barriers, but stops far short of genuine equal treatment so long as the basic norms (characterized as neutral standards of evaluation) are in fact biased. So many feminists have moved to more radical critique of law as a critique of discriminatory norms. I use the evolution of sex discrimination law and the continuing problem of violence against women to illustrate the progress and potential of this critique.

Smith, Patricia. Individualism and Social Responsibility: Reflections on Recent Work by French and May. *Soc Theor Pract*, 20(3), 363-380, Fall 94.

Smith, Patrick Nowell. "The Right to Die" in *Ethics on the Frontiers of Human Existence, Badham, Paul (ed)*, 209-221. New York, Paragon House, 1992.

Smith, Quentin. A Defense of a Principle of Sufficient Reason. *Metaphilosophy*, 26(1-2), 97-106, Ja-Ap 95.

Smith, Quentin. Anthropic Explanations in Cosmology. *Austl J Phil*, 72(3), 371-382, S 94.

Smith, Quentin. Can Everything Come to Be Without a Cause?. *Dialogue (Canada)*, 33(2), 313-324, Spr 94.

Smith, Quentin. Explanatory Rationalism and Contingent Truths. *Relig Stud*, 31(2), 237-242, Je 95.

This paper extends the orthodox bounds of explanatory rationalism by showing there can be an explanation of why there are positive contingent truths. A positive contingent truth is a true proposition that entails that at least one contingent concrete object exists. It is widely thought that it is impossible to explain why there are positive contingent truths. For example, it is thought by Rowe that 'God created the universe' is a positive contingent truth and therefore cannot explain why there are positive truths. I show, however, that the reasoning behind this orthodox view is unsound and that it is possible to explain why there are positive contingent truths.

Smith, Quentin. Internal and External Causal Explanations of the Universe. *Phil Stud*, 79(3), 283-310, S 95.

Smith, Quentin. Stephen Hawking's Cosmology and Theism. *Analysis*, 54(4), 236-243, O 94.

Smith, Quentin and Oaklander, L Nathan. *Time, Change, and Freedom: An Introduction to Metaphysics*. New York, Routledge, 1995.

Smith, Robin. "Logic" in *The Cambridge Companion to Aristotle, Barnes, Jonathan (ed)*, 27-65. New York, Cambridge Univ Pr, 1995.

Smith, Robin. Dialectic and the Syllogism. *Ancient Phil*, 14, 133-151, 1994.

Smith, Robin. What Use is Aristotle's *Organon*?. *Proc Boston Colloq Anc Phil*, 9, 261-285, 1993.

Smith, Steven B. At the Crossroads: Hegel and the Ethics of *bürgerliche Gesellschaft*. *Laval Theol Phil*, 51(2), 345-362, Je 95.

Hegel's concept of civil society (*bürgerliche Gesellschaft*) is widely used but not well understood by contemporary political theorists. Civil society was for Hegel the domain of a new kind of individual with a distinctive set of character traits, namely, the burgher or bourgeois. The term *bürgerliche Gesellschaft* was not for him one of contempt or derision but marked a new, even heroic, form of civilization. Hegel's claim to our attention is as the greatest analyst and defender of the bourgeois experience in its manifold aspects.

Smith, Steven B. Spinoza's Democratic Turn: Chapter 16 of the *Theologico-Political Treatise*. *Rev Metaph*, 48(2), 359-388, D 94.

This essay examines Spinoza's much neglected defense of democracy as the regime most likely to foster the intellectual and rational capacities of its citizens. Democracy is desirable not only because of its ability to solve the Hobbesian problem of peace but because it is the regime most consistent with Spinoza's vision of the autonomous individual or the liberated self. The essay considers further the necessary disproportion between the life of the democratic citizen and the intensely personal, even solitary character, of the philosophic life which remains the individual's highest end.

Smith, Steven M. "Getting Into and Out of Mental Ruts: A Theory of Fixation, Incubation, and Insight" in *The Nature of Insight, Sternberg, Robert J (ed)*, 229-251. Cambridge, MIT Pr, 1995.

Smolarski, Dennis C. Finding Meaning in Mathematics. *Ultim Real Mean*, 17(4), 249-260, D 94.

Mathematicians experience mathematics as an art in which ultimate reality is found, not in numerical intangibles or in proven theorems, but in doing mathematics. Mathematics contains reality and meaning aside from any verification through experience. Past mathematical discoveries may have been delayed when the cultural climate demanded experiential validation of results. Computers have not changed mathematical reality but merely decreased the time needed to come to certain conclusions. Since the reality associated with mathematics and computers differs from that associated with much in human life, one should avoid unfounded connections between mathematical results and human experiences.

Smolensky, Paul. "Connectionism, Constituency, and the Language of Thought" in *Connectionism: Debates on Psychological Explanation, Macdonald, Cynthia (ed)*, 164-198. Cambridge, Blackwell, 1995.

Smolensky, Paul. "Constituent Structure and Explanation in..Cognitive Architecture" in *Connectionism: Debates on Psychological Explanation, Macdonald, Cynthia (ed)*, 223-290. Cambridge, Blackwell, 1995.

Smolensky, Paul. "On the Projectable Predicates of Connectionist Psychology" in *Connectionism: Debates on Psychological Explanation, Macdonald, Cynthia (ed)*, 357-394. Cambridge, Blackwell, 1995.

Smolensky, Paul. "On the Proper Treatment of Connectionism" in *Connectionism: Debates on Psychological Explanation, Macdonald, Cynthia (ed)*, 28-89. Cambridge, Blackwell, 1995.

Smythies, John R. Requiem for the Identity Theory. *Inquiry*, 37(3), 311-329, S 94.

This paper examines the impact that recent advances in clinical neurology, introspectionist psychology and neuroscience have upon the philosophical psychoneural Identity Theory. My conclusion is that the Identity Theory is incompatible with the scientific evidence from an integrated approach to modern introspection is psychology, clinical neurology, and neuroscience. However,

Cartesian Dualism is even more incompatible with the evidence. This leaves only two viable theories. The first is Bohr's theory of brain-consciousness complementarity. The second is the Broad-Price-Smythies theory of extension, which is a topological theory of the relation between phenomenal space and physical space. (edited)

Snow, Nancy E. Humility. *J Value Inq*, 29(2), 203-216, Je 95.

Humility is a complex virtue with more than one variety. Analyzing humility shows its role in the moral psychology of agents, why it is worth having, and how it relates to other virtues. In section one, I examine a sample of statements that attest to the diversity of situations in which we experience humility. In section two, two senses of humility are developed, narrow and existential humility. The aim of section three is to argue toward a unifying conception of humility broad enough to apply to both senses. In four, I answer the question, "Why be humble?"

Snyder, Douglas M. On the Quantum Mechanical Wave Function as a Link Between Cognition and the Physical World: A Role for Psychology. *J Mind Behav*, 16(2), 151-179, Spr 95.

A straightforward explanation of fundamental tenets concerning the quantum mechanical wave function results in the thesis that the quantum mechanical wave function is a link between human cognition and the physical world. The way in which physicists have not accepted this explanation is discussed, and some of the roots of the problem are explored. The basis for an empirical test as to whether the wave function is a link between human cognition and the physical world is provided through developing an experiment incorporating methodology from psychology and physics. Research in psychology and physics that relied on this methodology indicates that it is likely that Einstein, Podolsky, and Rosen's theoretical result that mutually exclusive wave functions can simultaneously apply to the same concrete physical circumstances can be implemented on an empirical level.

Snyder, Laura J. It's *All* Necessarily So: William Whewell on Scientific Truth. *Stud Hist Phil Sci*, 25(5), 785-807, O 94.

One particularly intriguing claim made by the nineteenth-century polymath William Whewell is that empirical science can lead to the "a priori intuition" of necessary truths. Self-evident truths can *become* self-evident. In this paper I explicate Whewell's position by formulating an original interpretation of his notion of necessity. My interpretation demonstrates the importance of Whewell's "theological deduction" for his claim that necessary truths are analytic consequences of the Divine Ideas exemplified in the universe. I show that this interpretation has important consequences for Whewell's conception of the aims and methods of scientific inquiry. In particular, Whewell is led to the conclusion that all empirical laws are, in fact, necessary truths.

Soames, Scott. "T-Sentences" in *Modality, Morality, and Belief, Sinnott-Armstrong, Walter (ed)*, 250-270. New York, Cambridge Univ Pr, 1994.

Soare, Robert I and Jockusch Jr, Carl G. Boolean Algebras, Stone Spaces, and the Iterated Turing Jump. *J Sym Log*, 59(4), 1121-1138, D 94.

Soare, Robert I and Lachlan, Alistair H. Models of Arithmetic and Upper Bounds for Arithmetic Sets. *J Sym Log*, 59(3), 977-983, S 94.

We settle on a question in the literature about degrees of models of true arithmetic and upper bounds for the arithmetic sets. We prove that there is a model of true arithmetic whose degree is not a uniform upper bound for the arithmetic sets. The proof involves two forcing constructions.

Sobel, Jordan Howard. Nether Logic. *Teach Phil*, 17(2), 161-171, Je 94.

Nether logic is an axiom-free system for precisely the arguments in the language of sentential logic whose conclusions must be false if their premises are all false. Rules and forms are set out. Several theorems are derived. Proofs of completeness and correctness are sketched. And pedagogic uses of the exercise are indicated.

Sobel, Jordan Howard. Newcomblike Problems. *Midwest Stud Phil*, 15, 224-255, 1990.

Newcomb-like problems are catalogued and defended as coherent challenges to evidential decision theories, even elaborate theories that are "enhanced with metatickles". Criticism of arguments to the contrary feature not only nondominance and third-person Newcomb-like decision problems concerning what to do, but also nonaction Newcombesque desire problems concerning what to want and hope.

Sober, Elliott. "Did Evolution Make Us Psychological Egoists?" in *From a Biological Point of View, Sober, Elliott*, 8-27. New York, Cambridge Univ Pr, 1994.

The concepts of evolutionary altruism and egoism describe the fitness consequences of actions, not the motives that individuals have in producing them. The psychological concepts that go by the same names describe motives, not fitness effects. This paper describes what the two pairs of concepts mean and asks whether the evolutionary ideas provide a way of resolving the psychological problem.

Sober, Elliott. "The Adaptive Advantage of Learning and *A Priori* Prejudice" in *From a Biological Point of View, Sober, Elliott*, 50-70. New York, Cambridge Univ Pr, 1994.

When you see a tiger, you must decide whether the tiger is dangerous. The policy of "*a priori* prejudice" dictates that you should believe without further ado that the tiger is dangerous. A policy of learning dictates that your decision about this matter should be based on some observable feature of the tiger. This paper analyzes a quantitative model in which these epistemic policies have fitness consequences and so evolve by the process of individual natural selection.

Sober, Elliott. "The Primacy of Truth-Telling and the Evolution of Lying" in *From a Biological Point of View, Sober, Elliott*, 71-92. New York, Cambridge Univ Pr, 1994.

When there is communication among the members of a population, individuals must adopt policies about whether they will lie or tell the truth, and also about whether they will believe what they hear from others. This paper presents a quantitative model in which these policies of senders and receivers have fitness consequences and evolve by the process of individual natural selection. Views of Kant, Davidson, and Lewis are discussed.

Sober, Elliott. "When Natural Selection and Culture Conflict" in *Biology, Ethics, and the Origins of Life, Rolston III, Holmes (ed)*, 137-162. Boston, Jones & Bartlett, 1995.

If natural selection favors the evolution of trait A rather than B, whereas cultural traditions promote the adoption of trait B rather than trait A, what will happen? This paper explores the relationship between biological evolution and cultural evolution.

Sober, Elliott. *From a Biological Point of View*. New York, Cambridge Univ Pr, 1994.

This book assembles twelve essays on a variety of topics in philosophy of mind, epistemology, ethics, philosophy of science, and metaphysics. The essays try to show that ideas from evolutionary biology throw light on a range of traditional philosophical problems.

Sober, Elliott. Why Not Solipsism?. *Phil Phenomenol Res*, 55(3), 547-566, S 95.

This paper addresses a problem of explanation, not a problem of justification. The question is not why we are entitled to think that there are objects that exist outside our own minds, but why we in fact do so. This is interpreted as an issue about evolutionary adaptation: What advantage does an organism receive by formulating beliefs about such mind-independent entities, rather than confining its beliefs to the description and prediction of its own mental states? This question is connected with problems in the philosophy of science concerning operationalism and the eliminability of theoretical terms.

Sober, Elliott and Barrett, Màrtin. The Second Law of Probability Dynamics. *Brit J Phil Sci*, 45(4), 941-953, D 94.

When the probability of causes, and the probability of effects, given causes, are each randomly assigned, entropy 'usually' increases.

Sober, Elliott and Mougin, Gregory. Betting Against Pascal's Wager. *Nous*, 28(3), 382-395, S 94.

Only one traditional objection to Pascal's wager is telling: Pascal assumes a particular theology, but without justification. We produce two new objections that go deeper. We show that even if Pascal's theology is assumed to be probable, Pascal's argument does not go through. In addition, we describe a wager that Pascal never considered, which leads away from Pascal's conclusion. We then consider the impact of these considerations on other prudential arguments concerning what one should believe, and on the more general question of when and why belief formation ought to be based solely on the evidence.

Sober, Elliott and Wilson, David Sloan. A Critical Review of Philosophical Work on the Units of Selection Problem. *Phil Sci*, 61(4), 534-555, D 94.

The evolutionary problem of the units of selection has elicited a good deal of conceptual work from philosophers. We review this work to determine where the issues now stand.

Soble, Alan. Gender, Objectivity, and Realism. *Monist*, 77(4), 509-530, O 94.

This essay examines the significance of the thought of Evelyn Fox Keller (author of *Reflections on Gender and Science* and *Secrets of Life, Secrets of Death*) for the feminist epistemology project. Three topics are addressed: 1) the existence and nature of gender differences in cognitive ability and style; 2) the impact of these differences on both objectivity and the concept of objectivity; and 3) the upshot in the philosophy of science (the relativism vs. realism debate) of the purported gendered nature of science. I argue, *in media res*, that Keller's dichotomy (bad men's science, potentially good women's science) is overblown, and that gender considerations do not entail we should radically overhaul science.

Soble, Alan. In Defense of Bacon. *Phil Soc Sci*, 25(2), 192-215, Je 95.

Feminist science critics, in particular Sandra Harding, Carolyn Merchant, and Evelyn Fox Keller, claim that misogynous sexual metaphors played an important role in the rise of modern science. The writings of Francis Bacon have been singled out as an especially egregious instance of the use of misogynous metaphors in scientific philosophy. This paper offers a defense of Bacon.

Sodipo, J O and Hallen, Barry. "Excerpts from Knowledge, Belief, and Witchcraft" in *African Philosophy: Selected Readings, Mosley, Albert G (ed)*, 350-356. Englewood Cliffs, Prentice Hall, 1995.

Sodipo, Olubi and Hallen, Barry. The House of the "INU": Keys to the Structure of a Yoruba Theory of the Self. *Quest*, 8(1), 2-23, Je 94.

La méthode utilisée parles auteurs pour rechercher l'explication du concept de la "personne" formulée par un médecin (onísègùn) Yoruba est impruntée à la tradition analytique en philosophie. Le concept Yoruba de "inú" est supposé être l'équivalent du "self" en Anglais. Il est identifi comme la source de l'intellect (opolo), de la sagesse (ogbón)—ici interprété comme incluant la tradition orale—de la moralité personnelle (iwà), et de la patience (sùùrù). Les auteurs analysent aussi la possibilité de corrélations physiques, organiques, avec les aptitudes psychologiques. La théorie du moi, comme il est expliquée par l'onísègùn, semble être plus compatible avec la théorie "double-aspect" qu'avec le "dualism". Le concept de la personne deviendrait plus fondamental, capable d'avoir des attributs soit mentaux, soit physiques. (edited)

Sokolova, R I. Toward a Nontraditional Understanding. *Russian Stud Phil*, 33(4), 82-94, Spr 95.

Social values as universal formula are rather uncertain in sense. Uncertainty of sense is a very important characteristic in logical pragmatical psychological and scientific respect. It makes the limits of interpretation more extensive and indefinitely wide addressee—the whole mankind—expands the limits of interpretation even more. Another characteristic of social values is contradictoriness. Firstly, it comes from semantic confusion of transcendental and conventional senses. In different context social values also imply transcendental values which are maximum and nonlocalizable historically and conventional values which are therefore more forced nature and which in turn promote amalgamation of people only. Secondly, it comes from the fact that social values can be characterized both as highly dangerous and as highly saving phenomena. The twentieth century greatly contributed to that social values started to lose significance of an ideal or a pattern. That is why it became necessary to modify the definition of social values, rank them hierarchically, and analyse them more thoroughly.

Solana Dueso, José. Un ensayo de recomposición del protagorismo. *Convivium*, 6, 53-71, 1994.

Being the age of Pericles so great in cultural manifestations, why is it characterized by a philosophy so degrated as the Sophistic? Why did Plato and Aristotle attack their antagonists so obsessively? Facing such questions, this paper attempts to overcome and surpass what is still the norm in the sophistic studies today, that is to say, to understand these thinkers in the light of the academy or the lyceum. Taking as a starting point the hypothesis that the refuted Protagoras is not the historical one, this paper tries to set up the basic theoretical points of the sophist of Abdera, both in his political theory and in his more complex philosophical nucleus, namely, logic and epistemology. The protagoric philosophy, anchored to a relational linguistic system, constitutes the earlier milestone of the contractualistic theory and leads us to consider this author as a deep thinker on "relation".

Solberg, Joseph and Strong, Kelly C and McGuire Jr, Charles. Living (Not Learning) Ethics. *J Bus Ethics*, 14(1), 71-81, Ja 95.

The results of our survey of AACSB member schools confirm prior reports of similar surveys: The teaching of business ethics is indiscriminate, unorganized, and undisciplined in most North American schools of business. If universities are to be taken seriously in their efforts to create more ethical awareness and better moral decision-making skills among their graduates, they must provide a rigorous and well-developed system in which students can "live ethics" instead of merely learn ethics. (edited)

Soldati, Gianfranco and Bruns, Manfred. Object-Dependent and Property-Dependent Contents. *Dialectica*, 48(3-4), 185-208, 1994.

In a theory of representational or intentional states content is generally supposed to play various roles. It has to be the bearer of a truth-value, it has to determine the way a representation is about something (its mode of presentation), and finally it has to be used in order to give intra- and interpersonal psychological explanations. It has been argued that no unique kind of content can play all these roles. What criterion should one adopt in order to draw the dividing line? We suggest that the divide be based on ontological considerations related to the way content depends on external factors. There is a fundamental difference, we submit, between object-dependent and property-dependent contents. The requirements concerning modes of presentation as well as cognitive significance can be met by one kind of content. This content, it will appear, is property-dependent, but never object dependent.

Solecki, Slawomir. Covering Analytic Sets by Families of Closed Sets. *J Sym Log*, 59(3), 1022-1031, S 94.

Soles, David E. An Objectivist Account of Theory Change. *Method Sci*, 26(4), 195-206, 1993.

In a series of articles and books Alan Chalmers develops what he calls an objectivist account of theory change, an account "in terms of properties that theories possess independently of the beliefs, attitudes, or other 'subjective' properties of theories." I argue that Chalmers' theory does not live up to his objectivist aspirations.

Soliday, Elizabeth and Stanton, Annette L. Deceived Versus Nondeceived Participants' Perceptions of Scientific and Applied Psychology. *Ethics Behavior*, 5(1), 87-104, 1995.

Research examining the possible effects of deceptive research participation on participants' perception of psychology has yielded equivocal results. The present study's goal was to clarify the possible effects of participation in mildly deceptive research on participants' impressions of scientific and applied psychology. Participants (N = 112) were randomly assigned to one of six experimental conditions: active groups receiving negative, positive, or no feedback, or passive groups receiving negative, positive, or no feedback. Following participation, participants completed measures of impressions of psychotherapy and psychotherapists, researchers, and instructors. The manipulation did not affect attitudes toward psychology on any of the dependent measures, although gender effects resulted on one measure. Participants in general reported very positive attitudes toward the science and practice of psychology. Recommendations are offered for future research on the effects of more extensive deceptions.

Soller, Alois K. Die Unbegreiflichkeit der Wechselwirkung der Geister: Das Problem einer "Interpersonalitätslehre" bei Fichte. *Fichte-Studien*, 6, 215-227, 1994.

In Fichte's philosophy the meaning of call ("Aufforderung") for the formation of self-consciousness contrasts with the incomprehensibility of communication between men. The essay primarily wants to clear, why communication is incomprehensible for Fichte, whether this problem is peculiar to his whole philosophy and which solutions are offered by Fichte. The incomprehensibility develops from Fichte's theory of cognition and turns out as a permanent problem. Fichte therefore was obliged to go to harmonie préétablie at first, after that to occasional mediation by God. The solution of the problem in Fichte's late philosophy is vague.

Soller, Alois K. Fichtes Lehre vom nicht bewussten Vernunfthandeln. *Daimon Rev Filosof*, 9, 155-162, 1994.

Fichte does not deny the realistic view of the natural consciousness, as a decided critic of realism he understands it for reasons of the theory of cognition and moral as a mere appearance. Hence the question of its genesis is put. As to Fichte the finite form of self is also a mere datum of the consciousness and a mere appearance which does not know that it is produced, Fichte has to assume an unconscious activity of the spirit. His systematical claim leads him to conceive all contents and objects of consciousness as produced and to deduce them from unconscious and original activities of reason. Therefore Fichte is one of the most important founders of the doctrine of the unconscious, but not in the meaning of the empirical psychology, although he does touch its questions. Fichte's doctrine of the unconscious still stands in the tradition of rational psychology which becomes his philosophia prima in the frame of his transcendental philosophy.

Soller, Alois K. Nationale Erziehung und sittliche Bestimmung. *Fichte-Studien*, 2, 89-110, 1990.

Im ersten Teil meiner Ausführungen versuche ich, die Bedeutung der Erziehung im Gesamtwerk Fichtes, insbesondere hinsichtlich der Themenstellung dieser Tagung, darzustellen. Anschliessend werden dazu einige, Fichtes Denken immatent bleitende, kritische Fragen aufzuwerfen sein.

Solomon, Graham and DeVidi, David. Geometric Conventionalism and Carnap's Principle of Tolerance. *Stud Hist Phil Sci*, 25(5), 773-783, O 94.

We discuss in this paper the question of the scope of the principle of tolerance about languages promoted in Carnap's *The Logical Syntax of Language* and the nature of the analogy between it and the rudimentary conventionalism purportly exhibited in the work of Poincaré and Hilbert. We take it more or less for granted that Poincaré and Hilbert do argue for conventionalism. We begin by sketching Coffa's historical account, which suggests that tolerance be interpreted as a conventionalism that allows us complete freedom to select whatever language we wish—an interpretation that generalizes the conventionalism promoted by Poincaré and Hilbert which allows us complete freedom to select whatever axiom system we wish for geometry. We argue that such an interpretation saddles Carnap with a theory of meaning that has unhappy consequences, a theory we believe he did not hold. We suggest that the principle of linguistic tolerance in fact has a more limited scope; but within that scope the analogy between tolerance and geometric conventionalism is quite right.

Solomon, Graham and DeVidi, David. Tolerance and Metalanguages in Carnap's *Logical Syntax of Language*. *Synthese*, 103(1), 123-139, Ap 95.

Michael Friedman has recently argued that Carnap's *Logical Syntax of Language* is fundamentally flawed in a way that reveals "the ultimate failure of logical positivism". Friedman's argument depends crucially on two claims: 1) That Carnap was committed to the view that there is a universal metalanguage and 2) That given what Carnap wanted from a metalanguage, in particular given that he wanted a definition of "analytic" for an object language, he was in fact committed to a hierarchy of stronger and stronger metalanguages. We argue that neither of these claims need be accepted. We show that there is not textual evidence for (1) and that if metalanguages are to be used for merely descriptive and not also justificatory purposes, Carnap does not need to define analyticity sufficiently for proving consistency, and so could have given definition that does not entail a hierarchy of metalanguages.

Solomon, Miriam. "A More Social Epistemology" in *Socializing Epistemology: The Social Dimensions of Knowledge, Schmitt, Frederick F (ed), 217-233. Lanham, Rowman & Littlefield, 1994.

The paper argues that social groups can work to attain and even recognize epistemic goals without individual rationality or individual cognizance of the overall epistemic situation. Two case studies—the plate tectonics revolution and the development of genetics—suggest that scientific decisions are best assessed from a social perspective, both during times of dissent (as Goldman, Kitcher, Thagard and others have argued) and during consensus (not previously argued). A new normative perspective, called *social empiricism*, provides the more thoroughgoing social perspective needed.

Solomon, Miriam. Sizing Up Science: A Reply to Fuller. *Inform Log*, 16(1), 55-58, Wint 94.

Fuller claims that epistemic properties of scientific activity are size-sensitive. I agree with Fuller that size belongs as a variable in epistemological accounts of science. I offer reasons to doubt that it is as pivotal a variable as he claims. I suggest that Fuller is more influenced by ethical than by epistemological considerations.

Solomon, Miriam. Social Empiricism. *Nous*, 28(3), 325-343, S 94.

Philosophical accounts of scientific reasoning (both naturalistic and nonnaturalistic) have typically made normative assessments of decisions taken by *individual* scientists. Through examination of the motivational, cognitive, social and institutional factors which produced dissent and consensus in the late tectonics revolution, I argue that the only normative account that has a chance of being applicable to scientific change evaluates decision processes in the social network, rather than the individual cognizer. The normative account I develop is called *social empiricism*.

Solomon, Robert C. "The Cross-Cultural Comparison of Emotion" in *Emotions in Asian Thought, Marks, Joel (ed), 253-308. Albany, SUNY Pr, 1995.

This is a commentary and discussion of the essays in this book on Indian, Chinese and other cultures and their emotional differences. I discuss the relationship between various conceptions and theories of emotions and the understanding of these cultural differences. I also give special attention to certain (Buddhist) views of compassion and the special place of metaphors of the body in the cross-cultural understanding of emotion.

Solomon, Robert C. Marketing Heidegger: Entrepreneurship and Corporate Practices. *Inquiry*, 38(1-2), 75-81, Je 95.

Spinosa, Flores, and Dreyfus have made some valuable suggestions about the important but (in philosophy) much neglected concept of *entrepreneurship*. An entrepreneur, in the classical economists' lexicon, is a person who founds, organizes, and manages a business. In more modern conversation, he or she is a business hero or heroine. Nowhere is the new emphasis on entrepreneurship more evident than in our largest corporations. The authors analyse the entrepreneur not as an eccentric or a maverick but in terms a specific way of operating within existing social practices. They reject the still prevalent caricature of the avaricious entrepreneur in the grip of greed as well as the too "genius"-oriented conception of the inventor who cannot manage his own affairs, much less a corporation. An entrepreneur, on their account, is someone who knows how to notice and "hold on to" an anomaly and creates a market, sometimes where there was no market at all. They argue that entrepreneurship essentially involves *conversation*. It is not mere inventiveness. This "reconfiguration" of entrepreneurship explains a great deal about what many corporations—at considerable expense—are learning about their own activities and operations, and many established and successful companies are struggling to transform themselves in just the direction that Spinosa, Flores, and Dreyfus have outlined.

Solomon, Robert C. Some Notes on Emotion, "East and West". *Phil East West*, 45(2), 171-202, Ap 95.

It is said that all people are, in their basic emotions, alike. Psychologists have made this claim on the basis of cross-cultural comparisons of facial expressions of emotion. Neurologists have made similar claims based on the common structure and functions of the brain. Philosophers have long made similar claims concerning "human nature". There may be considerable embellishment and admirable verbal creativity, but the thesis remains, as psychologist Gardiner Lindzey insisted in 1954, "emotions, as biological events, are the same the world over". In this essay, I explore and challenge this idea, particularly with reference to East and South Asia.

Solomon, Robert C and Higgins, Kathleen M. "Atomism, Art, and Arthur: Danto's Hegelian Turn" in *Danto and his Critics, Rollins, Mark (ed)*, 107-126. Cambridge, Blackwell, 1993.

In this chapter, we discuss Arthur Danto's transformation from epistemological atomist and "analytic" philosopher into one of this country's premier art critics and theorists. What is perhaps most surprising is the "Hegelian" structure of his recent philosophy, including, notoriously, his speculations about "the end of art." We suggest, however, that Danto's criticism is taking and should take a further turn, more in the model of a philosopher he helped bring into the American philosophical mainstream, namely Nietzsche.

Solovyov, Vladimir. *Lectures on Divine Humanity*. Hudson, Lindisfarne Pr, 1995.

Sols Lucía, Ignacio and Pérez Camacho, Juan José. Domingo de Soto en el Origen de la Ciencia Moderna. *Rev Filosof (Spain)*, 7(12), 455-475, 1994.

Solum, Lawrence B. Inclusive Public Reason. *Pac Phil Quart*, 75(3-4), 217-231, S-D 94.

Sommerville, Johann P (ed) and James VI and James I. *Political Writings: King James VI and I*. New York, Cambridge Univ Pr, 1994.

Somos, Róbert. Origenes and Numenios. *Magyar Filozof Szemle*, 1-2, 33-46, 1994.

Origenes ist ein christlicher Denker, er baut sein theologisches System auf die "traditio apostolica" und äussert sich nicht zu optimistisch über die Möglichkeiten der Anwendung der griechischen Philosophie. Wir finden bei ihm jedoch viele Elemente, die den Tatbestand bezeugen, dass er ein allgemeines, philosophisches Normensystem und spezifisch platonische Ideen adaptierte. Zwischen den Richtungen der platonischen Philosophie ist für Origenes nicht die mittelplatonische Schulphilosophie die wichtigste, sondern der Protoneuplatoniker Numenios von Apameia. Origenes lobt Numenios in seinem Buch "Contra Celsum" wegen seiner Sympathie für die jüdische Religion und Moses mehrmals, aber diese Bemerkungen beweisen auch, dass er die Schriften des Numenios sehr gut kannte und dass Origenes den Philosophen als"... einen ausgezeichneten Erklärer der platonischen Schriften" und als "einen tüchtigen Vertreter der pythagoreischen Lehren..." bewertet. Origenes verwendet die Lehre des Numenios in der Theologie in engerem und in seiner Seelenlehre. (edited)

Sonderegger, Erwin. Boethius und die Tradition. *Z Phil Forsch*, 48(4), 558-571, 1994.

In the past Boethius was primarily considered as the author of the Consolatio, the theologician or the logician. But as philosopher he was the first to reflect on the concept of person, while Augustinus and others only made use of it. It is the purpose of this article, to show that exactly Boethius' situation in the late antiquity with its many differing traditions, urged and enabled him, to ask himself about what person essentially is. His concept of person (naturae rationabilis individua substantia) reverses the old relation between individual and tradition and strengthens—problematically—the position of substance.

Soper, Kate. Feminism and Ecology: Realism and Rhetoric in the Discourses of Nature. *Sci Tech Human Values*, 20(3), 311-331, Sum 95.

Ecology and constructivism are motivated by broadly shared political aspirations and subscribe to similar critiques of technocratism, patriarchy, and "instrumental rationality." But they diverge considerably in respect to the discourses they offer on "nature." By staging an encounter between ecological argument and feminist constructivist theory, this article seeks to illuminate, and to indicate the means of resolving, the ontological tensions between these respective critiques of modernity. It recognizes that the constructivist emphasis on the "discursivity" of nature offers an important corrective to the more simplistic, and potentially reactionary, aspects of ecological rhetoric but defends a realist perspective as essential to the coherence of any gender theory and politics.

Soper, Kate. Heterosexual Utopianism. *Rad Phil*, 69, 5-15, Ja-F 95.

Centered around the shifts that have taken place in the utopian discourses of the feminist movement from the mid-nineteenth century to the present day, notably in respect of the claims made about the potential of female emancipation to transform heterosexual relations, this paper explores the disjunctures between utopian projections and actual achievements. In the process, it outlines a conceptual framework for considering the effects of the feminist movement on relations between the sexes, and the significance of the varying degrees of concern it has expressed at differing stages with their amelioration. It also explores issues bearing on the historical relativity of utopian projections and the means of evaluating the 'progress' of an emancipatory movement such as feminism.

Sorell, Tom. The Customer Is Not Always Right. *J Bus Ethics*, 13(11), 913-918, N 94.

Consumers can sustain markets that are morally questionable. They can make immoral or morally suspect demands of individual businesses, especially small businesses. Even when they do not, the costs to firms of consumer protection can sometimes drive them to ruin. This paper presents cases where deference to the consumer is variously unwarranted, cases that may prompt second thoughts about some kinds of consumerism.

Sorensen, Roy. "Infinite Decision Theory" in *Gambling on God: Essays on Pascal's Wager, Jordan, Jeffrey (ed)*, 139-159. Lanham, Rowman & Littlefield, 1994.

This paper motivates the extension of decision theory to infinite quantities. Since there are various quantitative aspects of decision making, choices can have a variety of transfinite aspects. Perhaps the choice situation recurs endlessly (as in Nietzsche's eternal return and the infinite prisoner's dilemma). Maybe there is an infinite list of options (as in Michael Slote's optimizer dilemmas and George

Schlesinger's solution to the problem of evil). Or perhaps the utilities are infinite (as in Pascal's Wager and the St Petersburg paradox). A systematic approach unifies these aspects and bears on a range of topics: satisficing, moral dilemmas, sorites, and the problem of evil.

Sorensen, Roy. Commentary: The Epistemic Conception of Vagueness: Comments on Wright. *S J Phil*, 33(Supp), 161-170, 1995.

According to epistemicism, vagueness is just a special form of ignorance about conceptual boundaries. Crispin Wright's objections are countered with four theses: 1) "This a borderline F but I believe it is an F" is as unbelievable as the sentence posing Moore's problem: "This is F but I believe it is not F". 2) "Definitely F" only differs pragmatically from "F". 3) Belief that vagueness (of the sort driving the sorites paradox) serves the function of hedging claims is due to an equivocation with vagueness as underspecificity. 4) Belief that indeterminacy can be created by stipulation is due misplaced loyalty to semantic voluntarism—the belief that the speaker chooses the meanings of his words.

Soria, Belén and Romero, Esther. Metáforas y Convención. *Rev Filosof (Spain)*, 7(12), 383-402, 1994.

Soricelli, Elisabetta. *Il Trapianto d'Organi: Contributi per un'analisi etica, psicologica e sociale del problema*. Genova, Pantograf, 1994.

Soroos, Marvin S. Environmental Security: Choices for the Twenty-First Century. *Nat Forum*, 75(1), 20-24, Wint 95.

Sosa, David. Dónde se Encuentra el Enigma Sobre la Creencia?. *Critica*, 26(76-77), 7-50, Ap-Ag 94.

This paper investigates S Kripke's, "A Puzzle about Belief". I focus on three areas. First, it is not always clear where the puzzle lies. In what does the puzzle consist, exactly? A second focus is the methodology of Kripke's paper. I believe Kripke's use of the puzzle to defend Millianism involves an interesting methodology which has not received the attention it deserves. Third, I discuss relations between rationality, semantic value and reference. The current unfashionability of Fregean theories may be sustained by insensitivity to these relations. Toward the end I consider and reject a challenge to the Fregean position defended.

Sosa, Ernest. "De Re Belief, Action Explanations, and the Essential Indexical" in *Modality, Morality, and Belief, Sinnott-Armstrong, Walter (ed)*, 235-249. New York, Cambridge Univ Pr, 1994.

Latitudinarianism may be described briefly and sketchily as the doctrine that reference is always through an individuating concept, that thought about an entity is always "under a description" or anyhow "under an individuating concept" which uniquely specifies that entity. This paper tries to defend it from several objections. This defense reveals the natural alliance between such latitudinarianism and a view of concepts and propositions as (at least sometimes) perspectival rather than (always) absolute: i.e., as satisfied (concepts) or true (propositions) not absolutely but in a perspective. The paper also tries to defend this alliance from several objections, and to highlight some of its advantages.

Sosa, Ernest. Perspectives in Virtue Epistemology: A Response to Dancy and BonJour. *Phil Stud*, 78(3), 221-235, Je 95.

A reply to critiques by Jonathan Dancy and Lawrence Bonjour of *Knowledge in Perspective: Selected Essays in Epistemology* (Cambridge University Press, 1991).

Sosa, Ernest. Proper Functionalism and Virtue Epistemology. *Nous*, 27(1), 51-65, Mr 93.

As part of a book symposium on Alvin Plantinga's two volumes, *Warrant: the Current Debate*, and *Warrant and Proper Function* (both OUP, 1993), this paper sketches and considers critically Plantinga's main positive proposals, and then compares these with some alternative proposals by Alvin Goldman and Ernest Sosa, respectively. The relative advantages and disadvantages of the three are discussed. In conclusion, it is suggested that the differences are outweighed by the similarities, and that the three might well be viewed as varieties of "virtue epistemology", although there are significant features that distinguish them: the role of design Plantinga's, for example, and the role of epistemic perspective Sosa's.

Sosa, Ernest (ed) and Kim, Jaegwon (ed). *A Companion to Metaphysics*. Cambridge, Blackwell, 1995.

This reference work provides exhaustive coverage of main topics and areas, positions, movements, concepts, distinctions, arguments, and historical and contemporary figures in metaphysics and related fields. It includes more than 260 entries ranging from brief definitions of common terms to major discursive essays and reflects the most recent and sophisticated treatment of metaphysics. Alphabetically arranged with a comprehensive index and extensive and up-to-date bibliographical information, the *Companion* should be a highly useful reference source relevant to all fields of philosophy.

Soskice, Janet Martin. "Creation and Relation" in *Medicine and Moral Reasoning, Fulford, K W M (ed)*, 19-28. New York, Cambridge Univ Pr, 1994.

Soskice, Janet Martin (ed) and Gillett, Grant (ed) and Fulford, K W M (ed). *Medicine and Moral Reasoning*. New York, Cambridge Univ Pr, 1994.

The unifying theme of this edited collection is that moral reasoning in medicine should draw on a wide variety of sources, both philosophical and empirical articles include: Midgley on Darwinism; Soskice on creation and relation; Hare on embryo experimentation; Brandton on genetic testing; Lockwood on identity; William May on the suicide; Gillett on children; Oddie on moral uncertainty; Urmson on invention and discovery in morality; Crisp on quality of life; Campbell on dependency; and Fulford on involuntary psychiatric treatment.

Sosoe, Lukas K. Peut-on Parler de Théories en Éthique?. *Philosopher*, 16, 89-100, 1994.

Sotnak, Eric and Nayak, Abhaya C. Kant on the Impossibility of the "Soft Sciences". *Phil Phenomenol Res*, 55(1), 133-151, Mr 95.

In the *Metaphysical Foundations* Kant declares that every discipline is a science only to the extent that it can be mathematized and he refuses the status of science to chemistry and psychology. In the *First Critique* he suggests that qualities can be mathematized. Since chemistry and psychology are traditionally taken to be the study of certain qualities, Kant's claims seem to be conflicting. We resolve this conflict by suggesting that although mathematics can be applied to chemistry or psychology in some measure, it cannot be applied enough or in the right manner.

Soto, José Cercós. El problema de la nada: aproximación metafísica. *Dialogos*, 30(65), 7-32, Ja 95.

This article aims at the analysis of one of the most important concepts in the history of the philosophy: nothingness. From the point of view which somehow considers at an element or ingredient of the individual being. The first thing to be done is a historical survey: what some Greek, medieval and modern philosophers have thought about nothingness. Then, this point is systematically dealt with, concluding that the constitutive character of the human being, the being-within-its-limits, which provokes the something-to-do—either to-be-done or to-be-undone—that is the proof of the presence of nothingness in the being.

Sottomayor-Cardía, M. O interesse geral o e interesse de cada um. *Telos (Spain)*, 1(2), 9-35, Je 92.

The approach in this paper departs from classical utilitarianism in many ways. In the first place emphasis is laid on the concept of *interest* rather than in *happiness*. At the same time there is a vindication of a certain sort of preference for our own interest when confronted with the maximizing principle in its most radical form, as this radical maximizing principle could lead to a sort of "pathological Kantism". Exception is made in cases of "negative" utilitarianism, that is, when great greatest common *evil*. In such cases the author would even allow for some "unjust acts", so that suffering, and every sort of evil for the greatest number could be avoided.

Soudek, Ingrid H and Neeley, Kathryn A. The Match and Other Agents of Liberation: The Role of Technology in the Social Thought of Louise Otto. *Res Phil Technol*, 14, 119-137, 1994.

In *The Life of Women in the German Empire* (1876), the German feminist Louise Otto (1819-95) assesses the impact of the match and other technological developments on the lives of middle-class German women of her day. Through her very detailed and concrete treatments, Otto shows us that technology has great impact not so much because of its inherent power or incorporation into large systems but because it thoroughly permeates our everyday lives. Otto's work demonstrates the value of an approach that is simultaneously material, social, and emotional and uses the lived experience of individuals to expand our understanding of technological change.

Soulez, Antonia. How to Finish with Philosophy According to Wittgenstein?. *Filozof Cas*, 42(4), 560-582, 1994.

This French essay demonstrates the fundamental continuity in the development of Wittgenstein's philosophical project, which was characterised by its anti-socratic strategy of replacing questions with answers. In the *Philosophical Investigations* this project became a form of therapy of language, based on the analysis, case by case, of those formations of speech which are mismatched in their relationship to our ideas and our way of living. The act of philosophical thought is therefore always a one-off and repeated act.

Soutar, Geoffrey N (& others). A Management Perspective on Business Ethics. *J Bus Ethics*, 14(8), 603-611, Ag 95.

In recent years the institutionalisation of ethics as a means of enhancing the ethical nature of business operations has received widespread empirical coverage. To date, however, few studies have been conducted in the Australian business context. This paper examines the institutionalisation of ethics by a sample of companies based in Perth, Western Australia. In particular, company representatives were asked if their company was instiutionalising ethics, why this initiative was undertaken, how this was taking place and what specific issues were being addressed in the institutionalisation process. The results suggest that perceptions of external parties were the primary motivation for ethics institutionalisation efforts although there was also considerable focus on trying to internalise ethical values. In terms of how ethics were being institutionalised the responding compaines were more likely to have conducted ethics training programs than to have written Codes of Conduct and in general it appears that few companies were developing comprehensive formal ethics programs. The primary issue covered by these institutionalisation efforts was the observance of laws.

Spade, Paul Vincent. How to Start and Stop: Walter Burley on the Instant of Transition. *J Phil Res*, 19, 193-221, 1994.

Mediaeval logicians often wrote about changes between contradictory states, for example a switch's changing from being on to not being on. One of the questions discussed in these writings was whether at the moment the change occurs the changing thing is in the earlier or the later state. The present paper investigates the general setting for that question, and discusses the answer given by Walter Burley, an important early-fourteenth century author whose theory was a standard one. Burley's theory at first seems arbitrary, and moreover, committed to serious theoretical problems. The last part of the paper therefore considers what unspoken factors may have motivated Burley. Certain causal principles are suggested that would remove the apparent arbitrariness and avoid the theoretical problems with his theory, but only at the expense of revising it in a substantive way.

Spade, Paul Vincent (trans) and Abelard, Peter. *Ethical Writings: Ethics and Dialogue between a Philosopher, a Jew, and a Christian*. Indianapolis, Hackett, 1995.

Spader, Peter. Max Scheler's Practical Ethics and the Model Person. *Amer Cath Phil Quart*, 69(1), 63-81, Wint 95.

Max Scheler is probably best known for his attempt to show the possibility of an ethics of values that could surmount Kant's rational formalism. Although Scheler never developed a detailed practical ethics, some elements are clear. One of the more intriguing is Scheler's use of the "model person." Despite his belief in an absolute hierarchy of values, Scheler turns away from laws and norms and suggests the "model person" as the best source of moral direction. This paper explores why Scheler does so, develops some of the problems presented by Scheler's "model person", and suggests possible solutions to these problems.

Spader, Peter. Phenomenology and the Claiming of Essential Knowledge. *Husserl Stud*, 11(3), 169-199, 1994-95.

There is a need for a reliable phenomenological method of testing claims to knowledge of the essential elements of a phenomenon. Husserl's method of random, "infinite" variation is an excellent way of seeing essences, but due to its open-endedness it is a poor way to make and test any claims about them. For this new task I suggest we use deliberately focused, finite variations. I test this approach using the phenomenon "triangle", explore how it can be used on more obscure phenomena, and develop and meet a number of possible objections to this method of "closed" variation.

Spangler, G A. The Ends of Argument. *Teach Phil*, 17(4), 311-, D 94.

Assessing arguments for success or failure by attending to the purposes of arguers is the topic of this paper. Employing a version of Aristotle's Doctrine of the Mean I claim that an argument maybe regarded as a success or a failure depending on what purposes are taken into view, since what is excessive say, for one end may be adequate for another. I adduce several rules of thumb to guide a teleological critique of arguments.

Spanio, Davide. Idealismo e Dialettica dell'Idea nell'Attualismo di Giovanni Gentile. *G Crit Filosof Ital*, 73(2-3), 428-462, My-D 94.

Sparshott, Francis. "The Aesthetics of Architecture and the Politics of Space" in *Philosophy and Architecture, Mitias, Michael H (ed)*, 3-20. Amsterdam, Rodopi, 1994.

Architecture has to do with the coercive organization of social space, in ways that are advantageous to some and disadvantageous to others. The aesthetics of architecture, however conceived, is compromised by the diversity of the ways buildings impinge on the lives of different groups of users and observers, whose divergent interests are indisputable relevant. The paper explores some of the intricacies of the relationships concerned, and concludes that order can be introduced into architectural criticism only by political decisions without intellectual warrant.

Sparshott, Francis. Aesthetics and the End of Civilization. *Phil Exch*, 24-25, 15-26, 1993-94.

Why do writers on aesthetics emphasize acknowledged masterpieces of art? Because such masterpieces uniquely manifest aesthetic value, or because aesthetics represents the ideology of a social elite? Perhaps rather because the art in question is associated with the educational system to which aesthetics itself belongs. Contemporary critiques of that system, and of Western civilization, and of civilization as such, seem to threaten the credentials of aesthetics. However, those critiques are parasitic on the system they attack, and the basic concerns of aesthetics as a philosophical discipline remain untouched.

Spaulding, Will and Von Eckardt, Barbara and Poland, Jeffrey. "Problems with the *DSM* Approach to Classifying Psychopathology" in *Philosophical Psychopathology, Graham, George (ed)*, 235-260. Cambridge, MIT Pr, 1993.

Speaks, Michael (ed) and Boyman, Anne (trans) and Cache, Bernard. *Earth Moves: The Furnishing of Territories*. Cambridge, MIT Pr, 1995.

Spellman, James and Schmitt, Frederick F. "Socializing Epistemology: A Bibliography" in *Socializing Epistemology: The Social Dimensions of Knowledge, Schmitt, Frederick F (ed)*, 289-310. Lanham, Rowman & Littlefield, 1994.

This is a comprehensive bibliography of books and articles on social epistemology by philosophers. It includes classical writings as well as contemporary writings.

Spellman, Lynne. *Substance and Separation in Aristotle*. New York, Cambridge Univ Pr, 1995.

This book is a study of Aristotle's metaphysics in which the central argument is that Aristotle's views on substance are a direct response to Plato's Theory of Forms. The claim is that Aristotle believes that many of Plato's views are tenable once one has rejected Plato's notion of separation. In support of the view that Aristotle's substances are specimens of natural kinds, Aristotle's views on numerical sameness, his epistemology, and his account of teleology are examined.

Spencer-Smith, Richard. Reductionism and Emergent Properties. *Proc Aris Soc*, 95, 113-129, 1994-95.

Speranza, J L. "The Feast of Conversational Reason, o la Cuestión Fundamental de Grice en Torno del Immanuel Conversacional" in *Temas Actuales de Filosofía, Palacios, María Julia (ed)*, 591-597. Buenos Aires, Univ Nacional Salta, 1993.

Speranza, J L. Materia prima y cmabio substancial, Hoy. *Rev Filosof (Mexico)*, 27(81), 405-431, S-D 94.

Sperduto, D. L'eternità dell'essere nel pensiero di Emanuele Severino. *Sapienza*, 47(2), 173-210, 1994.

This essay explains Severino's thought and his evolution. The Italian philosopher relates 'nihilism' and 'time': beginning with the Greek Metaphysics (Plato, Aristotle), for each philosopher things are temporal. But for Severino as for Parmenides the becoming of beings is impossible (it is not possible not to be). Introducing a new concept of time, Severino affirms the eternity *and* the 'temporality' of all things. This essay demonstrates the not-contradiction of becoming and the not-necessity of the being of things (things can be or not be). It also demonstrates the wrongness of Severino's interpretation of Empedocles, for whom all things are forever.

Spiecker, Ben and Steutel, Jan. "Moral Identity and Education in a Multicultural Society" in *Identity, Culture, and Education, Smeyers, Paul (ed)*, 305-315. Leuven, Leuven Univ Pr, 1994.

The issue that is raised concerns the moral identity of persons in a pluralistic liberal-democracy. Democracies often are multicultural societies as well. Given such a pluralistic society, we pose the question which requirements, if any, apply to the moral identity of persons, not only with regard to their more personal sphere of life, but also concerning their role as citizens. This question must be understood as a typical educational question. What we aim at in education is the cultivation and development of a certain moral identity. Our question is: if we want to prepare our children for a life in a multicultural society, which moral identity should be our aim of education?

Spiecker, Ben and Steutel, Jan. Rationele passies en intellectuele deugden: Een conceptuele analyse. *Alg Ned Tijdschr Wijs*, 87(1), 1-14, Ja 95.

Intellectual virtues like open-mindedness, clarity, intellectual honesty and the willingness to participate in rational discussions, are important aims of education. In this paper an attempt is made to clarify the specific nature of intellectual virtues. Firstly, the intellectual virtues are systematically compared with moral virtues. The upshot is that considering a trait of character an intellectual virtue comes down to assuming that such a trait can be derived from, or is a specification of, the cardinal virtue of concern and respect for truth. Secondly, several (possible) misconceptions of intellectual virtues are removed by making the required distinctions. It is argued that our concept of an intellectual virtue should not be confused with a normative conception of intellectual virtuousness.

Spielman, Bethany. Futility and Bargaining Power. *J Clin Ethics*, 6(1), 44-52, Spr 95.

Physicians and families who disagree about the futility of medical treatments engage in bargaining. Regardless of whether the case ever enters the legal system, bargaining among the parties is shaped by the result the participants expect the legal system will yield. Thus, bargaining takes place "in the shadow of" the law. Bargaining power is a social power, used only under certain circumstances. Bargaining endowments that participants in futility disputes hold by virtue of the law will be as critical to solutions to futility problems as are normative ethical judgments.

Spinas, Otmar. Dominating Projective Sets in the Baire Space. *Annals Pure Applied Log*, 68(3), 327-342, Ag 94.

Spinas, Otmar and Hjorth, Greg and Rosado Haddock, Guillermo E. El Frege Kantiano. *Dialogos*, 30(65), 189-212, Ja 95.

Spinelli, Emidio (trans). *Contro Gli Etici*. Naples, Bibliopolis, 1995.

Spinello, Richard A. *Ethical Aspects of Information Technology*. Englewood Cliffs, Prentice Hall, 1995.

The purpose of this book is to highlight and analyze ethical issues related to the use of information technology and the management of information. The core of the book considers the following issues: anti-competitive practices and the use of technology as a competitive weapon, vendor/client relations, privacy, intellectual property, and security. The book also includes an extensive discussion of ethical theory and how it can be used to facilitate tenable resolutions to some of the moral dilemmas that arise in these areas. In addition to an analysis of these issues, twelve case studies are also included.

Spinosa, Charles (& others). Disclosing New Worlds: Entrepreneurship, Democratic Action, and the Cultivation of Solidarity. *Inquiry*, 38(1-2), 3-63, Je 95.

Both the commonsensical and leading theoretical accounts of entrepreneurship, democracy, and solidarity fail to describe adequately entrepreneurial, democratic, and solidarity-building *practices*. These accounts are inadequate because they assume a faulty description of human being. In this article we develop an interpretation of entrepreneurship, democratic action, and solidarity-building that relies on understanding human beings as neither primarily thinking nor desiring but as skillful beings.

Spinosa, Charles (& others). Skills, Historical Disclosing, and the End of History: A Response to Our Critics. *Inquiry*, 38(1-2), 157-197, Je 95.

We appreciate the thoughtful responses we have received on "Disclosing New Worlds". We will respond to the concerns raised by grouping them under three general themes. First, a number of questions arise from lack of clarity about how the matters we undertook to discuss—especially solidarity—appear when one starts by thinking about the primacy of skills and practices. Under this heading we consider 1) whether we need more case studies to make our points, and 2) whether national and other solidarities require willingness to die for the values that produce that solidarity. Second, we take up questions concerning the historical character of the skills of entrepreneurs, virtuous citizens, and culture figures. Here we shall 1) emphasize how we distinguish ourselves from earlier writers on these subjects, 2) consider essentialism, relational identities, and exclusion, 3) answer a number of Habermasian concerns raised by Hoy, 4) speak to Taylor's concern regarding the contingency of solidarity and forgetting, and 5) take up Grant's objection that we are both formalists and relativists. Third, we shall take up the concern, raised mostly by Borgmann, that historical disclosing, that is to say history as the West has known it, is over, and that now all that can be done by those who transform the practices is to make them more and more technological.

Spitta, Arnold. Raíces ideológicas de la "guerra suicia" en América latina (en especial Argentina). *Rev Filosof (Costa Rica)*, 31(75-76), 157-172, D 93.

In the discussion about semi-official violence and repression, special emphasis has been given to the Doctrine of National Security, originated in the United States and brought about by the Cold War, as their main ideological justification. This work states that other ideological justifications of an endogenous origin, partially coming from colonial times, have the same or greater importance, like the Catholic traditionalism of Spanish origin and exacerbated nationalism, the worship of militarism, mesianic militarism and others.

Spitz, Jean-Fabien. The Concept of Liberty in "A Theory of Justice" and Its Republican Version. *Ratio Juris*, 7(3), 331-347, D 94.

The author offers three interpretations of the Rawlsian conception of liberty. At the same time he compares this formal version of civil and political liberty with the substantive version produced by the republican theory of liberty. The first question is this: Can liberties be unequal? Here the liberal concept of liberty is discussed linking human will of liberty and equality. The second question is: Can liberties be equal when their respective values are not? The author stresses the Rawlsian distinction between liberty and the value of liberty showing the risk of reducing the less powerful to dependency. The third question is: Can political liberty be limited for the sake of personal liberties? From a republican perspective the answer to the Rawlsian instrumental conception of political liberty is that all personal liberties are necessarily founded on political liberty.

Spitzer, Manfred. Key Concepts: Associationism. *Phil Psychiat Psych*, 1(2), 135-137, Je 94.

Associationism can be broadly defined as a school of thought in philosophy and psychology that holds that mental activity can be accounted for by processes that combine simple elements or ideas. The concept of association, with its biological, psychological, and computational connotations, provides the framework needed for further experimental research. Its potential for contributing to our understanding of psychopathology can hardly be overestimated. (edited)

Spivak, Gayatri Chakravorty. "Supplementing Marxism" in *Whither Marxism?, Magnus, Bernd (ed)*, 109-119. New York, Routledge, 1994.

The purpose of the essay is to see what we can do with and for Marxism after the fall of international Communism. Six points are made: 1) the difference between the two uses of "social" in Marx; 2) class-consciousness as critique of reification theory; 3) deconstructive interpretation of the relationship between socialism and capitalism; 4) the role of the new immigrant; 5) internalizing Marxism; 6) globe-girdling New Social Movements.

Splett, Jörg. Das Argernis der Menschlichkeit Gottes. *Frei Z Phil Theol*, 42(1-2), 49-68, 1995.

Seit Xenophanes: Kampf dem Anthropomorphismus. Doch ist der nicht selber (negativ) anthropomorphistisch? Die Bibel kennt weder negative Theologie (die braucht nur, wer Erkennen als Beherrschen, Benennen als Beschreiben sieht) noch Anthropomorphismen; denn (F Rosenzweig) sie erzählt und bezeugt. Falsch ist die übliche Ausweitung des—kultischen—Bilderverbotes. Falsch ist auch die Rede von Abbild, Ebenbild, da Gott nicht aussieht. Der mensch ist Bild=Erscheinung= Versichtbarung des Unsichtbaren. Erscheinung aber wird stets auch vom Medium des Erscheinens geprägt. Gott erscheint in unserer Menschlichkeit *und* Unmenschlichkeit, und so ("Ecce homo") "zuletzt" im Menschen Jesus. Steht hinter dem Kampf dagegen nicht Misanthropie (darum—S Kierkegaard—das Ärgernis)? Gott aber *liebt* den Menschen (fòlie divine?).

Splett, Jörg. Wahrheit in Herrlichkeit: Auf Balthasar hören. *Theol Phil*, 69(3), 411-421, 1994.

Gegen neuscholastische und besonders moderne Abstraktion wie Reduktion wird die Wahrheits-Hehre H U v Balthasars vermittelt. Grundlage ist vor allem "Wahrheit der Welt", 1947 = Theologik I (1985). Das Wahrheits-Geschehen zeigt sich als Freiheits-Ereignis in der wechselseitigen Erschlossenheit von Subjekt und Objekt und ihrer wechselseitigen "Zuvor-kommenheit". Darüber hinaus macht Verf. Einen Vorschlag, Geheimnis neu zu verstehen: nicht als Verschlossenheit und Ausschliessung, sondern als Umschliessen und Bergen (Geheimnis-Ge-heim-nis). Unbegreiflich ist es, weil es seinerseits umgreift. Darum zeigt sich schon das Reden von Unbegreiflichkeit als unangemessen (Wer käme auf die Idee vgl. J Pieper, Unaüstrinkbares Licht, eine Dusche als, unaustrinkbar zu bezeichnen?).

Spoerl, Joseph. Justice and the Case for School Vouchers. *Pub Affairs Quart*, 9(1), 75-86, Ja 95.

Freedom is essential to human flourishing. Therefore, freedom ought not to be restricted unless the common good (i.e., conditions essential to the flourishing of all) requires such restriction. Public education in the US severely restricts the freedom of parents to select schools. Yet such restriction is not required by the common good. A voucher system is the best way of rectifying this injustice. Hence, justice requires the replacement of our current system of public schools with a voucher system. Standard objections to school vouchers do not withstand critical scrutiny.

Sponsel, Leslie E and Natadecha-Sponsel, Poranee. "The Potential Contribution of Buddhism in Developing an Environmental Ethic..." in *Ethics, Religion and Biodiversity, Hamilton, Lawrence S (ed)*, 75-97. Cambridge, White Horse, 1994.

The environmental ideas, actions, and consequences of Buddhism in Thailand are explored. While environmental ethics for a sustainable society are inherent in Buddhism, Westernization has weakened Thai adherence to Buddhism. Only when the actions of the populace adhere more closely to the ideals of Buddhism is the environmental crisis likely to be resolved or at least reduced in Thailand. Some hope is offered by forest monks who have applied Buddhist principles as environmental activitists. In recent years they have provided leadership among villagers to try to conserve some of the remaining forest and restore some of the deforested areas.

Sposito, Frank Andreas and Strong, Tracy B. "Habermas's Significant Other" in *The Cambridge Companion to Habermas, White, Stephen K (ed)*, 263-288. New York, Cambridge Univ Pr, 1995.

Springborg, Patricia. Hobbes's Biblical Beasts: *Leviathan* and *Behemoth*. *Polit Theory*, 23(2), 353-375, My 95.

Springborg, Patricia. Hobbes, Heresy, and the *Historia Ecclesiastica*. *J Hist Ideas*, 55(4), 553-571, O 94.

Hobbes's religious doctrines set an insoluble puzzle because of his insistence on official conformity but private freedom of belief. Charged with heresy on these grounds alone, he sought to defend himself in a series of works, among them the neglected 2242 line Latin poem, the *Historia Ecclesiastica*. Hobbes's defense is a history of heresy defined as private belief that lacks the sovereign's sanction. Cataloguing doctrinal disputes of the first four Church Councils, Hobbes also gives a history of "gentilism", pagan beliefs from ancient Egypt, Oriental, Greek and Roman sources that infected Christianity. This defense, needless to say, proved more inflammatory than the original doctrines for which he was charged, and was published posthumously in 1688.

Spruyt, Joke. Thirteenth-Century Discussions on Modal Terms. *Vivarium*, 32(2), 196-226, N 94.

Spurway, Neil. *Humanity, Environment, and God*. Cambridge, Blackwell, 1993.

Spurway writes about Lord Gifford, and 100 years' lectures on his foundation. Cupitt considers how the concepts of 'nature', 'culture', and 'environment' have changed in the century. Barrow, as physicist/cosmologist, assesses the quests for ultimate explanation by 'the cosmic bougoisie'. Dawkins presents living organisms as models

AUTHOR INDEX WITH ABSTRACTS 755 Stamou, G P

of the world in which each lives. Roberts considers 'history as environment', the essentiality of myth, and the unacceptable concept of 'historical guilt'. Kenny explores 'the kingdom of the mind', and the paradox of attempting to discuss the inconceivable. Finally Habgood contends that there is adequately reliable, though not certain, knowledge about God.

Squires, E J. "Quantum Theory—A Window to the World Beyond Physics" in *Philosophy, Mathematics and Modern Physics, Rudolph, Enno (ed)*, 92-103. New York, Springer-Verlag, 1994.

The measurement and locality problems of quantum theory are explained and discussed. It is suggested that they lead naturally to a dualistic understanding of reality with, on one hand, a world of quantum physics and, on the other, a consciousness which, it is shown, must have some features which are universal.

Squires, Roger. Dream Time. *Proc Aris Soc*, 95, 83-91, 1994-95.

On a no-recollected-experience account of dreaming such as that inspired by remarks of Wittgenstein (Macdonald, Bouwsma, Malcolm, Hunter, Dennett, McFee) are there adequate reasons for supposing that dreams occur *during sleep?* The following suggestions are considered: 1) External behavior. 2) The word of the reporter. 3) Occurrence of the process that causes the waking report (and perhaps from which its content could in theory be predicted). 4) Acquisition of the disposition to tell the dream. I suggest these fail and the Wittgensteinian account is revisionary.

St-Arnaud, Jocelyne. L'euthanasie: Enjeux Ethiques et Politiques. *Philosopher*, 13, 93-105, 1992.

This article defines the term *euthanasia* and its main qualifiers as used in the field of medical ethics since 1950s. It shows how the relevant terminology has evolved, on the one hand, with the advancement of science and medical technology and, on the other hand, with the ethical and political issues from which it cannot be separated. This contextual analysis leads into an account of the various trends marking current debate on the subject.

Staab, Janice. The Laboratory-Trained Believer: Peirce on the Scientific Character of Belief. *Trans Peirce Soc*, 30(4), 939-957, Fall 94.

Staal, Frits. Changing One's Mind. *J Indian Phil*, 23(1), 53-55, Mr 95.

Paul Hacker's hypothesis that Sankara wrote a gloss on the commentary on the *Yogasutra* may not be well-founded but has not been refuted by the very competent articles devoted to it by T S Rukmani (*J Indian Phil*, 20, 419-423 and 21, 395-404). Sankara could, as a youth, have fallen under the spells of a Yogi, and later reformulate the Vedanta (concerned with what is *siddha* "established"), as a higher synthesis of Yoga and Mcmamsa (concerned with what is *sadhya* "to-be-established").

Staal, Frits. The Sanskrit of Science. *J Indian Phil*, 23(1), 73-127, Mr 95.

Stabile, Carol A. "Feminism Without Guarantees" in *Marxism in the Postmodern Age, Callari, Antonio (ed)*, 283-291. New York, Guilford, 1994.

Through an analysis of postmodernist social theory, feminist theory, and the erasure of racism and economic oppression effected by Dan Quayle's articulation of "Murphy Brown" with the LA uprising, this essay illustrates how a politics of discourse operates at the expense of a materialist understanding social relations. Against the discursive idealism of contemporary critical theory, the essay argues that establishing class as a central category of analysis does not mean relinquishing the theoretical and practical gains of feminist analyses of gender and race, but provides a more comprehensive understanding of how oppressions are intertwined within the capitalist mode of production.

Stack, George J. The Concept of Dialectic. *Dialogos*, 30(65), 75-109, Ja 95.

The concept of dialectic is traced in a brief historical account beginning with Plato and proceeding to Sartre's account of a *raison dialectique*. Hegel's conception of a dialectic of thought and a dialectic in the world is discussed and related to the later variations of dialectical theory in the works of Marx, Kierkegaard, and Sartre. It is argued that a dialectical *interpretation* is particularly appropriate both for an understanding of the dynamics of the self and for a comprehension of social phenomena and interactions. As a theoretical model of reflexive thought processes and social dynamics, dialectic remains a valuable tool for interpretation of the human world, independent of its previous embodiment in the system of Hegel or its role in Marxism.

Stadler, Friedrich. "Heinrich Gomperz und Karl Popper im Kontext..." in *Heinrich Gomperz, Karl Popper und die österreichische Philosophie, Seiler, Martin (ed)*, 1-29. Amsterdam, Rodopi, 1994.

Stadler, Friedrich (ed) and Seiler, Martin (ed). *Heinrich Gomperz, Karl Popper und die österreichische Philosophie*. Amsterdam, Rodopi, 1994.

Stagno, Susan J (& others). Reconsidering "Psychosurgery": Issues of Informed Consent and Physician Responsibility. *J Clin Ethics*, 5(3), 217-223, Fall 94.

This paper explores several issues relative to the use of surgical intervention for psychiatric illness: 1) the capacity of severely and chronically mentally ill patients to consent to "psychosurgery"; 2) the standards which should be used to assess a patient's capacity; 3) who is qualified to perform the assessment; and 4) whether physicians should include the option of surgery for patients with severe and treatment-resistant mental illness. The authors conclude that, in most cases, patients who would be considered candidates for surgery are able to give informed consent and that, because of recent technological improvements (such as stereotaxis), neurosurgery provides a relatively safe and effective option in the care of patients with otherwise intractable illness.

Stahl, Jürgen. Fichtes Wissenschaftslehre im Aufbrechen der Paradigmen mechanizistischen Denkens. *Fichte-Studien*, 5, 149-158, 1993.

Stahl, Jürgen. Philosophiegeschichte als Problemfeld der Wissenschaftslehre Fichtes. *Daimon Rev Filosof*, 9, 163-170, 1994.

The article brings out the deeping of the immanent historical tendency emerging in Fichte's transcendental philosophy in the specific viewpoint of methodical approaches of historical-philosophical analysis. The debate with philosophical teaching is an integral moment of the structure of his system. In this way Fichte came to a series of insights into the historicity and logic in the development of philosophy which thereby prove themselves to be a step of formation of the unity of the logical and the historical through the classical German Idealism.

Stake, Robert and Kerr, Dale. René Magritte, Constructivism, and the Researcher as Interpreter. *Educ Theor*, 45(1), 55-62, Wint 95.

In this brief illustrated paper, we reflect upon the increasing legitimacy of direct interpretation in educational research. We draw upon the paintings of René Magritte, the Belgian surrealist of middle century, to cast the qualitative researcher also as bricoleur and provocateur, providing ingredients and stimulus to personal construction of knowledge by the reader. The responsibility of research becomes less the representation and explanation of phenomena and more the drawing of attention to what is worth pondering. This science is robust not because it can predict and prescribe but because it can develop a gallery of alternative perspectives.

Stalley, R F. Persuasion in Plato's *Laws*. *Hist Polit Thought*, 15(2), 157-177, Sum 94.

There is a dispute as to whether the persuasive preludes advocated in the *Laws* do or do not appeal to reason. The answer is that they are rational in the sense that they embody principles of reason but they do not call upon the citizens to exercise their own individual powers of reason. Plato believes that the lives of the citizens should conform to the requirements of the divine reason but he attaches no particular value to individual rational choice. His view of rationality is thus very different from that of most post-Kantian thinkers.

Stalley, R F. Punishment in Plato's *Protagoras*. *Phronesis*, 40(1), 1-19, 1995.

Plato's *Protagoras* 324a-b has been taken to establish that the sophist Protagoras was an enlightened pioneer in penal theory, whose views differ in some respects from those of Plato himself. But it is not clear to what extent the passage contains the thought of the historical Protagoras; the doctrine put into his mouth is not necessarily enlightened; and he sees punishment primarily as a matter of education. In this repect his view of punishment is close to that found in Plato's later dialogues. The account of punishment in the *Protagoras* should thus be seen as Platonic rather than Protagorean.

Stalnaker, Robert. "Letter to Brian Skyrms" in *Probability and Conditionals, Eells, Ellery (ed)*, 27-29. New York, Cambridge Univ Pr, 1994.

Stalnaker, Robert. "The Interaction of Modality with Quantification and Identity" in *Modality, Morality, and Belief, Sinnott-Armstrong, Walter (ed)*, 12-28. New York, Cambridge Univ Pr, 1994.

Stalnaker, Robert and Jeffrey, Richard. "Conditionals as Random Variables" in *Probability and Conditionals, Eells, Ellery (ed)*, 31-46. New York, Cambridge Univ Pr, 1994.

Stam, Henderikus J (ed) and Radtke, H Lorraine (ed). *Power/Gender*. Newbury Park, Sage, 1994.

This is a multidisciplinary collection focussed on the interrelations of power and gender. Some chapters explicate the gendered nature of power, while others analyze how the social construction of gender reflects the workings of power. Both micro- and macro-processes are discussed. The central thesis is that gender and power are inextricably connected such that a full understanding of one can only be achieved through consideration of the other. Drawing from a variety of theoretical frameworks and definitions of power, the contributors include R Connell, Marilyn French, Wendy Hollway, and Jean Lipman-Blumen.

Stamatescu, I O. "On Renormalization in Quantum Field Theory and the Structure of Space-Time" in *Philosophy, Mathematics and Modern Physics, Rudolph, Enno (ed)*, 67-91. New York, Springer-Verlag, 1994.

We discuss Renormalized Quantum Field Theory and its impact on our understanding of space and time. The renormalization procedure is a constitutive part of a quantum field theory since it turns the arbitrariness in the introduction of certain symbols ("bare" parameters) into a well defined relation to measurable quantities (physical masses and couplings). Since the fields and their correlations are space-time distributions it is suggested that they should be considered as probes of the physical space-time continuum. Then it is argued, that the observed intimate and non-trivial connection which renormalization provides between the short distance behaviour of these quantities and the interaction structure of the theory, should be considered as witnessing for a further step in the redefinition of the concepts of space and time induced by modern physics.

Stamatescu, I O. "Questions Concerning Theory and Experience and the Role of Mathematics..." in *Philosophy, Mathematics and Modern Physics, Rudolph, Enno (ed)*, 18-31. New York, Springer-Verlag, 1994.

We consider questions related to the interplay of theoretical input and empirical knowledge in building up the symbolic structure of modern physics. It is argued that a rigid a priori scheme is just as inappropriate as a naive reality hypothesis for describing the theoretical progress. An alternative approach based on strengthening the role of the signification network in the frame of the symbolic structure and of its dynamics could allow one to understand both its stability and flexibility. This dynamics is to be understood as taking place in the progress from theory to theory (historically) as well as in the process of turning empirical information in theoretical structures. It is argued that mathematics plays a very complex role in this dynamics, both in helping the stability of knowledge and in helping formulating hypotheses or giving hints or new points of view.

Stamatescu, I O and Rudolph, Enno. "On the Dialogue Between Physics and Philosophy" in *Philosophy, Mathematics and Modern Physics, Rudolph, Enno (ed)*, 2-17. New York, Springer-Verlag, 1994.

Stamatescu, I O (ed) and Rudolph, Enno (ed). *Philosophy, Mathematics and Modern Physics*. New York, Springer-Verlag, 1994.

Stamm, Marcelo. Das Programm des methodologischen Monismus Subjekttheoretische und methodologische Aspekte der Elementarphilosophie K L Reinholds. *Neue Hefte Phil*, 35, 18-31, 1995.

Stamou, G P and Korfiatis, K J. Emergence of New Fields in Ecology: The Case of Life History Studies. *Hist Phil Life Sci*, 16(1), 97-116, Ja 94.

We examine the emergence of the field of life-history strategies during the 1950s. (We consider a 'field' an area of scientific activity consisting of a theoretical core, a subject of research, a vocabulary and research tools). During the late 1940s and early 1950s, population ecology faced many problems, concerning its conceptual framework, its mathematical models, experimental deficiencies, etc. Research on life-history characteristics remained descriptive, lacking explanations about the causes and significance of phenomena. This was due to the deficiencies of the theoretical framework of population ecology up to the 1950s. The catalyzing factor for the emergence of the new field was the interdisciplinary impacts, and especially the impact of neo-Darwinism. The elaboration of a new theoretical core, invoking also methodological shifts, was the triggering factor, conditioning the emergence of the new field.

Standish, Paul. Knowledge, Practice, Truth. *J Phil Educ*, 28(2), 245-255, Wint 94.

This is a review article on *Beyond Liberal Education: Essays in Honour of Paul H Hirst*, edited by Robin Barrow and Patricia White, London: Routledge (1993). This varied collection deals with different aspects of Hirst's widely influential writings on the nature of knowledge, the relationship between theory and practice, and the place of philosophy in teacher education, and in aesthetic, moral, and religious education. The review critically discusses each chapter, including the concluding essay by Hirst himself, in which he makes an important retraction regarding the practical implications of his widely renowned forms of knowledge thesis.

Standish, Paul. Postmodernism and the Education of the Whole Person. *J Phil Educ*, 29(1), 121-135, March 95.

In some recent discussions the implications of postmodernism for education have been wrongly conceived. An alternative approach is offered and this is used as a means for challenging any grand design in the provision of schooling and in the conception of education. Through this, ideas of the whole person implicit in much educational theory and practice (including personal and social education) are questioned. With some reference to the work of Stanley Cavell an attempt is made to show the sort of thinking which might inform education, avoiding both the relativistic and complacent excesses of postmodernism and the explicit systematic planning of the grand design.

Stanford, P Kyle. For Pluralism and Against Realism About Species. *Phil Sci*, 62(1), 70-91, Mr 95.

I argue for accepting a pluralist approach to species, while rejecting the realism about species espoused by P Kitcher and a number of other philosophers of biology. I develop an alternative view of species concepts as divisions of organisms into groups for study which are relative to the systematic explanatory interests of biologists of a particular time. I also show how this conception resolves a number of difficult puzzles which plague the application of particular species concepts.

Stanley, Marjorie Thines. Multinational Capital Budgeting, Emerging Markets, and Managerial Agency: A Proposal for an Ethically Constrained Capital Budgeting Model. *Bus Prof Ethics J*, 12(4), 87-107, Wint 93.

The purpose of the paper is to provide suggestions for the development of an ethically constrained capital budgeting model for use by multinational corporations in emerging-market environments. Such a model is needed because the consistency between shareholder wealth maximization and welfare maximization, assumed by existing capital budgeting models, is greatly weakened in these environments. The paper evaluates several alternative theoretical approaches (managerial agency, stakeholder, and social contract theory), and recommends a model employing sensitivity analysis reflecting differing ethical states of the world, and a nexus-of-contracts view of the firm and of managerial agency.

Stanton, Annette L and Soliday, Elizabeth. Deceived Versus Nondeceived Participants' Perceptions of Scientific and Applied Psychology. *Ethics Behavior*, 5(1), 87-104, 1995.

Research examining the possible effects of deceptive research participation on participants' perception of psychology has yielded equivocal results. The present study's goal was to clarify the possible effects of participation in mildly deceptive research on participants' impressions of scientific and applied psychology. Participants (N = 112) were randomly assigned to one of six experimental conditions: active groups receiving negative, positive, or no feedback, or passive groups receiving negative, positive, or no feedback. Following participation, participants completed measures of impressions of psychotherapy and psychotherapists, researchers, and instructors. The manipulation did not affect attitudes toward psychology on any of the dependent measures, although gender effects resulted on one measure. Participants in general reported very positive attitudes toward the science and practice of psychology. Recommendations are offered for future research on the effects of more extensive deceptions.

Staples, Peter. Ultimates as Paradoxical Limits in Christian Ecumenical Science. *Ultim Real Mean*, 18(2), 139-150, Je 95.

In ecumenical science, the ultimate ideal is an ecclesial entity in which 'all' are 'one'. But how is this ecclesial entity conceived; and can it ultimately be socially constructed? So we must examine the 'models of unity' now under discussion in the Ecumenical Movement and also consider the paradoxical limits in the ecumenical process itself: e.g., 1) Ecumenism as an ideology sometimes divides denominations; 2) The classical voting paradoxes; 3) The exponential multiplication of ecumenical dialogues; and 4) The problematical processes of ecumenical 'reception'. Given such paradoxical limits, it is still unclear whether any of the 'models' can ultimately be socially constructed in practice.

Stapp, Henry P. Comment on 'Stapp's Theorem Without Counterfactual Commitment'. *Stud Hist Phil Sci*, 25(6), 959-964, D 95.

Michael Dickson has examined the 'could' version of my nonlocality theorem, and claims to have found a flaw. Several errors in his argument are pointed out. The main problem is that he replaces my locality criterion by a substitute that is too weak to do the job. His justification for making this change is critically flawed by a failure to differentiate my sufficient condition from the converse necessary condition. Nevertheless, Dickson succeeds in deriving all but the final step of my argument. My justification for this final crucial step is discussed here in some detail.

Stapp, Henry P. *Mind, Matter, and Quantum Mechanics*. New York, Springer-Verlag, 1993.

Classical physics entails that mind, the experiential aspect of nature, is, to the extent that it influences matter, controlled by the local deterministic laws that govern matter. The differing attitudes of Bohr, Heisenberg, von Neumann, and Einstein on this problem are described, and it is shown how their ideas lead naturally to a quantum mechanical conception of the mind/brain in which mind becomes complementary to, and interactive with, the material aspects of nature, rather than subservient to them.

Stapp, Henry P and Bedford, Donald. Bell's Theorem in an Indeterministic Universe. *Synthese*, 102(1), 139-164, Ja 95.

A variation of Bell's theorem that deals with the indeterministic case is formulated and proved within the logical framework of Lewis's theory of counterfactuals. The no-faster-than-light-influence condition is expressed in terms of Lewis 'would' counterfactual conditionals. Objections to this procedure raised by certain philosophers of science are examined and answered. The theorem shows that the incompatibility between the predictions of quantum theory and the idea of no faster-than-light-influence cannot be ascribed to any auxiliary or tacit assumption of either determinism or the related idea that outcomes of unperformed measurements are determinate within nature. In addition, the theorem provides an example of an application of Lewis's theory of counterfactuals in a rigorous scientific context.

Starchenko, S and Hart, B. Superstable Quasi-Varieties. *Annals Pure Applied Log*, 69(1), 53-71, S 94.

We present a structure theorem for superstable quasi-varieties without DOP. We show that every algebra in such a quasi-variety weakly decomposes as the product of an affine algebra and a combinatorial algebra, that is, it is bi-interpretable with a two sorted structure where one sort is an affine algebra, the other sort is a combinatorial algebra and the only nontrivial polynomials between the two sorts are certain actions of the affine sort on the combinatorial sort.

Starik, Mark. Should Trees Have Managerial Standing? Toward Stakeholder Status for Non-Human Nature. *J Bus Ethics*, 14(3), 207-217, Mr 95.

Most definitions of the concept of "stakeholder" include only human entities. This paper advances the argument that the nonhuman natural environment can be integrated into the stakeholder management concept. This argument includes the observations that the natural environment is finally becoming recognized as a vital component of the business environment, that the stakeholder concept is more than a human political/economic one, and that nonhuman nature currently is not adequately represented by other stakeholder groups. In addition, this paper asserts that any of several stakeholder management processes can readily include the natural environment as one or more stakeholders of organizations. Finally, the point is made that this integration would provide a more holistic, value-oriented, focused and strategic approach to stakeholder management, potentially benefitting both nature and organizations.

Stark, Andrew. The Appearance of Official Impropriety and the Concept of Political Crime. *Ethics*, 105(2), 326-351, Ja 95.

Stastny, Peter (trans) and Foucault, Michel and Sengel, Deniz (trans). Madness, the Absence of Work. *Crit Inquiry*, 21(2), 290-298, Wint 95.

Stastny, Roland. *Philosophische Praxis*. Vienna, Passagen, 1995.

Statham Jr, E Robert. Political Philosophy as Political Action: A Response to Mark Blasius. *Polit Theory*, 23(3), 517-519, Ag 95.

This research is a critique of the "Post-Modern" tendency to ground the activity of political theorizing in political action proper. The essay responds to this tendency by suggesting that the traditional "Classical" activity of political philosophy is rooted in the primary desire, not to act politically, but to obtain understanding of politics. The research recommends that genuine philosophizing about politics is fundamentally contemplative, and that the disparity that exists between the contemporary view of political theorizing as utilizing the mind to further interested goals in political practice constitutes a crisis regarding the status and meaning of political philosophy.

Statman, Daniel. Gossip and Morality (in Hebrew). *Iyyun*, 43, 399-416, O 94.

It has recently been suggested that gossip is not as morally bad as we used to think and, furthermore, that it has significant social and epistemic advantages. The purpose of my paper is to argue against this new evaluation of gossip. I argue that most people have an interest not to be an object of gossip; that gossip harms the relationships between members of society; and that a tendency to gossip reflects a bad character. Though gossip is far from being the worst activity from a moral point of view, there are still good reasons for reducing it which clearly override the reasons for engaging in it.

Statman, Daniel. Virtue Ethics and Psychology. *Int J Applied Phil*, 9(2), 43-49, Wint-Spr 95.

Recently it has been suggested that virtue ethics can help in solving some of the dilemmas of professional psychology. I express doubts about this idea, arguing that as virtue ethics is mainly concerned with judgments of character and not of particular actions, its ability to help solve practical dilemmas is rather limited. But while virtue ethics' contribution to professional psychology is limited, psychology might be able to contribute to the theoretical justification of virtue ethics. If the value of the virtues is assumed to rely on their connection to one's notion of well-being, then psychological work is called for to help explain this connection.

Staton, Scott (trans) and Moravia, Sergio. *The Enigma of the Mind: The Mind-Body Problem in Contemporary Thought*. New York, Cambridge Univ Pr, 1995.

The author analyzes the debate on the mind-body problem in the last 50 years. His approach is essentially theoretical: it examines the interpretations of the mental offered by the main contemporary philosophies of mind. Moravia's central theses are that both materialism and mentalism are untenable and that the true "subject" of the psychophysical experiences is the concrete person in-the-world. As to the mental, it should be viewed as a peculiar language which gives voice to some aspects (subjective, existential) of human being and human acting that no other language could express adequately.

Staude, John-Raphael. Language, Narration and the Self. *Hist Human Sci*, 7(2), 141-149, My 94.

Stauth, Georg. Critical Theory and Pre-Fascist Social Thought. *Hist Euro Ideas*, 18(5), 711-727, S 94.

The relation between the Frankfurt School critical theorists and pre-fascist social thought has often been characterised as "kommunikations verweigerung" (repudiation of communication). Both Adorno's aesthetics and his theory of knowledge, however, remain dependent on Kluges' dualism between mind and soul in an attempt to overcome it. The article concludes that much of post modernist theory activates issues which have been anticipated and conceptualised by pre-fascist social thought. A cautious re-reading of such conceptualisations of the 1920's is needed in order to understand the philosophical discourse of the 1950's and 1960's.

Stearns, James M and Borna, Shaheen. The Ethics of Lottery Advertising: Issues and Evidence. *J Bus Ethics*, 14(1), 43-51, Ja 95.

After a discussion of the evolution and criticisms of state run lotteries, this article examines the ethics of lottery advertising. A discussion of the appeals used by lottery advertisers is followed by evidence concerning the impact of expected value information on lottery purchase intentions. Findings point toward less emphasis on the lottery as a solution to financial and job problems and more emphasis on information about the actual value of a lottery bet. Using accepted standards from the marketing literature, lottery advertising is found to be deceptive.

Stebbins, J Michael. What Did Lonergan Really Say about Aquinas's Theory of the Will?. *Method*, 12(2), 281-305, Fall 94.

Stecker, Robert. Objectivity and Interpretation. *Phil Lit*, 19(1), 48-59, Ap 95.

Gregory Currie has argued that literary interpretation suffers from a failure of objectivity. I try to show both the faultiness of the conception of interpretation on which his argument is based, and that the argument should not be accepted even if we take his conception of interpretation for granted. I also argue that the same standard of objectivity ought not to be applied to all literary interpretations.

Stecker, Robert. Relativism About Interpretation. *J Aes Art Crit*, 53(1), 14-18, Wint 95.

Stecker, Robert and Adams, Fred. Vacuous Singular Terms. *Mind Lang*, 9(4), 387-401, D 94.

We offer direct reference solutions to two problems presented by vacuous singular terms: the semantics of sentences or thoughts containing vacuous terms and the explanation of behavior employing vacuous terms. We argue that the content of "Fa", where 'a' is vacuous, is the content of the open sentence 'x is F', and the content of "a exists" is the content of 'there is an x such that x = y' where y cannot be identified. We also argue that the syntax of sentences or thoughts plus the semantics of the associated thoughts or sentences explains behavior involving vacuous terms. We contrast our view with those of Braun, Burge, Donnellan, and Segal.

Steel, Carlos. Does Evil Have a Cause? Augustine's Perplexity and Thomas' Answer. *Rev Metaph*, 48(2), 251-273, D 94.

Steel, J R. Projectively Well-Ordered Inner Models. *Annals Pure Applied Log*, 74(1), 77-104, Je 95.

Steenbakkers, Piet. *Spinoza's Ethica From Manuscript to Print: Studies on Text, Form, and Related Topics*. Assen, Van Gorcum, 1994.

The different studies in this volume derive from a common source: an enquiry into the vicissitudes of Spinoza's *Ethica*. Chapter 1 reconstructs the editorial history of the *Opera posthuma* (1677). Chapter 2 is the first comprehensive account of accent-marks in Latin in the early modern period. Chapter 3 compares *Ethica* 3 (on the passions) with a text written by Lodewijk Meyer in 1670. Chapter 4 analyses the relationship between the Latin version of *Ethica* 5 and its contemporary Dutch translation. Chapter 5 argues that the controversial geometrical layout of the *Ethica* is connected with the foundation of Spinoza's philosophy.

Steeves, H Peter. Phenomenology and the Possibility of Narrative. *Clio*, 24(1), 21-36, Fall 94.

In an effort to understand how it is that we experience narrative and what it is that we experience narrative to be, I offer a phenomenological description to both the mechanisms and the necessary preconditions of the narrative experience. I suggest 1) that narrative represents a mediated world in motion and thus calls on us to adopt a new "narrative-horizon" in an attempt to understand; 2) that my personal lifestory and external examples of narrative arise together in sense, and thus 3) that one of the necessary preconditions of narrative is a community in which such recognition and constitution is possible.

Steger, Manfred. A Perspective on Solidarity in a 'Post-Socialist' World. *Hist Euro Ideas*, 19(1-3), 325-331, Jl 94.

Arguing that socialism understood as "abolition of the commodity form" has indeed come to an end after 1989, the author nonetheless maintains that the socialist ethos defined as "a movement toward a cooperative order of society" still retains relevance in a "post-socialist" world. Its appeal lies in its liberal demand to extend the democratic promise of the French Revolution. Understood as a "regulative idea" guiding political practice, an ethic of solidarity contests the disparities of wealth and well-being in capitalist society by formulating social democratic objectives within a language of rights.

Steiger, Karsten. Liebe, Tod, Erlösung: Richard Wagners "Tristan" und der Einfluss Schopenhauers. *Schopenhauer Jahr*, 76, 103-132, 1995.

Stein, Dan J and Hollander, Eric. A Neural Network Approach to Obsessive-Compulsive Disorder. *J Mind Behav*, 15(3), 223-237, Sum 94.

A central methodological innovation in cognitive science has been the development of connectionist or neural network models of psychological phenomena. These models may also comprise a theoretically integrative and methodologically rigourous approach to psychiatric phenomena. In this paper we employ connectionist theory to conceptualize obsessive-compulsive disorder (OCD). We discuss salient phenomenological and neurobiological findings of the illness, and then reformulate these using neural network models. Several features and mechanisms of OCD may be explicated in terms of disordered networks. Neural network modeling appears to constitute a novel and potentially fertile approach to psychiatric disorders such as OCD.

Stein, Edward. "The Relevance of Scientific Research About Sexual Orientation to Lesbian and Gay Rights" in *Gay Ethics*, Murphy, Timothy F (ed), 269-308. New York, Haworth Pr, 1994.

This essay considers the way in which scientific research is relevant to questions of lesbian and gay rights. It is specifically argued that such research is not relevant to these kinds of arguments because its results about the origins of sexual orientation do not necessarily—and should not be taken to—imply conclusions about moral entitlements. Questions about the moral and civic entitlements of gay men and lesbians are not bolstered or advanced by reference to biological accounts of sexual orientation. This is not to suggest, however, that research into the origins of sexual orientation is objectionable, only that it does not have the significance for moral rights that some have claimed.

Steinbock, A J. Phenomenological Concepts of Normality and Abnormality. *Man World*, 28(3), 241-260, Jl 95.

This article examines the problems of normality and abnormality from a phenomenological perspective by using Edmund Husserl's analyses found in his unpublished manuscripts on "primordial constitution." I focus on only two modes of normality and abnormality in this article: concordance and discordance, and optimality and nonoptimality. Husserl's approach is motivated by *constitutional* concerns rather than medicinal, diagnostic or therapeutic ones. As a result, these phenomenological notions challenge many traditional conceptions of normality and abnormality assumed by the theory and practice of physiology, psychology and therapeutics, and is suggestive for fields as diverse as somatic pathology and normative sociology.

Steinbock, Anthony J. The Project of Ethical Renewal and Critique: Edmund Husserl's Early Phenomenology of Culture. *S J Phil*, 32(4), 449-464, Wint 94.

"Renewal" is the expression Edmund Husserl used for the social, political, and ethical transformation of human culture (1922-1924). Considering the concept of renewal in the *generative* becoming of a culture, I first explain the phenomenological background in which Husserl approached the enterprise of renewal. I then describe Husserl's concept of renewal as an ethical task. Next, I take up the process of renewal as accomplishing "the best possible." Following this, I discuss the concept of critique advanced in the *Kaizo* articles. My conclusion interprets Husserl's emphases on the urgency of critique and renewal in relation to the generation of a culture.

Steinbock, Bonnie. Coercion and Long-Term Contraceptives. *Hastings Center Rep*, 25(1), S19-S22, Jan-Feb 95.

An objection to Norplant is its potential for coercion, particularly as applied to poor and minority women. The article analyzes the concept of coercion, and applies this analysis to the question of whether offering financial incentives for using Norplant is coercive. This depends on whether the program is more plausibly seen as liberty-limiting or liberty-enhancing. However, the potential for coercion is not the only objection to Norplant. An overemphasis on coercion may mask other important objections, such as those based on autonomy, informed consent, equal protection, and the reinforcement of inequality.

Steinbock, Bonnie and McClamrock, Ron. When Is Birth Unfair to the Child?. *Hastings Center Rep*, 24(6), 15-21, N-D 94.

We argue that having children under extremely adverse conditions may be unfair to the children, even if their lives are not so bad as to qualify as "wrongful." Instead, we appeal to a principle of parental responsibility to show how the child is wronged.

Steiner, Gary (trans) and Wolin, Richard (ed) and Löwith, Karl. *Martin Heidegger and European Nihilism*. New York, Columbia Univ Pr, 1995.

Steiner, Hillel. Persons of Lesser Value: Moral Argument and the 'Final Solution'. *J Applied Phil*, 12(2), 129-141, 1995.

For many persons, "Holocaust-abomination" is a fixed point on their moral compass: if anything can be evil, it was. Yet at least one of the justifications deployed by its perpetrators (the eugenics argument) invokes widely-held values concerning human health and procreation. Hence persons endorsing many current activities based on those values (e.g., genetic counselling) have been charged with being on a morally deplorable slippery slope. This paper sketches the necessary structure of a moral position capable of consistently embracing those values without placing its occupants on that slippery slope.

Steiner, Mark. The Applicabilities of Mathematics. *Phil Math*, 3(2), 129-156, My 95.

There are multiple issues concerning the applicability of mathematics in the physical sciences. The semantic issue, of showing how pure mathematics can be integrated in physical reasoning, was solved by Frege. The metaphysical issue, of showing how mathematical entities could be relevant to physical entities, was also solved by Frege. There are epistemological issues concerning the aptness of mathematical concepts to the nomological description of nature, which were raised first by Wigner, but have never been satisfactorily resolved.

Steiner, Peter. Metabole and Revolution: The Myth of the Platonic *Statesman* and the Modern Concept of Revolution. *Polis*, 12(1-2), 134-153, 1993.

The purpose of this essay is, to give an outline of the concept of Platonic rationality as a reasonable argument in contemporary philosophical discussion. It is reached within three steps: 1) An examination of "metabole" (change) in the myth of "The Statesman" and it's meaning in the Platonic dialogues. 2) A comparison between the modern concept of revolution (historically: the French revolution of 1789; philosophically: the concept of revolution in the mode of thinking by Immanuel Kant, 1781) and the Platonic concept of metabole. 3) The Platonic concept of rationality is not merely a logic concept, but includes "philosophy" as a "way of life".

Steiner, Rudolf. *Anthroposophy in Everyday Life*. Hudson, Anthroposophic Pr, 1995.

Steiner, Rudolf. *Intuitive Thinking as a Spiritual Path*. Hudson, Anthroposophic Pr, 1995.

Steiner, Rudolf. *The Genius of Language: Observations for Teachers*. Hudson, Anthroposophic Pr, 1995.

Steiner, Rudolf and Lathe, Robert F (trans) and Whittaker, Nancy Parsons (trans). *The Spirit of the Waldorf School*. Hudson, Anthroposophic Pr, 1995.

Steiner, Uwe. "Überwindung von Schwierigem durch Häufung Desselben". *Phil Rundsch*, 41(4), 315-320, D 94.

Steinhoff, Gordon. Kant's Argument for Causality in the Second Analogy. *Int Phil Quart*, 34(4), 465-480, D 94.

In this paper I show that Kant's single argument for causality in the Second Analogy is based on "the nature of time." Kant is arguing that *only* our presupposition of the causal determination of all events enables events to represent unified time. In support of this interpretation, I appeal to the general argument Kant offers in the Deduction, section 25, for the necessity of applying the "categories" in our thought of objects in space and time. I defend my interpretation against criticisms of an earlier version that has been offered and rejected by several of Kant's commentators.

Steinhorst, Kirk and Hallaq, John H. Business Intelligence Methods—How Ethical. *J Bus Ethics*, 13(10), 787-794, O 94.

An empirical study was conducted during Spring and Summer of 1991 about information gathering methods by businesses regarding operations of competitors. Respondents were employed in a variety of different industries. A convenience sample was administered in two adjoining states, with one group residing in an urban city and the other in smaller predominantly rural communities. Analysis of perceptions held by these two groups supports the hypothesis that rural residents tend to be more conservative and less approving of questionable methods of information gathering. Similarly, within each group and in the sample as a whole, differences in condoning or disapproving information gathering methods were discovered on the basis of demographic characteristics of respondents. (edited)

Steinitz, Yuval. Contradictions are Ontological Arguments. *Relig Stud*, 30(4), 505-509, D 94.

Although ontological arguments had provoked many objections, most of them boil down to the claim that a purely conceptual analysis must be devoid of factual content. Thus, instead of rebutting each of these objections separately, this paper intends to convince those who deny ontological arguments to admit the existence, from their own perspectives, of at least *negative* ontological arguments. The paper argues that conceptual contradictions constitute arguments of this type, showing what necessarily does not exist.

Steinitz, Yuval. Failing to Beg the Question. *Phil Quart*, 45(179), 202-204, Ap 95.

Steinitz, Yuval. Necessary Beings. *Amer Phil Quart*, 31(2), 177-182, Ap 94.

A sound ontological argument can be constructed by either of the following strategies: A) by arguing that the proposition "necessary beings, e.g., God, do not exist" is self-contradictory (the classical strategy of Descartes, Leibniz, etc.); or B) by arguing for the coherence of the concept of *necessary beings*. The second strategy is based on the fact that necessary beings, *ipso facto*, either necessarily exist or are necessarily absent. But if the concept of such beings is not self-contradictory, then there can be no reason for their *necessary* absence. By a process of elimination the second alternative obtains: such beings do necessarily exist. Hartshorne, Malcom and Plantinga indeed took the last route, but not without difficulties. However, these difficulties can be avoided by applying strategy (B) to the mere concept of *necessary beings*—rather than to concepts such as *God*, or of *an unsurpassable greatness* as they did.

Steinitz, Yuval. Prediction Versus Retrodiction in Mill. *Int Phil Quart*, 34(4), 481-483, D 94.

This paper demonstrates a most significant, yet largely unnoticed, entailment of Mill's plurality-of-causes thesis. This is the fact that the combination of this unique view of causation (or a modal version of it), with the more common view of the inductive nature of science, yields a surprising result about prediction versus retrodiction: That the future is *in principle* more accessible to scientific inference than the past. Thus, even if we were lucky enough to obtain the complete, ultimate encyclopedia of all the laws of nature—under a Millean perspective we would be able to deduce only future events.

Steinle, Friedrich. Experiment, Speculation and Law: Faraday's Analysis of Arago's Wheel. *Proc Phil Sci Ass*, 1, 293-303, 1994.

Faraday's view of the mutual relation of speculative theories and laws of nature implies that there should be a procedure, leading from speculative considerations to a system of facts and laws in which theories do no longer play any role. In order to make out the degree in which Faraday's claims correspond to his practice, the way in which he gains an explanation of Arago's effect is analyzed. The thesis is proposed that he indeed has a procedure of leaving theories aside. It is intimately connected with certain methodological guidelines of his experimentation.

Stekeler-Weithofer, Pirmin. Ideation und Projektion. *Deut Z Phil*, 42(5), 783-798, 1994.

How do we connect empirical discourse about shapes and 'spatial' relations of bodies with abstract propositions about 'geometrical forms' as given in 'analytical' and 'axiomatized' geometries? Because empirical congruence depends heavily on contextually given margins of precision, geometrical forms cannot be constituted by mere abstraction in the way rational numbers are. Ideal congruence is already defined by *formal* truth or provability conditions for *formal* sentences containing certain names for ideal forms. These conditions, however, are no arbitrary conventions but systematically connected with deep grounded empirical knowledge by principles of 'ideation', as the converse relation of 'projection' is called.

Stella, Vittorio. Il Sogno, la Fanciullezza e l'Arte nel Pensiero di Giovanni Gentile. *Filosofia*, 45(3), 329-356, S-D 94.

Stella, Vittorio. La Prospettiva Estetica di Augusto Guzzo. *Filosofia*, 45(1), 27-62, Ja-Ap 94.

Stella, Vittorio. La Riflessione sul Mito in Leopardi. *Stud Filosofici*, 321-339, 1991-92.

Stellardi, Giuseppe A. The Death of Philosophy and the Future of Thought. *Hist Euro Ideas*, 20(1-3), 553-557, Ja 95.

The article describes philosophy as the attempt to think beyond the limits of the immediately and legitimately thinkable. This attempt, as proven by deconstruction, is suicidal: in the death of philosophy, however, and thanks to it, the innermost essence of thought survives. In this process, metaphor, defined as a "displacement of meaning", inevitably plays a central part.

Stemmer, Nathan. A Behaviorist Alternative to *Theory* a n d *Simulation* Theories of Folk Psychology. *Behavior Phil*, 23(1), 29-41, Spr-Sum 95.

According to cognitivists, folk psychology hypotheses are intentional, and it is this feature that explains why these hypotheses are predictively successful. Two types of cognitivist theories are discussed. The *theory* theory assumes that the hypotheses derive from an explicit or implicit intentional theory. The *simulation* theory assumes that people arrive at their intentional hypotheses by a process of simulation. Both theories face serious problems. All these problems are avoided by the present behaviorist theory. According to this well-supported theory, folk psychology hypotheses are not intentional. They are inductive generalizations, and their predictive success derives from the adaptive value of human generalizing dispositions and from the intraspecies uniformity of these dispositions.

Stempsey, William E and Veatch, Robert M. Incommensurability: Its Implications for the Patient/Physician Relation. *J Med Phil*, 20(3), 253-268, Je 95.

Scientific authority and physician authority are both challenged by Thomas Kuhn's concept of incommensurability. If competing "paradigms" or "world views" cannot rationally be compared, we have no means to judge the truth of any particular view. We distinguish four steps in the process of translating medical science onto clinical decisions: the doing of the science, the appropriation of the scientific findings by the clinician, the transfer of the findings from the clinician to the patient, and the choice of a treatment regimen. Incommensurability can play a role in each stage. There is at least some theory- and value-ladenness in science that is dependent on the world view of those who construct the scientific theories. Clinicians who must use the results of scientific research will inevitably interpret the research from the standpoint of their own world view. There may be further incommensurability when these data are communicated to the patient. Finally, clinician and patient values must come into play in any decision about choice of treatment. No stage of medical research or practice is value-free.

Stenstad, Gail. The Last God—A Reading. *Res Phenomenol*, 23, 172-184, 1993.

Stephens, G Lynn and Graham, George. "An Introduction to Philosophical Psychopathology: Its Nature, Scope, and Emergence" in *Philosophical Psychopathology, Graham, George (ed)*, 1-23. Cambridge, MIT Pr, 1993.

Surveys the topics and literature of the field of philosophical psychopathology with emphasis upon the field's most recent areas of activity.

Stephens, G Lynn and Graham, George. "Mind and Mine" in *Philosophical Psychopathology, Graham, George (ed)*, 91-109. Cambridge, MIT Pr, 1993.

Examine introspective alienation as this phenomenon occurs in a variety of different psychopathological states or conditions. Distinguishes between two aspects of self-consciousness operative in such states or conditions. One is being conscious of one's own stream of consciousness; the other is being conscious of one's own mental agency.

Stephens, G Lynn and Graham, George. Commentary on "Kant, Thought Insertion, and Mental Unity". *Phil Psychiat Psych*, 1(2), 115-116, Je 94.

Stephens, G Lynn (ed) and Graham, George (ed). *Philosophical Psychopathology*. Cambridge, MIT Pr, 1993.

Collection of mostly original papers by more than a dozen philosophers and psychopathologists on topics at the intersection of philosophy of mind and psychopathology.

Stephens, G Lynn and Graham, George. Self-Consciousness, Mental Agency, and the Clinical Psychopathology of Thought-Insertion. *Phil Psychiat Psych*, 1(1), 1-10, Mr 94.

This paper shows that self-consciousness actually contains two distinct experiences: the sense of being the subject of consciousness, and the sense of being the agent of mental events within one's psychological history. This claim is based mainly on an analysis of psychopathological data concerning thought insertion, or thought alienation. These data may also seem to support the separability of self-consciousness from introspection. It is shown, however, that the data do not support separability. The experience of thought insertion requires the sense of being the subject of consciousness.

Stephens, G Lynn and Pence, Gregory. *Seven Dilemmas in World Religions*. New York, Paragon House, 1994.

Stephens, William O and Feezell, Randolph M. The Argument from Marginal Cases: Is Speciesism Defensible?. *Cont Phil*, 16(4), 7-16, Jl-Ag 94.

We discuss various attempts to resist the conclusions offered by critics of speciesism who argue that many criteria of moral concern actually raise many nonhuman animals above some "marginal cases" of human beings. The appeal to ridicule, the appeal to ignorance, the argument from no-consciousness, the argument from self-interest, and the argument from religious appeals we contend are popular, but less philosophically serious responses. The more serious responses are the argument from kinds/norms, the argument from moral sentiments, and the argument from rule utility. We conclude that none of these responses refutes the argument from marginal cases.

Stephenson, Harriet Buckman and Galbraith, Sharon and Grimm, Robert B. Ethical Congruency of Constituent Groups. *J Bus Ethics*, 14(2), 145-158, F 95.

This research investigates the perceptions of five constituent groups of an accredited business school—their perceptions of others' ethics, of their own ethics and ideal values, and of how business ethics can be improved. Self-described behavior from the constituent groups is quite similar, yet is decidedly different from that which respondents felt others would do. (edited)

Stepien, Teodor. A Note on Formalisations of First-Order Theories. *Rep Math Log*, 27, 19-28, 1993.

Sterba, James P (ed). *Earth Ethics: Environmental Ethics, Animal Rights, and Practical Applications*. Englewood Cliffs, Prentice Hall, 1995.

Sterba, James P. From Biocentric Individualism to Biocentric Pluralism. *Environ Ethics*, 17(2), 191-207, Sum 95.

Drawing on and inspired by Paul Taylor's *Respect for Nature*, I develop a view which I call "biocentric pluralism," which, I claim, avoids the major criticisms that have been directed at Taylor's account. In addition, I show that biocentric pluralism has certain advantages over biocentric utilitarianism (VanDeVeer) and concentric circle theories (Wenz and Callicott).

Sterba, James P. Reconciling Anthropocentric and Nonanthropocentric Environmental Ethics. *Environ Values*, 3(3), 229-244, Autumn 94.

I propose to show that when the most morally defensible versions of an anthropocentric environmental ethics and a nonanthropocentric ethics are laid out, they would lead us to accept the same principles of environmental justice.

Sterba, James P. Reconciling Conceptions of Justice: A Path to Universal Justice. *Dialogue Hum*, 2(3-4), 123-137, 1992.

Sterba, James P. Reconciling Pacifists and Just War Theorists Revisited (Response to Reitan). *Soc Theor Pract*, 20(2), 135-142, Sum 94.

Sterba, James P. Toward a Universal Environmental Ethics. *Dialogue Hum*, 3(4), 113-126, 1993.

Sterelny, Kim. Understanding Life: Recent Work in Philosophy of Biology. *Brit J Phil Sci*, 46(2), 155-183, Je 95.

This paper surveys recent philosophy of biology. It aims to introduce outsiders to the field to the recent literature (which is reviewed in the footnotes) and the main recent debates. I concentrate on three of these: recent critiques of the replicator/vehicle distinction and its application to the idea of the gene as the unit of section; the recent defences of group selection and the idea that standard alternatives to group selection are in fact no more than a disguised form of group selection; and recent ideas on the role of selection in evolution, especially the role of selection in structuring the large-scale history of life. The paper connects philosophy of biology to some more general problems in the philosophy of science, and concludes with a few suggestions about unfinished business.

Stern, David G. A New Exposition of the 'Private Language Argument': Wittgenstein's 'Notes for the "Philosophical Lecture"'. *Phil Invest*, 17(3), 552-565, Jl 94.

A recently published Wittgenstein manuscript from the early 1940s, which contains some unusually explicit notes for a public lecture on private language, helps to clarify the nature of Wittgenstein's argument that a private definition is impossible because ostension always depends on a "technique of use." It also strongly supports the view that Wittgenstein was not arguing for a positive theory of mind and helps us to see how the treatment of training and practice in the opening sections of the *Investigations* is the basis for the subsequent discussion of both rule-following and privacy.

Stern, David G. *Wittgenstein on Mind and Language*. New York, Oxford Univ Pr, 1995.

Stern, David S. "Transcendental Apperception and Subjective Logic: Kant and Hegel on the Role of the Subject" in *Hegel on the Modern World, Collins, Ardis B (ed)*, 159-175. Albany, SUNY Pr, 1995.

Stern, Karl. *The Flight from Woman (New Edition)*. New York, Paragon House, 1985.

The Flight from Woman is a study of the polarity of the sexes as reflected in the conflict between two modes of knowledge—scientific or rational, as contrasted with intuitive or poetic. The scientific revolution of the last 300 years has yielded a de-feminization and de-humanization of society, in the sense that it is a rejection of the kind of wisdom, called *sophia*, that man comprehends intuitively. (edited)

Stern, Robert. British Hegelianism: A Non-Metaphysical View?. *Bull Hegel Soc Gt Brit*, 31, 17-38, Spr-Sum 95.

This article puts forward a revisionary reading of Hegel's reception in Britain at the turn of the nineteenth century, in suggesting that the stance of the British Hegelians is very close to the sort of non-metaphysical or category-theory interpretation currently in vogue amongst contemporary commentators like Klaus Hartman, J N Findlay, Alan White and Terry Pinkard. (This article is a shortened version of one with the same title that appeared in the *European Journal of Philosophy*, vol 2, no 3, December 1994, pp. 293-321.)

Stern, Robert. British Hegelianism: A Non-Metaphysical View?. *Euro J Phil*, 2(3), 293-321, D 94.

This article puts forward a revisionary reading of Hegel's reception in Britain at the turn of the nineteenth century, in suggesting that the stance of the British Hegelians is very close to the sort of nonmetaphysical or category theory interpretation currently in vogue amongst contemporary commentators. It is shown that the British Hegelians arrived at this position as a way of responding to the hostile existentialist reaction to Hegel begun by Schelling in the 1840s, which led them to abandon the standard Neoplatonic reading of his idealism, and arrive at the sort of nonmetaphysical account which is most fully developed by J M E McTaggart in his interpretation of Hegel's *Logic*.

Stern-Gillet, Suzanne. *Aristotle's Philosophy of Friendship*. Albany, SUNY Pr, 1995.

Sternberg, Robert J. "An Investment Perspective on Creative Insight" in *The Nature of Insight, Sternberg, Robert J (ed)*, 535-558. Cambridge, MIT Pr, 1995.

Sternberg, Robert J (ed) and Davidson, Janet E (ed). *The Nature of Insight*. Cambridge, MIT Pr, 1995.

Steutel, Jan and Spiecker, Ben. "Moral Identity and Education in a Multicultural Society" in *Identity, Culture, and Education, Smeyers, Paul (ed)*, 305-315. Leuven, Leuven Univ Pr, 1994.

The issue that is raised concerns the moral identity of persons in a pluralistic liberal-democracy. Democracies often are multicultural societies as well. Given such a pluralistic society, we pose the question which requirements, if any, apply to the moral identity of persons, not only with regard to their more personal sphere of life, but also concerning their role as citizens. This question must be understood as a typical educational question. What we aim at in education is the cultivation and development of a certain moral identity. Our question is: if we want to prepare our children for a life in a multicultural society, which moral identity should be our aim of education?

Steutel, Jan and Spiecker, Ben. Rationele passies en intellectuele deugden: Een conceptuele analyse. *Alg Ned Tijdschr Wijs*, 87(1), 1-14, Ja 95.

Intellectual virtues like open-mindedness, clarity, intellectual honesty and the willingness to participate in rational discussions, are important aims of education. In this paper an attempt is made to clarify the specific nature of intellectual virtues. Firstly, the intellectual virtues are systematically compared with moral virtues. The upshot is that considering a trait of character an intellectual virtue comes down to assuming that such a trait can be derived from, or is a specification of, the cardinal virtue of concern and respect for truth. Secondly, several (possible) misconceptions of intellectual virtues are removed by making the required distinctions. It is argued that our concept of an intellectual virtue should not be confused with a normative conception of intellectual virtuousness.

Stevens, Bernard. "On Ricoeur's Analysis of Time and Narration" in *The Philosophy of Paul Ricoeur, Hahn, Lewis Edwin (ed)*, 499-506. Peru, Open Court, 1994.

The purpose of this essay is to show in which way Ricoeur's analysis of time and narration is complementary to Heidegger's ontology of time. Three main points are stressed in order to explain the issue. First, Ricoeur shows how Heidegger's basically existential understanding of time needs to be enriched by an "objective" notion, narration being the mediative function between the two. Second, Ricoeur's thematisation of the Western understanding of time shows in a remarkable way how such a notion manifests the blending of our double heritage: the Greek cosmo-temporal intuition of *phusis* and the narrative-historical self-understanding of the Jewish people. Third, such an interpretation of our double heritage is a preparation to the dialogue which has still to take place today: the historical meeting (and possibly blending) of Western ontology with Far-Eastern ontology (where the cosmo-temporal *kalpa* will be the main object of hermeneutic analysis).

Stevens, Bernard. Karl Löwith et le nihilisme japonais. *Rev Phil Louvain*, 92(4), 508-545, N 94.

Löwith was one of the last thinkers to live from the powerful oxygen that wafted German philosophy from Leibniz to Heidegger. If—at the time of his meeting with Nishida, at the most crucial moment for the formation of contemporary Japanese consciousness—he had grasped the importance of what was at stake, he would have had the opportunity to turn his philosophical research in a new direction. But—because in his Eurocentrism there was more refusal of the East than there was refusal of Europe on the part of Japanese thinkers—he saw only the Nihilist aspect of Japanese culture, and hence he remained insensitive to the remarkable development of thought that was taking place virtually before his eyes. (edited)

Stevens, John A. "Friendship and Profit in Xenophon's *Oecomicus*" in *The Socratic Movement, Vander Waerdt, Paul A (ed)*, 209-237. Ithaca, Cornell Univ Pr, 1994.

Socrates' interlocutor, Critobulus, desires to become a gentleman, and requires instruction in *eros* and *philia*. Socrates narrates the story of how an Ischomachus trained his wife to run his household. This wife is actually the infamous mother of the second son of Callias mentioned in Plato *Apology* 20A, the most celebrated scandal of adultery and sacrilege in Athens. This possibility and overt references to Aristophanes' *Clouds* encourage an ironic reading. Ischomachus is actually a negative *exemplum* for Critobulus and the *Oeconomicus* is Xenophon's comic reply to the *Clouds*. This dialogue is the locus for the Xenophontic Socrates' conceptions of *eros, kalokagathia* the basilikê technê, and *paideia*.

Stevenson, John. Pragmatism, Truth, and Social Reflexivity. *SW Phil Rev*, 11(1), 169-176, Ja 95.

Stevenson, Leslie. External and Internal Private Language Arguments. *Wittgenstein Stud*, n.a., 1994.

The external version of the PLA (private language argument) argues that there can be no such thing as x using 'K' meaningfully unless it is logically possible for any other person y to acquire reason to believe that x is doing so. The internal version claims that it must be logically possible for x himself to acquire reason for belief in the meaningfulness of his own usage. Both versions of Wittgenstein's argument are here set out explicitly, and defended against various objections that have been made over the last forty years.

Stevenson, Leslie F. Experiences in the Cave, the Closet, and the Vat—and in Bed. *Philosophy*, 70(272), 167-189, Ap 95.

We are haunted by images of the supposed indirectness and passivity of perceptual experience, from Plato's prisoners in the cave, and Locke's mind in the closet, to Putnam's brain in a vat. These make it seem possible for there to be a completely passive course of experience involving nothing but illusory representations of the external world—like a permanent dream or hallucination. But is this really possible? Focusing on the active nature of normal perception can throw some new light on these questions. The issues turn out to be different in detail for each of the thought experiments mentioned.

Steverson, Brian K. Contextualism and Norton's Convergence Hypothesis. *Environ Ethics*, 17(2), 135-150, Sum 95.

Toward Unity among Environmentalists is Bryan Norton's most developed effort to surmount the frequently intractable debate between anthropocentrists and nonanthropocentrists. Norton argues that the basic axiological differences between the two position have become irrelevant at the level of policy formation. His thesis is that the two camps converge when dealing with practical goals and aims for environmental management. I argue that Norton's approach falls significantly short of establishing such a convergence because of the overall methodological framework for policy formation that he defends. The key problem with that framework is that it fails to provide for the degree of species protection most suitable to the nonanthropocentrist position.

Stewart, David. "Ricoeur on Religious Language" in *The Philosophy of Paul Ricoeur, Hahn, Lewis Edwin (ed)*, 423-442. Peru, Open Court, 1994.

Stewart, Hamish. A Critique of Instrumental Reason in Economics. *Econ Phil*, 11(1), 57-83, Ap 95.

The standard view of rationality in economics treats all actions as instrumental and all goals as commensurable. This view fails to recognize that instrumentally chosen means can play back upon and modify the goals that they were meant to serve, and that people can and do reason about their goals. A broader concept of rationality that recognized the possibility of reasoning about ends would be a superior alternative to the standard view, because it would enable these effects to be analyzed and would restore the legitimacy of certain kinds of arguments in economics.

Stewart, J. Cognition without Neurones: Adaptation, Leanring and Memory in the Immune System. *Commun Cog—AI*, 11(1-2), 7-30, 1994.

This paper proposes a definition of cognition as a system capable of both action and perception, in which the coupling of action and perception is such that the emergent behaviour of the system in its environment satisfies a meaningful constraint. (edited)

Stewart, Jon. Hegel and the Myth of Reason. *Owl Minerva*, 26(2), 187-200, Spr 95.

The *oeuvre* of Hegel has been subject to a number of misrepresentations that have until recently rendered Hegel's reception in the Anglo-American philosophical world extremely problematic. One of the most pervasive of the famous Hegelian myths is the claim that Hegel was the last spokesman for reason before the full-scale attack on rationality by, for example, existentialism and poststructuralism. In this paper I argue that Hegel is very aware of the pernicious aspects of reason and thus is best seen not as the last *Aufklärer* but rather as a forerunner of the so-called "irrationalist tradition".

Stewart, M A. "An Early Fragment of Evil" in *Hume and Hume's Connexions, Stewart, M A (ed)*, 160-170. University Park, Penn St Univ Pr, 1995.

Stewart, M A. "Hume's Historical View of Miracles" in *Hume and Hume's Connexions, Stewart, M A (ed)*, 171-200. University Park, Penn St Univ Pr, 1995.

Stewart, M A. Critical Notice of 'Questions concerning the Law of Nature'. *Locke News*, 23, 145-165, 1992.

Robert Horwitz and his collaborators restore Locke's numeration of his Latin narratives on the Law of Nature, and relate them to the form of traditional disputations. But they exaggerate the errors in Von Leyden's previous edition. Neither edition is based on Locke's autograph, so neither is textually reliable, or any guide to the strata of composition. Horwitz confuses the relationship between "divine", "natural" and "revealed" law. J Clay has not sufficiently distinguished Locke's corrections, or understood his Greek. D Clay's translation is poorly nuanced. The new editors all misdescribe the manuscripts, and confuse Christian with Roman nomenclature, in an ill-formed critique of those who locate Lockean natural law within a Western monotheistic framework.

Stewart, M A. Locke's 'Observations' on Boyle. *Locke News*, 24, 21-34, 1993.

In a short, single leaf, manuscript of 1681, Locke comments on an unidentified manuscript by Boyle on the relations of sense, reason, and revelation. He accepts that in "natural and civil history" we may be persuaded of antecedently improbable events, but he is chary of accepting that beliefs essential to salvation should be revealed by such means. Locke's likeliest target is a paginated draft (no longer extant) of Boyle's *Christian Virtuoso*, 1690. But evidence is also supplied that Boyle discussed the reliability of testimony to miracles in other manuscripts over many years, one of which is partially transcribed here.

Stewart, M A (ed) and Wright, John P (ed). *Hume and Hume's Connexions*. University Park, Penn St Univ Pr, 1995.

Stich, Stephen. The Virtues, Challenges and Implications of Connectionism. *Brit J Phil Sci*, 45(4), 1047-1058, D 94.

Stich, Stephen and Ramsey, William and Garon, Joseph. "Connectionism, Eliminativism, and the Future of Folk Psychology" in *Connectionism: Debates on Psychological Explanation, Macdonald, Cynthia (ed)*, 311-338. Cambridge, Blackwell, 1995.

Stich, Stephen and Warfield, Ted A. "Reply to Clark and Smolensky: Do Connectionist Minds Have Beliefs?" in *Connectionism: Debates on Psychological Explanation, Macdonald, Cynthia (ed)*, 395-411. Cambridge, Blackwell, 1995.

We reply to papers by Andy Clark and Paul Smolensky on the issue of whether connectionist theories of the mind lend support to eliminativism about the propositional attitudes. We also discuss the general form of eliminativist arguments and identify some implausible hidden premises of such arguments.

Stich, Stephen P (ed) and Warfield, Ted A (ed). *Mental Representation: A Reader*. Cambridge, Blackwell, 1994.

This anthology collects new and recent work on mental representation and theories of mental content. The volume includes work from Fodor, Dretske, Field, Dennet and others as well as essays critically evaluating the most popular theories of mental content.

Stidd, Benton M and Wade, David L. Is Species Selection Dependent Upon Emergent Characters?. *Biol Phil*, 10(1), 55-76, Ja 95.

The architects of punctuated equilibrium and species selection as well as more recent workers (Vrba) have narrowed the original formulation of species selection and made it dependent upon so-called emergent characters. One criticism of this narrow version is the dearth of emergent characters with a consequent diminution in the robustness of species selection as an important evolutionary process. We argue that monomorphic species characters may at times be the focus of selection and that under these circumstances selection at the organism level is by-passed due to the absence of critical variance. Selection therefore shifts to the species level where variability reemerges in a clade. The absence of critical variance among organisms prevents effect macroevolution from operating. If species-wide properties are important in macroevolutionary processes, as we contend, systematists should pay more attention to their elucidation.

Stiening, Gideon and Euler, Werner. "...und nie der Pluralität widersprach"? Zur Bedeutung von Immanuel Kants Amtsgeschäften. *Kantstudien*, 86(1), 54-69, 1995.

Usually in philosophic-historical research Kant's official business at the University of Königsberg is described as being of less importance in relation either to his biography or to his scientific work. In contrast to this prepossession it's designed a new portrait of Kant that shows, how he was acting for some periods of universitary administration: he didn't deny responsibility, labour and democratic exposition in this context, concerning a great variety of universitary, cultural and political aspects; on the contrary he constructively made replies to the most important questions that had to be discussed and decided by the committees of the Albertina. Kant did not only influence his colleagues with innovative ideas but also produced plurality in the republic of letters that protected the autonomy of university and science against the authorities of the Prussian state. The thesis is demonstrated by help of unknown archival materials about the history of the University of Königsberg, recently discovered and explored in archives of Germany and Poland.

Stigliano, Tony. The Moral Construction of the Self. *J Theor Phil Psych*, 13(1), 48-61, Spr 93.

Social constructionist theory has been criticized as being relativistic. This paper addresses this criticism and draws out conclusions for the theory and for psychotherapy. A nonrelativistic basis for the self is its moral constitution. People need to trust, make promises, follow through on obligations in order to be in the society which is constructing them. These moral and ethical constituents of the socially constructed self are historically necessary without being universal. One important praxis affected by this conclusion is psychotherapy which, because its articulation of the constituents of self also constitute them, becomes a moral and political praxis.

Stigol, Nora. "Predicados y Propiedades" in *Temas Actuales de Filosofía, Palacios, María Julia (ed)*, 599-605. Buenos Aires, Univ Nacional Salta, 1993.

Traditionally, an asymmetry between singular terms and general terms concerning its relationship with subject-predicate distinction has been maintained. This asymmetry is connected with the long-standing thesis on the logical priority of particulars. P Strawson in *Individuals* intends to provide a rational explanation for thesis. In this paper, I intend to focus on a difficulty in Strawson's proposition which I call "Primacy of Universals". I maintain that both the expressions pertaining to the subject and to the predicate eventually involve universals. From my personal point of view this seems strange considering both the Strawsonian notion of "completeness" that is used to explain the identification of particulars in conversation and Strawson's thesis on the ontological priority of particulars.

Stigol, Nora and Rabossi, Eduardo A and González, María Cristina. "Los Seminarios en la Enseñanza de la Filosofía" in *Temas Actuales de Filosofía, Palacios, María Julia (ed)*, 521-524. Buenos Aires, Univ Nacional Salta, 1993.

Seminars as successful learning situations for philosophical goals are considered. It is mentioned some special features in our university classrooms that hinder teachers from getting the main aim: to learn to philosophize. Strategies used during a seminar are described: a preparatory stage and a discussion stage. The experience is evaluated.

Still, Judith. What Foucault Fails to Acknowledge...: Feminists and *The History of Sexuality*. *Hist Human Sci*, 7(2), 150-157, My 94.

An investigation of reading responses to Foucault, in particular that of feminists who want him 'on their side', but fear that he may have cut away the ground they judge necessary for a meaningful struggle against power. Despite the androcentrism and orientalism of some of Foucault's works, Sawicki finds it enabling for the feminist historian. McNay wishes that Foucault were more like Habermas; this article suggests that it may be more fruitful to relate him to Derrida. The rational demand that contradictions be resolved may entail an inappropriate, if not totalitarian, reading strategy.

Stirton, William R. The Logical Status of 'Exists'. *Proc Aris Soc*, 95, 37-50, 1994-95.

Stock, Guy (ed) and Allard, James W (ed) and Bradley, F H. *Writings on Logic and Metaphysics*. New York, Oxford Univ Pr, 1994.

Stocker, Michael. Some Comments on *Perfectionism*. *Ethics*, 105(2), 386-400, Ja 95.

Stockreiter, Karl. "Die Verführerische Marionette" in *Die besten Geister der Nation, Korotin, Ilse (ed)*, 328-349. Vienna, Picus, 1994.

Thomas Mann's novel "Mario und der Zauberer", which offers an attempt to the "psychology of Fascism", is used as an example to demonstrate the different roles of "myth as a vehicle": On one hand, myth is a medium of illusion to provide a reflection hostile esthetization of politics. In that sense an irrational Dionysos-image—derivated from Nietzsche—has been instaured. On the other hand, myth is a medium of reflection that the artist Thomas Mann has integrated in his narrative technique and that helps him to analyse certain psychic constellations of fascism.

Stöckler, Manfred. "Selbstorganisation und Reduktionismus" in *Schelling und die Selbstorganisation, Heuser-Kessler, Marie-Luise (ed)*, 149-160. Berlin, Duncker Humblot, 1994.

Three theories of self-organization are analyzed: thermodynamics of irreversible processes far from equilibrium (Prigogine), synergetics (Haken), theories of molecular evolution (Eigen), I argue that these theories support ontological reductionism. At the same time various examples of analyzing self-organizing systems show why methodological reductionism cannot hold. Finally I reject any claims of serious similarities to ideas developed by F W J Schelling in his speculative philosophy of nature.

Stokes, Michael. Formalism, Realism, and the Concept of Law. *Law Phil*, 13(2), 115-159, My 94.

Stolzenberg, Jürgen. Fichtes Satz *Ich bin*: Argumentanalytische Überlegungen zu Paragraph 1 der *Grundlage der gesamten Wissenschaftslehre* von 1794-95. *Fichte-Studien*, 6, 1-34, 1994.

In this article the first attempt is made to give a step for step reconstruction of the argument in Paragraph 1 of J G Fichte's "Doctrine of Science" from 1794/95. The main thesis is, that Fichte's argument shows, that the proposition "I am" cannot be understood by an empirical-psychological theory of consciousness, but that it can only be introduced and explained in starting from an empirical standpoint. Both the development of Fichte's idea of 'proof' for his main principle and the relationship to Karl Leonhard Reinhold's new philosophical position in 1792 (published in 1794) are taken in consideration.

Stolzenberg, Jürgen. Selbstbewusstsein: Ein Problem der Philosophie nach Kant. *Zum Verhältnis Reinhold-Hölderlin-Fichte. Daimon Rev Filosof*, 9, 63-79, 1994.

In this paper an attempt is made to elucidate the relationship between the different theories of self-consciousness of Karl Leonard Reinhold, Friedrich Hölderlin and Johann Gottlieb Fichte. It is shown, that Reinhold was the first of the post-Kantian philosophers remarking a problem in the concept of self-consciousness and whose theory of consciousness and self-consciousness must be considered as the theoretical background of Hölderlin's Fichte-Critique in his famous paper on *Judgment and Being* from 1795. It is then shown, that there is an implicit answer of Fichte to Hölderlin's Critique in Fichte's *System of Morals* from 1798, where Fichte developed a new systematic interpretation of that concepts of self-consciousness, which Reinhold and Hölderlin had in view.

Stone, Alan A. Iatrogenic Ethical Problems: A Commentary on "Can a Patient Refuse a Psychiatric Consultation to Evaluate Decision Making Capacity?". *J Clin Ethics*, 5(3), 234-237, Fall 94.

Stone, George C. Dewey on Causation in Social Science. *Educ Theor*, 44(4), 417-428, Fall 94.

Stone, Jerome A. Broadening Care, Discerning Worth: The Environmental Contributions of Minimalist Religious Naturalism. *Process Stud*, 22(4), 194-203, Winter 93.

Stone, Jim. Abortion as Murder?: A Response. *J Soc Phil*, 26(1), 129-146, Spr 95.

Abortion statutes are often called 'incoherent' because they affirm that fetuses are persons, but punish abortionists far less than murderers and provide no penalty for the woman. I argue that this is essential to giving unborn persons the full protection of the law. Remorseful women are unlikely to identify an abortionist if they too can be prosecuted; and they will invoke their fifth amendment right to refuse to testify. The law becomes unenforceable if women are punished. If doctors who perform abortions are going to be punished by death, say, juries are unlikely to convict them, whatever the evidence. Stronger penalties have a counter-deterrent value.

Stone, Lynda. "Misreading Dewey: A Thesis and Exemplar" in *Identity, Culture, and Education, Smeyers, Paul (ed)*, 317-331. Leuven, Leuven Univ Pr, 1994.

This paper takes seriously John Dewey's assertion that new times require new philosophy: a reconstruction in his terms, a misreading in those of Harold Bloom. Rationale for the new philosophy is a thesis that Dewey's work sits in a modernist-postmodernist tension of two forms. The first is syntactical requiring a change in method and the second is substantive requiring new content. The method is set out as are two central notions, organicism and situation. In turn these concepts are applied to a reconstruction of "multiculturalism," from Dewey for his time and then for the present.

Stone, Tony (ed) and Davies, Martin (ed). *Folk Psychology: The Theory of Mind Debate*. Cambridge, Blackwell, 1995.

With little or no formal teaching, human beings develop the capacity to deploy psychological concepts in predicting and explaining the actions and mental states of other members of the species. Many philosophers and psychologists argue that this everyday ability reflects the fact that normal adult human beings possess a primitive or 'folk' psychological theory. Recently, however, this *theory theory* has come under challenge from the *simulation alternative* which says that human beings are able to predict and explain each others' actions by using the resources of their own minds to simulate the psychological aetiology of the actions of others. The thirteen essays in this volume present the foundations of the theory of mind debate, and are accompanied by an extensive Introduction.

Storr, Anthony. Nietzsche and Music. *Philosophy*, 37(Supp), 213-227, 1994.

Nietzsche's life-long involvement with music dated from his infancy, when his father would play the piano to him to calm his temper tantrums. Nietzsche himself became a skilled improviser on the piano, and a less-skilled composer of songs, piano duets, and other pieces. His music was more influenced by Schumann than by Wagner. Long after his terminal illness had deprived him of the use of words, he was still able to play the piano. Nietzsche's philosophy was an attempt to replace religion with aesthetic values; and music, like Greek tragedy, was a way of reconciling Apollo with Dionysus.

Stramel, James S. *How to Write a Philosophy Paper*. Lanham, Univ Pr of America, 1995.

Strasser, Mark. Hutchenson and Mill on Evaluating Actions and Characters. *Philosophia (Israel)*, 24(1-2), 115-126, D 94.

Strauss, D F M. Thought and Language: On the Line of Demarcation between Animal and Human Abilities. *S Afr J Phil*, 13(4), 175-182, N 94.

Although an anthropomorphic mode of expression may easily tempt us to attribute typical human abilities to animals, a closer investigation shows that animals are neither able to think logically (by forming logical concepts), nor do they share in the dimension of human language. It is argued that if animals did have logical concepts at their disposal, then they should have been able to express logical judgments —something explicitly denied by prominent advocates of the idea that animals possess a-verbal concepts. In conclusion the way in which animals are largely determined by their instincts is contrasted with our unique human ability to exercise a freedom of choice within the matrix of *normative* considerations. (edited)

Strauss, Leo and Hartje, Hans (trans) and Guglielmina, Pierre (trans). Le problème de la connaissance dans la doctrine philosophique de Fr H Jacobi (II). *Rev Metaph Morale*, 99(4), 505-532, O-D 94.

Strawinski, Witold. How Unified is Physics Itself?: Comments on Józef Werle's Paper "How the Physical Sciences Discovered the Unity of Nature". *Dialogue Hum*, 3(3), 137-138, 1993.

Strawser, Michael. Kierkegaardian Meditations on First Philosophy: A Reading of *Johannes Climacus*. *J Hist Phil*, 32(4), 623-643, O 94.

What significance does this less familiar text have for a comprehensive interpretation of Kierkegaard's total life-view? First doubt and irony are contrasted. Then the historical conditions surrounding *Johannes Climacus* are discussed. These show that this text is most fruitfully read in connection with Kierkegaard's earlier works, rather than the later writings by Johannes Climacus. Finally, it is argued that Kierkegaard's early reflections on the nature of consciousness and the determinations of language constitute the philosophical grounds behind his method of indirect communication, and that this method structures the ensuing authorship, both pseudonymous and veronymous writings included.

Strawser, Michael. The Indirectness of Kierkegaard's Signed Writings. *Int J Phil Stud*, 3(1), 73-90, Mr 95.

Strawser, Michael J. Reading Heidegger after Derrida. *Topicos*, 4(6), 17-29, 1994.

This essay attempts to broach .the complex difference between Martin Heidegger and Jacques Derrida. It focuses on the fundamental assumptions involved in the reading of Heidegger's *Being and Time* and Derrida's early "noted" attention to this text. Is Heidegger's early work essentially tainted by "the metaphysics of presence," as Derrida wishes to suggest? After sketching Derrida's interpretation, the author attempts to show how readers of *Being and Time* need not succumb to Derrida's criticism.

Strawson, Galen. "The Experiential and the Non-Experiential" in *The Mind-Body Problem: A Guide to the Current Debate, Warner, Richard (ed)*, 69-86. Cambridge, Blackwell, 1994.

Strawson, Galen. *Mental Reality*. Cambridge, MIT Pr, 1993.

Mental Reality asks the following question: What part, exactly, does reference to 1) nonmental phenomena, 2) publicly observable phenomena, and 3) behavioral phenomena play in a satisfactory account of the nature of mental phenomena? I challenge the standard *neo-behaviorist* response, which answers 'A large and essential part' in all three cases. The main foci of discussion are as follows: chapter 1, the character and reality of conscious experience; chapters 3-4, the 'mind-body' problem; chapter 5, idealism and immaterialism; chapter 6, the definition of 'mental'; chapter 7, intentionality; chapter 8, sensation; chapter 9, propositional attitudes; chapter 10, the concept of behavior.

Strehle, Peter. Wittgenstein—Ein Wegbereiter der Mehrwertigen Logik?. *Wittgenstein Stud*, n.a., 1994.

Wittgensteins Denkansaetze enhalten Impulse fuer die Diskussion um die Rechtfertigung der mehrwertigen Logik und Mengenlehre (fuzzy logic, fuzzy sets). Mindestens der aeltere Wittgenstein kann als einer der Vordenker einer methodologisch begruendeten mehrwertigen und mehrdimensionalen Logik gelten. (edited)

Striker, Gisela. "Plato's Socrates and the Stoics" in *The Socratic Movement, Vander Waerdt, Paul A (ed)*, 241-251. Ithaca, Cornell Univ Pr, 1994.

This paper argues that Socrates of Plato's early dialogues was part of the Socratic heritage of the Stoic school, and that the Stoics developed their own distinctive conception of virtue as a craft partly as a reply to Platonic objections.

Striker, Gisela. Assertoric vs Modal Syllogistic. *Ancient Phil*, 14, 39-51, 1994.

An attempt to answer the question why Aristotle failed to do for modal syllogistic what he succeeded in doing for assertoric syllogistic, namely develop a consistent and—within its limits—complete deductive system.

Striker, Gisela. Commentary on Furley's "Some Points About Stoic Dynamics". *Proc Boston Colloq Anc Phil*, 9, 76-82, 1993.

Strikwerda, Robert and May, Larry. Reply to Victoria Davion's Comments on May and Strikwerda. *Hypatia*, 10(2), 157-158, Spr 95.

This is a very brief response to a largely positive review of our paper "Men in Groups: Collective Responsibility for Rape" Hypatia 9/2 (Spring 1994).

Ströker, Elisabeth. "Fiktive Welt im literarischen Kunstwerk" in *Kunst und Ontologie, Wlodzimierz, Galewicz (ed)*, 141-165. Amsterdam, Rodopi, 1994.

This article deals with a chief problem in Roman Ingarden's philosophy: the logical and ontological status of statements in that sort of literature in which a 'fictive world' is constituted. Referring to a long and vivid controversy on this topic between Ingarden and Käte Hamburger I tried to show that, notwithstanding Hamburger's sagacious criteria for determining 'fictive' elements in novels, etc., Ingarden's investigation of fictive worlds is more satisfying. By way of his phenomenological approach, based upon Husserl's *Logical Investigations*, he has thoroughly analyzed different modes of being and meanings of the term 'being' and aimed at a sharp distinction of the 'fictive' from the real and ideal, defining it as 'quasi-real'.

Ströker, Elisabeth. "Natur u. ihre Wissenschaft in der Philosophie des 19.Jhr." in *Naturauffassungen in Philosophie, Wissenschaft, Technik: Band III, Schäfer, Lothar (ed)*, 255-292. Freiburg, Alber, 1995.

This paper elucidates the origins of epistemology and modern philosophy of science at the beginning of the 19th century. The understanding of nature, as determined by the positive sciences in this period of their rapid development, turned out to become a particular challenge for continental philosophy, especially after the decline of 'German Idealism'. New philosophical approaches then entailed new analyses of human knowledge in focussing explicitly on scientific knowledge, thus leading to what then was called 'epistemology'. Philosophy of science then started from it with positivism under the influence of J S Mill and A Comte. Thus, even in philosophy, the concept of nature remained the scientific one.

Ströker, Elisabeth. "Wissenschaft und Technik" in *Naturauffassungen in Philosophie, Wissenschaft, Technik: Band I, Schäfer, Lothar (ed)*, 15-47. Freiburg, Alber, 1993.

This essay deals with the sources of modern sciences in ancient philosophy, in order to show that basic scientific strategies—claims and procedures of rational argumentation, the conception of the relationship between theory and observation, norms of objectivity and truth—are rooted in certain Presocratic, Platonian, and Aristotelian concepts of nature and in those of philosophical self-understanding of man in the early Greek culture. Special emphasis is laid on the fact that the scientific revolution in the 17th century was due to a radical change of those two concepts, rather than to a change of the above mentioned strategies for gaining knowledge of nature.

Ströker, Elisabeth. Edith Stein—Anlässe und Anfänge einer philosophischen Neubesinnung. *Z Phil Forsch*, 48(3), 448-454, Jl-S 94.

Edith Stein was one of the outstanding pupils of Husserl. However, little is known so far about the excellent work she did in phenomenology, on Husserl as well as on Heidegger. This is certainly due to the fact that in 1922 she entered a monastery and turned more and more to theology—until she became one of the victims of Nazi-barbarism in the holocost of Auschwitz (in August 1942). My essay is based upon recently published articles on Edith Stein in order to show how effective she was not only in her early phenomenological works, but also in her offering new perspectives in modern theology by means of Husserlian and other phenomenological methods.

Ströker, Elisabeth (ed) and Schäfer, Lothar (ed). *Naturauffassungen in Philosophie, Wissenschaft, Technik: Band I*. Freiburg, Alber, 1993.

Ströker, Elisabeth (ed) and Schäfer, Lothar (ed). *Naturauffassungen in Philosophie, Wissenschaft, Technik: Band II*. Freiburg, Alber, 1994.

Ströker, Elisabeth (ed) and Schäfer, Lothar (ed). *Naturauffassungen in Philosophie, Wissenschaft, Technik: Band III*. Freiburg, Alber, 1995.

Ströker, Elisabeth (ed) and Wlodzimierz, Galewicz (ed) and Strozewski, Wladyslaw (ed). *Kunst und Ontologie*. Amsterdam, Rodopi, 1994.

Strohmetz, David B and Rosnow, Ralph L. "A Mediational Model of Research Artifacts" in *Probability in Theory-Building, Brzezinski, Jerzy (ed)*, 177-196. Amsterdam, Rodopi, 1994.

Because humans are sentient and active participants in behavioral research, they present unique problems of researchers. This chapter focuses on these systematic, uncontrolled biases (i.e., research artifacts). A model is proposed to conceptualize how artifacts can be introduced at different stages in the research process. By identifying potential sources of artifacts, researchers can employ strategies to circumvent these threats, thereby increasing confidence in the validity of the study's outcomes and implications. The chapter elaborates on each part of the model, focusing on these potential artifacts as well as making suggestions on how to minimize these potential biases.

Strong, David. Challenging Technology. *Res Phil Technol*, 14, 69-92, 1994.

To be consequential, an environmental ethic needs a comprehensive and incisive critique of technological culture. Both natural and built things have been set upon and transformed into devices. This transformation entails as a consequence an impoverishment of our experiences. We experience things as *bringing the world near*. These experiences of things when the world is brought home to us make us at home, enlightening and enabling us to affirm life in a profound way. Pivotal here is the technological society's giving over the goal of consumption on behalf of things, including wilderness, for then, things, not technology, order the world.

Strong, David. *Crazy Mountains: Learning from Wilderness to Weigh Technology*. Albany, SUNY Pr, 1995.

By focusing on the Crazy Mountains in Montana and the threat of harm to them, this book shows concretely and generally that, because our culture believes that technological devices and commodities can make our lives positively good, we are transforming the Earth in increasingly extensive ways. It challenges this belief by using the theories of Heidegger and A Brogmann, and by evoking the importance of wilderness as a focal thing that is threatened by technology. It shows that if such centering things, rather than consumption, ordered our lives and communities, it would be better for both humans and the Earth.

Strong, Kelly C and Carlin, William B. A Critique of Western Philosophical Ethics: Multidisciplinary Alternatives for Framing Ethical Dilemmas. *J Bus Ethics*, 14(5), 387-396, My 95.

American discourse in business ethics is steeped in the traditional ethical theories of Western philosophies, specifically the Greek classics, Kant, and the British Utilitarians. These theories may be largely uninterpretable or unacceptable to non-Western populations owing to different traditions, religious beliefs, or cultural histories. As economic boundaries collapse and markets become more global in scope, traditional Western ethical thought may lead to clashes among Western ethical thought may lead to clashes among Western organizations and companies from differing cultural settings. Such clashes could lead to alienation of foreign customers, firms and governments and resultant competitive disadvantage, or to an abandonment of ethical considerations altogether in the struggle to compete internationally. This paper puts forward two general alternatives to Western ethical philosophies as useful frameworks for the analysis of international ethical dilemmas. The first alternative uses new organizational economics, while the second emphasizes role relationships and organizational citizenship.

Strong, Kelly C and Solberg, Joseph and McGuire Jr, Charles. Living (Not Learning) Ethics. *J Bus Ethics*, 14(1), 71-81, Ja 95.

The results of our survey of AACSB member schools confirm prior reports of similar surveys: The teaching of business ethics is indiscriminate, unorganized, and undisciplined in most North American schools of business. If universities are to be taken seriously in their efforts to create more ethical awareness and better moral decision-making skills among their graduates, they must provide a rigorous and well-developed system in which students can "live ethics" instead of merely learn ethics. (edited)

Strong, Tracy B. "Max Weber and the Bourgeoisie" in *The Barbarism of Reason, Horowitz, Asher (ed)*, 113-138. Toronto, Univ of Toronto Pr, 1994.

The essay argues that Weber thought the "scientific objectivity" (properly understood) could only be achieved by the knower accepting his or her position as

an "historical individual". In modern times, this means to accept the stance of a bourgeois—subject to the division of labor, disenchanted and rationalized. The essay concludes with an examination of Weber's hopes and fears for political leadership.

Strong, Tracy B and Sposito, Frank Andreas. "Habermas's Significant Other" in *The Cambridge Companion to Habermas, White, Stephen K (ed)*, 263-288. New York, Cambridge Univ Pr, 1995.

Strozewski, Wladyslaw. "Art and Participation" in *Kunst und Ontologie, Wlodzimierz, Galewicz (ed)*, 167-181. Amsterdam, Rodopi, 1994.

Strozewski, Wladyslaw (ed) and Ströker, Elisabeth (ed) and Wlodzimierz, Galewicz (ed). *Kunst und Ontologie*. Amsterdam, Rodopi, 1994.

Strudler, Alan. The Social Construction of Genetic Abnormality: Ethical Implications for Managerial Decisions in the Workplace. *J Bus Ethics*, 13(11), 839-848, N 94.

This paper examines moral issues concerning a firm's use of genetic information about a prospective employee's predisposition to contract occupational and other illnesses. It critically reviews leading social construction literature on genetic abnormality and genetic screening, and it examines the relevance of arguments from justice and meritocratic principles. It concludes that there is a strong moral presumption against genetic screening in employment.

Strutton, David and Hamilton III, J Brooke. Two Practical Guidelines for Resolving Truth-Telling Problems. *J Bus Ethics*, 13(11), 899-912, N 94.

The news reminds us almost daily that the "truth" is apparently not highly valued by many in business. This paper develops two prescriptive standards—the expectation and reputation guidelines—that may help businesspeople avoid violating clearly accepted truth standards. The guidelines also assist in determining whether truth is required in circumstances where honesty seems in conflict with the practical demands of business. A discussion of why, when and how these guidelines may be applied to facilitate truth-telling by business organizations follows, along with illustrative examples.

Strutton, David and Rawwas, Mohammed Y A and Pelton, Lou. Ethical Attitudes of Mental Health Practitioners: Balancing Therapeutic Practices and Treatments. *J Bus Ethics*, 13(8), 597-608, Ag 94.

This paper reports the responses of 251 mental health care practitioners to a mail survey examining their views concerning ethical conflicts and practices within their work environments. Besides identifying the sources and types of conflicts they experience, respondents were asked how ethical standards have changed over the last 10 years as well as the factors influencing these changes. Conclusions and implications are outlined and future research needs are described.

Stueber, Karsten R. "Understanding Truth and Objectivity: A Dialogue between Davidson and Gadamer" in *Hermeneutics and Truth, Wachterhauser, Brice (ed)*, 172-189. Evanston, Northwestern Univ Pr, 1994.

This article attempts to open the way for a better appreciation of the hermeneutic tradition within the analytic context. It argues that even though Gadamer developed his conception of truth in discussing the status of the humanities, his work is similar to Davidson's understanding of truth in important respects. Recognizing the similarities between these two philosopers does not imply that truth is a relativistic or subjective notion. Rather, in abandoning the representational picture of language, both Davidson and Gadamer develop a notion of truth which lies beyond the attack of relativism and skepticism.

Stuhr, John. Philosophical Night Vision. *Trans Peirce Soc*, 31(1), 1-10, Wint 95.

This article critically analyzes the far-reaching and influential interpretations of American pragmatism set forth in the work of John E Smith. Concentrating on Smith's new *America's Philosophical Vision*, I explicate the spirit, thought, and relevance of pragmatism. In addition, I examine the relation of theory to practice in pragmatism, and the place of pragmatism as *American* thought in the context of multiculturalism and concerns with diversity.

Stump, Eleonore and Kretzmann, Norman. Blindingly Obvious Christian Anti-Semitism. *Faith Phil*, 11(2), 279-285, Ap 94.

This article is part of an on-going public discussion between philosophers and theologians, prompted by Gordon Kaufman's "Evidentialism: A Theologian's Response", which tried to explain and defend the neglect of philosophy on the part of theologians. Part of what is at issue is the degree to which a religion is responsible for the evils committed in its name by its adherents. We make a distinction between sociological and doctrinal understandings of religion and religious claims. If a religion is defined only sociologically, then (if, in fact, any determination can be made) every major worldview is responsible for serious evil. This conclusion does not hold, however, if religion is taken doctrinally.

Sturlese, Rita. Le Fonti del "Sigillus Sigillorum" del Bruno, Ossia: Il Confronto con Ficino a Oxford Sull'anima Umana. *G Crit Filosof Ital*, 73(1), 33-72, Ja-Ap 94.

Stypinski, Andrew B. Teaching Philosophical Analysis with Nota Bene 3.0. *Teach Phil*, 17(3), 271-274, S 94.

The article demonstrates how a multilingual retrieval and word processing program such as NOTA BENE 3.0 opens a new vista in teaching philosophical analysis to college-level students. A ready made application, a TEXT-BASE in NOTA BENE, can be used for a new approach to research and analysis of philosophical text and concepts. This article provides many examples of how the program for academics can be used by a philosopher in research and teaching. The conclusion reached in the paper claims that a TEXT-BASE in NOTA BENE can be applied to further new methods in research and teaching philosophy.

Suárez, Francisco and Doyle, John P (trans). *On Beings of Reason (De Entibus Rationis) Metaphysical Disputation LIV*. Milwaukee, Marquette Univ Pr, 1995.

Subramanian, S. A Paretian Liberal Dilemma without Collective Rationality. *Theor Decis*, 37(3), 323-332, N 94.

This note proposes a principle of liberalism which is a simple and plausible variant of Sen's principle of 'minimal liberalism'. The former principle is shown to be incompatible with the weak Pareto principle; and this impossibility result is not dependent on the preference-aggregating rule being restricted by any collective rationality condition.

Suchocki, Marjorie Hewitt. The Idea of God in Feminist Philosophy. *Hypatia*, 9(4), 57-68, Fall 94.

The marginal position of women within the Western tradition provides a critical vantage point for feminist redevelopment of the notion of God. Feminists tend to replace the classical categories of substance philosophies traditionally used for God with relational categories often drawn from organic philosophies. They also project the dynamic character of language itself into the discussion of God. This essay focuses on these issues as they are developed by Mary Daly and Rebecca Chopp.

Suchodolski, Bogdan. The Manifold Attitude to Time and Eternity in a Single Culture. *Dialogue Hum*, 4(1), 9-15, 1994.

Suckiel, Ellen Kappy. "Radiance and Religious Belief" in *Contributors to the Philosophy of Humanism, Hillar, Marian (ed)*, 17-30. Pasadena, Humanists Houston, 1994.

In honor of Konstantin Kolenda, this paper examines the concept of "radiance" as the emanation of spiritual value. The key question is whether the "radiant" or spiritual dimension of existence is independent of human constitution. Two forms of humanism are examined: narrow or reductive humanism on the one hand, which is shown to be unacceptable; and Kolenda's broader and more subtle emergentist humanism on the other—under which human beings are regarded as the participants but not the sole participants in the creation of spiritual value. An objectivist concept of spiritual value is defended as an alternative to Kolenda's position.

Suddith, Michael L Czapkay. Bi-Level Evidentialism and Reformed Apologetics. *Faith Phil*, 11(3), 379-396, Jl 94.

In this paper I apply William Alston's "epistemic level distinctions" to the debate between evidentialist and anti-evidentialist approaches to Christian apologetics in the Reformed tradition. I first clarify the nature of this debate by showing that it rests fundamentally on a tension between the desire to have a comprehensive Christian apologetic and the belief that the Holy Spirit plays a special epistemic role in belief-

formation, such that certain beliefs are formed and justified by conditions unique to Christian religious experience. Secondly, I argue that even if S's belief that p is immediately justified (through such priviledged modes of belief-formation), (1) an evidentialist requirement can be placed on the higher-level belief that P* (p is immediately justified) and (2) apologetics can draw on the reasons which confer justification on P*, thereby providing indirect support for p.

Sudduth, Michael L Czapkay. Alstonian Foundationalism and Higher-Level Theistic Evidentialism. *Int J Phil Relig*, 37(1), 25-44, F 95.

I present a case for the compatibility of reformed epistemology (RE) and evidentialism based on the multi-level foundationalism of William P Alston. Alston's foundationalism entails an evidentialist requirement for every higher-level belief about the epistemic status of some putative belief that p. Distinguishing between the belief that Pt (where Pt = theistic belief) and the belief that Pt is justified, even if the former is and/or ought to be basic on a person's noetic structure, an evidentialist requirement can be imposed on the latter without conflicting with the claims of RE. I further argue that Alston's evidentialism entails an epistemically adequate form of evidentialism—*higher-level theistic evidentialism*.

Sugarman, Jeremy. Hawkeye Pierce and the Questionable Relevance of Medical Etiquette to Contemporary Medical Ethics and Practice. *J Clin Ethics*, 5(3), 224-230, Fall 94.

Do health care practitioners have a moral obligation to heed rules of medical etiquette? Answering this requires an understanding of the relationship between medical etiquette and ethics. Therefore, I 1) review historical texts in medical ethics that intertwine discussions of ethics and etiquette; 2) describe empirical research evaluating medical etiquette; 3) present some opposing views to these works; 4) consider a functional taxonomy for medical etiquette; 5) examine the conceptual relationship of medical ethics and etiquette; and 6) explore some of the implications of this relationship. I argue that there is a *prima facie* obligation for health care practitioners to adhere to rules of medical etiquette.

Sugarman, Jeremy. Should Hospital Ethics Committees Do Research?. *J Clin Ethics*, 5(2), 121-125, Sum 94.

Hospital ethics committees typically engage in three normative activities: case discussion and consultation, education, and policy formulation. The common promise of these activities is providing morally sound solutions to clinical problems. However, it is unclear whether such promises are met. Determining this requires descriptive ethics where good empirical data is essential. Empirical data, however, requires research. Accordingly, I argue that ethics committees ought to conduct empirical research and I discuss several related topics: 1) potential benefits of this research; 2) potential costs of this research; 3) barriers to research by ethics committees; and 4) questions regarding the publication of research by such committees.

Sugunasiri, Suwanda H J. The Whole Body, not Heart, as 'Seat of Consciousness': The Buddha's View. *Phil East West*, 45(3), 409-430, Jl 95.

The traditional view in Theravada Buddhism of the heart (*hadaya*) as the "seat of consciousness" is explored. Evidence is sought in the Nikayas, the Abhidhamma and commentaries, Buddhaghosa's *Visuddhimagga* (5th century), and Kassapa's *Mohavicchedani* (12th century). Some possible sources of error are identified. The view is challenged on the basis of the early teachings of the Buddha and the alternative view, that it is the whole body that is the seat of consciousness, is reconstructed. Some possible future comparative research and applications are suggested.

Suhamy, Ariel. Style épicurien, style spinoziste. *Arch Phil*, 57(3), 513-522, Jl-S 94.

Suleiman, Susan Rubin. Bataille in the Street: The Search for Virility in the 1930s. *Crit Inquiry*, 21(1), 61-79, Autumn 94.

Virility—how to acquire it, how to define it—was a major preoccupation of many political writers of the 1930's, both on the Right and the Left. Georges Bataille, allied

with the Left, grappled with this question in his novels as well as his political and philosophical essays between 1929 and 1941. I argued that Bataille moved from an outward, action-oriented definition of virility to an inward one, and that this move was intimately related to the evolution of European politics during that decade; furthermore, that it acquired a particular relevance and resonance in Nazi-occupied France.

Sullivan, Michael (trans) and Agamben, Giorgio and Whitsitt, Sam (trans). *Idea of Prose*. Albany, SUNY Pr, 1985.

Sullivan, Philip R. Contentless Consciousness and Information-Processing Theories of Mind. *Phil Psychiat Psych*, 2(1), 51-59, Mr 95.

Functionalist theories of mind sometimes have viewed consciousness as emerging simply from the computational activity of extremely complex information-processing systems. Empirical evidence suggests strongly, however, that experience without content ("pure consciousness" events, or "core mystical experience") and devoid of subjectivity (no sense of agency or ownership) do happen. The occurrence of such consciousness, lacking all informational content, counts against any theory that equates consciousness with the mere "flow of information," no matter how intricate.

Sullivan, Phillip R. The Natural Ought. *Behavior Phil*, 23(1), 1-12, Spr-Sum 95.

The traditional *ought* was derived from the relationship between human nature *and* supernature. Compliance was required to the Will of God and derivatively to his legitimately appointed spokesmen, religious and lay. For naturalists, *ought* obviously cannot have that same command context. Yet *ought* still speaks with a voice of command, one derived from natural selection in an extremely sophisticated social species, manifested in our *sense-of-fairness*, and mediated by subtly intense and inexorable pleasure/pain mechanisms. Like language, the *sense-of-fairness* is inborn; like language, its exact specification is shaped by experience.

Sullivan, Stephen J. Relativism, Evil, and Disagreement: A Reply to Hocutt. *Philosophia (Israel)*, 24(1-2), 191-201, D 94.

Sullivan, Thomas D. On the Alleged Causeless Beginning of the Universe: A Reply to Quentin Smith. *Dialogue (Canada)*, 33(2), 325-336, Spr 94.

In reply to Quentin Smith and others, I attempted in "Coming To Be Without A Cause" (*Philosophy*, 65: 1990) to show that modern cosmology does not prove the world began to be without a cause, and that it couldn't possibly do any such thing. Part of my original argument involved a defense of a weak version of The Principle of Sufficient Reason: whatever comes to be has a cause. In this sequel I elaborate that defense against Smith's new objections.

Sullivan, Thomas D and Pannier, Russell. Aquinas's Solution to the Problem of Universals in *De Ente et Essentia*.... *Amer Cath Phil Quart*, 68(Supp), 159-172, 1994.

It is sometimes said that in *De Ente et Essentia* Aquinas dissolves the problem of universals. We agree that the Aquinas attempts a dissolution, but argue that the attempt fails. Aquinas's argument is set out in detail.

Sullivan, Timothy. Identité et nationalisme irlandais. *Horiz Phil*, 5(1), 96-104, Autumn 94.

Irish national identity became problematic under a colonial administration. New forms of political, social, and economic organization uprooted families and lives, which led to a loss of contact with their heritage, and undermined traditional character. Nationalism surpassed the previous base of identity in the family and region, and spoke of the "people" with their common values as an order transmitting traditional culture. But Ireland's political liberation has not been synonymous with the achievement of Irish cultural objectives. The identity of a people established in the nation-state, its tricolor, and national currency, finds that identity again problematic.

Sulmasy, Daniel P (& others). Patients' Perceptions of the Quality of Informed Consent for Common Medical Procedures. *J Clin Ethics*, 5(3), 189-194, Fall 94.

To study patient perceptions of the quality of informed consent obtained by resident physicians, 105 inpatients or their surrogates were interviewed soon after common bedside procedures such as spinal taps. Almost all reported feeling that they had genuinely been asked to give permission. Only 53% reported that had been given alternatives. While 86% said that risks were explained, only 57% could remember at least one risk. Sixty-four percent rated explanations of the procedure as excellent; 57% rated explanations of the risks as excellent. The uninsured were less likely to know that they could refuse. These results highlight target areas for ethics education.

Sumner, L W. The Subjectivity of Welfare. *Ethics*, 105(4), 764-790, Jl 95.

An adequate theory about the nature of welfare must account for the subject-relativity of prudential value: the fact that this particular mode of value for a life (as opposed to others it might exemplify) is its value *for the individual whose life it is*. Subjective theories explain subject-relativity by rooting it in the interests or attitudes or concerns of the welfare subject. Objective theories, by definition, cannot appeal to this resource, and the best attempts (by Aristotle and Moore) to find some alternative are unsuccessful. No objective theory of welfare, therefore, can be correct.

Sumwalt, Vernon. Peirce on the Relation of Logic and Mathematics. *Dialogue (PST)*, 37(1), 15-24, O 94.

This article demonstrates Charles Peirce's different conceptions of "mathematics" and "logic". After summarizing the development of Peirce's logical system (in order to illustrate his replacement of an algebraic system of notation with a more iconic, graphical system), the difference between logic and mathematics emerges through an examination of Peirce's definitions of "mathematics" and "logic", his distinction between corollarial and theoremic reasoning, and his views towards logicism.

Sundararajan, Louise. Comment on Professor Johnson's Article on Computer Language. *Ultim Real Mean*, 17(4), 316, D 94.

Johnson's analysis of computer sublanguages is evaluated in light of Heidegger's theory of language. The evaluation shows that Johnson's article is an important extension of Heidegger, that contrary to Johnson's claim, computer language speaks "inauthentically" in many ways, that computer's potential to approximate "authentic" language is manifest in the limit it imposes on human efforts towards disambiguation.

Sundholm, Göran. Existence, Proof and Truth-Making: A Perspective on the Intuitionistic Conception of Truth. *Topoi*, 13(2), 117-126, S 94.

Truth-maker analyses construe truth as existence of proof, a well-known example being that offered by Wittgenstein in the *Tractatus*. The paper subsumes the intuitionistic view of truth as existence of proof under the general truth-maker scheme. Two generic constraints on truth-maker analysis are noted and positioned with respect to the writings of Michael Dummett and the *Tractatus*. Examination of the writings of Brouwer, Heyting and Weyl indicates the specific notions of truth-maker and existence that are at issue in the intuitionistic truth-maker analysis, namely that of proof in the sense of proof-object (Brouwer, Heyting) and existence in the nonpropositional sense of a judgment abstract (Weyl). Furthermore, possible anticipations in the writings of Schlick and Pfänder are noted.

Sundholm, Göran. Proof-Theoretical Semantics and Fregean Identity Criteria for Propositions. *Monist*, 77(3), 294-313, Jl 94.

Sunic, Tomislav. Marx, Moses, and the Pagans in the Secular City. *Clio*, 24(2), 169-188, Wint 95.

The main thesis of this essay is that over the last two thousand years, Judeo-Christian monotheism has been the source of theological and ideological disputes. Ever since the break-down of the Roman empire, the newly emerged Christian culture has lead to a mono-linear vision of history and to a wide-spread belief of one undisputed truth. With the gradual "securalisation" of Western societies, i.e., after the American and the French Revolutions, the Judeo-Christian dogma became supplanted by the liberal and socialist dogmas. Both socialism and liberalism, each from its own point of view, also posit a linear concept of history, assuming that eventually there will be the "end of history." In this essay, the author argues that the post-modern return to the pre-Christian and pre-Platonic spheric and circular view of history, may be the best remedy against totalitarian nightmares that have rocked our modernity.

Sunstein, Cass R. On Costs, Benefits, and Regulatory Success: Reply to Crandall. *Crit Rev*, 8(4), 623-633, Fall 94.

Sunstein, Cass R. Same-Sex Relations and the Law. *Metaphilosophy*, 25(4), 262-284, O 94.

Superson, Anita. Michael Slote and Barbara Herman. *Soc Theor Pract*, 20(2), 221-244, Sum 94.

I examine two new defenses of familiar theories: Slote's "common sense virtue ethics," and Herman's Kantian moral theory. Slote defends his theory by demonstrating failures of Kantianism, commonsense morality, and act utilitarianism. My main objection is that his defense at crucial points relies too heavily on intuition. I examine some of the main features of Herman's plausible and coherent version of Kantianism, including the motive of duty, the Categorical Imperative procedure, how Kantianism can accommodate relationships yet still be an impartialist theory, and the "rules of moral salience" which aid the agent in identifying moral issues and knowing what duty requires.

Suppe, Frederick. "Explaining Homosexuality: Philosophical Issues, and Who Cares Anyhow?" in *Gay Ethics, Murphy, Timothy F (ed)*, 223-268. New York, Haworth Pr, 1994.

Standard behavioral and biological attempts to explain the etiology of homosexuality are surveyed. These include genetic, physiological (e.g., hormonal), constitutional (e.g., wrong pubic hair configurations), childhood experience, parenting, and psychoanalytic accounts. These are criticized from a number of perspectives, including inadequate conceptualization of homosexuality and heterosexuality. The use of path analysis to assess etiological accounts is examined, with particular attention being paid to the Kinsey Institute's *Sexual Preference* efforts. Drawing from the sociology of science, recent philosophical work on the growth of scientific knowledge, and historical considerations, the legitimacy of homosexual etiology as a scientific research question is examined. It is argued that homosexual etiology is a degenerative research program. The research program's conceptual crudity with respect to sexual identity and sexual orientation precludes it from making any scientific contribution. Thus the claim that homosexual etiology is a legitimate scientific issue is plausible only against the backgound of a set of late Victorian normative assumptions about "normal love," some surrogate thereof, or a political agenda. Implications of the homosexuality etiology case study for more general philosophical treatments of explanation are considered briefly.

Suppes, Patrick. "A Brief Survey of Adams' Contributions to Philosophy" in *Probability and Conditionals, Eells, Ellery (ed)*, 201-204. New York, Cambridge Univ Pr, 1994.

Suppes, Patrick. "Some Questions about Adams' Conditionals" in *Probability and Conditionals, Eells, Ellery (ed)*, 5-11. New York, Cambridge Univ Pr, 1994.

Surber, Jere Paul. "German Idealism Under Fire: Fichte, Hegel, and 'Metacriticism'" in *Hegel on the Modern World, Collins, Ardis B (ed)*, 93-109. Albany, SUNY Pr, 1995.

Surber, Jere Paul. Kant, Levinas, and the Thought of the "Other". *Phil Today*, 38(3-4), 294-316, Fall 94.

Surette, Leon. Is Art Worth More Than the Truth?. *J Value Inq*, 28(2), 181-192, Je 94.

Heidegger builds his formalist, mimetic and contemplative aesthetic on the unpromising ground of Nietzsche's expressive, affective and ecstatic aesthetic by locating truth in the sensuous, thereby correcting Nietzsche's metaphysical error, leading him to think that art was worth more than the truth. For Heidegger art is the *naming* of earth, the bringing of earth into language, into the house of Being, and thereby constituting a world. This world is history, the destiny of a world-historical people. The work of art, then, is the historical rapture of an entire people, race, or nation, especially the German nation.

Surma, S J. A Generalisation of the Tarski-Herbrand Deduction Theorem. *Log Anal*, 34, 319-331, S-D 91.

The paper provides a condition which characterizes the implicational fragment of classical sentential logic in the same way as the Tarski-Herbrand deduction theorem together with its conversion characterizes the implicational fragment of intuitionistic logic.

Susse, Jennifer. Obeying a Rule: Wittgenstein's Stress on Obedience in Sections 198-202 of the *Philosophical Investigations*. *Conference*, 5(2), 15-28, Wint 94-95.

This article is directed at Kripke's 1982 claim that the fundamental problem of Wittgenstein's *Philosophical Investigations* is a 'skeptical paradox' concerning rule following, of which 202 is an explicit statement. It is my contention that an analysis of the largely ignored sections 198-201 is crucial for a proper understanding of both 202 specifically and the private language argument generally. Through a close exegetical reading of the text, I try to show that in these sections Wittgenstein intends to preempt skepticism with his point that paradigmatically rules are obeyed rather than interpreted. I conclude that section 202 is only one step in Wittgenstein's total private language argument.

Sutherland, Heather J and Meslin, Eric M and Till, James E. What's Missing from Current Clinical Trial Guidelines? A Framework for Integrating Science, Ethics, and the Community Context. *J Clin Ethics*, 5(4), 297-303, Wint 94.

The purpose of the work was to produce a framework to guide the development of meritorious clinical trial proposals. The framework consists of essential features of rigourous methodology, ethical acceptability, and a component referred to as "community context". These three domains were woven together in a checklist format under the headings of general, scientific and ethical considerations. Since texts concerning clinical trial methodology do not integrate ethics criteria and ethics guidelines do not provide detailed scientific criteria in obvious and practical ways, we outline a more contemporary and comprehensive set of guidelines.

Sutton, Agneta. Response to the HFEA Consultation Document on Research and Fertility Treatment. *Ethics Med*, 11(2), 33-36, 1995.

The response is based on the understanding that life is a gift and that the child is not a possession to which adults have a right. Assisted conception involving research entailing the destruction of the human embryo or fetus is socially and morally unacceptable. Ovum donation violates natural order. Procedures involving donation of egg or ovarian tissue from cadavers or aborted fetuses are particularly disturbing. But any child who is not conceived as the fruit of marriage will lack the full sense of kinship identity that anchors a person in the present by providing him with roots in the past.

Suvorov, Aleksandr V. Not the "Human Factor" but the Person. *Russian Stud Phil*, 33(4), 66-81, Spr 95.

Svedin, Uno (ed) and Karlqvist, Anders (ed) and Haken, Hermann (ed). *The Machine as Metaphor and Tool*. New York, Springer-Verlag, 1993.

Swanson, Judith A. The Political Philosophy of Aeschylus's *Prometheus Bound*. *Interpretation*, 22(2), 215-245, Wint 94-95.

Swanton, Christine. Profiles of the Virtues. *Pac Phil Quart*, 76(1), 47-72, Mr 95.

Swazo, Norman K. Gnōthi Sauton: Heidegger's Problem Ours. *J Brit Soc Phenomenol*, 25(3), 263-287, O 94.

This paper seeks to explain and understand Heidegger's entanglement with National Socialism in the context of his post-Rectorate meditations on the ontological-moral instruction of Sophoclean tragedy. Heidegger himself is "political" in his turn to Sophocles insofar as this turn represents his need/quest to come to terms with the problem of leadership, i.e., with the deformation he experienced in Hitler's leadership. Heidegger recognizes something paradigmatic in the character and fate of Oedipus, and so points out for our instruction some lessons about moral agency and political responsibility. Centrally at issue is the modern supposition of an autonomous moral agency.

Sweeney, Jill and Armstrong, Robert W. Industry Type, Culture, Mode of Entry and Perceptions of International Marketing Ethics Problems: A Cross-Cultural Comparison. *J Bus Ethics*, 13(10), 775-785, O 94.

The authors investigate the differences in ethical perceptions of Australian and Hong Kong international managers. Ethical perceptions are measured with respect to different industry types, cultures and modes of entry into international markets. Mode of entry refers to how firms select to enter foreign markets. Modes of entry include: exporting (indirect or direct), contractual methods (licensing and franchising) and via direct foreign investment (joint ventures and wholly-owned subsidiaries). It was determined that culture and mode of entry have a significant effect on the perception of ethical problems.

Sweet, Dennis. *Heraclitus: Translation and Analysis*. Lanham, Univ Pr of America, 1995.

Sweet, William. Anti-foundationalism, Hendrick Hart, and the Nature and Function of Religious Belief. *Phil Theol*, 8(2), 167-191, Wint 93.

In a number of recent essays, Hendrik Hart has elaborated an account of the nature and function of religious belief that, he believes, is post-modern in inspiration and anti-foundationalist in character. In this paper, I reconstruct what I take to be Hart's central claims. While Hart does remind us of some important aspects of the nature of religious belief—aspects often overlooked by many critics—I suggest that there are several problems in the account he provides, that there are tensions between his view of religious belief and his claims about how it can function, and that it is not clear that he ultimately avoids adopting a variant of the foundationalism he explicitly rejects.

Sweet, William. Rationality and the Humanities and Social Sciences. *Indian Phil Quart*, 21(3), 257-270, Jl 94.

In this paper I argue that there is no universal form of "rationality' applicable to academic study in the humanities and social sciences, and that the norms for what counts as appropriate to a field of study are, fundamentally, context dependent. In order to show the grounds for, and to provide an illustration of the consequences of, such an argument, I appeal to the example of the academic study of history which, I suggest, exhibits a number of the characteristic of humanities and social sciences.

AUTHOR INDEX WITH ABSTRACTS 765 **Szombath, Attila**

Sweet, William. Was Bosanquet a Hegelian?. *Bull Hegel Soc Gt Brit*, 31, 39-60, Spr-Sum 95.

Several recent studies have challenged the received view that British Idealism was "Hegelian". In light of this, I examine the work of Bernard Bosanquet (1848-1923). I argue that Bosanquet's and Hegel's respective analyses and methods are quite distinct and that, particularly in his accounts of the individual, the 'real will' and the state, Bosanquet's debt to Hegel is more to the latter's illustrations than to his original insights. I conclude that the best statement of the relation between them is that Bosanquet drew on Hegel for an elaboration of principles found in earlier authors, particularly Plato and Aristotle.

Sweetman, B. The Pseudo-Problem of Scepticism. *Phil Inq*, 16(1-2), 32-43, Wint-Spr 94.

This article argues that the problem of skepticism is a pseudo-problem. I attempt to illustrate by means of a detailed example that if we *do* take the problem seriously, we will *never* be able to solve it. This is an excellent reason in itself for dismissing the problem, since it is not a problem which has been raised on the basis of evidence. I also argue that the claim that skepticism is a *logical possibility* is not a good reason to take the problem seriously, and that there are no other good reasons to take the problem seriously.

Swiderski, Edward M. "Individual Essence in Ingarden's Ontology" in *Kunst und Ontologie, Galewicz, Wlodzimierz (ed)*, 183-205. Amsterdam, Rodopi, 1994.

Swidler, Leonard. Toward a Universal Declaration of a Global Ethic. *Dialogue Hum*, 4(4), 51-64, 1994.

Swidorski, Carl. "Constituting the Modern State" in *Radical Philosophy of Law, Caudill, David S (ed)*, 162-178. Atlantic Highlands, Humanities Pr, 1995.

This article first theoretically assesses the way the law ultimately reflects and sustains the existing social order yet has its own relative autonomy and internal logic. It then traces the post-New Deal record of the Supreme Court in legitimating the changes that occurred in the modern capitalist economy centering around the social contract among corporations, the government, and organized labor. The article concludes that labor law serves as a model of the contradictions faced by the Court, and the law in general, in fulfilling its constitutive role.

Swierstra, Tsjalling. Wetenschapsfilosofieën: op weg naar een vruchtbare rivaliteit. *Kennis Methode*, 18(2-3), 173-178, 1994.

Swift, Adam. Response to Spitz's "The Concept of Liberty in 'A Theory of Justice' and Its Republican Version". *Ratio Juris*, 7(3), 348-352, D 94.

Swift, Adam and Mulhall, Stephen. *Liberals and Communitarians*. Cambridge, Blackwell, 1992.

This book provides an overview of recent and contemporary debates between liberal political theorists and their communitarian critics. Structured by an agenda of five key themes, it examines the work of Sandel, MacIntyre, Taylor and Walzer, and evaluates their criticisms of Rawls (both early and late), Rorty and Raz.

Swift, Paul. In-Jestion: Intestinal Laughter in Kant and Nietzsche. *Int Stud Phil*, 27(1), 97-103, 1995.

Although not often thought of as contributing to a genealogy of digestion, Kant's laughter as a "tense expectation (which) is suddenly transformed into nothing" proves itself by promoting health "far better than the physician's wisdom." By tracing the incongruity theory of laughter as it emerges in Aristotle, Kant, and Schopenhauer, the *Erschütterung* is reconsidered as philosophic method to reconnect to corporeality. Nietzsche's attempt to read philosophy as a misunderstanding of the body demands an overcoming of dyspeptic ideals. By exploring the tense expectations of metaphysics as "transformed into nothing" by Nietzsche and Kant, the *Critique of Judgment* (i.e., the "end" of the critical enterprise) is connected with the recurring concern of health and the body in the Nietzschean corpus.

Swigart, Valerie. Recognizing and Respecting Family Judgment. *J Clin Ethics*, 6(1), 85-87, Spr 95.

This commentary proposes that in the absence of a clear and reliable autonomous expression from the patient, family members are in the best position to make judgments regarding what the patient would want in regard to life-preserving medical treatment. The validity of vague communication from a critically ill and medicated patient interpreted by staff as a request for continuing treatment is questioned. Life support decision making is an interpersonal as well as intrapsychic process. Intimacy and caring within the family provide the best link to understanding both the values of the patient and the context of any prior informal or formal request regarding end-of-life support.

Swinburne, Richard. "Body and Soul" in *The Mind-Body Problem: A Guide to the Current Debate, Warner, Richard (ed)*, 311-316. Cambridge, Blackwell, 1994.

I defend soft dualism. This holds that humans on Earth consist of two separate substances—body and soul—in interaction; but the soul has no necessary immortality, and it depends for its present functioning on the body. It would not be logically possible for a person to continue to exist after the destruction of his body (as it clearly is) unless he currently has a soul.

Swoyer, Chris. Leibniz on Intension and Extension. *Nous*, 29(1), 96-114, Mr 95.

Leibniz is well-known for his intensional interpretation of logic, but he also discusses, and sometimes even employs, an extensional approach. I examine Leibniz's views on intension, extension, and the connections between them. I show that Leibnizian intensions and extensions share a common structure that explains the relationships among the various interpretations he proposes for his logics, that because of this common structure extensions express intensions in Leibniz's important, technical sense of expression, and that Leibniz's views on intension and extension (in conjunction with his views about truth) require that Leibnizian concepts be extensional.

Swoyer, Chris. Leibniz's Calculus of Real Addition. *Stud Leibniz*, 26(1), 1-30, 1994.

I examine what is probably Leibniz's most complete logical system and show that it is well-developed formal logic with a number of original and important features. Among other things, Leibniz discusses alternative interpretations of his system, provides detailed proofs of over twenty theorems about (what are now known as) semilattices and shows their relevance to logic, and he develops what is probably the first formal theory of the part-whole relation. I then show how Leibniz's system illuminates other aspects of his logic and philosophy, including his views on the structure of concepts and on infinite analysis.

Swoyer, Chris. Zalta's *Intensional Logic and the Metaphysics of Intentionality*. *Nous*, 27(2), 243-247, Je 93.

Sylvan, Richard and Bennett, David. *The Greening of Ethics: From Human Chauvinism to Deep-Green Theory*. Cambridge, White Horse, 1994.

This text sets out what environmental ethics is and is not, tracks main movements in environmental ethics is proceeding and developing, provides suggestions on how environmental ethics can reach a wider audience, and recommends methods and actions of inculcating and promoting environmental ethics. The unifying theme is a greening of ethics and applications of this greening. The text also plays with the conception of an environmental ethic as good, as a focus of an intellectual business venture, theoretical ethics becoming a branch of economics. This suggests that there is no neat boundary between ethics and economics.

Synowiecki, Adam. From Scientific Myths to Pure Science. *Stud Phil Christ*, 30(2), 245-271, 1994.

The present paper is a philosophical essay which analyzes the origin, development and changes affecting learnedness. The author grants it a designation of scientific myths which are contrary to—as distinguished by Prigogign—"pure science". Mythology of learnedness is determined by two principles, of which one generalizes studied value of sciences or generally natural science while the other overestimates their value in the issue of development. Both principles were impaired in present days. For the development of natural history revealed the weakness of the faith in infinite cognitive possibilities of aforementioned sciences as well as expodes the human being to threats in existential aspect. According to the author natural history may not omit "human matters" which should be incorporated into metatheoretical level of science and expanded into the area of "antropophilic" solutions. There is a chance and hope that we are in the eve of such paradigm of biological sciences which responds to the demand. The science will retain its identity upon the horizontal approach; however, it will be transformed from vertical point of view.

Sytsma, Sharon E. Ethical Internalism and Moral Indifference. *J Value Inq*, 29(2), 193-201, Je 95.

I examine the argument that Ethical Internalism (the theory that moral judgment entails or guarantees motivation to act morally) must be false because of the fact of moral indifference. I argue that no facts of moral indifference can be adduced as evidence against the internalism. I begin by distinguishing two main versions of internalism. Then I identify and characterize four common forms of moral indifference and explain why each form fails to offer evidence against internalism. Only what I call Authentic Moral Indifference could provide a refutation of internalism; however, this type of moral indifference cannot be shown to exist.

Szabados, Béla. Autobiography and Philosophy: Variations on a Theme of Wittgenstein. *Metaphilosophy*, 26(1-2), 63-80, Ja-Ap 95.

Szabó, Zoltán. Berkeley's Triangle. *Hist Phil Quart*, 12(1), 41-63, Ja 95.

I argue that despite the centrality of the rejection of abstract ideas to Berkeley's philosophy, his attempt to bring anti-abstractionism into harmony with immaterialism ultimately fails. My discussion focuses on Berkeley's philosophy of geometry. I present his account of geometrical objects nd his theory about how we understand words and diagrams in a geometrical demonstration. I propose three simple criteria that any philosophical theory about geometry must meet, and argue that Berkeley's attempts to accommodate them fail as a result of his commitment to the 'ese est percipi' principle.

Szahaj, Andrzej. The Task of Philosophy. *Hist Euro Ideas*, 20(1-3), 559-566, Ja 95.

Szczepanski, Jan. Florian Znaniecki's Concept of a Humanist All-Mankind Civilization. *Dialogue Hum*, 4(5), 21-25, 1994.

Szegó, Katalin. Bódog Somló's Theory of Values. *Magyar Filozof Szemle*, 3-4, 343-364, 1994.

Bódog Somló was an outstanding Hungarian intellectual and university professor at the faculty of law. He joined the circle around the famous journal of progressive Hungarian intellectuals *'Huszadik Század'* as well as the *'Society for Social Sciences'*. The paper deals with his developments, i.e., the unfolding of his theory of values in laws and humanities.

Székely, László. Space-time in Philosophy and Physics (Melchior Palágyi's Theory on Space-time and the Einstein-Minkowski Theory of Relativity). *Magyar Filozof Szemle*, 3-4, 323-342, 1994.

'Does Palágyi's space-time concept really preceed the space-time theory of modern physics?' 'Can we really say with Ludwig Klages and Werner Deuble that the "Paradestück" of Relativity Theory was his discovery?' In order to answer these questions, the first part of our paper scrutinizes the metatheoretical and philosophical (metaphysical and epistemological) deliberations, in the context of which the Hungarian philosopher elaborated his concept of four-dimensional space-time. The second part analyses the parallels and contrasts between the Einsteinian-Minkowskian and Palágyi's theory and shows that despite of all their formal similarities in respect of their contents they are not identical. Consequently, we can look at Palágyi's work as the predecessor of the space-time concept of modern physics only in a very restricted sense. (edited)

Szlezák, T A. Tre lezioni su Platone e la scrittura della filosofia. *Riv Filosof Neo-Scolas*, 86(1), 3-43, Ja-Mr 94.

Szombath, Attila. The Metaphysics of Death. *Magyar Filozof Szemle*, 5-6, 633-670, 1994.

The author of the essay tries to analyze the problem of death from a philosophical standpoint. He argues that although death is something outside of our reach it attacks us from inside, it is always present in our life.

Szubka, Tadesz (ed) and Warner, Richard (ed). *The Mind-Body Problem: A Guide to the Current Debate*. Cambridge, Blackwell, 1994.

T-Kalogirou, E. Platon et Eschyle: la Relativité intérieure en tant que Recherche de l'origine. La Mimésis. *Philosophia (Athens)*, 23-24, 114-143, 1993-94.

Pourtant, chez Eschyle, la vision de la vérité survient comme processus de connaissance et, comme chez Platon, la transition du stade de la doxa à celui de la science s'effectue grâce à l'enchaînement. L'analogie entre les *Lois* de Platon et les *Euménides* et les *Suppliantes* d'Eschyle est surprenante: nous pourrons constater comment la solution de la dualité se fait au moyen du rattachement d'un des deux termes avec une Idée qui les dépasse. D'ailleurs, Eschyle aussi propose la connaissance de l'acte juste impliquant l'élévation au-delà de la réalité, au moyen d'une contemplation de l'origine. (edited)

Tabachnick, Barbara G and Bernsen, Ann and Pope, Kenneth S. National Survey of Social Workers' Sexual Attraction to Their Clients: Results, Implications, and Comparison to Psychologists. *Ethics Behavior*, 4(4), 369-388, 1994.

A survey form sent to psychologists (Pope, Keith-Spiegel, and Tabachnick, 1986) was adapted and sent to 1,000 clinical social workers (return rate = 45%). Most participants reported sexual attraction to a client, causing (for most) guilt, anxiety, or confusion. Some reported having sexual fantasies about a client while engaging in sex with someone other than a client. Relatively few (3.6% men; 0.5% women) reported sex with a client; training was related to likelihood of offending, though the effect is small and complex. An analysis of eight national studies (data from 5,148 therapists) found significant effects for gender (more male offenders) and year of study (about 10% annual decrease in reported offenses since 1977) but not profession (i.e., no difference among psychiatrists, psychologists, and social workers). Most social workers reported no graduate training whatsoever about sexual attraction; only 10% reported adequate training.

Tacq, Jacques. "Causality as Virtual Finality" in *Historiography Between Modernism and Postmodernism, Topolski, Jerzy (ed)*, 145-177. Amsterdam, Rodopi, 1994.

The historical writings on the concept of causality (Aristotle's *causa efficiens*) are astonishingly primitive. In the definitions of our predecessors, there is no reference to a causal field, to nonrealized possibilities nor to the equilibrium of a system, let alone values or ends. It is not so for the concept of finality (Aristotle's *causa finalis*), where value-orientations and complex system-thinking have always dominated the scene, an emphasis which is paramount in functionalism, interpretative sociology, decision-making and policy research. This has cost these domains dearly. The many problems associated with final causation are outlined and it is argued that causality and finality are nearer each other than it is shown in the history of causal writings.

Tadd, Win. "Accountability and Nursing" in *Ethics and the Professions, Chadwick, Ruth (ed)*, 88-103. Brookfield, Avebury, 1994.

Tännsjö, Torbjörn. The Secular Model of the Multi-cultural State. *Inquiry*, 38(1-2), 109-117, Je 95.

On what model should a modern multi-cultural democracy work? Spinosa *et al*. have argued that the political order should be sustained by a set of common values instilled in the citizens, without, however, any common rank order among these values. I argue that the multi-cultural state should rather conform to what I call the Secular Model, according to which the citizens need not share any basic values at all. On the Secular Model, people individually stick to the existing constitution (only) as long as they each feel that they have good reasons to do so. To be sure, each citizen of a multi-cultural state does need a feeling of community identity, a "we" ideology, but it is desirable that each individual can have more than one such identity. It is also important that each individual can shift as he or she pleases, from one such identity to another. So this kind of identity should not be moulded by the state, but by various different free associations, independent of the state.

Tagliacozzo, Giorgio. Giambattista Vico: Olvido y Resurrección. *Cuad Vico*, 3, 115-130, 1993.

Many causes contributed to the neglect of Vico for over two hundred years. Other causes have recently made possible an increasing recognition of the significance of Vico's thought. My intention here is to attempt to single out and assess both these sets of causes (principally in the English speaking world).

Tagliavia, Grazia. Il Cominciamento e la Costituzione della Fattualità. *G Metaf*, 16(3), 397-408, S-D 94.

"Womit muss der Anfang der Wissenscaft gemacht werden?", this is the question used as a title for the chapter about the beginning, placed by Hegel before his *Science of Logic*: "What has the beginning to be made with?" The subjective making (das subjective Tun) is an essential moment of the objective truth itself. However it's not this making that's present in the beginning-related question (gemacht-machen). The Hegelian attempt to an absolute beginning, pursued just through the dialectic of pure knowledge as an element-principle, attains to a "being made of the principle" which is "the always having to still make itself of the beginning".

Tagore, Saranindra N. Husserl's Conception of Hume's Problem: Toward a Transcendental Hermeneutic of Hume's *Treatise*. *Man World*, 27(3), 257-269, Jl 94.

Husserl made the remarkable claim that Hume was the first transcendentally motivated philosopher in the Western tradition. In this paper, I develop a transcendental interpretation of Hume's *Treatise* that is anchored in Husserl's conception of transcendental philosophy. Moreover, it is shown that the Husserlian-transcendental interpretation is consistent with Kant's posture regarding Hume.

Tai, Hua Terence. Strawson's Analytic Salvage of Kant's Transcendental Deduction of the Categories. *Phil Hist Sci*, 2(1), 51-95, Ap 93.

In *The Bounds of Sense* Peter F Strawson seeks to reconstruct Kant's argument in the transcendental deduction of the categories (TDC) independently of the doctrine of synthesis. Strawson's task may be viewed as an attempt to break apart what Kant once in the preface to the first edition of the *Critique of Pure Reason* referred to as two "sides" of TDC, namely, the objective and subjective deductions (OD and SD). This paper tries to dissect the kind of OD that Strawson has disentangled from SD. (edited)

Taka, Iwao. Business Ethics: A Japanese View. *Bus Ethics Quart*, 4(1), 53-78, Ja 94.

Although "fairness" and "social responsibilities" form part of the business ethics agenda of Japanese corporations, the meaning of these terms must be understood in the context of the distinctive Japanese approach to ethics. In Japan, ethics is inextricably bound up with religious dimension (two normative environments) and social dimension (framework of concentric circles). The normative environments, influenced by Confucianism, Buddhism, and other traditional and modern Japanese religions, emphasize that not only individuals but also groups have their own spirit (numen) which is connected to the ultimate reality. The framework of concentric circles lets moral agents apply different ethical rules to the respective circles. The dynamics of these religious and social dimensions lead to a different view of both individuals and corporations from that dominant in the West.

Takano, Mitio. Subformula Property in Many-Valued Modal Logics. *J Sym Log*, 59(4), 1263-1273, D 94.

The author discusses finitely valued modal logics which are characterized using Kripke model with a two-valued or many-valued accessibility relation. Deductive systems for these logics enjoying the subformula property are exhibited.

Takeuti, Gaisi. Grzegorcyk's Hierarchy and *Iep* E 1. *J Sym Log*, 59(4), 1274-1284, D 94.

Takeuti, Gaisi. Separations of Theories in Weak Bounded Arithmetic. *Annals Pure Applied Log*, 71(1), 47-67, Ja 95.

Takeuti, Gaisi. The Critical Number of a Variable in a Function. *J Sym Log*, 59(4), 1228-1244, D 94.

Talayco, Daniel E. Applications of Cohomology to Set Theory I: Hausdorff Gaps. *Annals Pure Applied Log*, 71(1), 69-106, Ja 95.

Talbot, Pierre. Formation Fondamentale et Culture Humaniste dans les Études Collégiales. *Philosopher*, 13, 205-216, 1992.

Talbott, W J. Intentional Self-Deception in a Single Coherent Self. *Phil Phenomenol Res*, 55(1), 27-74, Mr 95.

The author proposes a new theory of self-deception that explains how intentional self-deception is possible in a single, coherent, Bayesian agent. On the author's account, self-deception is intentional in the sense that it is caused or sustained by the agent's intentionally interfering with her otherwise reliable cognitive processes—for example, her attention, memory, reasoning, and evidence-gathering—to bias them in favor of believing a proposition that which she desires to believe regardless of whether it is true. Thus, self-deception involves intentional biasing, not intentional lying. The author compares his intentionalist account to the anti-intentionalist accounts of Elster, Mele, and Johnston, and argues that the anti-intentionalist accounts do not satisfactorily resolve what Nisbett and Ross refer to as the "Basic Antinomy".

Tallet, J A. A Search for Ultimate Reality and Meaning in a Universe of Possibilities. *Ultim Real Mean*, 17(4), 261-276, D 94.

Taken to its last consequences, a quest for ultimate reality and meaning would have to cover the largest conceivable domain—the realm of the possible, instead of limiting itself to a partial world that may happen to be actualized. This possible universe is both a contextual horizon and a monistic ultimate in the sense that all specific possibilities as such, even mutually contradictory contingencies, coalesce into the universe as possibility *per se*. Beyond its logico-ontological representation, the 'meaning' of such a 'reality' would be its own subsistence. Its 'value'—apart from the human aspiration to an absolute handhold—formal necessity.

Talmy, Leonard. The Cognitive Culture System. *Monist*, 78(1), 80-114, Ja 95.

Tam, Henry. "Crime and Responsibility" in *Introducing Applied Ethics, Almond, Brenda (ed)*, 169-184. Cambridge, Blackwell, 1995.

Tamir, Yael. "The Quest for Identity" in *Identity, Culture, and Education, Smeyers, Paul (ed)*, 49-84. Leuven, Leuven Univ Pr, 1994.

This paper offers an analysis of the notion "the quest for identity." The discussion emphasizes the importance of communal belonging, but rejects the view that one ought to belong to the community one was born to. It suggests that the quest for identity may lead individuals to follow many avenues: while some individuals might affirm their "inherent" affiliations and traditions, others may remain within their community of origin and strive to change its ways, or choose to leave their social group and opt for membership in a new one. This analysis suggests that choice characteristic of the liberal conception of the person and rootedness characteristic of the communitarian conception of the person both play an important role in the formation of personal identity.

Tan, Kok-Chor. Military Intervention as a Moral Duty. *Pub Affairs Quart*, 9(1), 29-46, Ja 95.

From the moral point of view, duty has to presuppose permissibility. But not all morally permissible acts are moral duties. With regard to military intervention, the just war doctrine has been primarily concerned with whether intervention is permissible and has said little on whether it can be a moral duty. While many scholars concede that interventions are sometimes permissible, they balk when it comes to deciding whether they are ever a moral duty. I argue in this paper that intervention under certain conditions is not only permissible but also a moral duty.

Tanaka, Kazuyuki and Kikuchi, Makoto. On Formalization of Model-Theoretic Proofs of Gödel's Theorems. *Notre Dame J Form Log*, 35(3), 403-412, Sum 94.

Tancredi, Laurence R. The Limits of Empirical Studies on Research Ethics. *Ethics Behavior*, 5(3), 217-236, 1995.

The results of empirical research in psychology and psychiatry are increasingly being used to formulate as well as understand problems at the interface of law and psychiatry. There has been a proliferation of studies, such as the determinants of individual competence or threat to self or others, the results of which are influencing policy and legislative decisions as well as buttressing holdings in court cases. In this article, I explore the issues of interpretation of epidemiological studies, particularly the role of ideological positions on the design and results of empirical findings, the importance of the way data are interpreted, and the role of ideologies in the way research findings are presented to provide support for policy positions.

Tanesini, Alessandra. "The 'Spider's Web' and the 'Tool': Nietzsche *vis-à-vis* Rorty on Metaphor" in *Nietzsche: A Critical Reader*, Sedgwick, Peter R (ed), 276-293. Cambridge, Blackwell, 1995.

The essay contrasts and compares Nietzsche's and Rorty's theories of metaphor. It argues that both oppose representationalists theories of language, and take metaphors to be at the center of cognition. Rorty's view that language is a tool which is used to fulfill preestablished needs if found lacking when compared with Nietzsche's position on this issue.

Tanner, Michael. *Nietzsche (Past Masters)*. New York, Oxford Univ Pr, 1994.

Tanner, R G. How Far Was Plato Concerned to Rebut the Claims of Cyrus the Great and Pisistratus to the Title of *Statesman*?. *Polis*, 12(1-2), 213-217, 1993.

Tanney, Julia. De-Individualizing Norms of Rationality. *Phil Stud*, 79(3), 237-258, S 95.

The possibility of irrationality invites questions about the substance, the nature, and the explanatory role of psychological norms. In this article, I consider explicitly the status of these norms, using Davidson's discussion of akrasia as a backdrop. In particular, I consider whether it makes sense to posit them as objects of cognition to explain our rational abilities. After considering various ways of attributing the norms as objects of cognition, I argue that none leaves us with a satisfactory account of the role of these norms. I propose instead that they be understood as constitutive of our ascriptive practices.

Tanzella-Nitti, Giuseppe. Nature as Creation. *Phil Sci (Tucson)*, 6, 77-95, 1995.

What is characteristic of the concept of nature, when nature is considered as *created*? Does that involve any implications for the natural sciences, despite the different facets the term nature has been endowed with along the centuries? Based on the content of Judaeo-Christian Revelation, theology of creation seems to contain implications for science on two major themes: the epistemology to be adopted for the study of nature and the meaning of scientific activity as human activity. The first theme concerns the specific view offered by Revelation on the epistemological-ontological structure of the world; the second one, more anthropological in character, concerns the attitude the scientist, as a man/woman who makes science, is expected to show or to feel toward nature, when performing his/her research work. The present paper briefly summarizes these implications following three guidelines: a) epistemological realism, b) nature as an open system, c) nature as bearer of significance.

Tappenden, Jamie. Commentary: Some Remarks on Vagueness and a Dynamic Conception of Language. *S J Phil*, 33(Supp), 193-201, 1995.

Tappenden, Jamie. Geometry and Generality in Frege's Philosophy of Arithmetic. *Synthese*, 102(3), 319-361, Ma 95.

This paper develops some respects in which the philosophy of mathematics can fruitfully be informed by mathematical practice, through examining Frege's *Grundlagen* in its historical setting. The first sections of the paper are devoted to elaborating some aspects of nineteenth century mathematics which informed Frege's early work. (These events are of considerable philosophical significance even apart from the connection with Frege.) In the middle sections, some minor themes of *Grundlagen* are developed: the relationship Frege envisions between arithmetic and geometry and the way in which the study of reasoning is to illuminate this. In the final section, it is argued that the sorts of issues Frege attempted to address concerning the character of mathematical reasoning are still in need of a satisfying answer.

Taranczewski, Pawel. "What Ingarden Has to Say to Painters" in *Kunst und Ontologie*, Galewicz, Wlodzimierz (ed), 207-217. Amsterdam, Rodopi, 1994.

Taroni, Paolo. *Tempo e Intuizione: Alle origini dello slancio vitale nel pensiero di Henri Bergson*. Ravenna, Ed Coop Lib Inform, 1993.

Tarrant, Harold A S. "The *Hippias Major* and Socratic Theories of Pleasure" in *The Socratic Movement*, Vander Waerdt, Paul A (ed), 107-126. Ithaca, Cornell Univ Pr, 1994.

I shed light on Socrates' attitudes towards pleasure by an examination of the *Hippias Major*. This concludes by examining a hedonistic explanation of 'the fine' whose refutation is usually interpreted anti-hedonistically. But aporetic dialogues usually conclude with the examination of quasi-Socratic theses. The alter ego is a more credible Socrates than his spokesman, and he is well disposed to hedonism. This fits the Polus arguments, if not the later Callicles arguments, in *Gorgias*, as well as *Protagoras*. I conclude by explaining how the same Socrates could inspire both hedonism (Aristippus) and cynicism (Antisthenes).

Taschek, William. Belief, Substitution, and Logical Structure. *Nous*, 29(1), 71-95, Mr 95.

I outline a proposal about the semantics of propositional attitude ascriptions. In virtue of the way that it blocks counter-intuitive substitutions in the content-clauses of attitude ascription, it respects the semantic relevance of differences in cognitive significance (*pace* certain strict Millian versions of the direct reference theory) without needing to assume (*pace* Frege) any sense like semantic value. For proper names, the felt need for sense arises from a joint commitment to i) the semantic relevance of differences in cognitive significance and ii) an unrestricted principle of compositionality for semantically relevant content. Taking my lead from a suggestion of Putnam's, I propose a restricted principle of compositionality that permits only substitutions that preserve what I call "global logical structure". I explain this latter notion and show how my proposal avoids Scott Soames' powerful objections to Putnam's original proposal.

Tasset, José Luis. Suicidio y fiesta del yo: el suicidio como transgresión moral definitiva: A propósito de "On Suicide" de David Hume. *Telos (Spain)*, 1(1), 149-166, F 92.

By way of a lecture and assessment of Hume's "On Suicide" (written in 1755-1757, posthumously published in 1777 edition of the withdrawn essays), a defense of the right to commit suicide or autonomotanasia is offered. Being translated this essay into Spanish in four different editions—and being included into contemporary British practical ethics readings—, we have up to this moment almost no study of its value

and main theses. A coherent empirist, atheological and utilitarianist view of this work is provided, connecting its main and central ideas with present debate on individual rights and providing a specifically ethical—neither medical nor pathological—lecture of the suicide problem.

Tasset, José Luis. Utilitarismo y Teoría del Desarrollo Moral (I): Análisis crítico de las teorías cognitivas del desarrollo moral y de sus fundamentos Kantianos. *Telos (Spain)*, 3(1), 49-83, Je 94.

Utilitarianism has, in general, despised moral development. This has resulted in a complete dominion of this important researching field by "the cognitive-developmental approach", a Kantian path to moral development, represented by Jean Piaget and Lawrence Kohlberg. Other forms of looking on moral growth are possible. May be an utilitarian view? Perhaps. In any case, empiricism (David Hume) and utilitarianism (J S Mill) could enlarge the foundations of moral development theories in an integral view that is so far away from Kant and his moral person concept. In the first part of this paper Kantian theories are assessed. In the second one (forthcoming issue of *Telos*) an approach to an utilitarianist scope of moral development and education is argued.

Taube, Volkmar. Bildliche Sprechakte. *Protosoz*, 2, 63-70, Ja 92.

How operates communication with pictures? S Kjörup has elaborated—follow up the analysis of pictorial symbolization in N Goodman's "languages of art"—a speech/act/theory of picturing. The problem of this approach is that Kjörup has no answer of pictorial fiction.

Tauber, Alfred I. *The Immune Self: Theory or Metaphor?*. New York, Cambridge Univ Pr, 1994.

The Immune Self is a critical study of immunology from its origins at the end of the nineteenth century to its contemporary formulation. The book offers the first extended philosophical critique of immunology, in which the function of the term *self*, which underlies the structure of current immune theory, is analyzed. However, this analysis is carefully integrated into a broad survey of the major scientific developments in immunology, a discussion of their historical context, and a review of the conceptual arguments that have molded this sophisticated modern science.

Tauer, Carol A. Human Growth Hormone: A Case Study in Treatment Priorities. *Hastings Center Rep*, 25(3), S18-S20, My-Je 95.

Prescription of growth hormone (GH) to short children who are not growth hormone deficient (GHD) represents an application of medicine for enhancement purposes. I argue that GH should be provided only to children who are GHD, who have medical conditions impinging on growth, or whose growth velocity is pathological. Children who are simply short, or have constitutional growth delay, are not entitled to GH. I refute the claim that fairness requires that all equally short children have equal access to GH, and the claim that short stature is a disability or is disadvantaging, and hence mandates access to GH.

Tauste Alcocer, Francisco. La Lectura del Timeo en Chartres: Teodorico de Chartres y Guillermo de Conches. *Rev Espan Filosof Med*, 0, 213-224, 1993.

The reading of the Timaeus at Chartres attempts to ideal with the Christian creation "secundum physicam" and appears as an exercise of doctrinal concord who takes into account too the Genesis's story of the origin of the world. Thus Thierry of Chartres and William of Conches carry out this task: the former starts from biblical text and to adapt it to the physical explanation and William, who seeks to interpret that Timaeus in the light of the Christian Weltanschauung.

Taylor, C C W. "Politics" in *The Cambridge Companion to Aristotle*, Barnes, Jonathan (ed), 233-258. New York, Cambridge Univ Pr, 1995.

The chapter contains a critical exposition of a number of central themes in Aristotle's *Politics*, including the theses that human beings are naturally political beings and that the *polis* is a natural entity, the account of the ideal state and the analysis and justification of slavery. These themes are discussed in relation to Aristotle's ethical theory and his philosophy of nature.

Taylor, Charles. Can Liberalism Be Communitarian?. *Crit Rev*, 8(2), 257-262, Spr 94.

In *Liberalism, Community and Culture*, Will Kymlicka suggests that the cultural resources with which communitarians have been concerned, inasmuch as they are prerequisites for the individual choice of the good, are appropriate objects of liberal protection. But Kymlicka's liberalism fails to fully meet the concerns of those who see their communities as intrinsically valuable—not merely as necessary means for the clarification of their options. Ultimately Kymlicka's approach shares in the tendency of liberalism to reduce manifold values to the single standard of equal concern for individuals—which results in a paternalistic disregard for those individuals' actual motivations.

Taylor, Charles. On 'Disclosing New Worlds'. *Inquiry*, 38(1-2), 119-122, Je 95.

The framework presented by Spinosa, Flores, and Dreyfus (henceforth SFD) centres on a new view of entrepreneurship. This sees the entrepreneur not simply as the instrumentally rational agent of economic maximization, but as someone committed to new modes of practice. This rescues the entrepreneur from the misleading stereotype which both right and left have conspired to accredit in our society. It allows us to see that there is more than one type of entrepreneur, and it defines one which is potentially very benign in democratic society (and also social-democratic societies). SFD propose to see political initiative-taking in democratic societies as analogous to this kind of entrepreneurship, and they extend their analysis to deal with the maintenance and fostering of solidarity. The framework is very illuminating for the first case, and partially, although less so, for the second.

Taylor, Charles. *Philosophical Arguments*. Cambridge, Harvard Univ Pr, 1995.

This is a collection of articles published formerly in different places, dealing with issues of epistemology, philosophy of language, social theory and political philosophy.

Taylor, Charles. Two Theories of Modernity. *Hastings Center Rep*, 25(2), 24-33, Mr-Ap 95.

Taylor, Craig. Moral Incapacity. *Philosophy*, 70(272), 273-285, Ap 95.

Bernard Williams has suggested that moral incapacities expressed in such first personal claims as "I can't" are best understood to be conclusions of practical deliberations by an agent. Against this I present an example where an agent might coherently claim that he morally can't act on the basis of his deliberative conclusion. My conclusion is then that we need to understand the connection Williams sees between deliberative reasoning and moral incapacity as qualified in ways he has not adequately brought out.

Taylor, Eugene. Radical Empiricism and the New Science of Consciousness. *Hist Human Sci*, 8(1), 47-60, F 95.

Taylor, Gabriele. Vices and the Self. *Philosophy*, 37(Supp), 145-157, 1994.

The thesis is that there are some vices, traditionally labelled 'deadly sins', which are quite literally corruptive of the self in that they point to a contradiction in the relevant structure of the will. The vices selected in illustration of the thesis are envy, avarice and pride; these are shown to be protective of a false self. These vices are therefore fundamentally harmful and so it must be in every agent's own interest to cultivate such virtues which should prevent their occurrence or at least mitigate their impact.

Taylor, Mark C. Denegating God. *Crit Inquiry*, 20(4), 592-610, Sum 94.

Taylor, Paul Christopher. So Black and Blue: Response to Rudinow. *J Aes Art Crit*, 53(3), 313-316, Sum 95.

"So Black and Blue" builds on Joel Rudinow's attempt to examine the connections between performance authenticity in blues music and racial authenticity. My primary motivating assumptions are pragmatic: that utterances of "white people can't play the blues" are historical events with formative and sustaining conditions, and that we accomplish more by inquiring into those conditions than by moving directly to moral condemnation. My aim is not to defend the claim that white people cannot play the blues, but to show that the claim is neither as simple nor as obviously a moral error as it seems.

Tazbir. Time in Old Polish Culture. *Dialogue Hum*, 4(1), 125-136, 1994.

te Velde, R. Repliek op Kal. *Tijdschr Filosof*, 57(2), 325-330, Je 95.

Teehan, John. What's A Philosopher To Do? A Deweyan Response. *Metaphilosophy*, 25(4), 376-391, O 94.

Teghrarian, Souren. "Wittgenstein, Kripke, and the 'Paradox' of Meaning" in *Wittgenstein and Contemporary Philosophy, Teghrarian, Souren (ed)*, 223-259. Bristol, Thoemmes, 1994.

Teghrarian, Souren (ed). *Wittgenstein and Contemporary Philosophy*. Bristol, Thoemmes, 1994.

Teichman, Jenny and Evans, Katherine C. *Philosophy: A Beginner's Guide (Second Edition)*. Cambridge, Blackwell, 1995.

Teichmann, Roger. Clocks and the Passage of Time. *Monist*, 78(2), 189-206, Ap 95.

What is the connection between statements about the passage of time and statements about clock-readings? A constitutive but nonreductive connection is argued for relying on the notion of a true clock (analogous to that of a normal-sighted observer when it comes to colour-statements). Two questions are tackled in the light of this account: 1) Would time pass in "situations" or "worlds" of horological confusion or stasis? 2) Is it *a priori* decidable whether time is continuous or dense, in the mathematical sense of these words?

Teichmann, Roger. Truth, Assertion and Warrant. *Phil Quart*, 45(178), 78-83, Ja 95.

In *Truth and Objectivity*, Wright argues that truth is a norm for assertoric discourse, and that this undermines deflationist theories of truth. A way in which truth is normative with respect to other speech-acts, e.g., question-asking, is spelled out, casting doubt on any special normative link between truth and assertion. The thesis that truth is normative for speech-acts generally would, however, seem not to force us to conclude that truth is a 'substantial property'. The phenomenon of defeasible criteria forces us to recognize a distinction between truth and warrant; but this also fails to establish the 'substantial property' view.

Tejera, Victorino. Plato's Ironies: Textural, Structural, and Allusional, On the Mathematical Humor in *Republic* Books VIII and IX. *Int Stud Phil*, 26(4), 85-99, 1994.

Telfer, Barbara and Jones, D Gareth. Before I Was an Embryo, I Was a Pre-Embryo: Or Was I?. *Bioethics*, 9(1), 32-49, Ja 95.

In this paper we look critically at the term 'pre-embryo', and we shall present the case for an alternative set of terms, namely, embryo-placenta and embryo-fetus. We consider this latter to be biologically-based terminology, that does not have any connotation of restricted moral value as the term pre-embryo does for some. (edited)

Temkin, Larry S. Weighing Goods: Some Questions and Comments. *Phil Pub Affairs*, 23(4), 350-380, Fall 94.

Temkine, Pierre. Le modèle de l'homme libre. *Rev Metaph Morale*, 99(4), 437-448, O-D 94.

The way Spinoza uses an *exemplar humanae naturae in Ethics IV* allows him to establish the image of the Wiseman as the centerpiece of his philosophy without lapsing into one of these three illusions: transcendence, finality, and free will. His system is indeed able to explain the mechanism by means of which an individual comes to project his desire upon an ideal figure; it thus explains how different effects follow different kinds of desires. Accordingly referring oneself to a "free man" model appears to be a central feature of ethical progress; it is a manifestation of the reason's desire generating rational effects and the model itself is an expression of man's essence.

Tempels, Placide. "Bantu Philosophy" in *African Philosophy: Selected Readings, Mosley, Albert G (ed)*, 62-86. Englewood Cliffs, Prentice Hall, 1995.

Temple, Dennis. Kant's Vision of the Moral Hero and the 'Laws of Arithmetic'. *Ultim Real Mean*, 17(2), 108-117, Ju 94.

Kant has two visions of the ideal moral character: that of virtue or the good will, and that of purity or the holy will. Kant seems to think that these ideals differ only in degree. For him, the holy will is simply a more virtuous version of the good will. But I argue here that if we look at them carefully, the good will and the holy will really represent ideals that are different in kind and not altogether compatible with each other. The good will is a human ideal; the holy will is something else.

Temporal Oleart, Josep. *Il.luminar-te el Rostre, Estimat*: Ressons de la Caverna al Cicle Rondallístic de l'Animal-Nuvi. *Convivium*, 7, 103-117, 1995.

The intention of this article is to specify a particular aspect—or suggest, at least, some specific traits—about Apuleius' Platonism. To be exact, I intend to emphasize Apuleiu's structural-scenic and content loans from Plato's Cavern ??? in his allegoric tale of Eros and Psyche—true archetype in the cycle of tales depending on this myth—which is included in the wider allegory of the whole story *Metamorphoses (Asinus Aureus)*.

Ten Have, Henk. The Anthropological Tradition in the Philosophy of Medicine. *Theor Med*, 16(1), 3-14, Mr 94.

The tradition of anthropological medicine in philosophy of medicine is analyzed in relation to the earlier interest in epistemological issues in medicine around the turn of the century as well as to the current interest in medical ethics. It is argued that there is a continuity between epistemological, anthropological, and ethical approaches in philosophy of medicine. Three basic ideas of anthropologically-oriented medicine are discussed: the rejection of Cartesian dualism, the notion of medicine as science of the human person, and the necessity of a comprehensive understanding of disease. Next, it is discussed why the anthropological movement has been superseded by the increasing interest in medical ethics. It is concluded that the present-day moral issues cannot be interpreted and resolved without clarification of the underlying anthropological images.

Tenbruck, Friedrich and Bleicher, J (trans). Internal History of Science or Universal History?. *Theor Cult Soc*, 11(1), 75-93, F 94.

Tenenbaum, Sergio and Lottenbach, Hans. Hegel's Critique of Kant in the Philosophy of Right. *Kantstudien*, 86(2), 211-230, 1995.

There is general agreement among commentators that in the *Philosophy of Right* Hegel misunderstands important aspects of Kant's practical philosophy. It is often claimed that Hegel entirely misses the point of Kant's universal law test and the mode of its application. We argue that these charges rest on misreadings of the *Philosophy of Right* in which Hegel's conception of the will is not taken into account. We show that Hegel's critique of Kant can be defended if it is interpreted as arising in response to Kant's own question of how the self-determination of a rational will can have determinate content.

Tengelyi, Lászlo. Der allgemeine Begriff des Bösen bei Jean Nabert. *Theol Phil*, 70(2), 259-267, 1995.

The unduly forgotten French philosopher Jean Nabert is considered in the article as a thinker who tried first to complete, then to overcome what was called by Ricoeur 'the ethical world view'. It is shown, first, how Nabert developed an *elementary ethics* which was neither teleological nor deontological in its structure; secondly, how he deepened Kant's doctrine of *radical evil*; thirdly, how he elaborated a *general concept of evil* by discovering a particular connection between guilt and suffering.

Tennant, Neil. Changing the Theory of Theory Change: Towards a Computational Approach. *Brit J Phil Sci*, 45(3), 865-897, S 94.

The theory of theory change has contraction and revision as its central notions. Of these, contraction is the more fundamental. The best-known theory, due to Alchourrón, Gärdenfors, and Makinson, is based on a few central postulates. The most fundamental of these is the principle of recovery: if one contracts a theory with respect to a sentence, and then adds that sentence back again, one recovers the whole theory. Recovery is demonstrably false. This paper shows why, and investigates how one can nevertheless characterize contraction in a theoretically fruitful way. (edited)

Tennant, Neil. Intuitionistic Mathematics Does Not Need *Ex Falso Quodlibet*. *Topoi*, 13(2), 127-134, S 94.

We define a system IR of first-order intuitionistic relevant logic. We show that intuitionistic mathematics (on the assumption that it is consistent) can be relevantized, by virtue of the following metatheorem: any intuitionistic proof of A from a set X of premisses can be converted into a proof in IR of either A or absurdity from some subset of X. Thus IR establishes the same inconsistencies and theorems as intuitionistic logic, and allows one to prove every intuitionistic consequence of any consistent set of premises.

Tennant, Neil. On Negation, Truth, and Warranted Assertibility. *Analysis*, 55(2), 98-104, Ap 95.

Wright's argument in Chapter 1 of *Truth and Objectivity* for the claim that truth and warranted assertibility are not the same is shown to make unwarranted use of non-constructive negation.

Tennant, Neil. Paradoxes of Pure Curiosity. *Theor Decis*, 38(3), 321-330, My 95.

We consider how a rational decision theorist would justify committing resources to an investigation designed to satisfy pure curiosity. We derive a strange result about the need to be completely open-minded about the outcome.

Tennekes, Henk. "The Limits of Science" in *Ecology, Technology, and Culture,* Zweers, Wim (ed), 72-88. Cambridge, White Horse, 1994.

This paper charts the conversion of professional meteorologist to a position similar to that of deep ecology. The intrinsic limits to the predictability of the weather and the philosophical implications of chaos theory are incompatible with the traditional hubris of scientists; the author's views have evolved toward the kind of humility advocated by Gregory Bateson in "Angels Fear". The limited access of rational analysis to the health of biological and mental ecosystems requires a thorough re-assessment of worldwide plans for planetary ecosystem management.

Teno, Joan M and Hill, T Patrick and O'Connor, Mary Ann. Advance Care Planning: Priorities for Ethical and Empirical Research. *Hastings Center Rep*, 24(6), Supp 1-36, N-D 94.

Federal statute endorses advance directives as one means for patients to control medical decisions in advance of incompetence. We invited investigators from multiple disciplines to develop priorities for conceptual and empirical research. Conference participants noted research should focus on the merits of a process of communication which we titled "advance care planning". Priorities for conceptual research included: 1) the moral weight of autonomy; 2) what preferences should be voiced in advance (considering importance, authenticity and stability); and 3) appropriate safeguards. Multidisciplinary empirical research utilizing both quantitative and qualitative research methodologies should describe the current process and outcomes of decision-making generally.

ter Meulen, Alice. "Semantic Constraints on Type-Shifting Anaphora" in *The Generic Book*, Carlson, Gregory N (ed), 339-357. Chicago, Univ of Chicago Pr, 1995.

Semantic operations in typed denotational domains constrain the dependencies between antecedents NPs and personal pronouns that differ in semantic type. Generic quantification admits of exceptions, which are modelled by default type-shifting operations between the kind and its members. Some observations are made concerning linguistic variance of such dependencies in the Germanic languages.

Ter Meulen, Ruud. Are There Limits to Solidarity with the Elderly?. *Hastings Center Rep*, 24(5), 36-38, S-O 94.

In most European countries the care for the elderly is based on the principle of solidarity; the young contribute to the costs of care for the old who have a greater risk on disease and handicaps. The increasing demand for care by the elderly puts this solidarity under strain. Particularly the medicalization of old age is a threat to the preparedness of the younger generations to take care of the needs of older persons. The process of medicalization should be stopped by introducing a two-tier system, based on the principle of humanitarian solidarity.

Térézis, Christos. Formes Métaphysiques et Etres Empiriques Selon Proclus. *Diotima*, 23, 162-164, 1995.

According to the Neoplatonic philosopher Proclus the forms are neither simple names nor the theoretical equipment of human consciousness. On the contrary, they are metaphysical realities having a specific existence. They appear in a specific level of the metaphysical development and are archetypes of the perceivable beings in which they coexist. Their mission is to cover the ontologic vacuums which exist between the metaphysical and the empirical world and to make their communication more functional.

Térézis, Christos. La Vie, Catégorie Ontologique chez Proclus et Denys. *Diotima*, 23, 60-63, 1995.

According to the Neoplatonic philosopher Proclus life is a self-existing ontologic reality, represents the class of the intelligible and intellective deities and is the second in the rank of the metaphysical generative causes. According to the Christian thinker Dionisious Aeropagitis life belongs to the actions of God which are at his will and which are not classified, does not owe its existence to superior cause. The difference between the two thinkers is due to the fact that the Neoplatonic believes in polyarchy while the Christian believes in monarchy with its numerous expressions.

Térézis, Christos. The Idea of Time in Work: "Elements of Theology" of Neoplatonic Proclus. *Philosophia (Athens)*, 23-24, 196-212, 1993-94.

Neoplatonic philosopher, Proclus (412-485), in his work *The Elements of Theology* treats time as a basic ontologic category and examines it in view of stable forms in which it appears as well in view of the general processes it establishes. More specifically, according to Proclus, time: 1) Is an objective reality with its own development terms and expresses a situation independent of the forms of man's surveilances; 2) Provides the conditions for a continuous cosmic harmony and introduces such proportions, in the area of perceptible beings, that articulate an interconnected system of laws; 3) Operates as a dymanics of changes, excludes static cosmic systems, is connected with motion and appears initually as an absolute collective measure which is articulated in succesive nonreversible periods.

Térézis, Christos. The Metaphysical Foundation of Gnosiology in Neoplatonic Proclus (412-485). *Phil Inq*, 16(3-4), 62-73, Sum-Fall 94.

Proclus, the Neoplatonic philosopher attempting to organize a convincingly articulated ontologic system in a firm way as well as to provide it with theologic orientation, thinks it is proper to present the dominant principles of his theory and the governing perspectives of his developments, in his first twelve chapters of his work, Platonic Theology. More specifically, based on Plato's works and interpreting them according to his estimations: 1) Suggests an objective and not arbitrary interpretation of what Gods reveal to Man as an epistemologic obligation; 2) Introduces a genuine agnosticism emphasizing his incredulity to the capacity of Man to comprehend gnostically the deep substance of divine cause of Beings; 3) Excludes every version of sceptistic orginality of the metaphysic world; 4) Articulates a hierarchical scale of the gnostic powers and gnostic actions of Man, restricting aesthisiocracy and underlining the potentialities of mental processes.

Terlouw, Jan. Strong Normalization in Type Systems: A Model Theoretic Approach. *Annals Pure Applied Log*, 73(1), 53-78, May 95.

Terpstra, Robert H and Giacalone, Robert A and Ralston, David A. Ethical Perceptions of Organizational Politics: A Comparative Evaluation of American and Hong Kong Managers. *J Bus Ethics*, 13(12), 989-999, D 94.

This paper presents a cross-cultural analysis of ethics with US and Hong Kong Chinese managers as subjects. These managers were given the Strategies of Upward Influence instrument and asked to evaluate the ethics of using various political strategies to attain influence within their organizations. Differences were found between Hong Kong and US managers on a variety of dimensions, indicating important differences between these two groups on their perceptions of ethical behavior. In the paper, we identify potential reasons for the findings, and suggest directions for future work in this area.

Terré, François. L'Orientamento della Filosofia del Diritto in Francia. *Riv Int Filosof Diritto*, 71(4), 741-751, 1994.

Tertulian, Nicolas. Benedetto Croce Critico dell'Irrazionalismo. *G Crit Filosof Ital*, 73(2-3), 238-252, My-D 94.

Terwee, Sybe and Peterson, Roland. Can Functionalism Provide the Proper Basis for a Core Theory of Psychoanalysis?. *Phil Psych*, 7(4), 463-469, 1994.

Before embarking upon the project of reformulating psychoanalysis in the 'scientific' terminology of cognitive science, we should first clearly define what psychoanalysis is about and what it is not about. Cognitive science is based upon a functionalistic philosophy of the mind. As a consequence such a project would require a functionalistic core theory of psychoanalysis. But Freud's claim of the therapeutic effect of psychoanalysis, attained through the rendering conscious of what is unconscious or the making personal of what is experienced by the neurotic patient as impersonal, cannot be explained by a functionalistic theory of the mind. We examine Freud's claim and conclude that there ought to be a philosophy of qualia at the core of psychoanalysis.

Terzis, George N. Human Flourishings: A Psychological Critique of Virtue Ethics. *Amer Phil Quart*, 31(4), 333-342, O 94.

According to the trait-relative view of flourishing this discussion defends, a person seeks to live a more coherent version of the life she is already motivated to seek owing to her individual core traits. Because this view implies that traits she ought to have must be framed in light of her actual traits, it questions the usefulness of the much more general conception of ideal traits associated with virtue ethics. Indeed, the discussion maintains that it belongs to psychology proper, rather than to virtue ethics' philosophical psychology, to determine the framework within which trait-relative flourishing is possible.

Teske, Roland J. The Will as King over the Powers of the Soul: Uses and Sources of an Image in the Thirteenth Century. *Vivarium*, 32(1), 62-71, My 94.

The article examines the image of the will as king and ruler over the other powers of the soul—an image that implies a strong version of voluntarism. The image is found in Henry of Ghent and Walter of Bruges, but it did not originate in the reaction to Aristotelianism late in the thirteenth century. Rather, it is already present in a highly developed form in the writings of William of Auvergne much earlier in the century. It seems likely that William was the source of the image in the later thinkers.

Teske, Roland J. Ultimate Reality According to Augustine of Hippo. *Ultim Real Mean*, 18(1), 20-33, Mr 95.

After sketching Augustine's life and major works, the article attempts to state what he took to be ultimately real and the source of meaning. It points out the hierarchical view of reality which he derived from the Neoplatonists and spells out on the basis of what he attributes to the Neoplatonists in Book Eight of *The City of God* Augustine's view of God as "the cause of existing, the source of understanding, and the order of living," that is, his view of God as creator of the universe, as the light of minds, and the source of our happiness.

Tessman, Lisa. Who Are My People? Communitarianism and the Interlocking of Oppressions. *Int Stud Phil*, 27(1), 105-117, 1995.

Tetens, Holm. "Natur und Erhaltungssätze" in *Naturauffassungen in Philosophie, Wissenschaft, Technik: Band III*, Schäfer, Lothar (ed), 13-40. Freiburg, Alber, 1995.

Tevzadze, Natia. National Identity and National Consciousness. *Hist Euro Ideas*, 19(1-3), 437-440, Jl 94.

Thagard, Paul. Mind, Society, the Growth of Knowledge. *Phil Sci*, 61(4), 629-645, D 94.

Explanations of the growth of scientific knowledge can be characterized in terms of logical, cognitive, and social schemas. But cognitive and social schemas are complementary rather than competitive, and purely social explanations of scientific changes are as inadequate as purely cognitive explanations. For example, cognitive explanations of the chemical revolution must be supplemented by and combined with social explanations, and social explanations of the rise of the mechanical worldview must be supplemented by and combined with cognitive explanations. Rational appraisal of cognitive and social strategies for improving knowledge should appreciate the interdependence of mind and society.

Thalos, Mariam. The Common Need for Classical Epistemological Foundations: Against a Feminist Alternative. *Monist*, 77(4), 531-553, O 94.

Thandeka. *The Embodied Self: Friedrich Schleiermacher's Solution to Kant's Problem of the Empirical Self*. Albany, SUNY Pr, 1995.

Thayer-Bacon, Barbara. Constructive Thinking: Personal Voice. *J Thought*, 30(1), 55-70, Spr 95.

Relying on current philosophical work by feminists, postmodernists, and pragmatists, the author redescribes critical thinking as an activity performed by a specific fallible unique person who is embedded and embodied. This redescription is called "constructive thinking". Given that thinkers are not neutral objective beings but have a 'personal voice' which actively contributes to any knowing, what are some of the important questions and concerns that arise? The author examines what others have to say on personal voice, and applies that examination to constructive thinking theory. The article concludes with suggestions concerning the development of personal voice in the classroom.

Thelwall, John and Claeys, Gregory (ed). *The Politics of English Jacobinism: Writings of John Thelwall*. University Park, Penn St Univ Pr, 1995.

Thero, Daniel P. Rawls and Environmental Ethics: A Critical Examination of the Literature. *Environ Ethics*, 17(1), 93-105, Spr 95.

The original position contractarian model of ethical reasoning put forth by John Rawls has been examined as a basis for an environmental ethic on three previous occasions in this journal and in Peter Wenz's *Environmental Justice*. In this article, I critically examine each of these treatments, analyzing the proposals offered and identifying their shortcomings. I find a total of seven different proposals in this literature for modifying Rawls' theory to augment its adequacy or as a ground for environmental ethics. The diverse difficulties that arise in attempting to apply Rawls suggest the conclusion that Rawlsian ethics may not be a suitable foundation for an adequate long-term environmental ethics.

Thérrien, Jean-Marie. L'Humanitaire Entre l'Éthique et la Politique. *Philosopher*, 16, 215-228, 1994.

Thérrien, Jean-Marie. La Notion de *Personne* Selon Lucien Sève. *Philosopher*, 17, 263-280, 1995.

Thérrien, Jean-Marie. Les Séquences d'ADN Humain Peuvent-Elles Etre Brevetées?. *Philosopher*, 14, 51-66, 1993.

Thesing, Josef. Democrazia e sviluppo—La Democrazia alla prova. *Aquinas*, 36(3), 593-606, S-D 93.

Thie, Marilyn. Epilogue: Prolegomenon to Future Feminist* Philosophies of Religion. *Hypatia*, 9(4), 229-239, Fall 94.

Thiel, Detlef. *Platons Hypomnemata: Die Genese des Platonismus aus dem Gedächtnis der Schrift*. Freiburg, Alber, 1993.

Thiele, Leslie Paul. Nature and Freeom: A Heideggerian Critique of Biocentric and Sociocentric Environmentalism. *Environ Ethics*, 17(2), 171-190, Sum 95.

A reformulation of our understanding of freedom is required if we are adequately to confront the environmental crisis. Engaging the debate between biocentric ecologists and sociocentric ecologists, I argue that the biocentric effort to ascribe rights (negative liberty) to nature is misbegotten. In turn, I suggest that the sociocentric effort to seek ecological realignment through the extension of human reason (positive liberty) is equally problematic. Martin Heidegger, who rejects both "negative" and "positive" notions of liberty, offers an understanding of human freedom that constitutes an ecologically attuned alternative.

Thiele, Leslie Paul. Out from the Shadows of God: Nietzschean Scepticism and Political Practice. *Int Stud Phil*, 27(3), 55-72, 1995.

Nietzsche's perspectivism leads him to a radical scepticism. Following Copernicus and Darwin and presaging Freud, Nietzsche displaces us from the center of the universe, from the pinnacle of earthly creation, and finally, from the throne of our own souls. Such a "schooling in suspicion" leads one to reject all teleologies. Taking Nietzsche's scepticism farther than even he allowed, however, produces a justification for social engagement that is grounded in an ironic, aestheticized politics. Even the most radical sceptic, indeed primarily the most radical sceptic, cannot maintain his doubt without pursuing that self-knowledge which reveals the psycho-social and biological origins of, and motivations for, his values and beliefs. Seeking this self-knowledge thrusts one into the political world.

Thinès, Georges. "Une rhétorique optimale du discours scientifique" in *Rhétoriques de la science, De Coorebyter, Vincent (ed)*, 117-130. Paris, Pr Univ France, 1994.

Thivel, Antoine. Prométhée, Personnage Romantique. *Diotima*, 22, 14-27, 1994.

Thom, Martina. "Natur—Ästhetische Kultur—Humanitätsförderung" in *Naturzweckmässigkeit und ästhetische Kultur, Schwabe, Karl-Heinz (ed)*, 7-29. Sankt Augustin, Academia, 1993.

Thom, Martina (ed) and Schwabe, Karl-Heinz (ed). *Naturzweckmässigkeit und ästhetische Kultur*. Sankt Augustin, Academia, 1993.

For the present discussion on the relationship between man and nature and on the matters of mental acquisition of the "world" Kant's philosophical approaches are not renouncable. The authors of the studies to the "Kritik der Urteilskraft" collected in this volume turn to Kant's problems and their reception from different points of view. In this connection they pursue both the problems of reasoning in modern aesthetics in connection with reflections on anthropology and philosophy of life and epistemological questions of modern science, e.g., physics, which were paid less attention to in the literature to Kant's third Critique. This volume makes a contribution to the current discussion on enlightening and modernity.

Thom, René. Le Référentiel selon Ferdinand Gonseth, et ses aspects philosophiques. *Dialectica*, 48(2), 157-168, 1994.

Cet exposé comporte deux parties: la premiére rappelle comment Ferdinand Gonseth comprenati ce terme de Référentiel qu'il avait auparavant introduit. La deuxième s'efforcera de préciser quelque peu cette notion par une interprétation topologico-dynamique.

Thomä, Dieter. Multikulturalismus, Demokratie, Nation: Zur Philosophie der deutschen Einheit. *Deut Z Phil*, 43(2), 349-363, 1995.

The author describes and criticizes the philosophical renaissance of the concept of "nation" in Germany since 1989. While the "nation" remains an abstract construction of social homogeneity, liberalism and democracy are based on individual capacities; but they underestimate their impact on particular life-forms and the peculiar relation between political motivation and personal integrity. By transferring the current debate on multiculturalism to the German situation, the author analyzes the new social conflicts between East and West as 'homemade' multiculturalism. The recognition of cultural identities turns out to be a constitutive condition (and not a denial) of individual participation.

Thomä, Dieter. Tugendhat, der Prinz und die Moral. *Deut Z Phil*, 42(1), 35-58, 1994.

Thomas, Bruce M. Abstraction and the Real Distinction Between Mind and Body. *Can J Phil*, 25(1), 83-102, Mr 95.

Descartes's argument for the real distinction between mind and body rests on the assumption that conceivability provides a reliable guide to possibility. Descartes concedes to Arnauld that inferences from what we can conceive to what is possible cannot be grounded in thoughts that have been "made *inadequate* by an abstraction of the intellect" (AT VII 221 : CSM II 156). This paper examines Descartes's account of the nature of abstraction, explains what it means to render a thought inadequate by abstraction and explains why Descartes *can* claim that his conception of himself as a thinking, nonextended thing has *not* been rendered inadequate by abstraction.

Thomas, Holly. Modal Realism and Inductive Scepticism. *Nous*, 27(3), 331-354, S 93.

Thomas, Laurence. Must We Care About Morality?. *Phil Psych*, 7(3), 383-394, 1994.

Moral philosophy is at its best when it takes human psychology seriously. Such are the instincts of Thomas Wren. His engaging book *Caring About Morality* is an

attempt to offer an account of human motivation that is true to human psychology, but which captures the spirit of Kantian morality without Kantian metaphysics. I argue that there are some fundamental psychological considerations which Wren does not take into account, and which are an obstacle to the success of his project. Moral motivation, I suggest, is much more tied to the psychological histories of persons than Wren allows.

Thomas, Simon and Sharp, James D. Uniformization Problems and the Cofinality of the Infinite Symmetric Group. *Notre Dame J Form Log*, 35(3), 328-345, Sum 94.

Assuming Martin's Axiom, we compute the value of the cofinality of the symmetric group on the natural numbers. We also show that Martin's Axiom does not decide the value of the covering number of a related Mycielski ideal.

Thomasma, David C. Beyond Autonomy to the Person Coping with Illness. *Cambridge Quart Healthcare Ethics*, 4(1), 12-22, Wint 95.

Thomasma, David C. The Ethical Challenge of Providing Healthcare for the Elderly. *Cambridge Quart Healthcare Ethics*, 4(2), 148-162, Spr 95.

Thomason, Neil. Philosophy Discussions with Less B.S.. *Teach Phil*, 18(1), 15-30, Mr 95.

Thomason, Neil. Sherlock Holmes, Galileo, and the Missing History of Science. *Proc Phil Sci Ass*, 1, 323-333, 1994.

There is a common (although not universal) claim among historians and philosophers that Copernican theory predicted the phases of Venus. This claim ignores a prominent feature of the writings of, among others, Copernicus, Galileo and Kepler—the possibility that Venus might be self-illuminating or translucent. I propose that such over-simplifications of the history of science merges from "psychological predictivism", the tendency to infer from "E is good evidence for H" to "H predicts E". If this explanation is correct, then in cases where evidence is less blatant the history of science (and philosophies of science that rely on it) has probably been seriously distorted in a predictivist direction.

Thompson, Audrey and Gitlin, Andrew. Creating Spaces for Reconstructing Knowledge in Feminist Pedagogy. *Educ Theor*, 45(2), 125-150, Spr 95.

This paper argues for a feminist pedagogy in which classroom relationships are foregrounded and problematized. Changing relations of power within spaces created for inquiry makes it possible to call into question assumptions regarding relevance, appropriateness, and legitimacy—assumptions that usually dictate what counts as knowledge. To move away from those framings, knowledge must be reconstructed through power shifts within relationships. We argue that intentional shifts within pedagogical power relations can at once reveal and alter prevailing local relations of power. Such a pedagogy does not escape institutional power relations but rather addresses them as sites of experimental and emergent inquiry.

Thompson, Janna. Aesthetics and the Value of Nature. *Environ Ethics*, 17(3), 291-305, Fall 95.

Like many environmental philosophers, I find the idea that the beauty of wildernesses makes them valuable in their own right and gives us a moral duty to preserve and protect them to be attractive. However, this appeal to aesthetic value encounters a number of serious problems. I argue that these problems can best be met and overcome by recognizing that the application of natural environments and the appreciation of great works of arts are activities more similar than many people have supposed.

Thompson, Janna. What Do Women Want? Rewriting the Social Contract. *Int J Moral Soc Stud*, 8(3), 257-272, Autumn 93.

Social contract theory, including that of Rawls, has almost always presupposed that the social contract which founds political society or determines principles of justice is made by male heads of families. What changes in the theory, if any, would be required if women were to be incorporated more centrally into the social contract story? I consider and criticize Susan Okin's attempt to revise Rawls's theory so that it can underwrite feminist demands for justice for women. I argue that more radical changes to the social contract story are required in order to take into account the concerns and needs to women and men who regard their obligations to their children, and others who depend upon them, as central to their lives.

Thompson, Manley. Things in Themselves. *Proc Amer Phil Ass*, 57(1), 33-48, S 83.

Thompson, Nicholas S. The Many Perils of Ejective Anthropomorphism. *Behavior Phil*, 22(2), 59-70, Fall-Wint 94.

Thompson, Patricia J. Dismantling the Master's House: A Hestian/ Hermean Deconstruction of Classic Texts. *Hypatia*, 9(4), 38-56, Fall 94.

Classical philosophy adopts the standpoint of males in the Greek *polis*. The consequent adumbration of the standpoint of women and noncitizen men in the *oikos*, the household, has implications for feminist philosophy. Two systems of action are differentiated: the domestic economy protected by the goddess Hestia, and the political economy protected by Hermes. Shifting one's standpoint to include both the *oikos* and the *polis* offers an alternative to gender as the defining issue in feminist theory.

Thompson, Paul (ed). *Issues in Evolutionary Ethics*. Albany, SUNY Pr, 1995.

Thompson, Walter J. Aristotle: Philosophy and Politics, Theory and Practice. *Amer Cath Phil Quart*, 68(Supp), 109-124, 1994.

Thompson, Walter J. Perspectivism: Aquinas and Nietzsche on Intellect and Will. *Amer Cath Phil Quart*, 68(4), 451-473, Autumn 94.

Thomson, Ernie and Osbrun, Jerry R. Discussion: Just Another Simi Valley Jury: The Supreme Court and the Death Penalty. *Phil Forum*, 26(1), 78-83, Fall 94.

This paper challenges an argument by C Meyers that the Supreme Court ruling in *McCleskey v. Kemp* (1987) was "just" despite clear evidence of death sentencing discrimination in Georgia. Meyers argues that McCleskey deserved his sentence and the fact that others similarly situated were not so sentenced did not change that fact. We argue that the evidence of racial discrimination was clear, and that the conservative Court majority distorted this evidence in reaching a blatantly *unjust* decision. *McCleskey* (1987) is clearly in the racist tradition of Dred Scott (1857) and *Plessey v. Ferguson* (1896) and represents a reversal of the attempt to remove racial discrimination from our legal system.

Thorkildsen, Theresa A. Toward a Fair Community of Scholars: Moral Education as the Negotiation of Classroom Practices. *J Moral Educ*, 23(4), 371-385, 1994.

This paper reviews research on student's concepts and theories of fair and effective educational practices and casts them as insightful critics of schooling who should be included in the negotiation of academic practices. Formal interviews show that students consider the goal or definition of the situation when evaluating the fairness of practices, and that conceptions of fairness develop differently for each type of situation. Students also hold different theories about how school should be defined and which situations should predominate. Moral education programmes could encourage students and teachers to negotiate fair classroom practices, creating a community of scholars who collaborate to build more fair and effective schools.

Thorne, Debbie M and Fraedrich, John and Ferrell, O C. Assessing the Application of Cognitive Moral Development Theory to Business Ethics. *J Bus Ethics*, 13(10), 829-838, O 94.

Cognitive moral development (CMD) theory has been accepted as a construct to help explain business ethics, social responsibility and other organizational phenomena. This article critically assesses CMD as a construct in business ethics by presenting the history and criticisms of CMD. The value of CMD is evaluated and problems with using CMD as one predictor of ethical decisions are addressed. Researchers are made aware of the major criticisms of CMD theory including disguised value judgments, invariance of stages, and gender bias in the initial scale development. Implications for business ethics research are discussed and opportunities for future research delineated.

Thorp Jr, John M (& others). Integrity, Abortion, and the Pro-Life Perinatologist. *Hastings Center Rep*, 25(1), 27-28, Jan-Feb 95.

Thurman, Robert A F. "Social and Cultural Rights in Buddhism" in *Human Rights and the World's Religions, Rouner, Leroy (ed)*, 148-163. Notre Dame, Univ Notre Dame Pr, 1988.

Thurnher, Rainer. "Der Rückgang in den Grund des Eigenen als Bedingung für ein Verstehen des Anderen im Denken Heideggers" in *Europa und die Philosophie, Gander, Hans-Helmuth (ed)*, 129-141. Frankfurt/M, Klostermann, 1993.

Tidman, Paul. Conceivability as a Test for Possibility. *Amer Phil Quart*, 31(4), 297-309, O 94.

Tidman, Paul. Logic and Modal Intuitions. *Monist*, 77(3), 389-398, Jl 94.

Tienson, John and Horgan, Terence. A Nonclassical Framework for Cognitive Science. *Synthese*, 101(3), 305-345, D 94.

David Marr provided a useful framework for theorizing about cognition within classical, AI-style cognitive science, in terms of three levels of description: the levels of i) cognitive function, ii) algorithm and iii) physical implementation. We generalize this framework: i) cognitive state transitions, ii) mathematical/functional design and iii) physical implementation or realization. Specifying the middle, design level to be the theory of dynamical systems yields a nonclassical, alternative framework that suits (but is not committed to) connectionism. We consider how a brain's (or a network's) being a dynamical system might be the key both to its realizing various essential features of cognition—productivity, systematicity, structure-sensitive processing, syntax—and also to a nonclassical solution of (frame-type) problems plaguing classical cognitive science.

Tienson, John and Horgan, Terence. Soft Laws. *Midwest Stud Phil*, 15, 256-279, 1990.

According to the standard philosophical conception of scienctific law, proper laws permit no exceptions within their own domain. We argue, to the contrary, that proper laws in intentional psychology virtually always have exceptions within their own domain—psychological exceptions, as opposed to "had a stroke" or "hit by a bus" exceptions. These soft laws, as we call them, have ineliminable *ceteris paribus* clauses. The argument draws on a critique of classical cognitive science, which embodies the standard conception of law. We also argue that, given the proper understanding of law, psychological explanation requires laws.

Tieszen, Richard. "Mathematics" in *The Cambridge Companion to Husserl, Smith, Barry (ed)*, 438-462. New York, Cambridge Univ Pr, 1995.

Tietz, Udo. Zur hermeneutischen Transformation der Sprachanalyse. *Deut Z Phil*, 42(5), 861-881, 1994.

Tijmes, Pieter. "The Technological Universe" in *Ecology, Technology, and Culture*, Zweers, Wim (ed), 247-261. Cambridge, White Horse, 1994.

Tiles, J E. Applying the Term 'Mental' in a World without a Within: Dewey's Realism. *Trans Peirce Soc*, 31(1), 137-166, Wint 95.

Dewey proposed a criterion for the application of the term 'mental' which can be fruitfully compared to the criterion proposed by Franz Brentano. Dewey's criterion clearly avoids the pitfalls of Cartesianism in a way that Brentano's criterion clearly does not, explains how 'intentional objects' can exist in mental states ('intentional inexistence') without inviting the toils of subjective idealism, and clarifies Dewey's self-proclaimed 'naive realism.'

Tiles, J E. Education for Democracy. *Stud Phil Educ*, 13(3-4), 261-271, 1994-95.

Using as an illustration the special features of the Hawai'i program for philosophy in the schools, this article argues that certain oral skills ("disciplined conversation") deserve a place in the curriculum alongside the traditional "Three R's". The theoretical basis for this argument draws on the social and political theories of John Dewey (this, above all, is the skill needed by members of a democratic culture) but, it is noted, the proposal amounts to a reintroduction into the curriculum of a skill highly prized in the ancient and medieval world, dialectic.

Tiles, Jim and Tiles, Mary. *An Introduction to Historical Epistemology: The Authority of Knowledge*. Cambridge, Blackwell, 1993.

The issues of epistemology are introduced in historical context by relating them to authority disputes. After a comparison between Francis Bacon and Plato, the remainder of the book is structured around Bacon's four idols, or obstacles to knowledge. Successive chapters thus discuss the relation of knowledge to language (idols of the market), speculation (idols of the theater), perception (idols of the tribe), and social formation (idols of the cave). Placed in its historical context, epistemology is seen to be something which philosophy should not abandon, for it is an important part of the arena in which questions of cultural authority are worked out.

Tiles, Mary and Tiles, Jim. *An Introduction to Historical Epistemology: The Authority of Knowledge*. Cambridge, Blackwell, 1993.

The issues of epistemology are introduced in historical context by relating them to authority disputes. After a comparison between Francis Bacon and Plato, the remainder of the book is structured around Bacon's four idols, or obstacles to knowledge. Successive chapters thus discuss the relation of knowledge to language (idols of the market), speculation (idols of the theater), perception (idols of the tribe), and social formation (idols of the cave). Placed in its historical context, epistemology is seen to be something which philosophy should not abandon, for it is an important part of the arena in which questions of cultural authority are worked out.

Tilghman, B R. "Architecture, Expression, and the Understanding of a Culture" in *Philosophy and Architecture, Mitias, Michael H (ed)*, 51-66. Amsterdam, Rodopi, 1994.

The eighteenth century included architecture among the fine arts, but was embarrassed by its connection with utility. The eighteenth century defined art in terms of beauty and the nineteenth century turned beauty into expression. The problem for architecture is to connect its utility with expression. Philosophical and ontological theories of the 'aesthetic object' are no help in understanding expression in art. Expressiveness in architecture can be understood in part as the way a building shows an understanding of the culture it is constructed to serve. The North American railroad station and the fast food restaurant serve as examples.

Tilghman, B R. *An Introduction to the Philosophy of Religion*. Cambridge, Blackwell, 1994.

This book is intended for students with no previous training in philosophy. Its topics are confined to issues arising primarily out of Judaism and Christianity and include the traditional arguments for the existence of God, the question of biblical truth and the doctrine of biblical inerrancy, the relation between religion and science and religion and ethics. It is argued that religion is best understood as a way of life rather than as a matter of believing various doctrines. Remarks about logic and philosophical method are made in course.

Tilghman, B R. Reply to Professor Cebik's "Secondary Language and Secondary Art". *J Aes Art Crit*, 52(4), 464-466, Fall 94.

Professor Cebik has argued that my contention in *But is it Art?* that many aesthetic descriptions are best understood as examples of words used in secondary senses is mistaken. In this brief reply I argue that he has misunderstood much of what I say about secondary sense, that he has failed to take account of the setting of the notion of secondary sense in *Philosophical Investigations* II, xi, and that he has failed to take account of the philosophical problems I invoked it to resolve.

Till, James E and Meslin, Eric M and Sutherland, Heather J. What's Missing from Current Clinical Trial Guidelines? A Framework for Integrating Science, Ethics, and the Community Context. *J Clin Ethics*, 5(4), 297-303, Wint 94.

The purpose of the work was to produce a framework to guide the development of meritorious clinical trial proposals. The framework consists of essential features of rigourous methodology, ethical acceptability, and a component referred to as "community context". These three domains were woven together in a checklist format under the headings of general, scientific and ethical considerations. Since texts concerning clinical trial methodology do not integrate ethics criteria and ethics guidelines do not provide detailed scientific criteria in obvious and practical ways, we outline a more contemporary and comprehensive set of guidelines.

Tillemans, Tom J F. Dharmakirti and Tibetans on *Adrsyanupalabdhihetu*. *J Indian Phil*, 23(2), 129-149, Je 95.

The article investigates Dharmakirti's (7th century Buddhist logician) position on arguments which invoke nonperception (anupalabdhi) in order to prove nonexistence. There is one variety of anupalabdhi known as nonperception of imperceptible things (adrsyanupalabdhi) which is particularly controversial. Generally, modern writers have taken Dharmakirti to assert that this variety of anupalabdhi is always fallacious, but we argue that this is not the best reading of Dharmakirti, nor is it that of the Tibetan commentators. In the last part of the article we try to trace when and where this Tibetan interpretation of adrsyanupalabdhi was developed.

Tilley, John. Two Kinds of Moral Relativism. *J Value Inq*, 29(2), 187-192, Je 95.

Tilley, John. Virtue and Choice in Aristotle's *Ethics*. *Philosophia (Athens)*, 23-24, 173-179, 1993-94.

In this study—divided into three parts—the writer tackles with the problem of "acrasia" (nic Ethics VIII). Firstly, a separation of actions into voluntary and involuntary is made with reference to the concept of "acrates". Secondly, four arguments from the same work are examined by means of which it is proved that "acrates" does not choose his own action. Thirdly, the way by which passion influences "acrates" is displayed and the relation between passion and knowledge is examined. In the end, the three stages existing between the "acrates" and the carrying out of his own action are examined. Conclusion refers to the questions and explanations provided by Aristotle himself.

Tilley, Terrence W. *The Wisdom of Religious Commitment*. Washington, Georgetown Univ Pr, 1995.

This text argues that the mainstream approach in modern philosophy of religion in general and religious epistemology in particular is engaging in rational theology rather than philosophy of religion. It claims that the key issue is not the rationality of religious belief or the entitlement to hold specific religious propositions, but the wisdom of making or keeping a commitment to specific religious traditions. After arguing for a "practical" philosophy of religion, for a broadened definition of religion, and against the sufficiency of the epistemologies of R Swinburne, A Plantinga, and W Alston, the text goes on to display an articulated account of *phronesis* in general and in particular with regard to religious commitment.

Tilliette, Xavier. Claudel philosophe. *Gregorianum*, 75(4), 705-721, 1994.

Tilliette, Xavier. La filosofia cristiana secondo Edith Stein. *Aquinas*, 37(2), 389-394, My-Ag 94.

Timmermans, Benoît. Descartes et Spinoza: de l' admiration au désir. *Rev Int Phil*, 48(189), 327-339, 1994.

Why is admiration the first passion according to Descartes, while it is desire which is the first of affects according to Spinoza? This apparent opposition hides an evolution from a concept of *difference* between man and the object of his passion as "exterior", to a concept of the same difference, this time considered as "interior".

Tindale, Christopher W. Totipotency and the Value of Embryonic Cells. *J Value Inq*, 28(4), 519-528, D 94.

Much of the debate surrounding human embryo experimentation takes its departure from positions in the abortion debate, but the opportunity that *in vitro* fertilization has provided for the laboratory observation of dividing embryonic cells has prompted further arguments founded on a new understanding of the nature of the human embryo. One argument centers on the use of the term "pre-embryo" and claims made about the totipotency of each embryonic cell, that is, its potential in the early stages of growth to develop into a complete organism. I examine whether "pre-embryo" does refer to an identifiable entity and discuss the significance which totipotency has to each side of the experimentation debate.

Tindemans, Klaas. Verhaal en beslissing: Notities bij Bert van Roermunds *Recht, verhaal en werkelijkheid*. *Alg Ned Tijdschr Wijs*, 86(3), 224-238, Jl 94.

The central theme of *Recht, verhaal en werkelijkheid*, by Bert van Roermund, is the 'interception-hypothesis': any narrative unit in the legal discourse can be read in two directions. Facts lead to interpretation, but this interpretation leads equally to a restatement of the facts. Between these two strategies of reading, no hierarchy can be installed; any choice is 'political'. Van Roermund's hypothesis is confronted with Derrida's notion of 'indecidability' in justice and law (see *Force de loi*). Derrida's observations shed a revealing light on Van Roermund's interpretation of Hans Kelsen's *Staatslehre*, which he sees as a radically democratic political theology.

Tinnin, Louis. Conscious Forgetting and Subconscious Remembering of Pain. *J Clin Ethics*, 5(2), 151-152, Sum 94.

The author of this commentary on "Informed Consent to Amnestics" (in the same journal) agrees that physicians use amnestic medication as anesthesia deceptively, allowing patients to believe they have been spared pain when they have only been spared the conscious memory of the pain. The author gives a theoretical explanation of how subconsciously remembered pain can cause later harm and warns physicians about this consequence of the use of benzodiazepine drugs to replace true anesthetics. It should be possible to alleviate the felt pain by some method that would influence the patient's subconscious appraisal of the sensations during the procedure.

Tipton, Paul and Haight, Catherine and Whitman, Jeffrey P. Citizens and Soldiers: Teaching Just War Theory. *Teach Phil*, 17(1), 29-39, Mr 94.

Using the core curriculum course on ethics and just war theory taught at the US Military Academy as an example, this paper offers some guidelines on how to incorporate instruction in just war theory into similar ethics courses at other colleges and universities. Furthermore, arguing that there is a real need for the public to understand just war concepts, this paper presents an overview and prescription for informed citizenship in the post-cold war age.

Titiev, Robert. Causal Troubles. *J Phil Res*, 20, 281-286, 1995.

The focus of this article is upon just one particularly problematic condition among seven espoused by Honderich in *A Theory of Determinism*, where he sets forth a counterfactual theory of causality using certain kinds of nomic conditionals. Analysis of his fifth requirement shows it not only to be subject to a variety of counterexamples, but also to be in conflict with Honderich's remarks about experimental testability in connection with claims expressed using nomic conditionals. Honderich has acknowledged that some fine tuning is needed in order to reach a suitable formal rendition of his requirement, but the nature of the new troubles pointed out here indicates that serious flaws lie at the heart of his requirement.

Tiwari, D N. Bhartrhari's Philosophy of Relation between Word and Meaning. *J Indian Counc Phil Res*, 11(2), 43-54, Ja-Ap 94.

The purpose of the paper is to elucidate Bhartrhari's philosophy of relation specifically on the ground of cognition as accomplished by language in communication. To accept relation as eternally dependent natural-fitness of the word is logically justified since his philosophy assumes a language as the only given reality and takes meaning as that revealed nondifferently by it in the mind. Cognizably and communicatively relation is not a relatation. It is neither a signified nor a signifier but is the fitness of the latter. The word is naturally fit to express all meanings and convention restrains the natural-fitness on account of which fixed meaning is cognized by a fixed word. As per expectancy of cognition as revealed and as caused by language the natural-fitness is explained by Vaiyakaranas as expressor-expressed and as cause-caused relation respectively.

Tiwary, N P. Gandhian Conception of Brahrmacharya. *Darshana Int*, 32(3/127), 40-43, Jl 92.

Todd, D D. The Fine Awareness of Martha Nussbaum. *Dialogue (Canada)*, 33(2), 305-312, Spr 94.

Toeplitz, Karol. On Some Paradigms of Ecumenical Dialogue. *Dialogue Hum*, 3(3), 59-71, 1993.

Tokarczyk, Roman A. *Bibliografia Prac: Romana Andrzeja Tokarczyka*. Lublin, Daimonion, 1992.

The main purpose of the work is presentation a short biography of Roman Andrzej Tokarczyk b.1942 and complete list of his publications from 1966-1991. Continuation on separate attached pages. The work is written in Polish and English. The results of Roman Tokarczyk's research which have been published in many countries of the world can be divided into five thematic groups: 1) methodology and history of doctrines of natural law, 2) methodology and history of political doctrines, 3) comparative law and political thought, 4) theory of law, politics and management, 5) works on the history of Maria Curie-Sklodowska University in Lublin, and especially of the Law Faculty.

Tokarczyk, Roman A. Universal Dimensions of Natural Law. *Dialogue Hum*, 4(2-3), 127-137, 1994.

The purpose of the work is to explain how the principal message of natural law would be realized by the establishment of a universal, global and ethically good social order. Natural law in many respects is essentially characterized by universalism. Among all other functions, that it has performed in human history, its influence on the formation of social order deserves special attention. Conceptions of natural law developed first in the European tradition and were transferred to the tradition of American thought. Natural law in other great traditions—Africanism, Judaism, Islam, Hinduism, Confucianism, and Buddhism—is studied from European and, above all, American point of view.

Tolhurst, William E. Moral Experience and the Internalist Argument Against Moral Realism. *Amer Phil Quart*, 32(2), 187-194, Ap 95.

Anti-realists have argued that moral realism cannot adequately account for the reason-giving status of moral beliefs. They claim that the putative objectivity of moral facts would prevent them from having the universal motivational power which their status as moral reasons for action would seem to require. This article aims to show that this argument is not a compelling reason for rejecting moral realism. I begin by developing a full statement of the argument that exposes the key theoretical assumptions. It is then argued that there is a crucial ambiguity in two of these assumptions. I conclude by showing that a proper appreciation of the motivational efficacy of moral experience provides the moral realist with good reason to reject the only plausible nonequivical interpretation of the argument.

Tolle, Susan W and Buchan, Melissa L. Pain Relief for Dying Persons: Dealing with Physicians' Fears and Concerns. *J Clin Ethics*, 6(1), 53-61, Spr 95.

Tomar Romero, Francisca. La Concepción de la Metafísica en Gabriel Marcel. *Sapientia*, 49(193-4), 273-295, 1994.

The object of this article is to analyze the peculiar concept of the metaphysics of Gabriel Marcel. Secondly, we examine the content of two of his most important works on metaphysics: *Journal Metaphysique* and *Position et approches concrètes du mystère ontologique*. Finally, in an attempt to expound Marcelian metaphysics in an orderly and systematic fashion, we explore the meaning and content of such key ideas in Marcel's metaphysics as the concept of "problem", "mystery", "ontological mystery", "being", "ontological exigency", "having", "primary reflection", "secondary reflection", "God", "liberty", "fidelity", "hope", and "love", among others.

Tomar Romero, Francisca. La Escala de los Seres en la Filosofía de Tomás de Aquino. *Rev Espan Filosof Med*, 0, 225-238, 1993.

Tomasi, John. Community in the Minimal State. *Crit Rev*, 8(2), 285-296, Spr 94.

If communitarian political philosophers such as Michael Sandel are right about the importance of genuine community commitment, then it is the liberal minimal state, rather than the more expansive state implied both by communitarianism and by Rawlsian welfare liberalism, that should be preferred. It is contended that Sandel's antiliberal arguments, while inadequate as a criticism of Rawls's particular formulation of liberalism, nonetheless contain an important challenge to rights-based political theories generally. However, by considering the various senses in which individual rights can be said to draw lines between persons, it is shown how the classical liberal might meet Sandel's challenge.

Tomasi, John. Kymlicka, Liberalism, and Respect for Cultural Minorities. *Ethics*, 105(3), 580-603, Ap 95.

Tomasini Bassols, Alejandro. Contrafácticos. *Analogia*, 4(2), 87-100, 1990.

In this paper I argue that no single theory of counterfactuals is possible, for they fulfill a variety of linguistic functions. I examine their utility in logic, empirical theories and natural language and try to show that their roles are completely different in each case.

Tomasini Bassols, Alejandro. Dos Concepciones del Lenguaje. *Analogia*, 8(2), 37-72, 1994.

My aim here is to criticize Chomksy's views on language from the point of view of Wittgenstein's later work. I first present their respective positions and then carry out a critical examination of some fundamental Chomskian assumptions (it makes sense to speak of unconscious knowledge, thoughts are in the head, etc.) and principles, like the Fregean composition principle according to which the sense of a sentence is a function of the senses of its parts. Against Chomsky I raise substantial, conceptual and methodological objections. I try to make clear why innatism cannot satisfy the Wittgensteinian requirement that language be learnable (or teachable). I contrast Chomsky's "mythological explanations" with the grammatical analyses on the same topics carried out by Wittgenstein.

Tomasini Bassols, Alejandro. Dos Nociones de Objeto en el *Tractatus*. *Analogia*, 7(2), 101-114, 1993.

My aim in this paper is to criticize and contrast the traditional interpretation of Tractarian objects as metaphysical (mysterious and unknowable) entities, with another interpretation, inspired both by Wittgenstein's own *dicta* in the 30 and by an idea of B F McGuinness, according to which the first part of the book contains a myth and not an "ontology". In this interpretation, the idea of an object is a presupposition of language since, through induction, it enables us to connect experience (appearances) and meaning in a regular way. Thus an object is rather like a law for the systematic construction of statements about what we know by acquaintance.

Tombs, David. 'Shame' as a Neglected Value in Schooling. *J Phil Educ*, 29(1), 23-32, March 95.

The first part of the paper examines the significance of shame values in South Asian societies and the implications of this for schools. The second section considers the common anthropological distinction and disjunction between "shame culture" and "guilt culture". The third section draws on the recent study of Ancient Greece by Bernard Williams. Williams suggests that the conflict between shame values and may have much to contribute to ethical thought, exposing weaknesses in contemporary Kantian moral outlooks and contributing to fuller conceptions of personal autonomy and personal identity, thus holding, as the final section indicates, important educational implications.

Tomek, Václav. The Historical Experience of Czech Anarchism. *Filozof Cas*, 42(5), 805-820, 1994.

This historical and intellectual wandering of Czech anarchism in the last decades of the 19th century and the early 20th century are a definite part of modern Czech history. At first dynamic and active, it was eventually frittered away by its own ranks and amended in the light of an assumed practical extent and historical reality. In order to bring this idea of political reality into effect, the idea itself was eventually so amended in the light of historical reality that even its supporters declared it to be a distant dream, an aging theory, while the authoritative reality of the communist dictatorship in Russia after the first World War was accepted as the path of acts and deeds in the right direction. Those who supported the idea of freedom as opposition to all authority felt that it was possible to temporarily sacrifice their own principles, to allow a temporary denial of freedom on the path to liberation. The historical experience of Czech anarchism has shown that such an idea of freedom can have consequences in the historical content that reach far beyond the direct present and can have a general validity for the historical experience of society.

Tomlinson, Thomas and Czlonka, Diane. Futility and Hospital Policy. *Hastings Center Rep*, 25(3), 28-35, My-Je 95.

Decisions to withhold futile resuscitation without the consent of patients or families are defensible on ethical grounds, but the concerns frequently expressed against such authority suggest a number of safeguards necessary for implementing a trustworthy hospital policy on futile CPR. The article concludes with an outline of an ideal policy.

Tondl, Ladislav. Time Direction, Philosophy of Technology, and Technology Assessment. *Filozof Cas*, 43(1), 65-79, 1995.

The presented study emphasizes the significance of time order and chronological problems in the sphere of philosophy of technology and technology assessment. The present conceptions of time order and time metrics are connected with causal processes which are asymmetrical and irreversible and are linked to the changes of entropy. This conception was developed—particularly from the philosophical point of view—by H Reichenbach. The author introduces Reichenbach's concept of "time direction" into the conception of the origin, development and function of technical artefacts. The introduction of time metrics is particularly significant in the projects of technology assessment. The dynamical behaviour of technical artefacts is connected with the tendency of the growth of entropy level and, therefore, also with the decrease of the value of utility function of the technical artefact.

Tonelli, Giorgio and Chandler, David H (ed). *Kant's "Critique of Pure Reason" within the Tradition of Modern Logic: A Commentary on its History*. Hildesheim, Olms, 1995.

The world of Kant scholarship was electrified in 1974, when Giorgio Tonelli presented a brief summary of his life's work. His was a meticulous study; the plethora of sources shaping Kant's world, particularly the nature and scope of logic. Tonelli found widely held interpretations of Kant to be inadequate, even wrong. At the end of that brief summary, given at the Fourth International Kant Congress in Mainz, Tonelli promised to publish a book with the detailed justification for this rethinking of Kant. Here is that book. Tragically Tonelli's life was cut short. Though he had hoped to include more chapters, the evidence Tonelli provides is ample in the three he was able to complete. Kant scholars will find it necessary to reconsider received interpretations and assumptions in light of this ground-breaking work.

Toney, Howard. Consent of the Citizen: A Discussion on Distinguishing Enforced Tendance from Tendance Voluntarily Accepted. *Polis*, 12(1-2), 188-203, 1993.

For Plato only the leadership of wisdom, controlling appetites and desires, enables individual or community to achieve man's end purpose of a virtuous life. The *Statesman* surmises the emergence of an 'ideal' ruler who needs neither laws nor people's willing consent. The idea remains a philosophical dream. Plato exposes its impractibility then introduces the cultural concept of politically educated, well-informed and experienced citizens having equal rights and opportunities to argue for change. Enlightened citizens can consent to wise self-leadership validated by prior knowledge. Plato's definition of political consent remains a target for citizenship rights.

Tong, Lik Kuen. "Act, Sign, and Consciousness: Thinking Along with Ricoeur" in *The Philosophy of Paul Ricoeur, Hahn, Lewis Edwin (ed)*, 511-527. Peru, Open Court, 1994.

This essay is an attempt to engage Ricoeur in a creative dialogue by thinking along with him on the central theme of his reflective philosophy—the theme of appropriation. Focusing on Ricoeur's notion of the founding act of selfhood and in terms of the interrelationships of act, sign, and consciousness, the discussion explores the presuppositions and fundamental implications, and assesses the strengths and weaknesses, of his hermeneutic phenomenology not only against the tradition of reflective thought in the West but also from the vantage point of a salient contrast between Eastern and Western philosophies on the perennial problematics of selfhood.

Tong, Rosemarie. Towards a Just, Courageous, and Honest Resolution of the Futility Debate. *J Med Phil*, 20(2), 165-189, Ap 95.

This essay discusses the history of the "futility debate" and the motives that sometimes prompt health care professionals, health care providers, patients, and surrogates to take different sides in it. Changes in the health care system, financial responsibility shifts, technical medical advances, and medical care rationing are analyzed as contributors to the futility debate. So too are variations in the definition of futility examined as part of the current controversy. The respective attitudes of professionals, providers, patients and surrogates in accepting the goals, capabilities, and limits of medicine are also explored. In particular, the lack of honest communication between health care professionals/health care providers on the one hand and patients/surrogates on the other is acknowledged as a major roadblock in the building of care-focused futility policies. Finally, various initial attempts of hospitals to create futility guidelines are evaluated in order to detect problem areas and to suggest lines of improvement.

Tong, Rosemarie (ed) and Tuana, Nancy (ed). *Feminism and Philosophy: Essential Readings in Theory, Reinterpretation, and Application*. Boulder, Westview Pr, 1994.

A collection of articles covering both theoretical and practical discussions of key issues in contemporary feminist philosophy. The anthology is designed to enable readers to understand what differentiates each of the feminist perspectives Liberal, Marxist, radical, socialist, psychoanalytic, ecological, phenomenological, postmodern, and anarcha feminists. Each feminist perspective sheds light on what is absent as well as what is present in traditional philosophy. The essays also illustrate the ways in which feminist philosophers make the kinds of distinctions that matter in women's everyday lives.

Tongqi, Lin and Minghua, Li. Subjectivity: Marxism and "The Spiritual" in China Since Mao. *Phil East West*, 44(4), 609-646, O 94.

Toombs, S K. The Lived Experience of Disability. *Human Stud*, 18(1), 9-23, Ja 95.

In this paper I reflect upon my personal experience of multiple sclerosis in order to provide a phenomenological account of disability. The phenomenological notion of lived body provides important insights into the profound disruptions of space and time that occur with loss of mobility. In addition, phenomenology discloses the emotional dimension of physical disorder. Loss of upright posture is particularly significant since it diminishes autonomy and affects relations with others. A phenomenological account of the lived body disruption engenderd by disability has important implication with respect to the clinical and social challenges posed by chroneic disabling disorders.

Topolski, Jerzy. "A Non-Postmodernist Analysis of Historical Narratives" in *Historiography Between Modernism and Postmodernism, Topolski, Jerzy (ed)*, 9-85. Amsterdam, Rodopi, 1994.

The main claim of the work is that the concept of truth is indispensable in historiography, with the proviso that one cannot speak about truth or falsehood of a single sentence because it cannot be extracted from a given narrative without the destruction of the latter. One may accordingly either completely discard realism with respect to historical narratives or else accept some of its nonnaive versions. It is further claimed that from such a point of view both narrative wholes which we encounter in historical narratives and similar concepts found in natural science have the same cognitive status. Truth in historiography is always involved in the context of a given historian's beliefs, and the narrative itself is an intricate structure in which one can single out three layers (aspects): the informative, the persuasive (rhetorical), and the ideological (controlling). This implies the necessity of accepting the existence of many truths in historical narratives, the value of which is determined by empirical practice. (edited)

Topolski, Jerzy (ed). *Historiography Between Modernism and Postmodernism*. Amsterdam, Rodopi, 1994.

The volume deals with fundamental problems of the philosophy of history discussed by experienced authors. The practice of historians is confronted with the postmodernist philosophical project. The main thesis of the column can be subsumed under the statement of one of its authors F R Ankersmit that owing to the attention on text we have lost our naivety with regard to the historical text and have become aware, for the first time, of the extent to which the representation of the past is structured by the hidden deep structure of the historian text. In particular studies or papers such problems as truth, metaphor, causality, paradigms, time in historiography and didactic of history are analyzed.

Topolski, Jerzy. The Kinds of Time in Historical Narration. *Dialogue Hum*, 4(1), 101-109, 1994.

Torbert, William R and Smith, Beverly A and Lichtenstein, Benyamin M. Leadership and Ethical Development: Balancing Light and Shadow. *Bus Ethics Quart*, 5(1), 97-116, Ja 95.

What makes a leader ethical? This paper critically examines the answer given by developmental theory, which argues that individuals can develop through cumulative stages of ethical orientation and behavior (e.g., Hobbesian, Kantian, Rawlsian), such that leaders at later developmental stages (of whom there are empirically very few today) are more ethical. By contrast to a simple progressive model of ethical development, this paper shows that each developmental stage has both positive (light) and negative (shadow) aspects, which affect the ethical behaviors of leaders at that stage. It also explores an unexpected result: later stage leaders can have more significantly negative effects than earlier stage leadership.

Torek, Paul. Liberties, Not Rights: Gauthier and Nozick on Property. *Soc Theor Pract*, 20(3), 343-361, Fall 94.

In *Morals by Agreement*, David Gauthier attempts to derive property rights from a moral principle called the Lockean proviso. The derivation fails, and the true implications of the moral principles which Gauthier invokes are quite different. These principles imply that persons have extensive liberties to use physical materials, but relatively few rights against interference by others in this use. Robert Nozick argues for an extensive system of property rights in *Anarchy, State, and Utopia*; his argument fails for similar reasons.

Toribio, Josefa. Causal Efficacy, Content and Levels of Explanation. *Log Anal*, 34, 297-318, S-D 91.

The aim of this paper is to develop an account of the causal efficacy of content that both avoids epiphenomenalist objections and that doesn't require the discovery of inner symbols in the computational modelling of such contentful mental states. A sufficient condition to guarantee the causal efficacy of semantic properties is formulated. It is shown that, when analyzed at the proper level of description, connectionist models can be vindicated as causally efficacious semantic engines.

Toribio, Josefa. Une crítica al realismo desde la teoría del significado. *Rev Filosof (Spain)*, 4(5), 13-29, 1991.

Toribio, Josefa and Clark, Andy. Doing without Representing?. *Synthese*, 101(3), 401-431, D 94.

Connectionism and classicism, it generally appears, have at least this much in common: both place some notion of internal representation at the heart of a scientific study of mind. In recent years, however, a much more radical view has gained increasing popularity. This view calls into question the commitment to internal representation itself. More strikingly still, this new wave of anti-representationalism is rooted not in 'armchair' theorizing but in practical attempts to model and understand intelligent, adaptive behavior. In this paper we first present, and then critically assess, a variety of recent anti-representationalist treatments. We suggest that so far, at least, the sceptical rhetoric outpaces both evidence and argument. Some probable causes of this premature scepticism are isolated. Nonetheless, the anti-representationalist challenge is shown to be both important and progressive insofar as it forces us to see beyond the bare representational/nonrepresentational dichotomy and to recognize instead a rich continuum of degrees and types of representationality.

Toribio Mateas, Josefa. De causalidad mental y conexionismo. *An Seminar Metaf*, 27, 39-58, 1993.

The aim of the paper is to develop an account of the causal efficacy of content that both avoids epiphenomenalist objections and that doesn't require the discovery of inner symbols in the computational modeling of such contentful mental states. A sufficient condition to guarantee the causal efficacy of semantic properties is formulated. It is shown that, when analyzed at the proper level of description, connectionist models can be vindicated as causally efficacious semantic engines.

Torok, Maria (ed) and Rand, Nicholas T (ed). *Rhythms: On the Work, Translation, and Psychoanalysis of Nicolas Abraham*. Stanford, Stanford Univ Pr, 1995.

Rhythms outlines in four essays a phenomenology of poetic consciousness; the creation of temporality through poetic rhythm; a literary esthetics based on psychoanalytic and phenomenological principles; a field of research concerned at once with literary criticism, translation, and psychoanalysis. The essays offer a new approach to the problem of literary creation an psychoanalytic definition of temporality, both seen in terms of a dynamic interplay between expectation and surprise, between unforeseen incidents and the modes of their integration. *Rhythms* forms a sequel to Abraham's previous work in *The Wolf Man's Magic Word* and *The Shell and the Kernel*.

Torralba Roselló, Francesc. Metafísica del ser y de la Vida en Santo Tomás. *Rev Espan Filosof Med*, 0, 239-250, 1993.

En este trabajo vamos a estudiar el significado del término "ser" y del término "vida" en los textos de Santo Tomás de Aquino. Vamos a tratar de descifrar el contenido semántico de estos vocablos y poner de relieve la relación significativa entre ambos. Qué es el ser? Qué es la vida? Qué vínculo existe entre ser y vida? Qué es primero desde el punto de vista ontológico? Qué es más perfecto? Estas son algunas de las cuestiones que planteamos en el presente artículo.

Torrance, John. *Karl Marx's Theory of Ideas*. New York, Cambridge Univ Pr, 1995.

Torres, Carlos Alberto. Education and the Archeology of Consciousness: Freire and Hegel. *Educ Theor*, 44(4), 429-446, Fall 94.

A key influence in Freire's philosophy is that of Hegel. This article analyzes the links between Hegelian thought and the political philosophy of education developed by Freire, especially in his seminal work Pedagogy of the Oppressed. The main thesis advanced in this article is that the dialectics of Pedagogy of the Oppressed have been deeply influenced by the logical structure of Hegel's dialectics. However, Freire's pedagogical and political utopia has transformed the epistemological principles in Hegel's logical structure, producing Freire's "Aufhebung" of Hegelian dialectics.

Torres, Fernando. Poder Político e Imperio en Dante Alighieri. *Analogia*, 9(1), 79-99, 1995.

Cuál fue el camino conceptual que dirigió y dio consistencia lógica a las argumentaciones de Dante para defender el principio de la unidad política teriamente resqueboajado en la Europa del s. XIII? Le trata de dilucidar las razones que llevaron al guan poeta florentino a defender el Imperio cristiano universal como continuación, síntesis y plenitud de la construcción estatal del genio romano clásico. En este trabajo se procura cotejar y contrastar las tesis imperiales en el ámbito del Derecho político con las posturas reacias contrarias al poder político supremo enconruado en el Emperador legítimo. Tembién se procura esbozar cuál es la significación meta-histórica y cultural del divino vertice de unidad equilibrada representado por el Eón o constante filosófica de la Unidad Imperial del Poder Supremo como instrumento de pacificación impoviendo la Justicia.

Torrico, Vitaliano. Marxismo y Hermenéutica. *Analogia*, 4(2), 69-86, 1990.

Toshimitsu, Isao. Is Aesthetics Dreary?—Scope and Limit of Analytic Aesthetics (in Japanese). *Bigaku*, 45(3), 1-11, Wint 94.

From the second half of the 1940's to the first half of the 1960's, as is generally known, the linguistic analytic method has dominated over Anglo-American aesthetics. Recently this aesthetics, now called analytic aesthetics, has been retrospected and reexamined by the various sides. Then, we also would like to analyze and loom up its primitive figure, focussing on the William Elton (ed); *Aesthetics and Language* (1954). In our view, analytic aesthetics can be characterized by the following three aspects, that is, its presupposition, theme and aim. 1) Analytic aesthetics presupposes that the aesthetic discourse must be fundamentally empirical scientific, and based on the fact or its experience. 2) Its main theme is to analyze the ambiguous concepts and propositions, and to clarify the aesthetic discourse. 3) Its final aim is to take up the position that there is no such thing as essence in art and, therefore, no criterion for the judicial criticism. And J A Passmore once called aesthetics which searches for essence or the general properties dreary. Our conclusions, however, is that not aesthetics proper but analytic aesthetics is dreary, for the latter never affords any insights about aesthetic or artistic phenomena.

Tosi, Lucía. Lavoisier e a Revoluçao Química. *Cad Hist Filosof Cie*, 4(1), 117-138, Ja-Je 94.

Tóth, Cvetka. Adornos Modellanalyse der Freiheit: Metakritik der praktischen Vernunft. *Filozof Istraz*, 14(1), 153-166, 1994.

Die vorliegende Abhandlung befasst sich mit dem Vertändnis Adornos von der Kantschen Freiheitsidee. Das Freiheitsmodell als das erste von drei Modellen der negativen Dialektik weist auf die sog. negative Auffassung der Freiheit hin, die Adorno mit Hilfe Kants zu reflektieren vermag. Dabei zeight Adorno, worin und warum die Kantsche autonome Ethik trotz einiger ihrer irrationalen, abstrakten oder sogar repressiven Aspekte heute noch immer so aktuell ist.

Tóth, Cvetka. Negative Dialektik als begriffliche Antithese zum Begriff. *Filozof Istraz*, 13(4), 939-953, 1993.

Die vorliegende Abhandlung bezieht sich auf die Ansichten Adornos über die Kritik des philosophischen Systems und des methodischen erkenntnistheoretischen Ideals in der Philosophie. In bezug auf seine bekannte Forderung, nach der das philosophische Ergründen auf das Einzelne und Besondere zu übertragen sei, wird in dieser Studie ausführlich auf seine Auffassung der Konstellation und Konfiguration der Wahrheit eingegangen. In diesem Kontext arbeitet Adorno ein sehr spezifisches Verständnis des Essays aus, jedoch in der Bedeutung der begrifflichen Antithese zum Begriff. Abgesehen von Adornos zahlreichen Kritiken des traditionellen Begriffs müsse das Denken die Anstrengung des Begriffs Aufbewahren.

Toulmin, Stephen. "From Clocks to Chaos: Humanizing the Mechanistic World-View" in *The Machine as Metaphor and Tool, Haken, Hermann (ed)*, 139-153. New York, Springer-Verlag, 1993.

Townsend, Dabney. "Metaphor, Hermeneutics, and Situations" in *The Philosophy of Paul Ricoeur, Hähn, Lewis Edwin (ed)*, 193-209. Peru, Open Court, 1994.

This paper is a two part response to Paul Ricoeur's influential hermeneutics of metaphor. Part one considers Ricoeur's position in *The Rule of Metaphor*. Ricoeur uses both analytical and mythopoetic theories to present metaphor as an interaction of text and audience. However, Ricoeur's theory does not provide a way to deal hermeneutically with actual metaphors. Part two attempts to remedy this by applying the situation semantics of Jon Barwise and John Perry to metaphor. The realism of situation semantics allows metaphors to be understood as interactions in which the situation itself is the interpretation. Situation semantics satisfies Ricoeur's hermeneutic requirements concretely.

Townsend, Lucy and Franklin, Betty. Relational Ethics in Writing a Woman's Life. *J Thought*, 30(1), 71-83, Spr 95.

The authors address relational ethics as developed and practiced in scholarly work. The piece documents the unfolding consciousness of the relation between collaborators, and includes an example of work which embodies ethical concerns in biographical research and writing. The authors also track the mentoring relationship which supports this delicate work of reframing the conventions of research and writing to move beyond positivist practice and an assumed static relation between participants in scholarly work.

Toyama, Kikuko. On Discourses on the "Failure of the Avant-garde". *Bigaku*, 45(4), 45-55, Spr 95.

This is an attempt to decipher some representative discourses on the "failure of the avant-garde" and presume a latent structure of denial/repression/exclusion under the origin of modern art, a structure as the other side of self-formation of art with a newly gained myth of autonomy. In order to establish itself as a sublimated domain of high culture, art might have had to throw away everything that could not comfortably fit in with its self-definition. Since modernized "arts" fell into a generic category "Art," this Art seems to have been increasingly marginalized and impoverished, and at the same time given more privileges (if only symbolic ones) in compensation. While the dualism between "high culture" and "low culture" is no longer grounded in reality as firmly as it was once, a renewed device, modernism, was invented to secure imaginary boundaries and to continue the process of autonomization; a more refined and reinforced device of repression, which also is to include the rebellious avant-garde as a momentary release of the repressed. The interrelatedness of modernism and the avant-garde, then, will appear as a conflict between an aesthetics for control and an aesthetics for anarchy.

Tozzi, Michel. Analyse d'Une Expérience de Pédagogie. *Philosopher*, 15, 209-230, 1994.

Tozzi, Michel. Réflexion sur *La Philosophie pour Enfants*. *Philosopher*, 17, 177-190, 1995.

Trabucco, Oreste. Il "Traicté du Feu et du Sel" di Blaise de Vigenère e una sua Sconosciuta Traduzione Italiana. *G Crit Filosof Ital*, 72(3), 418-436, S-D 93.

Trabuchi, Mariela. "Los Acontecimientos en la Filosofía de Wittgenstein" in *Temas Actuales de Filosofía, Palacios, María Julia (ed)*, 607-613. Buenos Aires, Univ Nacional Salta, 1993.

Tracy, David. *On Naming the Present: God, Hermeneutics, and Church*. Hertfordshire, Orbis, 1994.

Traiger, Saul. The Secret Operations of the Mind. *Mind Mach*, 4(3), 303-315, Ag 94.

David Hume is widely believed to be one of the founders of functionalism. His principles of association are seen as an early attempt to articulate a mechanics of the mind akin to Newtonian mechanics. It is argued that this view is based on a failure to appreciate that Hume's skepticism about reason extends to our ability to understand the representation for everyday knowledge. For Hume there are "secret operations" of the mind, operations for which functional explanations are not forthcoming. Hume's place in the history of cognitive science is reevaluated in light of his views on common sense knowledge and belief formation.

Traub, Hartmut. Realität und System: Das Realitätsproblem in Fichtes Theorie der Fünffachheit. *Fichte-Studien*, 6, 435-448, 1994.

Fichte's philosophy is known as a systematical theory of knowledge. The early "Wissenschaftslehre" shows that all categories of understanding, all forms of perception and every consciousness of reality are based on the fundamental experience of the transcendental Ego constituted by itself. Later versions of the

"Wissenschaftslehre" include a more different conception of reality. From the structure of pure reason Fichte deduces five principally possible conceptions of reality and five basic conceptions of feeling and happiness. Materialism, legalism, moralism, religion, and science are the ascending steps to an understanding of reality in its completeness. Speaking of reality in Fichte's philosophy makes it now necessary to point out the systematical context in which the term is used.

Trauzettel, Rolf. Eine grundlegende konzeptionelle Denkfigur der altchinesischen Philosophie. *Convivium*, 7, 15-30, 1995.

Starting with one of Gongsun Long's known sophisms, a pattern of thought is discussed, which underlies certain fundamental discourses in old Chinese philosophy. In that pattern, the whole and their parts are being added. Comparatistical remarks are brought up in this discussion, to show that Western philosophy is not entirely alien to such forms of thinking. It is concluded, firstly, that such a pattern responds to a social logic of political power; and secondly, it appears to be a form of sensegiving and an interpretation of the world proper to the monist conception of the universe.

Traversa, Guido. Il carattere illusorio della critica di Jacques Derrida alla metafisica. *Aquinas*, 36(3), 667-681, S-D 93.

Traversa, Guido. *L'Ente Intermedio: Percepire e Giudicare la Singola Cosa*. L'Aquila, Japadre, 1995.

Travis, Charles. Order Out of Messes: Akeel Bilgrami's *Belief and Meaning*. *Mind*, 104(413), 133-144, Ja 95.

Trejos, Susana. Las apariencias en Vladimir Jankélévitch. *Rev Filosof (Costa Rica)*, 31(75-76), 255-261, D 93.

The problem of appearances in the philosophy of Vladimir Jankélévitch is the problem of reality and validity of perception, and he treats it in 'impressionist' manner. We analyze two positions supposed to be opposed: the exaltation of the appearances in Baltasar Gracian and the statute of appearances in Plato. A new reading on Plato about this topic, based on the sixth book of the *Republic*, is effected, in which a lot of interpretations are contradicted. Beyond the dualism 'to be—to appear', Jankélévitch thinks that reality is situated in becoming.

Tremblay, Bruno. A propos d'un important *prooemium* de S Thomas. *Frei Z Phil Theol*, 41(1-2), 65-90, 1994.

Aquinas' commentary on the *Nicomachean Ethics* begins with a quote from Aristotle: *sapientis est ordinare*. Why did Thomas choose this particular quotation? In answer to this question, I first explore the general intention which guided Aquinas in the writing of his various *prooemia* through a brief consideration of the nature and the purposes of such a discourse, as he conceived it. Next I examine how Aquinas relates *sapientis est ordinare* to the whole of the subject of moral philosophy, and evince the sapiential character which moral philosophy and, especially prudence, assume in the thought of Aquinas.

Tremblay, Jacynthe. La logique de l'auto-Identité absolument contradictoire de Nishida. *Dialogue (Canada)*, 33(4), 595-610, Fall 94.

Trennert-Helwig, Mathias. The Church as the Axis of Convergence in Teilhard's Theology and Life. *Zygon*, 30(1), 73-89, Mr 95.

During the lifetime of Pierre Teilhard de Chardin, the Roman Catholic Church passed through deep changes of doctrines as well as ecclesiastical structures, marked by the First and Second Vatican Councils. In that historical period, the perceived threat of the more and more encompassing theory of universal evolution was the main reason that Teilhard was forbidden to publish anything about its theological or philosophical significance. Teilhard survived these lifelong restrictions within his beloved church by embracing the paradigm of the church as "the axis of universal convergence." His scientific background as a geobiologist gave him the necessary distance from the temporary statements of the magisterium of the Church. Over the whole of human history, however, he believed the Church to be the "phylum" whose development leads to the cosmic Christ as a guidance beam leads to a goal.

Trethowan, Illtyd (trans) and Dru, Alexander (trans) and Blondel, Maurice. *The Letter of Apologetics and History and Dogma*. Grand Rapids, Eerdmans, 1994.

Trias, Susana. La Máxima Hermenéutica "Comprender a un Autor..." en el Pensamiento de Dilthey. *Rev Filosof (Venezuela)*, 19, 41-58, 1994.

The main goal of this article is to establish the meaning that the maxim "to understand an author better..." has in Dilthey's work. In order to achieve this goal, the problems that the maxim generates are presented and its content is established in the previous hermeneutical literature. At last, the meaning of the maxim applied to Dilthey is related to the criticism that the "philosophical hermeneutics" makes toward the "methodological hermeneutics".

Trigeaud, Jean-Marc. La Funzione Legislativa. *Riv Int Filosof Diritto*, 71(4), 620-665, 1994.

Certes, il n'est pas de loi qui n'envisage un ressemblant et par là un genre ou un sous-genre. Mais une chose est une loi qui en fait sa justification, autre chose est une loi qui n'en fait que sa base, son assise, et *justification* n'est pas *fondement*. L'idéal *directif* inscrit dans la connaissance dont procède toute loi doit annoncer la présence de l'altérité, *de cette altérité qui est solidaire de l'intentionalité*. Autrement dit, elle doit accepter que chacun puisse être un "tu", libre et imprévisible, et protégeable en tant que tel, sans suspicion empiriste d'individualisme, avant de le traiter, dans le prolongement, comme un "lui", ce que ne l'enferme donc pas davantage dans une généricité, ou ce qui oblige du moins à considérer cette généricité comme acceptable parce qu'elle est "seconde". Le langage du "tu" n'est pas celui d'un législateur, mais c'est celui *du seul pouvoir qui le fait législateur*, celui de la vérité qui l'investit d'une autorité spécifique.

Trigeaud, Jean-Marc. *Métaphysique et Éthique au Fondement du Droit*. Bordeaux, Biere, 1995.

Il s'agit précisément ici de récuser ensemble le positivisme, les théories de la justice et les droits naturels en une acception abusivement limitative, et de se tourner *vers le donné radical et existentiel de la personne singulière sous la nature abstraite*. Tel est l'ordre du "fondationnel" où l'on peut se placer. Le "fondationnel" indique ce qui est vrai et juste sans avoir à dépendre d'une utilité pratique: il n'est pas exactement "fondateur" come un principe ou un axiome mais il est plutôt causal comme un présupposé. C'est cet ordre qu'explore une enquête à la fois métaphysique et éthique. Elle fuie les doutes des uns et les certitudes des autres, elle se libère de leur formalisme commun, car elle le juge générateur d'exclusion, et elle soustraie ainsi le droit à son essence en le rattachant à une justice qui le dépasse: ele soumet le pouvoir de la volonté et de la raison à l'inconditionnalité de l'être et de l'esprit.

Trigg, Roger. *Rationality and Science: Can Science Explain Everything?*. Cambridge, Blackwell, 1993.

This book defends a realist position, and argues that only on such a basis can reasons be given for trusting science. At the same time, science cannot explain everything, but must itself be given metaphysical foundations in the sense that the nature of reality underlies the possibility of our knowledge. The views of thinkers such as Rorty, Wittgenstein, Quine, and Putnam are considered. The threat of relativism is resisted, whilst the role of reason is firmly upheld.

Trigg, Roger. *Understanding Social Science: A Philosophical Introduction to the Social Sciences*. Cambridge, Blackwell, 1993.

This is intended as an introduction to the philosophy of social science. Its theme is that philosophical presuppositions are a necessary starting point for the study of society. The book uses examples from different areas of social science, and examines controversies about the character of social reality. Throughout the book runs the theme of the relationship of individual to society, and attention is given to the role of human nature, particularly as viewed by sociobiology. Relativism in all its forms is firmly resisted, and the role of rationality emphasized.

Tripathy, Laximan Kumar. Husserl, Heidegger and Wittgenstein: A Crusade Against Scientism. *Indian Phil Quart*, 21/2(Supp), 1-10, Ap 94.

The brief argument which I want to develop in this paper is the suggestion that the thematic of the life-world in Husserlian phenomenology has more or less similar philosophical functions within the tradition of phenomenology as the concept of 'forms of life' has in the philosophy of later Wittgenstein and the concept of 'Everydayness' in the Heideggerian existential epistemology.

Troelstra, A S. Natural Deduction for Intuitionistic Linear Logic. *Annals Pure Applied Log*, 73(1), 79-108, May 95.

The paper deals with two versions of the fragment with unit, tensor, linear implication and storage operator (the exponential!) of intuitionistic linear logic. The first version, ILL, appears in a paper by Benton, Bierman, Hyland and de Paiva; the second one, ILL^{+}, is described in this paper. ILL has a contraction rule, multiple occurences of labels for assumptions are permitted under certain conditions; moreover, there is a different introduction rule for the exponential, $!I^{+}$, which is closer in spirit to the necessitation rule for the normalizable version of S4 discussed by Prawitz in his monograph "Natural Deduction".

Trognon, Alain and Brassac, Christian. Formalizing the Theory of Intentionality. *J Prag*, 23(5), 555-562, My 95.

Troim, David. The Autonomy of Pure Reason in Kant. *Iyyun*, 44, 149-173, Ap 95.

This article analyzes three subjects in Kant's transcendental philosophy: The pure knowledge and its components, the term "a priori", and the status of the definitions of empirical concepts. These three subjects lead, each from a different direction, towards the necessary conclusion summarized in the title of this article. The critique of pure reason does not lead knowledge towards the empirical contents but towards pure self-revelation: An elementary embodiment of the interest of consciousness in its unconditional selfhood, which demands overcoming its interest in what is empirically given, its own nature.

Troncarelli, Barbara. L'Obiezione di Coscienza: A Proposito di un Recente Convegno. *Riv Int Filosof Diritto*, 71(4), 326-335, 1994.

Tronto, Joan C. Care as a Basis for Radical Political Judgements. *Hypatia*, 10(2), 141-149, Spr 95.

The best framework for moral and political thought is the one that creates the best climate for good political judgments. I argue that universalistic theories of justice fall short in this regard because they cannot distinguish idealization from abstraction. After describing how an ethic of care guides judgments, I suggest the practical effects that make this approach preferable. The ethic of care includes more aspects of human life in making political judgments.

Trosborg, Anna. Statutes and Contracts: An Analysis of Legal Speech Acts in the English Language of the Law. *J Prag*, 23(1), 31-53, Ja 95.

This paper is concerned with the language used in legal speech acts in legislative texts and contracts in the field of English contract Law. The central objects of study are regulative functions with a particular view to establishing realization patterns of the rhetorical functions of directive and commissive acts. The findings show that the language of the law characteristically selects patterns of regulatives distinct from, for example, the patterns typically selected in everyday conversational English. The characteristics of the language of the law can be interpreted within the adherence to legal institutions, as well as in terms of the face redress required by the socio-pragmatic situation.

Trout, J D. Austere Realism and the Worldly Assumptions of Inferential Statistics. *Proc Phil Sci Ass*, 1, 190-199, 1994.

I will consider the role of one statistical concept (statistical power) and two statistical principles or assumptions (homogeneity of variance and the independence of random error), in the reliable application of selected statistical methods. I defend a tacit but widely-deployed naturalistic principle of explanation (E): Philosophers should not treat as inexplicable or basic those correlational facts that scientists themselves do not treat as irreducible. In light of (E), I contend that the conformity of epistemically reliable statistical tests to these concepts and assumptions entails at least the following modest or austere realist commitment: (C) The Populations under study have a stable theoretical or unobserved structure that metaphysically grounds the observed values; the objects therefore have a fixed value independent of our efforts to measure them. (C) provides the best explanation for the correlation between the joint use of statistical assumptions and statistical tests, on the one hand, and methodological success on the other.

Trout, J D and Burian, Richard M. Ontological Progress in Science. *Can J Phil*, 25(2), 177-201, Je 95.

In this paper we advance and defend four theses: 1) The ontology of science is intensely compositional and hierarchical; 2) Although much science is reductionistic, the reductionism in question is generally not eliminative; 3) Current philosophers' treatment of the ontology (or ontologies) of science are far too intimately tied to the latest or the "best" theory; and 4) A central form of ontological progress in science consists in obtaining significant contact with, and accurate characterizations of, theoretical entities further and further removed from those that are perceptually available to us. We believe that the fragmentary arguments we advance cumulate to an explanatory potent version of scientific realism.

Trout, Lara M. Can Justice as Fairness Accommodate Diversity? An Examination of the Representation of Minorities and Women in *A Theory of Justice*. *Phil Cont World*, 1(3), 39-45, Fall 94.

The purpose of this paper is to expose a problem of application in John Rawls's theory of justice. An examination of his treatment of the application of his principles in *A Theory of Justice* reveals an insensitivity toward the proper representation of minorities and women. This problem, which is rooted in Rawls's conception of the relevant social position is not properly addressed by him, yet is grounded in inconsistencies which undermine the just practical implementation of his theory. A provisional solution to this problem is to provide the original position with historical information, as well as to place within its jurisdiction the application of the two principles of justice.

Troxell, Eugene A. On Having a Sense of Responsibility. *J Soc Phil*, 25(2), 5-28, Fall 94.

Philosophical discussions of responsibility have dealt with holding persons responsible for untoward events, rather than the proactive exercise of responsibility. Exercise of responsibility has two components: personal autonomy and attention to the "sphere of responsibility." Personal autonomy derives from practical understanding and self consciousness, both of which are also essential to the sphere of responsibility. Sphere of responsibility is composed of: 1) Orientation dimension, or long-range goals; and 2) Collateral dimension, or prediction and avoidance of side-effects of goal directed behavior. Ability to exercise responsibility is regarded as a recent development of human evolution which can be enhanced through education.

Trundle, Robert C. *Ancient Greek Philosophy: Its Development and Relevance to Our Time*. Brookfield, Ashgate, 1994.

In highlighting only the major philosophers of ancient Greece, this book (xvi + 328 pages) not only reveals an overlooked continuity in philosophical development but its astonishing impact on the dynamic ideas and events of our time. The book is a lucid history of philosophy, designed for both students and scholars, with discussions ranging from norms of politeness and changing conceptions of ourselves as men and women to scientific methodologies, moral theories, a metaphysics underlying conservatism and liberalism, and theology. It gives voice to our increasing awareness of the perennial relationship between science, morality, politics, and religion.

Trundle, Robert C. Extraterrestrial Intelligence and UFOs: Challenges to Physics, Metaphysics, and Theology?. *Method Sci*, 27(2), 73-98, 1994.

Are such things as the *Search For Extraterrestrial Intelligence (SETI)* and deep-space probe *Pioneer 10* congruous with the scientific community's cavalier dismissal of vastly superior extraterrestrial technologies and UFOs afforded by them? Without accepting the untarnished veracity of increasing UFO reports, this paper explores them in light of the fallibility of scientific theories and the challenges to theology with respect to both its universality and a revitalized metaphysics of physics.

Trundle, Robert C. Quantum Fluctuation, Self-Organizing Biological Systems, and Human Freedom. *Ideal Stud*, 24(3), 269-281, Fall 94.

COBE-satellite data recently strengthened, if not corroborated, an inflationary model of the Big Bang Theory in which a submicroscopic black hole's fluctuation yields a "chaos" interpretation of the evolution of physical and biological systems. This interpretation of the systems is compared to both a "Block Universe" cosmology articulated by Russell and a "Real Possibilities" view of James and Whitehead. Besides indicating that the latter view allows for the interpretation and that it is consistent with such epistemic notions as Neil Bohr's *correspondence principle*, it is argued that the evolving systems are consistent with novel teleological ideas of freedom and choice once mistakenly associated with quantum mechanics.

Truog, Robert D and Waisel, David. Amnesia Instead of Anesthesia: Not Always a Question of Consent. *J Clin Ethics*, 5(2), 153-155, Sum 94.

Some of the medications used in the practice of anesthesiology primarily produce amnesia, with little or no pain-relieving effect (analgesia). In rare cases, physicians use these agents *instead* of adequate analgesia, and rely on the amnestic effects to avoid patient complaints. In other cases, the best possible anesthesia has been achieved, but is not sufficient to make the patient comfortable. While we believe that the former use of these medications is simply bad medical practice, we argue that in the latter case the decision of whether to use amnestic agents should be based upon the patient's choice and informed consent.

Truss, J K. The Structure of Amorphous Sets. *Annals Pure Applied Log*, 73(2), 191-233, Je 95.

A set is said to be *amorphous* if it is infinite, but is not the disjoint union of two infinite subsets. Thus amorphous sets can exist only if the axiom of choice is false. We give a general study of the structure which an amorphous set can carry, with the object of eventually obtaining a complete classification. The principle types of amorphous set we distinguish are the following: amorphous sets not of projective type, either bounded or unbounded and amorphous sets of projective type. The hope is that all amorphous sets will be of one of these types. Examples of each sort are constructed, and a reconstruction result for bounded amorphous sets is presented, indication that (under certain set-theoretic assumptions) the amorphous sets of this kind constructed in the paper are the only possible ones. The final section examines some questions concerned with the resulting cardinal arithmetic.

Trusted, Jennifer. "Rich and Poor" in *Introducing Applied Ethics*, Almond, Brenda (ed), 289-304. Cambridge, Blackwell, 1995.

This paper addresses the extent to which the affluent have an obligation to help the poor, at home and abroad. There is discussion of the concept of poverty in different societies. Compassion of the poor and guilt regarding their situation is related to notions of benevolence and duty. It is suggested that private charity is inadequate and there must be national and international action. Nevertheless help for the distressed should not eclipse patronage of learning and the Arts; in this respect we have a debt to the future to preserve and develop our cultural heritage.

Tsalikis, John and LaTour, Michael S. Bribery and Extortion in International Business: Ethical Perceptions of Greeks Compared to Americans. *J Bus Ethics*, 14(4), 249-264, Ap 95.

This study investigates the differences in the way bribery and extortion is perceived by two different cultures—American and Greek. Two hundred and forty American business students and two hundred and four Greek business students were presented with three scenarios describing a businessmen offering a bribe to a government official and three scenarios describing a businessman being forced to pay a bribe to an official in order to do business. The Reidenbach-Robin instrument was used to measure the ethical reactions of the two samples to these scenarios. Results indicate that ethical reactions to bribery and extortion vary by (a) the nationality of the person offering the bribe, and (b) the country where the bribe is offered. In addition, Greeks perceived some of the scenarios as being less unethical than did Americans.

Tschumi, Raymond. Résurgences Grecques au fil du Romantisme Anglais. *Diotima*, 22, 66-70, 1994.

Tseëlon, Efrat. "Fashion and Signification in Baudrillard" in *Baudrillard: A Critical Reader, Kellner, Douglas M (ed)*, 119-132. Cambridge, Blackwell, 1994.

Tsouyopoulos, Nelly. Postmodernist Theory and the Physician-Patient Relationship. *Theor Med*, 15(3), 267-275, S 94.

The author discusses the postmodernist claim that the "grand theories" have lost credibility, even in the field to medical science and practice. Rather than representing a shared reality among physician and patient, illness represents two quite distinct realities—the meaning of one being significantly and distinctively different from the meaning of the other. However, existential clinical narratives can function as important bridges between the world of the patient and the world of the physician. Such narratives provide important information regarding the patient's biographical situation and, particularly, the personal and cultural meanings which are a function of the biographical situation. At the same time, these narratives provide physicians with useful information for the practice of medicine.

Tsuboi, Akito and Kikyo, Hirotaka. On Reduction Properties. *J Sym Log*, 59(3), 900-911, S 94.

Tsuji, Marcelo and Doria, Francisco A and da Costa, Newton C A. The Undecidability of Formal Definitions in the Theory of Finite Groups. *Bull Sec Log*, 24(2), 56-63, Je 95.

In this paper a set of *explicit* expressions for a family of finite groups will be constructed in the language of Zermelo-Fraenkel *plus* the Axiom of Choice set theory in such a way that there is no general procedure to decide whether a given expression of this set is representing a finite solvable group or not.

Tuana, Nancy. *Woman and the History of Philosophy*. New York, Paragon House, 1992.

Tuana, Nancy (ed) and Tong, Rosemarie (ed). *Feminism and Philosophy: Essential Readings in Theory, Reinterpretation, and Application*. Boulder, Westview Pr, 1994.

A collection of articles covering both theoretical and practical discussions of key issues in contemporary feminist philosophy. The anthology is designed to enable readers to understand what differentiates each of the feminist perspectives Liberal, Marxist, radical, socialist, psychoanalytic, ecological, phenomenological, postmodern, and anarcha feminists. Each feminist perspective sheds light on what is absent as well as what is present in traditional philosophy. The essays also illustrate the ways in which feminist philosophers make the kinds of distinctions that matter in women's everyday lives.

Tucker, Aviezer. In Search of Home. *J Applied Phil*, 11(2), 181-188, 1994.

This is a philosophical treatment of the phenomenon of *home*. A distinction is drawn between home and permanent residence and birthplace. Through discussion of the philosophy of Vaclav Havel, home is discovered to be a multi-level structure that may contain several homes on different and identical levels. Exclusionist concepts of home such as nationalism and fundamentalist monotheism deny this. Home is conditions that allow personal self fulfillment. Our actual home is the result of our efforts to reach our ideal home, departing from our natural home. Hospitality, personal and collective, is extension of conditions of home to a guest who may be homeless or in exile. The current use of 'home' by inhospitable, excluding, territorial monopolies such as the European Community, the US immigration service, and Hong Kong officials, as in 'returning refugees back home', is an Orwellian misuse of the linguistically assumed, positive relations between person and home to legitimize morally abhorrent policies.

Tucker, Aviezer. Platone e Vico: Una Reinterpretazione Platonica di Vico. *Boll Centro Stud Vichiani*, 24-25, 97-115, 1994-95.

Tucker, J V and Bergstra, J A. The Data Type of Stack Algebras. *Annals Pure Applied Log*, 73(1), 11-36, May 95.

We define and study the class of all stack algebras as the class of all minimal algebras in a variety defined by an infinite recursively enumerable set of equations. Among a number of results, we show that the initial model of the variety is computable, that its equational theory is decidable, but that its equational deduction problem is undecidable. We show that it cannot be finitely axiomatised by equations, but it can be finitely axiomatised by equations with a hidden sort and functions. This class of all stack algebras, together with its specifications, can be used to survey the many models in the literature on stacks in a systematic way, and hence give the study of the stack some mathematical coherence.

Tugendhat, Ernst. "Heidegger's Idea of Truth" in *Hermeneutics and Truth*, *Wachterhauser, Brice (ed)*, 83-97. Evanston, Northwestern Univ Pr, 1994.

Tugendhat, Ernst. La Pregunta de Heidegger por el Ser. *Rev Filosof (Spain)*, 7(11), 3-26, 1994.

Tugendhat, Ernst. Notes on Some Methodological Aspects of Rawls' Theory of Justice. *Filozof Cas*, 42(6), 966-980, 1994.

Tula Molina, Fernando. Del Empirismo al Humanismo: Clave de Lectura y Crítica de la Obra de P K Feyerabend. *Rev Latin de Filosof*, 21(1), 83-104, Fall 95.

I point out a double knowledge ideal in Feyerabend's work. The one that corresponds with his early articles is *empiricist*; the other, related to Mill's pluralistic conception, is *humanist*. In this paper I show critically the consequences of them in several epistemological matters. I reconstruct also the argumentative continuity between those ideals and I propose this *continuity* as a rich comprehension's clue of Feyerabend's work.

Tulipani, S and Cintioli, P. -Completeness of a Fragment of the Theory of Trees with Subtree Relation. *Notre Dame J Form Log*, 35(3), 426-432, Sum 94.

Tully, James. "Rediscovering America: The *Two Treatises* and Aboriginal Rights" in *Locke's Philosophy, Rogers, G A J (ed)*, 165-196. New York, Oxford Univ Pr, 1994.

A study of the chapter 'Of Property' (Ch 5) in the *Two Treatises* to show how it explains and justifies the right of English colonists to settle and acquire land in North America without the consent of the Aboriginal peoples. The justification fails.

Tully, James. *Strange Multiplicity: Constitutionalism in an Age of Diversity*. New York, Cambridge Univ Pr, 1995.

The distinguished political philosopher James Tully addresses the demands for cultural recognition that constitute the major conflicts of today, such as nationalism and federalism, the claims of Aboriginal peoples, feminism, linguistic and ethnic minorities. Tully's survey of four hundred years of constitutional practice shows that neither modern nor postmodern constitutionalism can adjudicate such claims justly, and in *Strange Multiplicity* he instead develops a post-imperial philosophy of constitutionalism capable of bringing peace to the twenty-first century.

Tully, R E. "Sub-Tractatus". *Wittgenstein Stud*, n.a., 1994.

Explicit references to Russell's ideas are numerous in the *Tractatus*. I am less interested in discussing these than the themes which lie just beneath the surface of the text where, I suggest, Wittgenstein was engaged in either correcting or modifying a number of the epistemological and metaphysical views he had encountered in Russell's writings. Chief among these, of course, is the concept of a proposition, a topic which they approached in sharply different ways. But no less interesting are the topics of logical form, internal relations, belief, the Self, the correspondence between Realism and Solipsism, and even the mystical attitude towards the world. (edited)

Tunick, Mark. "Are There Natural Rights?—Hegel's Break with Kant" in *Hegel on the Modern World, Collins, Ardis B (ed)*, 219-235. Albany, SUNY Pr, 1995.

Hegel criticizes Kant's categorical imperative and social contract theory of political obligation, but these criticisms miss the mark, for Kant is not really a consent theorist, nor is his categorical imperative empty. The most distinct break Hegel makes with Kant's philosophy of right is rather his rejection of a theory of natural rights, a theory central to Kant's *Metaphysics of Morals*. While Hegel offers a theory of natural right in some sense, he does not think individuals have natural rights, contrary to what recent commentators (Wood, Smith) suggest.

Tuohey, John F. Moving From Autonomy to Responsibility in HIV-Related Healthcare. *Cambridge Quart Healthcare Ethics*, 4(1), 64-70, Wint 95.

In the first years of the AIDS epidemic, most persons who were HIV positive entered a healthcare system that was HIV negative seeking care. Today, the demographics have changed. This makes it necessary to shift the ethical focus. There is a need to shift from an individual ethic with its emphasis on autonomy and confidentiality, toward a social ethic which emphasizes responsibility: acceptance of the reality of risk in healthcare, acceptance of one's own role in minimizing risks, and holding that the greatest burden for minimizing risk belongs to those who, in the last instance, are capable of doing so.

Tuohey, John F. The Gender Distinctions of Primeval History and a Christian Sexual Ethic. *Heythrop J*, 36(2), 173-189, Ap 95.

Most theories of sexual ethics use the creation narratives of Genesis to argue that the gender distinction necessary for procreation is to be the basis for a Christian sexual ethic. Through an examination of the purpose as well as the nuances of the Hebrew in these texts, this work argues that these narratives seek to minimize all human distinctions. The work concludes that gender complementarity is simply a biological fact. Just as racial distinctions cannot be the basis upon which normative social behavior is prescribed, gender distinctions should not be the basis upon which normative sexual behavior is prescribed.

Tuomivaara, Timo and Kuokkanen, Martti. The Threshold Model of Scientific Change and the Continuity of Scientific Knowledge. *J Gen Phil Sci*, 25(2), 327-335, 1994.

The continuity thesis of the Poznan school threshold model of the growth of scientific knowledge is considered in the light of the example of Van der Waals' and Boyle-Mariotte's laws. It is argued—using both traditional logical means and the structuralist reconstruction of the example—that the continuity thesis does not hold. (edited)

Tuozzo, Thomas M. Commentary on Rowe's "Philosophy and Literature: The Arguments of Plato's *Phaedo*". *Proc Boston Colloq Anc Phil*, 7, 182-191, 1991.

I agree with Rowe that the dramatic context is crucial to an understanding of the dialogues in the *Phaedo*, but understand that context rather differently, especially as concerns the characters of Simmias and Cebes. They are not the philosophical equals of Socrates. Their objections show insight, but their thought is dependent on images (lyre, weaver); their fears do not respond to rational argument. Because the discussion is not among three Socratic philosophers, the arguments in the *Phaedo* cannot simply be divided into those Plato thinks examples of sound philosophical reasoning (recollection and final) and those that Plato includes merely to depict philosophical collaboration and the detection of error (cyclical, affinity). (edited)

Tuozzo, Thomas M. Conceptualized and Unconceptualized Desire in Aristotle. *J Hist Phil*, 32(4), 525-549, O 94.

This essay locates Aristotle's theory of desire within his theory of cognition. Desire, it is argued, is predicative cognition (cognition that 'X is Y') where the predicate is *conative*. When this conative predicate is conceptualized, it is 'good' and the desire is a *boulesis*; when the conative predicate is sensed or "phantasized", it is 'pleasant' and the desire is an *epithumia*. A desire with a conceptualized *subject* can give rise to deliberation, whether the predicate is conceptualized or not. This interpretation proves useful in elucidating Aristotle's account of two important topics in moral psychology: weakness of will and moral education.

Tur, Richard H S. "Accountability and Lawyers" in *Ethics and the Professions, Chadwick, Ruth (ed)*, 58-87. Brookfield, Avebury, 1994.

Turgeon, Marc. L'enseignement de la Philosophie Devant l'approche-Programme et l'éducation Interculturelle. *Philosopher*, 13, 197-204, 1992.

Turiel, Elliot. Making Sense of Social Experiences and Moral Judgments. *Crim Just Ethics*, 13(2), 69-76, Sum-Fall 94.

Turnbull, Kenneth. Aristotle on Imagination: *De anima* iii 3. *Ancient Phil*, 14(2), 319-334, Fall 94.

I interpret three difficult points of Aristotle's doctrine of *phantasia*: whether it is a separate faculty of the soul, its relation to the common sense, and the sense of the analogy between *phantasia* and light. In the third and speculative part of the paper, I discuss how *phantasia* makes possible two sorts of seeing, one practical, one theoretical. I conclude by distinguishing *phantasia* from a modern sense of imagination.

Turner, Charles (ed) and Hrachovec, Herbert. Blumenberg: Truly Memorable Memories. *Hist Human Sci*, 7(4), 61-72, N 94.

An investigation of Hans Blumenberg's "dynamic Platonism" is attempted. It is situated in relation to Husserl's "Mistiftung" and to Wittgenstein's considerations concerning rule-following.

Turner, David H. Transcending Race: Further Reflections on Australian Aboriginal Culture. *Sophia (Australia)*, 34(1), 173-187, Mr-Ap 95.

Turner, J F (& others). Physicians' Ethical Responsibilities under Co-Pay Insurance: Should Potential Fiscal Liability Become Part of Informed Consent?. *J Clin Ethics*, 6(1), 68-72, Spr 95.

Turner, Stephen. Relativism Hot and Cold. *Hist Human Sci*, 7(1), 109-115, F 94.

Two forms of relativism are distinguished from social constructionism. "Cold" relativism appeals to background objects, such as cultures or world-views that have a high degree of stability; hot relativism involves objects such as paradigms that are replaced more frequently. Each object is used in the explanation of belief; neither object is easily reconciled with change in belief. Social constructionism purports to provide an internal account of belief change, based on the concept of practices: practices enable new facts to become accepted, and, through being used in a standard way, become taken for granted. Thus new practices are created through use.

Turner, Stephen P and Factor, Regis A. The Disappearance of Tradition in Weber. *Midwest Stud Phil*, 15, 400-424, 1990.

Late nineteenth century thinkers like Durkheim and Tönnies had the idea that morality was a societal force that impinged on individuals but was experienced as conscience or a sense of obligation. The idea is not found in Weber, who was an individualist. But it is instructive to ask what Weber did with the phenomena that these thinkers took to prove the insufficiency of individualism. The answer is to be found in Weber's classification of action. The phenomena are divided up, and each is explained under different individualist headings, such as habit, but in such a way that nothing remains.

Turoldo, Fabrizio. Omaggio a Bontadini: Osservazioni sulla Coerenza Interna e sugli Sviluppi del Pensiero Bontadininano. *Riv Filosof Neo-Scolas*, 87(1), 137-153, Ja-Mr 95.

Turpia, Piero. Il fantasma di Turing e l'incancellabilità del soggetto. *Aquinas*, 37(2), 417-423, My-Ag 94.

Tuschling, Burkhard. System des transzendentalen Idealismus bei Kant? Offene Fragen der—und an die—Kritik der Urteilskraft. *Kantstudien*, 86(2), 196-210, 1995.

Tuttle, Howard N. *The Dawn of Historical Reason: The Historicality of Human Existence in the Thought of Dilthey, Heidegger and Ortega y Gasset*. New York, Lang, 1994.

This book is a philosophical delineation, analysis, and comparison of the historicality (*Geschichtlichkeit*) of human existence in the thought of Wilhelm Dilthey (1833-1911), Martin Heidegger (1889-1976), and José Ortega y Gasset (1883-1955). Historicality is fundamental for the structure and content of their thought. These thinkers are interdependent and self-consciously interrelated. All of them presuppose that human existence in history requires a discursive thought form that is uniquely appropriate to it. The author labels the birth and development of this form as the dawn of historical reason.

Tweney, Ryan D and Ippolito, Maria F. "The Inception of Insight" in *The Nature of Insight, Sternberg, Robert J (ed)*, 433-462. Cambridge, MIT Pr, 1995.

Insightful discoveries are characterized as emerging from a dynamic blend of context and behavior and this discussion of insight centers on the unfolding of individual process in context. Specifically, the focus is on the resolution of a specific class of optical deceptions by the physicist Michael Faraday. The primary features of the proposed model of insight which emerges include repeated observation of key perceptual events, the generation and selection of inceptions (reconstructed perceptions which operate in ways veridical to reality that can be manipulated independently of the physical world), and the active construction of a workable mental model.

Tye, Michael. Vagueness: Welcome to the Quicksand. *S J Phil*, 33(Supp), 1-22, 1995.

An introduction to the problems, paradoxes, and major theories of vagueness.

Tye, Michael. What What It's Like is Really Like. *Analysis*, 55(2), 125-126, Ap 95.

It is argued, on the basis of some everyday examples, that what it's like is representational in nature.

Tygat, Wim. Learning from the Bell-Inequalities: Causality, Locality and Realism. *Philosophica*, 53(1), 105-122, 1994.

Tyler, Tom R and Kerstetter, Wayne. Moral Authority in Law and Criminal Justice: Some Reflections on Wilson's *The Moral Sense*. *Crim Just Ethics*, 13(2), 44-53, Sum-Fall 94.

Tyman, Stephen. Nietzsche's Passion: The Distraught Spirit and Archetypal Phenomenology. *Int Phil Quart*, 35(1), 5-24, Mr 95.

Tyman, Stephen T. "Ricoeur and the Problem of Evil" in *The Philosophy of Paul Ricoeur, Hahn, Lewis Edwin (ed)*, 451-471. Peru, Open Court, 1994.

Paul Ricoeur is one of the few contemporary philosophers who has faced the problem of evil head-on, without succumbing to a posture dark and tragic. He represents an attempt to assimilate a sense of this most hyperbolically negative human possibility with the hermeneutics of hope and faith. Does he succeed, however, in reaching to the concept of evil as a *position*, rather than, say, a "privation", in the manner of much monotheistic theology? What are the ontological implications of this question?

Tzamalikos, Panayiotis. The Religious Claim of Technology. *Philosophia (Athens)*, 23-24, 62-86, 1993-94.

The question pondered upon in this paper is whether science and technology could be claimed to be a sort of religion. In order to answer this, it is necessary to define what in fact constitutes the religious character of certain manifestations of human life outside the action and function of religion *per se*. That is, in what sense and in what respect, apparently nonreligious actions, institutions and symbols could in essence have a religious character and function. The conditions for this to happen are, first, a conception of religion as a *dimension*, rather than a sphere of human being; secondly, a quasi-religion should be understood within secularism; thirdly, this should be distinguished from pseudo-religion; and fourthly, this should encompass a transcendent ideology. Given these, it is not in fact science, and technology that could be seen as religious forces today. It is rather a distorted conception and function of them, appearing as scientism and technisism. Only in this respect science and technology qualify as quasi-religions. (edited)

Ubel, Peter A and Arnold, Robert M. The Euthanasia Debate and Empirical Evidence: Separating Burdens to Others from One's Own Quality of Life. *J Clin Ethics*, 5(2), 155-158, Sum 94.

Uebel, Thomas E. Otto Neurath's Idealist Inheritance: *The Social and Economic Thought of Wilhelm Neurath*. *Synthese*, 103(1), 87-121, Ap 95.

This paper provides a description and analysis of Wilhelm Neurath's economics and theory of value. Otto Neurath's rejection of a distinct methodology for social science and his insistence on the political partisanship of scientific sociology, I argue, represent his attempt to both continue the practical orientation of his father's theorizing and answer the normative problem his father's theories faced.

Uebel, Thomas E. The Importance of Being Austrian. *Stud Hist Phil Sci*, 25(4), 631-636, Ag 94.

Uffenheimer, Benjamin. "Buber's Socialist and Political Views: A Critique" in *Thinkers and Teachers of Modern Judaism, Goldsmith, Emanuel S (ed)*, 67-82. New York, Paragon House, 1994.

Ujlaki, Gabriella. The "Tacit" and the "Personal": An Aesthetical Approach to the Nature of Knowledge. *Tradition Discovery*, 21(2), 8-10, 1994-95.

Polanyi's post-critical epistemology is empirical and not transcendental but it grounds knowledge in perception; knowledge is thus primarily aesthetical and only partly conceptual. The conceptual is always embedded in the perceptual and comprehension or judgment always has an integrative structure. Polanyi's tacit knowledge is pre-conscious and must be distinguished from the personal which implies conscious commitment. If knowledge produces a cathartic effect, then it is more than merely tacit. The Polanyian revolution in epistemology argues that the human ability to reach truth through use of our cognitive powers is an art.

Ulanowicz, Robert E. Beyond the Material and the Mechanical: Occam's Razor Is a Double-Edged Blade. *Zygon*, 30(2), 249-266, Je 95.

To confine scientific narrative to only material and mechanical causes is to ensure incomplete and at times contrived descriptions of phenomena. In the life sciences, and particularly in the field of ecology, causality takes on qualitatively distinct forms at different hierarchical levels. The notion of formal cause provides for entirely natural and quantitative explanations of ecosystem behavior.

Ule, Andrej. Wille und Wunsch in der Handlung bei Wittgenstein. *Wittgenstein Stud*, n.a., 1994.

Wittgenstein befasste sich mit der Problematik von Wille und Wunsch in allen Phasen seiner Philosophie, besonders in der Betrachtug der "psychologischen Begriffe (Verben)" ('denken', 'vorstellen', 'meinen', 'verstehen', 'erinnern', 'glauben', 'sehen', 'fuehlen', 'beabsichtigen',...). In allen seinen Schriften findet man wichtige Bemerkungen zur Problematik von Wollen und Wuenschen. Oft betrachtet Wittgenstein Wille und Wunsch zugleich, insbesondere bei der Betrachtung der Handlung, aber auch selbstaendig als eigene "Phaenomene". Offensichtlich war diese Problematik fuer Wittgenstein sehr wichtig, doch nirgends hat er sie systematisch ausgebaut oder "in einem Stueck" dargestellt. Ich stelle hier darum nur einige Kennzeichnungen der Auffassung von Wille und Wunsch bei Wittgenstein dar, naemlich ihre grundlegende Differnz, wenn man beide in ihrem Verhaeltnis zur menschlicher Handlung (dem Tun) vergleicht. (edited)

Ulfig, Alexander. Protosoziologie und Diskurstheorie. *Protosoz*, 1, 50-59, Ap 91.

For Protosociology the "Diskurs"-theory has a special significance. Validity-dimensions of speech and their evaluation in the procedure of argumentation indicate generalized presuppositions of interactive processes. These validity-dimensions can be reconstructed in linguistic characterization of "normative language" (P W Taylor). Thus it is possible to make first steps of a theory of validity. Protosociology prove a special reconstruction of argumentative speech on the level "interpersonality, structure of communicative acting and collective identity". The aim of Protosociology within a context of problems of "Diskurs"-theory would have to establish normative values for an evaluation of such validity-dimensions. A logic of "Diskurs" would have to be developed as a kind of logic of "relevance".

Ulfig, Alexander. Was sind reflexive Sprechhandlungen? Bemerkungen zum Verhältnis von Reflexion und Sprache. *Protosoz*, 2, 47-62, Ja 92.

The relationship between reflection and language has become of main interest, not only in the area of philosophy. How is reflection by means of language on language possible? Firstly, I want to discuss the possibility of linguistic reflexivity within the late philosophy of L Wittgenstein. The next step will be a critical analysis of G Frey's "linguistic theory of reflection". This will be followed by an outline of the importance of reflection in context of the speech/act/theory (J L Austin, J R Searle). Finally, I will analyze the problems around linguistic reflexivity within a discourse theoretical framework (J Habermas, K O Apel). It will be questioned if the "discourse" would have to be understood as the linguistic equivalent to "reflection". Then I will be looking at the relationship between discourse and metacommunication. The analysis will end in the attempt of a typology of discoursive-reflexive predicats.

Ulkan, Maria and Meggle, Georg. Grices Doppelfehler: Ein Nachtrag zum Griceschen Modell. *Protosoz*, 2, 16-23, Ja 92.

This paper takes up again Grice's Basic Model (GBM) for analysing communicative acts. We draw attention to a 'new' fault in GBM, i.e., a fault not yet noticed in the literature: Grice's definiens for CA (=communicative attempt) is not only too weak (as it is not satisfying the reflexivity-condition according to which any CA implies the speaker's intention of CA's being understood by the hearer); it is also too strong—and just for the same reason.

Ullian, Joseph S. "On Peirce on Induction: A Response to Levi" in *Peirce and Contemporary Thought: Philosophical Inquiries, Ketner, Kenneth Laine (ed)*, 94-99. New York, Fordham Univ Pr, 1995.

I argue that Peirce had more to offer on the question of induction's justification than Levi has acknowledged. I agree with Levi that Peirce's view of probabilities left him with some problems, but express doubt that he would have welcomed the injection of subjectivism that Levi favors. I contrast Peirce's view of induction with that of Donald C Williams, which it superficially resembles. It is noted that Peirce was the first to use the concept of weight of evidence. I indicate where Peirce anticipated some of Nelson Goodman's worries about regularities and how Peirce's doctrine is equipped to deal with Goodman's new riddle of induction.

Ullmann-Margalit, Edna. On R Dworkin, *Life's Dominion* (in Hebrew). *Iyyun*, 43, 453-464, O 94.

Ulrich, Dolph E. On the Independence of B from I, C, W, K'$_1$, and Karpenko's Formula X. *Bull Sec Log*, 23(3), 96-97, O 94.

Unger, Peter. Contextual Analysis in Ethics. *Phil Phenomenol Res*, 55(1), 1-26, Mr 95.

Already seen successful in other domains of thought and talk, a context-sensitive semantics is provided for the ethical domain. In particular, for the sentence "What you did was morally all right" roughly this indexical analysis is offered? What you did was, in respect of the conditions for acceptability prevalent in this very context, close enough to being in complete conformity with morality. Through the likes of UNICEF, how much vital aid must you provide for your conduct to be morally acceptable? With a very lenient context, providing nothing may be close enough to complete conformity; but, when tough contexts are set, much more must be done for conduct to be *correctly assessed as* morally acceptable.

Unno, Taitetsu. "Personal Rights and Contemporary Buddhism" in *Human Rights and the World's Religions, Rouner, Leroy (ed)*, 129-147. Notre Dame, Univ Notre Dame Pr, 1988.

The article explores the historical expressions of "not-self" (*anatman*) in Early Indian Buddhism, Chinese Hua-yen thought, and Japanese Pure Land Buddhism and raises questions concerning contemporary discussions of personal rights. The teaching of not-self negates anthropocentric and egocentric assertions of the conventional self and advocates interdependence and interconnectedness of all life as more basic than what is ordinarily conceivable by man. Thus, it asks whether it is sufficient to speak of "rights" only for human beings; perhaps there is room to include nature and all forms of animate and inanimate life. Ultimately, when asserting personal rights, we need to deal with the massive self-centeredness at the core of every human enterprise, however noble and desirable.

Urbanek, Adam. Contemporary Non-Conventional Evolutionary Theories. *Dialogue Hum*, 2(1), 133-153, 1992.

Urbani Ulivi, L. Nota sullo scetticismo. *Riv Filosof Neo-Scolas*, 86(1), 154-169, Ja-Mr 94.

Urbas, Igor. A Note on "Carnot's Logic". *Bull Sec Log*, 23(3), 118-125, O 94.

Urmson, James O. "Morality: Invention or Discovery?" in *Medicine and Moral Reasoning, Fulford, K W M (ed)*, 162-170. New York, Cambridge Univ Pr, 1994.

Uroh, Chris. Colonialism and the Language Question: A Reply to Godfrey Tangwa. *Quest*, 8(2), 130-140, D 94.

The basic arguments of this paper is that language, as a means of mutual communication of experience of a people, is their memory-bank. It is the repository of their collective achievements and failures. Thus, language becomes, to a people, the crystal ball with which to reflect or recollect the past, interpret the present, and project into the future. It follows that to deny a people their native language and impose one with different cultural roots on them is to sentence them to a life of perpetual ciris of identity. The paper concludes that, Africa must disentangle itself from the linguistic trap it was caught in through colonisation.

Ursúa, Nicanor. Algunas Vías de Acceso a la Teoría Evolucionista del Conocimiento/Epistemología Evolucionista. *An Seminar Metaf*, 28, 197-208, 1994.

Evolutionäre Erkenntnistheorie/Evolutionary Epistemology is a research field that tries to combine philosophical and scientific elements to approach and to solve old epistemological problems. The EE, dealing with human cognition, includes facts, laws and theories of organic evolution and this trait justifies the epithet "evolutionary". There are some ways that lead, according to G Vollmer, a German representative of EE, to this approach, that is, the ethological, Kantian, psicobiological, linguistic, functionalistic, and philosophical way. All these ways are described in the essay. At the end there are two tables describing: 1) the differences between the EE and the Evolutionary Theory of Science and 2) the answers that the EE gives to some old epistemological questions.

Usberti, Gabriele and Martino, Enrico. Temporal and Atemporal Truth in Intuitionistic Mathematics. *Topoi*, 13(2), 83-92, S 94.

In section 1 we argue that the adoption of a tenseless notion of truth entails a realistic view of propositions and provability. This view, in turn, opens the way to the intelligibility of the *classical* meaning of the logical constants, and consequently is incompatible with the antirealism of orthodox intuitionism. In section 2 we show how what we call the "potential" intuitionistic meaning of the logical constants can be defined, on the one hand, by means of the notion of atemporal provability and, on the other, by means of the operator K of epistemic logic. Intuitionistic logic, as reconstructed within this perspective, turns out to be a part of epistemic logic, so that it loses its traditional foundational role, antithetic to that of classical logic. In section 3 we uphold the view that certain consequences of the adoption of a *temporal* notion of truth, despite their apparent oddity, are quite acceptable from an antirealist point of view.

Uscatescu, Jorge. Actualidad y Perennidad de Vico. *Cuad Vico*, 3, 131-140, 1993.

Turning again to the definitive moment in Vichian studies which was the anniversary of Vico's birth (1968), we investigate the importance of the principle moments before and after the anniversary. Principally, the contemporariness of Vico is shown by his position as the founder of the Philosophy of History, which can be presented as being of eschatological conception of the dynamics of history, in which religion and history are united, an invaluable step in understanding contemporary historical and post-historicist thought. The very contemporariness of Vico is evident by him surviving historicism.

Utke, Allen R. Michael Faraday's Concept of Ultimate Reality and Meaning. *Ultim Real Mean*, 17(3), 167-183, S 94.

Current science textbooks usually rather blandly depict Michael Faraday as having been merely a kindly, introverted, 19th century arch-empiricist who discovered electromagnetism and Faraday's Laws of Electrolysis among several significant scientific discoveries. This paper, however, after a unique, in-depth examination of Faraday's scientific accomplishments, character, paradigm, and concept of ultimate reality and meaning, uniquely concludes that he deserves nominations of being history's greatest scientist, most loved and respected scientist, greatest scientific educator, and most influential person in history, but also consideration as an appropriate modern model for both scientific endeavor and life.

Uus, Undo. *Blindness of Modern Science*. Estonia, APT Ltd, 1994.

Argues that certain methodological principles of modern natural sciences are antiscientific as they preclude the examination of important empirical data: the qualia and the modes of connectedness of components of conscious experiences. Analyzing those data concludes that 1) the seat of mind, the source of activity, and the basis of personal identity of a sentient-volitional being is the immaterial soul, 2) the cognitive abilities of live and artificial intelligence differ radically, 3) the possibilities for exploring the most fundamental aspects of brain functioning are nowadays entirely ignored, and 4) it may prove rather easy to build artificial animating brains.

Uyanne, Frank. Truth, Ethics and Divination in Igbo and Yoruba Traditions: A Reply to Emmanuel Eze. *Quest*, 8(1), 90-96, Je 94.

V Arregui, Jorge. "Yo Pienso" y "Yo Quiero": Razones de una Asimetría. *An Seminar Metaf*, 28, 211-226, 1994.

Vadas, Melinda. Reply to Patrick Hopkins. *Hypatia*, 10(2), 159-161, Spr 95.

Patrick Hopkins has claimed that SM is compatible with feminist principles. I argue that his account relies on both mistaken analogies and an untenable account of the allegedly changed meaning of SM scenes.

Vaden House, David. *Without God or His Doubles: Realism, Relativism and Rorty*. Leiden, Brill, 1994.

Vadnjal, Dan and O'Connor, Martin. What is the Value of Rangitoto Island?. *Environ Values*, 3(4), 369-380, Wint 94.

Contingent valuation has been promoted as a catch-all approach to environmental valuation. While there have been numerous attempts in recent years to place monetary values on environmental amenities, studies have often reported a high frequency of protest, zero or inordinately large dollar-value responses. This paper reports on the results of a survey designed to obtain information on how people actually interpret questions of paying to avoid changes in their views of Rangitoto Island. Evidence suggests that the meaning respondents attach to the actual dollar values they offer or bid are inconsistent with the conventional logic that underlies contingent valuation. Instead, respondents might be seen to be expressing views about how things ought to be in society, and that it is simply not right to develop Rangitoto Island.

Vahid, Hamid. Deductive Closure, Scepticism and the Paradoxes of Confirmation. *Ratio*, 8(1), 70-86, Ap 95.

To undermine much of what we ordinarily claim to know, sceptics have often appealed to a principle (known as the principle of closure) according to which knowledge (justification) is closed under known entailment. In this paper after expounding the views of Stein, Klein and others, I shall argue that they all fail to take note of different contexts in which the principle of closure is applied. The relevance of the principle of closure for scepticism is then analyzed in the light of, what I call, the 'infectious' character of epistemic contexts. I shall also highlight the similarities in the behavior of the concepts of justification and confirmation and appeal to certain solutions to the paradoxes of confirmation to provide a comprehensive account of the different instances of the principle of closure.

Vahid, Hamid. Experience and Justification: In Search of the Epistemic Pineal Gland. *Philosophica*, 53(1), 91-104, 1994.

Faced with the dualism of nondoxastic experiential states and the beliefs they cause, some philosophers have suggested various explanatory and normative mechanisms to bridge the gap between the causal and justificatory roles of experience. In this paper I try to show that these attempts all fail and that their failure in reminiscent of the (failed) Cartesian attempt to identify a point (the pineal gland) whereby mind comes into contact with the body.

Vaidman, Lev. On the Paradoxical Aspects of New Quantum Experiments. *Proc Phil Sci Ass*, 1, 211-217, 1994.

Two recently proposed quantum experiments are analyzed. The first allows to find an object without "touching" it. The second allows to teleport quantum states, transmitting a very small amount of information. It is shown that in the standard approach these experiments are in conflict with the intuitive notions of causality and locality. It is argued that the situation is less paradoxical in the framework of the many-worlds interpretation of quantum theory.

Valadez, Jorge M. The Sociopolitical Implications of Multiculturalism. *Phil Cont World*, 1(2), 41-47, Sum 94.

In this essay, I propose a definition of multiculturalism and provide pragmatic and theoretical reasons for accepting the multicultural perspective when it is defined in this manner. In addition, I discuss and defend three sociopolitical principles to which we are committed in adopting the multicultural perspective and discuss some of the concrete social and institutional changes needed for implementing these principles.

Valadez, Leticia. La subalternación y la conversión aristotélica de las proposiciones. *Topicos*, 4(6), 9-16, 1994.

The author demonstrates the validity of the inference of particular sentences from universal sentences through the Aristotelian simple conversion and accidental conversion of categorical propositions.

Valdés, Margarita M. Cómo es posible aceptar sin contradecirse "debo hacer X" y no aceptar "se debe hacer X"?. *Rev Latin de Filosof*, 20(2), 311-318, 1994.

Valdés, Mario J. "Paul Ricoeur and Literary Theory" in *The Philosophy of Paul Ricoeur*, Hahn, Lewis Edwin (ed), 259-280. Peru, Open Court, 1994.

This essay traces the work of Paul Ricoeur from 1970 to 1990 with concentration on the development of a post-structural hermeneutics and its bearing on contemporary literary theory. Two major books *The Rule of Metaphor* 1975 and *Time and Narrative* 1985 are closely examined in addressing the major issues of literary theory today: relative validity and authority, the function of criticism to provoke a redescription of the reader's values and world-making as a contemporary update to reader response theory.

Valdivia, Benjamín. Ockham: Suposición y Ontología. *Analogia*, 7(2), 141-151, 1993.

Based on Ockham's *Summa Logicae*, this article is intended to present the terms classification related to individual entities and inserted in propositions. Essence of signs is discussed, the same as reference to the world. Ockham states that sign is that which supposes a thing making it comprehensible. Supposition is made clear only in a sentence as a whole, for it is the smallest signification unit (and not the separated terms). It presents, too, conceptions of significativity and truth as qualities of sentences, composed by terms which suppose for an individualized reality.

Valdivia, Benjamín. Sobre Complejidad e Interdisciplina en el Objeto y Método de los Estudios Estéticos Actuales. *Analogia*, 8(1), 151-159, 1994.

Unlike most philosophical fields, Aesthetics is strongly linked to sciences. In this sense, it has been developed both in scientific and philosophic branches. This text affirms that it is possible to connect both. In this aim, it analyzes the whole art process (structured by authors, works and receivers situated all of them in several historic-social circumstances) and analyzes eight outstanding compositional elements. The essay states, against specialized approaches, the fusion of particular procedures and results. To the couple simplicity-unilaterality, it opposes the couple complexity-interdiscipline for a better understanding of the object and method in the Aesthetic field.

Valenza, Robert J and Henry, Granville C. Whitehead's Early Philosophy of Mathematics. *Process Stud*, 22(1), 21-36, Spr 93.

This article examines Whitehead's philosophy of mathematics as revealed by his early works, especially *An Introduction to Mathematics* (1911), *Universal Algebra* (1898), and the first volume of *Principia Mathematica* (1910). The authors argue that Whitehead was mainly an empiricist, perhaps tainted with Platonism, and indicate how his approaches to mathematical generality failed to anticipate the direction of twentieth century mathematics, although—surprisingly—his mature philosophy did.

Valkovic, Marijan. Freedom in Christian Theological Ethics. *Filozof Istraz*, 14(1), 59-66, 1994.

Man's freedom is an essential part of Jewish-Christian anthropology, which is testified to by numerous texts of the Old and New Testaments. Nevertheless, consciousness of the dynamics of sin in human existence leads to many things, already beginning with St Paul, which, from a theological perspective, speaks not only of the limits but also of the internal powerlessness of man's free will (Augustine, Luther, Calvin, 'Jansenism'). Modern determinism, transferring the natural-scientific method to the psychological and sociological area of man's life, closes the door to freedom of this type (e.g., Sartre). In Catholic theological ethics freedom is not only the freedom of choice, but is also so-called 'foundational' freedom, through which man determines his own self, even though there are certain internal 'constants' which, without harm, cannot be ignored. Freedom 'from something' finds its more perfect shape in freedom 'for something'. Freedom is not only a given condition, but is also a task (process), it is integral and encompasses the spiritual and bodily, the personal and social, and even the cosmic in man. It is, finally, a free 'response' to God's 'word'.

Vallance, Elizabeth. *Business Ethics at Work*. New York, Cambridge Univ Pr, 1995.

The book looks at business ethics from the perspective of the business practitioner, but with the rigour of the moral philosopher. It begins by setting business clearly in the context of creating value for its owners and develops a practiced ethical decision model which can be applied to business's hard moral choices. Against this background, some of the major ethical issues which arise in business are explored—in human resource management which arise in business are explored—in human resource management finance, marketing and advertising, the management for the environment and corporate governance. Finally, the book looks at the nature of ethical audit and argues that, in the future, the identification of its ethical values and their integration into its policies and practices, will be a crucial ingredient of a business's success.

Vallée, Richard. Descriptions, référence et anaphore. *Dialogue (Canada)*, 33(4), 611-634, Fall 94.

I examine Strawson's argument from anaphora against the Russellian theory of descriptions, reject some recently proposed solutions (Evans, Neale) and suggest my own account. The latter preserves the Russellian theory of descriptions by introducing text-pronouns, a type of referring terms anaphoric to descriptions, rather than bound by them. The syntax and the semantics of these pronouns is also discussed. In addition, I explore at length the problem of pronomial contradictions and the occurrence of text-pronouns like "he" in sentences like "A man called earlier. Mary believes that he will call back." My claim is that text-pronouns can solve most problems Strawson's argument raises against Russell's views on descriptions. However, as my concluding remarks show, one cannot accept both text-pronouns and Russell's empiricist considerations on referring expressions: using text-pronouns does not require acquaintance with the object referred to.

Vallentyne, Peter. Infinite Utility and Temporal Neutrality. *Utilitas*, 6(2), 193-199, N 94.

Mark Nelson has recently argued that if the future is infinitely long, then utilitarianism loses much of its normative bite. For many actions will produce an infinite amount of utility, and be judged permissible. I have defended a version of utilitarianism that plausibly preserves much of the normative bite in infinite cases. In the present article I defend this version against the criticism, raised by Mark Nelson and Jorge Garcia, that it is not temporally neutral (i.e., indifferent to the distribution of utility over time for any fixed total), and that temporal neutrality is a core commitment of utilitarianism.

Vallicella, William F. Do Individuals Exist?. *J Phil Res*, 20, 195-220, 1995.

Is there room for a metaphysics of existence above and beyond the logic of 'exists'? This paper defends an affirmative answer. It takes its point of departure from a recent polemic of Paul Edwards against Heidegger. According to Edwards, following Frege and Russell, Heidegger mistakenly assumes that existence belongs to individuals. I argue that although Heidegger does indeed make this assumption, he is not mistaken in so doing. My main concern, however, is neither to defend Heidegger nor to reply to Edwards; it is to vindicate the metaphysics of existence against the most damaging objection it faces.

Vallicella, William F. On Property Self-Exemplification: Rejoinder to Miller. *Faith Phil*, 11(3), 478-481, Jl 94.

My defense of the divine simplicity depends crucially on the possibility of property self-exemplification. Barry Miller, though a friend of the simplicity doctrine, rejects the possibility in question. This note provides some considerations in favor of property self-exemplification as well as a response to Miller's objection.

Vallins, David. Production and Existence: Coleridge's Unification of Nature. *J Hist Ideas*, 56(1), 107-124, Ja 95.

Valois, Raynald. La définition et la démonstration dans la logique d'Aristote. *Laval Theol Phil*, 50(2), 349-361, Ju 94.

La définition est l'opération logique qui permet d'expliquer ce qu'est une chose. Cette explication se fait d'abord par la découverte des prédicats essentiels. Mais en ce qui concerne les propriétés des choses, et, d'une certaine façon, la substance elle-même, c'est dans la démonstration qu'on montre ce qu'elles sont. Il y a donc un lien étroit de dépendance entre la définition et la démonstration.

Van Buren, John. Critical Environmental Hermeneutics. *Environ Ethics*, 17(3), 259-275, Fall 95.

Local, national, and international conflicts over the use of forests between logging companies, governments, environmentalists, native peoples, local residents, recreationalists, and others—e.g., the controversy over the spotted owl in the old-growth forests of the Northwestern United States and over the rain forests in South America—have shown the need for philosophical reflection to help clarify the basic issues involved. Joining other philosophers who are addressing this problem, my own response takes the form of a sketch of the rough outlines of a *critical environmental hermeneutics*. I apply hermeneutics, narrative theory, and critical theory to environmental ethics, and use this hermeneutical theory as a method to illuminate the "deep" underlying issues relating to the perception and use of forests. In applying this method, I first take up the analytical problem of identifying, clarifying, and ordering the different interpretive narratives about forests in terms of the underlying epistemological, ethical, and political issues involved. I then address the critical problem of deciding conflicts between these different interpretations of forests by working out a set of legitimation critera to which all parties concerned would ideally be able to subscribe.

Van Buren, John. Heidegger's Early Freiburg Courses, 1915-1923. *Res Phenomenol*, 23, 132-152, 1993.

Van Buren, E John. *The Young Heidegger: Rumor of the Hidden King*. Bloomington, Indiana Univ Pr, 1994.

Part One deconstructs Heidegger's later autobiographical accounts of his early period, demonstrating that the philosopher's famous "turn" after *Being and Time* was in fact also a re-turn to his youthful thought. Part Two examines Heidegger's student years, showing the influences of scholasticism, medieval mysticism, neo-Kantianism, and phenomenology on his thinking during this period. Part Three focuses on Heidegger's early Freiburg period, sketching his project of demythologizing metaphysics and effecting the end of philosophy. Part Four traces the young Heidegger's anarchic, personalist formulations of his new postmetaphysical beginning. Van Buren employs Heidegger's youthful thought to work out strategies for demythologizing problematic aspects of his later thought (such as the eclipse of the personal other, essentialism, ethnocentrism, genderism, and anthropocentrism) and to liberate its more radical countertendencies within contemporary debates.

Van Buren, John. The Ethics of *Formale Anzeige* in Heidegger. *Amer Cath Phil Quart*, 69(2), 157-170, Spr 95.

van Dalen, Dirk. Herman Weyl's Intuitionistic Mathematics. *Bull Sym Log*, 1(2), 145-169, Je 95.

The paper treats the history of Weyl's role in the foundational discussions, his personal contributions to intuitionism and the relation to Brouwer's views. In particular Weyl's views on choice sequences and on logic (quantification) are discussed.

Van De Poel, Ibo. De wereld van de legbatterij. *Kennis Methode*, 18(4), 315-340, 1994.

In dit artikel wordt beschreven hoe het ontwerp van legsystemem voor kippen vanaf eind jaren zestig beïnvloed is door maatschappelijke groepen als de dierenbescherming. Deze poging tot beïnvloeding wordt gezien als een ingreep in de bestaande manier van ontwerpen, zoals die plaatsvond in de ontwerpwereld van de legbatterij. Het concept ontwerpwereld wordt uitgewerkt, en ook wordt aangegeven hoe op basis van dit concept normaliteit en verandering in ontwerpen te begrijpen zijn. Op basis van de case-studie naar veranderingen in het ontwerp van legsystemen wordt een fasemodel voor beïnvloeding van ontwerpen ontwikkeld. Ten slotte wordt deze benadering—die uitgaat van de ontwerpwereld als centraal concept—geplaatst tegenover het SCOT (Social Construction of Technology)-model van Bijker.

Van de Vate, Dwight. Browning's Ontology. *SW Phil Rev*, 11(Supp), 83-91, Mr 95.

Van de Vate, Dwight. Some Notes on Browning's *Ethical Notes*. *SW Phil Rev*, 11(Supp), 63-73, Mr 95.

van den Bossche, Frank. Existence and Non-Existence in Haribhadra Suri's Anekanta-Jaya-Pataka. *J Indian Phil*, 23(4), 429-468, D 95.

In part I of the article the author explains how the problem of negation has led the Jains to accept Nonexistence as well as Existence as constituents or *dharmas* of every real object in the world and to formulate the first dialectical principle of the *Anekanta-vada* doctrine: *sad-asad-rupam vastu* or 'Every real object possesses a mode as an existent and as a nonexistent'. In part II of the article the author explains, using Mereology as a logical tool, how *Haribhadra Suri* defends the Jain viewpoint in his *Anekanta-jaya-pataka*.

Van Den Dungen, Peter. "Justified Warfare and the Relative Value of Human Life" in *Ethics on the Frontiers of Human Existence, Badham, Paul (ed)*, 223-252. New York, Paragon House, 1992.

Van Den Hengel, John. God with/out Being. *Method*, 12(2), 251-279, Fall 94.

The article forms part of a Symposium Issue discussing a draft of a 1978 paper by Bernard Lonergan entitled "Philosophy and the Religious Phenomenon." The article views the problematic relationship between philosophy and theology using the post-modern prism of Jean-Luc Marion's *God without Being*. Marion's refusal of a metaphysical/ontological framework for discourse about God provides a sharpened focus for Lonergan's theological principle of conversion by God's love. The article ends with Ricoeur's attempt to show that the theology-philosophy debate as accentuated by Thomas Aquinas is remarkable similar to the metaphorical-speculative debate of current philosophy.

Van Den Hengel, John and Rigby, Paul and O'Grady, Paul. Must a Hermeneutical Psychoanalysis Exclude Science?. *Man World*, 28(2), 115-128, Ap 95.

Van Der Burg, Wiltbren. *Slippery Slope Arguments* by Douglas Walton. *Inform Log*, 15(3), 221-229, Fall 93.

This is a critical study of Douglas Walton's book 'Slippery Slope Arguments'. I argue that his analysis, though an important contribution to the subject, is unconvincing in three major points. First, the definition of slippery slope arguments is too broad. Second, his pragma-dialectical analysis of fallacies is not very helpful for practical uses, as it only addresses the superficial structure of the argument and neglects the deep structure. Third, the exclusion of emotional and psychologic factors neglect crucial problems, like the question how these factors determine one's perception of empirical processes and of the likelihood of future developments.

van der Dussen, Jan. The Philosophical Context of Collingwood's Re-Enactment Theory. *Int Stud Phil*, 27(2), 81-99, 1995.

Van der Leeuw, Karel L. De studie der Chinese wijsbegeerte in het Westen: Een bibliografisch overzicht. *Tijdschr Filosof*, 57(1), 67-90, Mr 95.

The article contains a short introduction to the historiography of Chinese Philosophy in which the one-sidedness of Western attention for it is stressed, and a critical survey of literature in Western languages. Reviewed are mainly books in English, French, German and Dutch, translations and secundary literature. The literature reviewed is ordered according to main periods in the history of Chinese philosophy and to schools.

Van Der Merwe, W L. Facing the Challenges of Diversity—A Reflection on the Role of Philosophy in South Africa Today. *S Afr J Phil*, 13(4), 190-198, N 94.

The main argument of this article is that one of the primary tasks and challenges of the practice of philosophy in South Africa today entails a thorough and extensive philosophical encounter with the realities of diversity and conflict within the immediate social and intellectual context of our society. Such an encounter may entail a transformation of our practice of philosophy from an almost exclusive 'eurocentric' to a truly 'indigenous' South African one. In this regard reference is made to the importance of certain postmodern appreciations of the nature and importance of sociocultural diversity. Lastly, attention is also drawn to certain valuable possibilities for the mediation of cross-cultural assimilation and intercultural communication, as well as to the role of an 'indigenous', self-reflexively contextualized South African practice of philosophy in this regard.

AUTHOR INDEX WITH ABSTRACTS 781 **Van Fraassen, Bas C**

Van Der Poel, Marc. Rudolf Agricola's *De inventione dialectica libri tres*. *Vivarium*, 32(1), 102-114, My 94.

Van Der Steen, Wim J. Egoism and Altruism in Ethics: Dispensing with Spurious Generality. *J Value Inq*, 29(1), 31-44, Mr 95.

"Egoism" and "altruism" are unprofitable concepts for methodological reasons. by implication psychological egoism and ethical egoism are deeply problematic theses. The article defends the thesis that ethics must be infused with science and allied methodology.

Van Der Steen, Wim J. New Ways to Look at Fitness. *Hist Phil Life Sci*, 16(3), 479-492, D 94.

Many authors have argued that the core of evolutionary biology as represented by the catchphrase 'The fittest survive' is tautological. Concerning the fitness concept of population genetics it is easy to rebut this charge by a proper explication of the term 'survival'. In biology and in the philosophy of biology, various fitness concepts over and above that of population genetics have been elaborated. These concepts, which are called 'supervenient' by some philosophers, have a limited usefulness. On some interpretations they do lead to unacceptable tautologies and circular reasoning. The so-called propensity concept of fitness is problematic in this respect. If interpreted in a proper way, supervenient concepts appear not to allow the formulation of highly general explanations and theories; at best they reveal common patterns among diverse nongeneral explanations and theories. Philosophers cherishing supervenient fitness concepts are apparently motivated by a mistaken search for general theory. The fitness concept of population genetics may play a role in relatively general theories and explanations. Supervenient concepts cannot play such a role. They should rather help us recognize the value of natural history in biology.

Van Der Steen, Wim J. The Demise of Monism and Pluralism in Environmental Ethics. *Environ Ethics*, 17(2), 209-220, Sum 95.

Peter Wenz has recently distinguished various forms of moral pluralism in an effort to dissolve the controversy over monism and pluralism. I argue that the distinctions are not really helpful once the methodology and the substance of science are brought to bear on ethics. Theories in ethics and science alike are subject to context-dependent methodological trade-offs. Hence, the category of theories should be heterogeneous. Monism and pluralism are at cross-purposes since they endorse different unanalyzed notions of theory. Awareness of heterogeneity among theories is helpful in dismissing the controversy.

van der Straaten, Jan. "An Economic Theory of Natural Resources" in *Ecology, Technology, and Culture,* Zweers, Wim (ed), 204-214. Cambridge, White Horse, 1994.

In traditional neoclassical economic theories, environmental problems are defined as negative external effects. It is argued in these theories that the social costs, resulting from polluting production, have to be paid by the polluting industry. However, in most cases it is not possible to calculate these costs. This implies that new starting points have to be developed which can cope with these types of problems. In the paper, a sketch is given of such an approach giving full attention to the functioning of the ecosystem as a guideline for economic theories which means recycling of organic materials and a reduction in the use of fossil energy and raw materials.

Van der Veken, J. *Denken aan al wat is: Een hedendaagse fundamentele wijsbegeerte*. Assen, Van Gorcum, 1994.

van der Wal, Koo. "Technology and the Ecological Crisis" in *Ecology, Technology, and Culture,* Zweers, Wim (ed), 215-246. Cambridge, White Horse, 1994.

From a philosophical perspective the relation between the environmental issue and technology is not an accidental but an internal one: both these phenomena presuppose the symbolic universe that is characteristic of modern culture. Main components of this framework are a mechanistic, disenchanted world view, an operative, activistic ('poietic') model of knowledge and a privileged position (especially in an axiological respect) of man. Into and at the least implicitly 'technical' frame of reference like this the environmental problem is built in. A 'solution' requires an alternative framework in which nature once more can be read symbolistically, nonpoietic forms of contact with reality are rehabilitated and man takes a participatory attitude with regard to nature. For that purpose an appeal can be made to suppressed forms of experience.

van Dijk, Paul. "Theological-Anthropological Reflections on the Environmental Issue" in *Ecology, Technology, and Culture,* Zweers, Wim (ed), 56-62. Cambridge, White Horse, 1994.

It is becoming increasingly more apparent that we cannot keep abreast of the high speed of environmental destruction by healing symptoms from case to case. Besides all the necessary technical, economical and political measures, and regarding just these, it is of great importance to pose a question concerning man's nature: hence the anthropological and ethical question. These elementary basic attitudes are often determined by religion; in our context they are closely related to the cultural tradition of European Christianity. In order to understand the present life-threatening crisis which we face, we should become aware of the way which has led us into the crisis. A cultural-historical analysis of the hidden and often suppressed factors, which have played a role in the development of our attitude towards the surrounding reality, may be of use.

Van Eck, Job. Falsity without Negative Predication: On *Sophistes* 255e-263d. *Phronesis*, 40(1), 20-47, 1995.

There is virtually a consensus of opinion that, whereas in 255e8-257a12 Plato deals with 'not being' in the sense of nonidentity, in 257b1-258c5 he treats negative predication. This last notion of not being is believed to be needed or presupposed in his analysis of falsity in 263. But thus understood the text saddles us with a lot of difficulties. We defend the claim that there is no treatment or negative predication in 257b1-258c5. Thus an interpretation of 255e-263d becomes possible which removes the difficulties. And Plato neither presupposes, nor needs the notion of negative predication in his analysis of falsity in 263.

van Eemeren, Frans H and Grootendorst, Rob. Frans H van Eemeren and Rob Grootendorst Perelman and the Fallacies. *Phil Rhet*, 28(2), 122-133, 1995.

The authors argue that in Perelman and Olbrechts-Tyteca's New Rhetoric no critical analysis of fallacies is to be found, due to its extremely relativistic concept of reasonableness. They discuss a pragma-dialectical alternative approach to argumentation in which a critical-rationalist concept of reasonableness is adopted. Fallacies are pragma-dialectically analysed as incorrect discussion moves because they violate one or more of the rules of a critical discussion aimed at resolving a dispute. The authors argue for the integration of the New Rhetoric and Pragma-Dialectics as a result of which Perelman and Olbrechts-Tyteca's lengthy and detailed discussion of argumentation schemes and techniques is used as a rich source for the analysis of fallacies.

van Egmond, Aad. "Calvinist Thought and Human Rights" in *Human Rights and Religious Values, An-Na'im, Abdullahi A (& other eds)*, 192-202. Grand Rapids, Eerdmans, 1995.

Van Eijck, Jan and De Vries, Fer-Jan. Reasoning about Update Logic. *J Phil Log*, 24(1), 19-45, F 95.

Van Eijk, A H C. Ethics and the Eucharist. *Bijdragen*, 55(4), 350-375, 1994.

The Lima (or BEM) report was praised for the way it tried to connect baptism, ministry and especially, the Eucharist with ethics. In this connection the unity of the two poles of the ecumenical movement. "Faith and Order" on the one hand, "Life and Work" on the other, is at stake. As a matter of fact, quite a few theologians have, in the recent past, concerned themselves with the link between the Eucharist and (social) ethics. The names of many of them appear in the footnotes of this article. In the text the views of two of them are presented and discussed. They are Markus Barth and Louis-Marie Chauvet. It is shown that, in spite of the different Christian traditions to which they belong (Reformed and Roman Catholic respectively), of the different methods they use and of their rather divergent conceptions of the Eucharist, their concern is very much the same.

Van El, Carla. Sociale theorie en wetenschapsonderzoek: hebben die wat aan elkaar?. *Kennis Methode*, 18(2-3), 205-221, 1994.

In October 1993, a Round Table was organized on reciprocal animations between science studies and social theory. Nine Dutch participants, who work in the field of science studies, discussed the issue with Steven Yearley from the University of Ulster, who at the time was visiting-lecturer on behalf of the Netherlands Graduate School in Science and Technology Studies. Though most participants agreed that science studies run the risk of getting more and more isolated from both society and the academia, they disagreed on the need for a more intimate relation with social theory to solve this problem.

Van Engelen, Fons. On Borel Ideals. *Annals Pure Applied Log*, 70(2), 177-203, D 94.

Van Erp, Herman. Nationalisme versus republikeinse burgerschapszin. *Alg Ned Tijdschr Wijs*, 86(4), 251-269, O 94.

This article advocates a sharp distinction between the vague notion of nation as used by nationalist ideas and the political concepts of civil society and nation as implied by the principle of self-determination of nation states. Nationalism should not be identified with love for ones own nation nor with the promotion of national interests. It can be characterized as a special kind of modern political chauvinism, the causes of which are explained by Gellner's theory of the origin of the modern state. But his concept of nationalism is too wide and neutral for a normative evaluation of nationalism both in its aggressive and in its more gentle emotional forms.

Van Evra, James. Quine and Logical Positivism. *J Phil Res*, 19, 263-271, 1994.

The work of W V O Quine is often held to follow the logical positivism of the Vienna Circle in broad outline, but to diverge from it in crucial particulars. On the basis of recent evaluations of the latter, I argue that the philosophical distance between Quine and the Vienna Circle is less than ordinarily thought, or, most importantly, than Quine himself admits.

Van Eynde, L. Ontological Connivance (in French). *Tijdschr Filosof*, 56(3), 494-525, S 94.

In his *Discourse on Metaphysics*, Leibniz appears to have been thinking of a real and anti-predicative logic which would coincide with the world's inner *logos*. An analysis of Leibniz's teleology exposes the relevance of an intramundane rationality, establishing an epistemology of ontological connivance between the knowing subject and his world. At the same time, this philosophy of the universe of life, thanks to an Aristotelian understanding of force and qualitative interpretation of individuality. The present review of the *Discourse on Metaphysics* draws on phenomenological inspiration as well as particular interest in the interpretations of Leibnizian thought by Herder and Goethe.

Van Fraassen, Bas. Belief and the Problem of Ulysses and the Sirens. *Phil Stud*, 77(1), 7-37, Ja 95.

Van Fraassen, Bas. 'World' is not a Count Noun. *Nous*, 29(2), 139-157, Je 95.

The word "world" has ordinary uses as a count noun, but also a distinctive philosophical use in recent ontology. As to this philosophical use, I shall argue that there is no reason to think that it refers to anything, if indeed it is intelligible at all. The question addressed is not simply whether other possible worlds are real, but also whether the real, actual world exists. If my argument is correct, then there is no reason to think so—or to think that ontology of this kind addresses any real question successfully.

Van Fraassen, Bas C. Fine-Grained Opinion, Probability, and the Logic of Full Belief. *J Phil Log*, 24(4), 349-377, Ag 95.

Personal or subjective probability entered epistemology as a cure for certain perceived inadequacies in the traditional notion of belief. But there are severe strains in the relationship between probability and belief. They seem too intimately related to exist as separate but equal; yet if either is taken as the more basic, the other may suffer. After explaining the difficulties in some detail I will propose a single unified account which takes conditional personal probability as basic. Full belief is therefore a defined, derivative notion. Yet it is easiest to explain the resulting picture of opinion as follows: my subjective probability is only a grading of the possibilities left open by my beliefs. My conditional probabilities generally derive from the strongest belief I can maintain when admitting the relevant condition Appendices will survey the literature.

van Gelder, Tim. What Might Cognition Be, If Not Computation?. *J Phil*, 92(7), 345-381, Jl 95.

This paper refutes the "What else could it be?" argument for the computational conception of cognition by articulating and defending a viable alternative, the dynamical conception. The dynamical conception is introduced by means of a discussion of the watt centrifugal governor for steam engines.

Van Gulick, Robert. "Deficit Studies and the Function of Phenomenal Consciousness" in *Philosophical Psychopathology, Graham, George (ed)*, 25-49. Cambridge, MIT Pr, 1993.

Van Gulick, Robert. Are Beliefs Brain-States? And If They Are What Might That Explain?. *Phil Stud*, 76(2-3), 205-215, D 94.

Van Gulick, Robert. Why the Connection Argument Doesn't Work. *Phil Phenomenol Res*, 55(1), 201-207, Mr 95.

Van Haute, Philippe. Tussen relativisme en absolutisme: Democratie en mensenrechten. *Alg Ned Tijdschr Wijs*, 86(3), 165-182, Jl 94.

The work of Lefort, Lacan and Derrida allows to develop a theory of democracy that avoids a relativistic interpretation of the positions that are defended in the democracy debate, without falling back in an absolutist interpretation of our moral and political values. Lefort's theory of the declarations of human rights, just like Lacan's and Derrida's reflections on the status of the law, makes it possible to describe the democratic experience of the law in such a way that it both obliges and leaves room for essential and legitimate conflict. In this context we characterize democratic politics as essentially determined by a dynamic of rights. In this way it becomes clear why and in what sense democracy has to be understood as both an institution and a way of life (an ethos). In our conclusion we return to the Rushdie case which functioned as our starting point, formulating an alternative line of defense of Rushdie.

van Hooft, Stan. *Caring: An Essay in the Philosophy of Ethics*. Niwot, Univ Pr Colorado, 1995.

Relevant to debates in ethics about virtue and particularism, the central thesis of this book is that caring is a primordial structure of human existence that takes two forms: caring for self and caring for others. This dual form of caring is expressed in a variety of ways including instincts for survival and nurturing; emotions and the cultural construction of our world; pragmatic projects and social forms of solidarity; and religion, ethics and morality. This leads to an argument that the traditional centrality of obligation in morality should give way to commitment understood as a form given to our caring about ourselves and others.

Van Inwagen, Peter. *God, Knowledge, and Mystery: Essays in Philosophical Theology*. Ithaca, Cornell Univ Pr, 1995.

This book contains nine previously published essays, plus a general introduction and a separate introduction for each of its three sections. The introductions are attempts to tie the themes of the essays together and to show how the arguments of the various essays are related to one another. The central topic of the first section is the problem of evil. The second section discussed the confrontation of traditional Christian belief and modern knowledge: evolutionary biology, biblical criticism, and the comparative study of religions. The third section addresses logical problems raised by the doctrines of the Trinity and the incarnation.

Van Inwagen, Peter. Naive Mereology, Admissable Valuations, and Other Matters. *Nous*, 27(2), 229-234, Je 93.

This is a reply to David Sanford's "The Problem of the Many, Many Composition Questions, and Naive Mereology", which appeared in the same issue of *Nous*. Sanford's paper is a criticism of certain presuppositions and conclusions of my book *Material Beings*.

Van Inwagen, Peter. Unger's *Identity, Consciousness and Value*. *Nous*, 27(3), 373-379, S 93.

van Laak, Dirk. Der Nachlass von Carl Schmitt. *Deut Z Phil*, 42(1), 141-154, 1994.

Van Laarhoven, Jan. Titles and Subtitles of the *Policraticus*: A Proposal. *Vivarium*, 32(2), 131-160, N 94.

John of Salisbury's masterpiece (1159) contains an introductory poem, Entheticus, eight books (with prologues), and 166 chapters. Only the last ones have superscriptions which are, however, not headings in our modern sense, but rather a selection of some rubrics, probably made by a scribe or reader. In order to procure a real index of contents, new modern titles are given to the three main parts, the eight books, their subdivisions, and to all the chapters. Moreover, the sections of all the chapters are summarized by short clauses. The proposal may serve as a practical reader's guide to this rich store-house.

Van Langenhove, Luk and Harré, Rom. Cultural Stereotypes and Positioning Theory. *J Theor Soc Behav*, 24(4), 359-372, D 94.

This paper addresses the application of *positioning theory*, a new emerging theoretical scheme on the issue of cultural stereotyping. First, a critical conceptual analysis of the words 'cultural stereotype' is presented. Secondly, the basic tenets of positioning theory are outlined. Finally, it will be demonstrated how the framework of positioning theory can be used to analytically refine the concept of cultural stereotype. The main upshot of the article is that within social psychology, the concept of cultural stereotype is used in a conceptually vague and blurred way and that, with the necessary conceptual refinements, other research-agendas on stereotypes will have to be tackled if social psychologists want to contribute anything to the societal efforts of changing stereotypes.

Van Lente, Harro. Utopie in actie: wat verwachtingen in technologie doen. *Kennis Methode*, 19(1), 41-63, 1995.

Whereas traditional utopia seems to have lost its force in our postmodern age, utopian technologies like the information highway are increasingly powerful. These utopias 'new style' are no longer visions about the good life, but have the status of realistic assessments of our future. The article investigates the efficacy of these expectations and promises in the development of technology from two complementary perspectives. First, it is discussed how actors use expectations as a resource: to mobilize others, to legitimate their actions, to reduce the uncertainty of their complex environment. Second, one can reverse the perspective and ask what expectations do with actors. A key concept is the script of expectations: a description of the world with rolės for actors and artifacts. When the script is 'read', promises are articulated and converted into requirements and other guidelines for action. In this way, expectations coordinate the heterogeneous activities that together create technology.

van Luijk, Henk. Rights and Interests in a Participatory Market Society. *Bus Ethics Quart*, 4(1), 79-96, Ja 94.

In this paper I try to enlarge the scope of the questions commonly treated in business ethics. I first argue that not motives but action structures should form the basis of our analytical endeavours. I then distinguish three basic structures in human action: self-directed, other-including and other-directed actions. These structures, when linked with the concepts of interests and legitimate claims or rights, lead to a taxonomy of moral behaviour, each characterized by a specific set of moral principles and participatory ethics, three distinct realms of moral principles and a special relation between moral agents. My contention is that, up to now, analysis in business ethics has largely been focused on issues in the field of recognitional ethics. The discipline itself as well as ethical practices in business may greatly profit by paying explicit attention to market morality and transactional ethics as well as to the nonenforcable we-alliances of a participatory ethics, increasingly possible and needed in present-day civil society.

Van Luipen, Hans. Teleologie en fysica, en een reactie van A A Derksen op Th Kuipers over waarheidsbenadering. *Alg Ned Tijdschr Wijs*, 86(4), 291-293, O 94.

This article is a comment on a discussion of the strong notion of teleological explanations in nature by Peirce. By this strong notion teleological explanations are really teleologic if they cannot be reduced to causal ones. In this paper it is argued that if the behaviour of a closed system can be described in causal terms, it can also be described in final terms and vice versa. Furthermore an example is given of a closed system which shows the absurdity of the assertion that all statistical explanations are essentially teleologic in the strong sense. It is concluded that the strong notion of teleologic explanations make only sense for open systems.

Van McCrary, S (& others). Physicians' Quantitative Assessments of Medical Futility. *J Clin Ethics*, 5(2), 100-105, Sum 94.

Van Oosten, Jaap. Axiomatizing Higher-Order Kleene Realizability. *Annals Pure Applied Log*, 70(1), 87-111, N 94.

Van Parijs, Philippe. Social Justice and Individual Ethics. *Philosophica*, 52(2), 75-103, 1993.

If one is committed to a "Rawlsian" conception of social justice, is one not also necessarily committed to a "Christian" personal ethics? The paper offers a very partial answer to this question by arguing for two claims 1) Rawls's idea of a well-ordered society does not require maximin-guided individual choice and hence leaves room for legitimate incentive payments. 2) A limited form of patriotism does constitute an individual duty following from a commitment to maximin social justice.

Van Parijs, Philippe. Social Justice and Individual Ethics. *Ratio Juris*, 8(1), 40-63, Mr 95.

If one is committed to a "Rawlsian" conception of justice, is one not also necessarily committed to a "Christian" personal ethics? More explicitly, if one believes that social justice requires the maximinning of material conditions, should one not use one's time and resources as well as one can in order to assist the poorest? The paper offers a very partial answer to these questions by arguing for the following two claims: 1) Contrary to what is implied by some egalitarian critics of Rawls, the idea of a well-ordered society does not require maximin-guided choices at the individual level, and hence leaves room for legitimate incentive payments. 2) Despite Rawls's own neglect of this fact, a limited form of patriotism does constitute an individual "natural duty" following from a commitment to maximin social justice.

van Patten, James. Reflections on the Assessment of the Professoriate. *J Thought*, 30(3), 33-44, Fall 95.

The article explores the accountability movement in higher education with consequent use of multiple forms of faculty evaluation and assessment. Faculty assessment and evaluation originally utilized for improvement of instruction is now being used for promotion, salary appraisal, reappointment, and tenure. Legal factors, a factory model, negative implications of current assessment procedures, and future trends in faculty evaluation are explored. Threats to academic freedom through attacks on tenure in many states require more effective articulation of the philosophical aims and mission of higher education by the faculty and administration in our colleges and universities.

Van Reijen, Willem. Derrida—Ein unvollendeter Habermas?. *Deut Z Phil*, 42(6), 1037-1044, 1994.

In his essay "Das Andere der Gerechtigkeit" (*Deut Z Phil*, 42 (1992) 2, 795-220). Axel Honneth tries to reduce Derrida's philosophy to a supplement to Habermas' philosophy. Van Reijen is arguing that postmodern philosophy (Derrida, Lyotard) cannot be understood as filling the gaps Habermas' philosophy is leaving. Taken seriously post-modern philosophy reveals itself has a negative ontology. The ontological stains of its premisses forbids to integrate it in the pragmatic options of the theory of communicative action.

van Roojen, Mark. Humean Motivation and Humean Rationality. *Phil Stud*, 79(1), 37-57, Jl 95.

The paper examines the Humean Theory of Motivation as a reason to accept an instrumental conception of rationality, and Michael Smith's "direction of fit" arguments for the Humean theory. These arguments must show that there can be no besires, attitudes that combine the functional roles of belief and desire by both responding to evidence and motivating action. Because of rationality constraints on the proper attribution of attitudes the issue turns on the correct theory of rationality. Thus, arguments for the Humean Theory of Motivation must presuppose a Humean or instrumental theory of rationality.

van Veldhuijsen, Peter. Kant and the Eternity of the World: A Historico-critical Reading of the First Antinomy. *Bijdragen*, 56(1), 19-39, 1995.

The question of this article concerns the following problem: How strong is the position of the so-called first antinomy for Kant's thesis, that reason tangles itself up in unsoluble discrepancies when it is occupied with questions that exceed experience? Kant holds the view that regarding the ancient question on the eternity of the world are taken up always two positions (the world is finite contra the world is infinite) that are mutually exclusive, because each for itself claims apodictic argumentation. But from discussions that Thomas Aquinas made with Aristotle and Bonaventure on time and the infinite appears that the argumentation in the first antimony is not so apodictic as Kant imagined. So it seems that there are reasons to doubt if reason gets entangled when it is engaged in matters that exceed experience.

van Veuren, Pieter and Hattingh, Herselman. Identity and the Narrative Structure of Life. *S Afr J Phil*, 14(2), 60-71, My 95.

In this essay the relationship between narrative structure and identity formation is explored. Starting with a discussion of the notion on narratives as MacIntyre uses it in an attempt to provide a more solid basis for moral discussion and meaningful identity formation, the argument progresses to the work of Ricoeur, in an attempt to undermine the usefulness of the teleological narrative (advanced by MacIntyre) and finally to support the idea that much value is to be derived from the nontelelogical narrative, especially in view of our situatedness in a postmodern era.

van Wensveen, Louke M. Is Toughness a Business Virtue?. *Int J Applied Phil*, 9(2), 15-25, Wint-Spr 95.

This article investigates whether the aggregate of so-called "tough" business dispositions and actions is appropriately categorized as a virtue, and if so, whether this virtue is best called "toughness". The author observes that the term "toughness" functions both as a special virtue and as a cardinal virtue in business discourse. As a cardinal virtue it tends to be contrasted to "softness." The strategic benefits of using soft/tough imagery are highlighted, but shown to be undermined by problematic gender connotations. Hence the author proposes the use of alternative terms such as "boldness" and "effectiveness."

Van Woudenberg, René. Alston on Direct Perception and Interpretation. *Int J Phil Relig*, 36(2), 117-124, O 94.

Van Woundenberg, René. Rede, Religie en de Mogelijkheid van Christelijke Filosofie. *Tijdschr Filosof*, 57(2), 267-296, Je 95.

This paper deals with Dooyeweerd's radical thesis, i.e., his thesis that reason necessarily has a 'religious root'. First I argue that the arguments Dooyeweerd puts forward do not warrant his radical thesis. Secondly, I argue that Dooyeweerd's thesis itself is ambivalent between the theses. Secondly, I argue that Dooyeweerd's thesis itself is ambivalent between the theses 1) That religious commitments form the transcendental conditions for philosophical thinking, 2) That religious commitments are constitutive for philosophy, and 3) That religious commitments are regulative for philosophy. Each of three interpretations, I argue, is exposed to serious objections and leads to what Vincent Brümmer has called 'the dilemma of a Christian philosophy'. Since Dooyeweerd's radical thesis is untenable as it stands, so is his justification of this project of a 'Christian philosophy'; and since Brümmers solution to the dilemma is untenable as well, so is his justification of that project. In the last section of this paper I offer an alternative justification for such a project. (edited)

Van Wyk, Robert N. Liberalism, Religion, and Politics Again: A Reply to Gordon Graham. *J Soc Phil*, 25(3), 153-164, Wint 94.

Van Zyl Smit, Dirk. Degrees of Freedom. *Crim Just Ethics*, 13(1), 31-38, Wint-Spr 94.

The increased range of sanctions in modern penal systems means that the loss of freedom suffered by sentenced offenders cannot be characterized by a simple dichotomy between imprisonment and noncustodial sanctions. The implication for the imposition of sentences is that systematic attention must be paid to the equivalence between custodial and noncustodial sentencing options. During the implementation of sentence offenders may be moved administratively from one form of sanction to another. Judicial supervision of this process is of growing importance as administrative decisions determine the degree to which the freedom of sentenced offenders is restricted.

Vance, Robert D. Fiction and the *De Se* Self. *Phil Papers*, 23(2), 89-107, Ag 94.

I argue, against Kendall Walton's attempt to preserve a unified account of fictionality, that propositions which are to be imagined need not be fictional truths, and fictional truths need not be propositions whose imagining is prescribed. I then focus on *de se* imaginings and particularly on a kind of nonpropositional imagining that guarantees self-awareness without thereby representing the self. The *de se* self is this self *qua* unrepresented subject of imaginings. I examine various kinds of art works and nonart objects, arguing that they can all be construed as alluding to appreciators in such a way as to generate fictional truths about them without prescribing imaginings of those propositions. We appreciators, who as unrepresented subjects of experience initiate imaginative projects, thereby belong to a variety of fictional worlds.

Vance, Robert D. Sculpture. *Brit J Aes*, 35(3), 217-226, Jl 95.

Sculptors and art critics emphasize features of sculpture generally ignored by philosophers of art, such as sculpture's dependency on the human body. I examine Walton's account of art and find no good reason to regard sculptures as essentially generators of fictional truths or prescribers of propositional imaginings. In opposition to Wollheim's account, I hold that seeing-in is not wholly appropriate for sculpture and is less fundamental that feeling-in or, more generally, somatic sensation. I conclude that proper appreciation of something *qua* sculpture involves exercising nonpropositional somatic imaginings that generate identification with (some part or aspect of) the sculpture.

VandeCreek, Leon and Bricklin, Patricia M and Bennett, Bruce E. Response to Lazarus's "How Certain Boundaries and Ethics Diminish Therapeutic Effectiveness". *Ethics Behavior*, 4(3), 263-266, 1994.

Vandenberg, Brian. Ripples of Newtonian Mechanics: Science, Theology, and the Emergence of the Idea of Development. *J Mind Behav*, 16(1), 21-33, Wint 95.

The field of developmental psychology has typically traced its history to Darwin or to changes in view about the nature of childhood. What has been generally neglected is how the core assumptions of contemporary theories were forged in the early history of modern science. In particular, the rise of Newtonian mechanics precipitated similar perspectives in geology and then biology. They all converged on a shared set of assumptions about the nature of change in the physical world. Theology also played a key role in this process, serving not only as a foil, but also as a source of important insights for the emerging scientific, and developmental, world view. The field of developmental psychology is a child of this complex and often stormy relationship between science and theology that has shaped Western thought.

Vander Waerdt, Paul A. "Socrates in the Clouds" in *The Socratic Movement, Vander Waerdt, Paul A (ed)*, 48-86. Ithaca, Cornell Univ Pr, 1994.

Vander Waerdt, Paul A. "Zeno's *Republic* and the Origins of Natural Law" in *The Socratic Movement, Vander Waerdt, Paul A (ed)*, 272-308. Ithaca, Cornell Univ Pr, 1994.

Vander Waerdt, Paul A (ed). *The Socratic Movement*. Ithaca, Cornell Univ Pr, 1994.

Vanderschraaf, Peter. Convention as Correlated Equilibrium. *Erkenntnis*, 42(1), 65-87, Ja 95.

This paper presents a new game theoretic definition of conventions, which formalizes the notion of salience and which also generalizes the class of conventions Lewis discusses in his work. I define a convention as a *correlated equilibrium* (Aumann 1974, 1987) satisfying a *public intentions criterion*: Every agent wants his intended action to be *common knowledge*. I argue that many conventions correspond to correlated equilibria that are not Nash equilibria, and that this is consistent with Lewis's general viewpoint. Finally, I argue that game theoretic characterizations of convention, such as Lewis's and my own, help to explain a convention's stability, but that a fully satisfactory account of the emergence of convention requires a theory of equilibrium selection beyond the scope of Lewis's work. (edited)

Vanderschraaf, Peter. Endogenous Correlated Equilibria in Noncooperative Games. *Theor Decis*, 38(1), 61-84, Ja 95.

Most of the results of modern game theory presuppose that the choices rational agents make in noncooperative games are probabilistically independent. In this paper I argue that there is no *a priori* reason for rational agents to assume probabilistic independence. I introduce a solution concept for noncooperative games called an *endogenous correlated equilibrium*, which generalizes the Nash equilibrium concept by dropping probabilistic independence. I contrast the endogenous correlated equilibrium with the correlated equilibrium defined by Aumann (1974, 1987). I conclude that in general the endogenous correlated equilibrium concept is a more appropriate solution concept for noncooperative game theory than the less general Nash equilibrium concept. I close by discussing the relationship between endogenous correlated equilibrium and the game solution concept called *rationalizability* introduced by Bernheim (1984) and Pearce (1984).

Vanderveken, Daniel. On the Ramification of the Fundamental Notions of Meaning, Analyticity, Consistency, Entailment, and Commitment to Speech Acts in Formal Semantics. *J Prag*, 23(5), 563-576, My 95.

The purpose of this reply is to further explain the fundamental semantic notions of linguistic meaning, meaning in context, entailment and commitment. I will show that it is important to distinguish between, on one hand, weak and strong illocutionary entailment between sentences and, on the other hand, weak and strong illocutionary commitments to speech acts. Moreover, I also formulate new bridge principles between propositional and illocutionary logics that enable the semantic theory of speech acts to explicate weak illocutionary commitments.

Vandervennen, Robert E (ed) and Marshall, Paul A (ed). *Social Science in Christian Perspective*. Lanham, Univ Pr of America, 1988.

Vandervert, Larry R. How the Brain Gives Rise to Mathematics in Ontogeny and in Culture. *J Mind Behav*, 15(4), 343-349, Autumn 94.

Within the framework of Neurological Positivism (NP) this article describes how brain algorithms are translated into mathematics in ontogeny and in culture. The purpose is to address seemingly contradictory research findings that suggest that while mathematical axioms are innate, they are not the direct result of processes of selection. It is proposed that self-referencing feedback processes of maximum-power evolution guide the construction of algorithmic isomorphies between preadapted brain algorithms and mathematics. It is concluded that maximum-power evolution as described in NP offers mechanisms that make sense of findings that suggest that mathematical axioms are innate, yet not directly the result of selection as traditionally understood. It is concluded also that these mechanisms provide insight into the often intuitive nature of mathematical discovery.

Vandevelde, Pol. L'aeuvre d'art comme Discours: Heidegger et la Question de la Discursivité. *Heidegger Stud*, 9, 125-136, 1993.

Vannoy, Russell C. "Loving, Appraising, and Bestowing" in *The Nature and Pursuit of Love, Goicoechea, David (ed)*, 73-82. Buffalo, Prometheus, 1995.

Vansina, Frans D and Ricoeur, Paul. "Bibliography of Paul Ricoeur" in *The Philosophy of Paul Ricoeur, Hahn, Lewis Edwin (ed)*, 605-815. Peru, Open Court, 1994.

The bibliography opens with the list of Paul Ricoeur's Honorary Degrees, Awards and memberships in Learned Societies (p 609). Then the primary bibliography offers a quasi exhaustive listing of the books and articles written by Paul Ricoeur and published in fifteen different languages from 1947 up to 1994 (pp 611-735). The secondary bibliography lists the books and only the main articles on Paul Ricoeur's writing published in sixteen languages and covering years 1947 up to 1993 (pp 735-815). Both bibliographies retake and complete an early bibliographical publication: *A Primary and Secondary Systematic Bibliography of Paul Ricoeur 1935-1948* by Faus D Vansina (Louvain-la-Neuve Editions Peeters, 1985). This bibliographical work could only be achieved thanks to the substantial and precious help of Paul Ricoeur himself.

Varikas, Eleni and Löwy, Michael. 'The World Spirit on the Fins of a Rocket': Adorno's Critique of Progress. *Rad Phil*, 70, 9-15, Mr-Ap 95.

Apart from a lecture given in 1962, Adorno never offered a "systematic" or detailed account of his views on progress. Nonetheless, the critique of "progressivist" illusions runs right through his work. It is central to his historical vision and decisively important in the development of his ideas in art, literature and culture. His writings are marked not so much by a vacillation between positive and negative judgments as by a true "dialectic of progress" which both draws upon and participates in the dialectic of Enlightenment. In spite of his melancholy and pessimism, he does not give up the hope in a future humankind emancipated from the fateful magic of interlocking "progress" and "regression".

Varzi, Achille C. Vagueness, Indiscernibility, and Pragmatics: Comments on Burns. *S J Phil*, 33(Supp), 49-62, 1995.

In "Something to do With Vagueness," Linda Burns sustains a deep analogy between the informational and the borderline case variety of vagueness. To this end she argues that the latter is in fact less extraordinary and less disastrous than people in the tradition of Michael Dummett and Crispin Wright have told us. However, the proposed account involves presuppositions which cannot be taken for granted. My purpose here is to take a closer look at some of these presuppositions to weigh them against the arguments, and to show that they may—when left ungrounded—undermine much of Burns's general account.

Vasconcelos, Júlio C R. Um Teorema de Inércia e o Conceito de Velocidade nos *Discorsi* de Galileu. *Cad Hist Filosof Cie*, 3(1-2), 67-83, Ja-D 93.

Unlike tradition, this paper doesn't see any principle of inertia in 1683 Galileo's "Discorsi" ("Two New Sciences"). Though it is possible to find there a pioneer conception of the Newtonian law of inertia, this conception does not act in the "Discorsi" as a principle or as any kind of demonstrative tool, except inside a "scholium", in which Galileo argues, in mathematical terms and through two different "ways", for truth of the so-called "double-distance rule". (edited)

Vasiliu, Florin and Benea, Stefan (trans). *Paradoxism's Main Roots*. Phoenix, Xiquan Pub House, 1994.

Vasoli, Cesare. Sul Vico di Piovani. *Boll Centro Stud Vichiani*, 24-25, 131-161, 1994-95.

Vassallo, Nicla. Interpretations of Boole's Alleged Psychologism. *Epistemologia*, 17(2), 295-328, Ju-De 94.

The aim of this paper is to dispute the thesis according to which Boole is a psychologistic philosopher. That thesis has a long tradition and might have some *prima facie* reasons because Boole thinks it is possible 1) To deduce logical laws from the laws of the operations of the human mind and 2) To discover them by means of consciousness. But I claim that 1) and 2) are not good enough reasons to argue for his psychologism.

Vassallo, Nicla. *La Depsicologizzazione della Logica: Un confronto tra Boole e Frege*. Milano, FrancoAngeli, 1995.

Vasylchenko, Andriy. Interpreting Action as an Answer. *Synthese*, 100(1), 39-48, Jl 94.

The aim of this paper is to introduce a logically grounded approach to action semantics and action interpretation. The main ideal is to present the context of action as a set of questions demanding action to answer. I introduce 1) a basic procedure of action interpretation, which is a reformulation of Hilpinen's semantical procedure for imperatives; 2) a procedure of what-interpretation; 3) a procedure of why-interpretation. The conditions of mutual reducibility of interpretation procedures are explicated. The paper concludes by putting forth the problem of interpretive bounds of moral responsibility.

Vasyukov, Vladimir L. From Ternary to Tetrary?. *Bull Sec Log*, 23(4), 163-167, D 94.

In order to avoid 'suspicious' for logicians ternary accessibility relation in the semantic for R the author has previously proposed its 'bibinary', that is binary plus binary, version (*Bull Sec Log*, 15, 1986, 109-116). Unfortunately, the incompleteness of such a semantic was proved by J M Dunn (*Bull Sec Log*, 16, 1987, 107-110). A new proposal is to exploit another sense of 'bibinariness': now a binary relation is defined on the set of pairs of possible worlds. The equivalence of both semantics is proved and the results have been checked with the help of the computer program.

Vattanky, John. Semantic Competency (Yogyata). *J Indian Phil*, 23(2), 151-178, Je 95.

Vayda, Andrew P. Failures of Explanation in Darwinian Ecological Anthropology: Part I. *Phil Soc Sci*, 25(2), 219-249, Je 95.

In a consideration of explanatory issues raised by their work, Darwinian ecological anthropologists are criticized for their neglect of proximate causes and causal mechanisms; their obliviousness to the importance of causality in current conceptions of explanation; their reduction of Darwinian theory to predictions of fitness enhancement or reproductive success; their "naive functionalism" about fitness benefits as explanations of variations in human behavior; their offhanded presumptions of correlation between fitness and so-called proxy currencies; and their misconstruing confirmation of predictions derived from micro-economic models as constituting explanation and attesting to the power of their version of Darwinian theory.

Vázquez García, Francisco. "Nuestro más actual pasado": Foucault y la Ilustración. *Rev Filosof (Daimon)*, 7, 133-144, 1993.

The reception of the *Aufklärung* in Foucault's work is placed beyond other typical options of the modern thought self-defined as a continuation or rejection of the enlightened rationality. In Foucault's texts, the *Lumières* do not form a legacy of principles that should be prolonged or contested; it is, like the very reason, an event, that is why its condition is polivalent and cannot be set into a purely substantive definition. It may not be relevant the alternative election for or against Enlightenment. The present philosophy continues in the horizon which was opened by the *Lumières*, not because it maintains some supposed conquests, but because it keeps on thinking from the event that inaugurates it.

Vázquez García, Francisco. *Foucault: La Historia como Crítica de la Razón*. Barcelona, Montesinos, 1995.

This book is a general introduction to Foucault's thought and provides an easy understanding of the French philosopher's work. The book is divided into eight chapters. The first three chapters present a synopsis of the major Foucaultian concepts. This philosophical framework is placed in the tradition of a reason's criticism and is founded, not on a formal or trascendental reflection, but on a historical research. The last five chapters present diachronically the philosophical project of Foucault, with an evaluation of this internal rectifications and constants. The book includes a commented bibliography and a selection of fragments from the philosopher.

Vázquez Lobeiras, María Jesús. Nueva Propuesta para una Lectura Genética de la Obra de Kant. *Daimon Rev Filosof*, 8, 189-194, 1994.

Veatch, Robert M. Abandoning Informed Consent. *Hastings Center Rep*, 25(2), 5-12, Mr-Ap 95.

The concept of consent is often viewed as a challenge to the more traditional, paternalistic practice of medicine supported by the Hippocratic Oath. This essay challenges that assumption claiming that *consent* is a concept within the tradition of medicine that assumes that the physician is capable of determining what is in a patient's best interest. Consent involves asking for permission, condoning, or approval, but still based on physician judgments of what is best for the patient. The history of the consent doctrine is examined, alternative theories of the good are explored, and the reasons are given why experts should not be capable of estimating which treatment plans are best for patients. Two alternatives to consent are presented, each designed to facilitate treatments that will better reflect the patient's own values: 1) The liberal alternative based on patients given information about all plausible treatments and choosing among them and, 2) pairing of physicians and patients based on the "deep values".

Veatch, Robert M. Bioethics and Philosophy of Science. *J Med Phil*, 20(3), 227-231, Je 95.

This article introduces a special issue of the *Journal of Medicine and Philosophy* devoted to the relation of contemporary philosophy of science to bioethics. The authors collectively acknowledge the fundamental importance of some version of the necessity of world view or paradigm in shaping the doing of medical science and the practice of medicine that is based on that science. Most of the authors see the inevitable shaping carried out by world view to extend beyond clinical judgment to the doing of the medical science itself. They disagree on how serious a problem this creates. Most authors in this issue are worried about why lay people should be dependent on the practitioners' norms.

Veatch, Robert M. Healthcare Rationing through Global Budgeting: The Ethical Choices. *J Clin Ethics*, 5(4), 291-296, Wint 94.

Increasingly health care is being managed through global budgets by which a health system (national, state, institutional, or departmental) is given a flat, fixed budget and expected to allocate that budget among its patients in some appropriate manner. This means that the allocation decisions are diverted from governmental or executive authorities to managers of health care programs. Almost no attention is being given to the principles upon which these allocations are made. Physicians have been trained to do what is best for the patient and thus resist any attempt to allocate scarce resources. Administrators, on the other hand, are often trained in the techniques of cost-benefit analysis and assume they should allocate so as to maximize the aggregate net benefit per unit of cost. They are practicing utilitarians. This essay looks at a total of six different philosophical principles for allocating a global budget and explores who has the moral and political legitimacy to choose among the principles.

Veatch, Robert M and Stempsey, William E. Incommensurability: Its Implications for the Patient/Physician Relation. *J Med Phil*, 20(3), 253-268, Je 95.

Scientific authority and physician authority are both challenged by Thomas Kuhn's concept of incommensurability. If competing "paradigms" or "world views" cannot rationally be compared, we have no means to judge the truth of any particular view. We distinguish four steps in the process of translating medical science onto clinical decisions: the doing of the science, the appropriation of the scientific findings by the clinician, the transfer of the findings from the clinician to the patient, and the choice of a treatment regimen. Incommensurability can play a role in each stage. There is at least some theory- and value-ladenness in science that is dependent on the world view of those who construct the scientific theories. Clinicians who must use the results of scientific research will inevitably interpret the research from the standpoint of their own world view. There may be further incommensurability when these data are communicated to the patient. Finally, clinician and patient values must come into play in any decision about choice of treatment. No stage of medical research or practice is value-free.

Vecerka, Kazmír. E Kohák, J Pesek, and R Palous on Ontology. *Filozof Cas*, 42(5), 837-840, 1994.

Vedder, Ben. A Metaphysical Motivation of Hermeneutics: On the Metaphysical Consciousness in Man According to Dilthey (in Dutch). *Bijdragen*, 55(3), 249-268, 1994.

The author of this article investigates the position of metaphysics in Dilthey's work. At first sight Dilthey seems to destroy metaphysics because in the consciousness of the 19th century, man is aware of the historicality of thinking. Historicality of thinking and metaphysics are incompatible. After it is shown that hermeneutics, introspection as selfcontemplation and vision of life are involved in an endless process, the reason for this endlessness is discussed. The author points out that the metaphysical feeling in man is directed towards the infinity of the universe which cannot be caught in words reflection and visions of life. Every attempt to try to grasp the whole of life must necessarily fail because of the primary position of the infinite universe, which was Kilthey's foremost concern till the end of his life.

Veenhoven, Ruut. Is Happiness a Trait? Tests of the Theory That a Better Society Does Not Make People Any Happier. *Soc Indic Res*, 32(2), 101-160, Je 94.

Happiness can be regarded as a trait if it meets three criteria: 1) temporal stability, 2) cross-situational consistency, and 3) inner causation. This paper checks whether

AUTHOR INDEX WITH ABSTRACTS 785 **Verbrugge, Rineke**

that is, indeed, the case. The theory that happiness is a personal-character-trait is tested in a (meta) analysis of longitudinal studies. The results are: 1) happiness is quite stable on the short term, but not in the long run, neither relatively nor absolutely. 2) Happiness is not insensitive to fortune or adversity. 3) Happiness is not entirely built-in: its genetic basis is at best modest and psychological factors explain only part of its variance. The theory that happiness is a national-character-trait is tested in an analysis of differences in average happiness between nations. The results point in the same direction. It is concluded that happiness is no immutable trait. There is thus still sense in striving for greater happiness for a greater number. (edited)

Veenhoven, Ruut and Ehrhardt, Joop. Test of Predictions Implied in Three Theories of Happiness: The Cross-National Pattern of Happiness. *Soc Indic Res*, 34(1), 33-68, Ja 95.

Predictions about level and dispersion of happiness in nations are derived from three theories of happiness: comparison-theory, folklore-theory and livability-theory. The predictions are tested on two cross national data-sets: a comparative survey among university students in 38 nations in 1985 and a collection of comparable general population surveys in 28 nations around 1980. Most predictions of comparison-theory and folklore-theory are defied by the data. The predictions of livability-theory are all confirmed.

Vega, Jesús Fernández. Las "ciencias normativas" y la "ciencia del derecho". *El Basilisco*, 16, 3-18, Ap-Je 94.

Vega, Jose Fernandez. Tocqueville y la dinámica de la democracia moderna: Entre la escisión individualista y la ética republicana. *Cuad Etica*, 14, 21-51, D 92.

Starting from a critical explanation of Tocqueville's understanding of modern "individualism" in his major work *Democracy in America*, this article focuses the implications of that concept for the analysis of some political attitudes in contemporary democracies. Tocqueville's proposal of a "patriotic" behavior to overcome civil indifference is approached here as a peculiar political interpretation of the term "*patrie*" in the light of the Enlightenment tradition. Some references to the reception of Tocqueville's thought in last century Argentina are also made.

Vega, Luis. La Recucción al Absurdo: Una Aproximación Histórica. *Analogia*, 4(2), 3-35, 1990.

Reduction to absurdity is a discoursive procedure that has given rise to both admiration and mistrust. In philosophy, the admiration has been due to its dialectic thoroughness, in informal versions (Eleatic reduction), or in conclusive versions (reduction to contradiction or the impossible). The mistrust has arisen due to its contrast to direct and explanatory proof in the traditional programme of demonstrative science, or to mathematical constructive proofs in Proof General Theory. Its history reveals the strength of its logic (in infinite domains), and its inventive capacity (as in Cantorian proof by diagonalization), but also a dubious epistemological statute.

Vegas, José M. Juventud, valores y crisis de nuestro tiempo. *Dialogo Filosof*, 10(3), 411-424, S-D 94.

Este breve trabajo trata de presentar a personad poco expertas en temas filosóficos esa realidad cotidiana y misteriosa que es el valor. Se pone en relación la dimensión axiológica con las etapas biográficas del ser humano, en especial, con la de la juventud—a quien esta comunicación se dirigía. Y, puesto que hoy es un tema recurrente el de la crisis de los valores, se trata de entender en qué estriba esa famosa crisis.

Vegetti, Mario. "Quand la science parle à vide: procédés dialectiques et métaphoriques chez Aristote" in *Rhétoriques de la science, De Coorebyter, Vincent (ed)*, 7-32. Paris, Pr Univ France, 1994.

Aristotle often deplores the use of dialectical arguments and metaphors in philosophy and science, attributing it to Presocratics and Platonics. However, the article shows that dialectic and rhetorics are widely employed in the Aristotelian biological treatises. There are three main reasons for this: to protect the scientific discourse against his opponents in a competitive context; to fill the gaps in the scientific demonstration due to theoretical or observational difficulties; and above all to convey to its audience the general image of a world hierarchically ordered that is beyond the methodological limits of any scientific discipline.

Vejs, Janis. Transition of Society, Transformation of Philosophy. *Metaphilosophy*, 25(2-3), 143-155, Ap-Jl 94.

The article deals with the status of philosophy in a situation of rapid social change. The background information is drawn from the condition obtaining in newly= independent Latvia. The historical vicissitudes of the Latvian nation—cultural marginality, institutional developments under the totalitarian regime and the present intellectual situation is briefly sketched. Closer discussion of the subject=matter and role of philosophy in relation to science, religion and culture in general is undertaken. Notions of spirituality, quasi=religiosity, absolute values, occidental civilization are employed. The chief conclusion consists in holding that philosophy as a *sui generis* language game of cultivated reflection should embrace the totality of human condition.

Velarde Lombraña, Julián. Ingeniería del Conocimiento y Conocimiento Ordinario. *An Seminar Metaf*, 28, 299-316, 1994.

This paper presents an overview of the two methodologies in A I: the "logistic approach" and the "cognitive (or psychological) approach", as they are applied to model systems for management of commonsense knowledge. The objections to monotonic logic are analyzed; a survey of the theoretical results and applications of nonmonotonic logics is provided. The paper closes with a short account of the basic concepts and properties of fuzzy sets and fuzzy reasoning, and its applications to the analysis and designing of fuzzy expert systems.

Velarde-Mayol, Víctor. El Sentido del Concepto: Un Estudio a Través de Santo Tomás. *Rev Espan Filosof Med*, 0, 251-261, 1993.

El término "concepto" tiene múltiples significados, aquí me limitaré al sentido restringido de lo que posteriormente a Tomás de Aquino se ha llamado "concepto formal". En este sentido, el concepto es algo producido y dicho cuando la operación intelectual llega a término en el logro de una verdad. El presente estudio se ceñirá a dos breves cuestiones clásicas: 1) En qué sentido el concepto es lo preconocido, y 2) En qué sentido el concepto es alteridad, por el que se conoce al otro en calidad de otro.

Velasco, Marisa. "Confirmación Bootstrap y Descubrimiento Científico" in *Temas Actuales de Filosofía, Palacios, María Julia (ed)*, 615-618. Buenos Aires, Univ Nacional Salta, 1993.

Velasco N, Ignacio Ruiz. K Popper: Racionalismo Critico, Metafisica y Metodologia de lo Inverificable. *Topicos*, 1(1), 99-135, 1991.

Velásquez, Lorena. Precedentes Ockhamistas de la Significación. *Rev Filosof (Venezuela)*, 19, 21-33, 1994.

Velázquez, Lorena. El Concepto, Como Signo Natural: Una Polémica Acerca de Ockham. *Analogia*, 7(2), 125-139, 1993.

Velek, Josef. Justice and Good in the Political Liberalism of John Rawls. *Filozof Cas*, 42(6), 925-937, 1994.

Velema, Wyger (ed) and Melching, Willem (ed). *Main Trends in Cultural History*. Amsterdam, Rodopi, 1994.

Veley, Carl. "Isaac Asimov's Contribution to Humanism" in *Contributors to the Philosophy of Humanism, Hillar, Marian (ed)*, 129-132. Pasadena, Humanists Houston, 1994.

This essay critically evaluates the contribution of Isaac Asimov or rather lack of his contribution to Humanism as a movement. In spite of all his writings heavily flavored by his Humanism beliefs, he was never recognized by the media as the Humanist or the president of the AHA. Some explanations for this situation include the opinion that he was a "closet atheist" trying not to antagonize the public. Moreover, very few of his works had any clearly thought-out objectives. If he had consciously focused on those hidden meanings he subconsciously addressed, he mights have written half as many books with a thousand times the impact.

Velody, Irving. Introduction: Unnatural Acts—Or Nature Expelled from Her Garden. *Hist Human Sci*, 7(1), 81-85, F 94.

Velody, Irving. Policing the Frontiers of Science. *Hist Human Sci*, 8(2), 91-95, My 95.

Veltman, Frank. Semántica de actualización. *Rev Filosof (Spain)*, 4(6), 271-284, 1991.

Vencovská, A and Paris, J B and Wilmers, G M. A Natural Prior Probability Distribution Derived from the Propositional Calculus. *Annals Pure Applied Log*, 70(3), 243-285, D 94.

A σ-additive probability measure on the real interval [0, 1] is defined by considering the expected values of "randomly chosen" large formulae of the propositional calculus, where the propositional variables are treated as independent random variables on {0, 1} with expected value 1/2. Although arising naturally from logical and/or cognitive considerations, this measure is extremely complex and displays certain formally pathological features, including infinite density at all points of a certain dense subset of [0, 1]. Certain variants of the construction are also considered. The introduction includes an account of motivation for the study of such measures arising from a fundamental problem in inexact reasoning.

Vendemiati, Aldo. Analogia della legge: Uno studio su S Tommaso d'Aquino. *Riv Filosof Neo-Scolas*, 86(3), 468-490, Jl-S 94.

Vendler, Zeno. "The Ineffable Soul" in *The Mind-Body Problem: A Guide to the Current Debate, Warner, Richard (ed)*, 317-328. Cambridge, Blackwell, 1994.

Since the qualia of sensation, such as pain and sensuous color, are strictly subjective, they cannot be reached by science, and do not play a role in the language game; their *esse* is only *esse pro*. My purpose is to show that in spite of this we can talk about them by using analogy. Much the same way as the medieval doctors used analogy to talk about other "ineffables": God, angels, etc. Consequently although materialism is inadequate because it fails to deal with qualia, dualism makes no sense since it ignores the fact of analogy in counting substances or properties.

Venema, Yde. Cylindric Modal Logic. *J Sym Log*, 60(2), 591-623, Je 95.

We study restricted versions of first order logic as if they were modal formalisms. This approach is closely related to algebraic logic, as the Kripke frames of our system have the type of the atom structure of cylindric algebras; the full cylindric set algebras are the complex algebras of the intended multidimensional frames called cubes. The main contribution of the paper is a characterization of these cube frames for the finite-dimensional case and, as a consequence of the special form of this characterization, a completeness theorem for this class. These results lead to finite, though unorthodox, derivation systems for several related formalisms, e.g. for the valid *n*-variable first order formulas, for type-free valid formulas and for the equational theory of representable cylindric algebras. The result for type-free valid formulas indicates a positive solution to Problem 4.16 of Henkin, Monk and Tarski (16). (edited)

Ventimiglia, Giovanni. Il Trattato Tomista sulle Proprietà Trascendentali dell'Essere. *Riv Filosof Neo-Scolas*, 87(1), 51-82, Ja-Mr 95.

Ver Eecke, Wilfried. Hegelian Reflections on the Free Market Democracy. *Dialogue Hum*, 3(4), 75-86, 1993.

In this paper I propose to analyze the hopes that one may entertain about the contribution that both the free market and a constitutional democracy (monarchy) can make toward the good society. For that purpose I use Hegel's analysis of the modern society as he presents it in its mature form in his *Philosophy of Right*. Hegel distinguishes the contribution he expects from the economic order and the one he expects from the political order. We will therefore devote a section to each of these two orders. In our conclusion we will have to affirm that Hegel's insistence upon a hereditary monarch and a hereditary upper house are historically regressive requirements that cannot any more be looked upon to guarantee the proper relation between the economic and the political domain. This will leave us with the question as to what one can propose as an alternative.

Verbeek, Theo. Regius's *Fundamenta Physices*. *J Hist Ideas*, 55(4), 533-551, O 94.

Verbrugge, Rineke and Visser, Albert. A Small Reflection Principle for Bounded Arithmetic. *J Sym Log*, 59(3), 785-812, S 94.

Verene, Donald Phillip (ed) and Levi, Albert William and Verene, Molly Black (ed). *The High Road of Humanity: The Seven Ethical Ages of Western Man*. Amsterdam, Rodopi, 1995.

Verene, Molly Black. *Vico: A Bibliography of Works in English from 1884 to 1994*. Bowling Green, Philosophy Doc Ctr, 1994.

An updated bibliography of scholarship in English on Giambattista Vico is an ongoing project of the Institute for Vico Studies. This complete reorganization of the published lists, plus additions through 1993, contains all books and essays, with reviews; dissertations; English reviews of works on Vico in other languages; entries on Vico in reference works; all translations of Vico's works into English, with reviews; reviews of other translations of Vico; 75 pages of works citing Vico; an appendix of all Vico bibliographies; and a name index. The bibliography is a working list and does not claim to be inclusive or without error.

Verene, Molly Black (ed) and Verene, Donald Phillip (ed) and Levi, Albert William. *The High Road of Humanity: The Seven Ethical Ages of Western Man*. Amsterdam, Rodopi, 1995.

Vergara, Julia. La Distinción *Narrow Content-Wide Content*. *Rev Latin de Filosof*, 21(1), 131-144, Fall 95.

The notion of content establishes a close connection between intentionality and meaning. In the last twenty years several theories have made a bifurcation which is known as the narrow/wide content distinction. This topic has being broadly discussed in the area of mind, cognition and language. The intention of this paper is to outline what the issue is about. First, its origins linked to the semantical thesis known as externalism are examined. Second, following Akeel Bilgrami's analysis [Belief and Meaning (1991)] the motivations that give rise to the idea of wide content are discussed. Bilgrami has shed light on the problem of bifurcation in revealing its relation with Putnam, Kripke and Burge's causal views on reference. On the basis of this critique the paper places the narrow/wide content distinction in a broader philosophical context by noticing the profound motivations that lie under each notion as well as its connections with some epistemological questions.

Vergílio G Cuter, Joao. Wittgenstein e o Domínio da Gramática: A Ruptura com o Tractatus. *Educ Filosof*, 8(16), 173-181, Jl-D 94.

Verhey, Allen D. Cloning: Revisiting an Old Debate. *Kennedy Inst Ethics J*, 4(3), 227-234, S 94.

The debate about cloning that took place 25 years ago, although directed toward a different sort of cloning, elucidates fundamental issues currently at stake in reproductive technologies and research. Paul Ramsey and Joseph Fletcher were participants in this early debate. The differences between Ramsey and Fletcher about the meaning and sufficiency of freedom, the understanding and weighing of good and evil, the connection between embodiment and personhood, the relationship of humans with nature, and the meaning of parenthood suggest both a broader agenda for the debate about cloning and a cautious move forward in the development of embryo splitting.

Verhoogt, Jan (ed) and Griffioen, Sander (ed). *Norm and Context in the Social Sciences*. Lanham, Univ Pr of America, 1990.

Verley, Xavier. Logique et existence. *Rev Phil Fr*, 3, 295-315, Jl-S 94.

Vermazen, Bruce. Carlos Moya's Regress-Problem. *Pac Phil Quart*, 76(1), 73-81, Mr 95.

In *The Philosophy of Action: An Introduction* (Oxford, 1990), Carlos J Moya rejects analyses of action due to Arthur Danto, Hugh McCann, Brian O'Shaughnessy, and Jennifer Hornsby on the ground that they fail to solve "the regress-problem," unlike Moya's own view. I try to show that Moya sketches three distinct versions of this problem, that none of the versions involves a real infinite regress, and that the third version, used against McCann and O'Shaughnessy, is equally damaging to Moya's view.

Vermeersch, Etienne. "The Future of Environmental Philosophy" in *Ecology, Technology, and Culture,* Zweers, Wim (ed), 272-286. Cambridge, White Horse, 1994.

Vermeulen, C F M. Incremental Semantics for Propositional Texts. *Notre Dame J Form Log*, 35(2), 243-271, Spr 94.

Vermeulen, C F M. Merging without Mystery or: Variables in Dynamics Semantics. *J Phil Log*, 24(4), 405-450, Ag 95.

In this paper we discuss the treatment of variables in dynamic semantics. Referent systems are introduced as a flexible mechanism for working with variables. In a referent system we carefully distinguish the variables themselves both from the machinery by which we manipulate them—their names—and from the information that we store in them—their values. It is shown that the referent systems provide a natural basis for dynamic semantics. The semantics with referent systems is compared with the familiar formalisms in dynamics semantics, *DRT* and *DPL*.

Vernon, Richard. Locke's Antagonist, Jonas Proast. *Locke News*, 24, 95-106, 1993.

Veroli, Nicolas. Richard Rorty and Solidarity, or the Inconsequence of a Certain Capacity. *Int Stud Phil*, 27(1), 119-125, 1995.

Vertin, Michael. Lonergan on Consciousness: Is There a Fifth Level?. *Method*, 12(1), 1-36, Spr 94.

In his later writings, Bernard Lonergan often assets an experience of being in love without restriction. A few times he characterizes this experience as situated on the "fifth level" of consciousness. Do these characterizations indicate an important departure from Lonergan's usual affirmation of just four levels of consciousness? The correct answer to this question requires that one distinguish two senses in which Lonergan employs the word "level". On a wide but atypical Lonerganian sense of the word, there may indeed be five levels of consciousness. But on the strict and typical Lonerganian sense, there are only four.

Vesey, Godfrey. "Wittgenstein on Psychological Verbs" in *Wittgenstein and Contemporary Philosophy, Teghrarian, Souren (ed)*, 89-107. Bristol, Thoemmes, 1994.

Consider the verbs 'believe', 'expect', 'hope', 'intend', 'know', 'mean', 'remember', 'understand', 'wish', 'wonder'. Locke and Brentano held that there is a perfectly proper epistemological question, 'How is it that a person can say what he himself believes, expects, hopes, etc.?' to which the answer is that he must have observed in himself a mental operation, process, state, or whatever, of believing, expecting, hoping, etc. Wittgenstein rejected all such answers. That someone else believes something, expects something, etc. is something I find out about by observation. But that I believe something, etc., is not something I find out about by observation.

Vetere, Lucia. La Musica in Aristotele. *Stud Filosofici*, 107-124, 1991-92.

Vetlesen, Arne Johan. Relations with Others in Sartre and Levinas: Assessing Some Implications for an Ethics of Proximity. *Constellations*, 1(3), 358-382, Jan 95.

What is our original and most fundamental relation to others? The positions of Sartre and Levinas are examined. Early Sartre holds conflict to be the essence of inter-personal relationships. This pessimistic conclusion is challenged by Levinas, who seeks for a novel understanding of freedom and ethical responsibility. Levinas uncouples ethical responsibility from freedom (Sartre) as well as from reciprocity (Rawls, Habermas). In insisting that responsibility for the Other is not an option but instead absolute and unconditional, Levinas offers a bold approach to contemporary society's ethical challenges.

Vetter, Helmuth. "Ursprung und Wiederholung" in *Europa und die Philosophie, Gander, Hans-Helmuth (ed)*, 175-184. Frankfurt/M, Klostermann, 1993.

Vicenik, J and Cernik, V and Hanzel, I. What is a Category?. *Metaphilosophy*, 25(2-3), 181-193, Ap-Jl 94.

The task of this paper is to analyze the problems connected with philosophical categories as well as with systems of philosophical categories. We begin with some meta-reflections on the internal structure of philosophy. We then scrutinize the logical categories of cognition. Finally we explicate the concepts "philosophical category" and "system of philosophical categories", as well as the relation of categories to the history of human thinking.

Vico, G and Gómez, Francisco Navarro (trans). Oración II Pronunciada el 18 de Octubre de 1700. *Cuad Vico*, 3, 211-218, 1993.

Vico, G and Gómez, Francisco Navarro (trans). Oración III Pronunciada el 18 de Octubre de 1701. *Cuad Vico*, 4, 191-198, 1994.

Vico, G and Gómez, Francisco Navarro (trans). Oración IV Pronunciada el 18 de Octubre de 1704. *Cuad Vico*, 4, 201-208, 1994.

Vidal, Fernando. "Les mystères de la douleur divine": Une "prière" du jeune Jean Piaget pour l'année 1916. *Rev Theol Phil*, 126(2), 97-118, 1994.

En février 1916, le futur psychologue et épistémologue Jean Piaget (1896-1980) publia "Les mystères de la douleur divine", texte absent de toute bibliographie piagétienne. "Les mystères de la douleur divine" éclaire le passage, chez le jeune Piaget, d'une attitude religieuse et métaphysique liée à la recherche d'un absolu transcendant, à une attitude immanentiste annonçant le point de vue caractéristique de son oeuvre scientifique et philosophique ultérieure.

Vidiella, Graciela. "La Razón Práctica en la Teoría de Rawls" in *Temas Actuales de Filosofía, Palacios, María Julia (ed)*, 619-623. Buenos Aires, Univ Nacional Salta, 1993.

Vidiella, Graciela and Cabrera, Mónica. "La Cuestión del Género en la Cultura Popular: Del Tango al Rock" in *Temas Actuales de Filosofía, Palacios, María Julia (ed)*, 93-98. Buenos Aires, Univ Nacional Salta, 1993.

This paper intends to establish a comparison between the way of developing the gender subject in two significant expressions of the popular art in Buenos Aires city: the "tango" (1900-1940) and the Argentine rock (since 1960). The "tango" conforms the femininity with a suspicious glance: the woman is the other, the intruder in the male universe. She always provokes infidelity, abandon, deceit, or perdition. Since the 1960's, the female presence in the Argentine rock is not a question (matter) and the women conforms an integral image that inspires friendships, maternal tenderness, and sexuality. By these comparisons on try to bild the women as subjectivity and to get her recognition, but not her objectivity.

Vidrányi, Katalin. Imitatio Christi: Ethical Problems of Some Christological Standpoints. *Magyar Filozof Szemle*, 1-2, 1-9, 1994.

L'auteur de cet essai met en lumière la différence entre deux traditions christologiques, notamment, entre le type latin et le type grec de la doctrine néochalcèdonienne. L'une se fonde sur une anthropologie, laquelle, tout en affirmant l'unité du genre humaine, présente la chute de l'homme, qui néanmoins porte en soi l'image de Dieu, essentiellement comme une individualisation. Selon cette tradition, le Christ incarné sanctifie tout le genre humain, et imiter le Christ, c'est surtout dépasser l'individualité, par le moyen de la prière et de bonnes oeuvres. Quant à l'autre tradition, elle se fonde sur une anthropologie plus pessimiste, élaborée par saint Augustin, selon laquelle la distance entre l'homme et Dieu, à cause du péché originel, est extrêmement immense. Par conséquent, la nature humaine dans la personne de Christ ne peut pas comprendre rien de positif. Christ l'homme, selon cette tradition, est charactérisé exclusivement par la Passion. D'où résulte que l'imitation de Christ est présentée aussi comme une passivité: imiter le Christ, c'est, avant tout, souffrir. L'auteur, en opposant une à l'autre les deux traditions christologiques étudiées, qualifie d'égoïsme la deuxième, représentée par exemple par saint Augustin et Juan de la Cruz, parce qu'elle a une tendance de regarder l'autrui, et même le péché commis par lui, comme un pour obtenir la souffrance, conséquence, le salut individuel.

Viederman, Milton and Fins, Joseph J. Commentary on "But Is It Assisted Suicide?". *Hastings Center Rep*, 25(3), 24-25, My-Je 95.

Vieillard-Baron, Jean-Louis. Hegel et la Grèce. *Diotima*, 22, 55-61, 1994.

Vieillard-Baron, Jean-Louis. Instants fondateurs et image de soi dans l'oeuvre de Proust. *Rev Phil Fr*, 4, 421-438, O-D 94.

L'oeuvre de Prouste se fonde sur la discontinuité des instants; l'instant mondain est èphémère et superficiel; les instants privilégiés sont surtout les émotions esthétiques fortes; les instants fondateurs sont ceux de la résurgence involontaire de souvenirs qui donne son sens à la vie de l'auteur, en l'incitant à se consacrer à son oeuvre. La

AUTHOR INDEX WITH ABSTRACTS 787 Voigts, Manfred

Recherche du temps perdu manifeste la nature créatrice du narcissisme, le moi psychologique est discontinu. La création littéraire unifie les instants discontinus de la vie en restaurant une continuité qui vient de l'intemporalité du moi créateur, et atteint par la l'universalité, mieux que la pensée conceptuelle.

Vieillard-Baron, Jean-Louis. La notion d'Espace Cosmique et des origines de l'Univers. *Philosophia (Athens)*, 23-24, 9-13, 1993-94.

Vieillard-Baron, Jean-Louis. Nature, coutume et droit chez Hegel. *Laval Theol Phil*, 51(2), 363-370, Je 95.

S'opposant radicalement à la conception aristotélicienne de la nature, Hegel est le philosophe de l'universalité concrète de l'Esprit qui se détache de la nature; Montaigne, philosophe de la culture, et non de la nature, semble au contraire fasciné par la diversité des coutumes. Et cependant, Hegel ne néglige pas les <moeurs>, puisqu'il leur donne un statut spéculatif dans l'analyse de la *Sittlichkeit* dans sa *Philosophie du droit*. La réalité morale implique la prise en compte de la diversité des besoins des individus dans la société civile bourgeoise; et l'histoire montre à Hegel la diversité irréductible des États. La naturalité reste présente dans le droit, avec l'individualité et la contingence. Et l'universalité n'est vraie que lorsqu'elle pénètre et dépasse cette naturalité, sans la supprimer.

Vieira, Luiz Renato. Entre o Sociologismo e o Individualismo: Consideraçoes sobre a Sociologia de Pierre Bourdieu. *Educ Filosof*, 8(16), 285-300, Jl-D 94.

Vigna, Carmelo. "Contraddizione pratica, desiderio, coerenza" in *L'etica e il suo Altro, Vigna, Carmelo (ed)*, 15-40. Milano, FrancoAngeli, 1994.

Il saggio istituisce la differenza tra contraddizione speculativa e contraddizione pratica e indaga sulla loro relazione nella vita della coscienza. Mostra soprattutto come la contraddizione pratica sia la modalità secondo cui il desiderio umano vive. Indica, infine, il senso della possibile risoluzione della contraddizione pratica, utilizzando anche la figura della "coerenza" dell'agire.

Vigna, Carmelo (ed). *L'etica e il suo Altro*. Milano, FrancoAngeli, 1994.

Questo libro, scritto a più mani, cioè da un gruppo di studiosi che prendono parte al Seminario di Filosofia della pratica, attivo presso il Dipartimento di Filosofia e Teoria delle scienze dell'Università di Venezia, intende recare un contributo al dibattito contemporaneo sui problemi dell'etica, sostenendo che l'etica deve restare fermamente rapportata al proprio "altro", ossia che l'etica non deve essere "isolata" astrattamente dalla contestualità che le compete: il rimando alle strutture fondative della verità.

Vilas Nogueira, J. Identidad cultural, conflicto cultural y violencia. *Telos (Spain)*, 3(1), 109-124, Je 94.

This article examines, from a political point of view, the relationship between cultural identity and conflict, and violence. The diffusion of a certain stress in conspicuous legitimacy of cultural identity is the starting point of an inquiry into the possible meanings of the concept and into its practical consequences. Obviously they are not new-comer, but anti-individualist conceptions have proliferated in recent years in political science. I suggest, as a more appropriate alternative, to rescue the utilitarian approach. I contend that this outlook explains the necessary institutional features of democratic systems, because there are essential connections between the individual determination of interests and preferences and actual practices of free and rational government. My conclusion is a plea for a conception of the cultural identity as a function of the individual.

Villacañas, José L. Fichte und die charismatische Verklärung der Vernuntt. *Fichte-Studien*, 5, 117-148, 1993.

Villacañas, José L. Kant: Ilustración jurídica versus razón de Estado. *Rev Filosof (Daimon)*, 7, 35-53, 1993.

Villacañas, José L. La Especulación de Fichte: Ser y el Problema del Nihilismo. *Daimon Rev Filosof*, 9, 135-154, 1994.

El presente artículo quiere situar la metafísica de Fichte, centrada en la diferencia entre Sein y Dasein, como una respuesta a la experiencia del nihilismo que irrumpe con la filosofía kantiana y la reducción del Dasein a fenómeno. La filosofía de Fichte sería un intento continuo de contestar la pregunta que irrumpe en este texto: "Was wäre denn das wahre Mittel, diesem Sturze der Realität, diesem Nihilismus zu entgehen?"

Villacañas, José L. Química y Salvación. *Daimon Rev Filosof*, 8, 145-153, 1994.

Villalobos, Carlos Manuel. La mo(n)stración abaddónica de Ernesto Sábato. *Rev Filosof (Costa Rica)*, 31(75-76), 203-209, D 93.

This paper is taking into account Rafael Angel Herra's concept of "the monstrous". This proposal has been used as a theoretical frame in order to read Ernesto Sabato's novels. We study how the personages, in an unsatisfied context, see themselves in the need of putting the blame on monsters. Among which the most important is the monsters creation, which are masks that both show and hide the mentioned personages's identity.

Villalobos, José. El hacha niveladora: Donoso Cortés y Vico. *Cuad Vico*, 1, 55-67, 1991.

It is necessary to find out the causes that impel Donso to his interpretation to the thought of Vico, to understand his philosophical perspective that makes him consider Vico as the founder of the philosophy of history. The basic interest lies in the aim of that "philosophy of history" that thanks to Vico receives scientific consistency: Science of the human world. But even more, Vico offers Donoso the method of the philosophy of history. Nevertheless, one has to wonder why the "mature" Donoso (more theological) separates from the Vico embraced by the "young" Donoso and having achieved this, one will fully understand not only the development of the historical thought of Donoso but also Vico's reception in Spain.

Villani, Arnaud. Hölderlin et la Question du Centre. *Diotima*, 22, 46-54, 1994.

Vincenzo, Joseph P. Nietzsche and Epicurus. *Man World*, 27(4), 383-397, O 94.

In Epicurus, Nietzsche did not see merely a proponent of hedonist philosophy, but a countermovement against the latent, pre-existing form of Christianity which came into the world for the first time in Hellenistic Greece with the rise of Platonism. With Epicurus's rejection of guilt, punishment, and immortality, Nietzsche envisaged the overturning of Platonism, and with it an elimination of the spirit of revenge. This eradication of revenge amounts to a partial redemption of lived time. For Nietzsche, however, the Epicurian overturning of Platonism was not yet its overcoming. Beyond the Epicurian delight of inverted Platonism, Nietzsche calls for the higher affirmation of tragic joy. The article shows further how Epicurus's philosophy does not succumb to Nietzsche's assertion that Epicurus's thought is rooted in a flight from being. It shows finally an essential philosophical parallel between Nietzsche and Epicurus.

Vinci, Tom. Why Is There Analytic Epistemology?. *Dialogue (Canada)*, 33(3), 517-532, Sum 94.

Vinicky, Janicemarie K and Orlowski, James P. The Quantifiability of Medical Futility. *J Clin Ethics*, 5(2), 147-149, Sum 94.

Vintges, Karen. "The Second Sex and Philosophy" in *Feminist Interpretations of Simone de Beauvoir, Simons, Margaret A (ed)*, 45-58. University Park, Penn St Univ Pr, 1995.

The article concerns the question whether Simone de Beauvior's *The Second Sex* comprises a systematic philosophy. At first it is shown that, far from being a clumsy eclectic work, *The Second Sex* is structured systematically as a philosophical phenomenological enterprise. Then it is argued that its proper philosophical character has been denied by feminist theoreticians who state that the work constitutes a masculine view of women, due to Beauvoir's use of Sartre's inherently masculine concepts. Beauvoir's theory of woman as the historical Other is in fact a radical break with Sartrean theory.

Visker, Rudi. Dropping: The "Subject" of Authenticity. *Being and Time* on Disappearing Existentials and True Friendship with Being. *Res Phenomenol*, 24, 133-158, 1994.

Visser, A. A Course on Bimodal Provability Logic. *Annals Pure Applied Log*, 73(1), 109-142, May 95.

In this paper we study 1) the frame-theory of certain bimodal provability logics involving the reflection principle and we study 2) certain specific bimodal logics with a provability predicate for a subtheory of Peano arithmetic axiomatized by a nonstandardly finite number of axioms.

Visser, Albert and Verbrugge, Rineke. A Small Reflection Principle for Bounded Arithmetic. *J Sym Log*, 59(3), 785-812, S 94.

Vitoria, María Angeles. El Dominio Racional del Siglo XIII: Consideración Histórico-Epistemológica. *Rev Espan Filosof Med*, 0, 263-271, 1993.

In the course of the history, the relationship between philosophy, science and theology has been changing continuously. In the ancient times the philosophy treated the most important questions, and the science the particular ones. During the Middle Ages the science lived submerged in a philosophical-theological atmosphere; however, in the thirteenth century the philosophy was conscious of its limits comparing with the science. That's why it began looking for a wider comprehensive horizon: the transcendental one.

Vjecsner, Paul. Can the Existence of God Be Found Revealed By Way of the Common Capabilities Given Us, Those of Experience and Reason?. *Darshana Int*, 32(1/125), 48-51, Ja 92.

The article intends to disclose how knowledge of the existence of God can be derived from ordinary worldly phenomena. The attainment of the knowledge through inference from what may be known has long been the object of natural theology, but these efforts have engaged in either conjectures or elaborate and esoteric twists of logic. To sidestep the difficulties, lately that knowledge has even been by fiat declared possessed, although the existence of God is universally recognized to have been a matter of belief, not of verification. The present article affirms that that belief can by overlooked simple inference become certainty.

Vlachos, Georges. La Vision de la Mort en Tant que Principe d'une Éthique de l'action chez Homére. *Philosophia (Athens)*, 23-24, 105-111, 1993-94.

Selon les Grecs de l'époque classique la poésie homérique formait un ensemble de morale et de pédagogie. Dans cette poésie, l'accomplossement du but suprême, qu'est la vertu, consiste au sacrifice et à la mort du héros. Et, c'est à partir de cette idée principale que se manifeste une philosophie fondamentale de la vie et de la mort.

Vogel, Jeffrey S. Is Marx a Moral Consequentialist?. *Can J Phil*, 24(4), 541-563, D 94.

Vogel, Lawrence. Hans Jonas's Diagnosis of Nihilism: The Case of Heidegger. *Int J Phil Stud*, 3(1), 55-72, Mr 95.

I show how Hans Jonas, one of Heidegger's most distinguished Jewish students, traces his mentor's susceptibility to Nazism to a moral nihilism at the heart of Heidegger's teaching in *Being and Time*. I then demonstrate how Jonas's own "existential interpretation of the biological facts" and metaphysical grounding of "an imperative of responsibility" provide one of the most systematic and challenging rejoinders to the moral failings of Heidegger's thought.

Vogeley, Kai. *Repräsentation und Identität*. Berlin, Duncker Humblot, 1995.

Vogt, Erik Michael. *Sartres Wieder-Holung*. Vienna, Passagen, 1995.

Given the premise that Sartre's thought is still of value for the contemporary context of philosophy, the aim of this work is to relate Sartrian theorems to postmodernist approaches to philosophy by opening up the limits of certain discursive formations. Without levelling out the considerable differences, a kind of epoche is employed in order to defuse the official oppositions between existentialism and post-structuralism, between phenomenology and deconstruction, at least as those oppositions are connected with Sartre.

Voice, Paul. What Do Animals Deserve?. *S Afr J Phil*, 14(1), 34-38, F 95.

I argue that the failure of contractarianism to assign substantive moral weight to the interests of nonhuman animals does not count against contractarianism as a moral theory. I show why contractarianism excludes animals from the moral domain, and go on to argue that when proper attention is paid to the scope of moral theory, it is easily seen why animals lack full moral standing.

Voigts, Manfred. *Das geheimnisvolle Verschwinden des Geheimnisses*. Vienna, Passagen, 1995.

Volk, Carol 788 AUTHOR INDEX WITH ABSTRACTS

Volk, Carol (trans) and Ferry, Luc. *The New Ecological Order*. Chicago, Univ of Chicago Pr, 1995.

Volk, Tyler. *Metapatterns: Across Space, Time, and Mind*. New York, Columbia Univ Pr, 1995.

This book presents a synthesis of science, philosophy, and psychology in the universal patterns that underlie our lives and the world around us. (The word "metapattern" was coined by Gregory Bateson.) As much visual as verbal ideas, metapatterns facilitate explorations about the architecture of existence at all levels. Metapatterns are grand attractors—functional universals for forms in space, processes in time, and concepts in mind. The book identifies 10 such archetypes: spheres, borders, sheets and tubes, binaries, centers, layers, calendars, arrows, breaks, cycles.

Vollmer, Fred. The Control of Actions by Agents. *J Theor Soc Behav*, 25(2), 175-190, Je 95.

The aim of this paper is to clarify the assumption that actions are controlled by persons. Persons are in control of their actions in virtue of reflective consciousness (which is a property of the brain). Reflective consciousness consists in a primary, intrinsic, non-observational awareness of own activity, and a capacity to form second order thoughts about such activity. And having this property, or both aspects of it, is what makes a being a person. There is nothing that does the controlling in addition to reflective consciousness itself.

Volosinov, Valentin N. Das Wort im Leben und das Wort in der Poesie. *Deut Z Phil*, 43(1), 109-130, 1995.

V N Voloshinov (1895-1936), a member of the M M Bakhtin Circle, in this first of a series of articles (for the first time translated into German) thought to lay of the foundations of a sociological poetics. Comparing everyday speech acts and poetical expressions he finds the immanent social nature of poetics in intonation, choice and composition of words. These *material* forms of the word carry social evaluations, they are realizations of an aesthetical intercourse connecting author, listener and "hero" with one another and so the word with its external social context.

Von Eckardt, Barbara and Poland, Jeffrey and Spaulding, Will. "Problems with the *DSM* Approach to Classifying Psychopathology" in *Philosophical Psychopathology, Graham, George (ed)*, 235-260. Cambridge, MIT Pr, 1993.

von Engelhardt, Dietrich. "Verzeitlichung der Natur und Historisierung.." in *Naturauffassungen in Philosophie, Wissenschaft, Technik: Band III, Schäfer, Lothar (ed)*, 225-253. Freiburg, Alber, 1995.

von Gebsattel, Victor E and Welie, Jos V M (trans). The Meaning of Medical Practice. *Theor Med*, 16(1), 59-72, Mr 94.

Victor Von Gebsattel (1883-1974) was one of the primary representatives of the medical-anthropological movement, aimed at enriching and "humanizing" medicine by borrowing from early 20th century philosophical anthropology. Little of his work has been translated into English. In his last article from 1963 on the meaning of medical practice, Von Gebsattel outlines his views on the doctor-patient relationship. He discerns 3 stages: an initial sympathic or immediate stage; a diagnostic-therapeutic stage; and a personal stage. (For a critical analysis, see the translator's accompanying article in the same issue of theoretical medicine).

Von Graevenitz, Gerhart. Der Grund im Bewusstsein. *Phil Rundsch*, 41(3), 222-234, Je 94.

von Helmholtz, Hermann and Cahan, David (ed). *Science and Culture: Popular and Philosophical Essays*. Chicago, Univ of Chicago Pr, 1995.

Science and Culture: Popular and Philosophical Essays presents a new edition of Hermann von Helmholtz's essays. As physiologist, physicist, and philosopher Helmholtz was one of the leading figures of nineteenth-century European intellectual life. From the 1850 to the 1890s, he delivered more than two dozen popular and general academic lectures. The editor, David Cahan, has selected fifteen of these lectures, including those on the origins of the planetary system, the relation of natural science to science in general, the aim and progress of the physical sciences, the problems of perception, and academic freedom in German universities. Cahan has also introduced these essays by setting them in their broader context.

Von Hippel, William. A Social Psychological Perspective. *Ethics Behavior*, 4(4), 397-399, 1994.

von Manz, Hans Georg. Selbstgewissheit und Fremdgewissheit. *Fichte-Studien*, 6, 195-213, 1994.

It is examined how the notion of the other is essential for the notion of the self. Fichte showed through a transcendental deduction that consciousness of the world and of the self can only be constituted on the basis of an interpersonal relationship. The concept of the other is a fundamental component of the structure of subjectivity. The perception of the other is the result of an ethical action in which the other is being recognized and respected as being of free will. This concept is met by Levinas's concept of the other grounded on a relationship of absolute responsibility.

von Schomberg, René. "Wertsphären, argumentative Vernunft und die gesellschaftliche Bewältigung von wissenschaftlicher und moralisch-ethischer Unsicherheit " in *Mythos Wertfreiheit?, Apel, Karl Otto (ed)*, 235-255. Frankfurt, Campus Verlag, 1994.

The current social reaction to the ecological crisis can be understood as a reaction to scientific and ethical uncertainty, I contrast Max Weber's differentiation of the value spheres science, justice and morality in the modern world with the actual process of de-differentiation of these spheres. Therefore social contradictions emerge in the functional relationships between these value spheres. Science becomes a strategic resource for politics, justice becomes a basic constituent of an immoral form of negotiation and morality is transformed into fear. In conclusion I outline a solution with the help of the discourse theory of Apel and Habermas.

von Uexküll, Thure. Anthropology and the Theory of Medicine. *Theor Med*, 16(1), 93-114, Mr 94.

Instead of presupposing reality as the "realist" do, a genetic theory of knowledge attempts to understand scientific knowledge through the psychological origins of both the concepts, and the operations on which these concepts are based. Adopting the viewpoint of genetic epistemology, the envisaged theory of medicine will have to perform a threefold task: 1) A revision and reformulation of the psycho-physical problem and the development of a model for the living body; 2) A revision of our views concerning the relationship between humans and the inanimate and animate environment; and 3) The development of a concept for the construction of individual reality and its consequences for the patient-physician relationship.

von Weizsäcker, Carl Friedrich F. El Significado de la Teoría Cuántica. *Analogia*, 5(2), 3-34, 1991.

von Weizsäcker, Carl Friedrich F. Ideas Sobre la Filosofía de la Ciencia. *Analogia*, 4(1), 3-32, 1990.

von Weizsäcker, Carl Friedrich F. Las Consecuencias Políticas y Morales de la Ciencia. *Analogia*, 7(2), 3-38, 1993.

von Wright, Georg Henrik (ed) and Malcolm, Norman. *Wittgensteinian Themes: Essays 1978-1989*. Ithaca, Cornell Univ Pr, 1995.

These are essays by the late Norman Malcolm (1911-1990) from the last twelve years of his life, a companion volume to his two earlier collections of essays *Knowledge and Certainty* and *Thought and Knowledge*. Some essays deal directly with aspects of Wittgenstein's thought—defending Wittgenstein's position against what the author considers misunderstandings or distortions. Others deal in what may be called a Wittgensteinian spirit with topics in the writings of Anscombe and Kripke—the last one, published posthumously, treats of Moore's Paradox. The essays are of high quality and stylistic elegance and testify to the originality and forcefulness of Malcolm's mind.

Vorenkamp, Dirck. B-Series Temporal Order in Dogen's Theory of Time. *Phil East West*, 45(3), 387-408, Jl 95.

Dogen's views of time are descriptively compared to the modern Western philosophical view called "B-theory" and found to contain elements of each of the four main tenets of the B-theory. Furthermore, a fundamental incongruency is discovered. Even accounting for traditional Buddhist approaches to apparent contradictions, Dogen's problems in this regard call into question the assumption of consistency that has characterized modern interpretations of his views on time.

Vorobej, Mark. Pacifism and Wartime Innocence. *Soc Theor Pract*, 20(2), 171-191, Sum 94.

Do modern wars inevitably involve the killing of inocents? No, since 1) all morally relevant (intentional or foreseeable) killing in some modern wars can be restricted to the killing of combatants, and 2) combatants in a morally unjustified war are noninnocent in virtue of their functional role within such a war. If so, then Robert Holmes's recent attempt, in *On War and Morality*, to ground a defence of anti-war pacifism exclusively upon moral claims about the treatment of innocents is not compelling.

Vossenkuhl, Wilhelm. Spontaneität. *Z Phil Forsch*, 48(3), 329-349, Jl-S 94.

Vroom, Hendrik M. "Religious Ways of Life and Human Rights" in *Human Rights and Religious Values, An-Na'im, Abdullahi A (& other eds)*, 24-42. Grand Rapids, Eerdmans, 1995.

Wachbroit, Robert. Normality as a Biological Concept. *Phil Sci*, 61(4), 579-591, D 94.

The biological sciences employ a concept of normality that must be distinguished from statistical or value concepts. The concept of normality is presupposed in the standard explications of biological functions, and it is crucial to the strategy of explanation by approximations in, for example, physiology. Nevertheless, this concept of normality does not seem to be captured in the language of physics. Thus attempts at explaining the methodological relationship between the biological sciences and the physical sciences by concentrating only on the concept of biological function cannot go very far. An analysis of the concept of normality is also necessary.

Wachterhauser, Brice. "Gadamer's Realism: The 'Belongingness' of Word and Reality" in *Hermeneutics and Truth, Wachterhauser, Brice (ed)*, 148-171. Evanston, Northwestern Univ Pr, 1994.

Wachterhauser, Brice. "Introduction: Is There Truth after Interpretation?" in *Hermeneutics and Truth, Wachterhauser, Brice (ed)*, 1-31. Evanston, Northwestern Univ Pr, 1994.

Wachterhauser, Brice (ed). *Hermeneutics and Truth*. Evanston, Northwestern Univ Pr, 1994.

Wada, Toshihiro. Gangesa and Mathuranatha on Simhavyaghralaksana of *Vyapti*. *J Indian Phil*, 23(3), 273-294, S 95.

Wade, David L and Stidd, Benton M. Is Species Selection Dependent Upon Emergent Characters?. *Biol Phil*, 10(1), 55-76, Ja 95.

The architects of punctuated equilibrium and species selection as well as more recent workers (Vrba) have narrowed the original formulation of species selection and made it dependent upon so-called emergent characters. One criticism of this narrow version is the dearth of emergent characters with a consequent diminution in the robustness of species selection as an important evolutionary process. We argue that monomorphic species characters may at times be the focus of selection and that under these circumstances selection at the organism level is by-passed due to the absence of critical variance. Selection therefore shifts to the species level where variability reemerges in a clade. The absence of critical variance among organisms prevents effect macroevolution from operating. If species-wide properties are important in macroevolutionary processes, as we contend, systematists should pay more attention to their elucidation.

Waechter, Kay. *Studien zum Gedanken der Einheit des Staates: Über die rechtsphilosophische Auflösung der Einheit des Subjektes*. Berlin, Duncker Humblot, 1994.

Wälde, Martin. What Time Is Not: Critical Remarks on Husserl's Analysis of Time. *J Indian Counc Phil Res*, 11(2), 29-41, Ja-Ap 94.

Wagman, Morton. *The Sciences of Cognition: Theory and Research in Psychology and Artificial Intelligence*. New York, Praeger, 1995.

This book examines the nature of intelligence and intelligent systems as revealed by the sciences of psychology and artificial intelligence. The central and detailed aspects of a general unified theory of intelligence are presented. Theories of

AUTHOR INDEX WITH ABSTRACTS 789 Walker, Margaret Urban

reasoning and its computational modeling are considered. Problem solving and its computational modeling are considered. The nature of analogical thinking is discussed. Scientific discovery processes in the context of artificial intelligence and human psychology are discussed.

Wagner, Hans. Kants Konzept von hypothetischen Imperativen. *Kantstudien*, 85(1), 78-84, 1994.

Wagner, Stephen. Descartes' Wax: Discovering the Nature of Mind. *Hist Phil Quart*, 12(2), 165-183, Ap 95.

Descartes' procedure in *Meditation II* must be brought into line with his claim that "we must never ask about the existence of anything until we first understand its essence." And Descartes' *Meditation III* claim that he is aware of his mind's power to cause ideas must be grounded in a prior discovery of this power. Both demands are met by reading *Meditation II* as a progressive clarification of the nature of mind, with the investigation of the wax providing the discovery of the mind's generative power. This process of discovery also provides the meanings of "thinking" and "existing"—as "causing ideas" and "exercising causal power", respectively. Thus the discovery of the mind's nature also grounds the cogito. I provide a close reading of the wax investigation which supports this view.

Wagner, Steven J. "Supervenience, Recognition, and Consciousness" in *The Mind-Body Problem: A Guide to the Current Debate, Warner, Richard (ed)*, 87-98. Cambridge, Blackwell, 1994.

While some forms of the mind-body problem are solved and other ill-posed (e.g., those assuming a definite notion of the "physical"), the question whether science can explain mentality is real. It is connected to the question how mental processes are brought about by "submental" ones—as they clearly are. The epistemological ills of folk-psychological language make both questions hard. So do our first-person ways of access to conscious states. These issues are philosophical, not just technical; but they do not support the outlandish responses known from the literature.

Wagner, Wolfgang. The Fallacy of Misplaced Intentionality in Social Representation Research. *J Theor Soc Behav*, 24(3), 243-265, S 94.

This paper argues that social representations cannot be used as independent variables in causal explanations of social behaviour. It is shown that the structure of investigations often follows a causally explanatory design despite explicit statements to the contrary by the researchers. This fact is analyzed with three investigations. (edited)

Wahl, Russell. How Can What I Perceive Be True?. *Hist Phil Quart*, 12(2), 185-194, Ap 95.

Wahl, Russell. Impossible Propositions and the Forms of Objects in Wittgenstein's *Tractatus*. *Phil Quart*, 45(179), 190-198, Ap 95.

Wahlsten, Douglas. "Probability and the Understanding of Individual Differences" in *Probability in Theory-Building, Brzezinski, Jerzy (ed)*, 47-60. Amsterdam, Rodopi, 1994.

Wahsner, Renate. "Mechanism—Technizism—Organism" in *Naturzweckmässigkeit und ästhetische Kultur, Schwabe, Karl-Heinz (ed)*, 63-76. Sankt Augustin, Academia, 1993.

Wahsner, Renate. "'Ich bin der Apostel und Märtyrer der Engländer gewesen'" in *Naturauffassungen in Philosophie, Wissenschaft, Technik: Band II, Schäfer, Lothar (ed)*, 243-271. Freiburg, Alber, 1994.

Wain, Kenneth. Competing Conceptions of the Educated Public. *J Phil Educ*, 28(2), 149-159, Wint 94.

Alasdair MacIntyre's paper 'The idea of an educated public' followed on his frontal attack in *After Virtue* on the 'failed' intellectual project of the Enlightenment and on its liberal heritage. His argument, in the paper, was that the only way we can save ourselves from that failure is by restoring the idea of an educated public modelled on the type found in eighteenth century Scotland. This article takes up the issue of the 'crisis' of modernity, and argues that MacIntyre's 'public' is just one possible one and not necessarily the best. Other, competing conceptions of an educated public have been proposed, among others by Dewey and Habermas, that do not necessitate the conservative solution of going back to the past.

Wain, Kenneth. MacIntyre and the Idea of an Educated Public. *Stud Phil Educ*, 14(1), 105-123, 1995.

Some years ago, 1985, Alasdair MacIntyre wrote a paper on *The Idea of an Educated Public* in which he argued that the only route open for educators for the future, in order to emerge out of the current moral 'crisis' created by the 'emotivist' modernist culture is to bring back the idea of an 'educated public' from the Scottish Enlightenment and to regard education as education into such a public. The notion of an 'educated public', in effect, reappears in all his later books on moral philosophy, particularly his latest, *Three Rival Series of Moral Enquiry*, where he takes up his original proposal that educated publics should grow around universities and canvasses the new idea that under contemporary conditions what we may need is not one universal university but three kinds contextualized within the three rival kinds of cultural and moral programmes he identifies, and, correspondingly, three kinds of educated public. This paper tries to trace the evolution of MacIntyre's idea of an educated public throughout his work, 1) arguing that there is one particular perspective on the idea which he strangely omits, that represented by Dewey/Habermas, and 2) critiquing his final solution on the basis of its possibility and political desirability.

Wainer, S S and Handley, W G. Equational Derivation vs Computation. *Annals Pure Applied Log*, 70(1), 17-49, N 94.

Subrecursive hierarchy classifications are used to compare the complexities of recursive functions according to 1) their derivations in a version of Kleen's equation calculus, and 2) their computations by term-rewriting. In each case ordinal bounds are assigned, and it turns out that the respective complexity measures are given by 1) a version of the Fast Growing Hierarchy, and 2) the Slow Growing Hierarchy. Known comparisons between the two hierarchies then provide ordinal trade-offs between 1) derivation and 2) computation. Characteristics of some well-known subrecursive classes are also read off.

Waisel, David and Truog, Robert D. Amnesia Instead of Anesthesia: Not Always a Question of Consent. *J Clin Ethics*, 5(2), 153-155, Sum 94.

Some of the medications used in the practice of anesthesiology primarily produce amnesia, with little or no pain-relieving effect (analgesia). In rare cases, physicians use these agents *instead* of adequate analgesia, and rely on the amnestic effects to avoid patient complaints. In other cases, the best possible anesthesia has been achieved, but is not sufficient to make the patient comfortable. While we believe that the former use of these medications is simply bad medical practice, we argue that in the latter case the decision of whether to use amnestic agents should be based upon the patient's choice and informed consent.

Wajszczyk, Józef. The Logic of Dichotomic Changes. *Bull Sec Log*, 24(2), 89-97, Je 95.

Waldenfels, Bernhard. Ein menschlicher Traum für Wachende: Zur Natürlichkeit und Künstlichkeit der Erfahrung. *Filozof Istraz*, 13(4), 879-891, 1993.

In diesem Text versucht der Autor eine neue Problemkonfiguration hinsichtlich des Verhältnisses von Natürlichkeit und Künstlichkeit der menschlichen Erfahrung der Welt zu eröffnen. Der Autor geht davon aus, dass die bisherige Deutung der Welterfahrung, die als Bilderfahrung vermittelt wird, einen "Platonismus" voraussetzt, d.h. eine Spaltung der wahren Wirklichkeit und der Wirklichkeit, die durch das Bild der Wirklichkeit vermittelt wird. Aus dieser Spaltung geht auch die Unterscheidung der Natürlichkeit der Erfahrung und der Erfahrung von hergestellter, künstlicher, sozusagen derivierter Welt hervor. Die wahre Natürlichkeit als sich-selbst-herstellendes und selbstbewegendes Selbst wird im Gegensatz zur Welt des Künstlichen als "erste Natur" verstanden. Der Autor versucht aber diese Spaltung in Frage zu stellen, indem er die gewohnte Gegenüberstellung der Natürlichkeit der Erfahrung und der Künstlichkeit ablehnt. (edited)

Waldron, Jeremy. Family Justice and Social Justice. *Pac Phil Quart*, 75(3-4), 353-371, S-D 94.

Waldron, Jeremy. Why Law—Efficacy, Freedom, or Fidelity?. *Law Phil*, 13(3), 259-284, Ag 94.

Waldron, William S. How Innovative is the *Alayavijnana*?, Part II. *J Indian Phil*, 23(1), 9-51, Mr 95.

Walicki, Andrzej. The Idea of Universalism in the Polish Romantic Tradition. *Dialogue Hum*, 3(4), 19-38, 1993.

Walker, Brian. John Rawls, Mikhail Bakhtin, and the Praxis of Toleration. *Polit Theory*, 23(1), 101-127, F 95.

Walker, Chris. Karl Jaspers and Edmund Husserl—I: The Perceived Convergence. *Phil Psychiat Psych*, 1(2), 117-134, Je 94.

This is the first of three papers that examine the relationship between the psychopathological phenomenology of Karl Jaspers, the early philosophical phenomenology of Edmund Husserl (papers 1 and 2), and the role of phenomenology in the philosophy of Immanuel Kant (paper 3). The paper traces the development of Husserl's phenomenology from his earliest work in the philosophy of mathematics (1891) to the beginning of his transcendental phenomenology (1913), with a strong emphasis on *Logical Investigations*—the only work of any concern to Jaspers. (edited)

Walker, Chris. Karl Jaspers and Edmund Husserl—II: The Divergence. *Phil Psychiat Psych*, 1(4), 245-265, D 94.

This is the second of three papers exploring the philosophical influences on Jaspers's psychopathology. It examines Jaspers's work in the light of five themes from Husserl's early phenomenology in his *Logical Investigations*. The five themes are: 1) Phenomenology must begin with experience. 2) Consciousness is intrinsically intentional, i.e., it is necessarily directed toward an object. 3) Phenomenology is concerned with real meanings; only Husserl's later phenomenology is concerned with meaning as ideal, a priori essence. 4) Phenomenology is a scientific methodology for the investigation of subjective experience but not a scientific philosophy; only Husserl's later phenomenology claimed to be such a scientific philosophy. 5) Phenomenology is descriptive psychology.

Walker, Chris. Karl Jaspers and Edmund Husserl—III: Jaspers as a Kantian Phenomenologist. *Phil Psychiat Psych*, 2(1), 65-82, Mr 95.

This paper argues that specifically Kantian concepts of "appearance", "representation," and "form and content" are crucial to Jaspers's phenomenology. Phenomenology appears first in Kant's early correspondence and then in *The Metaphysical Foundations of Natural Science* (1786), where he uses it to mean the "theory of appearance." In order to become experience or knowledge, appearance must be "represented" in our intellect or understanding. Kant's theory of knowledge entails that such "representation" must divide into an intuitive content given from without and conceptual form imposed from within. Jaspers's phenomenology, correspondingly, is the description, definition, differentiation, and classification of subjective experience as appearance by the form or mode of its representation in consciousness. These concepts, it will be argued, as they are used in Jaspers's phenomenology, are essentially Kantian. They are completely absent from Husserl's phenomenology. It is concluded, therefore, that Jaspers himself radically misunderstood Husserl to be a descriptive psychologist. The real philosophical origins of Jaspers's phenomenology are to be found not in Husserl's philosophical phenomenology but in Kant's theory of knowledge. (edited)

Walker, Jeff. Was Ayn Rand a Humanist?. *Free Inq*, 14(3), 51-55, Sum 94.

Walker, Margaret Urban. Where Do Moral Theories Come From?. *Phil Forum*, 26(3), 242-257, Spr 95.

I analyze the specific conception of morality and moral philosophy—a "theoretical-juridical" one—constructed in nineteenth century utilitarian philosopher Henry Sidwick's *The Methods of Ethics*. I argue that this conception is the proximate historical source and conceptual template of the project of moral theory that has dominated Anglo-American ethics in the twentieth century. My account is intended to show how uncritical acceptance of this conception shields moral philosophers from important and uncomfortable questions about their positions to know and purposes in saying what morality "is."

Walker, Nigel. The Quiddity of Mercy. *Philosophy*, 70(271), 27-37, Ja 95.

Anselm and Aquinas had difficulty in reconciling God's mercy with his justice. Eighteenth-century thinkers had a similar difficulty with secular justice: if the law is right mercy cannot be, and vice versa. The problem was revived in the nineteen-sixties by Alwynne Smart, who claimed to have found a proper role for mercy in special cases. So have other philosophers in recent years, though less persuasively. Most recently, Ross Harrison has argued that mercy can have no place in the rules of a consistently rational penal code. It seems, however, that he has ignored more than one possibility. Finally, the assumption that a utilitarian code would rule out merciful decisions is also criticized.

Walker, Steven F. *Jung and the Jungians on Myth: An Introduction*. Hamden, Garland, 1995.

Wallace, Gerry. "War, Terrorism, and Ethical Consistency" in *Introducing Applied Ethics*, Almond, Brenda (ed), 305-317. Cambridge, Blackwell, 1995.

According to moral orthodoxy war can sometimes be justified but terrorism is always wrong. Whether the conventional view is ethically consistent is the subject of this essay. Orthodoxy insists that whatever justifies war cannot justify terrorism. So we must ask: what is the moral basis of the conventional attitude to war? Is terrorism a form of war? What concept of terrorism underpins the orthodox position? Does terrorism involve an evil in addition to those of war? It is argued that an examination of what is uncontroversially regarded as terrorism does not offer complete support for the orthodox view.

Wallace, Gerry. Wild Justice. *Philosophy*, 70(273), 363-375, Jl 95.

The nature and morality of revenge are explored in this paper. What is revenge? How is it related to self-defence, retribution and retaliation? Is there a right to revenge? What are we to make of the Christian's absolute prohibition on the taking of revenge? A number of literary examples of revenge are analysed alongside the characterisations of revenge offered by Schopenhauer and Bacon. It is argued that for the purposes of moral discussion malicious and non-malicious revenge must be distinguished and that although sometimes revenge may be justified there cannot be a general moral right to revenge.

Wallace, James D. Morality, Practical Knowledge, and Will. *J Phil Res*, 19, 23-36, 1994.

In *Quandaries and Virtues*, Edmund Pincoffs maintains that we observe a multiplicity of moral norms. A common life in which we participate supplies a context in which many virtues play diverse functional roles. He suggests, without developing the idea, that such a common life provides us with a structure for organizing and harmonizing the many moral norms we attempt to pursue. This essay explores that idea. Bodies of shared practical knowledge, such as medicine and scientific research, provide examples of empirically grounded practices in which people simultaneously observe a plurality of norms that guide them in right practice. The essay develops the idea that morality is in important ways like these bodies of technical practical knowledge. It maintains that the origin and source of authority of moral norms is appreciably like that of technical norms and that the motivation for observing such norms is fundamentally similar.

Wallace, Kathleen. John Smith's *America's Philosophical Vision*: American and/or Philosophical?. *Trans Peirce Soc*, 31(1), 11-19, Wint 95.

The article focuses on two main issues raised by Smith's work: one, the interpretation of philosophy as a discipline on the one hand and as representative of a culture on the other; two, the tension in Smith's treatment of American philosophy between an emphasis on the recovery of tradition and the propulsion to move forward to the cutting edge in philosophical thought. The author argues that the disciplinary and cutting edge features of American philosophy are somewhat underemphasized in Smith's work, while his interpretations of classical American philosophy continue to be oases of clarity in locating this philosophical tradition in a historical and cultural milieu.

Wallace, R Jay. *Responsibility and the Moral Sentiments*. Cambridge, Harvard Univ Pr, 1994.

The book defends the view that moral responsibility is a matter of normative competence, not freedom of the will. It involves the power to grasp moral reasons and to control one's behavior accordingly. The book connects the practice of holding people responsible to the reactive emotions of resentment, indignation, and guilt. It interprets the debate about responsibility as turning centrally on the question when it is *fair* to hold people morally responsible in this way, and argues that this normative condition is fulfilled by those agents who are competent to understand moral principles and to govern their actions accordingly.

Wallace, William A. Circularity and the Paduan *Regressus*: From Pietro d'Abano to Galileo Galilei. *Vivarium*, 33(1), 76-97, My 95.

The charge of circularity has often been made against the demonstrative regress, an Aristotelian logical methodology of discovery and proof. The article traces the history of its use in the Paduan tradition from Pietro d'Abano to Galileo, with particular attention to the teachings of Girolamo Balduino and Jacopo Zabarella and Zabarella's influence on Galileo. It argues that Galileo's use of the method—in his arguments for the existence of mountains on the moons, of Jupiter's satellites, and Venus's phases—was the first to show in a graphic way that the reasoning it employs is not circular.

Waller, Bruce N. Abortion and In Vitro Fertilization. *J Soc Phil*, 26(1), 119-128, Spr 95.

Opponents of elective abortion typically claim that because the rights of the fetus begin at conception, and the fetus' right to life takes precedence over any other rights involved, therefore it is legitimate to require a pregnant woman to carry her fetus to term. But that position would legitimize the coercive implantation of embryos produced by in vitro fertilization, including coercive implantation into women having no biological relation to the embryo. Examination of these implications leads to an improved interpretation of Judith Jarvis Thomson's violinist analogy: an interpretation that can withstand John Martin Fischer's critique.

Waller, Bruce N. Authenticity Naturalized. *Behavior Phil*, 23(1), 21-28, Spr-Sum 95.

Theories of autonomy divide into two conflicting categories: theories that emphasize freedom to choose among alternatives and theories that focus on personal authenticity. This conflict can be resolved by recognizing the basic function of natural authenticity, and its deep roots in human and animal behavior. Authenticity functions to keep options open that might be too hastily abandoned. Thus forms a natural symbiotic union with autonomy as alternatives. Human authenticity is a special adaptation, but it is not different in kind from the authenticity of may other species. My naturalistic account of authenticity avoids traditional problems concerning willing addicts and happy slaves and reaffirms the traditional link between authenticity and autonomous choices among alternatives.

Waller, Bruce N. Noncognitivist Moral Realism. *Philosophia (Israel)*, 24(1-2), 57-75, D 94.

Wallis, Charles. Ceteris Paribus Laws and Psychological Explanations. *Proc Phil Sci Ass*, 1, 388-397, 1994.

I argue that Fodor's (1991) analysis of ceteris paribus laws fails to underwrite his appeal to such laws in his sufficient conditions for representation. It also renders his appeal to ceteris paribus laws impotent against the major problem for this theory of representation. Finally, Fodor's analysis fails to provide useful solutions to the traditional problems associated with a thoroughgoing understanding of ceteris paribus clauses. The analysis, therefore, fails to bolster Fodor's (1975, 1990) position that special science laws are of necessity ceteris paribus laws and that one must recognize them as scientifically legitimate.

Wallis, Charles. Representation and the Imperfect Ideal. *Phil Sci*, 61(3), 407-428, S 94.

This paper examines the nomic covariationist strategy of using idealization to define representation. While the literature has focused upon the possibility of defining ideal conditions for perception, I argue that nomic covariationist appeals to idealization are pseudoscientific and contrary to a foundational and empirically well-supported methodological presupposition in cognitive science. Moreover, one major figure in this camp fails to come to grips with its role and its problems in mainstream science. Thus he forwards a false dichotomy of the sciences and treats idealization as a blank check written by scientists on an unknown bank. Finally, I consider and reject alternative formulations of the nomic covariationists's idealization strategy.

Walliser, Bernard. "Three Generalization Processes for Economic Models" in *Idealization VI: Idealization in Economics*, Hamminga, Bert (ed), 55-69. Amsterdam, Rodopi, 1994.

When considering how economic models evolve, the main operation appearing at work is generalization, which can itself be decomposed into three basic processes, conceptually distinct although not formally independent, but more and more ambitious. The enlarging process simply consists in extending the application domain of a model without modifying its formal structure, in order to transfer its properties from one field to another. The weakening process consists in constructing a model with a less stringent specification of one or more of its assumptions, in order to account for a larger set of situations. The rooting process consists in finding out some grounding propositions which infer one or more of the model's assumptions, in order to have a deeper explanation of its properties. Each process can be logically defined and illustrated by basic examples, may be considered at different levels and gives rise to model taxonomies, and fulfills as well a formal and an empirical role.

Wallulis, Jerald T. The Complexity of Bodily Feeling. *Human Stud*, 17(3), 373-380, Jl 94.

The experimental psychology of Eugene Gendlin offers a complex description of bodily feeling in terms of a full inward bodily sensing of one's situation. This essay examines positively Gendlin's descriptions of the "carrying forward" of feeling into the future and of the "focaling" or sensing of a whole bodily direction. It then endorses his account of the modern intricacy of bodily feeling expressed in the New Awareness Movement. Finally, it raises a critical question concerning social formation and whether Gendlin treats it with the same nuanced complexity as his important account of bodily feeling.

Walsh, Brian J. *Langdon Gilkey: Theologian for a Culture in Decline*. Lanham, Univ Pr of America, 1991.

Walsh, John-Pierre. École et Pédagogie. *Philosopher*, 13, 181-196, 1992.

Walsh, Peter (trans) and Froment-Meurice, Marc. *Solitudes: From Rimbaud to Heidegger*. Albany, SUNY Pr, 1995.

Walsh, Sylvia. Living Poetically: Kierkegaard and German Romanticism. *Hist Euro Ideas*, 20(1-3), 189-194, Ja 95.

Walter, Gerry and Reisner, Ann. Journalists' Views of Advertiser Pressures on Agricultural News. *J Agr Environ Ethics*, 7(2), 157-172, 1994.

All major journalism ethical codes explicitly state that journalists should protect editorial copy from undue influence by outside sources. A study of newspaper reporters who cover agricultural news found that the most pressing ethical concern is the effect of advertiser (agri-business) pressure on editorial copy, and that their concerns in general parallel those of farm magazine writers and editors. The majority reported being in situations in which they might be exposed to advertiser pressure, including pressures to change or withhold editorial copy. The newspaper reporters who cover agricultural beats showed slightly more resistance to advertiser pressure than did farm magazine editors in a parallel study. (edited)

Walters, Bruce and Hardin, Tim and Schick, James. Top Executive Compensation: Equity or Excess? Implications for Regaining American Competitiveness. *J Bus Ethics*, 14(3), 227-234, Mr 95.

The debate over compensation packages for top executives is discussed. Particular emphasis is placed on the decoupling of CEO pay and organizational performance. A contrast is drawn between firms that are owner-controlled and those that are manager-controlled. Owner-controlled firms tend to be more market-driven. In manager-controlled firms, however, ownership can become diluted to the point where decisions may not always be in the best interest of shareholders. The process of determining CEO compensation packages is examined, and special attention is given to the handling of stock options. In order to stem the threat of increased government intervention, suggestions are made for increasing the leverage of compensation committees and of shareholders in general.

Walters, LeRoy and Murphy, Timothy F. The Moral Significance of AIDS. *J Med Phil*, 19(6), 519-524, D 94.

Walton, Douglas N. Begging the Question as a Pragmatic Fallacy. *Synthese*, 100(1), 95-131, Jl 94.

The aim of this paper is to make it clear how and why begging the question should be seen as a pragmatic fallacy which can only be properly evaluated in a context of dialogue. Included in the paper is a review of the contemporary literature on begging the question that shows the gradual emergence over the past twenty years or so of the dialectical conception of this fallacy. A second aim of the paper is to investigate a number of general problems raised by the pragmatic framework.

Walton, Douglas N and Krabbe, Erik C W. *Commitment in Dialogue: Basic Concepts of Interpersonal Reasoning*. Albany, SUNY Pr, 1995.

This book develops a logical analysis of dialogue in which two or more parties attempt to advance their own arguments. It includes a classification of the major types of dialogues and a discussion of several important informal fallacies. The authors define the concept of commitment in a way that makes it useful in evaluating arguments. In traditional logic, a proposition is either true or false, and that is the end of it. In this new framework, an arguer can be held to his or her commitments in some cases, but in other cases, he or she can retract them without violating any rule of the dialogue. "Commitment in Dialogue" studies the conditions under which commitments should be held or may be retracted within an argument.

Walton, Gertrud. Cohen on Einstein on Simultaneity. *Philosophy*, 70(271), 114-118, Ja 95.

The debate has failed to consider content and validity of Einstein's mathematical arguments. I draw attention to elementary errors which invalidate Einstein's derivations, which show that his logic is seriously flawed, and which are responsible for the paradoxical implications of supposedly counter-intuitive mathematical truths. While the 'simple derivation' in an Appendix to *Relativity: The Special and The General Theory* constitutes an exercise in surrealist algebra, the argument central to the 1905 paper contains the proof that frames of reference moving in opposite directions are at rest with each other. The disenfranchisement of reason by mathematics must be contested.

Walton, Gertrud. Hanfling on Loving My Neighbour, Loving Myself. *Philosophy*, 69(270), 491-496, O 94.

The philosophical debate about the 'Christian' (biblical) command to love is inadequate. First, it ignores historical studies into the origin and subsequent development of Christian teaching, as well as a substantial Jewish literature which emphasizes the fundamental difference between the Christian and Jewish conceptions of human nature. Second, the uniquely Jewish belief in rational autonomy is confirmed by neurophysiological studies which show that cortical structures responsible for specifically human function grow in response to voluntary action. We arrive at a radical revaluation of human potential and of the metaphysical significance of the evolution of rational autonomy.

Walzer, Michael. Moralischer Minimalismus. *Deut Z Phil*, 42(1), 3-13, 1994.

Walzer, Michael. Response to Veit Bader. *Polit Theory*, 23(2), 247-249, My 95.

Wang, Hao. Time in Philosophy and in Physics: From Kant and Einstein to Gödel. *Synthese*, 102(2), 215-234, F 95.

The essay centers on Gödel's views on the place of our intuitive concept of time in philosophy and in physics. It presents my interpretation of his work on the theory of relativity, his observations on the relationship between Einstein's theory and Kantian philosophy, as well as some of the scattered remarks in his conversations with me in the seventies—namely, those of the philosophies of Leibniz, Hegel and Husserl—as a successor of Kant—in relation to their conceptions of time.

Wang, Hao. What is Logic?. *Monist*, 77(3), 261-277, Jl 94.

Wangerin, Paul T. Four Problems of Professional Ethics. *Prof Ethics*, 2(3-4), 39-58, Fall-Wint 93.

Ward, Andrew. Is Gerwin's Natural-Agency Theory a Viable Alternative to Hume?. *Dialogue (Canada)*, 33(4), 733-742, Fall 94.

Ward, David. The Solution of the Problem of Personal Identity *via* Locke, Butler, and Hume. *Locke News*, 25, 53 63, 1994.

Ward, Fritz R. 18th-Century Supplements to the Yolton and Attig Bibliographies. *Locke News*, 24, 107-114, 1993.

Ward, Graham. *Barth, Derrida, and the Language of Theology*. New York, Cambridge Univ Pr, 1995.

The book sets out to map the philosophy of language context within which Karl Barth's theology of language (the *analogia fidei* emerges. It then proceeds to show how the problematic Barth is wrestling with parallels the economy of *differance* as Jacques Derrida expounds it. In a series of comparisons between Barth and Levinas, Levinas and Derrida, Derrida and Barth the book argues how Derrida's work unlocks what have appeared to be contradictions within Barth's, while Bart's work unveils why Derrida continually returns to theological questions in his discussions and analyses of language.

Ward, J S K. The Question of Truth in Religion. *J Dharma*, 19(3), 209-223, Jl-S 94.

Ward, Julie K. "Beauvoir's Two Senses of 'Body' in *The Second Sex*" in *Feminist Interpretations of Simone de Beauvoir, Simons, Margaret A (ed)*, 223-242. University Park, Penn St Univ Pr, 1995.

Ward, Steven C. In the Shadow of the Deconstructed Metanarratives: Baudrillard, Latour and the End of Realist Epistemology. *Hist Human Sci*, 7(4), 73-94, N 94.

This paper explores the relationship between J Baudrillard's postmodern theory and B Latour's sociological constructionism with regard to the end of (realist) epistemology debate. While both lines of thought claim epistemology to be at an end,

they differ on what this means for contemporary theory. Postmodernists, such as Baudrillard, claim that in the current post-epistemological environment the only appropriate model available for intellectual activity is some form of literary criticism or analysis. However, from the constructionist position, such a move means that postmodernists are still operating under a modern epistemological dualism. This dualism leads post-modernists to conclude that if we cannot have fact we can only have fiction. For the constructionists, truth and reality are not simply textual and ideation, but socially constructed human products. As such, they have a social meaning and facticity which survives the figurative death of epistemology. Finally, it is argued that the constructionist critique makes the postmodern "literary turn" problematic.

Wardlaw, Harry. Theological Study and the Pursuit of Truth. *Sophia (Australia)*, 34(1), 233-240, Mr-Ap 95.

Warenski, Lisa. A Rebuttal To Shelly Kagan's Attack on Options. *Conference*, 4(1), 64-76, Spr 93.

Warfield, Ted A. Knowing the World and Knowing Our Minds. *Phil Phenomenol Res*, 55(3), 525-545, S 95.

Hilary Putnam argued that externalism about mental content can be combined with standard views about privileged access in an argument showing that at least certain forms of skepticism are false. The standard reply claims that in assuming externalism, Putnam undercuts privileged access and thus cannot refute the skeptic. I show that this reply is a clear failure. I also argue that philosophers should either accept that skepticism is provably false or should embrace skepticism. The moderate position which holds that skepticism is false but not provably so is, I argue, demonstrably false.

Warfield, Ted A and McLaughlin, B P. The Allure of Connectionism Reexamined. *Synthese*, 101(3), 365-400, D 94.

There is currently a debate over whether cognitive architecture is classical or connectionist in nature. One finds the following three comparisons between classical architecture and connectionist architecture made in the pro-connectionist literature in this debate: 1) connectionist architecture is neurally plausible and classical architecture is not; 2) connectionist architecture is far better suited to model pattern recognition capacities than is classical architecture; and 3) connectionist architecture is far better suited to model the acquisition of pattern recognition capacities by learning than is classical architecture. If true, 1)-3) would yield a compelling case against the view that cognitive architecture is classical, and would offer some reason to think that cognitive architecture may be connectionist. We first present the case for 1)-3) in the very works of connectionist enthusiasts. We then argue that the currently available evidence fails to support any of 1)-3).

Warfield, Ted A and Stich, Stephen. "Reply to Clark and Smolensky: Do Connectionist Minds Have Beliefs?" in *Connectionism: Debates on Psychological Explanation, Macdonald, Cynthia (ed)*, 395-411. Cambridge, Blackwell, 1995.

We reply to papers by Andy Clark and Paul Smolensky on the issue of whether connectionist theories of the mind lend support to eliminativism about the propositional attitudes. We also discuss the general form of eliminativist arguments and identify some implausible hidden premises of such arguments.

Warfield, Ted A (ed) and Stich, Stephen P (ed). *Mental Representation: A Reader*. Cambridge, Blackwell, 1994

This anthology collects new and recent work on mental representation and theories of mental content. The volume includes work from Fodor, Dretske, Field, Dennet and others as well as essays critically evaluating the most popular theories of mental content.

Warnek, Peter (trans) and Brogan, Walter (trans) and Heidegger, Martin. *Aristotle's Metaphysics* Theta 1-3: On the Essence and Actuality of Force. Bloomington, Indiana Univ Pr, 1995.

Warner, Martin. Rhetoric and Philosophy. *Phil Lit*, 19(1), 106-115, Ap 95.

Failure to distinguish stylistic from persuasive conceptions of rhetoric has confused recent discussions. Philosophical analysis of rhetoric (understood stylistically) has focussed on the tropes, while analysis of the art of persuasion leads, *inter alia*, into jurisprudence. Stylistic analysis of philosophy can reveal "metaphor in the text of philosophy" without deconstructing it, but analysis of philosophical argument in terms of rational persuasiveness provides a more promising tool for philosophical self-analysis.

Warner, Richard. "In Defense of a Dualism" in *The Mind-Body Problem: A Guide to the Current Debate, Warner, Richard (ed)*, 343-354. Cambridge, Blackwell, 1994.

Warner, Richard (ed) and Szubka, Tadesz (ed). *The Mind-Body Problem: A Guide to the Current Debate*. Cambridge, Blackwell, 1994.

Warnke, Georgia. "Communicative Rationality and Cultural Values" in *The Cambridge Companion to Habermas, White, Stephen K (ed)*, 120-142. New York, Cambridge Univ Pr, 1995.

Warnke, Georgia. "Hermeneutics, Tradition, and the Standpoint of Women" in *Hermeneutics and Truth, Wachterhauser, Brice (ed)*, 206-226. Evanston, Northwestern Univ Pr, 1994.

Warnock, Mary. *Imagination and Time*. Cambridge, Blackwell, 1994.

This book explores certain closely related ideas: personal identity, time, history and our commitment to the future, and the interpretative and cognitive role of the imagination. Warnock argues that the notion of personal immortality, as it appears in Christian dogma, cannot be taken literally. Nevertheless, as a metapor, immortality may illuminate both our relation with the past, our values and our responsibility for the future.

Warren, Mark E. "Nietzsche and Weber: When Does Reason Become Power?" in *The Barbarism of Reason, Horowitz, Asher (ed)*, 68-98. Toronto, Univ of Toronto Pr, 1994.

An examination of Nietzsche's and Weber's views that Enlightenment conceptions of reason are implicated in power. By distinguishing between reason locus of expression (thought, action, institution) and its mode (consistency, instrumentality, autonomy), the article shows (1) which forms of reason disappoint the Enlightenment view that reason might contain and ground power; (2) which forms of reason combine with power to produce domination; and (3) the extent and limitations of Nietzsche's and Weber's critiques.

Warren, Mark E. "The Self in Discursive Democracy" in *The Cambridge Companion to Habermas, White, Stephen K (ed)*, 167-200. New York, Cambridge Univ Pr, 1995.

Wartofsky, Marx. Science and Art: Heuristic and Aesthetic Dimensions of Scientific Discovery. *Phil Exch*, 24-25, 5-12, 1993-94.

Wartofsky, Marx W. "*Homo Homini Deus Est*: Feuerbach's Religious Materialism" in *Meaning, Truth, and God, Rouner, Leroy (ed)*, 154-173. Notre Dame, Univ Notre Dame Pr, 1982.

Waser, Ruedi. *Autonomie des Selbstbewusstseins: Eine Untersuchung zum Verhältnis von Bruno Bauer und Karl Marx (1835-1843)*. Tubingen, Francke, 1994.

Interpreting the relation Bauer/Marx 1835-43 based since 150 years on a misunderstood lampoon Bauer's against Hegel in 1841, which was taken as basic text of Bauer's Hegel-Revision whereas his substantial Revision—"Die Philosophie des Selbstbewusstseins"—was never looked through to its core with its ruinous philosophical consequences. Against the "opinio communis" Marx did not follow Bauer on this wrong way. Characteristic of this relation therefore are differences in problems of religion, state, emancipation and of theory and practice. Marx's way to *feuerbach* did not lead over the "Philosophie des Selbstbewusstseins" but was a complex transformation-process outgoing from Hegel's objective idealism itself.

Washburn, Jimmy. Kierkegaard, la recuperación del individuo existente y el discurso sobre lo histórico. *Rev Filosof (Costa Rica)*, 32(77), 117-121, Jl 94.

The reflection around history faces the distinction between the objective history and the subjective one, that is, the challenge between the changing and the logos (understood as permanent). Kierkegaard talks about change given in each individual existence and he points out how difficult it is to match this with the historical speech that is made in universal terms (permanent).

Wasserman, David. Impairment, Disadvantage, and Equality: A Reply to Anita Silvers. *J Soc Phil*, 25(3), 181-188, Wint 94.

Wasserman, Larry and Seidenfeld, Teddy and Herron, Timothy. The Extent of Dilation of Sets of Probabilities and the Asymptotics of Robust Bayesian Inference. *Proc Phil Sci Ass*, 1, 250-259, 1994.

We experience the phenomenon of dilation, where updating using sets of Bayesian conditional probabilities always causes the upper (and lower) probability of an event to increase (and decrease), thereby causing more uncertainty with regards to the event's truth. First, we contrast short-run dilation with standard long-run convergence of opinion results. Second, we note when dilation occurs and how dilation is connected to the independence of the conditioned and conditioning events. Third, we use sets of probabilities and asymptotic (increasing sample size) dilation to provide an interpretation of the difference between standard Neyman-Pearson hypothesis testing and Harold Jeffrey's Bayesian hypothesis testing.

Wassermann, Gerhard D. *A Philosophy of Matter and Mind: A New Look at an Old Major Topic in Philosophy*. Brookfield, Avebury, 1994.

A new foundation of a (nondialectical) mechanistic materialism is proposed. It is claimed that parts of the backbone of mechanistic materialism are 'scientific hypothetico-deductive theories', such as Newtonian mechanics, continuum mechanics, classical electromagnetic theory, quantum mechanics, quantum electrodynamics and thermodynamics. Much of the book gives a new characterization of the typical structure of 'scientific hypothetico-deductive theories', which shows what is typical of mechanistic materialism, since 'scientific hypthetico-deductive theories' try to explain many properties of matter. Mentality is also dealt with within the present mechanistic materialism. Attacks on mechanistic materialism by Aristotle, Martha Nussbaum and Bryan Magee are rebutted, and A Olding's mistaken views are dealt with.

Waterfield, Robin (trans) and Annas, Julia (& other eds) and Plato. *Statesman*. New York, Cambridge Univ Pr, 1995.

Waterman, Craig M. The Turing Test and the Argument from Analogy for Other Minds. *SW Phil Rev*, 11(1), 15-22, Ja 95.

In his 1950 paper "Computing Machinery and Intelligence" (A M Turing, *Mind*, LIX, 1950, pp. 433-60) Alan Turing proposed a test for machine intelligence that has come to be known as the "Turing test". I argue that we can understand the Turing test on the model of an argument from analogy for other minds, and so the test is not inherently behavioristic. I also argue that Turing's presentation of his test does not obviously favor either a behavioristic or an analogistic interpretation. I do not defend the Turing test itself under either interpretation.

Waters, Raphael T. Capital Punishment: An Act of Murder, Revenge, or Justice. *Cont Phil*, 16(6), 2-8, N-D 94.

In this article the author argues that modern society has focused almost exclusively on the physical descriptions of violent acts, to the detriment of their moral dimensions. This is a key reason that capital punishment is (erroneously) viewed as an act of revenge, rather than (correctly) as the just and authorized removal of a dangerous person from society.

Watkins, John. How I Almost Solved the Problem of Induction. *Philosophy*, 70(273), 429-435, Jl 95.

In his *Science and Scepticism* that author had proposed a new solution to the pragmatic problem of induction. The idea was to justify a pragmatic preference for IP (inductive principle) over CIP (counter-inductive principle) without justifying IP itself. Let IP and CIP be of the same logical strength, and E be evidence of past successes of IP. It was argued that the conjunction E-and-CIP has an excess content which has no counterpart in E-and-IP. The present Note points out that this argument, though correct, is covertly inductive since 'weaker' implies 'more probable'.

Watson, Gary. Freedom and Strength of Will in Hoffman and Albritton. *Phil Stud*, 77(2-3), 261-271, Mr 95.

Watson, Graham. A Comparison of Social Constructionist and Ethnomethodological Descriptions of How a Judge Distinguished Between the Erotic and the Obscene. *Phil Soc Sci*, 24(4), 405-425, D 94.

In 1985, a member of the Canadian judiciary handed down a written judgment in which he distinguished between erotica and obscene matter. The judgment attracted the scorn of some normative sociologists, who complained of the insufficiency of the social psychological research on which it was based. Their reaction prompts a review of the judgment in the light of social constructionism and of ethnomethodology; this, in turn, prompts a comparison of social constructionist and ethnomethodological methodologies, in which the legal judgment serves merely as a test case. It is argued that normative sociology and social constructionism, both being of an essentially ironic cast, occlude the judge's sense-making procedures, the very phenomena they purport to describe. Ethnomethodology, on the other hand, being nonironic, promises to capture those procedures.

Watson, James R. The End of Philosophy, the Time of Auschwitz, and the Bound Transcendence of Communities of Differences. *Hist Euro Ideas*, 20(1-3), 567-573, Ja 95.

The end of philosophy is reached with the accomplished nihilism of the Nazi death camps. The transitional period following this transformative event is marked by a stubborn and often studied rejection of the contention that the essence of the West was revealed in Auschwitz. The positions adopted by this paper is that repetitions of metaphysics attempt to transcend the event by tacitly denying that transcendence has been irreversibly altered by it. The task is that of "overcoming" metaphysics, meaning the orienting of thought within the transformative event and thus "binding" transcendence. Bound trascendence is both contextual and dialectical and cannot appeal to any standard or principle capable of subsuming the plurality of responses.

Watson, Richard A. Malebranche and Arnauld on Ideas. *Mod Sch*, 71(4), 259-270, My 94.

I examine the answers of Malebranche and Arnauld to two questions: What is an idea? and How does an idea represent its object? I give textual arguments for the conclusion that despite their standard Cartesian denial that mental ideas can be in any way like material objects, for both Malebranche and Arnauld, ideas represent their objects by resembling them. This is a major reinterpretation in opposition to more traditional views.

Waugh, Joanne B and Bochner, Arthur P. "Talking-With as a Model for Writing-About: Implications of Rortyean Pragmatism" in *Recovering Pragmatism's Voice, Langsdorf, Lenore (ed)*, 211-233. Albany, SUNY Pr, 1995.

This essay takes issue with traditional social science conceptions of communication as a research object and questions the validity of appropriations of writing as a model for speaking. The authors focus on ways in which the exemplary status of the scientist as a "moral exemplar" hinges on fixing language as an object out of which meaning can be found. The authors trace how from Plato on philosophical speech became parasitic on a conception of writing that claims a power external to our own. In response to the failed notion that nature can inscribe itself as an object, the authors propose an interpretative conception of language based on Davidson's notion of a "passing theory" that inspires a quite different conception of communication, one that blurs divisions between the narrative genres of literature and social science.

Waugh, Linda R. Degrees of Iconicity in the Lexicon. *J Prag*, 22(1), 55-70, Jl 94.

Iconicity is an important part of language: e.g., there is substantial diagrammatic iconicity in the lexicon due to recurrences of form-meaning connections in morphemes, submorphemes, phonesthemes, and word-affinity relations. However, the term morpheme has been applied to phenomena which do not exhibit iconicity. And, differential polysemy across words constrains cross-lexical recurrence of meaning. It emerges that the lexicon exhibits degrees of iconicity, as defined by two competing tendencies for sound: one towards total iconicity, the other towards total noniconicity (arbitrariness).

Wautischer, Helmut. On Love and Awareness. *Dialogue Hum*, 4(2-3), 31-40, 1994.

In this paper I will discuss some aspects of a humanistic perspective on love which include both elements, idealistic (e.g., concepts of oneness) as well as realistic (e.g., social anthropology) ones. I will argue, that any experience of love is directly affected by an individual's love of self-awareness that enables a person to recognize the origins of his feelings and allows him to act upon them in an intentional manner. Through such realizations, an individual can remain an autonomous actor, utilizing his knowledge of oneself to explore one's emotions beyond the limits of social restraints. For it is the authentic experience of one's awareness that enables a rational person to master the existential absurdity of one's existence. I will claim that the origin of love does not reside in the realm of emotionality. Instead, love relates directly to an individual's state of self-awareness.

Wawrykow, Joseph. The *Summa Contra Gentiles*: On the Contribution of the *De Trinitate* of Hilary of Poitiers. *Thomist*, 58(4), 617-634, O 94.

Waxman, Wayne. Kant on the Possibility of Thought: Universals without Language. *Rev Metaph*, 48(4), 809-858, Je 95.

A consideration of Kant's theory of general representation, focusing on certain passages in the Transcendental Deduction (esp. B133n) and the Paralogisms. Two obstacles Kant had to overcome are considered. First, given his insistence on the radical heterogeneity between sensibility and understanding, how can the advent of thought (concepts, judgments) be explained without surreptitiously intellectualizing the sensible or sensibilizing the intellectual (transcendental amphiboly)? Second, why, in the wake of Hume's reduction of understanding and reasoning to associative imagination, is it necessary to suppose the existence of an intellectual faculty over and above imagination? The article concludes with a consideration of the transition from thought as such (conceptus communis) to cognitive thought in conformity with the categories (concepts of objects).

Way, Eileen Cornell and Harré, Rom and Aronson, Jerrold L. *Realism Rescued: How Scientific Progress Is Possible*. Peru, Open Court, 1995.

A full-blown version of convergent realism is defined and defended by replacing the logicist technique for analyzing scientific theories with one found in knowledge representation, the dynamic type hierarchy. The authors use these hierarchies to provide an analysis of models that displays their indispensable role in science. They go on to use this analysis to develop a semantics for verisimilitude, truth and modalities. An inductive justification for convergent realism is then presented, one which, the authors contend, is not open to the objections that anti-realists have made against the inference to the best explanation defense.

Wayne, Andrew. Bayesianism and Diverse Evidence. *Phil Sci*, 62(1), 111-121, Mr 95.

A common methodological adage holds that diverse evidence better confirms a hypothesis than does the same amount of similar evidence. Proponents of Bayesian approaches to scientific reasoning such as Horwich, Howson and Urbach, and Earman claim to offer both a precise rendering of this maxim in probabilistic terms and an explanation of why the maxim should be a part of the methodological canon of good science. This paper contends that these claims are mistaken and that, at best, Bayesian accounts of diverse evidence are crucially incomplete. This failure should lend renewed force to a long-neglected global worry about Bayesian approaches.

Wear, Stephen and Logue, Gerald. A Desperate Solution: Individual Autonomy and the Double-Blind Controlled Experiment. *J Med Phil*, 20(1), 57-64, F 95.

The randomization ingredient in double-blind controlled experiments may be objectionable to patients who, in their desperation, come to such trials seeking a last chance of cure. Minogue *et al*, who view such a situation as inherently exploitive and undermining of patient autonomy, propose that such "desperate volunteers" instead be enrolled in the active arm, while other patients, less desperate and more committed to medical progress, continue to be randomized. Their view is critiqued as destructive of medical progress, inappropriate in its lack of clinical response to such patients, and fatally flawed by unrealistic notions of autonomy and voluntariness.

Weaver, Gary R. Does Ethics Code Design Matter? Effects of Ethics Code Rationales and Sanctions on Recipients' Justice Perceptions and Content Recall. *J Bus Ethics*, 14(5), 367-385, My 95.

Prior research on ethics codes has suggested, but rarely tested, the effects of code design alternatives on the impact of codes. This study considers whether the presence of explanatory rationales and descriptions of sanctions in ethics codes affects recipients' responses to a code. Theories of organizational justice and persuasive communication support an expectation that rationales and sanctions will be positively related to code recipients' recall of code content and perceptions of organizational justice. Content recall is an obvious precondition of code compliance; justice perceptions have multiple implications for the attitudes and actions of organizational members. Results show that explanatory rationales are associated with a statistically significant increase in perceptions of organizational procedural justice, but that rationales and sanctions generally show no relationship to distributive justice perceptions and accurate content recall. These results suggest that common prescriptions regarding ethics code design are of uncertain value apart from further research which unearths the relationships among the intended and perceived purposes of codes, the organizational settings in which they are applied, and a wide variety of code designs.

Weaver, George. A Note on Definability in Equational Logic. *Hist Phil Log*, 15(2), 189-199, 1994.

After an introduction which demonstrates the failure of the equational analogue of Beth's definability theorem, the first two sections of this paper are devoted to an elementary exposition of a proof that a functional constant is equationally definable in an equational theory if and only if every model of the set of those consequences of the theory that do not contain the functional constant is uniquely extendible to a model of the theory itself. Sections three, four and five are devoted to applications and extensions of this result. Topics considered here include equational definability in first order logic, an extended notion of definability in equational logic and the synonymy of equational theories. The final two sections briefly review some of the history of equational logic.

Webb, Mark Owen. Does the Sanctity of Christian Mystics Corroborate their Claims?. *Int J Phil Relig*, 37(2), 63-71, Ap 95.

In the Christian mystical tradition it is sometimes supposed that the moral and spiritual improvement of mystics is evidence of the veridicality of their experiences, and hence of Christianity in general. I argue that it is not because 1) mere perceptual contact is not sufficient to cause moral improvement, and so is not the best explanation for that improvement, and 2) even if it were, this would not support Christian doctrine more than any other religion's.

Webb, Mark Owen. Nota sobre *Sophismata* 8.4 de Buridán. *Pat Med*, 15, 39-44, 1994.

John Buridan's *Sophismata* chapter eight is a well-known and heroic attempt to deal with the problems of propositions that are paradoxical because of self-reference. In the midst of his discussion of such propositions (which discussion includes the famous "liar" paradox), we find *sophisma* 4, the proposition 'I say that a man is a donkey'. The question is whether a person uttering that proposition says something true or something false. Buridan seems to come to exactly the wrong conclusion about the solution to this *sophisma*, and it is a bit of a puzzle why. The answer is that his own theory of propositions invited him to slip back and forth between two interpretations of the *sophisma*.

Weber, Frank P. Initial Segments of the Lattice of Ideals of R E Degrees. *J Sym Log*, 59(4), 1326-1350, D 94.

Weber, Leonard J and Campbell, Margaret L. Procuring Organs From a Non-Heart-Beating Cadaver: Commentary on a Case Report. *Kennedy Inst Ethics J*, 5(1), 35-42, Mr 95.

Procurement of organs from non-heart-beating cadaver donors raises concerns. Standards for optimal patient care during withdrawal of life-sustaining therapy are evolving and continue to be debated and studied. Consensus on specific procedures and methods has not been attained, however, and protocols for the procurement of organs from patients following the withdrawal of life-sustaining therapies may compromise the evolving standards and harm the patient and the attendant family. In addition, there is little evidence to suggest that such protocols will significantly increase the number of organs procured. "Non-heart-beating cadaver" protocols that do not give comprehensive attention to optimal patient/family care at the time of withdrawal of life-sustaining therapy ought not to be endorsed.

Weber, Ralf. "The Myth of Meaningful Forms" in *Philosophy and Architecture, Mitias, Michael H (ed)*, 109-119. Amsterdam, Rodopi, 1994.

A return to an architecture of traditional forms has been propagated recently by a number of movements which have aimed at creating a more "meaningful" architecture. Starting with the question of whether meaning is innate in form, this article discusses various kinds of meaning in architecture as well as the notion of architecture as a language. It determines that meaning is principally inferred into architecture by individual subjects, but that this can occur at different levels of intersubjectivity. It argues that the development of a vernacular architectural tradition is characterized by the parallel evolution of architectural forms and the intersubjective cognitive schemes that allow different people to infer similar meanings from them. By contrast, the emergence of classical architecture (defined broadly as architecture produced by architects) is characterized by a process of formal ritualization that results in a steadily decreasing intersubjectivity of meaning. The article concludes by noting how both classical and vernacular architecture eventually undergo a process of stylization by which original meanings become less and less accessible to the public.

Wéber, É H. Jalons pour poursuivre l'effort d'Étienne Gilson en noétique. *Rev Thomiste*, 94(3), 396-412, Jl-S 94.

Weberman, David. Foucault's Reconception of Power. *Phil Forum*, 26(3), 189-217, Spr 95.

Foucault's statements about the nature of social power are dispersed among various works and interviews. They are sometimes metaphorical and obscure. In this paper I pull together, reconstruct, and assess his claims that power is omnipresent, positive (not repressive), non-substantive, and non-subjective. In the end I conclude that although his theory does not itself distinguish between normatively acceptable and unacceptable forms of power and although it is somewhat less novel than it pretends, it does advance a coherent and original conception which can support a social criticism free of the ideas of objective interests and values.

Weed, Laura E. Freud and the Torah. *Int Stud Phil*, 27(1), 127-135, 1995.

I believe that Freud should have credited his Jewishness, and the ethical injunctions of the Torah, for some of his most basic psychological insights. And, whatever their respective sources, whether from Torah or Freud or elsewhere, I believe that these ethical themes are worth revisiting at this juncture in the twentieth century, in their own right. In this paper I will argue that some of Freud's insights on Eros and Thanatos were derived, albeit indirectly, from certain themes in the Torah, or in the Talmudic interpretations of the Torah, and that these themes represent a form of nonrational ethical claim. To argue for this claim I will first, present an interpretation of selected prominent themes in the Hebrew Law; second, argue that these themes have an important psychological and ethical impact in human life, of a nonrational type, and third, point out that Freud's interpretation of Eros and Thanatos is an extrapolation of that psychological and ethical impact. I will conclude with a proposal for further study of this important topic, from my novel point of view.

Wegeler, Cornelia. "Österreichische Wissenschaftsgeschichte: Erkenntnisprozess oder Verdrängung?" in *Der geistige Anschluss, Fischer, Kurt R (ed)*, 179-205. Wien, WUV Univ, 1993.

Wegrzecki, Adam. "The Function of Ontology and Experience in Roman Ingarden's Axiological Investigations" in *Kunst und Ontologie, Galewicz, Wlodzimierz (ed)*, 219-228. Amsterdam, Rodopi, 1994.

Wehrle, Walter E. The Definition of Soul in Aristotle's *De anima* ii 1 Is Not Analogous to the Definition of Snub. *Ancient Phil*, 14(2), 297-317, Fall 94.

In this paper I challenge the view that the definition of soul is analogous to the definition of snub, for if it were analogous, the soul could not be a primary substance. In particular I attack the "story" in which Aristotle, supposedly having found at *Meta*. Z.10-11 that primary substances cannot be defined without their matter, salvages his hylomorphism by *identifying* matter and form at H.6. Also, I give direct arguments for the implausibility of the analogy, thus removing obstacles to the soul's being primary substance.

Wei-Hsun Fu, Charles. Critical Comments. *Asian Phil*, 4(2), 173-175, 1994.

Wei-Ming, Tu. The Mirror of Modernity and Spiritual Resources for the Global Community. *Sophia (Australia)*, 34(1), 79-91, Mr-Ap 95.

Weidemann, Hermann. Tiempo, Verdad y Posibilidad en Aristóteles y la Filosofía Helenística. *Daimon Rev Filosof*, 8, 5-21, 1994.

In this article three arguments are examined in which the notions of time, truth and possibility play an important part. They are due to Aristotle, Alexander of Aphrodisias and Diodorus Cronus, respectively. All three arguments are valid, because their conclusions logically follow from their premises. But whereas in the case of the first two their soundness depends on which sort of truth-conditions a future-tensed proposition is taken to have, the third is unsound, no matter whether we take a future-tensed proposition to have strong or weak conditions of truth.

Weier, Winfried. Geist und Psyche in tiefenpsychologischer und phänomenologischer Perspektive. *Frei Z Phil Theol*, 41(1-2), 155-187, 1994.

Die phänomenologische Analyse geht ein auf die wesentliche und fundamentale Differenz zwischen psychischer Sinnesvorstellung und geistiger Intuition: sie beziehen sich auf unbedingt zu unterscheidende Dimensionen der Wirklichkeit und realisieren demgemäss eine verschiedene Grundhaltung dieser gegenüber. Entsprechend heben sie sich in ihrem Aktcharakter voneinander ab. Ist die Sinnesvorstellung zeitlich, räumlich, zuständlich, veränderlich, bedingt, ableitbar usw., so ist der Inhalt der geistigen Intuition und mithin auch sie selbst zeitüberlegen, überräumlich, überzuständlich, werdelos, unbedingt, urphänomenal use. Diese in der Phänomenologie E Husserls und M Schelers sehr beachteten Differenzen werden jedoch in der Psychoanalyse S Freuds und C G Jungs ignoriert, und an die Stelle der bezeichneten Zweidimensionalität tritt eine undimensionale Gleichsetzung des Geistes mit der psyche und ihrer völlig anderen Gesetzlichkeit. In Zusammenhang damit ist zu sehen die progressive und phänomenvergessene Vereinnahmung des Geistes durch die Psyche im hetigen Wissenschaftsbewusstsein.

Weiermann, Andreas. A Functorial Property of the Aczel-Buchholz-Feferman Function. *J Sym Log*, 59(3), 945-955, S 94.

Weigart, Andrew J. José Ortega y Gasset on Understanding Life as Ultimate Reality and Meaning. *Ultim Real Mean*, 18(1), 54-65, Mr 95.

This essay presents four basic concepts in Ortega's understanding of human life. Without falling into empiricism or rationalism, he characterized thinking as a form of "vital reason." As such, Ortega understood human life: 1) as ultimate reality and meaning, based on his originary principle, "I am myself plus my circumstance, and if I do not save it, I cannot save myself;" 2) as circumstantial, which requires continual interpretation, the task of culture; 3) as historical, since a person "has no nature but, instead, a history" exemplified in his method of studying the dynamics of human generations; 4) as reflexive responsibility so that persons move from being shipwrecked to self understanding (*ensimismamiento*) and back to action in the world. Human life is a heroic quest for authentic "ultranational" solidarity with others amidst saved circumstances.

Weigert, Andrew J and Gecas, Viktor. Multiplicity and Dialogue in Social Psychology: An Essay in Metatheorizing. *J Theor Soc Behav*, 25(2), 141-174, Je 95.

This paper suggests moving the premise of dialogue among social psychologists from the historical "fact" of different social psychological traditions to metatheoretical constructs in the service of further theorizing. Based on the writings of George H Mead, a metatheoretical space is presented for the symbolic realm and similarities and differences are noted for selected illustrations. The discussion leads to the illuminating power of works that bridge previously separated domains. Reference is made to the importance of developments in the physical realm and their links to the symbolic, e.g., dialectic of a neural and symbolic self. The fruitfulness of the schema is portrayed in clarifying the idea of "risk". Continual metatheorizing is needed, since shared metatheoretical constructs make productive dialogue possible even among theoretically diverse traditions.

Weijers, Ido. "Intellectuals and their Education" in *Identity, Culture, and Education, Smeyers, Paul (ed)*, 333-338. Leuven, Leuven Univ Pr, 1994.

Weikart, Richard. Marx, Engels, and the Abolition of the Family. *Hist Euro Ideas*, 18(5), 657-672, S 94.

Marx and Engels forthrightly advocated the abolition of the family. Their critique of the family consisted of three main elements: 1) a depiction of the hypocrisy and inhumanity of the contemporary bourgeois family; 2) the historicization of the family, i.e., a historical account of the origins and development of the family in the past; and 3) a vision of the future "family" in communist society. Although some naturalism remained in their thought, this did not blunt their radicalism, since they made no provision for natural bonds in the communist "family".

Weimer, Wolfgang. Ist eine Deutung der Welt als Wille und Vorstellung heute noch möglich? Schopenhauer nach der Sprachanalytischen Philosophie. *Schopenhauer Jahr*, 76, 11-51, 1995.

This treatise intends to analyze to what extent Schopenhauer's central statement is touched by the findings of the analytic philosophy and in how far this thesis appears outmoded by these findings. Theses: 1) Schopenhauer's fundamental idea contains a number of terms (particularly 'Wille' and 'Vorstellung') whose sense is questioned in the linguistic approach and must presumably defined in a way divergent from Schopenhauer's. 2) On the other hand Schopenhauer's transcendental approach can be considered a possible shortcoming of the analytical philosophy (demonstrated in Kripke's interpretation of Wittgenstein). 3) A tangentiality of both philosophic conceptions is effected by Schopenhauer's own linguistic approach. 4) One advantage of Schopenhauer's philosophy bases on his attempt at giving life a means of orientation which cannot be achieved by analyzing man's speech in the common manner.

Weiming, Tu. "Toward the Possibility of a Global Community" in *Ethics, Religion and Biodiversity, Hamilton, Lawrence S (ed)*, 65-74. Cambridge, White Horse, 1994.

Weinberger, Ota. Argumentation in Law and Politics. *Commun Cog*, 28(1), 37-54, 1995.

The paper contains a critique of Discourse Philosophy (DP) in the sense of Habermas, Apel, Alexy: DP mixes up objective and pragmatic argumentation. Habermas's consensus theory of truth is misleading, because there is no path from opinion to objective truth or objective validity. DP turns away research from the aim to find effective methods and proofs to the unsound aim of getting assent. DP leads to a kind of collectivization of rationality by conceiving rationality as an effect of an (ideal) intersubjective discourse. The concept of an ideal discourse is an inappropriate idealization. Fictitious discourses by themselves do not provide the supposition that everybody would assent to the opinion because it has been proven or made very plausible by objective arguments.

Weiner, Joan. Burge's Literal Interpretation of Frege. *Mind*, 104(415), 585-597, Jl 95.

Weiner, Joan. Realism *bei* Frege: Reply to Burge. *Synthese*, 102(3), 363-382, Ma 95.

Frege is celebrated as an arch-Platonist and arch-realist. He is renowned for claiming that truths of arithmetic are eternally true and independent of us, our judgments and our thoughts; that there is a 'third realm' containing nonphysical objects that are not ideas. Until recently, there were few attempts to explicate these renowned claims, for most philosophers thought the clarity of Frege's prose rendered explication unnecessary. But the last ten years have seen the publication of several revisionist interpretations of Frege's writings—interpretations on which these claims receive a

very different reading. In 'Frege on Knowing the Third Realism', Tyler Burge attempts to undermine this trend. Burge argues that Frege is the very Platonist most have thought him—that revisionist interpretations of Frege's Platonism, mine among them, run afoul of the words on Frege's pages. This paper is a response to Burge's criticisms. I argue that my interpretation is more faithful than Burge's to Frege's texts.

Weinert, Friedel. The Correspondence Principle and the Closure of Theories: Two Incompatible Aspects of Heisenberg's Philosophy of Science. *Erkenntnis*, 40(3), 303-323, My 94.

Heisenberg holds 'that closed theories are valid for all time' and describes the relation between closed theories in terms of the correspondence principle so that, for instance, classical mechanics becomes a limiting case of quantum mechanics. This paper argues that Heisenberg's closed-systems view is incompatible with this use of the correspondence principle for he fails to distinguish the theoretical validity of a theory (the theoretical justification of its empirical limits) from its mere empirical validity (the agreement with its empirical domain). Systems can only be regarded as closed if they have both theoretical and empirical validity. The correspondence principle shows that none of Heisenberg's paradigm examples satisfy this requirement.

Weinert, Regina and Miller, Jim. The Function of LIKE in Dialogue. *J Prag*, 23(4), 365-393, Ap 95.

Two bodies of Scottish English data are analyzed. There are two major constructions with LIKE. The one with clause-final LIKE is used to (anticipate and) counter (possible) objections and assumptions; the second one, with LIKE in other positions, is analyzed as noncontrastive focus, a highlighting devise. The structures are not verbal tics but follow regular patterns with regular functions. They are not associated with hesitations and poor syntactic planning. There are far more frequent than clefts, possibly because they do not disrupt the syntax of a given construction. The structure is far from new but previous accounts either limit themselves to one particular function absent from the Scottish English data (see Romaine and Lange, 1991) or operate with a rather vague analytical concept (see Schourup, 1985).

Weingard, Robert and Callender, Craig. The Bohmian Model of Quantum Cosmology. *Proc Phil Sci Ass*, 1, 218-227, 1994.

A realist causal model of quantum cosmology (QC) is developed. By applying the de Broglie-Bohm interpretation of quantum mechanics to QC, we resolve the notorious 'problem of time' in QC, and derive exact equations of motion for cosmological dynamical variables. Due to this success, it is argued that if the situation in QC is used as a yardstick by which other interpretations are measured, the de Broglie-Bohm theory seems uniquely fit as an interpretation of quantum mechanics.

Weingard, Robert and Huggett, Nick. Interpretations of Quantum Field Theory. *Phil Sci*, 61(3), 370-388, S 94.

In this paper we critically review the various attempts that have been made to understand quantum field theory. We focus of Teller's (1990) harmonic oscillator interpretation, and Bohm et al.'s (1987) causal interpretation. The former unabashedly aims to be a purely heuristic account, but we show that it is only interestingly applicable to the free bosonic field. Along the way we suggest alternative models. Bohm's interpretation provides an ontology for the theory—a classical field, with a quantum equation of motion. This too has problems; it is not Lorentz invariant.

Weingard, Robert and Huggett, Nick. On the Field Aspect of Quantum Fields. *Erkenntnis*, 40(3), 293-301, My 94.

In this paper we contrast the idea of a field as a system with an infinite number of degrees of freedom with a recent alternative proposed by Paul Teller in Teller (1990). We show that, although our characterization lacks the immediate appeal of Teller's it has more success producing agreement with intuitive categorizations than his does. We go on to extend the distinction to quantum mechanics, explaining the important role that it plays there. Finally, we take some time to investigate the way in which strings are to be considered fields, and the important differences with scalar fields. Overall, we aim to show that many types of systems may be viewed as fields, and to point out significant distinctions amongst them, thereby expanding our understanding of what it is to fall in this category.

Weingard, Robert and Huggett, Nick. The Renormalisation Group and Effective Field Theories. *Synthese*, 102(1), 171-194, Ja 95.

Much apprehension has been expressed by philosophers about the method of renormalisation in quantum field theory, as it apparently requires illegitimate procedure of infinite cancellation. This has lead to various speculations, in particular in Teller (1989). We examine Teller's discussion of perturbative renormalisation of quantum fields, and show why it is inadequate. To really approach the matter one needs to understand the ideas and results of the 'renormalisation group', so we give a simple but comprehensive account of this topic. With this in hand, we explain how renormalisation can and should be understood. One thing that is revealed is that apparently very successful theories such as quantum electro-dynamics cannot be universally true; resolving the tension between success and falsity leads to a picture in which any theory may be viewed as irreducibly phenomenological. We explain how, and argue that the support for this view is tenuous at best.

Weingart, Peter. "Eugenische Utopien: Entwürfe für die Rationalisierung der menschlichen Entwicklung" in *Nationalsozialismus und Moderne, Welzer, Harald (ed)*, 166-183. Tübingen, Ed Diskord, 1993.

Weingartner, Paul. "Das Problem der Sprache in der Philosophie" in *Die Sprache in den Wissenschaften, Weingartner, Paul (ed)*, 221-276. Freiburg, Alber, 1993.

The essay starts with two claims: 1) That philosophers didn't develop a special language comparable to that of mathematicians, physicists or the legal language. 2) That philosophers do not have a common background-knowledge (except history of philosophy) comparable to that of scientists. 1) and 2) explain partially that the community of all philosophers is not an epistemic authority in contradiction to mathematicians, physicists, lawyers, or physicians. Certain groups however like logicians or philosophers of science may be an exception to some extent. Further chapters deal with problematic issues of signs (reference, meaning, "the unspeakable"), formal language, coding devices (like Gödel numbering) and antinomies.

Weingartner, Paul (ed). *Die Sprache in den Wissenschaften*. Freiburg, Alber, 1993.

The purpose of the conference was to ask scientists, philosophers and theologians to describe the specific language they use when doing research in their subject and when communicating with colleagues. The language of mathematics is described in different of its developmental stages, that of physics mainly since Newton's and Maxwell's conceptions together with recent problems that of neurobiology and brain-research, that of anthropology in the early history of mankind, and that of theology with the focus of its symbolic and mediating function. As an example of a special language of illiterates behavioural scientists describe a pearl-button-language of Zulus.

Weingartner, Rudolph H. Is Reading Plato Educational? Thoughts on Education, Prompted by a Reading of Plato's *Meno*. *Teach Phil*, 17(4), 335-, D 94.

Weinrib, Ernest J. *The Idea of Private Law*. Cambridge, Harvard Univ Pr, 1995.

Private law embodies a special morality that links the doer and sufferer of harm. Drawing on Aristotle's account of corrective justice and on Kant's principle of right, Weinrib elucidates the standpoint internal to this morality, in opposition to instrumentalists who view private law as an instrument in the service of external goals. He traces the implication of this special morality for our ideas of the structure, coherence, normative grounding, leading doctrines and of private law. The book combines philosophical exposition and legal analysis, and pays special attention to issues of tort law.

Weinstein, David. Entre el Kantismo y el Consecuencialismo en la Filosofía Moral de T H Green. *Telos (Spain)*, 3(2), 31-58, D 94.

Green's moral philosophy was profoundly consequentialist insofar as it was a genuine good-maximizing theory. But because Green defined the good to be maximized in a nonutilitarian way, he was not a utilitarian consequentialist. Though defining good differently than most of his utilitarian adversaries, Green nevertheless confessed that utilitarianism often mirrored his own theory by recommending the same practical strategies. Thus, maximizing or promoting good would seldom mean using people except in midly redistributionist and 'new liberal' ways.

Weinstein, Jami. On the Leveling of the Genre Distinction Between Theory and Fiction. *Conference*, 5(1), 35-47, Spr 94.

Weinstein, Scott and Osherson, Daniel. On the Danger of Half-Truths. *J Phil Log*, 24(1), 85-115, F 95.

Criteria of approximate scientific success are defined within a formal paradigm of empirical inquiry. One consequence of aiming for less than perfect truth is examined.

Weinstock, Daniel M. Notes sur le Relativisme et le Monisme en Éthique. *Philosopher*, 16, 189-196, 1994.

I argue that rival ethical theories (utilitarianism, deontology, virtue ethics) ought not to be viewed as mutually exclusive. The presentation of these theories in pedagogical contexts ought to emphasize the different contexts in which one or the other of these theories is most appropriate.

Weinstock, Daniel M. The Justification of Political Liberalism. *Pac Phil Quart*, 75(3-4), 165-185, S-D 94.

I outline Rawls's theory of justification, highlighting its philosophical and pragmatic conditions. I argue that the theory has remained essentially unchanged since his earliest methodological writings, and that his recent writings have sought to show how "justice as fairness" can satisfy these conditions, given Rawls's new construal of the "fact of pluralism" which theories of justice designed for modern Western liberal democracies must address. I argue that neither Rawls's revised conception of reflective equilibrium, based on the "fixed points" of such societies' political cultures rather than on individuals' "considered moral judgments" nor the newer notion of "overlapping consensus", succeed in justifying "justice as fairness" according to the terms of Rawls's theory of justification.

Weir, Alan. Gruesome Perceptual Spaces. *Analysis*, 55(1), 27-36, Ja 95.

It is widely held that significant asymmetries hold between Goodman's bent grue predicate and ordinary color predicates, asymmetries which obtain whether one views the problem from our perspective *or* from a putative 'Grueman's' perspective. Utilizing the idea of a bent perceptual space, I set out a version of the paradox immune to this objection and consider the problems thereby generated for confirmation theory and inductive logic. I also relate the discussion to some influential comments by Mary Hesse and conclude with some morals to be drawn for scientific rationality.

Weir, Jack L. Radical Translation and Animals: An Argument from the Principle of Humanity. *SW Phil Rev*, 11(1), 23-40, Ja 95.

In this paper, I argue for the attribution of simple beliefs, desires, interests, and understandings to higher animals, and that animals actually have such beliefs. In our common experience with animals, we do make belief attributions and rely upon such a principle of humanity, which was introduced by Richard E Grandy in an application of W V O Quine to animals. I discuss Grandy and Quine. I argue that such attributions are holistically and pragmatically effective. Similar neurophysiologies support such attribution. Moreover, such attributions provide the best holistic fit with the facts of our situation in the world and what we observe in the animal subjects.

Weir, Lorraine. "Post-Modernizing Gender: From Adrienne Rich to Judith Butler" in *Power/Gender, Radtke, H Lorraine (ed)*, 210-218. Newbury Park, Sage, 1994.

Weis, Gregory F. Grading. *Teach Phil*, 18(1), 3-13, Mr 95.

At the end of each academic term, we assign each student a grade for the course. What exactly are we doing when we grade? What is a grade? What is being graded? I show that these questions involve difficult conceptual and normative issues. I criticize the conventional view that grading is, in some simple and straightforward sense, a measure of a student's comprehension of, or competence in, the subject matter of the course. Finally, I argue that since what grading is must be stipulated, we each bear a responsibility to clarify what it is to ourselves and, most importantly, to our students.

Weisberg, Robert W. "Prolegomena to Theories of Insight in Problem Solving: A Taxonomy of Problems" in *The Nature of Insight, Sternberg, Robert J (ed)*, 157-196. Cambridge, MIT Pr, 1995.

Weishi, Yuan. A Few Problems Related to Nineteenth Century Chinese and Western Philosophies and their Cultural Interaction. *J Chin Phil*, 22(2), 153-192, Je 95.

Weismann, Francisco J. Primera aproximación al lenguaje. *Stromata*, 50(1-2), 105-117, Ja-Je 94.

Weiss, Bardo. Mechthild von Magdeburg und der frühe Meister Eckhart. *Theol Phil*, 70(1), 1-40, 1995.

In part one I have shown that Eckhart probably did get to know Mechthild's *Fliessendes Licht der Gottheit* while he was superior in Erfurt. The second part deals with a summing up of basic discrepancies between Mechthild (Brautmystik) and Eckhart himself (Mystik der Gottesburt). Part three shows in what way the early Eckhart (Buch der Unterweisung) deals with Mechthild's mysticism. He does take over thoughts of hers (e.g., Gott "muss"). He differs, however, distinctly from her, too. He holds reservations against her experiencing "God-alienation" (Gottesfremde): man may not set God at a distance. The background of his thinking is an image of God that stems more intensively from metaphysics.

Weiss, Bernhard. On Russell's Argument for Restricting Modes of Specification and Domains of Quantification. *Hist Phil Log*, 15(2), 173-188, 1994.

Russell takes his paper 'On denoting' to have achieved the repudiation of the theory of denoting concepts and Frege's theory of sense, and the invention of the notion of incomplete symbols. This means that Russell attempts to solve the set theoretic and semantic paradoxes without making use of a theory of sense. Instead, his strategy is to revise his logical ontology by arguing that certain symbols should be treated as incomplete. In constructing such arguments Russell, at various points, makes use of epistemological and metaphysical considerations. These arguments do not form themselves into a systemic set of considerations to be used in appraising a logical system. Finally, the vicious circle principle is argued for on the basis of considerations, which are presumed evident, about the nature of propositional functions. The stringency of this principle is a basic problem for the system of *Principia mathematica*. However, even given the terms of the argument, 'On denoting' does not offer a complete repudiation of the notion of sense. This allows the possibility of retaining some of the insights of *Principia mathematica* whilst rejecting the stringency of the vicious circle principle. The basis of such a system is the theory of sense.

Weiss, Daniel A. The Reflections of Linus: The Contradictions of Plato. *J Thought*, 29(4), 77-80, Wint 94.

Weiss, Gail. Ambiguity, Absurdity, and Reversibility: Responses to Indeterminacy. *J Brit Soc Phenomenol*, 26(1), 43-51, Ja 95.

This essay traces the influence of Husserl's notion of the "zone of indeterminacy" that serves as the omnipresent horizon for all of our noetic acts in the work of three French philosophers: Simone de Beauvoir, Albert Camus, and Maurice Merleau-Ponty. Although Husserl was somewhat ambivalent about the existence of this zone of indeterminacy as it inevitably seemed to undermine the phenomenological search for pure essences, his French successors viewed indeterminacy as a source of freedom, significance, and human possibility. More specifically, they transform Husserlian indeterminacy from a consequence of intentionality to a constitutive feature of human existence that characterizes the human situation as such.

Weiss, Gail. Creative Agency and Fluid Images: A Revew of Iris Young's *Throwing Like a Girl and Other Essays in Feminist Philosophy and Social Theory*. *Human Stud*, 17(4), 471-478, 1994-95.

This article explores Young's "embodied feminist social theorizing" as it is revealed within and across her collected essays. It is, I argue, through Young's understanding of individual and social bodies as creative agencies, that she is able to demonstrate the importance of self-articulation as well as social autonomy. Moreover, the very notion of a creative agency is itself a fluid image, one that seeks to do justice to individual differences by refusing to endorse any form of essentialism. As a material potency, this creative agency is, I claim, "forever caught up in a dialectic of making and being made, remaking and being remade."

Weiss, Gail. Sex-Selective Abortion: A Relational Approach. *Hypatia*, 10(1), 202-217, Wint 95.

A critical application of Ruddick's model of maternal thinking is the best way to grapple with the ethical dilemmas posed by sex-selective abortion which I view as a "moral mistake". Chief among these is the need to be sensitive to local cultural practices in countries where sex-selective abortion is prevalent, while simultaneously developing consistent international standards to deal with the dangers posed by the use of sex-selective abortion to eliminate female fetuses.

Weiss, Roslyn. Virtue without Knowledge: Socrates' Conception of Holiness in Plato's *Euthyphro*. *Ancient Phil*, 14(2), 263-282, Fall 94.

It is contended that in the *Euthyphro* Euthyphro and Socrates are antagonists, Euthyphro holding a view of holiness which Socrates regards as odious and from which he therefore attempts repeatedly in the dialogue to extricate Euthyphro. Socrates' own partial view of holiness is that it consists of service to the gods (rather than exchange with them), and that as service it requires of the pious person that he lack expertise with respect to good and evil, expertise that is the province of the gods he serves.

Weithman, Paul. Waldron on Political Legitimacy and the Social Minimum. *Phil Quart*, 45(179), 218-224, Ap 95.

Jeremy Waldron argues that liberalism's most fundamental commitment is to what he calls the 'transparency' of social institutions. They treat this demand as a necessary condition of political legitimacy. Liberals, Waldron concludes, think the social order legitimate only if it can satisfy the transparency requirement by withstanding rational scrutiny. Various essays gathered in the recently issued collection of Waldron's papers suggest his attempt to develop a more refined conception of political legitimacy, one that includes but goes beyond the transparency requirement. Thus in an essay on John Rawls, Waldron argues, in effect, that the political legitimacy of a 'social order' depends upon its sufficiently satisfying citizens' basic material needs that consider themselves full members of their society. I argue that the conception of political legitimacy Waldron's essays suggest leads to circularity; the circle can be removed only if Waldron gives up the transparency requirement.

Weithman, Paul J. Taking Rites Seriously. *Pac Phil Quart*, 75(3-4), 272-294, S-D 94.

The distinctively political character of Rawls's liberalism as articulated in *Political Liberalism* might seem to make Rawls's view especially congenial, for political liberalism rests upon toleration of comprehensive doctrines but not on skepticism about the claims they express. I examine Rawls's new discussion of public reason and argue that it rests upon mistaken claims about the relationship of religious and political aims. This view, if embodied in practice, could help to foster a "culture of disbelief". I propose a view of religious aims that would, if endorsed, address the problem I locate in Rawls's view.

Welch, Don. Just Another Day at the Office: The Ordinariness of Professional Ethics. *Prof Ethics*, 2(3-4), 3-14, Fall-Wint 93.

This article examines some of the efforts that have been made to distinguish the norms and methods of professional ethics from those of "ordinary morality." The author finds unpersuasive arguments for distinctiveness based on the following claims: professionals provide services that are important to society; professionals are committed to some good larger than their self-interest; the professions are granted a degree of autonomy by the community; the nature of professional services requires skills and knowledge not possessed by the population at large. He concludes by drawing on role morality to demonstrate the continuity that exists among various types of ethics.

Welch, John R. Science and Ethics: Toward a Theory of Ethical Value. *J Gen Phil Sci*, 25(2), 279-292, 1994.

What is the difference between the just and the unjust, the courageous and the cowardly, the ethically valuable and the ethically not valuable? To answer these and similar questions, a critical theory of ethical value is advanced. Using sample sentences that include ethical value terms, normative and descriptive components of the theory are identified, and the normative component is developed in some detail. Three levels of normative ethical discourse, adapted from Laudan's levels of scientific discourse, are then distinguished: descriptive, methodological, and axiological. Each sample sentence is assigned to a level, and the subsequent discussion illustrates how to proceed rationally at that level. The rational techniques appropriate to each level include inductive inference, falsification, and causal inference. These techniques are likewise appropriate to the corresponding level of the sciences.

Welch, P D. Characterising Subjects of ω_1 Constructible from a Real. *J Sym Log*, 59(4), 1420-1432, D 94.

A large cardinal upper bound is given for proving when certain sets of countable ordinals (including the universally Baire sets) and precisely those constructible (in the sense of Gödel) from a real number. In the core model, K, we find an exact equivalence in terms of the mouse ordering: the property that every set B of countable ordinals is U B iff B is in such an L(r) is presented under set forcing extensions if and only if there are arbitrarily large "admissibly measurable" cardinals.

Welchman, Jennifer. *Dewey's Ethical Thought*. Ithaca, Cornell Univ Pr, 1995.

Welchman, Jennifer. Locke on Slavery and Inalienable Rights. *Can J Phil*, 25(1), 67-82, Mr 95.

Some have argued that Locke's failure to condemn contemporary slavery is best viewed as a personal moral lapse which does not reflect on his political theory. I argue to the contrary.

Welie, Jos V M. Authenticity as a Foundational Principle of Medical Ethics. *Theor Med*, 15(3), 211-225, S 94.

Increasingly, contemporary medical ethicists have become aware of the need to expicate a foundation for their various models of applied ethics. Many of these theories are inspired by the apparent incompatibility of patient autonomy and provider beneficence. The principle of patient autonomy derives its current primacy to a large extent from its legal origins. However, this principle seems at odds with the clinical reality. In the bioethical literature, the notion of authenticity has been proposed as an alternative foundational principle to autonomy. This article examines this proposal in reference to various existentialist philosophers. It is concluded that the principle of autonomy fails to do what it is commonly supposed to do: provide a criterion of distinction that can be invoked to settle moral controversies between patients and providers. The existentialist concept of authenticity is more promising in at least one crucial respect: It acknowledges that the essence of human life disappears from sight if life's temporal character is reduced to a series of present decisions and actions. This also implies that the very quest for a criterion that allows physicians to distinguish between sudden, unexpected decisions of their patients to be or not to be respected, without recourse to the patient's past or future, is erroneous.

Welie, Jos V M. Viktor Emil von Gebsattel on the Doctor-Patient Relationship. *Theor Med*, 16(1), 41-72, Mr 94.

This article provides a summary overview of the ideas on medical anthropology and anthropological medicine of the German philosopher-psychiatrist Viktor Emil von Gebsattel (1883-1974), and discusses in more detail his views on the doctor-patient relationship. It is argued that Von Gebsattel's warning against a dehumanization of medicine when the "person" of both patient and physician are not explicitly present in their relationship remains valid notwithstanding the modern emphasis on respect for patient (and provider) autonomy.

Welie, Jos V M (trans) and von Gebsattel, Victor E. The Meaning of Medical Practice. *Theor Med*, 16(1), 59-72, Mr 94.

Victor Von Gebsattel (1883-1974) was one of the primary representatives of the medical-anthropological movement, aimed at enriching and "humanizing" medicine by borrowing from early 20th century philosophical anthropology. Little of his work has been translated into English. In his last article from 1963 on the meaning of medical practice, Von Gebsattel outlines his views on the doctor-patient relationship. He discerns 3 stages: an initial sympathic or immediate stage; a diagnostic-therapeutic stage; and a personal stage. (For a critical analysis, see the translator's accompanying article in the same issue of theoretical medicine).

Wellman, Carl P. *Real Rights*. New York, Oxford Univ Pr, 1995.

Real Rights provides the theoretical resources to determine whether some alleged right is real and what duties, if any, are actually implied by some specific right. It describes the grounds of legal rights and advances a new conception of moral reasons capable of grounding moral rights. The author argues that only agents could be right-holders, that children and the mentally limited can have only limited rights, and that fetuses, the dead and groups can have none. *Real Rights* also describes how rights imply duties, how rights conflicts can be resolved and what considerations could override a right.

Wellman, Carl P. The Inalienable Right to Life and the Durable Power of Attorney. *Law Phil*, 14(2), 245-269, My 95.

If one has an inalienable right to life, how is it possible to authorize someone else to make life-or-death medical decisions for one? One's right to life is a rights-package including the claim-right that others not endanger one's life. When a patient refuses life-prolonging medical treatment, she is not divesting herself of her claim-right that others not endanger her life but only waiving this right against her physician. When someone executes a durable power of attorney, one does not transfer to another one's right to life but merely delegates to a health care attorney one's power to refuse medical treatment.

Wells, Douglas. "Relational Persons and Ethical Paradigms" in *Identity, Culture, and Education, Smeyers, Paul (ed)*, 339-349. Leuven, Leuven Univ Pr, 1994.

This paper argues that using a relational view of persons to undergird a four dimensional basis to describe moral behavior will help us to avoid unnecessarily truncating our ethical thinking. Moral behavior is anchored upon four dimensions, namely that persons: have inalienable rights via their intentional consciousness; acquire rights via informal and formal relations; acquire duties within the epistemological basis within which the persons are engaged. The work argues that the relational view allows that acting ethically is a complex process involving the balancing factors along four dimensions. Ethical behavior cannot be described in any a priori fashion.

Wells, Kelley J. Contra Margolis' Peircean Constructivism: A Peircean Pragmatic *Logos*. *Trans Peirce Soc*, 30(4), 839-860, Fall 94.

Wells, Norman J. Javelli and Suárez on the Eternal Truths. *Mod Sch*, 72(1), 13-35, N 94.

An examination of Suárez's position on the Eternal Truths by bringing to bear upon it a controversy between Chrysostomus Javelli, O P (+1538) (who is defending Harvey Nedellec, a.k.a. Hervaeus Natalis, O P (+1323) and Paulus Barbus Soncinas, O P (+1494) on the issue of efficient causality with respect to necessary essential propositions and the distinction between a nonexistential use of the copula *est* vs an existential use thereof.

Wells, Norman J. John Poinsot on Created Eternal Truths vs Vasquez, Suárez and Descartes. *Amer Cath Phil Quart*, 68(3), 425-446, Sum 94.

An examination of John Poinsot's discussion of created eternal truths wherein he criticizes Gabriel Vasquez's interpretation of Aquinas' position on the eternal truths. What is taken to task is Vasquez's insistence upon a positive eternal aptitudinal truth on the part of necessary as well as contingent truths with regard to creatures. This is such that these truths are not eternal because known by God's eternal intellect. Rather, they are eternally true (aptitudinally) in themselves apart from the divine intellect. Linkage to Suárez's and Descartes' positions on created eternal truths is also considered.

Welsh, Ian. Green Anarchism: Peter Marshall's *Nature's Web*. *Environ Values*, 4(1), 73-78, F 95.

This review article engages with the arguments advanced in Peter Marshall's book Nature's Web. In particular the basis of an environmentally credible 'Green Anarchism' is critically contrasted with postmodernist and poststructuralist positions which emphasize a decentered self: It is argued that this poses major problems for all nineteenth century anarchisms which depend upon a self constituted through rational categories.

Welzer, Harald. "Männer der Praxis: Zur Sozialpsychologie des Verwaltungsmassenmordes" in *Nationalsozialismus und Moderne, Welzer, Harald (ed)*, 105-127. Tübingen, Ed Diskord, 1993.

First the article discusses different approaches to the socio-psychological reasons for becoming a perpetrator in the time of the so-called "Third Reich". The author discusses dispositional approaches as the "authoritarian personality" and situational approaches, which give more weight to the normative and social frames of authoritarian and violent behavior. By the case study of Rudolf Höss, the commander of Auschwitz, the author elaborates a type of specifically modern perpetrator who is just doing his job under the paradigms of optimal functionality in a given setting, which itself never is asked upon. Höss comes out as a perverted kind of social engineer who is using everyday routines as role-distance to image himself as a good man though being responsible for the killing of hundreds of thousands of people.

Welzer, Harald (ed). *Nationalsozialismus und Moderne*. Tübingen, Ed Diskord, 1993.

The book deals with attempts to identify lines of traditions and transformations of Nazi-ideologies and programmatics, which are related to specific impacts of modernity. Authors of philosophical, sociological and psychological professions discuss these relations on different subjects as by the case of Rudolf Höss, the commander of Auschwitz, by the development of eugenics or by studying female members of Neo-Nazi groups in Germany.

Wenger, Neil S and Halpern, Jodi. Can A Patient Refuse a Psychiatric Consultation to Evaluate Decision-Making Capacity?. *J Clin Ethics*, 5(3), 230-234, Fall 94.

AUTHOR INDEX WITH ABSTRACTS 797 Wheary, Jennifer

Wenger, Neil S and Halpern, Jodi. The Physician's Role in Completing Advance Directives: Ensuring Patients' Capacity to Make Healthcare Decisions in Advance. *J Clin Ethics*, 5(4), 320-323, Wint 94.

Wennemann, Daryl J. Middle Level Theory in Ellul's Thought: Where Theory and Practice Meet. *Res Phil Technol*, 14, 1994.

Wenzel, U J. "Beziehung ohne Beziehung": Bemerkungen zur Gesellschafts- und Gemeinschaftskritik von Emmanuel Lévinas. *Stud Phil (Switzerland)*, 53, 177-199, 1994.

Werle, Jozef. How the Physical Sciences Discovered the Unity of Nature. *Dialogue Hum*, 2(3-4), 19-47, 1992.

This essay presents the astounding progress of integration of the natural sciences. Though the knowledge of the empirical data is indispensable, Nature can be understood only with the help of suitable theories that synthesize but also transcend these data. The quantitative physical theories form an impressive hierarchy of increasing generality, accuracy and profoundness. The theories of lower level usually follow from the theories of higher level as special cases or approximations. The fact that the same concepts and theories describe not only phenomena belonging traditionally to proper physics, but also to astronomy, cosmology, chemistry, crystallography, geology, as well as physiology, medicine, etc. bears a convincing testimony to the profound unity of Nature. The advent of molicular biology opened a new path of integration of biology with exact sciences, i.e., with mathematics, physics and chemistry.

Wernecke, Jörg. *Denken im Modell: Theorie und Erfahrung im Paradigma eines pragmatischen Modellbegriffs*. Berlin, Duncker Humblot, 1994.

Wertheimer, Jürgen (ed). *Suchbild Europa—künstlerische Konzepte der Moderne*. Amsterdam, Rodopi, 1995.

This collection of essays documents and develops different constructs of the European scenario on a textual and poetological level. It takes into account voices not only from philology, but also philosophy, cultural semiotics, and literature, voices from the center and the periphery of Europe. The contributors of this volume share a critical perspective towards a Europe perceived alternately as myth, chimera or utopia. The goal is to show Europe's many facets, but also and more importantly the reflections and refractions of its vision. That is why authors *and* scholars have been joined to an unconventional review of "Europe" today.

Werther, David. Leibniz on Cartesian Omnipotence and Contingency. *Relig Stud*, 31(1), 23-36, Mr 95.

Leibniz contrasted his views of necessity, possibility, and impossibility with those of Descartes and Spinoza. On the one hand, he argued that Descartes erred by allowing that God has the ability to make contradictory claims true. On the other hand, Leibniz found Spinoza's commitment to fatalism to be counterintuitive. I show that, given his *in-esse* account of truth, Leibniz could not have avoided a commitment to fatalism, without affirming one of the most objectionable features of Descartes' divine voluntarism, the contingency of the law of noncontradiction.

Wertz, Frederick J. Cognitive Psychology: A Phenomenological Critique. *J Theor Phil Psych*, 13(1), 2-24, Spr 93.

In evaluating cognitive psychology from a phenomenological perspective, this work reviews the general orientation of cognitive psychology, some contemporary difficulties and problems noted by cognitive psychologists, and a number of apparent commonalities between phenomenological and cognitive psychologies. It is argued that the problems of cognitive psychology are inevitable consequences of its natural scientific orientation, which is far more traditional than it is revolutionary. A phenomenologically based, human science approach to psychology is offered as a solution of fundamental disciplinary problems.

Wertz, S K. The Hypergame Paradox: Smullyan's Version. *Darshana Int*, 32(3/127), 17-21, Jl 92.

Wertz, S K. The Role of Practice in Collingwood's Theory of Art. *SW Phil Rev*, 11(1), 143-150, Ja 95.

In The Principles of Art, R G Collingwood anticipates the institutional theory of art and, additionally, his theory has striking similarities with several other contemporary theories. This paper attempts to bring some of these features into sharp relief so that they can be better appreciated. A philosophy of art, Collingwood insists, should have the "practical consequences bearing on the way in which we ought to approach the practice of art (whether as artists or as audience) and hence, because a philosophy of art is a theory as to the place of art in life as a whole, the practice of life." This emphasis upon practice is frequently overlooked in treatments of Collingwood's aesthetic idealism. How this idea of practice plays an important role in his theory is traced and analyzed.

Wessell, L P. Comentario kafkiano en torno a la obra *Realidad y Verdad* de Antonio Pintor-Ramos. *Dialogo Filosof*, 11(1), 61-72, Ja-Ap 95.

Wessell Jr, Leonard P. Contrarréplica a una Valoración Sobre mi Crítica al Realismo Radical de Xavier Zubiri. *Themata*, 13, 249-274, 1995.

According to Isabel Aísa the interpretation and evaluation of the "radical realism" of X Zubiri by this author entails a misunderstanding of Zubiri's "reism". This paper accepts the essence of Aísa's criticism, but contends that the same antinomies follow and that, without an idealistic foundation, Zubiri "reism" collapses from lack of semanticity.

Wesson, Robert (ed) and Williams, Patricia A (ed). *Evolution and Human Values*. Amsterdam, Rodopi, 1995.

West, Cornel. "Theory, Pragmatisms, and Politics" in *Pragmatism: From Progressivism to Postmodernism, Hollinger, Robert (ed)*, 314-325. Westport, Praeger, 1995.

Westberg, Daniel. Thomistic Law and the Moral Theory of Richard Hooker. *Amer Cath Phil Quart*, 68(Supp), 203-214, 1994.

Westerman, Pauline C. "Hume and the Natural Lawyers: A Change of Landscape" in *Hume and Hume's Connexions, Stewart, M A (ed)*, 83-104. University Park, Penn St Univ Pr, 1995.

Contrary to the claims of several recent commentators, Hume's moral philosophy cannot be interpreted as a continuation of natural-law theory. Comparison of Grotius and Hume reveals that despite the similarity in vocabulary, Grotius seeks *justifying* principles that should regulate human behavior, whereas Hume tries to *explain* why people actually follow the rules. Although both purposes of justification and explanation had always been present in natural-law theory, the demand for a more empirical approach made it increasingly hard to reconcile both purposes. Hume univocally opted for explanation, but the enterprise of natural law was undermined in the process.

Westhelle, Vítor. Scientific Sight and Embodied Knowledges: Social Circumstances in Science and Theology. *Mod Theol*, 11(3), 341-361, Jl 95.

The essay establishes a peculiar difference between theology and science in the modern age. Knowledge, in modernity, is gained in an "agonistic situation" in which a new inscriptional practice (optical consistency) becomes the norm by which information is disseminated and "reality" defined and controlled. Having taken advantage of the new printing technic, theology became increasingly aware of its optical inconsistency being unable to be a hegemonic form of institutionalized knowledge. But instead of striving for scientific normativity, theology's promise lies exactly in its capability of recasting local and embodied knowledges that transgress the accepted canons of scientific inscription.

Westphal, Jonathan (ed). *Certainty*. Indianapolis, Hackett, 1995.

Westphal, Kenneth A. Kants Urteilstafel Zur Deutung von Reinhard Brandt. *Z Phil Forsch*, 49(1), 84-91, Ja-Mr 95.

Reinhard Brandt attempts to show that Kant's Table of Judgments is complete by demonstrating how it corresponds to the elements of traditional logic, the components of a judgment, the kinds of syllogism, and the main sections of the first *Critique*. I present these correspondences in a Table and summarize Brandt's evidence for them. Brandt's interpretation does not meet his own adequacy conditions and quantitative equivocations in Kant's discussion of the Table of Judgments show that he did not intend Brandt's kind of combinatoric completeness proof. (Printer's errors in my Table are corrected in the North American Kant Society *Newsletter* XI No 2 1995.)

Westphal, Kenneth R. Does Kant's *Metaphysical Foundations of Natural Science* Fill a Gap in the *Critique of Pure Reason*?. *Synthese*, 103(1), 43-86, Ap 95.

In 1792 and 1798 Kant noticed two basic problems with his *Metaphysical Foundations of Natural Science (MAdN)* which opened a crucial gap in the Critical system as a whole. Why is the *MAdN* so important? I show that the Analogies of Experience form a integrated proof of transeunt causality. This is central to Kant's "answer" to Hume. This proof requires explicating the empirical concept of matter as "the moveable in space", it requires the specifically metaphysical principle that every physical event has an external cause, and it requires a metaphysical principle regarding the individuation of spatio-temporal things. These three doctrines are not defended in the first *Critique*, but only in the *MAdN*. Kant's transcendental analysis of the conditions of experience thus requires the "special metaphysics" of the *MAdN*. This marks an important shift in Kant's view of the metaphysical basis of the transcendental philosophy.

Westphal, Kenneth R. Kant's Dynamic Constructions. *J Phil Res*, 20, 381-429, 1995.

According to Kant, justifying the application of mathematics to objects in natural science requires metaphysically constructing the concept of matter. Kant develops these constructions in the *Metaphysical Foundations of Natural Science (MAdN).*) In his Preface Kant claims completely to exhaust the metaphysical doctrine of body, but in the General Remark to *MAdN* chapter 2, "Dynamics," Kant admits that once matter is reconceived as basic forces, it is no longer possible to construct the concept of matter. I argue that Kant's admission is only the tip of the problem, and that none of Kant's commentators has fully grasped the problems infecting the *MAdN* that underlie Kant's admission. (edited)

Westra, Laura S. Corporate Responsibility and Hazardous Products. *Bus Ethics Quart*, 4(1), 97-110, Ja 94.

Wettersten, John. Styles of Rationality. *Phil Soc Sci*, 25(1), 69-98, Mr 95.

This article discusses the following: 1) The acceptability of diverse styles of rationality suggests replacing concern for uniqueness with that for coordination, 2) Popper's lowering of the standard of rationality increases its scope insufficiently, 3) Bartley's making the standard comprehensive increases its scope excessively, 4) the pluralist view of rationality as partial (i.e., of Jarvie and Agassi) is better, but its ranking of all rationality eliminates choice of styles, 5) styles diversify the standards of rationality, 8) rationality is not merely a matter of style, 6) 7) diversity raises new, interesting problems, allowing diversity permits reconciling differences better than does the absent unique standard, and 9) cultural heritage and rationality are complementary.

Wetzel, Marc. Action et passion. *Rev Int Phil*, 48(189), 303-326, 1994.

Weyembergh, M. The Liberal Ironist, Philosophy, and the Dialogue of Cultures. *Hist Euro Ideas*, 20(1-3), 575-580, Ja 95.

Wheale, Peter and McNally, Ruth. "Environmental and Medical Bioethics in Late Modernity" in *Philosophy and the Natural Environment, Attfield, Robin (ed)*, 211-225. New York, Cambridge Univ Pr, 1994.

Wheary, Jennifer and Ennis, Robert H. Gender Bias in Critical Thinking: Continuing the Dialogue. *Educ Theor*, 45(2), 213-224, Spr 95.

This paper reviews three sorts of claims that current conceptions of critical thinking reflect a male bias. The types discussed are 1) discrimination against females in educational settings where critical thinking is taught or observed; 2) neglect of females in research about thinking; and 3) an emphasis on typically male characteristics (such as rationality, judgment, and guidance by a set of universal principles) over typically female characteristics (such as emotion, attention to contextuality, a link between self and object, caring, and personal voice). The paper seeks to initiate dialogue about these claims by discussing: 1) their meaning, 2) their implications for conceptions of critical thinking and for critical thinking instruction, and 3) ways in which the claims need to be clarified or amended in order to be more helpful to those working in the area of critical thinking.

Wheeler, David L. Toward a Process-Relational Christian Eschatology. *Process Stud*, 22(4), 227-237, Winter 93.

Many Christian theologians have used Whiteheadian process-relational philosophy to clarify the ontological status of doctrinal assertions. It would seem that this strategy would not be helpful in the field of eschatology, which deals with scenarios of human and cosmic consummation. Process-relational thought denies traditional understandings of divine sovereignty and describes an open-ended cosmic process in which no final, determinate outcome is envisioned. However, process thought *does* describe God as guiding and encouraging a universal urge toward novelty and harmony, and exercising a species of judgment towards the world's achievements. I argue that these features of process thought can shed light on a nonmythological rendering of Christian eschatology which describes a proximate outcome of human hopes and striving.

Wheeler, Mark. The Uniformity of the Causal Connection in the Second Analogy, or How Not to Dodge Beck. *Kantstudien*, 85(3), 341-351, 1994.

Kant, in Second Analogy, argues that every state of affairs has some cause which immediately precedes it in time. Dodge claims that Kant's argument for this principle tacitly involves the premise that similar causes necessarily have similar effects. Crucial to Dodge's interpretation is the assertion that the subject be able to distinguish among enduring states of affairs, causal pairs, and causal half-pairs. I argue Kant does not presuppose this claim. Rather, Kant assumes only that objective representations of successive states of affairs are possible, not that the subject be able to recognize them as successive.

Whicher, Ian. Cessation and Integration in Classical Yoga. *Asian Phil*, 5(1), 47-58, 1995.

In this paper I challenge and attempt to correct conclusions about classical *Yoga* philosophy drawn by traditional and modern interpretations of Patañjali's *Yoga-sutras*. My interpretation of Patañjali's *Yoga*—which focuses on the meaning of "cessation" (nirodha) as given in Patañjali's central definition of *Yoga* (YS 1.2)—counters the radically dualistic and ontologically-oriented interpretations of *Yoga* presented by many scholars, and offers an open-ended, epistemologically-oriented hermeneutic which, I maintain, is more appropriate for arriving at a genuine assessment of Patañjali's system *(darsana)* of Yoga.

Whimster, Sam. Liberal Eugenics and the Vitalist Life Sciences: Incongruities in the German Human Sciences in the 19th Century. *Hist Human Sci*, 8(1), 107-114, F 95.

This is a review essay of Woodruff Smith *Politics and the Sciences of Culture in Germany, 1840-1920*. It discusses the monistic project of cultural sciences based on Leipzig and Berlin. It indicates the liberal origins of eugenic thought in the nineteenth century.

White, Alan. Hegel or Schelling?. *Bull Hegel Soc Gt Brit*, 30, 14-22, Autumn-Wint 94.

White, John. "Liberalism, Nationality, and Education" in *Identity, Culture, and Education*, Smeyers, Paul (ed), 85-93. Leuven, Leuven Univ Pr, 1994.

Yael Tamir's (1993) book *Liberal Nationalism* seeks to show that liberalism and nationalism are not incompatible political philosophies. Nationalism need not take the closed, authoritarian form it has so often taken; and liberalism is premised on certain national ideas, including national self-determination. This critical discussion of her account is broadly sympathetic to the compatibility thesis, but takes issue both with her notion of nationalism, with her account of a nation as a self-conscious cultural community, and with the sharp line she draws between civic and cultural concerns. Although her book does not deal with education, this paper concludes with remarks about what the role of nationality should be in education, in both a Tamirian and a non-Tamirian framework. The latter is applied to education in Britain.

White, John. The Dishwasher's Child: Education and the End of Egalitarianism. *J Phil Educ*, 28(2), 173-181, Wint 94.

This paper argues that egalitarianism, in itself and as a basis for educational policy, is unacceptable. Three recent defenses of it are examined and rejected. Three anti-egalitarian positions, however, all of which stress sufficiency rather than equality pass muster. Educational implications are followed through, with reference to mixed ability grouping, selection, equal opportunities in education and conflicting views about the minimum content of a common school curriculum.

White, Judith and Dobson, John. Toward the Feminine Firm: An Extension to Thomas White. *Bus Ethics Quart*, 5(3), 463-478, Jl 95.

This paper concerns the influence of gender on a firm's moral and economic performance. It supports Thomas White's intimation of a male gender bias in the value system underlying extant business theory. We suggest that this gender bias may be corrected by drawing on the concept of substantive rationality inherent in virtue-ethics theory. This feminine-oriented relationship-based value system complements the essential nature of the firm as a nexus of relationships between stakeholders. Not only is this feminine firm morally desirable, but it also economically more efficient in that trust becomes a more feasible implicit contractual enforcement mechanism. In an organizational context, therefore, from both a moral and an economic perspective, long established economic man is dominated by nascent economic woman.

White, Nicholas P. Conflicting Parts of Happiness in Aristotle's Ethics. *Ethics*, 105(2), 258-283, Ja 95.

White, Patricia. "Having a Voice and Getting a Hearing" in *Identity, Culture, and Education*, Smeyers, Paul (ed), 351-364. Leuven, Leuven Univ Pr, 1994.

Ronald Dworkin's claim that the right to free speech does not include a right to circumstances that encourage citizens to speak nor a right to competent and sympathetic understanding on the part of listeners is examined. Drawing on arguments for the existence of other human rights, Dworkin's claim is challenged. If, however, the challenge fails, that is not the end of the story. Democratic societies should try to foster conditions in which citizens are encouraged to speak and are listened to sympathetically in the interests of the well-being and flourishing of the polity. The role of education in this is explored.

White, Richard J. Georges Bataille and the Philosophy of the Sacred. *J Brit Soc Phenomenol*, 26(1), 52-64, Ja 95.

In this essay, I argue that the sheer variety of Bataille's work is focused upon the problem of the sacred. I then propose a reading of Bataille's theory of the sacred, and I show how on a *performative* level too, Bataille's work is intended as a sacred provocation. This suggests a way beyond the post-modern impasse, a way which contemporary philosophy still hesitates to take.

White, Richard J. Zarathustra and the Progress of Sovereignty: From the Overman to the External Recurrence. *Int Stud Phil*, 26(3), 107-115, 1994.

In *Thus Spoke Zarathustra*, there is an apparent contradiction between the doctrine of the Overman and the thought of Eternal Recurrence. For while the first idea looks forward to something which goes *beyond* man, the latter celebrates the return of everything, including "the lost man," which the Overman was supposed to consign to oblivion. In this essay, I suggest, however, that these two thoughts are finally not incompatible with each other, and that in some way they perform a mutual illumination: this helps us to understand Nietzsche's philosophical perspective on "sovereignty."

White, Stephen K. "Reason, Modernity, and Democracy" in *The Cambridge Companion to Habermas*, White, Stephen K (ed), 3-16. New York, Cambridge Univ Pr, 1995.

White, Stephen K. Diskursethik, schwere Fürsorge und leichte Fürsorge. *Deut Z Phil*, 42(6), 1051-1056, 1994.

White, Stephen K (ed). *The Cambridge Companion to Habermas*. New York, Cambridge Univ Pr, 1995.

Whitebook, Joel. Hypostatizing Thanatos: Lacan's Analysis of the Ego. *Constellation*, 1(2), 214-230, O 94.

Whitebook, Joel. *Perversion and Utopia: A Study in Psychoanalysis and Critical Theory*. Cambridge, MIT Pr, 1995.

Whitehouse, Peter J and Dresser, Rebecca. The Incompetent Patient on the Slippery Slope. *Hastings Center Rep*, 24(4), 6-12, Jl-Ag 94.

This paper focuses on issues arising in decisions on life-sustaining treatment for conscious incompetent patients when there is no clear evidence of their former preferences and values as competent persons. Using persons diagnosed with dementia as an example, the authors analyze the steps involved in applying the so-called best interests test (also known as the benefit-burden or reasonable person test). They discuss ways to improve the observer's ability to assess the subjective experiences of individual dementia patients and describe situations in which treatment could be withheld or withdrawn under a best interests approach.

Whiten, Andrew (ed). *Natural Theories of Mind: Evolution, Development, and Simulation of Everyday Mindreading*. Cambridge, Blackwell, 1991.

In developmental psychology researchers have begun to trace the child's developing understanding of such concepts as other's desires, emotional states and intentions. Ethologists and comparative psychologists have asked how and why an ability to read the mind of another might emerge in the course of evolution. In computer science, the question is how to shape the emergence within computational systems of representations of the minds of others. This volume brings together contributions from these three disciplines, with others from philosophy and anthropology, on the central topic of the emergence of theories of mind.

Whiteside, Kerry H. Hannah Arendt and Ecological Politics. *Environ Ethics*, 16(4), 339-358, Wint 94.

I argue that Arendt's understanding of "society" deepens Green critiques of productivism. By avoiding subjectivist or objectivist modes of thought, Arendt uncovers hidden links between life-sustaining labor and a world-destroying drive to consume. Checking environmentally destructive desires to produce and consume requires structuring communities around an optimal configuration of public deliberation, work and labor. I conclude that an Arendt-inspired ecological politics stresses the interdependence of human values and an all-encompassing natural order.

Whitford, Margaret (ed). *The Irigaray Reader*. Cambridge, Blackwell, 1994.

The Irigaray Reader consists of a selection of extracts from the work of Luce Irigaray, translated into English. There is a general editor's introduction, plus introductions to the three individual sections entitled: 1) The Critique of Patriarchy; 2) Psychoanalysis and Language; 3) Ethics and Subjectivity: Towards the Future. The *Reader* includes a brief glossary of Irigarayan terms and a bibliography.

Whitman, Jeffrey P. The Soldier as Conscientious Objector. *Pub Affairs Quart*, 9(1), 87-100, Ja 95.

This work examines the moral duties of professional soldiers, arguing that soldiers are not morally responsible for the justness of the wars they wage. While it may be morally permissible for a soldier to claim conscientious objector status in order to avoid fighting in an unjust war, the soldier must discharge a heavy burden of proof demonstrating the moral wrongness of the particular war she finds objectionable. For that reason, among others, the professional soldier rarely has a moral obligation to refuse service in a morally unjust war.

Whitman, Jeffrey P and Haight, Catherine and Tipton, Paul. Citizens and Soldiers: Teaching Just War Theory. *Teach Phil*, 17(1), 29-39, Mr 94.

Using the core curriculum course on ethics and just war theory taught at the US Military Academy as an example, this paper offers some guidelines on how to incorporate instruction in just war theory into similar ethics courses at other colleges and universities. Furthermore, arguing that there is a real need for the public to understand just war concepts, this paper presents an overview and prescription for informed citizenship in the post-cold war age.

Whitsitt, Sam (trans) and Sullivan, Michael (trans) and Agamben, Giorgio. *Idea of Prose*. Albany, SUNY Pr, 1985.

Whittaker, Nancy Parsons (trans) and Lathe, Robert F (trans) and Steiner, Rudolf. *The Spirit of the Waldorf School*. Hudson, Anthroposophic Pr, 1995.

Wible, James R. The Economic Organization of Science, the Firm, and the Marketplace. *Phil Soc Sci*, 25(1), 35-68, Mr 95.

Among the various institutional structures of an economy like the firm and the marketplace is one that is like no other. Science is unique. This uniqueness raises an important question: why does science exist? From an economic perspective, there are two potentially meaningful approaches to the existence of science. They both encompass institutional pluralism. A substitutes theory of comparative institutions presupposes the primacy of the commercial marketplace over firms—that firms substitute for the market when markets fail. This theory has not been used to explain the existence of science. A complements theory postulates that many simultaneous institutional responses, including science, are necessary for creating an efficient and equitable economy. The economic function of science is to produce fundamental theoretical abstractions about our world. Scientific theories are public goods that would not likely be produced within the governance structures of commercial markets and firms. The aim is to complement but not supplant traditional philosophical answers that science exists to discover truth and knowledge.

Wichmann, Heinz. Probleme der Kantischen Ethik: Überlegungen im Anschluss an Paul Menzers kritische Betrachtung. *Kantstudien*, 85(3), 303-308, 1994.

Nach Kant ist der Mensch in zwiefacher Hinsicht zu betrachten: Als Urheber des Moralgesetzes gehört er als mit Freiheit begabtes Wesen vermittels der Vernunft der intelligiblen Welt an. Als der Empirie zugehörig jedoch soll er, obwohl mit Vernunft begabt, als ein anderer betrachtet werden, da Kant keine Möglichkeit sieht, eine Beeinflussung des Empirischen durch das Intelligible nachzuweisen. Dieser Aufsatz versucht dagegen aufzuzeigen, dass eine gegenseitige Beeinflussbarkeit möglich sein muss. Die Bedingung dafür liegt in dem in der Kritik der reinen Vernunft B 567 angeführten "Subjekt der Sinnenwelt". Der Massstab, nach dem jedes Individuum seine Neigungen und Triebe vermittels de Vernunft vereinigen kann, ist in der Harmonie zu suchen, die durch Angleichung der Neigungen und Triebe an das Vernunftgesetz eines jeden handelnden empirischen Subjekts zur individuellen Zufriedenheit führt.

Wickham, Gary and Hunt, Alan. *Foucault and Law: Towards a Sociology of Law as Governance*. Boulder, Westview Pr, 1994.

This book explores what Foucault had to say about law and then goes on to use in the construction of a new framework for the sociology of law. It does not set out to construct a 'Foucaultian theory of law'. But it does contend that an exploration of his work can contribute to the construction of new and fruitful approach to the exploration of legal phenomena. This book has three parts. Part 1 provides a general introduction Foucault's thought to a readership which is familiar with law as a significant focus on inquiry, but is not familiar with Foucault's writing. Part 2 provides an exposition of the treatment of law in his texts. Rather it offers a critical commentary and evaluation of Foucault's treatment of legal themes. The argument advanced is that Foucault's equation of law with absolutism and sovereignty seriously undermines his capacity to engage with the role of law in modernity. In Part 3 a new framework for the sociology of law is advanced in which law is treated as a form of governance. Four principles of governance and some methodological rules for such a project.

Wicks, Andrew C. Albert Schweitzer or Ivan Boesky? Why We Should Reject the Dichotomy Between Medicine and Business. *J Bus Ethics*, 14(5), 339-351, My 95.

Several critics have maintained that there are some critical differences between the ethics of medicine and the ethics of business such that health care should remain as free as possible from the influence of business. In particular, it has been suggested that the core moral identity of those in medical practice, and their accompanying institutions, are not only antagonistic, but effectively opposed to their counterparts in business. This paper attempts to challenge such a sharp contrast and suggests that a reformulation, where the two are seen as fundamentally similar is both appropriate and compelling. Indeed, as we contemplate the direction of proposed comprehensive reforms in health care, such an understanding of the moral framework of medicine and business is essential.

Wicks, Andrew C. The Business Ethics Movement: Where are We Headed and What Can We Learn From Our Colleagues in Bioethics?. *Bus Ethics Quart*, 5(3), 603-620, Jl 95.

There is a long and distinguished history of ethical thought in both business and medicine dating back to ancient times. Yet, the emergence of distinct academic disciplines ("business ethics" and "bioethics") which are also tied to broader social movements is a very recent phenomenon. In spite of the apparent affinities that would seem to emerge from this connection, many have argued that the differences between business and medicine make any constructive interaction between business ethics and bioethics minimal. Indeed, little has been done to specifically examine the potential for collaboration and interdisciplinary research. This paper argues that there is considerable potential for constructive interaction between these two movements based on three major arguments: that the differences between medicine and business have been exaggerated, that both the fields face a number of urgent problems that are common to each, and that the model of bioethics can serve as a useful guide for business ethicists.

Wicks, Robert. Kant on Fine Art: Artistic Sublimity Shaped by Beauty. *J Aes Art Crit*, 53(2), 189-193, Spr 95.

This essay critically examines the view recently set forth by Paul Guyer that Kant's theories of artistic beauty and artistic creativity exclusively coincide with this theory of natural beauty. I note that very great works of art, although they may indeed be beautiful, also tend to be sublime. To acknowledge the sense of awe which attends those great works of art which are also beautiful, I argue that Kant's theory of sublimity must also be included within an accurate interpretation of Kant's account of artistic beauty, and maintain that Guyer's exclusive reference to Kant's theory of natural beauty will not suffice.

Wider, Kathleen. Truth and Existence: The Idealism in Sartre's Theory of Truth. *Int J Phil Stud*, 3(1), 91-109, Mr 95.

Although Sartre rejects a certain kind of idealism in *Truth and Existence*, I argue that a commitment to a kind of transcendental idealism remains. I explore the expression of this idealism in *Truth and Existence* and how it enhances an idealist tradition which begins with Kant. More importantly, I examine Sartre's divergence from Kantian idealism and his blending of pragmatism with idealism, in a way most similar to Wittgenstein's. Unlike Wittgenstein's idealism, however, Sartre's idealism, I argue, brings him dangerously close to solipsism and creates for his theory of truth a serious problem of cognitive splintering.

Widerker, David. Providence, Eternity, and Human Freedom: A Reply to Stump and Kretzmann. *Faith Phil*, 11(2), 242-254, Ap 94.

In this paper, I respond to Eleonore Stump's and Norman Kretzmann's defense of eternalism against an objection of mine in 'A Problem For the Eternity Solution.' There I argued that, insofar as eternalism is intended as a strategy of avoiding the conclusion of the argument against freedom from divine foreknowledge to the effect that the traditional theist is committed to the violation of the principle of the fixity of the past, it does not succeed. I discuss two attempts by Stump and Kretzmann to reject this claim and argue that they are unsatisfactory. Finally, I sketch what seems to me the most promising line of defense that an eternalist might adopt in order to deal with the problem I raise.

Widerker, David and Katzoff, Charlotte. Zimmerman on Moral Responsibility, Obligation and Alternate Possibilities. *Analysis*, 54(4), 285-287, O 94.

In "Obligation, Responsibility and Alternate Possibilities", (*Analysis*, 53, 1993, 51-53) Michael Zimmerman rejects the alleged link between the Kantian principle that "ought" implies "can" and the Principle of Alternate Possibilities as applied to moral blame, argued for by Widerker in 'Frankfurt on "Ought Implies Can" and Alternative Possibilities', (*Analysis*, 51, 1991, 222-224). We show that the principle upon which Zimmerman bases his argument—that one's blameworthiness for an action is a function of what one believes one's obligations to be—is false.

Wieand, Jeffrey. Hume's True Judges. *J Aes Art Crit*, 53(3), 318-319, Sum 95.

Wiehl, Reiner. "Schellings Naturphilosophie—eine Philosophie des Organismus?" in *Schelling und die Selbstorganisation, Heuser-Kessler, Marie-Luise (ed)*, 113-134. Berlin, Duncker Humblot, 1994.

Wiehl, Reiner. De la Teología a la Teología Aporía o camino? En relación a un debate central de la filosofía moderna. *An Seminar Metaf*, 27, 217-241, 1993.

Wielema, M R. The Historiography of Dutch Philosophy: Problems and Perspectives (in Dutch). *Tijdschr Filosof*, 56(3), 526-551, S 94.

This article contains a critical survey of the attempts that have been made to write a comprehensive history of philosophy in the Netherlands. Three historiographical types can be distinguished. In the early nineteenth century, Dutch philosophers became increasingly aware of the peculiarities of their national tradition in philosophy—as distinct from the traditions of France, Germany or Britain. The result was what might be called a 'patriotic historiography', which tended to glorify the Dutch intellectual past. In the second half of the century, however, a 'critical historiography' emerged, which tended to stress what was taken to be the lack of originality and relative unimportance of the Dutch contribution to philosophy. In recent years, research has tended to concentrate on bringing out the unique intermediary position of the Netherlands, which on many occasions has enabled it to play an influential role in various philosophical developments throughout Europe. (edited)

Wiercinski, Andrzej. Philosophy of Universalism and the Concept of Human Nature. *Dialogue Hum*, 4(2-3), 255-267, 1994.

Wiesing, Urban. Style and Responsibility: Medicine in Postmodernity. *Theor Med*, 15(3), 277-290, S 94.

To what extent can postmodern developments be observed in modern medicine and which theories of postmodern philosophy can we draw on with regard to medicine's theoretical problem? This article explores these questions with special emphasis on the epistemological status of medicine, the concept of disease, and the anthropological model. It is examined whether medicine's inherent duty to act can be questioned in the light of the plurality that characterizes postmodernity. It is concluded that, according to postmodern philosophy, medicine should be characterized by a justified variety of paradigms. Cooperation within the variety must continue to be guaranteed, always in favor of the constitutive moral duty of medicine.

Wiggins, David. "Putnam's Doctrine of Natural Kind Words and Frege's Doctrines of Sense, Reference, and Extension" in *Reading Putnam, Clark, Peter (ed)*, 201-215. Cambridge, Blackwell, 1995.

Wiggins, David. "The Kant-Frege-Russell View of Existence" in *Modality, Morality, and Belief, Sinnott-Armstrong, Walter (ed)*, 93-113. New York, Cambridge Univ Pr, 1994.

The paper defends the view mentioned in the title by developing it to the same point of explicitness as its recent rival, the first level view, and then pays particular attention to the problem of sentences of the forms: "Vienna exists", "Vienna does not necessarily exist", Vulcan does not exist". The paper shows how naturally the insights of the late Gareth Evans, in chapter ten of *The Varieties of Reference*, may be adapted to the second level of conception of existence.

Wiggins, Osborne P. Commentary on "Self-Consciousness, Mental Agency, and the Clinical Psychopathology of Thought Insertion". *Phil Psychiat Psych*, 1(1), 11-12, Mr 94.

Wike, Victoria S. *Kant on Happiness in Ethics*. Albany, SUNY Pr, 1995.

The book provides a comprehensive analysis of Immanuel Kant's treatment of happiness in ethics. It considers the meaning of happiness for Kant and the role of happiness in his ethics. The book argues that Kant's treatment of happiness is positive and coherent once it is recognized that Kant distinguishes four possible tasks for happiness. Happiness may be taken to be a principle of ethics, a natural end of human beings, a means to a moral end, or a component of the highest good. Kant rejects happiness as a principle but speaks positively about the other three tasks of happiness.

Wilbur, Ronnie B. Foregrounding Structures in American Sign Language. *J Prag*, 22(6), 647-672, D 94.

Foregrounding structures serve the primary function of highlighting information by clause-external placement. Foley and Van Valin (1985) identify five such structures: topicalization, clefts, pseudoclefts, left dislocation, and right dislocation. This paper will argue that there is strong evidence that ASL has the first four of these structures, but that evidence for the existence of right dislocation is weak. While topicalization and left dislocation in ASL have already been discussed in the literature, the contribution of the present discussion is to provide pragmatic evidence primarily for pseudoclefts and secondarily for clefts. Of significance is the argument that the prevailing view of the ASL pseudocleft as a 'rhetorical question-answer' sequence fails to account for both syntactic and pragmatic aspects of pseudocleft behavior. The final constituent in the pseudocleft is shown to be a focused phrase that provides the value of a variable in an open proposition; it is not an afterthought nor right dislocation.

Wildes, Kevin William. A Memo from the Central Office: The "Ethical and Religious Directives for Catholic Health Care Services". *Kennedy Inst Ethics J*, 5(2), 133-139, Je 95.

In 1994, the National Conference of Catholic Bishops revised the "Ethical and Religious Directives for Catholic Health Care Services." A goal of the Directives is to maintain the moral integrity of Catholic health care institutions and to address controversies in bioethics and healthcare. The Directives represent a shift to an exclusively principle-based approach to moral reason. This shift threatens to undermine the very tradition that the bishops seek to protect.

Wiley, Norbert. *The Semiotic Self*. Chicago, Univ of Chicago Pr, 1994.

Drawing on a synthesis of the writings of Charles Sanders Peirce and George Herbert Mead, this book argues that the self can be seen as a "trialogue" in which the present self ("I") talks to the future self ("you") about the past self ("me"). Wiley applies this view to the evolution of the self in the primates (phylogenesis), the origin of the self in the human infant (ontogenesis), and the ongoing self in the mature person. A distinctive feature is that there is a mutually supportive relation between the self and democracy, a view which Wiley traces through American history. In finding a way to decenter the self without eliminating it, Wiley supplies a way of giving closure to classical pragmatism, while also suggesting a new direction for neopragmatism.

Wilfond, Benjamin S. Screening Policy for Cystic Fibrosis: The Role of Evidence. *Hastings Center Rep*, 25(3), S21-S23, My-Je 95.

This paper describes an evidentiary model for making health policy decisions which includes the evaluation of clinical research, the identification of underlying normative issues, and public participation in a process to make allocation decisions. While the least controversial aspect of this model is the analysis of clinical data, screening policy for cystic fibrosis is used to show that even this is problematic. The State of Wisconsin embarked on a routine newborn screening program for cystic fibrosis, even though a nine year prospective study had not yet shown any pulmonary benefit. A recent OTA report on cystic fibrosis carrier screening suggested that such screening was inevitable, regardless of the outcome of clinical studies. These examples demonstrate that even the evaluation of clinical evidence cannot be assumed to be an objective activity.

Wilfred, Felix. Liberating Dialogue: An Indian Perspective. *J Dharma*, 19(3), 235-247, Jl-S 94.

Wilkerson, Abby. "Homophobia and the Moral Authority of Medicine" in *Gay Ethics*, Murphy, Timothy F (ed), 329-347. New York, Haworth Pr, 1994.

This essay identifies ways in which medicine expresses and legitimizes homophobic values. Examples of such homophobia are identified in the treatment of people with HIV, moralistic intepretations of people with AIDS, certain conceptions about ways in which HIV is transmitted, media representations of AIDS, and even in the way in which medicine's "objectivity" reinforces a moral view inimical to gay men, lesbians, and bisexuals. It is concluded that the notion of medical objectivity and traditional conceptions of ethics of health care hinder an appreciation of the ways in which medicine presumes and perpetuates homophobic values.

Wilkerson, Terence. Akrasia. *Ratio*, 7(2), 164-182, D 94.

Aristotle's account of *akrasia* is unsatisfactory for a number of reasons. First, his account of the problem is colored by a number of unattractive assumptions and preoccupations; second, his central claim, that *akrasia* involves a temporary displacement of knowledge, deals at best with only a small number of cases; third, he is wrong to suppose that the *akrates* is typically someone overwhelmed by passion. We need to follow Davidson in recognizing that the central problem consists in a failure to convert intention into action. Any solution must involve a recognition that we are dealing with a range of very different kinds of case, which demand different kinds of treatment. For example sometimes agents are overtaken by passion; sometimes they coolly and calmly do the wrong thing; sometimes they are insincere; sometimes they are suffering from a weakness of will; sometimes they are guilty of some kind of self deception; and sometimes they may have difficulty in comparing the goods and evils available.

Wilkes, K V. Psychology and Politics: Lies, Damned Lies and Self-Deception. *Philosophy*, 37(Supp), 115-129, 1994.

Wilkie, Sean. Searle's Theory of Visual Experience. *Phil Quart*, 45(178), 70-78, Ja 95.

The term 'visual experience' is central to contemporary philosophy of perception. The term 'sense-data', itself a successor to 'ideas' and 'impressions', has almost completely fallen out of fashion. John Searle offers an explanation for this preference. What he says about sense-data, however, is based upon a misunderstanding of traditional theories. There is, consequently, a good deal to be suspicious of in his assumption that 'visual experience' is not subject to the criticisms which brought 'sense-data' into disrepute. I am primarily interested in the similarities between the ways in which the terms 'sense-data' and 'visual experience' are introduced by their respective proponents. My main task will be to show that, in Searle's account at least, the intellectual distance between these two notions is very small indeed.

Wilkins, Burleigh T. The Moral *Prima Facie* Obligation to Obey the Law. *J Soc Phil*, 25(2), 92-96, Fall 94.

Wilkinson, Jennifer. "Not Exactly Making Believe: An Essay in the Philosophy of Literature" in *Life, World and Meaning*, Roux, A P J (ed), 93-107. Pretoria, Univ of S Africa, 1990.

The make-believe account of emotional response to fictional characters and their plight as presented by Walton and which takes making believe to be a benign form of pretending is challenged. Barrett's analysis of Austin's notion of pretending as a

way of not-exactly doing things allows the idea of pretending to be extended. By then applying the notion to both contexts, the analogy between the fictional situation and a game of mud-pies on which the make-believe explanation depends, is shown not only to be incomplete but also to break down in several important ways.

Wilkinson, Karina. "The Semantics of the Common Noun *Kind*" in *The Generic Book*, Carlson, Gregory N (ed), 383-397. Chicago, Univ of Chicago Pr, 1995.

Noun phrases containing the nouns *kind, type*, or *sort* can have an indefinite (existential) interpretation even with a definite determiner. They occur in *there*-sentences: *There are those kinds of books in the library*. Carlson (1977) analyzes *kind* as a transitive noun. Noun phrases such as *a book of that kind* do not have an obvious analysis if *kind* is transitive. Wilkinson proposes that there is a structural ambiguity in the definite noun phrases, which accounts for both the generic and existential interpretations. The author also examines the possibility of making *kind* ambiguous between a relation and a one-place predicate.

Wilks, Ian. Aquinas on the Past Possibility of the World's Having Existed Forever. *Rev Metaph*, 48(2), 299-329, D 94.

Willard, Dallas. "Knowledge" in *The Cambridge Companion to Husserl*, Smith, Barry (ed), 138-167. New York, Cambridge Univ Pr, 1995.

This essay specifies the exact structure of the state of mind and object which Husserl termed "knowledge". That state is a complicated structure in which an object of consciousness is found to be as it is thought to be. Husserl's special term for this is "fulfillment". Cases would be finding your keys to be in the table where you thought they were or deriving a formula by the distributive laws as you thought you could. Elaboration of "fulfillment" permits Husserl to provide an eidetic analysis of "the possibility of knowledge", which, for him, means how consciousness manages to grasp an object that is neither part of nor dependent upon the act which grasps it. Objects are not modified by the 'touch' of the mind. Hence, Husserl provides a reconciliation of the subjectivity of the act of consciousness and the objectivity of its subject matter that constitutes a straightforward epistemological realism.

Willard, Dallas. "The Unhinging of the American Mind: Derrida as Pretext" in *European Philosophy and the American Academy*, Smith, Barry (ed), 3-20. Peru, Open Court, 1994.

Willard, Ross. Hereditary Undecidability of Some Theories of Finite Structures. *J Sym Log*, 59(4), 1254-1262, D 94.

Using a result of Gurevich and Lewis on the word problem for finite semigroups, we give short proofs that the following theories are hereditarily undecidable: 1) finite graphs of vertex-degree at most 3; 2) finite nonvoid sets with two distinguished permutations; 3) finite-dimensional vector spaces over a finite field with two distinguished endomorphisms.

Willems, Klaas. Das neue Erkenntnisproblem: Erkenntniskritische Überlegungen zum "anthropoischen Prinzip" in der neueren Physik. *Kantstudien*, 85(2), 179-197, 1994.

What are the philosophical presuppositions of the so-called "anthropic cosmological principle" in modern physics, put forward by Stephen Hawking, John D Barrow, etc.? The paper gives a critique of this principle on the basis of transcendental philosophy (Immanuel Kant, Edmund Husserl, and mainly Ernst Cassirer). It is argued that the principle reduces the possibility of knowledge about the external world to the evolutionary fact that mankind came into existence in the universe at a given time. The "anthropic principle" does not, however, solve the epistemological problem but rather neutralizes it by naturalizing the old Protagorian motto "homo mensura".

Williams, Andrew D. The Revisionist Difference Principle. *Can J Phil*, 25(2), 257-281, Je 95.

One formulation of Rawls' difference principle favours the most egalitarian member of the set of pareto efficient distributions, and is revisionist since, under some circumstances, it prohibits maximising the expectations of the least advantaged. The revisionist principle withstands Raz's important critique of the intrinsic value of equality, but is objectionable because of its inability to satisfy the requirements of transitivity and contraction consistency. That conclusion may have political significance when, due to the absence of chain connection, the interests of the most and least advantaged diverge from those of the middle classes.

Williams, Bernard. *Making Sense of Humanity and Other Philosophical Papers 1982-1993*. New York, Cambridge Univ Pr, 1995.

Williams, Bernard. Pagan Justice and Christian Love. *Apeiron*, 26(3-4), 195-207, S-D 93.

Williams, Clifford. Kierkegaardian Suspicion and Properly Basic Beliefs. *Relig Stud*, 30(3), 261-267, S 94.

Reformed epistemologists claim that a properly basic belief in God is grounded in some triggering condition. Kierkegaard thought that people sometimes believe in God as a result of psychological and sociological conditions that have no legitimate triggering power, such as unconscious identification with the Christian church one has grown up in. If Kierkegaard is right, then Reformed epistemologists must distinguish legitimate triggering conditions for belief in God from illegitimate ones, and must concede that we have to rule out the presence of illegitimate ones before we can be justified in believing we possess a properly basic belief in God. Reformed epistemology must, in short, admit the necessity of "Kierkegaardian discriminatory evidence".

Williams, Howard. Democracy and Right in Habermas's Theory of Facticity and Value. *Hist Polit Thought*, 15(2), 269-282, Sum 94.

This is a discussion of Habermas's new book on Fact and Value from the standpoint of his theory of democracy. It is argued that a critical view of democratic procedures may lead to a more problematic view of right and law than Habermas suggests.

Williams, Kevin. "Education for European Citizenship: A Philosophical Critique" in *Identity, Culture, and Education*, Smeyers, Paul (ed), 365-374. Leuven, Leuven Univ Pr, 1994.

The target of the critique offered in this article is the attempt to use education to engineer political allegiance to an artificial notion of 'European citizenship'. In the first section of the paper the proselytizing, manipulative and even indoctrinatory character of the education envisaged is elaborated. The second part of the article raise some important difficulties in conceptualizing the shared identity which would be required in order to animate and sustain a sense of 'European citizenship' among inhabitants of nations who have long civic traditions of their own.

Williams, Mark and Simpson, Evan. The Ideal of Social Disillusionment. *Phil Forum*, 26(1), 63-77, Fall 94.

In this paper we argue that individuals in modern societies can share a general appreciation of the contingency of moral and political engagement without endangering these purposeful attachments. Depending upon the acceptance of various cognitive conventions, social practices and institutions cannot be sustained by appeals to advantage alone, but these conventions do not demand ontological commitment. Transparent fictions rather than ideological illusions can suffice to sustain valued forms of life. In contrast to Rorty's ironic society in which "only the intellectuals would be ironists", we suggest the benign disillusionment can characterize the public generally.

Williams, Melissa S. Justice toward Groups: Political Not Juridical. *Polit Theory*, 23(1), 67-91, F 95.

The recent literature on equality and difference evinces two distinct approaches to the task of defining justice in a manner responsive to social difference. The "juridical" approach, exemplified by Susan Okin and Will Kymlicka, accepts the liberal ideal of impartiality and presupposes that justice, defined in the abstract, should be interpreted and enforced by agents of an impartial state. The "political" approach, exemplified by Iris Young, maintains that standards of justice can avoid reproducing inequality only if they are defined through a discursive process that includes marginilized groups. This article defends the "political" approach but stops short of abandoning the ideal of impartiality altogether.

Williams, Meredith. Social Norms and Narrow Content. *Midwest Stud Phil*, 15, 425-462, 1990.

Williams, Patricia A (ed) and Wesson, Robert (ed). *Evolution and Human Values*. Amsterdam, Rodopi, 1995.

Williams, Quentin. Projected Actuality. *Brit J Aes*, 35(3), 273-277, Jl 95.

From my recognition of close (and elsewhere absent) similarities between the camera painting of Vermeer and Canaletto, I conclude, in "Projected Actuality" that too little reference has been made, in art-historical writing, to the effect of camera painting on the handling of paint, to the "modernising" effect, on later painting, of this particular kind of achieved surface appearance—and to the differences between camera painting and painting from the subject, from drawings or other information.

Williams, Rhonda M. "Consenting to Whiteness" in *Marxism in the Postmodern Age, Callari, Antonio (ed)*, 301-308. New York, Guilford, 1994.

This essay critiques recent Marxist economic discourse on discrimination. I argue that, our substantive differences notwithstanding, Marxian economists share a common tendency to undertheorize race. Neither side has accorded sufficient significance either to the economic and extraeconomic practices that create gendered, race-conscious workers or to the historical specificity of those practices. Hence our understanding of discrimination remains incomplete, our antiracist politics contorted. I suggest that both poststructuralist and feminist theories provide analytic means to the end of developing a richer theory of race and gender subjectification, agency, and "class interests".

Williams, Richard N. Temporality and Psychological Action at a Distance. *J Mind Behav*, 16(1), 63-75, Wint 95.

This paper discusses the manner in which Isaac Newton proposed to account for the phenomenon of action at a distance. His struggles arose from the attempt to maintain the corpuscular metaphysics (or, "metaphysic of things") common in his day. In psychology the same difficulty arises in accounting for the effects of past events on present behaviors. Traditional theories account for this "psychological action at a distance" by proposing various constructs and structures that serve the same function that aether served in the physical explanations of Newton's day. The paper argues that such explanations are unsatisfactory, and unnecessary once the assumptions of the metaphysics is presented to account for the subtle relationship of past events to present old ones.

Williams, Robert. "Hegel and Schleiermacher on Theological Truth" in *Meaning, Truth, and God, Rouner, Leroy (ed)*, 52-69. Notre Dame, Univ Notre Dame Pr, 1982.

Williams, Robert R. "The Other: F H Jacobi and German Idealism" in *Hegel on the Modern World, Collins, Ardis B (ed)*, 73-92. Albany, SUNY Pr, 1995.

Williams, Robert R. Discernment in the Realm of Shadows: Absolute Knowing and Otherness. *Owl Minerva*, 26(2), 133-148, Spr 95.

I wish to thank Professor Houlgate for his thoughtful article, especially in view of his agreement with so much of the argument of *Recognition*. I welcome his concurrence with many of my theses: that there is an account of intersubjectivity in German idealism, that reason is social, that love is the most important form of reciprocal recognition, and that Hegel does not reduce the other to the same. His analysis of both Fichte and Hegel is sophisticated and perceptive. Before responding directly to his criticisms, which focus chiefly on the topic of absolute knowledge, I should like to indicate briefly my objectives in writing *Recognition*, and how and at what levels the question of the other comes to be posed, and its significance for basic issues in Hegel interpretation.

Williams, Robin. Disciplinary Subjects and the Human Sciences. *Hist Human Sci*, 7(2), 1-5, My 94.

Williams, Rowan D. "Between Politics and Metaphysics: Reflections in the Wake of Gillian Rose" in *Rethinking Metaphysics, Jones, L Gregory (ed)*, 3-22. Cambridge, Blackwell, 1995.

Williams, Rowan D. Between Politics and Metaphysics: Reflections in the Wake of Gillian Rose. *Mod Theol*, 11(1), 3-22, Ja 95.

Williams, Stephen and Parfitt, Barbara. Models of Nursing and Theories of Humanity: A Christian Perspective. *Ethics Med*, 11(1), 12-17, Spr 95.

Williamson, Timothy. Definiteness and Knowability. *S J Phil*, 33(Supp), 171-191, 1995.

The paper argues against attempts to combine classical logic and a disquotational principle for truth with a denial that vagueness is an epistemic phenomenon, a matter of unknowable truths as to the location of sharp cut-off points. The notion of definiteness needed to characterize borderline cases cannot be substantiated in a nonepistemic way. Of course, not all kinds of unknowability involve vagueness. An account is given of the linguistic and conceptual sources of unknowability in borderline cases that distinguishes them from other cases of unknowability.

Williamson, Timothy. Is Knowing a State of Mind?. *Mind*, 104(415), 533-565, Jl 95.

The paper argues that knowing is a factive mental state, by an extension of externalism from the contents of propositional attitudes to the attitudes themselves. The claim that what knowledge adds to belief is psychologically irrelevant is refuted. The difference between knowing and believing is shown to be relevant to psychological explanation. The failure of attempts to analyze knowledge as true belief plus other factors is accounted for. The view is extended to other factive mental states, such as perceiving and remembering. Knowing may be the most general factive mental state. The inference from knowledge to belief is discussed.

Williamson, Timothy. Never Say Never. *Topoi*, 13(2), 135-145, S 94.

I) An argument is presented for the conclusion that the hypothesis that no one will ever decide a given proposition is intuitionistically inconsistent. II) A distinction between sentences and statements blocks a similar argument for the stronger conclusion that the hypothesis that I have not yet decided a given proposition is intuitionistically inconsistent, but does not block the original argument. III) A distinction between empirical and mathematical negation might block the original argument, and empirical negation might be modelled on Nelson's strong negation, but only on intuitionistically unacceptable assumptions. IV) Intuitionists may have to accept the original argument, and therefore be committed to a dubious view of time on which there cannot be merely inductive evidence for statements about the infinite future.

Willmott, Hugh and Kjonstad, Bjorn. Business Ethics: Restrictive or Empowering?. *J Bus Ethics*, 14(6), 445-464, Je 95.

There is a tendency in the business ethics literature to think of ethics in restrictive terms: what one should not do, and how to control this. Drawing on Lawrence Kohlberg's theory of moral development, the paper focuses on, and draws attention to, another more positive aspect of ethics: the capacity of ethics to inspire and empower individuals, as well as groups. To understand and facilitate such empowerment, it is argued that it is necessary to move beyond Kohlberg's justice reasoning so as to appreciate the value and importance of feeling and care. Accordingly, we draw upon case study material to review the meaning of Kohlberg's higher stages—5, 6 and 7—to question the meaning of ethical "reasoning". With such deeper understanding of particular ethical codes or practices, it is thought that members of organisations may come closer to the *spirit*, as opposed to the letter, of ethical conduct in organisations. This, we argue, is consistent with the degree of trust and integrity demanded by leaner, post-bureaucratic ways of organizing and conducting business as well as being personally beneficial to the people involved.

Wills, David (trans) and Derrida, Jacques. *The Gift of Death*. Chicago, Univ of Chicago Pr, 1995.

This book is the translation of an essay first published in French in 1992. It deals with questions raised in a number of earlier texts concerning the gift, sacrifice and responsibility, examining those issues through the work of Patocka, Heidegger, Kierkegaard, and the New Testament. Responsibility is discussed as a form of *aporia* whose complexity is represented by the French phrase *donner la mort*, meaning "to grant death" in the senses of putting to death and offering a gift of death. The text amounts to Derrida's most sustained consideration of religion to date.

Wilmers, G M and Vencovská, A and Paris, J B. A Natural Prior Probability Distribution Derived from the Propositional Calculus. *Annals Pure Applied Log*, 70(3), 243-285, D 94.

A σ-additive probability measure on the real interval [0, 1] is defined by considering the expected values of "randomly chosen" large formulae of the propositional calculus, where the propositional variables are treated as independent random variables on {0, 1} with expected value 1/2. Although arising naturally from logical and/or cognitive considerations, this measure is extremely complex and displays certain formally pathological features, including infinite density at all points of a certain dense subset of [0, 1]. Certain variants of the construction are also considered. The introduction includes an account of motivation for the study of such measures arising from a fundamental problem in inexact reasoning.

Wilson, Bradley E. A (Not-so-radical) Solution to the Species Problem. *Biol Phil*, 10(3), 339-356, July 95.

What are species? One popular answer is that species are individuals. Here I develop another approach to thinking about species, an approach based on the notion of lineage. A lineage is a sequence of reproducing entities, individuated in terms of its components. I argue that one can conceive of species as groups of lineages, either organism lineages or population lineages. Conceiving of species as groups of lineages resolves the problems that the individual conception of species is supposed to resolve. It has added the virtue of focusing attention on the characteristic of species that is most relevant to understanding their role in evolutionary processes, namely, the lineage structure of species.

Wilson, Catherine. "The Reception of Leibniz in the Eighteenth Century" in *The Cambridge Companion to Leibniz, Jolley, Nicholas (ed)*, 442-474. New York, Cambridge Univ Pr, 1994.

This article discusses the controversies over Leibniz-interpretation and Leibniz-Wolffian rationalism of the eighteenth century, some aspects of the reception of the *Theodicy* and the *New Essays* and the renewed popularity of Leibniz with the Plato renaissance in the 1700s.

Wilson, Catherine. Leibniz and the Logic of Life. *Rev Int Phil*, 48(188), 237-253, 1994.

The paper discusses the alleged absence (Foucault) of biology in the eighteenth century with special reference to Leibniz's views on continuity and analogies between plants and animals.

Wilson, Daniel J. "Fertile Ground: Pragmatism, Science, and Logical Positivism" in *Pragmatism: From Progressivism to Postmodernism, Hollinger, Robert (ed)*, 122-141. Westport, Praeger, 1995.

The distinct philosophical traditions of pragmatism and logical positivism experienced an uneasy convergence in the 1930s. The convergence was fostered primarily by young American philosophers knowledgeable in the pragmatic tradition who saw in logical positivism the possibility of strengthening pragmatic tendencies of empirical verification and scientific method. Logical positivism was seen as a way to move the philosophical project forward. The emigre logical positivists saw pragmatism as one of their empiricist and realistic predecessors. Logical positivism delivered what pragmatism had only promised. Pragmatism thus paved the way for the favorable reception of logical positivism in the United States.

Wilson, David Sloan. Language as a Community of Interacting Belief Systems: A Case Study Involving Conduct Toward Self and Others. *Biol Phil*, 10(1), 77-97, Ja 95.

Words such as "selfish" and "altruistic" that describe conduct toward self and others are notoriously ambiguous in everyday language. I argue that the ambiguity is caused, in part, by the coexistence of multiple belief systems that use the same words in different ways. Each belief system is a relatively coherent linguistic entity that provides a guide for human behavior. It is therefore a functional entity with design features that dictate specific word meaning. Since different belief systems guide human behavior in different directions, specific word meanings cannot be maintained across belief systems. Other sources of linguistic ambiguity include i) functional ambiguity that increases the effectiveness of a belief system, ii) ambiguity between belief systems that are functionally identical but historically distinct, and iii) active interference between belief systems. I illustrate these points with a natural history study of the word "selfish" and related words in everyday language. In general, language and the thought that it represents should be studied in the same way that ecologists study multi-species communities.

Wilson, David Sloan and Sober, Elliott. A Critical Review of Philosophical Work on the Units of Selection Problem. *Phil Sci*, 61(4), 534-555, D 94.

The evolutionary problem of the units of selection has elicited a good deal of conceptual work from philosophers. We review this work to determine where the issues now stand.

Wilson, Eddy. Practical Expressions of Natural Piety: Emerson and Dewey. *Topicos*, 3(4), 85-107, 1993.

The author explores the ways that natural piety would be expressed if one were persuaded to adopt the naturalism of Emerson or Dewey.

Wilson, Fred. Empiricism and the Epistemology of Instruments. *Monist*, 78(2), 207-229, Ap 95.

Wilson, Fred. On *Hume's Theory of Consciousness*. *Grad Fac Phil J*, 18(1), 271-275, 1995.

Wilson, George M. Edward Said on Contrapuntal Reading. *Phil Lit*, 18(2), 265-273, O 94.

Wilson, James Q. Emotions, Reason, and Character. *Crim Just Ethics*, 13(2), 83-92, Sum-Fall 94.

Wilson, James Q. Wealth and Happiness. *Crit Rev*, 8(4), 555-564, Fall 94.

Wilson, P Eddy. Corporations, Minors, and Other Innocents—A Reply to R E Ewin. *J Bus Ethics*, 13(10), 761-774, O 94.

R E Ewin has argued that corporations are moral persons, but Ewin describes them as being unable to think or to act in virtuous and vicious ways. Ewin thinks that their impoverished emotional life would not allow them to act in these ways. In this brief essay I want to challenge the idea that corporations cannot act virtuously. I begin by examining deficiencies in Ewin's notion of corporate personhood. I argue that he effectively reduces corporations to the status of incompetent patients. I make use of a richer notion of corporate personhood as I explore the logical relationship between corporate action and the quality of the corporate emotional life. (edited)

Wilson, Robert A. *Cartesian Psychology and Physical Minds: Individualism and the Sciences of the Mind*. New York, Cambridge Univ Pr, 1995.

This book offers a sustained critique of individualism in psychology, which has been the subject of debate between philosophers of mind for many years. The author approaches individualism from the perspective of the philosophy of science, and by discussing issues such as computationalism and the modularity of the mind, he also shows the relevance of his rejection of individualism for those working in cognitive science. The book has implications for a broad range of issues in the philosophy of mind, including the naturalization of intentionality, psychophysical supervenience, the nature of mental causation, and the viability of folk psychology.

Wilson, W Kent and Dickie, George T. The Intentional Fallacy: Defending Beardsley. *J Aes Art Crit*, 53(3), 233-250, Sum 95.

Wimbush, James C and Shepard, Jon M. Toward an Understanding of Ethical Climate: Its Relationship to Ethical Behavior and Supervisory Influence. *J Bus Ethics*, 13(8), 637-647, Ag 94.

In recent years, theoretical and empirical developments in the area of organizational climate has provided the impetus for research concerning ethical climate. According to this latter research, ethical climate is a multi-dimensional construct which is manifested in organizations. Studies, however, have not focused on the relationship between ethical climate and ethical behavior. Furthermore, an enhanced understanding of the multi-dimensionality of ethical climate will likely advance what we know about organizational climate and culture in general. We propose further examination of ethical climate by: 1) showing the conceptual relationship between ethical climate and ethical (or unethical) behavior in organizations; and 2) examining supervision as one of the principle influences on ethical climate and concomitant subordinate behavior. Finally, we explore the implications for future research on ethical climate.

Wimmer, Franz M (ed) and Dethloff, Klaus. *"Konservative Revolution und Philosophie in Österreich" in Der geistige Anschluss, Fischer, Kurt R (ed)*. Wien, WUV Univ, 1993.

Wimmer, Franz M (ed) and Fischer, Kurt R (ed). *Der geistige Anschluss*. Wien, WUV Univ, 1993.

Winch, Peter G. Mind, Body, and Ethics in Spinoza. *Phil Invest*, 18(3), 216-234, Jl 95.

Winchester, James J. *Nietzsche's Aesthetic Turn: Reading Nietzsche after Heidegger, Deleuze, Derrida*. Albany, SUNY Pr, 1994.

Analyzing the Nietzsche-interpretations of Heidegger, Deleuze, Mueller-Lauter, Derrida, and Nehamas, this book strives to find coherence in Nietzsche's later works. Although these authors struggle to avoid over-systemizing Nietzsche's writings, they often do precisely that. This book argues that the coherence of Nietzsche's thought can be traced through loosely-defined aesthetic criteria. Nietzsche moderates his relativism by claiming that some fictions are necessary for life. Finally, while criticizing Nietzsche's lack of social concern the book maintains that Nietzsche's general strategy of seeing our "truths" as questions of taste is not, as Rorty contends, inimical to liberal society.

Winfield, Richard Dien. Hegel on Classical Art: a Reexamination. *Clio*, 24(2), 147-167, Wint 95.

Hegel's account of classical art provides a key resource for reconceiving the art forms, provided their conceptual ordering is not conflated with their historical succession. To this end Hegel's concept of the classical artform is critiqued and reconstructed, removing certain anthropological assumptions, and rethinking the connection between symbolic and classical art and the dissolution of the classical style.

Winfield, Richard Dien. Natural Beauty and the Philosophy of Art. *J Speculative Phil*, 9(1), 48-62, 1995.

Beauty's joining of meaning and configuration involves a concrete universality exhibiting the logic of self-determination distinguishing the reality of rational agency. Consequently, natural beauty presents a challenge to aesthetics. An examination of the ordering principles commonly ascribed to nature (the abstract universality of efficient causality, the generic universality of species being, and the reciprocal functionality of organic unity) shows that they all lack concrete universality, establishing that aesthetics must be the philosophy of art and that natural beauty has aesthetic value only as a derivative projection of artistic beauty.

Winkler, Earl. Reflections on the State of Current Debate Over Physician-Assisted Suicide and Euthanasia. *Bioethics*, 9(3-4), 313-326, Jl 95.

This paper is part of a larger project. My overall aim is to argue that the evolution of familiar forms of termination of life sustaining treatment, constituting so-called passive euthanasia, has severely undercut the logic of every form of reasoning that has traditionally been used to oppose active euthanasia and assistance in suicide. Basically, there are two forms of traditional opposition, each represented in a range of different versions. There is the inevitable argument concerning social utilities—that permitting euthanasia and assisted suicide will have bad social consequences. But more fundamentally, the idea persists that killing is intrinsically worse than letting-die in some sense that justifies the current practice of prohibiting the first while allowing the latter. In this paper, I first consider this latter claim. My ultimate strategy, as I have said, is to show that the nature of certain things we have all come to approve regarding termination of treatment makes it next to impossible to convincingly explain, in either of these ways, what is wrong with certain forms of assistance in suicide and euthanasia. In the second part of this paper I take another step in this direction by discussing, in a preliminary way, a special case of the argument from social risks.

Winston, Kenneth. Legislators and Liberty. *Law Phil*, 13(3), 389-418, Ag 94.

This essay offers an account of Lon Fuller's conception of freedom, based on existing published and as yet unpublished archival materials. Fuller's analysis is carried out from the perspective of legislators, that is, experts in social structure who have the task of devising and managing mechanisms for facilitating human collaboration. From this perspective, the conventional debate about negative versus positive freedom is unhelpful. Instead, Fuller develops an "affirmative" conception of freedom which provides guidance to legislators attempting to meet the responsibilities of their office.

Winston, Robert. "The Value of In-vitro Research" in *Ethics on the Frontiers of Human Existence, Badham, Paul (ed)*, 45-49. New York, Paragon House, 1992.

Wippel, John F. *Mediaeval Reactions to the Encounter Between Faith and Reason*. Milwaukee, Marquette Univ Pr, 1994.

Wiredu, Kwasi. "Custom and Morality" in *African Philosophy: Selected Readings, Mosley, Albert G (ed)*, 389-406. Englewood Cliffs, Prentice Hall, 1995.

Wiredu, Kwasi. "How Not to Compare African Thought with Western Thought" in *African Philosophy: Selected Readings, Mosley, Albert G (ed)*, 159-171. Englewood Cliffs, Prentice Hall, 1995.

Wiredu, Kwasi. Are There Cultural Universals?. *Monist*, 78(1), 52-64, Ja 95.

Wirzba, Norman. From Maieutics to Metanoia: Levinas's Understanding of the Philosophical Task. *Man World*, 28(2), 129-144, Ap 95.

Levinas's description of the teaching-learning relation provides us with an opportunity to rethink the nature of the philosophical task. Rather than being a naive or dogmatic enterprise that reinforces or justifies previously held or accepted positions, philosophy becomes genuinely critical as its ideas are put into question by the transcendence of the human other. Teaching is the event, not of appropriation, but of transformation, brought on by the encounter with transcendence. Via a discussion of this encounter, an encounter made possible by the intersubjective realm, we are given a glimpse of the transformation of the ways of thought.

Wise, Thomas N. Commentary on "Normal Grief: Good or Bad? Health or Disease?". *Phil Psychiat Psych*, 1(4), 223-224, D 94.

Wisniewski, Andrzej and Kuipers, Theo A F. An Erotetic Approach to Explanation by Specification. *Erkenntnis*, 40(3), 377-402, My 94.

In the present paper it is shown that four kinds of erotetic argumentative steps occurring in the train of thought of explanation by specification are valid arguments in the sense of inferential erotetic logic. Hence, in view of the fact that other argumentative steps were already shown to be valid, it may be concluded that the logical structure of explanation by specification can be as well-established as that of explanation by nomological subsumption. Moreover, explanation by specification provides some illustrations of the applicability of erotetic logic in everyday life and some empirical sciences. (edited)

Witschen, Dieter. Können Kollektive Berechtigte von Menschenrechten sein? Ein Aspekt des Themas "Extensionen von Menschenrechten". *Theol Phil*, 70(2), 245-258, 1995.

Witt, Richard. La Fonction de la Musique chez les Contemporains du Denys Authentique. *Diotima*, 23, 109-120, 1995.

Wittgenstein, Ludwig. What is a Thought?. *Iyyun*, 44, 201-224, Ap 95.

Wittgenstein, Ludwig and Kenny, Anthony (ed). *The Wittgenstein Reader*. Cambridge, Blackwell, 1994.

Wittgenstein, Ludwig and Nedo, Michael (ed). *Ludwig Wittgenstein: Wiener Ausgabe/Vienna Edition—Band 1: Philosophische Bemerkungen*. New York, Springer-Verlag, 1994.

Wittgenstein, Ludwig and Nedo, Michael (ed). *Ludwig Wittgenstein: Wiener Ausgabe/Vienna Edition—Band 2: Philosophische Betrachtungen, Philosophische Bemerkungen*. New York, Springer-Verlag, 1994.

Witzany, Jirí. Possible Behaviours of the Reflection Ordering of Stationary Sets. *J Sym Log*, 60(2), 534-547, Je 95.

If S and T are stationary subsets of a regular uncountable cardinal, we say that S reflects fully in T, if S is stationary in all except nonstationary many ordinals in T. This relation is known to be a well-founded partial ordering. The purpose of the paper is to show under appropriate large cardinal assumptions that given a regular uncountable cardinal and a well-founded poset P of cardinality at most the successor of the cardinal there is a generic extension where the reflection ordering looks as the poset P in a natural sense.

Wlodzimierz, Galewicz (ed) and Ströker, Elisabeth (ed) and Strozewski, Wladyslaw (ed). *Kunst und Ontologie*. Amsterdam, Rodopi, 1994.

Wölflingseder, Maria. "Biologistische und Rassistische Tendenzen im spirituellen Öko-Feminismus" in *Der feministische "Sündenfall"?, Kohn-Ley, Charlotte (ed)*, 231-260. Vienna, Picus, 1994.

Wojciechowski, Tadeusz. Mono- und poligenischer Ursprung des Lebens. *Stud Phil Christ*, 30(2), 273-285, 1994.

Der Ursprung des Lebens erscheint vielen Wissenschaftlern als ein einziges Ereignis in der ganzen Geschichte der Erde. Nur wenige meinen, dass es keine einzige Urform, Urzelle des Lebens gab. Es gibt aber viele Hinweise darauf, dass alle irdische Lebewesen von einer gemeinsamen Urform stammen. Der Hintergrund dieser Aussage beruht auf den biophysikalischen und biochemischen Fakten. Vor allem weist darauf die Universalität des genetischen Codes und damit verbundene Vewandschaft aller Organismen, von der Bäckerhefe bis hinauf zum Menschen. Darauf weist auch die Zusammensetzung des Cytochroms-c, 1-Konfiguration der Proteinen, Anatomie u.a. Ähnlich, von dem naturwissenschaftlichen und philosophichen Standpunkt, kann man über die Abstammung der Menscheit von dem einzigen Vorfahr-Adam sprechen.

Wokler, Robert. *Rousseau (Past Masters)*. New York, Oxford Univ Pr, 1995.

In this study of Rousseau's life and works Robert Wokler shows how his philosophy of history, his theories of music and politics, his fiction, educational and religious writings, and even his botany, were all inspired by visionary ideals of mankind's self-realization in a condition of unfettered freedom. He explains how, in regressing to classical republicanism, ancient mythology, direct communion with God, and solitude, Rousseau anticipated some post-modernist rejections of the Enlightenment as well. (edited)

Wokler, Robert. Rousseau's Pufendorf: Natural Law and the Foundations of Commercial Society. *Hist Polit Thought*, 15(3), 373-402, Autumn 94.

Rousseau's apparent rejection of a natural law foundation for his theory of the social contract forms one of the principal subjects of controversy among his interpreters. This article identifies several dimensions of natural law to which Rousseau objected and in particular offers the fullest account available of his critique of Pufendorf's doctrine of natural sociability. In rejecting a Pufendorfian conception of human needs and timidity as the impetus for commerce, Rousseau took issue with the main jurisprudential social science of his day. Contrary to Grotius, Hobbes, and Pufendorf as well, he insisted that there could be no representation of liberty in the state.

Wolenski, Jan. "Sentences, Propositions and *Quasi*-Propositions" in *Kunst und Ontologie, Galewicz, Wlodzimierz (ed)*, 229-235. Amsterdam, Rodopi, 1994.

This paper tries to give formal-semantical account of sentences, propositions and quasi-propositions in Roman Ingarden's understanding. Since Ingarden understands these categories in a semantic way, the concept of model is used in the proposed explication. If L is a language, than a sentence is simply a formula of L. Now propositions correlated with sentences of L are truths in the model being a formal counterpart of the real world. Finally, quasi-propositions are sentences interpreted in semi-models.

Wolenski, Jan. Logical Content of Two Legal Principles. *Commun Cog*, 28(1), 87-90, 1995.

This paper proposes a logical analysis of two legal principles: 1) What is unavoidable is permitted, and 2) Everybody is innocent or acts bona fidae, unless it is proven otherwise. Both principles have an explicit logical content. The principle (1) is a special case of a principle of deontic logic: if something is necessary, it is permitted. The principle (2) is connected with a metalogical rule: negative existential statements are in general unprovable.

Wolf, Charles (trans) and Negri, Antonio. On Gilles Deleuze and Félix Guattari, *A Thousand Plateaus*. *Grad Fac Phil J*, 18(1), 93-109, 1995.

Wolf, Clark. Contemporary Property Rights, Lockean Provisos, and the Interests of Future Generations. *Ethics*, 105(4), 791-818, Jl 95.

This paper develops a Lockean theory of property which takes into account the interests of the future. It offers a novel interpretation of the Lockean Proviso, arguing that it represents a sufficient condition for justified appropriation by labor mixing. I argue that a necessary and sufficient condition of justified appropriation is that it must cause no harm to others, including members of future generations. This leads to a limited conception of property rights in crucial resources as usufructuary rights to harmless use of these resources, accompanied by obligations to protect and conserve them for the benefit of future generations.

Wolf, Jürgen and Neckel, Sighard. The Fascination of Amorality: Luhmann's Theory of Morality and its Resonances among German Intellectuals. *Theor Cult Soc*, 11(2), 69-99, My 94.

Wolff, Jonathan. Democratic Voting and The Mixed-Motivation Problem. *Analysis*, 54(4), 193-196, O 94.

Is democratic voting a matter of expressing a preference, or of expressing a moral belief? Either model can be used as part of an instrumental justification of democracy, but if some voters vote on self-interested grounds and others on moral grounds it is easily possible to achieve an outcome which is neither in the majority interest nor in accordance with majority beliefs about the common good.

Wolff, Jonathan. Political Obligation, Fairness and Independence. *Ratio*, 8(1), 87-99, Ap 95.

In the first section the problem of political obligation is motivated, and in Section 2 the core structure of the problem is laid bare. The problem will appear very different to different thinkers, depending on their moral theories. However this picture is seen to be too crude, and in the third section it is shown how a solution has been proposed by advocates of the 'theory of fairness'. In Section 4 this theory is evaluated, concentrating particularly on George Klosko's version. However it is argued that no version of the thoory is able to guarantee universal political obligations. In Section 5 it is argued that this is an unnoticed advantage of the theory, for it may well be that we should allow those who do not benefit from the existence of the state to escape political obligations. (edited)

Wolff, Michael. "'Neutrale Bewegung' beim jungen Galilei " in *Naturauffassungen in Philosophie, Wissenschaft, Technik: Band II, Schäfer, Lothar (ed)*, 139-148. Freiburg, Alber, 1994.

Wolff, Michael. *Die Vollständigkeit der kantischen Urteilstafel*. Frankfurt/M, Klostermann, 1995.

This book gives an analysis of Kant's table of judgments, reconstructs his proof (given in the *Critique of Pure Reason*) of its completeness and shows that it is conclusive. Formal logic, however, as Kant conceives it has to be demarcated from modern formal logic. The appended essay on Frege refutes all arguments raised by him in his *Begriffsschrift* against Kant's table.

Wolff, Richard and Resnick, Stephen. "Lessons from the USSR: Taking Marxian Theory the Next Step" in *Whither Marxism?, Magnus, Bernd (ed)*, 207-234. New York, Routledge, 1994.

A surplus labor rather than a power or property definition of class is deployed to ask what was the class structure of the USSR. Individuals other than the workers in state enterprises were always the appropriators and distributors of the surplus produced by those workers. The former used the appropriated surplus to secure a specific kind of property, power, cultural, and economic structure that kept them in their class position in the Soviet state. This distinctive surplus labor approach suggests that what collapsed in the Soviet Union was not socialism, but rather state capitalism, now being replaced by private capitalism.

Wolff, Robert Paul. Narrative Time: The Inherently Perspectival Structure of the Human World. *Midwest Stud Phil*, 15, 210-223, 1990.

Wolgast, Elizabeth. Moral Paradigms. *Philosophy*, 70(272), 143-155, Ap 95.

Extreme examples in moral philosophy, while they protect against skepticism, suggest that wrongdoing is a rare feature of our lives. Yet everyday examples seem to lack force and invite skepticism. The same tendency to look to extreme cases is shown in theory of knowledge. However awful deeds have different moral significance from everday wrongs, where we say, "There but for the grace of God go I." Agents of awful deeds we call a beast or devil, distancing ourselves from him. Our affinity with everyday wrongdoers and their lives is an important feature of moral discourse, and something moral philosophy should not neglect.

Wolin, Richard (ed). *The Heidegger Controversy: A Critical Reader*. New York, Columbia Univ Pr, 1991.

Wolin, Richard (ed) and Löwith, Karl and Steiner, Gary (trans). *Martin Heidegger and European Nihilism*. New York, Columbia Univ Pr, 1995.

Wolin, Sheldon. Fugitive Democracy. *Constellations*, 1(1), 11-25, Ap 94.

Wollheim, Richard. "Danto's Gallery of Indiscernibles" in *Danto and his Critics, Rollins, Mark (ed)*, 28-38. Cambridge, Blackwell, 1993.

Wolter, Frank. Decidability of Tense Logics. *Bull Sec Log*, 24(1), 46-50, Mr 95.

Wolterstorff, Nicholas. "Locke's Philosophy of Religion" in *The Cambridge Companion to Locke, Chappell, Vere (ed)*, 172-198. New York, Cambridge Univ Pr, 1994.

Wolterstorff, Nicholas. John Locke's Epistemological Piety: Reason is the Candle of the Lord. *Faith Phil*, 11(4), 572-591, Oct 94.

Not only is John Locke's *thought* shaped by Christian conviction; interspersed in his writings on politics and epistemology are suggestions as to how his conclusions on these matters are to be incorporated into lives of Christian piety. In this paper I focus on Locke's views as to how his epistemology, with its peculiar blend of skepticism and confidence, is to be incorporated into a life of gratitude and obedience. The theme of Reason, as an indistinguishable source of light given from God, is prominent in the discussion.

Wolterstorff, Nicholas. Tradition, Insight and Constraint. *Proc Amer Phil Ass*, 66(3), 43-57, N 92.

Wood, Ellen Meiksins. Radicalism, Capitalism and Historical Contexts: Not Only a Reply to Richard Ashcraft on John Locke. *Hist Polit Thought*, 15(3), 323-372, Autumn 94.

Wood, Gillen. "At the Crossroads of Positivism and Magic:" Benjamin, Baudelaire, and the Shock of the Sublime. *Conference*, 5(2), 59-70, Wint 94-95.

The author takes up Adorno's criticism of Benjamin, seeking a basis for the former's intuition of a "romantic element" in Benjamin's putatively materialist readings of Baudelaire. He discovers it in the rhetorical proximity of Kant's formulation of the sublime in the third *Critique* and Benjamin's definition of "shock" as the experiential condition of a specifically modern artistic consciousness. This proximity casts doubt on the "historicizing" quality of Benjamin's project, as the historical divide he marks between the "auratic" experience of bourgeois romanticism and the shock experience of modernity simply rehearses the ahistorical distinction Kant makes between the aesthetics of the beautiful and the sublime.

Wood, P B. "Hume, Reid and the Science of the Mind" in *Hume and Hume's Connexions*, Stewart, M A (ed), 119-139. University Park, Penn St Univ Pr, 1995.

Wood, Paul (ed) and Harrison, Charles (ed). *Art in Theory 1900-1990: An Anthology of Changing Ideas*. Cambridge, Blackwell, 1994.

Current debates about the status of Modernism have led to an increasing interest in critical and aesthetic theories, and to a questioning of some of the traditional assumptions and limits of art history. The aims of this substantial anthology is to equip the student, teacher and interested general reader with the materials for an up-to-date understanding of twentieth-century art. Beside the writings of the century's major artists, *Art in Theory* includes relevant texts by critics, philosophers, politicians and literary figures. It is organized into eight sections, from the legacy of Symbolism at the turn of the century to contemporary debates about the postmodern. Each section is prefaced by a brief essay. There are introductions for all of the 300-plus texts, so that theories and critical approaches are placed in context. The volume also includes an extensive bibliography. The result is both a comprehensive collection of documents on twentieth-century art and an encyclopedic history of relevant theory.

Wood, Robert E. Six Heideggerian Figures. *Amer Cath Phil Quart*, 69(2), 311-331, Spr 95.

Throughout Heidegger's work six different ways of thought appeared in near chronological order: the peasant, the artist-poet, the philosopher, the scientist, the man-in-the-street, and the thinker. The first two antedate the rise of philosophy and, together with the thinker, operate in the medium of the lifeworld. They are given to meditative thinking, appreciatively "letting things be," sensitive to mystery. The middle three operate in different modes of abstraction from the lifeworld. Driven by the will-to-power, philosophy emerges as critic of poetry, science as specialization within philosophy and modern everydayness as structured by scientific technology. "Thought" leads back to the lifeworld.

Woodruff, Paul (trans) and Plato and Nehamas, Alexander (trans). *Phaedrus*. Indianapolis, Hackett, 1994.

Woodruff, Peter and Parsons, Terence. Worldly Indeterminacy of Identity. *Proc Aris Soc*, 95, 171-191, 1994-95.

Woody, J Melvin and Phillips, James. Commentary on "Connectionist Hysteria". *Phil Psychiat Psych*, 1(2), 89-90, Je 94.

Woolfolk, Alan (ed) and Imber, Jonathan B (ed) and Masaryk, Thomas G. *Constructive Sociological Theory*. New Brunswick, Transaction Books, 1994.

This volume is a selection of major writings by Thomas G Masaryk (1850-1937), first president of the state of Czechoslovakia and a forgotten but distinguished founder of the discipline of sociology in central Europe. These writings and the introduction reveal the intertwining of politics and social theory that is characteristic of Masaryk's philosophical sociology—with chapters on modern suicide, Comte, religion, the problems of Marxism, nationalism, democracy, and other topics. The volume aims to introduce students and teachers of sociology to Masaryk's unified theory, which opposed the separation of facts and values, knowledge and belief, feeling and reason, and theory and practice that became dominant in sociological theory.

Woolgar, Steve and Grint, Keith. On Some Failures of Nerve in Constructivist and Feminist Analyses of Technology. *Sci Tech Human Values*, 20(3), 286-310, Sum 95.

Whereas many constructivist and feminist approaches to the social study of technology share an antipathy to technological determinism, they offer an insufficiently radical critique of technology. Three main problems in "anti-essentialist" critiques of technological determinism are identified, all of which mean that such critiques remain committed to a form of essentialism. These characteristics recur in many recent feminist arguments about technology, illustrated by the example of reproductive technologies. To overcome weaknesses in political radicalism based on anti-essentialism, it is necessary to move to a "post-essentialist" approach. The unwillingness to do so is shown to be based on unfounded objections to "excessive" relativism.

Woolhouse, Roger. "Locke's Theory of Knowledge" in *The Cambridge Companion to Locke*, Chappell, Vere (ed), 146-171. New York, Cambridge Univ Pr, 1994.

A short account of Locke's theory of knowledge.

Woolhouse, Roger S and Francks, Richard. Leibniz, Lamy, and 'The Way of Pre-Established Harmony'. *Stud Leibniz*, 26(1), 76-90, 1994.

Die Kontroverse mit François Lamy ist unter denen von Leibniz' *Système nouveau* (1695) hervorgerufenen eine der am wenigsten diskutierten. Die wenigen neueren Quellen sind schlecht dokumentiert und in wichtigen Details nicht korrekt. Wir versuchen hier, die Bibliographie richtigzustellen. Da Lamys Arbeit äusserst selten ist, fügen wir englische Übersetzungen der relevanten Stellen bei. Nach Pierre Bayle war eher Lamy als Leibniz der erste, der den Begriff 'prästabilierte Harmonie' verwendete. Es stellt sich heraus, dass dem nicht so ist.

Wootton, David. Narrative, Irony, and Faith in Gibbon's *Decline and Fall*. *Hist Theor*, 33(4), 77-105, 1994.

This article is divided into three sections. The first argues that the significance of David Hume's *History of England* as an inspiration for Gibbon's *Decline and Fall* has been underestimated, and that Momigliano's famous account of Gibbon's originality

needs to be adapted to take account of the fact that Gibbon was, in effect, a disciple of Hume. The second section analyzes the argument of chapter fifteen of the *Decline and Fall*, the first chapter on Christianity. (edited)

Worral, John. How to Remain (Reasonably) Optimistic: Scientific Realism and the "Luminiferous Ether". *Proc Phil Sci Ass*, 1, 334-342, 1994.

Fresnel's theory of light was a) impressively predictively successful yet b) was based on an "entity" (the elastic-solid ether) that we now "know" does not exist. Does this case "confute" scientific realism as Laudan suggested? Previous attempts (by Hardin and Rosenberg and by Kitcher) to defuse the episode's anti-realist impact. The strongest form of realism compatible with this case of theory-rejection is in fact *structural* realism. This view was developed by Poincaré who also provided reasons to think that it is the only realist view of theories that really makes sense.

Worthington, Glenn. Michael Oakeshott on Life: Waiting with Godot. *Hist Polit Thought*, 16(1), 105-119, Spr 95.

Samuel Beckett's presentation of life as a "meaningless" tragicomedy resonates with some of the themes encountered in Michael Oakeshott's account of human conduct. Beckett's characters are always "waiting for" the arrival of their purpose personified in Godot. Oakeshott's civil philosophy provides the basis of a critique of this type of activity as inauthentic, preferring the authentic activity of "waiting with" or "in" one's world of present experience. Oakeshott's idea of authenticity has its roots in the resolution of Hegel's master-slave dialectic in the recognition of oneself in a world of other selves. Oakeshott's account of authenticity is developed in terms of the subjective motives of an action. A self's recognition of its situation in its world is a condition of authenticity in moral activity.

Wright, Charles W (ed) and Honneth, Axel. *The Fragmented World of the Social: Essays in Social and Political Philosophy*. Albany, SUNY Pr, 1995.

The essays in this volume weave together arguments and insights drawn from German critical theory, diverse traditions of French philosophy and social theory, and recent Anglo-American moral and political theory. Pursuing the problem of sources of normative insight that emerges through his analysis of classical Marxism and early critical theory, Honneth canvasses these other traditions in an effort to identify more refined conceptual tools by which it might fruitfully be addressed. Ending the volume with careful discussions of modernism and postmodernism as well as of liberalism and communitarianism, the author points toward a conception of human sociability that promises to evade the familiar entrapments of contemporary social and ethical thought.

Wright, Crispin. "On Putnam's Proof that We Are Not Brains in a Vat" in *Reading Putnam*, Clark, Peter (ed), 216-241. Cambridge, Blackwell, 1995.

Wright, Crispin. Intuitionists Are Not (Turing) Machines. *Phil Math*, 3(1), 86-102, Ja 95.

Lucas and Penrose have contended that, by displaying how any characterization of arithmetical proof programmable into a machine allows of diagonalization, generating a humanly recognizable proof which eludes that characterization, Gödel's incompleteness theorem rules out any purely mechanical model of the human intellect. The main criticisms of this argument have been that the proof generated by diagonalization i) will not be humanly recognizable unless humans can grasp the specification of the object-system (Benacerraf); and ii) counts as a proof only on the (unproven) hypothesis that the object system is consistent (Putnam). The present paper argues that criticism ii) may be met head-on by an intuitionistic proponent of the anti-mechanist argument; and that criticism i) is simply mistaken. However the paper concludes by questioning the sufficiency of the situation for an interesting anti-mechanist conclusion.

Wright, Crispin. Ralph C S Walker, *The Coherence Theory of Truth: Realism, Anti-Realism, Idealism*. *Synthese*, 103(2), 279-302, My 95.

Wright, Crispin. *Realism, Meaning, and Truth (Second Edition)*. Cambridge, Blackwell, 1993.

Wright, Crispin. The Epistemic Conception of Vagueness. *S J Phil*, 33(Supp), 133-159, 1995.

Wright, Darryl F. Diagnosing the Naturalistic Fallacy: Principia Ethica Revisited. *S J Phil*, 32(4), 465-482, Wint 94.

Although Moore's *Principia Ethica* is a classic of moral philosophy, its important chapter on "Metaphysical Ethics" has escaped intensive study, because it has been believed merely to replay the book's earlier arguments about the "naturalistic fallacy". But the chapter actually presents something new: Moore's diagnosis of the naturalistic fallacy's intellectual causes. I reconstruct, and briefly assess, part of this neglected diagnosis, focusing on Moore's contention that "the *logical* doctrine that all propositions assert a relation between existents" is partly responsible for the "naturalistic fallacy" among idealist and empiricist moral philosophers.

Wright, John P. "Butler and Hume on Habit and Moral Character" in *Hume and Hume's Connexions*, Stewart, M A (ed), 105-118. University Park, Penn St Univ Pr, 1995.

Hume derives from Butler a psychological account of the development of moral character which he applies in a distinctive way in his moral philosophy. Butler's idea is that as we become accustomed to act in a certain way, the feelings which lead us to act become less sensible. This lies at the essence of Hume's account of calm passion in Book II of the *Treatise*, but differs from Hutcheson's account of calm desires. It is argued that Butler's analysis of the development of habits lies in the background of Hume's account of justice and the development of moral character.

Wright, John P (ed) and Stewart, M A (ed). *Hume and Hume's Connexions*. University Park, Penn St Univ Pr, 1995.

Wright, M R. Presocratics and Sophists. *Phronesis*, 40(1), 118-121, 1995.

Wright, Richard D and Dawson, Michael R W. To What Extent Do Beliefs Affect Apparent Motion?. *Phil Psych*, 7(4), 471-491, 1994.

A number of studies in the apparent motion literature were examined using the cognitive penetrability criterion to determine the extent to which beliefs affect the perception of apparent motion. It was found that the interaction between the perceptual processes mediating apparent notion and higher order processes appears to be limited. In addition, perceptual and inferential beliefs appear to have different effects on perceived notion optimality and direction. Our findings suggest that the system underlying apparent motion perception has more than one stage and is informationally encapsulated from cognitive factors.

Wright, Terrence C. Heidegger and Heaney: Poetry and Possibility. *Phil Today*, 38(4), 390-399, Wint 94.

This article considers how Heidegger's philosophy of language and poetic expression can serve to illuminate the work of the contemporary Irish poet Seamus Heaney. Also, it argues that Heaney's poetry illustrates well key aspects of the Heideggerian theory. In particular, it relates the dominant themes of Heaney's poetry to Heidegger's central notion that poetic expression is essentially temporal and distinguished by its ability to project possibilities for language, thought and action.

Wrong, Dennis H. *Power: Its Forms, Bases, and Uses*. New Brunswick, Transaction Books, 1995.

This is a new edition of a book originally published in 1979 and reissued with a new preface in 1988. It is an anatomy of power, a history of the ways it has been defined, and a study of its forms (force, manipulation, persuasion, and authority), their subtypes, its bases (individual and collective resources, political mobilization), and its uses. Issues addressed range from the philosophical to the psychological, from the micro-relations of everyday life to the macro-sphere of major social institutions. The work contains detailed examples from modern history and politics. Thinkers and writers discussed include Weber, Machiavelli, Hobbes, Marx, Freud, Aristotle, Dostoevsky, Orwell, Parsons, and Arendt. A new introduction to the 1995 edition reconsiders the concept of power in light of its often indiscriminate uses by contemporaries in the social sciences and humanities. The distinction between "power to" and "power over" is reviewed in new detail.

Wrzosek, Wojciech. "The Problem of Cultural Imputation in History: Cultures Versus History" in *Historiography Between Modernism and Postmodernism, Topolski, Jerzy (ed)*, 135-144. Amsterdam, Rodopi, 1994.

The formula stating that "one culture studies another culture" adequately describes the epistemological situation of a historian. Like an ethnologist or an ethnographer, in the name of his own culture he penetrates a sometimes diametrally different social reality. In the course of his investigations the historian, like any carrier of a given culture (an artist or a researcher), ascribes to the culture he studies logic, the concepts of time and space, and, above all, fundamental historiographical metaphors (dominant metaphors in the sense used by P Ricoeur). These include the ideas of genesis, development, linear time, causal nexus, etc. The impossibility of avoiding such imputation is the specific principle of indeterminacy in culture. It is so because the researcher cannot abstract from the constitutive characteristics of his thinking; he does not face the reality he studied as if he were a *tabula rasa*. Hence, he can at most only control the scope of the mentioned imputation.

Wrzosek, Wojciech. In Search for "Historical Time": Time—Culture—History. *Dialogue Hum*, 4(1), 79-89, 1994.

Wuketits, Franz M. Discussion: A Comment on Some Recent Arguments in Evolutionary Epistemology—and Some Counterarguments. *Biol Phil*, 10(3), 357-363, July 95.

Wulff, Henrik R. The Inherent Paternalism in Clinical Practice. *J Med Phil*, 20(3), 299-310, Je 95.

It is sometimes suggested that the physician should offer the patient "just the facts", preferably in a "value-free manner," explain the different options, and then leave it to the patient to make the choice. This paper explores the extent to which this *adviser model* is realistic. The clinical decision process and the various components of clinical reasoning are discussed, and a distinction is made between the biological, empirical, empathic/hermeneutic and ethical components. The discussion is based on the ethical norms of the public health services in the Nordic countries, and the problems are illustrated by a clinical example. It is concluded that the adviser model is unrealistic. Patient information is important, but the complexity of clinical reasoning makes it impossible to separate facts and value judgments.

Wurgaft, Lewis. Identity in World History: A Post-Modern Perspective. *Hist Theor*, 34(2), 67-85, 1995.

A parallel line of criticism has developed at the cultural or historical level. Writers such as Benedict Anderson and Ernest Gellner have effectively contrasted the shallow ideological and historical roots of nationalism with the effort to base national identity on the appeal to tradition and continuity. Other writers have emphasized the heterogeneous condition of the contemporary nation in a postcolonial world. They contrast a static concept of cultural or national identity to a more fluid notion which incorporates the ongoing process of displacement that, they argue, characterizes national discourse. The identity structures that emerge from this critique, both within a clinical and a historical setting, are more ambiguous and unstable, and reflect the heterogeneous experience of contemporary culture. World historians such as William McNeill and Theodore von Laue have cited the boundedness of historians within their own cultural identities as a significant obstacle to the development of an intercultural approach to world history. These postmodern reformulations of identity theory challenge the notion of cultural boundedness by emphasizing the discontinuities endemic to modern life and the inescapably plural character of contemporary identity.

Wyatt, Gail Elizabeth and Martin, Tony and Brant, Renée. Child Abuse or Acceptable Cultural Norms. *Ethics Behavior*, 5(3), 283-292, 1995.

Wyller, Egil A. *Henologische Perspektiven I/I-II: Platon—Johannes—Cusanus*. Amsterdam, Rodopi, 1995.

This collection of studies aims at working out henology (Gr.*hen*=one) as a Platonic inspired discipline of thought and at showing its faculty to combine philosophical and theological thought-structures, thus offering a new approach to the question of the relation between Platonism and Christianity. By Plato it develops his vision of principles: the Beautiful (*Symposium/Phaedrus*), the Good (*Politeia/Nomoi*) and especially the One (*Parmenides*), by St. John it works out the henological structure of the three main biblical works under his name, by Nicholas of Cusa it concentrates mainly upon his late theory of the *non aliud* or not-Other.

Wyller, Egil A. Sokrates und Christus in der Verfasserschaft Soren Kierkegaards: Eine Henologische Ganzheitsinterpretation. *Philosophia (Athens)*, 23-24, 347-356, 1993-94.

The author undertakes an inquiry into the parallel presence of Socrates and Jesus Christ in the Works of S Kierkegaard under the perspective of the "theory of henology". After an introduction into this theory the author determines the phases which follows Kierkegaard's thought on this topic: 1) Turn to Socrates. 2) Overcoming of Socrates and turn to faith. 3) Turn to Jesus Christ and fulfillment of His love, which entails *anabasis* to God and katabasis to (the inner-psychical life of) man. 4) Never overcoming of Jesus Christ.

Wyller, Truls. First Person Authority and Singular Thoughts. *Z Phil Forsch*, 48(4), 585-594, 1994.

After sketching the outline of an externalist theory of the mental, the author states the general problem of first person knowledge and the solutions to be found in Burge and Davidson. It is argued that these solutions do not work for singular thoughts. Therefore, given externalism, one seems forced to give up either the concept of singular thoughts, or first person authority for these kinds of thoughts. A solution to this problem might be found in the indexical character of human action directed at regions of space and time. Moreover, the solution offered evades normal classification as being either "externalist" or "internalist".

Wyller, Truls. *Indexikalische Gedanken: Über den Gegenstandsbezug in der raumzeitlichen Erkenntnis*. Freiburg, Alber, 1994.

This book deals with a problem that has been the object of much attention in recent philosophy of language: How are we to account for the existence of indexical thoughts, i.e., thoughts whose content both is determined through the subjective position of the thinker and has an objective truth-content? In opposition to the dominant "externalist", causal approach of much of the literature, the author claims that even thoughts about objective space and time have an indexical and intersubjective character.

Xin, Katherine R and Derong, Pan. On Chung-Ying Cheng's Onto-Hermeneutics. *J Chin Phil*, 22(2), 215-231, Je 95.

Chung-Ying Cheng's onto-hermeneutics not only embraced traditional Chinese thinking, but also assimilated ideas from the Western hermeneutical tradition and analytical thought. It is the offspring of the conflicts between and combination of Chinese and Western cultures. The very existence of onto-hermeneutics declares the possibility of the mutual understanding, penetration, and combination of Chinese and Western cultural systems. Society's important issues forces us to regard the world as globalizes totality. Onto-hermeneutics, with roots in both Chinese and Western cultures, provides a path for philosophical retrospection and reflection, helping improve our understanding.

Xu, Ming. Doing and Refraining from Refraining. *J Phil Log*, 23(6), 621-632, D 94.

The main purpose of this paper is to prove that in every *stit* semantic structure that contains a busy choice sequence, neither does doing imply refraining from refraining from doing, nor does refraining from refraining from doing imply doing.

Xu, Ming. On the Basic Logic of STIT with a Single Agent. *J Sym Log*, 60(2), 459-483, Je 95.

We present in this paper an axiomatization of Belnap and Perloff's *stit* theory (a logic of "seeing to it that") with a single agent. The idea of the proof is to apply the notion of companion sets—the same notion as used in another paper by the author that showed the decidability of *stit* theory with a single agent and *Refref* equivalence.

Yadav, Bibhuti S. The Coin and the Mirror. *Asian Phil*, 4(2), 177-181, 1994.

Yadav, Bibhuti S. Vallabha's Positive Response to Buddhism. *J Dharma*, 19(2), 113-137, Ap-Je 94.

Yaffe, Gideon. Velleman on Intentions as Reasons for Action. *Analysis*, 55(2), 107-115, Ap 95.

Yagisawa, Takashi. "The Cost of Meaning Solipsism" in *Holism: A Consumer Update, Fodor, Jerry (ed)*, 213-230. Amsterdam, Rodopi, 1993.

Meaning solipsism says that it is possible for there to be a meaningful state without any other meaningful state. The meaning of such a solo meaningful state should be nonnatural. The best strategy for establishing meaning solipsism is to argue for the determination of the meaning of a possible solo meaningful state via the set of entities the meaning of the state fits. Embracing merely possible and impossible entities is the most straightforward way to do so. Also, a good way to honor analyticities the meaning of a solo meaningful state gives rise to is to insist on certain facts about impossible entities as non-negotiable brute facts.

Yagisawa, Takashi. Logic Purified. *Nous*, 27(4), 470-486, D 93.

According to the classical model-theoretic first-order semantics, truth is defined relative to an ordered triple <ID, *O*, *R*, where *D* is a nonempty set of objects, *O* is a function from individual constants to objects in *D*, and *R* is a function from n-place predicates to n-tuples of objects in *D*. I claim that a single domain will not do for a general definition of truth for quantified sentences. My proposal has the consequence that many sentences which are classically judged logically true are no longer so judged and that many arguments which are classically judged valid are no longer so judged.

Yagisawa, Takashi. Thinking in Neurons: Comments on Stephen Schiffer's "The Language-of-Thought Relation and Its Implications". *Phil Stud*, 76(2-3), 287-296, D 94.

This is the comments delivered on Schiffer's talk at the Oberlin conference in 1993. Nine points are made. Among them are: Schiffer's assumption that the only source of divergence between meaning and proposition is indexicality is open to doubt; the notion of neural English may be problematic; language of thought may not have a compositional syntax; there is no guarantee that the portion of Shmenglish which diverges from English defies a compositional supervenience theory; the compositional supervenience theory for language of thought does not metaphysically entail systematicity; it is doubtful that each of infinitely many neural sentences means some particular proposition.

Yamagata, Hiroshi. Expérience Esthétique: La Volonté d'Exprimer et la Volonté d'Expliquer. *Aesthetics*, 3, 23-32, Mr 88.

Nous remarquons les deux tendances chez les hommes: la volonté d'exprimer et la volonté d'expliquer. Alors que l'explication se fait toujours avec les mots (ce qui veut dire que dans la volonté d'expliquer, il s'agit toujours de la compréhension de l'objet par le sujet), la volonté d'exprimer se réalise par le sens et non par les mots d'entendement. Le mot "sens" est ambigu (ce qui est sensible, est-ce le sujet ou l'objet?), mais c'est sans doute cette ambiguïté même qui rend possible l'expression. Dans l'expérience esthétique, nous vivons le moment où une chose s'exprime à travers l'artiste pour devenir l'oeuvre.

Yanal, Robert J. The Paradox of Emotion and Fiction. *Pac Phil Quart*, 75(1), 54-75, Mr 94.

I present and argue against several solutions to the paradox of emotion and fiction: factualism (Michael Weston, Peter McCormick, early Noël Carroll), counterfactualism (Ralph Clark), and fictionalism (Kendall Walton), with arguments against Walton making up the bulk of the essay. I defend a view that our emotions are real (are not quasi-emotions), though I indicate some systematic ways in which our emotions towards fictions differ from our emotions towards real things.

Yandell, Keith E. A Gross and Palpable Contradiction?: Incarnation and Consistency. *Sophia (Australia)*, 33(3), 30-45, N 94.

Yaneva, Dominika A. History and Philosophy of Science Rapprochement: Shared Methodological Framework. *J Gen Phil Sci*, 26(1), 143-152, 1995.

The paper intends to identify some particular basic assumptions, approaches and means of proceeding, which are spontaneously shared by philosophers, sociologists and historians of science, besides the common interchange of meta-notions describing science. To this end, the specific subject matter, scope, meta-cognitive goals and methodological background of each of the three domains of science study is first outlined. Only two shared proceedings are further discussed in details: the objective attitude, called 'playing a stranger', and the historiographers' involvement in demarcational problem resolution. A far-reaching prospect is finally suggested for philosophers and historiographers: methodological partnership, leading towards the elaboration of an impending integral metatheory of science.

Yang, Yue. The Thickness Lemma..... *J Sym Log*, 60(2), 505-511, Je 95.

This paper is part of the reverse recursion theory project, which studies the proof theoretic strength of theorems in recursion theory. In this paper the theorem of the existence of an incomplete recursively enumerable high set is considered. It is known that Sigma two induction is sufficient to prove the theorem, whereas Sigma one is not. His paper shows that over Sigma one induction, the theorem does not imply Sigma two induction.

Yang-Lewis, Tony. Commentary on "The Forgetful Mourner". *Hastings Center Rep*, 25(1), 32-33, Jan-Feb 95.

Yasenchuk, Ken. Assimilative Moral Realism and Supervenience. *Dialogue (Canada)*, 34(1), 75-97, Wint 95.

This paper examines the conception of moral facts advocated by David Brink in his book, *Moral Realism and the Foundations of Ethics*. In the course of defending naturalistic moral realism against objections based on the assumption that reductionism is false, Brink applies the concepts of supervenience and constitution to moral properties. While this seems to support the desired parity of morality and science, I argue that it should be rejected in favour of a modal analysis of moral claims that is compatible with Brink's realism only if there are sound moral explanations of certain nonmoral facts.

Yasenchuk, Ken. Sturgeon and Brink on Moral Explanations. *S J Phil*, 32(4), 483-502, Wint 94.

This paper examines some arguments contained in Nicholas Sturgeon's paper "Moral Explanations", and David Brink's *Moral Realism and the Foundations of Ethics*. Against these writers, I provide a number of technical reasons to suppose that moral principles cannot be tested empirically using the Duhemian method they favor. I also give a critique of their main arguments for the relevance and indispensability of assumptions about moral facts to explanations of moral judgments and other items. I conclude that these arguments establish neither the explanatory relevance nor the necessity of moral assumptions.

Yates, David J. Biases in the Perception of Mirror-Image Reversal. *Philosophy*, 70(272), 289, Ap 95.

Mirrors create images that are enantiomorphs of objects. Such images can correctly be seen as objective, geometrical reversals of the objects on any axis. However, human beings are biased to see their own images as left/right reversals of themselves. Psychologists have studied this bias, and have found different biases in other situations. There seem to be many possible reasons for bias, and further study is needed. Nevertheless, it has been shown to be a function both of the structural properties of objects (that is, their symmetries) and of the canonical axes and orientations defined by social usage.

Yearley, Lee H. Theories, Virtues, and the Comparative Philosophy of Human Flourishings: A Response to Professor Allan. *Phil East West*, 44(4), 711-720, O 94.

Yeo, Michael (& others). *Concepts and Cases in Nursing Ethics*. Peterborough, Broadview Pr, 1991.

Yeo, Michael and Dalziel, Jean. "Autonomy" in *Concepts and Cases in Nursing Ethics, Yeo, Michael (& others)*, 54-85. Peterborough, Broadview Pr, 1991.

Yeo, Michael and Donner, Gail. "Justice" in *Concepts and Cases in Nursing Ethics, Yeo, Michael (& others)*, 147-183. Peterborough, Broadview Pr, 1991.

Yeo, Michael and Ford, Ann. "Integrity" in *Concepts and Cases in Nursing Ethics, Yeo, Michael (& others)*, 184-218. Peterborough, Broadview Pr, 1991.

Yeo, Michael and Krahn, Irene. "Confidentiality" in *Concepts and Cases in Nursing Ethics, Yeo, Michael (& others)*, 117-146. Peterborough, Broadview Pr, 1991.

Yeo, Michael and Mitchell, Sandra. "Truthfulness" in *Concepts and Cases in Nursing Ethics, Yeo, Michael (& others)*, 86-116. Peterborough, Broadview Pr, 1991.

Yeo, Michael and Molke, Trudy. "Beneficence" in *Concepts and Cases in Nursing Ethics, Yeo, Michael (& others)*, 25-53. Peterborough, Broadview Pr, 1991.

Yhap, Jennifer. Pascal and Descartes on First Ideas. *Amer Cath Phil Quart*, 69(1), 39-50, Wint 95.

In this article, I compare the Cartesian first ideas with the Pascalian first principles of nature. Toward this end, I examine each philosophy using two considerations, the dialectical consideration of consistency and the scientific consideration of criteria for truth. Concerning Descartes, I find that the first ideas are innate, simple, and intrinsically act, their cognitive agency being that of a division into simple parts. Meanwhile concerning Pascal, I suggest that the first principles provide a true understanding of the object based on the unitary cognition of a whole, their actuality being exercised in combinations and repetitions of number. Finally I suggest a way of understanding the modern problem of a common world through the use of the Pascalian first principles.

Yi, Byeonguk. Glymour on Explanation. *Brit J Phil Sci*, 45(3), 914-917, S 94.

In his "Explanation and realism", Clark Glymour offers an account of explanation as unification: "many explanations ... demonstrate that one phenomenon is really just a variant of ... another phenomenon". To clarify this idea of explanation as unification, he gives a formal characterization of the condition under which a theory *explains* a phenomenon *as a variant of* another phenomenon. The present paper shows that the characterization fails to support the idea; it is incapable of distinguishing a mere conjunction of independent laws from a (genuine) unification.

Yijie, Tang. The "Zhi Yan" in Feng Youlan's *Xin Zhi Yan*. *J Chin Phil*, 21(3-4), 269-279, S-D 94.

Ying, Mingsheng. A Logic for Approximate Reasoning. *J Sym Log*, 59(3), 830-837, S 94.

Classical logic is not adequate to face the essential vagueness of human reasoning, which is approximate rather than precise in nature. Consequently, many logicians have proposed different systems of many-valued logic as a formalization of approximate reasoning. All the proposals are obtained by extending the range of truth values of propositions. In these logical systems reasoning is still exact and to make a conclusion the antecedent clause of its rule must match its premise exactly. The purpose of this paper is, unlike all the previous proposals, to develop a propositional calculus, a predicate calculus in which the truth values of propositions are still true or false exactly and in which the reasoning may be approximate and allow the antecedent clause of a rule to match its premise only approximately.

Yob, Iris M. The Form of Feeling. *Phil Music Educ Rev*, 1(1), 18-32, Spr 93.

Yoes Jr, M G. When Is If?. *Sorites*, 96-99, Ap 95.

This paper deals with examples offered by Adams, Austin and others which seem to show that "if" does not conform to all of the laws of the conditional. These are reconciled by treating them as conjunctions with embedded modalities.

Yokoyama, Olga T. Iconic Manifestation of Interlocutor Distance in Russian. *J Prag*, 22(1), 83-102, Jl 94.

Assuming that every utterance has some sort of syntactic 'deep structure', data from Coloquial Russian suggest that a restrained interlocutor relationship results, iconically, in a 'grammar of restraint'; the 'grammar of closeness', on the contrary, operates as a creative superstructure above the well-established and obligatory 'grammar of restraint'. An alternative solution would be to posit two different sub-grammars: 1) an analytic and explicit 'grammar of restraint', generating primarily hypotactic structures, and 2) an undifferentiated 'grammar of closeness', generating primarily paratactic structures. Whichever approach one takes, the data show that the speaker's perception of interlocutor distance is systematically encoded in the language. (edited)

Yolton, John W (& other eds). *The Blackwell Companion to the Enlightenment*. Cambridge, Blackwell, 1995.

Yonah, Yossi. Categorical Desires and the Future. *Dialogue (Canada)*, 33(4), 581-594, Fall 94.

Yonah, Yossi. Well-Being, Categorical Deprivation and the Role of Education. *J Phil Educ*, 28(2), 191-203, Wint 94.

"How should a person lead her life?" The purpose of this paper is to suggest some principles (not a complete list) which will serve as 'intellectual instruments' for assessing forms of life. These principles are utilitarian in nature, and, as I will argue, essential to a reasonably rich account of personal well-being. The principles suggested are not instrumental, that is, they determine the worthiness of a form of life led by an agent irrespective of whether it satisfies her existing desires and meet her actual preferences. Hence, I will argue that a person can be deprived, that is, categorically deprived, even when most of her desires are satisfied. In the last section of the paper I will argue for the role of education in 'initiating' the agent into worthy forms of life, and hence evading the charge of categorical deprivation and that of irrationality.

You, Sung-Keun. Why are There Sinners? Augustine's Response to Mackie. *Int J Phil Relig*, 37(1), 1-12, F 95.

Youguang, Tu. Universals and Individuals: A Brief Discussion of New *Lixue*. *J Chin Phil*, 21(3-4), 431-449, S-D 94.

The center of Professor Feng Youlan's New Lixue is a doctrine of the realm of Heaven and Earth. The metaphysical foundation of this doctrine takes universal as the basis. The paper shows that the difficulties in taking universal as the basis cannot be overcome and that universal is derived from, or stands for, individuals which should be taken as the basis. Such a change does not lessen the value of Feng's doctrine, but rather strengthens it.

Young, A H and Park, S B G. Connectionism and Psychiatry: A Brief Review. *Phil Psychiat Psych*, 1(1), 51-58, Mr 94.

Connectionist models have been developed in diverse areas of psychiatric inquiry. Their span is from low-level biologically inspired models of the effects of synaptic pathology and drug action on mental function to attempts to implement higher levels of description such as psychodynamic psychopathology within a brainlike framework. This article reviews a number of the models relevant to psychiatry and argues that the connectionist approach, particularly because of its ability to model failures in psychological function, offers a powerful new tool in the exploration of the substrate of mental disorder.

Young, Iris Marion. Mothers, Citizenship, and Independence: A Critique of Pure Family Values. *Ethics*, 105(3), 535-579, Ap 95.

Young, James O. Between Rock and a Harp Place. *J Aes Art Crit*, 53(1), 78-81, Wint 95.

I argue, contrary to what Bruce Baugh has held, that there are no criteria of aesthetic excellence specific to rock music. The criteria by which Baugh has proposed to judge rock performances have always been applied to performances of classical music.

Young, James O. *Global Anti-realism*. Brookfield, Ashgate, 1995.

This book investigates the possibility of and argues for an anti-realist account of all classes of sentences. According to global anti-realism, the truth values of all sentences depend on what users of the sentences can know. The version of global anti-realism developed here has much in common with the coherence theory of truth. Global anti-realism depends on a holist theory of meaning. It leads to a qualified relativism about truth.

Young, Julian. Being and Value: Heidegger contra Nietzsche. *Int Stud Phil*, 27(3), 105-116, 1995.

The essay presents and supports Heidegger's critique of Nietzsche as the objections of an ethical naturalist to an ethical voluntarist. Some conclusions are drawn with respect to the different meaning "nihilism" has for Heidegger and Nietzsche respectively.

Yu, Jiyuan. *Tode Ti* and *Toionde* in Metaphysics Z. *Phil Inq*, 16(3-4), 1-25, Sum-Fall 94.

Yuanhua, Wang. A Philosophical Correspondence with Li Rui. *J Chin Phil*, 22(2), 233-238, Je 95.

Mao Zedong's call to serve the people, like the 'common will' proclaimed by Jean Jacques Rousseau, is a universality drained of individuality, but it has been declared to be a more accurate way to give expression to a right which should be enjoyed by all members of the society, in spite of their falling short of fully recognizing it.

Yuktanandana, Aksak. Musical Beauty and Levels of Hearing. *Brit J Aes*, 35(1), 49-60, Ja 95.

Yulina, N S. Philosophy in Russian Today. *Metaphilosophy*, 25(2-3), 117-131, Ap-Jl 94.

Zabierowski, Miroslaw. The Diagram H-R of Stars Displacement: Real Fact or Useful Research Instrument?. *Stud Phil Christ*, 30(2), 287-298, 1994.

The standard approach in philosophy of astronomy is described as satisfied only on the level of selected facts and is criticized by myself as evidently insufficient. An additional nonstandard philosophical approach seems to be indispensable in order to explain the complicated history of observations and astrophysical theories (shortly speaking—modern astronomy). The proper reconstruction of space processes must be based on a completely new ontology.

Zacarés Pamblanco, Amparo. La Presenza di Vico nella Poetica Spagnola del XVIII Secolo. *Boll Centro Stud Vichiani*, 24-25, 230-236, 1994-95.

Zacarés Pamblanco, Amparo. Vico y la Poética de la Modernidad. *Cuad Vico*, 1, 165-176, 1991.

Vico does not only reopen in modernity the dispute for the truth, but emerges again in today's discourse of the Postmodern, reminding us of the dearth of the precarious insular concept of man centered in scientific reason, of an incomplete rationality. There is a debt of modernity towards the genetic epistemology and the hermeneutic of the *Scienza Nuova* that considers *poetry* a way of access to the truth and recognizes in poetical fictions the nature of truths. This subject becomes decisive to appreciate the open controversy between modernity and postmodernism, centered in an explanatory restatement of *reason*. In search of a foundation of reason from itself, *poetical reason* opens new perspectives and acknowledged possibilities. Such is the actual project of F Rella, recovering the sense of Vico.

Zack, Naomi (ed). *American Mixed Race: The Culture of Microdiversity*. Lanham, Rowman & Littlefield, 1995.

Mixed-race identities are descriptively and normatively explored on the premises that the American concept of race lacks scientific foundation and contradicts individual experience. Perspectives from literature, public policy and social science, as well as philosophy, structure analyses of black, Indian, Asian and white racial mixture in European, Hispanic and Native American cultures. Conclusions range over reaffirmations of pure racial categories, suggestions for new multiracial identities and arguments for eliminating "race".

Zack, Naomi. Locke's Identity Meaning of Ownership. *Locke News*, 23, 105-113, 1992.

I suggest that Locke assumed that normative ownership, or justified possession, can be derived from another kind of ownership, which in present usage, would be called identity. I argue that according to Locke, the foundational meaning of ownership in both Chapter V of the *Second Treatise*, and Chapter XXVII of the *Essay* (Book II), is that if X owns P, then P is a part of X or P is X.

Zack, Naomi. Mixed Black and White Race and Public Policy. *Hypatia*, 10(1), 120-132, Wint 95.

The American folk concept of race assumes the factual existence of races. However, biological science does not furnish empirical support for this assumption. Public policy derived from nineteenth century slave-owning patriarchy is the only foundation of the "one-drop rule" for black and white racial inheritance. In principle, Americans who are both black and white have a right to identify themselves racially. In fact, recent demographic changes and multiracial academic scholarship support this right.

Zack, Naomi. *Race and Mixed Race*. Philadelphia, Temple Univ Pr, 1993.

A critical analysis of black and white racial categories in the United States and of the concept of race in general. I explain how the "one-drop" rule, originally a rationalization for slavery, persists today even though there never have been pure races and blacks and whites share racial genes. I argue throughout that American racial categories are themselves racist. Existential problems of race are explored with a focus on mixed race, a category that has never been acknowledged, on a par with white or black, in American history.

Zadrozny, Wlodek. From Compositional to Systematic Semantics. *Ling Phil*, 17(4), 329-342, Ag 94.

We prove a theorem stating that any semantics can be encoded as a compositional semantics, which means that, essentially, the standard definition of compositionality is formally vacuous. We then show that when compositional semantics is required to be "systematic" (that is, the meaning function cannot be arbitrary, but must belong to some class), it is possible to distinguish between compositional and noncompositional semantics. As a result, we believe that the paper clarifies the concept of compositionality and opens the possibility of making systematic formal comparisons of different systems of grammar.

Zagal, Héctor. Nous y Phronesis: Un comentario a EN 1143a 35ss. *Topicos*, 3(4), 109-121, 1993.

The aim of this paper is to show some difficulties in the grasping of the first principles of practical reason.

Zagal A, Héctor. Versatilidad Argumentativa en Santo Tomas de Aquino. *Topicos*, 1(1), 79-87, 1991.

This article is a short commentary to the preface in Aristotle's *Posteriorum Libros Expositio* written by Thoman Aquinas. The aim of the paper is to show the many senses and meaning of argumentation in Aquinas.

Zagare, F C and Kilgour, D M. Uncertainty and the Role of the Pawn in Extended Deterrence. *Synthese*, 100(3), 379-412, S 94.

This paper develops an incomplete information model of extended deterrence relationships. It postulates layers who are fully informed about the costs of war and all other relevant variables, save for the values their opponents place on the issues at stake, i.e., the pawn. We provide consistent and intuitively satisfying parallel definitions for two types of players, Hard and Soft, in terms of the parameters of our model. We also answer several particular questions about the strategy choices of players in an extended deterrence relationship and, by identifying all the Perfect Bayesian Equilibria of the game model we construct, specify typical behavior patterns. Our most general finding is that an extended deterrence game always has a unique perfect Bayesian equilibrium with a rather simple form. (edited)

Zagzebski, Linda. Religious Luck. *Faith Phil*, 11(3), 397-413, Jl 94.

Recently the problem of moral luck identified by Joel Feinberg, Thomas Nagel, and Bernard Williams has captured a lot of attention in ethics. In this paper I argue that the problem exists for Christian moral theory and practice as well, and that the problem is magnified by certain aspects of Christian theology, including the doctrines of grace and of an eternal heaven and hell. I then consider five solutions to the problem, all of which involve modifying in one way or another either traditional Christian doctrines or common views on the grounds for moral evaluation.

Zaitseva, Valentina. The Metaphoric Nature of Coding: Toward a Theory of Utterance. *J Prag*, 22(1), 103-126, Jl 94.

This paper offers a theoretical framework which treats in a systematic fashion properties of the code related to iconicity, metaphorization and the speaker's view of the discourse situation. The framework elaborates on Fillmore's (1977) prototypical scenes (taking into consideration other works within the cognitive approach employing Rosch's (1977) Prototype theory) and Yokoyama's (1986) Transactional Discourse Model (TDM). Viewing metaphorization as mapping components from one PS onto another the present research provides evidence that the process of coding itself has a metaphoric nature. (edited)

Zajonc, Arthur. "The Two Lights" in *Homage to Pythagoras, Bamford, Christopher (ed)*, 213-242. Hudson, Lindisfarne Pr, 1994.

Zakharyaschev, Michael. A New Solution to a Problem of Hosoi and Ono. *Notre Dame J Form Log*, 35(3), 450-457, Sum 94.

This paper gives a new, purely semantic proof of the following theorem: if an intermediate propositional logic *L* has the disjunction property then a disjunction free formula is provable in *L* if it is provable in intuitionistic logic. The main idea of the proof is to use the well-known semantic criterion of the disjunction property for "simulating" finite binary trees (which characterize the disjunction free fragment of intuitionistic logic) by general frames.

Zalejko, Gwidon. "Soviet Historiography as a 'Normal Science'" in *Historiography Between Modernism and Postmodernism, Topolski, Jerzy (ed)*, 179-190. Amsterdam, Rodopi, 1994.

Soviet Marxist historiography was often treated as an ideology-dominated and dogmatic pseudoscience deviating from the binding standards of rationality. The difference of procedures and results from those accepted in the West made its comprehension difficult and inclined people to treat it lightly. Yet treating that historiographical activity as scholarly increases our knowledge of science as such and of the external conditions of its functioning. One can apply to it the conception of paradigms, advanced by Thomas Kuhn. It helps us understand that Soviet historiography was a normal—also in the specific sense formulated by Kuhn—discipline pursued under abnormal conditions. The ontological assumptions resulting from the Soviet interpretation of Marxism predetermined the results of the research carried out by historians. But this research itself was conducted in accordance with the methodological rules binding all over the world.

Zalta, Edward N. Two (Related) World Views. *Nous*, 29(2), 189-211, Je 95.

One of the most challenging criticisms of Castaneda's guise theory was offered by Plantinga, who identifies fundamental intuitions that guise theory gives up and develops several objections to the guise-theoretic world view. In this paper, the author contrasts his own the theory of abstract objects with Castaneda's guise theory in light of Plantinga's criticisms of the latter. The two theories can be fruitfully compared because they share a common intellectual heritage—both follow Ernst Mally (1912) in postulating a special realm of objects distinguished by their 'internal' or 'encoded' properties. Despite this common heritage, however, the theories organize, develop, and apply these special objects in distinctive ways. It is shown that the theory of abstract objects anticipates and addresses most of Plantinga's concerns about guise theory by preserving intuitions guise theory has abandoned.

Zangari, Mark and Rhook, Graeme. Should We Believe in the Big Bang?: A Critique of the Integrity of Modern Cosmology. *Proc Phil Sci Ass*, 1, 228-237, 1994.

We analyze aspects of the Big Bang program in modern cosmology, with special focus on the strategies employed by its adherents both in defending the theory against anomalous data and in dismissing rival accounts. We illustrate this by critically examining four aspects of Big Bang cosmology: the interpretation of the cosmic red-shift, the explanation of the cosmic background radiation, the inflation hypothesis and the search for dark matter. We conclude that the Big Bang's dominance of contemporary cosmology is not justified by the degree of experimental support it receives relative to rival theories.

Zangwill, Nick. Kant on Pleasure in the Agreeable. *J Aes Art Crit*, 53(2), 167-176, Spr 95.

At one point in the *Critique of Judgment*, Kant is concerned to argue that pleasure in the agreeable is "interested". Many commentators have found Kant's account problematic if not completely unintelligible. I do not want to spend much time picking apart what the various commentators have said. They have mostly thrown up their hands in desperation. But we must understand a position before we criticize it. With Kant, it is often worth trying a little harder than usual. I shall offer an interpretation of the text and then consider various problems for that interpretation. I aim to clarify and restore Kant's account. Readers can then construct my reply to the commentators if they wish. I then go on to consider problems for Kant's view. I end up defending much of what Kant says, while pointing out where I think he runs into trouble.

Zangwill, Nick. Supervenience Unthwarted: Rejoinder to Wicks. *J Aes Art Crit*, 52(4), 466-469, Fall 94.

I argue that aesthetic/nonaesthetic supervenience is a metaphysical relation between properties rather than an epistemological matter of what we can *know* about aesthetic properties on the basis of what we know about nonaesthetic properties. And I agree that aesthetic properties are very sensitive to alterations in nonaesthetic properties. Supervenience is not incompatible with that. Thus I defuse Wick's objections.

Zantema, Hans and Middeldorp, Aart. Simple Termination of Rewrite Systems. *Bull Sec Log*, 24(1), 31-36, Mr 95.

In this paper we investigate the concept of simple termination. A term rewriting system (TRS for short) is called simply terminating if its termination can be proved by means of a simplification order. We propose a new definition of simplification order and we investigate the properties of the resulting class of simply terminating systems.

Zapata, Martha. "Die Rezeption der Philosophie Friedrich Nietzsches im deutschen Faschismus" in *Die besten Geister der Nation, Korotin, Ilse (ed)*, 186-220. Vienna, Picus, 1994.

In diesem Beitrag werden die unterschiedlichen Nietzsche-Bilder der deutschen Philosophie skizziert und insbesondere wird nach ihrer Bedeutung für die NS-Herrschaft gefragt. Zuerst wird auf die "Entnazifizierung" der Philosophie Nietzsches eingegangen, die unmittelbar nach der Zerschlagung des NS-Staates im besetzten Deutschland staatfand. Dann wird ein kurzer Überblick über die Nietzsche-Rezeption in der Weimarer Republick gegeben, um auf die wichtigsten Schnittstellen für die Faschisierung der Nietzsche-Rezeption hinzuweisen. Schliesslich wird gezeigt, wie die Nietzsche-Deutung zwischen 1933 und 1945 an der Konstitution eines faschistischen Subjekts und an der Reproduktion der NS-Herrschaft gearbeitet hat.

Zapater, José María. El Siglo XIII de París: Nuevo Rumbo para la Filosofía Occidental. *Rev Espan Filosof Med*, 0, 273-278, 1993.

Plato's philosophy inspired Occidental thought until XIIth Century AC—Aristotle was meanwhile unknown. Several of his works were known and brought to Occident by Arabs and Hebrews during Xth and XIIth Centuries. But it was during XIIIth Century when Thomas Aquine spread Aristotle's work in Paris. Thomas Aquine's renewal was: 1) Authority is no argument in philosophy; 2) Essential distinction between theology and philosophy; 3) Reason's autonomy establishment; 4) Aristotle's metaphysics from the being's necessity, is radically changed by Thomas Aquine from the being's contingency as well as from freedom; 5) Aristotle's "man" keeps himself closed contemplating truth, where as from Thomas's point of view is a transcendent "being": 'he's got his feet on Earth' (he is "aliquid civitatis"), but his mind tends unto God (he is "aliquid Dei"). Thomas's conception of man and reason was three centuries in advance to the Renaissance, and five centuries to Kant's "audere sapere" in the XVIII Century....

Zárate, Marla. Los Creadores de Ficciones Sublimes. *An Seminar Hist Filosof*, 11, 129-136, 1994.

Setting off from the Kantian distinction between the beautiful and the sublime, that the philosopher attributes, respectively, to the feminine and male nature, in this article is supported by the thesis that there are no specific differences between the literary creations written by women and those whose authors are men and, from this presupposition, it is broached by the *ontology* of fiction (sublime, because the contemporary art has given up the classic criteria of beauty): the internal logic of reading and its imaginary-real characters.

Zarka, Yves-Charles. "Das Erbe der Freiheit" in *Das geistige Erbe Europas, Buhr, Manfred (ed)*, 477-488. Napoli, Vivarium, 1994.

Zarka, Yves-Charles. Leibniz et le droit subjectif. *Rev Metaph Morale*, 98(1), 83-94, Ja-Mr 95.

This paper intends to question Leibniz's original position in the history of the conceptions of natural right. On the one hand, Leibniz tries to conciliate modern natural right theories with ancient natural right theories, i.e., the ideas of Grotius and Hobbes with those of Aristotle. On the other hand, he also endeavors to conciliate the notion of a rational natural right with the religious perspective of Augustine's City of God. Hence, two questions: what happens to modern natural right, as subjective right, when it is taken up within a doctrine that endeavors to rehabilitate ancient or objective natural right? Or rather, what happens to subjective right within a conception of natural right that eventually aims—beyond the rehabilitation of objective right—at the revival of the theological perspective of a universal divine justice? Though the first formulations of subjective right were historically connected to an individualistic ontology, the fact that this notion bears a quite different meaning within the Leibnizian theory of natural right is sufficiently declared by our twofold question.

Zawadowski, M W. Descent and Duality. *Annals Pure Applied Log*, 71(2), 131-188, F 95.

Using the Makkai's duality for first-order logic, we characterize effective descent morphisms in 2-categories of pretoposes and Barr-exact categories. In both cases they coincide with conservative morphisms. We show that in those 2-categories the 2-coregular factorizations are exactly quotient-conservative factorizations. We also prove a generalization of the Makkai duality for pseudoelementary categories.

Zawidzski Jr, Tad and Ross, Don. Information and Teleosemantics. *S J Phil*, 32(4), 393-419, Wint 94.

This essay seeks to reconcile the information-based account of representation due to Dretske and Lloyd with the position of the 'teleosemanticists' (Dennett, Millikan, etc.) who analyze intentionality in terms of 'proper function' determined by natural selection. We argue that the analysis of intentionality in terms of information flow, if properly understood in the context of thermodynamics, is not only compatible with appealing to adaptations in fixing representational content, but actually helps to explain the utility of doing so in psychology and ethology.

Zehou, Li. Mourning Professor Feng Youlan by Engaging in Serious Philosophical Discussion Today. *J Chin Phil*, 21(3-4), 471-480, S-D 94.

Zeis, John. The Epistemic Passage of the Five Ways. *Amer Cath Phil Quart*, 68(Supp), 73-84, 1994.

The five ways are a progressive series of argumentations, each ending with its own distinctive conclusion leading epistemically to the next way in the series. The five ways are hence not simply five separate argumentations with the same conclusion, nor are they a simple cumulative case set of argumentations for God's existence. Rather, each is a unique demonstration and the five are deliberately ordered in an epistemic or pedagogical structure.

Zeis, John. Truth-Warranted Manifestation Beliefs. *Faith Phil*, 11(3), 436-451, Jl 94.

In *Perceiving God*, William Alston has argued that manifestation beliefs (M-beliefs) are warranted or justified in a way analogous to the justification of perceptual beliefs. However, there seems to be a sort of M-belief reported by the Carmelite mystics, Saints Teresa and John of the Cross, which are self-authenticating (SAM-beliefs). In this paper, I argue for an alternative view concerning the warrant of SAM-beliefs. I will suggest that SAM-beliefs are justified in a way analogous to the way in which Alston has suggested that privileged-access beliefs are justified: namely, they are truth-warranted.

Zelechow, Bernard. Biblical Speech and Modern Consciousness in the Post-Modern Age: The Double Paradox of Modernism. *Hist Euro Ideas*, 18(6), 885-900, N 94.

This paper in the history of ideas demonstrates the relationship between biblical presuppositions and modern conceptions of knowledge which emerge out of the quest for secular autonomy. The odyssey of modernity demonstrates the impossibility of grounding knowledge and morality autonomously. Implicitly, in displaced form the biblical notions of covenant, divine platform (sacred historicity), and prophecy are called into play to ground relational knowing, critique, and history.

Zellner, Harold. Is Relativism Self-Defeating?. *J Phil Res*, 20, 287-295, 1995.

Plato seems to have claimed that epistemological relativism is self-defeating in two ways. As reformulated by Siegel: arguments for relativism must be advanced as either relativistically or nonrelativistically sound. In either case they are dialectically ineffective for the relativist. Second, relativism is either relativistically or nonrelativistically true. Either choice commits the relativist to major concessions to her opponent, or so the story goes. But the relativist can advance her arguments as nonrelativistically sound, for the consumption of the nonrelativist. Moreover, relativists can claim that relativism is true not only for the relativist, but for her nonrelativist opponent as well. Relativism is not self-defeating in either of these ways, for much the same reasons that skepticism is not self-defeating. But we cannot live as relativists, because relativism leads to epistemic paralysis, as the example of prediction shows.

Zenkert, Georg. Hegel und das Problem der Macht. *Deut Z Phil*, 43(3), 435-451, 1995.

This study corrects a widespread misinterpretation of Hegel's political philosophy, *claiming that power may not be reduced to authority (Herrschaft) in the sense* of Max Weber. The crucial point is the relation between power and violence, both refering to each other and yet strictly different. It is Hegel's concept of constitution which leads beyond the paradoxical connection of subordination and consent.

Zeppi, Stelio. Metafisica e *Archè*, nel Pensiero Greco più Antico: Causalità e Temporalità in Quanto Categorie Presocratiche. *G Metaf*, 16(3), 299-325, S-D 94.

Zhixue, Liang. Interpersonalität beim jungen Fichte. *Fichte-Studien*, 3, 219-229, 1991.

Die Interpersonalität ist ein wichtiges Thema der gegenwärtigen Philosophie geworden. Und es war Fichte, der den bedeutendsten Beitrag zur Lösung dieser Aufgabe geleistet hat! Die Darlegung der von ihm vertretenen Ansichten über die Interpersonalität hat deshalb für die heutige philosophische Erforschung dieses Verhältnisses heuristischen Wert. Wenn wir uns auf seine Jugendzeit beschränken, so soll dies deutlich machen, dass Fichte das Problem der Interpersonalität schon in der Zeit von 1792 bis 1794 in seinen Grundlagen durchdacht und viele glänzende Ideen darüber vorgetragen hat.

Zhonghua, Li. Feng Youlan's Views on Chinese and Western Culture. *J Chin Phil*, 21(3-4), 255-262, S-D 94.

Zhou, Yiyun. The Unity of Heaven and Man versus Absolute Unlikeness—Kierkegaard, European Thinker, Contra Chinese Philosophy. *Hist Euro Ideas*, 20(1-3), 195-200, Ja 95.

Zhukov, V N. The Social Philosophy of P I Novgorodtsev. *Russian Stud Phil*, 33(3), 26-42, Wint 94-95.

Ziarek, Krzysztof. Semiosis of Listening: The Other in Heidegger's Writings on Hölderlin and Celan's "The Meridian". *Res Phenomenol*, 24, 113-132, 1994.

"Semiosis of Listening" explores the role of the other in Heidegger's thought in the context of Celan's reworking of the Heideggerian approach to poetry in "The Meridian." Against the widespread opinion about the absence of others in Heidegger's work, it argues that Heidegger, especially in his engagement with the problem of listening in poetry, outlines an ethical inscription of the other in language. Celan's preoccupation with both the ontological and the ethical signification of alterity, his emphasis on the "inverted breath" with which the other marks language, provides the parameters for the discussion of the ethical in Heidegger's "Letter on Humanism" and essays on Hölderlin.

Zieba, Maciej. Two or Even Three Liberalisms. *Dialogue Hum*, 4(5), 89-97, 1994.

Ziegler, Meinrad and Kannonier-Finster, Waltraud. "Erinnern ohne Gedenken" in *Nationalsozialismus und Moderne, Welzer, Harald (ed)*, 61-104. Tübingen, Ed Diskord, 1993.

Ziemke, Axel. *Was ist Wahrnehmung?*. Berlin, Duncker Humblot, 1994.

Zimmer, R M and Ali, S M. Discourse on Artificiality: A Unifying Framework for the Artificial Sciences. *Ideal Stud*, 24(3), 201-226, Fall 94.

This paper presents a unifying framework for the study of artificial life, intelligence and reality. By providing this framework we can give a clear and concise introduction to the fundamental arguments of all three artificial sciences and facilitate the translation of arguments from any one domain to the other two. The framework is based on a variant of functionalism that does not exclude the role of the observer.

Zimmerli, Walther Christoph. The Bullying of an Untheoretical History of Philosophy—Eclecticism Instead of Ideology. *Magyar Filozof Szemle*, 5-6, 855-858, 1994.

Zimmerman, Andrew D. Toward a More Democratic Ethic of Technological Governance. *Sci Tech Human Values*, 20(1), 86-107, Wint 95.

Recent scholarship in technology and society studies has given attention to the notion of technological citizenship. This article seeks to further integrate perspectives on this topic with theoretical contributions about the development of moral autonomy. The author challenges the presumption that the strategy of expanding opportunities of participation in technological decision making will in itself develop people's autonomy and citizenship. He argues that concurrent efforts must be made to democratize the political-economic structures of key technologies and to help people prepare morally for citizenship roles in governing these technologies. On this basis, a series of initiatives are suggested.

Zimmerman, Dean. Theories of Masses and Problems of Constitution. *Phil Rev*, 104(1), 53-110, Ja 95.

Concrete mass terms are often preceded by definite and indefinite articles—e.g., "the water in Heraclitus's tub" (where the unstressed "some" functions as the indefinite article for mass terms). What sorts of entities are referred to by such expressions? A "theory of masses" is an attempt to answer this question by describing the metaphysical status and most general properties of the referents of these terms. Exploration of alternative theories of masses turns up some radical consequences for the metaphysics of artifacts, organisms, and anything else supposed capable of persisting through changes in parts.

Zimmerman, Michael. Actions and Events. *J Phil Res*, 20, 585-594, 1995.

Kent Bach has argued that certain traditional problems of action theory (concerning the individuation of actions, their timing, their location, and the manner in which they enter into causal relations) arise only on the supposition that actions are events, and he has argued further that actions are not events. In this paper these arguments are examined and rejected.

Zimmerman, Michael J. Compensation and Culpability. *Philosophia (Israel)*, 24(1-2), 29-48, D 94.

Zimmerman, Michael J. French's *Responsibility Matters*, Murphy's *Retribution Reconsidered*, and Sher's *Desert*. *Nous*, 29(2), 248-259, Je 95.

A theme that is common to all three books and which is the main focus of this review is the justification of punishment. French's view, that corporations are moral persons in their own right and hence may be blamed and punished, is criticized primarily on the grounds that corporations are not capable of grasping moral concepts. Murphy's departure from his former Kantian type of retributivism, in the grounds that such retributivism is difficult to reconcile with liberalism, is discussed. Sher's attempt to ground desert of punishment in the benefit a wrongdoer derives from wrongdoing is criticized primarily on the grounds that it fails to distinguish satisfactorily between wrongdoing and culpability.

Zimmerman, Michael J. Prima Facie Obligation and Doing the Best One Can. *Phil Stud*, 78(2), 87-123, My 95.

Analyses are given of the concepts of absolute and prima facie obligation. The former is a maximizing analysis: roughly, one ought absolutely to perform those actions which are performed in the best worlds accessible to one. The latter analysis is roughly this: one ought prima facie to perform those actions which are such that those accessible worlds in which they are performed are better than the closest accessible worlds in which they are not performed. Accounts of conditional obligation, both absolute and prima facie, are also given, and the issue of the detachment of unconditional from conditional obligation is addressed.

Zimmerman, Michael J. Rights, Compensation, and Culpability. *Law Phil*, 13(4), 419-450, N 94.

It is frequently claimed that someone who has infringed a right owes compensation of some sort to the right-holder, even when the person who has committed the infringement is innocent, that is, not culpable for the infringement. In this paper, this claim is first refined and clarified and then challenged. One challenge involves comparing an innocent adult with an innocent child and an innocent gorilla. The main challenge involves an appeal to the repugnance of strict liability. It is argued that this repugnance implies that the claim in question is false.

Zinnes, D A and Muncaster, R G and Lee, S C. 'The Friend of My Enemy is My Enemy': Modeling Triadic Internation Relationships. *Synthese*, 100(3), 333-358, S 94.

The evolution of internation relationships is studied by means of a mathematical model based on a popular rule of triadic interaction: "the friend of my friend is my friend, the friend of my enemy is my enemy, the enemy of my enemy is my friend, the enemy of my friend is my enemy". The rule is shown to lead to the formation and preservation of unipolar and bipolar configurations of nations, with the strengths of relationships, both friendly and conflictual, intensifying through time. These results confirm speculations originally made in static, graph theoretic studies of the balancing of relationships within individuals, small groups and systems of nations.

Zizek, Slavoj. Der audio-visuelle Kontrakt—der Lärm um das Reale. *Deut Z Phil*, 43(3), 521-538, 1995.

The development of sound cinema permits us to reach important conclusions as to the relationship between gaze and voice, between what we see and what we hear. In its most radical dimension, voice does not simply belong to objects in reality, but points towards a kind of ontological "blind spot" in them: ultimately, we hear things because we cannot see everything, because there is something in them which structurally eludes our eyes. In our encounter with another speaking being, there is thus always a minimum of ventriloquism at work: her voice points towards another, spectral, "undead" dimension (the Lacanian Real) which cuts a hole in reality.

Znoj, Milan. Hegel and Our Democracy. *Filozof Cas*, 43(1), 111-125, 1995.

The article lays out the main topics of the debate between liberalism and communitarianism on the field of political philosophy and considers the extent to which the Czech tradition of Hegelian consideration can play a part in this debate. The analysis of Milan Sobotka's latest work devoted to Hegel's *Phenomenology of Mind* and *Philosophy of Law* concludes that Sobotka, following the analysis of Joachim Ritter, succeeds in interpreting Hegel's concept of morality and his critique of Kantian morality in a way which accepts the key themes of the debate between liberalism and communitarianism, removing Hegel from the neomarxist field.

Zöller, Günter. Schopenhauer and the Problem of Metaphysics: Critical Reflections on Rudolf Malter's Interpretation. *Man World*, 28(1), 1-10, Ja 95.

The essay examines the place of Schopenhauer in the classical German philosophical tradition from Kant to Heidegger. Building on Malter's recent interpretation of Schopenhauer as a proto-existentialist transcendental philosopher, I examine Schopenhauer's contributions to five central concerns of Kantian, post-Kantian and neo-Kantian philosophy: transcendental idealism, a post-critical metaphysics, the unity of subjectivity, the phenomenological method, and the dialectic of facticity and freedom. I argue that what distinguishes Schopenhauer from the Kantian mainstream, to which he otherwise belongs, is the lack of systematic concern with practical reason and intersubjectivity.

Zoloth-Dorfman, Laurie. One of These Mornings I'm Going to Rise Up Singing: The Necessity of the Prophetic Voice in Jewish Bioethics. *J Clin Ethics*, 5(4), 348-353, Wint 94.

Zonneveld, Leo W and Kidd, James W. The Energetics of Spirituality and Human Sexuality. *Dialogue Hum*, 3(2), 147-155, 1993.

Zoumbos, A N. Ein Kommentar zum Heraklit. *Philosophia (Athens)*, 23-24, 112-113, 1993-94.

In den herklitischen Fragmenten 43 und 94 betonen wir die Bedeutung des Begriffes "uetpov", welches einen ethischen Charakter hat.

Zovko, Jure. Philologische Barbarismen. *Filozof Istraz*, 13(4), 967-982, 1993.

Auffallend am philologischen Kommentar zum sechsten und siebten Buch der Platonischen *Politeia* von Damir Barbaric ist Barbarics Weigerung, sich auf die sonst als Interpretationsgrundlage erforderliche semantisch-linguistische Analyse des Platonsichen Textes einzulassen. Vielmehr nimmt er sich vor, "die Sprache auf das lebendige Philosophieren" selbst "vorzubereiten". Zu diesem Zweck bemüht sich der Kommentator sogar, den Platonischen Text gemäss seinen eigenen "philosophischen Anstrengungen" neu zu edieren und zu übersetzen. Neben dem grundsätzlich wissenschaftlich Unhaltbaren eines solches Ansatzes ist an Barbarics Unternehmen vor allem das auszusetzen, dass dabei das klassische Werk von James Adam *The Republic of Plato* mit nur geringfügiger eigener Anstrengung und ohne ausreichende Anerkennung de Adamschen Leistungen weitgehend nachgebildet oder bloss übertragen wurde.

Zuber, R. A Note on the Logical Dependence of Simple Quantifiers. *Bull Sec Log*, 23(4), 168-172, D 94.

It is shown that the specific property of *conservativity* known from the study of natural language quantifiers entails an algebraic version of logical dependence.

Zubiri, Xavier. Las fuentes espirituales de la anguistia y de la esperanza. *Rev Filosof (Spain)*, 4(6), 239-245, 1991.

Zubiri, Xavier. Sobre el problema de la filosofia. *Convivium*, 5, 81-98, 1993.

Zubiri, Xavier. Sobre el Problema de la Filosofía (II). *Convivium*, 7, 118-136, 1995.

Zubiría, Martín. Poetizar y Pensar? Desde la Meditación Heideggeriana Hacia el *Topos* Histórico de Hölderlin. *Themata*, 13, 211-228, 1995.

The Heideggerian thinking knows itself in the neighborhood of poetizing. For this reason it removes Hölderlin from our history, which is metaphysics, to place him within the horizont of the "other beginning". Hölderlin however, together with Rousseau and Schiller, appertain to a epochal figure of wisdom: that of civic knowledge. What does this mean? And why, besides the Heideggarian position, the relation between thinking and poetizing appear now entirely transformed? How does it become possible?

Zucker, Mark J and Gottlieb, Lawrence. Organs for Undocumented Aliens? A Transplantation Dilemma. *Cambridge Quart Healthcare Ethics*, 4(2), 229-232, Spr 95.

Undocumented aliens may appear in United States transplantation programs without any mechanism to pay for their treatment. Our institution, Newark Beth Israel Medical Center, Newark, New Jersey, faced the decision and developed a policy in order to try to approach the problem fairly and in compliance with all appropriate unos policies.

Zuesse, Evan M. "The Gate to God's Presence in Heschel, Buber, and Soloveitchik" in *Thinkers and Teachers of Modern Judaism, Goldsmith, Emanuel S (ed)*, 141-149. New York, Paragon House, 1994.

This essay analyses three major Jewish philosophers' attempts to develop a Jewish understanding of the world and Reality/God in terms of the non-Judaic, basically Protestant-Christian Kantian categories (e.g., in Rudolf Otto) prevalent in their formative years in early twentieth-century Germany. Since Buber, Heschel, and Soloveitchik are paradigmatic reform, conservative and modern orthodox thinkers, respectively, their differing responses tell us a great deal about the intellectual differences between these Jewish movements. Tacitly influencing all three's dissent from prevailing metaphysical systems was the Jewish halakha, or normative commandments, which gives a value to bodily life lacking in general thought.

Zurbrugg, Nicholas. "Baudrillard, Modernism, and Postmodernism" in *Baudrillard: A Critical Reader, Kellner, Douglas (ed)*, 227-255. Cambridge, Blackwell, 1994.

Zweers, Wim. "In Search of an Ecological Culture: Environmental Philosophy in the 1990's" in *Ecology, Technology, and Culture, Zweers, Wim (ed)*, 1-19. Cambridge, White Horse, 1994.

Zweers, Wim. "Radicalism or Historical Consciousness: On Breaks and Continuity in the Discussion of Basic Attitudes" in *Ecology, Technology, and Culture,* Zweers, Wim (ed), 63-71. Cambridge, White Horse, 1994.

Zweers, Wim (ed) and Boersema, Jan J (ed). *Ecology, Technology, and Culture*. Cambridge, White Horse, 1994.

Zwiauer, Charlotte. "Der Antike Dionysos bei Friedrich Nietzsche und Walter Friedrich Otto" in *Die besten Geister der Nation, Korotin, Ilse (ed)*, 221-239. Vienna, Picus, 1994.

Zycinski, Jósef. Postmodern Criticism of the Rationality of Science. *Stud Phil Christ*, 30(2), 299-312, 1994.

In the approach of contemporary postmodernism, the philosophy inspired by ideas of J P Lyotard and J Derrida, the traditional notion of rationality is regarded as a merely social-cultural phenomenon. Consequently, the natural sciences are treated as a form of literary narrative to which one cannot apply the traditional epistemic category of truthlikeness. To reinterpret scientific theories in this new perspective, the postmodernists refer very often to recent physical research dealing with the so-called chaotic phenomena. In their attempts to confirm this new philosophy at the level of nuclear physics, the famous experiment by Pons and Fleischmann is presented as a form of narrative in which the alleged cold fusion plays the role similar to Cervantes's Don Quichote. After criticizing new attempts at postmodern reinterpretation of physics and mathematics, the author points out that postmodernism itself remains nothing but a form of ideological poetry in which one a priori assumes very strong axioms of the reducibility of epistemic factors to social-cultural determinants.

Zynda, Lyle. Old Evidence and New Theories. *Phil Stud*, 77(1), 67-95, Ja 95.

I discuss two problems implicit in the problem of old evidence, a challenge to the orthodox Bayesian account of confirmation: first, explaining how on Bayesian grounds scientists can become more confident in hypotheses based on evidence they already know to be true; and second, explaining how known evidence can support theories. I argue that appeals to counterfactual conditioning cannot account for actual increases in confidence, and that appeals to logical-mathematical learning cannot address many problematic cases, e.g., those where hypotheses do not logically imply the evidence. I conclude that solving the problem will require significant departures from orthodox Bayesianism.

Guidance on the Use of the Book Review Index

The Book Review Index lists, in alphabetical order, the authors of books reviewed in philosophy journals. Each entry includes the author's name, the title of the book, the publisher, and the place and date of publication. Under each entry is listed the name of the reviewer, the journal in which the review appeared, along with the volume, pagination and date.

Aristoteles. *Retórica*. Madrid, Ed Gredos, 1990.
Narcy, Michel. *Arch Phil*, 58(1), 145-148, Ja-Mr 95.

Aristóteles. *Protréptico*. Buenos Aires, Ed Cultura Labor, 1993.
Torres, Eugenio. *Analogía*, 8(1), 199-200, 1994.

Aristotle and Gallop, David (trans). *Aristotle on Sleep and Dreams*. Peterborough, Broadview Pr, 1991.
Hankinson, R J. *Dialogue (Canada)*, 33(2), 340-343, Spr 94.

Armella, Aspe. *El concepto de técnica, arte y producción en la filosofía de Aristóteles*. Madrid, Fondo de Cultura, 1993.
Bay, Tatiana Aguilar-Alv. *Topicos*, 4(7), 77-80, 1994.

Armour, Leslie. *Being and Idea*. Hildesheim, Olms, 1992.
Warnke, Georgia. *Rev Metaph*, 48(2), 389-390, D 94.

Arnau, Hilari, Gutiérrez, José M and Navarro, Ginés. *Qué es el utilitarismo?*. Barcelona, Prom Pub Univ, 1993.
Diego, Carmen Verde. *Telos*, 2(1), 139-140, Je 93.

Arndt, Andreas. *Dialektik und Reflexion*. Hamburg, Meiner, 1994.
Hong, Yun-Gi. *Das Argument*, 208, 115-116, Ja-F 95.

Aronowitz, Stanley. *Science as Power*. Minneapolis, Univ of Minn Pr, 1988.
Mitcham, Carl. *Res Phil Technol*, 14, 306-312, 1994.

Arpád, Szakolczai. *A fejlödés megkérdöjelezése*. Budapest, Akad Kiado, 1990.
Darab, Tamás. *Magyar Filozof Szemle*, 5-6, 887-891, 1994.

Arregui, J V. *El horror de morir*. Barcelona, Tibidabo Ed, 1992.
Lluesma, Carlos Rodríguez. *Themata*, 13, 299-301, 1995.

Arregui, J V and Choza, J. *Filosofía del hombre*. Madrid, Rialp, 1991.
Lluesma, Carlos Rodríguez. *Themata*, 13, 301-302, 1995.

Aschheim, Steven E. *The Nietzsche Legacy in Germany 1890-1990*. Berkeley, Univ of Calif Pr, 1993.
Diethe, Carol. *Hist Euro Ideas*, 18(6), 954-955, N 94.
Pettey, John Carson. *Int Stud Phil*, 27(2), 109-111, 1995.

Aspin, David N, Chapman, Judith D and Wilkinson, Vernon R. *Quality Schooling*. London, Cassell, 1994.
Hyland, Terry. *J Moral Educ*, 24(2), 202-204, 1995.

Atherton, Margaret. *Berkeley's Revolution in Vision*. Ithaca, Cornell Univ Pr, 1990.
Brykman, Geneviève. *Rev Metaph Morale*, 99(4), 571-573, O-D 94.

Atran, Scott. *Cognitive Foundations of Natural History*. New York, Cambridge Univ Pr, 1993.
Landen, Laura. *Rev Metaph*, 48(2), 390-392, D 94.

Aubenque, Pierre and Tordesillas, Alonso. *Aristote politique*. Paris, Pr Univ France, 1993.
Kerkhoff, Manfred. *Dialogos*, 30(65), 224-230, Ja 95.

Audi, Robert. *Action, Intention, and Reason*. Ithaca, Cornell Univ Pr, 1993.
Bratman, Michael E. *Ethics*, 105(4), 927-930, Jl 95.
Dutton, Alan. *Phil Books*, 36(3), 191-192, Jl 95.
Kaye, Lawrence J. *Can Phil Rev*, 14(6), 379-381, D 94.
Mele, Alfred R. *Mind*, 104(413), 145-148, Ja 95.

Audi, Robert. *The Structure of Justification*. New York, Cambridge Univ Pr, 1993.
King-Farlow, John. *Can Phil Rev*, 15(1), 4-6, F 95.
Paxson, Jr, Thomas D. *Mind*, 104(413), 148-151, Ja 95.
Sinnott-Armstrong, Walter. *Phil Quart*, 45(180), 394-397, Jl 95.

Augé, Marc. *Orte und Nicht-Orte*. Frankfurt, Fischer, 1994.
Horák, Petr. *Filozof Cas*, 42(6), 1059-1061, 1994.

Aurelianensis, Aegidius. *Quaestiones super De generatione et corruptione*. Amsterdam, Zdzislaw Kuksewicz, 1993.
Flüeler, Christoph. *Frei Z Phil Theol*, 42(1-2), 214-218, 1995.

Austin, David F (ed). *Philosophical Analysis*. Dordrecht, Kluwer, 1988.
Tomberlin, James E. *Nous*, 27(2), 249-258, Je 93.

Avineri, Shlomo (ed) and De-Shalit, Avner (ed). *Communitarianism and Individualism*. New York, Oxford Univ Pr, 1992.
Bates Jr, Clifford A. *Hist Euro Ideas*, 18(5), 769-770, S 94.

Ayers, Michael. *Locke (Volume I)*. New York, Routledge, 1991.
Lyon, Ardon. *Philosophy*, 70(271), 123-125, Ja 95.

Babich, Babette E. *Nietzsche's Philosophy of Science*. Albany, SUNY Pr, 1994.
Cox, Christoph. *Rev Metaph*, 48(4), 886-887, Je 95.

Babolin, Albino. *Dai platonici di Cambridge a Joseph Butler*. Perugia, Ed Benucci, 1993.
Micheletti, Mario. *Riv Filosof Neo-Scolas*, 86(3), 605-606, Jl-S 94.

Bacca, Juan David García. *De magia a técnica*. Barcelona, Anthropos, 1989.
Lynch, James A. *Res Phil Technol*, 14, 294-297, 1994.

Bachmann, I. *La ricezione critica della filosofia esistenziale di Martin Heidegger*. Napoli, Guida, 1992.
Perrotta, Romolo. *G Metaf*, 16(1-2), 258-260, Ja-Ag 94.

Bacon, John (ed), Campbell, Keith (ed) and Reinhardt, Lloyd (ed). *Ontology, Causality and Mind*. New York, Cambridge Univ Pr, 1993.
Over, D E. *Phil Books*, 36(3), 183-185, Jl 95.

Badhwar, Neera Kapur (ed). *Friendship: A Philosophical Reader*. Ithaca, Cornell Univ Pr, 1993.
Burns, Steven. *Can Phil Rev*, 15(1), 6-9, F 95.

Baertschi, Bernard. *Les rapports de l'âme et du corps*. Paris, Vrin, 1992.
Bouckaert, Bertrand. *Rev Phil Louvain*, 92(4), 602-604, N 94.

Bahm, Archie J. *Axiology: The Science of Values*. Amsterdam, Rodopi, 1993.
Grünberg, Ludwig. *J Value Inq*, 29(1), 143-147, Mr 95.

Baier, Annette C. *A Progress of Sentiments*. Cambridge, Harvard Univ Pr, 1991.
Winkler, Kenneth P. *Phil Rev*, 103(4), 755-762, O 94.

Baier, Annette C. *Moral Prejudices*. Cambridge, Harvard Univ Pr, 1994.
Dunn, John. *J Phil*, 92(1), 44-47, Ja 95.

Baird, Robert M (ed) and Rosenbaum, Stuart E (ed). *Euthanasia*. Barcelona, Ed Martinez Roca, 1992.
Sánchez, Elías Pérez. *Telos*, 3(1), 129-130, Je 94.

Baird, Robert M. (ed) and Rosenbaum, Stuart E. (ed). *The Ethics of Abortion*. Buffalo, Prometheus, 1993.
Tacelli, S J, Ronald K. *Amer Cath Phil Quart*, 69(1), 97-98, Wint 95.

Baird Saenger, Elizabeth. *Exploring Ethics through Children's Literature*. Pacific Grove, Critical Think Pr, 1993.
Winston, Joe. *J Moral Educ*, 23(4), 475-477, 1994.

Baker, Lynne Rudder. *Saving Belief*. Princeton, Princeton Univ Pr, 1987.
Richardson, Robert C. *Nous*, 27(4), 536-539, D 93.

Bakhurst, David. *Consciousness and Revolution in Soviet Philosophy*. New York, Cambridge Univ Pr, 1991.
Jones, Peter E. *Hist Human Sci*, 7(4), 105-118, N 94.
Nemeth, Thomas. *Stud East Euro Thought*, 47(1-2), 144-148, Je 95.

Balasubramanian, R (ed). *Tolerance in Indian Culture*. New Delhi, Indian Coun Phil Res, 1992.
Mukerjee, Asha. *J Indian Counc Phil Res*, 11(2), 142-145, Ja-Ap 94.

Balcázar, José Luis, Díaz, Josep and Gabarró, Joaquim. *Structural Complexity I*. New York, Springer-Verlag, 1988.
Allender, Eric. *J Sym Log*, 59(4), 1436-1437, D 94.

Balcázar, José Luis, Díaz, Josep and Gabarró, Joaquim. *Structural Complexity II*. New York, Springer-Verlag, 1990.
Allender, Eric. *J Sym Log*, 59(4), 1436-1437, D 94.

Baldini, A Enzo (ed). *Botero e la 'Ragion di Stato'*. Florence, Olschki, 1992.
Black, Antony. *Hist Polit Thought*, 15(2), 299-303, Sum 94.

Baldwin, Thomas. *G E Moore*. London, Routledge, 1990.
Wetterström, Thomas. *Theoria*, 58(1), 223-227, 1992.

Balibar, Étienne. *La philosophie de Marx*. Paris, La Découverte, 1993.
Jean, Michel. *Philosopher*, 15, 237-239, 1994.

Balke, Friedrich, Méchoulan, Eric and Wagner, Benno. *Zeit des Ereignisses - Ende der Geschichte?*. Munchen, Wilhelm Fink, 1992.
Hinz, Manfred. *Das Argument*, 208, 120-121, Ja-F 95.

Baltes, Peter. *Lebenstechnik*. Darmstadt, Wiss Buchgesell, 1993.
Rösser, Hans-Otto. *Das Argument*, 207, 984-985, N-D 94.

Balzer, Noel. *The Human Being as a Logical Thinker*. Amsterdam, Rodopi, 1993.
Henry, D P. *Hist Phil Log*, 15(2), 254-255, 1994.

Barat, Michel. *La conversion du regard*. Paris cedex 14, Albin Michel, 1992.
Collin, Claude. *Philosopher*, 14, 221-227, 1993.

Barber, Michael D. *Guardian of Dialogue*. Lewisburg, Bucknell Univ Pr, 1993.
Dunlop, Francis. *J Brit Soc Phenomenol*, 26(1), 99-101, Ja 95.
Schalow, Frank. *Hist Euro Ideas*, 18(6), 993-995, N 94.

Barcalow, Emmett. *Open Questions*. Belmont, Wadsworth, 1992.
Athanasopoulos, Constantinos. *Can Phil Rev*, 14(4), 232-233, Ag 94.
Katz, Jonathan. *Can Phil Rev*, 14(3), 159-162, Je 94.

Barcellona, Pietro. *Postmodernidad y comunidad*. Madrid, Ed Trotta, 1992.
Cambrón, Ascensión. *Telos*, 2(1), 140-144, Je 93.

Barham, Peter. *Schizophrenia and Human Value*. London, Free Assoc Books, 1993.
New, Caroline. *Rad Phil*, 71, 45-46, My-Je 95.

Barilli, Renato and Pinkus, Karen E (trans). *A Course on Aesthetics*. Minneapolis, Univ of Minn Pr, 1993.
Wilkinson, Robert. *Brit J Aes*, 35(2), 173-174, Ap 95.

Barineau, R Maurice. *The Theodicy of Alfred North Whitehead*. Lanham, Univ Pr of America, 1991.
Cobb Jr, John B. *Int Stud Phil*, 26(4), 107-108, 1994.
McCutcheon, Russell T. *Process Stud*, 22(1), 51-54, Spr 93.

Barker, Peter (ed) and Ariew, Roger (ed). *Revolution and Continuity*. Washington, Cath Univ Amer Pr, 1991.
Lu, Yan. *Phil Hist Sci*, 2(1), 97-99, Ap 93.

Barker, Philip. *Michel Foucault: Subversions of the Subject*. Hertfordshire, Harvester-Wheatsheaf, 1993.
Anchor, Robert. *Hist Theor*, 34(1), 122-132, 1995.
Hadfield, Andrew. *Rad Phil*, 70, 38-40, Mr-Ap 95.

Barker, Stephen. *Autoaesthetics*. Atlantic Highlands, Humanities Pr, 1992.
Altizer, Thomas J J. *Int Stud Phil*, 27(2), 111-112, 1995.

Barkow, J H (ed) and Tooby, J (ed). *The Adapted Mind: Evolutionary Psychology and the Generation of Culture*. New York, Oxford Univ Pr, 1992.
Sterenly, Kim. *Biol Phil*, 10(3), 365-380, July 95.

Barnard, F M. *Pluralism, Socialism and Political Legitimacy*. New York, Cambridge Univ Pr, 1991.
Velímsky, Vitezslav. *Hist Euro Ideas*, 18(6), 973-975, N 94.

Barnes, Jonathan. *The Toils of Scepticism*. New York, Cambridge Univ Pr, 1990.
Silverman, Allan. *Phoenix*, 48(2), 165-170, Sum 94.

Barney, Gerald O. *Global 200C Revisited*. Arlington, Millennium, 1993.
Rue, Loyal D. *Zygon*, 30(2), 331-332, Je 95.

Barooshian, Vahan D. *V V Vereshchagin*. Gainesville, Univ Pr of Florida, 1993.
James, Helen. *Brit J Aes*, 34(4), 412-414, O 94.

Barr, Ian (ed). *A Sense of Belonging*. Dundee, Scot Consult Cncl, 1994.
Hyland, Terry. *J Moral Educ*, 24(1), 81-83, 1995.

Barrett, Michele. *The Politics of Truth*. Oxford, Polity Pr, 1991.
Stevenson, Nicholas. *Theor Cult Soc*, 11(2), 169-173, My 94.

Barrow, John D. *Pi in the Sky*. New York, Clarendon/Oxford Pr, 1992.
Espinoza, Miguel. *Dialogos*, 30(65), 230-237, Ja 95.
Espinoza, Miguel. *Rev Phil Fr*, 1, 119-121, Ja-Mr 95.

Barry, Brian (ed) and Goodin, Robert E (ed). *Free Movement*. University Park, Penn St Univ Pr, 1992.
Carmichael, Don. *Can Phil Rev*, 14(1), 7-9, F 94.

Barth, Ulrich. *Christentum und Selbstbewusstsein*. Göttingen, Vandenhoeck, 1983.
Moxter, Michael. *Phil Rundsch*, 41(2), 133-158, 1994.

Barwise, Jon and Etchemendy, John. *The Language of First-Order Logic (Third Edition)*. Chicago, Univ of Chicago Pr, 1992.
Marinoff, Louis. *Can Phil Rev*, 14(3), 162-164, Je 94.

Basalla, George. *The Evolution of Technology*. New York, Cambridge Univ Pr, 1988.
Ilerbaig, Juan F. *Res Phil Technol*, 14, 302-306, 1994.

Bataille, Georges. *On Nietzsche*. New York, Paragon House, 1994.
Reinert, Thomas. *Phil Lit*, 19(1), 169-170, Ap 95.
Richey, Lance Byron. *Dialogue (PST)*, 37(1), 36-37, O 94.

Battaglia, Luisella. *Lo specchio oscuro*. Torino, Satyagraha Ed, 1993.
Bazzicalupo, Laura. *Riv Int Filosof Diritto*, 71(3), 517-518, 1994.

Baudrillard, Jean. *L'illusion de la fin ou la grève des événements*. Parigi, Ed Galilee, 1992.
López, José Ramón Romero. *Daimon Rev Filosof*, 7, 195-196, 1993.

Baudrillard, Jean and Benedict, James (trans). *The Transparency of Evil*. New York, Verso, 1993.
O'Reilly, John. *Rad Phil*, 68, 57, Autumn 94.

Baudrillard, Jean and Gane, Mike (ed). *Baudrillard Live*. New York, Routledge, 1993.
O'Reilly, John. *Rad Phil*, 68, 57, Autumn 94.

Bauman, Zygmunt. *Postmodern Ethics*. Oxford, Blackwell, 1993.
Gilbert, Paul. *J Applied Phil*, 12(2), 207-209, 1995.

Bausch, Thomas. *Gerechtigkeit und Ungleichheit*. Berlin, Duncker Humblot, 1993.
Kissling, Christian. *Frei Z Phil Theol*, 41(1-2), 278-279, 1994.

Bausola, Adriano (ed) and Reale, Giovanni (ed). *AAVV, Aristotele: Perqué la metafisica*. Milano, Vita Pensiero, 1994.
Velázquez, Héctor. *Topicos*, 4(6), 178-181, 1994.

Baxter, Timothy M S. *The Cratylus*. Leiden, Brill, 1992.
Anagnostopoulos, Georgios. *J Hist Phil*, 32(4), 661-663, O 94.
Lavery, Jonathan. *Can Phil Rev*, 14(1), 9-11, F 94.

Bayerová, Marie. *Bernard Bolzano*. Praha, Nakladatelstvi, 1994.
Snebergová, Irena. *Filozof Cas*, 42(6), 1052-1055, 1994.

Bayle, Pierre. *De la tolérance*. Pr Pocket, 1992.
Solasse, Marie-Anne. *Laval Theol Phil*, 51(1), 201-204, F 95.

Bayles, Michael D. *Hart's Legal Philosophy*. Dordrecht, Kluwer, 1992.
Waluchow, W J. *Can Phil Rev*, 14(4), 234-235, Ag 94.

Bazán, Francisco García. *Plotino: Sobre la trascendencia divina*. Mendoza, Univ Nacional Cuyo, 1992.
Ritacco de Gayoso, Graciela L.. *Sapientia*, 49(193-4), 385-387, 1994.

Beakley, Brian (ed) and Ludlow, Peter (ed). *Philosophy of Mind*. Cambridge, MIT Pr, 1992.
Matthews, Gareth B. *Behavior Phil*, 22(1), 75-77, Spr-Sum 94.

Becker, Jill S, Breedlove, S Marc and Crews, David. *Behavioral Endocrinology*. Cambridge, MIT Pr, 1992.
Longino, Helen E. *Phil Psych*, 7(3), 401-404, 1994.

Beckermann, Ansgar (ed), Flohr, Hans (ed) and Kim, Jaegwon (ed). *Emergence or Reduction?*. Hawthorne, de Gruyter, 1992.
Stoecker, Ralf. *Phil Phenomenol Res*, 55(3), 701-706, S 95.

Beckwith, Francis J. *Politically Correct Death*. Grand Rapids, Baker Book, 1993.
Conley, John J. *Int Phil Quart*, 34(4), 509-511, D 94.

Bedani, Gino. *Vico Revisited, Orthodoxy, Naturalism and Science in the 'Scienza Nuova'*. Oxford, Berg, 1989.
Mazzola, Roberto. *Boll Centro Stud Vichiani*, 24-25, 275-277, 1994-95.

Beiner, Ronald. *What's the Matter With Liberalism?*. Berkeley, Univ of Calif Pr, 1992.
McLeod, N T. *Can Phil Rev*, 14(3), 165-166, Je 94.

Beiner, Ronald (ed) and Booth, William James (ed). *Kant and Political Philosophy*. New Haven, Yale Univ Pr, 1993.
McCarty, Richard. *Rev Metaph*, 48(2), 392-393, D 94.

Beiser, Frederick C. *Enlightenment, Revolution and Romanticism*. Cambridge, Harvard Univ Pr, 1992.
Deligiorgi, Katerina. *Rad Phil*, 69, 49-50, Ja-F 95.

Beiser, Frederick C (ed). *The Cambridge Companion to Hegel*. New York, Cambridge Univ Pr, 1993.
Inwood, M J. *Bull Hegel Soc Gt Brit*, 30, 45-49, Autumn-Wint 94.
O'Connor, Brian. *Phil Books*, 35(3), 179-180, Jl 94.

Belfiore, Elizabeth. *Tragic Pleasures*. Princeton, Princeton Univ Pr, 1992.
Seale, David. *Phoenix*, 48(4), 351-359, Winter 94.

Bell, Daniel. *Communitarianism and its Critics*. New York, Clarendon/Oxford Pr, 1993.
Edgar, Andrew. *Phil Books*, 36(1), 66-67, Ja 95.
Forst, Rainer. *Euro J Phil*, 3(1), 97-100, Ap 95.
Forst, Rainer. *J Phil Educ*, 29(1), 97-104, March 95.
MacIntyre, Alasdair. *Rad Phil*, 70, 34-35, Mr-Ap 95.

Bell, David (ed) and Vossenkuhl, Wilhelm (ed). *Wissenschaft und Subjektivität*. Berlin, Akademie, 1992.
Mormann, Thomas. *Z Phil Forsch*, 48(4), 631-637, 1994.

Bell, Richard H (ed). *Simone Weil's Philosophy of Culture*. New York, Cambridge Univ Pr, 1993.
Gealy, Walford. *Phil Invest*, 18(1), 92-96, Ja 95.

Bellamy, Richard (ed) and Cox, Virginia (trans). *Antonio Gramsci: Pre-Prison Writings*. New York, Cambridge Univ Pr, 1994.
Hoffman, John. *Bull Hegel Soc Gt Brit*, 30, 87-90, Autumn-Wint 94.
Martin, James. *Hist Polit Thought*, 15(2), 290-291, Sum 94.

Bellamy, Richard and Schecter, Darrow. *Gramsci and the Italian State*. Manchester, Manchester Univ Pr, 1993.
Hoffman, John. *Bull Hegel Soc Gt Brit*, 30, 87-90, Autumn-Wint 94.
Martin, James. *Hist Polit Thought*, 16(1), 144-148, Spr 95.

Belliotti, Raymond A. *Good Sex*. Lawrence, Univ Pr Kansas, 1993.
Archard, David. *Phil Quart*, 45(180), 407-408, Jl 95.

Belsey, A (ed) and Chadwick, R (ed). *Ethical Issues in Journalism and the Media*. New York, Routledge, 1992.
Kieran, Matthew. *Phil Quart*, 45(180), 408-410, Jl 95.

Ben-Ze'ev, Aaron. *The Perceptual System*. New York, Lang, 1993.
Cogan, Ross. *Can Phil Rev*, 14(5), 308-310, O 94.

Benardete, Seth. *Socrates' Second Sailing*. Chicago, Univ of Chicago Pr, 1992.
Held, Dirk T D. *Can Phil Rev*, 15(1), 9-11, F 95.

Benardete, Seth. *The Rhetoric of Morality and Philosophy*. Chicago, Univ of Chicago Pr, 1991.
Vaughan, Frederick. *Phil Rhet*, 28(2), 160-162, 1995.

Bencivenga, Ermanno. *Kant's Copernican Revolution*. New York, Oxford Univ Pr, 1987.
George, Rolf. *Kantstudien*, 86(1), 87-89, 1995.

Bencivenga, Ermanno. *Logic and Other Nonsense: The Case of Anselm and His God*. Princeton, Princeton Univ Pr, 1993.
Dore, Clement. *Notre Dame J Form Log*, 35(3), 464-468, Sum 94.

Bencivenga, Ermanno. *Oltre la tolleranza*. Milano, Feltrinelli, 1992.
Parasiliti, Sandro. *Riv Int Filosof Diritto*, 71(2), 349-350, 1994.

Bencivenga, Ermanno. *The Discipline of Subjectivity*. Princeton, Princeton Univ Pr, 1990.
Bond, Daniel Berthold. *Nous*, 27(3), 403-406, S 93.

Bender, John (ed). *The Current State of the Coherence Theory*. Dordrecht, Kluwer, 1989.
Greco, John. *Nous*, 27(1), 111-113, Mr 93.

Benedikt, Michael. *Heideggers Halbwelt*. Vienna, Turia & Kant, 1992.
Cristin, Renato. *Filosofia*, 45(3), 401-405, S-D 94.

Bengoa Ruiz de Azua, Javier. *De Heidegger a Habermas*. Barcelona, Herder, 1992.
Gil Martín, Francisco Javier. *Dialogo Filosof*, 11(1), 109-112, Ja-Ap 95.

Benhabib, Seyla. *Situating the Self*. New York, Routledge, 1992.
Funk, Nanette. *Phil Rev*, 103(3), 562-564, Jl 94.

Benjamin, Andrew (ed) and Osborne, Peter (ed). *Walter Benjamin's Philosophy*. New York, Routledge, 1994.
Rampley, Matthew. *Brit J Aes*, 35(2), 180-181, Ap 95.

Benjamin, Martin. *Splitting the Difference*. Lawrence, Univ Pr Kansas, 1990.
Forrester, James. *Nous*, 27(1), 85-89, Mr 93.

Bennett, Jane (ed) and Chaloupka, William (ed). *In the Nature of Things*. Minneapolis, Univ of Minn Pr, 1993.
Welsh, Michael. *Environ Ethics*, 17(3), 327-330, Fall 95.

Bennett, Jonathan. *Events and Their Names*. Indianapolis, Hackett, 1988.
Cleland, Carol E. *Nous*, 28(1), 103-109, Mr 94.

Benoit, Michèle, Carré, Michel and Tozzi, Michel. *Étude philosophique d'une notion, d'un texte*. Montpellier, l'Acad Montpellier, 1993.
Jean, Michel. *Philosopher*, 17, 321-324, 1995.

Brown, Stuart (ed). *Nicolas Malebranche: His Philosophical Critics and Successors*. Assen, Gorcum, 1991.
Cottingham, John. *Locke News*, 25, 120-124, 1994.

Browning, Don S (ed) and Evison, Ian S (ed). *Does Psychiatry Need a Public Philosophy?*. Chicago, Nelson Hall, 1991.
Elliott, Carl. *J Value Inq*, 28(2), 357-359, Je 94.

Brümmer, Vincent (ed). *Interpreting the Universe as Creation*. Kampen, Kok, 1991.
Koltermann, R. *Theol Phil*, 70(1), 149-150, 1995.

Brümmer, Vincent. *The Model of Love*. New York, Cambridge Univ Pr, 1993.
Grey, Mary. *Relig Stud*, 30(4), 536-537, D 94.

Brugger, Bill and Kelly, David. *Chinese Marxism in the Post-Mao Era*. Stanford, Stanford Univ Pr, 1990.
Phil East West, 45(1), 135-136, Ja 95.
Breslin, Shaun. *Hist Polit Thought*, 15(2), 305-306, Sum 94.

Brulé, James F and Blount, Alexander. *Knowledge Acquisition*. New York, McGraw-Hill, 1989.
Shalin, Valerie L. *Mind Mach*, 5(2), 257-261, My 95.

Brumbaugh, Robert S. *Western Philosophic Systems and Their Cyclic Transformations*. Carbondale, So Illinois Univ Pr, 1992.
Baird, Robert M. *Rev Metaph*, 48(4), 887-889, Je 95.

Brun, Jean. *La Philosophie de Pascal*. Paris, Pr Univ France, 1992.
Moreau, Denis. *Rev Thomiste*, 94(2), 336-338, Ap-Je 94.

Bruno, G. *Del infinito: el universo y los mundos*. Madrid, Alianza, 1993.
Gutiérrez Soler, Julio A. *Daimon Rev Filosof*, 8, 235-236, 1994.
Gutiérrez Soler, Julio A. *Rev Filosof (Spain)*, 8, 235-236, 1994.

Bruns, Gerald L. *Ancient and Modern Hermeneutics*. New Haven, Yale Univ Pr, 1992.
Halliburton, David. *Phil Lit*, 19(1), 158-160, Ap 95.

Bruns, Gerald L. *Hermeneutics Ancient and Modern*. New Haven, Yale Univ Pr, 1992.
Warnke, Georgia. *Metaphilosophy*, 26(1-2), 161-165, Ja-Ap 95.

Brykman, Geneviève. *Berkeley et le voile des mots*. Paris, Vrin, 1993.
Berlioz, Dominique. *Rev Metaph Morale*, 99(4), 573-574, O-D 94.

Buarque, Cristovam. *The End of Economics*. London, Zed Books, 1993.
Zadek, Simon. *Environ Values*, 3(3), 273-274, Autumn 94.

Buchdahl, Gerd. *Kant and the Dynamics of Reason*. Cambridge, Blackwell, 1992.
Adair-Toteff, Christopher. *Brit J Hist Phil*, 3(1), 192-194, F 95.
Neiman, Susan. *Phil Rev*, 103(4), 763-765, O 94.

Buchman, Margret and Floden, Robert. *Detachment and Concern*. London, Cassell, 1993.
Sullivan, John. *Heythrop J*, 36(2), 236-237, Ap 95.

Buckle, Stephen. *Natural Law and the Theory of Property*. New York, Clarendon/Oxford Pr, 1991.
Jarvad, Ib Martin. *Hist Euro Ideas*, 21(3), 469-470, My 95.

Buckler, Steve. *Dirty Hands*. Brookfield, Avebury, 1993.
Williams, John R. *Heythrop J*, 36(1), 102-103, Ja 95.

Buckley, R Philip. *Husserl, Heidegger, and the Crisis of Philosophical Responsibility*. Dordrecht, Kluwer, 1992.
Aylesworth, Gary E. *Can Phil Rev*, 15(1), 11-13, F 95.
Hanas, James C. *Husserl Stud*, 11(3), 219-224, 1994-95.
Vedder, Ben. *Tijdschr Filosof*, 57(1), 146-147, Mr 95.

Büchner, Hartmut (ed). *Japan und Heidegger*. Sigmaringen, 1989.
Osier, Jean-Pierre. *Rev Metaph Morale*, 99(4), 557-558, O-D 94.

Buela, Alberto. *Epítome de Antropología*. Buenos Aires, Ed Cultura Labor, 1993.
Torres, Eugenio. *Analogía*, 8(1), 201-202, 1994.

Buhr, Manfred and Losurdo, Domenico. *Fichte: die französische Revolution und das Ideal vom ewigen Frieden*. Berlin, Akademie, 1991.
Radrizzani, Ives. *Arch Phil*, 58(1), 157-158, Ja-Mr 95.

Bukatman, Scott. *Terminal Identity*. Durham, Duke Univ Pr, 1993.
Armitage, John. *Rad Phil*, 68, 58, Autumn 94.

Bulger, R E (ed), Heitman, E (ed) and Reiser, S J (ed). *The Ethical Dimensions of the Biological Sciences*. New York, Cambridge Univ Pr, 1993.
Beckwith, Francis J. *Can Phil Rev*, 14(4), 242-243, Ag 94.
Gilman, Daniel. *J Med Human*, 16(2), 141-146, Sum 95.

Bulhof, Ilse N. *The Language of Science*. Leiden, Brill, 1992.
Curtis, Ronald. *Phil Soc Sci*, 24(4), 510-516, D 94.

Bullough, Vern L (ed) and Madigan, Timothy J (ed). *Toward a New Enlightenment*. New Brunswick, Transaction Books, 1994.
Rockler, Michael J. *Free Inq*, 14(3), 58-59, Sum 94.

Bungies, W (& other eds). *Sämtliche Schriften und Briefe*. Berlin, Akademie, 1990.
De Salas, Jaime. *Rev Filosof (Spain)*, 4(6), 437-439, 1991.

Burbidge, John W. *Hegel on Logic and Religion*. Albany, SUNY Pr, 1992.
Dahlstrom, Daniel O. *Rev Metaph*, 48(2), 395-397, D 94.
Westphal, Merold. *Int Stud Phil*, 26(4), 113, 1994.

Burke, Peter. *A Revoluçao Francesa da Historiografia*. Sao Paulo, UNESP, 1991.
Reis, Andréa Ermantina. *Educ Filosof*, 8(16), 303-308, Jl-D 94.

Burnyeat, Myles. *The Theaetetus of Plato*. Indianapolis, Hackett, 1990.
Glidden, David K. *Nous*, 27(3), 408-409, S 93.

Burrell, David B. *Freedom and Creation in Three Traditions*. Notre Dame, Univ Notre Dame Pr, 1993.
Idziak, Janine Marie. *Int J Phil Relig*, 37(3), 181-183, Je 95.
Koterski, Joseph W. *Int Phil Quart*, 35(1), 102-103, Mr 95.

Burton, Steven. *Judging in Good Faith*. New York, Cambridge Univ Pr, 1992.
Macleod, Colin. *Phil Rev*, 103(3), 559-562, Jl 94.

Busch, Thomas W. *The Power of Consciousness and the Force of Circumstances in Sartre's Philosophy*. Bloomington, Indiana Univ Pr, 1990.
Santoni, Ronald E. *J Brit Soc Phenomenol*, 26(1), 105-108, Ja 95.

Busch, Thomas W (ed) and Gallagher, Shaun (ed). *Merleau-Ponty, Hermeneutics, and Postmodernism*. Albany, SUNY Pr, 1992.
Gauthier, Jeffrey. *Can Phil Rev*, 14(5), 312-315, O 94.

Butler, Judith. *Bodies That Matter*. New York, Routledge, 1993.
Watts, Carol. *Rad Phil*, 71, 41-42, My-Je 95.

C, Molina Petit. *Dialéctiva feminista de la Ilustración*. Barcelona, Anthropos, 1994.
Cano López, Antonio José. *Rev Filosof (Spain)*, 8, 240-241, 1994.

Cabanchik, Samuel. *El revés de la filosofía*. Padua, Biblos, 1993.
Leclerq, Mariano Garreta. *Rev Filosof (Argentina)*, 9(1-2), 113-116, N 94.

Cabral, R (& other eds). *Portugalsko-brazilská filosofická encyklopedie, Vol III*. Verbo, Lisabon-Sao Paulo, 1991.
Kourím, Zdenek. *Filozof Cas*, 43(1), 153-156, 1994.

Cabral, R (& other eds). *Portugalsko-brazilská filosofická encyklopedie, Vol IV*. Verbo, Lisabon-Sao Paulo, 1992.
Kourím, Zdenek. *Filozof Cas*, 43(1), 153-156, 1994.

Caffarena, Jose Gomez (ed). *Enciclopedia Iberoamericana de Filosofia. Vol 3*. Madrid, Trotta, 1993.
Capanna, Pablo. *Rev Latin de Filosof*, 21(1), 174-176, Fall 95.

Cahn, Steven M (ed). *Affirmative Action and the University*. Philadelphia, Temple Univ Pr, 1993.
Boxill, Bernard R. *Ethics*, 105(3), 672-674, April.

Cairns, Douglas L. *Aidos: The Psychology and Ethics of Honour and Shame in Ancient Greek Literature*. New York, Clarendon/Oxford Pr, 1993.
Belfiore, Elizabeth. *Amer J Philo*, 115(4), 609-612, Wint 94.

Caleo, Marcello. *Kant e il suo doppio*. Salerno, Ed Dottrinari, 1994.
Carrano, Andrea. *Sapienza*, 47(4), 491-494, O-D 94.

Calhoun, Craig. *Bourdieu: Critical Perspectives*. Chicago, Univ of Chicago Pr, 1993.
De Greiff, Pablo. *Ethics*, 105(4), 957-959, Jl 95.

Calhoun, Craig (ed). *Habermas and the Public Sphere*. Cambridge, MIT Pr, 1992.
Hirschkind, Charles. *Conference*, 4(2), 90-99, Fall 93.

Callahan, Daniel. *The Troubled Dream of Life*. New York, Simon & Schuster, 1993.
Purdy, Laura M. *Bioethics*, 9(2), 175-178, Ap 95.

Callicott, J Baird. *Earth's Insights*. Berkeley, Univ of Calif Pr, 1994.
Tucker, Mary Evelyn. *Environ Ethics*, 17(3), 321-325, Fall 95.

Calvo Martízen, Tomás (ed) and Crespo, Avila (ed). *Paur Ricoeur: los caminos de la interpretación*. Barcelona, Anthropos, 1991.
Cabrera Sánchez, Carlos. *An Seminar Metaf*, 27, 307-313, 1993.

Campbell, John. *Past, Space and Self*. Cambridge, MIT Pr, 1994.
Cockburn, David. *Phil Invest*, 18(3), 297-300, Jl 95.
de Gaynesford, R M. *Phil Quart*, 45(179), 243-245, Ap 95.

Campbell, Richard. *Truth and Historicity*. New York, Oxford Univ Pr, 1992.
Stoothoff, Robert. *Austl J Phil*, 72(4), 532-534, D 94.

Camps, Victoria, Guariglia, Osvaldo and Salmeron, Fernando (ed). *Enciclopedia Iberoamericana de Filosofia. Vol II*. Madrid, Trotta, 1992.
Bertomeu, María Julia. *Rev Latin de Filosof*, 21(1), 173-174, Fall 95.

Canfield, John V (ed) and Shanker, Stuart G (ed). *Wittgenstein's Intentions*. Hamden, Garland, 1993.
Cohen, Michael. *Phil Books*, 35(3), 182-183, Jl 94.

Cannon, Betty. *Sartre et la psychanalyse*. Paris, PUF, 1993.
Guilbert, Jean-Luc. *Philosopher*, 17, 304-306, 1995.

Canovan, Margaret. *Hannah Arendt: A Reinterpretation of Her Political Thought*. New York, Cambridge Univ Pr, 1992.
De Greiff, Pablo. *Int J Phil Stud*, 3(1), 179-182, Mr 95.
Disch, Lisa J. *Hist Polit Thought*, 15(3), 462-464, Autumn 94.
Knauer, James T. *Int Stud Phil*, 26(4), 114, 1994.

Caplan, Arthur L. *If I Were a Rich Man Could I Buy a Pancreas?*. Bloomington, Indiana Univ Pr, 1992.
Menzel, Paul T. *J Clin Ethics*, 5(2), 172-173, Sum 94.

Caporali, Riccardo. *Heroes gentium*. Bologna, Il Mulino, 1992.
Lomonaco, Fabrizio. *Boll Centro Stud Vichiani*, 24-25, 286-289, 1994-95.

Caporaso, James A and Levine, David P. *Theories of Political Economy*. New York, Cambridge Univ Pr, 1992.
Baker, Dean. *Econ Phil*, 10(2), 354-359, O 94.

Capozzi, Gino. *Filosofia, scienza e "praxis" del diritto*. Napoli, Jovene Ed, 1992.
Parasiliti, Sandro. *Riv Int Filosof Diritto*, 71(3), 520-521, 1994.

Coffa, J Alberto. *The Semantic Tradition from Kant to Carnap*. New York, Cambridge Univ Pr, 1991.
George, Rolf. *Kantstudien*, 86(1), 102-105, 1995.
Pigden, Charles. *Phil Soc Sci*, 24(4), 522-525, D 94.
Rumfitt, Ian. *Brit J Hist Phil*, 3(1), 205-207, F 95.

Cohen, Avner and Dascal, Marcelo. *The Institution of Philosophy*. Peru, Open Court, 1989.
Cremaschi, Sergio. *Riv Filosof Neo-Scolas*, 86(3), 609-613, Jl-S 94.

Cohen, Hermann (ed). *Helmut Holzhey (Auslegungen 4)*. New York, Lang, 1994.
Ollig, H L. *Theol Phil*, 70(1), 113-114, 1995.

Cohen, Jean and Arato, Andrew. *Civil Society and Political Theory*. Cambridge, MIT Pr, 1992.
Axtmann, Roland. *Theor Cult Soc*, 12(1), 175-179, F 95.

Cohen, L Jonathan. *An Essay on Belief and Acceptance*. New York, Clarendon/Oxford Pr, 1992.
Moore, Joseph. *Phil Rev*, 103(4), 705-709, O 94.
Radford, Colin. *Mind*, 104(413), 154-162, Ja 95.

Cohen, Morris R, Nagel, Ernest and Corcoran, John (ed). *An Introduction To Logic*. Indianapolis, Hackett, 1993.
Dipert, Randall R. *Trans Peirce Soc*, 30(4), 1064-1068, Fall 94.

Cohen, Ted (ed), Guyer, Paul (ed) and Putnam, Hilary (ed). *Pursuits of Reason*. Lubbock, Texas Tech Univ Pr, 1993.
Lyas, Colin. *Can Phil Rev*, 14(4), 244-245, Ag 94.

Colburn, Timothy R (ed), Fetzer, James H (ed) and Rankin, Terry L (ed). *Program Verification*. Dordrecht, Kluwer, 1993.
Burkholder, Leslie. *Can Phil Rev*, 15(1), 22-25, F 95.

Cole, John R. *The Olympian Dreams and Youthful Rebellion of René Descartes*. Champaign, Univ of Illinois Pr, 1992.
Watson, Richard A. *Int Stud Phil*, 26(4), 116-117, 1994.

Cole, Thomas. *The Origins of Rhetoric in Ancient Greece*. Baltimore, Johns Hopkins U Pr, 1991.
Murray, James S. *Phoenix*, 48(3), 262-264, Autumn 94.

Cole-Turner, Ronald. *Alexander Response to Cole-Turner (The New Genesis: Theology and the Genetic Revolution)*. 1994.
Alexander, Denis R. *Zygon*, 30(2), 345-346, Je 95.

Cole-Turner, Ronald. *The New Genesis*. Louisville, Westminster Pr, 1993.
Mitchell, C Ben. *Ethics Med*, 11(2), 47-48, .

Collier, Andrew. *Critical Realism*. New York, Verso, 1994.
Elliott, Gregory. *Rad Phil*, 69, 48-49, Ja-F 95.

Collingwood, R G and van der Dussen, J (ed). *The Idea of History*. Oxford, Clarendon/Oxford Pr, 1993.
Adam, A M. *Phil Soc Sci*, 25(2), 256-258, Je 95.

Collins, Harry and Pinch, Trevor. *The Golem*. New York, Cambridge Univ Pr, 1993.
Hull, David L. *Phil Sci*, 62(3), 487-488, S 95.
Nickles, Thomas. *Brit J Phil Sci*, 46(2), 261-266, Je 95.
Wilde, Rein de. *Kennis Methode*, 18(2-3), 279-285, 1994.

Collomb, Michel and Raulet, Gérard (ed). *Critique de l'ornement, de Vienne à la postmodernité*. Paris, Ed Klincksieck, 1992.
Ruelland, Jacques G. *Philosopher*, 14, 241-244, 1993.

Colomer, Eusebi. *El idealismo*. Barcelona, Herder, 1986.
Caimi, Mario. *Kantstudien*, 85(4), 473-477, 1994.

Colomer, Eusebi. *El pensamiento alemán de Kant a Heidegger*. Barcelona, Herder, 1986.
Caimi, Mario. *Kantstudien*, 85(4), 473-477, 1994.

Come, Arnold B. *Trendelenburg's Influence on Kierkegaard's Modal Categories*. Montreal, InterEditions, 1991.
McLelland, Joseph C. *Dialogue (Canada)*, 33(4), 772-773, Fall 94.

Cometti, Jean-Pierre. *Lire Rorty*. Combas, Ed l'Eclat, 1992.
Engel, Pascal. *Rev Phil Fr*, 4, 474-476, O-D 94.

Compagni, V Perrone. *Cornelius Agrippa, 'De occulta philosophia libri tres'*. Leiden, Brill, 1992.
Hamilton, Alastair. *Heythrop J*, 35(3), 333-334, Jl 94.

Composta, Dario. *Filosofia del diritto. II*. Roma, Pont Univ Urbaniana, 1994.
Ancona, Elvio. *Riv Int Filosof Diritto*, 71(4), 788-790, 1994.

Coniglione, F (ed), Poli, R (ed) and Wolenski, J (ed). *Polish Scientific Philosophy*. Amsterdam, Rodopi, 1993.
Misiuna, K. *Hist Phil Log*, 15(2), 242-243, 1994.

Connolly, William E. *The Augustinian Imperative*. Newbury Park, Sage, 1993.
Bruyneel, Kevin. *Conference*, 4(2), 102-105, Fall 93.

Conrad, Elfriede. *Kants Logikvorlesungen als neuer Schlüssel zur Architektonik der Kritik der reinen Vernunft*. Stuttgart, Frommann-Holzboog, 1994.
Schwaiger, Clemens. *Kantstudien*, 86(2), 248-251, 1995.

Contreras, Enrique and Pena, Roberto. *Introducción al estudio de los Padres Latinos de Nicea a Calcedonia*. Madrid, Ed Monasterio Trap, 1994.
Bergada, María Mercedes. *Pat Med*, 15, 93-95, 1994.

Conway, Gertrude D. *Wittgenstein on Foundations*. Atlantic Highlands, Humanities Pr, 1989.
Creegan, Charles. *Can Phil Rev*, 14(2), 82-84, Ap 94.

Cook, Deborah. *The Subject Finds a Voice*. New York, Lang, 1993.
Owen, David. *J Brit Soc Phenomenol*, 26(1), 101-103, Ja 95.

Cook, Patricia (ed). *Philosophical Imagination and Cultural Memory*. Durham, Duke Univ Pr, 1993.
Hamlyn, D W. *Hist Euro Ideas*, 18(6), 981-982, N 94.

Coolen, Maarten. *De Machine Voorbij*. Meppel, Boom, 1992.
Fleischhacker, L. *Alg Ned Tijdschr Wijs*, 87(1), 54-58, Ja 95.

Cooper, David (ed). *A Companion to Aesthetics*. Cambridge, Blackwell, 1992.
Wilkinson, Robert. *Hist Euro Ideas*, 18(5), 832-833, S 94.

Cooper, David E. *Metaphor*. Cambridge, Blackwell, 1986.
Roche, J P. *Lit Aes*, 1, 103, Spr 91.

Cooper, Ron L. *Heidegger and Whitehead*. Athens, Ohio Univ Pr, 1993.
Ford, Lewis S. *Mod Sch*, 72(1), 85-86, N 94.
Shade, Patrick. *Trans Peirce Soc*, 31(1), 246-253, Wint 95.

Copeland, Jack. *Artificial Intelligence: A Philosophical Introduction*. Cambridge, Blackwell, 1994.
Ross, Don. *Phil Books*, 36(3), 194-196, Jl 95.

Copenhaver, Brian P and Schmitt, Charles B. *Renaissance Philosophy*. New York, Oxford Univ Pr, 1992.
Burke, Peter. *Hist Euro Ideas*, 18(5), 811-812, S 94.
Hamilton, Alastair. *Heythrop J*, 36(1), 88-89, Ja 95.

Copp, David (ed), Hampton, Jean (ed) and Roemer, John E (ed). *The Idea of Democracy*. New York, Cambridge Univ Pr, 1993.
Archard, David. *Rad Phil*, 68, 48-50, Autumn 94.
Goodin, Robert E. *Ethics*, 105(2), 425-426, Ja 95.

Corazza, Eros and Dokic, Jérôme. *Penser en contexte*. Combas, Ed l'Eclat, 1993.
Vallée, Richard. *Dialogue (Canada)*, 33(3), 556-559, Sum 94.

Corbin, Michel. *L'aeuvre de S Anselme de Cantorbéry*. Paris, Cerf, 1988.
Benoist, Jocelyn. *Arch Phil*, 58(2), 268-271, Ap-Je 95.

Corbin, Michel. *Prière et raison de la foi*. Paris, Cerf, 1992.
Bastit, Michel. *Rev Thomiste*, 94(2), 332-333, Ap-Je 94.

Cordón, Juan Manuel Navarro and Rodríguez, Ramon. *Heidegger o el final de la filosofía*. Madrid, Ed Complutense, 1993.
Pascual, Andrés Sánchez. *Convivium*, 6, 129-133, 1994.

Corey, M A. *God and the New Cosmology*. Lanham, Rowman & Littlefield, 1993.
Jeffery, Andrew V. *Can Phil Rev*, 14(4), 246-248, Ag 94.
Krettek, Thomas. *Int Phil Quart*, 34(4), 505-507, D 94.
Wilson, Patrick A. *Amer Cath Phil Quart*, 68(4), 548-553, Autumn 94.

Cori, René and Lascar, Daniel. *Logique Mathématique I*. Paris, Masson Ed, 1993.
Bélair, Luc. *J Sym Log*, 60(2), 691-692, Je 95.

Cori, René and Lascar, Daniel. *Logique Mathématique II*. Paris, Masson Ed, 1993.
Bélair, Luc. *J Sym Log*, 60(2), 691-692, Je 95.

Correas, Carlos I M. *Ecología y filosofía*. Mendoza, Eulum, 1993.
Crespo, Ricardo F. *Sapientia*, 49(193-4), 396-398, 1994.

Correas, Carlos I M. *Filosofía del derecho*. Buenos Aires, Abeledo Perrot, 1994.
Crespo, Ricardo F. *Sapientia*, 49(193-4), 399-400, 1994.

Corrington, Robert S. *Nature and Spirit*. Bronx, Fordham Univ Pr, 1992.
Neville, Robert Cummings. *Int Phil Quart*, 34(4), 504-505, D 94.
Ryder, John. *Metaphilosophy*, 26(1-2), 138-146, Ja-Ap 95.

Cortina, Adela. *Ética aplicada y democracia radical*. Madrid, Tecnos, 1993.
López, M Teresa. *Telos*, 3(1), 130-134, Je 94.

Cosi, Giovanni. *Il Logos del diritto*. Turin, Giappichelli, 1993.
Palazzani, Laura. *Riv Int Filosof Diritto*, 71(2), 352-354, 1994.

Costanzo, Angelo. *Condizioni di incoerenza*. Milano, Giuffre, 1992.
Amato, Salvatore. *Riv Int Filosof Diritto*, 71(3), 524-526, 1994.

Costello, Paul. *World Historians and Their Goals*. DeKalb, No Illinois Univ Pr, 1993.
Breisach, Ernst A. *Clio*, 24(1), 91-94, Fall 94.

Cottingham, John. *A Descartes Dictionary*. Cambridge, Blackwell, 1993.
Buroker, Jill Vance. *Phil Books*, 35(3), 175-177, Jl 94.

Couloubaritsis, Lambros. *Aux origines de la philosophie européenne*. Bruxelles, De Boeck-Wesmael, 1992.
Montenot, Jean. *Rev Phil Fr*, 2, 223-224, Ap-Je 94.

Coval, S C and Campbell, P G. *Agency in Action*. Dordrecht, Kluwer, 1992.
Wyatt, Richard. *Mind Mach*, 5(2), 298-302, My 95.

Covell, Charles. *The Defense of Natural Law*. New York, Macmillan, 1992.
Lisska, Anthony J. *Heythrop J*, 35(3), 347-349, Jl 94.
Murphy Jr, Cornelius F. *Phil Quart*, 45(180), 399-400, Jl 95.

Coyle, J K (& others). *'De moribus ecclesiae catholicae et de moribus Manichaeorum'*. Palermo, Augustinus, 1991.
Bettetini, Maria. *Riv Filosof Neo-Scolas*, 86(3), 599-605, Jl-S 94.

Cozzo, C. *Teoria del significato e filosofia della logica*. Bologna, CLUEB, 1994.
Moriconi, Enrico. *Teoria*, 14(2), 148-149, 1994.

Craemer-Ruegenberg, Ingrid (ed) and Speer, Andreas (ed). *Scientia und Ars im Hoch- und Spätmittelalter*. Hawthorne, de Gruyter, 1994.
Gallagher, David M. *Rev Metaph*, 48(4), 891-892, Je 95.

Craig, Edward. *Was wir wissen können*. Frankfurt, Suhrkamp, 1993.
Willmann, T. *Theol Phil*, 70(1), 129-131, 1995.

Dummett, Michael. *Origins of Analytical Philosophy*. London, Duckworth, 1993.
Engel, Pascal. *Phil Quart*, 45(179), 268-271, Ap 95.

Dummett, Michael. *The Logical Basis of Metaphysics*. Cambridge, Harvard Univ Pr, 1991.
Purtill, Richard L. *Hist Euro Ideas*, 21(2), 297-298, Mr 95.

Dummett, Michael. *The Seas of Language*. New York, Clarendon/Oxford Pr, 1993.
Frapolli, Maria J. *Hist Phil Log*, 15(2), 245-246, 1994.
Taylor, Barry. *Austl J Phil*, 73(1), 157-159, Mr 95.
Wagner, Steven J. *Rev Metaph*, 48(4), 892-894, Je 95.
Williams, C J F. *Int Phil Quart*, 35(2), 230-231, Ju 95.

Dummett, Michael. *Ursprünge der analytischen Philosophie*. Frankfurt, Suhrkamp, 1988.
Cramm, Wolf-Jürgen. *Protosoz*, 1, 128-133, Ap 91.

Duncan, Carol. *The Aesthetics of Power*. New York, Cambridge Univ Pr, 1993.
Harris, Jonathan. *Brit J Aes*, 34(4), 411-412, O 94.

Dunlop, Charles (ed) and Kling, Rob (ed). *Computerization and Controversy*. Boston, Academic Pr, 1991.
Johnson, Deborah G. *Mind Mach*, 5(1), 142-144, F 95.

Dunlop, Francis. *Scheler (Thinkers of Our Time)*. London, Claridge Pr, 1991.
Coady, C A J. *Phil Quart*, 45(179), 273-275, Ap 95.

Dunn, John (ed). *Democracy: The Unfinished Journey*. New York, Oxford Univ Pr, 1992.
Ryan, Alan. *Ethics*, 105(2), 423-425, Ja 95.

Dunn, Robert. *The Possibility of Weakness of Will*. Indianapolis, Hackett, 1987.
Mele, Alfred R. *Nous*, 27(3), 384-385, S 93.

Dunne, Joseph. *Back to the Rough Ground*. Notre Dame, Univ Notre Dame Pr, 1993.
Fodor, Jim. *Mod Theol*, 11(2), 274-276, Ap 95.
Madigan, Arthur. *Int Phil Quart*, 35(1), 103-105, Mr 95.
Stuhr, John J. *Phil Lit*, 18(2), 360-361, O 94.
Woerner, Markus H. *Int J Phil Stud*, 3(1), 182-185, Mr 95.

Duponcheele, Joseph. *L'être de l'alliance*. Paris, Cerf, 1992.
Bedouelle, Thierry. *Rev Phil Louvain*, 92(4), 640-642, N 94.

Dupré, John. *The Disorder of Things*. Cambridge, Harvard Univ Pr, 1993.
Dowe, Phil. *Can Phil Rev*, 14(6), 387-389, D 94.
Hull, David L. *Phil Rev*, 103(4), 701-705, O 94.
Sklar, Lawrence. *Rev Metaph*, 48(2), 400-401, D 94.
Stent, Gunther S. *Biol Phil*, 9(4), 497-506, O 94.
Thalos, Mariam. *Phil Sci*, 62(2), 351-353, Je 95.

Dupré, Louis. *Metaphysics and Culture*. Milwaukee, Marquette Univ Pr, 1994.
Johnston, Suzie. *Laval Theol Phil*, 51(1), 216-218, F 95.

Dupré, Louis. *Passage to Modernity*. New Haven, Yale Univ Pr, 1993.
Kow, James Paul. *Can Phil Rev*, 14(4), 251-254, Ag 94.
Scharlemann, Robert P. *Mod Theol*, 11(2), 272-274, Ap 95.

Duque, Félix (ed). *El mal: irradiación y fascinación*. Barcelona, Pub Univ Murcia, 1993.
Bello, Eduardo. *Daimon Rev Filosof*, 8, 236-238, 1994.
Bello, Eduardo. *Rev Filosof (Spain)*, 8, 236-238, 1994.

Dvoráková, Vladimíra and Kunc, Jirí. *O Prechodech k Demokracii*. Praha, SLON, 1994.
Ríchová, Blanka. *Filozof Cas*, 43(1), 139-142, 1994.

Dworkin, Gerald (ed). *Morality, Harm and the Law*. Boulder, Westview Pr, 1994.
Dwyer, Susan. *Can Phil Rev*, 15(1), 29-32, F 95.

Dworkin, Ronald. *El Dominio de la Vida*. Barcelona, Ariel Pr, 1994.
Sánchez, Elías Pérez. *Telos (Spain)*, 3(2), 135-137, D 94.

Dworkin, Ronald. *Life's Dominion*. New York, HarperCollins, 1993.
Belshaw, Christopher. *Mind*, 104(415), 632-637, Jl 95.
Heyd, David. *Euro J Phil*, 3(1), 105-109, Ap 95.
Heyd, David. *J Phil Educ*, 29(1), 105-109, March 95.
Schiavello, Aldo. *Riv Int Filosof Diritto*, 71(2), 355-358, 1994.

Eagleton, Terry. *The Ideology of the Aesthetic*. Cambridge, Blackwell, 1990.
Christie, William. *Lit Aes*, 1, 100-102, Spr 91.

Earman, John. *Bayes or Bust?*. Cambridge, MIT Pr, 1992.
Castell, Paul. *Phil Quart*, 45(180), 377-379, Jl 95.

Earman, John (ed), Janis, Allen I (ed) and Massey, J (ed). *Philosophical Problems of the Internal and External Worlds*. Pittsburgh, Univ of Pitt Pr, 1993.
Pauri, Massimo. *Phil Sci*, 62(3), 484-487, S 95.

Easthope, Antony (ed). *Contemporary Film Theory*. White Plains, Longman, 1993.
Butler, Alison. *Brit J Aes*, 35(3), 311-312, Jl 95.

Ebert, Theodor. *Dialektiker und frühe Stoiker bei Sextus Empiricus*. Göttingen, Vandenhoeck, 1991.
Gasser, James. *Hist Phil Log*, 15(2), 252-253, 1994.

Eckert, Michael. *Gott — Glauben und Wissen*. Hawthorne, de Gruyter, 1987.
Moxter, Michael. *Phil Rundsch*, 41(2), 133-158, 1994.

Eckstein, Jerome. *Metaphysical Drift*. New York, Lang, 1991.
Wyschogrod, Michael. *Int Stud Phil*, 26(4), 123-124, 1994.

Eco, Umberto. *Die Suche nach der vollkommenen Sprache*. Munich, Beck, 1994.
Nieragden, Göran. *Das Argument*, 208, 121-123, Ja-F 95.

Eco, Umberto. *I limiti dell'interpretazione*. Milan, Bompiani, 1990.
Osorio, Carlos Rojas. *Dialogos*, 30(65), 216-221, Ja 95.

Eco, Umberto. *Interpretation and Overinterpretation*. New York, Cambridge Univ Pr, 1990.
Patton, Paul. *Lit Aes*, 4, 128-130, O 94.

Eco, Umberto. *The Limits of Interpretation*. Bloomington, Indiana Univ Pr, 1990.
Gorman, Michael. *Nous*, 28(1), 119-122, Mr 94.

École, Jean. *La métaphysique de Christian Wolff*. Hildesheim, Olms, 1990.
Soto, M Jesús. *Anu Filosof*, 28(1), 166-168, 1995.

Edgar, David. *Citizen Locke (Television Show)*. 1994.
Goldie, Mark. *Locke News*, 25, 125-129, 1994.

Edwards, Ward (ed). *Utility Theories*. Dordrecht, Kluwer, 1992.
Mullen, John D. *Phil Sci*, 61(3), 489-490, S 94.

Eells, Ellery (ed) and Maruszewski, Tomasz (ed). *Probability and Rationality*. Amsterdam, Rodopi, 1991.
Harré, Rom. *Int Stud Phil*, 26(4), 124-125, 1994.

Eichel, Christine. *Vom Ermatten der Avantgarde zur Vernetzung der Künste*. Frankfurt, Suhrkamp, 1993.
Giacomazzi, Giorgio. *Das Argument*, 207, 980-983, N-D 94.
Ricard, Marie-Andrée. *Z Phil Forsch*, 49(2), 336-339, Ap-Je 95.

Eisenman, Peter (& others). *Reworking Eisenman*. London, Academy Ed, 1993.
Williams, James. *Phil Quart*, 45(178), 109-110, Ja 95.

Eklof, Paul C and Mekler, Alan H. *Almost Free Modules*. Amsterdam, North-Holland, 1990.
Dow, Alan. *J Sym Log*, 60(2), 696-698, Je 95.

Elders, Leo J. *The Metaphysics of Being of St. Thomas in a Historical Perspective*. Leiden, Brill, 1993.
Baur, Michael. *Amer Cath Phil Quart*, 69(1), 101-109, Wint 95.

Elders, Léon. *La Philosophie de la nature de saint Thomas d'Aquin*. Paris, Téqui, 1994.
Hubert, Bernard. *Rev Thomiste*, 95(2), 326-334, Ap-Je 95.

Ellis, John M. *Language, Thought, and Logic*. Evanston, Northwestern Univ Pr, 1993.
Poole, Gabriele. *Phil Lit*, 19(1), 142-143, Ap 95.

Elsner, Gary. *Nietzsche: A Philosophical Biography*. Lanham, Univ Pr of America, 1992.
Breazeale, Daniel. *Int Stud Phil*, 27(2), 112-113, 1995.

Elsner, John (ed) and Cardinal, Roger (ed). *The Cultures of Collecting*. Reaktion Books, Undated.
Wadley, Nick. *Brit J Aes*, 35(3), 299-300, Jl 95.

Elster, Jon. *Local Justice*. New York, Cambridge Univ Pr, 1992.
McPherson, Mike. *Econ Phil*, 11(1), 177-182, Ap 95.

Elster, Jon. *Political Psychology*. New York, Cambridge Univ Pr, 1993.
Cloots, A. *Tijdschr Filosof*, 56(3), 605-607, S 94.
Roberts, Marcus. *Rad Phil*, 68, 42-45, Autumn 94.

Elster, Jon (ed) and Slagstad, Rune (ed). *Constitutionalism and Democracy*. New York, Cambridge Univ Pr, 1988.
Richards, David A J. *Ethics*, 105(4), 945-947, Jl 95.

Emmet, Dorothy. *The Role of the Unrealizable*. New York, St Martin's Pr, 1994.
Wilburn, Ron. *Mind*, 104(414), 413-419, Ap 95.

Engel, Pascal. *États d'esprit*. Aix-en-Provence, Alinea, 1992.
Verley, Xavier. *Rev Phil Fr*, 4, 514-516, O-D 94.

Engelhardt Jr, H Tristram. *Manuale di Bioetica*. Milan, Saggiatore, 1991.
Reichlin, Massimo. *Riv Filosof Neo-Scolas*, 86(2), 396-401, Ap-Je 94.

Enos, Richard Leo. *Greek Rhetoric before Aristotle*. Prospect Heights, Waveland Pr, 1993.
Fortenbaugh, William W. *Phil Rhet*, 28(2), 162-164, 1995.

Enrico, Berti. *Introduzione alla metafisica*. Torino, UTET, 1992.
Malatesti, Luca. *Aquinas*, 37(3), 689-694, S-D 94.

Ereshefsky, Marc (ed). *The Units of Evolution*. Cambridge, MIT Pr, 1992.
Blackburn, Pierre. *Can Phil Rev*, 14(2), 92-94, Ap 94.
James, Peter. *Hist Phil Life Sci*, 16(2), 395-396, Ag 94.

Erhard, Johann Benjamin. *Du droit du peuple à faire la révolution*. Lausanne, L'Age d'Homme, 1993.
Chauvier, S. *Rev Metaph Morale*, 98(1), 130-132, Ja-Mr 95.

Espinoza, Miguel. *Théorie de l'intelligibilité*. Arles, Actes, 1994.
Beuchot, Mauricio. *Analogía*, 9(1), 215-216, 1995.
Largeault, Jean. *Dialogos*, 30(65), 213-216, Ja 95.

Esposito, Costantino. *Heidegger: Storia e fenomenologia del possibile*. Bari, Levante Ed, 1992.
Augello, Giuseppe. *G Metaf*, 16(1-2), 265-267, Ja-Ag 94.
Roviello, Anne-Marie. *Rev Metaph Morale*, 98(1), 134-136, Ja-Mr 95.

Estévez, A Pérez. *Religión, moral y política*. Maracaibo, Univ Zulia, 1991.
Beuchot, Mauricio. *Analogía*, 7(1), 209-211, 1993.

Goodman, Michael F (ed) and Snyder, Robert A (ed). *Contemporary Readings in Epistemology*. Englewood Cliffs, Prentice Hall, 1993.
Pappas, George S. *Teach Phil*, 17(4), 362-364, D 94.

Gorlée, Dinda L. *Semiotics and the Problem of Translation with Special Reference to the Semiotics of Charles S Peirce*. Alblasserdam, Offsetdrukkerij K BV, 1993.
Llamas, Carmen. *Anu Filosof*, 28(1), 168-169, 1995.

Gormally, Luke (ed). *Euthanasia, Clinical Practice and the Law*. London, Linacre Ctr, 1994.
Fergusson, Andrew. *Ethics Med*, 11(2), 44-45, .

Gottfried, Paul. *Carl Schmitt (Thinkers of Our Time)*. London, Claridge Pr, 1990.
Coady, C A J. *Phil Quart*, 45(179), 273-275, Ap 95.

Gottfried, Paul Edward. *Carl Schmitt: Politics and Theory*. Westport, Greenwood Pr, 1990.
Sweet, William. *Dialogue (Canada)*, 33(4), 770-771, Fall 94.

Gouinlock, James. *Rediscovering the Moral Life*. Buffalo, Prometheus, 1993.
Dwyer, Philip. *Phil Books*, 36(3), 198-201, Jl 95.
Sauer, James B. *Can Phil Rev*, 14(4), 259-261, Ag 94.
Teichert, Lucille L. *J Speculative Phil*, 9(2), 163-168, 1995.

Gould, Carol C. *Rethinking Democracy*. New York, Cambridge Univ Pr, Undated.
Lemos, Ramon M. *Nous*, 27(4), 525-527, D 93.

Gould, Carol C (ed). *The Information Web*. Boulder, Westview Pr, 1989.
Feenberg, Andrew. *Mind Mach*, 5(1), 138-142, F 95.

Goulet, Richard. *La Philosophie de Moise*. Paris, Vrin, 1987.
Dillon, John. *Dialogue (Canada)*, 33(4), 749-750, Fall 94.

Goutier, Klaus. *Rechtsphilosophische und juristische Methodenlehre im Lichte der evolutionären Erkenntnistheorie*. New York, Lang, 1989.
Brieskorn, N. *Theol Phil*, 69(3), 473-475, 1994.

Govinda, Lama Anagarika. *The Psychological Attitude of Early Buddhist Philosophy*. Delhi, Motilal Banarsidass, 1991.
Putney, David. *Asian Phil*, 5(1), 75-78, 1995.

Gowans, Christopher W. *Innocence Lost*. New York, Oxford Univ Pr, 1994.
Nelson, James Lindemann. *Hastings Center Rep*, 25(3), 48-49, My-Je 95.

Goyard-Fabre, Simone. *Les fondements de l'ordre juridique*. Paris, PUF, 1992.
Blais, François. *Dialogue (Canada)*, 34(1), 166-168, Wint 95.

Gracia, Jorge J E. *Individuality: An Essay on the Foundations of Metaphysics*. Albany, SUNY Pr, 1988.
Gill, Kate. *Nous*, 27(1), 94-97, Mr 93.

Gracia, Jorge J E. *Philosophy and Its History*. Albany, SUNY Pr, 1991.
Alvarez-Castellanos, Juan José Sánchez. *Dialogos*, 30(66), 200-209, Jl 95.

Grafstein, Robert. *Institutional Realism*. New Haven, Yale Univ Pr, 1992.
Saraydar, Edward. *Econ Phil*, 11(1), 208-216, Ap 95.

Graham, A C. *Two Chinese Philosophers*. Peru, Open Court, 1992.
Berkson, Mark. *Phil East West*, 45(2), 292-297, Ap 95.

Graham, George. *Philosophy of Mind: An Introduction*. Cambridge, Blackwell, 1992.
Thomas, Janice. *Heythrop J*, 36(1), 113-114, Ja 95.

Graham, Keith. *Karl Marx, Our Contemporary*. Hertfordshire, Harvester-Wheatsheaf, 1992.
Smith, Tony. *Int Stud Phil*, 27(2), 116-117, 1995.

Grandpont House. *Grandpont Papers, The Past and the Present*. Oxford, Grandpont House, 1993.
Hamlyn, D W. *Phil Invest*, 18(2), 177-179, Ap 95.

Grant, Robert. *Oakeshott (Thinkers of Our Time)*. London, Claridge Pr, 1990.
Coady, C A J. *Phil Quart*, 45(179), 273-275, Ap 95.

Grassi, E. *La filosofia del humanismo*. Barcelona, Anthropos, 1993.
Quintanilla Navarro, Ignacio. *An Seminar Metaf*, 28, 374-377, 1994.

Grassi, Ernesto. *Vico and Humanism*. New York, Lang, 1990.
Verene, Donald Philip. *Cuad Vico*, 3, 197-198, 1993.

Grawe, Klaus (ed), Donati, Ruth (ed) and Bernauer, Friederike (ed). *Psychotherapie im Wandel*. Seattle, Hogrefe, 1994.
Ricken, F. *Theol Phil*, 69(3), 477-480, 1994.

Green, Georgia M. *Pragmatics and Natural Language Understanding*. East Sussex, Erlbaum, 1989.
Ter Meulen, Alice G B. *Nous*, 27(4), 550-553, D 93.

Green, O H. *The Emotions*. Dordrecht, Kluwer, 1992.
Priest, Stephen. *Mind*, 104(413), 166-168, Ja 95.
Van Eechaute, Ann. *Tijdschr Filosof*, 56(4), 794-796, D 94.

Greenawalt, Kent. *Law and Objectivity*. New York, Oxford Univ Pr, 1992.
Bedau, H A. *Phil Rev*, 103(3), 551-553, Jl 94.

Greenfeld, Liah. *Nationalism: Five Roads to Modernity*. Cambridge, Harvard Univ Pr, 1992.
Yack, Bernard. *Polit Theory*, 23(1), 166-182, F 95.

Greenspan, Louis (ed) and Nicholson, Graeme (ed). *Fackenheim*. Toronto, Univ of Toronto Pr, 1992.
Gillman, Neil. *Dialogue (Canada)*, 34(1), 181-184, Wint 95.

Greenstone, J David. *The Lincoln Persuasion*. Princeton, Princeton Univ Pr, 1993.
Eisenach, Eldon J. *Hist Polit Thought*, 16(1), 151-154, Spr 95.

Greppi, A and Moietta, E. *Giochi con carte truccate*. Roma, A Pelicani, 1994.
Pezzella, Anna Maria. *Aquinas*, 37(3), 681-684, S-D 94.

Griffin, James. *Well-Being: Its Meaning, Measurement and Moral Importance*. New York, Clarendon/Oxford Pr, 1986.
Simpson, Evan. *Nous*, 27(1), 83-85, Mr 93.

Griffiths, A Phillips (ed). *A J Ayer*. New York, Cambridge Univ Pr, 1991.
Mackenzie, Patrick. *Can Phil Rev*, 14(2), 96-97, Ap 94.
Magill, Kevin. *Rad Phil*, 68, 50-52, Autumn 94.

Griffiths, A Phillips. *Ethics*. New York, Cambridge Univ Pr, 1993.
Boddington, Paula. *Phil Books*, 36(3), 201-203, Jl 95.

Griffiths, A Phillips. *Wittgenstein's Centenary Essays*. New York, Cambridge Univ Pr, 1991.
Tanney, Julia. *Hist Euro Ideas*, 18(6), 970-973, N 94.

Grim, Patrick. *The Incomplete Universe*. Cambridge, MIT Pr, 1991.
Kirk, Robert. *Hist Phil Log*, 15(2), 237-238, 1994.

Groarke, Leo. *Greek Scepticism*. Montreal, McGill-Queens U Pr, 1990.
Nalezinski, Alix. *Eidos*, 12(1), 169-173, Je 94.
Silverman, Allan. *Phoenix*, 48(2), 165-170, Sum 94.

Grondin, Jean. *Einführung in die philosophische Hermeneutik*. Darmstadt, Wiss Buchgesell, 1991.
Kaegi, Dominic. *Phil Rundsch*, 41(2), 116-132, 1994.
Rocque, André. *Dialogue (Canada)*, 33(3), 550-553, Sum 94.

Grondin, Jean. *L'universalité de l'herméneutique*. Paris, Pr Univ France, 1993.
Rocque, André. *Dialogue (Canada)*, 33(3), 550-553, Sum 94.

Gross, Paul R and Levitt, Norman. *A Reply to Steve Fuller's Review of "Higher Superstition: The Academic Left and Its Quarrels with Science"*. Baltimore, Johns Hopkins U Pr, 1994.
Gross, Paul R. *Hist Human Sci*, 8(2), 125-129, My 95.

Gross, Paul R and Levitt, Norman. *Higher Superstition*. Baltimore, Johns Hopkins U Pr, 1994.
Hist Human Sci, 8(2), My 95.

Grossheim, Michael. *Ludwig Klages und die Phänomenologie*. Berlin, Akademie, 1994.
Fabeck, Hans v. *Phil Rundsch*, 42(1), 91-96, Mr 95.

Grossheim, Michael (ed) and Waschkies, Hans-Joachim (ed). *Rehabilitierung des Subjektiven*. Bonn, Bouvier, 1993.
Ollig, H L. *Theol Phil*, 70(1), 135-138, 1995.

Grossmann, Reinhardt. *The Fourth Way*. Bloomington, Indiana Univ Pr, 1990.
Moser, Paul K. *Nous*, 27(3), 395-397, S 93.

Grosz, Elizabeth. *Volatile Bodies*. St Leonards, Allen and Unwin, 1994.
Wei Leng, Kwok. *Austl J Phil*, 73(2), 301-303, Je 95.

Grube, G M A (trans). *Plato's Republic*. Indianapolis, Hackett, 1992.
Dorter, Kenneth. *Teach Phil*, 17(1), 69-71, Mr 94.

Grube, G M A (trans). *Plato's Republic (Response to Dorter's Review)*. Indianapolis, Hackett, 1992.
Reeve, C D C. *Teach Phil*, 17(1), 71-72, Mr 94.

Grünbaum, Adolf. *Validation in the Clinical Theory of Psychoanalysis*. Madison, Intl Univ Pr, 1993.
Kitcher, Patricia. *Phil Sci*, 62(1), 166-167, Mr 95.

Guadaño, E Bustos. *Filosofía contemporánea del lenguaje I*. Madrid, Cuad UNED, 1987.
Beuchot, Mauricio. *Analogía*, 7(2), 211-213, 1993.

Guerrero, Luis. *Kierkegaard: Los límites de la razón en la existencia humana*. Mexico, Pub Cruz O, 1993.
Valadez, Leticia. *Topicos*, 4(6), 181-183, 1994.

Guerrière, Daniel (ed). *Phenomenology of the Truth Proper to Religion*. Albany, SUNY Pr, 1990.
Ricken, F. *Theol Phil*, 70(1), 134-135, 1995.

Guest, Stephen. *Ronald Dworkin*. Edinburgh, Edinburgh Univ Pr, 1992.
Postema, Gerald J. *Utilitas*, 6(2), 328-332, N 94.

Guetti, James. *Wittgenstein and the Grammar of Literary Experience*. Athens, Univ of Georgia Pr, 1993.
Robinson, Ian. *Phil Invest*, 18(2), 179-183, Ap 95.

Guignon, Charles (ed). *The Cambridge Companion to Heidegger*. New York, Cambridge Univ Pr, 1993.
Inwood, M J. *Phil Books*, 35(3), 183-185, Jl 94.
Murphy, Paul N. *Can Phil Rev*, 14(2), 98-100, Ap 94.
Polt, Richard. *Phil Phenomenol Res*, 55(3), 725-728, S 95.
Williams, John R. *Heythrop J*, 35(3), 354-355, Jl 94.

Guisán, Esperanza. *Esplendor y miseria de la ética kantiana*. Barcelona, Anthropos, 1988.
Caimi, Mario. *Kantstudien*, 85(3), 364-366, 1994.

Guisán, Esperanza. *Ética sin religión*. Madrid, Alianza, 1993.
Tasset, José Luis. *Telos*, 2(2), 151-154, D 93.

Guisán, Esperanza. *La Ética mira a la izquierda*. Madrid, Tecnos, 1992.
López, María Teresa. *Telos*, 2(1), 136-139, Je 93.

Gunn, Giles. *Thinking Across the American Grain*. Chicago, Univ of Chicago Pr, 1992.
Elkins, William Wesley. *J Speculative Phil*, 9(1), 68-73, 1995.

Gunther, Poltner. *Evolutionare Vernunft*. Stuttgart, Kohlhammer, 1993.
Esterbauer, Reinhold. *Deut Z Phil*, 42(1), 179-182, 1994.

Gupta, Anil and Belnap, Nuel. *Reply to Robert Koons*. Notre Dame, Univ Notre Dame Pr, 1994.
Gupta, Anil. *Notre Dame J Form Log*, 35(4), 632-636, Fall 94.

Gupta, Anil and Belnap, Nuel. *The Revision Theory of Truth*. Cambridge, MIT Pr, 1993.
Gargile, James. *Phil Books*, 36(3), 165-173, Jl 95.
Koons, Robert C. *Notre Dame J Form Log*, 35(4), 606-631, Fall 94.
Kremer, Philip. *Can Phil Rev*, 15(1), 39-42, F 95.

Gupta, Som Raj. *The Word Speaks to the Faustian Man*. Delhi, Motilal Banarsidass, Undated.
Dallmayr, Fred. *Phil East West*, 45(2), 286-292, Ap 95.

Gustason, William. *Reasoning from Evidence*. New York, Macmillan, 1994.
Burnor, Richard N. *Teach Phil*, 18(2), 188-190, Je 95.

Guy, Alain. *Femmes-Philosophes en Espagne et en Amérique Latine*. Meudon, CNRS, 1989.
Despilho, P X. *Rev Metaph Morale*, 99(4), 555-557, O-D 94.
Santo-Thomas, Jean-Julien de. *Rev Thomiste*, 94(2), 338-339, Ap-Je 94.

Guyer, Paul. *Kant and the Experience of Freedom*. New York, Cambridge Univ Pr, 1993.
Baldner, Kent. *Can Phil Rev*, 14(1), 19-21, F 94.
Krasnoff, Larry. *Phil Rev*, 103(4), 765-768, O 94.
Marshall, John. *Phil Books*, 36(2), 105-107, Ap 95.
Scarre, Geoffrey. *Brit J Aes*, 34(4), 401-403, O 94.
Wicks, Robert. *J Aes Art Crit*, 53(3), 336-338, Sum 95.

Guyer, Paul (ed). *The Cambridge Companion to Kant*. New York, Cambridge Univ Pr, 1991.
Freydberg, Bernard D. *Hist Euro Ideas*, 21(1), 75-80, Ja 95.
Walker, Ralph C S. *Brit J Hist Phil*, 3(1), 189-191, F 95.

Haack, Susan. *Evidence and Inquiry*. Cambridge, Blackwell, 1993.
Clendinnen, F John. *Austl J Phil*, 72(4), 536-537, D 94.

Haar, Michel. *Heidegger and the Essence of Man*. Albany, SUNY Pr, 1993.
Russon, John. *Rev Metaph*, 48(2), 405-406, D 94.

Habermas, Jürgen. *Nachmetaphysisches Denken*. Frankfurt, Suhrkamp, 1988.
Schmidt, Thomas M. *Protosoz*, 1, 116-120, Ap 91.

Habermas, Jürgen, Lenhardt, Christian (trans) and Nicholsen, Shierry Weber (trans). *Moral Consciousness and Communicative Action*. Cambridge, MIT Pr, 1990.
Hudson, Hud. *J Speculative Phil*, 9(1), 74-77, 1995.

Hacker, P M S. *Wittgenstein: Meaning and Mind, Volume III*. Cambridge, Blackwell, 1990.
Churchill, John. *Thomist*, 59(1), 161-167, Ja 95.

Hackler, Chris (ed). *Health Care for an Aging Population*. Albany, SUNY Pr, 1994.
Waymack, Mark H. *Cambridge Quart Healthcare Ethics*, 4(2), 250-251, Spr 95.

Hahn, Lewis Edwin (ed). *The Philosophy of A J Ayer*. Peru, Open Court, 1992.
Van Evra, James. *Can Phil Rev*, 14(5), 327-329, O 94.

Hahn, Lewis Edwin (ed). *The Philosophy of Charles Hartshorne*. Peru, Open Court, 1991.
Cooper, Ron. *Vera Lex*, 13(1-2), 59-61, 1993.
Shields, George W. *Int J Phil Relig*, 36(3), 190-192, D 94.
Valady, Mohammad. *Int Stud Phil*, 26(4), 133-135, 1994.

Hahn, Robert. *Kant's Newtonian Revolution in Philosophy*. Carbondale, South Ill Univ Pr, 1988.
Watkins, Eric. *Kantstudien*, 86(2), 231-234, 1995.

Haines, Charles Grove. *The Revival of Natural Law Concepts*. Cambridge, Harvard Univ Pr, 1930.
Kelly, Robert. *Vera Lex*, 13(1-2), 61-62, 1993.

Hakken, David and Andrews, Barbara. *Computing Myths, Class Realities*. Boulder, Westview Pr, 1993.
Hess, David J. *Sci Tech Human Values*, 19(4), 528-530, Autumn 94.

Halbertal, Moshe and Margalit, Avishai. *Idolatry*. Cambridge, Harvard Univ Pr, 1992.
Eckstein, Jerome. *Int Stud Phil*, 26(4), 135-136, 1994.
Helm, Paul. *Mind*, 104(414), 419-422, Ap 95.

Haldane, John (ed) and Wright, Crispin (ed). *Reality, Representation, and Projection*. New York, Oxford Univ Pr, 1993.
Heil, John. *Phil Books*, 36(2), 116-120, Ap 95.

Halfon, Mark S. *Integrity*. Philadelphia, Temple Univ Pr, 1989.
Lauer, Henle. *Nous*, 27(3), 399-401, S 93.

Hall, David L. *Richard Rorty: Prophet and Poet of the New Pragmatism*. Albany, SUNY Pr, 1994.
Rumana, Richard. *Phil Lit*, 19(1), 144-145, Ap 95.

Hall, John A (ed) and Jarvie, I C (ed). *Transition to Modernity*. New York, Cambridge Univ Pr, 1992.
Collins, Randall. *Phil Soc Sci*, 25(1), 120-125, Mr 95.

Hall, Ronald L. *Word and Spirit*. Bloomington, Indiana Univ Pr, 1993.
Power, W L. *Int J Phil Relig*, 36(2), 125-126, O 94.

Hall, William D. *Making the Right Decision*. New York, Wiley & Sons, 1993.
Smith, David C. *Bus Ethics Quart*, 5(1), 157-161, Ja 95.

Haller, Rudolf (ed) and Brandl, Johannes (ed). *Wittgenstein: Eine Neubewertung/ Towards a Re-evaluation*. Vienna, Hoelder-Pich-Temp, 1990.
Hund, John. *S Afr J Phil*, 13(4), 204-205, N 94.

Halper, Edward. *Form and Reason*. Albany, SUNY Pr, 1993.
Geirsson, Heimir. *Teach Phil*, 18(2), 185-186, Je 95.

Hanák, Tibor. *Geschichte der Philosophie in Ungarn*. München, Trofenik, 1990.
Péter, Egyed. *Magyar Filozof Szemle*, 3-4, 577-582, 1994.

Hanfling, Oswald (ed). *Philosophical Aesthetics*. Cambridge, Blackwell, 1992.
Shaw, Daniel J. *Phil Books*, 35(3), 217-219, Jl 94.
Zangwill, Nick. *Phil Quart*, 45(180), 410-412, Jl 95.

Hans, James S. *Contextual Authority and Aesthetic Truth*. Albany, SUNY Pr, 1992.
Young, Julian. *Int Stud Phil*, 27(2), 117-118, 1995.

Hansen, Chad. *A Daoist Theory of Chinese Thought*. New York, Oxford Univ Pr, 1992.
Van Norden, Bryan W. *Ethics*, 105(2), 433-435, Ja 95.

Hansen, Phillip. *Hannah Arendt: Politics, History and Citizenship*. Oxford, Polity Pr, 1993.
Caterino, Brian. *Constellation*, 2(1), 148-151, Ap 95.
d'Entrèves, Maurizio Passerin. *Euro J Phil*, 2(3), 361-366, D 94.
De Greiff, Pablo. *Int J Phil Stud*, 3(1), 179-182, Mr 95.
Hadfield, Andrew. *Rad Phil*, 69, 50-51, Ja-F 95.

Haraway, Donna J. *Simians, Cyborgs, and Women*. New York, Routledge, 1991.
Woody, Andrea. *Phil Sci*, 62(2), 346-348, Je 95.

Hardin, Garrett. *Living Within Limits*. New York, Oxford Univ Pr, 1993.
Stücker, Harald. *Frei Z Phil Theol*, 41(1-2), 282-284, 1994.
Trout, Paul A. *Environ Ethics*, 17(3), 331-336, Fall 95.

Harding, Sandra (ed). *The "Racial" Economy of Science*. Bloomington, Indiana Univ Pr, 1993.
Honig, Carlye. *Sci Tech Human Values*, 19(4), 523-526, Autumn 94.

Hardt, Michael. *Gilles Deleuze*. London, UCL Pr Ltd, 1993.
Lecercle, Jean-Jacques. *Rad Phil*, 71, 48-49, My-Je 95.

Hare, R M. *Essays in Ethical Theory*. New York, Oxford Univ Pr, 1989.
Price, A W. *J Applied Phil*, 11(2), 239-241, 1994.

Hare, R M. *Essays on Bioethics*. New York, Clarendon/Oxford Pr, 1993.
Price, A W. *J Applied Phil*, 11(2), 239-241, 1994.

Harkin, Patricia (ed) and Schilb, John (ed). *Contending with Words*. New York, Modern Lang Assoc, 1991.
Larson, Richard L. *Phil Rhet*, 28(2), 175-179, 1995.

Harland, Richard. *Beyond Superstructuralism*. New York, Routledge, 1993.
McDonald Meidner, Olga. *Brit J Aes*, 35(2), 181-183, Ap 95.

Harras, Gisela. *Handlungssprache und Sprechhandlung*. Hawthorne, de Gruyter, 1983.
Mumme, Angela. *Protosoz*, 2, 117-119, Ja 92.

Harris, Errol E. *Atheism and Theism*. Atlantic Highlands, Humanities Pr, 1993.
Rinaldi, Giacomo. *Ideal Stud*, 24(3), 285-288, Fall 94.

Harris, Ian. *The Continuity of Madhyamaka and Yogacara in Indian Mahayana Buddhism*. Leiden, Brill, 1991.
King, Richard. *Asian Phil*, 4(2), 183-187, 1994.

Harris, Ian. *The Mind of John Locke*. Cambridge, Cambridge Univ Pr, 1994.
Pringle, Helen. *Austl J Phil*, 73(2), 303-305, Je 95.

Harris, James F. *Against Relativism*. Peru, Open Court, 1992.
Baghramian, Maria. *Phil Books*, 35(3), 185-187, Jl 94.
Holland, Robert Aa. *Metaphilosophy*, 26(1-2), 147-153, Ja-Ap 95.

Harris, James Franklin (ed). *Logic, God, and Metaphysics*. Dordrecht, Kluwer, 1992.
Keller, James A. *Process Stud*, 22(4), 239-242, Winter 93.

Harrison, Ross. *Democracy*. New York, Routledge, 1993.
Archard, David. *Rad Phil*, 68, 48-50, Autumn 94.
Fullinwider, Robert K. *Phil Books*, 36(1), 69-70, Ja 95.

Harwood, Jonathan. *Styles of Scientific Thought*. Chicago, Univ of Chicago Pr, 1993.
Fässler, Peter E. *Hist Phil Life Sci*, 16(1), 173-175, Ja 94.

Hatfield, Gary. *The Natural and the Normative*. Cambridge, MIT Pr, 1991.
Kitchener, Richard F. *Phil Sci*, 62(2), 334-335, Je 95.

Hauser, Christian. *Selbstbewusstsein und personale Identität*. Stuttgart, Frommann-Holzboog, 1994.
Champlin, T S. *Locke News*, 25, 106-109, 1994.

Hausman, Carl R. *Charles S Peirce's Evolutionary Philosophy*. New York, Cambridge Univ Pr, 1993.
Colapietro, Vincent. *J Hist Phil*, 32(4), 682-685, O 94.

Hausman, Daniel M. *Essays on Philosophy and Economic Methodology*. New York, Cambridge Univ Pr, 1992.
Shaw, Patrick. *Phil Books*, 36(2), 141-142, Ap 95.

Hausman, Daniel M. *The Inexact and Separate Science of Economics*. New York, Cambridge Univ Pr, 1992.
Hammond, J Daniel. *Econ Phil*, 10(2), 338-342, O 94.

Hjort, Mette. *The Strategy of Letters*. Cambridge, Harvard Univ Pr, 1993.
Newton, K M. *Brit J Aes*, 35(3), 309-311, JI 95.
Payne, Michael. *Hist Euro Ideas*, 18(6), 1040-1041, N 94.

Hobbes, Thomas and Tuck, Richard (ed). *Leviathan*. New York, Cambridge Univ Pr, 1991.
Garrett, Aaron V. *Grad Fac Phil J*, 18(1), 277-282, 1995.

Hobhouse, Leonard Trelawny and Meadowcroft, James (ed). *Liberalism and Other Writings*. New York, Cambridge Univ Pr, 1994.
Taylor, Michael W. *Utilitas*, 6(2), 339-341, N 94.

Hodge, M J S. *Origins and Species*. Hamden, Garland, 1991.
Gregorio, Mario di. *Hist Phil Life Sci*, 16(1), 163-164, Ja 94.

Hodges, Wilfrid. *Model Theory*. New York, Cambridge Univ Pr, 1993.
Pillay, Anand. *J Sym Log*, 60(2), 689-691, Je 95.

Hodgson, David. *The Mind Matters*. New York, Clarendon/Oxford Pr, 1991.
Campbell, Keith. *Austl J Phil*, 72(3), 396-400, S 94.

Höffe, Otfried. *Principes du droit*. Paris, Cerf, 1993.
Chauvier, Stéphane. *Rev Metaph Morale*, 99(4), 539-540, O-D 94.

Hölker, Klaus. *Zur Analyse von Markern*. Stuttgart, Steiner Verlag, 1988.
Cadiot, Pierre. *J Prag*, 22(6), 687-689, D 94.

Hösle, Vittorio. *Philosophie der Ökologischen Krise*. München, C H Beck, 1991.
Kamaryt, Jan. *Filozof Cas*, 42(4), 693-695, 1994.

Hoffe, Otfried. *Persino un popolo di diavoli ha bisogno dello Stato*. Turin, Giappichelli, 1993.
Iagulli, Paolo. *Riv Int Filosof Diritto*, 71(2), 362-363, 1994.

Hoitenga Jr, Dewey J. *Faith and Reason from Plato to Plantinga*. Albany, SUNY Pr, 1991.
Sennett, James F. *Faith Phil*, 11(2), 342-348, Ap 94.

Holmes, George. *The Florentine Enlightenment 1400-1450*. New York, Clarendon/Oxford Pr, 1992.
Brackett, John K. *Hist Euro Ideas*, 21(3), 477-479, My 95.

Holmes, Stephen. *The Anatomy of Antiliberalism*. Cambridge, Harvard Univ Pr, 1993.
MacIntyre, Alasdair. *Rad Phil*, 70, 34-35, Mr-Ap 95.
McClure, Kirstie M. *Polit Theory*, 22(4), 698-705, N 94.
Moore, Margaret. *Hist Euro Ideas*, 21(3), 467-468, My 95.

Holub, Robert C. *Crossing Borders*. Madison, Univ of Wisconsin Pr, 1992.
Tobin, Robert. *Phil Lit*, 18(2), 397-398, O 94.

Honderich, Ted. *How Free Are You?*. New York, Oxford Univ Pr, 1993.
Trampota, A. *Theol Phil*, 69(3), 462-466, 1994.
Wilkinson, Stephen. *Phil Quart*, 45(179), 249-251, Ap 95.

Honig, Bonnie. *Political Theory and the Displacement of Politics*. Ithaca, Cornell Univ Pr, 1993.
Mackenzie, Craig. *Hist Human Sci*, 7(3), 113-116, Ag 94.

Honneth, Axel. *Kampf um Anerkennung*. Frankfurt, Suhrkamp, 1992.
Jurist, Elliot J. *Constellation*, 1(1), 171-180, Ap 94.
Velek, Josef. *Filozof Cas*, 43(1), 143-146, 1994.

Hooker, Brad (ed). *Rationality, Rules, and Utility*. Boulder, Westview Pr, 1993.
Hoag, Robert W. *Phil Books*, 36(3), 203-204, JI 95.

Horgan, Terrence (ed) and Tienson, John (ed). *Connectionism and the Philosophy of Mind*. Dordrecht, Kluwer, 1991.
Munsat, Stanley. *Phil Psych*, 7(4), 509-512, 1994.

Horowitz, Asher. *Rousseau, Nature, and History*. Toronto, Univ of Toronto Pr, 1992.
Chisick, Harvey. *Int Stud Phil*, 26(4), 138-139, 1994.

Horton, John (ed) and Mendus, Susan (ed). *John Locke: A Letter Concerning Toleration - In Focus*. New York, Routledge, 1991.
Yolton, John W. *Teach Phil*, 17(2), 188-190, Je 94.

Horton, John (ed) and Nicholson, Peter (ed). *Toleration*. Brookfield, Avebury, 1992.
Reid, Eileen. *J Applied Phil*, 11(2), 247-249, 1994.

Horwich, Paul (ed). *World Changes*. Cambridge, MIT Pr, 1993.
Andersen, Hanne. *Erkenntnis*, 40(3), 411-415, My 94.
Psillos, Stathis. *Brit J Phil Sci*, 45(3), 923-926, S 94.

Hosinski, Thomas E. *Stubborn Fact and Creative Advance*. Lanham, Rowman & Littlefield, 1993.
Boulting, N E. *Trans Peirce Soc*, 30(4), 1081-1091, Fall 94.

Hosle, V. *Die Krise der Gegenwart und die Verantwortung der Philosophie*. München, C H Beck, 1990.
Acebes Jiménez, Ricardo. *An Seminar Metaf*, 28, 357-361, 1994.

Hottois, Gilbert. *Simondon et la philosophie de la "culture technique"*. Bruxelles, De Boeck-Wesmael, 1993.
Pénel, Jean-Dominique. *Rev Phil Fr*, 4, 486-487, O-D 94.

Houlgate, Stephen. *Freedom, Truth and History*. New York, Routledge, 1991.
Harris, H S. *Phil Soc Sci*, 24(4), 517-519, D 94.
Kolb, David. *Owl Minerva*, 26(2), 221-224, Spr 95.

Hourani, Albert. *Der Islam im europäischen Denken*. Frankfurt, Fischer, 1994.
Kropácek, Lubos. *Filozof Cas*, 42(6), 1065-1067, 1994.

Houston, Joseph. *Reported Miracles*. Cambridge, Cambridge Univ Pr, 1994.
Schoen, Edward L. *Relig Stud*, 31(2), 275-276, Je 95.

Howard, V A. *Learning By All Means*. New York, Lang, 1992.
Smith, Ralph A. *Phil Music Educ Rev*, 2(1), 53-56, Spr 94.

Howell, Robert. *Kant's Transcendental Deduction*. Dordrecht, Kluwer, 1992.
Ess, Charles. *Can Phil Rev*, 14(5), 332-334, O 94.

Howells, Christina (ed). *The Cambridge Companion to Sartre*. New York, Cambridge Univ Pr, 1992.
Mahon, Joseph. *Hist Euro Ideas*, 21(3), 401-410, My 95.
Pellauer, David. *Can Phil Rev*, 14(2), 101-102, Ap 94.

Hoyningen-Huene, Paul. *Reconstructing Scientific Revolutions*. Chicago, Univ of Chicago Pr, 1993.
Psillos, Stathis. *Brit J Phil Sci*, 45(3), 923-926, S 94.
Rueger, Alexander. *Can Phil Rev*, 15(1), 46-48, F 95.

Huber, James M (ed) and Almeder, Robert F (ed). *Biomedical Ethics Reviews: 1992*. Clifton, Humana Pr, 1993.
McNeill, Paul M. *Bioethics*, 9(1), 87-89, Ja 95.

Hülsen, C Reinhard. *Zur Semantik anaphorischer Pronomina*. Leiden, Brill, 1994.
Boh, Ivan. *Rev Metaph*, 48(4), 899-900, Je 95.

Huffman, Carl A. *Philolaus of Croton*. New York, Cambridge Univ Pr, 1993.
Bussanich, John. *Rev Metaph*, 48(4), 897-898, Je 95.

Hughes, R I G (ed). *A Philosophical Companion to First-Order Logic*. Indianapolis, Hackett, 1993.
Lowe, E J. *Hist Phil Log*, 15(2), 255-256, 1994.
Schumm, George F. *J Sym Log*, 60(2), 684-685, Je 95.

Hull, David. *Science as a Process*. Chicago, Univ of Chicago Pr, 1988.
Kyburg Jr, Henry E. *Nous*, 27(1), 107-109, Mr 93.

Hultbert, H (ed). *Schleiermacher im besonderen Hinblick auf seine Wirkungsgeschichte in Dänemark*. Munchen, Wilhelm Fink, 1986.
Moxter, Michael. *Phil Rundsch*, 41(2), 133-158, 1994.

Hunt, Geoffrey (ed). *Ethical Issues in Nursing*. London, Routledge, 1994.
Singleton, Jane. *J Applied Phil*, 12(2), 203-205, 1995.

Hunter, Kathryn Montgomery. *Doctors' Stories*. Princeton, Princeton Univ Pr, 1991.
Hess, Volker. *Hist Phil Life Sci*, 16(1), 155-156, Ja 94.

Hurka, Thomas. *Perfectionism*. New York, Oxford Univ Pr, 1993.
Carr, David. *Phil Quart*, 45(178), 115-117, Ja 95.
Carson, Thomas L. *Phil Phenomenol Res*, 55(3), 719-723, S 95.
Hooker, Brad. *Phil Books*, 35(3), 200-202, JI 94.
Kumar, Rahul. *Ratio*, 7(2), 191-197, D 94.
Moore, Andrew. *Austl J Phil*, 72(4), 520-530, D 94.
Wueste, Daniel E. *Rev Metaph*, 48(2), 409-410, D 94.

Husserl, Edmund. *Die Krisis der europäischen Wissenschaften und die transzendentale Phänomenologie. Ergänzungsband*. Dordrecht, Kluwer, 1993.
Buckley, R Philip. *Res Phenomenol*, 24, 245-251, 1994.
Sokolowski, Robert. *Rev Metaph*, 48(4), 900-902, Je 95.

Hutcheson, F. *Una investigación sobre el origen de nuestra idea de belleza*. Madrid, Tecnos, 1992.
Fontán, Manuel. *Themata*, 13, 310-312, 1995.

Hutchison, Ross. *Locke in France 1688-1734*. Oxford, Voltaire Taylor Inst, 1991.
Schosler, Jorn. *Brit J Hist Phil*, 3(1), 177-185, F 95.

Ineichen, Hans. *Philosophische Hermeneutik*. Freiburg, Alber, 1991.
Kaegi, Dominic. *Phil Rundsch*, 41(2), 116-132, 1994.

Ingardia, Richard (ed). *Thomas Aquinas International Bibliography 1977-1990*. Bowling Green, Philosophy Doc Ctr, 1993.
González, Ana Marta. *Anu Filosof*, 28(1), 170, 1995.

Inness, Julie C. *Privacy, Intimacy and Isolation*. New York, Oxford Univ Pr, 1992.
Parent, William A. *Phil Phenomenol Res*, 55(1), 242-246, Mr 95.

Invitto, G. *Esistenza/estetica*. Capone, Cavallino Lecce, 1994.
Papa, Alessandra. *Sapienza*, 47(4), 489-491, O-D 94.

Inwood, Brad. *The Poem of Empedocles*. Toronto, Univ of Toronto Pr, 1992.
Osborne, Catherine. *Phil Rev*, 103(3), 565-567, JI 94.

Inwood, Michael. *A Hegel Dictionary*. Cambridge, Blackwell, 1992.
Gervais, Richard. *Dialogue (Canada)*, 34(1), 169-171, Wint 95.
Zimmerman, Carita M. *Hist Euro Ideas*, 18(6), 977-978, N 94.

Irigaray, Luce and Gill, Gillian C (trans). *Marine Lover of Friedrich Nietzsche*. New York, Columbia Univ Pr, 1991.
Large, William. *Rad Phil*, 71, 50-51, My-Je 95.

Irrgang, Bernhard. *Lehrbuch der Evolutionären Erkenntnistheorie*. Munchen, Reinhardt, 1993.
Erbrich, P. *Theol Phil*, 69(3), 461-462, 1994.

Irvine, A D and Wedeking, G A. *Russell and Analytic Philosophy*. Toronto, Univ of Toronto Pr, 1993.
Monk, Ray. *Russell*, 14(1), 87-97, Sum 94.

Irwin, Kevin W (ed) and Pellegrino, Edmund D (ed). *Preserving the Creation*. Washington, Georgetown Univ Pr, 1994.
Deane-Drummond, Celia. *Heythrop J*, 36(2), 225-226, Ap 95.

Irwin, Terence. *Aristotle's First Principles (Volume I)*. New York, Oxford Univ Pr, 1988.
Dahl, Norman O. *Nous*, 27(1), 127-133, Mr 93.

Levine, George (ed). *Realism and Representation*. Madison, Univ of Wisconsin Pr, 1993.
Woller, Raymond. *Rev Metaph*, 48(4), 909-910, Je 95.

Levine, Michael P. *Pantheism*. New York, Routledge, 1994.
Helm, Paul. *Philosophy*, 70(271), 129-131, Ja 95.

Levinson, Henry Samuel. *Santayana: Pragmatism and the Spiritual Life*. Chapel Hill, Univ N Carolina Pr, 1992.
Brüntrup, G. *Theol Phil*, 70(1), 126-128, 1995.

Levinson, Jerold. *Music, Art, and Metaphysics*. Ithaca, Cornell Univ Pr, 1990.
Lorraine, Renée. *Phil Music Educ Rev*, 1(1), 75-78, Spr 93.

Levy, David J. *Political Order*. Praha, SLON, 1993.
Marada, Radim. *Filozof Cas*, 42(4), 683-693, 1994.

Lewis, H W. *Technological Risk*. New York, Norton, 1990.
Thompson, Paul B. *Res Phil Technol*, 14, 312-320, 1994.

Leyvraz, J P (ed) and Mulligan, K (ed). *Wittgenstein analysè*. Nimes, Chambon, 1993.
Voizard, Alain. *Dialogue (Canada)*, 34(1), 187-190, Wint 95.

Librová, Hana. *Pestrí a Zelení*. Brno, Veronica, 1994.
Valach, Milan. *Filozof Cas*, 42(6), 1055-1059, 1994.

Lichtenstein, Jacqueline. *La couleur éloquente*. Paris, Flammarion, 1989.
Hénaff, Marcel. *Rev Metaph Morale*, 99(4), 559-561, O-D 94.

Liessmann, Konrad Paul. *Philَsophie der modernen Kunst*. Wien, WUV Univ, 1993.
Themann, Thorsten. *Das Argument*, 207, 983-984, N-D 94.

Lilla, Mark. *G B Vico: The Making of an Anti-Modern*. Cambridge, Harvard Univ Pr, 1993.
Martin, Raymond. *Hist Euro Ideas*, 18(6), 1035-1037, N 94.

Lilla, Mark (ed). *New French Thought*. Princeton, Princeton Univ Pr, 1994.
Kurtz, Paul. *Free Inq*, 15(1), 57-58, Wint 94-95.

Lin, Cheng-Hung (ed) and Fu, Daiwie (ed). *Philosophy and Conceptual History of Science in Taiwan*. Dordrecht, Kluwer, 1993.
Dauben, Joseph W. *Phil Hist Sci*, 3(1), 85-106, Ap 94.

Lindberg, David C. *The Beginnings of Western Science*. Chicago, Univ of Chicago Pr, 1992.
Kaiser, Christopher B. *Zygon*, 29(4), 667-668, D 94.

Link-Salinger, Ruth. *Torah and Wisdom*. New York, Shengold, 1992.
Ewbank, Michael. *Rev Metaph*, 48(2), 415-417, D 94.

Lipovetsky, Gilles. *El crepúsculo del deber*. Barcelona, Anagrama, 1994.
Aznar, Hugo. *Telos*, 3(1), 135-139, Je 94.

Lippman, Edward. *A History of Western Musical Aesthetics*. Lincoln, Univ of Nebraska Pr, 1992.
Niblock, Howard. *J Aes Art Crit*, 53(2), 219-222, Spr 95.

Lipton, Peter. *Inference to the Best Explanation*. New York, Routledge, 1991.
Gibson, Roger F. *Rev Metaph*, 48(2), 417-418, D 94.

Liss, Per-Erik. *Health Care Need*. Brookfield, Avebury, 1993.
Van Der Wilt, Gert Jan. *Theor Med*, 15(4), 457-460, D 94.

List, Peter C (ed). *Radical Environmentalism*. Belmont, Wadsworth, 1993.
Brennan, Andrew. *Can Phil Rev*, 14(1), 29-31, F 94.

Little, Daniel. *Varieties of Social Explanation*. Boulder, Westview Pr, 1991.
Cooper, Wesley E. *Can Phil Rev*, 14(3), 186-189, Je 94.

Livingston, Paisley. *Literature and Rationality*. New York, Cambridge Univ Pr, 1991.
Reiner, Richard. *Phil Soc Sci*, 24(4), 519-522, D 94.
Seamon, Roger. *Dialogue (Canada)*, 33(4), 773-776, Fall 94.

Llewelyn, John. *The Middle Voice of Ecological Conscience*. New York, Macmillan, 1991.
Hatley, James. *Environ Ethics*, 17(1), 109-111, Spr 95.

Lloyd, A C. *The Anatomy of Neoplatonism*. New York, Clarendon/Oxford Pr, 1990.
Preus, Anthony. *J Neoplatonic Stud*, 1(1), 141-145, Fall 92.

Lloyd, Dan. *Simple Minds*. Cambridge, MIT Pr, 1989.
Kazez, Jean R. *Phil Rev*, 103(4), 718-720, O 94.

Lloyd, Genevieve. *Being In Time*. New York, Routledge, 1993.
Losin, Peter. *Phil Lit*, 18(2), 409-410, O 94.

Lloyd, Genevieve. *Being In Time: Selves and Narrators in Philosophy and Literature*. New York, Routledge, 1993.
Grimshaw, Jean. *Rad Phil*, 69, 43-44, Ja-F 95.

Lloyd, S A. *Ideals as Interests in Hobbes's 'Leviathan'*. New York, Cambridge Univ Pr, 1992.
Anderson, Elizabeth. *Int Stud Phil*, 27(2), 123-124, 1995.
Darwall, Stephen. *Phil Rev*, 103(4), 748-752, O 94.

Lob-Hüdepohl, Andreas. *Kommunikative Vernunft und theologische Ethik*. Basel, Herder Pr, 1993.
Möhring-Hesse, M. *Theol Phil*, 69(4), 619-624, 1994.

Lobto, A (ed). *Littera, sensus, sententia*. Milano, Massimo, 1992.
Beuchot, Mauricio. *Analogía*, 8(1), 185-187, 1994.

Locke, J. *La conducta del entendimiento y otros ensayos póstumos*. Barcelona, Anthropos, 1992.
Martínez M, José A. *An Seminar Metaf*, 27, 340-342, 1993.

Löhr, Gebhard. *Das Problem des Einen und Vielen in Platons "Philebos"*. Göttingen, Vandenhoeck, 1990.
Robinson, Thomas M. *Phoenix*, 48(3), 264-266, Autumn 94.

Lötter, Hennie P P. *Justice for an Unjust Society*. Amsterdam, Rodopi, 1993.
Ramose, Mogobe B. *Quest*, 8(1), 112-125, Je 94.

Lohse, Eduard. *Theological Ethics of the New Testament*. Minneapolis, Fortress Pr, 1991.
Kotva Jr, Joseph J. *Heythrop J*, 36(2), 215-216, Ap 95.

Lonergan, Bernard and Lambert, Pierre (trans). *Pour une méthodologie philosophique*. Montreal, Bellarmin, 1991.
Naud, Julien. *Dialogue (Canada)*, 33(2), 343-346, Spr 94.

Lonergan, Bernard J F. *Collected Works of Bernard Lonergan*. Toronto, Univ of Toronto Pr, 1993.
Walters, Gregory J. *Can Phil Rev*, 15(1), 56-58, F 95.

Lopez Aranguren, José Luis. *Obras completas (volumen 1)*. Madrid, Ed Trotta, 1994.
Murillo, Ildefonso. *Dialogo Filosof*, 10(3), 444-445, S-D 94.

Lorenz, Dietrich. *Studi 1994*. Rome, Pont U Aquinas Urbe, 1994.
Castelbranco, Maria J. *Acta Phil*, 4(1), 149-152, 1995.

Lorenz, Edward N. *The Essence of Chaos*. London, UCL Pr Ltd, 1993.
Montequi, J M. *Anu Filosof*, 28(1), 171-172, 1995.

Lorenzen, Paul. *Lehrbuch der konstruktiven Wissenschaftstheorie*. Munster, BI-Wissenschafts, 1987.
Ulfig, Alexander. *Protosoz*, 2, 100-105, Ja 92.

Lucas, J R. *Responsibility*. New York, Clarendon/Oxford Pr, 1993.
Gowans, Christopher W. *Phil Books*, 35(3), 203-206, Jl 94.
Helm, Paul. *J Applied Phil*, 11(2), 242-243, 1994.
McMahon, Christopher. *Ethics*, 105(2), 404-407, Ja 95.
Melchert, Norman. *Rev Metaph*, 48(4), 910-911, Je 95.
Postow, B C. *Mind*, 104(413), 175-178, Ja 95.

Luckmann, Thomas. *Die unsichtbare Religion*. Frankfurt, Suhrkamp, 1991.
Kühnlein, Michael. *Protosoz*, 2, 111-113, Ja 92.

Ludwig, Bernd. *Kants Rechtslehre*. Hamburg, Meiner, 1988.
Schottky, Richard. *Fichte-Studien*, 1, 242-250, 1990.

Lütterfelds, W. *Fichte und Wittgenstein*. Stuttgart, Klett-Cotta, 1989.
Jergius, Holger. *Fichte-Studien*, 3, 279-307, 1991.

Lütz, Dietmar. *Homo Viator*. Zurich, Theol Verlag, 1988.
Moxter, Michael. *Phil Rundsch*, 41(2), 133-158, 1994.

Luhmann, Niklas. *Die Wissenschaft der Gesellschaft*. Frankfurt, Suhrkamp, 1990.
Martin, Dirk. *Protosoz*, 1, 120-124, Ap 91.

Lukács, Georg, Gaines, Jeremy (trans) and Keast, Paul (trans). *German Realists in the Nineteenth Century*. London, Libris, 1993.
Giles, Steve. *Brit J Aes*, 34(4), 407-408, O 94.

Lycan, William G. *Judgement and Justification*. New York, Cambridge Univ Pr, 1988.
Stich, Stephen. *Nous*, 27(3), 380-383, S 93.

Lyons, David. *Moral Aspects of Legal Theory*. New York, Cambridge Univ Pr, 1993.
Lo, M C. *Can Phil Rev*, 14(1), 31-33, F 94.
Rakowski, Eric. *Phil Books*, 36(2), 133-134, Ap 95.
Ten, C L. *Utilitas*, 6(2), 313-317, N 94.

Lyotard, Jean-François. *The Postmodern Explained*. Minneapolis, Univ of Minn Pr, 1993.
Eisenstein, Gabe. *Int Stud Phil*, 27(1), 139-140, 1995.

Lyotard, Jean-François, Harvey, Robert (ed) and Roberts, Mark (ed). *Toward the Postmodern*. Atlantic Highlands, Humanities Pr, 1992.
Lingis, Alphonso. *Int Stud Phil*, 26(4), 142-143, 1994.

Lyotard, Jean-François and Rottenberg, Elizabeth (trans). *Lessons on the Analytic of the Sublime*. Stanford, Stanford Univ Pr, 1994.
Huhn, Thomas. *J Aes Art Crit*, 53(1), 89-91, Wint 95.

Macann, Christopher (ed). *Martin Heidegger*. New York, Routledge, 1992.
Marlin, Randal. *Can Phil Rev*, 14(4), 275-277, Ag 94.

Macann, Christopher (ed). *Martin Heidegger: Critical Assessments (Volume II)*. New York, Routledge, 1992.
Marlin, Randal. *Can Phil Rev*, 14(6), 399-401, D 94.

Macann, Christopher (ed). *Martin Heidegger: Critical Assessments (Volume III)*. New York, Routledge, 1992.
Marlin, Randal. *Can Phil Rev*, 14(6), 402-404, D 94.

Macann, Christopher (ed). *Martin Heidegger: Critical Assessments (Volume IV)*. New York, Routledge, 1992.
Marlin, Randal. *Can Phil Rev*, 14(6), 405-408, D 94.

Macaulay, Ronald K S. *Locating Dialect in Discourse*. New York, Oxford Univ Pr, 1991.
Moller, Erik. *J Prag*, 22(2), 223-227, Ag 94.

MacCormick, Neal (ed) and Bankowski, Zenon (ed). *Enlightenment, Rights and Revolution*. Aberdeen, Aberdeen Univ Pr, 1989.
Pois, Robert A. *Hist Euro Ideas*, 18(6), 985-988, N 94.

Mason, Andrew. *Political Disagreement*. New York, Cambridge Univ Pr, 1993.
Gorman, J L. *Phil Books*, 36(3), 206-207, Jl 95.

Mason, John Hope (ed) and Wokler, Robert (ed). *Political Writings—Diderot*. New York, Cambridge Univ Pr, 1992.
Kelly, Christopher. *Hist Euro Ideas*, 18(6), 1012-1013, N 94.

Mason, Roger (ed). *John Knox: On Rebellion*. New York, Cambridge Univ Pr, 1994.
Nederman, Cary J. *Hist Euro Ideas*, 21(1), 159-160, Ja 95.

Massumi, B. *A User's Guide to Capitalism and Schizophrenia*. Cambridge, MIT Pr, 1992.
Buchanan, Ian. *Theor Cult Soc*, 11(3), 166-168, Ag 94.

Masters, Roger D. *Beyond Relativism*. Hanover, Univ Pr New England, 1993.
Wood Jr, Forrest. *Rev Metaph*, 48(4), 911-912, Je 95.

Matassi, Elio. *Eredità hegeliane*. Napoli, Morano, 1991.
S, M. *G Crit Filosof Ital*, 73(1), 159-162, Ja-Ap 94.

Mather, Cotton and Solberg, William U (ed). *The Christian Philosopher*. Champaign, Univ of Illinois Pr, 1994.
Walters, Kerry S. *Phil Lit*, 19(1), 167-168, Ap 95.

Mathieu, Vittorio. *Perché leggere Plotino*. Milano, Rusconi, 1992.
Marcellino, Claudio. *Riv Filosof Neo-Scolas*, 86(2), 408-411, Ap-Je 94.

Matthews, Gareth B. *Thought's Ego in Augustine and Descartes*. Ithaca, Cornell Univ Pr, 1992.
Loeb, Louis E. *Mind*, 104(413), 182-186, Ja 95.
Martin, Christopher. *Phil Quart*, 45(179), 265-266, Ap 95.

Mattick Jr, Paul (ed). *Eighteenth-Century Aesthetics and the Reconstruction of Art*. New York, Cambridge Univ Pr, 1993.
Symmons, Sarah. *Brit J Aes*, 35(1), 75-77, Ja 95.
Townsend, Dabney. *Phil Quart*, 45(180), 412-415, Jl 95.

Matustík, Martin J. *Postnational Identity*. New York, Guilford, 1993.
Brown, Alison Leigh. *Man World*, 28(1), 181-184, Ja 95.
Velek, Josef. *Filozof Cas*, 42(6), 1061-1065, 1994.

Maudlin, Tim. *Quantum Non-Locality and Relativity*. Cambridge, Blackwell, 1994.
Sklar, Lawrence. *Brit J Phil Sci*, 45(3), 933-934, S 94.

May, Larry. *Sharing Responsibility*. Chicago, Univ of Chicago Pr, 1992.
Pence, Gregory. *Can Phil Rev*, 14(3), 189-190, Je 94.

May, Larry (ed) and Sharratt, Shari Collins (ed). *Applied Ethics: A Multicultural Approach*. Englewood Cliffs, Prentice Hall, 1994.
Palmer, Clare. *Can Phil Rev*, 15(1), 58-60, F 95.

Mayo, Deborah G (ed) and Hollander, Rachelle D (ed). *Acceptable Evidence*. New York, Oxford Univ Pr, 1991.
Thompson, Paul B. *Res Phil Technol*, 14, 312-320, 1994.

Mazlish, Bruce. *The Fourth Discontinuity*. New Haven, Yale Univ Pr, 1993.
Donald, Merlin. *Hist Theor*, 33(3), 367-374, 1994.

Mazzotta, Giuseppe. *Dante's Vision and the Circle of Knowledge*. Princeton, Princeton Univ Pr, 1993.
Roda, Anthony. *Phil Lit*, 19(1), 194-195, Ap 95.

McBride, William L. *Sartre's Political Theory*. Bloomington, Indiana Univ Pr, 1991.
Flay, Joseph C. *Res Phenomenol*, 23, 212-221, 1993.

McCall, Storrs. *A Model of the Universe*. New York, Clarendon/Oxford Pr, 1994.
Smart, J J C. *Austl J Phil*, 73(1), 161-163, Mr 95.
Vallentyne, Peter. *Mind*, 104(415), 658-661, Jl 95.

McCawley, James D. *Everything That Linguists Have Always Wanted To Know About Logic But Were Ashamed To Ask*. Chicago, Univ of Chicago Pr, 1993.
Valencia, Victor Sánchez. *Hist Phil Log*, 15(2), 248-252, 1994.

McCloskey, Donald N. *Knowledge and Persuasion in Economics*. New York, Cambridge Univ Pr, 1994.
Weintraub, E Roy. *Econ Phil*, 11(1), 221-224, Ap 95.

McConnell, Terrance. *Gratitude*. Philadelphia, Temple Univ Pr, 1993.
Barron, Guillermo. *Can Phil Rev*, 14(3), 191-193, Je 94.
Care, Norman S. *Ethics*, 105(3), 657-659, April.
Hughes, Gerard J. *Phil Quart*, 45(180), 403-405, Jl 95.

McCormick, Peter J. *Modernity, Aesthetics, and the Bounds of Art*. Ithaca, Cornell Univ Pr, 1990.
Carvalho, John M. *Can Phil Rev*, 14(2), 106-110, Ap 94.

McCumber, John. *The Company of Words*. Evanston, Northwestern Univ Pr, 1993.
Burbidge, John W. *Can Phil Rev*, 14(2), 110-112, Ap 94.
Dove, K R. *J Hist Phil*, 32(4), 681-682, O 94.

McDonald, Lynn. *The Early Origins of the Social Sciences*. Montreal, McGill-Queens U Pr, 1993.
Trompf, Garry W. *Phil Soc Sci*, 25(2), 261-264, Je 95.

McGhee, Michael (ed). *Philosophy, Religion and the Spiritual Life*. New York, Cambridge Univ Pr, 1992.
King-Farlow, John. *Can Phil Rev*, 14(1), 35-37, F 94.

McGinn, Colin. *Mental Content*. Cambridge, Blackwell, 1989.
Agar, Nicholas. *Austl J Phil*, 73(1), 164-165, Mr 95.
Levin, Michael. *Nous*, 27(1), 137-139, Mr 93.

McHale, Jean V. *Medical Confidentiality and Legal Privilege*. New York, Routledge, 1993.
Dickens, Bernard M. *Bioethics*, 9(2), 167-169, Ap 95.
Draper, Heather. *J Applied Phil*, 11(2), 241-242, 1994.

McInerny, Ralph. *Aquinas Against the Averroists*. West Lafayette, Purdue Univ Pr, 1993.
McCabe, Herbert. *Int Phil Quart*, 35(2), 224-225, Ju 95.

McInerny, Ralph. *The Question of Christian Ethics*. Washington, Cath Univ Amer Pr, 1993.
Inglis, Brian D. *Can Phil Rev*, 14(4), 278-279, Ag 94.

McKenna, Andrew J. *Violence and Difference*. Champaign, Univ of Illinois Pr, 1992.
Youngerman, Mark. *Int Stud Phil*, 26(4), 149-150, 1994.

McLaughlin, Andrew. *Regarding Nature*. Albany, SUNY Pr, 1993.
Gault, Richard. *Environ Values*, 4(1), 79-81, F 95.
Johnson, Gregory R. *Agr Human Values*, 12(1), 64-67, Winter 95.

McLean, Edward B. *Law and Civilization, The Legal Thought of Roscoe Pound*. Lanham, Univ Pr of America, 1992.
Murphy, Jr, Cornelius F. *Vera Lex*, 13(1-2), 53-55, 1993.

McLeod, Mark S. *Rationality and Theistic Belief*. Ithaca, Cornell Univ Pr, 1993.
Everitt, Nicholas. *Phil Books*, 36(1), 71-72, Ja 95.
Helm, Paul. *Int Phil Quart*, 35(1), 98-100, Mr 95.
Willard, Julian. *Relig Stud*, 31(2), 272-274, Je 95.

McNeill, Paul M. *The Ethics and Politics of Human Experimentation*. New York, Cambridge Univ Pr, 1993.
Dodds, Susan. *Austl J Phil*, 72(3), 400-401, S 94.

Meadowcroft, James (ed). *L T Hobbhouse: Liberalism and Other Writings*. New York, Cambridge Univ Pr, 1994.
Stapleton, Julia. *Hist Polit Thought*, 15(2), 304-305, Sum 94.

Meckenstock, G (ed). *Schleiermacher und die wissenschaftliche Kultur des Christentums*. Hawthorne, de Gruyter, 1991.
Moxter, Michael. *Phil Rundsch*, 41(2), 133-158, 1994.

Meeks, Wayne. *The Origins of Christian Morality*. New Haven, Yale Univ Pr, 1993.
Barclay, John M G. *Mod Theol*, 11(2), 261-262, Ap 95.

Meier-Oeser, Stephen. *Die Präsenz des Vergessenen*. Munster, Aschendorff, 1989.
de Gandillac, Maurice. *Arch Phil*, 58(1), 152-153, Ja-Mr 95.

Meinwald, Constance C. *Plato's 'Parmenides'*. New York, Oxford Univ Pr, 1991.
Sayre, Kenneth. *Nous*, 28(1), 114-116, Mr 94.

Mele, A R. *Springs of Action*. New York, Oxford Univ Pr, 1992.
McCann, Hugh J. *Phil Phenomenol Res*, 54(4), 979-982, D 94.
Tracy, Thomas F. *Thomist*, 59(2), 332-335, Ap 95.

Melnick, Arthur. *Space, Time, and Thought in Kant*. Dordrecht, Kluwer, 1989.
Guyer, Paul. *Kantstudien*, 85(4), 477-482, 1994.

Melzer, Arthur M (ed), Weinberger, Jerry (ed) and Zinman, M. Richard (ed). *Technology in the Western Political Tradition*. Ithaca, Cornell Univ Pr, 1993.
O'Donnell, Brian. *Int Phil Quart*, 35(2), 232-233, Ju 95.

Menczer, Béla. *Tensions of Order and Freedom*. New Brunswick, Transaction Books, 1994.
Wegierski, Mark. *Rev Metaph*, 48(4), 912-914, Je 95.

Mensching, Günther. *Das Allgemeine und das Besondere*. Stuttgart, Metzler, 1992.
Enders, Markus. *Z Phil Forsch*, 48(4), 623-628, 1994.

Merklinger, Philip M. *Philosophy, Theology, and Hegel's Berlin Philosophy of Religion*. Albany, SUNY Pr, 1993.
Harris, H S. *Rev Metaph*, 48(4), 914-915, Je 95.
Shanks, Andrew. *Bull Hegel Soc Gt Brit*, 30, 74-76, Autumn-Wint 94.

Messer, Richard. *Does God's Existence Need Proof?*. New York, Clarendon/Oxford Pr, 1993.
Kvanvig, Jonathan. *Phil Books*, 36(3), 213-215, Jl 95.
Taylor, James E. *Int J Phil Relig*, 37(3), 183-185, Je 95.

Mestrovic, Stjepan G. *The Barbarian Temperament*. New York, Routledge, 1993.
Armitage, John. *Rad Phil*, 70, 48, Mr-Ap 95.

Metzger, Dieter. *Thomas Hobbes und die Englische Revolution 1640-1660*. Stuttgart, Frommann-Holzboog, 1991.
Hespe, Franz. *Z Phil Forsch*, 48(3), 480-484, Jl-S 94.

Mey, Jacob L. *Pragmatics: An Introduction*. Oxford, Blackwell, 1993.
Mao, LuMing R. *J Prag*, 23(5), 577-589, My 95.

Meyer, Michel. *Le philosophe et les passions*. Paris, Lib Gen Francaise, 1991.
Gabaude, Jean-Marc. *Rev Phil Fr*, 4, 531-533, O-D 94.

Meyer, Thomas Ludof. *Das Problems eines höchsten Grundsatzes der Philosophie bei Jacob Sigismund Beck*. Amsterdam, Rodopi, 1991.
Chico, Gabriel. *Analogía*, 5(2), 205-208, 1991.

Meyers, Diana Tietjens (ed), Kipnis, Kenneth (ed) and Murphy Jr, Cornelius F (ed). *Kindred Matters*. Ithaca, Cornell Univ Pr, 1993.
Coady, Margaret. *Phil Quart*, 45(180), 405-406, Jl 95.

Meynell, Hugo (ed). *Grace, Politics and Desire*. Calgary, Univ of Calgary Pr, 1990.
Horban, Peter. *Dialogue (Canada)*, 33(3), 544-549, Sum 94.

Midgley, Mary. *Can't We Make Moral Judgments?*. New York, St Martin's Pr, 1991.
Suttle, Bruce B. *J Value Inq*, 28(2), 355-356, Je 94.

Midgley, Mary. *Science as Salvation*. New York, Routledge, 1992.
Avis, Paul. *Heythrop J*, 35(3), 355-356, Jl 94.
Rodrigues da Cruz, Eduardo. *Zygon*, 30(2), 333-336, Je 95.

Miethe, Terry L and Flew, Antony G N. *"Existe Dios?" El debate entre un creyente y un ateo*. Madrid, Catedra, 1994.
Bono, José Luis Caballero. *Dialogo Filosof*, 10(3), 445-447, S-D 94.

Miethe, Terry L and Flew, Antony G N. *Does God Exist? A Believer and an Atheist Debate*. New York, HarperCollins, 1991.
Burgess-Jackson, Keith. *Teach Phil*, 17(4), 359-362, D 94.

Miethke, Jürgen. *Las ideas políticas de la Edad Media*. Buenos Aires, Ed Biblos, 1993.
Tursi, Antonio D. *Pat Med*, 15, 96-97, 1994.

Mignini, Filippo. *Romolo Murri*. Ancona, Transeuropa, 1993.
S, A. *G Crit Filosof Ital*, 73(1), 171-172, Ja-Ap 94.

Milbank, John. *The Religious Dimension in the Thought of Giambattista Vico Volumes 1 and 2*. Lewiston, Mellen Pr, 1992.
Mazzola, Robert. *Boll Centro Stud Vichiani*, 24-25, 277-282, 1994-95.

Millán Puelles, Antonio. *La libre afirmación de nuestro ser*. Madrid, Rialp, 1994.
Manssini-Correas, Carlos I. *Analogía*, 9(1), 209-212, 1995.

Miller, Barry. *From Existence to God*. New York, Routledge, 1992.
Schlesinger, George N. *Int J Phil Relig*, 37(1), 61-62, F 95.

Miller, James. *The Passion of Michel Foucault*. New York, HarperCollins, 1993.
Kelly, Michael. *Constellation*, 1(1), 158-163, Ap 94.

Miller, Mara. *The Garden as an Art*. Albany, SUNY Pr, 1993.
Giles, Gordon J. *Brit J Aes*, 35(1), 77 79, Ja 95.

Miller, Richard W. *Moral Differences*. Princeton, Princeton Univ Pr, 1992.
Copp, David. *Phil Rev*, 103(4), 723-726, O 94.

Millikan, Ruth Garrett. *White Queen Psychology and Other Essays for Alice*. Cambridge, MIT Pr, 1993.
Martin, Michael. *Phil Books*, 36(1), 59-62, Ja 95.
Tanney, Julia. *Phil Quart*, 45(178), 137-139, Ja 95.

Milton, Kay (ed). *Environmentalism: The View from Anthropology*. New York, Routledge, 1993.
Rival, Laura. *Environ Values*, 4(1), 83-84, F 95.

Minas, Anne (ed). *Gender Basics*. Belmont, Wadsworth, 1993.
Damico, Linda H. *Can Phil Rev*, 14(3), 193-195, Je 94.

Minowitz, Peter. *Profits, Priests, and Princes*. Stanford, Stanford Univ Pr, 1993.
Heath, Eugene. *Rev Metaph*, 48(4), 915-916, Je 95.
Teichgraeber III, Richard F. *Polit Theory*, 23(1), 147-165, F 95.

Misgeld, Dieter. *Toward a New Humanism*. Santiago, Nunoa, 1993.
Canon, Carlos. *J Moral Educ*, 23(3), 362-363, 1994.

Missa, Jean-Noël. *L'esprit-cerveau, la philosophie de l'esprit à la lumière des sciences cognitives*. Paris, Vrin, 1993.
Fuchs, Edith. *Rev Phil Fr*, 1, 111-114, Ja-Mr 95.

Mitcham, Carl. *Philosophy of Technology in Spanish Speaking Countries*. Dordrecht, Kluwer, 1993.
Huyke, Héctor José. *Man World*, 28(3), 307-311, Jl 95.

Mitchell, Joshua. *Not By Reason Alone*. Chicago, Univ of Chicago Pr, 1993.
Eisenach, Eldon J. *Hist Polit Thought*, 16(1), 148-151, Spr 95.
Farr, James. *Polit Theory*, 23(2), 386-388, My 95.

Mitra, M N. *Language, Truth and Predication*. New Delhi, New Statesman, 1988.
Pradhan, R C. *J Indian Counc Phil Res*, 11(2), 131-134, Ja-Ap 94.

Modica, G. *Fede libertà peccato*. Palermo, Palumbo, 1992.
Ercoleo, Marisa. *G Metaf*, 16(1-2), 272-274, Ja-Ag 94.

Moggridge, D E. *Maynard Keynes*. New York, Routledge, 1992.
Davis, John. *Econ Phil*, 10(2), 359-364, O 94.

Mohanty, Jitendra Nath. *Reason and Tradition in Indian Thought*. New York, Clarendon/Oxford Pr, 1992.
Oldmeadow, Harry. *Asian Phil*, 5(1), 90-93, 1995.

Mohanty, Saroj Kumar. *The Concept of Action*. New Delhi, Indus, 1992.
Chhabra, Raj Kumar. *J Indian Counc Phil Res*, 11(2), 138-141, Ja-Ap 94.

Mojsisch, B (ed) and Pluta, O (ed). *Historia Philosophiae Medii Aevi*. Amsterdam, Gruner, 1992.
Winkler, Norbert. *Deut Z Phil*, 43(1), 187-188, 1995.

Molina Petit, C. *Dialéctica feminista de la Ilustración*. Barcelona, Anthropos, 1994.
Cano López, Antonio José. *Daimon Rev Filosof*, 8, 240-241, 1994.
Cano López, Antonio José. *Rev Filosof (Spain)*, 8, 240-241, 1994.

Monk, Ray. *Ludwig Wittgenstein, The Duty of Genius*. New York, Penguin USA, 1991.
Tejedor Palau, María Asunción. *An Seminar Metaf*, 28, 366-369, 1994.

Monk, Ray. *Wittgenstein: Le devoir de génie*. Paris, Odile Jacob, 1993.
Largeault, Jean. *Rev Phil Fr*, 4, 492-496, O-D 94.

Montague, Phillip. *In the Interests of Others*. Dordrecht, Kluwer, 1992.
Hahn, Carl. *Can Phil Rev*, 14(1), 38-39, F 94.
Pybus, Elizabeth. *Mind*, 104(414), 422-425, Ap 95.
Wellman, Carl. *Int Stud Phil*, 27(2), 125-126, 1995.

Moody, Harry R. *Ethics in an Aging Society*. Baltimore, Johns Hopkins U Pr, 1992.
Holstein, Martha. *J Med Human*, 15(3), 185-193, Fall 94.

Moon, J Donald. *Constructing Community*. Princeton, Princeton Univ Pr, 1993.
Kuhlman, Sherryl. *Can Phil Rev*, 14(5), 334-336, O 94.
Macedo, Stephen. *Polit Theory*, 23(2), 389-393, My 95.

Moonan, Lawrence. *Divine Power*. New York, Clarendon/Oxford Pr, 1994.
Hughes, Gerard J. *Relig Stud*, 31(2), 269-271, Je 95.
Reynolds, Philip Lyndon. *Heythrop J*, 36(2), 224-225, Ap 95.

Mooney, Edward F. *Knights of Faith and Resignation*. Albany, SUNY Pr, 1991.
Perkins, Robert L. *Int Stud Phil*, 26(4), 150-151, 1994.

Moore, A W. *The Infinite*. New York, Routledge, 1990.
Robles, José Antonio. *Critica*, 26(78), 119-122, D 94.

Moore, Brooke Noel and Bruder, Kenneth. *Philosophy: The Power of Ideas (Second Edition)*. Mountain View, Mayfield, 1993.
Sauvé, Kevin. *Can Phil Rev*, 14(4), 280-281, Ag 94.

Moore, Edward C (ed). *Charles S Peirce and the Philosophy of Science*. Tuscaloosa, Univ of Alabama Pr, 1993.
Harris, H S. *Trans Peirce Soc*, 30(4), 1046-1054, Fall 94.

Moore, Margaret. *Foundations of Liberalism*. New York, Clarendon/Oxford Pr, 1993.
Milde, Michael. *Can Phil Rev*, 14(2), 112-115, Ap 94.

Moore, Stanley. *Marx versus Markets*. University Park, Penn St Univ Pr, 1993.
McMurtry, John. *Can Phil Rev*, 14(1), 40-43, F 94.

Moran, Dermot (ed). *International Journal of Philosophical Studies*. New York, Routledge, 1993.
Champlin, T S. *Phil Books*, 36(1), 33-35, Ja 95.

Moran, Dermot. *The Philosophy of John Scottus Eriugena*. New York, Cambridge Univ Pr, 1989.
Jarka-Sellers, Hannes. *Phil Rev*, 103(3), 577-580, Jl 94.

Moravcsik, Julius. *Plato and Platonism*. Cambridge, Blackwell, 1992.
Baltzly, Dirk. *Mind*, 104(413), 186-193, Ja 95.
Kraut, Richard. *Nous*, 28(4), 547-555, D 94.
Tessin, Timothy. *Phil Invest*, 17(3), 566-570, Jl 94.

Moreland, J P and Nielsen, Kai. *Does God Exist?*. Buffalo, Prometheus, 1993.
Dickson, Gwen Griffith. *Heythrop J*, 36(1), 114-115, Ja 95.

Morewedge, Parviz (ed). *Neoplatonism and Islamic Thought*. Albany, SUNY Pr, 1992.
Netton, Ian Richard. *Asian Phil*, 4(2), 191-192, 1994.

Moriconi, Enrico. *Discorso e Significato*. Roma, La Nuova Ital Sci, 1994.
Cepparello, Giovanna. *Teoria*, 14(2), 151-152, 1994.

Morin, Edgar. *Science Avec Conscience*. Paris, Fayard, 1990.
Holzbachová, Ivana. *Filozof Cas*, 42(4), 696-698, 1994.

Morin-Aguilar, Eric (trans). *Entre la logique et la foi*. Montricher, Ed Noir Blanc, 1990.
Gasser, James. *Hist Phil Log*, 15(2), 253-254, 1994.

Morreim, E Haavi. *Balancing Act*. Dordrecht, Kluwer, 1991.
Carroll, Mary Ann. *J Value Inq*, 29(1), 149-152, Mr 95.

Morris, David B. *The Culture of Pain*. Berkeley, Univ of Calif Pr, 1991.
Cobbs, Elizabeth Lipton. *J Clin Ethics*, 5(2), 164-165, Sum 94.

Morris, Debra (ed) and Shapiro, Ian (ed). *The Political Writings*. Indianapolis, Hackett, 1993.
Campbell, James. *Trans Peirce Soc*, 30(4), 1072-1077, Fall 94.

Morris, Michael. *The Good and the True*. New York, Clarendon/Oxford Pr, 1992.
Millar, Alan. *Phil Books*, 36(3), 188-190, Jl 95.

Moseley, Fred (ed). *Marx's Method in Capital*. Atlantic Highlands, Humanities Pr, 1993.
Albritton, Robert R. *Rad Phil*, 70, 41-42, Mr-Ap 95.

Moser, Paul K. *Philosophy After Objectivity*. New York, Oxford Univ Pr, 1993.
Elugardo, Reinaldo. *Rev Metaph*, 48(2), 418-419, D 94.

Moss, Jean Dietz. *Novelties in the Heavens*. Chicago, Univ of Chicago Pr, 1993.
Cloudsley, Tim. *Hist Euro Ideas*, 21(1), 89-91, Ja 95.

Mostefaï, Ourida. *Lectures de "La Nouvelle Héloïse"*. Ottawa, Coll Pensee Libre, 1993.
Larochelle, Élaine. *Laval Theol Phil*, 50(3), 657-660, O 94.

Mosterin, J. *Filosofía de la cultura*. Madrid, Alianza, 1993.
Amilburu, María García. *Dialogo Filosof*, 10(2), 273-275, My-Ag 94.

Mouffe, Chantal. *The Return of the Political*. New York, Verso, 1993.
Anderson, Brian. *Austl J Phil*, 72(4), 538-539, D 94.
Squires, Judith. *Rad Phil*, 69, 41-43, Ja-F 95.

Moulines, C U. *Pluralidad y recursión*. Madrid, Alianza, 1991.
Falguera, José-Luis. *Critica*, 26(76-77), 248-266, Ap-Ag 94.

Mourelatos, Alexander P D (ed). *The Presocratics*. Princeton, Princeton Univ Pr, 1993.
Ferber, Rafael. *Frei Z Phil Theol*, 41(3), 575-576, 1994.

Mowitt, John. *Text: the Genealogy of an Antidisciplinarian Object*. Durham, Duke Univ Pr, 1992.
Brown, Andrew. *Hist Euro Ideas*, 18(6), 1019-1020, N 94.

Moya, Patricia. *El principio del conocimiento en Tomás de Aquino*. Pamplona, EUNSA, 1994.
Fernández, Héctor Velázquez. *Topicos*, 4(7), 84-86, 1994.

Moyaert, Paul. *Ethiek en sublimatie*. Nigmegen, Uitgeverij SUN, 1994.
Ijsseling, Hester. *Alg Ned Tijdschr Wijs*, 87(1), 58-60, Ja 95.
Rosemann, Philipp W. *Int J Phil Stud*, 3(1), 199-201, Mr 95.

Muehlmann, Robert G. *Berkeley's Ontology*. Indianapolis, Hackett, 1992.
Cummins, Phillip D. *Phil Rev*, 103(3), 580-582, Jl 94.

Müller, Christof. *Geschichtsbewusstsein bei Augustinus*. Wurzburg, Augustinus Verlag, 1993.
Sieben, H J. *Theol Phil*, 69(4), 582-584, 1994.

Müller, Erich Wolfgang. *Albert Schweitzers Kulturphilosophie im Horizont säkularer Ethik*. Hawthorne, de Gruyter, 1993.
Wolf, Jean-Claud. *Frei Z Phil Theol*, 41(3), 576-578, 1994.

Münch, Dieter. *Intention und Zeichen*. Frankfurt, Suhrkamp, 1993.
Soldati, Gianfranco. *Phil Rundsch*, 41(3), 269-275, Je 94.

Mues, Albert. *Transzendentalphilosophie als System*. Hamburg, Meiner, 1987.
Soller, Alois K. *Fichte-Studien*, 3, 250-278, 1991.

Mulhall, Stephen. *Stanley Cavell: Philosophy's Recounting of the Ordinary*. New York, Clarendon/Oxford Pr, 1994.
McFee, Graham. *Brit J Aes*, 35(2), 177-180, Ap 95.

Mulhall, Stephen and Swift, Adam. *Liberals and Communitarians*. Cambridge, Blackwell, 1992.
Forst, Rainer. *J Phil Educ*, 29(1), 97-104, March 95.
Simpson, Evan. *Can Phil Rev*, 14(2), 115-117, Ap 94.

Muller, Jerry Z. *Adam Smith in His Time and Ours*. New York, Free Pr, 1993.
Brown, Vivienne. *Hist Euro Ideas*, 21(1), 116-117, Ja 95.

Mulligan, Kevin. *Language, Truth and Ontology*. Dordrecht, Kluwer, 1992.
Gaeta, Rodolfo. *Rev Latin de Filosof*, 21(1), 186-190, Fall 95.

Mulligan, Kevin (ed). *Speech Act and Sachverhalt*. Dordrecht, Kluwer, 1987.
Kienzle, Bertram. *Nous*, 27(1), 101-102, Mr 93.

Mumford, M J and Peasnell, K V. *Philosophical Perspectives on Accounting*. London, Routledge, 1993.
Hurley, G M. *J Applied Phil*, 12(1), 120-121, 1995.

Muratore, S. *L'evoluzione cosmologica e il problema di Dio*. Rome, Ed Ave, 1993.
Giustiniani, Pasquale. *Sapienza*, 47(4), 485-489, O-D 94.

Murdoch, Iris. *Metaphysics as a Guide to Morals*. London, Viking, 1992.
Beauchamp, Richard A. *J Speculative Phil*, 9(1), 78-81, 1995.
Hepburn, R W. *Phil Books*, 36(2), 124-127, Ap 95.

Murphy, James Bernard. *The Moral Economy of Labour*. New Haven, Yale Univ Pr, 1993.
Hunt, I E. *Can Phil Rev*, 14(6), 413-415, D 94.

Murphy, Kevin R. *Honesty in the Workplace*. Pacific Grove, Brooks/Cole, 1993.
Tobin, R James. *Can Phil Rev*, 14(2), 117-118, Ap 94.

Musgrave, Alan. *Common Sense, Science and Scepticism*. New York, Cambridge Univ Pr, 1993.
Baird, Davis. *Rev Metaph*, 48(4), 917-918, Je 95.
Legg, Cathy. *Can Phil Rev*, 14(5), 336-339, O 94.
Milne, Peter. *Phil Quart*, 45(180), 379-384, Jl 95.
Tebbit, Mark. *Phil Books*, 35(3), 219-221, Jl 94.

Nachtsheim, Stephan. *Emil Lasks Grundlehre*. Tübingen, Mohr, 1992.
Hammacher, Klaus. *Fichte-Studien*, 5, 233-236, 1993.

Nadin, Mihai. *Mind: Anticipation and Chaos*. Stuttgart, Belser Pr, 1991.
Smith, Philip L. *Phil East West*, 45(1), 123-131, Ja 95.

Nadler, Steven. *Malebranche and Ideas*. New York, Oxford Univ Pr, 1992.
Doney, Willis. *Mind*, 104(413), 193-196, Ja 95.
Pyle, Andrew. *Phil Books*, 36(3), 177-179, Jl 95.

Nägele, Rainer. *Theater, Theory, Speculation*. Baltimore, Johns Hopkins U Pr, 1991.
Brown, Hilda Meldrum. *Hist Euro Ideas*, 18(5), 789-791, S 94.

Nagl-Docekal, Herta and Pauer-Studer, Herlinde. *Jenseits der Geschlechtermoral*. Frankfurt, Fischer Taschenbuch, 1993.
Stoller, Silvia. *Deut Z Phil*, 43(1), 191-194, 1995.

Nancy, Jean-Luc and Holmes, Brian (trans). *The Birth of Presence*. Stanford, Univ Pr, 1993.
Armour, Leslie. *Rev Metaph*, 48(4), 918-920, Je 95.

Nancy, Jean-Luc and McDonald, Bridget (trans). *The Experience of Freedom*. Stanford, Stanford Univ Pr, 1993.
Polit Theory, 23(2), My 95.
Villa, Dana R. *Polit Theory*, 23(2), 382-386, My 95.

Nannini, Sandro. *Cause e Ragioni*. Rome, Ed Riuniti, 1992.
Sanguineti, Juan José. *Acta Phil*, 2(3), 371-373, 1994.

Nardi, Massimo. *Pensare nella verità*. Rome, Studium, 1993.
Nebuloni, Roberto. *Riv Filosof Neo-Scolas*, 87(1), 185-186, Ja-Mr 95.

Nation, R Craig. *War on War*. Durham, Duke Univ Pr, 1989.
Stud East Euro Thought, 47(1-2), 119-122, Ja 95.

Naumann, Ralf. *Das Realismusproblem in der analytischen Philosophie*. Freiburg, Alber, 1993.
Quante, Michael. *Protosoz*, 6, 260-265, 1994.

Naval, Concepción. *Educación, Retórica y Poética*. Pamplona, EUNSA, 1992.
Laspalas, F J. *Topicos*, 4(7), 87-90, 1994.

Navarro Cordón, Juan Manuel and Rodríguez, Ramon. *Heidegger o el final de la filosofía*. Madrid, Ed Complutense, 1993.
Fabris, Adriano. *Teoria*, 14(2), 145-146, 1994.
Munoz Delgado, Mercedes. *An Seminar Metaf*, 27, 326-329, 1993.

Nayak, G C. *Evil and Retributive Hypothesis*. Delhi, Motilal Banarsidass, 1993.
Marathe, M P. *Indian Phil Quart*, 21(3), 273-275, Jl 94.

Ndiaye, A R. *La philosophie d'Antoine Arnauld*. Paris, Vrin, 1991.
Bedouelle, Thierry. *Rev Phil Louvain*, 92(4), 596-597, N 94.

Ndjimbi-Tshiende, Olivier. *Réciprocité-Coopération et le Système Palabrique Africain*. St Ottilien, EOS, 1992.
Ngoma-Binda, P. *Quest*, 8(2), 152-159, D 94.

Nead, Lynda. *The Female Nude*. New York, Routledge, 1992.
Markowitz, Sally. *J Aes Art Crit*, 53(2), 216-218, Spr 95.

Nedo, M (ed). *Ludwig Wittgenstein*. New York, Springer, 1993.
Simons, Peter. *Frei Z Phil Theol*, 42(1-2), 226-229, 1995.

Nef, Frédéric. *Le langage: Une approche philosophique*. Paris, Bordas, 1993.
Engel, Pascal. *Rev Phil Fr*, 4, 533-536, O-D 94.

Negri, Antimo. *Pensiero materialistico e filosofia del lavoro*. Milanese, Marzorati Ed, 1992.
Ferri, Enrico. *Riv Int Filosof Diritto*, 71(2), 365-368, 1994.

Negri, Maurizio. *Elementi di Logica*. Milano, L E D, 1994.
Moriconi, Enrico. *Teoria*, 14(2), 147-148, 1994.

Neiman, Susan. *The Unity of Reason*. New York, Oxford Univ Pr, 1994.
Taylor, Robin. *Phil Books*, 36(3), 179-181, Jl 95.

Nelson, Daniel Mark. *The Priority of Prudence*. University Park, Penn St Univ Pr, 1992.
Kennedy, Terence. *Gregorianum*, 76(1), 176-177, 1995.
Kennedy, Terence. *Heythrop J*, 35(3), 350-351, Jl 94.

Nelson, R J. *Naming and Reference*. New York, Routledge, 1992.
Martens, David B. *Phil Quart*, 45(180), 389-391, Jl 95.

Nerlich, Graham. *Values and Valuing*. Oxford, Clarendon/Oxford Pr, 1989.
Anderberg, Thomas. *Theoria*, 58(1), 230-234, 1992.

Neumann, Harry. *Liberalism*. Durham, Carolina Acad Pr, 1991.
Basinski, Paul A. *Interpretation*, 22(1), 143-149, Fall 94.

Neumann, Harry. *Liberalism (Reply to Basinski's Review)*. Durham, Carolina Acad Pr, 1991.
Neumann, Harry. *Interpretation*, 22(1), 151-154, Fall 94.

Neville, Robert C. *The Puritan Smile*. Albany, SUNY Pr, 1978.
Jones, Judith A. *Man World*, 27(3), 335-341, Jl 94.

Neville, Robert Cummings. *Behind the Masks of God*. Albany, SUNY Pr, 1991.
Ives, Christopher. *Process Stud*, 22(2), 107-108, Sum 93.

Neville, Robert Cummings. *Eternity and Time's Flow*. Albany, SUNY Pr, 1993.
Ford, Lewis S. *Mod Sch*, 71(4), 317-319, My 94.
Helm, Bert P. *Process Stud*, 22(4), 242-244, Winter 93.

Newell, Allen. *Unified Theories of Cognitions*. Cambridge, Harvard Univ Pr, 1990.
Facione, Peter A. *Mind Mach*, 5(1), 127-131, F 95.

Nichols, Mary P. *Citizens and Statesmen*. Lanham, Rowman & Littlefield, 1992.
Miller Jr, Fred D. *Teach Phil*, 17(1), 81-84, Mr 94.

Nicholson, Graeme. *Illustrations of Being*. Atlantic Highlands, Humanities Pr, 1992.
Tietz, John. *Dialogue (Canada)*, 34(1), 171-173, Wint 95.

Nicholson, Marjorie Hope (ed) and Hutton, Sarah (ed). *The Conway Letters*. New York, Oxford Univ Pr, 1992.
Southgate, Beverley. *Hist Euro Ideas*, 21(1), 123-124, Ja 95.

Nida-Rümelin, Julian. *Kritik des Konsequentialismus*. München, Verlag Oldenburg, 1993.
Edmüller, Andreas. *Z Phil Forsch*, 49(1), 141-145, Ja-Mr 95.
Nortmann, Ulrich. *Erkenntnis*, 42(3), 419-422, My 95.

Nielsen, Kai. *God, Scepticism and Modernity*. Ottawa, Univ of Ottawa Pr, 1989.
King-Farlow, John. *Dialogue (Canada)*, 34(1), 196-201, Wint 95.

Niethammer, Lutz and Camiller, Patrick (trans). *Posthistoire: Has History Come to an End?*. New York, Verso, 1993.
McCarney, Joseph. *Rad Phil*, 69, 39-41, Ja-F 95.

Nisters, Thomas. *Kants Kategorischer Imperativ als Leitfaden humaner Praxis*. Freiburg, Alber, 1989.
Soller, Alois K. *Fichte-Studien*, 5, 205-212, 1993.

Nitecki, Matthew H (ed) and Nitecki, Doris V (ed). *History and Evolution*. Albany, SUNY Pr, 1992.
Ghiselin, Michael T. *Hist Phil Life Sci*, 16(1), 175-176, Ja 94.

Norman, Richard. *Free and Equal*. New York, Oxford Univ Pr, Undated.
Oldenquist, Andrew. *Nous*, 27(3), 388-391, S 93.

Norris, Christopher. *The Truth About Postmodernism*. Cambridge, Blackwell, 1993.
O'Hagan, Timothy. *Phil Quart*, 45(178), 106-109, Ja 95.
Payne, Michael. *Hist Human Sci*, 7(3), 117-120, Ag 94.

Norton, David Fate (ed). *The Cambridge Companion to Hume*. New York, Cambridge Univ Pr, 1993.
Coleman, Dorothy. *Rev Metaph*, 48(4), 920-921, Je 95.
O'Shea, James. *Int J Phil Stud*, 3(1), 185-188, Mr 95.
Singer, Ira. *Ethics*, 105(4), 959-961, Jl 95.

Norwood, Vera. *Made From This Earth*. Chapel Hill, Univ N Carolina Pr, 1993.
Maienschein, Jane. *Hist Phil Life Sci*, 16(3), 496-497, D 94.

Novak, Michael. *The Catholic Ethic and the Spirit of Capitalism*. New York, Macmillan, 1993.
Rasmussen, Douglas B. *Amer Cath Phil Quart*, 68(4), 557-561, Autumn 94.

Novitz, David. *The Boundaries of Art*. Philadelphia, Temple Univ Pr, 1992.
Couvalis, George. *Austl J Phil*, 72(3), 401-403, S 94.

Nozick, Robert. *The Nature of Rationality*. Princeton, Princeton Univ Pr, 1993.
Cooper, Wesley E. *Can Phil Rev*, 14(3), 195-198, Je 94.
Hubin, Donald C. *Ethics*, 105(3), 659-662, April.
Lowe, E J. *Phil Quart*, 45(180), 397-399, Jl 95.
Wüstehube, Axel. *Protosoz*, 6, 247-251, 1994.

Nubiola, J. *La renovación pragmatista de la filosofía analítica*. Pamplona, EUNSA, 1994.
Arregui, Jorge V. *Themata*, 13, 316-318, 1995.

Nuland, Sherwin B. *How We Die*. New York, Knopf, 1994.
Fins, Joseph J. *Hastings Center Rep*, 25(2), 38, Mr-Ap 95.

Nussbaum, Martha. *Love's Knowledge*. New York, Oxford Univ Pr, 1990.
Roncalli, Elvira. *Rev Phil Louvain*, 92(4), 629-631, N 94.

Nussbaum, Martha (ed) and Sen, Amartya (ed). *The Quality of Life*. New York, Clarendon/Oxford Pr, 1993.
Baker, John. *Int J Phil Stud*, 3(1), 201-203, Mr 95.
Brennan, Samantha. *Can Phil Rev*, 14(5), 340-342, O 94.

Nussbaum, Martha C. *The Therapy of Desire*. Princeton, Princeton Univ Pr, 1994.
James, Susan. *J Applied Phil*, 12(2), 201-203, 1995.

Nussbaum, Martha C (ed) and Rorty, Amélie Oksenberg. *Essays on Aristotle's 'De Anima'*. New York, Clarendon/Oxford Pr, 1992.
Modrar, Deborah K W. *Ethics*, 105(2), 413-416, Ja 95.
Witt, Charlotte. *Phil Books*, 36(2). 81-89, Ap 95.

NY State Task Force, On Life and the Law. *When Others Must Choose*. Albany, Health Educ Srv, 1992.
Gasner, M Rose. *J Clin Ethics*, 5(2), 165-167, Sum 94.

Nye, Andrea. *Philosophia*. New York, Routledge, 1994.
d'Entrèves, Maurizio Passerin. *Euro J Phil*, 2(3), 361-366, D 94.

O'Brien, Denis. *Théodicée plotinienne*. Leiden, Brill, 1993.
Esposito Buckley, Lisa Marie. *Tijdschr Filosof*, 56(4), 764-766, D 94.
Etienne, Alexandre. *Frei Z Phil Theol*, 41(1-2), 269-273, 1994.
Lassègue, Monique. *Rev Phil Fr*, 2, 226-229, Ap-Je 94.

O'Connell, Robert J. *Soundings in St Augustine's Imagination*. Bronx, Fordham Univ Pr, 1994.
Teske, Roland. *Mod Sch*, 72(1), 83-85, N 94.

O'Daly, Gerard. *La filosofia della mente in Agostino*. Palermo, Ed Augustinus, 1990.
Bettetini, Maria. *Riv Filosof Neo-Scolas*, 86(1), 197-201, Ja-Mr 94.

O'Donnell, James J (ed). *Augustine: Confessions*. New York, Clarendon/Oxford Pr, 1992.
Solignac, Aimé. *Arch Phil*, 58(1), 149-152, Ja-Mr 95.

O'Donohue, John. *Person als Vermittlung*. Mainz, Gruenewald, 1993.
Schmidt, J. *Theol Phil*, 70(1), 108-110, 1995.

O'Donovan, Oliver. *Résurrection et expérience morale*. Paris, PUF, 1992.
Bourguet, Vincent. *Rev Metaph Morale*, 98(1), 138-140, Ja-Mr 95.

O'Hear, Anthony and Groves, Judy. *Jesus For Beginners*. Cambridge, Icon Books, 1993.
Butcher, Barry W. *Sophia (Australia)*, 34(1), 279-282, Mr-Ap 95.

O'Leary, Joseph Stephen. *La vérité chrétienne à l'âge du pluralisme religieux*. Paris, Cerf, 1994.
Nault, François. *Laval Theol Phil*, 51(1), 212-216, F 95.

O'Meara, Dominic J. *Plotinus: An Introduction to the Enneads*. New York, Oxford Univ Pr, 1993.
Meredith, Anthony A. *Heythrop J*, 35(3), 326-327, Jl 94.

O'Meara, Dominique. *Plotin, une introduction aux Ennéades*. Paris, Cerf, 1992.
De Gandillac, Maurice. *Rev Metaph Morale*, 99(4), 575-576, O-D 94.
Lassègue, Monique. *Rev Phil Fr*, 2, 229-232, Ap-Je 94.

O'Neill, John. *Ecology, Policy and Politics*. New York, Routledge, 1993.
Barry, Brian. *Environ Values*, 4(2), 181-182, May 95.
Hughes, Jonathan. *Rad Phil*, 70, 45-46, Mr-Ap 95.
Knowles, Dudley. *Phil Books*, 36(2), 127-129, Ap 95.

O'Neill, John. *Worlds Without Content*. New York, Routledge, 1991.
Tieszen, Richard. *Husserl Stud*, 10(3), 253-259, 1993-94.

O'Neill, Onora. *Constructions of Reason*. New York, Cambridge Univ Pr, 1989.
Potter, Nelson. *Nous*, 27(3), 386-388, S 93.

O'Regan, Cyril. *The Heterodox Hegel*. Albany, SUNY Pr, 1994.
Hodgson, Peter C. *Mod Theol*, 11(3), 385-386, Jl 95.

O'Rourke, Kevin D and Boyle, Philip. *Medical Ethics: Sources of Catholic Teachings*. Washington, Georgetown Univ Pr, 1993.
Skeel, Joy D. *Cambridge Quart Healthcare Ethics*, 4(1), 122-123, Wint 95.

O'Sullivan, Noël. *Santayana (Thinkers of Our Time)*. London, Claridge Pr, 1992.
Coady, C A J. *Phil Quart*, 45(179), 273-275, Ap 95.

Oakley, Justin. *Morality and the Emotions*. New York, Routledge, 1992.
Buss, Sarah. *Phil Rev*, 103(4), 726-728, O 94.
Szabados, Béla. *Can Phil Rev*, 15(1), 60-63, F 95.
Van Eechaute, Ann. *Tijdschr Filosof*, 56(3), 598-600, S 94.

Oberkrome, Willi. *Volksgeschichte*. Göttingen, Vandenhoeck, 1993.
Iggers, Georg G. *Hist Theor*, 33(3), 395-400, 1994.

Obiols, G A and Rabossi, E. *La filosofía y el filosofar*. Buenos Aires, Centro Ed Amer Latin, 1993.
Di Camilo, S G. *Rev Latin de Filosof*, 20(2), 373-376, 1994.

Obiols, Guillermo A and Segni de Obiols, Silvia di. *Adolescencia, posmodernidad y escuela secundaria*. Buenos Aires, Kapelusz, 1993.
Joyal, Achille. *Philosopher*, 15, 248-253, 1994.

Oderberg, David S. *The Metaphysics of Identity over Time*. New York, Macmillan, 1993.
Garrett, Brian. *Austl J Phil*, 73(2), 306-307, Je 95.

Odifreddi, Piergiorgio. *Logic and Computer Science*. San Diego, Academic Pr, 1990.
Mints, Grigori. *J Sym Log*, 59(4), 1111-1114, D 94.

Oelkers, Jürgen (ed); Schulz, Wolfgang K (ed) and Tenorth, Heinz-Elmar (ed). *Neukantianismus*. Weinheim, Deut Stud, 1989.
Ollig, H L. *Theol Phil*, 69(3), 444-445, 1994.

Oelschlaeger, Max. *Caring for Creation*. New Haven, Yale Univ Pr, 1994.
Glasser, Harold. *Environ Ethics*, 17(2), 221-224, Sum 95.

Ohnuki-Tierney, Emiko (ed). *Culture Through Time*. Stanford, Stanford Univ Pr, 1991.
Ulin, Robert C. *Int Stud Phil*, 27(1), 141-143, 1995.

Ohst, Martin. *Schleiermacher und die Bekenntnisschriften*. Tübingen, Mohr, 1989.
Moxter, Michael. *Phil Rundsch*, 41(2), 133-158, 1994.

Okonta, Ike. *Nietzsche: The Politics of Power*. New York, Lang, 1992.
Golomb, Jacob. *Int Stud Phil*, 27(2), 126-127, 1995.

Olivé, L. *Knowledge, Sociality and Reality*. Amsterdam, Rodopi, 1993.
Beuchot, Mauricio. *Analogía*, 8(2), 193-196, 1994.

Olivetti, Marco M. *Analogia del soggetto*. Bari, Laterza, 1992.
Gentile, Andrea. *Acta Phil*, 4(1), 153-156, 1995.

Ollman, Bertell. *Dialectical Investigations*. New York, Routledge, 1993.
Walker, David. *Rad Phil*, 68, 59-60, Autumn 94.

Olson, Alan M. *Hegel and the Spirit*. Princeton, Princeton Univ Pr, 1992.
Khushf, George. *Owl Minerva*, 26(1), 71-77, Fall 94.

Olson, Alan M. *Heidegger and Jaspers*. Philadelphia, Temple Univ Pr, 1994.
Samay, Sebastian. *Int Phil Quart*, 35(2), 235-238, Ju 95.

Oppenraaij, Aafke M I (trans). *Aristotle "De Animalibus"*. Leiden, Brill, 1992.
Pellegrin, Pierre. *Rev Phil Fr*, 2, 218-220, Ap-Je 94.

Ortega y Gasset, José. *Mission of the University*. New Brunswick, Transaction Books, 1992.
Casement, William. *J Value Inq*, 28(4), 573-575, D 94.

Oruka, H Odera (ed). *Sage Philosophy*. Nairobi, Africa Ctr Tech Stud, 1991.
Bewaji, J A I. *Quest*, 8(1), 104-111, Je 94.

Osorio Romero, Ignacio. *Antonio Rubio en la filosofía novohispana*. Mexico, UNAM, 1988.
Beuchot, Mauricio. *Analogía*, 7(2), 215-216, 1993.

Otto, Stephen. *Giambattista Vico*. Napoli, Guida, 1992.
Cacciatore, Giuseppe. *Boll Centro Stud Vichiani*, 24-25, 269-275, 1994-95.

Outka, Gene (ed) and Reeder Jr, John P (ed). *Prospects for a Common Morality*. Princeton, Princeton Univ Pr, 1992.
Williams, John R. *Heythrop J*, 35(3), 349-350, Jl 94.

Overall, Christine. *Human Reproduction*. New York, Oxford Univ Pr, 1993.
Peach, Lucinda Joy. *Can Phil Rev*, 14(5), 347-349, O 94.

Owens, D Alfred (ed) and Wagner, Mark (ed). *Progress in Modern Psychology*. New York, Praeger, Undated.
Innis, Nancy K. *Behavior Phil*, 22(1), 71-73, Spr-Sum 94.

Owens, David. *Causes and Coincidences*. New York, Cambridge Univ Pr, 1992.
Oderberg, David S. *Ratio*, 8(1), 108-112, Ap 95.
Tooley, Michael. *Phil Rev*, 103(3), 546-549, Jl 94.

Paddison, Max. *Adorno's Aesthetics of Music*. New York, Cambridge Univ Pr, 1993.
Brown, Lee B. *J Aes Art Crit*, 53(2), 212-216, Spr 95.
Ridley, Aaron. *Brit J Aes*, 35(2), 193-194, Ap 95.

Padgett, Alan G. *God, Eternity, and the Nature of Time*. New York, St Martin's Pr, 1992.
Gowen, Julie. *Phil Books*, 35(3), 206-207, Jl 94.

Pagano, Maurizio. *Hegel: La religione e l'ermeneutica del concetto*. Napoli, E S I, 1992.
Cuniberto, Flavio. *Filosofia*, 45(2), 265-269, My-Ag 94.
Mancini, Sandro. *Riv Filosof Neo-Scolas*, 87(1), 183 185, Ja-Mr 95.

Page, Benjamin B (ed). *Marxism and Spirituality*. New York, Bergin & Garvey, 1993.
Jirásek, Ivo. *Filozof Cas*, 42(6), 1067-1071, 1994.

Pajon, E. *El ser y la libertad*. Madrid, Fundamentos, 1992.
Zárate, Marla. *Dialogo Filosof*, 10(2), 268-271, My-Ag 94.

Palmer, Frank. *Literature and Moral Understanding*. New York, Clarendon/Oxford Pr, 1992.
Kaminsky, Alice R. *Int Stud Phil*, 27(2), 127-128, 1995.
Stern-Gillet, Suzanne. *Brit J Aes*, 34(4), 406-407, O 94.

Palmquist, Stephen. *Kant's System of Perspectives*. Lanham, Univ Pr of America, 1993.
Krantz, Susan F. *Rev Metaph*, 48(2), 419-421, D 94.
McRobert, Jennifer. *Can Phil Rev*, 14(2), 119-121, Ap 94.

Panaccio, Claude. *Les mots, les concepts et les choses*. Paris, Vrin, 1992.
Biard, Joël. *Vivarium*, 32(2), 273-275, N 94.

Panchen, Alec. *Evolution*. London, Duckworth, 1993.
Smithurst, Michael. *Phil Books*, 36(2), 138-139, Ap 95.

Pangle, Thomas L (ed). *The Roots of Political Philosophy*. Ithaca, Cornell Univ Pr, 1987.
Glidden, David K. *Nous*, 27(1), 99-101, Mr 93.

Pániker, Salvador. *Filosofía y Mística*. Barcelona, Anagrama, 1992.
Galán, Ilia. *Rev Filosof (Mexico)*, 28(82), 105-111, Ja-Ap 95.

Pannenberg, Wolfhart and Peters, Ted (ed). *Toward a Theology of Nature*. Louisville, Westminster Pr, 1993.
Ward, Keith. *Zygon*, 30(2), 343-345, Je 95.

Papineau, David. *Philosophical Naturalism*. Cambridge, Blackwell, 1993.
Browne, Derek. *Austl J Phil*, 73(2), 307-309, Je 95.
Kapitan, Tomis. *Mind*, 104(414), 426-430, Ap 95.

Pappin, Joseph L. *The Metaphysics of Edmund Burke*. Bronx, Fordham Univ Pr, 1993.
Asselin, Don T. *Int Phil Quart*, 35(1), 112-114, Mr 95.
Townsend, Dabney. *Rev Metaph*, 48(2), 421-422, D 94.

Parangimalil, Bastin J. *Toward Integral Holism in Psychology*. New Delhi, Inter India Pub, 1990.
Jain, Uday. *J Indian Counc Phil Res*, 12(1), 182-185, S-D 94.

Paris, Cécile L. *User Modelling in Text Generation*. London, Pinter, 1993.
Schütz, Jörg. *J Prag*, 22(6), 684-686, D 94.

Park, Chan-Young. *Untersuchungen zur Werttheorie bei Franz Brentano*. Dettelbach, J H Roll, 1991.
Hála, Vlastimil. *Filozof Cas*, 42(6), 1048-1052, 1994.

Park, Jung Soon. *Contractarian Liberal Ethics and the Theory of Rational Choice*. New York, Lang, 1992.
Tenenbaum, Sergio. *Can Phil Rev*, 14(5), 349-353, O 94.

Park, Sung-Bong. *An Aesthetics of the Popular Arts*. Stockholm, Almqvist & Wiksell, 1993.
McAdoo, Nick. *Brit J Aes*, 34(4), 401, O 94.

Parsons, Michael J and Blocker, H Gene. *Aesthetics and Education*. Champaign, Univ of Illinois Pr, 1993.
Simpson, Alan. *Brit J Aes*, 35(1), 73-74, Ja 95.

Passerin d'Entreves, Maurizio. *The Political Philosophy of Hannah Arendt*. New York, Routledge, 1994.
De Greiff, Pablo. *Int J Phil Stud*, 3(1), 179-182, Mr 95.

Patterson, Dennis M (ed). *Wittgenstein and Legal Theory*. Boulder, Westview Pr, 1992.
Belliotti, Raymond A. *J Value Inq*, 28(4), 577-580, D 94.

Patterson, Wayne A. *Bertrand Russell's Philosophy of Logical Atomism*. New York, Lang, 1993.
Agassi, Joseph. *Can Phil Rev*, 14(1), 44-45, F 94.

Patton, Paul (ed). *Nietzsche, Feminism and Political Theory*. New York, Routledge, 1993.
Nutt, Kathleen. *Int J Phil Stud*, 3(1), 203-205, Mr 95.
Owen, David. *Hist Human Sci*, 7(4), 121-123, N 94.

Paty, Michel. *Einstein philosophe*. Paris, Pr Univ France, 1993.
Marchildon, Louis. *Dialogue (Canada)*, 34(1), 178-181, Wint 95.

Patzig, Günther (ed). *Aristoteles' "Politik"*. Göttingen, Vandenhoeck, 1990.
Ricken, F. *Theol Phil*, 69(3), 423-424, 1994.

Paul, Ellen Frankel (ed), Miller Jr, Fred D (ed) and Paul, Jeffrey (ed). *Altruism*. New York, Cambridge Univ Pr, 1993.
Heath, Eugene. *Rev Metaph*, 48(4), 921-923, Je 95.

Paul, William. *Laughing Screaming*. New York, Columbia Univ Pr, 1994.
Plantinga, Carl. *J Aes Art Crit*, 53(3), 332-334, Sum 95.

Paul II. *Crossing the Threshold of Hope*. London, Random House, Undated.
Zan, Myint. *Sophia (Australia)*, 34(1), 259-268, Mr-Ap 95.

Pavel, Thomas. *Le mirage linguistique*. Parigi, Les Ed Minuit, 1988.
Largeault, Jean. *Arch Phil*, 57(3), 597-599, Jl-S 94.

Payne, Michael. *Reading Theory*. Cambridge, Blackwell, 1993.
Nash, Jesse W. *Hist Euro Ideas*, 21(1), 130-132, Ja 95.

Peach, W Bernard. *The Correspondence of Richard Price Volume III: March 1786-February 1791*. Durham, Duke Univ Pr, 1994.
Sell, Alan P F. *Int J Phil Stud*, 3(1), 213-215, Mr 95.

Peacocke, Christopher. *A Study of Concepts*. Cambridge, MIT Pr, 1992.
Crane, Tim. *Euro J Phil*, 2(3), 352-356, D 94.
Hanna, Robert. *Phil Rev*, 103(3), 541-544, Jl 94.
Niclauss, Norbert. *Erkenntnis*, 42(3), 409-412, My 95.
Pessin, Andrew. *J Mind Behav*, 15(3), 295-298, Sum 94.

Peacocke, Christopher (ed). *Objectivity, Simulation and the Unity of Consciousness*. New York, Oxford Univ Pr, 1994.
Robinson, Howard. *Philosophy*, 70(273), 469-472, Jl 95.

Pears, David. *Hume's System*. New York, Oxford Univ Pr, 1990.
Winkler, Kenneth P. *Phil Rev*, 103(4), 755-762, O 94.

Pearsall, Marilyn. *Women and Values*. Belmont, Wadsworth, 1993.
Burton, Wendy E. *Can Phil Rev*, 14(4), 281-283, Ag 94.

Pearson, Roger. *The Fables of Reason*. New York, Clarendon/Oxford Pr, 1993.
Weber, Michael J. *Phil Lit*, 18(2), 390-392, O 94.

Pecham, John and Potter, Vincent G (trans). *Questions Concerning the Eternity of the World*. Bronx, Fordham Univ Pr, 1993.
Etzkorn, Girard J. *Int Phil Quart*, 34(4), 499-500, D 94.

Pejovic, Danilo. *Oprostaj od Moderne*. Dubrovnik, Matica-Ogranak, 1993.
Bosto, Sulejman. *Filozof Istraz*, 13(4), 983-986, 1993.

Pelikan, Jaroslav. *Christianity and Classical Culture*. New Haven, Yale Univ Pr, 1993.
Helleman, Wendy Elgersma. *Phoenix*, 48(2), 179-180, Sum 94.

Pellegrino, Edmund D and Thomasma, David C. *The Virtues in Medical Practice*. New York, Oxford Univ Pr, 1993.
Kuczewski, Mark G. *Theor Med*, 15(4), 460-463, D 94.
Sutton, Agneta. *Ethics Med*, 11(2), 45, .

Pellegrino, Edmund D (ed), Veatch, Robert M (ed) and Langan, John P (ed). *Ethics, Trust, and the Professions*. Washington, Georgetown Univ Pr, 1991.
Flores, Albert. *Teach Phil*, 17(2), 177-179, Je 94.

Pelletier, Frances Jeffry. *Parmenides, Plato, and the Semantics of Not-Being*. Chicago, Univ of Chicago Pr, 1990.
Keyt, David. *Nous*, 28(1), 117-119, Mr 94.

Penzo, Giorgio. *Nietzsche allo specchio*. Bari, Laterza, 1993.
Fazio, Domenico M. *Riv Int Filosof Diritto*, 71(2), 368-371, 1994.
Penati, Giancarlo. *Riv Filosof Neo-Scolas*, 86(1), 205-207, Ja-Mr 94.

Pepper, David. *Eco-socialism: From Deep Ecology to Social Justice*. New York, Routledge, 1993.
Meadowcroft, James. *Environ Values*, 4(1), 85-86, F 95.

Pera, Marcello and Mandelbaum, Jonathan (trans). *The Ambiguous Frog*. Princeton, Princeton Univ Pr, 1992.
Salmon, Wesley C. *Phil Sci*, 62(1), 164-166, Mr 95.

Pereda, Carlos. *Razón e Incertidumbre*. 1994.
Lafont, Cristina. *Logos (Mexico)*, 23(67), 87-89, Ja-Ap 95.

Perkins, Revere D. *Deixis Grammar and Culture*. Amsterdam, J Benjamins, 1992.
Ariel, Mira. *J Prag*, 23(4), 455-459, Ap 95.

Peroli, Enrico. *Il Platonismo e l'antropologia filosofica di Gregorio di Nissa*. Milano, Vita Pensiero, 1993.
Cerbelaud, Dominique. *Rev Thomiste*, 94(2), 340-342, Ap-Je 94.

Perry, John. *The Problem of the Essential Indexical and Other Essays*. New York, Oxford Univ Pr, 1993.
Harcourt, Edward. *Phil Books*, 36(1), 53-55, Ja 95.
Vallée, Richard. *Dialogue (Canada)*, 33(3), 553-556, Sum 94.

Pessa, Eliano. *Intelligenza artificiale*. Torino, Bollati Boringhieri, 1992.
Morchio, Renzo. *Epistemologia*, 17(1), 157-158, Ja-Je 94.

Peters, Bernhard. *Die Integration moderner Gesellschaften*. Frankfurt, Suhrkamp, 1993.
Bohman, James. *Constellations*, 1(3), 422-427, Jan 95.

Petruccioli, Sandro. *Atoms, Metaphors and Paradoxes*. Cambridge, Cambridge Univ Pr, 1993.
Faye, Jan. *Brit J Phil Sci*, 46(2), 275-279, Je 95.

Pettit, Philip. *The Common Mind*. New York, Oxford Univ Pr, 1993.
Thomas, Alan. *Phil Quart*, 45(179), 237-240, Ap 95.
Vincent, Andrew. *Utilitas*, 6(2), 319-324, N 94.
Wilson, Rob. *Phil Rev*, 103(4), 715-718, O 94.

Pettit, Philip (ed) and McDowell, John (ed). *Subject, Thought and Context*. New York, Clarendon/Oxford Pr, 1986.
Liz, Manuel. *Philosophia (Israel)*, 24(1-2), 235-248, D 94.
Peña, Lorenzo. *Philosophia (Israel)*, 24(1-2), 235-248, D 94.

Petzet, Heinrich Wiegand, Emad, Parvis (trans) and Maly, Kenneth (trans). *Encounters and Dialogues with Martin Heidegger, 1929-1976*. Chicago, Univ of Chicago Pr, 1993.
Ahern, Daniel R. *Rev Metaph*, 48(4), 923-925, Je 95.

Pfeifer, Karl. *Actions and Other Events*. New York, Lang, 1989.
Ripley, Charles. *Dialogue (Canada)*, 34(1), 190-194, Wint 95.

Philipp, Peter and Raatzsch, Richard. *Essays on Wittgenstein*. Bergen, Wittgenstein Arch, 1993.
Ammereller, Erich. *Phil Invest*, 18(2), 173-177, Ap 95.

Press, Gerald A (ed). *Plato's Dialogues*. Lanham, Rowman & Littlefield, 1993.
Stalley, R F. *Phil Books*, 36(1), 37-38, Ja 95.

Preston, Paul. *The Politics of Revenge*. Scranton, Unwin Hyman, 1990.
Moradiellos, Enrique. *El Basilisco*, 15, 96-97, Ja-Mr 94.

Price, A W. *Love and Friendship in Plato and Aristotle*. New York, Oxford Univ Pr, 1989.
Glidden, David. *Nous*, 27(1), 109-110, Mr 93.

Priest, Stephen (ed). *Hegel's Critique of Kant*. New York, Clarendon/Oxford Pr, 1987.
Fulda, Hans Friedrich. *Nous*, 27(1), 118-121, Mr 93.

Prilleltensky, Isaac. *The Morals and Politics of Psychology*. Albany, SUNY Pr, 1994.
Barney, Ken. *J Mind Behav*, 16(2), 211-214, Spr 95.

Prini, Pietro. *Plotino e la fondazione dell'umanesimo interiore*. Milano, Vita Pensiero, 1993.
Gatti, Maria Luisa. *Riv Filosof Neo-Scolas*, 87(1), 169-171, Ja-Mr 95.

Prinz, Wolfgang and Weingart, Peter (ed). *Die sogenannten Geisteswissenschaften: Innenansichten*. Frankfurt, Suhrkamp, 1990.
Rentsch, Thomas. *Phil Rundsch*, 41(2), 166-191, 1994.

Prokhovnik, Raia. *Rhetoric and Philosophy in Hobbes' Leviathan*. New York, Garland, 1991.
Slomp, Gabriella. *Hist Polit Thought*, 16(1), 155-156, Spr 95.

Pufendorf, Samuel, Tully, James (ed) and Silverthorne, Michael (trans). *On the Duty of Man and Citizen*. New York, Cambridge Univ Pr, 1991.
Diamond, Peter J. *Hist Euro Ideas*, 18(5), 847-848, S 94.

Puntel, Lorenz B. *Wahrheitstheorien in der neueren Philosophie*. Darmstadt, Wiss Buchgesell, 1993.
Brüntrup, G. *Theol Phil*, 69(3), 458-460, 1994.

Purdie, Susan. *Comedy*. Hertfordshire, Harvester-Wheatsheaf, 1993.
Hadfield, Andrew. *Rad Phil*, 68, 52-53, Autumn 94.

Puster, Rolf W. *Britische Gassendi-Rezeption am Beispiel John Lockes*. Stuttgart, Frommann-Holzboog, 1991.
Champlin, T S. *Locke News*, 23, 175-180, 1992.

Putnam, Hilary. *Il pragmatismo: una questione aperta*. Bari, Laterza, 1992.
Marsonet, Michele. *Epistemologia*, 17(1), 149-152, Ja-Je 94.

Putnam, Hilary. *Renewing Philosophy*. Cambridge, Harvard Univ Pr, 1992.
Alston, William P. *Phil Rev*, 103(3), 533-535, Jl 94.
Burri, Alex. *Erkenntnis*, 42(3), 405-408, My 95.
Willaschek, Marcus. *Z Phil Forsch*, 48(3), 484-488, Jl-S 94.

Putnam, Hilary. *Representation and Reality*. Cambridge, MIT Pr, 1988.
Hannon, Barbara. *Nous*, 27(1), 102-106, Mr 93.

Putnam, Hilary. *Von einem realistischen Standpunkt*. Reinbeck, Rowohlt, 1993.
Burri, Alex. *Erkenntnis*, 42(3), 403-404, My 95.

Putnam, Hilary and Conant, James (ed). *Words and Life*. Cambridge, Harvard Univ Pr, 1994.
Hookway, Christopher. *Philosophy*, 70(273), 460-463, Jl 95.

Pyke, Steve. *Philosophers*. Manchester, Cornerhouse, 1993.
Quinton, Anthony. *Mind*, 104(413), 196-197, Ja 95.

Quaglioni, Diego. *I Limiti della Sovranita*. Padova, Cedam, 1992.
Black, Antony. *Hist Polit Thought*, 15(2), 299-303, Sum 94.

Quay, Paul. *Final Causality in Contemporary Physics*. Toronto, Univ of Toronto Pr, 1995.
Kovacs, George. *Ultim Real Mean*, 18(1), 66-67, Mr 95.

Queraltó, Ramón. *Mundo, tecnología, y razón en el fin de la Modernidad*. Barcelona, Prom Pub Univ, 1993.
Rojas, José Baena. *Themata*, 13, 320-322, 1995.

Quine, W V (ed). *Pursuit of Truth*. Cambridge, Harvard Univ Pr, 1992.
Ebbs, Gary. *Phil Rev*, 103(3), 535-541, Jl 94.
Kaminsky, Jack. *Int Stud Phil*, 27(2), 131-132, 1995.

Quine, W V, Carnap, Rudolf and Creath, Richard (ed). *Dear Carnap, Dear Van*. Berkeley, Univ of Calif Pr, 1991.
Uebel, Thomas. *Int Stud Phil*, 27(2), 133-134, 1995.

Quinn, Warren. *Morality and Action*. Cambridge, Cambridge Univ Pr, 1993.
Lane, Melissa. *Mind*, 104(415), 662-664, Jl 95.

Rabade Romeo, Sergio. *La razón y lo irracional*. Madrid, Ed Complutense, 1994.
Murillo, Ildefonso. *Dialogo Filosof*, 10(3), 447-448, S-D 94.

Radder, Hans. *The Material Realization of Science*. Assen, Gorcum, 1988.
Rowlands, Mark. *Philosophia (Israel)*, 24(1-2), 249-252, D 94.

Radrizzani, Ives. *Vers la fondation de l'intersubjectivité chez Fichte*. Paris, Vrin, 1993.
Ivaldo, Marco. *Teoria*, 14(1), 146-148, 1994.

Raffman, Diana. *Language, Music, and Mind*. Cambridge, MIT Pr, 1993.
Higgins, Kathleen Marie. *Phil Phenomenol Res*, 55(3), 734-737, S 95.
Levinson, Jerrold. *Mind*, 104(413) 197-202, Ja 95.
Sloboda, John. *Mind Lang*, 9(3), 377-385, S 94.

Rahman, Shahid. *Über Dialoge Protologische Kategorien und andere Seltenheiten*. New York, Lang, 1993.
Bertotti, Gabriel. *Analogía*, 8(1), 177-183, 1994.
Böttcher, Guillermo. *Hist Phil Log*, 15(2), 256-259, 1994.

Rajchman, John. *Philosophical Events*. New York, Columbia Univ Pr, 1991.
Carvalho, John M. *Can Phil Rev*, 14(2), 106-110, Ap 94.

Ramazanoglu, Caroline (ed). *Up Against Foucault*. New York, Routledge, 1993.
Hadfield, Andrew. *Rad Phil*, 70, 38-40, Mr-Ap 95.

Ramirez, Mario Teodore. *El quiasmo*. Morelia, Univ Michoacana, 1994.
Boburg, Felipe. *Rev Filosof (Mexico)*, 27(81), 530-534, S-D 94.

Ramos, Francisco José. *Hacer: Pensar*. San Juan, Univ Puerto Rico Pr, 1994.
Rubio, Andrés Rodríguez. *Dialogos*, 30(66), 191-199, Jl 95.

Ramsey, Bennett. *Submitting to Freedom*. New York, Oxford Univ Pr, 1993.
Skrupskelis, I K. *Int J Phil Relig*, 36(2), 126-128, O 94.

Ramsey, F P and Galavotti, Maria Carla (ed). *Notes on Philosophy, Probability and Mathematics*. Naples, Bibliopolis, 1991.
Armendt, Brad. *Phil Rev*, 103(4), 713-715, O 94.
Di Maio, Maria Concetta. *Phil Sci*, 61(3), 487-489, S 94.
Wolenski, Jan. *Synthese*, 101(1), 121-127, O 94.

Ramsey, Frank Plumpton, Rescher, Nicholas (ed) and Majer, Ulrich (ed). *On Truth*. Dordrecht, Kluwer, 1991.
Wolenski, Jan. *Synthese*, 101(1), 121-127, O 94.

Rand, Richard (ed). *Logomachia*. Lincoln, Univ of Nebraska Pr, 1992.
Payne, Michael. *Hist Human Sci*, 7(3), 117-120, Ag 94.

Rankin, Kenneth. *The Recovery of the Soul*. Montreal, McGill-Queens U Pr, 1991.
Reidy, Martin Francis. *Dialogue (Canada)*, 33(3), 539-542, Sum 94.
Russon, John. *Phoenix*, 48(3), 269-271, Autumn 94.

Rao, K Ramakrishna (ed). *Cultivating Consciousness*. New York, Praeger, 1993.
Laakso, Aarre. *Can Phil Rev*, 14(3), 206-208, Je 94.

Rasmussen, Douglas B and Den, Douglas J. *Liberty and Nature*. Peru, Open Court, 1991.
Williams, E L. *Can Phil Rev*, 14(2), 128-130, Ap 94.

Rastier, F. *Sémantique et recherches cognitives*. Paris, PUF, 1991.
Van de Vijver, Gertrudis. *Commun Cog—AI*, 11(1-2), 207-210, 1994.

Rauche, Gerhard A. *Knowledge and Experience*. Alice, Fort Hare Univ Pr, 1990.
Lichtigfeld, A. *Int Stud Phil*, 27(1), 140-141, 1995.

Raven, Diederick (ed), van Vucht Tijssen, Lieteke (ed) and de Wolf, Jan (ed). *Cognitive Relativism and Social Science*. New Brunswick, Transaction Books, 1992.
Fox, John F. *Phil Soc Sci*, 24(4), 506-510, D 94.

Ravetz, J R. *The Merger of Knowledge with Power*. London, Mansell, 1990.
Mitcham, Carl. *Res Phil Technol*, 14, 306-312, 1994.

Rawls, John. *Political Liberalism*. New York, Columbia Univ Pr, 1993.
Forst, Rainer. *Constellation*, 1(1), 163-171, Ap 94.
Riek, Anna. *Protosoz*, 6, 252-256, 1994.
Samar, Vincent J. *Bus Ethics Quart*, 5(3), 629-645, Jl 95.

Raz, Joseph. *The Morality of Freedom*. New York, Clarendon/Oxford Pr, 1989.
Marshall, Ernest. *Nous*, 28(1), 96-98, Mr 94.

Read, Stephen (ed). *Sophisms in Medieval Logic and Grammar*. Dordrecht, Kluwer, 1993.
Perreiah, Alan R. *Hist Phil Log*, 15(2), 246-247, 1994.

Reale, G, Hölscher, Ludger (trans) and Seifert, Josef (ed). *Zu einer neuen Interpretation Platons*. Paderborn, Ferdinand Schöningh, 1993.
Lichtigfeld, A. *Tijdschr Filosof*, 57(1), 129-130, Mr 95.

Reale, Mario. *La Difficile Eguaglianza: Hobbes e gli animali politici*. Rome, Ed Riuniti, 1991.
Baccelli, Luca. *Teoria*, 14(2), 135-137, 1994.

Recanati, Francois. *Direct Reference*. Cambridge, Blackwell, 1993.
Saul, Jennifer M. *Phil Quart*, 45(178), 134-135, Ja 95.
Smith, David. *Phil Books*, 36(1), 56-57, Ja 95.

Reck, Andrew (ed), Harvath, Tibor (ed) and Krettek, Thomas (ed). *American Philosophers' Ideas of Ultimate Reality and Meaning*. Toronto, Univ of Toronto Pr, 1994.
Prendergast, Thomas L. *Trans Peirce Soc*, 31(1), 239-245, Wint 95.

Redeker, Hans. *Helmuth Plessner oder Die verkörperte Philosophie*. Berlin, Duncker Humblot, 1993.
Arlt, Gerhard. *Phil Rundsch*, 41(2), 159-165, 1994.

Reeve, C D C. *Practices of Reason*. New York, Oxford Univ Pr, 1992.
Bobonich, Christopher. *Phil Rev*, 103(3), 567-569, Jl 94.
Dahl, Norman O. *Ethics*, 105(2), 411-412, Ja 95.

Rehg, William. *Insight and Solidarity*. Berkeley, Univ of Calif Pr, 1994.
Swindal, James. *Mod Sch*, 72(1), 81-83, N 94.

Reibnitz, B. *Ein Kommentar zu Friedrich Nietzsche 'Die Geburt der Tragödie aus dem Geiste der Musik'*. Stuttgart, Metzler, 1992.
López, Héctor Julio Pérez. *Daimon Rev Filosof*, 7, 199-200, 1993.

Reich, Klaus, Kneller, Jane (trans) and Losonsky, Michael (trans). *The Completeness of Kant's Table of Judgments*. Stanford, Stanford Univ Pr, 1992.
Dahlstrom, Daniel O. *Rev Metaph*, 48(2), 423-425, D 94.

Reichenbach, Bruce R. *The Law of Karma*. Honolulu, Univ of Hawaii Pr, 1990.
King, Richard. *Asian Phil*, 5(1), 78-81, 1995.

Reid, Thomas and Haakonssen, Knud (ed). *Practical Ethics*. Princeton, Princeton Univ Pr, 1990.
Raphael, D D. *Brit J Hist Phil*, 3(1), 186-188, F 95.

Seech, Zachary. *Open Minds and Everyday Reasoning*. Belmont, Wadsworth, 1992.
Johnson, Fred. *Can Phil Rev*, 14(3), 211-212, Je 94.

Seks, Vladimir. *Ogledi o slobodi savjesti*. Zagreb, Globus, 1994.
Barisic, Pavo. *Filozof Istraz*, 14(1), 221-223, 1994.

Semerari, Furio. *Potenza come diritto*. Bari, Dedalo, 1992.
Nosari, Sara. *Filosofia*, 45(3), 406-409, S-D 94.

Sen, A and Hawthorne, G (ed). *Standard of Living*. New York, Cambridge Univ Pr, 1991.
Lacroix, André. *Eidos*, 11(1-2), 143-147, Je-D 93.

Sen, Amartya. *Inequality Reexamined*. Cambridge, Harvard Univ Pr, 1992.
Anderson, Elizabeth. *Econ Phil*, 11(1), 182-188, Ap 95.
Cohen, Joshua. *J Phil*, 92(5), 275-288, My 95.
Roemer, John. *Phil Rev*, 103(3), 554-557, Jl 94.
Schramme, Thomas. *Z Phil Forsch*, 49(1), 138-141, Ja-Mr 95.

Sennett, James F. *Modality, Probability, and Rationality*. New York, Lang, 1992.
McLeod, Mark S. *Faith Phil*, 11(2), 339-342, Ap 94.

Sentis, Laurent. *Saint Thomas d'Aquin et le mal*. Paris, Beauchesne, 1992.
de Gandillac, Maurice. *Rev Metaph Morale*, 98(1), 128-130, Ja-Mr 95.

Seppmann, Werner. *Subjekt und System*. Luneburg, Klampen, 1993.
Bay, Hansjörg. *Das Argument*, 208, 118-120, Ja-F 95.

Serequeberhan, Tseney. *African Philosophy*. New York, Paragon House, 1991.
Bewaji, J A I. *Quest*, 8(2), 140-147, D 94.

Sergeny, Scott J. *Russian Teachers and Peasant Revolution*. Bloomington, Indiana Univ Pr, 1989.
Stud East Euro Thought, 47(1-2), 122-126, Je 95.

Serra, Maurizio. *La Ferita della Modernità*. Bologna, Il Mulino, 1992.
Bosworth, Richard. *Hist Euro Ideas*, 18(5), 774-775, S 94.

Serra, Teresa. *Il disagio nel diritto*. Turin, Giappichelli, 1993.
Caserta, Marco. *Riv Int Filosof Diritto*, 71(3), 536-542, 1994.

Serres, Michel. *Die fünf Sinne*. Frankfurt, Suhrkamp, 1993.
Feldmann, Carsten. *Das Argument*, 207, 977-979, N-D 94.
Friedrich, Clemens. *Deut Z Phil*, 43(2), 393-395, 1995.

Seung, T K. *Intuition and Construction*. New Haven, Yale Univ Pr, 1993.
Schultz, David. *Int Stud Phil*, 27(2), 135-136, 1995.

Sevilla, José M (ed). *Cuadernos sobre Vico II*. Sevilla, Univ de Sevilla, 1992.
Cacciatore, Giuseppe. *Boll Centro Stud Vichiani*, 24-25, 320-324, 1994-95.

Shalom, Albert. *The Body/Mind Conceptual Framework and the Problem of Personal Identity*. Atlantic Highlands, Humanities Pr, 1985.
Laakso, Aarre. *Can Phil Rev*, 14(2), 137-139, Ap 94.

Shanks, Andrew. *Hegel's Political Theology*. New York, Cambridge Univ Pr, 1991.
Harris, H S. *Phil Soc Sci*, 25(1), 135-137, Mr 95.

Shapin, Steven. *A Social History of Truth*. Chicago, Univ of Chicago Pr, 1994.
Chalmers, Alan. *Brit J Phil Sci*, 46(1), 142-144, Mr 95.
Daston, Lorraine. *J Phil*, 92(7), 388-392, Jl 95.

Shapiro, Gary. *Alcyone*. Albany, SUNY Pr, 1991.
Banham, Gary. *J Brit Soc Phenomenol*, 25(3), 306-309, O 94.

Shapiro, Michael. *Reading "Adam Smith"*. Newbury Park, Sage, 1993.
Teichgraeber III, Richard F. *Polit Theory*, 23(1), 147-165, F 95.

Shapiro, Stewart. *Foundations without Foundationalism*. New York, Clarendon/Oxford Pr, 1991.
Largeault, Jean. *Arch Phil*, 57(3), 595-597, Jl-S 94.
Steiner, M. *Iyyun*, 44, 225-226, Ap 95.

Sharma, Arvind (ed). *God, Truth and Reality*. New York, Macmillan, 1993.
Loughlin, Gerard. *Heythrop J*, 36(2), 232-233, Ap 95.

Sharma, Arvind (ed) and Young, Katherine K (ed). *The Annual Review of Women in World Religions*. Albany, New York Univ Pr, 1994.
Andersen, Ruth E. *Phil East West*, 45(3), 439-445, Jl 95.

Sharples, R W (ed). *Modern Thinkers and Ancient Thinkers*. London, UCL Pr Ltd, 1993.
Crivelli, Paolo. *Phil Books*, 36(1), 35-37, Ja 95.

Shaw, William (ed). *Social and Personal Ethics*. Belmont, Wadsworth, 1993.
Tomsons, Sandra. *Can Phil Rev*, 14(5), 360-362, O 94.

Shea, William R. *The Magic of Numbers and Motion*. Canton, Science History Pub, 1991.
Manders, Kenneth L. *Phil Sci*, 62(1), 162-164, Mr 95.

Sheed, F J (trans). *Augustine's Confessions*. Indianapolis, Hackett, 1993.
Henderson, Lynnette. *Can Phil Rev*, 14(5), 363-364, O 94.

Sheets-Johnstone, Maxine (ed). *Giving the Body Its Due*. Albany, New York Univ Pr, 1992.
Fields, Gregory P. *Phil East West*, 45(3), 431-437, Jl 95.

Sheets-Johnstone, Maxine. *The Roots of Thinking*. Philadelphia, Temple Univ Pr, 1990.
Fetzer, James H. *Phil Psych*, 7(3), 397-399, 1994.

Sheffler Manning, Robert John. *Interpreting Otherwise than Heidegger*. Pittsburgh, Duquesne Univ Pr, 1993.
Gorczyca, Jakub. *Int Phil Quart*, 35(2), 225-226, Ju 95.

Shelton, George. *Morality and Sovereignty in the Philosophy of Hobbes*. New York, St Martin's Pr, 1992.
Martinich, A P. *Int Stud Phil*, 27(2), 136-137, 1995.

Sherwin, Susan. *No Longer Patient*. Philadelphia, Temple Univ Pr, 1992.
Crosthwaite, Jan. *Bioethics*, 9(1), 72-79, Ja 95.
Wendell, Susan. *Dialogue (Canada)*, 33(4), 783-785, Fall 94.

Shields, Philip R. *Logic and Sin in the Writings of Ludwig Wittgenstein*. Chicago, Univ of Chicago Pr, 1993.
von der Ruhr, Mario. *Phil Invest*, 18(1), 74-81, Ja 95.

Shotter, John. *Cultural Politics of Everyday Life*. Milton Keynes, Open Univ Pr, 1993.
Glover, David. *Rad Phil*, 69, 46-47, Ja-F 95.

Shrader-Frechette, K S. *Risk and Rationality*. Berkeley, Univ of Calif Pr, 1991.
Thompson, Paul B. *Res Phil Technol*, 14, 312-320, 1994.

Shute, Michael. *The Origins of Lonergan's Notion of the Dialectic of History*. Lanham, Univ Pr of America, 1993.
Melchin, Kenneth R. *Can Phil Rev*, 14(5), 365-367, O 94.

Shwayder, D S. *Statement and Reference*. Dordrecht, Kluwer, 1992.
Colter, I W. *Can Phil Rev*, 14(2), 139-141, Ap 94.

Sifianou, Maria. *Politeness Phenomena in England and Greece*. New York, Clarendon/Oxford Pr, 1992.
Preisler, Bent. *J Prag*, 22(2), 227-232, Ag 94.

Silberman, Bernard S. *Cages of Reason*. Chicago, Univ of Chicago Pr, 1993.
Gilbert, Paul. *Hist Euro Ideas*, 18(6), 1025-1027, N 94.

Silverman, Alexander E. *Mind, Machine, and Metaphor*. Boulder, Westview Pr, 1993.
Goldstein, Laurence. *Phil Books*, 36(2), 134-136, Ap 95.

Sim, Stuart. *Beyond Aesthetics*. Toronto, Univ of Toronto Pr, 1992.
Mullin, Amy. *Can Phil Rev*, 14(4), 293-295, Ag 94.

Simm, Christopher. *Kants Ablehnung jeglicher Erbsündenlehre*. Münster, Lit Verlag, 1990.
Cavallar, Georg. *Kantstudien*, 86(1), 90-93, 1995.

Simmons, A John. *On the Edge of Anarchy*. Princeton, Princeton Univ Pr, 1993.
Selegzi, Noel S. *Can Phil Rev*, 14(6), 421-423, D 94.

Simmons, A John. *The Lockean Theory of Rights*. Princeton, Princeton Univ Pr, 1992.
Ashcraft, Richard. *Brit J Hist Phil*, 3(1), 173-176, F 95.
Dunn, John. *Int Stud Phil*, 27(2), 137-138, 1995.

Simmons, Keith. *Universality and the Liar*. New York, Cambridge Univ Pr, 1993.
Drozdek, Adam. *Mind*, 104(413), 208-210, Ja 95.

Simons, Peter. *Philosophy and Logic in Central Europe from Bolzano to Tarski*. Dordrecht, Kluwer, 1992.
Falkenberg, Gabriel. *Erkenntnis*, 41(2), 275-279, S 94.

Simplicius and Hagen, Charles (trans). *On Aristotle Physics 7*. London, Duckworth, 1993.
Gerson, Lloyd P. *Phil Quart*, 45(179), 260-264, Ap 95.

Simplicius and Urmson, J O (trans). *On Aristotle on the Void*. London, Duckworth, 1993.
Gerson, Lloyd P. *Phil Quart*, 45(179), 260-264, Ap 95.

Simpson, David. *Romanticism, Nationalism, and the Revolt Against Theory*. Chicago, Univ of Chicago Pr, 1993.
Polan, Dana. *J Aes Art Crit*, 53(1), 96-98, Wint 95.

Singer, Peter (ed). *A Companion to Ethics*. Cambridge, Blackwell, 1991.
Farrell, Daniel M. *Ethics*, 105(4), 930-932, Jl 95.
Tasset, José Luis. *Telos*, 2(1), 127-135, Je 93.

Singer, Peter (ed). *Ethics (Oxford Readers)*. New York, Oxford Univ Pr, 1994.
Farrelly-Jackson, Steven. *Heythrop J*, 36(2), 221-222, Ap 95.

Singer, Peter. *La libération animale*. Paris, Bernard Grasset, 1993.
Blackburn, Pierre. *Philosopher*, 15, 254-258, 1994.

Sinha, Harendra Prasad. *Religious Philosophy of Tagore and Radhakrishnan*. Delhi, Motilal Banarsidass, 1993.
Oldmeadow, Harry. *Asian Phil*, 5(1), 82-84, 1995.

Sklar, Lawrence. *Philosophy of Physics*. Boulder, Westview Pr, 1992.
Clark, Peter. *Mind*, 104(415), 664-671, Jl 95.
MacCallum, David. *Phil Books*, 35(3), 221-223, Jl 94.
Maudlin, Tim. *Brit J Phil Sci*, 46(1), 145-149, Mr 95.

Sklar, Lawrence. *Physics and Chance*. New York, Cambridge Univ Pr, 1993.
Clark, Peter. *Mind*, 104(415), 664-671, Jl 95.
Maudlin, Tim. *Brit J Phil Sci*, 46(1), 145-149, Mr 95.
Rynasiewicz, Robert. *Phil Sci*, 62(2), 337-338, Je 95.
Torretti, Roberto. *Dialogos*, 30(65), 243-249, Ja 95.

Skledar, Nikola. *Obzorje suvremenosti*. Zapresic, Matica Hrvatska, 1994.
Despot, Blazenka. *Filozof Istraz*, 14(2-3), 607-608, 1994.

Skordev, Dimiter G. *Computability in Combinatory Spaces*. Dordrecht, Kluwer, 1992.
Normann, Dag. *J Sym Log*, 60(2), 695-696, Je 95.

Skorupski, John. *English Language Philosophy 1750-1945*. New York, Oxford Univ Pr, 1993.
Gustason, William. *Rev Metaph*, 48(2), 426-428, D 94.
Levine, James. *Int J Phil Stud*, 3(1), 209-212, Mr 95.
Wilkerson, T E. *Phil Books*, 36(1), 47-48, Ja 95.

Stone, Christopher D. *The Gnat Is Older than Man*. Princeton, Princeton Univ Pr, 1993.
Gillespie, Alexander. *Environ Values*, 4(2), 182-185, May 95.
Weston, Anthony. *Environ Ethics*, 16(4), 441-444, Wint 94.

Stone, E L. *Pleasura and Realitas*. Buffalo, Prometheus, 1993.
Maundrell, Richard. *Can Phil Rev*, 14(3), 213-214, Je 94.

Stone, Jerome A. *The Minimalist Vision of Transcendence*. Albany, SUNY Pr, 1992.
Shaw, Marvin C. *J Speculative Phil*, 9(2), 159-163, 1995.

Stove, David. *The Plato Cult and Other Philosophical Follies*. Cambridge, Blackwell, 1991.
Irvine, A D. *Can Phil Rev*, 14(1), 59-63, F 94.

Strawson, P F. *Analysis and Metaphysics*. New York, Oxford Univ Pr, 1992.
Preston, John. *Austl J Phil*, 73(1), 168-170, Mr 95.

Streminger, Gerhard. *David Hume: Sein Leben und Sein Werk*. Paderborn, Schoeningh, 1994.
Bonk, S. *Theol Phil*, 70(1), 106-108, 1995.

Ströker, Elisabeth and Hardy, Lee (trans). *Husserl's Transcendental Phenomenology*. Stanford, Stanford Univ Pr, 1993.
Mohanty, J N. *Phil Quart*, 45(179), 266-268, Ap 95.

Stroll, Avrum. *Moore and Wittgenstein on Certainty*. New York, Oxford Univ Pr, 1994.
Champlin, T S. *Philosophy*, 70(273), 466-469, Jl 95.

Struever, N S. *Theory as Practice*. Chicago, Univ of Chicago Pr, 1992.
Panizza, Letizia A. *J Hist Phil*, 32(4), 669-671, O 94.

Stuart, Robert. *Marxism at Work*. New York, Cambridge Univ Pr, 1992.
Hause, Steven C. *Hist Polit Thought*, 16(1), 139-143, Spr 95.

Stuhr, John J (ed). *Philosophy and the Reconstruction of Culture*. Albany, SUNY Pr, 1993.
Mitchell, Jeff. *Phil Lit*, 18(2), 403-404, O 94.

Stump, Eleonore (ed). *Reasoned Faith*. Ithaca, Cornell Univ Pr, 1993.
Clark, Kelly James. *Phil Rev*, 103(4), 743-745, O 94.
Godfrey, Joseph J. *Int Phil Quart*, 35(2), 239-241, Ju 95.
Grover, Stephen. *Phil Books*, 35(3), 209-211, Jl 94.
Lockey, Paul. *Rev Metaph*, 48(2), 429-431, D 94.

Stump, Eleonore (ed) and Flint, Thomas P (ed). *Hermes and Athena*. Notre Dame, Univ Notre Dame Pr, 1993.
Zagzebski, Linda. *Phil Books*, 36(1), 74-77, Ja 95.

Sublon, Roland. *La Lettre ou l'Esprit*. Paris, Cerf, 1993.
Lacas, Pierre-Paul. *Rev Thomiste*, 94(2), 329-331, Ap-Je 94.

Sukale, Michael. *Denken, Sprechen und Wissen*. Tübingen, Mohr, 1988.
Motzkin, Gabriel. *Iyyun*, 43, 349-351, Jl 94.

Sunstein, Cass R. *The Partial Constitution*. Cambridge, Harvard Univ Pr, 1993.
Meister, Robert. *Polit Theory*, 23(1), 182-195, F 95.

Suppe, Frederick. *The Semantic Conception of Theories and Scientific Realism*. Champaign, Univ of Illinois Pr, 1989.
Diederich, Werner. *Erkenntnis*, 41(3), 421-426, N 94.

Surber, Jere Paul. *Language and German Idealism, Fichte's Linguistic Philosophy*. Atlantic Highlands, Humanities Pr, 1994.
Köddermann, Achim. *Daimon Rev Filosof*, 9, 361-363, 1994.
Köddermann, Achim. *Rev Filosof (Spain)*, 9, 361-363, 1994.

Swartz, Norman. *Beyond Experience*. Toronto, Univ of Toronto Pr, 1991.
Reese, William L. *Dialogue (Canada)*, 33(4), 776-779, Fall 94.

Sweeney, Leo. *Divine Infinity in Greek and Medieval Thought*. New York, Lang, 1992.
Madigan, Arthur. *Amer Cath Phil Quart*, 68(4), 562-564, Autumn 94.

Swinburne, Richard. *Responsibility and Atonement*. New York, Clarendon/Oxford Pr, 1989.
Stump, Eleonore. *Faith Phil*, 11(2), 321-328, Ap 94.

Swinburne, Richard. *Revelation: From Metaphor to Analogy*. New York, Clarendon/Oxford Pr, 1992.
Spradley, Garey B. *Faith Phil*, 11(2), 328-333, Ap 94.
Stump, Eleonore. *Phil Rev*, 103(4), 739-743, O 94.

Swinburne, Richard. *The Coherence of Theism (Revised Edition)*. New York, Clarendon/Oxford Pr, 1993.
Hughes, Gerard J. *Heythrop J*, 36(1), 115-116, Ja 95.

Swinburne, Richard. *The Existence of God (Revised Edition)*. New York, Clarendon/Oxford Pr, 1991.
Löffler, W. *Theol Phil*, 70(1), 138-143, 1995.

Szporluk, Roman. *Communism and Nationalism*. New York, Oxford Univ Pr, 1991.
Lovell, David W. *Hist Euro Ideas*, 21(1), 142-143, Ja 95.

Tabernero del Río, Serafín M. *Filosofía y educación en Ortega y Gasset*. Salamanca, Univ Pont Salamanca, 1993.
Quesada, Paz. *Anu Filosof*, 28(1), 179-180, 1995.

Tagliacozzo, Giorgio (ed). *New Vico Studies Vol. IX*. 1991.
Nuzzo, Enrico. *Boll Centro Stud Vichiani*, 24-25, 294-308, 1994-95.

Tagliacozzo, Giorgio (ed). *New Vico Studies Vol. VII*. 1989.
Nuzzo, Enrico. *Boll Centro Stud Vichiani*, 24-25, 294-308, 1994-95.

Tagliacozzo, Giorgio (ed). *New Vico Studies Vol. VIII*. 1990.
Nuzzo, Enrico. *Boll Centro Stud Vichiani*, 24-25, 294-308, 1994-95.

Tagliacozzo, Giorgio. *The Arbor Scientiae Reconceived and the History of Vico's Resurrection*. Atlantic Highlands, Humanities Pr, 1993.
Kelley, Donald R. *Rev Metaph*, 48(2), 431-432, D 94.

Tamás, Vay. *A posztmodern Amerikában*. Budapest, Tematikus napló, 1991.
Endre, Kiss. *Magyar Filozof Szemle*, 1-2, 309-316, 1994.

Tamir, Yael. *Liberal Nationalism*. Princeton, Princeton Univ Pr, 1993.
Kymlicka, Will. *Can Phil Rev*, 14(1), 64-67, F 94.
Yack, Bernard. *Polit Theory*, 23(1), 166-182, F 95.

Tarca, Luigi. *Ragione e paradosso nella filosofia contemporanea*. Genova, Marietti, 1993.
Fabris, Adriano. *Teoria*, 14(1), 154-159, 1994.

Tarrant, Harold. *Thrasyllan Platonism*. Ithaca, Cornell Univ Pr, 1993.
Rist, John M. *Rev Metaph*, 48(4), 933-934, Je 95.

Tauber, Alfred I (ed). *Organism and the Origins of Self*. Dordrecht, Kluwer, 1991.
Khalil, Elias L. *Hist Phil Life Sci*, 16(2), 390-392, Ag 94.

Taussig, Michael. *Mimesis and Alterity*. New York, Routledge, 1993.
Hadfield, Andrew. *Rad Phil*, 68, 52-53, Autumn 94.

Taylor, Charles. *La ética de la autenticidad*. Barcelona, Ed Paidos, 1994.
del Junco, Manuel Fontán. *Themata*, 13, 322-324, 1995.

Taylor, Charles. *Multiculturalism and "The Politics of Recognition"*. Princeton, Princeton Univ Pr, 1992.
Halvorson, Jonathan. *Conference*, 5(1), 100-104, Spr 94.
Jaggar, Alison M. *Hastings Center Rep*, 24(5), 44-45, S-O 94.
Reidy, David A. *Auslegung*, 20(1), 43-46, Wint 95.

Taylor, Charles. *Multikulturalismus und die Politik der Anerkennung*. Frankfurt, Fischer, 1993.
Velek, Josef. *Filozof Cas*, 42(4), 703-706, 1994.

Taylor, Charles. *Quellen des Selbst*. Frankfurt, Suhrkamp, 1994.
Horster, Detlef. *Z Phil Forsch*, 49(2), 324-327, Ap-Je 95.

Taylor, Charles. *Rapprocher les solitudes*. Sainte-Foy, Pr Univ Laval, 1992.
Roy, Yves. *Dialogue (Canada)*, 33(3), 563-565, Sum 94.

Taylor, Charles. *The Ethics of Authenticity*. Cambridge, Harvard Univ Pr, 1992.
Keshen, Richard. *Can Phil Rev*, 14(6), 423-425, D 94.
Sullivan, John. *Heythrop J*, 35(3), 346-347, Jl 94.

Taylor, Charles. *The Malaise of Modernity*. Concord, Anansi, 1991.
Groarke, Louis. *Eidos*, 12(1), 175-178, Je 94.

Taylor, Mark C. *nOts*. Chicago, Univ of Chicago Pr, 1993.
King-Farlow, John. *Can Phil Rev*, 14(3), 215-217, Je 94.

Taylor, Monica (ed). *Values Education in Europe*. Berkshire, Ntl Fndtn Educ Res, 1993.
Torney-Purta, Judith. *J Moral Educ*, 24(1), 83-85, 1995.

Taylor, Seth. *Left-wing Nietzscheans*. Hawthorne, de Gruyter, 1990.
Diethe, Carol. *Hist Euro Ideas*, 21(1), 96-97, Ja 95.

Te Velde, Rudi. *Thomas over goed en kwaad*. Baarn, Ambo, 1993.
Lippens, Elisabeth. *Tijdschr Filosof*, 56(4), 770, D 94.

Teichman, Jenny. *Pacifism and the Just War*. Cambridge, Blackwell, 1986.
Lackey, Douglas P. *Nous*, 27(4), 546-548, D 93.

Tekippe, Terry J. *Lonergan and Thomas on the Will*. Lanham, Univ Pr of America, 1993.
Barry, Robert J. *Can Phil Rev*, 14(5), 369-370, O 94.

Temkin, Larry S. *Inequality*. New York, Oxford Univ Pr, 1993.
Moore, Andrew. *Phil Quart*, 45(178), 114-115, Ja 95.
Sikora, R I. *Ethics*, 105(3), 663-665, April.

Templeton, John Marks. *Evidence of Purpose*. New York, Continuum, 1994.
Stein, Gordon. *Free Inq*, 15(1), 61, Wint 94-95.

Templeton, John Marks and Herrmann, Robert L. *Is God the Only Reality?*. New York, Continuum, 1994.
Stein, Gordon. *Free Inq*, 15(1), 61, Wint 94-95.

Tennant, Neil. *Autologic*. Edinburgh, Edinburgh Univ Pr, 1992.
Frápolli, Maria J. *Phil Books*, 36(2), 113-114, Ap 95.

Tenodi, Damir. *Yin i Yang*. Zagreb, Anan Pr, 1990.
Premur, Ksenija. *Filozof Istraz*, 14(2-3), 615-618, 1994.

Theissen, Gerd and Kohl, Margaret (trans). *Social Reality and the Early Christians*. Minneapolis, Fortress Pr, 1993.
Turner, Geoffrey. *Heythrop J*, 35(3), 324-325, Jl 94.

Thélot, Jérôme. *Baudelaire*. Paris, Gallimard, 1993.
Carraud, Christophe. *Arch Phil*, 58(2), 261-265, Ap-Je 95.

Thiel, Manfred. *Method, Volume III: G W F Hegel (2 Volumes)*. Heidelberg, Elpis, 1992.
Lichtigfeld, A. *Int Stud Phil*, 27(1), 149, 1995.

Thiessen, Elmer John. *Teaching for Commitment*. Montreal, McGill-Queens U Pr, 1993.
Colwell, Gary. *Can Phil Rev*, 15(1), 68-70, F 95.

Thody, Philip. *The Conservative Imagination*. New York, St Martin's Pr, Undated.
Stocker, Mark. *Phil Lit*, 18(2), 387-388, O 94.